Author-Title Index
to
Joseph Sabin's

Dictionary of Books
Relating to America

compiled by

JOHN EDGAR MOLNAR

Vol. I: A-F

The Scarecrow Press, Inc.
Metuchen, N.J.   1974

Library of Congress Cataloging in Publication Data

Molnar, John Edgar.
    Author-title index to Joseph Sabin's Dictionary of
books relating to America.

    1. Sabin, Joseph, 1821-1881. A dictionary of books
relating to America--Indexes. I. Sabin, Joseph, 1821-
1881. A dictionary of books relating to America.
II. Title.
Z1201.S222   016.9173   74-6291
ISBN 0-8108-0652-5

INTRODUCTION

That the Dictionary of Books Relating to America contains a treasure of bibliographic information cannot be denied. Unfortunately, the scholar searching for this wealth of materials finds it as elusive as the Seven Cities of Cibola, and, like Coronado, is vanquished by the inhospitable wilderness. Sabin's method of arrangement, as outlined in his "Prospectus," complied with contemporary usage, but it becomes both obscure and impractical in the light of the more refined bibliographical cataloging practices of our own times. The latter volumes of the Dictionary, issued in the early nineteen hundreds, attempted to correct some of the more glaring inconsistencies through the use of frequent cross-references. Due to the limits of space and the urge to complete the Dictionary, even this attempt fell far short of removing the difficulties imposed by Sabin's arrangement, and often added to the confusion. Hence this author-title index.

There are 106,413 numbered entries in the Dictionary. Appended to many of the numbered entries are bibliographic descriptions of the works cited, titles of other works by the same author, and short citations to ancillary or critical works on the same subject. In the initial compilation of the authors and titles mentioned in the Dictionary, 520,000 entries were produced. A large number were duplicated title entries; perhaps a tenth of the Sabin entries proved to be duplicate citations of the same work, listed under both author and title or subject; and almost all sets and collections were found to have analytic entries under the contributing authors. Nevertheless, this index contains over 270,000 separate author and title entries.

The terms "author" and "title" are broad in scope. Included in this index are: authors, joint authors, editors, compilers, illustrators, engravers and cartographers; publishers, if the firm compiled the work issued; private and public corporate agencies; and governing bodies, both political and ecclesiastical. In addition to main, series, and running titles, selected alternate titles and subtitles are also entered, generally for works published before 1800, the latter included to facilitate comparison of Sabin entries with variants found in such bibliographies as Pollard and Redgrave, Wing, Evans, and the early volumes of the American Bibliography.

Apart from arranging in alphabetical order the authors and titles found in the Dictionary, this index has several other useful features. A large proportion of the pseudonymous authors have been identified, and many authors of anonymous works have been brought to light. Liberal use has been made of cross-references in the entry of foreign multiple surnames, and whenever possible the surnames conform to the practices used in the Catalogue of Books Represented by Library of Congress Printed Cards. Sabin numbers for all the listed tracts in numerous pamphlet wars have been entered under the author and title of each work in a particular controversy. A number of generic entries have been used: "election sermon," "constitution," "laws, statutes, etc.," and the like, may be found under both national and state governments; and "almanac" draws together all the numerous issues of this type of publication. All entries for parts of series or collections have been given duplicate entry under the inclusive titles.

The index should not be used to ascertain exact wording of titles. Title entries are generally given in short-title form, and when two or more Sabin numbers are given for individual citations, they generally correct or complement each other. Also, Sabin deleted "words of a title regarded as unimportant" by the frequent use of ellipses, thus creating a large number of incomplete and/or totally misleading entries. Although no attempt has been made to verify and reinstate the omitted phrases, there are very few catchword or meaningless titles in the index. In all cases, the user should verify index citations by consulting the Dictionary itself.

Acknowledgments

This work could not have been completed without the assistance of many individuals. They generously offered information and advice which prevented or corrected many errors; those which remain are mine alone.

Mr. Leon K. Smith, Acting Chief, General Legal Division, Organization of American States, and Mr. Shirley A. Victor, Assistant Curator, Library, Hispanic Society of America, gave valuable information concerning the proper entry form for Latin-American judicial reports.

Numerous members of the faculty of Longwood College, Farmville, Virginia, freely gave of their time and knowledge in answering questions and providing details in their fields of study.

Mrs. J. W. Dunnington (Kathryn Chamberlin Dunnington) provided information which clarified entries in the Cherokee language.

Mr. Donald Houpe provided expert assistance in translating entries in the non-romance languages, and was invaluable in explicating obsolete and dialectic phrases in all the foreign languages.

My aunt, Miss Ethel R. Molnar, translated the Hungarian entries.

Mr. Richard Vettese, of the Detroit Public Library, searched for answers to numerous questions, and offered much advice and encouragement.

To all these individuals go my most grateful thanks.

In solving bibliographical puzzles many libraries were consulted. The staff of the Boatwright Library, University of Richmond, Richmond, Virginia; the staff of the Library, Union Theological Seminary, Richmond, Virginia; and the staff of the Reference and Circulation Division, Virginia State Library, Richmond, were all most helpful.

Mr. Paul Grier, Librarian, and the staff of the Eggleston Library, Hampden-Sydney College, Hampden-Sydney, Virginia, were of great assistance. They provided not only free access to the Eggleston Library's fine bibliographical facilities, but also cheerfully answered my numeroud questions and suggested solutions to my problems. To them I am most grateful.

To Mr. Charles E. Butler, Librarian, and my colleagues of the Lancaster Library at Longwood College I owe a debt of thanks which can never be repaid. For six years they have listened to my problems and complaints, and lived with my preoccupation with this index.

Special thanks are due to Mrs. George H. LeStourgeon (Martha Holman LeStourgeon), now Acting Librarian of the Lancaster Library. Her masterful grasp of the techniques of cataloging and bibliography, as well as her tactful suggestions of many improvements in the structure of this work, have made her advice invaluable. Whatever merits this index may possess are in large part due to her.

I received two small grants from the Longwood College Committee on Faculty Research, and for these I am most grateful. The grant monies provided partial support for a number of Longwood students employed to alphabetize and file the cards which formed the basis of this index. My thanks are due to Mrs. Gail Douglas Bates, and Mrs. Shirley George Lynn; and to the then Misses Linda Adamee, Chena Allison, Agnes Lee Barnes, Nancy Barrett, Ava Beasley, Patricia Benze, Chryl Cassada, Mary Anne Chandler, Karen Elaine Cheney, Joann Clabo, Karen DeBord, Terri d'Emilio, Elaine Dowdy, Ann Earman, Linda Featherston, Fran Garlser, Karen Gibson, Sandra Marie Goodman, Cindy Hardisan, Dottie Harry, Margaret Lantz, Julia H. Lewis, Diane Livick, Judy Luffsey, Kathy Luttrell, Carole Menefee, Connie Metcalf, Libby Nicar, Susan Margaret Scantling, Margaret Anne Schaefer, Ellen Smith, Victoria Smith, Frances Nell Snead, Nancy H. Stansbury, Claire Marie Tavel, Susan Jeanette Thrasher, Sherry Tomlin, Mary Beth Underwood, Rebecca Rose Vimpeny, Janet Walsh, Joy Walston, Martha Whitehurst, Peggy Ann Winn, Gail Womack, Elizabeth Blair Wooding, and Vicki York.

Finally, my greatest debt is to my family. My sister and brother-in-law, Mary and James R. Collins, provided occasional assistance during the final editing and typing. My parents coped with my incessant monologues on the vagaries of Sabin, and their encouragement sustained me in the completion of the work. Moreover, they took time from their own research and writing to assist me in the final arranging, editing, and proof-reading of the manuscript. It is to them that this index is dedicated.

Farmville, Virginia
May, 1972

Key to original volumes of Sabin

v.	1.	A - Bedford, Pennsylvania
v.	2.	Bedinger - Brownell, H. H.
v.	3.	Brownell, H. H. - Chesbrough
v.	4.	Cheshire, New Hampshire - Costa Pereira
v.	5.	Costa Rica - Dumorter
v.	6.	Du Moulin - Franklin, A. W.
v.	7.	Franklin, Benjamin - Hall, Joseph
v.	8.	Hall, Joseph - Huntington, Jedediah V.
v.	9.	Huntington, Joseph - Lacroix, Francois J. P. de.
v.	10.	Lacroix, Frederic - M'Clary
v.	11.	McClean - Memoire justificatif
v.	12.	Memoire justificatif des hommes - Nederland (Articulen)
v.	13.	Nederland (Besoignes) - Omai
v.	14.	Omana y Sotomayor - Philadelphia City Tract Society
v.	15.	Philadelphia Club - Providence, Rhode Island (Measures)
v.	16.	Providence Mechanics' and Apprentices' Library - Remarks relative
v.	17.	Remarks respecting - Ross, C. K.
v.	18.	Ross, D. B. - Schedae
v.	19.	Schedel - Simms, W. G.
v.	20.	Simms, W. G. - Smith, Seba.
v.	21.	Smith, Sebastian Bach - Solis y Valenzuela, Bruno de.
v.	22.	Solis y Valenzuela, Pedro de - Spiritual manifestations
v.	23.	Spiritual maxims - Storrs, R. S.
v.	24.	Storrs, R. S. - Ternaux-Compans, H.
v.	25.	Ternaux-Compans, H. - Tucker, J.
v.	26.	Tucker, J. - Vindex, pseud.
v.	27.	Vindex, pseud. - Weeks, Levi.
v.	28.	Weeks, William Raymond - Witherspoon, J.
v.	29.	Witherspoon, J. - Z.

Key to numbered entries in Sabin

A	1 - 2546	N	51671 - 56364
B	2547 - 9740	O	56365 - (58050)
C	9741 - (18220)	P	58051 - 66883
D	18221 - 21607	Q	(66884) - 67372
E	21608 - 23576	R	67373 - (74601)
F	(23577) - 26265	S	74602 - 94141
G	26266 - 29387	T	94142 - 97659
H	(29388) - 34140	U	97660 - 98253
I	34141 - 35325	V	98254 - 100860
J	(35326) - 36967	W	100861 - 105711
K	36968 - 38373	X	105712 - 105742
L	(38374) - 42894	Y	105743 - 106228A
M	42895 - 51670	Z	106229 - 106413

v

Free Church Circular. Oneida Reserve. 1848. 8vo.

Free Churches. *New York.* 1843. 12mo, pp. 12. 25707

The Free Enquirer. *New York.* 1828–32. 5 vols., 4to. c.
A continuation of the "New Harmony Gazette." Edited by Frances Wright, Robert Dale Owen, R. L. Jennings, and Amos Gilbert.

A Free Enquiry into the Causes, both Real and Pretended, for Laying on the Embargo. By a Citizen of Vermont. *Windsor, (Vt.): Printed by Charles Spear.* 1808. 8vo, pp. 28.

Free Grace Maintained. *See* [Mather (C.)]

Free Labor in the Colonies. 1852. 25710

Free Military School for Applicants for Commands of Colored Troops ... . *Philadelphia: King & Baird.* 1863. 8vo, pp. 12.

The Free Negro Question in Maryland. *Baltimore: John W. Woods, Printer.* 1859. 8vo, pp. 28. 25712

Free Negroism; or, Results of Emancipation in the North, and West India Islands; with Statistics of the Decay of Commerce, Idleness of the Negro, his Return to Savageism, and the Effect of Emancipation upon the Farming, Mechanical and Laboring Classes. *New York: Van Eyrie, Horton & Co.* 1862. 12mo, pp. 32. B., C. 25713

Free Public Libraries; Suggestions on their Foundation and Administration. ... *Boston.* 1871. Post 8vo, pp. 59. 25714

Free Religion. Report of Addresses at a Meeting ... in Boston, May 30, 1867 ... . *Boston: Adams & Co.* 1867. 8vo, pp. 55. B., H. 25715

Free Remarks on the Spirit of the Federal Constitution, the Practice of the Federal Government, and the Obligations of the Union, respecting the Exclusion of Slavery from the Territories and New States. ... By a Philadelphian. *Philadelphia: A. Finley.* 1819. 8vo, pp. 116. BA., C. 25716

Free Soil Minstrel. *New York.* 1846. 12mo, pp. 228. + [*Ibid.*] 1846. 25717
A republication of the "Liberty Minstrel," with considerable additions.

Free Soil Songs for the People. *Boston.* 1848. 25718

Free Thoughts. *See* [Anderson (James)], Vol. 1., No. 1399.

The ———.' No. I. 95279
——, Lieut. Col. pseud. Jack Mosby.
51039
——, Lieut. Col. pseud. John Y. Beall.
4110
——, Lieut. Col. pseud. Semmes, the
pirate. 79084
——, Reverend. Fast sermon. (23905)
-----, -----, a native of the province, pseud.
Sermon preached at Litchfield. see
Andrews, Samuel.
-----, Bishop of. pseud. Rise, progress,
and present state. see Jackson William,
Bishop of Oxford, 1751-1815.
-----, Mr. pseud. Speech of Mr. -----.
see Pitt, William, 1st Earl of Chatham,
1708-1778.
----- Anonymous. pseud. Age of steam. see
Whiting, Henry.
. . ., Heer. pseud. Brieve van den Heer.
see Murk van Fhelgum, -------.
*r. pseud. tr. 16467, 16504, 16535
**, M. E. pseud. tr. see Eidous, Marc
Antoine. tr.
***. pseud. tr. 17494, 77688, 95803,
96433
***. pseud. Address to the representatives
in Parliament. 440
***. pseud. Bibliotheca Mexicana. see
Fischer, Augustin.
***. pseud. Briefe aus den Vereinigten
Staaten von Nord Amerika. see Joerg, E.
***. pseud. Choix des lettres edifiantes.
see Montmignon, Jean Baptiste.
***. pseud. Diccionario Portuguez e Brasili-
ana. see Velloso Xavier, Jose Mariano
da Conceicao.
***. pseud. Guerra do Paraguay. see Souza
Bocayuva, Quintino de.
***. pseud. Lettres critiques et politiques.
see Dubuc, Jean Baptiste.
***. pseud. Life and times of Sam. see
Sam. pseud.
***. pseud. Memoires et observations geo-
graphiques. see Engel, Samuel.
***. pseud. Memoires sur la Louisiane.
see Wante, Charles Etienne Pierre.
Supposed Author.
***. pseud. Relations curieuses. see Du
Fresne de Francheville, Joseph.
***. pseud. Voto de America. see Indarte,
Jose Rivera.
, **. pseud. True pleasure. 97136
***, Adrien. pseud. Savanes. see Rouquette,
Adrien E.
***, Americano. pseud. tr. see Formaleoni,
Vincenzio.
***, Ancien Capitaine de Vaisseau. pseud.
Decouvertes des Francois. see Fleurieu,
Charles Pierre Claret de, Comte de.
***, Chevalier de. pseud. Voyages et avantures.
100839-100840
***, De. pseud. Jeune Ameriquaine. see
Villeneuve, Gabrielle Suzanne Barbot
Gallon de.
***, Formerly a Captain in the French Navy.
pseud. Discoveries of the French. see
Fleurieu, Charles Pierre Claret de,
Comte de.

***, M. pseud. tr. see Le Febvre de
Villebrune, -------. tr.
***, M., pseud. tr. see Raulin, Joseph.
tr.
***, M. pseud. Memoires sur la Louisi-
ane. see Le Page du Pratz, -------.
***, M., Americain. pseud. Abrege de la
revolution de l'Amerique Angloise. see
Buisson, Paul Ulric du.
***, Madame de. pseud. Jeune Ameriquaine.
see Villeneuve, Gabrielle Suzanne Barbot
Gallon de.
***, Maxan. pseud. Military reflections.
46998
***, Monsieur. pseud. Carte. 23342
***, Theresia, Baronesse van. pseud.
Grootmoedige en heldhaftige Hollandsche
Amasoon. see Hoog, Theresia, Baronness van.
****. pseud. see Frere ****. pseud.
****, ***** *. pseud. Spirit. see Ehle,
George L. supposed author
****, Right Hon. the Countess of. pseud.
Story of Inkle and Yarrico. 92340
*****. pseud. tr. 64827, 2d note after
96457
*****. pseud. Lettre. see Pinto, Isaac
de, 1715-1787.
*****. pseud. ed. Memorial most humbly
addressed. See Pownall, Thomas.
*****. pseud. Premiere lettre. see Pinto,
Isaac de, 1715-1787.
*****, J. M. B. de. pseud. Briefe. see
Saint Victor, Jacques Maximilien Benjamin Bins de.
*****, J. M. B. de. pseud. Lettres. see
Saint Victor, Jacques Maximilien Benjamin Bins de.
*****, Madame. pseud. Relation d'un voy-
age. see Hoven, ------ (van Uitenhage
de Mist) de.
***** * ****. pseud. Spirit. see Ehle,
George L. supposed author
***** ***. pseud. True pleasure. 97136
***** *********. pseud. Address to the
people. 435
******* *********. pseud. Narrative of
the United States' Brig Vixen. see
One of the Vixen's crew. pseud.
********, in London. pseud. Letter.
(40313)
*********, *******. pseud. Narrative of
the capture of the United States' Brig
Vixen. see One of the Vixen's crew.
pseud.
*********, John. Alias see Syllavan,
Owen. Defendant
+. pseud. Answer to an invidious pamphlet.
see Cross, -----, fl. 1755.

A

A. pseud. Dialogue between A and B.
19924
A. pseud. Dialogue on cheap postage.
64478
A. pseud. Notes on the army of the United
States. 97924

A. _pseud_. Occasional reverberator. _see_ Smith, William, 1728-1793.

A. _pseud_. Party in power, and the new constitution. 58970

A. _pseud_. Thoughts on the entertainment of the stage. 95703

A. _pseud_. El traves de la razon. 96506

A. and B. _pseud_. Proposals for traffick and commerce. 66039

A., A. O., _pseud_. see Andrews, A. O.

A., Ad. d'., _pseud_. _see_ D'A , Ad., _pseud_.

A. . ., Antoine, _pseud_. Lettres d'un membre du congres. _see_ Vincent, N.

A., B., _pseud_. Some buds and blossoms. _see_ Antrobus, Benjamin.

A., C., _pseud_. Thoughts on the Baptist controversy. 95691

A., C. C., _pseud_. tr. (8784)

A., E., _pseud_. New-England loyal publication society _see_ Atkinson, Edward.

A., E. H. M., _pseud_. Present way of the country. 65334

A., F., _pseud_. Considerations on behalf of the colonists. _see_ Dummer, Jeremiah. supposed author and Otis, James. supposed author

A——n, F——s., _pseud_. _see_ Alison, Francis.

A., G., _pseud_., tr. 8744

A., G., Author of "Portugal," _pseud_. Young traveller in South America. I, 87318, 106195

A., G. A., _pseud_. Tecumseh. _see_ Aynge, G. A. supposed author

A., H. G., _pseud_. Histoire du pays nomme Spitsberghe. _see_ Assum, Hessel Gerritz.

A., J., _pseud_. Their majesties colony of Connecticut. _see_ Allyn, John. supposed author

A., J., _pseud_. Some miscellaneous observations. _see_ Willard, Samuel, 1640-1707. supposed author

A., J. H. L., _pseud_. Plea for practical heraldry. (63387)

A., J. P. F. N., _pseud_. Dialogo constitucional brasileiro. _see_ Nabuco de Araujo, Jose Paulo de Figueiroa.

A., J. R., _pseud_. Legion of Liberty. _see_ Ames, Julius Rubens. supposed author

A., J. S. de., _pseud_. tr. 49980

A., J. V., _pseud_. Manifiesto. _see_ Arguelles, Jose Vazquez.

A., L. C. D. L., _pseud_. L'Amerique delivree. 38759

A., M. A. L. V., _pseud_. Recueil des plusieurs cartes. 68451

A., M. E., _pseud_. Comentario o anotacion de las leyes. _see_ Acevedo, M. E.

A., N., _pseud_. Brief chronological table. 87749

A., P., _pseud_. Freeholder's address. _see_ Wise, John.

A., P., _pseud_. Voyages and adventures of Capt. Barth. Sharp. _see_ Ayres, Philip.

A., P., in Boston, _pseud_. Three curious pieces. 95734

A., R., _pseud_. Congratulatory peom. 78297

A., R., _pseud_. Narrative of the proceedings. _see_ Allen, Richard.

A., R. B., _pseud_. Short notice of Ariel. _see_ Anderson, R. B. supposed author

A., S. y, _pseud_. Triunfo de la religion. _see_ Sul y Amira, -------.

A., T., _pseud_. _see_ Abbay, Thomas.

A., T., Gent, _pseud_. Carolina. _see_ Ash, Thomas.

A., T., _pseud_. Chaine de scripture chronologie. _see_ Allen, Thomas.

A., V. R., _pseud_. Songs of the Washingtonians. 86942

A., W., a minister in Virginia, _pseud_. Letter. 40349

A., Z. O., _pseud_. Saudade pela sentidissima morte. _see_ Villeia Barbosa, Francisco.

A. y N., G., _pseud_. Ojeada sobre la campana. 57078, 57522

A. y Pineda, J. _see_ Pineda, J. A. y.

A. B., _pseud_. _see_ Appleton, Nathaniel.

A. B., _pseud_. _see_ B., A., _pseud_.

A. B., _pseud_. _see_ Bussaeus, A. tr.

A. B., _pseud_. _see_ Byfield, Nathanael.

A. B., _pseud_. _see_ Franklin, Benjamin. supposed author

A. B., _pseud_. _see_ Tucker, Josiah, [ ] 1712-1799.

A. B., _pseud_. see Weymouth, Mass. South Parish. Committee of Inquiry.

A. B., _pseud_. see Wharton, Samuel. supposed author

A——B——, _pseud_. see B——, A——, _pseud_.

A. B. C., _pseud_. see C., A. B., _pseud_.

A. B. C. D. E., _pseud_. see Hopkinson, Francis.

ABCFM _see_ American Board of Commissioners for Foreign Missions.

A. B. H., _pseud_. see Hassan, A. B.

A. B. M., _pseud_. see M., A. B. _pseud_.

A Brandis, G. Brender. see Brender a Brandis, G.

A. C., _pseud_. see Chute, Anthony.

A. C——d, _pseud_. see Cleveland, Aaron. supposed author

A. D... ., _pseud_. see D. . . ., A., _pseud_.

A. E., _pseud_. see E., A., _pseud_.

A. E. L., _pseud_. see Level, Andreas E.

A. E. Wright's Boston, New York, Philadelphia & Baltimore commercial directory. 105529

A. F., _pseud_. see F., A., _pseud_.

A. F***, _pseud_. see F***, A., _pseud_.

A. Fishe Shelly, _pseud_. see Gerard, James Watson.

A. G. D., _pseud_. see Dole, Anna Greenleaf.

A. G. U., _pseud_., tr. see U., A. G., _pseud_., tr.

A Goes, Damiano. see Goes, Damiao de, 1501-ca. 1573.

A. H., _pseud_. see H., A., _pseud_.

A. H., _pseud_. see Holmes, Alexander. supposed author and petitioner

A——ld H——son, _pseud_. see Hutcheson, Archibald.

A. Hoyt's acquittal from the anonymous charges. 33398

A. I., _pseud_. see Islip, Adam.

A. J., _pseud_. see Jones, Absalom.

A. J., _pseud_. see Justice, Alexander.

A. J. F., _pseud_. see F., A. J., _pseud_.

A. J. W., _pseud_. tr. see W., A. J., _pseud_., tr.

A. Kempis, Thomas. see Kempis, Thomas a.

A——a known to the A——ts. 66232

A. L., _pseud_. see L., A., _pseud_.

A. L., _pseud_. see Linton, Anthonie.

A. L., _pseud_. see Longworthy, A. supposed author

A. L. S. & M. Academy, Middletown, Conn. see American Literary, Scientific and Military Academy, Middletown, Conn.

A. L. Scovill & Co.'s Framers' and Mechanics' Almanac. 78461

A. L. V. A., pseud. see A., M. A. L. V., pseud.
A. M., pseud. see M., A., pseud.
A. M., pseud. see Morris, Apollos.
A. M. D. G. 89827
A. M. D. G. Potewateme Missinoi-kan Catechisme. 64577
A. M. D. G. St. John's College, Fordham. 75291
A. M. de Mirbech. 39545
A. M. R. T., pseud. see T., A. M. R., pseud.
A. M'Elroy's Philadelphia directory, for 1837. 61606
A Malo de Villavicencio, Johannes. see Villavicencio, Johannes a Malo de.
A Mendizabal, Gregorius Lopez. see Lopez a Memdizabal, Gregorius.
A. O., pseud. see Exquemelin, Alexandre Olivier.
A. O. A., pseud. see Andrews, A. O.
A. O. F., pseud. see Van der Kemp, Francis Adrian.
A. P., pseud. see P., A., pseud.
A. P., pseud., tr. see P., A., pseud., tr.
A. P., pseud. see Pember, Arthur.
A. P., pseud. see Peniston, Arthur.
A. P., pseud. see Pike, Albert.
A. P. Upshur, of Richmond, to the citizens of Philadelphia. 98099
A. R. see Gt. Brit. Sovereigns, etc., 1702-1714 (Anne)
A. R., pseud. see Roche, Alfred R.
A. R., pseud. see Ross, A.
A. R. Castelmanns Reisen. 12557
A. R. F., pseud. see F., A. R., pseud.
A. R. y C. L., pseud., tr. see L., A. R. y C., pseud., tr.
A. Rifleman, Esq., Gent, pseud. see Keiley, A. M.
A. S., pseud. see S., A., pseud.
A. S., pseud. see Steuart, Adam.
A. S., pseud. see Steuart, Andrew.
A. S. P., pseud. see P., A. S., pseud.
A Saa, Jacobus. see Saa, Jacobus a.
A San Augustino Macedo, Francisco. see Macedo, Francisco a San Augustino.
A. T. Myrthe, pseud. see Ganihl, Anthony.
A Thuessink, Evert Jan Thomassen. see Thomassen A. Thuessink, Evert Jan.
A. V., pseud. see V., A., pseud.
A. V., el Mexicano, pseud. see V., A., el Mexicano, pseud.
A Varea, Alphonso Lasor. see Lasor a Varea, Alphonso.
A Veracruce, Alphonsus. see Gutierrez, Alonso.
A Veracruse, Illephonsus. see Gutierrez, Alonso.
A. W., pseud. see Wilkins, A.
A--- W-----, pseud. see W-----, A---, pseud.
A*** W*****, pseud. see W*****, A***, pseud.
A. W. Farmer, pseud. see Seabury, Samuel, 1729-1796; Wilkins, Isaac; and Chandler, Thomas Bradbury, incorrectly supposed author; Cooper, Myles, incorrectly supposed author; and Inglis, Charles, incorrectly supposed author.
A. W. M., pseud. see Mitchell, Agnes Woods.
A. Wagstaffe, pseud. see Wagstaffe, A., pseud.
A Westchester Farmer, pseud. see Seabury, Samuel, 1729-1796; Wilkins, Isaac; and Chandler, Thomas Bradbury, incorrectly supposed author; Cooper, Myles, incorrectly supposed author; and Inglis, Charles, incorrectly supposed author.

A Westhuysen, Abrahamus. see Westhuysen, Abrahamus a.
A Wood, Anthony. see Wood, Anthony a, 1632-1695.
A. Y., Esq.; author of the Theatre of the present war in North America, pseud. see Young, Arthur.
A. Z., pseud. see Z., A. pseud.
A. Z., pseud. see Gales, Benjamin. supposed author
A——r Z——h, pseud. see Z——h, A——r, pseud.
A.——Z., pseud. 100774
A Abraham Lincoln. (72971)
A Arthur Dillon. 20170, 85807
A Atalanta. 88832
A, B, C, des Chretiens. (11497)
A, B, C, of religion. (46211)
A batalha de Campo-Grande. 88731
A bord et a terre. 15411
A cantora brazileira. 88802
A caca no Brazil. 7546
A comedia constitucional. 88733
A constitucao de Portugal. 38387
A coroa e a emancipacao do elemento servil. 81110
A crise de lavoura. 88735
A. D. P. E. P. 23580
A Dakota nyelv. 33832
A deos omnipotente. 98708
A devocion del Bachiller Miguel Sanchez Presbitero. 76289
A Don Francisco de Roxas y Sandoual. (24317), 93311
A donzalla da Mangueira. 81300
A Escravidao no Brasil. 60873
A fidelidade Maranhense. 24259
A garganta do inferno. 29237
A gloria dos brasileiros. 22807
A gloria y loor de Dios. note after 27585, 40960, note after 47850
A gratidao Parnambucana ao seu bemfeitor. 47860
A gratidao Parnambucana o seu Bemfeitor. 17952
A hildago. 106222
A ihreja no Brazil. 98828
A ilha de Fernando de Noronha. 72773
A J. B. Louvet. 58164
A Javier Little, homme de couleur. 39611
A Iesu Christo S. N. 36133
A Jose Francisco Barrundia. 24325
A Justicia. 7506
A la Chambre de Pairs. 5653
A la Chambre de Pairs. Petition additionnelle. 5655
A la Chine. 17033
A la Convention Nationale. 39871, 40930, 87124, 99739
A la Convention Nationale, sur les derniers evenemens. 15908
A la grata memoria de Iturbide. 99712
A la grata memoria de Iturbide. Segunda parte. 99712
A la magestad catholica del rey nuestro senor. (74854)
A la memoire de Mme Faubert. 12881
A la memoria de Morazan. 50527
A la mer. 69017
A la nacion. (49408), 64877, 99241
A la nacion Espanola. 48508
A la nacion Espanola el Pensador del Peru. 38782
A la nacion Guatemalana. 98379
A la societe des amis de la Convention Nationale. 87113
A la societe des amis de la liberte & de l'egalite. 87125

A la Zoutmans victorie. 106379
A l'Abri, or the tent pitch'd. 104504, 104509
A las Camaras del Congreso. 56374, 95106
A las cortes constituyentes. 85711
A las ilustres victimas del Sur. 99695
A las reverendas madres preladas. 55934
A l'Assemblee Nationale. 75048, 93792, 93815
A l'assomption et la conspiration para-guayenne. 58528
A leur patrie a ses representans. 40181
A libertade no Brasil. 47455
A los Colombianos. 96351
A los Cubanos. 29047
A los cvras benificaidos. 74863
A los habitantes de esta capital. 98859
A los habitantes de la isla. 36417
A los habitantes de los pueblos del Sur. 98860
A los habitantes de ultramar. (70383)
A los hijos del 27 de Febrero. 75046
A los Honorables el Senado. 70168
A los Ives. diputados y senadores. 48257
A los liberales de corazon. 42106
A los libres del Nuevo Mundo. 98120
A los manes de Rivadavia. 71607
A los Mexicanos. 76733
A los pensadores de Venezuela. Num. I°. 98868
A los pueblos de Centro-America. 55160
A los pueblos del Salvador. 76189
A los Salvadorenos. 65346
A los semi-eruditos. 94342
A los sensatos y ciudadanos pacificos. 97049
A los Venezolanos. 87257
A los VV. y en Christo amados PP. Pro-vinciales. 98718
A luneta magica. 43213
A mes compatriotes. 5652
A mes concitoyens . . . Haytiens! 98666
A MM. les Commissaires Nationaux Civils. 46950
A messieurs les electeurs de la Division de Rougemont. 19767
A M. M. les membres de la Chambre des Deputes. 4513
A Messieurs les Membres de la Chambre de Deputes. 73508
A Messire Iaqves Amproux. 72314
A mis compatriotas. 73856
A mis conciudadanos. 41141
A missao paranhos e a paz do Uruguay. 88772
A Monseigneur le Controlleur General. 40126
A monseignevr Monseignevr dv Vair. 77952
A M. de Lac Charriere. 5653
A M. Dupin, depute de la Nievre. 5652
A M. J. K. Polk, President des Etats-Unis. 3706
A M. le baron de Mackau. 5652
A M. Washington, President des Etats-Unis. 101723
A mulher a familia e a civilisacao. 81109
A mulher perante a historia. 88796
A N. R. mo P. M. Fr. Ivan de Lvzriaga. 76007
A nostre ame & feal conseiller. 42389
A nova phase. 88736
A nuestros compatriotas. 98022
A opiniao e a corora por Philemon. 88738
A parte de los veynte. . . [y un libros rituales] 96213
A Paul Alliot, Maire de Levroux. (58163)
A posteridade. 7617

A primavera: cantata. 99734
A propos de la guerre contre le Paraguay. (44340)
A propos d'un articule du journal "Le Figaro." 76522
A questao financeira em 1856. 47822
A. S. A. R. le Prince de Joinville. Le tremblement de terre. 38460
A salvacao do Brasil. 22511
A ses collegues de la Chambre des Deputes. 38583
A ses collegues du corps legislatif. 87126
A ses collegues, membres des deux Conseils. 87122
A ses compatriotas. 38718
A ses concitoyens. 39286
A ses concitoyens de la ville de Cap. 96346
A ses concitoyens des parties de l'Ouest et du Sud. 41140
A su censores. 94343
A sua Alteza Real o Principe Regente nosso Senhor. 98709
A Suas Altezas Reaes. 57897
A succedaneum to the grand Theriaca Andromachi. 30785
A sus comitentes. 76209
A sus compatriotas. 8782, 30412, 38717, 76731, 76732, 94225
A sus conciudadanos. 15160, 35544, 50228
A sus fieles habitantes. 67101
A sus habitantes, Abril 18 de 1854. 76160
A todo el mundo entero dice la Habana. 29460
A todos los corregidores. 98795
A todos que habitan las islas, y el vasto contiente de la America Espanola. 96118
A todos que habitan las islas y el vasto contiente de las Americas. 48270
A todos su habitantes. 98861
A todos sus habitantes pas y salud. (67080)
A todos sus habitantes salud y paz. (67080)
A tomada de Cayana pelos Portuguezes aos Francezes. 96138
A tous les bons Francais. 96349
A tous les Francais de Saint-Domingue. 87114
A tous presens et aduenir. 75015
A travers l'Amerique Central. 4580
A travers l'Amerique du Sud. 18241
A travers l'Amerique par Julius Froebel. 25993
A travers l'Atlantique. 58979
A travers les Etats-Unis. 81306
A un militar. 97048
A Venezuela. 44899
A voz da verdade de sancta Igreja catholica. 76330
Aa, Pieter van der, 1659-1733. 3, 127, 3960, 4806, 4807, 4850, 5073, 5905, (6036), (10690), 10813, (11608), 12528, 17874, 20014, 20856, 22329, 25062, 25998, 26367, (30154), 30297, 31353, 31362, 31551, 31552, 32805, 39910, 44666, (67556), 77683, 82817, 82818, 82822, 82838, 82853, 82854, 86427, 86428, 90056, 90057, 95332, note be-fore 96440, 99281, 100847, 1st note after 103943
Aan de Hoog Mog. Heeren Staaten Generaal. 102889A
Aan de lesser. (20593), note after 98474
Aan de Seconde Kamer aangaande de Koloni-satie in Suriname. 67993
Aan den Eerwaarden D°. Joannes Leydt. (71602)

Aan het volk van Nederland. 52219
Aan 't Volk van Nederland. 52220
Aan zihne medereeders. 68631
Aanbiddelyke wegens Gods. 98491
Aanhangsel behelzende een reyze.
(10757), 31360, 63706
Aankomst van Jean d'Ezquebel ter
Bevolking van Jamaica. 31556
Aanleiding tot de regte gebruik van he
compas. 31731
Aanmerkelyke voyagie gedaan na 't gedeelde
van Noorder America. 4806, 31362
Aanmerkens-waardige voyagien. 90057,
99281
Aanmerking over den Koophandel en het
Geldt. 39307
Aanmerkinge op de Briev van een
Amsterdams Koopman. 99757
Aanmerkinge wegens de cultuur der
heidegronden. 69632
Aanmerkingen op de sware aardbevinge
geweest den 18 Sept. (41077)
Aanmerkingen op eene verhandeling
betreffende de kolonie Suriname.
93849, 98822
Aanmerkingen over de gewigtigheid der
staatsomwenteling in Noord-Amerika.
(65451)
Aanmerkingen over den aart der burgerlyke
Vryheid. 65445, 65455
Aanmerkingen van eener Reiziger. 7500
Aanmerkingen van Johann Reinhold Forster.
(31184)
Aanmerkingen van Will. Penn Sec.,
Quaker. 30708
Aanmerkingen wegens Noord-America.
106, 102647
Aanmerklyk verhaal van een zonderling
werk. 7341
Aanpryzende Voorrede van de Gecommitteerde
des Classis van Amsteldam. (77643)
Aanspraak van den Generaal Washington.
5361, 101777
Aanteekening gehouden op het schip de
Vrouw Maria. 62799
Aanteekeningen betrekkelijk de kolonie
Suriname. 31225, note before
93848
Aanteekeningen en Brieven van de gedagten
Heer Melton. 47472
Aanteekeningen en een voorbericht. 62424
Aanteekeningen, gehouden gedurende mijn
verblijf in de West-Indien. (40031)
Aanteekeningen gehouden op eene Reis om
de Wereld. 97052
Aanteekeningen op mijne reis om de
wereld. 35820
Aanteekeningen op vorenstaande reize van
G. Willinck. 104497
Aanteekeningen van Dr. M. A. N. Rovers.
58739
Aar i Groenland. 35507
Aar i Utah. 34723
Aarde en hare bewoners volgens. 106334
Aardenburg, of de onbekende volkplanting
in Zuid-Amerika. 49827
Aardrijks- en natuurkundige beschrijving
van Kantschatka. 38300
Aardrijkskundig handboek. 74752
Aaron, A Slave pseud?? 41041,
(82009)-82010
Aaron's history. 41041, (82009)-82010
Ab Amana, Nicolao. see Amana,
Nicolao ab.
Ab Orto, Garcia. see Orta, Garcia de,
16th cent.

Ab Isselt, Michaelis. see Isselt,
Michaelis ab.
Ab inclinatione Romani Imperii. 74659
Aba reta y caray ey baecue Tupa upe
ynemboaguiye uca hague Pay de
la Comp.a de Iha. 74029
Abad, Diego Jose. supposed author
106237
Abad Queipo, Manuel. see Queipo,
Manuel Abad, Bp. of Michoacan.
Abad y Lasserra, Inigo. 6, 66594,
98367
Abad y Queipo, Manuel de. see Queipo,
Manuel Abad, Bp. of Michoacan.
Abanderung der Constitution. (36269)
Abanico con visos de Espejo. 75769
Abarca, Joseph Mariano de. see Mariano
de Abarca, Joseph.
Abarca, Nicolas Blanco. 76161
Abarca de Bolea, Ambrosio Funes
Villapando, Conde de Ricla. 29454,
(71240)
see also Cuba. Gobernador,
1763-1765 (Abarca de Bolea)
Abarca y Tiendra, Geronymo Chacon.
(16146)
Abascal y Sousa, Jose Fernandez de.
44541, (68243)
see also Peru (Viceroyalty) Virrey,
1806 - 1816 (Abascal y Sousa)
Abattoirs. 19823
Abbad, Inigo. see Abad y Lasserra,
Inigo.
Abbadie, J. 4931-4934
Abbay, Thomas. 82832
Abbaye des Vignerons. 16437
Abbe Brasseur and his labors. 7441
Abbeville, Adrien Sanson d'. see Sanson
d'Abbeville, Adrien, d. 1708.
Abbeville, Claude d'. 4-5, 13505, 106227
Abbeville, Guillaume Sanson d'. see
Sanson d'Abbeville, Guillaume, d.
1703.
Abbeville, Nicolas Sanson d'. see Sanson
d'Abbeville, Nicolas, 1600-1667.
Abbeville, Nicolas Sanson d'. see Sanson
d'Abbeville, Nicolas, 1626-1648.
Abbeville Court House, S. C. Anti-tariff
Meeting, 1827. see Anti-tariff
meeting, Abbeville Court House, S. C.,
1827.
Abbeville District, S. C. Anti-tariff
meeting, 1828. 87914
Abbeville District, S. C. Citizens.
Petitioners 47658
Abbey, Father. pseud. see Seccome,
John, 1708-1793.
Abbey, Matthew. pseud. see Seccome,
John, 1708-1793.
Abbey, R. 88403-88404
see also Southern Methodist
Publishing House. Agent.
Abbildung der indianischen Niederlassung.
86874
Abbildung Nordamericanischer Lander und
Eingebohrner Wilden. 55453
Abbildung verschiedener Fische schlangen
Insecten. 11512
Abbildungen zu Assal. 57819
Abbildungen zur Naturgeschichte
Brasiliens. 47011
Abbot, -------, fl. 1753. (1838)
Abbot, -------, fl. 1850. 19909
Abbot, Abiel. 8-16, 18, 32127, 3d note
after 96123, 97257, 101686
Abbot, Abiel, fl. 1847. 19

Abbot, C. G.   85010, 85015
    see also Smithsonian Institution.
    Assistant Secretary.
Abbot, Daniel.   20
Abbot, Edward F.   plaintiff
    21006
Abbot, Ephraim.   19
Abbot, Ezra.   ed.   76852
Abbot, Ezra, Jr.   10136
Abbot, G. J.   (11866)
Abbott, George, Abp. of Canterbury
    21
Abbot, Henry L.   (33797), 69946
Abbot, Hull.   22-23
Abbot, Jean.   see Abbot, John.
Abbot, Jeffra.   82832, note after 92664,
    2d note after 100510
Abbot, Joel, USN, complainant   5465
Abbot, Joel, USN, defendant at court
    martial   24, 96807, 1st note
    after 101000
Abbot, John.   25, 82789, (82789A)
Abbot, John, of Westford, Mass.
    103030
Abbot, Moses.   (16628)
Abbot Alainval.   see Deslisle de la
    Drevetiere, Louis Francois.
Abbot Collegiate Institution for Young
    Ladies, New York.   (54199)
Abbot's geography.   21
Abbotsford.   35141
Abbott, --------   27863
Abbott, Abbott A.   26-27
Abbott, Austin.   28
Abbott, Charles.   see Colchester, Charles
    Abbott, 2d Baron.
Abbott, G. D.   ed.   69352
Abbott, J. ed.   69352
Abbott, J.   29-30
Abbott, Jacob.   31-34, 25610, 51181
Abbott, John Stevens Cabot.   35-41
Abbott, Josiah G. 55049, 70996
Abbott, Lyman.   70121
Abbott, Nehemiah.   42-43
Abbott, Orrin.   supposed author   86269
Abbott, Simon C.   44
Abbott Lawrence.   (39344)
Abbreviations of some few of the many
    (later and former) testimonys from
    the inhabitants of New-Jersey.
    53031
Abbring, H. J.   7
Abby, Thomas.   82832, note after 92664,
    2d note after 100510
Abdalla the Moor, and the Spanish knight.
    5549
Abdallah and Sebat.   84137
Abdruck aus dem Bremer Handelsblatt.
    93771
Abdruck einiger wahrhafften Berichte aus
    Germanton.   27153
Abduction and murder of William Morgan.
    97955, note after 103826
Abduction of Mary Ann Smith.   46901
Abduction of William Morgan.   4919
Abdy, Edward Strutt, 1791-1846.   45-46
Abdy, Matthew.   pseud.   see Seccombe,
    John.   Supposed Author
Abecedaire Haytien.   (29563)
Abeille, J.   47
L'Abeille Americaine, journal historique.
    48
La abeja.   94191, 97049
La abeja de Michoacan.   (63971)
Abeja republicana.   61132, 76157
Abel, Henry J.   49
Abel, Twarns.   22867

Abel being dead yet speaketh.   41005,
    55881, 55885
Abelin, Jean Philippe.   3, 50, (8784),
    16962, 19952, (26070), note
    before 90036, 92665
Abell, Truman.   52681
Abenaki Indians.   see Abnaki Indians.
Abenaki Indians; their treaties of 1713
    & 1717.   37710
Abenaqui Springs.   51
Abencerage.   Melanges litteraires.   12248
Abencerages.   12248
Les abencerrages.   12248
Abenteuer des Captain Bonneville.   35127
Abenteuer des Letzten der Abenceragen.
    (12250)
Abenteuer eines deutschen Auswanderers.
    20129
Abenteuer im fernen Sudwesten.   (4724)
Abenteuer in den Gebirgen und Waldern
    von Canada.   35133
Abentheuer des Ambrosius Dalfinger.
    38057
Abentheuerinnen im Lande der Esquimaux.
    22845
Abentheuerliche Ereignisse aus dem Leben
    der ersten Ansiedler.   65721
Aberdeen, George Hamilton Gordon, 4th
    Earl of, 1784-1860.   50859
Aberdeen, Bishop of.   see Skinner, John,
    Bishop of Aberdeen, 1744-1816.
Aberdeen, Scotland.   Court of Sessions.
    104482
Aberdeen, Scotland.   Magistrates.
    104482
Aberdeen Anti-slavery Society.   81712
Aberdeen University.   84677
Abercrombie, James.   52-53
Abercrombie, Sir Ralph.   44131
Abercrombie, Robert.   54-55, 50462,
    58896
Abernethy, Andrew.   (63509)
Abert, J. W.   56-59
Abert, John J.   (12500), 12508, 45098
Abertura do Amazonas.   67539
Abe's policy.   8447
Abgerissene Nachrichten.   6015
Abhandlung der naturforsch. Gesellschaft
    zu Halle.   9350-9351
Abhandlung der K. Bayerischen Akademie
    der Wissenschaften.   99363
Abhandlung uber dem Kropf.   3814
Abhandlung: Ueber die altesten Karten des
    neuen Continents.   (27261)
Abhandlung uber die vermeinte Zauberkraft.
    1287, (3818)
Abhandlung von der sitten der Regierungsart.
    32547
Abhandlung von Dr. C. F. Ph.   von Martius.
    44999
Abhandlung von eben demselben uber die
    Nordwestkuste von Amerika.   47264
Abhandlung, vorgetragen vor der Nationalen
    Sonntags-Convention zu Saratoga.
    77492
Abhandlungen der Konigl.   Akademie der
    Wissenschaften zu Berlin.   9521-9531
Abhandlungen der philosophisch-historischen
    klasse der koniglichen Akademie der
    Wissenschaften zu Berlin.   60
Abhandlungen uber die Kolonien uberhaupt.
    38231
Abienza, -------- d'.   see D'Abienza, --------.
Ability of the government to redeem its
    paper.   91016
Ability to, and fidelity in, the ministry
    derived from Christ.   8938

Abimelech Coody. pseud. see Verplanck,
Gulian Crommelin.
Abingdon, Willoughby Bertie, 4th Earl of,
1740-1799. 61-67, (5006)-5007, 9291,
11158, (11767), 41293
Abingdon, Md. Cokesbury College. see
Cokesbury College, Abingdon, Md.
Abingdon, Mass. Overseers of the Poor.
68
Abingdon, Mass. School Committee. 68
Abingdon, Mass. Selectmen. 68
Abingdon Baptist Association. see
Baptists. Massachusetts. Abingdon
Baptist Association.
Abingdon collection of sacred musick.
64022
Abingdon, Mass. Rev. H. D. Walker's
address. 69
Abinoji aki Tibajimouin. 57080
Abinodjiag Omasinaiganiwan. 57881
Abiponer in Sudamerika. 78011
Abismo de la gracia. 76161
Abispa de Chilpancingo. 50599
Abjir, drame en 4 actes. 5387
Ablancourt, Francois Fremont d'. see
D'Ablancourt, Francois Fremont.
Able and faithful ministers very needful.
103732
Ablijn, Cornelis. see Ablyn, Cornelis.
Ablijn, Jean Philippe. see Abelin, Jean
Philippe.
Ablin, Claude d'. see Dablon, Claude.
Ablyn, Cornelis. tr. 16961, 34107,
note after 99383C
Abnaki Indians. Treaties, etc. 37710
Abnormal address to the pupils of the
normal school. (69425)
Abogado. pseud.
Dialogo entre un abogado y un
capitan. 76747
Abogado. pseud.
Patronato dialogo entre un Cura y
un Abogado. 59113
Abogado de la imprenta. pseud. (59512)
Abogado de los tribunales nacionales.
pseud. 49454
Abolicion de la esclavitud en el Peru.
61073
Abolicion de la esclavitud en Puerto-Rico.
85710
Abolicion en Cuba. 85711
Abolicion en Puerto-Rico. 85712
Abolition a sedition. 81713
Abolition a sedition, and abolition and
colonization contrasted. 14784
Abolition and colonization contrasted.
14784
Abolition and secession. 81714-81715
Abolition and sedition. 55809
Abolition, and the relation of races. 4029
Abolition cause eventually triumphant.
(73118)
Abolition conspiracy to destroy the union.
26712, 81716-81717
Abolition de la traite des noirs. 12348
Abolition de la traite et de l'esclavage
dans les colonies francaises. 5407
Abolition de l'esclavage. 14062
Abolition de l'esclavage a la Guadeloupe.
26761
Abolition de l'esclavage, civilization du
centre de l'Afrique. 21488
Abolition de l'esclavage dans les colonies
anglaises. (81719)-81721
Abolition de l'esclavage dans les colonies
francaises. 39639

Abolition de l'esclavage, division des
terres. (81718), 100617
Abolition de l'esclavage: examen
critique. (77740)
Abolition de l'esclavage par Abraham
Lincoln. (20096)
Abolition de l'esclavage reflexions
sur le libre de M. Cochin. 27501
Abolition immediate de l'esclavage.
77745
Abolition intolerance and religious
intolerance combined. 81970
Abolition is national death. 81722
Abolition leaders convicted out of their
own mouths. 23626
Abolition of American slavery considered.
65743
Abolition of slave-trade. 36442
Abolition of slavery. (79766)
Abolition of slavery as a war measure.
82179
Abolition of slavery in Cuba and Porto
Rico. 81723
Abolition of slavery the right of the
government. 81724
Abolition of the African slave trade.
(81725)
Abolition of the [Negro] Apprenticeship.
95495
Abolition of the Negro apprenticeship,
March 30, 1838. (27530)
Abolition of the postal system. (82595)
Abolition of the slave trade. 8414
Abolition of the slave trade, a poem in
four parts. 50143
Abolition of the slave trade considered.
533
Abolition of the slave-trade in the District
of Columbia. 26126, 65915
Abolition of the slave trade; peace; and
a temperate reform. 81726
Abolition philanthropy! (81727)
Abolition scheme taken into cool and
candid consideration. 68268
Abolition schemes of Negro equality,
exposed. 71090
Abolition sermon preached by Rev. Wm.
H. Furness. 81851
Abolition Society of Delaware. see
Delaware Abolition Society.
Abolition Society of Massachusetts. see
Massachusetts Abolition Society.
Abolition Society of New Jersey. see
New Jersey Abolition Society.
Abolitionist tract. No. I. 81728
Abolition unveiled. 35700
Abolitionism exposed, corrected. 81729
Abolitionism exposed! proving that the
principles of abolitionism are
injurious to the slaves themselves.
82128
Abolitionism in its fruits. 18300
Abolitionism in its morals. 18300
Abolitionism reviewed. 40849
Abolitionism unveiled! 81730
Abolitionist. pseud.
Epitome of the West India question.
81964, 4th note after 102832
Abolitionist. pseud.
Extracts from "Remarks on Dr.
Channing's Slavery." (11920)
Abolitionist. pseud.
Few observations on the importation
of slave grown sugar. 24236
Abolitionist. pseud.
Negro's memorial. 52275

Abolitionist and colonizationist.　pseud.
　　Liberian colonization.　40927
Abolitionist and the land pirate.　82029
Abolitionist: or record of the New
　　England Anti-slavery Society.
　　52655, 81731
Abolitionist; published under the direction
　　of the British and Foreign Society
　　for the Universal Abolition of Negro
　　Slavery.　(81732)
Abolitioniste francais.　81733, 85816
Abolitionistics.　81734
Abolitionists, and their relation to the war.
　　26712
Abolitionist's catechism.　52275
Abolitionist's library.　90429, 103812
Abominations of Mormonism exposed.
　　29858
Aboriginal monuments of the state of New
　　York.　85072, 89950
Aboriginal names of New York.　54476
Aboriginal port-folio.　30813
Aboriginal races of North America.
　　20866, 20868, 20873
Aboriginal shell-money.　90931
Aborigines, a drama.　62447
Aborigines' friend.　(14687)
Aborigines or Indian natives of New
　　England.　95151
Aborigines Protection Society.　(14687),
　　33540, 34612, 34649, 34675
Aborigines Protection Society.　Committee.
　　(51124)
Aborigines Protection Society.　Sub-
　　Committee.　10469
About 12 o'Clock his excellency the
　　governor was pleased . . .　100504
About woman, love, and marriage.
　　77174
Above fac-simile of a rare copy of the
　　original.　105963
Abraca, J. M. de.　24157
Abrahall, Chandos Hoskyns.　71
Abrahall, John Hoskyns.　72
Abraham.　pseud.
　　Acts of the elders.　see Norwood,
　　Abraham.　supposed author
Abraham.　pseud.
　　Revelations.　70160, 103445
Abraham Africanus I.　(41163)
Abraham and Lot.　105246
Abraham Bishop unmask'd.　5598, 102396
Abraham evangelico.　76173
Abraham in arms.　56206
Abraham Lincoln.　14061, 40205, 41164,
　　83959, 84064, 84067
Abraham Lincoln: a eulogy delivered, at
　　Anamisa, Iowa.　30117
Abraham Lincoln.　A memoir.　41169
Abraham Lincoln.　A memorial address.
　　21817, (51633)
Abraham Lincoln.　A study.　41165
Abraham Lincoln.　A threnody.　41166
Abraham Lincoln and Ulysses S. Grant.
　　41170, 72867
Abraham Lincoln, assassinated at
　　Washington.　(41192)
Abraham Lincoln, born February 12,
　　1809.　30161
Abraham Lincoln, der Befreier der Neger-
　　Sclaven.　32411
Abraham Lincoln, der grosse Staatsman.
　　28999
Abraham Lincoln der Wiederhersteller der
　　Nordamerikanischen Union.　(38877)
Abraham Lincoln, foully assassinated
　　April 14, 1865.　41167, note before
　　94542

Abraham Lincoln geschetst in zijn leven
　　en daden.　2651
Abraham Lincoln, his great funeral
　　cortege.　64767
Abraham Lincoln:　his life and its lessons.
　　41219, 95516
Abraham Lincoln:　his life and public
　　services.　30157
Abraham Lincoln.　His life, public
　　services, death, and great funeral
　　cortege.　64768
Abraham Lincoln, late president . . .
　　41168
Abraham Lincoln.　Military order of the
　　Loyal Legion of the United States,
　　Commandery of the State of
　　Pennsylvania.　84508
Abraham Lincoln.　President of the
　　United States.　84508
Abraham Lincoln, prisoner at the bar.
　　(41234)
Abraham Lincoln, private citizen.　34180
Abraham Lincoln.　Proceedings at the
　　Athenaeum Club.　(51640)
Abraham Lincoln.　Rede beim
　　Trauergottesdienst in der Zions
　　Kirche zu Philadelphia.　88842
Abraham Lincoln sa naissance, sa vie,
　　sa mort.　2056
Abraham Lincoln.　Sa vie, son caractere,
　　son administration.　48978
Abraham Lincoln, sein Leben und sein
　　offentlichen Dienste.　30158
Abraham Lincoln.　Sein leben, wirken
　　und Sterhen.　41169
Abraham Lincoln: the just magistrate.
　　9133
Abraham Lincoln.　The value to the
　　nation of his exalted character.
　　10844
Abraham Lincoln.　Two discourses.　47177
Abraham Lincoln's character.　2562
Abraham Lincoln's character, sketched
　　by English travellers.　8376
Abraham Panther.　pseud.　see Panther,
　　Abraham.　pseud.
Abraham Rogers Offne Thur zu dem
　　verborgenen Heydenthum.　72603
Abraham the passenger.　21665, 23023
Abraham Weatherwise.　pseud.　see
　　Weatherwise, Abraham.　pseud.
Abrahami Ortelii Antverpiani Thesavrvs
　　geograhicvs.　(57709)
Abrahami Ortelii Geographiae veteris
　　tabvlae aliqvot.　66497
Abrahami Ortelii Theatri orbis terrarvm
　　parergon.　66494
Abrahami Saurii Statte-Buch.　77201
Abrahams, -------.　89204
Abraham's humble intercession for Sodom.
　　103704
Abraham's offering up his son Isaac.
　　103573
Abram Lincoln and South Carolina.　36059
Abramo Lincoln com' ei visse, qual'
　　opera compie.　9166, (41172)
Abramo Lincoln e la guerra fra i Federali
　　ed i Confederati degli Stati-Uniti.
　　59171
Abramo Lincoln presidente della Rupublica
　　Stati-Uniti d'America.　41171
Abrams, Isaac.　supposed author
　　97118, 97273
Abranches, Antonio Manuel do Rego.　see
　　Rego Abranches, Antonio Manuel do.
Abrantes, M. de.　73
Abrege chronologique.　3656

Abrege de la foi catholique. 11502
Abrege de la geographie moderne. 62959
Abrege de la requeste presentee au Roy. 39609
Abrege de la revolution de l'Amerique Angloise. 9080, 21037, 29197, 100776
Abrege de la vie d'aucunes filles de S. Vrsvle. 38619, 98167
Abrege de la vie de Franklin. 25585, 78116
Abrege de la vie de la B. Soevr Rose de Sainte Marie. 24227, 73176
Abrege de l'histoire de l'Oncle Tom. 92537
Abrege de l'histoire des decouvertes et conquetes de l'Amerique. 89461
Abrege de l'histoire des establissements et du commerce des deux Indes. 68082
Abrege de l'histoire des Indiens. 3246
Abrege de l'histoire des revolutions de l'Amerique Meridionale. 21124
Abrege de l'histoire des revolutions de l'Amerique Septentrionale. 21125
Abrege de l'histoire des traites de paix. 38201
Abrege de l'histoire du Canada. 61005
Abrege de l'histoire du Canada depuis sa decouverte jusqu'a 1840. 26676
Abrege de l'histoire generale des voyages. 9846, 22023, 38632
Abrege d'histoire naturelle. 73491
Abrege de l'histoire et philosophique. 68082
Abrege de tous les voyages au pole du Nord, depuis les Freres Zeno. (39620)
Abrege de tous les voyages au pole du Nord, depuis Nicolo Zeno. (39620)
Abrege de tout ce qui s'y est passe. 47929
Abrege des fruits aguis. 74
Abrege des plantes usuelles de Saint Domingue. 64730
Abrege des preuves donnees devant un comite de la chambre des communes. 81735
Abrege des principaux traites. 43889
Abrege des voyages modernes. 9846
Abrege historique . . . 36812, 2d note after 97689, 4th note after 97689
Abrege historique des navigations. 24748
Abrege historique des troubles de la Martinique. (20671)
Abrege historique et chronologique des principaux voyages. (2814)
Abreu, Antonio Joseph Alvarez de, Marquis de la Regalia. 76
Abreu, Joao Capistrano de. see Capistrano de Abreu, Joao.
Abreu, Juan de. 48267
Abreu de Galineo, Juan de. 79, note after 27546
Abreu e Lima, J. J. de. 78
Abreu Medeiros, F. L. d'. see Medeiros, F. L. d'Abreu.
Abreu y Bertodano, Joseph Antonio. 77
Abreu y Valdes, Miguel Anselmo Alvarez de, Bp. 75, 58297
    see also Antequera (Diocese) Bishop (Abreu y Valdes)
Abridged blue book. 20325
Abridged history of the principal treaties of peace. 26229
Abridged history of the United States. 104041

Abridged history of the United States. For the use of schools. (31763)
Abridged life of Thomas Pain. [sic] 57169
Abridged memoir of . . . George Whitefield. 103614
Abridged reports of General De Peyster. 19634
Abridged statement of differences with the Detroit and Milwaukee Railroad Company. (33280)
Abridged view of the alien question unmasked. 14436
Abridgement see Abridgment
Abridgment and collection of the acts of assembly. 5643
Abridgment of all the public acts of assembly, of Virginia. 100387
Abridgement [sic] from the New-England psalm-singer. (5419)
Abridgment of Captain Cook's last voyage. (16257), 37133
Abridgment of . . . his [i. e., Anghiera's] 5. 6. 7. and 8. decades. 1562
Abridgment of Humboldt's statistical essay on New Spain. (33716)
Abridgment of Mr. David Brainerd's journal. 7339
Abridgment of Mr. Edwards' civil and commercial history. (21904)
Abridgment of Mr. Hopkins' historical memoirs. 32947, 2d note after 102507
Abridgment [sic] of Portlock's and Dixon's voyage. 20365
Abridgement [sic] of several acts and clauses. 80
Abridgment of Sir Walter Raleigh's history of the world. 67542-67544
Abridgment of Smellie's practice of midwifery. 82252
Abridgment of such of the colonial laws. 23301, (81744)
Abridgment of the acts of assembly passed in the Island of St. Christopher. 74007
Abridgment [of the acts of assembly passed in the Island of Jamaica.] 35617
Abridgment of the acts of assembly, passed in the Island of Montserrat. (50224)
Abridgment of the acts of congress now in force. 34738
Abridgment of the American gazetteer. 50922
Abridgment of the arts and sciences. 83403
Abridgment of the Assembly's catechism. 46534
Abridgment of the criminal law of the United States. 40798
Abridgment of the debates of congress. 4783
Abridgment of the English military discipline. 49999
Abridgment of the evidence delivered before a select committee. 93600
Abridgment of the general history of the Baptist denomination in America. 4646
Abridgment of the history of New England. 207
Abridgement [sic] of the history of the United States. 104041
Abridgement [sic] of the laws in force and use in her majesty's plantations. 81, note before 87563, note after 100381

Abridgment of the laws in force in Jamaica.
(35609)
Abridgment of the laws of Jamaica.
35611
Abridgment of the laws of Jamaica, etc.
(35615)
Abridgment of the laws of Jamaica, in
manner of an index. (35610)
Abridgment of the laws of Maryland,
now in force. 45043
Abridgment of the laws of Pennsylvania.
59769
Abridgment of the laws of Pennsylvania,
from 1700. 59768, 60652
Abridgment of the laws of the province
of the Massachusetts-Bay. 45700
Abridgment of the laws of the United
States. 28421
Abridgement [sic] of the laws of Virginia
compiled in 1694. 100381
Abridgement [sic] of the life [of Samuel
Thomson.] 95567
Abridgment of the life of the late reverend
and learned Dr. Cotton Mather.
36038
Abridgment of the minutes of the evidence,
taken before a Committee of the
whole House, to whom it was referred
to consider of the slave trade, 1790.
81736, 81737
Abridgment of the minutes of the evidence,
taken before a committee of the
whole House, to whom it was
referred to consider of the slave
trade, 1791. 81738
Abridgment of the practice of midwifery.
(82253)
Abridgement [sic] of the publick laws of
Virginia. 5119, 100382
Abridgment of the public permanent laws
of Virginia. 100405
Abridgment of two discourses. (59317)
Abridgment of universal geography.
(73602)
Abris von Nordamerika. 69142
Abriss der Geschichte der Kaiser-reichs.
(31258)
Abriss der Gesetze betreffend die
Sklaverei in Verschiedenen Staaten.
93096
Abriss der physicalischen Erdbeschrei-
bung. 4853A
Abriss der Staatsverfassung der vornehmsten
Lander in America. 3987
Abriss einer Geschichte der
geographischen Entdeckungen. 4853
Abrisz der merkwurdigsten neuen Welt-
Begebenheiten enthaltend for 1784
bie Geschichte der Revolution von
Nord-Amerika. 89755
Abroad and at home. 3794
Abrogation of the seventh commandment.
81739
Abrrege des annales ecclesiastiqves et
·politiqves de l'ancien. 12294
Ab-sa-ra-ka Home of the Crows. (11061)
Abschieds Addresse an das Volk der
Vereinigten Staaten. 101670, 101672,
101673, 101676, 101682
Abschieds-Rede an seine lutherische
Gemeinden in Pennsylvanien. 100956
Abschiedsadresse [an das Volk der
Vereinigten Staaten] 9672
Abschrifft etlicher Brieffe. 72321
Absconditorum a constitutione mundi.
64521
Absence of the Comforter described and
lamented. (32306)

Absolon, John. illus. 41908, 41922
Absolute dependence on God. 91115
Absolute equality of all men before
the law. (20097)
Absolute necessity of salvation through
Christ. 104929
Absolute submission to a rebel
conspiracy. 39514
Abstract and argument of Platt Smith
for defendant. 83725
Abstract, exhibiting the condition of
the banks, 1853. 46108
Abstract exhibiting the condition of the
banks in Massachusetts. 45540
Abstract exhibiting the condition of the
banks in Rhode-Island. 70496
Abstract exhibiting the condition of the
institutions for savings in Rhode-
Island. 70496
Abstract exhibiting the condition of the
institutions for savings of
Massachusetts. 45540
Abstract from a report of a committee.
85957
Abstract from David Paul Brown's
speech. 8466
Abstract from the journal of the Rev'd
Mr. Frisbie. 103212
Abstract from the returns of agricultural
societies in Massachusetts. 45541
Abstract from the returns of banks in
the commonwealth. 59770
Abstract from the statement of the
condition of the several banks in
Connecticut. 15676
Abstract log. 46974
Abstract of a bill for uniting the legislative
councils and assemblies. 10474
Abstract of a correspondence with the
executive. 78403
Abstract of a journal kept by E. Bacon.
81742
Abstract of a journal of E. Bacon.
2641, 81740, 81741
Abstract of a letter from a person of
eminency and worth. 78197
Abstract of a letter from Thomas
Paskell. 58991
Abstract of a letter to Cotton Mather.
46932
Abstract of a number of sermons preached.
104275
Abstract of a paper on gold mining in
Nova Scotia. 31936
Abstract of a printed newspaper. 6377
Abstract of a report on Illinois coal.
34252
Abstract of a report on the coal and
iron estate. (60219)
Abstract of a report on the practicability
of forming a communication between
the Atlantic and Pacific Oceans. 50767
Abstract of a system of exercise and
instruction. 104659
Abstract of a system of military discipline.
91396
Abstract of all the discoveries. 20404
Abstract of all the statutes. 31045
Abstract of an address by Edward Crane.
17397
Abstract of an address delivered before
the Young Men's Christian Association,
of Chicago. 77563
Abstract of Bp. Berkeley's treatise on tar
water. 4876
Abstract of captain Middleton's journal.
20404
Abstract of consul Dean's narrative. 104686

Abstract of criminal laws of Massachusetts. 45542

Abstract of drafts of members. (15224)

Abstract of each preceding census. 11667

Abstract . . . of eighth annual report [of the Society for the Promotion of Collegiate and Theological Education at the West.] 85911

Abstract of evidence. (78878)

Abstract of exports. 53430

Abstract of George Keith's letter to Thomas Maule. 62420

Abstract of his [i.e. George Washington's] last will and testament. 101636

Abstract of historical events. 70497

Abstract of land certificates. 95045

Abstract of laws and government. 17043

Abstract of laws regulating state and municipal elections. 56859

Abstract of laws relating to the assessment and collection of taxes. 54014

Abstract of magnetical observations. (37898)

Abstract of manufacturing establishments. 53431

Abstract of Massachusetts school returns. (5312)

Abstract of military discipline. 5857

Abstract of . . . ninth annual report [of the Society for the Promotion of Collegiate and Theological Education at the West.] 85911

Abstract of Philippine mining laws and regulations. 84529

Abstract of private acts and joint resolutions. 95000

Abstract of remarks of William D. Northend. 55784

Abstract of returns of criminal cases [of Massachusetts.] 1st note after (19871)

Abstract of returns of inspectors and keepers of jails. 45543

Abstract of returns of joint-stock companies. 45549

Abstract of returns showing the amount of money. 43895

Abstract of royal edicts. 82

Abstract of school returns. 45544

Abstract of several clauses of the acts of Parliament. 6036, 97160

Abstract of some passages of divers letters. 41762, 63318

Abstract of Stirling's rhetorick. 80654

Abstract of the argument . . . , made by Gerrit Smith. (82596)

Abstract of the argument on the fugitive slave law. 82597

Abstract of the arguments of . . . the petitioners. 12860

Abstract of the art of gunnery. 82841-82843

Abstract of the Assiento. 40319, 1st note after 102785

Abstract of the author's [i.e., Thomas Hooker's] life. 32846

Abstract of the bill, entitled An act for settling and better regulation of the militia. (50851)

Abstract of the bill of mortality for the town of Salem. 75623

Abstract of the British West Indian statutes. 81743, note before 102812

Abstract of the by-laws of the town of Boston. 6611

Abstract of the case of the Royal African Company. 73756

Abstract of the case of the West India Dock Company. 31684-31685

Abstract of the cases of capture made by France. 83

Abstract of the cause. 103162

Abstract of the census of Canada. 10400

Abstract of the census of . . . Massachusetts. (45545)

Abstract of the census of the population. 65626

Abstract of the charter, and of the proceedings of the Society [for the Propagation of the Gospel in Foreign Parts.] 96797, 101276

Abstract of the charter, and proceedings, Feb. 1786-Feb. 1787 [of the Society for the Propagation of the Gospel in Foreign Parts.] 101468

Abstract of the charter granted to the Society for the Propagation of the Gospel in Foreign Parts. 84

Abstract of the charter of the Governour and Company of Merchants of Great Britain. 88166

Abstract of the charter [of the Society for the Propagation of the Gospel in Foreign Parts.] 103964

Abstract of the constitutions of the United States. 59771

Abstract of the criminal laws. 67061

Abstract of the currency debates. (15533)

Abstract of the decisions of the Supreme Court of Louisiana. 42251

Abstract of the decisions of the Supreme Court of Massachusetts. 65979

Abstract of the discussion upon the paper. (41693)

Abstract of the evidence contained in the report of the Lords of the Committee of Council. 23301, (81744)

Abstract of the evidence delivered before a select committee of the House of Commons. 81745-81746, 93600

Abstract of the evidence given before the committee of Privy Council. 102851

Abstract of the evidence lately taken in the House of Commons. 85

Abstract of the fifth annual report of the Newfoundland School Society. 54974

Abstract of the first annual report of the directors [of the General Theological Seminary of the Protestant Episcopal Church.] 26910

Abstract of the form of prayer. 66982, (67003)

Abstract of the general tax. 87730

Abstract of the history of the order. 22588

Abstract of the information. (81979)

Abstract of the journal of a mission to the Delaware Indians west of the Ohio. 19372, 103211

Abstract of the journal, of the Rev. J. B. Cates. 81740

Abstract of the journals of the Convention [of the Connecticut Medical Society.] 15783

Abstract of the law of March 6th, 1818. 61561

Abstract of the laws of Jamaica. 42682

Abstract of the laws of New England. 17042, 45652

Abstract of the laws of Pennsylvania. 59772

Abstract of the laws of the colony of Massachusetts. 45546

Abstract of the last official report of Sir J. P. Grant. 35605

Abstract of the life of Mr. Thumb.
96133-96134

Abstract of the loix de police. (66983)

Abstract of the Massachusetts school
returns. 44324

Abstract of the most useful and
necessary articles. 6466

Abstract of the most useful parts
of a later treatise. (44476)

Abstract of the Norfolk exercise.
45547, 104750, 104751, 104753

Abstract of the number of convicts.
45902

Abstract of the ordination prayers.
79410

Abstract of the original titles of
record. 94980

Abstract of the population and
statistics of New Jersey. (53030)

Abstract of the present French king's
edict. 25882

Abstract of the principal expeditions.
16244

Abstract of the proceedings against
the Rev. J. Smith. 82898

Abstract of the proceedings [and] list
of the members [of the Society
for the Propagation of the Gospel
in Foreign Parts.] 100900

Abstract of the proceedings at the
annual meeting of the Chamber
of Commerce of San Francisco.
76036

Abstract of the proceedings at the two
meetings. 29705

Abstract of the proceedings before
the Land Commissioners' Court.
65627

Abstract of the proceedings, Feb. 1721
[i.e. 1722]-Feb. 1722 [i.e. 1723,
of the Society for the Propagation
of the Gospel in Foreign Parts.]
102178

Abstract of the proceedings . . . for the
year ending October, 1865 [of the
Massachusetts Grand Encampment
of Knights Templars.] 38133

Abstract of the proceedings of a meeting
held by deaf-mutes. 74996, note
before 90783

Abstract of the proceedings of Dr. Bray.
7470

Abstract of the proceedings of the Anti-
Masonic State Convention of
Massachusetts. 45548

Abstract of the proceedings of the
Baptist Convention of Illinois.
(34210)

Abstract of the proceedings of the Board
of Supervisors of the County of
Rensselaer. 69633

Abstract of the proceedings of the Board
of Trustees of the General
Theological Seminary. (66153)

Abstract of the proceedings of the
[Chicago] Convention, for the
Improvement of Rivers and
Harbors. 12632

Abstract of the proceedings of the Church
Society of the Archdeaconry of
New-Brunswick. 52525

Abstract of the proceedings of the
Corporation for the Relief of
Widows and Children of Clergymen
in the Communion of the Church
of England in America. 86

Abstract of the proceedings of the
Corporation for the Relief of
Widows and Children of Clergymen
of the Protestant Episcopal Church
in Maryland. (45298)

Abstract of the proceedings of the
Corporation [of the Butler Hospital
for the Insane.] 66243

Abstract of the proceedings of the 88th
and 89th general meetings [of the
Society for Propagating the Gospel
among the Heathen.] 86172

Abstract of the proceedings of the first
annual session, . . . 1860 [of the
New Brunswick Provincial Board
of Agriculture.] 52551

Abstract of the proceedings of the Grand
Lodge in June, A. L. 5827. (53692)

Abstract of the proceedings of the Grand
Lodge of Ancient Free-Masons of
South-Carolina. 87834

Abstract of the proceedings of the Grand
Lodge of Pennsylvania. 60128

Abstract of the proceedings of the
National Lord's Day Convention.
51998

Abstract of the . . . Proceedings . . . of
the Society [for the Propagation of the
Gospel in Foreign Parts.] 90218-
90218, 103964

Abstract of the proceedings of the Society
from the 18th of February 1731, to
the 16th of February 1732. 82194

Abstract of the proceedings relative to
the Union of Free Masons in South
Carolina. 87835

Abstract of the proceedings . . . within
the year last past [of the Society
for the Propagation of the Gospel
in Foreign Parts.] 37448

Abstract of the public documents. 97901

Abstract of the quarantine laws. 53433

Abstract of the report of the joint
committee of the legislature.
59773

Abstract of the report of the Lords
Committees on the condition and
treatment of the colonial slaves.
(81747)

Abstract of the reports of the foreign
insurance companies. (70498)

Abstract of the return of paupers.
45549

Abstract of the returns and statements
of foreign insurance companies.
(45550)

Abstract of the returns from banks.
70496

Abstract of the returns of corporations.
(43896)

Abstract of the returns of insurance
companies. 45551

Abstract of the returns of meteorological
observations. 53434

Abstract of the 5th census. 11666

Abstract of the returns of the insurance
companies. (70499)

Abstract of the returns of the Overseers
of the Poor. 45552

Abstract of the returns of the public
schools. 70500

Abstract of the returns of the Selectmen.
43931

Abstract of the revenue laws of America.
91089

Abstract of the revised statutes of . . .
New York. 53432
Abstract of the same [i.e. evidence
before the House of Commons,
1790-91, respecting the slave
trade.] 23525
Abstract of the scheme of government.
(56101)
Abstract of the seventh annual report
of the Society for the Promotion
of Collegiate and Theological
Education at the West. 85911
Abstract of the several acts of
Parliament. 88167
Abstract of the several royal edicts.
17852
Abstract of the slave laws of Jamaica.
35612
Abstract of the statements of the
several banks. 45553
Abstract of the sufferings of the people
call'd Quakers. 66904
Abstract of the supplement to the reports
of the Committee of Secrecy.
88168, 88187
Abstract of the third annual report . . .
[of the National Life Insurance
Company of the United States.]
51996
Abstract of the title of John Stevens.
54495
Abstract of the valuation of real and
personal property. 68203
Abstract of the valuation of real
property in . . . Ohio. (56860)
Abstract of the voyage and discoveries
of the late Capt. G. Vancouver.
38966, 98444
Abstract of those parts of the custom
of the Viscounty and Provostship
of Paris. (66985), 67061
Abstract of transactions of the Grand
Lodge of Free . . . Masons of the
State of New York. (53692)
Abstract of Unitarian belief. 89002
Abstract, or abbreviation of some few
of the many (later and former)
testimonys from the inhabitants of
New-Jersey. 53031
Abstract or [sic] the lawes of New
England. 52595
Abstract . . . prepared by Oliver
Warner. 45963
Abstract taken out of certain Spanyardes
letters. (67551)
Abstracted Indian trust bonds. 50835
Abstracted Indian trust bonds. Report
of the select committee. 24913
Abstraction of moneys from the public
treasury. 40985
Abstracts from reports and epistles
from America. 34596
Abstracts from the annual reports of
the School Committee. 54290
Abstracts of acts of Parliament.
35612
Abstracts of calculations. (38738)
Abstracts of laws relating to army
and navy pensions. 60807
Abstracts of observations to 1855
inclusive. (74707)
Abstracts of proceedings of
Massachusetts State Council
of the Order of Sovereigns of
Industry. 88816
Abstracts of returns [from the
agricultural societies in Maine.]
43908

Abstracts of returns of assessors.
45554
Abstracts of some letters written by
Mr. Robert Rich. 70896
Abstracts of such parts of the acts
of Parliament. (1791)
Abstracts of the acts of the
legislature. 50865, 84620-84621
Abstracts of the authorities. 32968,
1st note after 97146
Abstracts of the barometer. 12078
Abstracts of the laws of the American
states. 42561
Abstracts of the observations from 1841
to 1848. 74711
Abstracts of the principal regulations. 87
Abstracts of the reports of the benevolent
societies. (12515)
Abstracts of the returns from the banks.
45555
Abstracts of the several royal edicts.
17852, (66984)
Abstracts of testimony of Charles H.
Dalton. 83856
Absurdities of immaterialism. 64949
Absurdity and blasphemy of depreciating
moral virtue. 7789
Absurdity and blasphemy of substituting
the personal righteousness of men.
64274
Abth. Handbuch der allgemeinen Geographie
und Statistik. 91197
Abth. Handbuch der Geographie und
Statistik. Brasilien. 91197
Abth. Handbuch der Geographie und
Statistik des ehemaligen spanischen
Mittel- und Sud-Amerika. 91197
Abth. Handuch der Geographie und
Statistik von Nord-Amerika. 91197
Abtruck ains lateinischen Sandtbrieues
an bapstliche Heiligkeit. 22405
abu-'Ali al-Hasan ibn-al-Haytham. see
Alhazen, 965?-1039?
Abuse of army ambulances. 6990
Abuse of pastoral influence. 91303
Abuses and scandal of some late
pamphlets. 20720, (34791), 64570
Abuses in the army. 8557
Abuses in the navy. 24657
Abuses stript and whipt. 39820, 1st
note after 94666
Abusos se radican si se toleran los
errores. 62936
Acacia les Butterfly. 2244
Academia, Rio de Janeiro. see
Rio de Janeiro. Academia.
Academia Cubana de Literatura. 74769
Acedemia de Derocho Espanol, Mexico
(City) 48520, 48649
Academia de Jurisprudencia, Caracas.
68853
Academia de Jurisprudencia, Mexico
(City) (48455)
R. Academia de la Historia, Madrid.
(10814), 24834, 38826, (44650),
47633, 47750, 51347, (52099),
57990, 73992
Academia de la Historia de Cuba.
98164, 98165
Academia de Medicina de Buenos Aires.
(8992A)
R. Academia de San Carlos de Nueva-
Espana. 68220
Academia de San Felipe Neri, Mexico
(City) 76027
Academia Imperial das Bellas Artes,
Rio de Janeiro. 71465

13

Academia Imperial das Bellas Artes,
Rio de Janeiro. Exposicao,
1862. 71465
Academia Imperiale della Scienze,
Torino. see Torino, Italy.
Academia Imperiale della
Scienze.
Academia Medico Quirurgica, Puebla,
Mex. 48210
Academia Medico-Quirurgica, Mexico
(City) Comision. 48449
Academia mexicana. (75565), 75566
Academia Nacional de S. Carlos de
Mexico. see Mexico (City)
Academia Nacional de S. Carlos
de Mexico.
Academia Real de Sciencias, Madrid.
70794
Academia Real dos Sciencias, Lisbon.
see Lisbon. Academia Real
dos Sciencias.
Academia Reale della Scienze, Torino.
see Torino, Italy. Academia
Imperiale della Scienze.
Academic addresses. 1808
Academic college and the scientific
college. 18427
Academic pioneer. 102990
Academic recreations. 14801
Academical and Theological Institution,
New Hampton, N. H. see New
Hampton, N. H. Academical and
Theological Institution.
Academical discourse. 95559
Academical education. 23271
Academician. 62661
Academician's magazine. 58927, 97799
Academiciens envoyes sous l'equateur.
pseud. Histoire des pyramides
de Quito. see La Condamine,
Charles Marie de.
Academico de la Real Academica
Espanola. pseud. Ensayo
chronologica. see Barcia,
Andres Gonzalez.
Academicus. pseud.
Friendly debate; or, A dialogue
between Academicus; and Sawny
& Mundungus. see Walter,
Thomas, 1696-1725.
Academicus. pseud.
Friendly debate; or, A dialogue
between Rusticus and Academicus.
(74419)
Academie, Lyon, France. see Lyon,
France. Academie.
Academie, Marseille, France. see
Marseille, France. Academie.
Academie Classique et Militaire,
Mantua, Pa. see Mantua, Pa.
Academie Classique et Militaire.
Academie de Medecine, Paris. 25579,
(63712), 65984, 92135
Academie de Medecine, Paris.
Commissaires. 11624
Academie des Sciences, Lyon, France.
see Lyon, France. Academie
des Sciences.
Academie des Sciences, Paris. 6877,
8831-(8833), (11723), 38483, 71110,
101364, 101365, 104999, 105014A
Academie des Sciences et Beaux Artes
des Etats-Unis de l'Amerique,
Richmond, Va. see Academy
of Sciences and Fine Arts,
Richmond, Va.
Academie des sciences et des artes.
9123

Academie des Sciences Morales et
Politiques, Paris. (14064), 48903
Academie Royale de Londre. see
Royal Academy, London.
Academie Royale de Suede. see
Sweden. Academie Royale.
Academie Royale des Sciences,
Bordeaux. 58826
Academie Royale des Sciences, Paris.
see Academie des Sciences, Paris.
Academie Royale des Sciences de France.
see France. Academie Royale
des Sciences.
Academies of arts. 50957, 50960
Academie, Great Barrington, Mass.
see Great Barrington Academy.
Academy, Kingsville, Ohio. see
Kingsville Academy, Kingsville, Ohio.
Academy, Milwaukee, Wisc. see
Milwaukee Academy.
Academy, Monson, Mass. see Monson
Academy, Monson, Mass.
Academy, New Salem, Mass. see New
Salem Academy, New Salem, Mass.
Academy, Newark, N. J. see Newark
Academy, Newark, N. J.
Academy, St. Johnbury, Vt. see
St. Johnbury Academy, St. Johnbury,
Vt.
Academy, Utica, N. Y. see Utica
Academy.
Academy, Wilton, N. H. see Wilton,
N. H. Academy (Proposed)
Academy, Worcester, Mass. see
Worcester Academy, Worcester,
Mass.
Academy at Little Falls, Herkimer
County, N. Y. 41534
Academy of Arts, New York (City)
see New York (City) Academy
of Arts.
Academy of arts and Sciences of
Connecticut. see Connecticut
Academy of Arts and Sciences.
Academy of Arts of Pennsylvania. see
Pennsylvania Academy of Arts.
Academy of Medicine, New York (City)
see New York Academy of
Medicine.
Academy of Medicine, Philadelphia.
62097
Academy of Music, Boston. see Boston
Academy of Music.
Academy of Natural Sciences, Philadelphia.
47390-(47391), 61404-61405, (77377),
77389, 98579, 103061
Academy of Natural Sciences, Philadelphia.
Charter. 61405
Academy of Natural Sciences, Philadelphia.
Library. 61405
Academy of Natural Sciences of California.
see California Academy of Natural
Sciences.
Academy of Natural Sciences of Minnesota.
see Minnesota Academy of Natural
Sciences.
Academy of Sacred Music, New York
(City) see New York Academy
of Sacred Music.
Academy of Science and Literature of
Maryland. see Maryland Academy
of Science and Literature.
Academy of Science of Kansas. see
Kansas Academy of Science.
Academy of Science of New York. see
New York Academy of Science.
Academy of Science of St. Louis. see
St. Louis Academy of Sciences.

Academy of Sciences, Chicago. see
Chicago Academy of Sciences.
Academy of Sciences, New Orleans. see
New Orleans Academy of Sciences.
Academy of Sciences, New York (City)
see New York Academy of
Sciences.
Academy of Sciences, St. Louis. see
St. Louis Academy of Sciences.
Academy of Sciences and Fine Arts,
Richmond, Va. 67128-(67129)
Academy of the Fine Arts, Philadelphia.
see Pennsylvania Academy of the
Fine Arts, Philadelphia.
Academy of the Fine Arts of South
Carolina. see South Carolina
Academy of the Fine Arts.
Academy of the fine arts. (68186)
Academy of the Protestant Episcopal
Church, Philadelphia. 62102
Academy of the Protestant Episcopal
Church, Philadelphia. Charter.
62102
Academy of the Protestant Episcopal
Church, Phialdelphia. Trustees.
62102
Acadia. see Nova Scotia.
Acadia. A lost chapter in American
history. 83715, 83719
Acadia College. 33072
Acadia: or, A month with the blue noses.
17321
L'Acadiade. 12610, 18221, 18222
Acadian geology. 18948-18949
Acadian recorder. 40607, 106083
Acadie. see Nova Scotia.
L'Acadie. 733
Acadiens et Canadiens. 67622
Acadiensis. 84422
Acambaro, Mex. Justicia ordinaria.
76223
Acarete du Biscay, -----. 88, 152,
95333, note after 100824
Acarette de Biscaie, ------. see
Acarete du Biscay, ------.
Accademico della Crusca. pseud.,
tr. see Corsini, Filippo.
supposed tr.
Accarias de Serionne, Joseph, 1706-1792.
14966A, 32521, 48905, (79233)-
79236
Accentos morales. 16753
Acceptable delivery before large
audiences. 105789
Acceptable fast. 18429
Acceptances of the war department.
(24914)
Accepted of the multitude of his
brethren. 70915
Accepted time and day of salvation.
74292
Access to an open polar sea. 37003
Accidence for the sea. 82814
Accidence for young seamen. 82855
Accidence, or the path-way to
experience. 82812, 82813, 82839
Accioli de Cerqueira e Silva, Ignacio,
1808-1865. 89, 11703-(11707),
47459
Accion de gracias del Convento de
N. P. S. Augustin. 106228A
Accion de gracias que la Academia de
Derocho Espanol. 48520
Accion solemne de gracias que
tributaron al todo-poderoso. 48251
Acclimatement et l'acclimatation de
l'homme. 81318

Accompaniment to Mitchell's map of
the world. (49713)
Accompaniment to Mitchell's new
map of Texas. 49714
Accompaniment to Mitchell's reference
and distance map. (49715)
Accompanying a bill making appropriations.
96629
Accomplished demagogue. 49774
Accomplished Dr. Theodore Wilson.
102470
Accomplished gentleman. 90235
Accomplished judge. (26776)
Accomplished singer. 36212
Accoord met de Staaten van Zeeland.
93834
Accoord tussen de Gemagtidge van de
Ed. Mog: Heeren Staaten van
Zeeland. 93834
Accoord van Brasilien. 7501
Accoort ende Articulen tusschen de
Croone van Portugael. 102875
According to my promise I shall now
lay before the reader such
alterations. 94092
Accords-Puncta. 102876
Account and history of the Oregon
Territory. 8807, 57544
Account and instruction relating to
the colony. 102509
Account and observations on their
conferences. 71406
Account [by Gaspar Correa.] 62806,
note after 90319
Account concerning the present state
of Christianity. 47151-47152
Account given by General Bowles.
104277
Account, historical, political, and
statistical. 56330
Account how George Keith became a
Quaker. 103703
Account in the Boston Evening-Post.
360, 11967, 3d note after 96741
Account of a beautiful young lady. 93891
Account of a call to the ministry. 64624
Account of a celebrated philosophical
farmer. (74176), 3d note after
98684
Account of a celebrated race. 60395
Account of a collection of plants.
28374
Account of a conference between the
late Mr. Grenville. 46922
Account of a contagious fever. 9383
Account of a cruise. 24863
Account of a faithful Negro slave. 85819
Account of a geographical and astronomical
expedition. (77152)
Account of a hail storm. (19863)
Account of a humorous political print.
90136
Account of a journey through North-Eastern
Texas. 82444
Account of a journey to Niagara, Montreal
and Quebec, in 1765. (35322)
Account of a journey to Niagara, Montreal
and Quebec, in 1766. 55111
Account of a kettle. 84411
Account of a late conference. 90, 91132
Account of a late revival at Plymouth.
73140
Account of a most extraordinary work
of God. 8981
Account of a national church and the
clergy. 37177
Account of a new Indian sect. 23167

15

Account of a new society for the
benefit of the Indians. 34597,
(53400)
Account of a plan for civilizing the
North American Indians. 17703
Account of a pleasure tour to Lake
Superior. 4048
Account of a plot. 62743
Account of a . . . revival among the
state prisoners. 70418
Account of a second voyage. 102431
Account of a seizure made at English
Manchac. 104017
Account of a shooting excursion. 35556
Account of a steamboat excursion.
71618
Account of a strange appearance in
the heavens. 65575
Account of a successful attempt to
domesticate the vicuna. 101223
Account of a surprising phenomenon.
61406
Account of a temperance meeting.
5071
Account of a tornado near New Harmony.
12008, 85072
Account of a visit lately made to the
people called Quakers. (58493)
Account of a visit made to it [i.e. Devil's
Hole]. (14762)
Account of a voyage, etc. by Mons.
Acarete du Biscay. 152, note
after 100824
Account of a voyage for the discovery
of a North-West passage. 20808,
82549, 1st note after 94082
Account of a voyage from Spain to
Paraquaria. (79164)
Account of a voyage in search of La
Perouse. 38423
Account of a voyage of discovery in the
north-east of Siberia. 62506-62507,
77126
Account of a voyage to Guiana and
Trinidad. 36636
Account of a voyage to Jamaica. 99423
Account of a voyage to Spitzbergen.
(38653)
Account of a voyage up the Mississippi
River. 62835
Account of Abimelech Coody. 13709,
2d note after 96480, 99260
Account of Admiral Vernon's taking
of Porto Bello. 99249
Account of affairs at Hudson's Bay.
40707, note after 96500
Account of all the affairs in Orange-
Country. 68970
Account of all the ships. 91091
Account of America, or the New World.
1427
Account of an ancient structure in
Newport. (67486)
Account of an ancient inscription in
North America. (42105)
Account of an aurora borealis. 28689
Account of an embassy to the kingdom
of Ava. (59572)
Account of an expedition from Pittsburgh.
35682, 77390
Account of an expedition to the Dead Sea,
under Lieut. Lynch. 36014
Account of an intended voyage. 98124
Account of Anneke Janes and of her
family. 35766
Account of Atlantic steam ships. (91)

Account of Bar Harbor. 6260, 2d
note after 96993
Account of California and the
wonderful gold regions. (9991)
Account of Canada. 6007
Account of Captain Estill's defeat.
(24793)
Account of chrystallized basaltes.
84411
Account of coffee. 57160, 1st-2d notes
after 103078
Account of Col. Crockett's glorious
death. 17570
Account of Col. Crockett's tour. 17565
Account of conferences held. 36337
Account of discoveries in the South
Pacific Ocean. 92
Account of discoveries in the West
until 1519. 72063
Account of Dr. . . . Franklin's
autobiography. 28557
Account of Dr. John Wilson. (44901)
Account of Dr. Smith's life. 82304-
(82305)
Account of East-Florida. 24840,
92220-92221, 92223
Account of expenses during the
revolutionary war. 101546, 101546A
Account of experiments to ascertain the
length of the seconds pendulum.
(74699)
Account of experiments to determine the
figure of the earth. (74699)
Account of extraordinary services
incurred and paid. 71318-71319
Account of former projects. 99553
Account of fourteen years' transportation.
(24024)
Account of Francis Adam Joseph Phyle.
(2283), 31920, 62589
Account [of Gaspar Correa.] 62806,
note after 90319
Account of Greenland. 13015
Account of Harper's Ferry. 9917, 1st
note after 96334, 4th note after 100532
Account of Haverford School. 30904
Account of her [i.e. Elizabeth Smith's]
life and character. 82505
Account of her [i.e. Mary Clarke Lloyd's]
life and character. 41694
Account of his [i.e. Robert Finley's]
agency. 8490
Account of his [i.e. Thomas Ellwood's]
birth. 22352, 105653
Account of his [i.e. William Tennant's]
being three days in a trance. 6854
Account of his captivity, by A. Guinnard.
29242
Account of his [i.e. George Johnstone's]
engagement with a French squadron.
5792, 36395
Account of his [i.e. George Whitefield's]
interment. 58891
Account of his [i.e. George Berkeley's]
life. 4881
Account of his [i.e. Alexander Selkirk's]
life and conversation. (79017)
Account of his [i.e. James Cook's] life
and public services. (16257)
Account of his [i.e. Benjamin Holme's]
life and travels. 32573
Account of his [i.e. Adam Smith's] life
and writings. 82318
Account of his [i.e. William Robertson's]
life and writings. 72007, 72011

Account of his [i.e. David Brainerd's]
life, character, &c. 21965
Account of his [i.e. Sir William
Howe's] proceedings. 46919
Account of his [i.e. John Ash's]
reception. 2168
Account of his [i.e. Eleazar Wheelock's]
receipts. 103207
Account of his [i.e. John Paul Jones']
services. 36558
Account of his [i.e. Stephen Merril
Clark's] short life. (13370)
Account of his [i.e. Captain Parker's]
taking the town. 11030, 27799
Account of his [i.e. Peter Henry Bruce's]
travels. 8726
Account of his [i.e. William Wills']
trial at Guild-Hall. 104543
Account of his [i.e. Calvin Galpine's]
trial for perjury. 26451
Account of his [i.e. Sir Francis
Drake's] valorous exploits.
20849, 100842
Account of his [i.e. Charles I. S.
Hazzard's] very early enjoyment
of the Grace of God. 90200
Account of humbugs. 3563
Account of Iceland. 13015, 38975
Account of it [i.e. an earthquake] in
Hampton. 27960, 30153, note
after 95748
Account of its [i.e. the Humane Society
of Cambridge's] origin. 10152
Account of its [i.e. the Santa Fe
expedition's] journey. 23724
Account of its [i.e. Rutgers University's]
union. 74439
Account of Jamaica. (35557), note after
91690
Account of Jane C. Rider. 4411
Account of Japan. 69381
Account of . . . Jennet B. Mott. 51115
Account of John Forsyth. 106030
Account of John Glover. (27601)
Account of John Plantain. 20777
Account of Knoepfel's Schoharie cave.
38136
Account of laying the corner stone.
73623
Account of Leslie's retreat. 22559
Account of Louisiana. 17384-17386
Account of Louisiana; being an abstract
of documents delivered. (42178)
Account of Louisiana, being an abstract
of documents, in the offices of the
Department of State, and of the
Treasury. 42177
Account of Louisiana, being an abstract
of documents in the . . . [Offices
of the] Departments of State, and
of the Treasury. 42192
Account of Louisiana, exhibiting a
compendious sketch. 40125,
42180
Account of Louisiana, laid before
Congress. 42179
Account of Magellan's voyage.
34100-34107
Account of many other adjacent
islands. (1948)
Account of memorials presented to
Congress. 64474
Account of Mr. How's death at
Canada. 33220
Account of Mr. Vandeleur's being
left behind. 98468

Account of money received and
disbursed. 103492
Account of money, receiv'd and
expended. 103493
Account of Monsieur de la Salle's
last expedition. 96171
Account of Natal in Africk. 18375
Account of new discoveries. 57181
Account of New England agents.
(52596)
Account of New Haven. (15702), 24273
Account of New Netherland in 1643-4.
36144, (80023)
Account of New Switzerland. 75372,
93793
Account of Odessa. 91553
Account of Oregon. 59648
Account of other depredations. 5676
Account of others left there. (35704),
79018
Account of our late troubles in Virginia.
17039
Account of Papal operations in our
country. 13365
Account of Paraguay. 67094
Account of parties in the United States.
16038, 16610
Account of patients. (54480)
Account of Pedro de la Gasca. 92228
Account of Persia. 66686
Account of pleas of late made. 92100
Account of Priester John's country.
26870
Account of Prince Edward Island.
note after 93185
Account of Prince Edward Island,
addressed to intending emigrants.
40768
Account of Prince Edward Island, in the
Gulph of St. Lawrence. 91696
Account of proceedings between Messrs.
Fordyce, Grant & Co. 91598
Account of proceedings in an expedition
from Virginia. 77448
Account of Quebec. 95, 10330, 12143
Account of receipts and payments.
61407
Account of recent archeological,
philological and geographical
researches. 3747, 54476
Account of recent transactions. 6331
Account of Robert Morris' property.
50869
Account of Rose Butler. 71496
Account of St. Luke's Hospital. 75413
Account of several actions by sea. (5613)
Account of several daring attempts. 6517
Account of several estates for sale. 72113
Account of several large fires. (4442)
Account of several late voyages &
discoveries. (72185)
Account of several late voyages and
discoveries. (72186)-(72187)
Account of several meteoric stones. 83003
Account of several observables in
Virginia. (13575)
Account of several passages and letters.
53435
Account of several remarkable vestiges.
3820
Account of Sir Francis Drake's first
voyage. 6024
Account of Sir Francis Drake's voyage
round the world. 22187, 41006
Account of six years residence in
Hudson's-Bay. (72259)

Account of some experiments. 2612
Account of some investigations.
75792
Account of some late attempts.
34598
Account of some of the bridges.
12031, 41573
Account of some of the descendants of
Capt. Thomas Brattle. (30469)
Account of some of the fossil shells
of Maryland. (77367)
Account of some of the labours. 94478
Account of some of the most striking
scenes. 21716
Account of some of the principal slave
insurrections. 14176
Account of some of the proceedings of
the legislatures. 37486, 79711
Account of some of the steam-boats.
69651
Account of some of the traditions.
37705
Account of some particulars relative
to the meeting held at York,
on Thursday, Dec. 30, 1779.
79624
Account of some particulars relative
to the meeting held at York,
on Thursday the 30th of December,
1779. 82257
Account of some particulars, which
passed at the meeting held at
York, on Thursday, the 30th
December, 1779. 82256
Account of some parts of the Brazils.
36813, 6th note after 97689
Account of some recent feats. (13876)
Account of some schools in Great
Britain. 5245
Account of Spain. (27689)
Account of statues, busts, etc. (54016)
Account of successful advertisers.
(47793), 73551
Account of sundry goods imported, and
of sundry goods of this province
exported. 87732
Account of sundry goods imported and
of sundry goods the produce of
this province exported. 12064
Account of sundry missions performed.
701
Account of surveys and examinations.
80753
Account of Texas and Yucatan. (24968)
Account of that wonderful pedestrian.
(21734)
Account of the abduction and murder
of William Morgan. 50682,
97958
Account of the Abipones. (20414)
Account of the aborigines of Nova
Scotia. 56102
Account of the act. 32125
Account of the action at Lake George.
16603
Account of the actual state of the
country. 43665
Account of the agreement which took
place. 93, (59400), 65121
Account of the alteration and present
state of the penal laws. (42533)
Account of the American Baptist
mission. 38153
Account of the American expedition.
81152
Account of the annual religious
ceremony. (11528)

Account of the ancestors and descendants
of G. L. Clark. 81386
Account of the archipelago of Chiloe.
49894
Account of the Arctic regions. 78167
Account of the arraignments and tryals.
(37982)-37983 note after 99766,
note after 100901
Account of the art of breeding. 81008
Account of the . . . Asylum, . . .
established, near Philadelphia.
59900
Account of the asylum for the insane.
101133
Account of the asylum for the relief of
persons deprived of . . . reason.
(23142), 59900
Account of the attack and engagement
at Quebec. 36728
Account of the attempts of the Company
of Scotland. 6428
Account of the author's [i.e. John
Witherspoon's] life. 104946
Account of the author's [i.e. Sir Walter
Raleigh's] life, tryal, and death.
67544
Account of the author's [i.e. Pierre F. X.
de Charlevoix's] shipwreck. 12140
Account of the . . . author's [i.e. Stephen
Chapin's] trial on those points.
11958
Account of the baneful effects. 4678
Account of the banquet. 75448
Account of the baptisms and burials.
61408
Account of the Bartram Garden. 3869
Account of the battle of Bunker Hill,
compiled from authentic sources.
66634
Account of the battle of Bunker Hill.
Written for the Portfolio. 19071
Account of the battle of Bunker's-Hill.
66771
Account of the battle of Gettysburg.
45385
Account of the battle of Lundy's Lane.
(42696)
Account of the battle of Point Pleasant.
33301
Account of the battle of Prescott. 42847
Account of the battle of Ridgeway. 19566
Account of the beginning, transactions
and discovery. 72720, 106070
Account of the beginnings and advances
of a spiritual life. (78444)-(78445)
Account of the behavior and sentiments
of some well disposed Indians. 34599
Account of the Benevolent Christian
Society. 54114
Account of the best places of resort for
invalids. 13302
Account of the bilious remitting and
intermitting yellow fever. 74227
Account of the bilious remitting yellow
fever. 18000, (74198), (74226)
Account of the births and burials in
Christ-Church Parish. 61409
Account of the black Charaibs. 106124
Account of the Bloomingdale Asylum.
17214
Account of the Boston Asylum for
Indigent Boys. 6576
Account of the British African Colonization
Society. 32351
Account of the British expedition. 64940
Account of the British settlement of
Honduras. 31308

Account of the British settlement of
Honduras, with sketches of the
Musquito Indians.   32752

Account of the British settlements
on the Musquito shore.   21907

Account of the Bunker Hill battle and
monument.   9171

Account of the Bunker Hill monument.
(26082)

Account of the burning of John Rogers.
note after 65546

Account of the burning of Royalton.
91164

Account of the Cambridge Humane
Society.   10152

Account of the campaign in the West
Indies.   104563

Account of the campaign in western
Virginia.   43010, 43018

Account of the captivity and death of
his [i.e. Isaac Jogues'] companion,
Rene Goupil.   (80023)

Account of the captivity . . . &
deliverance of Mrs. Jemima
Howe.   (28378)

Account of the captivity and sufferings
of Mrs. Barber.   (51835)

Account of the captivity of Elizabeth
Hanson.   (30265)

Account of the captivity of Mrs. Jemimah
Howe.   30178

Account of the capture of Buenos
Ayres.   8999

Account of the capture of Davis.   (37300)

Account of the capture of the Spanish
schooner Amistad.   12054, 82003

Account of the castles of Cibola.   (7162)

Account of the celebration by the
Minnesota Historical Society.
11192

Account of the celebration commemorative
of the opening of railroad
communication between Boston and
Canada.   6766

Account of the celebration of American
independence, at Clay Lick.
13573, (40970), 85133

Account of the celebration of its [i.e. the
Cape Cod Association's] first
anniversary.   10734

Account of the celebration of the
anniversary of the battle of
Plattsburgh.   (63363)

Account of the . . . celebration [of the
centennial of St. John's Lodge.]
23317

Account of the celebration [of the
eighty-second anniversary of the
battle of Hubbardton.]   13295

Account of the celebration of the 55th
anniversary of American
independence.   20917

Account of the celebration of the first-
centennial anniversary of the
incorporation of Columbia
College.   14802

Account of the celebration of the two
hundredth anniversary of the first
settlement of Salem.   (75624)

Account of the celebration of the 200th
anniversary of the settlement of
the town of Salem.   75625

Account of the centennial celebration
in Danvers.   18513

Account of the ceremonies at the laying
of the corner-stone of the New
York Asylum for Idiots at Syracuse.
53802

Account of the ceremony of laying the
corner stone of St. Thomas'
Church.   (75496)

Account of the ceremony of the laying
of the corner stone of the new
church.   45357, 75214

Account of the change in his [i.e. William
Henry Brisbane's] views on the
subject of slavery.   8010

Account of the character of Washington.
101547

Account of the charter-oak.   (12161)

Account of the Cherokees.   73389

Account of the chief national
improvements.   (70402)

Account of the Christian denomination.
13778

Account of the churches in Rhode-
Island.   35414

Account of the Cinchona forests of
South America.   38728

Account of circumstances between
Governor Hinslop and Thomas
Talboys.   31995

Account of the city of Philadelphia.
59712

Account of the city treasurer.   73716

Account of the Classical School in
Granville.   28326

Account of the climate.   (10013)

Account of the Coal Bank disaster
at Blue Rock.   56861

Account of the College and Academy of
Philadelphia.   84599-84600, 84678C

Account of the College of New-Jersey.
53032

Account of the colony of Nova Scotia.
56103

Account of the colony of the Lord
Baron of Baltimore.   103353

Account of the commencement and
progress of an institution.   (9848)

Account of the commencement in the
College of Philadelphia.   61546

Account of the commencement of
hostilities.   90943

Account of the commitment, arraignment,
tryal and condemnation of Nicholas
Bayard.   4033, 53436

Account of the conduct of the council.
7663, 21967

Account of the conduct of the people
called Shakers.   (11975)

Account of the conduct of the war.
26420, 102645

Account of the Conewago Canal.   (15223)

Account of the conflagration of the
principal part of the first ward
of the city of New York.   25201

Account of the conflagration of the
Ursuline Convent.   12093, 1st note
after 98167

Account of the conquest of California.
48575

Account of the constitution and government
of Harvard-College.   30722

Account of the contagious epidemic
yellow fever.   (57968), 58980

Account of the controversy between
Mackinac and the Mormons.
48805, 92674

Account of the controversy between New
York and Vermont.   12819

Account of the controversy between . . .
S. Weller . . . and B. Mills.   102565

Account of the controversy between the
warrantees and actual settlers.
56862

Account of the controversy in the First
Parish Church. 10125
Account of the conversion of an Indian.
(30395), 97269
Account of the conversion of J. Thayer.
95239
Account of the conversion of Rev.
John Thayer. 95242
Account of the conversion of the Rev.
John Thayer. 95241
Account of the conversion of the
Reverend John Thayer. 95244
Account of the conversion of the Rev.
Mr. John Thayer. 95232, 95238,
95243
[A]ccount of the conversion of the
Reverend Mr. John Thayer. 95231
Account of the conversion of the
Reverend Mr. John Thayer.
95233-95237, 95240, 95246, 95252
Account of the convincement. 18756
Account of the countries adjoining to
Hudson's Bay. 20404
Account of the country of Accadie.
40707, note after 96500
Account of the county of Addison. (27857)
Account of the creation. 79196
Account of the cruelties. 53402
Account of the cruise of the St. George.
19602
Account of the crustacea of the United
States. 77388
Account of the customs and manners. 94
Account of the dedication of Morgan
School Building. 90432
Account of the descendants of John
Pease. (59460)
Account of the descendants of Robert
Fletcher. 24721
Account of the descent of the Spaniards.
32760
Account of the design, origin, and
present state. 61991
Account of the designs and proceedings
of the Associates [of the late
Dr. Bray.] 83977
Account of the designs of the Associates
of the late Dr. Bray. 7470
Account of the destruction of Fayetteville.
73568
Account of the destruction of the great
fleet. 22187, 41006
Account of the destruction of the
settlement of Wyoming. 44258,
105687-note after 105690
Account of the different societies.
61604, 91312
Account of the difficulties in the church
of Haverhill. 30908
Account of the dinner given to Charles
Dickens. 20005, 69854
Account of the dinner given to
Professor List. 41427
Account of the discoveries made in
the South Pacifick Ocean. 18334
Account of the discovery of America.
13015
Account of the discovery of an ancient
ship. 57848
Account of the discovery of Hogarths
Sound. 43142
Account of the disease. 8553
Account of the deceased [i.e. Nathaniel
Byfield.] 12325
Account of the distances from the city
of Philadelphia. 61410
Account of the donations. (3257)

Account of the dreadful havock. (4674)
Account of the Dummer Academy. 21201
Account of the dysentery. (80427)
Account of the Earl of Macartney's
embassy. (59572)
Account of the early laws of Massachusetts.
17042
Account of the early settlement of Kentucky.
6374
Account of the early voyages. 37952
Account of the earthquake, in Hampton.
27960, 30153, note after 95748
Account of the earthquake that occurred
on the island of Juan Fernandez.
93945
Account of the earthquakes which occurred
in the United States. 21635
Account of the ecclesiastical affairs.
24183
Account of the edifying behaviour. 106391
Account of the eleven thousand schools.
(74300)
Account of the emancipation of the slaves.
(3357)
Account of the emigrant aid companies.
(29624)
Account of the emperor's life after his
abdication. 65295
Account of the endeavours used. 33800
Account of the endowments for education.
93126
Account of the engagement between the
Chesapeake and Shannon. 39355,
92320
Account of the English and foreign
railways. 25179
Account of the English settlements in
Newfoundland. 14414
Account of the English settlements in
the Illinois. 34730
Account of the epidemic cholera. 20825
Account of the epidemic fever of
Jamaica. 2037
Account of the epidemic fever which
prevailed in New York in 1795.
54018
Account of the epidemic fever which
prevailed in the city of New-York.
4056
Account of the epidemic yellow fever.
78614, 102346
Account of the escape of six federal
prisoners. (55004)
Account of the European settlements in
America. 9282-9283, 9289, 92196
Account of the events. 63881
Account of the execution of Col. R. Kirby.
note after 100901
Account of the execution of the six
militia-men. 35391
Account of the executive organization.
76586, 76647
Account, of the exercise and experience.
104518
Account of the exercises at a Methodist
camp-meeting. 48207
Account of the exercises on the occasion.
84997
Account of the expedition from Pittsburg.
(35683)
Account of the expedition of Captains
Lewis and Clark. 40834
Account of the expedition to Carthagena.
11128, 1st note after 99245, 102632
Account of the expedition to the West Indies,
against Martinico, Guadelupe, and other
the Leeward Islands. 26627

Account of the expedition to the West
  Indies, against Martinico, with
  the reduction of Guadelupe. 26628
Account of the expeditions to the sources
  of the Mississippi. 62836
Account of the expenditures. 51901
Account of the extraordinary degrees.
  48858
Account of the extraordinary doings.
  7897
Account of the extraordinary revival.
  37485
Account of the fair and impartial
  proceedings. 87359, 87805
Account of the family meeting. 4570
Account of the Farmington . . .
  Hampshire and Hampden . . .
  and New Haven and Northampton
  [Canal] Compan[ies.] 52854
Account of the fatal hurricane. (3258)
Account of the febrile diseases of
  Sheffield. 102346
Account of the Field Relief Corps.
  (76598), 76647
Account of the fiftieth anniversary of the
  American Bible Missionary Union.
  (49470)
Account of the fifty-year jubilee. 51171
Account [of the fire at Newburyport.]
  54925
Account of the first commencement
  of Rhode Island College. 70716
Account of the first confederacy of
  the Six Nations. 60737, 2d note
  after 100005
Account of the first discoveries of the
  New World. 32147, 106120
Account of the first discovery, and
  natural history of Florida.
  24841, 71926
Account of the first discovery of gold.
  93971
Account of the first exhibition of the
  blind pupils. 60339
Account of the first settlement. 9245,
  note after 98483
Account of the first voyages and
  discoveries. 11227-11230, 11233,
  11234, 11289
Account of the fishes of New York.
  54362
Account of the five Rotterdam ships.
  14401
Account of the formation and action
  of the Vigilance Committee.
  37808, 97098
Account of the formation and proceedings
  of the Auxiliary Foreign Mission
  Society. 105337
Account of the formation, constitution
  and regulation of the Eastern
  Diocese. 20207, 52631
Account of the formation of the Eliot
  Church. 55086
Account of the formation of the Upper
  Canada Religious Tract and Book
  Society. 98094
Account of the foundation. 3572, 10955
Account of the fourth annual meeting
  of the . . . Friends. 24512
Account of the Free-School Society
  of New-York. 54285, 84700
Account of the French prophets.
  105012
Account of the French settlements in
  North America. 95, 10330, 12143
Account of the French usurpation. 2554

Account of the Fund for the Relief of
  East Tennessee. 23271
Account of the funds. 85991
Account of the funeral honours. 39355,
  92320
Account of the gaol and penitentiary
  house. 7265
Account of the garden at St. Vincent.
  22319
Account of the geography of Texas. 82347
Account of the geological structure. 18948
Account [of the Genoese Pilot.] 62806,
  note after 90319
Account of the giants lately discovered.
  9732, 59030, 101143
Account of the gold regions. 9999
Account of the gospel labours. 13025
Account of the Grammar School. 75465
Account of the Grand Canal. 99559
Account of the grand canals. 27855, 53550
Account of the grand celebration. (56696)
Account of the grand Federal procession.
  (61411), 104632
Account of the grants. 6209
Account of . . . the great awakening of
  1857-'58. 15096
Account of the great battle of August
  20th. (7132)
Account of the great conflagration in
  Portland. 52148
Account of the great dangers and
  distresses. 59552
Account of the great divisions. 37178,
  37205
Account of the great earthquakes in the
  western states. 21636, 62746
Account of the great fire in Broad Street
  in 1821. 54019
Account of the great fire in New York.
  54020
Account of the great fire of 1843. 25315
Account of the great revival in
  Middleborough, Mass. 65576
Account of the great revival of religion.
  14252
Account of the great Whig Festival.
  3007, 103271
Account of the habits of the birds. 2366
Account of the High School for Girls,
  Boston. (6713)
Account of the high school re-union. 64427
Account of the history and condition of the
  colored population. (20931)
Account of the history, manners and
  customs of the Indian nations. 1183
Account of the Home for Discharged
  Female Convicts. 37989
Account of the illegal prosecution. 4034
Account of the impeachment and trial.
  32976, 1st note after 96883
Account of the impeachment, trial, and
  acquittal. 55255, 1st note after 96909
Account of the importation of American
  cochineal insects. 1402A
Account of the imprisonment and sufferings
  of Robert Fuller. 26172
Account of the . . . inauguration. 16798
Account of the incidents. (11757)
Account of the Indian chief Black Hawk.
  5676
Account of the Indian nations inhabiting
  within the limits of the thirteen
  United States. 24336, 34355
Account of the Indian nations inhabiting
  within the limits of the XIII states.
  (34358)
Account of the Indian nations within the
  limits of the United States. 24337

Account of the Indian tribes. 6317

Account of the Indians. 102511

Account of the institutions. 7471

Account of the insurrection in St. Domingo. 32990

Account of the insurrection of the Negro slaves. 8809

Account of the intended rebellion of the Negroes. (52623), 63524

Account of the interest and conduct of the Jamaica planters. 35558

Account of the interment of the remains of American patriots. 91754

Account of the interment of the remains of 11,500 American seamen. 54021, 91754, 94298

Account of the interviews. 45817

Account of the introduction of woolen manufactures. 37289

Account of the iron railway bridge across the Mississippi. 13465

Account of the island and government of Jamaica. (35624)

Account of the island of Jamaica. 44717

Account of the island of Newfoundland. 104226

Account of the island of Prince Edward. 34706

Account of the island of Ratan. 89248

Account of the islands of Bermudas. 17334

Account of the Isthmus of Tehuantepec. (26546), note after 95491

Account of the jubilee of Monson Academy. 50041, 92272

Account of the landed estate. 36820

Account of the last expedition to Port Egmont. 60798

Account of the last illness and death of the Hon. William Wirt. 104865

Account of the last illness of the late Hon. Daniel Webster. (35974)

Account of the late action of the New-Englanders. 77246

Account of the late earthquake in Boston. 97585

Account of the late earthquake in Jamaica. (35559), 97172

Account of the late expedition. 102202

Account of the late intended insurrection. 12033, (30013)

Account of the late invasion of Georgia. 93962

Account of the late remarkable religious impressions. (18762)

Account of the late revolution in New England. 9708, 9709, 52597, 52598

Account of the late revolutions in New England. 2547

Account of the late success of the Gospel. 8986

Account of the late wonderful American vision. 90934

Account of the law-suit. 70848

Account of the laying of the corner stone of the Holmesburg Public School. 61723

Account of the . . . laying the corner-stone of the new building. 75284

Account of the laying the first stone of the monument to Wolfe. (80871)

Account of the leading policy. 7146

[Account of the] letter of Columbus. (40041)

Account of the life and character of Christopher Ludwick. 74199

Account of the life and character of the author [i.e. Samuel Fothergill.] 25272

Account of the life and military services of Maj. Gen. John Stark. 72730, note after 90518

Account of the life and travels in the work of the ministry. 25270

Account of the life and works of fifteen Negroes. (28728)

Account of the life and writings of Dr. John Shebbeare. 80062

Account of the life and writings of the author [i.e. James Thomson.] 95574

Account of the life and writings of the author [i.e. William Robertson.] 72015

Account of the life and writings of William Robertson. 91674

Account of the life, character, &c., of the Rev. Samuel Parris. 25320

Account of the life, manners, and customs of the inhabitants. 9970, 26787

Account of the life, ministry, last sickness, and death of Elias Hicks. 31716

Account of the life of David Brainerd. 93291

Account of the life of George Berkeley. 91871

Account of the life of Mr. David Brainerd. 21928

Account of the life of that ancient servant of Jesus Christ, John Richardson. 71023

Account of the life of that ancient servant of Jesus Christ, John Richarsn [sic]. 71024

Account of the life of the late Reverend Mr. David Brainerd. 21927, 64945, 102653

Account of the life of William Parsons. 58922

Account of the life, personal appearance, character, and manners, of Charles S. Stratton. 92792

Account of the life, travels, and Christian experiences in the work of the ministry of Samuel Bownas. 7097, 71024

Account of the lives, sufferings, and printed works, of the two thousand ministers. (9868)

Account of the loss of His Majesty's ship Deal Castle. 30953, (64000), 106094

Account of the loss of H. M. Sloop "Swift." 28172

Account of the loss of the Lady Hobart Packet. 38547

Account of the loss of the ship Omartal. 6244

Account of the loss of the Wesleyan missionaries. (36585)

Account of the Louisville city-school. 42311

Account of the Lyme dispute. 101216

Account of the Maine Charity School. 43967

Account of the malignant fever, lately prevalent in the city of New-York. 30314

Account of the malignant fever, which prevailed in the city of New-York. 30315

Account of the management of certain estates. 36648

Account of the manner in which the Protestant Church of the Unitas Fratrum, or United Brethren, preach the Gospel. 88925-88926
Account of the manner in which the said manuscript was discovered. 90251, 90259-90281, 90283, 90285-90286
Account of the manner in which the slave dealers take free people. 96283
Account of the manners and customs of the inhabitants. 16772
Account of the manners and customs of the savage inhabitants of Brazil. 11724
Account of the manners of the German inhabitants. 74200
Account of the manners of the inhabitants. (9920), 18556, 78218
Account of the manure Guano. 29054
Account of the manuscript papers of George Washington. 88963
Account of the Massachusetts Society for Promoting Christian Knowledge. 45897
Account of the Massachusetts State Prison. 45902
Account of the matter, form, and manner of a new and strange religion. 67954
Account of the medical properties of the Grey Sulphur Springs. 100419
Account of the medical school in Boston. 45846
Account of the medicinal plants growing in Jamaica. 105626
Account of the meeting of the class. 105879
Account of the meetings in March, 1907. 83896
Account of the method and further success of inoculating. (46213)
Account of the methods used. 32945
Account of the mining and metallurgical industry. 68067
Account of the mischief done by the enemy. 104268
Account of the miserable lives and woful deaths. 89465
Account of the missionary labors. 15812
Account of the missions the last year. 103212
Account of the Mississippi. 25853
Account of the money he received. 103494
Account of the Mormon campaign. 16214
Account of the most cruel treatment. (35447)
Account of the most material transactions. (3256)
Account of the most remarkable and memorable deliverances. 104261
Account of the most valuable varieties of fruit. 37463
Account of the murder of Gen. Roland Chester. 72707
Account of the murder of Jacob Gould. 19042
Account of the murder of Madame Beaumont de la Coste. 98515
Account of the Murrinitish plague. 90149
Account of the Muscle Shoals. (13299)
Account of the mutiny and massacre of the ship Globe. 15078

Account of the mutiny in the Anderson cavalry. (39551)
Account of the native tribes. 49894
Account of the naval engagement. 21842
Account of the new discoveries. 23781
Account of the New Hampshire Society. 6949
Account of the New-Haven city meeting and resolutions. (52970)
Account of the new invented Pennsylvanian fire-places. 25490
Account of the new northern archipelago. 90063
Account of the New World. 66686
Account of the New York Clearing House. 13599
Account of the New-York Hospital. (54480)
Account of the New York Institution for the Blind. 54499
Account of the newspapers and other periodicals. 92784
Account of the noblesse or gentry in Canada. 45417
Account of the North American Indians. (34600), 46943
Account of the North Carolina Gold Mine Company. 55651
Account of the number of inhabitants. (15631)
Account of the number of slaves employed. 75510
Account of the number of the inhabitants. (15631)
Account of the numbers that have died. 24573
Account of the obsequies observed by the city [of Portsmouth, N.H.] (59128), 64412
Account of the obsequies of Abraham Lincoln. 64412
Account of the observation of Venus upon the sun. 102715
Account of the operations against Buenos Ayres. (2453), 9000, 9002
Account of the operations of the Indiana Brigade. 82742
Account of the order in Ireland. (80023)
Account of the organization & proceedings of the Battle of Lake Erie Monument Association. 3967, 38658
Account of the organization of the army of the United States. 72069
Account of the origin and design of the Society for Promoting Christian Knowledge. (59436)
Account of the origin and designs of the Society for Promoting Christian Knowledge. 95421, 95422
Account of the origin and doings of the Society for the Promotion of Temperance in Haverhill and vicinity. 85927
Account of the origin and formation of the New-York Protestant Episcopal City-Mission Society. 54526
Account of the origin and practice of monkery. 73924
Account of the origin and progress of the Pennsylvania Institution for the Deaf and Dumb. 60337
Account of the origin of the cabinet. 84793
Account of the origin of the Mississippi doctrine of repudiation. 2407, 43609
Account of the origin of the Woodhull Monument Association. 44756
Account of the origin, progress, and actual state of the war. 58265

23

Account of the origin, progress, and present state of the Episcopal Church. 50977

Account of the origin, progress, . . . and statistics of the Methodist Episcopal Church. (28035)

Account of the origin, progress, relation to the state, and present condition of the evangelical churches. (2792)

Account of the . . . original inhabitants of America. 49819

Account of the orphan-house in Georgia. 103513

Account of the orphan-House in Georgia, from January $174\frac{0}{1}$ to 1742. 103495

Account of the orphan-house in Georgia, from January $174\frac{0}{1}$, to January $174\frac{2}{3}$. 103496

Account of the orphan-house in Georgia, to the time of his [i.e George Whitefield's] death. 103579

Account of the outlaw Rande. 84246

Account of the Palo de Vaca, the cow tree of Caracas. 18731

Account of the Patagonians. 6870

Account of the penitentiary and penal code of Pennsylvania. 59775

Account of the Pennsylvania Hospital. 25588, 86582

Account of the people and institutions of the United States. 24946

Account of the people called Quakers. 93601

Account of the people called Shakers. (8567)

Account of the persecution of G. Keith, in Pennsylvania. 9072

Account of the persons. 25620

Account of the Philadelphia Dispensary. 61991

Account of the Pilgrim celebration at Plymouth. 63471

Account of the piracies and cruelties of John Augur. 32182, (32197), (36191)

Account of the pirates. 55027

Account of the plan. 3721

Account of the plenary councils. 80008

Account of the political meeting. 54015

Account of the poor fund. 57145

Account of the Port Society. 6732

Account of the Portage Railroad. 71920

Account of the present condition of the Asylum for the Relief of Persons Deprived of their Reason. (30903)

Account of the present condition of the South Sea Islands. 16268

Account of the present state and strength of Canada. 4035

Account of the present state of Brazil. 9871

Account of the present state of Nova Scotia. 32543

Account of the present state of Nova Scotia: in two letters. 56104

Account of the present state of religion. 72052

Account of the present state of the island. 32051

Account of the present state of the Sandwich Islands. 10210

Account of the preservation of eight men in Greenland. 13015

Account of the principal articles of the Quakers faith. 64973, 72688

Account of the principal woolen manufactures. 4779

Account of the principle and effects of the American air-stove grates. 79838

Account of the proceedings at the Countess of Huntington's College. 27007

Account of the proceedings [at the dedication of the granite monument on Acton Common.] (6977)

Account of the proceedings at the dinner. 59367, 1st note after 91507

Account of the proceedings at the inauguration. 38788, 72649

Account of the proceedings at the laying of the corner-stone of Hospital of the Protestant Episcopal Church. 61726

Account of the proceedings at the laying of the corner-stone of the State Emigrant Hospital. 53964

Account of the proceedings had in the Superior Court. 56303

Account of the proceedings in Dorchester. (20618)

Account of the proceedings in France. (12811)

Account of the proceedings in the House of Representatives. 24383

Account of the proceedings, July 4, 1833. 5236

Account of the proceedings of Abraham Van Vleet. 57844, note after 97893, note after 105575

Account of the proceedings of the British. (45411), (66986), 66989

Account of the proceedings of the Corporation. 54022

Account of the proceedings of the Earl of Bellamont. 16653

Account of the proceedings [of the first triennial meeting of the Society of the Alumni of Dartmouth College.] 8555

Account of the proceedings of the General Synod of the Reformed Dutch Church. 68763

Account of the proceedings of the governor and assembly of Jamaica. (21893), note after (35559)

Account of the proceedings of the Grand Lodge. 60129

Account of the proceedings of the Illinois and Ouabache Land Companies. 96, 84577-84578, 2d-3d notes after 97876

Account of the proceedings of the magistrates. 104482

Account of the proceedings of the meeting at Auburn. 2354

Account of the proceedings of the presbytery. 54

Account of the proceedings of the squadron. 57346

Account of the proceedings of the town. 5361, 12114, (50842), 101777, 101841, 101874

Account of the proceedings of the laying the corner-stone. 27491

Account of the proceedings on this occasion [i.e. the installation of the second National Congress of Venezuela.] 6189

Account of the proceedings preliminary to the organization. (45867)

Account of the proceedings upon the transfer. 75626

Account of the procession, dinner, and ball. 54023

Account of the procession, together with copious extracts. (54024)

Account of the produce of the gold-washings. 7627

Account of the progress of a detachment. 25628

Account of the progress of a reformation of manners. 97

Account of the propagation of the Gospel in foreign parts. 99, 85932, 93233

Account of the propagation of the Gospel in the English dominions. 98

Account of the proposed canal. 5700, note after 105386

Account of the proposed Providence and Worcester Canal. (66236)

Account of the pro-slavery mob. 90890

Account of the providential preservation of Eliz. Woodcock. (57098)

Account of the province of Carolina in America. 10963, 104685

Account of the province of New Brunswick. 2763

Account of the public festival. 88852

Account of the publications. 41176

Account of the purchase from the Indians. 15689

Account of the putrid Murrinitish plague. 90147, 90149

Account of the quantity of sugars. 81738

Account of the quarter centennial celebration. 9058

Account of the reasons. 42778, 78621, (78622), 95166

Account of the receipts and expenditures . . . of North Brookfield. 55579

Account of the receipts and expenditures of the Merrimack County Agricultural Society. (48011)

Account of the receipts and expenditures of the town of Newton. (55087)

Account of the receipts and expenditures of the Union Canal Company. 97767

Account of the reception. 54025

Account of the Red River in Louisiana. 25787

Account of the regular graduation in man. 103356

Account of the religious experience and some of the trials. (41049)

Account of the religious experience of an Indian man. 104518

Account of the remains of a fossil extinct reptile. 53033

Account of the remarkable conversion of Jachiel Hirshel. 106382

Account of the remarkable occurrences in the life and travels of Col. James Smith. 82763, 82764

Account of the remarkable occurrences in the life and travels of Colonel James Smith. 82764-82765

Account of the remonstrances of the Church in Exeter. 72616

Account of the resources of the state of Honduras. 54828

Account of the revival . . . in Bridgehampton. 8983

Account of the revival of religion in Boston. 65577

Account of the revival of the Company. 88103

Account of the revolution in California. 33595

Account of the rise and present state of the inquisitions. (53403)

Account of the rise and progress of the American war. 102646

Account of the rise and progress of the malignant fever. 3722

Account of the rise and progress of the scheme. 6163

Account of the rise, doctrines and principles. 66905

Account of the rise of the Antipedo-Baptist persqasion. [sic] 9105

Account of the rise of the colonies. 1968

Account of the rise, progress, and consequences of the land bank. 45556

Account of the rise, progress, and present state, of the Boston Female Asylum. 6705

Account of the rise, progress, & present state, of the Pennsylvania Hospital. 60327

Account of the rise, progress, and termination, of the malignant fever. 61412

Account of the robbery and piracy. (51797)

Account of the Russian discoveries. 17309

Account of the sad sufferings. 6377

Account of the said conflagration [i.e. of London, 1666.] 35753

Account of the Salem Female Charitable Society. (75725), 93211

Account of the Salmo Otsego. (13710)

Account of the salt springs of Salina. 4227

Account of the same fever. 10883

Account of the savage treatment. 27331

Account of . . . the Scotch settlement. 33198, 33199

Account of the Schuylkill navigation. 59776

Account of the sea-fights and victories. 8074

Account of the seizure and enslavement. 26125

Account of the services of colored men. 1425

Account of the settlement, commerce, and riches. (25926)

Account of the settlement of the town of Bristol. 8054, 1st note after 91736

Account of the seventy-first anniversary. 66305, 92046

Account of the several cruises. 31456

Account of the several religious societies. 702

Account of the several treatises in print. 37199

Account of the several voyages round the globe. 16244

Account of the several voyages undertaken. (62573)

Account of the Shakers. 79693

Account of the shameful miscarriage. (19639), note after 31743

Account of the skeleton of the mammoth. 59422

Account of the slave trade. 23721

Account of the slavery times. (50717)

Account of the Smithsonian Institution, . . . Aug. 10th, 1853. 31403

Account of the Smithsonian Institution, its founder, building, operations, etc. 70474, 85090

Account of the Smithsonian Institution. Its origin, history, objects and achievements. 85091-85092

Account of the Society for Promoting Christian Knowledge. 85848, 97361

Account of the Society for Propagating the Gospel in Foreign Parts. 101

Account of the Society for the Encouragement of the British Troops in Germany and North America. 100, 30276

Account of the "Society for the Promotion of Theological Education in Harvard University." (30723)

Account of the Society for the Propagation of the Gospel in America. (37449)

Account of the Society in Scotland for Propagating Christian Knowledge. 85992

Account of the soil, growing timber, and other productions of several lands, particularly the Genesee Tract. (34358)

Account of the soil, growing timber, and other productions, of the lands in the back parts of the states. (53437)

Account of the soil, growing timber, and other productions, of the lands . . . in North America. 26926

Account of the Spanish butcheries. 30525, 39120

Account of the Spanish settlements in America. 40709, 1st note after 96502

Account of the Spanish settlements in America. In four parts. 102

Account of the state of religion. (27522), 65122

Account of the state of the schools. 85933

Account of the state of the treasury. 45557

Account of the state prison. 21816, 54026, 86586

Account of the struggle for liberty. 4125

Account of the subsequent proceedings. (9435)

Account of the success of inoculation. 31198, 34792

Account of the success of two Danish missionaries. 44086

Account of the sufferings and Christian experience. (66671)

Account of the sufferings and persecution. 11849

Account of the sufferings of Margaret Rule. 9926

Account of the sufferings of Richard Sellers, of Keinsey. 79031

Account of the sufferings of Richard Seller, of Kiensey. 82871

Account of the sugar maple-tree. 74201

Account of the Sunbury Water-Power Canal. 93737

Account of the supplies sent to Savannah. 77265

Account of the surprising revivals of religion. 59066

Account of the surveys of Florida, &c. 26763, 42070

Account of the Swan River settlement. 7295

Account of the taking of Carthagena by the French and buccaniers. 11129

Account of the taking of Carthagena by the French in the year 1697. 63702

Account of the taking of the East and West-India fleet. 102812

Account of the taking of the said Major Bonnet. 6326, 1st note after 97284, 1st note after 96956

Account of the tempest. (11757)

Account of the ten deserters. 30356

Account of the ten tribes of Israel. (44190)

Account of the terrestrial measurement. 84678C

Account of the terrible effects. 90935, 90937

Account of the terrific and fatal riot. 54027

Account of the time. 61175

Account of the time of holding the yearly, quarterly, and monthly meetings of Friends. 86020

Account of the times and places of holding the monthly, quarterly and preparative meetings. 86021

Account of the total eclipse. 27419, 85072

Account of the tract. 62481

Account of the trade in India. 98781

Account of the trade-winds. 19726

Account of the trade with Great Britain. 18685

Account of the trades, manners, and customs. 7800

Account of the transit of Mercury over the sun. 84678C

Account of the transit of Venus over the sun. 84678C

Account of the treatment of Mr. Fairchild. 23681

Account of the treatment of the natives. 12998

Account of the treaty between his excellency Benjamin Fletcher. 24712

Account of the treaty held at the city of Albany. 34601

Account of the Trenchara and Costilla estates. 14735

Account of the trial of Doctor Joseph Priestley. 90148

Account of the trial of Edward Smyth. 85207

Account of the trial of Francis Delap. 19355

Account of the trial of Jesse Wood. 105040

Account of the trial of John Edwards. 21923

Account of the trial of Thomas Cooper. 16608

Account of the trial of Winslow Russell. 74409

Account of the true nature and object of the late Protestant Episcopal Clerical Association. 7883, (54611), 66116, note after 97492

Account of the turbulent and factious proceedings. (13895), (14009), note after 101847

Account of the typhoid fever. 84403

Account of the United Brethren at Bethlehem. 68992

Account of the United Brethrens' missions. 50514

Account of the U. S. Naval Observatory. 27419

Account of the United States of America. 32602

Account of the unparalleled fires. 25695, 65016

Account of the unparalleled sufferings. 101521

Account of the very important debate. 103

Account of the viceroyalty of Buenos-Ayres. 8990

Account of the views and principles. 104

Account of the visit of General Lafayette. 38583

Account of the voyage and treatise on navigation. 62806, note after 90319

Account of the voyage of discovery. 77126

Account of the voyage of the Ursulines. (80023)

Account of the voyage of Thomas Candish. 66686

Account of the voyages and cruizes of Capt. Walker. 101043

Account of the voyages of W. Barents. 66686

Account of the voyages undertaken. 16275, 30934-30935, 30937-30939

Account of the Wapeti. 49570

Account of the war with Algiers. 7045

Account of the weather. 11772

Account of the West Indies and the American islands. 32147, 106120

Account of the whale fishery. (40201), 51787

Account of the wheat moth. (21802), 42526

Account of the Whitten plaster. 82939

Account of the witchcraft delusion at Salem. 96149

Account of the wonderful apparition. 9110

Account of the wonderful preservation of the ship Terra Nova. 13015

Account of the work of God at Georgia. 103550

Account of the work of God at New-York. 103549

Account of the work of God, in Newfoundland. (17139)

Account of the wreck of the transport Premier. 56105

Account of the writings of Roger Williams. 29221

Account of the yellow fever, as it appeared in Philadelphia. 74228

Account of the yellow fever as it prevailed in Philadelphia. 68520

Account of the yellow fever, as it prevailed in the city of New-York. 96390

Account of the yellow . . . fever, . . . in . . . Philadelphia. 35458

Account of the yellow fever, which appeared in the city of Galveston. (82341)

Account of the yellow fever which occurred in the city of New York. 30316

Account of their manners. 42165, 101219

Account of their tragical deaths. 94466

Account of this celebration. 98050

Account of those who died in Philadelphia. 3722

Account of three camp-meetings. 101292

[Account of tobacco sales.] 100048

Account of two missionary voyages. 38223, 95529

Account of two remarkable trains of angular erratic blocks. 72670

Account of two terrible fires. (61413)

Account of two voyages to New-England. (36672)

Account of two voyages to New-England, made during the years 1638, 1663. (36673)

Account of various interesting contemporaneous events. 3233

Account of W. Penn's travails. 59674

Account of Warner Mifflin. 48895

Account of Washington College. 84579, note after 101995

Account of Waymouth's voyage. 66686

Account of which is given in the Life of the Rev. Mr. John Wesley: 102683

Account shewing the progress of the colony of Georgia. 45000

Account shewing what money has been received. 27008, 91307

Account stated in respect to the province. 53438

Account which attends on a spirit. 4677

Account with the United States. 101546A

Account written by Jordan Seaman of Jericho. 78612

Account written by the hand of Mormon. 83071

Accounts and papers for 1847. (17769)

Accounts and papers for 1852-53. 17761

Accounts and papers relating to the late . . . accident. 10162

Accounts and papers, v. 35, 1850. 85560

Accounts . . . from . . . March 1780, until . . . 1781. 36970

Accounts, from June, 1775, to June, 1783. 101546-101546A

Accounts historical, biographical, and amusing. 91838

Accounts of expenses. 101546A

Accounts of gold hunters. (9991)

Accounts of Griffith Owen and descendants. 49327, 2d note after 95449

Accounts of Iceland and Greenland. 66686

Accounts of marches. 3536

Accounts of recent shipwrecks. (33386), 90853

Accounts of religious revivals. 7281

Accounts of shipwreck and other disasters. 885

Accounts of some Negroes. 20094

Accounts of some proceedings of committees. 34602

Accounts of the civil war. 10462

Accounts of the Corporation. (61414)

Accounts of the East and West Indies. 66686

Accounts of the Mexicans. 66686

Accounts of the receipts and payments of the mayor. (27494)

Accounts of the River Ob. 66686

Accounts of the state treasurer. 59927

Accounts of the treasury of . . . Pennsylvania. 59777

Accounts of the Turkish empire and the east. 66686

Accounts of the war, &c. 14389

Accounts of two attempts. 34603, 34617

Accounts of voyages. 66686

Accrostick. Washington. 101768

Accrostics, a number of original pieces. 80197

Accurate account of the battle of Lake Erie. 9187

Accurate account of the blockade of Boston. 11124

Accurate account of the important debate. 25337

Accurate account of the life of James M'Gowan. 96889

Accurate accounts of the capture of Groton Fort. (2489)

Accurate and authentic account of the taking of Cape Breton. 10723

Accurate and authentic journal of the siege of Quebec. 66987

Accurate and authentic report of the proceedings. 94964

Accurate and copious account of the debates.
81932
Accurate and interesting account of the
hardships. 31400
Accurate and particular account of the
establishment of the Missisippi
Company in France. 39311
Accurate Beschreibung aller vornehmsten
in der ganzen Welt. 79636
Accurate Beschreibung derer beruhmsten
Berge. 28738
Accurate description of Cape Breton.
10724
Accurate description of Niagara Falls.
(10617)
Accurate description of the ceremonies.
(34131)
Accurate description of the Liverpool
and Manchester Rail-way. 101061
Accurate description of those . . .
regions. 92355
Accurate descriptive table of the several
countries. 15116, 1st note after
102507
Accurate discourse ispremised [sic] of
Mr. John Elliot. 95652
Accurate history of the city. (21040)
Accurate journal and account. 42173,
60841
Accurate journal of one who has seen
the elephant. (10035)
Accurate list of the names. 18862
Accurate map of the West-Indies.
26973, 2d note after 102833
Accurate narrative of the sufferings.
92355
Accurate naval history. 10236
Accurate report of the argument. 30254,
3d note after 96883
Accurate report of the case of James
Maurice. (46955), 75951, 2d
note after 96891
Accurate statement of the maritime
forces. 91092
Accurate synopsis of the sixth census.
49722
Accurate table. 87369
Accurate tables for finding the mean-
diameters. 105474
Accursed thing must be taken away
from a people. (12309)
Accusatie ende conclusie overgegeven.
77999
Acerra exoticorum. 25460
Acevedo, Gaspar de Zuniga y. see
Zuniga y Acevedo, Gaspar de,
Conde de Monterey.
Acevedo, M. E. 56269
Acevedo, Rafael. 104391
Acevedo, Rafael Antunez y. see
Antunez y Acevedo, Rafael.
Acha, Jose Maria. 94914
Achat, loyer et reparations de Spencer
Wood. (10453)
Achates. pseud.
Reflections. see Pinckney,
Thomas.
Achenbach, H. 105
Achenwall, D. Gottfried. see
Achenwall, Gottfried, 1719-1772.
Achenwall, Gottfried, 1719-1772.
106-108, 102647
Achievements of the western naval
flotilla. (28852)
Achilles (Brig) in admiralty 60180,
60582, 94236
Achte Schiffart. Kurze Beschreibung.
33662

Achter Theil Americae. (8784)
Achter-volgens den 24sten articul
vanden octroy. 102929
Achtzehen Monate in Sud-Amerika.
27169
Achtzehender Theil der newen Welt.
33671
Achtzehn Predigten. 91201
Achushnet, Mass. Selectmen. 154
Ackermann, F. X. 109
Acknowledgement of receipts from the
Pacific coast. 76625
Aclamacion y pendones. 110
Acland, John Dyke, d. 1778. 89210
Aclaracion al arancel general. 48257
Aclaracion al articulo 38 del arancel. 48257
Aclaracion de las maldades del
administrador. 79091
Acoluthia. 26561
Acontecimientos de Cartagena con Ad.
Barrott. 11130
Acorn Club, Hartford, Conn. 92114
Acosta, ---------. ed. 132
Acosta, Blas de. 111-112
Acosta, Cecilio. 16990
Acosta, Christoval. 113-115, 13801,
14355, 57666
Acosta, Elias. tr. 58429
Acosta, Francisco. 116
Acosta, Gaspar. 21003
Acosta, Gioseffo di. see Acosta,
Joseph de.
Acosta, J. tr. 6941
Acosta, J. J. de. ed. 6
Acosta, Joaquin, 1799-1852. 117,
6941
Acosta, Joseph de. 118-131, 5039,
(8784), 26981, note after (41373),
(43784), 57458, 57459, 66686, 94838
Acoubar, ou la loyaute trahie. 29938
Acoubar, tragedie. 29939
Acquest of dominion. 6209
Acquisition of Cuba. (20611)
Acquisition of territory. 20031
Acreedores al Peage de Veracruz. see
Acreedores al Ramo de Peages
Del Camino de Vera-Cruz.
Acreedores al Ramo de Peages del
Camino de Vera-Cruz. Petitioners
98900-98901
Acrelius, Israel. (133)
Across America and Asia. 66652
Across Mexico in 1864-65. (9146)
Across the Atlantic. 134
Across the continent: a summer's journey.
(7077)
Across the continent. Atlantic and
Pacific Railway. (64356)
Across the continent of South America.
57727
Across the Rocky Mountains. (37320)
Acrostic. 17261
Acrostic on the memory of the Rev. Mr.
George Whitefield. 103637
Acrostics. 12393, 103736
Acsiomas militaires. 11466
Act altering the several acts. 94989
Act amendatory of the internal revenue
laws. 34909
Act amendatory of the militia law. 94763
Act amending the statute of limitations.
100462
Act and recommendation of the General
Assembly. 94691
Act and resolutions of the General Assembly.
87666
Act and testimony. 63121

Act and testimony of the General Assembly and others. 65123
[Act appropriating the public revenue.] 100364
[Act arranging counties into districts for representation in congress.] 100362
[Act "arranging the counties into districts to choose representatives."] 100367
Act assessing a tax. 99125
Act authorizing a subscription of stock. 47200
Act authorizing the Board of Education. 54121
Act authorizing the formation of corporations. 53439
Act authorizing the governor to incorporate the Susquehanna and Delaware Canal and Rail Road Company. 93918
Act authorizing the governor to incorporate the West-Chester Rail Road Company. 102760
Act authorizing the survey. 10009
Act codifying the laws of Massachusetts. (45558)
Act concerning aliens. (69843)
[Act concerning elections.] 100376
[Act "concerning executions and for the relief of insolvent debtors."] 100368
[Act concerning executions and insolvent debtors.] 100373
[Act concerning fees of certain officers.] 100363
[Act concerning officers.] 100323
Act concerning preaching lately made. 94922, note after 103402
[Act concerning taxes for 1791.] 100360
Act concerning the admission of church members. 65125
Act concerning the Catholic churches. 95027
Act concerning the city of San Francisco. 76032
Act concerning the convention. 100351
[Act concerning the erection of the district.] 100355-100356
[Act "concerning the fees of certain officers."] 100369
Act concerning the location and possession of mining claims. 52407
Act concerning the manufacture and sale of spirituous . . . liquors. (45559)
Act concerning the schools. 23701
Act concerning the students of Yale College. 105844
Act creating a general post office. 94985
Act directing the mode of proceeding. 100357
Act directing the treasurer to issue state notes. 99091-99092
Act directing what money and bills of credit shall be a legal currency. 99079
Act dividing the state into districts. 99120
Act . . . 1863. (51964)
Act empowering municipal corporations to subscribe. 28478
Act encouraging the importation of naval stores. 135
Act entitled An act for the establishment of common schools. 54029
Act entitled An act to incorporate the Union Insurance Company. 97808
Act entitled "An act to reduce into one act." 94988

Act . . . "establishing a supreme judicial court." 52891
Act establishing an equitable mode of levying the taxes. 56863
Act establishing county courts. (52780)
Act establishing fees. 99127
Act establishing general regulations. 100430
Act establishing religious freedom. 16118, 35914, 74622, 100342, 100344, 100427, 3d note after 100486
Act establishing the municipal court. 74777
Act establishing the New Bedford Fire Department. 52457
Act establishing town courts. (42780)
[Act exempting artificers from militia.] 100332
Act extending the charter of the Bank of Virginia. 100429
Act extending the privilege. 15239
Act for a Company Trading to Africa and the Indies. 136, 18544
Act for a fast. 98181
Act for allowing further time. 87603
Act for amending an act. 87627
Act for amending the several acts. 60651
[Act for appointing commissioners to liquidate and settle the expenses.] 100348
Act for appointing commissioners to take down the church. 87627
Act for appointing deputies. 100345
[Act "for appointing electors."] 100366
[Act "for appropriating the public revenue."] 100370
Act, for ascertaining certain taxes and duties. 100336
Act for ascertaining . . . the citizens. (53440)
[Act for ascertaining the number of militia.] 100333
Act for ascertaining the rates of money. (59876)
Act for better regulating the province. 45564
Act for better settling and regulating the militia. 53034
Act for carrying into effect on the part of the state of New-Jersey. 94222
Act for charging of tobacco. (52599)
Act for cleansing and making navigable Tulisinny Creek. 87627
Act for compleating the quota of troops. 87627
Act for disposing of certain estates. 137, 87634
Act for dividing the township of Orangeburgh. 87627
Act for emitting fifty thousand pounds in bills. 60124
Act for encorporating the Bank of Virginia. 100429
Act for encouraging the people known by the name of Unitas Fratrum. 1st note after 97845
Act for enlisting soldiers. 100335
Act . . . for enrolling and calling out the national forces. (57407)
Act for enrolling and calling out the national forces, and for other purposes. 25735
Act for establishing a board of commissioners. 87628
Act for establishing a court of civil jurisdiction. 54975
Act for establishing a ferry. 87627

[Act for establishing a land office.]
100324
Act for establishing a parish in Craven
County.   87627
Act for establishing an agreement.
87355
Act for establishing an health office.
59778, 61717
Act for establishing and opening lock
navigation.   102981
Act for establishing Knoxville.   (34358)
Act for establishing ministerial
libraries.   (65124)
[Act, for establishing public schools.]
100374
Act for establishing religious freedom.
35914, 100341-100344
Act, for establishing rules and articles.
94983
Act for establishing several ferries.
87627
Act for establishing six state banks.
53035
Act for establishing the constitution.
87414
Act for forming and regulating the
militia in New-Hampshire.   91429
Act for forming and regulating the
militia of the province of
Pennsylvania.   59779
Act for founding a college at Chester.
101996
Act, for giving further time to enter
certificates.   100349
Act for granting a supply.   45044
Act for granting and applying certain stamp
duties.   138, 90132
Act for granting His Majesty the sum of
one hundred thousand pounds.   59781
Act for granting liberty to carry rice.
70813
Act for granting to His Majesty an
excise upon wines.   86684
Act for granting to Their Majesties the
rate of one penny per pound.   53441
[Act "for imposing a public tax for
1792."]   100371
Act for incorporating a society.   87627
Act for incorporating certain persons.
75627
Act for incorporating the company.
(15223)
Act for incorporating the free port of
Perth-Amboy.   (61071)
Act for incorporating the Protestant
Episcopal Church.   100347
Act for incorporating the St. David's
Society.   87627
Act for incorporating the Salem Bank.
75712
Act for incorporating the Salem
Society.   87627
Act, for incorporating the Society, formed
for the Relief of Poor, Aged, and
Infirm Masters of Ships, their
Widows and Children.   59782,
85968
Act, for incorporating the Society, formed
for the Relief of Poor, Aged, and
Infirm Masters of Ships, their
Widows and Children.   Together
with the bye-laws of the society.
85969
Act for incorporating the society, known
by the name and stile of the
Philadelphia Contributionship.   61986
Act for inflicting penalties.   87635

Act for laying an excise.   53442
Act for laying out a road.   87627
Act for levying a tax.   99086
Act for making good deficiencies.   88171
Act for making more effectual provision.
95690
Act for making provision for the support
of public credit.   (29981)
Act for opening and extending the
navigation of Potomack River.   100339
Act for opening and extending the
navigation of the Potomack River.
96005
Act for opening the navigation of Lynch's
and Clark's Creeks.   87627
Act for propagating the Gospel in New
England.   52600
[Act for raising a corps of invalids.]
100330
Act for raising a fund.   (61415)
Act for raising and paying into the public
treasury of the state, a tax for the
uses therein mentioned.   87631
Act for raising and paying into the public
treasury of this state, the tax
therein mentioned.   87636
Act for raising and paying into the public
treasury . . . the tax . . . passed
March 28, 1778.   87627
Act for raising six thousand pounds.
53443
Act for raising volunteers to join the
grand army.   100319, 100322
Act for recruiting this state's quota.
100329
Act for reducing the number of directors.
88173
Act for regulating and ascertaining the
rates.   87607, 87627
Act, "for regulating and disciplining the
militia."   100350
Act for regulating and governing the
militia of the state of Vermont, and
repealing all laws heretofore passed.
99114
Act for regulating and governing the
militia of the state of Vermont.
Passed by the legislature.   99122
Act for regulating and governing the
militia of the state of Vermont,
passed in October, 1793.   91421
Act for regulating and governing the
militia, 1778.   45560
Act for regulating and ordering the
troops.   15632, 15674
Act for regulating elections.   53445
Act for regulating, governing, and training
the militia of the commonwealth of
Massachusetts.   45560, 91456
Act for regulating pilots fees.   100338
Act for regulating the fees.   53445
Act for regulating the militia of
Pennsylvania.   60653
[Act "for regulating the militia of the
commonwealth."]   100372
[Act for regulating the militia of Virginia.]
100365
Act . . . for regulating the militia;
together with the acts of the . . .
United States.   100375
Act for repealing certain parts of an act.
(139), (45561)
Act for restraining and punishing
privateers.   53444
Act for reviving and amending several
acts.   87627

[Act, "for reviving, continuing, and amending an act."]   100349

Act for settling and better regulation of the militia. (50851)

Act for speedily recruiting the quota. 100325

Act for supplying the army.   100328

Act for supplying the city of Boston with pure water.   6780

Act for suppressing immorality.   53664

Act for testablishing [sic] county courts. 87640

Act for the abolition of feudal rights. (42507)

Act for the abolition of slavery.   93260

Act for the admission of emigrants. 100337

Act for the admission of the state of Tennessee.   note after 94725

Act for the better employment, relief and support of the poor.   59783

Act for the better regulating of pilots. 87627

Act for the better regulation of the several banking and savings institutions and loan companies. 60510

Act for the better security of Charlestown. 87627

Act for the better settling of intestate estates.   27012

Act for the consolidation & amendment of the laws.   59784

Act for the consolidation of the railroad state debt.   (49571)

[Act for the defence of the eastern frontier.]   100331

Act . . . for the due training of teachers.   60380

Act for the encouragement and enlargement of the whale fishery. 1st note after 97845

Act for the encouragement of fisheries. 48941

Act for the establishment and organization of the army.   2054

Act for the establishment and support of public schools.   3008

Act for the establishment of a college.   70716

Act for the establishment of common schools.   54029

Act, for the establishment of district courts.   10043

Act for the establishment of religious freedom.   94024, note after 100447, note after 102401

Act for the establishment of religious worship.   10956, (10958), (10968), 10980, 87347, 87355, 87805, 1st note after 97553

Act for the final adjustment of land titles.   55951

Act for the formation of corporations. 53446

Act, for the general valuation and assessment.   89277

Act for the government of slaves.   35619

Act for the government of the territory. note after 94720

Act . . . for the improvement of the internal navigation.   50833

Act for the improvement of the navigation of the river Susquehannah.   93938

Act for the improvement of the state. 60750, note after 97766

Act for the incorporation of the Salem Iron Foundry Company.   75727

Act for the limitation of actions. 99018, 99022

Act for the military organization of this state.   83854

Act for the more effectual preservation of the government of the province of Carolina.   10956, (10958), 10980, 87347, 87355, 87805, 1st note after 97553

Act for the more effectual prevention of the desertion.   87618

Act for the more effectual suppression of drinking houses.   70502, (70576)

Act for the more effectual suppression of piracy.   96954, 96955, 96957

Act for the more speedily completing the quota of troops.   100320

Act . . . for the organizing, arming, and disciplining the militia.   59785

Act for the organization, . . . of common schools.   37027

Act for the preservation of white and other pine trees.   (42780)

Act for the protection of the creditors. 78077

Act for the purpose of procuring provisions for the troops.   99078, 99085

Act for the purpose of raising three hundred able-bodied effective men. 99088

Act for the regulation of banks in . . . Pennsylvania.   (59786)

Act for the regulation of fees.   99094

Act for the regulation of the militia of . . . Pennsylvania.   91457

Act for the regulation of the militia of . . . Pennsylvania, passed the second day of April.   59788

Act for the regulation of the militia of the commonwealth of Pennsylvania. 58787

Act for the regulation of the militia of this state.   87627

Act for the regulation of the post-offices. 87627

Act for the regulation of the staple of tobacco.   99908

Act for the relief of debtors.   56107

Act for the relief of insolvent debtors. 87569

Act for the relief of the banks.   49574

Act for the relief of the insolvent debtors. 59789

Act for the sequestration of the estate. 5380, (27106)

Act for the subsistence, clothing, and the better regulation and government of slaves.   35619, 81748

Act for the support of common schools; Assembly, Feb. 25, 1819.   53447

Act for the support of common schools, passed April 17, 1822.   53454

Act for the suppression of drinking-houses and tippling-shops.   43980

Act for the suppression of drinking houses and tippling shops. Passed at the January session.   70502

Act for the suppression of drinking houses and tippling shops, passed at the May session, 1852.   70501

Act for the suppression of drinking houses and tippling shops, passed . . . 1851. 43898

Act for the suppression of intemperance.
52902

Act for the trial of certain offenders. 36185

Act for vesting in James Rumsey. 74124

Act for vesting 600 acres of land. 87627

Act, further supplementary to an act. 89277

Act further to amend the charter of the city of
Brooklyn. 8270

Act further to amend the charter of the city of
New York. 54028

Act, further to establish and to incorporate a
college. 84558

Act giving effect to the laws of the United
States. note after 94725

Act, giving further time to enter certificates.
100340

[Act "giving further time to owners of
surveys."] 100359

Act granting a rate, &c. 53726

Act granting certain powers to the Bank of
Kentucky. 37492

Act granting lands to aid in the construction
of a railroad. 88607

[Act imposing certain taxes on law process.]
100378

Act imposing taxes for the support of
government. 15225

Act imposing taxes on distilled spirits. 20925

Act in addition to an act for forming and
regulating the militia within the
commonwealth of Massachusetts.
45560

Act in addition to an act intitled "An act to
prevent monopoly and oppression."
45564

Act in addition to an act to establish the city
of Cambridge. (10139)

Act, in addition to an act, to establish the city
of New Bedford. 52457

Act in addition to an act to incorporate the
Metropolitan Railway Company. 73653

Act in aid of the construction. 45367

Act, in alteration to an act, entitled, An act
regulating proprietors meetings. 99096

Act in relation to schools. 56826

Act in relation to the engraving of bank notes.
53539

Act in relation to the Medical Institution of
Yale College. 15783

Act in relation to the monies. (53448)

Act incorporating the city of Cincinnati.
13061

Act incorporating the city [of Cleveland.]
13676

Act . . . incorporating the . . . company.
(62617)

Act incorporating the House of Refuge.
61728

Act incorporating the Little Schuylkill and
Susquehanna Rail-Road Company.
(60218)

Act incorporating the Little Schuylkill
Navigation Rail Road and Coal Company.
(60219)

Act incorporating the Magdalen Society.
(61801)

Act . . . incorporating the Philadelphia,
Germantown, and Norristown Railroad
Company. 62001

Act incorporating the proprietors of the locks.
48015

Act incorporating the Weymouth and Braintree
Institution for Savings. 103087

Act incorporating the Wyoming and Lehigh
Rail Road Company. 105686

Act lately pass'd in Carolina. (10968),
10980, 16728, 87347

Act laying duties on household furniture.
59790

[Act laying taxes for the support of government.]
100377

Act made by Charles Gookin, Esq; 60399

[Act, "making further provision for the erection
of the district of Kentucky, into an
independent state."] 100353

Act more effectually to provide for the support.
75008

Act of Assembly. 60358

Act of Assembly ceding to the United States
the then territory southwest of the river
Ohio. 94777

Act of Assembly, passed in the island of
Antigua. 1694

Act of confederation defective. 97439

Act of Congress approved April 20, 1862.
(32743)

Act of Congress establishing the Smithsonian
Institution. 85018

Act of Congress for the admission of Tennessee
into the Union. 94777

Act of Congress granting lands. (8599)

Act of incorporating of the New Jersey
Navigation Company. 53036

Act of incorporation, additional acts and by-laws
[of the Massachusetts Charitable Fire
Society.] 45828

Act of incorporation, and by-laws and
ordinances of the . . . [Pennsylvania]
Academy [of the Fine Arts.] 60294

Act of incorporation and by-laws [of East
Boston.] 6556

Act of incorporation and by laws, of the Bank
of Wooster. 105224

Act of incorporation and by-laws of the Boott
Cotton Mills. 6397

Act of incorporation and by laws of the Boston
and Worcester Rail Road Corporation.
6768

Act of incorporation and by-laws of the Demilt
Dispensary. 54236

Act of incorporation and by-laws of the East
India Marine Society. 75656

Act of incorporation and by-laws of the Eastern
Dispensary. 54255

Act of incorporation and by-laws of the Eastern
Railroad Company. (21666)

Act of incorporation and by-laws [of the
Herkimer County Mutual Insurance
Company.] (31492)

Act of incorporation . . . and by-laws of the
Kane Monument Association. 37005

Act of incorporation and by-laws of the . . .
[Lowell Hosiery] Company. 42490

Act of incorporation and by-laws of the
Maryland State Colonization Society.
45243

Act of incorporation and by-laws of the
Massachusetts Charitable Eye and Ear
Infirmary. 45827

Act of incorporation and by-laws [of the
Massachusetts College of Pharmacy.]
45831

Act of incorporation and by-laws of the
Massachusetts Congregational
Charitable Society. 45835

Act of incorporation and by-laws of the . . .
[Massachusetts Historical] Society.
(45850)

Act of incorporation and by-laws of the
Massachusetts Medical Society. 45873

Act of incorporation and by-laws of the Mount
Carbon Rail Road Company. (60265)

Act of incorporation and by-laws of the New
England Coal Mining Company. 52665

Act of incorporation, and by-laws of the New England Society for the Promotion of Manufacturers and the Mechanic Arts. (52744)

Act of incorporation and by-laws of the Northern Dispensary of . . . New York. (55793)

Act of incorporation and by-laws of the Northern Railroad. (55825)

Act of incorporation and by-laws of the Old South Society. 57145

Act of incorporation and by-laws of the Pennsylvania Horticultural Society. 60326

Act of incorporation and by-laws of the . . . [Pennsylvania] Training School. 60385

Act of incorporation, and bye laws of the Proprietors of the Second Turnpike Road in New-Hampshire. (52780)

Act of incorporation and by-laws of the Proprietors of the Social Law Library. 85692

Act of incorporation, and by-laws, of the Rutgers Female Institute. 74445

Act of incorporation and by-laws of the Salem Dispensary. 75723

Act of incorporation and by-laws of the Second and Third Street Passenger Railway Co. (62235)

Act of incorporation and by-laws of the Second Congregational Unitarian Church. (54214)

Act of incorporation and bye-laws [of the Society for the Promotion of Agriculture and Domestic Manufactures In and For Cumberland.] 85910

Act of incorporation and by-laws of the Sullivan Railroad Company. 93562

Act of incorporation and by-laws of the Trustees [of the Astor Library.] 2249

Act of incorporation and by-laws of the village of Rutland. 74465

Act of incorporation and by-laws of the Western Clinical Infirmary. 62386

Act of incorporation and bye-laws of the Williamsburgh Fire Insurance Company. 104439

Act of incorporation and by-laws of the Worcester County Institute for Savings. 105420

Act of incorporation and by-laws, together with the laws of Massachusetts. 75802

Act of incorporation, and constitution and by-laws of the Kentucky Historical Society. 37521

Act of incorporation and constitution of the New York Society, for Promoting the Manumission of Slaves. (54851)

Act of incorporation and constitution [of the Pennsylvania Society for Promoting the Abolition of Slavery.] 60364

Act of incorporation and constitution of the Philadelphia Society for Alleviating the Miseries of Public Prisons. 62034

Act of incorporation, and documents relating to the city of Cairo. 9862

Act of incorporation, and laws of the Philadelphia Medical Society. 62017

Act of incorporation and laws relative to the New-York House of Refuge. 54486

Act of incorporation and minutes of the Baptist Convention of the State of Rhode Island and Vicinity. 70554

Act of incorporation, and organization [of the Boston Athenaeum.] 6593

Act of incorporation, and ordinances for the establishment of a house of refuge, in the county of St. Louis. 75405

Act of incorporation and report of the Mecklenburgh Gold Mining Company. 47289

Act of incorporation and reports of the Rochester Water Works Company. 72369

Act of incorporation, and rules and regulations of the Proprietors of Neponset Bridge. 52336

Act of incorporation and settlements thereto. 93920

Act of incorporation, and standing regulations of the Pennsylvania Academy of the Fine Arts. 60294

Act of incorporation and supplement [of the city of Baltimore.] 3053

Act of incorporation and the bye laws of the Boston and Montreal Turnpike Company. 50238

Act of incorporation and the by-laws of the South Reading Mechanic and Agricultural Institution. 88162

Act of incorporation, and the ordinances and regulations [of Marietta, Ohio.] (44564)

Act of incorporation . . . and the supplements . . . [of the Philadelphia, Easton and Water-Gap Railroad Company.] (61993)

Act of incorporation and the supplements thereto, passed by the legislature of Maryland. 93920

Act of incorporation, by-laws, and a list of the original members [of the Bunker Hill Monument Association.] (9174)

Act of incorporation, by-laws and catalogue of the Brooklyn City Library. 8266

Act of incorporation, by-laws and orchestral regulations of the musical Fund Society. 61853

Act of incorporation, by-laws and standing rules, of the Detroit Young Men's Society. 19782

Act of incorporation, by-laws, &c. [of the American Institute of Instruction.] 1108

Act of incorporation, by-laws &c. of the Hibernian Provident Society, for the Relief of Emigrants. 61720

Act of incorporation, by-laws, &c., of the Hibernian Society. 86147

Act of incorporation, by-laws, ordinances, rules and regulations of the Board of Water Commissioners of the city of Detroit. 19783

Act of incorporation, by-laws, rules, and regulations of Dummer Academy. (21202)

Act of incorporation, by-laws, rules and regulations . . . of the Grand Lodge of Massachusetts. 45760

Act of Incorporation, by-laws, rules and regulations of the Monument Cemetery. 50234

Act of incorporation, by-laws, rules and regulations, officers and members, of the monument cemetery. 61846

Act of incorporation, . . . catalogue of members, and circular letter of the Massachusetts Historical Society. (45850)

Act of incorporation, constitution and by-laws, and lists of the officers and members [of the Essex Institute.] 23015

Act of incorporation, constitution and by-laws of the Chamber of Commerce, Milwaukee, Wis. 49153

Act of incorporation, constitution and by-laws of the Essex Institute. 23012

Act of incorporation, constitution and by-laws of the Lowell Dispensary. 42486

Act of incorporation, constitution, and by-laws of the New-Hampshire Historical Society. 52872

33

Act of incorporation, constitution, and by-laws, of the Northern Baptist Society. 3236

Act of incorporation, constitution, and by-laws, of the Salem Society for the Moral and Religious Instruction of the Poor. (75735)

Act of incorporation, constitution and by-laws, of the Salem Young Men's Union. 75738

Act of incorporation, constitution and statutes [of the General Theological Seminary.] 26910

Act of incorporation &c., &c. [of the Massachusetts Horticultural Society.] 45862

Act of incorporation, etc. . . . [of the Herkimer County Mutual Insurance Company.] (31492)

Act of incorporation, . . . &c. of the Hibernian Society. 60135

Act of incorporation, . . . &c. of the Hibernian Society, for the relief of Emigrants. 61720

Act of incorporation, &c. of New York Manumission Society. 82024

Act of incorporation, for that part of the Northern Liberties, lying between the middle of Sixth Street. (59791)

Act of incorporation, for that part of the Northern Liberties, lying between the west of Sixth Street. (59791)

Act of incorporation for the Kensington District of the Northern Liberties. 59792

Act of incorporation, laws and regulations, catalogue, &c., of the Massachusetts Charitable Fire Society. 45828

Act of incorporation, laws and regulations of "The Colored Home." 85981

Act of incorporation of Lafayette College. 38586

Act of incorporation . . . of the Academy of Natural Sciences. 61405

Act of incorporation of the American Academy of Music. 61458

Act of incorporation of the Benevolent Congregational Society. 66242

Act of incorporation [of the Boston Female Asylum.] 6705

Act of incorporation of the Catholic Congregational Society. 8054, 1st note after 91736

Act of incorporation [of the Cincinnati Astronomical Society.] 9373

Act of incorporation of the city of Camden. 10160

Act of incorporation, . . . of the Franklin Fire Insurance Company. 61675

Act of incorporation of the Franklin Library Association. 39391

Act of incorporation of the Kentucky Coal Mining Company. (37518)

Act of incorporation [of the McKean and Elk Land Improvement Company.] (43381)

Act of incorporation of the Manhattan Company. 44255

Act of incorporation of the Massachusetts Fire and Marine Insurance Company. (45845)

Act of incorporation of the Mine Hill & Schuylkill Haven Rail Road Company. 60252

Act of incorporation [of the Missionary Society of Connecticut.] 15806

Act of incorporation of the New York Juvenile Asylum. 54503

Act of incorporation of the North Pennsylvania Railroad Company. 60277

Act of incorporation . . . of the Northern Dispensary for the . . . Poor. 61869

Act of incorporation of the Northern Liberties Gas Works. 59793

Act of incorporation [of the People's College of the State of New York.] 60820

Act of incorporation of the Philadelphia and Reading Rail Road Company. 61948

Act of incorporation [of the Reading & Lehigh Rail Road.] 68214

Act of incorporation . . . of the St. Lawrence University and Universalist Theological School. 75323

Act of incorporation of the Summit Branch Rail Road Company. 93633

Act of incorporation, of the United Society of St. John's Church. 97899

Act of incorporation of the village of Brooklyn. 8269

Act of incorporation of the village of Mineral Point. 49208

Act of incorporation, regulations, and members of the . . . [Massachusetts Congregational Charitable] Society. 45835

Act of incorporation, supplementary acts, and by-laws of the Lykens Valley Rail-Road and Coal Company. 60225

Act of incorporation, the laws, and the circular letter of the Massachusetts Historical Society. (45850)

Act of incorporation, with the additional acts, and by-laws [of the Massachusetts Historical Society.] (45850)

Act of incorporation . . . with the by-laws and orders, of the Massachusetts Medical Society. 45874

Act of incorporation; with the by-laws and rules of the Louisville Gas and Water Company. 42328

Act of incorporation, with the medical police, by-laws and rules, of the Rhode-Island Medical Society. 70727

Act of incorporation, with the rules and regulations [of Newton Theological Institution.] (55095)

Act of Independence [of Venezuela.] 10775, (34898), note after 98877

Act of Parliament appointing commissioners. 140

Act of Parliament for an agreement. 87697, 1st note after 97056

Act of Parliament for ascertaining the rates. 53449

Act of Parliament for encouraging the Scots African and Indian Company. 141, (78198)

Act of Parliament for establishing an agreement. 87697

Act for Parliament for repealing the stamp duties. 142

Act of Parliament for reversing the attainder. (53719)

Act of Parliament, offering rewards of £20,000 for the North Passage. 55725

Act of Parliament relating to the government. (143)

Act of Parliament 1644. 80715, 86364

Act of Parliament 1649. 80715, 86358

Act of perpetual insolvency. 78664

Act of registering ships to prevent fraud. 144

Act of that synod for a fast. 93, (59400), 65121

Act of the Associate Presbytery of Pennsylvania, against occasional communion. (59899)

Act of the Associate Presbytery of Pennsylvania concerning public covenanting. 65125

Act of the Commission of the General Assembly. 80715, 86358

Act of the commonwealth of Massachusetts. 28959

Act of the General Assembly confirming the same [i.e. the charter of the city of New York.] 54165

Act of the General Assembly for raising
£100,000. (53663)
Act of the General Assembly of New York
for raising a supply of £100,000. 23508
Act of the General Assembly of South-Carolina.
87666
Act of the General Assembly of the Governour,
Council and Representatives of New-
England. 52601
Act of the General Assembly of the state of
Missouri. 49573
Act of the General Assembly, 1643. 80715,
86364
Act of the King's Council of State. 10485
Act of the legislature . . . and a patent to
incorporate a Company For Erecting a
. . . Bridge. (59794)
Act of the legislature and ordinances of the
city council. (6692)
Act of the legislature establishing a fire
department. (10140)
Act of the legislature . . . for regulating the
practice of physick. 45874
Act of the legislature . . . incorporating the
Eastern Market Company. 60077
Act of the legislature of New-Hampshire.
28446
Act of the legislature of New Jersey. 53037
Act of the legislature of New York, entitled
"An act for suppressing immorality."
53664
Act of the legislature of New York to provide
for the indigent deaf and dumb. 53450
Act of the legislature of the state of
Pennsylvania. 64250
Act of the legislature, . . . relating to the
. . . [Union Canal Company of Philadel-
phia.] note after 97766
Act of the legislature to remove the dam
across the Concord River. 90771
Act of the legislature to unite said cities [of
Roxbury and Boston.] 6770
Act of the Parliament of Scotland. (18545)
Act of the Particular Synod of New York.
53854
Act of the state of Maryland. 45809
Act of the Synod of Philadelphia. 104741
Act of William and Mary laying a tax. 59795
Act passed by the General Assembly of the
State of South Carolina. 87677
Act passed by the legislature of the state of
Vermont, the 8th instant. 99104
Act passed by the legislature of the state of
Vermont, 29th October last. 99098
Act pass'd in Carolina. 10956, (10958), 10980,
87347, 87355, 87805, 1st note after 97553
Act [passed in Pennsylvania, Nov. 27, 1755.]
59780
Act passed in the General Assembly, held at
Philadelphia. 59796
Act pass'd in the General Assembly . . . of
Pennsylvania. 59797
Act, passed in the year 1774. 56462, note
after 63734
Act passed March 12 1805. 53451
Act passed, Nov. 19, 1778. (52780)
Act prohibiting slavery. 52179
Act prohibiting trade. 145
Act proposed by a New York state banker.
51962
Act providing a uniform system of free public
schools. 45132
[Act providing against invasion.] 100327
Act providing for the appointment of inspectors.
(61988)
Act providing for the assessment of taxes.
6537

Act providing for the enumeration of the
inhabitants. 70144, (70145)
Act providing for the more easy payment.
45562
Act providing for the resumption of specie
payments. 59798
Act providing for the second census. 70146
Act providing remedy for bankrupts. 45563
Act regulating and stating the fines. 99084
Act regulating general elections. 34572
Act regulating proprietors meetings. 99096
Act regulating the choice of a Council of
Censors. 99098
Act regulating the grants of land. 86169
Act, . . . regulating the militia. (53060)
Act regulating the militia of the state of New
York. 53452
Act regulating the militia of the state of
Vermont. 99104
Act reincorporating the village of Little Falls.
41533
Act relating to a public cemetery. 73626
Act relating to banks. 59799
Act relating . . . to estates. 65432
Act relating to insurance companies. (52780)
Act relating to public schools. 70503, 70748
Act relating to the gold fields. 56107
Act [relating to] the militia. 37550
Act relating to the Society of the Lying-In
Hospital. (54508)
Act reorganizing the judiciary. (52780)
[Act respecting executions.] 100352
Act respecting the government of the territories.
94720
Act supplementary to an act entitled An act for
the establishment of common schools.
54029
Act supplementary to an act entitled An act to
establish a general land office for the
Republic of Texas. 94987
Act supplementary to an act to establish a
general system of education. (59800)
Act supplementary to . . . an act to incorporate
the Philadelphia, Germantown and Norris-
town Rail Road Company. 62001
Act the more effectually to prevent and punish
desertion. 100326
Act to abolish imprisonment for debt. 91819
Act to accept a cession of the claims. note
after 94720
Act to aid the construction. 15798
Act to allow the commodore of this state a
share. 87627
Act to alter and amend certain provisions of
the act. 10485
Act to alter and amend the slave laws. 35619
Act to alter the name of the Corporation of
Trinity Church. 90661
Act to alter the organization of the common
council. 54030
[Act to amend an act directing the mode of
proceeding under certain executions.]
100357
Act to amend an act entitled "An act to amend
and reduce to one act, the several acts
. . . for regulating the militia." 100379
Act to amend [an act for incorporating the
Society, known by the name and stile of
the Philadelphia Contributionship.] 61986
Act to amend . . . "An act to establish a
metropolitan police district." 53453
Act to amend an act to improve the New York
police. 54031
Act to amend "An act to revise and amend the
several acts relating to the city of Brooklyn,
passed April 4, 1850." 8271

[Act to amend and continue two acts passed in 1788.] 100361

Act to amend, and reduce into one act, the militia laws. 10518

Act to amend and reduce into one the several laws. 94990

Act to amend and reduce to one act, the several acts. 100379

[Act "to amend an act, 'for regulating and disciplining the militia'."] 100350

Act to amend the act for the support of common schools. 53454

Act to amend the act incorporating the "Texas Rail-Road Navigation and Banking Company." 94991

Act to amend the act relating to the gold fields. 56107

Act to amend the charter of . . . New York. 54032

Act to amend the city charter. 73627

Act to amend the jury of this province. 10502

Act to amend the laws. 42508

Act to amend the same [i.e. an act passed by the General Assembly of the state of South Carolina.] 87677

Act to amend the several acts of Assembly concerning naval-officers. 100084

Act to amend the several acts relating to the city. 613

Act to amend . . . the . . . statutes. 53990

Act to amend the 3d section of the 10th article of the constitution. 87452-87453

Act to apportion and assess a tax. 43897

Act to appropriate the income of the United States Deposite Fund. 21879

Act to authorize a loan to defray the expenses. 60308

Act to authorize life insurance companies. 53455

Act to authorize the congress of the United States to adopt certain regulations. 100337

Act to authorize the formation of a corporation. (53456)

Act to authorize the governour to incorporate a company. 59801

Act to authorize the governor to incorporate the Erie Canal Company. 60089

Act to authorize the licencing of vessels. 18095

Act to charter the Bank, of . . . Missouri. 49574

Act to charter the Union Bank of the State of Tennessee. 94812, note after 97760

Act to compensate the services. note after 94720

Act to consolidate and amend an act, entitled, "An act to incorporate the city of Madison." 43734

Act to consolidate and amend several acts relating to the city of Brooklyn. 8273

Act to consolidate and amend the act entitled "An act to incorporate the city of Brooklyn, passed April 8, 1834." 8272

Act to consolidate the cities of Brooklyn and Williamsburgh. 8274

Act to construct a ship canal. 55112

Act to create a fund. 23352, 91879

Act to create a metropolitan sanitary district and board of health. 53457, 54399

Act to declare certain trespasses felony. 45162

Act to define and limit the issue of promissory notes. 95013

Act to define seigniorial rights in Lower Canada. 21291

Act to detect fradulent land certificates. 95045

Act to direct executors and administrators. 87643

Act to discontinue . . . the landing and discharging . . . of goods. 94142

Act to dispose of the Southwest Pacific Railroad. 49572

Act to empower justices of the peace. 84575

Act to empower the Court of Admirlaty. 87622

Act to empower the inhabitants of Salem. 75628

Act to enable persons who have entered into and made improvements on lands. 99019

Act to enable persons who have settled and made improvements on lands. 99020

Act to enable the citizens of this commonwealth to discharge certain taxes. 100358

Act to enable the governor . . . to incorporate a company for making an artificial road from . . . Philadelphia. (59802)

Act to enable the governor to incorporate a company for making an artificial road . . . Vine and Tenth Streets, Philadelphia. 62195

Act to enable the governor of this commonwealth, to make an artifical road. 104537

Act to enable the inhabitants of the colony to discharge their publick dues. 40537, 1st note after 100484

Act, to enable the judges of the Admiralty. 100045

Act to enable the masters of ships. 100318

Act to enable the members of the United Church of England and Ireland in Canada to meet in synod. 10331

Act to enable the President and Managers of the Schuylkill and Susquehanna Navigation. 84621

Act to enable the Savannah & Charleston Railroad Co. 87678

Act to enable . . . the Schuylkill and Susquehanna Navigation. 78068

Act to enable the South Sea Company. 88172

Act to encourage the destroying beasts of prey. 87570

Act to encourage the manufacture of iron. 28476, (35091)

Act to encourage to trade to America. (24157)

Act to enforce the thirteenth article of the constitution. 62890

Act to establish a bank in the Mississippi Territory. (49487)

Act, to establish a general land office. 94986, 94987

Act to establish a general system of education. (59800)

Act to establish a lazaretto or quarantine hospital. 87677

Act to establish a medium of circulation. 87641

Act to establish a metropolitan police district. 53453

Act to establish a new proportion for the assessment of public taxes. (52780)

Act to establish a police court. (73628)

Act to establish a state board of health. 82470

Act to establish a system of common schools. 10001

Act to establish a system of public instruction. 53038

Act to establish an uniform system of bankruptcy. 3194

Act to establish and maintain a system of free schools. 34248

Act to establish free schools. 70689

Act to establish . . . free schools . . . February 15, 1855. 34224

Act to establish . . . free schools . . . February 21, 1859. 34247

Act to establish . . . in New Orleans the University of Louisiana. 42310

Act to establish regulations. (54033)

Act to establish the Boston and Worcester
Railroad Corporation. 6768
Act to establish the city of Cambridge. (10139)
Act to establish the city of Lynn. (42830)
Act to establish the city of Manchester.
44204
Act to establish the city of New-Bedford.
52471
Act to establish the city of Portsmouth. 64413
Act to establish the city of Roxbury. 73629
Act to establish the city of Salem. 75629
Act to establish the Office of Superintendent of
Public Instruction. (52780)
Act to establish . . . "The Philadelphia, Dover
and Norfolk Steam-Boat and Transport
Company." 61992
Act to establish the Smithsonian Institution.
84998
Act to establish the Superior Court in the city
of Boston. (6777), 67235, 67254
Act to exempt the inhabitants. 95974
Act to facilitate the raising of troops. (52780)
Act to found a state woman's hospital. 53978
Act to further provide for the public defence.
15228
Act to impose regulations. 15226
Act to impower certain commissioners. 87599
Act to improve the New York police. 54031
Act to improve the public health. 64618
Act to incorporate . . . a rail road. 59804
Act to incorporate . . . a society. 45765
Act to incorporate and vest certain powers in
the free-holders and inhabitants of the
village of Brooklyn. (8275)
Act to incorporate and vest certain powers in
the freeholders and inhabitants of the
village of Williamsburgh. 104436
Act to incorporate certain persons by the name
of the Massachusetts General Hospital.
45846
Act to incorporate certain persons, by the name
of the Society for Propagating the Gospel
among the Indians and Others. 85864
Act to incorporate Charleston. 87637
Act to incorporate medical societies . . . in
this state. 53458
Act to incorporate medical societies, . . .
regulating the practice of physic and
surgery in Ohio. (56864)
Act . . . to incorporate . . . Philadelphia.
60114
Act to incorporate Saint-Andrew's Church,
Montreal. 50286
Act to incorporate sundry persons. 98079
Act to incorporate the Bangor and Piscataquis
Canal and Railroad Company. 3154
Act to incorporate the Bank of Ohio and other
banks. (56865)
Act to incorporate . . . [the Buffalo Juvenile
Asylum.] 9063
Act to incorporate the Cairo City and Canal
Company. 9859
Act to incorporate the Carpenters' Company
of . . . Philadelphia. 61518
Act to incorporate the city bank of New Haven.
(52955)
Act to incorporate the city of Brooklyn. 8276
Act to incorporate the city of Brooklyn, passed
April 8, 1834. 8272
Act to incorporate the city of Madison. 43734
Act to incorporate the city of Philadelphia.
59805
Act to incorporate the city of Philadelphia,
with enlarged boundaries. 59806
Act to incorporate the city of Rochester.
72338
Act to incorporate the city of St. Louis.
75404

Act to incorporate the city of Utica. 98225
Act to incorporate the Commercial Bank of
New-Orleans. 53300
Act to incorporate the Connecticut Medical
Society. 15783
Act to incorporate the Delaware and Schuylkill
Basin Company. 61569
Act to incorporate the District of Spring Garden.
60650
Act to incorporate the District of Spring
Garden, . . . extending the bounds of the
corporation. (59807)
Act to incorporate . . . the District of Spring
Garden, lying between Vine Street and
the middle of Hickory Lane. (59807)
Act to incorporate the Dundee Manufacturing
Company. 21272
Act to incorporate . . . the Eagle Fire Company.
54251
Act to incorporate the East River Fire Insurance
Company. 54253
Act to incorporate the Freedman's Saving and
Trust Company. 25737
Act to incorporate the . . . Fulton Bank. 54034
Act to incorporate the Girard Bank. 27490
Act to incorporate the Jeffersonville and New-
Albany Canal Company. (35951)
Act to incorporate the Library Company of
Wilmington. 104581
Act to incorporate the Lodi Manufacturing
Company. 41767
Act to incorporate the Long-Island Rail-Road
Company. 41899
Act, to incorporate . . . the Massachusetts
Manufacturing Company. 45871
Act to incorporate the Mechanics' and Traders'
Bank of New Orleans. 53300
Act to incorporate the members of the New-York
Institution for the Instruction of the Deaf
and Dumb. 54500
Act to incorporate the Metropolitan Railroad
Company. 73653
Act to incorporate the Mohawk and Hudson
Railroad Company. 49853
Act to incorporate the Mutual Assurance
Company. 54410
Act to incorporate the National Safe Deposit
Company. 54416
Act to incorporate the New Bedford and
Fairhaven Railway Company. 52458
Act to incorporate the New England Emigrant
Aid Society. (52673)
Act to incorporate the New England Society of
Louisiana. 42181
Act to incorporate . . . the New Hampshire
Iron Factory Company. (42873)
Act to incorporate the New York and Stonington
Railroad Company. 54741
Act to incorporate the New York, Providence
and Boston Railroad Company. 54839
Act to incorporate the New York Washington
Mutual Assurance Company. 54865
Act, to incorporate the North American Mining
Company. (55554)
Act to incorporate the Ohio River Improvement
Company. 57069
Act to incorporate the owners and proprietors.
97255
Act to incorporate the Pennsylvania, Delaware
and Maryland Steam Navigation Company.
60316
Act to incorporate the Pennsylvania Fire
Insurance Company. 60322
Act to incorporate the Pennsylvania Railroad
Company. 60356
Act to incorporate the People's Pacific Railroad
Company. 60828

Act to incorporate the Philadelphia Board of Trade. 61970

Act to incorporate the Philadelphia, Easton and Water-Gap Railroad Company. (61993)

Act to incorporate the Philadelphia, Germantown and Norristown Rail Road Company. 62001

Act to incorporate the Philadelphia Time Lock Company. (62045)

Act to incorporate the Portland Dry-Dock and Insurance Company. 64338

Act to incorporate the President, Directors & Company of the Westchester County Bank. 102955

Act, to incorporate the Proprietors of the West Boston Bridge. 102758

Act to incorporate the Savannah and Charleston Railroad Company. 87679

Act to incorporate the Society for the Relief of Poor Widows with Small Children. 85970

Act to incorporate the Society Instituted in the State of New-York, for the Promotion of Agriculture, Arts and Manufactures. 96743

Act to incorporate the Society of Mechanics and Tradesmen. 54676

Act to incorporate the Society of Teachers of . . . New York for Benevolent and Literary Purposes. 54677

Act to incorporate the Society [of the Lying-In Hospital.] (54508)

Act to incorporate the South Wharf Corporation. 88215

Act to incorporate the Southern Railroad Company. 88455

Act to incorporate the Spot Pond Aqueduct Company. 89642

Act to incorporate the State Bank of Ohio. (56866)

Act to incorporate the stockholders in the Union Bank of Maryland. 97760

Act to incorporate the stockholders of the New York Insurance Company. (54782)

Act to incorporate the stockholders of the Philadelphia Arcade. 61953

Act to incorporate the stockholders of the Pleasant Valley Manufacturing Company. 63407

Act to incorporate the stockholders of the United Insurance Company. 97878

Act to incorporate the subscribers of the Union Bank of Louisiana. 97758

Act to incorporate the subscribers to the Bank of Louisiana. 42195

Act to incorporate the subscribers to the Bank of Pennsylvania. 59908, 60308

Act to incorporate the subscribers to the Bank of the United States. 3189

Act to incorporate the Suffolk Insurance Company. 93437

Act to incorporate the Susquehanna Rail Road Company. 93932

Act to incorporate the town of Belvidere. 4612

Act to incorporate the Tredegar Iron Company. 96760

Act to incorporate the trustees of the Missionary Society of Connecticut. 15633

Act to incorporate the Tuscarora and Cold Run Tunnel and Rail Road Company. 97505

Act to incorporate the Union Bank of Florida. 24842

Act to incorporate the Union Canal Company. 60750, note after 97766

Act to incorporate Union Canal Company of Pennsylvania. (60749), note after 97766

Act to incorporate "The Union Insurance Company of Philadelphia." 62351, 97806, 97808

Act to incorporate the Union Marine Insurance Company. 97812

Act to incorporate the United States Insurance Company. 97967

Act to incorporate the vestry of the Parish of St. James. 87627

Act to incorporate the Washington Insurance Company. 102021

Act to incorporate the Washington Mutual Assurance Company. 102027

Act to incorporate the Watervliet Turnpike Company. 102109

Act to incorporate the West Philadelphia Passenger Railway Company. 62383

Act to incorporate the West Philadelphia Rail Road Company. 62384, note after 102944

Act to incorporate the Wilmington and Susquehanna Rail Road Company. 104586

Act to incorporate the Worcester and Hartford Railroad Company. 105446

Act to incorporate the Zoological Society of Philadelphia. 62407

Act to incorporate various societies in Schenectady. (77589)

Act to incorporate Washington Lodge No. 3. 101493

Act to increase the number of fire-masters. 87616

Act to indemnify Colonels John Thomas and Ezekiel Polk. 87627

Act to make and keep in repair a road. 87627

Act to oblige every free male inhabitant. 87627

Act to oblige the free male inhabitants. 100321

Act to oblige the inhabitants of Jamaica. 81749

Act to oblige the several inhabitants. 35613

Act to organize, govern, and discipline the militia. 43997

Act to organize the militia of . . . New York. (53459)

Act to organize the militia of the state of New-York. 91462

Act to organize the several fire companies. 101955

Act to organize the territories of Newbraska and Kansas. 52180, 52189

Act to prevent frauds and perjuries. 53460

Act to prevent monopolies and oppression. 70504

Act to prevent monopoly and oppression. 45564

Act to prevent monopoly and oppression, . . . [General Assembly, May 1777.] (70505)

Act to prevent Negro slaves. 87665

Act to prevent sedition. 87621

Act to prevent unlawful gaming. 100069

Act to prohibit all trade and intercourse. (52780)

Act to prohibit the sale of goods. 87627

Act to promote the efficency of the navy. 70250

Act to promote the more certain and equal assessment. 59808

Act to provide a more expeditious mode. 87452, 87453

Act to provide a national currency secured by a pledge of United States bonds. 32694, 51965

Act to provide a national currency, secured by a pledge of the United States stocks. 3192, (24796)

Act to provide against infectious and pestilential diseases. 53461

Act to provide an armed military force. 87371, 87680

Act to provide and establish a warehousing system. 94989

Act to provide for a general system of common schools. 34506

Act to provide for supplying the city. 102952

Act to provide for the better organization. 42508

Act to provide for the construction. 49523

Act to provide for the . . . Department of Alms. 54035

Act to provide for the education of youth. 43932

Act to provide for the enactment of certain laws. 35570

Act to provide for the enrolment of the militia. 53462

Act to provide for the funded debt. 34526

Act to provide for the improvement of the internal navigation. 53463

Act to provide for the military organization. 87704

Act to provide for the national defence. 91429

Act, to provide for the national defence, by organizing the militia. 94984

Act to provide for the opening of Washington Park. 8317

Act to provide for the organization and discipline of the militia. 45262

Act to provide for the organization . . . of common schools. (37030)

Act to provide for the public defence. 15227

Act to provide for the punishment of persons. 87856

Act to provide for the relief of the families of the soldiers. 87681

Act to provide for the valuation of lands. 69815

Act to provide internal revenue. 23379

Act to provide township organization. 49234

[Act to punish bribery and extortion.] 100354

Act to punish offences against slave property. 37063

Act to punish those who shall counterfeit. 87617

Act to raise an additional military force. (22541), 92381-92382

Act to re-charter certain banks. 59809

Act to reduce internal taxation. 34911

Act to reduce internal taxation, . . . approved, June 30, 1864. 34910

Act to reduce into one act. 94988

Act to reduce the law incorporating the village of Brooklyn. 8277

Act to reduce the state debt. 60498

Act to regulate and discipline the militia. 45262, 91422

Act to regulate and restrain paper-bills of credit. 58440, 70506

Act to regulate banks and banking institutions. 49574

Act to regulate civil proceedings. 97892

Act to regulate elections. 53239

Act to regulate institutions for savings. 105420

Act to regulate intercourse. 61206

Act to regulate the general elections of this commonwealth. 59810

Act to regulate the general elections, within this commonwealth. 59811

Act to regulate the militia of . . . New-York. 53464

Act to regulate the militia of the commonwealth of Pennsylvania. 59812, (60098)

Act to regulate the sale of intoxicating liquors. (59813)

Act to regulate the sale of intoxicating liquors, within the Metropolitan Police District. 53465

Act to regulate the sale of lottery tickets. 105998

[Act to remedy the inconveniences.] 100334

Act to repeal an act entitled, "An act to prohibit the sale of goods." 87627

Act to repeal certain acts. 2658, 27376-27377, note after 89216

Act to repeal several acts. 87627

[Act to repeal the act for incorporating the Protestant Episcopal Church.] 100347

Act to repeal title XXXIV of the revised statutes. 70507

Act to restrain the sale of intoxicating liquors. 10485

Act to restrain the trade and commerce of Massachusetts. 45564

Act to restrain the trade and commerce of New Jersey. 55039

Act to restrict the sale of intoxicating drinks. 43898

Act to reverse and annul the judgment. 70508

Act to revise and amend the militia laws. 94762

Act to revise and amend the several acts relating to the city of Brooklyn, passed Feb. 19, 1849. (8278)

Act to revise and amend the several acts relating to the city of Brooklyn, passed April 4, 1850. 8271

Act, "to revive and amend in part, an act." 100340, 100349

Act to revive and continue "An act for establishing." 87628

Act to revive and continue, for the time therein mentioned. 87623

Act to supply the treasury. 45564

Act to suppress the riots. 45564

Act upon that solemn affirmation. 53040, 53069

Act zur Einladung des unter den Anmen Unitas Fratrum. 97851

Acta capitali generalis Bononiae. (20580), 29497

Acta capituli generalis Romae. 20581

Acta capituli provincialis celebrati die 24 Julii 1776. 61074

Acta capituli provincialis celebrati in hoc Imperiali S. Dominici Mexiceo Ceoneobio die 6 Maij, 1809. 20581

Acta capitvli provincialis . . . celebrati 24 Julij Anni Dni 1748. 61074

Acta capitvli provincialis celebrati 24 Julij 1760. 61074

Acta capituli provincialis celebrati 24 Julii 1768. 61074

Acta capituli provincialis celebrati 24 Julij 1772. 61074

Acta capitvli provincialis hvivs provinciae S. Joannis Baptistae del Perv. 61074

Acta capitvli provincialis Limae. 61074

Acta celebrada por las autoridades de esta plaza. 98903

Acta Columbiana, 1875-6. 86933

Acta constitucional. 48252

Acta de contricion. 96269

Acta de la Junta. 98904

Acta del Tribunal del Protomedicato. 98382

Acta et decreta concilii plenarii Baltimorensis. 72900

Acta et decreta primi concilii provincialis Halifaxiensis. 29698

Acta et decreta synodorum provincialium Baltimori. 72904

Acta & statuta synodi dioecesanae Roffensis. 72966

Acta synodi dioecesanae Baltimorensis. 72929

Acta synodi dioecesanae Philadelphiensis. (72960)

Acta y documentos relativos a la exposicion general de industria. (48453)

Actas capitulares desde el 21 hasta el 25 Mayo de 1810. 8991

Actas de la Sociedad Mexicana. 85766

Actas de las juntas generales que celebro la
  Real Sociedad Economica de Amigos del
  Pais de la Habana. 17746, 29412
Actas de las sesiones de las Camaras.
  (48254)
Actas del Congreso Constituyente del estado
  libre de Mexico. 48255
Actas del Congreso Constituyente Mexicano.
  48255
Actas formadas en el capitulo general de N.
  Sagrado Orden Bethlemitico. (42856)
Actas [of the American Philosophical Society.]
  52130
Acte constitutionel de Haut et Bas Canada.
  31337
Acte constitutionnel de la Confederation
  Mexicaine. 70352
Acte de la Republique de Virginie. 100342,
  100344
Acte d'independence des Etats-Unis. (146)
Acte de l'ouverture des cortes a Lisbonne.
  7646, 101228
Acte pour l'organization de la Millice de
  Michigan. 48712
Acte qui regle plus solidement le
  gouvernement. 66988
Acte van Subsidie van de Provintie van
  Groningen en Ommelanden. 93834
Acte van Subsidie van de Provintie van
  Gelderland. 93834
Acte van Subsidie van de Provintie van
  Holland en West-Vriesland. 93834
Acte van Subsidie van de Provintie van
  Utrecht. 93834
Acte van Subsidie van de Provintie van
  Zeeland. 93834
Acte vande Staten van Groeningen Ende
  Ommelanden. 78000
Acte zur Anordnung der Militz der Republik
  Pennsylvanien. 59814
Acte zur Einrichtung der Militiz der Republick
  Pennsylvanien. 91419
Acte, zur incorporirung zur Unterstutzung
  nothleidender Deutschen beysteurenden
  Deutschen Gesellschaft in Pennsylvanien.
  59815
Achtenmassige Darstellung der Bedruckungen.
  5889
Actes de la legislature de la Caroline du Sud.
  16847
Actes de la sesiones de la Camara del
  Representantes. 14555
Actes de la Societe d'Ethnographie Americaine
  et Orientale. 70374, 85791
Actes de la Societe Philologique. (72812),
  85823
Actes du Conseil Legislatif. 53301
Actes et memoires concernant les negociations.
  147, 26821
Actes et ordonnances revises du Bas-Canada.
  10475
Actes passes a un congres des Etats-Unis.
  15495
Actes relatifs aux townships. 48713
Acting edition of plays. 92409, note after 93950
Acting edition. 102. 84785
Acting Gibbs Association of Vermont. see also
  Gibson Association of Vermont.
Acting Gibbs Association of Vermont. Agent.
  82407 see also Smith, Columbus.
Acting Gibbs Association of Vermont.
  Directors. 82407
Acting plays (Number 263) 84786
Actings of faith in moral reforms. (44749)
Action of Board of Trade of Chicago. 12668
Action of ecclesiastical bodies. 13003
Action of legislatures. (55108)

Action of the Chamber of Commerce, New-
  York. 90585
Action of the First Church. 22327
Action of the General Assembly of the Presby-
  terian Church in the United States.
  (65126)
Action of the legislature of . . . Texas. 50350
Action of the Ohio regiments. 73254
Action of the several yearly meeting of Friends.
  52602
Action of the stockholders of the South-Carolina
  Railroad Company. 88022
Action of trespass for levying a fine. (34042)
Actionnaire desillusionne. pseud. Lettre
  adresse a l'auteur. 19729
Actions of the councils vindicated. 88660
Acto de contricion. 96268-96269, 100643
Acto de contricion dispuesto en cincuenta y
  ocho decemas. 98784
Acto de contricion, en idioma Mexicana.
  (48328)
Acton, Me. York County Conference of Churches
  Semi-Annual Meeting, 1839. see Congre-
  gational Churches in Maine. York County
  Conference of Churches. Semi-Annual
  Meeting, Acton, 1839.
Actor's regalio. 95283-95284
Actos administrativos del Gobernador de
  Guanajuato. 29052
Actos de fee. 106243
Actos de los principales virtudes. 76774
Actos legislativos del Congreso Constitucional.
  20576
Actos legislativos. 10768
Actress of Padua. 83777-83788
Actress of Padua, and other tales. 83777
Acts and amendments relating to the public
  schools. 70509
Acts and by-laws, and reports of the Directors
  of the . . . Institution [for the Instruction
  of the Deaf and Dumb.] 54500
Acts and debates of the General Assembly of
  the Presbyterian Church. 65127
Acts and joint resolutions [of the General
  Assembly of the state of South Carolina.]
  87500
Acts and joint resolutions of the General
  Assembly of the state of South Carolina,
  passed at the regular session of 1868-69.
  87676
Acts and joint resolutions, relating to education.
  87682
Acts and laws. 99077-99078, 99088-99089,
  99091
Acts and laws. Building meeting-houses, and
  supporting ministers. 99093
Acts and laws. Castleton Grammar School.
  99105
Acts and laws. Commissioners to make
  reprisal. 99097
Acts and laws: County of Addison. 99100
Acts and laws. Emitting and redeeming money.
  99082
Acts and laws. Establishing the currency.
  99083
[Acts and laws. Feb. 1783.] 99092
Acts and laws. Form of passing laws. 99095
Acts and laws, made and passed by the General
  Assembly of the Representatives of the
  Freemen of the State of Vermont. 99076
Acts and laws . . . made and passed since the
  revision of June, 1767. 70515
[Acts and laws. March, 1784.] 99096
[Acts and laws, October 1780 and June 1781.]
  99084
[Acts and laws. Oct. 1783.] 99094

Acts and laws of His Majesties colony of
Connecticut in New England. (15757)
Acts and laws, of His Majesties colony of
Rhode-Island. 70510
Acts and laws of His Majesty's colony of
Connecticut. 15756
Acts and laws, of His Majesty's colony of North
Carolina. 55582
Acts and laws, of His Majesty's colony of
Rhode-Island, and Providence-Plantations,
in America. 70511
Acts and laws, of His Majesty's colony of
Rhode-Island, and Providence-Plantations,
in New-England. 70512-70513
Acts and laws of His Majesty's English colony
of Connecticut. 15634, 15758
Acts and laws of His Majesty's province of the
Massachusetts-Bay. (45566), 45568
Acts and laws of His Majesty's province of
New-Hampshire. 52782
Acts and laws [of the colony of Massachusetts.]
(45673)
Acts and laws of the colony of New-Hampshire.
52783-52784, 1st note after 52940
Acts and laws of the commonwealth of
Massachusetts. 45570
Acts and laws of the English colony of Rhode-
Island. 70514
Acts and laws [of the province of Massachusetts
Bay, 1764.] 97546
Acts and laws [of the province of Massachusetts
Bay, 1766.] 97546
Acts and laws of the province of New Jersey.
53041
Acts and laws of the state of Connecticut.
15635, 15760
Acts and laws of the state of New Hampshire.
52783-52784, 1st note after 52940
Acts and laws of the state of Vermont. 99075
Acts and laws, of the state of Vermont. Passed
at the session of the General Assembly
holden in Rutland. 99102
Acts & laws of the state of Vermont, passed by
the legislature at 9 Rutland. 99113, 99119
Acts and laws [of Vermont.] note after 99131
Acts and laws [of Vermont, 1779.] 99051
Acts and laws, passed by the General Assembly
of the Representatives of the Freemen of
the state of Vermont, at their session at
Bennington, October 1780. 99078
Acts and laws, passed by the General Assembly
of the Representatives of the Freemen of
the state of Vermont, at their session at
Manchester, October 1779. 99077
Acts and laws, passed by the General Assembly
of the Representatives of the Freemen of
the state of Vermont, at their session at
Windsor, February 1781. 99080
[Acts and laws, passed by the General Assembly
of the Representatives of the Freemen of
Vermont, at their session at Windsor,
April 1781.] 99081
Acts and laws, passed by the General Assembly
of the Representatives of the state of
Vermont, at their session at Bennington,
June 1781. 99083
Acts and laws, passed by the General Assembly
of the Representatives of the state of
Vermont, at their session at Bennington,
October 1780. 99079
Acts and laws, passed by the General Assembly
of the Representatives of the state of
Vermont, at their session at Windsor,
April 1781. 99082
Acts and laws, passed by the General Assembly
of the state of Vermont. 99089

Acts and laws, passed by the General Assembly
of the state of Vermont, at their session
at Charlestown, October 1781. 99087
Acts and laws, passed by the General Assembly
of the state of Vermont, at their session
at Rutland, in October, 1784. 99097
Acts and laws; passed by the General Assembly
of the state of Vermont, at their session
at Windsor, February 1783. 99091
Acts and laws, passed by the General Assembly
of the state of Vermont, at their session
in Windsor, October 1796. 99110, 99115,
99117, 99119
Acts and laws, passed by the General Assembly
of the state of Vermont, at their sessions
at Bennington, in February & March, 1784.
99095
Acts and laws, passed by the General Assembly
of the state of Vermont, at their sessions
at Norwich, in June, 1785. 99099
Acts and laws, passed by the General Assembly
of the state of Vermont, at their sessions
at Westminster, October, 1783. 99093
Acts and laws, passed by the General Assembly
of the state of Vermont, at their sessions
at Windsor, in October, 1785. 99100
Acts and laws, passed by the General Assembly
of the state of Vermont, at their stated
session, at Rutland, in October 1786.
99101
Acts and laws passed by the General Court or
Assembly of His Majesties province of
New-Hampshire. 52781
Acts and laws, passed by the Great and General
Court . . . of the Massachusetts-Bay, in
New-England. 45565
Acts and laws, passed by the Great and General
Court . . . of the province of the Massa-
chusetts Bay in New-England. 45567
Acts and laws passed by the Great and General
Court or Assembly of the colony of the
Massachusetts Bay in New-England.
(45569)
Acts and laws passed by the legislature of the
state of Vermont. 99126, 99131
Acts and laws, passed by the legislature of the
state of Vermont, at their adjourned
session at Bennington, January 1791.
99109
Acts and laws, passed at the legislature of the
state of Vermont, at their adjourned
session holden at Rutland. 99123
Acts and laws, passed by the legislature of the
state of Vermont, at their session at
Castleton. 99108
Acts and laws, passed by the legislature of the
state of Vermont, at their session at
Manchester. 99106
Acts and laws, passed by the legislature of the
state of Vermont, at their session at
Newbury. 99105
Acts and laws, passed by the legislature of the
state of Vermont, at their session at
Rutland. 99112
Acts and laws, passed by the legislature of the
state of Vermont, at their session at
Westminster. 99107
Acts and laws, passed by the legislature of the
state of Vermont, at their session at
Windsor, October [-November], one
thousand seven hundred and ninety-seven.
99124
Acts and laws, passed by the legislature of the
state of Vermont, at their session at
Windsor, October 1791. 99111

Acts and laws. Passed by the legislature of
the state of Vermont, at their session at
Windsor, October, 1793. 99113, 99116
Acts and laws passed by the legislature of the
state of Vermont, at their session at
Windsor, October, one thousand seven
hundred and ninety-three. 99115, 99119
Acts and laws passed by the legislature of the
state of Vermont, at their session holden
at Middlebury. 99130
Acts and laws, passed by the legislature of the
state of Vermont, at their session holden
at Rutland, on the second Thursday of
October 1784. 99117, 99119
Acts and laws, passed by the legislature of the
state of Vermont, at their session holden
at Rutland, on the second Thursday of
October, one thousand seven hundred and
ninety-six. 99121
Acts and laws passed by the legislature of the
state of Vermont. At their session holden
at Vergennes. 99128
Acts and laws, passed by the legislature of the
state of Vermont, at their session holden
at Windsor, in October, A. D. one
thousand seven hundred & ninety nine.
99129
Acts and laws, passed by the legislature of the
state of Vermont, at their session holden
at Windsor, on the second Thursday of
October, one thousand seven hundred and
ninety-five. 99118
Acts and laws passed in New England. (52603)
Acts and laws. Probate division. 99106
Acts and laws. Proprietors meetings. 99096
Acts and laws. Regulating fines and premiums.
99084
Acts and laws. Regulation of fees. 99094
Acts and laws. Settlement of grants. 99101
Acts and laws. State securities. 99107
Acts and laws. Taxes. 99099
Acts and laws. Vacancies in offices. 99108
Acts and monuments of our late Parliament.
35560
Acts and ordinances of the city of Brooklyn.
8279
Acts and ordinances of the General Assembly
of the state of South-Carolina: passed
February 20th, 1790. 87649
Acts and ordinances of the General Assembly
of the state of South-Carolina. Passed
in April, 1776. note before 17613
Acts and ordinances of the General Assembly
of the state of South-Carolina, passed in
February, 1788. 87646
Acts and ordinances of the General Assembly
of the state of South-Carolina, passed
in October and November 1788. 87647
Acts and ordinances of the General Assembly
of the state of South Carolina, passed in
October, 1785. 87641
Acts and ordinances of the General Assembly
of the state of South-Carolina. Passed
in the year 1778. 87627
Acts and ordinances of the General Assembly
of the state of South Carolina, passed in
the year 1783. 87636
Acts and ordinances of the Governor and Judges
of the Territory . . . South of the River
Ohio. 94764
Acts and ordinances passed in March [1783.]
87636
Acts and proceedings . . . at Reading, Pa.
27150
Acts and proceedings of the Central Synod of
the Reformed Dutch Church in North
America. 68764

Acts and proceedings of the Classis and
General Synod of the True Reformed
Dutch Church in the United States of
America. 97138
Acts and proceedings of the Classis of Albany
of the Reformed Dutch Church. 68765
Acts and proceedings of the General Assembly
of the Presbyterian Church. 65128
Acts and proceedings of the General Association
of Connecticut. 15803
Acts and proceedings of the General Synod of
the Reformed Dutch Church in America.
68766
Acts and proceedings of the General Synod, of
the Reformed Dutch Church in North
America. 68767
Acts and proceedings of the General Synod of
the Reformed Protestant Dutch Church in
North America. 68775-(68776)
Acts and proceedings of the General Synod of
the Reformed Protestant Dutch Church in
North America, from June, 1846, to June,
1849, inclusive. 68777
Acts and proceedings of the government of
. . . Ohio. 56867
Acts and proceedings of the Particular Synod
of Albany. 68768
Acts and proceedings of the Synod of New York
and Philadelphia. 65163
Acts and resolutions adopted at the 1st session
of the 12th General Assembly of Florida.
(24845)
Acts and resolutions, 1868 [of the Legislature
of Iowa.] 93882
Acts and resolutions, from October, 1817, to
February, 1819. 49488
Acts and resolutions granting medals, swords,
&c. 32687
Acts and resolutions of the first session of the
Provisional Congress of the Confederate
States. 15229
[Acts and resolutions of the fourth session of
the Provisional Congress of the Confederate
States.] 15229
Acts and resolutions of the General Assembly
of . . . North Carolina. (55584)
Acts and resolutions of the General Assembly
of the state of Florida. 24844
Acts and resolutions [of the General Assembly
of the state of South Carolina.] 87500
[Acts and resolutions of the General Assembly
of the state of South Carolina, 1801-1830.]
87666
[Acts and resolutions of the General Assembly
of the state of South Carolina, 1832-1838.]
87667
Acts and resolutions of the General Assembly,
of the state of South-Carolina, from
December, 1794 [i. e. 1795], to December,
1797, inclusive. 87658-87660
Acts and resolutions of the General Assembly
of the state of South Carolina. Passed
at the extra session, June, 1838. 87669
Acts and resolutions of the General Assembly,
of the state of South-Carolina, passed in
April, 1794. 87655
Acts and resolutions of the General Assembly
of the state of South-Carolina, passed in
December, 1791. 87652
Acts and resolutions, of the General Assembly
of the state of South-Carolina. Passed
in December, 1792. 87653
Acts and resolutions of the General Assembly,
of the state of South-Carolina, passed in
December, 1793. 87654
Acts and resolutions of the General Assembly,
of the state of South-Carolina. Passed in
December, MDCCXCIV. 87656

Acts and resolutions of the General Assembly,
of the state of South-Carolina. Passed
in December, 1796. 87659
Acts and resolutions of the General Assembly,
of the state of South-Carolina. Passed
in December, 1797. 87660
Acts and resolutions of the General Assembly,
of the State of South-Carolina, passed
in December, 1798. 87661-87662
Acts and resolutions of the General Assembly,
of the state of South-Carolina. Passed
in December, 1799. 87663
Acts and resolutions of the Geeneral Assembly,
of the state of South-Carolina. Passed
in December, 1800. 87664
Acts and resolutions of the General Assembly
of the state of South-Carolina. Passed
in December, 1801. 87666
Acts and resolutions of the General Assembly
of the state of South-Carolina. Passed
in December, 1809. 87666
Acts and resolutions of the General Assembly
of the state of South Carolina. Passed
in December 1831. 87667
Acts and resolutions of the General Assembly,
of the state of South Carolina, passed in
December, 1834. 87668
Acts and resolutions of the General Assembly,
of the state of South-Carolina. Passed
in Nov. and Dec. 1795. 87657
Acts and resolutions of the General Council of
the Choctaw Nation. 12862
Acts and resolutions of the Legislative Assembly
of the state of Oregon. 57545
[Acts and resolutions of the third session, held
at Richmond, Virginia, of the Provisional
Congress of the Confederate States.]
15229
[Acts and resolutions of the second session of
the Provisional Congress of the Confederate States.] 15229
Acts and resolutions passed at the first session
of the General Assembly, convened at
Iowa City. 35014
Acts and resolves [of the General Assembly of
the state of Rhode Island.] 70684
Acts and resolves of the General Assembly of
the state of Rhode Island and Providence
Plantations. 70517
Acts and resolves [of the General Assembly of
the state of Rhode Island, January session,
1869.] 84975
Acts and resolves of the General Assembly
relating to public schools in Rhode
Island. 70518
Acts and resolves . . . of the province of
Massachusetts Bay. 45571
Acts and resolves passed by the legislatre of
Massachusetts. 45572
Acts and resolves, passed by the twentieth
legislature of the state of Maine. (43899)
Acts and resolves . . . with the by-laws [of
the Massachusetts Charitable Eye and Ear
Infirmary.] 45827
Acts and statutes of the island of Barbados.
3259
Acts and supplemental acts of the legislatures
of Louisiana and Mississippi. 102763
[Acts concerning county and other inferior
courts.] 100396
[Acts concerning district courts.] 100397
[Acts "concerning the erection of the District
of Kentucky into an independent state."]
100393
Acts concerning the Territory of Columbia.
(20297)
[Acts for imposing duties, etc.] 100394
[Acts "for re-forming the county courts."]
100346

Acts for the government of the territories.
1270
Acts for the promotion of education in Lower
Canada. (42514)
Acts . . . for the protection of the said canal
[i. e. the Union Canal of Pennsylvania.]
60750
Acts in regard to passengers in vessels.
(53522)
Acts incorporating . . . act empowering
municipal corporations to subscribe to the
Great Western Railway. 28478
Acts incorporating the Delaware and Raritan
Railway Company. 53042
Acts incorporating the Milwaukee, Fond du Lac
& Green Bay R. R. Co. 49173
Acts incorporating the Milwaukee, Waukesha,
and Miss. R. R. Co. 49177
Acts, joint resolutions and memorials passed by
the first Legislative Assembly [of
Minnesota.] 49235
Acts of a general nature. 56868
Acts of a local or private nature. (37528)
Acts of Assembly. 53467, (53731)
Acts of Assembly and ordinances, passed by
the Council of the Borough of West
Philadelphia. 62379
Acts of Assembly and ordinances relating to
the water works. 62369
Acts of Assembly in relation to common-schools
in North-Carolina. 55586
Acts of Assembly, made and enacted in the
Bermuda, or Summer-Islands. (4906)
Acts of Assembly, now in force, in the colony
of Virginia. 100388, 100391
Acts of Assembly, now in force, in Virginia.
100389
Acts of Assembly . . . occasioned by the repeal
of sundry acts made in . . . 1748. 100245
Acts of Assembly of . . . New York. 53466
Acts of Assembly of the island of Jamaica.
35618
Acts of Assembly, of the province of Maryland.
45046
Acts of Assembly of the province of Pennsylvania.
59820
Acts of Assembly of the sixth year of Her
Majesty's reign. (39408)
Acts of Assembly, passed in the Charibbee
Leeward Islands. 12025
Acts of Assembly passed in the Charibee
Leeward Islands. (10891)
Acts of Assembly, passed in the colony of
Virginia, from the year 1662. 100384
Acts of Assembly, passed in the colony of
Virginia, from 1662, to 1715. 100383
Acts of Assembly, passed in the island of
Antigua. 1695
Acts of Assembly, passed in the island of
Jamaica, from 1770, to 1783. 35617
Acts of Assembly, passed in the island of
Jamaica; from 1681, to 1737. 35614
Acts of Assembly, passed in the island of
Jamaica; from 1681, to 1754. (35615)
Acts of Assembly, passed in the island of
Jamaica; from the year 1681 to the year
1768 inclusive. 35616
Acts of Assembly, passed in the Island of
Montserrat. (50224)-50225
Acts of Assembly, passed in the island of
Nevis. 52425
Acts of Assembly, passed in the island of St.
Christopher; from 1711, to 1735,
inclusive. 75009
Acts of Assembly, passed in the island of St.
Christopher, from 1711 to 1740
inclusive. 75007
Acts of Assembly, passed in the island of St.
Christopher; from the year 1711, to 1769.
75010

Acts of Assembly, passed in the province of
Maryland. 45045
Acts of Assembly, passed in the province of
New-York, from 1691, to 1718. (53467)
Acts of Assembly passed in the province of
New-York, from 1691, to 1725. 53468
Acts of Assembly, printed since the revised
code. 100399
Acts of Assembly relating to Fairmount Park.
61650
Acts of Assembly relative to the Board of
Health. 60061
Acts of Assembly relative to the Board of
Wardens of the Port of Philadelphia.
59822
Acts of cession from Maryland and Virginia.
(9198)
Acts of Congress in relation to the District
of Columbia, from July 16th, 1790, to
March 4th, 1831. (20299)
Acts of Congress in relation to the District
of Columbia, from June 19th, 1790, to
March 4th, 1831. (18789)
Acts of Congress in respect to copyrights.
15490
Acts of Congress now in force. 34738
Acts of Congress of June 3, 1864. 13600
Acts of Congress organizing said territory and
other acts. (37065)
Acts of Congress relating to loans and
currency. 15507
Acts of Congress relating to loans and the
currency, from 1847 to 1868. 15491
Acts of Congress relating to loans and the
currency, from 1790 to 1867. 41707
Acts of Congress relating to the direct tax.
15506
Acts of Dr. Bray's visitation. 7472
Acts of General Assembly for . . . improving
the navigation of James River. 100400
Acts of incorporation, and by-laws of the
Marine Society of Newburyport. 54919
Acts of incorporation and by-laws of the
Merchants' and Miners' Transportation
Company. 47915
Acts of incorporation and by-laws of the Old
Colony and Fall River Railroad Company.
57119
Acts of incorporation, by-laws, rules and
regulations of the Odd Fellows' Cemetery
Company of Philadelphia. 61882
Acts of incorporation [of the South Baltimore
Company.] 3961
Acts of June 1838. 87669
Acts of kings. 30230
Acts of Maryland and Virginia. 20298
Acts of naturalization. 16114
Acts of October, 1779. 99076
Acts of Parliament relating to the army.
(1791)
Acts . . . of Pennsylvania, . . . 1726. 59819
Acts of 1726. 45046
Acts of 1793 and 1850. (69606)
Acts of the Apostles; and the epistles of Paul.
18291, 71336
Acts of the Apostles, in the Mohawk language.
49837
Acts of the Apostles, translated into the
Arrawack tongue. 2099, 80762
Acts of the Apostles, translated into the
Cherokee language. 12433
Acts of the Apostles translated into the
Choctaw language. 12863
Acts of the Assembly relative to the
incorporation of the township of
Moyamensing, &c. (59823)
Acts of the British worthies. 56808

Acts of the Commissioners of the United
Colonies of New England. 53388, 63488
Acts of the Council and General Assembly of
the state of New-Jersey. 53048
Acts of the elders. 148, (55932)
Acts . . . of the fifth Congress. (39424)
Acts of the first Assembly of Montana
Territory. (50079)
Acts of the 1st session of the Provisional
Congress [of the Confederate States.]
15341
Acts of the General Assembly and ordinances
of the Trustees, for the organization and
government of the University of North
Carolina. 55700
Acts of the General Assembly, and ordinances
of the Trustees . . . of the University of
North Carolina. 55700
Acts of the General Assembly, 1801 [of Georgia.]
27010
Acts of the General Assembly . . . for the
gradual abolition of slavery. 60364
Acts of the General Assembly of Arkansas.
1987
Acts of the General Assembly . . . of . . .
Georgia. (27009)
Acts of the General Assembly, of His Majesty's
province, of New-Brunswick, in the year
1786. 52526
Acts of the General Assembly of . . . New
Brunswick. 52527
Acts of the General Assembly of North
Carolina. 55585
Acts of the General Assembly of . . . Pennsyl-
vania: passed at a session. (59824)
Acts of the General Assembly of Pennsylvania,
relating to the Eastern State Penitentiary.
59825
Acts of the General Assembly of Pennsylvania,
respecting the gradual abolition of slavery.
62255
Acts of the General Assembly of Prince Edward
Island. 65628-65629
Acts of the General Assembly of Prince Edward
Island. From 1853 to 1862. (65630)
Acts of the General Assembly of Prince Edward
Island. From . . . 1773 to . . . 1852.
(65630)
Acts of the General Assembly of South-Carolina,
at a session begun to be holden at Charles-
Town. 87586
[Acts of the General Assembly of South Carolina,
1839-1849.] 87670
[Acts of the General Assembly of South Carolina,
1868-1871.] 87676
Acts of the General Assembly of South-Carolina,
passed in September and October, 1776.
87624
Acts of the General Assembly of South-Carolina,
passed in the year 1760. 87594
Acts of the General Assembly of South-Carolina,
passed in the year 1761. 87596
Acts of the General Assembly of South-Carolina,
passed in the year 1762. 87597
Acts of the General Assembly of South-Carolina,
passed in the year 1764. 87600
Acts of the General Assembly of South-Carolina,
passed in the year 1765. 87602
Acts of the General Assembly of South-Carolina,
passed in the year 1769. 87608
Acts of the General Assembly, of South-Carolina,
passed the 7th of April, 1759. 87592
Acts of the General Assembly of South-Carolina.
Passed the 7th of April, 1770. 87610
Acts of the General Assembly of South-Carolina.
Passed the 12th of April, 1768. 87606
Acts of the General Assembly of South-Carolina.
Passed the 20th of March, 1771. 87611

Acts of the General Assembly of South-Carolina. Passed the 22d and 23d day of August, 1777. 87626

Acts of the General Assembly of the commonwealth of Pennsylvania. (59821)

Acts of the General Assembly of the province of New-Jersey. 83979

Acts of the General Assembly of the province of New-Jersey, from the surrender of the government to Queen Anne. 53046

Acts of the General Assembly of the province of New-Jersey, from the time of the surrender of the government in the second year of the reign of Queen Anne. 53044

Acts of the General Assembly of the province of New-Jersey, from the time of the surrender of the surrender of the government of the said province. 53043

Acts of the General Assembly of the province of New-Jersey, from the year 1753. 53045

Acts of the General Assembly of the state of Georgia. 27011

Acts of the General Assembly of the state of Louisiana. 42184

Acts of the General Assembly of the state of Missouri. 49575

Acts of the General Assembly of the state of New Jersey. 53947

Acts of the General Assembly of the state of North Carolina. 55583

[Acts of the General Assembly of the state of South Carolina, 1850-1860.] 87671

[Acts of the General Assembly of the state of South Carolina, 1861-1867.] 87672

[Acts of the General Assembly of the state of South-Carolina, from December, 1795, to December, 1804.] 87683

Acts of the General Assembly of the state of South-Carolina, from February, 1791, to December, 1794. 87683

Acts of the General Assembly of the state of South Carolina, passed at the sessions of 1864-65. 87672-87674

Acts of the General Assembly of the state of South Carolina, passed at the special session of 1868. 87675

Acts of the General Assembly of the state of South Carolina, passed in December, 1841. 37670

Acts of the General Assembly of the state of South Carolina, passed in December, 1850. 87671

Acts of the General Assembly of the state of South Carolina, passed in December, 1861. 87672

Acts of the general Assembly of the state of South Carolina, passed in December, 1864. 87672-87673

Acts of the General Assembly of the state of South-Carolina, ratified in February, 1791. 87651

Acts of the General Assembly of Virginia for regulating pilots. 100406

Acts of the Legislative Assembly of the Territory of Washington. 101915

Acts of the Legislative Council of the Territory of Florida. 24843

Act of the legislature altering and amending the same [i. e. the charter of Columbia College.] 14831

Acts of the legislature . . . and ordinances of the Common Council . . . in relation to the . . . introduction of water. (54036)

Acts of the legislature . . . and ordinances . . . of the Common Council, with the rules . . . of the Croton Aqueduct Board. (54232)

Acts of the legislature of New-Hampshire. 52785

Acts of the legislature of New York. 54073

Acts of the legislature of Pennsylvania. 78078

Acts of the legislature of South-Carolina. 12044

Acts of the legislature of the island of Tobago, containing the whole of the laws up to the 1st August 1800. 96045

Acts of the legislature of the island of Tobago; from 1768, to 1775. 96044

Acts of the legislature of the state of Michigan. (48715)

Acts of the legislature of the Territory of Orleans. 42183

Acts of the legislature of Wisconsin. 75032

Acts of the legislature relating to the city [of Boston.] 6540

Acts of the legislature . . . relating to the Union Canal Company. 60750, note after 97766

Acts of the legislature respecting navigable communications between the great western and northern lakes, and the Atlantic Ocean. 22749

Acts of the legislature . . . respecting navigable communications between the great western and northern lakes and the Hudson River. 22739, 53469

Acts of the legislatures of Rhode Island and Connecticut, relating to the New York, Providence, and Boston Railroad Company. 54839

Acts, of the province of Maryland. 45047

Acts of the province of Pennsylvania. 59816

Acts of the rebels. 68026

Acts of the second session of the fourth Congress. note after 94725

Acts of the state legislature . . . as relate to . . . Baltimore. 3053

Acts of the state of Georgia. 27013

Acts of the state of Ohio. 56869

Acts of trade of the British plantations. 87

Acts of Virginia and Maryland concerning the Potomac Company. 12501

Acts of Virginia, Maryland, and of the United States. 100398

Acts of Virginia, Maryland and Pennsylvania. 12501

Acts of Virginia relating to land titles. (37533)

Acts . . . ordered to be left out. 45572

Acts, ordinances, and resolve, of the General Assembly, of the state of South-Carolina. 87642

Acts, ordinances, and resolves . . . [of the General Assembly of the state of South Carolina.] 87500

Acts, ordinances, and resolves of the General Assembly of the state of South-Carolina; passed in March, 1785. 87639

Acts, ordinances, and resolves, of the General Assembly of the state of South-Carolina; passed in March, 1787. 87644

Acts, ordinances, and resolves, of the General Assembly of the state of South-Carolina, passed in March, 1789. 87648

Acts, ordinances, and resolves of the General Assembly of the state of South Carolina, passed in the year 1784. 87638

Acts passed at a Congress. 15493

ACTS

Acts passed at a Congress of the United States.
    (15494)
Acts passed at a Congress of the United States
    of America begun and held at . . . New-
    York. 15608
Acts passed at a Congress of the United States
    of America begun and held at the city of
    New York. 15492, 15493
Acts passed at a General Assembly. 87633
Acts passed at different sessions. 45048
[Acts passed at the] first [and] second session
    . . . fifteenth Congress, 1817-19. 15505
[Acts passed at the] first [and] second session
    . . . tenth Congress, 1807-9. 15505
[Acts passed at the] first [and] second session
    . . . twelfth Congress, 1811-13. 15505
[Acts passed at the] first and second sessions
    . . . eighth Congress. 15505
[Acts passed at the] first and second sessions
    . . . ninth Congress. 15505
Acts passed at the first and second sessions
    of the Legislative Council of the
    Territory of Orleans. 42182
[Acts passed at the] first and second sessions
    . . . seventh Congress. 15505
[Acts passed at the] first and second sessions
    . . . sixth Congress. 15505
Acts passed at the first General Assembly of
    the state of Tennessee. 94766
Acts passed at the first [second and third]
    Congress. 15500
[Acts passed at the] first . . . second [and]
    third sessions . . . thirtieth [i. e.
    thirteenth] Congress. 15505
Acts passed at the first-[second] session of the
    [5th-14th] General Assembly of the state
    of Tennessee. 94771
[Acts passed at the] first session . . .
    fourteenth Congress. 15505
Acts passed at the first session of the fifth
    Congress. 15502
Acts passed at the first session of the first
    legislature of the Territory of Orleans.
    42183, 53302
Acts passed at the first session of the fourth
    Congress. 15501, note after 94725
Acts passed at the first session of the fourth
    General Assembly of the state of
    Tennessee. 94771
Acts passed at the first session of the General
    Assembly of the Territory of the United
    States, South of the River Ohio. 94764
Acts passed at the first session of the second
    Congress. 15497
Acts passed at the first session of the second
    General Assembly of the state of
    Tennessee. 94768
Acts passed at the first session of the seventh
    General Assembly, 1798. (37527)
Acts passed at the first session of the sixth
    Congress. 15505
Acts passed at the first session of the third
    General Assembly of the state of
    Tennessee. 94770
[Acts passed at the] first . . . third session
    . . . eleventh Congress. 15505
Acts passed at the second Congress of the
    United States. 15499
[Acts passed at the] second session . . .
    fourteenth Congress. 15505
Acts passed at the second session of the
    Congress of the United States . . . held
    at . . . New-York. 15496, note after
    94720
Acts passed at the second session of the first
    General Assembly of the state of
    Tennessee. 94767

Acts passed at the second session of the first
    General Assembly of the Territory of the
    United States of America, South of the
    River Ohio. 94765
Acts passed at the second session of the first
    Legislative Council of the Territory of
    Michigan. 48714
Acts passed at the second session [of the first
    Legislature of the Territory of Orleans.]
    101604
Acts passed at the second session of the second
    Congress. 15498
Acts passed at the second session of the second
    General Assembly of the state of
    Tennessee. 94769
[Acts passed at the] second session [of the] sixth
    Congress. 15505
Acts passed at the third session of the Congress.
    15493
Acts passed at the third session of the fifth
    Congress. 15504
Acts . . . passed by the . . . Borough of West
    Philadelphia. 61565
Acts passed by the commonwealth of Kentucky.
    37529
Acts passed by the General Assembly of South-
    Carolina. 87571
Acts passed by the General Assembly of South-
    Carolina. At a session begun to be holden
    at Charles-Town, on Tuesday the fourteenth
    day of September. 87568
Acts passed by the General Assembly of South-
    Carolina, at a sessions begun and holden
    at Charles-Town, on Tuesday the fourteenth
    day of September. 87567
Acts passed by the General Assembly of South-
    Carolina, at a sessions begun and holden
    at Charles-Town, on Tuesday the tenth day
    of September. 87572
Acts passed by the General Assembly of South-
    Carolina, at a sessions begun and holden
    at Charles-Town, on Tuesday the tenth of
    November. 87565
Acts passed by the General Assembly of South-
    Carolina, at a sessions begun and holden
    at Charles-Town the fifteenth day of
    November. 87563
Acts passed by the General Assembly of South-
    Carolina, at a sessions begun and holden
    at Charles-Town, the tenth day of
    November. 87564
Acts passed by the General Assembly of South-
    Carolina, at a sessions begun to be holden
    at Charles-Town, on Thursday the fourteenth
    day of November. 87580-87581, 87583-
    87584
Acts passed by the General Assembly of South-
    Carolina, at a sessions begun to be holden
    at Charles-Town, on Tuesday the twenty-
    eighth day of March. 87579
Acts passed by the General Assembly of South-
    Carolina, at a sessions begun to be holden
    at Charles-Town on Wednesday the tenth
    day of September. 87573-87574
[Acts passed by the General Assembly of South-
    Carolina. May, 1740-July, 1742.] 87566
Acts passed by the General Assembly of South-
    Carolina, on the 23d day of August, 1769.
    87608
[Acts passed by] the General Assembly of the
    province of Nova-Scotia. 56108
Acts passed by the General Assembly of the
    province of South-Carolina, at a sessions
    begun and holden at Charles-Town, on
    Tuesday the nineteenth day of January.
    87576

Acts passed by the General Assembly of the province of South-Carolina, at a sessions begun and holden at Charles-Town, on Tuesday the twenty-eighth day of March. 87578

Acts passed by the General Assembly of the province of South-Carolina, in the years 1755, 1756, 1757, and 1758. 87587

Acts passed by the General Assembly, 1682-1727. 87697, 1st note after 97056

Acts passed . . . [by] the legislature respecting the canals. 53470

[Acts passed in 1732 at a session May 18-July 1.] 100234

Acts passed in the General Assembly . . . . Held at Philadelphia. 59818

Acts passed in the General Assembly of the province of Pennsylvania. 59817

Acts passed in the island of Barbados. 29840

Acts passed 1731-1734. 87697, 1st note after 97056

Acts regulating banks and banking. (45573)

Acts relating to patents. 10485

Acts relating to public schools. 31101

Acts . . . relating to the circuit courts. 59826

Acts . . . relating to the existing war. (37530)

Acts relating to the Germantown and Norris-town Railroad. 27154

Acts relating to the . . . [Milwaukee and Rock River Canal] Company. (49169)

Acts relating to the powers, duties and protection of justice of the peace in Lower Canada. 10485

Acts relating to the public schools of Rhode Island. 70519

Acts relating to the public schools of Rhode Island, with remarks and forms. 70520, (70695), 70743

Acts relative to Bowdoin College. 7018

Acts, resolutions, and memorials adopted by the Arizona legislature. 1983

Acts, resolves, by-laws, and rules and regulations [of the Massachusetts General Hospital.] 45846

Acts to amend the charter of the Philadelphia, Wilmington and Baltimore Railroad Company. 62051

Acts to amend the municipal & agricultural acts of Lower Canada. 42508

Acts which the Baltimore platform approves. 41126

Actuaciones literarias. 41078

Actual commencement of hostilities against this continent. 87366

Actual estado del Asunto del Ferrocarril Interoceanico. note just before (73261)

Actual life. 41007

Actual Settler. pseud. Life in Santo Domingo. 75158

Actual Settler. pseud. Suggestions on the propriety. see Read, H. Y.

Actual state of the Mexican mines. 350

Actual survey of the sea coast from New York. 88221

Actzen, James. alias see Hill, James. defendant

Acuerdo de la Real Sociedad Patriotica de la Habana. 1874

Acuerdo del Illmo. Cabildo Metropolitano de Mexico. 50096

Acuerdo del Ve. Cabildo Metropolitano de la Catedral de Caracas. (47807)

Acuerdos generales e interesantes. 29432

Acuerdos hechos en el Ayuntamiento de la Habana. 17747

Acugna, Christophe d'. see Acuna, Christoval de.

Acugna, Christopher. see Acuna, Christoval de.

Acuna, Antonio Gonzalez de. 149, 27793, (73180), (73189)

Acuna, Christoval de. 150-153, 44614, 52380, 58141, 72524, 72757, (72759), note after 93778, 1st note after 100824

Acuna, Juan de, Marques de Casafuente. 11224 see also Mexico (Viceroyalty) Virrey, 1722-1734 (Acuna)

Acuna, Juan de, Marques de Casafuente. complainant 26122 see also Mexico (Viceroyalty) Virrey, 1722-1734 (Acuna) complainant

Acuna, Rodrigo de Aguiar y. see Aguiar y Acuna, Rodrigo de.

Acuna Bonal, Maria de. plaintiff 74517

Acusacion contra el Director del Estado. 99459

Acusacion fiscal en la causa contra J. M. Aviles. 11294

Acusacion fiscal en la Tercera Sala de la Suprema Corte de Justicia. 11295

Acusacion presentada al Gran Jurado. 67646

Acusacion presentada en la Camara de Diputados. 67326

Acusacion que eleva al Soberno Congreso Nacional. 74888

Acworth, N. H. Centennial anniversary, 1869. 47998

Ad articvlos Calvinianae. 99724

Ad ea quae Hugo Grotius et Joan. Lahetius de origine gentium Peruvianarum et Mexicanarum scripserunt. (63711)

Ad illvstrissivm. 41366

Ad Io. Hvg. Linscotvm. 41356

Ad Iulium II. 43763

Ad librum. 52646, note after 62743

Ad Myrtacearum Americanarum aequinoctialium. (4841)

Ad Rvdolphvm Agricolam rhetvm epistola. 63957

Ad sapie[n]tissimu[m] Ludouicu[m] Maria[m] Sfortia[m] Anglu[m] septimu[m] Medico lani Duce[m]. 94095

Ad Sixtum V., Philippi II. 91231

Adair, -------. USA (35374)

Adair, James. 155-156

Adair, James Makittrick, 1728-1802. 157, 95343

Adair, James Makittrick 1728-1802. supposed author 97580

Adair, John. 5906, 74878

Adalaska. 5224

Adalbert, Prince of Prussia, 1811-1873. 159-162, 38050

Adalbert, Heinrich Wilhelm, Prince of Prussia. see Adalbert, Prince of Prussia, 1811-1873.

Adam, -------. 7052

Adam, L. 163

Adam, Thomas. 164-165

Adam, Victor. illus. 48916, 73935

Adam, William, b. 1799. 166, 26861

Adam, William Jackson. 167

Adam Bede. 40774

Adame y Arriaga, Joseph. 48494

Adamic race. 74626

Adams, -------. cartographer 91496

Adams, -------. defendant (49956)

Adams, A. C. 174

Adams, Abigail. see Smith, Abigail (Adams) 1765-1813.

Adams, Abigail (Smith) 1744-1818. 264

Adams, Alvin. plaintiff 90320

Adams, Amos. 169-173

Adams, Arthur. 28400

Adams, Caleb. defendant 102075

Adams, Charles. 46070
see also Massachusetts. Attorney General.

Adams, Charles Baker, 1814-1853. 175-178, 28364, 68476
Adams, Charles Francis, 1807-1886. 179-188, 189, 246, 253, 264, 16887, 20256, 39206, 45451, 45711, (55531), 84633, 102321, 103268 see also U. S. Legation. Great Britain.
Adams, Charles Francis, 1835-1915. 89572, 89699, 104848
Adams, Clement. 66686
Adams, Daniel, 1773-1864. 190-191, 47305, 83958
Adams, E. E. (192)-193
Adams, Ebenezer. 62830
Adams, Edwin G. 194
Adams, Eliphalet. 195-200, 103707
Adams, Elisha. respondent 83493
Adams, Francis. pseud.
Voyages et adventures. see Cabet, Etienne.
Adams, Francis Colburn. 201-204, (36945), 57941, 92624
Adams, G. J. 90488
Adams, George. 601, 6696, 10117, 15706, 23746, 39394, 42477, 42837, (44215), 45825, 45886, 52661, 70734, 73724, 73729, (75722), 87340
Adams, George, 1807-1865. 205, 26862
Adams, George, fl. 1841. 104719
Adams, George Washington. 206, 23841, 92191
Adams, H. G. 216, 27628
Adams, Hannah, 1755-1831. 207-215, 31651, 42461, 50928, 50971, 70204
Adams, Henry, 1838-1918. 55562, 84787
Adams, Israel. 217
Adams, J. 98181
Adams, J. G. 54813
Adams, J. J. USA 5625
Adams, J. S. 24862
Adams, James. 96132
Adams, James Hopkins, 1812-1861. 87508, 87519, 87521, 87523-87524, 87530, 87792 see also South Carolina. Governor, 1854-1856 (Adams)
Adams, Jasper. 218-221
Adams, John. pseud. To the Hon. John Quincy Adams. 95129
Adams, John, Of Waltham-Abbey. tr. 36813, 6th note after 97689
Adams, John, 1704-1740. 222, (14513), 97451
Adams, John, Pres. U.S., 1735-1826. 183, 227-249, 251-253, 259, 263, (445)-449, 1016, (1230), 2446, 3431, 9672, 14008, (14151), 14388, 14990, 15456, (15934), 18005, 24886, 25876, 25886, 26445, 26810, 29974, 31947, 32362, (32551), (32634), 34865, 35302, 37712, 40696, (41645), 41646, 47760, (48051)-48056, 48141, 48148, 59593, 62656, 62658, 62702, (63799), 63811, 65359, (67288), 69837-69838, 69866, 78647, 78743, 79000, 79369, 79391, 79399, (79402), note after 79538, (80310), 80405, 81394, 82974, 82976, 82979, 84678C, 84832, 84904, 84906, 88969, 89198, 90629, note after 91540, 92762, 93712, 94261, 5th note after 95677, 96590, 7th note after 97146, 97147, 98504, 98505, note after 99292, 101482, 101709, 101712-101716, note after 101839, 103848, 104204-104205 see also U. S. Legation. Netherlands; U. S. President, 1797-1801 (Adams)
Adams, John Pres. U. S., 1735-1826. mediumistic author 71149
Adams, John, 1750?-1814. 223-226

Adams, John, 1778-1854. 3189
Adams, John, fl. 1812. 721, 94568
Adams, John A. 84974
Adams, John G. 84292
Adams, John Greenleaf, 1810-1887. 226
Adams, John J. 255
Adams, John Jay. 265
Adams, John Milton. 327
Adams, John Quincy, Pres. U. S., 1767-1848. 185, 267-271, 273-276, 278-283, 285-313, 325, (445)-448, (14151), 14313, 15489, 18005, 23258, 24052, 24892, 25876, 31091, 31577, 35376, 40482, 42459, 43375, 48087-48095, 48148, 48580, (50398), 2d note after 52014, 56524, 57356, 58405, 63694-63695, 63697, 63911, 64402, 68728, 2d note after (69432), 69903, 71712, 74262, 78403, 78647, 82979, 84904, 84905, 85069, 85070, 85076, 85198, 88496, 88939, 89595, 89629, 92136, 93573, 96261, 96636-96657, 97913, 97925, note after 99796, 103434, 103819, 104204-104205, 104874, note after 105101 see also U. S. Department of State; U. S. President, 1825-1829 (J. Q. Adams)
Adams, John Quincy, Pres. U. S., 1767-1848. supposed author 272, 29659, 52798, 80855, 96933
Adams, John Quincy, Pres. U. S., 1767-1848. mediumistic author 91766
Adams, John Quincy, fl. 1913-1919. ed. 104533
Adams, John S. 326
Adams, Joseph. 328-330
Adams, Josiah. 331-334
Adams, Julius W. 335
Adams, Moses. defendant (9089), 96808
Adams, Nathaniel. 337
Adams, Nehemiah, 1806-1878. 338-341, 23684, 41599, 63162, 74741, 80198, 82243
Adams, R. S. 343
Adams, Randolph G. ed. 104627
Adams, Robert Huntington, 1792-1830. 336
Adams, Samuel, fl. 1765. 342
Adams, Samuel, fl. 1783-1785. 23954 see also Fayette County, Pa. Collector of Excise.
Adams, Samuel, 1722-1803. 242, 344, 6478, 6566, 29974, (32551), 57866, 58231, 7th note after 97146, 97147
Adams, Samuel, 1722-1803. supposed author 1792A, (31912)
Adams, Seth. Defendant (13756)
Adams, Sherman Wolcott, 1836-1898. 91754
Adams, T. M. 346
Adams, Thomas. 345
Adams, Will. pseud. Errata. see Neal, John.
Adams, William. 348-349
Adams, William, 1575?-1620. 66686
Adams, Sir William, 1783-1827. see Rawson, Sir William, originally William Adams, 1783-1827.
Adams, William, 1807-1880. 351-355, (17268), (45438)
Adams, William Bridges, 1797-1872. supposed author 36927, 2d note after 94241
Adams, William Edwin, 1832- 356
Adams, William H. 86204 see also Sodus Canal Company. President.
Adams, William Henry Davenport, 1828-1891. tr. 70333
Adams, William Taylor, 1822-1897. 357-359, 57216, 86266
Adams, Ymant. pseud see Middelgeest, Simon van. supposed author
Adams, Zabdiel. 360-366, 11967, 11968, 3d note after 96741

Adams. see also Addoms.
Adams. firm see Hunt and Adams. firm
Adams. firm see Sidney & Adams. firm
Adams & Co. firm see Wilcox, Adams &
    Co. firm
Adams & Co. firm plaintiffs 90320
Adams and Wilder. firm publishers 93900
Adams, Sampson & Co. firm publishers
    42477, 42837, (44215), 53814, 73729,
    (75722)
Adams Academy, Quincy, Mass. (67283)
Adams Academy, (Founded by President John
    Adams.) Quincy, Mass. [Catalogue for]
    1873. (67283)
Adams and liberty. 15024, 58200, 97402
Adams Express Company. firm petitioners
    37167
Adams ode. 89656
Adamsen, Ymant. pseud. see Middelgeest,
    Simon van. supposed author
Adamson, John. 367-369
Adamson, M. pseud. Friendly epistle to
    neighbour John Taylor. 370
Adamson, Thomas. 371
Adamson, W. Agar. 372
Adams's Boston directory for 1852. 6696
Adams's new directory of the city of Boston.
    6696
Adanson, Michel, 1727-1806. 67461
Adda, Gerolamo d'. 14640
Addeman, Joshua M. 3741, 70510, 70589 see
    also Rhode Island. Secretary of State.
Addenda. 82402
Addenda, being a reply to "Truth, in plain
    English." 98979
Addenda, from the Weekly Journal. 30174
Addenda from the 'Weekly Journal,' No. XL.
    46265
Addenda to the Bibliotheca Americana. 73095
Addenda to the Carpenter family. 82402
Addenda to the Lloyd genealogy. 82402
Addenda to the Municipalist. 51330, note after
    71222
Adderley, Charles Bowyer. see Norton,
    Charles Bowyer Adderley, 1st Baron,
    1814-1905.
Adderley, William. 80199, 80200
Adder's den. (21579)
Adderup, Andrew. pseud. Lincolniana. 41207
Addey, Markinfield. 374-375
Addicion a los festexos. 99400
Addicion de otros cinco Jesuitas originarios, y
    naturales paysanos del P. Viana. 94574
Addington, ------. 63082
Addington, Henry Unwin, 1790-1870. 58475 see
    also Great Britain, Legation. U. S.
Addington, I. 78202 see also Massachusetts
    (Colony) Council. Secretary.
Addington, L. 15524
Addison, ------, fl. 1738. 92802
Addison, ------, fl. 1740. 103502
Addison, Alexander. 376-380, 100081, 105045
Addison, Alexander. defendant at impeachment
    381, 96809
Addison County, Vt. Court. 95518
Addison County, Vt. Convention of Republican
    Citizens, 1814. see Democratic Party.
    Vermont. Addison County. Convention,
    1814.
Addison County, Vt. Democratic Party Con-
    vention, 1814. see Democratic Party.
    Vermont. Addison County. Convention,
    1814.
Addison Consociation. see Congregational
    Churches in Vermont. Addison
    Consociation.
Additamentum. (8784)

Additamentum nonae partis Americae, hoc est
    descriptio. (8784)
Additamentum oder Anhang desz neundten
    Theils Americae. (8784)
Additamentvm theatri orbis terrarvm.
    (57694)
Addition. 44505
Addition aux memoires. 4935, 4936
Addition, in a second conference. 20057
    (20271)
Addition or postscript to the vindication.
    33497
Addition to Fairmount Park. 62128
Addition to the book, entituled, The spirit of
    the martyrs revived. 89501
Addition to the present melancholy circum-
    stances. (45574)
Addition to what I presented to the ministry.
    72682
Additional act to alter the law. 7018
Additional acts of the legislature. 60750, note
    after 97766
Additional appendix. 101891
Additional articles of the bye-laws. 99193
Additional by-laws of the town of Portland.
    64343
Additional catalogue—May 1840. 72355
Additional catalogue of the Territorial Library
    of Colorado. 14737
Additional causes of appeal. 85212
Additional chapter on cotton seed and its uses.
    (42792)
Additional charter granted to the Governors
    of the College of New-York, in America.
    14818, 54198
Additional charter of the College, Academy,
    and Charitable School of Philadelphia,
    in Pennsylvania. (61416)
Additional convention to the Convention . . .
    [of] November, 1868. 64517
Additional declaration. 104143
Additional discourses. 84614, 84615, 84626,
    84678C
Additional discourses and essays. 84580,
    84597, 84598, 84600
Additional documents. 61057
Additional estimates. 15230
Additional facts and observations. 61548
Additional facts, observations, and conjectures.
    3802
Additional facts, remarks, and arguments.
    382
Additional hymns. 36593
Additional information for Joseph Knight.
    102434
Additional information for John Wedderburn.
    102435
Additional inquiries. 34588
Additional instances of navigators. 3631
Additional lecture on the constitution. (65513)
Additional letters on some questions of inter-
    national law. (30298)
Additional notes by Thomas Park. 30394
Additional notes of a discussion of tidal
    observations. 2587
Additional notes on the history of slavery.
    50381
Additional notices of his [i.e. Thomas
    Shepard's] life and character. 80198
Additional notices of miss Hannah Adams.
    213
Additional number of letters from the
    Federal Farmer. 383, (39783)-39784,
    40583
Additional observations. 65457
Additional observations applicable to Hon.
    E. G. Stanley's plan. 9398

Additional observations on certain passages in Dr. Chauncey's [sic] remarks, &c. 12318-12319, 23319, (41644), 2d note after 99800

Additional observations on civil liberty, &c. 20483

Additional observations on hybridity in animals. (51024)

Additional observations on the American treaty. 17184

Additional observations on the nature and value of civil liberty. 65444, 65461, 91600, 104706

Additional observations to a Short narrative of the horrid massacre in Boston. 6741, 80669, 80673, 101479

Additional observations to the report. 50786

Additional papers concerning the province of Quebec. 45415

Additional papers concerning the province of Quebeck. (66986), 66989

Additional papers on the Nova Scotia gold fields. 56109

Additional papers relative to the Arctic expedition. 1920

Additional piece by Hamilton. 30050, 2d note after 105926

Additional postscript from another hand. 28344

Additional proposals for convictions from the churches. 92095

Additional reasons, &c. 105036

Additional reasons for our immediately emancipating South America. 9315, 100594

Additional regulations concerning commercial intercourse. 74077

Additional remarks on a topic of importance. 6989

Additional remarks on the currency. 56812

Additional remarks [on the Gulf Stream.] (2588)

Additional report of the commissioner. 59827, 60562

Additional report on water power. 62371

Additional resolves respecting the north-eastern boundary. 43900

Additional sketches, by a few friends. 27429

Additional sketches of adventure. 43053

Additional speeches, addresses, and occasional sermons. (58737)

Additional statements by the Agents of the Illinois and Wabash Land Companies. 34294, 84577-84578, 2d-3d notes after 97876

Additional supplement to the catalogue. 15568

Additiones ad singula capita historiam illustrantes. (8784)

Additiones constitutionum nouae impressionis. 98913

Additions and amendments to the civil code of . . . Louisiana. 42205

Additions and corrections to the first and second editions. 82303

Additions and corrections to the former editions. 71989

Additions and reflections. 92027

Additions. By Aristides. 35362, 2d note after 98528

Additions by Herman S. Noble. 51853

Additions by Professor W. W. Turner. 49668

Additions made to the Library of Congress. 15574

Additions, Nov., 1837 [to the Library of the Worcester Lyceum.] 105430

Additions of 1838 & 1839 [to the Library of the Worcester Lyceum.] 105430

Additions to Common sense. 58215

Additions to Plain truth. 15526, note after 63244, 84642, 2d note after 96428

Additions to the catalogue . . . from 1821 to the present. 40881

Additions to the first edition of the Reply, etc. 26443

Additions [to the] Nouveau dictionnaire historique. 27789

Additions to the Life and designs of Dr. Bray. 89377

Addoms, J. S. 384

Address. 5403, 20623, 20657, 25850, 27550, 27850, 28428, 30972, 32397, 32807, 32881, 34310, 35801, 38544, 39383, 41793, 43345, 43664, 45694, 46840, (50948), (51120), 55737, 56236, 58693, (59158), (63025), 68641, 73015, (78937), 81351, 85485, 94388, 96761, 97258, 101514, 1st note after 101877, 104872, 105497, 105995

Address ad fratres in Eremo. 46324

Address adopted at a meeting of citizens of Philadelphia. (61417)

Address adopted at the annual meeting of the State Council. 53523

Address adopted by the Democratic Convention. (70521)

Address adopted by the Democratic State Convention. (34523)

Address adopted by the Whig State Convention. 45577

Address . . . against immediate emancipation. 33387

Address . . . Agricultural Society of Loudon County. (29913)

Address . . . Agricultural Society of Montgomery County. (29913)

Address . . . agriculture of Maryland. 51561

Address . . . American Antiquarian Society. 36030

Address . . . Amicable Lodge, October 18, 1855. (58176)

Address and accompanying documents. 31180

Address and annual reports of the several departments. 64351

Address and caution to the public. 10456

Address and constitution of the Evangelical Missionary Society. (45724)

Address and constitution of the New York Missionary Society. 54516

Address, and constitution of the [Schenectady County Bible] Society. 77605

Address and correspondence. 24092

Address and discourse. 11938, 37466

Address and draft of a proposed constitution. 53471

Address and instructions. 89652

Address and petition of the clergy. 61418

Address and petition of the people called Quakers. 61936

Address and poem before the Association of the Alumni. 74379

Address and poem delivered before the associate chapters. (80907)

Address and poem delivered before the chapters. 80908

Address and poem, delivered before the Columbia College Alumni Association. 78838

Address and poem delivered before the Mechanic Apprentices' Library Association. 89082

Address and prayer. 90176

Address and proceedings of the Democratic State Convention. 53472

Address and proceedings of the masters and past masters. 54037

Address and proclamation of Andrew Jackson. 35391
Address and reasons of dissent. 59829
Address and recommendations to the states. 385, 15508
Address and reply on the presentation. 12200, 27969
Address and reply to his worthy representatives. 98911
Address and report of a Select Com. 2992
Address and report upon the practicability of manufacturing railroad iron. (35091), 75328
Address and resignation of his excellency George Washington. 101593
Address and resolutions adopted at the meeting of the Southern Rights Convention of Maryland. 45049, note before 88481
Address and resolutions, adopted at the Whig State Convention. 45575
Address and resolutions adopted by a meeting of workingmen and others. 82355, 104222
Address and resolutions adopted by the said convention [i.e. Republican Convention, Rockingham County, N. H.] 3772
Address and resolutions adopted by the State Rights and Free Trade Party at Charleston. 39144, 88065
Address and resolutions adopted on war. 72390
Address and resolutions [of the Anti Masonic Convention.] 65819
Address and resolutions of the Connecticut soldiers. 55834
Address and resolutions of the convention. 105425
Address and resolutions of the Grant National Republican Meeting. 54038
Address; and resolutions [of the State Temperance Committee of Massachusetts.] 46143
Address and resolutions of the Union League. 62352
Address and resolves of the Democratic members. 45576
Address and rules of the South-Carolina Society. 88039
Address and select discourses of Rev. Samuel H. Stearns. 90988
Address and supplement. 93796
Address and suppressed report. 53049
Address and testimonials. (77205)
Address and the constitution of the Bible and Common Prayer-Book Society. (54116)
Address . . . Annapolis. (31467)
Address. . . . anniversary . . . of the Newark Institute for Young Ladies. 64798
Address . . . annual commencement of Dickinson College. 9912
Address . . . annual convention of the Protestant Episcopal Church. (32301)
Address . . . annual fair of the Hampden Co. Agricultural Society. 24766
Address, . . . April 5th, 1831. 50437
Address . . . April 1, 1835. 9899
Address, . . . April 24, 1865. 14344
Address . . . Association of Alumni of Connecticut State Normal School. 60947
Address at a meeting of the descendants of Richard Haven. (58628)
Address at a religious celebration in Salem. (12406)
Address at Acton. 331
Address . . . at Albany, Feb'y 12, 1868. 17229
Address . . . at Albany, February 22, 1858. 35477

Address . . . at Amherst College. 33794
Address at Amesbury, Mass. 18364
Address . . . at Athens. (27440)
Address at Athol, Mass. 55893
Address at Aurora, Cayuga County, New York. 77834
Address at Bennington. 37127
Address . . . at Bloody Brook. 41182
Address, . . . at . . . Buffalo. 51128
Address at Burlington College, July 4, 1853. 20390
Address at Burlington College, July 4, 1855. 20391
Address at Burlington College, on the seventy-eighth anniversary of American independence. 20391
Address, at Burlington College, on the seventy-second anniversary of American independence. 20384
Address, . . . at Canandaigua. 13749
Address at Charleston, . . . March 29, 1831. 28862
Address at Charleston, S. C., May 3, 1870. 81257
Address . . . at Charleston, S. C., . . . November 4th, 1852. 43447
Address . . . at Charleston, S. C., on March 23, A.'.O.'.737. 28135
Address . . . at Charleston, [S. C.] Sep. 19, 1834. 25675
Address . . . at Cherry Valley. 50955
Address at Columbus, Ohio. 2333
Address at Copperstown. (43157)
Address . . . at Evans. 80125
Address . . . at Faneuil Hall, Boston. 65567
Address at Fitchburg, Mass. 32287
Address [at] Genesee Wesleyan Seminary. 91102
Address . . . at Greenfield. 24766
Address . . . [at] Hanover College. (49833)
Address at Hartford before the delegates. 3114
Address at Hatfield, Mass. 7497
Address at Harve de Gras. 386
Address at her [i.e. Martha Day's] funeral. 18972
Address at his [i.e. Edward Hitchcock's] inauguration. 32250
Address . . . at Hombourg-les-Bains, Germany. 37948
Address . . . at Irving Hall. 32653
Address . . . at Jefferson College. (41639)
Address at Koskonong, Wisconsin. 78165
Address, at laying corner-stone of Calvanistic Society. 16327
Address at laying the corner stone of the Girard College. 5236, 71856
Address at Leominster. 15086
Address at Lockport. 37681
Address at Loudon Park Cemetery. (47106)
Address . . . at Louisville. 32650
Address . . . at Lynn. 18095
Address at Mendon, Mass. 90463
Address . . . [at] Mount Saint Mary's College. 42809
Address . . . at Nantucket. 36029
Address . . . at . . . Nashville, October 4, 1826. 41315
Address . . . at Nashville, Ten. Feb. 22, 1832. 41315
Address . . . at . . . Needham. (56233)
Address, . . . at New Bordeaux, . . . S. C. (50488)
Address at New Fane, Vt. 22241
Address . . . at New Haven. 33983
Address . . . at New Platz. 1240, 44747
Address at Northampton. 20612

ADDRESS

Address at Oswego. 34092
Address . . . [at] Oxford Female College. (43647)
Address . . . at Pembroke, Mass. 50416
Address at Philadelphia at the laying of the corner stone of All Soul's Church. 20391
Address . . . at Philadelphia, March 15, 1866. 37272
Address . . . at Philadelphia, October 29, 1863. 4575
Address . . . at Pittsfield. 43369
Address . . . at Plessis. 44804
Address . . . at Pomfret, Con. (44749)
Address . . . at Portland before the Cumber. County Temperance Society. 37779
Address . . . at Portland, before the Grand Lodge. 80301
Address . . . at Portland, February 6, 1834. 38528
Address at Portsmouth, July 4th. (23149)
Address . . . at Portsmouth, N. H. (63452)
Address at Princeton. 55361
Address . . . at Rochester. 3389
Address . . . at Saco. 32605
Address . . . at . . . St. Louis. (43859)
Address at Southern Convention. 34039
Address at Sparta, Wisc. 30827
Address . . . at Sterling. (31806)
Address . . . at the anniversary meeting of the Massachusetts Colonization Society. 39226
Address . . . at the anniversary meeting of the New York State Colonization Society. 39226
Address . . . at the anniversary . . . of the American Colonization Society. 39226
Address at the anniversary of the American Peace Society. 59347
Address . . . at the annual commencement of the Medical School. 79872
Address, . . . at the annual communication of the Grand Lodge. 24208
Address.. . . . at the annual Conference of Christian Ministers. 17357
Address at the annual examination of Ohio Female College. 92178
Address . . . at the . . . annual fair of the American Institute. 47389
Address . . . at the annual fair of the New-York State Agricultural Society. 20693
Address, . . . at the annual meeting of the American Temperance Society. (38027)
Address . . . at the annual meeting of the Historical Society of Pennsylvania. 36510
Address at the annual meeting of the Maine Colonization Society. 6045
Address . . . at the annual meeting of the N. Y. State Agricultural Society. (55905)
Address . . . at the annual meeting of the N. Y. State Agricultural Society, Albany, February 9, 1865. (80128)
Address at the annual meeting of the Pennsyl- vania Colonization Society. (29303)
Address at the bar of the Legislative Assembly of Canada. 21291
Address at the celebration of the Sunday School Jubilee. 28862
Address at the centennial celebration in Hard- wich, Mass. (58176)
Address, . . . at the centennial celebration, in Peterborough, N. H. 50710
Address . . . at the centennial celebration of the birth day of Washington. 18024
Address at the centennial celebration of the settlement of . . . Lancaster, N. H. 45431

Address, at the centennial celebration, of the town of Fitchburg. 85491
Address . . . at the centennial celebration of Warren, N. H. (41529)
Address . . . at the ceremony of laying the corner-stone. (33333)
Address at the citizens' celebration, Woonsocket. 91185
Address, . . . at the Collegiate Institution in Amherst. 33788
Address . . . at the commencement, in the General Theological Seminary. 43105
Address at the commencement of the General Theological Seminary. 37338
Address . . . at the commencement of the General Theological Seminary of the Protestant Episcopal Church. 17581
Address . . . at the Conference of Churches. 44745
Address at the consecration of Dell Park Cemetery. 2681
Address at the consecration of Plymouth Lodge. 11117
Address at the consecration of the Cambridge Cemetery. (10121)
Address . . . at the consecration of the Grand Lodge of Maine. 80299
Address . . . at the consecration of the Pine Grove Cemetery. 79676
Address . . . at the consecration of the room. 98471
Address . . . at the consecration of the Spring- field Cemetery. 59384
Address . . . at the consecration of the Union Cemetery. (33946)
Address, at the convention . . . Cincinnati, Ohio. 12194
Address at the dedication and opening of Bristol Academy. (20529)
Address at the dedication and opening of the New-England Normal Institute. 74386
Address . . . at the dedication of a school house. 50893
Address . . . at the dedication of Lancaster Memorial Hall. 38790
Address at the dedication of Pardee Hall. 68064
Address at the dedication of the astronomical observatory. (49665)
Address at the dedication of the building in Chalmers Street. 28862
Address at the dedication of the Cave Hill Cemetery. (33786)
Address at the dedication of the Free Academy. (29271)
Address, . . . at the dedication of the Green Hill Cemetery. 47175
Address at the dedication of the Hinesdale Academy. 89744
Address at the dedication of the new building. 70406
[Address] at the dedication of the new city hall. 32512
Address . . . at the dedication of the new hall. 33205
Address at the dedication of the Punchard Free School. 26174
Address at the dedication of the second hall. 91204
Address, . . . at the dedication of the Smith School House. 49320
Address at the dedication of the Soldiers' Monument. 78823
Address at the dedication of the town hall. 18846
Address at the dedication of the Washington County Soldiers' Monument. 84385

Address . . . at the . . . eighth triennial festival. (8902)

Address . . . at the eleventh anniversary of the Massachusetts Peace Society. (26185)

Address . . . at the erection of a monumental stone. 64061

Address . . . at the fair of the Erie County Agricultural Society. (33100)

Address at the Federal Republican meeting. 34360

Address . . . at the Federal-Street Theatre, Boston. 26525

Address at the first anniversary of the Free Academy. 4651

Address at the first annual exhibition. 19480

Address . . . at the formation of the Blackstone Monument Association. 55016

Address at the fourth annual commencement of the Washington Business College. 89378

Address . . . at the fourth convention of the graduates. 26536

Address at the funeral of Bishop T. C. Brownell. 9243

Address at the funeral of Caleb Ticknor. 69000

Address at the funeral of Capt. Lorenzo D. Gove. 39825

Address . . . at the funeral of Capt. William F. Brigham. 43139

Address . . . at the funeral of Daniel Campbell. (58368)

Address at the funeral of Deacon Anson Moody. 92902

Address at the funeral of Deacon Nathan Beers. 21469

Address at the funeral of Deacon William P. Ripley. 7944

Address at the funeral of Eli Ives. 21471

Address at the funeral of Hon. Henry Wyles Cushman. 28543

Address at the funeral of Hon. Roger Sherman Baldwin. (21470)

Address at the funeral of Hon. Simeon Baldwin. 21471

Address, . . . at the funeral of John Johnston. (43224)

Address at the funeral of John R. Kane. 80463

Address at the funeral of Lieut. Col. A. R. Thompson. (24191)

Address at the funeral of Mrs. Elizabeth Thompson. 47254

Address at the funeral of Mrs. [L. O. B.] Thompson. 2675

Address . . . at the funeral of Mrs. Martha Freme. 51123

Address at the funeral of Mrs. Sarah Griffing. 84900

Address at the funeral of Mrs. Susan E. Musser. (78936)

Address at the funeral of N. H. Cobbs. 22283

Address . . . at the funeral of Rev. Benjamin Tappan. 43419

Address at the funeral of Rev. John Lovejoy Abbot. 23271

Address at the funeral of Rev. John R. M'Dowall. 39562

Address at the funeral of Rev. Samuel Abbot Smith. 31864, 84013, 91049

Address . . . at the funeral of Rev. William Ellery Channing. 26436

Address at the funeral of Robert C. Goodhue. 4575

Address at the funeral of . . . Sergeant Henry Todd. 48930

Address . . . at the funeral of Sophia, wife of Major Gen. Towson. 36930

Address . . . at the funeral of the Hon. Dennis Kimberly. 13589

Address at the funeral of the Hon. Jacob Axson. 18066

Address at the funeral of the Hon. Thomas A. Davis. 62733

Address at the funeral of the Reverend and beloved Dr. John Lord Taylor. 85208

Address . . . at the funeral of the Rev. Dr. Milnor. 92082

Address . . . at the funeral of the Rev. Dr. William M. Tennent. (28505)

Address, at the funeral of the Rev. John David Ogilby. 20391

Address . . . at the funeral of the Rt. Rev. Benjamin Moore. (32301)

Address at the funeral of Timothy Phelps Beers. 38119

Address at the Humboldt Celebration. 40985

Address at the Ichthyon feast. (25221)

Address at the inauguration of Cornelius Conway Felton. (24040)

Address at the inauguration of Joseph G. Hoyt. 33409

Address at the inauguration of Mr. Charles King. 14804

Address at the inauguration of the author as professor. 41869

Address at the inauguration of the Hatborough Monument. 4613, 30832

Address . . . at the inauguration of the Hon. Theodore Frelinghuysen. 74434

Address at the inauguration of the Young Men's Christian Association. 71114

Address . . . at the installation of Columbian Lodge, Boston. (80303)

Address . . . at the installation of the officers of St. Paul's Royal Arch Chapter, Boston. (33308)

Address at the installation of the officers of the Mount Zion Royal Arch Chapter, Stoughton. 33983

Address . . . at the interment of Professor Frisbie. (55861)

Address at the interment of R. W. James Davenport. 30521

Address at the interment of Robert Ralston. (28505)

Address at the interment of Sylv. Bourne. 43329

Address at the laying of the corner stone of a house of worship for the Allen Street Congregational Society. 64104

Address . . . at the laying of the corner-stone of a house of worship for the First Congregational Society. (32344)

Address . . . at the laying of the corner stone of St. Matthew's Church, New-York. 77482

Address at the laying of the corner stone of the Church of the Advent. 28667

Address . . . at the laying of the corner stone of the city hall. 39226

Address at the laying of the corner-stone of the Douglas Monument. 20337

Address at the laying of the corner stone [of the fifth house of worship of the First Church.] 22327

Address at the laying of the corner-stone of the Holmesburgh Public School. 17250

Address at the laying of the corner-stone of the Lake Erie Female Seminary. (5658)

Address at the laying of the corner-stone of the library edifice. 15471

Address . . . at the laying of the corner-stone of the new chapel. 62533

Address . . . at the laying of the corner-stone of the new Masonic Temple. 39226

Address . . . at the laying of the corner stone of the University of Nashville. 43233

Address at the laying of the corner stone of Trinity Church. 20391

Address . . . at the . . . meeting of the Maryland State Colonization Society. 30419

Address at the meeting of the Massachusetts General Conference. 85218

Address . . . at the . . . N. York State Agricultural Society. 37816

Address . . . at . . . the nineteenth annual fair of the American Institute, of the city of New York. 11851

Address at the 19th triennial festival of the Massachusetts Charitable Mechanic Association. (13231)

Address at the opening and dedication of the Winchester Home for Aged Indigent Women. 23286

Address . . . at the opening celebration, May 9, 1863. 62352

Address . . . at the opening of Portsmouth Academy. 56813

Address . . . at the opening of the Agricultural College. (34971)

Address . . . at the opening of the American State Council. 75906

Address at the opening of the Eastern Rail Road. 59365

Address, . . . at the opening of the Genesee Wesleyan Seminary. 57174

Address . . . at the opening of the hall. 65535

Address at the opening of the Law Academy. 21383

Address . . . at the opening of the Law Department. (24191)

Address at the opening of the new clinical lecture room. 42652

Address at the opening of the new edifice. 89744

Address . . . at the opening of the new Female Academy. 42651

Address . . . at the opening of the new Medical College. 23271

Address . . . at the opening of the New-York High-School. 28878

Address, at the opening of the observatory of Williams College. 32906

Address at the opening of the Rhode Island State Normal School. (64637)

Address . . . at the opening of the Rock-Island Medical School. (38068)

Address . . . at the opening of the rooms. 42149

Address at [the opening of the Stuyvesant Institute.] 101338

Address at the opening of the town hall. (62723)

Address at the ordination of Mr. M'Keen. (43391)

Address at the organization of the city government. 73649

Address, at the place of execution. 102075

Address at the public exercises of Albany Academy. (30980)

Address . . . at the reception by the Seventh Regiment. 20342

Address . . . at the request of the Massachusetts Charitable Fire Society. 38005

Address, . . . at the request of the Union and Jefferson Societies. 43516

Address at the second anniversary of the U. S. Christian Commission. (33273)

Address . . . at the 64th convention of the Protestant Episcopal Church in . . . Pennsylvania. 64617

Address at the sixty-third anniversary of the New-York Historical Society, Dec. 19, 1867. 31386

Address at the spring soiree. 89286

Address at the thirty-ninth annual session of the New York Eastern Christian Conference. 54767

Address, at the thirty-fifth commencement of Hartwick Seminary. 39176

Address . . . at the thirty-third anniversary of the South Parish Sunday School in Portsmouth, N. .H 59354

Address . . . at the triennial convention . . . of Chicago Theological Seminary. 43844

Address at the twenty-second anniversary of the American Peace Society. 92015

Address . . . at the University of Pennsylvania before the Society of the Alumni, . . . November 15, 1852. 64677

Address . . . at the University of Pennsylvania, before the Society of the Alumni, on the . . . 109th annual celebration. 82715

Address . . . at the Washington University. 64471

Address at the Western Baptist Theological Institution. 59156

Address at Troy, N. Y. (71891)

Address . . . at Troy, on the celebration of the abolition of slavery. 59180

Address . . . [at] West Point. 9609

Address, . . . at . . . Wilkes-Barre, Penn. 49201

Address . . . at Wilton . . . July 4, 1828. 41574

Address . . . at Wiscasset. (80298)

Address . . . at Worcester, August 24, 1820. 27945

Address . . . at Worcester, (Mass.) (41257)

Address at Worcester, Oct. 21, 1807. (41257)

Address, . . . August 8, 1860. (47166)

Address . . . Aug. 1, 1850. (11866)

Address . . . August 14, 1828. (24040)

Address . . . August 2, 1850. 32933

Address . . . August 22, 1860. 23678

Address before a convention of loyal women of Iowa. 64797

Address before Annapolis Lodge. (24923)

Address . . . before . . . Antioch College. (47179)

Address, before . . . Burlington College. 20391

Address before Essex Lodge. 10922

Address before Hampshire, Franklin and Hampden Agricultural Society. (25221)

Address before Howard Lodge. (67750)

Address . . . before . . . Jordan Lodge. (55188)

Address . . . before . . . Lafayette College. 43340

Address, before Lodge No. 5. 68149

Address before Marshall College. (11866)

Address before . . . Masons . . . June 24, 1868. 31010

Address before . . . Masons of . . . Massachusetts. 31010

Address . . . before . . . State Normal School. 47181

Address . . . before the Abolition Society at New York. (12406)

Address . . . before the Agricultural Society of the County of Oneida. 27704

Address before the Agricultural Society of Albemarle, Va. 91586

Address before the Agricultural Society of Chester County. 22432

Address before the Agricultural Society of Genesee County. (32962)

Address before the Agricultural Society of New Castle County. 24506

Address before the Agricultural Society of Rutland County. 44737

Address . . . before the Agricultural Society of the County of Missisquoi at Bedford. 33977

Address before the Agricultural Society of Warren County. 68170

Address . . . before the Agricultural Society of Westborough and vicinity. 82115

Address . . . before the Alabama University. 47368

Address before the Albany Medical College. 22518

Address, before the Albany Typographical Society. 13014

Address before the Alexandrian Society. 13269

Address . . . before the Alpha Phi Delta & H. H. H. Societies. 33244

Address . . . before the Alpha Phi Omega and Euglossian Societies. 20341

Address before the Alpha Pi Delta Society. 91771

Address, . . . before the Alumni Association of Columbia College. (55256)

Address . . . before the Alumni Association . . . of Dartmouth College. 3777

Address, . . . before the Alumni Association of Friends' New England Yearly Meeting School. (64668)

Address . . . before the Alumni Association of Nassau Hall. (79199)

Address . . . before the Alumni Association of Nassau-Hall, . . . September 30, 1835. 5237

Address before the Alumni Association of Pennsylvania Cent. High School. (47391)

Address, before the Alumni Association of Rutgers College. (25153)

Address . . . before the Alumni Association of Rutgers College, July 23, 1853. (58651)

Address . . . before the Alumni Association of Rutger's College, July 27th, 1852. 63733

Address . . . before the Alumni Association of the College of New Jersey, September 26, 1838. (43194)

Address . . . before the Alumni Association of the College of Physicians. (46947)

Address before the Alumni Association of the University of North Carolina. 45467

Address before the Alumni Association of Washington College. 85476

Address before the alumni of Atkinson Academy. 24037

Address . . . before the alumni of Cambridge. 26074

Address . . . before the . . . alumni of Columbia College, . . . 4th of May, 1825. 50339

Address . . . before the . . . alumni of Columbia College, . . . May 4, 1831. 44301

Address . . . before the alumni of Columbia College, on the seventh of May, 1828. 48998

Address before the alumni of East Tenn. University. 68664

Address before the . . . alumni of Hanover College. 55324

Address before the alumni of Hobart College. 24472

Address . . . before the . . . alumni of Middlebury College. 44128

Address . . . before the alumni of Pennsylvania College. (46939)

Address . . . before the alumni . . . of St. John's College. 62972

Address . . . before the . . . alumni of the College of Charleston. 43115

Address . . . before the alumni of the Norwich Free Academy. 82465

Address . . . before the alumni of the University of Alabama, at their fourteenth anniversary. 83004

Address . . . before the alumni of the University of Alabama, July 13th, 1858. 43582

Address, . . . before the alumni of the University of North-Carolina. 32881

Address before the alumni of the University of Pennsylvania; by William B. Reed. (68597)

Address before the alumni of the University of Pennsylvania, November, . . . 1851. 27458

Address before the . . . alumni of the University of the City of New-York, June 28, 1852. (31388)

Address . . . before the . . . alumni of the University of Virginia. 32467

Address . . . before the alumni of Waterville College. 52161

Address . . . before the alumni . . . of Western Reserve College. 31127

Address before the . . . alumni of William & Mary College. (36617)

Address before the alumni of Yale College. 18427

Address, . . . before the Alumni Society of the University of Nashville, October 7, 1846. 51880

Address . . . before the Alumni Society of the University of Nashville. . . . On the 3d of October, 1854. 41313

Address . . . before the American Academy of Fine Arts. 39383

Address . . . before the American Antiquarian Society. 32588

Address, . . . before the American Association for the Advancement of Learning. (49958)

Address before the American Association for the Advancement of Science, August, 1855. 18427

Address before the American Association for the Advancement of Science, August, 1859. 11480

Address . . . before the American Association for the Advancement of Science, August, 1867. 54896

Address before the American Colonization Society. 13385

Address before the American Colonization Society, Washington, D. C. 26169

Address before the American Education Society, at Boston. 28818

Address . . . before the American Education Society, . . . Boston, May 30, 1865. 58625

Address before the American Geographical and Statistical Society, by Sylvester Mowry. 51211

Address . . . before the American Geographical and Statistical Society, January 24, 1870. 18358

Address . . . before the American Institute. . . . October 14, 1850. (31890)

Address . . . before the American Institute, October 9, 1845. 47389

Address . . . before the American Institute . . . Oct. 17th, 1833. (37423)

Address . . . before the American Institute of Instruction, at Portland, Me. 55782

Address . . . before the American Institute of Instruction . . . Boston, August 31st, 1867. 41251

Address . . . before the American Institute . . . of New-York. 42812

Address . . . before the American Institute of the City of New York. 18095

Address before the American Iron Association. 33337

Address . . . before the American Medical Association. 44481

Address . . . before the American Medical Association, at St. Louis. 58921

Address . . . before the American Medical Association, . . . in . . . New Haven, Conn. 49021

Address before the American Peace Society. 93687

Address before the American Peace Society, at its anniversary in Boston. 93687

Address . . . before the American Peace Society, at its thirtieth anniversary. 82653

Address before the American Peace Society, at its twenty-ninth anniversary. 91047

Address before the American Peace Society: delivered in Park Street Church. 92105

Address . . . before the American Peace Society, in . . . Boston. 47078

Address . . . before the American Peace Society . . . May 20, 1869. 49196

Address before the American Peace Society . . . May 23, 1842. (17138)

Address before the American Peace Society, . . . May 26, 1862. 44096

Address before the American Social Science Association. (22172)

Address, . . . before the American Temperance Society . . . Boston. (38027)

Address before the American Temperance Society, New York. 82668

Address before the American Whig and Cliosophic Societies of the College of New Jersey. June 23d, 1846. (8440)

Address . . . before the American Whig and Cliosophic Societies of the College of New Jersey. September 29, 1835. 26752

Address . . . before . . . [the] Ancient Free Masons. 20706

Address before the Art Union of Philadelphia. (68545)

Address before the Anti-masonic Convention. 3315

Address before the Anti-slavery Society. 28943

Address . . . before the assembly of citizens. (31425)

Address before the Associated Instrucers [sic] of Boston. 59318

Address . . . before the Associated Lodges of Free and Accepted Masons . . . at Buffalo. 81594

Address . . . before the Association in Keene. (58703)

Address before the Athenian Society of Indiana University. 78273

Address . . . before the Athenian Society of the University of Ohio. 60955

Address before the Attleborough Agricultural Society. 104380

Address, . . . before the . . . Bar of the County of Bristol. 32590

Address before the Beaufort Volunteer Artillery. 22267

Address . . . before the Benevolent Society of Bowdoin College. (55021)

Address, before the Berkshire Agricultural Association. 27961

Address before the Berkshire Agricultural Society, at Pittsfield. 19077

Address . . . before the Berkshire Agricultural Society, October 8th, 1868. 27866

Address, . . . before the Berkshire Association . . . of Agriculture. 43369

Address . . . before the . . . Bible and Prayer Book Society. 43679

Address before the Bible Society at Mount Kisco. 35849

Address, . . . [before] the Bible Society of the District of Columbia. 51261

Address . . . before the Bible Society of the University of Virginia. 62904

Address before the Boston Academy of Music. (22174)

Address . . . before the Boston Encampment of Knights Templars. (50333)

Address . . . before the Boston Mercantile Library Association. (30800)

Address before the Boston Young Men's Christian Association. (74306)

Address . . . before the Bridgewater Society for the Promotion of Temperance. (79927)

Address before the Bristol Association for the Promotion of Temperance. 20977

Address before the Brooklyn Common Council. 8772

Address before the Brunswick . . . Society for the Suppression of Intemperance. 13610

Address before the Caledonian County Agricultural Society. 91506

Address . . . before the Cayuga County Agricultural Society. (28114)

Address . . . [before] the Central High School. 47105

Address before the Chamber of Commerce, N. Y. 42936

Address . . . before the Charitable Irish Society. 7110

Address before the Charleston Temperance Society, and the Young Men's Temperance Society of Charleston. 28862

Address . . . before the Charlestown Temperance Society. 24220

Address . . . before the Chester County Agricultural Society. 24506

Address before the Chester County Horticultural Society, 1847. 20165

Address before the Chester County Horticultural Society, West Chester, September 11, 1846. 18600

Address before the Chester Co., Penn., Horticultural Society. 39808

Address before the citizens and schools of Quincy, Mass. 42714

Address before the citizens of Cambridge. 58702

Address before the . . . citizens of Charlottesville, N. Y. 4243

Address . . . before the citizens of North-Yarmouth. (47442)

Address before the citizens of Union, Conn. 30092

Address before the city authorities in Salem. (7945)

Address . . . before the . . . College of Physicians. 43277

Address . . . before the . . . College of St. James. 43865

Address before the Colonization Society of Kentucky. 13550

Address . . . before the Columbian Association. 16297

Address . . . before the Columbian Institute. note after 39323

Address before the Columbian Society of Columbia College. 76440

Address . . . before the Columbian Society, of Marblehead, on the eighth of January, 1839. 65567

Address . . . before the Columbian Society of Marblehead, on the eighth of January, 1856. 42083

Address . . . before the Concord Temperance Society. 24667

Address before the Connecticut Peace Society. (31707)

Address before the Convention of American Women. (81752)

Address before the . . . Convention of the Protestant Episcopal Church. 37950

Address before the Cortland County, N. Y., Teachers' Institute. 37681

Address before the Cotton Planters' Convention of Georgia. 36575

Address . . . before the Cumberland County Agricultural Society. 39226

Address before the Delaware Horticultural Society. 22432

Address before the Democratic Central Club. 56854

Address . . . before the Diagnothian and Goethean Literary Societies. (66653)

Address . . . before the Dialectic and Franklin Societies. 61400

Address before the Dialectic Society of the Corps of Cadents. 987

Address . . . before the Dorchester Temperance Society. 39824

Address before the encampment. (23910)

Address before the Essex Agricultural Society. 42083, 64100

Address before the Essex Agricultural Society, at Danvers. 31122

Address before the Essex Agricultural Society, at Georgetown. 28365

Address before the Essex Agricultural Society, at Topsfield. 26297

Address before the Essex Agricultural Society, by Hon. Leverett Saltonstall, September 27, 1843. 75855

Address . . . before the Essex Agricultural Society, by James R. Nichols. 55204

Address before the Essex Agricultural Society, by John L. Russell. 74345

Address before the Essex Agricultural Society, (Mass.) 77173

Address . . . before the Essex Agricultural Society . . . October 17, 1821. 97257

Address before the Euphradian and Clariosophic Societies. 65371

Address before the Female Benezet Philanthropic Society. (40758)

Address before the Female Charitable Society at Worcester. 27875

Address . . . before the First Christian Church in Boston. 42092

Address . . . before the Franklin County Agricultural Society. (6977)

Address . . . before the Franklin Institute. 71921

Address before the Franklin Institute . . . the fourth of December, 1856. 27455

Address, before the "Franklin R. A. Chapter." 30330

Address . . . before the Franklin Typographical Association. 54283

Address . . . before the Gamma Sigma Society. 42033

Address, before the . . . General Assembly. (39192)

Address before the General Association of New-York. (20158)

Address . . . before the General Society of Mechanics and Tradesmen of the City of New-York. 55375

Address, . . . before the . . . General Theological Seminary. 57308

Address . . . [before] the General Theological Seminary . . . December, 1847. 56836

Address . . . before the General Trades Union. 50347

Address . . . before the Georgia Historical Society. (36478)

Address before the "Girard Brotherhood." (11866)

Address . . . before the Goethean Literary Society of Marshall College . . . August 28, 1844. 52423

Address . . . before the Goethean Literary Society, of Marshall College, . . . August 29, 1842. 52422

Address . . . before the Golden Branch Society. 50716

Address, . . . before the graduating class, in the Medical Department of the University of Vermont. (59456)

Address . . . before the graduating class of the Albany Medical College. (58647)

Address . . . before the graduating class of the Law Department of Hamilton College. 56237

Address . . . before the graduating class of the Law School of Columbia College. 81067

Address before the Grand Division of the Sons of Temperance. 47290

Address . . . before the Grand Lodge of Iowa. 36139

Address . . . before the Grand Lodge of Massachusetts. 41420

Address before the Grand Lodge of Rhode Island. 4647

Address . . . before the Grand Lodge . . . on the . . . dedication of Freemasons' Hall, in Boston. 31180

Address before the Grant and Colfax Club. 35849

Address before the Great Barrington Branch of the Washington Benevolent Society. (32239)

Address before the Halifax Mechanic's Institute. (33315)

Address . . . before the Hampshire, Franklin & Hampden Agricultural Society. 32250

Address before the Hampshire, Franklin, and Hampden Agricultural Society, at Northampton, Mass. (55905)

Address . . . before the Hampshire, Franklin and Hampden Agricultural Society, at Northampton, Oct. 14, 1858. 42083

Address before the Hampshire, Franklin, and Hampden Agricultural Society; . . . Greenfield, Oct. 23, 1833. 14535

Address . . . before the Hampshire, Franklin and Hampden Agricultural Society, Northampton, Oct. 24, 1832. 39365

Address before the Hampshire, Franklin, and Hampden Agricultural Society . . . October 12, 1853. 37859

Address before the Hartford County Agricultural Society, October 3, 1845. 93162

Address before the Hartford Co. Agricultural Society, Oct. 2, 1846. 9549

Address before the Hartford County Agricultural Society, Oct. 12, 1826. 27875

Address before the Hartford County Peace Society; delivered on the evening of November 11, 1832. 105752

Address [before the Hartford County Peace Society, in Christ Church.] 103166

Address, . . . before the Hartford County Peace Society, May, 1831. 32515

Address, . . . before the Hartford Peace Society, March 18, 1829. 41378

Address before the Harvard Natural History Society. 31864

Address before the Hastings Invincibles. 30827

Address . . . before the Hibernian Relief Society. 43790

Address before the Hillsborough Agricultural and Mechanical Society. (6977)

Address before the Hillsborough Society for the Promotion of Agriculture. (50391)

Address before the Historical Society of Pennsylvania. 68598

Address . . . before the Historical Society of the Lutheran Church. (63683)

Address . . . before the Hollis Branch of Massachusetts Peace Society. (50391)

Address before the Housatonic Agricultural Society. (6977)

Address before the House of Convocation of
Hobart Free College, Geneva, July 19,
1854. 46877
Address before the House of Convocation, of
Hobart Free College, pronounced at the
annual commencement. (78051)
Address, . . . before the House of Convocation
of Trinity College . . . Hartford, July
26th, 1854. 32933
Address, . . . before the House of Convocation
of Trinity College, in . . . Hartford, July
28th, 1852. 50690
Address . . . before the Independent Company
of Cadets. 42139
Address before the Indiana State Agricultural
Society. 28492
Address, before the Jefferson County Agricul-
tural Society. (37959)
Address before the Jefferson Literary Society.
(71766)
Address . . . before the Junior Anti-slavery
Society. 61243
Address . . . before the Kansas City Republican
Club. 36237
Address before the Kappa Alpha Phi Society.
43595
Address . . . before the Law Academy of Phila-
delphia. 34727
Address . . . before the Legislature of Michigan.
24287
Address before the legislature to the people of
. . . Massachusetts. 45578
Address . . . before the Leicester Temperance
Society. (24796)
Address before the Linnaean Association. 91781
Address before the Literary and Historical So-
ciety of Quebec. 38901
Address before the literary societies in Marietta
College. 78857
Address before the literary societies of Amherst
College. 93654
Address . . . before the literary societies of
Cumberland University. 43233
Address before the literary societies of Dela-
ware College. 29855
Address . . . before the literary societies of
Erskine College. 57655
Address before the literary societies of Hamil-
ton College, Clinton, N. Y., July 23, 1844.
28492
Address . . . before the literary societies of
Hamilton College, July 22, 1845. (28803)
Address . . . before the literary societies of
Lafayette College. 34750
Address: . . . before the literary societies of
Mossy Creek Baptist College. 47164
Address before the literary societies of Rutgers
College. 25827
Address before the literary societies of the
University of Georgia, Aug. 5, 1847. 34750
Address . . . before the literary societies of
the University of Georgia . . . August 2,
1860. 33244
Address . . . before the literary societies of
the University of Virginia. 46974
Address . . . before the literary societies of
the Wesleyan University. 43790
Address . . . before the literary societies of
Washington College. (43168)
Address before the Literary Society of Wash-
ington Coll., Pa. 17221
Address . . . before the . . . Lodges of St.
John, St. Peter and St. Mark. (18435)
Address . . . before the Long Island Historical
Society. (82176)
Address before the Lyceum of Natural History.
(72745)
Address . . . before the Maine Board of Agri-
culture. 39617

Address . . . before the Maine Charitable
Mechanic Association. (47442)
Address . . . before the Malden Temperance
Society. 28529
Address . . . before the Marine Temperance
Society. (44749)
Address . . . before the Maryland Institute.
(37423)
Address . . . [before] the Maryland State Tem-
perance Society. (47106)
Address . . . before the Masonic Fraternity.
42816
Address . . . before the Massachusetts Agricul-
tural Society, at . . . Brighton. 67255
Address, before the Massachusetts Agricultural
Society, at the Brighton Cattle Show.
62659
Address . . . before the Massachusetts Agri-
cultural Society . . . October 13, 1818.
(42463)
Address . . . before the Massachusetts Chari-
table Fire Society, . . . May 31, 1799.
18846
Address . . . before the . . . Massachusetts
Charitable Fire Society, . . . May 27,
1808. 58182
Address before the Massachusetts Charitable
Mechanic Association at Boston, . . .
October 10, 1833. 28608
Address . . . before the Massachusetts Chari-
table Mechanic Association, on its first
semi-centennial anniversary. 41248
Address before the Massachusetts Charitable
Mechanic Association, on occasion of their
seventh exhibition. (74329)
Address . . . before the Mass. Charitable
Mechanic Association . . . September 24,
1856. 33964
Address . . . before the Massachusetts Coloniza-
tion Society. 80072
Address . . . before the Massachusetts Horti-
cultural Society, on the dedication of Horti-
cultural Hall. 42708
Address . . . before the Massachusetts Horti-
cultural Society . . . September 20, 1837.
41267
Address before the Massachusetts Horticultural
Society, . . . sixth anniversary, September
17, 1834. 28399
Address . . . before the Massachusetts Lyceum.
77232
Address before the Massachusetts Medical So-
ciety. (13297)
Address before the Mass. Soc. for Sup. of
Intemperance. 1808
Address before the Massachusetts Society for
the Suppression of Intemperance, delivered
May 27, 1833. (76995)
Address . . . before the Massachusetts State
Temperance Society, May 31, 1835. 42149
Address before the Massachusetts Temperance
Society, . . . May 27, 1838. 13385
Address . . . before the Massachusetts Temper-
ance Union. 37749
Address . . . before the Masters and Brethren
of the Lodges of St. Peter and St. Paul.
58627
Address . . . before the Mechanic Apprentices'
Library Association. 41248
Address . . . before the Mechanical Association.
32250
Address . . . before the mechanics and other
citizens. 17292
Address before the Mechanics' Institute. 8385
Address . . . before the mechanics of Troy.
32538
Address . . . before the medical graduating
class. (65257)

Address . . . before the Medical Society of Maine. 44307

Address . . . before the Medical Society of . . . New-York, February 8, 1837. 43595

Address . . . before the Medical Society of . . . New-York, . . . 25th . . . July, 1831. 59565

Address . . . before the Medical Society of the County of New York. 44301

Address before the Medical Society of the State of New York. 73015

Address before the Medical Society of the State of New York, and the . . . legislature. 58661

Address [before the Medical Society of the State of New-York, 1817.] 103419

Address . . . before the Medical Society of the State of New York, February 6, 1839. (33639)

Address before the Medical Society of the State of North Carolina. 93109

Address . . . before the members and friends of the Pennsylvania Anti-slavery Society. (26240)

Address . . . before the members of St. Alban's Lodge. (25258)

Address before the members of St. John's Lodge. 14333

Address . . . before the members of the Massachusetts Charitable Fire Society. 28381

Address before the members of the Taunton Lyceum. 4060

Address . . . before the Mercantile Library Association, at its thirtieth anniversary. 31875

Address before the Mercantile-Library Association, Boston. 11219

Address . . . before the Mercantile Library Association . . . in Boston. 32774

Address, . . . before the Mercantile Library Association . . . January 8, 1839. 28145

Address, . . . before the Mercantile Library Association, January 11, 1836. 55860

Address before the Mercantile Library Association of Boston. 93669

Address before the . . . Mercantile Library Association of Cincinnati. 29800

Address before the Mercantile Library Association of the City of New-York. 89783

Address before the Merrimack County Agricultural Society. 42083

Address . . . [before] the Miami Chapter of the Alpha Delta Phi Society. (66615)

Address before the Middlesex Association. 78976

Address before the Middlesex County Agricultural Society at Concord. 22309

Address . . . before the Middlesex County Agricultural Society . . . October 9th, 1846. 36374

Address . . . before the Middlesex County Agricultural Society . . . October 13th, 1842. 35405

Address . . . before the Middlesex County Agricultural Society, . . . October 13th, 1843. 46808

Address . . . before the Middlesex North Agricultural Society. 31930

Address . . . before the Middlesex North District Medical Society. 28545

Address . . . before the Middlesex Society of Husbandmen and Manufacturers. 62567

Address . . . before the Minnesota State Bible Society. 55378

Address . . . before the Montgomery County, Maryland, Agricultural Society. 32459

Address . . . before the Mount Desert Temperance Society. (27426)

Address . . . before the National Association of Knit Goods Manufacturers. 31026

Address before the National Association of Wool Manufacturers. 31026

Address before the National Equal Suffrage Association. 6395

Address before the Natural History Club of Philadelphia. 33877

Address before the Naumkeag Mutual Trading and Mining Company. 105322

Address . . . before the Needham Temperance Society. (37748)

Address before the New Bedford Port Society. 22175

Address before the New Castle County Agricultural Society and Institute. 81610

Address before the New England Historic-Genealogical Society, in the hall of the House of Representatives. 74731

Address . . . before the New England Historic-Genealogical Society, . . . January 1, 1862. (40863)

Address [before the New England Historic-Genealogical Society.] . . . January 4, 1865. (40863)

Address [before the New England Historic-Genealogical Society.] . . . January 7, 1863. (40863)

Address [before the New England Historic-Genealogical Society.] . . . January 6th, 1864. (40863)

Address . . . before the . . . New-England Society, in Charleston. 34001

Address . . . before the New England Society of . . . Montreal. 82340

Address, . . . before the New England Society of . . . New-York, December 24, 1844. (44734)

Address before the New-England Society of New York, Dec. 22, 1852. 351

Address . . . before the New England Society of San Francisco. 33896

Address before the New England Society of the City of New York, December 22, 1842. 12398

Address before the New-England Society of the City of New York, on Forefather's Day. 2659

Address . . . before the New Hampshire Agricultural Society. 37859

Address, . . . before the New Hampshire, Franklin and Hampden Agricultural Society. 42785

Address, . . . before the New-Hampshire Medical Society. 57202

Address . . . before the New Haven Horticultural Society, May 25, 1843. 50039

Address . . . before the New Haven Horticultural Society, September 25, 1838. 80164

Address before the New-Jersey Historical Society, at their meeting. 20391

Address, . . . before the New Jersey Historical Society, . . . Jan'y 19th, 1854. 49022

Address . . . before the New-Jersey Historical Society, January 17, 1867. (58651)

Address . . . before the New York Alpha of the Phi Beta Kappa. 64622

Address . . . before the New York City Antislavery Society. note after (58767)

Address before the New York High School for Females. 35117

Address . . . before the New York Historical Society, . . . December 16, 1868. 51107

Address before the New York Historical Society, Nov. 21st, 1865. 19626

Address before the New York Peace Society. 56527

Address . . . before the New-York Protestant Episcopal Missionary Society. (32301)

Address before the New York State Agricultural Society. (23937)

Address . . . before the New York State Agricultural Society, at Albany. 39306

Address before the New-York State Agricultural Society, at the fair. 36078

Address before the New York State Agricultural Society . . . at Utica. 24498

Address before the New-York State Medical Society. 43595

Address, . . . before the Newark Bible Society. (49080)

Address . . . before the Newark Mechanics' Association. 28873

Address . . . before the Newport Democratic Union Club. 39383

Address . . . before the Newton Temperance Society. (28706)

Address . . . before the Norfolk Agricultural Society, at Dedham, September 30, 1857. 38776

Address before the Norfolk Agricultural Society, at Dedham, September 24, 1851. 74330

Address before the Norfolk Agricultural Society, at Dedham, Sept. 26, 1860. 31875

Address . . . before the North Carolina University. 62904

Address before the North Kingstown Temperance Society. (80409)

Address before the officers and students of the Indiana Medical College. 55317

Address before the Ohio Agricultural Convention. (38054)

Address . . . before the Ohio County Medical Society. 33188

Address before the Ohio Society Sons of the ₹ Revolution. 83964

Address . . . before the Old Bay State Association. (6977)

Address . . . before the Old Colony Anti-slavery Society. 26712

Address, before the Old Settlers Society. 67391

Address, before the Ontario Agricultural Society. 12829, (29891)

Address . . . before the Ontario Agricultural Society, at its first annual meeting, Oct. 13, 1819. (55168), (57369)

Address . . . before the Ontario Co. Agricultural Society. (55905)

Address before the Otsego County Agricultural Society. 50387, 102136

Address before the Pawcatuck Temperance Society. 31101

Address before the Peace Convention. 42359

Address . . . before the Peace Society of Amherst College. 42028

Address . . . before the Peace Society, of Exeter, N. H. 59376

Address . . . before the Peace Socety of Windham County at its annual meeting in Brooklin. (60943)

Address . . . before the Peace Society of Windham County, at . . . Pomfret, February 14, 1827. 60972

Address ·. . . before the Peithessophian and Philoclean Societies. 64684

Address before the Pennsylvania Agricultural Society. 18600

Address before the Pennsylvania State Teachers' Association. 77761

Address before the people of New York. 93640

Address before the people of Orange, N. J. 8348

Address before the Phi Beta Kappa at Yale College. 79498

Address before the Phi Beta Kappa Society, at Amherst College. 44489

Address before the Phi Beta Kappa Society of Dartmouth College. (58703)

Address before the Phi Beta Kappa Society of Harvard University, at their anniversary. 93673

Address . . . before the Phi Beta Kappa Society of Harvard University, 28 August, 1834. 26633

Address . . . before the Phi Beta Kappa Society of Harvard University, 27 August, 1835. 58907

Address . . . before the Phi Beta Kappa Society of Union College. 37481

Address before the Phi Beta Kappa Society of Yale College. 82710

Address before the Philadelphia Society for Promoting Agriculture. 18600

Address before the Philanthropic and Dialectic Societies. 26752

Address before the Philo and Franklin Societies. 82174

Address . . . before the Philoclean and Peithessophian Societies, of Rutgers College. 25829

Address, before the Philoclean and Peithessophian Societies of Rutgers College: July 27, 1847. 73059

Address . . . before the Philoclean Society of Rutgers College. 56836

Address before the Philological Institute . . . on its fourteenth anniversary. 80498

Address before the Philological Institute . . . thirteenth anniversary. 71731

Address before the Philomathean Society, August 5, 1856. 68047

Address before the Philomathean Society of the Ohio University. 74877

Address before the Philomathean Society of the University of Pennsylvania. 27458

Address before the Philomathic Society. 8743

Address before the Pittsburgh Total Abstinence Society. 102174

Address . . . before the Plymouth County Agricultural Society. 35597

Address before the Porter Rhetorical Society. 103194

Address . . . before the Portland Association for the Promotion of Temperance. 55202

Address . . . before the Portsmouth Anti-slavery Society. 13188

Address before the Presbyterian Church in Brockport. 73128

Address [before the Protestant Episcopal Society.] 87933

Address . . . before the Providence Association for the Promotion of Temperance. 58921

Address . . . before the Providence Association of Mechanicks and Manufacturers. 33385

Address . . . before the Providence Association of Mechanics and Manufacturers. 33383

Address . . . before the Providence Union Temperance Society. 63054

Address . . . before the Public School Teachers' Association. 17464

Address . . . before the public schools. 79928

Address . . . before the Pynxian Club. 64943

Address before the Queen's County Agricultural Society. 26220

Address before the Queens County Agricultural Society, at Flushing. 37789

Address . . . before the Queen's County Agricultural Society, . . . October 13th, 1842. (43106)

Address before the Quincy Homestead Association. 67265

Address . . . before the Railroad Convention. (29484)

Address . . . before the Reading Room. 39226

Address . . . before the Republican Association. 20666

Address before the Republican citizens of Berkshire. 2643

Address, . . . before the Republican citizens of Newburyport. 27371

Address . . . before the Rhode-Island Historical Society. 64628

Address before the Rhode Island Peace Society at its twenty-seventh annual meeting. (29753)

Address before the Rhode Island Peace Society, June 29, 1819. 9235

Address before the Rhode-Island Society, for the Encouragement of Domestic Industry, and the Rhode-Island Horticultural Society. 74331

Address, . . . before the Rhode-Island Society for the Encouragement of Domestic Industry, October 21, 1828. 63054

Address . . . before the Rockingham Sacred Music Society. 25875

Address . . . before the . . . Royal Arch Masons. 57200

Address before the Sabbath School. 83031

Address before the St. Lawrence County Agricultural Society. (33633)

Address . . . before the St. Louis Literary and Philosophical Association. 71549

Address . . . before the St. Louis Total Abstinence Society. 64692

Address before the Salem Female Anti-slavery Society. 92117

Address . . . before the Saratoga Baptist Association. 43502

Address before the Saratoga County Agricultural Society. 91830

Address, before the Saratoga Society for Promoting Agriculture and Domestic Manufactures. 78061

Address . . . before the Scituate Auxiliary Society. 35694

Address . . . before the senior class in Divinity School. 22460

Address before the Senior class of Kimball Union Academy. 42033

Address . . . before . . . the Sigma Phi Fraternity. 29713

Address before the Sigma Phi Society. 28948

Address before the sixth anniversary of the Erodelphian Society. 20812

Address before the Social Fraternity. 13631

Address before the . . . societies of Rugers College . . . July 18th, 1837. 3454

Address, . . . before the . . . societies of Rutgers College. . . . 26th July, 1848. (25153)

Address, . . . before the Society for Promoting Temperance. 61031

Address . . . before the Society for Promoting Theological Education. 58325

Address . . . before the Society for the Prevention of Pauperism. (33345)

Address, . . . before the Society for the Promotion of Collegiate and Theological Education at the West. 32943

Address before the Society for the Promotion of Collegiate . . . Education at the West . . . October 30, 1851. 37976

Address . . . before the Society of Alumni. 35242

Address . . . before the Society of California Volunteers. (50886)

Address . . . before the Society of Inquiry on Missions. (12406)

Address before the Society of Inquiry, Wabash College. 13602

Address . . . before the Society of Moral and Religious Inquiry. 70857

Address before the Society of Moral Philanthropists. 70766

Address before the Society of Natural History. 29808

Address before the Society of the Mystical Seven. 8717

Address . . . before the South-Carolina Institute. (42677)

Address before the South-Carolina Society for the Promotion of Temperance. 20093, note after 88042

Address before the South Carolina Society, on the . . . opening of the Male Academy. 68190

Address before the State Agricultural Society of Wisconsin. (39192)

Address before the State Historical Society of Wisconsin. 92950

Address before the State Historical Society of Wisconsin, . . . January 30th, 1868. 11729

Address before the State Historical Society of Wisconsin, . . . January 30, 1873. 72058

Address . . . before the State Historical Society of Wisconsin, Madison. 44904

Address before the State Historical Society of Wisconsin . . . 23 February, 1869. 57726

Address before the State Teacher's Association. 5939

Address . . . before the Strafford Agricultural Society. 42766

Address . . . before the students of Amherst College. 30889

Address . . . before the Suffolk District Medical Society . . . April 27, 1850. (35974)

Address . . . before the Suffolk District Medical Society . . . Boston, April 24, 1852. (13297)

Address . . . before the Suffolk Masonic Society. 82804

Address . . . before the . . . Sunday Schools. 49131

Address before the surviving members. 24291

Address before the Synod of New Jersey. 67889

Address . . . before the Tammany Society. 41790

Address . . . before the teachers and pupils. 42714

Address before the teachers of the Hancock Sunday School. 28390, note after 93744

Address, . . . before the Temperance Society at Ashfield. (54935)

Address . . . before the Temperance Society in Pembroke. (50391)

Address . . . before the Temperance Society of Franklinville. 42784

Address . . . before the Temperance Society of Pittsburgh. 63356

Address, . . . before the Temperance Society of Plymouth. (38027)

Address . . . before the Temperance Society of the medical class in Dartmouth College. 57202

Address, before the Theological Society. 29893

Address before the Travellers' Club. 21229

Address . . . before the two literary societies of the University of North Carolina. 62904

Address . . . before the two literary societies, of the University of North Carolina: in Gerard Hall. 80186

Address . . . before the two literary societies of the University of North-Carolina, June 1, 1853. 55219

Address . . . before the two literary societies of the University of North Carolina, June 6th, 1860. (64023)

Address before the Union Association of Working Men. 42731

Address . . . before the Union Literary Society. 64692

Address before the Universalist Anti-slavery Convention. 89075

Address . . . before the University of South Carolina. 43640

Address . . . before the Utica Lyceum. 36162

Address, . . . before the Vermont Historical Society. 29513

Address before the Vermont Historical Society delivered at Montpelier, Vt. 88830

Address . . . before the Vincennes Historical and Antiquarian Society. 39317

Address before the Virginia Agricultural Society. 73909

Address . . . before the . . . Virginia Military Institute. 46184

Address . . . before the Virginia State Agricultural Society. 32467

Address before the Washington and Jefferson Societies. 64372

Address . . . before the Washington Benevolent Societies of Cranbury and Princeton. 28531

Address before the Washington Benevolent Society. 3765, (33880)

Address, . . . before the Washington Benevolent Society at Cambridge. 32588

Address, . . . before the Washington Benevolent Society . . . by William Hay, Junr. 31001

Address before the Washington Benevolent Society, in Newburyport. 1494

Address before the Washington County Association. 31101

Address . . . before the Washington Independent Temperance Society. 2848

Address . . . before the Washingtonian Societies of Belfast. 36165

Address . . . before the Wayne County Education Society, (8541)

Address . . . before the Wesleyan Literary Association. (50157)

Address, before the Westchester Agricultural Society. 30087

Address before the Westchester County (N. Y.) Medical Society. 35999

Address before the Western Institute. 49012

Address before the Whig and conservative citizens. 98543

Address before the Whitewater and Miami Valley Pioneer Association. 30562

Address . . . before the Wilberforce Association. 80860

Address . . . before the Windsor County Agricultural Society. (18206)

Address . . . before the Wisconsin State Agricultural Society. (69001)

Address . . . before the Wisconsin State Teachers' Association. 33337

Address . . . before the Worcester Agricultural Society, October 8, 1823. 24554

Address . . . before the Worcester Agricultural Society, October 7, 1819. (41254)

Address. . . . before the Worcester Agricultural Society, October 10, 1832. (24796)

Address . . . before the Worcester Agricultural Society, October 13, 1824. 27945

Address . . . before the Worcester Agricultural Society, October 12, 1820. 5319

Address . . . before the Worcester Temperance Society. 76996

Address . . . before the Working Man's National League. 969

Address before the Working-Men's Society of Dedham. 103347

Address . . . before the young men of Boston. 38084

Address . . . before the Young Men's Association of . . . Buffalo. (30983)

Address before the Young Men's Mercantile Library Association of Cincinnati. 58024

Address before the Young Men's State Association of . . . New York. 19017

Address before the Zelosophic Society. 15898

Address . . . before . . . Virginia Military Institute. (33929)

Address . . . before . . . Virginia State Agricultural Society. 32467

Address before Washington Lodge, Burlington, Vt. 80316

Address . . . Berkshire Agricultural Society. 27704

Address . . . Berkshire Association for the Promotion of Agriculture and Manufactures. 27704

Address . . . Boston, May 29, 1850. 58625

Address . . . Boston . . . May 27th. (12406)

Address . . . Boston Union Club, 23271

Address by A. A. Low. 42391

Address by a catholic layman. (62214)

Address by a Committee of the Trustees. 34517

Address, by a female visitor. 60080

Address by A. Hazeltine. 35734

Address [by A. J. Gordon.] 12200

Address by a member of the club. 89214

Address by a minister of the Church of Jesus Christ of Latter-Day Saints. 50726

Address, by A. Oakey Hall. 80908

Address [by Alexander Cummings.] 17912

Address . . . by Alexander Vattemare. 34931, 65799

Address by Allen T. Graves. 28347

Address [by Bell.] 63244

Address, . . . by Bro. Joseph Henry Nisbet. (55352)

Address [by Burt.] 57749

Address by C. T. Russell. 23280

Address by Charles Mason. 40114

Address by Col. Claiborne Snead. 85373

Address by David D. Demarest. 19460

Address by Deacon Samuel Goodhue. (27858)

Address by . . . Derby. (19667)

Address, by Dr. Coulter. 13573, (40970), 85133

Address by Dr. J. G. Holland. 89859

Address by Dr. Samuel Cartwright. 49650

Address by Edward Crane. 17397

Address, . . . by Elder Jonas Hartzell. 34585

Address, by G. W. Hosmer. 9063

Address by Gen. Jubal A. Early. 88369

Address by Gen. Lewis Cass. 11349

Address by General William Sooy Smith. 84897

Address by George B. Wood. 60332

Address by Geo. C. S. Southworth. 88664

Address by George Washington. 101573

Address . . . by Guy H. Salisbury. 9056, note after 95451

Adess . . . by Henry I. Bowditch. 6991

Address, by Hon. Benjamin Seaver. 78674

Address, by Hon. Charles Hudson. 103035

Address . . . by Hon. E. Newton. 55075

Address by Hon. Emory Washburn. 7827

Address by Hon. G. W. Clinton. 9063

Address by Hon. Isaac Davis. 41258

Address by Hon. James Gallatin. 26400

Address by Hon. James T. Morehead. 37519

Address by Hon. Levi Lincoln. 41258

Address, by Hon. N. R. Middleton. 87738

Address by Hon. Noah Davis. 9477

Address, by Hon. S. W. Barker. 87738

Address . . . by Hon. William P. Cutler. 18189

Address . . . by J. E. Teschemacher. 45862

Address, by J. Jenkins Mikell. 87738

Address . . . by J. Miller M'Kim. 43455
Address by J. W. Taylor. 76930
Address by J. W. Tucker, Esq. 49651
Address [by J. E. Wallace.] note after 7264
Address by James A. Dorr. 20643
Address, by James B. Congdon. 15471
Address by James Barron Hope. 86161
Address, by James R. Spalding. 99213
Address by James Underwood. 97738
Address . . . by John Johnson. 75284
Address . . . by John S. Moore. 37339
Address, by Joseph Cook. 16284
Address, by Joseph White. 103419
Address . . . by Levi Lincoln. (41257)
Address by Major General George G. Meade.
51019
Address [by Mr. Harold.] 47236
Address by Nehemiah Strong. (28908)
Address . . . by Nicholas Biddle. 27491
Address by Oliver G. Steele. 91135
Address by Parson Brownlow. 8706
Address by Philip B. Streit. 92796
Address. By Prof. Egbert C. Smyth. 85218
Address by Prof. Lewis H. Steiner. 91206
Address, by Rev. Alonzo Hill. 39902
Address, by Rev. Carlton A. Staples. 47819,
note after 90463
Address by Rev. E. O. Haven. 41215
Address, by Rev. Henry Neill. 63156
Address by Rev. J. D. Fulton. 65899
Address by Rev. John Carroll Perkins. 84353
Address, by Rev. Justin Spaulding. 89049
Address by Rev. Lyman Beecher. 94296
Address by Rev. Prof. F. D. Huntington. 29492
Address by Rev. Robert F. Burns. (44452)
Address by Rev. W. F. Morgan. 30972, 5th
note after 96966
Address by Rev. William Preston. 63118
Address [by Robert B. Caverly.] (11611)
Address by S. Blydenburgh. 69637
Address, by S. S. Laws. 39404
Address by Samuel Miller. 9918
Address by Stephen Smith. 84256
Address by the Citizens Association of
Pennsylvania. 59976
Address by the colored people of Missouri.
81750
Address by the Committee [of the Upper Canada
Religious Tract and Book Society.] 98094
Address by the Directors of the Albany and
Susquehanna R. R. Co. 592
Address by the [Free Trade and State Rights
Association.] 87827
Address of the General Committee of the Federal
Republicans. 54039
Address by the Hampshire Convention. (30135)
Address by the Hon. A. Bruyn Hasbrouck.
30791
Address by the Hon. Daniel S. Dickinson. 20031
Address, by the Hon. George Muter and Benjamin
Sebastian. (44778)
Address . . . by the Hon. John J. Monell.
49964
Address by the Hon. Joseph Holt. 32650
Address by the Hon. Samuel B. Ruggles. 73975
Address by the Hon. Thomas B. Reed. 68587
Address by the Honorable Walter I. Smith.
84520
Address by the Lackawanna Coal Mine and
Navigation Company. (38465)
Address by the late Rev. Timothy B. Hudson.
(33499)
Address by the Mayor of New York. 59218
Address, by the ministers of the original
Association. 104759
Address by the pastor. 49723
Address [by the Pennsylvania Seamen's Friend
Society.] 60362

Address, by the President [of Woodward College.]
105174
Address by the Republican State Convention.
87940
Address, by the Rev. A. Alexander. (43195)
Address by the Rev. A. Fletcher. 92477
Address by the Rev. Doctor Inglis. 65922
Address by the Rev. Henry Ward Beecher. 4308
Address by the Rev. Joseph T. Smith. 83390
Address by the Rev. Kingston Goddard. 60336
Address by the Rev. Peter Whitney. 58686,
103771
Address by the Rev. S. A. Crane. 65828
Address, by the Rev. Samuel Starr. 90561
Address . . . by the Rev. T. Ralston Smith.
18959
Address, by the Rev. W. A. Muhlenberg. 51256
Address by the Rev. William Goodfellow. 41236,
6th note after 96964
Address by the Rev. William Henry Channing.
11931
Address . . . by the students. 60758
Address by the Washington Benevolent Society.
54928
Address [by the Yearly Meeting of Friends of
Baltimore.] (70201)
Address by Thomas Erving. (56974)
Address by Thomas Henderson. 101961
Address by Thomas Neil. 85307
Address . . . by Thomas R. Mercein. 54093
Address by Turner H. Foster. (51874)
Address by Verannus Morse. 50973
Address by W. A. Stearns. 90991
Address [by Wallace.] (66038)
Address by Walter George Smith. 84509
Address by Walter George Smith, Esq. 84516
Address by Walter George Smith. Read before
the Society of the Alumni. 84511
Address . . . by William Darlington. 54929
Address. By William Henry Smith. 84790
Address . . . by William J. Mullen. 42359
Address, by William M. Dickson. (20097)
Address by Wm. S. Pennington. 54881
Address by William Slocomb. 56962
Address . . . Calvert College. 28170
Address, . . . Chicago . . . September 31st,
1859. 24274
Address, . . . Columbia College. 68068
Address commemorative of Nathan Ryno Smith.
83664
Address commemorative of Rufus Choate. 58912
Address, commemorative of seven young men
of Danvers. 37791
Address commemorative of the battle of Bunker
Hill. 22533
Address commemorative of the life and services
of Isaac Sherman. 83569
Address commemorative of the services of the
alumni and former students. 39758
Address commemorative of the two hundredth
anniversary of the incorporation of
Lancaster, Massachusetts. 38789
Address . . . commencement . . . June 30, 1869.
68147
Address . . . commencement June 29, 1870.
68147
Address, commencement of Hamilton College.
18826
Address . . . consolidated Business College.
26664
Address, constitution and by-laws of the
Unconditional Union Central Committee.
54040
Address, constitution and by-laws . . . of the
Young Men's Christian Union. 9063
Address, constitution, and subscription proposal.
15705

Address, constitution, . . . [of the Buffalo Association for the Relief of the Poor.] 9063
Address containing a review of the times. 105588, 105596
Address, containing a review of the times, as first delivered in the Hall of Science, New-York. 105581, 105588
Address . . . Dartmouth College, N. H. 65093
Address . . . Dartmouth College upon the induction of the author. 57201
Address . . . December, 1831. 16621, 87968
Address . . . December 9th, 1835. 64617
Address . . . Dec. 28, 1803. 30521
Address . . . December 22, 1834. 42651
Address . . . December 22, 1837. 37161
Address, declining a re-election to the Presidency. 32784
Address . . . dedication of the new building of Bristol Academy. 24039
Address . . . dedication of the Ohio Female College. 24503
Address, delivered April 11, 1845. 89744
Address, delivered April 9, 1871. (17833)
Address delivered April 17th, 1830. 92364
Address delivered as the introduction to the Franklin Lectures. 23271
Address delivered at a meeting of the citizens of Trenton. 91886
Address delivered at a meeting of the descendants of Major-General Israel Putnam. 28950
Address delivered at a public meeting, in the City Hall, Glasgow. 89282
Address delivered at a public meeting of the citizens of Mason. 99548
Address delivered at a public meeting of the Young Men's Benevolent Society. 106161
Address delivered at a reunion of the Sons of Weston. (82331)
Address delivered at a town-meeting of the Anti-masonic citizens. 36545
Address delivered at Amherst, Hartford, etc. 33791, 34474
Address delivered at an interior town in Nevada. 67422
Address delivered at Andover. 81638
Address: delivered at Augusta. 3719
Address, delivered at Bedford, New Hampshire. 3515
Address, delivered at Beersheba Springs. 20353
Address delivered at Bethel Church. 77186
Address delivered at Bloody Brook. (23245)
Address delivered at Bloomington. 105658
Address delivered at Boston, before the Boston Society of Natural History. 95554
Address delivered at . . . Boston, January 8, 1828. 28608
Address delivered at Brewster's Hall. 7780
Address delivered at Brunswick. 24963
Address, delivered at Cambridge. 89628
Address delivered at Camden. 12168
Address delivered at Camp McRae. 35678
Address delivered at Canandaigua. 8774
Address delivered at Castle Garden. 8373
Address delivered at Charlestown, August 1, 1826. 23244
Address delivered at Charlestown, . . . 17th of June, 1836. 23222
Address delivered at Chester. 2018
Address delivered at . . . Columbia College. 18139
Address delivered at Columbus. 11059
Address delivered at Concord, before the New-Hampshire Historical Society. (2269)
Address delivered at Concord, N. H., December 25, 1835. 66818

Address, delivered at Concord, N. H., January 8, 1828. (31829)
Address delivered at Concord [N. H.], July the fourth, 1825. 6951
Address delivered at Concord, October 4, 1848. 28399
Address, delivered at Corinth. 76233
Address delivered at Crawfordsville. 92394
Address delivered at Cumming. 73845
Address, delivered at Cummington. 72173
Address, delivered at Dedham. 8709
Address delivered at Dorchester. 74537
Address delivered, at Fairfield. 88902
Address delivered at Fitchburg. (80302)
Address delivered at Glen Cove L. I. 78518
Address delivered at Gorham. 51889
Address delivered at Halifax. (3396)
Address delivered at Hanover. 42045
Address delivered at Hanson. 32262
Address delivered at Hartford. 20031
Address delivered at Haverford College. 83490
Address delivered at Haverhill, N. H. 88871
Address, delivered at his [i. e. Henry Vethake's] inauguration. 99392
Address delivered at Hope Chapel. 9533
Address, delivered at Ikesburg. 24935
Address, delivered at Ipswich. 103361
Address: delivered at Jefferson College. 23237
Address delivered at Lancaster. 78636
Address delivered at Laurel Hill Cemetery. 22430
Address, delivered at Leicester. 105617
Address delivered at Lenox. 11924
Address, delivered at Lexington. 23246
Address delivered at Limerick. 25782
Address delivered at Lyme. 77314
Address . . . delivered at McSherrysville. (13069)
Address delivered at Middletown. 29816
Address, delivered at Mt. Kisco, . . . 4th of July, 1861. 35843
Address, delivered at Mt. Kisco, New York. 35838
Address delivered at Nashville, Oct. 5, 1820. 4461
Address delivered at New Haven. 37475
Address delivered at New-Castle. 68160
Address delivered at New York. 35849
Address delivered at Newburyport. (13609)
Address delivered at North Springfield. 90901
Address delivered at Northampton, before the Hampshire, Hampden, and Franklin, Agricultural Society. (20074)
Address delivered at Northampton, Mass. 887
Address, delivered at Paoli Massacre Ground. 17467
Address delivered at Pittsfield, Mass. 88883
Address delivered at Plainfield. 36039
Address delivered at Plattsburg. 105214
Address, delivered at Plymouth. 71752
Address delivered at Port Townsend. 23146
Address delivered at Portland, before the Grand Lodge. 25850
Address delivered at Portland, on the decease of John Adams. 18680
Address delivered . . . at Princeton. 18320
Address delivered at Roxbury. 101467
Address, delivered at Saint Johns. 103835
Address delivered at St. Louis, December 6, 1871. 25419
Address . . . delivered at . . . St. Louis, Mo. 8453
Address delivered at St. Louis, 22d April, 1857. 23271
Address delivered at Salem, on the eighth of January, 1836. 23223
Address delivered at Sanford. 102591

Address delivered at Smith & Nixon's Hall.
92179

Address delivered at South Coventry. (36855)

Address delivered at South Deerfield. 41261

Address delivered at Southampton. 21889

Address delivered at Springfield. (59380)

Address delivered at Tammany Hall. 98336

Address delivered at the . . . Amicable Lodge.
31896

Address delivered at the anniversary
celebration. 13305

Address delivered at the anniversary meeting.
29803

Address delivered at the anniversary of the
Associated Alumni. 18405

Address delivered at the anniversary of the
New York Female Auxiliary Bible
Society. 89783

Address delivered at the anniversary of the
Philomathaean Society. 905

Address delivered at the anniversary of the
Young Men's Christian Union of New
York. 69336

Address delivered at the annual commencement
of East Tennessee College. 23024

Address delivered at the annual commencement
of the Theological Seminary of the
Protestant Episcopal Church of the
Diocese of Virginia, June 24, 1869. 89019

Address delivered at the annual commencement
of the Theological Seminary of the
Protestant Episcopal Church of the
Diocese of Virginia, June 27, 1872. 89023

Address delivered at the annual examination.
84279

Address delivered at the annual exercises.
(11438)

Address delivered at the annual exhibition of
the N. Y. State Agricultural Society, at
Buffalo. 89344

Address delivered at the annual exhibition of
the N. Y. State Agricultural Society; at
Utica. (67256)

Address delivered at the annual fair. 58905

Address delivered at the annual meeting of the
Convocation of Bishop's College. 76252

Address delivered at the annual meeting of the
Louisiana State Colonization Society.
78396

Address delivered at the annual meeting of the
New England Historical and Genealogical
Society. 20884

Address delivered at the annual meeting of the
New York State Agricultural Society.
(28113)

Address, delivered at the annual meeting of the
Rice Family. 70814

Address delivered at the Anti-slavery Picnic.
2967

Address delivered at the Beneficent Congregational Meeting House. (76998)

Address delivered at the Broadway House.
20602

Address delivered at the celebration by the
New York Historical Society, May 20,
1863. note after 7263, 53671-53672,
(66038)

Address delivered at the celebration of the
anniversary of St. John the Baptist.
84063

Address . . . delivered at the celebration of
the close of the second century from the
time Exeter was settled. 82801

Address delivered at the celebration of the
third anniversary in honor of the martyrs
for Cuban freedom. (5059)

Address delivered at the centennial celebration
at Cherry Valley. 10277

Address delivered at the centennial celebration
in Merrimack. 870

Address delivered at the centennial celebration
in Wilton. 59359

Address delivered at the centennial celebration
of the incorporation of New Boston. 14074

Address delivered at the close of the anniversary
exercises. 89744

Address delivered at the close of the annual
examination. 89744

Address delivered at the close of the Crimean
War. 77426

Address delivered at the Colored Department
of the House of Refuge. 37272

Address delivered at the commencement held
in Queen's College. (41630)

Address delivered at the commencement of La
Grange Female College. (31890)

Address delivered at the commencement of the
Albany Medical College. 13365

Address, delivered at the commencement of the
lectures. (73014)

Address delivered at the consecration and
installation of Mount Zion Royal Arch
Chapter. 71049

Address delivered at the consecration, by the
Hon. John M'Lean. 89824

Address delivered at the consecration of Lowell
Cemetery. 5816

Address delivered at the consecration of Oak
Hill Cemetery. 90912

Address, delivered at the consecration of Oakwood
Cemetery. 8974

Address delivered at the consecration of the
cemetery. (5920), note after 89877

Address, delivered at the consecration of the
Harmony Grove Cemetery. 103363

Address delivered at the consecration of the
Lake Grove Cemetery. 6114

Address, delivered at the consecration of the
Linden Grove Cemetery. 92180

Address delivered at the consecration of the
new cemetery in West Cambridge. 18364

Address, delivered at the consecration of the Oak
Grove Cemetery. (15465)

Address delivered at the consecration of the
Soldiers' Cemetery. 23271

Address delivered at the consecration of the
Woodlawn Cemetery. 22309

Address delivered at the dedication of Dane Law
College. 67194

Address delivered at the dedication of Loring
Hall. 90928

Address delivered at the dedication of Mount
Hope Cemetery. 12991

Address delivered at the dedication of the
American Academy. 101472

Address delivered at the dedication of the
Athens Cemetery. (64936)

Address delivered at the dedication of the City
Hospital. 1345

Address, delivered at the dedication of the new
hall. 72750

Address delivered at the dedication of the new
rooms. 75931

Address delivered at the dedication of the new
school house. 4720

Address delivered at the dedication of the
school house called Eliot Hall. 104168

Address delivered at the dedication of the
school-house . . . in Salem. 57204

Address delivered at the dedication of the
school house in the Fifth District of San
Francisco. 5412

Address . . . delivered at the dedication of the
Spencertown Academy. 64983

Address delivered at the dedication of Williston
Academy. 32943

Address delivered at the Democratic town meeting. 37267

Address, delivered at the eighth anniversary of the Massachusetts Peace Society. 5330

Address, delivered at the Elm Tree. 28427

Address delivered at the erection of a monument. 23271

Address delivered at the examination. 90977

Address, delivered at the Exchange Coffee-House Hall. 3757

Address delivered at the fair. 64983

Address delivered at the fifteenth anniversary of the Massachusetts Peace Society. 93637

Address delivered at the fifth anniversary of the Massachusetts Peace Society. 67195

Address delivered at the fifth anniversary of the Peace Society of Minot. (36492)

Address delivered at the fifty-second annual meeting of the American Colonization Society. 71903

Address delivered at the first anniversary meeting of the United Agricultural Society of South Carolina. 78547

Address, delivered at the first anniversary of the Lake Eire Female Seminary. 92232

Address delivered at the first anniversary of the New York City Temperance Society. 33089

Address delivered at the first anniversary of the Orphan Asylum Society of San Francisco. (5413)

Address delivered at the first anniversary of the Porter Rhetorical Society. 21979

Address delivered at the First Baptist Church. 66237

Address delivered at the first medical commencement. 92189

Address delivered at the First Reformed Church of Passaic. 83526

Address delivered at the first session of the Teachers' Institute. 92913

Address delivered at the formation of the Blackstone Monument Association. 5702

Address, delivered at the formation of the Lycurgan Association. 105907

Address, delivered at the formation of the Seamen's Bethel Temperance Society. 85485

Address delivered at the fourth anniversary of the Massachusetts Peace Society. (26419)

Address delivered at the Free Mason's Hall. 8193, 8198

Address, delivered at the funeral of Henry Payson. 9364

Address, delivered at the funeral of John Gorham. (35424)

Address delivered at the funeral of Nathaniel Fillmore. 33099

Address delivered at the funeral of Rev. Bernard Whitman. 71531

Address delivered at the funeral of the Hon. George Partridge. 37468

Address delivered at the funeral of the Rev. Benjamin H. Pitman. 89744

Address delivered at the funeral [of the Rev. Edward D. Allen.] 89744

Address delivered at the funeral services in memory of Dr. Samuel Bancroft Barlow. 72625

Address delivered at the funeral solemnities of the late President Lincoln. 37236

Address, delivered at the general meeting of the schools. 79797

Address delivered at the Grand Convention of the Free Masons. 17437

Address delivered at the house of Capt. Joseph Chaplin. 105035

Address delivered at the inauguration of the author [i. e. Asa Dodge Smith.] 82332

Address delivered at the inauguration of the Charlottetown Young Men's Christian Association. 85469

Address delivered at the inauguration of the faculty of Bristol College. 14785

Address . . . delivered at the inauguration of the public schools. 20093

Address delivered at the inauguration of the Union Club. 23271

Address, delivered at the installation of President Simpson. 101099

Address delivered at the installation of Social Harmony Lodge. 47987

Address delivered at the installation of the Worcester County Encampment of Knights Templars. 105020

Address delivered at the . . . Institution . . . [for the Instruction of the Deaf and Dumb.] 54500

Address delivered at the interment of Mrs. Sarah Burger. 90177

Address, delivered at the interment [of the Rev. Benjamin Carpenter.] 78278

Address, delivered at the interment of the . . . Rev. Richard Price. 37958

Address delivered at the late anniversary meeting. 104620

Address delivered at the laying of the cap stone. 17958

Address delivered at the laying of the corner stone of Antioch College. 65738

Address delivered at the laying of the corner stone of the building. 1314, note after 102377

Address delivered at the laying of the corner stone of the Bunker Hill Monument. 102266

Address delivered at the laying of the cornerstone of the Evangelical Congregational Church. 98296

Address, delivered at the laying of the corner stone of the House of Refuge for Colored Juvenile Delinquents. 3360

Address delivered at the laying of the corner stone of the Insane Hospital, at Northampton, Massachusetts. 35805

Address delivered at the laying of the cornerstone of the Preston Retreat. 65391

Address delivered at the laying of the cornerstone of the Second Church. (71767)

Address delivered at the meeting of the Agricultural Society. 12299

Address delivered at the meeting of the Association of American Geologists and Naturalists. (72654)-72655

Address delivered at the meeting of the General Synod. 83338

Address delivered at the Merchants' Exchange. (73948)

Address delivered at the Normal School. 13749

Address delivered at the nineteenth annual fair. 24967

Address delivered at the opening of an edifice. 77987

Address delivered at the opening of Eames and Putnam's English and Classical Hall. 21620

Address delivered at the opening of session 1864-65. 85473

Address, delivered at the opening of the Boston Mechanics' Institute. 22429

Address delivered at the opening of the Brooklyn Female Academy. 89744

Address, delivered at the opening of the Charlestown Lyceum. 101079

Address delivered at the opening of the Church of the Transfiguration. 33161

Address delivered at the opening of the Colburn Grammar School. (21876)

Address delivered at the opening of the Columbian College. 90834

Address delivered at the opening of the new court house. 79941

Address, delivered at the opening of the new Diagnothian Hall. (27135)

Address delivered at the opening of the New Home for Aged Indigent Females. (72650)

Address, delivered at the opening of the New Theatre. 88634

Address delivered at the opening of the new town hall. 34126

Address delivered at the opening of the nineteenth annual fair. 20019

Address delivered at the opening of the session. 84276

Address . . . delivered at the opening of the Supreme Judicial Court at Boston. 58681

Address delivered at the opening of the tenth exhibition. 99262

Address delivered at the opening of the town hall. 5919, 11951

Address, delivered at the opening of the twenty-first annual fair. 12890

Address, delivered at the opening of Williams Hall. 5322

Address delivered at the . . . organization of the Boston Phrenological Society. 28529

Address, delivered at the organization of the Hopkinton Abstinence Society. 104320

Address delivered at the organization of the Normal School. (3361)

Address, delivered at the organization of the Oxford Temperance Society. 92120

Address, delivered at the Pittsfield Young Ladies' Institute. (72441)

Address, delivered at the Provincial Industrial Exhibition. 18962

Address delivered at the re-dedication of Monson Academy. 30092

Address delivered at the request of a committee. 267, (50398)

Address, delivered, at the request of the Board of Managers. 97641

Address delivered at the request of the citizens of Hartford. 30920

Address delivered at the request of the city government. 9456

Address delivered at the request of the Franklin Temperance Society. 78354

Address delivered at the request of the Managers. 79198

Address, delivered at the request of the military. 17395

Address, delivered at the request of the Philanthropic Society. 92703

Address, delivered at the request of the Washington Benevolent Society. 94359

Address delivered at the Retreat for the Insane. 71839

Address delivered at the second anniversary celebration. 28917

Address, delivered at the seventh anniversary of the Massachusetts Peace Society. 93539

Address delivered at the seventh anniversary of the Mount Holyoke Female Seminary. 37976

Address delivered at . . . the Sheffield Scientific School. 42777

Address, delivered at the Temperance Meeting. 102580

Address delivered at the tenth anniversary of the Massachusetts Peace Society. 38528

Address delivered at the third anniversary of Barnstable Peace Society. (27938)

Address delivered at the thirteenth anniversary of the Massachusetts Peace Society. 5831

Address delivered at the thirty-second National Conference on Charities and Correction. 84069

Address, delivered at the time of laying the corner stone. 79019

Address delivered at the town meeting in Plymouth. 72697

Address, delivered at the twelfth anniversary of the Massachusetts Peace Society. 105316

Address delivered at the twenty-first annual commencement. 89018, 89025

Address delivered at the Union Celebration of Independence. 32281

Address delivered at the United States Naval Academy. 42623

Address delivered at the University of Pennsylvania, before the Society of the Alumni, at their 119th annual celebration. 79861

Address delivered at the University of Pennsylvania, before the Society of the Alumni, on the occasion of their annual celebration. 79860

Address delivered at the University of Pennsylvania, December 4, 1865. 55082

Address, delivered at the Western Reserve College. 92229

Address delivered at the Whig Convention, held at Utica, the 10th of September, by Chandler Starr. 90544

Address delivered at the Whig Convention held at Utica, the tenth of September, one thousand eight hundred and thirty-four. 90545 ·

Address delivered at Topsfield. 13604

Address delivered at Tremont Temple, Boston. 11947

Address delivered at Trenton. 100988

Address delivered at Union-Village. 78402

Address: delivered at Warren Hall, in Charlestown. 3766

Address delivered at Washington, D. C., January 21, 1851. 26169

Address delivered at Washington, July 4, 1821. 24052, 2d note after (69432), 93573

Address delivered at Watertown. (12703)

Address delivered at West Springfield. 89729

Address, delivered at Westfield. 90559

Address delivered at Weymouth. 23229

Address, delivered at Weymouth, South Parish. 95156

Address delivered at Whitesborough. 28512

Address delivered at Whitsborough. 28602

Address delivered at Windsor. 11785

Address delivered at Worcester. 4242

Address delivered August 5, 1846. 89744

Address delivered August 14, 1844. 29864

Address delivered August 16, 1843. 89744

Address delivered Aug. 23, 1843. 22429

Address delivered before a meeting of the citizens of Nassau County, Florida. 78630

Address delivered before a meeting of the friends of Sunday-Schools. 85262

Address delivered before a number of military companies. 71838

Address delivered before Massachusetts Lodge. 103749

Address delivered before Montgomery Lodge. 95158

Address delivered before Mount Vernon Lodge. (13395)

Address delivered before Mount Zion Lodge. 47986

Address delivered before . . . Oglethorpe University. 12149

Address delivered before Philip H. Sheridan Post. 76974

Address delivered before Richmond Encampment of Knights Templars. 25850

Address delivered before St. Paul's Lodge. 83484

Address delivered before the Adelphian Society. 21721

Address delivered before the Adelphic Union Society of Williams College, August 20, 1850. 90430

Address delivered before the Adelphic Union Society of Williams College, on commencement day, August 16, 1837. 23271

Address, delivered before the African Grand Lodge. (31916)

Address delivered before the Agricultural and Horticultural Societies. 8976

Address delivered before the Agricultural Society of Albemarle. (43721)

Address delivered before the Agricultural Society of South Carolina. 87738

Address delivered before the Agricultural Society of the County of West Chester, New York. 30087

Address delivered before the Agricultural Society of Westborough and Vicinity. 74307

Address delivered before the Albany Institute, April, 1838. 24091

Address delivered before the Albany Institute, April 3, 1833. 19017

Address delivered before the Albany Institute, April 28th, 1837. 102331

Address delivered before the alumni and graduating class. 8724

Address delivered before the Alumni Association of Columbian College. 90409

Address, delivered before the Alumni Association of Jefferson College. 71266

Address delivered before the Alumni Association of Nassau-Hall. 88240

Address, delivered before the Alumni Association of the Columbian College. 74593

Address delivered before the Alumni Association of the University of North Carolina. (20087)

Address delivered before the Alumni Association of Washington College. 85476

Address delivered before the alumni of Bowdoin College. (18682)

Address delivered before the . . . alumni of Columbia College, May 2, 1832. (32406)

Address, delivered before the alumni of Columbia College, on the evening of the 5th October, 1842. 82731

Address, delivered before the alumni of Columbia College, on the third day of May, 1826. (3372)

Address delivered before the alumni of Jefferson College. 79761

Address delivered before the . . . alumni of Newton Theological Institution. (29524)

Address delivered before the alumni of the High School. 7771

Address delivered before the alumni of the University of Alabama. 84879

Address delivered before the alumni of Union College. 105997

Address, delivered before the . . . alumni of Williams College, at the celebration of the semi-centennial anniversary. 32943

Address delivered before the alumni of Williams, College by Hon. William Bross. 8386

Address, delivered before the Alumni Society of the University of Nashville. 4458

Address, delivered before the American Academy of Fine Arts. 99261

Address, delivered before the American Academy of Fine Arts, November 17, 1825. 68033

Address delivered before the American Antiquarian Society. 41267

Address delivered before the American Geographical and Statistical Society. 23588

Address delivered before the American Institute . . . during the sixteenth annual fair. 26220

Address delivered before the American Institute of Instruction, at Portland, Me. 92391

Address delivered before the American Institute of the City of New York, at their fourth annual fair. 23271

Address, delivered before the American Institute of the City of New York, . . . October 17, 1845. 22175

Address delivered before the American Peace Society, at its annual meeting, May 27, 1844. (11905)

Address delivered before the American Peace Society, at its annual meeting, May 26th, 1851. 13356

Address delivered before the American Peace Society, Boston, May, 1848. 19862

Address delivered before the American Peace Society, Boston, May 29, 1854. 906

Address delivered before the American Peace Society, . . . May 29, 1843. 59354

Address delivered before the American Peace Society, . . . May 26, 1845. 35855

Address delivered before the American Whig and Cliosophic Societies of the College of New Jersey. September 24, 1839. (18999)

Address delivered before the American Whig and Cliosophic Societies of the College of New Jersey, September 29, 1840. (36157)

Address delivered before the American Whig and Cliosophic Societies of the College of New Jersey, Sept. 26, 1843. 19003

Address delivered before the American Whig and Cliosophic Societies of the College of New Jersey. September 26, 1837. 88241

Address delivered before the American Whig and Cliosophic Societies of the College of New Jersey, 23d June, 1846. 8638

Address delivered before the Amoskeag Vetrans. (64619)

Address delivered before the Amphisbeteon Literary Society. 83879

Address delivered before the Anti-masonic Convention holden at Middlebury, Vt. 3316

Address, delivered before the Anti-masonic Convention of Delegates, for Plymouth County. 95158

Address, delivered before the Anti-masonic Convention of Reading, Mass. 76255

Address, delivered before the Anti-masonic Meeting at Faneuil Hall. 95158

Address delivered before the Archaean Society. 78020

Address delivered before the Art-Union of Philadelphia. (26240)

Address delivered before the Associate Alumni of the Merrimack Normal Institute, at their first annual meeting. 74388

Address delivered before the Associate Alumni of the Merrimack Normal Institute, at their second annual meeting. 76245

Address delivered before the Associate Alumni of the University of Vermont. 68054

Address delivered before the Associated Alumni Castleton Medical College. (21724)

Address delivered before the Associated Instructors of Youth. 39190

Address delivered before the Association of Alumni of Yale College. (21571)

Address delivered before the Association of American Geologists and Naturalists. 80130

Address, delivered before the Association of Teachers. 5795

Address delivered before the Association of the Alumni of Bowdoin College, . . . August 8, 1861. 65093

Address delivered before the Association of the Alumni of Bowdoin College, . . . August 5, 1858. 58096

Address delivered before the Association Alumni of the University of the City of New-York. 32994

Address delivered before the Association of the Alumni of Yale College. 81031

Address delivered before the Association of the Manufacturers of Berkshire County. 37289

Address delivered before the Auxiliary New-York Bible and Common Prayer Book Society. (32301)

Address delivered before the Auxiliary New-York Bible and Common Prayer Book Society, in St. Paul's Chapel. (33226)

Address delivered before the Baltimore Democratic Association. 32619

Address delivered before the Bar of Berkshire. (79940)

Address delivered before the Bedford, N. H., Farmers' Club. 72171

Address, delivered before the Berkshire Agricultural Society. 78831

Address delivered before the Board of Trade of . . . Pittsburgh. 63110

Address delivered before the Boston Board of Trade. 67270

Address delivered before the Boston Board of Trade, October 16, 1867. 67269

Address delivered before the Boston Mercantile Library Association. 11215

Address delivered before the . . . [Boston Social Science] Association. (67262)

Address delivered before the Boston Society of the New Jerusalem and the . . . Sabbath and Week-Day Schools. 68581

Address delivered before the Boston Society of the New Jerusalem, July 4, 1837. 68540

Address delivered before the Boston Young Men's Christian Union. (16374)

Address, delivered before the Bretheren [sic] of Zion Lodge. 104777

Address, delivered before the Birdgewater Society for the Promotion of Temperance. 32345

Address delivered before the Buffalo Historical Society. (33100)

Address delivered before the Buffalo Young Men's Temperance Society. 24764

Address delivered before the Cadets of Norwich University. 13342

Address delivered before the Cadets of the Norwich University. 24536

Address, delivered before the Cambridge Temperance Society. 104956

Address delivered before the candidates for the Baccalaureate in Union College, at the anniversary commencement, July 30th, 1806. 56036

Address delivered before the candidates for the Baccalaureate in Union College, at the anniversary commencement, July 24, 1811. 56036

Address delivered before the candidates for the Baccalaureate in Union College, at the anniversary commencement, July 29, 1807. 56036

Address delivered before the Candidates for the Baccalaureate in Union College, at the anniversary commencement, May 18th, 1805. 56036

Address, delivered before the Canterbury Temperance Society. 26018

Address delivered before the Chicago Historical Society. 84788

Address delivered before the Chippewa County Temperance Society. (77832)

Address delivered before the Cincinnati Astronomical Society. 44376

Address delivered before the Cincinnati Temperance Society. 92181

Address, delivered before the citizens of Becket, Mass. 93266

Address delivered before the citizens of Boston. 757

Address delivered before the citizens of Bristol, R. I. 19882

Address, delivered before the citizens of Charleston. 25675

Address delivered before the citizens of Ithaca. 82687

Address delivered before the citizens of Livingston County. (68051)

Address delivered before the citizens of Oxford. 47185

Address delivered before the citizens of Philadelphia. 79197

Address delivered before the citizens of Pittsfield. 33794

Address delivered before the citizens of Providence. 62625

Address delivered before the citizens of the town of Hingham. 41263

Address delivered before the citizens of Worcester. 23271

Address delivered before the city government and citizens of Roxbury, at the consecration of the cemetery at Forest Hills. (66775)

Address delivered before the city government, and citizens of Roxbury, on occasion of the death of Abraham Lincoln. 66777

Address, delivered before the city government and citizens of Roxbury, on the life and character of the late Henry A. S. Dearborn. (66776)

Address, delivered before the Cleosophic Society. 91105

Address delivered before the Colonization Society of Kentucky. 7674

Address delivered before the colored citizens of Boston. 84410

Address delivered before the Columbian Horticultural Society. 102157

Address delivered before the Columbian Institute for the Promotion of Arts and Sciences. 18158

Address delivered before the Columbian Society. 22250

Address delivered before the Concord Female Anti-slavery Society. 72714

Address delivered before the Connecticut River Valley Agricultural Society. 76237

Address delivered before the contributors. (14175)

Address delivered before the convention, by Jonathan A. Allen. 99176

Address delivered before the convention by the Hon. John W. Taylor. 65760, 94516

Address delivered before the Convention of the Diocese of Pennsylvania. 91575

Address delivered before the Convention of the Friends of Peace of the State of New-Jersey. 91887

Address delivered before the convention of the Protestant Episcopal Church, Springfield, Illinois. 12190

Address delivered before the Coos Agricultural Society. 7194

Address delivered before the Corps of Cadets of the United States Military Academy. 2408

Address delivered before the Corps of Cadets of the United States Military Academy, at West-Point. 71586

Address delivered before the Corps, on the semi-centennial anniversary. 92697

Address, delivered before the Dedham Auxiliary Society. 103408

Address delivered before the De Molay and Virginia Encampments. 97781

ADDRESS

Address delivered before the Delta Phi and
Athenaean Literary Societies of Newark
College. 63997
Address, delivered before the Dialectick
Society. 104286
Address, delivered before the Domestic Horti-
cultural Society. 92360
Address, delivered before the "East Tennessee
Historical and Antiquarian Society." 67728
Address delivered before the eighth graduating
class. (81427)
Address delivered before the Enosinian Society.
85576
Address delivered before the Equitable Union.
91721
Address delivered before the Essex Agricultural
Society, at . . . Topsfield. 21737
Address delivered before the Essex Agricultural
Society, October, 1862. (14261)
Address delivered before the Essex County
Natural History Society. 74347
Address delivered before the Euglossian and
Alpha Phi Delta Societies. 103666
Address delivered before the Eumenean and
Philanthropick Societies. 89016
Address delivered before the Euphemian Society.
84486
Address delivered before the Female Anti-slavery
Society. 2314
Address delivered before the Franklin Debating
Society. (7995)
Address delivered before the Franklin Society
of St. Louis. (22178)
Address, delivered before the Franklin Typo-
graphical Association. 71429
Address, delivered before the free people of
color. 26704
Address, delivered before the General Society
of Mechanics. 91133
Address, delivered before the Georgia Demo-
cratic State Convention. 91769
Address delivered before the German Societies
of Cincinnati. 83962
Address delivered before the Goethean and
Diagnothian Societies. 92011
Address delivered before the Governour and
Council. 93540
Address delivered before the graduates. 49090
Address delivered before the graduating class
of the Medical College of Georgia. 67333
Address delivered before the graduating class
of the United States Military Academy.
68119
Address delivered before the graduating class
of Union Female College. 90999
Address delivered before the Grand Chapter of
. . . New York. 65095
Address delivered before the Grand Lodge F. A.
A. M. 90366
Address, delivered before the Grand Lodge of
Iowa at Muscatine. 76489
Address, delivered before the . . . Grand Lodge
of Iowa . . . June 4, 1863. 58974
Address delivered before the Grand Lodge of
Massachusetts . . . December 28, 1829.
36016
Address delivered before the Grand Lodge of
Massachusetts, . . . December 25, 5802.
29297
Address delivered before the Grand Lodge of
Rhode Island, at their anniversary. 25968
Address delivered before the Grand Lodge of
Rhode-Island . . . in Providence. 67953
Address delivered before the . . . Grand Lodge
of the District of Columbia. 25849
Address delivered before the Hamilton County
Agricultural Society. 92182
Address . . . delivered before the . . . Hampden
Sidney [sic] College. 26678

Address delivered before the Hampshire Co.
Agricultural Society. 24766
Address, delivered before the Hampshire, Frank-
lin and Hampden Agricultural Society.
102332
Address delivered before the Harmonick Club.
103750
Address delivered before the Hartford County
Peace Society. 103166
Address delivered before the Harvard Musical
Association. 17389
Address delivered before the Hibernian Society.
23685
Address delivered before the High School. 29946
Address delivered before the Historical Society
of Galveston. 82346
Address delivered before the Historical Society
of Pennsylvania. 15895
Address delivered before the Historical Society
of the University of North-Carolina. 2286
Address delivered before the Holland Lodge.
13711
Address delivered before the Horticultural So-
ciety of Charleston. 20093
Address delivered before the Howard Musical
Association. (13660)
Address delivered before the inhabitants of
Grafton. 7961
Address, delivered before the inhabitants of
Stratford. 74482
Address delivered before . . . the inhabitants of
the town of Carolina, N. Y. 89234
Address delivered before the inhabitants of the
town of Milton. (71821)
Address delivered before the Institute of Natural
History. 91042
Address delivered before the Irving Society of
the College of St. James. 77488
Address delivered before the Jackson Convention.
(17400)
Address delivered before the Jacksonville Me-
chanic's Union. 93278
Address delivered before the Jefferson Society.
91321
Address, delivered before the Keeseville Tem-
perance Society. 92378
Address, delivered before the King Solomon's
Lodge. 39190
Address delivered before the Ladies' Anti-
slavery Society. 25170
Address delivered before the Law Academy of
Philadelphia, at the opening of the session
of 1826-7. 32985
Address delivered before the Law Academy of
Philadelphia, session 1828-29. 34772
Address delivered before the Law Association
of the City of New-York. 37475
Address delivered before the law class of the
University of Wisconsin. 74528
Address delivered before the Law Department
of the University of Louisville. 82185
Address delivered before the Legislature of
California. 10009
Address delivered before the Legislature of
Tennessee. 97050
Address delivered before the Legislature of
the state of Vermont. 33160
Address delivered before the Library Association
of Hudson. 25754
Address delivered before the Library Societies
of Dartmouth College. (15180)
Address, delivered before Lincoln Lodge. 80300
Address delivered before the Linnaean Associa-
tion. 85182
Address delivered before the Literary Associa-
tion. 27308
Address delivered before the Literary Societies
of Amherst College. 23271

70

Address delivered before the Literary Societies of Hamilton College. 25026

Address delivered before the Literary Societies of Jefferson College. 104020

Address delivered before the Literary Societies of Lafayette College. 20677

Address delivered before the Literary Societies of Pennsylvania College. 15898

Address delivered before the Literary Societies of the Rochester University. 68056

Address, delivered before the Literary Societies of the University of Virginia. 97606

Address delivered before the Literary Societies of the Virginia Military Institute. 3339

Address delivered before the Literary Societies of the Wesleyan Academy. 38841

Address, delivered before the literary Societies of the Wesleyan University. 89744

Address, delivered before the Literary Society of Granville College. 92183

Address delivered before the Literary Society of the University of Vermont. 34743

Address delivered before the Local Preachers' Association. (71891)

Address . . . delivered before the Macomb County Agricultural Society. (24527)

Address delivered before the Maryland Historical Society. 27378

Address delivered before the Massachusetts Agricultural Society. (14535)

Address delivered before the Massachusetts Charitable Fire Society. 23237

Address, delivered before the Massachusetts Charitable Mechanic Association, at the celebration of their twelfth triennial anniversary. 82589

Address delivered before the Massachusetts Charitable Mechanic Association, at the public celebration. (8902)

Address delivered before the Massachusetts Charitable Mechanic Association, at the . . . tenth triennial festival. 32721

Address delivered before the Massachusetts Charitable Mechanic Association, October 4, 1821. 102605

Address delivered before the Massachusetts Charitable Mechanic Association, October 4, 1827. 31896

Address delivered before the Massachusetts Chraitable Mechanic Association, October 7th, 1824. (11199)

Address, delivered before the Massachusetts Charitable Mechanic Association, . . . October 3, 1839. 2415

Address delivered before the Massachusetts Charitable Mechanic Association, on its 14th triennial festival. 77917

Address delivered before the Massachusetts Charitable Mechanic Association, on the occasion of their fifteenth triennial festival. 8901

Address delivered before the Massachusetts Charitable Mechanic Association, on the occasion of their sixth exhibition. 81611

Address, delivered before the Massachusetts Charitable Mechanic Association, September 26, 1844. 42708

Address delivered before the Massachusetts Charitable Mechanic Association, 20th September, 1837. 23271

Address delivered before the Massachusetts Charitable Mechanick Association, December 17, 1818. 36016

Address delivered before the Massachusetts Charitable Mechanick Association, December 21, 1809. 74302

Address delivered before the Massachusetts Christian Charitable Mechanic Association. 23674

Address delivered before the Massachusetts Horticultural Society, at their eighth anniversary. 103044

Address delivered before the Massachusetts Horticultural Society, at their fifth annual festival. 23237

Address delivered before the Massachusetts Horticultural Society, on the celebration of their first anniversary. 19077

Address delivered before the Massachusetts Peace Society. 101401

Address delivered before the Massachusetts Society for the Suppression of Intemperance, May 31, 1827. 89657

Address delivered before the Massachusetts Society for the Suppression of Intemperance, May 29, 1828. 24782

Address delivered before the Massachusetts Temperance Society. (11905)

Address, delivered before the Mayor and Common Council. 103880

Address delivered before the Mechanic Apprentices' Library Association, in the Hall of the Lowell Institute. 89083

Address delivered before the Mechanic Apprentices' Library Association, . . . thirty-fourth anniversary. 12542

Address delivered before the Mechanics' Institute of the City of New York. 64983

Address, delivered . . . before the mechanics of Boston. 24536

Address, delivered before the Medical Society of Tennessee. 105948

Address, delivered before the Medical Society of the City and County of New York. (65241)

Address delivered before the members of the Anti-masonic State Convention. 95158

Address, delivered before the members of the Frederick Lyceum. 16208

Address delivered before the members of the Kensington Institute. 102729

Address, delivered before the members of the Massachusetts Charitable Fire Society. (71009)

Address, delivered before the members of the New-England Society. (21290)

Address delivered before the members of the Norfolk Bar. 71010

Address, delivered before the members of the Northern Indiana Editorial Association. 83768

Address delivered before the members of the schools and citizens of Quincy. 179

Address, delivered before the Mercantile Library Association, . . . Boston. 23271

Address delivered before the Mercantile Library Association . . . March 20th, 1837. 64990

Address delivered before the Mercantile Library Association of Boston, December, 1845. 11219

Address delivered before the Mercantile Library Association of Boston, Massachusetts. 5739

Address delivered before the Mercantile Library Association of Boston on the evening of their sixteenth anniversary. 97600

Address, delivered before the Mercantile Library Company, of Philadelphia. 11924

Address delivered before the Middletown Colonization Society, at their annual meeting. 103171

Address delivered before the Middletown Colonization Society, . . . July 4, 1835. (24537)

Address delivered before the Minnesota Historical Society. 80819

Address, delivered before the Missionary Fraternity. 88574

Address delivered before the Missouri Historical Society. 79991

Address delivered before the Moral Reform Society of Salem. 102588

Address, delivered before the Moral Society in Brookfield. 92085

Address delivered before the National Teachers' Association. 68147

Address delivered before the National Union Association. 1297

Address, delivered before the New-Bedford Auxiliary Society, for the Suppression of Intemperance, at their annual meeting. 104524

Address, delivered before the New-Bedford Auxiliary Society, for the Suppression of Intemperance, . . . January 6, 1817. 68139

Address, delivered before the New Bedford Dorcas Society. 65089

Address, delivered before the . . . New Bedford Lyceum. 28615

Address delivered before the New-Bedford Port Society for the Moral Improvement of Seamen. 85545

Address delivered before the New Bedford Port Society, on the occasion of its twenty-eighth anniversary. 27505

Address delivered before the New Bedford Port Society, on the occasion of its twenty-seventh anniversary. 17371

Address, delivered before the New England Society, in the City of New York. 104860

Address delivered before the New-England Society of Brooklyn. (13609)

Address delivered before the N. E. Society of Michigan. 11349

Address delivered before the New England Society of Philadelphia; at its semi-annual meeting. 6281

Address delivered before the New England Society of Philadelphia, May 1, 1820. 51747

Address delivered before the New-England Society of South-Carolina. 17339

Address delivered before the New Hampshire Lyceum. 13631

Address, delivered before the New-Hampshire State Lyceum. 28709

Address delivered before the New Jersey Militia Association. 74145

Address delivered before the New-Jersey-State Agricultural Society. 49022

Address delivered before the New York African Society. 81751

Address delivered before the New York Historical Society, at its fortieth anniversary. 8174

Address, delivered before the New-York Historical Society, at its forty-second anniversary. 77851

Address delivered before the New York Historical Society, by the Hon. Edward Everett. 23271

Address delivered before the New York Historical Society, on its sixtieth anniversary. 19623

Address delivered before the New York Horticultural Society, . . . August 29th, 1826. 49749

Address delivered before the New-York Horticultural Society, . . . on the eighth of September, 1829. 25448

Address delivered before the New York Medical Society. 13247

Address delivered before the New York State Agricultural Society, . . . at Buffalo. 23271

Address delivered before the New-York State Agricultural Society, at the capitol. 99533

Address delivered before the N. Y. State Agricultural Society, by Josiah Quincy, Jr. (67257)

Address delivered before the New York State Medical Society, and members of the Legislature. 91481

Address, delivered before the New York State Medical Society in . . . Albany. (42974)

Address delivered before the New York State Society of the Cincinnati. 86117

Address delivered before the New York State Teachers' Association. 72868

Address delivered before the New York Young men's Christian Association. 2955

Address delivered before the Newark Mechanics' Association. 88242

Address, delivered before the Newburgh Library Association. 104549

Address, delivered before the Newburgh Lyceum of the Natural Sciences. 104549A

Address delivered before the Niagara County Anti-slavery Society. 91103

Address delivered before the Norfolk District Medical Society. 693

Address delivered before the Norfolk District Medical Society, at the annual meeting. 75797

Address delivered before the North Carolina State Agricultural Society. 68120

Address delivered before the Northern Lyceum. 27286

Address delivered before the officers and inmates. 90886

Address delivered before the Ohio Wool Growers' Association. 67790

Address delivered before the Ontario Agricultural Society. (28283)

Address delivered before the Peace Society of Amherst College. 91038

Address delivered before the Peace Society of Hartford and the Vicinity. 28780

Address delivered before the Peace Society of Hartford County. 103233

Address delivered before the Peithesophian Society of Rutger's College. 23237

Address delivered before the Peithesophian and Philoclean Societies of Rutgers College, by the Hon. Robert Strange. 92695

Address, delivered before the Peithesophian and Philoclean Societies of Rutgers College. . . . By William Wirt. 104869

Address delivered before the Peithesophian and Philoclean Society of Rutgers College, July 23, 1844. 17292

Address delivered before the Pelo-Paidensian Society. (17485)

Address delivered before the Penn'a State Agricultural Society. 91586

Address, delivered before the Pennsylvania Temperance Society. 21803

Address delivered before the Penobscot Association of Teachers. 10988

Address delivered before the People's College Association. 93219

Address delivered before the Phi Alpha Society. 63934

Address delivered before the Phi Beta Kappa Society, Alpha of Maine. 34750

Address delivered . . . [before] the ΦBK Society, Dartmouth College. 18399

Address delivered before the Phi Beta Kappa Society in Yale College. 23271

Address delivered before the Phi Beta Kappa Society of Harvard College. 31864

Address delivered before the Phi Kappa and Demosthenian Societies. 91770

Address delivered before the Philadelphia Society for Promoting Agriculture; at its anniversary meeting, January 18, 1820. 95821

Address delivered before the Philadelphia
Society for Promoting Agriculture: at its
anniversary meeting, January 19, 1819.
67998
Address delivered before the Philadelphia
Society for Promoting Agriculture, at its
annual meeting on the eighteenth of
January, 1825. 98698
Address delivered before the Philadelphia
Society for Promoting Agriculture . . .
on the fifteenth of January, 1822. 5328
Address delivered before the Philadelphia
Society for Promoting Agriculture . . .
twentieth of July, 1824. 10889
Address delivered before the Philodemic
Society. 43499
Address delivered before the Philolexian and
Peithologian Societies. 99263
Address delivered before the Philolexian
Society in New-York. 43475
Address delivered before the Philolexian
Society of Columbia College. (29538)
Address delivered before the Philomathaean
and Phrenakosmian Societies. (70451)
Address delivered before the Philomathaean
Society. 85181
Address delivered before the Philomathean and
Phrenakosmian Societies. (5234)
Address delivered before the Philomathean
Literary Institute. (71565)
Address delivered before the Philomathean
Society of the University of Pennsylvania.
105027
Address delivered before the Philomathean
Society of the University of Pennsylvania,
. . . November 1st, A. D. 1838. 68599
Address delivered before the Philomathean
Society of Troy Conference Academy.
92921
Address delivered before the Philomathean
Society of Union College. 89467
Address delivered before the Philomathic
Society. 27505
Address, delivered before the Philosophical
Institute. (5337)
Address delivered before the Phrenakosmian
Society. 82716
Address delivered before the Pilgrim Society
of Plymouth, December 22, 1834. 5723
Address delivered before the Pilgrim Society
of Plymouth, December 22, 1835. 89696
Address delivered before the Plattsburg Lyceum.
(81635)
Address delivered before the Portland Associ-
ation. 52161
Address delivered before the Portland Temper-
ance Society. 12677
Address, delivered before the Portsmouth
Temperance Society. 92365
Address delivered before the Presbyterian
Historical Society. (32330)
Address delivered . . . before the professors
and tutors of Marion College. 64692
Address delivered before the Pro-slavery
Convention. 79763
Address delivered before the public schools.
4699
Address delivered before the Readfield Temper-
ance Society. 9912
Address delivered before the Reading Peace
Society. 60973
Address delivered before the Rensselaer
Agricultural Society. 95780
Address, delivered before the Republican
citizens of Concord. 102086
Address delivered before the Republicans of
Newport. 3831

Address delivered before the Rhode-Island
Historical Society. 26517
Address delivered before the Rhode Island
Homoeopathic Society. 57100
Address delivered before the Rhode-Island
Society for the Encouragement of Domestic
Industry, at their anniversary. 95827
Address delivered before the Rhode Island
Society for the Encouragement of Domestic
Industry, October 15, 1823. 20967
Address delivered before the Rhode Island
Society for the Encouragement of Domestic
Industry, October 19, 1825. 71125
Address, delivered before the Rhode Island
Society for the Encouragement of Domestic
Industry, October 20, 1824. 33934
[Address delivered] before the Rochester
Anthenaeum. 12991
Address delivered before the Rockingham Agri-
cultural Society. 63451
Address delivered before the Rockingham Tem-
perance Society. 92366
Address, delivered before the Roxbury Charitable
Society, 71073
Address delivered before the Sabbath Schools.
17274
Address delivered before the Salem Charitable
Mechanic Association. 89689
Address delivered before the Saratoga County
Convention. 9114
Address delivered before the Savannah Lodge.
69619
Address delivered before the School Society.
71076
Address delivered before the schools and citizens
of Quincy. 8340
Address delivered before the Seamen's Bethel
Temperance Society. 76994
Address delivered before the Senate of Union
College. 9611
Address delivered before the Singing Society.
(70847)
Address delivered before the Social Union.
22327
Address, delivered before the Society, at Argyle.
101974
Address delivered before the Society, at their
celebration of the twelfth anniversary of
the admission of . . . California. 86010
Address, delivered before the Society, by N. R.
Smith. 83663
Address delivered . . . before the Society for
the Prevention of Pauperism. 28390
Address delivered before the Society for the
Reformation of Morals. 24307
Address delivered before the Society of Adelphi.
41261
Address delivered before the Society of Agri-
culture and Horticulture of Westchester
County. 17227
Address delivered before the Society of Alumni
of Miami University. 1385
Address delivered before the Society of Alumni
of the University of Virginia. 71684
Address, delivered before the Society of Alumni
of Williams College, at Williamstown, Mass.
19519
Address delivered before the Society of Alumni
of Williams College, . . . August 16, 1843.
71840
Address delivered before the Society of Middle-
sex Husbandmen and Manufacturers. 12426
Address, delivered before the Society of the
Alumni of Dartmouth College. 8555
Address delivered before the Society of the
Alumni of Franklin College. 13859
Address delivered before the Society of the
Alumni of the University of Alabama. 64946

ADDRESS

Address delivered before the Sons of
Temperance. 104792
Address delivered before the South Carolina
Historical Society. 82988
Address delivered before the South-Carolina
Institute, at its first annual fair. 30101,
88006
Address delivered before the Strafford Agri-
cultural Society. 101065
Address, delivered before the Tallmadge
Colonization Society. 103826
Address delivered before the Tammany Society.
64622
Address delivered before the Temperance
Society of Harvard University. 76997
Address, delivered before the Temperance
Society of South Berwick, (Maine.)
92367
Address delivered before the Temperance
Society of . . . Washington. 62904
Address delivered before the Temperate
Society, at Plymouth. 67873
Address, delivered before the Thalian and
Phi-Delta Societies of Oglethorpe Uni-
versity. 85278
Address delivered before the Thalian and Phi
Delta Societies of Oglethorpe University,
Georgia. 91776
Address delivered before the Tippecanoe Club
of New York. 98104
Address, delivered before the trustees, faculty,
and students, of La Fayette College.
67999
Address, delivered before the trustees, faculty,
and students of the University of Penn-
sylvania. 19345
Address delivered before the two literary
societies of Davidson College. 83635
Address delivered before the two literary
societies of Randolph-Macon College.
97605
Address delivered before the two literary
societies of the University of North
Carolina, by Hon. Robert Strange.
92696
Address delivered before the two literary
societies of the University of North
Carolina . . . in June 1839. 8450
Address delivered before the two literary
societies of the University of North
Carolina, May 31st, 1854. 8432
Address delivered before the Union Agricultural
Society. 23271
Address delivered before the Union Campaign
Club. 35849
Address delivered before the Union League of
Philadelphia, October 31, 1864. 47388
Address delivered before the Union League of
Philadelphia on Saturday Evening,
January 20, 1906. 83320
Address delivered before the Union League . . .
Philadelphia. 8668
Address delivered before the Union Literary
Society. 106084
Address delivered before the Union Temper-
ance Society. 104954
Address delivered before the United States
Naval Academy. 23271
Address delivered before the University of
Nashville. (33352)
Address delivered before the . . . University
of Virginia. 9513
Address delivered before the Vermont Histori-
cal and Antiquarian Society. (9643)
Address delivered before the Vermont State
Agricultural Society and Wool Growers'
Association. (63727)

Address delivered before the Vermont State
Agricultural Society, at Brattleboro'.
74310
Address delivered before the Vincennes
Historical and Antiquarian Society. 39316
Address delivered before the Was-ah Ho-de-no-
son-ne. 77933
Address delivered before the Washington Benev-
olent Societies of Hampstead and London-
derry. 89559
Address delivered before the Washington Be-
nevolent Societies of Princeton &
Cranbury. (4038)
Address delivered before the Washington Be-
nevolent Society, at Portsmouth. 102258
Address delivered before the Washington Be-
nevolent Society, Brimfield. 101769
Address delivered before the Washington Be-
nevolent Society, in Dorchester. 30504
Address, delivered before the Washington Be-
nevolent Society of Lancaster and
Sterling. (4629)
Address delivered before the Washington Chap-
ter. 37832
Address delivered before the Washington City
Temperance Society. 79465
Address delivered before the Windham County
Peace Society. 102517
Address, delivered before the Worcester
Agricultural Society, October 11, 1826·
101513
Address, delivered before the Wrocester
Agricultural Society, October 12,. 1825.
97415
Address delivered before the Worcester
Agricultural Society, October 20, 1831.
24554
Address delivered before the Worcester
Agricultural Society, September 28,
1855. 7963
Address delivered before the Worcester
Agricultural Society, September 25,
1822. 19600
Address delivered before the Worcester
Agricultural Society, September 27,
1821. 74353
Address delivered before the Worcester
& Middlesex Temperance Union. 2201
Address delivered before the York County
Agricultural Society. (25861)
Address delivered before the Yorkville Lodge.
42863
Address, delivered before the Young Ladies'
Literary Society. 91884
Address delivered before the young men of
Boston. 101035
[Address] delivered before the Young Men's
Association of Buffalo. 3845
Address delivered before the Young Men's
Association, of the city of Albany.
64280
Address delivered before the Young Mens'
Christian Association, of Baltimore.
83386
Address delivered before the Young Men's
Christian Association, of Chicago.
77563
Address delivered before the Young Men's
Christian Association of San Fran-
cisco. (1423)
Address delivered before the Young Men's
Jefferson Society. (35948)
Address delivered before the Young Men's
Mercantile Library and Mechanic's
Institute of Pittsburgh. (71922)
Address delivered before the Young Men's
Temperance Association. 90563

Address delivered before the Young Men's Temperance Society of Middlebury, Vermont. 81678

Address delivered before the Young Men's Temperance Society, of New Haven, Conn. 92072

Address delivered before the Young Men's Temperance Society of St. Louis. 64689

Address delivered before Wirt Institute. (82358)

Address delivered by a member of the Manumission Society. 94800

Address, delivered by appointment, at Morristown. (15172)

Address, delivered by appointment, in the Episcopal Church. 88635

Address delivered by B. Alden Bidlack. 5251

Address delivered by Benjamin Crowninshield. 17707

Address delivered by Bvt. Col. Ben. P. Runkle. (74134)

Address; delivered by Charles F. Stansbury. 90367

Address delivered by Charles W. Peale. 59417

Address delivered by Col. R. Penn Smith. 83789

Address delivered by Companion James Reiley. 69104

Address delivered by ex-gov. Alexander Ramsey. 67725

Address delivered by George Wm. Brown. (8482)

Address delivered by Henry Ward Beecher. 4325

Address delivered by His Excellency Daniel D. Tompkins. 96149

Address delivered by His Exc'y John Tyler. 67607

Address delivered by Hon. Henry Winter Davis. 18828

Address delivered by Hon. J. V. C. Smith. 82805

Address delivered by Hon. John N. Conyngham. 16230

Address delivered by Hon. John Q. Adams, at Washington. 89629

Address. Delivered by Hon. John Y. Smith. 83026

Address delivered by Hon. Joseph J. Roberts. (71904)

Address delivered by Hon. Marshal Cram. 17377

Address, delivered, by invitation. 88636

Address delivered by J. M. Sturtevant. 93276

Address, delivered by John H. B. Latrobe. 39223

Address delivered by L. Tinelli. 95846

Address delivered by Maj. General N. P. Banks. 3206

Address delivered by Mr. Fred. P. Stanton. 90406

Address delivered by Mrs. [A. H.] Hoge. 32427, (76614), 76647

Address, delivered by O. de A. Santangelo. 76823

Address, delivered, by request, before the Literary Societies of Lafayette College. (78317)

Address, delivered by request of the Humane Impartial Society. 24377

Address, delivered by request of the students of Dartmouth College. 76238

Address delivered by Rev. Clement M. Butler. 9627

Address delivered by Rev. J. Steele. 91119

Address delivered by Rev. L. L. Hamline. 30076

Address delivered by Robert MacFarlane. 43250

Address delivered by S. F. Austin. 2426

Address delivered by the Hon. John Q. Adams at Washington. 268, 89629

Address delivered by the Hon. Robert Strange. 92697

Address, delivered by the Rev. E. N. Kirk. 37976, 85967

Address, delivered by the Rev. Ferdinand De W. Ward. 101291

Address, delivered by the Rev. S. B. How. (33221)

Address delivered by the Reverend Walter E. Clifton Smith. 84507

Address delivered by W. S. Scarborough. 77447

Address, delivered by William H. Seward. 79499

Address delivered December 4, 1860. 29781

Address delivered . . . 1880. 88005

Address, delivered February 4, 1806. 105371

Address delivered February 28, 1825. 17340

Address . . . 1st August, 1856. 59765

Address delivered 14th April, 1841. 14535

Address delivered . . . Gerard College. 15898

Address delivered in behalf of the Ladies' Soldiers' Aid Society of West Cambridge. 84013

Address delivered in behalf of the Society for the Promotion of Collegiate and Theological Education at the West. 93274

Address, delivered in . . . Boston, February 26th, 1861. 37660

Address delivered in Boston, Mass., May, 1857. 82705

Address delivered in . . . Boston, . . . October 24, 1832. 82471

Address, delivered in Braintree. 92242

Address delivered in . . . Camden, N. J. 26702

Address delivered in Charleston, before the Agricultural Society of So. Caro. at its anniversary meeting. 103314

Address delivered in Charleston, before the Agricultural Society of South Carolina, 19th August, 1828. 33043

Address delivered in Charleston, before the Agricultural Society of South Carolina, . . . on 18th of August, 1829. 62900

Address delivered in Christ Church, Gardiner. 13380

Address delivered in Columbia. 73142

Address delivered in . . . Concord. 22453

Address delivered in . . . Dorchester. (25375)

Address delivered in Fanueil Hall. 23271

Address delivered in . . . Foxborough, Mass. 82744

Address, delivered in Free-Mason Hall. 104165

Address, delivered in Hallowell. 89694

Address, delivered in Ipswich, Mass. 92041

Address delivered in Ithaca. 89233

Address delivered in Jacksonville. 42647

Address delivered in Lansingburgh. 89083

Address, delivered in Medfield. 76350

Address, delivered in New York. (33352)

Address delivered in Oak-Grove Cemetery. 8336

Address, delivered in Parkersburg. (12990)

Address delivered in Philadelphia. 64676

Address delivered in Princeton. 43164

Address delivered in Saco. 21517

Address, delivered in St. George's Church, Flushing. 82933

Address, delivered in St. Paul's Church, Richmond. 36156

Address delivered in St. Peter's Church, Cheshire. (4129)

Address delivered in Sherburne. 76351

Address, delivered in . . . Syracuse. 47078

Address delivered . . . in Tremont Temple. (6977)

Address delivered in the Academy of Music. (23266)

Address delivered in the Capitol. 102545

Address delivered in the Central Presbyterian Church. 8473

Address delivered in the Chapel of the State Prison. (65559)

Address, delivered in the Chapel of the University. 21590

Address delivered in the city of Galveston. 82342

Address delivered in the Congregational Church, Milton. 78623

Address, delivered in the Congregational Meeting House, in Chatham. (72416)

Address delivered in the convention of the two houses. 37792, 3d note after 103271

Address delivered in the Essex Lodge. 4772

Address delivered in the Evangelical Lutheran Ebenezer Church. 89744

Address delivered in the First Church, Dorchester. (29830)

Address, delivered in the First Congregational Church, in Middletown. 66874

Address delivered in the First Parish, Beverly. 95227

Address, delivered in the Lodge Room at Schenectady. 106000

Address, delivered in the Mercer Street Church. 89744

Address delivered in the Methodist Episcopal Church in Easton. 91913

Address delivered in the M. E. Church, Nassau. 87266

Address, delivered in the Middle Dutch Church, Albany. 89744

Address delivered in the New Meeting-House in Brattleborough. 102609

Address delivered in the New-York Free School. 98473

Address, delivered in the Orphan Asylum. 90178

Address delivered in the Presbyterian Church, at Tuscumbia. 91068

Address, delivered in the Presbyterian Church, at Wilmington. 91069

Address delivered in the Reformed Dutch Church. 81649

Address delivered in the Representatives Hall. 9644

Address delivered in the Second Presbyterian Church. 97368

Address delivered . . . in the Senate Chamber. 68146

Address, delivered in the South Congregational Church. 13365

Address delivered in the South Dutch Church, Albany. 89744

Address delivered in Tremont Temple, Boston. 62528

Address, delivered in . . . Troy. 4614

Address, delivered in Wales, Mass. 26610

Address delivered in Windsor, Conn. 27405

Address delivered Jan. 1, 1833. 81641

Address . . . delivered . . . January 14, 1862. 26712

Address delivered July 4th, 1849. 82746, 82747

Address, delivered July 4, 1832. 14422

Address, delivered July 12, 1826. 73531

Address delivered July 20, 1830. 104869

Address delivered July 24, 1849. 89744

Address, . . . delivered . . . July 23, 1847. 26358

Address, delivered, June 28, at the laying of the corner-stone. 103827

Address, delivered June 24, 1812. (70945)

Address delivered March 8, 1825. 70469

Address delivered, March 31, 1864. 10256, 89744

Address delivered May 17, 1901. 84907

Address delivered May 30, A. D. 1832. 103722

Address . . . delivered May 30th, 1872. 76974

Address delivered May 20, 1837. 94264

Address, delivered October, 1807. 90835

Address delivered October 5, 1842. 45809

Address, delivered, October 20, 1863. 19637

Address delivered on Edisto Island. 96378

Address delivered . . . on Franklin's birth-day. 2844

Address delivered on . . . laying the corner stone of a Free Church at Fort Edward. (64645)

Address delivered on occasion of laying the corner stone of the Smithsonian Institution. 18320

Address delivered on the occasion of the funeral of the Rev. William James. 89744

Address delivered on occasion of the raising of the national flag. 89744

Address, delivered on request of the managers. 90179

Address delivered on several occasions during . . . 1860. 32269

Address, delivered on Sunday evening, July 7, 1850. 18924

Address delivered on the anniversary of the birth-day of Thomas Paine. 19613

Address delivered on the anniversary of the Philolexian Society. 25442

Address delivered on the anniversary of the Union Literary Society. 90832

Address delivered on the celebration of the centennial anniversary of St. John's Lodge, no. 2. 67780

Address, delivered on the centennial anniversary of St. John's Lodge, No. I., at Portsmouth, N. H. (50322)

Address, delivered on the centennial celebration, to the people of Hollis, N. H. 64791

Address delivered on the commemoration at Fryeburg. (18679)

Address delivered on the consecration of the Worcester Rural Cemetery. (41257)

Address delivered on the day of his [i.e. Rev. James Flint's] funeral. 13224

Address delivered on the day of the national fast. 21888

Address delivered on the dedication of the cemetery. 29983

Address delivered on the VIII of October MDCCCXXX. 19073

Address delivered on the evening of December 4, 1838. 89744

Address delivered on the evening of the twenty-second of February, MDCCCXLVII. 89744

Address delivered on the first anniversary of Van Doren's Collegiate Institute. (47119)

Address delivered on the 1st of August, 1831. 41619

Address, delivered on the first public exhibition. 17252

Address delivered on the fourth July, 1835. 79730

Address, delivered on the fourth of July, 1835. 91560

Address, delivered on the fourth of July, 1820. (67709)

Address delivered on the fourth of July, 1828. 25440

Address delivered on the Gun-House Square, at Gloucester. 36610

Address delivered on the morning of May 31, 1826. 101378

Address, delivered on the 9th of August, 1865. 89744

Address delivered on the occasion by Rev. S. Granby Spees. 89264

Address, delivered on the occasion of assuming the chair as President. 90892

Address, delivered on the occasion of his [i. e. Joseph Few Smith's] inauguration. 83343

Address delivered on the occasion of laying the corner-stone of the Church of the Epiphany, Philadelphia. 97624

Address delivered on the occasion of laying the corner stone of the new medical hall of Transylvania University. 103876

Address delivered on the occasion of placing the crowning stone of the main building of the Girard College. (11866)

Address delivered on the occasion of the funeral solemnities of the late President of the United States. 21331

Address delivered on the occasion of the graduation of the first class of colored nurses. 84259

Address delivered on the occasion of the inauguration of the New South Building. 83357

Address, delivered on the occasion of the opening of Marshall Cemetery. (8977)

Address delivered on the second anniversary of Van Doren's Collegiate Institute. 50581

Address delivered on the third anniversary of the Washington Benevolent Society. 5323

Address delivered on the 28th of June, 1830. 23271

Address, delivered on the 20th of December, 1849. 31221

Address delivered on Tuesday evening, June 15, 1869. 89744

Address, delivered September 5, 1839. (26322)

Address delivered September 6, 1831. 3454

Address delivered September 28th, 1854. 42847

Address, delivered September 25, 1834. 38660

Address delivered Sunday, June 20th, 1869. 89744

Address, delivered . . . the evening before the annual commencement, 17292

Address delivered the twenty-eighth June, 1853. 7769

Address delivered to the American Union Academy. 20899

Address, delivered to the Auxiliary New-York Bible Society. 8052

Address delivered to the Biological Section of the British Association. 78144

Address delivered to the candidates for Baccalaureate of Wittenberg College. 89751

Address delivered to the Colonization Society of Kentucky. 97739

Address delivered to the Companies of California Adventurers. (7958)

Address delivered to the graduates of the Union Literary Society of Maimi University. 85518

Address: delivered to the graduating class in the Medical Department of Yale College. 90887

Address delivered to the Grand Lodge of North-Carolina. 94508

Address delivered to the inhabitants of Bath. 93952

Address delivered to the Massachusetts Peace Society. 71556

Address delivered to the members of the Bar of Suffolk. 21472

Address, delivered to the members of the Berkshire Agricultural Society. 102134

Address delivered to the Oneida Indians. 5880, 104213

Address delivered to the pastors. 18814, 30130

Address delivered to the people of Goshen. 64790

Address delivered to the Philanthropic Society. 2842

Address delivered to the pupils of Henry Dean's Writing School. (24480)

Address delivered to the singing schools. 37925

Address delivered to the students of Phillips Academy in Andover, immediately after the yearly examination and exhibition. 94362

Address delivered to the students of Phillips' Academy, in Andover, . . . July 18, 1791. 62535, note after 94362

Address delivered to the students of the Philadelphia Association for Medical Instruction. 91782

Address, delivered to the students of theology. 66228

Address, delivered to the Third Division of Massachusetts Militia. 98641

Address delivered to the voters in Manchester. 105675

Address delivered to the Ware-Village Temperance Society. 16338

Address delivered . . . 28th November, 1866. 19627

Address delivered 27th April, 1839. (24191)

Address delivered under the Old Elm Tree. 19852

Address delivered upon the installation of Rev. Lucien W. Berry. 34995

Address, Denmark, Iowa, July 3, 1867. 43844

Address . . . Derry, N. H. (4470)

Address . . . Dickinson College. 9364

Address directed to the citizens. 95576

Address . . . Dorchester, February 1, 1863. (29830)

Address . . . Dorchester, June 19th, 1864. (29830)

Address . . . Eclectic Institute, at Hiram, Ohio. 26664

Address . . . 1877. 88005

Address . . . 1876. 88005

Address . . . 1830. 16621, 87968

Address, embracing the early history of Delaware. 25001

Address, . . . Elizabethtown, Nov. 24, 1845. (49064)

Address . . . Essex, July 4, 1865. 82349

Address, etc. (80090)

Address, etc., of the Charitable Society. 30140

Address, &c. upon the subject. 95490

Address explanatory of the principles. 33185

Address . . . Feb., 1840. (33639)

Address . . . February 2nd, 1863. 3895

Address . . . February 7th, 1854. 37481

Address . . . Feb. 7, 1830. (37747)

Address . . . Feb. 6, 1850. 91481

Address . . . February 24, 1859. 4457

Address . . . Female Medical College of Pennsylvania. (13655)

Address, first anniversary of the abolition of slavery. 91697

Address . . . Flushing, Long Island. (43102)

Address for names of persons. 10598

Address . . . for the education of indigent pious young men. 26694

Address . . . for the promotion of collegiate and theological education at the west. (29484)

Address for the removal of Edward G. Loring. (29841)

Address for the year 1833. 77148

Address, . . . fourth July, A. D. 1822. 42097

Address [4 July, 1861] by Edward Everett. 23271

Address . . . 4th October, 1837. 43679

Address . . . 4th of July, 1844. (20159)

Address [fourth of July, 1800,] at New York. 49749

Address . . . fourth of July, 1835. 43503

[Address] . . . Franklin and Marshall College. 20677

Address . . . Franklin College. 22588

Address, . . . Franklin Institute and Union Literary Societies. 25020

Address . . . Franklin Institute . . . 1842. (2588)

Address, . . . Free High School-House. (64106)

Address from a committee. 60275

Address from a farmer. 70523

Address from a junto of members. 19456

Address from a minister in Virginia. 100420

Address from Henry Peckwell. 27548

Address from Mrs. Harriet Beecher Stowe. 59532, 92506, 92522

Address from one of the secretaries. 54041

Address from Rhode Island Quarterly Meeting of Friends. 70522

Address from Robert Goodloe Harper. (30423)

Address from Scipio Quarterly Meeting of Friends. 86022

Address from some of the ministers. 94926, 6th note after 103650

Address from the alumni. 64946

Address from the Baptist Church in Philadelphia. (3237), 69519, note after 104732

Address from the Brethren's Society. 387

Address from the church on the occasion. 101381

Address from the clergy of New-York and New-Jersey. 16585, note after 100420

Address from the colored citizens of Norfolk. 55476

Address from the committee appointed at Mrs. Vanderwater's. 53473, 54042, 83604

Address from the Committee of Friends. (79113)

Address from the Committee of the New-York Athenaeum. 54432

Address from the Convention of Congregational Ministers. 45579

Address from the Corporation of Albany. 4035

Address from the delegates. 97533

Address, from the delegates, to the people of Great-Britain. 22624, note after 41286

Address from the Directors of the Peruvian Mining Company. 61074

Address from the General Court. 45580

Address from the Grafton and Coos Counsellor Convention. 28201

Address from the Hon. Richard Jackson. (35451)

Address from the inhabitants of Wyoming and others. (59830), 105686A

Address from the Irish Emancipation Society. 68191

Address from the Legislative Assembly. 25176

Address from the Legislature of the state of New-York. 53474

Address from the Managers of the House of Refuge. 61729

Address from the Manumission Society. 94801

Address from the members of the constitutional body. 388

Address from the Monthly Meeting of Friends of Philadelphia. (61419)

Address from the Pennsylvania Society for Promoting the Abolition of Slavery. 81753

Address from the people of Ireland to their clergymen. (81754)

Address from the people of Ireland to their countrymen. (56653)

Address from the Philadelphia Society for Promoting Agriculture. 62036

Address from the Presbytery of New-Castle. 52562, 84850

Address from the Presbytery of New York. (53475)

Address from the President and Directors of the Pennsylvania Company for Insurances on Lives. 60315

Address from the Roman Catholics of America. 11071, note after 101769

Address from the Session of the Second Presbyterian Church. 71163

Address from the Trustees and Treasurer of "The Friendly Association." 34589, 59831

Address from the . . . Trustees of the Farmers' High School. (60097)

Address from the Trustees [of the Missionary Society of Connecticut.] 15811

Address from the Trustees of the New-York Homoeopathic Dispensary Association. (54478)

Address, from the Trustees . . . to the people. (45724)

Address from the Twelve United Colonies. 19159A

Address from the Yearly Meeting of Friends of North Carolina. 55587

Address from the Yearly Meeting of New-England. 52604

Address from Trinity Lodge. 98474

Address from William Smith. 84816, 84817

Address . . . Geneva College. 25009

Address given at . . . St. Paul. 30984

Address, giving the early history of Hennepin County. 91543

Address . . . Grand Lodge of Kentucky. 37921

Address . . . Grand Lodge of the District of Columbia. 25850

Address . . . Hanover College. 43569

Address . . . Horticultural Society of Maryland. (37423)

Address, Hudson Literary Society. 24530

Address illustrative of the nature and power of the slave states. 67196

Address in a letter to the Seceding Masons. 87836

Address, . . . in Amherst. (18453)

Address, in answer to a pamphlet. 74207

Address in answer to the speech. 250

Address in behalf of Rev. Charles Spear. 37848

Address in behalf of . . . temperance. 52421

Address . . . in behalf of the . . . American Union. 37817

Address in behalf of the Columbia Institution. 26404

Address in behalf of the Juvenile Library Company. 71164, 3d note after 104862

Address . . . in behalf of the New-York Institution. 49074

Address in behalf of the Society for the Promotion of Collegiate and Theological Education at the West. 17270

Address, . . . in Belleville. 59486

Address . . . in . . . Boston. 38156

Address . . . in Brighton. (33308)

Address . . . in Burlington. 44739

Address . . in Castleton. 3940

Address in celebration of the nativity of St. John the Baptist. (71050)

Address in Christian love. 8565

Address in commemoration of Abraham Lincoln. 6061

Address in commemoration of Alexander Dallas Bache. 28097

Address, in commemoration of American independence. 101459

Address in commemoration of . . . Ledyard. (28882)

Address in commemoration of Lexington battle. 22531

Address in commemoration of Professor J. W. Bailey. 28089

Address in commemoration of Sears Cook Walker. 28097

Address in commemoration of the Boston Massacre. 22533

Address in commemoration of the death of William Henry Harrison. 27649

Address in commemoration of the first settlement of Kentucky. 50583

Address, in commemoration of the 4th July, 1776. 76352

Address in commemoration of the reestablishment of the national flag at Fort Sumter. 6059

Address in commemoration of the sixth of September, 1781. (7333)

Address in commemoration of Washington's birth day. 13381

Address in commemoration of . . . William Henry Harrison. 5524

Address, . . . in Danvers, before the Society. (55190)

Address, in Danvers, [on] intemperance. 57782

Address in defence of J. Cushing Edmands. 21861

Address in favor of the Broadway Railroad. 54135

Address in favor of universal suffrage. 90395

Address in five numbers. 71069

Address . . . in Groton. 3794

Address . . . in Hanover College. 43565

Address . . . in Haverhill. (61370)

Address in Latin. 94368

Address in Latin, by Joseph Willard. 104054

Address . . . in Leicester. 52313

Address . . . in . . . Lime. (38027)

Address . . . in Marlboro' Chapel. 26712

Address in memory of Miss Sarah Paul. 37848

Address in memory of Rebecca G. Elliot. 72624

Address . . . in Middlebury. 36258

Address . . . in Nashville. 41314

Address . . . in New-Haven. (81045)

Address . . . in . . . [New York] January 15, 1851. 51539

Address . . . in North Wrentham. 62479

Address, in opposition to the projected union. 50959

Address . . . in . . . Philadelphia. 6075, 42979

Address . . . in Raleigh. 59535

Address in refutation of the Thomsonian system. 91052

Address in regard to the memorial. 389

Address in relation to the epizootic disease. 85493

Address . . . in Roxbury. 41420

Address . . . in Senate Chamber of Maryland. 29521

Address in support of Mr. Clinton's election. 35111

Address in support of the . . . temperance reformation. 56215

Address . . . in the Chapel. 26139

Address in the Virginia Gazette. 23500, 100465

Address . . . in Townshend. 61368

Address intended to have been delivered. 8053

Address, intended to promote a geological and mineralogical survey. 8672

Address . . . interment of Mrs. Harriet Storrs. 14137

Address introductory to a course of lectures. 20391

Address, introductory to a course of lectures delivered in . . . New York. 4276

Address, intorductory to a course of lectures, delivered in the hall of the Medical College of South Carolina. (70491)

Address introductory to a course of lectures on the theory and practice of medicine. 83661

Address, introductory to opening the Southern Botanico-Medical College. 88855

Address, introductory to the course of instruction. 70493

Address introductory to the fourth course. 24953

Address, intorductory to the second course. (62519)

Address, investigating society. 13371

Address . . . Iowa State University. 21818

Address . . . January 1, 1866. 72055

Address . . . January 25, 1853. 31221

Address . . . Jan. 24, 1830. (61370)

Address, Jan. 26 and 27, 1852. 23684

Address . . . Jefferson College. 50449

Address, . . . July 4, 1853. 12973

Address . . . July 4, 1828. 38156

Address, . . . July 2d, 1856. 43567

Address . . . July 13th, 1836. 2888

Address . . . July 24, 1848. (21117)

Address . . . July 22d, 1851. (37318)

Address . . . June 7, 1841. 12194

Address, . . . June 30, 1858. 57791

Address June 30, 1819. (35746)

Address . . . June 22, 1865. 37272

Address . . . June 23rd, 1852. 8748

Address . . . Lafayette College, Easton, Pennsylvania. 64317

Address . . . Lafayette College . . . September 14, 1847. 38315

Address lately presented. 59832

Address . . . Law Department of Hamilton College. 20031

Address, laying the corner stone. 21979

Address left with His Excellency, Gov. Tryon. 53630, 97291

Address . . . Louisville Medical Institute. 24782

Address . . . Lynn, June 24, 1821. 24007

Address, made at Union, (Maine). 103475

Address made by Thomas Donaldson. 20590

Address made in New Haven. 30787

Address, . . . Marshall College, . . . September 28, 1841. (26054)

Address . . . Marshall College . . . Sept. 25, 1838. 64273

Address . . . Massachusetts Charitable Fire Society. 26624

Address . . . Massachusetts Medical Society. 28544

Address . . . May 1840. 5028

Address . . . May 28, 1862. 33964

Address . . . May 21, 1840. 45448

Address, May 26, 1829. 28818

Address, Mechanic's Institute. (27530)

Address . . . Mercer University. 80429

Address . . . Mount Moriah Lodge. 32538

Address . . . Naval Academy, Newport. 30019

Address never before published. 2397

Address. . . . New Bedford Port Society. 22100

Address . . . New-England Historic-Genealogical Society. 36035

Address, . . . New-York Agricultural Society. 12412

Address . . . New York, August 1, 1838. 26712

Address, New-York, Feb. 14, 1854. 26712

Address, New York, November 1, 1864. (14120)

Address, New York State Agricultural Society. 19017

Address . . . New York State Agricultural Society, Albany, Feb. 15, 1855. 37322

Address . . . N. Y. State Agricultural Society, Albany, February 3, 1862. 26824

Address . . . New York Young Men's Christian Association. 42019

Address . . . Newport, R. I., on St. John's
Day. 33820
Address . . . November 5th, 1865. (46867)
Address . . . November 15, 1835. 4277
Address . . . November 14, 1832. 38156
Address . . . November 17, 1833. 94557
Address, Nov. 13, 1814. (16750)
Address . . . Nov. 10, 1860. 25958
Address, Nov. 24, 1863. 21628
Address occasioned by the death of Aaron
Bean. (33308)
Address, occasioned by the death of David
Mould. 33042
Address occasioned by the death of General
Lingan. 18151
Address, occasioned by the death of Nathan
Smith. 83654
Address, occasioned by the late invasion.
94718
Address, occasioned by the peace between
America and Great Britian. 51125
Address . . . October, 1844. (54729)
Address . . . October, 1838. 14535
Address . . . Oct. 11, 1871. (64308)
Address . . . October 2d, 1851. 20341
Address . . . October 2, 1856. 24766
Address . . . October 21, 1858. (13707)
Address . . . Oct. 24, 1820. (49080)
Address . . . October 26, 1842. 50030
Address of a back settler. 390
Address of a central committee. 314
Address of a committee appointed by a public
meeting. 6473
Address of a committee appointed by the
citizens of Pittsburgh. (59833)
Address of a committee of the Board of
Missions. (66127)
Address of a convention of Worcester. 45581
Address of a convention of delegates from the
Abolition Society. 81755
Address of a convention of delegates from
twenty towns. 43901, 1st note after
106023
Address of a convention of delegates of the
people of New-Jersey. 53050
Address of a faction there. 46756, 2d note
after 99797
Address of a minister . . . [inquiring] "Whether
a church is obliged . . . . " 2703
Address of a minister to the church under his
care. 52605
Address of a part of the Democratic delegation.
53476
Address of a portion of the members of the
General Assembly of Georgia. 27093,
27102, 87436, 87443
Address of Abraham Johnstone. 36390
Address of Ajax. (4024)
Address of Albert Gallatin. 78844, note before
95127, note after 95722, note after 99394
Address of Alderman Parker. (58646)
Address of . . . [Alexander Dallas] Bache.
(2588)
Address of Anti-greenbacks. 70126
Address of B. Gratz Brown. 8453
Address of B. P. Johnson. 28622
Address of Brig.-Gen. E. W. Gantt. 26543
Address of C. A. Wickliffe. 103855
Address of C. F. Adams. 20256, 45711
Address of Capt. R. F. Stockton. 106236
Address of Captain Stockton. 91890
Address of certain members [of the Quebec
Assembly.] 58489
Address of Charles D. Drake. (20814)
Address of Charles L. Chaplain. 11963
Address of Charles Robinson. 72055
Address of Chief Justice Parker. (58678)

Address of Chief Justice Robertson. 13550
Address of Christian counsel. 391
Address of Col. C. C. Crow. 17689
Address of Col. Crittendon. 56422
Address of Col. Ebenezer Dumont. (21205)
[Address of] Col. Marshall. 56422
[Address of] Col. O'Hara. 56422
Address of Col. Samuel R. Curtis. (38476),
58089
Address of Commodore R. F. Stockton. 91891
Address of condolence. 46436
Address of Congress to the people of the
Confederate States. 15231
Address [of Cotton Mather.] (37215)
Address of counsel. (74135)
Address of D. F. Boyd. 42310
Address of David T. Riley. 71392
Address of David Trimble. 96970
Address of Democratic members of Congress.
392
Address of divers minsters. 45633
Address of Dr. A. P. Dostie. 20665
Address of Dr. D. P. Gardner. (26642)
Address of Dr. Winslow Lewis. 40864
Address of E. Fontaine. 24984
Address of . . . Edmund Pendleton. (59641)
Address [of Edward A. Raymond.] 11299
Address of . . . [Edward Everett.] 23271
Address of . . . Edward Fontaine. 24984
Address of Edward O. Stevenson. 91593
Address of Elizabeth Cady Stanton. 90396
Address of Elkanah Watson, Esq. 27961, 50837
Address of Elkanah Watson, Esq. delivered before
the Berkshire Agricultural Society. 102129
Address of Epaminondas. 22679, 28282, 53477
Address of Ex.-Gov. Aaron V. Brown. (8429)
Address of Ex-Governor Bigler. 72036
Address of Ex-Gov. Hunt. 33898
Address of Ezra Cornell. 26824
Address of Francis E. Rives. 71658
Address of Friends of the Yearly Meeting of
New-York. 86023
Address of G. Burton Thompson. 65489
Address of G. Washington, on his declining a
re-election to the Presidency. 101541,
101591
Address of Gabriel Moore. (50375)
Address of General A. B. R. Sprague. 89655
Address of General Association of Pastors.
15804
Address of General H. H. Heath. 31187
Address of General James Lloyd. 41587
Address of Gen. Jacob Morris. 50837
Address of General Leslie Combs. 14927
Address of Gen. Peter B. Porter. 4061
Address of General Washington, on his resigning
the Presidency. 101559
Address of General Washington, to the United
States of America. 101556
Address of Geo. N. Sanders. 46962
Address of George W. Clinton. 13748
Address of George Washington. (61900), 101686
Address of George Washington on declining being
considered a candidate. 101686
Address of George Washington, President of the
United States, and late Commander in
Chief of the American Army. 101551,
101587
Address of George Washington, President of the
United States, Commander in Chief of their
armies. 101549
Address of George Washington, President of the
United States, to his fellow citizens.
101553, 101574, 101586, 101592, 101595
Address of George Washington, President of the
United States, to the people of America.
101552

Address of George Washington, to the people of the United States, announcing his resolution to retire from public life. 101582

Address of George Washington, to the United States of America, on his resignation. 101561

Address of Gerrit Smith. 32532

Address of Gov. Boutwell at the dedication of the Davis Monument. 6972

Address of Governor Boutwell at the dedication of the monument to the memory of Capt. Wadsworth. (6973), 93405

Address of Governor Hamilton. 66067, 88068

Address of Gov. Hamlin to the Legislature. (43944)

Address of Gov. Robert M. Patton. 59163

Address of Governor Washburn. 43943

Address of Hampden County Society. 30128

Address of Harvey Lindsly. 41317

Address of Henry B. Stanton. 90428

Address of Henry Clay. (13537), 13538

Address of Henry Clay Dean. 19021

Address of Henry S. Jennings. 36040

Address of Henry Stanbury. 90143

Address of His Excellency Edward Everett. 45582

Address of His Excellency George Washington. 101548

Address of His Excellency Governor Trumbull. 97251

Address of His Excellency John A. Andrew. 1467

Address of His Excellency Mirabeau B. Lamar. 95025

Address of His Excellency Nathaniel P. Banks, to the . . . Legislature of Massachusetts, January 7, 1858. 3206

[Address of His Excellency Nathaniel P. Banks, to the . . . Legislature of Massachusetts,] January 7, 1859. 3206

[Address of His Excellency Nathaniel P. Banks, to the . . . Legislature of Massachusetts,] January 6, 1860. 3206

Address of His Honor the Mayor. (73687)

Address of Hon. A. T. Akerman. 84808

Address of Hon. Abel Rawson. 67012

Address of Hon. Albert G. Brown. 8434

Address of Hon. Alexander H. H. Stuart. 93119

Address of Hon. Alexander H. Stephens, before the Few and Phi Gamma Societies. 91251

Address of Hon. Alexander H. Stephens, of Georgia. 91252

Address of Hon. Charles B. Penrose. 30546

Address of Hon. Charles Holden. 32471

Address of Hon. Chas. J. Jenckins. 71214

Address of Hon. Charles Theodore Russell. 65648

Address of Hon. Daniel Needham. (52231)

Address of Hon. E. Everett. 60592

Address of Hon. Edward Everett, at the consecration of the National Cemetery at Gettysburg. 27231

Address of Hon. F. W. Bird. 5533

Address of Hon. G. F. Bailey. 2730

Address of Hon. George E. Spencer. 89316

Address of Hon. George Ticknor Curtis. 18033

Address of Hon. Henry A. Reeves. 68668

Address of Hon. Henry Winter Davis. 18830

Address of Hon. Hugh McCulloch. 43124

Address of Hon. I. A. Lapham. 38979

Address of Hon. Jacob M'Lellan. 64351

Address of Hon. John C. Breckenridge. 7671

Address of Hon. John E. Bouligny. 6886

Address of Hon. John Slidell. (82136)

Address of Hon. Joseph H. Speed. 89235

Address of Hon. Myron Lawrence. 39364

Address of Hon. N. P. Banks . . . [at New York.] 3206

Address of Hon. N. P. Banks . . . from the steps of the Merchant's Exchange. 3206

Address of Hon. Nathaniel B. Borden, Mayor, at the last regular meeting of the Board of Aldermen, April, 1858. 23742

Address of Hon. Nathaniel B. Borden, Mayor . . . at the last regular meeting of the Board of Aldermen, for . . . 1858. 6406

Address of Hon. Noel Jones. (27492)

Address of Hon. Oliver Miller. (49042)

Address of Hon. R. Barnwell Rhett. 70477

Address of Hon. R. F. Stockton. 91892

Address of Hon. R. King Cutler. 18180

Address of Hon. Robert C. Winthrop. (45858)

Address of Hon. T. E. Wales. (9338)

Address of Hon. Thomas J. Hudson. 33498

Address of Hon. William Bigler. 5340

Address of Hon. William D. Murphy. 51477

Address of Hon. William H. Haywood, Jr. 31089

Address of Hon. Wm. L. Harris. 30532

Address of Hon. Zadock Pratt. (64981)

Address of Horatio Seymour at the opening of the Prison Reform Congress. 79646

Address of Horatio Seymour, before the Alumni of Madison University. 79647

Address of Hugh N. Smith. 82733

Address of investiture of . . . Ashbel P. Willard. 34518

Address of Isaac Serrill. (30907)

Address of J. Clayton Jennyns. 36052

Address of J. W. Schuckers. 77993

Address of James J. Voorkers. 100771

Address of James W. Gerard. 1679

Address of John A. Andrew. 52645

Address [of John Caldwell Calhoun.] (22237), note after 100545A

Address of John Hillyard Cameron. 10167

Address of John Lothrop Motley. 51106

Address of John G. Watmough. 102125

Address of John Prescott Bigelow. 5313

Address of . . . John Quincy Admas, delivered at Washington, July 4, 1821. 24052, 2d note after (69432), 93573

Address of John Quincy Adams to his constituents. 270

Address of Jonas Platt. 63355

Address of . . . Jonathan Roberts. 60297

Address of Joseph Parrish. 58845

Address of Joseph R. Chandler. (27492)

Address [of Joseph Wanton.] 95980

Address of Judge A. P. Upshur. 98100

Address of L. C. Norvell. (55916)

Address of L. W. Powell. (37488)

Address of Lewis Cass. 11349

Address of Major A. S. Cushman. 18124

Address of Marcus Morton at Taunton. 20256, 45711

Address of . . . Marcus Morton to the . . . Legislature. 51010

Address of . . . Mayor of . . . Lowell. 42469

Address of members of the House of Representatives of the Congress of the United States. 393, 67197, note after 93482

Address of Memucan Hunt. (33881)

Address of Messrs. Spooner, Wilson, Alley, and Miner. 89627

Address of Mr. Chambers. (11794)

Address of Mr. Everett. 23271

Address of Mr. Justice Livingston. 41635

Address of Mr. M'Lane. 43486

Address [of Mr. Ryan.] (10998)

Address of Mr. T. P. Chandler. 11884

Address of Mrs. Elizabeth Cady Stanton, delivered at Seneca Falls & Rochester, N. Y. 90397

Address of Mrs. Elizabeth Cady Stanton to the women of the republic. 65869, 90405

ADDRESS

Address of natives of Ireland to American friends. (35061)
Address of Ohio Yearly Meeting. 56876
Address of Philan. 101891
Address of Philip R. Fendall. 98425, 101950
Address of . . . President, at the laying of the corner stone. 61496
Address of Professor Benjamin Peirce. 59541
Address of Professor C. E. Stowe. 92386
Address of Prof. N. R. Smith before the Medical and Chirurgical Faculty of Maryland. 83662
Address of Professor N. R. Smith, concerning the late Dr. Jno. H. O'Donovan. 83662
Address of Republican members of the Senate and Assembly. (53478)
Address of Rev. C. P. Krauth. 60313
Address of Rev. Dr. Anderson. 76104
Address of Rev. H. E. Niles. 55310
Address of Rev. James F. Chalfant. 56377
Address of Rev. James H. Johnston. 36371
Address of Rev. John C. Young. 106085
Address of Rev. Joseph C. Stiles. 61761
Address of Rev. Joshua Bates. 3938
Address [of Rev. Mr. Hoppins.] 63467
Address of Rev. Mr. O'Gorman. (70079)
Address of Rev. President Lord. 52887
Address of Rev. W. R. de Witt. 30544
Address of Robert J. Walker. 101066
Address of Robert Wickliffe. 103863
Address of Samuel Hoar. 45711
Address of September, 1796. 70626-70628
Address of sixteen members of the Assembly of Pennsylvania. 102415
Address of Southern delegates in Congress. 402, 33930, 88335
Address of State Campaign Committee of the Republican Party of Louisiana. 42186
Address of students in Union College. 97773
Address of sundry citizens of Colleton District. 83853
Address of Teyoninhokarawen. 49846
Address of thanks to the wardens of Christ Church and St. Peters. 61420
Address of the accused. 82437
Address of the Administration Convention. 55588
Address of the Albany Republican Corresponding Committee. 586
Address of the . . . Alumni to the . . . Trustees. 54198
Address of the American Society for the Encouragement of Domestic Manufactures. 394
Address [of the Anti-masonic Convention of the County of Cayuga, N. Y.] (65820)
Address of the Antimasonic Republicans of Massachusetts. 45591
Address of the Assembly of Lower Canada. 93175
Address of the Associated Pastors of Boston. (14497)
Address of the Association of Mechanics and Other Working Men. 83655, 101926
Address of the Atlanta Register. 2292, 15232
Address of the Baptist Anti-slavery Convention held at Waterbury. 81756
Address [of the Bible and Common-Prayer Book Society of New York City.] (54116)
Address of the Bishop of New York. (64646)
Address of the Board of Direction of the . . . [New York Mercantile Library] Association. 54391
Address of the Board of Directors of the Delaware and Raritan Canal and Camden and Amboy Railroad Companies. (19406)
Address of the Board of Directors of the Presbyterian Education Society. 65194

Address of the Board of Education established by the . . . Presbyterian Church in the United States. 65141
Address of the Board of Education, to the Reformed Dutch Churches. 68769
Address of the Board of Health. 54124
Address of the Board of Managers of the American Society for Colonizing the Free People of Color. 14732
Address of the Board of Managers of the American Colonization Society. 81757
Address of the Board of Managers of the Colonization Society of the State of Maine. (43916)
Address of the Board of Managers of the Society for Improving the Condition, and Elevating the Character of Industrious Females. 85843
Address of the Board of Managers of the Washington National Monument Society. 102069
Address of the Board of Missions. 65143
Address of the Board of Trustees of the . . . [Massachusetts General] Hospital to the public. 45846
Address of the Board of Trustees of the Protestant Episcopal Theological Seminary of Maryland. 36155
Address [of the British and Foreign Freed-men's Aid Society.] 8086
Address of the Bunker Hill Monument Association. (9174)
Address of the Cameron and Lincoln Club of the City of Chicago. 12662
Address of the candidates of the American Party. 3009
Address of the carriers. 75385
Address of the Catholic lay citizens. 61421
Address of the central committee, appointed by . . . the Legislature. (45583)
Address of the Central Committee of Correspondence. 59834
Address of the Central Committee of Fauquier. 23930, 78721, 103287, note after 103287
Address of the Central Committee [of the Anti-masonic party.] 65760, 94516
Address of the Central Executive Committee of Irish Citizens. 35083
Address of the Central Finance Committee. 76535, 76647
Address of the Cherokee delegation. 12435
Address of the Cherokee Nation. 12434
Address [of the Christian Alliance.] 12900
Address of the citizens of . . . Ohio. 56871
Address of the citizens of . . . Philadelphia. 61422
Address of the citizens of Richland District. 71117
Address of the city of Baltimore. (3010)
Address of the city of Bristol. 9372, 81492
Address of the colonists. 40925
Address of the Commissioners of the Gulf and Ship Island Railroad. (49489)
Address of the committee, appointed, April 19th, 1843. 89246
Address of the committee appointed by a public meeting, held at Faneuil Hall. 81758
Address of the committee appointed at a public meeting held in Boston, December 19, 1823. 23271, 104863
Address of the committee appointed [by the Democratic meeting of delegates of Washington County, Pa.] 102011
Address of the Committee appointed by the . . . [Pennsylvania] Society [for the Prevention of Cruelty of Animals.] (60368)
Address of the committee appointed for the purpose. 45817

Address of the Committee from the State of Missouri. 20817, (49576)

Address of the Committee . . . 9th of October, 1852. (61993)

Address of the Committee of Correspondence for . . . Philadelphia. 61423

Address of the Committee of Democratic Delegates. 61424

Address of the Committee of Health. 54124

Address of the Committee of Mechanics. 54044

Address of the Committee of Safety. 53479

Address of the Committee of St. Mary's Church. (62214)

Address of the Committee of Seven. 60358

Address of the Committee of the City of New-York. 13725

Address of the Committee of the Delaware and Schuylkill Canal Company to a Committee of the Senate and House of . . . . Representatives. (19418)

Address of the Committee of the Delaware and Schuylkill Canal Company to the Committee of the Senate and House of Representatives. 39219, 60451, 62116, 84648

Address of the Committee of the Delaware and Schuylkill Canal Company, to the Committees of the Senate and House. 60046

Address of the Committee of the Grand Lodge of South-Carolina. 87846

Address of the Committee of the Greek Fund. 54045

Address of the Committee of the Pennsylvania Society for the Promotion of Internal Improvement. 60370

Address of the Committee of the State Rights, Union and Jackson Party of Kershaw District. 90644

Address of the Committee of the Town of Portsmouth. 64414

Address of the Committee of Vigilance. 54046

Address of the Committee on Premiums and Exhibitions. 25656

Address of the Committee to the people of Pennsylvania. 62090

Address of the Committee to Promote the Passage of a Metropolitan Health Bill. 54047

Address of the Commons of Lower Canada. 99597

Address of the Confederate Congress. 57656

Address of the Congregational Union in Scotland. 81759

Address of the Congress to the inhabitants. 15510

Address of the Congress to the people. 395

Address [of the Connecticut Medical Society.] 15783

Address of the Constitutional Reform Association. (10332)

Address of the Convention for Framing a Constitution. (52789)

Address of the Convention, for Framing a New Constitution of Government. 45584

Address of the Convention for Framing a New Constitution or Form of Government. 52788, 2d note after 52940

Address of the Convention of National republicans. (45050)

Address of the Convention of the Representatives of the State of New-York. 53480

Address of the Convention of 27th June, 1827. 59835

Address of the Convention to the free electors of New Jersey. 53050

Address of the Convention to the legislature. (53481)

Address of the Corporation for Relief of Poor and Distressed Presbyterian Ministers. 65129

Address of the Correspondence Committee for . . . Philadelphia. 61425

Address of the Council of Censors. 61394

Address of the Council of Censors to the freemen of Pennsylvania. 59836

Address of the Council of Censors, to the people of Vermont. 99015

Address of the Council of the Massachusetts Temperance Society. 45909

Address of the Councils and Conferences of the Society of St. Vincent de Paul. 86085

Address of the Counsellors to the Fellows. 45874

Address of the delegates in convention. (53482)

Address of the Democratic Association at Washington. 88496

Address of the Democratic Association, Washington, D. C. 96362, 101069

Address of the Democratic Central Committee of Correspondence to the people of Pennsylvania. 59837

Address of the Democratic Committee of Philadelphia. 61844

Address of the . . . Democratic Committee of Virginia. (23627)

Address of the Democratic Hickory Club. 61572

Address of the Democratic members of the legislature, to the Democratic Party in . . . Maine. (43902)

Address of the Democratic members of the legislature to the people of Maryland. 45051

Address of the Democratic members of the legislature to the people of Virginia. 100421

Address of the Democratic members of the Massachusetts Legislature. 45585

Address of the Democratic Republican Association. 54048

Address of the Democratic Republican Committee of New Castle County. 52563

Address of the Democratic Republican Committee of Pittsburgh. 13726

Address of the Democratic Republican Young Men's General Committee. 53483

Address of the Democratic State Central Committee. 59837

Address of the Democratic State Central Committee, September 19, 1863. 60619

Address of the Democratic State Convention, . . . at Utica. 53484

Address, of the Democratic State Convention, held at Syracuse. 53862

Address of the Democratic Whig Association. (61576)

Address of the Democratic Young Men's General Committee. 54049

Address of the Directing President of the Western District Agricultural and Horticultural Society. 102974

Address of the directors and commissioners. 33535

Address of the Directors [of the New-Hampshire Branch of the American Education Society.] 52862

Address of the Directors of the New York and Erie Railroad Company. (54729)

Address of the Directors of the New York Cheap Postage Association. 54756

Address of the Directors . . . [of the New York Institution for the Instruction of the Deaf and Dumb.] 54500

Address of the Directors . . . [of the Pennsylvania Institution for the Deaf and Dumb.] 60338

Address of the . . . Directors of the Preston Retreat. 65391

Address of the Directors of the Society for Promoting Theological Education. 30765

ADDRESS

Address of the Episcopal Clergy of Connecticut
to Bishop Seabury with his answer. 78556
Address of the Episcopal Clergy of Connecticut,
to the Right Reverend Bishop Seabury.
(15654), 39529, 78555
Address of the Executive Committee of the
African Mission School Society. 15717
Address of the Executive Committee, of the
American Missionary Association. (65832)
Address of the Executive Committee of the
American Tract Society, Boston. 81760
Address of the Executive Committee of the
American Tract Society to the Christian
public. 1247
Address of the Executive Committee of the
Democratic Party. 55589
Address of the Executive Committee of the
New-York State Temperance Society.
43975, 53843
Address of the Executive Committee of the
Providence Association of the Friends of
Moral Reform. 66306
Address of the Executive Committee . . . [of
the Young Men's Association for the
Suppression of Intemperance.] 106157
Address of the Executive Committee to the
people of the state. 88090
Address of the Executive Committee, with
record of proceedings. (30661)
Address of the Faneuil Hall Committee. 6781
Address of the Fayette County Corresponding
Committee. 93806
Address of the Federal Republicans. 97413
Address of the fifty-eight members of the
Virginia Legislature. 100422
Address of the Finance Committee [of the
Martyrs' Monument Association.] 94461
Address of the First Presbyterian . . . Congre-
gation. 61665
Address of the Free Constitutionalists. 397,
89604
Address of the Free Soil Association of the
District of Columbia. 20314, (81761)
Address of the Free Trade Convention. 30052
Address of the Free Trade Convention. No. III.
10889
Address of the Friends of Domestic Industry.
398, (53675), 104020
Address of the Friends of the National Adminis-
tration. 100661
Address of the General Assembly of the Presby-
terian Church in the Confederate States of
America. 396, 65130
[Address of the General Assembly to the
people.] 100072
Address of the General Association of
Connecticut to the Congregational churches.
15804
Address of the General Association of
Connecticut to the Congregational ministers
and churches. (15636)
Address of the General Association of
Connecticut to the District Associations.
15637
Address of the General Association of New
Hampshire. (52836)
Address of the General Association of New-
Hampshire, on the doctrine of the Trinity.
(52836), 105328
Address [of the General Committee appointed
by the World's Temperance Convention.]
65850
Address of the General Committee of
Correspondence. 59838
Address of the General Committee of Republican
Young Men. 54050
Address of the General Committee of the Board
of Agriculture. (53543)

Address of the General Committee of the
Federal Republicans. 54051
Address of the General Committee of the
Republicans. 15638
Address of the General Committee of Whig
Young Men, of New-York City. 103283
Address of the General Committee of Whig
Young Men of . . . New York to the
young men of the state. 54052
Address of the General Executive Committee
of the American Republican Party of . . .
New York. 54053
Address of the General Executive Committee of
the Mechanics and Other Workingmen of
. . . New York. 54054
Address of the General Union for Promoting
the Observance of the Christian Sabbath.
(26914)
Address [of the Genesee Missionary Society.]
(26923)
Address of the gentry and merchants of Boston.
6474, 95946
Address of the government of the Massachusetts
Washington Total Abstinence Society. 45913
Address of the Governor and Council of Jamaica.
35561
Address of . . . the Governor, to . . . the
General Court of New Hampshire. 52786
Address of the Governors of the . . . [New York]
Hospital to the public. (54480)
Address of the Governors of the . . . [New York]
Hospital, to their fellow citizens. (54480)
Address of the Grand Jury. 3011, 93214
Address of the Grand Lodge. 70584
Address of the Great State Convention of Friends
of the Administration. 52790
Address of the Harmonia Sacred Music Society.
(61716)
Address [of the Harrisburg National Democratic
Union Club.] 30547
Address of the Health Committee of Danvers.
(55189)
Address of the heirs, &c. 17180
Address of the Home League. 399, 32710
Address of the Hon. Abraham Lincoln. 41162
Address of the Honorable Abram P. Maury.
46959
Address of the Hon. Benj. F. Perry. 61026
Address of the Hon. C. G. Memminger. 47489
Address of the Hon. Charles B. Penrose. 60799
Address of the Hon. Charles F. Mayer. 3084
Address of the Hon. Charles L. Scott. 78248
Address of the Hon. David G. Burnet, pronounced
over the remains of the late John A.
Wharton. 94962
Address of the Honorable David G. Burnet, to
the senate. 94969
Address of the Hon. Dr. Rolph. 72873
Address of the Hon. Elbridge Gerry Spaulding,
at the Bank Officers and Bankers' Building.
89030
Address of the Hon. Elbridge Gerry Spaulding,
at the meeting of the Bankers' Association.
89031
Address of the Hon. George W. Woodward.
60755
Address of the Hon. H. A. S. Dearborn. 73630
Address of the Hon. James Dixon. 20368
Address of the Hon. John Pool. 64024
Address of the Hon. John S. Preston. 11652
Address of the Hon. John S. Sleeper. 82116
Address of the Hon. Joseph R. Chandler. 11864
Address of the Hon. Josiah Quincy. (67198)
Address of the Honourable Judge Putnam. 66841
Address of the Hon. Mr. Banks. 73947
Address of the Hon. Oliver H. Smith. 83688
[Address of the Hon. Richard Hawes.] 30927
Address of the Honourable S. F. Austin, one of
the Commissioners of Texas. 2426

Address of the Honorable Stephen F. Austin, delivered in Louisville. 95114
Address of the Honorable the Congress. 97233
Address of the Hon. the House of Commons. 31338
Address of the Honorable the Lieutenant Governour Stoughton. 92349
Address of the Hon. Timothy C. Day. (18993)
Address of the Hon. Waddy Thompson. 95536
Address of the Hon. William B. Reed. 68614
Address of the Hon. William Branch Giles. 27372
Address of the Hon. William Bross. 8385
Address of the Honorable Wm. H. Wharton. 95114
Address of the Hon. William Marvin. 45035
Address of the House of Commons. 10571
Address of the House of Representatives to the inhabitants. 45586
Address of the House of Representatives to the people of Massachusetts. 45587
Address of the inhabitants of Newfoundland. 11089
Address of the inhabitants of the towns. 52791, note after 98998
Address of the Irish liberator. (56653)
Address of the Jackson Central Committee. 45052
Address of the Jackson Convention. (50396)
Address of the Jackson State Convention. 45053
Address of the Joint Board of Directors. 10828
Address of the ladies of St. Mary's Congregation. (62214)
Address of the late George Washington, when President. 101686
Address of the late George Washington, when President, to the people of the United States. 12114, 20623, 50942, 101594, 101602
Address of the Lay Association. 72574
Address of the Lay Trustees of St. Mary's Church. (62214)
Address of the Lay Trustees to the Congregation of St. Mary's Church. (62214)
Address of the Legislative Assembly. 10601, 10602
Address of the . . . Legislative Assembly for copies of charters. 33551
Address of the Legislative Assembly, for correspondence. 10469
Address of the Legislative Council. 66990, 67007
Address of . . . the Legislative Council to Her Majesty. 10333
Address of the Legislature of the state of Tennessee. 94745
Address of the Legislature of Virginia. 100073
Address of the Legislature to the inhabitants. 45588
Address [of the Legislature] to the people of Massachusetts. 45609
Address of the Legislature to the people of . . . Massachusetts: . . . reports . . . on the late Treasury's accounts. (45589)
Address of the liquor dealers. 54055
Address of the [Literary and Philosophical Society of South Carolina.] 87868
Address of the London Anti-slavery Society. 69690, 81762
Address of the Lord Mayor and Livery of London. 15583, 98439
Address of the Lords Spiritual, and Temporal, and Commons. 104144
Address of the Louisiana Native American Association. (42185)
Address of the Loyal Leagues, Utica. 42549

Address of the Loyal National League of . . . New York, to the people of . . . New York. 53485
Address of the Loyal National League of the state of New York, . . . to the American people. 42552
Address of the M. W. Grand Master. 87841
Address of the Macedon Convention. 27850
Address of the Managers of the American Colonization Society. 14732, 81763
Address of the . . . Managers [of the American Society for Colonizing the Free People of Color.] 14732
Address of the Managers of the Apprentices' Library Company. 61475
Address of the Managers of the Bible Soceity of Virginia. 100436
Address of the Managers of the Mission Tract and Book Society. 61638
Address of the Managers of the Pennsylvania Lying-In and Foundling Hospital. 60345
Address of the Managers of the Philadelphia Bible Society. 61966
Address of the Mayor, and annual reports of the city auditor. 52957
Address of the Mayor and Commonalty of the city of Philadelphia. 62323
Address of the Mayor at the organization of the city government. 74777
Address of the Mayor, . . . of . . . New York. 54056
Address [of the Mayor of Rockland, Me.] (72398)
Address [of the Mayor] to the City Council at the organization of the city government. (75630)
Address of the Mayor to the City Council of Boston. (67258)
Address of the . . . Mayor, to the City Council of New Bedford. 52472
Address of the Mayor upon the first organization of the city government. (10141)
Address of the Mayor upon the organization of the city government, March 25, 1850. 81072
Address of the Mayor, upon the organization of the city government, March 22, 1841. 75631
Address of the members of the Assembly. 68710
Address of the members of the Constitutional Convention. (54043)
Address of the members of the General Assembly. 59839
Address of the members of the House of Representatives. 15509
Address of the merchants of the city of Norfolk. 55477
Address of the ministers of the Northern Association. 30142
Address of the minority in Congress. 70200
Address of the minority in the Virginia legislature. 100423
Address of the minority of the Council of Censors. 10662, 59956
Address of the minority of the Legislature of South Carolina. 87476
Address of the Missionary Society. 70470
Address of the National Anti-masonic Convention. 45492, 97956
Address, of the National Anti-slavery Convention. (23624)
Address of the National Compensation Emancipation Society. 51951
Address of the National Convention of Business Men. 61856
Address of the National Democratic . . . Committee of . . . New York. 54057
Address of the National Democratic Committee to the people. 2325

Address of the National Democratic Executive
Committee. 51971
Address of the National Democratic State
Central Committee. 34197
Address of the National Democratic Volunteers.
53486
Address of the . . . [National Johnson] Club.
51993
Address of the National Union Executive
Committee. 53487
Address of the Native American Conventions.
52038
Address of the New England Anti-slavery
Convention. 52655
Address of the New-York City Anti-slavery
Society. 54436
Address of the . . . [New York City Temper-
ance] Society. 54448
Address of the New-York City Young Men's
Moral Reform Society. 54450
Address of the New York . . . Colonization
Society. 54437
Address of the New York Democratic Associ-
ation of Washington. 54762
Address of the New-York Protestant Episcopal
City-Mission Society. 54526
Address of the New-York State Auxiliary Clay
Monument Association. 53813
Address of the New York Temperance Society.
54550
Address of the New York Yearly Meeting of
Friends. (54559)
Address of the New-York Young Men's Anti-
slavery Society. 54560, note after
106153
Address of the nonconformist ministers of
London. 9372, 81492
Address of the Northern Rail-Road Company.
55826
Address of the Officers and Standing Committee
of the New Jersey Monument Association.
53051
Address of the Officers of the Metropolitan
Museum of Art. (54404)
Address of the Ohio soldiers in the Army of
the Cumberland. 15877
Address of the Ohio soldiers . . . with the
correspondence. 57046
Address of the Pastor. 22327
Address of the Pennsylvania Convention, 1845.
52038
Address of the Pennsylvania Seamen's Friend
Society. 60362
Address "of the Pennsylvania Society for the
Promotion of Manufactures and the
Mechanic Arts." 60371
Address of the Pennsylvania Society for the
Promotion of Manufactures and the
Mechanic Arts, to the public. 10889
Address of the Pennsylvania State Temperance
Society. 60383
Address of the people call'd Quakers. 59840
Address of the people of Great Britain. 400,
18346
Address of the [people] of South-Carolina.
87509
Address of the People's Club of Philadelphia,
in favor of Gen. Simon Cameron for
President. (61426)
Address of the People's Club of Philadelphia,
in favor of General Simon Cameron for
the next Presidency of the U. S. 10169
Address of the Philadelphia Baptist Orphan
Society. 61964
[Address of the Philadelphia Democratic
Committee.] 60603
Address of the Philadelphia Society for the
Promotion of Domestic Industry. 51992,
62040

Address [of the Philadelphia Young Men's
Bible Society.] 62052
Address of the Postal Reform Committee.
(64518)
Address of the Presbyterian Ministers of the
city of Philadelphia. 65132
Address of the Presbytery of Elizabethtown.
22189
Address of the Presbytery of New Jersey.
(53052)
Address of the President and Managers of the
Schuylkill Navigation Company. 78079
Address of the President and Managers, of the
. . . [Union Canal] Company. 60750, note
after 97766
Address of the President, and reports of the
Treasurer. 59390
Address of the President June 23, 1866. 35849
Address of the President . . . of the Northern
Central Railway Company. (60280)
Address of the President of the Republic. 95029
Address of the President of the South-Carolina
College. 16621
Address of the President . . . on the organization
59390
Address of the President, to the people of the
United States. 101570
Address of the President to the people of the
United States on his declining being con-
sidered a candidate. 101558
Address of the Presiding Bishop. 57318
Address of the Protestant Episcopal Society in
Western New York for the Promotion of
Evangelical Knowledge. 66201
Address of the protestant pastors of France.
8124, 37781
Address of the Rector [of Christ Church.] 22193,
32397
Address of the religious society called Quakers.
66906
Address of the representatives of the counties
of New-Castle, Kent, and Sussex upon
Delaware. 52564
Address of the representatives of the religious
society of Friends called Quakers. 59841,
note after 66906, 81764
Address of the Republican and Union Democratic
Members. 53488
Address of the Republican Committee of Corre-
spondence of Philadelphia. 61427
Address of the Republican Committee. The
Second Congressional District of Minn.
(49236)
Address of the Republican convention. 59842
Address of the Republican General Committee
of the Republican electors of the state.
53489
Address of the Republican General Committee
of Young Men. 35391
Address of the Republican members of the
Legislature, of the state of New-York.
96417
Address of the Republican members of the
Legislature to the electors of . . . New
York. (53490)
Address of the Republican State Central
Committee. 70524
Address of the Republicans of . . . New York.
54058
Address of the Retiring President. 45862
Address of the Rev. Dr. Tyng. 49131
Address of the Rev. George Montgomery West.
102720
Address of the Rev. Horace James. 35702
Address of the Rev. J. McCarrell. 95313
Address of the Rev. Robert Heys. 94505A
Address of the Rhode Island State Republican
Committee. 70525

Address of the Rhode-Island State Temperance Society. 70737
Address of the Right Rev. Bishop Hobart. 103464
Address of the Right Rev. Henry U. Onderdonk. 57317
Address of the Rt. Rev. . . . Jas. H. Otey. 65790
Address of the Roman Catholics [of New York.] 54615
Address of the Roman Catholics to their fellow-citizens. (54059)
Address of the St. Louis Capital Committee. 75337
Address of the Schuylkill and Delaware Canal Company. 78069
Address of the Scott Corresponding Club of Maryland. 89275
Address of the Senate to the people. 46031
Address of the seventeenth of September, 1796. 96800
Address of the . . . Society [for the Conversion and Religious Instruction and Education of the Negroe Slaves.] 85878
Address of the Society for the Encouragement of American Manufactures. 15649
Address of the Society of Constitutional Republicans. 62258
Address of the . . . Society to the citizens of Pennsylvania. 62036
Address of the Southern and Western Liberty Convention held at Cincinnati, June 11 & 12, 1845. 88294
Address of the Southern and Western Liberty Convention, held at Cincinnati, June 11, 1845. 88296
Address of the Southern and Western Liberty Convention, to the people of the United States. (81765), 88295
Address of the Southern delegates in Congress. 402
Address of the Southern Rights Association of South Carolina College. 87967
Address of the Southern Rights Association of Yazoo County. 88480
Address of the Starksborough and Lincoln Anti-slavery Society. 81766, note after 90530
Address of the State Central Committee of the National Union Democracy. 45145
Address of the State Committee of Correspondence. 39888, 59843
Address of the State Committee of Republicans. 59844
Address of the state convention, held at Trenton. 96771
Address of the state convention, Middletown. (15650)
Address of the state convention of delegates. 53491, 82598
Address of the State Convention of Teachers and Friends of Education. 53492
Address of the State Temperance Alliance. 46142
Address of the State Temperance Committee. 46143
Address of the Synod of Kentucky. (81767)
Address of the Synod of New York and Philadelphia. 65133
Address of the Tammany Society of New-York. 104984
[Address of the teacher, M. Miner.] (77813)
Address of the Temporary Home Association. (62303)
Address of the True Republican Party. 87941
Address of the Trustees and Treasurer. 60729
Address of the Trustees; [of Burlington College, N. J.] 9337

Address of the Trustees . . . [of St. Mary's Church] to the congregation. (62214)
Address of the Trustees of St. Mary's Church to their fellow-citizens. (62214)
Address of the Trustees of the College of New-Jersey. (53087)
Address of the Trustees of the Evangelical Missionary Society. (45724)
Address of the Trustees . . . [of the Massachusetts General Hospital.] 45846
Address of the Trustees of the New-England Institution for the Education of the Blind. 52691
Address of the Trustees of the New York Society Library. 54542
Address of the Trustees of the Public School Society. 54615
Address of the Trustees of the University of Pennsylvania. 60758
Address of the Trustees of the Washington Monument Association. 102025
Address of the Trustees of Williams College. 104414
Address of the Twelve United Colonies of North America, by their representatives in Congress. 403, 15512, (35062), (41651)
Address of the Twelve United Colonies to the inhabitants of Great Britain. (404)
Address of the Unconditional Union State Central Committee. 31867
Address of the Union Electorial Committee. 53493
Address of the Union League . . . to the citizens of Pennsylvania. 62352
Address of the Union League . . . to the citizens of Philadelphia. 62352
Address of the Union members of the Legislature. 56870
Address of the Union State Central Committee of Maryland. (47091)
Address of the Union State Central Committee of Pennsylvania. 59845, 60751
Address of the Union State Central Committee, with the proceedings of the meeting. 45054
Address of the United States Anti-masonic Convention. 32529, 97957
Address of "The United Whig Club." 43614
Address of the University of Free Medicine & Popular Knowledge. 62360
Address of the University of Maryland. (45386)
Address of the Vestry of Christ Church, Hagerstown. 45055
Address of the Virginia Anti-Jackson Convention. 100500
Address of the Visitors and Governors of St. John's College. 75285
Address [of the Washington Monument Association, Boston.] 65821, 102026
Address of the Washington Monument Association of the First School District of Pennsylvania. 62376
Address of the Washington Society. 102035, 102036
Address of the Western Association of New-Haven County. 102965
Address of the Whig Central Committee of Vigilance. 23930, 78721, 103287, note after 103287
Address of the Whig Convention at Concord. 48852
Address of the Whig Convention for the Nomination of Electors. 100574, note after 103285
Address of the Whig members of the Legislature. 103281
Address of the Whig members of the Senate. (67260)

Address of the Whig State Convention. 70526
Address of the Whig Young Men's Convention.
2nd note after 103271, 104861
Address of the women of England. 13864
Address of the women of England to their
sisters of America. 43335
Address of the Worcester Convention. 45590
Address of the Yearly Meeting of Friends for
New England. 52606
Address of the Yearly Meeting of the religious
society of Friends, held in the city of
New York. 54060, 81768
Address of the Yearly Meeting of the religious
society of Friends, on the slave-trade
and slavery. 65774
Address of the young men of Philadelphia.
61428
Address of the Young Men of the National
Republican Party. 45056
Address of the Young Men's Colonization
Society. 81769
Address of the . . . [Young Men's Moral Reform
Society.] 106180
Address [of the Young Men's Society for the
Promotion of Temperance.] 106182
Address of the Young Men's Temperance Society.
106187
Address of Theodore Sedgwick. (78832)
Address of Thomas Bodley. 6113
Address of Thomas D. Eliot. 22175
Address of Thomas Gales Forster. 25145
Address of Thomas L. Clingman. (13707)
Address of Thomas Melvill. (47477)
Address of Thomas Swann, Esq. May 1 [1850.]
2992
Address of Thomas Swann, Esq. (President).
2992
Address of thousands. 62652, note before 93501
Address of Trustees, narrative of missions, &c.
15806
Address of Valentine Mott. (51120)
Address of W. C. Rives. 71659
Address of W. H. Trescott. (22284), 87514
Address of Wm. Bacon Stevens. 91580
Address of William Leigh. 39932
Address of William M. Dickson. 20098
Address of William Smith. 84705
Address of William T. Barry. (3692)
Address of working men of Pittsburgh. 63105
Address on African slavery. 58631
Address on agriculture. (9202)
Address on American independence. 4721
Address on American literature. 17652
Address on American Odd-Fellowship. (71287)
Address on American slavery. 61244
Address on an outline of a system of public
schools. 67766
Address on ardent spirit. 51594
Address on behalf of the Deinologian Society.
71947
Address on behalf of the Infant School Society.
103178
Address on behalf of the Seamen's Widow and
Orphans' Association. 51192
Address on Christian education. 92184
Address on church music. 45472
Address on confederation. 64124
Address on education, as connected with the
permanence of our republican institutions.
49315
Address on education before the two houses of
the General Assembly. 79762
Address on embalming. 18731
Address on . . . establishing a pattern farm.
47270
Address on female education. 28365
Address on female education. Delivered at
Newark. 105239

Address on female education, . . . Nov. 21st,
1827. 26406
Address on free medical schools. 18872
Address on giving the right hand of fellowship.
85263
Address on his [i. e. Washington Irving's] life
and genius. 35221
Address on imprisoning the unfortunate debtor.
22533
Address . . . on Indian affairs. 37354
Address on infant schools. (74387)
Address on intemperance. 865
Address . . . on laying the corner stone of the
Academy of Natural Sciences of Phila-
delphia. 36334
Address on laying the corner stone of the
Masonic Hall. 51277
Address on legal tenders. (12372)
Address on . . . Manual Labor School. 39226
Address on medical jurisprudence. 92190
Address on music. 104717
Address on national art. 92061
Address on occasion of the bi-centennial services.
89044
Address on occasion of the funeral of John T.
McCoun. 37395
Address, on occasion of the gathering of his
[Col. Benjamin Bellows'] descendants. 4570
Address on our destiny. 72645
Address on pauperism. 76981
Address on . . . peace, . . . and war. 28862
Address on peace. Issued by the Yearly Meeting
of Friends. (52607)
Address on popular education. 8710
Address on religious intollerance. 25102
Address on re-opening the slave trade. 49014
Address on sacred musick. 105300
Address on sacred music at Hampton, N. H.
18405
Address on sacred Music . . . Princeton, N. J.
52422
Address, on St. John's Day. (30402)
Address on secession. 28676
Address on secession. Delivered in South
Carolina in . . . 1851. 40985
Address on secession written in the year 1851.
40985
Address on slavery, and against immediate
emancipation. 31645, 73942, 81770
Address on slavery. Delivered in Danvers, Mass.
25207
Address on slavery in Cuba. (43697)
Address on slavery, Sabbath protection, and
church reform. 20688
Address on some of the duties of the American
citizen. 44234
Address on success in business. 28492
Address on "suffrage and reconstruction." 29994
Address on temperance. 11906
Address on temperance . . . at West Sandwich,
Mass. 44753
Address on temperance; delivered at the Court
House in Lexington. 106086
Address on temperance, . . . May 16, 1842.
44812
Address on temperance, . . . Salem, January 14,
1830. 59559
Address on Thanksgiving Day. 77425
Address on Thanksgiving Day, November 20, 1845.
56947
Address, on that occasion, by W. Gilmore Simms.
81266
Address on the acts and deliverances of the
General Assembly. 83385
Address on the advantages and disadvantages to
America. 19571
Address, on the advantages and facilities. 9899
Address . . . on the advantages of low fares.
19305

Address on the amelioration of the social state. 10206

Address on the Anglo Saxon destiny. 1386

Address . . . on the annexation of Texas. (64637)

Address on the annexation of Texas, and the aspect of slavery. 62518

Address on the anniversary of American independence. 19811

Address . . . on the anniversary of the birth-day of Washington. (13176)

Address . . . on the anniversary of the constitution. 20817

Address on the anniversary of Washington's birth-day. 77715

Address, on the annual commencement of the College of New Jersey. 34750

Address . . . on the . . . anti-masonic excitement. 39191

Address on the aspect of national affairs. 36345

Address on the birth-day of General Washington. 25675

Address . . . on the birthday of Linnaeus. 35816

Address on the botany of the United States. 28526

Address . . . on the celebration of the abolition of slavery. 59180

Address . . . on the celebration of the fiftieth anniversary of the Sunday School Institution. 26536

Address . . . on the centennial anniversary of St. John's Lodge. 50332

Address on "the changes of a century." 23938

Address on the character and example of President Lincoln. 12211

Address on the character and services of De Witt Clinton. 33904

Address on the character and services of George Washington. (24770)

Address on the character of the colony. 6913

Address on the character . . . of the late Daniel Seymour. (37317)

Address . . . on the . . . close of the second century. 89659

Address on the condition and office of the Agricultural College. (24527)

Address on the consecration, and installation of the officers of Olive Branch Lodge. 84859

Address on the consecration of the Spring Grove Cemetery. 43516

Address on the constitution. 21867

Address on the death of Abraham Lincoln . . . delivered by J. W. Ricks. (71245)

Address on the death of Abraham Lincoln, President of the United States. 18733

Address on the death of Alfred Mason. 12388

Address on the death of Austin Stowell. (35748)

Address on the death of Charles Carroll. (39267)

Address on the death of General Nathaniel Lyon. 31311

Address on the death of President Lincoln, delivered at the request of the citizens of New Rochelle. 25311

Address on the death of President Lincoln, . . . in . . . North Attleboro'. 59551

Address on the death of the Hon. James A. Pearce. 59433

Address, on the death of the venerable and illustrious Adams and Jefferson. 105568

Address on the death of William Moore De Rham. 43679

Address . . . on the dedication of Magnolia Cemetery. 25675

Address on the deplorable state of the Indians. 8195, 8198

Address on the duties of government. (3441)

Address on the early history of St. Lawrence County. 33154

Address on the early reminiscences. 3845

Address on the education of woman. 58372, 92771

Address on the encroachments of the slave power. (50417)

Address on the Epizooty. 85493

Address on the errors of husbandry. 41790

Address on the formation of the Society. 36035

Address, on the 4th of July, 1807. 51595

Address on the free-soil question. 51440

Address on the history, authority and influence of slavery. 24093

Address on the history of California. 67820

Address on the immorality of the traffic. 88815

Address on the importance and best method. 105659

Address on the importance of a well regulated militia. 18451

Address, . . . on the importance of encouraging agricultural and domestic manufactures. 18152

Address on the improvement of baptism. 90192

Address on the influence of the federative and republican system. 19836

Address, on the introduction of historical studies. 92118

Address on the Iroquois. 54476

Address on the land policy of the United States. 23925

Address . . . on the late frauds. 26797

Address on the laying of the foundation stone. (77428)

Address on the life and character of Abraham Howard Quincy. (16652)

Address on the life and character of Abraham Lincoln. 24289

Address on the life and character of Andrew Wylie. 58976

Address on the life and character of Colonel Edward D. Baker. 24590

Address on the life and character of Gen. William Henry Harrison. 17288

Address on the life and character of James Dean. 6988

Address on the life and character of Rev. Dr. A. B. Longstreet. 84992

Address on the life and character of the late Francis R. Shunk. 11847

Address on the life and character of Washington. 81495

Address on the life and character of William Smyth. 58096, 85345

Address on the life and public services of Hon. Edwin M. Stanton. 36387

Address on the life, character and public services of B. W. Leigh. 42344

Address on the life, character and public services of Henry Clay. 50330

Address on the life . . . of Elisha Bartlett. (33952)

Address on the life . . . of Robert M. Porter. 41312

Address on the maritime rights of Great Birtain. 21823

Address on the means of opening new sources of wealth. (26931)

Address on the means of promoting common school education. 68147

Address on the necessity of education. 92916

Address on the Northwest. 91521

Address on the occasion of dedicating the monument. 1466

Address, . . . on the occasion of his [i. e. Calvin Pease's] inauguration. 59457

Address . . . on the occasion of his [i. e. William G. T. Shedd's] inauguration. (80080)

Address on the occasion of the annual commencement. 82353

Address on the occasion of the centennial celebration. 60330

Address on the occasion of the dedication of the New York Conference Academy. 30097

Address on the occasion of the funeral obsequies. 67778

Address on the occasion of the laying of the corner stone. 31429

Address on the occasion of the return of the Kentish Guards. (17406)

Address on the one hundredth and thirtieth anniversary. 29678

Address . . . on the opening of the Apprentices' Library. 47897

Address . . . on the . . . opening of the Collegiate Department. (37423)

Address on the opening of the new Town Hall in Braintree. 180

Address . . . on the organization of city government. 6742

Address on the past, present and eventual relations. 405, (20042)

Address on the patent laws . . . before the Franklin Institute. 37006

Address on the patent laws delivered on invitation. 27335

Address on the patriot character. 28862

Address on the peninsula of Sabino. 59139

Address on the position in regard to slavery. (61360)

Address on the present condition and prospects of the aboriginal inhabitants of North America. 62737

Address on the present condition, prospects and duties of the medical profession. (70407)

Address on the present condition, resources, and prospects of British North America. 29679

Address . . . on the present state of polite learning. 23237

Address on the presentation of the Gold Medal. 19363

Address on the prevention of pauperism. (11905)

Address on the progress of agriculture. 47270

Address on the progress of manufactures. 36616

Address on the progress of popular science. (80466)

Address on the proposed bill. 67711

Address on the proposed federation. 29678

Address on the propriety of continuing the state geological survey. 10009

Address on the recent progress of geological research. 72655

Address on the recognition of the church. 12121, (50948), 91812

Address on the religious history of the college. 85224

Address on the "religious test." 26790

Address . . . on the removal of the municipal government. 57860, 89659

Address, on the return of peace. 90967

Address on the right of free suffrage. 42730

Address on the scientific life and labors of William C. Redfield. (57238)

Address on the seventy-fifth anniversary. (25243)

Address on the several subjects of science. (26931)

Address on the slave trade and slavery. 10675, 51822

Address on the slave trade and slavery, to sovereigns. 86024

Address . . . on the state of slavery. 81771

Address on the state of the colonies. 10599

Address on the state of the country, at the Assembly Chamber. 83025

Address on the state of the country. Delivered by John Jay. 35836

Address on the state of the public mind. 105582, 105588, 105596

Address, on the state of the union. 12823

Address on the subject of a free library. 53353

Address on the subject of a mariner's church. 54061

Address, on the subject of a surveying and exploring expedition. 70430, 70432

Address, on the subject of African slavery. 104550

Address, on the subject of an "American Academy of Language and Belles-Lettres." 10801

Address on the subject of a common school education. 105660

Address on the subject of democracy. 88223

Address on the subject of education. 94042

Address on the subject of missions. 15639

Address on the subject of peace. 91039

Address on the subject of petitioning the General Assembly. 84920

Address on the subject of the approaching presidential election. 88084

Address on the subject of the late presidential election. (13547)

Address on the subject of the Southwestern Railroad. (64119)

Address on the subject of the usury laws. 26403

Address on the subject of theatrical amusements. 86025

Address on the teacher's calling. 43340

Address on the tendency of our system of intercourse. 30049

Address on the time. 80455

Address . . . on the 26th . . . May, 1836. 62734

Address on the unveiling of the statue of Columbus. 72198

Address on the visit of the Prince of Wales. 77429

Address on this subject. 24274

Address on university progress. 33408

Address on West India emancipation. 104551

Address . . . opening of the Convention of Teachers and of the Friends of Education. 33794

Address, . . . opening of the Medical College. 22276

Address . . . opening of the Wills Hospital. 34750

Address or resignation of our worthy President. 101581

Address, Palmyra, Missouri. 27325

Address . . . Pennsylvania Colonization Society. 34750

Address . . . Pennsylvania Peace Society. (11866)

Address, petition, and memorial of the representatives of the freeholders of Nova Scotia. 56110

Address, petition and memorial, to the King's Most Excellent Majesty. (56128)

Address. Philadelphia, Oct. 1, 1772. 61443

Address . . . Philadelphia, on September 9th, 1856. 37272

Address, poem, and other proceedings. 64620

Address . . . Portsmouth . . . July 4, 1828. (31832)

Address prefixed, as adopted by the State Rights' and Free Trade Party of Charleston. 88063

Address preparatory to opening the Department of the Arts and Sciences. 25935
Address prepared at the request of the Ministerial Union. 91915
Address prepared by order of the Anti-masonic Convention. 79255
Address, prepared by Rev. Joseph I. Foot. 25005
Address . . . presented . . . December 31, 1834. 66306
Address . . . presented to a Mutual Council. 39771
Address presented to John Lord Lovelace. 86960
Address, presented to the members of the Faustus Association. (74399)
Address, pronounced at the opening of the New-York Athenaeum. 103151
Address pronounced at Worcester. 7496
Address pronounced before the House of Convocation. 3454
Address pronounced before the Massachusetts Horticultural Society. 101315
Address, pronounced before the Massachusetts Horticultural Society . . . 10th of September, 1830. 16300
Address pronounced before the medical graduates of the University of Maryland, April 7th, 1828. 83658
Address pronounced before the medical graduates of the University of Maryland, April 6th, 1829. 83659
Address pronounced before the Order of the United States of America. 8373
Address pronounced . . . 1857. 88005
Address pronounced in the Representatives' Hall. 95473
Address, pronounced in Worcester, (Mass.) 2421
Address pronounced on the anniversary of the Concord Lyceneum. (24040)
Address, pronounced on the first Tuesday of March, 1831. 95184
Address, proposing a plan of common school education. 69634
Address . . . public schools, . . . New Orleans. 42969
Address, read at the close of the autumn term. 74389
Address read at the last meeting. 82675
Address read at the opening of the Pennsylvania Hall. 103804
Address read before the Conference of Baptist Ministers. 79784
Address read before the Directors of the American Academy of Fine Arts. 97241
Address read before the Long Island Historical Society. 7754
Address, read before the Religious Historical Society. 105668
Address read before the Western New Church Convention. 93184
Address read before the Young Ladies' Literary Society. 78593
Address read by James Biddle. 5233
Address recommending the society to public patronage. 54674
Address. Rectitude in national policy essential. 106084
Address . . . Red Hook, September 11th, 1864. 63353
Address, Rensselaer County Agricultural Society. 18822
Address, reported by Mr. Van Buren. 55414
Address, reports, and memorials to Congress. (16200)
Address, resolution, and proceedings of the County Law Reform and Working Men's Convention. 52792

Address, resolutions, and other proceedings of a public meeting. 35391
Address, resolutions & proceedings of the Anti-monopoly State Convention. (53053)
Address . . . Richmond, on the occasion of the funeral of Rev. William Meade. (36157)
Address, . . . Richmond, Va. 24710
Address. Rochester, N. Y. 14535
Address . . . Rogersville, Tenn. 42960
Address, St. John's Day. 42940
Address . . . St. Mary's College. (39807)
Address . . . Salem, March 13, 1863. (58703)
Address . . . Savannah Medical College. 22276
Address, . . . September, 1845. 56971
Address . . . Sept. 18th, 1850. 37272
Address . . . September 18, 1850, before the Middlesex Society of Husbandmen and Manufacturers. (6977)
Address, Sept. 4, 1849. (82711)
Address, . . . September 20th, 1828. 7666
Address . . . September 20, 1865. 9133
Address . . . September 22, 1864. 17921
Address . . . September 26, 1850. 18095
Address, showing the means to prevent wars. 24444
Address . . . Society of Associated Mechanics and Manufacturers. 28660
Address, spoken at the funeral of the Rev. George Whitney. 66778
Address spoken before the New England Society of Montreal. 16761
Address, spoken before the Society at an adjourned anniversary meeting. 100556
Address spoken in the College Chapel, Cambridge. 66779
Address. Subject: General Washington. 62671
Address . . . Sunday School Union. 24377
Address, . . . Temperance Society of Bath. (38027)
Address. The claims of the Academy of Natural Sciences of Philadelphia to public favor. 74181
[Address, the constitution, and the first annual report of the Virginia Religious Tract Society.] 100564
Address . . . the Sabbath following the assassination of President Lincoln. 51548
Address to a friend in the country. 95382
Address to a horse chestnut. 97621
Address to a meeting of the citizens of Philadelphia. 23356, 98626, 104632
Address to a Presbyterian Church. 89259
Address to a provincial Bashaw. 12978
Address to all believers in Christ. 83147
Address to all honorably discharged soldiers. 86322
Address to all impartial men. (31176)
Address to all play-actors. 21923
Address to all the churches. 6920
Address to all the good people of England. 97153
Address to an assembly of the friends of American manufactures. 406
Address to an enterprising public. 104289
Address to and by Schuyler Hamilton. 30031
Address to, and expostulation with, the public. 18348, 90092
Address to anti-slavery societies. 81772
Address to Baptist ministers. 81773
Address to Brian Edwards. 91599
Address to Brigadier General D. Henrique Martinez. 94859
Address to British emigrants. 5565
Address to Calliopean Society of Wabash College. 4299
Address to candid men of all parties. 63796
Address to Capt. Evelyn Sutton. 91598
Address to chambers of commerce. 42187
Address to Christian parents. 99161

Address to Christians. 25250
Address to Christians of all denominations. 40802
Address to Christians of every denomination. 407
Address to Christians throughout the world. (15233)
Address to Christians throughout the world, by a convention of ministers. 81774
Address to Congress. (13897), note after 101860
Address to Congress: being a view of the ruinous consequences. 10889
Address to Congress, on the resignation of his [i. e. George Washington's] commission. 101530
Address to contributors. 5470
Address, to Dr. Ley. 29592
Address to Edmund Burke. 96183
Address to Edward Purse. 95439
Address to emigrants. 15643
Address to Episcopalians, on the subject of the American Bible Society. (32301)
Address to every Britain. 81775
Address to every class of British subject. 69003
Address to every free-man. (4478)
Address to federal clergymen. 537
Address to Friends in North America. 86026
Address to Friends on the order and discipline. (14954)
Address to Friends; or, can all professing to be Friends become united? 65434
Address to Friends prepared by the Committees of the Yearly Meetings. 86027
Address to Friends within the compass of the Yearly Meeting held in Philadelphia. 59846
Address to Friends within the compass of the Yearly Meetings held in Philadelphia. 61429
Address to General Lafayette. 38583
Address to General William Tyron. 15642
Address to Governor Gordon. 59847
Address to her [i. e. the Virginia girl's] Maryland lover. 88492
Address to his [i. e. Joseph Huntington's] Anabaptist brethren. 92930
Address . . . to his [i. e. Richard Goodloe Harper's] constituents. 30424
Address . . . to his [i. e. T. Chilton's] constitutents, Feb. 27, 1837. 12809
Address to his [i. e. Samuel Taggart's] constituents, on the subject of impeachments. 94207
Address to his [i. e. Richard Fletcher's] constitutents, relative to the speech delivered by him in Faneuil Hall. 24735
Address to his [i. e. English freeholder's] countrymen. 22612, 106378A
Address to his [i. e. Tradesman's] countrymen. 60730, 62341, note after 96429
Address to His Excellency Sir Charles Hardy. (30352), (41640)
Address to his [i. e. Citizen of New York's] fellow-citizens. 53494
Address to his [i. e. John Stannage's] friends in Jersey. 90354
Address to his [i. e. Henry W. Bellows'] own congregation. 4572
Address to his [i. e. Samuel Thayer Spear's] people. 89087, 89093
Address to his [i. e. Robert Heys'] society in Douglas. 94505
Address to holders of Minnesota state bonds. 49237
Address to Hon. Admiral Augustus Keppel. 91598

Address to its [i. e. the Society of Worcester County and Vicinity's] patrons. 105392
Address to J. Sayre. (77412)
Address to John Hancock. 47955
Address to Joseph Fish. 2627
Address to King Cotton. 59582
Address to . . . Lord Glenelg. 71390
Address (to Ld. H. P., and) to the British Parliament. 85250
Address to Major-General Tryon. 53495, 97291
Address to manufacturers, traders, and others. (409)
Address to mechanics. 71544
Address to medical graduates. (21278)
Address to men of all parties. 410
Address to members of Congress. 73753, 81776
Address to members of the United Church of England and Ireland. 39761
Address to Miss Phillis Wheatley. 103142
Address to Mr. Silas Deane. (19067), 86193
Address to Mr. Wilberforce. 32747
Address to my [i. e. Isaac Wikoff's] fellow citizens. (61430), 7th note after 103943
Address to our congregations. 99543
Address to our landed, trading and funded interests. 72150
Address to parents and the public. (52483)
Address to parents, upon the importance of religiously educating their children. 104529
Address to persons of fashion. 411
Address to persons who entertain the wish to better themselves. 10434
Address to philanthropists. 43109
Address to physicians. 54448, 54550
Address to President Tyler. 52655
Address to protestant dissenters. 65500
Address to protestants of all perswasions. 59675
Address to protestants upon the present conjuncture. 59675
Address to sailors. 51233
Address to . . . seamen. 54373
Address to seamen, . . . in Portland. (59309)
Address to several distinct classes of professors. 103569
Address to several of the cabinet ministers. 58411
Address to Silas Deane. (19067)
Address to Sir John Cust. 78127
Address [to some in New-England.] 12914
Address to sovereigns, &c. (49341)
Address to sovereigns on slave trade. (81777)
Address to students. 97799
Address to such as wish to avail themselves. 703
Address to such of the Quakers as are desirous of supporting the testimony of their ancestors. 66907
Address to the abolitionists of Massachusetts. 45817
Address to the Agricultural Society of Maryland. 47010
Address to the Agricultural Society of Portage County. 96424
Address to the Agricultural Society of the County of Oneida. 17213
Address to the alumni and graduates of St. John's College. 33822
Address to the alumni and students of St. John's College. 67775
Address to the Alumni Association of Brown University. 63048
Address to the alumni of Columbia College. 50429
Address to the alumni . . . of St. John's College. 41834
Address to the alumni of the University of the City of New York. 20897

Address to the Alumni Society of Nashville University. 91250

Address to the . . . American Antiquarian Soceity. (52955)

Address to the American Association for the Advancement of Science. 83003

Address to the American Association . . . on retiring from the office of President. 28097

Address . . . to the American Friendly Association. 33839

Address to the American people. 15927

Address to the American people [by the National Convention of Colored Men, Syracuse, 1864.] 65883

Address to the American people, upon the subject of rotation to public office. 95856

Address to the American Society for Colonizing the Free People of Colour of the United States. (9239), 81778

Address to the Americans at Edinburgh. 22789

Address to the Ancient and Honorable Society of Free and Accepted Masons. 97622

Address to the annual convention of the Medical Society. 49202

Address to the annual subscribers. 14251

Address to the anti-masons of Lancaster County. 65808

Address to the anti-slavery Christians. 81779, 1st note after 95774

Address to the armies of the United States. 33804

Address to the army and navy. 78745

Address to the army; in reply to strictures by Roderick M'Kenzie. 30226

Address to the Assembly of Jamaica. 23530

Address to the Assembly of Pennsylvania. 59848

Address to the Assembly of the Friends of American Manufactures. 17293

Address to the Association of the Southern Part of Litchfield County. 93066

Address to the author of a pamphlet. (26423), 26442

Address to the authorities of the town of Kingston-upon-Hull. 30693

Address to the Baptist Church in Middletown, Vt. 103460

Address to the Baptists of the United States. (79362)

Address to the benefactors and friends. 13724

Address to the Beneficient, Richmond-Street and High-Street Congregational Churches. 97800

Address to the Benevolent Fraternity of Churches. 42149

Address to the biennial convention. (28881)

Address to the Board of Aldermen, and members of the Common Council of Boston, on the organization of the city government at Faneuil Hall. 67199

Address to the Board of Aldermen, and members of the Common Council, of Boston, on the organization of the city government, January 1, 1827. 67201

Address to the Board of Aldermen, and members of the Common Council of Boston, on the organization of the city government, January 2, 1826. 67200

Address to the Board of Aldermen and members of the Common Council on the organization of the city government, January 1, 1828. 67202

Address to the Board of Aldermen, of the city of Boston. (67203)

Address to the Board of Supervisors. 28444

Address to the Board of Trade. 74304

Address to the booksellers of the United States. 61431

Address to the brethren of Hiram Lodge No. 7. 103124

Address to the British public, on the case of Brigadier Picton. 20894

Address to the British public respecting Col. Fremont's leasing powers. (32393)

Address, to the Calvinistic Society in Springfield. 89883

Address to the candidates for degrees and licences. 49202, 105918

Address . . . to the candidates for the Baccalaureate. 47005

Address to the candidates for the degree of Doctor of Medicine. 103784

Address to . . . the catholic bishop of Pennsylvania. 10899, 30414

Address to the catholic citizens of Baltimore. 104445

Address, to the Charitable Fire Society. 96374

Address to the Charlestown Artillery Company. 93719

Address to the chiefs and people of that [i. e. Seneca] nation. 79108

Address to the children. 20903

Address to the Christian churches in Kentucky. 92025

Address to the Christian Negroes in Virginia. 23931

Address to the Christian public, by the Trustees of the Western Missionary Society. 60780, 102995

Address to the Christian public, in two parts. 28628, 42791, 104113, 104117

Address to the "Christian reader." 18475, 18476, 24579, (44077), 80263, 95195, 104654

Address to the Christians throughout the world. 408

Address to the church and congregation. 95154

Address, to the churches and congregations. (23696)

Address, to the churches of Jesus Christ. 23134, 54264, (81780)

Address to the churches of the Middlesex Consocation. 48843

Address to the churchmen of the United States. 102584

Address "To the citizens of Alabama" by the Trustees. 64946

Address to the citizens of Alabama, on the constitution and laws of the Confederate States of America. 83870

Address to the citizens of Albany, and the donors and friends of the Dudley Observatory. 21094

Address to the citizens of Albany, on the Albany & Susquehanna R. R. 593

Address to the citizens of America. 5183, 2d note after 97146

Address to citizens of Arkansas. 36288

Address to citizens of Boston, and memorials to the city government. 6475

Address to the citizens of Boston and vicinity. 6476

Address to "The citizens of Boston," by Mr. H. Williams. (11905)

Address to the citizens of Boston [December, 1816.] 45846

Address to the citizens of Boston . . . on poison. 82493

Address to the citizens of Boston, on the XVIIth of September. 67204

Address to the citizens of Connecticut. 12279, (15640), 102333

Address to the citizens of Kent. 40245

Address to the citizens of Louisiana, on the subject of the recent election in New Orleans. 11598

Address to the citizens of Louisiana. Proceedings in Congress. 18181

Address to the citizens of Massachusetts, on the approaching state elections. (45592)

Address to the citizens of Massachusetts on the causes and remedy of our national distresses. 45593, 58627

Address to the citizens of New Hampshire. 52793

Address to the citizens of New Hampshire, on the approaching election. 52794

Address to the citizens of New Hampshire upon a subject of the greatest importance. 52795

Address to the citizens of New Orleans. 37272

Address to the citizens of New Orleans, on . . . temperance. (53304)

Address to the citizens of New York. (42855)

Address to the citizens of New-York, on the claims of Columbia College. 14803

Address to the citizens of Norfolk County, exposing the absurdity of the arguments most commonly urged. (73945)

Address to the citizens of Norfolk County, exposing the absurdity of the present war. (73946)

Address to the citizens of Pennsylvania. 59849

Address to the citizens of Pennsylvania, in favor of a railroad. 61950

Address to the citizens of Pennsylvania on the . . . more liberal encouragement of agriculture. 59850

Address to the citizens of Pennsylvania, on the situation of our country. 60787

Address to the citizens of Pennsylvania relative to the election. 30360

Address to the citizens of Pennsylania, upon . . . a life insurance company. 59851

Address to the citizens of . . . Philadelphia, and constitution [of the Provident Society for the Employment of the Poor.] (62107)

Address to the citizens of Philadelphia; containing additional proofs. 74239

Address to the citizens of Philadelphia, in favor of Texas. 61432

Address to the citizens of Philadelphia, in favor of the Philadelphia, Easton and Water Gap Rail-Road. (61951)

Address to the citizens of Philadelphia, on . . . establishing an asylum. 61435

Address to the citizens of Philadelphia, on the advantages from the trade of the western country. (61433)

Address to the citizens of Philadelphia, on the great advantages which arise from the trade of the western country. 94381

Address to the citizens of Philadelphia, on the subject of fancy fairs. 61434, 62192

Address to the citizens of Philadelphia, on the subject of slavery. 2315

Address to the citizens of Philadelphia, respecting the better government of youth. 13474

Address to the citizens of Pittsburgh. 102284

Address to the citizens of Providence. 28581

Address to the citizens of Rhode Island, in answer to their call. 9235

Address, to the citizens of Rhode-Island, on the choice of electors. 70527

Address to the citizens of Rhode Island who are denied the right of suffrage. 70528

Address to the citizens of Richmond. 6827

Address to the citizens of Salem and vicinity. 85508

Address to the citizens of South Bend. 87334

Address to the citizens of South Carolina. 19682, 3d note before 97733

Address to the citizens of Taunton. 51009

Address to the citizens of the colony of Plymouth. 63489

Address to the citizens of the District of York. (58150)

Address . . . to the citizens of the Fifth Congressional District. (33482)

Address to the citizens of the state of Tennessee. 94787

Address to the citizens of the United States. 44897

Address to the citizens of the United States; and extracts from Jack Tar's journals. 59477

Address to the citizens of the United States, but more particularly those of the middle and eastern states. 82151

Address to the citizens of the United States of America on the subject of slavery. (81781)

Address to the citizens of the United States, on national representation. 104564

Address to the citizens of the U. States, on the effects of war. 103716

Address to the citizens of the United States, proposing a new system of national instruction. 96285

Address to the citizens of the United States, September 17th, 1796. 101569

Address to the citizens of the United States. Written by himself [i. e. William Hull.] (33642)

Address to the citizens of Westchester County, New York. 35849

Address to the citizens of Westchester County, on the approaching state election. 35849

Address to the City Council. 75856

Address to the city of London. 412, 41852

Address to the clergy. 16127

Address to the clergy and laity. 66117

Address to the clergy and the people of . . . Middlesex. 48844

Address to the clergy of all denominations. 14732

Address to the clergy of Massachusetts. (13870)

Address to the clergy of New-England. 63447

Address to the clergy of the established church. 52268, (56479)

Address to the cocoa-tree. 97161

Address to the College of Physicians at Philadelphia. (31032)

Address to the colonies. 84599, 84600

Address to the colonists of British Guiana. 8102

Address to the colored citizens of Ohio. (56418)

Address to the coloured people of Philadelphia. 97638

Address to the colored population of Louisiana. 72462

Address to the Columbian Institute, on a moneyed system. note after 39323

Address to the Columbian Institute, on the question, "What ought to be the circulating medium of a nation?" 14866, (39322)

Address to the Committee acting under the authority of a meeting at Mechanic-Hall. (32301), 54062

Address to the Committee of Association for the County of York. (30686)

Address to the Committee of Association of the County of York. 30685

Address to the Committee of Correspondence in Barbados. 3262, (20037), 20038

Address to the Committee of the County of York. (30686)

Address to the . . . Common Council. 78674

Address to the . . . Common Council, of Boston, on the organization of the city government, January 5, 1829. 57860

Address to the . . . Common Council, of Boston, on the organization of the city government, January 4, 1830. 57860

Address to the community. 45874

Address to the conductors of the New York periodical press. 105583

Address to the congregation of St. Anne's Church. (21878)

Address to the congregation of St. John's Church. 30985

Address to the congregation of St. Mary's Church. 32424, 32426

Address to the Congress of the United States. 413, 8456, 15513

Address to the Congressional District. 13771

Address to the consociated pastors and churches. 15641

Address . . . to the Constitutional Convention. 78632

Address to the Convention of Sunday School Teachers. 37976

Address to the Convention of the Colony and Ancient Dominion of Virginia. 7466, note before 100424

Address to the Convention of the Diocese of Ohio. 43324

Address to the Convention of the Protestant Episcopal Church in Pennsylvania. 64617

Address . . . to the . . . Convention of the Protestant Episcopal Church, in the Diocese of Georgia. 22283

Address to the Convention of the Two Republican Parties. (28283)

Address . . . to the Convocation of the Protestant Episcopal Church of Va. 47242

Address to the Council [of Jamaica.] 26155

Address to the country. 1979

Address to the countrymen. 60730

Address to the Danvers Auxiliary Society. 65949

Address to the Democracy and the people of the United States. 414, 19490, note after 91521

Address to the Democracy of Indiana. 34483

Address to the Democracy of the Northwest. 76383

Address to the Democracy of the United States. 415, 19489

Address to the Democratic Party. 51441

Address . . . to the Democratic Republican Celebration. 43504

Address to the Democrats of Massachusetts. 79135

Address [to the Democrats of Pennsylvania.] 59828

Address to the deputies of North America. (15511)

Address to the Diocesan Convention. (28881)

Address to the Directors of the Society for the Circulation of Dr. Channing's Works. 85874

Address to the Earls of Pembroke, Lindsey, and Dover. 82851

Address to the East Haverhill Temperance Society. 21650

Address to the electors, and other free subjects. 416, 72044

Address to the electors and people. 22590, 91237, 95563

Address to the electors of Charleston [Congressional] District. 62904

Address to the electors of Charleston District. 62904

Address. . . . to the electors of Dutchess County. (59574)

Address to the electors of Great Britain. 36301, note after 69480, 78302

Address to the electors of Kingston. 43161

Address to the electors of Massachusetts. 45594

Address to the electors of Massachusetts, in favor of his [i. e. Mr. Dexter's] election. 19900

Address to the electors of New-Hampshire. (63448)

Address to the electors of New Hampshire on the choice of representatives to Congress. 52941

Address to the electors of . . . New York. 53499

Address to the electors of . . . New York, by the Republican members of the Legislature. 53500

Address to the electors of . . . New York in favor of Judge Yates's election as governor. 53496

Address to the electors of . . . New York on the ensuing charter election. 53498

Address to the electors of . . . New York. Published by order of the Republican General Committee. 53497

Address to the electors of South Oxford. 10418

Address . . . to the electors of the counties of Huntington and St. Maurice. 58489

Address to the electors of the county of Plymouth [Mass.], by a Committee of Federal Republicans. (63491)

Address to the electors of the county of Plymouth, May 7, 1811. 63490

Address to the electors of the Ninth Congressional District. 45595

Address to the electors of the Ninth Ward. 54063

Address to the electors of the Second Congressional District. 18945

Address to the electors of the state of New York. 29947

Address to the . . . electors of the state of New York. (59574)

Address to the electors of the Third District. 106066

Address to the electors of the Western District. 71148

Address to the emigrants from Connecticut. 15643, 21546

Address to the emigrants, upon embarking. 106169

Address to the Episcopalians in the United States. 54433

Address to the Episcopalians in Virginia. 29381

Address to the Episcopalians of the United States. (52956)

Address to the Essex Agricultural Society, at Danvers. 37791

Address to the Essex Agricultural Society . . . at Topsfield. 33357

Address to the Essex Agricultural Society, May 5, 1818. 62659

Address to the Essex Agricultural Society, September 15, 1844. 65949

Address to the Essex County Agricultural Society, at New-Rowley. 89560

Address to the Essex County Agricultural Society, . . . September 25, 1834. 51051

Address to the fair daughters of the United States. 417

Address to the farmer. 47276, 97107

Address to the farmers and mechanics. 65949

Address to the farmers of Great Britain. (5563)

Address to the farmers of Pennsylvania. 59852

Address to the farmers of Rhode Island. 70529

Address to the farmers of the United States. 10889

Address to the Federal electors of New York. (53501)

Address to the Federal Republicans of Burlington County. 254, 5674

Address to the Federal Republicans of the state of New Jersey. 53054

Address to the females of Ohio. 95459

Address . . . to . . . the Fenian Brotherhood. 57348

Address to the first graduating class. 62719

Address to the fourth annual convention. 30038

Address to the Fredes. 49749

Address to the free and independent citizens of Maryland. 45057

Address to the free and independent citizens of the United States. (19063)

Address to the free and independent people of Massachusetts. 45596

Address to the free and independent people of Massachusetts. With a protest. 45596

Address to the free colored people, advising them to remove to Liberia. (5576)

Address to the free colored people of the United States. (81782)

Address to the free people of color. 29802

Address to the free people of colour. 81783

Address to the freeholders and inhabitants of the province of Pennsylvania. 59853

Address to the freeholders and inhabitants of the province of the Massachusetts-Bay. 45597

Address to the freeholders of New-Jersey. 53055

Address to the freeholders of . . . New York. 53502

Address to the freeholders of Philadelphia. 61436

Address to the freeholders of the Southern District. 25752

Address to the freemen, citizens of Philadelphia. 61437

Address to the freemen, freeholders and inhabitants. 53503

Address to the freemen of Connecticut. 15644, note after 102333

Address to the freemen of Connecticut, May 24, 1806. 15645, 102334

Address to the freemen of Massachusetts. 813, 45598

Address to the freemen of New England. (30196), 74359, 103849

Address to the freemen of New-Hampshire. 93509

Address to the freemen of Rhode Island. (64630)

Address to the freemen of Rhode Island. By a freeman. 70530

Address to the freemen of Rhode Island, by a Republican farmer. 70531

Address to the freemen of Rhode Island, on the annual election. 70532

Address to the freemen of Rhode Island, on the subject of the spring elections, 1832. 70533

Address to the freemen of South-Carolina. 67681, 2d note before 87733

Address to the freemen of the agricultural and manufacturing interests. 70534

Address to the freemen of the colony. 80456

Address to the freemen of the counties. 105118

Address to the freemen of the state of Rhode Island. By a citizen. 70535

Address to the freemen of the state of Rhode-Island; by Elisha R. Potter. 64629

Address to the freemen of the state of South-Carolina. 9278, note immediately before 87733

Address to the freemen of Vermont. 99136, 99174

Address to the freemen of Vermont, by a farmer. 99200

Address to the freemen of vermont, by a soldier. 99137

Address to the freemen of Vermont, by their delegation. 99198

Address to the Friendly Sons of St. Patrick. 29733

Address to the friends of constitutional liberty. (81784)

Address: to the friends of free institutions. 33296, 95092

Address to the friends of Grace Church. 6647

Address to the friends of liberty. 81785

Address to the friends of Sabbath schools. 30141

Address to the "Gamma Theta Society." 92723

Address to the Guardians of the Washington Asylum. 101961

Address to the General Assembly of Pennsylvania. 84581

Address to the General Conference. 78344

Address to the General Convention. 91031

Address to the genius of America. 102585

Address to the gentlemen of the provinces of America. 1037, 81585

Address to the government of the United States, on the cession of Louisiana to the French. 8457, 42188, 50022

Address to the government, the merchants, manufacturers, and the colonists in America. 418

Address to the Governor, Council, and Assembly of Albany. 587

Address to the graduates at the commencement of Rhode-Island College. 47005

Address, . . . to the graduates of Brown University. 48151

Address, . . . to the graduates of Rhode-Island College, at the . . . commencement. 47005

Address . . . to the graduates of Rhode-Island College, at the public commencement. 47005

Address . . . to the graduates of Rhode Island College, . . . Sept. 7, 1803. 48151

Address . . . to the graduates of Rutgers College. 48998

Address to the graduates of the Medical College of South-Carolina. 81327

Address to the graduates of the Medical Department of the St. Louis University. 58330

Address to the graduates of the Medical Institution of Geneva College. 89385

Address to the graduates of the South-Carolina College. 87968

Address . . . to the . . . graduates of Williams College. 28818

Address . . . to the graduating class at the Massachusetts Medical College. 31864

Address . . . to the graduating class in Union Theological Seminary. 80078

Address to the graduating class of Carroll College. 77240

Address to the graduating class of Geneva Medical College. (39716)

Address to the graduating class of the Albany Law School. 64622

Address . . . to the graduating class of the Indiana Medical College. (38068)

Address to the graduating class of the Law Department. 24006

Address to the graduating class of the Law School of Columbia College, of May, 1861. 32405

Address to the graduating class of the Law School of Columbia University. 37997

Address to the graduating class of the Medical School of Georgia. 62718

Address to the graduating class of the Memphis Medical College. 67335
Address to the graduating class of the State and National Law School. 58175
Address to the graduating class of the State Normal School. 72628
Address to the graduating class of the United States Naval Academy. 18807
Address to the graduating class . . . University of Albany. 58175
Address to the grand jury of Wexford. 24731
Address to the great man. 63079
Address to the holders of bonds. (63106)
Address to the honorable American Congress. 7286, 4th note after 99005
Address to the honourable House of Representatives. 104898
[Address] to the honorable the Legislature of the state of New-York. 37787
Address to the House of Lords. 31131
Address to the House of Representatives from the Meeting for Sufferings, 10. mo. 26. (59854)
Address to the House of Representatives of the United States. 10883, 28775, 97902
Address to the impartial public. 88908
Address to the independent citizens of Massachusetts. on the . . . approaching election. 45600
Address to the independent electors of Massachusetts, 45599, 62705, 103783
Address to the independent electors of . . . New York. (53504)
Address to the independent electors of the county of Washington. 102009
Address, to the independent electors of the Hampshire North District. 94203
Address to the independent Federal electors. 54064
Address to the industrial classes. 105583
Address to the inhabitants . . . by the . . . Managers of the New-York . . . Temperance Society. 54448
Address to the inhabitants, in general. (81786)
Address to the inhabitants in the new settlements. 104533
Address to the inhabitants of Alexandria. 746, 66065
Address to the inhabitants of Charleston. 722
Address to the inhabitants of Europe. 81787
Address to the inhabitants of Jamaica. 104930
Address to the inhabitants of London. 97996
Address to the inhabitants of Maine. 43904
Address to the inhabitants of Massachusetts Bay. 45601
Address to the inhabitants of Marblehead. 68593
Address to the inhabitants of Nantucket. 59546
Address to the inhabitants of New Brunswick. 7252
Address to the inhabitants of New-Jersey. 17151
Address to the inhabitants of New Mexico and California on territorial governments. 53275
Address to the inhabitants of New Mexico and California, on the omission by Congress to provide them with territorial governments. 419, 35868
Address to the inhabitants of North Carolina. 55590
Address to the inhabitants of Pennsylvania. By John Freeman. 25779
Address to the inhabitants of Pennsylvania, by those freemen. 59610
Address to the inhabitants of . . . Philadelphia [by a Friend to Mankind.] 61438

Address to the inhabitants of Philadelphia [by Andrew Marvell.] 45022
Address to the inhabitants of Quebec. (15528), note after 23535
Address to the inhabitants of Rhode Island. 70536
Address to the inhabitants of the British colonies in America. (74205)
Address to the inhabitants of the British settlements in America. 55354, 74202-74204, 74206, (82106), note after 99798, 2d note after 102803
Address, to the inhabitants of the British settlements, on the slavery of the Negroes. 74206-74207, note after 99798
Address to the inhabitants of the colony of New York. 55371
Address to the inhabitants of the County of Berkshire. 4894
Address to the inhabitants of the District of Gore. 104557
Address to the inhabitants of the District of Maine. (43903)
Address to the inhabitants of the Miami County lands. 56948
Address to the inhabitants of the New-Hampshire Grants. 101077
Address to the inhabitants of the new settlements. 420, 15646, 2d note after 91736
Address to the inhabitants of the province of Quebec. 15526, (15528), 15544, 84642.
Address to the inhabitants of the province of Quebec, from the forty-nine delegates. 13584, 15516, 48860
Address to the inhabitants of the province of the Massachusetts-Bay. (45602)
Address to the inhabitants of the state of Delaware. (81788)
Address to the inhabitants of the towns and parishes. (52796)
Address to the inhabitants of Wales. 104195
Address to the inhabitants . . . of Washington. 58151
Address to the inhabitants of Westchester County. 35867
Address to the interior cabinet. 421
Address to the Irish inhabitants of Quebec. 97123
Address to the Irish members of the Imperial Parliament. 81961
Address to the Ladies' Grande Ligne Missionary Society. 37976
Address to the ladies of Glasgow. 95505
Address to the landed, trading and funded interests. 72149
Address to the landholders and farmers of Newport County. 9235
Address to the landholders & inhabitants of the Holland Purchase. 84221
Address to the . . . Law School of the University of Albany. 45027
Address to the Lawyers' Club of Buffalo. 84516
Address to the legislature and people of New York. 47181
Address to the legislature and people of the state of Connecticut. 9479, 15648
Address to the legislature and the citizens of Ohio. 85111
Address to the legislature in June last. 99133
Address to the legislature of Indiana, December 6th, 1847. 34506, 57327
Address to the legislature of Indiana on education. 34506
Address to the legislature of Kentucky. 17577
Address to the legislature of Mass. Jan, 11, 1848. 7943

Address . . . to the . . . legislature of
Massachusetts . . . [on] "The annexation
of part of Deerfield to Greenfield."
45603, 1st note after 94663

Address to the legislature of . . . Missouri.
(43198)

Address to the legislature of New-Jersey.
101084

Address to the legislature [of New York.]
19126

Address to the legislature of New-York, adopted
by the State Woman's Rights Convention.
90398

Address to the legislature of South Carolina.
87737

Address to the legislature on the reception of
the news. 1468

Address to the liberal and humane. 10889,
61439

Address to the Literary and Philosophical
Society of South-Carolina. (36245)

Address to the Literary and Philosophical
Society of South Carolina; . . . Charleston, . . . the 10th of August, 1814. 22276

Address to the living. 72710

Address to the loyal part of the British empire.
17720

Address to the loyal people of Tennessee. 8701

Address to the Maryland State Bar Association.
84516

Address to the Massachusetts Charitable Fire
Society . . . May 31, 1811. 63852

Address to the Massachusetts Charitable Fire
Society, . . . Oct. 10, 1817. (28387)

Address to the Massachusetts Peace Society.
18924

Address to the Mayor and City Council. 104737

Address to the Mayor and Corporation, and
advice to the police. 21923

Address to the . . . Mayor and Corporation
. . . the Wardens . . . of Trinity House.
30687

Address to the Mayor, the Aldermen, and
inhabitants of New York. 93511

Address to the mechanics and laborers of all
classes. 35532

Address to the mechanics and laboring classes.
54065

Address to the mechanics and working men
of New York. (53505)

Address to the mechanics of Easton, Pennsylvania. 64270

Address to the medical graduates. 105028

Address to the members and friends of the
Wesleyan Methodist Church. (74543)

Address to the members . . . at their late
convention. (38425)

Address to the members of both houses of
Parliament. 43172, 97578

Address to the members of the Assembly.
1792, note after 45640, 81891

Address to the members of the Attleborough
Society. 103980

Address to the members of the Bar of Suffolk,
Mass. 93548

Address to the members of the Bar of the
counties of Hampshire, Franklin and
Hampden. 5918

Address to the members of the Bar of Worcester
County. 104058

Address to the Members of the Charitable Fire
Association. 271

Address to the members of the Church of
England. 92632

Address to the members of the congregation of
Grace Church. 6648

Address to the members of the Congress. 422

Address to the members of the Cumberland Bar.
32920

Address to the members of the Diligent Engine
Co. 90548

Address to the members of the Episcopal
Church. (45842)

Address to the members of the Episcopal
separation. (32311)

Address to the members of the First Presbyterian Congregation. 61665

Address to the members of the Historical
Society. (47111)

Address to the members of the House of Representatives. 100971

Address to the members of the Labor Reform
League. 15187

Address to the members of the Massachusetts
Charitable Fire Society, at their annual
meeting, in Boston. 95185

Address, to the members, of the Massachusetts
Charitable Fire Society, at their annual
meeting, June 2, 1797. 102567

Address to the members of the Massachusetts
Charitable Fire Society; at their annual
meeting, May 27, 1814. 103830

Address to the members of the Massachusetts
Charitable Fire Society, . . . May 29,
1795. (49325)

Address to the members of the . . . [Massa-
chusetts Medical Society.] 45874

Address to the members of the Massachusetts
Society for Promoting Agriculture. 71011

Address to the members of the Merrimack
Humane Society, at their anniversary
meeting in Newburyport, Sept. 1, 1807.
89787

Address, to the members of the Merrimack
Humane Society, at their anniversary
meeting, in Newburyport, Sept. 3, 1805.
103364

Address to the members of the Merrimack
Humane Society . . . Newburyport,
September 7th, 1813. 18405

Address to the members of the Merrimack
Humane Society . . . Newburyport, Sept.
2, 1806. 11204

Address to the members of the Merrimack
Humane Society, . . . Sept. 6, 1808. 32333

Address to the members of the new Parliament
on the proceedings of the Colonial Department, for ameliorating the condition of the
slaves, &c. (81789)

Address to the members of the new Parliament,
on the proceedings of the Colonial Department on the West India question. 93796

Address to the members of the new Parliament,
on the proceedings of the Colonial Department, with respect to the West India
question. (69410), (69491), 102863

Address to the members of the Philadelphia
Yearly Meeting. 61440

Address to the members of the Protestant
Episcopal Church, in . . . America. 35816

Address to the members of the Protestant
Episcopal Church in Maryland. 45048

Address to the members of the Protestant
Episcopal Church, in . . . New-York. 41348

Address to the members of the Protestant
Episcopal Church in the United States of
America. 66118, 66672

Address, to the members of the Protestant
Episcopal Church, in Virginia. 43705

Address to the members of the Protestant
Episcopal Church of Maryland. 84582

Address to the members of the Quarterly Meeting
of Westbury. 97735

Address to the members of the religious society
of Friends on . . . slavery and the slave
trade. 61997

Address to the members of the religious society of Friends, on the duty of declining the use of products. 44685

Address to the members of the senior class at St. Mary's Hall. 75435

Address to the members of the senior class, at the closing exercises. 20391

Address to the members of the society of Friends. 59855

Address to the members of the Suffolk Bar. 92284

Address . . . to the members of the Union Club. 67255

Address to the members of the "United Church of England and Ireland." 44509

Address to the merchants of Great Britain. 423

Address to the merchants of New York. 78557, 78581

Address to the merchants of the mercantile navy. (33889)

Address to the merchants, traders, and liverymen. 35661

Address to the Mexican nation. 57679

Address to the Middlesex Society of Husbandmen and Manufacturers. (14535)

Address to the ministers and congregations. 78558

Address to the ministers and members. 52582

Address to the ministers, elders, and members. 62534

Address to the ministers of England and Wales. 34590

Address to the ministers of the Gospel. (58037)

Address to the most worshipful Grand Lodge. 95399

Address to the natives of Scotland residing in America. 104931, 104934

Address to the Negroes in . . . New York. 53506

Address to the Negroes in the state of New York. 30085

Address to the New-York African Society for Mutual Relief. 30038

Address to the non-slaveholders of Kentucky. (42312), 81790

Address to the non-slaveholders of the South. 81791, 2d note after 94368

Address to the Normal Association. 47078

Address to the North Americans. (25789)

Address to the officers composing the medical staff. 49749

Address to the officers of the N. Y. S. Militia. 65911

Address to the officers of the New-York state troops. 19638

Address . . . to the Ontario Bar Association. 84516

Address to the owners of slaves. 19939, (32948), (81956)

Address to the "Pacific Pioneers." 60952

Address to the Palestine Missionary Society. 92259

Address to the parents and guardians of children. 104757

Address: to the parents and guardians of the children. 35673

Address to the parishioners of St. Peter's Church. 9268

Address to the parishioners of the Church of the Ascension. 82940

Address to the Parliament and people of Great Britain. 106327

Address to the . . . Parliament . . . with respect to the West-India question. (59410)

Address to the patriotism of the country. 65389

Address to the patrons of the Manufacturer's and Farmer's Journal. 28582

Address to the patrons of the [Northport, Ala.] Spectator. 84896

Address, to the patrons of the Ogdensburgh Sentinel. 56827

Address to the patrons of the "Tuscaloosa Observer." 84896

Address to the patrons of the Whig. 35111

Address to the . . . peers of Scotland. (33824), 91840

Address to the Pennsylvania Militia. 52344

Address to the Pennsylvania Volunteers. 78318

Address to the people. 48670

Address to the people. Anti-masonic state convention. 95158

Address . . . to the people, . . . at the close of the session. 45585

Address to the people, by a citizen of Massachusetts. 95843

Address to the people, by Rev. Convers Francis. 91372

Address to the people, by Rev. George W. Blagden. 95263

Address to the people [by the Colored People's Convention.] 87808

Address to the people. By the General Court. 45614

Address to the people, by the Rev. E. Halley. 89744

Address to the people [by the Second United States Anti-masonic Convention.] 97960

Address to the people called Methodists, concerning the criminality of encouraging slavery. 7203

Address to the people called Methodists concerning the evil of encouraging the slave trade. 7202

Address to the people called Quakers, concerning the manner in which they treated Timothy Davis. 18893, 94170

Address to the people called Quakers, on their testimony concerning kings and government. 58212-(58214)

"Address to the people," delivered at the installation. 62772

Address to the people of Alabama. (33816)

Address to the people of America. 17432

Address to the people of America on the prospect of a war. 424

Address to the people of Anne Arundell County. (13506)

Address to the people of Arkansas. 103269

Address to the people of Barnwell District. 96177

Address to the people of Beaufort and Colleton Districts. (70478)

Address . . . to the people of Berlin. (6977)

Address to the people of Cambridge. 10135

Address to the people of Canada. 10334

Address to the people of Charles, Calvert, and St. Mary's Counties. 45059

Address to the people of Chester District, S. C., assembled to discuss the question of nullification, &c. (12548)

Address to the people of Chester District, S. C., on nullification. 22342

Address to the people of color of Pennsylvania. 50818

Address to the people of Connecticut. 15647, 41474, 81493, 97175

Address to the people of Connecticut, adopted by the state convention. 15652

Address to the people of Connecticut by the Board of Commissioners of Common Schools. 15718

Address to the people of Connecticut on sundry political subjects. (15651), (15716), note after 90846

ADDRESS

Address to the people of . . . Connecticut on
the . . . removal. 36846
Address to the people of Cumberland County.
327
Address to the people of Darlington District.
87828
Address to the people of England, being a
protest. 22599
Address to the people of England. By Peter
Porcupine. 14013
Address to the people of England. By William
Cobbett. 14021
Address to the people of England on the
necessity of a convention. 27164
Address to the people of England, Scotland,
and Ireland. 42944
Address to the people of Florida. 10049
Address to the people of Franklin County.
103407
Address to the people of Great Britain. 427,
93600, 95959
Address to the people of Great Britain, America,
and Ireland. (4151)
Address to the people of Great Britain [by the
American Continental Congress.] (15528),
15544
Address to the people of Great Britain: con-
taining a new, and more powerful
argument. 102865
Address to the people of Great Britain, containing thoughts entertained during the
Christmas recess. 425
Address to the people of Great Britain in
general. 426
Address to the people of Great Britain . . .
occasioned by the dismission of William
Pitt. 63080
Address to the people of Great Britain on the
consumption of West-India produce.
102813
Address to the people of Great Britain, on the
meeting of Parliament. 428
Address to the people of Great Britain, on the
propriety of abstaining from West India
sugar and rum. 429, (17335), 80582,
80691-80692, 102868
Address to the people of Great Britain on the
propriety of abstaining from West India
sugar and rum. 25378, 1st note after
102813
Address to the people of Great Britain.
September 6, 1864. 65066
Address to the people of Iowa, April 8, 1854.
(28851)
Address to the people of Ireland. 19160, 23530
Address to the people of Ireland, July 28. 403,
(41651)
Address to the people of Kentucky. By H.
Marshall. 44774
Address to the people of Kentucky. Dated
Bowling Green. 7671, 46962
Address to the people of Kentucky, on the
subject of emancipation. 81792
Address to the people of Kentucky, on the
subject of the Charleston & Ohio Rail-road.
103864
Address to the people of Litchfield County.
8561
Address to the people of Louisiana. 26797
Address to the people of Maine from M. Kinsley.
43906
Address to the people of Maine, from the
convention of delegates. 43905
Address to the people of Maine, on . . .
separation. 40786
Address to the people of Maryland, by a farmer
and landholder. 45060

Address to the people of Maryland by the
General Assembly. 45061
Address to the people of Maryland, by the
National Republican Central Committee of
Baltimore. 95810
Address to the people of Maryland, by the Whig
Central Committee. (45062)
Address to the people of Maryland, [December
20, 1860.] 14455
Address to the people of Maryland, from their
delegates. 37479, 45063
Address to the people of Maryland, on the origin,
progress and present state of French
aggression. 45064
Address to the people of Maryland, on the subject
of the presidential election. 45065
Address to the people of Maryland, respecting
some abuses. 45066
Address to the people of Massachusetts.
45607-45608, 93639
Address to the people of Massachusetts, adopted
at the Union Convention. 91605
Address to the people of Massachusetts. By a
Washington Federalist. 41944
Address to the people of Massachusetts. [By
B. R. Curtis.] 18025
Address to the people of Massachusetts, by the
Friends of Temperance. 45615
Address to the people of Massachusetts. By
members of the legislature. 45613
Address to the people of Massachusetts by the
House of Representatives. (45616)
Address to the people of Massachusetts [by the
Whig members of the legislature.] 45611
Address to the people of Massachusetts.
February, 1805. 45604-45605
Address to the people of Massachusetts,
February 15, 1812. 45610
Address to the people of Massachusetts, in
relation to the political influence of
freemasonry. 29890
Address to the people of Massachusetts on the
electors. 45612
Address to the people of Massachusetts on the
justice and importance of a law. 45617
Address to the people of Massachusetts, on the
present condition. 32944
Address to the people of Massachusetts, on the
subject of human rights. 20538
Address to the people of Massachusetts, on the
subject of the licence law of 1838. 20539
Address to the people of Massachusetts, on the
. . . temperance reformation. 45910
Address to the people of Mississippi. 90643
Address to the people of Missouri. 49577
Address to the people of New England. 20757
Address to the people of New-England. 32133
Address to the people of New-England, by
Algernon Sidney. (28281), (39911), 80854
Address to the people of New-England: occasioned
by the preaching and publishing. 1759,
43663, (52608)
Address to the people of New-England. Repre-
senting the very great importance of
attaching the Indians to their interest.
32946
Address to the people of New England, with
remarks on the plans. 62551
Address to the people of New-Hampshire. 102322
Address to the people of New-Jersey. 10162
Address to the people of New Jersey on the
present crisis. (53056)
Address to the people of New Jersey, on the
subject of common schools. 20383
Address to the people of New-Jersey, on the
subject of the Delaware and Raritan Canal
and Camden and Amboy Rail Road. 91895

Address to the people of New Mexico. 13682
Address to the people of . . . New York, by
the Federal Republican members of the
Legislature. (53507)
Address to the people of North Carolina.
(55591)
Address to the people of Ohio. 11211
Address to the people of Ohio, on the
important subject of the next presidency.
56872
Address to the people of Pennsylvania, adopted
at a meeting. (40566)
Address to the people of Pennsylvania and the
United States. 59856, 60374
Address to the people of Pennsylvania; con-
taining a narrative of the proceedings.
55226
Address to the people of Pennsylvania, issued
by authority. 59857
Address to the people of Pennsylvania on the
approaching election. 59858
Address to the people of Pennsylvania over the
signature of Franklin. 59859
Address to the people of Pennsylvania, read to
the Anti-masonic Convention, Feb. 25.
13427
Address to the people of Pennsylvania, upon
a great public question. (59860)
Address to the people of Philadelphia. 105584
Address to the people of Rhode-Island,
delivered in Newport. 27647
Address to the people of Rhode-Island, from
the convention. 70537
Address to the people of Rhode Island proving
that more than eight millions of the
public money has been wasted. 70538,
note after 98028
Address to the people of Rhode-Island,
published in the Providence Journal. 30058
Address to the people of Rhode Island, upon
the course of the Hon. Elisha R. Potter.
70539, 106194
Address to the people of St. Helena Parish.
22287
Address to the people of South Carolina. 39144,
87436
Address to the people of South Carolina. 46140,
48097, 87423, 87426, 87428, note after
90638
Address to the people of South-Carolina; and
more particularly to the members of the
legislature. 104660
Address to the people of South Carolina,
assembled in convention. 87432
Address to the people of South-Carolina, by the
General Committee of the Representative
Reform Association. 87733
Address to the people of South Carolina, by
their delegates in convention. 87420
Address to the people of South Carolina by
their Senators and Representatives in
Congress. 39144, 88065
Address to the people of Texas. By A. J.
Hamilton. 29993
Address to the people of Texas, on the protection
of slave property. 65482
Address to the people of the American states.
430
Address to the people of the commonwealth.
45618
Address to the people of the commonwealth of
Massachusetts. 103004
Address to the people of the commonwealth
. . . relative to the licence question.
59861
Address to the people of the Congressional
District of Charleston. 20917

Address to the people of the counties of Accomac
and Northampton. 64683
Address to the people of the counties of Colum-
biana, Starke and Wayne. 82170
Address to the people of the county of Hampshire.
30139
Address to the people of the county of Hanover.
103288
Address to the people of the eastern states.
81793, 88423
Address to the people of the First Congressional
District. (18993)
Address to the people of the free states. 18837
Address to the people of the Mississippi
Territory. 94673
Address to the people of the North. 19668
Address to the people of the Second Congressional
District. 84896
Address to the "people" of the several sovereign
states. 431, 72122
Address to the people of the slave holding states.
81794, 94790
Address to the people of the southern and western
states. 88298
Address to the people of the southern states.
5225
Address to the people of the state of New York.
31687
Address to the people of the state of New York.
By Hon. Erastus Root. 73124
Address to the people of the state of N. Y.,
dated Albany. 100669
Address to the people of the state of New-York,
on the subject of the constitution, agreed
upon at Philadelphia. 35830, 83604
Address to the people of the state of New-York:
shewing the necessity of making amendments
to the constitution. (53508), 83604
Address to the people of the state of South
Carolina. 83853
Address to the people of the state of Vermont.
99226
Address to the people of the Third Congressional
District. 96148
Address to the people of the 21st Congressional
District. 104020
Address to the people of the United States. 432,
93914
Address to the people of the United States,
adopted at a conference of colored citizens.
87734
Address to the people of the United States, and
of Kansas Territory. 37016
Address to the people of the United States, and
particularly of the slave states. (50880)
Address to the people of the United States, and
to the members of Congress in particular.
34591
Address to the people of the United States, by
a committee. 52635
Address to the people of the United States [by
Amos Kendall.] 37348
Address to the people of the United States. By
Dr. Samuel Thomson. 95598
Address to the people of the United States, by
George Washington, Esquire. 101557
Address to the people of the United States by
George Washington, Esq. Expressing his
determination not to be considered a
candidate. 101563
Address to the people of the United States by
John Beeson. 4359
Address to the people of the United States [by
Lajos Kossuth.] 38265, 38269
Address. To the people of the United States.
[By Nehemiah R. Knight.] (38121)
Address to the people of the United States [by
Robert Smith.] 83818-83823, 83827-83828

Address to the people of the United States [by the American Bible Society.] (54075)

Address to the people of the United States [by the American Society for the Encouragement of Domestic Manufactures.] 1219

Address to the people of the United States, by the Convention of the people of South Carolina. 46140, 48097, 87421, 87423, 87426, 87428, note after 90623

Address to the people of the United States [by the Free Trade Convention.] 36724

Address to the people of the United States. By the Hon. Robert Smith. 83825-83826

Address to the people of the United States [by the National Institution for Promoting Industry in the United States.] 51991

Address . . . to the people of the United States [by the United States Anti-masonic Convention.] 97959

Address [to the people of the United States, by the United States Sanitary Commission.] 76526, 76647

Address to the people of the United States, calling a national convention. 88622

Address to the people of the United States. . . . —Democracy, constructive and pacific. 27672

Address to the people of the United States, drawn up by order. 433

Address to the people of the United States. From George Washington. 101568

Address to the people of the United states, from the late Secretary of State. 83824

Address to the people of the United States in behalf of the American Copyright Club. 434, 8812, 16740

Address to the people of the United States. New-York, Oct. 25, 1837. 8898

Address to the people of the United States of America. 101567

Address to the people of the United States (of members of Congress who opposed the passage of the bill.) 37015

Address to the people of the United States, on declining a re-election to the presidency. 101530

Address to the people of the United States [on slavery.] 81795

Address to the people of the United States, on the measures pursued by the Executive. 41609

Address to the people of the United States, on the policy of maintaining a permanent navy. 97903

Address to the people of the United States on the presidential election. (4781)

Address to the people of the United States, on the . . . presidential election: with . . . reference to the nomination. 35391

Address to the people of the United States on the subject of slavery. (81796)

Address to the people of the United States, on the subject of the anti-masonic excitement. 32530

Address to the people of the United States on the subject of the presidential election. 436

Address to the people of the United States on the subject of the presidential election, comprising a comparative view. 35391

Address, to the people of the United States, on the subject of the report of a committee of the House of Representatives. 104982

Address to the people of the U. States; shewing that, P. P. F. Degrand's plan is the only one. 19303, 58089, (65854), (76066)

Address to the people of the United States. The great rebellion. 32458

Address to the people of the U. States. To which is added, a letter. 62647, 62652, note before 93501

Address to the people of the United states who choose electors. 13741

Address to the people of the United States: with an epitome and vindication. (35920), 97904

Address to the people of the United States, with the proclamation. 40880

Address to the people of this commonwealth. 45626

Address to the people of this country. 32945

Address to the people of Virginia. 71188

Address to the people of Virginia, by the members of the General Assembly. 100424

Address to the people of Virginia, May 19, 1865. (62753)

Address to the people of Virginia on the alien and sedition law. 23177

Address to the people of Virginia, respecting the alien & sedition laws. 100425

Address to the people of West Virginia. 73922-73923, 81797

Address to the people of Winchester. 92873

Address to the people, on the subject of the contest. 435

Address to the people, representatives and President. 437

Address to the people . . . with the report. 45606

Address to the Phi Beta Kappa Society of Brown University. (48167)

Address to the Phi Beta Kappa Society of Dartmouth College. 17626

Address to the Phi Beta Kappa Society of Rhode Island. 27649

Address to the Philadelphia Annual Conference. (59285)

Address to the Philermenian Society of Brown University. 23237

Address to the physicians of Philadelphia. 61441

Address to the planters and farmers of South-Carolina. 87735

Address to the Presbyterian Church. 6916

Address to the Presbyterian Congregation in that place [i. e. Morristown, N. J.] 24497

Address to the Presbyterians of Kentucky. 37487, 81798

Address to the Prescott Guards. 3145

Address to the President of the United States, adopted by said House [i. e. Pennsylvania House of Representatives.] 60070

Address to the President of the United States, on the subject of his administration. 102369

Address to the President, Senate and House of Representatives. 94002

Address to the principal inhabitants. 8507

Address to the protestant clergy of the United States. 4291

Address to the protestants of the United States. 64129

Address to the public. 438, 25341

Address to the public, accounting for the large sum of money. 43851

Address to the public, and constitution, of the Roxbury Charitable Society. (73726)

Address to the public, and especially the printers. 50456, 97950

Address to the public at the first exhibition. 25938, 60339

Address to the public authorities. 91841

Address to the public. By Doctor Sylvester Gardiner. 26630A

Address to the public [by James Pope.] 64108
Address to the public. By Jonathan Parsons. 58888
Address to the public [by the Berkshire County Meeting.] 104433
Address to the public [by the Bible Society of Union College.] 97791
Address to the public, by the Board of Managers. 69891, note before 101926
Address to the public [by the Colby College Manual Labour Association.] 102106
Address to the public [by the Connecticut Historical Society.] (15710)
Address to the public [by the Greene and Delaware Society for the Promotion of Good Morals.] 28624
Address to the public by the Managers of the Colonization Society of Connecticut. 81799
Address to the public [by the meeting in Charleston.] (12071)
Address to the public [by the New-England Anti-slavery Society.] 52655
Address to the public [by the New Hampshire Missionary Society.] (52879)
Address to the public [by the New-York State Colonization Society.] 53816
Address to the public [by the Young Men's Temperance Society.] 106188
Address to the public [by William Matthews.] 46894
Address to the public; constitution and by-laws; and visitor's manual. 54099
Address to the public, constitution, and list of officers. 60785, 106171
Address to the public, constitution, and visitor's manual. (73726)
Address to the public, containing some remarks. 439, 1336, 95773
Address to the public from the Trustees of the Gardiner Lyceum. 26634
Address to the public, issued by the Executive Committee. 81824
Address to the public, May 5, 1766. 43638
Address to the public, occasioned by "Methodism anatomized." 59871
Address to the public of Great Britain and Ireland. (81800)
Address to the public of Pennsylvania. 34759
Address to the public on Amherst Collegiate Institution. (50459)
Address to the public on the African School. 53509
Address to the public, on the first exhibition. 25821
Address to the public on the Home for the Industrious Blind. 60339
Address to the public on the importance of educating pious young men. 105410
Address to the public, on the importance of restoring health. 103690
Address to the public, on the occasion. 54066
Address to the public, on the present peace. 90093
Address to the public, on the present state of the question. 81801
Address to the public on the subject of the African School. 65134
Address to the public over the signature of Franklin. 15653
Address to the public; (particularly) to the members of the legislature of New-York. 104042
Address to the public relative to the progress of the monument. (9174)
Address to the public; together with a copy of a letter. 28228, 82775
Address to the public; upon the present civil war. 97729

Address to the pupils of Sharon Boarding School. 62240
Address to the Quakers. 86636, 104522
Address to the quarterly, monthly and preparative meetings. 81802
Address . . . to the Radical Union men of Missouri. 20817
Address to the reader. 24678, 52445, 96899, 102447
Address to the reader of the documents. 26474, 93710, 95086, 105111
Address to the representatives in Parliament. 440
Address to the Republican citizens of New York. 642, (53510)
Address to the Republican citizens of . . . New-York. 53511
Address, to the Republican citizens of New-York, on the inauguration of Thomas Jefferson. 105511
Address to the Republican Club of Buffalo. 92874
Address: to the Republican electors of the Middle District. 88649
Address to the Republican electors of the Southern District. 53512
Address to the Republican people of Tennessee. 94790
Address to the Republicans and people of New York. 441, 53513
Address to the Republicans of Massachusetts. 18823
Address to the Republicans of the state of New-York. 93603
Address to the respective collectors. 99133
Address to the Rev. Dr. Alison. (42384), 66908
Address to the Rev. Moses C. Welch. 94074, 94077, 102518, 102523
Address to the Rhode-Island Society for the Encouragement of Domestic Industry, delivered at Pawtucket. 71740
Address to the Rhode-Island Society for the Encouragement of Domestick Industry . . . at Pawtuxet. 9235
Address to the Right Honourable L—d M—sf—d. 51544
Address to the Right Rev. Bishop Conwell. (62214)
Address to the Right Rev. the Bishop of Pennsylvania. (62214)
Address to the right reverend the prelates. 30555, 78722
Address to the Roman Catholics of . . . Philadelphia. 47236
Address to the Roman Catholics of the United States, by a layman. (62214)
Address to the Roman Catholics of the United States of America. 442, 11072, 30955, 103090, 103092, 103095
Address to the rulers of state. 443
Address to the Secretary of War. 76523, 76549, 76647
Address to the Selectmen and others. 7983
Address to the Senate and House of Representatives of the United States, on the question of an inquiry. 94003
Address to the Senate and House of Representatives of the United States, on the . . . tariff. 60788
Address to the Senators and Representatives of the free states. 81803
Address to the senior class, delivered at the commencement. 106087
Address to the senior class in Nassau Hall. 18770
Address to the senior class in Yale-College. 91029
Address to the senior class of students. 104932-104933, 104947

Address to the senior class [of the University of North Carolina.] 9910

Address to the serious Christians among ourselves. 27312

Address to the seventy-second annual convention. (64646)

Address to the several churches: and a letter. 92825

Address to the several churches of Christ. 97311

Address to the shareholders. 94406

Address to the singing society and choir. 97478

Address to the Six Nations. 49849, 95145

Address to the slaveholders of Tennessee. (47164)

Address to the slaves. 101039

Address to the society, by the Rev. Charles Briggs. 106051

Address to the Society for Promotion of Collegiate Education. (4307)

Address to the Society for the Promotion of Agriculture. (71739)

Address to the Society of Friends. (3369)

Address to the Society of Middlesex Husbandmen and Manufacturers. 58325

Address to the Society of the Constitutional Republicans. 401

Address to the soldiers of New Hampshire. 444, 52797

Address to the . . . Sons of Temperance. 43450

Address to the South Americans and Mexicans. 31316

Address to the state of Ohio. 97881

Address to the stock and loan holders. 78081

Address to the stockholders and creditors. 8722

Address to the stockholders and friends. (13225)

Address to the stockholders of the Bank of Pennsylvania. 59910

Address to the stockholders of the City Library. 54067

Address to the stockholders of the . . . [New York Society] Library. 54542

Address to the stockholders of the Schuylkill Navigation Company. 78080

Address to the stockholders of the Southern Pacific Railroad Company. 88429

Address to the stockholders of the Winnisimmet Company. 46893

Address to the students and faculty. (28505)

Address, to the students at Phillips Academy. (50953)

Address to the students in the Independent Academy. 58879

Address to the students in the University of Vermont. 76353

Address to the students of Dickinson College. 55351, 73361

Address to the students of law in Transylvania University. (47119)

Address to the students of Miami University. 40985

Address to the students of the College of New-Jersey. 10942

Address to the students of the General Theological Seminary. (29538)

Address to the students of the National Academy of Design. 21309

Address to the students of the South Carolina College. 65387

Address to the Suffolk North Association. 40185

Address to the Supreme Being. 84678C

Address to the Texian troops. 95077

Address to the three thousand colored citizens. 82599

Address to the throne of grace. 2403

Address to the tories. 42402

Address to the two branches of the legislature. 23271

Address to the Unitarian Congregation. (65513)

Address to the united administration. 101260

Address to the . . . United States Agricultural Society. 33454

Address to the U. S. Military Philosophical Society. 104295

Address to the United States of America. 101575

Address to the United States of North America. 19064

Address to the United Whig Club. 57785

Address to the unregenerate. 79272

Address to the Utica Forum. 36162

Address to the Utica Lyceum. 26162

Address to the Vestry of Trinity Church. (32301)

Address to the voters of Maryland. 89275

Address to the voters of Philadelphia. 61442

Address to the voters of the Fifth Congressional District. 72073-72074

Address to the voters of the First Congressional District of Maryland. 20658

Address . . . to the voters of the First District of Georgia. (37840)

Address to the voters of the Fourth Congressional District. 45619

Address to the voters of the Sixth Congressional District. 84896

Address to the voters of the Third Congressional District. 31755

Address to the voters . . . residing within the first five wards. (45067)

Address to the voting classes . . . of Philadelphia. 60290

Address to the well disposed. (4039), note after 98548, note after 102951

Address to the Whigs of Flushing. 25918

Address to the Whigs of Rhode Island. (70540)

Address to the Whigs of Vermont. (23282)

Address to the whites. (6858)

Address . . . to the Worcester County Agricultural Society. 48928

Address to the working-men of New-England. 5318, 42731

Address to the workingmen of the United States of America. 67900

Address to the young ladies. (44808)

Address to the young men of the United States. 106186

Address to the young men of Worcester County. 105417

Address to their anti-masonic fellow-citizens. 46091

Address to their brethren. 66119

Address . . . to their constituents. 45585

Address to those captives in spirit. 74499

Address to those persons at Elizabeth-Town. 56822

Address, to those presbyterians. 19938, 60057, 64448

Address to those Quakers. 66909

Address to those who may be disposed to remove. (17175), 87307

Address, to unite all good people. 22182, 59045

Address to Washington City. 104975

Address to William Tudor. (10850), 97407

Address to workingmen. 54068

Address to young mechanics. 105585, 105588, 105596

Address to . . . young men . . . and . . . other matter. (14151)

Address to young men: . . . delivered before the Wide-Awakes. 14204

Address to young men of the United States. 53514, 106183

Address to young people. 103197

Address to youth. 105175

Address . . . Trinity College, Hartford. (22172)

Address . . . 23d June 1841. 18248

Address . . . two hundredth anniversary. 52168
Address . . . Union College. 20677
Address, Union-Springs Female Seminary. 12002
Address . . . University of Albany. 24274
Address . . . University of Nashville. 29922
Address . . . University of North Carolina. 44303
Address unto those parts of New-England. (46389)
Address upon a proposed railroad. 62051, 92812
Address upon education and common schools. (31396)
Address upon Henry Price. (26656)
Address . . . upon his [i. e. Stephen Taylor's] inauguration. 94538
Address upon our national affairs. 35
Address upon secession. (6977)
Address upon the ceremony of dedicating the new Masonic Hall. (24047)
Address upon the character of the late Hon. Isaac H. Williamson. 29928
Address upon the effects of ardent spirits. (38209)
Address upon the general changes. (4700)
Address upon the industrial school movement. 7156
Address upon the late . . . Dr. Fredrick Dorsey. 45466
Address upon the life and character of Washington. 9332
Address upon the life and services of Edward Everett. 18442
Address . . . upon the opening of Baltimore College. 81408
Address . . . Utica Musical Academy. 55513
Address vindicating the right of woman. (18053)
Address was read at a meeting of the merchants. 61670
Address Washington Benevolent Society, 1815. 32527
Address . . . Washington Benevolent Society of Leominster. 37368
[Address] . . . Washington, February 27th. 1823. 96971
Address . . . Washington Lodge. (33308)
Address . . . William and Mary College. 14103
Address . . . Williams College. 9133
Address . . . with a narrative. 15633
Address, with appendix. 33072
Address written by Mr. Clerc. 13636
Address written by Parley P. Pratt. (64968)
Addresse a toutes les puissances de l'Europe. 28298
Addresse an das Volk der Vereinigten Staaten. 101542
Addresse an die democratischen Republikaner in Adams County. 59862
Addresses. (26529), (39941), 45909, 50433
Addresses and discourse at the inauguration. 34985, 43844
Addresses and documents. (57591), 93510
Addresses and letters. 30688
Addresses and memorial. 35562
Addresses and messages of George Washington. 101529
Addresses and messages of the Presidents of the United States, from 1789 to 1839. (446)
Addresses and messages of the Presidents of the United States, from Washington to Harrison. 447
Addresses and messages of the Presidents of the United States, from Washington to Tyler. 448

Addresses and messages of the Presidents of the United States, inaugural, annual, and special, from 1789 to 1849. 104205
Addresses and messages of the Presidents of the United States, inaugural, annual, and special, from 1789 to 1846. 104197
Addresses and messages of the Presidents of the U. S. to Congress. (445)
Addresses and miscellaneous writings. (29484)
Addresses and other proceedings. 54911
Addresses and poems. 85224
Addresses and proceedings at the centennial anniversary. 74142
Addresses and proceedings at the semi-centennial celebration. 48832
Addresses and proceedings of the State Independent Free Territory Convention of the People of Ohio. 56873
Addresses and recommendations of Congress. 101534
Addresses and remonstrances. 61444
Addresses and reports read before the Bunker Hill Soldiers' Relief Society April 19th, 1861, & April 20, 1863. 12094
Addresses and reports read before the Bunker Hill Soldiers' Relief Society, April 19, 1862 & April 20, 1863. 9172
Addresses and resolutions. 85173
Addresses and sermon at the dedication. 13701
Addresses and sermons by Joseph Wilberforce Richardson. 71072
Addresses at the annual meeting. 85386
Address at the commencement of Rutgers Female College. 74442
Addresses . . . at the inauguration [of A. Bruyn Hasbrouck.] 30791
Addresses at the inauguration of Charles William Eliot. 22131, (30724)
Addresses at the inauguration of Israel W. Andrews. 44568
Addresses at the inauguration of Jared Sparks. (30724), 89014
Addresses at the inauguration of Rev. Alonzo A. Miner. (49197)
Addresses at the inauguration of Rev. E. D. MacMaster. 48682
Addresses at the inauguration of Rev. H. D. Kitchel. 48832
Addresses at the inauguration of Rev. L. Clarke Seelye. 84961
Addresses at the inauguration of the Hon. Edward Everett. 23272, (30724)
Addresses . . . at the inauguration of the professors. 48832
Addresses at the inauguration of the Rev. G. Wilson McPhail. 43623
Addresses at the inauguration of the Rev. Robert G. Wilson. 57015
Addresses at the inauguration of William W. Folwell. 49312
Addresses . . . [at] the opening of the Free Academy. 54284
Addresses before the . . . [Free School] Society. 54285
Addresses before the members of the Bar. 104058
Addresses . . . before the Philomathean Society. 60390
Addresses before the Virginia state convention. 1395
Addresses before the Washington Art Association. 92061
Addresses before the Young Men's Temperance Society. 11991
Addresses by H. B. Rogers. 38788, 72649
Addresses by His Excellency Governor John A. Andrew. 1469, 6477
Addresses by J. Young Scammon. 12621

Addresses [by John Codman.] 14135
Addresses by John T. Hilton. (6765), note after 97006
Addresses by Major General O. O. Howard. (33274)
Addresses by Prof. B. F. Greene. 69638
Addresses by Rev. J. P. Langworthy. 45890
Addresses by Rev. Jesse Appleton. 1802
Addresses by the Lord Bishop of Huron. 5574, 34009
Addresses by the President of Columbia College. 14805
Addresses commemorative of the late Lieut. Enos Dickinson. 90998
Addresses delivered at the celebration. 35391, 53305
Addresses delivered at the dedication of the Clinton Cemetery. 13758
Addresses delivered at the dedication of the edifice. 2926
Addresses delivered at the dedication of the Indian Hill Cemetery. 48870
Addresses delivered at the inauguration of Rev. William H. Campbell. 74435
Addresses delivered at the inauguration of the professors. 18520
Addresses delivered at the inauguration of the Rev. Robert G. Wilson. 57015, 104682
Addresses delivered at the opening of the Pennsyvlania Female College. 5341
Addresses delivered at the presentation. (53057)
Addresses delivered at the sixth anniversary meeting. 45244
Addresses delivered at the stated communication. 13455
Addresses delivered at the thirty-fifth commencement. 34025
Addresses delivered before the Pennsylvania State Agricultural Society. 60376
Addresses, delivered by Governor Wallace. 101100
Addresses delivered in . . . Philadelphia. 6058
Addresses delivered in the Chapel at West Point. (82343)
Addresses delivered in the Hall. (61307)
Addresses, delivered in the Senate and House of Representatives. 74305
Addresses delivered on laying the corner stone. 90180
Addresses, delivered on Thursday, December 18, 1851. 90437
Addresses delivered on various public occasions. 27665
Addresses, delivered to the candidates for the Baccalaureate. 56033
Addresses for blood and devastation. 50452
Addresses from the Committee. 8085
Addresses in recognition of his public services. 84277
Addresses in the Congress of the U. S. 324
Addresses . . . in Washington, D. C. 39226
Addresses, inaugurals and charges. 79014
Addresses . . . inauguration of Charles Conway Felton. (30724)
Addresses . . . inauguration of the Rev. James Walker. (30724)
Addresses . . . inauguration of Thomas Hill. (30724)
Addresses, lectures, and reviews. 33410
Addresses [of Amos Twitchell.] 6993
Addresses of Benj. B. Edsall. 21874, 93939, note after 97514
Addresses [of Cassius Marcellus Clay.] 13536
Addresses of Drs. Wm. Hague and E. N. Kirk. 29530
Addresses of George H. Calvert. 55028
Addresses of H. H. Childs. 12733

Addresses of Hon. G. M. G. Leonard. 72402
Addresses of John Romeyn Brodhead. (8175)
Addresses of Prof. Morse. 50958
Addresses of Rev. A. D. Mayo. (47182)
Addresses of Rev. Dr. Perkins. 97393
Addresses of Rev. Drs. Park, Post, & Bacon. 58616
Addresses of Revs. Drs. Hopkins, E. Beecher, Bacon, and L. Beecher. 85922
Addresses of Revs. Drs. Sturtevant and Stearns. 93275
Addresses of the city of New York to George Washington. 53515, 54069
Addresses of the Governor and Council. 35660, 105080
Addresses of the Hon. W. D. Kelley. 61445
Addresses of the liberator. 6206
Addresses of the Lords and Commons to the King. (10335)
Addresses of the newly appointed professors. 14806
Addresses of the Philadelphia Society for the Promotion of National Industry. 10889, 22987, 62041
Addresses of the Right Rev. Alonzo Potter. 61535, 62093
Addresses of the Society [of the First Church in Mansfield.] (80370), 80371, 102522
Addresses of the Soldiers' and Sailors' State Central Committee. 86328
Addresses of the successive Presidents of the United States. 449
Addresses of W. P. Phillips. 75626
Addresses of W. W. Campbell. 12480
Addresses on the battle of Bennington. 9645
Addresses on the consideration of resolutions. 59863
Addresses on the death of Hon. Edward D. Baker. 2822
Addresses on the death of Hon. Owen Lovejoy. 42370
Addresses on the death of Hon. Stephen A. Douglas. (20696)
Addresses on the death of Hon. T. H. Hicks. 31723
Addresses . . . on the dedication of the Hartford Hospital. 30652
Addresses on the inauguration of the first president. 22360
Addresses on the occasion, by Messrs. Hamersley, Stuart, and Deming. (12161), 14763, 30669, 65765
Addresses on the occasion of opening the Girard College. (27494)
Addresses on the occasion of the death of the Hon. John C. Bell. 4464
Addresses on the occasion of the death of the Hon. Robert R. Reed. (59864), 68577
Addresses on the presentation of the sword. 35391
Addresses on the presidential election. 450
Addresses on the social and religious questions. 50454
Addresses presented to General Washington. (13897), note after 101860
Addresses, presented to His Excellency Major General Sir John Colborne. 98066
Addresses, remonstrances, and petitions. 451
Addresses, resolutions, and treasurer's report. 81820
Addresses to his Excellency [George, Earl of Dalhousie] the Governor in Chief. (10336)
Addresses to His Royal Highness the Prince Regent. 98096
Addresses to Lord Aylmer. (2518)
Addresses to old men. 46214
Addresses . . . to Sir Arthur Rumbold. 52426
Addresses to Sir Charles Metcalfe. 48168

Addresses to Sir Francis B. Head. 31137, 98067
Addresses to the citizens of the southern states. 10889
Addresses to the graduates. (39716)
Addresses to the public. 93382
Addresses to the Right Rev. the bishops, the clergy, and lay members. 35789
Addresses to the society. (80370), 80371, note after 100602, 102522
Addresses to the whites. 20094
Addressor addressed. 94074, 94075, 94077, 102518
Addums, Mozis. pseud New letters. see Bagby, George William.
Adelaide. 99838
Adelbert College, Cleveland, Ohio. see Western Reserve University, Cleveland, Ohio.
Adelbert von Chamisso's Werke. 11817
Adele Dubois. 77254
Adele y Matilde. 74608
Adeline. pseud. Scenes in the West Indies. see Sergeant, Mrs. R. A.
Adelphi School, Philadelphia. see Philadelphia Association of Friends for the Instruction of Poor Children. Adelphi School.
Adelphic-Union, Williams College. see Williams College, Williamstown, Mass. Adelphic Union.
Adelung, Johann Christoph, 1732-1806. 453, 5269, 8389, 11042, 31600, 52411, 98846
Adept. pseud. Chrysal. see Johnstone, Charles.
Adequacy of the constitution. (23888)
Ader, Israel Ben. pseud. see Ben Ader, Israel. pseud.
Adet, ------. tr. 38014
Adet, Carlos Emilio. ed. 88808
Adet, Pierre Auguste, 1763-1832. 454-456, 2460, 13884, 14004, 16878, 23919, 34900, 62659, (70219), 2d note after 101709 see also France. Legation. U. S.
Adfywiad cvefydd Lloegr Newdd. (457)
Adgate, Andrew. ed. 89423
Adger, John B. (458)-459, 82027, 87524
Adhemar, ------. 67156
Adiawando. Indian Chief. 4391, 15429
Adicional al manifiesto legal. 86377
Adicionada con el mensajo al Congreso Nacional. (12753)
Adiciones al libro de las glorias de Queretaro. 80974
Adiciones y rectificaciones a La historia de Mexico. 40962
Adiev a la France. 40166
Adirondack. pseud. National finances. 51979
Adirondack. 31147
Adirondack Iron and Steel Company. 460
Adis, H. 462
Adison, ------. 91585
Adioynder of svndry other particvlar wicked plots. 78364
Adjourned Meeting of Delegates of Various Banks, from Different States in the Union, New York, 1838. see Bank Convention, New York, 1838.
An adjourned meeting of the citizens of Kershaw District was held. 88076, note after 94393
Adjourned Meeting of the Freeholders and Inhabitants of the Village of Brooklyn, 1825. see Brooklyn, N. Y. Citizens.
Adjutant General's report, 1862. (37551)
Adjutant General's report of Missouri State Militia. 49578
Adjutant Stearns. 90979
Adlard, ------. illus. 3784, 8899, note after 104504-104505

Adlard, George. 464
Adler, ------. 69673
Adler, Cyrus, 1863-1940. 85092
see also Smithsonian Institution. Librarian.
Adler, N. tr. (36972)
Adm------I V------n. pseud. Genuine speech. see Vernon, Edward, 1684-1757.
Administracao local. 85636
Administracion de justicia. 99482
Administracion General, Caracas. see Caracas, Venezuela. Administracion General de Tobaco.
Administration and its assailants. 43631
Administration and regulation of the colonies. 71379
Administration and the opposition. 272, 29659, 52798, 80855
Administration and the war. 68057
Administration Convention, Baltimore, 1827. see Maryland Administration Convention, Baltimore, 1827.
Administration Convention, Raleigh, N. C., 1827. 55588
Administration de Sabastien-Joseph de Carvalho et Melo. 63911
Administration dissected. 465
Administration du Marquis de Pombal. 19912
Administration of Abraham Lincoln sustained. 16299
Administration of the British colonies. 64818-64820
Administration of the colonies. 64814-64817, 64821
Administration reviewed. 43440
Administrations of parochial bishops valid. 40318, 80391
Administrations of the United States. 89053
Administrative rules and regulations. 84999
Admiraal Piet Hein. 51278
Admirabilis vita S. Rosae a Sancta Maria virginis Peruanae. 73177
Admirabilis vita, virtus, gloria S, Rosae a S. Maria virginis Limanae. (67808)
Admirabilis vita, virtus, gloria S. Rosae a S. Maria virginis Limanae ordinis Praedicatorum primi. 73178
Admirable blessings. 79444, 91940, 104083
Admirable deliverances from danger. 9502
Admiral Jeremy Squib. pseud. see Squib, Jeremy, Admiral. pseud.
Admiral Lowe's last cruise. 59184
Admiral Morgan's expedition against Panama. 79781
Admiral Porter and President Grant. (64224)
Admiral Rodney's victory. 66539
Admiral Russel's letter. 74287
Admiral Sir P. B. V. Broke, Bart., KCB. 7973
Admiral Squib. pseud. see Squib, Admiral. pseud.
Ad^m. V---n. pseud. Opinion. see Vernon, Edward, 1684-1757.
Ad^m. V---n's opinion upon the present state of the British navy. 99243
Admiral Vernon's ghost. 99249
Admiral Vernon's resolution. 99249
Admiranda narratio. 5112, (5784)
Admiranda vita, gloria S. Ludovici Bertrundi Valentini. (67808)
Admiranda navigationis. (8784)
Admirari, Nil. pseud. Trollopiad. see Shelton, Frederick William, 1814-1881.
Admired new song. 92174C
Admirer of Chivalry. pseud. Poltroonius. see Head, Edward Francis.
Admission of Alabama. 7130
Admission of California. Remarks of Mr. Cass. 11349

Admission of California. Speech . . . in the
Senate. 4787
Admission of California. Speech of Mr. Bocock.
6109
Admission of California: speech of Willard P.
Hall. (29856)
Admission of Georgia. Speech . . . in the
Senate. 64024
Admission of Georgia. Speech . . . March 5,
1870. (39276)
Admission of Georgia. Speech of Hon. George
E. Spencer. 89317
Admission of Georgia. Speech of Hon. Hiram
R. Revels. 70167
Admission of Georgia. Two speeches. 78021
Admission of Kansas. Speech . . . March 27,
1858. (29841)
Admission of Kansas. . . . Speech . . . March
26, 1858. 50817
Admission of Kansas. Speech of Hon. G. A.
Grow. 28993
Admission of Kansas. Speech of Hon. James
Harlan. 30386
Admission of Kansas. Speech of Hon. L. F. S.
Foster. 25252
Admission of Kansas. Speech of Hon. Marcus
J. Parrott. 58851
Admission of Kansas. Speech of Hon. W.
Porcher Miles. (48942)
Admission of Kansas. Speech of the Hon.
Henry M. Phillips. 62492
Admission of Kansas. Speech of William H.
Seward. (79500)
Admission of Oregon. 91253
Admission of West Virginia. 5744
Admit to the assembly. 93359
Admonish crime. pseud. Midsummer's day-
dream. see Richmond, James Cook.
Admonition of Poor Richard. (25598)
Admonition to the reader. 66430
Admonition to youth. 83999
Admonitions against disunion. 6953
Admonitions from "the depths of the earth."
64662
Admonitorie preface. 10199
Admonitory epistles. 41496
Admonitory letter to those brethren. 99820
Admonitory picture and solemn warning. 21394
Adolenscens Evropaevs ab Indo moribvs
Christianis informatus. 55273
Adolff, -----. tr. 63176
Adolph, and other poems. 79986
Adolphe, J. C. R. Milliet de Saint. see
Milliet de Saint-Adolphe, J. C. R.
Adolphus, John 1768-1845. 466
Adonde las dan las toman. 105743
Adonis, ou le bon Negre. 62676
Adopted citizen. pseud. American slavery.
see Scholte, Henry P.
Adopted citizen. pseud. Texas question. see
Santangelo, Orazio Donato Gideon de
Attelis.
Adopted citizen of the republic. pseud. Letters.
Letters. see Treviranus. pseud.
Adopted son of America. 96169
Adoptirten Mitgliede der Oneida-Nation. pseud.
Reise in Ober-Penslyvanien. see
Crevecoeur, J. Hector St. John, 1735-
1813.
Adorable ways of God. 98492
Adresse a l'Assemblee Nationale de France.
96078, 96079
Adresse a l'Assemblee Nationale [par l'Assem-
blee Provinciale de la Partie du Nord de
Saint-Domingue.] 75036
Adresse a l'Assemblee Nationale [par les colons
de Saint-Domingue.] (75035)

Adresse a l'Assemblee Nationale par les
proprietaires de Saint-Domingue. (75037)
Adresse a l'Assemblee Nationale pour
l'abolition de la traite des noirs. 8014,
81804
Adresse a la Convention. 58165
Adresse a la Convention Nationale. 75038,
75121
Adresse a MM. de l'Assemble Nationale. (34352)
Adresse au corps legislatif. 100905
Addresse au Conseil Legislatif du Territoire
d'Orleans. 42189, (53303), 65745
Adresse au people Francais. 19654
Adresse au Roi Coton. 59581
Adresse au Roi, et discours a Sa Majeste.
75039
Adresse au sujet d' une entendue de terre.
69718
Adresse aux amis de l'humanite. 81805
Adresse aux nations de l'Europe. 81806
Adresse ci-jointe de l'Assemblee Legislative.
10538, 10611
Addresse de Guillaume Thomas Raynal. (68072)
Adresse de la Garde Nationale. 64177
Adresse de la jeunesse de Cap-Francaise.
10750
Adresse de la Societe de la Morale Chretienne.
(81807)
Adresse de la Societe der [sic] Amis des Noirs,
a l'Assemblee Nationale. 13515
Adresse de la Societe des Amis des Noirs, en
faveur des hommes de couleur. 85808
Adresse de l'Assemblee Generale de la partie
Francoise de Saint-Domingue a Paris.
75102
Adresse de l'Assemblee Legislative. 67055
Adresse de l'Assemblee Provinciale de la
Partie du Nord de Saint-Domingue. 75040
Adresse de MM. les Maire et Officiers
Municipaux de Bordeaux. (6405)
Adresse de Pinchinat aux hommes de couleur.
94901
Adresse de Polverel et Sontonax. 99242
Adresse des capitaines. 10751
Adresse des citoyens de couleur. 36424
Adresse des citoyens des Etats-Unis de
l'Amerique. 99253
Adresse des colons de l'ile de Saint-Domingue.
75041
Adresse des habitants de la Partie du Nord de
Saint-Domingue. 75042
Adresse des membres de l'Assemblee
Provinciale du Nord de Saint-Domingue.
75043
Adresse des planteurs et citoyens de l'isle
Sainte Lucie. 75408
Adresse pour les noms des personnes nommees
a des charges. 10575
Adresses de l'Assemblee Provinciale du Nord
de St. Domingue. 29564
Adresses des Icariens de Nauvoo a citoyen
Cabet. 9788
Adresses le 4 Juin 1854. (57399)
Adriaanszoon, Petrus Loosjes. tr. 5361, 101777
Adrian, -----. 467
Adrian city (Mich.) directory and advertiser. 468
Adrian Gottlieb Volckarts Chirurgi zu Halbau in
Ober-Lausitz Reisen und Schiffahrten.
100685A
Adrian van Berkel's Beschreibung seiner Reisen.
4875
Adriance, Isaac. appellant 89349
Adrien ***. pseud. Les Savanes. see
Roquette, Adrien E.
Adrift in Dixie. (23026)
Aduana martima de Manzanillo. 48431
Aduanas maritimas. 48257

Aduard, O. A. Lewe van. see Lewe van
Audard, O. A.
Adulateur. 101480
Adult School Union, Philadelphia. see
Philadelphia Academy and Adult School
Union.
Advance almanac for 1862. 75315
Advance Light Brigade. see U. S. Army.
Advance Light Brigade.
Advance of the Anglo-Americans to the South-
West. 25019
Advance of the United States. 38308
Advanced value of gold. 36159
Advancement of female education. 104043
Advancement of the common school. 22429
Advantage of testing our principles. 4575
Advantageous situation of the city of Washington.
101929
Advantages and disadvantages of the marriage
state. 102452
Advantages and obligations. 13345
Advantages and the dangers of the American
scholar. 99264
Advantages as a manufacturing and commercial
point. 67278
Advantages of a settlement upon the Ohio.
(56875)
Advantages of an increase of the West Indian
Corps considered. 80564
Advantages of direct steam communication.
48935
Advantages of early religion. 10073
Advantages of education. 79358
Advantages of emigration to Canada. 11557
Advantages of League Island. 39516, 39517,
69684
Advantages of life insurance. 51610
Advantages of national repentance. 20099
Advantages of Negro slavery. 72123
Advantages of ocean steam navigation. 48936
Advantages of Ralston. 67613
Advantages of the definitive treaty. (469)
Advantages of the proposed canal. 22740,
50826
Advantages of the revolution illustrated. 470
Advantages of unity. 8641
Advantages thereof in preventing and curing
many distempers. 82869-82870
Advantages to Great Britain from the
approaching war. 471
Advantages which America derives from her
commerce. 472, 3683
Advantages which have accrued to the publick.
88170
Advantages which ministers in the colonies may
enjoy. 473
Advenimiento de SS. MM. I. I. Maximiliano y
Carlota. 47032
Advent review and Sabbath herald. 84477
Adventidas en los monarchas antiguos. 80985
Adventism, millennarianism, and a gross
materialism exposed. 14947
Adventure in Vermont. 99138-99139
Adventure on a frozen lake. (33869)
Adventure on the banks of the Ohio. 104447
Adventurers in the second class of the New-
Ark Land and Cash Lottery. (12927)
Adventurers to Prosecute the Discovery of the
Passage to the Western Ocean of America,
London. Committee. see Committee
Appointed by the Adventurers to Prosecute
the Discovery of the Passage to the
Western Ocean of America, and Extend
the Trade, and Settle the Countries
Beyond Hudson's Bay, London, 1749.
Adventures. American anecdotes. 91505
Adventures among the corsairs of the Levant.
29473

Adventures among the Indians and beavers.
10906
Adventures among the spiritualists and freelovers.
(40021)
Adventures among the trappers. (69070)
Adventures and achievements of Americans.
33297
Adventvres and discovrses of Captain Iohn
Smith. 82859
Adventures and discoveries of the first explorers.
3229
Adventures and escapes of Harvey Robbins and
family. 71819
Adventures and observations. 82830
Adventures and observations in Southern
California. 64804
Adventures and providential deliverances. 23120
Adventures and sufferings of Peter Wilkinson
[i. e. Williamson.] 44258, 105687-note
after 105690
Adventures and surprizing deliverances of James
Dorbourdieu. 20411
Adventures by sea and land; a cruise in a whale
boat. 70761
Adventures by sea and land of the Count De
Ganay. (12573)
Adventures d'Arthur Gordon Pym. 63528
Adventures in America. 30227
Adventures in Americana. 100510
Adventures in California and its gold fields.
9992
Adventures in California and Nicaragua. 103938
Adventures in Canada. 26841, note after 90307
Adventures in Mexico. 20600
Adventures in Mexico and the Rocky Mountains.
74501
Adventures in search of a white buffalo. 69022
Adventures in Texas. 64533
Adventures in Texas, chiefly in the spring and
summer of 1840. 42979
Adventures in the Apache country. (8656)
Adventures in the Camanche country. 102247,
102249
Adventures in the far South-West. (4724)
Adventures in the far West. 2952, (4724),
69064
Adventures in the far West, a story for boys.
64917
Adventures in the far West and the far South
West. (4719)
Adventures in the fur countries of the far North.
69085
Adventures in the gold region. 5350
Adventures in the Pacific. 17142
Adventures in the path of empire. 94440
Adventures in the polar regions. 2952, 23906
Adventures in the South Pacific. 480
Adventures in the South-West. (4723)
Adventures in the wilderness. 51549
Adventures in the wilds of North America.
(38912), 38914
Adventures in the wilds of the United States.
38913
Adventures in the woods. 16408
Adventures of a bale of goods from America.
(474)
Adventures of a Baltimore trader. 90166
Adventures of a Cotton-Tree. 104177
Adventures of a family lost in the great
desert. 4426
Adventures of a gold-digger. 80339
Adventures of a gold finder. 476
Adventures of a gold-seeker in California.
79971
Adventures of a guinea. 36391
Adventvres of a human boy. 80482
Adventures of a lawyer. 95391
Adventures of a lost family. 69037

Adventures of a New Bedford boy. 29745
Adventures of a Peruvian family. (69045)
Adventures of a sugar plantation. 104178
Adventures of a wanderer. 51771, 59548
Adventures of Alexander Vendchurch. 20411
Adventures of an African slave trader. 47093
Adventures of an angler in Canada. 38915, 38926
Adventures of an army officer. 57216
Adventures of an atom. 85104
Adventures of an East-India rupee. (78271)
Adventures of an emigrant. 73538
Adventures of an English gentleman's family. (5056)
Adventures of an officer in Southern Mexico. 69068
Adventures of Audubon. 59544
Adventures of Billy Bump. 27922
Adventures of British seamen. 51503
Adventures of Canadian emigrants. 75260
Adventures of Captain Bonneville. 35125
Adventures of Captain Bonneville in the Rocky Mountains. 35126, 35195
Adventures of Captain Huestis. (33564)
Adventures of Capt. Isaac Stewart. 44258, 105687-note after 105690
Adventures of Captain John Smith. 82858
Adventures of Christopher Hawkins. (30948)
Adventures of Col. Daniel Boon. 24336, 34355
Adventures of Col. Gracchus Vanderbomb. (36527)
Adventures of Congo in search of his master. (81808)
Adventures of Daniel Boone. 30971
Adventures of Daniel Boone; and the power of virtuous and refined beauty. 8787
Adventures of Daniel Boone, the Kentucky rifleman. (6372)
Adventures of Dick Onslow. 4215, (37902)
Adventures of Ebenezer Fox. 25343
Adventures of Emmera. 106061
Adventures of five hours. (62861), 86904
Adventures of four Russian sailors. 89544
Adventures of G. Whillikens, C. S. A. 88322
Adventures of Hector Wigler. 103943, 1st note after 105973
Adventures of Henry Hudson. 33492
Adventures of Hercules Hardy. 93408
Adventures of hunters and travellers. 475
Adventures of James Capen Adams. (32275)
Adventures of James Sharan. (79772)
Adventures of John R. Jewett. 27922
Adventures [of John Wesley.] (27219)
Adventures of Jonathan Corncob. 477
Adventures of Leather Stocking. 16541
Adventures of Louisa Baker. 102739
Adventures of Louisa Baker, a native of Massachusetts. 102739
Adventures of Lucy Brewer, (alias) Louisa Baker. note after 102739
Adventures of Lucy Brewer, who served as a marine. 7758, note after 102739
Adventures of M. P. Viaud. 99416
Adventures of Miles Wallingford. 16409
Adventures of Miss Clementia Shoddy. 91058
Adventures of Miss Harriet Simper. 97238
Adventures of Miss Lucy Brewer. 102742
Adventures of Miss Lucy Brewer, a native of Plymouth County, Mass. 102742
Adventures of Mr. George Edwards. 21921
Adventures of Mr. Thomas Freeman. (25780)
Adventures of Mrs. West. 102741
Adventures of my grandfather. 61320
Adventures of Parson Handy. 75737
Adventures of Pomponious. 478
Adventures of Porte Crayon and his cousins. 93092, 1st note after 100557
Adventures of Richard Pengelley. 37907

Adventures of Robert Chevalier. 40158
Adventures of Roderick Random. 85104A
Adventures of Sieur de Montavban. 96171
Adventures of Sir John Franklin. 25632
Adventures of Sir Lyon Bourse. 6937
Adventures of the Barnabys in America. 97035
Adventures of the Chevalier du Faublas. 42357
Adventures of the crew of the Wager. 10205
Adventures of the first settlers. (73326)
Adventures of the forefathers of New-England. 17682
Adventures of the Ojibbeway and Ioway Indians. 11529
Adventures of the widow wedded. 97035
Adventures of Theresia, Baroness van Hoog. 95323
Adventures of three Southerners. (11172), 5th note after 100577
Adventures of Timothy Peacock. 95474, note before 99222
Adventures of Triptolemus Snooks. 14112
Adventures of twenty-two scouts. (56973)
Adventures of Unca Eliza Winkfield. 104781
Adventures of Uncle Sam. 479, 24260
Adventures on the Columbia River. 17267
Adventures on the frontier. 41902, 69084
Adventures on the grand hunting grounds. 48225
Adventures on the Mosquito Shore. 89951, 90002
Adventures on the prairie. 34592
Adventures on the western coast of South America. 17143
Adventures, sufferings and observations of James Wood. 105038
Adventures with the gold diggers. 81347
Adventures within and beyond the Union lines. (8666)
Adversus Libertinos. 46215
Advertencia. (76008)
Advertencia aos senhores deputados as Cortes de Lisboa. 88836
Advertencia del traductor. 63697, 97913
Advertencias a los confesores de Indios. 3993
Advertencias de danos qve se sigven. 93320
Advertencias importantes. 81095
Advertencias. Para los confessores de los naturales. 3242
Advertencias qve el presentado Fr. Diego de Velasco. 98789
Advertencias y preceptos para la Classe de Menores. 52204
Advertencias y preceptos utiles para la Classe de Menores. 47867
Advertisment. 6978, 17481, (23941), 26421, 27642, (27643), (33445), 33446, 46550, (61447), 61930, note after 95360, 2d note after 97091, 99279, 102685, 104028, 104237, 104355, 104986, 106052
Advertisement and circular. 102346
Advertisement, and not a joke. 481
Advertisement: as the present state of our funds. 102690
Advertisement. Boston. January 15. 1752. 85839
Advertisement by C. B. Coventry. (3909)
Advertisement concerning this work in general. 91537-91538
Advertisement. For the satisfaction of the adventurers. 46191
Advertisement having appeared at the Coffee-House. 95985
Advertisement I beg leave to take this opportunity. 59867
Advertisement in the Boston Gazette, Feb. 20, 1721. 54635
Advertisement of a proposition. 20225, note before 93512
Advertisement of December 31, 1862. (15234)
Advertisement of December 12, 1860. (64475)

Advertisement of the Commissioners for Designs. 6759
Advertisement [of the Commissioners of Property.] 59866
Advertisement of the Committee for the Abolition of the Slave Trade. 69434
Advertisement of the . . . [New England Female Medical] College. (52683)
Advertisement. Philadelphia, the 22d of May, 1775 [i. e. 1755]. 7210
Advertisement. Proposals to all such people. 64856
Advertisement signed W, X, Y, Z. 91499
Advertisement . . . to supply the city of New-York with rock water. (54070)
Advertisement to the powers and people of this nation. 86627, note after 104031
Advertisement. To the students of Yale-College. 105894-105895
Advertisement. Whereas an advertisement was yesterday dispers'd. 98696
Advertisement. . . . William Masters. 46192
Advertisements for the unexperienced planters of New-England or any where. 82815, 82823-82824, 82855
Advertisements for the unexperienced planters of New England, or anywhere. 82816
Advertisements from the Boston Chronicle. 6558
Advertiser's guide: containing a complete list of all the newspapers in Canada. (47403)
Advertiser's guide, containing a short description of those towns. 24478
Advertiser's hand-book. 61294
Advertisers' manual. 87127
Advertising gazetteer of Michigan. 19786
Advertising hand-book. 23187
Advertissement certain contenant les pertes aduenues en l'Armee d'Espagne. 11603
Advertissement for men inclyned to plantasions in America. 86845, 1st note after 93596
Advice and caution from our Monthly Meeting at Philadelphia. 61449
Advice and exhortation. 28500
Advice and information to the freeholders and freemen of the province of Pensilvania. 59868, (60012), 60693, 65887
Advice and instruction for German emigrants. (6131)
Advice as to camping. 76552, 76647
Advance concerning bills of exchange. (71909)
Advice from a clock. 93034
Advice from Taberah. (46216)
Advice from the watch tower. (46217)
Advice in the pursuits of literature. 38084
Advice of a father to a son. 22435
Advice [of John Wesley.] (52054)
Advice of William Penn to his children. 59698-59699
Advice to a child. 62517
Advice to a young man. 46472
Advice to a young tradesman. (25598)
Advice to emigrants. 21604
Advice to emigrants on the best routes. 26033
Advice to his [i. e. William Penn's] children. 59698-59699
Advice to his [i. e. Thomas Symmes'] children, to his servants. 94115
Advice to his [i. e. Hugh Peters'] daughter. 61192
Advice to his [i. e. Hugh Peters'] daughter written by his own hand. 61191
Advice to his [i. e. William Hobby's] people from the grave. 32317
Advice to his [i. e. Sir Walter Raleigh's] son. 67577-67584
Advice to his [i. e. the Earl of Chesterfield's] son, on men and manners. 90230, 90233, 90236-90237, 90243

Advice to servants. 482, 28934
Advice to soldiers. 29863
Advice to the children of Godly ancestors. 46629
Advice, to the churches of the faithful. 46218
Advice to the colonies. 70128
Advice to the commanders and officers. 27394
Advice to the free-holders and electors of Pennsylvania. 59869
Advice to the freeholders, &c. 60456, (69525)
Advice to the inhabitants of the northern colonies. 483
Advice to the King of Spain. 10199
Advice to the lovely Cyprians. 30227
Advice to the million upon emigration. 7701
Advice to the officers and soldiers. 48970
Advice to the officers of the British army. 482, 28934
Advice to the parents and guardians of pupils. 62201
Advice to the privileged orders. 3414, 3426
Advice to tale-bearers. 101370
Advijs door een Lief-hebber. 7545, (7981)
Advijs van den Raedt van Staten. 484
Aduis tres-necessaire a tous ceux qui veulent habiter. 7133
Advise [sic] and information to the freeholders and freemen. (60012)
Aduise [sic] concerning the philosophy of these late discoueryes. 35711, note after 92708
Advisive narrative concerning Virginia. 26274, 2d note after 100571
Advisory Board of Aeronautics. 85000
Advisory Committee on the Langley Aerodynamical Laboratory. see Smithsonian Institution. Advisory Committee on the Langley Aerodynamical Laboratory.
Advocate for peace. pseud. War with England. 101268
Advocate for water. 8327
Advocate of education. (77823)
Advocate of equality. 67421
Advocate of freedom. 85345
Advocate of liberty. 85345
Advocate of peace. 91047, 92015, 93687
Advocate of peace. By Henry Holcombe. 32462
Advocate's Library, Montreal. 50253
Advogado da justicia. pseud. Nova forma de apreciar. (26593)
Advys op de Presentatie van Portugael. Het tweed Deel. 60987
Advys op de Presentatie van Portugal. Het eerste Deel. 7503
Aduarte, Diego, Bp. 76772
Adye, Stephen Payne. 485
Adynasius. pseud. Essays on lay representation. see Snethen, Nicholas, 1769-1845.
Aegidius, Petrus. ed. 50542
Aegles. pseud. Letter of Aegles. see Watkins, Tobias.
Aegles. pseud. Letters. see Watkins, Tobias.
AEgyptiaca servitus. 72227
Aegyptian. pseud. Acts of the rebels. see Ray, James.
AEgyptus, Tiphys. pseud. see Tiphys AEgyptus. pseud.
Aelij Antonij Nebrissensis Gra[m]matici in cosmographiae libros introductoriũ[m] incipitur foeliciter ad lectorem. 52205
AElii Antonii Nebrissensis Grammatici in cosmographiae libros introductorium, multo quae antea castigatus. 52206
Aelteste Geschichte der Entdeckung und Erforschung des Golfs von Mexico. 38210
Aelwyd f'Ewythr Robert. 92620
Aen alle Koninghen, Potentaten en Natien. 36131
Aen d'Edele Gr: Mog: Heeren Staten van Hollandt. 4275, note after 102883

Aen de Edele Groot-Mogende Heeren Staten
van Hollant. 15929, note after 102887
Aen de Heeren Staten Generael. 102913
Aen de Hoogh-Mogende Heeren Staten Generael
der Verrenighde Nederlanden. 16738,
102890
Aen de Hoogh Moog: Heeren Staten Generael
der Vereenighde Nederlanden. 486,
102877
Aen-Spraeck aen den Getrouwen Hollander.
7504
Aende Hooghende Vvelghe borene. 41356
Aende Vvelgheborene. 41356
Aeneas Silvius. see Pius II, Pope, 1405-1464.
Aeneid. 73932, 92337-92338
Aeneis. 57984, 73932, 76458, 92337-92338,
2d note after 102599
Aengemerckte voorvallen op de Vreden Articulen
met Portugael. 487
Aenmerckelycke Historische Reys-Beschryvinge.
31358
Aenmerkelyke Voyagie gedaan na't Gedeelte van
Noorder America. 31361
Aenmerkenswaardige en Zeldzame West-Indische
Zee- en Land-Reizen. (488), 47474, 2d
note after 102813
Aenmerkingen op Price's Leer- en
Grondbeginsellen van Burgerlijke Vryheit
en Regeering enz. (27927)
Aenshangsel van de Veranderingen van Visschen
in Kikvorschen en van de Kikvorschen in
Visschen. (47959)
Aenspraeck van de Heetgebaeckerden Hollander
Vrienden. 7515
Aenumerantur que in hoc opera, dicto Margarita
philosophica. 69121
Aenwysinge: datmen vande Oost en West-Indische
Compagnien. 102878
Aeolus, or the constitutional politician. 489
Τα Ἀεθλαᾶγγλαμερίκανα ἄρα δὴ Προγυμνας μάτα
τῆς Φραγκίνης νέης Πελατγίκης Μονό-
βιβλὸς 23964, 80733
Aepitoma omnis phylosophiae alias Margarita
Phylosophica. (69122)
AErae: a poem. (81599)
Aerial navigation. 64312
Aerial navigation and the patent laws. 80133
Aeronaute Hollandais. 63530
Aerssen, Francois van. see Sommelsdick,
Francois van Aerssen, Heer van.
Aesculapius non Vinetus. pseud. Jeannette.
35875
Aesop. pseud. Hypocrite. 34140
Aesop, Junior, in America. 490
Aesthetics at Washington. 28672
Aethiopian. pseud. Sermon on the evacuation
of Charleston. 79274
Aetna, a discourse. 90181
Aeusserung uber Chevalier's nord-amerikanischen
Briefe. 21074
Af de Gamle Kiendt. 7129
Afara. (13435)
Afectisimo del bien comun. pseud. Modo
facil. see Truxillo, Ildefonso.
Afer Baptizatus. (31807)
Affair at Grey Town. 90479
Affair on the River Plate considered. 44126
Affaire de la Plata. Notes statistiques et
commerciales. 4514
Affaire de la Plata. Protestation. 38986
Affaire de Tabago. 8015
Affaire des deportes de la Martinique. (44970)
Affaire d'Haiti. 29565
Affaire d'or. (34129)
Affaire du Canada. 10337
Affaire prieux contre le gouvernement du
Bresil. 65519
Affaires de la Plata; compte-rendu. 4516

Affaires de la Plata. La traite Le Predour et
les interets de la France. (5813)
Affaires de la Plata. Petition et documens.
38987
Addaires de la Plata. Refutations. 4515
Affaires de l'Angleterre et de l'Amerique. (491)
Affaires des Jesuites en Amerique. 94126
Affaires du pays. 10338
Affaires entrangeres. 48258
Affairs and men of New Amsterdam. 59217
Affairs at Fort Chartres. 25161
Affairs of Great Britain and America. 36915
Affairs of Rhode Island. (70542)
Affairs of the Canadas. 10339, 74544
Affairs of the Second Church in Boston. 6673
Affecting account of the death of Miss Polly &
Hannah Watts. 15664
Affecting and thrilling anecdotes. 34458
Affecting history of the dreadful distresses.
44258, 105687-note after 105690, 105692
Affecting letter. 96873
Affecting narrative of a lady. 5676
Affecting narrative of facts. 86262
Affecting narrative of Louisa Baker. 2839,
note after 102739, 102740
Affecting narrative of Mr. William Warland.
101428
Affecting narrative of the captivity and sufferings
of Mrs. Mary Smith. 83535, 83537, 83540-
83543
Affecting narrative of the captivity & sufferings
of Mrs. Mary Smith. 83536, 83538-83539
Affecting narrative of the captivity and sufferings
of Thomas Nicholson. (55232)
Affecting narrative of the tragical death. 99424
Affecting narrative of the unfortunate voyage.
1634
Affecting story. 87171
Affection for the house of God recommended.
Sermon . . . at Yarmouth, Jan. 1, 1795,
at the opening of a new meeting-house.
47449
Affection for the house of God recommended.
Sermon delivered at Yarmouth, Jan. 1, 1795
occasioned by the opening of a new
meeting-house. 704
Affectionate address to the inhabitants. 492
Affectionate address to the members. 37741
Affectionate address to young people. 99818
Affectionate caution. 86028
Affectionate farewell address. 104957
Affectionate father's dying advice. (49449)
Affectionate letter. 40314
Affectionately addressed to Robt. J. Walker.
16286
Affection's gift. 73252
Affiches Americaines. 493, (75044)-75045,
75123-75124
Affiches de Brunswick. 494
Affidavit made by Captain Robert Williams.
102652
Affidavit of Andrew Jackson. 47186
Affidavit of G. M. Dodge. (20496)
Affidavit [of General Myers.] 51630
Affidavit of John London. 33149
Affidavit of Mrs. Jane Smith. 82899
Affidavit of the appellant. 56235
Affidavit of the falsity of the first charge.
47084
Affidavits and depositions relative to the
commencement of hostilities in the pro-
vince of Massachusetts Bay. 45622
Affidavits and depositions relative to the
commencements of hostilities at Concord
and Lexington. 502
Affidavits concerning depredations upon
Spanish ships. 96404

Affidavits disproving the charge of misconduct
  against the master. 51814, 103355
Affidavits of . . . Ferrin and . . . Abbey.
  88403
Affidavits showing the treatment of Governor
  Door. (20647), note after 96509
Affinite de quelques legendes americaines.
  12018
Affleck, Thomas. ed. 102979
Afflicted and deserted wife. 91289
Affranchissement des Negres. 77149
Affrighted officers. 5945, 101481
Afhandling om de Norskes. (77809)
Afhandling oms Islands. 99466
Afloat and ashore. 16409, 16471, 16475
Afloat in the forest. 69018
Afonso IV, King of Portugal, 1643-1683. 17452,
  51710, 99522 see also Portugal.
  Sovereigns, etc., 1656-1683 (Afonso VI)
Afoot and alone. 64804
Africa. A poem. 23137
Africa and America. 25030
Africa and America described. 50984
Africa and colonization. 80072
Africa and her children. 63884
Africa and the American flag. (25013)
Africa as she was. 68154
Africa given to Christ. 83756
African, a tale. 50345
African a trust from God to the American.
  17927
African American. pseud. Sermon on the
  capture of Lord Cornwallis. 16816
African captives. 1337, 81809
African colonization. 10889
African colonization. An address . . . at the
  anniversary meeting of the Massachusetts
  Colonization Society. 39226
African colonization. An address . . . at the
  anniversary . . . of the American
  Colonization Society. 39226
African colonization. An address delivered at
  the fifty-second meeting of the American
  Colonization Society. 71903
African colonization. An enquiry into the
  origin of the American Colonization
  Society. 81810
African colonization. [Dated Washington,
  December 19, 1862.] 9068
African colonization—its principles and aims.
  39226
African colonization. Proceedings of a meeting
  of the Friends of African Colonization.
  14732, 45245
African colonization. Proceedings, on the
  formation of the New-York State Coloni-
  zation Society. 53816
African colonization—slave trade—commerce.
  37404
African colonization unveiled. 73910
African Company's property to the forts. (495)
African Education and Civilization Society, New
  York. 69862
African Education Society, Washington, D. C.
  69891, note before 101926
African Education Society, Washington, D. C.
  Board of Managers. 69891, note before
  101926
African history. 27913
African Institution, London. 496, 7891, 44706,
  46857, (81914), (81979), 95656, 95657,
  95661, 95689
African Institution, London. Committee. (68265),
  70254, 91242, 95689
African Institution, London. Committee on a
  General Registry of Slaves. 44709
African Institution, London. Directors. 81966,
  95560, 95656, 95657, 95659

African Institution, London. Directors.
  Committee. 497, 70222, (81979), 95659
African Institution, report. 496
African merchant. pseud. treatise. 96753
African Methodist Episcopal Church. 48181
African Methodist Episcopal Church. New
  England Annual Conference. 52643
African Methodist Episcopal Church. South
  Carolina Branch. 87736
African Methodist Episcopal Church. Trustees.
  48181
African minstrels. 39469
African Mission-School Society, Hartford, Conn.
  (30661)
African Mission-School Society, Hartford, Conn.
  Executive Committee. 15717, (30661)
African monitor. 88338
African observer. 40801
African prince. pseud. Narrative. 51783
African race in America. 43308
African relations by George Sandys. 66686
African relations by J. B. Gramaye. 66686
African repository and colonial journal. (498)
African servitude: what is it, and what its moral
  character? 13666
African servitude: when, why and by whom
  instituted? 500
African slave trade. 4703, 9691, 9695, 13357,
  17225, 18413, 81812
African slave trade and its remedy. 9686,
  (9687)
African slave-trade in Jamaica. 35563, (45211A),
  80327
African slave trade; or, a short view of the
  evidence. 81811
African slave trade. The secret proposal of the
  insurgents. 4703, 81812
African slave trade to Cuba. (81813)
African slavery regarded from an unusual
  stand-point. 29605, (81814)
African Society, Boston. see Sons of the
  African Society, Boston.
African squadron. 24014
African trade for Negro-slaves. 79823, 95530
African trade, the great pillar and support. 501
African Union Meeting and School-House,
  Providence, Rhode Island. see Providence,
  R. I. African Union Meeting and School
  House.
Africani, Ioannis Leonis. see Leo Africanus,
  Joannes.
Africans, living in Boston. petitioners 1792,
  note after 45640, 81891
Africans revenge. 105631
African's right to citizenship. 499, 81815
Africanus, Jean Leo. see Leo Africanus,
  Joannes.
Africanus, P. Scipio. see Scipio Africanus, P.
Africanus, Philo. pseud. see Philo Africanus.
  pseud.
Africa's redemption, a discourse. 73925
Africa's redemption the salvation of our country.
  25758
Afrika, Amerika und Atlantis. 20605
Afrikaners merkwurdige Lebensgeschichte. 98664
Afrikanische Sklavenhandel. 3148
Afrikanische Sklavenhanden und seine Abhulfe.
  (9688)
Afrique. 76712
Afrique interieure. (21011)
Afrus, Dionysius. see Dionysius Periegetes.
Afschaffing der Slavernij in de Nederlandsche
  West Indische Kolonien. 80988
Afschieds-Reden tot de Gemeinte op Batavia.
  (32437)
After icebergs with a painter. 55380
After many days. 25877
After souls by death are separated from their
  bodies. 10226

After the defeat at the Chesapeak. 34135, 102677-102679
After the storm. (81604)
After the war. 69091
After-thought. (79098)-79100
Afterpiece of the comedy of convocation. 90877
Afterthoughts on college and school education. (64298)
Against covetousness. 79358
Against infant baptism. 22141
Against revenge. 79358
Against the degredation of the states. 16922
Against the force bill. 9936
Agaisnt the right of the federal government. 22101
Agala, Marcelo. 32756
Agapito Canelo y Cachuto, Juan. see Canelo y Cachuto, Juan Agapito.
Agar, ʀ----. 94155
Agassiz, Alexander, 1835-1910. 503
Agassiz, Louis, 1807-1873. 504-508, 1120, 2612, 5806, (30524), 30714, 42706, 44505, (81481), 82393, 85056, 85072, 85336, 85337, 87532, 89533 see also Committee on Spiritualism, Boston, 1857.
Agassiz and spiritualism. (66767)
Agathangelus. 46261
Agathocles. pseud. Popish hierarchy. 7985
Agathodaemon, of Alexandria. cartographer 66470, 66497
Agatone the renegade. (64922)
Agawam, John. pseud. Miscellaneous poems. see Story, Joseph. supposed author
Age. 32930, 33320
Age. see Richmond age.
Age of benevolence. 103967
Age of black. 53379
Age of error. 509
Age of God. 42702
Age of inquiry. 510
Age of liberty. 102453
Age of paper. 103713
Age of print. (47442)
Age of reason. (71242), 84827, 85600, 91818, 92856, 97656, 98338, 100977
Age of reason unreasonable. 85600
Age of steam. 103691
Age of superstition. 104713
Age of the world. 80492
Age of U. S. volunteer soldiery. (76696)
Age of Washington. (39807)
Age to come. (49001)
Aged and retired citizen of Boston. pseud. Letter. see Otis, Harrison Gray, 1765-1848.
Aged Christian. 47181
Aged Christian's cabinet. 90182
Aged Christian's companion. 90182
Aged clergyman of Massachusetts. pseud. "Short and easy method." see Norton, John. supposed author
Aged friend of the author (John Rutledge) of the United States Constitution. pseud. Statesman's manual. see Cruger, Lewis.
"Aged guard of '62." pseud. Voice. 3089
Aged layman. pseud. Letter to the clergy. 15817, 20063
Aged minister. pseud. Answer to a letter. see Dickinson, Moses.
Aged minister commending his people to God. 39193, 39198
Aged minister of the everlasting Gospel. pseud. Dying legacy. see Mather, Samuel 1706-1785.
Aged minister's review of the events and duties. 54957
Aged minister's solemn appeal to God. 42007

Aged non-conforming ministers. pseud. see Some aged non-conforming ministers. pseud.
Agency and providence of God acknowledged. 92952
Agency of God, illustrated. 6055
Agency of God, in raising up important characters. 104530
Agency of God in the elevation of man. 66224
Agency of steam power. 13365
Agency of the American Tract Society, Philadelphia. see American Tract Society. Pennsylvania Agency, Philadelphia.
Agent for Petitioners for Union of Upper and Lower Canada. see Stuart, Sir James, Bart., 1780-1853.
Agent of the Foreign Holders of Indiana State Bonds. 34526
Agent of the Heirs at Law of William James. see Heirs at Law of William James. Agent.
Agent of the Houghton Association. see Houghton Association. Agent to England.
Agent of the State of New York, to Procure and Transcribe Documents in Europe. see New York (State) Agent to Procure and Transcribe Documents in Europe.
Agent of the Virginia Yazoo Company. see Virginia Yazoo Company. Agent.
Agent to England of the Houghton Association. see Houghton Association. Agent to England.
Agent to purchase arms for the state of Indiana. Report of Robert Dale Owen. 34565
Agent to the Settlers on the Coast of Yucatan; and the Late Settlers on the Mosquito Shore. petitioner see Mosquito Shore (British Colony) Inhabitants. Agent. petitioner
Agents of the American Loyalists. see American Loyalists. Agents.
Agents and Commissioners of the McDonogh Estate. see McDonogh Educational Fund and Institute, Baltimore. Trustees.
Agents Appointed to Establish a School for Heathen Youth, New York. 51790, (76453)
Agent's manual of life assurance. 24436
Agents of the Hampshire and Hampden Canal Company. see Hampshire and Hampden Canal Company.
Agents of the Massachusetts Board of Education. (67316)
Ages of Michigan. 77876, 103695
Agg, John. 511, 56637
Agg, John. reporter 60401
Aggionte fatte alla Margarita filosofica. 69132
Aggiunta dell' Istria, & altre isole, scogli, e nuove suciosita. 64153
Aggiunta di molte isole. (64149)-64151
Aggivnta . . . . Di mostri, & vsanze . . . con le sue figure. 6806
Aggregate amount of each description of persons. 43907
Aggregate amount of persons in the United States. 512
Aggregate and valuation of the exports of produce. 72992, 101211
Aggregates of polls, property, taxes, &c. (45683)
Aggressions and usurpations of slavery. 85608
Aggrieved member. pseud. Short correspondence see Prince, Thomas.
Agia, Miguel de. 513
Agitation of slavery. 81816
Agitation—the doom of slavery. 81817
Aglaeksimasut kavlunait pelleseena illaennit. 91172
Aglio, Augustin. illus. 16938, (37800)

Agnes Farriday. 90648
Agnes Paschal. 58985
Agnew, C. R. 76545, 76602, 76613, 76647
  see also United States Sanitary Com-
  mission. Committee to Visit the Military
  General Hospitals, In and Around Wash-
  ington.
Agnew, Daniel. 514
Agnew, J. Holmes. 515
Agnew, J. L. 39733
Agnew, M. 516
Agnew, Margaret. see Blennerhasset,
  Margaret (Agnew)
Agonies of Mother Goose. 46917
Agoult, --------, Comte d', fl. 1790.
  75041
Agreeable admonitions for old and young.
  46219
Agreeable to previous notice. 83853
Agreeable to the order of the day. 99047
Agreement and rules of the Southern Railway
  and Steamship Association. 88459-88460
Agreement at Cambridge. 106052
Agreement between the Albany and Schenectady
  Rail Road Company. 53517
Agreement between Lord Baltimore and
  Messieurs Penn. (45073), 60743, note
  after 97106
Agreement between William Smith and others.
  84583
Agreement made among lawyers. 84558
Agreement of the New York and Harlem R. R.
  Co. (54732)
Agreements . . . between the . . . citizens of
  Philadelphia. 61451
Agregado, J. M. 43816
Agrelo, Pedro Jose. (47615) see also Buenos
  Aires (Province) Fiscal General.
Agresiones y hazandas de tres Apaches.
  (34155)
Agression de l'Espagne contre le Chile. 17160
Agrestis. pseud. Short review. see Allston,
  Joseph.
Agricola. pseud. Address to the legislature
  of South Carolina. 87737
Agricola. pseud. Hints to emigrants. see
  Spafford, Horatio Gates.
Agricola. pseud. Letter to the inhabitants.
  40488
Agricola. pseud. Letters and essays. see
  Whitehouse, W. F.
Agricola. pseud. Letters of Agricola on the
  principles. see Young, John, of Halifax.
Agricola. pseud. Squabble. 89940
Agricola. pseud. To the legislature of South
  Carolina. 88082
Agricola. pseud. Two letters from Agricola
  to Sir William Howe. 33344
Agricola. pseud. Virginia doctrines, not
  nullification. 100555
Agricola, P. pseud.?? 54776
Agricola, Rudolphus, 1443-1485. 63956-63960,
  98283
Agricola. 46220
Agricola's address to the legislature of South
  Carolina. 87737
Agricola's letters and essays on sugar farming.
  103667
Agricultor Venezolano. 19972
Agricultura de la zona torrida. 4561
Agricultura y comercio de la Habana. 29413
Agricultural address. 23964
Agricultural address of Ex.-Gov. Aaron V.
  Brown. 8430
Agricultural and horticultural advertiser. 64918
Agricultural and Horticultural Society, Hingham,
  Mass. 21588, 31956

Agricultural and Horticultural Society, Marsh-
  field, Mass. see Marshfield Agricultural
  and Horticultural Society.
Agricultural and Horticultural Society of
  Cattaraugus County, N. Y. see Cattaraugus
  County Agricultural and Horticultural
  Society.
Agricultural and horticultural society transactions.
  31956
Agricultural and Mechanical Association of
  Missouri. see Missouri Agricultural and
  Mechanical Association.
Agricultural and Mechanical Association of St.
  Louis. see St. Louis Agricultural and
  Mechanical Association.
Agricultural & Mechanical Society of South
  Carolina. see State Agricultural &
  Mechanical Society of South Carolina.
Agricultural Association, Rio de la Plata. see
  Rio de la Plata Agricultural Association.
Agricultural Association of Lower Canada. 10347
Agricultural botany. (18593)-18594
Agricultural College, Albany, N. Y. see New
  York (State) Agricultural College, Albany.
Agricultural College of Massachusetts. see
  Massachusetts Agricultural College.
Agricultural College of Michigan. see Michigan.
  State Agricultural College.
Agricultural College of New Hampshire, Durham.
  see New Hampshire. College of Agri-
  culture and the Mechanic Arts, Durham.
Agricultural College of the state of Michigan.
  (48716)
Agricultural correspondence. 101722
Agricultural Convention, Bloomington, Ind., 1860.
  1605
Agricultural Convention, Harrisburg, Pa., 1851.
  60408
Agricultural Convention of South Carolina. see
  State Agricultural Society of South Carolina
  (1839-1845)
Agricultural enquiries on plaister of Paris. 61204
Agricultural Exhibition, Halifax, 1853. see Nova
  Scotia. Agricultural Exhibition, Halifax,
  1853.
Agricultural exhibition of Nova Scotia. . . . at
  Halifax . . . October 5th and 6th, 1853.
  (56111)
Agricultural, geological, and descriptive sketches
  of lower North Carolina. (73911)
Agricultural interest, as affected by the
  reciprocity treaty. 517
Agricultural interests, &c. (72131)
Agricultural life in some of its intellectual
  aspects. 38776
Agricultural, Mechanical, and Educational
  Association of Canada West. 10340
Agricultural Meeting, Boston, 1840. 14535,
  (69758), 102319
Agricultural observations. 8918
Agricultural progress in Massachusetts. 74307
Agricultural property and products. 73971
Agricultural reports. (70736)
Agricultural repository for the year of Our Lord
  1804. 14858, 44316
Agricultural resources of Georgia. 36575
Agricultural Society, Columbus, Ga. 86214
Agricultural Society, Litchfield, Conn. see
  Litchfield Agricultural Society.
Agricultural Society, Martha's Vineyard, Mass.
  see Martha's Vineyard Agricultural
  Society.
Agricultural Society, Middlesex, Mass. see
  Middlesex Agricultural Society.
Agricultural Society, Nantucket, Mass. see
  Nantucket Agricultural Society.
Agricultural Society, Norfolk, Mass. see
  Norfolk Agricultural Society.

Agricultural Society, Westchester, N. Y. see
Westchester Agricultural Society.
Agricultural Society, Worcester, Mass. see
Worcester Agricultural Society.
Agricultural Society and Institute of Newcastle
County, Delaware. see Newcastle County
Agricultural Society and Institute,
Wilmington, Del.
Agricultural Society and Mechanics' Institute,
Rock County, Wisc. see Rock County
Agricultural Society and Mechanics'
Institute.
Agricultural Society of Albany County, N. Y.
see Albany County Agricultural Society.
Agricultural Society of Berkshire County, Mass.
see Berkshire Agricultural Society.
Agricultural Society of California. see
California State Agricultural Society.
Agricultural Society of Canada. 10347, 58447
Agricultural Society of Essex County, Mass.
see Essex Agricultural Society.
Agricultural Society of Franklin County, Mass.
see Franklin County Agricultural
Society.
Agricultural Society of Frederick County, Md.
see Frederick County Agricultural
Society.
Agricultural Society of Grenada. see Grenada
Agricultural Society.
Agricultural Society of Greene County, N. Y.
see Greene County Agricultural Society.
Agricultural Society of Hamilton County, Ohio.
see Hamilton County Agricultural
Society.
Agricultural Society of Hampden County, Mass.
see Hampden County Agricultural
Society.
Agricultural Society of Hampshire, Franklin
and Hampden. see Hampshire, Franklin
and Hampden Agricultural Society.
Agricultural Society of Hartford County, Conn.
see Hartford County Agricultural
Society.
Agricultural Society of Herkimer County, N. Y.
see Herkimer County Agricultural
Society.
Agricultural Society of Jefferson County, N. Y.
see Jefferson County Agricultural
Society.
Agricultural Society of Kentucky. see Kentucky
State Agricultural Society.
Agricultural Society of Lower Canada. see
Quebec Agricultural Society.
Agricultural Society of Massachusetts. 45774
Agricultural Society of Minnesota. see
Minnesota State Agricultural Society.
Agricultural Society of Monroe County, N. Y.
see Monroe County Agricultural Society.
Agricultural Society of New England. see
New England Agricultural Society.
Agricultural Society of New Hampshire. see
New Hampshire Agricultural Society.
Agricultural Society of New Haven County, Conn.
see New Haven County Agricultural
Society.
Agricultural Society of New Jersey. 53062
Agricultural Society of New York State. see
New York State Agricultural Society.
Agricultural Society of Oneida County, N. Y.
see Oneida County Agricultural Society.
Agricultural Society of Onondaga County, N. Y.
see Onondaga County Agricultural
Society.
Agricultural Society of Oregon. see State
Agricultural Society of Oregon.
Agricultural Society of Pennsylvania. see
Pennsylvania State Agricultural Society.

Agricultural Society of Pike County, Ill. see
Pike County Agricultural Society.
Agricultural Society of Queens County, N. Y.
see Queens County Agricultural Society.
Agricultural Society of Rensselaer County, N. Y.
see Rensselaer County Agricultural
Society.
Agricultural Society of Restigouche, New
Brunswick. see Restigouche Agricultural
Society.
Agricultural Society of Rockingham County, N. H.
see Rockingham Agricultural Society.
Agricultural Society of Rutland County, Vt. see
Rutland County Agricultural Society.
Agricultural Society of St. John's Colleton, S. C.
78548, 78551, 87534
Agricultural Society of South Carolina. see
State Agricultural & Mechanical Society of
South Carolina and State Agricultural
Society of South Carolina.
Agricultural Society of South Carolina (1855-1861)
see State Agricultural & Mechanical
Society of South Carolina
Agricultural Society of South Carolina (1839-1845
see State Agricultural Society of South
Carolina (1839-1845)
Agricultural Society of Tennessee. see Ten-
nessee State Agricultural Society.
Agricultural Society of the Connecticut River
Valley. see Connecticut River Valley
Agricultural Society.
Agricultural Society of the County of Plymouth,
Mass. see Plymouth County Agricultural
Society.
Agricultural Society of the State of New York.
see New York State Agricultural Society.
Agricultural Society of the United States. see
United States Agricultural Society.
Agricultural Society of Vermont. see Vermont
State Agricultural Society.
Agricultural Society of Windham County, Conn.
see Windham County Agricultural Society.
Agricultural statistics of Massachusetts. 45623
Agricultural statistics of the state of New York.
33154
Agricultural survey of Somerset Co., Me. 6090
Agricultural survey of the county of Steuben.
(19594)
Agricultural tour in the United States. 3368,
72876
Agriculturalist, and journal of the state and
county societies. 94808
Agriculture. 55619
Agriculture and industry of Kennebec County
Maine. 6089
Agriculture, commerce, revenus et appendice.
74922
Agriculture—its dignity and progress. 17227
Agriculture: its past, present, and future. 24766
Agriculture of Massachusetts. (24765)
Agriculture of New-York. 53794
Agriculture of North Carolina. 55592
Agriculture of the United States, an address.
14535
Agriculture of the United States in 1860. 11673,
37425
Agriculture of the United States, or an essay.
(55313)
Agrimensura aplicada al sistema de medidas.
31562
Agrippa, Cornelius. pseud.?? (11679), 45641
Agua ligada para ayudar al unico especifico.
86395
Aguado, Juan Lopez. see Lopez Aguada, Juan.
Agueda de San Ignacio, Maria Anna. see San
Ignacio, Maria Anna Agueda de.

Aguero, Christobal. see Aguero, Christoual de.
Aguero, Christoual de. 552, 106254
Aguero, Gaspar de Escalona. 520-521, 22819-22820
Aguero, Gaspar de Scalona. 520, 22819-22820
Aguero, Jose de la Riva. see Riva Aguero, Jose de la.
Aguero, Juan Francisco de Castaniza Gonzalez de. see Gonzalez de Aguero, Juan Francisco de Castaniza.
Aguero, P. de. 519
Agueros, Pedro Gonzalez de. 524, 27822
Aguglia, -----. 76897
Aguiar, Diego de. 6809, 69240
Aguiar, Diego Pardo y. see Pardo y Aguiar, Diego.
Aguiar, Jose Francisco d'. ed. 99523
Aguiar, Lucas da Lylva de. see Lylva de Aguiar, Lucas de.
Aguiar y Acuna, Rodrigo de. 525
Aguila, Melchor Xufre de. see Xufre de Aguila, Melchor.
Aguila, Melchora del. defendant 86410
Aguila mexicana. 48259, 48348, 70090
Aguilar, G. de. 10712
Aguilar, J. de Ayala y. see Ayala y Aguilar, J. de.
Aguilar, Jose de. 526
Aguilar, Jose Mateo. 99499
Aguilar, Nic. Flores y. see Flores y Aguilar, Nic.
Aguilar, Pedro Sanchez de. see Sanchez de Aguilar, Pedro.
Aguilar, Sanchez de. see Sanchez de Aguilar, Pedro.
Aguilar del Rio, Jaun de. see Rio, Juan de Aguilar del.
Aguilera, ------- Pluma y. see Pluma y Aguilera, ------.
Aguinaldo. (72521)
Aguinaldo Habanero. 50701
Aguira y Mayora, Jose Mariano de. 44558
Aguirre, ------. 36800
Aguirre, Ambrosio de Solis. see Solis Aguirre, Ambrosio de.
Aguirre, D. C. ed. 70012
Aguirre, J. Sanchez de. 528-531, (14367)
Aguirre, Joseph Saenz de. see Saenz de Aguirre, Joseph.
Aguirre, Manuel. 20419, 57386
Aguirre, Miguel de. 532
Aguirre Gomendio, Francisco de. see Gomendio, Francisco de Aguirre.
Aguirre y Espinosa, Joseph Francisco de. see Cuevas Aguirre y Espinosa, Joseph Francisco de.
Aguirre y Espinosa, Joseph Francisco de Cuevas. see Cuevas Aguirre y Espinosa, Joseph Francisco de.
Agurto, Pedro de. see Pedro de Agurto.
Agutter, William. 533
Ah can I cease to love her. 92169
Ah! Lovely appearance of death! 102643, 103604
Ahiman rezon. 102460
Ahiman rezon abridged and digested. 84584, 84668
Ahiman rezon, containing a view of the history. 59870
Ahiman rezon, for the use of the Grand Lodge of Ancient Free-Masons of South-Carolina. 87837
Ahiman rezon, for the use of the Grand Lodge of South-Carolina. 87845
Ahiman rezon; or, book of constitutions. (43445), 87838

Ahiman rezon, prepared under the direction of the Grand Lodge of Georgia. 72447
Ahna, Charles H. de. see De Ahna, Charles H.
Ahrens, H. 73164
Ahuma, S. R. B. Attoh. see Attoh Ahuma, S. R. B.
Ahumada, Juan Antonio de. petitioner 69984
Aiamie Kushkushkutu Mishinaigan. 21436
Aiamie Tipadjimo8in Masinaigan. (34593)
Aianrie Tipadjimo8in Masinaigan. 36939
Aid-de-camp. 15235
Aid-de-camp; a romance of the war. 42962
Aid Society, Providence, R. I. see Providence Aid Society.
Aid to Ireland. 54324
Aid to preaching and hearing. 81639
Aid to the Union prisoners in Richmond. 76626
Ἀιέν αριθτενέιν 14842
Aigremont, Jean de Laon, Sieur d'. see Laon, Jean de, Sieur d'Aigremont.
Aiken, George L., 1830-1876. 91288, 92513
Aiken, John. 534
Aiken, P. F. 535
Aiken, Samuel C. 43419, 56947
Aiken, Silas. 536
Aiken, Solomon. 537-538, 89813, 105240
Aiken, S. C. Southern Vine Growers' Convention, 1860. see Southern Vine Growers' Convention, Aiken, S. C., 1860.
Aikens, Andrew J. (49156)
Aikin, ------. 47368
Aikin, John. 539
Aikman, William. 540-542
Ailhaud, ------. see also France. Commission Aux Isles Sous les Vent.
Aillaud, J. P. 49085, 76846
Ailly, Pierre d'. 66508, 76838
Aimard, Gustave. 543
Aime, J.-J. see Ayme, Jean Jacqves.
Aime-Martin, M. see Martin, Louis Aime.
Aimie Tipadjimo8in Masinaigan. 46820
Aims and purposes of the founders of Massa-chusetts. 22300
Aims, antecedents, and principles. 40026
Ainsa, A. 1982
Ainsworth, Calvin. 52810
Ainsworth, William Harrison, 1805-1882. 546, 773, 5556
Ainsworth & Co. Firm see Woolworth, Ainsworth & Co. firm, publishers
Airbreathers of the coal period. 18950
Airs of Palestine; a poem. 62758
Airs of Palestine, and other poems. 62759
Airvault, Marie Charles du Chilleau, Marquis d'. 3312A, 12062-12063, (68372), 75059, 75060, 75141, 75149 see also Santo Domingo (French Colony) Governor General, 1788-1789 (Airvault)
Aislabie, John. 547-548, 80328, 88168
Aislabie, John. defendant 547-548, 65862, 80329, 88190
Aitken, James, 1752-1777. defendant 31834-31841, 39363
Aitken, James, fl. 1856. 99546
Aitken, R. 550
Aitken's general American register. 550
Aitkin, -----. 32496
Aitkin, W. B. 549
Aitzinger, M. (69296)
Aix de la Chaise, Francois d'. see La Chaise, Francois d'Aix de.
Aix, France (Diocese) Bishop (De Boisgelin de Cuce) 68433 see also De Boisgelin de Cuce, Jean de Dieu Raymond, Bp.
Ajax. pseud. Address of Ajax. (4024)
Ajokaersutit illuartut Gudimik pekkorsejniglo innungnut. (22847)

Ajokoersoirsun Atuagekseit Nalagbingne
 Grondlandme. 22846
Ajuria, D. M. (67640), 67643
Akademie der Wissenschaften, Berlin. 60,
 9521-9523, (9527), 49949
Akademie der Wissenschaften, Munich. 2313,
 4000, 38347, 38348, 99363
K. Akademie der Wissenschaften, Vienna.
 5209-5210, 5217, 6862, 25823
K. Akademie der Wissenschaften, Vienna.
 Philosophisch-Historischen Klasse.
 (77616), 77622
Akerly, Samuel. 551
Akerman, Amos Tappan, 1821-1880. 84808
Aket missigssuissut avguasavalit. (22866),
 63723
Akins, Thomas B. 552-553, 56166, (56184),
 56190 see also Nova Scotia. Com-
 missioner of Public Records.
Akron, Ohio. Ohio Women's Rights Convention,
 1851. see Ohio Women's Rights Con-
 vention, Akron, Ohio, 1851.
Akten, welche in der General Assembly.
 100404
Aktenstucke Brasilischer Seite. 7505
Aktenstucke, Gesammelte, des Vereins zum
 Schutze deutscher Einwanderer in Texas.
 (554), 95131
Akts ov the Apostelz. (67763), note after
 94300
Al Aaraaf, Tamerlane, and minor poems.
 (63518)
Al Congreso Nacional. 57847
Al "Curioso." 58435
Al Defensor de Tontos. 98909
Al eccellentiss. M. Hieronimo Fracastoro.
 67731
Al editor. 86238
Al excelentissimo Senor Don Fernando de
 Torres Portugal. 32492, 100643
Al excmo Snor Don Joseph Manso de Velasco.
 (69983)
Al exmo. Senor General Jose Antonio Paez.
 67662, 98869
Al excellentissimo Senor Conde de Salvatierra.
 98804
Al historiador de Buenos Ayres. 44174
Al Jeneral D. Justo Jose de Urquiza. 77087
Al lector. 32492, 100643
Al publico. (79313)
Al publico imparcial de esta isla. 1870
Al publico imparcial de Trinidad. 67121
Al publico por D. Nicolas Ruiz. 74011
Al pueblo catolico. 66578
Al pueblo Centro-americano. 50527
Al pueblo Mexicano. 48633, 69189
Al que le venga el saco que se lo ponga.
 96265-96266
Al que le wenga el saco que se le ponga.
 93445
Al rector. 56324
Al Rey Ferdinando VI. 71451
Al Rey nvestro Senor Don Felipe III. 74599
Al Rey nvestro Senor, en su Real y Supremo
 Consejo de las Indias. 75785
Al Rey nvestro Senor, por la provincia de la
 Compania de Jesus de la Nueua Espana.
 58279, 72777, (73620)
Al Rey nvestro Senor. Satisfacion al memorial
 de los religiosos de la Compania del
 nombre de Iesus. 56265, 58280, (77142)
Al Senor Doct. D. Ioseph del Corral. (72290)
Al Sr. General D. Melchor Muzquiz. 99713
Al Senor Ministro de Estado del Despacho de
 Gobierno. 61161
Al Soberano Congreso dirige este discurso.
 86396

Al suo amicissimo Ioanimaria Anzolello
 Vicentino. S. 50050
Al verdadero constitucional dos palabras y
 perdone V. 68416
Alabado sea el Santissimo Sacramento. 98741
Alabama (Territory) Convention, 1819. 558
Alabama (Territory) General Assembly. 555
Alabama (Territory) General Assembly. House
 of Representatives. 559
Alabama (Territory) General Assembly.
 Legislative Council. 560
Alabama. Agent to Adjust the Claims of Deceased
 Soldiers. (25331) see also Fowler,
 William C.
Alabama. Census, 1838. 26699
Alabama. Census, 1840. 26699
Alabama. Census, 1844. 26699
Alabama. Commissioners to examine the Bank
 of Mobile. (49785)
Alabama. Commissioners to Examine the
 Branch of the Bank of the State of
 Alabama at Decatur. 24071 see also
 Fenner, Robert.
Alabama. Commissioners to Examine the
 Planters and Merchants Bank of Mobile.
 (49785)
Alabama. Commissioners to Examine the
 Southern Bank of Alabama. (567)
Alabama. Commissioners to the Slave-holding
 States. 84877
Alabama. Constitution. 557, 1269, 1271, 2071,
 5316, 6360, 16103, 16107, 16113, 16133,
 33137, (47188), (57514), 59771, (66397),
 104198
Alabama. Constitutional Convention, Montgomery,
 1867. 56770
Alabama. Convention, Montgomery, 1861. 84877
Alabama. Financial Agents. see also Clews,
 Habicht & Co. firm and Clews (Henry)
 & Co. firm
Alabama. General Assembly. 15841, (50375)
Alabama. General Assembly. Joint Committee
 on the Alleged Election of Geo. E. Spencer,
 as U. S. Senator. 89323
Alabama. General Assembly. House of Representatives. 561, 568, (49785)
Alabama. General Assembly. Senate. 562,
 84806
Alabama. Governor, 1857-1861 (Moore) 33150
 see also Moore, Andrew Barry, 1807-1873.
Alabama. Governor, 1868-1870 (Smith) 84803-
 84809 see also Smith, William Hugh,
 1826-1899.
Alabama. Governor, 1907-1911 (Comer) 83629
 see also Comer, Braxton Bragg, 1848-
Alabama. Laws, statutes, etc. 564, 23765,
 39414, 47368, 49777, 49779, 52051,
 (57514), 57632, 70820-70821, 82438,
 84880-84881, 84883, 88455, 87327, 89066,
 96328
Alabama. Southern Rights Convention, Mont-
 gomery, 1852. see Southern Rights
 Convention, Montgomery, Ala., 1852.
Alabama. State Bank. see Bank of Alabama.
Alabama. Superintendent of Public Instruction
 89235 see also Speed, Joseph H.
Alabama. Supreme Court. 80280, 84896
Alabama. University. 83004
Alabama. University. Alumni. 64946
Alabama. University. Library. 571
Alabama. University. Trustees. (570), 64946
Alabama. Confederate Armed Cruiser. 79080
"Alabama." 90066
Alabama and Chattanooga Railroad Company.
 83871
Alabama and the Kearsarge. 21842
Alabama Anti-masonic Convention, Cahawba,
 1830. 556

Alabama Anti-masonic Convention, Tuscaloosa County, 1830. 556
Alabama Baptists State Convention. see Baptists. Alabama. State Convention.
Alabama Central Railroad. see South and North Alabama Railroad Company.
'Alabama' claims and arbitration. 7047
Alabama. Correspondence respecting the "Alabama." 573, (16898)
Alabama Infantry. 14th Regiment Volunteers (1861-1865) 34013
Alabama, Florida and Georgia Railroad Company. 572
Alabama Historical Society. 569
Alabama, or here we rest. 34594
Alabama state gazetteer and business directory. 83903
Alabama und Mississippi. 8200
Alabama Wesleyan University, Florence, Ala. see Florence Wesleyan University, Florence, Ala.
Alabanza poetica. 11031
Alaethophilus. pseud. Breedvoerige Verhandeling. (42749)
Alagoas (Brazilian Province) Presidente (Cunhae Figueiredo) 69314, 69327 see also Cunhae Figueiredo, Jose Bento da.
Alagoas (Brazilian Province) Presidente (Nactividade e Silva) 69316 see also Nactividade e Silva, Galdino Augusto.
Alagoas (Brazilian Province) Presidente (Pimentel) 62876 see also Pimentel, Esperidiao Eloy de Barros.
Alagoas (Brazilian Province) Presidente (Saraiva) 69312 see also Saraiva, Jose Antonio.
Alagoas (Brazilian Province) Vice-Presidente (Natividade Silva) 60888 see also Natividade Silva, Galdino Augusto da.
Alagoas (Brazilian Province) Vice-Presidente (Mello) 69309 see also Mello, Roberto Calheiros de.
Alagon, ---------, Duke of. claimant 103427
Alaham,------. RN 21313
Alainval, Abbot. see Deslisle de la Drevetiere, Louis Francois.
Alaire, M. M. see Allaire, M. M.
Alala ou les habitans du desert. 12239
Alaman, Lucas, 1792-1853. 579-581, 6834, 34188, 40962, 48429, 48599, (65266), 69982, 71448
Alaman, Lucas, 1792-1853. defendant 582, 48417, (65925) see also Mexico. Ministro de Relaciones. defendant
Alamo, and other poems. 37623
Alamoth. 37925
Alantse, -----. 63957
Alarcon, Hernando de. 16951, 67740, 84379
Alarm bell. No. I. 583, 16146
Alarm-bell: or, considerations on the present dangerous state. 102814
Alarm bell published in 1863. 28466
Alarm; or a plan of pacification. (582A)
Alarm, or three sermons. 77279
Alarm to American patriots. 91472
Alarm to Christian partiots. 13270
Alarm to Lord N---h. 102051-102052
Alarm to Pennsylvania. (48178), 59871
Alarm to the legislature of New York. 78581
Alarm to the legislature of the province of New-York. 11882, 16590-16591, 78559, 2d note after 103119, 1st note after 104016
Alarm to Zion. 103592
Alarm trumpet. 97075
Alarming Boston Port-Act. 6751, 75632

Alarming developments. 13255, 33944
Alarming law case. 22182, 59045
Alarming portraiture. 102137-102139
Alasco. 584
Alaska and its resources. 18308
Alaska and the polar regions. 37010
Alaska. Lecture I. 83599
Alaska. Speech of William H. Seward. 79501
Alaska. Speech of William Higby. 31735
Alaska-Yukon-Pacific Exposition, Seattle, 1909. 85021
Alatorre, Juan Jose Flores. see Flores Alatorre, Juan Jose.
Alaux, Gustave d', 1816-1885. 8075, 20574, 20579
Alaves, Diego Zepada. defendant 86405
Alazon, and other poems. 84916
Alba, Jose M. Gutierrez de. see Gutierrez de Alba, Jose M.
Albacea de D. Agustin de Iturbide. see Navarrete, Juan Gomez.
Albaceta de S. Arzobispo Ortega Montanes. defendant see Patino, Andres. defendant
Albacea Fiduciario del Ilmo. Sr. Dr. Don Luis de Penalver. see Echeverria y Penalver, Manuel de.
Albaceas y Herederos de D. Francisco Linares. plaintiffs (76224)
Albaceas y Herederos de D. Francisco de la Pena. plaintiffs 74860
Albach, James R. (585), 60955
Alban. A tale. 33969-33970
Alban. A tale of the new world. 33969
Alban: or, the history of a young Puritan. 33969
Albani, Giovanni Francesco. see Clement XI, Pope, 1649-1721.
Albans, Francis Bacon, Viscount St. see Bacon, Francis, Viscount St. Albans.
Albany, N. Y. 612, 4035, 65486, 79642
Albany. Aldermen and Commonalty. 628, 66062
Albany. Antimasonic State Convention of New York, 1829. see Antimasonic State Convention of New York, Albany, 1829.
Albany. Army Relief Bazaar, 1864. see Army Relief Bazaar, Albany, 1864.
Albany. Associate Presbytery. see Presbyterian Church in the U. S. A. Associate Presbytery of Albany.
Albany. Bar. 18585
Albany. Central Synod of the Reformed Dutch Church. see Reformed Church in America. Central Synod of Albany.
Albany. Charters, etc. 613, 621-622
Albany. Circuit Court. 19369, note after 94503, 102448
Albany. Citizens. petitioners 47642
Albany. Classis. see Reformed Church in America. Classis of Albany.
Albany. Common Council. 22753, 22763, 77597, note after 97071
Albany. Common Council. Committee of Arrangements. 88644
Albany. Congress, 1754. see Albany Congress, 1754.
Albany. Constitutional Convention, 1821. see New York (State) Constitutional Convention, Albany, 1821.
Albany. Constitutional Convention, 1846. see New York (State) Constitutional Convention, Albany, 1846.
Albany. Constitutional Convention, 1867-1868. see New York (State) Constitutional Convention, Albany, 1867-1868.
Albany. Convention for Bible Missions, 1846. see Convention for Bible Missions, 2d, Albany, 1846.

Albany. Convention of Delegates, from Several Moral Societies in the State of New York, 1819. see Convention of Delegates, From Several Moral Societies in the State of New York, Albany, 1819.

Albany. Convention of Delegates, from the Different Counties in the State of New York, Opposed to Free-masonry, 1829. see Antimasonic State Convention of New York, Albany, 1829.

Albany. Convention of Delegates of the Several Moral Societies in the State of New York, 1820. see Convention of Delegates of the Several Moral Societies in the State of New York, Albany, 1820.

Albany. Convention of Delegates of the Several Moral Societies in the State of New York, 1821. see Convention of Delegates of the Several Moral Societies in the State of New York, Albany, 1821.

Albany. Convention of Iron Workers, 1849. see Convention of Iron Workers, Albany, 1849.

Albany. Court. 64283

Albany. Court of Arbitrators. (35991), 98547

Albany. Democratic Legislative Meeting, 1834. see Democratic Party. New York. Albany. Legislative Meeting, 1834.

Albany, N. Y. Democratic State Convention, 1848. see Democratic Party. New York. Convention, Albany, 1848.

Albany. Democratic State Convention, 1861. see Democratic Party. New York. Convention, Albany, 1861.

Albany. Dudley Observatory. 21095, 21098, 28093, 92774

Albany. Dudley Observatory. Astronomer in Charge. 21100

Albany. Dudley Observatory. Directors. 21100

Albany. Dudley Observatory. Scientific Council. 21096, 28093

Albany. Dudley Observatory. Trustees. 21097, 21100, (28096)

Albany. Dudley Observatory. Trustees. Majority. 28097

Albany. Evangelical Lutheran Ebenezer Church. 23130

Albany. Federal Committee. see Federal Party. New York. Albany. Committee.

Albany. Federal Party Convention, 1812. see Federal Party. New York. Convention, Albany, 1812.

Albany. Female Academy. see Albany Female Academy.

Albany. First Lutheran Church. 89754

Albany. First Presbyterian Church. Member of the Congregation. pseud. see Member of the Congregation. pseud.

Albany. First Presbyterian Church. Trustees. 10256, 89744

Albany. General Convention of Congregational Ministers and Delegates in the United States, 1852. see Congregational Churches in the U. S.

Albany. General Republican Corresponding Committee. see Democratic Party. New York. Albany. General Corresponding Committee.

Albany. General Synod of the Reformed Dutch Church in North America. see Reformed Church in America. General Synod, Albany, 1812.

Albany. Grace Church. 28186

Albany. Hartwick Theological and Classical Seminary. see Hartwick Theological and Classical Seminary, Albany.

Alabany. Hospital. (63292)

Albany. Inhabitants. petitioners see Albany. Citizens. petititoners

Albany. Institute. see Albany Institute.

Albany. Maple Grove Cemetery Association. 44451

Albany. Mayor, 1690 (Schuyler) 628, 66062 see also Schuyler, Pieter.

Albany. Meeting for Promoting a Plan Proposed by M. A. Vattemare, 1847. 34931

Albany. Meeting of the General Committee Appointed by the World's Temperance Convention, 1st, 1854. see General Committee Appointed by the World's Temperance Convention, New York, 1853. Meeting, 1st, Albany, 1854.

Albany. Meeting of the Officers of Colleges and Academies, 1853. see New York (State) University.

Albany. Meeting of Working-men and Other Persons Favorable to Political Principle, 1830. see Meeting of Working-men and Other Persons Favorable to Political Principle, Albany, 1830.

Albany. Meeting of Workingmen and Others, 1830. see Meeting of Working-men and Other Persons Favorable to Political Principle, Albany, 1830.

Albany, N. Y. Meeting to Promote the Election of Clinton and Tallmadge, 1824. see Democratic Party. New York. Albany.

Albany. Military Officers. 628, 66062

Albany. Mrs. Loveridge's School. see Mrs. Loveridge's School, Albany.

Albany. National Republican Party Convention, 1828. see National Republican Party. New York. Convention, Albany, 1828.

Albany. New York State Agricultural College. see New York (State) Agricultural College, Albany.

Albany. New York State Agricultural Rooms. see New York (State) Agricultural College, Albany.

Albany. New York State Agricultural Convention, 1832. see New York State Agricultural Convention, Albany, 1832.

Albany. New York State Convention of Colored Citizens, 1840. see New York State Convention of Colored Citizens, Albany, 1840.

Albany. New York State Convention of Colored People, 1851. see New York State Convention of Colored People, Albany, 1851.

Albany. New York State Museum. see New York State Museum, Albany.

Albany. Normal School. see New York (State) State College for Teachers, Albany.

Albany. North Dutch Church. 101867

Albany. Ordinances, etc. 620-622

Albany. Particular Synod. see Reformed Church in America. Particular Synod of Albany.

Albany. Philomathean Society. see Philomathean Society, Albany.

Albany. Presbytery. see Presbyterian Church in the U. S. A. Presbytery of Albany.

Albany. Public Meeting, 1840. 615

Albany. Republican Legislative Meeting, 1834. see Democratic Party. New York. Albany. Legislative Meeting, 1834.

Albany. Rural Cemetery. 24611

Albany. St. Andrew's Society. see St. Andrew's Society of Albany.

Albany. St. Peter's Church. 635, 638, 13786

Albany. St. Peter's Church. Vestry. Delegates to the Diocesan Convention, 1849. 89354 see also Spencer, John Canfield.

Albany. St. Peter's Church. Vestry. Lay Delegates to the Diocesan Convention, 1845. 637, 35847, 89353 see also Spencer, John Canfield.

Albany. St. Petrus-Vereins. see St. Petrus-Vereins, Albany.

Albany. Scientific Commission, 1852. see Scientific Commission, Albany, 1852.

Albany. Second Presbyterian Church. 89744

Albany. Soldiers' and Sailors' State Convention, 1866. see Soldiers' and Sailors' State Convention, Albany, 1866.

Albany. Star-Spangled Banner Chapter, No. 96, Order of United Americans. see Order of United Americans. Star-Spangled Banner Chapter, No. 96, Albany.

Albany. State Convention of Delegates from the Several Counties of . . . New York, 1828. see National Republican Party. New York. Convention, Albany, 1828.

Albany. State Normal School. see New York (State) Normal School, Albany.

Albany. State Street Presbyterian Church. 90651-90652

Albany. State Street Presbyterian Church. Sunday School. Library. 90649-90650

Albany. State Street Presbyterian Church. Young People's Society. 90653

Albany. State Woman's Rights Convention, 1854. see New York State Woman's Rights Convention, Albany, 1854.

Albany. Trinity Church. 643

Albany. University. see Union College, Schenectady, N. Y.

Albany. Washington Benevolent Society. see Washington Benevolent Society. New York (State) Albany.

Alabany. Young Men's Association. see Young Men's Association of the City of Albany.

Albany. Young Men's Association for Mutual Improvement. see Young Men's Association for Mutual Improvement, of the City of Albany.

Albany. Young Men's Temperance Society. see Young Men's Temperance Society, Albany.

Albany. Zouave Cadets. 53518

Albany County, N. Y. 641

Albany County, N. Y. Circuit Court. 19369

Albany County, N. Y. Court of Sessions. 83638

Albany County, N. Y. Democratic Meeting, 1810. see Democratic Party. New York. Albany County. Meeting. 1810.

Albany County, N. Y. Democratic Meeting, 1853. see Democratic Party. New York. Albany County. Meeting, 1853.

Albany County, N. Y. Republican Convention, 1828. see Democratic Party. New York. Albany County. Convention, 1828.

Albany County, N. Y. Special Court of Oyer and Terminer. 92688-92693, 103301

Albany (Diocese) Bishop (Conroy) 72022 see also Conroy, John Joseph, Bp.

Albany (Diocese) Bishop (McNeirny) 72923 see also McNeirny, Francis, Bp.

Albany (Diocese) Synod, 1869. 72922

Albany (Diocese) Synod, 1884. 72923

Albany Academy. 588

Albany almanac, for . . . 1844. (41376)

Albany almanac, for the year of Our Lord, 1842. 81598

Albany almanack. 64075

Albany and Harlem Railroad Company. 590

Albany and Rensselaer Anti-Rent Association. (60837)

Albany and Schenectady Rail Road Company. 591, 53517

Albany and Susquehanna R. R. Company. Directors. 592

Albany and West-Stockbridge R. R. Company. Superintendent. 595

Albany annual register. 596, (51357)

Albany argus. 317, 4061, (53524), 73464, 89357, 89359, 94302, 97964, 98425, 100676, 102337, 103072

Albany argus and rough-hewer. 73464

Albany atlas. 598, (70118)

Albany basin and Erie Canal. 597

Albany Brewers. 19369, note after 94503

Albany Bridge case. 31850, 79505

Albany Bridge question. Speech of the Hon. Daniel E. Sickles. 80841

Albany Bridge question. Speech of the Hon. Joshua A. Spencer. 89364

Albany centinel. (13743), (14375), 40570, 41349, 95451

Albany centinel & register. 25000, 89297

Albany citizens advertiser and general directory. 41956

Albany city guide. 599

Albany City Temperance Society. Ex-Committee. 19369, note after 94503

Albany Coal Company. Directors. 101464

Albany commercial directory, for 1848-9. 33900

Albany Congress, 1754. 32968, 1st note after 97146

Albany Corresponding Committee. see Democratic Party. New York. Albany. Corresponding Committee.

Albany County Agricultural Society. 617, 21710, 26985

Albany Democratic reformer. 600

Albany directory. 601

Albany directory and city register. 51368

Albany evening journal. 10190, 93644, 94510

Albany Federal Committee. see Federal Party. New York. Albany. Committee.

Albany Female Academy. 50201

Albany Female Academy. Young Ladies. see Young Ladies of the Albany Female Academy. eds.

Albany Gallery of Fine Arts. 603

Albany gazette. (80023), 96006, 101549

Albany Institute. 606-607, 32733, 33145, (33148), 64933 see also Society for the Promotion of Useful Arts, New York.

Albany Institute. Committee to Continue the Meteorological Observations. 604

Albany Liberty National Nominating Convention, 1841. 608

Albany Lyceum of Natural History. see Albany Institute.

Albany Medical School. 23699, 53605

Albany minerva. (51358)

Albany morning express. 629

Albany morning express. Carrier. pseud. New year's address. see McCall, H. S.

Albany Northern Railroad Company. (609)

Albany Particular Synod. see Reformed Church in America. Particular Synod of Albany.

Albany pocket almanack. 610

Albany Presbytery. see Presbyterian Church in the U. S. A. Presbytery of Albany.

Albany quarterly. 91688

Albany ratification meeting. 611

Albany register. 642, (53510), 88640

Albany register—extra. 13724
Albany register. Supplement. 642, (53510)
Albany Religious Tract Society. 104212
Albany Republican Corresponding Committee.
see Democratic Party. New York.
Albany. Corresponding Committee.
Albany Republican County Convention. see
Democratic Party. New York.
Albany County. Convention, 1828.
Albany Republican Meeting, 1810. see Demo-
cratic Party. New York. Albany
County. Meeting, 1810.
Albany Society for the Relief of Orphan and
Destitute Children. see Society for the
Relief of Orphan and Destitute Children,
Albany.
Albany Temperance Society. see Albany City
Temperance Society.
Albany Young Men's Temperance Society. see
Young Men's Temperance Society, of the
City of Albany.
Albany Zouave Cadets to the Rochester Union
Blues. 53518
Albaredes Portal, Pierre-Barthelemy d'. see
Portal, Pierre-Barthelemy d'Albaredes.
Albares, Juana. see Pinto de Ulloa, Juana
(Albares de Rosal) de Valverde.
Albares de Rosal, Juana. see Pinto de Ulloa,
Juana (Albares de Rosal) de Valverde.
Albares Serrano, Iuan de. see Serrano,
Juan de Albares.
Albarez de Toledo, Domingo. 644
Albarracin, M. Santiago. (645)
Albemarle County, Va. Citizens. petitioners
100532
Albemarle County, Va. Public Dinner Given
to Mr. William C. Rives, 1834. 71667
Albemarle Female Institute, Staunton, Va.
60845
Albemarle Street. pseud. Letter from
Albemarle Street to the Coca-Tree.
40320
Albenino, Nicolao. 647, note after 98944
Alberdi, Juan Bautista, 1814?-1886. 648-655,
26273
Albericus Vespuccius Laurencio Petri
Francisci de Medicis vir grus[s] [et]c.
99342
Alberic[us] Vespucci[us] Laure[n]tio Petri
Francisci de Medicis Salutem plurima[m]
dicit. note before 99327, 99327
Albericus Vespucius Laurentio Petri de Medicis
salutem plurimam dicit. note before
99327, 99328-99330, 99332-99339, 99378-
99379, note after 99383C
Albericus Vespucius sageth vil heyles vnd gutes
Laurencio Petri de Medicis. 99346
Albericus Vespuctius Laurencio Petri
Francisci de Medicis vir grus[s]. 99341
Albericus Vespuctius Laurentio Petri
Francisci de Medicis vir Gruses[s].
99340, 99344
Albericus Vespuctius Laurentio Petri
Franciscij vil grues mit glucklicher fart.
99360
ALBERICVS VESPVTIVS LAVRENTIO PETRI
DE MEDICIS SALVTEM PLVRIMAM
DICIT. note before 99327, 99331
Albericus Vesputi[us] sagt vil heyls vnd gutes
Laurentio Petri de Medicis. 99348-
99349
Albers, J. A. 656
Albert. pseud. Review of the history. 70236
Albert, J. W. 22536
Albert-Montemont, -------. 4349, 9140
Albert Barnes on the Maine liquor law. (3496)

Albert J. Beveridge Memorial Fund Series.
see American Historical Association.
Albert J. Beveridge Memorial Fund Series.
Albert Newsam. 55067
Alberthoma, Robert. 65677
Alberti, George F. defendant 70275
Alberti, Leandro. 659-660
Alberti, Michael. 25474, 46805
Albertinis, Francisco de. 661-668, 72884
Albertino, Francisco. see Albertinis, Francisco
de.
Albertinus, Aeg. tr. 6808
Alberto, Joseph Antonio de San. see San
Alberto, Joseph Antonio de, Abp., 1727-
1804.
Albertus Magnus. 671-673
Albertus, Joannes. 68521
Albertvs Pi Ghius Campensis de Oequinoctiorvm
solstitioruque inuentione. 62809
Albertvs Pighivs Campensis, De ratione
paschalis celebrationis. (62810)
Alberykus Wespucius Wawrzin tzy Petrowi de
Medicis pozdrawenije. 99367
Albin, Jacques de St. pseud. Voyage au centre
de la terre. see Collin de Plancy,
Jacques A. S.
Albin, J. Saint. pseud. Voyage au centre de
la terre. see Collin de Plancy, Jacques
A. S.
Albin Berville, Saint. see Berville, Saint-
Albin.
Albinus. Petrus. see Petrus Albinus.
Albion, -------- Plowden, Earl of, fl. 1784.
52434
Albion, N. Y. Phipps Union Female Seminary.
see Phipps Union Female Seminary,
Albion, N. Y.
Albion. 8543
Albion: in twelve books. 674
Albion Society, Philadelphia. (61452)
Albion triumphant. 66539
Alboise, Albig. 19750
Albornos, Mariana de la Puenta Carrillo de.
see Carrillo de Albornos, Mariana de
la Puenta.
Alboroto y motin de los Indios de Mexico.
80987
Albro, John A. (675), (10121), 41599, 80262
Albubather. et centiloquium Diui Germetis.
99328
Albuerne, Manuel de. 44422, (57599)
Album de Ayachucho. 31566
Album de fotografias de Emilio Manuel du
Mensil. 56026
Album de la sombra 1874. 86559
Album de los voluntarios. 86227
Album d'Eleonore. 4738
Album des souvenirs Canadiens. 23609
Album du Canadien. (10348)
Album fotographico di Caracas. (40210)
Album historique. 38985, 98298
Album Mejicano tributo de gratitud. 48260
Album mexicano. 48261
Album of a literary lounger. 104499
Album of language. (51756)
Album of Long Branch. 77561
Album of Virginia. 5125
Album pintoresco de la isla de Cuba. 17748
Album pittoresque de la fregate la Thetis. 6874
Album universal. 132
Album von Combe-Varin. 47115
Albuquerque, A. C. de Sa e. see Sa e
Albuquerque, A. C. de.
Albuquerque, Affonso de, 1453-1515. 66686
Albuquerque, Antonio de. 677, 26874-26875

Albuquerque, Francisco de Paula d'Almeida e.
see Almeida e Albuquerque, Francisco
de Paula d'.
Albuquerque Coello, Duarte de, Marques de
Basto. 676, 14153
Alcabalatorio de la isla de Cuba. 17749,
(44951)
Alcaforado, Francisco. 679-680, 32051, 69287
Alcala, Domingo de. supposed author 93399
Alcala, Josef Maria de. see Maria de Alcala,
Josef.
Alcala-Galiano, Dionysio. supposed author
681, 2312, (69221)
Alcalde. pseud. Tertulia de la aldea. 94895
Alcalde, Neo. defendant 67639
Alcance al Num. I° del organo del pueblo.
97275
Alcantara, Juan de Larrea del de. see Larrea
del de Alcantara, Juan de.
Alcazar, Francisco de Solis y. see Solis y
Alcazar, Francisco de.
Alcazar, Ignacio Antonio de. 97720
Alcedo, Antonio de. 682-684, 95512
Alcedo y Herrera, Dionisio de. 685-687
Alcocer, Jose Miguel Guridi. see Guridi y
Alcozer, Jose Miguel, 1763-1828.
Alcock, T. St. Leger. 688
Alcock, Thomas. tr. 69278
Alcohol and the commonwealth. (3679)
Alcoholic liquors. 87019
Alcon, Juan Jose. (689)
Alconcle, Antoine Felix. 959
Alcott, Louisa May, 1832-1888. 690-691,
52305, 57942, 76692
Alcott, William Alexander. 102194
Alcozer, J. M. Guridi y. see Guridi y Alcozer,
Jose Miguel, 1763-1828.
Alcune lettere . . . dalle Damigelle della sua
triplice classe. 64014
Alcune lettere scritte alcuni giorni addietro e
sparse per l'Italia. 71553
Alcune lettre scritti gli anni 1590. & 1591.
18658, 89537
Alcune osservazioni sopra la struttura primitiva
del corpo animale. (24990)
Alcune osservazioni sull'articulo quarto
pubblicato nel North American Review.
64014
Alcune osservazioni sui vegetabili piu utili di
quel paese. 11413
Alcune parole che usano le genti della terra di
Bressil. 67730
Alcuni avisi scritti gli anni 1690 et 1691.
44964, 89536, 89538
Aldaiturreaga, C. Juan. (48811)
Aldama y Guevara, Joseph Augustin de. 692
Alday y Aspee, Manuel de. 57423
Aldeano amante de su patria. 86396
Alden. pseud. Notes on the sea-shore. see
Shade of "Alden." pseud.
Alden, -----. publisher 53187
Alden, Ebenezer. 693-(695)
Alden, Edward K. 696
Alden, Henry M. 29113
Alden, J. Dean. (12161), 14763, 30669, 65765
Alden, Joseph. 698-700
Alden, T. J. Fox. 49498
Alden, Timothy. 701-709, (780), 54470
Aldenburgk, Johann Gregor. 710
Alden's New-Jersey register . . . for . . . 1811.
53187
Alderbrook. 36863
Alderete, Juan Sarria y. see Sarria y
Alderete, Juan.
Alderick, ------. 32787
Alderman Rooney. pseud. Alderman Rooney at
the Cable banquet. see Townley, Daniel
O'Connell.

Alderman Rooney at the Cable banquet. 54071,
96372
Aldermanic wisdom. 33098
Alderson, John. (711)
Aldis, A. O. 88829
Aldobrandini, Ippolito. see Clement VIII, Pope,
1536-1605.
Aldovera, Miguel de Azero y. see Azero y
Aldovera, Miguel de.
Aldrete, Martin Carrillo de, Bp. defendant
51043 see also Oviedo (Diocese) Bishop
(Aldrete) defendant
Aldrey, F. T. de. ed. 69664
Aldrich, J. P. 87451
Aldridge, J. 44677, 44679
Aldridge, W. 44678
Aldvs Manvtivs Romanvs, Iacobo Sanazaro
patritio Neapolitano et eqviti clariss.
S. P. D. 67736
Alegacion canonica. 86399
Alegacion de los derechos. 94348
Alegacion de sus meritos. 34150
Alegacion en derecho en competencia de
jurisdicion. 51041
Alegacion en derecho por el que asiste. 75561
Alegacion en derecho por el R^mo. Padre
Predicador. 42627
Alegacion en favor de la fabrica espiritual.
75584
Alegacion en favor de los herederos. 86400
Alegacion en favor de los religiosos. 86401
Alegacion en justicia. 94279
Alegacion juridica en defensa del Capitan Don
Joseph Diego de Medina y Saraviz. 26122
Alegacion juridica por Andres Lopez Moscoso.
93314
Alegacion juridica por D. Fernando de Ortega.
57674, 74858
Alegacion juridica por D. Miguel Perez de Santa
Cruz. 75583
Alegacion juridica por el Sargento Mayor.
74857
Alegacion juridica por Jeronimo Victoria. 86402
Alegacion juridica por la Provincia de la
Caridad. 76303
Alegacion juridica, que dio al publico. 77141
Alegacion por el Alferez, Manuel Baroja. (76304)
Alegacion por el Capitan Francisco Nicolas.
86403
Alegacion por el Conde del Valle de Orizaba.
76305
Alegacion por el Dr. y Mtro. D. Agustin Cabanas.
75585
Alegacion por el Provincial y Difinitorio de los
PP. Agustinos. 86404
Alegacion por la justicia de Diego Ortiz
Sepulveda. 86405
Alegacion por la Provincia de la Compania de
Jesus. (76336)
Alegacion por la Provincia de PP. Agustinos de
Mechoacan. 86406
Alegacion por los herederos de Alvarez Fuentes.
86407
Alegacion por los hijos y herederos de Andres
Arias Tenorio. 86408
Alegacion por los religiosos Dominicos de
Oaxaca. 86409
Alegacion por Miguel Gonzalez. 86410
Alegaciones en favor del clerco del obispado de
la Puebla. 66544
Alegaciones en favor del clero, estado
eclesiastico, i secular. 99441
Alegambe, Philip. 712-713, 70776-70777
Alegate en defensa de Dona Neo. Alcalde. 67639
Alegatio que conforme a las constituciones.
(41079)
Alegato de biene probado. (44966)
Alegato de buena prueba. 88728

Alegato de defensa en favor de los Srs.
Esteves. 25480
Alegato de defensa, que D. Manuel
Posadas. 64444
Alegato de puena prueba. (44966)
Alegato en favor del presbit. 10060
Alegato hecho ante el Juez Primero.
76747, note after 93338
Alegato por el Colegio Mayor. 48262
Alegato por el Dean y Cabillo
Sedevacante. 56396, 79138
Alegato por el General D. Domingo Ruyz
de Tagle. 74517
Alegato por el Obispo de la Puebla.
35266
Alegato presentado. 93344
Alegato pronunciado. 99435
Alegato, que conforme a las constitucionfs.
[sic] 98659
Alegato que huzo el ciudadano Anjel
Mariano Toro. 96209
Alegorias de Don Pedro de Castro.
(6797)
Alegorical discription. 89515
Alegre, Francisco Javier. 714, 9574,
32718-32719
Alegre, Manoel de Araujo Porto. see
Porto-Alegre, Manoel de Araujo.
Alexsandr I Pavlovich, Emperor of
Russia, 1777-1825. 93988 see also
Russia. Sovereigns, etc., 1801-1825
(Aleksandr I)
Aleman, Mateo, 1547?-1610. 715
Alembert, Alfred d'. see Almbert,
Alfred d', 1813-1887.
Alemparte, Jose Antonio. (717)
Alencar, J. Martiniano de. see Martiniano
de Alencar, J.
Alencar Araripe, Tristao de. see Araripe,
Tristao de Alencar.
Alencastre, Jose Martins Pereira de. see
Pereira de Alencastre, Jose Martins.
Alencastro Marona y Silva, Fernando de,
Marques de Valdafuentes. 57479
see also Mexico (Viceroyalty) Virrey,
1711-1716 (Alencastro Marona y Silva)
Aleph. pseud. The old city. 57118
Alethe. 72133
Aleutian abecedarium. 718
Alexander. pseud. Letter of Alexander.
13731
Alexander, pseud. Thoughts on the ensuing
election. 95702
Alexander VI, Pope, 1431?-1503. 745, 1561,
39893, 57542, 65990, (79179), 79179,
90296-90297 see also Catholic Church.
Pope, 1492-1503 (Alexander VI)
Alexander VII, Pope, 1599-1667. 56057, 73990
see also Catholic Church. Pope, 1665-
1667 (Alexander VII)
Alexander, The Great, 356-323 B. C. 69333,
105218
Alexander, -----. CSA (14283), 23304
Alexander, -----. defendant 30365
Alexander, ----. publisher 83787-83788
Alexander, A. 722
Alexander, Alexander. 719
Alexander, Alexander Humphreys. see
Humphreys-Alexander, Alexander,
Calling himself Earl of Stirling,
1783-1859.
Alexander, Alexander John. 101114
Alexander, Anne (Tuke) 1767-1849. 727,
(20180), (71189)
Alexander, Archibald. 720-(721), (38228),
(43195), (49064), 68473, 89736,
94568

Alexander, Caleb. 723, 56204
Alexander, Charles. ed. (38549), 83513,
84162
Alexander, Charles A. (724)
Alexander, Catharine. (10676)
Alexander, E. 71666
Alexander, Gabriel. 31719
Alexander, George William. (725)-726, 728
Alexander, J. G. 2992
Alexander, James. 729-732, 30380, 54421,
84554, 84558, 98429
Alexander, James. supposed author 19341,
84577
Alexander, James. defendant 53075 see also
Board of Proprietors of the Eastern
Division of New Jersey. defendants
Alexander, Sir James Edward, 1803-1885.
733-735, 6331, 75833
Alexander, James W. 738
Alexander, John Henry. (736)-737, 45127,
45155-(45156), 45158, 45339, 45346,
(45348)-45349
Alexander, Julian J. 45107
Alexander, Stephen. 85072
Alexander, William. ed. 742, 25318
Alexander, William, of Texas. 744
Alexander, Sir William, 1567?-1641. see
Stirling, William Alexander, 1st earl of,
1567?-1641.
Alexander, William, 1726-1783. see Stirling,
William Alexander, Calling himself 6th
Earl of, 1726-1783.
Alexander, William, fl. 1824-1840. 472-473,
81801, 92326
Alexander, William, fl. 1861. 10329
Alexander, William C. ed. 65652
Alexander (William) & Sons. firm defendants
101149
Alex. Graf. von Bonreval. 9809
Alexander H. Stephens. 13658
Alexander Hamilton. A historical study.
79983
Alexander Hamilton and his contemporaries.
71312
Alexander Hamilton Post no. 182, G. A. R.
see Grand Army of the Republic.
Department of New York. Alexander
Hamilton Post no. 182.
Alexander Hamilton's report on the subject of
manufactures. 29979
Alexander McRae, plaintiff; Thomas Morton,
defendant. 96904
Alexander Rossen's Unterschiedliche
Gotterdienste. 73321
Alex. Selkirchs sallsamma afventyr. (3984)
Alexander Selkirchs Schicksale zu Wasser und
zu Lande. 3983
Alexander T. Blakeley, claimant of part of the
cargo. 89224
Alexander von Humboldt. 78100
Alexander von Humboldt: a biographical
monument. 38046
Alexander von Humboldt. Ein biographisches
Denkmal. (38045)
Alexander von Humboldt. Ein Lebensbild fur
Jung und Alt. 77668
Alexander von Humboldt on two attempts to
ascend the Chimborazo. 33701
Alexander von Humboldt's Ansichten der Natur.
33702
Alexander von Humboldt's Leben und Wirken.
(38044)
Alexander von Humboldt's Reisen in Amerika.
38241
Alexander von Humboldt's Reisen in Amerika
und Asien. 38049, 41777
Alexandri Sardi Ferrariensis, De moribus ac
ritibus gentium libr. III. 24162

Alexandria, La. State Seminary. see
 Louisiana. State University.
Alexandria, Va. 74256-74257, (74270), 74271,
 99301, 2d note after 101951
Alexandria, Va. Convention of the Colored
 People of Virginia, 1865. see
 Convention of the Colored People of
 Virginia, Alexandria, 1865.
Alexandria, Va. Protestant Episcopal
 Theological Seminary in Virginia. 23689,
 100515
Alexandria, Va. Protestant Episcopal
 Theological Seminary in Virginia.
 Board of Managers. 100516
Alexandria (Ship) in Admiralty 34419
Alexandria Sentinel. 83775
Alexandria Tammany Society. see Tammany
 Society, Alexandria.
Alexandrias. 32718, 32719
Alexo de Orrio, Francisco Xavier. 750
Alexipharmacon. 12335
Alfandega do Rio de Janeiro. 59236
Alfaro, -------, Marques de Villahermosa
 de. see Villahermosa de Alfaro,
 ------, Marques de.
Alfaro, Diego de. 61165, (75985) see also
 Hospitallers of St. John of God.
 Province of the Archangel San Rafael
 de los Reynos del Peru y Chile.
 Comissario General.
Alfaro y Beaumont, Isidro Sainz de. see
 Sainz de Alfaro y Beaumont, Isidro.
Alfaro y Pina, L. 48647
Alferes, Barao do Paty de. see Paty de
 Alferes, Barao do.
Alferez, ----- La Monja. see La Monja
 Alferez, -----.
Alfieri da Asti, Vittorio. 751
Alfonce, Ian. see Fonteneau, Jean.
Alfonse de Saintonge. see Fonteneau, Jean.
Alfonso Maria de Liguori, Saint. see
 Liguori, Alfonso Maria de, Saint,
 1696-1787.
Alfonso, Pedro Antonio. (752)
Alfred, King of England. spirit author.
 1081A, 101770
Alfred. pseud. Letter to the Hon. John
 Quincy Adams. 283
Alfred. pseud. Letter to the Hon. John
 Quincey Adams. 40482
Alfred, Maine. Convention, 1812. see York
 County, Me. Convention, Alfred, 1812.
Alfred: a masque. 84678C
Alfred: an historical poem. 105785
Alfred Crowquill. pseud. Goodnatured hints.
 see Forrester, Alfred Henry.
Alfred the Great. An historical tragedy.
 106135
Alfriend, F. H. ed. 88393
Algarotti, Francesco, Conte, 1712-1764. 753
Algemeen Letterlievend Maandschrift. 95455
Algemeen Verslag van derzelver Grenzen.
 50925
Algemeene Armenschool, Heilige Rosa,
 Curacao. see Heilige Rosa, Curacao.
 Algemeene Armenschool.
Algemeene, Beschrijving, van Vreemde
 Havens. 24945
Algemeene Natuurkunde. 33737
Algemeene Weereld-Beschryving. (38504)
Algemeene Wereldt-Beschryving. (38504)
Algemeine Geschichte der Lander und
 Volcker von America. (38594A), (77989)
Algemeyne Oprekeninge van de Huyzen.
 36080
Alger, Francis. 35402
Alger, Horatio, 1832-1899. 754, 44636, 55977

Alger, William Rounseville, 1822-1905. 757-
 761, 88820
Algerie agricole. 70367
Algerine captive. 97615
Algerine spy in Pennsylvania. 763, 44623
Algernon Sidney. pseud. Vindication of the
 measures. see Granger, Gideon. and
 Leigh, Benjamin Watkins. incorrectly
 supposed author
Algernon Sydney. pseud. Principles and men.
 see Richmond, William E.
Algic researches. 77835
Algic Society for Encouraging Missionary
 Effort in Evangelizing the North American
 Tribes. 77843
Algiers. Sovereigns, etc. (Hassan Bashaw)
 96586 see also Hassan Bashaw, Dey of
 Algiers.
Algiers. Treaties, etc. (6361), 18875, 96562,
 96586
Algo de masones. 94577
Algo mas que cuatro palabras al declamador.
 72257
Algo sobre cierto discurso. 98176
Algodon-Bay in Bolivien. 5209
Algora, Juan. 767
Algumas observacoes acerca do commercio
 das carnes. 81079
Algumas reflexoes sobre a historia natural
 do Brasil. 34840
Algumas vergalhadas dadas em prosa. 88704
Algunas cuestiones de actualidad. 62996
Algunas declaraciones en el asunto. 56291
Algunas hazanas de las nuchas. (4587)
Algunas ideas sobre la historia. 20101,
 (39076)
Algunas ideas sobre organizacion de la
 hacienda. 65517
Algunas indicaciones acerca de la intervenciona
 europa. 48263
Algunas indicaciones sobre los deberes mas
 esenciales. 57724
Algunas notas de la correspondencia. 19268,
 93785
Algunas obras raras sobre la lengua
 Cumanagota. 94346, 94424, 105954
Algunas observaciones arregladas a los
 principios. 12740
Algunas observaciones de Mr. I. Bailey.
 45019
Algunas observaciones sobre el opusculo.
 48264
Algunas poesias ineditas. (57229)
Algunas reflecsiones acerca de los dolorosos.
 29353
Alguno, Senor. pseud. The baby and the
 bards. see Ames, Nathan.
Alguno, Senor. pseud. Childe Harvard. see
 Ames, Nathan.
Algunos Aviados de la Mina de Jacal.
 plaintiffs (44966)
Algunos Catolicos Amantes de su Religion y
 de su Patria. eds. 99656
Algunos documentos que se hallan en la
 propia coleccion de Nunoz. 94352
Algunos Mexicanos Afectos a la Tierna
 Ninez. tr. 74969
Algunos planos levantados por los oficiales.
 12743
Algunos Proprietarios de Fincas Rusticas.
 pseud. Respuesta. 70094
Algunos Proprietarios de Fundos Colindantes
 con las Riberas del Mar, Valparaiso,
 Chile. petitioners 23439
Alguns capitulos tirados das cartas. 68328
Alhalla. (77836)
Alhazen, 965?-1039? 66686

Ali Bey. pseud. Extracts from a journal.
see Knapp, Samuel Lorenzo, 1783-1838.
Aliander de Cosco. tr. 14628-14633, 77902
Alice Lee. 88666
Alice of Monmouth. 91060
Alice Roy. 29670
Alice Singleton. 84133
Alida; or, miscellaneous sketches of incidents.
14943
Alida; or, Town and country. 78828
Alida: sketches of the late American war.
49767
Alien and sedition laws. (23627)
Alien laws of the state of New-York. 52051
Alienation of affections. 26780
Alienigenae of the United States. 5471
Alienist and neurologist. 84246
Aliens, a patriotic poem. 44775
Alien's guide to citizenship. 78269
Aliens. [Whether aliens are rateable polls.]
45624
Alient Baptist Dissenter. pseud. Plowman's
complaint. see Brooks, Seth.
Aliquis. pseud. Midwinter's day dream.
(48878)
Aliqvot opvscula. 27690
Alison, Alexander. 769
Alison, Archibald. 770
Alison, Francis. 771, (42384), 61420, 66908,
70716, 90607 see also Corporation for
the Relief of Poor and Distressed Presby-
terian Ministers. Trustees.
Alison, W. P. 772
Aliste y de Villaflor, Luis Henriquez de Guzman,
Code de Alva de. see Henriquez de
Guzman, Luis, Conde de Alva de Aliste
y de Villaflor.
All able bodied seamen. 95342
All about little Eva. 92502
All about petroleum. (49081)
All about poor little Topsy. 92503
All about southern California. 77424
All about the draft. 20805
All barkers are not biters. 94543, note before
95353
All Canada in the hands of the English. 10349
All' Ear, Milord. pseud. see Milord All'Ear.
pseud.
All' eccellentiss. M. Hieronimo Fracastoro.
67730, 67732-67735
All' Eye, Milord. pseud. see Milord All'Eye.
pseud.
All flesh is as grass. (79404)
All gentlemen sailors. 41388
All gentlemen sailors . . . let them repair on
board. (12899), 99601A
All gentlemen volunteers. 19140
All good wishes in one. 46325
All governments derive their just powers.
28160
All' Illustriss. et Eccellentiss. Signora Givlia
Sforza Pallavicina. 1559, 2d note after
45010
All impressments unlawful. 34409
All is not gold that glitters. 67599
All loyal seamen. 61453
All men are born equal. 29618
All mens place. 103510
All nations of the earth blessed in Christ.
12331
All persons having in their possession. 61454
All plots against God and his people detected.
104073
All power in heaven. 59604
All religions and religious ceremonies. 71841
All rights to all men! 17355
All round the world. 773

All Saints' Church, New York. see New York
(City) All Saints' Church.
All Saints' Memorial Church, Navesink, N. J.
see Navesink, N. J. All Saints' Memorial
Church.
All slave-keepers that keep the innocent in
bondage. 39465, 79446
All the members of the Council. pseud.
Vindication. see Spring, Samuel.
All the memorials. (774), note after (47740),
note after 96403
All the polemical works of Lorenzo Dow. 20757
All the proceedings in relation to the New South
Ferry. 8291, (54072)
All the publick acts. 100233
All the suppressed facts. 7360
All the treaties. 775
All the voyages round the world. 65699
All the world's a stage. 92277
All things for Christ. (26166)
All true ministers of the Gospel are called.
2624
All who are out of commons. 105832
Alla illvstrissima et excellentissima Signora la
S. Contessa di Albi. 67730
Alla va eso y tope donde topare. 99676
Allaire, M. M. 776, 48702
Allais, Denis Vairasse d'. see Vairasse
d'Allais, Denis.
Allan, -----. 54023
Allan, George H. 47493
Allan, Henry. 72121
Allan, John, 1746-1805. 37715, 47493
Allan, John, d. 186-? 74681
Allan, William. publisher (21542)
Allan, William, 1837-1889. 33131
Allans, --------. illus. 81134
Allanson, ------. engr. 84779
Allard, Carel. ed. 57460
Allard, Isaac T. petitioner 73706
Allardice, Samuel. engr. 85105
Allardt, Hugo. cartographer 73418
Allardt, M. L. ed. 48756
Allde, John. 79343
Alleganiad, and other original poems. 97705
Allegany County, N. Y. petitioners 53979,
note after 90676
Allegations de MM. les docteurs Hosack et
Townsend. 12483, 13645
Allegations made against proprietary govern-
ments. (59676)
Allegations made by Stephen Codman. 98562
Allegations of certain presbyters. 90690
Alleged corrupt combination. 15514
Alleged "objectionable features" in the religion.
90846
Alleged relations of the American Board of C. F.
Missions. 9063
Alleghan. 27990
Alleghania. 62910
Allegheny, Pa. 89246
Allegheny, Pa. Western Theological Seminary
of the Presbyterian Church. see Western
Theological Seminary of the Presbyterian
Church, Alleghany, Pa.
Allegheny County, Pa. Commissioners.
defendants 60287
Allegheny County, Pa. Sundry Citizens.
petitioners 47650
Allegheny Cemetery, Pittsburgh. see Pittsburgh.
Allegheny Cemetery.
Alleghany College, Meadville, Pa. 777, 101710
Alleghany College, Meadville, Pa. Library. 777,
(59987)
Alleghany magazine; or repository of useful
knowledge. (780)
Alleghany Portage Railroad. 778

Alleghany Portage Railroad. Superintendent of Motive Power. 85465 see also Snodgrass, John.

Alleghany Railroad and Coal Company. 779, 59872

Alleghany Railroad and Coal Company. Charter. 59872

Alleghany Valley Rail Road. Chief Engineer. 59873

Alleghany Valley Rail Road. President. 59873

Alleghany Valley Rail Road. Treasurer. 59873

Allegiance and patronage. 26079

Allegoric memoir of the Boston Exchange Office. 6513, (11890)

Allegorical dialogue on John's baptism. 70281

Allegorical memoir of the Boston Exchange Office. 6513

Allegorical poem. (56840)

Allegorical representation. 105614

Allegory. 16362, 79371, 82973, 88478, 89058, 89532

Allegory addressed to the Dialectic Society. 22545

Allegory on life and futurity. (74635)

Allemand, ------- l'. see L'Allemand, -------.

Allemant, Charles l'. see Lallemant, Charles.

Allemao, F. Freire. see Freire Allemao, F.

Allen, -------. ed. 1614

Allen, ------, of Pittsfield. 104136

Allen, ------. plaintiff 36136

Allen, ------. supposed author 6215

Allen, ------, fl. 1777. 60662

Allen, ------, fl. 1834. (77847)

Allen, A. J. ed. 781, 103377

Allen, Alfred. (70981)

Allen, Anson. 55101

Allen, Andrew. claimant 782, 84842

Allen, B. 783

Allen, Benjamin, 1789-1829. 902, 36819, 57739, 1st note after 97993

Allen, Benjamin F. 784

Allen, Bird. 785

Allen, Charles, 1797-1869. 786-787

Allen, Charles, 1827-1913. 83881, 85212

Allen, Diarca Howe, 1808-1870. 788

Allen, E. G. 790

Allen, Ebenezer. 789

Allen, Edward Archibald, 1843- 85374

Allen, Elizabeth Ann (Chase) Akers, 1832-1911. 60871

Allen, Ethan, 1737-1789. 791-803, 806, 20987, 57424, 66514, 74327, 79287, 90629, 4th-5th notes after 98997, 1st note after 99000, 1st note after 99003, 2d-3d notes after 99005, 6th note after 99005

Allen, Ethan, 1737-1789. supposed author 98998

Allen, Ethan, of Pennsylvania, fl. 1786. (59830), 105586A, 105693A

Allen, Ethan, 1796-1879. 807-812, (45211A), 45339, (45347)

Allen, Frank J. 96675-99676, 96679, 96683, see also U. S. Commissioners to the Kaskaskia and Peoria Indians; U. S. Commissioners to the Kickapoo Indians; U. S. Commissioners to the Piankeshaw and Wea Indians; U. S. Commissioners to the Shawnee and Delaware Indians.

Allen, Fordyce A. 79897

Allen, George, 1792-1883. 813-815, 45596, 45598, (45639), (62666), 69438, 70068, 95070, 95705

Allen, George, 1792-1883. supposed author 15048, note after 95073

Allen, George, 1808-1876. ed. 28242

Allen, Harrison, 1841-1897. 816

Allen, Heman. plaintiff 65098, 69392, 96810, 99008

Allen, Henry B. 88820

Allen, Henry W. defendant 82597

Allen, Henry Watkins, 1820-1866. 42271, (42307), 83921 see also Louisiana. Governor, 1864-1865 (Allen)

Allen, Horatio, 1802-1889. 87962, 87965 see also South Carolina Railroad Company. Chief Engineer.

Allen, Hugh. ed. 65903

Allen, Ira, 1751-1814. 795, 817-825, (12851), 97536, 98999-99000, 1st note after 99000, 99002, 99004-99005, 1st note after 99005, 4th note after 99005, 99008, 99023, 99045-99046, 99073, 99133-99134 see also Vermont. Treasurer.

Allen, Ira, 1751-1814. incorrectly supposed author 7286, 4th note after 99005

Allen, Ira M., d. 1849 ed. 97961

Allen, Ira Wilder, 1827- 69157

Allen, James. defendant 101214

Allen, James, 1632-1710. 826-829, (36851), 37209, (44077), (46466), (46631), 46695, 97190, note after 94098 see also Ministers of the Gospel in Boston. pseud.

Allen, James, 1691-1747. 830-832, 917-919.

Allen, James, 1739-1808. 833, 6738, (82501)

Allen, James, fl. 1784. 834, 91599, 102789 see also Meeting of the West-India Merchants and Planters, London, 1784. Secretary.

Allen, Joel. illus. 36666, 92083

Allen, John. of Hackney 9353

Allen, John. supposed author 1037, 81585

Allen, John. plaintiff 96811

Allen, John. publisher 28052, 28506, 65689

Allen, John, 1763-1812. 837

Allen, John, fl. 1764. supposed author 36919, 81586-81588, 94006

Allen, John, 1771-1843. 839

Allen, John, fl. 1772. supposed author 94006

Allen, John, fl. 1773. incorrectly supposed author 836, 81586

Allen, John. fl. 1826. 838

Allen, John Fisk. 840

Allen, Jonathan, 1749-1827. 841

Allen, Jonathan Adams, 1825-1890. 99176

Allen, Joseph, of Western, Mass. 842, 845

Allen, Joseph, fl. 1776-1817. 105397, 105401-105403, 105405

Allen, Joseph, 1790-1873. 843-844, 846

Allen, Joseph, 1810?-1864. 847-848

Allen, Joseph D. 54723, 57833

Allen, Joseph Henry, 1820-1898. 849-850

Allen, Lewis Falley, 1800-1890. 9056, (82391), note after 95451

Allen, Lewis Leonidas. 851-852, 97295

Allen, Myron Oliver. 853

Allen, Paul, 1775-1826. 854-(858), 1358, (40828), 86129, note after 102121

Allen, Rev. Richard. 859, 36442

Allen, Richard, fl. 1841. 36383

Allen, Richard Howe, 1820?-1892. ed. 61772, 61886 see also Philadelphia. Pine Street Church. Pastor.

Allen, Richard L., 1808-1873. 860-861, 76916

Allen, Richard N. defendant 45070

Allen, Robert, late of Peru. 862-863, 19277, 22969

Allen, Rev. S. 866

Allen, S., fl. 1821. 54124

Allen, Samuel. 865

Allen, Samuel Clesson, 1772-1842. 867-868
Allen, Silas. supposed author 93205, 101203
Allen, Stephen, 1767-1852. 869, 96876
Allen, Stephen Merrill, 1819-1894. 90169, 90173
see also Standish Memorial Association.
Corresponding Secretary.
Allen, Stephen Thompson. 870
Allen, T. S. 49209
Allen, Thaddeus. 871
Allen, Thomas, 1608-1673. (872), 3213, 17059,
17085, note before 92797, note after
92800, 3d note after 103687
Allen, Thomas, 1743-1810. 873-875
Allen, Thomas, fl. 1768. cartographer 63476
Allen, Thomas, 1813-1882. 876-878, 75331,
102208
Allen, Thomas G. 879
Allen, Timothy, 1715-1806. 880-881
Allen, W. 84975
Allen, Wilkes, 1775-1845. 882-883
Allen, William. United we Stand. see Allen,
Benjamin, 1789-1829.
Allen, William. ed. 21873, 22352, 79612,
note before 91980, 105653
Allen, William, 1710 (ca)-1780. 884, 84586
Allen, William, 1780-1873. (894)
Allen, William, 1784-1868. 885-893, (7141)-
7142, 72110, 83654, 101636
Allen, William, 1784-1868. plaintiff 7036,
92313
Allen, William, 1793-1864. 899
Allen, William, 1806-1879. 896-898, 901
Allen, William Francis, 1830-1889. 82067
Allen, William G. (903)
Allen William Henry, 1808-1882. 904-906,
60376
Allen, William Joshua, 1828-1901. 907
Allen, William S. 908
Allen (B.) & Co. Agricultural Warehouse, N. Y.
firm publisher 88276
Allen de genen die desen sullen sien oft hooren
lesen saluyt. 16664, 102889
Allen Prescott. 909, 78828-78829
Allen teutschen Eltern. 106350
Allen trials. 36136
Allen versus Gunter. 36136
Allen's exposition of the controversy. 69392
Allende, Ignacio. (66521)
Allentown, Pa. Muhlenberg College. see
Muhlenberg College, Allentown, Pa.
Allentown, Pa. Sonntags-Schul-Verein. see
Sonntags-Schul-Verein fur Deutschen
Gemeinden, Allentown, Pa.
Alleralteste Nachricht von der neuen Welt. 910,
note before 99327, 99358
Allerhand so Lehr-als Geistreiche Brief.
(52376), 91981-91982
Allerneueste Beschreibung der Provintz
Carolina. 10957, 39453
Allerneueste Reise nach der Sud See. (25928)
Allerneuester Kriegsstaat. 911
Allestree, Richard, 1619-1681. 26596, 103557,
103557A
Alley, Jerome. 912
Alley, John. defendant 70276, 79895
Alley, John B. 912, 912A
Alleye de Cyprey, --------, Baron. 57840
Alleyne, J. S. B. ed. (47326), 91829
Allgemeine Beschreibung der englandischen
Colonien. 26980
Allgemeine Cultur-Geschichte. 38043
Allgemeine deutsche Volks-bibliothek. 92554
Allgemeine Erdkunde. 104704
Allgemeine geographie. (4858)
Allgemeine Geschichte der geograph.
Entdeckungsreizen. 104702, 104703
Allgemeine Geschichte der ost und west-indischen
Handlungsgesellschaften in Europa. 79072

Allgemeine Geschichte und Beschreibung von
Neu-Frankreich. (12138)
Allgemeine Geschichte der neuesten Zeit. (38278)
Allgemeine Geschichte der Vereinigten Staaten.
94444
Allgemeine Geschichte, von Alfang der historischen
Kenntniss. 73443
Allgemeine Historie der Reisen zu Wasser und
Zu Lande. 913, 36810, 65406, 84560,
85380, 1st note after 97689
Allgemeine historische Weltbeschreibung. 6808
Allgemeine Lander und Volkerkunde. 4853A
Allgemeine Schaubuhne der Welt. 42659
Allgemeine See-Atlas. 4857A
Allgemeine Sprachenkunde mit dem Vater Unser
als Sprachprobe. 453, 5269, 11042
Allgemeine Ueebersicht Frankreichs von Franz
I. 106337
Allgemeinen Uebersicht von Amerika. 91197
Allgemeiner Ueberblick der politischen Lage.
23226
Allgemeines historisches Taschenbuch . . . fur
1787. 89755
Allgemeines historisches Taschenbuch oder
Abrisz der merkwurdigsten neuen Welt-
Begebenheiten enthaltend for 1784. 89755
Alliance between Brazil, the Argentine Con-
federation and Uruguay. (58526)
Alliance du Bresil et des republiques de la
Palata. 39980
Alliance of British cotton spinners. 91007
Alliance of Jehoshaphat and Ahab. 42367
Alliance Russo-Americaine. 2355
Alliance weekly news. 28082
Alliance with the Negro. 4229
Alliances dans lesquelles les ministre de la
Grande-Bretagne ont engage la nation.
68284, 80054
Allias, Nicolas Vinton de Saint. see Saint-
Allias, Nicolas Vinton de, 1773-1842.
Allibone, Samuel Austin, 1816-1889. (914),
18320, 35221, (36998)
Allid. pseud. National ballads of Canada. see
Lanigan, G. F.
Allies and the late ministry defended. 915
Alligator. 7386
Alli letteri. 67731
Allin, Abby. see Carter, Abby (Allin)
Allin, J., fl. 1684. 33442
Allin, James, 1691-1747. 917-919
Allin, John, 1596-1671. 920-922, (21090),
33698, 66059, 78431, 104846
Alline, Rev. Henry. 924
Alline, Henry, 1748-1784. 923, 78322
Alling, Jeremiah. 925
Allison, Samuel. 53046, 83979
Allison, ------. 84678C
Allison, Burgiss. 90836
Allison, John. 926
Allison, Joseph. 927
Allison, Patrick. (928)-929, 5746, 22337,
99771
Allison, W. J. ed. 36597
Allison, William Boyd. 930
Allison, William L. 85146
Allman's edition. 105010
Allocutio Exc. D. D. Antonii M. Bucareli, et
Ursua. 8836
Allouard, Emma. tr. 69019, 69052, 69055
Allouez, Claude. (18247), 25853, 39998, (44664),
note after 69259, 80002
Allowing soldiers to vote. (2723)
All's well. 59871
All's well that ends well. 91829
Allsop, Robert. 931
Allston, Col. pseud. Life, adventures and
opinions. see Hines, David Theodore.

Allston, ------. illus. 69409
Allston, Joseph. 80684-80685
Allston, Robert Francis Withers, 1801-1864.
  932-933, 61297, 87499 see also South
  Carolina. Governor, 1856-1858 (Allston)
Allston, Washington. 101411
Allumeur de reverberes. 17940
Allyn, John. supposed author (15860), note
  after 95296 see also Connecticut.
  (Colony) Secretary.
Allyn, Rev. John. 934-938
Allyn, Robert. 70565 see also Rhode Island.
  Office of Commissioner of Education.
Alm, Jacob. 939
Almacen universal. 48265
Almada, Bartolome E. 26519 see also
  Sonora, Mexico. Apoderado.
Almanac. HERE ARE ENTERED ALL
  ALMANACS. DUPLICATE ENTRIES
  WILL BE FOUND UNDER RESPECTIVE
  AUTHORS AND TITLES 940-(944),
  958, (1038)-1039, 1309, 1952, 3143,
  (3211), 3885-3885A, 4206, 4260, 4354,
  4388, 4718, 4857A, 4908, 5220, 6134,
  6492, 7507-7511, 7977, 8001, 8265, 8494,
  8680, 8992, 9215, 9994, 10118, 10622,
  (10624), 10769-10770, 10907, 10981,
  11416, 11521, 11617, 12036, 12423,
  12619, 12901-12902, (13000), 13027,
  13073, 13077, 13103, 13405, 13640,
  13668, (13777), (14683), 14857-14858,
  14890, 14701, 14995, 15143, 15256-15258,
  15476-15477, 15659-15663, 15828-(15829),
  (15661), 15663, 15664, 15883-15884, 17473,
  (17576), 17728, 17957, (18062), 18232,
  18473, (19217), 19383-(19384), 19449,
  19496, (19739), 20325, 20769, 21284,
  21289, (21717), 21833, 22238, 22321,
  23006, 23126, (23241), 23762, 23297,
  23844, 23846-23848, (23850), 23858,
  23909-23911, 24220, 24596, (24687)-(24688),
  24950, 24972, 25375, 25564, 25566-25568,
  25642, 25643, 25667, (25776), 25791,
  25957, 26331, 27050, 27332, (27594),
  27617, 27656, 27835, 28453, 28475, 28560,
  28671, 28783, (28805)-28806, (28931),
  (29037), 29064, 29070, 29156, 29566,
  29567, (30200), 30302, 30579, 30784,
  31448, (32698), (32766), 32776, 33158,
  33587, 33878, 34049, 34330-34332, 34334,
  34338, 35564, 35593, 35637, 36028, (36058),
  36981, 37125, 37497, (37520), 37698,
  38097, 38131, 38140, 38548, 38552, 38792,
  (38846), 39328, (39555), 39689, (39809),
  39815, (39816), 39822, (39826)-39827,
  40934, (41081), (41376), 41561, 41768,
  41939, 41950, 41959, 42394, 42402,
  (42520), 42733, (42849), 42937, 43070,
  (43125), 43243, (43494), 43969, 44258,
  44316, 45201, (45235), 45251, 45509,
  45625, 45813-45814, 45826, 45844, 45887,
  46239, 46774, 47053, 47160, (47161),
  47209-47210, 47256, 47280, 47407-47408,
  47776, 47910, 47912, 47921, 48026, 48189,
  48217, 48266, 48486, 48757, (48830),
  49009, 49096, (49154), (49190), 49221-
  49222, 49231, 49615, 50142, 50258, 50269,
  50432, 50434, 50441-50443, (50492),
  (50592), 51089, 51373, 51601, 51686,
  51709, (51849), 51900, 51917, (51949),
  52005, 52031, 52063, 52221, (52244),
  52542, 52578, 52646-52655, 52670, 52679,
  52681, 52690, 52752, 52767, 52811, 52864,
  (52870), 52884, (52889), 52971, 53164-
  53167, 53267, (53306), 53619, 53674,
  53799, 54298, 54456, 54459, (54719)-(54721),
  54730, 54739, 54759, 54774, (54833),

(54837), 54984, 55009-(55010), (55015), 55029,
  (55039), 55048, 55101, 55536, 55540,
  55544, (55567), 55796, 55871, 55868,
  (55923), 56155, 56207, 56266, 56305,
  56965, 57131, 57142, 58079, 58202, 58328,
  58381, 58496, 58576, 58669, 58874, 58965,
  59306, 59399, 59555, (60182), (60298),
  60300-60301, 60347, 60348, (60350), 60818,
  60825, 61002, 61076, 61940, 61941,
  (61942), (61999), 62021, 62505, 62540,
  62553, 62557, 62569, 62591, 62743, note
  after 62743, 63014, 63114, 63123, 63143,
  63323, 63432, 63506-63508, (63483), 63506-
  63508, 63823, (64069)-64071, (64074)-64079,
  64081, 64083, 64089-64091, 64094-64096,
  64103, 64179, 64254, 64324, 64424, 64712,
  64721, (64958), 65136, 65191, (65195),
  65196, 65549, (65637), 65680, (65974),
  66121, 66187-66188, 66298, 66391, (66428),
  (66440), 66457, (66518), 66741, 67040,
  67076, 67508, 66741, 68215, 68349, 68410,
  70701-(70707), 70733, 70997-(71001), 71457,
  (71540), 71621, 71688, 71689, (71720),
  71917, 72025-72027, 72065, 72239, 72380,
  73066, 73715, 73724, 73729, (73795), 74053,
  74325, 74327, 74340, 74476, 74827-74828,
  (75013), (75047), 75271, 75511, 75315,
  (75722), 76088, 76092, 76487, (77542),
  78150, 78427, 76088, 76092, 76487, (77542),
  78150, 78427, 78461, (78760), (79028),
  79388, 79472, 79775-79779, 79780, 79844,
  79845, 79910, 79999, 80089, 80157, 80281,
  80282, 80395, 80396-80403, 80439, 80788,
  81360, 81598, 81821, 81835, 82291, 82376,
  82377, 82378, 82811, 82914, 82974, 82976,
  84218-84219, 84552, 84799, 84948-84950,
  86276, 86318-86319, 87745-87789, 88257,
  88276-88287, 88306, 88400, 88401, 88500A,
  88631-88633, 88654, 88705, 89573-89591,
  89838, 89855, 90071-90076, 90571-90572,
  90594, 90642, 90796, 90937-90958, 91386,
  91618, 91832, 91970-91979, 92363, note
  after 92979-93065, 93075, 93229-93232,
  93242, 93245, 93831, 93848, 83857, 93869,
  93870, 93891, note after 94610, 95078,
  2d note after 95414, 95416, note after
  95426, 95447, 95555-95556, 95611, 95820,
  95853, note after 96057, 96482, 96921,
  96979, 97284, 97438, 97961, 97963, 97968,
  97977, 97985-97986, 97988, 97991, 97997-
  97998, 98014, note after 99139-99143,
  99160, 5th note after 99205, 99233, 99236-
  99237, 101212, 101213, 101230, note after
  101426, 101426, 102182, 102495, 102496,
  102530, 102788, 103176, 103263, 103264,
  103607, 104200, 104206, 104391-104395,
  105008, 105444, 105687, note after 105687,
  note after 105846, 106404
Almanac, agreeable to the new-stile. 87752
Almanac and city record. 10118
Almanac, and ephemeris. 70703
Almanac and register for the island of Jamaica.
  35564
Almanack and register, for the state of
  Connecticut. 15668, (15829)
Almanack, and register, for the state of Vermont.
  99140
Almanack by George Andrews, Esq. 87753
Almanack . . . by George Andrews . . . for . . .
  1774. 87760
Almanac calculated for the island of St. Vincent.
  75511
Almanack . . . calculated for the meridian of
  Harvard College. 72027
Almanack. Containing an account of the
  coelestial motions, aspects, &c. For the
  year of the Christian empire. 1690. 55009,
  62743

Almanack containing an account of the coelestial
motions, aspects, &c. For the year of
the Christian empire, 1691. (55010),
62743
Almanac. 1857. 8494
Almanac 1867. (73795)
Almanack . . . fitted to the meridian of
Boston. 72027
Almanac for . . . 1800. 97284
Almanac . . . for 1805. 76487
Almanack, for 1817. 89575
Almanack for 1820. 89582
Almanac for . . . 1827. 64076
Almanack . . . for 1829. 75271
Almanac for 1821. 51373
Almanac, for 1848. (75013)
Almanac for 1850. 7977
Almanac for 1866. 19449
Almanac for New England. 25791, 59555
Almanack for 1720. 51089
Almanac for 1724. 96482
Almanack for . . . 1725. 52670
Almanac for 1726. (33587)
Almanac for 1732. (78760)
Almanac for 1741. 103607
Almanac for 1747. 51900
Almanack, for . . . 1755. 80400
Almanac for 1757. 62743
Almanack for . . . 1761. 93242, note after
105846
Almanac for 1767. 62557, 62743
Almanack for . . . MDCCLXVII. 47407
Almanack for 1768. 47408
Almanack for 1772. 24685
Almanack for 1773. 87759
Almanac for 1775. 62553
Almanack, for . . . 1777. 26989
Almanack, for . . . 1778. 93029
Almanack for 1780. 45251
Almanack, for . . . 1780. 55540, 70703, 93031
Almanack, for . . . 1781. 93032
Almanac, for . . . 1782. 93033
Almanack for . . . 1783. 93034
Almanack, for . . . 1783. 56155
Almanack, for . . . 1784. 93035
Almanack, for . . . 1785. 93036
Almanack, for . . . 1786. 93037, 93054
Almanack, for . . . 1787. 92997, 93038, 93055
Almanack for . . . 1788. 93000
Almanack, for . . . 1788. 93039
Almanack for . . . 1790. 93004
Almanack, for . . . 1791. 93042
Almanack, for . . . 1792. 93043
Almanack, for . . . 1795. 52864, 93017
Almanack, for . . . 1796. 93019
Almanack, for . . . 1797. 41561, 93048
Almanack, for . . . 1797. (52870)
Almanack, for . . . 1797. 93049
Almanac for 1669. 45625
Almanack . . . for . . . 1695. 62743
Almanac for 1697. 53519
Almanack for the dyonisian year of the
Christian AEra. M.DC.LXXXIII.
46239
Almanack for the state of Connecticut. (15829)
Almanack for the year of Christ 1733. 25566
Almanack, for the year of Christian account,
1770. 87756
Almanack, for the year of Christian account,
1771. 87757
Almanack, for the year of Christian account,
1772. 87758
Almanack for the year of Christian account
1687. 39815
Almanack. For the year of Christian AEra,
1777. 42402
Almanack, for the year of Christian AEra,
1783. 79388

Almanack for the year of grace, 1686. 36981,
(60182)
Almanack for the year of our Lord Christ,
1739. 90074
Almanack for the year of our Lord Christ,
1750. 80396
Almanack, for the year of our Lord Christ,
1750. 80395
Almanack for the year of our Lord Christ,
1753. (80397)
Almanack, for the year of our Lord Christ,
1753. (80398)
Almanack, for the year of our Lord Christ,
1754. 80399
Almanack for the year of our Lord Christ
1756. 80401
Almanack for the year of our Lord Christ,
1760. 80402
Almanack for the year of our Lord Christ,
1761. 80403
Almanac, for the year of our Lord, 1801. 88631
Almanac, for the year of our Lord, 1806. 88632
Almanac for the year of our Lord 1840. 12440
Almanack for the year of our Lord 1847. 18473
Almanack for the year of our Lord, 1740. 90075
Almanack for the year of our Lord, 1744. 90076
Almanack for the year of our Lord 1750. 80281
Almanack for the year of our Lord 1752.
(64069), 80282
Almanack for the year of our Lord, 1769. 87754
Almanack, for the year of our Lord 1793. 64103
Almanack for the year of our Lord 1839. 25791,
59555, 62743, (66428)
Almanack for the year of our Lord 1646. 47209
Almanack for the year of our Lord 1647. 18473
Almanack for the year of our Lord 1648. 62743
Almanack for the year of our Lord 1649. 62743
Almanack for the year of our Lord 1650. 47210,
62743
Almanack for the year of our Lord 1656. 62743
Almanack for the year of our Lord 1657. 62743
Almanack for the year of our Lord 1660. 62743
Almanack for the year of our Lord, 1661. 62743
Almanack for the year of our Lord, 1662. 62743
Almanack for the year of our Lord 1667. 62743
Almanack for the year of our Lord, MDCLXXXVII.
62743, 97437
Almanack . . . for the year of the Christian
AEra 1685. 46774
Almanack for the year 1703. 66740
Almanack for the year 1705. 58965
Almanack, for the year, 1718. 58202
Almanack . . . for the year . . . 1720. (24687)
Almanac for the year 1731. 47053
Almanack for the year . . . 1756. 52971
Almanack for the year 1761. 87747
Almanack, for the year 1799. 90071
Almanac for the year 1679. 18232
Almanack for the year 1683. 10118
Almanack for the year M.DC.LXXXIII. 6492
Almanack for the year MDCLXXIV. 62743
Almanack for the Jear [sic] 1695. 66741
Almanac of British North America. 10622
Almanack of coelestial motions and configurations
for the year of the Christian epocha, 1687.
62743
Almanack of coelestiall motions and configurations
for the year of the Christian epocha, 1687.
104395
Almanack of coelestiall motions, and configu-
rations &c. for the year of the Christian
AEra, 1684. 62743
Almanack of coelestiall motions for the year
of the Christian AEra, 1669. 62743
Almanack of coelestiall motions for the year
of the Christian AEra, 1670. 62743
Almanack of coelestial motions for the year
of the Christian AEra, 1671. 62743

Almanack of coelestial motions for the year of
the Christian AEra. 1673. 62743
Almanack of coelestial motions for the year of
the Christian AEra 1675. 62743
Almanack fo coelestial motions for the year of
the Christian epoch 1665. 56207
Almanack of coelestial motions for the year of
the Christian epocha 1678. 62743
Almanack of coelestial motions for the year of
the Christian epocha 1679. 62743
Almanack of coelestial motions for the year of
the Christian AEpocha, 1680. 62743
Almanack of coelestial motions for the year of
the Christian epocha, 1681. 62743
Almanac of celestial motions, for the year
1680. 940
Almanack of coelestial motions of the sun &
planets, with some of the principal
aspects for the year of the Christian
AEra MDCLXXXV. 46774, 62743
Almanack of coelestial motions of the sun &
planets, with some of the principal
aspects for the year of the Christian
AEra MDCLXXXVI. 62743
Almanack of coelestial motions of the sun and
planets, with some of their principal
aspects. For the year of the Christian
AEra 1676. 62743
Almanack of coelestial motions of the sun and
planets, with some of their principal
aspects. For the year of the Christian
AEra 1677. 62743
Almanack of coelestial motions of the sun and
planets, with their principal aspects, for
the year of the Christian AEra 1678.
62743
Almanac of celestial motions, viz., of the sun
and planets, &c., for the year 1674. 940
Almanack of coelestial motions viz. of the sun
and planets, with some of the principal
aspects, for the year of the Christian
AEra 1674. 62743
Almanac of Poor Richard the Second. 64077
Almanack of the coelestiall motions, aspects
and eclipses, &c. For the year of our
Lord God, MDCXCIV. 62743
Almanack of the coelestial motions, aspects &
eclipses, for the year of the Christian
AEra, 1712. 62743
Almanack of the coelestial motions, aspects
and eclipses, for the year of the Christian
AEra, 1716. 72027
Almanack of the coelestial motions, aspects,
and eclipses . . . for the year . . .
1714. 72026
Almanac of the coelestiall motions, &c., for the
year of our Lord God M.DC.XCIV. 940
Almanack of the coelestial motions for the
year of the Christian AEra 1663. 62743
Almanack of the coelestial motions for the
year of the Christian AEra 1664. 62743
Almanack of the coelestial motions, for the
year of the Christian AEra, 1685. 62743,
104394
Almanack of the coelestial motions for the
year of the Christian epocha. 1688. 62743
Almanack of the coelestial motions for this
present year of the Christian AEra 1659.
62743
Almanack or astronomical calculations of the
most remarkable celestial revolutions.
62743
Almanack or register of coelestial configu-
rations &c. For the year of our Lord
God 1679. 62743
Almanack . . . 1702. 62743
Almanack. 1760. 21809
Almanac, . . . 1798. 62505

Almanach administrativo, mercantil e industrial
da corte e provincia do Rio de Janeiro.
38552
Almanach administrativo, mercantil, industrial e
noticoso da provincia do Para. 58496
Almanach americain. 941
Almanach americain, asiatique et africain. 941
Almanach californien. 9994
Almanach civil, ecclesiastico, historico-
administrativo da provincia de Mocambique.
(26488)
Almanach de Cayenne. (11617)
Almanach de commerce pour la Nouvelle-Orleans.
(53306)
Almanach de Guyane Franciase. 29156
Almanach de la Guadeloupe et dependance.
(29037)
Almanach de lembrancas Brasileiras. 7507
Almanach de lembrancas luso-brasileiro para o
anno de 1863. 11416
Almanach de lembrancas luso-brasileiro para o
anno de 1866. 7508
Almanach de Quebec. 67040
Almanach . . . . Den Freunden der Erdkunde
gewidmet. 4857A
Almanach des colonies. 14701
Almanach des colonies, 1788. 942
Almanach et directorum francais de Etats-Unis.
943
Almanach interessant dans les circonstances
presentes. 8001
Almanach litteraire. (42849)
Almanach national de la republique d'Haiti. 29566
Almanach pour 1854. 92525
Almanach royal d'Hayti pour l'annee 1814. 73515,
(75047)
Almanach royal d'Hayti pour l'annee 1815. 29567
A[l]manach royal d'Haity. 3885
Almanacque nacional. 56266
Almanak administrativo, civil industrial da
provincia de Minas-Geraes do anno de
1869. (49190)
Almanak administrativo, mercantil e industrial
da corte e provincia do Rio de Janeiro.
71457
Almanak de ministerio da marinha. 7510
Almanak do ministerio da guerra. (7509)
Almanak dos eleitores da provincia de Minas
Geraes. 88705
Almanak geral do imperio do Brasil. 93831
Almanak militar para o anno de 1865. 7511
Almanak voor de Nederlandsche West-Indische
Bezittingen en de kust van Guinea van
1856. 52221
Almanak voor de Nederlandsche West-Indische
Bezittingen, en de kust van Guinea, voor
het jaar 1859. 93848
Almanak y kalendario general diario de quarto
de luna. 8992
Almanaque agricola, pastoril e industrial de la
republica Argentina y de Buenos-Ayres.
1952
Almanaque de Bogota i guia de forasteros para
1867. 6134
Almanaque de la corte. (42866)
Almanaque imperial para el ano de 1866. (42866)
Almanaque para el ano de 1837. 29064
Almanaque para el ano de 1863. 21796
Almanaque para el ano de 1867. 10769
Almanaque peruano y guia de forasteros. 58576,
61076
Almanaque portatil para el ano de 1869. 10770
Almanaque universal hispano-americano. (944)
Almarez, Gregorio de. pseud. Restauracao de
Portugal prodigiosa. see Escobar, Manoel
de.
Almaraz, Ramon. 945, 47589
Almbert, Aldred d', 1813-1887. (716), 946

Almedo y Torre, Antonio de. ed. 26748, 1st
note after 98659
Almeida, Antonio Lopes da Costa. see Costa
Almeida, Antonio Lopes da.
Almeida, Candido Mendes de. see Mendes de
Almeida, Candido.
Almeida, Manuel Antonio de. 47753
Almeida, Miguel Calmon du Pin e. see Pin e
Almeida, Miguel Calmon du.
Almeida, Teodoro de. 26506
Almeida, Tito Franco de. 26244
Almeida Carvalhaes, Rodrigo Pinto Pizarro de.
see Carvalhaes, Rodrigo Pinto Pizarro
de Almeida.
Almeida de Carvalho, Manuel de. see
Carvalho, Manuel de Almeida de, Bp,
1749-1818.
Almeida de Menezes, Jorge de. see Menezes,
Jorge de Almeida de.
Almeida e Albuquerque, Francisco de Paula d'.
947
Almeida e Sa, Luis de Franca. see Franca
Almeida e Sa, Luis de.
Almeida Nogueira, Baptista Caetano de. tr.
74029
Almighty dollar. 93095
Almirante, en consideracion de los seruicios.
102815
Almiron, Miguel Nieto de. see Nieto de
Almiron, Miguel.
Almodovar del Rio, Pedro Jiminez de Gongara
y Lujan, Duque de, d. 1794. (68084),
88944
Almofadas sem frankas. 22511
Almoguerra, Joannes de. (948)
Almoloyan, Mexico. Sub-prefectura. 48814,
(57235)
Almon, John, 1738-1805. 241, 243, 255, (491),
806, 949-955, 14392, (15202)-(15203),
25704, 26829, 32177, 36909, 37244,
34087, 38180, 39706, (47395), 50830,
(52446), 63784, 64832, 66015, 70256,
84642, 86745, 91132, note after 92858,
95750, 97575, 101150, 2d note after
103122, 104003, 106311
Almon, John, 1738-1805. supposed author
(34374), (70207), 70211-70213
Almond & Redgate. firm claimants 80449
Almonte, Juan Nepomuceno. see Nepomuceno
Almonte, Juan.
Almost Christian. 103497, 103530, 103605
Almost Obsolete Loyalist. pseud. England's
western, or America's eastern shore?
22597
Alms House, Bridgewater, Mass. see Massa-
chusetts. State Alms House, Bridgewater.
Alms House, Monson, Mass. see Massa-
chusetts. State Alms House, Monson.
Almshouse, New York (City) see New York
(City) Hospital and Alms House.
Almshouse, Philadelphia. see Philadelphia.
Almshouse.
Alms House, Tewksbury, Mass. see Massa-
chusetts. State Alms House, Tewksbury.
Almshouse women. 83566
Almy, John. 957, 48803
Alnambay 1859. Almanac. 958
Alnwick castle with other poems. (29867)-29868
Alocucion de Pio IX. 39284
Alocucion del Supremo Delegado a los centro-
americanos. 49416
Alocucion patriotica pronunciado en die 20
Sept. de 1853. 22659
Alocucion que Pio. VI. tuvo. 11377
Alocuciones cartas oficiales e instrucciones.
47033
Alone. 94840
Along the Madawaska. (52154)

Alonso Decalves. pseud. see Vandeleur,
John. pseud??
Alonso de Jesus. supposed author 86367
Alonso de Veracruz. see Gutierrez, Alonso.
Alonso, Juan Bautista, b. 1821. 85710
Alonso y Pantiga, Angel. 68806
Alonso and Melissa. 49688
Alonso Geronimo de Salas Brabadillo. (69551)
Alonzo, - - - - - - - - - . 80342
Alonzo; or, the cave of vice. 97548
Alonzo's dream. 105614
A'Lord, G. 960
Alouette. pseud. Quantrell. 66942
Alpass, Thomas. tr. 12592
Alpha. pseud., tr. 6307
Alpha (Ship) 59584, 93383
Alpha Delta Phi Fraternity. 86930-86931
Alphab⁹. Rivulus obeundus. 2118
Alphabet of Omahaw syllables. 57262
Alphabet of syllables of the Cherokee Language.
34481
Alphabet of verses. 97494
Alphabetical analysis of the constitution. 16111
Alphabetical and analytical catalogue of the
American Institute Library. (1107)
Alphabetical and analytical catalogue of the New-
York Society Library. 54543
Alphabetical and chronological catalogue. 6636
Alphabetical and numerical list of proprietors.
51146
Alphabetical army register. 961
Alphabetical arrangement. 61604, 91312
Alphabetical atlas. 19023
Alphabetical catalogue of authors. 44718
Alphabetical catalogue of books proposed to be
purchased. 50845, (59393)
Alphabetical catalogue of books published in this
country. (5763)
Alphabetical catalogue of the forest trees and shrubs.
44776
Alphabetical catalogue of the Library of Congress.
Authors. 15577
Alphabetical catalogue of the Library of Congress,
1864. 10053
Alphabetical catalogue of the Library of Congress.
Subjects. 15577
Alphabetical catalogue of the Library of Parlia-
ment. 10393, 10398
Alphabetical compendium of the various sects. 208
Alphabetical digest of the public statute law.
87684
Alphabetical index of the births. (66238)
Alphabetical index to American genealogies.
(21438)
Alphabetical index to places of interment. 72831
Alphabetical index to subjects. 64040
Alphabetical index to the Astor Library. 2250,
14218
Alphabetical index to the four sheet map. 94310
Alphabetical index to the laws of Texas. 94999
Alphabetical index to the laws of Texas, arranged
by a member of the bar. 95001
Alphabetical index to the laws of Texas: of fourth
and fifth Congress. 95000
Alphabetical index to the laws of the republic
of Texas. 95002
Alphabetical list of all the wards. (59263)
Alphabetical list of applicants. 53520
Alphabetical list of members. 87338
Alphabetical list of patented models. (33909)
Alphabetical list of persons deceased. (66238)
Alphabetical list of post-offices. 20325, 53389
Alphabetical list of private claims. 11443
Alphabetical list of senators and representatives.
37859
Alphabetical list of the laws of Canada. 27521
Alphabetical list of the proprietors. 105437
Alphabetical list of the streets. 61456

Alphabetical register of all the authors. 70153
Alphabetical roll of the General Assembly. 65135
Alphabetical table. 42400
Alphabetical vocabularies of the Clallam and Lummi. 27300
Alphabetical vocabulary of the Chinook language. 27299
Alphabetical vocabulary, or dictionary of words. 78993
Alphabetische Naam-Lijst van alle de Groenlandsche en Straat-Davissche Commandeurs. 76854
Alphabetische Naamlijst van Boeken. 94467
Alpheus Spring Packard. A commemorative address. 85209
Alphonsus Liguori, Saint. see Liguori, Alfonso Maria de, Saint, 1696-1787.
Alpine and arctic plants. 18955
Alpuche, Jose Maria. defendant 64444
Alpizar, -----. (47807)
Alranado, Leon. 32759, 55142
Alrich y Elias, D. A. tr. 16944
Als Handbuch fur Reisende und Beytrag zur Landerkunde. (42662)
Alsedo y Herrera, Dionysio de. see Alcedo y Herrera, Dionisio de.
Alsinet, Josef. (962)
Alsographia americana. 67437
Alsop, George. 963, (80023)
Alsop, John. 96022
Alsop, Richard, 1761-1815. 964-(966), 15791, 16964, 21534, (21778), 36123, 49893-49894
Alsop, Richard, 1761-1815. supposed author 98003
Alsop y Compania. Socio Director. defendant 47811 see also Bispham, Carlos. defendant
Alspach, S. (78071)
Alstine, John van. see Van Alstine, John, 1778-1819.
Alston, Joseph. 5906, 74878
Alston, Theodosia (Burr) 5906, 74878
Alston, William J. 967
Alstyn, Matthew van. see Van Alstyn, Matthew.
Alsufficient physician. 95161
Alt, George. tr. 77523
Alta, Miguel de Salcedo y Sierra. see Salcedo y Sierra Alta, Miguel de.
Alta California. see California (Alta California)
Alta California. 102640
Altamira, Antonio Joseph Ortiz de Casqueta, Marques de. see Casqueta, Antonio Joseph Ortiz de, Marques de Altamira.
Altamira, Bartholome Antonio Joseph Ortiz de Casqueta, Marques de. see Casqueta, Bartholome Antonio Joseph Ortiz de, Marques de Altamira.
Altamirano, Diego. 99436
Altamirono, Ignacio M. ed. 69596, 71636
Altamirano y Castilla, Lope. 87157 see also Catholic Church. Commissario General de la Sancta Cruzada.
Altar de Nuestra Senora la Antigva. 86429
Altar of Baal thrown down. 93492-93493
Altar of peace. 70470
Altare Christianum. 63515
Altars of sacrifice. 23136
Alte Germantown Calendar, 1854. 27162
Alte in der neuen Welt. 106316
Alte Mexico. 2002A
Alte Reisen und Abenteuer. 91218
Alte und neue Bruder-Historie. 17410
Alte und neue Gronlandische Fischerei und Wallfischfang. 106373
Alte und neue Heimath. 93101

Altemont Lodge, Peterborough, N. H. see Freemasons. New Hampshire. Altemont Lodge, Peterborough.
Alten Gronlands neue Perlustration. 22019, 22024
Alteration of the coyn. 33163
Alterations and amendments of the laws of the Scots Thistle Society. (62233)
Alterations and amendments to the articles and plan of association. 61908
Altercation. 95788
Alternative. 32468
Alterta Dominicanos! 75046
Alteste Bekannte Abbildung sudamerikanischer Indianer. 99362
Alteste Karte mit dem Namen Amerika. 101017
Altham, John. 103352-103353
Althorpe, Lord -----. (15052)
Althought private disputes afford but little entertainment. 96442
Altieri, Emiliero. see Clement X, Pope, 1590-1676.
Altman, C. Koning. tr. (43434)
Alton, Davis. 969
Alton, Ill. Common Council. petitioners 968
Alton, Ill. Court. 41268, note after 97069
Alton, Ill. Shurtleff College. see Shurtleff College, Alton, Ill.
Alton city directory for 1868-9. 32518
Alton observer--Extra. (34313), 81818
Alton trials. 41268, note after 97069
Altorf. A tragedy. 105586
Los Altos (Guatamalan State) Supremo Gobierno Provisorio. 44283
Altowan. 91392
Altperuanisches Drama. 57224
Altra relation fatta per Pietro Dalvarado. 67740
Altruria. 84436
Alumni address. 58148
Alumni Association, Dartmouth College. see Dartmouth College. Alumni Association.
Alumni hall. 30765
Alumni of King's College, Windsor. (37871)
Alumni records, 1833 to 1869. (36839)
Alumni Society of the University of Nashville. see Nashville, Tenn. University. Alumni Society.
Alumnos del establecimiento de educacion publica de la Cabecera de Huejutla. see Huejutla, Mexico. Establecimiento de Educacion Publica. Alumnos.
Alumnus. pseud. Brown University under the presidency of Asa Messer. 8600
Alumnus. pseud. Letter to Andrews Norton. 55865
Alumnus. pseud. Letter to the corporation and overseers of Harvard College. note just before (30750), 58321
Alumnus. pseud. Plea for Harvard. see Quincy, Josiah, 1772-1864.
Alumnus. pseud. Remarks on a pamphlet. see Lowell, John, 1769-1840.
Alumnus Brunensis. pseud. Letter to the corporation of Brown University. 8626
Alumnus of that college. pseud. Further remarks. see Lowell, John, 1769-1840.
Alumnus of that college. pseud. Remarks on a pamphlet. see Lowell, John, 1769-1840.
Alumnus of that school. pseud. "Latest form of infidelity," examined. see Ripley, George, 1802-1880.
Alva, Bartholome de. 970, 48375
Alva, Bartolini. see Alva, Bartholome de.
Alva de Aliste y de Villaflor, Luis Henriquez de Guzman, Conde de. see Henriquez de Guzman, Luis, Conde de Alva de Aliste y de Villaflor.

Alva Ixtlilxuchitl, Fernando de. see
   Ixtlilxuchitl, Fernando de Alva, ca.
   1568-1648.
Alva y Astoraga, Pedro de. 87133
Alvado de Abranches. 43301
Alvah. (57792)
Alvarado, Antonio. 105953 see also Mexico.
   Fiscal.
Alvarado, Francisco. 32770 see also
   Honduras. Ministro jeneral.
Alvarado, Francisco de. (971), 49652
Alvarado, Juan de. see Juan de Alvarado,
   Fray.
Alvarado, Leon. tr. 89956
Alvarado, Pedro de. defendant 67646
Alvarado, Pedro de, 1495?-1541. 3350, 16936-
   16937, 16951, 67740, 94854
Alvarado, Pietro de. see Alvarado, Pedro de,
   1495?-1641.
Alvarado y de la Pena, S. de. tr. 16266
Alvares, Bernardino. see Alvarez,
   Bernardino.
Alvares, Domingo de. (972)
Alvares, Pedro. 67730
Alvares Caal, Pedro. see Caal, Pedro
   Alvares.
Alvares d'Andrada, Francisco Ladislau. see
   Andrada, Francisco Ladislau Alvares d'.
Alvares de Oliveira, Jose. see Oliveira,
   Jose Alvares de.
Alvares Pereira Coruja, Antonio. see
   Pereira Coruja, Antonio Alvares.
Alvarez, A. 44273
Alvarez, Bernardino. 16061, 68849
Alvarez, Francisco, 16th cent. 674, 66686,
   67730 see also Ethiopia. Ambassador
   to the Vatican.
Alvarez, Francisco, fl. 1778. 975
Alvarez, J. J. 976
Alvarez, Jose. see Toledo y Dubois, Jose
   Alvarez de.
Alvarez, Jose Maria. 979
Alvarez, Juan. 48527
Alvarez, M. 93394
Alvarez, Nicholas. (980)
Alvarez, R. 981, 54300
Alvarez Cabral, Pedro. see Cabral, Pedro
   Alvarez.
Alvarez Chana, Diego. see Chana, Diego
   Alvarez.
Alvarez de Abreu, Antonio Joseph. see Abreu,
   Antonio Joseph Alvarez de, Marques de
   la Regalia.
Alvarez de Abreu y Valdes, Miguel Anselmo.
   see Abreu y Valdes, Miguel Anselmo
   Alvarez de, Bp.
Alvarez de Faria Rios Sanchez y Zarzosa,
   Manuel de Godoy. see Godoy Alvarez
   de Faria Rios Sanchez y Zarzosa,
   Manuel de, Principe de la Paz, 1767-
   1851.
Alvarez de Ron, Antonio Joseph. petitioner
   (69983)
Alvarez de Sobrino, Rodrigo. 48812
Alvarez de Toledo, F. 973
Alvarez de Toledo, Jose. see Toledo y
   Dubois, Jose Alvarez de.
Alvarez de Toledo, Juan Baptista, Bp. 72531
   see also Guatemala (Archdiocese)
   Bishop (Alvarez de Toledo)
Alvarez de Toledo y Dubois, Jose. see
   Toledo y Dubois, Jose Alvarez de.
Alvarez Fuentes, ----. 68497
Alvaro, Francisco. 62806, note after 90319
Alvear, Carlos. 982-983
Alvear, Diego de. 984, 9010
Alvensleben, Ludwig von. tr. 5889
Alverna seraphico. 48267

Alves, Robert. 985
Alves Branco Moniz Barreto, Domingos. see
   Barreto, Domingos Alves Branco Moniz.
Alves da Silva, Manuel. see Silva, Manuel
   Alvas da, 1793-
Alves Massa, Joao. see Massa, Joao Alves.
Alves Serrao, Custodio. 88782
Alvim, Francisco Cordeiro da Silva Torres e.
   see Torres e Alvim, Francisco Cordeiro
   da Silva.
Alvim, Miguel de Souza Mello e. see Souza
   Mello e Alvim, Miguel de.
Alvires, -----. 73159
Alvirey, Alexo de. 986
Alvirez, J. M. 10097
Alvise, Querini. (22416), 29112
Alvo, Francisco. see Alvaro, Francisco.
Alvord, Benjamin. 987, 85072
Alvord, C. supposed author. (59003)
Alvord, John Watson, 1807-1880. 988, (9217),
   25743 see also U. S. Bureau of
   Refugees, Freedmen and Abandoned Lands.
   General Superintendent of Schools for
   Freedmen.
Alwaise, John. 29539
Always abounding in the work of the Lord. 92243
Always thankful. 78459
Aly Bey. pseud.? Historia de la revolucion de
   1854. 32034
Alyhabet [sic] Yakama. 75449
Alzate, Jose. 79327
Alzate, Josef Antonio de. see Alzate Ramirez,
   Jose Antonio, 1738-1799.
Alzate Ramirez, Jose Antonio, 1738-1799.
   (989)-991, (39083), 40059, 48426
Alizde, oder die Amerikaner. 100720, 100722
Alzír, vagy az Amerikanusok. 100723
Alzira. A tragedy. 100710-100719
Alzira. Or Spanish insult repented. 100719
Alzira, ovvero gli Americani. 100724
Alzira tragedia di Voltaire. 100725
Alzire. 100727-100728
Alzire, oder der Americaner. 100720-100721
Alzire, of de Amerikanen. 100709
Alzire, ou les Americains. 100696-100708
Alzirette. 100728
Am I not a man, and a brother? (992)
Amada del senor. (72293)
Amadeo Bonpland. 22776
Amador, Augustin de Souza y. see Souza y
   Amador, Augustin de.
Amador de los Rios, Jose. see De los Rios,
   Jose Amador.
Amador bueno. 93587
Amana. pseud. Catholic question at Boston.
   see Savage, George.
Amana, Nicolao ab. 993
Amanach royal d'Haity. 3885
Amand, ------ Saint. see Saint-Amand,
   -------.
Amanda. 8006
Amandus Zierixeensis. 994, 106399
Amant, Charles de Saint. see Saint-Amant,
   Charles de.
Amante de la justicia y de que se publique.
   98267
Amante de la paz. pseud. Triunfo de la
   constitucion. 97017
Amante de la religion y de su patria. pseud.
   publisher 34177, 47417, 86398
Amante de su patria. pseud. Causas para
   declarar la guerra. 11577, 48332
Amante de su patria. pseud. El triunfo de los
   escritores. 97023
Amante de su patria. pseud. Todavia
   arrastramos las cadenas. 96081
Amante del Christianismo. pseud. Viva la
   patria. see Morales, Francisco Jose de.

Amantes do deserto. (12243)
Amaral, Delfim Augusto Maciel do. 43301
Amaral e Silva, Antonio Luiz do. (995)
Amaral Gurgel, Manoel Joaquim do. see
   Gurgel, Manoel Joaquim do Amaral.
Amaranth: being a collection of original pieces.
   97080
Amaranth, or masonic garland. (50333)
Amarilla, Bernabe de la Higuera y. see
   Higuera y Amarilla, Bernabe de la.
Amarillas, ----------, Marquesa de la. 48427
Amaro, Juan Romualdo. 996
Amartelado Amigo Suyo. pseud. ed. 99732
Amartigena. (66411)
Amaru, Jose Gabriel de Tupac. see Tupac-
   Amaru, Jose Gabriel de.
Amaru, Juan Tupac. see Tupac-Amaru, Juan.
Amassa, Juan de. defendant 51043
Amasa Stetson's claim. 91366
Amat, Manuel. 98150
Amateur. pseud. Crayon sketches. see Cox,
   W.
Amateur. pseud. ed. New book of a thousand.
   52512
Amateur. pseud. New mirror for travellers.
   see Paulding, James K.
Amateur. pseud. Union and liberty. 97755
Amateur casual. pseud. Sketches of society
   and others. (81568)
Amateur traveller. pseud. Altowan. see
   Steuart, Sir William Drummond, Bart.
Amati, Bernardino de. tr. 72000
Amati, G. 997
Amatolos. pseud. Friendly dialogue. see
   Spring, Samuel, 1746-1819.
Amator, Clementiae. pseud. see Clementiae
   Amator. pseud.
Amator Virtutis. pseud. Youth's companion.
   see Witherspoon, John.
Amaty y reglamento. 63899
Amazon, and the Atlantic slopes. 46961
Amazonas, Lourenco da Silva Araujo e. see
   Silva Araujo e Amazonas, Lourenco da.
Amazonas und seine Confluenten. 35524
Amazone. 5135
Amazone. Les metis de la savane. (11044)
Amazone. Les revoltes du Para. 11045
Amazonian republic recently discovered. 77250
Amazons and the coast. 82720
Ambach, Ed. von. (37114)
Ambassadeur de Dieu et le Pape Pie XX.
   73265
Ambassadors tears. (46221)
Amberteuil, H. see Hilliard d'Auberteuil,
   Michel Rene.
Ambigu, ----. 92542
Ambition des Anglais demasquee par leur
   pirateries. (63831)
Ambitious shepherd. 86825
Ambler, Jaquelin. 96005, 100414-100417 see
   also Virginia. Treasurer.
Ambrister, R. C. defendant at court martial
   1893-1895, 48077, 51782, 56758
Ambrose, Paul. pseud. Letters on the
   rebellion. see Kennedy, John Pendleton,
   1795-1870.
Ambrosij Richszhoffers, Braszilianisch- und
   West Indianische Reisze Beschreibung.
   71219
Ambrosil de Vria, Nicolas. see Uria, Nicolas
   Ambrosial de.
Ambrosio de Letinez. 51651, 95143
Ambulance system. 58314
Amelia. pseud. Poems. see Welby, Amelia
   B. (Coppuck)
Amelia, or malevolence defeated. (79484)
Amelia; or, the bower of virtue. 97548
Amelia; or, the faithless Briton. (79484)

Amelia; or, the influence of virtue. 105056,
   105058
A-me-li-ke ho chung kwo che leo. 7834
Amelot, ----. 75057
Amelot de Lacroix, Irenee. see Lacroix,
   Irenee Amelot de.
Amemategui, Miguel Luis. (1002A)
Amenability of Northern incendiaries. 106004
Amende honorable de Nicolas Durand. 99725
Amended act of incorporation and ordinances of
   Rutland. 74466
Amended articles of association [of the New York
   and Lake Superior Mining Company.] 54735
Amended by-laws of the Southern Protection
   Insurance Company. 88449
Amended by-laws, rules and regulations for the
   State Reform Farm. 57053
Amended canons reported to the General
   Convention of 1871. (66120)
Amended charter of the city of St. Louis. 75329
Amended charter of the village of Sing-Sing.
   (81415)
Amended constitution of . . . New York. 53521
Amended constitution of the state of New
   Hampshire. (52799)
Amended ordinances of the city of New Bedford.
   52459
Amended treaty with the New York Indians.
   54781
Amendment of Mr. Porter. (60516)
Amendment to the constitution of the United
   States. 78601
Amendment to the militia laws. 94772
Amendment to the siegniorial act, of 1854. 10495
Amendments of the by-laws of the . . . [Massa-
   chusetts Medical] Society. 45874
Amendments of the by-laws of the South Carolina
   College. 87969
Amendments of the constitution of Massachusetts.
   45626
Amendments of the constitution proposed by the
   Council of Censors. 16144, note after
   99172, note after 104629
Amendments of the constitution submitted to the
   consideration of the American people.
   1003*, 40985
Amendments of the constitution to prohibit
   slavery. (78157)
Amendments proposed for the constitution. 45127
Amendments proposed to be added to the federal
   constitution. 1004
Amendments proposed to the constitution of the
   state of Vermont. 44727
Amendments to acts in regard to passengers.
   (53522)
Amendments to our national constitution. 1005
Amendments to the charter of . . . New York.
   (54074)
Amendments to the charter of the St. Louis
   Gas-Light Company. 75387
Amendemnts to the constitution of Pennsylvania.
   59874
Amendments to the constitution of the United
   States. 31884
Amendments to the internal improvement laws.
   34278
Amendments to the militia law. 53778
Amendments to the report of the Commissioners
   Appointed to Revise the General Statutes
   of the Commonwealth. (45627)
Amenite Lodge, no. 73, Philadelphia. see
   Freemasons. Pennsylvania. Amenite
   Lodge, no. 73, Philadelphia.
Ameno, Juan Moreno y Castro, Marques de Valle.
   see Moreno y Castro, Juan, Marques de
   Valle-Ameno.
Ament. 1006
Amerescoggin Indians. see Pequawket Indians.

Amerescogging Indians. see Pequawket Indians.
Americ Vespuce. 99383A-note after 99383C
America. 3827, 27214, 29050, 30861, 39147, 50086, 70922
America. 14637
America (Song) 84041-84042, 84047, 84058, 84060, 105959, 105966
America. A dramatic poem. 96299
America, a four years' residence. 8575
America—a land preeminently blessed. 91153
America, . . . a lecture. 33817
America. A most singular woodcut or broadside. 1031
America. A poem. (23882)
America; a poem in the style of Pope's Windsor Forest. 21547
America, a prophecy. 5797
America; a series of historical tableaux. 89455
America. A sketch of the political, social, and religious character. 77491
America adolorida. 67082
America. An epistle in verse. 1008, 94401
America, an ode; and other poems. 14180
America, an ode; to the people of England. 1009
America and Africa. 1015
America, and American methodism. 36137
America and Europe. 29318
America and France. 1016, (1230)
America and Great Britain. 20384
America and her army. (43432)
"America and her destiny." 30340
America and her resources. 8050
America and her slave-system. (81819)
America and the American church. 11473
Ameirca, and the American people. 67972
America and the Americans. "Audi alteram partem." 6087
America and the Americans. By the late Achille Murat. 51409
America and the Americans. By W. E. Baxter. 4018
America and the Americans versus the Papacy and the catholics. 93183
America and the British colonies. 37865
America and the corn laws. 18054
America and the Stockholm Society for Emigrants. 1281
America and the West Indies. 41875, 97307
America ante-Colombiana. (39102)
America ante Columbum verteribus rabbinis nota. 29485
America as a field for the exertions of the Christian scholar. 8386
America as I found it. 1017, 21262, 42691
America before Europe. 26726
America: being an accurate description of the New World. 24081, 50088
America: being the latest, and most accurate description of the New World. (50089)
America by river and rail. 24100
America Central reclamacion de la intervencion del Coronel Sr. Alejandro Macdonald. (43143)
America compared with England. 1018, 74364
America. Correspondence between the Marquess Wellesley and Mr. Foster. 1010, note after 102574
America. Correspondence between the Marquess Wellesley and Mr. Morris. 1010, note after 102574
America. Correspondence of the Marquess Wellesley. 1010, note after 102574
America. Correspondence relative to the French decrees. 1014, 16895
America. Cronica hispano-Americana. (38393)
America contrasted with England. 93226

America, das ist, Erfindung und Offenbahrung der Newen Welt. (8784), note after 106331
America de Centro. Memoria dirigida por el Ministerio de Estado a la Assemblea Constitugente. 32773
America del Centro memoria dirijida por el Ministerio de Estado a la Asemblea Constiguente. (55137)
America del Sur ante la ciencia del deracho de gentes moderno. (10092)
America descriptio nova impresia. 71908
America di Raffaello Gualterotti. 90088
America discovered: a poem. 33970
America discovered. A poem, in twelve books. (1020)
America discovered in the tenth century. 67466
America dissected. 43662, 82976, 98029
America, disputatio publica. 1021
America en peligro. (23065)
America, &c., and other poems. 94401
America, Europa und die politischen Gesichtspunkte der Gegenwart. 25987
America for free working men! (55459)
America free, or America slave. 35836
America, from the Atlantic to the Pacific. 68008
America geografico-storico politica. 1022
America heeft veel baden. 37968
America heeft veel goud. 37968
America, historical, statistic, and descriptive. 8892
America hoedanige waterholen daar zijn. 37968
America illuminata. 94034
America in arms. 1023
America in 1819. 95351
America in fifty hours. 8467
America in its relation to Irish emigration. 43854
America in the tenth century. 83424
America invincible. 1024
America invoked to praise the Lord. 100917
America islands and continent. 26659
America, its history and resources. 16747
America libra. 751
America libre. 10098
America llorando. 1025, (24145), 76216
America lost. 1026
America, maps. 104830
America. My country, 'tis of thee. 84042
America, nach siener ehemaligen und jetzigen Verfassung. 38369
America: o examen general. 23225
America oder wie Man es zu teutsch nennt. 130
America, ofte de Nievwe Wereld. 5721
America, om af de Gamel Kiendt. 7129
America: or a general survey of the political situation. 23224
America: or an exact description of the West-Indies. 51678, 102816
America or the hope of mankind. 38307
America. Our national hymn. 84041
America painted to the life. 28020, (36203)
America poema eroico. 3797
America poetica. 1027
America pois'd in the balance of justice. (1028)
America, printed for the purchasers. (41634)
America, qvae est geographiae Blavianae pars qvinta. 5714
America revisited. 84000
America saved. 8168
America. Senate of the United States. 101712
America seu novvs orbis descriptio. 57687
America, sive novvs orbis. 48170
America socorrida. 39082
"America' Testimonial, Boston, 1895. 84058, 84062
'America' Testimonial, Boston, 1895. Executive Committee. 84062

America the land of Emanuel. 28148, (28951)
America: the origin of her present conflict.
46185
America threatened. 28466
America to Columbia. (16907)
America. Translated from the French. 1007
America, un tempo spagnuola. 3091
America und seine jetzige Bewegung. 1029
America viewed physically, politically, religiously. (74954)
America vindicada. 76308
America vindicated from the high charge.
(1030)
America y Espana consideradas en sus intereses
de raza. 24175
Americaansche Mercurius. 1032, 47938
Americae achter theil. (8784)
Americae das funffte Buch. (8784)
Americae nona & postrema pars. (8784)
Americae pars decima. (8784)
Americae pars VIII. (8784)
Americae pars qvarta. (8784)
Americae pars qvinta. (8784)
Americae pars VII. (8784)
Americae pars sexta. (8784)
Americae pars vndecima. (8784)
Americae retectio. 92665
Americae, sive novi orbis nova descriptio.
86424
Americae tertia pars. (8784)
Americae tomi vndecimi appendix. (8784)
Americaensche oorlog beweend. 96330
Americaensche Zee-Roovers. 23468
Americain. pseud. Christophe Colomb. see
Bourgeois, Auguste Anicet.
Americain. pseud. Considerations sur
l'Amerique Espagnole. 16022
Americain. pseud. Examen de la question.
see Cass, Lewis, 1782-1866.
Americain. pseud. Frankliniana. (25668)
Americain. pseud. Lettres. see Lacroix,
Jacques Vincent de.
Americain. pseud. Memoires. see Lacroix,
Jacques Vincent de.
Americain. pseud. Observations. (64903)
Americain. pseud. Projet d'un constitution
religieuse. (65985)
Americain. pseud. Travail. see Morhard,
------.
Americain. pseud. L'union de l'eglise et de
l'etat. 97802
Americain. pseud. Voeux patriotique d'un
Americain. 100658
Americain. 17876
Americain des isles neutres. pseud. Observations. see Maillet Duclairon, Antoine.
Americain naturalise ancien eleve ingenieur.
pseud. Manual guide des voyageurs. see
Gernagus de Gelone, -----.
Americain retourne d'Europe depuis peu. pseud.
Letter. see Walsh, Robert, 1784-1859.
Americain, Sange-mele. pseud. see C., J.
M., American sang-mele. pseud.
Americains. 100696-100708
Americains coureurs des bois. (23577)
Americains d'aujourd'hui. 12888
Americains, ou, le preuve de la religion
Chretienne. 1033
Americains Reunis a Paris, 1791. see Santo
Domingo (French Colony) Assemblee
Generale.
American. pseud. 103262
American. pseud. tr. 63732, 1st note after
97687
American. pseud. tr. see Doane, A. Sidney.
American. pseud. America discovered. (1020)
American. pseud. American anecdotes. see
Hunt, Freeman.

American. pseud. American churches. see
Birney, James G.
American. pseud. American husbandry. see
Young, Arthur.
American. pseud. American pioneer. 1185
American. pseud. American tears. see
Mather, Cotton, 1663-1728.
American. pseud. Americans defended. 1267
American. pseud. America's future. (1277)
American. pseud. America's misfortune. 81845
American. pseud. Annals of blood. see
Cobbett, William, 1763-1835.
American. pseud. At anchor. 2261
American. pseud. Captain Hall in America.
see Biddle, Richard.
American. pseud. Carta de un Americano.
11094
American. pseud. Causes and origin of slavery.
11580
American. pseud. Collection of state-papers.
14388
American. pseud. Columbian harp. 14864
American. pseud. Considerations on the
commencement of the civil war. 15977
American. pseud. The constitutionalist. see
Barton, William.
American. pseud. Cotton is king. see
Christy, David.
American. pseud. Discourses, on the public
revenue. (22976)
American. pseud. Enquiry into the condition
and prospects. (22635)
American. pseud. Eoneguski. see Strange,
Robert.
American. pseud. Essay in vindication of the
continental colonies. 22933
American. pseud. Essay on the rights and
duties of nations. see Everett, Charles
Carroll.
American. pseud. Essay upon the government.
(22976)
American. pseud. Examination of the question.
see Cass, Lewis, 1782-1866.
American. pseud. France; its king, court, and
government. see Cass, Lewis, 1782-1866.
American. pseud. Geography epitomized.
(26983)
American. pseud. Hints to my countrymen.
see Sedgwick, Theodore, 1780-1839.
American. pseud. Historical sketches. (38571)
American. pseud. Hobomok. see Child,
Lydia Maria.
American. pseud. Imminent dangers. see
Morse, Samuel Finley Breese, 1791-1872.
American. pseud. Impartial review. see
Sullivan, James, 1744-1808.
American. pseud. Inquiry into the condition
and prospects. (34804)
American. pseud. International copyright.
see Smith, Robert Pearsall, 1827-
American. pseud. Letter on American slavery.
see Morse, Sidney Edwards.
American. pseud. Letter on South America
and Mexico. 69702
American. pseud. Letter to Lord Brougham.
40443
American. pseud. Letter to the Edinburgh
reviewers. 105610
American. pseud. Letter to the people of
America. see Galloway, Joseph, 1729?-
1803, supposed editor.
American. pseud. Letters of an American.
(40606)
American. pseud. Life in California. see
Robinson, Alfred.
American. pseud. Maximilian and the Mexican
empire. 47029
American. pseud. Memoirs. (47566)

American. pseud. New system of philosophy.
53407

American. pseud. Observations on the trial by
jury. see Barton, William.

American. pseud. Oppression. (57415)

American. pseud. Plea for authors and the
rights of literary property. see Sockett,
Grenville A.

American. pseud. Poems. see Pickering,
Henry.

American. pseud. Political character of
John Adams. 229, 14388

American. pseud. Political character of the
said John Adams. 241

American. pseud. Political character of the
said John Adams, Esquire. (32634)

American. pseud. Political economy. (63766)

American. pseud. Political reflections. see
Galloway, Joseph, 1729?-1803.

American. pseud. Politician out-witted. see
Low, Samuel.

American. pseud. Remarks on Lord Sheffield's
observations. see Ruston, Thomas.
supposed author

American. pseud. Remarks on the British
treaty. 69440

American. pseud. Remarks on the governor's
speech. see Everett, Alexander H.

American. pseud. Review of Capt. Basil Hall's
travels. see Biddle, Richard.

American. pseud. Revolution in France. see
Webster, Noah, 1758-1843.

American. pseud. tr. Secret expedition to
Peru. note after 97687

American. pseud. Serious Christian. see
Mather, Cotton, 1663-1728.

American. pseud. Sons of the sires. see
Anspach, F. R. supposed author

American. pseud. South America. see
Brackenridge, Henry Marie.

American. pseud. Spanish America. 64904,
note after 88938

American. pseud. Theatrical censor. 95285

American. pseud. The times. see
Church, Benjamin.

American. pseud. To the independent electors
of Pennsylvania. 60705

American. pseud. To the people of the United
States. 97948

American. pseud. To the merchants committee. 62331

American. pseud. Tonnewonte. see Hart,
Julia Catharine Beckwith.

American. pseud. Tour in Holland. see
Watson, Elkanah.

American. pseud. Tracts on the Oregon
question. 57573

American. pseud. True interest of the United
States. see Barton, William.

American. pseud. United States and England.
see Green, Duff, 1791-1875.

American. pseud. Very short and candid
appeal. 99321

American. pseud. Vindication of the conduct
and character of John Adams, Esq. 261,
29961, 99802

American. pseud. What is our situation. see
Hopkinson, Joseph. supposed author

American. pseud. William and Ellen. see
Smith, Englesfield. supposed author

American. pseud. Winter display'd. see Low,
Samuel.

American. pseud. Wonderful narrative of two
families. see Telemachus. pseud.

American. pseud. Yankies war-hoop. 105974

American Abolition Society. 82103

American abolitionism. 24985

American aboriginal portfolio. 21682

American Academy of Arts and Sciences. 1034-
(1035), 6288, 7017, 18807, 18428, 18845,
32241, 35402, 42442, 47572, 62631, 62637-
62638, 67942, 72746, 104351

American Academy of Arts and Sciences.
Council. 67187

American Academy of Fine Arts, New York.
31577, 54017

American Academy of Fine Arts, New York.
Barclay Street Gallery. 97243

American Academy of Fine Arts, New York.
Chambers Street Gallery. 97245

American Academy of Fine Arts, New York.
Charter. 54017

American Academy of Fine Arts, New York.
President. 97241 see also Trumbull,
John, 1756-1843.

American Academy of Fine Arts, Philadelphia.
see Columbianum.

American Academy of Music, Philadelphia. see
Philadelphia. Opera House.

American Academy of Sciences. 83303, 83368,
83383, 84514

American accomptant. 39719

American accountant. 105474

American Adoptive Rite. see Mosaic Templars
of America, Europe, Asia and America.
American Adoptive Rite.

American adventure, by land and sea. 1036,
(76949)

American advocate. 84162

American advocate of peace. 31385

American alarm. 1037, 81585

American almanac. (1038)

American almanac and repository of useful
knowledge. 1039

American almanack, . . . and city directory.
54459

American almanac [for 1847.] 93075

American almanack [for 1700. (39816)

American almanack [for 1733.] 84552

American almanack for 1749. (36058)

American almanack for the year of our redemption, 1780. 74327

American almanack, for the year of our redemption, 1782. 74327

American almanack for the year 1714. (39826)

American almanack for the year . . . 1731.
39827

American almanack, New York register and city
directory. 41939

American anachron. 6376

American, and a citizen of Philadelphia. pseud.
Politicians. 63819

American, and a citizen of Philadelphia. pseud.
Triumphs of love. see Murdock, John.

American and British chronicle. 1040

American and British Joint Commission for the
Final Settlement of the Claims of the
Hudson's Bay and Puget's Sound Agricul-
tural Companies. see British and
American Joint Commission for the Final
Settlement of the Claims of the Hudson's
Bay and Puget's Sound Agricultural
Companies.

American and British kalendar. 26332

American and commercial daily advertiser.
93801

American and English oppression. 1041

American and European harmony. 64022

American and European railway and steamship
guide. 20316

American and European railway practice.
32526

American and Foreign Anti-slavery Society.
81779, 81820, 1st note after 95774

American and Foreign Anti-slavery Society.
Executive Committee. 81785

American and Foreign Anti-slavery Society.
Secretary. 81791, 2d note after 94368
see also Tappan, Lewis, 1788-1873.
American and Foreign Anti-slavery Society.
Treasurer. 81820
American and Foreign Bible Society. (14757)
American and Foreign Bible Society. Washington D. C. Auxiliary. see Washington
Bible Society.
American and Foreign Bible Society. Young
Men's City Bible Society, New York.
see Young Men's City Bible Society,
New York.
American and foreign statistician. 54202
American and French Institute. 97480
American and Indian transit. 3689
American and Mexican Railroad and Telegraph
Company. (66074)
American and Mexican Railroad and Telegraph
Company. Charter. (66074)
American and West-Indian gazetteer. 1042
American anecdotes. 91505
American anecdotes: original and select. 1043,
33848
American angler's book. 55508
American annals; or a chronological history of
America. 32576-(32577)
American annals; or, hints and questions.
(59756)
American annals of education. 1112
American annual cyclopaedia. 1044
American annual monitor. 1045, (71006), 86029
American annual register. (1046), (6037)
American annual register for the year 1833.
1047, (6037)
American annual register of public events.
1047, (6037)
American annual register, or, historical memoirs. 10062
American anthems. 57594
American antiquarian. 85139
American Antiquarian Society. 1049-1049,
1051-1053, 2225, 19050-19051, 23274,
23971, 24961, 26399, 27958, 31374,
(52625), 57819, 65936, 67234, 83980,
85144, 85211, 85214, 85222, 85224,
89542, 91853, 85404, 85406, 96481A,
99841-99853
American Antiquarian Society. Library. 1050
American Antiquarian Society. President.
1052, 95404 see also Thomas, Isaiah,
1749-1831.
American Antiquarian Society. Special Committee. 95406
American antiquities. 13703, 15076
American antiquities, and discoveries in the
west. 65484
American antiquities, and researches. 7233
American antiquities, or the new world the
old. (31196)
American antiquities. Read before . . . the
Pioneer Association. 58635
American anti-slavery almanac. 81821
American anti-slavery conventions. 81822
American Anti-slavery Society, New York.
419, (4298), 8522, 9324, 9330, 9805,
11924, 11996, (12127), 14400, (20309),
24955, 25908, 26079, 26128, 26712,
30676, 31755, (31792), 32338, 34697,
35868, 37331, 53275, 53391, 55369,
56652, 58325, 62528, (63345), (68652),
(70347), 81823-(81828), 81856, 81861-
81862, note after 81865, 81919, 81987,
88237, 92452, 95593, 102547-102548,
102550, 103299, 103812, 103814
American Anti-Slavery Society, New York
Executive Committee. (81784), 81823-81824

American Anti-slavery Society at war with the
church. 13469
American Apollo. 1054
American apology for American accession to
Negro slavery. 28246
American archaeological researches. 89994
American architect. 71554
American architecture. (13660)
American archives. 25053
American archives: fourth series. 25053
American arguments for British rights. 29948,
84818, 84828
American arithmetick. 72087
American art and art unions. 102091
American Art Association. (62421), 1st note
after 96964, 101452
American art: its awful altitude. 25486
American art museums. (60940)
American Art Union. (1055), 1760
American artillerist's companion. 96339
American artists and American authors. (38848)
American Association for the Advancement of
Science. 1057, 82997, 83003, 85386
American Association for the Advancement of
Science. Committee of Twenty. (1056),
69932
American Association for the Promotion of
Social Science. 1058
American Association in London. 41853
American Association of Agricultural Colleges
and Experiment Stations. 85061
American Association of Social Science. (36714)
American Asylum for the Education and
Instruction of the Deaf and Dumb, Hartford,
Conn. Directors. 30653
American Athenaeum. 41485
American Atlantic and Pacific Ship Canal
Company. 1059
American Atlantic and Pacific Ship Canal
Company. Chief Engineer. 34940 see
also Childs, Orville W.
American atlas. 104830
American atlas. A complete historical,
chronological and geographical American
atlas. (1062)
American atlas, consisting of twenty one large
maps. 1060
American atlas; containing the following maps.
1061, (69016)
American atlas: containing twenty maps and one
chart. 10855
American atlas. Exhibiting the post offices.
9438
American atlas: or, a geographical description
of the whole continent of America. 35953,
35962
American babes instructed. 94439
American Baptist Anti-slavery Convention.
36715
American Baptist Board of Foreign Missions.
12891, 84358-84362, 84365
American Baptist Board of Foreign Missions.
Missionaries. 79978
American Baptist Home Missionary Society.
3241
American Baptist Missionary Union. (49470),
(49472)
American Baptist register. 9473
American Bar Association. President. 84516
see also Smith, Walter George, 1854-1926.
American Bar Association. Advance information
for newspaper use only. 84516
American bards. 1063
American bards: a modern poem. 105496
American bards. A satire. 101134, 101140
American bastile. 44798
American battles. 99434

American bee. 1064
American bee keeper's manual. (49205)
American bible. 32496
American Bible Society. 18289, 18291, (49847),
(54075), 69646-69647, 69649, 71336
American Bible Society. Board of Managers.
54593
American Bible Society. Employees. 90772
American Bible Society. New Haven County
Auxiliary. see New Haven County Bible
Society.
American Bible Society. Young Men's New-
York Bible Society. see New York Bible
Society.
American biblical repository. 92387
American biblical repository. (Indexes) 5202
American bibliographer. 91520, 99362
American bibliographer's manual. 74692
American bibliographical guide. 607
American bibliopolist. 61196, 74695
American biographical and historical dictionary.
888-889, 101636
American biographical dictionary. 890
American biographical panorama. (33899)
American biographical sketch book. 33899-
33900
American biography. 88980
American biography. By Jeremy Belknap. 4430
American biography, containing biographical
sketches. (1065)
American biography; or, an historical account.
4429
American biography, . . . of distinguished
Americans. 38069
American bird fancier. 8648
American bird-keeper's manual. 44329
American bloody register. 1066, 3625, note
before 93509, 103349A
American blooms. 83972
American Board and slaveholding. (59166)
American Board and the American Missionary
Association. 34467
American Board of Commissioners for Foreign
Missions. 12878, 12891, 18288, 18292,
(19992), 22610, 27550, 32124, (69360)-
(69361), 69645, 69646, 69648-69649,
71322, 76454, 83458, 84358-84368, 90107,
96418-96419, 97874, 99564-99567, 104306,
104308, 105534
American Board of Commissioners for Foreign
Missions. Committee on Anti-slavery
Memorials. (81829)
American Board of Commissioners for Foreign
Missions. Deputation to the Indian
Missions. 69851
American Board of Commissioners for Foreign
Missions. Missionaries. tr. 12878,
18285, 69645, 105540 see also Byington,
Cyrus. and Wright, Alfred.
American Board of Commissioners for Foreign
Missions. Missionaries at Constantinople.
88572
American Board of Commissioners for Foreign
Missions. Oregon Mission. 88874
American Board of Commissioners for Foreign
Missions. Prudential Committee. 34858
American Board of Commissioners for Foreign
Missions. Secretary. 90808
American Board of Commissioners for Foreign
Missions. Western Reserve Foreign
Missionary Society. see Western
Reserve Foreign Missionary Society.
American Board of Commissioners for Foreign
Missions and the Rev. Dr. Chalmers.
27550
American Board of Commissioners for Foreign
Missions. Report of the Committee on
Anti-slavery Memorials. (81829)

American book of flowers and sentiments.
29670
American booksellers' complete reference
trade-list. (5763)
American botanist. 50026
American boy's life of Washington. 34118
American bravery displayed. 9641
American broadside verse. 104850, 104864,
105959
American budget, 1794. 29949
American buccaneer. 51532
American Bureau of Mines. Union Pacific
Railroad. 1067, (22054)
American business series. 83375
American calendar. 1122, 97905
American candour. 1068
American Cannel Coal Company. 10689
American captive. 63647, note after 94220
American captives in Havana. (13277)
American captives in Tripoli. 17226
American catalogue of books for 1869. 40906
American catalogue of books; or English guide
to American literature. (42403)
American catalogue of books (original and
reprints.) 37310
American catholic almanac. 11521
American catholic almanac for 1858. 21289
American catholic historical magazine. 101884
American catholic historical researches. 85257
American catholic quarterly review. 84192
American catholicity. 33979
American cause in England. 4308
American cemetery. 47175
American chancery digest. 103189
American charters. 1069
American Chess Congress, New York, 1857.
24544
American Chesterfield. 90221
American chorister. 5417
American Christian record. 1070
American chronological tablets. 1071
American chronology, from the discovery by
Columbus. 98395
American chronology from the discovery of the
western world. 13376
American chronology; or a summary of events.
1072
American church almanack. 66121
American church and the African slave trade.
35837
American church and the American union. 11474
American church in the protestant disruption.
66122
American church monthly. 33483, 3d note after
96986
American churches. (81830)
American circular. 29892, (34686)
American circular. pseud. tr. see Lawrence,
William B.
American citizen. pseud. Address to the
people of the United States. see Bronson,
Enos. supposed author and Gallatin,
Albert, 1761-1849. supposed author
American citizen. pseud. American rebellion.
see Victor, Orville James.
American citizen. pseud. Appeal to the
government. 1781
American citizen. pseud. Discourses on
Davila. see Adams, John, Pres. U. S.,
1735-1826.
American citizen. pseud. Examination of the
constitution. see Coxe, Tench.
American citizen. pseud. Inquiry into the
causes and origin of slavery. 34799
American citizen. pseud. Ireland and America.
35059

American citizen. pseud. Letter addressed to the President of the United States. 22934, 40262

American citizen. pseud. Letter to Thomas Paine. (58249), note after 101837

American citizen. pseud. Oration written. 57446

American citizen. pseud. Philanthropic results. see Brockett, L. P.

American citizen. pseud. Plain facts and considerations. 8864

American citizen. pseud. Pope and the Presbyterians. 64127

American citizen. pseud. Pope's stratagem. 64129

American citizen. pseud. Rejoinder to "The replies from England, etc." (43652), 69158

American citizen. pseud. Remedy. 69547

American citizen. pseud. ed. and tr. Shahmah in pursuit of freedom. see Gneene, Frances.

American citizen. pseud. Slavery in Great Britain and the United States. (82092)

American citizen. pseud. To Daniel O'Connell. (56653)

American citizen. 97948

American citizen. A discourse. 38314

American citizen and emigrant adviser. 61615

American citizen: his rights and duties. 32926, (32927)

American citizen: his true position. 78839

American Citizens at Paris. 30592 see also Paris. Meeting of the Citizens of the United States, 1843.

American Citizens in Melbourne, Australia. see Melbourne, Australia. American Citizens.

American citizen's manual of reference. 1073, 29490

American Citizens on the Mobile. see Washington County, Ala. Citizens.

American Citizens Resident in Buenos Aires. see Buenos Aires. American Citizens.

American Citizens Resident in Peru. see Peru. American Citizens.

American citizen's sure guide. 1074

American citizens' text-book. 15626

American citizenship. (47898)

American civil war. 1075

American claim of rights. (1076)

American Classical and Military Academy, Mt. Airy, Pa. 27161

American coast pilot. (2588), 6025, 26218-26219, 101284

American code of marine signals. 72674

American code of signals. 72673, 72676

American coins and coinage. 21786

American College and Education Society. see American Education Society. Congregational Education Society of Boston. Society for the Promotion of Collegiate and Theological Education at the West.

American colleges. An address. 93276

American colleges and the American public. (64298)

American colonial history: an address. 20590, (45211A)

American colonial tracts. 36284-(36286), 51810, 53249, 56098, 82820, 82836, 86574, 91316, 94218, 1st note after 99856, note after 99867, 100464, 2d note after 100494, 103397

American colonies previous to the Declaration of Independence. 20797

American colonization scheme examined and exposed. 93139

American colonization scheme further unravelled. 93132

American Colonization Society. 14732, 69887, 81831-(81833), 81842, 81977, 90427, 90703, 99544, 104011

American Colonization Society. petitioners 14732

American Colonization Society. Board of Directors. 81831

American Colonization Society. Board of Managers. 14732, 81757

American Colonization Society. Executive Committee. 104012

American Colonization Society. Hartford Auxiliary. see Hartford Colonization Society.

American Colonization Society. Managers. 14732, 81763

American Colonization Society. Semi-centennial Anniversary, Washington, D. C., 1867. 47688

American Colonization Society, Philadelphia. Ladies' Association. see Ladies' Association, Auxiliary to the American Colonization Society, Philadelphia.

American Colonization Society. Addresses . . . in Washington, D. C. 39226

American Colonization Society, and the colony of Liberia. 45832, (81833), 90307

American Colonization Society, for Colonizing the Free People of Color in the United States. see American Colonization Society.

American Colonization Society. The proceedings of a public meeting. 81832

American colony in Paris in 1867. (40043)

American colporteur system. (14757)

American comedies. 59188

American comic annual. 24399, 36356

American comic melodist. 50860

American commerce. 42815

American commerce & American union. 73947-(73948), 73977

American commerce—southern emigration. (47352)

American commercial claims. 40580

American commercial regulations. 97906

American Commissioners of Claims at Paris. (1077)

American common-place book of poetry. 12395

American common-place book of prose. 12394

American commonwealth series. 84342

American conchology. 77368

American conflict: a history of the great rebellion. 28482

American conflict. A lecture. (20157)

American conflict: an address. 16761

American conflict as seen from a European point of view. 23664

American conflict. By A. W. Clason. (13503)

American Congregational Association. Corresponding Secretary. 65767

American Congregational Society, Boston. 15479

American Congregational Society, Boston. Directors. 15483

American Congregational Union. 1078, 15479

American congregational year book. 15482

American congregationalism. 90890

American constitutionalist. pseud. Address to men of all parties. 410

American consummation of equality. 49002

American continent. (21276)

Americna controversy considered. 79187

American Convention for Promoting the Abolition of Slavery, and Improving the Condition of the African Race. 49358, (49379), (65782), 81755, 81783, 81795, 82015-82019, 95921, 95922

American Convention for Promoting the Abolition
of Slavery, and Improving the Condition
of the African Race. Committee to Draft
a Plan for the General Emancipation of
Slaves. 82048

American Convention for Promoting the Abolition
of Slavery, and Improving the Condition
of the African Race. President. 95921
see also Foster, Theodore.

American Convention for Promoting the Abolition
of Slavery, and Improving the Condition
of the African Race. Secretary. 95921
see also Cope, Thomas P., fl. 1797.

American Convention to Form a Liturgy for the
Episcopal Churches in the United States.
see Protestant Episcopal Church in the
U. S. A. Convention to Form a Liturgy,
1789.

American cottage and villa architecture. (80858)
American cottage library. 25489
American cotton planter. 86214
American cotton planter and the soil of the
South. 86214
American country almanack. 50443
American country almanack, for the year of
Christian account 1756. 64082
American criminal trials. 11868, 32362,
(33060), 83423, 96946
American crisis. (46925), (58206)-58208,
92853-92854, 95996
American crisis; a discourse. 10685
American crisis: a letter, addressed by
permission to the Earl Gower. 884
American crisis, and a letter to Sir Guy
Carleton. 58209, 93776
American crisis, by a citizen of the world.
1079
American crisis, by Americus. 1080
American crisis considered. 40015
American crisis, in relation to the anti-slavery
cause. 46186
American crisis; or pages from the note-book.
61321
American crisis; or, sketches in North America.
69004
American crisis; or, trial and triumph of
democracy. 12214
American criticism on American literature.
28101
American criticisms on Mrs. Trollope's
"Domestic manners of the Americans."
97028
American Cruikshank. sobriquet see Johnston,
D. C. illus.
American cruiser. (41512)
American cruiser's own book. (41512)
American customs vindicated. 93745
American cyclops. 9620, 43499
American cyclopaedia. 52439, 71523
American daily advertiser. see Claypoole's
American daily advertiser.
American dangers and duties. 47181
American debater. (43221)
American defence of the Christian golden rule.
31441
American democrat. 16412
American depository of arts and sciences.
104129
American deputy. pseud. 25339
American destiny. (1081)
American diadem. 79907
American dialogues of the dead. 1081A, 101770
American dictionary of the English language.
(20541), 37892, 102335
American diplomatic code. 22231
American discovery and conquest. (1083)
American dispensatory. 37813
American disruption. 32895

American distiller. 38294
American dis-union. 68009
American documents. 31405
American domination. 26793
American drama. In five acts. 81241
American drama. No. I. 85169
American Dutch. 6176, note after 92721
American ecclesiastical almanac. (77542)
American eclectic materia medica. 32524
American editor. pseud. Brief enquiry into
the real name. 97028
American editor. pseud. Notice, critical and
biographical of the author. 50445
American education. An address. 8748
American education, its principles and elements.
(44364)
American education; or strictures. (59533)
American Education Society. 1198, 21880
see also Congregational Education Society
of Boston. Joint Committee from the
American Education Society, and the
Society for the Promotion of Collegiate
and Theological Education at the West.
American Education Society. Directors. 104503
American Education Society. Illinois Branch.
Directors. (34232)
American Education Society. New Hampshire
Branch. 52862
American Education Society. New Hampshire
Branch. Directors. 52862
American Education Society. Northwestern
Branch. Directors. 101037
American Education Society. Western Reserve
Branch. see Western Reserve Education
Society.
American Education Society of Norfolk County,
Mass. 14224
American education monthly. (54859)
American education year-book. 1082
American electro magnetic telegraph. 98290-
98291
American eloquence: a collection of speeches and
addresses. 39749, 50354, 92297, 92299,
104873
American eloquence, consisting of orations,
addresses and sermons. 46999
American Emigrant's Friend Society, Phila-
delphia. 61459
American emigration. 93277
American encroachments on British rights. 2262
American encyclopedia of history, biography and
travel. 65254
American encyclopaedia of printing. 71428
American Englishman, Pastor of a Church in
Boston, New England. pseud. Attempt to
shew. see Mather, Samuel, 1706-1785.
American entomologist. 71391
American entomology. 77369-77371
American Equal Rights Association. 65815,
90395
American Ethnological Society. 1084, 4608,
29636, 89983, 106326
American ethnology. A paper on a general
Society for the study of American anti-
quities. 46863
American ehtnology: being a summary. 89952
American evangelist. 91594
American evidences. 12484
American exiles. pseud. petitioners Memorial.
85534
American exiles' memorial to Congress. 85534
American exploring expedition: a personal
narrative. 3746
American Exploring, Mining and Manufacturing
Company. (38670)
American exports and imports. (1085)
American expositor. 13185

American—. . . extracts . . . from American authors. 81673

American eyes. pseud. Yankee travels. 17816, 62423

American fable. 17463, 84671, 84673

American fables. 34476, 84624

American facts. 66795

American factories and their female operatives. 78168

American family keepsake. 81600

American family Robinson. 4426

American farmer. pseud. Letters. see Crevecoeur, J. Hector St. John, 1735-1813.

American Farmer. pseud. Notes on American gardening. see Cobbett, William, 1763-1835.

American farmer. pseud. Peace without dishonor. see Lowell, John.

American farmer. 81612, 95746

American farmers. 105183

American farmers' magazine. 10842, 63429

American farmer's markets. 22097

American Female Education Society, Philadelphia. (61460)

American Female Guardian Society, New York. 54076

American Female Guardian Society, New York. Home for the Friendless. 54076

American female poets. (47061)

American fire-alarm telegraph. 11930

American fish-culture. 55508

American fixings of English humanity. 95867

American flag. 20859

American Flint Glass Manufactory, Pettie's-Island Cash Lottery, Philadelphia, 1773. (41454)

American florist. 67438

American flower garden companion. 77397

American flower garden directory. 31683

American, forest. 30962, 1st note after 97724

American, formerly member of Congress. pseud. Influences of democracy. see Ames, Fisher, 1758-1808.

American Free Trade League. 25726

American freedman. 1086

American Freedman's Aid Commission. Its origin. (25738)

American Freedmen's Inquiry Commission. see U. S. American Freedmen's Inquiry Commission.

American Freedmen's Union Commission. Committee. 70121

American Freedman's Union Commission. New York Branch. 25746, 51981, 51983, 53803, 54827

American freeman's chronicle for 1840. 10981

American freemason. 37544

American friend. see Friend.

American friends' library. (59616), 77453

American fruit book. (14291)

American fruit garden companion. (77398)

American fruit-grower's guide, for the orchard and fruit-garden. (22266)

American fruit-grower's guide, in orchard and garden. 22264

American fugitive in Europe. 8586

American gallery of art from the works of the best artists. (77106)

American game in its seasons. (31459)

American gardener. [By John Gardiner and David Hepburn.] 26621

American gardener. By William Cobbett. 13871

American gardener's calendar. (43560), 82987

American gardener's magazine. 1089, 33207, 43809, 54771

American gazette. 1088

American gazetteer; containing a distinct account of all the parts of the new world. (1090), 26814

American gazetteer, exhibiting, . . . a much more full and accurate account. 50922-50923, 50934, 50943

American genealogy. (32489)

American generals. 26022

American gentleman. pseud. tr. see Alsop, Richard, 1761-1815.

American gentleman. pseud. tr. see Irving, Washington, 1783-1859.

American gentleman. pseud. Letter. 42945

American gentleman. pseud. New critical pronouncing dictionary. 52585

American gentleman. pseud. Patriot muse. see Prime, Benjamin Young.

American gentleman. pseud. Poems. 103885

American gentleman. pseud. Poems moral and divine. 63616

American gentleman. pseud. Voice from America to England. see Colton, Calvin.

American gentleman and lady. pseud. Hand book of practical receipts. 30210

American Geographical and Statistical Society of New York. see American Geographical Society of New York.

American Geographical Society of New York. 1092, (54077), 65816, 80586, 91521, 1st note after 100521 see also Joint Special Committee of the New York Chamber of Commerce and American Geographical and Statistical Society on the Decimal System.

American Geographical Society of New York. Library. 1091, note after 92754

American geography. (50924), 50926, 97086, 101841, 101874, 2d note after 101887

American geological history. 18427

American geology, containing a statement. 22518

American geology. Letter on . . . the geology of Texas. 44500

American Germans. 6176, note after 92721

American gift book. 43828

American gift-book, containing Washington's farewell address. 1093

American glory. 25722, 1st note after 99448

American Gold Mining Company, on the Portage River. 41808

American gold quotations. 27706

American grammar: adapted to the national language. 31586

American grammar: or, a complete introduction. 73403

American grape grower's guide. 12886

American grenadier. pseud. Poem. 100963

American grove of new or revised trees and shrubs. 67437

American grove, or, an alphabetical catalogue. 44776

American guide. 41689

American guide book. 1094, 31113

American Gymnastic Union. 85707

American handbook and tourist's guide. 73507

American handbook of ornamental trees. (47365)

American harmonist. (43813)

American harmony. 32475

American harmony; containing the rules of singing. 80766

American harmony; or, royal melody complete. 94335-94339

American Health Convention. 2d, New York, 1839. 69896

American herbal. 90959

American hero. 11304

American herpetology. (30388)

American historian. pseud. New and complete history. 71986

American historical and literary curiosities. 82974-82979, 102143

American Historical Association. 85455, 87328, note before 95044, 95075, 98409, 98425, 103113, 104845
American Historical Association. Albert J. Beveridge Memorial Fund Series. 102550
American historical magazine. (1836) 1095, 22456
American historical magazine. (1850-) 1096
American historical magazine and Tennessee quarterly. 94720
American historical record. 85144
American historical register. 84866
American historical review. 83761, 83976, 83978, 86573, 86574, 96788, 4th note after 99888, 103756
American historical school. 44737
American Historical Society. 1097, 11345, 51810, 84791, 86574, note before 87347, 91316, 2d note after 100494
American historical tales. (1098)
American historical tales for youth. 1099
American history. 31, 27368, 27913
American history and biography. 1100
American history and literature. 38069
American history leaflets. 82850, 93611
American home book. 20902
American Home Missionary Society. see Congregational Home Missionary Society.
American Home Missionary Society and slavery. 81834
American Home Missionary Society report. 1101
American homoeopathic review. 82717
American Hose Company, Philadelphia. see Philadelphia. American Hose Company.
American houses. (82160)
American hunter. 1102
American husbandry; being a series of essays. 26803
American husbandry. Containing an account of the soil. 106062
American idea, and what grows out of it. 11944
American idea of defence. 8642
American impressions. (27723)
American in Algiers. 1103
American in England. pseud. Private letters. (65726)
American in England. (43420)
American in Europe. 17578
American in his fatherland. pseud. American and English oppression. 1041
American in London. pseud. The Americans. 14766
American in Paris. 76397
American independence. 75960
American independence, an everlasting deliverance. 96502
American independence: an oration. 9235
American independence, and tribute. 54881
American independence the interest and glory of Great Britain. 11152-11154
American independence vindicated. 103766
American independence, written and published at Washington. (74252), 103155
American independency. 104302
American independency defended. 58212-58213
American Indian Missionary Association. 65914
American Indian, no. 12. 94682
American Indian; or virtues of nature. 2654
American Indians. 92299
American Indians. Their history, condition and prospects. 77837, 77867, (77882)
American industrial opportunity. 83368
American Institute of Instruction. 1108, (39668), 42484, (52489), 52983, (55765), 64348, 66275, 85202
American Institute of Instruction. Board of Censors. 1108, (39668), 42484

American Institute of Instruction. Charter. 1108
American Institute of the City of New York. 1105-1106, (36716), (54079), 65796
American Institute of the City of New York. Annual Fair, 3d, 1830. (54080)
American Institute of the City of New York. Charter. (54079)
American Institute of the City of New York. Library. (1107)
American institutions. 84001, 84009
American instructor. 24459, 94713
American Instructors of the Deaf and Dumb. Convention, 5th, Jacksonville, Ill., 1858. see Convention of American Instructors of the Deaf and Dumb, 5th, Jacksonville, Ill., 1858.
American insurance manual. 36609
American intelligencer. (22609)
American interests in Asia. (50603)
American interests in Borneo. 38308
American International Relief Committee for the Suffering Operatives of Great Britain. 1109
American jest book. 1110, 48027
American Jewish advocate. 56633
American journal. 90227, 90229
American journal of conchology. 1111
American journal of education (1826-1829) see American annals of education.
American journal of education (1855-1882) 1113-1114, (2726), 3464-3465, 3467, (7057), 11117, 14255, 18955, (21878), (24040), 25330, 42799, 44376, (69001), 47392, 92267, 92392, 92394, 94559
American journal of education and college review. 1113-1114, 92267
American journal of geology and natural science. 1115
American journal of improvements in the useful arts. (1116), 81602
American journal of indigenous materia medica. (1117)
American journal of insanity. 1118, 4474, 35805, 68024, 84253
American journal of medical jurisprudence. 52311
American journal of medical sciences. 1121, 52126, 83664, 92191
American journal of numismatics. 1119
American journal of science. 507-508, 1120, 7845, 18427, 35402, 41376, 51022, 55337, (68512), 72476, 72671, 80168, 81048, 82810, 82993, 82996, 82997, 82999, 83003, 85078, 89978, 89986, 89996, 93529, 98042
American journal of science and arts. see American journal of science.
American journal of theology. 85213
American jurisprudence. A digest of the law. (74252), 103155
American jurisprudence in contrast with the doctrine. 27851
American jurisprudence, written and published at Washington. 103155
American jurist. see American jurist and law magazine.
American jurist and law magazine. 22975, 72064, (79940), 93692, 98560, 100461, 103304
American jute. 33393
American kalendar. 1122, 97905
American keepsake. 1123
American keystone. 45518
American kitchen gardener. 24220
American labor: its necessities and prospects. 20368
American labor versus British free trade. 10827
American laborer. 1124

American lady. pseud. Change for the American notes. see Wood, Henry, Yorkshire journalist. supposed author
American lady. pseud. Drum for the ear of the drowsy. 20969
American lady. pseud. Sketches of the lives. 81577
American lancet. 69824, 100796
American Land Company, Arkansas. (11489)
American Land Company, New York. 11488
American landlord. pseud. Tales. 94245
American landscape. 1125, 8813
American Latin grammar. 73404
American Latin grammar: or a compleat introduction to the Latin tongue. (73402)
American Latin grammar, or a complete introduction to the Latin tongue. 73401
American law directory. 29555
American law journal. (60342)
American law journal and miscellaneous repertory. 29812
American law register. 21468, 21545, 84398, 84515
American law review. (79094)
American lawyer. 4100
American leaves. 57787
American Legal Association. 1126, 41629
American Letter Mail Company. 89619
American liberties and American slavery. 96512
American liberty, a poem. 1127, 6571
American liberty almanac. 81835
American liberty and government questioned. 74596
American liberty and independence. 105159
American liberty and its obligations. 16697
American liberty. Fourth of July. 19526
American liberty, its sources. (22379)
American liberty of the press. 14013
American liberty song. 97557
American liberty triumphant. 39512
American liberty vindicated. 15880
American Library Association. (64045), 84980
American library of useful knowledge. 92303
American life at home. 11363
American literature. (70451)
American Literary Association. Constitution. 1128
American literary gazette and publishers' circular. 1190, 55867, 66532, 86368, note after 85148
American literary magazine. 1129, 89719
American Literary, Scientific and Military Academy, Middletown, Conn. 36694, (48871), note after (58963)
American Literary, Scientific and Military Academy, Norwich, Vt. 36701, note after (54963), 55931
American Literary Union, Philadelphia. 81123
American Lloyd's register of American and foreign shipping. 30711
American loyalist. pseud. Address. 388
American loyalist. pseud. Memoirs. 47567
American loyalist in Upper Canada. pseud. Letters. 35438
American loyalists. (19156), (19176), 24847, 42563, 102767 see also His Majesty's Loyal Associated Refugees Assembled at Newport, R. I. petitioners His Majesty's Loyal Subjects, late West Florida. petitioners Loyalists Confined in Mason's Lodge, 1777. petitioners
American loyalists. claimants 11306, 27082, note after 42561 see also General Agent for Claimants Before the Board of Commissioners Under Article 6th of the Treaty Between Great Britain and the United States, 1794.

American loyalists. Agents. 68294
American loyalists. 74732
American Lutheran church, historically, doctrinally, and practically delineated. (77716)
American Lutheran mission, with an appeal in its behalf. 83338
American lycaeum in Paris. 101445
American Lyceum of Science and the Arts. 1129A
American Lyceum, or Society for the Improvement of Schools, and Diffusion of Useful Knowledge. (1130)
American Lyceum, or Society for the Improvement of Schools, and Diffusion of Useful Knowledge. Convention, New York, 1831. (1130)
American lyrics. (36483)
American magazine, a monthly miscellany. (1131)
American magazine and historical chronicle. 1132
American magazine and monthly chronicle of the British colonies. (1133), 52440, 84585, 84678C
American magazine and repository of useful knowledge. 1134
American magazine. Containing a miscellaneous collection of original and other valuable essays. 1135, 102401
American magazine, devoted to the interests . . . of the young men of the country. 58123
American magazine for 1769. 1136
American magazine of useful and entertaining knowledge. 1137
American magazine of wit. (1138)
American magazine of wonders. 25676
American magazine; or monthly view of the political state of the British colonies. 1139, 102246
American mail. 21116
American mail-bag. 1140
American manual. 79385
American manual, containing a brief outline. (9325)
American manual of the grape vines. 67439
American manual of the mulberry trees. 67440
American mariners. (18847)
American masonic register. 45493
American measurer's guide. 71912
American mechanic. 67170
American mechanic's magazine: containing useful original matter. (1141)
American mechanics' magazine; devoted to the useful arts. (25655)
American medical almanac. 82811
American medical and philosophical register. 33083
American Medical Association. (1142)-1143, (61461), 62125, 83363, 83503, 90467, 93978-93980
American medical biography. 35459, 104378
American medical biography; or memoirs. 95147
American medical botany. 5294
American medical recorder. 1144
American medical review. 47328, 83654, 83664
American Medical Society. 89946
American medical times. 1145, 84276
American melodies; containing a . . . selection. 50820
American melodies, in three parts. 17859
American memoranda. 42679
American merchant. pseud. Independance absolue des Americains. 23919, (34441)
American merchant. pseud. Remarks on British relations. see Vaughan, Benjamin. supposed author

145

American mercury. 92804, 93013, 93017,
93019, 93025, 93063, 93065
American mercury. Carrier. pseud. Vision
of the printer's boy. 100602
American messenger. 85341
American methodism. 78524
American Methodist Episcopal Missionary
Society. 12891, 84358-84362, 84365
American military biography. 1146
American military library. 20994
American military pocket atlas. 1147, 7326
American militia officer's manual. (21576)
American mineralogical journal. 1148
American minerva. 102401
American mines and mining. 68067
American mines, shewing their importance.
29390
American minister. pseud. Records of the
Bubbleton Parish. 68406
American miscellany of popular tales. (1149)
American mission in the Sandwich Islands.
22335
American missionary. 34457
American Missionary Association. see also
Convention for Bible Missions, 1st,
Syracuse, 1846. Convention for Bible
Missions, 2nd, Albany, 1846.
American Missionary Association. Executive
Committee. (65832)
American missionary memorial. 62791
American Missionary Society. 1149A
American minstrel. 47217
American mock-bird. 1150
American monitor. A political, historical and
commercial magazine. 1151
American monitor. Containing elegant extracts.
77831
American monitor, or the Republican magazine.
1152
American monthly magazine. (1824) 1156,
95294, 101159
American monthly magazine. (1829-1831) 1157,
(69590)
American monthly magazine. (1833-1838) 1153,
52698, (65973), 85144
American monthly magazine and critical review.
1154
American monthly magazine and review. 1155
American monthly museum. see Pennsylvania
Magazine; or, American monthly review.
American monthly review. 1158
American monthly review; or literary journal.
1159
American moral and sentimental magazine.
1160
American museum. 67443
American museum, and repository of arts and
sciences. 22245
American museum: antiquities, curiosities,
beauties and varieties of nature and art
in America. (1161)
American museum, illustrated. (3571)
American museum of literature and the arts.
85466
American museum of science, literature, and
the arts. A monthly magazine. 85466
American museum: or, annual register of
fugitive pieces. 1162A
American museum, or repository of ancient
and modern fugitive pieces. 1162, 14869,
(17294), 21971, 74210, 85685, 97216,
note after 97998, 104450
American museum, or universal magazine.
1162
American Musical Convention, New York, 1845.
65817
American musical miscellany. 1163

American Mutual Life Insurance Company, of
New Haven, Connecticut. 52958
American nation: a history. 84340
American nation: lives of the fallen braves and
living heroes. 79992
American national intelligencer. 1687
American national lyrics. 31879
American national preacher. 92779
American nationality. A sermon delivered in
Lexington. 18466
American nationality. An address. 77488
American nationality. An oration. 37848
American nationality. By J. H. McIlvaine.
43325
American nationality. From the Biblical
repository and Princeton review. 1164
American nations. 67441
American natural history. 27663
American naturalist. 58097, 89989
American naval battles. 1165, 2696
American naval biography. (2732)
American naval biography; comprising lives of
the commodores. 26023
American navy. 61228
American naval officer. pseud. Narrative.
see Fanning, Nathaniel. USN
American negotiator. 105606-105607
American nepos. 1166, 101778, note after
104564
American neutrality. 30299
American neutrality: its honourable past. 4624
American News Company. publisher 103923
American newspaper directory. (47793), 73548,
73551
American newspaper directory and record of
the press. 37457
American newspaper rate-book. (47793), 73551
American nights' entertainments. 28613
American nomination. 45841
American Normal School Association. 1167,
51974
American normal schools. 1167
American notes. 20004, note after 105032
American notes and pictures from Italy. 19997
American notes and queries. 1168, 8394, 50786
American notes, for general circulation. 19996
American novel. 6946, 70064, 73474
American, now resident in London. pseud.
Letter. see Bingham, William.
American nuggets. 91508, 91511
American nuggets. Bibliotheca Americana.
91509
American nuggets, or a catalogue of rare and
valuable books. 91509
American Numismatic and Archaeological
Society. 1119
American numismatic manual. (20021)
American Numismatic Society. (1169)
American nun. 39042
American Odd-Fellows Museum. 1170
American officer. pseud. Civil and military
life of Andrew Jackson. 35363
American officer. pseud. Prospect. (66070)
American officer. pseud. Rough and ready
songster. 73463
American officer in the service of France.
pseud. Letters. see Eustace, Jean-Skey
American oracle. 90934, 90960-90961, 90965
American orator: containing two hundred
specimens. 1171
American orator, or elegant extracts. 16311
American orator; with appendix. 51337
American orator appendix. 51338
American orator's own book. 1172
American oratory. 1173, 92297
American ornithology. 6264, 6266, 16045,
(57467), 104597-104598, 104600, 104603-
104604

American orphan in Germany. 38279
American orthographer. Book II. 102445
American orthographer, in three books. 102445
American outlaws. 28534
American part of the collection. 65582
American Party. 3008, 28493, 52038
American Party. Convention, Philadelphia, 1845. 19179
American Party. Louisiana. (42185) see also Louisiana Native American Association.
American Party. New York (State) State Council. 53523
American Party. Pennsylvania. Convention, Harrisburg, 1845. 60422, 52038
American Party. Pennsylvania. Philadelphia. 61540, (61860), 61862, (62315) see also Native American Association of the Unincorporated Northern Liberties, Philadelphia.
American Party. Pennsylvania. Philadelphia. Native American Hall Company of Cedar Ward. 61861
American Party. Rhode Island. Filmore State Committee, 1856. 24333
American Party. Vermont. 99144
American Party, and its mission. 84867
American Party: its principles, its objects, and its hopes. (71948)
American Party of New York. Address adopted. 53523
American pastor. pseud. Two sermons. see Bacon, Thomas.
American pastor's journal. 32711, 59026
American patriot. pseud. Prayer. see Paine, Thomas, 1737-1809.
American patriot. (32907)
American patriot and hero. 47050
American patriotism. 23140
American patriotism farther confronted with reason. (24724)
American patriot's prayer. 58212-58213
American Peace Society. 10081, (54421), 91839, 98051
American Peace Society. petitioners 1174
American Pharmaceutical Association. 1192-1193
American pharos. 49112
American Philological Association. (65818)
American philosopher. 24925, 83790
American Philosophical Society, Philadelphia. 1136, (1175), 1177-1183, 3816, (3821), 7668, 10915, (13179), 13821, 30818, 31206, 39489, 39666, (40206), 51022, 52130, 52131, 62622, (68512), 74201, 77038, 77376, 77381, (77387), 79731, 84079, 84411, 84678C, note before 91856, 95646, 104297, 104300, 106301
American Philosophical Society, Philadelphia. petitioners 47653, 61824
American Philosophical Society, Philadelphia. Charter. 1178
American Philosophical Society, Philadelphia. Corresponding Secretary. 21383
American Philosophical Society, Philadelphia. Historical and Literary Committee. 1183, 7668, 31206
American Philosophical Society, Philadelphia. Library. 1178
American Philosophical Society, Philadelphia. President. 59143
American physician. pseud. Victims of gambling. 99427
American physician. (72622)
American physician, and family assistant. (82472)
American physitian. 33605
American picture. 36537
American pilot. 26219

American pioneer. (1184), 31798, 104378
American pioneer: with a new and useful plan. 1185
American pioneering. 21229
American piracy. 27326
American plan of street cleansing. 83845
American planter. 36869
American pleader's assistant. 68144
American pocket atlas. 10856
American poem. 50165, 101341
American poems. 1186
American poems, selected and original. (82501)
American poetical and prose miscellany. 20994
American poetical miscellany. 1187
American poets. A poem. 23247
American policy. 75194
American policy—its benefits to the west. 91008 (1188)
American political and military biography. (1188)
American political manual. 1189
American politician. 78647
American politics. (30222)
American politics, no. 6. 84801
American Popular Life Insurance Company of New York. (54081)
American popular lessons. 71806-71807, 71809
American portrait gallery; containing correct portraits. 36451
American portrait gallery. . . . containing portraits. 41622
American postage stamp album. 78277
American practice of surgery. 84276
American prayer. (63615)
American preacher. 2401, 78983, 83802, 84096
American precedents of declarations. 1677
American preceptor. 5430
American prejudice against colour. (903)
American Presbyterian. 102562
American Presbyterian almanac for 1863. 65136
American Presbyterian and theological review. (82704), (82712) see also Theological review.
American press. 13799
American primer. note after 65546
American primer. Improved. note after 65546
American principles. 66817
American principles, a review of the works of Fisher Ames. 273
American principles on national prosperity. 51536
American Print Works. firm plaintiffs 39347
American Print Works, vs. Cornelius W. Lawrence. 39347
American progress. 2729
American progress—Judge Davis and the presidency. 44770
American prophecy. 78870
American prosperity. 13684
American Protestant Association. 1199, 66967
American Protestant Association of Ohio. Ohio Lodge, No. I. (56988)
American Public Health Association. 83367, 84252, 84260, 84276
American Public Health Association. Advisory Committee. New York Member. 84252 see also Smith, Stephen, 1823-1922.
American Public Health Association. Semi-centennial Meeting in Honor of the Approaching Centennial of Dr. Smith, 1921. 84254
American publications. 95450
American publisher's circular. see American literary gazette and publishers' circular.
American publishers' circular and literary gazette. see American literary gazette and publishers' circular.
American pulpit. 1194, 25305, 66197

American quarterly church review and ecclesiastical register. see Church review.
American quarterly journal of agriculture. 24563
American quarterly observer. 1195, 1196, 11904
American quarterly register. 1198, 84359, 92886, 103911, 104059, 105031
American quarterly register and magazine. 1197, 93116
American quarterly review. 3138, 25805, 34801, 39383, 44941, 70270, 95806, 97028, 98687, 2d note after 100580, 101154, 101157, 101166, 102276
American quarterly review. plaintiff 20341
American quarterly review, and . . . New-York, on the banking system. (53524)
American quarterly review of the American Protestant Association. 1199
American quarterly review vs. the state of New-York. 20341
American querist. 16586
American question. A letter from a calm observer. 1200, 36779
American question, and how to settle it. 1201
American question considered. 15110, 3d note after 103852
American question in a nut-shell. 69005
American question in its national aspects. 59563
American question. I. English opinion. 2138
American question. . . . Reprinted . . . from "The daily news." 92333
American question. Secession. Tariff. Slavery. 1202
American question. . . . Translated by Thomas Ray. (29507)
American race-turf register. 21841
American railroad and steam navigation guide. (20204)
American railroad journal. 1203, 5984, 80445
American railway and steam navigation guide. (23197)
American rail-way, and the Winans Carriage. 93512
American railway guide, and pocket companion. (13839)
American railway guide, 1851. 1204
American railway register. 68498
American reader . . . a selection of lessons. note just before 71069
American reader: containing a selection of narration. 33433
American reader: containing selections in prose. 85536
American ready reckoner. 104037
American rebellion: its history. 35838
American rebellion. Letters on the American rebellion. 27638
American rebellion. Report of speeches. 4309
American rebellion. Some facts and reflections. 99433
American recently returned from France. pseud. Letter. see Walsh, Robert, 1784-1859.
American recognition of Irish independence. 84393
American Reform Tract and Book Society, Cincinnati. 57280, 82030
American register. see Literary magazine, and American register.
American register. see Military monitor and American register.
American register and magazine. 93116
American register for 1775. (1206)
American register: or general repository of history. (1205), 8457

American register, or summary review of history. 1207, 3302, 101155
American rejected addresses. 5295
American rejected addresses on the opening of the Park Theatre. (54082)
American relations with Mexico. 83478
American remembrancer, and universal tablet of memory. 30317
American remembrancer; or, an impartial collection of essays. 1208
American repository, and annual register. 1210
American repository of arts, sciences, and manufactures. (1209)
American repository of useful information. 1210
American republic. (12990)
American republic and human liberty. (62484)
American republic; its constitution, tendencies, and destiny. 8711
American republic the bane and ruin of despotism. 4838
American republican. 18598, 19772, 49587
American Republican Party of the City of New York. 17522, 54053
American republican politics. 3206
American republicanism. 25072
American resident in China. pseud. Our commercial and political relations with China. (57912)
American resistance indefensible. 1211, 79280
American review; a Whig journal. 1212, 1261, 28566, 41911, 50182, 89952, 89965, 89979 see also American Whig review.
American review, and literary journal. 1213
American review of history and politics. 101156, 101163
American reviews of Mrs. Trollope's Domestic manners of the Americans. 97028
American revolution. 3116
American revolution; a lecture. 9855
American revolution, from the commencement. 95148
American revolution, including also the beauties of American history. 5783
American revolution or national journal. (70770)
American Revolution Society. South Carolina. see Joint Committee of the South-Carolina State Society of Cincinnati, and the American Revolution Society. petitioners
American revolution: written in scriptural, or ancient historical style. 85590, 85592
American revolution; written in the style of ancient history. 85589
American revolutionary tale. 43310
American revolutionary war. (4465), 11487
American rural sports. 9795
American rush-light. 13872, 14015
American sailor. 8944
American savage. A dramatic entertainment. 13616, 2d note after 96139
American savage, or Orab and Phoebe. 3495
American Scenic and Historic Preservation Society. 99281
American scenery, art, and literature. 32707
American scenery. Illustrated by T. Addison Richards. 70958
American scenery; or land, lake, and river illustrations. 3784, 8899, note after 104504, 104505
American scenes and Christian slavery. 18752
American School for the Deaf, Hartford, Conn. Committee. 15693
American school library. 95217
American Scientific, Educational and Philosophical Society. 18725

American seaman, prisoner of war. pseud.
  Oration. (57441)
American seaman's vocabulary. 44590, 50410
American seamen. (50916)
American Seamen's Friend Society. 74973,
  74975
American selection of lessons. 102336
American semaphoric signal book. 72676
American senator. 11006
American Shandy-ism. 23912
American shepherd. 50781
American shipping. 31822
American ships and ship-builders. 51468
American silk grower's guide. 37462
American Silk Society. 36717, 82674
American singing book. 68145
American sketches. 1214
American sketches. By a native of the United
  States. 1215
American sketches. By Thomas C. Upham.
  98048
American sketches. Farmer's fireside. A
  poem. 1216, 98049
American sky lark. 97818
American slave. pseud. Life of an American
  slave. see Bibb, Henry.
American slave code. (27846)
American slave trade. 96283
American slavery. (42656), 78151
American slavery. A formidable obsticle.
  27850
American slavery. A lecture. 95491
American slavery, a prayer for its removal.
  82737
American slavery. A protest. 81836
American slavery. . . . A reply to the letter.
  (2278)
American slavery: a reprint of an article.
  79130-79131, (81837), note after 92624,
  93648
American slavery. A sermon. 91214
American slavery and colour. 11806
American slavery, and its Christian cure.
  47176
American slavery and the Kansas question.
  1217, 37018
American slavery, and the means of its
  abolition. 101309
American slavery, and the means of its
  removal. 92244
American slavery and the war. 46841
American slavery as it is. 11575, 102547
American slavery as viewed and acted on.
  43270
American slavery. Demonstrations in favor
  of Dr. Cheever. (12406)
American slavery distinguished. 78582
American slavery, essentially sinful. 92794
American slavery. From the London eclectic
  review. 81838
American slavery, in reference to the present
  agitation. 77771
American slavery. Organic sins. (81839)
American slavery. Remarks occasioned by
  strictures. 81840
American slavery. Report of a meeting of
  members of the Unitarian Body. (81841)
American slavery. Report of a public meeting
  held at Finsbury Chapel. 20716
American Social Science Association. 30206
American Society for Colonizing the Free
  People of Color in the United States.
  see American Colonization Society.
American Society for Educating Pious Youth for
  the Gospel Ministry. Middlesex Auxiliary.
  see Middlesex Auxiliary Society for the
  Education of Pious Youth.

American Society for Educating Pious Youth
  for the Gospel Ministry. North-Western
  Branch. 55737
American Society for Educating Pious Youth
  for the Ministry. 12680
American Society for Encouraging the Settle-
  ment of the Oregon Territory. 26871,
  37260, 57551
American Society for Meliorating the Condition
  of the Jews. 36120, 89744
American Society for Promoting National Unity.
  (1218)
American Society for Promoting the Civilization
  and General Improvement of the Indian
  Tribes Within the United States. 34595,
  94606
American Society for the Diffusion of Useful
  Knowledge. 66083
American Society for the Diffusion of Useful
  Knowledge. petitioners 47654
American Society for the Encouragement of
  Domestic Manufactures. 394, 1219
American Society for the Encouragement of
  Domestic Manufactures. petitioners
  47655
American Society for the Promotion of Tem-
  perance. see American Temperance
  Society.
American society in the days of Washington.
  28897
American Society of Church History. 84390
American Society of Free Persons of Colour,
  For Improving their Condition. 81843
American Society of United Irishmen. 19161
American soldier. pseud. Recollections of the
  United States Army. 68379
American songster. 97989
American songster: being a select collection.
  1220
American spectator. 1221
American spelling-book. 70494, 102338
American sportsman. (40796)
American spy. pseud. Letters. 1222, 40659
American spy. 94043
American spy, a collection of XXXVI letters.
  1223
American spy: letters written in London. 1222,
  40659
American spy, or freedom's early sacrifice.
  81179-81181
American standard. Editor. 71168
American standard—extra. 101066
American star. 94306
American star (Song) 86955, 101830
American star, being a choice collection. 1224
American star. From the 20 of September
  1847 to the 30 of May 1848. (48268),
  83867
American star songster. 90495
American state. 85450
American state papers. 13821, 82881, 90637-
  90638, 103237
American state papers, and correspondence.
  1225
American state papers, being a collection.
  101731
American state papers. Claims. 82939
American state papers; containing authentic
  documents. 1226, 21247, (40825)
American state papers, containing the corre-
  spondence. 1127
American state papers delivered by the Presi-
  dent. 94261
American state papers. Documents. 1228
American state papers, foreign relations. 83817
American state papers. Important documents
  and dispatches. 1016, (1230)

American state papers, miscellaneous. 82883, 82939
American state papers. Second series. 1229
American states acting over the part. 92777
American states, churches, and slavery. 2977
American states; or the principles of the American constitutions. 102399
American statesman. 106060
American statesman extra sheet. (1231), note after 93362
American statesman; or illustrations of the life and character of Daniel Webster. 3226
American statesman's kalendar. 1232
American statesmen. General index to the American statesmen series. With a selected bibliography. 84335
American statesmen. General index to the American statesmen series. With an epitome of United States history. 84336
American statesmen series. 84335-84336, 90460, 98425
American statistical annual. 24494
American Statistical Association. 1233, 24037, 83566
American steam navigation. Speech of Hon. George E. Badger. 2697
American steam navigation. Speech of William H. Seward. 79502
American Steamship Company. (31825), 65806
American steamship lines. 43144
American story. 32512
American struggle. 1234, 62543
American stud book. 8728
American Sunday school spelling book. 104976
American Sunday School Union. (27829), 59875, 88342, 97756, 99629, note after 104633
American Sunday School Union. Charter. (1235)
American Sunday School Union. Committee of Publication. 27502, (34615), 86285, 90543, 97861, 101840, 101845, 101888, 101904, 102787
American Sunday School Union. Western Board of Agency. see Western Sunday School Board of Agency.
American superiority at the World's Fair. 72472
American supplement. (73795)
American syren. 92226
American system. 1237
American system of government. 78602
American system, or the effects of high duties on imports. 29648
American system. Speeches on the tariff question. 91648
American tale. 8467, 36125, (42155), 83784, 89476, 92719, 101204, 103888, 104230
American tale: being a sequel to the history of John Bull. 4433
American tale containing a true account. (81808)
American tale: founded on a recent fact. 64088, note after 90519
American tale, founded on fact. 49688
American tale; in two volumes. 98341
American tars in Tripoli. 68034
American taxation. 94431
American teacher's lessons. 27712
American tears. 46222
American telegraph and signal book. 4969
American Telegraph Company. Remarks of R. W. Russell. 74365
American telegraph magazine. 1237A
American temperance intelligencer. 89744
American Temperance Society. 1240, 44747, 60986, 89491

American Temperance Society. Corresponding Secretary. 21979 see also Edwards, Justin, 1787-1853.
American Temperance Society. Executive Committee. 1238
American Temperance Union. 1239-1240, 47223, 44747, 86307, 86335
American text book. 1241
American text-books of art education. 84491, 84499-84500
American Thanksgiving Celebration, Paris, 1865. see Paris. American Thanksgiving Celebration, 1865.
American thanksgiving celebration in Paris. 1242
American thanksgiving dinner in St. James's Hall. 1243
American theatre. 90520
American theological review. 82706
American theory of government. 9382
American times, a satire. 1244, 1449, 14111
American tourist's pocket companion. 94661
American Tract Society, Boston. 1245, (1248), 22148, 74655, 86283, 86299, 99139, 102475
American Tract Society, Boston. Executive Committee. 81760
American Tract Society, Boston. Secretary. (5935) see also Bliss, Seth.
American Tract Society, New York. 1249, 35867, (47241), 64085, (69644), 70243, (81844), 86295, 86864, 89770, 93816, 97859, 100833, 102189, 102476, 103984, 103985, 105546, 105751
American Tract Society, New York. plaintiff 68499
American Tract Society, New York. Executive Committee. 1247
American Tract Society, New York. Public Deliberative Meeting, 1842. 65801, 73047
American Tract Society, New York. Secretary. see One of the Secretaries of the American Tract Society. pseud.
American Tract Society, New York. Superintendent of Colportage. (14757), 17656 see also Cross, Jonathan.
American Tract Society. New England Branch. see New England Tract Society.
American Tract Society. New York City Auxiliary. see New York City Mission and Tract Society.
American Tract Society. Philadelphia Agency, Philadelphia. 60295
American Tract Society, Boston. 103299
American Tract Society. Documents relating to the publication of anti-slavery tracts. (81844)
American trade balance and probable tendencies. 83369
American trader's compendium. (50099)
American traveller. pseud. Poems. see Lyttleton of Frankley, Thomas Lyttleton, 2d Baron, 1744-1779.
American traveller. 2707, 90084
American traveller; being a new historical collection. 1250
American traveller; or, guide through the United States. 94311
American traveller; or national directory. 31633
American traveller; or, observations on the present state. 13796, 69142
American Trenck. 101340
American trooper's pocket companion. 58596
American turf register. 1251, 81613
American tune. 103526
American underwriters' manual. 21756

American uniform commercial acts. 84516
American union. A discourse delivered . . .
  December 12, 1850. 6065
American union. A discourse delivered in
  Concord. 42991
American union. An address, delivered before
  the Alumni Association. 74593
American union, and the birth of Gen. Wash-
  ington. 101771
American Union Breakfast, Paris, May 29,
  1861. 16076
American Union Commission. petitioners
  1254
American Union Commission: its origin. 1252
American Union Commission. Speeches of
  Hon. W. Dennison. 1253, 19593
American Union for the Relief and Improve-
  ment of the Colored Race. 23459, 69860
American union; its effect on national character
  and policy. 5708, 68009, 89279, 89281
American Union of Associationists. 30289
American union shown to be the new heaven.
  33870
American union. Tune—Rule Britannia. 101771
American Unitarian Association. 1255, 11584,
  55875, 71531, 71771, (71773), 71781,
  79392, 89045, 91044, 93473, 97390,
  101053, 101386, 101396, 101410
American Unitarian Association. Minister at
  Large, Boston. 97393-97395 see also
  Tuckerman, Joseph, 1778-1840.
American Unitarian biography. 101409
American Unitarianism. 4596, 50946, 96412
American universal geography, for schools and
  academies. (5779)
American universal geography; or a view of
  the present state of all empires. 25764,
  40517, 50926, 2d note after 97378, note
  after 104434
American universal magazine. 1256, 84079
American university. 28097
American view of the causes. 86030
American village. 96502
American village, and other poems. 1257,
  19560, 19562
American vine, a sermon, preached in Christ-
  Church, Philadelphia, before the Honourable
  Continental Congress. 21047
American vine. A sermon preached in Christ's
  Church, Philadelphia, Friday, January 4,
  1861. 20635
American vine dresser's guide. 42160
American wanderer. 1258, 1st note after
  100576
American war. A lecture. 24730
American war. A letter to an English friend.
  1259
American war. A poem. 68324
American war—a poem, by the same author.
  85590
American war, a poem; in six books. 14108
American war, an ode. 14289
American war and American slavery. 58713
American war and slavery. 8475
American war, by Newman Hall. 29832
American war examined. 10666, 84564-84565
American war: facts and fallacies. 16998
American war, from 1775 to 1783. 82375
American war in favor of liberty. 37649
American war lamented. 96331
American war. Secession and slavery. 64121
American war: the aims, antecedents, and
  principles. 40026
American war, the whole question explained.
  (23752)
American war: with some suggestions. 38126
American weeds and useful plants. 18594

American weekly mercury. 60181, 82975-82976,
  84552, 96321, note after 97166, 100560
American weekly messenger. (1260)
American whig. (11876), (14394)-14395
American whig review. 1212, 1261, 89962
  see also American review; a whig journal.
American Whig Society, Princeton University.
  see Princeton University. American
  Whig Society.
American whites and blacks. 46
American: who has had an opportunity of being
  conversant with the facts herein related.
  pseud. tr. see Stevens, Robert. tr.
American who resided in London during most
  of the war. pseud. Reminiscences.
  69566
American Widows Relief Association, New York.
  Secretary. (54083) see also Robinson,
  Solon.
American wild flowers. 22414
American wit and humor. 1262
American woman. pseud. Letter. see Cutler,
  Mrs. H. M. Tracy.
American woman. pseud. Sentiments. 79154
American womanhood. 35430
American women responsible. 25015
American wonder. 92709-92710
American writers. pseud. Our country. 57913,
  61356
American year-book and national register. 10175
American young man's best companion. 1263
American youth. pseud. Battle of Plattsburgh.
  see Woodworth, John.
American Youth. pseud. Spunkiad. see
  Woodworth, John. supposed author
American youth. pseud. Yankee in London.
  see Tyler, Royall.
American youth. 91361-91362
Americana. pseud. Privilegi della ignoranza.
  12616
Americana. pseud. Proclama. 65929
Americana. 84583
Americana ramminga. (38757), 67064
Americana Series of the Massachusetts His-
  torical Society. 47648, 54946, (59707),
  65936, 66039, 86843, 88961, 92349,
  99328-99329, 99332, 99335-99339, 99341,
  99345, 99347, 99352, 99353, 99363,
  99366, 99849, 1st note after 100478,
  100486, 100502, 100572, 100575, 102227,
  104844, 3d note after 106221, 106401
Americaner. 100720-100721
Americani. 100724
Americanische Annalen der Arzneykunde
  Naturgeschichte Chemie und Physik. 656
Americanische Freybeuter. 62752
Americanische Reisz-Beschreibung. 1139,
  89554A, 99534
Americanische Seerauber. 23470
Americanische Volkerwanderung. 31257
Americanischen neuen Welt Beschreibung.
  90039, 105680
Americanischer Wegweiser. 56647
Americanisches Ackerwerk Gottes. note after
  98130-98131
Americanism. Address. 46840
Americanism and other isms. 89306
Americanism conquers panics, socialism and
  war. 83883, 83888
Americanism. Speech of Hon. Lewis D.
  Campbell. 10261
Americano. pseud. Carta de un Americano
  a un amigo suyo. 17757
Americano. pseud. Carta de un Americano
  a un diputado. see Inana y Torre, Jose
  Isidro.

Americano. pseud. Carta de un Americano al Espanol sobre su numero XIX. see Mier, Manual de. incorrectly supposed author and Mier Noriega y Guerra, Jose Servando Teresa de. supposed author

Americano. pseud. Explicacion, y reflexiones. 87314

Americano. pseud. Manifiesto. see Moreno, Francisco Javier.

Americano. pseud. Prima y segunda carta. 65525

Americano. pseud. Proclama. see V., J. pseud.

Americano. pseud. Proyecto de una constitucion religiosa. see Llorente, -----.

Americano. pseud. Segunda carta. 78907

Americano. pseud. Vindicacion al R. P. Gutierrez. 99783

Americano, Amante de la religion, y patria. pseud. Clamor de la verdad. see Velasco, Ignacio Alonso de.

Americano, argonauta de las costas. 1264

Americano em Londres. 67319

Americano seraphico llanto de esta provincia. 57818

Americano sincero. pseud. El Americano sincero en defensa. see Zaida Guntisu. pseud.

Americano sincero en defensa del Excmo. Sr. Virey. 106242

Americano Y. O. S. pseud. Anecdota. see S., Y. O. pseud.

Americanos: trageda francessa. 10095, 100726

Americans against liberty. 79269

Americans as they are. 1265

Americans at home; or, byeways, backwoods, and prairies. 1266, 29680

Americans at home: pen-and-ink sketches. 43646

Americans. By an American in London. 14766, note after 97028

American's defence of his government. 4183

American defended by an American. 1267

American's dream. 1268, 2d note after 95453

"American's examination" of the "Right of search." 11346, 23369, (69691), 71353

Americans! Friends of Washington! Look here!! 101772

American's guide. 1269-1271

Americans in 1841. 63371

Americans in England. 73603

Americans in Rome. 39965

Americans in their moral, social, and political relations. 29002

Americans mistaken. 23758

American's offering. 1272

Americans no Jewes. (40231)

American's own book, containing the constitutions. 5316

American's own book. The Declaration of Independence. 1273

Americans repudiate fusion. 66813

Americans roused. 1274, 17982, (79396), 79397

Americans triumphant. 101263

Americans warned of Jesuitism. 63062

Americanus. pseud. 95768

Americanus. pseud. (23141), 97367

Americanus. pseud. Address to the people of the United States. see Beckley, John. supposed author and Beckley, John James. supposed author

Americanus. pseud. Constitutionalist. see Ford, Timothy.

Americanus. pseud. Eight letters. 20704, (22080)

Americanus. pseud. False alarm. 23758

Americanus. pseud. Letter. 18239

Americanus. pseud. Letter to the freeholders. see Quincy, Edmund, 1703-1788. supposed author

Americanus. pseud. Letter to the Rev. Mr. John Wesley. see Evans, Caleb.

Americanus. pseud. Military Academy at West Point, unmasked. 48952, note after 102946

Americanus. pseud. Sketches of the life. (17445)

Americanus, Junius. pseud. Political detection. see Lee, Arthur.

Americanus, Junius. pseud. Review of "A discourse." see Stearns, George Osborne.

Americanus, Scipio. pseud. see Scipio Americanus. pseud.

Americanus, Scotus. pseud. see Scotus Americanus. pseud.

Americanus, Silvanus. pseud. History of North America. see Nevill, Samuel.

Americanus, Sylvanus. pseud. History of North-America. see Nevill, Samuel.

Americanus, Sylvanus. pseud. ed. New American magazine. see Nevill, Samuel. ed.

Americanus Aurelius Prodentius. pseud. Sacred minister. see Mather, Samuel, 1706-1785

Americanus examined. 1275

America's appeal to the impartial world. 1276, 46770

Americas Arctiske Landes gamle geographie. (67467)

America's blessings and obligations. 15892

America's future. (1277)

America's lamentation. 101773, 101790, 101823, 101833, 101834, 101850

America's lamentations on the death of Gen. Washington. 101773

America's lecacy [sic]: being the address of G. Washington. 101541, 101591

America's legacy: containing General Washington's farewell address. 101530

America's messinger. 36981, (60182)

America's misfortune. 81845

America's offering. 47274

Americas opdagelse i det tiende Aarhundrede. 67468

America's remembrancer. 30642

America's tomorrow. 84235

Americi Vespucci navigationis tertiae. note before 99327, 99368

Americologia ossia osservazioni storiche e fisologiche. 24997

Americus. pseud. The American crisis. 1080

Americus. pseud. Eight letters. 20704, (22080)

Americus. pseud. Executive power of appointment and removal. 1277A

Americus. pseud. Spain, Cuba and the United States. see Kingsley, Vine Wright.

Americus. pseud. Thoughts for the times. 1278, note before 95669

Americus Club, Philadelphia. 61462

Americus Patriar. pseud. Friendly check. 25948

Americus Vespucci eines florenzischen Edelmannes. 3150, note after 99383C

Americus Vespuccius. A critical and documentary review. 99363

Americus Vespucius. (40044)

Amerigo. Canti Venti. 73264

Amerigo Vespucci. 99353, 99374, 99379

Amerigo Vespucci. [By Alberto Magnaghi.] 99383A, 99383C-note after 99383C

Amerigo Vespucci, by Frederick A. Ober.
99383A, 99383C-note after 99383C
Amerigo Vespucci. Son caractere. note before
99327, 99369, 99383A-99383C
Amerigo Vespucci's account of his first voyage.
99373
Amerigo Vespucci's account of his third voyage.
note before 99327, 99376
Amerigo Vespuzzi vier Seereisen. note before
99327, 99359
Amerika. 9321, 19998
Amerika, benevens de omliggende Eilanden.
24945
Amerika. [Brasilien (Mitte Dezember.)] 1282
Amerika dargestellt durch sich selbst. 1279,
28049
Amerika. De staatkundige, maatschappelijke
en kerkelijk-godsdienstige toestand.
77490
Amerika. Die politischen, socialen und
kirchlick-religiosen Zustande. 77489
Amerika. Erster Band. Brasilien. Columbien
und Guyana. 102622
Amerika, i sin forhen voerende og nu voerende
Forfatning. 38370
Amerika im Jahre 1825. 72841
Amerika, in alle zyne byzonderheden beschouwd.
1280
Amerika in geographischen und geschichtlichen
Umrissen. 1461
Amerika in seiner gegenwartigen politischen
Gestalt. 72480
Amerika-Mude. 38352
Amerika, oder allgemeiner Ueberblick. 23226
Amerika ohne Schminke. (22042)
Amerika samt om Emigrant-Foreningen i
Stockholm. 1271
Amerika! Treuer Rathgeber und Fuhrer. 1284
Amerika und Australien. 10687, 37164
Amerika und die Auswanderung dahin. 1284
Amerika und die moderne Volkerwanderung.
(7449), 67916
Amerika und die Sklaverei. 56413
Amerika. Zeitschrift fur Auswanderer. 1285
Amerkiaansch verhall. 16432
Amerikaansche hefboom tot opbeuring van ons
lager onderwijs. 5268
Amerikaansche voyagien. (4874), note before
98408
Amerikaenschen Landman. pseud. Brieven.
see Crevecoeur, J. Hector St. John,
1735-1813.
Amerikanen. 100709
Amerikaner. pseud. Historischer Abriss.
see Buisson, P. U. du.
Amerikaner. pseud. Vorstellung der
Staatsveranderung in Nordamerika. see
Buisson, P. U. du.
Amerikaner. 100720, 100722
Amerikaner in ihren moralischen, politischen
und gesellschaftlichen Verhaltnissen.
29003
Amerikaner in Mexico. 93107
Amerikaner. Lustspiel in einem Aufzuge.
63415
Amerikaner, Scenen aus dem Volksleben.
77155
Amerikanisch-Asiatisch Etymologien. 63364
Amerikanische Anekdoten. 1285A
Amerikanische Bibliothek. 3566, (4724), 17936,
92561
Amerikanische Bibliothek. Herausgegeben von
C. D. Ebeling. 21747
Amerikanische Burgerkrieg. Geschichte des
Volks. 77667
Amerikanische Burgerkrieg von seinem Beginn.
76345

Amerikanische Criminalgeschichte. (4724)
Amerikanische Eisenbahnen. 64733
Amerikanische Erzahlung. 27177
Amerikanische Erzahlungen und Geschichten.
2304
Amerikanische Federalist. (37726)
Amerikanische Jagd- und Reiseabenteuer. 93102
Amerikanische Kolonisation. 8163
Amerikanische Kriegsbilder. 31625
Amerikanische Miscellen. 14891, 72481
Amerikanische Nachrichten. 55239
Amerikanische Reisebemerkungen. 19999
Amerikanische Reisebilder fur die Jugend. 20122
Amerikanische Reisen. 5129
Amerikanische Reisenovellen. (4538)
Amerikanische Reise-Skizzen aus dem Gebiete
der Technik. 29498
Amerikanische Romane. 16413
Amerikanische Sachwalter. 4101
Amerikanische Skizzen und Erzahlungen. 92434
Amerikanische Staatensystem. 4853A
Amerikanische Union. 89280
Amerikanische Wald- und Strombilder. 27170
Amerikanische Weinbauschule. 51305
Amerikan. Zeitgemalde mit Gesang u. Tanz in
3 Abthlgn. 92574
Amerikanischen Besserungs-Systeme. (36889)
Amerikanischen Guthsbesitzers. pseud.
Sittlichen Schilderungen von Amerika.
see Crevecouer, J. Hector St. John,
1735-1813.
Amerikanisches Archiv. 1286, 9259, 39709,
41285, 65454, 69549, 97350
Amerikanisches Charakterbild. 3976
Amerikanisches Culturbild. 38352
Amerikanisches Lebensbild. 37180
Amerikanisches Les-Cabinet. 2567
Amerikanisches Magazin. Herausgegeben von
Karl Niedhard. 1288
Amerikanisches Magazin oder authentische
Beitrage. 1287, (3818), (31235)
Amerikanske Antegnelser af Charl. Dickens.
20000
Amerikanusok. 100723
Amerika's Besserungs-system. 4192, note
after 96059
Amerikas forenede Staters Historie. (77966)
Amerikas grosse Urstadt. 71447
Amerikas Opdagelse og Erobring af Columbus.
10291
Amerikas wichtigste Charakterstik nach Land
und Leuten. 8732
Ameriquain aux Anglois. 1288A, note before
99759
Amerique. 5715, 6269
Amerique actuelle. 36638
Amerique angloise. (5969), 57158
Amerique centrale. (56735)
Amerique centrale. Colonisation du district de
Santo-Thomas. (11681), 76882
Amerique centrale. La republique du Honduras
et son chemin inter-oceanique. 4594
Amerique chrestienne. 12294
Amerique, d'apres les voyageurs les plus
celebres. 1289, 38759
Amerique decouverte. 1289, six livres. (39253)
Amerique decouverte; poeme en XXIV chants.
6896
Amerique delivree. 1290, 38759
Amerique devant l'Europe. 26725
Amerique du Nord. Lettre au Corps Legislatif.
59504
Amerique du Nord; ou, le correspondant des
Etats-Unis. 1291
Amerique en 1826. 106320

Ameriqve en plvsievrs cartes, & en divers
traittes de geographie. 76708
Amerique en plvsievrs cartes, etc., en divers
traites de geographie. 76715
Amerique en plusieurs cartes nouvelles et
exactes. 76712-76714
Ameriqve en plvsievrs cartes, novvelles, et
exactes. 76709
Ameriqve en plvsievrs cartes novvelles, et
exactes, etc. 76710
Ameriqve en plvsievrs cartes novvelles et
exactes, &c. (76711)
Amerique equatoriale. 57352
Amerique Espagnole en 1830. 7396
Amerique Espagnole, ou lettres civiques.
55405
Amerique et l'Europe en 1846. (38383)
Amerique et ses hommes d'etat. 37112
Amerique histoire des voyages dans cette
parte monde. 21121
Amerique il y a soixante ans. 78771
Amerique independante. (19476), 19478
Amerique Latine. 10090
Amerique meridionale iles diverses. 1293,
(24403)
Amerique. Notice historique et geographique.
44168
Amerique pittoresque. 104505
Amerique protestante. 70384
Amerique septentrionale et meridionale. 1295
Amerique septentrionalis. 31359
Amerique sous le nom de Pays de Fou-Sang.
58549
Amerique telle qu'elle est. 14936
Ameriquiade. Poeme. 38760
Ames, ------. defendant 36388
Ames, B. D. ed. 25162, 38853
Ames, Benjamin. 1296
Ames, Benjamin. supposed author (20226),
(37853), 37856, 104779
Ames, Charles G. 1297
Ames, D. defendant 102587
Ames, Edgar Willey, 1870- 82850
Ames, Ellis. 1298, 66939
Ames, Fisher, 1758-1808. 273-274, (1299)-
1304, 11005, 29992, 42459, 43375,
45459, 78997, 89220, 101749, 101803,
note after 101883
Ames, Fisher, 1758-1808. spirit author
1081A, 101770
Ames, Joseph Sweetman, 1864-1943. 85010
Ames, Julius. 89477
Ames, Julius Rubens. 1305-1306, 29062
Ames, Julius Rubens. supposed author
39867-(39868), 95097
Ames, Levi, d. 1773. 1307, 91809
Ames, Nathan. 1308, (12728)
Ames, Nathaniel. 1309, 62743, 95966
Ames, Samuel. ed. 70700
Ames, Samuel. plaintiff 5786
Ames, Samuel. reporter 1310, 5785, 70697
Ames, Seth. ed. 1304
Ames, William. 72103, 72110
Ames. firm see Mitchell, Ames and White.
firm publishers
Amesbury, Mass. Young Men's Temperance
Association. see Young Men's Tem-
perance Association in Salisbury and
Amesbury, Mass.
Amherst, Jeffrey Amherst, 1st Baron, 1717-
1797. 34891, 36727, 38164, 42175
Amherst, William, 1732-1781. 38164
Amherst, Mass. Amherst College. see
Amherst College, Amherst, Mass.
Amherst, Mass. Massachusetts Agricultural
College. see Massachusetts. Uni-
versity, Amherst.

Amherst, Mass. Mount Pleasant Boarding
School for Boys. see Mount Pleasant
Institute, Amherst, Mass.
Amherst, Mass. Mount Pleasant Classical
Institution. see Mount Pleasant Institute,
Amherst, Mass.
Amherst, Mass. Mount Pleasant Institute. see
Mount Pleasant Institute, Amherst, Mass.
Amherst, Mass. University of Massachusetts.
see Massachusetts. University, Amherst.
Amherst College, Amherst, Mass. 1312-1314,
89907, 90716, 90991, 90998, note after
102377
Amherst College, Amherst, Mass. petitioners
1315, 23271, 30765, 89138, 1st note after
104432
Amherst College, Amherst, Mass. Alumni.
85386
Amherst College, Amherst, Mass. Board of
Trustees. 1332, note after 93378
Amherst College, Amherst, Mass. Board of
Trustees. petitioners (45895)
Amherst College, Amherst, Mass. Class of
1831. 64977
Amherst College, Amherst, Mass. Class of
1854. 73936
Amherst College, Amherst, Mass. Faculty.
1332, note after 93378
Amherst College. Decennial meeting of the
class of 1854, with a biographical record.
73936
Amherst Collegiate Institution, Amherst, Mass.
see Amherst College, Amherst, Mass.
Amherst Collegiate Institution. A plea for a
miserable world. 1314, note after 102377
Amherst Collegiate Institution. March 1, 1823.
1313
Amherst Institution, Amherst, Mass. see
Amherst College, Amherst, Mass.
Amherst Institution. . . . January 17, 1825.
1315
Amherst journal. 100595
Amherstburg, Ontario. General Convention for
the Improvement of the Colored Inhabitants
of Canada. see General Convention for
the Improvement of the Colored Inhabitants
of Canada, Amherstburg, Ontario, 1853.
Amherstburg, Ontario. Uncle Tom's Cabin and
Relief Society. see Uncle Tom's Cabin
and Relief Society, Amherstburg, Ontario.
Amhurst, Nicholas. 101167
Amhurst, Nicholas. supposed author 1335A,
17351, 18510-18511, 56514, 66643, 86644,
101167
Ami de la religion. 19202
Ami de la verite. pseud. tr. (7935), 6th note
after 97845, 97851
Ami de l'ordre. pseud. Question des fabriques.
67140
Ami des hommes de toutes les couleurs. pseud.
De la traite des Negres. see Gregoire,
Henri.
Ami du corps social. pseud. Triomphe du
nouveau monde. see Brun, Jean B.
Ami du jeune age. 98964
Amicable Fire Company, Philadelphia. see
Philadelphia. Amicable Fire Company.
Amicable Fire Company are requested to meet.
61463
Amice lector Alberti Magni Germani principis
philosophi. 673
Amice lectori Alberti Magni Germani principis
philosophi. 671
Amici justitiae. pseud. Verdict unsealed.
98955
Amico. pseud. Vita. see Stuart, D. sup-
posed author

Amicum. pseud. Sermon. see Kent, Benjamin.
Amicum cleri, et populi. pseud. Plea for the ministers. see Fitch, Jabez.
Amicus. pseud. Rebel states. 68321
Amicus. pseud. Slavery among the Puritans. 82074, 93197
Amicus curiae. pseud. Excursion on the River Connecticut. (15865)
Amicus mundi. pseud. Defence of the colonies. (19242), 75099
Amicus patriae. pseud. Address to the inhabitants. see Lover of his country. pseud.
Amicus patriae. pseud. Friendly check. see Wise, John.
Amicus patriae. pseud. Proposals for traffick and commerce. 66039
Amicus reipublicae. pseud. Address to the public. see Thurston, Benjamin.
Amid Rowe Hills. 83505
Amid the many private and public distresses. 99050
Amines, France. Commercants et Fabricants. 40675
Amigo. pseud. Carta de un amigo a otro. 11095
Amigo. pseud. Sustos a los regatones. 93942
Amigo de la academia. pseud. ed. 74769
Amigo de la justicia. pseud. Ultimo golpe. 96208
Amigo de la patria. (48269), 72267
Amigo de la patria dado en Guatemala. 98377
Amigo de la religion, agricultura, politica, comercio. 59628
Amigo de la verdad y enemigo del desorden. pseud. Mexico por dentro y fuera. see Villarroel, Hipolito. supposed author
Amigo de las leyes. 69628
Amigo de liberato anti-servilio. pseud. Respuesta al duelo vindicado. 70093
Amigo de los hombres. pseud. Amigo de los hombres: a todos que habitan las islas. see Toledo y Dubois, Jose Alvarez de. supposed author
Amigo de los hombres: a todos que habitan los islas. 48270, 96118
Amigo del orden. pseud. El protector nominal de los pueblos libres. 9030
Amigo del pueblo. Periodico de religion, variedades y anuncios. 48272
Amigo del pueblo. Periodico seminario literario. (48271)
Amigo suyo. pseud. Prontuario e instruccion. 65995
Amigos de la libertad. pseud. Impugnacion al articulo. 76157
Amigos del Bien Publico. see Sociedad de Socorros Mutuos "Los Amigos del Bien Publico," San Juan.
Amigos del Pais, Panama. see Sociedad Amigos del Pais, Panama.
Aminadab Sledgehammer. pseud. see Sledgehammer, Aminadab. pseud.
Amir Khan, and other poems. 18734
Amira, ------. Sul y. see Sul y Amira, -------.
Amira de Narte, Sejo. pseud. Clamores de la America. see Teran, Jose Maria.
Amirola, Eugenio de Llaguno. see Llaguno Amirola, Eugenio de.
Amirucius, Georgius. see Amirutzes, Georgius.
Amirutzes, Georgius. 66479
Amis de la Bienfaisance, Baltimore. 43350, 96962 see also Entertainment given in Honor of Duncan McIntosh, Baltimore, 1809.

Amis & freres. 101689
Amiscogging Indians. see Pequawket Indians.
Amistad (Sloop) in Admiralty 274, 81809
Amistad captives. 1337, 81809
Amistad captives. Africans taken in the Amistad. 1338
Amistad claim. History of the case. 27329
Amistad claim. Speech . . . . in the Senate. 20368
Amistead, Wilson. ed. 4694
Amite Presbytery. see Presbyterian Church in the U. S. Presbytery of Amite.
Amman, Hans Jacob. 1339, 99534
Ammann, Hans Jacob. see Amman, Hans Jacob.
Ammans, Hans Jacob. see Amman, Hans Jacob.
eumerrikan-standard or pronunsieshon. 102445
eumerrikanz-diksoerian standard. 102445
eumerrikanz jeograffikal standard. 102445
Ammiraglio dell'Indie. (22416), 29112
Amnesty proclamation, and third annual message. 41162
Amnesty. Remarks . . . December 19, 21, and 22, 1870. 36615
Amnesty. Speech of Hon. Charles H. Porter, of Virginia. (64204)
Amo y Figueroa, Juan de Cara. see Cara Amo y Figueroa, Juan de.
Amoenitates academicae. (41352), 93764
Among my books. 68600, (68612)
Among the birds. 75967
Among the guerillas. 27447
Among the Indians. 6221
Among the lilies, and elsewhere. 82389
Among the Mormons. 8645
Among the pines. 27448
Among the trees. 42072
Amor a la Patria. 75572
Amor patriae. pseud. Blasphemy of abolitionism exposed. 1341
Amor patriae. pseud. Comparison of slavery with abolitionism. 1340
Amor patriae. pseud. Dissertations on the grand dispute. 20290
Amor patriae. pseud. Letters and dissertations. see Crowley, Thomas.
Amor patriae. pseud. Slavery. Con and pro. 82087
Amor patriae; or, the disruption and fall of these states. 1342
Amor y patria. 11711
Amores de dos salvages en el desierto. 12242
Amores de dous salvagens no o deserto. 12244
Amores de una Guajira. 98827
Amoretti, Carlo, 1741-1816. tr. 44109-44111, (62804)-62805, 62807
Amori di due selvaggi nel deserto. 12245
Amorosa contienda de Francia, Italia, y Espana. 44958
Amorosas respiraciones y alegres regocijos. (55349)
Amory, Thomas Coffin. 1343-1344.
Amory, Thomas Coffin, Jr. 1345
Amos, Andrew. (1346)
Amoskeag Veterans, of Manchester, N. H. (64619)
Amours de deux sauvages dans le desert. 12237
Amours de l'auteur. 99428
Amours of Dr. Post and Mrs. Peweetle. 12967, 61198, 84400
Amours of two savages in the desert. 12240
Ampel en breed Verhaal. (64184)
Ampere, Jean Jacques Antoine, 1800-1864. 1347
Amphi-theatrum, Worinnen III. 1348
Amphiaraus. pseud. Sermon. 13736
Amphlett, William. 1349

Ample confirmation of the foregoing discourse. (46655)
Ample refutation of all the objections. 56825
Ample traite du naturel. (12605), 71102
Ampliatio oder Erweiterung dess Privilegii. 98186
Amplissimis, prudentissimis, ornatissimis D. D. Domino Praetori. 77958
Amplissimos simul et consultissimos viros. 78199
Ampuero, Jose. petitioner 93813
Ampullariidae. (5503)
Ampzing, Samuel. 1350
Amric. pseud. Songs of the powow. 86938
Amstelophilus. pseud. Op de onafhankelykheid van Noord-America. 57381
Amsterdam. (39804), 42747-42748, (42749), 66217
Amsterdam. Achtbaren Magistret. 27123
Amsterdam. Burgeren. petitioners (16680), (57320), 1st note after 102889A
Amsterdam. Burgermeesteren. (15186), 16732-(16734), 20594, 23344, 55280-55281, note after 98474, note after 99310, 102887, 3d note after 102889A, 7th note after 102890
Amsterdam. Burgermeesters ende Raden. 16732-(16734)
Amsterdam. Burgerije. petitioners (16680), (57320), 1st note after 102889A
Amsterdam. Classis. see Nederlandsche Hervormde Kerk. Classis van Amsterdam.
Amsterdam. English Presbyterian Church. 72110
Amsterdam. Gereformeerde Ghemeente. see Nederlandsche Gereformeerde Ghemeente, Amsterdam.
Amsterdam. Mennonite Church. Archives. 77532
Amsterdam. K. Nederlandsche Instituut van Wetenschappen, Letterkunde en Schoone Kunsten. see K. Nederlandsch Instituut van Wetenschappen, Letterkunde en Schoone Kunsten, Amsterdam.
Amsterdam. Negotianten. petitioners (16680), (57320), 1st note after 102889A
Amsterdam. Raden. 16732-(16734), 23344, 3d note after 102889A, 7th note after 102890
Amsterdam. Societeit van Suriname. see Societeit van Suriname.
Amsterdam. West-Indische Maatschappij. see West-Indische Maatschappij, Amsterdam.
Amsterdam. A poem. 89673
Amsterdam aan zyne Regenten. 94081
Amsterdammian definition of a familist. 94477
Amsterdams Dam-Praetje. 1351
Amsterdams koopman. pseud. Briev. 99757
Amsterdams Tafel-Praetje. 1352
Amsterdams Vuur-Praetje. 1353
Amsterdamsch burger. pseud. Missive. (49566)
Amsterdamsche rechtgeleerden. pseud. Reflexien. 68729
Amsterdamsche Veerman op Middelburgh. 1354, note after 102878
Amsterdamse kapitein. pseud. Reys-Journael. 70461
Amthor, E. 35205
Amulet. 89492
Amulet; a tale of Spanish California. 1355
Amulet, or Christian and literary remembrance. 104614
Amunategui, Manuel. ed. (12753)
Amunategui, Miguel Luis. 56857
Amusement for a winter's evening. 1274, 17982, (79396), 79397
Amusement for the mess. 10182

Amusement in the said postscript. 95963
Amusements for youth. 78768
Amusements geographiques et historiques, ou les memoires de M***. 52091
Amusements geographiques et historiques, ou voyages. 52092, note after 100836
Amusing and memorable of American country life. (6243)
Amusing and thrilling adventures of a California artist. (20342)
Amusing companion. 95293
Amusing instructive and entertaining tales. 97513
Amusing scenes from the revolution. 82979
Amusing trial. 81846
Amy, Jean Baptiste l'. see Lamy, John Baptist, Abp., 1814-1888.
Amy Lawrence. 84328
Amy Lothrop. pseud. Dollars and cents. see Warner, Anna Bartlett.
Amy Moss. 75247
Amy Warwick (Ship) in Admiralty (18446), 89704
Amyot, F. ed. 1912
An den gunstigen Leser. (8784)
An den gutwilligen Leser. (8784)
An den Nordpol. 38038
An der Indianer-Grenze. 93103
An 2440. 35487, 1st note after 100816
An die Deutschen. (61464)
An die Farmer. 85897, 91010
An die Freunde. 95929
An die Freyhalter und Einwohner. 61465, 102512
An seine liebe Teutsche. 42642, note after 106351, 106359
Anabaptism. 2762
Anabaptists. Barbican Meeting, London, 1674. 59718
Anabaptists. New England. 104097
Anabaptists. Munster. 95739
Anacalypsis. 31737
Anachoreta. pseud. Hand-book of civil rights. 30203
Anacreon in heaven. 86897, 90497
Anacreontic ode. (5343)
Anacreontic Society, New York. 101880
Anaesthesia and Asepsis. 84267
Anaesthesia! The greatest discovery of the age! 84441, 84446
Anaesthesia. Who is entitled to the credit of making the great discovery? 84442
Anagnosia o arte de cer. 77131
Anagr. John Winthrop, Oh Print Wo nih. 104850
Anagram, leave old arm's. 98056
Anagrammas en aplauso y gloria. 50478
Anahuac. 72567
Analectic history. 20751
Analectic journal. 47238
Analectic magazine. 19134, 41486, 78991
Analectic magazine and naval chronicle. 1358, 19357
Anales de Aragon. 1950
Anales de ciencias. (74904)
Anales de historia natural. 74005
Anales de la Academia de Medicina de Buenos Ayres. (8992A)
Anales de la dictadura. 61077, 64879
Anales de la educacion comun. 44395
Anales de la iglesia de Puno. 62750
Anales de la Junta de Fomento y memorias de la Sociedad Patriotica. 17750
Anales de la minera Mexicana. 48273
Anales de las Reales Junta de Fomento y Sociedad Economica. 29414
Anales del Ministerio de Fomento. (1359), (48274)
Anales del Museo Publico de Buenos Aires. 8993

Anales Mexicanos de ciencias. 48275
Anales universitarios del Peru. 59322
Analisis de la aguas de la fuente de Madruga. 69568
Analisis de la oracion Dominical. 73155
Analisis de la platica Mexicana del Padre Jesuita Ignacio Paredes sobre el misterio de la Santisima Trinidad. 73156
Analisis de la platica Mexicana del Padre Jesuita Ignacio Paredes sobre la vida, pasion y muerte de Ntro. Sr. Jesu-Cristo. 73157
Analisis de la "Salve" en Mexicano. 73158
Analisis de las aguas terminales de Yura. 67523
Analisis del idioma Yucateco al Castellano. 74518
Analisis del papel titulado "Lo mas y lo 49406
Analisis del romance de Veracruz. 94154
Analisis estadistico de la Provincia de Michuacan. 38385, (39945)
Analisis que ofrece a este publico. 51767
Analogical discourse on earthquakes. 73496
Analum samantekin og a Latinski. 2058, (28646), 74880
Analyse da constitucao do imperio. 8989
Analyse de la carte generale de l'ocean Atlantique. 1360
Analyse de la discussion de la Chambre des Deputes. 85816
Analyse de la discussion generale du projet de loi. 36414
Analyse de l'histoire philosophique et politique. 1361, 4928, 60873
Analyse de la nature. 67465
Analyse de l'ordonnance du Conseil Special. 38609
Analyse des discussions qui se sont elevees. 49983
Analyse des hypotheses anciennes et modernes. 63667
Analyse des loix commerciales. 21056
Analyse des notes des Conseils Coloniaux. 1362
Analyse des pieces par Page et Brulley. 16043, 58164
Analyse dos factos praticados em Inglatera. 98776
Analyse du journal de la navigation. 76833
Analyse d'un entretien. 10350, note after 99595
Analyse d'un memoire sur les bois d'Amerique. 101347
Analyse e refutacao do libello accusatorio. 17006
Analyse et rapprochement des operations. 40740
Analyse raisonne de la carte. 33700
Analyses and essays. (35584)
Analyses de materia medica Brasileira. 59503
Analysis and estimate of the character of General Grant. 82158
Analysis and refutation of the "Statement of facts." 17653
Analysis by Prof. S. P. Duffield. (75394)
Analysis [by Town.] 102370
Analysis of American law. (51132)
Analysis of four hundred and thirty-nine recovered amputations. 84276
Analysis of Jackson County Springs. 82991
Analysis of marls from the vicinity of Charleston. 87534
Analysis of memorial of the Delaware & Hudson Canal Co. 19409
Analysis of meteoric iron. 81032

Analysis of Mr. R. Pearsall Smith's scheme. 83876
Analysis of patriotism. 1363
Analysis of Saratoga waters. 55522
Analysis of Sharon Waters, Schoharie County. 24976
Analysis of some of the . . . iron ores. 36334
Analysis of the apple. 75793
Analysis of the Australian colonies government bill. 43349
Analysis of the authorities. 6026
Analysis of the Bible. 19488
Analysis of the Book of Mormon. 11478
Analysis of the Book of Mormon; with prefatory remarks. 10206
Analysis of the character and conduct of Rev. J. N. Maffitt. 43790, note after 95312
Analysis of the Congress Spring. 91095
Analysis of the constitution of Georgia. 27014
Analysis of the evidence given before the Select Committee. 81847
Analysis of the explanatory article. 23355, (26388), 2d note after 101806
Analysis of the foreign trade. 83369
Analysis of the hydrant and well waters of the city of Troy. 22098
Analysis of the late correspondence. 1068, 42443-42444, 1st note after 93806
Analysis of the memorial. (48276)
Analysis of the mineral water from the Plantagenet Spring. 63313
Analysis of the mineral waters of Afton. 75795
Analysis of the mineral waters of Saratoga and Ballston, containing some general remarks. 91096
Analysis of the mineral waters of Saratoga and Ballston, with practical remarks. 91097
Analysis of the mineral waters of Saratoga and Ballston, with practical remarks on their use in various diseases. 91098
Analysis of the principal mineral fountains. 860
Analysis of the proposed tax levy. (54188)
Analysis of the report of a Committee of the House of Commons. 81848
Analysis of the report of the Committee of the General Assembly. 100081
Analysis of the rhubarb. 75793
Analysis of the Rockbridge Alum Springs. (72376)
Analysis of the Seneca language. 79117
Analysis of the statutes of Georgia. 13842
Analysis of the testimony taken at the trial. 97773
Analysis of the third article of the Treaty of Cession. 42190
Analysis of the traveling route. 72139
Analysis of the water of the Jamaica Resevoir. 8331
Analysis of the waters of Bedford Mineral Springs. 12999
Analysis of theology. 73131
Analysis verbi. 6103
Analyst: a collection of miscellaneous papers. 36627
Analytic digest of the laws of the United States. 7971
Analytica. pseud. Problem of government. 65742
Analytical abridgment of Kent's commentaries. 36231
Analytical and comparative view. 15166
Analytical and sanitary observations. 6026
Analytical class-book of botany. 28523
Analytical digest of the law of Marine insurance. 80359, (80361)
Analytical digest of the laws of the United States. 7972

ANALYTICAL

Analytical index of the whole of the documents.
 25125
Analytical index to the civil code of Lower
 Canada. 10477
Analytical index to the colonial documents.
 53058, note before 91508
Analytical magazine. 7143
Analytical parallel and criticism. 19628
Analytical parliamentary digest. 30246
Analytical repository. 83808
Analytical statement of the case. 3208
Analytical synopsis of the natural history of
 man. 62624
Anamihe-masinahigan. 12831
Anamnesis. pseud. Civil war in America.
 13166
Anania, Giovanni Lorenzo d'. 1364
Anania, Lorenzo. tr. 78166
Anarchiad. 1365, 71321, 97204
Anarchy and despotism. 7199
Anarchy of the ranters. 3363, 95752, 103062
"Anas" of Thomas Jefferson. 4030
Anastaf de Morales, C. D. C. pseud. Vida de
 Hernan-Cortes. see San Rafael, Tomas
 de.
Anastaris, Ramon Perez de.
 see Perez de Anastaris, Ramon.
Anastasio, Juan de San. see San Anastasio,
 Juan de.
Anatomia, fisiologis y patologia vegetal. 67525
Anatomia racional de los miembros. 29420
Anatomical illustrations. 79471
Anatomie. 33773
Anatomist. 14395, 84678C
Anatomy of an American Whig. 29955, 6th
 note after 104016
Anatomy of an opossum. 97637
Anatomy of independency. (27953)
Anatomy of the controversed ceremonies.
 97128
Anatomy of the nervous system of Rana
 Pipiens. 85072, 105674
Anaya, Cirilo Gomez y. see Gomez y Anaya,
 Cirilo.
Anaya, Francisco Garcia. 48810
Anbange [sic] uber das Unchristiliche des
 Papstthumes. 85108
Anburey, Thomas. 1366-1370, 69146, 2d note
 after 96502, 100835
Anbury, Thomas. see Anburey, Thomas.
Ancestors of Moses Belcher Bass. 84298
Ancestry and childhood of James J. Strang.
 92687
Ancestry of General Grant. (44769)
Ancestry of Mary Oliver. 57208
Anchieta, Jose de, 1533-1597. 1371-1371A,
 7588, 63028, 98651
Anchieta, Joseph de. see Anchieta, Jose de,
 1533-1597.
Anchor. pseud. Chancellorsville and its
 results. see De Peyster, John Watts.
Anchor Lines Agents Excursion, 1872. 88690
Anchor stones. 85041
Anchoret. 97371
Anchoret reclaimed. 96083, note after 105147
Ancien avocat soussigne. 5401
Ancien capitaine de vaisseau. pseud.
 Decouvertes des Francois. see Fleurieu,
 Charles Pierre Claret de, Comte de.
Ancien colon. pseud. Tableau de l'esclavage.
 see Macaulay, Zachary. supposed
 author and Reveridi, A. supposed
 author.
Ancien consul. pseud. Etudes historiques.
 see L***, F., Ancien consul. pseud.
Ancien fonctionnaire des Indes Neerlandaises.
 pseud. La question de l'esclavage.
 67138

Ancien intendant de cette isle. pseud. Essai
 sur la colonie de Sainte Lucie. see
 Chardon, Daniel Marc Antoine.
Ancien magistrat condamne le 14 mai 1830.
 pseud. Plainte portee. 63252
Ancien Missionaire. pseud. De Montcalm en
 Canada. see Martin, Felix.
Ancien Missionaire. pseud. Etudes
 philologiques. see Cuoq, A.
Ancien officier de Dragons. pseud. tr. see
 Raulin, Joseph. tr.
Ancien syndic de la Chambre de Commerce de
 Lyon. pseud. Dissertation. 20288
Anciennes archives Francaises. 10352
Anciens Canadiens. 26735
Ancient aboriginal trade in North America.
 67966
Ancient America. 18792
Ancient and Honourable Artillery Company,
 Boston. see Massachusetts. Ancient
 and Honorable Artillery Company.
Ancient and Honorable Artillery Company of
 Massachusetts. see Massachusetts.
 Ancient and Honourable Artillery Company.
Ancient and modern history of the Brethren.
 17411
Ancient and modern Michilimackinac. 48805,
 92674
Antient and modern state of the parish of
 Cramond. 105051
Ancient and modern teacher of politics. 40985
Ancient and modern things contrasted. 82475-
 82476
Ancient and Most Benevolent Order of the
 Friendly Brothers of Saint Patrick,
 Boston. 75450
Ancient annals of Kentucky. 44780
Ancient architecture of America. (41884), 54476
Ancient book of destiny. 83735
Ancient Bramin. pseud. see Chesterfield,
 Philip Domer Stanhope, 4th Earl of,
 1694-1773.
Ancient Briton's Benefit Society, New York.
 54084
Ancient charters and papers. 15670
Ancient constitution. 35022
Ancient dialogue. 104218
Ancient doucments. 66239
Ancient dominions of Maine. 79437
Ancient fauna of Nebraska. 39903, 85072
Ancient French archives. 10351
Ancient Gospel pleaded. 12333, 104184
Ancient historical record of Norwalk, Conn.
 (29763) '
Ancient history and the discovery of America.
 55012
Ancient history, or annals of Kentucky. (67442)
Ancient lady. pseud. Peep into the past. see
 Poyas, Elizabeth Anne.
Ancient lady, author of "Our forefathers."
 pseud. Days of yore. see Poyas,
 Elizabeth Anne.
Ancient lady, of Charleston. pseud. Peep into
 the past. see Poyas, Elizabeth Anne.
Ancient landmark. 82293
Ancient landmark and masonic digest. (82292)
Ancient men which came out of Holland and Old
 England. pseud. Dialogues. 52630
Ancient mining on the shores of Lake Superior.
 85072, 103821
Ancient missionary of Chili. 7084
Ancient monuments, and the aboriginal, semi-
 civilized nations. 89979
Ancient monuments of North and South America.
 67443
Ancient monuments of the Mississippi Valley.
 47813, 70307, 85072, 89953-89955
Ancient mounds and earth-works. 85041

Ancient mounds in Iowa and Wisconsin. 85041
Ancient mounds in Jackson County, Iowa. 85041
Ancient Order of Six Principles of the Doctrine
of Christ (Baptist) Yearly Meeting,
Coventry, R. I., 1812. see Baptist
Yearly Meeting of the Ancient Order of
Six Principles of the Doctrine of Christ,
Coventry, R. I., 1812.
Ancient Pemaquid. 95632
Ancient picture writing in America. 47578
Ancient platforms of the Congregational
Churches of New England. 52621
Ancient population of the new world. 47578
Ancient preface. 94109
Ancient promise improved. (50913)
Ancient psalmody revived. (48842)
Ancient records. 1376
Ancient right of the English nation. (6208)
Ancient slavery disapproved of God. (50882)
Ancient story of the Negro race. 52256
Ancient testimony and principles. 59614, note
after 66909
Antient testimony of the people called Quakers,
reviv'd. 61469, 66912
Ancient testimony of the religious society of
Friends. 86031
Ancient testimony of the said people, revived.
3366
Ancient things as they stand in the scripture.
82476
Ancient things as they stand in the scriptures.
82475
Ancient tumuli in Georgia. (36473)
Ancient tumuli on the Savannah River. (36472)
Ancient universal history. 96144
Ancient waymarks. 52959
"Ye ancient-Wrecke." 41560, (42112), note
after 89026
Ancient Ynca drama. 57224
Ancizar. 1377
Ancona, S. E. defendant at court martial
(1378)
Ancone, Freduci d'. see D'Ancone, Freduci.
Ancora sulla quistione se Cristoforo colombo
studio a Pavia. 76522
And their raised cain. (65945)
And, whereas, the name of my friend is
unknown. 83713
Andagoya, Pascual de. 18782-18783, 56338
Andalusia. 19810
Anden, forkortede udgave, efter overeenskomst
med forfatteren besorget ved W. v. Rosen.
5399
Ander Schiffart. In dir orientalische Indien.
(33654)
Ander Theil dieses Weltbuchs von Schifffahrten.
25472, 77677, 90039
Ander Theyl, der newlich erfundenen
Landtschafft Americae. (8784)
Anderde Discovers, by Forma van Messieve.
102879
Andere Andrede an die deutschen Freyhalter.
102512
Andere Declaratie van Iean de Vierde. 36131
Andere Reyse. 6340
Andere Vorrede des Verfassers und Ueber-
setzers. 102874
Anderson, ------. (28249)
Anderson, ------, fl. 1794. 64397
Anderson, ------, fl. 1861. 49247
Anderson, ------, of Pennsylvania. (59800)
Anderson, Mr. ------. 1380-1381
Anderson, Dr. A. 1383
Anderson, Adam, 1692?-1765. 1382
Anderson, Alexander. defendant 72374
Anderson, Alexander, 1775-1870. 9538, 36666,
83998, 84237, 84568, 97512, 98539

Anderson, Benjamin M. defendant before
military commission 9381
Anderson, Charles. RA 1384
Anderson, Charles, 1814-1895. 1385-1389A,
11579
Anderson, Charles Frederick. (1390)
Anderson, David, Bp of Rupert's land, 1814-1885.
1391-1393, (52345), 74147, (74148)
Anderson, Edward. 1394
Anderson, Edward C. 77261 see also Savan-
nah, Ga. Mayor, 1855 (Anderson)
Anderson, Elbert, fl. 1824. 53600 see also
New York (State) Contractor. claimant
Anderson, Eliza. tr. 46998
Anderson, Fulton, 1820-1874. 1395
Anderson, G. W. ed. 52455
Anderson, George Campbell. (39408)
Anderson, George W. 1396
Anderson, Hugh, d. 1848. 94215-94218
Anderson, Isaac, 1780-1857. supposed author
94800
Anderson, J. W. defendant 97773
Anderson, Rev. James, of Edinburgh. 1403
Anderson, James, 1680?-1739. 1397-1398,
25797
Anderson, James, 1739-1808. 1399-1401,
101735-101736
Anderson, James d. 1809. 1402-1402A
Anderson, James Stuart Murray, 1800-1869.
1404
Anderson, Johann, 1673-1743. 1405-1408A
Anderson, John. 55029, 55540, 62743, 70703
Anderson, John, 1792-1853. 1409
Anderson, John E. 27034
Anderson, John Jacob, 1821-1906. 1410, 18693
Anderson, Joseph, 1757-1837. 1411, 27377
Anderson, Joshua. 8974 see also Bucks Co.,
Pa. Sub-Lieutenant.
Anderson, Leroy. (65036)
Anderson, Lucien, 1824-1898. 1412
Anderson, Martin Brewer, 1815-1890. 55844
Anderson, Mary E. 1413
Anderson, Melville Best, 1851- tr. 96172
Anderson, Osborne Perry, 1830-1872. 1414
Anderson, Peter. tr. 83119
Anderson, R. B. supposed author. 80674
Anderson, R. P. 83655, 101926 see also
Association of Mechanics and Other
Working Men, Washington, D. C. Cor-
responding Secretary.
Anderson, R. W. 1416
Anderson, Rufus, 1796-1880. 1417-(1420), 47732,
90107
Anderson, Thomas Davis, 1819-1883. 1421-1422
Anderson, W. C. (1423), 76104
Anderson, William, M. D. defendant 96824,
100796
Anderson, William. reporter 1424, 29836,
40940
Anderson, William Clayton, 1826-1861. 8529
Anderson, Wiliam J. 1425
Anderson, William Wemyss. 1426-1428
Anderson (W. H.) Company. firm publishers
94882
Anderson improved. 55029
Anderson revived. 70703
Andersonville. (82600)
Andersonville prison. 30073
Anders, Rudolph. 1379
Andes and Pampas. 27419
Andes and the Amazon. 57727
Andet brev til mine venner og Bekjendte i
Danmark. 87139
Andilly, Arnavld d'. tr. 42582
Andiron Club, New York. 97234
Andover, Henry Howard, Viscount. see Suffolk,
Henry Howard, 12th Earl of, d. 1779.

Andover, Mass. 26178, 66656
Andover, Mass. Convention for Suppressing
  Violations of the Lord's Day, 1814. see
  Middlesex County, Mass. Convention for
  Suppressing Violations of the Lord's Day,
  Andover, 1814.
Andover, Mass. Phillips Academy. see
  Phillips Academy, Andover, Mass.
Andover, Mass. South Church. 15451
Andover, Mass. Theological Seminary. see
  Andover Theological Seminary.
Andover and Wilmington Railroad. 1443
Andover case. 85212
Andover creed. 77393
Andover defence. 85212
Andover heresy. 85212
Andover husking. 1431
Andover review. 85210, 85212
Andover speech. 93208
Andover Theological Seminary. 1433-1434,
  (1436)-1437, 1439-1441, 70224, 85222,
  note after 94525, 95158, 95190
Andover Theological Seminary. Class of 1859.
  (1442)
Andover Theological Seminary. Class of 1859.
  Secretary. (1442) see also Palmer,
  Charles Ray.
Andover Theological Seminary. Library.
  1432-1433
Andover Theological Seminary. Semi-centennial
  Celebration, 1859. 1440, note after 94507
Andover Theological Seminary. Society of
  Inquiry Respecting Missions. 41954
Andover Theological Seminary. Visitors.
  85212
Andover Theological Seminary. Visitors.
  defendants 85212
Andover Theological Seminary. Visitors.
  respondents 85212
Andover trial. 85212
Andrada, -------, Conde de Lemos y. see
  Lemos y Andrada, -----, Conde de.
Andrada, ----- Paes de. see Paes de
  Andrada, -----.
Andrada, Antonio Carlos Ribeiro de. see
  Ribeiro de Andrada, Antonio Carlos.
Andrada, Beatris Bernardina de. see Ser-
  vantes Casaus, Beatris Bernardina (De
  Andrada) de.
Andrada, Francisco Ladislau Alvares d'. 92598
Andrada, Gomes Freire de. 63895, (69168)
Andrada, Martin Francisco Ribeiro de. see
  Ribeiro de Andrada, Martin Francisco.
Andrada e Silva, Jose Bonifacio de. 1444-1446
Andrada Machado e Silva, Antonio Carlos
  Ribeiro. see Ribeiro de Andrada
  Machado e Silva, Antonio Carlos.
Andrade, Alfonso de. 93330
Andrade, Alonzo de. 1447, 11360
Andrade, Antonio Carlos Ribeiro de. see
  Ribeiro de Andrade, Antonio Carlos.
Andrade, Francisco Rojas y. see Rojas y
  Andrade, Francisco.
Andrade, Jose Maria, 1807-1883. 579, 6834,
  47037, 48429, 48599
Andrade, Navarro d'. 28293
Andrade e Silva, Jose Maria de. 1448
Andrade Figueira, Antonio Agostinho de. see
  Figueira, Antonio Agostinho de Andrade.
Andrade Leitao, Francisco de. see Leitao,
  Francisco de Andrade.
Andrade y Portugal, Pedro Fernandez de Castro.
  see Castro Andrade y Portugal, Pedro
  Fernandez de, Conde de Lemos, 1634-1672..
Andre, -------, le Pere. (1459)-(1460)
Andre, Dupin de Saint. see Saint-Andre,
  Dupin de.
Andre, J. F. tr. 225, 36559

Andre, John, 1751-1780. (1065), 1163, 1449-1452,
  4746-4748, (13744), 18775, 21296-21297,
  69750, 70350, 79477-(79483), 79485-79486,
  (79488), 82974, 82976, 82979, 4th note
  after 99800 see also Great Britain.
  Army. Commissioners for Settling a
  Cartel for the Exchange of Prisoners,
  1779.
Andre, John, 1751-1780. defendant at court
  martial. 1453-(1458), 83423, 96812
Andre; a tragedy, in five acts: as now performed.
  21297
Andre; a tragedy, in five acts; as performed.
  21296
Andre: a tragedy in five acts. By W. W. Lord.
  (42051)
Andre Conscience a la convention Nationale.
  15908
Andrea, D. W. tr. 11282
Andrea, Francisco Jose de Souza Soares de.
  see Souza Soares de Andrea, Francisco
  Jose de.
Andrea Caluo ad Paulo Uerrano. 16950, 56052
Andrea Corsali Fiorentino . . . ella nauigatione
  del mar. 67730
Andreana. (1458)
Andreas Michaux Geschichte der Amerikanischen
  Eichen. 48692
Andreas Philopatrus. pseud. Responsione. see
  Parsons, Robert, 1546-1610.
Andree, Karl, 1808-1875. 1461-1464, 2615,
  2618, 35685, 94328
Andres Lamas a sus compatriotas. 38717
Andres van Ravenswaay . . . aan de Seconde
  Kamer. 67993
Andreu, Felipe. 29088 see also Sociedad Econo-
  mica de Amigos de Guatemala. Secretario.
Andrew, ------. engr. 92485
Andrew, ------. publisher 93937
Andrew, John. engr. 4711
Andrew, John Albion, 1818-1867. 1465-1481,
  6477, (8636)-8637, 9616, 9801, (46033),
  46125, (49198), 52645, 70235, 79454,
  81525 see also Massachusetts. Governor,
  1861-1866 (Andrew) New England His-
  toric-Genealogical Society. President.
Andrew, W. 1482
And. Battell's voyage to the River of Plate.
  66686
Andrew Bradford. 36510
Andrew College, Trenton, Tenn. 1483
Andrew Fresneau's Executors. see Executors
  of Andrew Fresneau.
Andrew Frey's account and observations. 71406
Andrew Jackson, President of the United States
  of America, to all and singular to whom
  these presents shall come, greeting.
  96659-96663, 96665
Andrew Jackson's Negro speculations. 93797
Andrew Johnson Club. see National Andrew
  Jackson Club.
Andrew Johnson Club. Inaugural address of the
  president. 59481
Andrew Johnson, President of the United States.
  25253
Andrew Marvell's second address. 45022
Andrew Trueman. pseud. see Trueman,
  Andrew. pseud.
Andrew Wiggin, and others,—Petitioners.
  103894
Andrew Wiggin, and six other gentlemen. 103894
Andrewes, ------, fl. 1603. 67545
Andrews, A. O. 88110
Andrews, Charles. 1484, 65713
Andrews, Charles, 1814-1852. 1485
Andrews, Charles C. 1487
Andrews, Charles Maclean, 1863- 46731-46732,
  note after 70346, 92350

Andrews, Charles Wesley, 1807-1865. 1490, 1763
Andrews, Christopher Columbus, 1829-1922. 1486, 1488, 1489, 57405
Andrews, David. 1491-1492, 60842 see also Pepperell, Mass. Committee to Reply to Caleb Butler's History of the Ecclesiastical Affairs of Pepperell.
Andrews, Ebenezer Baldwin, 1821-1880. 1493, 56923-(56924), 56926
Andrews, Ebenezer T. 95449-95451 see also Andrews & Company. firm publishers Thomas and Andrews. firm booksellers Thomas, Andrews & Penniman. firm booksellers
Andrews, Edward Wigglesworth, d. 1825. 1494
Andrews, Elisha. 1495
Andrews, Erastus. (1496)
Andrews, Ethan Allen, 1787-1858. 1497, 69353
Andrews, Ethan Allen, 1859- 85072
Andrews, Ferdinand. publisher 89136
Andrews, George. 87746-87751, 87753-87754, 87760, 87763
Andrews, Israel D. 1498
Andrews, Israel Ward, 1815-1888. 1499
Andrews, J. engr. 84352, 84359, 89664
Andrews, James D. ed. 104632
Andrews, John. engr. 79332
Andrews, John, 1736-1809. 1500-1501, 32227
Andrews, John, 1743-1822. 1502
Andrews, John, 1746-1813. 80346
Andrews, John, 1764?-1845. 1503-1507
Andrews, John L. 1508
Andrews, Joseph. 1509
Andrews, Judson B. 90900
Andrews, Lorrin, 1795-1868. 100646
Andrews, P. engr. 79332
Andrews, Rufus F. 1510
Andrews, S. P. tr. 94976
Andrews, Samuel, 1737-1818. 1511-1513
Andrews, Samuel, b. 1809. 1514
Andrews, Samuel George, 1796-1863. 1515
Andrews, Samuel M., b. 1830. defendant. (18802), 1st note after 96812
Andrews, Sidney. 1516
Andrews, T. F. reporter 49245
Andrews, W. S. 1517
Andrews, William. tr. 57488-57489
Andrews, William, of Windham. 90704
Andrews, William Loring, 1837-1920. ed. 91167-91169
Andrews, William Watson, 1810-1897. 1518- (1519), 82937, 105886
Andrews & Company. firm publishers 1520, 61466, 95451 see also Andrews, Ebenezer T.
Andrews & Co.'s stranger's guide in . . . Philadelphia. 61466
Andrews & Co's stranger's guide in the city of Boston. 1520
Andrews & Penniman. firm see Thomas, Andrews & Penniman. firm
Andrews's almanack for the year of Our Lord, 1769. 87754
Andrews's South Carolina and Georgia almanack and ephemeris. 87763
Andriaensz. van Ulissinghen, Pieter. see Ulissinghen, Pieter Andriaensz van.
Andrieux, ------. illus. 92536
Andrieux, Francois Guillaume Jean Stanislas, 1759-1833. 17876
Andros, Sir Edmund, 1637-1713. 1523, (45953) see also Massachusetts (Colony) Governor, 1687-1689 (Andros)
Andros, Richard Salter Stoors, 1817-1868. 1524-1525
Andros, Thomas, 1759-1845. (1526)-1527, 51574

Andros, Thomas, 1759-1845. supposed author 92834
Andros tracts. 9708, (46637), 46642, 46689, 46709, 46712, 46723-46725, 46731-46732, (46749), 46756, 52598, 52611, (65323), 1st note after 65324, 65646, note after 90346, 80621, 92350, 103755, 104068
Androvicini Melisone. pseud. Secchia poema eroicomico. see Tassoni, Alessandro.
Andrus, Albert. 1528-1529
Andrus, Judson B. see Andrews, Judson B.
Andueza, D. J. M. de. 1530
Andy's trip to the west. 41721, 86183, 2d note after 94082
Ane parliamente. 105937
Ane poemme. 105937
Ane songe. 105937
Aneages mas comunes en America. 47848
Anecdota de la Havana. (29415)
Anecdota historica del siglo XVII. (16974)
Anecdota importante. 74637
Anecdotas do ministerio do Marquez de Pombal. 63910
Anecdote coloniale. 62676, (62678)
Anecdote du nouveau monde. 62677
Anecdotes Americaines. 33039
Anecdotes [and] copious notes. 10018
Anecdotes and illustrations. 82424
Anecdotes and incidents. 11533
Anecdotes and letters of Zachary Taylor. 58025, note after 95665
Anecdotes and memories. 6121
Anecdotes and personal reminiscences. 68049
Anecdotes Anglaises et Americaines. 1531, (38878)
Anecdotes by Phazma. 84237
Anecdotes curieuses. 5946
Anecdotes du ministere de Sebastien-Joseph Carvalho. (63909)
Anecdotes for our soldiers. 88043A
Anecdotes for the family. 81549
Anecdotes for the young. 82425
Anecdotes, historical and literary. (1532)
Anecdotes illustrative of the character of ministers. 4399, (13638)
Anecdotes, incidents, and sketches. (74538)
Anecdotes inedites. 93988
Anecdotes of Africans. 81849
Anecdotes of an enterprise. 35129
Anecdotes of eminent persons. 104609
Anecdotes of gamblers. 102463
Anecdotes of Harper's Ferrians. (36667)
Anecdotes of missionary worthies. 50515
Anecdotes of painting in England. 82823
Anecdotes of the American Indians. (5780), (34604)
Anecdotes of the American revolution. 1533
Anecdotes of the American revolution, illustrative of the talents and virtues of the heroes and patriots. 26598
Anecdotes of the American revolution, illustrative of the talents and virtues of the heroes of the revolution. 26599
Anecdotes of the late American and present French war. 14208
Anecdotes of the late Charles Lee. 38902
Anecdotes of the late Lieut.-Gov. Villettes. 7013
Anecdotes of the life of the Right Hon. William Pitt. 949, 63081
Anecdotes of the Reverend Andrew and John Eliot. 6660
Anecdotes of the revolutionary war in America. (26597)
Anecdotes, poetry and incidents of the war. (50355)
Anecdotes; political, historical, and miscellaneous. (5507)

Anecdotes secretes sur la revolution du 18 Fructidor. (1534), (27337)
Anecdotes secretes sur le 18 Fructidor et nouveaux memoires. 29157, 67625
Anecdotes sur les Indiens de l'Amerique du Nord. 1535
Anecdotial, personal, and descriptive sketches. (32740), (38848)
Anegada Island and reef. note after 77796
Anelay, H. illus. 92487-92488, 92572
Anent the North American continent. 1535A
Anent the United States. 1535B
Anexo Num. 2 a la memoria del Ministerio de Relaciones. (73028)
Anexos a la memoria del Ministerio de Relaciones Exteriores. 8996, 38988
Anfichter von Louisiana. 7178
Anfugung des Tagbuchs eines die Durchfahrt zwischen Gronland und Amerika. 25997, 38974, note after 100853
Angabe der indianischen Volkerstamme. 34359
Angakordlo palasimik napitsivdlune agssortuissok. (22886), 63723
Ange des prairies. 70331
Angekok. (22866)
Angel, Antonio de Barroetta y. see Barroetta y Angel, Antonio de.
Angel, Gaspar de los Reyes. see Reyes Angel, Gaspar de los.
Angel, Joseph Kinnikut, 1794-1857. 1543, 70537
Angel, Joseph Kinnikut, 1794-1857. reporter 70696
Angel, Myron. 2429
Angel, William G., 1790-1858. 1536
Angel of Bethesda. (46223)
Angel of the battle-field. 7291
Angel of the little ones. 46228
Angel of the waters. 46228
Angel voices. (71275)
Angelic ministrations. 62772
Angelical life. 79955-79957
Angelini, Batista. pseud. Letters. see Shebbeare, John, 1708-1778.
Angelis, Pedro de, 1784-1859. 984, 1537-1542, (2535), 3371, 9811, (11677), 23788, 60843, 67347, 68385, 69228, 73211, 87305-87306, 94272, 96247, 96547, 96556, 97447, 97742, 99399, 99515-99517, 99665-99666, 106365
Angell, Pardon. 84974
Angelo, C. Aubrey. 1544
Angelo, Jacopo d'. tr. 66469-(66478), 66481-(66482)
Angelographia. 46630
Angeloni, Batista. pseud. Letters. see Shebbeare, John, 1709-1778.
Angeloni, Batista. pseud. Select letters. see Shebbeare, John, 1709-1788.
Angels' address. 35706
Angels of the churches. 12210
Angels' salutation to the shepherds. 64798
Angenehme opfer . . . Johann Bunian. 62849
Angenehmer Geruch der Rosen und Lilien Die im Thal der Demuth unter den Dornen Hervor gewachsen alles aus der Bruderlichen Gesellschafft in Bethania. 1546
Angenehmer Geruch der Rosen und Lilien Die im Thal der Demuth unter den Dornen Hervor gewachsen alles aus der Schwesterlichen Gesellschaft in Saron. 1545
Angers, Francois Real, d. 1860. 10495, 34041, 69661, 70360

Anghiera, Pietro Martire d', 1455-1526. 1547-1565, 4798, 8150, 16947-16949, 16957, (27689), 29600, 32018, 34100-34107, (34715), (36789), 40995, 44983, (45009)-45013, 57994, 62803, 67740, 1st-3d notes after 93588, note after 99383C, 2d note after 102836, 102837, 2d note after 104134, 106294, 106330-106331
Angiadelo, Jean Marie. see Angiolello, Giouanmaria.
Angier, Ames. 1566
Angier, John. 1567
Angier, Joseph. 1569
Angier, Samuel. defendant (41559), 95666
Angina exantematica de Mexico. 14143
Angiolello, Giouanmaria. incorrectly supposed author (50054), 99379
Anglais en Amerique. 11742
Angle-Canadian. pseud. Notes. see Smyth, David William.
Anglerius. see Anghiera, Pietro Martire d', 1455-1526.
Angles y Gortari, Mathias de. 10803
Anglesey, Richard Annesley, 6th Earl of, 1694-1761. defendant 1602, 63222
Angleterre, Etats-Unis d'Amerique, et France. 34061
Angliara, Johan von. see Anghiera, Pietro Martire d', 1455-1526.
Angliara, Juan de. see Anghiera, Pietro Martire d', 1455-1526.
Anglicano, Jacobus. see Annesley, James, 1715-1760.
Anglicus, Civis. pseud. see Civis Anglicus. pseud.
Angling Club, Cincinnati. see Cincinnati Angling Club.
Anglivel de la Beaumelle, Victor Laurent Suzanne Moise. 1570, (76324)
Anglo-African magazine. (81850)
Anglo-American. pseud. The national crisis. 1573
Anglo-American. 84984
Anglo-American. A journal of literature. 59131
Anglo-American Beneficial Society, Philadelphia. 61467
Anglo-American Church Emigrants' Aid Society. 1571
Anglo-American copyright. 83876
Anglo-American journal of literature, science, art. 28477
Anglo-American literature and manners. 12219
Anglo-American magazine for 1844. 70327
Anglo-American magazine. July 1852 to Dec. 1855. 1572, 2356
Anglo-American of several years' residence. pseud. Letters from the United States of America. 40600
Anglo-American; or, memoirs of Capt. Henry Gardiner. 26616
Anglo-American Sabbath. 77493
Anglo-American sympathy with continental reform. 61060
Anglo-amerikanische Sonntag. 77492
Anglo-Brazilian times. 7512
Anglo Britannoae. pseud. Herwologia Anglica. see Holland, Henry.
Anglo-Californian. pseud. National crisis. 1573, 51969
Anglo-Canadian. pseud. Ten letters. see Townley, Adam.
Anglo-Columbian. pseud. Columbia in 1826. 14569
Anglo-French intervention in the River Plate. 61344

Anglo-Irishman. pseud. Some thoughts.
86776
Anglo-Mexican Mining Association. Directors.
48277, 69855
Anglo-Saxon colonies. 92348
Anglo Saxons; their origin. 1386
Anglois. pseud. Fragment de Xenophon. see
Brizard, Gabriel.
Anglois. pseud. Lettre. 40670
Anglois, Creanciers des Habitans de Tabago.
petitioners see Francklyn, Gilbert.
petitioner and Tod, William. petitioner
Anglus. pseud. Series of letters. 99774
Angola (Colony) Laws, statutes, etc. 7619
Anguiano, Mateo. 1574, 66579
Anguis flagellatus. 40197, 103655, 105650
Angus, John. defendant 60180
Anhang aus der in dem Jahren 1740 bis 1744.
25929
Anhang beygefuget von dem erstaunens-
wurdigen Schiff-brucht. 8547, (9501),
(20827)
Anhang Chr. Arnolds und zahlreichen Kupfren.
73320
Anhang desz neundten Theils Americae. (8784)
Anhang: Die vereinigten Staaten und das
Seekriegsrecht. 37901
Anhang I. Nachricht von den Sprachen der
Volker. 51480, (51482), 98777
Anhang om Tiids-Regningen i dem gamle
Nordiske Historie. (77809)
Anhang uber Brasilien. 7929, 89763, 91304
Anhang uber versteinerte Holzer der arctischen
Zone. (31229)
Anhang von dem Wegnehmen der englischen
Schiffe. 52383
Anhang von William Flemmings Trubsalen.
20016
Anhang zu Doctor Price's Schrift. 69549
Anhang II. Des Herrn P. Anselm Eckart.
51480, (51482), 98777
Anhang zwoer Reisen. (1575)
Anhange. 78695
Anhange uber die Entdeckung von Neuholland.
98025
Anhange, vieler denckwardigkeiten. 6441, 7407,
note after 98470
Anhange von . . . Amerika. 11656
Anhange von der Nordlichen Polarlanden. 3987
Anhange von noch ungedruckten Briefen und
Berichten. (69369)
Anhange, welcher eine Geschichte des
Ursprunges und des Fortganges. (74384)
Anharenda. Indian chief. 628, 66062 see also
Three Maquas Castles Indians. Sachems.
Aniceto de Lara, Mariano. see Lara, Mariano
Aniceto de.
Anicetus. pseud. The cannonade. see Clark,
W. A.
Anicetus. pseud. Our modern Athens. see
Clark, W. A.
Anichinabek amisinahikaniwa, kicheanameatchik.
19315
Anichinabek amisinahikaniwa, the Indian book.
34605
Anichinabek amisinaki-kaniwa. 19317, 34605
Animadversions contained in the prefatory
remarks. (32305), 99815
Animadversions of an hour. 101127
Animadversions of Secretary Stanton and
General Halleck. 80414
Animadversions on a book called A plea for
non-scriblers. 22093
Animadversions on a late publication. 102752
Animadversions on a pamphlet entitled
"Thoughts on the examination and trials
of candidates for the sacred ministry."
5746

Animadversions on a pamphlet . . . published by
. . . J. Brooks. 96507
Animadversions on a reply to a letter. 1576
Animadversions on an article in the "New York
evangelist." 80493
Animadversions on certain remarks on the first
edition. 84106
Animadversions on Mr. Crosswell's sermon.
17671
Animadversions on Mr. Hart's late dialogue.
32955
Animadversions on Mr. Ilmstone's epistle.
17051
Animadversions on sundry flagrant untruths.
71409
Animadversions on the Albany quarterly. 91688
Animadversions on the doctrines and pretentions
of the Latter-Day Saints. 79628
Animadversions on the past and present state
of public affairs. 63818, 67815
Animadversions on the proceedings of the
Regents. 2087
Animadversions on the reasons of Mr. Alexander
Creaghead's receding from the judicatures
of this church. (5753)
Animadversions on the Rev. Mr. Croswell's
late letter. (17905)
Animadversions on "The substance of two
sermons." 92887
Animadversions to G. K.'s answer to his own
queries. 24278
Animadversions upon, and refutations of sundry
gross errors. 82289
Animadversions upon some late arguments.
23895, (26248)
Animadversions upon the Antisynodalia Americana.
920, 66059
Animadversions upon . . . [T. Walker's] Essay
upon that paradox. 12362
Animadversory address to the inhabitants. 791,
1st note after 99000
Animal and vegetable products of America.
(71911)
Animal kingdom. 27913
Animal magnetism in New England. (59371)
Animal magnetism. Report of Benjamin
Franklin. 82987, 92135
Animales en cortes. 23607, 97045
Animalia Mexicana descriptionibus. (31515)-31516
Animals desired for the National Zoological
Park. 85001
Animals of North America. 82195-82196
Animaux articules a pieds articules. 29110,
74922
Aningait & Ajutt: a Greenland tale. 36295A,
60793
Anishinabe enuet anikunotabiung. 56723
Anitsalagi tsunalenvtodi tsu adeloquasdi. 12448
Aniversario de la entrada de los restos del
inmortal Bolivar. 99492
Aniversario de la Sociedad Literaria de Buenos
Aires. 8995
Aniversario de su glorioso grito en 16 de
Setiembre de 1826. 99680
Aniversario del primer grito de independencia.
(34445)
Aniversario del primer grito de nuestra
independencia. 95874
Anketell, John. 105980, 105985
Anklage-Acte gegen Stephen A. Douglas. 78022
Ankunft der Deutschen aus Amerika. (42725)
Anleihen in Frankreich, England und Northamerika.
4789
Anleitung: welcher Gestalt die Einzeichnung zu
der newen Suder Compagnie. 98196
Anmaerkninger over de tre forste Boger af Hr.
David Crantze. 17420

Anmerckungen uber ein ohnlangst
  herausgekommenes Protestations-Schreiben.
  25576-25577, (59888), 84587
Anmerkungen begleitet von Dieterich Tiedemann.
  (17502), 69136
Anmerkungen herausgegeben von Matthias
  Christ. Sprengel. 7929, 91304
Anmerkungen uber den Theil von Cap. Cooks
  Reise-relation. 22567
Anmerkungen uber die Abschaffung des
  Sclavenhandels. 32547
Anmerkungen uber die Natur der burgerlichen
  Freyheit. 65454, 69549
Anmerkungen uber die vornehmsten Acten
  des dreyzehnten Parlements von
  Groszbritannien. 41285, 69549
Anmerkungen uber eine neuliche Protestation.
  (66215), 84586
Anmerkungen uber Nord-Amerika. 107, 102647
Anmerkungen und Vorword von F. A. Ruder.
  73892, 101301
Anmerkungen und Zusatzen durch E. A. W. von
  Zimmerman. 59760
Anmerkungen und Zusatzen von J. C. Adelung.
  8389
Anmerkungen vermehret von Friedrich Eberhard
  Rambach. 90027
Anmerkungen von Fr. Dieffenbach. 18650
Anmerkungen von J. R. Foster. 8033
Anmerkungen zum ersten Theile. 97689
Ann (Ship) in Admiralty. 23532, 39925, 1st
  note after 87356, note after 87824, note
  after 96924
Ann and Good. (Ship) see Ann (Ship) in
  Admiralty
Ann Arbor, Mich. Convention, 1836. see
  Michigan (Territory) Convention, Ann
  Arbor, 1836.
Ann Arbor, Mich. Young Men's State Tem-
  perance Convention, 1836. see Young
  Men's State Temperance Convention, Ann
  Arbor, Mich., 1836.
Ann Arbor, Mich. Memorial Proceedings in
  Honor of Abraham Lincoln, 1865. 41215
Ann Arbor, Mich. Nineteenth Annual Con-
  ference of the Methodist Episcopal Church
  in Michigan, 1854. see Methodist
  Episcopal Church. Michigan. Annual
  Conference, 19th, Ann Arbor, 1854.
Ann Arbor journal. 78501
Anna, --------. 1577
Anna, Antonio Lopez de Santa. see Santa
  Anna, Antonio Lopez de, Pres. Mexico,
  1795-1876.
Anna, Joaquim de Sancta. see Sancta Anna,
  Joaquim de.
Anna, Jose Manuel de Castro Santa. see
  Castro Santa Anna, Jose Manuel de.
Anna Esbarra, Joaquim Jose de Sancta. see
  Esbarra, Joaquim Jose de Sancta Anna.
Annaes da Bibliotheca Nacional do Rio de
  Janeiro. 74029
Annaes da Capitania de S. Pedro. 62952
Annaes da marinha Portugueza. (67342)
Annaes da Provincia de S. Pedro. 40118,
  62953
Annaes do Rio do Janeiro. 41410
Annaes ecclesiasticos. 43300
Annaes Fluminenses de sciencias, artes e
  litteratura. 98828
Annaes maritimos e coloniaes. 1577A
Annaeus, Teucrius. tr. (8784)
Annalen der Erd- Volker- und Staatenkunde.
  4857A
Annalen der Verbreitung des Glaubens. 1579A
Annaler for Nordsk oldkyndighed. 28659
Annales Canadiennes. 5150

Annales d'Afrique. 96345
Annales d'agriculture. 101347
Annales de Curita. 38949
Annales d'Espagne et de Portugal. 14541
Annales d'horticulture et de botanique. 1580
Annales de la Academia de la Historia, Madrid.
  51347
Annales de la monarqvia de Espana. (59587)
Annales de la revolucion. 60900
Annales de la Societe d'Agriculture et d'Economie
  Politique a la Martinique. 44971
Annales de la societe des soi-disans Jesuites.
  26806
Annales de la Societe Entomologique de France.
  (6154)
Annales de la temperance. 39217, 50239
Annales de la Universidad de Chile. 12741
Annales de la vertu. (81024)-81025
Annales de l'Association de la Propagation de
  la Foi. 1578
Annales de philosophie Chretienne. 1582,
  (12019)-(12020)
Annales des choses . . . sous le regne
  d'Elizabeth. 10159
Annales des sciences naturelles. 5901
Annales des voyages. 27788, 31802, 56093,
  94228
Annales des voyages, de la geographie, de
  l'histoire et de l'archeologie. 44167
Annales des voyages, de la geographie et de
  l'histoire. (44156)-44157
Annales de l'histoire de l'institution. 1581
Annales d'hygiene publique. 6853
Annales du Cabinet de Lecture de Montreal.
  73520
Annales du commerce exterieur. (48278)
Annales du Conseil Souverain de la Martinique.
  19735
Annales du Museum d'Histoire Naturelle. 1583
Annales ecclesiastiqves et politiqves de l'ancien.
  12294
Annales eclesiasticos, y secvlares de la mvy
  noble y mvy leal civdad de Sevilla.
  57716-57717
Annales et historiae de rebus Belgicus. 28956
Annales generales des sciences physiques.
  67458
Annales historiques de la revolution. 10087,
  10091
Annales historiques du College de l'Assomption.
  18506
Annales hydrographiques. 6836, 46972
Annales maritimes. 3583, 86355
Annales maritimes et coloniales. 1584
Annales maritimes et coloniales ou recueil de
  lois et ordonnances royales. 1585, 11503,
  42504, 47535, (68447), 70357
Annales medicales del Peru. 7397
Annales, or the historie of . . . Elizabeth. 10158
Annales patriotiques de St. Domingue. 75049
Annales philosophiques, politiques, et literaires.
  1586
Annales politiques, civiles et litteraires du 18me
  siecle. 9267, 41332, 69717
Annales religieuses de Roma. (24703)
Annales rervm Anglicarvm, et Hibernicarvm.
  10157-10158
Annales scientifiques d'Auvergne. (1587)
Annales statistiques des Etats-Unis. 79632
Annali di Genova, de secolo sedicesimo. 11341
Annals. 74144
Annals and occurrences of New York city and
  state. 102141
Annals and recollections of Oneida County.
  (36596)
Annals: comprising memoirs, incidents, and
  statistics. 50642

Annals, &c. published in 1753. 89126
Annals of a western missionary. 1588
Annals of America. (32578)
Annals of Amherst College. 1316
Annals of Administration. 1589, (26993)
Annals of Albany. (51357), 51359, (51365)
Annals of Alexander Hamilton Post No. 182.
  84423
Annals of Annapolis. (71282)
Annals of Baltimore. 28827
Annals of Barnstable County. (25760)
Annals of Binghamton. 104024
Annals of blood. (13874)
Annals of Boston. 7043
Annals of British legislation. 40752
Annals of Chicago. 2928
Annals of commerce. 43626
Annals of Congress. 1229, 4783, 84822,
  84835
Annals of deceased preachers. 84756, 84756A
Annals of early Moravian settlement. 68992
Annals of Europe for 1739. 1590
Annals of George the Third. (28564)
Annals of Great Britain. 10267
Annals of Harper's Ferry. (36667)
Annals of historical and natural sciences.
  67452
Annals of industry and genius. 7978
Annals of Iowa. 34973, 83725, 83882
Annals of Jamaica. 7820
Annals of Kentucky. (67442)
Annals of liberty, generousity, public spirit,
  &c. 1591, 10889
Annals of Louisiana. (25854)
Annals of Luzerne County. 59434
Annals of medicine, natural history, agriculture,
  and the arts. 33083
Annals of medicine, natural history and the
  arts. (62562)
Annals of Melrose. 28056
Annals of methodism. 68036-68037
Annals of nature. 67444, (67448)
Annals of New-England. 28020, 65585
Annals of Newberry. 57330
Annals of Newtown, in Queens County, New-
  York. (71386)
Annals of Pennsylvania. (31102)
Annals of Philadelphia. 102140-102141
Annals of Philadelphia and Pennsylvania.
  102140
Annals of philosophy. 48985
Annals of Phoenixville and its vicinity. 60796
Annals of pioneer settlers. 71159
Annals of Portsmouth. 337
Annals of public education. 64931
Annals of Salem. 24029
Annals of Salem, from its first settlement.
  24028
Annals of San Francisco. 87268
Annals of southern methodism. 19230
Annals of Tennessee. 67729
Annals of the American Academy of Political
  and Social Science. 83368, 83383, 84514
Annals of the American Associate pulpit.
  89730
Annals of the American Associate Reformed
  pulpit. 89730
Annals of the American Baptist pulpit. 89730
Annals of the American Episcopal pulpit.
  89730
Annals of the American Lutheran pulpit. 89730
Annals of the American Methodist pulpit.
  89730
Annals of the American Presbyterian pulpit.
  89730
Annals of the American pulpit. 70950, 78581,
  84062, 84620, 85439, 85443, 89730

Annals of the American Reformed Dutch pulpit.
  89730
Annals of the American Reformed Presbyterian
  pulpit. 89730
Annals of the American revolution. 1592, 50927
Annals of the American . . . turf. 54857
Annals of the American Unitarian pulpit. 89730
Annals of the Army of the Cumberland. (24567),
  24585-24586
Annals of the Astronomical Observatory of
  Harvard College. 30725
Annals of the Baptist Churches in New-Hamp-
  shire. 17920
Annals of the church in Brimfield. 50921
Annals of the Cincinnati Historical Society.
  13062
Annals of the city of Kansas. 88862
Annals of the city of Trenton. 30872
Annals of the Classis of Bergen. 94442
Annals of the coinage of Britain. 73897-73898
Annals of the colonial church. 1593
Annals of the Congress of the United States.
  15519
Annals of the corporation, relative to the late
  contested elections. 12373, 42881
Annals of the Diocese of Toronto [and] Quebec.
  30951
Annals of the Dudley Observatory. 21095
Annals of the Empire City. 54085
Annals of the Hebrew race. 85154
Annals of the Housatonic. 89148
Annals of the industry of the United States.
  5606
Annals of the Lyceum of Natural History of
  New York. 6267, (54365), 84126-84127,
  89984
Annals of the Massachusetts Charitable Mechanic
  Association. 8904
Annals of the Minnesota Historical Society.
  (49264), (49274), 85433
Annales of the Minnestoa Historical Society:
  1852, containing the annual address. 81351
Annals of the Missouri Conference. 42937
Annals of the Missouri Historical and Philo-
  sophical Society. 49616
Annals of the New York Academy of Science.
  84536
Annals of the New York stage from A. D. 1798
  to A. D. 1848. (18231), 35057
Annals of the New-York stage, from 1798 to
  1848. 24310
Annals of the . . . Observatory [of Harvard
  University.] 6288
Annals of the Propagation of the Faith. (1579)
Annals of the Protestant Episcopal Church of
  the Evangelists, Southwark, Philadelphia.
  62103
Annals of the reign of King George the Third.
  539
Annals of the revolution. 8243
Annals of the Sixth Pennsylvania Cavalry.
  (28188)
Annals of the State Historical Society of Iowa.
  (34972)
Annals of the Swedes on the Delaware. (13570)
Annals of the town of Concord. 23818, 50392
Annals of the town of Dorchester. 5777
Annals of the town of Hillsborough. 82398
Annals of the town of Keene. 29660
Annals of the town of Providence. 70719, 90475
Annals of the town of Warren. (21713)
Annals of the troubles in the Netherlands.
  (72991)
Annals of the United States. 25056
Annals of the United States Christian Com-
  mission. 51091
Annals of the wars of the eighteenth century.
  18145

Annals of the wars of the nineteenth century.
18146
Annals of the west. (585), 60954-60955
Annals of the Zoological Society, London.
78148
Annals of Tyron County. 10275-10276
Annals of virtue. 26952, 81027
Annales of virtue, a selection. 35681
Annals of witchcraft in New England. 20867
Annals of Yale College, from its foundation.
2882
Annals of Yale College, in New Haven. 2881,
(2883), 2d note after 97444
Annals or history of Yale-College. (13212),
105760
Annand, Alexander. defendant 6326, 1st note
after 96956, 1st note after 97284
Annand, William. ed. (33315)
Annandale, N. Y. St. Stephen's College. see
Columbia University. St. Stephen's
College, Annandale, N. Y.
Annapolis, Md. Constitutional Convention,
1850-1851. see Maryland. Constitutional
Convention, Annapolis, 1850-1851.
Annapolis, Md. Constitutional Convention,
1864. see Maryland. Constitutional
Convention, Annapolis, 1864.
Annapolis, Md. Convention, 1774. see
Maryland (Colony) Convention, Annapolis,
1774.
Annapolis, Md. Convention, 1774-1775. see
Maryland (Colony) Convention, Annapolis,
1774-1775.
Annapolis, Md. Convention, 1775. see
Maryland (Colony) Convention, Annapolis,
1775.
Annapolis, Md. Convention, 1776. see
Maryland (Colony) Convention, Annapolis,
1776.
Annapolis, Md. Dinner given to the Hon.
Daniel Webster by the Reform Convention
of Maryland, 1851. see Maryland.
Constitutional Convention, Annapolis,
1850-1851. Webster Dinner, 1851.
Annapolis, Md. Freedmen's Convention, 1864.
see Freedmen's Convention, Annapolis,
1864.
Annapolis, Md. Reform Convention, 1850-1851.
see Maryland. Constitutional Convention,
Annapolis, 1850-1851.
Annapolis, Md. St. John's College. see
St. John's College, Annapolis, Md.
Annapolis, Md. United States Naval Institute.
see United States Naval Institute,
Annapolis, Md.
Annapolis and Elkridge Rail Road Company.
1595
Annapolis considered as a suitable situation.
33577
Annapolis-Royal. 99539
Anne, Queen Consort of James I, King of Great
Britain. spirit author 78374-78375,
100799
Anne, Queen of Great Britain, 1665-1714.
10972, 39527, 87805, 89425, 96537-96538,
96541 see also Great Britain. Sover-
eigns, etc., 1702-1714 (Anne)
Annee de sejour a Londres. 73377
Anneke, Fritz. 1597
Anneke, Mathilde Franziska. (1598)
Anneke Jans and Trinity Church. 35765, 5th
note after 96979
Anner' lab innungorsimasub parinek 'arneranik.
73900
Annerch ir Cymru. (66607)
Annesley, James, 1715-1760. 1599-1601, 1603
Annesley, James, 1715-1760. plaintiff 1602,
63222

Annesley, Richard, 1694-1761. see Anglesey,
Richard Annesley, 6th Earl of, 1694-1761.
Annesley, William. 93516
Annet, Peter. 1604, 85685
Annexation of Cuba. 7100
Annexation of Louisiana. 102017
Annexation of Roxbury and Boston. Argument on
behalf of the remonstrants. 2481
Annexation of Roxbury and Boston. Remonstrance
of Bostonians against the measure. (50626)
Annexation of San Domingo. (75050)
Annexation of San Domingo. Speech of Hon.
Carl Schurz. 78023
Annexation of Texas. 14775, note after 95065
Annexation of Texas, a case of war. 98141
Annexation of Texas. A sermon. (13409)
Annexation of Texas and seperation of the
United States. 95068
Annexation of Texas. By Justin H. Smith.
83466, 83470
Annexation of Texas. By the editor [i. e. B. B.
Minor.] 95066
Annexation of Texas. Opinions of Messrs. Clay,
Polk, Benton & Van Buren. 95067
Annexation of Texas—the war on Texas by Henry
Clay. 95128
Annexation question. 30465
Annexation to the United States. 56112
Annexed address of the Legislative Assembly.
10538
Annexed addressed [sic] of the Legislative
Assembly. 10538, 10611
Annexed remarks and estimates. 101501
Annexed result of an ecclesiastical council.
25038
Annexes. 3308
Annexion du Texas; emancipation des noirs.
(36415)
Annexion du Texas, l'Oregon. 36416
Annexo ao relatorio do Ministerio dos Negocios
Estrangeiros. 85648
Annexos do relatorio apresentado a Assemblea
Legislativa Provincial. 85620
Annie Grayson. 39136
Annie Nelles. 52304
Annin, W. B. engr. 93996
Anningait and Ajutt, a Greenland tale. 36295A,
60793
Anniversaries of Strafford County. 92668
Anniversary address . . . at the Lyceum. 56810
Anniversary address . . . before the Alumni
Association. (46947)
Anniversary address, before the American
Institute, New York, . . . on the 16th
. . . of October, 1851. 35401
Anniversary address before the American
Institute of the City of New-York, at the
Broadway Tabernacle. 93118
Anniversary address before the American
Institute of the City of New York, . . .
October 20, 1842. 14262
Anniversary address before the American
Institute of the City of New-York . . .
October 28th, 1856. (2588)
Anniversary address . . . before the American
Institute . . . 20th October, 1843. 3454
Anniversary address before the American
Unitarian Association. 19862
Anniversary address before the Association of
American Geologists. 32250
Anniversary address before the Franklin Society.
(82172)
Anniversary address before the Mount Holyoke
Female Seminary. 32250
Anniversary address [before the Protestant
Episcopal Society, For the Advancement
of Christianity in South-Carolina.]
87933

Anniversary address, . . . before the Theological Society. 58625

Anniversary address, delivered before the American Institute of the City of New York, . . . October 17, 1845. 22175

Anniversary address, delivered before the Columbian Institute. 88243

Anniversary address, delivered before the Federal gentlemen. 102256

Anniversary address delivered before the Historical Society of New Mexico. 4660

Anniversary address delivered before the St. Nicholas Society of New-York, December 3d, 1850. 5098

Anniversary address delivered before the St. Nicholas Society of the City of New York, Dec. 1st, 1848. (21114)

Anniversary address delivered before the Southern Central Agricultural Society. 93613

Anniversary address, delivered by William J. Stevenson. 91615

Anniversary address, delivered to the First Regiment. 101040

Anniversary address . . . February 1st, 1814. 72477

Anniversary address . . . February 7, 1815. 72477

Anniversary address, New York, Season of Bloom. 72889

Anniversary address on the progress of the natural sciences. 19319

Anniversary address to the . . . graduates. (58348)

Anniversary address to the New York Medical and Surgical Society. 91678

Anniversary addresses of the priests and people. 66673

Anniversary and farewell sermon. 25184

Anniversary and historical discourse. (67858)

Anniversary celebration of the Christ Church Parish School Association. 54179

Anniversary Celebration of the Landing of the Pilgrims, St. Louis, 1845. see St. Louis. Anniversary Celebration of the Landing of the Pilgrims, 1845.

Anniversary discourse. (17406)

Anniversary discourse before the New-York Academy of Medicine. 25448

Anniversary discourse, before the New-York Academy of Medicine, delivered in the chapel of the University. 83358

Anniversary discourse before the New York Academy of Medicine, Nov. 8, 1848. 44301

Anniversary discourse before the Philadelphia Forum. 31993

Anniversary discourse, . . . before the Society for the Education of Orphan Children. 59565

Anniversary discourse, delivered at Dudley, Massachusetts. 3939

Anniversary discourse, delivered before the Albany Institute. 9608

Anniversary discourse delivered before the Columbian Institute. 102118

Anniversary discourse, delivered before the Historical Society of New-York. (75947)

Anniversary discourse, delivered before the Lyceum of Natural History of New-York. 96391

Anniversary discourse, delivered before the New-York Historical Society, December 7, 1818. 99265

Anniversary discourse, delivered before the New-York Historical Society, December 6, 1828. (37472)

Anniversary discourse delivered before the New York Historical Society, December 6th, 1828. 54469

Anniversary discourse, delivered before the New-York Historical Society . . . Dec. 13, 1837. (6037)

Anniversary discourse, delivered before the New York Historical Society, (November 17, 1857). (25446)

Anniversary discourse, delivered before the New-York Historical Society, on Thursday, December 28, 1820. 103152

Anniversary discourse delivered before the St. Nicolas Society of Manhattan. 32390

Anniversary discourse, delivered in . . . New Haven. (4130)

Anniversary discourse, delivered in St. Thomas' Church. 4129A

Anniversary discourse for 1826, delivered in the chapel of the University. 82921

Anniversary discourse, . . . November 19, 1847. 9610

Anniversary discourse occasioned by the death of four children. 64212

Anniversary discourse, on the state and prospects of the Western Museum Society. 20818

Anniversary discourse, pronounced before the New York Horticultural Society. 77981

Anniversary Dudleian-Lecture. 103907

Anniversary . . . 1815 [of the Hudson River Baptist Association.] 33531

Anniversary exercises at the parsonage. 35533

Anniversary Festival of the Mitchell Family, South Britain, Conn., 1858. see Mitchell Family Festival, South Britain, Conn., 1858.

Anniversary lecture; . . . Nov. 27, 1810. (49136)

Anniversary lecture, pronounced before the Historical Society of the County of Vigo, Indiana. 17582

Anniversary ode, by Rev. Brother Harris. 101870

Anniversary of the Home for Jewish Widows and Orphans of New Orleans. 53329

Anniversary of the Hudson River Baptist Association North. 33552

Anniversary of the Massachusetts Temperance Society. Annual address. 101514

Anniversary of Washington's birthday. 90379

Anniversary oration at the Buckeye Celebration. (68172)

Anniversary oration before the Corporate Society of the California Pioneer Association. 32270

Anniversary oration. . . . before the faculty and students. 55083

Anniversary oration . . . before the Federal Republicans of Hallowell. 60981

Anniversary oration before the New Jersey State Society. 20391

Anniversary oration before the New Jersey State Society of the Cincinnati. 86114

Anniversary oration before the New-York Academy of Medicine. 64452

Anniversary oration . . . before the Tammany Society. 49745

Anniversary oration, by Dr. J. P. Barratt. 88017

Anniversary oration . . . Charlestown, July 5, 1819. 27562

Anniversary oration; delivered before the Philokrisean Society. 91673

Anniversary oration delivered before the South Carolina Medical Association. 14161

Anniversary oration; delivered by the Hon. William Harper. 30446, 88041

Anniversary oration, delivered May 21, [1782.]
6286
Anniversary oration of the Cincinnati of New
Jersey. 86115
Anniversary oration of the Demosthenian
Society. 89245
Anniversary oration of the Philadelphia
Philological Society. 82750
Anniversary oration on the subject of quarentines.
9899
Anniversary oration, pronounced before the
Society of Artists of the United States.
(39220), 86005
Anniversary oration, . . . 13th of April 1836.
56821
Anniversary poem, delivered before the
Mechanic Apprentices' Library Associ-
ation. 16372
Anniversary poem, . . . Mercantile Library
Association of Boston. 24301
Anniversary poem pronounced before the
Philhermenian Society. 28582
Anniversary poem recited before the Young
Men's Mercantile Library Association of
Cincinnati. 68179
Anniversary report of the Directors of the
. . . [Young Men's Auxiliary Education
Society of the City of New-York.] 106160
Anniversary report of the Managers of the
Pennsylvania Society for Discouraging
the Use of Ardent Spirits. (60363)
Anniversary report of the Managers of the
. . . [Pennsylvania State Temperance]
Society for 1834. 60383
Anniversary sermon and report . . . sixteenth
anniversary [of the Church of the Advent,
Boston.] 6223
Anniversary sermon and report of Committee
of Proceedings of the Society for
Educating the Poor of Newfoundland.
8950, 54987
Anniversary sermon at Plymouth, Mass. 7213
Anniversary sermon before the Brainerd
Evangelical Society. 72192
Anniversary sermon [before the Protestant
Episcopal Association for the Promotion
of Christianity among the Jews.] (66186)
Anniversary sermon before the St. Andrew's
Society. 46853
Anniversary sermon by the Rev. Henry Budd.
8950, 54987
Anniversary sermon, Dec. 1, 1816. 47005
Anniversary sermon, delivered June 14, 1846.
24519
Anniversary sermon for Emanuel Church.
33964
Anniversary sermon, in Christ Church,
Cambridge. 32999
Anniversary sermon, preached at Plymouth,
December 22d, 1777. 102743
Anniversary sermon preached at Plymouth,
Dec. 23, 1776. 15090
Anniversary sermon, preached in St. James
Church. 85853
Anniversary sermon, presented in the Third
Congregational Church. 13589, 64304
Anniversary sermon, to the memory of . . .
G. Whitefield. 104821
Anniversary sermon . . . Winsted, Conn.,
December 5th, 1858. (9100)
Anniversary week in Bloomington. 1605
Anno millesimo septingentesimo septuagesimo
sexto. 19379
Anno regni Annae reginae. 53525
Anno regni Annae reginae Magnae Britanniae,
Franciae & Hiberniae, nono. 88171
Anno regni Annae reginae octavo. (59876)

Anno regni Georgii regis Magnae Britanniae
. . . . 53059
Anno regni Georgii regis Magnae Britanniae,
Franciae, & Hiberniae, decimo tertio.
88172
Anno regni Georgii II. . . . at a General
Assembly of the Province of Pennsylvania,
begun and holden at Philadelphia, the
fifteenth day of October, . . . 1759.
(59880)
Anno regni Georgii II. . . . at a General
Assembly of the Province of Pennsylvania,
begun and holden at Philadelphia, the
fourteenth day of October, Anno Dom.
1734. 59878
Anno regni Georgii II. . . . At a General
Assembly of the Province of Pennsylvania,
begun and holden at Philadelphia, the
fourteenth day of October, 1743. 59879
Anno regni Georgii II. Magnae Britanniae,
Franciae, & Hiberniae, tricesimo-secundo.
87593
Anno regni Georgii II. . . . octavo. 100235
Anno regni Georgii II. regis . . . . At a session
of the General Assembly of the colony of
New-York, held at . . . New-York. (53527)
Anno regni Georgii II. regis . . . . At a session
of the General Assembly of the colony of
New York, . . . in New York. 53526
Anno regni Georgii II. Regis Magna [sic]
Britanniae. 87575
Anno regni Georgii II. regis Magnae Britaniae.
[sic] 87590
Anno regni Georgii II. regis Magnae Britanniae
. . . . (53060)
Anno regni Georgii II. regis Magnae Britanniae,
Franciae, & Hiberniae, secundo. 87355
Anno regni Georgie II. regis Magnae Britanniae,
Franciae, & Hiberniae, tertius. 59877
Anno regni Georgii II. regis Magnae Britanniae,
Franciae, & Hiberniae, tricesimo. 87589
Anno regni Georgii II. regis Magnae Britanniae,
Franciae, & Hiberniae, tricesimo-primo.
87591
Anno regni Georgii II. regis Magnae Britanniae,
Franciae, & Hiberniae, tricesimo-tertio.
87595
Anno regni Georgii II. regis Magnae Britanniae,
Franciae, & Hiberniae, vicesimo-octavo.
87588
Anno regni Georgii II. regis Magnae Britanniae,
Franciae & Hiberniae, vicesimo-quinto.
87582
Anno regni Georgii II. regis Magnae Britanniae,
Franciae, & Hiberniae, vicesimo-septimo.
87585
Anno regni Georgii II. regis Magnae Britanniae,
Franciae, & Hiberniae, vicesimo sexto.
88173
Anno regni Georgii II. regis Magnae Britanniae,
Franciae & Hiberniae, vicesimo-tertio.
87577
Anno regni Georgii II. . . . vicesimo secundo.
1st note after 97845
Anno regni Georgii III. . . . At a General
Assembly of the Province of Pennsylvania.
59881
Anno regni Georgii III. Regis Magna Britanniae.
138
Anno regni Georgii III. regis Magnae Britanniae
. . . . At a session begun at Burlington.
53061
Anno regni Georgii III. regis Magnae Britanniae,
Franciae & Hiberniae, quarto. 87601
Anno regni George III. regis Magnae Britanniae,
Franciae, & Hiberniae, quinto. 1606,
90131-90133, 90135

Anno regni Georgii III. regis Magnae Britanniae, Franciae, & Hiberniae, secundo. 87598
Anno regni Georgii III. regis Magnae Britanniae, Franciae & Hiberniae, septimo. 87605
Anno regni Georgii III. regis Magnae Britanniae, Franciae & Hiberniae, sexto. 87604
Annone. see Hanno.
Annotaciones. 32492, 100643
Annotacoes do Dr. Sallustino Orlando de Aranjo Costa. 70793
Annotated bibliography of bibliographies. note before 99008
Annotated catalogue of the principal mineral species. 5801
Annotationi sopra la lettione della Sfra del Sacro-Bosco. 74810
Annotations and original documents. (10076)
Annotations historiques. 73520
Annotations upon a short account. (36054), 103591
Annotazioni posteriori alla pubblicazione. 79309
Announcement and catalogue of the Medical Department of the University of Buffalo. 9063
Announcement and catalogue of the Rush Medical College. (74279)
Announcement and circular of the Memphis Medical College. 47780
Announcement for 1873-74 [of the Southern University.] 88512
Announcement for 1866-67 [of the Southern University.] 88512
Announcement of Kentucky University, 1859. 37508
Announcement of lectures, . . . by the Trustees. 61746
Announcement of lectures, &c. &c., for . . . 1840-1. 60313
Announcement of the autumnal course of lectures. 11440
Announcement . . . of the Bellevue Hospital Medical College. 54113
Announcement of the Eclectic Medical College of . . . New York. (54256)
Announcement of the Eclectic Medical College of Pennsylvania. 60081
Announcement of the Female Medical College. 60100
Announcement of the fifty-second semi-annual session. 69641
Announcement of the . . . [Homoeopathic Medical] College. 60147
Announcement of the Independent Medical School of Pennsylvania. 60158
Announcement of the Kansas City College of Physicians and Surgeons. 37093
Announcement [of the Law Department of the University of New York.] 54708
Announcement of the Law, Literary, and Medical Departments, of the University of Nashville. 51880
Announcement of the Louisville Medical Institute. 42331
Announcement of the Medical Department of the Lind University. (41287)
Announcement of the Medical Department of the St. Louis University. 75401
Announcement of the Medical Department of the University of Iowa. 34994
Announcement of the Medical Department of the University . . . [of Nashville.] 51880
Announcement of the Medical Department, University of Buffalo. 9063
Announcement of the Medical Faculty, 1851-52. 43273
Announcement of the Medical School of Maine. 7019

Announcement of the Metropolitan Medical College. 54403
Announcement of the National Medical College. 52006
Announcement of the New York College of Dental Surgery. (54758)
Announcement of the New York Medical College for Women. (54806)
Announcement of the Pennsylvania Polytechnic College. 60531
Announcement of the Philadelphia College of Medicine. 61982
Announcement of the Polytechnic College, of . . . Pennsylvania. 60396
Announcement of the Southern Medical School. 88399
Announcement of the Wagner Free Institute of Science. 62372
Announcement. This souvenir is published in connection with the 'America' Testimonial tendered to Rev. Dr. S. F. Smith. 84062
Announcements, circulars, and catalogues. 87871
Announcements of lectures. 54710
Annua do Brasil sendo provincial. 68329, 72499
Annvae litterae Societatis Jesu anni 1581. 1607
Annuaire de la Guyane Franciase. 29158
Annuaire de la marine et des colonies. (1608)
Annuaire de la Societe des Antiquites de France. 19648
Annuaire des deux mondes. 1609
Annuaire du Comite d'Archeologie Americaine. 14953
Annuaire historique universel. 1610, 40234
Annuaire de la Ville-Marie. 39217
Annuaire des voyages et de la geographie. 1611
Annuaire oriental et Americain. 1612
Annual account of his [i. e. Eleazar Wheelock's] receipts and disbursements. 103207
Annual account of the missionary labors. 15812
Annual address and accompanying documents. 31180
Annual address at Troy, N. Y. (71891)
Annual address before the Agricultural Society of Warren County. 68170
Annual address . . . before the American Geographical and Statistical Society. 18358
Annual address . . . before the American peace Society. 49196
Annual address before the Buffalo Historical Society, Jan. 13, 1864. 9056, (33100), note after 95451
Annual address . . . before the Diagnothian and Goethean Literary Societies. (66653)
Annual address before the Euphradian and Clariosophic Societies. 65371
Annual address [before the Hartford County Peace Society.] 103166
Annual address, . . . before the Hartford Peace Society. 41378
Annual address before the Harvard Natural History Society. 31864
Annual address before the Massachusetts Medical Society. (13297)
Annual address before the Massachusetts Temperance Society. 13385
Annual address before the Medical Society of the State of New York, and the . . . legislature. 58661
Annual address . . . before the Medical Society of the State of New York, February 6, 1839. (33639)
Annual address before the Medical Society of the State of New York [1809.] 73015
Annual address . . . [before the Medical Society of the State of New York, 1810.] 73015
Annual address before the New-Jersey Historical Society. 20391

Annual address before the New-York State
Medical Society. 43595
Annual address . . . before the Public School
Teachers' Association. 17464
Annual address, . . . before the Rhode Island
Society for the Encouragement of
Domestic Industry. 63054
Annual address before the State Historical
Society of Wisconsin. 92950
Annual address before the State Historical
Society of Wisconsin, . . . January 30,
1873. 72058
Annual address before the State Historical
Society of Wisconsin, . . . January 30th,
1868. 11729
Annual address before the Vermont Historical
Society. 88830
Annual address before the Westchester County
(N. Y.) Medical Society. 35999
Annual address, by Emory Washburn. 101514
Annual address, by J. H. Simpson. 81351
Annual address, by Joseph White. 103419
Annual address delivered before the Albany
Institute, April, 1838. 24091
Annual address delivered before the Albany
Institute, April 28th, 1837. 102331
Annual address delivered before the Board of
Trade. 63110
Annual address delivered before the Buffalo
Historical Society. (33100)
Annual address delivered before the Cincinnati
Astronomical Society, June, 1845. 44376
Annual address, delivered before the Cincinnati
Astronomical Society, June 3, 1844. 9373
Annual address delivered before the Historical
Society of Galveston. 82346
Annual address delivered before the Maryland
Historical Society. 27378, (45211A)
Annual address delivered before the Massa-
chusetts Temperance Society. (11905)
Annual address delivered before the New York
State Medical Society, and members of
the legislature, at the Capitol. 91481
Annual address delivered before the New-York
State Medical Society and members of
the legislature . . . February, 1853.
13247
Annual address delivered before the Rhode
Island Society for the Encouragement of
Domestic Industry, October 15, 1823.
20967
Annual address delivered before the Rhode
Island Society for the Encouragement of
Domestic Industry, October 19, 1825.
71155
Annual address, delivered before the Rhode
Island Society for the Encouragement of
Domestic Industry, October 20, 1824.
33934
Annual address. Delivered by Hon. John.Y.
Smith. 83026
Annual address, delivered, October 20, 1863.
19637
Annual address . . . 1856. 32397
Annual address . . . Feb., 1840. (33639)
Annual address . . . Feb. 6, 1850. 91481
Annual address . . . October 21, 1858. (13707)
Annual address of the Bishop of New York.
(64646)
Annual address [of the Connecticut Medical
Society.] 15783
Annual address of the Rector [of Christ Church,
Elizabeth, N. J.] 22193
Annual address . . . [of the Rector of Christ
Church, Elizabeth, N. J.] 32397
Annual address of the Rector of Christ Church,
New Haven, Conn. (7783)

Annual address, read before the Religious
Historical Society. 105668
Annual address, Rensselaer County Agricultural
Society. 18822
Annual address to his [i. e. John Stannage's]
friends in Jersey. 90354
Annual address to the candidates for degrees
and licences. 49202, 105918
Annual address to the Convention of the Protes-
tant Episcopal Church in Pennsylvania.
64617
Annual address to the Franklin and Philo
Literary Societies. 91636
Annual address to the graduates of the Medical
College of South-Carolina. 81327
Annual address to the Medical Society of the
State of New York, 1819. 90893
Annual address to the Medical Society of the
State of New York, 1820. 90893
Annual address to the medical Society of the
State of New York, 1821. 90893
Annual address to the Medical Society of the
State of New York, Feb. 4th, 1818. 90893
Annual address to the parishioners of the Church
of the Ascension. 82940
Annual address to the Philadelphia Annual
Conference of the A. M. E. Church.
(59285)
Annual address to the . . . United States Agri-
cultural Society. 33454
Annual addresses and reports read before the
Bunker Hill Soldiers' Relief Society April
19th, 1861, & April 20, 1863. 12094
Annual addresses and reports read before the
Bunker Hill Soldiers' Relief Society.
April 19, 1862, & April 20, 1863. 9172
Annual advertisement of the . . . [New England
Female Medical] College. (52683)
Annual advertiser, Bridgeport, Conn. see
Bridgeport Directory and annual advertiser.
Annual almanac. The United States almanac.
(19739)
Annual and special messages of Gov. William H.
Smith. 84803
Annual announcement . . . see Announcement
. . .
Annual announcements . . . see Announcements
. . .
Annual appeal of the Domestic Committee of the
Board of Missions. 66123
Annual appropriations, 1847 and '48. (73631)
Annual biography and obituary. 1613
Annual book-list for 1856. 55871
Annual catalogue . . . see Catalogue . . .
Annual catalogues . . . see Catalogues . . .
Annual circular . . . see Circular . . .
Annual commencement and distribution of
premiums. 75515
Annual commencement of Columbia College.
14809
Annual commencement of Kentucky University.
37508
Annual commencement of St. Joseph's College,
Bardstown, Ky. 75302
Annual commencement of St. Joseph's College,
Perry County, Ohio. (75304)
Annual commencement, of St. Mary's College,
Marion County, Kentucky. 75425
Annual communication of the Grand Lodge Of
Massachusetts. 45760
Annual communications of the Grand Lodge of
the State of Maine. (43992)
Annual communication of the mayor. (42313)
Annual Connecticut register & United States
calendar. (15829)
Annual Connecticut register, and United-States
calendar, for the year 1823. 15660

Annual Convention of the Diocese of Connecticut, Middletown, 1835. see Protestant Episcopal Church in the U. S. A. Connecticut (Diocese) Convention, Middletown, 1835.
Annual digest for 1847. 66825
Annual digest of the laws of Pennsylvania. 59882
Annual Dinner of the Hide and Leather Trade of the City of New York, 1859. 69755
Annual director . . . 1868-9 [of Milwaukee, Wisc.] (49154)
Annual director of the inhabitants, etc. of Lafayette. 38584
Annual director of the inhabitants, etc. of Madison. 43725
Annual director to Indianapolis. 34582
Annual director to . . . Milwaukee. (49154)
Annual director to the city of Indianapolis. 34582
Annual director to the inhabitants, etc., in Freeport. 25818
Annual director to the inhabitants, etc., in the cities of New Albany and Jeffersonville. 52432
Annual director to the inhabitants, institutions, incorporated companies, manufacturing establishments, business, business firms, &c. 75346
Annual directory . . . for 1867 [of Indianapolis.] 34582
Annual directory of the inhabitants, etc., in the city of Chicago. 12641
Annual discourse . . . see Discourse . . .
Annual discourses . . . see Discourses . . .
Annual eclipse of May 26, 1854. 85003
Annual exhibit of the manufacturing and commercial industry. 49233, note before 96959
Annual exhibition of the Columbian Society of Artists. 14881
Annual exhibition of the Lawrence Academy. 39388
Annual exhibition of the Society of Artists of the United States. 86006
Annual exhibition of the Society of Artists of the United States, and the Pennsylvania Academy. 60616
Annual exhibition of the University Grammar School. 66377
Annual fair of the Rutland County Agricultural Society. (74475)
Annual financial report of the Auditor of the Canal Department. 53557
Annual financial statement of the city of Chicago. (12649)
Annual . . . for 1870. 33494
Annual guide with a treatise on the mineral waters. 76921
Annual law register of the United States. 28832
Annual legislative statistics. (15739)
Annual letter of the Nashotah Mission. 51855
Annual masonic register for 5812. 30305
Annual medical advertiser for 1844. 10990
Annual medical statistical report. 96106
Annual meeting of the Association for the Improvement of Common Schools in Indiana. 34506
Annual meeting of the Chicago Historical Society. 12621
Annual meeting of the Convention [of Baptists of Vermont.] 99151
Annual meeting of the Illinois Natural History Society. 1605
Annual meeting of the Ladies' Tract and City Missionary Society. 52460

Annual meeting of the Massachusetts Episcopal Society for the Religious Instruction of Freedmen. (45843)
Annual meeting of the New York . . . Maternal Association. 54443
Annual meeting of the Tract Society will be held in New-York. (47241), 93816
Annual meeting of the Trustees of the Granville Literary and Theological Institution. 28328
Annual meeting . . . proceedings of the Commissioners of the Soldiers' National Cemetery Assocation. 27233
Annual message . . . see Message . . .
Annual messages of several governors to the legislature. 933, 87499
Annual messages, veto messages, proclamation, &c. 35342
Annual minutes of the Illinois Conference of the Methodist Episcopal Church. 34215
Annual monitor. (33884), 53779, 98705
Annual narrative of missions performed. 15812
Annual obituary noticies of eminent persons. 17644
Annual of the National Academy of Sciences. 51915
Annual opening and concluding addresses. 45221
Annual oration . . . see Oration . . .
Annual parliaments, the ancient and most salutary right. 79808
Annual proceedings of the [Bunker Hill monument] Association. (9174)
Annual record of horticultural and agricultural statistics. 80329
Annual regattas of the New York Yacht Club. (54558)
Annual register. 6839, 13978, 84832
Annual register and circular of the State Normal School. 53966
Annual register, and military roster. 95209
Annual register, and Virginian repository. 1615
Annual register, from 1789 to 1848. 15659
Annual register [of De Veaux College for Orphan and Destitute Children.] 19806
Annual register of fugitive pieces. 1162A
Annual register of Indian affairs. 43110
Annual register of Indian affairs within the Indian (or Western) Territory. (43111)
Annual register of its rise, progress, and events. 32180, 105602-105605
Annual register of the Baptist denomination in North America. 2222
Annual register of the Executive and Legislative Departments of the government of Massachusetts. 45628, 64028
Annual register of the . . . Metropolitan Academy and Gymnasium. 54396
Annual register of the Military Order of the Loyal Legion. (45833)
Annual register of the officers and students for 1854-5. 61061
Annual register of the proceedings. 102989
Annual register of the Rensselaer Polytechnic Institute of the city of Troy. 69641
Annual register of the Rensselaer Polytechnic Institute, Troy, N. Y. 69641
Annual register of the state of Mississippi. 5033
Annual register of the United States Naval Academy. 1594
Annual register, or a view of history. 1614
Annual remembrancer of the church. 65196
Annual report . . . see Report . . .
Annual reports . . . see Reports . . .
Annual retrospect of public affairs for 1831. 1616
Annual returns of trade and navigation. 52530

171

Annual review. History of St. Louis. 878, 75331
Annual review of Pierce County, Wisc. 62748
Annual review of the commerce, manufactures, public and private improvements of Chicago. 12628
Annual review of the commerce of Cincinnati. 13066
Annual review of the commerce of St. Louis, for the year 1852. 75330
Annual review [of the commerce of St. Louis,] for [the year] 1854. 75331
Annual review of the commerce of St. Louis, together with a list of steamboat disasters, for the year 1856. 75332
Annual review of the commerce of St. Louis, together with a very full list of steamboat disasters. 75333
Annual review of the trade and commerce and of the condition and traffic of the railways. 12629
Annual review of the trade and commerce of Detroit. 19784
Annual reward book for youth. 58858
Annual sermon before the American Sunday-School Union. 17404
Annual sermon, before the bishops, clergy and laity. 92073
Annual sermon, . . . before the . . . Diocese of New Jersey. 56835
Annual sermon . . . by Phil. P. Neely. 49357
Annual sermon for the Boston Prison Discipline Society. 92016
Annual sermon for the Presbyterian Sunday School Society of St. Louis. 64692
Annual sermon, in behalf of the American Sunday-School Union. 5084
Annual sermon, preached before the American Society for Meliorating the Condition of the Jews. 89744
Annual session of the Grand Lodge of the State of Vermont. 99185
Annual session of the R. W. Grand Encampment of Northern New York. (53692)
Annual session of the Teachers' Institute. 50030
Annual state register. 74340
Annual statement . . . see Statement . . .
Annual souvenir gallery. 88683
Annual synopsis [of Ingham University.] 34756
Annual synopsis of new genera and species of animals. 67444
Annual visiter. pseud. Introduction. see Perkins, Thomas H.
Annual Visiting Committee of the Public Schools, Boston. see Boston. Public Schools. Annual Visiting Committee.
Annual visitor. 97284
Annual volunteer and service militia list of Canada. 10519
Annuario de las ordenes imperiales. 74036
Annuario del Observatorio Fisico-Meteorico de la Habana. 63657
Annuario historico braziliense. 7513, 94425
Annuario politico, historico y estatistico do Brazil. 7514
Annve litterae Societatis Iesv. (41508)
Annuncio do manual de deputados. 88831, 88836
Annus mirabilis. 75269
Ano, ------. defendant. 97700
Ano de 1827. 76804
Ano feliz y jublio particular. 94862
(*) Ano (*) politico allegoricamente reformado. 96245
Anonymous. pseud. Sketches of American orators. 81552

Anonymous. pseud. Vaderlandsche merkwaerdigheden in het merkwaerdig Jaar 1782. 98277
Anonymous, ----. pseud. Age of steam. see Whiting, Henry.
Anonymous diary. (48440)
Anonymous emigrant. pseud. Address to the inhabitants of Wales. 104195
Anonymous piece published in the New-Hampshire Sentinel. 92785
Anonymous Portuguese. pseud. see Knight of Elvas. pseud.
Anotaciones a la memoria. 94148
Anotaciones al informe. 41080
Anotaciones criticas. 80987
Anotaciones que publico. 26577
Anotaciones y concordancias. 99633
Anotationes in Ptholemaei geographiam. (66477)
Another account of a transaction. 63082, 63084
Another account of the incidents. (11757)
Another act for the establishment of religious worship. 10956, (10968), 10980, 87347, 87355, 87805, 1st note after 97553
Another and better country. 91548
Another author. pseud. Eulogy. (24390)
Another candid address. 63240-63241
Another case of Jeronimy Clifford. 13688
Another cry of the innocent and oppressed for justice. (1618)
Another cry of the innocent for justice. 1617
Another declaration of His Majesties Councell for Virginia. 99879
Another Episcopalian. pseud. Reply to "An answer." see Hobart, John Henry, Bp., 1775-1830.
Another essay for the investigation of truth. (18703)-18704, (46778)
Another essay, to recommend & inculcate the maxims of early religion. 46614
Another essay, to warn young people against rebellions that must be repented of. (46485)
Another Friend. pseud. Prayer. 86045
Another hand. pseud. Appendix. 46581, note after 100591
Another hand. pseud. Appendix. see Walter, Thomas.
Another hand. pseud. Brief sketches from the narrative. 35869
Another hand. pseud. Character of the Reverend Mr. John Wise. 103398
Another hand. pseud. Conformists reasons for joining with the nonconformists. 46301
Another hand. pseud. Considerations relative to the subject. 23895, (26248)
Another hand. pseud. Further account of that young gentleman. (46578), 3d note after 99448
Another hand. pseud. Letter. 104901
Another hand. pseud. ed. Memoirs of Miss Lucy Richards. (70956)
Another hand. pseud. Narrative of one lately converted. 9105, 103941
Another hand. pseud. Notes and observations. 47004
Another hand. pseud. Postscript by another hand. 2602
Another hand. pseud. Postscript by another hand, wherein those several texts generally reverted. 21657
Another hand. pseud. Reasons for adhering to our platform. 68261, 103400
Another hand. pseud. ed. Some improvements thereof. (35559), 35665, 97172
Another hand. pseud. Some remarks. 17829
Another helper from North Carolina. (30961)

Another high road to Hell. 1619
Another layman. pseud. Remarks on the
recent ordination. see Palfray,
Warwick.
Another letter, from One In the Country.
(45631)
Another masonic murder. 45535
Another memorial. (12466)
Another of the people. pseud. Reply to "The
crisis." 60458, 69704
Another pamphlet for the friends of Senator
Pomeroy. 63935
Another Poyais humbug. 64840
Another proof that the nation is ruined.
(82608)
Another Republican. pseud. Letters to James
Fenner. (24070)
Another sketch of the reign of George III.
27000-(27001), (81534)
Another Spaniard. pseud. tr. 56512, note
before 88936, 106218
Another tongue brought in. 35103, 46224
Another vision. 77366
Another voice from the watchtower. 57267
Another who also knows. pseud. Strictures.
12216
Anquetil, Louis Pierre. 1620
Ansaldo de Vera, Juan. defendant 98730
Anschauungen in den Jahren 1834, 1835, und
1836. 36891
Anschauungen und Erfahrungen in Nord-
Amerika. 1621
Ansdale Hall. 26267
Ansel, ------- Ben. see Ben-Ansel, -------.
Ansicht von Philadelphia. (55456)
Ansichten aus dem Innern von Mexico und
Californien. 104891
Ansichten der Natur. 33702-33703
Ansichten von Louisiana. 7178
Ansiedler. 16504
Ansiedler David Cover und seine Sohne. 38241
Ansiedler im Missouri-Staate. 3974
Ansiedler im Westen. 1624
Ansiedler in Amerika. 44332
Ansiedlerleben in der Kolonie Blumenau.
65364
Ansiedlungen in den Urwaldern von Canada.
1622, 96440
Anslijn, P. D. tr. 21215
Anson, George Anson, Baron, 1697-1762. 1625-
1630, (1632)-1633, 1637-1641, 21211-
21215, 25929, 31389, (50834), 52455,
(54897), 56064, 64396, 69135, 69381,
100803 101175-101192
Anson Guards, Company C. 84734
Anson's voyage to the South Seas. 1633
Anson's voyages round the world. 69381
Anspach, F. R. 1643
Anspach, F. R. supposed author (32207),
87110
Anspach, Lewis Amadeus. 1644-1646, 54991
Ansted, David T. 1647-1648
Answeer to the Hampshire narrative. 7656,
(30136)
Answer. 105016
Answer and arguments of the Synod. (46778)
Answer and pleas of Samuel Chase. 12203
Answer and report. 54793
Answer at large to Mr P--tt's speech. 63083
Answer by a citizen. 17359, 90874
Answer [by J. Sayre.] (77412)
Answer, by way of letter. 98837
Answer, delivered to the Mayor. 53630, 97291
Answer for the messengers of the nation.
63622

Answer from a Gentleman in Connecticut.
68969
Answer from the electors of Bristol. 11758
Answer from the Minister [for Foreign Affairs.]
9028
Answer given to the charges. (14600), 99485
Answer of a committee from the congregation.
75209
Answer [of Bishop Abraham Jarvis.] 35801
Answer [of Bishop Samuel Seabury.] (15654),
39529, 78555-78556
Answer of Charles Naylor. 52136
Answer of Daniel Adams. 83958
Answer of Deacon James G. Carter. 11117,
95259
Answer of Earl Cornwallis. 13754
Answer [of General Burgoyne.] 39708
Answer of George Thomas. 95398
Answer [of George Whitefield.] 103645
Answer [of Governor Sullivan.] 62652, note
before 93501
Answer [of Governor Wentworth.] 41656, note
after 102630
Answer of . . . [Governor] William W. Holden.
55594
Answer of His Excellency William Franklin.
25636
Answer [of Mr. Greenhow.] 23725
Answer of Mr. John Cotton. 104331
Answer of Mr. Sullivan. 93513-93514
Answer [of Peter Porcupine.] 14007
Answer of President Buchanan. 52997
Answer of Robert F. Stockton. 91893
Answer of St. Peter's Church. 13786
Answer of Samuel Chase. 12207
Answer [of Secretary Van Tienhoven.] 20597,
note after 98474
Answer of several ministers in and near Boston.
(46631)
Answer of the Assembly of Divines. 1649
Answer of the Committee of the . . . Directors.
62229
Answer of the Company of Royal Adventurers
of England. 1650
Answer of the dissenting brethren and mes-
sengers. 49662, 66059
Answer of the elders and other messengers of
the churches assembled at Boston in the
year 1662. 45632, (52609), 63342
Answer of the elders and other messengers of
the churches assembled at Boston, 1662.
1651
Answer of the elders of the several churches
in New-England. 18710
Answer of the Elders of the severall churches
in New-England. 46776
Answer of the Friend in the West, to a letter.
13213, 26353-(26354), (38374), note after
105924, 3d note after 105937
Answer of the generality of the creditors of the
Royal African Company. 73757
Answer of the House of Representatives of
Mass., and the Governor's speech, June,
1823. 97413
Answer of the House of Representatives [of
Massachusetts, 1812.] 46129, 92886
Answer of the House of Representatives [of
the Massachusetts-Bay Colony.] 92349
Answer of the House of Representatives, to the
same. (46131), 2d note after 89220
Answer of the House of Representatives to the
speech of Governor Dudley. 45633
Answer of "The members of the congregation
of St. Peter's Church." 635

Answer of the Pastor & Brethren of the Third Church in Windham. 104756

Answer of the President of the United-States. 79399, (79402), note after 99292

Answer of the Prince, Jan. 23. 1688-89. 104144

Answer of the Senate to the Governor's speech. 53530

Answer of the state of Rhode Island and Providence Plantations. 70753

Answer of the States General. 1652

Answer of the Trustees of Union College. 97779

Answer of the Whig members of the Legislature. 37792, 3d note after 103271

Answer of William Rector. 68415

Answer, printed by order of the Second Church in Ipswich. 13592

Answer thereto, by a person to whom it was communicated. 78904

Answer thereunto; by Jacob Johnson. 6225

Answer thereunto [by Thomas Barnard.] 329

Answer to a bill in the Chancery of New-Jersey. (53066)

Answer to a book entitled, A brief discourse. 104255, 104257

Answer to a book, entituled, Quakerism no Christianity. 59727

Answer to a book entituled The Christian Sabbath. 6227

Answer to a book entituled The holy table. 31653

Answ[er] to a book lately [written] by Peter Pratt. 64973, 72688

Answer to a calumny. 1653, note after 35564

Answer to a censorious epistle. 29818, 72088, 72110

Answer to a circular letter. 8526

Answer to a clandestine address. (22680), 97067

Answer to a colonel's letter. 1654

Answer to a dialogue between a Federalist and a Republican. 1655, 19683

Answer to a dialogue concerning the half way covenant. 4497

Answer to a dialogue entituled The meritorious price. 55882

Answer to a discourse. 42986

Answer to a late pamphlet, entitled Taxation no tyranny. 36309, 97635

Answer to a late pamphlet, intitled, A letter to a friend. 104242

Answer to a late pamphlet, intitled, An attempt, &c. 4497

Answer to a letter addressed to a Republican member of the House of Representatives of . . . Massachusetts. 40255, (45634), 45970

Answer to a letter addressed to him [i. e. Charles Pinkney Summer.] 93694

Answer to a letter from a gentleman in the country. 1656

Answer to a letter from a son of candor. 99813

Answer to a letter from an aged layman. 20063

Answer to a letter from Dr. Bray. 105651

Answer to a letter from the Hon. F. H. Elmore. 89311

Answer to a letter from the Reverend Association. 7655

Answer to a letter inferring publique communion. 72102

Answer to a letter sent from Mr. Coddington. 104330

Answer to a letter to the freemen, etc. (34613)

Answer to a letter to the right honourable the Earl of B***. (40527)

Answer to a libel entituled A defence of the Scots abdicating Darien. (18552), 78206, 78209, (78215)

Ansvver to a libell intituled, A coole conference. 91381

Answer to a most false and scandalous pamphlet. 18229, 52757, 55060

Answer to a pamphlet, called, A second letter. 80056

Answer to a pamphlet, call'd The conduct of the ministry. (80038)

Answer to a pamphlet, containing the correspondence. (35833), 41549

Answer to a pamphlet, entitled "Considerations on the public expediency." 6596, (6600), note after 97401

Answer to a pamphlet, entitled "Strictures on Mr. Pattison's reply." 59151

Answer to a pamphlet, entitled Taxation on tyranny. 1657

Answer to a pamphlet entitled, The causes and consequences of the late emigration to the Brazils. 34780, 41329

Answer to a pamphlet, entitled, The groans of the plantations. 20242

Answer to a pamphlet, entituled, A skirmish made upon Quakerism. 59732

Answer to a pamphlet intitled The divine right of Presbyterian ordination. 78494

Answer to a pamphlet, intituled, The divine right of Presbyterian ordination, &c., argued. (25392), 103067

Answer to a pamphlet, lately published, entitled, "A treatise on church government." 360, 11967-11968, 3d note after 96741

Answer to a pamphlet of Mr. John A. Lowell. (8345)

Answer to a pamphlet, recently addressed to the Episcopalians of Pennsylvania. 63217, 63239-63241

Answer to a petition of the General Court of Boston. 9462

Answer to a piece, entitled, "An appeal to the impartial publick." 1658, 27591-27592

Answer to a piece intitled Some friendly remarks on said sermon. (64276)

Answer to a postscript. (24469)

Answer to a printed letter. 43663, (55031), (65578), 96298

Answer to a publication of a Friend in Rhode-Island. 80193

Answer to a question, "The Pennsylvania Museum and School of Industrial Art, Philadelphia, Penn.:" 84497

Answer to a reformed Quaker. 106106

Answer to a scandalous pamphlet, called "News from New England." 7855

Answer to a scandalous pamphlet, entituled, A word for the armie. 101330, note after 105462

Answer to a scandalous paper. 66910

Answer to a scurrilous libel. 25859

Answer to a scurrilous pamphlet. 14018, note after 95866

Answer to a small pamphlet entituled, A monitory letter. 72689

Answer to a small treatise. 28041

Answer to a tax payer. 8327

Answer to a treatise of Mr. J. Paget. 18708

Answer to a very new pamphlet indeed (57146), 99320, note after 99776

Answer to an abolition sermon. 81851

Answer to an "Address by a catholic layman." (62214)

Answer to an address presented to John Lord Lovelace. 86960
Answer to an address to Silas Deane. (19067), 86193
Answer to an advertisement in the Boston Gazette. 45635
Answer to an anonymous pamphlet, entitled, Articles exhibited. 29998
Answer to an anonymous pamphlet, intituled A reply to Col. Clap's vindication. 13210, 13211
Answer to an attack made by Rev. J. L. Hodge. 70281
Answer to an examination of the British doctrine. 4549
Answer to an invidious pamphlet, intituled, A brief state. (17666), 84589
Answer to Bishop Hobart's pastoral letter. 32296
Answer to Capt. Dampier's vindication of his voyage. (26213), 102513
Answer to certain objections. 8252
Answer to certain parts of a work. 10879
Answer to certain queries. 46954
Answer to "Colonel Choate's reasons of dissent." 2602, 12857, 29853
Answer to Col. Wanton's address. 95980
Answer to considerations on certain political transactions. 39923-39924, 87790
Answer to Cotton Mather (a priest in Boston) his calumnies. 5631
Answer to Cotton Mather's abuses of the said people. 5631
Answer to Dr. Blackstone's reply. (65513)
Answer to Dr. Inglis's defence of his character. (34763), 58833-(58834), 99410-99411
Answer to Dr. Mayhew's Observations on the charter and conduct of the Society for the Propagation of the Gospel. (47141), 47144-(47145), 78713-78714, 78719
Answer to Dr. Price's Observations on the nature of civil liberty. 23409
Answer to Dr. Price's system of fanatical liberty. 21476
Answer to Dr. Tappan's remarks. 7241
Answer to Dr. Wood's reply. 101375, 105135
Answer to each question. 81490
Answer to 'Eliphalet Pearson's letter to the candid.' 103723
Answer to enquiries relative to middle Florida. (43612)
Answer to Gen. Nathan Heard and Col. Gardner Burbank. 47987
Answer to George Keith's libel. (44077)
Answer to His Excellency George Washington. 101591
Answer to Increase Mather's "Order to the Gospel." 28052
Answer to it [i. e. Jacob Duche's letter to Washington.] 101739-101740
Answer to J. B. Moreton's Manners and customs in the West Indies. 46847
Answer to Jeremy Belknap's discourse. 77436
Answer to John Plimpton's dis-ingenuous paper. 59726
Answer to letter from Rev. L. Strong. 92944
Answer to Lewis Evans' letter. 100426
Answer to Lord Sheffield's pamphlet. 14085
Answer to Master Roger Williams. 17044
Answer to Messrs. Burges, Duer, and Mackenzie. (16415)
Answer to Mr. Blatchford's letter. 84692
Answer to Mr. Broadstreete. 9095
Answer to Mr. Burke's letter. (11767)
Answer to Mr. Cotton's letter. 17045

Answer to Mr. Franklin's remarks. 25576-25577, 84586
Answer to Mr. Frothingham's late letter. 2632
Answer to Mr. Gales' pamphlet. 28220
Answer to Mr. George Dixon. 20362, (47257)
Answer to Mr. Gillett's letter. 28884
Answer to Mr. Jefferson's justification. 41610
Answer to Mr. John L. Sullivan's report. 93532, 93535
Answer to Mr. John Lee's remarks. 97454
Answer to Mr. Jonathan Edwards' sermon. 12316, (21935), 67768
Answer to Mr. Paine's letter to Gen. Washington. (37437)
Answer to Mr. Samuel Willard. (37179), 37211, 104070
Answer to Mr. Tucker's letter. (11858), 97315, 97322
Answer to Mr. Wadsworth's book. 4287
Answer to Mr. Wilberforce's appeal. (22402)
Answer to Nathaniel Morton of New Plimouth. (28046)
Answer to Nat. Stone's (of Harwich) cautions. 30081
Answer to nine positions about Church government. 46776
Answer to O'Kelley's rejoinder. 85439
Answer to one of the people. 68274
Answer to Paine's Rights of man. 43429, 94025
Answer to part of a book. 66911
Answer to Pilate's question. 881
Answer to "Questions addressed to Rev. T. Parker." 76982
Answer to remarks upon a message. 45069, 45318
Answer to Rev. Jonathan Ward's "Brief statement." 94522-94523
Answer to Rev. Mr. Davidson's pamphlet. 94159
Answer to Richard Harden's reply to John Earle's letter. 21622, 81461
Answer to Robert Smith's address to the people. 83827
Answer to Roger Williams. 51773
Answer to S. A. Douglas, on popular sovereignty. (18039)
Answer to Samuel Finley. 86739
Answer to several new laws and orders. 25345
Answer to Six months in a convent. 12097, 45038, 75208, 2d note after 98167-98168
Answer to Slaveholding not sinful. (33223)
Answer to some cases of conscience respecting the country. 79444, 91940, 104083
Answer to some false and malicious objections. (24957), 35565
Answer to some false statements and misrepresentations. 94505
Answer to some late papers. 90011
Answer to some observations. 9906
Answer to strictures on a pamphlet entitled a "Friendly address." (3684)
Answer to "Taxation of learning." 62119, 95434
Answer to that common objection. 86627, note after 104031
Answer to that part of the narrative. (16811)
Answer to that question. 1703
Answer to the address. 87846
Answer to the apologetical preface. 18704
Answer to the appendix. 9907
Answer to the assertions. 5913
Answer to the Baltimore millers' memorial. 96991
Answer to the Bishop of Derry. 78732

Answer. To the Bishop of London's last
pastoral letter. 103577
Answ[er] to the book lately [written] by Peter
Pratt. 72688
Answer to the Budget. 1659
Answer to the committee. 93364
Answer to the common objections. 89252
Answer to the complaint. 78203
Answer to the confutation. 97128
Answer to the considerations. 18510
Answer to the Council of Proprietors two
publications. 53067
Answer to the Declaration of the American
Congress. 15589, 41280-41281
Answer to the Declaration of the general
Congress. 18347, 27145, note after
41286, note after 71369
Answer to the declaration of the King of
England. 86077
Answer to the defence of the Scots settlement
there. 78209-78210
Answer to the exposition of a pamphlet. 1660
Answer to the exposition of Thomas H. Lewis.
(7067)
Answer to the first and second part of an
anonymous pamphlet. 103498
Answer to the first part. 103498
Answer to the Governor of Washington Terri-
tory. 101922
Answer to the greatest falsehood ever told.
104381-104382
Answer to the gross abuses, lies and slanders,
of Increase Mather, and Nath. Morton,
&c. 37208
Answer to the gross abuses, lyes and slanders
of Increase Mather and Samuel Norton,
&c. 37207
Answer to the Hon. J. Whipple. 26403
Answer to the inquiry "Is it expedient to
introduce slavery into Kansas." (27864),
92867
Answer to the inquiry, why do the contracts
ask for more than the tunnel costs?
30859
Answer to the interrogatories. 25641
Answer to the introduction to the Observations.
66990
Answer to the Joint Committee of the . . .
Councils. 62369
Answer to the late Archbishop Carroll's
reply. 103090
Answer to the letter addressed to the author.
57317
Answer to the letter of Edmund Burke, Esq.
9291
Answer to the letter of Mr. Duer. (14282)
Answer to the letter to two great men. 1661
Answer to the notes and observations.
(53068)
Answer to the objections contained in the
French memorials. (47547), (56129),
note after 96403
Answer to the objections raised in the report.
103439
Answer to the objections urged. 95123
Answer to the observations on the papers.
1662
Answer to the pamphlet entitled The conduct
of the Paxton men. 1663
Answer to the pamphlet entitled The duty of
Columbia College. 70247
Answer to the plea of T. B. Chandler, D. D.
12319
Answer to the preceding reply. 105132
Answer to the preface of Mr. Caldwell's
sermon. 43293

Answer to the printed speech. 80039
Answer to the proprietors of the South-Sea
capital. 88169
Answer to the publications of Messieurs
Thurston, Woodman, and Coe. 80190
Answer to the queries, contained in a letter to
Dr. Shebbeare. 80040
Answer to the queries on the proprietary
government of Maryland. 45069
Answer to the question, whether are not the
Brethren, and not the elders of the church
only. 99805
Answer to the question, whether the use of
distilled liquors. 93199
Answer to the question "Who are the Plymouth
brethren?" (29244)
Answer to the question, why does the Sanitary
Commission need so much money?
(76604), 76647
Answer to the questions. 67206, 92886
Answer to the reasons. 39936
Answer to the reasons against an African
Company. 1664
Answer to the reasons against Leisler's bill.
68285
Answer to the reasons given by a number of
ministers conven'd at Taunton. (22007),
94921, note after 103633, 5th note after
103650
Answer to the "Rejoinder." 44324
Answer to the remarks of the Plymouth Com-
pany. (8764), 63498
Answer to the remarks of the Rev. Messieurs
Wigglesworth and Chipman. 2873, 103934
Answer to the remarks on his [i. e. Captain
Middleton's] vindication. 20407
Answer to "The reply of the Trustees." 20708
Answer to the report of Allan Campbell.
22763, note after 97071
Answer to the report of the Committee of the
House of Representatives. (18453)
Answer to the resolutions and address of the
American Congress. 106-107, 1657,
2760, 15523, (19253), 36302-36303,
36306-36309, 50452, 56060, 58399,
63216, 63771, 78302, (80441), 90317,
note before 94431, note before 94434,
96184, 97635, 102647
Answer to the Rev. Chandler Robbin's reply.
(17101)
Answer to the Rev. Mr. Clarkson's essay.
(25478)
Answer to the Rev. Mr. Garden's three first
letters to the Rev. Mr. Whitefield.
(17668), note after 103614
Answer to the Rev. Mr. Harris's "Scriptural
researches." (33606)
Answer to the Rev'd Mr. Hobart's principles,
&c. 96094
Answer to the Reverend Mr. Jonathan Edwards's
sermon. 67768
Answer, to the Rev. Mr. Leaming's disser-
tations. 80391
Answer to the Rev. Mr. Prescott's examination.
8505, (65240)
Answer to the Rev. Mr. Prince's letter.
104854
Answer to the Rev. Mr. Thompson's tract.
79823, 95530
Answer to the Reverend Mr. White's three
letters. 96357, 103403
Answer to the Rev. Mr. William Hart's
remarks. 32955
Answer to the Rt. Rev. P. Chase. 2511
Answer to the same [i. e. Circular of the
Directors of the Philadelphia & Atlantic
Steam Navigation Company.] 61943

Answer to the scurrilous invectives. 103336
Answer to the second part. 103498
Answer to the seditious and scandalous pamphlet. 90540, 97265
Answer to the southern pastoral of April 18, 1867. 49690
Answer to the Spanish memorial against it. 18549, 18571, 78211-78213, 78234
Answer to the speech of William Wilberforce. 34789, 82068, 4th note after 102785
Answer to the statements contained. 49684
Answer to the strictures of Mr. Thomas Falconer. (28630)
Answer to the summary discussion, &c. 69463
Answer to the supplementary bill in equity. 70546
Answer to the tears of the Foot Guards, in which that respectable Corps are vindicated. 94569
Answer to the tears of the Foot Guards upon their departure for America. 1664A
Answer to the "Vindication of the official conduct." (21281)
Answer to the vindication of the Rev. Commission. 31293, 31297
Answer to the vindicatory address and appeal. 76498, 95779, 102207
Answer to the vote of the Church of Christ. 11117
Answer to the white-washing committee. (1665)
Answer to this question. 4395
Answer to Thomas Paine's letter. 90446
Answer to those two late pamphlets. 59728
Answer to two treatises. (2937)
Answer to Vamp Overreach's letter. 36027
Answer to W. R. his narration. (67947), 102551
Answer to War in disguise. 50827, 91246-91247, 101270
Answer to what has been offer'd as argument. 53040, 53069
Answer unto nine positions. 46776
Answer unto the Maquas Sachims propositions. 66062
Answers, by Elias Hicks to the six queries. 31710, 104521
Answers, by Jonas Coe. 43156
Answers filed by the defendants. (8482)
Answers given by the Judges of the Supreme Court of Nova Scotia. 91357, note after 94546
Answers of David B. McComb, Esq. 43082
Answers of the Committee . . . of "The President, . . . and Company for Erecting a Permanent Bridge." (61468)
Answers of the immediate government. 30765
Answers of the President of the Colonization Society. 45331
Answers of the Senate and House of Representatives. (13897), note after 101860
Answers to all the objections. 102817
Answers to circular on immigration. (10435)
Answers to enquiries concerning the books. 11217, 40392
Answers to Mr. Toriano's objections. 2195
Answers to questions contained in Mr. Parker's letter. 58738
Answers to Rev. Albert Barnes' questions. 8883
Answers to strictures on a pamphlet. (3684)
Answers to the articles of impeachment. (65249)
Answers to the Lords of Trade. 103051
Answers to the objections against the proposals. 73758

Answers, to the queries, in a letter. 103560, 103622
Answers to the queries of the Abolition Society. (13081)
Answers to the question "Where in Florida shall we locate?" 24862
Answers to the questions proposed to him [i. e. William Cooper.] 14516
Answers to the questions: what constitutes currency? 10827
Ant. M. pseud. Histoire. see Magini, Giovanni Antonio.
Antagonism of war to Christianity. 92015
Antagonisme et solidante des etats orientaux. 1665A
Antagonisms in the moral and political world. 4615
Antapologia. 21991, 27952
Antarctic mariner's song. 58356
Antarcticus. pseud. Letter to the President of the Royal Geographical Society. (1666)
Antarctike. 95339
Ante bellum. 40036
Antecedentes del Marscal de Campo Francisco Narvaez. 51843
Antecedentes i documentos de la apertura del canal. 85736
Antelope (Ship) in Admiralty 274
Antenor. pseud. Letters. (23712)
Antepara, Jose Maria. 1667
Antequera Enriquez y Castro, Jose de. 1668, 10803, 58393 see also Paraguay (Province) Gobernador, 1721-1725 (Antequera Enriquez y Castro)
Antequera, Mexico. 24155
Antequera (Diocese) Bishop (Abreu y Valdes) 75, 58297 see also Abreu y Valdes, Miguel Anselmo Alvares de. Bp.
Antequera (Diocese) Bishop (Zarate) 94854 see also Zarate, J. de. Bp.
Antersen, Johann Peter von. 1669
Antes, Frederick. 33351, 60026 see also Pennsylvania. Commissioners Appointed to Explore the Head-waters of the Rivers Delaware, Lehigh, and Schuylkill, and the North-east Branch of the Susquehanna.
Antes, Henry, 1701?-1755. 2462-2463, 60766, 4th note after 97845
Antes, William. 62279 see also Philadelphia County, Pa. Sub-Lieutenant.
Antezana, Jose Ventura. see Ventura Antezana, Jose.
Antheil der Deutschen an der Entdeckung von Sud-Amerika. 23997, 38057
Anthem for thanksgiving day. 16642
Anthoine de Saint-Joseph, Francois, Baron. 1670-(1762)
Anthology: an annual reward book for youth. 58858
Anthology of New Netherland. 51460, 51464, 91169
Anthon, Charles, 1797-1867. 83048, (85481)
Anthon, George C. 1672A
Anthon, Henry. 1673-1675, 82732
Anthon, Henry. supposed author 4973, 2d note after 96984
Anthon, John, d. 1865. 1677-(1678), 54723
Anthon, William Henry. 1680
Anthonii Thysii JC Historia navalis. 95777
Anthony, Elliott. 1681-1683
Anthony, H. B. 65336
Anthony, James. defendant 1684
Anthony, John. 95990
Anthony, Joseph B. 59827, 60562 see also Pennsylvania. Commission on the Leins of the Commonwealth Upon the Lands of John Nicholson and Peter Baynton.

Anthony, Susan Brownell, 1820-1906. ed.
90405
Anthony, Susan Brownell, 1820-1906. petitioner
90404
Anthony, Susanna, d. 1791. 32951, 57757,
63988
Anthony, V. S. engr. (46832)
Anthony Benezet. 4694, 98704
Anthony Burns. A history. 91490
Anthony (E.) firm 85414
Anthony Grumbler of Grumbleton Hall. pseud.
Miscellaneous thoughts. see Hoffman,
David.
Anthony Oldbuck. pseud. see Oldbuck,
Anthony. pseud.
Anthony Pasquin. pseud. see Williams, John,
1761-1818.
Anthony Sharp, philom. pseud. see Ritten-
house, David.
Anthony Stoddard, of Boston, Mass. 91929-
91930, 91932
Anthony Thatcher's narrative. 106052
Anthracite coal, and the proposed tax. 84443
Anthracite coal fields of Pennsylvania. 80024
Anthropological Society, London. (6207)
Anthropologie. 21216
Anthropophagi frequentes in novo orbe. 61257
Anthropos. pseud. Connecticut's flood. 98058
Anti-abolition sermon. 103896
Anti-abolition tracts. 25713, 26712, 81487,
81715-81717, 81722, (81982)
Anti-abolitionist. pseud. Facts and arguments.
see Jarvis, Russell.
Anti-Argos. 61078
Anti-bullionist. pseud. Enquiry into the
causes. 22633
Anti-Brissot. 2764
Anti-bureaucrat. pseud. Remarks on the
petition. see Thom, Adam.
Antiburgher Seceders. see Associate-
Reformed Synod of North America.
Antichrist of New-England. 4296
Anti-Christian conspiracy against the true
republicanism. 85122
Antichristian conspiracy detected. 105684
Anti-Christian religion discovered. 18893
Anti-Christs and sadducees detected. (37180)
Anti-Christ's kingdom. 18608, 79727, note
after 97880, note after 94924, note after
106196
Anticipation. pseud. Address on the past.
see Dickinson, John, 1732-1808.
Anticipation: containing the substance of His
M-----y's most gracious speech.
95788-95789
Anticipation. Containing the substance of His
Majesty's most gracious speech. 95790
Anticipation continued. 1685, note after 95790-
95791
(Anticipation.) Disunited States, January 1,
1834. 56315, 96073
Anticipation: (For the year MDCCLXXIX.)
1686, 95792
Anticipation of marginal notes. 1687
Anticipation; or the voyage of an American to
England. 1688
Anticipations of the future. 1689, 73912
Anticipator. pseud. Essays. see Snethen,
Nicholas, 1769-1845.
Anticipatory epitaph on the constitution.
(10878)
Anti-compromise speech . . . of Mr. Benton.
4787
Anti-Corn-Law League and the cotton trade.
79842
Anti-Dariensi. pseud. New Darien artifice
laid open. 18562

Anti Decius. pseud. (50137), (55169), 100451
Antidotael-memorie, betreffende de prysen.
100948, 100950, 102818
Antidotael memorie tot nadere Verdediging.
(47759)
Antidote. 59887, 71913
Antidote against, and reward of, Toryism.
103317
Antidote against distractions. 91147
Antidote against Popery. (5988), 44493
Antidote against the common plague of the world.
28041
Antidote against the venome of the snake.
103655
Antidote against Toryism. 103317-103318
Antidote analyzed. 71913
Antidote au Congres de Radstadt. 64887
Antidote for a poisonous combination. (73941)
Antidote for popular public opinion. 66775
Antidote in some remarks on a paper of David
Lloyd's. 37241, (41792)
Antidote. Rev. E. Spencer's defence. 89314
Antidote to Deism. 56825
Antidote to expell the poison. 73768
Antidote to John Wood's poison. 12374, note
after 101455
Antidote to Mormonism. (43002)
Antidote to popular frenzy. 77450
Antidote to Rev. H. J. Van Dyke's pro-slavery
discourse. 6369
Antidote to the Merino-mania. 1690
Antidote to the poison now vending. 33866
Antidote to West-Indian sketches. 81852, 102819
Antidoto catholico contra a veneno methodista.
(76318)
Antidoto contra as maximas do Governador e
Capitao-General de Mocambique. 45536
Antidoto eficaz contra el mal frances hallado.
35250, note after 74024
Antidotum Cecillianum. 78189
Antidotum Licolniense. 31653
Anti-Duelling Association of New York. 4337
Anti-duelling Convention, Pittsburgh, 1827.
5673
Anti-duelling resolutions. 5673
Antienne & l'oracion de cette bienheureuse.
24227, 73176
Antient . . . see Ancient . . .
Anti-enthusiasticus. pseud. Appendix. see
Chauncy, Charles, 1592-1672. supposed
author and Colman, Benjamin, 1673-1747.
supposed author
Anti-episcopal methodist. pseud. Exposition of
the government. 23454
Antietam. pseud. McClellan and Fremont.
43025
Antietam National Cemetery. see U. S.
Antietam National Cemetery.
Antietam National Monument. Trustees. see
Rhode Island. Trustees of the Antietam
National Monument.
Anti-federal objections refuted. 602
Anti-gallic letters. 95369
Antigallican. 84585
Antigallican; or, the lover of his country. 1691,
14021
Antigallicus, Titus. pseud. see Titus
Antigallicus. pseud.
Anti-Greenbacks, of the Thirty-Eleventh Con-
gressional District. pseud. Resumption
specie payments. 70126
Antigionian and Bostonian beauties. 2561,
12310

Antigua. Branch Association of the Society for the Conversion and Religions Instruction and Education of the Negro Slaves. see Society for the Convension and Religious Instruction and Education of the Negro Slaves. Branch Association of Antigua and St. Christopher.
Antigua. Court of Vice Admiralty. 29517, 1st note after 92630, 101262
Antigua. Laws, statutes, etc. 1694-1695, (1699), 8448, 39416, 85361
Antigua. Legislature. 1697A
Antigua. A poem. 1692, 63577
Antigua and the Antiguans. 1693
Antigua gazette. 84678C
Antigua planter. 63624
Antiguedad de las bubas. 77092
Antiguedades Americanos. (2607)
Antiguedades Peruanas. 71641-71643
Anti-guillotine. pseud. Five letters to Governor Hamilton. 30016
Antiguo mercurio Peruano. (26114), 47936
Antiguos labradores Venezolanos. pseud.
Observaciones. see L., J. M. pseud.
Antiguos redactores del Museo Mejicano. pseud. eds. Revista cientifica y literaria. 70300
Anti-Intemperance Society of South-Carolina. see South Carolina Anti-Intemperance Society.
Anti-Jackson Convention, Richmond, Va., 1827-1828. see National Republican Party. Virginia. Convention, Richmond, 1827-1828.
Anti-Jackson Convention of Missouri. see National Republican Party. Missouri. Convention, 1828.
Anti-Jackson Men of Franklin County, Pa. see National Republican Party. Pennsylvania. Franklin County.
Anti-Jesuit. 55560
Anti-Junius. pseud. Few words about John Tyler. 63777, 63816
Anti-Junius. pseud. Political facts for the times. 63777, 63816
Anti-Junius. pseud. Tap of the drum. 63777, 63816
Anti-kaulen, oder mythische Vorstellungen. (64599)
Anti-Lecompton Meeting, New York, 1858. see Democratic Party. New York. New York (City)
Antilia. 81086
Antillas Espanolas ante las naciones civilzadas. 17817
Antillen. 77741
Antilles. 73927
Antilles; Cuba; Jamaique. 101350
Antilles. Etudes d'ethnographie et d'archeologie Americaines. 73310
Antilles Francaises, particulierement la Guadeloupe. 7135
Antilles Francaises.—Question monetaire. 40129
Antilles. Par M. Ferdinand Denis. 19540
Antillion, Is. 1702
Antimanifeste du Seigneur Fernando Telles de Faro. 94621
Anti-masonic almanac, for . . . 1837. (45494)
Anti-masonic almanac for . . . 1829. 27332
Anti-masonic almanac, for New England. (45494)
Anti-masonic Committee of Suffolk County, Mass. see Anti-masonic Party. Massachusetts. Suffolk County. Committee.

Anti-masonic Committee of York County, Pa. see Anti-masonic Party. Pennsylvania. York County. Committee.
Anti-masonic Convention, Baltimore, 1831. see United States Anti-masonic Convention, Baltimore, 1831.
Anti-masonic Convention, Philadelphia, 1830. see United States Anti-masonic Convention, Philadelphia. 1830.
Anti-masonic Convention, Utica, N. Y., 1830. 65819
Anti-masonic Convention, Woodstock, Conn., 1829. 79255
Anti-masonic Convention of the County of Cayuga, N. Y., 1830. see Anti-masonic Party. New York (State) Cayuga County. Convention, 1830.
Antimasonic Convention of Young Men of the County of Washington, Hartford, N. Y., 1830. (65791), 102010
Anti-masonic Meeting, Boston, 1836. see Anti-masonic Party. Massachusetts. Boston.
Anti-masonic Meeting, Lampter Square, Pa., 1839. see Anti-masonic Party. Pennsylvania. Lancaster County.
Antimasonic pamphlets. 64402, 104874
Anti-masonic Party. 28493
Anti-masonic Party. Massachusetts. 45591, 46091
Anti-masonic Party. Massachusetts. Boston. 46091
Anti-masonic Party. Massachusetts. Suffolk County. Committee. 93694, 95158
Anti-masonic Party. New York (State) 50677
Anti-masonic Party. New York (State) Convention, Utica, 1832. 53531
Anti-masonic Party. New York (State) Cayuga County. Convention, 1830. (65820)
Anti-masonic Party. New York (State) Genesee County. 50677
Anti-masonic Party. New York (State) Livingston County. 50677
Anti-masonic Party. New York (State) Monroe County. 50677
Anti-masonic Party. New York (State) Niagara County. 50677
Anti-masonic Party. New York (State) Ontario County. 50677
Anti-masonic Party. New York (State) Saratoga County. Central Committee. 65760, 94516
Anti-masonic Party. New York (State) Saratoga County. Convention, Ballston Spa, 1831. 65760, 94516
Anti-masonic Party. Pennsylvania. Convention, Harrisburg, 1832. (60411)
Anti-masonic Party. Pennsylvania. Lancaster County. 65808
Anti-masonic Party. Pennsylvania. York County. Committee. 74259
Anti-masonic party. Vermont. General Committee. 99145
Antimasonic Republicans of . . . Massachusetts. see Anti-masonic Party. Massachusetts.
Anti-masonic Republican State Convention, Utica, N. Y., 1832. see Anti-masonic Party. New York (State) Convention, Utica, 1832.
Anti-masonic Republican State Convention. Proceedings. 53531
Anti-masonic review, and magazine. 54844, 101298
Anti-masonic review and monthly magazine. (45495)

Anti-masonic State Convention of Connecticut, Hartford, 1830. 15795

Anti-masonic State Convention of Massachusetts, Boston, 1829. 45548, 45659, 45941, 95158

Anti-masonic State Convention of Massachusetts, Boston, 1830. 45548

Anti-masonic State Convention of Massachusetts, Boston, 1831. 45548

Anti-masonic State Convention of New York, Albany, 1829. 65784

Anti-masonic State Convention of Rhode Island, Providence, 1830. petitioners 70600

Anti-masonic State Convention of Rhode Island, Providence, 1831, (70618)

Anti-masonic State Convention of Rhode Island, Providence, 1835. 70615-70616

Anti-masonic State Convention of Rhode Island, Providence, 1835. Nominating Committee. 70615

Anti-masonic State Convention of Vermont, Montpelier, 1829. 99146

Anti-masonic State Convention of Vermont, Montpelier, 1830. 99147

Anti-masonic State Convention of Vermont, Montpelier, 1831. 99148

Anti-masonic State Convention of Vermont, Montpelier, 1833. 99145, 99149

Antimasonic Tract Association of Connecticut. see Connecticut Anti-masonic Tract Association.

Anti-masonic tracts. 45496, (46628), 72851, 95158

Anti-masonry. 25805

Anti-masonry, first published in the American quarterly review. 101157

Anti-masons of Massachusetts, listen to the voice. 47987

Anti-ministerial objections considered. 1703, (37480), note after 97417

Antimonian [sic] sermon. 19051

Anti-monopoly State Convention, Trenton, N. J., 1868. (53053)

Anti-Nebraska Meetings, New Haven, Conn., 1854. 89199

Anti-Negro emancipation. 73077

Antinomian pleas for licentiousness considered. 20059

Antinomianism in the colony of Massachusetts Bay. 104848

Antinomianisme anatomized. 78825

Antinomians and Familists condemned. 104843

Antioch College, Yellow Springs, Ohio. 1705, 1707, (19223), 44324

Antioch College, Yellow Springs, Ohio. President. (19223), 44324 see also Mann, Horace, 1796-1859.

Antioch College, its parentage, organization, finances. 1704

Anti-paedo-rantism. 50633

Anti-Pater, Theophilus. 1708

Anti-pierna-seca. pseud. see Masson, E.

Anti-piti-lista de los toros. (41081)

Antipode to AEsop. 78189

Antipoedorantism. 24391

Antiquarian. pseud. Article on continental money. 16163, 62490

Antiquarian. pseud. Review of the article. see Phillips, Henry, Jr.

Antiquarian and general review. 1709

Antiquarian and Historical Society of Dorchester, Mass. see Dorchester Antiquarian and Historical Society.

Antiquarian and Historical Society of Illinois. 34310

Antiquarian, ethnological and other researches. (6207)

Antiquarian . . . found the following original paper. 6717

Antiquarian library. 8677

Antiquarian miscellany. (22548)

Antiquarian researches among the early printers. 86033

Antiquarian researches: comprising a history of the Indian wars. 33402

Antiquarian researches (on American antiquities.) 82808, 97196

Antiquario noticiosa general de Espana y sus Indios. 78902

Antiquarisk tidsskrift. 55464

Antiquariske efterretninger fra Groenland. 28659

Antiquary. pseud. Origin, history, and character. see Livermore, George.

Antiquary. pseud. Sketch of the olden times. 81529

Antiqui orbis tabulae xxvii. et tabulae xxviii. 43822

Antiquitates Americanae. (4117), (67469)-67470, (67486), 81698, 83424

Antiquites Americaines au point de vue des progres de la geographie. 36431

Antiquites Americaines d'apres les monuments historiques. 67471

Antiquites de la vallee du Mississipi. 88841

Antiquites des Incas et autres peuples anciens. 11411

Antiquites Mexicaines. 23795, 40038, 101364

Antiquites Mexicaines; a propos d'une memoir. (7419)

Antiquites Peruviennes. 71644

Antiquities of America. (18793), (31828), 31963, 35320, (37800), (42065), 81283, 81286, 95146, 99397

Antiquities of America, by S. B. Evans. 85041

Antiquities of the southern Indians. (36474)

Antiquities of the state of New York. 89955

Antiquities of the west. 13153

Antiquites of Wisconsin. 38976, 85072

Antiquities. To the editor of the Advertiser. 19200

Antiquity and revival of Unitarian Christianity. 101410

Antiquity of the name of Scott. 78336

Antiquity of the Quakers. 105683-105684

Antiquity revived. 102531

Antiquo codice di Boturino. 9570

Anti-rent movement and out-break in New York. 3446

Anti-rent satanstoe. 16422

Anti-Sabbath Convention, Boston, 1848. 1710

Anti-secret Association, Southport, Wisc. see Southport Anti-secret Association.

Anti-secret Confederation. (1711)

Anti-secret Society Convention, Syracuse, N. Y., 1870. see New-York Anti-secret Society Convention, Syracuse, 1870.

Anti-sectarian. pseud. Introduction and notes. see Richmond, James C.

Anti-sectarian tendency of Congregational Church policy. 93275

Anti-shepherd-crat. 105542

Antisell, Thomas. (1712), 69946

Anti-slavery address. 14198

Anti-slavery advocate. 81853

Anti-slavery and Abolition Societies of the United Kingdom. petitioners 96026

Anti-slavery and pro-slavery. 36316

Anti-slavery argument. (8493)

Anti-slavery Association, Hull, England. see Hull and East-Riding Anti-slavery Association.

Anti-slavery Association, Leeds, England. see
Leeds Antislavery Association.
Anti-slavery Association of the East-Riding of
Yorkshire. see Hull and East-Riding
Anti-slavery Association.
Anti-slavery catechism. 12710
Anti-slavery Cent-a-Week Society. General
Agent. 88238-88239, 4th note after
103852 see also Southard, Nathaniel.
Anti-slavery Church, Philadelphia. see
Philadelphia. Anti-slavery church.
Anti-slavery Conference, Manchester, England,
1854. 82055
Anti-slavery Convention, Concord, N. H.,
1834. see New Hampshire Anti-slavery
Convention, Concord, 1834.
Anti-slaevry Convention, London, 1840. see
General Anti-slavery Convention, London,
1840.
Anti-slavery Convention, London, 1843. see
General Anti-slavery Convention, London,
1843.
Anti-slavery Convention, Milton, Indiana, 1838.
see Indiana Convention to Organize a
State Anti-slavery Society, Milton, 1838.
Anti-slavery Convention, Philadelphia, 1833.
82036
Anti-slavery Convention, Providence, R. I.,
1836. see Rhode Island Anti-slavery
Convention, Providence, 1836.
Anti-slavery Convention, Upper Alton, Ill.,
1837. see Illinois Anti-slavery Con-
vention, Upper Alton, 1837.
Anti-slavery Convention of American Women,
New York, 1837. 82037
Anti-slavery Convention of American Women,
Philadelphia. 1838. 81772, (81782),
81803, 82038
Anti-slavery Convention of American Women,
Philadelphia, 1838. Delegate. 82049
see also Lovell, Laura H.
Anti-slavery Convention of American Women,
Boston, 1838-1839. 81888
Anti-slavery Convention of American Women,
Philadelphia, 1839. 82039
Anti-slavery Convention of Illinois, Upper Alton,
1837. see Illinois Anti-slavery Con-
vention, Upper Alton, 1837.
Anti-slavery Convention of New England,
Boston, 1843. see New England Anti-
slavery Convention, Boston, 1843.
Anti-slavery Convention of Ohio, Putnam, 1835.
see Ohio Anti-slavery Convention,
Putnam, 1835.
Anti-slavery crisis. (81854), note after 95491
Anti-slavery enterprise. 93640-93641
Anti-slavery examiner. (20309), (22361),
62528, (81784), (81855), 81919, (82643),
82645, 95460, 102547, 102548, 102550,
103812
Anti-slavery examiner—extra. (81960), 2d
note after 102832
Anti-slavery harp. 8587
Anti-slavery history of the John-Brown year.
81856
Anti-slavery hymns. 90031
Anti-slavery in Virginia. 81857
Anti-slavery lecturer. pseud. American
women responsible. see Foote, C. C.
Anti-slavery letter of Dr. Duncan. 90334
Anti-slavery magazine. 81858
Anti-slavery manual, being an examination.
24003
Anti-slavery manual, containing a collection of
facts. 93752

Anti-slavery Meeting, Birmingham, England,
1835. see Great Anti-slavery Meeting,
Birmingham, England, 1835.
Anti-slavery Meeting, Boston, 1855. see
Boston. Anti-slavery Meeting, 1855.
Anti-slavery Meeting, Leeds, England, 1855.
29236, (39292)
Anti-slavery Meeting, Spafield's Chapel, London,
1859. see London Emancipation Society.
Anti-slavery Meeting, Spafield's Chapel,
1859.
Anti-slavery melodies. 41252
Anti-slavery monthly reporter. 81859, 95533
Anti-slavery movement. 20709
Anti-slavery opinions before the year 1800.
45241, (64041)
Anti-slavery picknick. 14443
Anti-slavery pilot. 81860
Anti-slavery poems. 81861
Anti-slavery poems of John Pierpont. 62760
Antislavery recollections. 91233
Anti-slavery record. 81862
Anti-slavery record of Hon. S. C. Pomeroy.
63936
Anti-slavery reform. 7005
Anti-slavery reporter. 81859, (81863), 81864,
93138, 93459, 93610, 103670, 103806
Anti-slavery review. 45363
Anti-slavery societies of Whitestown and Oneida
Institute. see Whitestown and Oneida
Institute Anti-slavery Societies.
Anti-slavery Society, Aberdeen. see Aberdeen
Anti-slavery Society.
Anti-slavery Society, Boston. see Boston
Anti-slavery Society.
Anti-slavery Society, Chatham, England. see
Rochester and Chatham Anti-slavery
Society.
Anti-slavery Society, Holden, Mass. see
Holden Anti-slavery Society.
Anti-slavery Society, Leicester, England. see
Leicester Auxiliary Anti-slavery Society.
Antislavery Society, Liverpool, England. see
Liverpool Antislavery Society.
Anti-slavery Society, London. see London
Anti-slavery Society.
Anti-slavery Society, Mansfield, Mass. see
Mansfield Anti-slavery Society.
Anti-slavery Society, New York City. see
New York Anti-slavery Society.
Anti-slavery Society, Philadelphia. see Phila-
delphia Anti-slavery Society.
Anti-slavery Society, Providence, R. I. see
Providence Anti-slavery Society.
Anti-slavery Society, Rochester, England. see
Rochester and Chatham Anti-slavery
Society.
Anti-slavery Society, Union College, N. Y. see
Union College, Schenectady, N. Y. Anti-
slavery Society.
Anti-slavery Society of Canada. Executive
Committee. 81865
Anti-slavery Society of Kentucky. see Ken-
tucky Anti-slavery Society.
Anti-slavery Society of Massachusetts. see
Massachusetts Anti-slavery Society.
Anti-slavery Society of Meriden, Conn. see
Meriden Anti-slavery Society.
Anti-slavery Society of New England. see
New England Anti-slavery Society.
Anti-slavery Society of New Hampshire. see
New Hampshire Anti-slavery Society.
Anti-slavery Society of New York State. see
New York State Anti-slavery Society.
Anti-slavery Society of Ohio. see Ohio Anti-
slavery Society.

Anti-slavery Society of Pennsylvania. see
Pennsylvania Anti-slavery Society.
Anti-slavery Society of Salem and vicinity.
see Salem Anti-slavery Society.
Anti-slavery Society of Union College. see
Union College, Schenectady, N. Y.
Anti-slavery Society.
Anti-slavery Society of Vermont. see
Vermont Anti-slavery Society.
Anti-slavery standard. 62524
Anti-slavery state convention proposed 8487
Anti-slavery tract. 88264-88265
Anti-slavery Tract Association of New England.
see New England Anti-Salvery Tract
Association.
Anti-slavery tracts. (4298), 9324, 9805, 11996,
24955, 26079, 26128, 30676, 31755,
(31792), 32338, 34697, 58325, (70347),
note after 81865, 92452, 103299
Anti-slavery tracts. New series. 8522, 11924,
(12727), 25908, 26128, 26712, 53391,
56652, 62528, 81861, note after 81865
Anti-slavery watchman. (81866)
Anti-supernaturalism. 59354
Antisynodalia Americana. 920, 66059
Anti synodalia scripta Americana. 12304,
49662, 66059
Anti-tariff Convention, Milledgeville, Ga., 1832.
27086
Anti-tariff Meeting, Abbeville Court-House,
S. C., 1827. (47733)
Anti-tariff Meeting, Abbeville Court-House,
S. C., 1827. petitioners (47733)
Anti-tariff Meeting, Sumter District, South
Carolina, 1827. see Sumter District,
S. C. Anti-tariff Metting, 1827.
Anti-tariff Meeting of the People of Abbeville
District, S. C., 1828. see Abbeville
District, S. C. Anti-tariff Meeting, 1828.
Anti-texass legion. 95068-95069
Antithelemite. 46954
Anti-tobacco Society, New York. see New
York Anti-tobacco Society.
Antitraditionist. 78322
Anti-tyther. 100427
Anti-universalist. 65496
Antoine, A., de Saint Jervais. 1713
Antoine, Joseph. 97091
Antoine A . . . pseud. Lettres d'un membre
du Congres Ameriquain. see Vincent, N.
Antoine and Marie. 81867
Antoinette de Mirecourt; . . . a Canadian tale.
40132
Antologia. 64005, 99406
Antologia de los comentarios reales. 98755
Anton Munon Chimalpain, Juan Bautista de San.
see Chimalpain, Juan Bautista de San
Anton Munon.
Anton in Amerika. 86384-86385
Anton von Solis Geschichte von der Eroberung
Mexico. 86493
Antonet, C. M. 1714
Antonii, Andre Joao. 1715
Antonii Bertolonii . . . Florula Guatimalensis.
5015
Antonii Psaevinii Cultura ingeniorum. 58989
Antonii Possevini Mantvani . . . Cultvra in
geniorvm. 64450
Antonini Ponti consentini rhomitypion. 64020
Antonio de Jesu. see Jesu, Antonio de.
Antonio de la Colancha. 40072
Antonio del Espiritu Santo. ed. 86443
Antonio, Agustin San. see San Antonio,
Agustin.
Antonio, Francisco de San. see San Antonio,
Francisco de.

Antonio, Joseph. 1716
Antonio, Juan Francisco de San. see San
Antonio, Juan Francisco de.
Antonio, Luis. ed. 55262
Antonio, Marco. pseud. see Macro-Antonio.
pseud.
Antonio, Nicholas, 1617-1684. 1717-(1720),
80987
Antonio Moreno, Martin de San. see San
Antonio Moreno, Martin de.
Antonio Ortega, J. de San. see Ortega, J.
de San Antonio.
Antonio Saenz, Matias San. see San Antonio
Saenz, Matias.
Antonio Jose ou o poeta e a inquisicao. 43792
Antonio Perez and Philip II. (48904)
Antonius Musa. see Musa, Antonius, fl. 23
B. C.
Antony, Henry B. 1723
Antrittsprogramm von Matthias Christian
Sprengel. 89763
Antrittsrede . . . bey seiner Einsetzung in die
theologische Professur. 77717
Antritts-Rede in der Kapelle des Columbia
College. 77672
Antrobus, Benjamin. 1721
Ants. A rhapsody. 1722
Antunez y Acevedo, Rafael. 1724, 47756
Antwerp, Bragg & Co. firm see Van Antwerp,
Bragg & Co. firm
Antwoord aan den Generaal Buonaparte. 42348
Antwoord op dezen aanmerkingen. 93849
Antwoorde vande Heeren Staten Generael. 7516
Antwoordt der Heeren Bewinthebbers. 4275,
note after 102883
Antwoordt, op sekeren Brief Evlaly. 23103-
23104
Antwoordt op sekeren Brieff Evlalii. 23105
Antwoort-Brief van een onpartydigh Coopman.
52222
Antvvoort vanden Ghetrouwen Gollander. 7415
Antwort auf diesen Aufsatz. 99303
Antwort auf Hrn. Franklins Anmerckungen.
25577, (59888), 84587
Antwort aus Amerika an Freiligrath. 25822
Antwort der Herren Agenor de Gasparin. 26734
Antwort der Herrn Franklin auf das gerichtl.
Befragen. 96161
Anuario de correos de la republica Arjentina.
8998
Anuario de la Administracion General de
Correos. 8997
Anuario de la Provincia de Caracas. 85740
Anuario del Colegio Nacional de Mineria.
48273
Anuario estadistico de la republica de Chile.
(12742)
Anuario nacional. 40726
Anuario publicado por D. Andres Poey. 29445
Anunciacion, Domingo de la. see Domingo de
la Anunciacion.
Anunciacion, Juan de la. see Juan de la
Anunciacion.
Anvers, Caleb d', of Gray's-Inn. pseud. see
Amhurst, Nicholas.
Anville, J. B. Bourguignon d'. see Bourguignon
d'Anville, J. B.
Anweisung, wie man hoch hier. (73908)
Any compromise a surrender. 27828
Anzeiger des westens Besonders. 85702
Anzorena, Jose Mariano de. 34187, 34189
Ao imperador. Cartas politicas de Erasmo.
7517
Apache als eine athapaskische Sprache erwiesen.
9521
Apalachicola Indians. Treaties, etc. 96669,
96690

Apalachicola Land Company. 1727
Apalachicola Land Company. Board of Directors. President. 5878 see also Blatchford, Richard M.
Aparicio, Manuel Ramirez. see Ramirez Aparicio, Manuel.
Aparicion de la Santisima Virgen de Ocotlan. 93327
Aparicion de N.^tra Senora de Guadalupe de Mexico. 9567, 74945
Aparicion y milagros de la prodigiosa imagen del patriarcha. 63888
Apela de la sentencia del Jurado del Canton de Caracas. 59636
Apelacion a la nacion Peruana. 68789, 94833
Apelacion a S. A. la Regencia del Reyno. 10680
Apelacion al buen criterio de los nacionales. 76725
Apelacion al pueblo Colombiano. 14556
Apelacion al tribunal de la opinion publica. 106380-1 [sic]
Apello Corbulacho, Juan Carlos de. see Corbulacho, Juan Carlos de Apello.
Apendice a la memoria. 61139
Apendice a la relacion. 1729, note after 98611
Apendice a las reflexiones historico criticas. 10771
Apendice a los documentos oficiales. 44177
Apendice al diccionario universal. 579, 6834, 48429, 48599
Apendice al nuevo Colon. 2583
Apendice concerniente las minas del Peru. 57476
Apendice de la historia de la masoneria. 102243
Apendice de monumentos pertenecientes. 10803
Apendice de sus robos llamados confiscaciones. 73218
Apendice del traductor. 65276
Apendice, en que se da razon del origen de dicha santa imagen. 69229, 72519
Apendice: memoria sobre las observaciones astronomicas. 681, (69221)
Apendice relativo al de Bogota. (56455)
Apendice sobre la decadencio del Paraguay. (20367)
Apendice sobre las orografia y la poblacion de la Confederacion. (74914)
Apendix a la historia de las missiones que entre gentes barbaras. 70789
Apendix. Containing reflections on gold. 65678, 103121
Apercu de la grammaire Maya. 73307
Apercu de la situation interieure. 63731
Apercu de l'ancienne geographie. (67472)
Apercu de l'etat actuel de ces etablissemens. 68082
Apercu de l'etat des noirs en esclavage. 63434
Apercu des dernieres revolutions. 1730
Apercu des Etats-Unis. 1731, 4172
Apercu d'un voyage dans les etats. 7420
Apercu d'un voyage dans l'interieur du Brasil. (75216)
Apercu general du climat des Antilles. 75522
Apercu general sur l'etat actuel du Texas. 5832, 79139
Apercu geographique. 71686
Apercu historique de geologie. (46975)
Apercu moral et politique. 44341
Apercu sur le chemin de fer. 1732
Apercu sur la constitution de Saint Domingue. 14048, 14052

Apercu sur la situation politique. 97501
Apercu sur les moeurs les institutions Americaines. 23932
Apercu sur l'isthme de Suez. 12584
Apercu topographique de la Louisiane. 42191
Apercu topographique de la Virginie. 43358
Apercue statistique de l'ile de Cuba. 33471
Apercus sur les institutions et les moeurs. 49094
Apercus sur les poetes des Etats-Unis. (70379)
Apersoutingoello koekkorsunnut illinniegaekset. 95618
Apertura del Amazonas. 7518
Apertura del Establecimiento de Educacion 66592
Apertura del istom Americano. 4577
Apes, William. (1733)-1737, 85433
Apess, William. see Apes, William.
Aphelia; and other poems. 63410
Aphorismes of state. 78379
Aphorisms of the war. 5300
Aphorisms . . . physiognomy . . . and the blessings of poverty. 3760
Apianus, Petrus, 1501?-1552. 1738-1757, 5260, 27724, 63957, 76838, 86390
Aplavso reverente y afectuoso. 29145
Aplicacion rara de la ley. 71482
Aplin, ------. 97091
Aplin, John. 1758, 43664, 47142, (52608), note after 99295
Apocalypse Britannique. 1759
Apocalypse de Chiokvyhikoy. 12816, (35102)
Apocalyptic gnomon. 93574
Apocatastasis. (44755)
Apodaca, Juan Ruiz de. see Ruiz de Apodaca, Juan.
Apoderado. pseud. Alegato. see Suraez y Navarro, Juan.
Apodous holothurians. 85072
Apographum descriptionis regionum Siberiae. 67355
Apollinario de Conceicao. 1759A-1759B, 15099
Apollo Association for the Promotion of the Fine Arts in the United States. see American Art Union
Apollonius, Guilianmus. 55888
Apollonius, Levinus. 1761-1762A, 4798, note after (40758)
Apologetical answer unto some letters and papers. 103441
Apologetical discourse on Italy. 64014
Apologetical narration. 56461
Apologetical preface set before the essay. (18703)-18704, (46778)
Apologeticall narration, hvmbly svbmitted to the Honourable Houses of Parliament. 21991, 27952-(27953), (69679), 74624, 91383
Apologia a favor do R. P. Ant. Vieyra. 34186
Apologia catolica del mismo proyecto. 41674
Apologia de la aparicion de Nuestra Senora de Guadalupe. 29289
Apologia de la conducto militar. 36129
Apologia de la del A. L. de Santa-Anna. 76735
Apologia de la Margileida. (39083)
Apologia de los palos. 11092
Apologia de Victoria en los dias de la accordada. 99440
Apologia del cuarto Congreso Constitucional. 94277
Apologia del Diario de Veracruz. 94154
Apologia del manifiesto del Senor Agar. 94155
Apologia del metodo. 98311

Apologia del Pichon Palomino. 39096, 58388
Apologia del poema intitulado: Primavera Indiana. 80987
Apologia delle ricerche istorico-critiche. 3799
Apologia dos bens dos religiosos, e religiosas. 76319
Apologia en defensa del ingenio y fortalez de las Indios. 39140
Apologia Ioannis Genesii Sepvlvedae pro libro. (79175), 79176, (79178)
Apologia ivsta, et necessaria. (72089)
Apologia por los doctrinas y curatos. 73850
Apologia por todos los criollos de la America. 75782
Apologia pro libro de Iustis belli causis. 79179
Apologia . . . pro libro de Justis belli causis. 79180
Apologiae, ofte vvaerachtighe verantvvoordinghe. 40988
Apologias y discurssos de las conquistas occidentales. 98604
Apologie de Barthelemy de Las Casas. 28723
Apologie de constitutions des Etats-Unis d'Amerique. 41646
Apologie de J. de Mosquera. 51067
Apologie de la conduite de la France. 4182
Apologie de la vie solitaire. 73478
Apologie des franc-macons. 25793
Apologie des orders der freimaurer. 90509
Apologie for his voyage to Guiana. 67561, 67587, 67598
Apologie oder Vertheidigungs-Schrift. 3365
Apologie of the churches in New England. 52610
Apologie of the said elders of New-England. 46776
Apologies for the crime. 93647
Apologo de la ociosidad el trabajo. 75568
Apologvs vanden Krijch der Gansen. (59074)
Apology. 1490
Apology for abolitionists. 47965
Apology for anti-abolitionists. 13300
Apology for apostolic order and its advocates. (32301)
Apology for Calvinism. 92031
Apology for collegiate education. (36934)
Apology for congregational divines. 106097A
Apology for Great Britain. 1764, 16024, 18160
Apology for having imported some stockings. 3866
Apology for his unlucky voyage to Guiana. (67543)-67544
Apology for Negro slavery. 97461, note after 102819
Apology for new principles in education. 101404
Apology for protesting against the Methodist Episcopal government. 85439
Apology for rational and evangelical Christianity ity. 95189
Apology for religious conferences. 63992
Apology for renouncing the jurisdiction. 65137, 92031
Apology for slavery. 26823, 81868
Apology for the author's withdrawing his fellowship. 88665
Apology for the Bible. 92836
Apology for the builder. 1765
Apology for the Church of England in the Canadas. 10353
Apology for the colonial clergy. 105066
Apology for the discipline of the ancient church. 55261
Apology for the friends of peace. 82885
Apology for the last voyage to Guiana. 67560

Apology for the liberties of the churches. 46791
Apology for the life and actions of General Wolfe. 46914
Apology for the life of James Fennell. 24065
Apology for the life of Mr. Bampfylde-Moor Carew. 27615
Apology for the life of Mrs. Bellamy. 4484
Apology for the ministers who subscribed. 104184
Apology for the people called Quakers. 59613
Apology for the for the religious society, called Free Quakers. 103062
Apology for the right of ordination. 62582
Apology for the times. 1766
Apology for the translator. 106354
Apology for the true Christian divinity. 3364
Apology for the United States of America. 1767, 97907
Apology for the view of Halifax. 29687
Apology for voting for the fugitive slave bill. 19890, (30195)
Apology for West Indians. 85226
Apology in behalf of the Revd. Dr. Whitefield. 25386
Apology, in justification of Mrs. -----'s friendship. 29316
Apology of patriots. 2422
Apology of Stephen Thurston. 95776
Apology of the Presbytery of New-Brunswick. 94700
Apology or vindication of Francis Nicholson, Esq. 55221
Apology. The Protestant Episcopal Society for the Promotion of Evangelical Knowledge. 1763
Apology to the printer. 80677
Apology to the Rev. Nathan S. S. Beman. 8166
Apolonius, Levinus. see Appollonius, Levinus, 16th cent.
Apontamentos biographicos do Barao de Cayru. 47456
Apontamentos de Direito Financeiro Brasileiro. 3649, 60890
Apontamentos extrahidos de Mr. John Quincey [sic] Adams. 96261
Apontamentos juridicos sobre contractos. 81115
Apontamentos para a historia do cholera-morbus no Para. 11451
Apontamentos para a historia financeira do Brasil. 85622
Apontamentos para o diccionario historico. (44663)
Apontamentos relativos a botanica. 52357
Apontamentos sobre a colleccao de plantas. 88781
Apontamentos sobre o systema monetario e resgate do cobre. 96262
Apontamentos para o direito internacional. 62986
Apostacy from the primitave church. 89369
Apostate exposed. 59663
Apostate further convicted. 103703
Apostel de los Indios. (9887)
Apostle of liberty. 77161
Apostle's advice to the jaylor improved. 17675
Apostles neither impostors nore inthusiasts. 23880
Apostles of St. Paul and St. James reconciled. 2873
Apostol de la paz. (41989)
Apostol de las gentes de Indias. (76898)
Apostol de las Indias. 60847
Apostol Mariano representado en la vida. 98842
Apostolic church government displayed. 104634
Apostolic commission. 90385

Apostolic letter concerning the African slave trade. 22587
Apostolic preaching considered. 91788
Apostolicae literae in forma brevis. 76315
Apostolick charity. 7473
Apostolick mode of preaching. 79782
Apostolico Congregacion de N. G. P. Sr. S. Pedro. see Congregacion de San Pedro.
Apostolicos Afanes de la Compania de Jesus. 1768, 38234, 57680
Apotheosis. (66411)
Apotheosis of the heroes of the antirent war. 77848
Appalachicola Indians. see Apalachicola Indians.
Apparent tendencies of political thought. 4572
Apparentia. 65940-65941
Apparitionist. 77633
Appeal against the abuses in the local government. 54186
Appeal against the proposed transfer. 70009
Appeal and caution. 81869
Appeal and protest. (59889)
Appeal and remonstrance. 14338, 103663
Appeal, by Dr. Bushnell. 10001
Appeal . . . by Elmer Cushing. 18101
Appeal by husband and wife. (77302)
Appeal by the Convention of Michigan. 48723
Appeal . . . . Commended to the readers. 61558
Appeal defended. 11874, (12326)
Appeal farther defended. 11875
Appeal for a free Episcopal Church in . . . Boston. 57391
Appeal for aid. 6838
Appeal for co-operation. 19369
Appeal for freedom. 89307
[Appeal for funds, July 4, 1862.] 76569, 76647
Appeal for gospel love and unity. 86034
Appeal for justice. 84080
Appeal for Mount Vernon. 51177
Appeal for peace. 28542
Appeal for rectitude in primary politics. 105564, 105566
Appeal for suffering genius. 8785
Appeal for the American Sunday-School Union. 6076
Appeal for the ancient doctrines. 86035
Appeal for the establishment of a free library. 3018
Appeal for the floating church. 87261
Appeal for the purchase and future preservation. 17968
Appeal for the rights of conscience. 34485
Appeal for the union. 1770
Appeal for the union of parties. 1769
Appeal for the Young Men's Institute. 106174
Appeal for water line from Norfolk, Va. 5589
Appeal (for which several were imprisoned, &c.) 37200, 97113
Appeal from a countryman to the union men. 33325
Appeal from an order of the Circuit Court. 8481
(Appeal from Antigua.) Joint appendix. 101262
Appeal from Antigua. The respondent's case. 101262
Appeal from Bermuda. 100576
Appeal from Gibraltar. 104160
Appeal from our present divided times. (39070)
Appeal from Portland. (64340)
Appeal from the American press. 52161
Appeal from the colored men of Philadelphia. 18856, 81870
Appeal from the country to the city. (30463)

Appeal from the Court of Chancery. 96896, 97879
Appeal from the Court of the First Judicial Circuit. 96920
Appeal from the denunciation. 45465
Appeal from the District Court of the United States. 9615
Appeal from the judgments of Great Britain. 101158
Appeal from the madness of disunion. 13704
Appeal from the misrepresentations of James Hall. 9652
Appeal from the missionaries at the Sandwich Islands. 21477, 76451
Appeal from the new to the old Whigs. 181, 102321, 103268
Appeal from the politicians to the people. (63576)
Appeal from the sentence. 57309
Appeal from the southern states. 20604
Appeal from the Synod of New-York and Philadelphia. 30383
Appeal from the twenty-eight judges. (1771), 37181
Appeal from William Wilberforce. 44880
Appeal, . . . in behalf of a Protestant Episcopal Theological Seminary. 12194
Appeal in behalf of Antioch College. 1706
Appeal in behalf of common schools. 16359
Appeal in behalf of missions. 64617
Appeal in behalf of Negro slaves. 14021
Appeal in behalf of Oglethorpe University. 56850
Appeal in behalf of our country. 20498
Appeal in behalf of the Boston Athenaeum. 67207
Appeal in behalf of the church in California. 33475
Appeal in behalf of the Diocese of Ohio. (56878)
Appeal in behalf of the Illinois College. 34227
Appeal in behalf of the Indiana Theological Seminary. 88131
Appeal in behalf of the Methodist Episcopal Church. 65683
Appeal in behalf of the New York Infant Asylum. (54496)
Appeal in behalf of the . . . [Philadelphia City] Institute. 61978
Appeal in behalf of the proposed church and hospital. 54068
Appeal . . . in behalf of the Protestant Episcopal Church. 57317
Appeal in behalf of the South-Carolina College. 87970
Appeal in favor of female education. 104043
Appeal in favor of that class of Americans. 12711
Appeal, in four articles. 101039
Appeal, in verse. 31197
Appeal in vindication of peace principles. 42359
Appeal, Morristown, N. J. 64249
"Appeal," not to the romantic sensibility, but the good sense. 7821
Appeal no. 1. (22402)
Appeal of A. J. Blackbird. (5636)
Appeal of a soldier of 1812. 86269
Appeal of Charles Gould. 28098
Appeal of civilization and liberty. 1772
Appeal of Commodore Charles Stewart to Congress. 91651
Appeal of Commodore R. F. Stockton. 91891
Appeal of Commodore R. F. Stockton to the people. 91894
Appeal [of Harriet B. Stowe.] 13175

Appeal of Hugh B. Mosier. 51062
Appeal of John Lorimer Graham. (28233)
Appeal of Joseph Wheaton. 103163
Appeal of L. Louaillier. (42158)
Appeal of Maj. Gen. Fitz John Porter. 64246, 64249
Appeal of Moses M. Strong. 92947
Appeal of religion to men in power. 19862
Appeal of Rev. Reeder Smith. 93752
Appeal of Samuel D. Greene. (28610)
Appeal [of Samuel Vaughan.] (51453)
Appeal [of Senator Phelps.] 61394, 81679
Appeal, of some of the unlearned. 91941
Appeal of the American citizens resident in Peru. 83711
Appeal of the Association of Fairfield West. (23698)
Appeal of the boatmen of the Schuylkill Canal. 78070
Appeal of the Boston Consulting Committee. 85912
Appeal of the . . . Directors on behalf of the Pennsylvania Training School for Idiotic and Feeble-Minded Children. 60385
Appeal of the Domestic Committee of the Board of Missions. 66123
Appeal of the Executive Finance Committee. (76538), 76549, 76647
Appeal of the Independent Democrats in Congress. (52182)
Appeal of the Managers of St. Luke's Hospital. (75414)
Appeal of the Managers of the . . . [Philadelphia Lying-in] Charity. 62012
Appeal of the old elm on Boston Common. 6686
Appeal of the people of West Virginia. 81871
Appeal of the prosecutor, Alonzo P. Bacon. 89304
Appeal of the religious society of Friends. 1773
Appeal [of William Wilberforce.] 102770
Appeal on behalf of fugitives from slavery. 81872
Appeal on behalf of Kenyon College, Ohio. 43320
Appeal on behalf of the British factory population. 78168
Appeal on behalf of the British subjects. (38989)
Appeal on behalf of the sick. 59890
Appeal on the common school law. 13814
Appeal on the contemptible and malignant article. 4603
Appeal on the iniquity of slavery. (81873)
Appeal on the subject of slavery. 93753
Appeal on the subject of slavery; addressed to the members. 104561
Appeal on truth's behalf. 72110
Appeal to a candid world. 37651
Appeal to all the followers of Christ. (13532)
Appeal to all the followers of Jesus. 87952
[Appeal] to all those citizens of Cambridge. 10153
Appeal to all who in any way promote the traffic. 51733
Appeal to American authors. 46840
Appeal to American Christians. (58093)
Appeal to American patriots. 94589
Appeal to American youth. 20028
Appeal to Americans. 102338
Appeal to an impartial public. 105233
Appeal to banks in particular. 7768
Appeal to candour and common sense. 81874
Appeal to Christians, in behalf of state prisoners. 70418

Appeal to Christians, on the subject of slavery. 31590
Appeal to citizens of Baltimore. 82777
Appeal to citizens of the U. S. 71919
Appeal to common sense and common justice. 10889
Appeal to common sense . . . occasioned by the late trial. 38091
Appeal to Congress and to the people of the United States. 1774
Appeal to Congress by the citizens of Rock Island and Moline. 51925
Appeal to . . . Congress . . . concerning the relative rank. 62967
Appeal to Congress for a revision. 20296
Appeal to Congress in behalf of the northwest. 67726
Appeal to Democrats and Union men. 45636, 81875
Appeal to England. 104035
Appeal to Englishmen of every class and party. 71812
Appeal to Episcopalians. 17525
Appeal to facts. 15538, 34447
Appeal to history. 80419
Appeal to honest inquirers. 1775
Appeal to honest Republicans. 105542
Appeal to knowledge. 1776
Appeal to liquor makers. 85144
Appeal to loyal religious people. 2756
Appeal to Maryland. (37423)
Appeal to matters of fact. 62437
Appeal to merchants and ship owners. 25051
Appeal to Mr. Wilberforce. 73077
Appeal to our countrymen. 17522
Appeal to our country's loyalty. 42016
Appeal to Philadelphians. 61640
Appeal to parents for female education. 20391, (75434)
Appeal to patriots. 9333
Appeal to Pennsylvania. 68601
Appeal to reason and justice. 1777
Appeal . . . to the abolitionists. (12703)
Appeal to the abolitionists of Great Britain. 28853, 95492
Appeal to the alumni and friends. 30765
Appeal to the American Board of Commisioners for Foreign Missions. (47984)
Appeal to the American Board of C. F. Missions, from the unjust and oppressive measures. 59264
Appeal to the American churches. 40749
Appeal to the American churches, with a plan. 77718
Appeal to the American people. (50727)
Appeal to the bar and the freemen of Maryland. 45070
Appeal to the British nation on the affairs of South America. 1778, 52773
Appeal to the British nation, on the greatest reform. 8893
Appeal to the British nation to think for themselves. 68557
Appeal to the candid of all parties. 62471
Appeal to the candid, or the Trinitarian review. 105247
Appeal to the candid, upon the present state. (15671), 97176, 105925
Appeal to the candid world. 14897
Appeal to the candour and justice. 1779, 5th note after 102788
Appeal to the capitalists and others. 53312
Appeal to the Christian community. 26253, 79105, 79110, 92978
Appeal to the Christian philanthropy. 96798

Appeal to the Christian public. Containing the discipline of the Trinitarian Church in Concord, Mass. 28551

Appeal to the Christian public, on the evil and impolicy. 32818

Appeal to the Christian women of America. 81876

Appeal to the Christian women of the south. 28853, 95492

Appeal to the Christian world. 94127

Appeal to the Christians in America. 35854

Appeal to the church, in behalf of a dying race. 52306

Appeal to the churches. 105240

Appeal to the churches of Christ. 97076

Appeal to the citizens of Boston. (21285)

Appeal to the citizens of Connecticut. 102708

Appeal to the citizens of Davidson County. 41313

Appeal to the citizens of Maryland. 8692

Appeal to the citizens of New Hampshire. 52942

Appeal to the citizens of New-York, by a tax payer. 94429

Appeal to the citizens of New York for the organization. 4622

Appeal to the citizens of New-York, on behalf of the Christian Sabbath. 89783

Appeal to the citizens of Newton. 18884

Appeal to the citizens of Pennsylvania for . . . additional accomodations. 37980

Appeal to the citizens of Pennsylvania on behalf of the Historical Society of Pennsylvania. 60144, 85578

Appeal to the citizens of Philadelphia. 61611, 64617

Appeal to the citizens of . . . Philadelphia against the City Councils. 61472

Appeal to the citizens of Philadelphia, for means to purchase a lot. 61470

Appeal to the citizens of Philadelphia, in behalf of domestic missions. 61471

Appeal to the citizens of the commonwealth of Maryland. 45071

Appeal to the citizens of the United States. 48376

Appeal to the clergy and laity. (66124)

Appeal to the colored people of the United States. 37305

Appeal to the common sense and patriotism of the people. (77472)

Appeal to the common sense of the country. 42393

Appeal to the common sense of the people. 33990

Appeal to the Congress of the United States, by a Committee of New Jersey Bank Officers. 3176, 53070

Appeal to the Congress of the United States, concerning the relative rank. (62908)

Appeal to the Congress of the United States on the subject of bank tax. 3176, (8148), 53070

Appeal to the conscience of the Rev. Solomon Aiken. 105240

Appeal to the consciences of a degenerate people. (24926)

Appeal to the conservative men of all parties. 1780

Appeal to the country people of Massachusetts. 45655

Appeal to the Court for the Trial of Impeachments. 96762

Appeal to the creditors of the Bank of Maryland. 64722

Appeal to the Democracy of Indiana. 34484

Appeal to the Democracy of the south. 37060, 62815

Appeal to the Democracy of Wisconsin. 46852

Appeal to the documents. (33231)

Appeal to the females of the African Methodist Episcopal Church. 91780

Appeal to the females of the north. 81877

Appeal to the free and independent people. 45596, 92886

Appeal to the freemen. 61473

Appeal to the friends of education. (24016)

Appeal to the friends of humanity. 89064

Appeal to the friends of religion and literature. 92633

Appeal to the friends of temperance. 19844

Appeal to the German-American citizens. 51311

Appeal to the Germans in America. 40979

Appeal to the good sense of a great people. 81878

Appeal to the good sense of a great people, on the subject of slavery. (81879)

Appeal to the good sense of the Democrats. 62529

Appeal to the good sense of the legislature and the community. 6597

Appeal to the good sense of the nation. 10861

Appeal to the good sense of the people. 24308

Appeal to the good sense of the people of Massachusetts. 45637

Appeal to the good sense of the people of South Carolina. 87936

Appeal to the government and Congress of the United States. 1781

Appeal to the government and people of the United States. 87312, 97908

Appeal to the government of the United States. 1782

Appeal to the government to change its by-laws. 58105

Appeal to the government to emancipate the slaves. (58104)

Appeal to the government to protect the rights. 58105

Appeal to the governors and people of the northern states. (36117)

Appeal to the Green Mountain Boys. 83241, 83288

Appeal to the honour and good sense of persons. 105463

[Appeal] to the Honourable Levi Woodbury. (43454)

Appeal to the honourable the members of the Senate and House of Assembly. 53533

Appeal to the honourable the Senate of the United States. 30152, 87791

Appeal to the honourable the Senate of the United States, in behalf of the conservative people of South Carolina. 30152, 87791

Appeal to the impartial public, by an association. 1658

Appeal to the impartial publick, by the Society of Christian Independents congregating in Glocester. 1658, 27591-27592, 93506

Appeal to the impartial public, in behalf of the oppressed. 51516

Appeal to the Imperial Parliament. (76396)

Appeal to the industrial classes of the United States. 90489

Appeal to the inhabitants of Europe. (81880)

Appeal to the inhabitants of Her Majesty's Canadian provinces. 8563

Appeal, to the inhabitants of the state of Vermont. 99176

Appeal to the inhabitants of Vermont. 99182

Appeal to the justice and humanity. 10889

Appeal to the justice and interests. 1783, (39697)-39698, 98179
Appeal to the ladies of Canada. 37896
Appeal to the ladies of Great Britain. 81881
Appeal to the laity of Maryland. 34098
Appeal to the Latter-Day Saints. 55078
Appeal to the lay members. (60438)
Appeal to the learned. (46669), 91941, 91954
Appeal to the Legislative Council. 53071
Appeal to the legislators of Massachusetts. (12727)
Appeal to the legislature and the people. 19841
Appeal to the legislature in behalf of Martenet's map. 44830
Appeal to the Legislature of the commonwealth of Pennsylvania. 19839
Appeal to the Legislature of the state of Maryland. 91823
Appeal to the Legislature of the United States. 25688
Appeal to the legislatures of the United States. 8340
Appeal to the Medical Society of Rhode Island, in behalf of female physicians. 70727
Appeal to the Medical Society of Rhode Island, in behalf of woman . . . as "midwife." 70547
Appeal to the members of the Protestant Episcopal Church. 66125
Appeal to the men of New-England. 52611
Appeal to the merchants of New York. 54089
Appeal to the Methodist Episcopal Church. 78345
Appeal to the Methodist Episcopal Church concerning what its next general conference should do. 91473, 103172
Appeal to the Methodist Episcopal Church, North and South. (25690)
Appeal to the ministers and members of the Methodist Episcopal Church. 81882, 103844
Appeal to the nation. 34108
Appeal to the north. (47166)
Appeal to the old Whigs of Massachusetts. 45638, 92886
Appeal to the old Whigs of New-Hampshire. 52801, 63449, note after 102255
Appeal to the Parliament of England. 10822
Appeal to the patriot and the Christian. 97077
Appeal to the patriotic National Republican members of Congress. 20153
Appeal to the patriotism of the citizens of Missouri. 49581
Appeal to the patrons of science. 51032
Appeal to the people and Legislature of Massachusetts. 9330, 55369
Appeal to the people, being a brief statement. 102126
Appeal to the people; being a brief review. 14310
Appeal to the people for the suppression of the liquor traffic. (38019)
Appeal to the people, from the decision of the Senate. 78315
Appeal to the people of Illinois. 5564
Appeal to the people of Ireland. 81883
Appeal to the people of Maine. (43909)
Appeal to the people of Maryland. 45072
Appeal to the people of Massachusetts. 30858
Appeal to the people of Massachusetts, on the Texas Question. (45639), 95070
Appeal to the people of . . . New York, on the expediency of abolishing the Council of Appointment. (29546), (53532)
Appeal to the people of Pennsylvania for the decision. 59892

Appeal to the people of Pennyslvania for the sick and wounded soldiers. 62358, 76693
Appeal to the people of Pennsylvania on the . . . Asylum for the Insane Poor. 59891
Appeal to the people of Rhode Island. 31109
Appeal to the people of the city of New-York. (54091), 78818
Appeal to the people of the late province of Upper Canada. 24615
Appeal to the people of the north. 1234, 62543
Appeal to the people of the north. 1783A, 14315
Appeal to the people of the northern and eastern states. 81884, note before 88112
Appeal to the people of the south. 32412
Appeal to the people of the state of New York, adopted by the Executive Committee. 54090
Appeal to the people of the state of New-York; being a report of the Executive Committee. (32516), 84221
Appeal to the people of the state of New York in favor of constructing the Genesee and Alleghany Canal. 26927
Appeal to the people of the state of New-York, in favor of the construction of the Chenango Canal. 96352
Appeal to the people of the state of New York to legalize the dissection of the dead. 20899
Appeal to the people of the United States against J. K. Paulding. 23913
Appeal to the people of the United States, by a freeholder. 1784, 25751
Appeal to the people of the United States, by citizens of the District of Columbia. 48962
Appeal to the people of the United States, in behalf of art. 89624
Appeal to the people of the United States; with a plan. 69547
Appeal to the people of Vermont. (61393)
Appeal to the people, on the causes and consequences. 42445, (62502)
Appeal to the people on the conduct of a certain public body. 51137
Appeal to the people on the question. (56312), 87829
Appeal to the people. Proof of an alliance. 36676
Appeal to the Presbyterians of New Brunswick. 41652, 104681
Appeal to the President of the United States. 64246, 64249
Appeal to the professors of Christianity. 52612, (81886)
Appeal to the protestant evangelical churches. 80495, note after 90579
Appeal to the public. 61474, 103825
Appeal to the public, and especially the medical public. 17282
Appeal to the public answered. 12311
Appeal to the public, by Joseph Healy. 31173
Appeal to the public [by the Douglas Monument Association.] (20696)
Appeal to the public, by William Vans. 98550
Appeal to the public, especially to the learned. 97177
Appeal to the public, &c. 86741
Appeal to the public for religious liberty. 1786, 2625
Appeal to the public. From . . . results of the Maine law. 43898
Appeal to the public, in behalf of George Johnstone. (36397)

APPEAL

Appeal to the public in behalf of Samuel
Vaughan. 98689
Appeal to the public, in behalf of the Church
of England in America. 1785, 11873,
(11876)
Appeal to the public in behalf of the Philadelphia City Institute. 61978
Appeal to the public, in behalf of the Theological Institute of Connecticut. 105891,
105892
Appeal to the public, in consequence of an
attack by the Rev: Nathan H. Hall.
25172, 33905, 96466
Appeal to the public in its [i. e. Plummer
Farm School's] behalf. 63466
Appeal to the public in relation to the charges.
89744
Appeal to the public, in which the misrepresentations and calumnies, contained in a
pamphlet. 6935
Appeal to the public, occasioned by proceedings
of the Hopkinton Association. 105327
Appeal to the public on behalf of a House of
Refuge. 52236, (61730)
Appeal to the public on the conduct of the
banks. 54092
Appeal to the public, on the controversy.
31751, 42461, 50928, 50971, 70204
Appeal to the public. Operations and results.
76627
Appeal to the public; or, a story without fiction.
(77613)
Appeal to the public, or an exposition of the
conduct. 43507
Appeal to the public, relative to an act of the
General Association. 104760
Appeal to the public, relative to the unlawful-
ness. 66410, 97178
[Appeal to the public, September 11, 1862.]
76671
Appeal to the public; stating and considering
the objections. 4947, (66991)
Appeal to the public whether certain pen-
marked, half-formed spurious interest
tables. 73596
[Appeal to the public, with letters.] 76573,
76647
Appeal to the public, with respect to the un-
lawfulness of divorces. 97179
Appeal to the religion. 103951
Appeal to the reason and religion. (73941),
(81887)
Appeal to the representatives of the British
nation. 11198
Appeal to the representatives of the people of
the state of New-York. (22741), (22766),
92863
Appeal to the Republicans of Massachusetts.
45640
Appeal to the respectable tribunal of the pub-
lic. 98982
Appeal to the Senate of Rhode Island. 70548
Appeal to the Senate to modify its policy.
(20611)
Appeal to the sense of the people. 1787
Appeal to the society of Friends. 3463, 25264
Appeal to the society of Friends, in behalf of
the Bible Association of Friends in
America. 86036
Appeal to the soldiers of the American armies.
(40853)
Appeal to the south. 54596
Appeal to the state. 87792
Appeal to the state, continued. 87792
Appeal to the State Rights Party of South
Carolina. 87793

Appeal to the Synod of New York and New
Jersey. 37628
Appeal to the temperate. 56050
Appeal to thinking men. 1790
Appeal to the tribunal of public justice. (32969)
Appeal to the two counties of Lincoln and Han-
cock. 98021
Appeal to the unerring tribunal of the impartial
public. 104328
Appeal to the unprejudiced, concerning the
present discontents. 1788
Appeal to the unprejudiced from the injurious
and uncharitable reflections. 4095,
(20062)
Appeal to the unprejudiced judgment. 99150
Appeal to the unprejudiced; or, a vindication.
1789
Appeal to the virtue and good sense of the
inhabitants. 8194
Appeal to the voluntary citizens of the United
States. 71303
Appeal to the wealthy of the land. 10889
Appeal to the Whigs of Cambridge. 10148
Appeal to the women of the nominally free
states. 81888
Appeal to the women of America. 44611
Appeal to the women of New York. 90399
Appeal to the world on the controversy. 212
Appeal to the world; or, a vindication of the
town of Boston. 6478
Appeal to those members. 40805
Appeal to those who oppose the union of Texas.
37627
Appeal to young soldiers. 88043B
Appeale on truths behalfe. 72090
Appeals from the decrees of the District Court.
89224
Appeals to President Lincoln. (36119)
Appel a la justice. 94175
Appel a la justice de l'etat. 21044
Appel a la justice de sa majeste. 81654
Appel a l'opinion publique. Par Martial Besse.
54051
Appeal a l'opinion publique sur l'indemnite.
75052
Appel a l'union. 75053
Appel au gouvernement imperial. 5847
Appel au Parlement imperial. 10354
Appel aux abolitionistes. (24009)
Appel aux chambres. 19479
Appel aux habitants de l'Europe. (81889)
Appel aux municipalites du Bas Canada. 20888
Appel aux nations Hispano-Amercaines. 63667
Appel aux populations laborieuses de France.
39984
Appel de la capitale de l'Ecosse aux Etats-Unis.
57178, 81890
Appel des etrangers dans nos colonies. 97459
Appel d'un Americain. 50695
Appel interjette par l'Assemblee Generale.
75054
Appellant and mediator. (28136)
Appellant's brief on the question raised. 85212
Appellant's case. 101262, 104157, 104160
Appellant's case. To be heard at the bar of
the House of Lords. 105082
Appendex to the book, entitled, New England
judged. 5629, 91318
Appendice a la correspondance particuliere.
9043, 93807
Appendice a la memoria presentada. 58418
Appendice al num. 26, del Archivo Americano.
34437
Appendice alla memoria. 76522
Appendice contenant diverses addresses, cor-
respondances, etc. 658, 69284

189

Appendice contenant les actes publies. 40234
Appendice contenant les opinions de l'Empereur Napoleon 1er. 42355, (75482)
Appendice de Tapuyis, et Chilensibus. 7588, 63028
Appendice dell'avvacato Giambattista Belloro. 4565
Appendice. Par le Superintendant des Ecoles du Haut-Canada. 10428, (74569)
Appendice sobre o voto separado. 76321
Appendice sur le coton. 4568, 67131
Appendices, containing historical notices. 18205
Appendices in Margaritam philosophicam. 69130
Appendices (including report upon a route.) 69946
Appendices Ioannis Schoner Charolipolitani in opusculum globi astriferi nuper ab eodem aeditum. (77799)
Appendices Joannis Schoner Charolipolitani in opusculum globi astriferi nuper ab eodē[m] editū[m]. 77798
Appendix. 2738, 23168, 28608, 29656, 29892, 33798, (34686), 38188, 43314, 45488, 46581, 46927, 56521, 57611, 63342, 72620, 79652, 80673, 84750, note after 89883, 93538, 94073, 95144, 2d note after 95742, note before 96272, note after 96880, 1st note after 96936, note after 100591, 104695, note before 105987
Appendix A. Company's monthly report. 96481
Appendix. A full account of the late dereadful earthquake. (42593), 64185, 97102
Appendix A [of Head's narrative.] 98067
Appendix A added by the American Colonization Society. 69887, 90427
Appendix addressed to the public. 70750
Appendix, and a further appendix. (46541), note after 94885
Appendix and illustration of a memoir. 95782, 95785
Appendix, . . . and other papers. (41630)
Appendix ao dialogo constitucional. 51687
Appendix B [of Head's narrative.] 31137, 98067
Appendix, being the Registrar's book. 68004
Appendix, by a citizen of northern Pennsylvania. 60275
Appendix, by a gentleman of North Carolina. 98530
Appendix by another hand. 46515
Appendix by B. Colman. 16640
Appendix, by Dr. William Whiting. 79373, note after 103712
Appendix, by E. W. Stoddard. 91932
Appendix, by Elizur Wright. 45888
Appendix by James Blake. 13208
Appendix by John Bacon, A. M. 102755
Appendix by John Delavall. 37209
Appendix by John Martin. 44889
Appendix by Lieut. Campbell Hardy. 38913
Appendix by Mr. Dunbar. (40825)
Appendix by Mr. Foxcroft. 21946
Appendix [by Nathan Bassett.] (24469)
Appendix by one of the attestators. (64276)
Appendix, by Peter Porcupine. 63374
Appendix by Rev. Stephen Parks. 58809, note after 97074
Appendix, by . . . Rev. T. Y. Howe. 32294
Appendix by Robert Etheridge. (35584)
Appendix, by the Rev. Mr. Taylor. 104268-104271
Appendix, by the Rev. Mr. Williams. 104268-104271
Appendix by the Rev. William H. Furness. 62614

Appendix, by the same author. 103322
Appendix by way of supplication to Almighty God. 9743
Appendix. Camp stories and tales. 86308
Appendix, compiled as a manual of reference. 38917
Appendix, compiled in 1862. 32917
Appendix, comprehending a list. 90295
Appendix, comprising a supplementary memoir. 22352
Appendix, comprising all his [i. e. George Washington's] most valuable public papers. 36361, note after 101900
Appendix, comprising biographical sketches. 55320
Appendix, comprising brief memoirs. 86856
Appendix concerning longitude. 35711, note after 92708
Appendix concerning Mr. Garden's treatment of Mr. Whitefield. (17668), note after 103614
Appendix, concerning the American colonies. 46792
Appendix concerning the essays that are made. 46238
Appendix concerning the longitude. 35712
Appendix, concerning the revolutions. 104857
Appendix, consisting of extracts from an essay. 28790, 79243
Appendix consisting of Gen. Foster's report. 51720
Appendix, consisting of Mr. Jefferson's bill. (35937)
Appendix, consisting of official reports of the battle. 5223
Appendix consisting of Secretary Monroe's letter. (69090)
Appendix . . . containing a brief account of the question. 49881
Appendix, containing a brief account of two former expeditions. (47149)
Appendix containing . . . a brief memoir. 77572
Appendix, containing a brief notice. (8318), 24445, note after 93743
Appendix, containing a brief sketch of the history. 73879
Appendix, containing a brief sketch of the revolutionary services. (33643)
Appendix, containing a catalogue of the alumni. 51880
Appendix, containing a chemical analysis. 47237
Appendix, containing a concise dissertation. 104634
Appendix, containing a concise history of the prisoner's life. 96919
Appendix, containing a concise history of the war in Canada. 83623
Appendix, containing a detail of the Seminole War. 51782
Appendix, containing a discussion with Rev. Mr. Wilcott. (39673)
Appendix, containing a farther review. 70213
Appendix, containing a full account. 2992, 84847
Appendix, containing a full analysis. 64056
Appendix, containing a further account. 16637
Appendix containing a genealogy of his family. (80317)
Appendix, containing a general history of the town. 31221
Appendix, containing a historical notice and description. 92283
Appendix containing a history of reconstruction. 17597

Appendix, containing a history of the college, etc. 33072

Appendix, containing a letter from Mr. Keene. 416, 72044

Appendix, containing a list of officers and members. 90890

Appendix containing a memoir of the parish. 55201

Appendix, containing a memorial. 5926, 102854

Appendix containing a narration of wonderful passages. (46363)

Appendix; containing a number of interesting papers. 30072

Appendix, containing a plan. 33365

Appendix, containing a remonstrance. 95503

Appendix, containing a report. 4823, 95700

Appendix, containing a reprint of a work now extremely rare. 98029

Appendix, containing a selection of papers. 10067

Appendix, containing a short account. 78748

Appendix, containing a short address. 72869

Appendix containing a short history of the lodge. 103749

Appendix containing a short sketch of the history. 105037

Appendix, containing a sketch of the late war. 95133, 6th note after 100603

Appendix, containing a sketch of the mission. 17418

Appendix, containing a statement of facts. 105523

Appendix, containing a statement of the peculiar doctrines. 88822

Appendix, containing a statistical account of the valley. (11986)

Appendix; containing a summary of such acts of Assembly. 59982

Appendix, containing a summary of the laws of the nation. (30647), 96092

Appendix, containing a summary view of the principles. 105989

Appendix, containing a translation of the will. 65450

Appendix, containing a variety of other matters. 84350

Appendix: containing a view of those countries. 65330

Appendix, containing, abstracts of such parts of the acts. (1791), 53072

Appendix, containing abstracts of the acts. 50865, 84620

Appendix, containing accounts of the disorders. 27271, 103647

Appendix, containing accounts of the effects. 81741

Appendix, containing among other things, a description. 104728

Appendix, containing an abstract of the finances. 45623

Appendix, containing an abstract of the last official report. 35605

Appendix, containing an abstract of the steward's accounts. 80825

Appendix, containing an account of Admiral Vernon's success. 40190

Appendix containing an account of conferences. 36337

Appendix, containing an account of Louisiana. 17386

Appendix, containing an account of the . . . catastrophe. 102524

Appendix, containing an account of the church Methodists. 72144

Appendix, containing an account of the Church of Christ. 71830

Appendix, containing an account of the epidemic cholera. (80425)

Appendix, containing an account of the fatal and bloody effects of enthusiasm. (28793), (79238)

Appendix, containing an account of the real causes of the transaction. 5913, 49380

Appendix, containing an account of the schools. 86577-86578

Appendix, containing an account of the several daring attempts. 6517, 39183

Appendix, containing an account of the tragedy. 78678

Appendix, containing an account of the voyages. 58788

Appendix: containing an account of those taken captive at Deerfield. 104264

Appendix, containing an account of those taken captive at Deerfield. 104265-104267

Appendix, containing an address of the Right Rev. Bishop Hobart. 103464

Appendix, containing an essay on the natural history. 78259

Appendix, containing an extract of a letter. 103776

Appendix, containing an historical and topographical sketch. 33805

Appendix, containing an index to the documents. 14204

Appendix, containing an obituary notice of Mrs. Anna E. Horton. 33079

Appendix containing an ode on science and liberty. 34091

Appendix, containing animadversions upon the conduct. (79257), 85660, 97597

Appendix, containing attestations of the principal facts in the letter. 69400, 90595, 103594, 3d note after 103650

Appendix containing biographical sketches of several deceased members. 88036, note after 96180

Appendix, containing biographical sketches of several general officers. 95152

Appendix, containing brief notices of his grandfathers and parents. 104793

Appendix containing brief notices of Mr. Gilbert. (71798)

Appendix, containing brief sketches. 36509

Appendix, containing Capt. Parker's own account of his taking the town of Porto Bello. 11030, 27799

Appendix, containing certain articles. 7904, 84842

Appendix containing certain documents relating thereto. 12403, 45184

Appendix, containing characteristic traits. 44314, note after 75924

Appendix containing characters of the Rev. Messrs. John and Charles Wesley. 103663

Appendix, containing . . . commercial laws. 73153

Appendix, containing decisions in the Admiralty Court. 87456

Appendix, containing descriptions of portions of the collection. 5806

Appendix containing descriptions of the plants. 41241

Appendix, containing directions for the institution. 96289

Appendix, containing documents. (15815), 101999

Appendix containing Dr. Rolph's speech. 41309

Appendix containing essays. 82925

Appendix, containing extracts from proceedings. 81740

APPENDIX

Appendix, containing extracts from the log of Capt. Middleton. 3664, 13833

Appendix, containing extracts from the writings. (5080)

Appendix, containing facts and arguments. 82179

Appendix, containing fifty-one substantial reasons against any alteration what-ever. 10889, note after 97536, 97537

Appendix containing full instructions to emigrants. 36329

Appendix containing geognostical observations. 25626

Appendix containing grants. 51825-51826, 90629, 5th note after 98997

Appendix, containing his remarks. 96841

Appendix, containing histories of the plague. 97656

Appendix, containing illustrations of ancient and South American arts. (23313)

Appendix, containing important statistics. (37766)

Appendix, containing John Stuart Mill's letter. (20097)

Appendix, containing letters from Generals Fitzhugh Lee. (19568)

Appendix, containing letters from Maj.-General John A. Dix. 70242

Appendix containing lists. 74154

Appendix, containing many original letters. 11879

Appendix containing many valuable records. 71652, 1st note after 87949

Appendix, containing, memoirs of his life. 102521

Appendix: containing memorial. 102854

Appendix, containing memorials of the dying sayings. 79857

Appendix, containing Mr. Patrick Kennedy's journal. (34053)-34054

Appendix, containing notes on Lake Champlain. 19193

Appendix, containing notices of the Jones Family. 36627

Appendix, containing obituary notices. 78510

Appendix; containing observations on the seventh trumpet. 104729

Appendix containing official documents and letters. 100641

Appendix, containing olden time researches. 102140

Appendix: containing particular accounts of the lives. 61813

Appendix, containing proofs of the principal facts. 69400, 90596, 103594, 3d note after 103650

Appendix, containing public documents &c. 95487

Appendix. Containing reflections on gold. 65678

Appendix, containing remarks on a late memoir. 97657

Appendix, containing remarks on Dr. Solander and Mr. Bank's voyage. 53025

Appendix, containing remarks on sundry members. (73820)

Appendix containing replies to the statements. (74581)

Appendix, containing report of Admiral R. Fitzroy. 89971

Appendix, containing revolutionary reminiscences and incidents. 71842

Appendix, containing rules and orders. (68770)

Appendix containing rules in equity. 70820

Appendix, containing sermons. 36327

Appendix, containing several interesting letters. 93994

Appendix, containing several new and popular songs. 86950

Appendix, containing several of Mr. Paine's unpublished pieces. (80429)

Appendix, containing several papers on the subject. 27524

Appendix, containing sketches of all the coloured churches. 11558

Appendix, containing sketches of some of the western counties. 8558

Appendix, containing sketches of the civil and ecclesiastical history. 103781

Appendix, containing some account of proceedings. (9201)

Appendix, containing some account of the society. 106161

Appendix, containing some account of their conversion. (13895), 103350

Appendix containing some animadversions and remarks. (14943)

Appendix, containing some animadversions on the new work. 90107

Appendix, containing, some general observations. 94075, 102523

Appendix, containing some hints on the means. 35455

Appendix containing some important documents relating to the subject. 102728

Appendix, containing some important documents relative to the subject. 102727

Appendix, containing some miscellaneous papers. 32673

Appendix, containing some observations on a pamphlet. 36305

Appendix, containing some of the more common and useful forms. 94773

Appendix, containing some remarks on a book. 46747

Appendix containing some remarks on the works. (11893)

Appendix, containing such regulations. 10471

Appendix, containing sundry documents concerning Jonathan Robbins. 62898

Appendix, containing sundry documents in relation to the management of affairs on the Boston Station. 24, 96807, 1st note after 101000

Appendix, containing the action of Congress. 65011

Appendix, containing the acts of Parliament. 102636

Appendix, containing the advice and resolution. 103631

Appendix, containing the arguments and evidence. 9434

Appendix, containing the author's [i. e. Thomas Paine's] life. 58234

Appendix, containing the case of Passmore Williamson. 31770

Appendix, containing the character of Dr. Franklin. 50766

Appendix, containing "The coalition." 62851

Appendix containing the concurrence of some other ministers. 80797

Appendix, containing the constitution. 52031

Appendix, containing the correspondence. 88652

Appendix, containing the counter statement. 9943, 57565

Appendix, containing the entire correspondence. 65437, 91765

Appendix, containing the evidence. 98052

Appendix, containing the history and management. 35701

Appendix, containing the journal. 104378
Appendix; containing the latest reports. 73228
Appendix containing the laws of the United
    States. (71820)
Appendix, containing the letters of Mr.
    Ingersoll. 34735, 92851
Appendix, containing the letters which passed.
    (35827)
Appendix, containing the library regulations.
    (66309)
Appendix, containing the minutes of the court
    martial. 91842
Appendix containing the national banking act.
    50954
Appendix containing the neutralization and
    passenger laws. 8226
Appendix: containing, the new method of inocu-
    lating. 74208, (74226)
Appendix containing the old charters. (8280),
    8286
Appendix, containing the opinion of Chancellor
    Kent. 61206
Appendix, containing the opinions of Judge
    Marvin. 61179
Appendix, containing the original patent. 97182
Appendix containing the performances of Dexter.
    81364
Appendix; containing the position. 72118
Appendix, containing the present state. 17117,
    2d note after 100818
Appendix containing the President's inaugural
    speech. 14312, (23365), 97440
Appendix, containing the proceedings at the
    dedication. 54500
Appendix, containing the proceedings of the
    Congress. 39414
Appendix, containing the proceedings of the
    Naval Court of Enquiry. 75957, note
    after 96922
Appendix, containing the proceedings of the old
    Congress. 34481, note after 96593
Appendix containing the public and private
    instructions. (13287)
Appendix. Containing the reasons of the ordi-
    nation. (78694)
Appendix containing the relation of the conver-
    sion. 46222
Appendix, containing the resolutions of the
    missionaries. 106096
Appendix, containing the result of the Council
    at Bradford, and Mr. Balch's reply.
    7268, 27584, 103399
Appendix containing the rules. 98084
Appendix; containing the several acts of Parlia-
    ment. 53045
Appendix, containing the several depositions.
    (80671)
Appendix, containing the state of the national
    debt. 65452
Appendix, containing the story of "The fox."
    (27416)
Appendix, containing the testimony. 101433A
Appendix, containing the treaty of armed
    neutrality. 93572
Appendix: containing the true preparation.
    80573-80574
Appendix, containing the views of John Wesley.
    (41882)
Appendix, containing the views of T. Ellicott.
    45368
Appendix, containing the western traveller.
    (55833)
Appendix, containing the whole documentary
    evidence. 33827, 91841A
Appendix, containing the writings of several of
    the sufferers. 5631

Appendix, containing three letters. 17725,
    93270
Appendix, containing two essays. 35237
Appendix, containing various interesting and
    valuable papers. 104831
Appendix, containing various matters. 46357,
    75214
Appendix, containing various notes. 68972,
    95524
Appendix, containing various remarks. 74966
Appendix contains the history. 46976
Appendix de Congo. (8784)
Appendix. Descriptive list of carboniferous
    plants. 18954
Appendix desz eilfften Theils Americae. (8784)
Appendix embodying the recent report. (30527)
Appendix embracing a report of the testimony.
    93965
Appendix, embracing historical, statistical, and
    ecclesiastical information. 84049
Appendix, embracing . . . letters. 50781
Appendix, embracing sketches of the town of
    Alstead. 16168
Appendix, embracing the first annual catalogue.
    14785
Appendix, embracing the researches. 82808
Appendix, evincing George Keith's self-
    condemnation. 103658
Appendix. Exhibit L. 85212
Appendix, exhibiting some account of their con-
    version. (31895)
Appendix, exhibiting the present state and
    influence. 2665
Appendix explanatory of the peculiarities.
    92068
Appendix: first address. 23930, 78721, note
    after 103287
Appendix V. of the geological survey of Jamaica.
    (35584)
Appendix from . . . E. Everett. 69537
Appendix from election sermons. 12313
Appendix. From the Boston evening-post.
    12331
Appendix from the National Academy of
    Sciences. 72024
Appendix from the Washington globe. 81794,
    94790
Appendix. From the Weekly news-letter.
    (12323)
Appendix, furnishing a brief historical sketch.
    37942
Appendix geographica. 66484, 66486-(66488)
Appendix, giving a concise account. 106388
Appendix, giving a faithful account. 102221
Appendix, giving a particular account. 105116
Appendix, giving a short account. 95426
Appendix, giving an account of the Boston and
    Hingham Pecks. 59474
Appendix, giving an account of the formation of
    the mission. 51186
Appendix, giving an historical account. 21234
Appendix, giving biographical sketches. 66730
Appendix, giving some account of the captives.
    27348, note after 101219
Appendix, giving some account of the ground of
    difficulty. 37851
Appendix, giving some account of the Methodist
    Protestant Church. 104657A
Appendix, giving some account of the particu-
    lars. 104963
Appendix, giving . . . the late disturbances.
    50755
Appendix, in answer to a dialogue. 103327
Appendix, in answer to a pamphlet. 7192A,
    (31912)

Appendix, in answer to an expensive publication. 9002, 103675
Appendix, in answer to two common, but unreasonable complaints. 28792
Appendix, in three parts. 97189
Appendix. In which are published some of Major Downing's letters. 84148
Appendix, including the affidavit. 82899
Appendix, including the scheme. 102613
Appendix, intended to illustrate the merits. 37156, 37158
Appendix—laws of Mississippi. 84882
Appendix Mathesoes in Margarita philosophicam. 69128
Appendix no. 15. Mines. 56172
Appendix no. 14. Crown lands. 56144
Appendix no. 16. Indian affairs. 56178
Appendix, N⁰. III, containing, considerations. 64816
Appendix, obviating the objections offered. 82722
Appendix of anecdotes and reminiscences. 52293
Appendix of astronomical, magnetic, climatological and barometric observations, etc. 69946
Appendix of biography, genealogy and statistick. (8232)
Appendix of Captain Parry's voyage. 58860-58861
Appendix of documents relating to the clergy reserves. 10571
Appendix of documents [sic] referred to in the speech. 13550
Appendix of emblems. 24611
Appendix of facts. 51187
Appendix of forms. 98080
Appendix of historical memoranda. (80442)
Appendix of illustrative notes. 82766
Appendix of important documents. 23186, 94189
Appendix of laws. 6025
Appendix of letters, &c. 96361
Appendix of original documents, correspondence, and other evidence. 14138, 2d note after 98553
Appendix of original documents, relating to the history. (39750)
Appendix of practical instructions. (28480)
Appendix of state papers. 17184
Appendix of the journals. 30963, 30967, 1st note after 100494, 100513
Appendix of the rules and orders. 20148
Appendix of the rules and regulations. 12846
Appendix of the useful cultivated plants. 18595
Appendix, on camp and military hospitals. 36524, 94063
Appendix on the aborigines. (27916)
Appendix, on the bars at the mouth of the Mississippi. 22207
Appendix on the chronology of Wisconsin. 38979
Appendix on the excellent and admirable in Mr. Burke's second printed speech. 80042
Appendix on the free trade and tariff question. 57922
Appendix on the influence of education. 3469
Appendix, on the means of emancipating slaves. 22980
Appendix on the politics of the New Testament. 14912
Appendix, on the principles and character of Washington. (56044)
Appendix on the subject of colonization. 94472
Appendix on the subject of the great lakes. 63370
Appendix on the voyages of the Cabots. (43971)
Appendix on various subjects. (25624)

Appendix: or, some observations. 1792, note after 45640, 81891
Appendix, or voices in American history. 66757
Appendix: papers relating to the great industrial exhibition. 73841
Appendix personal to the author. 8703
Appendix regnum Congo. (8784)
Appendix, relating to the case of the Rev. Cave Jones. 65042, 99772
Appendix relating to the Charleston Union Presbytery. (65228), 2d note after 90734
Appendix relating to the Huguenots in America. 82281
Appendix relative to the murder of Logan's family. 35905
Appendix: shewing . . . necessary matters. 103055
Appendix, shewing some scripture ground to hope. 46737
Appendix, shewing the action of the court. 71578
Appendix, shewing what has been the constant doctrine. 106390
Appendix, showing that freemasonry is responsible. 90897
Appendix, showing the origin and evils of intemperance. 20311, note after 94656
Appendix. Some essays to fit that excellent portion. (66440)-(66441)
Appendix: specification and description of the anthracite coal furnace. 33521, 93530
Appendix, stating the heavy grievances. 80456
Appendix. The speech of Mr. Pitt. 63064
Appendix to a late essay. 1793, 2d note after 98175
Appendix to a letter from James Stuart. 93171
Appendix to a letter to Dr. Shebbeare. 2760, 36304, (80041)
Appendix to a sermon preached. 104931
Appendix to a treatise. 94707
Appendix to an account of Louisiana. 42192
Appendix to "An inquiry into the nature and tendency." 90894
Appendix to Aristides's vindication. 35921, 98530
Appendix to Captain Parry's journal. 58865
Appendix to Captain Synge's pamphlet. 24181
Appendix to Common sense. 58212-(58214)
Appendix to discourse on the 4th commandment. 3105
Appendix to Dr. Watts's psalms and hymns. 71539
Appendix to Hayward's New England gazetteer. 31075
Appendix to Haywood's revised laws. 94775
Appendix to John Norton's book. 59659
Appendix to M. Perkins his six principles. 72099
Appendix to Massachusetts in agony. (11679), 45641
Appendix to Mr. Perkins his six principles. 72091, 72093
Appendix to Mr. Perkins' six principles. 72092
Appendix to Mr. Samuel Vaughan's appeal. (51453)
Appendix to render this work more compleat. 20726, 3d note after 93596
Appendix to Stolberg's travels. (59572)
Appendix to the address. (62214)
Appendix to the American code. (72676)
Appendix to the American edition. (11877), 64328, (78715)
Appendix to the book, entituled, New England judged. 5629
Appendix to the Canada papers. 10355
Appendix to the catalogue of books. 55053

Appendix to the catholic question. 103090, 103098

Appendix to the civil and political history. (22729)

Appendix. To the cleargie of the foure great parties. 104333

Appendix to the concise statement. 8404, 15120, (81892)

Appendix to the Congressional globe. 83833-83835, 84370-84371

Appendix to the considerations. 1794, 72152-72153

Appendix to the crustacea of the United States. 77372

Appendix to the defence of Dr. Price. 105704

Appendix to the Defence of the Modest proof. (25402), 25407, 99800, 103904

Appendix to the Dutch in Maine. 19636

Appendix to the eighth edition of The olive branch. 10851

Appendix to the essays on capital punishments. 62431

Appendix to the exposition. 98551

Appendix to the Field genealogy. 24276

Appendix to the first part of The history of Virginia. 91860-91861

Appendix to the foregoing: being remarks. 101447

Appendix to the foregoing letters. (22152), note before 92797, note after 104794

Appendix to the fourth annual report of the Board of Regents. 36107

Appendix to the fourth annual report to the Legislature. 79886

Appendix to the General Assembly's state of the right. 90629

Appendix to the history of Vermont. 95544

Appendix to the history of William Stevens. 91306

Appendix to the impartial statement of the controversy. 1795, (34385), note after 53697, note after 83791

Appendix to the laws of Pennsylvania. 60281

Appendix to the life and times. 76384

Appendix to the memoirs. 71536

Appendix to the Modest proof. 25407, 99800

Appendix to the narrative. 73384

Appendix to The notes on Virginia. (35880)

Appendix to the present state of the nation. (28769), 69436, 103123

Appendix to the report of the Central Board of Health. 35566

Appendix to the report of the Committee. 87351

Appendix to the report on state certificates. (70549)

Appendix to the report on the accounts. 6675

Appendix to the representation. 79809

Appendix to the review of Mr. Pitt's administration. 70213

Appendix to the second edition of Mr. McGregorie's sermon. 9907

Appendix to the Senate journal of the session of 1826-27. 27015

Appendix to the sermon on divine decrees. 91999

Appendix to the sober remarks. 25407, 99800

Appendix to the . . . trial of John Francis Knapp. 38066

Appendix to the true economy of human life. 90279

Appendix to volume I. of the Friend of peace. 105269

Appendix; together with an address. (58214)

Appendix touching the Indian affairs. 59608

Appendix, treating of its antiquities. 104285

Appendix upon studies for practical men. 93558

"Appendix" with a letter dated Boston, May 4, 1818. 21002, 56521, 93538

Appendix, with a protest and appeal. 20391, note after 104574

Appendix, with copies of letters which passed. 35723

Appendix, with information relative to the institution. 93620

Appendixes, comprising the original report. 77878

Appercu des crimes commis par les Anglo-Americains. 48900

Appercu hazarde sur l'exportation dans les colonies. (23031)

Appius. pseud. Letters. see Harper, Robert Goodloe. supposed author

Apple, Christian. 60168, 103236

Apple, T. A. 77731

Applegate, ------. plaintiff (5162)

Applegate vs. Lexington and Ohio Railroad Company. (5162)

Appleton, Elizabeth Haven. 8459, 93422

Appleton, Frank Parker. 1799

Appleton, J. H. 1800

Appleton, James. 1801

Appleton, Jesse. 1802-1808

Appleton, John, M. D. 1809-1811, 50237

Appleton, John, of Maine. 1812

Appleton, Nathan. 1813-1815, 19245, (69692), 82083

Appleton, Nathaniel. 1826-1845, 12313, 18110, 22126, 27166, 69400, 90595-90596, 94517, 95737, 100915, 103594, 3d note after 103650, 103899, 104056

Appleton, Nathaniel, of Boston. 1846, 81939

Appleton, Samuel. 1847

Appleton, William H. 1848

Appleton, William S. 36036, 57208, 86790

Appleton (D.) & Co. firm publishers 1796-1798, 30971, (70868), (70959)-70962, 104392

Appleton, Wisc. Lawrence University. see Lawrence University, Appleton, Wisc.

Appleton Academy, New Ipswich, H. N. 53027

Appleton, and Burlingame. (68200)

Appletons' companion hand-book of travel. (70959)

Appleton's cyclopedia of biography. 30971, (70868)

Appletons' hand-book of American travel, northern and eastern tour. 70962

Appleton's handbook of American travel: northern tour. 29755

Appleton's handbook of Amercian travel. The southern tour. 29756

Appleton's illustrated hand-book of American travel. 70960

Appletons' illustrated hand-book of American travel. Part I. 70961

Appleton's literary bulletin. 1796

Appleton's magazine. 93147

Appletons' popular science monthly. see Popular science monthly.

Appletons' railroad and steam-boat companion. 104392

Appleton's railway and steam navigation guide. 1797

Appleton's United States postal guide. 1798

Applewhite, J. 17436, note before 90804 see also Committee on Railroads in Austin and Washington Counties, Texas.

Appleyard. firm publishers 92463

Appleyard's pocket edution. 92463

Applicants for the Incorporation of the Tomkins County Bank. see Tomkins County Bank. petitioners

Application for habeas corpus. 82206
Application for the office of Paymaster of
  Marines. 104235
Application has been made to the Legislature.
  105361
Application having been made to the merchants.
  95989
Application of his majesty's licenses. 8514
Application of John C. Tucker. 51664.
Application of redemption. 32828-32829
Application of Robert Codman and others. 12860
Application of $7,300,000, etc. 69817
Application of some general political rules. 1849
Application of the Bank of Mutual Redemption.
  (69526)
Application of the Bishop and clergy of London.
  9372, 81492
Application of the geological observations.
  6385
Application of the Hudson and Delaware Canal
  Company. 33507
Application . . . of the New York Protestant
  Episcopal Public School. 73977
Application of the Orthodox Party. (53637)
Application of the Scots to foreign trade.
  78200
Application of the Troy and Greenfield Rail-
  road. 32889, 103002
Application to the Governor and Senate of New-
  York. 96510
Application to the Legislature of Pennsylvania.
  (1235)
Application to the Legislature of the Haver-
  hill Aqueduct Company. 51615
Application which the West India Planters
  intend to make. 56506, note after 102851
Applications of chemistry to the arts. 69654
Applications of some general laws. 75474
Application of the science of mechanics. 69654
Appointment of a clothier having . . . altered.
  100409
Appointment of the general fast vindicated.
  5183, 2d note after 97146
Appointments of auditors. 43495
Appollonius, Levinus, 16th cent. (27730)
Appologo de la ociosidad y el trabajo intitulado
  Labricio portundo. 75567
Appomatox. pseud. Letter. see Leigh,
  Benjamin Watkins. supposed author
Apportionment of representation. 36838
Appreciation by S. R. Smith. 84087
Appreciation of the life of William Pryor
  Letchworth. 84251
Apprehension, and examination of Savle. 65421
Apprentice system for the United States
  Merchant Service. 27701
Apprenticed labourer's manual. 44389
Apprentices' Library, New York. 54093-54904
Apprentices' Library Company, Dyottsville, Pa.
  see Dyottsville Apprentices' Library
  Company.
Apprentices Library Company, Philadelphia.
  61475
Apprentices Library Company, Philadelphia.
  Managers. 61475
Apprentices Library Society, Charleston, S. C.
  12040
Approach of every important election, gives
  cause. 94674
Approaching change of national empire. 68309
Approaching presidential election. 36162
Approbation de la Societe Royale d'Agriculture
  de Lyon. 26013
Appropriation of the public money. 31446
Appropriation to western rivers. 1850
Appropriations, 1848-89. (73631)

Appropriations, 1847 and '48. (73631)
Appropriations of public lands. 38819
Approved directions, from the best artists.
  98399
Approved minister of God. 24391
Approved minister. Sermon preached at the
  ordination. 30521
Approximate cotidal lines. (2588)
Approximate estimate of that portion. 45098
Appun, Carl Ferdinand. 1851
Aprendix. 98950
Apreciacao da revolta praieira em Pernambuco.
  47463
Apresentacao Campellos, Joao da. see
  Campellos, Joao da Apresentacao.
Apricius, Jonathan Price. (38248) see also
  Gt. Brit. Legation. Netherlands.
April 18th, 1757. To the Honorable Robert
  Dinwiddie. 99923
April 1, 1863. 34182
(April 16, 1807.) No I. of the new-milk cheese.
  77018, note after 98576
April 16th, 1757. To the Honorable Robert
  Dinwiddie. 99905
April, 13, 1830. Report: 3189
April 12, 1777. Your committee have obtained.
  106119
Aprilhefte der Sitzungsberichte der Philos-.-
  Histor. Classe. (77616)
Aprobacion. (76300)
Aprobacion del Br. Juan Gomez Brizeno.
  76007
Aprobacion del Doctor D. Ioseph del Corral.
  (72290)
Aprobacion del Doctor Don Ivan de Morales
  Valverde. (72290)
Aprobacion del R. P. Fr. Juan de Torres.
  76007
Aprosio, P. A. 91728
Aprovacion. 81286
Apthorp, East. 1852-1857, 47140-47142, 47144-
  47145
Apthorp, R. E. 89630
Apulche, Jose Maria. 29137
Apuntaciones. 70399, 99402
Apuntaciones para su defensa. 21766
Apuntaciones sobre el origen de la poblacion de
  America. 87194
Apuntador Semanario de teatros. 48279
Apvntamiento, en qve breuemente se sunda el
  derecho. 96050
Apuntamientos amplificando los fundamento de
  hecho. (67640)
Apuntamientos critico-historicos. (67127)
Apuntamientos para la biografia del Senor
  Licenciado. 58132
Apuntamientos para la historia de lo occurido.
  76726
Apuntamientos para la historia natural de los
  paxaros. 2532
Apuntamientos para la historia natural de los
  quadrupedos. (2531)
Apuntamientos para la historia politica i social.
  75909
Apuntamientos para la historia por el General
  Jose Maria Obando. 56404
Apuntamientos para manifestacion de la
  persecucion. 56405
Apuntamientos sobre Centro-Americana. 89956
Apuntamientos sobre derecho publico ecclesias-
  tico. 48280, (48664)
Apuntaciones sobre el Habanero. 29416
Apuntamientos sobre la vida publica. 39089
Apuntes. 74864
Apuntes biograficos. 49931

Apuntes biograficos de D. Ignacio Valdivielso.
31727
Apuntes biograficos de Don Francisco Antonio
Marciel. 44538
Apuntes biograficos de escritores. 29338
Apuntes biograficos de la Senora Da. Maria
Ana. 16976
Apuntes biograficos del General de la nacion.
57723
Apuntes biograficos del ilustre quimico
Mexicano. 87163
Apuntes biograficos del Mayor General Juan
Antonio Quitman. (67339)
Apuntes biograficos del V. P. Fray Jose de la
Cruz Espi. 62608
Apuntes biograficos ficos leidos. 22776
Apuntes boigraficos sobre el Jeneral Frai
Felix Aldao. 77087
Apuntes canonico-regulares de lo que debe
observarse. 93298
Apuntes cronologicos para servir a la historia.
33486
Apuntes de algunas de las gloriosas acciones.
98309, 98317
Apuntes de mi cartera. 48338
Apuntes de un viagero. 15084
Apuntes del diario de la Princesa Ines de
Salm. 75809
Apuntes del Distrito de Texcoco. 30995
Apuntes destinatos a illustrar la discusion.
(74905)
Apuntes hidrograficos. 12743
Apuntes historicos con algunas observaciones.
98866
Apuntes historicos de la heroica ciudad de
Vera-Cruz. 40138
Apuntes historicos sobre la banda oriental. 38990
Apuntes interesantes para la historia. (19757)
Apuntes para escribir la historia de los
projectos. 31726
Apuntes para formar un bosquejo historico.
73022
Apuntes para la biografia de D. Ignacio Lopez
Rayon. 68130
Apuntes para la corografia y la estadistica.
63010
Apuntes para la estadistica del Departamento
de Orizava. 78928
Apuntes para la historia. 104391
Apuntes para la historia de la guerra. 1858,
48281
Apuntes para la historia de la isle de Cuba.
(752)
Apuntes para la historia de la libertad. 24325
Apuntes para la historia de la republica
oriental del' Uruguay. 58051
Apuntes para la historia de las letras. 2608
Apuntes para la historia de Mexico. (16767)
Apuntes para la historia del gobierno. 9568,
76727
Apuntes para la immigraciones de las tribus
en Mexico. 57641
Apuntes para servir a la historia. 67646
Apuntes para un catalogo de escritores. 34152
Apuntes poeticos. (74015)
Apuntes sobre Chile. (73203)
Apuntes sobre la provincia litoral de Loreto.
67524
Apuntes sobre las islas del delta Arjentino.
(645)
Apuntes sobre las mejores materiales. (61332)
Apuntes sobre los principales sucesos. 1859,
98284
Apuntes sobre su vida y sus obras. 39280
Apure (Venezuelan State) Laws, statutes, etc.
68787

Aquae Homo. pseud. Sermon. see Waterman,
Jotham.
Aquarelles: or summer sketches. 86564
Aquaviva, Claudio. 49980
Aquenses, Fabricius. tr. 93888
Aquerrigui, Pedro Sugada y. see Sugada y
Aquerrigui, Pedro.
Aqui comienca vn vocabulario. (49866)
Aqui comienza una doctrina Xpiana. 24105
Aqui se contiene treynta proposiciones. 11233,
11235, 11239, (11249), 11267, 11289
Aq[ui] seco[n]tiene un sermon. (36795)
Aqui se contiene vna disputa. 11234-11245,
11248, 11267, 11283, 11289, 39115
Aqui se co[n]tiene vnos auisos y reglas.
(11232)
Aquidneck. A poem. 8341
Aquignispicium. 78189
Aquiline Nimble-Chops, Democrat. pseud.
Democracy. see Livingston, Brockholst,
1757-1823.
Aquino, Thomas de. 1861
Aquino e Castro, Olegario Herculano de. 29288
Aquitanus. see Prosper, Tiro, Aquitanus,
Saint.
Ara de Apollo. 96246
Ara poru aguiyey haba yaoca ymomocoinda.
34818
Arabia Petraea. 106294, 106330-106331
Arabia Petraea (Diocese) Bishop. (67499)
Arabians; or the power of Christianity. 84136-
84137
Araburu, Andres de. plaintiff 94351
Araeth y Barnwe Burneet o dalaeth Ohio. 65436
Araeth yr anrhyd. 93682
Aragao Morato, Francisco Manuel Trigoso de.
see Morato, Francisco Manuel Trigoso
de Aragao.
Arago, Dominique Francois Jean, 1786-1853.
1862, 1865-1866
Arago, Jacques Etienne Victor, 1790-1855.
1863-1867
Arago, M. F. ed. 15194
Aragon, Francisco de Borja y. see Borja y
Aragon, Francisco de, Principe de
Esquilache, 1582-1658.
Aragon, Luis de Mendoca Catano y. see
Mendoca Catano y Aragon, Luis de.
Aragon, Manuel Lopez de. see Lopez de
Aragon, Manuel.
Aragon, Phelipe de. defendant 62881
Aragon (Viceroyalty) Virrey (Solis) see also
Solis, Francisco de, Bp. 86398
Araguaya, Domingos Jose Goncalves de Magal-
hanes, Visconde de. see Goncalves de
Magalhanes, Domingos Jose, Visconde de
Araguaya, 1811-1882.
Arana, Diego Barros. see Barros Arana,
Diego, 1830-1907.
Arancel de la republica del Peru. 61079
Arancel de los derechos que deben llevar los
Corregidores. 59324
Arancel de los honorarios y derechos judiciales
que se han de cobrar en el Departamento
de Chiapas. 84282
Arancel de los honorarios y derechos judiciales
que se han de cobrar en el Departamento
de Puebla. (66545)
Arancel general de aduanas maritimas y
fronterizas. 1868
Arancel general de aduanas maritimas y
fronterizas y panta de comisos. 48283
Arancel general interino e instruccion para
gobierno. 48284
Arancel para el cobro de derechos judiciales.
35543

Arancel provisional para las aduanas de
Guatemala. 29066
Arancel que para la esaccion del derecho de
alcabala debe observarse. 48660
Aranceles formados de orden de la Real
Audiencia. 29065
Aranceles generales para el cobro de derechos
de importacion. 66593
Aranceles generales para el cobro de derechos
de introduccion. (17752)
Aranceles—importaciones—contrabando. 7797
Arancels.—Prohibiciones. 56442
Arango, D. A. J. d'. 1869
Arango, Francisco de. 1870-1873, 1887, 3611-
3612, (17778)
Arango, Jose de. 1872, 1882, 1884-1887,
3612, 29107, 62937
Arango, Jose Agustin. 85720
Arango, Manuel de Zequeira y. see Zequeira
y Arango, Manuel de.
Arango y Escandor, Alejandro. 40079
Arango y Parreno, Francisco de. 96307
Aranguren, Ignacio de Soto Zevallos. see
Soto Zevallos Aranguren, Ignacio de.
Aranjo Costa, Sallustiano Orlando de. see
Costa, Sallustiano Orlando de Aranjo.
Aranjo Lima, Andre Cordeiro de. (69328)
see also Santa Catharina (Brazilian
State) Presidente (Aranjo Lima)
Aranzel de derechos eclesiasticos. 51045
Aranzel de derechos parrochiales. 73867
Aranzel, de los derechos. 56242
Aranzel para todos los curas. 42066, 48285
Araoz de Lamadrid, Gregorio. see Lamadrid,
Gregorio Araoz de.
Araque, Blas Maria. tr. 16521
Araque Ponze de Leon, Christoual. ed. 96242
Ararat. pseud. Cubbeer Burr. see Thom,
Adam. supposed author
Araripe, Tristao de Alencar. tr. note before
90061
Arator. pseud. Attack. 60297
Arator; being a series of agricultural essays.
94483-94484, 94486
Aratus Solensis. 65940-65941
Araucana. 22718-22727, 49893, 56299, 57300,
57629, (57801)-57803, 93311
Araucania i sus habitantes. 20558
Araucanians. 82443
Araucano. 86251
Arauco domado. 57300-57303, 98772
Araujo, Antonio de. 1889-1890, 5065
Araujo, C. ed. 70308
Araujo, Jose de Sousa Azevedo Pizarro y.
see Azevedo Pizarro y Araujo, Jose de
Sousa.
Araujo, Jose Paulo de Figueiroa Nabuco de.
see Nabuco de Araujo, Jose Paulo de
Figueiroa.
Araujo, Juan Martinez de. see Martinez de
Araujo, Juan.
Araujo, Leonardo de. 98809 see also
Augustinians. Provincia del Peru.
Provincial.
Araujo, Manuel do Monte Rodrigues de. see
Monte Rodrigues de Araujo, Manuel do,
Bp., 1798-1863.
Araujo, Pedro Gonzalez. see Gonzalez Araujo,
Pedro.
Araujo Brusque, Francisco Carlos de. see
Brusque, Francisco Carlos de Araujo.
Araujo e Amazonas, Lourenco da Silva. see
Silva Araujo e Amazonas, Lourenco da.
Araujo e Castro, Felipe Ferreira de. tr.
(12243)
Araujo e Silva, Domingos de. 1892

Araujo e Silva, Luis Ferreira de. ed. 73432
Araujo Porto-Alegre, Manoel de. see Porto-
Alegre, Manoel de Araujo de Araujo.
Araujo y Rio, Joseph de. see Rio, Joseph de
Araujo y.
Aravia, Miguel Gonzalez. 76932
Arbeiterband, New York. publisher 85704
Arber, Edward, 1836-1912. 35675, (67585),
82812, 82815, 82819, 82823, 82824,
82830, 82831-82834, 82837, 82850, 82851-
82852, 82855-82857, 99366, note after
99383C, 104795
Arbitrament of national disputes. 39853
Arbitration Tribunal, Geneva, 1871-1872. see
Geneva Arbitration Tribunal, 1871-1872.
Arbitration Tribunal Under the Treaty of
Washington. see Geneva Arbitration
Tribunal, 1871-1872.
Arbitrary arrest of a judge!! 48958
Arbitrary arrests. 68057
Arbitrary arrests. Speech in the House of
Assembly. (30902)
Arbitrary arrests; speech of Hon. Edson B.
Olds. (57165)
Arbitrary arrests. Speech of Hon. George I.
Post. 64455
"Arbitrary arrests." Speech of Hon. Mr.
Prindle. 65679
Arbizu, Miguel Romero Lopez. see Robero
Lopez Arbizu, Miguel.
Arbol genealogico. (78929)
Arbol que produce el cafe. 38431
Arboleya, Jose G. Garcia de. see Garcia de
Arboleya, Jose G.
Arbrisselle, J. B. d'. 1893
Arbuckle, M. USA 96697, 96732-96733 see
also U. S. Commissioner to the Great
and Little Osage Indinans. U.S. Com-
missioners to the Comanche and Wichita
Indians. U. S. Commissioners to the
Creek Tribe of Indians.
Arbustrum Americanum. 44776
Arbuthnot, Alexander. defendant at court
martial 1893-1895, 48077, 51782,
56758
Arca, Juan de. 40957
Arca noe. 33013
Arcade Hotel guide . . . Philadelphia. 8502,
61476
Arcano del mare. 21089
Arcanum opened. 98123, 100670
Arce, Francisco Saraza y. see Saraza y
Arce, Francisco.
Arce, Gonzales Andres Menesis y. see
Menesis y Arce, Gonzales Andres.
Arce, Juan Dias de. see Dias de Arce, Juan.
Arce, Manuel de la Barcera y. see Barcera
y Arce, Manuel de la.
Arce, Manuel Jose. (1900)
Arce, Pascual de Gayangos y. see Gayangos
y Arce, Pascual de, 1809-1897.
Arce de Otalora, Francisca. see Otalora,
Francisca Arce de.
Arce Limesis gazophilacium regium Peruvicum.
521
Arch, John. 1901
Arch Street Presbyterian Church, Philadelphia.
see Philadelphia. Arch Street Pres-
byterian Church.
Archaeologia. 44070, 67599, 103054A
Archaeologia Aeliana. 86004
Archaeologia Americana. 1049, 2225, 19051,
23971, 27958, 50537, 57819, 95406
Archaeologiae Americanae Telluris collectanae
et specimina. (3803)

Archaeological and Historical Society of Ohio.
see Ohio State Archaeological and
Historical Society.
Archaeological collections of the United States
National Museum. 85072
Archaeological researches in Nicaragua. 85072
Archaeology of the United States. 30893, 85072
Archaios, Mathetees. pseud. see Mathetees
Archaios. pseud.
Archbishop of Armagh. see Boulter, Hugh,
Archbishop of Armagh, 1672-1742.
Ussher, James, Archbishop of Armagh,
1581-1656.
Archbishop of Cambray. see Fenelon,
Francois de Salignac de la Mothe-,
Abp., 1751-1715.
Archbishop of Canterbury. see Abbot, George,
Archbishop of Canterbury, 1562-1633.
Cornwallis, Frederick, Archbishop of
Canterbury, 1713-1783. Herring, Thomas,
Archbishop of Canterbury, 1693-1757.
Hutton, Mathew, Archbishop of Canterbury,
1693-1758. Manners-Sutton, Charles,
Archbishop of Canterbury, 1755-1828.
Moore, John, Archbishop of Canterbury,
1730-1805. Secker, Thomas, Archbishop
of Canterbury, 1693-1768. Sumner, John
Bird, Archbishop of Canterbury, 1780-
1862. Tenison, Thomas, Archbishop of
Canterbury, 1636-1715.
Archbishop of Cashel. see Nicolson, William,
Archbishop of Cashel, 1655-1727.
Archbishop of Dublin. see Browne, George,
Archbishop of Dublin, d. 1556.
Archbishop of Glasgow. see Leighton, Robert,
Archbishop of Glasgow, 1611-1684.
Archbishop of Huron. see Bishop of Huron.
Archbishop of York. see Dawes, Sir William,
Bart., Archbishop of York, 1671-1724.
Drummond, Robert Hay, Archbishop of
York, 1711-1776. Gilbert, John, Arch-
bishop of York, 1693-1761. Harcourt,
Edward, Archbishop of York, 1757-1847.
Harsnet, Samuel, Archbishop of York,
1561-1631. Herring, Thomas, Archbishop
of Canterbury, 1693-1757. Hutton,
Mathew, Archbishop of Canterbury, 1693-
1758. Markham, William, Archbishop of
York, 1719-1807. Monteigne, George,
Archbishop of York, d. 1628.
Archbishop. 4428
Archbishop Hughes in reply to General Cass.
33593
Archbishop of Cambray's dissertation on pure
love. (24054)
Archdale, John. 1902, 49010, 87903
Archdeacon, Peter. 1903
Archdeacon of Colchester. see Lyall, William
Rowe, 1788-1857.
Archdeacon of Rochester. see Denne, John.
Archenholtz, Johann Wilehlm von. 1904-(1906)
Archeologie Canadienne. 99601
Archer, Armstrong. 1907
Archer, Gabriel. 66686
Archer, John Rose. defendant 46271
Archer, Ornon. 53681
Archer, P. J. 71578
Archer, Thomas. 1908
Archer, William S. (1909)-1911
Archibald M'Intyre, John B. Yates, Henry
Yates, James M'Intyre, and John Ely, Jr.
vs. the Trustees of Union College. 97781
Archicofradia de Arcangel San Miguel, Mexico
(City) see San Miguel (Parroquia),
Mexico (City) Archicofradia de San
Miguel.

Archicofradia de Ciudadanos de la Santa
Veracruz. Mexico. 76804
Archi-Cofradia de la Minerva de la Santa
Ciudad de Roma. 93581
Archicofradia de San Miguel, Mexico (City)
see San Miguel (Parroquia), Mexico
(City) Archicofradia de San Miguel.
Archilochus, jun. pseud. Volunteer laureate.
100757
Archiloge Sophie. 76838
Architect: series of original designs. 67893
Architects' and builders' guide. 37453
Architect's reports and plans. (1390)
Architectural illustrations. 22178A
Architecture and Christian principle. 43844
Architecture in the United States. 6533, 52586
Architecture of country houses. 20772
Archiv der Franckenschen Stiftungen zu Halle.
78014
Archiv fur das Studium der neueren Sprachen.
10269
Archiv fur die neuesten und merkwurdigsten
Reisebeschreibungen. 102538
Archiv fur wissenschaftlichen Kenntniss von
Russland. 22770
Archives curieuses de l'histoire de France.
24855, 40178
Archives de commerce. 55983
Archives de la Commission Scientifique du
Mexique. 48286
Archives de la Societe Americaine de France.
85781
Archives des voyages. (7559), 11140, 94843,
99728
Archives diplomatiques pour l'histoire du temps.
20216
Archives diplomatiques recueil de diplomatie
et d'histoire. 1912
Archives des indigens. 7421
Archives du Bureau de la Marine, Paris. see
France. Bureau de la Marine. Archives,
Paris.
Archives du Museum d'Histoire Naturelle.
1913
Archives historiques et politiques. 77752
Archives litteraires de l'Europe. (1914), 6902
Archives of aboriginal knowledge. 77839
Archives of . . . Massachusetts. 45965
Archives of science. (57625)
Archives paleographiques de l'Orient et de
l'Amerique. 73299-73300
Archivo Americano y espiritu de la prensa del
mundo. (1915), 34437, 38991
Archivo de la Habana. 29417
Archivo dos conhecimentos uteis. 16047
Archivo General de Buenos Aires. see Buenos
Aires. Archivo General.
Archivo medico Brasileiro. 38953
Archivo Mexicano. Coleccion de leyes y
decretos circulares. (48288)
Archivo Mexicano. Documentos para la historia
de Mexico. 48287, 93580
Archivo Palmskioldiano. see Palmskiold.
Archivo.
Archivo storico Italiana. 10908
Archivos da Palestra Scientifica do Rio de
Janeiro. 71458
Archivos do Museu Nacional do Rio de Janeiro.
(71459), 98833
Archivs geographiques et historiques du XIX[e]
siecle. 70364
Archontologia cosmica, das is Beschreibung
aller Kaiserthumer. 1917
Archontologia cosmica; sive, imperiorvm,
regnorvm, principatvvm. (28070)
Archy Moore, the white slave. 31791

Arco, Francisco Sanchez del. see Sanchez del Arco, Francisco.
Arco del Pueblo. 63737
Arco triunfal magnifico. 78903
Arcobispos y obispos de las Indias occidentales. 102866
Arco-iris Mexicano. (48289)
Arctic adventure by sea and land. 76950
Arctic adventurers. (75259)
Arctic boat journey. 31019
Arctic Crusoe a tale of the Polar Seas. 75248
Arctic current around Greenland. 35086
Arctic dispathces. 1918, (43072)
Arctic discovery and adventure. 1919
Arctic enterprise, a poem. 71
Arctic expeditions. A poem. 64167
Arctic expeditions from British and foreign shores. 82419
Arctic expeditions. Report of the Committee. 1920
Arctic expeditions. Return . . . 5 February, 1850. 25633
Arctic explorations and discoveries. (77700), 85145-85146, 85151-85153, 85158-85159, 85162, 85164
Arctic explorations: the second Grinnell expedition. 37001
Arctic geography and ethnology. 73792, 78998
Arctic miscellanies. (1924)
Arctic news. 1921
Arctic papers. 72048
Arctic queen. 1922
Arctic regions: a narrative. 1923
Arctic regions and polar discoveries. 81145
Arctic regions by sea and land. (76951)
Arctic regions; their situation. 78169
Arctic regions, voyages to Davis' Straits. 21253
Arctic researches and life among the Esquimaux. 29738
Arctic rewards. 1925
Arctic rovings. 29745
Arctic searching expedition: a journal of a boat-voyage. 71025
Arctic searching expeditions. Papers and dispatches. 1926
Arctic travels. 100841
Arctic voyage; explanatory of a pictorial illustration. 36999
Arctic voyage to Baffin's Bay. 27931
Arctic voyages. 3659
Arctic zoology. (59757), (59759)-59760
Arcturus, a journal of books and opinion. 1927, 46840
Arcularius, Philip I. plaintiff 75950, 2d note after 96812
Arcy, Uriah Derick d'. see D'Arcy, Uriah Derick.
Ardagh, Bishop of. see Werenhall, Edward, Bishop of Kilmore and Ardagh, 1636-1713.
Arden, James. appellant 91365
Arden, Richard D. appellant 91365
Ardoino, Antonio, Marques de Lorito. 3350
Ardouin, B. 1928-(1929)
Are four men to rule New York with a rod of iron? 73114
Are North Carolinians freemen? 31224
Are the five-twenty bonds redeemable in coin? (5730)
Are the southern privateersmen pirates? 18355
Are the West India colonies to be preserved? 102820
Are the West Point graduates loyal? 44770
Are they no longer the representatives of their fellow citizens at home? 84387
Are we bound in honor to pay for them? 58943

Are we obliged in this government of the Massachusetts? 67133
Are ye fair as op'ning roses, a favorite song. 92170
Areanas, Pedro de. 1937
Arellano, Diego de. 48295
Arellano, Emmanuele Garcia de. see Garcia de Arellano, Emmanuele.
Arellano, Jose Luis Velasco y. see Velasco y Arellano, Jose Luis.
Arellano, Lorenzo. 29052 see also Guanajuato (Mexican State) Gobernador, 1848 (Arellano)
Arellano, Miguel de Luna y. see Luna y Arellano, Miguel de.
Arellano, R. Ramires de. see Ramires de Arellano, R.
Arellano y Salas, Diego, see Salas, Diego Arellano y.
Arena, Thomas Ignacio de. see Ignacio de Arena, Thomas.
Arenales, Jose. 1930-1931
Arenas, ---------. 1932, 99720-99721
Arenas, Pedro de. (1933)-1937
Arenas del Uruguay. 23714, 23716
Arends, Fr. 1938
Arenga civica el 11 de Sept. 1854. 80889
Arenga que debio pronunciar. 99470
Arenga . . . sobre la victoria de Ayacucho. 26211
Arent, -----. pseud.? 98973
Arequipa, Peru. Colegio de la Independencia America. see Colegio de la Independencia America, Arequipa, Peru.
Arequipa, Peru. Corte Superior. defendants 29258
Arequipa, Peru. Gobierno eclesiastico. see Catholic Church in Peru.
Arequipa (Diocese) Bishop [ca 1720] 97671
Arequipa (Diocese) Bishop [ca 1832] plaintiff 29258
Arequipa (Diocese) Bishop (Leon) 16069 see also Leon, Antonio de, Bp.
Arequipa (Diocese) Bishop (Perea) 60877 see also Perea, Pedro de, Bp.
Arequipa (Diocese) Synod, 1684. 16069
Arevalo, Juan Francisco Sahagum de. see Sahagum de Arevalo, Juan Francisco.
Arevalo, Rafael de. 29072, 76860 see also Guatemala (City) Secretario de la Municipalidad.
Arey, Mrs. H. E. G. (32712)
Arey, Henry W. 1939-1940, (27494)
Areytos; or songs and ballads of the south. 81188
Areytos, or, songs of the south. 81187
Arfwedson, Carl David. 1941-(1943)
Argais, Gregorio de. see Gregorio de Argaiz.
Argaiz, Gregorio de. see Gregorio de Argaiz.
Argal, Samuel. 66686
Argander, F. 1945
Argeant, Mandar. anagram see Gatereau, Armand.
Argeaut, ----- Armand. incorrectly supposed author see Gaterau, Armand.
Argensola, Bartolome Leonardo de. 1946-1950, 91538
Argentiada poema historico descriptivo. 97004
Argentina. see Argentine Republic.
Argentina o la conquista de Rio Plata. 3371, (11677)
Argentina y conquista del Rio de la Plata. 3350, 3370
Argentine Confederation. see Argentine Republic.

Argentina (Viceroyalty) see Rio de la Plata (Viceroyalty)
Argentine Republic. 1951, 1959, 9009, 9022, 17841, (20441), 38719, 44177, 52247, 61112, 68830, 68832, (70048), 71230, 87189
Argentine Republic. Administrador General de Correos. 8997
Argentine Republic. Census, 1851-1861. 24170
Argentine Republic. Census, 1869. 26109
Argentine Republic. Comision Militar, Buenos Aires. 70124
Argentine Republic. Comision Nombrada para Establecer la Nueva Linea de Frontera al Sud de Buenos Aires. 73211
Argentine Republic. Congreso. 44292, 77105
Argentine Republic. Congreso. Senado. 76127
Argentine Republic. Constitucion. 1951, 9005, 9012, 16059, 27801, 38995, 66392, 77071
Argentine Republic. Convencion Encargada del Examen de la Constitucion Federal, 1859-1860. see Buenos Aires (Province) Convencion Encargada del Examen de la Constitucion Federal, 1859-1860.
Argentine Republic. Convencion Nacional Santa Fe, 1860. 38995
Argentine Republic. Director General de Correos. 8998
Argentine Republic Director Provisorio, 1852. see Argentine Republic. Presidente, 1862-1868 (Mitre)
Argentine Republic. Gefe Supreme, 1835-1852 (Rosas) 34437 see also Rosas, Juan Manuel de, 1793-1877.
Argentine Republic. Gobierno, Encargado de las Relaciones Exteriores de la Confederacion. see Buenos Aires (Province) Gobierno Encargado de las Relaciones Exteriores de la Confederacion.
Argentine Republic. Justica Nacional, Buenos Aires. 9004
Argentine Republic. Laws, statutes, etc. 1955, 65549, 68385, (68887), 70014, 77105
Argentine Republic. Legation. France. 1956
Argentine Republic. Legation. Great Britain. 1956, 38996 see also Moreno, Manuel, 1782-1857.
Argentine Republic. Legation. Spain. 1956
Argentine Republic. Legation. U. S. 77062 see also Sarmiento, Domingo Faustino, Pres. Argentina, 1811-1888.
Argentine Republic. Ministro de Guerra y Marina. 9021
Argentine Republic. Ministro de Hacienda. 9021
Argentine Republic. Ministro de Justicia, Culto e Instruccion Publica. 9021
Argentine Republic. Ministro de Relaciones Exteriores. 9027-9028
Argentine Republic. Ministro del Interior. 9021, 70011, 93807 see also Rosas, Juan Manuel de, 1793-1877.
Argentine Republic. Presidente, 1862-1868 (Mitre) 9022, 44287 see also Mitre, Bartolome, Pres. Argentina, 1821-1906.
Argentine Republic. Presidente, 1868-1874 (Sarmiento) (77081) see also Sarmiento, Domingo Faustino, Pres. Argentina, 1811-1888.
Argentine Republic. Treaties, etc. (14302), 58062, 98596
Argentine Republic. Universidad Nacional, Buenos Aires. see Buenos Aires. Universidad Nacional.

Argentine republic. 77062
Argibuy, Virgilio. 88728
Argilite and Greeup Coal and Iron Company. (1960)
Argimon; an Indian tale. (34113)
Argo Batava. 3407
Argo Belgica. 9153
Argomenti in ottaua rima. 27473
Argomenti del Can. Alber. Baris. 94402
Argon. 85072
Argonaut. pseud. Authentic statement. see Etches, John.
Argonaut. pseud. Continuation of an authentic statement. see Etches, John.
Argonaut (Ship) in Admiralty 92294
Argonaut series. 90060
Argonauta de las costas de Nueva-Espana. (16165)
Argonautica Gustaviana. 44661, 98187, 98216
Arog-navta Batavvs. 44968
Argos. Editores. 61128
Argos constitucional de Lima. 61078, 61080
Argote, Francisco Agustin. 97720
Argote y Gorostiza, R. J. 64573
Argoult, Charlotte des Cossas (du Vivier-Bourgogne) d'. defendant 75162
Argoult, Robert d'. defendant 75162
Argudin, Jose Suarez. see Suarez Argudin, Jose.
Arguelles, -----. 1962
Arguelles, Anacleto Rodriguez y. see Rodrigues y Arguelles, Anacleto.
Arguelles, Jose Ganga. 1663
Arguelles, Jose Vazquez. (1964)
Arguello, Francisco Suarez de. see Suarez de Arguello, Francisco.
Arguello, Maria de la Soledad Ortega de. see Soledad Ortega de Arguello, Maria de la.
Arguinaldo coleccion de recriminaciones. 39481
Arguleta, ------. 40733
Argumens avancees de la parte de M^{rs} les Directeurs. 102442
Argument addressed especially to American statesmen. 91839
Argument addressed to . . . the Governor of Pennsylvania. 59893
Argument against rebellion. 14204
Argument against the abolition of the constitution. (1965)
Argument against the constitutional validity. 18034
Argument against the expediency of a war. 64165
Argument against the policy of re-opening the African slave trade. (30425)
Argument against the power of Congress. 64622
Argument . . . against the repeal of the personal liberty law. 62528
Argument against war with Great Britain. 42455
Argument and appeal in behalf of the remains. 29539
Argument and observations. 105163
Argument . . . as to the right. 82439
Argument at a court of Grand Sessions. 1966, 10892
Argument at the close of the petition. 89697
Argument . . . at the hearing of the petition. 42078
Argument before a . . . committee of the Massachusetts Legislature. 49195
Argument before a Joint Committee of the Wisconsin Legislature. 83753
Argument before the Committee of the Legislature of Massachusetts. (20933)

Argument before the Committee of the Legislature, on the subject. 89877

Argument before the Committee on the District of Columbia. 89376

Argument . . . before the Court of Appeals. 68042

Argument, before the General Assembly of . . . Connecticut. (18262)

Argument before the General Synod of the Reformed Protestant Dutch Church. (33223)

Argument before the Hon. J. D. Cox. 55195

Argument before . . . the Legislature of Massachusetts. 31812

Argument . . . before the New York Canal Appraisers. 64285

Argument before the Select Committee of the U. S. Senate. 90391

Argument before the Supreme Court of the U. S., in the case of the U. S., appellants, vs. Cinque and others. 274

Argument before the Supreme Court of the United States, March 10, 1818. 102261

Argument before the United States Supreme Court. 2067

Argument by Charles Theodore Russell. 85212

Argument by Col. S. C. Stambaugh. 90113

Argument by John C. Gray. 85212

Argument by N. P. Chipman. (12825)

Argument by O. B. Hart. 30641

Argument delivered at Annapolis, by William Wirt. 104870

Argument delivered . . . in Richmond, Virginia. (18203)

Argument delivered in the Court of Appeals. 28862

Argument delivered in the Supreme Court of the United States. (18036)

Argument delivered on the part of New-York. 1967

Argument . . . District Court of the U. States. (42615)

Argument for a Catholic Church on the jail-lands. 6997

Argument for American consistency. 24043

Argument for, and persuasive unto the great and important duty of family worship. (14525)

Argument for cheap trains. 67265

Argument for Christian colleges. 82705

Argument . . . for . . . Christian education. 39171

Argument for cleansing the sanctuary. 59894

Argument for constitutional guarantees. 59651

Argument for construing largely the right of an appellee. 37357

Argument for defence by Benjamin F. Thomas. 95377

Argument for defendant. 93489, 98429

Argument for government. 16147

Argument for home missions. 104812

Argument, for opening the reading room. (22293)

Argument for Professor Egbert C. Smyth. 85212

Argument for securing Christian education in Southern Illinois. 21401

Argument for the abolition of sects. 98495

Argument for the complainant, in the case of the state of Pennsylvania, vs. the Wheeling and Belmont Bridge Co., and others, by Mr. Edwin M. Stanton. 90390

Argument for the complainant, in the case of the state of Pennsylvania, vs. the Wheeling and Belmont Bridge Company . . . . In reply to Mr Russell. 30333

Argument for the defence by A. G. Riddle. 71258

Argument for the defendant in error. 68567

Argument for the defendant, submitted to the Supreme Court. 12197

Argument for the extension of the Old Colony and Fall River Railroad. 55049

Argument for the heirs at law in the Halsey will case. 17996

Argument for the heirs of Stephen Girard. 58857

Argument for the legal proscription of the traffic. 11301

Argument for the plaintiffs in the Dartmouth-College case. 18613

Argument for the Supreme Court of the United States. 104413

Argument from the Bible. 36931

Argument general du dernier des manifestes. 93605

Argument in behalf of the East Boston Ferry Company. 78515

Argument in behalf of the Eastern Rail-Road Company. 19662

Argument in behalf of the intervenors. 82145

Argument . . . in case of Duncan, Sherman & Co. 64285

Argument . . . in defence of Capt. Schaumburg. 13620

Argument in defence of Edwin T. Grayson. 28422

Argument in defence of the exclusive right. 1968

Argument in defence of the principle. 8544

Argument in defence of the Rev. Eliphalet Nott. 89345

Argument in defence of W. Kenny. (37458)

Argument . . . in favor of "A bill for the relief." 28038

Argument in favor of a land grant. 38546

Argument . . . in favor of a state loan. 19662

Argument, in favor of the constitutionality of the general banking law. 25009

Argument in favor of the constitutionality of the legal tender clause. 72589

Argument in favor of the proposed consolidation. 11869

Argument in favor of the repeal of the excise law. (25734)

Argument in favor of the removal of the national capital. (68305)

Argument in opposition to annexing Roxbury to Boston. 74876

Argument . . . in support to his claim. 23893

Argument in support of the memorial. 94531

Argument in support of the right. 33609

Argument . . . in the Albany Bridge case. 31850

Argument in the case of Ebenezer Smith Platt. 63352

Argument . . . in the case of Francis O. J. Smith. 18028

Argument in the case of James Sommersett. 30374

Argument . . . in the case of R. W. Meade. 47236

Argument, in the case of Rhode-Island against Massachusetts. 70550

Argument . . . in the case of the arrest of the person. 33839

Argument in the case of the carriage duties. 103854

Argument in the case of the ship Hunter. 33939, 103717

Argument in the case of the United States vs. Philemon T. Herbert. 65388

Argument, . . . in the case of the United
States vs. Richard C. Bristol. 59159
Argument in the case Rhode Island against
Massachusetts. (31093)
Argument in the Circuit Court of the U. States
79585
Argument in the De Lux case. 35849
Argument . . . in the discussion of the ques-
tion. 82601
Argument . . . in the Eliot School case. 21414
Argument in the House of Assembly. 31595
Argument . . . in the Massachusetts Legislature.
(51850)
Argument in the matter of application by
Randolph Coyle. 20266
Argument in the matter of the arbitration
between the United States and the Green
Bay and Mississippi Canal Company.
37679
Argument . . . in the Methodist Church
property case. (16986)
Argument in the Rhode Island causes. 29889
Argument in the Supreme Court of Louisiana.
(51560)
Argument, in the Supreme Court of the United
States, in the cases of Colin Mitchell
and others. 103431
Argument in the Supreme Court of the United
States, March, 1866. 31317
Argument . . . in the Vallandigham Habeas
Corpus case. (61025)
Argument intended to induce the people and
public men. 14419
Argument . . . involving the question of the
power. 50836
Argument . . . March 14th, 1854. 56238
Argument . . . November 17th, 1863. 56238
Argument of A. C. Davis. 18797
Argument of [Alexander Hamilton]. (29950)
Argument of Alexander Smyth. 85190
Argument of Benjamin F. Butler. 9612
Argument of Benjamin F. Hallett. 29890
Argument of Benjamin F. Porter. 64201
Argument of Byron Paine. 58181
Argument of C. F. Southmayd. 88591
Argument of Charles D. Drake. 20817
Argument of Charles P. Shaw. (79901)
Argument of Charles Sumner. 93642
Argument of Charles W. Russell. 74316
Argument of counsel, and the decision of the
court. (20647), note after 96509
Argument of counsel in the case of R. W.
Meade. 47236
Argument of Daniel E. Sickles. 80842
Argument of Daniel S. Richardson. 70996
Argument of E. C. Seamen. 78603
Argument of E. Delafield Smith. 82452
Argument of E. R. Hoar. 85212
Argument of Edgar Ketchum. (33273)
Argument of Edward G. Ryan. 74529
Argument of Ed. Graham Haywood. (31083)
Argument of Edward Sanford. 76407
Argument of Edwin R. Mason. 45434
Argument of F. P. Stanton. 90407
Argument of Francis O. J. Smith. 82559
Argument of G. B. Duncan. (21256)
Argument of George B. Cheever. (12406)
Argument of Henry Stanbery. 90145
Argument of Henry W. Muzzey. 51615
Argument of Hon. Charles Robinson. 72056
Argument of Hon. Chas. Theo. Russell in
behalf of the Boston and New York Central
Railroad Co. 74309
Argument of Hon. Chas. Theo. Russell in behalf
of the town of Danvers. 74308

Argument of Hon. Daniel S. Richardson.
70995
Argument of Hon. Edwards Pierrepont. 62783
Argument of Hon. Emory Washburn. 101515
Argument of Hon. George Marston. 44823
Argument of Hon. John M. Read. 68162
Argument of Hon. Roscoe Conkling. (15628)
Argument of Hon. W. D. Porter. 64321
Argument of Horace Binney. 5472
Argument of Ivers J. Austin. 2409
Argument of J. M. Patton. 59161
Argument of James T. Austin. 96843
Argument of John A. Bingham, Chairman of
the Managers. 5438
Argument of John A. Bingham, Special Judge
Advocate. 5451
Argument of John A. Logan. 41800
Argument of John C. Spencer. 89349
Argument of John C. Vaughan. 98688
Argument of John Jay. 37977
Argument of John K. Porter, counsel for the
disfranchised corporators. 64281
Argument of John K. Porter, in the Court of
Appeals. 64285
Argument of John K. Porter, . . . January 10,
1862. 58611
Argument of John K, Porter, on the trial at
Albany. 64283
Argument of John K. Porter on the trial of
. . . J. C. Mather. 64282
Argument of John R. Pater on the trial of
William Landon. 59050
Argument of John T. Montgomery. 50152
Argument of Joseph Mason. 45470
Argument of L. Madison Day. 18970
Argument of Matt. H. Carpenter. 10995
Argument of Milton H. Smith. 83630
Argument of Mr. Armstrong. (59766)
Argument of Mr. Carlisle. 10927
Argument of Mr. Hambly. 65520
Argument [of Mr. Stanton.] 90394
Argument of Mr. Wickliffe. 103856
Argument of Montgomery Blair. 5751
Argument of N. P. Chipman in the trial of Col.
Edmund E. Paulding. 59185
Argument of N. P. Chipman in the trial of
Edmund E. Paulding. (12825)
Argument of N. Richardson. (71078)
Argument of Peleg Sprague. 89698
Argument of Peter Y. Cutler. 18179
Argument of Philip R. Fendall. (24051)
Argument [of President Burnet.] 95107
Argument of President Lincoln. (55179)
Argument of R. C. L. Moncure. (49956)
Argument of R. Barnwell Smith. 83854
Argument of R. D. Smith. 83856
Argument of respondent's counsel. 78856
Argument of Richard H. Dana. 18450
Argument of Robert C. Pitman. 63056
Argument of Robert D. Smith. 83860
Argument of Roger S. Baldwin. 2908
Argument of Rufus B. Smith. 83961
Argument of Rufus Choate. 18906
Argument of Samuel B. Ruggles. 73955
Argument of Samuel L. Southard. 19205,
88244
Argument of Samuel T. Glover. 27614
Argument of the Bishop of New Jersey. (20385),
88253
Argument of the counsel for the plaintiffs.
89380
Argument of the Hon. Thos. Johnson. 95005
Argument of the Judges-Advocate. 82572
Argument of the opening counsel in the case of
the Providence Bank vs. the state of
Rhode Island. 66240

Argument of the opening counsel, in the case of the Providence Bank vs. Thomas G. Pitman. 66240
Argument of the questions. 103717
Argument of the secessionists. 41162
Argument of the United States. 18083
Argument of Thomas C. Amory. 1343
Argument of Thomas Hopkinson. (32988)
Argument of Titian J. Coffey. 14156
Argument of Wendell Phillips. (62520)
Argument of William H. Seward, in defence of William Freeman. (79503)
Argument of William H. Seward in the Albany Bridge case. 79505
Argument of William H. Seward in the Circuit Court. 79546
Argument of William H. Seward on the law. 79504
Argument of William Henry Anthon. 1680
Argument of William Johnston. 36388
Argument of William Orton. 57729
Argument on behalf of Thaddeus Hyatt. 79454
Argument on behalf of the American Tract Society. 68499
Argument on behalf of the complainants in the Andover case. 85212
Argument on behalf of the complainants, in the matter. 85212
Argument . . . on behalf of the Eastern Railroad Company. 42078
Argument . . . on Indian affairs. 50836
Argument on the act requiring attorneys. 89363
Argument on the . . . annexation of Roxbury to Boston. 13689
Argument on the chancery powers. 7183, note after 105507
Argument on the constitutionality and construction. 7336
Argument on the constitutionality of the act of Congress. 24274
Argument on the . . . constitutionality of the general banking law. 56238
Argument on the fugitive slave law. 82597
Argument on the Houmas land claim. 30624
Argument on the liabilities of bankers and brokers. 40778
Argument on the memorials from the county of Allegany. 53979, note after 90676
Argument on the petitions. (6977)
Argument on the popular sovereignty. 50383
Argument on the powers. 31408
Argument on the question of slavery. 91888
Argument on the question of the constitutionality. 102594
Argument on the questions whether the loss. 33939, 103717
Argument on the unconstitutionality of slavery. 47438
Argument or speech of John Gardiner. 26618
Argument presented by the Committee of the Convention of the Diocese of New Jersey. 47243
Argument presented to the Finance Committee. 84909
Argument proving that the South-Sea Company are able. 88174
Argument . . . relating to the . . . Central Branch Union Pacific R. R. Co. (55196)
Argument respecting the constitutionality of the carriage tax. 94485
Argument, showing the legal status of the Memphis, El Paso, and Pacific Railroad Company. 88506
Argument, submitted to the Committee of the Senate. 101956

Argument submitted to the Committee on Printing. 72850
Argument submitted to the Secretary of the Treasury. 78970
Argument. The town being collected in Faneuil-Hall. 95280
Argument to establish the illegality. 36261
Argument to shew the disadvantages. 69523, 88175, 88179, 96768
Argument to the Court for the Correction of Errors. 89386
Argument upon the Alabama Claims. (58709)
Argument vs. the Baltimore and Ohio Railroad Company. (74315)
Argument was pleaded. 97177
Argument which His Excellency Alexander G. McNutt. 2407, 43609
Argument, with map. 88428
Argumentative petition. 93241
Argumento [de De Soto.] 11234, 39115
Argumento [de Las Casas.] 11234, 11283
Argumento del editor. 99482
Argumento del editor sobre la atribucion 30 arte 90. 99482
Argumento ministerial. 99482
Argumento negativo. 9567
Argumentorum quae a D. D. Directoribus Societatis. 68792
Arguments against imposition of hands in ordination. 24401
Arguments and decisions in the Indiana conspiracy case. 49087
Arguments and judgment of the Mayor's Court. 74432
Arguments and statements addressed to the members. 6782, note after 9785
Arguments before the Committee on Elections. (5541)
Arguments entered into. 21313
Arguments for defendants. 35314
Arguments for the defendant before the President. 9622
Arguments for the defendant, on a special verdict. 46875, 95436
Arguments . . . Girls Reform School. 89377
Arguments in behalf of the United States in the matter of the claims. 18095
Arguments in behalf of the United States, with supplement. 18082
Arguments in favor of the International Submarine Telegraph. 93976
Arguments in favor of the ladies. 103336
Arguments in support of the proposed bill. (81893), note after 102820
Arguments in support of the supremacy of the British legislature. (1969)
Arguments in the case of Isaac H. Burch vs. Mary W. Burch. 4256
Arguments in the case of John D. Minor et al. 49314
Arguments in the case of Shotwell vs. Henrickson. 80738
Arguments in the case of the Eliot School rebellion. 21414
Arguments in the Court of Appeals. 21543
Arguments of counsel. 64285
Arguments of counsel in the cases of the Snipe. 29308
Arguments of counsel in the close of the trial. (2482)
Arguments of counsel in the New York Court of Appeals. 59502
Arguments of counsel, in the West Washington market case. 6021
Arguments of Franklin Dexter & B. F. Hallett. 34959

Arguments of Gerrit Smith and David J. Mitchell. (82602)
Arguments of Messrs. Adam N. Riddle, Judge Lane, and Thomas Ewing. 84743
Arguments of Messrs. Choate and Webster. 7127
Arguments of Messrs. Whipple and Webster. 70732
Arguments of Rev. Drs. Joshua W. Wellman. 85212
Arguments of Robert D. Smith and Albert E. Pissbury. 83858
Arguments of secessionists. 40985
Arguments of the council for the defendant. 19341, 84557-84558, 98429
Arguments of the counsel of Joseph Hendrickson. 105025
Arguments of the defendants' counsel. 27488
Arguments of the Hon. Edward Stanly. 90320
Arguments of the Hon. James R. Doolittle. 20609
Arguments of . . . the petitioners. 12860
Arguments offered to the Right Honorable the Lords Commissioners. 53534
Arguments, pro and con. 20717
Arguments proving the inconsistency and impolicy. 1970
Arguments submitted to the Judiciary Committee. 53189
Arguments to prove, that not only in taxation. 11152-(11153)
Arguments to prove the policy and necessity. 50857
Arguments . . . upon the power of Congress. 42048
Arguments upon the secularization. 86697
Argumentum ad hominem. 59677
Argumentum operis. 26561
Argumossa y Gandara, Theodoro Ventura de. see Ventura de Argumossa y Gandara, Theodoro.
Argus. pseud. A tale of Lowell. 1971
Argus. 103867
Argus of Western America. 37351
Argy, Louis Henri Marthe, Marquis de Gouy d'. see Gouy d'Arsy, Louis Henri Marthe, Marquis de, 1753-1794.
Argyle's advice to Sir R——t W——p——e. 99249
Argyll, Archibald Campbell, 9th Earl of, 1629-1685. defendant 47571, 78227
Argyll, George Douglas Campbell, 8th Duke of, 1823-1900. 83876
Argyll, John Campbell, 2d Duke of, 1678-1743. 10227-10229, 89188
Argyll, John George Edward Henry Douglas Sutherland Campbell, 9th Duke of, 1845-1914. 10251
Argyropolis. 77064-(77066)
Arias, Anselmo de Paula. 1972
Arias, C. Juan de Dios. see Juan de Dios Arias, C.
Arias, Fernando de. 98718
Arias, Francisco Gavino. 1973
Arias, Puetro. 1974
Arias de Ugarte, Fernando. see Ugarte, Fernando Arias de, Abp.
Arias Montano, Benito. see Montano, Benito Arias.
Arias Saavedra, Francisco. see Saavedra, Francisco Arias.
Arias Tenorio, Danres. see Tenorio, Danres Arias.
Aribau, Buenaventura Carlos. (9890), 32043
Ariel. pseud. The Negro. see Payne, Buckner H., 1799-1883.

Ariel [i. e. H. B. Bayne] dissected and the Negro resurrected. 81894
Ariel refuted. (78545)
Arieta & Co. firm see Caricaburu, Arieta & Co. firm
Arillaga, B. J. 48636
Ariquipa (Diocese) Bishop (Ugarte y Sarabia) 25487 see also Ugarte y Sarabia, Augustin de, Bp.
Aris, ------. ed. 90024
Arispe, Miguel Ramos de. see Ramos de Arispe, Miguel.
Aris's Birmingham gazette. 90024
Aristander. pseud. Treatise on political economy. see Stirrat, David.
Aristarque Francais. 93825
Aristides. pseud. 84642, 2d note after 96428
Aristides. pseud. Address to the country. 1979
Aristides. pseud. Appendix to Aristides's vindication. see Van Ness, William Peter.
Aristides. pseud., ed. Celebrated letters of Philo-Cato. 62545
Aristides. pseud. Concise narrative. see Van Ness, William Peter.
Aristides. pseud. Considerations on the proposed removal. see Hanson, Alexander Contee.
Aristides. pseud. Essays on the spirit of Jacksonism. see McKenney, T. L.
Aristides. pseud. Examination of the various charges. see Van Ness, William Peter.
Aristides. pseud. Letter to General Hamilton. see Van Ness, William Peter. supposed author and Webster, Noah, 1758-1843. supposed author
Aristides. pseud. Letter to the Secretary of the Treasury. see Van Ness, William Peter. supposed author and Webster, supposed author
Aristides. pseud. Observations upon the late proceedings. 1976
Aristides. pseud. Political frauds exposed. 20650, 63778
Aristides. pseud. Prospect before us. 66067, 88068
Aristides. pseud. Remarks on the proposed plan of a federal government. see Hanson, Alexander Contee.
Aristides. pseud. Remarks on the proposed plan of an emission of paper. see Hanson, Alexander Contee.
Aristides. pseud. Strictures on the case. 2485, note after 92848
Aristides. pseud. To John Cruger. 95897
Aristides. pseud. Vindication of the Vice President. see Van Ness, William Peter.
Aristides. pseud. Virginia edition, of the various charges exhibited. see Van Ness, William Peter.
Aristo. pseud. see Unanue, Jose Hipolito.
Aristo. pseud. Coloquio de Aristo y Timandro. 14734
Aristocles. (20062), 23091, 36294
Aristocles letter to Authades. (20062)
Aristocracy. 94491
Aristocracy. An epic poem. (1980)
Aristocracy, aristocratic government. 8413
Aristocracy exposed. 1981
Aristocracy in America. 29004
Aristocracy of America. A short sketch. 93634
Aristocracy of Boston. 6479
Aristocracy of New York. 54095

Aristocracy, or the Holbey family. 104170
Aristocrat: an American tale. 36125
Aristocrat and trades union advocat. 105473
Aristocratie negriere. 80818
Aristodemus. pseud. Brieven. 7936, 22991
Aristokratie in Amerika. 29005
Aristoteles. 27266, (31564), (73860), 96108, 98912
Arithmetic on the productive system. 83911
Arithmetica della nazioni e divisione. 31600
Arithmetica of Cyffer-Konst. 98862
Arithmetical rules. 11970
Arithmetick vulgar and decimal. 28689
Arizcorreta, Mariano. 70094 see also Mexico (State) Gobernador (Arizcorreta)
Arizona (Territory) Laws, statutes, etc. 1983
Arizona (Territory) Legislative Assembly. 36754
Arizona and Sonora. 51210
Arizona Historical Society. 1984
Arizona: its resources and prospects. 43101
Arizpe, Pedro Joseph Rodriguez de. see Rodriguez de Arzipe, Pedro Joseph.
Arjiropolis o la capital. (38992), 77063
Arjona, Francisco de. 1985
Ark of God on a new cart. 83572
Ark of liberty. 40749
Arkansas (Territory) Laws, statutes, etc. 1990-1991
Arkansas. Auditor. (69761)
Arkansas. Commissioner of Public Works and Internal Improvements. (69761)
Arkansas. Commissioner of State Lands. 84962A see also Smithee, James Newton, 1842-1905?
Arkansas. Constitution. 1269, 1988, 5316, 16113, 33137, (47188), 59771, 63923, (66397)
Arkansas. Convention, Little Rock, 1861. 36706, 57511
Arkansas. County Clerks. 84962A
Arkansas. Governor, 1852-1860 (Conway) 33150 see also Conway, Elias Nelson, 1812-1894.
Arkansas. Governor, 1874-1876 (Garland) 84485 see also Garland, Augustus Hill, 1832-1899.
Arkansas. Laws, statutes, etc. 1987, 23765, 28115, 52051, 63921-63922, 70820-70821, 82438, 89066
Arkansas. Legislature. petitioners (1992)
Arkansas. Legislature. Committee on Federal Relations. 1995
Arkansas. Treasurer. (69761)
Arkansas. 73481
Arkansas in 1875. 84962A
Arkansas Immigrant Aid Society. 1986
Arkansas! The home for immigrants. 1986
Arkansaw doctor. (67620)
Arktische Erforschungen und Entdeckungen. 85148
Arktische Fahrten und Entdeckungen. 36999
Arlach, H. de T. d'. 1997
Arlegui, Joseph. 1998, (52106)
Arlequin sauvage. 13616, 2d note after 96139
Arlington. Resolution and speech. 43119
Arlington Street Church, Boston. see Boston. Arlington Street Church.
Arlovi, Benito Garret y. see Garret y Arlovi, Benito, Bp.
Armageddon. (2910)
Armagh, Archbishop of. see Boutler, Hugh, Abp. of Armagh, 1672-1742. Ussher, James, Abp. of Armagh, 1581-1656.
Arman, -----. defendant 50564
Arman, H. M. van. see Van Arman, H. M.

Armand. pseud. see Strubberg, Friedrich Armand.
Armand-Aubert, -----. (1999)
Armand-Argeaut, -----. incorrectly supposed author see Gatereau, Armand.
Armand's Ausgewahlte Romane. 93103
Armas, Francisco de. 2000
Armas, Juan Ignacio de. supposed author 86257
Armas, Luis Umpierres y. see Umpierres y Armas, Luis.
Armas y Cespedes, Francisco de. 2001
Armazem de conhecimentos uteis. 16048
Armazem literario. 7563
Armazen de novellas escolhidas. 46198
Armbruster, Anthony. supposed author 32053, 60137-(60138), 60145, 97114, 2d note after 102552
Armee and Flotte und ihre ruhmreichen Thaten. 94085
Armee son histoire. 29364
Armeni, Haithoni. see Hethum, Prince of Korghos, d. 1308.
Armeno, Hayton. see Hethum, Prince of Korghos, d. 1308.
Armies of Europe. 43020
Armin, Th. 2002-2002A
Arming, Friedrich Wilhelm. (2003)
Armistead, Wilson, 1819?-1868. 216, 2003A-2007, 2186, 17850, 25352, 27628, (26672), 40946, 104325
Armistice. 28467
Armitage, John. 2008
Armitage, Thomas. 2009
Armitage, William E. 2010
Armor, Thomas. 106024 see also York County, Pa. Collector of Excise.
Armour of Christianity. 46225
Armrisch, E. 2011
Armroyd, George. supposed author 2012-2013, 10860
Armroyd (George) & Co. firm petitioners 2014
Arms, Hiram P. 2015
Armsby, J. H. 2016, 99217
Armsmear; the house, the arms, and the armory. 14763
Armstrong, -----. (59766)
Armstrong, -----. cartographer 6516
Armstrong, ------. plaintiff (5576)
Armstrong, Sir Alexander, 1818-1899. 2017
Armstrong, Edward. 2018-2019, 60143, 68399
Armstrong, George Dodd, 1813-1899. 2020-2021, 20255
Armstrong, J. W. 96697 see also U.S. Commissioners to the Comanche and Wichita Indians.
Armstrong, Jacob D. 2022
Armstrong, John, B. A. 2026
Armstrong, John, of New York. supposed author 106216
Armstrong, John, 1709-1779. 2023
Armstrong, John, 1758-1843. 2024-2025, 14379, 15508, (31987), 58478, 98548
Armstrong, John, 1758-1843. supposed author 13819, (22650), 40569, 62841, 89139, 89296, note after 101937, 104746
Armstrong, John, fl. 1814-1819. 25642, 63143
Armstrong, John L. 2027-2028
Armstrong, John W. (2029)
Armstrong, Kosciusko. 2030, 43405
Armstrong, Lebbeus, 1775-1860. 2031-2035, 70281
Armstrong, Price. 2036
Armstrong, Robert. 2037
Armstrong, Robert G. 2038

Armstrong, Samuel. 46036 see also Massachusetts. Governor, 1835-1836 (Armstrong)
Armstrong, W. C. 2041
Armstrong, William. defendant 88828
Armstrong, William. petitioner 2040
Armstrong, William. USA 96732 see also U. S. Commissioners to the Creek Tribe of Indians. U. S. Superintendent. Western Territory (Acting)
Armstrong, William, fl. 1848. 2039, note before before 91886
Armstrong (Brig) see General Armstrong (Brig)
Army abuses. 79174
Army and navy almanac. 64096
Army and navy chronicle. 2043
Army and navy chronicle, and scientific repository. 2042
Army and navy chronicle of the United States. 25060
Army and Navy Claim Agency of the United States Sanitary Commission. see United States Sanitary Commission. Army and Navy Claim Agency.
Army and navy gazette. (2044)
Army and navy melodies. (18259)
Army and navy of America. 52241, 2d note after 95758
Army and navy of the United States. 2d note after 95758
Army and navy official gazette. 2045
Army and navy pension laws. 47193
Army and navy prayer book. (2046)
Army and navy register. 97968
Army and Navy Union of Massachusetts. see Massachusetts Army And Navy Union.
Army Association of Massachusetts. see Massachusetts Army Association.
Army chaplain. (8597)
Army chaplains' manual. (30103)
Army Committee of the Boston Young Men's Christian Association. see Young Men's Christian Association, Boston. Army Committee.
Army Committee of the United States Christian Commission, Pittsburgh. see United States Christian Commission. Army Committee, Pittsburgh.
Army correspondence. 39260
Army hymn book. (2047)
Army life in a black regiment. 31752
Army life on the Pacific. 37944
Army life; or, incidents from the prayer meeting. 2048
Army list. 41456
Army medical reports. 83367
Army memoir. 44490
Army meteorological register for twelve years. 2051
Army meteorological register . . . from 1831 to 1842. 2050
Army, navy and militia volunteer guide. 30025
Army notes. 67314
Army of the Potomac. 69869
Army of the Potomac, and its mismanagement. 22203
Army of the Potomac, battle of Petersburg. 69870
Army of the Potomac. Behind the scenes. 11434
Army of the Potomac; Gen. McClellan's report. (43011)
Army of the Potomac; its organization. 36407, 1st note after 97024

Army of the Potomac. Report of Maj. Gen. Geo. B. McClellan. 43010, 43018
Army of the Potomac. The defence of Richmond against the Federal Army under General McClellan. 2052A, 19241
Army of the United States not to be employed. 79506
Army of the Valley of Virginia. see Confederate States of America. Army. Army of the Valley of Virginia.
Army ration. 33050
Army register of Ohio volunteers. 56879
Army register of the United States. 2053
Army regulations, adopted for the use of the army of the Confederate States. 15236
Army regulations, adopted for the use of the army of the Confederate States, in accordance with late acts of Congress. 2054
Army Relief Bazaar, Albany, N. Y., 1864. (76646)
Army reunion. 86094
Army series. 1255, 55875
Arnall, William. 80700, 101167
Arnao, Vincente Gonzalez. tr. 33718
Arnaud, A. see Arnauld, A.
Arnaud, Achille. 2056
Arnaud, Leopold. 2057
Arnauld, A. 2055, (58293)
Arnault de la Boirie, ------. tr. (43782)
Arnay, ------ d'. see D'Arnay, -----.
Arne, Thomas Augustus, 1710-1778. 84678C
Arngrime, Jonssije Fordum. see Vidalin, Arngrimur Jonsson, 1568-1648.
Arnold, -------. plaintiff 96813
Arnold, Augustus C. L. ed. 53290
Arnold, Benedict, 1741-1801. 2059, (2063), 4746-4748, 60433, 82978, 83467, 4th note after 99800
Arnold, Benedict, 1741-1801. defendant 2060-2061
Arnold, Benedict, 1741-1801. incorrectly supposed author 69508, 81137
Arnold, Benedict, 1741-1801. spurious author Poem on door-keeping. see Wills, Archibald.
Arnold, Benjamin. 51752
Arnold, Charles Henry. 2064
Arnold, Christoph. 72603, 73320, 102615
Arnold, E. G. (2065)
Arnold, G. B. 2066
Arnold, George. defendant 96815
Arnold, George. plaintiff 96814
Arnold, George W. supposed author 92809
Arnold, Gottfried, 1666-1741. 72590
Arnold, Isaac N. 2067-2073, 12621
Arnold, Josias Lyndon, 1768-1796. 2074
Arnold, Lemuel H. (1665), 2075, 2077
Arnold, Matthew, 1822-1888. 83876
Arnold, R. Arthur. 2078
Arnold, Samuel, 1622?-1693. 2079, 98056
Arnold, Samuel, 1740-1802. 86925
Arnold, Samuel, fl. 1865. defendant 41180-41182, 41235
Arnold, Samuel Greene, 1821-1880. 2080-2084
Arnold, Seth S. 2085
Arnold, Stephen. defendant 96816-96817
Arnold, Theodor. tr. 57161
Arnold, Thomas Dickens, 1798-1870. 2086
Arnold, William. M. D. 35601
Arnold, William. of Barbadoes 3278, 3290
Arnold a model teacher. 72868
Arnold and Andre. (10084)
Arnold and Ramsay, vs. the United Insurance Co. 96813

Arnold at Saratoga. 61231
Arnold Brown's Indian voyage. 66686
Arnold, or the treason of West Point. 33458
Arnold prize essay. 20797
Arnold's march from Cambrdige to Quebec.
83467
Arnot, ------. 26845, 83796
Arnot, David Henry. 2087
Arnot, Hugo. supposed author 95453
Arnould, Ambroise Marie. 2088-2091
Arnoult, N. E. 2092
Arnout, ------. tr. 628, 66062
Arnstedt, Friedrich. 2093
Arny, William Frederick Milton, 1813-1881.
53276-53277 see also New Mexico
(Territory) Governor, 1861-1866 (Arny)
Aromatum & medicamentorum in orientali
India. 57666
Aromatvm, et simplicivm aliqvot medicamen-
torvm. 57663-57666
Aromatvm, frvctvvm, et simplicivm aliqvot
medicamentorvm. (25418), 26005
Aron. an Eskimo. engr. 22860, 36977
Aronsson, J. E. ed. (27350)
Arooawr. pseud.? Trenton falls. 96778,
101233
Arosemena, Juste. 2094, 58404
Arossemena, Blas. 85720
Around the world; a narrative of a voyage.
2095, (31430)
Arozarena, Ramon. 2096
Arp, Bill. pseud. see Smith, Charles Henry,
1826-1903.
Arquellada, Ventura de. tr. 72329
Arquellada Mendoza, Domingo Joseph de. see
Mendoza, Domingo Joseph de Arquellada.
Arqueta, Pedro de. 76007
Arraignment and conviction of Sᵣ Walter
Rawleigh. 67545
Arraignment of abuses. 90506
Arraignment, trial, and condemnation of Capt.
John Quelch. 67085-67086
Arraignment, tryal and condemnation of
Captain William Kidd. 37701-37702
Arrana, Juan Antonio Guerrero y Davila
Urrutia y. see Guerrero y Davila
Urrutia y Arana, Juan Antonio.
Arrangement, for the grand & solemn funeral
procession. 2097
Arrangement of medals and tokens. 77144
Arrangement of provincial coins. 15165
Arrangement of the music for the funeral
solemnities. 61479
Arrangement of the music, to be performed.
101774
Arrangement of the Pennsylvania line, Jan-
uary 17, 1781. (59895)
Arrangement of the tradesmen's cards.
(9537)
Arrangements for diffusing agricultural
knowledge. 53811
Arrangements for the inauguration of the Hon.
Josiah Quincy. 67208
Arrangements to be observed on the 22d day
of February next. 101775
Arrangoiz y Berzabal, F. de. 47036
Arrearage of taxes due. 99016
Arrebatado de Dios. 106220
Arredono, Fernando de la Maza. claimant
83356, 103431
Arredondo, Miguel Joseph Cortes de. see
Cortes de Arredondo, Miguel Joseph.
Arredondo, Nicolas de. 2101
Arreglamento mandado observar con los dos
fragatas. 56243

Arreglo a los decretos del Senor Provisor.
41665
Arreglo del Cuerpo Permanente de Artilleria.
48290
Arreglo del Cuerpo Permanente de Ingenieros.
48290
Arrest and trial of Rev. George Storrs. 92230
Arrest de la Cour de Parlement. 68074
Arrest de verification de la Cour de Aydes.
56086
Arrest du Conseil d'Estat du Roy, du dix-
huitieme Juillet 1682. 56072
Arrest du Conseil d'Estat du Roy. Du douzieme
Aoust 1671. (56069)
Arrest du Conseil d'Estat du Roy du 12 Fevrier
1726. 2103, 10356
Arrest du Conseil d'Estat du Roy, du premier
Decembre 1722. 15914
Arrest du Conseil d'Estat du Roy, du quatre
Juillet 1722. 15914
Arrest du Conseil d'Estat du Roy du 30
Decembre 1713. (73809)
Arrest du Conseil d'Estat du Roy, portant
qu'il sera estably. 73813
Arrest du Conseil d'Estat du Roy, qui decharge
les morues. 73810
Arrest du Conseil d'Estat du Roy, qui declare
en faveur. 15914
Arrest du Conseil d'Estat du Roy, qui exempte
du tous droits. 56071
Arrest du Conseil d'Estat du Roy, qui ordonne
aux negociants. (73712)
Arrest du Conseil d'Estat du Roy. Qui ordonne
que, conformement. 15914
Arrest du Conseil d'Estat du Roy, qui ordonne
que dans six mois. 75011
Arrest du Conseil d'Estat du Roy, qui ordonne
que les droits. 56075
Arrest du Conseil d'Estat du Roy. Qui ordonne
que pendant dix annees. 73811
Arrest du Conseil d'Estat du Roy qui ordonne
qu'il ne sera plus envoye. 15914
Arrest du Conseil d'Estat du Roy, qui permet
aux Sieurs Bergier. 56077
Arrest du Conseil d'Estat du Roy, qui prescrit
les formalites. 73814
Arrest du Conseil d'Estat: pour faire rendre
compte. 56070
Arrest du Conseil d'Estat: qvi permet aux
habitans de Canada. 56068
Arrest du Conseil d'Estat, Sa Majeste y estant,
pour le retablissement de la fabrique de
purs castors de Canada. Du 12 Avril
1685. 56074
Arrest du Conseil d'Estat, Sa Majeste y estant,
pour le retablissement de la fabrique des
purs castors de Canada. Du 8 Fevrier
1865. 56073
Arrest . . . [du Conseil d'Etat du Roi.]
(2105)
Arrest du Conseil d'Etat du Roi. 2102
Arrest du Conseil d'Etat du Roy. Du 9 Fevrier
1700. 56076
Arrest du Conseil d'Etat du Roy qui ordonne
l'infeodation de l'isle. 4510
Arrest du Conseil d'Etat du Roy qui ordonne
que les marchandises du cru. 73816
Arrest du Conseil d'Etat du Roy qui ordonne
que les marchandises qui seront apportees.
15914
Arrest du Conseil d'Etat du Roy, qui ordonne
que pendant dix annees. 73815
Arrest du Conseil d'Etat, &c. (2102A)
Arrest du Conseil du 30 Aout 1784. 56472
Arrest du Roy concernant le commerce. 10357

Arrest of William Walker. 82137
Arrest qui permet a tous Francois. 75055
Arret du Conseil de'Etat, qui ordonne. (14704)
Arret du Conseil d'Etat, concernant le commerce etranger. 14702
Arret du Conseil d'Etat concernant le commerce interlope. 14705
Arret du Conseil d'Etat, concernant les armemens. 14703
Arret du Conseil d'Etat du Roi. 2104
Arret du Conseil d'Etat du Roi, concernant le retour des noirs. 15914
Arret du Conseil d'Etat du Roi, concernant l'etablissement des paquebots. 14706
Arret du Conseil d'Etat du Roi, portant cassation. 75060
Arret du Conseil d'Etat du Roi, portant suppression des 24 paquebots. 56078
Arret du Conseil d'Etat du Roi portant suppression d'un memoire. 75057
Arret du Conseil d'Etat du Roi, pour le renouvellement. 75056
Arret du Conseil d'Etat du Roi, qui casse & annulle un ordonance. 75059
Arret du Conseil d'Etat du Roi qui declare le Sieur Fournier. 75058
Arret du Conseil d'Etat du Roi qui ordonne l'establissement. 75409
Arret du Conseil d'Etat, qui prolonge. 29159
Arret du Conseil d'Etat, qui proroge. 15914
Arret du Conseil du 30 Aout dernier. 40001
Arret du Conseil du 30 Aout 1784. (40681)
Arret du Conseil Superieur du Cap-Francois. 75061
Arret du Roi concernant l'etablissement des paquebots. (2105)
Arret du 29 Juillet 1786. 73469, 96048
Arret of the King's Council of State. (38735)
Arret portant suppression d'un ouvrage. 75062
Arrete de l'Assemblee Provinciale du Nord de St. Domingue. 75064
Arrete de l'Assemblee Provinciale du Nord de Saint Domingue, le 4 Janvier, 1790. 75063
Arrete des agens particuliers du Directoire Executif. 99746
Arrete du Conseil-General de Liquidation. 81658
Arrete Gueydon a la Martinique. 77742
Arrete relatif aux secours a envoyer a Saint-Domingue. 75065
Arretes du Directoire et des ses agens. 99745
Arrets du Conseil Superieur de Quebec. 10486
Arrets et commission des 6 et 18 Mai 1628. 10442
Arrets et reglements du Conseil Superieur de Quebec. 10476
Arriaga, Joseph Adame y. see Adame y Arriaga, Joseph.
Arriaga, Pablo Joseph de. 2106
Arrian. see Arrianus, Flavius.
Arrianus, Flavius. 22682, 67730, 67736
Arricertia. 2107
Arricivita, Juan Domingo. 22896
Arrieta, Francisco Sales de, Abp. 99499 see also Lima (Archdiocese) Archbishop (Arrieta)
Arrilaga, ------ Bas. see Bas Arrilaga, ----------.
Arrilaga, Blas. 67111 see also Jesuits. Mexico. Provincial.
Arrillaga, Basilio Jose. (2108), 48636
Arrillaga, Mariano Paredes y. see Paredes y Arrillaga, Mariano.
Arrillaga y Barcarcel, Basilio Manuel, 1791-1867. (48374)
Arrindell, ------. 82905

Arrington, Alfred W. supposed author 2108A, 93617-note after 93619
Arrington, Mrs. Alfred W. 93617
Arrival, description, and departure. 96363
Arrival of the Britannia. 26536
Arrival of the first colony in Charlestown. 85505
Arrivee a San-Francisco. 74988, note after 100812
Arrivee des ambassadeurs de Patagonce. (10358)
Arrivee des ambassadevrs dv royavme de Patagoce. (10358)
Arrivee des peres Capucins et la conversion. 5
Arrivee des peres Capvcins en l'Inde Nouuelle. 13505
Arroniz, Marcos. 2109-(2111)
Arrow against profane and promiscuous dancing. (2112), 46632
Arrow poison of the Indians of Guiana. (77790)
Arrowsick Island, Mass. Indian Conference, 1717. see Massachusetts (Colony) Indian Conference, Arrowsick Island, 1717.
Arrowsmith, Aaron, 1750-1823. 2113-2114, 50939
Arroyo de la Cuesta, Felipe. 2116-2118
Arroyo Ladron de Guevara, J. de. see Ladron de Guevara, J. de Arroyo.
Arroyo y Daza, Diago de. 2115, 69197
Arruda da Camara, Manoel. see Camara, Manoel Arruda da.
Ars et vocabularium Mexicanum. 57231
Arscot, Alexander. 2118A-(2118B)
Arsdale, Elias van. 53082
Arsdale, John van. USA 71388
Arseos. pseud. Historico y analyse. see Soares, Sebastiao Ferreira, 1820-1887.
Arseos historico e analyse esthetigraphica. 24315, 85628A
Arsy, Louis Henri Marthe, Marquis de Gouy d'. see Gouy d'Arsy, Louis Henri Marthe, Marquis de, 1753-1794.
Art and industry. 84499
Art and industry, as represented in the exhibition. (28484)
Art Association of Philadelphia. 83320
Art Association of Rhode Island. see Rhode Island Art Association.
Art culture. 3457
Art de navigeur. (47345)
Art de tirer et purifier les metaux. 3255A
Art de verifier les dates. 25173, 101348-101351, 101359
Art du cultivateur. 2767
Art education. 84491
Art education, scholastic and industrial. 84490
Art Exhibition, New Bedford, Mass., 1858. see New Bedford Art Exhibition, 1858.
Art Gallery, Providence, R. I. see Providence R. I. Free Public Library, Art Gallery, and Museum.
Art idea. 35795
Art in education. (60940)
Art journal. 42118
Art, literature, and the drama. 57816
Art of beautifying suburban home grounds. 78264
Art of contentment. 78657
Art of domestic happiness. 2119
Art of excelling. 9235
Art of fly catching. 23300
Art of fortune-telling unveiled. 62891
Art of healing disclosed. 91620
Art of lying and swearing, made easy. 97263
Art of making breeches. 35008

Art of making common salt. (2120)
Art of making sugar. 2120A
Art of painting. 105184
Art of photography. 85414-85415
Art of planting and cultivating the vine. 67782, 75475
Art of pleading. 2121
Art of pleasing. 90227-90228
Art of polite correspondence. 40557
Art of preaching. 82223-(82225)
Art of preserving health. 2023
Art of printing incorrectly. 22785, 91385
Art of raising the mulberry and silk. 37462
Art of reading. 90295
Art of refining silver. 3254
Art of rhetorick made easy. 91848
Art of speaking. 2123
Art of speaking and holding one's tongue. (2122)
Art of speculation. 83884, 83886
Art of travel. 26461
Art of travelling. 11289, 39119
Art of war lawful and necessary. 24426
Art of war the gift of God. (15091)
Art Union of Philadelphia. 61480
Arte bocabulario tesoro, y catecismo. 74034
Arte breve de la lengua Aymara. (5017)
Arte da grammatica da lingua do Brasil. 24313
Arte de adquirirla por la traduccion de los autores. 57578
Arte de bien morir. (40080)
Arte de cer. 77131
Arte de el idioma Maya. 4608
Arte de el idioma Mexicano. 60911
Arte de grammatica da lingoa mas usada. 1371, 7588, 63028
Arte de grammatica da lingua Brasilica. 44178
Arte de la gramatica de la lengua Zapoteca. 17843
Arte de la lengua Aymara, con una silva de sus frases. (29049)
Arte de la lengua Aymara, con una sylva de phrases. 5019
Arte de la lengua Cahita. (9841)
Arte de la lengua Chahita. 11738
Arte de la lengua de Michoacan. 7461
Arte de la lengua general de los Indios de los reynos del Peru. 20564
Arte de la lengua general de los Indios de Peru. 48232
Arte de la lengua general del reyno de Chile. 23968
Arte de la lengua general del Ynga. 47424
Arte de la lengua Guarani. 74033, 74035
Arte de la lengua Guarani, o mas bien Tupi. 74040
Arte de la lengua Kakchiquel. 24823
Arte de la lengua Japona. 58044
Arte de la lengua Mame. 39035
Arte de la lengua Maya. 76007-(76008)
Arte [de la lengua Maya.] 2d note after 99650
Arte de la lengua Mexicana, 29119
Arte de la lengua Mexicana. 692, 24312, 26746-26748, 76430, 1st note after 98659
Arte de la lengua Mexicana con la declaracion de los adverbios. 10953
Arte de la lengua Mexicana, corregido segun l'original. 57227
Arte de la lengua Mexicana, dispvesto. 99384-99385
Arte de la lengua Mexicana. Grammaire de la lengue Nahuatl. 57232
Arte de la lengua Mexicana segun la acostumbran hablar los Indios. 29118

Arte de la lengua Mexicana, y breves platicas. 2492
Arte de la lengua Mexicana y Castellana. 49868-49869
Arte de la lengva Moxa. 44465
Arte de la lengua Nevome. 2124, 84380
Arte de la lengua Quechua general. 33559
Arte de la lengva Qvichua. 96268-96270, 100643
Arte de la lengua Tagala. 43814
Arte de la lengua Tarasca. 3875A
Arte de la lengua Teguima. 41841
Arte de la lengua Tepeguana. 71411
Arte de la lengua Totonaca. 106244
Arte de la lengua Yunga. 11042
Arte de la verdadera navegacion. 94133
Arte de las lenguas Chippa, Zoque, Celdales, y Cinacanteca. 11692
Arte de lengua Mexicana. 26746-26748
Arte de lengua Totonaca. (6304)
Arte de los metales. (3253)
Arte de nauegar en que se contienen todas las reglas. 47344
Arte de navegar . . . & roteiro das viagens. 62883
Arte de Nebrixa. 58044
Arte del idioma Maya. (4609)
Arte del navegar. (47346)
Arte dela lengva general del Peru. 32492, 100643
Arte di verificare le date. 101352
Arte doctrinal y modo general. 29146
Arte en lengua de Michoacan. 27357
Arte en lengva Mixteca. 70393-70394
Arte en lengva Zapoteca. 16766, 106253
Arte grammatica, vocabulario, catecismo y confessionario. 42670
Arte i vocabulario de la lengua de Guatemala. 16828
Arte i vocabulario de la lengua de Kacchiquel. 16828
Arte menor de arithmetica. 59336
Arte Mexicana. (71412)-71413
Arte Mexicano, o grammatica de la lengua Mexicana. 29372
Arte novissima de lengua Mexicana. 94353
Arte o cartilla del nuevo beneficio de la plata. 96225
Arte o neuvo modo de beneficiar los metales. (50075)
Arte o rudimentos de gramatica en lengua indigena del Peru. 98763
Arte of navigation. (16967)-16968, 94220
Arte of navigation, translated out of the Spanish. 47347
Arte para aprender la lengua de los Indios. 74650
Arte para criar sede. 11290
Arte para entender la lengua comun de los Indios. (7749), 67369
Arte para sangrar, y examen de barberos. 41970
Arte practica de navegar & roteiro das viagens. 62882
Arte vocabulario, confessionario, y modo de administrar. 70459
Arte vocabulario, y confessionario. 16971
Arte, y bocabvlario de la lengva de los Indios Chaymas. 94423
Arte, y bocabvlario de la lengua Gvarani. 74026
Arte y diccionario de la lengua Tarasca. 767
Arte y dictionario: con otras obras. 38627
Arte y gramatica general de la lengva. 42669, 98324-98325
Arte y grammatica copiosa de la lengua Aymara. (5018)

Arte y vocabulario de la lengua de los Indios. 3328
Arte y vocabulario de la lengua Dohema. 28252, 84381
Arte, y vocabulario de la lengua Quichua. 96271
Arte, y vocabulario en la lengva general del Perv llamada Quichua. 5020, 10710, 20565, (67160), 100643
Arte y vocabulario de la lengua Lule, y Tonocote. 11697, (43315)
Arte y vocabulario de la lengua Mocorosi. 49789
Arte, y vocabulario de la lengua Morocosi. Compvesto por vn Padre de la Compagnia de Jesvs. 51218
Arte, y vocabulario en lengva Mame. 70459
Arteaga, C. (66591)
Artega, Manuel del Carmen. see Carmen Artega, Manuel del.
Artemus Ward among the Mormons. (8643)
Artemus Ward: his book. 8647, 84185-84187
Artemus Ward; his travels. 8645
Artemus Ward (his travels) among the Mormons. 8647
Artemus Ward in London. 8644
Arteta de Monteseguro, Ant. 2125
Arteta y Berganza, ------. 65931
Arthaud, Charles. 95349
Arthaud, M. 2126-(2127)
Arthur, a Negro. defendant 105349
Arthur, ------. defendant 72063
Arthur, Alexander H. 2128
Arthur, George. (32758), 32760
Arthur, John. 2129
Arthur, M. ed. (69966)
Arthur, O. R. reporter 2130, 29931
Arthur, T. 2131
Arthur, Timothy Shay, 1809-1885. 2132-2137, 2997, 3002, (11011)-(11015), 28676, 25568, 87105-87106
Arthur, William. ed. 1709
Arthur, Rev. William. 2138, 24416, 48919
Arthur Carryl, a novel. 57752
Arthur de Bretagne, tragedie. 12348
Arthur Gordon Pym. 63571
Arthur Merwyn. 8457
Arthur Middleton. pseud. Arthur Middleton to his brother. see Wakefield, Priscilla (Bell)
Arthur Middleton to his brother Edwin. 100982, 100983
Arthur Sketchley. pseud. see Rose, George.
Arthus, Gottard, 1570-1630? 2139, (8784), (33666), 37691, 55433, 55437, 67546, 92539
Artickel vnd Satzungen. 102923
Article by the Rev. Mr. Verot. 47103
Article containing facts connected with slavery. 19580, note after 92624
Article from the American monthly magazine. (69490)
Article from the Boston quarterly review. 8714
Article from the Christian examiner. 2290, 58757
Article from the Independent of Feb. 21, 1850. 63826
Article from the London "Times" on slavery. (31378)
Article from the North American review. 68344, 70632
Article in the Bible repository and Princeton review. 58624
Article in the Edinburgh review. 35663, note after 90597

Article in the North American review for January, 1824. 88971, 88973
Article in the North American review, in which that gentleman is branded as an impostor. 55485
Article in the North American review, October, 1834. 102208
Article in the sixty-sixth number of the North American review. 90745
Article of agreement between the Trustees, Ministers & Stewards of the Methodist Episcopal Society of Newark. 96141
Article of faith and church covenant. (21207)
Article on continental money in Harper's magazine. 16163, 62490
Article on the charities of Boston. (22174)
Article on the debts of the states. 18026
Article on the Latimer case. 39208
Article on the law of copyright. (5763)
Article on the slave trade. 82027
Article on "Uncle Tom's cabin." 79130-79131
Article particulier, retire du text. 105643
Article published in the Boston recorder. 22381
Article published in the Worcester daily spy. 92867
Article reprinted from the North American review. 39383
Articles accordes par le Roi a la Compagnie de la Nouvelle-France. 10360
Articles accordez par le Roy. A la Compagnie de la Nouuelle France. 56079
Articles accordez entre les Directevrs et Associez en la Compagnie de la Novvelle France. 41844
Articles acordes entre les Directeurs et Associes en la Companie de la Nouvelle-France. 10359
Articles agreed on. (2140)
Articles and by-laws of the Philadelphia Hose Company. 62004
Articles and covenant of the Tabernacle Church. (75753)
Articles and discourses. 13781
Articles and regulations of the Relief Fire Society. 54926
Articles and rules of the New-York Association for the Improvement of the Breed of Horses. 54846
Articles: containing the rules and regulations. 105428
Articles de la capitulation de l'isle Martinique. 44972
Articles de la Compagnie de Canada. (10361)
Articles drawn up by the members of the Church of Malden. 44098
Articles exhibited against Lord Archibald Hamilton. 29997-29998
Articles exhibited by Mr. Freeman. 14144
Articles for the better government of the troops. 2143
Articles for the government of the Second Battalion. 61989
Articles from the Biblical Repertory. (32330)
Articles from the "London times." (12729)
Articles from the Metropolitan record. 48222
Articles in addition to, and amendment of, the constitution. 42802
Articles, lawes, and orders. 99866
Articles of a constitution. 70551
Articles of a treaty between the United States of America, and the Chiefs and Head Men of the Indian Tribe called the Cherokees. Concluded on the 25th day of October, A. D. 1805. 96621

ARTICLES

Articles of a treaty between the United States
of America, and the Chiefs and Head
Men of the Indian Tribe called the
Cherokees. Concluded on the 27th day of
October, A. D. 1805. 96622
Articles of a treaty between the United States
of America, and the . . . Piankeshaws.
96626
Articles of a treaty between the United States
of America, and the Sachems, Chiefs,
and warriors of the Ottaway. 96630
Articles of a treaty between the United States
of America and the Tuscorora nation of
Indians. 96612
Articl[e]s of a treaty, concluded at Fort
M'Intosh. 96599
Articles of a treaty, concluded at Fort Stanwix.
96598
Articles of a treaty, concluded at Hopewell, on
the Keowee, between Benjamin Hawkins.
96600, 96602
Articles of a treaty concluded at Hopewell, on
the Keowee, near Seneca Old Town,
between Benjamin Hawkins, Andrew
Pickens and Joseph Martin, Commis-
sioners Plenipotentiary of the United
States of America on the one part, and
Piomingo. 96601
Articles of a treaty, concluded at Hopewell,
on the Keowee, near Seneca Old Town,
between Benjamin Hawkins, Andrew
Pickens and Joseph Martin, Commis-
sioners Plenipotentiary of the United
States of America on the one part; and
Yockanahoma. 96601
Articles of a treaty, concluded at the mouth of
the Great Miami. 96600, 96602
Articles of a treaty made and concluded at
Buffalo Creek. 96726
Articles of Addison Consociation. 99165
Articles of agreement and association of the
Florida Peninsula Land Company.
24846
Articles of agreement and association of the
United States Land Company. 97969
Articles of agreement and association of the
Wisconsin Mining Company. 104889
Articles of agreement, and by-laws of the
[Belmont Coal Mining] Company. 4583
Articles of agreement and cession, between
the United States and Georgia. (49547)
Articles of agreement and convention between
the United States of America, and the
Seneca Tribe of Indians. 96665
Articles of agreement between the General
Conference of the Methodist Episcopal
Church. 48181
Articles of agreement &c. (61481)
Articles of agreement, for carrying on the
expedition. (2141)
Articles of agreement made and concluded.
34416, (45073), 59896, 60743, note after
97106
Articles of agreement made the 10th day of
October. 16654
Articles of agreement [of the Cyprus River
Mining Company.] 18218
Articles of agreement of the South Brooklyn
Building Association. 87343
Articles of agreement [of the Territorial
Company, Philadelphia.] 63287, 94879
Articles of amendment, adopted by the Con-
gress. (16096)
Articles of an association by the name of the
Ohio Company. 56976-56977
Articles of arrangement. 96619

Articles of association, act of incorporation,
and . . . transactions of the . . .
[Philadelphia Female Hospital] Society.
(61656)
Articles of association and agreement constitut-
ing the Connecticut Land Company. 15712
Articles of association and agreement, constitut-
ing the New England Mississippi Land
Company. (52708)
Articles of association and by-laws of the
Massachusetts Medical Benevolent Society.
45875
Articles of association and by-laws of the
North American Trust and Banking Com-
pany. 55566
Articles of association and by-laws . . . [of
the Union League of Philadelphia.] 62352
Articles of association and by-laws of the
United States and New York Foreign
and Domestic Exchange Company. 97954
Articles of association, and by-laws of the
United States Trust and Banking Company.
97993
Articles of association and by-laws of the
Williamsburgh Bank. 104438
Articles of association and constitution of the
National Union Club of . . . Philadelphia.
52035, 61858
Articles of association, and other documents.
19188
Articles of association and rules of the
Philadelphia Chamber of Commerce.
61974
Articles of association and systems of organiza-
tion. 54879
Articles of association, by-laws, and catalogue
of books. 89852
Articles of association, by-laws, etc., of the
Agricultural Society. 41468
Articles of association, by-laws, rules and
regulations. (8264)
Articles of association "for carrying on the
linen manufactory." 61482
Articles of association for forming a company.
102987
Articles of association of a mortgage stock
banking company. 89613
Articles of association [of Buffalo General
Hospital.] 9063
Articles of association . . . of the Bank of
Commerce. 54109, 73977
Articles of association of the Bank of Upper
Canada. 98068
Articles of association [of the Bank of Utica.]
98223
Articles of association of the Batopilas Mining
Co. 3959
Articles of association of the Cincinnati and
Lake Superior Copper and Silver Mining
Company. (13115)
Articles of association of the city of Galveston.
26472
Articles of association [of the Cleveland Mining
Company.] 13674
Articles of association of the Commercial
Bank of Troy. 97071
Articles of association of the Connecticut Land
Company. (15680)
Articles of association of the Copper Rock
Mining Company. 16704
Articles of association of the Edgeworth
Association. (44099)
Articles of association of the Farmers' Bank
of Geneva. 26935
Articles of association of the Female Hospital
Society. (61656)

212

Articles of association [of the Galveston Bay and Texas Land Company.] 93710, 95086, 105111

Articles of association [of the Green Bay and Lake Superior Railroad Company.] 28573

Articles of association of the Mohawk Valley Railroad Company. 49855

Articles of association of the Montreal River Mining Company. 50270

Articles of association of the Monument Cemetery. 61846

Articles of association of the New Bedford and California Joint Stock Mining and Trading Company. 52461

Articles of association of the New England and Michigan Mining Company. 52653

Articles of association of the Ogdensburgh, Clayton and Rome Railroad Company. 56830

Articles of association of the Philadelphia Board of Trade. 61970

Articles of association of the Phoenix Insurance Company. 62057

Articles of association of the Sandusky City and Cedar Point Company. 76444

Articles of association of the Saving Fund Society. 62225

Articles of association of the Sherman Institute. 80421

Articles of association of the Spooner Copyright Company. 89630

Articles of association of the Stuyvesant Square Home Guard. 54685, note after 93290

Articles of association of the Suffolk Bank. 93428

Articles of association of the Washington Bank. 101980

Articles of association of the Worcester Society of Mutual Aid in Detecting Thieves. 105380

Articles of association of the Worthington Manufacturing Company. 105509

Articles of association, report of the committee, and schedule of property. 104494

Articles of capitulation. 50155

Articles of Christian doctrine and church covenant. 55086

Articles of confederation and perpetual union. 2142

Articles of confederation; the declaration of rights. 100039

Articles of confederation vs. the constitution. 65568

Articles of confession, and covenant. 20742

Articles of consociation, adopted A. D. 1798. 99165

Articles of consociation, adopted by the Congregational Churches. 99164

Articles of consociation, recommended to a number of churches. 99162

Articles of consociation, revised, and with some additions. 99163, 99172

Articles of faith. 83035

Articles of faith and covenant, adopted by several Baptist churches. 105390

Articles of faith and covenant, adopted by the Calvinist Church in Worcester. 105340

Articles of faith and covenant adopted by the First Church of Christ in Worcester. 105357

Articles of faith and covenant adopted by the First Congregational Church, in Saint John. 75272

Articles of faith and covenant, adopted by the South Church in South Hadley. 88125

Articles of faith, and covenant of the Baptist Church, in Southwick, Mass. 88658

Articles of faith and covenant of the Baptist Church in Waterville, Me. 102098

Articles of faith and covenant of the Eliot Church. 73640

Articles of faith and covenant of the Evangelical Church. (67284)

Articles of faith and covenant of the First Baptist Church in South Kingstown, R. I. 88143

Articles of faith, and covenant, of the First Church, Charlestown. 12098

Articles of faith and covenant of the First Congregational Church in Westbrook. 102949

Articles of faith and covenant of the Maverick Church. 6657

Articles of faith and covenant of the Orthodox Congregational Church, Walpole. 101151

Articles of faith and covenant of the Pine-Street Church, Boston. (6670)

Articles of faith and covenant of the St. Lawrence Street Church, Portland. (64377)

Articles of faith and covenant, of the Salem Church, Boston. 75761

Articles of faith and covenant of the South Church, South Danvers. 88120

Articles of faith and covenant of the Trinitarian Congregational Church in Waltham. 101206

Articles of faith and covenant, rules, and list of members. 6646

Articles of faith and covenant, together with a historical sketch of the East Evangelical Church in Ware. 101412

Articles of faith, and form of covenant, adopted by the Calvinistic Congregational Church in Sandwich. (76446)

Articles of faith and form of covenant adopted by the Church in Williamstown. 104495

Articles of faith and form of covenant, adopted by the Congregational Church in Leicester. (39897)

Articles of faith, and form of covenant, adopted by the Phillips Church in South Boston. 87337

Articles of faith and form of covenant of the Third Congregational Church of Plymouth. 63473

Articles of faith and form of government adopted by the Congregational Church in ———. 99166

Articles of faith and government, of the First Baptist Church. 52462

Articles of faith . . . and names of members. 6645

Articles of faith and of the covenant. 14227

Articles of faith and plan of church government. 61483, 98010

Articles of faith and practice. 79161

Articles of faith, and the covenant, of Park-Street Church, Boston. 6668

Articles of faith, and the covenant, of the West Congregational Church in Taunton. 94421A

Articles of faith, covenant, and extracts from the rules and regulations. 93982

Articles of faith, covenant, and standing rules. 89396

Articles of faith, covenant, &c. [of the Boston First Free Congregational Church.] 6644

Articles of faith, covenant, etc. [of the Bowdoin Square Church, Boston.] 18137

Articles of faith . . . of the Bowdoin Street
Church. 6637
Articles of faith [of the Canadian Anti-Slavery
Baptist Association.] 10404
Articles of faith of the Church of Jesus Christ
of the Latter-Day Saints. 83036
Articles of faith, of the Holy Evangelical
Church. 51735
Articles of faith submitted. 55086
Articles of impeachment. (65249)
Articles of organization of the Union for
Christian Work. (66376)
Articles of peace and alliance between the
Most Serene and Mighty Prince Charles
II. . . . and the Most Serene and
Mighty Lords the States General of the
United Netherlands. 2147
Articles of peace and alliance between the
Most Serene and Mighty Prince Charles
II. . . . and the Most Serene and Mighty
Prince Lewis XIV. 2144, 96526
Articles of peace between . . . Charles II. . . .
and several Indian kings and queens, &c.
(34614)
Articles of peace between . . . Charles II . . .
and the . . . States General of the United
Netherlands. 2146
Articles of peace between the Common-wealth
of England, and that of the United
Provinces of the Netherlands. 2150
Articles of peace between the most Serene and
Mighty Prince Charles II. . . . and the
Most Serene and Mighty Prince Lewis
XIV. 2144
Articles of peace between the most Serene and
Mighty Prince Charles II. . . . and
several Indian kings and queens, &c.
2145, 10005
Articles of peace between William III. and
Louis XIV. 2148, 96536
Articles of peace, friendship, and entercourse.
2149
Articles of perpetual union, commerce, and
friendship. 63301
Articles of religion, as established by . . . the
Protestant Episcopal Church of the
United States. 23413
Articles of religion, of the Protestant Episcopal
Church, supported by reference to the
scriptures. 74483
Articles of religion of the Protestant Episcopal
Church . . . together with the canons.
45299
Articles [of the Association for the Suppres-
sion of Vice and Immorality.] 85985
Articles of the company, with the names.
26353, 2d note after 97808
Articles of the Massachusetts Constitutional
Society. 45836
Articles of the New Bedford Reform and
Relief Association. 52463
Articles of the [New Bedford Women's Reform
and Relief] Association. 52484
Articles . . . of the New Brighton Association.
(52515)
Articles of the Star Fire Society. 90487
Articles of the treaty of peace betwixt England
and France. 2151, note before 96521
Articles of the true religion. 46316
Articles of the Union Library Society of New-
York. 97809
Articles of the United Fire Club. 97871
Articles of the Washington Fire Club. 75758
[Articles of war.] 100410-100411

Articles of war for the government of the
armies of the Confederate States. 2153,
15237
Articles of war, for the government of the
army of the Confederate States of
America. 2054, 15236
Articles of war of the Confederate States of
America. 2152
Articles on the American Education Society.
93200
Articles on the laboring classes. 8715
[Articles on] the tariff. 44376
Articles on which duties will be levied.
(53409)
Articles, or by-laws, for the government of the
Associated Independent Philadelphia Troop
of Volunteer Greens. 61485
Articles, published by Congress. 96566
Articles sett downe for the second lottery.
99864
Articles, settlement and offices. 59897
Articles touching navigation and commerce.
2154
Articles, where-upon a most happy union.
46235
Articles which will be brought over the Western
Rail-way. 103011
Articles written by the Prophet Joseph Smith.
83252
Articles written by the Prophet Joseph Smith
and President John Taylor. 83253
Articul-Bref. 7519
Articul-Brief van de Generael Nederlandsche
Geoctrooirde West-Indische Compagnie.
1254A, 102880
Articul-Brief van de Generael Nederlandtsche
Geoctroyeerde West-Indische Compagnie.
2154A, 102880
Articul-Brief van de Generael Nederlandtse
Geoctroyeerde West-Indische Compagnie.
102881
Articule du journal "Le Figaro" sur la partie.
76522
Articulen en conditien van den eeuwigen vrede.
52223
Articulen ende conditien gemaeckt by het over-
leveren van Brasilien. 2155A, 7520
Articvlen, met approbatie vande Ho: Mo: Heeren
Staten Generael. 102920-102921, 102924
Articulen van de Vreed. 2146
Articulen van het tractaet. 2149
Articulen van het tractaet van bestant ende
ophoudinge. 23508, 102891
Articulen van vrede ende confederatie tusschen
de Republique van Engelandt. 2156
Articulen van vrede ende confederatie tusschen
den Koning van Portugael. 52224
Articulen van vrede ende confoederatie,
gheslooten tusschen den Doorluchtingsten
Coningh van Portugael. 2157, 96522-
96523
Articulen van vrede ende verbondt. 2158
Articuli pacis. 2146
Articuli pacis et confoederationis inter . . .
Lusitaniae Regem. 2154B
Articuli pacis inter . . . Carolum . . . II. . . .
et . . . Ordines Gener. Foeder. Belgii
Provinc. 2154C
Articulo comunicado del Senor Coronel Don
Pablo Victor Unda. 87167
Articulo de la Revista de los dos mundos.
(70341), 4th note after 99402
Articulo del Cosmopolitia. 40066
Articulo del Jose Z. Gonzalez del Valle. 48162
Articulo della civita cattolica. 76522

Articulo en la Miscelanea. 50476
Articulo publicado en la Voz de pueblo. 95083
Articulo publicado por "El Veracruzano."
    48514
Articulos publicados en El diario de la marina
    de la Habana. 50527
Articulo sacado del Diario de Veracruz. 95851
Articulo sobre la republica de Chile. 12758
Articulo sobre los fundamentos. (48291)
Articulo tomado del "Atlantico." (48578)
Articulos constitucionales. 99471
Articulos de costumbres, etc. (23072)
Articulos de historia, geografia, viajos, litera-
    tura y variedades. 48265
Articulos insertos en El diario de la marina.
    11465
Articulos preliminares. 96558
Articulos publicados en La revista de Buenos-
    Aires. (67124)
Articulos publicados por La gaceta de Guate-
    mala. 66101
Articulos reales para el gobierno. (38993)
Articulos tomados del "Diccionario universal
    de historia y de geografia." 48599
Artificial shell-deposits in New Jersey. 67966
Artigo priemiro, Antilia. 81086
Artikel der Patriotischen Gesellschaft der
    Stadt und Caunty Philadelphia. 61915
Artikel . . . tusschen Carel de II. 2155
Artikelen van regeering, gemackt in 1638.
    36925, 98478
Artikelen von vrede. 2151
Artikler hvorefter Commandeurerne og
    Mandskabet paa Skibere. 29636
Artillero. pseud. Relacion verdadera. see
    Munoz, Bernardo.
Artillero Americano. pseud. Canonagos. see
    Solano, Vicente, 1791 or 2-1865.
Artillery Company, Boston. see Massachu-
    setts. Ancient and Honourable Artillery
    Company.
Artillery Company, Newport, R. I. see
    Newport, R. I. Artillery Company.
Artillery election sermon. here are entered
    all artillery election sermons. Duplicate
    entries will be found under respective
    authors and titles. 8, 15, 23, 171, 919,
    1833, 2734, 2870, 2915, 4398, (4776),
    6008, 7806, 7812, 9711, (11207), 17106,
    17107, 12312, 13347, (13383), 13430,
    (14471), 14538, (16597), 19038, (21246),
    (21792), 22309, 22465, 23324, (25039),
    25238, 26069, 26624, 26785, 27304,
    28687, 30521, (30884), 31218, 31444,
    32317, 32726, 33278, 37336, (37845),
    38005, 39186, 42140, (42147), 42422,
    42710, (46415), 46548, (46658), 46807,
    47253, 48928, 50299, (50953), 51614,
    56206, 56384-56385, 57778, 58825, 58899,
    59374, 59602, 59609, 62515, 62772,
    64245, 67784, 68014, 71021, (71022),
    (71795), (71826), (73981), 76372, (77244),
    (79789), 80801, 81621, 82945, 90996,
    91375, 91806, 94106, 95163, 95177,
    95262, 97398, 98037, 100910, 101169,
    101173, 102745, 103727, 103928, 104084,
    104093, 104408
Artillery election sermon at Boston, June 6, 1763.
    2870
Artillery election sermon, Boston, June 7th,
    1812. 8
[Artillery-election] . . . sermon, . . . 1805.
    30521
Artillery-election sermon, 1834. 31218
Artillery-election sermon, 1837. 51614
artillery election sermon, 1802. 15

Artillery election sermon, 1735. 23
Artillery for the United States Land Service.
    50531
Artillery officer. pseud. Few thoughts on the
    artillery. 24243
Artillery officers. petitioners see U. S.
    Army. Artillery. Officers. petitioners
Artis analyticae praxis ad aequationes alge-
    braicas nova. 30376
Artis rethoricae syntagma ad usum tironum.
    72536
Artiste. pseud. Indiens de la Baie d'Hudson.
    see Kane, Paul.
Artists and Manufacturers of Philadelphia.
    petitioners 44431
Artists' Fund Society, Philadelphia. Exhibition,
    1st, 1835. (61484)
Artists of America. 40218
Arts of design. An address before the Art
    Union of Philadelphia. (68545)
Arts of design, by T. Addison Richards. 22085
Arts of design, especially as related to female
    education. (78937)
Arts of empire. 67599
Arts of empire, and mysteries of state. 67599
Art's true mission in America. 21156
Artus, Gotard. see Arthus, Gotthard, 1570-
    1630?
Artyckel-Brief, van de Generale Geoctroyeerde
    West-Indische Compagnie. 102881
Artykelen, van't overgaen van Nieuw-Nederlandt.
    102883
Arusmont, Frances Wright d'. see
    D'Arusmont, Frances (Wright) 1795-1852.
Arvelo, Carlos. 68875 see also Venezuela.
    Ejercito. Medico Cirujano Mayor e
    Inspector de los Hospitales.
Arwed, ou les represailles. 23093, note after
    98620
As a matter of history. 74550
As an answer to several church meetings.
    (73874)
As Doctor Chandler, and those of his brethren.
    95977
As expedients are no longer wise. 105347
As few vices are attended. 101699
As good as a comedy. (81279)
As great a man as Nelson! 16815
As it is. 2159, 84868
As it is generally imagined. 95970
As it was intimated in a pamphlet. 89138,
    1st note after 104432
As the claim of Cornelius C. Bogardus and
    others. 96000
As the great business of the polite world.
    2160, 101482
As the merchants of this city. 95988
As the present state of our funds. 102690
As the President of the United States will
    honor this town. 101784
As the public have had much writing. 94662
As this town is shortly to be honoured.
    101875-101876
As we hope that the time is not far distant.
    101764
As you like it. 100893
As you sow, so must you reap. 62772
As you were! 2161
Asa-Asa. an African 65569
Asa Stoddard's composition. 91931
Asahel Smith, of Topsfield, Massachusetts.
    83348
Asamblea Popular, Caracas, 1869. see
    Caracas. Asamblea Popular, 1869.
Asamblea popular el 5 de Julio de 1869, en
    Caracas. 17817

Asaph, ------. 76838
Asbjornsson, Kolskeggr. 74880
Asbury, Daniel B. 51584
Asbury, Francis, Bp., 1745-1816. 2162-(2163),
 14251,. 48182, 48200
Asbury and his caojutors. 39071
Ascanio, Nicolas de Herrera. see Herrera
 Ascanio, Nicolas de.
Ascension Association, New York. see New
 York (City) Church of the Ascension.
 Association.
Ascension dans les montagnes Rocheuses.
 44501
Ascension du Pichincha en 1856. 69593
Ascensione al volcano Popocatepetl. 64139
Ascham, ------. 77887
Ascoli, Cecco d'. see Cesso d'Ascoli.
Ascot Heath. 78471
Ascot Mining Company. 2164
Aschenfeldt, Friedrich. 2165
Aschlund, Arent. 2166, (4819)-4820
Aschmann, Rudolf. (2167)
Asemblea General Constituyente de Bolivia,
 1831. see Bolivia. Asemblea General
 Constituyente, 1831.
Asenjo, Ignacio. supposed author 76777
Asesinatos y matanzas del Degollador Juan
 Manuel Rosas. 34435
Asgill, ou desordres des guerres civiles.
 47107
Asgill, tire de l'histoire de la revolution
 Americaine. 5387
Ash, Horace F. 87028
Ash, John. 2168-2169
Ash, St. George, successively Bishop of Cloyne,
 Clogher, and Derry. (2170)
Ash, Simeon. 2171, 3213, 33630, (40355),
 80205, 80212, note before 92797, note
 after 92800, 3d note after 103687
Ash, Thomas. 2172
Ashbee, ------. ed. 67599
Ashburn, Rebecca. 34434, 105172
Ashburnham, Mass. 2174
Ashburnham, Mass. School Committee. 2173
Ashburton, Alexander Baring, 1st Baron, 1774-
 1848. 3384-3387, 64812, 17184
Ashburton Coal Company. 2175
Ashburton treaty. 25014
Ashcroft, John. 2176
Ashcroft's railway director for 1866. 2176
Ashe, Samuel, 1725-1813. 14745 see also
 North Carolina. Governor, 1795-1798
 (Ashe)
Ashe, Simeon. see Ash, Simeon.
Ashe, Simon. see Ash, Simeon.
Ashe, Thomas. 2177-2180, 62506-62507, 96496
Asher, Adolph. 2181-2182
Asher, C. W. 2183
Asher, G. M. 2184-2185, 13037, note before
 100436
Asher, J. 2186
Ashes of southern homes. 59495
Ashfield, Redford. defendant 53542
Ashland, N. Y. Hedding Literary Institute.
 see Hedding Literary Institute, Ashland,
 N. Y.
Ashland, Va. Randolph Macon College. see
 Randolph Macon College, Ashland, Va.
Ashland text book. 13539
Ashley, Chester. 2187
Ashley, F. B. 2188
Ashley, James M. (2189)-2191
Ashley, John. 2192-2196, 1st note after 93460
Ashley, John. supposed author 65327
Ashley, Jonathan. 2197-2200, (23584)
Ashley, S. S. 2201

Ashley-Cooper, Anthony, 1st Earl of Shaftes-
 bury. see Shaftesbury, Anthony Ashley
 Cooper, 1st Earl of, 1621-1683.
Ashmead, John W. 2202, 47236
Ashmead, William. 2203
Ashmore, Francis. tr. 100749
Ashmun, George. 2205
Ashmun, Jehudi. 2204, (2206), (29303)
Ashton, John. 82859
Ashton, Philip. 2207
Ashton, Robert, ed. 72091, 72110
Ashton, Thomas B. illus. 85466
Ashton's memorial. 2207
Ashurst, Sir Henry, Bart. petitioner 97547
Ashurst, Sir William Henry. 31834
Ashworth, Henry. 2208
Asia. 30861
Asia de Joam de Barros. 3646
Asia de Ioao de Barros e de Diogo de Couto.
 (3648)
Asia del Sig. Giovanni di Barros. 3647
Asia Portugueza. 23801
Asiae Europaeque elegentissima descriptio.
 63164
Asiatic cholera. 52318
Asiatic history. 27913
Asiatic review. 81150
Asiatisches, Africanisches und Americanisches
 Heydenthum. 72603
Asie. 76712
Asie et Amerique. (2209)
Asie, l'Amerique . . . par ordre chronologique.
 19486
Asignaciones eclesiasticas. 10772
Asilo a los criminales estranjeros. 99482
Asmodee a New-York. 54098
Asmodeus. pseud. Asmodee a New-York.
 54098
Asmodeus. pseud. Jenny Lind mania in
 Boston. (41279)
Asmodeus in New York. 54097
Asmodeus; or, legends of New-York. 8846
Asmodeus; or the iniquities of New York.
 54096
Asociacion Medico-Quirurgica 'Larrey'. 87163
Aspasio. pseud. Letters and dialogues. see
 Bellamy, Joseph.
Aspden, Matthias. 2210
Aspect of the times, a political poem, &c.
 2212
Aspecto fisico. 77069, 77087
Aspects of nature. 33707
Aspects of religion in the United States of
 America. 2213, (5544), 44724
Aspee, Manuel de Alday y. see Alday y Aspee,
 Manuel de.
Aspen, John. appellant 2210
Aspersions on the character of Dr. Benjamin
 Rush. 36242
Aspin, Jehoshaphate. 39125
Aspinall, Joseph. 2214
Aspinwall, G. illus. 48975
Aspinwall, Thomas. 2215-2217, 35221
Aspinwall, William. 2218-(2219), 17043
Aspinwall, William. petitioner 8252, 68298
Aspland, Alfred. 2220
Aspland, Robert. 2221
Asplund, John. 2222-2223, 100434, 103017
Asquerino, Eduardo. ed. (38393)
Ass in the lyon's skin. 22785, 91385
Ass: or, the serpent. 7208
Assaigns of W. Courten. defendants 17179
Assalini, Paolo. 2224
Assall, Friedrich Wilhelm. 2225, 50537
Assas, ------ Guillon-d'Assas, -------.
Assassinated president. 78938

Assassination and death of Abraham Lincoln.
26
Assassination and history of the conspiracy.
2226, (41173)
Assassination and insanity. 84869
Assassination de la fille du President Geffrand.
12968
Assassination, its lessons to young men. 21332
Assassination of Abraham Lincoln. A lecture.
(29833)
Assassination of Abraham Lincoln, late President of the United States. 41174
Assassination of Abraham Lincoln, President of the United States. 20970
Assassination of Joseph & Hiram Smith. 42828
Assassination of Lincoln. 41175
Assassination of President Lincoln. 41233
Assassination of President Lincoln. A sermon.
11780
Assassination of President Lincoln, and trial.
41182
Assassination of the President. (14527)
Assassination of the President of the United States. (58642)
Assassination plot in New-York in 1776. 23122
Assault and battery. (35991), 98547
Assault on Mr. Sumner. 81157
Assault on Senator Sumner. 38059
Assaults on the national credit. 71885
Assaults upon freedom. (28380)
Assayer's guide. (40986)
Assemblee Coloniale de la partie Francaise de Saint-Domingue. 75066
Assemblee de Colons Americains, Paris, 1789. (75118)
Assemblee des Citoyens-Libres et Proprietaires de Couler des Isles et Colonies Francoises, Paris, 1789. see Assemblee de Colons Americains, Paris, 1789.
Assemblee des Noirs. (75067)
Assemblee des Piankashaws au Post Saint Vincent. 24338
Assemblee Generale de la Partie Francoise de Saint-Domingue aux Francois. 75068
Assemblee Generale de la Partie Francoise de Saint Domingue aux quatre-vingt-trois departemens. 75070
Assemblee Generale de la Partie Francoise de Saint-Domingue, aux representants de la nacion. 75069
Assemblee nationale. 19434
Assembly, Convened for the Purpose of Adopting Resolutions Against Duelling, Pittsburgh, 1827. see Anti-Duelling Convention, Pittsburgh, 1827.
Assembly. John Dickinson, (etc) ***. 20039
Assembly of Christians the temple of God. (79299), 92272
Assembly of Divines, Boston, 1657. see Convention of Congregational Ministers of Massachusetts, Boston, 1657.
Assembly of Divines, and Mr. Cotton's catechism. 52714, 52730, note after 65546
Assembly of Divines at Westminister. see Westminister Assembly of Divines.
Assembly of Divines' catechism. (52713), 52716, note after 65546
Assembly of Divines catechism, &c. note after 65546
Assembly of Pastors of Churches in New-England, Boston, 1743. see Boston.
Assembly of Pastors of Churches in New England, 1743. and Convention of Congregational Ministers of Massachusetts, Boston, 1743.

Assembly Room, Federal Street, Boston. see Boston. Assembly Room, Federal Street.
Assembly's address. 34072
Assembley's address and message to his excellency. (50851)
Assembly's catechism. 46534, 80720
Assembly's shorter catechism. 49859, 52726, 80716, 103037
Assembly-man in Carolina. pseud. see N----, J----. pseud.
Assent for allowing the subjects of England. 14371
Asserto historial apologetico. 40733
Assessors' report of the valuation and taxes. 41550
Assiento. 2227, 40319, 96541, 1st note after 102785
Assiento contract consider'd. 2228, note after 105078, 105079
Assiento. En el nombre de Dios. 2234
Assiento, or, contract. 2227
Assiento que se tomo con Antonio Fernandez Delbas. (2229), 19422
Assiento treaty for the importation of Negroes. 14399
Assiento y capitulacion con Don J. Velez de Guevara y Salamanca. 98825
Assiento y capitvlacion, qve los Senores Presidente, y del Consejo Real de las Indias tomaron con Adriano de Legaso. 2232
Assiento y capitvlacion, qve los Senores Presidente, y del Consejo Real de las Indias. tomaron con el Prior. 2233
Assiento, y capitvlacion qve los Senores Presidente y del Consejo Real de las Indias tomaron con los vezinos. 2231
Assiento, y capitvlacion que por mandado de Su Magestad se ha tomado con diuersas personas. 2230
Assiento y capitvlacion qve se tomo con Manvel Rodrigvez Lamego. 72556
Assientos de Averia. 36952
Assimilated rank of the civil branch of the navy. 74182
Assimismo copia de la carta respuesta. 100637
Assinniboine and Saskatchewan Exploring Expedition. see Canada. Assinniboine and Saskatchewan Exploring Expedition.
Assistance (H. M. Ship) 73784
Assistant. pseud. Few facts. see Lesley, Joseph Peter.
Assistant of the ministry at large. 73622
Assistant to the evangelical psalmodist. 84679-84680
Assize sermon. 92097
Assize sermon preached before the Honourable Her Majesties Superiour Court. 4403
Asso y del Rio, Ignacio Jordan, 1742-1804. 103429
Associacao Commercial da Praca da Bahia. Junta Directora. 69320
Associacao Maritima e Colonial, Lisboa. 1577A
Associate Alumni of the General Theological Seminary of the Protestant Episcopal Church, New York. see New York (City) General Theological Seminary of the Protestant Episcopal Church in the U. S. Associate Alumni.
Associate Church in North America. 72118, 98181
Associate Church in North America. Ministers. 49024
Associate Library Company, Worcester, Mass. see Worcester Associate Library Company, Worcester, Mass.

Associate members . . . December 7th, 1861.
76558, 76647
[Associate members, June 26, 1861.] 76533,
76647
Associate members . . . March 15th, 1862.
76557, 76647
Associate members of the U. S. Sanitary
Commission. March 15th, 1864. 76600,
76647
Associate members of the U. S. Sanitary
Commission, June 29, 1861. 76534,
76647
Associate Mission for Minnesota. see Bishop
Seabury Mission, Faribault, Minn.
Associate of said Society. pseud. Return of
departed spirits. (70140)
Associate Presbyterian magazine. 65138
Associate Presbytery of Albany. see Presby-
terian Church in the U. S. A. Associate
Presbytery of Albany.
Associate Presbytery of Cambridge. see
Presbyterian Church in the U. S. A.
Associate Presbytery of Cambridge.
Associate Presbytery of Morris County. see
Presbyterian Church in the U. S. A.
Associate Presbytery of Morris County.
Associate Presbytery of Pennsylvania. see
Presbyterian Church in the U. S. A.
Associate Presbytery of Pennsylvania.
Associate Presbytery of Westchester. see
Presbyterian Church in the U. S. A.
Associate Presbytery of Westchester.
Associate Reformed Church. see Presbyterian
Church.
Associate Reformed Church in North America.
65150, 65155, 65170, 72118
Associate Reformed Church in North America.
Committee to Prepare a Draught of a
Plan for a Seminary. 65213
Associate Reformed Church in North America.
Constitutional Presbytery. 98181
Associate Reformed Church in North America.
Delegates. 63265
Associate Reformed Church in North America.
General Synod. (65124), 65161, 65172,
67874
Associate Reformed Presbyterian Church. 93,
13689, (59400), (59899), 65121, 65125,
65160, 86365
Associate Reformed Presbyterian Church.
Theological Seminary, Newburgh, N. Y.
95313
Associate Reformed Presbyterian Church, Little
Britain, N. Y. see Little Britain, N. Y.
Associate Reformed Presbyterian Church.
Associate Reformed Presbyterian Synod. see
Associate Reformed Presbyterian Church.
Associate Reformed Synod, Philadelphia. see
Associate Reformed Presbyterian Church.
Associate Reformed Synod of North America.
see Reformed Presbyterian Church in
North America. General Synod.
Associate Reformed Synod of the West. 90744,
101446
Associate Synod of North America. 65162,
(65174), 90512, 90514, 90516, note after
96840, 1st note after 97091, 98181
Associated Banks of Massachusetts for the
Suppression of Counterfeiting. 45642
Associated Banks of Massachusetts, for the
Suppression of Counterfeiting. Board of
Managers. (3178)
Associated Banks of New York City. Loan
Committee. (54363)
Associated Body of House Carpenters, New
York City. 54220

Associated Churches of Litchfield, Conn. see
Congregational Churches in Connecticut.
Litchfield Association.
Associated Executive Committee of Friends on
Indian Affairs. see Friends, Society of.
Associated Executive Committee on Indian
Affairs.
Associated Independent Philadelphia Troop of
Volunteer Greens. see Pennsylvania.
Militia. Associated Independent Troop of
Volunteer Greens, Philadelphia.
Associated Mechanics, New York City. (1141)
Associated Mechanics and Manufacturers of
Massachusetts. 45643
Associated Members of the Bar of Philadelphia.
see Philadelphia. Bar.
Associated Ministers of the County of Windham,
Conn. see Congregational Churches in
Connecticut. Windham County Associa-
tion.
Associated Pastors in Boston, New England.
see Congregational Churches in Massa-
chusetts. Boston Association.
Associated Pastors of Boston. see Congrega-
tional Churches in Massachusetts.
Boston Association.
Associated Pastors of Boston and Charlestown.
see Congregational Churches in Mas-
sachusetts. Boston Association.
Associated Pastors of New Haven Center.
see Congregational Churches in Con-
necticut. New Haven Center Association.
Associates of the Government of New-Plymouth.
see Massachusetts (Colony)
Associates of the Late Dr. Thomas Bray, For
Converting the Negroes in the British
Plantations. 29673, 83976-83977, 95612
Associates of the Jersey Company of Powles
Hook. Charter (53089)
Association. pseud. eds. Geographical and
commercial gazette. 26970
Association. pseud. eds. Western examiner.
102978
Association. (15528), 15544
Association and articles of agreement of the
Sun Fire Society. 93728
Association and reorganization of industry.
8004
Association de la Propagation de la Foi. see
Society For the Propagation of the Faith.
Association de Secours pour Venir en Aide
aux Defricheurs du Sol. 20892
Association Diocesaine de Ville-Marie,
Montreal. see Montreal (Diocese)
Association Diocesaine de Ville-Marie.
Association discussed. 28494
Association du Sou par Semaine en Faveur des
Esclaves. 2236
Association entered into last Friday. 100503
Association, &c., of the delegates of the colonies
2238
Association for Aged Indigent Women, Cincin-
nati. Managers. 13089
Association for Carrying On the Linen Manu-
factory, Philadelphia. 61482
Association for Colored Volunteers, New York.
see New York Association for Colored
Volunteers.
Association for Establishing a School for the
Education of the Blind in Philadelphia.
60339, 61487 see also Pennsylvania
Institution for the Instruction of the Blind,
Philadelphia.
Association for Freedmen, Rhode Island. see
Rhode Island Association for Freedmen.

Association for Improving the Condition of the Poor, New York City. 54099

Association for Improving the Condition of the Poor, New York City. Committee on the Sanitary Condition of the Laboring Classes. 54099

Association for Improving the Condition of the Poor. First report of the Committee. 54099

Association for Improving the Navigation of Connecticut River Above Hartford. Directors. Committees. (15874), 3d note after 97578

Association for Restoration of American Shipping Intersts, New York. see New York Association for Restoration of American Shipping Interests.

Association for the Advancement of Science and Art, New York. see New York Association for the Advancement of Science and Art.

Association for the Benefit of Colored Orphans, New York. 54100

Association for the Benefit of Colored Orphans, Providence, R. I. see Providence Association for the Benefit of Colored Orphans.

Association for the Care of Colored Orphans, Philadelphia. (61488)

Association for the Exhibition of the Industry of All Nations, New York. 2239-2241, 4862, 23399, 90674 see New York (City) Exhibition of the Industry of All Nations, 1853-1854.

Association for the Improved Instruction of Deaf Mutes, New York. 54101

Association for the Improved Instruction of Deaf Mutes. First annual report, . . . 1868. 54101

Association for the Improvement of Common Schools in Indiana. 34506

Association for the Improvement of Indigent Girls, Chelsea, Mass. see Chelsea Association for the Improvement of Indigent Girls.

Association for the Improvement of the Condition of the Poor, New York. see New York Association for the Improvement of the Condition of the Poor.

Association for the Increase and Extension of American Commerce. 69925

Association for the Promotion of Internal Improvements in the State of Kentucky. Engineer. 104291 see also Williams, John C.

Association for the Promotion of Temperance, Providence, R. I. see Providence Association for the Promotion of Temperance.

Association for the Reformation of Morals, Charlestown, Mass. see Charlestown Association for the Reformation of Morals.

Association for the Relief of Aged and Destitute Women, Salem, Mass. 75635

Association for the Relief of Aged and Destitute Women, Salem, Mass. Charter. 75635

Association for the Relief of Aged, Indigent Women, Portland, Me. (64341)

Association for the Relief of Disabled Firemen, Philadelphia. see Philadelphia Association for the Relief of Disabled Firemen.

Association for the Relief of Jewish Widows & Orphans, New Orleans. (53307)

Association for the Relief of Respectable Indigent Aged Females, New York. (54102)

Association for the Relief of the Industrious Poor, New York. (54103)

Association for the Relief of the Poor, Buffalo, N. Y. see Buffalo Association for the Relief of the Poor.

Association for the Suppression of Gambling, New York. see New York Association for the Suppression of Gambling.

Association for Working the Mines of Tlalpuxahua and Others in Mexico. 95875

Association in Aid of the Grand-Ligne Mission, Brooklyn. 8334

Association in Aid of the Swiss Mission to Canada, Philadelphia. see Philadelphia Association in Aid of the Swiss Mission to Canada.

Association in Tolland County. see Congregational Churches in Connecticut. Tolland County Association.

Association International des Travailleurs. see International Workingmen's Association.

Association letter. 61497

Association Library Company of Philadelphia. 61489

Association monthly. 66964

Association of American Geologists and Naturalists. 2235, (72654)

Association of Banks for the Suppression of Counterfeiting. see Associated Banks of Massachusetts, for the Suppression of Counterfeiting.

Association of Baptist Churches in the State of South Carolina, Charleston. see Baptists. South Carolina. Charleston Association.

Association of Boston School Masters. 44324

Association of Bowdoin Students. see Bowdoin College, Brunswick, Me. Students Association.

Association of Christian Ministers. 15103

Association of Citizens of Massachusetts to Erect a Monument in Honor of Gen. George Washington. see Washington Monument Association, Boston.

Association of Citizens, to Erect a Monument in Honor of Gen. George Washington, Boston. see Washington Monument Association, Boston.

Association of clergymen. pseud. eds. Protestant Episcopalian and church register. 66210

Association of clergymen in New-York. pseud. eds. Evangelical guardian and review. 23133

Association of Congregational Ministers, Boston. see Congregational Churches in Massachusetts. Boston Association.

Association of Cotton Manufacturers. Commercial Correspondent. see Commercial Correspondent of an Association of Cotton Manufacturers. pseud.

Association of Delegates from the Benevolent Societies of Boston. 6574, 97387 see also Committee of Delegates from the Benevolent Societies of Boston.

Association of Delegates from the Benevolent Societes of Boston. President. 6574, 97387 see also Tuckerman, Joseph, 1778-1840.

Association of Delegates from the Benevolent Societies of Boston. Secretary. 6574, 97387 see also Rogers, Henry B.

Association of Fairfield West, Connecticut.
see Congregational Churches in Connecticut. Fairfield West Association.
Association of Franklin Medal Scholars, Boston.
2237, 6575
Association of Friends at Philadelphia and Vi-
cinity, for the Relief of Colored Freed-
men. see Friends' Association of
Philadelphia for the Relief of Colored
Freedmen.
Association of Friends for the Education of
Poor Children, Philadelphia. see
Philadelphia Association of Friends for
the Education of Poor Children.
Association of Friends for the Free Instruc-
tion of Adult Colored Persons. Board
of Managers. 86032
Association of Friends for the Instruction of
Poor Children, Philadelphia. see Phila-
delphia Association for the Education of
Poor Children.
Association of Friends for the Relief of Those
Held in Slavery, New York. see New
York Association of Friends for the
Relief of Those Held in Slavery.
Association of gentlemen. pseud. eds.
Biblical repository. 65654
Association of gentlemen. pseud. Christian
spectator. (12925)
Association of gentlemen. pseud. eds.
Quarterly Christian spectator. (12925),
66955, (70214)
Association of gentlemen. pseud. eds. South-
ern pioneer, and Gospel visiter. 88444
Association of gentlemen. pseud. eds. Spirit
of the forum and Hudson recorder.
89499
Association of gentlemen. pseud. eds. Uni-
tarian advocate, and religious miscellany.
97829
Association of gentlemen. pseud. publishers
Virginia lyceum. 100558
Association of Housewrights, Salem, Mass.
75705
Association of individuals. pseud. eds.
Truth's advocate. 97272
Association of Jamaica Proprietors. petitioners
(35621)
Association of Lake Underwriters. Board of
Marine Inspectors. 65823
Association of Laymen, Boston. 6563, 94924
Association of literary men. pseud. eds.
Gallery of illustrious Americans. 26415
Association of Mechanics and Manufacturers,
Newport, R. I. see Newport Association
of Mechanics and Manufacturers.
Association of Mechanics and Manufacturers,
Providence, R. I. see Providence Asso-
ciation of Mechanics and Manufacturers.
Association of Mechanics and other Working
Men, Washington, D. C. 83655, 101926
Association of Mechanics and Other Working
Men, Washington, D. C. Corresponding
Secretary. 83655, 101926 see also
Anderson, R. P.
Association of Mechanics and Other Working
Men, Washington, D. C. President.
83655, 101926 see also Smith, Nathan.
Association of Medical Superintendents of
American Institutions for the Insane.
Committee on the Distribution of Lunatic
Hospital Reports. (2242)
Association of members of the bar. pseud.
eds. Journal of law. 36712

Association of Ministers Convened at Marl-
borough, Mass. see Congregational
Churches in Massachusetts. Marlborough
Association.
Association of Ministers Convened at Weymouth,
Mass. see Congregational Churches in
Massachusetts. Weymouth Association.
Association of Ministers in the County of Tol-
land, Conn. see Congregational Churches
in Connecticut. Tolland County Associa-
tion.
Association of Ministers on Piscataqua River,
N. H. see Congregational Churches in
New Hampshire. Piscataqua River
Association.
Association of Mutual Aid in Detecting Thieves,
Worcester, Mass. see Worcester As-
sociation of Mutual Aid in Detecting
Thieves.
Association of New Haven County, Conn. see
Congregational Churches in Connecticut.
New Haven County Association.
Association of Perfectionists, Putney, Vt.
89516
Association of physicians. pseud. eds.
Monthly journal of medicine. 50178
Association of Practical Farmers of Cumber-
land County, Pa. 74164
Association of Students of Yale College. see
Yale University. Class of 1834. eds.
Association of the Alumni, Columbia College.
see Columbia University. Association
of the Alumni.
Association of the County of New Haven, Conn.
see Congregational Churches in Con-
necticut. New Haven County Association.
Association of the Defencers of the County in
the War of 1812, Pennsylvania. see
Society of the War of 1812. Pennsylvania.
Association of the Fifth Presbyterian Church
in Philadelphia. see Philadelphia.
Fifth Presbyterian Church.
Association of the Friends of Moral Reform,
Providence, R. I. see Providence
Association of the Friends of Moral
Reform.
Association of the Girls' Industrial School,
New York City. 54104
Association of the Members of the Federal
Street Society for Benevolent Purposes,
Boston. see Boston. Federal Street
Society. Association for Benevolent
Purposes.
Association of the New Orphan Asylum, Cincin-
nati. see Cincinnati Orphan Asylum
Association.
Association of the Principal Inhabitants of
Jamaica. see Jamaica. Citizens.
Association of the Propagation of the Faith.
see Society For the Propagation of the
Faith.
Association of the South Part of Litchfield
County, Conn. see Congregational
Churches in Connecticut. Litchfield South
Association.
Association of Underwriters of Rutland, Vt.
74470
Association of the Western District of New
Haven County, Conn. see Congregational
Churches in Connecticut. New Haven
County Western Association.
Association of Windham County. see Congre-
gational Churches in Connecticut. Wind-
ham County Association.

Association or Club of Laymen, Conven'd at Boston. see Association of Laymen, Boston.
Association Pour la Possession et Exploration de 600,000 Acres de Terre Concedees par l'Etat de New-York. 12220
Association, Signed by 89 Members of the Late House of Burgesses, 1774. see Non-Importation Association of Virginia, 1774.
Association to Protect the Interests of King William Against King James. 82979
Associative manual. 93567
Assollant, Alfred. 2243-2244
Assu, Francisco Echave y. see Echave y Assu, Francisco.
Assault on Mr. Sumner. (18391)
Assault on Senator Sumner. (14950)
Assault on Stony Point. 18930
Assum, Hessel Gerritz. (32028)
Assumpto moral. 22063
Assur Re d'Ormus. 64014
Assurances au Canada. 25290
Asta-Buruaga, Francisco Solano. see Solano Asta-Buruaga, Francisco, 1817-1892.
Astarte. pseud. Poems. 63609
Asten, Abraham. 105192
Asteroid supplement to new tables. 85072
Astete de Ulloa, Gonzalo. 2245, 35238
Asti, Felice. 2246
Asti, Vittorio Alfieri da. see Alfieri da Asti, Vittorio.
Astie, J. F. 2247-2248A
Astley, Thomas. 28539, 65402, 65406, 84559-84560, 84562, 85380
Astley (Thomas) publisher 28539, 65402
Astley's collection of voyages. see Green, John. New general collection of voyages and travels.
Aston, Edward. tr. 6120
Astonishing affair! 62426
Astonishing development. 35314
Astonishing visit. 10607
Astor, Diego de. illus. (69550)
Astor, John Jacob, 1763-1848. 58956, 88487, 90663
Astor, John Jacob, 1763-1848. claimant 88951
Astor, John Jacob, 1763-1848. defendant 96888
Astor Library, New York City. see New York (City) Public Library. Astor Library.
Astor Mining Company. 2256
Astorga, Pedro de Alva y. see Alva y Astorga, Pedro de.
Astoria, oder Abenteuer in den Gebirgen und Waldern von Canada. 35133
Astoria, oder die Unternehmung jenseits des Felsengebirges. 35132
Astoria or anecdotes of an enterprise. (5522), 25432, 35129
Astoria; or, enterprise beyond the Rocky Mountains. 35130
Astounding disclosures and frauds in the liquor traffic. 2257
Astounding disclosures! Three years in a mad house. 33867, 92057
Astraea: . . . a poem. 32621
Astraea, et tidsskrift. 77648
Astraldi, Miguel Anjel. ed. 23969-23971
Astrea. 76321
Astria, Gio. Battista. (4831)
Astro brillante en el nuevo mundo. 27342
Astrologer of the nineteenth century. 83735
Astrological almanack. (71720)

Astrological journal. 8426
Astro-magnetic almanac. 80439
Astronomical and meteorological observations made at the United States Naval Observatory, during the year 1861. 2259
Astronomical and meteorological observations, made at the United States Naval Observatory during the year 1862. 27419
Astronomical and meteorological observations made at the United States Naval Observatory during the year 1866. 18803
Astronomical calculations by N. Daboll, J. Gallup, etc. 15665
Astronomical calculations of the most remarkable celestial revolutions, &c. 62743
Astronomical calendar. 9050
Astronomical calendar, for the year of Our Lord 1822. 65680
Astronomical description of the late comet. 18474
Astronomical diary. 62743, 93025, 93051
Astronomical diary, calendar, or almanack, for . . . 1800. 93025
Astronomical diary, calendar, or almanack, for . . . 1807. 93051
Astronomical diary, calendar, or almanac, for . . . 1811. (48830)
Astronomical diary, kalendar, or almanack, for . . . 1788. 92999, 93056
Astronomical diary, kalendar, or almanack, for . . . 1789. 93001, 93002, 93040, 93057
Astronomical diary, kalander or almanack for . . . 1790. 93041
Astronomical diary, kalendar, or almanack, for . . . 1790. 93003, 93058-93059
Astronomical diary, kalendar, or almanac, for . . . 1791. 93005-93006, 93060
Astronomical diary, calendar, or almanac, for . . . 1792. 93008
Astronomical diary, kalendar, or almanack, for . . . 1792. 93007, 93009, 93061
Astronomical diary, calendar, or, almanack, for . . . 1793. 93010
Astronomical diary, kalendar, or almanack, for . . . 1793. 93011, 93044, 93062
Astronomical diary, calendar, or almanack, for . . . 1794. 93012, 93014, 93045
Astronomical diary, kalendar, or almanack, for . . . 1794. 93013, 93063
Astronomical diary, calendar, or almanack, for . . . 1795. 93046
Astronomical diary, kalendar, or almanack for . . . 1795. 93015
Astronomical diary, calendar, or almanack, for . . . 1796. 93018, 93047
Astronomical diary, calendar, or almanack, for . . . 1797. 93020-93021
Astronomical diary, calendar, or almanack, for . . . 1798. 93022-93023
Astronomical diary, calendar, or almanack, for . . . 1799. 93024, 93050
Astronomical diary [for 1803.] 93025
Astronomical diary . . . for 1805. 76488
Astronomical diary for 1828. The New-York almanack. 89583
Astronomical diary for 1828. Vo. 2, no. 4. The Yankee. 89578
Astronomical diary for 1829. 89585
Astronomical diary for 1831. 89586
Astronomical diary for 1839. 89588
Astronomical diary for 1840. 89579
Astronomical diary for 1841. 89589
Astronomical diary for 1842. 89574
Astronomical diary for 1843. 89590
Astronomical diary for 1845. 89591

Astronomical diary, for . . . 1772. 70773
Astronomical diary . . . for . . . 1776. 90943
Astronomical diary for 1787. 93055
Astronomical diary for . . . 1787. 87764
Astronomical diary, of, and almanack, for the
 year of our Lord Christ, 1754. 80399
Astronomical diary . . . or almanac [for 1801.]
 93025
Astronomical diary, or almanack, for 1817.
 89575
Astronomical diary, or almanack, for . . .
 1819. 89576
Astronomical diary, or almanack for . . .
 1820. 89582
Astronomical diary, or almanack, for . . .
 1783. 92990
Astronomical diary, or almanack for . . .
 1787. 92994, 92996
Astronomical diary: or almanack, for . . .
 1795. 93064
Astronomical diary: or almanack, for 1796.
 93065
Astronomical diary: or almanack, for 1797.
 93065
Astronomical diary; or almanack, for the year
 of Christian AEra, 1793. 79388
Astronomical diary; or almanack, for the year
 of Our Lord 1793. 64103
Astronomical diary, or an almanack, for . . .
 1755. 80400
Astronomical diary; or an almanack for . . .
 1761. 93242, note after 105846
Astronomical diary, or, an almanack for the
 year of our Lord Christ, 1750. 80396
Astronomical diary, or, an almanack, for the
 year of our Lord Christ, 1753. (83097),
 (83098)
Astronomical diary, or, an almanack, for the
 year of our Lord Christ, 1760. 80402
Astronomical diary; or, an almanack. For the
 year of the Christian AEra, 1777. 42402
Astronomical diary; or, an almanack for the
 year 1726. 1309
Astronomical ephemeris, kalendar, or almanack,
 for . . . 1776. 93027
Astronomical ephemeris, kalendar, or almanack,
 for . . . 1777. 93028
Astronomical ephemeris, calendar, or almanack,
 for . . . 1782. 92988
Astronomical ephemeris, calendar, or almanack,
 for . . . 1783. 92989
Astronomical ephemeris, calendar, or almanack,
 for . . . 1784. 92991
Astronomical ephemeris, calendar, or almanack,
 for . . . 1785. 92992
Astronomical ephemeris, calendar, or almanack,
 for . . . 1786. 92993
Astronomical ephemeris, calendar, or almanack,
 for . . . 1787. 92995
Astronomical ephemeris for . . . 1812. 52063
Astronomical museum, for . . . 1802. 64077
Astronomical observations. 35308
Astronomical observations in the Arctic seas.
 (77905), 85072
Astronomical observations made at the island
 of Barbados. (45422)
Astronomical observations made during the
 year 1845. 2258
Astronomical observations, made during the
 years 1845-50. 46974
Astronomical observations, made in the voyages
 which were undertaken by order of His
 Present Majesty. 101029
Astronomical observatory of Harvard University.
 49728

Astronomical Society, Cincinnati. see Cincin-
 nati Astronomical Society.
Astronomical tables. 27419
Astronomical tables, which will serve as a
 constant diary. 5972
Astronomy improved. 93066
Astronomy of the red men of the New World.
 47578
Astroscepium. 38722
Asuwisi ageyo. 44088, 3d note after 94085
Asylum, Pa. First Presbyterian Church. 2260
Asylum. 49688
Asylum, Washington, D. C. see Washington,
 D. C. Asylum.
Asylum and Farm School for Indigent Boys,
 Boston. see Boston Asylum and Farm
 School for Indigent Boys, Thompson's
 Island.
Asylum for . . . Idiotic and Imbecile Youth
 of Ohio. see Ohio. State Hospital,
 Columbus.
Asylum for Idiots, Syracuse, N. Y. see New
 York (State) Institution for Feeble Minded
 Children, Syracuse.
Asylum for Insane Convicts, Matteawan, N. Y.
 see New York (State) State Hospital.
 Matteawan.
Asylum for Insane Convicts. First annual
 report, 1860. 53535
Asylum for Lying-in Women, New York City.
 see New York Asylum for Lying-in
 Women.
Asylum for the Deaf and Dumb, Philadelphia.
 see Philadelphia Asylum for the Deaf
 and Dumb.
Asylum for the Education of the Deaf and Dumb
 of Illinois. see Illinois Asylum for the
 Education of the Deaf and Dumb.
Asylum for the Insane, Charlestown, Mass.
 see Charlestown, Mass. Asylum for the
 Insane.
Asylum for the Insane, Concord, N. H. see
 New Hampshire. State Hospital, Concord.
Asylum for the Insane Poor, Philadelphia. see
 Pennsylvania. Asylum for the Insane
 Poor, Philadelphia.
Asylum for the Relief of Persons Deprived of
 . . . Reason, Frankford, Pa. see Phila-
 delphia. Friends' Asylum for the Insane.
At a committee of the Society Instituted for the
 Purpose of Effecting the Abolition of the
 Slave Trade. London, April 26th, 1791.
 85996
[At a Convention of Committees for the County
 of Worcester, convened at the court-
 house in Worcester, January 27, 1775,
 the following resolve (among others)
 passed, viz.] 105395
At a Convention of Committees for the County
 of Worcester, convened at the court-house
 in Worcester, January 27, 1775, the
 following resolves (among others) passed,
 viz. 105396
At a convention of delegates . . . at Richmond.
 100009
At a convention of the antimasonic members of
 the legislature. 99145
At a council held at Philadelphia, May 17th.
 1742. 61491
At a court held at Punch-Hall, in the colony
 of Bacchus. 34683, (74118)-74121
At a Court of General Sessions of the Peace,
 Oyer and Terminer, Assize and General
 Goal Delivery, holden at Charles-Town.
 87356

At a Court of General Sessions of the Peace within and for the County of Worcester. 105397

At a Court of Vice-Admiralty. 81390

At a General Assembly begun and held at the capitol. 99928

At a General Assembly, begun and held at . . . Williamsburg, the first day of February, in the first year of the reign of . . . George II. 100318

At a General Assembly, begun and held at Williamsburg, the first day of February, in the first year of the reign of our sovereign Lord George II. 100235

At a General Assembly begun and holden at Charleston. 87630

At a General Assembly begun and holden at Charles-Town, on Friday the sixth day of December. 87625A

At a General Assembly begun and holden at Charlestown on Monday the fourth day of January. 87629, 87631

At a General Assembly, begun and holden at Charles-Town on Monday the twenty-eighth day of October. 87604-87605

At a General Assembly begun and holden at Charles-Town, on Monday the twenty-fifth day of October. 87601, 87603

At a General Assembly, begun and holden at Charles-Town, on Saturday the sixth day of February. 87598

At a general Assembly begun and holden at Charles-Town, on Thursday the sixth day of October. 87591, 87593, 87595

At a General Assembly begun and holden at Charles-Town, on Tuesday the 12th day of November. 87589

At a General Assembly begun and holden at Charles-Town, on Tuesday the twelfth day of November. 87590

At a General Assembly begun and holden at Columbia. 87665

At a General Assembly begun to be holden at Charles-Town, on Thursday. 87585

At a General Assembly begun to be holden at Charles-Town, on Tuesday the twelfth day of November. 87588

At a General Assembly, begun to be holden at Charles-Town, on Tuesday the 28th of March. 87577

At a General Assembly begun to be holden at Charles-Town on Wednesday. 87575

At a General Assembly begun to be holden in Charles-Town, on Thursday. 87582

At a General Assembly of the Governor and Company of the English colony of Connecticut. 15674

At a General Assembly of the province of Pennsylvania, begun and holden at Philadelphia, the fifteenth day of October. (59880)

At a General Assembly of the province of Pennsylvania, begun and holden at Philadelphia, the fourteenth day of October, Anno Dom. 1734. 59878.

At a General Assembly of the Province of Pennsylvania, begun and holden at Philadelphia, the fourteenth day of October, Anno Dom. 1729. 59877

At a General Assembly of the province of Pennsylvania, begun and holden at Philadelphia, the fourteeenth day of October 1743. 54879

At a General Assembly of the province of Pennsylvania, begun and holden at Philadelphia, the fourteenth day of October, . . . 1769. 59881

At a General Court of Proprietors of the West-India Dock Company. 102777

At a meeting held by public notice. 105693A

At a general meeting of the citizens of Philadelphia. 61492

At a general meeting of the merchants and traders of this city. 61918

At a legal meeting of the freeholders. 6615

At a meeting of a large number of gentlemen. 104433

At a meeting of a number of the citizens. 61493

At a meeting . . . of citizens of Philadelphia. 97643

At a meeting of clergymen and lay-delegates. 59901

At a meeting of delegates from Newburn. 101972

At a meeting of delegates from the several towns. (23007)

At a meeting of our class. 105885

At a meeting of sundry citizens. 93925

At a meeting of the Board of Managers. 60785, 106171

At a meeting of the Chamber of Commerce. 75342

At a meeting of the Class of 1822 at New-Haven. 105884

At a meeting of the "Class of 1822," held at commencement. 105884

At a meeting of the committee appointed by. the several counties. 45074

At a meeting of the Corporation of Trinity Church. 96980

At a meeting of the delegates of every town. 93430

At a meeting of the delegates . . . of the province. 45075

At a meeting of the deputies. 45076

At a meeting of the Directors and Agents of the Ohio Company, at Mr. Bracket's Tavern. 56978

At a meeting of the Directors and Agents of the Ohio Company, at Mr. Rice's Tavern. (56979)

At a meeting of the friends of the present administration. 100495

At a meeting of the inhabitants of Washington County. 102008

At a meeting of "The Maryland Society for Promoting the Abolition of Slavery." 45241

At a meeting of the National Republican Young Men of Worcester. 105363

At a meeting of 'The Pennsylvania Society for the Promotion of Internal Improvement.' 95381

At a meeting of the . . . [Pennsylvania] Society [for the Promotion of Manufactures and the Mechanic Arts.] 60371

At a meeting of the Pennsylvania State Society of the Cincinnati. 60382

At a meeting of the Proprietors of the Middle-sex Canal. 93536

At a meeting of the Soldiers Memorial Society. 86340

At a meeting of the stockholders of the company. 88438

At a meeting of the stockholders of the Insurance Company. 60163

At a meeting of the subscribers to the Emmet Monument. 22510

At a meeting of the true sons of liberty. 86983

At a meeting of the West-India Planters and Merchants. 834, 102789

At a meeting of the Whig members of the legislature. 103272
At a meeting of thirty-four members. 105419
At a meeting of working-men and other persons. 82355, 104222
At a Parliament begun and holden at Westminster. 90131-90133, 90135
At a Parliament begun . . . at Westminister. 1st note after 97845
At a Republican convention. 105425
At a session begun at Burlington. 53061
At a session of the General Assembly of Maryland. 45191
At a session of the General Assembly of the colony of New-Jersey. 53059
At a session of the General Assembly of the colony of New-York, held at . . . New-York. (53527)
At a session of the General Assembly of the colony of New York, . . . in New York. 53526
At a session of the General Assembly of the province of New-Jersey. (53060)
At a special meeting this day. 33032
At a special session of the Gederal [sic] Assembly. 15675
At a Sub-Committee for Managing the Donation Fund, containing a letter. 61494
At a Sub-Committee for Managing the Donation Fund for the Relief of Friends in America America. 81895
At a term of the Circuit Court of the United States of America. 84738
At a time of great awakenings. 7300
At a very large and respectable meeting. 102013
At a yearly meeting at Philadelphia. 61495
At a yearly meeting for Pennsylvania. 86037
At a yearly meeting of the religious society of Friends. 86070, 3d note after 94928
At an adjourned meeting of merchants. 104579
At anchor. 2261
At home and abroad. 57813
At home in the wilderness. 42034
At home with the Patagonians. (51600)
At the annual session of the President and Fellows of Yale-College. 105817
At the Court of General Sessions of the peace. 87468
At the Court of St. James's. 99252
At the dedication of the new City Hall. 32512
At the [first] annual meeting of the Worcester County Institution for Savings. 105423
At the following session, 1821-22. 90725
At the General Assembly of the Governor and Company of the English colony of Rhode-Island and Providence Plantations in New-England in America, begun and held at South-Kingstown. 70516
At the General Assembly of the Governor and Company of the English colony of Rhode-Island, and Providence Plantations, in New-England in America; begun and holden, by adjournment, at East-Greenwich. 70716
At the Parliament begun and holden at Westminster, the ninth day of October. 88172
At the Parliament begun and holden at Westminster, the tenth day of November. 88173
At the Parliament begun and holden at Westminster, the twenty fifth day of November. 88171
At the South Pole. 37907
At the suit of John Earl of Stair. 5378
At the Supreme Judicial Court. 3527

At this alarming crisis. 97900
At this important crisis. 101783
At this juncture. 95771
Atala. 12238-12242, 12246-12247, 12251, (12261)-12262
Atala. . . . Abencerage melanges litteraires. 12248
Atala. Die Indische Hutte. (12250)
Atala. El Rene. El ultimo Abencerrage. 12249
Atala et Chactas. 12248
Atala, o gli amori di due selvaggi nel deserto. 12245
Atala, o los amores de dos salvages en el desierto. 12242
Atala, of de gelieven in de woestigen. 12248
Atala; or, the amours of two savages in the desert. 12240
Atala; or the love and constancy of two savages. 12240
Atala, ou les amours de deux sauvages. 12237
Atala, ou os amantes do deserto. (12243)
Atala ou os amores de dous salvagens no o deserto. 12244
Atala. Rene. 12249-(12250), (12261)
Atala. Rene. . . . Abencerages. 12248
Atala. Rene, le dernier des Abencerrages. (12250)
Atala. Rene. Les abencerrages. 12248
Atala: Rene: les aventures du dernier Abencerrage. 12248
Atala. Rene. Les aventures du derniere Abencerage. Les Natchez. 12248
Atala. Rene. Les Natchez. 12248, 12251, (12261)
Atala. Rene. Notes et critiques de diverses personnes sur Atala. (12261)
Atala. Rene und der Letzte der Abencerrages. 12251
Atala, the beautiful Indian of the Mississippi. 12240
Atala und die Abenteuer des Letzten der Abenceragen. (12250)
Atala y Rene. 12249
Atalantis. 81197, 81206, 81215-81216, 81264
Atalantis. A story of the sea. 81189-81190
Atalaya, -------- d', Cardinal. 63905 see also Lisbon (Archdiocese) Archbishop (Atalaya)
Atall, Peter. pseud. see Waln, Robert, 1794-1825.
Ataque brusco. 1876
Atar Gull. 93409-93410
Atcheson, Nathaniel. 2262-(2265)
Atchison, David R. 2266
Atchison & St. Joseph Rail Road. President. 49607
Ateneo di Treviso. 5133
Ateneo Mexicano. 48292
Athanasia. 78644
Athanasion, an ode. 17277
Athapaskische Sprachstamm. 9522, (9527)
Athenae Oxonienses. 27351, 67599
Athenaean Library, Bowdoin College. see Bowdoin College, Brunswick, Me. Athenaean Library.
Athenaean Society of Bowdoin College. see Bowdoin College, Brunswick, Me. Athenaean Society.
Athenaeum, Boston. see Boston Athenaeum.
Athenaeum, Fall River, Mass. see Fall River Athenaeum.
Athenaeum, Manchester, N. H. see Manchester Athenaeum.
Athenaeum, New Bedford, Mass. see New Bedford Athenaeum.

Athenaeum, New York City. see New York
   Athenaeum.
Athenaeum, Newport, R. I. see Newport,
   R. I. Redwood Library Company.
Athenaeum, Newton, Mass. see Newton
   Athenaeum.
Athenaeum, Philadelphia. see Philadelphia
   Athenaeum.
Athenaeum, Portland, Me. see Portland
   Athenaeum.
Athenaeum, Portsmouth, N. H. see
   Portsmouth Athenaeum.
Athenaeum, Providence, R. I. see Providence
   Athenaeum.
Athenaeum, Richmond, Va. see Richmond
   Athenaeum.
Athenaeum, Rochester, N. Y. see Rochester
   Athenaeum and Mechanics' Association.
Athenaeum, Roxbury, Mass. see Roxbury
   Athenaeum.
Athenaeum, Salem, Mass. see Salem
   Athenaeum.
Athenaeum, Toronto. see Toronto Athenaeum.
Athenaeum. 30599, 54847, 105846
Athenaeum and Mechanics' Association,
   Rochester, N. Y. see Rochester, N. Y.
   Athenaeum and Mechanics' Association.
Athenaeum and Reading Room, Brooklyn, N. Y.
   see Brooklyn Athenaeum and Reading
   Room.
Athenaeum Association, New York City. 54432
Athenaeum Association, New York City.
   Charter. 54432
Athenaeum Club, New York City. (51640),
   54105
Athenaeum Gallery, Boston. see Boston
   Athenaeum. Gallery.
Athenaeum Society of Trinity College, Hart-
   ford, Conn. see Trinity College, Hart-
   ford, Conn. Athenaeum Society.
Athenaeum—Young Men's Association, Ro-
   chester, N. Y. see Rochester. N. Y.
   Athenaeum—Young Men's Association.
Athenee Oriental, Paris. 70375
Athenian. pseud. Life in town. 41016
Athenian and literary gazette. 89936
Athenian oracle. 79440, 79446
Athens, Ga. Franklin College. see Franklin
   College, Athens, Ga.
Athens, Ohio. University. see Ohio. Uni-
   versity, Athens.
Athens and other poems. 62627
Atheos. 2267
Atherton, Booz M. 102584
Atherton, C. G. 2268
Atherton, Charles Humphrey. (2269)-2270,
   2272, 78997, 2d note after 101883
Atherton, Joshua. 2271
Atherton, William. 2273
Athol, Mass. Committee. 68395
Atienca, Joan de. see Atienza, Juan d'.
Atienza, Giovanni d'. see Atienza, Juan d'.
Atienza, Juan d'. 18658, 44963-44965, 89536-
   note after 89538, 94838
Atienza, Terrero. 17817
Atitlan Indians. Chiefs. 94854
Atkins, Charles G. 25257
Atkins, Dudley. ed. (69947)
Atkins, Dudley. see Tying, Dudley Atkins,
   1760-1829.
Atkins, John. 2274-2275, 28539
Atkins, John. appellant 2276, 56235, 76505
Atkins, Samuel. 36981, (60182)
Atkins, Smith D. (2277)
Atkins, Thomas. (2278)
Atkinson, Archibald. 2279

Atkinson, C. F. (42082)
Atkinson, Charles. 88469
Atkinson, Edward, 1827-1905. 2280-2282,
   80389
Atkinson, Henry. USA 96639-96646, 96648-
   96650 see also U. S. Commissioners
   to the Belantse-etoa or Minnetaree
   Indians. U. S. Commissioners to the
   Crow Indians. U. S. Commissioners to
   the Hunkpapa Sioux. U. S. Commission-
   ers to the Maha Indians. U. S. Com-
   missioners to the Mandan Indians. U. S.
   Commissioners to the Oto and Missouri
   Indians. U. S. Commissioners to the
   Pawnee Indians. U. S. Commissioners
   to the Ponca Indians. U. S. Commis-
   sioners to the Ricara Indians. U. S.
   Commissioners to the Sioune and Oglala
   Indians. U. S. Commissioners to the
   Teton, Yancton, and Yanctonai Sioux
   Indians.
Atkinson, John. supposed author (2283), 31920,
   62589
Atkinson, Joseph. 2284
Atkinson, Richard. 99854 see also Virginia
   Company of London. Clerk.
Atkinson, S. 2285
Atkinson, Thomas, Bp., 1807-1881. 2286-2287
Atkinson, W. Christopher. (2288)
Atkinson, William King. 2289
Atkinson, William P. 2290, 58757
Atkinson's casket. 11335
Atlanta. Convention of the Southern Railway
   and Steamship Association, 1875. see
   Southern Railway and Steamship Associa-
   tion. Convention, Atlanta, 1875.
Atlanta. Convention of the Trustees of a Pro-
   posed University for the Southern States,
   1857. see Convention of the Trustees of
   a Proposed University for the Southern
   States, Under the Auspices of the Pro-
   testant Episcopal Church, Atlanta, 1857.
Atlanta. Cotton States Exposition, 1895. see
   Cotton States Exposition, Atlanta, 1895.
Atlanta. Mayor. 80417-(80418)
Atlanta. Oglethorpe University. see Ogle-
   thorpe University, Atlanta.
Atlanta. Ordinances, etc. 44352
Atlanta. Southern Baptist Publication Society
   Meeting, 1853. see Southern Baptist
   Publication Society. Meeting, Atlanta,
   1853.
Atlanta register. 2292, 15232
Atlanta southern confederacy. see Southern
   confederacy.
Atlante dell' America contenente le migliore
   carte geografiche. 35955
Atlante novissimo. 106276
Atlantes. 72775
Atlantiade. 39999
Atlantic and Great Western Railway. Banquet
   to Thomas W. Kennard. 37379
Atlantic and Great Western Railway Company
   of the States of Ohio, New York, and
   Pennsylvania. 37379, 59964
Atlantic and Great Western Railway Company
   of the States of Ohio, New York, and
   Pennsylvania. defendant 68169
Atlantic and Michigan Railway. 2293
Atlantic and Mississippi Railroad. 2295A,
   68511
Atlantic and Pacific Canal Company. Report
   of the survey. (38855)
Atlantic and Pacific Gold & Silver Mining Co.
   66084

225

Atlantic and Pacific International Ship-Canal Company (Limited.) Isthmus of Nicaragua, Central America. 55138
Atlantic & Pacific Railroad Company. 2294, 88607
Atlantic & Pacific Railroad Company. appellant 88584
Atlantic and Pacific Railroad. Route to the Pacific Ocean. 88607
Atlantic and Pacific Railroad to Costa Rica. 38354
Atlantic and Pacific railway. (64356)
Atlantic & Pacific Ship Canal Company. (55162)
Atlantic and Pacific Telegraph Company. plaintiff 88290
Atlantic and Pacific telegraph. 2295
Atlantic and St. Lawrence Railroad Company. 2296
Atlantic and transatlantic sketches. (43461)
Atlantic and West-Indian navigator. 91090
Atlantic Avenue. 67261
Atlantic City. Its early and modern history. 10948
Atlantic club-book. 2298
Atlantic DeLaine Company. defendant 35680
Atlantic Dock Company. (8314)
Atlantic group. 73544
Atlantic journal, and friend of knowledge. 67445
Atlantic magazine. (2298A), 69492, 76442
Atlantic monthly. 2299, (20504), 55367, 62710, 67189, 92440, 97070
Atlantic navigator. 2300
Atlantic neptune. 3606
Atlantic-Pacific canal for all nations. (2307), 34938
Atlantic pilot. (7324)
Atlantic souvenir. 83788
Atlantic steam-ships. 96363
Atlantic telegraph. (74396)
Atlantic telegraph: a discourse . . . August 8, 1858. 26527
Atlantic telegraph. A discourse preached in Chelsea, 1858. 16698
Atlantic telegraph. A history of preliminary experimental proceedings. 2301
Atlantic telegraph; its history from the commencement of the undertaking in 1854, to the final success in 1866. 2303
Atlantic telegraph; its history from the commencement of the undertaking in 1854, to the sailing of the Great Eastern in 1866. 2303
Atlantic telegraph. Report of the proceedings. 24265
Atlantic voyage. A moral poem. (18847)
Atlantico. (48578)
Atlantis. 20123
Atlantis. Amerikanischen Erzahlungen und Geschichten. 2304
Atlantis. Amerikanischen Erzahlungen und Geschichten. Serie II. 2304
Atlantis. Journal des Neuesten und Wissenwurdigsten aus dem Gebiete der Politik. 2305
Atlantis retecta. 63203
Atlantis. Zeitschrift fur Leben und Literatur in England und Amerika. 2306
Atlanto-Pacific Canal. For all nations. (2307), 34938
Atlas. 25916, 26330, (26779), 27775, 28368, 32750, 39614, 69599, note before 83906, 83922, 83929-83935
Atlas, Boston. see Boston Atlas.
Atlas accompanying Greenleaf's map. 28666

Atlas Ameriquain septentrional. 35954, (40141) (40141)
Atlas and map to accompany the geology of Canada. 41811
Atlas [by Adams.] 91496
Atlas carcelario o coleccion de laminas. 74906
Atlas compose de cartes. 76834, 76851
Atlas, compose de mappemondes, de portulans, et de cartes hydrographiques et historiques, depuis le VIe jusqu'au XVIIe siecle, pour la pluspart inedites, devant servir de preuves a l'histoire. 76835, 76838
Atlas compose de mappemondes, de portulans et de cartes hydrographiques et historiques depuis le VIe jusqu'au XVIIe siecle, pour la plupart inedites, et tirees de plusieurs bibliotheques de l'Europe. (76837)
Atlas compose de mappemondes et de cartes hydrographiques et historiques du XIe au XVIIe siecle. 76835, 76838
Atlas compose de mappemondes et de cartes hydrographiques et historiques depuis le XIe. jusqu'au XVIIe. siecle. 76836
Atlas compose de mappe-mondes et de portulans. (76837)
Atlas de botanique. 21354
Atlas de 14 cartes. 14718
Atlas de Joan Martines. 76838
Atlas de la navigation et du commerce. 69598
Atlas de M. le Vicomte de Santarem. 76846
Atlas de plusieurs cartes de cette ile. 50002
Atlas de zoologie. 21354
Atlas . . . designed for schools and academies. 104049
Atlas d'etude. 71870
Atlas do imperio do brazil. 47801
Atlas du mer. 5715
Atlas du voyage. 22672
Atlas du voyage de decouvertes. 98442
Atlas du voyage de Vancouver. 98441
Atlas e relatorio concernente a exploracao do Rio de S. Francisco. 29675
Atlas, enthaltend Umrisse von Vulkanen. (33725)
Atlas ethnographique du globe. 2856
Atlas fisico y politico de la republica de Venezuela. 14114
Atlas, for schools, academies, and families. note before 83906, 83928
Atlas for Winterbotham's history of America. 104830
Atlas francois. 35538
Atlas geografico del Peru. (59325)
Atlas geografico de la America septerntrional y meridional. 41999
Atlas, geographico, estadistico e historico. 26554
Atlas geographicus. 2308
Atlas geographique. (15055), 33768
Atlas geographique de la republique du Perou. 59326
Atlas geographique et physique. 33753
Atlas geographique et universel. 35252
Atlas geographus. (49902)
Atlas, grave par Ambroise Tardieu. 94228
Atlas Guatemalteco en ocho cartas. 71631
Atlas historique. 29141
Atlas historique et geographique. 33722
Atlas historique genealogique chronologique et geographique. (15055), (39124)
Atlas historique, geographique, geologique, palenontologique, et botanique. 57457
Atlas hydrographique. 38985
Atlas Insurance Comapny. defendant 102600

Atlas lithographie. (42739)
Atlas magnus. 5718
Atlas maior. 35773
Atlas manuale. (49903)
Atlas Marianus. 77606
Atlas maritimus. Describing the sea coasts. (79023)
Atlas maritimus et commercialis. 29894
Atlas maritimus. Or a book of charts. 79024
Atlas maritimus or the sea-atlas. 95631
Atlas mayor, geographia Blaviana. (5717)
Atlas Mercatoris per Franciscum Halma. 66498
Atlas minimus. (79025)
Atlas minor. 47889
Atlas minor Gerardi Mercatoris. (47887)
Atlas minor, ou briefve, & vive description de tout le monde. 47888
Atlas nouveau, contenant toutes les parties du monde. 76716-76718
Atlas nouveau, des empires, monarchies, royaumes, republiques, &c. 35252
Atlas nouveau et curieaux des plus celebres itineraires. 3
Atlas novus. 5720
Atlas novus sive descriptio geographica totius orbis terrarum. 47883
Atlas of America. 14787
Atlas of American history. (32490)
Atlas of battles of the American revolution. 2309
Atlas of Champaign Co. Ohio. 90555
Atlas of Herkimer County, New York. 55191
Atlas of Licking Co., Ohio. (4356)
Atlas of modern and ancient geography. note before 83906, 83936
Atlas of Montgomery and Fulton Counties, New York. 55191
Atlas of Muskingum Co., Ohio. 4357
Atlas of North America. 3717
Atlas of plates. 28089
Atlas of plates, illustrating the geology of the state of Maine. (43938)
Atlas of the cities of Pittsburgh. 63108
Atlas of the North West passage. 55734
Atlas of the oil region of Pennsylvania. 4355
Atlas of the state of New York. 19873
Atlas of the state of Rhode Island and Providence Plantations. (70552)
Atlas of the state of South Carolina. 49113
Atlas of the union. 14788
Atlas of the United States. 50964
Atlas of the United States, containing separate maps. 94312
Atlas of the United States for the use of the blind. 2311
Atlas of the United States of North America, 2310
Atlas of the United States of North America, Canada, New Brunswick. 72669
Atlas of the world. 14787, 57345, 88947
Atlas of Wereldts-Water-Deel en desselfs Zee-Custen. 14548
Atlas; or, a geographicke description of the regions. (47886)
Atlas ou representation du monde universel. 47884
Atlas para el viage. 2312
Atlas physique et geographique. (33756)
Atlas portatif, universel. 71862-71863
Atlas portatif, universel et militaire. 71861
Atlas series, no. 7. 82806
Atlas showing battles, engagements, and important localities. 4222
Atlas sive cosmographicae meditationes de fabrica mundi. (47881)

Atlas sive cosmographicae meditationes de fabrici mundi. 35773, 47882, 82829
Atlas, to accompany a system of universal history. 104049
Atlas to accompany Geography for beginners. 104045
Atlas universal de geographie physique. (43762)
Atlas universal y cosmographico de los orbes. (5717)
Atlas universel. 71864-71866, 71871
Atlas van Zeevaert en Koophandel. 69599
Atlas von Amerika. 69599, (77654)
Atlas y catecismo de geografia y estadistica. 71630
Atlas zoologique. 57457
Atlas zu A. von Humboldt's Kosmos in zwei und vierzig Tafeln. 8201
Atlas zur Entdeckungs-Geschichte Amerikas. 2313, 38348
Atlas zur Reise in Brasilien. 44996, 89549
Atlas zur seiner Reise durch die Provinzen von Rio de Janeiro. 9346
Atlee, E. P. 2314-2315
Atlee, Edwin A. ed. 91877
Atlee, Samuel J. 99005
Atlee, Samuel Yorke. (2316)
Atlee, Washington L. 2317
Atleta. (48293)
Atmore, Charles. ed. 11870
Atmospheric actinometry. 85072
Atocha, Alexander J. 2318
Atondo, Isidore d'. 98928
Atonement. 92026
Atonement of Christ. 2632
Atotarho of the Iroquois. 92768
Atoyac: egloga. 97038
Atrato and San Juan Canal and Transportation Co. in New Granada. (2319)
Atrato River Mining and Trading Company. (2320)
Atristain, Miguel. (44966)
Atrocidades cometidas. 10795
Atrocious judges. 31770
Atrocities of the pirates. 82297-82298
Atson, William. 2321
Attache; or Sam Slick in England. 29696
Attack [by Arator.] 60297
Attack of C. J. Ingersoll upon Daniel Webster. 2205
Attack of Sheriff Miller. 92687
Attack on New Orleans and its defences. 23879
Attack on Porcupine's answer. 102401, 104007
Attack on the political opinions of Mr. Buchanan. 36542
Attaque de Brimstonhill. 27650, (63966), 68421
Attar Gull. 93418
Attelis Santangelo, Orazio Donato Gideon de. see Santangelo, Orazio Donato Gideon de Attelis, b. 1774.
Attempt at scurrility. 35339
Attempt of the North to subdue the southerners. 2322, 69680
Attempt to balance the income and expeditures of the state. 18348, 81396, 90094
Attempt to classify the longicorn coleoptera. 39666
Attempt to collect and preserve some of the speeches. (55312)
Attempt to delineate the character and reward of the faithful servants of Christ. (77585)
Attempt to delineate the character of William Ellery Channing. 2221

Attempt to demonstrate the practicability of emancipating the slaves. 52700, 81896
Attempt to discriminate and describe the animals. 32241
Attempt to display some of the glories. 79496
Attempt to draw aside the veil. 31737
Attempt to elucidate the pernicious consequences. 2323
Attempt to equalize the races. 81722
Attempt to establish an identity of interest. 10873
Attempt to explain the real issues. 9856
Attempt to fix the date of Dr. Franklin's observations. (2588)
Attempt to furnish some hints. 48823, 1st note after 102599
Attempt to illustrate and confirm the ecclesiastical constitution. 32307
Attempt to nip in the bud. (13597)
Attempt to point out the fatal and pernicious consequences. 4497-4498
Attempt to present the claims of Long Lake. 19016
Attempt to preserve the memory. (50313)
Attempt to prove, from the prophetic writings. (26354)
Attempt to prove that a Calvinist is a Christian. (77230)
Attempt to prove that God is a rewarder. 4095
Attempt to prove that pro-slavery interpretations. 59167
Attempt to prove . . . that the abolition of the British trade. 55364
Attempt to prove, that the lues venerea was not introduced. 96161
Attemtp to prove that the Mosaic law furnishes. 37401, (81990)
Attempt to recommend justice. 64138
Attempt to shew, that America must be known. 46792
Attempt to strip Negro emancipation. 2324, 81897
Attempt to vindicate the American character. 50446
Attempt towards laying the foundation. 37447
Attempted speculation of Lemuel H. Arnold. 2076
Attention of the public is solicited. 49231, 97399
Attention! or, new thoughts on a serious subject. 15672, 102339
Attention, voters! 2325
Atterbury, John C. 2326
Atterley, Joseph. pseud. Voyage to the moon. see Tucker, George.
Attestation. 46209, 64274, 67164, 103136
Attestation, by several ministers of Boston. 20057, (20271)
Attestation from some of the ministers of Hampshire. 21939
Attestation of Nicholas Decasse. 95299
Attestations contain'd in letters. 16199, 94918, 4th note after 103650
Attestations from a number of their brethren. 16199, 94918
Attfield, W. 2327
Attibert, Fr. 2328-2329
Atticus. pseud. Essays. see Clayton, Augustin Smith.
Atticus. pseud. Few considerations. 24229
Atticus. pseud. Hints on the subject. 61721
Atticus. pseud. Remarks on the proposed canal. see Clinton, De Witt, 1768-1828. supposed author and Williamson, Hugh. supposed author

Attitude of Iowa cooperheads towards the soldier. 64797
Attleborough, Mass. Society for Detecting Horse-Thieves, and Recovering Stolen Horses. see Society for Detecting Horse-Thieves, and Recovering Stolen Horses, Wrentham, Franklin, Medway, Medfield, Walpole, Foxborough, Mansfield, and Attleborough, Mass.
Attleborough, Mass. Society for the Encouragement of Agriculture, Arts, and Social Intercourse. see Society for the Encouragement of Agriculture, Arts, and Social Intercourse, Attleborough, Mass.
Attoh Ahuma, S. R. B. 98661
Attorney General ex relatione Rector, Wardens and Vestry of St. Anne's Church, in Lowell. (48013)
Attorney General v. Sillem and others. 34419
Attorney; or the correspondence of John Quod. 35114
Attractions of New Haven. 22244
Attractions of Poultney. 64725
Attree, William H. reporter 63916, 72162-72163
Atuagagdliutit. 22848
Atwater, Caleb, 1778-1867. 2225, 2332-(2336), 12272, 50537, 96659 see also U. S. Commissioners to the Winnebago Indians.
Atwarter, Caleb, 1778-1867. supposed author (51657)
Atwater, Dorance. 1429
Atwater, E. 83852
Atwater, H. Cowles. 2337
Atwater, Jesse. 2338
Atwater, Jeremiah. 2339
Atwater, Lyman H. ed. 65654
Atwater, Noah. 2340-2341
Atwater, Noah. supposed author 93245, note after 105846
Atwel & Co. firm 64369
Atwell, Amos Mawe. (13395)
Atwell, S. Y. (70653)
Atwood, E. S. 2342
Atwood, Thomas. 2343-2345A
Atwood Family Reunion, 1866. see Family Reunion of the Descendants of Waitstill Ranney and Jeremiah Atwood. 8th, Chester, Vt., 1866.
Atzerodt, George A. defendant 41180-41182, 41235
Au calomniateur Therou. 39597
Au citoyen Creuse Pascal. (75100)
Au clerge Francais. 5652
Au Congres et au peuple des Etats-Unis. (69603)
Au coq qui chante. 16741
Au corps electoral. 15194
Au Directoire Executif. 96347-96348
Au Directoire Executif et au Corps Legislatif. 6322
Av lectevr. 74883, 74885
Au lecteur Chrestien. 99727-99728
Av lecteur, salvt. 77952
Au profit des victimes de la Guadelupe. 72256
Au public. 101152
Au Roi, et a mos Seigneurs les Commissaires Generaux. 101149
Au Roi. Raisons que font voir combéin il est important. 10362
Au Roi sur la necessite et la possibilite de reconquerir. 4267
Au Roi, sur la Nouvelle France. 10363
Au Roy. 98928
Av Roy des Roys. 74883

Au Roy et a Nosseigneurs de son Conseil.
39278
Au Roy raisons qui font voir combien il est
important. (56080)
Av Roy svr la Novvelle France. 56081
Au Texas. 15925
Au Texas. 2^e ed. 15926
Auanzo, Francesco. tr. 22279, 27778, 47828
Aubanus, J. Boemus. see Boemus, Johann,
fl. 1500.
Aub-ba-nauba. Potawatomi Indian chief. 96701
Aub-ba-nauba Band of Potawatomi Indians. see
Potawatomi Indians (Aub-ba-nauba Band)
Aube, ------. (21460)
Aubert, ------. tr. 6123
Aubert, ----- Armand. see Armand-Aubert,
------.
Auberteuil, Michel Rene Hilliard d'. see
Hilliard d'Auberteuil, Michel Rene, 1751-
1789.
Aubigny, ------ d'. pseud. Washington. see
Baudouin, Jean Marie Theodore.
Aubigny, Charles d'. see D'Aubigny, Charles.
Aubigny, Charles Francois d'. see D'Aubigny,
Charles Francois, 1817-1878.
Aubin, ------. ed. 70377-(70378), 85781,
85791
Aubin, J. M. A. (7419)
Aubin, N. 23789, 34041, 69661
Aubin, Penelope. 2347
Aubin, Stephanie Felicite Ducrest de Saint.
see Saint-Aubin, Stephanie Felicite
Ducrest de, Comtesse de Genlis.
Aublet, Jean Baptiste Christophe Fusee. 2348
Aubonneau, ------ d'. 2349, 19084
Auborn, A. d'. see D'Auborn, A.
Aubouin, Carlos. 66590
Aubre, Paul d'. (2350), (18663)
Aubree, Paul d'. see Aubre, Paul d'.
Aubree, Pierre. 2351
Aubrey, ------. (15052)
Aubry, ------. 2352
Auburn, N. Y. Auburn and Oswego Canal
Celebration, 1835. see Auburn and
Oswego Canal Celebration, Auburn, N. Y.,
1835.
Auburn, N. Y. Cayuga County Democratic
Convention, 1819. see Democratic
Party. New York. Cayuga County.
Convention, Auburn, 1819.
Auburn, N. Y. Court. (79503)
Auburn, N. Y. Meeting in Relation to the Mea-
sures Taken to Enforce the Sabbath, and
the Attempt to Establish A Christian
Party in Politics, 1828. see Meeting
in Relation to the Measures Taken to
Enforce the Sabbath and the Attempt to
Establish a Christian Party in Politics,
Auburn, N. Y., 1828.
Auburn, N. Y. Meeting of citizens, 1838. 97124
Auburn, N. Y. Prison. see New York (State)
Prison, Auburn.
Auburn, N. Y. St. Peter's Church. defendants
64810
Auburn, N. Y. State Prison. see New York
(State) State Prison, Auburn.
Auburn, N. Y. Veteran Association. see
Veteran Association of Auburn.
Auburn and Oswego Canal Celebration, Auburn,
N. Y., 1835. 79499
Auburn and Pennsylvania systems compared.
65704
Auburn directory. 7104
Auburn free press. 105472

Auburndale, Mass. Lasell Female Seminary.
see Lasell Female Seminary, Auburn-
dale, Mass.
Aucaigne, Felix. 2355
Auch fragmente. 77662
Auch Patagonische Reisen Moglich. 89836
Auchinleck, G. 2356
Auchmuty, Robert. 2357
Auchmuty, Samuel. 2358-2359, (35326)
Auckland, William Eden, 1st Baron, 1744-1814.
(10924)-(10925), (14380), (21827)-21828
see also Great Britain. Commissioners
to Treat, Consult, and Agree Upon the
Means of Quieting the Disorders Now
Subsisting in Certain of the Colonies,
1778.
Auctentijck verhael. 7522
Auction record. 89111
Auctioneers of New York. see New York
(City) Auctioneers.
Auctioneers of Philadelphia. see Philadelphia.
Auctioneers.
Auctions inconsistent with regular trade.
54106
Auctuarium Indicum. 2476
Aucun. pseud. Sketch of the history of
Framington. see Ballard, William.
Aucuparius, ------. 66481
Audain, L. 2360
Audebard, Andre E. J. P. J. F. d'. see
Ferussac, Andre E. J. P. J. F. d'Aude-
bard, Baron de.
Audi alteram partem. 6087
Audi alteram partem, or a counter-letter.
2361, 28749
Audi et alteram partem. 95983
Audibert Roubard, J. L. see Roubard, J. L.
Audibert.
Audinet-Serville, -------. (58327)
Audit Office records. 85247
Auditor General's report on public accounts.
52531
Auditor's annual report, for the fiscal year
1866-7. 76033
Auditor's annual report of the receipts and
expenditures of the city of Salem. 75636
Auditors' annual report of the receipts and
expenditures of the town of Braintree.
7354
Auditor's annual report of the receipts and
expenditures of the town of Quincy.
67285
Auditor's fifth annual report of the receipts
and expenditures. 64351
Auditor's report, for . . . 1863. 37019
Auditor's report of receipts and expenditures.
49146
Auditor's report of the receipts and expenditures
of the town of East Kingston, N. H.
21651
Auditor's report of the receipts and expendi-
tures of the town of Lexington. 40887
Auditor's report of the receipts and expendi-
tures, with the School Committee's
report of the town of Oxford. 58039
Auditor's report on the estate of Charles F.
Sibbald. 80813
Auditor's report to the State Constitutional
Convention. (42276)
Auditor's second annual report. 64342
Auditor's second printed report. (20628)
Auditor's seventh annual report. 42470
Auditors' third report. 73633
Audoenus. see Owen, John, 1560?-1622.
Audoin, ------. ed. 78689
Audubon, J. V. 2363-2365, 2372

Audubon, John James, 1785-1851. 2362-2371, 92341
Audubon, Mrs. John James. (8869), 92341
Audubon, the naturalist of the New World. 75242
Auellaneda, Barnardino Delgadillo de. 77289
Auendano y Vilela, Francisco de. (69222), 69293, 69294
Auer, Alois. 2373, 57438
Auf nach West Canada! 21753
Aufenthalt und Reisen in Mexico. 9275
Aufforderung an das Volk Gottes in Amerika. 38350
Aufforderung an Teutsche Auswanderer. 2374
Aufforderung und Erklarung in Betreff einer Auswanderung. 2375
Aufgesetzt in Carlstown von vier Schweizen. 87855
Aufrichtige Nachricht aus Publicum. 106351
Aufruf an die Deutschen in Amerika. 40979
Aufruf an die Deutschen Wahler. 29006, 62715
Aufsatze betreffend das Eisenbahnwesen in Nord-Amerika. 4643
Aufsatze vermischen Inhalts. 25556A
Aufsatze, Zeitungscorrespondenzen und Briefauszuge von Ansiedlern. (6013)
Aufsatze zur Kunde ungebildeter Volker. 78011
Aufschlusse uber die Lage. 30704
Aufstand der vier westlichen grafschaften Pennsylvaniens. 69107
Aufuhrliche Nachricht von dem Saltzburgischen Emigranten. 98132
Auger, Edouard. 2376
Aughey, John Hill. 2377
Aughey, Samuel. 2378
Augsburg confession. 51735
Augspurger, Johann Paul. 2379
Auguecheek, Andrew. 97997
Auguis, P. R. 11816
Augur, John, d. 1718. defendant 32182, (32197)
Augur's choice. 43050
Aug. 1, 1831. Dear Sir: 105883
August Ludwig Schlozers Briefwechsel meist historischen und politischen Inhalts. 77658
Augusta, Ga. Congress of the Four Southern Governors, and the Superintendent of that District, with the Five Nations of Indians, 1763. see Congress of the Four Southern Governors, and the Superintendent of that District, with the Five Nations of Indians, Augusta, Ga., 1763.
Augusta, Ga. Grand Committee of Twenty. 2381
Augusta, Ga. St. James' Methodist Episcopal Sabbath School. 2381
Augusta, Ga. Southern Baptist Convention, 1845. see Southern Baptist Convention, Augusta, Ga., 1845.
Augusta, Me. Court. 47985, note after 96896
Augusta, Me. Insane Hospital. see Maine. State Hospital, Augusta.
Augusta, Me. South Parish Congregational Church. 103042
Augusta, Me. State Hospital. see Maine. State Hospital, Augusta.
Augusta, Me. State Temperance Convention, 1852. see State Temperance Convention, Augusta, Me., 1852.
Augusta, N. Y. Washington Benevolent Society. see Washington Benevolent Society. New York (State) Augusta.
Augusta County, Va. Meeting of Freeholders, 1775. (65797)

Augusta Colonization Society. 2380
Augusta directory for 1861. 2382
Augusta Georgia chronicle. 101783
Augusta, Hallowell, and Gardiner directory. 38892
Augusta intelligencer. 93899
Augusta mirror. 50487
Augustin, Andres de San. see San Augustin, Andres de.
Augustin, Antonio. 79176
Augustin, Gaspar de San. see San Augustin, Gaspar de.
Augustine, Saint, of Hippo. 24150
Augustinian confession of faith. 92757
Augustinians. 16063, 24150, (42603), 48392, 57517, 57519, (68842), (68936), note after (68936), 98913, note after 98913
Augustinians. petitioners 69973
Augustinians. plaintiffs 86421
Augustinians. Provincia de Mexico. (17606), 48392, 66544, 86411
Augustinians. Provincia de Mexico. Procurador General. petitioner 106408
Augustinians. Provincia de Mexico. Provincial y Difinitorio. plaintiffs 86404
Augustinians. Provincia de Michoacan. Visitador. 86406, 86414 see also Pedro de Santa Maria.
Augustinians. Provincia del Nuevo Reyno de Granada. 56282
Augustinians. Provincia del Nuevo Reyno de Granada. Procurador General. plaintiff 56282 see also Canizares, Martin de. plaintiff
Augustinians. Provincia del Peru. 8740
Augustinians. Provincia del Peru. Procurador y Difinidor General. 87175 see also Sosa, Diego de, 1696-1767.
Augustinians. Provincia del Peru. Provincial. 98809 see also Araujo, Leonardo de.
Augustino Macedo, Francisco a San. see Macedo, Francisco a San Augustino.
Avgvstino Barbadico serenissimo Venetiarvm principi et senatvi felicitatem. 74658
Augusto Congreso Nacional reunido en cortes extraordinarias. 76886
Augusto iluminado. 24154, 72532
Augusto Revilo Elippihw. pseud. Nine letters. see Whipple, Augustus Oliver.
Augustus, Hieronymus Oliberius. 2383
Augustus, John. (2384)
Augy, -----d'. 2386
Auld, Jacob. 50164
Aulicus coquinariae. 31654
Aulnaye, F. H. S. de l'. 4933
Aulne, Anne Robert Jacques Turgot, Baron de l'. see Turgot, Anne Robert Jacques, Baron de l'Aulne, 1727-1781.
Aun las cuestiones de limites del Ecuador. (21797), 58054
Aun porfian esos comprados defendieno gachupinos. 98111
Aunay, Mosneron de l'. see L'Aunay, Mosneron de.
Aungerville Society, Edinburgh. see Aungervyle Society, Edinburgh.
Aungervyle Society, Edinburgh. 91318, 100460
Aunis, France. Chambre de Commerce. petitioners 47513
Aunon, Alfonso Carrio y Morcillo Rubio de. see Carrio y Morcillo Rubio de Aunon, Alfonso.
Aunon, Miguel de Zavala y. see Zavala y Aunon, Miguel de.
Aunon, Pedro Morcillo Rubio de. see Morcillo Rubio de Aunon, Pedro.

Aunt Friendly. pseud. Picket-guard. 62664
Aunt Leanna. 72572
Aunt Mary. pseud. Peep into Uncle Tom's
cabin. see Stowe, Harriet Elizabeth
(Beecher) 1811-1896.
Aunt Phillis's cabin. 21683
Aunt Phillis's cabin reviewed. (28800)
Aunt Sally come up. (28485)
Aunt Sophie's stories. 81368
Aura; or, the slave. 2387, 11023, 92782
Aurele, De la Guadeloupe Poirie de Saint.
see Poirie de Saint-Aurele, de la
Guadeloupe.
Aurelien et Asterie. (4959)
Aurelius. pseud. Brief consideration. see
Gardner, John.
Aurelius, Macrobius. see Macrobius Aurelius.
Aurelius Prodentius, Americanus. pseud.
Sacred minister. see Mather, Samuel,
1706-1785.
Auren, Joen. 89173-89175
Auriac, Jules Berlioz d', 1820- 2388-2389,
4900-4903F
Auricular confession and popish nunneries.
32426
Aurifodina. 5350
Aurora, Ill. Christian Convention, 1867. see
Christian Convention, Aurora, Ill., 1867.
Aurora. (20991), 20994, (23921), 97270
Aurora en Copacabana. (9890)
Aurore boreal-orientale observee a la Havana.
63667
Aus Amerika. Erfahrungen, Reisen und Studien.
25988
Aus Amerika uber Schule. 21174
Aus Chili, Peru und Brasilien. 5211
Aus Columbien an seine Freunde. 14557
Aus dem Soldatenleben in Mexico. 4526
Aus dem westen Amerika's. 74167
Aus den Schatzen der Schriftgelehrten zum
Hillemreich. 77506
Aus der Geschichte der ersten Ansiedelungen.
72188, 2d note after 94271
Aus meinem Leben. (47027)
Aus meinen Tagebuch. 159
Aus zwei Welttheilen. 27194
Auserlesenen Zugaben. 72603
Ausflug auf die Prairien. 35144
Ausflug nach den Felsen-Gebirgen im Jahre
1839. 104905
Ausfluge nach Canada. 69142-69143, 102502
Ausfuhrlich und glaubwurdige Geschichte.
(30943)
Ausfuhrliche Beschreibung der insel Surinam.
93850
Ausfuhrliche Beschreibung des Theils. 25997,
38974, note after 100853
Ausfuhrliche Beschreibung von der unglucklic-
hen Reise. 2390, 32377, 98990
Ausfuhrliche historisch-physikalische Beschrei-
bung. (34115)
Ausfuhrliche Nachrichten. 98133-98136, 98138-
98139
Ausfuhrliche und accurate geographische
Beschreibung. 51690, 100494
Ausfuhrliche und wahrhafte Nachricht. 22023
Ausfuhrlichen Abhandlung. 89957
Ausfuhrlichen Bericht. 12835, 24138, 1st note
after 98488
Ausfuhrlichen Beschreibung. 51690, 100494
Ausfuhrlichen Beschreibung von dessen Leben.
8547, (9501), (20827)
Ausfuhrlichen EbenEzerichen Nachrichten zu
Lesen. 98135
Ausfuhrlichen historische und geographische
Beschreibung. (32104), note after 42194

Ausfuhrlichen Nachrichten. 98133
Ausfuhrlichen Vorsichtsregeln fur Auswanderer.
104960
Ausfuhrlicher Worterbuche. 35184
Ausfuhrlicher Bericht vber den Manifest.
98188
Ausfuhrlicher Bericht von der beruhmten
Landschaft Carolina. (2391)
Ausfuhrlicheren Bemerkungen. 64603
Ausgewhalte Amerikanische Romane. 5555
Ausgewahlte Offenbarungen. 83275
Ausgewahlte Romane [von F. A. Strubberg.]
93103
Ausgewahlte Romane [von J. C. Cooper.]
16414
Ausgewahlte Sammlung. 83274
Ausgewahlte Schriften der Konigl. Geographi-
schen Gesellschaft. 4857A
Ausgewahlte Schriften [von Alexandre Dumas.]
21187
Ausgewahlte Schriften [von Thomas Carlyle.]
(10933)
Ausgewahlte Werke [von Chateaubriand.] 12251
Ausgewahlte Werke von E. A. Poe. 63552
Ausgewandertem. pseud. Beschlusse der
Kongresses der Vereinigten Staaten.
5037
Ausilios del Ecuador. 2392
Auslegung der Mercarthen. 25964, 1st note
after 98183
Auspices of war. (2393)
Asseren und inneren politischen Zustande.
71225
Aussfuhrliche und aus vielen . . . alten und
neuen Schribenten. 77201
Aussfuhrlicher Bericht von Sud und Nord
Carolina. 52362
Aussprache des . . . Chs. C. Leigh. (39920)
Aussichten fur gebildete Deutsche in Nordame-
rika. 41826
Austen, C. A. tr. 55362
Austin, Arthur W. 2394
Austin, Benjamin. 2395-2398
Austin, C. H. 2399-2400
Austin, David. 2401-2405, 78983, 83802,
84096, 97766, note after 101874
Austin, Elbridge Gerry. 2406
Austin, Horace, 1831- 49302 see also Min-
nesota. Governor, 1870-1874 (Austin)
Austin, Isaac. petitioner 61563
Austin, Iver James. 2407-2410, 43609
Austin, James Trecothick, 1784-1870. 2411-
2415, 11917, (11920), 64948, 81162,
85430, 94057-94058, 96843 see also
Massachusetts. Attorney General.
Austin, Jonathan Loring. 2416
Austin, Jonathan Williams. 2417
Austin, L. A. 2418
Austin, Moses, 1761-1821. 2419
Austin, Robert F. 2420
Austin, Samuel. 2421-2425, 95888 see also
Massachusetts Missionary Society.
Secretary.
Austin, Stephen Fuller, 1793-1836. 2426,
26474, 93710, 94938, 94945, 94950,
95086, 95114, 105111
Austin, Walter. note after 92840
Austin, William. (2428), (20062)
Austin, William. supposed author (30763),
note after 92840
Austin, Texas. Constitutional Convention,
1845. see Texas. Constitutional Con-
vention, Austin, 1845.
Austin, Texas. Constitutional Convention,
1866. see Texas. Constitutional Con-
vention, Austin, 1866.

Austin, Texas. Constitutional Convention, 1868-1869. see Texas. Constitutional Convention, Austin, 1868-1869.

Austin, Texas. Consultation, 1836. see Texas (Provisional Government) Consultation, Austin, 1835.

Austin, Texas. Convention, 1832. see Coahuila and Texas (Mexican State) Convention, Austin, 1832.

Austin, Texas. Convention, 1833. see Coahuila and Texas (Mexican State) Convention, Austin, 1833.

Austin, Texas. Reconstruction Convention, 1866. see Texas. Constitutional Convention, Austin, 1866.

Austin, Texas. State Library. see Texas. State Library, Austin.

Austin County, Texas. Committee on Railroads. see Committee on Railroads in Austin and Washington Counties, Texas.

Austin city gazette. 94965

Austin Presbyterian Theological Seminary. 85132

Austin state gazette. 10842

Australia a mistake. 52545

Australian and Californian gold discoveries. 91851

Australien. 27186

Australien. Californien. Mexiko. 21184

Australische Navigatien. 89444-89445

Australischen oder Suder Compagney im Konigreich Schweden. see Soder Compagniet.

Austria, Jose de. 2430

Austria, Juan. 50206

Austria. (16890), 33651, 44605

Austria. Charge d'Affaires. U. S. (33650) see also Hulsemann, Johann Georg.

Austria. Gesandtschaft, Rio de Janeiro. 7607, (77973)

Austria. K. Hofnaturalienkabinets Director. 7607, (77973) see also Schreibers, Carl Franz Anton von, 1775-1852.

Austria. Laws, statutes, etc. 40712, 68792, 102442

Austria. Ministerium der Auswartigen Angelegenheitem, Vienna. 7607, (77973)

Austria. K. Naturforschen in Brazilien. 7607, (77973)

Austria. Sovereigns, etc., 1711-1740 (Charles VI) 40712, 68792, 102442 see also Charles VI, Emperor of Austria, 1685-1740.

Austria. Sovereigns, etc., 1740-1780 (Maria Theresa) 96543-96544 see also Maria Theresa, Empress of Austria, 1717-1780.

Austria. Sovereigns, etc., 1780-1790 (Joseph II) see also Joseph II, Emperor of Austria, 1741-1790. suprious author

Austria. Sovereigns, etc., 1790-1792 (Leopold II) (69722) see also Leopold II, Emperor of Austria, 1747-1792.

Austria. Treaties, etc. 19274, 68792, 96543-96545, 102442

Austria and its polity. 20511

Austrian government comprised by its officials. 85453

Austro-Hungarian question. (33650)

Auswahl der besten auslandischen geographischen und statistischen Nachrichten. 89763, 91079, 98444

Auswahl kleiner Reisebeschreibungen und anderer statistischen und geographischen Nachrichten. 2439

Auswahl schoner seltener Gewachse. 2440

Auswahl von Ansichten der interessantesten Gegenden. 55455

Auswanderer. 2d note after 94271

Auswanderer am Niederrhein. 2431

Auswanderer-Bibliothek. 2432

Auswanderer-Calender fur 1854 und 1855. 2433

Auswanderer in Amerika. 2434

Auswanderer nach Amerika. 92760

Auswanderer nach Texas. 29494, note after 95070

Auswanderer, zunachst Organ der Sammtlichen Auswanderungsvereine Sachsens. 2435

Auswanderers Schutz. 86195

Auswanderung der Deutschen nach Texas. 2436

Auswanderung nach Amerika. 2437

Auswanderung nach Brasilien und Colonisation daselbst. 7927

Auswanderung nach der Tropenwelt. 23100

Auswanderung nach Mexico. 48294

Auswanderung und Colonisation im Interesse des Deutschen Handels. 9150

Auswanderung und Deutsch-Nationale Kolonisation von Sud-Amerika. 81280

Auswanderungsbuch. 5126

Ausz America. 1019

Auszfuhrlicher Bericht vber den Manifest. 98189

Auszfuhrung allerhand wolbedencklicher Argumenten. 98190

Auszug aus dem Criminal-Process. 51426

Auswug aus dem Englischen Original. 91080

Auszug aus dem Heidelberger Catechismus. (80900)

Auszug aus dem Tagebuch des Konigl. Schiffs The Endeavour. 16243

Auszug aus der grosseren Sammlung. 20367

Auszug aus Petit trate sur le gouvernement des esclaves. 68977

Auszug der Nachrichten. 41771

Auszug der Totalsummen. (55595)

Auszug ettlicher Sendbrieff. 2442, 22086

Auszug fur das Grossere Publikum. 92808

Auszug von General Waschington's Circular-Schreiben. 101542

Auszuge aus Briefen aus Nord-Amerika. (2441)

Auszuge aus dem Briefen und Papieren. (71299)

Autenrieth, A. tr. 20000

Autenrieth, J. F. H. tr. (74209)

Autentijck Verhael. 2443

Avtentyck verhael van 't gene in Brasiel. 7521

Auteroche, Jean Chappe de. see Chappe d'Auteroche, Jean.

Auteur anonyme probablement natif d'Espagne. pseud. Manuscrit qui contient un commentaire. 76838

Auteur de l'Antidote au Congres de Radstadt. pseud. Du Congres de Vienne. see Pradt, Dominique Georges Frederic de Riom de Prolhiac de Fourt de, Abp., 1759-1837.

Auteur de la Bibliotheca Americana vetustissima. pseud. Fernand Colomb. see Harrisse, Henry.

Auteur de la Bibliotheca Americana vetustissima. pseud. Notes pour servir a l'histoire. see Harrisse, Henry.

Auteur de La paix en Europe par l'alliance Anglo-Franciase. pseud. Blancs et les noirs en Amerique. 5856

Auteur de La reponse au Patriote Hollandois. pseud. Reponse au Patriote Hollandois. 40660

Auteur de "Une annee de sejour a Londres."
pseud. Voyage vers le pol Arctique.
see Defauconpret, A. J. B.
Auteur des Interets des nations de l'Europe.
pseud. Commerce de la Hollande. see
Serionne, Jacques Accarias de.
Auteur des Lettres d'Affi a Zurac. pseud.
Memoires d'un Americain. see Lacroix,
Jacques Vincent de.
Auteur des Lettres d'un Cultivateur Americain.
pseud. Voyage dans la houte Pensylvanie.
see Crevecoeur, J. Hector St. John,
1735-1813.
Auteur des Melages interssans & curieux.
pseud. Memoires geographiques. see
Rousselot de Surgy, Jacques Philibert.
Auteur des Nouvelles ecclesiastiques. pseud.
ed. Extraits de la relation abregee.
63907, 1st note after 98174
Auteur des Soeurs jumelles; ou, la vocation.
pseud. Seraphine. 79191
Author des Souvenirs des Antilles. pseud.
Voyage fait dans les annees 1816 et 1817.
see Montlezun, --------, Baron de.
Auteur des "Vues politiques." pseud. Reflex-
ions du bon citoyen. see Chachereau,
------.
Auteur d'Olesia. pseud. tr. 16552
Auteur du Congres de Vienne, etc. pseud.
Memoires historiques. see Pradt,
Dominique-Dufour de.
Auteur du Memoire. pseud. Examen de la
reponse. see Morellet, Andre.
Auteur du Mercure politique. pseud. Mercure
politique. 40661
Auteur du "Mot a l'oreille." pseud. Confes-
sion generale faite au public. 15444
Auteur du Theatre d'education. pseud. Annales
de la vertu. see Sillery, Stephanie
Felicite Brularet de, Comtesse de, 1746-
1830.
Auteur du Triumvirat. pseud. tr. 86476-
86478, 86480
Auteur impartial, ami de la verite. pseud.
tr. (7935), 6th note after 97845, 97851
Auteur natif & habitant du pais. pseud. His-
toire de la Virginie. see Beverley,
Robert.
Auteurs de traite intitule: De la France et
des Etats-Unis. pseud. Lettre a l'auteur
du Mercure politique. see Brissot de
Warville, Jacques Pierre, 1754-1793.
and Claviere, Etienne, 1735-1793.
Authentic. 96572, 96578
Authentic account of all the proceedings. 3019,
101776
Authentic account of an embassy. 90843
Authentic account of Commodore Anson's
expedition. (1631)
Authentic account of the appearance of a ghost.
67065
Authentic account of the barbarity of the
Russians. 87145
Authentic account of the death of Miss Jane
M'Crea. 11304
Authentic account of the fatal duel. 33911
Authentic account of the first discoverers of
those islands. 65333, 4th note after
102858
Authentic account of the first discovery and
settlement. 81166
Authentic account of the last hours of John
Francis Knapp. 38065
Authentic account of the massacre of Joseph
Smith. 18824

Authentic account of the most remarkable
events. 95441
Authentic account of the mutiny of the Ship
Bounty. 3663
Authentic account of the outrages in Kansas.
37056
Authentic account of the part taken by the late
Earl of Chatham. 63082, 63084
Authentic account of the proceedings. (2444),
53537
Authentic copies of the provisional articles and
definitive treaty with America; and the
preliminary articles. 91093
Authentic copies of the provisional articles
and definitive treaty with America; the
preliminary articles and definitive
treaties. 91092
Authentic account of the reduction of Louis-
bourg. 42174
Authentic account of the reduction of the
Havana. 2450, 29418
Authentic account of the rise and progress of
the present contest in America. 2445
Authentick account of the slave trade. 81898
Authentic account of the whole insurrection.
97487
Authentic account of Puerto Bello's being taken.
97661
Authentic and complete history of popular
shipwrecks. 21252
Authentic and complete history of shipwrecks.
21252
Authentic and complete trial of Lieut. Gen.
Whitelocke. 103671
Authentic and comprehensive history of Buffalo.
37648
Authentic and descriptive narrative of the latest
discoveries. 105656
Authentic and impartial narrative. 101444
Authentic and interesting description. 8999
Authentic and interesting narrative in three
parts. 52266
Authentic and interesting narrative of Nathaniel
Price. 65441
Authentic and particular account of the life of
Francis Burdett Personnel. 61069
Authentick and particular account of the taking
of Carthagena. 63705
Authentic and thrilling narrative. 33023
Authentic anecdotes of American history.
(12727)
Authentic anecdotes of American slavery.
(81899)
Authentic biography of Col. Richard M. Johnson.
36274
Authentic biography of General La Fayette.
38568
Authentic biography of Richard W. Johnson.
22532
Authentic confession of Jesse Strang. 92688
Authentic copies of the correspondence of
Charles Cotesworth Pinckney. 2446
Authentic copies of the correspondence of
Thomas Jefferson. 35881
Authentic copies of the preliminary articles
of peace. 2447
Authentic copies of the provisional and pre-
liminary articles of peace between Great
Britain and the United States. 2449
Authentic copies of the provisional and pre-
liminary articles of peace signed between
Great Britain. (2448)
Authentic copy of Lord Ch——m's speech.
63065
Authentic copy of the memorial. 47258

Authentic copy of the minutes. 82899
Authentic copy of the petition to the King.
  15544
Authentic copy of the result. 7894
Authentic daily record. (7132)
Authentic exposition of the "K. G. C." 38132
Authentic exposition of the origin. 36968
Authentic historical memoir. 49133
Authentic history. 68986
Authentic history of Lancaster County.
  49926
Authentic history of remarkable persons.
  (50728)
Authentic history of the celebrated horse
  American Eclipse. 98539
Authentic history of the English West Indies.
  (22621), 101821
Authentic history of the Harper's Ferry
  tragedy. 8518, (20935)
Authentic history of the late war. 18875
Authentic history of the Lawrence calamity.
  (39392)
Authentic history of the missions. 3165
Authentic history of the peopling of America.
  55012
Authentic history of the second war for inde-
  pendence. (8556)
Authentic history of the Vermont State Prison.
  74289
Authentic incidents. 26099
Authentic journal of the late expedition. 62458
Authentick journal of the proceedings. 10349
Authentic journal of the siege of the Havana.
  2450
Authentic letters from Upper Canada. 43846
Authentic life of His Excellency Louis Kossuth.
  38265
Authentic life of John C. Colt. 14760
Authentic life of Mrs. Mary Ann (Dunn)
  Bickford. 5221
Authentic memoir of the life of the late Rev.
  G. Whitefield. 103615
Authentic memoirs of Capt. Paul Jones. 82237
Authentic memoirs of John Eliot. note after
  22167
Authentic memoirs of Phebe Phillips. 104995
Authentic memoirs of the early life of Benja-
  min West. 102716
Authentic memoirs of the Right Honourable the
  late Earl of Chatham. 63085
Authentic memoirs of William Augustus Bowles.
  7082
Authentic narrative. 60845, 104172
Authentic narrative and record. 62739
Authentic narrative of a voyage from the Cape
  of Good Hope to Brasil. (41295)
Authentic narrative of a voyage performed by
  Captain Cook. 22333
Authentic narrative of a voyage to the Pacific
  Ocean. 16224
Authentic narrative of a young Negro. 52266
Authentic narrative of facts. 2451
Authentic narrative of James Williams. 103812
Authentic . . . narrative of . . . Miss Pauline
  D'Estraye. 59220
Authentic narrative of Mrs. Simeon Hays.
  49126
Authentic narrative of the Baltimore mob of
  1812. 3020
Authentic narrative of the captivity of John
  Stover. 34477
Authentic narrative of the causes. 79487,
  83421-83422
Authentic narrative of the life and surprising
  adventures of Peter Williamson. 36555,
  104463-104464

Authentic narrative of the life of James S.
  Stedman. 91070
Authentic narrative of the life of Joshua Slocum.
  82177
Authentic narrative of the loss of the American
  brig Commerce. 71397
Authentic narrative of the loss of the Dodding-
  ton Indiaman. 2452, (20487)
Authentic narrative of the memorable achieve-
  ments. 35371
Authentic narrative of the mutiny. 5672
Authentic narrative of the Negro insurrection
  in 1831. 35594
Authentic narrative of the parentage. (31814)
Authentic narrative of the proceedings. 2453,
  9000, 13672
Authentic narrative of the recent loss. 98124,
  102204
Authentic narrative of the Seminole War.
  24901, (27655), (79063)-79064, 4th note
  after 97085
Authentic narrative of the success of tar water.
  65700
Authentic narrative of the voyages and hardships of John Hoxes. 33394
Authentic narrative; to which are added some
  interesting letters. 16794, 41538
Authentic narratives of the lives. 63015
Authentic papers. 58932, note after 75175
Authentic papers from America. 2454
Authentic papers relating to the expedition
  against Carthagena: being the resolutions
  of the councils of war. 2455, 11131, 1st
  note after 99245
Authentic papers relating to the expedition
  against Carthagena. Containing original
  letters. 11132, 1st note after 99245
Authentic papers relative to the expedition
  against the Charibbs. 2456
Authentic particulars respecting the gold region.
  (10013)
Authentic proceedings of the French King.
  (2457)
Authentic rebel papers. 2458, (75198)
Authentic record of startling adventures. 34162
Authentic register of the British successes.
  2459, 30930
Authentic relation of the horrid barbarity.
  (13874)
Authentic relation of the many hardships.
  21451
Authentic report of a trial. 96895
Authentic report of the debate. 2459A, 3261
Authentic report of the testimony. 80737
Authentic sketch of San Francisco. 10002
Authentic Spanish map of America. 28460,
  1st note after 94082
Authentic speeches of S. P. Chase. 12200
Authentic statement of all the facts. 23087-
  23088
Authentic statement of the case and conduct.
  90183
Authentic story. 104699
Authentic translation of a note. 454, 2460
Authentic view of the progress of . . . Penn-
  sylvania. (59906)
Authenticated account of monies received and
  expended. 103212
Authenticated copy of the proceedings. 14092
Authentick . . . see Authentic . . .
Authentiek tractaet van vriendschap, commercie
  en navigatie. 2461, 96585
Authentische Beitrage zur Erdbeschreibung.
  1287
Avthentische Nachricht von der Verhandlung.
  2462, 4th note after 97845

Avthentische Relation von dem Anlass, Fortgang
und Schlusse. 2463, 4th note after 97845
Autheroche, Jean Chappe d'. see Chappe
d'Auteroche, Jean.
Authes, Hermann Adolphum. ed. 77201
Autheur au lecteur. 38635
Autheur tot sijn boeck. (72762)
Author. pseud. Address to the citizens. see
Cogswell, Thomas.
Author. pseud. Negro a man, but not a
brother. 82022
Author. pseud. Strictures on Montgomery on
the cotton manufactures. 50150
Author. 19010
Author, as yet, unknown. pseud. Manual of
religious liberty. 44411
Author for the first time. pseud. Falls of
Niagara. 55118
Author of "A defence of the Earl of Shelburne."
pseud. Postscript addressed to the Earl
of Stair. see O'Bryen, Denis.
Author of "A disquisition on faith," and "A
dialogue on commonwealths." pseud.
Radical. see Brown, Paul.
Author of a dramatic piece on the battle of
Bunker's Hill. pseud. Death of General
Montgomery. see Brackenridge, Hugh
Henry.
Author of A journal of travels in England,
Holland, and America, pseud. Remarks
made on a short tour. see Silliman,
Benjamin, 1779-1864.
Author of a "History of the temperance reform-
ation." pseud. Temperance anecdotes.
94641
Author of A letter to the Duke of Grafton
vindicated from the charge of democracy.
48939-(48940)
Author of A letter to the Roman Catholics of
the city of Worcester. pseud. Reply to
an address. see Wharton, Charles
Henry.
Author of A New England tale. pseud. Red-
wood; a tale. see Sedgwick, Catharine
Maria, 1789-1867.
Author of "A South-side view of slavery."
pseud. Sable cloud. see Adams,
Nehemiah.
Author of A true picture of America. pseud.
Softly, brave Yankees!!! 86210, 1st note
after 102867
Author of "A word on behalf of the slave."
pseud. Beloved crime. (81904)
Author of a "View of the state of parties in
America." pseud. Comparative view.
see M'Cormick, Samuel. supposed
author
Author of a weekly paper, entitled, The watch-
tower. pseud. Address to His Excel-
lency Sir Charles Hardy. see Livingston,
William. supposed author and Zenger,
John Peter. supposed author
Author of "A year in Spain." pseud. Sea-
service. see Mackenzie, Alexander
Slidell.
Author of "Adam Bede." pseud. Silas Marner.
see Eliot, George. pseud.
Author of Adeliade. pseud. Viola. see
Botsford, Margaret.
Author of "Allen Prescott." pseud. Alida.
see Sedgwick, Susan Ann (Livingston)
Ridley, 1789-1867.
Author of "American bards." pseud. Sisyphi
opus. see Waln, Robert, 1794-1825.

Author of American liberty, a poem, General
Gage's coliloquy, &c. psued. Voyage to
Boston. see Freneau, Philip Morin,
1752-1832.
Author of American popular lessons. pseud.
Tales from American history. see
Robbins, Eliza.
Author of An address to the government of the
United States. pseud. Monroe's embassy.
see Poplicola. pseud.
Author of An appeal to the justice and interests
of Great Britain. pseud. Speech,
intended to have been delivered. see
Lee, Arthur, 1740-1792.
Author of "Atalantis," "Southern passages and
pictures," &c. pseud. Donna Florida.
see Simms, William Gilmore, 1806-1870.
Author of "Atalantis," "Southern passages and
pictures," &c. pseud. Grouped thoughts.
see Simms, William Gilmore, 1806-1870.
Author of "Atalantis," "The Yemassee," "Guy
Rivers," "Carl Werner," &c. pseud.
Southern passages and pictures. see
Simms, William Gilmore, 1806-1870.
Author of "Austria as it is." pseud. Ameri-
cans as they are. 1265
Author of Barnes' Brief history of the United
States for schools. pseud. Barnes'
Centenary history. see Steele, Joel
Dorman.
Author of "Beasts at law." pseud. Quarter-
day. see Woodworth, Samuel.
Author of "Behemouth." pseud. Motley book.
see Mathews, Cornelius.
Author of "Beulah." pseud. Marcaria. see
Evans, A. J.
Author of "Blackbeard." pseud. Printz Hall.
65692
Author of "Brazil, &c." pseud. Arctic dis-
covery and adventure. 1919
Author of "Caius Marius," "The deformed,"
&c. &c. pseud. The forsaken. see
Smith, Richard Penn, 1799-1854.
Author of Campaigns and cruises in Venezuela.
pseud. Earthquake of Caraccas. see
Mahoney, William D. supposed author
and Vowell, Richard Longeville. supposed
author
Author of "Carolina in the olden time." pseud.
Our forefathers. see Poyas, Elizabeth
Anne.
Author of "Caste." pseud. Bond and free.
see Pike, Mary H.
Author of "Chestnut Hill." pseud. The springs.
89904
Author of "Clinton Brandshaw." pseud. East
and west. see Thomas, Frederick
William.
Author of Common sense. see Paine, Thomas, 1737-1809.
American crisis. see Paine, Thomas, 1737-1809.
Author of Common sense. pseud. Public good.
see Paine, Thomas, 1737-1809
Author of Considerations on the measures.
pseud. Further examination. see
Robinson, Matthew.
Author of Contempt on revenge. pseud.
Mysterious nothing. see S., W. pseud.
Author of conversations and letters on the
Sandwich Island Mission. pseud. Con-
versations on the mission to the Arkansas
Cherokees. see Tuttle, Sarah.
Author of Conversations and letters on the
Sandwich Islands. pseud. Village pastor.
see Tuttle, Sarah. and Lawson, J.
incorrectly supposed author

Author of Conversations on the Bombay Mission. pseud. Conversations on the Choctaw Mission. see Tuttle, Sarah.

Author of Conversations on the Bombay Mission. pseud. Letters and conversations on the Cherokee Mission. see Tuttle, Sarah.

Author of Conversations on the Indian Missions. pseud. History of the American mission. see Tuttle, Sarah.

Author of Conversations on the Sandwich Island, Bombay, and Ceylon Missions. pseud. Letters on the Chickasaw and Osage Missions. see Tuttle, Sarah.

Author of "Conversations on the Sandwich Islands." pseud. Letters on the Chickasaw Mission. see Tuttle, Sarah.

Author of Conversations on the Sandwich Islands Mission. pseud. Conversations on the Mackinaw and Green-Bay Indian Missions. see Tuttle, Sarah.

Author of Conversations on the Sandwich Islands Mission. pseud. Hugh Clifford. see Tuttle, Sarah.

Author of Cyril Thornton. pseud. Men and manners in America. see Hamilton, Thomas.

Author of "Ecarte." pseud. Wacousta. see Richardson, John.

Author of Edwin and Eltrude. pseud. Ode on the peace. see Williams, Helen Maria.

Author of "Elfie Grafton." pseud. Henry Roberts. (31421)

Author of Ethel Somers. pseud. Mary Clifton. see Smythe, James M.

Author of "Europe," &c. pseud. America. see Everett, Alexander H.

Author of "Evenings in Boston." pseud. Ramon, the rover of Cuba. see Blake, J. L.

Author of Evenings in Boston, etc. pseud. Beauties of American history. see Blake, J. L.

Author of four former letters to the people of England. pseud. Fifth letter. see Shebbeare, John, 1709-1778.

Author of 'Francis Berrian.' pseud. George Mason. see Flint, Timothy.

Author of "Francis Berrian." pseud. Shoshonee Valley. see Flint, Timothy.

Author of Free thoughts, &c. pseud. Congress canvassed. see Seabury, Samuel, Bp., 1729-1796. and Wilkins, Isaac.

Author of Free Thoughts, &c. pseud. View of the controversy. see Seabury, Samuel, Bp., 1729-1796. and Wilkins, Isaac.

Author of "Green Mountain boys." pseud. Centeola. see Thompson, Daniel Pierce.

Author of "Green Mountain boys." pseud. May Martin. see Thompson, Daniel Pierce.

Author of "Guy Livingstone." pseud. Border and battle. see Lawrence, George Alfred.

Author of "Guy Rivers." pseud. Count Julian. see Simms, William Gilmore, 1806-1870.

Author of "Guy Rivers," "Martin Faber," &c. pseud. The Yemassee. see Simms, William Gilmore, 1806-1870.

Author of "Guy Rivers," "The Yemassee," "Richard Hurdis," &c. pseud. Castle Dismal. see Simms, William Gilmore, 1806-1870.

Author of "Hard knocks, or who is first?" pseud. State Street. see Clark, William Adolphus.

Author of "Hochelaga." pseud. Conquest of Canada. see Warburton, George Drought.

Author of Homeward bound, The pioneers, &c. pseud. Home as found. see Cooper, James Fenimore, 1789-1851.

Author of "Honesty the best policy." pseud. Plain facts. 63218

Author of "Hope Leslie." pseud. see Sedgwick, Catharine Maria, 1789-1867.

Author of "Indian wars." pseud. Tales of the revolution. see Sanders, D. S. supposed author

Author of Jane and her teacher. pseud. George Wilson and his friend. 104618

Author of Julia, etc. pseud. Tales of the night. see Wood, Sally Sayward Barrell Keating.

Author of Julia, The speculator, and Amelia. pseud. Ferdinand & Elmira. see Wood, Sally Sayward Barrell Keating.

Author of "Johnny Wright," etc. pseud. Homes of the west. 32742

Author of "Leah, the forsaken." pseud. Patriot highwayman. 59083

Author of Letters and conversations on the Sandwich Island . . . Missions, pseud. Letters and conversations on the Indian Missions. see Tuttle, Sarah.

Author of Letters concerning the present state of Poland. pseud. Remarks on the principal acts. see Lind, John.

Author of "Letters from Cuba." pseud. Cuba and the Cubans. see Kimball, Richard Burleigh.

Author of Letters from Paraguay. pseud. Letters from Buenos Ayres and Chili. see Davie, John Constanse.

Author of "Letters from the mountains." pseud. Memoirs of an American lady. see Grant, Anne.

Author of "Letters from the south, . . . &c. pseud. Dutchman's fireside. see Paulding, James K.

Author of "Letters on the eastern states." pseud. Miscellanies. see Tudor, William, 1779-1830.

Author of Letters to a nobleman. pseud. Plain truth. see Galloway, Joseph, 1729?-1803.

Author of Letters to a nobleman. pseud. Reply to the observations. see Galloway, Joseph, 1729?-1803.

Author of Letters to a nobleman on the conduct of the American war. pseud. Candid examination of the mutual claims. see Galloway, Joseph, 1729?-1803.

Author of Letters to a nobleman, on the conduct of the American war. pseud. Historical and political reflections. see Galloway, Joseph, 1729?-1803.

Author of Letters to a young planter. pseud. Apology for Negro slavery. see Turnbull, Gordon.

Author of Liberal opinions. pseud. Emma Corbett. see Pratt, Samuel Jackson.

Author of Life and writings of Samuel Crothers, etc. pseud. Soldier, the battle, and the victory. see Ritchie, Andrew. supposed author

Author of "Life in the south." pseud. Stonewall" Jackson. see Hopley, Catherine C.

Author of "Life of Boone," "Kit Carson," etc. pseud. Life and adventures of Colonel David Crockett. (17469)

Author of "Lights and shadows of factory life."
pseud. Jenny Ambrose. 36050
Author of "Lights and shadows of factory life."
pseud. Rural life in New England. 74170
Author of "Long-Legged Joe." pseud. Squint-
eyed Bob. 90009
Author of Lyteria. psued. Charicles. see
Quincy, Josiah Phillips.
Author of "Martin Faber," "Atalantis." pseud.
Guy Rivers. see Simms, William
Gilmore, 1806-1870
Author of "May Martin." pseud. Locke
Amsden. see Thompson, Daniel Pierce.
Author of "May Martin, or the money diggers."
pseud. Green Mountain boys. see
Thompson, Daniel Pierce.
Author of "Mellichampe." pseud. Pelayo.
see Simms, William Gilmore, 1806-1870.
Author of Memoir of Mary Lundi Duncan.
pseud. America as I found it. see
Lundie, Mrs. J. C.
Author of Memoirs of Goerge Frederick Cooke.
pseud. Thirty years ago. see Dunlap,
William.
Author of Millenial institutions. pseud.
Millennium. 49003
Author of Monmouth, The Danish massacre,
&c. pseud. Slavery. 82108
Author of "Moral and scientific dialogues."
pseud. ed. Narrative of O. M. Spencer.
see K., P. pseud. ed.
Author of "Moral pieces in prose and verse,"
pseud. Poems. see Sigourney, Lydia
(Huntley) 1791-1865.
Author of Morals of pleasure. see Sedgwick,
Susan Ann (Livingston) Ridley, 1789-1867.
Author of "Morgan, the buccaneer." pseud.
Seven brothers of Wyoming. 79354,
105692
Author of "Mosquito, Nicaragua, and Costa
Rica." pseud. State of the great ship
canal question. 90614
Author of "My mother's gold ring," &c. &c.
pseud. Legal remedy. see Sargent,
Lucius M.
Author of nothing. pseud. The experiment.
see Ranken, ------.
Author of Observations on the means. pseud.
Interest of Great Britain. see Anderson,
James.
Author of "Our forefathers; their homes and
their churches." &c. &c. pseud. Days
of yore. see Poyas, Elizabeth Anne.
Author of "Patriotic effusions." pseud. Olio.
see Gilley, William B.
Author of "Peep of day," F. L. M. pseud.
Banished count. see Mortimer, F. L.
Author of "Pen and ink sketches." pseud.
Hand-book of Newport and Rhode Island.
see Dix, John Ross.
Author of "Pencillings by the way." pseud.
Inklings of adventure. see Willis,
Nathaniel Parker, 1806-1867.
Author of Pencilings along the way. pseud.
Romance of travel. see Willis,
Nathaniel Parker, 1806-1867.
Author of "Percy's masque." pseud. Judgment,
a vision. (36850)
Author of Picciola. pseud. Solitary of Juan
Fernandez. see Boniface, Joseph Xavier.
Author of Plain facts. pseud. The crisis.
17521
Author of Plain truth. pseud. Additions to
Plain truth. see Smith, William, 1727-
1803.
Author of Plain truth strip'd stark naked. 2464

Author of "Portraits of my married friends."
pseud. Mary Staunton. see White,
Rhoda Elizabeth (Waterman)
Author of "Precaution." pseud. Pioneers.
see Cooper, James Fenimore, 1789-1851.
Author of "Precaution." pseud. Spy. see
Cooper, James Fenimore, 1789-1851.
Author of Quaker unmasked, strip'd stark
naked. 2464A
Author of Quozziana. pseud. Daw's doings.
see Kettell, Samuel.
Author of "Random recollections of Albany."
pseud. Recollections of Cincinnati. see
Worth, Gorham A.
Author of Redwood. pseud. see Sedgwick,
Catharine Maria, 1789-1867.
Author of Regulus. pseud. Defence of the
American Congress. see Nourse, Mr.
Author of Regulus. pseud. Defence of the
resolutions and address. (19253)
Author of "Richard Hurdis." pseud. Beau-
champe. see Simms, William Gilmore,
1806-1870.
Author of Richards's Botanical dictionary.
pseud. Manual of botany. see Eaton,
Amos.
Author of Ruth's sacrifice, or life on the
Rappahannock. pseud. Poor white.
64092
Author of Royal perseverance. pseud.
Tyranny the worst taxation. 97634
Author of "Salad for the solitary." pseud.
Mosaics. see Saunders, Frederic.
Author of "Salad for the solitary," "Mosaics,"
etc. pseud. Festival of song. see
Saunders, Frederic.
Author of "Sam Slick." pseud. Americans at
home. see Haliburton, Thomas Chandler.
Author of "Sam Slick." pseud. Bubbles of
Canada. see Haliburton, Thomas Burton.
Author of "Scenes and narratives from German
history." pseud. Scenes and narratives
from the early history of the United
States of America. see Donne, M. A.
Author of "Scenes in Chusan." pseud. Scenes
in the Indian country. 77463
Author of sermons to asses. pseud. Sermons
to ministers of state. see Murray, James.
Author of "Seven years on the slave-coast of
Africa." pseud. California: its gold
and its inhabitants. see Huntley, Sir
Henry V.
Author of Siris. pseud. Two letters. 65700
Author of "Sketches and incidents." pseud.
Sketches from the study. see Stevens,
Abel.
Author of Sketches of Cantabs. pseud. Across
the Atlantic. 134
Author of Sketches of the south-west. pseud.
Rangers and regulators of the Yanaha.
see Arrington, A. W.
Author of some late pieces in the Delaware
gazette. see Coram, Robert.
"Author of some remarks, &c." pseud. 52933
Author of "Sophia Morton," and "Esther."
pseud. New year's day. (53426)
Author of Sot's paradise. pseud. Trip to
Jamaica. see Ward, Edward.
Author of "Souvenirs of a residence in Europe."
pseud. Home and the world. (32705)
Author of "Souvenirs of a summer in Germany."
pseud. Scenes on the shores of the
Atlantic. see Dickson, M. F.
Author of "Spotted Dan," etc. pseud. Sharp-
snout. 79851

Author of "Stars and stripes." pseud. The refugee. 68784

Author of Statisticus. pseud. Paradox solved. (58508)

Author of "Stories about Gen. Lafayette." pseud. Story of a revolutionary patriot. 92335

Author of Stories about the elephant. pseud. Stories about whale catching. see Tuttle, George.

Author of "Straws." pseud. Deesse. (19237)

Author [of Strictures on Montgomery on the cotton manufactures.] pseud. Strictures. 50150

Author of "Tales and sketches, such as they are." pseud. Ups and downs. see Stone, William Leete, 1792-1844.

Author of "Tales, National revolutionary," &c. &c. pseud. Fall River. see Williams, Catherine R. (Arnold)

Author of that book. pseud. Defence of the dialogue. see Dickinson, Jonathan.

Author of that work. pseud. Few notices. see Everett, Alexander H.

Author of the address to the people of Great Britain. pseud. Summary of the evidence. see Fox, William.

Author of The American fables. pseud. Indian songs of peace. see Smith, William, 1727-1803.

Author of The answer to Dr. Shebbeare and Dr. Johnson. pseud. Some observations on a pamphlet. see Baillie, Hugh.

Author of The answer to Mr. Burke's letter. pseud. Second thoughts. see Chalmers, George.

Author of the "Arkansaw doctor." pseud. Rambles of Fudge Fumble. (67620)

Author of "The attempt of the North to subdue the southerners, &c. pseud. Reply to a critique. 69680 see also Author of "Uncle John's cabin, next door to Uncle Tom's cabin." pseud.

Author of "The bethroted of Wyoming." pseud. Meredith. 47950

Author of "The backwoodsman." pseud. Chronicles of the city of Gotham. see Paulding, James Kirke, 1778-1860.

Author of the Bloody buoy, etc. etc. pseud. Bone to gnaw for the Democrats. see Cobbett, William, 1763-1835.

Author of the "Bloody charter." pseud. Age of paper. see Whiting, William.

Author of The candid examination. pseud. Reply to an address. see Galloway, Joseph, 1729?-1803.

Author of The "Cavaliers of Virginia." &c. &c. pseud. Knights of the Horse Shoe. see Carruthers, William Alexander.

Author of The cave of Morar. pseud. Poetical legends. see Tait, John.

Author of the "Child of song." pseud. Germantown. 27159

Author of the "Children's Robinson Crusoe." pseud. Story of the life of Lafayette. see Farrar, Eliza Ware (Rotch)

Author of "The church cause and the church party." pseud. American church in the protestant disruption. see Hope, A. J. B. Beresford.

Author of "The church, Rome and dissent." pseud. Bible and the common schools. see Smythe, William Herbert.

Author of The city farce, The voyage up the Thames, &c. pseud. Incle and Yarico. see. Weddell, -------. supposed author

Author of "The clockmaker." pseud. Bubbles of Canada. see Haliburton, Thomas Chandler.

Author of The comparison between the proposals. pseud. Letter of thanks. see Trenchard, John.

Author of The compendious extract, &c. pseud. Compendious extract containing the chiefest articles. 106361

Author of The compleat library. pseud. Observations on the late tryals. 97495

Author of The conduct of the allies. pseud. Some remarks on the barrier treaty. see Swift, Jonathan, 1667-1745.

Author of the Constitution of '76. pseud. Virginia convention question in 1827. see Member of the Staunton Convention. pseud.

Author of "The cruise." pseud. The caraguin. 10787

Author of The curious maid. pseud. Genuine dialogue. 26961

Author of the defence of the American congress. pseud. Letter to the Rev. Dr. Price. see Nourse, ------.

Author of The defence of the Earl of Shelburne. pseud. Remarks upon the report of a peace. see O'Bryen, Denis.

Author of The Democratiad. pseud. The guillotina. see Cobbett, William, 1763-1835.

Author of The detection of the state and situation. pseud. Enquiry into the methods. see Inhabitant of one of His Majesty's Leward Caribbee Islands. pseud.

Author of "The discovery of the sources of the Mississippi." pseud. To the public of New York. see Beltrami, Giacomo Constantino.

Author of "The district school as it was." pseud. White slavery. see Burton, Warren.

Author of "The elegy written among the ruins of an abbey. pseud. Yarico to Inkle. see Jerningham, Edward.

Author of "The Dutchman's fireside," &c. pseud. Westward ho! see Paulding, James Kirke, 1778-1860.

Author of The English empire in America. pseud. Vievv of the English acquisitions in Guinea. see Crouch, Nathaniel.

Author of "The Englishwoman in America." pseud. Aspects of religion in the United States of America. see Bird, Isabella. and Marsh, Miss C. incorrectly supposed author

Author of The essay on the treatment and conversion of African slaves. pseud. Inquiry into the effects. see Ramsay, James.

Author of The essay on ways and means. pseud. Essay upon the government. see Digges, Sir D. supposed author and Raleigh, Sir Walter, 1552?-1618. supposed author

Author of The evidence of the existence of God. pseud. Some advice to governesses and teachers. see Fenelon, ------.

Author of 'The fall of the Indian,' &c. pseud. Year, and other poems. see McLellan, Isaac.

Author of "The fall of the Nau Soung." pseud. Mohawk chief. 49856

Author of the first. pseud. Second and third letter to the whigs. 40548

Author of the first. pseud. Second appeal to the justice. see Lee, Arthur, 1740-1792.

Author of the following, about a twelve-month since. 95841

Author of the former review of the speeches, &c. &c. pseud. Second defence. see Lorimer, John G.

Author of "The forsaken." pseud. Actress of Padua. see Smith, Richard Penn, 1799-1854.

Author of "The fortunes of a colonist." pseud. Pilgrimage over the prairies. 62846

Author of the four letters to the people of England. pseud. Answer to a pamphlet. see Shebbeare, John, 1709-1788.

Author of the four letters to the people of England. pseud. Prophetic fragment. see Shebbeare, John, 1709-1788.

Author of "The Green Mountain boys." pseud. Doomed chief. see Thompson, Daniel Pierce.

Author of "The Green Mountain boys." pseud. Rangers. see Thompson, Daniel Pierce.

Author of "The historical essay on the English constitution." pseud. Plan of reconciliation. see Ramsay, Allan.

Author of the 'History of the American Board of Commissioners.' pseud. Refutation of the charges. see Tracy, Joseph.

Author of The impartial account. pseud. Fully reply. see Oglethorpe, James.

Author of "The Kentuckian in New-York." pseud. Cavaliers of Virginia. see Carruthers, William Alexander.

Author of "The kinsman." pseud. Confession. see Simms, William Gilmore, 1806-1870.

Author of The last of the Mohicans. pseud. Deerslayer. see Cooper, James Fenimore, 1789-1851.

Author of "The Leighton children." pseud. Snarly or Sharly. see Guernsey, Clara Florida.

Author of The letters of Junius. pseud. Miscellaneous works. see Boyd, Hugh.

Author of The life of God in the soul of man. pseud. Sermon preach'd on the 25th of December. see Scougal, Henry, 1650-1678.

Author of the letters signed Scipio Americanus in the Gazetteer. pseud. Address to Sir John Cust. see Scipio Americanus. pseud.

Author of The life of the ever-memorable Mr. John Hales, &c. pseud. ed. Collection of several pieces of Mr. John Locke. (41726)

Author of "The limner." pseud. Phantom barge. see Thomson, Charles West.

Author of "The Linwoods." pseud. see Sedwick, Catharine Maria, 1789-1867.

Author of The London spy. pseud. Writings. see Ward, Edward.

Author of "The magician's own book." pseud. Sociable. see Williams, Henry Llewellyn.

Author of The man of the mountain. pseud. Adventures on the banks of the Ohio. see Farnsworth, Frederick. supposed author

Author of The marriage act a novel. pseud. tr. Letters on the English nation. see Shebbeare, John, 1709-1788.

Author of The memoir of Mary Lundie Duncan. pseud. America as I found it. see Lundie, Mrs. J. C.

Author of the moral drama of the same name. pseud. Drunkard. see Smith, William Henry, 1806-1872.

Author of the 'Mountain wild flower.' pseud. Chains and freedom. see Lester, Charles Edwards.

Author of the "Narrative." pseud. View of the political conduct of Aaron Burr. see Cheetham, James.

Author of the "Northern traveller." pseud. Sketches of scenery and manners in the United States. see Dwight, Theodore, 1796-1866.

Author of the "Observations." pseud. 19251

Author of the "Observations." pseud. "Observations." see Person who Resided Several Years at Jamaica. pseud.

Author of "The old house by the river." pseud. Later years. see Prime, W. C.

Author of "The old white meeting-house." pseud. Life in New York. see Prime, Samuel Irenaeus.

Author of The olive branch. pseud. Calm address. see Carey, Mathew, 1760-1839.

Author of "The olive branch." pseud. "Look before you leap." see Carey, Mathew, 1760-1839.

Author of The olive branch. pseud. Prospects on the Rubicon. Part II. see Carey, Mathew, 1760-1839.

Author of The Owl Creek letters. pseud. Old house by the river. see Prime, W. C.

Author of the pamphlet called An answer to the Hampshire narrative. pseud. Answer to the Hampshire narrative. (30136)

Author of the "Philippiad." pseud. Boston city measured. 6490

Author of "The pilgrimage of Osmond." pseud. Lay of the last pilgrim. see Riley, William. supposed author

Author of The pilgrim's progress. pseud. News from Pensilvania. see Bugg, Francis.

Author of The plough-jogger. pseud. Political wars of Otsego. see Peck, Jedediah.

Author of the "Political crisis." pseud. Letters on the present state of England and America. see Stoddard, Amos.

Author of The political looking-glass. pseud. Duty of the king and subject. 21476

Author of "The puritan, or lay-essayist." pseud. Belle of Zion. see Withington, Leonard.

Author of The religion of science. pseud. Life of Thomas Paine. see Blanchard, Calvin.

Author of The remarks. pseud. Examiner examin'd. see Brown, John, of Higham.

Author of The remarks. pseud. Reply to the "Vindication" of "the land agent." (43948)

Author of The republic of the United States. pseud. History of democracy in the United States. see Capen, Nahum.

Author of The review. pseud. Appendix to the review of Mr. Pitt's administration. see Almon, John, 1738-1805. supposed author.

Author of The review. pseud. Essay on the south sea trade. see Allen, Robert. supposed author and Defoe Daniel, 1659?-1631.

Author of The right of the British legislature vindicated. pseud. Remarks on the new essay. 20047

Author of The ruins of Paestum. pseud. Athens and other poems. see Pickering, Henry.

Author of "The scout." pseud. Quaker partisans. see Simms, William Gilmore, 1806-1870.

Author of "The serf." pseud. Rip van Winkle. see Irving, Washington, 1783-1859.

Author of "The shoebinders of New York," etc. pseud. New York needlewoman. 54829

Author of the Snake in the grass discovered, to be a publisher of lyes. 78185

Author of "The silver bugle." pseud. Quindaro. see Hazeltine, -------.

Author of The sketch book. pseud. Letters of Jonathan Oldstyle, gent. see Irving, Washington, 1783-1859.

Author of "The sketch-book." pseud. Tour on the prairies. see Irving, Washington, 1783-1859.

Author of The sketches of the life of Greene. pseud. Remarks, critical and historical. see Johnson, William.

Author of "The spy." pseud. Monikins. see Cooper, James Fenimore, 1789-1851.

Author of The subaltern. pseud. Campaigns of the British army. see Gleig, George Robert.

Author of The theatre of the present war in North America. pseud. Reflections on the present state of affairs. see Young, Arthur.

Author of The thirty years; view. pseud. Abridgment of the debates. see Benton, Thomas Hart, 1782-1858.

Author of The thirty years' view. pseud. Historical and legal examination. see Benton, Thomas Hart, 1782-1858.

Author of "The tory outwitted." pseud. Giant spy of Bunker Hill. 27268

Author of The tours through England. pseud. Observations on the present state. see Young, Arthur.

Author of the Vindication of the government, doctrine and worship, of the Church of England, established in the reign of Queen Elizabeth. pseud. see Maddox, Isaac, successively Bishop of St. Asaph, and Worcester, 1697-1759.

Author of the voyage to Boston. pseud. General Gage's confession. see Freneau, Philip Morin, 1752-1832.

Author of the "Watch tower." pseud. ed. Narrative of a new and unusual American imprisonment. see Livingston, William, 1723-1790.

Author of The way to wealth. pseud. Countryman's companion. see Tryon, Thomas.

Author of "The wilderness." pseud. Spectre of the forest. see McHenry, James.

Author of 'Win and wear." pseud. My new home. (51620)

Author of The winter evening conversation. pseud. Winter evening conversation vindicated. see Webster, Samuel, 1719-1796.

Author of "The Yemassee." pseud. Carl Werner. see Simms, William Gilmore, 1806-1870.

Author of "The Yemassee." pseud. Mellichampe. see Simms, William Gilmore, 1806-1870.

Author of "The Yemassee." pseud. Partisan. see Simms, William Gilmore, 1806-1870.

Author of "The Yemassee," "Guy Rivers," &c. pseud. Atalantis. see Simms, William Gilmore, 1806-1870.

Author of "The Yemassee," "Guy Rivers," &c. pseud. Wigwam and the cabin. see Simms, William Gilmore, 1806-1870.

Author of "The Yemassee," "Guy Rivers," "Mellichampe," &c. pseud. Damsel of Darien. see Simms, William Gilmore, 1806-1870.

Author of "The Yemassee," "Life of Marion," "History of South Carolina." pseud Views and reviews. see Simms, William Gilmore, 1806-1870.

Author of "The Yemassee," "Life of Marion," "Life of Bayard," etc. pseud. Lily and the totem. see Simms, William Gilmore, 1806-1870.

Author of The young man's guide. pseud. Ways of living on small means. see Alcott, William Alexander.

Author of "The young man's own book." pseud. Yound lady's book. 106143

Author of "Thomas Jackson." pseud. Lilias and her cousins. 41065

Author of Thomason's men, etc. pseud. Men and things in America. see Bell, Andrew.

Author of those reasons. pseud. Remarks on the late printed answer. see Choate, John.

Author of "Thoughts on a new order of Missionaries," etc. pseud. Tribute to the memory of Fitzhugh Smith. 82548, 13th note after 96964

Author of "Three experiments of living." pseud. Tales. see Lee, Hannah F.

Author of "Tom Cringle's log." pseud. Cruise of the Midge. see Scott, Michael.

Author of Two discourses and a prayer. pseud. Prayer of Agur. see Fothergill, Samuel.

Author of "Two years and a half in the navy." pseud. Trip to Boston. see Wines, Enoch Cobb.

Author of "Uncle John's Cabin, next door to Uncle Tom's cabin." pseud. Attempt of the North to subdue the southerners. 2322 see also Author of "The attempt of the North to subdue the southerners, &c." pseud.

Author of "Uncle Philip's conversation." pseud. Adventures of Captain John Smith. see Hawks, Francis Lister.

Author of Uncle Philip's conversations. pseud. Adventures of Daniel Boone. see Hawks, Francis Lister.

Author of "Village missionaries," &c. pseud. Soldier's return. 86306

Author of "Wanted, a male cook." pseud. Stand by the flag. see Baker, George Melville.

Author of War in disguise. pseud. Dangers of the country. see Stephen, Sir James. and Brown, John. incorrectly supposed author

Author of Way marks of a wanderer. pseud. North and the south. see Rush, Caroline E.

Author of "Winter studies in the country." pseud. Rustic rhymes. 74417

Author of "Zoe," etc. pseud. Aristocrat. see Jewsbury, Geraldine Endsor.

Author turned critic. 19357

Author wishing it may be improved and enlarged. 103143

Author, who never held office under the government. pseud. Sorehead war. 87136
Authorities cited antagonistic to Horace Binney's conclusions. (35462)
Authorities given by the several governments. 32968, 1st note after 97146
Authorities on which metre psalmody stands. 84696
Authority. 94491
Authority and free will. 78380
Authority of the nation supreme and absolute. 33334
Authority of tradition considered. 103908
Authorized Agents of Seventeen of the Twenty-three Towns Proposed to be Set Off Into a New County. see Middlesex County, Mass. and Worcester County, Mass.
Authorized report of the proceedings. 66126
Author's apology for printing the same. 18554
Author's apology to the printer. 80677
Author's being absent by reason of the smallpox. 103149
Author's edition. 92467
Author's epitaph, made by himself. 67577
Author's jewel. 81370
Author's last sermon. 101171
Authors of "The West Indies in 1837." pseud. Reply. see Harvey, Thomas. and Sturge, Joseph.
Author's petition to this present Parliament. 11398, 57765
Author's philosophical contemplations, &c. 90955
Author's reasons. 90896
Author's recollections. 10616
Author's thoughts. 92802
Author's visit to Palos. 35183
Authorship, a tale. (52149)
Autikon botanikon. 67446, 67461
Auto. 98800
Auto de bueno gobierno. (56858)
Auto de la fe celebrado en Lima. (50124)
Auto del gobierno y capitania general. 52109
Auto del Provisor de Mexico. (74861)
Auto general de la fee. 48295
Auto-biografia. 98596
Autobiografia del General Jose Antonio Paez. (58136)
Autobiographical discourse. 80069
Autobiographical memoir of George Laval Chesterton. 12551
Auto-biographical memoir of Sir John Barrow, Bart. 3659
Autobiographical narrative. (24621)
Autobiographical notes, letters and reflections. 85264
Autobiographical notes [of Rev. Thomas Smyth.] 85265, 85272, 85275, 85286, 85290, 85294, 85296, 85298, 85300, 85309, 85312, 85315, 85317, 85321, 85325, 85328, 85330, 85332, 85335-85337, 85339, 85340-85341
Auto-biographical novel. 101419
Autobiographical recollections. (40198)
Autobiographical sketch [of Alfred Johnson Cotton.] 16038
Autobiographical sketch of J. B. Whitridge. 103785
Autobiographical sketches and recollections. 13227
Autobiographical sketches, in a series of letters. 10852
Autobiographie von Frederick Douglass. (20715)
Auto-biography. 28586, (37306), note after 105956

Autobiography. (29388), (44749), 51109, 52160, 52304, (55210), 72132, (79352), 80034
Autobiography. A collection of the most instructive and amusing lives. 103541
Autobiography and memorial of Captain Obadiah Conger. 12407, 15461
Autobiography and ministerial life of Rev. John Johnson. (36375)
Autobiography and personal recollections. 28082
Autobiography and reminiscences of Rev. John Graham. 28226
Autobiography, containing incidents of voyages and travels. 32457
Autobiography, correspondence, etc., of Lyman Beecher. (4328)
Autobiography, edited and supplemented by Rev. James R. Boyd. 90004
Autobiography for boys. 69067
Autobiography in verse. 7412
Autobiography of a criminal, Henry Tufts. 97416
Autobiography of a female slave. 28836
Autobiography of a new churchman. 41519
Autobiography of a New England farm-house. 11781
Autobiography of a pioneer. 62615
Autobiography of a seaman. 21273
Autobiography of a Shaker, and revelation of the Apocalypse. 23151
Autobiography of a Shaker, etc. 23193
Autobiography of a Wesleyan Methodist missionary. 16398
Autobiography [of Abel Charles Thomas.] 2d note after 95375
Autobiography of Alfred Newman. 55005
Autobiography of an actress. 51206
Autobiography of an adventurer. 18121
Autobiography of an English soldier. 2465
Autobiography of Archibald Hamilton Rowan. 73527
Autobiography [of Arthur Young.] note after 106063
Autobiography of Benjamin Franklin. 25491, 25492, 25537, (25538), 25587, 70604; 76966, 88982, 88984
Autobiography of Capt. Richard Drake. 20865
Autobiography of Charles Caldwell. 9893
Autobiography [of Chateaubriand.] 12256
Autobiography [of Colonel Boone.] 30683
Autobiography of Daniel Merrill. (47993)
Autobiography [of Daniel Webster.] note after 102255, 102257
Autobiography of David Russell. 74320
Autobiography of Dr. J. J. Polk. 63844
Autobiography of Elder Jacob Knapp. 38064
Autobiography of Elder Soborn. (57747)
Autobiography of Elihu H. Shepard. 80175
Autobiography of Elizabeth Oakes Smith. 84162
Autobiography of his son, Rev. Henry Fry. 81708
Autobiography of James Silk Buckingham. 8894
Autobiography of Jane Fairfield. (23692)
Autobiography [of John Adams.] 5th note after 95677
Autobiography of John B. Gough. 28079
Autobiography of John B. Gough, with continuation to the present time. 28080
Autobiography of John B. Gough, with orations. 28081
Autobiography of John Galt. 26455
Autobiography of Jonathan Romer. 74197
Autobiography of Joseph Smith III. 83302
Auto-biography of Lemuel Norton. 55908
Autobiography of Lemuel Sawyer. 77319
Autobiography of Levi Hutchins. 34050

Autobiography of M. W. Louie Philipps. 62453
Autobiography of Martin Van Buren. 98409, 98425
Autobiography [of Michael Wigglesworth.] 19034-19035, 103928
Autobiography of Mrs. Harriet B. Cooke. 16310
Autobiography of Parley P. Pratt. 64964
Autobiography of Peter Cartwright. 11160-11161
Autobiography of . . . Rev. Edward Mathews. 46852
Autobiography of Rev. James B. Finley. (29378), (49704), 92378, 92824
Autobiography of Rev. Tobias Spicer. 89426
Auto-biography of Sam Simple. 103961
Autobiography [of Samuel Hobart Turner.] 97492-97493
Autobiography of Samuel S. Hildebrand. 31761
Autobiography of the backwoods preacher. 11162
Autobiography of the first forty-one years. (13857)
Autobiography of the Rev. V. P. Mayerhoffer. 47116
Autobiography of Thomas Douglas. 20705
Autobiography of Thomas Shepard. 80198, 106052
[Autobiography of Thurlow Weed.] 102448
[Autobiography [of Toussaint l'Ouverture.] (42356)
Autobiography of William H. Seward. (79507)
Autobiography of William Neill. 52292
Autobiography, reminiscences and letters. 97249
Autobiography, 1787-1808. 84862
Autobiography, with appendix. (35882)
Autocrat of the breakfast table. 32621, 84185
Autodicus. pseud. Critique of The vision of Rubeta. 2466, 57755
Autograph leaves of our country's authors. 2467
Autograph miscellany. 52346
Autograph holographiani. 8394
Autographs of freedom. 28835, 92395, 92452
Autographs. The American orator appendix. 51338
Autor Americano de nombre incierto. pseud. Flores Guadalupanas. 63305
Autor da Escola mercantil. pseud. Analyse dos factos praticados. see Veiga, Manuel Luis da.
Autor de Civilizacion y barbaria. pseud. Recuerdos de Provincia. see Sarmiento, Domingo Faustino, Pres. Argentina, 1811-1888.
Autor de la "Apologia de los palos." pseud. Carta. 11092
Autor de La idea del valor de la isla Espana. pseud. America vindicada de calumnia. see Sanchez Valverde, Antonio.
Autor de La oracion funebre. pseud. Fama postuma. see Bermudez, Joseph Manuel.
Autor de Sume. pseud. Amador bueno. see Indio Moranducara. pseud.
Autor del Duelo de la inquisicion. pseud. Respuesta. see San Bartolome, Jose de.
Autor del Habanero. pseud. Recuerdo. 17802
Autor del Pacto social. pseud. Fanal. 23773
Autor del Nuevo Robinson. pseud. Descubrimiento y conquesta de la America. see Campe, J. H.
Autor des Kurzen extracts, &c. pseud. Kurzen extracts. 106352
Autora. 83788

Autores de unos papeles publicados contra el poder ejercutivo. defendants 99481
Autores dignos de eterna fama. 3646
Autorite divine, ou reponse a cette question. 5027
Autos, acuerdos y decretos de govierno del Real y Supremo Consejo de las Indias. 40050
Autos de fe, celebrades por la Inquisicion de Mexico. 93348
Autre monde. 24996
Autre officier. pseud. Journal. 23923, 73377
Autumn hours and fireside reading. 37984
Autumn in America. 46885
Autumn in Nova Scotia. 36037
Autumn leaves. (26653)
Autumn leaf. (71235)
Autumnal leaves. (12727)
Autun, Honore d'. see D'Autun, Honore.
Aux Canadiens Francais soldats de Pie IX. 39010
Aux colonies de Saint-Domingue. 75071
Aux colons de Saint-Domingue. 21483
Aux constituans de l'Assemblee Generale. 75072
Aux emigres de toutes les contrees de l'Europe. 60086
Aux Francais. 3916, 58930
Aux Francais. Le parti republicain, ses doctrines et ses hommes. 3916
Aux habitans de Saint Domingue. 75053
Aux habitans du Comte de Berthier. 62609
Aux habitants de la province du Canada. 10364
Aux Haitiens. 51704
Aux membres de la Convention Nationale. 59091
Aux pasteurs et ministres de toutes les denominations. (81900)
Aux peuples de Canada. 101689
Aux vrais amis de la patrie. 20168
Auxiliador. 5091
Auxiliador da industria nacional. 56370
Auxiliar commercial do Rio de Janeiro. 71460
Auxiliary Anti-slavery Society, Leicester, England. see Leicester Auxiliary Anti-slavery Society.
Auxiliary Bible Society, Montreal. see Montreal Auxiliary Bible Society.
Auxiliary Bible Society, Providence, R. I. see Providence Auxiliary Bible Society.
Auxiliary Bible Society, Westchester County, N. Y. see Westchester County Auxiliary Bible Society.
Auxiliary Bible Society in the County of Worcester, Mass. see Worcester County Auxiliary Bible Society.
Auxiliary Bible Society of New Brunswick. see New Brunswick Auxiliary Bible Society.
Auxiliary Bible Society of Rutland. see Rutland and Stamford Auxiliary Bible Society.
Auxiliary Bible Society of Stamford. see Rutland and Stamford Auxiliary Bible Society.
Auxiliary Bible Society of the Counties of Montgomery, Fulton and Hamilton, N. Y. 50163
Auxiliary Clay Monument Association of New York State Auxiliary Clay Monument Association.
Auxiliary Colonization Society of New Hampshire. see New Hampshire Colonization Society.
Auxiliary Colonization Society of Worcester County, Mass. see Worcester County Auxiliary Colonization Society.

Auxiliary Education Society of Strafford County, N. H. see Strafford Auxiliary Education Society.
Auxiliary Foreign Mission Society of the Worcester Central Association. see Congregational Churches in Massachusetts. Worcester Central Association. Auxiliary Foreign Mission Society.
Auxiliary Foreign Mission Society of Worcester North Association. see Congregational Churches in Massachusetts. Worcester North Association. Auxiliary Foreign Mission Society.
Auxiliary New York Bible and Common Prayer Book Society. see New York Auxiliary Bible and Common Prayer Book Society.
Auxiliary Protestant Episcopal Society, New York. see Protestant Episcopal Society for Promoting Religion and Learning in the State of New York.
Auxiliary Society, Brooklyn. see New York and Brooklyn Auxiliary Society.
Auxiliary Society, New York. see New York and Brooklyn Auxiliary Society.
Auxiliary Society for the Education of Pious Youth, Middlesex, Mass. see Middlesex Auxiliary Society for the Education of Pious Youth.
Auxiliary Society, for the Suppression of Intemperance, New Bedford, Mass. New Bedford Auxiliary Society, for the Suppression of Intemperance.
Auxiliary Unitarian Association, In the County of Worcester, Mass. see Unitarian Churches. Massachusetts. Worcester Association.
Auxiliary Unitarian Association in Providence, R. I. see Providence Auxiliary Unitarian Association.
A'Vache, Haiti. 58472
Aval, Charles Yvres Cousin d'. see Cousin d'Aval, Charles Yvres, called Cousin d'Avalon.
Avalanche, Sir Anthony. pseud. Fashion's analysis. see Blauvelt, -------.
Avalle, -------. 2468
Avalon, ------. 103331
Avalon, Cousin d'. see Cousin d'Aval, Charles Yvres, called Cousin d'Avalon.
Avalos, Felice Antonio de Christoforo d'. see Christoforo d'Avalos, Felice Antonio de.
Avalos y Bracamont, Pedro Alonso de, Conde de Miravalles. plaintiff 98966
Avalos y Chauca, Jose Joaquin de. (11454)
Avalos y Figueroa, Diego d'. 2469
Avant-propos et notes par M. Fs. Barruere. 78916
Avanteurs de M. Robert Chevalier. 40157
Avanturen van de kleine Scipio. 78126
Avantures du Sr. C. Le Beau. 39582
Avary, Myrta Lockett. 91279
Avaugour, le Comte ------- Du Parc d'. see Du Parc d'Avaugour, -------, le Comte.
Avaux, ------d'. (39804)
Ave-Lallemant, Friedrich Christian Benedict, 1809-1892. 2470
Ave-Lallemant, Robert Christian Berthold. 2471-2474, 38690
Avecilla, Pablo de. see Pablo de Avecilla.
Aveledo, Agustin. (76782)
Avellan, Juan de. 16185, (43392)
Avellaneda, Gertrudis Gomez de. see Gomez de Avellaneda, Gertrudis.
Avellino Ferreira e Souza, Bernardo. see Ferreira e Souza, Bernardo Avellino.

Avenant, Charles d'. see Davenant, Charles, 1656-1714.
Avenant, Sir William d'. see Davenant, Sir William, 1606-1668.
Avendano, Diego de. 2376
Avenger of blood. 70907, 81250
Avenging brother; or, the two maidens. 34776
Avenia. 7375
Avenir du monde. 12264
Aventuras de Aristonoo. (12268)
Aventura de Arturo Gordon Pym. 63529
Aventuras de Carlos y Fanny. 38402
Aventuras y conquistas de Hernan Cortes en Mejico. 16944-16945
Aventures chez les sauvages. 11189
Aventures de Don Juan de Vargas. 36794
Aventures de guerre. 50551
Aventures de Jacques Sadeur. 74820-74822
Aventures de Monsieur Robert Chevalier. 4163
Aventures de Miles Vallingford. 16410
Aventures de quelques naufrages dans des pays inconnus. 100806
Aventures de Robinson Crusoe. 72219
Aventures de terre. 69052
Aventures de terre et de mer. 69019
Aventures d'Hercule Hardi. 93411-93414
Aventures diverses de Clairancy. 100805
Aventures du Chevalier Dumirail. 19534
Aventures de dernier Abencerrage. 12248
Aventures du derniere Abencerage. 12248
Aventures d'un jeune emigre Francais en 1830. 44699
Aventures d'un officier Americain. 69020
Aventures d'une colonie d'emigrants en Amerique. 27194
Aventures d'une famille Allemande emigree en Amerique. 19530
Aventures d'une famille perdue dans les solitudes de l'Amerique. 69048
Aventures et conquetes de Cortes au Mexique. (16952)
Aventures et conquetes de Fernand Cortez au Mexique. 39621
Aventures les plus curieuses des voyageurs. 32701
Aventures Mexicaines. 21367
Aventures tragi-comiques d'Amb. Gwinett. 10668
Aventurier. 93417
Aventurier Parisien. 96171-96172
Aventuriers et corsaires. 23546
Averay, -------. 2477, 8067
Averill, Leonard B. 2478
Avertimenti amichevoli all'erudito tradottore romano. 9763
Avertissement a la Grande-Bretagne et a ses colonies. (4667)
Advertissement sur les manoeuvres. (61271)
Avery, -----. 84616-84617, 84647
Avery, Benjamin. 84566
Avery, David. 2479-2480
Avery, Edward. 2481
Avery, Elizabeth (Parker) 58769
Avery, Ephraim K. defendant (2482)-2483, 2485-2486, 29887, (31792), note after 92848, 96818, 1st note after 99826
Avery, John. 2487
Avery, Joseph, fl. 1806. 2488
Avery, Joseph, fl. 1845. 94923
Avery, Robert. USA (31083)
Avery, Rufus. (2489), (67952)
Avery (William L.) firm publisher 75273
Avery Glibun. 54960
Avery's business directory for the city of Saint John. 75273

Aves, Thomas. 2490
Aves. 74921
Aves de la isla de Cuba. (39988)
Avezac-Macaya, Armand d', 1800-1875. 2491-
2493A, 11139, 27788, 30604, (43971),
68443
Avezac-Macaya, Marie Armand Pascal d'. see
Avezac-Macaya, Armand d', 1800-1875.
Aviados De la Mina de Jagal, Martinique.
plaintiffs (44966)
Aviendo entendido la materia que se contro-
vierte. 61081
Aviendo prevenido en el papel antecedente.
61081
Aviendo representado el Conde de Monterey a
Su Majestad. (22181)
Avignon, ------d'. see D'Avignon, -------.
Avignon, Francis J. D. ed. 55804
Avila, Francisco de. 2494-2495
Avila, Juan de. see Juan de Avila.
Aviles, J. M. defendant 11294
Avis. 95332
Avis a ceux qui se proposent de passer dans
les Etats-Unis d'Amerique. 7802
Avis a ceux qui voudroient aller s'etablir sur
l'Amerique. 25596
Avis a l'auteur de la lettre. 106045
Avis a particolari delle Indie di Portugallo.
7523
Avis au Canada. 99596
Avis au relieur. 95349
Avis Au Roi sur les affaires de la Nouvelle-
France. 10363
Avis au Roi sur les affaires de la Nouvelle
France en 1620. 56082
Avis aux habitants des colonies. 38611
Avis aux Hessois. 2496, (49392)
Avis aux ordres privilegies. 3415
Avis de . . . [A. de Mendoza] sur les pres-
tations. 94854
Avis de la Compagnie du Scioto. 78123
Avis de l'editeur. 73511
Avis de M. le Baron van des Capellen. 97254
Avis des Conseils Coloniaux. 67154
Avis des Conseils Speciaux et Coloniaux.
22831
Avis divers. 75123
Avis divers et petites affiches Americaines.
(75044), 75073
Avis du Cap. (75044)
Avis du libraire. 100708
Avis du Roi sur les affaires de la Nouvelle-
France en 1620. 10365
Avis d'un bon patriote. (2497)
Avis pour elever le prince destine a regner.
98983
Avis sur la vente de 1180 actions de la Com-
pagnie de Colonisation. 94004
Avis sur les maladies de St. Domingue. 38566
Aviso al pueblo. 97039
Aviso al pueblo sobre las proximas elecciones.
(17753)
Aviso de 15 de Marco de 1870. 88805
Aviso del ciudadano Mariano Tramarria.
96448
Aviso-eIecciones, Feb. 16, 1826. 14558
Aviso historico, politico, geographico con las
noticias del Peru. 685
Avitium, Petrum d'. see Avity, Pierre d',
Sieur de Montmartin, 1573-1635.
Avity, -------, Sieur d'. Avity, Pierre d',
Sieur de Montmartin, 1573-1635.
Avity, Pierre d', Sieur de Montmartin, 1673-
1635. 2498, 18911-18913, 26858, (28070),
41288, note after 69259, note after 105742

Avocat. pseud. Traite sur la politique colon-
iale du Bas-Canada. see Mondelet,
Dominique.
Avocat au Parlement de Paris. pseud. Pat-
riote Anglois. see Le Blanc, Jean
Bernard. supposed author
Avocat pour et contre. 39299
Avondschemering. (5370)
Avontuerlijcke vreemde ende waerachtige
beschrijving. 90043
Avonturen, gedurende een tweejarig verblijk in
Californie. 74533
Avonturen in de wouden en prairien van Amerika.
4432A
Avontuurlijke reys-togten van Johan Smith.
82817-82818, 82854
Avontuurlijke reyze en Raven's reyze na
Groenland. 6337
Avowals of a republican. 103477
Avrainville, Arthur d'. tr. 67081
Avrigny, C. J. Loeuillard d'. 2500
Awake from your slumber's let gratitude kindle.
103149
Awake, my fair, the morning springs. (63893)
Awake O spirit of the north. (6424)
Awakener, making a brief essay. 46580, 2d
note after 99604
Awakening for the unregenerate. 46568
Awakening soul-saving truths. (46633)
Awakening thoughts on the sleep of death.
46226, 46619
Awakening truths tending to conversion. (46634)
Award of premiums. 57341
Awards, 1857. (37488)
Away to the wilderness. 2501
Away with the colonies. (27830), 96075
Awbron's nationair. 8447
Awe-ful po'm by Awe-thur the Capt'n. 41452
Awe-thur the Capt'n. pseud. Awe-ful po'm.
41452
Awful beacon. 102741-102742
Awful calamities. 2502, 80539
Awful calamity! 95282
Awful calamity at Richmond. 71168
Awful crisis. 100428
"Awful disclosures," a hum-bug. (49996)
Awful disclosures of Maria Monk. (49992),
84021, 92145
Awful exposures of the atrocious plot. 49994
Awful murder. 89626
Awful sentence. 35973
Awful treason against the will of God. 85129
Awful view. 102465
Awful warning to the youth of America. (75023)
Ayala, Juan de Mendoza. see Mendoza Ayala,
Juan de.
Ayala, Pedro de. 10807
Ayala, Pedro Lopez de. see Lopez de Ayala,
Pedro
Ayala, Sebastian Lopez de Guzman y. see
Lopez de Guzman y Ayala, Sebastian.
Ayala, T. Oritz de. see Oritz de Ayala, T.
Ayala i Mendrano, -----. 44280
Ayala y Aguilar, J. de. 44279
Ayamo moyolpachihuitia in Totlatocatzin. 98850
Ayanque, Simon. pseud. Lima por dentro y
fuera. see Terralla y Landa, Esteban de.
Ayanques, Simon. pseud. Lima por dentro y
fuera. see Terralla y Landa, Esteban de.
Ayanz, Geronimo de. 70095 see also Spain.
Comendador de Ballesteros.
Aycinena, Juan. 2505-2506
Aycinena, Mariano, Pres. Guatemala. 29079
see also Guatemala. Presidente, 1827-
1829 (Aycinena)

Aycrigg, B. 2507
Aycrigg, B. B. 2508
Aydelott, B. P. (2509)-2511
Aydelott, William J. 45090
Ayer, James C. 2512
Ayer, J. Winslow. 2513
Ayer, Samuel H. 52810
Ayers, Elisha. (2514)
Ayes de la aguila Mexicana. 75607, note after 98317-98318
Ayeta, Francisco. 76776
Ayeta, Francisco de. 73859
Ayguals de Izo, Wenceslao. see Izco, Wenceslao Ayguals de.
Ayllon, Cecilio. 79183
Ayllon, Juan de. (2414)
Ayllon Laynez, Juan de. see Laynez, Juan de Ayllon.
Aylmer, -------. 1st note after 97148, 105081
Aylmer, F. (2516)
Aylmer, Louisa Anne. (2517)
Aylmer, Matthew Whitmore, 5th Baron. 1775-1850. 2519, (5218)-5219, (10535), note after (10557), 4th note after 42522, 67113, 93716 see also Canada. Governor General, 1830-1835 (Aylmer)
Ayme, Jean Jacques. 544-545, 2521, 9369
Aynge, G. A. supposed author 2, note after 94577
Ayrault, Charles. 2523
Ayres, J. A. 2524
Ayres, Philip. 79781
Ayres de Casal, Manuel, b. 1754? (2525), 2526, 11640, 31314
Ayes de Cazal, Manoel. see Ayres de Casal, Manuel, b. 1754?
Ayscough, George Edward. ed. (42890)
Ayscough, S. 50198
Ayscough, Samuel. 2527, (17497), 1st note after 69470
Ayton, the Armenian. 66686
Ayuntamiento constitucional de Nuevitas. (17751)
Ayuntamiento de Puebla. 66546
Ayuntamiento . . . de Tlaxcala. 95878
Azais, Jean Pierre Hyacinthe. 2528
Azambuja, Joaquim Maria Nascentes de. 53590
Azambuja, Jose Bonifacio Nascentes d'. see Nascentes d'Azambuja, Jose Bonifacio.
Azana, Jose de. (2529)
Azaph, -----. 76838
Azara, Agustin de. 2543, 2539
Azara, Felix de. (2531)-(2544)
Azcarate, M. M. defendant 65926
Azebedo, Balthasar de. 12974
Azeredo Coutinho, Jose Joaquim da Cuna de. see Cuna de Azeredo Coutinho, Jose Joaquim da.
Azero y Aldovera, Miguel de. 2545
Azevedo, J. Lucio de. 99519, 99524
Azevedo, Joao Ignacio d'. 85772
Azevedo, Leonardo de Souza Leitte. see Souza Leitte Azevedo, Leonardo de.
Azevedo Pizarro y Araujo, Jose de Sousa. 2546, 63186
Azilia. 51193
Azo, -----. see Asso y del Rio, Ignacio Jordan de, 1742-1804.
Azor, ou les Peruviens. 23859, 73846
Azotan, Berdugo. 94286
Azote literario por el democratia. 23716
Aztec city of Sumai. 55012
Aztec Club. 48390
Aztecas. 61171

Azua e Yturgoyen, Pedro Phelipe de, Abp. 65553 see also La Concepcion, Chile (Diocese) Bishop (Azua e Yturgoyen) and Santa Fe, Colombia (Archdiocese) Archbishop (Azua e Yturgoyen)
Azvcena de Qvito. 9665, 50508
Azurara, -----. 76843
Azuzena entre espinas. (63972)

B

B. pseud. Dialogue between A and B. 19924
B. pseud. Dialogue on cheap postage. 64478
B. pseud. In the eleventh month. see Browne, John, of Nevis.
B. pseud. Observations relative to the establishment. 102769
B. pseud. Present attempt. see Morse, Samuel Finley Breese, 1791-1872.
B. pseud. Proposals of traffick and commerce. see A. and B. pseud.
B. pseud. Reconstruction. see Bourne, William Oland.
B. pseud. Reise nach den unbekandten Sud-Landen. see Behrens, Karl Friedrich.
B. pseud. Some miscellaneous observations. see Willard, Samuel, 1640-1707.
B. pseud. Supplement to the essay. see Bordley, John Beale. supposed author
B. pseud. Tavares de la razon. 96506
B. pseud. Yellow fever. see Bordley, John Beale. supposed author
B . . . pseud. Washington. 101889
B-----, Prof. pseud. ed. Up country letters. 44384
B-----nd, Mr. supposed author Rights of the English colonies. 71380
B-----r, -----. pseud. Letters. see Barber, Jonathan.
B., ----- de. pseud. tr. see Barentin de Montchal, Charles Paul Nicolas, Vicomte, 1737-1824.
B***, ----- de. pseud. Histoire de l'expedition de trois vaisseaux. see Behrens, Karl Friedrich.
B., -------- Le, Sieur. see Le B., --------, Sieur.
B., A. pseud. Account of the late revolution[s] in New England. see Byfield, Nathanael.
B., A. pseud. Brief representation of the case. 43663, (45031), (65578), 96298
B., A. pseud. Considerations on slavery. see Appleton, Nathaniel, of Boston.
B., A. pseud. Considerations on the agreement of the Lords Commissioners. see Franklin, Benjamin, 1706-1790. supposed author and Wharton, Samuel. supposed author
B., A. pseud. Impartial enquiry. 88183
B., A. pseud. Letter from a merchant in London. see Tucker, Josiah, 1712-1799.
B., A. pseud. Letter strongly opposed to emancipation. (40376)
B., A. pseud. Rawleigh, his ghost. 67599
B., A. pseud. Report. see Weymouth, Mass. South Parish. Committee of Inquiry.
B., A. pseud. Six letters. 2549
B-----, A-----. pseud. State of the island of Jamaica. 35663, 90615
B., A. pseud. tr. see Bussaeus, A. tr.
B . . . . . ., A.-J. pseud. Notice sur l'ile Saint-Lucie. 2550
B., B. pseud. Coast survey. (13824)

B

B., B. pseud. Entertainment for a winter's evening. see Green, Joseph.
B., B. pseud. Lines sacred to the memory. 101479
B., B. pseud. Modest enquiry. see Franklin, Benjamin, 1706-1790.
B., B. pseud. Strictures. 92859
B., B. B. pseud. tr. 77470
B., C. pseud. ed. Reliquiae Haenkeanae. 29503
B., C. pseud. tr. 88946
B., C., Gent. pseud. Poem on the late massacre in Virginia. see Brooke, Christopher.
B., C. B. pseud. Wieland. see Brown, Charles Brockden, 1771-1810.
B., C. de. pseud. ed. see Beauregard, Couvray de.
B***, C. de. pseud. Histoire des navigations. see Brosses, Charles de, 1709-1777.
B——, C—— de la. pseud. Life in Mexico. see Calderon de la Barca, Frances Erskine Inglis.
B., C. F. pseud. Poems. see Briggs, Charles F.
B., C.-G.-D. pseud. De la necessite. see Beaulieu, Charles Gillston de.
B . . . ., Constantia von. pseud. tr. 105591
B., D. pseud. tr. see Dubourg, ------. tr.
B . . . . d, D . . S . . pseud. Treatise on the law and the Gospel. 96748
B., D. de P. y. pseud. Sobre-carta al ciudadano Pacifico de San Francisco. see Vera y Pintado, Bernardo.
B . . . . de S., M. pseud. see S., M.
B. . . . de. pseud.
B . . . . -Duvallon, ------. pseud. Vue de la colonie. see Berquin-Duvallon, -------.
B., E. pseud. Declaration of the sad and great persecution. see Burrough, Edward.
B——, E. pseud. Honor of the University of Oxford defended. see Bentham, Edward.
B——, E——. pseud Mr. E— B——'s answer. see Burke, Edmund. spurious author
B., E. pseud. tr. 63697, 97913
B----g---l, E----ce. pseud. Vindication. see Budgel, Eustace, 1686-1737.
B--g-ll, E-st-ce. pseud. Speech. see Budgel, Eustace, 1686-1737.
B., F. pseud. Causes of the present distractions. see Bernard, Sir Francis, 1712-1779.
B——, F——. pseud. Causes of the present distractions. see Bernard, Sir Francis, 1712-1779.
B--t, F---l. pseud. Letter, from one in Boston. see Dudley, Paul.
B., F. pseud. see Fisher, Benjamin. supposed author
B., F. pseud. tr. see Brooke, Francis. tr.
B., G. pseud. Revived puritan. 103578
B., G. B. D. pseud. Sphere des deux mondes. see Boileau de Bouillon, Giles, 16th cent.
B., G. H. pseud. Uses and value of congress. see Bates, G. H.
B., H. pseud. Boston almanack. 6481, 92743
B., H. pseud. Leaders. see Binney, Horace.
B., H. pseud. tr. 92624
B., I. pseud. Description of the province. see Blackwell, Isaac.

B., I. N. C. pseud. Grundriss von Nordamerika. 29012
B., J. pseud. Account of the French usurpation. 2554
B., J. pseud. Account of the present state of Nova Scotia. 56104
B., J. pseud. Almanac for 1669. see Brown, J.
B., J. pseud. Leaves from the note-book of a New York detective. 39553
B., J. pseud. Letter to a member of Parliament. 2555, 40403
B., J. pseud. Life of Jeremy Belknap. see Marcou, Jane (Belknap)
B., J. pseud. Merchants' avizo. see Browne, John, fl. 1589.
B., J. pseud. Plaine and true relation. see Baers, Joannem.
B., J. pseud. Poem occasioned by the rise and fall. 2556
B., J. pseud. What is a ghost? see Brent, H. J.
B., J., Curate of N—th—t. pseud. Remarks on the continuation. 103535
B., J., Friend of the Aborigines Protection Society. pseud. Young patriot. see Burtt, John.
B., J., Middletown, Conn. pseud. To the reader. see Barrat, Joseph.
B., J., Philomathemat. pseud. 1669. An almanack of coelestial motions. see Browne, Joseph. supposed author
B., J. F. pseud. tr. 35540
B., J. M. A. pseud. Sobre eleccion de compromisarios. 85672
B., J. W. pseud. Triunfo de la religion. see Barquera, Juan Wenceslao.
B., L. pseud. ed. Kalifornien, das Goldland. 10015
B., L. pseud. National currency. 51961
B., L. M. pseud. Voyage a la Guyane. see Barbe-Marbois, Francois de, Marquis, 1745-1837.
B . . . . . , L . . . . . M . . . . . , Armateur. pseud. Voyage a la guiane. see Prudhomme, Louis.
B., M. pseud. Letter to the West India merchants. 40546, 3d note after 102846
B., M. pseud. Marcha patriotica. 98906
B**, M. pseud. tr. see Bourrit, Marc Theod. tr.
B***, M. pseud. Voyages interessans. see Bourgeois, Auguste Anicet.
B., M. A. G. pseud. Notice sur la republique orientale de l'Uruguay. see Bellemare, M. A. G.
B***, M. D. pseud. Novelles considerations sur Saint-Domingue. see Buisson, Paul Ulrich de.
B***, M. D. pseud. tr. 1288A, note before 99759
B., M. E. pseud. Poems and tales. see Blake, Mary E.
B., M. R. F. de la. pseud. Kalendario manuel Americano. 48509
B., N. pseud. Constables pocket book. 2557, 16004
B., N. pseud. Copie de qvelqves letres. see Barre, Nicolas.
B., N. L. pseud. Canal de Nicaragua. see Napoleon III, Emperor of the French, 1808-1873.
B., O. pseud. Five letters to my neighbor Smith. see Goodrich, Samuel Griswold, 1793-1860.

246

B., Oct. pseud. Histoire de la conquete du Mexique. see D'Exauvillez, Octave Boistel.
B., P. pseud. ed. Brief account. 96179
B., P. pseud. tr. see Bolona, Pablo. tr.
B., R. pseud. tr. see Crouch, Nathaniel, 1632?-1725?
B., R. pseud. English heroe. see Burton, Robert.
B., R. pseud. History and present state of Virginia. see Beverley, Robert.
B., R. pseud. Vievv of the English acquisition in Guinea. see Crouch, Nathaniel.
B., R. pseud. View of the valley of the Mississippi. see Bache, Richard. supposed author and Baird, Robert. supposed author
B., R. pseud. William B. Reed. see Rush, Benjamin.
B., R. C. pseud. Essais politiques. see Rutledge, Jean Jacques.
B., S., Philomathemat. pseud. Almanack for the year of Our Lord 1657. 62743
B., S. C. pseud. tr. 80288
B., S. G. pseud. Biography of self-taught men. Continuation. 21890
B., S. O. pseud. Memoir of Sidney Smith. see Beeton, S. O.
B., T. pseud. Observations upon Prince Rupert's white dogge. (2558)
B., T. pseud. Sic in se sua per vestigia volvitur annuc. see Brattle, Thomas.
B., T. T. pseud. Observations on American independency. 2559
B., V. D. pseud. Leeven en Daden. see Bos or Bosch, in Latin Sylvius, Lambertus van den.
B., W. pseud. see Broedleth, Wilhelm. publisher
B., W. pseud. Discourse of the variation of the campas. see Burroughs, W.
B., W. pseud. Commemoration of those poems. see Bradford, William. supposed author
B., W. pseud. Proceedings relative to the Danish brig Hope. see Bingham, William.
B., W. pseud. To the reader. see Bradford, William.
B., W. pseud. Voyage round the world. 64390
B., W. pseud. tr. 67357
B., W., Gent. pseud. Militia discipline. see Breton, William.
B., W. B. pseud. Abraham Lincoln's character. 2562
B., W. B. pseud. Baltimore: or long long time ago. see Buchanan, W. B.
B., W. D. pseud. Roscrans' campaign. see Bickham, William D.
B., W. H. M. pseud. tr. 98670, 98674
B., W. S. pseud. Memoir. 7495
B., W. S. A. pseud. Antigonian and Bostonian beauties. see Chauncy, Charles, 1705-1787.
B., W. W. pseud. Tribute. see Beldene, W. W.
B. D. B., G. pseud. Sphere des deux mondes. see Boileau de Bouillon, Gilles, 16th cent.
B. de *****, J. M. pseud. Lettres. see Saint Victor, Jacques Maximilien Benjamin Bins de.
B. d'E., E. pseud. Essai sur cette question. see Enqel, Samuel.
B . . . . de S., M. pseud. see S., M.
B . . . . de. pseud.

B . . . .-Duvallon, --------. pseud. Vue de la Colonie. see Berquin-Duvallon, ---------.
B. A. S. pseud. reporter see S., A. B. pseud. reporter
B. B. pseud. see B., B. pseud.
B. B. pseud. see Franklin, Benjamin, 1706-1790.
B. B. pseud. see Green, Joseph.
B. B. B. pseud. tr. see B., B. B. pseud. tr.
B. B. D. V. pseud. tr. see V., B. B. D. pseud. tr.
B. C. pseud. see C., B. pseud.
B. C. pseud. see Colman, Benjamin, 1673-1747.
B. C. D. Surinamensia Grilliana cum consensu Ampliss. Facult. Med. 93764
B*** D. pseud. see Buisson, Paul Ulric de.
B*** D***. pseud. see Baudry des Lozieres, Louis Narcisse.
B. Ey. O. pseud. see O., B. Ey. pseud.
B. F. pseud. see Franklin, Benjamin, 1706-1790.
B. G. D. pseud. see Gerbier, Sir Baltazar, 1592?-1667.
B. I. D. P. E. pseud. see Boulanger, Nicolas Antoine.
B. J. D. pseud. see Desmaulants, J. B.
B. J. L. et E. pseud. see M. B. J. L. et E. pseud.
B. K. pseud. see Keach, Benjamin.
B. K. L. pseud. see L., B. K. pseud.
B. K. Z. pseud. see Hall, Frederick.
B. L. M. de V. pseud. see Villarroel, Hipolito. supposed author
B. Ludewig. pseud. see Zinzendorff, Nicolaus Ludwig, Graf von, 1700-1760.
B. Ludewig's wahrer Bericht de dato Germantown. 42642, note after 106351, 106359
B. M. pseud. see M., B. pseud.
B. Mendel, Moses. see Moses B. Mendel.
B. N. pseud. see N., B. pseud.
B. S. pseud. see S., B. pseud.
B. T. pseud. see T., B. pseud.
B. T. pseud. see Teall, Benjamin.
B. T. pseud. see Tompson, Benjamin.
B. V. pseud. see Vera y Pintado, Bernardo.
B. V. O. pseud. see O., B. V. pseud.
B. van L. pseud. see L., B. van. pseud.
B. W. pseud. see W., B. pseud.
Baader, Friedrich. 2563
Baaius, G. 2564
Baarle, Casper. see Baerle, Kaspar van, 1584-1648.
Baars, J. (2565)
Babbidge, Charles. 2566
Babbit, E. B. USN defendant at court martial 2568
Babbitt, Benjamin B. 2567
Babbitt, E. D. ed. 66962
Babbitt, Elijah. 2569-2570
Babbitt, Nathan G. 99554
Babcock, Adam. plaintiff 90433
Babcock, Charles. 2571
Babcock, Elisha. 93017, 93019, 93025
Babcock, George R. 2572
Babcock, J. S. (2573)
Babcock, James F. 89199
Babcock, O. M. (72397)
Babcock, Rufus. 2574, 59487, 88856
Babcock, Samuel B. 2572-(2577)
Babcock, William G. (2578)
Babcock family. (2579)
Babeuf, Julius. 89849
Babeuf's directory of Springfield, Illinois. 89849
Babi, Antonio Garcia. tr. 64902

Babie, F. 2580, 70904
Babilon, ----. 58566
Babin, ------. defendant 47527
Babinet, -----. cartographer 73429
Babo, Franz Joseph Maria. 2581, 104839
Babson, John J. (2582)
Baby and the bards. 1308
Babylons fall in Maryland, &c. 38886, 92940
Baca, Alvar Nunez Cabaza de. see Cabeza de
    Vaca, Alvar Nunez, 1490?-1557.
Bacan, Alvaro de, Marques de Santa Cruz.
    see Santa Cruz, Álvaro de Bacan,
    Marques de.
Bacardi, Alejandro. 2583
Baccalaureate address . . . at . . . Geneva
    College. 29615
Baccalaureate address, . . . at . . . Lagrange
    College. 58195
Baccalaureate address . . . August 7, 1839.
    29615
Baccalaureate address . . . before . . .
    Antioch College. 31864
Baccalaureate address, by the president of the
    college. 87991
Baccalaureate address . . . Geneva College,
    August 1, 1838. 29615
Baccalaureate address . . . October 3, 1832.
    41315
Baccalaureate address, . . . on the sixth
    anniversary commencement. 41315
Baccluareate address . . . September 15, 1850.
    38310
Baccalaureate address to the graduating class.
    62719
Baccalaureate addresses. 105121
Baccalaureate delivered at Antioch College.
    44324
Baccalaureate discourse. 66229
Baccalaureate discourse . . . at Dartmouth
    College. 82340
Baccalaureate discourse . . . at Dartmouth
    College, July 17, 1870. 82333
Baccalaureate discourse . . . at Middlebury,
    Vermont. 38401
Baccalaureate discourse to the class of 1858.
    42045
Baccalaureate discourse, . . . to the senior
    class. 43324
Baccalaureate in Miami University . . .
    August 8th, 1844. (36934)
Baccalaureate in Miami University . . .
    August 11th, 1842. (36934)
Baccalaureate in Miami University . . .
    August 10th, 1843. (36934)
Baccalaureate sermon. 103173
Baccalaureate sermon and ordination and poem.
    59346
Baccalaureate sermon and ordination and poem.
    Class of 1870. 59354
Baccalaureate sermon [at] . . . Indiana State
    University. (56346)
Baccalaureate sermon, delivered at Williams-
    town, Mass. 32940
Baccalaureate sermon . . . June 23, 1867.
    (30876)
Baccalaureate sermon preached in Calvary
    Church. 17277
Baccalaureate sermon, to the graduating class
    of Washington College. 78321
Baccalaureate sermons and occasional dis-
    courses. 32937
Bacchiani, Alessandro. 99281
Bacco in America. (44091)
Bacellar, Antonio Barbosa. 2584
Bach, Moritz. 2585, 2586, 38319, 57902

Bacharel. pseud. ed. Peculio do Procurador
    de segunda instância. 59507
Bache, Alexander Dallas, 1806-1867. 2587-
    (2588), 6723, 12081, 13821, (56465),
    61561, 76554, 76647, 85072, 87396 see
    also U. S. Coast and Geodetic Survey.
    Superindentent.
Bache, Benjamin Franklin, 1769-1798. 2589,
    31759, 96575, 101878
Bache, Benjamin Franklin, 1769-1798. supposed
    author 20994, (69388), 97270, 101878
Bache, Franklin. 2590
Bache, Hartman. note after 60249, note after
    104493
Bache, Louis. USA defendant at court martial
    (2591)
Bache, Richard. (2592), 60398, note after 95821
    see also Constitutional Society of Penn-
    sylvania, Philadelphia. Chairman.
Bache, Richard. USA 2593-2594, 99586
Bache, Richard Meade. 2595
Bache, William. 2596
Bachelder, Samuel. 2597
Bacheler, Origen. (2598), 82130, note after
    98777
Bacheler, Origen. defendant 2599, 4th note
    after 103741
Bacheler, W. reporter (2600)
Bachelet, Louis. 2601
Bachelier de Salamanque. 40159
Bacheller, Samuel. defendant before church
    council 2603-2604, 29853, 31052, 99795
Bachelor of Salamanca. 40160
Bachelors, and other tales. 38084
Bachelor's button. 84870
Bachelor's Christmas. 81199
Bachelor's journal. 105956
Bachelor's reverie. 49672, 49677
Bachelor de la Pylaie, A. J. M. 2605-2606,
    24802
Bachiler, John. 17091
Bachiller y Morales, Antonio. (2607)-2611
Bachiller D. Diego de Valladolid, Presbitero.
    98368
Bachiller Gabriel de Soria, hijo de padres
    nobles y principales. 87156
Bachman, John, 1790-1874. 2367-2368, 2612,
    (51024), 82393, 85298, 87373
Bachschmid, Paul. 81144
Back, Sir George, 1796-1878. 2613-2618,
    (25624), 31601, 37963, 85145-85146,
    85619
Back Bay improvement. (58853)
Back-bone. 20358
Back from the dead. 84128
Back-Inhabitants of the Province of Pennsylvania.
    see Pennsylvania (Colony) Citizens
    Petitioners.
Back settler. pseud. Address of a back settler.
    389
Back settler. pseud. Some fugitive thoughts on
    a letter signed Freeman. 86648
Backer, ------- de. 1st note after 98488
Backer, Alois de. (2619)
Backer, Augustin de. (2619)
Backhaus, Johann Gottlieb. 2620
Backsettler. pseud. [Pamphlet.] 14963
Backus, Azel. 2622
Backus, Charles. 2623, 104963-104964
Backus, G. B. 90708
Backus, Isaac, 1724-1806. 1786, 2624-2632,
    24439, (45801), 86855, 91795, 92165,
    93622, 97263, 104716
Backus, J. S. 2636, 37583
Backus, John C. 2633-2634

Backus, Joseph. 2635
Backus, L. S. 51601
Backus, Samuel. 104764
Backus, Samuel D. 13591
Backus, Simon. 2637
Backus, William. 13591
Backus and Kenyon on secret societies. 2636, 37583
Backward glances. 84375
Backwood leaves. 41020
Backwood rangers. 75249
Backwoods and prairies. 69798-68799
Backwoods boy who became a minister. 63038
Backwoods expedition. 39072
Backwoods of Canada. 96441
Backwoods preacher. (11163)
Backwoodsman. pseud. Crown and the confederation. (43162)
Backwoodsman. pseud. Statistical sketches of Upper Canada. see Dunlop, William.
Backwoodsman. 54182, (59189), 59194
Bacmeister, Hartwig Ludwig Christian. 2638A
Bacon, -------. attorney 104412
Bacon, ------. intervenor 82145
Bacon, Alonzo P. 89304
Bacon, Anthony. 2638, 80592
Bacon, Anthony. supposed author 97121
Bacon, Asa. 96033
Bacon, Austin. 51904, 88148
Bacon, Benjamin C. 2639, 2682, 62293
Bacon, C. 2652, 36174
Bacon, D. ed. 54788
Bacon, David. reporter 29514
Bacon, David Francis. 2640, 93246, note after 105852
Bacon, Delia Salter, 1811-1859. 4295, 94250
Bacon, E. 2641, 81740-81742 see also U. S. Assistant Agent for the Reception of Recaptured Negroes on the Western Coast of Africa.
Bacon, E. petitioner 46164
Bacon, Edmund. 62792
Bacon, Edward. 102843
Bacon, Eliza Ann (Munroe) 2642
Bacon, Ezekiel. 2643-2647
Bacon, Francis, Viscount St. Albans, 1561-1626. (29819), 39820, 78992, 1st note after 94666
Bacon, Francis, Viscount St. Albans, 1561-1626. supposed author 67548-67550
Bacon, George Washington. 2648-2652, 36174
Bacon, George Washington. supposed author 18839, note after 88114
Bacon, H. W. supposed author 18839, note after 88114
Bacon, Henry. 2653
Bacon, Rev. James. (2655)
Bacon, James, fl. 1795. 2654
Bacon, John, 1737-1820. 2656-2657, 102755
Bacon, John, 1738-1820. 2658, note after 89216
Bacon, L. 94271
Bacon, L. B. Stetson. 2676
Bacon, Leonard, 1802-1881. 2659-2675, 52959, 58616, (70214), 85922, 89199, 93138
Bacon, Leonard Woolsey, 1830-1907. (2677)
Bacon, Math. 2678, 89463-89465
Bacon, Nathaniel. 89463
Bacon, Nathaniel A. 2680
Bacon, Oliver N. 2681
Bacon, R. C. see Bacon, Benjamin C.
Bacon, Roger, 1214?-1294. 66686
Bacon, Samuel. (2683)
Bacon, Samuel P. 92675
Bacon, Thomas, 1700?-1768. 2684-2687, 45186
Bacon, Thomas. defendant 2688
Bacon, W. 57317

Bacon, William J. 41548, 17641
Bacon, William J. defendant 104412
Bacon, William Johnson. 2689
Bacon, William Thompson. 2690
Bacon de Lachevalerie, ------. 2691, 38421
Baconian Biblist. pseud. Practical view of the common causes. 97930
Bacon's descriptive handbook of America. 2648
Bacon's guide to American politics. 2649
Bacon's rebellion. 16234, note after 80002
Bacquere, Rumoldus de. tr. 106257
Bacqueville de la Potherie, Claude Charles le Roy, b. ca. 1668. 2692, 84779, 100808
Bad effects of speculative theology. 2693
Bad omen to the churches of New-England. (35046)-35047, 62644
Bad wife's looking glass. 102464
Bade, Th. 2694, (69072)
Badeau & Bros. firm illus. (39832)
Badeaux, M. J. B. 67023
Badger, Mrs. ------, d. 1822? 2276, 56235, 76505
Badger, Barber. 2696
Badger, Barber. supposed author 1165
Badger, George Edmund, 1795-1866. 2697, 52200, 84463, 90323, 93663
Badger, Henry C. 2698-(2700), 7906, 76636
Badger, Joseph. 47496
Badger, Sarah. 2701, note after 90697
Badger, Stephen. 2703-2705
Badger, W. 4107
Badger, William, 1779-1852. 52790 see also National Republican Party. New Hampshire. Convention, Concord, 1828. President.
Badger, William Whittlesey. 2706
Badger & Porter. firm publishers 2707, 90084
Badger & Porter's stage register. 2707, 90084
Badgley, William. 2708
Badgley, William. supposed author 93126
Badia, Marc. Ant. 2709
Badin, Stephen Theodore. 2710, 37562, 88911A
Baeca, G. de. tr. (36775)
Baena, Antonio Ladislau Monteiro. see Monteiro Baena, Antonio Ladislau.
Baer, Karl Er. von. (2711), 105519
Baerle, Kaspar van, 1584-1648. 3407-3412, (14350)-(14351), 31539-31543, 44057, 63319
Baers, Joannem. (2712)
Baers, Joannem. supposed author 2553, 76215
Baert, Alexandre Balthasar Francois de Paule, Baron de. 2713, 2d note after 94174
Baeyle, Hyp. 2714
Baffin, William, 1584-1622. 66686, (74131)
Bagby, A. P. 57632
Bagby, George William, 1828-1883. (51225), 88393
Bagert, J. see Begert, J.
Bagg, E. N. 89735
Bagg, J. N. 89735
Bagger, J. K. ed. 72595
Baggett & Co. firm publishers 76092
Bagot, Sir Charles, 1781-1843. 72879 see also Canada. Governor General, 1842-1843 (Bagot)
Bagot, Lewis, successively Bishop of Bristol, Norwich, and St. Asaph, 1740-1802. 2715
Bagster (B.) firm 103669
Bahamas. Attorney-General. (39408) see also Anderson, George Campbell.
Bahamas. Charter. Chapter 2716
Bahamas. Commissioners of Correspondence. (2719)

Bahamas. Governor, 1864-1869 (Rawson)
(68017) see also Rawson, Sir Rawson
William, 1812-1899.
Bahamas. House of Assembly. 2721, 11768,
(81893), note after 102820
Bahamas. Laws, statutes, etc. (39408)
Bahamonde, Nicolas de la Cruz y. see Cruz
y Bahamonde, Nicolas de la.
Bahia (Brazilian Province) Assemblea Legis-
lativa. 68810
Bahia (Brazilian Province) Laws, statutes, etc.
68810, 81084
Bahia (Brazilian Province) Presidente (Sin-
imbu) (69326) see also Sinimbu, Joao
Lins Vieira Casancao, Visconde de,
1810-1906.
Bahia (Archdiocese) Archbishop (Seixas)
47590, 72503, 78952-78959 see also
Seixas, Romualdo Antonio de, Abp.
Bahia (Archdiocese) Archbishop (Soledade e
Castro) 86357 see also Soledade e
Castro, Vicente da, Abp.
Bahia Associacao Commercial da Praca. see
Associacao Commercial da Praca da
Bahia.
Bahia Sociedade Commercio. see Sociedade
Commercio da Bahia.
Bahia Sociedade de Vehiculos Economicos.
see Sociedade de Vehiculos Economicos
da Bahia.
Bahia Sociedade em Commandita Transportes
Urbanos. see Sociedade em Comman-
dita Transportes Urbanos na Bahia.
Bahia Sociedade Portugueza de Beneficencia.
see Sociedade Portugueza de Bene-
ficencia da Bahia.
Baides, -------- Marques de. 12802
Baie d'Hudson. 69021
Baile en Caracas en 1854. 16155
Bailey, A. 21042, 38507, (49154), 67281
Bailey, A. H. (2723)
Bailey, Abigail (Abbot) 2722, 82534
Bailey, Adolphe. (7782)
Bailey, B. F. 2724
Bailey, Benjamin H. 2725
Bailey, Charles E. USA 70567
Bailey, Ebenezer. 2727
Bailey, Francis. ed. 13118
Bailey, Frederick Augustus Washington. see
Douglass, Frederick, 1817?-1895.
Bailey, G. 2728
Bailey, G. ed. 23625
Bailey, G. F. 2730
Bailey, G. S. (2731)
Bailey, Gamaliel. 2729
Bailey, Henry. 86133
Bailey, I. 45019
Bailey, Isaac. (2732), (70726)
Bailey, J. tr. (36818)
Bailey, J. C. W. 12641
Bailey, J. T. 2737
Bailey, J. W. 2738
Bailey, James. 2733
Bailey, John, of Natick. 2735
Bailey, John, of Watertown. 2734
Bailey, John C. W. 37013, 76504
Bailey, John J. (2736)
Bailey, John Whitman. 2739-2741, 85072
Bailey, Jonathan Jay. 75369 see also St.
Louis. Public School Library. Librarian.
Bailey, Joseph. 2742
Bailey, L. W. 2743
Bailey, Luther. 2744
Bailey, M. J. 2745
Bailey, P. G. 89246
Bailey, Philip James. 2746

Bailey, R. T. (2750)
Bailey, R. W. ed. 59073
Bailey, Richard. see Bayley, Richard.
Bailey, Robert. 2748
Bailey, Robert S. 2749
Bailey, Rufus William. 2751
Bailey, Silas. 2752
Bailey, Theodorus. 23879
Bailey, Thomas. 2753
Bailey, W. L. 2754
Bailey, William. 2755
Bailey, William Shreve. 2756
Bailey, Winthrop. 2757
Bailey. firm see Halpin & Bailey. firm
publishers
Bailey (J. C. W.) firm publishers 34263
Bailie, Robert. defendant see Baillie, Robert,
d. 1684. defendant
Baillard, Edme. supposed author 2758, 64875
Baillet, Adrien, 1649-1706. tr. 26303, 26308
Bailley, ------. 70492
Baillie, Hugh. 2759-2761, 36304, (80041)
Baillie, Robert, 1599-1662. 2762
Baillie, Robert, d. 1684. defendant 47571,
78227
Baillie, Thomas. 2763
Baillio, ------. 2764, 2766
Baillio, ------ petitioner (2765), 75163,
99242
Baillot de Saint-Martin, -----. 2767, (75418)-
75419
Bailly, Felipe. (26116)
Bailly, Felix. 2768-2769, 4577-4580, 26518,
note after 95460
Baily, -----. (60516) see also Pennsylvania.
Legislature. House of Representatives.
Committee on Inland Navigation. Chair-
man.
Baily, -----. plaintiff 33256
Baily, Francis. 2770
Baily, James. 2769, 99830
Baily, John, fl. 1693. (44077)
Baily, John, fl. 1850. 2771-(2772), 9152
Baily et al v. Poindexter's ex'r. 33256
Bain, J. W. 2773
Bainbridge, William, 1774-1833. 25722, 1st
note after 99448
Bainbridge, Joseph. 95955, 96014
Baines, Edward, 1774-1848. 2774-2776, 17925
Baines, Sir Edward, 1800-1890. 2776
Baines, R. supposed author (10621), 103118
Baines, Thomas. 2777
Baines' history of the late war. 2775, 17925
Baird, B. F. 69946
Baird, D. 2778
Baird, Henry Carey. (2780)-2782
Baird, Henry M. 2783
Baird, Robert. 2784-(2800), 9675, 26734,
(76492), note after 94327
Baird, Robert. supposed author. 2594, note
after 94327, 99586
Baird, Samuel J. (2801)-2803
Baird, Spencer Fullerton, 1823-1887. 2804-
2809, 22538, 27419, 27484, 35308, 68476,
69946, 81472-81473, 84229-84229, 84233,
85014 see also Smithsonian Institution.
Secretary. U. S. Bureau of Fisheries.
Baird, Thomas H. 2810, 100661
Baissas, Rene. tr. 74911
Bajamar, --------, Marques de. 2811
Bajon, ------. 2812-2813
Bajot, Louis Marin. 1585, (2814)-2815, 11484,
70357
Bake, H. A. 6294
Bake-pan for the dough-faces. (2816)
Baked meats of the funeral. (29918)

Baker, -------, fl. 1812. 1013, (16872)
Baker, -------, fl. 1869. 33586
Baker, -------. engr. 92459, 92485
Baker, Rev. Mr. pseud. see Hines, David
Theodore.
Baker, A. R. 29844
Baker, Charles. cartographer 103769
Baker, Conrad, 1817-1885. (34556) see also
Indiana. Governor, 1867-1783 (Baker)
Baker, Daniel, fl. 1650-1660. 2817
Baker, Delphine Paris. supposed author
(2818), 19455, 86512
Baker, E. C. 2819
Baker, Edmund. (20619)
Baker, Edward Dickinson, 1811-1861. (2820)-
2821
Baker, George A. 61563
Baker, George E. 2823, 79457, 79595, 79597
Baker, George Melville. 2824, 90153
Baker, Henry F. 2825
Baker, J. B. 2827
Baker, J. P. 2838
Baker, James. 2826
Baker, James Loring. 2828-(2833), 30304
Baker, Jehu. 2834
Baker, John. defendant 96819
Baker, John F. 2835
Baker, John Martin. 2836-2837
Baker, L. C. USA 2840-2841, 29386
Baker, Levi. petitioner (13254)
Baker, Louis. 2837
Baker, Louisa. see West, Lucy (Brewer)
Baker, Luther. 2842-2843
Baker, Morrell. petitioner 97891
Baker, Mosely. 76747, 94966
Baker, Peter C. 2844
Baker, Polly. pseud. Rede. see Franklin,
Benjamin, 1706-1790.
Baker, Polly, pseud. Speech. see Franklin,
Benjamin, 1706-1790.
Baker, R. P. 2845
Baker, Rachel. 2846
Baker, Richard. 2847
Baker, S. W. 2848
Baker, T. ed. 84416
Baker, W. B. 75332 see also St. Louis
Chamber of Commerce. Secretary.
Baker, W. D. (2849), note after (77147)
Baker, William M. 2851
Baker-Cumback correspondence. 33586
Baker Street Bazaar, London, 185-? see
London. Baker Street Bazaar, 185-?
Balaert, W. tr. 39681
Balance and Columbian repository. 2853,
32091, 75929-75930, note after 79739
Balance of our foreign trade. 44184
Balance of the sanctuary. (46227)
Balanco apresentado aos accionistas. 88706
Balanco da receita e despenza do imperio no
exercicio. (2854), 7524
Balanza de comercio por el puerto de Ve-
racruz. (79312)
Balanza general del comercio de la isla de
Cuba. 11754, (26701)
Balanza general del comercio maritimo por
los puertos de la republica Mexicana, en
el ano 1810. 48296
Balanza general del comercio meritimo por
los puertos de la republica Mexicana en
el ano de 1826. (2855)
Balanza mercantil de la isle de Puerto-Rico.
11699
Balanza mercantil de la plaza de Mexico.
48297
Balanza mercantil de las plazas. 48298
Balbi, Adriano, 1782-1848. 2856-2858, 52105

Balbi, Gasparo. 66686, 89452
Balbo, Cesare, Conte di Vinadio, 1789-1853.
99504
Balbo, J. P. 2859
Balboa, Miguel Cavello. 2860
Balboa, Vasco Nunez de. see Nunez de Bal-
boa, Vasco, 1475-1517.
Balbuena, Bernardo de. see Valbuena, Ber-
nardo de.
Balby, Caspar. see Balbi, Gasparo.
Balcarce, ------. (2865)
Balcarcel y Formento, Domingo. 38624, 96273
Balcarres, Alexander Lindsay, 6th Earl of,
1752-1825. (21893), (21908), note after
(35559) see also Jamaica. Governor,
1795-1801 (Balcarres)
Balch, B. 2866
Balch, F. V. ed. 69767, 2d note after 96936
Balch, L. P. W. 84296
Balch, Rev. Thomas. 2867-2870
Balch, Thomas. ed. 2871-2872, (26428), note
after 79366
Balch, Vistus. engr. 84154, 104205
Balch, William. 2873, 7269, 99830, 103934
see also Bradford, Mass. Second Church.
Pastor.
Balch, William. defendant before church
council 7268, 27584, 103399
Balch, William S. 2874, 2875
Balcom, D. A. 2876
Balcon, Juan Prudencio de Osorio y. see
Osorio y Balcon, Juan Prudencio de.
Bald eagle: a story of the American revolution.
82507
Bald eagle, or the last of the Ramapaughs.
82506
Baldani, Fulgentio. (57715)
Baldelli, Francesco. tr. 41068
Baldelli, G. B. 99383B
Baldillo, Jos. Ant. e. de Otero y. see Otero
y Baldillo, Jos. Ant. E. de.
Baldridge, S. C. 2877
Balduc, Z. B. Z. 2878
Balduini, Francisco. 93324
Baldwin, A. C. 70280, 90688
Baldwin, Angel E. Ribas. see Ribas Baldwin,
Angel E.
Baldwin, Aug. S. USN defendant at court of
enquiry (72747)
Baldwin, C. C. 1050, 105433
Baldwin, Charles N. 2880, 41493
Baldwin, Charles N. defendant 2879, 72619,
101441
Baldwin, Ebenezer. 2881-2886, 80456, 2d note
after 97444
Baldwin, Ebenezer. supposed author 105935
Baldwin, Elihu W. 2887-2888
Baldwin, George C. 2889, (29714)
Baldwin, George R. 2890-2891, note after
91588, 97058
Baldwin, Harvey. 86348
Baldwin, Henry. 2895-2896, 10889, 26916,
1st note after 92842
Baldwin, Henry. petitioner 2894
Baldwin, James. 104788
Baldwin, Jedun. 102457
Baldwin, John D. 2897
Baldwin, Joseph G. 2898-2899
Baldwin, L. 13738, 86734A
Baldwin, Lewis. 2900
Baldwin, Loammi. 2901-2904, 60750, note after
97756
Baldwin, Michael. 97255
Baldwin, Moses. 2905-2906
Baldwin, N. B. 2907

BALDWIN

Baldwin, Nathan. 105347 see also Worcester, Mass. Committee of Correspondence. Chairman.
Baldwin, R. S. supposed author 15720-15721, 36334, (69512), note after 101998, note before 101999, 103169
Baldwin, Roger S. 2908
Baldwin, Samuel. 2909
Baldwin, Samuel Davies. (2910)
Baldwin, Simeon. 2911
Baldwin, Simeon E. 85212
Baldwin, Stephen. petitioner 2894
Baldwin, Theron. 2912, 85914, 85917
Baldwin, Thomas, of Philadelphia. 2924-2925
Baldwin, Thomas, b. 1750? 2922
Baldwin, Thomas, 1753-1825. 2913-2921, 12121, (50948), 82483, 82488, 82492, 91795, 91812, 105248, 105266, 105313
Baldwin, Thomas, fl. 1832. (2923), 34229
Baldwin, William. USN 18599
Baldwin (H. A.) firm publishers 2892-2893
Baldwin (W. A.) firm publishers 103351
Baldwin, Me. Inhabitants. (2927), note after 103796
Baldwin Place Baptist Church, Boston. see Boston. Baldwin Place Baptist Church.
Baldwin School, St. Paul, Minn. 2926, 75453
Baldwin's consolidated business directory, 1866. 2892
Baldwin's handbook of Central Park. 2893
Balesdens, Joan. (64523)
Balestier, Joseph N. 2928-2929, 70182
Balfour, Jean. 2930-2931
Balfour, Walter. 93205
Balkam, U. 2932
Ball, Alexander M. W. 50955
Ball, Benjamin Lincoln. 2933
Ball, Charles, negro slave. 2934-2935
Ball, Charles, fl. 1854. 89199
Ball, Ebenezer. defendant 96820
Ball, Heman. 2936
Ball, J. P. 2940
Ball, John, 1585-1640. 921, 2937-2939, 17070, 80259
Ball, John. 75646, 75732 see also Salem City Mission, Salem, Mass. City Missionary.
Ball, L. Chandler. (2941)-2943, 69638
Ball, Mott. Dulany. (2944)
Ball, Richard. 2945, 64863
Ball, William. 53164, 87752
Ball, and Dr. Price's Observations on civil liberty. (4284)
Ballad. 79625, 80812, 92171, 98051, 101255
Ballad, . . . as performed at the concerts. 84156
Ballad concerning the fight between the English and French. 2946
Ballad in two parts. 74971
Ballad of Bull Run. 49807
Ballad of the abolition blunder-buss. 76999, 81901
Ballad of the times of enchantment. 62811
Ballad, to the tune of Chevy-chace. 64072
Ballads and other poems. (41906)
Ballads and songs. 51263
Ballads of the south. 2947
Ballads of the war. 2948, 21156, (31631)
Ballance, Charles. (2949)
Ballantine, John. 2950, 7655
Ballantyne, Robert Michael. 2951-2952, 97657
Ballantyne. firm publishers 86391
Ballard, Charles W. ed. (54765)
Ballard, E. 29474

Ballard, Edward, 1804-1870. 2953, 64133 see also Popham Celebration, 1862. Executive Committee. Secretary.
Ballard, Frank W. 2954-2956
Ballard, Joseph. 2957, 6667, 57145
Ballard, William. 2958, 81520
Ballarna, Santiago. 2959, 69174
Ballenstedt, C. W. T. 2960
Balleroy, J. B. 2961
Ballesteros, Lazaro de la Garza y. see Garza y Ballesteros, Lazaro de la, Abp.
Ballesteros, Tomas de. 2962, 61163-(61164)
Ballet en un acte. 94214
Ballon, Hosea. 98012
Ballot and the bullet. 90143
Ballot box a remedy for national crimes. 4330
Ballot box, the palladium of our liberties. (2963), 3391
Balloting-book, and other documents. 53538
Ballou, Adin. 2964-2967, (48948), 70103
Ballou, Hosea. 2968-2969, 93210
Ballou, John. 2970
Ballou, Maturin. 2972
Ballou, Maturin Murray, 1820-1895. 2971, 51532, 89640
Ballou's pictorial drawing-room companion. 89640
Ball's Bluff massacre. 33227
Ball's . . . mammoth pictorial tour of the United States. 2940
Ballston Spa, N. Y. Convention of Republican Antimasonic Delegates from the Several Towns in the County of Saratoga, 1831. see Anti-masonic Party. New York (State) Saratoga County. Convention, Ballston Spa, 1831.
Ballston Spa, N. Y. State and National Law School. see State and National Law School, Ballston Spa, N. Y.
Ballston springs. 2973
Bally, Victor. (2975)
Balm for the weary and the wounded. (67334)
Balm in Gilead to heal Sions wounds. 101120
Balm of Gilead. 70419
Balmanno, ------. (2976)
Balme, ----- de la. see De la Balme, ------.
Balme, Josua R. 2967-(2969)
Balmis, Francesco Saverio de. 2980-2982
Baltasar, Jean. 2983-2986, 11028
Baltasar de Somonte y Velasco, Jose. see Somonte y Velasco, Jose Baltasar de.
Balthasar de Medina, ------. see Medina, Balthasar de.
Balthasar Springers Indienfahrt 1505/06. 99363
Baltimore, Cecil Calvert, 2d Baron, 1606-1675. Proprietary. 69291 see also Maryland (Colony) Proprietary.
Baltimore, Cecil Calvert, 2d Baron, 1606-1675. incorrectly supposed author (45316), 69291-69292, note after 80002, 103353
Baltimore, Charles Calvert, 3d Baron, 1629-1714. 10083
Baltimore, Charles Calvert, 3d Baron, 1629-1714. defendant 95687 see also Maryland (Colony) Proprietary. defendant
Baltimore, Charles Calvert, 6th Baron, 1699-1751. (45073), 60743, note after 97106 see also Maryland (Colony) Proprietary.
Baltimore, Charles Calvert, 6th Baron, 1699-1751. defendant 34416 see also Maryland (Colony) Proprietary. defendant
Baltimore, Frederick Calvert, 7th Baron, 1731-1771. 34439
Baltimore. (3010), 3025, 13158, 31704
Baltimore. defendant 28247

252

Baltimore. American Convention for Promoting the Abolition of Slavery, and Improving the Condition of the African Race, 1828. see American Convention for Promoting the Abolition of Slavery, and Improving the Condition of the African Race.

Baltimore. Amis de la Bienfaisance. see Amis de la Bienfaisance, Baltimore.

Baltimore. Anti-masonic Convention, 1831. see United States Anti-masonic Convention, Baltimore, 1831.

Baltimore. Beinnial American Convention for Promoting the Abolition of Slavery, 1828. see American Convention for Promoting the Abolition of Slavery, and Improving the Condition of the African Race.

Baltimore. Board of Commissioners. 3070

Baltimore. Board of Commissioners. Engineer. (3074)

Baltimore. Board of Commissioners of Public Schools. see Baltimore. Commissioners of Public Schools.

Baltimore. Board of School Commissioners. see Baltimore. Commissioners of Public Schools.

Baltimore. Board of Trade. see Baltimore Board of Trade.

Baltimore. Celebration of the Triumph of Liberty in France, 1830. Committee of Arrangements. publishers 104872

Baltimore. Charter. 3053-3054, 45169

Baltimore. Church Home Society. see Church Home Society, Baltimore.

Baltimore. Citizens. petitioners 2992

Baltimore. Citizens' Meeting on the Claim of Louisa Browning, 1825. see Baltimore. Meeting of Citizens on the Claim of Louisa Browning, 1825.

Baltimore. City Council. 2992, 41227, 47487, 63216

Baltimore. City Council. appellants 8481

Baltimore. City Council. petitioners 3044

Baltimore. City Council. Committee on Ways and Means. 46396

Baltimore. City Council. First Branch. 63126

Baltimore. City Council. Joint Standing Committee on Jones' Falls. 36631

Baltimore. City Council. Joint Standing Committee on Water. 3060

Baltimore. City Court. 9308, 45070, 71401, 91710

Baltimore. Commissioners of Public Schools. (3015), 3071, 3082, 43340

Baltimore. Commissioners of Public Schools. Committee to Visit the Public Schools of Philadelphia, New York, Brooklyn and Boston, 1867. (69802)

Baltimore. Commissioners of Public Schools. Delegation to the National Convention of Friends of Common School Instruction, 1849. 69850

Baltimore. Committee Composing the Delegation, Appointed by the Citizens, to the Susquehanna Railroad Convention, Sunbury, Pa., 1851. see Susquehanna Railroad Convention, Sunbury, Pa., 1851. Baltimore Delegation.

Baltimore. Conference of Friends, 1849. see Friends, Society of. Conference, Baltimore, 1849.

Baltimore. Conference of the Committees of the Yearly Meetings of New York, New England, Baltimore, North Carolina, and Indiana, 1851. see Friends, Society of. Conference of the Committees of the

Yearly Meetings of New York, New England, Baltimore, North Carolina, and Indiana, Baltimore, 1851.

Baltimore. Convention of Delegates from Several States to Nominate a Candidate for Vice-President, 1832. see Democratic Party. National Convention, Baltimore, 1832.

Baltimore. Convention of the Friends of Domestic Industry, 1831. see Convention of the Friends of Domestic Industry, Baltimore, 1831.

Baltimore. Convention on Internal Improvements, 1825. see Convention on Internal Improvements, Baltimore, 1825.

Baltimore. Convention on Internal Improvements of Maryland, 1836. see Convention on Internal Improvements of Maryland, Baltimore, 1836.

Baltimore. Convention on the Recommendation to Reduce the Pay for Mail Service to Rail Road Companies, 1854. see Convention on the Recommendation to Reduce the Pay for Mail Service to Rail Road Companies, Baltimore, 1854.

Baltimore. Convention to Form a Supreme Grand Lodge for the United States, 1847. see Freemasons. U. S. Convention to Form a Supreme Grand Lodge for the United States, Baltimore, 1847.

Baltimore. Delegates Appointed at a Meeting of the Free Colored People to Visit British Guiana and the Island of Trinidad, 1839. see Baltimore. Meeting of the Free Colored People, 1839. Delegates to Visit British Guiana, and the Island of Trinidad, for the Purpose of Ascertaining the Advantages to be Derived by Colored People Migrating to Those Places.

Baltimore. Delegates to the Education Conventions of Buffalo and Boston, 1860. 43340 see also M'Jilton, John Nelson, 1805-1875.

Baltimore. Delegations, Appointed by the Citizens of Baltimore, to the Susquehanna Railroad Convention, Sunbury, Pa., 1851. see Susquehanna Railroad Convention, Sunbury, Pa., 1851. Baltimore Delegation.

Baltimore. Delegation to the National Convention of the Friends of Common School Instruction, 1849. see Baltimore. Commissioners of Public Schools. Delegation to the National Convention of the Friends of Common School Instruction, 1849.

Baltimore. Democratic Party National Convention, 1832. see Democratic Party. National Convention, Baltimore, 1832.

Baltimore. Democratic Party National Convention, 1835. see Democratic Party. National Convention, Baltimore, 1835.

Baltimore. Democratic Party National Convention, 1840. see Democratic Party. National Convention, Baltimore, 1840.

Baltimore. Democratic Party National Convention, 1852. see Democratic Party. National Convention, Baltimore, 1852.

Baltimore. Democratic Party National Convention, 1860. see Democratic Party. National Convention, Baltimore, 1860.

Baltimore. Democratic State Convention, 1827. see Democratic Party. Maryland. Convention, Baltimore, 1827.

Baltimore. Deutsch-Evangelischen Kirche. 91211

Baltimore. Emmanuel Church. 77565

Baltimore. Emmanuel Church. Vestry. 77565

Baltimore. Engineer. (3074), 45098 see also Trimble, I.

Baltimore. Entertainment Given in Honor of Duncan McIntosh, 1809. see Entertainment Given in Honor of Duncan McIntosh, Baltimore, 1809.

Baltimore. Fete Donnee a Mr. Duncan M'Intosh, 1809. see Entertainment Given in Honor of Duncan McIntosh, Baltimore, 1809.

Baltimore. First Battalion of Militia. see Maryland. Militia. First Baltimore Battalion.

Baltimore. Francais Refugies de Saint Domingue. see Francais Refugies De St. Domingue, Baltimore.

Baltimore. German Reformed Church. 3050

Baltimore. Great Meeting of the Friends of Civil and Religious Liberty, 1837. see Great Meeting of the Friends of Civil and Religious Liberty, Baltimore, 1837.

Baltimore. Great Whig Festival, 1835. see Whig Party. Maryland. Baltimore. Great Whig Festival, 1835.

Baltimore. Internal Improvement Convention, 1834. see Internal Improvement Convention, Baltimore, 1834.

Baltimore. Johns Hopkins Hospital. 84267, 84276

Baltimore. Loyola College. see Loyola College, Baltimore.

Baltimore. McDonogh Educational Fund and Institute. see McDonogh Educational Fund and Institute, Baltimore.

Baltimore. Marine Insurance Companies. see Marine Insurance Companies of Baltimore. petitioners

Baltimore. Maryland Administration Convention, 1827. see Maryland Administration Convention, Baltimore, 1827.

Baltimore. Maryland Club. 45206

Baltimore. Maryland Eye and Ear Infirmary. see Maryland Eye and Ear Institute, Baltimore.

Baltimore. Maryland Eye and Ear Institute. see Maryland Eye and Ear Institute, Baltimore.

Baltimore. Maryland Hospital. Board of Visiters. [sic] 45218

Baltimore. Maryland Hospital. President. 45218

Baltimore. Maryland Industrial School for Girls. see Maryland Industrial School for Girls, Baltimore.

Baltimore. Maryland Institute for the Promotion of the Mechanic Arts. see Maryland Institute for the Promotion of the Mechanic Arts, Baltimore.

Baltimore. Maryland State Fair, For the Christian and Sanitary Commissions, 1864. see Maryland State Fair, for the Christian and Sanitary Commissions, Baltimore, 1864.

Baltimore. Mass Meeting on the Sunday Law, 1866. 3080

Baltimore. Mayor. 2992, 3027, 26697, 45098, 70228

Baltimore. Mayor. appellant 8481

Baltimore. Mayor. petitioner 3044

Baltimore. Mayor. plaintiff 45396

Baltimore. Meeting of Citizens on the Claim of Louisa Browning, 1825. (45378)

Baltimore. Meeting of the Free Colored People, 1839. Delegates to visit British Guiana, and the Island of Trinidad, for the Purpose of Ascertaining the Advantages to be Derived by Colored People Migrating to those Places. 59489 see also Peck, -------. and Price, -------.

Baltimore. Meeting of the Friends of African Colonization, 1827. see Friends of African Colonization. Meeting, Baltimore, 1827.

Baltimore. Meeting of the Young Men of Maryland. 1831. see Meeting of the Young Men of Maryland, Baltimore, 1831.

Baltimore. Merchants. petitioners 3046, 62969

Baltimore. Merchants and Traders. petitioners 3045

Baltimore. Methodist Episcopal Church Conference, 1784. see Methodist Episcopal Church. Conferences. Conference, Baltimore, 1784.

Baltimore. Methodist Episcopal Church Conference, 1792. see Methodist Episcopal Church. Conferences. Conference, Baltimore, 1792.

Baltimore. Methodist Episcopal Church Meeting, 1828. see Methodist Episcopal Church Meeting, Baltimore, 1828.

Baltimore. Mount Hope Institution. see Mount Hope Institution, Baltimore.

Baltimore. Mount Oliver Cemetery. 3032, 51163

Baltimore. Mount St. Vincent's Hospital. Physician. 51172 see also Stokes, W. H.

Baltimore. National Lord's Day Convention, 1844. see National Lord's Day Convention, Baltimore, 1844.

Baltimore. National Masonic Convention, 1843. see Freemasons. U. S. National Masonic Convention, Baltimore, 1843.

Baltimore. National Republican Central Committee. see National Republican Party. Maryland. Central Committee of Baltimore.

Baltimore. National Republican Party Convention, 1830. see National Republican Party. Maryland. Convention, Baltimore, 1830.

Baltimore. National Republican Party Convention, 1831. see National Republican Party. Convention, Baltimore, 1831.

Baltimore. National Republican Party Convention, 1832. see National Republican Party. Convention, Baltimore, 1832.

Baltimore. National Union Convention, 1864. see Republican Party. National Convention, Baltimore, 1864.

Baltimore. Office of Discount and Deposit. 23396

Baltimore. Ordinances, etc. 3051-3054, 45396, (62080)

Baltimore. Peabody Institute. see Peabody Institute, Baltimore.

Baltimore. Pleinary Council of the Catholic Church in the United States, 1st, 1852. see Catholic Church in the United States. Plenary Council, 1st, Baltimore, 1852.

Baltimore. Plenary Council of the Catholic Church in the U. S., 2d, 1866. see Catholic Church in the U. S. Plenary Council. 2d, Baltimore, 1866.

Baltimore. Police Commissioners. 3075

Baltimore. Protestant Episcopal Society for the Increase of the Ministry Annual Meeting, 15th, 1871. see Protestant Episcopal Society for the Increase of the Ministry. Annual Meeting, 15th, Baltimore, 1871.

Baltimore. Public Meeting of the Friends of the Union, 1861. 3058, (65804)
Baltimore. Republican Party National Convention, 1864. see Republican Party. National Convention, Baltimore, 1864.
Baltimore. St. Mary's College. see St. Mary's College, Baltimore.
Baltimore. St. Peter's Church. Members. petitioners 18653, 45372
Baltimore. St. Peter's Church. Vestry. defendants 18653, 45372
Baltimore. St. Timothy's Hall. see St. Timothy's Hall, Baltimore, Md.
Baltimore. School for the Blind. see Maryland. School for the Blind, Baltimore.
Baltimore. Southern and Western Commercial Convention, 1832. see Southern and Western Commercial Convention, Baltimore, 1832.
Baltimore. Southern Rights Convention, 1861. see Southern Rights Convention, Baltimore, 1861.
Baltimore. State Convention on Internal Improvements, 1825. see Convention on Internal Improvements, Baltimore, 1825.
Baltimore. State Normal School. see Maryland. State Normal School, Baltimore.
Baltimore. Tallow Chandlers. 3043
Baltimore. Trade Convention, 1835. see Trade Convention, Baltimore, 1835.
Baltimore. Unconditional Union State Central Committee. see Unconditional Union Party. Maryland. State Central Committee, Baltimore.
Baltimore. Underwriters and Merchants. petitioners 3046
Baltimore. Union Prayer Meeting, 1863. see United States Christian Commission. Union Prayer Meeting, Baltimore, 1863.
Baltimore. United States Anti-masonic Convention, 1831. see United States Anti-masonic Convention, Baltimore, 1831.
Baltimore. Visitors of the Jail. 3076
Baltimore. Washington Medical College. see Washington University, Baltimore. Medical Department.
Baltimore. Washington Monument. 3019, 101776
Baltimore. Washington University. see Washington University, Baltimore.
Baltimore. Whig Party National Convention, 1852. see Whig Party. National Convention, Baltimore, 1852.
Baltimore (Archdiocese) 34863, 88912
Baltimore (Archdiocese) Archbishop (Bayley) (72931) see also Bayley, Jacob Roosevelt, Abp., 1814-1877.
Baltimore (Archdiocese) Archbishop (Carroll) 11071-11072, 22702, 30955, 85257, note after 101769, 103090, 103092 see also Carroll, John, Abp., 1735-1815.
Baltimore (Archdiocese) Archbishop (Eccleston) 3079, 70228 see also Eccleston, Samuel, Abp., 1801-1851.
Baltimore (Archdiocese) Archbishop (Gibbons) 72932 see also Gibbons, Jacob, Cardinal, 1834-1921.
Baltimore (Archdiocese) Archbishop (Mareschal) 44522 see also Mareschal, Ambrose, Abp., 1764-1828.
Baltimore (Archdiocese) Archbishop (Spalding) 88911 see also Spalding, Martin John, Abp., 1810-1872.
Baltimore (Archdiocese) Archbishop (Whitfield) (51839), 59019, 72925 see also Whitfield, James, Abp., 1770-1834.

Baltimore (Archdiocese) Clerical Benevolent Association. 3029
Baltimore (Archdiocese) Synod, 1791. 22702
Baltimore (Archdiocese) Synod, 1817. 72924
Baltimore (Archdiocese) Synod, 1831. 72925
Baltimore (Archdiocese) Synod, 1853. 72926
Baltimore (Archdiocese) Synod, 1857. 72927
Baltimore (Archdiocese) Synod, 1863. 72928
Baltimore (Archdiocese) Synod, 1865. 72929
Baltimore (Archdiocese) Synod, 1868. 72930
Baltimore (Archdiocese) Synod, 1875. (72931)
Baltimore (Archdiocese) Synod, 1886. 72932
Baltimore (Diocese) see Baltimore (Archdiocese)
Baltimore (Ecclesiastical Province) Council, 1829. (15105), 72901, (72903)-72904
Baltimore (Ecclesiastical Province) Council, 1833. (15105), (72903)
Baltimore (Ecclesiastical Province) Council, 1840. (15105), (72904)
Baltimore (Ecclesiastical Province) Council, 1843. (15105), 72905
Baltimore (Ecclesiastical Province) Council, 1846. (15105), 72906
Baltimore (Ecclesiastical Province) Council, 1849. (15105), 72907
Baltimore (Ecclesiastical Province) Council, 1855. (72908)
Baltimore (Ecclesiastical Province) Council, 1858. 72909
Baltimore (Ecclesiastical Province) Council, 1869. 72910
Baltimore (Ecclesiastical Province) Council, 1875. 72931
Baltimore County, Md. Circuit Court. 8481, 33012, 92013
Baltimore County, Md. Court of Oyer and Terminer. 3011, 32054, 35112, 93214, 3d note after 96883
Baltimore County, Md. Court of Oyer and Terminer. Chief Justice. 3011, 93214
Baltimore County, Md. Court of Oyer and Terminer. Grand Jury. 3011, 93214
Baltimore County, Md. Court of Oyer and Terminer. Grand Jury. Foreman. 3011, 93214 see also Stuart, Richardson.
Baltimore; a short account. (2990), 63433
Baltimore address directory. 2999
Baltimore American. (69888), 86625, note before 90497
Baltimore and Ohio Railroad Company. 2991-2992, 84847, 99409
Baltimore and Ohio Railroad Company. defendants 2992, 45396, 104870
Baltimore and Ohio Railroad Company. Assistant Master of Transportation. 84848 see also Smith, William Prescott, 1825?-1872.
Baltimore and Ohio Railroad Company. Chief Engineer. 2992, 84847 see also Knight, Jonathan. and Latrobe, Benjamin Henry, 1764-1820.
Baltimore and Ohio Railroad Company. Committee on Western Connections. 2992
Baltimore and Ohio Railroad Company. Committee to Confer with the Authorities of the City of Wheeling. 2992
Baltimore and Ohio Railroad Company. Directors. petitioners 2992
Baltimore and Ohio Railroad Company. Engineers. 2992
Baltimore and Ohio Railroad Company. Finance Committee. 32935
Baltimore and Ohio Railroad Company. President. 2992, 16868 see also Swann, Thomas.

Baltimore and Ohio Railroad Company. President. petitioner 2992

Baltimore and Ohio Railroad Company. Select Committee. 2992

Baltimore and Ohio Rail Road Company. An analysis of their reports. 99409

Baltimore and Susquehanna Railroad Company. 2993-2994

Baltimore and Susquehanna Railroad Company. petitioners (45258)

Baltimore and Susquehanna Railroad Company. Chief Engineer. 94071 see also Swift, Joseph Gardner.

Baltimore and Susquehanna Railroad Company. President and Directors. 94071

Baltimore, A. D. 1862; or how they act in Baltimore. 2988

Baltimore, A. D. 1862; or the volunteer zouave in Baltimore. 2989

Baltimore. April 26. 102195

Baltimore as it is. 2996

Baltimore Association for the Improvement of the Conditions of the Poor. 3057

Baltimore Association for the Moral and Educational Improvement of the Colored People. 3012

Baltimore Association of Friends to Advise and Assist Friends of the Southern States. 86061

Baltimore Baptist Association. see Baptists. Maryland. Baltimore Baptist Association.

Baltimore Board of Trade. 3006, 3014

Baltimore book. 2997

Baltimore Branch Bank of the United States Bank. see Bank of the United States. Baltimore Branch.

Baltimore business directory. 3000

Baltimore Canton Company. see Canton Company of Baltimore.

Baltimore Christian Association. 3065, 3069

Baltimore chronicle. 35384, (65342), 81514, note after 103429

Baltimore City Convention of the Union Party. see Union Party. Maryland. Baltimore. City Convention.

Baltimore club. 3081

Baltimore College. Trustees. petitioners (45389)

Baltimore, Dec. 31, 1776. 101693

Baltimore Democracy and independent Democracy. 12196

Baltimore director. 46199

Baltimore directory and citizen's register for 1807. 43311

Baltimore directory for 1802. 2998, 1st note after 90069

Baltimore directory for 1804. 2998

Baltimore directory for 1796. 2998

Baltimore directory for 1799. 2998

Baltimore evening post. (55313), note after 95351

Baltimore Humane Impartial Society and Aged Woman's Home. 3013

Baltimore Irish Emancipation Society. see Irish Emancipation Society, Baltimore.

Baltimore, January 29. 101697

Baltimore Ladies' Branch Bible Society. see Ladies' Branch Bible Society of Baltimore.

Baltimore Ladies' Southern Relief Association of Maryland. see Ladies' Southern Relief Association of Maryland, Baltimore.

Baltimore Ladies' Union Relief Association. see Ladies' Union Relief Association, Baltimore.

Baltimore Library Company. 3023

Baltimore literary and religious magazine. 3001, 85341, 89502

Baltimore literary monument. 3002

Baltimore Medical and Philosophical Lyceum. 64656

Baltimore Mercantile Library Association. see Mercantile Library Association of Baltimore.

Baltimore Millers. petitioners 96991

Baltimore monthly journal of medicine and surgery. 83664

Baltimore-Ohio-Eisenhahn uber das Alleghany-Gebirg. 27257

Baltimore: or long long time ago. 2560, 8870, (45211A)

Baltimore patriot. note before 90497

Baltimore patriot office, August—1827. 13552

Baltimore phoenix and budget. 3003

Baltimore physician. pseud. Series of letters and other documents. 3083, (79224)

Baltimore platforms—slavery question. 27329

Baltimore Presbytery. see Presbyterian Church in the U. S. A. Presbytery of Baltimore.

Baltimore Religious Tract Society. see Religious Tract Society of Baltimore.

Baltimore repertory of papers. 3004

Baltimore, September 13. 101701

Baltimore Society of Teachers. see Society of Teachers, Baltimore.

Baltimore Society of St. George. see Society of St. George, Baltimore.

Baltimore Southern and Western Commercial Convention, 1832. see Southern and Western Commercial Convention, Baltimore, 1832.

Baltimore Temperance Society. 83663

Baltimore town and Fell's Point Directory. 95556

Baltimore Union Relief Association. see Union Relief Association, Baltimore.

Baltimore Union Society. (3062)

Baltimore Unitarian Book Society. publisher 97833

Baltimore United Working-Men's Trading Society. see United Working-Men's Trading Society of Baltimore.

Baltimore weekly magazine. 3005

Baltimore Yearly Meeting. see Friends, Society of. Baltimore Yearly Meeting.

Baltimore Young Men's Bible Society. see Young Men's Bible Society of Baltimore.

Baltimore Young Men's Christian Association. see Young Men's Christian Association, Baltimore.

Baltimore Young Men's Colonization Society. see Young Men's Colonization Society, Baltimore.

Baltimore Young Men's Society. Committee on Lotteries. 3064

Baltimorean. pseud. Stranger's guide to Baltimore. 3085

Baltzell, John. 3090

Baluartes de Mexico. 21776, (24140), note after 99395

Baluffi, Gaetano. 3091-3092

Bambous. Fables de Lafontaine. 38608

Banchero, G. 3093

Banco de Guatemala. (29067)

Banco de Potosi. Charter. 68224

Banco de San Carlos. Charter. 68228

Banco Espanol, Havana. see Havana. Banco Espanol.

Banco Industrial, Havana. see Sociedad Anomina Denominada Banco Industrial, Havana.

Banco; or, the tenant of the spring. 103491
Bancos do Brazil, e sua historia. 25482
Bancroft, Aaron, 1755-1839. 3094-3105, (3700), 27695, 63992, 70115, 97296, 105243
Bancroft, Edgar A. 84518
Bancroft, Edward, 1744-1821. (1969), 3106-(3111), 38180, 50198, 56562, 4th note after 93855, 99584, 103107, 5th note after 103107, 2d note after 103122
Banfroft, Edward, 1744-1821. supposed author 25595, 34579-34580, 96769, 99584, note just before 103108
Bancroft, Edward Nathaniel. 3112-3113
Bancroft, George, 1800-1891. 3114-3134, 3136-3142, 13678, 14218, 28600, 31231, 33841, 35221, 35377, 36007, 36008, 37098, 41219, (41600), 67221, 67244, (68620), 77256, (78052), 79353, 88496, 2d note after 99889
Bancroft, Hubert Howe, 1832-1918. 3143, (76810)
Bancroft, Joseph. 3144
Bancroft, Luther S. 3145
Bancroft, W. L. 3146
Bancroft Davis, J. C. see Davis, J. C. Bancroft.
Bancroft naturalization treaties. 51311
Bancroft's hand-book almanac. 3143
Bancroft's speech in New-York. 88496
Banda de buen gobierno mandado observar en la ciudad. 66584
Banda oriental. 9001
Bandeira, Antonio Herculano de Souza. see Souza Bandeira, Antonio Herculano de.
Bandeira da constituicao. see Banner of the constitution.
Banderar roja. 48816
Banderilla. 72270
Bandetti. 82503
Bandiera, Domenico. see Vandiera, Dominico, of Siena.
Bandiera, Dominico. see Vandiera, Dominico, of Siena.
Bandinel, James. (3147)-3148
Bandini, Angelo Maria. 3149-3150, 99383A, note after 99383C
Bandini, Simon. 74033
Bandit californien. (34129)
Banditen. 16420
Banditti of the Rocky Mountains. 34162
Bandlier, Ad. Eug. 7859
Bando de buen gobierno del Excmo. Sr. D. Manuel Cagigal. 17755
Bando de buen gobierno para la ciudad de la Havana. (29419)
Bando publicado por D. Salvador Joseph de Muro y Salazar. 86816
Bane and antidote. 100577
Banecke, G. F. tr. 2345
Banet-Rivet, L. 41217
Banfield, -----. 86386
Bangbar, Barnaby. 95330
Bangor, Phileluth, V. E. B. pseud. see Foxcroft, Thomas.
Bangor, Bishop of. see Bayly, Lewis, Bp. of Bangor. Egerton, John, Bp. of Bangor. Herring, Thomas, Bp. of Bangor. Hutton, Mathew, Bp. of Bangor. Moore, John, Archbishop of Canterbury, 1730-1805. Warren, John, Bp. of Bangor, 1730-1800.
Bangor, Me. Bank of Bangor. see Bank of Bangor, Bangor, Maine.
Bangor, Me. Charter. (3155)-3156

Bangor, Me. Maine Charity School. see New Theological Seminary, Bangor, Me.
Bangor, Me. Meeting of the Church Association of Maine, 1853. see Unitarian Churches. Maine. Annual meeting, 1st, Bangor, 1853.
Bangor, Me. New Theological Seminary. see New Theological Seminary, Bangor, Me.
Bangor, Me. Ordinances, etc. (3155)-3156
Bangor, Me. Theological Institution. see Theological Institution, Bangor, Me.
Bangor city directory. (3152)
Bangor directory. (3151)
Bangor journal of literature, science, morals, and religion. 3153
Bangor, Orono and Oldtown Rail Road. 50993
Bangor register. 103307
Bangs, Edward. 3161-3162, 105411
Bangs, Edward. supposed author 105958-105959, 105963
Bangs, Edward Dillingham. 3163-3164
Bangs, Nathan. 3165-3168, 92823
Bangs, Stephen Beekman. 43852
Bangs & Co. firm 74687, (77842), 89731
Bangs, Brother & Co. firm (74675), (74691)
Bangs, Merwin & Co. firm (70839), 72313, 74677A, 74678, 74681, 74685, 74688, note after (74691)
Banier, -------. (4932)
Banished Briton. (28136)
Banished Briton and Neptunian. 28137
Banished count. 88927
Banister, Thomas. 3169-3171, 22966, 40532
Banister, William B. 3172
Banjo and bones' comic song book. 28496
Bank, Providence, R. I. see Providence Bank, Providence, R. I.
Bank, Salem, Mass. see Salem Bank, Salem, Mass.
Bank, Worcester, Mass. see Worcester Bank, Worcester, Mass. and Worcester County National Bank.
Bank. 16297
Bank bill, as it passed the Louisiana Legislature. 42195
Bank bill. Soldiers must be paid. 29294
Bank bills, or paper currency. 3173
Bank case. 87448
Bank contest. 103713
Bank Convention, New York, 1837. 49377
Bank Convention, New York, 1837. Delegates of the Banks of New York City. (54107)
Bank Convention, New York, 1838. (65807)
Bank Convention of the Confederate States, Richmond, Va., 1861. 65822
Bank crash, Esq. pseud. Present crisis. see Dutton, George.
Bank dinner. 3174
Bank director. pseud. Examination into the prospective effects. 23348
Bank for Savings, New York. 54108
Bank for Savings, New York. Charter. 54108
Bank for Savings, New York. Trustees. 54108
Bank guide. 13223
Bank note list and counterfeit detector. 18995
Bank note plate delineator. (21580)
Bank note reporter. 9385
Bank notes proved to be a robber on the public. 18749
Bank of Alabama. Decatur Branch. 19138
Bank of Alabama. Decatur Branch. President. 14922 see also Coman, J. M.
Bank of Alabama. Huntsville Branch. President. (23330) see also Ewing, Stephen S.

Bank of Alabama. Mobile Branch. (26335)
Bank of Alabama. Mobile Branch. President. (49785)
Bank of Alabama. Montgomery Branch. President. 23656 see also Fair, G. Y.
Bank of America, New York. petitioners 54109
Bank of Bangor, Bangor, Me. 3159
Bank of Charleston. defendants 87448
Bank of Charleston. Stockholders Meeting. 12066
Bank of Commerce, New York. 54109, 73977
Bank of Commerce, New York. Shareholders. 54109
Bank of credit erected in the Massachusetts-Bay. 104902, note after 105459
Bank of England. 15028, 65865, 88192, 15028
Bank of faith and works united. (71497)
Bank of Illinois. President. defendant 20630 see also Marshall, John. defendant
Bank of Kentucky. 37492, 37493
Bank of Kentucky. President and Directors. 37493
Bank of Kentucky. President and Directors. petitioners 37493
Bank of Louisiana. See Louisiana Bank, New Orleans.
Bank of Maryland. 22220, 45079
Bank of Maryland. plaintiffs 45079
Bank of Maryland. Trustees. 45078
Bank of Maryland conspiracy, as developed. 22220
Bank of Missouri. Charter. 49574
Bank of Missouri. Committee. 49574
Bank of Mutual Redemption. Boston. (69526)
Bank of Newburgh, Newburgh, N. Y. Charter. 54902
Bank of North America, Philadelphia. 84374
Bank of North America, Philadelphia. Charter. 15967, 69398, 104628
Bank of Ohio. Charter. (56865)-(56866)
Bank of Pennsylvania, Philadelphia. 59908-59910
Bank of Pennsylvania, Philadelphia. defendant 60288
Bank of Pennsylvania, Philadelphia. Charter. 59910
Bank of Pennsylvania, Philadelphia. Committee. 59910
Bank of Pennsylvania, Philadelphia. Directors. 59910
Bank of Pennsylvania, Philadelphia. Directors. petitioners 59910
Bank of Pennsylvania, Philadelphia. President. 59910
Bank of Pennsylvania, Philadelphia. President. defendant 42867
Bank of Pennsylvania, Philadelphia. State Directors. 59909-59910
Bank of Pennsylvania, Philadelphia. Stockholders. 59910
Bank of Pennsylvania. Philadelphia, November 14, 1829. 59909
Bank of Philadelphia. 61961
Bank of South Carolina. see Bank of the State of South Carolina.
Bank of the State of South Carolina, Charleston. 87500
Bank of the State of South Carolina, Charleston. defendants 87448
Bank of the State of South Carolina, Charleston. Charter. 87686
Bank of the State of South Carolina, Charleston. President. 87387 see also Bennett, Thomas.

Bank of the State of South Carolina, Charleston. President and Directors. 87386
Bank of the State of South Carolina, Charleston. President and Directors. defendants 87469-87470
Bank of the United States. 3189, 5104
Bank of the United States. defendants 82145
Bank of the United States. petitioners 26399
Bank of the United States. plaintiffs 30090, note after 90601
Bank of the United States. respondent 60774
Bank of the United States. Baltimore Branch. 104318
Bank of the United States. Committee of Inspection and Investigation. 3189
Bank of the United States. Committee of Investigation. see Bank of the United States. Committee of Inspection and Investigation.
Bank of the United States. Directors. Committee. 3189
Bank of the United States. Joint Committee of Valuation. 3189, note after 57037
Bank of the United States. Stockholders. 3189
Bank of the United States; an article. 39383
Bank of the United States. . . . April 13, 1830. 43205
Bank of the United States vs. Osborn and others. 3189
Bank of Upper Canada. 98068
Bank of Utica, Utica, N. Y. 98223
Bank of Virginia. 100429-100431
Bank of Virginia. plaintiffs (49956)
Bank of Virginia. Charter. 100429-100430
Bank of Washington, Washington, D. C. plaintiffs 72063
Bank of Wooster, Wooster, Ohio. 105224
Bank of Wooster, Wooster, Ohio. Charter. 105224
Bank officer. pseud. Some objections to government demand notes. 86669
Bank reformer. 73913
Bank report. 59905
Bank secrets of the Bank of Columbia. (3175), 14853
Bank statement. 45080
Bank Street Church, Philadelphia. see Philadelphia. Bank Street Church.
Bank tax and bank currency. 3176, 53070
Bank torpedo. 18749
Banka, J. Harrie. 90640
Banker. 94542
Banker's almanac, for 1851. 32691
Banker's almanac for 1852. 47910
Banker's code. 79903
Banker's commonplace book. 32692
Banker's magazine and statistical register. 3190, 24351, 103304
Banker's register for 1859. 47911
Banking. 94491
Banking and mercantile table. 8680
Banking association and uniform currency bill. 3191, 32874
Banking bubble burst. 24535
Banking laws of Massachusetts. (71091)
Banking system of the state of New York. 13599
Banking system of the state of New York, with notes. 13600
Banking systems of Louisiana. 42195
Bankrupt law of America. 16621
Bankrupt law of the United States, 1867. (35688)
Bankrupt law of the United States, etc. 3193
Bankrupt law of the United States, with an outline of the system. 11869

Bankrupt law, the fiscal agent, and auction duties. 68042
Bankrupt law. Speech of Thomas A. Jenckes. 35981
Bankrupt stories. 25484
Banks, -------. defendant 15617
Banks, Henry. 3196-3200, 97921
Banks, James. 43364
Banks, John. defendant 57357
Banks, Sir Joseph, Bart., 1743-1820. (3201)-3203, 6864, 6867, 30934-30945, 31389, 33196, (69276)
Banks, Nathaniel Prentiss, 1816-1894. 3206-3206A, 33150, 42305, 53372, 73947-(73948) see also Massachusetts. Governor, 1858-1861 (Banks)
Banks, Sir Robert. incorrectly supposed author 4246, 16242, note after 36695
Banks, Sir Thomas C. 741, 3207-3208, 16684, 91840, 91853
Banks, Sir Thomas C. supposed author 91841A, 91856
Banks and a paper currency. 73069
Banks and banking in New York. 24647
Banks and banking in the United States. 2825
Banks and paper currency. 3177
Banks, banking, and paper currencies. 29611, (31775)
Bank's bond-man answered. 21249
Banks in danger. 54110
Banks of New York City. 90733
Banks of New-York, their dealers, the clearing house. (27289)
Banks of Philadelphia. petitioners see Philadelphia. Banks. petitioners
Banks of Richmond, Va. see Richmond, Va. Banks.
Banks of the Hudson. 17688
Banks of the Ohio. 75247
Banks of the Ohio: a poem. 38521, 39022
Banks of the Ohio, or westward ho! 59190
Banks of the United States. 14917
Bankson, John. 84610
Bankson & Stuart. firm 93166
Bannan, Benjamin. 18257
Bannantine, James. 3209
Bannatyne Club. 73797, 91853
Bannatyne Club publications. 91853
Bannard, William. 3210
Banneker, Benjamin. (3211)
Banneker's almanac. (3211)
Banneling. 3211A
Banner of freedom. 58144
Banner of the church. 19244, 32933
Banner of the constitution. 3212, 31497, 67504, 94090, 96433
Banner of divine love displayed. 13350
Banner song of the Washington Light Infantry. 84344
Bannerman, Anne. supposed author (30010), 38570, 101802
Banners of a free people set up in the name of their God. 36218
Banners of grace and love displayed. 3213, note before 92797, note after 92800, 3d note after 103687
Bannissement des Jesuits de la Louisiane. (10790)
Bannister, H. M. 34253
Bannister, John W. 3214, note after 81503, note after 81567, 3d note after 98090
Bannister, N. H. 3214A
Bannister, S. ed. 59054
Bannister, Saxe. 3215-(3220), note just before 69467

Banos, Diego Antonio de Oviedo y. see Oviedo y Banos, Diego Antonio de.
Banos, Joseph de Oviedo y. see Oviedo y Banos, Joseph de.
Banos de Velasco, J. see Velasco, J. Banos de.
Banos y Sotomayor, Diego de. 3221
Banos de Catillo. 86436
Banque du Credit Foncier. 42947
Banque Francaise de l'Amerique et des Indies. (4633)
Banques coloniales. 3222
Banquet at the capital of Laputa. 38269, 84886
Banquet, Given to Mr. Cyrus W. Field, New York, 1866. see New York (State) Chamber of Commerce of the State of New York. Banquet Given to Mr. Cyrus W. Field, 1866.
Banquet Held in Honor of C. W. Field, London, 1868. 24265
Banquet to Senor Matias Romero, New York, 1867. see New York (City) Dinner to Senor Matias Romero, 1867.
Banquet to Senor Matias Romero, Envoy Extraordinary and Minister Plenipotenitary from Mexico. 73023
Banquet to Thomas W. Kennard, London, 1865. see London. Banquet to Thomas W. Kennard, 1865.
Banquet to Thos. W. Kennard, Esq., . . . at . . . London. 37379
Banquete dato al Ministro de la Republica Mejicana. 73024
Banquo. pseud. Hit at banking. 32231
Banvard, John. 3223, 3225-3233
Baptism. 79254
Baptism of believers only. 105313
Baptism of Christ. 78287
Baptism of Christ, a Gospel ordinance. 78281, 102638
Baptism of Jesus Christ not to be imitated by Christians. 24429
Baptism of slavery. 42367
Baptismal piety. 46228
Baptismus redivivus. 75445
Baptist. pseud. Three considerations proposed to Mr. William Pen. 8372, note after 14379, 81492
Baptist, J. (74457)
Baptist annual register. 71538
Baptist Anti-slavery Convention, Waterbury, Vt., 1841. 81756
Baptist anti-slavery correspondent. 81902
Baptist Association, Charleston, S. C. see Baptists. South Carolina. Charleston Baptist Association.
Baptist Association, Lafayette, Wisc. see Baptists. Wisconsin. Lafayette Baptist Association.
Baptist Association, Portsmouth, Va. see Baptists. Virginia. Portsmouth Baptist Association.
Baptist Association, Taunton, Mass. see Baptists. Massachusetts. Taunton Baptist Association.
Baptist Association . . . minutes of session of 1855. 44667
Baptist Association of New York City. see Baptists. New York. New York City Baptist Association.
Baptist Auxiliary Education Society, Boston. 6579
Baptist Board of Foreign Missions. Committee. 39229

Baptist Board of Foreign Missions for the United States. Auxiliary Society for Worcester County, Mass. see Society for Worcester County and Vicinity, Auxiliary to the Baptist Board of Foreign Missions for the United States.

Baptist Board of Missions. 35687

Baptist Book and Tract Society of Ohio. see Ohio Baptist Book and Tract Society.

Baptist catechism. 93596

Baptist Charitable Society of Massachusetts. see Massachusetts Baptist Charitable Society.

Baptist Church, Boston. see Boston. Baptist Church.

Baptist Church, Bristol, Conn. see Bristol, Conn. Baptist Church.

Baptist Church, Brookline, Mass. see Brookline, Mass. Baptist Church.

Baptist Church, Columbus, Miss. see Columbus, Miss. Baptist Church.

Baptist Church, Concord, N. H. see Concord, N. H. Baptist Church.

Baptist Church, Hardwick, Vt. see Hardwick, Vt. Baptist Church.

Baptist Church, Leverett, Mass. see Leverett, Mass. Baptist Church.

Baptist Church, Medfield, Mass. see Medfield, Mass. Baptist Church.

Baptist Church, Montague, Mass. see Montague, Mass. Baptist Church.

Baptist Church, Morristown, N. J. see Morristown, N. J. Baptist Church.

Baptist Church, Newton, Mass. see Newton, Mass. Baptist Church.

Baptist Church, North Attleborough, Mass. see North Attleborough, Mass. Baptist Church.

Baptist Church, North Haven, Conn. see North Haven, Conn. Baptist Church.

Baptist Church, Roxborough, Pa. see Roxborough, Pa. Baptist Church.

Baptist Church, Sandy Hill, N. Y. see Sandy Hill, N. Y. Baptist Church.

Baptist Church, South Abington, Mass. see South Abington, Mass. Baptist Church.

Baptist Church, South Reading, Mass. see South Reading, Mass. Baptist Church.

Baptist Church, Southington, Conn. see Southington, Connn Baptist Church.

Baptist Church, Southwick, Mass. see Southwick, Mass. Baptist Church.

Baptist Church, Stamford, Conn. see Stamford, Conn. Baptist Church.

Baptist Church, Warren, R. I. see Warren, R. I. Baptist Church.

Baptist church directory. 31994

Baptist Church in Philadelphia. see Baptists. Pennsylvania. Philadelphia.

Baptist Church of Christ, Newtown, N. H. see Newtown, N. H. Baptist Church of Christ.

Baptist Church of Christ, Salem, Mass. see Salem, Mass. Baptist Church of Christ.

Baptist Church of Christ, Willington, Conn. see Willington, Conn. Baptist Church of Christ.

Baptist church transplanted from the old world to the new one. 29525

Baptist Convention for Missionary Purposes, Philadelphia, 1814. see Baptists. Pennsylvania. Convention for Missionary Purposes, Philadelphia, 1814.

Baptist Convention of the State of Rhode Island. see Baptists. Rhode Island. State Convention.

Baptist cyclopaedia. (31058)

Baptist denomination. 31047

Baptist Domestick Mission Society of New Hampshire. see New Hampshire Baptist Domestic Mission Society.

Baptist Education Society, New York. see Society of Correspondence in New York, with the Baptist Education Society in Philadelphia.

Baptist Education Society, Philadelphia. Society of Correspondence in New York. see Society of Correspondence in New York, with the Baptist Education Society in Philadelphia.

Baptist Education Society of New Jersey. see New Jersey Education Society.

Baptist Education Society of New York. 53540

Baptist Education Society of . . . New York, thirty-ninth annual meeting, held at Hamilton. 53540

Baptist Education Society of Ohio. see Ohio Baptist Education Society.

Baptist Education Society of Pennsylvania. see Pennsylvania Baptist Education Society.

Baptist Education Commission. 53540

Baptist Educational Commission of New York. see Baptists. New York. Educational Commission.

Baptist Elders of Bristol, Conn. petitioners see Bristol, Conn. Baptist Church. Elders. petitioners

Baptist Female Institute, Staunton, Va. see Albemarle Female Institute, Staunton, Va.

Baptist General Committee of Virginia. see Baptists. Virginia. Baptist General Committee.

Baptist General Convention. see Baptists. U. S. General Convention.

Baptist General Convention for Missionary Purposes. 5th triennial Meeting, New York, 1826. see Baptists. New York. General Convention for Missionary Purposes. 5th Triennial Meeting, 1826.

Baptist General Tract Society. 3241

Baptist history. (17387)

Baptist library. 4664, 86855, 93622, note after 102109

Baptist Institute, Philadelphia. see Philadelphia Baptist Institute.

Baptist Meeting-House, Charlestown, Mass. see Charlestown, Mass. Baptist Meeting-House.

Baptist memorial and monthly record. 3234

Baptist minister. pseud. Slavery. 82073

Baptist mission in Jamiaca. 3624

Baptist Missionary Society of London. see London Baptist Missionary Society.

Baptist Missionary Society of Massachusetts. see Massachusetts Baptist Missionary Society.

Baptist Missionary Society of Pennsylvania. see Pennsylvania Baptist Missionary Society.

Baptist Missionary Union. see American Baptist Missionary Union.

Baptist Missionary Convention, New York. see New York Baptist Missionary Convention.

Baptist Orphan Society, Philadelphia. see Philadelphia Baptist Orphan Society.

Baptist People, Called Quakers, in New-London County, in Connecticut Colony. see Friends, Society of. New London Monthly Meeting.

Baptist pulpit of the United States. 4400

Baptist quarterly. 83495

Baptist register. 95431

Baptist Sabbath School Library, Worcester, Mass. see Worcester, Mass. Baptist Sabbath School Library.
Baptist Social Union. 84053
Baptist State Convention for Missionary Purposes, Pennsylvania. see Baptists. Pennsylvania. Baptist State Convention for Missionary Purposes.
Baptist State Convention of North Carolina. see Baptists. North Carolina. Baptist State Convention.
Baptist succession. 68023
Baptist Sunday School Convention of Rhode Island. see Rhode Island Baptist Sunday School Convention.
Baptist Theological Seminary, New York. see New York (City) Baptist Theological Seminary.
Baptist Union for the Ministerial Education. New York. see Rochester Theological Seminary, Rochester, N. Y.
Baptist Union in England. Deputation. (17256)
Baptist Yearly Meeting of the Ancient Order of Six Principles of the Doctrine of Christ, Coventry, R. I., 1812. 49360
Baptista, Elias de S. Iuan. see San Juan Bautista, Elias de, d. 1605.
Baptista, Joan, Fray. see San Juan Bautista, Elias de, d. 1605.
Baptista, Juan, Fray. see San Juan Bautista, Elias de, d. 1605.
Baptista de Oliveira, Candido. see Oliveira, Candido Baptista de.
Baptistae Fulgosi De dictis factils que memorabilibus collectanea. 26140
Baptiste, George de. ed. 87444
Baptistes. (46229)
Baptists. 31047, 72118 see also National Baptist Educational Convention, New York, 1870. Northern Baptist Society.
Baptists. Alabama. State Convention. 563
Baptists. California. San Francisco Baptist Association. 76089
Baptists. Connecticut. 92164
Baptists. Connecticut. Convention, Lebanon, 1833. 15821
Baptists. Connecticut. Danbury Baptist Association. (18458)
Baptists. Connecticut. Groton Union Conference. see Baptists. Connecticut. Stonington Union Association.
Baptists. Connecticut. New London Baptist Association. (53258)
Baptists. Connecticut. Stonington Baptist Association. see Baptists. Stonington Union Association.
Baptists. Connecticut. Stonington Union Association. 92164-92165, 105144
Baptists. Connnecticut. Union Baptist Association. 97762
Baptists. England. see Baptists. Great Britain.
Baptists. Georgia. Georgia Association. 27077
Baptists. Georgia. Sunbury Baptist Association. 93736
Baptists. Great Britain. 93596, 95431
Baptists. Illinois. Convention. (34210)
Baptists. Illinois. Edwardsville Baptist Association. 22000
Baptists. Illinois. General Association. 34212
Baptists. Illinois. Pastoral Union. 34211-34212
Baptists. Illinois. Rock River Baptist Association. 72414

Baptists. Illinois. South District Baptist Association. 49614, 88122
Baptists. Indiana. General Association. 34496
Baptists. Iowa. State Convention. 34979
Baptists. Ireland. 95431
Baptists. Kansas. Convention. (37073)
Baptists. Kentucky. (37559)
Baptists. Kentucky. General Association. 37558
Baptists. Kentucky. Long Run Association. (41903)
Baptists. Kentucky. South Kentucky District Association. 99142
Baptists. London. 61557, 87794
Baptists. Maine. Bowdoinham Baptist Association. (7040)
Baptists. Maine. Convention. 43963
Baptists. Maine. Cumberland Association. 17881
Baptists. Maine. Damariscotta Baptist Association. (18360)
Baptists. Maine. York Baptist Association. 106021
Baptists. Maryland. Baltimore Baptist Association. 3049
Baptists. Maryland. Union Association. 45204
Baptists. Maryland. Western Shore Association. 103017
Baptists. Massachusetts. Abingdon Baptist Association. 70
Baptists. Massachusetts. Barnstable Baptist Association. 3553
Baptists. Massachusetts. Berkshire Baptist Association. (4891)
Baptists. Massachusetts. Boston Union Committee of the Sunday Schools of the Three Baptist Societies. 79797
Baptists. Massachusetts. Charitable Society. see Massachusetts Baptist Charitable Society.
Baptists. Massachusetts. Convention for Organizing the Wachusett Baptist Association, Princeton, 1842. 65777 see also Baptists. Massachusetts. Wachusett Baptist Association.
Baptists. Massachusetts. Council, October, 1803. 85542
Baptists. Massachusetts. Massachusetts Baptist Convention, Boston, 1802. 45821
Baptists. Massachusetts. Massachusetts Baptist Convention, Boston, 1824. 45820
Baptists. Massachusetts. Massachusetts Baptist Convention, Worcester, 1825. 45821
Baptists. Massachusetts. Milford Baptist Association. 48947
Baptists. Massachusetts. Missionary Society. see Massachusetts Baptist Missionary Society.
Baptists. Massachusetts. Salem Baptist Association. 75713-75714
Baptists. Massachusetts. Salem Baptist Association. Sabbath School Convention. 75715
Baptists. Massachusetts. Sturbridge Baptist Association. 32160, 93255-93256, note after 93254
Baptists. Massachusetts. Taunton Baptist Association. 94420
Baptists. Massachusetts. Wachusett Baptist Association. 65777
Baptists. Massachusetts. Wendell Baptist Association. 102626
Baptists. Massachusetts. Westfield Baptist Association. 103029

Baptists. Massachusetts. Worcester Baptist Association. 105384

Baptists. Massachusetts. Worcester Baptist Association. Committee on the Worcester County High School. 105375

Baptists. Massachusetts. Worcester Baptist Association. Sabbath School Teachers Convention, West Boylston, Mass., 1836. 105385

Baptists. Massachusetts. Worcester County Association. 105390

Baptists. Michigan. Convention. 48722

Baptists. Minnesota. Baptist Association. 49270

Baptists. Mississippi. Convention. 49534

Baptists. Missouri. General Association. 49613

Baptists. New Brunswick. Baptist Association in Upper Granville. see Baptists. Nova Scotia. Baptist Association in Upper Granville.

Baptists. New Brunswick. Convention. 3239

Baptists. New Brunswick. Eastern New Brunswick Baptist Association. 52541

Baptists. New Hampshire. Convention. (52858), (52859)

Baptists. New Hampshire. Meredith Baptist Association. (47951)

Baptists. New Jersey. East New Jersey Baptist Association. 24435

Baptists. New Jersey. State Convention. 53168

Baptists. New Jersey. see also Baptists. Pennsylvania and New Jersey.

Baptists. New York. Berkshire Baptist Association. 4892

Baptists. New York. Black River Baptist Association. 5682

Baptists. New York. Cattaraugus Baptist Association. 11555

Baptists. New York. Cayuga Baptist Association. 11637

Baptists. New York. Chenango Baptist Association. 12424

Baptists. New York. Convention, Mount Pleasant, 1791. 51166

Baptists. New York. Convention for Forming the New York Association, New York, 1791. 49376 see also Baptists. New York. New York Association.

Baptists. New York. Ecclesiastical Council, Sandy Hill, 1860. 68873

Baptists. New York. Education Commission. 53540

Baptists. New York. Education Society. see New York Baptist Education Society.

Baptists. New York. Essex Baptist Association. 23018

Baptists. New York. Franklin Baptist Association. 25647

Baptists. New York. General Convention for Missionary Purposes. 5th Triennial Meeting, 1826. 65846

Baptists. New York. Holland Purchase Association. 32517

Baptists. New York. Hudson River Baptist Association. 33531

Baptists. New York. Hudson River Baptist Association North. 33532

Baptists. New York. Madison Baptist Association. 43729

Baptists. New York. Monroe Baptist Association. 50029

Baptists. New York. New Brighton Association. (52515)

Baptists. New York. New York Baptist Association. (54111), (54748)

Baptists. New York. Oneida Baptist Association. 57338

Baptists. New York. Onondaga Baptist Association. 57359

Baptists. New York. Ontario Baptist Association. (57369)

Baptists. New York. Otsego Baptist Association. (57876)

Baptists. New York. Rensselaerville Baptist Association. 69642

Baptists. New York. St. Lawrence Baptist Association. 75313

Baptists. New York. Saratoga Baptist Association. 76923

Baptists. New York. Stephenstown Association. 91326

Baptists. New York. Warwick Baptist Association. 101510

Baptists. North Carolina. Baptist State Convention. 55667

Baptists. North Carolina. Kehukee Baptist Association. see Baptists. North Carolina. United Baptist Association.

Baptists. North Carolina. Kehuky Baptist Association. see Baptists. North Carolina. United Baptist Association.

Baptists. North Carolina. United Baptist Association. 37166, 97839-97844

Baptists. Nova Scotia. Baptist Association in Upper Granville. 56153

Baptists. Nova Scotia. Convention. 3239

Baptists. Nova Scotia. Western Baptist Association. 56152

Baptists. Ohio. Maumee Baptist Association. 46938

Baptists. Ohio. Strait-Creek Baptist Association. 92672

Baptists. Ontario. Baptist Association. 10525

Baptists. Pennsylvania. Bridgewater Baptist Association. 7841

Baptists. Pennsylvania. Convention. 60603

Baptists. Pennsylvania. Convention for Missionary Purposes, Philadelphia, 1814. 51498

Baptists. Pennsylvania. Philadelphia. (3237), 61557, 69519, note after 104732

Baptists. Pennsylvania. Philadelphia Association. see Baptists. Pennsylvania. Philadelphia Baptist Association.

Baptists. Pennsylvania. Philadelphia Baptist Association. 23143, 27407, 36602, 61497, (61962), (62412), 72740

Baptists. Pennsylvania. Philadelphia General Association. 93596

Baptists. Pennsylvania. State Convention for Missionary Purposes. 60303

Baptists. Pennsylvania and New Jersey. 37929 see also Baptists. New Jersey.

Baptists. Prince Edward Island. Convention. 3239

Baptists. Rhode Island. Narragansett Association. 51772

Baptists. Rhode Island. Providence Baptist Association. (66313)

Baptists. Rhode Island. State Convention. 70554, 70711

Baptists. Rhode Island. State Convention. Charter. 70554

Baptists. Rhode Island. Warren Association. 2632, 3240, 49388, 82483, 101496, note after 101497-101498

Baptists. Rhode Island. Warren Association. Education Society. 101497

Baptists. South Carolina. Bethel Baptist Association. 5072

Baptists. South Carolina. Charleston Baptist Association. 26228, 49361, 87794-87796, 1st note after 93597

Baptists. South Carolina. Savannah Baptist Association. (77267), 87947

Baptists. South Carolina. State Convention. 87797

Baptists. South Carolina. Welsh Neck Baptist Association. 102619

Baptists. Tennessee. 94788

Baptists. Tennessee. Stone's River Association. 92158

Baptists. Tennessee. Tennessee Association. 94788

Baptists. United States. 2222-2223, 93596

Baptists. United States. Board of Foreign Missions. see American Baptist Board of Foreign Missions.

Baptists. United States. Board of Missions. 60931

Baptists. United States. General Convention. 3238, (14882)

Baptists. Vermont. Convention. 99151

Baptists. Vermont. Shaftsbury Association. 49383

Baptists. Vermont. Sunday School Union. see Vermont Baptist Sunday School Union.

Baptists. Vermont. Vermont Association. 99152-99158

Baptists. Vermont. Woodstock Baptist Association. 105143-105145

Baptists. Virginia. petitioners. 100101-100102

Baptists. Virginia. Committee, 1791. 49360

Baptists. Virginia. Dover Baptist Association. (49367)

Baptists. Virginia. Educational Society. see Virginia Baptist Educational Society.

Baptists. Virginia. General Association. 100432

Baptists. Virginia. General Committee. 2223, 49359, 97845, 100434

Baptists. Virginia. General Meeting of Correspondence. 100433

Baptists. Virginia. Kehukee Association. see Baptists. North Carolina. United Baptists Association.

Baptists. Virginia. Middle District Association. 48822

Baptists. Virginia. Portsmouth Baptists Association. 64437, 100435

Baptists. Virginia. Strawberry District Association. 92748

Baptists. Wales. 95431

Baptists. Western Baptist Education Association. see Western Baptist Education Association.

Baptists. Wisconsin. Dane Baptist Association. 18463

Baptists. Wisconsin. First Baptist Association of Central Wisconsin. 104887, 104889

Baptists. Wisconsin. La Crosse Valley Baptist Association. (38509)

Baptists. Wisconsin. Lafayette Baptist Association. (38587)

Baptists. Wisconsin. Marquette Baptist Association. 44667

Baptists. Wisconsin. Racine Baptist Association. 67393

Baptists (Free-Will) see Free-Will Baptists.

Baptists (Regular Baptists) Ohio. Miami Association. 48684

Baptists (Western Baptists) General Convention, Cincinnati, 1834. see General Convention of Western Baptists. 1st, Cincinnati, 1834.

Baptists and the national centenary. 83465, 83495

Baptists of Germantown, Philadelphia. 89310

Baptists of the north on the state of the country. 3235

Baptists in America. (17256)

Baptists in literary activity. 83495

Baptists in North America. (17387)

Baquer, Antonio. tr. 99455

Baqueiro, Serapio. 3244

Baquet, Camille. tr. 82528

Baquijano, J. B. (35821)

Baquijano y Carrillo, Jose. (11454)

Baquio, Francisco de Lorra. see Lorra Baquio, Francisco de.

Bar, George La. see La Bar, George.

Bar of the City of New York. see New York (City) Bar.

Bar of Erie County, N. Y. see Erie County, N. Y. Bar.

Bar of Indianapolis. see Indianapolis. Bar.

Bar of New Jersey. see New Jersey. Bar.

Bar of Philadelphia. see Philadelphia. Bar.

Bar of Worcester County, Mass. see Worcester County, Mass. Bar.

Bar rules of the County of Worcester. 105393

Baradere, Juan Maria Raymond. 3245-3245B, 23795, 29099, 40038, 44062, 44391

Baraga, Frederick. 3246-3248

Barahona, Francisco Vitoria. see Vitoria Barahona, Francisco.

Baralt, Rafael Maria. 3249-3251

Baranda, Pedro Sainz de. see Sainz de Baranda, Pedro.

Baranowski, J. tr. 33726

Barao, -----. 79217 see also Sergipe (Brazilian Province) Vice Presidente (Barao)

Baraona, Francisco de Vitoria. see Vitoria Barahona, Francisco.

Baratt, Joseph. see Barratt, Joseph.

Barazabal, Mariano. supposed author 93350

Barba, Alvaro Alonso. (3253)-3255D, (67375)

Barba, Antonio. tr. 79177

Barbacena, -------, Marques de. 96262

Barbacenia Alexandrinae und Alexandra Imperatricis Entdeckt und Beschrieben. note after 77796

Barbade. 101350

Barbadian. pseud. Essay towards the vindication of the Committee of Correspondence. 3262, 3267

Barbados. Attorney General. 27306 see also Beckles, John.

Barbados. Census, 1862. 75410

Barbados. Charter. 3259

Barbados. Citizens. 3263A, 19162

Barbados. Citizens. petitioners 25313, (80601), 96016

Barbados. Colonial Agent. 36646 see also Jordan, G. W.

Barbados. Committee of Correspondence. (20037)-20038

Barbados. Council. 3956

Barbados. Council. Committee to Inquire into the Actual Condition of the Slaves. 3283

Barbados. Court of Grand Sessions. 19598

Barbados. Governor, 1868-1875 (Rawson) 68018 see also Rawson, Sir Rawson William, 1812-1899.

Barbados. House of Assembly. 3269, 4731, 86734

Barbados. House of Assembly. Select Committee to Inquire into the Origin, Causes, and Progress of the Late Insurrection. 3284

Barbados. Inhabitants. see Barbados. Citizens.

Barbados. Laws, statutes, etc. 81, 3259-3260, 3274-3276, 3280, 29840, note after 100381

Barbados. Most Considerable Proprietors. see Barbados. Proprietors.

Barbados. Proprietors. 3273, 36405

Barbados. Several Planters and Other Inhabitants. petitioners see Barbados. Citizens. petitioners

Barbados (Diocese) 3292

Barbados, Bishop of. see Coleridge, William Hart, Bp. of Barbados, 1789-1849. and Parry, Thomas, Bp. of Barbados, 1795-1870.

Barbados a poem. 102451

Barbados almanack. 28783

Barbadoes and other poems. 11993

Barbadoes gazette. (37174)

Barbadoes girl. 32413

Barbadoes packet. (3256)

Barbados planter. pseud. Sugar trade. see Ashley, John.

Barbados seeds. 44639

Barbadoes Society for the Encouragement of Arts, Manufactures, and Commerce, see Society for the Encouragement of Arts, Manufactures, and Commerce, Barbados.

Barbacena, --------, Marques de. 3293-3294

Barao, --------. 17006

Barbara, F. 3295

Barbarini, Maffeo. see Urban VIII, Pope, 1568-1644.

Barbarism of Col. Bullock's chain gang slavery. 27019

Barbarism of slavery. 10190, 93643-93645

Barbarism of slavery. Speech of Hon. Owen Lovejoy. 42368

Barbarism the first danger. 9549

Barbarities of the enemy. 3296

Barbarities of the rebels, as shown in their cruelty. 33275

Barbarities of the rebels at Manassas. 3297

Barbaro, Iosafa. 67736

Barbarosa, Januario da Cunha. see Cunha Barbarosa, Januario da.

Barbarossa. pseud. Lost principle. see Scott, John. CSA

Barbarous capture and death of Gen. Nathaniel Woodhull. 57312

Barbaroux, Charles Oge. 3298, 38583, 38585, 100810-100811

Barbato, the Pirate. defendant 11223

Barbault, Anna Letitia (Aikin) 1743-1825. 3300, 71806, 81434

Barbault Royer, C. see Royer, C. Barbault.

Barbaz, A. L. 3301

Barbazan, E. de. ed. (68417)

Barbe-Marbois, François de, Marquis, 1745-1837. (1534), 3302-3312A, (11525), 21062, (27337), 44474, 75110, 75183, 2d note after 100802, 3d note after 101785

Barbe-Marbois, Francois de, Marquis, 1745-1837. supposed author 3312, 75129

Barbeau de la Bruyere, --------. 21149, (40027)

Barbee, William J. 3313

Barbeiro politico. (62985)

Barber, Daniel. 3314

Barber, E. D. 3315-3316

Barber, E. D. petitioner 99197

Barber, John Warner. 3317-3334, 57249, note after 99587

Barber, Jonathan. 103640

Barber, W. E. supposed ed. 22982

Barber & Southwick. firm publishers (64074)

Barber & Southwick's almanack. (64074)

Barberey, ------ de. 18509

Barbero, Antonio Domingo Thello y. see Thello y Barbero, Antonio Domingo.

Barbessa, Odoardo. 67730

Barbeu-Dubourg, Jacques. (3335), 20045, 20980, 25607, 61511

Barbey, Theodore. 3336

Barbichon, P. M. 3337

Barbier, -------, Chevalier de la Serre. 39129

Barbier, -------, Le. see Le Barbier, ---------.

Barbieri, Gaetano. 2542, 49921

Barbinais, Le Gentil de la. see La Barbinais, Le Gentil de.

Barboer, Jean. 3337A

Barbosa, Antonio Sebastian de Solis y. see Solis y Barbosa, Antonio Sebastian de.

Barbosa, Francisco Villela. see Villela Barbosa, Francisco.

Barbosa, Januario da Cunha. see Cunha Barbosa, Januario da.

Barbosa Machado, Diogo. see Machado, Diogo Barbosa.

Barbosa Machado, Ignacio. see Machado, Ignacio Barbosa.

Barbot, -----. 13015

Barbot, John. defendant 3338

Barbot Gallon de Villenueve, Gabrielle Suzanne. see Villeneuve, Gabrielle Suzanne Barbot Gallon de.

Barbot's description of North and South Guinea and Angola. 13015

Barbou, Jean. publisher 40707

Barbour, B. J. 3339

Barbour, I. Richmond. 3340

Barbour, James, 1775-1842. 3341-3342, 96656 see also U. S. Commissioner to the Cherokee Nation of Indians, West of the Mississippi. and U. S. War Department.

Barbour, John. see Barbour, James 1775-1842.

Barbour, John S. 3343

Barbour, Lucian. 3344

Barbour, Oliver Lorenzo, 1811-1889. reporter 3344A

Barbour, Philip Pendleton, 1783-1841. 3345-3347

Barbour, T. ed. 49620

Barbour's temperance table. 3340

Barca, Frances Erskine Inglis Calderon de la. see Calderon de la Barca, Frances Erskin (Inglis) 1804-1882.

Barca, Pedro Calderon de la. see Calderon de la Barca, Pedro, 1600-1681.

Barcarcel, Basilio Manuel Arrillaga y. see Arrillaga y Barcarcel, Basilio Manuel, 1791-1867.

Barcelo, -------- Narcisio y. see Narcisio y Barcelo, ------.

Barcelona, Francisco Xaviero de Meunrios, Comte de. pseud. Descripcion historique. see Louis XVIII, King of France, 1755-1824.

Barcelona, Spain (Province) Laws, statutes, etc. 48464

Barcelonne, Francisco Xaviero de Meunrios, Comte de. pseud. Descripcion historique. see Louis XVIII, King of France, 1755-1824.

Barcena, Alonzo de. 3348

Barcena, Jose Maria Roa. see Roa Barcena, Jose Maria.
Barcena, Manuel de la. see La Barcena, Manuel de.
Barcena, R. Roa. see Roa Barcena, R.
Barcena y Arce, Manuel de la. 34185, (48815), (76183) see also Michoacan (Archdiocese) Comisionados Para el Funeral y Exequias del Antonio de San Miguel Iglesias.
Barcia, Andres Gonzalez. 3349-3350, 3370, 9767, (14676), 16937, 27733, 31540-31541, 31545, 32043, 40053, 57987, 75577, 77684, 80971, 98745, 98758, 105720, 106269
Barcia Carballido y Zuniga, Andres Gonzalez de, 1673-1743. 18335
Barckhusen, Hermann. 99378
Barclay, --------. RA 9925
Barclay, -------, fl. 1839. 60546
Barclay, Alexander. (3351)-3353, (69413) see also Jamaica. Commissioner of Emigration.
Barclay, Allardyce. see Barclay, Robert, fl. 1842.
Barclay, Anthony. (3354)
Barclay, Charles. ed. 3355, 98083
Barclay, Cuthbert C. (3356)
Barclay, David. defendant before Presbytery 37628, 79376
Barclay, David, of London and Jamaica. (3557)
Barclay, David, fl. 1786. 81895
Barclay, David, 1823-1889. 3358
Barclay, G. L. ed. 47865
Barclay, Grace. pseud. Grace Barclay's diary. see Post, Lydia Minturn.
Barclay, Henry. petitioner 3359
Barclay, Henry. tr. 57488-57489
Barclay, James J. 3360-(3361)
Barclay, John. ed. 9416, 59674
Barclay, John M. (16106), 16117
Barclay, L. A. ed. 78285
Barclay, P. (25402)
Barclay, Patrick. 3362
Barclay, Robert. supposed tr. 86590-86591
Barclay, Robert, 1648-1690. 3363-3367, 59660, 78295, 95752, 103062, 103069
Barclay, Robert, fl. 1773. plaintiff 53074, 91855
Barclay, Robert, fl. 1786. 81895
Barclay, Robert, fl. 1842. 3368, 72876
Barclay, Robert. pseud. Address to the Society of Friends in the United States. (3369)
Barclay, Sidney. pseud. Grace Barclay's diary. see Post, Lydia Minturn.
Barclay, Sidney. pseud. Personal recollections. see Post, Lydia Minturn.
Barclay Street Gallery, New York. see American Academy of the Fine Arts, New York. Barclay Street Gallery.
Barclays, of Boston. 57861
Barco Centenera, Martin del. 3350, 3370-3371, (11677), 29379
Bard, Samuel A. pseud. Adventures on the Mosquito Shore. see Squier, Ephraim George, 1821-1888.
Bard, Samuel A. pseud. Waikna. see Squier, Ephraim George, 1821-1888.
Bard, William. (3372)
Bard of Baltimore. sobriquet see Preuss, Henry Clay.
Bard of "Classic Sheffield." pseud. Missionary's burial. see M., J. pseud.

Bardo Venezolano. sobriquet see Lezano, Abigail.
Bards of Lind. 1308
Bardsen, Ivar. 19198
Bardstown, Ky. St. Joseph's College. see St. Joseph's College, Bardstown, Ky.
Bardstown, October 1834. The St. Joseph's College Minerva. 75303
Bardwell, Horatio. 3373
Bardwell, J. plaintiff 102587
Bare fac'd lies. 105016
Barentin de Montchal, Charles A. Louis. see Barentin de Montchal, Charles Paul Nicolas, Vicomte, 1737-1824.
Barentin de Montchal, Charles Paul Nicolas, Vicomte, 1737-1824. 85256
Barentin de Montchal, Louis. see Barentin de Montchal, Charles Paul Nicolas, Vicomte, 1737-1824.
Barents, Willem, d. 1597. 98738
Baretus, -----. 66686
Bargain proved by the testimony. 13567
Barham, Henry. 3375-(3376)
Barham, J. T. supposed author 3377, 22590, 40358, 46855, 91237, 102797, 102845
Barham, William. 3378
Barhamville, S. C. Female Collegiate Institute. see South Carolina Female Collegiate Institute, Barhamville, S. C.
Barhydt, David Parish. 3379
Bariff, ------. 6375, 22368
Baril, V. L., Comte de la Hure. 3380-3382A
Barinetti, Charles. 3383
Baring, Alexander. see Ashburton, Alexander Baring, 1st Baron, 1774-1848.
Baring, Brothers, & Co. firm 3388
Barker, -------. 31799
Barker, A. 85819
Barker, Abigail. 10082
Barker, Colin. 3388A
Barker, David. 3389
Barker, E. H. ed. 26971
Barker, Edward John. ed. 10633
Barker, Francis. ed. 47377
Barker, George P. 8790
Barker, H. 3392
Barker, H. A. 89540
Barker, Jacob. (2693), (3390)-3392, 68326, 96431
Barker, Jacob. defendant 3392, 89217-89219, note after 96820, note after 98992
Barker, James Nelson, 1784-1858. 3393-3395
Barker, James Nelson, 1784-1858. supposed author 101091-101092
Barker, Joseph, 1751-1815. (3396)-3399, 34895
Barker, Joseph, 1806-1875. 3400-3401
Barker, Martha. 34895
Barker, Robert. 3403-(3404)
Barker, S. W. 87738
Barker, Thomas H. 3405
Barker, W. T. 3406
Barker vs. Barker. 3392
Barklay's digest of the rules of proceedings. (16106)
Barkley, George. 66686
Barkley, Sir Maurice. 99860
Barlaeus, Caspar. see Baerle, Kaspar van, 1584-1648.
Barlow, E. 3413
Barlow, Joel, 1754-1812. 1365, 3414-3437, (8016), 8030, 28734-(28735), note just before 30829, 71321, 78743, (82501), 97204, 97218-97219, 99253, 100597, 105785A
Barlow, Nathan. (3438), 94545

Barlow, S. L. M. 3440
Barlow, William. (3441)-3442
Barlow & Co. firm see Dun, Barlow & Co. firm publishers
Barman, G. N. see Barmann, Georg Nice.
Barmann, Georg Nice. tr. 16429, 16483
Barn-yard rhymes. 68651
Barn-yard statesmen of Podunk. 83716
Barn-yard statesmen: or, rum and dynamite. 83716
Barnaby or Barneby family. 59547
Barnaby, the sandtiller. 72133
Barnaby's in America. 97035
Barnard, C. H. 3445
Barnard, Charles. 85838
Barnard, Charles F. 3443-3444
Barnard, Daniel D. 3446-3454, 33902
Barnard, Edward. (3455)-3456
Barnard, F. C. 3460
Barnard, Frederick Augustus Porter, 1809-1889. (1056), 3457-3459, 14832, 40653, note after 68783, 69932
Barnard, Frederick Lamport. (3461)
Barnard, George G. plaintiff 96821
Barnard, George N. illus. 3462, (62587)
Barnard, Hannah (Jenkins) 3463, 25264
Barnard, Henry, 1811-1900. 1113-1114, (2726), 3464-3469, (7057), 11117, 14255, 15725, 15728, 18955, (21878), 22085, (24040), 25330, 42799, 44376, (69001), 70635, 70683, 70723, 70743, 74392, 92267, 92392, 92394, 94559 see also Rhode Island. Office of Commissioner of Education.
Barnard, J. 12313
Barnard, J. G. 85072
Barnard, Jethro. respondent 51752
Barnard, John, 1681-1770. 3470-3471, 62812, 69400, 90595-90596, 103594, 103631, 3d note after 103650
Barnard, John, 1690-1758. 3472-3476
Barnard, Jonathan G. 3477-3484
Barnard, Richard. 3485
Barnard, Thomas, 1716-1776. 329, 3486-3489
Barnard, Thomas, 1748-1814. (3490)-3493, 101882
Barnard & Callahan. publishers see Peoples, Barnard & Callahan. publishers
Barnard Freemen's Aid Society, Dorchester, Mass. Executive Committee. (20628)
Barnard's American journal of education. 1113-1114, (2726), 3464, 3465, 3467, (7057), 11117, 14255, 18955, (21878), (24040), 25330, 42799, 44376, (69001), 74392, 92267, 92392, 92394, 94559
Barnave, Antoine Pierre Joseph Marie, 1761-1793. 3494, 49083, 75111, 75184
Barnby, ------. 3495
Barnes, -------. plaintiff 45709, 58909
Barnes, Albert, 1798-1870. (3496)-(3508), 4107, 8883, 18766, 38837, 65203, 71285, (82606), 86870
Barnes, Albert, 1798-1870. defendant before Presbytery (36934), 65165, 96822
Barnes, David. 3510-(3512)
Barnes, David M. 3513
Barnes, David M. reporter 31331
Barnes, Edward. 3514
Barnes, G. H. ed. 102550
Barnes, Isaac O. 3515-3516
Barnes, J. 3517
Barnes, John. 3518
Barnes, John Harbeson. 3519-3520
Barnes, John W. Le. see Le Barnes, John W.
Barnes, Joseph. 3521-(3522)

Barrel, Joseph. supposed author 95868
Barnes, Joseph K. 3523, 47307 see also U. S. Surgeon General's Office.
Barnes, Melvin. 789, 3524-3525
Barnes, Oliver W. 60199
Barnes, R. L. cartographer 84983
Barnes, S. W. 3526
Barnes, Thomas. plaintiff 3527
Barnes, William. 3528-3529
Barnes, William H. (3530)-3532
Barnes. 80281
Barnes' Brief history of the United States. 91123
Barnes' Centennial history. 91123
Barnes' Map of Philadelphia. 84983
Barnes' One-term history. 91124
Barnet, James. 3533
Barnett, Francis. 3534
Barnett, Henry N. (3535)
Barneuvo Rocha y Benavides, Pedro de Peralta. see Peralta Barneuvo Rocha y Benavides, Pedro de.
Barnewell im Gefangniss und Yariko in der Sklaverei. 20617
Barney, ------. 66044 see also Committee of Merchants and Bankers of the City of New York.
Barney, C. 3536
Barney, C. W. (3537)
Barney, H. H. ed. (56986)
Barney, John. 3538-3540
Barney, Joshua. civil engineer 3542
Barney, Joshua, 1759-1818. 3541
Barney, Mary. 3541, (3543), (52004)
Barney, William C. (3544)
Barney Rooney's letters on confederation. 26717
Barnicou, ------. (3545)
Barnitz, Jacob. 3546-3548, 106025-106027 see also York County, Pa. Collector of Excise.
Barnoin, Theophile. 3549
Barns, David. see Barnes, David.
Barns, Thomas. (3550)
Barnstable, Mass. Cape Cod Centennial Celebration, 1839. 3555, 10734
Barnstable, Mass. Court of General Sessions of the Peace. (35771)
Barnstable, Mass. Manufacturers of Salt. 3552
Barnstable County, Mass. Ministers. see Congregational Churches in Massachusetts. Ministers in Barnstable County.
Barnstable County, Mass. Superior Court. see Massachusetts. Superior Court for the Counties of Plymouth, Barnstable, &c.
Barnstable Baptist Association. see Baptists. Massachusetts. Barnstable Baptist Association.
Barnstable congressional nomination. (28525)
Barnstable County Agricultural Society. 3556
Barnstable Conference of Evangelical Congregational Churches. 3551, 59462
Barnstable Conference of Evangelical Christian Churches. Committee. 3551, see also Pease, Giles. 59462
Barnstable Massachusetts. 18895, (25762)
Barnuevo, Pedro de Peralto. see Peralta Barnuevo Rocha y Benavides, Pedro de.
Barnuevo, Rodrigo. 3557
Barnum, E. M. 3558
Barnum, H. L. (3559)-3562, 35950
Barnum, Phineas Taylor, 1810-1891. 3563-(3571)
Barnum, der Kaufmann, Journalist und Raritatenmann. 3569

Barnum's American museum. (3571)
Barnum's baby show. 51671
Barnum's connection with the Yankee clock
business. (36063)
Barnum's Leben. 3566
Barnum's parnassus. 9661, (41279)
Barnwell. pseud. Game fish. see Roosevelt,
Robert Barnwell, 1829-1906.
Barnwell, John. 3572, 10955
Barnwell, Joseph W. 88005
Barnwell, Robert Gibbes. 3573, 19116
Barnwell, William H. 3374
Baroja, Manuel. defendant (76304)
Barometria. 29445
Baron, A. 3575
Baron, Richard, d. 1766. 47131
Baron, Richard, fl. 1858. 3576-3577
Baron Dupin's report. 21357
Baron Munchausen, Jr. pseud. Morganiana.
50692
Baron Steuben's regulations. 91405, 91407
Baroncourt, ------ Petit de. see Petit de
Baroncourt, ------.
Baronatage. 20832
Baronia Anglia concentrata. 3207
Baroux, L. 3578
Barquera, Juan Wenceslao. 48336, 76116,
97020
Barr, James. 3579
Barr, Joseph M. 3580
Barr, Mary. 3581
Barr, T. H. 3582
Barra, John. engr. 82824
Barra, Justo de la. see La Barra, Justo de.
Barraband, --------. illus. 40731, 1st note
after 98298
Barradall, Edward. reporter 99975
Barral, L. M. 3583
Barralet, ------. illus. 85105
Barranca, Jose S. ed. and tr. 57223
Barrande, J. 3584
Barrao do Castello de Paiva, A, Herculano
e o. see Paiva, A. Herculano e o
Barrao do Castello de.
Barras, ------ de. 27140
Barratariah chief. 83784
Barratt, B. F. (3585)
Barratt, J. P. 88017
Barratt, Joseph. 3586-3587, 94680-94682
Barrault, Emile. 3588
Barre, ------ de la. 13768, note after 98258
Barre, Isaac. (15052)
Barre, Le Febvre de la. see La Barre, Le
Febvre de.
Barre, Louis. tr. 92525
Barre, Nicolas. 3589, (8784), 99728
Barre, P. Y. 67417
Barre, W. L. 3590-3591, 44812
Barre Saint-Venant, Jean. 3592, 75506
Barre, Vt. Academy. see Barre Academy,
Barre, Vt.
Barre, Vt. Methodist Episcopal Church.
Official Board. 73833
Barre Academy, Barre, Vt. 3593
Barreda, Domingo. 65401 see also Dominic-
ans. Mexico. Provincial.
Barreda, Francisco de. 93335
Barreda, M. Perez de. see Perez de Barreda,
M.
Barreda, Nicholas de la. 3594
Barreda, Pedro Perez de. see Perez de
Barreda, Pedro.
Barreda y Vera, Francisco Sanchez de. see
Sanchez de Barreda y Vera, Francisco.
Barreiro, Antonio. 62980

Barreiros, Gaspar. 3595-3597, (34105), 64001
Barrell, Charles. 3598, 36777, 36778, 1st
note after 90696, 1st note after 97160
Barrell, George. 3598, 36777, 1st note after
90696
Barrell, Henry F. 3598, 36777, 1st note after
90696
Barrell, John. 3599, 27165, 90592
Barrell, Samuel Brown. 3598
Barren fig trees doom. 104065
Barrenechea, J. A. 61158
Barrenechea, Juan de. 3600
Barrera, Alonso de la. 3601, 40708, 98122
Barrera, Jose Maria. 48299
Barrera y Troncoso, M. de la. see La Bar-
rera y Troncoso, M. de.
Barreras, Juan Garcia. see Garcia Barreras,
Juan.
Barrere, B. 3602
Barrere, Pierre. 3603-3605, 62957, (65038),
69148
Barrere de Morlaix, Bernard. tr. 101356
Barres, Joseph F. W. des. see Desbarres,
Joseph Frederick Wallet.
Barret, J. R. 3609
Barreto, Domingo Alves Branco Moniz. 100793
Barreto, Francisco. 3610
Barreto, Luis do Rego. see Rego Barreto,
Luis do.
Barreto, Nicholas, Conde de Casa Barreto.
(1871), 1872, 3611-3612
Barreto, Nicholas Barreto, Conde de Casa. see
Barreto, Nicholas, Conde de Casa Barreto.
Barrett, ------, fl. 1857. (77442)
Barrett, ------, fl. 1851. 30449, 43545
Barrett, B. F. 3613, 31671
Barrett, Jonathan Fay. (3614), 15130
Barrett, Joseph C. 3615
Barrett, Joseph H. 3616-(3618)
Barrett, Lucas. (35584)
Barrett, S. A. 3623
Barrett, Samuel. 3619-3622, 64994
Barrett, Walter. pseud. Old merchants of
New York City. see Scoville, Joseph A.,
1811-1864.
Barrett, Walter. pseud. Vigor. A novel. see
Scoville, Joseph A., 1811-1864.
Barrett, William Garland. 3624
Barrett Lennard, C. E. see Lennard, C. E.
Barrett.
Barrett and Welford. firm 3753
Barretto, Francisco Moniz. see Moniz Bar-
retto, Francisco.
Barretto, Joao P. dos Santos. see Santos
Barretto, Joao P. dos.
Barreyrie, F. de la. see La Barreyrie, F. de.
Barrick, Richard, d. 1784. defendant 1066,
3625, (31895), note before 93509, 103349A
Barrie. firm see Gebbir & Barrie. firm
publishers
Barrientos, Antonio Joaquin de Ribadeneyra y.
see Ribadeneyra y Barrientos, Antonio
Joaquin de.
Barrier treaty, with the two separate articles.
86742, 94070
Barrillon, ------. 3626
Barringer, D. M. 3627
Barrington, Daines, 1727-1800. 3628-3632,
(22574), 46951, 66002, 78169
Barrington, Daines, 1727-1800. supposed author
93597
Barrington, Shute, successively Bishop of
Salisbury and Durham, 1734-1826. 3633
Barrington, William L. 3634
Barrio, Paulino del. 3635

267

Barrio y Lima, Lorenzo Phelipe Torre. see
    Torre Barrio y Lima, Lorenzo Phelipe.
Barrios, Gerardo, Pres. El Salvador, d. 1865.
    3636, 76189 see also El Salvador.
    Presidente, 1860-1862 (Barrios)
Barrios, J. H. de. (40086)-40088, (51894), 3d,
    6th-7th notes after 93855
Barrister. pseud. see Northcote, Sir Stafford.
Barrister. pseud. Analysis of the evidence.
    81847
Barrister. pseud. Englishman's right. see
    Hawles, Sir John.
Barrister. pseud. Few words on the subject
    of Canada. see Clark, Charles.
Barrister. pseud. Trip to Mexico. see
    Forbes, Alexander C. supposed author
Barrister. pseud. Two tracts. see Reeves,
    John.
Barrister at law. pseud. Short account of
    the Bahama Islands. see Graves, John.
    supposed author and Wylly, William.
    supposed author
Barrister of the Inner Temple. pseud.
    reporter 103671
Barrister of the State of Virginia. pseud.
    Summary review. 93606
Barritarian pirate. 47570
Barritt, ---------. illus. 30449
Barritt, Frances Fuller. 3637-3638
Barroetta y Angel, Antonio de, Abp. (41115)
    see also Lima (Archdiocese) Archbishop
    (Barroetta y Angel)
Barroilhet, Carlos. 3639-3642
Barron, Eustaquio. plaintiff 36872
Barron, Henry D. 10765
Barron, James. USN 19132
Barron, James. USN defendant at court
    martial 3644
Barron, James. USN defendant at court of
    inquiry 3643
Barron, William. 3644A, (47944), 94124
Barros, ------. 76897
Barros, Andre de, 1697-1794. 3645
Barros, Giovanni di. see Barros, Joao de,
    1496-1570.
Barros, Joao Borges de. (3650)
Barros, Joao de, 1496-1570. 3646-(3648),
    67731-(67733)
Barros, Jose Mauricio Fernandes Pereira. see
    Pereira de Barros, Jose Mauricio Fernandes.
Barros, Manuel Francisco de, 2d Visconde de
    Santarem. see Santarem, Manuel
    Francisco de Barros, 2d Visconde de,
    1791-1856.
Barros, Pedro Jose de Costa. see Costa
    Barros, Pedro Jose de.
Barros Arana, Diego, 1830-1907. 973, 39151
Barros e Sousa de Mesquita de Macedo Leitao
    e Carvalhosa, Manuel Francisco de.
    see Santarem, Manuel Francisco de
    Barros, 2d Visconde de, 1791-1856.
Barros Pimentel, Esperidiao Eloy de. see
    Pimentel, Esperidiao Eloy de Barros.
Barrot, Adolf. (3651), 11135, 62802 see also
    France. Consulat. Cartagena.
Barrow, Alexander. 3652
Barrow, C. 3653, 40502, 2d note after 102846
Barrow, David. supposed author 79723-79727,
    note after 94924, note after 97880, note
    after 106196
Barrow, E. P. 3675
Barrow, John. 3654-3658, 4858A
Barrow, Sir John, Bart., 1764-1848. 3659-
    3669, 13833, 23213, 73374, 101175

Barrow, John, fl. 1849. 3672
Barrow, John Henry. (49428)
Barrow, Robert. 7879
Barrow, Robert Ruffin. 3673
Barrow, Washington. 3674
Barrow. firm see Smith & Barrow. firm
Barrows, Charles H. 85212
Barrows, George B. 94112
Barrows, John. ed. 16270
Barrows, William. 3676-3680, 34653
Barruel, Augustin de, 1741-1820. 59316
Barruel-Beauvert, Philippe Auguste de. 3681,
    28797
Barruere, Fs. 78916
Barrundia, Jose. tr. 85674
Barrundia, Jose Francisco. 24325
Barrus, Hiram. 83541
Barry, ------. tr. 33701
Barry, David. ed. 36807, 1st note after
    97687
Barry, Edward. tr. 67698, 75576, 98767
Barry, Edmund D. 3682
Barry, Edmund L. du. see Du Barry, Edmund
    L.
Barry, Henry. supposed author 472, 3683-
    (3684), (11881), 16587-16588, 16867,
    26867, 39714, 92830-92831, 92850
Barry, J. J. tr. (73273)
Barry, John Stetson. 3685-3687
Barry, John Stewart, 1802-1870. 33150 see
    also Michigan. Governor, 1850-1852
    (Barry)
Barry, Joseph. (36667)
Barry, P., fl. 1848. ed. (33066)
Barry, P., fl. 1858. (3688)
Barry, Pat. 3689
Barry, S. F. 4779
Barry, Thomas. 3690
Barry, W. F. 3484
Barry, William. (3691)
Barry, William Taylor, 1785-1835. (3692)-3693,
    64498 see also U. S. Post Office
    Department.
Barry Cornwall. pseud. ed. see Procter,
    Bryan Waller, 1787-1874. ed.
Barstow, A. C. 3694, 8524, note after 89213
Barstow, Alfred. 10011 see also Union
    League of America. California. Grand
    Secretary.
Barstow, Benjamin. 3695-3696
Barstow, George. 3697-(3698)
Barstow, William Augustus, 1813-1865. see
    also 84866 Wisconsin. Governor, 1854-
    1856 (Barstow)
Barstow, William Augustus, 1813-1865. defendant 3699, 3883
Barstow, Zedekiah S. 3094, (3700), (72453)
Bart, T. M. 3701
Bart Ridgely, a story of northern Ohio. 71259
Bartas, Guillaume de Salluste, Seigneur du.
    see Du Bartas, Guillaume de Salluste,
    Seigneur, 1544-1590.
Bartels, A. tr. 20899
Barth, ------. ed. 6018
Barth, Christian Gottlieb. 3702-3703
Barthe, J. G. 3704-3705, 69661
Barthelemy, Auguste Marseille, 1796-1867.
    (1534), 3706, (27337)
Barthelemy, Francois de, Marquis, 1750?-1830.
    67626
Barthelemy, Peter. 3707-3708, 99283
Barthelemy-Hadot, Marie Adele. 3709-(3710)
Barthelmess, R. 3711
Barthema, Lewis. see Varthema, Ludovico.
Barthema, Lodovico. see Varthema, Ludovico.
Bartholomeus Las Casas. (55419)

Bartholomew, Andrew. 3712-3713
Bartholomew, Edward. 3714-3716 see also
Philadelphia County, Pa. Collector of
Excise.
Bartholomew, John, 1831-1893. 3717
Bartholomew, John G. 3718
Bartholomew, Orlo. 3719
Bartholomew, William N. 84500
Bartholomew's drawing-books. 84500-84503
Bartholow, -------. USMC 63393
Bartlet, William S. see Bartlett, William S.
Bartlett, Bailey. 3721
Bartlett, Benjamin Smith. 1287, (3818)
Bartlett, Charles R. 3722
Bartlett, Daniel. 68566
Bartlett, David W. 3723-3726, (15518)
Bartlett, Elisha. 3727-3730, 81336
Bartlett, Ichabod. (3731)-3732, 52790
Bartlett, Israel. 3733
Bartlett, J. E. (3754)
Bartlett, John. 3734
Bartlett, John Russell, 1805-1886. 3735-
3752, 15485, 22158, 27243, 38221,
51773, 52872, 54476, 54640, 70546,
70589, (70595), (70633), (70636), 70688,
70700, 95406 see also Rhode Island.
Commissioner on the Soldiers' National
Cemetery, at Gettysburg. Rhode Island.
Secretary of State.
Bartlett, John S. 3755
Bartlett, John Stephen. 3756
Bartlett, John Stephen. plaintiff 3756
Bartlett, Joseph. 3757-3761
Bartlett, Josiah, 1759-1820. 3762-3763
Bartlett, Josiah, 1768-1838. 3765-3773, 5361,
12114, (50942), 72390, 101594, 101777,
101841, 101874
Bartlett, Josiah, 1803-1853. 3764, 3773
Bartlett, M. R. 3774
Bartlett, Richard. 3775
Bartlett, Robert. 3776
Bartlett, Samuel Colcord, 1817-1898. 3777,
71339
Bartlett, S. R. 3778
Bartlett, Thomas. 3779
Bartlett, Washington A. 3781
Bartlett, Washington A. defendant 3780
Bartlett, William E. 3783
Bartlett, William Henry. 3784-3789, 8899,
note after 104504, 104505
Bartlett, William S. 3720, 66194
Bartlett, Zacheus. 95432
Bartlett. firm see Smith & Bartlett. firm
Bartlett and Welford's catalogue. 3753
Bartley, James Avis. (3790)
Bartol, C. A. 3791-3794
Bartol, George Murillo. 3795
Bartolache, Joseph Ignacio. (3796)
Bartolo, Tio. 68340
Bartolome, Jose de San. see San Bartolome,
Jose de.
Bartolomei, Giralamo. 3797
Bartolomeides, Ladislaw. (3798)
Bartolozzi, Francesco, 1727-1815. 5690,
12155, 21901, 76310
Bartolozzi, Francesco, fl. 1789. 3799-3800,
99383C
Barton, ------. 82744
Barton, Andrew. 3801
Barton, Benjamin Smith, 1766-1815. 3802-
3827, 62015, 62959, 67461, 77038
Barton, Charles Crillon. 3828
Barton, Clara Hurlow, 1821-1912. (3829)
Barton, Cyrus. 3820, 3831
Barton, David. 3832-3834, 68415
Barton, E. H. 3835-(3838), 53366

Barton, Ed. 66686
Barton, Elijah. defendant 3839
Barton, Hull. 3840-(3841)
Barton, Ira. 3842-3843
Barton, Ira M. 2668
Barton, James. 3844
Barton, James L. 3845-3848
Barton, Michael H. ed. 86839
Barton, R. T. ed. 99975
Barton, Seth. 104282
Barton, T. 84641
Barton, Thomas. 3849, (15209), 59268, 84678C
Barton, Thomas. supposed author 13782,
80049-80050
Barton, Titus Theodore. 3850-3851, 93905
Barton, William, 1748-1831. 51834
Barton, William, 1748-1831. plaintiff 51834
Barton, William, fl. 1775-1815. 3852-3855,
16143, 56536, (56570), 60744, 97122,
note after 102412
Barton, William, fl. 1806. 90727 see also
Rhode Island. Militia. Rhode Island
Brigade. Claims Agent.
Barton, William P. C. 3856-3863, 43500
Barton, William S. ed. 88502
Barton, William Sumner, 1824-1899. 3864
Barton. firm see Hill & Barton. firm
publishers
Barton Premium. pseud. see Premium,
Barton. pseud.
Bartow, Robert. (3865)
Bartram, Alexander. 3866, 95976
Bartram, F. S. 84423
Bartram, John, 1699-1777. (3867)-3869,
(41354), 80573-80574, 92221-92222
Bartram, William, 1739-1823. 3870-3873
Bartram (John) & Son. firm. (3867)
Bartreau, C. K. (3874)
Barus, Carl, 1856-1935. 85072
Barzena, Alfonso. 3875
Bas Arrilaga, -------. 22913, 76111 see also
Jesuits. Mexico. Provincial.
Basalenque, Diego. 3875A-3876
Basanier, ---------. tr. 69210
Basanier, Martin. ed. 39295
Bascom, -----. 23195
Bascom, Ezekiel L. 3877
Bascom, H. B. 3878-3879, 59472
Bascom, Henry B. plaintiff 48191, note after
93976
Bascom, J. H. 3879
Bascom, Jonathan. (3880)-3881
Bascom, William. 3882
Bascoso, Teresa Castaniza de. see Castaniza
de Bascoso, Teresa.
Bascunan, Franzisco Nunez de Pineda y. see
Pineda y Bascunan, Franzisco Nunez de.
Base de la prosperidad i de la republica en
los Estados Unidos. (77075)
Baseless fabric. 51310
Baseness and perniciousness of the sin of
slandering and backbiting. 100868
Bases de la contrata de limpias. 48299
Bases de organizacion politica de la republica.
48300
Bases d'un premier etablissement societaire.
15926
Bases et statuts de la Societe de Colonisation
Europe-Americaine. 15926
Bases organicas de la republica Mexicana.
48301
Bases sobre las que se ha formado un plan de
colonizacion. 48302, 94592
Bases y leyes constitucionales. 48303
Bases y puntos de parleda para la organizacion
politica. 648

Bashford, Alex. plaintiff 3699
Bashford, Coles. plaintiff 3883
Bashford vs. Barstow. 3883
Basilio de Castro, Jose. alias see Montenegro, Juan.
Basin, Jean. tr. 99354, 99356
Basin of the Mississippi. 17378
Basire, -------. engr. 84617
Basis of a proposed union. 98181
Basis of polygamy. 83284
Basis of sanitary reform. (54188)
Basis of union agreed upon. 98181
Baskerville, Sir Thomas. 77289
Basket, Sir James. 3884-3885, 36956-(36957), 75133 see also Gt. Brit. Agent in the Antilles.
Basler Landmann. pseud. Brief aus Amerika. 7858
Bascoso, Jose Maria. 579, 6834, 47429, 48599
Bason (W. P.) firm publishers 3885A
Bason's county almanack. 3885A
Basque, Benjamin. 3886
Bass, Edward, Bp., 1726-1803. (3887), 103240
Bass, John. 3888-3889, 55332
Bassentin, Jaques. 58546
Basset, -------. 75476
Basseterre, St. Christopher. Court of Oyer and Terminer. see St. Christopher (British Colony) Court of Over and Terminer, Basseterre.
Bassett, Miss -------. (41232)
Bassett, Allen L. ed. (53180), 55814, 85466
Bassett, Amos. (3891), 105896
Bassett, Francis. (3892), 86807
Bassett, George W. 3893-3895, 40948
Bassett, Nathan. (24469)
Bassett, William. (3896)
Bassett, William. supposed author 86067
Bassin du Mississipi au seizieme siecle. 11740
Basterot, -------, Vicomte de. 3897
Bastide, Jean Francois de. 3898, (10513), 47516, 69530
Bastide, Martin de la. see La Bastide, Martin de.
Bastiles of the north. 38900, 76521
Bastille in America. (3899)
Basto, Durate de Albuquerque Coello, Marques de. see Albuquerque Coello, Duarte de, Marques de Basto.
Bastos, A. C. Tavares. see Tavares Bastos, Aureliano Candido, 1839-1875.
Bastos, Francisco Xavier de Sancta Rita. see Sancta Rita Bastos, Francisco Xavier de.
Bastos, Jose De Reveira. 3900
Bastos, Jose Tavares. (69310) see also San Paulo (Brazilian Province) Presidente (Bastos)
Bastos, Manuel Jose de Oliveira. see Oliveira Bastos, Manuel Jose de.
Bastos do Solitario, A. C. Tavares. see Tavares Bastos, Aureliano Candido, 1839-1875.
Basuyne des Oorloghs. 3902
Batalla de Santa Ines. (22900)
Batalla de Tampico. 42107
Batalla de Yanacocha. 3903
Batavia, Netherlands. Societe des Arts et des Sciences. see Bataviaasch Genootschap van Kunsten en Wetenschappen.
Batavia, N. Y. Institution for the Blind. see New York (State) State School for the Blind, Batavia.
Batavia, N. Y. State School for the Blind. see New York (State) State School for the Blind, Batavia.

Batavia, as delineated in the intercepted letters. 8512
Bataviaasch Genootschap van Kunsten en Wetenschappen. 47476, 49982, 80864
Batavius, Cato. pseud. see Cato Batavius, de Jonge. pseud.
Batchelder, Eugene. 3904-3906
Batchelder, J. P. (3909)
Batchelder, John. 3907
Batchelder, John M. (3908)
Batchelder, Samuel, 1784-1879. 3910-3911, 17115, 17124, (70088)
Batchelder, Samuel, 1830-1888. 3912
Batchelder, William. 3913-3914
Batcheller, D. 3915
Batchellor, Albert Stillman, 1850-1913. 52791, 61280, 66514, 1st-2d notes after 98997, note after 98998, 1st note after 99003, 103894
Batchelor, G. 3916, 58930
Batchelor, George. 3917
Batchelor, H. (12406)
Batchelors-Hall; a poem. 102213
Bate, J. P. tr. 100621
Bate, Jesse Denison. see Denison, Jesse.
Bateaux a vapeur et les chemins de fer. 35758
Bateham, M. B. ed. 52770
Batemam, Edmund. 3918, 83978
Bateman, James. 3919
Bateman, Newton. (3920), 34248
Bates, Albert C. publisher 99541
Bates, Archibald L. defendant 96823
Bates, Barnabas. (3921)
Bates, Benjamin. 3922, 47619, 47687, 86043, 100522
Bates, Mrs. D. B. (3923)
Bates, David S. 96352
Bates, Edward, 1793-1869. 3924-(3928), 3929, (55179) see also U. S. Department of Justice.
Bates, Elisha. 3930-3931, 24455
Bates, G. H. 76925-76926
Bates, Henry Walter. 3932-3934
Bates, Isaac C. 3935-3936
Bates, Joseph. 3937
Bates, Joshua, d. 1854. 3938-3941
Bates, Mary. 3945
Bates, Paulina. 79704
Bates, Samuel P. 3946
Bates, Stephen. 85929
Bates, Tacy C. 100523
Bates, W. G. 89877, 90684
Bates, Walter. 3947-3948
Bates, William. (3949)
Bates, William C. 3950, note after 90573
Bates College, Lewistown, Me. 3951
Batesville, Ark. Soulesbury Male College. see Soulesbury Male College, Batesville, Ark.
Bath, William Pulteney, 1st Earl of, 1682-1764. 1777, 2548, 22636, 27614, 41263, 57614, (66641)-66648, 68296, 68700, 70199, 70269, 80700, 86751, 97352, note after 95717, 99249, 101147-101148, 101167
Bath, William Pulteney, 1st Earl of, 1682-1764. supposed author 20684, 23610, 60862, 69470, 70233, note after 96403
Bath, William Pulteney, 1st Earl of, 1682-1764. erroneously supposed author 1661, 26900, 29043, 40263, 40293, 40479
Bath, Me. (3952)
Bath, Me. Charter. (3952)
Bath, Me. City Council. (3952)
Bath, Me. Mayor. (3952)
Bath, Me. School Committee. (3952)
Bath, N. H. Citizens. 52791, note after 98998

Bath and Wells, Bishop of. see Beadon,
Richard, Bp. of Gloucester, afterwards
Bp. of Bath and Wells, 1737-1824. and
Wynne, John, Bp. of Bath and Wells.
Bather, James. 3954
Bath-kol. 3955, note after 104356
Bathurst, Edward Bathurst, 4th Earl. 3956
Bathurst, Henry Bathurst, 3d Earl, 1762-1834.
3956, 8005
Bathurst, Henry, Bp. of Norwich, 1744-1837.
3957
Batie, ------- Dejean de la. see Dejean de
la Batie, ------.
Batista Angeloni. pseud. Letters. see
Shebbeare, John, 1709-1788.
Batista Angeloni. pseud. Select letters. see
Shebbeare, John, 1709-1788.
Baton Rouge, La. Female Orphan Asylum.
3958
Baton Rouge Industrial Fair Association. 3958
Batopilas Mining Company. 3959
Batrachomyomachia. 104998
Battalia de Caa-Guaza poema. 34437
Battel, Andries. 3960, 66686
Battel van Leigh, Andries. see Battel,
Andries.
Battell, And. see Battel, Andries.
Batteries upon the kingdom of the devil.
46230, 46338
Battersby, ------. 50863
Battes, ------. 86700
Battes, John. 86700
Batteur d'Estrade. 21373
Battey, --------. illus. 3662, 23213
Battle, William H. 55689
Battle. 3961, (15209)
Battle! a battle! a battle a squirt. 3961
Battle and massacre at Frenchtown, Michigan.
21092
Battle-axe. 102097-102088
Battle between innkeepers and ecclesiastics.
38067
Battle between the Algonquins and Iroquois.
32470
Battle between truth and error. 95206
Battle cry of freedom. 83677
Battle echoes. 34170
Battle field of Shiloh. 3962, 80491
Battle fields and camp fires. 62739
Battle-fields of the republic. 30559
Battle-fields of the revolution. 70495
Battle fields of the revolution. A poem.
70836
Battle fields of the south. 3963
Battle fields of Virginia. 33131
Battle ground. 13568
Battle grounds of America. 3964, 92215
Battle history of the great rebellion. 41686
Battle hymn of the republic. 83677
Battle not man's, but God's. 67876
Battle of Brooklyn. (8282)
Battle of Buena Vista. 10905
Battle of Bull Run. By Edmund C. Stedman.
91061
Battle of Bull Run. By William Howard
Russell. 74397
Battle of Bunker Hill, or the temple of liberty.
(22527)
Battle of Bunker Hill. This song was composed
by the British. 86878
Battle of Bunkers Hill. 96437
Battle of Bunkers Hill; a dramatic piece.
7184-7185, 50155, 58640
Battle of Bunker's Hill. By a Lieutenant
Colonel. note after (9174)

Battle of Chancellorsville. 3965
Battle of 1862. 63150
Battle of Fort Sumter, and the first victory.
(3966)
Battle of Fort Sumter. Its mystery and
miracle. 85264A
Battle of Franklin. (57206)
Battle of Fredericksburg. 69849
Battle of Fredericksburgh. 15212
Battle of freedom. 25068
Battle of Gettysburgh and the Christian Com-
mission. 17651
Battle of Gettysburgh, and the part taken.
4657
Battle of Groton Heights. 30539
Battle of Hexham. (18997)
Battle of King's Mountain. 80116
Battle of Lake Erie. 38657
Battle of Lake Erie. A discourse. (58917)
Battle of Lake Erie Monument Association.
3967, 38658
Battle of Lake Erie, or answers to Messrs.
Burges, Duer, and Mackenzie. (16415)
Battle of Lake Erie, with notices of Commodore
Elliot's conduct. 9232
Battle of Lepanto. 100861
Battle of Lexington. 40888
Battle of Long-Island: a lecture. 101338
Battle of Long Island, with connected preceding
events. (24293)
Battle of Monterey. 45036
Battle of New Orleans, including the previous
engagements. 84934
Battle of New Orleans; or, Jackson's victory.
3968
Battle of Niagara. 3069, 52150
Battle of Plattsburgh: an address. (81635)
Battle of Plattsburgh: a poem. 63362, 105176
Battle of Plattsburgh, 11th September, 1814.
(63363)
Battle of Saratoga. 68635
Battle of the books. 20503
Battle of the Cambrians and mice. 32487
Battle of the Eutaw Springs. (23123), 34969
Battle of the kegs. 32977, 86955
Battle of the shells. 21782, 63005
Battle of the Sierra Morena. 94441
Battle of the Thames. 22530
Battle of the Thames, October 5, 1813. 3970
Battle of the Welsh and the mice. 65527
Battle of Thermopyle. 105726
Battle of Tippecanoe. (5895)
Battle of Tippecanoe, triumphs of science, and
other poems. 101109
Battle of Trenton. 33219
Battle of Valparaiso. 783
Battle of Williamsburg. (9405)
Battle-pieces and aspects of the war. 47480
Battle record of the American rebellion. 20925
Battle roll. 60859
Battlefield of Chattanooga. 84774
Battles and leaders of the Civil War. 83959,
84774, 85374
Battles between Tom Hyler and Country
M'Cleester. 93507
Battles during the great American rebellion.
3971
Battles of Lake Erie, and Champain. 103721
Battles of Mexico. 62686
Battles of Mexico. Survey of the line of
operations. 56771, 83867
Battles of the British navy from A. D. 1800 to
1840. 847
Battles of the United States. 18931
Battles of the war of the revolution. 18932

Battles of the world. 6434
Batton. 80281
Batvie, Anseleme Polycarpe. 3903A
Batwell, Daniel. 3972
Bauche, -------. 3973, 18344
Bauclas, L. de. tr. 104505
Baudelaire, Charles. tr. 63521, 63528,
  63560-63562, 63572
Baudenkmaler aller Volker der Erde. 7738
Baudin, -----. 35539-35540 see also France.
  Legation. Mexico.
Baudin, -----. traveller 21211-21215
Baudissin, Adelbert, Graf. 3974-3975
Baudissin, Ulrich. 3976
Bauditz, W. 43075
Baudoin, J. tr. 98743, 98750, 98752
Baudoin, Jean Marie Theodore. 3978, 101895
Baudouin, Alphonse. 3977
Baudous, Wilhelm de. 3978A
Baudrand, Michael Antonius. see Baudrand,
  Michel Antoine, 1633-1700.
Baudrand, Michel Antoine, 1633-1700. (2308),
  24163, 52769, 79124
Bavdrand e Cantelli, Sansone. 73418
Baudrillart, -------. ed. 82317
Baudry des Lozieres, Louis Narcisse. 3979-
  3980, 3d note after 100802
Bauduy, Pedro. 2096
Bauer, Edm. 3981
Bauer, Franz. 3982
Bauer, Juliette. tr. 38046-38047
Bauer, Johann Chr. August. 3983-3985
Bauer murder. 65253
Baugher, H. L. 3986
Bauhin, Kaspar, 1560-1624. 29512
Baum, C. H. 97848
Baumann, Ludwig Adolph. 3987
Baumbach, L. von. 3988
Baumgarten, G. ed. (75396)
Baumgarten, Siegmund Jacob. (38594A),
  (77989)
Baumont, Simon van. (3989), (4196), 29186
Baunet, ------. 75476
Baurand, ------. 79124
Baury, Alfred L. (3990)-3991, 97621
Bausman, B. 77731
Bausset-Roquefort, -------------, Marquis de.
  (3992)
Bautismo de Moteuhzoma II. (67641)
Bautista, Elias de San Juan. see San Juan
  Bautista, Elias de, d. 1605.
Bautista, Matias de San Juan. see San Juan
  Bautista, Matias de.
Bauza, Felipe. 4000
Bavaria. Akademie der Wissenschaften. see
  Akademie der Wissenschaften, Munich.
Bavaria. Armee. Hauptconservatorium. 2313,
  38348
Bavier, Urban. (4001)
Bavier's, des See-Capitans, merckwurdige
  Reisen und Begebenheiten. (4001)
Bawier, Urban. see Bavier, Urban.
Baxley, H. Willis. 4002
Baxter, -------. engr. 62051, 81541
Baxter, Benjamin. 4003
Baxter, G. A. 4004
Baxter, Joseph. 4005-4007
Baxter, M. 4008
Baxter, Richard, 1615-1691. 4009-4014, 22165,
  46375, note after 102501
Baxter, Simeon. pseud. Tyrannicide proved
  lawful. see Peters, Samuel. supposed
  author
Baxter, Th. (4016)
Baxter, William. 4017
Baxter, William Edward. 4018-4019

Baxter's directions to slaveholders revived.
  (4011)
Baxton, -------. tr. 69078
Bay, Elihu Hall. 87453
Bay, Elihu Hall. reporter 87455, 87458-87459
Bay fight, Mobile Bay, August 5, 1864. (4021)
Bay of Samara. (24246)
Bay-path. (32509)
Bay psalm book. 22155, 28050, 52736, (66428)-
  (66442), 1st note after 102552, 2d note
  after 103846
Bay psalm book being a facsimile reprint.
  2d note after 103846
Bay state forty-fourth. (74873)
Bay State Granite Company. 72407
Bay state monthly. 102254
Bay State Union, Chicago. 12662
Bayard, A. W. 27377
Bayard, Ferdinand-M. 4022
Bayard, James. 4023
Bayard, James A., d. 1815. 4025-4028
Bayard, James A. jr. 4029-4030, 4037, 20458
Bayard, Lewis P. (4031)
Bayard, Margaret. see Smith, Margaret
  (Smith) 1778-1844.
Bayard, Nicholas. 4035-(4036)
Bayard, Nicholas. defendant 4033-4034, 53436
Bayard, R. H. 4037, 20458
Bayard, Samuel. (4038)-4040, note after 98548,
  note after 102951
Bayard, Samuel J. ed. 91904
Bayard, William, 1764?-1826. 4041, 21108
Bayard, William, fl. 1769. (7884), 54368,
  63210, 95935 see also New York
  (Colony) Agents On the Boundary Line
  Between New-York and New-Jersey, 1769.
Bayard & Co. firm see Le Roy, Bayard
  & Co. firm
Bayard (William) & Co. firm 4042
Bayer, P. Wolfgang. 4043-4044
K. Bayerische Akademie der Wissenschaften.
  see Akademie der Wissenschaften,
  Munich.
Bayfield, Henry Wolsey. 4045-4048, 75246
Bayfield's chart. 75246
Bayless, -----. 9659
Bayless, Sol. D. ed. 50175, 51666
Bayley, ------, fl. 1753. 79922
Bayley, Abner. 4049
Bayley, Daniel. 4050, 94335, 101196
Bayley, F. W. N. 4051, 25287
Bayley, Jacob. 66514, 1st note after 99003
  see also Vermont. Committee to Draw
  Up a Public Defence of the Right of the
  New-Hampshire Grants.
Baylet, Jacob Roosevelt, Abp., 1814-1877.
  (72931) see also Baltimore (Archdio-
  cese) Archbishop (Bayley)
  Newark (Diocese) Bishop (Bayley)
Bayley, Job. defendant 6326, 1st note after
  96956, 1st note after 97284
Bayley, Kiah. 4054
Bayley, N. 4055
Bayley, Richard. 2747, 4056-4057
Bayley, Richard. supposed author 54018
Bayley, Solomon. 4058
Bayley, T. W. N. ed. 80949
Bayley, Thomas Henry. see Bayly, Thomas
  Henry.
Baylie, ------. 32861
Baylie, Robert. (4059), 17091
Baylies, Francis, 1784-1852. 4060-4069,
  (20871), 22472, 55848
Baylies, William. 4070-4071
Baylor, C. G. 4072
Baylor University, Waco, Texas. 4073

Bayly, -------, fl. 1822. 20461
Bayly, James. 4074
Bayly, Josiah. 45090 see also Maryland. Attorney General.
Bayly, Lewis, Bp. of Bangor, d. 1631. 4075-(4076), 22165
Bayly, Thomas Henry. 4077-4078
Bayly, William. 4079, 101030
Bayman, A. Phelps. 4080
Bayman, Robert. 4080
Bayne, Peter. 4081
Bayne, Thomas. 4082
Bayne, W. M. 4083
Baynes, E. D. 85361
Bayonet vs. freedom. (71941)
Bay's reports. 87455
Bazan, Estanislao de Vega. see Vega Bazan, Estanislao de.
Bazancourt, C. de. 4084
Bazeley, Charles W. 85594
Bazley, Thomas. 4086
Bazile, L. 4085
Bazin, Eugene. tr. 2371
Bazo, Manuel. tr. 16506
Bazquez Despinosa, A. see Vazquez de Espinsoa, Antonio.
Bazy, S. (4087)
Be followers of them. 65579
Be it enacted by the Senate and House of Representatives. 105844
Be it known that -------- is a subscriber. 85841
Be it known that this morning. 102195
Be natural! 82603
Be not deceived. 88440
Be patient! (13379)
Be thou clean. 67765
Beach, Alfred B. 4088
Beach, Bessie B. 83852
Beach, David. 4089
Beach, Ephraim. 93919
Beach, George. 4090
Beach, John. 4091-4095, (20062), (23211), 78730, 102569
Beach, Lazarus. (66077)
Beach, Lewis. 4096
Beach, M. S. 4097
Beach, Noah. defendant 103765
Beach, S. Ferguson. 102594
Beach, Samuel B. 4098
Beach, Samuel B. supposed author 15939, note after (63430)
Beach, W. 4099
Beacon Hill. A local poem. 51025
Beacon to the Society of Friends. 19187
Beaconsfield, Benjamin Disraeli, 1st Earl of, 1804-1881. 20276
Beadle, Delos W. 4100-4101
Beadle, Irwin P. 4101
Beadle, William A. 4102
Beadle and Company. firm publishers 4101, 22297, 90508, 91284, 99434
Beadle's American battles. 99434
Beadle's dime novels. 90508, 91284
Beadle's dime speakers. 4101
Beadle's dime tales. 4101, 22297
Beadon, Richard, Bp. of Gloucester, afterwards Bp. of Bath and Wells, 1737-1824. 4103
Beake, Richard. 103441
Beal, James H. 83857
Beale, -------. (42660), 43255
Beale, Charles L. 4104
Beale, Charles T. pseud. Colonel Crockett's exploits. see Smith, Richard Penn, 1799-1896.
Beale, E. F. 4105-4106, 88607

Beale, Robert. reporter 64222
Beale, Stephen T. 4107
Beale, Thomas. 4108
Beale pamphlet. (42660)
Beale's survey. 43255
Beall, John Y. defendant before military commission 4109
Beals, George B. complainant 2599
Beals, William. defendant 4111
Beaman, Charles C. 4112
Beaman, F. C. 4113-4115
Beames of eternal brightness. 4116
Beamish, North Ludlow. (4117), 81698
Beamten von Berks Caunty, fur jedes Jahr. 93110
Bean, -------. 81053
Bean, Charles. (4118)
Bean, Joseph. 4119
Bean, Tarleton H. 85072
Beantwortungs-Schreiben. 2390, 32377, 98990
Bear-hunters of the Rocky Mountains. 7092
Bear Valley Coal Company. (4121)
Bearcroft, Philip. 4122-4123, 83978
Beard, Henry. 90416
Beard, John R. 4124-4126, (42356)
Beard, Thomas. 4127
Beardslee, George W. 4128
Beardsley, E. Edwards. (4129)-4136
Beardsley, Levi. 4137-4139
Beardsley, Samuel. 4140
Bearings of modern commerce. 92073
Bearss family. 54934
Beasley, Frederic, A. M. see Beasley, Frederick, 1777-1845.
Beasley, Frederick, 1777-1845. 1081A, (4141), (14375), 40570, 41349, 84120, 101770
Beasley, M. 4142
Beasley, Robert E. (4143)
Beasley, T. 4142
Beasts and birds of America. (29906)
Beasts at law. 105177-105178, 105194
Beatificationis, et canonizationis ven. servi Dei Joannis de Palafox y Mendoza. 58289
Beatifick vision. (16628)
Beatson, John. 4144
Beatson, R. S. 4146
Beatson, Robert. (4145)
Beattie, Francis S. 90711
Beattie, Francis S. defendant 96898
Beatty, C. C. 14949
Beatty, Charles. 4147-4150, 21928
Beatty, George. ed. 55314
Beatty, John. 90828
Beatty, M. (4151)
Beatus Pius V. Pontifex Maximus ex ordine praedicatorum assumptus. (67808)
Beau, C. le. see Le Beau, C.
Beau, M. (4153)
Beaubien, Henry Des Rivieres. see Des Rivieres Beaubien, Henry.
Beauchamp, Alphonse de. 4154-4158
Beauchamp, Ann (Cook) 4159, 4167, 16231
Beauchamp, Jeroboam O. defendant 4159-4160, 18431, 41028, 79848
Beauchamp, William. ed. 102973
Beauchamp, William Lygon, 1st Earl of. 40458, 42768
Beauchamp, or the Kentucky tragedy. 31201, 81191-(81192)
Beauchamp tragedy, in Kentucky. 4160
Beauchamp. (81279)
Beauchamp's trial. 18431, 79848
Beauchene, Robert de. 4163, 40157-40158
Beauclerk, -------, fl. 1730-1745. 57614, 99249
Beauclerk, Charles. 4164

Beaudry, Hercules. 4165
Beaudry, Louis Napoleon, 1833-1892. 6292, 6891
Beaufain, John Henry de Berenger de. see Berenger de Beaufain, John Henry de.
Beaufe, Jacques. 35792, 35794
Beaufort District, S. C. Citizens. petitioners 4165A
Beaufort District, S. C. Grand Jury. 87450
Beaufoy, ---------. (4170)
Beaufoy, Henry. 4166-4167
Beaufoy, Mark, 1764-1827. 3629, 4168-4169, 2d note after 96334
Beauge, ------. 4171
Beauharnois, --------, Seigneur de. defendant 69718
Beauharnois County Agriculture Society. see Societe d'Agriculture du Comte de Beauharnois.
Beaujour, Louis Philippe Felix de, Baron. 1731, 4172-4173
Beaulieu, Charles Gillston de. 4174
Beaulieu Hues O'Neil, Sieur de. pseud. tr. see Baillet, Adrien, 1649-1706.
Beaumarchais, Amelie Eugenie Caron de. see Toussaint de la Rue, Amelie Eugenie (Caron de Beaumarchais)
Beaumarchais, Pierre Auguste Caron de, 1732-1799. 4178, 4182, 99513, 100657
Beaumarchais, Pierre Auguste Caron de, 1732-1799. supposed author 4177, 4182, note after 34694, 56580, 68123-68124
Beaumarchais and his times. 41846
Beaumarchais and the lost million. 91785
Beaumarchais et son temps. (41845)
Beaumelle, Victor Laurent Suzanne Moise Angliviel de la. see Angliviel de la Beaumelle, Victor Laurent Suzanne Moise.
Beaumont, ----------, Baron de. 4185-(4186)
Beaumont, Arthur J. 4183-4184
Beaumont, Elie de, 1798-1854. 67935
Beaumont, Francis, 1584-1616. note after 88547
Beaumont, Francisco Zavier de Lizana y. see Lizana y Beaumont, Francisco Zavier de.
Beaumont, George A. O. (4187)
Beaumont, Isidro Sainz de Alfaro y. see Sainz de Alfaro y Beaumont, Isidro.
Beaumont, J. A. B. 4194
Beaumont, Jean Baptist Armand Louis Leonce Elie de. see Beaumont, Elie de, 1798-1854.
Beaumont, S. van. see Baumont, Simon van.
Beaumont de Brivazac, -----. 4195
Beaumont de la Bonniniere, Gustave Auguste de, 1802-1866. 4188-4193, 19371, 96070, note after 96059, 1st-2d notes after 96068, note after 96069
Beauplan, Arthur de. 92544
Beauport, Quebec. Commissioners of the Temporary Lunatic Asylum. 4197
Beaupre, C. F. Beautemps. see Beautemps-Beaupre, C. F.
Beaupre, C. Gaudichaud. see Gaudichaud-Beaupre, C.
Beauregard, Couvray de. ed. 25823
Beauregard, Jean Brumauld de. see Brumauld de Beauregard, Jean.
Beauregard, Pierre Gustave Toutant, 1818-1893. (4198)-(4199), 15363, 56783
Beauregard songster. 4200, 77974
Beaurepaire, Alexandre Marie Quesnay de. see Quesnay de Beaurepaire, Alexandre Marie.
Beaurepaire-Rohan, Henrique de, Visconde, 1812-1894. 4201, 72773-72774
Beaurois, A. M. F. J. 59419

Beautemps-Beaupre, C. F. 22672
Beautes de l'histoire d'Amerique. (4202)
Beautes de l'histoire des Etats-Unis de l'Amerique septentrionale. 56055
Beautes de l'histoire des voyages. 5947, 11934
Beautes de l'histoire des voyages les plus fameux. (39986)
Beautes de l'histoire du Canada. (18283)
Beautes de l'histoire du Mexique. (20169)
Beautes de l'histoire du Perou. 66012
Beauties and celebrities of the nation. 22215
Beauties and deformities of Fox, North, and Burke. 4203, 25341
Beauties of American history. 4204, 5783
Beauties of American miscellanies. (9792)
Beauties of Anna Seward. 79473
Beauties of Brother Bull-us. 4205
Beauties of Captain Cook's voyages. 16253
Beauties of Cobbett. 14022
Beauties of diplomacy. 89840
Beauties of divine poetry. 83626
Beauties of Dr. Robertson. 72015
Beauties of going to law. (77011)
Beauties of history. 92804
Beauties of nature delineated. 30521
Beauties of philanthropy. 7376
Beauties of philanthropy: and guardian genius of the federal union. (7377)
Beauties of Poor Richard's almanack. 4206
Beauties of priestcraft. 103329
Beauties of Sterne. 91340-91341
Beauties of Story. 92317
Beauties of the American newspapers for 1805. 6921A, 7175, note after 89505
Beauties of the Bible. 75925
Beauties of the British senate. 4207
Beauties of the creation. 71393-(71394)
Beauties of the healing art. 100878
Beauties of the Hon. Daniel Webster. 68636, note after 102311-102312
Beauties of the Hon. Henry Clay. 13553
Beauties of the late Edmund Burke. 9304
Beauties of the monopoly system in New Jersey 10828
Beauties of tropical scenery. (21239)
Beauties of the study of nature. 75474
Beauties of Washington Irving. 35135, (35148)
Beauties of Wesley. 20757
Beautiful captive of the rebel camp. (31118)
Beautiful Indian of the Mississippi. 12240
Beautiful poem on providence. 103125
Beautiful plan to give each man. 16394
Beautiful spy. (9212)
Beautiful star. 12854
Beautiful tribute. 66789
Beauty and booty. 88659
Beauty and glory of the "patriarchal system" illustrated. 82113
Beauty & loveliness of Christ. 83435
Beauty of divine providence. 103912
Beauty of holiness. 20391
Beauty of virtue. 17022
Beauty of Willard's mill. 3637
Beauvais, Joseph Arthur. 4208
Beauvallet, Leon. 4209-4210
Beauvallon, Jean Baptiste Rosemond de. see Rosemond de Beauvallon, Jean Baptiste.
Beauvart, ------ de. supposed author 67020
Beauvert, P. A. de Barruel. see Barruel-Beauvert, P. A. de.
Beauvois, -----. 85791
Beauvois, A. M. F. J. see Palisot de Beauvois, Ambroise Marie Francois Joseph, Baron.
Beauvois, Ambroise Marie Francois Joseph Palisot de. see Palisot de Beauvois, Ambroise Marie Francois Joseph, Baron.

Beauvois, Eugene, 1835- (4212), 19204
Beaux traits de l'histoire des voyages. 5946
Beavan, Hugh J. C. ed. and tr. 64706
Beaven, James. 4213
Beaven, Samuel. 4214
Beaver, B. pseud. Adventures of Dick Onslow.
   see Kingston, William H. C.
Beaver County, Pa. Citizens. petitioners
   60387
Beaver & Conneaut Rail Road. 60007
Beaver Meadow Railroad and Coal Company.
   4214A
Beaver Meadow Railroad and Coal Company.
   Directors. 59911
Becerra, Hernando. 86411
Becerra, Ricardo. 49931
Becerra Moreno, Juan. see Moreno, Juan
   Becerra.
Becerra Tanco, Luis. 4216
Bechamel Francois, b. 1637. 151-152, 72757,
   (72759), note after 93778, 1st note after
   100824
Bechard, Ferdinand. 4217
Becharia, Antonio. 20210
Beche, H. T. de la. see De la Beche, H. T.
Becher, Arthur E. illus. 83556
Becher, A. B. 4218-4219, 6313
Becher, C. C. 4220
Becher, Johann Joachim. 4221
Bechervaise, John. supposed author 95361
Bechler, Gustavus R. 4222
Bechtel, John, 1690-1777. 4223, 80611
Bechteln, Joannes. see Bechtel, John, 1690-
   1777.
Beck, Abraham. 4224
Beck, Charles. 69917
Beck, J. B. plaintiff 96824, 100796
Beck, John B. 4225-4226
Beck, Lewis C. 4227-4334, 53789, 67461
Beck, Nicholas F. 4235, 15946
Beck, Paul. (4236)
Beck, R. (4239)
Beck, Robert. 104270
Beck, Theodoric Romeyn. 4237-4238, 21710,
   26985, 53434
Beck, William L. de. see De Beck, William L.
Beck-Bernard, Amelie Lina. 4240
Beck-Bernard, Charles. 4241
Beck, A. C. ed. 66957
Becker, A. (49963), 50372
Becker, Abraham. 4242-4243
Becker, George. 4244
Becker, Gottfried Wilhelm, 1778-1854. 4245,
   73387, 2d note before 93419
Becker, Matthias. (8784)
Beckerstaff, Isaac. see Bickerstaffe, Isaac,
   1735?-1812?
Becket, Thomas. 4246, 16242, note after
   36695
Beckett, C. E. 4247, (29198)
Beckett, James M. 85698
Beckett, S. B. 4247, (29198), 64359
Beckford, Charles A. publisher 89056
Beckford, William. 4248-4251
Beckford, William, 1709-1770. 451 see also
   London. Lord Mayor.
Beckles, John. 27306
Beckley, Hosea. (4252), 97417, 99161
Beckley, John, of Virginia. 20490, 96005,
   100358 see also Virginia. General
   Assembly. House of Delegates. Clerk.
Beckley, John, of Virginia. supposed author
   (35920), 97904
Beckley, John, fl. 1794. 19618
Beckley, John James, 1757-1807. supposed
   author (35920), 97904

Beckmann, Johann, 1739-1811. 4253-4254, 5902
Beckmann, Johann Christoph. 4255
Becks, Matthias. 49559, 2d note after 102897
Beckwith, C. 4256
Beckwith, E. G. USA 4257-4258, 69900, 69946
Beckwith, George. photographer 4260
Beckwith, George, 1703-1794. 4259
Beckwith, George Cone, 1800-1870. 4261-4263,
   38529
Beckwith, George Cone, 1800-1870. supposed
   author 63403
Beckwith, H. engr. 31643, 91035
Beckwith, Henry T. (4264)
Beckwith, N. W. (58595)
Beckwith's almanac. 4260
Beckwourth, James P. 4265-4266
Becmann, Johann Christoph. see Beckmann,
   Johann Christoph.
Becourt, R. de. 4267
Bedard, P. H. 4268
Bedard, Thomas. 4269-4270
Beddoes, Thomas. 103239
Bedell, Gregory Thurston, Bp., 1817-1892.
   4271-4274, 5574, 34009, 56024, (69359),
   97627 see also New York (City) Church
   of the Ascension. Rector.
Bedell, Richard. respondent 31299
Bedenckinge over d'antwoordt. 4275, note after
   102883
Bedenckinghen. 98201
Bedenckinghen over den staet vande Vereenichde
   Nederlanden. 98191
Bedenkingen en opmerkingen. 33121
Bedenkingen over Tartaryen en Japon. 67408
Bedenkingen van den Graaf de Mirabeau. (65451)
Bedenkingen wegen de nieuwe reglement onlangs
   ingevoerd in Suriname. 6453, 1st note
   after 93850
Bedernoton, David de Parra. pseud. Al defen-
   sor de tontos. see Vera y Pintado,
   Bernardo.
Bedford, Gunning S. 4276-4277
Bedford, John Russell, 4th Duke of, 1710-1771.
   74342
Bedford, Peter. (81880)
Bedford, Mass. St. Matthew's Church. Rector.
   (35840)
Bedford, Mass. School Committee. 4278
Bedford, N. H. (4279)
Bedford, N. Y. Society for the Suppression of
   Vice. see Society for the Suppression of
   Vice in the town of Bedford, N. Y.
Bedford mineral springs. (4281)
Bedinger, Daniel. 4282
Bedinger, Henry. 4283
Bedlam, a ball, and Dr. Price's Observations on
   civil liberty. (4284)
Bedlam garland. 103135
Bedlow, Henry. defendant (69914)
Bedolliere, Emile Gigault de la. see La
   Bedolliere, Emile Gigault de.
Bedortha, N. ed. 95608
Bee, Thomas. 87456
Bee. 102394
Bee. [Serial.] 51377
Bee-hunter. 16489
Bee, no. 1. 4285
Beebe, G. J. (4286), 43604
Beebee, Samuel. 4287
Beech, -------. 36679
Beech, E. D. 4288
Beecham, John. 13829
Beeche y Compania. firm see Uriburu,
   Beeche y Compania. firm
Beechenbrook; a rhyme of the war. 65375

Beecher, Catharine Esther, 1800-1878. 4289-
4295, 28854, (30661), 31771, 92435
Beecher, Charles, 1815-1900. 4296-4301, 4305,
4328
Beecher, Edward, 1803-1895. (4302)-4305,
85922
Beecher, Eunice White (Bullard) 1813-1897.
4327
Beecher, George. 4306
Beecher, Harriet Elizabeth. see Stowe,
Harriet Elizabeth (Beecher) 1811-1896.
Beecher, Henry Ward, 1813-1887. (4307)-4326,
8299, 8302, 15096, 18354, 26706, 50328,
76687, 98005
Beecher, Henry Ward, 1813-1887. imaginary
author. 13167
Beecher, Lyman, 1775-1863. (4328)-4345,
9623, 28965, 28976, 42460, 84296,
85922, 101057, 103798
Beecher, Lyman, 1775-1863. defendant before
Presbytery 96825
Beecher, Lyman, 1775-1863. defendant before
Synod 104676
Beecher, T. 4346
Beechey, Frederick William, 1796-1856. 4347-
4349, 21211-21215, 31601, 71031, 89540
Beeckeren, -------, Baron van. 31225, note
before 93848
Beede, Thomas. 4350-4351
Beedome, Thomas. 71906
Beeedigde verklaring van Andries Cornelissen
Vertholen. 47766, 3d note after 102895
Beek, J. ter. 4352
Beekman, Cornelia. appellant 98438
Beekman, Gerard G. appellant 98438
Beekman, James W. 89345
Beelden uit Amerika. 4353
Beelden uit het leven te New-York. 78463
Beelzebub. pseud. Sure guide to hell. see
Bourn, Benjamin. supposed author
Beems, ------. tr. (21177)
Beene, Jesse. petitioner 94813
Beers, Andrew. (4354), 23846, 62569, 73066,
91975-91978
Beers, F. W. 4355-4357
Beers, J. M. 4355
Beers, Joseph D. defendant 101435-101436
Beers, Nathan. 105859 see also Yale Uni-
versity. Steward.
Beers, Seth P. 105844
Beers, William P. (4358)
Beers' almanack for . . . 1818. (4354)
Bees. A poem. 98519
Bees, from the latin of J. Vaniere. 75949,
98520, 2d note after 96930A
Beeson, John, d. 1803. 4359-4361, 10080
Beeston, ------. 79781
Beet-root sugar. 28303
Beeton, Samuel Orchart, 1831-1877. ed.
79913, 84183, 84307, 84313
Beeton's books for all time. 84307
Beeton's humourous books. 79913, 84183
Beets, N. 4362
Before and after the battle. 52161
Before the after the battle: a day and night in
'Dixie." (66796)
Before the after the curtain. 55758
Before the behind the curtain. 51206, 71561
Before the Board of Visitors of Andover
Theological Seminary. Arguments on
behalf of the complaints. 85212
Before the Board of Visitors of Andover
Theological Seminary. In the matter of
the charges. 85212
Before the Court Martial trying the case of
Ben. P. Runkle. (74135)

Before the flood and after. 82389
Before the footlights and behind the scenes.
41804
Before the Mixed Commission on British and
American Claims. 88829
Before the Most Noble and Right Honourable
the Lords Commissioners of Appeals in
Prize Causes. The Virginia, Christopher
Lee, Master. 100576
Before the Most Noble and Right Honourable
the Lords Commissioners of Appeals in
Prize Causes. The War Hawk, John
Chamming, Master. 101262
Before the Most Noble and Right Honourable
the Lords Commissioners of Appeals in
Prize Causes. The William Tell, Henry
Jackways, Master. 104160
Before the Most Noble and Right Honorable the
Lords Commissioners of Appeals in Prize
Causes. William Tell, Henry Jackways,
Master. . . . Appeal from Gibraltar.
104160
Before the President of the United States.
19904
Befreiten Sclaven in Amerika. (39920)
Befreiungskampf der Nord-Amerikanischen
Staaten. 22366
Begebenheiten auf einer Reise in Yucatan.
91296
Begebenheiten und Reisen zu den Amerikanischen
Wilden. 39585
Begert, Jakob. (4363), note after 51694
Begg, -----. 4303
Beggar girl. 97284
Begin ende 31503
Begin ende Voortgang vande Vereenigde
Nederlandsche Geoctroyeerde Oost-Indische
Compagnie. (11608), 14957, 64582, 67558,
89447, 3d note after 100831
Begin ende Voortgangh, van de Vereenighde
Nederlantsche Geoctroyeerde Oost-Indische
Compagnie. (14958)-14960, 37691, 55448,
67558, 68454, 89447A, 3d note after
100831
Begin, midden en eynde der see-rooveryen.
23468
Begin, midden en eynde, der zee-rooveryen.
15016
Beginning and end. 89829
Beginning and progress of the war with the
Indians. 34621
Beginning and the end. 4364
Beginning of America. 4652
Beginning of the Sabbath. 80255-(80257)
Beginning of the year. (23209)
Beginning, progress and conclusion of Bacon's
rebellion in Virginia. 4366
Beginning, progress, and conclusion of the late
war. 4365
Beginnings of biography, &c. 94468
Beginnings of the Capuchin mission in Louisiana.
79993
Begouen, -------. 65033
Begriss de Mirakelen, met de VVelcke Godt de
onsterffelijcke Glorio van de H. Rosa.
(4367)
Begrypende zes Reyzen zo na Lybien. 49792
Beguerie, J. M. 4368
Behaim, Martin, 1459?-1506. (13179), 76838
Behandlung der Kolonisten in der Provinz St.
Paulo. 18677
Behandlung der Sklaven. 7927
Behemoth. 46828, 46836, 46840
Behind the scenes. 37141
Behind the scenes; by a nigger woman who took
in work. 81903

Behind the scenes; or, life in an insane asylum.
83501
Behm, Jacob. 39820
Behme, Ant. see Bohm, Antonius.
Behn, Aphra (Johnson) 1640-1689. 4369-4373
Behr, Ottomar von. 4374-4375
Behrend, Fr. J. 4376
Behrens, Karl Friedrich. 4377-4379
Beiden altesten General-Karten von Amerika.
38211
Beijer, E. see Beyer, E.
Beil, J. A. 4380
Beilage zu 10. 203 der Leipziger Zeitung von
1853. 85082
Being appointed by the Vice-Admiral Viscount
Howe 33326
"Being defamed, we entreat." 103745
Beissel, C. 100775, 106364
Beissel, Johann Conrad. 106363
Beitrag zu Ansons Reisen nebst Leben Ansons.
69135
Beitrag zur Charakteristik der Amerikanischen
Indianer. 38214
Beitrag zur Flora Brasiliens. 44999
Beitrag zur Geographie, Natur- und Volker-
geschichte von Westindien. 38369
Beitrag zur Geschichte der Deutsch-Amerikan-
erthums der letzten 25 Jahre. 77639
Beitrag zur Geschichte der Deutschen ausser
Deutschland. 92806
Beitrag zur Handelsgeschichte der Stadt
Augsburg. (69369)
Beitrag zur Kenntniss der geognostischen
Beschaffenheit Californiens. (28785)
Beitrag zur Kenntniss der orographischen und
geognostischen Beschaffenheit der Nord-
West-Kuste Amerikas. 28784
Beitrag zur Losung der Duetschen Verfas-
sungsfrage. 2563
Beitrag zur neuesten evangelischen Mission-
geschichte. 86874
Beitrag zur Tages und Sitten-Geschichte.
71471
Beitrage zu einer richtigen Kenntniss der
Vereinigten Staaten und ihrer Bewohner.
9671
Beitrage zur Allgem. Auswanderungs-Zeitung.
6826
Beitrage zur Charakteristik der Vereinigten
Staaten. 28880
Beitrage zur Ethnographie und Schrachenkunde
Brasiliens. 44984
Beitrage zur Ethnographie und Sprachen-Kunde
Amerika's zumal Braziliens. (65038)
note after (74627), 77220
Beitrage zur Gebirgskunde Brasiliens. 22829
Beitrage zur genauren Kenntniss seiner Bew-
honer und seines gegenwartigen Zustandes.
7452
Beitrage zur Geschichte der Heidenbekehrung.
(7445)
Beitrage zur Geschichte der Spanisch-
Americanischen Literatur. 35536
Beitrage zur Geschichte der Vereinigten Staaten.
69108
Beitrage zur Kenntniss der Amerikanischen
Muhlenwesens und der Mehlfabrikation.
(4383)
Beitrage zur Kenntniss der Mennoniten-
Gemeiden. 69149
Beitrage zur Kenntniss der Russichen Reichs
und der angrazenden Lander Asiens.
(2711)
Beitrage zur Kenntniss der Spanischen Besit-
zungen in Amerika. 4382

Beitrage zur Lebensgeschichte des Generals
Lafayette. 68928
Beitrage zur Mission der Lutherischen Kirchen.
20923
Beitrage zur naheren Kenntniss des Kraiser-
thums Brazilien. 25922
Beitrage zur Naturgeschichte von Brasilien.
44985, 47012
Beitrage zur Naturgeschichte von Chile. 5210
Beitrage zur Tages- und Sitten-Geschichte der
Hauptstadt von Brasilien. 71471, 77653
Beitrage zur Topographien. 8203
Beitrage zur Volker und Landerkunde. 89763
Beitragen von A. Erman. 32991
Bekanntmachung. 88823
Bekanntmachung! 104921
Bekenner der Wahrheit die Nach der Gottselig-
keit ist. pseud. tr. (46643)
Bekenner und Verehrer Jesu des Gekreuzigten.
pseud. Das Wunder ohen Massen. 105633
Bekker, Balth. tr. 33017
Beknopt en getrouw verhaal. 28927
Beknopte Beschrijving van de Nederlandsche
overzeesche Bezittingen. 94581
Beknopte Beschryving der Engelsche en Fransche
Bezittingen. (58310)
Beknopte en zakelyke Beschryving. 4385, 9285
Beknopte Historie en Tegenwoordigen Staat.
10234
Beknoptelijck getrocken. 100857
Bekort Verhaal. 38487
Belagerung von Boston. 16467, (16469)
Belain d'Esnambuc et les Normands aux
Antilles. 44533
Belanger, -----. 4386
Belangrijke Berigten uit Pella, Iowa. 81438
Belani, H. E. R. pseud. see Haeberlin, Carl
Ludwig.
Belarius of Cymbeline. pseud. First of a
series of a work in favor of the consti-
tutionality of a national bank. see Evans,
Estwick, 1787-1866.
Belarmino, Cardinal 51205
Belasco, Jose Ignacio de Toca. see Toca
Velasco, Jose Ignacio de.
Belcher, C. H. 4388
Belcher, Sir Edward, 1799-1877. 1918, 4389-
(4390), (43072)
Belcher, Jonathan, 1682-1757. 4391-4392, 15429,
(15440), 53200, 92694 see also Massa-
chusetts (Colony) Governor, 1730-1741
(Belcher) New Jersey (Colony) Governor,
1747-1757 (Belcher)
Belcher, Jonathan, 1682-1757. respondent
52454, 103894 see also New Hampshire
(Colony) Governor, 1730-1741 (Governor)
respondent
Belcher, Joseph, 1699-1723. 4393-4398, 95164
Belcher, Joseph, 1794-1859. 4399-4402, (13638)
Belcher, Samuel. 4403-4404
Belcher, William. (65019)
Belcher's farmer's almanack. 4388
Belchertown, Mass. Brainard Church. (14308),
52053
Belchertown, Mass. Ecclesiastical Council,
1723. see Congregational Churches in
Massachusetts. Ecclesiastical Council,
Belchertown, 1723.
Belcourt, George Antoine. 4406-4408
Belden, -----. 76092
Belden, E. P. 4409-4410
Belden, L. W. 4411
Beldene, W. W. 4412
Belding, H. H. ed. 4418, 55853
Belding, Keith and Co. firm (4417), 80487

Belding's northwestern review. see North-
western review, and commercial and
real estate reporter.
Belegering van Boston. 16468
Belena, ------- de Montemayor y. see
Montemayor y Belena, ------ de.
Belena, Eusebio Bentura. see Belena, Euse-
bio Buenaventura, 1736-1794.
Belena, Eusebio Buenaventura, 1736-1794.
4419, 50110, 56261, 58417
Belerofonte matematico contra la quimera
astrologica. 80976
Beleuchung der Sklaven- und Handels-
verhaltnisse der Vereinigten Staaten.
(4839)
Beleuchtung des Beweises. 85108
Belfast, Ireland. Chamber of Commerce.
petitioners (4420), (35060)
Belfast, Ireland. Harbour Commissioners.
petitioners (4420), (35060)
Belfast, Ireland. Town Council. petitioners
(4420), (35060)
Belfast news letter. 12969
Belfrey of Bruges. 41910
Belfrey of Bruges and other poems. (41932)
Belgian Colonization Company. see Com-
pagnie Belge de Colonisation.
Belgick-souldier. (78359)-78360, 78379
Belgick pismire. 78378
Belgicke pismire. 78357-78358, 78379
Belgische Compagnie zur Colonisation des
Districts Santo Thomas, Staat Guatemala.
4421
Belgische ofte Nederlantsche oorlogen ende
geschiedenissen. 48175
Belgischen Colonien in Guatemala und Brasilien.
4422, 29068
Belgium. Commission Belge de l'Exposition
Internal du Chile, 1875. (79351)
Belgium. Sovereigns, etc., 1831-1865
(Leopold I) (36119) see also Leopold
I, King of Belgium, 1790-1865.
Belgrano y Guemes. 49756
Belgrove, William. 4423
Belhaven, John Hamilton, 2d Baron, 1656-1708.
18572
Beliambe, ------ de. reporter 86843
Belieres, J. J. 4424
Believer. pseud. Practical language inter-
preted. see Smith, Eunice.
Believer asleep in Jesus. 66865
Believer healed. 104686
Believer magnifying Christ. 91569
Believers baptism vindicated. 92930
Believers encouraged to pray. 46684
Believers gain by death. 46635
Believers happy change by dying. 50295
Believers in Christ, only, the true Chrildren
of God. 42008
Believers invited to come to Christ. 79405
Believers most sure freedom purchased by
Jesus Christ. 97429
Believer's rest. (82423)
Believer's triumph over death, and the grave.
65075
Believing Jew. 84137
Belin, Oliberos. plaintiff 61110
Belin de Launay, Jules Henri Robert, 1814-
1883. 17940, 39248, 49144
Belin de Villeneuve, -------. 99737
Belinfante, G. tr. 73272
Beliot College, Beliot, Wisc. 4590
Beliot Rail Road Company. see Milwaukee
and Beliot Rail Road Company.
Belisario, A. M. reporter 4425, 32327
Belisarius. A tragedy. (23824)

Belisle, D. W. 4426-4427
Belisle, Guillaume. cartographer 6152
Belisle, Orvilla S. 4428, 66011
Belius, Robertus. see Bell, Robert, fl. 1570.
Belize, Honduras. British Superintendent. see
Gt. Brit. Superintendent, Belize, Honduras.
Belize. 55912
Belknap, Jeremy, 1744-1748. 4429-4441, 17907,
40952, 77436, 95410, 102747
Belknap, Rufus R. (4442)-4444 see also
Brooklyn. Fire Marshal.
Bell, ------. 84724
Bell, --------. defendant before military
commission 8979
Bell, ------, fl. 1860. 77402
Bell, A. N. 4445
Bell, A. W. 4446
Bell, Alexander Graham, 1847-1922. 84997
Bell, Andrew. 4447, 95454
Bell, Andrew. tr. 26676
Bell, Benjamin. 4449
Bell, Benjamin. defendant 4448
Bell, C. supposed author 89637-89639
Bell, Charles. 4450
Bell, Charles Henry, 1823-1893. 65646, 84704,
103223 see also New Hampshire.
Governor, 1881-1883 (Bell)
Bell, Deborah. 4451
Bell, E. Q. ed. 19116
Bell, F., of Kentucky. see Bell, Joshua F.
Bell, Hiram. 4452
Bell, J. B. ed. 103673 see also Bell and
De Camp. firm publisher
Bell, James. 4453-4454
Bell, James C. ed. 104304
Bell, James H. 4466
Bell, James Madison. 4467-4468
Bell, John. 94893, note after 101884, 103093
Bell, John, 1745-1831. 88534, 88537, 100719
Bell, John, 1762-1820. 4455
Bell, John, 1796-1872. 4455A-4457
Bell, John, 1796-1872. petitioner 35459
Bell, John, 1797-1869. 4458-4461, 28493,
34663, 103265
Bell, John Gray. (4465), 11487
Bell, Joshua F. 4469
Bell, L. A. 11651, 41183 see also Colored
People's Educational Monument Associ-
ation in Memory of Abraham Lincoln,
Washington, D. C. Recording Secretary.
Bell, Luther V. (4470)-4475
Bell, Manuel A. 4476
Bell, R. 98778
Bell, Robert fl. 1570. 4477, (32004)
Bell, Robert, 1732?-1784. (4478)-4480, 10671,
58215, 60286, (61751), 61925, note after
63244, 84642, 2d note after 96428, 97366,
99418
Bell, Robert, fl. 1766. ed. 4451
Bell, Robert, 1800-1867. ed. 23690
Bell, Samuel, 1770-1850. 52809 see also New
Hampshire. Governor, 1819-1823 (Bell)
Bell, Samuel B. (4481)
Bell, Samuel D. 52930
Bell, Samuel N. 52822
Bell, Sidney Smith. 4482
Bell, Solomon. pseud. Tales of travels. see
Snelling, William Joseph, 1804-1848.
Bell, Thomas, 1792-1880. 4389, 18649
Bell, William. 4483
Bell, William. plaintiff 96996, 4th note after
102623
Bell (J. B.) firm publisher see Bell and De
Camp. firm publishers
Bell (Thomas) & Co. firm 73048
Bell and De Camp. firm publishers 103673
Bell and De Camp's edition of the trial. 103673

Bell and Everett. 16142
Bell and Everett Club, Marian, Ala. Executive Committee. 69861 see also Constitutional Union Party. Alabama.
Bell, Lincoln, and Douglas. 65389
Bell of Zion. 104948
Bellamont, Richard Coote, 1st Earl of, 1636-1701. 16653-16654, 18563, 18574, 78201-78202, 78238, 92349 see also Massachusetts (Colony) Governor, 1697-1701 (Bellamont) New York (Colony) Governor, 1697-1701 (Bellamont)
Bellamy, ------. 17834
Bellamy, George Anne, 1731?-1788. 4484
Bellamy, Joseph, 1719-1790. (4485)-4497, 17671, 46770, 78734, 94524, 106390
Bellamy, Joseph, 1719-1790. supposed author 102425
Bellamy, Y. 99303
Bellamy Brownjohn. pseud. see Dunham, Robert Carr.
Bellardi, Luigi. (4499)
Bellarmino, Roberto, Cardinal. 4500
Belle-Forest, Francois de. 4506, 51400
Belle Boyd, in camp and prison. (30338)-30339
Belle Brittan on a tour. 26162
Belle et agreable narration. (23998)
Belle of Bayou Luie. 25778
Belle of Prairie Eden. (41399)
Belle of Washington. 39136
Belle Otis. pseud. Diary of a milliner. see Woods, Caroline H.
Belle Scott. 4501, (36412)
Bellecombe, Andre de. 4502
Bellefontaine and Indiana Railroad Company. 4503
Bellefontaine Cemetery, St. Louis. see St. Louis. Bellefontaine Cemetery.
Bellefontaine Railroad Line. 4505
Bellegarde, Charlotte (Ogletorpe) de. defendant 104125
Bellegarde, Henrique Luis de Neimeyer. see Neimeyer Bellegarde, Henrique Luis de.
Bellegarde, Jean Baptiste Morvan de. 4507-4508, 11273-(11274), 21349-21351
Bellegarde, Joseph-Francois de. defendant 104125
Bellegarrigue, A. 4509
Bellegent, Paul de. tr. 10159
Belleisle. Impartial narrative of the reduction of Belle-Isle. 4511, 34378
Bellemare, M. A. G. 98175
Bellemarre, Louis de. 4518-4540, 24196
Bellena, Eusebio Bentura. see Belena, Eusebio Buenaventura, 1736-1794.
Bellenger, Joseph M. 4541, 43887
Bellero, ------. 1561
Bellers, John. 4542
Belles of Broadway. (13435)
Belles-lettres repository; a monthly magazine. 4543, 54796
Belles Lettres Society, Dickinson College. see Dickinson College, Carlisle, Pa. Belles Lettres Society.
Bellet, Louis. 4544
Bellet, Paul Pecquet du. see Pecquet du Bellet, Paul.
Belletristische Ausland. 4539, 7710, 16429, 91283
Belletristische Welt. (4538)
Belletristischen Ausland. Kabinetsbibliothek. 29567
Belletristisches Lese-Cabinet. 92560
Belleville, Ontario. Wesleyan Methodist Chapel. defendants 48190, 74566

Bellevue, ------- Blanchetiere. see Blanchetiere-Bellevue, ------.
Bellevue Hospital, New York. see New York (City) Bellevue Hospital.
Bellevue Hospital Medical College, New York. 54413
Bellevue Medical College, New York. see Bellevue Hospital Medical College, New York.
Bellew, F. H. T. illus. 84886
Belley, ------. 4546, 99242
Belley de Saint-Domingue, representant du peuple, a ses collegues. 4546
Belleyme, Adolphe de. 4547
Bellgraves, Henrietta de. see De Bellgraves, Henrietta.
Bellido, Joseph. 4548
Belligerent rights asserted and vindicated. 4549
Belligerent rights of maritime capture. (30298), (30300)
Bellin, Jacques Nicolas. 4550-4559, 75103, 92197, 94571
Bellinger, E. ed. 87689
Bellingham, Mass. Society for Detecting Horse Thieves. see Society for Detecting Horse Thieves in the Towns of Mendon, Bellingham and Milford.
Bellinghausen, ------. 21211-21215
Bellini, Bernardo. (4560)
Bellisle, M. E. Poyen. see Poyen-Bellisle, M. E.
Bellmare, Alfred Gustave. 4513-4516
Bello, Andres. 4561, (12753), 70301
Belloc, Hippolyte. 4562-4563
Belloc, Louise (Swanton) 1796-1881. tr. 92526
Bellomont, Richard Coote, 1st Earl of. see Bellamont, Richard Coote, 1st Earl of, 1636-1701.
Bellon de Saint-Quentin, J. 4564, 81958
Belloro, Giambattista. 4565
Belloro, Giovanni Tommaso. 4565
Bellot, Joseph Rene. 4566-4567, 67131
Bellot des Minieres, Ernest. 4568
Bellows, C. W. 45681
Bellows, Henry Whitney, 1814-1882. 4569-4575, 8162, 76082, 76537, 76549-76550, 76574, 76579, (76589), 76622, 76647, 76669, 76672, (76675), 76687 see also United States Sanitary Commission. President.
Bellows Falls intelligencer. 96304
Belloy, Auguste, marquis de. 4576
Bell's address to every free-man. (4478)
Bell's Book-Store, Philadelphia. firm 61520
Bell's British theatre. 90520
Bell's memorial on the free sale of books. 4480
Bellvm Christianorvm principvm. 72023
Bellus, Robertus. see Bell, Robert, fl. 1570.
Belly, Felix. see Bailly, Felix.
Belmann, E. 4581
Belmont, ---------- de. 67020
Belmont Coal Mining Company. 4583
Belmont Gallery, on exhibition for the benefit of the U. S. Sanitary Commission. (4582)
Belmont Hospital, Philadelphia. see Philadelphia. Christ Church Hospital.
Belmont Medical Society. 4584
Belmont, the buccanneer and the bay. 34776
Belmonte, B. E. C. 4585-4586
Belmonte, B. E. Dolaco. see Belmonte, B. E. C.
Belmonte Bermudez, Luis de. (4587), 67359
Belmontet, Louis, 1799-1879, 4588
Belot, Charles. 4591
Belot, Gustave de. 4592-4594

Beloved crime. (81904)
Beloved disciple of Jesus characterized. 26781
Beloved of God. 103510
Beloved physician. A sermon occasioned by
    the death of Calvin Smith. 85201
"Beloved physician." A sermon preached in
    Canadaigua, N. Y. 18269
Beloved physician: a tribute to the memory of
    James C. Bliss. 58704
Belsches, Alexander. 85992
Belser, -----. 70481
Belsham, J. 4595
Belsham, Thomas. 4596-4599, 50946, 96412
Belsham, W. 4600
Belsham, W. J. (4601)
Belt, E. W. 4602
Belton, W. H. ed. 88324
Beltrami, Giacomo Constantino. 4603-4607,
    73166, 74948
Beltran de Santa Cruz, Gabriel. see Santa
    Cruz, Gabriel Beltran de.
Beltran de Santa Rosa Maria, Pedro. 4608-
    4610
Belu, C. (3611)
Belus auf den Anden. (25905)
Belvidere, N. J. Charter. 4612
Belville, Jacob. 4613, 30832
Belzoni, -------. 19582, 100825
Bem, -----. 59356, 59358
Beman, Rev. Mr. pseud. see Hines, David
    Theodore.
Beman, Nathan S. S. 4614-4618, 97073
Beman, Nathan S. S. defendant before
    Presbytery 97073
Bembo, Pietro, Cardinal, 1470-1547. 4619-4621
Bement, Ernest M. 4622
Bemerker de Denkund Handelweise der Mens-
    chen. pseud. Wunderthaetige Kraft der
    Kleider. 105637
Bemerkingen Betreffende de Nederlandsche
    West-Indische Eilanden. 5632, 28777
Bemerkungen auf einer Reise durch d. Innere
    der Verieinigten Staaten. 22781
Bemerkungen auf einer Reise durch die
    Vereinigten Staaten. 30534
Bemerkungen auf einer Reise in America.
    5570
Bemerkungen auf einer Reise um die Welt.
    25132
Bemerkungen auf einer Reise um die Welt in
    den Jahren 1803 bis 1807. (38895)
Bemerkungen uber Brasilien. 38898
Bemerkungen uber den Handels- und Schiffahrts-
    Verkehr Triest's 3981
Bemerkungen uber die Landschaften, welche
    ich kennen lernte. 92760
Bemerkungen uber die Missionsanstalten der
    Bruderunitat zu Paramaribo. 71305
Bemerkungen uber die nordlichen Staaten von
    Amerika. 86848
Bemerkungen uber die Sitten und Kunsten der
    Einwohner von Afrika. 63720
Bemerkungen uber Rio de Janeiro und Brasilien.
    42621
Bemerkungen und Ansichten auf einer
    Entdeckungs-Reise. (11818)
Bemis. pseud.? Clay and Frelinghuysen.
    4623
Bemis, George. 4624-4626
Bemis, George. reporter 4627, 5292
Bemis, Stephen. 4628-4630
Bemoaning letter of an ingenious quaker.
    35327
Ben, Uncle. pseud. Brief sketch of the life
    of Charles Baron Metcalfe. see Crofton,
    Walter Cavendish.

Ben Ader, Israel. pseud. Chronicles of B***g.
    12960
Ben-Ansel, ---------. 27016
Ben Israel, Manasseh ben Joseph. see Man-
    asseh ben Joseph ben Israel, 1604-1657.
Ben Jesse, David Marin. see Marin Ben
    Jesse, David.
Ben Joseph ben Israel, Manasseh. see Man-
    asseh ben Joseph ben Israel, 1604-1657.
Ben Saam, Moses. pseud. Speech of Mr. John
    Talbot Campo-bell. see Robertson,
    ------, of Nevis.
Ben Saddi, Nathan. pseud. Chronicles of the
    Kings of England. see Chesterfield,
    Philip Dormer Stanhope, 4th Earl of, 1694-
    1773. supposed author and Dodsley,
    Robert, 1703-1764. supposed author
Ben Saddi, Nathan. pseud. Fragment. see
    Dodsley, Robert, 1703-1764. supposed
    author
Ben Shadow. pseud. see Shadow, Ben. pseud.
Ben Smith. pseud. Motley book. see Mathews,
    Cornelius.
Ben Wade on McClellan. 43030
Benaduci, Lorenzo Boturini. see Boturini
    Benaduci, Lorenzo.
Benamati, Guid' Ubaldo. 4632
Benard, T. N. (4633)
Benavente, D. J. 4634
Benavente, Juan de. (4635)
Benavente, Toribio de. see Motolinia, Toribio,
    d. 1568.
Benavides, Alonso de. 4636-4638, 43826,
    (76810)-76814
Benauides, Alphonse de. see Benavides,
    Alonso de.
Benavides, Alphonsus de. see Benavides,
    Alonso de.
Benavides, I. A. F. 8133
Benavides, Pedrarias de. 4639
Benavides, Pedro de Peralta Barneuvo Rocha y.
    see Peralta Barneuvo Rocha y Benavides,
    Pedro de.
Benavides Cortes, Luis de, Marques de Fro-
    mesta. plaintiff 99436
Benavides y De la Cerda, Bort de. 4640
Benazech, -------. engr. 81486
Benazech, J. 4641
Bench and bar. (21131)
Bench and bar in Jurytown. 24282
Bench and bar of Cayuga County. 4642
Bench and bar of Georgia. 49072
Bench and bar of New-York. (65950)
Bench and bar of Wisconsin. 83961
Bendel, A. 4643
Bender, Benoit. RA defendant at court martial
    96826
Bender, Hastings R. 4645
Benderloch. 84737
Bending willow. 26165
Bendire, Charles. 85072
Benedict XII, Pope, 1285-1342. 62601, 62602
    see also Catholic Church. Popes, 1334-
    1342 (Benedict XII)
Benedict XIII, Pope, 1649-1730. 29148 see
    also Catholic Church. Popes, 1724-1730
    (Benedict XIII)
Benedict XIV, Pope, 1675-1758. 14365, (41115),
    (58529), (61164), (63902), 63904, 63907,
    note after 68444, (68842), 73871, 76315,
    1st note after 98174, 99324 see also
    Catholic Church. Pope, 1740-1758
    (Benedict XIV)
Benedict, Saint, Abbot of Monte Casino. 63367,
    66471

Benedict, David. 4646-4650, 4664, (72171), note after 102109
Benedict, Erastus Cornelius, 1800-1880. 4651-(4656)
Benedict, G. G. 4657
Benedict, George W. supposed author 99210-99211
Benedict, J. 4658
Benedict, James. 4665
Benedict, Joel. 4659
Benedict, Judson D. defendant 29831
Benedict, Kirby. 4660-4661
Benedict, Lewis. claimant 64285
Benedict, Noah. (4663), note after 102109
Benedict, Thomas. 4665
Benedict Arnold, a biography. 31816
Benedictines. 63367, 73871
Benedictines. Congregation de Saint-Maur. publishers 101348-101350, 101352
Benedicto, Josephum a S. see San Benito, Jose.
Benedictus. 46231
Benefactors of the Medical School of Harvard University. 32620
Benefactors of Yale-College, a poetical attempt. 33430, 105926
Beneficient bee. 64036
Beneficient ministries of an early Christian death. 58706
Beneficial influence of literary and scientific institutions. 98733
Beneficien voor de Soldaten gaende naer Brasil. 7525
Beneficio de . . . oro y plata. 26551
Beneficios que deben resultar a la monarquia Espanola. (60901)
Benefit of a well-ordered conversion. 19563, 33442
Benefit of afflictions. 32838
Benefit of afflictions illustrated. 92086
Benefit of plantations or colonies. 78992
Benefit of the writ of habeas corpus is naturally suspended. 29464
Benefit Street Central Congregational Society, Providence, R. I. see Providence, R. I. Benefit Street Central Congregational Society.
Benefits and claims of Sabbath schools. 104906
Benefits and influences of commerce. 28145
Benefits of the Gospel. (50978)
Benefits of the rebellion. 67782
Benemeritos vencedores de Junin y Ayachucho y sus contemporaneos. 93399
Benengeli, Cid Hamet. pseud. Dedication. 19224
Benes, Juan Botero. see Botero, Giovanni, 1540-1617.
Beneski, Charles de. 4666
Benevent, Charles Maurice de Talleyrand-Perigord, Prince de. see Talleyrand-Perigord, Charles Maurice de, Prince de Benevent, 1754-1838.
Beneventanus, Marcus. ed. 66475-(66476)
Benevente, Diego Jose. defendant 55997
Benevolence about righteousness. 82319
Benevolence and gratitude. 14111
Benevolence of the Deity. 12331
Benevolent Association of Hampden County, Mass. 30129
Benevolent Christian Society, New York. 54114
Benevolent Congregational Society, Providence, R. I. see Providence, R. I. Benevolent Congregational Society.
Benevolent Hebrew. 17878

Benevolent Societies in Cheshire County, N. H. (12515)
Benevolent Societies of Franklin County, Mass. (25658)
Benevolent Society, New York. 54114
Benevolent Society of Bloomfield, N. J. (5993)
Benevolent Society of Quebec. see Societe Bienveillante de Quebec.
Benevolent Society of St. James' Church, Roxbury, Mass. see Roxbury, Mass. St. James' Church. Benevolent Society.
Benevolent Society of the County of Orange, N. Y. 57429
Benevolent tar. 86928
Benevolo lectori. 33659, 67546
Benevolus, Hector. pseud. Hartford Convention in an uproar! 30662, note after 101993
Benezet, Anthony, 1713-1784. (4011), (4667)-4694, (17541), 40618, 63224, note just before 69475, 79260, 79264-(79265), 79818-79819, 80675, 82026, 86691, 89175, 93601, 95712, 101276, 102699
Benezet, Anthony, 1713-1784. supposed author 4692, 4694, 49750, 63221, 86662, 86762, 95710-95712, 1st note after 103107
Benger, Miss -------. 96057
Benger, E. 50145, 50147
Benham, Ashbel. 4695
Benians, E. A. ed. 82852
Benicia, Calif. St. Augustine's College. see St. Augustine's College, Benicia, Calif.
Benitez Coronel, Nicolas. plaintiff 24824, (70796)
Benighted Mexico. 83745
Benign influence of religion. 60965
Benincasa, Gratiosos. 76838
Benito, Jose San. see San Benito, Jose.
Benjamin, of Tudela. 66686
Benjamin, -------. USA 95664
Benjamin, J. J. 4698
Benjamin, Jonathan. 4697
Benjamin, Judah Philip, 1811-1884. 4699-4709, 15286, 15396, 15419, 81812 see also Confederate States of America. Department of State.
Benjamin, L. N. reporter 4710, 74983
Benjamin, Park, 1809-1864. 1153, 30290, (65973), 102215
Benjamin, Park, 1849-1922. 4711
Benjamin, S. G. W. 4712
Benjamin, Saint. pseud. New Gospel of peace. see White, Richard Grant.
Benjamin and American slaveholders. 91112
Benjamin Fletcher Captain General and Governour of the Province of New-York. 53671
Benjamin Franklin. 10719, 68643
Benjamin Franklin. A book for all. 25609
Benjamin Franklin: a book for the young and the old. 34051
Benjamin Franklin, docteur en droit. 23807
Benjamin Franklin. Eine Biographie. (48904)
Benjamin Franklin, his autobiography. 25493
Benjamin Franklin. Lebensbild eines Ehrenmannes in Amerika. 56736
Benjamin Franklin, sa vie, ses ouvrages, ses decouvertes. 39126
Benjamin Franklin. Sein Leben, Denken und Wirken. 5099
Benjamin Franklin's Leben und Schriften. 74168
Benjamin Tompson . . . first native-born poet of America. 96156
Benner, Enos. 4714, 39586
Bennet, G. J. ed. (43002)

Bennet, John. see Bennett, John.
Bennet, Moses. 63476
Bennet, Parker. 104245
Bennet, R. G. 4715-4716, 3d-4th notes after 103943
Bennet, William. 4717
Bennet and Walton's almanac, for 1813. 4718
Bennet en Hake. firm publishers 98506
Bennett, -------. engr. 168, 84905
Bennett, A. H. 4720
Bennett, Alfred. (4719)
Bennett, Benjamin. 4721
Bennett, Caleb P., 1758-1836. (45109) see also Delaware. Governor, 1833-1837 (Bennett)
Bennett, D. K. 4722
Bennett, E. T. 71031
Bennett, Emerson. (4723)-(4724)
Bennett, Emily T. B. 4725
Bennett, Frederick Debell. 4726
Bennett, Henry. 4727
Bennett, James. 6137
Bennett, James Arlington, 1841-1918. 83236, 83288
Bennett, James Gordon, 1795-1872. 4728, 33591, 56726
Bennett, John. (4730)-4732
Bennett, Rev. John. 92839
Bennett, John C. (4733)
Bennett, Joseph. 4734-4735
Bennett, Thomas. 87387 see also Bank of the State of South Carolina. President.
Bennett, Thomas H. supposed author 12215, (12749), 100814
Bennett, W. J. plaintiff 12045
Bennett & Walton firm publishers 4718
Bennewitz, Peter. see Apianus, Petrus, 1501?-1552.
Benning, Henry L. 1395
Bennington, Vt. Committee of Arrangement for the Funeral Observations on the Death of Washington, 1799. 101827
Bennington and its surroundings. 4736
Bennion de los tratados celebrados por el Peru. 61094
Benoit, Eulalie. 4738
Benoit, P. J. 4737
Benoit Dinouart, Chanoine de. S. see Dinouart, Chanoine de S. Benoit.
Benoist et Delamarre, P.-V. tr. 4484
Benque, W. 4739
Bensen, E. tr. 59748
Benson, Alfred G. 4740
Benson, Carl. pseud. Letter to Dr. Henry Halford Jones. see Bristed, Charles Astor.
Benson, Egbert. 4741-4748, (11323), 4th note after 99800
Benson, H. (4749)
Benson, Henry C. 4750
Benson, Joseph. ed. note after 102580, 102702
Benson, Martin, Bp. of Gloucester, 1689-1752. 4751
Benson family of Newport, Rhode Island. (26703)
Bent, John. 12416
Bent, Joseph. 4753
Bent, N. T. (4754)-4756
Bent, Silas. 4757
Bent, T. N. see Bent, N. T.
Bentalou, Paul. 4758-(4759)
Bentham, -------. 20832
Bentham, Edward. (4760)-4761
Bentham, George, 1800-1884. 4762-4764, 31944

Bentham, Jeremy, 1748-1832. 4765-4769, 99809
Bentinck, Henry. see Portland, Henry Bentinck, 1st Duke of, 1692-1726.
Bentinck, William Cavendish. see Portland, William Cavendish-Bentinck, 3d Duke of, 1738-1809.
Bentley, ---------. 19807
Bentley, Charles. illus. 3784, 4770, 77796, 85203
Bentley, John. defendant 4471, 44898
Bentley, William. 4772-(4776)
Bentley (Richard) firm publishers 4777, 29683, 97028
Bentley's miscellany. 4777
Bentley's standard library of popular modern literature. 97028
Benta da Cinha e Figueiredo, Jose. see Cinha e Figueiredo, Jose Bento da.
Bento da Cunhae Figueiredo, Jose. see Cunhae Figueiredo, Jose Bento da.
Bento da Silva, Carlos. see Silva, Carlos Bento da, 1812-
Bentom, Clark. defendant 4778, note after 90679
Benton, Col. pseud. see Hines, David Theodore.
Benton, C. 4779
Benton, C. S. 4780
Benton, Jesse. (4781)
Benton, Nathaniel S. 4782
Benton, Thomas Hart, 1782-1858. 297, 3929, 4783-4787, 15888, 83832, 84151, 86569, 86570, 95067, note after 95362
Benton's policy of selling and developing the mineral lands. 15622
Bentotes, George. tr. 72002
Bentuleio, Xysto. tr. 16957
Bentura Belena, Eusebio. see Belena, Eusebuo Buenaventura, 1736-1794.
Bentura de Portegueda, Juan. see Portegueda, Juan Bentura de.
Benutzung der Palmen am Amazonen-Strom. (2472)
Benutzung von noch ungedruckten Briefen. 8875
Benwell, J. (4788)
Benzenberg, Johann Friedrich. 4789
Benzoni, Girolamo. (4790)-4807, (8784), 11264-11265, 12959, 31362, 39630, 39632, 68346, (74830), 85347, 2d note after 84844
Benzoni, Hieronymo. see Benzoni, Girolamo.
Benzoni, Joannes. see Benzoni, Girolamo.
Benzonius, J. see Benzoni, Girolamo.
Borja, Rodrigo Lanzol y. see Alexander VI, Pope, 1431?-1503.
Benzos, Jerom. 66686
Beobachtungen aus der Zoologie und Berglie-chungen. 33773
Beobachtungen des Don. Alex. Malaspina. (57257)
Beobachtungen uber den gegenwartigen Zustand. 69142
Beobachtungen und Bemerkungen fur auswan-dernde Duetsche. 42529
Beoefening der Nederlandsche Geschiedenis in Noord-Amerika. 39268
Beoordeeling van het werk. 66948
Bequest of Silvia Ann Howland. 71130
Bequests to societies. 79870
Beranejos, Casandro Rueda. see Rueda Beranejos, Casandro.
Beranger, ------. 16262
Berard, A. B. 4808
Berard, S. tr. (65540)

Beratarrechea, D. J. B. de. tr. 65269
Berattelse fran Nya England. 92446
Berattelse skrifven med Mormons hand pa
 platar. 83143
Berattelse, skrifven med Mormons hand pa
 plater. 83142
Berbice. Coloniers. petitioners (36423)
Berbreugger, ------. incorrectly supposed
 author 4815, 69611
Berches, C. de. 9594
Berchon, Ernest. 4816-4817
Berckel, Engelbert Francois van. 27683,
 69607, 98407, 98509
Bercy, ------ Drouin de. see Drouin de
 Bercy, -------.
Berdenoton, David Parra y. pseud. Al defen-
 sor de tontos. see Vera y Pintado,
 Bernardo.
Berdugo, Francisco. 86517
Berdugo, Nicolas. 4818, 72246
Bere, Iver. (4819)-4820
Bereas. pseud. Brief remarks on some
 pamphlets. see Worcester, Noah.
Bereaved father. pseud. In memoriam. see
 Sheppard, John Hannibal, 1789-1873.
Bereaved urged, to eye and acknowledge God.
 (81637)
Beredeneerde Beschrijving der Asiatische en
 Amerikaansche Monumenten. (39830)
Bereisung der Verenigten Staaten von Nor-
 damerika. 21463
Berenger, J. P. 4822, 6897, note after 100841
Berenger, L. P. 68418
Berenger, L. P. supposed author 98983
Berenger de Beaufain, John Henry de. (4821)
Beresford, J. 4823, 95700
Beresford Hope, A. J. B. see Hope, A. J. B.
 Beresford.
Beretaire, Sebastien. see Berettari, Seb-
 astino.
Beretning om Californien og dets Guldrigdom.
 4825, 9995
Beretning om Corvetten Galathea's Reise.
 5399
Beretning om de Norske Nybyggeres Tilstand
 i Wisconsin. 13508
Beretning om de Norske Setlers i Amerika.
 3824
Beretning om det Danske Eiland St. Croix i
 Vestindien. 102730
Beretning, skreven ved Mormons haand paa
 plader. 83117, 83119
Beretning, skreven ved Mormons haand pas
 tavler. 83115, 83116
Berettari, Sebastiano. (1373), 4826-4833
Berford, Sebastino Gomes da Silva. see
 Silva Berford, Sebastiao Gomes da.
Berg, A. W. 90500
Berg, Albert. 4834
Berg, Jo. Rut. 22704
Berg, Joseph H. (4835)-4838, 50520, 91199
Berg, Olof. (4839)-4842A
Berg van Dussen Muilkerk, W. E. J. (4843)
Berg-Buchlein von den Metallen und Mineral.
 3255B
Berg-Predige Christi. 2390, 32377, 98990
Berghaus, Heinrich. ed. 11539
Bergamo. see Foresti, Jacobo Philippo.
Bergamo, Italy. 73166
Bergano y Villegas, Simon. 4844
Berganza, ------- Arteta y. see Arteta y
 Berganza, --------.
Bergen, Teunis G. 4845-4846, 66721
Bergen family. 4845
Berger, Frederich Ludwig von. 4847A-(4848)

Bergeries merinos-naz du Pichinango. 64696
Bergeron, J. J. 4849
Bergeron, Pierre. 4850, 39590-39591, note
 before 96440
Bergey, David Hendricks, 1860-1937. 85072
Bergh, Henry. 4851
Bergh, L. Ph. C. van den. 4852
Bergh, S. J. van den. tr. 19557, 92445
Berghaus, Heinrich Karl Wilhelm, 1797-1884.
 4853-(4858A), 7738, 31593
Bergk, J. K. 4858A
Bergman, G. 4859
Bergoing, -----------. 75540 see also
 France. Corps Legislarif. Conseil des
 Cinq-Cents. Commission des Colonies.
Bergomas. see Foresti, Jacobo Philippo.
Bergomate, Jacobo Philippo. see Foresti,
 Jacobo Philippo.
Bergomense, Jacobo Philippo. see Foresti,
 Jacobo Philippo.
Bergomensis. see Foresti, Jacobo Philippo.
Bergordnung fur Neuspanien. 4860
Bergstrasser, Wilhelm. 4861
Berguin, H. K. 4862
Bericht Amerigo Vespucci's an Lorenzo de
 Medici. note before 99327, 99378
Bericht an den Berliner Verein zur Centrali-
 sation Duetscher Auswanderung. 6138
Bericht an die Kaiserliche Akademie der
 Wissenschaften. 77615
Bericht, de dato Germantovvn, den 20, Febr.
 1748. 106359
Bericht der Association fur die Ausstellung der
 Industrie-Erzeugnisse aller Nationen in
 New-York im Jahr 1853. 5863
Bericht der Cochituate-Wasserleitungs-
 Commission an den Statrath von Boston
 im J. 1852. 6783
Bericht der Directoren der Societat zur
 Ausbreitung des Evangeliums under
 den Heiden. 86168
Bericht des Boards der Commissare fur
 Versorgung Invalider New Jersey
 Soldaten. 53073
Bericht des Direktoren-Rathes der offentlichen
 Schulen von St. Louis. 75366
Berichten des Kaiserl. Brasilianischen Staats-
 rathes Luiz Pedreira do Coutto Ferraz.
 38224
Bericht des Stadts Superintendenten des offent-
 lichen Schulwesens. 45137
Bericht door Directeuren van de Societeit van
 Suriname aan haar Hoog Mogenden over-
 gelevert. 93836
Bericht eines Englischen Amerikaners von
 Philadelphia. 4864
Bericht fur Diejenigen so sich nach Nordame-
 rika begehen wollen. 25515
Bericht geschreiben von der Hand Mormonis
 auf Tafeln den Platten Nephis entnommen.
 83130
Bericht geschreiben von der Hand Mormon's
 auf Tafeln Nephi's Tafeln entnommen.
 83124-83128
Bericht uber das Mosquitoland im Auftrag des
 Prinzen von Preussen. 161
Bericht uber die Expedition des Admirals Pedro
 Alvarez Cabral. (69369)
Bericht uber die im hochsten Auftrage des
 Prinzen Karl von Preussen und der
 Fursten von Schonburg-Waldenburg.
 24013, 51076
Bericht uber die Reise der Corvette Galathea
 um die Welt. 5400
Bericht uber eine Reise nach den Westlichen
 Staaten Nordamerika's. 21073

BERICHT

Bericht uber meine Reise nach Texas. 86847
Bericht von Beschaffenheit. 4866
Bericht von dem Strom derer Amazonen. 153
Bericht von dem Ursprunge, Fortgange und
Gegenwartigem Stande. 58267
Bericht von den Verrichtungen besagter
Synode. 94795
Bericht von den Verrichtungen der Evang.
Lutherischen Tennessee Synode. 94795
Bericht von den wunderharen bezoardischen
Steinen. 104966
Bericht von der beruhmten Landschaft
Caroolina. 10959
Bericht von der Landschafft Carolina. 4867
Bericht von einigen Lordlandern und
absorderlich von dem so genandten
Grunlande aus Schreibern. 10735
Bericht von Grohnland. 4865, 38972
Bericht, wie sine Reise . . . nach Indien
auzustellen sey. 105639
Berichte aus dem Vereiningten Staaten. 27196
Berichte, betreffend die Mucury-Colonie in de
Brasilianischen Provinz Minas Geraes.
51228
Berichte uber die Sitten und Gebrauche der
Einwohner und die Naturerzeugnisse von
Patagonien. 98613
Berichte uber die Sitten und gebrauche der
Einwohner von Patagonien. 16771
Berichte uber Ost-Tennessee und die Duetsche
Ansiedelung. (29287)
Berichten Aangaande de la Perouse en zijne
tochtgenooten. 38969
Berichten der General-Postamts. 8215
Berichten over Asie, Afrika, en Amerika.
36081
Berichtigungen. (43871)
Berichtigungen des Herrn Navarro d'Andrade.
28293
Berigt door de Societeit van Suriname. 93837
Berigt, door Directeuren van de Societeit van
Suriname, aan haar Hoog Mog. overge-
geven. 93836
Berigt door Directeuren van de Societeit van
Suriname, overgegevan aan de Hoog Mog.
Heeren Staaten Generaal der Vereenigde
Nederlanden tot justificatie van haar
gesustineerde. 93836
Berigt door Directeuren van de Societeit van
Suriname overgegeven aan de Hoog
Mogende Heeren Staaten Generaal der
Vereenigde Nederlanden tot justificatie
van deselver gehoudene conduites. 93836
Berigt door Directeuren van de Societeit van
Suriname . . . tegen de grievan van
eenige perssonen. 93835
Berigt door Directeurs van de Societeit van
Suriname aan de Staten Generaal. (4868)
Berigt, en Onderrigtinge, nopens en aan de
Colonie en Kerke van Pensylvanien.
49912, 102509
Berigt van Bewinthebberren der geoctroyeerte
West Indische Compagnie ter Kamer
Zeeland. 4869
Berigt van Christoffel Columbus over zyne
eerste Reize. 19793A
Berigt van de moederlijke Vereenigingen in
Amerika en Engeland. (4870)
Berigt van Directeuren van de Societeit hierop.
1775. 93841
Beristain de Souza, Jose Mariano, 1756-1817.
4871-4873, 18671, 22060, 72266, 88724
Beristain de Souza Fernandez de Lara, J. M.
see Beristain de Souza, Jose Mariano,
1756-1817.
Berk, Johan. see Capellen, Johan Berk,
Baron van der.

Berkel, Adriaan von. (4874)-4875, note before
98408
Berkeley, George, Bp. of Cloyne, 1685-1753.
4876-4882, 11879, 66021, 67144, 91871-
91872
Berkeley, George Charles Grantley Fitz-
Gardinge. 4883
Berkeley, Norborne, Baron de Botetourt. see
Botetourt, Norborne Berkeley, Baron de,
1718?-1770.
Berkeley, Sir William, Bart., 1606-1677.
4889A, 41460, 99976, 4th note after
100484 see also Virginia (Colony)
Governor, 1642-1652 (Berkeley) Virginia
(Colony) Governor, 1662-1677 (Berkeley)
Berkeley, Sir William, Bart., 1606-1677.
supposed author 4889, 51810, 100459,
2d note after 100494
Berkeley, S. C. Union And State Rights
Meeting, 1831. see Union & State Rights
Meeting, Berkeley, S. C., 1831.
Berkeley Divinity School, Middletown, Conn.
4884
Berkenhout, J. (4885), (10237)
Berkenmeyer, Willem Christoffel. 4886-4887
Berkely, George. 4888
Berkely, Sir William. see Berkeley, Sir
William, Bart., 1606-1677.
Berkley, Mass. Ecclesiastical Council, 1830.
see Congregational Churches in Massa-
chusetts. Ecclesiastical Council,
Berkeley, 1830.
Berks Co., Pa. Collector of Excise. 4890,
8383, (24998) see also Brosius, Nicholas.
and Foos, Conrad.
Berks Co., Pa. Lieutenant. 50649 see also
Morgan, Jacob.
Berks County officers. 93110
Berkshire. pseud. Brief remarks on the rail
roads. see Sedgwick, Theodore, 1780-
1839.
Berkshire County, Mass. Citizens. petitioners
69577
Berkshire County, Mass. Committee of the
Citizens on the Removal of Williams
College. see Berkshire County, Mass.
Meeting on the Removal of Williams
College, Pittsfield, 1819. Committee.
Berkshire County, Mass. Meeting of a Large
Number of Gentlemen from Various Towns
in the County, for the Purpose of Ex-
pressing the Views and Fellings of the
County in Relation to the Proposition to
Remove Williams College, Pittsfield, 1819.
see Berkshire County, Mass. Meeting
on the Removal of Williams College,
Pittsfield, 1819.
Berkshire County, Mass. Meeting on the
Removal of Williams College, Pittsfield,
1819. 104433
Berkshire County, Mass. Meeting on the
Removal of Williams College, Pittsfield,
1819. Committee. 69401, 2d note after
104432
Berkshire County, Mass. Washington Benevolent
Society. see Washington Benevolent
Society. Massachusetts. Berkshire
County.
Berkshire County, Mass. Wool Growers and
Manufacturers. petitioners see Wool
Growers and Manufacturers of Berkshire
County, Mass. petitioners
Berkshire County, N. Y. Washington Bene-
volent Society. see Washington Bene-
volent Society. New York. Berkshire
County.

Berkshire Agricultural Society. 4898, 102129
Berkshire Association of Congregational
Ministers. see Congregational
Churches in Massachusetts. Berkshire
Association.
Berkshire Baptist Association (Massachusetts)
see Baptists. Massachusetts. Berk-
shire Baptist Association.
Berkshire Baptist Association (New York)
see Baptists. New York. Berkshire
Baptist Association.
Berkshire County eagle. 83336
Berkshire County Mutual Life Insurance
Company. 4898
Berkshire Family School. 4898
Berkshire Jubilee, celebrated at Pittsfield,
Mass. 3893
Berkshire Medical Institution, Pittsfield, Mass.
4896, 4898
Berlandier manuscripts. 85008
Berlin, Germany. German, English and
American Ministers. see German,
English and American Ministers at
Berlin, Germany.
Berlin, Germany. International Statistical
Congress, 1863. American Delegate.
see U. S. Delegate to the International
Statistical Congress, Berlin, 1863.
Berlin, Germany. International Statistical
Congress, 1863. 5th Session. see
International Statistical Congress. 5th
Session, Berlin, 1863.
Berlin, Germany. International Statistical
Congress, 1863. 6th Session. see
International Statistical Congress. 6th
Session, Berlin, 1863.
Berlin, Germany. K. Preussischen Akademie
der Wissenschaften. see Akademie der
Wissenschaften, Berlin.
Berlin, Mass. Church of Christ. 32292
Berlin, Mass. First Congregational Church.
77301
Berlin, N. Y. Washington Benevolent Society.
see Washington Benevolent Society.
New York. Berlin.
Berlin-Falls Manufacturing Company of New
Hampshire. (4899)
Berliner Colonisations-Gesellschaft fur Central-
Amerika. 9151
Berliner Colonisations-Gesellschaft fur Central-
Amerika. Comite. 1623
Berliner Gesellschaft fur die Deutsch-
Evangelische Mission in Amerika. 1624
Berliner Vereins fur die Deutsche Mission in
Nordamerika. 1624
Berliner Vereins zur Centralisation Deutscher
Auswanderung und Colonisation. 37640
Berlingeri, Francesco. see Berlinghieri,
Francesco.
Berlinghieri, Francesco. ed. and tr.
66500-66501, 66508
Berlingske Tidende. 18274
Berlioz d'Auriac, Jules. see Auriac, Jules
Berlioz d', 1820-
Bermani, B. tr. 92591
Bermejo, Ildefonso. (4904)
Bermejo y Roldan, Francisco. see Roldan,
Francisco Bermejo y.
Bermerkungen auf einer Reise im Innern von
La Plata. 27392
Bermerkungen uber den gegenwartigen Zustand
Neu-Spaniens. 9144
Bermingham, Thomas. 4905
Bermond. firm see Liniers y Bermond.
firm
Bermuda. Assembly. petitioners 90605

Bermuda. Council. petitioners 90605
Bermuda. Court of Vice Admirality. 96934,
100576
Bermuda. Governor. petitioner 90605
Bermuda. Laws, statutes, etc. (4906)
Bermuda (Steamship) in admiralty 89224
Bermuda: a colony, a fortress, and a prison.
4907
Bermuda Company. (57499), 86698, 97057,
3d note after 99888, 100450, 101509,
105694
Bermuda Company. petitioners 100450,
104190, 104974, 105694
Bermuda Company. Charter. (57499), 3d note
after 99888
Bermuda Company. Governor and Company.
petitioners see Bermuda Company.
petitioners
Bermuda: its history, geology, climate. 27653
Bermuda pocket almanack for . . . 1861. 4908
Bermudas preacher proved a persecutor.
(23054)
Bermudez, Joseph de Rivera. see Rivera
Bermudez, Joseph de, Conde de Santiago
de la Laguna.
Bermudez, Joseph Manuel. 4911-4913, 27812,
39025
Bermudez, Luis de Belmonte. see Belmonte
Bermudez, Luis de.
Bermudez, Silverio. 4914
Bermudez de Castro, Carlos. 11448-11449
Bermudez de Castro, Manuel. see Castro,
Manuel Bermudez de.
Bermudez de la Torre, Pedro. see Bermudez
de la Torre y Solier, Pedro Joseph.
Bermudez de la Torre y Solier, Pedro Joseph.
86218-86219, 96224
Bermudian. A poem. 4916, 97371
Bern (Synod) 4223, 80611
Bernabeu, ------. 41968
Bernal, Antonio Joaquin de Urizar y. see
Urizar y Bernal, Antonio Joaquin de.
Bernal y Salvatierra, Andres. see Salvatierra,
Andres Vernal de.
Bernaldez, Andres. 4918
Bernard, Master, fl. 1639. 46776, 52610
Bernard, The Wise, 9th cent. 68443
Bernard, ---------. USA 96319
Bernard, Amelie Lina Beck. see Beck-
Bernard, Amelie Lina.
Bernard, Charles Beck. see Beck-Bernard,
Charles.
Bernard, David. 4919, 50683, 92847
Bernard, Sir Francis, 1712-1779. 2552, 4920-
4925, 4927-4928, (15954), 16683, 30754,
(32551), (46131), (49225), 78987, 2d note
after 89200, 90611, 95354, 7th note after
97146, 97147 see also Massachusetts
(Colony) Governor, 1760-1769 (Bernard)
New Jersey (Colony) Governor, 1758-1760
(Bernard)
Bernard, Francois. 1361, 4928, 48905, 68073,
79236
Bernard, J. A. 4930
Bernard, Jacques. ed. 68453
Bernard, Jean Frederic. 4931-4937A, 16782,
25299, 31355, 38970-38971, 38975, 62600,
68419, note after 68441-note after 68442,
69172, 69262, 69299, 96172
Bernard, John. 4929
Bernard, John Augustine. 6145
Bernard, Laure. 4938
Bernard, Louis. 4939-(4942)
Bernard, M. 4946
Bernard, Mountague. 4943-4945
Bernard, Richard. 72100-72101

Bernard, Samuel. 35633 see also Jamaica.
Assembly. Speaker.
Bernard, T. 4947-4948, (66991)
Bernard, Thomas J. plaintiff 67721
Bernard l'Hermite decrites & representees.
95332
Bernard Lile; an historical romance. 13617
Bernardes, Diogo. (4949)
Bernardes, I. de Rivera. see Rivera
Bernardez, Joseph de.
Bernardez, Joseph de Rivera. see Rivera
Bernardez, Joseph de.
Bernardin de Saint Pierre, Jacques Henri.
see Saint Pierre, Jacques Henri
Bernardin de.
Bernardino Botelho, Jose de S. see Bothelo,
Jose de S. Barnardino.
Bernardo de la Trinidad. Fray 23338, 96309
Bernardo de Nantes. see Nantes, Bernardo
de.
Bernardo de Santa Maria. Fray 23338, 96309
Bernardo, Juan de San. see Juan de San
Bernardo.
Bernardo, Juan San. see San Bernardo, Juan.
Bernardo, o victoria de Ronscesvalles. (2864)
Bernardus, Guidonis, Bp., 1261 or 2-1331
76838
Bernardston, Mass. Powers Institute. see
Powers Institute, Bernardston, Mass.
Bernau, J. H. 4952
Bernegy, J. A. Sprecher de. see Sprecher
de Bernegy, J. A.
Bernhard, Herzog zu Sachsen-Weimer-Eisenach.
see Karl Bernhard, Herzog zu Sachsen-
Weimer-Eisenach.
Bernhardi, Wolfgang. 4955
Bernice. (55211)
Berniere, Henry de. cartographer 19071
Beroa, Diego de. 4956
Beroaldus, Phillippus. ed. 66471
Beroemde Amerikanen. 58739
Berquen, R. de. 4957
Berquin-Duvallon, -------. (4958)-4966, 18853,
21487, 5th note after 100859
Berra, Manuel Orozco y. see Orozco y
Berra, Manuel.
Berredo, Bernardo Pereira de. 4967
Berrian, Hobart. 4968
Berrian, James. defendant 96827
Berrian, Richard. 4969
Berrian, Samuel. 4970-4971
Berrian, William. 4972-4977, 32297, 92677,
2d note after 96984
Berrien, John Macpherson. 4978-4985, 11349,
(21730), 69949, 77260
Berriman, J. 83978
Berriman, William. (4986), 83978
Berrio de Montalvo, Luis. see Montalvo,
Luis Berrio de.
Berro, Bernardo. 4988
Berruyer, -----. 75016
Berry, George. 4988A
Berry, Harrison. 4989
Berry, Henry. 4990
Berry, Ira. defendant 103041
Berry, J. Romeyn. 4991
Berry, Nathaniel Springer, 1796-1894. 52808
see also New Hampshire. Governor,
1861-1863 (Berry)
Berry, Philip. 4992-(4993)
Berry, R. T. 4994-4995
Berry, Salter & Co. firm publishers 4996
Berry-pickers of Wisconsin. 4997
Berry, Salter & Co.'s railway business
directory. 4996

Berryer, Pierre Antoine. 4996A-4996B
Bersabita, Francesco. pseud. tr. see
Castellani, Giacomo.
Berskett, Sir James. see Basket, Sir James.
Bert, Pierre. see Bertius, Petrus, 1565-1629.
Bertal, A. 5034
Bertal, A. J. 4998
Bertall, ------. illus. 16527
Bertaud, C. F. J. (4999)
Bertelli, ------. cartographer 5000
Berthelot, Amable. 5001
Berthelot, Sabin. (5002), 74922
Berthet, Elie. 5003-5004
Bethold, Arnold Adolf. 5005
Berthollet, ------. 88905
Berthoud (James) and Co. firm see Tarascon,
Jun., James Bethoud and Co. firm.
Bertie, Willoughby. see Abingdon, Willoughby
Bertie, 4th Earl of, 1740-1799.
Bertie, or life in the field. 78686
Bertier, Ferdinand de, Comte. 5009
Bertin, Antoine de. 5010-5011
Bertin, F. tr. 27451
Bertius, Petrus, 1565-1629. 5012-5014, 13805,
(14350)-(14351), 18911, 31539-31543,
66494, 66497
Bertodano, Joseph Antonio de Abreu y. see
Abreu y Bertodano, Joseph Antonio de.
Bertoloni, Antonio. 5015
Berton, Henri Montan. 5016, (70379)
Bertonio, Ludovico. (4017)-5019, 5021-5023,
note after 99728
Bertonio, Ludovico. incorrectly supposed
author 5020, 100643
Bertran, Felipe, Bp. 5024 see also Salamanca
(Diocese) Bishop (Bertran)
Bertrand, ------. (5025), (40682)
Bertrand, ------. illus. 10296
Bertrand, ------ de. 5028 see also France.
Ministre de Marine.
Bertrant, Arthus. publisher. 14460
Bertrand, Henri Gratien, Comte, 1773-1844.
5026
Bertrand, L. A. 5027, 5029
Bertuch, F. J. 1645, 18672, 22828, 40835,
42621, 47936, 61153, 91612, 98613,
101304
Bertulus, Evariste. 5030
Berty, L. Nigon de. see Nigon de Berty, L.
Berube, Cesaree (Theriault) defendant 65923
Berube, Joseph. defendant 65923
Berucksichtigung der Auswanderung dorthin.
10015
Berugung auf die Gerechtigkeit und den Vor-
theil. 69549
Berufs-Reise nach America. (71300), 89401
Beruhmten Herrn Baron la Hontan neueste
Reise nach Nord-Indien. 38647
Berville, Saint-Albin. 5031
Berwick, Sir Robert. 18570, 78196, 2d note
after 91386 see also Scotland. Lord
President of the Session.
Berwick Academy, Dover, Mass. 5032
Berzabal, F. de Arrangoiz y. see Arrangoiz y
Berzabal, F. de.
Besancon, L. A. publisher 5033
Besancon's annual register of the state of
Mississippi. 5033
Besant, Sir Walter, 1836-1901. 83876
Bescherelle, Louis Nicholas. 5034
Beschke, Wilhelm. tr. 94444
Beschke, William. 5035-5036
Beschlusse der Kongresses der Vereinigten
Staaten. 5037
Beschouwing der kontrakten in 1840. 38326

Beschouwing van den toestand der Surinaamsche plantigieslaven. (38338)
Beschouwing van het adres. 5038
Beschouwing ven het op 25 Oct. 1858. 52348
Beschouwingen over de emancipatie der slaven. (32378)
Beschouwingen over de kolonie Suriname. 82288
Beschreeven door een vorrnaam reysiger. 12528
Beschreibung aller beruhmten Stadte in der gantzen Welt. 79635
Beschreibung aller bewusten Religionen, Secten, und Ketzereyen. 73321
Beschreibung aller deren Landschafften. (22657), 1st note after 102874, note after 102948
Beschreibung aller Engellandischen Plantingen. 57159
Beschreibung aller Gottes- und Gotzendienste. 73322
Beschreibung aller Lander. 51386-(51395)
Beschreibung aller Lander der Funf Welttheile. 104704
Beschreibung aller Lender. [sic] 51384
Beschreibung aller Religionen und Ketzereyen. 73320
Beschreibung Americae 9. Thiele. 5039
Beschrebung darinnen deren Erfindung. 105680
Beschreibung der Antill-Insul. 5040
Beschreibung der Antillen Insuln. 72321
Beschrebiung der bevorstehenden Partial Monds-Finsterniss. 26090
Beschreibung der dreizehn unabhangigen Nordamerikanischen Staaten. (5041)
Beschreibung der Eilandes Pines. 35256, 82187
Beschreibung der Europaischen Kolonien in Amerika. (9286)
Beschreibung der gantzen Welt. (51396)
Beschreibung der gantzen Welt abgebildet mit sehr schonen cosmographischen Land-Tafeln. 5012
Beschreibung der grossesten durch die Franzosische und Englische Meer-Beuter. 23470
Beschreibung der in der grossen knochen Hohle. 30389
Beschreibung der Insel Cuba. (12007)
Beschreibung der Insel St. Miguel. 38398
Beschreibung der Lander von Brasilien. 51480, (51482), 98777
Beschreibung der Landschaft Louisiana. 31364
Beschreibung der Landschaft Sonora. 61334
Beschreibung der Moluckischen Inseln. 1949
Beschreibung der neuerfundenen Pensylvanischen Kamine oder Oefen. 59913
Beschreibung der Occidentalischen und Indianischen Landern. 12959
Beschreibung der Patagonischen Kusten. 9736
Beschreibung der Porto-Seguro und San Salvador. 41297
Beschreibung der Provinz Mojos in Sud Amerika. 11038
Beschreibung der Provinz Rio Grande do Sul. 33010
Beschreibung der Reise die er nach dem Nordlichen Amerika. 36987
Beschreibung der Reisen um die Welt und Entdeckungen in Sudmeere. 78097
Beschreibung der Rheisz vnd Schiffahrt ausz Engellandt. 20837, 93588
Beschreibung der Schiffart des Haubtmans Martini Frobisher. 25996, (79344)
Beschreibung der Sitten, Gebrauchen, Aberglaube, Debauden, und Kleidung. 38715

Beschreibung der Sitten, Lebensart der Einwohner. (23107)
Beschreibung der Sitten und Gebrauche der Nordamerikanischen Wilden. (64394)
Beschreibung der Spanischen Amalgamation. 86965
Beschreibung der Spanischen Macht in Nord-Amerika. 5052
Beschreibung der Vereinigten Staaten von Nord Amerika. 22048
Beschreibung der von Magellan unternommenen ersten Reise. 62807
Beschreibung der vornehmbesten Reiche in der Welt. 19361
Beschreibung der vornehmsten Weltgeschichte. 42659
Beschreibung der vornembsten Handeln und Geschichten. 93888
Beschreibung der Welt-Geschichte. 77517
Beschreibung der Welt-Teils Amerika und des Sud Landes. 5043
Beschreibung der West-Indischen Insel San Domingo. (44150)
Beschreibung der Westlichen Staaten. 94444
Beschreibung der wunderbaren Reise Wilhelm Schouten ausz Hollandt. 33669, 77956
Beschreibung der wunderbarlichen Reyse. (8784)
Beschreibung der zweyen Insuln Formosa vnd Japan. 33678
Beschreibung des Brittischen Amerika. 39937
Beschreibung des Eilandes Pines. 35256, 82187
Beschreibung des gegenwartigen Zustands. 10875
Beschreibung des gelben Fiebers. (75209)
Beschreibung des Gronlandischen Wallfisch-fangs und Fischery. 106377
Beschreibung des Inner von Neu Wallis. 97703
Beschreibung des Landes Kamtschatka. 38302
Beschreibung des landes, seines Klimas und Bodens. 48294
Beschreibung des Mississipischen Handels. 26837
Beschreibung des Missourium Theristocaulon. (38196)
Beschreibung des Portugiesischen Amerika. 17830
Beschreibung des Stats- oder Congress-Landes in Iowa. 52379, 77697
Beschreibung des Welt-Teils Amerika. 50087, 1st note after 97721
Beschreibung dreier neuen Pflanzen. note after 77796
Beschreibung einer alten Stadt. 71445
Beschreibung einer neuen Gronlandischen Thierpflanze. 51647
Beschreibung einer Reise die Vereinigten Staaten. 27195
Beschreibung einer Reise nach Surinam und des Aufenthaltes daselbst. 74749
Beschreibung eines behaarten Gurtenthiers Praopus Hirsutus. 9351
Beschreibung einiger Nordamericanischen Holz- und Buscharten. 101237
Beschreibung meiner Reise nach der Goldminen Californiens. 2960
Beschreibung meiner Reise von Hamburg nach Brasilien. 78019
Beschreibung nach Congo in Ethiopien. 106394
Beschreibung nouae Gvianeae. 77956
Beschreibung seiner Einkomens Krafften und . . . Regierung. 94185
Beschreibung seiner Reise nach der Nordsee. (37617)

Beschreibung seiner Reisen nach Rio de Berbice und Surinam. 4875
Beschreibung Tabago einer Amerikanischer Insel. 96046
Beschreibung und Kolonisation der Landenge von Tehuantepec. 27472
Beschreibung und Natur-Geschreichte von Gronland. 22025
Beschreibung von Amerika und West Indien. 77480
Beschreibung von Brasilien. 40968
Beschreibung von Brasilien, mit Berichtigungen des Herrn Navarro d'Andrade. 28293
Beschreibung von Carolina in Nord-America. 494
Beschreibung von dem Leben und medicinischen Erfindungen von Samuel Thomson. 95599
Beschreibung von der Schlacht und ganzlichen Ausrottung der Regulatorn. 51690, 100494
Beschreibung von der unglucklichen Reise. 10960, 32377
Beschreibung von Gronland, mit einter Karte. 4820
Beschreibung von Gronland und Spitzbergen. (29001)
Beschreibung von Guiana. (30713)
Beschreibung von . . . Kamtschatka. 91218
Beschreibung von Nees von Esenbeck und von Martius. 44999
Beschreibung von Patagonien und den angrenzenden Theilen. 23736
Beschreibung von St. Jago in Chili. 9737
Beschreibung von Sud-Carolina. (20915)
Beschreibung von Tabago. 72325-72326
Beschreibung von Versteinerungen aus Palaozoischen und Tertiaren Schichten. 72591
Beschreibung von Virginien. (35909)
Beschreibung von Wisconsin. 29410
Beschreibung, welcher Gestalt die Hauptstaat desz Konigreichs Brasilien. (41850)
Beschreibung zur Arzeney dienlicher Pflazen. 24226
Beschreibungen einer Hochst-Muhselingen vnd gantz gefahrlichen Reyse. 33679
Beschreibungen zweier . . . Konigreiche. 105639
Beschreijving van Suriname. 80989
Beschreven door Kastagnede. 57806
Beschrijvanghe van de wonderlijcke reyse. 77930
Beschrijving der nieuwe staten van Amerika. 86849
Beschrijving eener reis door Nieuq-Spanje. (9142)
Beschrijving, etc. (17983)
Beschrijving van alle landen, staten en rijken der Aarde. 74752
Beschrijving van dat land. 63328
Beschrijving van de expeditie der Franschen op Cartehena. (10757), 63706
Beschrijving van de Hooft-Stadt Philadelphia. 59716
Beschrijving van de kust van Guyana. 29160
Beschrijving van het eiland Curacao. 58127
Beschrijving van het eiland Curacao. 81320
Beschrijving van het eiland Sint Eustatius. 28778
Beschrijvinge der walvischvangst. 38222
Beschrijvinge van America. 90052, 90054-90055
Beschrijvinge van de gantsche custe van Guinea. (41362)
Beschrijvinge van de regeeringe van Peru. 31505
Beschrijvinge van de regeringhe van Peru. 31506
Beschrijvinge van de volkplantinge Zuriname. 31495, 38483, 2d note after 93850
Beschrijvinge van de voyagie om den geheelen werelt-kloot. 55439
Beschrijvinge van de wonderlijcke reyse. 77933, 77938-77939, 89448
Beschrijvinge van Guiana. 29161, note before 93851
Beschrijvinge van Pensilvania en Philadelphia. 55285, 1st note after 99428
Beschrijvinge vande gantsche custe van guinea. 41363
Beschrijvinge van de overtreffelijke ende wydtvermaerde see-vaert. (11608)
Beschrijvinfe vande reyse ghedaen by den Commandeur Dirck Albertsz. Raven. 67980
Beschrijvingen van Indien. 30680
Beschrijvingh van de voyagie om den gantschen Aerdt-Kloot. 31505-31506
Beschrijvingh van de inwoonderen seden. (38712), note after 100855
Beschrijvingh vande wonderlijcke voyagie. 77937
Beschrijvinghe des gantsche aert-bodem als Europa. (36639)
Beschrijvinghe van alle de rivieren. 104999
Beschrijvinghe van America. 90043-90049
Beschrijvinghe van de gantsche custe van Guinea. 41356-41357, 41360
Beschrijvinghe van de Noordtsche Landen. 55431
Beschrijvinghe van de wonderlicke reyse. 77920, (77922)-77923, 77925
Beschrijvinghe van Virginia. 5045, note before 100436
Beschrijvinghe van West-Indien. 38554-38555
Beschriving van Guyana. 29162
Beschrybung der welt. 99356-99357, 102623
Beschryving der haringvisschery. 101231
Beschryving der Rivier Potomack. 64584, 101944
Beschryving der zee en landreizen naar de Oost- en West-Indien. 5044
Beschryving van America. 50086
Beschryving van Brasil. (2565)
Beschryving van de importante en doordeeligheit van Kaap Breton. 6216, 10728
Beschryving van de Kaap-Breton. 10726
Beschryving van de kolonie Suriname. 93851
Beschryving van de nieuw uitgevonden Pensilvanischen schoorsteenen. 59914
Beschryving van de onderscheidene volken. 6467
Beschryving van de ontdekking. 57160, 1st-2d notes after 103078
Beschryving van de plechtigheden nevens. 93876
Beschryving van de rivier en colonie der Barbice. 4810, 93852
Beschryving van de Straat Davids. 29408
Beschryving van de Straat Davids, van de Zuydbay. 29407
Beschryving van de Amerikaanschen gebulten stier. 100783
Beschryving van Guiana. 3109
Beschryving van Guiana, of de wildekust, in Zuid-America. 30712
Beschryving van het eiland Curacao. (17983), 31486
Beschryving van Kaap Breton. (10727)

Beschryving van Kaap Breton, waar agter het vredes traktaat in 1713. (10725)
Beschryving van Louisiana. (31357)
Beschryving van Noord-America. (31357)
Beschryving van Oud-Groenland. (22026)
Beschryving van Surinam. 101461
Beschryving van Ysland. 1407
Beschryving vande wonderlijcke voyagie, ghedaen door VVillem Cornelisz Schouten. 77934-77935
Beschryving vande wonderlijcke voyagie, ghedan door Willem Cornelisz Schouten. 77936
Beschryvinge des gehelen Aertbodems. 25473
Beschryvinge ende vindinge van het Landt Canada. 10366
Beschryvinge van America. 90050-90051, 90055, 90058
Beschryvinge, van de avontuerlijcke reyse van Willem Ysbrandtz. Bontekoe van Hoorn. 74840
Beschryvinge van de Noordtsche landen. 74848
Beschryvinge van de obsertreffelijcke ende wijdtvermaerde zeevaerdt. 11605-(11606), note after 65395
Beschryvinge van de rivier en colonie van Berbice. 4810, 93852
Beschryvinge van de volk-plantinge Zuriname. 38384
Beschryvinge van eenige voorname kusten. 5046
Beschryvinge van het heerlijcke ende gezegende landt Guajana. (37674), note after 93852
Beschryvinge van het magtig koningrijk Krinke Kesmes. 82249
Beschryvinge van Moscovien ofte Ruslandt. (74847)
Beschryvinge van Nieuvv-Nederlandt. (15186), 20594, 55280-55281, 102887
Beschryvinge van Nieuvv-Nederlant. (15186), (20593)-20594, 83982, note after 98474, note after 99310, 102887
Beschryvinge van Oost en West-Indien. 5046
Beschryvinge van 't in-nemen van de stadt Salvador. 76212
Beschryvinge van verscheyde landen. 41365
Beschryvinge vande overtreffelijcke ende wydtvermaerde zeevaerdt. (11606)
Beschryvinge vande wonderlijcke reyse gedaen door Willem Cornelisz Schouten. 77928
Beschryvinge vande wonderlijcke reyse, ghedaen door VVillem Cornelisz Schouten. 77927
Beschryvingh van Yslandt en Groenlandt. 5903
Beschryvingh vande voyagie om den gantschen aerdt-kloot. 31503-31504, 31507
Beschryvinghe. 41356
Beschryvinghe, hoe, en op wat sijse men de walvisschen vanght. 28641, 51334
Beschryvinghe van de voyagie om den geheelen werelt cloot. 55435
Beschryvinghe van de wonderlijcke reyse. 77921, 77924, 77931-77932
Beschryvinghe van de wonderlijcke reysen. 77926, 77929
Beschryvinghe van het eylandt Eso. 8427, 33678
Beschryvinghe van Moscovien ofte Ruslandt. 74846
Beschryvinghe van Turckyen. 74849
Beschryvinghe van West-Indien. 4804, 11264, (74830), 2d note after 74844
Beschryvinghe vande regeringe van Peru. 31504, 43760

Beschryvinghe vande voyagie om den geheelen cloot. 55434
Beschryvinghe vander Samoyeden landt in Tartarien. 33489, 67355
Beschwerliche reise nach Gronland. 28653, 100785
Bescommonconty Indians. see Pequawket Indians.
Besddo, Christ. tr. 11238
Besiers, Ermengaud de. 76838
Beskrifning fer frente Staterna etc. 6235
Beskrifning ofver de Engelska colonierne i Nordamerika. 5047
Beskrifning om de Swenska Forsamlingars. (133)
Beskrivelse of Seigland og resa til Nova Dania. 51333
Beskrivelse over eylandet St. Croix i America i West-Indien. 29406
Beskrivelse over reisen gjennem Europa. 83007
Beskrivelse til det vorende situations-kart. 28177
Besnard, Julio. tr. 84736
Besoignes en Communicatien over de Ligue Garentie. 52225
Besoldo, Christoforo. see Besoltus, Christophorus.
Besoldus, Christophorus. 5048-5049
Besonderer Derucksichtigung des Gold- und Quecksilber-Distriktes. 9990
Besonderer Hinsicht auf den Charakter und die Lebensart der Seeleute. 99312
Besonderer Rucksicht auf Deutsche Auswanderer. 3988, 4855, (24693)
Besonderer Rucksicht auf die Ansiedelung. 10375
Besonderer Rucksicht auf die Mercury-Colonie in der Provinz Minas Geraes. 38276
Besonderer Rucksicht auf die Naturgeschichte der Gold- und Diamanten-districte. 9348
Besonderer Rucksicht auf die physiche Beschaffenheit und der Kulturzustand der Argentinischen Republik. 9347
Besonders merkwurdige Reise von Amsterdam nach Surinam. 61187
Besse, ------. 75051
Besse, Joseph. 7097, 66921
Besse, Antoney. 3213, note before 92797, note after 92800, 3d note after 103687
Bessey (M.) firm publisher 89856
Bessey's Springfield directory for 1851-1852. 89856
Bessie books. (46846)
Bessierre, J. F. 5050
Bessy Conway. 74824
Best, George. (5051)-5053, 25994, 79341, 79345, 2d note after 97116
Best, Thomas. 66686
Best, William. (5054)-5055, 83978
Best earthly conservative peace in our country. (24909)
Best form of report of diseases and wounds. 83367
Best means of promoting immigration. 8500
Best method of disposing of our pauper and vagrant children. 7157
Best method of putting an end to the American war. 27548
Best methods of conducting common schools. 82558
Best new-year's gift for a prime minister. 78384
Best New-year's gift for young people. 106212
Best new year's gift to a prime minister. 78385-78387

Best ornaments of youth. (46232)
Best priviledge. 104066
Best product of land. 52209
Best railway route from the North American
 seaboard to the Ohio River. 88155
Best sermons, as delivered in Brooklyn.
 83896
Best staple of commerce. 52209
Best talent of the east. pseud. Sketches of
 men of mark. 81562
Best way of living. 46233
Best way to stop the slave trade. 38843
Beste, George. see Best, George.
Beste, J. Richard. (5056)
Besten Quellen historisch-biographisch. 22366
Bestes, Peter. 81587
Besuch bei den Ruinen von Quirigua im
 Staate Guatemala. (77616)
Beswick, Samuel. ed. 70164
Beta, Heinrich Bettziech. see Bettziech—
 Beta, Heinrich.
Betagh, William. 4047, 62957, 80158
Betancourt, A. 5058
Betancourt, Jaspar. (5059)
Betancourt, J. Ramon de. 5060
Betancourt, Jose Victoriano. 5061
Betancur, Pedro de San Joseph. 68845
Betancur, S. Guiseppe. 5062
Betancurt, Augustin de. see Vetancurt,
 Augustin de.
Betancurt y Figueroa, Luis de. 5063-5064
Betancurt y Figueroa, Luis de. supposed
 author petitioner 47635
Betendorf, Joao Filippe. 5065
Beteta, Gregorio de. 24894, 84379, note after
 94854, 94856
Bethany College, Bethany, Va. 5066
Bethel, Jane. 5069
Bethel Baptist Association. see Baptists.
 South Carolina. Bethel Baptist Associ-
 ation.
Bethel Baptist Church, New York. see New
 York (City) Bethel Baptist Church.
Bethel College, Russellville, Ky. 5067
Bethel Female College, Hopkinsville, Ky.
 (5068)
Bethel Free School, New York. see New
 York (City) Bethel Free School.
Bethel Lodge, Peterborough, N. H. see
 Freemasons. New Hampshire. Bethel
 Lodge, Peterborough.
Bethel Temperance Society, Boston. 5071
Bethel Union, Charleston, S. C. see
 Charleston Bethel Union.
Bethell, Robert. 89817 see also Spring
 Garden (District) Philadelphia. Solicitor.
Bethencourt, Galien de. 5073, 32016, note
 before 96440
Bethencourt, Jean de, d. 1425? 4850
Bethencourt, Rene Robineau, Sieur de. see
 Robineau, Rene, Sieur de Bethencourt.
Bethesda Orphan House, Savannah. see
 Savannah. Bethesda Orphan House.
Bethiah. 46234
Bethlehem, N. Y. Court. 31331
Bethlehem, Pa. Female Seminary. see
 Moravian Seminary and College for
 Women, Bethlehem, Pa.
Bethlehem, Pa. Moravian College. see
 Moravian Seminary and College for
 Women, Bethlehem, Pa.
Bethlehem, Pa. Moravian Seminary for Young
 Ladies. see Moravian Seminary and
 College for Women, Bethlehem, Pa.

Bethlehem, Pa. Moravian Young Ladies'
 Semianry. see Moravian Seminary and
 College for Women, Bethlehem, Pa.
Bethlehem and Bethlehem School. 50983
Bethlehem Church and its pastor. 38837
Bethlehem Female Seminary, Bethlehem, Pa.
 see Moravian Seminary and College for
 Women, Bethlehem, Pa.
Bethlehemites. 9122, 68845
Bethlehemites. Mexico. Caputilo General.
 (42856)
Bethroted [sic] of Wyoming. 47950
Bethune, A. N. 5074-5075
Bethune, C. R. Drinkwater. see Drinkwater
 Bethune, C. R.
Bethune, George W. 5076-5085, 32707, (52746),
 85100
Bethune, Joanna (Graham) (5080), (28211)-
 28212
Bethune, John. 5086-5088
Betizy, Eugene de. defendant 104125
Betoog over het nadeel eener belasting op de
 publiek verkoop. 5089
Betrachlichen Zusatzen und Anmerkungen zur
 naturlichen Geschichte. 17414
Betrachtungen ueber das Laenderei-Vertheilungs-
 Gesetz. (5090), 7526
Betrachtungen uber den gegenwartigen Zustand.
 31898, 75074
Betrachtungen uber die Amerikanische Frage.
 46952
Betragtninger over Daniels Bog og Aabenharin-
 gen. 84476
Betrayal of the cause of freedom. (79596)
Betrayal of the Republican Party in Missouri.
 20817
Betri, Dominico Maria. incorrectly supposed
 author 100611
Betrothed of Wyoming. 105691
Betrothed; or, love in death. 79866, (79867)
Bettencourt, Jose de la. 5091
Better days of Joseph Barker. 28417
"Better edification" a good plea. 4889B
Better interests of the country. 46840
Betteridge, William. 89512
Betterment law. 77000
Bettinger, J. B. tr. 29203
Bettini, Antonio. 66470
Bettle, Jane. 5092
Bettoni, Nicolas. (5093)
Bettridge, William. 5094
Betts, Samuel Rossiter, 1786-1868. (5095)-5097,
 61179, 84738, 88951
Betts, William. 5098, 14802, 14806
Betty, an Indian woman. 104519-104520
Betty. pseud. Opposition mornings. see
 O'Neil, Elizabeth. supposed author and
 Tickell, Richard. supposed author
Betty's remarks. 57344, 95797
Bettziech-Beta, Heinrich. 5099
Between J. Bardwell et al., plaintiffs in equity,
 and D. Ames et al., defendants. 102587
Between James Jackson, ex. dem. Brockholst
 Livingston, and others, plaintiffs in error;
 and Anne Delancy & Abraham Russell,
 defendants in error. 96885
Between James Jackson ex dem. Brockholst
 Livingston, and others plaintiffs in error;
 and John Robins, defendant in error.
 96887
Between Nathaniel L. Griswold and George
 Griswold, plaintiffs in error, and Joshua
 Waddington, who is impleaded. 96881

Between Old John Uncas, Young John Uncas, and several other Mohegan Indians, on behalf of themselves and the rest of their tribe. 15750

Between Robert Pleasants, son and heir of John Pleasants, dec'd pltf. and Mary Logan, widow and administratrix of Charles Logan. 100231

Between Timothy Peaceable (on the demise of Dr. Fothergill and others, being the London Company) appellant. And Christian Stover, respondent. 92362

Between two fires. 54960

Between two parallels. 79749

Between William Yates and Sarah his wife, plaintiffs, and Abraham Salle, Bernard Markham, Edward Moseley, Benjamin Harris, and William Wager Harris, defendants. 105702

Beuckelaer, Cornelis. 5100

Beughem, Cornelius van. 5102

Beukma, K. Jz. 5103

Beulah. 23136

Beuve, Charles Auguste Sainte. see Sainte-Beuve, Charles Auguste, 1804-1869.

Bevan, Joseph Gurney. 81895

Bevan, Joseph Gurney. supposed author 91324, 93601

Bevan, Matthew L. 3189, 5104

Bevan, William. 5105-5106

Bevans, John. 99799

Bevans, William. defendant 5107

Bevattende een Verslag van de Luchtstreek. 10005

Bevel Faulcon. 87789

Beveridge, John. 5108-5109

Beveridge, William, Bp. of St. Asaph, 1637-1708. 5110, 86617

Beverley, John. 5111

Beverley, Peter. 100382

Beverley, Robert. 5112-5117, (74605)-74606, note after 91491, 97111, 100382, 2d note after 100478, 1st note after 100480, 3d note after 100480, 2d note after 100518

Beverley, T. 5118, 60870, 71966

Beverley, William. 5119, 100382

Beverley, Mass. 5123

Beverley, Mass. First Church. 22126

Beverley, Mass. Public Library. 5120-5121

Beverely, Mass. St. Peter's Church. 75667

Beverely, Mass. School Committee. 5123

Beverley, Mass. Second Social Library. 5122

Beverley, Mass. Social Library. see Social Library, Beverley, Mass.

Beverley's abridgment. 100382

Beverly, John. see Beverley, John.

Beverly, Robert. see Beverley, Robert.

Beverly, Mass. see Beverley, Mass.

Beverningk, H. van. 98926 see also Netherlands. Legatie. Great Britain.

Bevrijding der slaven. 4362

Beware of men. 78995

Beweis, dass die Amerikanischen Indianer. 55375

Bewert Recept von ainem Holtz Guaicanum. 68348

Bewert recept, wie man das holtz Guayaca fur die Kranckheyt der Frantzosen brauchen sol. 68347

Bewert recept, wie man das holtz Guayacan brauchen soll. 29155

Bewezen uit de memorie van d. Ridder Yorke. 106045

Bewick, -------. illus. 4689

Bewilligungen bey den Staten General. 102884

Bewinthebberen der Nederlandtsche West-Indische Compagnie. see Nederlandsche West-Indische Compagnie. Bewinthebberen.

Bewinthebberen der Westindische Compagnie. see Nederlandsche West-Indische Compagnie. Bewinthebberen.

Bewinthebberen van de Generale Geoctroyeerde West-Indische Compagnie deser landen maken bekent. 56018, 102296

Bewinthebberen van de Geoctroyeerde West-Indische Compagnie der Vereenighde Nederlenden. see Nederlandsche West-Indische Compagnie. Bewinthebberen.

Bewland, Enos. 94890

Bewohner Sachsens. eds. 45258

Bey, Ali. pseud. Extracts from a journal. see Knapp, Samuel Lorenzo, 1783-1838.

Bey, Aly. pseud.? see Aly Bey. pseud.?

Bey siener Excellenz G. Waschington. 101703

Beyard, Nicholas. see Bayard, Nicholas.

Beye Zisnores y Quixano, Emmanuel Ignatius. (44420)

Beyer, E. (5124), 93875

Beyer, Ed. 5125

Beyer, Mor. 5126-5129

Beygedrucktem Anhangder. (25461)

Beyhulfe von die Teutschen um Englisch zu Lernen. 56353, 77197

Beyhullfe vor die Tuetschen um Englisch zu Lernen. 88825, 88827

Beyhullfe vor Deutsche um Englisch zu Lernen. 88826

Beylaagen relatief tot het bericht door Directeuren. 93836

Beylage zum 150ten Stuck des Philadelphischen Staatsboten. 5130

Beylagen. 2462, 4th note after 97845

Beyond the breakers. 58024

Beyond the lines. 26835

Beyond the Mississippi. 70980

Beyond the west. (62923)

Beytrag zur Geschichte der Jesuiten in Paraguay. (59173)

Beytrag zur Geschichte von Paraguay. 56342

Beytrag zur Teutschen holzgerechten Forstwissenschaft. 101238

Beytragezur Beschreibung von St. Croix. 102731

Beytrage zur Gebirgskunde Brasiliens. 63677

Beytrage zur genauren Kenntniss. (24418)

Beytrage zur Kenntniss des gegenwartigen Zustandes. (5124)

Beytrage zur mineralogischen Kenntnisz. 77754

Beza, Theodore. 104655

Bezerra, Hernando. plaintiff 86417 see also Dominicans. Province of Santiago de Mexico. Procurador General. plaintiff

Bezerra de Menezes, Manuel Jacome. see Menezes, Manuel Jacome Bezerra de.

Bezerra e Lima, Joao Ant. 5131

Beziehung auf allgemeine Sudamerikanische Verhaltnisse. 38319

Beziehung auf die Brundsatze des Canningschen Ministeriums. 20218

Beziehungen zur grossen Sklavenfrage. 12720

Bezoek in de Vereenigde Staten van Noord-Amerika. 6427

Bezoni, Hieronymi. see Benzoni, Girolamo.

Biali i czarni. 92406

Biancani, Giuseppe. 5132

Bianchetti, Giuseppe. 5133

Bianchi, Isidorio. incorrectly supposed author 10911

Bianco, Andrea. cartographer 47934, 76838

Biard, Francois. 5134-5135

Biard, Pierre. 5136, 39958, (69300), note
after 69259, 69268
Biarnes, Adolphe. 5137
Biard, Lucian. 5138-5142
Bias, C. 5143
Bibaud, Francois Marie Uncas Maximilien,
1824- 5145-5146, 5157, 5206, 5207,
43799
Bibaud, Maximilien, 1824- see Bibaud,
Francois Marie Uncas Maximilien, 1824-
Bibaud, Michael. 4148-4160, 25431, 34041,
69661
Bibb, George Mortimer, 1776-1859. 5161-
(5162)
Bibb, George Mortimer, 1776-1859. petitioner
97928
Bibb, Henry. 5163, (46866)
Bibel voor kinders of bibels spreek. (58041)
Bibelimit ujarsimmassut okralluktuaet. 91165
Bibelingoak. (5164)
Bibelingoak. merdlainnut imaloneet. 23601
Bibibus. pseud. Tooth-ful of advice. 96182
Bible. Cherokee. 1860. 12477
Bible. Chippewa. 1839. 12831
Bible. Cree. 1861. 36973
Bible. English. 1614. 94477
Bible. English. 1648. (66434)
Bible. English. 1682. 66435
Bible. English. 1786. 5165
Bible. English. 1790. Authorized. 1568,
12929
Bible. English. 1790. Douay. (5166)
Bible. English. 1791. 5170, 1572-1573
Bible. English. 1791-1792. 5171
Bible. English. 1792. 5174-5176, 8511
Bible. English. 1793. 5177-5177A
Bible. English. 1794. 53019
Bible. English. 1796. 5178
Bible. English. 1797. 5180
Bible. English. 1798. 5181-5182
Bible. English. 1799. 5181
Bible. English. 1867. 83247
Bible. English. 1903. 83248
Bible. English. 1906. 83248
Bible. English. 1908. 83248
Bible. English. 1908. 83250
Bible. English. 1909. 83248
Bible. English. 1912. 83248
Bible. English. 1915. 83248
Bible. English. 1920. 83248
Bible. English. 1925. 83249
Bible. French. Douai. 18288, 18289, 69646,
69649
Bible. German. 1743. 5191
Bible. German. 1763. 5192
Bible. German. 1775. 5193
Bible. German. 1776. (5194)
Bible. Massachuset. 1663. (22154), (22156),
(65324), (66434), 82975-82976
Bible. Massachuset. (1663) 1675. 65324
Bible. Massachuset. (1663) 1847. 82975
Bible. Massachuset. (1663) 82976. 82976
Bible. Mohegan. 1749? 99196
Bible. Paraphrases. Choctaw. 1845-1850.
26409
Bible. Paraphrases. English. 1636. 76464
Bible. Paraphrases. English. 1638. 76465
Bible. Paraphrases. English. 1648. (76466)
Bible. Paraphrases. English. 1703. 84553
Bible. Paraphrases. English. 1716. 84553
Bible. Paraphrases. English. 1745. 84553
Bible. Paraphrases. English. 1747. 84553
Bible. Paraphrases. English. 1748. 84553
Bible. Paraphrases. English. 1749. 84553
Bible. Paraphrases. English. 1754. 84553

Bible. Paraphrases. English. 1762. 84663
Bible. Paraphrases. English. 1766. 84553
Bible. Paraphrases. English. 1767? 84553
Bible. Paraphrases. English. 1769. 84553
Bible. Paraphrases. English. 1771. 84553
Bible. Paraphrases. English. 1774. 84553
Bible. Paraphrases. English. 1779. 84553
Bible. Paraphrases. English. 1786. 84553
Bible. Paraphrases. English. 1790. 84553
Bible. Paraphrases. English. 1792. 84553
Bible. Paraphrases. English. 1793. 84553
Bible. Paraphrases. English. 1794. 84553
Bible. Paraphrases. English. 1795. 84553
Bible. Paraphrases. English. 1796. 84553
Bible. Paraphrases. English. 1804. 84553
Bible. Paraphrases. English. 1805? 84553
Bible. Paraphrases. English. 1806. 84553
Bible. Paraphrases. English. 1807. 84553
Bible. Paraphrases. English. 1813. 84553
Bible. Paraphrases. English. 1820? 84553
Bible. Selections. Abnaki. 1830. 105710
Bible. Selections. Algonquin. 1859. (34593)
Bible. Selections. Arawak. 17--? 67153
Bible. Selections. Carib Dialect. 17--? 67152
Bible. Selections. Cherokee. 1833. 105321
Bible. Selections. Cherokee. 1836? 78989
Bible. Selections. Cherokee. 1844. 12475
Bible. Selections. Chippewa. 1852. 12834
Bible. Selections. Choctaw. 1827. 105539
Bible. Selections. Dakota. 1839. 18288
Bible. Selections. English. 1782. 5167
Bible. Selections. English. 1785. 32496
Bible. Selections. English. 1788. (17990)
Bible. Selections. English. 1790. 5169
Bible. Selections. English. 1796. 5179
Bible. Selections. English. 1800. 75925
Bible. Selections. English. 1802. 75925
Bible. Selections. English. 1806. 75925
Bible. Selections. English. 1835. 93761
Bible. Selections. English. 1836. 93762
Bible. Selections. English. 1839. 93763
Bible. Selections. Malecite. 1863. 44123,
67764
Bible. Selections. Mohawk. 1715. 13180-
13181, (50765)
Bible. Selections. Mohawk. 1829. 49845
Bible. Selections. Nez Perce. 1843. 88878
Bible. Selections. Potawatomi. 1846. 61318
Bible. O. T. Eskimo. 1822-1836. 22865
Bible. O. T. Eskimo. 1832. 28657
Bible. O. T. Paraphrases. Choctaw. 1831.
21168
Bible. O. T. Selections. Dakota. 1839.
69646
Bible. O. T. Selections. Dakota. 1842.
63996
Bible. O. T. Selections. Dakota. 1842-1843.
18292
Bible. O. T. Selections. Delaware. 1838.
(19375)
Bible. O. T. Selections. Eskimo. 1820.
22864
Bible. O. T. Selections. Eskimo. 1822-1825.
(28637)
Bible. O. T. Selections. Eskimo. 1832.
(22851)
Bible. O. T. Selections. Latin. 1787.
78993
Bible. O. T. Selections. Latin. 1801. 78993
Bible. O. T. Selections. Latin. 1804. 78993
Bible. O. T. Selections. Latin. 1807. 78993
Bible. O. T. Selections. Ojibwe. 1835.
57089
Bible. O. T. Pentateuch. Ojibwe. 18--?
(57094)
Bible. O. T. Genesis. Cherokee. 1853.
12459

Bible. O. T. Genesis. Chipewa. 1835.
36593
Bible. O. T. Genesis. Dakota. 1839. 18288,
18290, 63995, 69646
Bible. O. T. Genesis. Eskimo. 1822. 22852
Bible. O. T. Genesis. Eskimo. 1834. 22852
Bible. O. T. Genesis. Massachuset. 1663.
69242
Bible. O. T. Genesis. Malecite. 18--?
44123
Bible. O. T. Genesis. Micmac. 1857. 67752
Bible. O. T. Genesis. Sioux. 1839. 18290
Bible. O. T. Exodus. Chipewa. 1833. 12833
Bible. O. T. Exodus. Cherokee. 1853.
12459
Bible. O. T. Exodus. English. 1767. 66448
Bible. O. T. Exodus. Micmac. 1870. 67765
Bible. O. T. Exodus. Ojibwe. 1847. 26378
Bible. O. T. Exodus. Potawatomi. 1846.
16318
Bible. O. T. Deuteronomy. English. 1651.
66431
Bible. O. T. Deuteronomy. English. 1658?
(66433)
Bible. O. T. Deuteronomy. English. 1665?
(66434)
Bible. O. T. Deuteronomy. English. 1671.
(66436)
Bible. O. T. Deuteronomy. English. 1682?
66435
Bible. O. T. Deuteronomy. English. 1698.
(66440)
Bible. O. T. Deuteronomy. English. 1706.
(66441)
Bible. O. T. Deuteronomy. English. 1709.
(66441)
Bible. O. T. Deuteronomy. English. 1713.
(66441)
Bible. O. T. Deuteronomy. English. 1715.
(66441)
Bible. O. T. Deuteronomy. English. 1716.
(66441)
Bible. O. T. Deuteronomy. English. 1717.
(66441)
Bible. O. T. Deuteronomy. English. 1718.
(66441)
Bible. O. T. Deuteronomy. English. 1719.
(66441)
Bible. O. T. Deuteronomy. English. 1720.
(66441)
Bible. O. T. Deuteronomy. English. 1722.
(66441)
Bible. O. T. Deuteronomy. English. 1725.
(66441)
Bible. O. T. Deuteronomy. English. 1726.
(66441)
Bible. O. T. Deuteronomy. English. 1729.
(66441)
Bible. O. T. Deuteronomy. English. 1730.
(66441)
Bible. O. T. Deuteronomy. English. 1733.
(66441)
Bible. O. T. Deuteronomy. English. 1737.
(66441)
Bible. O. T. Deuteronomy. English. 1741.
(66441)
Bible. O. T. Deuteronomy. English. 1742.
(66441)
Bible. O. T. Deuteronomy. English. 1744.
(66441)
Bible. O. T. Deuteronomy. English. 1754.
(66441)
Bible. O. T. Deuteronomy. English. 1757.
(66441)
Bible. O. T. Deuteronomy. English. 1762.
(66441)

Bible. O. T. Joshua. Choctaw. 1852. 12864
Bible. O. T. Judges. Choctaw. 1852. 12864
Bible. O. T. Judges. English. 1651. 66431
Bible. O. T. Judges. English. 1658? (66433)
Bible. O. T. Judges. English. 1665? (66434)
Bible. O. T. Judges. English. 1671. (66436)
Bible. O. T. Judges. English. 1698. (66440)
Bible. O. T. Judges. English. 1706. (66441)
Bible. O. T. Judges. English. 1709. (66441)
Bible. O. T. Judges. English. 1713. (66441)
Bible. O. T. Judges. English. 1715. (66441)
Bible. O. T. Judges. English. 1716. (66441)
Bible. O. T. Judges. English. 1717. (66441)
Bible. O. T. Judges. English. 1718. (66441)
Bible. O. T. Judges. English. 1719. (66441)
Bible. O. T. Judges. English. 1720. (66441)
Bible. O. T. Judges. English. 1722. (66441)
Bible. O. T. Judges. English. 1725. (66441)
Bible. O. T. Judges. English. 1726. (66441)
Bible. O. T. Judges. English. 1729. (66441)
Bible. O. T. Judges. English. 1730. (66441)
Bible. O. T. Judges. English. 1733. (66441)
Bible. O. T. Judges. English. 1737. (66441)
Bible. O. T. Judges. English. 1741. (66441)
Bible. O. T. Judges. English. 1742. (66441)
Bible. O. T. Judges. English. 1744. (66441)
Bible. O. T. Judges. English. 1754. (66441)
Bible. O. T. Judges. English. 1757. (66441)
Bible. O. T. Judges. English. 1762. (66441)
Bible. O. T. Ruth. Choctaw. 1852. 12864
Bible. O. T. Samuel I-II. Choctaw. 1852.
12872
Bible. O. T. Samuel I. English. 1651. 66431
Bible. O. T. Samuel I. English. 1658?
(66433)
Bible. O. T. Samuel I. English. 1665?
(66434)
Bible. O. T. Samuel I. English. 1671.
(66436)
Bible. O. T. Samuel I. English. 1698.
(66440)
Bible. O. T. Samuel I. English. 1706.
(66441)
Bible. O. T. Samuel I. English. 1709.
(66441)
Bible. O. T. Samuel I. English. 1713.
(66441)
Bible. O. T. Samuel I. English. 1715.
(66441)
Bible. O. T. Samuel I. English. 1716.
(66441)
Bible. O. T. Samuel I. English. 1717.
(66441)
Bible. O. T. Samuel I. English. 1718.
(66441)
Bible. O. T. Samuel I. English. 1719
(66441)
Bible. O. T. Samuel I. English. 1720.
(66441)
Bible. O. T. Samuel I. English. 1722.
(66441)
Bible. O. T. Samuel I. English. 1725.
(66441)
Bible. O. T. Samuel I. English. 1726.
(66441)
Bible. O. T. Samuel I. English. 1730.
(66441)
Bible. O. T. Samuel I. English. 1733.
(66441)
Bible. O. T. Samuel I. English. 1737.
(66441)
Bible. O. T. Samuel I. English. 1741.
(66441)
Bible. O. T. Samuel I. English. 1742.
(66441)
Bible. O. T. Samuel I. English. 1744. (66441)

Bible. O. T. Samuel I. English. 1754.
(66441)
Bible. O. T. Samuel I. English. 1759.
(66441)
Bible. O. T. Samuel I. English. 1762.
(66441)
Bible. O. T. Kings I. Choctaw. 1852.
12872
Bible. O. T. Job. English. 1637. 76465
Bible. O. T. Job. English. 1676. 76467
Bible. O. T. Psalms. Paraphrases. English.
1697. 79443
Bible. O. T. Psalms. Polyglot. 1516.
(66468)
Bible. O. T. Psalms. Dakota. 1839. 18288,
69646
Bible. O. T. Psalms. Dakota. 1869. 71342
Bible. O. T. Psalms. Dakota. 1871. 71342
Bible. O. T. Psalms. Dutch. 1688. 66454
Bible. O. T. Psalms. Dutch. 1784. 66423
Bible. O. T. Psalms. English. 1636. 76464
Bible. O. T. Psalms. English. 1637. 76465
Bible. O. T. Psalms. English. 1640. 22155,
28050, (66428), 1st note after 102552,
2d note after 103846
Bible. O. T. Psalms. English. 1647. 66430
Bible. O. T. Psalms. English. 1648.
(76466)
Bible. O. T. Psalms. English. 1651. 66431
Bible. O. T. Psalms. English. 1652. 66432
Bible. O. T. Psalms. English. 1658?
(66433)
Bible. O. T. Psalms. English. 1665?
(66434)
Bible. O. T. Psalms. English. 1671.
(66436)
Bible. O. T. Psalms. English. 1676. 76467
Bible. O. T. Psalms. English. 1680.
(66437)
Bible. O. T. Psalms. English. 1682? 66435
Bible. O. T. Psalms. English. 1682. 66457
Bible. O. T. Psalms. English. 1688. 66451-
(66452)
Bible. O. T. Psalms. English. 1694. 66438
Bible. O. T. Psalms. English. 1697. 66439
Bible. O. T. Psalms. English. 1698.
(66440)
Bible. O. T. Psalms. English. 1704. 66449
Bible. O. T. Psalms. English. 1706.
(66441)
Bible. O. T. Psalms. English. 1707. 52735
Bible. O. T. Psalms. English. 1709.
(66441)
Bible. O. T. Psalms. English. 1710. 64998-
65000, 66449
Bible. O. T. Psalms. English. 1713.
(66441), 66449
Bible. O. T. Psalms. English. 1715.
(66441)
Bible. O. T. Psalms. English. 1716. 46471,
(66441)
Bible. O. T. Psalms. English. 1717.
(66441)
Bible. O. T. Psalms. English. 1718.
(66441)
Bible. O. T. Psalms. English. 1719.
(66441)
Bible. O. T. Psalms. English. 1720.
(66441), 66449
Bible. O. T. Psalms. English. 1722.
(66441)
Bible. O. T. Psalms. English. 1725.
(66441)
Bible. O. T. Psalms. English. 1726.
(66441)

Bible. O. T. Psalms. English. 1729. 52735,
(66441)
Bible. O. T. Psalms. English. 1730. 52737,
(66441)
Bible. O. T. Psalms. English. 1733.
(66441), 66449
Bible. O. T. Psalms. English. 1734.
(66459)
Bible. O. T. Psalms. English. 1736. 66446
Bible. O. T. Psalms. English. 1737.
(66441), 66449
Bible. O. T. Psalms. English. 1741.
(66441)
Bible. O. T. Psalms. English. 1742. 52735
Bible. O. T. Psalms. English. 1744. 52735,
(66441)
Bible. O. T. Psalms. English. 1745. 52737
Bible. O. T. Psalms. English. 1754.
(66441), 66449
Bible. O. T. Psalms. English. 1755. 66449
Bible. O. T. Psalms. English. 1756. 17333,
66456
Bible. O. T. Psalms. English. 1757. 66449
Bible. O. T. Psalms. English. 1758. 52736,
(66442)
Bible. O. T. Psalms. English. 1759.
(66441)
Bible. O. T. Psalms. English. 1760. 66449
Bible. O. T. Psalms. English. 1761.
(66463)
Bible. O. T. Psalms. English. 1762.
(66441), 66449
Bible. O. T. Psalms. English. 1763. 66449-
66450
Bible. O. T. Psalms. English. 1764. 52736-
52737, (66463)
Bible. O. T. Psalms. English. 1765. 66449
Bible. O. T. Psalms. English. 1766. 66449
Bible. O. T. Psalms. English. 1767. 66448-
66449
Bible. O. T. Psalms. English. 1768. 52737,
52765, (66463)
Bible. O. T. Psalms. English. 1769. 66449
Bible. O. T. Psalms. English. 1770. 52737,
66449, (66463)
Bible. O. T. Psalms. English. 1771. 52737,
66449, (66463)
Bible. O. T. Psalms. English. 1773.
(66442), 66449
Bible. O. T. Psalms. English. 1774. 52737,
66449, (66463)
Bible. O. T. Psalms. English. 1784. 52737,
66460
Bible. O. T. Psalms. English. 1785.
(41553), (66442)
Bible. O. T. Psalms. English. 1787. 66449,
66461
Bible. O. T. Psalms. English. 1790. 66427
Bible. O. T. Psalms. English. 1791. 66449
Bible. O. T. Psalms. English. 1792. 66444,
71539
Bible. O. T. Psalms. English. 1793. 66449
Bible. O. T. Psalms. English. 1794. 66427
Bible. O. T. Psalms. English. 1795. 66449,
(66462)
Bible. O. T. Psalms. English. 1796. 53419,
66425, 66443, 87917
Bible. O. T. Psalms. English. 1797. 66427,
87917
Bible. O. T. Psalms. English. 1802. 66444
Bible. O. T. Psalms. English. 1804. 71539
Bible. O. T. Psalms. English. 1814. 66426
Bible. O. T. Psalms. English. 1815. 66447
Bible. O. T. Psalms. English. 1824. 66427
Bible. O. T. Psalms. English. 1829. 66426

Bible.	O. T.	Psalms.	English.	1835.	86859
Bible.	O. T.	Psalms.	English.	1854.	66458
Bible.	O. T.	Psalms.	English.	1862.	
(66429)					
Bible.	O. T.	Psalms.	English.	1903.	2d
note after 103846					
Bible.	O. T.	Psalms.	Eskimo.	n.d.	28651
Bible.	O. T.	Psalms.	Eskimo.	1824.	22868
Bible.	O. T.	Psalms.	Eskimo.	1834.	22868,
28644					
Bible.	O. T.	Psalms.	German.	1744.	66467
Bible.	O. T.	Psalms.	German.	1753.	52363,
60271					
Bible.	O. T.	Psalms.	German.	1757.	66464
Bible.	O. T.	Psalms.	German.	1760.	
(66465), 66467					
Bible.	O. T.	Psalms.	German.	1762.	42728,
(66465)-66466					
Bible.	O. T.	Psalms.	German.	1764.	66467,
93916					
Bible.	O. T.	Psalms.	German.	1772.	
52363, 60271					
Bible.	O. T.	Psalms.	German.	1777.	66467
Bible.	O. T.	Psalms.	German.	1781.	66467
Bible.	O. T.	Psalms.	German.	1784.	66467
Bible.	O. T.	Psalms.	German.	1791.	66467
Bible.	O. T.	Psalms.	German.	1795.	66467
Bible.	O. T.	Psalms.	German.	1796.	66467
Bible.	O. T.	Psalms.	German.	1797.	66467
Bible.	O. T.	Psalms.	German.	1808.	66467
Bible.	O. T.	Psalms.	German.	1813.	66467
Bible.	O. T.	Psalms.	German.	1821.	66467
Bible.	O. T.	Psalms.	German.	1825.	42728
Bible.	O. T.	Psalms.	Hebrew.	1688.	66451-
66454					
Bible.	O. T.	Psalms.	Hebrew.	1726.	66454
Bible.	O. T.	Psalms.	Hebrew.	1758.	66454
Bible.	O. T.	Psalms.	Hebrew.	1809.	
(66455)					
Bible.	O. T.	Psalms.	Latin.	1688.	66453-
66454					
Bible.	O. T.	Psalms.	Latin.	1726.	66454
Bible.	O. T.	Psalms.	Latin.	1758.	66454
Bible.	O. T.	Psalms.	Malecite.	185-?	
44123					
Bible.	O. T.	Psalms.	Massachuset.	1658.	
66445					
Bible.	O. T.	Psalms.	Massachuset.	1661.	
22155, (22164)					
Bible.	O. T.	Psalms.	Massachuset.	1663.	
82975-82976					
Bible.	O. T.	Psalms.	Massachuset.	1664.	
(22164)					
Bible.	O. T.	Psalms.	Massachuset.	1680.	
22157, (22164), note before 101232					
Bible.	O. T.	Psalms.	Massachuset.	1709.	
45537					
Bible.	O. T.	Psalms.	Micmac.	1859.	67753
Bible.	O. T.	Psalms.	Mintagnar.	1847.	
21436					
Bible.	O. T.	Psalms.	Mohawk.	1839.	49840
Bible.	O. T.	Psalms.	Ojibwe.	1853.	79689
Bible.	O. T.	Psalms.	Ojibwe.	1880.	79690
Bible.	O. T.	Proverbs.	Dakota.	1839.	18288,
69646					
Bible.	O. T.	Proverbs.	Dakota.	1869.	71342
Bible.	O. T.	Proverbs.	Dakota.	1871.	
71342					
Bible.	O. T.	Proverbs.	English.	1761.	
(66463)					
Bible.	O. T.	Proverbs.	English.	1764.	
(66463)					
Bible.	O. T.	Proverbs.	English.	1768.	
(66463)					
Bible.	O. T.	Proverbs.	English.	1770.	
(66463)					

Bible.	O. T.	Proverbs.	English.	1771.	
(66463)					
Bible.	O. T.	Proverbs.	English.	1774.	
(66463)					
Bible.	O. T.	Proverbs.	English.	1784.	
66460					
Bible.	O. T.	Proverbs.	Eskimo.	1828.	
22869					
Bible.	O. T.	Proverbs.	Eskimo.	1849.	
(75836)					
Bible.	O. T.	Ecclesiastes.	Dakota.	1869.	
71342					
Bible.	O. T.	Ecclesiastes.	Dakota.	1871.	
71342					
Bible.	O. T.	Ecclesiastes.	English.	1637.	
76465					
Bible.	O. T.	Ecclesiastes.	English.	1648.	
(76466)					
Bible.	O. T.	Song of Solomon.	Paraphrases.		
			English.	1741.	89526
Bible.	O. T.	Song of Solomon.	Paraphrases.		
			English.	1742.	89526-89527
Bible.	O. T.	Song of Solomon.	Paraphrases.		
			English.	1743.	89527
Bible.	O. T.	Song of Solomon.	Paraphrases.		
			English.	1764.	89527
Bible.	O. T.	Song of Solomon.	Paraphrases.		
			English.	1787.	89529
Bible.	O. T.	Song of Solomon.	Paraphrases.		
			English.	1790?	90530
Bible.	O. T.	Song of Solomon.	Dakota.	1869.	
71342					
Bible.	O. T.	Song of Solomon.	Dakota.	1871.	
71342					
Bible.	O. T.	Song of Solomon.	English.	1651.	
66431					
Bible.	O. T.	Song of Solomon.	English.	1658?	
(66433)					
Bible.	O. T.	Song of Solomon.	English.	1665?	
(66434)					
Bible.	O. T.	Song of Solomon.	English.	1671.	
(66436)					
Bible.	O. T.	Song of Solomon.	English.	1682?	
66435					
Bible.	O. T.	Song of Solomon.	English.	1698.	
(66440)					
Bible.	O. T.	Song of Solomon.	English.	1706.	
(66441)					
Bible.	O. T.	Song of Solomon.	English.	1709.	
(66441)					
Bible.	O. T.	Song of Solomon.	English.	1713.	
(66441)					
Bible.	O. T.	Song of Solomon.	English.	1715.	
(66441)					
Bible.	O. T.	Song of Solomon.	English.	1716.	
(66441)					
Bible.	O. T.	Song of Solomon.	English.	1717.	
(66441)					
Bible.	O. T.	Song of Solomon.	English.	1718.	
(66441)					
Bible.	O. T.	Song of Solomon.	English.	1719.	
(66441)					
Bible.	O. T.	Song of Solomon.	English.	1720.	
(66441)					
Bible.	O. T.	Song of Solomon.	English.	1722.	
(66441)					
Bible.	O. T.	Song of Solomon.	English.	1725.	
(66441)					
Bible.	O. T.	Song of Solomon.	English.	1726.	
(66441)					
Bible.	O. T.	Song of Solomon.	English.	1729.	
(66441)					
Bible.	O. T.	Song of Solomon.	English.	1730.	
(66441)					
Bible.	O. T.	Song of Solomon.	English.	1733.	
(66441)					

Bible. O. T. Song of Solomon. English. 1737. (66441)
Bible. O. T. Song of Solomon. English. 1741. (66441)
Bible. O. T. Song of Solomon. English. 1742. (66441)
Bible. O. T. Song of Solomon. English. 1744. (66441)
Bible. O. T. Song of Solomon. English. 1754. (66441)
Bible. O. T. Song of Solomon. English. 1759. (66441)
Bible. O. T. Song of Solomon. English. 1762. (66441)
Bible. O. T. Isaiah. Paraphrases. English. 1795. 58547, note after 93067
Bible. O. T. Isaiah. English. 1651. 66431
Bible. O. T. Isaiah. English. 1658? (66433)
Bible. O. T. Isaiah. English. 1665? (66434)
Bible. O. T. Isaiah. English. 1671. (66436)
Bible. O. T. Isaiah. English. 1682? 66435
Bible. O. T. Isaiah. English. 1698. (66440)
Bible. O. T. Isaiah. English. 1706. (66441)
Bible. O. T. Isaiah. English. 1709. (66441)
Bible. O. T. Isaiah. English. 1713. (66441)
Bible. O. T. Isaiah. English. 1715. (66441)
Bible. O. T. Isaiah. English. 1716. (66441)
Bible. O. T. Isaiah. English. 1717. (66441)
Bible. O. T. Isaiah. English. 1718. (66441)
Bible. O. T. Isaiah. English. 1719. (66441)
Bible. O. T. Isaiah. English. 1720. (66441)
Bible. O. T. Isaiah. English. 1722. (66441)
Bible. O. T. Isaiah. English. 1725. (66441)
Bible. O. T. Isaiah. English. 1726. (66441)
Bible. O. T. Isaiah. English. 1729. (66441)
Bible. O. T. Isaiah. English. 1730. (66441)
Bible. O. T. Isaiah. English. 1733. (66441)
Bible. O. T. Isaiah. English. 1737. (66441)
Bible. O. T. Isaiah. English. 1741. (66441)
Bible. O. T. Isaiah. English. 1742. (66441)
Bible. O. T. Isaiah. English. 1744. (66441)
Bible. O. T. Isaiah. English. 1754. (66441)
Bible. O. T. Isaiah. English. 1759. (66441)
Bible. O. T. Isaiah. English. 1762. (66441)
Bible. O. T. Isaiah. Eskimo. 1825. 22870
Bible. O. T. Isaiah. Eskimo. 1837. 22870
Bible. O. T. Isaiah. Mohawk. 1839. (49847)
Bible. O. T. Jeremiah. Dakota. 1877. 71335
Bible. O. T. Jeremiah. English. 1638. 76465
Bible. O. T. Jeremiah. English. 1648. (76466)
Bible. O. T. Jeremiah. English. 1651. 66431
Bible. O. T. Jeremiah. English. 1658? (66433)
Bible. O. T. Jeremiah. English. 1665? (66434)
Bible. O. T. Jeremiah. English. 1671. (66436)
Bible. O. T. Jeremiah. English. 1682? 66435
Bible. O. T. Jeremiah. English. 1698. (66440)
Bible. O. T. Jeremiah. English. 1706. (66441)
Bible. O. T. Jeremiah. English. 1709. (66441)
Bible. O. T. Jeremiah. English. 1713. (66441)
Bible. O. T. Jeremiah. English. 1715. (66441)
Bible. O. T. Jeremiah. English. 1716. (66441)

Bible. O. T. Jeremiah. English. 1717. (66441)
Bible. O. T. Jeremiah. English. 1718. (66441)
Bible. O. T. Jeremiah. English. 1719. (66441)
Bible. O. T. Jeremiah. English. 1720. (66441)
Bible. O. T. Jeremiah. English. 1722. (66441)
Bible. O. T. Jeremiah. English. 1725. (66441)
Bible. O. T. Jeremiah. English. 1726. (66441)
Bible. O. T. Jeremiah. English. 1729. (66441)
Bible. O. T. Jeremiah. English. 1730. (66441)
Bible. O. T. Jeremiah. English. 1733. (66441)
Bible. O. T. Jeremiah. English. 1737. (66441)
Bible. O. T. Jeremiah. English. 1741. (66441)
Bible. O. T. Jeremiah. English. 1742. (66441)
Bible. O. T. Jeremiah. English. 1744. (66441)
Bible. O. T. Jeremiah. English. 1754. (66441)
Bible. O. T. Jeremiah. English. 1759. (66441)
Bible. O. T. Jeremiah. English. 1762. (64421)
Bible. O. T. Jeremiah. Eskimo. 1849. (75836)
Bible. O. T. Ezekiel. Dakota. 1877. 71335
Bible. O. T. Ezekiel. Eskimo. 1849. (75836)
Bible. O. T. Daniel. Dakota. 1839. 18288, 69646
Bible. O. T. Daniel. Dakota. 1877. 71335
Bible. O. T. Daniel. Eskimo. 1829. (28658)
Bible. O. T. Daniel. Eskimo. 1849. (75836)
Bible. O. T. Minor Prophets. Dakota. 1877. 71335
Bible. O. T. Minor Prophets. Eskimo. 1829. 22871
Bible. O. T. Minor Prophets. Eskimo. 1849. (75836)
Bible. O. T. Jonah. English. 1651. 66431
Bible. O. T. Jonah. English. 1658? (66433)
Bible. O. T. Jonah. English. 1665? (66434)
Bible. O. T. Jonah. English. 1671. (66436)
Bible. O. T. Jonah. English. 1682? 66435
Bible. O. T. Jonah. English. 1698. (66440)
Bible. O. T. Jonah. English. 1706. (66441)
Bible. O. T. Jonah. English. 1709. (66441)
Bible. O. T. Jonah. English. 1713. (66441)
Bible. O. T. Jonah. English. 1715. (66441)
Bible. O. T. Jonah. English. 1716. (66441)
Bible. O. T. Jonah. English. 1717. (66441)
Bible. O. T. Jonah. English. 1718. (66441)
Bible. O. T. Jonah. English. 1719. (66441)
Bible. O. T. Jonah. English. 1720. (66441)
Bible. O. T. Jonah. English. 1722. (66441)
Bible. O. T. Jonah. English. 1725. (66441)
Bible. O. T. Jonah. English. 1726. (66441)
Bible. O. T. Jonah. English. 1729. (66441)
Bible. O. T. Jonah. English. 1730. (66441)
Bible. O. T. Jonah. English. 1733. (66441)
Bible. O. T. Jonah. English. 1737. (66441)
Bible. O. T. Jonah. English. 1741. (66441)
Bible. O. T. Jonah. English. 1742. (66441)
Bible. O. T. Jonah. English. 1744. (66441)
Bible. O. T. Jonah. English. 1754. (66441)
Bible. O. T. Jonah. English. 1754. (66441)

Bible. O. T. Jonah. English. 1759. (66441)
Bible. O. T. Jonah. English. 1762. (66441)
Bible. O. T. Habakkuk. English. 1651. 66431
Bible. O. T. Habakkuk. English. 1658? (66433)
Bible. O. T. Habakkuk. English. 1665? (66434)
Bible. O. T. Habakkuk. English. 1671. (66436)
Bible. O. T. Habakkuk. English. 1682? 66435
Bible. O. T. Habakkuk. English. 1698. (66440)
Bible. O. T. Habakkuk. English. 1706. (66441)
Bible. O. T. Habakkuk. English. 1709. (66441)
Bible. O. T. Habakkuk. English. 1713. (66441)
Bible. O. T. Habakkuk. English. 1715. (66441)
Bible. O. T. Habakkuk. English. 1716. (66441)
Bible. O. T. Habakkuk. English. 1717. (66441)
Bible. O. T. Habakkuk. English. 1718. (66441)
Bible. O. T. Habakkuk. English. 1719. (66441)
Bible. O. T. Habakkuk. English. 1720. (66441)
Bible. O. T. Habakkuk. English. 1722. (66441)
Bible. O. T. Habakkuk. English. 1725. (66441)
Bible. O. T. Habakkuk. English. 1726. (66441)
Bible. O. T. Habakkuk. English. 1729. (66441)
Bible. O. T. Habakkuk. English. 1730. (66441)
Bible. O. T. Habakkuk. English. 1733. (66441)
Bible. O. T. Habakkuk. English. 1737. (66441)
Bible. O. T. Habakkuk. English. 1741. (66441)
Bible. O. T. Habakkuk. English. 1742. (66441)
Bible. O. T. Habakkuk. English. 1744. (66441)
Bible. O. T. Habakkuk. English. 1754. (66441)
Bible. O. T. Habakkuk. English. 1759. (66441)
Bible. O. T. Habakkuk. English. 1762. (66441)
Bible. O. T. Apocrypha. English. 1790. 5170
Bible. O. T. Apocrypha. English. 1791. 5172-5173
Bible. O. T. Apocrypha. English. 1793. 5177
Bible. O. T. Apocrypha. English. 1796. 5178
Bible. O. T. Apocrypha. English. 1797. 5182
Bible. N. T. Chippewa. 1833. 12833
Bible. N. T. Choctaw. 1848. 12875
Bible. N. T. Choctaw. 1854. 12875
Bible. N. T. Cree. 1859. 17453
Bible. N. T. Dakota. 1866. 71332
Bible. N. T. Dakota. 1867. 71332
Bible. N. T. Dakota. 1871. 71332
Bible. N. T. Dakota. 1874. 71332

Bible. N. T. Dakota. 1878. 71332
Bible. N. T. Dakota. 1880. 71332
Bible. N. T. Delaware. 1821. (40989)
Bible. N. T. Dutch (Creole) 1781. 56364
Bible. N. T. Dutch (Creole) 1802. 56364
Bible. N. T. Dutch (Creole) 1818. 56364
Bible. N. T. English. 1777. 53410
Bible. N. T. English. 1778. 53411
Bible. N. T. English. 1779. 53411
Bible. N. T. English. 1780. 53411
Bible. N. T. English. 1786. 53411
Bible. N. T. English. 1788. 53411
Bible. N. T. English. 1790. 53411
Bible. N. T. English. 1791. 53412
Bible. N. T. English. 1792. 53412
Bible. N. T. English. 1794. 53412
Bible. N. T. English. 1797. 53412
Bible. N. T. English. 1798. (53413)
Bible. N. T. English. 1799. 53412
Bible. N. T. English. 1861. (53414)
Bible. N. T. English. 1862. (53414)
Bible. N. T. English. 1863. (53414)
Bible. N. T. English. 1867. 83250
Bible. N. T. English. 1892. 83251
Bible. N. T. Eskimo. 1766. 22041, 56343
Bible. N. T. Eskimo. 1799. 22873, 22876, 56343
Bible. N. T. Eskimo. 1810. (22872)
Bible. N. T. Eskimo. 1822. 22875
Bible. N. T. Eskimo. 1827. (22874)
Bible. N. T. Eskimo. 1840. 22875
Bible. N. T. German. 1745. 52371
Bible. N. T. German. 1755. (52372)
Bible. N. T. German. 1760. (52372)
Bible. N. T. German. 1763. (52372)
Bible. N. T. German. 1769. (52372)
Bible. N. T. German. 1775. 52373
Bible. N. T. German. 1795. 52374
Bible. N. T. German. 1796. 52375
Bible. N. T. German. 1803. 52374
Bible. N. T. German. 1807. 52374
Bible. N. T. Greek. 1800. 56204
Bible. N. T. Greenland. 1822. 22875
Bible. N. T. Massachuset. 1661. 22155
Bible. N. T. Massachuset. 1680. (22156)-22157
Bible. N. T. Ojibwe. 1844. 57090
Bible. N. T. Ojibwe. 1854. 57095
Bible. N. T. Ojibwe. 1856. 57091
Bible. N. T. Paraphrases. Ojibwe. 1835. 26409
Bible. N. T. Selections. Dakota. 1839. 18289, 69647-69648
Bible. N. T. Selections. Dakota. 1842-1843. 18282
Bible. N. T. Selections. Dakota. 1843. 18291
Bible. N. T. Selections. Eskimo. n. d. 79127
Bible. N. T. Selections. Micmac. 1872? 67765
Bible. N. T. Selections. Ojibwe. 1835. 57085
Bible. N. T. Selections. Sioux. 1839. 18289
Bible. N. T. Gospels. Arrawak. 1850. 2100
Bible. N. T. Gospels. Chippewa. 1850. 57265
Bible. N. T. Gospels. Choctaw. 1831. 12874, 105533
Bible. N. T. Gospels. Delaware. 1821? (19376), (40989), note after 106301
Bible. N. T. Gospels. Eskimo. 1744. (22849)
Bible. N. T. Gospels. Eskimo. 1810. 22862
Bible. N. T. Gospels. Eskimo. 1813. 22853
Bible. N. T. Gospels. Eskimo. 1848. 22853
Bible. N. T. Gospels. Malaya. 1677. 25281

Bible. N. T. Gospels. Selections. Delaware.
  1821. (19376)
Bible. N. T. Matthew. Paraphrases.
  English. 1796. 17434
Bible. N. T. Matthew. Polyglot. 1593.
  47384
Bible. N. T. Matthew. Polyglot. 1680.
  57448
Bible. N. T. Matthew. Polyglot. 1712.
  (57434)
Bible. N. T. Matthew. Polyglot. 1713.
  (57434)
Bible. N. T. Matthew. Polyglot. 1736.
  (57434)
Bible. N. T. Matthew. Polyglot. 1748.
  25986, 78007
Bible. N. T. Matthew. Polyglot. 1805.
  57436
Bible. N. T. Matthew. Polyglot. 1806.
  57437
Bible. N. T. Matthew. Polyglot. 1839.
  70903
Bible. N. T. Matthew. Polyglot. 185-?
  28134
Bible. N. T. Matthew. Polyglot. 1851.
  57438
Bible. N. T. Matthew. Polyglot. 1860.
  48367, 85759
Bible. N. T. Matthew. Polyglot. 1869.
  (51756)
Bible. N. T. Matthew. Polyglot. 1870.
  (57438)
Bible. N. T. Matthew. Charib. 1847. 31304
Bible. N. T. Matthew. Cherokee. 1832.
  105321
Bible. N. T. Matthew. Cherokee. 1843.
  12460
Bible. N. T. Matthew. Cherokee. 1844.
  12460
Bible. N. T. Matthew. Choctaw. 1842.
  (12873)
Bible. N. T. Matthew. Dakota. 1839. 18289,
  69649
Bible. N. T. Matthew. English. 1761.
  (66463)
Bible. N. T. Matthew. English. 1764.
  (66463)
Bible. N. T. Matthew. English. 1767. 66448
Bible. N. T. Matthew. English. 1768.
  (66463)
Bible. N. T. Matthew. English. 1770.
  (66463)
Bible. N. T. Matthew. English. 1771.
  (66463)
Bible. N. T. Matthew. English. 1774.
  (66463)
Bible. N. T. Matthew. English. 1784. 66460
Bible. N. T. Matthew. English. 1819?
  97504
Bible. N. T. Matthew. Latin. 1715. 57435
Bible. N. T. Matthew. Malecite. 1853.
  44123
Bible. N. T. Matthew. Micmac. 1853. 67756
Bible. N. T. Matthew. Micmac. 1871. 67760
Bible. N. T. Matthew. Mohawk. 1831. 49844
Bible. N. T. Matthew. Mohawk. 1835. 49844
Bible. N. T. Matthew. Muskokee. 1825.
  51582
Bible. N. T. Matthew. Nez Perce. 1845.
  88874
Bible. N. T. Matthew. Nez Perce. 1871.
  88875
Bible. N. T. Matthew. Ojibwe. 1829. 57081
Bible. N. T. Matthew. Ojibwe. 1839. 57083
Bible. N. T. Matthew. Ojibwe. 1844. 57083
Bible. N. T. Matthew. Ojibwe. 1847. 26378

Bible. N. T. Matthew. Ojibwe. 1850. 57981
Bible. N. T. Matthew. Ottawa. 1841. 57883
Bible. N. T. Matthew. Potawatomi. 1844.
  42770
Bible. N. T. Matthew. Potawatomi. 1846.
  16318
Bible. N. T. Matthew. Seneca. 1829. 79118
Bible. N. T. Matthew. Shawnee. 1836.
  (79977)
Bible. N. T. Matthew. Shawnee. 1842.
  42769
Bible. N. T. Matthew. Spanish (Mexican
  Dialect) 1859. 48367
Bible. N. T. Matthew. Tuscarora. 1819?
  97504
Bible. N. T. Mark. Abnaki. 1844? 105709
Bible. N. T. Mark. Creek. 1855. 17454
Bible. N. T. Mark. English. 1833. 85452
Bible. N. T. Mark. Micmac. 1872? 67765
Bible. N. T. Mark. Mohawk. 1787. 6351,
  49845
Bible. N. T. Mark. Mohawk. 1829. 49845
Bible. N. T. Luke. Aymara. 1829. 59345
Bible. N. T. Luke. Dakota. 1839. 18289,
  69649
Bible. N. T. Luke. English. 1651. 66431
Bible. N. T. Luke. English. 1658? (66433)
Bible. N. T. Luke. English. 1671. (66436)
Bible. N. T. Luke. English. 1698. (66440)
Bible. N. T. Luke. English. 1706. (66441)
Bible. N. T. Luke. English. 1709. (66441)
Bible. N. T. Luke. English. 1713. (66441)
Bible. N. T. Luke. English. 1715. (66441)
Bible. N. T. Luke. English. 1716. (66441)
Bible. N. T. Luke. English. 1717. (66441)
Bible. N. T. Luke. English. 1718. (66441)
Bible. N. T. Luke. English. 1719. (66441)
Bible. N. T. Luke. English. 1720. (66441)
Bible. N. T. Luke. English. 1722. (66441)
Bible. N. T. Luke. English. 1725. (66441)
Bible. N. T. Luke. English. 1726. (66441)
Bible. N. T. Luke. English. 1729. (66441)
Bible. N. T. Luke. English. 1730. (66441)
Bible. N. T. Luke. English. 1733. (66441)
Bible. N. T. Luke. English. 1737. (66441)
Bible. N. T. Luke. English. 1741. (66441)
Bible. N. T. Luke. English. 1742. (66441)
Bible. N. T. Luke. English. 1744. (66441)
Bible. N. T. Luke. English. 1754. (66441)
Bible. N. T. Luke. English. 1759. (66441)
Bible. N. T. Luke. English. 1762. (66441)
Bible. N. T. Luke. English. 1829. 79121
Bible. N. T. Luke. Maya. 187?. 74522
Bible. N. T. Luke. Maya (Yucatan Dialect)
  1865. 40246, 74524
Bible. N. T. Luke. Micmac. 1856. 67757
Bible. N. T. Luke. Micmac. 1872? 67765
Bible. N. T. Luke. Mohawk. 1827. 49850,
  3d note after 97291
Bible. N. T. Luke. Mohawk. 1833. 49848
Bible. N. T. Luke. Ojibwe. 1837. 57084
Bible. N. T. Luke. Ottawa. 1850. 47377
Bible. N. T. Luke. Seneca. 1829. 79121
Bible. N. T. Luke. Spanish. 1829. 59345
Bible. N. T. John. Chippewa. 1831. (12832)
Bible. N. T. John. Cherokee. 1838. 12461
Bible. N. T. John. Cherokee. 1841. 12461,
  105321
Bible. N. T. John. Cherokee. 1847. 12461
Bible. N. T. John. Creek. 1860. 8942,
  (17460)
Bible. N. T. John. Dakota. 1839. 18289,
  69649
Bible. N. T. John. English. 1805. 49846,
  95145

Bible. N. T. John. English. 1818. 49846, 95145
Bible. N. T. John. English. 1820. 22850
Bible. N. T. John. Eskimo. 1810. 22850
Bible. N. T. John. Eskimo. 1820. 22850
Bible. N. T. John. Maya. 1869. 40247
Bible. N. T. John. Malecite. 1855. 44123
Bible. N. T. John. Malecite. 1870. 67758
Bible. N. T. John. Massachuset. 1709. 45537
Bible. N. T. John. Micmac. 1854? 67765
Bible. N. T. John. Micmac. 1872. 67765
Bible. N. T. John. Mohawk. 1805. 49846, 95145
Bible. N. T. John. Mohawk. 1818. 49846, 95145
Bible. N. T. John. Ojibwe. 1850. 57981
Bible. N. T. John. Ottawa. 1844. 47377
Bible. N. T. Acts. Arawack. 1802. 2099, 80762
Bible. N. T. Acts. Arawack. 1807. 2099, 80762
Bible. N. T. Acts. Arawack. 1850. 2099, 80762
Bible. N. T. Acts. Cherokee. 1833. 105321
Bible. N. T. Acts. Cherokee. 1842. 12433
Bible. N. T. Acts. Choctaw. 1839. 12863
Bible. N. T. Acts. Dakota. 1839. 18289, 69649
Bible. N. T. Acts. Dakota. 1843. 18291, 71336
Bible. N. T. Acts. Malayan. 1677. 25281
Bible. N. T. Acts. Malecite. 185-? 44123
Bible. N. T. Acts. Micmac. 1863. (67763), note after 94300
Bible. N. T. Acts. Mohawk. 1835. 49837
Bible. N. T. Acts. Ojibwe. 1838. 56723
Bible. N. T. Acts. Potawantomi. 1844. 42770
Bible. N. T. Epistles. Eskimo. 1848. 22853
Bible. N. T. Epistles of Paul. Dakota. 1843. 18291, 71336
Bible. N. T. Epistles of Paul. English. 1678. 75445
Bible. N. T. Epistles of Paul. Mohawk. 1836. 49843
Bible. N. T. Romans. Mohawk. 1835. 49841
Bible. N. T. Corinthians I. Mohawk. 1834. 49851
Bible. N. T. Galatians. Mohawk. 1835. 49842
Bible. N. T. Ephesians. Cherokee. 1848. 12454
Bible. N. T. Ephesians. Mohawk. 1835. 49842
Bible. N. T. James. Cherokee. 1847. 12458
Bible. N. T. Epistles of John. Cherokee. 1840. 12453
Bible. N. T. Epistles of John. Choctaw. 1840. 105532
Bible. N. T. Epistles of John. Choctaw. 1841. 105532
Bible. N. T. Epistles of John. Delaware. 1818. 19377
Bible. N. T. Epistles of John I. Creek. 1855. 17455
Bible. N. T. Epistles of John I. Dakota. 1839. 18289, 69649
Bible. N. T. Revelation. Cherokee. 1850. 70158
Bible. N. T. Revelation. Dakota. 1843. 18291, 71336
Bible. N. T. Revelation. English. 1651. 66431

Bible. N. T. Revelation. English. 1658? (66433)
Bible. N. T. Revelation. English. 1671. (66436)
Bible. N. T. Revelation. English. 1698. (66440)
Bible. N. T. Revelation. English. 1706. (66441)
Bible. N. T. Revelation. English. 1709. (66441)
Bible. N. T. Revelation. English. 1713. (66441)
Bible. N. T. Revelation. English. 1715. (66441)
Bible. N. T. Revelation. English. 1716. (66441)
Bible. N. T. Revelation. English. 1717. (66441)
Bible. N. T. Revelation. English. 1718. (66441)
Bible. N. T. Revelation. English. 1719. (66441)
Bible. N. T. Revelation. English. 1720. (66441)
Bible. N. T. Revelation. English. 1722. (66441)
Bible. N. T. Revelation. English. 1725. (66441)
Bible. N. T. Revelation. English. 1726. (66441)
Bible. N. T. Revelation. English. 1729. (66441)
Bible. N. T. Revelation. English. 1730. (66441)
Bible. N. T. Revelation. English. 1733. (66441)
Bible. N. T. Revelation. English. 1737. (66441)
Bible. N. T. Revelation. English. 1741. (66441)
Bible. N. T. Revelation. English. 1742. (66441)
Bible. N. T. Revelation. English. 1744. (66441)
Bible. N. T. Revelation. English. 1754. (66441)
Bible. N. T. Revelation. English. 1759. (66441)
Bible. N. T. Revelation. English. 1762. (66441)
Bible. N. T. Revelation. Spanish. 1727. 42578
Bible against slavery. 102548
Bible and abolitionism. (28239)
Bible and American slavery. 7761
Bible and civil government. (46843)
Bible and its literature. 72067
Bible and national prosperity. 866
Bible and school fund. 13365
Bible and slavery. By Charles Elliott. 22254
Bible and slavery. By Sidney E. Morse. 50965
Bible and the common schools. 85359
Bible and the public schools. 89101
Bible and the sword. 5183, 2d note after 97146
Bible and Tract Society, Orange, N. Y. see Orange Bible and Tract Society.
Bible argument. 78345
Bible argument; or, slavery in the light of divine revelation. 92870
Bible Association of Friends in America. 5184, 86036, 86042
Bible boy taken captive by the Indians. (34615)
Bible communism. (57337)
Bible Communists. see Oneida Community.
Bible, confession of faith, and common sense. 84761

Bible Convention, Columbia, S. C., 1829. 87799
Bible Convention, Columbia, S. C., 1840. 87800
Bible Convention, Columbia, S. C., 1842. 87801
Bible Convention, Columbia, S. C., 1842.
    Executive Committee. 87801
Bible Convention, Columbia, S. C., 1843. 87801
Bible Convention, Columbia, S. C., 1843.
    Executive Committee. 87801
Bible Convention, Columbia, S. C., 1844. 87801
Bible Convention, Columbia, S. C., 1844.
    Executive Committee. 87801
Bible defence of slavery; and origin, fortunes,
    and history of the Negro race. (65497)
Bible defence of slavery, and the unity of
    mankind. 49692
Bible, history, and common sense. (67674)
Bible in the army. 5185, 54433
Bible in the public schools. A . . . discussion.
    70823
Bible in the public schools. A reply to the
    allegations and complaints. 14800
Bible in the public schools: a sermon preached
    by Rev. Samuel T. Spear. 89084
Bible in the public schools. Addresses.
    (47182)
Bible Mission, Providence, R. I. see Provi-
    dence Bible Mission, Providence, R. I.
Bible news. (82540), 105271
Bible of every land. 5186
Bible on the present crisis. 5187
Bible professor. pseud. On the ten tribes of
    Israel. 56744, 57298
Bible rights of the slave. (81904)
Bible servitude. 9367
Bible servitude re-examined. 30839
Bible slaveholding not sinful. 26542
Bible Society, Newark, N. J. see Newark
    Bible Society.
Bible Society in the County of Worcester, Mass.
    see Auxiliary Bible Society in the
    County of Worcester, Mass.
Bible Society: its designs and operations.
    60304
Bible Society of Charleston, S. C. see
    Charleston Bible Society.
Bible Society of Maryland. see Maryland
    State Bible Society.
Bible Society of Massachusetts. see Massachu-
    setts Bible Society.
Bible Society of Middlesex County, Mass. see
    Middlesex County Bible Society.
Bible Society of Minnesota. see Minnesota
    State Bible Society.
Bible Society of New Hampshire. see New
    Hampshire Bible Society.
Bible Society of New Haven County, Conn. see
    New Haven County Bible Society.
Bible Society of New Jersey. see New Jersey
    Bible Society.
Bible Society of New York City. See New
    York Bible Society.
Bible Society of Newark, N. J. see Newark
    Bible Society.
Bible Society of Norfolk County, Mass. see
    Norfolk County Bible Society.
Bible Society of North Carolina. see North
    Carolina Bible Society.
Bible Society of Ohio. see Ohio Bible Society.
Bible Society of Pennsylvania. see Pennsyl-
    vania Bible Society.
Bible Society of Philadelphia. see Philadelphia
    Bible Society.
Bible Society of Salem and Vicinity. see
    Salem Bible Society, Salem, Mass.
Bible Society of Saratoga County, N. Y. see
    Saratoga County Bible Society.

Bible Society of Schenectady County, N. Y.
    see Schenectady County Bible Society.
Bible Society of Schoharie County, N. Y. see
    Schoharie County Bible Society.
Bible Society of Strafford County, N. H. see
    Strafford Bible Society.
Bible Society of Suffolk County, N. Y. see
    Suffolk County Bible Society.
Bible Society of the Confederate States of
    America. see Confederate States
    Bible Society.
Bible Society of the Counties of Montgomery,
    Fulton, and Hamilton, N. Y. see Auxil-
    iary Bible Society of the Counties of
    Montgomery, Fulton, and Hamilton, N. Y.
Bible Society of the State of Rhode Island and
    Providence Plantations. see Rhode Island
    Bible Society.
Bible Society of Union College. see Union
    College, Schenectady, N. Y. Bible Society.
Bible Society of Vermont. see Vermont Bible
    Society.
Bible Society of Virginia. see Virginia Bible
    Society.
Bible Society of Washington, D. C. see
    Washington Bible Society.
Bible Society of Washington County, N. Y. see
    Washington County Bible Society.
Bible system. (58153)
Bible the basis of American liberty. 64692
Bible, the rod, and religion, in common schools.
    83572, 83579
Bible—the safe-guard of the nation. 91154
Bible Translation and Foreign Missionary
    Society, Salem, Mass. see Salem Bible
    Translation and Foreign Missionary
    Society.
Bible Union of Philadelphia. see Philadelphia
    Bible Union.
Bible versus polygamy. 82429
Bible view of polygamy. 5188, 39483
Bible view of slavery. 5189-(5190), 6231,
    20955, 27936, (32928), 39789, 42695,
    (44755), 47062, 55014
Bible view of slavery, by John H. Hopkins,
    D. D., Bishop of . . . Vermont, . . .
    examined. 20955
Bible view of slavery. [By Morris Jacob
    Raphael.] (8488)
Bible view of slavery; or, Bishop Hopkins re-
    viewed. 5189
Bible view of slavery reconsidered. (5190),
    55014
Bible view of slavery reviewed. (22088)
Bible without note or comment. (79494)
Bible-woman's record. 82948
Biblia, das ist: die ganze Gottliche Heilige
    Schrift. (5194)
Biblia, das ist: die ganze Heilige Schrift. 5193
Biblia, das ist: die Heilige Schrift. 5191
Biblia, das ist Heilige Schrift. 5192
Biblical dialogues between a father and his
    family. 73619
Biblical narrative of the acts of first and
    second kings. 30230
Biblical repertory. see Princeton review.
Biblical repertory and Princeton review. see
    Princeton review.
Biblical repertory and theological review. see
    Princeton review.
Biblical repository. see Bibliotheca sacra.
Biblical researches in Palestine. 72067
Biblical view of slavery. 67913
Biblicus. pseud. Bible view of slavery recon-
    sidered. see Newman, Lewis C.
    supposed author

Bibliografia de las lenguas Quechua y Aymara. 86268

Bibliographia Americana. 91519

Bibliographia Americana historico naturalis. 27481

Bibliographia de la primera imprenta de Buenos Aires. 29339

Bibliographia genealogica Americana. (21438)

Bibliographia historica. 5102

Bibliographia Lincolniana. 41176

Bibliographical account of Catholic Bibles. (79994)

Bibliographical account of early English literature. 67554

Bibliographical account of the sources of early American history. 91519

Bibliographical and critical account. 82833, 82847

Bibliographical catalogue of books. (77840)

Bibliographical catalogue of the Waltonian library. 74673

Bibliographical essay. 42644

Bibliographical essay on Governor Hutchinson's historical publications. 19044

Bibliographical essay on the collection of voyages and travels. 2182

Bibliographical essays. 83978, note before 99075

Bibliographical guide to American literature. (54365)

Bibliographical index of American surgical writers. (82714)

Bibliographical introduction to the writings of Roger Williams. 51773

Bibliographical list of books and pamphlets. 33136

Bibliographical memoirs of the American Academy of Political and Social Science. 83003

Bibliographical mirrour. 82823

Bibliographical miscellany. 5195, 61246

Bibliographical-spelling-book. 102445

Bibliographical tracts. (19046), 89927

Bibliographie biographique universelle. (56739)

Bibliographie de la Guyane Francaise. 94849

Bibliographie der Freimaurerei in Amerika. 3711

Bibliographie d'Haiti. (6309)

Bibliographie historique de la Compagnie de Jesus. (10791)

Bibliographie instructive. (8784)

Bibliographische Mittheilunger uber die Deutschen Ausgaben. (8784)

Bibliography of American natural history. 27481

Bibliography of bibliography. 74674

Bibliography of Hennepin's works. (79995)

Bibliography of miscellaneous literature. 83308

Bibliography of North American conchology. 5499

Bibliography of Philippine geology. 84529

Bibliography of Rhode Island. 3735

Bibliography of Sir Walter Raleigh. 67599

Bibliography of that ancient and honourable order of the Society of the Cincinnati. 83491

Bibliography of the Algonquin language. 39409, 96105

Bibliography of the first letter of Columbus. 44068

Bibliography of the historical literature of North Carolina. 85313

Bibliography of the Massachusetts Historical Society. 28557

Bibliography of the Society of the Cincinnati. 86111

Bibliography of the state of Maine. 55870

Bibliography of the state of New Hampshire. 55870

Bibliography of the state of Vermont. 55870

Bibliography of Vermont. 29736

Biblioteca Americana. 77130

Biblioteca Americana, por una Sociedad de Americanos. 5197

Biblioteca Ayacucho. 10193, 36807, note before 94254, 96235, 1st note after 97687, 98148, note after 98870

Biblioteca de autores Espanoles. (9890), 11402, 13055, 27733, 32043, 57302, 57987, 67324, (70780), 86472, 105724, 106269

Biblioteca de escritores Portugueses. 99519

Biblioteca de escritores Venezolanos contemporaneos. 72790

Biblioteca de historia Argentina y Americana. 94606

Biblioteca de instruccion primaria superior. 39066

Biblioteca de la Junta de Historia y Numismatica Americana. 94606

Biblioteca de las memorias de la Sociedad Economica de Santiago de Cuba. 98165

Biblioteca de viaje. 63564

Biblioteca de vulgarizacion de la ciencia Espanola. 100622

Biblioteca del boletin de la Sociedad Agricola Mexicana. 84332

Biblioteca del comercio del Plata. 63330

Biblioteca di scienza politische. 96067

Biblioteca economica de clasicos Castellanos. 98604

Biblioteca economico-portatile di educazione. 69330

Biblioteca glottica. 42643

Biblioteca Goathemala. 99643

Biblioteca Hispano-Americana septentrional. 4871, 22060, 38957

Biblioteca Hispano-Chilena. 98301

Biblioteca Hispano-ultramarina. 67359

Biblioteca historica de la Iberia. 99388

Biblioteca historica de Puerto-Rico. 94352

Biblioteca ilustrada de Gaspar y Roig. 86472

Biblioteca maritima Espanola. 52097

Biblioteca nacional economica. 86474

Biblioteca Peruana de historia ciencias y literatura. (26114), 47936, 61153

Biblioteca universal economica. 12242

Bibliotheca. 19612

Bibliotheca Americana. 55871, 91508

Bibliotheca Americana (Gowan's series) 8953, 19612, note after 28166, 49026

Bibliotheca Americana. A catalogue of a valuable collection of books and pamphlets, illustrating the history & geography. 82326

Bibliotheca Americana. A catalogue of a valuable collection of books & pamphlets relating to the history and geography. 83014

Bibliotheca Americana. A catalogue of a valuable collection of books, illustrating the history and geography. 83016

Bibliotheca Americana. A catalogue of a valuable collection of books, pamphlets, manuscripts, maps, engravings, and engraved portraits. 83015

Bibliotheca Americana. A catalogue of books relating to North and South America. 3736

Bibliotheca Americana. A catalogue of books relating to the history and literature of America. (5199), 91511

Bibliotheca Americana. A catalogue of the entire library of Andrew Wright. 74683

Bibliotheca Americana. A chronological catalogue. 83013
Bibliotheca Americana, being a choice collections. 31623, 40010, 101353
Bibliotheca Americana. Catalogo de los autores. 684
Bibliotheca Americana. Catalogue of American publications. 37310, 73091-(73096)
Bibliotheca Americana. Catalogue of . . . books relating to America. 6947
Bibliotheca Americana. Catalogue of the library belonging to Mr. Richard W. Roche. 72313, note after (74691)
Bibliotheca Americana. Catalogue raisone d'une tres-precieuse collection. 39647
Bibliotheca Americana et selectissima. (74675)
Bibliotheca Americana nova. 28306, 70875-70879, 70887
Bibliotheca Americana; or, a chronological catalogue. (5198)
Bibliotheca Americana or a descriptive account of my collection. 25567, 91509-91511
Bibliotheca Americana vetus. 70880
Bibliotheca Americana vetustissima. 24130, 24933, 30599-30601
Bibliotheca Americana vetustissima. . . . Additions. 63180
Bibliotheca Americano-septentraionalis. 101354
Bibliotheca Anglo-poetica. 1721
Bibliotheca anti-quakeriana. 83307-83308
Bibliotheca Barlowiana. 3440
Bibliotheca Brasilica. (7603)
Bibliotheca Canadensis. 50647
Bibliotheca chret de l'adolenscence. (23577)
Bibliotheca clericalis Americana. 85551
Bibliotheca Coisliniana, olim Sequeriana. 66508
Bibliotheca de la revista. 89995
Bibliotheca del ex-coronel Pineda. 62928
Bibliotheca dramatica. 74676
Bibliotheca Grenvilliana. (8784)
Bibliotheca Hispana nova. (1720)
Bibliotheca Hispana sive Hispanorvm. 1719
Bibliotheca Hispana vetus. 1717
Bibliotheca Hispana vetus, sive Hispani Scriptores. 1718
Bibliotheca historica. (20908), 30599
Bibliotheca historica; catalogue raisonne d'une collection. 39647
Bibliotheca historica de Portugal. 62994
Bibliotheca historica instructa a B. Burcardo Gotthelf Struvio. 93112
Bibliotheca historico-geographica. 22663
Bibliotheca litteraria. 7527
Bibliotheca Lusitana, historica, critica, e cronologica. 43298
Bibliotheca Lusitana; or a catalogue of books and tracts. 368
Bibliotheca Marsdeniana. 44718
Bibliotheca Mejicana. 24417
Bibliotheca Mexicana. 5200, 48304
Bibliotheca Mexicana sive eruditorum historia vivorum. 22060
Bibliotheca Munselliana. 51360, 86941
Bibliotheca Nacional, Rio de Janeiro. see Brazil. Bibliotheca Nacional, Rio de Janeiro.
Bibliotheca occidental. 70887
Bibliotheca Parisiana. (8784)
Bibliotheca parochialis. 7474
Bibliotheca populare. 6818
Bibliotheca quakeriana. 83308
Bibliotheca sacra. 5201-5202, 25122, 44327, 70190, 72067, 76243, 80073, 92393, 99583
Bibliotheca sacra (Indexes) 5202

Bibliotheca sacra and American biblical repository. see Bibliotheca sacra.
Bibliotheca sacra and theological review. see Bibliotheca sacra.
Bibliotheca scriptorvm Societatis Iesv opvs inchoatvm. 70777
Bibliotheca scriptorum Societatis Jesu, post excusum 1608, catalogum ad 1642. 712
Bibliotheca scriptorum Societatis Jesu, post excusum 1608 catalogum R. P. Petri Ribadeneirae. 70776
Bibliotheca siue thesavrvs virtvtis et gloriae. 6162
Bibliotheca splendidissima. (75677)
Bibliotheca symbolica ecclesiae universalis. 77494
Bibliotheca universalis Americana. (32720)
Bibliothecae Americanae primordia. 30599, 37447
Bibliothecae scriptorum Societatis Jesu supplementa. 70777
Bibliothek class. Romane der Auslandes. 12247
Bibliothek der Lander-und Volkerkunde. 92807
Bibliothek der Lander- und Volkerkunde, nach den neuesten politischen Gestaltungen. (4858)
Bibliothek der neuesten auslandischen Classiker. 16493
Bibliothek der neuesten Reisebeschreibungen. 4348, 16263, 17419, 19323, 19646, (20915), 30024
Bibliothek der neuesten und wichtigsten Reisebeschreibungen. 4964, 49480-49482, 89744, 100690, note after 104633
Bibliothek des litterarischen Vereins. 23997, 90039
Bibliothek Deutscher Originalromane. 27177
Bibliothek fur Morskabslaening. 16458
Bibliothek fur die reifere Christliche Jungd. 11659
Bibliothek fur meine Kinder. 5203
Bibliothek klassischer Schriftsteller Nordamerika's. 5204, 5555
Bibliothek Reichard, Leipzig. 95348
Bibliotheque Americaine, contenant des memoires. 5205
Bibliotheque American e ou catalogue des ouvrages. 94844
Bibliotheque Canadienne. 5206-5207
Bibliotheque Chretienne et morale. 86389
Bibliotheque conchyliologique. 12430, 15905
Bibliotheque de l'Arsenal, Paris. see Paris. Bibliotheque de l'Arsenal.
Bibliotheque de l'emigrant. (73456)
Bibliotheque des ecrivains de la Compagnie de Jesus. (2619)
Bibliotheque des meilleurs romans etrangers. 92443
Bibliotheque des merveilles. (81311)
Bibliotheque dramatique. 92544, 92546, 92549
Bibliotheque du theatre Francais. 29938
Bibliotheque d'un homme de gout. 92433
Bibliotheque geographique et instructive. 10305
Bibliotheque Heher. (8784)
Bibliotheque Mazarine, Paris. see Paris. Bibliotheque Mazarine.
Bibliotheque Nationale, Paris. see Paris. Bibliotheque Nationale.
Bibliotheque portative des voyages. 5208, 31406
Bibliotheque Royale, Paris. see Paris. Bibliotheque Nationale.
Bibliotheque Sainte-Genevieve, Paris. see Paris. Bibliotheque Sainte-Genevieve.
Bibliotheque universelle des historiens. 21361

Bibliotheque universelle des voyages effectues
  par mer ou par terre. 4349, 6865,
  9140, 14095, 16275, 23780, 50113,
  97033, 98442
Bibliotheque universelle des voyages, ou notice
  complete et raisonnee. 6847
Bibliotheque Willett. (8784)
Bibra, Ernst, Freiherr von. 5209-5217
Bibron, ------. 14113, 74921-74922
Bicard, M. illus. (79271)
Bicardo, Ariele. ed.? 32681
Bicentenary sermons. 72574
Bi-centennial book of Malden. 43060
Bi-centennial sermon. 73119
Bichebois, -------. illus. 48916, 73935
Bickell, R. (3352), 5218
Bicker, Laurens. 14349
Bickerstaff. pseud. Bickerstaff's town
  and country almanack. see Patten,
  Nathaniel. publisher and Strong,
  Nehemiah.
Bickerstaff, Isaac. pseud. Bickerstaff's
  Boston almanack. see West, Benjamin,
  1730-1813.
Bickerstaff, Isaac. pseud. Letter from a
  Gentleman in Transilvania. see Hunt,
  Isaac.
Bickerstaff, Isaac. pseud. New England
  almanac for 1781. see West, Benjamin,
  1730-1813.
Bickerstaff, Jacob. pseud. Memoirs. see
  Houstoun, James, b. ca. 1690.
Bickerstaffe, Isaac, 1735?-1812? ed. 84241
Bickerstaffe, Isaac, 1735?-1812? supposed
  author 10668, (29384)-29385, 89592-
  89593, 105634
Bickerstaff's almanack. 93891
Bickerstaff's Boston almanack. 5220, 62743
Bickerstaff's Boston almanack for 1788. 105008
Bickerstaff's genuine Boston almanack for
  1788. 102530
Bickerstaff's New-England almanack. 93053
Bickerstaff's town and country almanac. 44258,
  note after 105687
Bickersteth, Edward, 1786-1850. 105923
Bickford, James. 5221
Bickham, George. 5222, 80618
Bickham, William D. 5223
Bickley, George W. L. 5224-5226
Bickley, Lloyd Wharton. supposed author
  106369
Bicknell, John. 18987
Bida di Hesoe Kriestoe, noos dibienoe. (66745)
Biddeford, Me. 5227
Biddeford, Me. Church. 31842
Biddeford, Me. Mayor. 5227
Biddle, -------. defendant (73530)
Biddle, Charles. ed. 16964, 19071, 29813,
  (32499), (64182), 67377
Biddle, Charles, fl. 1836. 5228, 15000
Biddle, Charles John. 5229-(5231)
Biddle, Clement. 61602
Biddle, Clement C. ed. and tr. 77363
Biddle, George W. 5232
Biddle, J. B. ed. 47316
Biddle, James. 5233, 25636
Biddle, James C. (5234)-5235, 97768
Biddle, John. 32062
Biddle, Nicholas, 1786-1844. 856, 5236-5243,
  14981, 34735, (40828), 71856, 92851,
  92861
Biddle, Owen. 5244-5245, 84678C
Biddle, Richard. (5246)-5250
Biddulph, W. 66686
Bidlack, Benjamin Alden, 1804-1849. 5251
Bidlake, John. 5252

Bidrag til beskrivelse over St^e Croix. 102732
Bidrag til det Vestindiske origes. (69112)
Bidrag til kundskab om Brasiliens batrachia og
  sauru. 69113
Bidrag til kundskab om Brasiliens padder og
  krybdyr af J. Reinhardt. 69114
Bidwell, Barnabas. 5253-5256, 93937 see also
  Massachusetts. Attorney General.
Bidwell, Charles Toll. 5257
Bidwell, Marshall Spring. 5259, 72872
Biechte des Conincx van Spanjen. 70323
Biedma, Luis Hernandez de. 24858, 24894,
  87206, note after 94854, 94856
Bien (Julius) & Co. firm publishers 94172
Biena venturanzas del sant patriarca sen. San
  Joseph. 20569
Bienaventvrada Rosa Pervana de S. Maria.
  73179
Bienaventvrado Toribio Alfonso Mogroveio
  Arzobispo de Lima. 42055
Bienes i Herederos del Governador Don
  Francisco Vanegas. defendants 86523
Bienes y Herederos de Dona Gertrudis de la
  Pena. defendants (67401)
Bienes, y Herederos del Governador Don
  Francisco Vanegas. defendants 86524
Bienewitz, Peter. see Apianus, Petrus, 1501?-
  1552.
Biennial American Convention for Promoting
  the Abolition of Slavery. see American
  Convention for Promoting the Abolition
  of Slavery, and Improving the Condition
  of the African Race.
Biennial catalogue . . . see Catalogue . . .
Biennial digest for 1857 and 1859. 7972
Biennial message, delivered to the Iowa General
  Assembly. (34974)
Biennial register of all officers and agents.
  (5261)
Biennial register of federal officers. 20325
Biennial report . . . see Report . . .
Biennial reports . . . see Reports . . .
Bienvenida, L. de. 94854
Bier, George Henry. 5262
Bierce, L. V. 5263-5264
Bierfruend, Friedrich Ludvig. 5265
Bierstadt, Albert, 1830-1902. (5266)
Biervliet, Paul van. 5267
Bierwirth, Leopold. petitioner (23591)
Biesen, J. J. van der. 5268
Biet, Antoine. 5269, (65038), (77219)
Big Abel and the little Manhattan. 46829
Big bear of Arkansas. 95662
Big bull in a court house. 35509
Big fort, the guide. 30044
Big-shoe songster. 79667
Big sinner. pseud. On the vanity of human
  actions. see Smith, Michael. minister
  of the gospel
Big Springs, Kansas. Territorial Delegate
  Convention, 1855. see Kansas Territory
  Delegate Convention, Big Springs, 1855.
Big thing. 89230
Big Tree. Seneca Indian Chief 79109
Bigaurures d'un citoyen de Geneve. 5270, note
  after 14001
Bigelow, Abijah. 5271-5272, 63796
Bigelow, Albert. 89672
Bigelow, Andrew. 5273-5284
Bigelow, Eliza (Tappan) 5285
Bigelow, Erastus Brigham, 1814-1879. 5286-
  (5291)
Bigelow, George Tyler. reporter 5292
Bigelow, Henry Jacob. 5293
Bigelow, Jacob, 1786-1879. 5294-5301, 67461,
  80679

Bigelow, Jacob, 1786-1879. supposed author
  33647, 101507
Bigelow, John, 1817-1911. (5302)-5307, 25492,
  (37656)
Bigelow, John F. 5308
Bigelow, John M. 5309-5311, 69946
Bigelow, John Prescott. (5312)-5315
Bigelow, John R. 5316
Bigelow, Jonathan. 5317
Bigelow, Josiah. 5318, 106051
Bigelow, Lewis. 5319-(5320)
Bigelow, Liberty. 5321
Bigelow, Moses. (54875) see also Newark,
  N. J. Mayor, 1857 (Bigelow)
Bigelow, Timothy. 5322-(5328), 101803, 101870
Bigelow, Tyler. 5330
Bigelow, W. E. 5331
Bigelow (A.) & Co. firm 96495
Bigelow Association, Clinton, Mass. 13761
Bigger, Samuel. (34548)
Bigges, Walter. 9500, 20828, 20837, 20840-
  20843, note after 93587-93588
Biggs, Asa. (5332), (55688)
Biggs, James. supposed author 5333-5334,
  9117,
Biggs, Joseph. (5335)
Biggs, William. 5336, 7956
Bigham, T. J. (5337)
Bigland, John. 5338-(5339)
Bigler, John, 1805-1871. 76077 see also
  California. Governor, 1852-1856 (Bigler)
Bigler, William, 1814-1880. 5340-5342, 20498,
  (25648), note just before 60250, 62036,
  92909 see also Pennsylvania. Governor,
  1852-1855 (Bigler)
Bigler, William H. 68990
Biglow, H. ed. 1154
Biglow, William. (5343)-5349
Biglow papers. (42433), 84185-84187
Bigly, Cantell A. pseud. Aurifodina. 5350
Bigney, M. F. 5351
Bigot, Francois. 7650
Bigot, Francois. defendant (38696), 47528,
  98684
Bigot, Jacques. 5352-5356
Bigot, Vincent. (5357), 1st note after 93480
Bigotry exposed. (16145), 81905
Bigsby, John J. (5358)-5360
Bihang til Amiralen Lord Ansons resa. 100803
'Bijah in Pandemonium. (19522), note after
  93549
Bijdraagen tot eene meer naauwkeurige kennis.
  (24419)
Bijdrage ter aanwijzing van der grondslagen.
  52348
Bijdrage tot de kennis der kolonie Suriname.
  (38932)
Bijdrage tot de kennis der voormalige Neder-
  landsche kolonien. 38206
Bijdrage tot de ware beschouwing van de zoo
  hoog geroemde uitbreiding des Christen-
  doms. 94582
Bijdrage tot eene nadere beschouwing van den
  tegenwoordigen toestand der kolonie
  Suriname. 94584
Bijdragen ter gedachtniss van G. Washington.
  5361, 101777, 101874
Bijdragen tot de bevordering van de kenniss
  der Nederlandsch West Indische kolonien.
  (24937), 2d note after 93879
Bijdragen tot de geschiedenis onzer kolonisatie
  in Noord-Amerika. (4843)
Bijdragen tot de huishouding van staat in het
  koningrijk der Nederlanden. 98822
Bijdragen tot de kennis der Nederlandsche en
  vreemde kolonien. 5362

Bijlaagen. 5361, 101777
Bijzonderheden betrekkelijk den brand te
  Paramaribo. 94583
Bijzonderheden omtrent C. Pllari. 31487
Bijzonderheden uit de geschiedenis van Amerika.
  5363
Bilbao, Francisco. (5364), (23065)
Bilbao, Manuel. (5364), 73221
Bilbo, W. N. 5365-5366
Bild aus dem Leben der Auswandere. 91219
Bild aus der Missiongeschichte ber Bruder-
  gemeine. 39673
Bilde. (9208)
Bilder aus dem geselligen Leben der Nord-
  Amerikaner. 5367
Bilder aus dem militarischen Leben. 37102
Bilder aus dem Wald- und Prairieleben
  Amerika's. 20123
Bilder aus der Mission unter den Negern.
  32685
Bilder aus einer Reise nach Amerika 1852.
  7725
Bilder aus Rio de Janeiro und Umgebung. 5368
Bilder und Charaktere. 92436
Bilder und Skizzen aus Kansas. 27529
Bilder zum Anshauungs-Unterricht fur die
  Jugend. 5369
Bilderdijk, Willem. (5370)
Bildnisse des Verfassers. 100686
Biles-Island lottery. 5371
Bilious fever. 77438
Bilk op den vroegeren en tegenwaardigen
  toestand. 5914
Bill, Ledyard. 5372A-(5373)
Bill and answer. 96860
Bill and explanation of Preston King. 37830
Bill and report of John A. Bingham. 5439
Bill and report on the New Mexican slave codes.
  5440
Bill Arp. pseud. see Smith, Charles Henry,
  1826-1903.
Bill Arp, so called. 5384, (82394)
Bill Arp's letters. (82395)
Bill Arp's peace papers. (82396)
Bill Arp's scrap-book. (82397)
Bill authorizing mail steamship service. 43449
Bill [by Mr. Ingersoll.] 60273
Bill concerning the convention. 100049
Bill converning the judicial system. (5375)
Bill Deadeye, and the Anaconda. 82117
[Bill declaring tobacco receivable in payment
  for taxes.] 100044
Bill establishing a provision for teachers of the
  Christian religion. 100528
[Bill entitled "An act, to enable the judges of
  the Admiralty, to hold courts of oyer
  and terminer.] 100045
Bill for a complete system of education.
  (35937)
Bill for an act declaring the traffic in spirituous
  or intoxicating liquors unlawful. 84464
Bill for establishing religious freedom. 100041
Bill for establishing the constitution. 87477
[Bill, "For making lands subject to the payment
  of debts."] 100057
Bill for making more effectual provision for
  the government of the province of Quebec.
  (11601), 2d note after 105598-9 [sic]
Bill for raising a supply for His Majesty's
  service. (45085)
[Bill "For re-forming the county courts."]
  100042
Bill for relief of William Paterson. 59053
Bill for repealing several subsidies. (5356),
  (5374)

Bill for re-uniting to the crown the government of several colonies and plantations in America. 5377

[Bill for the appointment of electors to choose a president.] 100051

Bill for the better raising of money on the inhabitants of Philadelphia for publick uses. 61499

Bill for the better regulating the nightly watch. 61500

Bill for the construction of a national road. (71068)

Bill for the government of the navy. 52122

Bill for the incorporation of companies. 53541

Bill for the preservation and civilization of the Indian tribes. 65338

Bill for the relief of certain officers in the United States Navy. 28038

Bill for the relief of the heirs of John Paul Jones. 36561

Bill for the removal of the Indians. 89222

Bill for the suspension of the Jamaica constitution. 89153

Bill for uniting the legislative councils and assemblies of the provinces of Lower and Upper Canada. 10474

Bill in equity. 35680

Bill in equity, the commonwealth of Massachusetts vs. the state of Rhode Island. 46149

Bill in the Chancery of New Jersey. At the suit of John Earl of Stair, and others. 5378, (53066), 83982

Bill in the Chancery of New Jersey, at the suit of John Hunt. 5379, 33874, 91855

Bill in the Chancery of New Jersey at the suit of Robert Barclay. 53074, 91855

Bill in the Chancery of New-Jersey, at the suit of Samuel Smith. 83979

Bill in the Chancery of New York at the suit of Priscilla Bland. 53542

Bill incorporating the Southern Trans-Continental Railway Company. 88505

Bill intituled An act to amend the several acts. 100084

[Bill laying taxes for 1797.] 100068

Bill of chancery, filed in the Circuit Court of the United States. 27488

Bill of complaint in the Chancery of New Jersey. 53075

Bill of complaint of the state of Florida. 27048

Bill of indictment. 78033

Bill of mortality. (50900)

Bill of mortality for Kenington, N. H. (20747)

Bill of mortality, for Portsmouth, Newhampshire, for A. D. 1802. (64416)

Bill of mortality for the society of Friends, in Dover, N. H. 20743

Bill of mortality for the town of Salem from the 1st of January, 1818. 75623

Bill of mortality for the town of Salem, from the 1st of January, 1820. 75639

Bill of mortality of the city of Lowell. (42471)

Bill of rights, a list of grievances, occasional resolves. (15528), 15544

Bill of rights of the state of Virginia. 16102

Bill of wrongs and rights. 65883

[Bill on subject lands to be sold for payment of debts as amended.] 100061

Bill prohibiting slavery in Kansas. 57063

Bill prohibiting the importation of foreign distilled spirits. 100046

Bill . . . providing for the accomodation of the General Post Office and Patent Office. (64481)

Bill, regelende de afschaffing der slavernij. 5385

Bill seigneurial expose sous son vrai jour, et quelques avis. 5383

Bill seigneurial expose sous son vrai jour par le journal "Le patrie." 67614

Bill—synopsis—and explanatory remarks. 24343

Bill: the commonwealth of Massachusetts vs. the state of Rhode Island and Providence Plantations. 46152, 70752

[Bill to amend act entitled An act to prevent unlawful gaming.] 100069

[Bill, to amend and reduce into one act the several acts.] 100062

[Bill, to amend the penal laws of the commonwealth.] 100063-100064

Bill to authorize the establishment of a line of mail steamers. 95464

Bill to be entitled An act extending the privilege of purchasing clothing at government cost. 15239

Bill to be entitled An act for the sequestration of the estate. 5380

Bill to be entitled An act to amend the act. 94991

Bill to be entitled, An act to incorporate the Southern Railroad Company. 88455

Bill to close the operations of the Bank of the State of South Carolina. 87377

Bill to enforce the fifteenth amendment. 66092

Bill to establish a national system of finance. 24343

Bill to establish a territorial government for Utah. 70913, 85563

Bill to establish a uniform coinage. 34923

Bill to establish a uniform system of bankruptcy. 35980

Bill to establish an uniform system of bankruptcy. 5381

Bill . . . to establish permanently in . . . Alabama a common school fund. 64202

[Bill to establish public schools.] 100065

Bill to establish the New Hampshire Agricultural College. (52915)

Bill to guarantee to certain states, whose governments have been usurped or overthrown, a republican form of government. (6977)

Bill . . . to levy additional taxes. (31917)

Bill to organize the territories of Nebraska and Kansas. 52180

Bill to prevent officers of the army and navy, and other persons in the military and naval service of the United States, from interfering in elections in the states. 69739

Bill to promote the education of the deaf and dumb. 45976

Bill to provide a national currency. (51963)

Bill to provide for organizing, arming and disciplining the militia of the United States. (5382), 48978

Bill to provide for the ascertainment and satisfaction of claims. 17555

Bill to provide for the establishment of a state hospital for the insane. 55597

Bill to provide for the safe and expeditious transportation of troops and munitions of war. (15240)

[Bill to repeal certain acts.] 100070

Billard, Ed. 5386

Billardon de Sauvigny, Louis Edme. 5387-5389, 77221-77222, 87304

Billaud-Varennes, Jacques Nicolas. 5390-5391, (42899), note after 98597

Billault, Auguste Adolphe Marie. 5392-5394
Billberg, Gustaf Johan. 5395
Billberg, J. 5395
Billde, Nicholas. 27491
Bille, Steen Andersen, 1781- 5396-5398, 6399-6400
Bille, Steen Andersen, 1797- 5399-5400
Billecocq, Jean Baptiste Louis Joseph. 5401-5402, 41879, 47262, 95837
Billeder fra Gronland. 73901
Billerica, Mass. 5403-5405
Billerica, Mass. Committee on the Two Hundredth Anniversary Celebration, 1855. 5403
Billerica, Mass. School Committee. 5405
Billet, H. 5406
Billiard, Francois Jacques Marie Auguste. 5407-5408
Billings, --------. illus. 92459, 92485
Billings, Charles O. 83857
Billings, Edward. 53083
Billings, Eliza (Allen) 5411
Billings, Elkanah, 1820-1876. (5409)-5410, 10637
Billings, Frederick. 5412-(5413)
Billings, John. 5414
Billings, John Shaw, 1838-1813. 69920, 83367, 85072
Billings, Josh. pseud. see Shaw, Henry Wheeler, 1818-1855.
Billings, Joseph. explorer 77124, (77152)-77153
Billings, Rev. Joseph. ed. 51666
Billings, William. reporter 1066, 3625, note before 93509, 103349A
Billings, William, 1746-1800. 5415-5420
Billouard de Kerlerec de Kervasegan, Louis. see Kerlerec de Kervasegan, Louis Billouard de, Marquis.
Billow. (63893), 77008-77009
Billowy water. 77008-77009
Billroth, Albert. 5421
Billroth, Hermann. 5421
Billy Buck's visit with his master to England. 36595, 82069, note after 90541, note after 95543, note after 95665
Billy Pitt and the farmer. 50804
Billyke beweegreedenen om aen Spanje den oorlog. 5422
Bilton, Thomas. 5423
Biluao, Luys de. 5424
Bimbo. pseud. Pleasures of yachting. 5425
Bi-metallic money. 84002-84003
Bi-metallic question. 84003
Bimetallism. 84004
Bimetallists' catechism. 84801
Binckes, Jacob. 5426, (49564)
Binckum, ------- de. (66852)
Binder, Chr. 5427
Binder, Eduard. tr. 4010
Binder, Philipp Friedrich. ed. (42662)
Bindon, David. tr. 63773
Binet, G. see Hurt-Binet, Marc-Gabriel.
Binet, Marc-Gabriel Hurt. see Hurt-Binet, Marc-Gabriel.
Bingham, A. 5429
Bingham, Caleb. 5430-(5431)
Bingham, Caleb. tr. 12240
Bingham, Daniel H. 88471
Bingham, Hiram. 5432
Bingham, J. C. 5433
Bingham, John Armor, 1815-1900. 5438-5452, 9621
Bingham, Joel F. 5434-5437

Bingham, Kinsley Scott, 1808-1861. 5453-5454, 48740 see also Michigan. Governor, 1855-1859 (Bingham)
Bingham, L. D. 5455
Bingham, William. 5458-(5459), 32637, (40321)
Bingham's bill and report. 5440
Bingham, N. Y. Inebriate Asylum. see New York (State) State Hospital, Binghamton.
Binghamton, N. Y. State Hospital. see New York (State) State Hospital, Binghamton.
Bingley, William, fl. 1689. 5460
Bingley, William, fl. 1820. 5461-5464
Binnen- en buitenlandsche Kolonisatie. 31248
Binney, Amos. 5466-5467
Binney, Amos, defendant at court martial 5465, 48976, 8th note after 96930C
Binney, Barnabas. 5468
Binney, C. J. F. 5469
Binney, Horace. 5470-(5497), 9131, 14848, (28936), 30022, (35462), 48675, 61890, 62369, 65729, 91540, 97768
Binney, Horace. reporter (5497)
Binney, James. 33254
Binney, T. 48918
Binney, Thomas. (5498)
Binney, William. 66293
Binney, William G. 5499-5505, 28087, (67449), 69946, (77373)
Binns, John. (5506)-(5507), 23759, 42850, 91768, 96897, 97592
Binns, John. defendant 8466
Binns, John. plaintiff 42850, 91768, 96897
Binns, William. 5508
Binns (John) publisher 16117, 17446, note after 92827
Binot Paulmyer de Gonneville, Jean. see Paulmier, Jean, d. ca. 1669.
Bins de Saint Victor, Jacques Maximilien Benjamin. see Saint Victor, Jacques Maximilien Benjamin Bins de.
Binzer, A. ed. 25523
Biografia. 93345
Biografia de cota ilustra Cubana. (47979)
Biografia de Don Fray Bartolome de Las Casas. 39077
Biografia de D. Jose M. Justo Gomez de la Cortina. 16975, 27760
Biografia de esta ilustra Cubana [i. e. Condesa de Merlin.] 27757
Biografia de la actriz Dona Matilde Diez. 20132
Biografia del autor, escrita por el Coronel de Artilleria D. Bartolome Mitre. (34436)
Biografia del Brigadier Argentino Don Miguel Estanislas Soler. 38451
Biografia del Doctor D. Jose A. Rodriguez Aldea. 72565
Biografia del Doctor Jose Cecilio Avila. (27817)
Biografia del Gral. de Division C. Ignacio Zaragoza. 27769
Biografia del General de Division Mariano Montilla. 50206
Biografia del General San Martin. 62941
Biografia del General Santa Anna. 76747
Biografia del Gobernador y Capitan General Manuel Guillermo Pinto. 9589
Biografia del ilustre general Americano Don Jose de San Martin. 26110
Biografia del Jeneral Don Manuel Bulnes. (9148)
Biografia del Manuel Carpio. (11019)
Biografia del Senor General Jose Arenales. 1538
Biografia del Teniente Coronel . . . J. M. Sosa. 87182
Biografia e estudio de historia politica contemporaneo. 26244

Biografia, el Jeneral San Martin. 29046
Biografias de Cubanos distinguidos. 519
Biografias de los personas mas notables del
    Rio de la Plata. 49757
Biografias del ciudadano Licenciado General
    Vicente Riva Palacio. 87178
Biografia Americana. 25851
Biographia Britannica. 20832, 67599, 91871
Biographia do Exm. Conselheiro Joaquim
    Marcellino de Brito. 47459
Biographia do maior classico da lingua
    Portugueza. 99519
Biographia do Senador Diogo Antonio Feijo.
    47459
Biographia do Tenete-Coronel e Cirurgiao Mor
    Reformado do Exercito Dr. Manoel
    Joaquim de Menezes. 47459
Biographia e apreciacao dos trabalhos do
    botanico Brasileiro Frei Jose Marianno
    da Conceicao Velloso. 75615
Biographia e apreciacao dos trabalhos do
    botanico Brasileiro Frei Leandro do
    Sacramento. 75616
Biographia evangelica. 48859
Biographia nautica. 10230
Biographia navalis. 12155
Biographias de muitos delles. (7582)
Biographical account of those divines. 8235
Biographical and critical account of the rarest
    books. 14416
Biographical and critical dictionary of painters.
    89624
Biographical and critical essay. 13553
Biographical and critical introduction, by A. G.
    Bradley. 82857
Biographical & critical introduction: by Sir
    Egerton Brydges. 67599
Biographical and critical memoir of the author,
    by Dugald Stewart. 82314
Biographical and critical miscellanies. 65259
Biographical and critical notices. 14201
Biographical and critical sketches. 94389
Biographical and explanatory notes, by J. E.
    Hall. 29814, 62042
Biographical and historical memoirs. (31793)
Biographical and other extracts from the
    manuscript writings. 55359
Biographical and statistical history of the city
    of Oshkosh. 57794
Biographical annual. 5509, 28891
Biographical catalogue, being an account of the
    lives of Friends. 83315
Biographical catalogue descriptive of the
    portraits. 86151
Biographical catalogue of Princeton Theological
    Seminary. 83738
Biographical chart of the signers of the
    Declaration of Independence. 64769
Biographical conversations on celebrated
    travellers. 5461
Biographical conversations on the most eminent
    voyagers. 5462
Biographical dictionary, containing a brief
    account of the first settlers. 22168
Biographical dictionary of eminent living
    characters. (47791)
Biographical dictionary, or, sketches of . . .
    celebrated characters. 40017
Biographical history of Clermont or Livingston
    Manor. 13500
Biographical history of Dionysius, Tyrant of
    Delaware. 95833
Biographical history of England. 82823
Biographical history of the county of Litchfield,
    Connecticut. 37733

Biographical history of the Wesley family.
    20738
Biographical index, by G. P. Putnam. 31015
Biographical introduction. By Frank Moore.
    36170
Biographical introduction by Henry Kingsley.
    19286
Biographical, literary, and political anecdotes.
    950, 101150
Biographical magazine. 41624
Biographical magazine containing portraits of
    eminent and ingenious persons 5510
Biographical memoir by John Brazer. 32673
Biographical memoir by S. Gilman. 39777
Biographical memoir of Daniel Boone. 24784
Biographical memoir of Doctor James Wykes.
    94094
Biographical memoir of Dr. William D. Brinckle.
    26609
Biographical memoir of Gen. George Washington.
    101725
Biographical memoir of Gen. Washington. 63786,
    5th note after 101872, 101982
Biographical memoir of George Washington.
    24221
Biographical memoir of H. Hurlbert Eaton.
    80562
Biographical memoir [of Henry Clay.] 13546-
    (13547)
Biographical memoir of Hugh Williamson.
    (33084)
Biographical memoir of John C. Otto. 58843
Biographical memoir of Josiah Goodhue. 104377
Biographical memoir of officers killed in
    defence of the union. 80005
Biographical memoir of Rev. John Lothropp.
    [sic] 39187
Biographical memoir of Richard Jordan. (36650)
Biographical memoir of Samuel Bard. 21043
Biographical memoir of Sir Peter Parker.
    18315, (58726)
Biographical memoir of the deceased [i. e.
    Edmund D. Griffin.] (28816)
Biographical memoir of the late Commodore
    Joshua Barney. 3541
Biographical memoir of the late Ichabod Norton.
    36518
Biographical memoir of the late John Revere.
    51117
Biographical memoir of the late Sir Peter
    Parker. 18315, (58726)
Biographical memoir of the reverend author.
    104274
Biographical memoir of the Rev. Dr. West.
    95196
Biographical memoir of the Rev. Edmund D.
    Griffin. 43670
Biographical memoir of the Rev. John Williams.
    104378
Biographical memoir of William Grover. 28991
Biographical memoir of Wright Post. 51118
Biographical memoirs, of Adam Smith. 91675
Biographical memoirs of Albert Gallatin. 39383
Biographical memoirs of General George
    Washington. 15177
Biographical memoirs of James Oglethorpe.
    (30505)
Biographical memoirs of Lord Viscount Nelson.
    12155
Biographical memoirs of the illustrious Gen. G.
    Washington. 101779
Biographical memoirs of the illustrious Gen.
    Geo. Washington. 15176, 15678, 37899
Biographical memoirs of the illustrious General
    George Washington. 16916-(16917), 101778

Biographical memoirs of the late John Gano.
(26538)
Biographical memorial of the American
officers. 80005
Biographical monument. 38046
Biographical narrative of Joseph Octave Pleiss
Bishop of Quebec. 24106
Biographical notice and notes by Alice Wilmere.
11842
Biographical notice of Charles Caldwell. 13828
Biographical notice of Com. Jesse D. Elliott.
35809
Biographical notice of Daniel Drake. 47387
Biographical notice of Dr. Charles Milford
Crandall. 33154
Biographical notice of Dr. Sylvester D.
Willard. 33154
Biographical notice of Edward Livingston.
27458
Biographical notice of Henry Bond. (15174)
Biographical notice of James Melville Gilliss.
28091
Biographical notice of Joseph Hartshorne.
(23142)
Biographical notice of Mr. Haines. (29550)
Biographical notice of Peter Wraxall. 64932
Biographical notice of Prof. William Tully.
(8230)
Biographical notice of the author [i. e. David
Jones.] 36488
Biographical notice of the late Hon. Dudley
Atkins Tyng, Jr. (42463)
Biographical notice of the late J. Greely
Stevenson. 91602
Biographical notice of the late John Ryan.
6282
Biographical notice of the late Moses Sheppard.
55503
Biographical notices. 5619
Biographical notices, . . . edited by S. W.
Butler. 18872
Biographical notices of distinguished men in
New England. 7214
Biographical notices of Edward Livingston.
1183
Biographical notices of eminent divines. 77702,
note after 85148
Biographical notices of General Lafayette.
38568
Biographical notices of many American
loyalists. 18075
Biographical notices of many loyalists. 18076
Biographical notices of members of the society
of Friends. 21591, 97433
Biographical notices of Mr. Charles Hayward.
103179
Biographical notices of some of his [i. e. John
Callender's] distinguished contemporaries.
(10076)
Biographical notices of some of the members.
7852
Biographical notices of some of the most
illustrious blind. 54499
Biographical notices of the members of the
fifty-sixth General Assembly of . . .
Ohio. 56987
Biographical notices of the most prominent
public men. 4782
Biographical outline of Gen. George Washington.
101711
Biographical outline of his [i. e. George
Washington's] life and character. 101750
Biographical preface by the Rev. James Foote.
(80215)
Biographical preface by the Rev. James M.
Platt. 83456

Biographical record. (50365)
Biographical record of the class of 1827.
83743
Biographical register of the officers and
graduates. 17865
Biographical remains of Rev. George Beecher.
4306
Biographical sketch. 30353
Biographical sketch, and a copy of the will.
7127
Biographical sketch and character of George
Washington. 101981
Biographical sketch, and services of Commo-
dore Charles Stewart. 91652
Biographical sketch by A. J. Upson. 22520
Biographical sketch . . . by G. Shepard. 13269
Biographical sketch, by Hon. Richard Frothing-
ham. (37846)
Biographical sketch. By J. H. Powell. (64752)
Biographical sketch by Jedediah Morse. 101651
Biographical sketch [by L. W. Fitch.] 60868
Biographical sketch, by Orin B. Judd. 36848
Biographical sketch, by Rev. Dr. Blanchard.
16760
Biographical sketch by Rev. George F. Foot.
25008
Biographical sketch by Rev. Richard S. Edes.
47070
Biographical sketch, by Samuel F. B. Morse.
18734
Biographical sketch. By the author of "Life
in the South." 35469, note after 92160
Biographical sketch of . . . A. F. Holmes.
29716
Biographical sketch of . . . Abraham Lincoln.
30621
Biographical sketch of Adam Kuhn. 38337
Biographical sketch of all the most prominent
generals. 95148
Biographical sketch of Amos Pilsbury. 62866
Biographical sketch of Andrew Jackson. 101159
Biographical sketch of Caesar A. Rodney.
68189
Biographical sketch of Capt. Chipman. 103743
Biographical sketch of Col. Noah E. Smith.
83680
Biographical sketch of Col. Richard M. Johnson.
36275
Biographical sketch of Col. Solomon P. Sharp.
4160
Biographical sketch of Commodore Charles
Stewart. 91653
Biographical sketch [of David Coddington.]
14119
Biographical sketch of Dr. James W. Stone.
92068
Biographical sketch of Doctor Jonathan Potts.
(52280)
Biographical Sketch of Dr. Robinson. 72134
Biographical sketch of Edward Crafts Hopson.
13293
Biographical sketch of Ezekiel Cheever. 3464
Biographical sketch of General Bouquet. 84619
Biographical sketch of Gen. George Washington.
101634
Biographical sketch of Gen. Joseph Warren.
101477-101478
Biographical sketch of Gen Miranda. 83640
Biographical sketch of General Robert Adair.
158
Biographical sketch of Harvey Prindle Peet.
59536
Biographical sketch of Henry A. Wise. 29933
Biographical sketch of Henry Tuke. 51533
Biographical sketch of Herman Melville. 83323

Biographical sketch of Hon. Hannibal Hamlin. 3724

Biographical sketch of Hon. Henry Wilson. 61369

Biographical sketch of Hon. John Boyle. 71949

Biographical sketch of Hon. John C. Breckenridge. 7672

Biographical sketch of Hon. Linn Boyd. 7116, note after 95512

Biographical sketch of Hon. Schuyler Colfax. 61369

Biographical sketch of J. Fenimore Cooper. (41580)

Biographical sketch of J. Kearny Rodgers. 19331

Biographical sketch of James G. Carter. 11117

Biographical sketch of James Smithson. 84986

Biographical sketch of [John] Barnard. 103837

Biographical sketch of John Vanderlyn. 98481

Biographical sketch of [Luke] Whitcomb. 94717

Biographical sketch of Martin Van Buren. 48096

Biographical sketch of Mary Lion. (5658)

Biographical sketch of Mr. V. A. Stewart. 51552, note before 91708, 101209

Biographical sketch of Mrs. F. W. Lander. 38831

Biographical sketch of Mrs. Sarah Peck. 59490

Biographical sketch of Rev. Preserved Smith. 83729

Biographical sketch of Rev. Simeon Doggett. 7959

Biographical sketch of Rev. Thomas Davies. (18772)

Biographical sketch of Stephen A. Douglas. (20696)

Biographical sketch of that famous and diverting humorist. 23722, 37315

Biographical sketch of the author [i. e. Albert William Duy.] 21495

Biographical sketch of the author [i. e. Benjamin B. Bowen.] (7046)

Biographical sketch of the author [i. e. David How.] 33217

Biographical sketch of the author [i. e. David Tappan.] 94367

Biographical sketch of the author [i. e. Domingo Faustino Sarmiento.] 77078

Biographical sketch of the author [i. e. Edwin R. Purple.] 66714

Biographical sketch of the author [i. e. Francois Jean, Marquis de Chastellux.] 12230

Biographical sketch of the author [i. e. Francois Pierre Guillaume Guizot.] (29266)

Biographical sketch of the author [i. e. George D. Prentice.] 65065

Biographical sketch of the author [i. e. George Lippard.] (41399)

Biographical sketch of the author [i. e. Gregory T. Bedell.] 4273

Biographical sketch of the author [i. e. John D. Codman.] 27663

Biographical sketch of the author [i. e. John Shaw.] 79924

Biographical sketch of the author [i. e. Samuel Bartlett Parris.] 58842

Biographical sketch of the author [i. e. Samuel Porter.] 64315

Biographical sketch of the author [i. e. Samuel Woodworth.] 105192

Biographical sketch of the author [i. e. Thomas Campbell.] 92150

Biographical sketch of the author [i. e. Thomas Clarkson.] 13493

Biographical sketch of the author [i. e. William Sullivan.] 93559

Biographical sketch of the author's [i. e. Samuel Stillman's] life. 91798

Biographical sketch of the celebrated Salem murderer. 17712, 75640

Biographical sketch of the character of Governor [Jonathan] Trumbull [Junior.] 22392, 97205

Biographical sketch of the character of the author [i. e. Michael Wigglesworth.] 103922

Biographical sketch of the class of 1826. 29558

Biographical sketch of the Clinton family. 13708

Biographical sketch of the Honorable George Poindexter. 63683

Biographical sketch of the Hon. John L. Helm. 31261

Biographical sketch of the Hon. Lazarus W. Powell. 64755

Biographical sketch of the Hon. Samuel Dexter. 19903

Biographical sketch of the Hon. William Rufus King. (31511)

Biographical sketch of the late A. B. Shipman. 36112

Biographical sketch of the late Daniel Ayres. 85604

Biographical sketch of the late Dr. George Parkman. 32620

Biographical sketch of the late Hon. Harvey Putman. 66814

Biographical sketch of the late Rev. Schuyler Hoes. (4749)

Biographical sketch of the late Thomas Say. 13828

Biographical sketch of the life & character of His late Excellency Governor Hancock. 30180, note after 93493-93494

Biographical sketch of the life of Andrew Jackson. 35360, 101160

Biographical sketch of the life of the late Capt. Michael Cresap. 35488

Biographical sketch of the life of the late Captain Michael Cresap. (35489)

Biographical sketch of the . . . Marquis de La Fayette. 38568

Biographical sketch of the Most Rev. John Carroll. 11075

Biographical sketch of the Most Rev. John Hughes. 33588

Biographical sketch of the Rev. Thomas Davis. 18888

Biographical sketch of the Rev. Valentine Cook. 91591

Biographical sketch of Thomas Clarkson. 94541

Biographical sketch of Thomas Jefferson. 27458

Biographical sketch of William L. Knight. 82715

Biographical sketch or memoir of Lieutenant-Colonel Patrick Ferguson. 24088

Biographical sketch, read pursuant to appointment. 3856

Biographical sketch, words of the songs, ballads, &c. 46175

Biographical sketches. 44944

Biographical sketches and anecdotes of the most distinguished officers. (26045)

Biographical sketches and interesting anecdotes. (51111)

Biographical sketches and sermons. 49024

Biographical sketches by Fennings Taylor. (56025)

Biographical sketches. By H. F. Parker. 58672

Biographical sketches by Robert Parks. 59174

Biographical sketches of adherents to the British crown. 74732
Biographical sketches of all the most distinguished characters. 10259
Biographical sketches of Confederate generals. 13405
Biographical sketches of distinguished American naval heroes. 101006
Biographical sketches of distinguished Americans, now living. 41623
Biographical sketches of distinguished Jerseymen. 2080
Biographical sketches of distinguished New York surgeons. (25450)
Biographical sketches of eccentric characters. 5511
Biographical sketches of eminent American lawyers. 41624
Biographical sketches of eminent itinerant ministers. 93628
Biographical sketches of eminent lawyers. 38070
Biographical sketches of eminent living characters. (47791)
Biographical sketches of eminent persons. 38137
Biographical sketches of father and son. 38007
Biographical sketches of General Nathaniel Massie. 43160
Biographical sketches of graduates of Harvard University. 80825
Biographical sketches of Joseph Smith. 83496-83499
Biographical sketches of loyalists of the American revolution. 74733
Biographical sketches of Mrs. David Starr. 90546
Biographical sketches of parish priests of St. Louis. 83546
Biographical sketches of patriots. 8159
Biographical sketches of pioneer settlers. 13675
Biographical sketches of several of the most eminent of the New England fathers. 71847
Biographical sketches of Sheridan and Kotzebue. 8137, 80342
Biographical sketches of some of the more prominent [American women.] 13630
Biographical sketches of the authors. 13650
Biographical sketches of the bench and bar. 57331
Biographical sketches of the Bordley family. 27314
Biographical sketches of the Campbells. 33301
Biographical sketches of the distinguished men. 68069
Biographical sketches of the early physicians. (31794)
Biographical sketches of the early settlers of the township. 94271
Biographical sketches of the fathers of New England. 13336
Biographical sketches of the fifty-sixth Ohio House of Representatives. 90085
Biographical sketches of the fifty-sixth Ohio Senate. 90086
Biographical sketches of the founder and principal alumni. 720
Biographical sketches of the lives and characters of illustrious and eminent men. 21582
Biographical sketches of the members and licentiates. 5787
Biographical sketches of the members of the forty-first General Assembly of Indiana. (34492)

Biographical sketches of the men who signed the Declaration of Independence of America, &c. 72699
Biographical sketches of the military and naval heroes. (50358)
Biographical sketches of the ministers of the First Church. 20160
Biographical sketches of the Moody family. 50307
Biographical sketches of the Most Reverend John Carroll. 7719
Biographical sketches of the senators and representatives of Pennsylvania. (59915)
Biographical sketches of the signers of the Declaration of American Independence. 42114, 42123
Biographical sketches of the state officers and members of the Legislature of the state of New York. 51477
Biographical sketches of Yale graduates. 83743
Biographical sketches; with other literary remains. (10260)
Biographical studies. 28595
Biographical treasury. 46942
Biographie de deux Indiens de la Haute Californie. 5512
Biographie der jungen Amerikanischen Dichterin. 35136
Biographie der Verfasserin und einer Vorrede. 92558
Biographie des correspondants de Humboldt. 33709
Biographie des hommes du jour. 77104
Biographie des Sagamos illustrees. 5145
Biographie du General Andrew Jackson. 6881
Biographie et oraison funebre. 38419
Biographie etrangere. (5513)
Biographie Geo. Washington's. 101780
Biographie mythique. 35494
Biographie von F. A. Mignet. (48904)
Biographies and miscellanies. 35137
Biographies of deceased physicians. 24463
Biographies of Generals Butler [and others.] (47792), 99434
Biographies of Generals Halleck [and others.] (47792), 99434
Biographies of Generals Hooker [and others.] (47792), 99434
Biographies of good wives. (12717)
Biographies of Philip Trapnall. 89453
Biographies of Sophia J. St. John and Wm. Henry St. John. 75266
Biographies of successful Philadelphia merchants. 5514
Biographies of the immortal signers of the Declaration of Independence. 4427
Biographische Skizze. 28999, 63548
Biographische Skizze, und Dienste der Commondor Carl Stewart. 91654
Biographische Skizzen der durchlauchtigsten General George Washington. 101781
Biographisches Denkmal. (38045)
Biography and character of George Washington. 101982
Biography and family records of Lorenzo Snow. 85503
Biography and history of the Indians of North America. 20866, 20868, 20873
Biography, and notes of Francis Wright d'Arusmont. 18638, 105587
Biography and poetical remains of Margaret Miller Davidson. 18735
Biography and writings of Ann Maria Hyde. 80967
Biography, by his [i. e. D. S. Dickinson's] brother. 20030

Biography by John Uri Lloyd. 83710
Biography, by Miss Sedgwick. 18734
Biography, for the use of schools. 102340
Biography, notes, and political letters of
  Frances Wright D'Arusmont. 18637
Biography of a pioneer manufacturer. 83328
Biography of an American bondsman. 8532
Biography of Andrew Jackson. 27950
Biography of B. W. Stone. 72701
Biography [of] Benjamin Rush. 35459
Biography of Capt. Phineas Stevens. 90518
Biography of Chas. Lucas. 42614
Biography of Commodore Bainbridge. 19077
Biography of Deacon John Phillips. 62497
Biography of Dr. Elisha K. Kane. 27659,
  43043
Biography of Eld. Barton Warren Stone. 92027
Biography of Elder David Purviance. 66730
Biography of Elder J. T. Johnson. 72701
Biography of Elder Lott Cary. 94472
Biography of Eli Bruce. 50872
Biography of Elisha Kent Kane. 22094
Biography [of Father Mayhew.] 43855
Biography of females. 80967
Biography of Gen. George Clinton. 13741
Biography of General Lewis Cass. (11351)
Biography of Henry Clay. 65062, 103819
Biography of Hon. Fernando Wood. 43536
Biography of Isaac Hill. 31830
Biography of Isaac W. Ambler. 25786
Biography of J. S. Buckminster. 95191
Biography of James Lawrence. 39356
Biography of John Randolph. 77320
Biography of Louis Moreau Gottschalk. 18230
Biography of Martin Van Buren. 98425
Biography of Martin Van Buren, Vice President
  of the United States. 22533
Biography of Millard Fillmore. 24331
Biography of Millard Fillmore of Buffalo.
  24330
Biography of Mr. Edwin Forest. (25106)
Biography of Mr. Girard. 1940
[Biography of Mrs. Emma Willard.] 33900
Biography of Mrs. Lydia B. Bacon. 2676
Biography of Mrs. Rebecca Gair Webster.
  92131
Biography of Mrs. Sematha Mettler. 28522
Biography of Nahmeonitah. 51727
Biography of Nicholas Stoner & Nathaniel Foster.
  81185
Biography of pious persons. 80967
Biography of Prince Metternich. 85170
Biography of Rev. Elhanan Winchester. 92042
Biography of Rev. Hosea Ballou. 2971
Biography of Rev. W. H. Griswold. 87269
Biography of revolutionary heroes. 104171
Biography [of Richard Cobden.] (43269)
Biography of Samuel Lewis. (40862)
Biography of self-taught men. 21890
Biography of Sir Walter Raleigh. 67599
Biography of Stephen Girard. 81371
Biography of the author [i. e. Charles W.
  Russell.] 74317
Biography of the author [i. e. Henry Lee.]
  39743
Biography of the borthers Davenport. 55212
Biography of the first settlement of the family
  of the name of Goodhue. (27858)
Biography of the Hon. Caleb Strong. 7215
Biography of the Hon. Solomon W. Downs.
  20891
Biography of the principal American military
  and naval heroes. 104693
Biography of the Rev. Robert Finley. 8490,
  24384

Biography of the signers of the Declaration of
  Independence. (76398)-76403, 84866,
  101140
Biography of the signers of the Declaration of
  Independence, and of Washington and
  Patrick Henry. 36865
Biography of Thomas Jefferson. 9431, 12380,
  2d note after 92859, 105044, 2d note
  after 106011
Biography of William Austin. note after 92840
Biography [of William Cobbett.] 82445
Biography of Zadock Pratt. 64982
Biography, or memoirs of eminent Pennsyl-
  vanians. 59916
Biography, with sketches of important events
  in early New England. 51237
Biondelli, Bernard. (5515)-5516, 74948
Biondo, Michaele Angelo. 5517-(5518)
Bionne, Henri. 5519
Biorck, T. E. 89174
Bioren, John. 5520, 9199, 15531, 39425, 59917,
  60196, 64721
Bioren's Pennsylvania pocket remembrancer.
  59917
Bioren's town and country almanack. 5520
Biot, Edouard Constant. 5521
Biot, Jean Baptiste. (5521)
Birago, Giovanni Battista. 106333
Birbeck, --------. (17175)
Birch, Arthur N. (14694)
Birch, E. P. 5523
Birch, Harvey. see Crosby, Enoch.
Birch, James J. 5524-5527
Birch, Thomas, 1705-1766. 67598-67599
Birch, Thomas E. 5528
Birch, Thomas Ledie. 5529
Birch, W. 5531
Birch (W.) and Sons. firm engrs. 5530, 101820
Birckhead (James) and Co. firm 5532, (71467)
Bird, Benjamin. petitioner 73625
Bird, Francis W. 5533-(5541), (40235)
Bird, H. M. (5542), 1st note after 99578
Bird, I. ed. 58587
Bird, Mrs. I. ed. 58587
Bird, Isaac. 5543, 26863
Bird, Isabella Lucy. see Bishop, Isabella
  Lucy (Bird) 1831-1904.
Bird, James. (5546)
Bird, Jonathan. 5547
Bird, Joseph. 5548
Bird, Robert Montgomery. 5549-(5558), 61177,
  91912
Bird, Samuel. 5559
Bird, William A. 5560
Birds. 53784
Birds, by George Robert Gray and R. Bowdler
  Sharpe. 28401, 71032
Birds, by J. Cassin. 27419
Birds, by J. Gould. 31945
Birds, by John Gould. 18649
Birds, by Spencer F. Baird. 69946
Birds. By William Swainson. 71027
Birds coll. on an explor. exped. from the
  Missouri to Utah Lake. 2809
Bird's eye sketch of the military concerns.
  97909
Bird's eye view of city life. 73368
Bird's-eye views of slavery in Missouri. (39922)
Birds from Santa Fe. (78134)
Birds of America. 2366
Birds of America. From drawings made in the
  United States and their territories. 2363-
  2365
Birds of America from original drawings. 2362
Birds of Canada. 73329

Birds of Florida. 47162
Birds of Jamaica. 28060
Birds of Long Island. (27498)
Birds of New England. 75968
Birds of New Zealand. 28401, 71032
Birds of North America. 82196
Birds of North America. By D. G. Elliot. 22227
Birds of North America; the descriptions of species. 2809
Birds of the United States and Mexican boundary. 2809
Birds, I. Birds of New Zealand. 28401, 71032
Birdsall, Ausburn. 5561
Birdsall, John. 95009 see also Texas (Republic) Attorney General.
Birdseye, George W. 5562
Birkbeck, Morris. (5563)-5570, 23956, 87307
Birkenhead & Cheshire advertiser. 5508
Birkett, Mary. 5572
Birkett, William. 64094
Birkinbine, Henry P. M. 62369-62370 see also Philadelphia. City Engineer.
Birkinshaw, Maria Louisa. (5573)
Birks, T. R. 5574, 34009
Birmingham, England. Great Anti-slavery Meeting, 1835. see Great Anti-slavery Meeting, Birmingham, England, 1835.
Birmingham gazette. see Aris's Birmingham gazette.
Birmingham working man. pseud. Tour through the land of the west. see Smith, N.
Birney, James Gillespie, 1792-1857. 5575-5581, (22361), (81830)
Birney, William, 1819-1907. 37129
Birney's vindication of abolitionists. 5580
Birnstill, Joseph. ed. 66957
Biron, ------. see Byron, John, 1723-1786.
Biron, Armand Louis de Gontaut, Duc de Lauzun, afterwards Duc de, 1747-1793. 39271-(39272)
Biron, Claude. 5582
Birt, John. 5583
Birth and death of nations. 43370
Birth and early growth of toleration. (18821)
Birth-day, a dramatic entertainment. 60793
Birth-day memorial of seventy years. 61186
Birth-day of Washington. (66815)
Birth day sermon. 46684
Birth, fortunes, and general experiences. 11161
Birth of a day. (72111)
Birth of our Saviour. 23878
Birth of Washington. 105016
Birth, parentage and education of Praise-God Barebone. 5584
Birth-places of Americanism. 72058
Birthday of Washington. 14345
Birthplace and parentage of William Paterson. 58143
Birthright Church: a discourse. 36842
Births from 1851-1870. (66238)
Bis in die Wildniss. 93104
Bisbe, John. (5585)-5586
Bisbee, John H. (5587), 70837-70838
Bisbee, Noah. 5588
Bisbie, D. T. 5589
Biscaie, -------- Acarette de. see Acarete du Biscay, --------.
Biscay, ------- Acarete de. see Acarete du Biscay, -------.
Bischof Benjamin Onderdonk von New York und sein Verurtheilung. 57309
Bise, Mary Ann. 40226

Bishop. pseud. Looking-glass for high churchmen. (66176)
Bishop, -----. (76380)
Bishop, Abraham, 1763-1844. 5590-5598, 15875, 28903, 95742, 102396, 105939
Bishop, Abraham, 1763-1844. supposed author 44890, 1st note after 97010, 97440
Bishop, Albert Webb. 5599-5600
Bishop, Amasa W. ed. 45517
Bishop, Anna. 5601
Bishop, Francis A. 5602, 100930
Bishop, G. 5603
Bishop, George, d. 1668. 5628-5631, (70000), (73483), 91318-91319
Bishop, Harriet E., 1817-1883. 5604
Bishop, Henry Fitch. 5605
Bishop, Isabella Lucy (Bird) 1831-1904. 2213, (5544)-5545, 44724
Bishop, Joel Prentiss, 1814-1901. 5607-(5609)
Bishop, John, the reformed drunkard. 5610
Bishop, John Leander, 1820-1868. 5606
Bishop, John Soast, 1834-1915. 5611, 61015
Bishop, Judson Wade, 1831-1917. 5612
Bishop, Levi, 1815-1881. (19792)
Bishop, Matthew, fl. 1701-1744. (5613)
Bishop, Nathaniel Holmes, 1837-1902. 5614
Bishop, P. E. 5616
Bishop, Putnam P. 5615
Bishop, Richard M. defendant 90145
Bishop, Robert. 5617
Bishop, Robert Hamilton, 1777-1855. 5618-5619, 70826, 92031
Bishop, Rufus. 102602, 106199
Bishop, Samuel C. petitioner 5620
Bishop, Samuel G. 5621-5622
Bishop, W. W. USA 5625
Bishop, William. 5623
Bishop, William G. reporter 8300, 53916, 93624
Bishop, William S. 5624
Bishop and Clergy of London. see London (Diocese) Bishop and Clergy.
Bishop and Clergy of the Diocese of Pennsylvania. see Protestant Episcopal Church in the U. S. A. Pennsylvania (Diocese) Bishop and Clergy.
Bishop and the court at the bar of public opinion. 38651, 3d note after 98805
Bishop Berkeley's donation. 105841
Bishop Chase's address. 12190
Bishop Doane's sermon. 58846
Bishop Doane's words at the burial of Mrs. Bradford. 23091
Bishop Hopkin's letter on slavery ripped up. (32928)
Bishop Hopkins reviewed. 5189
Bishop in the church of God. 84746
Bishop Jarvis's charge to the clergy of his diocese. 35801
Bishop McIlvaine's address to the convention. 43324
Bishop McIlvaine's respectful address. 43321
Bishop Meade's second pamphlet. 47239
Bishop of ------. pseud. Rise, progress, and present state, of the dispute. see Jackson, William, Bishop of Oxford, 1751-1815.
Bishop of Aberdeen. see Skinner, John, Bishop of Aberdeen, 1744-1816.
Bishop of Bangor. see Bayly, Lewis, Bp. of Bangor, d. 1631. Cleaver, William, successively Bp. of Chester, Bangor, and St. Asaph, 1742-1815. Egerton, John, successively Bp. of Bangor, Lichfield and coventry, and Durham, 1721-1787.

Ewer, John, successively Bp. of Llandaff, and Bangor, d. 1774. Herring, Thomas, Abp. of Canterbury, 1693-1757. Hutton, Mathew, Abp. of Canterbury, 1693-1758. Moore, John, Abp. of Canterbury, 1730-1805. Reynolds, Richard, successively Bp. of Bangor, and Lincoln, 1674-1744. Warren, John, successively Bp. of St. Davids, and Bangor, 1730-1800.

Bishop of Barbados. see Coleridge, William Hart, Bp. of Barbados, 1789-1849. Parry, Thomas, Bp. of Barbados, 1795-1870.

Bishop of Bath and Wells. see Beadon, Richard, successively Bp. of Gloucester, and Bath and Wells, 1737-1824. Moss, Charles, successively Bp. of St. Davids, and Bath and Wells, 1711-1802. Wynne, John, successively Bp. of St. Asaph, and Bath and Wells, 1667-1743.

Bishop of Brechin. see Gleig, George, Bishop of Brechin, 1753-1840.

Bishop of Bristol. see Bagot, Lewis, successively Bp. of Bristol, Norwich, and St. Asaph, 1740-1802. Boulter, Hugh, Abp. of Armagh, 1672-1742. Butler, Joseph, successively Bishop of Bristol and Durham, 1692-1752. Felton, Nicholas, successively Bp. of Bristol, and Ely, 1556-1626. Gooch, Sir Thomas, Bart., successively Bishop of Bristol, Norwich, and Ely, d. 1754. Hume, John, successively Bp. of Bristol, Oxford, and Salisbury. Newton, Thomas, Bp. of Bristol, 1704-1782. Searchfield, Rowland, Bp. of Bristol, 1565?-1622. Secker, Thomas, Abp. of Canterbury, 1693-1768. Yonge, Philip, successively Bp. of Bristol, and Norwich, d. 1783.

Bishop of Calcutta. see Wilson, Daniel, Bishop of Calcutta, 1778-1858.

Bishop of Carlisle. see Bradford, Samuel, successively Bp. of Carlisle, and Rochester, 1652-1731. Douglas, John, successively Bp. of Carlisle, and Salisbury, 1721-1807. Harcourt, Edward, Abp. of York, 1757-1847. Law, Edmund, Bp. of Carlisle, 1703-1787. Nicolson, William, Archbishop of Cashel, 1655-1727. Osbaldistun, Richard, successively Bp. of Carlisle, and London, 1690-1764.

Bishop of Chester. see Blomfield, Charles James, successively Bp. of Chester, and London, 1786-1857. Cleaver, William, successively Bp. of Chester, Bangor, and St. Asaph, 1742-1815. Dawes, Sir William, Bart., Abp. of York, 1671-1724. Keene, Edmund, successively Bp. of Chester, and Ely, 1714-1781. Porteus, Beilby, successively Bp. of Chester, and London, 1731-1808.

Bishop of Chichester. see Buckner, John, Bishop of Chichester. Hare, Francis, successively Bp. of St. Asaph and Chichester, 1671-1740. Harsnet, Samuel, Abp. of York, 1561-1631. Mawson, Matthias, successively Bishop of Chichester, and Ely, 1683-1770. Williams, John, Bishop of Chichester, 1636-1709.

Bishop of Clogher. see Ash, St. George, successively Bp. of Cloyne, Clogher, and Derry. Garnett, John, Bishop of Clogher.

Bishop of Cloyne. see Ash, St. George, successively Bp. of Cloyne, Clogher, and Derry. Berkeley, George, Bp. of Cloyne, 1685-1753.

Bishop of Cloyne's exhortation to the Roman Catholick clergy of Ireland. 4880

Bishop of Cork. see Wetenhall, Edward, successively Bp. of Cork, and Kilmore and Ardagh, 1636-1713.

Bishop of Coventry. see Bishop of Lichfield and Coventry.

Bishop of Derry. see Ash, St. George, successively Bp. of Cloyne, Clogher, and Derry. Nicolson, William, Archbishop of Cashel, 1655-1727.

Bishop of Duresme. see Bishop of Durham.

Bishop of Durham. see Barrington, Shute, successively Bp. of Salisbury, and Durham, 1734-1826. Butler, Joseph, successively Bishop of Bristol and Durham, 1692-1752. Egerton, John, successively Bp. of Bangor, Litchfield and Coventry, and Durham, 1721-1787. Monteigne, George, Abp. of York, d. 1628. Thurlow, Thomas, successively Bp. of Lincoln, and Durham, 1721-1787. Trevor, Richard, successively Bp. of St. Davids, and Durham, 1707-1771. Van Mildert, William, successively Bp. of Llandaff, and Durham, 1765-1836.

Bishop of Ely. see Dampier, Thomas, successively Bp. of Rochester, and Ely, 1748-1812. Felton, Nicholas, successively Bp. of Bristol, and Ely, 1556-1626. Fleetwood, William, successively Bp. of St. Asaph, and Ely, 1656-1723. Gooch, Sir Thomas, Bart., successively Bishop of Bristol, Norwich, and Ely, d. 1754. Green, Thomas, successively Bp. of Norwich, and Ely, 1658-1738. Keene, Edmund, successively Bp. of Chester, and Ely, 1714-1781. Mawson, Matthias, successively Bishop of Chichester, and Ely, 1683-1770. Moore, John, successively Bishop of Norwich, and Ely, 1646-1714. Turner, Francis, successively Bp. of Rochester, and Ely, 1638?-1700. Yorke, James, successively Bp. of Gloucester, and Ely, d. 1808.

Bishop of Exeter. see Clagett, Nicholas, successively Bp. of St. Davids, and Exeter, d. 1746. Keppel, Frederick, Bp. of Exeter, 1729-1777. Ross, John, Bp. of Exeter, 1719-1792.

Bishop of Fredericton. see Medley, John, Bp. of Fredericton, 1804-1892.

Bishop of Gloucester. see Beadon, Richard, successively Bp. of Gloucester, and Bath and Wells, 1737-1824. Benson, Martin, Bp. of Gloucester, 1689-1752. Johnson, James, successively Bp. of Gloucester, and Worcester, 1705-1774. Warburton, William, Bp. of Gloucester, 1698-1779. Wilcocks, Joseph, successively Bp. of Gloucester, and Rochester, 1673-1756. Yorke, James, successively Bp. of Gloucester, and Ely, d. 1808.

Bishop of Guiana. see Percy, William, Bp. of Guiana.

Bishop of Hereford. see Bisse, Philip, successively Bp. of St. Davids, and Hereford, 1667-1721. Butler, John, successively Bishop of Oxford and Hereford, 1717-1802. Egerton, Henry, Bp. of Hereford, d. 1746.

Bishop of Honolulu. see Stanley, Thomas Nettleship, Bp. of Honolulu, 1823-1898.

Bishop of Huron. see Cronyn, Benjamin, Bp. of Huron, 1802-1871. Hellmuth, Isaac, Bp. of Huron.

Bishop of Jamaica. see Spencer, Aubrey George, successively Bp. of Newfoundland, and Jamaica, 1795-1872.
Bishop of Kilmore and Ardagh. see Wetenhall Edward, successively Bp. of Cork, and Kilmore and Ardagh, 1636-1713.
Bishop of Lichfield and Coventry. see Cornwallis, Frederick, Abp. of Canterbury, 1713-1783. Cornwallis, James Cornwallis, 4th Earl, Bp. of Lichfield and Coventry, 1742-1824. Egerton, John, successively Bp. of Bangor, Lichfield and Coventry, and Durham, 1721-1787. Hough, John, successively Bp. of Oxford, Lichfield and Coventry, and Worcester, 1651-1743. Hurd, Richard, successively Bp. of Lichfield and Coventry, and Worcester, 1720-1808. Smallbroke, Richard, successively Bp. of St. Davids, and Lichfield and Coventry, 1672-1749.
Bishop of Lincoln. see Gibson, Edmund, successively Bp. of Lincoln, and London, 1669-1748. Green, John, Bp. of Lincoln, 1706?-1779. Monteigne, George, Abp. of York, d. 1628. Reynolds, Richard, successively Bp. of Bangor, and Lincoln, 1674-1744. Tenison, Thomas, Archbishop of Canterbury, 1636-1715. Thomas, John, successively Bp. of Lincoln, and Salisbury, 1691-1766. Thurlow, Thomas, successively Bp. of Lincoln, and Durham 1737-1791. Tomline, Sir George Pretyman, Bart., successively Bp. of Lincoln, and Winchester, 1750-1827.
Bishop of Llandaff. see Copleston, Edward, Bp. of Llandaff, 1776-1849. Cresset, Edward, Bp. of Llandaff, d. 1755. Ewer, John, successively Bp. of Llandaff, and Bangor, d. 1774. Gilbert, John, Abp. of York, 1693-1761. Newcome, Richard, successively Bp. of Llandaff, and St. Asaph, d. 1769. Shipley, Jonathan, successively Bp. of Llandaff, and St. Asaph, 1714-1788. Sumner, Charles Richard, successively Bp. of Llandaff, and Winchester, 1790-1874. Van Mildert, William, successively Bp. of Llandaff, and Durham, 1765-1836. Watson, Richard, Bp. of Llandaff, 1737-1816.
Bishop of London. see Blomfield, Charles James, successively Bp. of Chester, and London, 1786-1857. Gibson, Edmund, successively Bp. of Lincoln, and London, 1669-1748. Hayter, Thomas, successively Bp. of Norwich, and London, 1702-1762. King, John, Bp. of London, 1559-1621. Lowth, Robert, successively Bp. of St. Davids, Oxford, and London, 1710-1787. Monteigne, George, Abp. of York, d. 1628. Osbaldistun, Richard, successively Bp. of Carlisle, and London, 1690-1764. Porteus, Beilby, successively Bp. of Chester, and London, 1731-1808. Sherlock, Thomas, successively Bp. of Salisbury, and London, 1678-1761. Terrick, John, successively Bp. of Peterborough, and London, 1710-1777.
Bishop of London, Ontario. see Pinsoneault, --------, Bp. of London, Ontario.
Bishop of London's pastoral letter to the people of his diocese. 27310
Bishop of Meath. see O'Beirne, Thomas Lewis, Bp. of Meath, 1748-1823.
Bishop of Montreal see Fulford, Francis, Bp. of Montreal, 1803-1868. Mountain, George Jehosaphat, successively Bishop of Montreal, and Quebec, 1789-1863.

Bishop of Newfoundland. see Field, Edward, Bp. of Newfoundland, 1801-1876. Spencer, Aubrey George, successively Bp. of Newfoundland, and Jamaica. 1795-1872.
Bishop of Norwich. see Bagot, Lewis, successively Bp. of Bristol, Norwich, and St. Asaph, 1740-1802. Bathurst, Henry, Bp. of Norwich, 1744-1837. Gooch, Sir Thomas Bart., successively Bishop of Bristol, Norwich, and Ely, d. 1754. Green, Thomas, successively Bp. of Norwich, and Ely, 1658-1738. Harsnet, Samuel, Abp. of York, 1561-1631. Hayter, Thomas, successively Bp. of Norwich, and London, 1702-1762. Leng, John, Bp. of Norwich, 1665-1727. Lisle, Samuel, successively Bp. of Norwich, and St. Asaph, 1683-1749. Manners-Sutton, Charles, Abp. of Canterbury, 1755-1828. Moore, John, successively Bishop of Norwich, and Ely, 1646-1714. Stanley, Edward, Bp. of Norwich, 1779-1849. Trumnell, Charles, successively Bp. of Norwich and Winchester, 1663-1723. Yonge, Philip, successively Bp. of Bristol and Norwich, d. 1783.
Bishop of Nova Scotia. see Inglis, Charles, Bp. of Nova Scotia, 1734-1816. Inglis, John, Bp. of Nova Scotia, 1777-1850.
Bishop of Oxford. see Butler, John, successively Bishop of Oxford, and Hereford, 1717-1802. Hough, John, successively Bp. of Oxford, Lichfield and Coventry, and Worcester, 1651-1743. Hume, John, successively Bp. of Bristol, Oxford, and Salisbury. Jackson, William, Bp. of Oxford, 1751-1815. Lowth, Robert, successively Bp. of St. Davids, Oxford, and London, 1710-1787. Secker, Thomas, Abp. of Canterbury, 1693-1768. Smallwell, Edward, successively Bp. of St. Davids, and Oxford, d. 1799. Wilberforce, Samuel, successively Bp. of Oxford, and Winchester, 1805-1873.
Bishop of Peterborough. see Hinchliffe, John Bp. of Peterborough, 1731-1794. Kennett, White, Bp. of Peterborough, 1660-1728. Terrick, John, successively Bp. of Peterborough, and London, 1710-1777. Thomas, John, successively Bp. of Peterborough, Salisbury, and Winchester, 1696-1781.
Bishop of Quebec. see Mountain, George Jehosaphat, successively Bishop of Montreal, and Quebec, 1789-1863. Mountain, Jacob, Bp. of Quebec, 1775-1837. Stewart, Charles James, Bp. of Quebec, 1775-1837.
Bishop of Quebec's Upper Canada Mission Fund. see Church of England in Canada. Quebec (Diocese) Bishop of Quebec's Upper Canada Mission Fund.
Bishop of Rochester. see Bradford, Samuel, successively Bp. of Carlisle, and Rochester, 1652-1731. Dampier, Thomas, successively Bp. of Rochester, and Ely, 1748-1812. Horsley, Samuel, successively Bp. of St. Davids, Rochester, and St. Asaph, 1733-1806. Thomas, John, Bp. of Rochester, 1712-1793. Turner, Francis, successively Bp. of Rochester, and Ely, 1638?-1700. Wilcocks, Joseph, successively Bp. of Gloucester, and Rochester, 1673-1756.
Bishop of Rupert's land. see Anderson, David, Bp. of Rupert's Land.
Bishop of St. Asaph. see Bagot, Lewis, successively Bp. of Bristol, Norwich, and St. Asaph, 1740-1802. Beveridge, William,

Bp. of St. Asaph, 1637-1708. Cleaver, William, successively Bp. of Chester, Bangor, and St. Asaph, 1742-1815. Drummond, Robert Hay, Abp. or York, 1711-1776. Fleetwood, William, successively Bp. of St. Asaph, and Ely, 1656-1723. Hare, Francis, successively, Bp. of St. Asaph, and Chichester, 1671-1740. Horsley, Samuel, successively Bp. of St. Davids, Rochester, and St. Asaph, 1733-1806. Lisle, Samuel, successively Bp. of Norwich, and St. Asaph, 1683-1749. Maddox, Isaac, successively Bp. of St. Asaph, and Worcester, 1697-1759. Newcome, Richard, successively Bp. of Llandaff, and St. Asaph, d. 1769. Shipley, Jonathan, successively Bp. of Llandaff, and St. Asaph, 1714-1788. Wynne, John, successively Bp. of St. Asaph, and Bath and Wells, 1667-1743.
Bishop of St. Davids. see Bisse, Philip, successively Bp. of St. Davids, and Hereford, 1667-1721. Burgess, Thomas, successively Bp. of St. Davids, and Salisbury, 1756-1837. Clagett, Nicholas, successively Bp. of St. Davids, and Exeter, d. 1746. Ellys, Anthony, Bp. of St. Davids, 1690-1761. Horsley, Samuel, successively Bp. of St. Davids, Rochester, and St. Asaph, 1733-1806. Jenkinson, John Banks, Bp. of St. Davids, 1781-1840. Lowth, Robert, successively Bp. of St. Davids, Oxford, and London, 1710-1787. Moss, Charles, successively Bp of St. Davids, and Bath and Wells, 1711-1802. Smallwell, Edward, successively Bp. of St. Davids, and Oxford, d. 1799. Trevor, Richard, successively Bp. of St. Davids, and Durham, 1707-1771. Warren, John, successively Bp. of St. Davids, and Bangor, 1730-1800.
Bishop of Salisbury. see Barrington, Shute, successively Bp. of Salisbury, and Durham, 1734-1826. Burgess, Thomas, successively Bp. of St. Davids, and Salisbury, 1756-1837. Burnet, Gilbert, Bp. of Salisbury, 1643-1715. Douglas, John, successively Bp. of Carlisle, and Salisbury, 1721-1807. Drummond, Robert Hay, Abp. of York, 1711-1776. Gilbert, John, Abp. of York, 1693-1761. Hume, John, successively Bp. of Bristol, Oxford, and Salisbury. Sherlock, Thomas, successively Bp. of Salisbury, and London, 1678-1761. Thomas, John, successively Bp. of Lincoln, and Salisbury, 1691-1766. Thomas, John, successively Bp. of Peterborough, Salisbury, and Winchester, 1696-1781. Ward, Seth, Bishop of Salisbury. 1617-1689.
Bishop of Sarum. see Bishop of Salisbury.
Bishop of Sierra Leone. see Bowen, John, Bp. of Sierra Leone, 1815-1859.
Bishop of Sodor and Man. see Wilson, Thomas, Bp. of Sodor and Man, 1663-1755.
Bishop of Strasbourg's observations. 92645
Bishop of the Leeward Islands. see Bishop of Barbados.
Bishop of Toronto. see Strachan, John, Bp. of Toronto, 1778-1867.
Bishop of Vermont's protest, and draft of a pastoral letter. 32929
Bishop of Wells. see Bishop of Bath and Wells.

Bishop of Winchester. see Sumner, Charles Richard, successively Bp. of Llandaff, and Winchester, 1790-1874. Thomas, John, successively Bp. of Peterborough, Salisbury, and Winchester, 1696-1781. Tomline, Sir George Pretyman, Bart., successively Bp. of Lincoln, and Winchester, 1750-1827. Trimnell, Charles, successively Bp. of Norwich, and Winchester, 1663-1723. Wilberforce, Samuel, successively Bp. of Oxford, and Winchester, 1805-1873.
Bishop of Worcester. see Hough, John, successively Bp. of Oxford, Lichfield and Coventry, and Worcester, 1651-1743. Hurd, Richard, successively Bp. of Lichfield and Coventry, and Worcester, 1720-1808. Johnson, James, successively Bp. of Gloucester, and Worcester, 1705-1774. Maddox, Isaac, successively Bp. of St. Asaph, and Worcester, 1697-1759.
Bishop Onderdonk's trial. 89137
Bishop Payne's first annual address. (59285)
Bishop Seabury and Bishop Provoost. 61050
Bishop Seabury and the "Episcopal recorder." 61060
Bishop Seabury Mission, Faribault, Minn. 49474, 78591, 90660
Bishop Seabury's communion office. 78561
Bishop Seabury's first charge. (15664), 39529, 78555
Bishop Seabury's second charge. 78560
Bishop Strachan's pastoral letter. 92634
Bishop White Prayer Book Society, Philadelphia. 91581
Bishop Whitehouse and the Diocese of Illinois. 37614
Bishope, George. see Bishop, George, d. 1668.
Bishop's address and charge. 37612
Bishop's address to the members of the senior class, at St. Mary's Hall. 75435
Bishop's address to the members of the senior class, at the closing exercises. 20391
Bishop's bonus, Seabury College, divine right of Presbyterianism. 96123, 1st note after 105926
Bishop's College, Lennoxville, Quebec. 5626
Bishop's council. 5627
Bishop's fund and phoenix bonus. 30050, 2d note after 105926
Biske, George. 101803
Bispham, Carlos. defendant 47811 see also Alsop y Compania. Socio Director. defendant
Bisschop-Grevelink, A. H. 5632
Bisse, Philip, successively Bp. of St. Davids, and Hereford, 1667-1721. 5633
Bisselin, Olivier. 100828-100834
Bissell, A. H. (49311)
Bissell, Champion. 5634
Bissell, J. 5635, 91754
Bissell, Johann. 99443-99444
Bissell, Samuel. (5636)
Bissell, William Henry, 1811-1860. 5637, 33150, 34269, see also illinois. Governor, 1857-1860 (Bissell)
Bisset, Charles. 5638
Bisset, George. 5639-5642
Bisset, James. 5643
Bisset, John. 5644
Bisset, Richard. (5645)
Bisset, Robert. 5646-5649
Bissette, Cyrille Charles Auguste. 5650-5656, 70362

Bissing, Friedrich. 5657
Bissonnais, ------ le. see Le Bissonnais, ------.
Biter bit. 49766
'Biter bit.' An allegory. 15362, 89058
Biters bit. 88199
Bitt and a knock for Vnder-Sheriffs. (39510)
Bitter-sweet. A poem. 32512
Bitterness and bigotry exposed. 96318
Bittinger, J. B. (5658)-5660
Biven, Rarey. 5661
Bivouac and the battle-field. 56214
Bivouac aux prairies d'Amerique. 6882
Bivouac des trappeurs. 70336
Bivouacs de Vera-Cruz a Mexico. 5662, 26417
Bizari, Petro. 5663
Bizco. Une passion au Mexique. 5138
Bjorck, Tobias Er. 5664, 28916, 89174
Bk ov Djenesis. 67752
Blaaw, Johan. see Blaue, Johan, 1596-1673.
Blach, F. V. ed. 69767
Blach, William. 27584, 103399
Blachford, M. 5665-5666, 102776
Black, pseud. Sermon, on the present situation of the affairs. 79275
Black, ------. 72676
Black, David. tr. 27176
Black, Helen. supposed author 90293
Black, James. 5667
Black, Jeremiah Sullivan, 1810-1883. 4107, 5668-5671, 20693, (20696), 36266, (36629), note after 69421, 88323 see also U. S. Department of Justice.
Black, John, officer of the ship Lady Shore. 5672
Black, John, 1752-1802. 254, 5674
Black, John, 1783-1855. tr. 33715
Black, John, fl. 1827. 5673
Black, William. 69520
Black (Adam and Charles) firm publisher 3717
Black and white. A journal of a three months' tour. 39161
Black and white. No party—no creed. (47795)
Black and white; or, the Jamaica question. 16692
Black and white rivals. 85170
Black bird. 105966
Black bondsman. 81906
Black book. 73818-73819, 73822-(73823)
Black Brigade, Cincinnati. see Ohio. Militia. Cincinnati Black Brigade.
Black brigade of Cincinnati. 13353
Black code of the District of Columbia. 85445
Black diamonds gathered in the darkey homes of the south. 63853, (63877)
Black diamonds; or humor, satire, and sentiment. 30237
Black eagle; a romance of days not far distant. 35697
Black eagle; a tale of times not long ago. 35697
Black gauntlet. 77883
Black Hawk, 1767-1838. Indian Chief 84861
Black Hawk, and scenes in the west. 82461, (82462)
Black Hawk Gold Mining Company. (5678)
Black Hawk journal. 82752
Black Heath Coal Company. 59918
Black-Hollow. 35317
Black Jeremiah. (81907)
Black laws of Illinois. 36526
Black list. 5679
Black man. 9344
Black man and black bird. 43490
Black man and the war. (79946)

Black man of the south, and the rebels. 90867
Black man's lament. 57397
Black of Guardaloupe [sic]. pseud. Speech. 40304
Black phantom. 80749
Black plume rifles. 33321
Black race in North America. 81908
Black record! 18021
Black Republican. 91358
Black Republican imposture exposed. (568)
Black riders of Congaree. 81225
Black River and Utica Rail Road Company. Chief Engineer. 5681
Black River Baptist Association. see Baptists. New York. Black River Baptist Association.
Black River Band of Chippewa Indians. see Chippewa Indians (Black River Band)
Black River Conference memorial. 28033
Black River Literary and Religious Institute, Watertown, N. Y. see Jefferson County Institute, Watertown, N. Y.
Black River Marble and Soapstone Manufacturing Company. 5683
Black sluggard. pseud. Proposed alteration of "the judicial tenure." 87927
Black trail of anthracite. 84085, 84087
Black vampyre. (18537)
Blackbeard. 65692
Blackbeard. A comedy, in four acts. 77321
Blackbeard. A page from the colonial history of Philadelphia. 5685
Blackbird, A. J. (5636)
Blackburn, --------, chief justice. 23561, 24368, 24371
Blackburn, --------, of Pennsylvania. (5686)
Blackburn, Alexander W. (61999)
Blackburn, George. supposed author 89787
Blackburn, W. M. ed. 38007
Blackburn, William W. 5687-5688
Blackburne, Francis. 5689-5690, 11868, 17550
Blackburne's works. 5689
Blackford, Dominique de. see Blackford, Thomas.
Blackford, Isaac. 84403
Blackford, Thomas. 5691, 65025, 96191
Blackie, George S. ed. 88491
Blackie, John Stuart, 1809-1895. 74626
Blackie, W. G. 5692
Blackledge, William. 90347
Blackley, Frederick R. 5693
Blacklock, Thomas. supposed author 69475
Blackman, Louisa. 5694
Blackman, his antecedents, his genius, and his achievements. 8589
Blackmore, R. D. 5695
Blackness of sins against light. (18469)
Black's atlas of North America. 3717
Blackstone, Sir William, 1723-1780. (5696)-5697, 18919, 25416, 39767, 40444, (65513), 68564, 97381
Blackstone, R. I. Library Association. see Blackstone Library Association, Blackstone, R. I.
Blackstone, R. I. School Committee. 5699
Blackstone Canal Committee, Worcester County, Mass. see Worcester County, Mass. Committee on the Blackstone Canal.
Blackstone Canal Corporation. 5700
Blackstone Family. 5701, (77001)
Blackstone Library Association, Blackstone, R. I. 5699
Blackstone monument. 5702
Blackstone Monument Association, Pawtucket, R. I. 5702, 55016
Blackstone's commentaries. (5696), 97381

Blackwater chronicle. 37405, 93092
Blackwell, -------. surveyor 54582
Blackwell, Isaac. 5705, 78214
Blackwell, John, fl. 1695. 52622, 86618
Blackwell, Robert. 5703
Blackwell, Robert S., 1823-1863. (5704), 34290
Blackwood, A. R. Ch. 13867
Blackwood, Isaac. see Blackwell, Isaac.
Blackwood, Thomas, of Scotland. 5706
Blackwood, Thomas, fl. 1833. 5707
Blackwood's Edinburgh magazine. 5708, 10645, 74502, 78339, 96128
Blackwood's magazine. see Blackwood's Edinburgh magazine.
Blada, V. pseud. Sketches from the Civil War. see Bolck, Adalbert John, 1828-
Bladen, Elizabeth L. petitioner 90404
Bladen uit mijn dagboek in Mexico. 75810
Bladensburg races. 5711
Bladensburg series, no. 2. 36045
Bladh, C. E. 5712-5713
Bladinger, E. G. ed. 51140
Blaeu, Cornelius. 5714, 35773
Blaeu, Johan, 1596-1673. 5714-(5717), 5719, 5721, 35773
Blaeu, Willem, d. 1638. 5714, 35773
Blaeu, Willem Janszoon, 1571-1638. (2308), 5718-5719, 5721, 52729, (71907), 77920-77964, 79124
Blagden, George Washington, 1802-1884. 5722-(5726), 85263
Blagdon, Francis William, 1778-1819. 5727
Blaikie, Alexander. 5728-5729
Blaine, E. (Veech) ed. 98736
Blaine, James Gillespie, 1830-1893. (5730)-5736
Blainville, H. M. Ducrotay de. see Ducrotay de Blainville, H. M.
Blair, -------. ed. (15607)
Blair, -------. plaintiff 5161
Blair, Archibald. 100037 see also Virginia. Council of State. Secretary.
Blair, Austin, 1818-1894. 20947, 27249, 48740, 48791 see also Michigan. Governor, 1861-1865 (Blair)
Blair, Bernard. 91610
Blair, Daniel. (5737)
Blair, David Boyle. 86976
Blair, Francis D. plaintiff 20817
Blair, Francis Preston, 1821-1875. 5738-5742, (25845), 51020, 79524, (80502)
Blair, Hugh, 1718-1800. 5743
Blair, Jacob B. 5744
Blair, James, 1655-1743. 5745, 30716, 55222-55223, note after 104154
Blair, John. 99907 see also Virginia (Colony) Council. Clerk.
Blair, John, 1720-1771. 5746, 94127
Blair, John, d. 1782. 5747, 73412
Blair, John Durbarrow, 1759-1823. 5748
Blair, Montgomery, 1813-1883. 5749-5751, 64249
Blair, Samuel. frontiersman 34461
Blair, Samuel, 1712-1751. (5752), 5758-5761, 79292
Blair, Samuel, 1741-1818. 5753-5757
Blair, Thomas. 5762
Blair, W. T. 17726
Blair, William W. 84549
Blair & Rives, Washington, D. C. firm defendants 47186
Blair investigation case. 5742
Blair vs. Williams. 5161
Blair's chronological and historical tables. 5747
Blaisdell, John. defendant 96828

Blaisdell, Sargent. defendant 12105, (12110), 96947, 96950, 4th note after 98168
Blake, Alexander V. (5763)
Blake, Charles. (5764)
Blake, Dominick T., d. 1839. 5765
Blake, Emma M. 69363
Blake, F. N. 34677
Blake, Francis, 1774-1817. (5766)-5768
Blake, George, 1768?-1841. 5769-5771
Blake, Harrison Gray, 1818-1876. 5772-(5774)
Blake, Henry Nichols, 1838- (5775)-(5776)
Blake, James, 1688-1753. 5777, 13208
Blake, John Falkner. see Falkner, John Blake, 1832-
Blake, John Lauris, 1788-1857. 4204, (5779)-5783, (34604), 67665, 80287-89288, 104687
Blake, Joseph. 5784
Blake, Joseph M., 1809-1879. 5785-5786
Blake, Mary Elizabeth (McGrath) 1840-1907. 63601
Blake, Mortimer, 1813-1884. 5787-5789
Blake, Nancy. pseud. Letters to a western cousin. see Cromwell, Ruth N. supposed author
Blake, Richard. 5792, 36395
Blake, S. H. 5794
Blake, Sophia Jex. see Jex-Blake, Sophia, 1840-
Blake, William, 1757-1827. 5797
Blake, William H. 5798
Blake, William J. 5799
Blake, William O. 5800, 6525-(65255)
Blake, William Phipps, 1826-1910. 5801-5810, 12526, 18278, (58595), 69946, 88362
Blake. firm see West & Blake. firm
Blake, Brothers, & Co. firm 5811
Blakeley, Alexander T. appellant 89224
Blakeney, -------. RA. 53271
Blakes and the Flanagans. 74825
Blake's remarks on Com. Johnstone's account. 5792
Blakslee, Solomon, 1762-1835. 5812
Blameless bishop. (23021)
Blamey, Jacob. cartographer 16278, 35966, 35968, (55557)
Blanc, ------ Le. see Le Blanc, ------.
Blanc, Edmond Adolphe. (5813)
Blanc, Hippolyte, b. 1820. (5814)
Blanc, Louis. 47292
Blanc, Vincent le. see Le Blanc, Vincent.
Blanc-Gilly, Matthew. 5815
Blanchard, ------. reporter 103678
Blanchard, ------. tr. 72232
Blanchard, Amos, 1801?-1869. 5816
Blanchard, Amos, 1807-1870. 16760
Blanchard, Calvin. 5817-5820
Blanchard, Charles. 5821
Blanchard, Edmund F. (63532)
Blanchard, Ira D. 19374
Blanchard, Ira Henry Thomas, d. 1845. 5822
Blanchard, John, 1787-1849. 5823
Blanchard, John, fl. 1842. 5824
Blanchard, John, fl. 1845. 5825
Blanchard, Joshua Pollard, 1782-1868. 5826-5831, (65665)
Blanchard, Louis. plaintiff 84409
Blanchard, P. 5832-5835, 10295
Blanchard, Rufus, 1821-1904. 5836-5837, 49252, 101710
Blanchard, Victor. 5838-5839
Blanchard, William Isaac, d. 1796. reporter 31841, 96176
Blanchardiere, Rene Courte de la. see Courte de la Blanchardiere, Rene.
Blanche, ------. 5840
Blanche of Brandywine. 41391
Blanchelande, ------- de. 5841-5845

Blanchelande, ex-Gouveneur de Saint-Domignue, convaincu de trahison. (58163)
Blanchet, -----. 5846
Blanchet, Francois. 5847
Blanchetiere-Bellevue, -----. 4545, 5848-5850, 68366
Blancius, Hieronymous. 28691, 51646
Blancke, G. 5851
Blanco, -------, fl. 1838. 22912
Blanco, ------- Salinsa del Penon. see Salinas del Penon Blanco, ------.
Blanco, J. Sabau y. see Sabau y Blanco, J.
Blanco, Jose Felix, 1782-1872, ed. 98879
Blanco, Matias Ruiz. see Ruiz Blanco, Matias, 1643-1705?
Blanco Abarca, Nicolas. see Abarca, Nicolas Blanco.
Blanco Solana, Juan. 5855
Blanco White, Joseph. see White, Joseph Blanco, 1775-1841.
Blanco y Crespo, Jose Maria. see White, Joseph Blanco, 1775-1841.
Blancs et les noirs en Amerique. 5856
Blancus, Hieronymous. 27691, 51646
Bland, ------. 5858
Bland, Edward, d. 1653. 52518-52519, note after 100459, 104191
Bland, Humphrey, 1686?-1763. 5857, 53271
Bland, Priscilla. plaintiff 53542
Bland, Richard, 1710-1776. (5859)-5861, 10173, 100444
Bland, T. A. ed. 55741
Bland, Theodric, 1742?-1790. 5863-5867, 72494, 1st note after 100788, 2d note after 104412 see also U. S. Legation. Buenos Aires (Province) U. S. Legation. Chile.
Bland, Theodoric, 1742?-1790. petitioner 5862, (45103) see also Maryland. Chancellor. petitioner
Bland, Thomas. 5868-5870
Bland, William. 95977
Bland papers. 5867
Blande, John. petitioner 100529
Blanding, Abraham, 1776-1839. 10964, 87408, 87726, 87729 see also South Carolina. Superintendent of Public Works.
Blanding, James D. 87973
Blane, Sir Gilbert, Bart., 1749-1834. 5871
Blane, William Newham, 1800-1825. (5872), 84305-84306, 84309, 84313, 96503
Blaney, Captain -----. see Blane, William Newham, 1800-1825.
Blank poem. 91182
Blanq-Deisisles, -----. 4873
Blanquel, Simon. publisher 71483
Blanqui, ------. (82311)
Blanvillain, J. F. C. tr. 12245
Blanquiere, Edward. ed. 18674-18675
Blanquiere, P. de. 100896
Blarney, J. see Blamey, Jacob.
Blarney O'Democrat. pseud. see O'Democrat, Blarney. pseud.
Blas, Caesario San. pseud. Voyage to the island of philosophers. see Woodruff, Sylvester. supposed author
Blaschke, Eduard Leontjevich. 5874
Blasco de Lanuza, V. see Lanuza, V. Blasco de.
Blascowitz, C. 3606
Blasius Vitalis Seywald's Welt-Spiegel. 79674
Blaskowitz, -----. 35969
Blascon Zacatecano coronado por el cielo. 106238
Blasphemers justly reproved. 78741
Blasphemy of abolitionism exposed. 1341
Blasquez, Ignacio. 5876

Blasquez, Pedro. 5876
Blast of a trumpet in Zion. 66629
Blatchford, E. W. (31431)
Blatchford, John. (5877), 9538
Blatchford, Richard M. 5878 see also Apalachicola Land Company. Board of Directors. President.
Blatchford, Samuel, 1767-1828. 5880-5883, 84692, 104213
Blatchford, Samuel, 1820-1893. reporter 5879, 53984, (79503)
Blatchford, Thomas W. 5884-5885
Blatchly, A. 5886
Blattides. 77211
Blauen und Gelben. (27171)
Blauvelt, -------. 5887, 1st note after 104829
Blavet, ------, Abbe. 82316
Blavet, ------, Abbe. tr. (82307), 82309
Bleak house. 19580, 91234, note after 92624
Bleakley & Co. firm see Smith, Bleakley & Co.
Bleau, ------. cartographer see Blaeu, Willem Janszoon, 1571-1638.
Bleby, Henry. 5888-5891
Bledsoe, Albert Taylor. 5892-5894, 22263, 74317, 79900
Bledsoe, Jesse. (5895)
Bleecker, Ann Eliza. 5896, (23924)
Bleecker, Anthony. ed. 71397
Bleecker, Anthony J. 5897
Bleecker, Leonard. 5899
Bleeker, P. 5900
Bleekrod, ------. 5901
Blefken, Dithmar. 5902-5905, 28929, 47383, 52359, 66686
Blenman, Jonathan. supposed author 6012, note just before (69427)
Blenman, Richard. supposed author 6012, note just before (69427)
Blennerhassett, Harman, 1765-1831. 5906, 74878
Blennerhassett, Harman, 1765-1831. defendant 9434
Blennerhassett, Margaret (Agnew) 5906, 74878
Blennerhassett, Margaret (Agnew) supposed author 103884
Blennerhassett papers. 5906, 74878
Blessed dead. 22788
Blessed dead. The funeral sermon of Hugh Aikman. 89085
Blessed hope. (46636)
Blessed unions. 46235
Blessedness. 28689
Blessedness of dying in the Lord. 64692
Blessedness of giving; a discourse preached in the Old South Church. 22327
Blessedness of giving. A sermon, preached in St. John's Church. 91709
Blessedness of peace-makers represented. 94685
Blessedness of such as trust in Christ. 103929
Blessedness of the dead who die in the Lord. A sermon preached . . . after the funeral of Mrs. Anna Foxcroft. 12331
Blessedness of the dead who die in the Lord. A sermon preached at the publick lecture. 103898
Blessedness of the dead who die in the Lord, illustrated in a sermon. 104312
Blessedness of the tried saint. 16629
Blessedness of those who die in the Lord. 22140
Blessedness of those who die in the Lord, considered. 102420
Blessing and honor of fruitful mothers. (14525)
Blessing of peace. 97601

Blessing of Zebulun & Issachar. 14470
Blessings and sins of the nation. 43104
Blessings of a soul in health. 25408
Blessings of America. (41342), 84845
Blessings of peace. 24334, 62859
Blessings of poverty. 3760
Blessings of the revolution. 26231
Blessings yet left us. 83573
Bleynie, Leon. 5907
Blick auf das Alpenland Guatemala. 71313
Blick auf Kanada. 102502
Blick in dasn Dunkel der Geisterwelt. 89424
Blick in's Thal des Ohio. 31375, 56883
Blicke, Charles. 5908
Blicke in die Geschichte der Vereinigten
    Staaten von Amerika. 23948
Blicker, Laurens. 31228
Blier, Paul. tr. 41915
Blifken, Ditmar. see Blefken, Dithmar.
Bligh, William, 1754-1817. 5908A-5913, 21211-
    21215, 52580, 64396
Blik op den vorigen en den tegenwoordigen
    toestand van Jamaica. 91692
Blik op zijne toekomst. (58524)
Blik paa Brasiliens dyreverden. 42687
Blin, ----- Duverger de Saint. see Saint
    Blin, ---- Duverger de.
Blind Bartimeus. 103515, 103593
Blind girl, and other poems. 17633
Blind heart. (81202), 81203
Blind-man. pseud. Dialogue between a blind-
    man and death. see Standfast, Richard.
Blind man's offering. (7046)
Blind sisters. 104175
Blinn, Henry C. 106199
Blish, J. K. 14265, 1st note after 94219
Blismon. pseud. Jeune voyager. see
    Blocquel, Simon.
Bliss, -------. ed. 601
Bliss, Charles R. 5915
Bliss, Daniel. 5916
Bliss, E. F. ed. note after 106301
Bliss, Edward. 5917
Bliss, George. 5918-5923, note after 89877,
    103010
Bliss, Henry. 5924-5929, 15975, 102854
Bliss, Leonard. 5930
Bliss, Philemon. (5931)-5932
Bliss, Porter Cornelius. 5933
Bliss, Porter Cornelius. petitioner 57711
Bliss, Sarah Ann. (5934)
Bliss, Seth. (5935) see also American Tract
    Society, Boston. Secretary.
Bliss, Sylvester. 5936-5937
Bliss, T. E. (5938)-5939
Bliss, Mrs. William Starkie. 5940
Bliss, Z. 5941
Bliss. firm publishers see Whitney & Bliss.
    firm publishers
Blithedale romance. 30994
Blocius, Johann. 5942
Block, -----. 13508
Block, Maurice, 1816-1901. 12590
Blockade. 101481
Blockade of Boston. 9260
Blockade of the American ports, &c. 101473
Blockaded British subject. pseud. Life in the
    South. see Jones, Sarah L.
Blockheads; or, the affrighted officers. 5945,
    101481
Blockheads, or, the fortunate contractor. 5944
Blockhoy, Pieter Corneliszoon. 91169, 63425
Blocquel, Simon. 5946-5948
Blocus Americain. 65413
Blodget, Lorin. 5949-5954, 61970 see also
    Philadelphia. Board of Trade. Secretary.

Blodget, Samuel, fl. 1755. 5955
Blodget, Samuel, fl. 1805. 5956-5958, 56594,
    95708
Blodget, Silas. 25232, 73562, 102947 see also
    West Stafford, Conn. Second Church.
    Committee.
Blodget, W. P. 72461
Blodget, William. incorrectly supposed author
    5959, (10096)
Blodget, William. supposed author 95678
Blodgett (J. W.) and Co. firm 5961
Bloem, Lvdovicvs Vlas. see Vlas-Bloem,
    Lvdovicvs.
Bloeyende opkomst de aloude en hedengaagsche
    Groenlandsche visschery. 106374-106376
Blois, John T. 5962
Blom, Anthony. 5963-5964
Blome, Anthony. see Blom, Anthony.
Blome, Richard. 4937A, (5965)-5972, note
    after 17686, 36944, note after 41144,
    68430, 76720
Blome, Robert. supposed author note after
    (28941), 57158
Blomfield, Charles James, successively Bishop
    of Chester, and London, 1786-1857. 14767
Blomfield, E. 5973
Blond, F. F. le. see Le Blond, F. F.
Blond, Frank C. le. see Le Blond, Frank C.
Blondeau, J. engr. 76182
Blondel van Cuelebrouk, Edouard. 5974, 17835
Blondel: a historical fancy. 70830
Blondin, der Held vom Niagra. Ein wahheitsge-
    treues Lebensbild. 2011
Blondin, der Held des Niagra. Seine Fahrten
    und Abenteuer zu Wasser und zu Lande.
    4955
Blondus, M. A. see Biondo, Michaele Angelo.
Blood, ------. comp. 53193
Blood, B. 5975
Blood, Caleb. 5976
Blood, Henry Ames. 5977, 102427
Blood, Mighill. (5978)
Blood, William. 5979-(5981)
Blood. firm publishers see Talbott and
    Blood. firm publishers
Blood Iago, blood. (39813)
Blood of Abel and the blood of Jesus. 15092
Blood of the Mohawk! (38449)
Blood will out. 42737, 88270
Bloodgood, Abraham. (5982)
Bloodgood, C. De Witt. see Bloodgood, Simeon
    de Witt, 1799-1866.
Bloodgood, Francis. defendant (35991), 98547
Bloodgood, Francis A. 5983, 35279
Bloodgood, Simeon de Witt, 1799-1866. 5984-
    5986, 33508, 80445
Bloodgood (John) & Co. firm 89898
Bloody buoy. 13873, 13877, 64159, 64161
Bloody butchery by the British troops. 40888
Bloody charter. 103713
Bloody news from Carolina. 87803
Bloody tenent yet more bloody. 51773, 104333
Bloody tragedy of the prize schooner Waring.
    68320
Bloody tribunal. (5988), 44493
Bloody week! 5987
Bloom of youth immortal by piety and glory.
    106212
Bloomfield, B. (5989)
Bloomfield, John W. 95135
Bloomfield, Joseph, 1755-1823. (5990), 53125,
    53148, 96030 see also New Jersey.
    Governor, 1803-1812 (Bloomfield)
Bloomfield, Obadiah Benjamin Franklin. 5991

Bloomfield, Me. Ecclesiastical Council, 1848.
see Congregational Churches in Maine.
Ecclesiastical Council, Bloomfield, 1848.
Bloomfield, N. J. Benevolent Society. see
Benevolent Society of Bloomfield, N. J.
Bloomingdale Asylum, White Plains, N. Y.
54117
Bloomington, Ill. Illinois Wesleyan University.
see Illinois Wesleyan University, Bloom-
ington, Ill.
Bloor, Alfred J. 5994-5995, 76606, 76624,
76647
Bloss, William C. 5996
Blosseville, Ernest de. tr. 35686, 50703,
94329, note after 96221
Blossom, ------. 38979
Bloudy newes from the Barbadoes. (5997)
Blovdy tenent of persecution. 17044-17046,
17056, 17077, 51773, 2d note after
103852, 104331-104332, 104341
Bloudy tenent, washed. 17045
Blouet, Abel. (5998), 19475
Blouin, Daniel. petitioner 104017
Blount, Charles, Earl of Devonshire. see
Devonshire, Charles Blount, Earl of,
1563-1606.
Blount, Sir Thomas Pope. 5999
Blount, William. defendant 36744
Blount, William, 1749-1800. 69834, note after
94720, 94725 see also Tennessee
(Territory) Governor, 1790-1796 (Blount)
Blount, Willie, 1768-1835. 6004, 33150, 94725,
94758-94761 see also Tennessee.
Governor, 1809-1816 (Blount)
Blount College, Knoxville, Tenn. see Tennes-
see. University.
Blow, Henry Taylor, 1817-1875. 6005-6006,
52127
Blow at the root. 24682
Blow at the root, being a fashionable fast-day
sermon. 39967
Blow at the root of aristocracy. 62437
Blow at the root of the refined antinominianism.
(4485)
Blow at the root of war. 59475
Blowe, Daniel. 6007
Blowers, Thomas. 6008-6009
Bloy, Johann. see Blocius, Johann.
Blue beard. (81173)-81174
Blue bell of Scotland. 105959
Blue book. (5261)
Blue book abridged. 20325
Blue book for 1866. 20325
Blue book for the county of Philadelphia.
38235
Blue book; or, register of officers and agents.
20316
Blue books [of Parliament.] 16885-16886,
37708, 39002
Blue-eyed Mary. 91162
Blue grass philosophy. 79916
Blue laws of Connecticut. 6010, (15761), 85170
Blue laws of New Haven Colony. 6010
Blue laws of New York, Maryland, Virginia and
South Carolina. 6010
Blue laws revived. 105339
Blue lights, or the convention. 78325
Blue-shop. 14003, 14023
Bluenose. pseud. Lady and the dressmaker.
see Fenety, George E.
Bluett, Thomas. 6011
Bluffton: a story of to-day. (77244)
Blume der Prairie. 4522
Blumeau, J. incorrectly attributed author
6012, note just before (69427)
Blumen-Busch. (25461)

Blumenau, Hermann. (6013)-6016
Blumenbach, -----. 82393
Blumencron, Leopold R. von. tr. 17936
Blumhardt, Christoph Gottlieb. 6017-6019
Blumhof, Johann Georg Ludwig. tr. (23107)
Blundell, B. 6020
Blundell, Joseph L. reporter 1680, 6021
Blundeville, Thomas. 6022-6024
Blunt, Edmund M. (2588), 6025-6033, 26218-
26219, (43847), 101284
Blunt, Edmund M. plaintiff 96829
Blunt, George M. 6025
Blunt, George W. (2588), 6025, 6031, 6034,
26218-26219, 101284
Blunt, Henry. 3, (6035)
Blunt, Sir John, fl. 1721. 65865, 88192
Blunt, Sir John, fl. 1721. supposed author
6036, 97160
Blunt, Joseph. (6037)-(6044)
Blunt, M. 101284
Blunt, Nathaniel B. reporter 18868, 84452
Blunt, W. B. reporter 71953
Blunt's new chart of the Atlantic. 6026
Blunt's stranger's guide to the city of New-
York. 6033
Blut-Fahne ausgesteckt zur Warnung politischer
Wegweiser in America. 64160
Blyden, Edward W. 6045-6047
Blydenburgh, S. 69637
Blydenburgh, Samuel. 6048
Blyth, Joseph. (6049), 83303, 101803
Blyth, Stephen C. (6050), 32225, 3d note after
96993
Blythe, James. 6051
Blythe, S. K. 40575, 94799
Boa Vista, Barao da. (60992) see also
Pernambuco. Presidente (Boa Vista)
Boadicea. (6052)
Boanerges. A short essay to preserve and
strengthen the good impressions. 46236
Boanerges, or the humble supplication of the
ministers of Scotland. 78379
Board having reason to believe. 98059G
Board of Agriculture and state farm. 24766
Board of Agriculture at Boston. see Boston.
Board of Agriculture.
Board of American Lloyds. 68837
Board of Censors of Suffolk District, Mass.
see Massachusetts Medical Society.
Suffolk District Medical Society. Board
of Censors.
Board of Civil Engineers to Consider the Sub-
ject of the Construction of a Rail and
Highway Bridge Across the Mississippi
River, 1867. see St. Louis. Board of
Civil Engineers to Consider the Subject
of a Rail and Highway Bridge Across the
Mississippi River, 1867.
Board of Clergy, Canonically Constituted for
Trying the Truth of Certain Charges
Against the Rev. John Ireland, of Brooklyn.
see Protestant Episcopal Church in the
U. S. A. New York (Diocese) Board of
Clergy Canonically Constituted for Trying
the Truth of Certain Charges Against the
Rev. John Ireland, of Brooklyn, 1810.
Board of Commissioners for Carrying into
Effect the Sixth Article of the Treaty of
Amity, Commerce and Navigation, Con-
cluded Between His Britannic Majesty and
the United States of America. see Board
of Commissioners Under Article 6th of
the Treaty Between Great Britain and the
United States, London, Nov. 19, 1794.

Board of Commissioners for the Adjustment of French Spoliation Claims. see U. S. Board of Commissioners For the Adjustment of French Spoliation Claims.

Board of Commissioners of Common Schools. Legal provision respecting the education and employment of children in factories. 15725

Board of Commissioners Under Article Sixth of the Treaty Between Great Britain and the United States, London, Nov. 19, 1794. 782, 7904, 10663, 13196, (14989)-14190, 17975-17976, 34761-34762, 43158, 53609, 56542, 62899, 84842, 93768-93769, 104368 see also General Agent for Claimants Before the Board of Commissioners Under Article 6th of the Treaty Between Great Britain and the United States, 1794.

Board of Commissioners Under Article Sixth of the Treaty Between Great Britain and the United States, London, Nov. 19, 1794. Agent for British Creditors. 782, 17976, 34761, 84842 see also Smith, William Moore, 1759-1821.

Board of Commissioners Under Article Sixth of the Treaty Between Great Britain and the United States, London, Nov. 19, 1794. United States Agent. 54542 see also Read, John.

Board of Commissioners Under the Convention with France, of the 4th of July, 1831. see U. S. Board of Commissioners for the Adjustment of French Spoliation Claims.

Board of Commissioners Under the Eleventh Article of the Treaty of Amity, Settlement, and Limits, Between the United States and His Catholic Majesty, Concluded at Washington, on the 22d of February, 1819. 33939, 78737, 103717

Board of Directors of the Delaware and Raritan Canal and Camden and Amboy Railroad Companies. see Joint Board of Directors of the Delaware and Raritan Canal, and Camden and Amboy Rail Road Transportation Companies.

Board of Education for Freedmen. see U. S. Bureau of Refugees, Freedmen and Abandoned Lands. Board of Education for Freedmen.

Board of Education. "University project." Report of special committee. (13088)

Board of Fire Underwriters, New York. see New York Board of Fire Underwriters.

Board of Management of Veterans of the National Guard, New York. see Veterans of the National Guard, New York. Board of Management.

Board of Managers for the Industrial School for Girls, Dorchester, Mass. see Dorchester, Mass. Industrial School for Girls. Board of Managers.

Board of Managers [of the Pennsylvania Seamen's Friend Society]. Preamble and resolutions . . . in relation to [the assassination of Lincoln.] 60362

Board of Managers of the Washington National Monument Society to the American people. 102030

Board of Marine Inspectors of the Association of Lake Underwriters. see Association of Lake Underwriters. Board of Marine Inspectors.

Board of Metropolitan Police of the District of Columbia. see District of Columbia Police Department.

Board of Missions. 35816

Board of Missions of the Protestant Episcopal Church. Twenty-third annual report of the Foreign Committee. (66127)

Board of National Popular Education. 6054, 21881, 56885

Board of National Popular Education. Constitution. 6054, 21811

Board of National Popular Education. General Agent. 6054, 21811, 56885

Board of Naval Officers Upon a Trial of an Amoskeag Steam Fire Engine, 1866. see U. S. Navy. Board of Naval Officers Upon a Trial of an Amoskeag Steam Fire Engine, 1866.

Board of Proprietors of the Eastern Division of New Jersey. 1000, 5378, 53067, (53078), (53091), (53236), (59679), (80693) see also Penn, William, 1644-1718. Rudyard, Thomas. West, Robert.

Board of Proprietors of the Eastern Division of New Jersey. defendants 5379, 33874, 53074-53075, 91855 see also Alexander, James. defendant and Stirling, William Alexander, calling himself 6th Earl of, 1726-1783. defendant

Board of Proprietors of the Eastern Division of New Jersey. petitioners 53053, 53203, 83982

Board of Proprietors of the Eastern Division of New Jersey. plaintiffs 5378, (53066) 53082, 53098 see also Stair, John Dalrymple, 5th Earl of, 1720-1789. plaintiff

Board of Proprietors of the Eastern Division of New Jersey. Counsel. 53082

Board of Proprietors of the Eastern Division of New Jersey. respondents 33874, 91855

Board of Proprietors of the Eastern Division of New Jersey. Scots Proprietors. 53079

Board of Survey of the Navy. 55106

Board of the Western Ladies of Philadelphia for the Relief . . . of the Poor. 62385

Board of Trade, Boston. see Boston. Board of Trade.

Board of Trade, Charleston, S. C. see Charleston. Board of Trade.

Board of Trade, Denver, Colorado. see Denver, Colo. Board of Trade.

Board of Trade, New York (City) see New York Board of Trade and Transportation.

Board of Trade, Oswego, N. Y. see Oswego, N. Y. Board of Trade.

Board of Trade, Philadelphia. see Philadelphia. Board of Trade.

Board of Trade, Pittsburgh. see Pittsburgh. Board of Trade.

Board of Trade, Portland, Me. see Portland, Me. Board of Trade.

Board of Trade, Salem, Mass. see Salem Board of Trade.

Board of Trade, Springfield, Ill. see Springfield, Ill. Board of Trade.

Board of Trade and Merchant's Exchange, Pittsburgh. see Pittsburgh. Board of Trade.

Board of Trade of Denver City, Colorado. see Denver, Colo. Board of Trade.

Board of Trade of Southern Colorado. (14743)

Board of treasury. 57785

Board of Trustees from the Old Thirteen
States, Philadelphia, 1860. see Conven-
tion of Delegates from the Thirteen
Original States, Philadelphia, 1852.
Board of Underwriters, New York. see New
York Board of Underwriters.
Board of War and Ordnance. Williamsburg,
August 17, 1779. 100408
Board of Wardens of the Port of Philadelphia.
see Philadelphia. Board of Wardens
of the Port.
Board of Works report. (56115)
Board proceeded to the consideration of the
letters of Colonel Clarke. 100036
Boarden, James. 94087
Boarding School, Greenfield, Mass. 28628
Boarding school. A poem. 96989
Boardman, Charles A. 6055-6056
Boardman, David S. 6067
Boardman, George Dana. 6058-6062
Boardman, George N. 6063-6064
Boardman, Henry A. 4107, 6065-6086, 20391,
42979, 68151
Boardman, James. 6087
Boardman, John. 6088
Boardman, S. L. 6089-(6091)
Boardman, William. 37385
Boardman, William W. 6092
Boards of Missions, Education Foreign Missions,
and Publication. 32704
Boat armament of the U. S. Navy. 18276
Boatman's magazine. 89500
Boatmen of the Schuylkill Canal. petitioners
78070
Boatmen's reporter. 89500
Boatswain's spell at Washington. (55298)
Boatswain's whistle. 6093
Bob Short. pseud. see Gilley, William B.
Bob Smith's clown song and joke book. 82357
Bob-Ad-Ill, Captain. pseud. Where are ye all
now? 103238
Bobadilla, Diego Lopez Pacheco y. see Lopez
Pacheco y Bobadilla, Diego.
Bobbett, -------. engr. 77176, 77182
Bobbett, Hooper, & Co. firm Engravers 91067
Bobin, Isaac. 6095
Bobo, S. 81266 see also Spartansburg Fe-
male College, Spartansburg, S. C. Board
of Trustees. President.
Bobo, William M. (27582), 2d note after 88112
Bobolink minstrel. 9161
Bob's letter. (6094)
Bobse, August. tr. 11282
Boca de la iglesia, Santo Domingo de Guzman.
78922
Bocabulario de la lengva Gvarani. 74036
Bocanegra, ------. 48336, 76116
Bocanegra, Juan Perez. 6096
Bocanegra, Matea de. 6097-6101
Bocangel y Vnzueta, Gabriel. 66104 see also
Lima. Tribunal del Consulado, y Junta
General de Comercio.
Bocayuva, Quintino de. see Souza Bocayuva,
Quintino de.
Boccage, Marie Anne du. see Duboccage,
Marie Anne.
Bocchi, Francesco. 6102
Bocina periodico. (48305)
Bock, Carl Wilhelm. 6103
Bock, Friedrich Samuel. 6104-6105
Bockett, Elias. 6106-6108, 73235, 92322
Bockett, Elias. supposed author 6108, 92329
Bocking, Ed. ed. (56021)
Bockwitz, H. H. ed. 54946, 3d note after
106221

Bocock, Thomas Stanhope, 1815-1891. 6109,
42822
Bocquet, Edward. illus. 36908
Bodano, Gualtero. 39587
Boddelen i Bern. 16438
Boddily, John. 6111
Bodemann, Friedrich Wilhelm. 6110
Bodley, Thomas. 6113
Bodman, Manoah. 83541
Bodmer, Charles. illus. 47014-47015
Bodwell, J. C. 6114
Body of divinity. 90029
Body of divinity for little children. 84553
Body of divinity versified. (46211), 46403,
46589
Body of liberties. (28387), 45652, 101330
Body of sermons. 84650, 84675A, 84678C
Body of the laws of the province of New Jersey.
53076
Body politic. (3530)
Bodye of lawes of the colonie of Rhode Island
and Providence Plantations. 70510
Boeck spreeckt. (72762)
Boeckh, -------. lithographer 84774
Boehm, Anthony William. see Boehme, Anton
Wilhelm, 1673-1722.
Boehm, Henry. (6115)
Boehm see also Bohm
Boehme, Anton Wilhelm, 1673-1722. 2390,
32377, 98990, 102211-102212
Boehmer, George H. 85093
Boek der landverhuizers. 5127
Boek der leer en verbonden. 83220
Boek van Mormon. 83120-83121
Boek voor den Zeeman. (40035)
Boekanier. 47400
Boeke di orasjon pa katolieka nan. 66746
Boel, ------. 25755, 25974, 98572
Boelen, J. 6116
Boem, Joannes. see Boemus, Johann, fl.
1500.
Boemus, Johann, fl. 1500. 6117-6120, 94273,
106330
Boen, William. 6121
Boero, Giuseppe. 6122-6123
Boesche, E. T. see Bosche, Eduard Theodor.
Boese, Thomas. 54614, 66516 see also New
York (City) Board of Education. Clerk.
Boesnier, ----. 6124, 86479
Boethius, d. 524. spurious and doubtful works
74801
Boetius, Severinius. 69130
Bogardus, J. P. 91919
Bogardus, W. E. 6125
Bogardus & Labatt. firm publishers see
Harris, Bogardus & Labatt. firm
publishers
Bogart, Alwyn. 74448
Bogart, David Schuyler. 6126
Bogart, William H. (6127)-6129
Bogen, F. W. 6130-6132
Bogert, Cornelius I. (34385), note after 53697,
(68287), note after 83791
Bogert, Cornelius I. defendant 96888
Bogg, F. see Bugg, F.
Boggs, John. 6133
Boggs, John. ed. (55738)
Bogle, Samuel. 61927
Bogota, Colombia. 6135-6136, 68874
Bogota, Colombia. Charter. 68874
Bogota, Colombia. Colegio Mayor de Nuestra
Senora del Rosario. 96242
Bogota, Colombia. Ordinances, etc. 6136,
68874
Bogota, Colombia. Sociedad Filotecnica. see
Sociedad Filotecnica, Bogota.

Bogota (Archdiocese) Archbishop (Mosquera) 51067 see also Mosquera, Manuel Jose, Abp.
Bogota in 1836-7. 91388
Bogtrykkeren Benjamin Franklins liv og levnet. 44496
Bogue, David. 6137
Boguslawski, B. von. 6138
Bogy, Lewis V. (6139)
Bohemia. Sovereigns, etc. 1617-1619, (Ferdinand II) petitioner 15930-15932, 69589, 95749, 102888 see also Ferdinand II, King of Bohemia, 1578-1637.
Bohemia. Treaties, etc. 19274, 96543-96545
Bohemian. 6140, 12945
Bohemian Brethren. see Moravians. and United Brethren.
Bohemian Mining Company. 6141
Bohemian Mining Company. Charter. 6141
Bohm, Antonus. 13015, 79162-79166
Bohm see also Boehm
Bohmen, Joh. Phil. 106351
Bohmisch-Mahrischen Bruder. see United Brethren.
Bohmische Robinson. (72225)
Bohn, Casimir. 6142
Bohn, Henry George, 1796-1884. 6183, 8677, 19284, 82400
Bohn, Henry George, 1796-1884. tr. (24241), (33708)
Bohn's hand-book of Washington 6142
Bohn's hand-book of Washington. Supplement. 6142
Bohn's illustrated edition. 92465, 92466
Bohn's library edition. 92466
Bohn's shilling edition. 92466
Bohn's standard library. 88562
Bohun, Edmund, 1645-1696. 6144-6145, 31655
Bohun, R. 6146
Boies, Charles Alfred. 6147
Boies, John. defendant 6148
Boies, Patrick. 6149
Boigne, Claude Pierre Joseph Leborgne de. see Leborgne de Boigne, Claude Pierre Joseph.
Boil, A. M. tr. 83145
Boileau, Lambert de. see De Boileau, Lambert.
Boileau, Virgile. tr. (69061)
Boileau de Bouillon, Gilles, 16th cent. 18576
Boiler explosion of the Martin boiler. 6150, 12422
Boilieu, Lambert de. 6151, 19110
Boimare, A. L. 6152
Boinod & Gaillard. firm 61519
Boirie, ------- Arnault de la. see Arnault de la Boirie, -------.
Bois, Gualterus du. see Du Bois, Gualterus, 1666-1751.
Bois, Henry A. du. see Du Bois, Henry A.
Bois, L. E. 81021
Bois, L. E. supposed author 77099
Bois, T. K. du. see Du Bois, T. K.
Bois, William E. du. see Du Bois, William E.
Bois-Mesle, Jean-Baptiste Torchet de. 6158
Bois-Robert, Joseph Lavallee, Marquis de. see Lavallee, Joseph, Marquis de Bois-Robert, 1747-1816.
Boisbriant, ------. 103422 see also Compagnie des Indes Occidentales. Conseil. Chief Judge.
Boisduval, -------. ed. 78689
Boisduval, Jean Alphonse. (6153)-6155, 21210

Boisgelin de Cuce, Jean-de-Dieu-Raymond de. see De Boisgelin de Cuce, Jean-de-Dieu-Raymond.
Boishebert, --------, Sieur de. 6156, 47525
Boislecomte, Andre Olivier Ernest Sain de, d. 1799. (6157), 74978
Boisneuf, ------ Payen de. see Payen de Boisneuf, -------.
Boisneuf, ------ Poyen de. see Payen de Boisneuf, ------.
Boisrond-Tonnerre, -----. (6159)-6160
Boissard, Jan. Jac. 6161-6162, 34160
Boissardo, Ian. Iac. see Boissard, Jan. Jac.
Boissier de Sauvages de la Croix, Pierre Augustin de. 6163, 20220
Boissiere, C. C. Tanguy de la. see Tanguy de la Boissiere, C. C.
Boistel d'Exauvillez, Andre Philippe Octave. 86482, 86484
Boisthibault, ------- Doublet de. see Doublet de Boisthibault, -------.
Boiteau, Paul. 4567
Boitel Amedee. 6165-6166
Boitel, Ch. 6167
Boitel, Pierre, Sieur de Gaubertin. 6164
Boix, Ignacio. ed. 68390
Bokee, David A. 6168
Boker, ------. (65665)
Boker, Charles S. 50152, 68169
Boker, George G. 51437
Boker, George Henry. 6169-6174, 41164, note after 94389
Bokkelen, Libertus van. see Van Bokkelen, Libertus.
Bokum, Hermann. 6175-6180, note after 92721 see also Tennessee. Commissioner of Immigration.
Bokum, Hermann. tr. (77017)
Bolander, --------. plaintiff 101436
Bolanos Mining Company. General Courts of Proprietors. (65769)
Bold buccaniers. 63516
Bold push. 102425
Bold scalp-hunter. 36582
Bolde, ------. 9463
Bolduc, J. B. Z. 6181
Bolea, Ambrosio Funes Villapando Abarca de. see Abarca de Bolea, Ambrosio Funes Villapando, Conde de Ricla.
Bolet, Ramon. 89285
Boletim da segunda classee. 99524
Boletin de la Sociedad de Agricultura. (12745)
Boletin de la Sociedad de Ciencias Fisicas y Naturales de Caracas. 10773
Boletin de la Sociedad Mexicana de Geografia y Estadistica. 48308, 59518, 73034, 94615
Boletin de las leges del imperio Mexicano. 48345
Boletin de las leyes del imperio Mexicano. 48306
Boletin de las leyes i decretos del gobierno. (76856)
Boletin de las leyes, ordenes y disposiciones particulares. 48306
Boletin de las leyes y de las ordenes y decretos del gobierno. 12744
Boletin del Instituto Nacional de Geografia y Estadistica de la republica Megicana. 85758
Boletin del Instituto Nacional de Geografia y Estadistica de la republica Mexicana. (48307)
Boletin oficial del govierno supremo de Honduras. 23753
Bolingbroke, Henry, 1785-1855. 6182-6183, 62506-62507

Bolingbroke, Henry Saint John, 1st Viscount,
   1678-1751. 75238-75240, 80700, 101167
Bolivar, Simon, 1783-1830. 6184-6186, 6188-
   (6190), 6205-6206, 14563, 14608, 14612,
   14578, 29369, note after 39087, (66401),
   93812, 96221, 99498 see also Colombia.
   President, 1819-1830 (Bolivar)
Bolivar MacCabe, Julius P. see MacCabe,
   Julius P. Bolivar.
Bolivar. 6311
Bolivar au congres de Venezeula. Ode. 19742
Bolivar i Washington. 98120
Bolivar's Denkwurdigkeiten. 6184, 21068
Bolivia. 6204, 44559
Bolivia. Assemblea General Constituyente de
   1831. 6195
Bolivia. Congreso Constitucional. 6432
Bolivia. Congreso Constitucional de 1834.
   6195
Bolivia. Congreso Jeneral Constituyente de
   1839. 6196
Bolivia. Constitution. 6194-6196, 6205-6206,
   (66401)
Bolivia, Laws, statutes, etc. 6192-(6193),
   6197, 90775, note after 103224
Bolivia. Ministro de Estato. 6198, (29335)
Bolivia. Ministro de Hacienda. 39015 see
   also Lara, Joseph M. de.
Bolivia. Ministro de la guerra. 6200-6201
Bolivia. Ministro de Relaciones Esteriores.
   (6199)
Bolivia. President, 1826-1828 (Sucre)
   (6202) see also Sucre, Antonio Jose de,
   Pres. Bolivia, 1795-1830.
Bolivia. President, 1829-1839 (Santa Cruz)
   6203, 76770-76771 see also Santa-Cruz,
   Andres, Pres. Bolivia, 1794-1865.
Bolivia. Secretario de Relaciones Esteriores
   i Majoras Internas. 6432
Bolivia; or, Upper Peru, its geographical
   position. 61082
Bolivian. pseud. see Peru-Bolivian. pseud.
Bollaert, William. (6207), 47578, 83033
Bollaert, William. tr. 81285
Bollaert's ancient population of the new world.
   47578
Bollan, William. (6208)-6214, 6216-6220, 8069,
   10728, 25748, 93387, 4th note after
   95843, 2d note after 103853
Bollan, William. supposed author 6215, 93387
Bollan, William. incorrectly supposed author
   6220, (68029)-68032
Boller, Henry A. 6221
Bolles, James A. 6222-6224, 43322, 91104,
   93750
Bolles, John. 6225-6227, 69290
Bolles, John Augustus, 1809-1878. 6228-6230,
   (70542)
Bolles, John R. 6231
Bolles, Joseph. 89501
Bolles, Lucius. 6232-6234
Bollettio della R. Societa Geografia Italiana.
   99281
Bollin, J. 6235
Bollman, Erick. 6236-6238, 58511
Bollman, Justus Eric, 1769-1821. defendant
   9426
Bollman, Lewis. 6239-6240
Bollo, Diego de Torres. see Torres Bollo,
   Diego de.
Bologne, Francesco de. see Francesco de
   Bologne.
Boloix, Pablo. 6241, 20217
Bolona, Pablo. tr. 38431
Boloxi, Pablo. see Boloix, Pablo.
Bolscherezk, Russia. Chancery. 90063

Bolton, A. M. 105575, 105577
Bolton, Curtis E. tr. 83122-83123
Bolton, Edward Chichester. 6242
Bolton, Henry Carrington. 85096
Bolton, James. (6243)
Bolton, John. 6244
Bolton, Richard. 15051
Bolton, Robert, 1814-1877. 6245-6248, 103068-
   103069
Bolton, Samuel. 80205
Bolton, Thomas. 6249
Bolton, William. (6250)
Bolton, William C. USN defendant at court
   martial 6251
Bolton, Mass. Ecclesiastical Council, 1773.
   see Congregational Churches in Massa-
   chusetts. Ecclesiastical Council, 1773.
Bolton, Mass. Evangelical Church. 15454
Bolton, Mass. First Congregational Church.
   6252
Bolton, Mass. Many persons. pseud. Testi-
   monies. 360, 6254, 11968, 3d note after
   96741
Bolton chronicle. 2208
Boltwood, Lucius M. 6255, 36843, 83336
Bolzius, -------. 68369
Bom, J. 6256
Bomare, Jacques Christophe Valmont de. see
   Valmont de Bomare, Jacques Christophe,
   1731-1807.
Bomb search'd and found stuff'd with false
   ingredients. 66735
Bomb thrown amongst the Quakers. 66735,
   66737
Bombardement de Valparaiso. Destruction
   d'une ville sans defense. 6258
Bombardement de Valparaiso (documents
   officiels). 6257
Bombardement et entiere destruction de Grey-
   Town. 3681, 28797
Bombardment of Algiers. 83788
Bombardment of Valparaiso. 4915
Bon, Elisabeth de. 6259
Bon advis. 47832
Bon citoyen. pseud. Reflexions du bon citoyen.
   see Chachereau, -------.
Bon citoyen. pseud. Reponse a la justification.
   69716
Bon Hollandais. pseud. Second discours.
   78728
Bon negre, anecdote coloniale. 62676
Bon patriote. pseud. Lettre. 106045
Bona, F. de. 6261
Bonafous, Louis A. supposed author 19359-
   19361, 3d note after 100846
Bonafous, Matthieu. 6262-6263
Bonal, Maria de Acuna. see Acuna Bonal,
   Maria de.
Bonaparte, Charles Jules Laurent Lucien,
   Prince de Canino, 1803-1857. 6264-6267,
   16045, 104598
Bonaparte, Charlotte Julie. see Survillier,
   Charlotte Julie (Bonaparte) Comtesse de.
Bonaparte, Jerome Napoleon, 1805-1870.
   plaintiff (6268)
Bonaparte, Joseph. see Joseph Bonaparte,
   King of Spain, 1768-1844.
Bonaparte, Louis Lucien, Prince, 1813-1891.
   ed. 6269, 76904
Bonaparte in the West Indies. 42349, 91235
Bonaparte-Patterson marriage in 1803.
   74868
Bonaparte soldier, eight years in the armies.
   11339
Bonar, Horatius, 1808-1889. 27414
Bonassus. 89599

Bonaventura, Saint, 1221-1274. 76003-76005, 76105, 98737
Bonaventura, F. G. de San. see San Bonaventura, F. G. de.
Bonaventure, Saint see Bonaventura, Saint, 1221-1274.
Bonaventure, Marie de Saint. see Marie de Saint Bonaventure, mere superieure.
Bonaventure de Jesus, Marie de Saint. see Marie de Saint Bonaventure, mere superieure.
Bond, -----. (33569)
Bond, Alvan. 6270-6280
Bond, Benjamin. defendant 5368, (53066)
Bond, Beverley W. 86620
Bond, Francis. 9535
Bond, Henry. 6281-(6283)
Bond, J. Wesley. 6284
Bond, Sampson. 6285, (21671), (23054)
Bond, Thomas. 6286
Bond, William. 6287
Bond, William Cranch, 1759-1859. 6288
Bond, William Key, 1792-1864. 6289-6290
Bond. firm see Whitwell & Bond. firm and Whitwell, Bond & Co. firm
Bond and free. 62827
Bond or free? 62815
Bondage a moral institution. 6291, (24909)
Bondholders of the Indiana State Bank for 1844-1845. petitioners 34526
Bondigh verhael. (74830)
Bondmaid. 66832
Bondrye, Louis N. see Beaudry, Louis Napoleon, 1833-1892.
Bonds of the covenant. 46237
Bonds of the United States outstanding. 20940
Bondt, Jacob de, 1592-1631. 7588, 63028
Bondt, Nicolaus, M. D. 6293-6294
Bondt, Nicolaus, 1732-1790. 22012
Bonduel, Fl. S. J. 6295-6297
Bone, J. H. A. 6298
Bone to gnaw for "A senior." 101339
Bone to gnaw, for Grant Thorburn. 11196
Bone to gnaw, for the Democrats. 13875-13877, (13897), 14032, 64161, (78988), 85597, 86176
Bonelli, L. Hugh de. 6299, 19111
Boner, Robert. 66686
Bones, Brudder. pseud. Brudder Bones' book of stump speeches. see Scott, John F.
Bones of Joseph. 14504
Bonet, de Lates, 16th century. 74801
Boneti de latis hebzei medici pzouenzalis amuli astromici vtilitatum. 74801
Bonfield. 34776
Bonham, J. Ellis. 6300
Bonham, Milledge Luke, 1813-1890. 6301, 87558 see also South Carolina. Governor, 1862-1864 (Bonham)
Boniface, Jose Xavier. 75542-75543, 100745
Bonifacio, Alonso. 11431
Bonifacius. 46238, 46306
Bonilla, ----------. defendant 67646
Bonilla, ---------, fl. 1730. 36800
Bonilla, A. A. Montero Prieto de. see Montero Prieto de Bonilla, A. A.
Bonilla, Alejandro. 6302-6303
Bonilla, Joaquin Ignacio Ximenez de. see Ximenez de Bonilla, Joaquin Ignacio.
Bonilla, Jose Zambrano. see Zambrano Bonilla, Jose.
Bonilla, Joseph Prieto de. see Prieto de Bonilla, Joseph.
Bonilla, Juan J. 32756
Bonilla, M. Diez de. see Diez de Bonilla, M.
Bonilla y San Juan, Alexandro. 6305

Bonilla, Ozaeta y Aguirre, segundo 15 de Enero de la corte Mexicana. 36800
Bonin, Theodore. 3606-3607
Bonington, -------. 73935
Bonitz, J. A. ed. 45522
Bonnard, F. A. 76092
Bonnaventure de Jesus, Marie de Sainte. see Marie de Saint Bonaventure, mere superieure.
Bonne-Maison, Alonso de. see Buena-Maison, Alonso de.
Bonne negresse, anecdote coloniale. (62678)
Bonneau, Alexandre. (6309)-(6310), (75136)
Bonneau, Marcel. 14936
Bonnechose, Francois Paul Emile Boisnormand de, 1801-1875. 6311-6312
Bonnefoux, L. 6314-6316, 16077
Bonnefoux, Pierre Marie Joseph, Baron de, 1782-1885. 4218, 6313
Bonnell, George W. 6317
Bonnell, Joseph Gatch, ed. 84749
Bonnemain, A. 6318
Bonner, -------, fl. 1830. engr. 88546
Bonner, John, ca. 1643?-1726. cartographer 85489
Bonner, John, 1828-1899. (6319)
Bonner, John, fl. 1852. 6308
Bonner, T. D. 4265
Bonnet, Auguste. 6320
Bonnet, Edmond. 6321
Bonnet, Guy-Joseph. 6321-6322, 87122
Bonnet, J. Espirit. 6323-6325
Bonnet, Stede. defendant 6326, 1st note after 97284, 1st note after 96956
Bonneville, Madame -------. 103191
Bonneville, Madame -------. plaintiff (75956)
Bonneville, Benjamin Louis Eulalie de, 1796-1878. 35125-35128, 35195
Bonneville, C. de. incorrectly supposed author 1292, 6327
Bonneville, Nicolas de, 1760-1828. incorrectly supposed author 1292, 6327
Bonneville, Zacharie de Pazzi de. supposed author 1292, 6327
Bonnie blue flag. 42942, 83677
Bonniniere, Gustave Auguste de Beaumont de la. see Beaumont de la Bonniniere, Gustave Auguste de, 1802-1866.
Bonnifield, M. S. 52399
Bonnot de Mably, Gabriel. see Mably, Gabriel Bonnot de, 1709-1785.
Bonnycastle, Sir Richard H. 6328-6333
Bonoeil, John. 31988, 35676, 99883, 99886
Bonpland, Alexander. see Bonpland, Aime Jacques Alexandre, 1773-1858.
Bonpland, Aime Jacques Alexandre, 1773-1858. 6334, 33738, (33752)-33773, 96501
Bonplandt, A. see Bonpland, Aime Jacques Alexandre, 1773-1858.
Bonrepos, ------ de. 6335
Bont, J. 6336
Bontekoe, Willem Ysebrandsz, 1587-1647? 6337-6340, (40035), 67980, 68455, 74839-74840
Bontekou, Guillaume Isbrantsz. see Bontekoe, Willem Ysebrandsz, 1587-1647?
Bontekuhe van Horn, Willem Isbrandtz. see Bontekoe, Willem Ysebrandsz, 1587-1647?
Bontemantel, ------. 100761
Bontems. pseud? Nouveau Nabuchodonosor. 56061, (68086)
Bontius, Jacob. 6341, 32884, (57377), (63029), 98930
Bonus, Petrus. ed. 66471
Bonynge, -----. reporter 97630
Bonynge, Francis. 6342

Boogher's repository. 82725
Book about "the show business" in all its branches. 41804
Book and Pamphlet Society, Boston. 6343
Book and slavery irreconcilable. 6917
Book buyer. 6344
Book Club, Northampton, Mass. see Northampton Book Club, Northampton, Mass.
Book Club of California. publisher 99381
Book, design'd to be lodg'd and left in their hands. 46449
Book for all. 25609
Book for Batavians. 93750
Book for boys. By "Carleton." 14168
Book for boys. By William H. G. Kingston. (37902)
Book for every body. (14291)
Book for every farmer. (14291)
Book for every soldier's knapsack. 20510
Book for Massachusetts children, in familiar letters, for the use of families and schools. (45654)
Book for Massachusetts children, in familiar letters from a father. 31764
Book for New Englanders. 916, 11113
Book for New-Hampshire children. 31765
Book for railway men and travelers. 84247-84248
Book for the cemetery. 43316
Book for the children of Maine. 43913
Book for the "impending crisis!" (77472)
Book for the nation and times. 6345
Book for the patriot, statesman, and student. 59093
Book for the time, and for all times. 28156, 67376
Book for the times. 78346
Book for the times; or shots from the monitor. 28762
Book for the winter evening fireside. 80994
Book for the young and the old. 34051
Book for youth. 11541
Book founded on fact. 74247
Book-hunter. 9495
Book-hunter's library. (73290)
Book needed for the times. 101210
Book of Abraham. 83037, 83258 see also Pearl of great price.
Book of Abraham; containing a revelation made to him. 148, (55932)
Book of Abraham. Its authenticity established as a divine and ancient record. 83037
Book of Ahiman Rezon. 100473
Book of allegiance. 87449
Book of Alma. 83038
Book of American Indians. 34616
Book of American pastimes. 61316
Book of American songs. 59175
Book of anecdotes, and joker's knapsack. 6346
Book of anecdotes; or, the moral of history. (26054)
Book of brothers. 34064
Book of bubbles. (6347)
Book of Canadian and American poems. 83530
Book of charts. 79024
Book of chronicles of the city of Lexington. (40894)
Book of chronicles of the land of Ecnarf [i. e. France.] 32046
Book of chronicles, part I. 1376
Book of commandments and book of doctrine and covenants. 83290
Book of commandments, for the government of the Church of Christ. 50729, 83147-83151, 83208
Book of commerce by sea and land. 6348

Book of common prayer. 86305
Book of common prayer, according to the use of the Church of England. 6352
Book of common prayer, . . . according to the use of the Protestant Episcopal Church in the United States of America. 65000
Book of common prayer, and administration of the sacraments, and other rites and ceremonies as revised and proposed to the use of the Protestant Episcopal Church. 6349
Book of common prayer, and administration of the sacraments, and other rites and ceremonies of the church, according to the use of the Church of England: together with a collection of occasional prayers. 6351
Book of common-prayer, and administration of the sacraments. And other rites and ceremonies of the church, according to the use of the Church of England. Together with the psalter. 64998-(64999)
Book of common prayer, and administration of the sacraments, and other rites and ceremonies of the church, according to the use of the Protestant Episcopal Church in the United States of America. 6350
Book of common prayer, and administration of the sacraments and other rites and ceremonies of the church . . . in the Confederate States of America. 6354
Book of common prayer, and selections from the psalms and hymns. 6353
Book of common prayer, containing a form of public worship. 86298
Book of common prayer, . . . of the Protestant Episcopal Church in the United States of America. 49838
Book of common prayer of the Reformed Episcopal Church compared with that of the Protestant Episcopal Church. 83518
Book of consolation for those who mourn. 28900
Book of constitutions, and the constitution, by-laws, and general regulations of the Grand Lodge of Iowa. 58975
Book of constitutions of Missouri. 49596
Book of constitutions of the Grand Lodge of Ancient Freemasons of South Carolina. (43445), 87838
Book of copperheads. 6356, 39962
Book of covenants. 94026
Book of days. 11801
Book of discipline agreed on by the Yearly Meeting of Friends for New-England. 52613
Book of doctrine and covenants. (50732), 80134, 83160, 83176, 83179-83180, 83184, 83187, 83190, 83195, 83199, 83202, 83205, 83206, 83210, 83212, 83232-83234, 83290
Book of doctrine & covenants, of the Church of Jesus Christ of Latter-Day Saints. 83155, 83157-83159
Book of doctrine and covenants, of the Church of Jesus Christ of Latter-Day Saints. 83160-83167, 83175
Book of Enos. 83038
Book of Esther and Moroni. 83038
Book of evergreens. 32871
Book of exhibition. (45223)
Book of Exodus in Micmac. 67765
Book of facts, incidents, and results. 50349
Book of fruits. (44353)

Book of general lawes and libertyes concerning the inhabitants of the Massachusetts. (45653)

Book of general reference. 48937

Book of Genesis, and a part of the psalms. 18292

Book of Genesis, Psalms, and Isaiah. (28537)

Book of Genesis, translated into the Esquimaux language. 22852

Book of geography shewing all the empires, monarchies, kingdoms, regions, dominions, principalities, and countries in the whole world. (79025)

Book of good examples. (26054)

Book of government and law. 27922

Book of grievances. 103970

Book of Hadborim and Maazim. (40893)

Book of Helaman. 83038

Book of home beauty. 37985

Book of human nature. 93754

Book of illustrious mechanics. (25274)

Book of Indian records for their lands. 53388, 63488

Book of Jacob. 83038

Book of Jarom. 83038

Book of John. 44123

Book of Judgment. 85540

Book of knaves. 25295

Book of knowledge. 59049

Book of lamentations. 103337

Book of laws. 87060

Book of legal forms and law manual. 71152

Book of legal forms, for the legal transaction of business. 71151

Book of Lehi. 83038

Book of literature. 27913

Book of Matthew translated into the Maliseet language. 44123

Book of meetings. 86038

Book of Mormon. Danish. 83115-83119

Book of Mormon. Dutch. 83120-83121

Book of Mormon. French. 83122-83123

Book of Mormon. English. 31922, 50748, 58915, 64951, 70628, 80134, 83038-83070, 83072-83114, 83152, 83176, 83209, 83213, 83251, 83270, 83283

Book of Mormon. German. 83124-83130

Book of Mormon. Hawaiian. 83131-83133

Book of Mormon. Hebrew. 83146

Book of Mormon. Hindostani. 83146

Book of Mormon. Italian. 83134

Book of Mormon. Japanese. 83135

Book of Mormon. Maori. 83136-83137

Book of Mormon. Samoan. 83138

Book of Mormon. Spanish. 83139-83141

Book of Mormon. Swedish. 83142-83143

Book of Mormon. Tahitian. 83144

Book of Mormon. Turkish. 83145

Book of Mormon. Welsh. 83146

Book of Mormon, translated into the Japanese language. 83135

Book of Mormon, translated into the Turkish language. 83145

Book of Mosiah. 83038

Book of my lady. 81193

Book of nature unfolded. 106069

Book of Nephi. 83038

Book of Niagara Falls. By Horatio A. Parsons. 58883

Book of Niagara Falls. [By Oliver Gray Steele.] 91137, 91140

Book of nullification. 6357, 56313, note after 87802, note after 89146

Book of Omni. 83038

Book of oratory. 44770

Book of Peace. 6358

Book of poems. 8576

Book of poems on the rising glory of the American empire. 94439

Book of psalmes with the new English translation. (66452)

Book of psalmody. 101196

Book of psalms, in a translation exactly conformed unto the original. 46471

Book of psalms, in the Dakota language. 71342

Book of psalms translated into the Esquimaux-language. 22868

Book of psalms with the new English translation. 66451

Book of public worship. 52575

Book of records of the town of Southampton. 88230

Book of reference for quartermasters. 36022

Book of reference, for regular and volunteer officers and soldiers of the Confederate States Army. 15241

Book of religions. 31065

Book of retrospections & anticipations. 6554, 79004, note after 102419

Book of revelations. 6359, 70160, 103445

Book of rhymes. 71423

Book of Saint Nicholas. (59191)

Book of savings. 79913

Book of stump speeches. 78316

Book of the army. (26024)

Book of the chronicles of Isaac the Scribe. 86610

Book of the colonies. 26025

Book of the constitution. 6360, 104198

Book of the continuation of forreign [sic] passages. (6361)

Book of the drama. 64987

Book of the first American Chess Congress. 24534

Book of the First Church of Christ, in Middleborough. 48224

Book of the general laws for the people within the jurisdiction of Connecticut. 15754

Book of the general laws of the inhabitants of the jurisdiction of New-Plimouth. (53384)-(53385)

Book of the great railway celebrations of 1857. 84846

Book of the heart. 49677

Book of the Hudson. (35138)

Book of the Indians of North America. 20868, 80315

Book of the Indians of North America; illustrating their manners. (26026)

Book of the law. Chapter I. The Decalogue. 92677

Book of the law of the Lord. 83147, 92675-92676, 92678-92680

Book of the Lockes. 41729

Book of the navy. 26027

Book of the ocean or sea-cocks. 42392

Book of the prophet Stephen, son of Douglas. 6362, 103445

Book of the revelation of Jesus Christ. 72680

Book of the revelation of Jesus Christ, which God gave unto Him. 72681

Book of the signers. 8395, 76403

Book of the spring. 55522

Book of the telegraph, Boston. 18810

Book of the United States, exhibiting its geography, 6363, 47439

Book of the United States, geographical, political, historical. 94243, 97927

Book of the world. 24485

Book of the Younger Nephi. 83038

Book of truth. 6364

Book of trade. 6365

Book of vagaries. 59192
Book of verses. 70830
Book of wealth. 33895
Book on capital and labor. 84523
Book I. Autobiography, with appendix. (35882)
Book peculiarly adapted to the times. 44252
Book Society, New York. see New-York Book Society.
Book the second . . . gunnery. 30275
Book trade, a monthly literary journal. 73097
Book Trade Association of the City of Philadelphia. 66532-66533
Bookbuyer's almanac. 55871
Bookbuyer's manual. 66801
Bookes and divers epistles of that faithful servant of the Lord, Josiah Coale. 13814
Books. 106123
Books added in . . . 1846 [to the Canadian Parliamentary Library.] 10396
Books added [to the Boston Athenaeum] since . . . 1827. 6590
Books added to the library since the year 1741. 61787
Books for sale, at William Young's book and stationery store. 106122
Books for the million! 91284
Books in the Philomathean Society Library, in Union College. 97797
Books lately printed and to be sold by William Bradford in Philadelphia, 1692. 37217, (37225)
Books more particularly fitted to the use of the several classes of catechumens. 7475
Books of Genesis, Psalms and Acts. 44123
Books of Joshua, Judges, and Ruth. 12864
Books of the chronicles of the land of Georgia. 27016
Books, places, and people. 49752
Books printed and sold by T. Sowle. 96142
Books printed by Humphrey Moseley. 67561
Books printed by Peter Cole. 63332
Books printed for J. Almon in Piccadilly. 64832
Books printed for . . . Joseph Watts. 67599
Books published and sold by W. W. Woodward. 105169A
Books relating to America. 70887
Books relating to America. 1493-1700. 70881
Books relating to America. 1493-1700. Supplement. 70882
Books to be sold by William Bradford in Philadelphia. (37223), 96113
Bookseller to the reader. 82865
Booksellers' advertiser. (6366)
Booksellers' and stationers' trade list. 6368
Booksellers' Company of Philadelphia. 61431
Booksellers' medium and publisher's advertiser. 73097
Booksellers to the town of Boston. see Boston. Booksellers.
Booksellers of the town of Boston, unwilling to impose on the publick by printing their private disputes in the newspapers. 95966
Booksellers' trade list and publisher's register. 6367
Boole, William H. 6369
Boon, Joseph. see Boone, Joseph.
Boon voyage intended for the sea. 100486
Boone, Daniel, 1734-1820. (6370), 24336-24338, 34355, 40997, 48166, 82975-82976
Boone, H. H. 30396
Boone, Joseph. petitioner 10967, 87359, 87805

Boone, Nicholas. 6375, 22368, (66440)
Boone, Thomas. (26151), (27056), 36718, note after 97347 see also South Carolina (Colony) Governor, 1761-1765 (Boone)
Boone, Thomas. petitioner 93593, 3d note after 105598-9 [sic]
Boone, W. T. 6376
Boone County, Ky. Court. 96852
Boorman, James. (6378), 33537
Boorne, Jesse. defendant 6379-6380, 31054, 96830-96831, 101012
Boorne, Stephen. defendant 6379-6380, 31054, 96830-96831, 101012
Boot, Thomas. 64572
Boot and shoe manufacturer's assistant and guide. 71096
Boot and shoe trade. 6382
Boot and Shoemakers of Philadelphia. defendants (41697), note before 96946
Boot on the other leg. (6381)
Booth, -------, plaintiff 26130
Booth, Abraham. 6383
Booth, David B. 15763
Booth, James. 52569 see also Delaware. Convention, Newcastle, 1776. Clerk.
Booth, James C. (6384)-6386
Booth, James C. defendant (43135)
Booth, John Wilkes, 1838-1865. 6387
Booth, John Wilkes, 1838-1865. supposed author 41225
Booth, Mary L. 6389-6391
Booth, Mary L. tr. 14065-14066, 26726, 26730, 38440, 44469
Booth, Robert Russell. 6392-6393
Booth, Samuel. defendant 6326, 1st note after 97284, 1st note after 96956
Booth, S. M. 83755
Booth, Sherman M. 6394-6395
Booth, Walter, 1791-1870. 6396
Boothbay, Mass. petitioners (61266)
Bootmaker of Fifth Avenue. 65376
Boott Cotton Mills, Boston. firm 6397
Boquette, ------ de la. 71995
Bor, Pieter Christiaanszoon, 1559-1635. 6398
Borandon, Saint. see Brendan, of Clonfert, Saint, 484-577.
Borbazza, Andrea. (51557)
Borch, Gerhard Frederik. 5397, 6399-6400
Borchardt, S. 7532, note after 92013
Borcke, Heros von. 6401
Borda, Andres de. see Bordas, Andres de.
Borda, Cypriano Geronimo Calatayud y. see Calatayud y Borda, Cypriano Geronimo.
Borda, Jean Charles de, 1733-1799. 98960
Borda, Jose Cornelio. (6503)
Borda, Leopoldo. tr. 96068
Borda y Orosco, ------. (6404)
Bordas, Andres de. (6402), 86550
Borde, ------ de la. see La Borde, ---, Sieur de.
Borde, Jean Benjamin de la. see La Borde, Jean Benjamin de.
Borde, M. la. see La Borde, M.
Bordeaux, France. Academie Royale des Sciences. see Academie Royale des Sciences de Bordeaux.
Bordeaux, France. Maire et Officiers Municipaux. (6405)
Bordeaux, France. Negocians. 56472
Bordeaux, France. Parlement. (40680)
Borden, Luther M. defendant 29889, 42729, 70560, 70732
Borden, Nathaniel B. 6406, 23742
Borden, Simeon. 6407-6408, (46053)
Borden, T. 6409

Bordentown, N. J. College. see Bordentown
Female College, Bordentown, N. J.
Bordentown, N. J. Spring-Villa Seminary for
Young Ladies. see Spring-Villa
Seminary for Young Ladies, Bordentown,
N. J.
Bordentown Female College, Bordentown, N. J.
6410
Border adventures. 3904
Border and bastile. 39351
Border beagles. 81194-81195, (81279)
Border chief. 39447
Border feud. (36220)
Border methodism and border slavery. (42988)
Border reminiscences. 44511
Border ruffian code in Kansas. 6411, 37020
Border spy. (31118)
Border state co-operation. 8348
Border states. (37407)
Border states; their power and duty. (6412),
37406
Border warfare of New-York during the revolu-
tion. 10275-10276
Border wars of the American revolution.
92132
Border wars of the west. 26028
Borderers. 16416, (16551), note after 102637
Bordier, Jacques. 6413, 39995, note after
69259
Bordillon, -----. 38608
Bordley, John Beale. (6414)-6416, 45373,
(58785), (81583), note after 93609
Bordley, John Beale. supposed author 57275,
623196, 93803, 106010
Bordman, William. 39374
Bordone, Benedetto. 6417-6421, (63177)
Bordonova, S. (6422)
Bord's Rome and Oneida County business
directory. 73019
Bore, ----. (6423)
Boreas. pseud. Slave representation. (6424)
Boreel Hofman, J. L. V. (6425)
Borger-Vennen. 18724
Borges, Abilio Cesar. 6426
Borges de Barros, Joao. see Barros, Joao
Borges de.
Borghi, -------. tr. 91081
Borgman, C. 6427
Borgne, Jeanne Francois le. see Le Borgne,
Jeanne Francois.
Borja, Francisco de, Saint, 1510-1572. 94819
Borja, Rodrigo Lanzol y. see Alexander VI,
Pope, 1431?-1503.
Borja y Aragon, Francisco de, Principe de
Esquilache, 1582-1658. (41092) see also
Peru (Viceroyalty) Virrey, 1615-1621
(Borja y Aragon)
Borja y Velasco, Gaspar de, Abp. 86443
see also Seville (Archdiocese) Arch-
bishop (Borja y Velasco)
Borland, Francis. supposed author 6428,
47571
Borland, Solon. (6429)-(6430)
Borneck, Adolar. (6431)
Bornecque, J. tr. 77534
Borough, Chr. 66686
Borrestein, D. A. 47862
Borrero, Eugenio. 6432
Borrero, Eusebio. 6432, 56277 see also
Colombia. Secretaria de Relaciones
Esteriores.
Borrett, George Tuthill. (6433)
Borrowed notes for home circulation. 32384

Borrowed plumes. 62916
Borrowers at the Worcester Bank will in
future be subjected to the following
regulations. 105382
Borscht, Joseph. tr. 11659
Borshardt, S. 7532
Borsieri, G. tr. 7165
Borthwick, J. Douglas. 6434-6436
Borthwick, Peter, 1804-1852. 38094, 95496-
95497, 95504, 96400
Bory, -----. 56581
Bory, Gabriel de. (6437), 22927, 47554
Bory de Saint Vincent, Jean Baptiste Georges,
1778?-1846. 6438, 21353, (23767),
75235
Bos or Bosch, in latin Sylvanius, Lambertus
van den. (6439)-6442, 6453, 7407, note
after 98470
Bosanquet, Charles. 6443-6444, 40364, 40553,
89293, 102847-102848
Bosc, ------. 776, 48702
Boscana, Geronimo. (10031), 72048
Boscawen, Edward, 1711-1761. 36727, 42175
Boscawen, N. H. 65442
Boscawen, N. H. Ecclesiastical Council, 1833.
see Congregational Churches in New
Hampshire. Ecclesiastical Council,
Boscawen, 1833.
Boscawen, N. H. Second Congregational
Church. 7779
Boscawen Moral Society. 6445
Bosch, ------ van den, fl. 1822. 6453, 1st
note after 93850
Bosch, D. W. 6447
Bosch, G. B. 6448-(6449)
Bosch, J. van den. 6454
Bosch, L. van. tr. 31472
Bosch, Lambertus van den. see Bos or
Bosch, in latin Sylvanius, Lambertus van
den.
Bosch, P. C. 5038
Bosch Spencer, Guillaume Henri. 6451-(6452),
note after 89323
Bosche, Eduard Theodor. 6450
Bosco, Joannes de Sacro. see Sacro Bosco,
Joannes de, fl. 1230.
Bosley, John. 34461
Bosque, --------, Sieur. (6455)
Bosque, ------ du. see Du Bosque, -------.
Bosquejo biografico de los generales Itrubide
y Teran. 59340
Bosquejo biografico del general D. Jose de
San Martin. 29340
Bosquejo de la Europa y de la America en
1900. 86234
Bosquejo de la historia civil y politica de
Buenos Ayres. (9590)
Bosquejo de la historia de los Incas. 74955
Bosquejo de la historia eclesiastica para el
Colegio de Na. Sa. de Guadalupe.
(75582)
Bosquejo de la historia militar de Venezuela.
2430
Bosquejo de la marcha de la republica y de la
influencia militar en sus destinos. (6457),
12746, (43796)
Bosquejo de la republica de Costa Rica. 49879
Bosquejo de la republica de los Estados Unidos
de Norte-America. 98364
Bosquejo de los viajes aereos de Eugenio
Robertson. 72286
Bosquejo del comercio en esclavos. 6458
Bosquejo del heroismo del Exmo. Senor Baylio
Fr. D. Antonio Maria Bucareli y Ursua.
75607, note after 98317-98318

Bosquejo historico de la constitucion del
gobierno de Chile. 39148
Bosquejo, historico de la revolucion de tres
dias. 6459
Bosquejo historico de las revoluciones de
Centro-America. 45017
Bosquejo historico e documentado das operacoes
militares da provincia do Rio Grande do
Sul. 88765
Bosquejo ligerisimo de la revolucion de Mejico.
6456, 1st note after 72267, 98947
Bosquejo politico e estadistico de Nicaragua.
76932
Bosquejo de la vida, costumbres, caracter y
aparencia personal de Carlos S. Stratton.
92730
Bosquet, John le. see Le Bosquet, John.
Boss, Peter. defendant 37203, (37226), 1st
note after 96931, 2d note after 96956,
2d note after 97284
"Boss" Richards. pseud. see Richards,
"Boss." pseud.
Bossange, Hector. 6460, 23541
Bossart, Johann Jakob. ed. and tr. (57152)
Bossay, P. A. Poulain de. see Poulain de
Bossay, P. A.
Bossert, G. 6461
Bosshard, H. ed. 1621
Bossi, Bartolome. 6462
Bossi, Luigi. (6463)-6464
Bossu, N. 6465-6470, 25133, 25135
Bossy, Chavalier. see Bossi, Luigi.
Bossy, Monsieur. see Bossu, N.
Bost, A. tr. 6019
Bosthwick, D. 771
Bostick, --------. 8984
Boston, --------, fl. 1749. (17673)
Boston, Patience, d. 1735. 6471-6472
Boston. 4471A, 6478, 6518, 6554, 6566, 6714,
6736, 6737, 6747, 6759, 6770, 6785,
12676, (13297), (23273), 79004, 78674,
79886, 82805, 82807, 93698, 94139, note
after 97575, 101477-101478
Boston. see also East Boston, Mass.
Boston. defendant 72744, 82581, 93643
Boston. petitioners 6498, 6782, 6785
Boston. Africans. see Africans Living in
Boston.
Boston. Agricultural Meeting, 1840. see
Agricultural Meeting, Boston, 1840.
Boston. 'America' Testimonial, 1895. see
'America' Testimonial, Boston, 1895.
Boston. American Congregational Association.
see American Congregational Associa-
tion, Boston.
Boston. American Institute of Instruction.
see American Institute of Instruction.
Boston. American Tract Society. see
American Tract Society, Boston.
Boston. American Unitarian Association. see
American Unitarian Association.
Boston. Ancient and Honorable Artillery
Company. see Massachusetts. Ancient
and Honorable Artillery Company.
Boston. Ancient and Most Benevolent Order
of the Friendly Sons of St. Patrict. see
Ancient and Most Benevolent Order of
the Friendly Brothers of St. Patrick,
Boston.
Boston. Annual Visiting Committee of the
Public Schools. see Boston. Public
Schools. Annual Visiting Committee.
Boston. Anti-masonic Meeting, 1836. see
Anti-masonic Party. Massachusetts.
Boston.

Boston. Anti-masonic State Covention, 1829.
see Anti-masonic State Convention of
Massachusetts, Boston. 1829.
Boston. Anti-masonic State Convention, 1830.
see Anti-masonic State Convention of
Massachusetts, Boston, 1830.
Boston. Anti-masonic State Convention, 1831.
see Anti-masonic State Convention of
Massachusetts, Boston, 1831.
Boston. Anti-sabbath Convention, 1848. see
Anti-sabbath Convention, Boston, 1848.
Boston. Anti-slavery Convention of American
Women, 1838-1839. see Anti-slavery
Convention of American Women, Boston,
1838-1839.
Boston. Anti-slavery Meeting, 1855. 6500
Boston. Arlington Street Church. 6642, 11924,
11926, 13689, 79324
Boston. Arlington Street Church. Association
for Benevolent Purposes. Committee.
30759
Boston. Arlington Street Church. Proprietors.
defendants 13689
Boston. Artillery Company. see Massachu-
setts. Ancient and Honorable Artillery
Company.
Boston. Assembly of Divines, 1657. see
Convention of Congregational Ministers in
Massachusetts, Boston, 1657.
Boston. Assembly Room, Federal Street.
93359
Boston. Assembly of Pastors of Churches in
New England, 1743. 16199, 94918, 4th
note after 103650 see also Congrega-
tional Churches in New England.
Boston. Assessing Department. 6615, 6617-
6620, 6634
Boston. Associated Pastors. see Congrega-
tional Churches in Massachusetts.
Boston Association.
Boston. Association of Citizens, To Erect a
Monument in Honor of Gen. George
Washington. see Washington Monument
Association, Boston.
Boston. Association of Delegates From the
Benevolent Societies. see Association of
Delegates From the Benevolent Societies
of Boston.
Boston. Association of Franklin Medal Scholars.
see Association of Franklin Medal
Scholars, Boston.
Boston. Association of Laymen. see Associa-
tion of Laymen, Boston.
Boston. Association of School Masters. see
Association of Boston School Masters.
Boston. Bakers. petitioners 103404
Boston. Baldwin Place Baptist Church. 6636
Boston. Bank of Mutual Redemption. see
Bank of Mutual Redemption, Boston.
Boston. Baptist Auxiliary Education Society.
see Baptist Auxiliary Education Society,
Boston.
Boston. Baptist Church. 93594
Boston. Bethel Temperance Society. see
Bethel Temperance Society, Boston.
Boston. Board of Aldermen. 6614
Boston. Board of Health. see Boston. Health
Department.
Boston. Board of Trade. 3911, 6581-6582,
6584-6587, 17115, 20807, 74734, note
after 90850
Boston. Board of Trade. Committee on the
Internal Revenue Bill. 34920

Boston. Board of Trade. Committee "To Make . . . Investigation Into the Causes of the Recent Monetary Difficulties and Mercantile Embarrassments." 6585

Boston. Board of Trade. Committee to Whom was Referred the Subject of Steam Communication Between Boston and New Orleans. 53312

Boston. Board of Trade. Committee Upon the Cotton Tax. 6584, 17129

Boston. Board of Trade. Secretary. 74734 see also Sabine, Lorenzo.

Boston. Board of Trade. Special Committee on the Prosecution of Franklin W. Smith by the United States Navy Department. (82573)

Boston. Board of Trade. Special Committee on the Reciprocity Treaty. (6582)

Boston. Book and Pamphlet Society. see Book and Pamphlet Society, Boston.

Boston. Booksellers. 11486, 95966

Boston. Boott Cotton Mills. see Boott Cotton Mills, Boston.

Boston. Bostonian Society. see Bostonian Society.

Boston. Bowditch Library. Proprietors. 7012

Boston. Bowdoin Street Church. 6637, 18137

Boston. Bowdoin Street Young Man's Peace Society. see Bowdoin Street Young Man's Peace Society, Boston.

Boston. Brothers of St. Patrick. see Ancient and Most Benevolent Order of the Friendly Brothers of St. Patrick, Boston.

Boston. Burns Club. see Burns Club of Boston.

Boston. Caledonia Division, No. 90, Sons of Temperance. see Sons of Temperance of North America. Massachusetts. Caledonia Division, No. 90, Boston.

Boston. Cape Cod Association. see Cape Cod Association in Boston.

Boston. Celebration of the Eighty-Third Anniversary of American Independence, 1859. 93699-93700

Boston. Censors. 6626

Boston. Census, 1845. 6625

Boston. Census, 1850. 6614

Boston. Census, 1855. 6626

Boston. Certain Merchants and Other Inhabitants. see Boston. Citizens.

Boston. Chamber of Commerce. 6628, 69754

Boston. Chapman Hall School. 12002A

Boston. Charles Street Baptist Church. 6638

Boston. Charter. (6629)-6631, 6633, 6690, 6718-6719, 6721-6722

Boston. Chauncy Hall School. 12340-12341, 18120, 18122

Boston. Chauncy Street Church. see Boston. First Church.

Boston. Chauncy Society for Mutual Improvement. see Chauncy Society for Mutual Improvement, Boston.

Boston. Cheap Postage Association. see Cheap Postage Association, Boston.

Boston. Christ Church. (6639)

Boston. Christ Church. Vestry. (6639)

Boston. Church of the Advent. 6440, 17276

Boston. Church of the Advent. Rector. 21663, 88581 see also Southgate, Horatio, 1812-1894.

Boston. Church of the Disciples. 13413

Boston. Church of the Holy Cross. Apostolic Vice-Regent. 6838

Boston. Church Reading Room. 66133

Boston. Citizens. 6473-6474, 9708, 23449, 27637, 46651, 46722, 46731-46732, 52597, 58359, (65323), 69743, note after 70346, 81758, 82060, 92350, 96754

Boston. Citizens. petitioners 6474, (6527)-6528, 23449, 39754, 47705-47707, (47659), (50626), 82014, 95946, 102319

Boston. Citizens. Committee For Considering the Recent Case of Kidnapping, 1846. 6473

Boston. Citizens. Committee to Prepare the Memorial. Chairman. (6927), 82014, 102319 see also Webster, Daniel, 1782-1852.

Boston. Citizens' Committee Opposed to a Further Increase of Duties on Importations, 1827. see Boston. Committee of Citizens Opposed to a Further Increase of Duties on Importations, 1827.

Boston. Citizens Favorable To a Revision of the Laws in Relation to Debtor and Creditor. see Society for the Promotion of the Rights and Interests of Bona Fide Creditors, and the Benefit and Relief of Honest Debtors, Boston.

Boston. City Council. 3942-(3943), 6330, 6718, 6749, 6768, (9069), 12513, (23273), 41228, 67233, 1st note after 94186, 104803

Boston. City Council. petitioners (67238)

Boston. City Council. Committee of Both Branches. 6702

Boston. City Council. Committee on Census of 1845. 6625

Boston. City Council. Committee on Census of 1850. 12676

Boston. City Council. Committee on the Library. 6759

Boston. City Council. Complimentary Banquet to Rear Admiral Lessoffsky and the Officers of the Russian Fleet, 1864. 40213

Boston. City Council. Joint Committee on Common and Public Grounds. 6754, (6755)

Boston. City Council. Joint Committee on Public Lands. see Boston. City Council. Joint Committee on Common and Public Grounds.

Boston. City Council. Joint Committee to Revise the City Charter. 6722

Boston. City Council. Joint Special Committee on Back Bay Streets. 6578

Boston. City Council. Joint Special Committee on Census of 1855. 6626

Boston. City Council. Joint Special Committee on the Petition of Albert Bowker, and Others. 78515

Boston. City Council. Joint Standing Committee on the Harbor. 6725

Boston. City Hall. 6684, 6691

Boston. City Hospital. (6692)-6693

Boston. City Hospital. Trustees. (6693)

Boston. City Missionary. 13648 see also Cleveland, Charles.

Boston. City Physician. see Boston. Health Department. City Physician.

Boston. City Registrar. see Boston. Registry Department.

Boston. City Solicitor's Office. 35406, 69886

Boston. Club. see Association of Laymen, Boston.

Boston. Cochituate Water Board. 6783

Boston. Colored Citizens. petitioners 84410

Boston. Comer's Commercial College. see Comer's Commercial College, Boston.

Boston. Commissioners Appointed on the Union of Roxbury and Boston. see Commissioners Appointed By the City Councils of the Cities of Roxbury and Boston, Respectively, On the Union of the Two Cities Under One Municipal Government.

Boston. Commissioners For the Library. see Boston. Public Library. Commissioners.

Boston. Commissioners of the Customs. see Gt. Brit. Customs Commissioners, Boston.

Boston. Commissioners on Bringing Water of Long Pond into the City. 6785

Boston. Commissioners to Devise a Plan for Supplying the City with Pure Water. 6785

Boston. Commissioners to Examine the Sources From Which Pure Water May be Obtained. 6785

Boston. Committee in Favor of the Union of Boston and Roxbury. see Committee in Favor of the Union of Boston and Roxbury.

Boston. Committee of Arrangements for the Visit of the President of the United States, 1789. 101875-101876

Boston. Committee of Citizens Opposed to a Further Increase of Duties on Importations, 1827. 23363, 27637, 39753, (39756), (56590), 1st note after 69741, 70258, 92843

Boston. Committee of Correspondence. 104294

Boston. Committee of Delegates From the Benevolent Societies of Boston. see Committee of Delegates From the Benevolent Societies of Boston.

Boston. Committee of Merchants and Manufacturers, On the Proposed Tariff, 1824. 69807, 2d note after 95623

Boston. Committee of Merchants and Others, 1820. 28386, 60953 see also Gray, Francis Calley, 1790-1856. Perkins, James. Webster, Daniel, 1782-1852.

Boston. Committee of One Hundred and Fifty. 1469, 6477

Boston. Committee of the Inhabitants on the Rights of the Colonists, 1772. see Boston. Citizens.

Boston. Committee of Valuation. see Boston. Assessing Department.

Boston. Committee on a System of Municipal Government, 1821. 6716

Boston. Committee on Aid to Complete the Bytown and Prescott Railway. 17398

Boston. Committee on Amendments to the City Charter. 6721

Boston. Committee on Spiritualism, 1857. see Committee on Spiritualism, Boston, 1857.

Boston. Committee on the Death of General Lafayette, 1834. 38583

Boston. Committee on the Petition of Isaac P. Davis and Others. 6748, 69912

Boston. Committee on Working Men. see Committee on the Working Men of Boston.

Boston. Committee to Adopt Such Measures as may Indicate the Public Sensibility on the Late Afflictive Event of the Death of General George Washington. 101782

Boston. Committee to Consider the Institution Proposed by Miss Emma Hardinge, for Homeless and Outcast Women. 90730

Boston. Committee to Prepare "A Short Narrative of the Horrid Massacre in Boston," 1770. 6739, 6741, 80668-80673, 101479 see also Bowdoin, James.

Pemberton, Samuel. Warren, Joseph, 1741-1775.

Boston. Committee to Revise the City Charter. 6632

Boston. Committee to Take Into Consideration the Expediency of Making an Alteration to the Municipal Government of the Town. 6720

Boston. Common Council. 6537, 6690-6691

Boston. Common Council. Committee on Internal Health. 6634

Boston. Common Council. Standing Committee on the House of Reformation. 6727

Boston. Congregational Board of Publication. see Congregational Board of Publication, Boston.

Boston. Congregational Education Society. see Congregational Education Society, Boston.

Boston. Congregational House. 65767

Boston. Congregational Library Association. see American Congregational Association, Boston.

Boston. Connecticut Association Festival, 1857. see Connecticut Association, Massachusetts. Festival, Boston, 1857.

Boston. Constitutional Convention, 1853. see Massachusetts. Constitutional Convention, Boston. 1853.

Boston. Constitutional Meeting, 1850. 6545

Boston. Consumptives' Home. (17876)

Boston. Convention, 1779. see Massachusetts. Convention, Boston, 1779.

Boston. Convention, 1788. see Massachusetts. Convention, Boston, 1788.

Boston. Convention, 1820. see Massachusetts. Convention, Boston, 1820.

Boston. Convention of Congregational Ministers of Massachusetts, 1657. see Convention of Congregational Ministers of Massachusetts, Boston, 1657.

Boston. Convention of Congregational Ministers of Massachusetts, 1697. see Convention of Congregational Ministers of Massachusetts, Boston, 1697.

Boston. Convention of Congregational Ministers of Massachusetts, 1743. see Convention of Congregational Ministers of Massachusetts, Boston, 1743.

Boston. Convention of Congregational Ministers of Massachusetts, 1773. see Convention of Congregational Ministers of Massachusetts, Boston, 1773.

Boston. Convention of Congregational Ministers of Massachusetts, 1795. see Convention of Congregational Ministers of Massachusetts, Boston, 1773.

Boston. Convention of Congregational Ministers of Massachusetts, 1799. see Convention of Congregational Ministers of Massachusetts, Boston, 1799.

Boston. Convention of Congregational Ministers of Massachusetts, 1830. see Convention of Congregational Ministers of Massachusetts, Boston, 1830.

Boston. Convention of Congregational Ministers of Massachusetts, 1849. see Convention of Congregational Ministers of Massachusetts, Boston, 1849.

Boston. Convention of Congregational Ministers of Massachusetts, 1860. see Convention of Congregational Ministers of Massachusetts, Boston, 1860.

Boston. Convention of Congregational Ministers of New England, 1743. see Boston. Assembly of Pastors of Churches in New England, 1743.

Boston. Convention of Congregational Ministers of New England, 1745. see Convention of Congregational Ministers of New England, Boston, 1745.
Boston. Convention of Ministers, 1759. see Convention of Congregational Ministers, Boston. 1759.
Boston. Convention of Delegates From Several of the New England States, 1780. 6543
Boston. Convention of Delegates on Proposed Annexation of Texas, 1845. 45939, 65780, note after 95109
Boston. Convention of New England States, 1780. see Boston. Convention of Delegates from Several of the New England States, 1780.
Boston. Convention of the Friends of American Industry, 1832. see Friends of Domestic Industry.
Boston. Convention of the Northern Lines of Railway, 1850-1851. see Convention of the Northern Lines of Railway, Boston, 1850-1851.
Boston. Convention of the People of Massachusetts, 1862. see People's Convention, Boston, 1862.
Boston. Convention on the Proposed Annexation of Texas, 1845. see Boston. Convention of Delegates on Proposed Annexation of Texas, 1845.
Boston. Convention to Improve the Condition of the Indians in the United States, 1861. see Convention to Improve the Condition of the Indians in the United States, Boston, 1861.
Boston. Court. (16326), (30359), 38091, 67085-67086, 79011, (79012) see also Boston. Superior Court.
Boston. Customs House. see Gt. Brit. Customs House, Boston.
Boston. Daniel Webster Statue. 102321
Boston. Democratic Legislative Convention, 1840. see Democratic Legislative Convention, Boston. 1840.
Boston. Democratic Party Convention, 1860. see Democratic Party. Massachusetts. Convention, Boston, 1860.
Boston. Dinner Given to Charles Dickens, 1842. see Dinner Given to Charles Dickens, Boston, 1842.
Boston. Dinner, July 5, 1858. 32614
Boston. Divers of the Gentry, Merchants, and Others. see Boston. Citizens.
Boston. Eastern Yacht Club. see Eastern Yacht Club, Boston.
Boston. Ecclesiastical Council, 1723. see Congregational Churches in Massachusetts. Ecclesiastical Council, Boston, 1723.
Boston. Ecclesiastical Council, 1841. see Congregational Churches in Massachusetts. Ecclesiastical Council, Boston, 1841.
Boston. Ecclesiastical Council, 1866. see Congregational Churches in Massachusetts. Ecclesiastical Council, Boston, 1866.
Boston. Education Society of the Young Men. see Education Society of the Young Men of Boston.
Boston. Educational Convention, 1860. see Educational Convention, Boston, 1860.
Boston. Eight Ministers Who Carry On the Thursday Lecture. pseud. see Eight Ministers Who Carry On the Thursday Lecture in Boston. pseud.
Boston. Eighty Second Anniversary of American Independence Celebration, 1858. 6519

Boston. Eleven Ministers. pseud. see Eleven Ministers in Boston. pseud.
Boston. Emancipation League. see Emancipation League, Boston.
Boston. Episcopal Charitable Society. see Episcopal Charitable Society, Boston.
Boston. Essex Street Chruch. 6641, 70116
Boston. Essex Street Religious Society. see Boston. Union Church.
Boston. Evening Lecture. see Evening Lecture, Boston.
Boston. Everett School. (23276)
Boston. Excelsior Division, No. 16, Sons of Temperance. see Sons of Temperance in North America. Massachusetts. Excelsior Division, No. 16, Boston.
Boston. Exchange. 86373
Boston. Exhibition of American Manufactures, 11th, 1869. see Massachusetts Charitable Mechanic Association. Exhibition of American Manufactures, 11th, Boston, 1869.
Boston. Experimental School For Teaching and Training Idiotic Children. see Massachusetts. Walter E. Fernald State School, Waltham.
Boston. Family Meeting of the Descendants of Charles Kellogg, 1858. see Family Meeting of the Descendants of Charles Kellogg, Boston, 1858.
Boston. Faneuil Hall Committee on Water Supply. 6781
Boston. Faneuil Hall Meeting, 1820. see Boston. Free Trade Meeting, 1820.
Boston. Faneuil Hall Meeting, 1821-1822. 26141
Boston. Faneuil Hall Meeting, 1854. 6505, 9400, 9404
Boston. Farm School. see Boston Asylum and Farm School for Indigent Boys, Thompson's Island.
Boston. Federal Street Meeting House. see Boston. Arlington Street Church.
Boston. Female Asylum. see Boston-Society for the Care of Girls.
Boston. Female Society for Missionary Purposes. see Female Society for Missionary Purposes, Boston.
Boston. Festival at the Exchange, In Honor of the Russian Achievements Over their French Invaders, 1813. 81513
Boston. Festival of the Connecticut Association, 1857. see Connecticut Association. Festival, Boston, 1857.
Boston. Festival of the Pilgrims, 1842. see Festival of the Pilgrims, Boston, 1842.
Boston. Festival of the Sons of New Hampshire, 1849. see Sons of New Hampshire. Festival, 1st, Boston, 1849.
Boston. Festival of the Sons of New Hampshire, 1853. see Sons of New Hampshire. Festival, 2d, Boston, 1853.
Boston. Firewards. 6537
Boston. First Baptist Church. 6643, 63596
Boston. First Church. 22327, 63335
Boston. First Church. Pastor. 22327 see also Ellis, Rufus.
Boston. First Church (Unitarian) Theological Library. 95311
Boston. First Church (Universalist) 101863
Boston. First Exhibition and Fair of the Massachusetts Charitable Mechanic Association. see Massachusetts Charitable Mechanic Association. Exhibition and Fair, 1st, Boston, 1837.

Boston. First Free Congregational Church.
6644

Boston. First State Exhibition by the Massachusetts Board of Agriculture, 1857.
see Massachusetts. State Board of Agriculture. Exhibition, 1st, Boston, 1857.

Boston. Franklin Fire Society (1792-1816)
see Franklin Fire Society, Boston.

Boston. First New England Temperance Convention, 1866. see New England Temperance Convention, 1st, Boston, 1866.

Boston. Fourth of July Celebration, 1860.
23271

Boston. Franklin Fund. see Franklin Fund, Boston.

Boston. Franklin Street Church. 6645

Boston. Franklin Typographical Society. see Franklin Typographical Society, Boston.

Boston. Franklin United Fire Society. see Franklin United Fire Society, Boston.

Boston. Fraternity. see The Fraternity, Boston.

Boston. Free Church of St. Mary, for Sailors.
75420

Boston. Free Church of St. Mary, for Sailors. Committee. 72137

Boston. Free Democratic Meeting, 1852. see Free Soil Party. Massachusetts. Boston.

Boston. Free Trade Convention, 1832. see Free Trade Convention, Boston, 1832.

Boston. Free Trade Meeting, 1820. 7256

Boston. Friday Lecture. see Friday Lecture, Boston.

Boston. Friendly Brothers of St. Patrick. see Ancient and Most Benevolent Order of the Friendly Brothers of St. Patrick, Boston.

Boston. Friendly Fire Society. see Friendly Fire Society, Boston.

Boston. Friends of a National Bank, 1841. see Friends of a National Bank, Boston, 1841.

Boston. Friends of a Railroad to San Francisco. see Friends of a Railroad to San Francisco, Boston.

Boston. Funeral Ceremonies for George Washington, 1799-1800. 101868

Boston. Garden Street Church. 6646

Boston. General Convention of the Methodist Protestant Church. see Methodist Protestant Church. General Convention, Boston, 1839.

Boston. Gentlemen, Merchants, and Inhabitants, and the Country Adjacent. see Boston. Citizens.

Boston. Gentry and Merchants. see Boston. Citizens.

Boston. German Evangelical Lutheran Zion's Church. 27148

Boston. Girls' High School. see Boston. High School for Girls.

Boston. Grand Consistory of the State of Massachusetts. see Grand Consistory of the State of Massachusetts. Valley of Boston.

Boston. Granite Club. see Granite Club, Boston.

Boston. Great National Peace Jubilee and Musical Festival, 1869. see Great National Peace Jubilee and Musical Festival, Boston, 1869.

Boston. Great Temperance Meeting, 1867.
89627

Boston. Great Whig Meeting of Citizens, 1838. see Whig Party. Massachusetts. Boston.

Boston. Great Whig Meetings, 1838. see Whig Party. Massachusetts. Boston.

Boston. Greene Foundation. see Boston. Trinity Church. Greene Foundation

Boston. Hanover Street Christian Church. 6674

Boston. Hawes-Place Congregational Church.
10743

Boston. Health Department. 6537, (6610), 6998, 45796

Boston. Health Department. City Physician.
6634, 68187-68188

Boston. High School for Girls. (6713)

Boston. Historic Genealogical Society of New England. see New England Historic Genealogical Society, Boston.

Boston. Hollis Street Church. 6654-6655, 62773

Boston. Hollis Street Church. Ex-parte Council, 1839. see Congregational Churches in Massachusetts. Ex-parte Council, Hollis Street Church, Boston, 1839.

Boston. Hollis Street Church. Meeting of Friends of Rev. John Pierpont, 1839. 62776 see also Friends of Rev. John Pierpont. pseud.

Boston. Hollis Street Church. Pastor. 62767, 62775 see also Pierpont, John, 1785-1866.

Boston. Hollis Street Church. Proprietors.
62775, 101515

Boston. Hollis Street Church. Proprietors. Committee. 6651, 6653, 6656, 62776, 62778-62779

Boston. Horace Mann Statue. (44325)

Boston. Hospital for the Insane. see Massachusetts. State Hospital, Boston.

Boston. House of Reformation for Juvenile Offenders. 6727

Boston. Howard Benevolent Society. see Howard Benevolent Society, Boston.

Boston. Hussars. see Massachusetts. Militia. Boston Hussars.

Boston. Immigrant Society. see Immigrant Society, Boston.

Boston. Industrial Aid Society for the Prevention of Pauperism. see Industrial Aid Society for the Prevention of Pauperism, Boston.

Boston. King's Chapel. (25021), (41555), 81513, 86373

Boston. Ladies' Collegiate Institute. see Ladies' Collegiate Institute, Boston.

Boston. Lancaster Memorial Hall. 38790

Boston. Latin School. see Boston. Public Latin School.

Boston. Lecture. see Boston lecture.

Boston. Liberty Tree Division, No. 47, Sons of Temperance. see Sons of Temperance of North America. Massachusetts. Liberty Tree Division, No. 47, Boston.

Boston. Light Artillery. see Massachusetts. Militia. Light Artillery, Boston.

Boston. Lincoln Guard. see Massachusetts. Militia. Lincoln Guard, Boston.

Boston. Lodge of the Iron Crown. see Independent Order of the Sons of Malta. Massachusetts. Lodge of the Iron Crown, Boston.

Boston. Lyceum Hall Christian Church. see Boston. Hanover Street Christian Church.

Boston. Marcus Latham's Mission on Fort Hill. (39162)

Boston. Marine Bible Society. see Marine Bible Society, Boston.

Boston. Marine Society. see Marine Society, Boston.

Boston. Mariner's Church. (44589)

Boston. Massachusetts Baptist Convention, 1824. see Baptists. Massachusetts. Massachusetts Baptist Convention, Boston, 1824.

Boston. Massachusetts Charitable Eye and Ear Infirmary. see Massachusetts Charitable Eye and Ear Infirmary, Boston.

Boston. Massachusetts General Hospital. see Massachusetts General Hospital, Boston.

Boston. Massachusetts Infant Asylum. see Massachusetts Infant Asylum, Jamaica Plain.

Boston. Massachusetts Tin-plate, Copper, and Sheet-iron Workers' Association. see Massachusetts Tin-plate, Copper, and Sheet-iron Workers' Association, Boston.

Boston. Mattapan Literary Association. see Mattapan Literary Association, Boston.

Boston. Maverick Church. 6657

Boston. Mayor, 1823-1829 (Quincy) 67199-(67203) see also Quincy, Josiah, 1772-1864.

Boston. Mayor, 1828-1831 (Otis) 6742 see also Otis, Harrison Gray, 1765-1848

Boston. Mayor, 1834-1835 (Lyman) 6785 see also Lyman, Theodore, 1792-1849.

Boston. Mayor, 1841. (11925), 67907

Boston. Mayor, 1845-1849 (Quincy) (67258) see also Quincy, Josiah, 1802-1882.

Boston. Mayor, 1850. 6614

Boston. Mayor, 1852-1853 (Seaver) 78674 see also Seaver, Benjamin.

Boston. Mayor, 1854 (Smith) 82805, 82807 see also Smith, Jerome Van Crownin-shield, 1800-1879.

Boston. Mayor, 1856-1857 (Rice) 70918 see also Rice, Alexander Hamilton, 1818-1895.

Boston. Mayor, 1868-1870 (Shurtleff) 80778 see also Shurtleff, Nathaniel Bradstreet, 1810-1874.

Boston. Mechanics. 102284

Boston. Meeting for the Purpose of Choosing Delegations to the Anti-tariff Convention, 1831. 65001

Boston. Meeting of Citizens from Every Part of the State, 1815. see Massachusetts. Meeting of Citizens from Every Part of the State, Boston, 1815.

Boston. Meeting of Citizens of Boston and Vicinity, Dec. 3, 1819, on Restraining the Further Extension of Slavery. see Boston. Citizens.

Boston. Meeting of New-England Ministers, 1745. see Convention of Congregational Ministers, Boston, 1745.

Boston. Meeting of Free Religion, 1867. see Meeting on Free Religion, Boston, 1867.

Boston. Meeting on the Rights of the Cherokee Indians, 1830. see Meeting on the Rights of the Cherokee Indians, Boston, 1830.

Boston. Meeting on the Subject of the Cases of Captain Abraham Wendell, Jr., and the Crew of the Ship William Engs, 1838-1839. see Meeting on the Subject of the Cases of Captain Abraham Wendell,

Jr., and the Crew of the Ship William Engs, Boston, 1838-1839.

Boston. Mein's Circulating Library. see Mein's Circulating Library, Boston.

Boston. Mercantile Library Association. 6744-6746, (47880), 75932

Boston. Merchants. 3944, 6536, (56501), 5th note after 96962

Boston. Merchants. petitioners 6524-6526, 69583, 47681-47682

Boston. Merchants and Manufacturers. Committee. see Boston. Committee of Merchants and Manufacturers.

Boston. Methodist General Biblical Institute. see Methodist General Biblical Institute, Boston.

Boston. Methodist Protestant Church General Convention. see Methodist Protestant Church. General Convention, Boston, 1839.

Boston. Minister at Large of the American Unitarian Association. see American Unitarian Association. Minister at Large, Boston.

Boston. Ministers from Divers Parts of Massachusetts, 1697. see Convention of Congregational Ministers of Massachusetts, Boston, 1697.

Boston. Mount Auburn Cemetery. 51146, 92283

Boston. Mount Auburn Cemetery. Trustees. 51146

Boston. Mount Vernon Classical School. 51181

Boston. Mount Vernon Congregational Church. see Boston. New Congregational Church.

Boston. Municipal Court. 2599, 8911, 21293, 50334, 95187, 95602, 96833, 96835, 96840, 96850, 4th note after 103741

Boston. Music Hall. 68768, 12th note after 96966

Boston. National Anti-slavery Bazaar, 21st, 1855. see National Anti-slavery Bazaar, 21st, Boston, 1855.

Boston. National Anti-slavery, Festival, 24th, 1858. see National Anti-slavery Festival, 24th, Boston, 1858.

Boston. National Commercial Convention, 1868. see National Commercial Convention, Boston, 1868.

Boston. National Congregational Council, 1865. see National Council of Congregational Churches, Boston, 1865.

Boston. National Council of Congregational Churches, 1865. see National Council of Congregational Churches, Boston, 1865.

Boston. National Musical Convention, 1841. see National Musical Convention, Boston, 1841.

Boston. National Musical Convention, 1845. see National Musical Convention, Boston, 1845.

Boston. National Quarantine and Sanitary Convention, 4th, 1860. see National Quarantine and Sanitary Convention, 4th, Boston, 1860.

Boston. National Sunday School Society. see Unitary Sunday School Society, Boston.

Boston. National Theological Institute and University. see National Theological Institute and University, Boston.

Boston. New Church. 6635

Boston. New Congregational Church. 6658, (51179)

Boston. New-England Anti-slavery Convention, 1834. see New England Anti-slavery Convention, Boston, 1834.

Boston. New-England Anti-slavery Convention, 1843. see New England Anti-slavery Convention, Boston, 1843.

Boston. New England Anti-slavery Convention, 1860. see New England Anti-slavery Convention, Boston, 1860.

Boston. New England Art Union. see New England Art Union, Boston.

Boston. New England Conservatory of Music. see New England Conservatory of Music, Boston.

Boston. New-England Emigrant Aid Company. see New-England Emigrant Aid Company, Boston.

Boston. New England Historic Genealogical Society. see New England Historic Genealogical Society, Boston.

Boston. New England Hospital for Women and Children. 52689

Boston. New England Inventors' and Mechanics' Association Industrial Festival, 1855. see New England Inventors' and Mechanics' Association. Industrial Exhibition, Boston, 1855.

Boston. New England Methodist Centenary Convention, 1866. see New England Methodist Centenary Convention, Boston, 1866.

Boston. New England Mutual Life Insurance Company. see New England Mutual Life Insurance Company of Boston.

Boston. New England Women's Auxiliary Association. see United States Sanitary Commission. New England Women's Auxiliary Association, Boston.

Boston. New Era Division, No. 175, Sons of Temperance. see Sons of Temperance of North America. Massachusetts. New Division, No. 175, Boston.

Boston. New North Church. 42778

Boston. New North Church. Dissatisfied Brethren. 42778, 78621-(78622), 95166

Boston. New North Church. Several Members. 42778, 78621-(78622), 95166 see also Lyman, Caleb. and Seares, Alexander.

Boston. New South Church. 95191

Boston. North Street Union Mission. 55731

Boston. Number of New England Ministers, 1745. see Convention of Congregational Ministers of New England, Boston, 1745.

Boston. Old North Church. see Boston. Second Church.

Boston. Old South Chapel Prayer Meeting. see Boston. Old South Church.

Boston. Old South Church. 6662-6666, 15453, 15912, 50025, 57145

Boston. Old South Church. petitioners 67274

Boston. Old South Church. Library. 65581-65582

Boston. Order of the Friendly Brothers of St. Patrick. see Ancient and Most Benevolent Order of the Friendly Brothers of St. Patrick, Boston.

Boston. Ordinances, etc. 6537, 6540, 6607-6613, 6690, (6692), 6733, 6749

Boston. Overseers of the Poor. 6537

Boston. Parish of the Advent. see Boston. Church of the Advent.

Boston. Park Street Church. 6668-(6669), 79061

Boston. Park Street Church. Public Meeting in Behalf of the Society for the Promotion of Collegiate and Theological Education at the West, 1845. see Public Meeting in Behalf of the Society for the Promotion

of Collegiate and Theological Education at the West, Boston, 1845.

Boston. Payson Church. Committee. 23684

Boston. Peace Convention, 1830. see Peace Convention, Boston, 1830.

Boston. Peace Convention, 1838. see Peace Convention, Boston, 1838.

Boston. Peace Convention, 1866. see Peace Convention, Boston, 1866.

Boston. Penitent Female's Refuge. see Refuge in the City of Boston.

Boston. People's Convention, 1862. see People's Convention, Boston, 1862.

Boston. People's Perpetual Loan Association. see People's Perpetual Loan Association, Boston.

Boston. Peirce Academy. (59556)

Boston. Peirce Academy. Semi-Centennial Jubilee, 1858. (59557)

Boston. Pilgrim Society. see Pilgrim Society, Boston.

Boston. Pine Street Church. (6670)

Boston. Pine Street Church. Public Meeting, 1851. see South End Provident Association, Boston. Public Meeting, 1851.

Boston. Pitts Street Chapel. 63162

Boston. Port Society. see Port Society of the City of Boston and its Vicinity.

Boston. Presentation Meeting, 1855. (6765), note after 97006

Boston. Primary School Board. Committee on the Caste Schools. Minority. 35406, 69886

Boston. Printers' Festival, 1848. see Franklin Typographical Society, Boston. Printers' Festival, 1848.

Boston. Prison Discipline Society. see Prison Discipline Society, Boston.

Boston. Protestant Episcopal Church Reading Room. see Boston. Church Reading Room.

Boston. Protestant Episcopal Church Union. see Protestant Episcopal Church Union, Boston.

Boston. Public Latin School. 6756-6758, 46206, 77133, 94136

Boston. Public Lecture. see Public Lecture, Boston.

Boston. Public Library. (6730), 6759, 65581-65582, 103242

Boston. Public Library. Commissioners. 6759

Boston. Public Library. Trustees. 6759

Boston. Public Meeting for the Relief of the Greeks, 1823. Committee. 23271, 104863

Boston. Public Meeting for the Relief of the Greeks, 1823. Committee. Chairman. 23271, 104863 see also Winthrop, Thomas Lindall.

Boston. Public Meeting for the Relief of the Greeks, 1823. Committee. Secretary. 23271, 104863 see also Everett, Edward, 1794-1865.

Boston. Public Meeting in Behalf of the Society for the Promotion of Collegiate and Theological Education at the West, Boston, 1845. see Public Meeting in Behalf of the Society for the Promotion of Collegiate and Theological Education at the West, Boston, 1845.

Boston. Public Meeting to Consider the Recent Case of Kidnapping from our Soil, 1846. see Boston. Citizens.

Boston. Public Schools. Annual Visiting Committee. 6762-6763, 77770

Boston. Public Schools. Director of Drawing. 84499 see also Smith, Walter, 1836-1886.

Boston. Purchase Street Congregational Church. Pastor. 71522 see also Ripley, George, 1802-1880.

Boston. Railroad Celebration, 1851. see Railroad Celebration, Boston, 1851.

Boston. Railroad Jubilee, 1851. see Railroad Celebration, Boston, 1851.

Boston. Rainsford Island Hospital. see Massachusetts. Rainsford Island Hospital, Boston.

Boston. Record Commissioners. see Boston. Registry Department.

Boston. Recruiting Committee. 6549

Boston. Refuge in the City of Boston. see Refuge in the City of Boston.

Boston. Registry Department. 6624, 6696, 6749, note after 102733

Boston. Religious Anti-slavery Convention, 1846. see Religious Anti-slavery Convention, Boston, 1846.

Boston. Revere Lodge. see Freemasons. Massachusetts. Revere Lodge, Boston.

Boston. Revere House. 70183

Boston. Rowe Street Baptist Church. 6671

Boston. Roxbury Young Men's Christian Association. see Roxbury Young Men's Christian Association of Boston.

Boston. Sailors' Snug Harbor. see Sailors' Snug Harbor, Boston.

Boston. St. Aloysius Sunday School. 106132

Boston. St. Andrew's Lodge. see Freemasons. Massachusetts. St. Andrew's Lodge, Boston.

Boston. St. Joseph's Home for Sick and Destitute Servant Girls. 75305

Boston. St. Mary's Mutual Benevolent Catholic T. A. Society. see St Mary's Mutual Benevolent Catholic T. A. Society, Boston.

Boston. St. Paul's Church. 35816

Boston. St. Paul's Church. Proprietors. 6672

Boston. St. Stephen's Brotherhood. see St. Stephen's Brotherhood, Boston.

Boston. Salem Church. 75761

Boston. Salem Street Academy. 75762

Boston. Samaritan Institute, No. 1, United Order of Independent Odd Ladies. see United Order of Independent Odd Ladies. Samaritan Institute, No. 1, Boston.

Boston. School Committee. 2237, 98395

Boston. School Committee. minority. 74313

Boston. School Committee. Committee Upon the Petitions of John T. Hilton and Others. minority. 74313

Boston. School Committee. Grammar School Board. Special Committee. 6760

Boston. School for Idiotic and Feeble-Minded Youth. see Massachusetts. Walter E. Fernald State School, Waltham

Boston. School Presentation Meeting, 1855. see Boston. Presentation Meeting, 1855.

Boston. Seamen's Aid Society. see Seamen's Aid Society, Boston.

Boston. Second Church. 6673

Boston. Second Church. Committee. 71777

Boston. Second Church. Pastor. 57935, 71783

Boston. Selectmen. 6612, 6615

Boston. Senior Pastors of the Town. see Senior Pastors of the Town of Boston.

Boston. Several Ministers of the Gospel. pseud. see Several Ministers of the Gospel, In and Near Boston. pseud.

Boston. Shakespeare Division No. 46, Sons of Temperance. see Sons of Temperance of North America. Massachusetts. Shakespeare Division, No. 46, Boston.

Boston. Shawmut Division, No. 1, Sons of Temperance. see Sons of Temperance of North America. Massachusetts. Shawmut Division, No. 1, Boston.

Boston. Siloam Lodge, No. 2. see Odd Fellows, Independent Order of. Boston. Siloam Lodge, No. 2.

Boston. Society for Employing the Female Poor. see Society for Employing the Female Poor, Boston.

Boston. Society for Employing the Poor. see Society for Employing the Female Poor, Boston.

Boston. Society for Encouraging Industry and Employing the Poor. see Society for Encouraging Industry and Employing the Poor, Boston.

Boston. Society for Improvement in Practical Piety. see Society for Improvement in Practical Piety, Boston.

Boston. Society for Ministerial Relief. see Society for Ministerial Relief, Boston.

Boston. Society for Promoting Christian Knowledge, Piety and Charity. see Society for Promoting Christian Knowledge, Piety and Charity, Boston.

Boston. Society for Promoting Regular & Good Singing. see Society for Promoting Regular & Good Singing, Boston.

Boston. Society for Propagating the Gospel Among the Indians and Others in North America. see Society for Propagating the Gospel Among the Indians and Others in North America.

Boston. Society for the Circulation of Dr. Channing's Works. see Society for the Circulation of Dr. Channing's Works, Boston.

Boston. Society for the Mutual Benefit of Female Domestics and Their Employers. see Society for the Mutual Benefit of Female Domestics and Their Employers, Boston.

Boston. Society for the Prevention of Pauperism. see Industrial Aid Society for the Prevention of Pauperism, Boston.

Boston. Society for the Promotion of the Rights and Interests of Bona Fide Creditors, and the Benefit and Relief of Honest Debtors. see Society for the Promotion of the Rights and Interests of Bona Fide Creditors, and the Benefit and Relief of Honest Debtors, Boston.

Boston. Society for the Relief of Aged and Destitute Clergymen, Boston. see Society for Ministerial Relief, Boston.

Boston. Society in Aid of Social Improvements. see Society in Aid of Social Improvements, Boston.

Boston. Soldiers' Memorial Society. see Soldiers' Memorial Society, Boston.

Boston. Social Law Library. (6773), 85692, 85693

Boston. Social Law Library. Charter. 85692

Boston. Social Library, No. 1. 85695

Boston. Somerset Club. see Somerset Club, Boston.

Boston. Sons of Columbia. see Sons of Columbia, Boston.

Boston. Sons of the African Society. see
Sons of the African Society, Boston.
Boston. South Church. 88116
Boston. South Cove Corporation. see South
Cove Corporation, Boston.
Boston. South End Provident Association.
see South End Provident Association,
Boston.
Boston. South Wharf Corporation. see
South Wharf Corporation, Boston.
Boston. Spring Lane School. 89828
Boston. State Hospital. see Massachusetts.
State Hospital, Boston.
Boston. State Library. see Massachusetts.
State Library, Boston.
Boston. Steam Boiler Makers' and Iron Ship
Builders' Benevolent & Protective
Association. see Steam Boiler Makers'
and Iron Ship Builders' Benevolent &
Protective Association, Boston.
Boston. Stone Chapel. see Boston. King's
Chapel.
Boston. Suffolk Club. see Suffolk Club,
Boston.
Boston. Suffolk District Medical Society see
Massachusetts Medical Society. Suffolk
District Medical Society.
Boston. Summer Street Christian Church.
6674
Boston. Sun Fire Society. see Sun Fire
Society, Boston.
Boston. Sunday School Society. see Unitarian
Sunday School Society, Boston.
Boston. Sundry Colored Citizens. petitioners
see Boston. Colored Citizens.
petitioners
Boston. Superintendent of Public Schools.
6761, (6764)
Boston. Superior Court. 12365, 24744,
32362, 37712, 67193, note before 90598,
96946, 96951, 2d note after 98664, 2d
note after 102632, 3d note after 102623
Boston. Synod, 1662. see Congregational
Churches in Massachusetts. Boston
Synod, 1662.
Boston. Synod, 1679. see Congregational
Churches in Massachusetts. Boston
Synod, 1679.
Boston. Synod, 1680. see Congregational
Churches in Massachusetts. Boston
Synod, 1680.
Boston. Synod, 1716. see Congregational
Churches in Massachusetts. Boston
Synod, 1716.
Boston. Tailors. petitioners (47638)
Boston. Temperance Committee. see Tem-
perance Committee, Boston.
Boston. Temperance Convention, 1835. see
Temperance Convention, Boston, 1835.
Boston. Tercentenary Celebration of the Birth
of Shakespeare, 1864. see New England
Historic Genealogical Society, Boston.
Tercentenary Celebration of the Birth of
Shakespeare, 1864.
Boston. Theological Library. see Boston.
First Church (Unitarian) Theological
Library.
Boston. Third Church. 104076
Boston. Third Gathered Church. see Boston.
Third Church.
Boston. Third Social Library. 95359
Boston. Thursday Evening Club. see Thurs-
day Evening Club, Boston.
Boston. Thursday Lecture. see Thursday
Lecture, Boston.
Boston. Town Convention, 1804. 6715

Boston. Town Meeting. 6612
Boston. Town Meeting, 1769. 6478
Boston. Town Meeting, 1770. 6741
Boston. Town Meeting, 1772. 6546, 6568-6569
Boston. Town Meeting, 1773. 6567
Boston. Town Meeting, 1774. 6570
Boston. Town Meeting, 1782. 6552
Boston. Town Meeting, 1785. 6609
Boston. Town Meeting, 1786. 6609
Boston. Town Meeting, 1801. (6610)
Boston. Town Meeting, 1814. 13158
Boston. Town Meeting, 1822. 6615
Boston. Tremont Temple. 73440
Boston. Trinity Church. Greene Foundation.
90734
Boston. Trinity Church. Greene Foundation.
Charter. 90734
Boston. Trinity Church. Greene Foundation.
Treasurer. 90734
Boston. Trinity Church. Greene Foundation.
Trustees. 6678-(6679), 69533, 90734
Boston. Trinity Church. Laity. 6680
Boston. Trinity Church. Proprietors. 6677
Boston. Trinity Church. Rector and Assistant
Minister. 6676
Boston. Trinity Church. Treasurer. 6675
Boston. Trinity Church. Vestry. 6676-6677
Boston. Trinity Church. Wardens. 6676
Boston. Tuesday Lecture. see Tuesday Lec-
ture, Boston.
Boston. Trinity Hall Sunday School. 57874
Boston. Twenty Eighth Congregational Society.
58768, 12th note after 96966
Boston. Twenty-Fourth National Anti-slavery
Festival, 1858. see National Anti-slavery
Festival, 24th, Boston, 1858.
Boston. Two Meetings, on the 7th & 14th July,
1852, To Protest Against the Nomination
of Gen. Scott. see Boston. Webster
Meetings, July, 1852. and Whig Party.
Massachusetts. Suffolk County.
Boston. Union Meeting, Dec. 8, 1859. 6491
Boston. Union Church. 97772-97772A
Boston. Union Committee of the Sunday Schools
of the Three Baptist Churches. see
Baptists. Massachusetts. Boston. Union
Committee of the Sunday Schools of the
Three Baptist Societies.
Boston. Union Society. see Union Society,
Boston.
Boston. Unitarian Association. see Unitarian
Churches. Massachusetts. Boston
Association.
Boston. Unitarian Sunday School Society. see
Unitarian Sunday School Society.
Boston. United Fire Society(1789-   ) see
United Fire Society, Boston (1789-   )
Boston. United Fire Society (1773-1816) see
Franklin United Fire Society, Boston.
Boston. Universalist Sabbath School Associa-
tion. see Universalist Sabbath School
Association, Boston.
Boston. Warren Street Chapel. 6681-(6682),
(41554)
Boston. Warren Street Chapel. Committee.
6683
Boston. Washington Artillery. see Massa-
chusetts. Militia. Washington Artillery,
Boston.
Boston. Washington Hotel Lottery. see
Washington Hotel Lottery, Boston.
Boston. Washington Mass Convention, 1845.
see Washington Mass Convention, Boston,
1845.
Boston. Washington Monument Association.
see Washington Monument Association,
Boston.

Boston. Washington Society. see Washington Society, Boston.

Boston. Webster Meetings, July, 1852. 6548, 78422

Boston. Weekly Lecture. see Weekly Lecture, Boston.

Boston. Wesleyan Juvenile Benevolent Society. see Wesleyan Juvenile Benevolent Society, Boston.

Boston. West Church. 3794, 42431

Boston. West Parish Association. see West Parish Association, Boston.

Boston. Whig Celebration, July 4, 1834. see Whig Party. Massachusetts. Boston.

Boston. Whig Republican Association. see Whig Republican Association, Boston.

Boston. Widows' Society. see Widows' Society, Boston.

Boston. Winslow Blues. see Massachusetts. Militia. Winslow Blues, Boston.

Boston. Working Men's Convention, 1833. see Working Men's Convention, Boston, 1833.

Boston. Young Catholics Friend Society. see Young Catholics Friend Society, Boston.

Boston. Young Men's Anti-masonic Association for the Diffusion of Truth. see Young Men's Anti-masonic Association for the Diffusion of Truth, Boston.

Boston. Young Men's Benevolent Society. see Young Men's Benevolent Society, Boston.

Boston. Young Men's Christian Association. see Young Men's Christian Association, Boston.

Boston. Young Men's Christian Association of Roxbury. see Young Men's Christian Association, Roxbury, Mass.

Boston. Young Men's Temperance Society. see Young Men's Temperance Society, Boston.

Boston (Archdiocese) Archbishop (Williams) 72934 see also Williams, John Joseph, Abp., 1822-

Boston (Archdiocese) Bishop (Cheverus) 72976 see also Cheverus, Jean Louis Anne Magdelene Lefebre de, Cardinal, 1768-1836.

Boston (Archdiocese) Bishop (Fenwick) 72885 see also Fenwick, Benedict Joseph, Bp., 1782-1846.

Boston (Archdiocese) Synod, 1842. 72933

Boston (Archdiocese) Synod, 1868. 72934

Boston, England. Mayor. 6588

Boston (Schooner) in admiralty 82312

Boston: a commercial metropolis in 1850. 19656

Boston: a peom [by Jane E. Locke.] 41724

Boston; a poem. By Winthrop Sargent. (6480), 77032-77033

Boston Academy of Music. 6573

Boston advertiser. 84037

Boston African Society. see Sons of the African Society, Boston.

Boston almanac for 1788. 105008

Boston almanack, for . . . 1768. 5220, 62743

Boston almanack, for the year 1836. 6482

Boston almanack for the year of our Lord God 1692. 6481, 62743

Boston amateur poet. pseud. Poet's offering. see Patch, John, 1807-1887.

Boston and Albany road-book. 6483

Boston and Boston people, in 1850. 33101

Boston and its environs. 61302

Boston and its environs; a poem. (6483A)

Boston and its vicinity, past and present. 6484, 6522

Boston and Liverpool. (31825)

Boston and Lowell Railroad Corporation. 6768

Boston and Lowell Railroad Corporation. Charter. 6768

Boston and Lowell Railroad Corporation. Directors. 6768

Boston and Maine Railroad. Committee of Investigation. 6768

Boston and Maine Railroad. Directors. 6768, 14047

Boston and Maine Railroad. Stockholders. 6768

Boston and Maine Railroad: a statement. (3754)

Boston and Missouri Land Company. 62501

Boston and Montreal Turnpike Company. 50238

Boston and Montreal Turnpike Company. Charter. 50238

Boston and New York Coal Company. (26056)

Boston and Portland Railroad Corporation. Committee of Stockholders. 6768

Boston and Providence Railroad Corporation. 6768

Boston and Providence Railroad Corporation. Directors. 6768

Boston and Providence Railroad Corporation. Engineer. 6768

Boston and Providence Railroad Corporation. Grantees. 6768

Boston and Providence Railroad Corporation. Report of the Board of Commissioners. 6768, 45996

Boston and Roxbury Mill Corporation. 6748, 17037, 69912

Boston and the west. 6485

Boston and Worcester Railroad Corporation. 6768 see also Committee of the Boston and Worcester and Western Railroad Corporations on Uniting the Two Railroads.

Boston and Worcester Railroad Corporation. petitioners 90774

Boston and Worcester Railroad Corporation. Charter. 6768

Boston Anti-slavery Society. 47291

Boston, April 22, 1779. 90227

Boston aqueduct and the city of Boston. 6784, 77002

Boston Aqueduct Corporation. 6785

Boston assemblage, or a peep at Caucus Hall. 6486, 96472

Boston Associates of the Sanitary Commission. see United States Sanitary Committion. Boston Branch.

Boston Association of Congregational Ministers. see Congregational Churches in Massachusetts. Boston Association.

Boston Asylum and Farm School for Indigent Boys, Thompson's Island. 86912

Boston Asylum and Farm School for Indigent Boys, Thompson's Island. Directors. 6577

Boston Asylum for Indigent Boys. 6576-6577

Boston Athenaeum. 6589-6590, 6593, (6595), 64049, 88964, 93160, 103911

Boston Athenaeum. Charter. 6593

Boston Athenaeum. Gallery. 6591-6592, 77108

Boston atlas. 40657, 58453, note after 95099

Boston atlas. Stenographer. see Stenographer of the atlas. pseud. reporter

Boston bard. pseud. Life of the Boston bard. see Coffin, Robert S.

Boston bard. pseud. Miscellaneous poems. see Coffin, Robert S.

Boston bard. pseud. Oriental harp. see Coffin, Robert S.

Boston bars and Boston boys. 21700
Boston before the revolution. 6487, 12725
Boston Board of Trade. see Boston. Board of Trade.
Boston Board of Trade. 74734
Boston Board of Trade, 1856. Report of the committee. 53312
Boston book. 6488, 85433, 92448, 95221
Boston book for 1837. 89001
Boston Branch, United States Sanitary Commission. see United States Sanitary Commission. Boston Branch.
Boston business and copartnership directory. 6694
Boston business-street directory. 6695
Boston bulletin. 14898
Boston by daylight and gaslight. 77227
Boston by daylight and gaslight for two hundred and forty years. 77228
Boston by-lays to hell. 6489
Boston chronicle. 9558, 96754
Boston city measured. 6490
Boston Civil Service Reform Association. 84505
Boston Clearing House Association. Tax Committee. 3188
Boston commercial gazette. 94090
Boston Committee in Canada. 32445
Boston Committee of Policy Holders of the Mutual Life Insurance Company of New York. see New York Mutual Life Insurance Company. Boston Committee of Policy Holders.
Boston Committee on the Removal of the United States Bank Deposites. 69766
Boston common. 6687
Boston common: a tale of our own times. 23890
Boston common. [Opinions.] 6688
Boston common, or rural walks in cities. 6689
Boston commonwealth. (12012), 24636
Boston conspiracy. (72126)
Boston courier. 6491, (18042), (18048), 23684, 42706, 58758, 67423, 70192, 77015, 82083, 87341, 89533, 93545, 2d note after 98269
Boston courier report of the proceedings of professed spiritual agents and mediums. 89533
Boston courier report of the Union Meeting in Faneuil Hall. 6491
Boston courier (Whig) 12860
Boston Cutta Peacha Company. petitioners 5620
Boston daily advertiser. 5196, 5994, (19046), (29619), 29632, 38444, 45704, 64046, 69487, 69657, 79874, 84957, 85083, 89927, 93527
Boston daily advertiser. Editor. pseud. Remarks. see Hale, Nathan, 1784-1863.
Boston daily advocate. 69705
Boston daily atlas. (11920), 13362, 93197
Boston daily evening transcript. 6784, 95641
Boston directory. 6696, 87340, note after 102733
Boston dispensary. 6698
Boston ephemeris. An almanac for the Dyonisian year of the Christian AEra. M.DC.LXXXIII. 46239
Boston ephemeris. An almanack . . . for the year of the Christian AEra 1685. 46774
Boston ephemeris. An almanack for the year MDCLXXXIV. 62743
Boston ephemeris. An almanack for the year M.DC.LXXXIII. 6492

Boston ephemeris. An almanack of coelestial motions of the sun & planets, with some of the principal aspects for the year of the Christian AEra MDCLXXXV. 46774, 62743
Boston ephemeris. An almanack of coelestial motions of the sun & planets, with some of the principal aspects for the year of the Christian AEra MDCLXXXVI. 62743
Boston evening post. 360, 1829, 11967, 12331, (13210), (15954), 86617, 94334, 94517, 95159, 3d note after 96741, 102066, 104056
Boston evening post. News boy. 100800
Boston evening transcript. 2831, 77021, 84041, 84505, 88221
Boston. February 22, 1792. 6717
Boston. February 27, 1777. 104294
Boston Female Anti-slavery Society. 6703-(6704), 11994, (44939), 81909-81912
Boston fire, November 9th and 10th, 1872. 26061
Boston galaxy. 102535
Boston Gas Light Company. plaintiffs 6712, note after 96867
Boston Gas Light Company versus William Gault. 6712, note after 96867
Boston gazette. 243, 2197, (14394)-14395, (32551), 45635, 56595, 91308, 91796, 94107, 95963, 97147, 7th note after 97146, 97208, 98445, 104854, 104899
Boston harbor. 28092
Boston, Hartford and Erie Railroad Company. petitioners 70605, 70657
Boston illustrated. 90459
Boston in colonial times. 51887
Boston in 1682 and 1699. 52641, note after 100866, 101286
Boston independent chronicle. 2395, 2397
Boston. January 15. 1752. 85839
Boston. January 6, 1800. 101782
Boston journal. 77382, 83597
Boston journal of natural history. 5505, (6775), (28088), 72670, 78528
Boston journal of natural history. New series. 47579
Boston journal of philosophy and the arts. 6493
Boston, July 14. & 17. 1766. 104852
Boston, July 21st, 1779. 101121
Boston kidnapping. (58740)
Boston law reporter. 35314
Boston lecture. 14481, 14484, 14486, (14489), (14497), 14504, 14506, 14521-(14522), (14525), (17040), 28005-(28006), 40773, 46269, 46280, 46296, 46352, (46358) - 46359, 46393, 46395, 46397, 46427, 46448, 46465, 46493, 46499, (46509), 46511-46512, 46540, (46565), 46600, 46711, 46736, 46758, 46798, 50298, 59602, (56500), 56503, 79405-(79407), 79422, 79431, (79448), 91942, 91966, 91948, 91964, 91956, 91967, 95642, 3d note after 97160, note after 98054, 100916, 104066, 104074, 104082, 104090-104091-2, 104095, 104099, 104102-104103, 104111, 104259, 104262, 104264-104270, 104405
Boston lecture, Sept. 24, 1713, before the execution of David Wallis. (14525)
Boston lights. (48874)
Boston literary gazette. see Yankee and Boston literary gazette.
Boston literary magazine. 6494
Boston Long Wharf. see Boston Pier, or the Long-Wharf.

Boston magazine (1805-   ) (6496), (41758)
Boston magazine (1783-1789) 6495
Boston Maratime Mission. Treasurer. 93547
Boston masonic mirror. see Masonic
  mirror and mechanics† intelligencer.
Boston, May 11, 8159. 91603
Boston Mechanics Association. 6743
Boston medical and surgical journal. 6497,
  75797, 82811, 91602
Boston medical intelligencer. 82811
Boston memorial for the repeal of the fugitive
  slave bill. 93649
Boston memorial of 1842. 6498
Boston memorial on the cotton manufacture.
  6498, (35448)
Boston memorial to Congress. 17114
Boston Mercantile Library. 64049
Boston merchant. pseud. Is our prosperity
  a delusion? 35233
Boston merchant of 1745. (36249)
Boston Mill Corporation. 6747
Boston miscellany and lady's monthly magazine.
  6499
Boston miscellany of literature and fashion.
  6499
Boston mob of gentlemen of property and
  standing. 6500
Boston monthly express list. 85515
Boston monthly magazine. 18084
Boston morning post. 4111, (69701), 1st note
  after 97258
Boston morning post. Reporter. 79005
Boston morning post—extra. 30663, 103290
Boston museum edition of American acting
  dramas. 84782
Boston, New York, Philadelphia & Baltimore
  commercial directory. 105529
Boston news letter. 198, 6377, (19639), note
  after 31743, (79447), 79457, 82975-
  82976, 84553, 88221, 91182, 94107,
  95966, 97421, 98055, 99808 see also
  Massachusetts gazette and Boston news
  letter.
Boston news letter, and city record. 7042
Boston, Norwich and New London Rail Road
  Company. Charter. 105447 see also
  Norwich and Worcester Rail Road
  Company.
Boston notion. 85411
Boston notions. (19078)
Boston, November 17th, 1858. 91604
Boston opposition to the new law for the sup-
  pression of rum shops. 6501, 45655
Boston: or a touch at the times. 105618
Boston orations. 30177
Boston patriot. 231, 19903, 83826
Boston patriotic song. 97402
Boston pearl. 102535
Boston Pier, or the Long-Wharf. (6731)
Boston Port and Seamen's Aid Society. 6753
Boston port bill. 6752, (67192)
Boston post. 35235, (81481), 81531
Boston Presbytery. see Presbyterian Church
  in the U. S. A.‾Presbytery of Boston.
Boston prize poems. 6502, 6758, 89665
Boston quarterly review. 3730, 6503, (8713)-
  8715
Boston railways, their condition and prospects.
  28303
Boston recorder. 22381, (62666), 83572,
  99610, note after 105324
Boston recorder. Proprietor. 104503 see
  also Willis, Nathaniel.
Boston recorder & telegraph. see Boston
  recorder.

Boston recorder. Proposal of the proprietor.
  104503
Boston report and mercantile memorials. 10889
Boston report on free trade. 10889
Boston review. 6504, 14876, 50167, 97327,
  1st note after 101785 see also Monthly
  Anthology, and Boston review.
Boston revival, 1842. 50420
Boston Sanitary Association. petitioners 35803,
  46043, 47656
Boston School Masters. see Association of
  Boston School Masters.
Boston sheet. 62743
Boston slave riot, and trial of Anthony Burns.
  6505, 9400, 9404
Boston Social Science Association. (67262)
Boston Social Science Association. Cheap food
  dependent on cheap transportation. (67262)
Boston Society for the Care of Girls. 6705
Boston Society of Natural History. 6774-6776,
  17196, 78527, 78529-78530
Boston Society of the New Jerusalem. see
  New Jerusalem Church. Boston Society.
Boston speaker. 83508
Boston spectator. 6506, 105628
Boston spy. 89933
Boston spy. Being a series of sketches. 41016
Boston statesman. (57637)
Boston telegraph. 105523
Boston theatre. 84786, 89398
Boston, Thursday Sept. 25th, 1690. 66526
Boston times. 3730
Boston token. 50639-50640
Boston Tontine Association. 6779, 16079
Boston tragedy. 5331
Boston transcript. 8881, (77001), 79449, 86917,
  note after 102442
Boston traveller. 6507, 45769, 90871
Boston traveller extra. 6507, 45769
Boston, 25 January, 1769. 16822
Boston, 25th of May, 1783. 94663
Boston, 24 Sept. 1796. 101783
Boston two hundred years ago. 39730
Boston weekly magazine (1743) 6508
Boston weekly magazine (1802-   ) 6509,
  (73614)
Boston weekly messenger. 6510
Boston weekly news-paper. see Massachusetts
  gazette.
Boston weekly report of public sales and of
  arrivals. 19305
Boston weekly symbol. 92751
Boston whig. 58325
Bostoniad. 40973
Bostonian. pseud. Biographical sketch of Gen.
  Joseph Warren. 101477-101478
Bostonian. pseud. Diplomatic policy of Mr.
  Madison unveiled. see Lowell, John.
Bostonian. pseud. Effects of the stage on the
  manners of a people. see Haliburton,
  William.
Bostonian. pseud. Interesting political discus-
  sion. see Lowell, John.
Bostonian. pseud. Scholiast schooled. 6763,
  77770
Bostonian. pseud. Tamerlane and other poems.
  see Poe, Edgar Allan, 1809-1849.
Bostonian. pseud. Traits of the tea party.
  see Thatcher, Benjamin Bussey.
Bostonian Ebenezer. (46240)
Bostonian plea. 81585
Bostonian prophet. 6511
Bostonian Society.
Boston's Old Planters and Some Others. pseud.
  Old men's tears. 57137

Bostwick, David, 1721-1763. 6788-(6789), 18765, 34598
Bostwick, E. B. 957
Bostwick, Erastus, 1767-1864. 6790
Bostwick, Henry, 1787-1836 or 7. 6791
Bostwick, Samuel. supposed author 15642, 53495, 97291
Bosworth, Alfred. (70667)
Bosworth, Benjamin, 1615?-1700. 6792, 80910
Bosworth, Joseph S. 45458
Bosworth, Newton. 6793
Botanic family physician. 95604-95605
Botanic family physician, or the secrets of curing diseases. 89408
Botanic Garden, Cambridge, Mass. see Cambridge, Mass. Botanic Garden.
Botanic Garden, Lexington, Ky. see Transylvania University, Lexington, Ky. Botanic Garden.
Botanica. (26779), 39066
Botanica criptogamia. 74921
Botanica fanerogamia. 74921
Botanica neglecta. 106129
Botanical account of all the . . . important plants. 41293
Botanical appendix by Dr. Hooker. 55303
Botanical class-book. 55410
Botanical description. 42683
Botanical descriptions. 31944
Botanical dictionary. 21706, 44408
Botanical harmony delineated. 75474
Botanical, historical, and practical treatise on the tobacco plant. 8183
Botanical illustrations. 67446
Botanical profile. 5309
Botanical report, by E. Durand and T. C. Hilgard. 69946
Botanical report (by J. G. Cooper and Prof. Asa Gray.) 69946
Botanical report (by J. S. Newberry and others.) 69946
Botanical report, by John Torrey. 69946
Botanical repository. see Floral magazine and botanical repository.
Botanical teacher for North America. 36247
Botanical text-book. 28368
Botanique. 11411
Botanique. Atlas de botanique. 21354
Botanique, cryptogamie. 21353
Botanique. 1844-1866. 98298
Botanique. La cryptogamie. 21216
Botanique, par M. Gaudichaud. 25916
Botanique, par M. J. Decaisne. (21355)
Botanique. Par MM. A. Lesson et A. Richard. 21210
Botanique.—Plantes cellulaires. 74922
Botanique, plantes cellulaires de l'ile de Cuba. 50042
Botanique.—Plantes vasculaires. 74922
Botanist. 102055
Botany. 69946
Botany; by A. Gray, J. Torrey, G. Thurber, and G. Engelmann. 35308
Botany, by Dr. J. Torrey. 68476
Botany; . . . by Rev. M. A. Curtis. 55620
Botany; containing a catalogue of the indigenous and naturalized plants. 18059
Botany: cryptogamia: filices. 7193
Botany for young people. 28368
Botany of Captain Beechey's voyage. 32863
Botany of the Antarctic voyage of H. M. discovery ships Erebus and Terror. 32822
Botany of the boundary. 22538
Botany of the northern and middle states. 4228

Botany of the northern parts of British America. (32865)
Botany of the southern states. 18525
Botany of the United States Exploring Expedition. (7692)
Botany of the United States north of Virginia. 4230
Botany of the United States of America. 4229
Botany of the voyage of H. M. S. Herald. 78865
Botany of the voyage of H. M. S. Sulphur. 31944
Botany. Phanerogamia. 28368
Boteler, Alexander H. 6794
Botelho, Jose de S. Bernardino. (6795)-6796
Botella, Josef. (48041)
Botello de Moraes y Vasconcelos, Francisco. (6797)-6798
Botero, Giovanni, 1540-1617. (6799)-6812, (36282), 36283, 36287, (66890)-66891, (68338), 69240, 94185, 1st note after 96483, 98222, 105491,
Botero, Juan. see Botero, Giovanni, 1540-1617.
Botero Benes, Juan. see Benes, Juan Botero.
Boterus, J. see Botero, Giovanni, 1540-1617.
Botetourt, Norborne Berkeley, Baron de, 1718?-1770. 99907, 104156 see also Virginia (Colony) Governor, 1768-1770 (Botetourt)
Both, ------. 14957-14960
Both sides of religious ceremonies. 83830
Both sides of the question. 6814, 27017, 56848
Both sides; or, a short chapter of facts. 6815, 11883
Both sides, or the real state of parties. 6816
Both sides reviewed. 104657A
Botschafft des groszmechtigsten Konigs Dauid. 106399
Botschaft des Gouveneur's Thomas C. Fletcher. (49584)
Botschaft uber den Vertrag zwischen den Vereinigten Staaten. 6817
Botschaft von Gouverneur David Butler. 52185
Botsford, Margaret. 99838
Botta, Carlo Giuseppe Guglielmo, 1766-1837. 6818-6821, 86841
Botta, Vincenzo. 6822
Bottarelli, Giovanni Gualberto. 6823
Botten-Hansen, Paul. 6824
Bottger, Adolf, 1815-1870. 6825
Bottger, C. 6826
Bottger, Gottfried Conrad. tr. 98744, 98747
Bottiger, C. A. tr. 43808, 101242
Bottle-Nose Ben, the Indian hater. (64200)
Botts, C. T. 70261, 88445 see also New Idria Mining Company of California. Counsel.
Botts, John Minor, 1802-1869. 6847-6832, 59004, 2d note after 100532, 103265
Boturini Benaduci, Lorenzo, ca. 1702-1750. 6834-6835, 80987
Boturino, ------. 9570
Boty, Iver. 66686
Boucaniers. 21368-21369
Boucarut, A. 6836
Bouchacourt, Charles. 6837
Bouchard de la Poterie, Claud Florent. 6838, 64575
Boucher, ------, fl. 1830. 27567
Boucher, Emile le. see Leboucher, Emile.
Boucher, Jonathan, 1734-1804. 6839, 6841
Boucher, Jonathan, 1734-1804. supposed author 40317, 7th note after 100577
Boucher, Jonathan, 1734-1804. incorrectly supposed author 6840, (39613)

Boucher, Odet-Julien le. see Le Boucher, Odet-Julien, 1744-1826.
Boucher, Pierre, Sieur de Boucherville, 1622?-1717. 6843-6844, (10348)
Boucher, Philippe. 6842, (26774)
Boucher de la Bruere, -------, fils. 6845-6846
Boucher de la Richarderie, Gilles, 1733-1810. 6857, 20828
Boucherville, C. B. de. 19113-19114
Boucherville, George Boucher de. 10456
Bouchette, Joseph. 6848-6851, 84779
Bouchot, Auguste. 6852
Boucly, Felix. 40956 see also France. Procureur du Roi.
Boudin, J. Ch. M. 6853
Boudinot, Elias, 1740-1821. 6854-6857, 94719
Boudinot, Elias, d. 1839. (6858)-6860, 12442, 12447, 12460-12461, 64084-(64086), 1st note after 97291, 97859, 105317-105321
Boudinot, Elisha. 1795, note after 53697, note after 83791
Boudrye, Louis Napoleon, 1833-1892. see Beaudry, Louis Napoleon, 1833-1892.
Boudry de Lozieres, Louis Narcisse. see Baudry de Lozieres, Louis Narcisse.
Boue, Ami, 1794-1881. 6862
Bouet-Willaumez, Louis Edouard, Comte, 1808-1871. 6863
Bougainville, Hyacinthe Yves Philippe Potentien, Baron de, 1781-1846. 6874-(6875)
Bougainville, Louis Antoine de, 1729-1811. 6864-6873, 21211-21215, 31389, 43415, (54897), 56064, 60997, 71252, 93292, note after 937294, 2d note after 100806
Bougainville de la jeunesse. 6873, 71252
Bouguer, Pierre. 3605, (6876)-6877, 38490, 62957, 69148
Bouille, Rene, i. e. Amour Louis Charles Rene, Marquis de, b. 1802. 6879-6880
Bouillon, Gilles Boileau de. see Boileau de Bouillon, Gilles, 16th cent.
Bouillus, Carolus. 69130
Bouis, Amedee Theodore. 6881-(6883)
Boulainvilliers, Henri, Comte de, 1658-1722. 4931-4934
Boulanger, Joseph Ignatius le. see Le Boulanger, Joseph Ignatius.
Boulanger, Nicolas Antoine, 1722-1759. 6884-6885
Boulbon, Gaston de, Comte Raousset. see Raousset-Boulbon, Gaston de, Comte.
Bouldin, Thomas Tyler, 1781-1834. (1819)
Boulingy, John Edward, 1824-1864. 6886
Boulonger, ------. cartographer 77803
Boulanger, Louis. 101023
Boulter, Hugh, Abp. of Armagh, 1672-1742. (6887)
Boulton, D'Arcy. 6888
Boulton, Henry John. 6889
Boulton, Richard. 6890, 15051
Boulton, Robert. 6248, 103068
Boulton, Thomas. 63582, 100804
Boumann, C. C. 6891
Bounce-about. 95868
Bound labor interest in the United States. 36869
Boundary line between the British provinces and the United States. 5560
Boundary question. 52777
Boundary question revived. 28340
Bouniol, Bathild. 6892
Bounty (H. M. Ship) 49380
Bounty Fund Commission, Philadelphia. see Philadelphia. Bounty Fund Commission.

Bounty lands to the surviving officers of the late war. (38814), 95954
Bounty plan. 48018
Bouquet, Henry. supposed author (74155), 84616-84619, 84676, 1st note after 101814
Bouquet of flowers. (25461)
Bouquet of flowers, from the garden of paradise. 17723
Bouquet's expedition against the Ohio Indians. 84619
Bourassa, N. ed. 70356
Bourbon, Armand de. see Conti, Armand de Bourbon, Prince de, 1629-1660.
Bourbon (French Colony) 44975
Bourbon County, Ky. Circuit Court. 79759
Bourbon conspiracy to rule or destroy the nation. 88453
Bourbourg, Charles Etienne Brassier de. see Brasseur de Bourbourg, Charles Etienne, 1814-1874.
Bourbourg, E. Beauvois Brasseur de. see Brasseur de Bourbourg, E. Beauvois.
Bourdier, Raoul. 3565, (47094), 69021, (69028), 69031, (69035), 69046, 69076
Bourdillon, Jacob. 104692
Bourdiol, H. 6893
Bourdon, Louis Gabriel. 6894, 4th note after 100806
Bourg, Edme Theodore. 75197, 77104
Bourgeois, Auguste Anicet. 4822, (6895), 6897-6898, (69144), 96336, note after 100841
Bourgeois, J. 6900
Bourgeois, Nicolas Louis. 6896-6899, 96336, 96487, 3d note after 100806
Bourgeois de New-Haven. pseud. Lettres. see Condorcet, Marie Jean Antoine Nicolas Caritat, Marquis de, 1743-1794.
Bourges, Florentin de. 6901
Bourgogne, Charlotte de Cossas du Vivier. see Argoult, Charlotte des Cossas (du Vivier-Bourgogne) d'.
Bourgogne, Marie-Anne (Godefroy) du Vivier-. defendant 75162
Bourgoing, Jean Francois, Baron de, 1748-1811. 1905, 6902
Bourgoing, Paul Charles Amable, Baron de, 1791-1864. 6903, 85791
Bourguignat, Auguste. 6904-6906
Bourguignon d'Anville, J. B. (38022), (38413), 47552
Bourignon, Haubold Xaverius, Graf von. 97746
Bourinot, John George. 6907
Bourke, Sir Richard, 1777-1855. ed. 9304
Bourke, William. supposed author 9282-9289
Bourlet de Vauxcelles, Simon-Jerome. see Vauxcelles, Simon-Jerome Bourlet de.
Bourlez, ------. tr. 82266
Bourne, Miss -----. see Campbell, ------- (Bourne)
Bourne, Benjamin. supposed author 93826-93827
Bourne, Benjamin. incorrectly supposed author 8054, 1st note after 91736
Bourne, Benjamin Franklin. 6910-6911, 72231
Bourne, Charles. defendant 6912
Bourne, Edward Emerson, 1797-1873. 6913
Bourne, Edward Gaylord, 1860-1908. ed. 87206, 104994
Bourne, Ezra A. plaintiff 72744
Bourne, George, 1780-1845. (6914)-6921, 6921A, 7175, (42069), 66115, (67033), note after 89505, 97929
Bourne, George, 1780-1845. supposed author 49811, 1st note after 98684

Bourne, H. 6494
Bourne, Henry Richard Fox, 1838-1909.
6922-6923
Bourne, Hugh. 6924
Bourne, S. 6926
Bourne, Silvanus. supposed author 6927,
12986, 18485,
Bourne, Stephen. 6925, 93471
Bourne, Thomas. 94688
Bourne, William Oland. 6928-6934, 86288
Bourne's views in . . . New York. 54129
Bournos, ------ Tausia. see Tausia-
Bournos, ------.
Bourreau de Berne. 16439
Bourrit, Marc Theodore, 1739-1819. tr.
23737
Bours, John. 6935
Boursier, Adolphe. (6936)
Bousell, John. 6938
Boussingault, Adam, fl. 1670. 6940
Boussingault, Jean Baptiste Joseph Dieudonne,
1802-1887. 6941, 57451
Boussole morale et politique des hommes et
des empires. (6939)
Boutelier, George Frederick. defendant 91682
Boutelier, John. defendant 91682
Boutelle, John Alonzo. 6942-6943
Boutelle, Thomas. 93952
Boutier, Pierre. 32016
Boutillier, T. 6944-6945, 10591
Bouton, J. W. 6947
Bouton, Jacques. 6948
Bouton, John Bell, 1830-1902. 6946, 73474
Bouton, Nathaniel, 1799-1878. ed. 6949-6969,
52791, 61280, 66514, 94112, 1st-2d notes
after 98997, note after 98998, 1st note
after 99003, 103894
Boutron-Charland, A. F. 6970
Bouttats, Gaspard, d. 1703. cartographer
31358, 31545
Boutwell, E. B. 6971
Boutwell, George Sewall, 1818-1905. 6972-
6977, 9615, 37326, 38788, 45923, 46148,
72649, (73795), 92038, 93405 see also
Massachusetts. Governor, 1851-1853
(Boutwell)
Bouvet de Cresse, Auguste Jean Baptiste,
1772-1839. 6978-6980, 17481
Bouvier, ------. engr. 85819
Bouvier, John, 1787-1851. 6981
Bouyer, ------. 2351
Bouyer, Frederic. 6982
Bovell, James. 6983-6984
Bovis, ------ de. 6985
Bovo de Revello, F. J. see Revello, F. J.
Bovo de.
Bow, James Dunworthy Brownson de. see
De Bow, James Dunworthy Brownson,
1820-1867.
Bowden, Andrew. plaintiff 96832
Bowden, James. 6986
Bowden, John, 1751-1817. 6987, 91745, 91749,
104638
Bowditch, Henry Ingersoll, 1808-1892. 6988-
6993, 35406
Bowditch, J. I. 93269
Bowditch, Nathaniel, 1773-1828. 6996
Bowditch, Nathaniel Ingersoll, 1805-1861.
1847, 6997-7004, 45846
Bowditch, William Ingersoll, 1819-1909. 7005-
7011
Bowditch family. 58325
Bowditch Library, Boston. see Boston.
Bowditch Library.
Bowdler, Henrietta Maria, 1754-1830. 82505
Bowdler, Thomas, 1754-1825. 7013-7014

Bowdoin, James, 1729-1790. 6739-6741, 7015-
7017, 15436, 36737, (45953), 80668-
80673, note after 97925, 101479 see also
Boston. Committee to Prepare "A Short
Narrative of the Horrid Massacre in
Boston," 1770. Massachusetts (Colony)
Commissioners to Treat with the Eastern
and Penobscot Indians, 1753. Massa-
chusetts. Governor, 1785-1787 (Bowdoin)
Bowdoin College, Brunswick, Me. 7029-7030,
7033, 7035, 7038, 58476
Bowdoin College, Brunswick, Me. Athenaean
Library. 7021-7022
Bowdoin College, Brunswick, Me. Board of
Trustees. 7036, 92313
Bowdoin College, Brunswick, Me. Centennial
Celebration, 1894. 85224
Bowdoin College, Brunswick, Me. Charter.
7031
Bowdoin College, Brunswick, Me. Library.
7024-7025
Bowdoin College, Brunswick, Me. Medical
School. 7019, 7029
Bowdoin College, Brunswick, Me. Medical
School. Library. 7026
Bowdoin College, Brunswick, Me. Overseers.
7018-7031
Bowdoin College, Brunswick, Me. Phi Beta
Kappa. Alpha of Maine. see Phi Beta
Kappa. Maine Alpha, Bowdoin College.
Bowdoin College, Brunswick, Me. Peucinian
Society. 7028
Bowdoin College, Brunswick, Me. Peucinian
Society. Library. 7027
Bowdoin College, Brunswick, Me. Students
Association. 86932
Bowdoin College, Brunswick, Me. Undergradu-
ates. 7020
Bowdoin College catalogue of the Fraternity
of ΦBK, Alpha of Maine. 7023
Bowdoin in the war. 7032
Bowdoin poets. 7039, 103043
Bowdoin port-folio. 7020
Bowdoin Square Church book. 18137
Bowdoin Street Church, Boston. see Boston.
Bowdoin Street Church.
Bowdoin Street Young Men's Peace Society,
Boston. 91039
Bowdoinham Baptist Association. see Baptists.
Maine. Bowdoinham Baptist Association.
Bowdon College, Bowdon, Ga. 7041
Bowdon Collegiate Institution, Bowdon, Ga.
see Bowdon College, Bowdon, Ga.
Bowells of compassion towards the scattered
seed. 62918
Bowen, ------. defendant 32192, (32197)
Bowen, Abel, 1790-1850. 7042-7045, 23839,
85489, 91536
Bowen, Benjamin B., 1819-1905. (7046)
Bowen, C. supposed author 5187
Bowen, Charles Synge Christopher Bowen,
Baron, 1835-1894. 7047
Bowen, Daniel, b. 1759 or 60. (7048)
Bowen, Ele. see Bowen, Eli, b. 1824.
Bowen, Eli, b. 1824. 7049-7055
Bowen, Francis, 1811-1890. 1039, (7056)-
7058, 55562, 96065
Bowen, George. defendant 7059
Bowen, Henry L., 1810-1865. 7060
Bowen, J. B. 103201
Bowen, Miss J. B. 7062
Bowen, James L. 7061
Bowen, John, Bp. of Sierra Leone, 1815-1859.
7062
Bowen, Nathan. 7063, 52670
Bowen, Nathaniel, 1779-1839. (7064)

Bowen, Noel H. (7065)
Bowen, Penuel. 7066
Bowen, Thomas J. 85072
Bowen, William W. (7067)
Bowen's Boston news-letter, and city record. 7042
Bowen's picture of Boston. 7043-7044
Bower of literature. (74165)
Bower of virtue. 97548
Bowers, Bathsheba, 1672?-1718. 7068
Bowers, James, fl. 1796-1830. (7069)
Bowers, John. 7070
Bowery Savings Bank, New York. 54109
Bowery songster. 59008
Bowery tragedy. 36101
Bowie, Richard Johns, 1807-1888. 7071
Bowie, Richard I. see Bowie, Richard Johns, 1807-1888.
Bowker, Albert. petitioner 78515
Bowker, J. 7072
Bowker, Joseph. 99047
Bowl de punch de Master Oliver Dreamer. (58262)
Bowlan, Elizabeth. defendant 96833
Bowler, Metcalf. 7073
Bowles, B. F. 7074
Bowles, Charles. 7075
Bowles, Charles S. P. (7076), (76649)
Bowles, Samuel, 1826-1878. (7077)-7080
Bowles, W. RN 7081
Bowles, William A. defendant before military commission 96953
Bowles, William Augustus, 1764-1805. 7082-7083, 104277
Bowles, William Leslie, 1762-1850. 7084-7086
Bowlin, James Butler, 1804-1874. 7087-7088
Bowling, William King, 1808-1885. (7089)-7090, (51878)
Bowly, Samuel. 7091
Bowman, A. H. (2588), 12081
Bowman, Anne. 7092-(7094)
Bowman, John. supposed author 87898
Bowman, Jonathan. defendant before church council 7095, (20624)-20625, 96500
Bowman, Joseph, fl. 1778-1779. USA (13287)
Bowman, Rev. Joseph, fl. 1791. 89793
Bowman, Samuel Millard, 1815-1885. 7096
Bowman on court of equity. 87898
Bownas, Samuel, 1676-1753. 7097, 30081, 30264-(30265), 71024
Bowrey, Thomas. see Bowrie, Thomas.
Bowrie, Thomas. 7098
Bowring, Sir John, 1792-1872. 4765-4766, 4769
Bowyer, John. of Virginia supposed author (7132), (35489)
Box. pseud. Tale of a box. 94238
Box, Henry W. ed. (41192)
Boxiana. 77402
Boy captive in Canada. 83556
Boy captive of Old Deerfield. 83556
Boy-hunters. 69022
Boy hunters in the North. 69086
Boy inventor. 9092
Boy-life among the Cherokees. 28130
Boy slaves. 69023
Boyce, Captain ------. 7099, 25368
Boyce, Joseph. (22426)
Boyce, William Waters, 1818-1890. 7100
Boyd, ------. 68198
Boyd, A. H. 7106-7107
Boyd, Adam, 1738-1803. (7101)
Boyd, Andrew. 7103-7105, 19380, 22191, 41167, 41214, 41743, 72340, 77599, note before 94542

Boyd, Andrew, fl. 1777-1780. 7102 see also Chester County, Pa. Sub Lieutenant.
Boyd, Belle, 1843-1800. (30338)-30339
Boyd, George. 7108
Boyd, H. tr. (22729)
Boyd, Henry. supposed author 98340
Boyd, Hugh, 1746-1794. 7109
Boyd, J. P. ed. 93937
Boyd, James. 7110, 46072, 67908
Boyd, James R. 90004
Boyd, John. (7111)
Boyd, Sir John Alexander, 1837-1916. 7112-7113
Boyd, John Parker, 1764-1830. 7114-(7115), 20453
Boyd, Joseph B. 13068
Boyd, Robert. defendant 6326, 1st note after 96956, 1st note after 97284
Boyd, Samuel Stillman, 1807-1867. 7118
Boyd, William. typographer 7121
Boyd, William, d. 1800. 7119-(7120)
Boyd, William Henry, 1825-1887. 7104-7105, 7122-7125, 13676, 19380, 22191, (22359), (37917), 38797, 53077, 53547, 54459, (54874), 55044, 55925, 59059, 59262, 59923, 59925, 61606, (71174), 73019, 76913, 77599
Boyd, William Kenneth, 1879-1938. 97092
Boyd. firm publishers see Edwards & Boyd. firm publishers
Boyd (A.) publisher 72340
Boyd (John T.) & Co. firm 93067
Boyden, Ebenezer, 1803-1891. (7126)
Boyden, James W. 7127
Boyd's Auburn directory. 7104
Boyd's business directory of . . . New Jersey. 53077
Boyd's business directory of over one hundred cities. 53547
Boyd's business directory of [ten] counties of . . . Pa. 59923
Boyd's business directory of the counties. 7105
Boyd's Delaware state directory. 19380
Boyd's directory of Elizabeth. 22191
Boyd's directory of Richmond city. (71174)
Boyd's directory of Richmond city, and a business directory of Norfolk, Lynchburg, Petersburg, and Richmond. (71174)
Boyd's directory of Saratoga Springs. 76913
Boyd's Elmira directory. (22359)
Body's hand-book of Cincinnati. 13068
Boyd's Lancaster County business directory. 38797
Boyd's Lockport City directory. 41743
Boyd's Newark business directory. (54874)
Boyd's Philadelphia city business directory. 61606
Boyd's pictorial directory of Broadway. 7124, 54459
Boyd's Rochester and Brockport directory. 72340
Boyd's Rochester directory. 72340
Boye, Emmanuel de. 7128
Boye, F. tr. (42739)
Boye, Johannes. 7129
Boyer, Lieutenant. (7132), (35489)
Boyer, Abel, 1667-1729. 5269, (65038), 1st note after (74627), (77219)-77220
Boyer, Benjamin Markley, 1823-1887. 7130-7131
Boyer, Jean Pierre, Pres. Haiti, 1776-1850. (16894), (29576)-(29577) see also Haiti. President, 1818-1843 (Boyer)
Boyer, Paul, b. 1615. 7133

Boyer de Peyreleau, Eugene Edouard, Baron
  de. 7134-7135
Boyer Fonfrede, J. B. 67927
Boyer's journal. (35489)
Boyga, Manuel. defendant 27309, (51797),
  69915, 93808, 96948
Boyle, Augustus F. ed. 54836
Boyle, E. 28693
Boyle, Frederick, 1841- 7136
Boyle, Henry. (7137), 75419
Boyle, Isaac. 6700, 7138
Boyle, Jacobo. see Boyle, James. supposed
  author
Boyle, James. supposed author 103993,
  105928
Boyle, John. defendant 96814
Boyle, Captain Robert. Voyages and adven-
  tures. see Chetwood, William Rufus,
  d. 1755.
Boyle, Hon. Robert, 1627-1671. 7139
Boylston, Thomas, 1720?-1798. 7140
Boylston, Ward Nicholas. 7140
Boylston, Zabdiel, 1679-1766. 7143, 86588
Boylston Medical School. see Harvard Uni-
  versity. Boylston Medical School.
Boylston Medical Society, Harvard University.
  see Harvard University. Boylston
  Medical Society.
Boylston prize dissertations for 1836-37.
  32621
Boylston prize essay, August, 1834. 9899
Boylston prize questions. 79871
Boylstone, Zabdiel. see Boylston, Zabdiel.
Boynton, Charles Brandon, 1806-1883. 7146-
  7151, 52032
Boynton, Eben Moody. 105074, 105077
Boynton, Edward Carlisle, 1824-1893. (7150)
Boynton, Thomas J. 7152
Boy's adventures in the forests of Brazil.
  2952
Boy's adventures in the gold regions. 27194
Boy's and girl's library. 30962, (30966),
  30970-30971, 95217, 1st note after 97724,
  3d note after 97724, 2d note after 97725,
  2d note after 97726, 2d note after 100480
Boys and girls of seventy-seven. 83556
Boys and girls stories of the war. (7153)
Boy's experience in the United States Navy.
  55461
Boy's High School, Providence, R. I. see
  Providence, R. I. Boy's High School.
Boys in blue. 32428
Boys' Industrial School, Lancaster, O. see
  Ohio. Boys' Industrial School, Lan-
  caster.
Boy's life and essays of Franklin. 25611
Boy's narrative of the adventures of a settler's
  family in Canada. 26841, note after
  90307
Boys of the border. 83556
Boy's reading-book. 80913
Boy's trip across the plains. 65373
Boz Ball, New York, 1842. 54715
Boz Ball. To be given under the direction of
  a committee. 54715
Boza y Garzes, Antonio. 98335 see also
  Lima. Universidad de San Marcos.
  Rector.
Bozman, John Leeds. 7154-7155, 45268, 45370
Braam Houckgeest, E. van. see Houckgeest,
  E. van Braam.
Brabourne, ------. 80255-(80256)
Bracamont, Pedro Alonso de Avalos y, Conde
  de Miravalles. see Avalos y Bracamont,
  Pedro Alonso de, Conde de Miravalles,

Bracamont y Orozco, Maria Catharina Davalos.
  see Davalos Bracamont y Orozco, Maria
  Catharina, Condesa de Miraville. plaintiff
Bracamonte, Alonso de Solis Valderabano i.
  see Solis Valderabano i Bracamonte,
  Alonso de.
Bracamonte, Bernardino de Meneses. see
  Meneses Bracamonte, Bernardino de.
Bracamonte y Espinosa, Pedro Alonso Davalos.
  see Davalos Bracamonte y Espinosa,
  Pedro Alonso, Conte de Mirvalle.
Bracciolini, Poggio. see Poggio-Bracciolini,
  1380-1459.
Brace, Charles Loring, 1826-1890. 7156-7158
Brace, J. ed. 96089
Brace, John Pierce, 1793-1872. 7160
Brace, Jonathan, 1810-1877. 7159
Brachiopoda, a division of annelida. 50915
Bracho, Luis. 48299
Bracht, Viktor. 7161
Brackenbridge, W. S. 31051, 46130, 1st note
  after 89210
Brackenridge, --------, fl. 1793. 63790
Brackenridge, H. B. 45362
Brackenridge, Henry Marie, 1786-1871. 6921A,
  (7162)-7183, 17362, 18333, 62509, 87319,
  note after 89505, 97972, note after 105507
Brackenridge, Hugh Henry, 1748-1816. 7184-
  7192, 25904, 50155, (56702), note after
  90154, 97972, note after 101861
Brackenridge, Hugh Henry, 1748-1816. supposed
  author 58640
Brackenridge, William Dunlop, 1810-1893.
  7193-27419
Bracket, Adino N. 7194
Brackett, Albert Gallatin, 1829-1896. 7195-
  7196
Brackett, Edward Augustus, 1818-1908. 7197
Brackett, Gilbert R. 85276, 85300, 85341
Brackett, James, 1782-1852. 7198
Brackett, Joseph W. petitioner 33939, 78737,
  103717
Brackett, Joseph Warren, 1775-1826. 7199-
  7200
Brackett, Loraina. 92135
Brackinridge, H. 38111
Bradburn, George, 1806-1880. 7201
Bradburn, Samuel, 1751-1816. 7202-7203
Bradbury, Charles, 1798-1864. 7204
Bradbury, James Ware, 1802-1901. 7205-7206
Bradbury, John, fl. 1809. 7207, 84303-84306,
  84320-84321
Bradbury, Thomas. 7208
Braddock, Edward, 1695?-1755. 15205, 17365,
  (41650), (47511)-47512, 51661, 101710
Braddock's defeat. 7209
Braddock's times. 43311, 1st note after 101905,
  103986
Bradfield, J. H. tr. 51409
Bradford, J. A. 90692
Bradford, Alden, 1765-1843. 7213-7232, 9180,
  (46131), 64775
Bradford, Alexander Warfield, 1815-1867.
  7233-7235 see also New York (County)
  Surrogate
Bradford, Andrew, 1686-1742. 78759-(78760),
  84552, 106148, 106351
Bradford, Augustus Williamson, 1806-1881.
  7236-7237, 45128, 45164, (45263), 45266
  see also Maryland. Governor, 1862-
  1865 (Bradford)
Bradford, Benjamin J. 94770
Bradford, Ebenezer, 1746-1801. 7238-7244,
  94361
Bradford, Ephraim Putnam, 1776-1845. 7245-
  7246

Bradford, Gamaliel, 1795-1839. 7247-7248, note after 90640, 105628
Bradford, George. 7251
Bradford, George W., 1796-1883. 7249-(7250)
Bradford, James. (26322)
Bradford, John, 1749-1830. 91838
Bradford, John, fl. 1788. 7252
Bradford, John, fl. 1815. (32170), 63650
Bradford, Moses. 7253
Bradford, Samuel, successively Bp. of Carlisle, and Rochester, 1652-1731. 7254
Bradford, Samuel Dexter. 7255-7257
Bradford, Samuel Fisher, 1776-1837. (7258), 14026, note after 95800, 12th note after 95843
Bradford, Samuel T. tr. 12289
Bradford, Sarah Elizabeth (Hopkins) 1818-7259
Bradford, Thomas G., fl. 1819. ed. 94730
Bradford, Thomas Gamaliel, 1802-1887. 7260-7261, 12596, 22556, 62635, (70885), 84062, 103911
Bradford, Vincent L. 60210
Bradford, William, 1588-1657. 7262-7263, 19051, 51012, 51017, (51198)-51201, note after 104797, 106053
Bradford, William, 1663-1752. 7264, 8957, 12914, 36981, 37181, 37185, 37202, 37216-37217, (37223), (37225), (60182), (66038), 78754-(78760), 82975-82976, 84556, 97113, 96790, 106148
Bradford, William, 1663-1752. supposed author (37125), note after 101268
Bradford, William, 1663-1752. defendant 37203, (37226), 1st note after 96931, 2d note after 96956, 2d note after 97284
Bradford, William, 1722-1791. 60325
Bradford, William, 1755-1795. 7265
Bradford, William John Alden, 1791-1858. 7267
Bradford, William M. (7266)
Bradford, Mass. Ecclesiastical Council, 1744. see Congregational Churches in Massachusetts. Ecclesiastical Council, Bradford, 1744.
Bradford, Mass. School Committee. 7268
Bradford, Mass. Second Church. 7268, 27584, 103399
Bradford, Mass. Second Church, Pastor. 7269, 99830 see also Balch, William.
Bradford County, Pa. Convention of Delegates, Tunkhannock, 1840. see Convention of Delegates from Luzerne, Susquehanna and Bradford Counties, Tunkhannock, Pa., 1840.
Bradford Club. note after 7269
Bradford Club series, no. 1. 58449
Bradford Club series, no. 2. 20862
Bradford Club series, no. 3. 28332, (80023)
Bradford Club series, no. 4. 51460, 51464, 91169
Bradford Club series, no. 5. 87206
Bradford Club series, no. 6. 33144
Bradford Club series, no. 7. 39360
Bradford family. (66719)
Bradford prayer book. 36508
Bradford's and Winslow's journal. (51198)-51201, note after 104797, 106053
Bradi, -------, Comtesse de. 85819
Bradish, Isaac. 1066, 3625, note before 93509, 103349A
Bradish, Luther, 1783-1863. (7270), (7272)-7273, 25641, 90661, 3d note after 96984
Bradlee, Caleb Davis, 1831-1897. 7274-7275, 29827
Bradlee, John E. 7276

Bradlee, Nathaniel J. 7277
Bradlee's pocket guide to the White Mountains. 7276
Bradley, Arthur Granville, 1850- 82857
Bradley, C. 7278
Bradley, C. W. (15829)
Bradley, Frank Howe, 1838-1879. 34527
Bradley, George S. (7279)
Bradley, Jesse. 7280
Bradley, Joseph P., 1813-1892. (7282)-7283, 74437
Bradley, Joshua. defendant 96834
Bradley, Joshua, 1773-1855. 7281
Bradley, Mary E. (7283A)
Bradley, Micah. 7284
Bradley, Stephen Row, 1754-1830. 7286, 4th note after 99005
Bradley, Thomas. 94291
Bradley, Thomas. supposed ed. 28078
Bradley, Thomas Bibb. 63410
Bradley, William A. plaintiff 101975
Bradley, William C. 7287
Bradman, Arthur. 7288
Bradshaw, G. (7289)
Bradshaw, S. 66686
Bradshaw, Thomas. 7290
Bradshaw, Wesley. 7291-7294
Bradshaw, William. 72103
Bradshaw, William S. 7295
Bradshaw's railway manual and directory. (7289)
Bradstreet, Anne (Dudley) 1612?-1672. 7296-7299, note after 94823
Bradstreet, Benjamin, d. 1762. 7300
Bradstreet, John, 1711-1774. 19788, 33138
Bradstreet, Martha, b. 1780. 7304-7306
Bradstreet, Martha, b. 1780. plaintiff 7307, (15620), 90686
Bradstreet, Nathan. 7308
Bradstreet, Simon, 1603-1697. (33445), 97547, 106052 see also Massachusetts (Colony) Governor, 1679-1686 (Bradstreet) Massachusetts (Colony) Governor, 1689-1692 (Bradstreet)
Bradstreet, Simon, fl. 1701. supposed author 28052, 28506, 65689, 91945-note after 91945, note after 105090
Bradstreet, Simon, fl. 1755-1762. 7309-7310
Bradstreet (John M.) and Sons. firm 7302-7303
Bradt, Henry Y. 77599
Bradwell, James Bolesworth, 1828-1907. 7311
Brady, -------, fl. 1863. 89223
Brady, Cyrus Townsend, 1861-1920. 95396
Brady, James T. 7313-(7314)
Brady, Jasper Ewing, 1797-1871. 7312
Brady, Matthew B., 1823-1896. 26415, (40221)
Brady, Nathaniel. (66441)
Brady, Nicholas, 1659-1726. 3471, 7315, 64998-(64999), (66440)-(66441), 66448-66449
Brady, William. 7316
Braemer, O. F. tr. 59187
Braga, Bernardo de, 1604-1662. (7317)-7318
Braga, Jose Cardoso. tr. 42607
Braganza, Miguel Evaristo de. see Miguel I, King of Portugal, 1802-1866.
Bragdon, C. D. 24683 50344
Bragdon, Joseph H., d. 1905. (7320)
Brager, ------- Durand. see Durand-Brager, -------.
Bragg, Arial, b. 1772. 7321
Bragg, Benjamin. pseud. Voyage to the North Pole. 7322, 5th note after 100818
Bragg, Braxton, 1817-1876. 12674, 15324
Bragg, Samuel A. B. 87031
Bragg, Samuel A. D. 87016

Bragg, Thomas, 1810-1872. 33150 see also
North Carolina. Governor, 1855-1859
(Bragg)
Bragg & Co. firm see Van Antwerp, Bragg
& Co. firm
Bragge, Robert. 7323
Brahm, John Gerar William de. 1147, (7324)-
7326, 72995, 93574, 103051
Brahm, William Gerard de. see Brahm,
John Gerar William de.
Brailsford, Edward, d. 1856. 7327-7328
Brailsford & Morris. firm 87920
Brain, Tudor. 78661
Brainard, Jeremiah Gates, 1760?-1830. 7330
Brainard, John. see Brainerd, John, 1720-
1781.
Brainard, John Gardner Calkins, 1796-1828.
7331-7332, 25160, 103819
Brainard, William Fowler, 1784-1844. (7333)
Brainard Church, Belchertown, Mass. see
Belchertown, Mass. Brainard Church.
Braine, Benjamin. 6106, 92322
Brainerd, C. N. (7337)
Brainerd, Cephas, 1831-1910. 7334-7336
Brainerd, D. S. 7338
Brainerd, David, 1718-1747. 4149, 4678,
7339-7343, 7346, 21927-21928, 21949,
21951, 21953, 59608, 64945, 85994,
93291, 102699
Brainerd, John, 1720-1781. 7329
Brainerd, Thomas, 1804-1866. 7347-7353,
65203, 78320
Brainerd's journal. 4149
Brainerd's remarks on the work of Grace.
7343
Braintree, Mass. Auditors. 7354
Braintree, Mass. Ecclesiastical Council,
1792. see Congregational Churches in
Massachusetts. Ecclesiastical Council,
Braintree, 1792.
Braintree, Mass. First Church. (7358)
Braintree, Mass. First Church. Committee.
(67191)
Braintree, Mass. School Committee. 7356
Braintree Institution for Savings. see Wey-
mouth and Braintree Institution for
Savings.
Braister, Margaret. 8654
Braithwaite, Anna. 7359, 103059
Braithwaite, John, 1797-1870. 7360, 73370
Braithwaite, Joseph Bevan, 1818-1905. 7361
Brakel, William a, 1635-1711. 7362
Brakeman, Nelson L. 7363
Brakenbury, Samuel. 62743
Braman, D. E. E. 7364
Braman, Isaac, 1770-1858. 7365-7367
Braman, Milton Palmer, Bp., b. 1799. 7368-
(7370), 103797, 103802
Braman's information about Texas. 7364
Bramham, James W. 7372, 104329
Bramhill, Frank G. 7371
Bramin. pseud. see Chesterfield, Philip
Dormer Stanhope, 4th Earl of, 1694-1773.
Bramston, William. 7373
Bramwell, -----. 7374
Branagan, Thomas, b. 1774. 7375-7384, 13890,
14011, (71368), 71369
Branch, ------. (21730)
Branch, North. pseud. see North Branch.
pseud.
Branch, Stephen. (70667)
Branch, Stephen H., b. 1813. 7385-7386.
Branch, William. 7387
Branch mint in Oregon. (31322)
Branch mint of the United States. 52341

Branch of Sanitary Commission. Final report.
76661
Branch of the Sanitary Commission. Third
annual report of the New-England Women's
Auxiliary Association. 76661
Branch of the United States Sanitary Commis-
sion. (76628)
Branch of the U. S. Sanitary Commission.
Final report of the General Aid Society
for the Army. 76629
Branch of the U. S. Sanitary Commission.
Fourth annual and final report of the
Woman's Central Association of Relief.
76634
Branch of the U. S. Sanitary Commission.
Second annual report of the Woman's
Central Association of Relief. 76632
Branch of the U. S. Sanitary Commission.
Second semi-annual report of the Women's
Central Association of Relief. 76630
Branch of the U. S. Sanitary Commission.
Third annual report of the Womans'
Central Association of Relief. 76633
Branch of the U. S. Sanitary Commission.
Third semi-annual report of the Womans'
Central Association of Relief. 76631
Branch of the Whitney family. 30487
Branches of everlasting blessings. 4116
Branciforte, Miguel de la Grua Talamanca,
Marques. see Grua Talamanca, Miguel
de la, Marques de Branciforte.
Branco Moniz Barreto, Domingos Alves. see
Barreto, Domingos Alves Branco Moniz.
Brand, --------. defendant (14087)
Brand, Charles. RN 7388-7389
Brand, G. 74514
Brand, W. 86574
Brand, W. F. 7390
Brand, W. H. 1528
Brand plucked out of the fire. 90184
Brandaines, Saint. see Brendan, of Clonfert,
Saint, 484-577.
Brandao, Luiz da Silva. see Silva Brandao,
Luiz da.
Brandao Montezuma, Francisco Gomes. 7391
Brandard, Robert, 1805-1862. 3784, 3787,
8899, note after 104504-104505
Branded hand. 28594, 79691
Branded hand. A dramatic sketch. (41525)
Brandegee, Augustus, 1828-1904. 7392
Branden, Marten Hans. 102893
Brandende veen. (72762)
Brandes, Fr. 7393
Brandes, Karl. 7392
Brandes, Karl. tr. 2794-2795
Brandhof Ez., A. van den. (7395)
Brandin, Abel Victorino. 7396-7398
Brandis, Bernhard. 9684
Brandis, G. Brender a. see Brender a
Brandis, G.
Brandis, J. D. tr. 49892
Brandligt, C. 7399
Brandon, Benjamin. supposed author 12982,
25296, 86684, 3d note after 95765, 2d
note after 102065
Brandon, Charles. tr. 44702
Brandon, Curris. (7400)
Brandon, Lorenco. (7401)
Brandon, Samuel Hoheb. (27218), (40086)-40088,
(51894), 3d 6th-7th notes after 93855
Brandreth, Dr. pseud. see Hines, David
Theodore.
Brandreth, George A. 7402
Brandsen, Carlos Luis Federico de. see
Brandsen, Federico, 1785-1827.

Brandsen, Federico, 1785-1827. 61127, 68789, 94833
Brandt, F. 7403-7404
Brandt, Geeraert, 1626-1685. 6441, 7405-7408, note after 98470
Brandt, R. J. (7409)
Brandt in Brasilian Gedruck in't jaer ons heeren. 7528
Brannan, -------. 10015
Brannan, Benjamin. 7410
Brannan, John. 7411
Brannan, William Penn, 1825-1866. 7412
Brano, Joseph. illus. 28527
Brason, David. (25261)
Brason & Jones. firm publishers 55599
Branson's North Carolina business directory. 55599
Brant, Joseph, 1742-1807. 6351, 49845
Brantly, William Theophilus, 1816-1882. 7414-7416
Brantz, Lewis. 7417
Braodwell, S. (8148)
Braschi, Giovanni Angelo. see Pius VI, Pope, 1717-1799.
Brasford, J. F. 85072
Brashear, ---------. defendant 5161
Brashear, John Alfred, 1840-1920. 84997
Brashears, Noah. 7418
Brasil, Thomas Pompeo de Sousa. see Pompeo de Sousa Brasil, Thomas.
Brasil historico. 7529
Brasil historico e a corographia historica do imperio do Brasil. 7616
Brasil salvo. 11708
Brasil visto por Cima. 7530, 56371, 68332
Brasile di Ferdinando Denis. 19544
Brasileiras celebres. 88801
Brasileiro. pseud. Historia universal. 32039
Brasileiro. pseud. Memoria sobre a nobreza no Brasil. see Gama e Castro, Jose de.
Brasileiro. pseud. Memorias de um Sargento de Milicias. see Almeida, Manuel Antonio de.
Brasileiro. pseud. Retrospecto dos erros da administracao do Brasil. see Souza Franca, Manoel Jose de.
Brasileiro. pseud. tr. see Sanctos, Luis Goncalves dos.
Brasileiro emigrado. 94612
Brasileiro impartial. 43882
Brasileiro veterano. pseud. Conselhos que da uno Brasileiro veterano. see D., M. pseud.
Brasilia durch Johann Staden. (8784)
Brasilia pontificae. 44664
Brasiliana. pseud. Scintille d'un brasiliana. 78122
Brasilian navigator. (66690)
Brasilianas. 64398
K. K. Brasilianer-Museum, Vienna. see Vienna. K. K. Brasilianer-Museum.
Brasilianische Geschichte. 3412
Brasilianische Geschichte Johann Moritz, Fursten zu Nassau. 7531
Brasilianische Handelsrecht. 7532, note after 92013
Brasilianische Organisationscharakter. 9345
Brasilianische Volkslieder und Indianischen Melodien. 44996, 89549
Brasilianische Zustande. 95813
Brasilianischen Geschichte. 3411
Brasilianisches Lebensbild. 27173
Brasilien. 19542, 70386
Brasilien als unabhangiges Reich in Historischer, Mercantilischer und Politischer Beziehung geschildert. 77486

Brasilien, Chili, etc. 106334
Brasilien, Chile und Patagonien. 106334
Brasilien. Columbien und Guyana. 102622
Brasilien, die neue Welt. 22825
Brasilien fur Deutsche und Schweizerische Auswanderer. 91188
Brasilien in seiner Entwicklung seit der Entdeckung bis auf unsere Zeit. 89547
Brasilien. Nachtrage, Berichtigungen und Zusatze. 47013
Brasilien und Deutschland. 25425
Brasilien und seine Bedeutung fur die Deutsche Auswanderung. 38276
Brasilien von Ferdinand Denys. 19542, 102622
Brasiliens gegenwartiger Zustand und Colonialsystem. 102443
Brasiliens Kriegs- und Revolutionsgeschichte seit dem Jahre 1825 bis auf unsere Zeit. 78934
Brasiliens uddode dyrskabning. 42688
Brasiliens vorzuglich lastige Insekten. (63678)
Brasilsche breede-byl. 7534
Brasilsche gelt-sack. 7535, 102885
Brasilsche oorloghs overwegingh. 7536
Brass, H. W. D. tr. 20617
Brasseur, ------ le. see Le Brasseur, ------.
Brasseur de Bourbourg, Charles Etienne, 1814-1874. (7419)-7441, (14676), 24110, 38826, (44433), 49464, 48436, 73299, 76007, 89976
Brasseur de Bourbourg, E. Beauvois. 85781
Brasyls schuyt-praetjen. 7537
Braszilianisch- und West Indianische Reisze Beschreibung. 71219
Brathwaite, Richard, 1588?-1673. 94165
Bratt, A. M. V:a. tr. 92407
Brattle, Thomas, 1658-1713. 62743
Brattle, Thomas, 1658-1713. supposed author 28052, 28506, 65689, 91945, note after 105090
Brattle, Thomas, fl. 1735. 15045
Brattle, William, 1662-1717. 62743, 66457, 95820
Brattle, William, 1706-1777. (7442)
Brattleboro, Vt. Fair of the New England and Vermont State Agricultural Societies, 1866. see Fair of the New England and Vermont State Agricultural Societies, Brattleboro, Vt., 1866.
Brattleboro, Vt. Lawrence Water-Cure. see Lawrence Water-Cure, Brattleboro, Vt.
Brattleboro semi-weekly eagle. 7286, 30798, 51825, 4th note after 99005, 102608
Bratton's Brigate, South Carolina Volunteers. see South Carolina Infantry. Bratton's Brigade.
Brattonsville, S. C. Celebration of Huck's Defeat, 1839. Committee of Arrangements. 87921
Brauer, Johann Hartwig. (7445)
Braun, Bartholome. 7446-7447, 27535
Braun, Georg, fl. 1593-1616. 7448, 73000
Braunfels, Carl, Prinz zu Solms-. see Carl, Prinz zu Solms-Braunfels.
Brauns, Ernest Ludwig. (7449)-7455
Brauns, J. Ernst Ludwig. tr. 47437
Brauns, Frederick William, 1830-1895. 7456
Braun's voyage to Congo. 67565
Braunschweig, Johann Daniel von. 7457
Brauw, J. de. 31487
Brave and happy soldier. 44725
Brave ballads for American children. 91067
Brave Lowewell, and several members of his company lamented. 94107
Brave old salt. 357
Brave patriot. 91067

Brave soldier, . . . defended. 36262
Brave yankee boys. 97283
Bravet, --------, Sieur. 7458
Bravo, ------. 93791
Bravo, Fernando. 7459
Bravo, Francisco. 7460
Bravo, Jose. supposed author 86182
Bravo, Juan. 7461
Bravo, Pedro Oliver y. see Oliver y Bravo, Pedro.
Bravo de Lagunas y Castilla, Pedro Joseph. 7462-7463, 38628-38630
Bravo de Rivero, Joseph. see Rivero, Joseph Bravo de.
Bravo de Rivero y Zavala, Diego Miguel. see Rivero y Zavala, Diego Miguel Bravo de.
Bravo del Ribero, Pedro. see Ribero, Pedro Bravo del.
Bravo. 83788
Bravo: a tale. 16417
Bravo . . . . Aus dem Englishchen. 16419
Bravo . . . . Traduit. 16418
Brawern, Heinrich. 8427, 13015, 33678
Brawern and Herckemann's voyage to Chili in 1642 and 1643. 13015
Braxton, Carter, 1736-1797. 7466, note before 100024
Braxton, Carter M. 7467, 44444
Bray, Caroline (Hennell) 7468
Bray, John E. 91109
Bray, Oliver, 1776-1823. 7669
Bray, Thomas, 1656-1730. 7473-7483, 83976, 83977, 105651-105652 see also Church of England in America. Maryland. Commissary.
Bray, Thomas, 1656-1730. petitioner 83978
Bray, Thomas, 1656-1730. supposed author 7470
Bray, Thomas Wells, 1738-1808. 7485-7486
Bray, William. 7487
Braydon, C. D. 24683, 50344
Brayer, Miguel. 7558
Brayman, James O., 1815-1887. 7488-7489
Brayman, M. 34289
Braynard, Selden. defendant 96835
Brayton, --------. reporter 69392
Brayton, J. A. 7490
Brayton, J. J. 7491
Brayton, Mary Clark. 76663, 86316
Brayton, Patience. (7492)
Brayton, William D. (70667)
Brazer, John, 1787-1846. 7494-7495, 32673
Brazer, Samuel, 1785-1823. 7496
Brazer, Samuel, Jr. 7497-7499
Brazil, Thomaz Pompeo de Souza. see Souza Brazil, Thomaz Pompeo de, 1852-
Brazil (Dutch Colony) 2155A, 7501, 7520
Brazil (Dutch Colony) Gesamentlijcke Aenwesende Gedeputeerdens. petitioners 7635
Brazil (Dutch Colony) Hoogen Raet. 7564 see also Haencx, Hendrick.
Brazil (Dutch Colony) Laws, statutes, etc. 7552, 7619, 7636-7637, note after 89149, note after 102886
Brazil (Dutch Colony) Militie. Luytenant Generael. 7564 see also Schoppe, Sigismondus van.
Brazil (Dutch Colony) Militie. Officieren. 7505
Brazil (Dutch Colony) President. 7564, 7578 see also Schonenburgh, Wouter van.
Brazil (Dutch Colony) Raden. 7579, 40988, 1st note after 102891
Brazil (Dutch Colony) Treaties, etc. 2155A, 7520, 63895

Brazil. (2854), (3901), 7524, 16903, 57463, 87189, 88770
Brazil. defendant 65519
Brazil. Academia Imperial das Bellas Artes, Rio de Janeiro. see Academia Imperial das Bellas Artes, Rio de Janeiro.
Brazil. Assemblea Geral Legislativo. see Brazil. Congresso.
Brazil. Bibliotheca Nacional, Rio de Janeiro. see Rio de Janeiro.
Brazil. Camara Legislativa. see Brazil. Congresso.
Brazil. Commissao Brazileira na Exposicao Internacional de Londres, 1862. Presidente. see London. International Exposition, 1862. Brazilian Commission. President.
Brazil. Commissao de Inquerito, Nomeda por Aviso do Ministerio da Fazenda, 1850. 7624
Brazil. Commissao Directora da 2a. Exposicao Nacional de 1866. Secretario. 88799 see also Souza Rego, Antonio Jose de.
Brazil. Commissao Encarregada da Revisao da Tarifa das Alfandegas. 7568
Brazil. Commissao Mixta Brasileira e Portugueza na Execucao dos Artigos 6.° e 7.° do Tractado de 29 de Agosto de 1825. see Commissao Mixta Brasileira e Portugueza na Execucao dos Artigos 6.° e 7.° do Tractado de 29 de Agosto de 1825.
Brazil. Commisao para Esse Fim Nomeada por Decreto de 8 de Janeiro de 1832. 96264
Brazil. Congresso. 67539, 68755
Brazil. Congresso. Camara dos Deputados. 7631
Brazil. Congresso. Camara dos Deputados. Commissao de Fazenda. 58571
Brazil. Conselho de Estado. 41713, 81094
Brazil. Conselho de Estado. Seccao de Fazenda. 85680
Brazil. Constitution. 7555-7557, 7611, 7617, 16052, 72497
Brazil. Consul-General, Philadelphia. 68331-68332 see also Gonsalves da Cruz, Antonio.
Brazil. Direito Financeiro Brasileiro. 3649
Brazil. Exercicio. (2854), 7524
Brazil. Exposicao Nacional, 1875. 71462
Brazil. Imperial Instituto dos Meninos Cegos, Rio de Janeiro. see Imperial Instituto dos Meninos Cegos, Rio de Janeiro.
Brazil. Instituto Brasileiro de Historico e Geographico. 7574, 7602, 7610, 7630, (11452), 14364, 24314, 35334, 47755, 56427, 60879, 2d note after 70319, 71464, 76904, 85635, 88806, note after 90061, 94595, 98828-98829, note after 99383C, 99522
Brazil. Instituto da Ordem dos Advogados. see Instituto da Ordem dos Advogados Brasileiros.
Brazil. Instituto Historico e Geographico Brasiliero. see Brasil. Instituto Brasileiro de Historico e Geographico.
Brazil. Instituto Historico Geographico e Ethnographico. see Brazil. Instituto Brasileiro de Historico e Geographico.
Brasil. Intendente Geral da Policia. 7621
Brazil. Junta de Porto. 57196
Brazil. Laws, statutes, etc. 7532, 7548-(7551), 7557, 7566, 7586, 7596, 16052, 16757, (17009), 24129, 24169, 25275, 26495, 41713, 42346, 44461, 51687, 51688,

(56023), 59507, 67668, 68335, 70793,
72302, 73432, 79306, 81077, 81091-
81094, 85637, 85679-85680, 88730,
88766, 88770, 88774, 88797, note after
92013, 100893
Brazil. Legation. U. S. 68331-68332 see
also Rebello, Jose Silvestre.
Brazil. Ministerio da Agricultura. 52358,
70454, 88783
Brazil. Ministerio da Fazenda. 7624, 21364,
49461, 66064, 69321 see also Castro
a Silva, Manoel de Nascimento. Pin e
Almeida, Miguel Calmon du.
Brazil. Ministerio da Guerra. (7509), 7623
Brazil. Ministerio da Justicia. 46906 see
also Mattoso Camara, Eusebio de
Queiroz Coitinho.
Brazil. Ministerio da Marinha. 7510
Brazil. Ministerio das Relacoes Exteriores.
7623, 14299, 16153, 24165, 38224, 38994,
39523, 69322, 85648, 88805, note after
93820 see also Ferraz, Luiz Pedreira
de Coutto. Silva Lisboa, Bento. Soares
de Souza, Paulino Jose, Visconde do
Uruguay, 1807-1866.
Brazil. Ministerio do Imperio. 9760 see
also Soares de Souza, Paulino Jose,
Visconde do Uruguay, 1807-1866. Soares
de Souza, Paulino Jose, 1834-
Brazil. Ministerio dos Negocios Estrangeiros.
see Brazil. Ministerio das Relacoes
Exteriores.
Brazil. Ministro a Quem Competia Fazer a
Ceremonia da Bencao e Coroacao de
S. M. o Imperador, 1841. 72503
Brazil. Museu Imperial e Nacional, Rio de
Janeiro. see Rio de Janeiro. Museu
Nacional.
Brazil. Museu Nacional, Rio de Janeiro.
see Rio de Janeiro. Museu Nacional.
Brazil. Negocians. petitioners. 7626, 16050
Brazil. Procurador dos Feitos da Fezenda
Nacional. 60873
Brazil. Sovereigns, etc. 1822-1831 (Pedro I)
59516 see also Pedro I, Emperor of
Brazil, 1798-1834.
Brazil. Supremo Tribunal de Justicia. 59507
Brazil. Thesouro Nacional. Chefe de Seccao.
85626 see also Soares, Sebastiao
Ferreira, 1820-1887.
Brazil. Treaties, etc. (21123), 28292, 38719,
47598, 62986, 68786, 85648
Brazil. Viceroy (Mascarenhas) 45409 see
also Mascarenhas, Jorge, Marquez de
Montalvao.
Brazil. 62957
Brazil agricola. 7539, 56372
Brazil, and Buenos Ayres. 15167, 49816
Brazil and La Plata. 91664
Brazil and River Plate route. 73800
Brazil and the Brazilians. 88910
Brazil and the Brazilians, portrayed in histori-
cal and descriptive sketches. 24723,
37709
Brazil and the River Plate in 1868. 29487
Brazil and the River Plate Mail. see South
American journal.
Brazil as a field for emigration. 21314
Brazil Company (Portuguese) 7590
Brazil historico escripto. (47457)
Brazil: its history. 7540
Brazil; its provinces and chief cities. 78536-
(78537)
Brazil pittoresco historica. (70809)-70810
Brazil pilot. 31674

Brazil por hum presbitero secular do gram
priorado do Crato. 7541
Brazil. The Amazons and the coast. 82720
Brazil the home for southerners. 21319
Brazil, the River Plate, and the Falkland Islands.
29486
Brazileiro devoto de S. Huberto. pseud. A
caca no Brazil. 7546
Braziliada. 76331
Brazilian and Latin vocabulary. 7588, 63028
Brazilian Association of Liverpool. Member.
pseud. see Member of the Brazilian
Association of Liverpool. pseud.
Brazilian improvements. 7542
Brazilian Mining Association. Directors. 7627
Brazilian pilot. 62884
Brazilie, als onafhankelijk rijk. (77487)
Brazilien. Canonisationis, seu declarationis
martyri servorum Dei Ignatii Azeuedi.
68434
Breach in Jerusalem's walls deplored. 62580
Bread cast upon the waters. 67765
Breakenrig, T. petitioner 91649
"Breaking of bread," . . . . Five sermons.
12331
Breaking the line. 9742
Breaking up of courts. 101107, 1st note after
101924
Breard, --------, Sieur. 7650
Breathedsville, Md. College of St. James.
51256, 75237
Breathedsville, Md. College of St. James.
Grammar School. 75237
Breathitt, John, 1786-1834. 87423 see also
Kentucky. Governor, 1832-1834
(Breathitt)
Breazeale, J. W. M. 7651
Brebe [sic] exorto para el entrego del Santo
Cristo a los enfermos. 74520
Brebeuf, Jean de, 1593-1649. 7652, 39950-
39952, note after 69259
Brebisson, Alphonse de, 1798-1872. 85415
Brechin, Bishop of. see Gleig, George,
Bishop of Brechin, 1753-1840.
Breck, Daniel, 1788-187. (7654)
Breck, Edward. 66910
Breck, Joseph. (7653)
Breck, Robert, 1713-1784. 7655-7659, 7662-
7664, 16640, 21967, (30136), 32317,
104270
Breck, Robert L. 7665
Breck, Samuel, 1771-1862. 1183, 7666-7670
Breckenridge, John. ed. (24016), 65141
Breckenridge, Robert Jefferson, 1800-1871.
7674-7689, (13564), 37548, (58346), 89502,
95493, 95494, 95500, 103871, 103873
Breckenridge, Robert Jefferson, 1800-1871.
defendant 7690
Breckenridge, S. M. 7691
Breckenridge, William D. (7692)
Breckenridge, William Lewis, 1803-1876.
7693-7695
Breckenridge, J. 33594
Breckinridge, John Campbell, 1821-1875.
7671, 11065, (15326), 28493, 46963
Breckinridge, R. T. 3001
Breckinridge and Lane campaign documents.
(7673), 19490, 20424, 29890, 54130, 91524
Breckinridge and Lane . . . documents no. 6.
54130
Breda. Gouverneur. 89457
Bredan, Daniel. 7696
Bredow, Gabriel Gottofried, 1773-1814. 32039
Breech-loaders versus muzzle-loaders. (20512)
Breeches. 86634

Breechiad, a poem. 95321
Breed, William Pratt, 1816-1889. 7697-7699
Breeden raedt aende Vereenichde Neder-
landsche Provintien. 20596, 23521,
26272, note after 98474, note after 99310
Breedvoerige Verhandeling waar in het
politicq systema onderzocht en de
rechtsgeleerde memoire. (42749)
Breen, Henry Hegart. 7700
Brees, Samuel Charles. 7701
Breese, Sidney, 1800-1878. 7702-7703
Breeze from the Great Salt Lake. 57226
Bref de Nostre S. Pere le Pape Clement IX.
24227, 73176
Bref de N. S. P. le Pape Innocent X. 7704,
34790
Bref discours d' aucunes missions. 44962
Bref du Pape sur le differend d'entre l'Eveque
d'Angelopolis. 56067
Bref om America till hemmevarande lands-
mann. 93985
Bref om de forente staterna forfattade under
en resa till America. 38053
Bref qui constitue le Cardinal Saldanha. 63907,
1st note after 98174
Bref recit du voyage du Sieur de Povtracovrt.
16212, 40167
Bref recueil de l'afflicition et dispersion de
l'eglise. 99728
Bref under en versa i Norra Amerika och pa
Cuba. 7709
Brega, George W. 7705
Bregethwyd yn Christ-Church, Mehefin y 23,
1775. 84645
Brehat, Alfred. pseud. Histoires d'amour
au Mexique. see Guezenac, Alfred,
1823-1866.
Brehier, Julie Delafaye. see Delafaye
Brehier, Julie.
Breiðfjord, Sigurður Eiriksson, 1798-1846.
7706
Breif summ of ye chief articles. 17107
Breitenbauch, Georg August von. 7707-7708
Breitmann ballads. (39963)
Bremen. Treaties, etc. 64516
Bremen. (59595)
Bremer, Fredrika, 1801-1865. 7709-7714,
20775, 16930, 92439
Bremer, Michael. 100775
Bremer Handelsblatt. 93771
Bremond, M. F. (7716)
Bremond, Marie Auguste. 7715
Brenainn, Saint. see Brendan, of Clonfert,
Saint, 484-577.
Brenan, Daniel. 7717
Brenchley, Julius. (69594)
Brend, W. 28041
Brendan, of Clonfert, Saint, 484-577. 39858
Brender a Brandis, G. 94163, note after
101819, 3d note after 101888
Brengger, Johann Georg. 73295
Brenham banner. 89305
Brennan, -------. defendant 6021
Brent, -------, fl. 1810. 105507
Brent, H. J. ed. 52000
Brent, Henry Johnson, 1811-1880. 7718
Brent, John Carroll. 7719-7721, 11075
Brent, Lind. (7722), note after 12718, 19232,
35501
Brent, Robert J. 7723-7724, 12928, (45321)
see also Maryland. Attorney General.
Brentano, Carl August von. 7725
Brenton, E. B. supposed author 65414
Brenton, Edward Pelham, 1774-1839. 7726-
7728

Brenton, James. defendant at impeachment
94546
Brents, John A. 7729
Brentwood, N. H. Convention, 1812. 72390,
93487, 102319
Brentwood, N. H. Convention, 1812. Committee
on elections. 93487, 102319
Brereton, John, fl. 1603. (7730)
Brereton, John A. 7731
Brerewood, Edward, 1565?-1613. (7732)-7733
Bresil. 19541, 70385, 101350
Bresil. A constitucao de Portugal. 38387
Bresil et France. 4738
Bresil, ou histoire, moeurs, usages et coutumes.
94416
Bresil. Quelques corrections indispensables.
(37023), 47024
Bresil tel qu'il est. 23410
Bresilien, etc. 36640
Bresiliennes. 16751
Bressani, Francesco Giuseppe. 7734-(7735),
80018
Bressany, F.-J. see Bressani, Francesco
Giuseppe.
Bresseau, -----. 2351
Brest, France. Municipalite. (7736)-7737,
40668
Brethren, at a grant convention of Ancient York
Masons. 87846
Brethren dwelling together in unity. 46241
Breton, -------. tr. 5208, 31406, (62838)
Breton, Adrien le. see Jarry de Mancy,
Adrien (Le Breton)
Breton, Ernst, 1812-1875. 7738
Breton, Guillaume le. see Guillaume, Le
Breton.
Breton, J.-B.-J. tr. 10305, 10309, 21896,
21899, note after 100811
Breton, Raymond, 1609-1679. (7739)-(7742),
21396, 72314
Breton, William. 7743
Brett, William Henry, 1818-1886. (7744)-7746
Breton. see Cape Breton.
Breugel, G. P. C. see Breugel, Gaspard
Philippe Charles van.
Breugel, Gaspard Philippe Charles van. 7747,
93855
Brev fra suebfersvend J.... D.... i America.
50751
Brev til Hr. Amtmand Moinichen. (18240)
Brevard, Joseph. ed. 87684
Breve analisis de la voluntad popular y bosquejo
del falso patriotismo. 1875
Breue apostolico de N. Santissimo Padre Inno-
cencio X. 56265, 58280, (77142)
Breve apostolico de Pio Sexto. 63168
Breve apostolico y estatutos generales. 7748
Breve bocabvlario [sic] qve comienca por los
uocablos Quichua al trocado del passado.
96268-96269, 100643
Breve catecismo de la doctrina Cristianà.
(26751), 2d note after 98659
Breve clara y precisa explicacion del sistema
metrico-decimal. (74021)
Breve compendio de la situacion y propriedad
de la tierra. 72765
Breve compendio de la sphera y de la arte de
nauegar. 16966
Breve compendio de la vida del V. Anachoreta
Fray Bartholome de Jesus Maria. 24805
Breve compendio de todo lo que debe saber.
67637
Breve compendio e narracam do funebre
espectaculo. 72299
Breve compendivm hostivm Haereticorvm
Olandensivm. (56326)

Breve contestacion en que el Dr. J. F. Madrid, satisface. 43757

Breve de Clemente XIV. de 12. de Septiembre del propio ano. 68232

Breve de Monsenor Clementi. 9586

Breve de N. Santissimo Padre el Senor Vrbano VIII. 98108

Breve de Su Santidad el Sr. Pio IX. (78909)

Breve de Su Santidad que se la dirige sobre el patronato. 68247

Breve defensa de las exenciones y privilegios regulares. 48309

Breve defensa del Coronel T. M. Jornel [i. e. Tornel.] 96208

Breve descripcion de la fabrica. 106237

Breve descripcion de la lapida de la constitucion. 57838

Breve descripcion de las solemne exequias en los dias 25 y 26 de Junio. 44893

Breve descripcion de los festivos sucesos de esta ciudad. (66547)

Breve descripcion del mapa. 49191, note after 98817

Breve descripcion del mundo. 47358

Breve descripcion del mundo o guia geographica de medrano. 47359

Breve descriptione del mondo. 41068

Breve devocionario. 31305

Breve di Nostro Signore P. P. Benedetto XIV. (63902), 63904

Breve discurso del motivo y principio de la guerra de Chile. 100631

Breve diseno critico de la emancipacion y libertad de la nacion Mexicana. 7750, 35287

Breve disertacion sobre la revista de Colombia y Venezeula. (70302)

Breve disseno de la festiva pompa. 87190

Breve e compendiosa descrittione del regno di Polonia. 67738

Breve e evccinta descrittione della Livonia tvtta. 67738

Breve en que Nuestro Santisimo Padre el Senor Pio IX. nombra su delegado apostolico. 48410

Breve epitome de la restavracion de la isle de Santa Catalina. 29376

Breve et svccinta narratione della nauigacion. 67740

Breve examen de esta cuestion. 100789, 105745

Breve examen del cuaderno publicado en Popayan. 14559

Breve exposicion de la enfermedad del Illmo. Sr. Benavente Arzobispo de Lima. (21277)

Breve exposicion de los principios y doctrinas de la ciencia social. 98867

Breve exposicion que hace Jose Antonio Alemparte. (717)

Breve fra Gronland. (36938A)

Breve historia do projecto da estrada de ferro. 14080

Breve historia dos felizes acontecimentos politicos. 23804

Breve idea de la administracion del comercio y de las rentas y gastos. 74907

Breve idea de Marruecos en 1822. 15084

Breve . . . informe . . . para desimpressionar los siniestros que se han hecho a los senores ministros de la corte de Madrid. 98717

Breve instruccion, o arte para entender la lengua comun de los Indios. (7749), 67369

Breve instruccion para el cultivo del algodon, en Centro-America. 57809

Breve instruccion sobre la contribuciones directas establecidas en la nacion. 63011

Breve manifestacion del que suscribe. 10099, (48310)

Breve manifestacion que hace al publico. 48039

Breve manifestacion que hace . . . Don Juan Vasco y Pascual. 98650

Breve memoria escrita por el Oidor Honorario de la Audiencia de Cuba. 93300, 94341

Breve narratione della vita et fatti del Signor Vassvncassano Fratta per Giouan'maria Angiolello. 67736

Breve noticia acerca del autor. 40985

Breve noticia de la biblioteca Hispano-Americana Septentrional. 38957

Breve noticia de la portentosa conversion, y admirable vida. 99612

Breve noticia de la prodigiosa imagen de Nuestra Senora de los Angeles. 60814

Breve noticia de la religiosa vida del P. Juan Tello de Siles. 81001

Breve noticia de la vida del autor. 72000

Breve noticia de las solemnes exequias de la Reina Madre Dona Maria Luisa de Borbon. 7751

Breve noticia de los enfermos, que se han curado. (68842)

Breve noticia de los primeros meses de mandado Exmo. Senor D. Miguel Tacon. 74908

Breve noticia de sa vida, que dirige a sa amada feligresia D. Joseph Antonio Eugenio Ponze de Leon. (63971)

Breve noticia del autor de esta obra. 75982

Breve noticia del recibimiento y permanencia de S. M. el Emperador y la Emperatriz de Mexico. 47036

Breve noticia del recibimiento y permanencia de SS. MM. II. en la ciudad de la Puebla. 66548

Breve noticia sobre a colleccao de madeiras do Brazil. 88782

Breve ojeada historica. 63658

Breve practica del confessionario de Indios. 10809, 98813

Breve practica, y regimen del confessionario de Indios. 10809, 98813

Breve ragguaglio della prodigiosa e rinomata immagine. 29036

Breve ragguaglio delle ultime scoperte fatte dai Russi nel Mar Pacifico. 24998

Breve rasgo de los meritos y servicios del Sr. D. Francisco Arango y Parreno. 1888

Breve relacao dos ultimos sucessos de guerra do Brasil. 16833

Breve relacion de la destruccion de las Indias Occidentales. (11236), 39114, 39116

Breve relacion de la invencion de S. Sagv. Cverpo. 76271

Breve relacion, de la peregrinacion qve ha hecho de la mayor parte del mvndo. (17819)

Breve relacion de la persecvcion. 7926, 1st note after 100872, note after 105625

Breve relacion de la plausible pompa, y cordial regocijo. (70797)

Breve relacion de la vida y muerte del Doctor D. Francisco de Aguiar, y Seyxas. 40909

Breve relacion de las acclamaciones festivas. 7752

Breve relacion de las Indias Occidentales. (11236)-11237

Breve relacion de los hechos mas publicas y
memorables. 34433
Breve relacion de los mas notables aconteci-
mientos de su gobierno. 75607, note
after 98317-98318
Breue relacion del fruto que se recoge de los
Indios del Peru. 96259
Breve relacion del origen y fundacion de los
siervos de Maria Santissima. 7753
Breve relatione d'alcvne missioni de' PP.
della Compagnia di Giesu. 7734
Breve relatione del P. Diego de Torres.
96253
Breve relazione della prodigiosa apparizione
di Maria Santissima. 94151
Breve relazione della virtu e morte del P.
Antonio Ripari. 71492
Breve resena biografica del Dr. Carlos Arvelo.
(64170)
Breve resena de los sucesos de Guadalajara.
26386
Breve resena historica de los acontecimientos
mas notables. 96197
Breve resposta, que ao relatorio da liquidacao
da Companhia do Mucury. (57900)
Breve resumen de las mas singulares indul-
gencias. 86494
Breve Santissimi Domini Nostri Vrbani Papae
VIII. 98109
Breve sobre la reduccion de asilos en todos
los dominios de Espana. 13626
Breve summa de la oracion mental y de su
exercicio. 43755
Breve teatro de las acciones mas notables.
50069
Breve tratado de derecho administrativo
Espanol general del reino. (50700)
Breve tratado de geographia. 47360
Breve tratado de la enfermedad venerea or
morbo galico. 61255
Breue tratado que ensena el camino de la vida
perfecta. 74799, 98897-98898
Breve trattado del mondo, et delle sve parti,
semplici, et miste. 19603, 55465
Breve y compendiosa narracion de la ciudad
de Mejico. 99535
Breve y particular noticia de toda la historia
Indiana. 28255
Breve y sommaria descrittione del gran Dvcato
di Litvania. 67738
Breve y sumaria relacion de los senores, y
maneras y diferencias que habia de ellos
en la Nueva Espana. 106405
Breves annotacoes a memoria que o Exmo.
Sr. Visconde de S. Leopoldo escreveu.
17012
Breves consideracoes acerca da epidemia que
no anno preterito e corrente (1849 e
1850) tem assolado. 88702
Breves noces para se estudar com methodo a
geographia do Brasil. 58073
Breves observacaes sobre o tractado concluido
em 1826. 24171
Breves observacoes sobre as annotacoes do
Dr. Sallustino Orlando de Aranjo Costa.
70793
Breves reflecsiones que varios cosecheros del
ramo de pulques hacen. 98621
Breves reflexiones sobre la censura de los
oficios dirigidos al Excmo. Ayuntamiento
de esta capital. 99651
Breves reflexoes retrospectivas. 947
Brevet Major Pindar Puff. pseud. State
triumvirate. see Verplanck, Gulian
Crommelin.
Brevi prolusione de Corticis. 89437

Brevi prolusione de siliquis convolvuli Ameri-
cani vulgo Vainigliis. 89436
Breviarum orbis terrarum. 13805
Breviarvm totivs orbis. 100955
Breviarum totius terrarum. 5013
Breviary of the history of England. 67599
Breviate. 43316
Brevier legislative reports. 34493
Breviloq, Dr. pseud. Curious and interesting
dialogue. see Valiniere, Pierre Huet de
la.
Brevis ac succincta Americae. 31540, 44057
Brevis . . . Americae . . . descriptio. 5014
Brevis de fortunatis insulis comentariolus.
(8784)
Brevis & admiranda descriptio regni Gvianae.
33659, 67546
Brevis et compendiosa narratio missionum
quarundam Orientis et Occidentis. 44963
Brevis et fida narratio. 101423
Brevis & succincta insulae hujus descriptio.
(58059), 64912, 96049
Brevis narratio eorvm quae in Florida Americae
provincia Gallis acciderunt. (8784)
Brevis relatio historica. 96256
Brevis relation missionum Soc. Jesu. 23062
Brevis repetitio omnium que excellentissimus
D. Legatus Portugalliae ad componendas
res Brasilicanas proposuit. 7543, 88754
Brevis summa. (8784)
Brevis summa earum rerum quae in tertia
Americae parte continentur. (8784)
Breuissima descrittione de Tartari Campestri.
67738
Brevissima narratione della seconda navigatione.
67742
Breuissima relacion de la destruycion de las
Indias. 11227, 11235-(11236), 11239,
11242-11243, 11244, (11249), 11267, 11283,
11289
Breuissima relatione della distrvttione dell'Indie
Occidentali. 11242-11244
Brevissimo compendio da vida e excellencias
de S. Francisco Xavier. 50103
Brevoort, James Carson, 1818-1887. 7754,
(30968)
Brewer, -------. 2852, 7763-7764, (19723)
Brewer, -------, M. D. 12041
Brewer, D. R. 7756
Brewer, Daniel. 7755
Brewer, Elisha. 1066, 3625, note before 93509,
103349A
Brewer, John M. 7757
Brewer, Lucy. see West, Lucy (Brewer)
Brewer, Stephen. defendant (7759)
Brewer, Thomas Mayo, 1814-1880. (7760),
85072
Brewer, Urban C. 7761
Brewer, William A. 7762, 86567, 89931
Brewer's panorama. 7763, (19723)
Brewerton, George Douglas, 1820-1901. 7765
Brewerton, George W. Douglas. see Brewerton,
George Douglas, 1820-1901.
Brewerton, John. 7766
Brewin, William. 30780
Brewster, Abel. 7768
Brewster, Benjamin Harris, 1816-1888. 7769-
7773
Brewster, C. K. 70838
Brewster, Charles Warren, 1802-1868. 7774
Brewster, Sir Francis, fl. 1674-1702. 7778
Brewster, Francis E. 7776-7777
Brewster, Frederick Carroll, 1825-1898. 7775,
15097
Brewster, H. B. 6446, 7779
Brewster, James. 7780, 52967

Brewster, James C. ed. 57190
Brewster, Jarvis. 7781, 23464
Brewster, Lyman D. (7782)-(7783) see also
  New Haven, Conn. Christ Church.
  Rector.
Brewster, Martha (Wadsworth) fl. 1757. 7784
Brewster, Sackford. 52518-52519, note after
  100459
Breydenbach, ------. 99367
Brez, Guy de. 7785, 78439
Brezila ou la tribu des femmes, ballet en un
  acte. 94214
Brialmont, Alexis Henri, 1821-1903. 7786
Briand de Verze, ------. 7787
Briano, Giorgio. 7788
Briant, Lemuel, d. 1754. 7789, 55332
Briant, Timothy. 7790
Briar-Hill lectures. 82941
Bribery and corruption!! 59924
Bribery and piracy. 29861
Brice, Andrew, 1690-1773. 7791
Brice, James R. 7792-7793
Brice, John, fl. 1775-1783. (65493)
Brice, John, fl. 1814. ed. 7794
Brice, Robert, fl. 1776-1783. (65493)
Briceno, Mariano de. 7795-7799, 70296
Brick Church memorial. 89767, 89775
Brick-dust. 63933
"Brick" Pomeroy. pseud. see Pomeroy,
  Mark M.
Brick Presbyterian Church, New York. see
  New York (City) Brick Presbyterian
  Church.
Brickell, John, 1710?-1745. 7800, 39452
Bricklayers Corporation, Philadelphia. 61505
Bricklayers Corporation, Philadelphia. Charter.
  61505
Bridal ballad. 67174
Bridal eve [by Eugene Sue.] 93410
Bridal eve [by William Russell Smith.] 84871
Bridal of Vaumond. 76441
Bride of Fort Edward. (7801)
Bride of Ossano. 100577
Bride of seven. 100372
Bride of the northern wilds: a tale. (18061)
Bride of the wilderness. (65066)
Bridel, Edd. P. tr. 59705
Bridel, Louis. 7802-7804
Bridge, Ebenezer. 7805-7806
Bridge, Hosiah. 7808-7809
Bridge, James. 7808
Bridge, Matthew, 1720?-1775. 7810
Bridge, Thomas, 1657-1715. 7811-7813, 46231
Bridge, William, 1600?-1670. 3213, 21991,
  27952-27954, (69679), 74724, 91383,
  note before 92797, note after 92800, 3d
  note after 103687, 104343 see also
  Church of Scotland. General Assembly.
  Commission.
Bridge across the Potomac. 64585
Bridge documents. (61506)
Bridgens, R. 7814
Bridgeport, Conn. Library Association. see
  Bridgeport Library Association.
Bridgeport, Conn. St. John's Lodge. see
  Freemasons. Connecticut. St. John's
  Lodge, Bridgeport.
Bridgeport, Conn. Soldiers' Aid Society. see
  Soldiers' Aid Society, Bridgeport, Conn.
Bridgeport and East Bridgeport directory.
  7815
Bridgeport directory and annual advertiser.
  7816
Bridgeport Library Association. 7817
Bridges, George Wilson. 7820-(7823)
Bridges, L. 7824

Bridges, Samuel Augustus, 1802-1884. 7826
Bridges, Sir Samuel Edgerton. 8829, 25999,
  79342
Bridges, William. cartographer 7825
Brigeton, N. J. South Jersey Institute. see
  South Jersey Institute, Bridgeton, N. J.
Bridgettines. 68844
Bridgewater, England. Citizens. 7828
Bridgewater, Mass. 7830
Bridgewater, Mass. Citizens. 7828
Bridgewater, Mass. Normal School. see
  Massachusetts. State Normal School,
  Bridgewater.
Bridgewater, Mass. Scotland Trinitarian Congre-
  gational Church. (7829)
Bridgewater, Mass. Selectmen. 7830
Bridgewater, Mass. State Alms House. see
  Massachusetts. State Alms House,
  Bridgewater.
Bridgewater, Mass. State Normal School. see
  Massachusetts. State Normal School,
  Bridgewater.
Bridgewater, Mass. Town Meeting, 1795. 7830
Bridgewater, Mass. Trinity Church. Clerk.
  90681
Bridgewater, Mass. Trinity Church. Wardens.
  90681
Bridgewater, Mass. Two Hundredth Anniversary
  Celebration, 1856. 7827
Bridgewater Baptist Association. see Baptists.
  Pennsylvania. Bridgewater Baptist
  Association.
Bridgewater's monitor. Two sermons. 37234
Bridgham, Samuel Willard, 1774-1840. 7831-
  7832, 66250
Bridging the Ohio & Mississippi Rivers. 13071
Bridgman, Charles De Witt, 1835-1899. 7833
Bridgman, Elijah Coleman. 7834
Bridgman, Laura. 7835
Bridgman, Lewis Jesse, 1857- illus. 83556,
  83560
Bridgman, Thomas, b. 1795. 7836-7840
Bridgman & Fanning. firm see Ensign,
  Bridgman & Fanning. firm publishers
Bridgwater's monitor. A sermon preached . . .
  at Bridgwater. (37235)
Bridle for disputants. 105299, 105455
Bridle for sinners and a spur for saints.
  105225-105227
Bridle for the ass. 47276, (78736), 97107
Bridle on the heart. 84440
Bridle to the French king. 75324
Brie, Jean de. (59572)
Brief. 45095, 94622, 106357
Brief aan de Europesche kolonisten te Groningen
  aan Saramacca. (7395)
Brief aan de Heer. N. H. Koopman in Nieuw-
  Nederland. 7362
Brief aan den Koning van Poolen. 59678
Brief aan den Lord Bisschop van Landaff.
  (41643)
Brief aan eenen vriend over de vermeende
  vorrechten. (27927)
Brief aan John Rogers. 40120
Brief abstract of remarks by Rev. William B.
  Hayden. 31013
Brief account concerning several of the agents
  of New-England. (46637)
Brief account of a religious scheme. 67955
Brief account of a strange & unusuall providence
  of God. 104111
Brief account of an ecclesiastical council, so
  called, convened in the first parish in
  Newbury, March 31, 1767; and again, by
  adjournment, April 21. following. 97312

Brief account of an ecclesiastical council, so called, convened in the first parish in Newbury, March 31. 1767. and of some occurrences and transactions relative thereto. 97311

Brief account of emissions of paper money. 64631

Brief account of General Jackson's dealing with Negroes. 35391

Brief account of his [i. e. Samuel J. May's] ministry 47078

Brief account of its [i. e. New York City's] first settlement by the Dutch. 30319

Brief account of many remarkable passages. 29389

Brief account of my exercises, from my childhood. (59668)

Brief account of persecutions in Boston and Connecticut governments. 6226

Brief account of religion in Virginia. 27677

Brief account of St. Paul's College, &c. 27325

Brief account of Sebastian Lewis. 7792

Brief account of Shakers and Shakerism. 79694

Brief account of some good & great things a doing for the Kingdom of God. 46434

Brief account of some Lent and other extraordinary processions. 103499

Brief account of some of the causes which seem to have led to the prosecution. 90516, note after 96840, 1st note after 97091

Brief account of some very uncommon occurrences. 82763-82765

Brief account of the African Christian Church, in New-Bedford. 16233

Brief account of the agency of the Honourable John Winthrop. 104986

Brief account of the Albany-County Penitentiary. 7843

Brief account of the Associated Presbyteries. 7844, (65144)

Brief account of the author's [i. e. Henry Sterne's] individual wrongs. 91339

Brief account of the author's [i. e. Samuel Heineke's] travels. 31243

Brief account of the buildings and dedication of the Wadsworth monument. 93405

Brief account of the captivity and cruel sufferings of Captain Deitz. 7792

Brief account of the case of William Trusdell. 30380, 84558

Brief account of the causes that have retarded the progress of the colony of Georgia, in America. (60861), 91305

Brief account of the collection of coins belonging to the mint. 21788

Brief account of the collection of coins belonging to the mint of the United States. 21014-21015

Brief account of the commissioners proceedings in the reducing of Maryland. 100546-100547

Brief account of the construction, management, & discipline &c. &c. 64788

Brief account of the Dana Hill Public Schools, Cambridge. 41563

Brief account of the debts provided for by the South-Sea Act. 88176

Brief account of the deluded Dutartres. 26594, 73406

Brief account of the difficulties in the Baptist Church in Hardwick. 94890

Brief account of the discoveries and results of the United States Exploring Expedition. 7845, 18427

Brief account of the dreadful occurrence at the laying of the corner stone. 43790

Brief account of the efforts of Senator Cooper. 40858

Brief account of the epidemical fever which lately prevailed. 18662

Brief account of the establishment of the colony of Georgia. (27018), 86574

Brief account of the evangelical work among the Christianized Indians. 46373

Brief account of the execution of the six militia men. 86569, 86570

Brief account of the finances and paper money of the revolutionary war. (77992)

Brief account of the first opening up of the Ottawa country. 72605

Brief account of the formation and settlement of the second church and congregation in Framingham. 27623

Brief account of the happy death of Mary Ann Clap. 3941

Brief account of the history, objects and condition of the Society. 61853

Brief account of the honourable society and present mission. 79410

Brief account of the Indian battles. 32174, 76367

Brief account of the island of Antigua. 42665

Brief account of the Lake Superior Mining Company. 38669

Brief account of the last house of Albert B. Dod. (32330)

Brief account of the late fire at Richmond Virg. 71175

Brief account of the late revivals of religion in a number of towns. 7847, 27588

Brief account of the life & adventures of William Healy. 31174

Brief account of the life and death of that noble of nature Thomas Paine. 103191

Brief account of the life and experience, call to the ministry, travels and afflictions of Peter Young. 106088-106089

Brief account of the life and political opinions of Martin Van Buren. 98425

Brief account of the life, character, and death, of the author [i. e. Samuel Davies.] 18765

Brief account of the life, experience, travels and gospel labors of George White an African. 103384

Brief account of the life, last sickness, and death of Robert Mott. 51115

Brief account of the life of the late Rev. Caleb Smith. 82362

Brief account of the life of the late Reverend Caleb Smith. 82363

Brief account of the life, sufferings, and memorable visit of General Lafayette. 22242, 22273

Brief account of the means and manner of the author's [i. e. Elhanan Winchester's] embracing these sentiments. 104735

Brief account of the methods used. 32947, 2d note after 102507

Brief account of the mineral waters of Frankfort, Ky. 38017

Brief account of the mission established among the Esquimaux Indians. 7846, 93386, 5th note after 97845, 1st note after 97862

Brief account of the new British settlement on the head-waters of the Susquehanna, in Philadelphia. 1349

Brief account of the New-York Hospital. (54481)

Brief account of the occasion, process, and issue of a late trial. 103500

Brief account of the origin and progress of the Boston Female Society for Missionary Purposes. (6706)

Brief account of the origin and progress of the divisions in the First Presbyterian Church in the city of Troy. 97073

Brief account of the origin and progress of the Tammany Society. 94289

Brief account of the origin and services of the First Union Relief Association of Baltimore. 3021

Brief account of the origin of the institution [i. e. Amherst College.] 1314, note after 102377

Brief account of the origin, progress, and present state of the colonial settlements of Texas. 103114

Brief account of the persecution in France. 25882

Brief account of the pious life and joyful death of Mrs. Elizabeth Pratt. (64935)

Brief account of the present declining state of the West Indies. 102785

Brief account of the present state, income, expenditures, &c. of the Society for Propagating the Gospel Among the Indians. (34619), 95170

Brief account of the present state of the Society for Propagating the Gospel Among the Indians and Other in North-America. 34618

Brief account of the proceedings of the Committee appointed by the Yearly Meeting of Friends, held in Baltimore. 7849

Brief account of the proceedings of the Committee, appointed in the year 1795, by the Yearly Meeting of Friends of Pennsylvania. 7848, (34617)

Brief account of the proceedings of the Potosi, La Par, [sic] and Peruvian Mining Association. 94659

Brief account of the prominent points and characteristic incidents. 94562

Brief account of the province of East Jersey, in America. (53078), (59679)

Brief account of the province of East "New" Jersey in America. 53079

Brief account of the province of Pennsilvania [sic] in America. 59681

Brief account of the province of Pennsilvania [sic] lately granted by the king. 59680

Brief account of the province of Pennsylvania. 21048

Brief account of the Quincy family. 103754

Brief account of the religious experience, sickness and death, of the late pious Miss Mary M. Tooker. 96179

Brief account of the revenues, pomp, and state of the bishops. (7850)

Brief account of the rise and progress of the people called Quakers. 59682, 59694, 59730, 95752

Brief account of the rise of the society [of Friends.] 23189

Brief account of the rise, principles, and discipline of the people called Quakers. 67793

Brief account of the rise, principles, and discipline of the people call'd Quakers, in America. 67792

Brief account of the rise, progress, & persecutions of the Church of Jesus Christ of Latter-Day Saints. 85534

Brief account of the rise, progress, and present situation of the orphan-house in Georgia. 103501, 103518, 103522, 103575

Brief account of the rise, progress, and present state of the paper currency in New-England. 7851, 52615

Brief account of the rise, progress and present state of the Theological Seminary of the Presbyterian Church. 65655

Brief account of the said Luther Gleason. (27566)

Brief account of the school for the liberal education of boys. 40816

Brief account of the sentiments of the first Baptist churches. 2628

Brief account of the services rendered by the Second Regiment Delaware Volunteers. 83864

Brief account of the singular circumstances attending the death of Mr. Joseph Morse. 50972

Brief account of the Society for Propagating the Gospel Among the Indians and Others in North America. 34620, note after 95170

Brief account of the Society of the Friendly Sons of St. Patrick. 7852, (25951), 32802

Brief account of the state of the province of Massachusetts Bay. 45657

Brief account of the successful labors of the New York Manumission Society. 1487

Brief account of the sufferings of the servants of the Lord. (38890)

Brief account of the various institutions and public objects in this metropolis. 62006, 62058

Brief account of the various institutions . . . in this metropolis. 62005

Brief account of the war in N. America. 104465

Brief account of the winds, weather, and currents. 4219

Brief account of the Yearly Meeting of Friends for New-England. 52614, 86039

Brief account of twenty-three campaigns. 82771

Brief account, together with observations. 72874, 72877

Brief address to the citizens of West Roxbury. 8460

Brief an einer Farmer in Ohio. 10829

Brief analysis of the Book of Mormon. 83112

Brief and candid answer to a late printed sheet. 74871, 79440, 79446

Brief and comprehensive view of the government of the United States. 80770-80772

Brief and correct account of an earthquake. (21637), 26615

Brief and general account of the first part of the life of the Reverend Mr. Geo. Whitefield. 103502

Brief and impartial history of the life and actions of Andrew Jackson. 85424

Brief and impartial review of the state of Great Britain. 7853

Brief and modest reply. 103939

Brief and perfect journal of the late proceedings. 7854, 74616

Brief and plain discourse. (32735)

Brief and plain essay on God's wonder-working providence. 55330

Brief and plain essay, upon, a life of religion. (46386)

Brief and plain essay, upon . . . good works. 46314

Brief and plain exhortation to his people. 97453

Brief and remarkable narrative of the life and extreme sufferings of Barnabas Downes. 20768

Brief and simple record of the Lord's gracious work. 92941

Brief and sorrowful account of the present
state of the churches. 55332
Brief and speech in the U. S. Court of Claims.
3392
Brief and true account of the persecution of
the church. 34621
Brief and true account of their persecution of
the Church of England. 7855, 18229,
52757
Brief and true narration of the late wars
risen in New-England. (52616)
Brief and true narrative of some remarkable
passages. (39442)
Brief and true narrative of the hostile con-
duct. 7856
Brief and true relation. 46687
Brief and true report of the new foundland
of Virginia. (8784)
Brief animadversions on the narrative of the
New England Baptists. 46638
Brief animadversions upon the New-England
Anabaptists late fallacious narrative.
104097
Brief annals of Northampton. 7838
Brief answer to a certain slanderous pamphlet.
(13865)
Brief answer to a false and foolish libell.
59683
Brief answer to a small book written by John
Norcot. 22141
Brief answer to an official reply to the Board
of Missions. 61186
Brief answer to John Rogers boasting of his
sufferings. 64973, 72688
Brief answer to some passages in a late book.
(12705), 1st note after 98664
Brief answer to the principal objections
opposed to the amendment of the
insolvent law. (7857)
Brief answer to two papers procured from
Friends in Maryland. 8951
Brief apology in behalf of the people in
derision call'd Quakers. 1185
Brief appeal in behalf of the special fund.
93354
Brief appeal to public opinion. 48191
Brief appeals for the loyal cause. 82447
Brief appendix on the mode of administering
the ordinance. 84099
Brief aus Amerika. 7858
Brief aus Californien von Moritz August
Richter. 71222
Brief aus England. 97667
Brief aus Highland im Staate Illinois. 7859
Brief aus und uber die Vereinigten Staaten
von Nord-Amerika. (77664)
Brief autobiography of the author [i. e. Anson
Jones.] 36455
Brief betreffende de Plantagien Waterland.
7860
Brief biographic memorial of Joh. Jonas Rupp.
74150
Brief biographical memoir [of Rev. Theophilus
Lindsay.] 4599
Brief biographical notice of the deceased.
104180
Brief biographical sketch, &c., &c. 18318
Brief biographical sketch, 1787-1868. 84862
Brief biographies. 82279
Brief, but faithful account of the proceedings
thereon. 101256
Brief but faithful account of this fine colony.
40769
Brief but general view of the history of the
world. 14904
Brief by den selven W. P. geschreven. 59710

Brief character of the antient Christian Quakers.
46809
Brief chronicle of the acts and gestes of the
Spaniardes in the West Indies. 11287, 1st
note after 39118
Brief chronological table of the most remarkable
events in, and relating to, the war. 87749
Brief circular relating to the counties of
Clinton, Cedar and Linn. (35010)
Brief commentary, and moderate discourse upon
the apologeticall narration. (27953)
Brief comparison of the Methodist Episcopal and
Methodist Protestant Churches. 82580
Brief compend of the history of the United
States. 83532
Brief consideration of the important services
and distinguished virtues and talents which
recommend Mr. Adams for the president
of the United States. 26649
Brief considerations on slavery. 4668
Brief considerations on the political and com-
mercial relations. 101269
Brief continuation, . . . by a friend. 51524
Brief course of . . . devotional exercises.
62844
Brief, decent, but free remarks. (7862)
Brief declaration of Mr. Peter Thacher. 95166
Brief deduction of the case between George
Carew. 10822
Brief defence of the late council's result against
the doctor's charges in his late brief
history. 13594, 103322
Brief demonstration that the doctrines of Grace
hitherto preserved. 46438
Brief des Herrn Francis P. Blair an den
Republikanischen Verein. 5741
Brief description and statistical sketch of
Georgia. 37170
Brief description of a gospel church. 102089
Brief description of New-Englands errand into
the wilderness. 18475
Brief description of New-York. 19611-19612
Brief description of Nova-Scotia. (41747)
Brief description of Phil-Ellena. 10991
Brief description of the canals and railroads
of Pennsylvania and New Jersey. 94313
Brief description of the canals and railroads
of the United States. 94314
Brief description of the fifth monarchy. 2218
Brief description of the gold region. 9969
Brief description of the Island of Jamaica.
35567
Brief description of the property belonging to
the Lycoming Coal Co. 42754
Brief description of the province of Carolina.
10961
Brief description of the said province. 66223
Brief description of the San Joaquin Valley.
76118
Brief description of the several varieties of
birds. 9502
Brief description of the skeleton of the gigantic
mastodon. 7863
Brief description of the territory and its
government. 26866
Brief description of the toil and sufferings of
slaves. 51733
Brief description of the whole world. 21
Brief directions to a young scholar. 104067
Brief discours des choses plus necessaires &
dignes. 94865
Brief discovrs et histoire d'vn voyage de
quelques Francois en la Floride. 4795,
39630
Brief discourse. 46639, 46747

Brief discourse about the dreadful justice of God. (46459)

Brief discourse concerning regular singing. 7864, 81421

Brief discourse concerning that ceremony of laying the hand on the Bible in swearing. 104068

Brief discourse concerning the lawfulness of worshipping God by the common-prayer. 46639, 46747, 104255-104257

Brief discourse concerning the name heathen, commonly given to the Indians. 104334

Brief discourse concerning the prayse due to God. 46757

Brief discourse concerning the unlawfulness of the common prayer worship. 46639, 46747, 104255-104257

Brief discourse deliver'd at North-Haven. 103786

Brief discourse, discovering the one thing wanting. 104095

Brief discourse . . . made on a solemn thanks-giving. 46255

Brief discourse on a passage by the North-Pole to Japan. 51219

Brief discourse of justification. 104069

Brief discourse, offered unto a religious society. 46482

Brief discourse on the methods and motives to pursue a victory. 4398

Brief discourse on the necessary properties & practices of a good servant. (46345)

Brief discourse on the practice of close communion. 105266

Brief discourse, on what fears, we may have. 46277

Brief discourse proving that the first day of the week is the Christian Sabbath. 24577

Brief discourse tending to direct the course of sea-men. 69355

Brief discourse to the inhabitants of a place. 46452

Brief discourse touching New England. 13308

Brief discourse upon the temptations which are the more ordinary devices of Satan. (46604)

Brief discourse, wherein Christs parable of the lost son found. 104094

Brief discourse wherein great sinners are encouraged. 104102

Brief discourse, wherein is asserted and declared, the great honour. 104090

Brief discourse wherein is set forth the woful danger. 104065

Brief discourse wherein is shewn the connexion where there is between the promise. 104076

Brief discoverye of some things best worth noteinge. 104095

Brief display of Mordecai's character. 25408

Brief disquisition concerning the early history of printing in America. 30601

Brief disquisition into the modern system of British politics. 9650

Brief dissertation on . . . the penitent thief on the cross. (46350)

Brief dissertation on the three first chapters of Genesis. (14525)

Brief enquiry. 78251

Brief enquiry into the causes of, and conduct pursued by, the colonial government, for quelling the insurrection. 7865, 104904

Brief enquiry into the prospective results that might follow. 75075

Brief enquiry into the true basis of the credit system. 98101

Brief enquiry into the true nature and character of our federal government. 7866, 92291, note after 98101, 1st note after 100577

Brief enquiry into the use of means. 32955

Brief epistle from Dr. Ziba Sproule. 77003, 89919, note after 96474

Brief essay. 46593

Brief essay on a merciful Saviour. 46250

Brief essay on, a soul passing from death to life. (46483)

Brief essay, on all supplied in an alsufficient Saviour. 46303

Brief essay on divine consolations. 46427

Brief essay on mans not knowing his time. 46365

Brief essay, on that case, what should be the behaviour of a Christian at a funeral? 46251

Brief essay on the advantages and disadvantages. 7867, 97328-97332

Brief . . . essay on the best of blessings. 46247

Brief essay, on the blessings of Abraham. (46539), 2d note after 94857

Brief essay on the blessings enjoy'd by a people. 46281

Brief essay on the civil service of the United States. 29544

Brief essay on the conduct exposed of such as have had their duty. 46424

Brief essay on the conspicuous blessings with which the people of God and their off-spring are known. 46560

Brief essay on the glory of aged piety. (27834), (46346)

Brief essay, on the good things. (46612)

Brief essay, on, the Grace of the Redeemer. 46423

Brief essay on the holy silence and Godly patience. 46512

Brief essay on the life of God. (46584), 78441-78443, 2d note after 100616

Brief essay on the nature and power of a true faith. 7813

Brief essay on the number seven. 7868

Brief essay on the signs of good growth and strength. 46399

Brief essay on the unsearchable riches of Christ. 46564, 5th note after 97146

Brief essay; or, an attempt to prove. (26354)

Brief essay, to awaken in a dying man, . . . a proper and a lively concern. 46594, 1st note after 103119

Brief essay to declare the danger & mischief of all evil customs. (46217)

Brief essay to demonstrate, that all men should hearken to reason. 46398

Brief essay to direct and excite family religion. (46323)

Brief essay, to discover the sin that slayes its ten thousands. 46576, note after 99319

Brief essay to do good unto the widow. 46401

Brief essay to illustrate the marriage. 46335

Brief essay to obtain from young people. 46372

Brief essay, to rebuke first the natural sleep which too often proves a dead fly. 46580, 2d note after 99604

Brief essay to rectify the mistakes of men. (46565), 3d note after 97160

Brief essay to serve the great interests of religion. 46329

Brief essay towards an apology for a play actor. 88637

Brief essay, upon a soul at ease. 46428
Brief essay upon falls into sins. (46557),
note after 96508
Brief essay upon the death of . . . Mrs.
Elizabeth Mather. (46480)
Brief essay upon the glorious designs &
methods of winning the minds. 46429
Brief essay upon the miracle of our Saviour
walking upon the water. 46390
Brief essay, upon those returns of thankfulness
and obedience. (46543)
Brief essay, . . . which apprehends the face
of . . . God. (46246)
Brief examination and exposition of the right
of detention. (17289)
Brief examination into the increase of the
revenue, commerce, and manufactures
of Great Britain, from 1792 to 1799.
73238
Brief examination into the increase of the
revenue, commerce, and navigation, of
Great-Britain, during the administration
of the Rt. Hon. William Pitt. 73239
Brief examination into the increase of the
revenue, commerce, and navigation of
Great Britain since the conclusion of
the peace of 1783. 7869-7870, 73237
Brief examination into the state of agriculture.
9493
Brief examination of Asa Rand's book. 34035
Brief examination of Col. James Monroe's
claims. 98363
Brief examination of Lord Sheffield's Observations on the commerce. (17294), 32635
Brief examination of MM. Say and Sismondi
on the same subject. (23230)
Brief examination of Rev. Mr. Sullivan's
reply. 72085
Brief examination of scripture testimony on the
institution of slavery. 40799, 92868-
92869
Brief examination of some of the most pre-
valent false doctrines. 16241
Brief examination of testimony. 104026
Brief examination of the author's second book.
103655
Brief examination of the expediency of repeal-
ing the naturalization laws. (7871)
Brief examination of the plan and conduct of
the northern expedition in America, in
1777. 7872, 9258
Brief examination of the practice of the times.
(76414)-76415
Brief examination of the relations between the
Cherokees. (6038)
Brief examination of . . . the Rev. Mr.
Boardman's . . . attempt. 20391
Brief examination of the right of jurisdiction
and soil. (59925)
[Brief examination] of the surrender of the
army. 7872
Brief exhortation to all who profess the truth.
104544
Brief, explained by a statement of the case.
78853
Brief explanation of some philosophical and
other instruments. (22732)
Brief explanation relative to the end of the
. . . missionaries. 59031
Brief explanatory correspondence. 7304
Brief exposition of matters relating to the
Bank of Maryland. (36271), 64723
Brief exposition of the character, operations,
and claims. 48205
Brief exposition of the claim of Ebenezer
Cooley. 16357

Brief exposition of the claims of the New-York
Indians. 54781
Brief exposition of the constitution of the United
States. For the use of common schools.
30627
Brief exposition of the Constitution of the United
States, with an appendix. 4023
Brief exposition of the established principles
and regulations of the United Society
called Shakers. 79695, note after 97880,
1st note after 102601
Brief exposition of the established principles
and regulations of the United Society of
Believers, called Shakers. 79696-79697
Brief exposition of the fanaticism. 79698, note
after 97880
Brief exposition of the injury done to the community. 30366
Brief exposition of the leading principles of a
bank. 45091
Brief exposition of the Lord's Prayer. 32830
Brief exposition of the philosophic principles
upon which the system of education for
the Girard College for Orphans is founded.
43067
Brief exposition of the rise, discipline, Christian
doctrines and testimonies of the religious
society of Friends. 66913
Brief exposition of the Stack-O'Hara controversy.
90025
Brief exposition of the views of John L. Sullivan.
(14282), 93513-93514
Brief exposition of the views of the Society for
the Colonization of Free Persons of
Colour, in Africa. 85875
Brief exposition of the whole Book of Canticles.
17047
Brief exposition with practical observations
upon the whole Book of Canticles. 17048
Brief exposition with practicall observations
upon the whole Book of Ecclesiastes.
17049
Brief exposure of Rev. Mr. Robinson's evasions.
72086
Brief extract, or summary of important argu-
ments. 7873
Brief extracts. 90462
Brief extracts from the journal of a voyage.
18063
Brief extracts from the works of Isaac Pening-
ton. 59658
Brief for appellant. 85212
Brief for claimants. 88829
Brief for defendants. 82144
Brief for Mr. White by Edwin L. Stanton.
90389
Brief for the appellees. 87287
Brief for the Trustees of Phillips Academy.
85212
Brief for the United States. 3924
Brief for the Visitors. 85212
Brief for the Visitors, on demurrer to the
bill. 85212
Brief genealogy of the Whipple family. 6942
Brief geschreiben aus Pensylvanien in Amerika.
39587
Brief geschreibung aus Pensylvanien in Amerika.
39587
Brief geschreven by Sigismvnd van Shoppe.
77897
Brief, gestiert tot de godvruchtige en genaedigen
ooren. 94350
Brief gheschreven in Maurits-Stadt de Pernam-
buco. 23511
Brief grammar and vocabulary of the Esquimaux
language. 1405

Brief historical abstracts. 50871
Brief historical account of sundry things.
  44764, 2d note after 95515
Brief historical noticies. 93254
Brief historical sketch, illustrative of a
  picture. 93192
Brief historical sketch [of Park Presbyterian
  Church.] (8301)
Brief historical sketch of the Howard Sunday
  School. 89744
Brief historical sketch of the Middletown
  Lyceum. 48872
Brief historical sketch of the rise and pro-
  gress of the cotton manufacture in
  America. 50149
Brief historical sketch of the town of West
  Boylston. (18716)
Brief historical sketches of the war in the
  North-West. 34429
Brief historical sketches of the Western
  Baptist Theological Institute. 69694
Brief historical, statistical, and descriptive
  review. 28398, 82755-82756
Brief historical view, of the several cases
  and trials. 90433
Brief histories of the Albany regiments.
  (13361)
Brief history. 46640, 46693
Brief history and vindication of the doctrines.
  13214
Brief history, articles of faith, covenant, and
  living members. (44201)
Brief history [by N. Whitaker.] 13594, 103322
Brief history, confession of faith, and covenant.
  88256
Brief history, constitution, rules, and members.
  91468
Brief history of an existing controversy on the
  subject. 74183
Brief history of Cambridgeport and East
  Cambridge. 81369
Brief history of epidemic and pestilential
  diseases. 102341
Brief history of Francis Fauvel Gouraud.
  7385
Brief history of his [i. e. George Thompson's]
  connection with the anti-slavery cause
  in England. 95497
Brief history of Joseph Smith. 83235
Brief history of St. George's Parish. 45357,
  75214
Brief history of the American Tract Society.
  1246
Brief history of the battle which was fought.
  94110
Brief history of the church [i. e. Charles
  Street Baptist Church, Boston.] 6638
Brief history of the church at Rockaway, New-
  Jersey. 72375
Brief history of the church in Upper Canada.
  5094, 89512
Brief history of the Cincinnati Horticultural
  Society. 13069
Brief history of the condition of women. 12712
Brief history of the country of humanity.
  50658
Brief history of the county from 1821 to 1871.
  63406
Brief history of the Duane Street late Cedar
  Street Presbyterian Church. (45429)
Brief history of the early settlement of Fair-
  field County. 76391
Brief history of the early visions of the pro-
  phet. 83280
Brief history of the establishment of the float-
  ing school. 3022

Brief history of the Evangelical Missionary
  Society of Massachusetts. 45658
Brief history of the First Baptist Church in
  Boston. 6643
Brief history of the First Baptist Church, in
  Cambridge. 10126
Brief history of the First Free Congregational
  Church. 6644
Brief history of the First Presbyterian Church
  & Society in Utica. 98226
Brief history of the formation and organization
  of the church. 18137
Brief history of the influenza. 71237
Brief history of the institution [i. e. Dartmouth
  College.] (11983)
Brief history of the late expedition against Fort
  San Juan. 18459
Brief history of the leading causes of the
  Hancock mob. 16227
Brief history of the life of the author [i. e.
  Josiah Shippey.] (80536)
Brief history of the Louisiana Territory. 84522
Brief history of the Massachusetts
  Sabbath School Society. 45890
Brief history of the missions and settlements.
  781, 103377
Brief history of the Mississippi Territory.
  29783
Brief history of the New England Historic-
  Genealogical Society. 80304
Brief history of the New-England historical &
  genealogical register. 19030
Brief history of the new gold regions in
  Colorado Territory. 5917
Brief history of the New Jersey congressional
  election. 53080, 102328
Brief history of the oldest city in Canada.
  72606
Brief history of the oldest city in Canada,
  from its foundation. 74408
Brief history of the organization and work of
  the [American Tract] Society. 1245
Brief history of the other ignivomous mountains.
  (46611), note after 105484
Brief history of the parish of Trinity Church.
  79020
Brief history of the Pennsylvania petroleum
  region. 15219
Brief history of the Pequot War. 15748, 36351,
  45454-45455
Brief history of the Pittsburgh and Connellsville
  Rail Road Company. (7875)
Brief history of the principles and views of
  the Federalists. 66527
Brief history of the proceedings of the Assembly
  [of Connecticut.] (18262)
Brief history of the proceedings of the Synod
  of Kentucky. (37496)
Brief history of "the progress and present
  state of the Unitarian Churches in
  America." 4596, 96412
Brief history of the proposed impeachment.
  (43380), 60772, note after 99586
Brief history of the Protestant Episcopal
  Church. 7874
Brief history of the Protestant Reformed Dutch
  Church. (38169)
Brief history of the rebellion. 70942
Brief history of the Reformed Dutch Church
  of Raritan. (48158)
Brief history of the revolution. 31646
Brief history of the Riker family. 71387
Brief history of the rise and progress of
  Mormonism. 18824
Brief history of the rise and progress of the
  charitable scheme. 7876, 84588

Brief history of the rise, growth, and progress of Quakerism. 9072
Brief history of the settlement of the Third Church in Salem. 13594, 103319
Brief history of the Society for one hundred years. 6734
Brief history of the state. (9668)
Brief history of the Strict Congregational Convention of Long Island. 92826
Brief history of . . . the temperance reform. 36331
Brief history of the territory north-west of the River Ohio. 85134
Brief history of the Theological Seminary of the Presbyterian Church. 65656
Brief history of the town of Norfolk. 73842
Brief history of the town of Stoneham, Mass. 19042
Brief history of the trial of the Rev. William A. Scott. 85178
Brief history of the United States. 91124
Brief history of the United States boundary question. 35695
Brief history of the United States of America. 7834
Brief history of the University of Michigan. (1142)
Brief history of the war with the Indians in New-England. (46641)
Brief history of the warr with the Indians in Nevv-England. 46640
Brief history of the wars and treaties. 7877
Brief history of the wars, revolutions, and events. 6209
Brief history of the Waterman Street Baptist Church. 66380
Brief history of Westtown Boarding School. 103058
Brief history of the whale fishery. 8658
Brief illustration and confirmation of the divine right of infant baptism. 13350, 20053
Brief illustration of the principles of war and peace. 38522, 2d note after 102601
Brief illustration of the prophecies and promises of God's word. 72852
Brief in behalf of the unborn. 84751
Brief in the case of Major Ben. P. Runkle. (74136)
Brief incidental review. 8466
Brief incidents in the war of Missouri. 58258
Brief inquiry into some of the objections urged. 35391
Brief inquiry into the condition of Jamaica. 35979
Brief inquiry into the origin and principles of free masonry. 28668
Brief inquiry into the real name and character of the author. 97028
Brief inquiry into the reasons. 14469
Brief introduction by the Rev. A. B. Lawrence. 95091
Brief introduction in the principles of the Christian religion. 93596
Brief introduction relating to the character of [Whitefield.] 11894
Brief introduction relating to the law of nature. 6219
Brief investigation of the causes. (54131)
Brief journal of the life, travels and labours of love. 104689
Brief life, by Tom Owen. 58025
Brief medical account of the middle regions of Georgia. 28030
Brief memento of Captain Henry Brooks O'Reilly. 57595
Brief memoir. 20778, 20789

Brief memoir by Miss L. C. Edgarton. (78334)
Brief memoir concerning Abel Thomas. 95375
Brief memoir explanatory of a new trace. 12216
Brief memoir of Andrew Underhill. 97731
Brief memoir of Dr. Winslow Lewis. 80305
Brief memoir of George Fox. 25360
Brief memoir of George Mifflin Dallas. 18320
Brief memoir of Harriet M. Gardiner. 26632
Brief memoir of . . . His Excellency George Washington. 47050
Brief memoir of his [i. e. Samuel Stanhope Smith's] life and writings. 84120
Brief memoir of his [i. e. Thomas Preistley's] life and writings. 4597
Brief memoir of his [i. e. Granville O. Haller's] military services. 29886
Brief memoir of Horace Bassett Morse. 50918
Brief memoir of Jane Bethel. 5069
Brief memoir of John Bouvier. 6981
Brief memoir of Joshua Fisher. 11900
Brief memoir of . . . Mrs. Lydia M. Malcom. 44095
Brief memoir of Mrs. Mary Brewster Park. (58633)
Brief memoir of Mrs. Place. 63204
Brief memoir of one of New Jersey's neglected sons. 82980
Brief memoir of Rev. Hezekiah Calvin Wooster. (57747)
Brief memoir of Rev. Joseph Bancroft Hill. 32353
Brief memoir of Robert Waterton. (19045)
Brief memoir of Sir Walter Raleigh. 20869
Brief memoir of Solomon Underhill. 97735
Brief memoir of the author [i. e. Erskin Mason.] (45438)
Brief memoir of the author [i. e. William Sewel.] 79614
Brief memoir of the family of Shelton. (20354)
Brief memoir of the life and public character of George Fox. 64457
Brief memoir of the life, labours, and death of John Stewart. (49704), note after 101083
Brief memoir of the life of George Fox. 25359
Brief memoir of the life of James Wilson. 104641
Brief memoir of the life of William Penn. 100979
Brief memoir of the Marquis de Chastellux. 101707
Brief memoir of the Rev. Giles Firmin. 19031
Brief memoir of the writer [i. e. Rev. Peter Jones.] (36590)
Brief memoirs of Daniel De Lisle Brock. (8152)
Brief memoirs of eminent Americans. 42127, note after 42135
Brief memoirs of John and Walter Deane. 19069
Brief memoirs of the class of 1797. 18991
Brief memoirs of the members of the class. 24266
Brief memoirs of Thomas Fowell Buxton and Elizabeth Fry. 9693, (29314)
Brief memorandum of his [i. e. John Stevens'] own experiences. 91541
Brief memorial of Rev. Henry Martyn Adams. 9536
Brief memorial on the origin and earlier history of the Tammany Society. 94290
Brief memorial, or matters, and methods for pastoral visits. 46242
Brief memorial representing the present state of religion. 7878

Brief memorials of an only son. 8442
Brief memorials of departed worth. 83561-83562
Brief memorials of the lives and dying sayings of several young Quakers. 7879
Brief memorials of the virtuous lives and dying sayings of several of the people called Quakers. (66914)
Brief narration of the captivity of Isaac Hollister. 32556
Brief narration of the practices of the churches in New-England. (52617)-52618, 102552
Brief narration of the sufferings of the people called Quakers. 28099
Brief narration of the unhappy disputes. 25232, 73562, 102947
Brief narrative. 20386
Brief narrative and deduction of the several remarkable cases. 7880, 17178
Brief narrative concerning that country. (28656), 92712
Brief narrative concerning the said criminals. 80794
Brief narrative, &c. 7269, 99830
Brief narrative of a late difference among the Quakers. (44077)
Brief narrative of a revival of religion. (67061)
Brief narrative of an unsuccessful attempt to reach Repulse Bay. (42851)
Brief narrative [of Edward Winslow.] 106053
Brief narrative of facts in the McGarrahan case. 43255
Brief narrative of incidents in the war in Missouri. 7881
Brief narrative [of Mr. Aylmer.] 1st note after 97148, 105081
Brief narrative, of New-Englands lamentable estate. 96155
Brief narrative of several remarkable passages. 9071
Brief narrative of some considerable passages. 74288
Brief narrative of some of the brethren. 4074
Brief narrative of the captivity and sufferings of Lt. Nathan'l Segar. 78895
Brief narrative of the case and trial of John Peter Zenger. 106310, 106312
Brief narrative of the case and tryal of John Zenger. 106304-106305, 106314
Brief narrative of the Indian Charity-School. 103202-103203
Brief narrative of the invention of reaping machines. 90021
Brief narrative of the origin, history, and dissolution of St. John's Grand Lodge. (53692)
Brief narrative of the practices of the Churches in New-England. (62517)
Brief narrative of the principal transactions of that day. 13316
Brief narrative of the proceedings of the Eastern Association. 103374
Brief narrative of the proceedings of the government of New York. 792, 20987, 90629, 4th-5th notes after 98997
Brief narrative of the progress of the Gospel among the Indians of New England. 22143
Brief narrative of the progress of the Gospel amongst the Indians of New-England. 22142, note just before 85867, note just before 85932
Brief narrative of the revival of religion in Virginia. 51829, (67887), 100437

Brief narrative of the Royal African-Company's proceedings. 73759
Brief narrative of the shipwreck of the transport "Premier." 18635
Brief narrative of the success which the Gospel hath had. 47151
Brief narrative of the trial for the bloody and mysterious murder. 7882, note before 96903A
Brief notes of a sermon. 80261
Brief notes and remarks, by Rev. E. Ryerson. 48190, 74566
Brief notice of a portion of a work by William Burke. 50470
Brief notice of American slavery. (23055), (81913)
Brief notice of an "account of the true nature and object of the late Protestant Episcopal Clerical Association of the City of New-York." 7883, (54611), 66116, note after 97492
Brief notice of his [i. e. A. Porter's] life. 64199
Brief notice of recent outrages committed by Isaac I. Stevens. 101107, 1st note after 101924
Brief notice of Rev. John Gloucester. 11558
Brief notice of the Evangelical Church of Lyons. 24414
Brief notice of the Iroquois Indians. 4782
Brief notice of the late Commodore Charles Morris. 20403, 50806
Brief notice of the manufactures of the city [of Buffalo.] 9054
Brief notice of the recent outrages committed by Isaac I. Stevens. 91530, 101107, 101911
Brief notice of the settlement of . . . Newton. 35475
Brief notice of William Shurtleff. 80773
Brief notices of a runic inscription found in North America. 77841
Brief notices of Hayti. 10673
Brief notices of the happy deaths of twenty six sabbath school scholars. 97013
Brief notices of the life and character of the late Moses Brown. 8538
Brief notices of the life and character of the late Nicholas Brown. 27649
Brief notices of the principal events in the public life of Governor Clarke. 13472
Brief observations on the management of the war. (46180)
Brief observations on the militia. 53548
Brief observations on the West India question. 102795
Brief of the authorities upon the law of impeachable crimes. (39376)
Brief of the case of Caricaburu, Arieta & Company. 105476
Brief of the Choctaws. (63037)
Brief of the claims, on the part of the province of New-Jersey. (7884)
Brief of the Governor and Council of Massachusetts. (45656)
Brief of the remarks made before the Committee on Rail-ways and Canals. 9235
Brief of the U. S. Solicitor before the United States Court of Claims. (69090)
Brief of title to a tract of land. 88157
Brief of war premium claimants. 89570
Brief outline for a national bank. (7885)
Brief outline of the faith . . . of the Latter Day Saints. 42828
Brief outline of the life of Henry Clay. (77027)

Brief outline of the origin and progress of political power. (9325)

Brief outline of the rise, progress, and failure of the revolutionary scheme. 7886

Brief outline of . . . [the work of] the U. S. Sanitary Commission. 57245

[Brief outline of what the United States Sanitary Commission has done and is doing.] 76635

Brief plea for the ambulance system for the Army of the United States. 6990

Brief popular account of all the financial panics. 7887

Brief reasons for repudiation. 9680

Brief recapitulation. 46458

Brief recit du voyage de Poutrincourt. 16212

Brief recit, & succincte narration. 11138

Brief recit et succincte narration de la navigation. 11139

Brief recollections of the late Rev. George W. Walker. (26284)

Brief record of events in Exeter, N. H., during . . . 1861. 51882

Brief record . . . [of events in Exeter, N. H.,] during . . . 1863. 51883

Brief record . . . [of events in Exeter, N. H.,] during . . . 1862. 51883

Brief relation of a credible intelligence of the present estate of Virginia. 104795

Brief relation of a strange impression from heaven. 46315

Brief relation [of John White.] 106052

Brief relation of patient and joyful sufferings. (46444)

Brief relation of remarkables in the shipwreck of above one hundred pirates. 46369

Brief relation of Sir W. Raleigh. 78994

Brief relation of Sir Walter Raleigh's troubles. 67598-67599

Brief relation of the cruel murder of Betsy Van Amburgh. 96816

Brief relation of the most memorable and remarkable passages. 51012-51014

Brief relation of the occasion of planting of this colony. 103397

Brief relation of the state of New England. 46642, (46749)

Brief relation of the sufferings of the people called Quakers in New-England. 5631

Brief relation of the sufferings of the people called Quakers in those parts of America. 4628

Brief relation of the voyage vnto Maryland. 103353

Brief remarker on the ways of man. (75926)

Brief remarks . . . March 11, 1837. 38937

Brief remarks on a number of false propositions. 30646

[Brief remarks] on a special report of the African Institution. 7891

Brief remarks on Dr. Channing's letter to Hon. Henry Clay. 11913, 95141

Brief remarks on Miss Catharine E. Beecher's Essay on slavery. 31771

Brief remarks on scriptural notices. 7888

Brief remarks on some of the leading topics of popular education. 41655, 99563

Brief remarks on some pamphlets, written by Dr. Moore and Dr. Linn. 105252

Brief remarks on the common arguments now used. 68301, 97584

Brief remarks on the defence of the Halifax libel. 7889, 69455

Brief remarks on the hygiene of Massachusetts. 18056

Brief remarks on the organization and action of the Board of Missions. 7890

Brief remarks on the projected reunion of Lower and Upper Canada. (82129)

Brief remarks on the rail roads. 78833

Brief remarks on the Rev. Mr. Fletcher's late tract. 23140

Brief remarks on the satyrical drollery at Cambridge. 17669-17670

Brief remarks on the slave registry bill. 7891, (81914), 98836

Brief remarks on the "wife" of Washington Irving. 4741

Breif remembrancer for Pennsylvania. 9743

Brief reply to a ludicrous pamphlet. (62214), note after 93765

Brief reply to a meer raposdie of lies. 90540, 97265

Brief reply to a pamphlet. 67143

Brief reply to an extraordinary publication. 95207

Brief reply to certain charges. 85556

Brief reply to Mr. George Kieth [sic]. 104070

Brief reply to Peter Porcupine. 14031, 94025

Brief reply to some part of the annexed letters. 2657

Brief reply to some statements of Joseph John Gurney. 9370

Brief reply to the late writings of Louisa Baker. 89409

Brief reply to the "observations" of friend Edward Cobb. (67748)

Brief reply to the report of the investigating committee. 19662

Brief reply to the Rev. James R. Wilson's pamphlet. 55373

Brief report of the debates in the Anti-masonic Convention. 45659

Brief report of the hearing of the Troy and Greenfield Railroad Company. 32888

Brief report of the operations of the Sanitary Commission in Tennessee. 54896

Brief report of the proceedings at the great inaugural mass meeting of the Loyal National League. 28461

Brief report of the rise, progress and condition of the Rochester Athenaeum—Young Men's Association. 72355

Brief report of the services rendered by the freed people. 7892, 14918

Brief report of the trials of several other persons. 25961, 96866

Brief report of some other Gospel-doctrines. 46770

Brief representation of the case. 43663, (55031), (65578), 96298

Brief resume of the history of the United States. 83531

Brief retrospect of the eighteenth century. 49048

Brief review of a book entitled, Testimony of God against slavery. 82203

Brief review of a historical sermon. 11852

Brief review of Bishop Doane's sermon. 20392

Brief review of "Considerations respectfully submitted." 7894

Brief review of forty years. 76507

Brief review of Miss Martineau on that subject. 82091, 7th note after 88114

Brief review of Mr. Calhoun's letter. (67132)

Brief review of the causes and course of the division. 25219, 40801

Brief reivew of the discovery of the continent of North America. 83516

Brief review of the Episcopal Church in Virginia. 47242

Brief review . . . of the errors. 30859
Brief review of the "First annual report of the American Anti-slavery Society." (68652)
Brief review of the navy yard question. 53251
Brief review of the origin, progress, and administration of the Bank of the United States. 3189, 7893
Brief review of the past sixty years. (43589)
Brief review of the plan and operations of the Association for the Relief of Maimed Soldiers. 7895, (15242)
Brief review of the political state of Lower Canada. 12935
Brief review of the previous transactions in Great Britain and Ireland. 3463, 25264
Brief review of the proceedings of the annual conference of the Methodist Episcopal Church. (43002)
Brief review of the revenue, resources and expenditures of Canada. 48023
Brief review of the rise and progress of English liberty. 16034
Brief review of the rise and progress, services and sufferings, of New England. 7896, note after 52619
Brief review of the settlement of Upper Canada. 43535
Brief review of the speech of Hon. Thomas G. Cary. 19662
Brief review of thirty years in the ministry. 30925
Brief rule to guide the common people of New-England. 95192-95194
Brief sermon preached to the Great & General Assembly. 4393
Brief sketch of a lecture. 103365
Brief sketch of a religious society of people called Shakers. 101368
Brief sketch of Commodore Samuel Tucker. 80306
Brief sketch of David Brainard. 4678
Brief sketch of events. (38102)
Brief sketch of his [i. e. Henry Anthon's] life. 1676, 11th note after 96966
Brief sketch of his [i. e. Isaac Stockton Keith's] life. (37232)
Brief sketch of its [i. e the tax system of Philadelphia's] unequal and unjust operation. 10863
Brief sketch of La Crosse, Wisconsin. (11025)
Brief sketch of Maryland. 45092
Brief sketch of Ohio. (18173), 18175
Brief sketch of parties. 7897
Brief sketch of Rev. Andrew Arnot. 28226
Brief sketch of some of the principal universities. 41317
Brief sketch of Spain. 88852
Brief sketch . . . of Stephen and Jesse Boorn. 31054, 96830, 101012
Brief sketch of the author's [i. e. Benjamin Morrell's] early life. 50778
Brief sketch of the author's [i. e. James Spencer's] life. 89333
Brief sketch of the author's [i. e. Thomas Paine's] life. 58235
Brief sketch of the birth, life & sufferings, of Capt. Francis Duclos. (21065)
Brief sketch of the causes and treatment of disease. 95600
Brief sketch of the character and services of Captain Josiah Sturgis. 93267
Brief sketch of the character of William M. Richardson. (58689)
Brief sketch of the characters and sufferings of the pilgrims. 63474

Brief sketch of the commerce on the great northern and western lakes. 3846
Brief sketch of the efforts of Philadelphia Yearly Meeting of the religious society of Friends. 34622
Brief sketch of the First Congregational Church in Milford. 48946
Brief sketch of the first settlement of Deerfield, Mass. 19234
Brief sketch of the first settlement of the county of Schoharie. 8526
Brief sketch of the frontier life. 56983
Brief sketch of the history of Leicester Academy. 101520
Brief sketch of the history of Lexington, Ky. 61176
Brief sketch of the history of the Catholic Church. 4053
Brief sketch of the life and character of Mrs. Elizabeth Adams. 93194
Brief sketch of the life and character of Rev. John Bruce. 11958
Brief sketch of the life and history of General McClellan. note after 43024
Brief sketch of the life and labors of the late Rev. John Keir. (59134)
Brief sketch of the life and military services of Arthur P. Hayne. (31038)
Brief sketch of the life and public services of William Henry Harrison. 30574
Brief sketch of the life and religious labours of Thomas Shillitow. 80489
Brief sketch of the life, character and services of Major General Andrew Jackson. 31831
Brief sketch of the life, character, and writings of William Charles Wells. 3727
Brief sketch of the life, civil and military, of John A. Quitman. 67365
Brief sketch of the life of Anna Backhouse. (2621)
Brief sketch of the life of Charles Baron Metcalfe. 17586
Brief sketch of the life of Horace Carter. 11114
Brief sketch of the life of Mary Smith. 83544
Brief sketch of the life of the deceased [i. e. John B. Preston.] 102458
Brief sketch of the life of the Rev. Lott Carey. (39303)
Brief sketch of the life of William Green. 81703
Brief sketch of the life of William Penn. 42717
Brief sketch of the military operations on the Delaware. 7898
Brief sketch of the national judiciary powers. 21380
Brief sketch of the origin and present state of . . . Philadelphia. 61507
Brief sketch of the origin and progress of the Virginia Baptist Education Society. 100500
Brief sketch of the origin and rise of the Workingmen's Party. 4968
Brief sketch of the plan and advantages of a sectional floating dry dock. 7899
Brief sketch of the political importance of the British colonies. 7900
Brief sketch of the present state of the province of Nova Scotia. 32725
Brief sketch of the property belonging to the North American Coal Company. 7901, 55545
Brief sketch of the property of the North American Coal Company. 7901, 55545
Brief sketch of the public services of Major Isaac Roach. 71708
Brief sketch of the remarks. 9235

Brief sketch of the republic of Costa Rica. (42908), (49883)

Brief sketch of the revival of religion in Boston. 2913

Brief sketch of the rise, progress, and present state of the Wesleyan-Methodist societies throughout the world. 35464

Brief sketch of the St. David's Benevolent Society. 36445

Brief sketch of the school system. 75461

Brief sketch of the services of John G. Watmough. 102127

Brief sketch of the state of Ohio. 47394, 101319-101320

Brief sketch of the state penitentiary for Eastern Pennsylvania. 59926

Brief sketch of the trial of William Lloyd Garrison. 26705

Brief sketch of the voyages and discoveries of Columbus and Cortez. 8137, 80342

Brief sketch of Whiteside Co. 26204

Brief sketches of Christian biography. 9912

Brief sketches of some of his [i. e Robert Finley's] contemporaries. 8492

Brief sketches of the moral and political character of this country. 10889

Brief sketches of the officers who were in the Battle of Lake Erie. 58921

Brief sketches of the present condition of the city of Rochester. (57593)

Brief, so als die tot onse handen quam. 91320

Brief, soo als die tot onse handen quam. 91319

Brief state of Pennsylvania. 84627

Brief state of the controversy between the colonies of New-York and New Jersey. 7902, 53549

Brief state of the province of Pennsylvania. (17666), 60742, 84589-84593, note after 97095

Brief state of the services and expenses of the province. 45660

Brief statement. 103000

Brief statement and examination of the sentiments of the Weslean Methodists. 101310, 101314

Brief statement and examination of the sentiments of the Wesleyan Methodists. 94522

Brief statement and examination of the sentiments of the Wesleyn Methodists. 94523

Brief statement of facts, as connected with . . . St. Jude's Protestant Episcopal Free Church. (54132)

Brief statement of facts for the consideration of the Democracy. 54790

Brief statement of facts in relation to the proposed railroad. (6767)

Brief statement of facts in relation to the Western Rail-Road. 102999

Brief statement of facts in relation to the Western Rail Road, February, 1839. 103000

Brief statement of facts, in support of the bill. 7903

Brief statement of facts, respecting the origin, persecutions, and successive steps to toleration. 66915

Brief statement of his [i. e. John Johnson's] religious experience. 96891

Brief statement of opinions given in the Board of Commissioners. 7904, (14989), 84842

Brief statement of proposed railroad. 24595

Brief statement of the causes which have led to the abandonment of the celebrated system of penitentiary discipline. 73226

Brief statement of the causes which led to a division of the Christian Church in Summer Street. 6674, 103983

Brief statement, of the claims of the trustees. 105067

Brief statement of the cost of the new hall. 60129

Brief statement of the dispute between Sir C. Metcalf. 23737

Brief statement of the exertions of the Friends of Cheap Postage. (3921)

Brief statement of the pleadings and argument. (16421)

Brief statement of the proceedings of the citizens of Utica. 98224

Brief statement of the rights of the Seneca Indians. 79104

Brief statement of the rise and progress of the testimony. 7905

Brief statement of the Romulus and Remus Silver Mine. 73065

Brief statement of the Sanitary Commission's work. 2698, 7906, 76636

Brief statement of the sufferings of Mary Dyer. 21594

Brief statement of the transactions and accounts. 95418

Brief statement relative to the claim on the Eastern Railroad Company. (21666)

Brief statement relative to the late election. (32301), 96981

Brief statement respecting the Roxbury church. 73634

Brief statement, support by original documents. 7907, (29069)

Brief statement touching the Revd Dr Schroeder's late publication. 77978, note after 96981

Brief statements and remarks respecting the present division. 62665

Brief statements of facts. 45093

Brief suggestions in the case of General Fitz John Porter. 64249

Brief summary of Christian doctrine and a form of covenant adopted by the First Presbyterian Church, Buffalo. 9049

Brief summary of Christian doctrine, and form of covenant, adopted in the First Church in Dedham. (19213)

Brief summary of some of the . . . incidents. (55023)

Brief survey. 66143

Brief survey of the great extent and evil tendencies of the lottery system. 7908, 42151, 97643

Brief survey of the prophetical and evangelical events. 8655

Brief survey of the temple mystical. 56220

Brief survey of the whole world delineated. (32367)

Brief synopsis of the doings of the Texas Navy. 50351

Brief testimony against tale-bearers. 90458

Brief. The Society for Propagating the Gospel Among the Indians and Others in North-America, . . . having requested. 87865

Brief, though fair and impartial history. 82580

Brief topographical and statistical manual. 27854-27855, 53550

Brief topographical description of the county of Washington. 19332

Brief tractate. 55883-55884

Brief treatise of the most principal fruits and herbs. 25947, note after 97286-97287

Brief treatise on manufacturing in the south. 90847

Brief . . . treatise on . . . plank roads. 58017

Brief treatise on the injuries offered unto the . . . Saviour. 46549
Brief treatise on the police of the city of New York. 12895, 54133
Brief treatise upon constitutional and party questions. 18207, (20690)
Brief treatise upon the evils of the union. 24299
Brief tribute to the life and character of Dr. Kane. 755
Brief van Comm. Hidde Dirks Kat. (35768)
Brief van de Vice-Admiraal de Ruyter. 74506
Brief van de Wel Eewarde Classis van Amsterdam. (36984), 53551
Brief van de Weleerwaarde Classis van Amsterdam. 7909
Brief van dem E. Generael Pieter Pietersz. Heyn. 31658
Brief van den Heere Admirael Spil-berghen. 89443
Brief van den Koningh van Portugael. 16730
Brief van een Amsterdams koopman te Petersburg. 95850
Brief van een burger van Amsterdam. 7910
Brief van een Heer te Londen. 7911
Brief van een koopman in Amsterdam. 7912
Brief van een koopman te Londen. 97367
Brief van een S[urinam]s Heer. 7913
Brief van een. zeker Heer aan William Penn. (59684), 59714
Brief van het Algemeene Synode der Hollandsche Gereformde Kerk. (7914)
Brief van Jan Regtuit. (77977)
Brief van Iohan Valckenburgh. 98302
Brief van land verhuizer zynvertrokken naar Pella, Iowa. 81439
Brief van Monsieur Soler. 86375
Brief van NN. aan zijnen vriend A. 51679
Brief van Z. Kon. Maj. van Denemarken. 7915
Brief van zijne excellentie Jonathan Trumbull. 36925, 98478
Brief vande politycque Raeden in Brasil. 7579, note after 102891
Brief view of a controversy. 105233
Brief view of constitutional powers. 7916, 34724
Brief view of ecclesiastical jurisdiction. 7917
Brief view of facts. 89768
Brief view of Methodist Episcopacy. 105158
Brief view of the accounts of the Treasury. 59927
Brief view of the actual condition and treatment of the Negro slaves. 31309
Brief view of the conduct of Pennsylvania, for the year 1755. (17666), 19370, 33694, 60742, 84594, note after 97095
Brief view of the constitution of the United States. 21377
Brief view of the . . . controversy. 46767
Brief view of the distresses. (11827)
Brief view of the enterprise. 22332
Brief view of the formation, government and discipline. 104770
Brief view of the friendly conduct of William Penn towards them. 35413
Brief view, of the great anti-Christian conspiracy. 85122
Brief view of the important relations of the Morris Canal. 81878
Brief view of the missionary proceedings in the western country. 60780, 102995
Brief view of the nature and effects of Negro slavery. 81915
Brief view of the origin and results of episcopacy. 78583

Brief view of the policy and resources of the United States. (30369), 1st note after 97909, 101165
Brief view of the policy of the founders of the colonies. 10871
Brief view of the political circumstances of the United States. 58034
Brief view of the proceedings of the Western Missionary Society. 60780, 102995
Brief view of the religious tenents and sentiments. 78322
Brief view of the system of internal improvement of the state of Pennsylvania. 10853
Brief view I. Of errors and obscurities in the common version. 102342
Brief vindication of the constitution. (17719)
Brief vindication of the doctrine of God's decrees. 102425
Brief vindication of the particular communion of the Baptist churches. 2914
Brief vindication of the proceedings of the Trustees relating to the college. 7918
Brief vindication of the proceedings of the Trustees relating to the Columbia College. 14811
Brief vindication of the purchassors [sic] against the proprietors. 7919, note just before 53081
Brief vocabulary of the Mosquito language. 90002
Brief von der Portogalesischen Meerfahrt. (69369)
Brief wegens eene uitstorting des Heigligen Geestes in de Vereenigde Staten van Amerika. 7920
Briefe and accvrate treatise. 98890
Briefe and true relation. (7730)
Briefe and true report of the new found land of Virginia. 20926, 30377, 82823, 103395
Briefe answer to a certaine declaration. 98500
Briefe aus America. (38220)
Briefe aus Amerika fur Deutsche Auswanderer. 7921
Briefe aus Bremen, Baltimore, a und St. Louis. (19443)
Briefe aus den Vereinigten Staaten von Nord Amerika. 7861, 36141
Briefe aus den Vereinigten Staaten von Nordamerika in die Heimath. 3988
Briefe aus Columbien an seine Freunde. 7922
Briefe aus Nord-Amerika. (59595)
Briefe aus Nord-Amerika von einem kathol Missionar. 7923
Briefe aus und uber Nordamerika. 9671
Briefe aus Wisconsin in Nord-Amerika. 27714
Briefe bey Gelegenhet der Ankunft. 39709
Briefe catechism concerning church government. 72094
Briefe chronicle of the acts and gestes of the Spaniardes. 11287
Briefe collection and compendious extract of straunge and memorable thinges, gathered out of the Cosmographeye of Sebastian Munster. (51406)
Briefe collection and compendious extract of straunge and memorable things gathered oute of the Cosmograupye of Sebastian Munster. 51405
Briefe declaration of the present state of things. 9873
Briefe den gegenwartigen Zustand von Nord Amerika betreffend. 89756
Briefe der Generalin von Riedesel. (71300)
Briefe der nach Amerika ausgenwanderten Familie Steines. (19443)
Briefe des Ferdinand Cortes. 16958

Briefe des Generals Lee. 9259, 69549
Briefe discourse dialoguewise. 18668
Briefe eines Deutschen aus Kalifornien. 78098
Briefe eines Deutschen aus Nord-Amerika.
  7924
Briefe eines Englischen Fraulein. 95250
Briefe eines Reisenden. 104707
Briefe eines unter dem Schutze des Mainzer
  Vereins. 87148
Briefe enarration of the ayre. 50786
Briefe in die Heimath, geschreiben zwischen
  October 1829. 7925
Briefe in die Heimath zwischen October 1829.
  38237
Briefe information of the affaires of the
  Palatinate. 78379
Briefe narration (occasioned by certain asper-
  sions). 104796, 106053
Briefe narration [of Las Casas.] 66686
Briefe narration of some church courses.
  (67947), 102551
Briefe narration of the originall undertakings.
  28020
Briefe relation of the discoverie and plantation
  of New England. 52619, 66686
Briefe relation of the late horrid rebellion.
  25260
Briefe relation of the persecvtion lately made
  against the Catholike Christians. 7926,
  1st note after 100872, note after 105625
Briefe uber Alexander von Humboldt's Kosmos.
  33731
Briefe uber Amerika. (10914)
Briefe uber Amerika nach der neuesten.
  31376
Briefe uber Brasilien. 7927
Briefe uber den Kampf und das Wiederaufleben.
  31375, 56883
Briefe uber den moralischen und politischen
  Zustand. 51410
Briefe uber die jetzige Uneingkeit. 7930
Briefe uber die Vereinigten Staaten von Nord-
  Amerika. 7928
Briefe uber die westlichen Theile der Verein-
  igten Staaten von Nord Amerika. 44828
Briefe uber Nord-Amerika und Mexico. 28919
Briefe uber Portugal. 7929, 89763, 91304
Briefe uber Portugal und Brasilien. 7544
Briefe uber schriftstellerisches Eigenthum.
  10830
Briefe von der Insel Teneriffa. 37778
Briefe von Deutschen aus Nord-America.
  (7931)
Briefe, welche Beobachtungen uber verschiedene
  Gegenstande. 21049
Briefe welche Kurzlich von Personen in PAris.
  (65501), 92070
Briefen an Freunde in England. 30534
Briefen an seine freunde beschreiben. 35243
Briefen an seine Freunde von Eduard Ludecus.
  42639
Briefen eines Rigaer's. (71470)
Briefen Skizzirt von J. M. K. 90510
Briefen von demselben. 94639
Briefen von Jonathan Slick. 91283
Brieff. (45749), (46643)
Brieff so ausz Hispania. 16663, 63176
Brieff van eenen vriendt. 16737
Brieff van eenen vrient. 16737, (57378)
Brieff von der Glucklichen Fortgang. (46643)
Briefless barrister. pseud. Golden Christmas.
  see Simms, William Gilmore, 1806-1870.
Briefs geschreven uyt West-Indien. 62613
Briefs in the controversy between Massa-
  chusetts Bay and New Hampshire. 45661
Briefs von New-Yorck. 103607

Briefs-wijse door den ontedekker opgesteld.
  99281
Briefsgewyse voorgedragen. 100948, 102818
Briefve deduction par laquelle est clairement
  monstre. 7932
Briefve, & vive description de tout le mond.
  47888
Briefwechsel, Heft XXIII und XXIV. 99311
Briefwechsel meist historischen und politischen
  Inhalts. 77658
Brier, William Wallace. 7933
Brierly, John. defendant 6326, 1st note after
  96956, last note after 97284
Briet, Philip. (7934), 52769, 79124
Brieto, Philippo. see Briet, Philip.
Brietius, P. see Briet, Philip.
Briev van Broeder Jedema. 35876
Briev van een Amsterdams koopman. 99757
Brieve et fidele exposition. (7935), 6th note
  after 97845, 97851
Brieve relation de l'estat de Phernambucq.
  29100
Brieve relation dv voyage de la Novvelle France.
  39946, note after 69259
Brieve relation du voyage des isles de l'
  l'Amerique. (58095), (66393)
Brieve van den Heer . . . aan den Heer . . . .
  51450
Brieven, behelzende der toestand. 17499
Brieven geschreven door gedeporteerde
  geestelyken. 99322
Brieven gewisselt tusschen den Engelschen
  Vice-Admiraal Joung. 7937, 75199,
  106077
Brieven over de Noord-Americaansche onlusten.
  51890, 95310
Brieven over de regeeringsvorm en wetten der
  Vereenigde Staten van Nord America.
  (42926)
Brieven over de tegenwoordige tijdsomstandighe-
  den. 98503
Brieven over de zeden en staatkunde der Vere-
  enigde Staten. 51411
Brieven over het bestuur den colonien Essequebo
  en Demerary. 7936, 22991
Brieven tusschen den Eng. Viceadm. Joung.
  7937, 106007
Brieven uit en over de Vereenigde Staaten van
  Noord-Amerika. 36439, note before 93999
Brieven uit Pella van een Gelderschman. 23520
Brieven uit . . . Sante-Fee. 96101, note after
  104997
Brieven van den 13. en 16 Maart uit Londen.
  97589
Brieven van eenen Amerkaenschen landman.
  17498, 98479
Brieven van Ferdinand Cortes. 16962
Brieven van hunne excellenties de Heeren
  Jonathan Trumbull. 97252
Brieven van K. Jz. Beukma. 5103
Brigadier-General Thomas Francis Meagher.
  42871
Brigands of the revolution. 79354, 105692
Brigant, Jacques le. see Le Brigant, Jacques,
  1720-1804.
Briganti, Annibale. tr. 49939, 57667, 57670
Brigantine; or Admiral Lowe's last cruise.
  59184
Brigden, Zech. 62743
Brigdon, Philip. 29767
Briggs, -------. 96304
Briggs, Carolina A. see Mason, Caroline A.
  (Briggs)
Briggs, Charles. 7938-7939, 106051
Briggs, Charles Frederick, 1804-1877. 7940,
  25484, (54134), 90507

Briggs, Clinton. 7941
Briggs, Ephraim. 7942
Briggs, George Nixon, 1796-1861. 7943,
45686, 45921-45922 see also Massa-
chusetts. Governor, 1844-1851 (Briggs)
Briggs, George Ware. 7944-7948
Briggs, Henry. 99885
Briggs, Hugh L. 7949
Briggs, Isaac, fl. 1799-1803. 87777, 87779-
87780
Briggs, Isaac, fl. 1810-1816. (7950)-7951
Briggs, Rev. Isaac, fl. 1855. 7952
Briggs, John. 7954
Briggs, John A. B. 7953
Briggs, L. 7955
Briggs, Nathan M. defendant 28621
Briggs, W. see Biggs, William.
Briggs, William. 84421
Brigges, ------. 66686
Brigham, Alasco Delancey. 26937, 41743,
57835
Brigham, Alasco Delany. see Brigham,
Alasco Delancey.
Brigham, C. A. G. (7957)
Brigham, C. S. ed. 104336
Brigham, Charles H. (7958)-7959
Brigham, David. defendant 96836
Brigham, H. H. 7960
Brigham, William. 7961-7963
Brighamism: its promises and their failures.
50730
Bright, Jesse David, 1812-1875. 7964
Bright, John, 1811-1889. 7965-7967, 14037,
(14040)
Bright, John M. 7968-7969
Bright, Jonathan Brown, 1800-1879. 7969
Bright, Michael. defendant 7970
Bright republic. 5434
Bright side of Indian character. 36183
Brighter age. 102053
Brightly, Frederick Charles, 1812-1888.
7971-7972, 60064, 60652
Brightly, H. A. illus. 83734, 83775, 84237
Brighton, J. G. 7973
Brighton, Mass. 7974
Brighton, Mass. Evergreen Cemetery. 23292
Brighton, Mass. School Committee. 7975
Brighton, Mass. Treasurer. 7976
Brighton and Brookline business directory.
7977
Brighton gazette. 10371
Bright's analytical digest of the laws. 7972
Brights of Suffolk, England. 7969
Brightwell, C. L. 7978-7979
Brignoles, --------, Marquis de. 7980
Brigstock, William. defendant 96837
Brij. Fz., H. de. tr. 83220
Brij, William J. de. see DeBrij, William J.
tr.
Brikbeck, M. 24911
Bril-gesicht voor de verblinde eyghen baetsuch-
tige handelaers op Brasil. 7545, (7981)
Brillante porvenir del Curzo. 70166
Brillante trisagio que a todas lices declara.
74853
Brilliant military record of Maj.-General
Hawley. (30982A)
Brim, a Quaker. pseud. Americans roused.
see Sewall, Jonathan, 1728-1796.
Brim, a Quaker. pseud. Cure for the spleen.
see Sewall, Jonathan, 1728-1796.
Brimblecom, Samuel. see Brimblecome,
Samuel.
Brimblecomb, Nicholas. pseud. Uncle Tom's
cabin in ruins. 7982, note after 92624

Brimblecome, Samuel. complainant at court
martial 27838, 96874
Brimfield, Mass. Ecclesiastical Council, 1801.
see Congregational Churches in Massa-
chusetts. Ecclesiastical Council, Brim-
field, 1801.
Brimfield, Mass. Washington Benevolent
Society. see Washington Benevolent
Society. Massachusetts. Brimfield.
Brinckle, W. D. 7986
Brinckmeier, E. tr. 35133
Bringas, Diego Miguel. see Bringas de
Manzaneda y Encinas, Diego Miguel.
Bringas de Manzaneda y Encinas, Diego Miguel.
7988-7989, 44440, 51558
Bringas de Manzaneda y Enzinas, Diego. see
Bringas de Manzaneda y Encinas, Diego
Miguel.
Bringhurst, Joseph. (7990)
Bringier, Louis. 18535
Bringing in sheaves. (21623)
Brink, Barend ten, 1803-1875. 27683
Brink, C. W. 20718, 76582, 76647
Brink, H. 42635
Brinkerhoff, Jacob, 1810-1880. 7991-7993
Brinley, Francis. 7994
Brinley, Francis, 1800-1889. (7995)
Brinley, George. 15765
Brinsley, John. 7996, 16037
Brinsmade, Thomas C. 7997
Brinton, Daniel Garrison. 7998-(7999)
Briolo, Giammichele. tr. 21899
Brion, ------. 8001
Brion de la Tour, Louis. 8000
Brisas del avila. 8002
Brisas del plata. 11712
Brisay, Jacques Rene de. see Denonvile,
Jacques Rene de Brisay, Marquis de, d.
1710.
Brisbane, A. H. 8003
Brisbane, Albert. 8004
Brisbane, Sir Charles, 1769?-1829. 8005,
(20578), 75512 see also St. Vincent.
Governor (Brisbane)
Brisbane, William Henry, ca. 1803-1878. 8006-
8010, 88307
Brisbin, James S. 8011-8012
Briseno, Ramon. 8013
Brissot de Warville, Anacharsis. 8040
Brissot de Warville, Jacques Pierre, 1754-1793.
8014-8039, 9078, 13479, 13513-13517,
25139, 25573, 40661, 52580, 64396, 81804,
85808, 94902, 104187 see also Societe
des Amis des Noirs, Paris. Secretaire.
Bristed, Charles Astor, 1820-1874. 8041-8047,
10156
Bristed, John, 1778-1855. 8048-8052, 50194
Brister, Peter W. supposed author 70760
Bristol, Augustus John Hervey, 3d Earl of, 1724-
1779. (31602)
Bristol, F. W. 9486, 38676
Bristol, Richard C. defendant 59159
Bristol, William. 8053
Bristol (Ship) 35571
Bristol, Bishop of. see Bagot, Lewis, succes-
sively Bp. of Bristol, Norwich, and St.
Asaph, 1740-1802. Boulter, Hugh, Abp. of
Armagh, 1672-1742. Butler, Joseph.
successively Bishop of Bristol, and Durham,
1692-1752. Felton, Nicholas, successively
Bp. of Bristol, and Ely, 1556-1626. Gooch,
Sir Thomas, Bart., successively Bishop
of Bristol, Norwich, and Ely, d. 1754.
Hume, John, successively Bp. of Bristol,
Oxford, and Salisbury. Newton, Thomas,
Bp. of Bristol, 1704-1782. Searchfield,

Rowland, Bp. of Bristol, 1565?-1622.
Secker, Thomas, Abp. of Canterbury,
1693-1768. Yonge, Philip, successively
Bp. of Bristol, and Norwich, d. 1783.
Bristol, England. 9372, 81492
Bristol, Conn. Baptist Church. Elders.
petitioners 8056, 15824
Bristol, Mass. petitioners (61266)
Bristol, R. I. Catholic Congregational Society.
see Catholic Congregational Society,
Bristol, R. I.
Bristol, R. I. Committee on the Providence
and Bristol Railroad. see Committee
appointed by the Citizens of Providence,
Warren and Bristol, on the Providence
and Bristol Railroad.
Bristol, R. I. School Committee. 8055
Bristol, R. I. Young Men's Christina Associa-
tion. see Young Men's Christian
Association, Bristol, R. I.
Bristol County, Mass. Convention, Taunton,
1837. see Whig Party. Massachusetts.
Bristol County.
Bristol County, Mass. Number of Ministers.
see Congregational Churches in Massa-
chusetts. Bristol County Ministers.
Bristol Academy, Taunton, Mass. 24039
Bristol Academy, Taunton, Mass. Board.
President. 94419
Bristol Academy, Taunton, Mass. Trustees.
94419
Bristol and Clifton Ladies' Anti-slavery
Society. 8062, 90783
Bristol College, Bucks County, Pa. 8061,
14785
Bristol County Agricultural Society. (8057)
Bristol County almanac for 1852. 8059
Bristol County Whig Convention, Taunton,
Mass., 1837. see Whig Party. Massa-
chusetts. Bristol County.
Britain, Philo. pseud. see Scots Sawney.
pseud.
Britain: a poem, in three books. 8063
Britain and her colonial dependencies. 3169
Britain and her colonies. (33994)
Britain preserved. A poem. (8063)
Britain the country, versus Britain the empire.
8847
Britain's commercial interest explained and
improved. 64562, 64564
Britain's glory or Gallic pride humble. (65526)
Britain's mercies, and Britain's duty. 103503,
103593
Britain's mistakes in the commencement and
conduct of the present war. (8065),
93798-93799
Britain's original right to all that part of the
American continent. 25883, note after
59581
Britain's refuge. 71114
Britain's remembrancer. Being some thoughts
on the proper improvement of the pre-
sent juncture. 8066
Britain's remembrancer . . . from 1600 to
1688. (32044)
Britain's scheme to make a new coin of gold
and silver. 64743
Britain's victory. 43248
Britan, Philo. pseud. see Philo-Britan.
pseud.
Britannia. pseud. Letter from Britannia to
the king. 40326
Britannia. pseud. Letter of congratulation
from Britannia to the king. (40353)
Britannia: a poem. 28076

Britannia and the Gods in council. 2477, 8067
Britannia in tears. 8068
Britannia lamenting the loss of her children.
15049
Britannia languens. (12707)
Britannia liberia. 6220, 8069
Britannia major. 8070
Britannia; or a geographical description of the
kingdoms. (5965)
Britannia to America. 8072
Britannia triumphans. 8073
Britannia triumphant; or, an account of the sea-
fights and victories. 8074
Britannia triumphant; or, an historical account
of some of the most signal naval victories.
(63699)
Britanniae speculum. 8071
Britannia's lamentations. 86511
Britannico, Mercurio. pseud. Mundus alter et
idem. see Hall, Joseph.
Britannicus. pseud. Columbus. see Smith,
Robert. of London
Britannicus. pseud. The Dominican Republic
and the Emperor Soulouque. 8075, 20574
Britannicus. pseud. Letter from Don Blas de
Lezo. 99249
Britannicus. pseud. Letter to the Right
Honourable William Pitt. see
Randolph, Francis.
Britannicus. pseud. Letters on the present
disturbances. see Ramsay, Allan.
Britannicus, Indus. pseud. see Indus Britan-
nicus. pseud.
Britannische ryk in Amerika. 57160, 1st-2d
notes after 103078
Britanno sed Dunensi. pseud. Defence of the
Scots abdicating Darien. see Hodges,
James. supposed author
Britische Reise in America. 57161
British aid to the confederates. 81916
British almanac of the Society for the Diffusion
of Useful Knowledge. 8076
British America. (43280), 43285
British American. pseud. Sentiments. see
Thacher, Oxenbridge.
British, American, and West-India interests
considered. 47301
British American, and West Indian magazine.
10625
British American Association and the Nova
Scotia baronets. 8070
British American federation a necessity. 8848
British American journal. 10429, 38463
British American journal of medical and
physical science. 8078
British American Land Company. 8079
British American League Convention, Kingston,
Ontario, 1849. see Convention of Dele-
gates of the British American League,
Kingston, Ontario, 1849.
British American magazine. 8080
British American medical journal. 10429,
38463
British American navigator. 66691
British American reader. 6435
British American royal kalendar. 67040
British and American compting-house. 103055
British and American counting-house. 103056
British and American Joint Commission for the
Final Settlement of the Claims of the
Hudson's Bay and Puget's Sound Agri-
cultural Companies. 18082-18083, 18095
British and American Joint Commission of the
Hudson's Bay and Puget's Sound Agri-
cultural Companies' Claims. In the
matter. 18083

British and American liturgy. 43797
British and American Steam Navigation
Company. 83462
British and Colonial magazine and East India
review. 81150, 90614
British and Foreign Anti-slavery Society.
8082-8084, 81917, 93459
British and Foreign Anti-slavery Society.
Committee. 8084-8085, note after
(65854), (82082)
British and Foreign Anti-slavery Society.
General Anti-slavery Convention, London,
1840. see General Anti-slavery
Convention, London, 1840.
British and Foreign Anti-slavery Society.
General Anti-slavery Convention, London,
1843. see General Anti-slavery Con-
vention, London, 1843.
British and Foreign Bible Society. 22875
British and Foreign Freed-men's Aid Society.
8086
British and foreign review. 106076
British and Foreign Society for the Universal
Abolition of Negro Slavery, and the
Slave Trade. (81732)
British and North American Mining Associa-
tion. 8087
British aristocratic plot. 50963
British army, as it was,-is,-and ought to be.
10222
British Association for the Advancement of
Science. 39167, 85555
British Association for the Advancement of
Science. Oxford, 1860. President, the
Right Hon. the Lord Wrottlesley. 85555
British barbarity and piracy!! 8088
British Bostonian. pseud. American alarm.
see Skillman, Isaac, 1740-1799. and
Allen, John, fl. 1764. supposed author
British Bostonian. pseud. Oration on the
beauties of liberty. see Skillman,
Isaac, 1740-1799. and Allen, John, fl.
1764. supposed author
British Bostonian. pseud. Oration upon the
beauties of liberty. see Skillman,
Isaac, 1740-1799. and Allen, John, fl.
1764. supposed author
British Bostonian. pseud. Watchman's alarm
to Lord N---h. 102051-102052
British Branch, United States Sanitary Com-
mission. see United States Sanitary
Commission. English Branch.
British butchers. pseud. Song. 86876-86877
British Canadian. pseud. Tour of H. R. H.,
Albert Edward. 657
British Chapel and Burial Ground, Caracas,
Venezuela. see Caracas, Venezuela.
British Chapel and Burial Ground.
British colonial library. 44907
British colonial register. 53390
British colonial slavery. 57601, 102790
British colonial slavery compared with that of
pagan antiquity. 8096, 81918
British colonies in North America. 85851
British colonies, their history, extent, condi-
tion, and resources. 44908
British colonist. 37903
British colonization and coloured tribes. 3215
British Columbia. 58446
British Columbia. Agent-General. 89908
see also Sproat, Gilbert Malcolm.
British Columbia. Columbia River Expedition,
1865. 49776
British Columbia. 16819
British Columbia. An essay. 8549

British Columbia and Vancouver's Island. 52772
British Columbia and Vancouver's Island. A
complete hand-book. 8089
British Columbia and Vancouver's Island;
comprising a description of these depen-
dencies. 43149
British Columbia and Vancouver's Island.
Comprising an historical sketch of the
British settlements. 31126
British Columbia. Columbia River exploration,
1865. Instructions, reports, and journals.
49776
British Columbia, emigration, and our colonies.
85552
British Columbia gold fields. 8092
British Columbia. Information for emigrants.
89908
British Columbia Mission. 8093
British Columbia. Williams Lake and Cariboo.
58355
British constitution. 106079
British Constitutional Society. 98074
British cruelty, oppression, and murder. 30178
British customs, containing an historical and
practical account. 77334
British diplomacy on the River Plate. 8097
British dominions in North America. 6848
British drama. 14526, 88543, 100719, note
after 105986
British emigrant's guide to the United States.
8098
British emigrant's "hand book," and guide to
the new states. 54996
British empire. 17818, note after 95370
British empire: a sketch of the geography.
7468
British empire; historical, biographical, and
geographical. 17451
British empire in America. 41877, (49907),
52140, (57156)-57157
British empire in America, considered. 8099
British engineers. pseud. Ship canal. 80501
British enterprise beyond the seas. 26264
British falsehoods detected by American truths.
70283
British fisheries. 8100
"British free trade," a delusion. 85895, 91009
British Freed-Men's Aid Societies. National
Committee. see National Committee
of British Freed-Men's Aid Societies.
British freeholder. 32775, 49987, 66909
British friend. 13493, 86035, 94129
"British friend" edition. 13493
British grenadier (Tune) 101859
British grenadiers (Tune) 101815, 101858
British Guiana. 76337
British Guiana. Combined Assembly. 83487
British Guiana. Court of Policy. 83487
British Guiana. Court of Policy. Secretary.
83487 see also Gloster, Henry.
British Guiana. Geological Survey. 83487
British Guiana. Governor (Smith) 83487 see
also Smith, Sir Lionel, Bart., 1778-1842.
British Guiana. 1835. Colonial taxes. 83487
British Guiana, Jamaica, and Trinidad. 58816
British Guiana. Speech delivered at the anti-
slavery meeting. 78152
British hero, and ignoble poltroon contrasted.
8107
British hero in captivity. 8108
British Honduras. Agent. petitioner (11313),
103448, 2d note after 106221 see also
White, Robert. petitioner
British Honduras. Citizens. petitioners 32365,
51077, note after 96027, 96028, note after
103446, 103447, note after 103448, 1st
note after 106221

British Honduras. Inhabitants. see British
Honduras. Citizens.
British Honduras. Principal Inhabitants. see
British Honduras. Principal Inhabitants.
see British Honduras. Citizens.
British Honduras: Central America. 2571
British Honduras Company. 8109
British honour and humanity. 8110, note after
94022
British imperial federation. 84855
British imperial legislation. 84855
British influence on the affairs of the United
States. 104983
British Inhabitants of the Province of Quebeck.
petitioners see Quebec (Province)
British Inhabitants. petitioners
British in Philadelphia. 41398
British librarian. 17971
British library. 52321
British lion rous'd. 56808
British mars. 72260
British mechanic. 8098, 8111
British merchant. pseud. Common sense.
14998
British merchant. pseud. Letter to Chas.
Jas. Fox. 29176
British merchant. pseud. Observations on the
report. see Cock, Simon.
British merchant: a collection of papers.
37783
British merchant. Observations on the present
state, culture, and commerce. 13798
British merchant long resident abroad. pseud.
Reflections on the domestic and foreign
policy. 68699
British Merchants and Others. Subjects of
his Britannic Majesty Within the United
States. petitioners see Sundry British
Merchants and Others, Subjects of His
Britannic Majesty Within the United States.
petitioners
British military biography. 8112
British ministry. 91092
British monarchy. 5222, 80618
British Museum. 86264, 91512-91517
British Museum. Department of Printed
Books. 77803
British naval officer. pseud. Service afloat.
79323
British navy vindicated. 8613
British North America at the Detroit Conven-
tion. 61032
British North America; comprising Canada.
8114
British North America. Copies or extracts of
correspondence. 8113
British North America; its condition, &c.
(29681)
British North America, its extent and future.
(50796)
British North American almanac, and annual
record. 8116
British North American act. 56120
British North American colonies. 106072
British officer. pseud. Battle of Bunker Hill.
86878
British officer. pseud. Gambler. 26508
British officer. pseud. To the people. 95958
British officers' monthly register, and mentor.
73801
British officers' monthly register, chronicle,
and military mentor. 73802
British opinions of the American Colonization
Society. 8117, 93138
British opinions on the protective system.
8118, 23237

British parliamentary Boston Port-Bill un-
wraped. 102051-102052
British partizan. 50487
British philanthropy and Jamaica distress. 8119
British planter. pseud. Brief remarks on
scriptural notices. 7888
British planter. pseud. Negro emancipation
made easy. 52262
British planter. pseud. West India claims on
the mother country. 102771
British poets. 78300
British pretentions and American rights. 97947
British pride humbled; a poem on the American
revolution. (65526)
British pride humbled, or Americans triumphant.
101263
British prison-ship: a poem. 25891
British prize ship; a poem. 8120
British relations with the Chinese empire in
1832. 8121
British remains. (58011)
British review. 104039
British review for 1788. (41491)
British sailor, a sincere wellwisher. pseud.
Specimen of naked truth. see Vernon,
Edward, 1684-1757.
British sailor's discovery. 8122
British sailors in America. 25884, note after
91499
British settler. pseud. Poetical annals of
Lower Canada. see Fleming, John.
British Society of Shipowners. see Society of
Shipowners (Gt. Brit.)
British soldiers. pseud. Song. 86878-86879
British spy. pseud. Letters. see Wirt,
William.
British spy: or, letters. 8123, 104871
British statutes relative to Upper Canada.
98063
British subject. pseud. Boundary question
revived. see Grattan, Thomas Colley.
British subject. pseud. Three letters to Lord
Brougham. see Head, Sir Francis Bond.
supposed author
British subject. pseud. Tour through parts of
the United States and Canada. see
Beaufoy, Mark.
British subject. pseud. True picture of the
United States of America. 97134-97135
British subjects. claimants see Gt. Brit.
Citizens. claimants
British Subscription Library, Rio de Janeiro.
71463
British sympathies in the American crisis.
8124, 37781
British sympathy with America. 82706
British system of education. 38785
British telegraph monopoly. (37349)
British Temperance Emigration Society and
Saving Fund. 8125, 104885
British Temperance Emigration Society and
Saving Fund. Committee. 104885-104886
British theatre (Cumberland's) 14526, note after
105986
British theatre (Inchbald's) 14526, 88540-88541,
note after 105986
British trade with North American Indians.
34623
British traveller. pseud. Colonial policy of
Great Britain considered. 14695
British treaty. 8126, 8457
British treaty with America. 8127
British treaty. Debates in the House of
Representatives. 8128
British trident. 21251

British West India colonies in connection with slavery. 6925, 93471
British West Indian statutes for the protection and government of slaves. 81743
British West Indies. Courts. 70241
British West Indies. Laws, statutes, etc. (10891), 12025, (22621), 23301, 70241, 81743-(81744), 93606, 101821, note before 102812
British West Indies, and foreign sugar growing countries. 93457
British West Indies. London. 1836. 85936
British worthies. 27586
Brito, Bernardo Gomes de. see Gomes de Brito, Bernardo.
Brito, Francisco Tavares de. 8129
Brito, Joao Rodgigues de. 8133
Brito, J. Jose Rodrigues de. 8134
Brito, Paulo Jose Miguel de. 8135
Brito Freire, Francisco de. 8130-8132
Briton. pseud. Considerations on certain remarks. note after 92630
Britons invited to rejoice. 96355
Brittan, Samuel Byron. ed. 80106, 89531, 94608
Brittan & Partridge. firm publishers see Partridge & Brittan. firm publishers
Brittische Reich in America. 8136
Brittische Reise in America. 57162
Britto, Anacleto de. defendant and claimant 96929
Britton, --------, fl. 1866. 90416
Britton, John, 1771-1857. 8137, 80342
Brivazac, ------- Beaumont de. see Beaumont de Brivazac, -------.
Briviesca, Alvaro de Soria. see Soria Briviesca, Alvaro de.
Brizard, Gabriel, d. 1793. 8138, 105719
Brizeno, Juan Gomez. 76007
Brizuela, Juan J. 57077
Broad, Amos. 8139-8140
Broad, Amos. defendant 8140
Broad pennant. 94455
Broad Street Baptist Church, Philadelphia. see Philadelphia. Broad Street Baptist Church.
Broadcloth, Dr. pseud. see Dr. Broadcloth. pseud.
Broaddus, William F. 8141
Broadhead, Garland Carr, 1827- 34253
Broadluch, Cephus. pseud. Races of mankind. see Gazlay, Allan W.
Broadside for the times. 8142
Broadside into Parker and the politicians. 8143
Broadway. 8144
Broadway idyl. 41776, note after 97370
Broadway journal. (8145), (54134)
Broadway Rail Road Company. defendants 57119
Broadway railroad. (8146)
Broadway Railway Association, New York. petitioners 54135, 79836
Broadway Tabernacle, New York. see New York (City) Broadway Tabernacle Church.
Broadway Tabernacle Anti-slavery Society, New York. 8147
Broadway travellers series. 90060
Broadwell, S. (8148), 53070
Broca, Philippe de. (8149)
Brocardus, ------. 1553, 8150, 34100-34107
Brocchus, P. E. 8151
Brochure. 91065
Brochure adressee par le General La Fayette aux membres de la Chambre des Deputes. 77163

Brochure de M. Fleuriau. 5652
Brochure de MM. les Abbes Laverdiere et Casgrain. 20892
Brochure imprimee a Salem, en Amerique en 1787. 18176
Brochure publiee en Mai 1836. 57178
Brochure sur l'ouvrage de M. Schoelcher. 5652
Brock, Daniel De Lisle. (8152)
Brock, Sir Isaac, 1769-1812. (8152)
Brock, John. 103352-103353
Brock, Robert Alonzo, 1839-1914. 4th note after 99888
Brock, Sallie A. 71204, 88288
Brockden, Charles. ed. 59972
Brockenbrough, William Henry, 1812-1850. (8154A), 44894
Brocket. firm see Kissingen and Brocket. firm
Brockett, Linus Pierpont, 1820-1893. 8155-8162, 46766, 57925, 62427, 77704, 85148, 85152, 85153, 91754
Brockett, Paul, 1872- 85067
Brockhaus, Heinrich, 1858- (26979)
Brockhaus. firm publishers 11482
Brockmann, Karl. 8163
Brockway, Diodate, 1776-1849. 8164-(8165)
Brockway, J. 8166-8167
Brockway, Thomas, 1744-1807. 8168-8169
Brockway, Thomas, 1744-1807. supposed author 23113
Brockwell, Charles. 8170-8171
Brockwell, Will. 8172
Brocq, Philip Le. see Le Brocq, Philip.
Brodhead, Edward H. 64590 see also Potsdam & Watertown Railroad. Chief Engineer.
Brodhead, Jacob. 8173
Brodhead, John Romeyn, 1814-1873. 8174-8179, (53606), 53653, 53669 see also New York (State) Agent to Procure and Transcribe Documents in Europe, Relative to the Colonial History of Said State.
Brodhead, Richard, 1811-1863. 8180
Brodie, Walter. 8181
Brodie, William. 8182
Brodigan, Thomas. 8183
Brodribb, Edward. 94778
Broe, S. de, Seigneur de Citry et de la Guette, 17th cent. tr. 24864, 28706, 86482, 96475
Broeck, Abraham Ten. 33523, 53480, 94674-94676
Broeck, Matheus van den. 8184, 14958-14960
Broeck, Pieter van den. see Broecke, Pieter van den, 1575-1641.
Broecke, Pieter van den, 1575-1641. 68455, 74837
Broeder Jedema. pseud. Briev. 35876
Broedleth, Wilhelm. publisher (46643)
Broek, Joachim George Le Sage ten, 1775-1847. (52239)
Broek, Reinier van den. see Van den Broek, Reinier.
Broek, Wilhelm van den. (36984), 53551
Brogden, William. 8185
Brogile, Achille Charles Leonce Victor, Duc de, 1785-1870. 8186-8187, (67930)
Broglie, Albert, i. e. Jacques Victor Albert, Duc de, 1821-1901. 8188
Broglie, Jacques Victor Albert. see Broglie, Albert, i. e. Jacques Victor Albert, Duc de, 1821-1901.
Brogniart, ------. 67935
Brokaw, Abraham. 8189, 97138
Broke, Sir Philip Bowes Vere, 1776-1841. (50044)
Broke goal, in Worcester. 105372

Broken harp. Poems. 38116
Broken heart. (32854)
Broken heart acceptable with God through
  Christ. 13202
Broken heart relieved. 83454
Broken pillars. 66756
Broken seal. (28611)
Brokesby, Francis, 1637-1714. 8190
Brome Mining Company. 8191
Bromey, T. 30696
Bromley, Clara Fitzroy (Kelly) 8199
Bromley, Thomas, d. 1691. 8192
Bromley, Walter. 8193-8198, 29686
Bromme, Th. 27194
Bromme, Traugott, 1802-1866. 8200-8222
Bromsgrove elegy. (24020)
Bromwell, H. R. 8223
Bromwell, William. 8224-8225, 41760, 56749
Bromwell, William Jeremy, 1834-1874. 8226,
  15266
Bronchorst, Johann. tr. 66508
Bronson, -------. 103464
Bronson, -------. plaintiff 64810
Bronson, A. 23751
Bronson, Arthur. complainant 2067
Bronson, Enos, d. 1824? 8227, 78991
Bronson, Enos, d. 1824? supposed author
  97903
Bronson, Greene Carrier, 1789-1863. 8228-
  8229, 21782, 34571, 53616, (55801),
  63005 see also New York (State)
  Attorney General.
Bronson, Henry, 1804-1893. (8230)-(8232)
Bronson, Tillotson. 8233
Bronson, William White, 1816- 8234
Brontologia sacra. 46243
Brook, Benjamin, 1776-1848. 8235-(8236)
Brook, Jehiel. 8237, 15047
Brook, Z. 83048, 83074
Brook Farm Association for Industry and
  Education, West Roxbury, Mass. 8238
Brook Farm Phalanx. publishers 30289
Brook Farm: the amusing and memorable of
  American country life. (6243)
Brooke, -------. (38449)
Brooke, C. W. 8239, 62120
Brooke, Christopher, d. 1628. 100510
Brooke, Frances (Moore) 1724-1789. 8240
Brooke, Francis. tr. 39593
Brooke, Francis Taliaferro, 1763-1851. 8241
Brooke, H. 100358 see also Virginia.
  General Assembly. Senate. Clerk.
Brooke, Henry, 1703?-1783. (8242)
Brooke, Henry K. 8243
Brooke, John R. USA 84774
Brooke, John T. 8244
Brooke, Robert. supposed author 16252,
  (69383)
Brooke, Robert, 1751-1799. 100225 see also
  Virginia. Governor, 1794-1796 (R.
  Brooke)
Brooke, Samuel. 8245
Brookes, Richard, fl. 1750. 8246, 12861,
  (78330)
Brookes's Universal gazetteer. 8246
Brookfield, Mass. Evangelical Church. 92092
Brookfield, Mass. School Committee. 8248
Brookfield, Mass. Washington Benevolent
  Society. see Washington Benevolent
  Society. Massachusetts. Brookfield.
Brookfield, N. Y. Washington Benevolent
  Society. see Washington Benevolent
  Society. New York. Brookfield.
Brookfield Association. see Congregational
  Churches in Massachusetts. Brookfield
  Association.

Brookhaven, N. Y. Congregational Convention
  of Long Island, 1808. see Congregational
  Convention of Long Island, Brookhaven,
  N. Y., 1808.
Brookhaven. 1665-1876. Historical sketch of
  the town. 82458
Brookline, Mass. 8255
Brookline, Mass. Baptist Church. 8254
Brookline, Mass. Committee for Building a
  Road. 8258
Brookline, Mass. Committee on New School-
  Houses. 8256
Brookline, Mass. Ordinances, etc. 8253
Brookline, Mass. Public Library. Board of
  Trustees. 8261
Brookline, Mass. Saint Paul's Church. 8257
Brookline, Mass. Treasurer. 8262
Brookline business directory. 7977
Brookline, Jamaica Plain and West Roxbury
  directory. 8251
Brookline jubilee. (62724)
Brooklyn. (8292), 8305, 8334, (54072), 54222
  see also New York (City)
Brooklyn. Abraham Lincoln Statue. 41231
Brooklyn. Adjourned Meeting of the Free-
  holders, 1825. see Brooklyn. Citizens.
Brooklyn. Association in Aid of the Grande-
  Ligne Mission. see Association in Aid
  of the Grande-Ligne Mission, Brooklyn.
Brooklyn. Atlantic Dry Dock Company. see
  Atlantic Dry Dock Company, Brooklyn.
Brooklyn. Board of Water Commissioners.
  see Brooklyn. Water Commissioners.
Brooklyn, Census, 1863. 8298
Brooklyn. Central Union Club. see Central
  Union Club of Brooklyn.
Brooklyn. Charter. 8269-(8275), 8277-(8278),
  (8280), 8286-8288, (8295)-8297, 8312
Brooklyn. Christian Union. see Christian
  Union of New York and Brooklyn.
Brooklyn. Church Charity Foundation. see
  Church Charity Foundation, Brooklyn.
Brooklyn. Church of the Pilgrims. 90662
Brooklyn. Church of the Saviour. 66758
Brooklyn. Citizens. 8276
Brooklyn. City Clerk. 8300
Brooklyn. City Surveyor. 8328, note after
  91935 see also Stoddard, John S.
Brooklyn. Clinton Avenue Church. 90662
Brooklyn. Commissioners of Prospect Park.
  8313
Brooklyn. Commissioners . . . to Provide for
  the Opening of Washington Park. see
  New York (State) Commissioners . . .
  to Provide for the Opening of Washington
  Park, on Fort Green, in the City of
  Brooklyn.
Brooklyn. Committee of Ten. see Committee
  of Ten on a Proposed University in
  Brooklyn.
Brooklyn. Committee on Public Health. 8334
Brooklyn. Common Council. 5603, 8287, 8291,
  8300, 8333, 65796, 94072
Brooklyn. Common Council. Special Committee
  on Communication of Henry Ruggles.
  8326
Brooklyn. Common Council. Special Committee
  on Supplying the City with Water. see
  Brooklyn. Water Committee.
Brooklyn. Common Council. Water Committee.
  see Brooklyn. Water Committee.
Brooklyn. Comptroller. 8281
Brooklyn. Dinner Given by the Citizens of
  Brooklyn to the Hon. Henry C. Murphy.
  see Dinner Given by the Citizens of
  Brooklyn to the Hon. Henry C. Murphy,
  1857.

Brooklyn. Ecclesiastical Council, 1854. see
Congregational Churches in New York.
Ecclesiastical Council, Brooklyn, 1854.
Brooklyn. Eighth Ward. 8315
Brooklyn. Fire Marshal. 4444 see also
Belknap, Rufus R.
Brooklyn. Foreign Missionary Society. see
Foreign Missionary Society of New York
and Brooklyn.
Brooklyn. Health Officer. 8334
Brooklyn. Home for Destitute Children. see
Brooklyn Industrial School Association
and Home for Destitute Children.
Brooklyn. Mansfield Academy. see Mans-
field Academy, Brooklyn.
Brooklyn. Mercantile Library Association.
see Brooklyn Library.
Brooklyn. Nassau Water Department. 8334
Brooklyn. Naval Retiring Board, 1863. see
U. S. Navy. Retiring Board, Brooklyn,
1863.
Brooklyn. Ninth Ward. 8315
Brooklyn. Ordinances, etc. 8279-(8280),
8286-8287, 8297, 8307-8309
Brooklyn. Packer Collegiate Institute. see
Packer Collegiate Institute, Brooklyn.
Brooklyn. Park Presbyterian Church. (8301)
Brooklyn. Plymouth Church. 8299, 90662
Brooklyn. Presbyterian Church. (76492)
Brooklyn. Prospect Park Commissioners.
see Brooklyn. Commissioners of
Prospect Park.
Brooklyn. Public Health Committee. see
Brooklyn. Committee on Public Health.
Brooklyn. Public Library. 8266
Brooklyn. St. Thomas's Church. 8319
Brooklyn. St. Thomas's Church. Trustees.
75498
Brooklyn. Sanitary Fair, 1864. 8263, 76679
Brooklyn. South Congregational Church. 32116
Brooklyn. Standing Committee on Water.
see Brooklyn. Water Committee.
Brooklyn. Superintendent of Schools. 8334
Brooklyn. Supreme Court of Errors. see
New York (State) Court for the Trial of
Impeachments and the Correction of
Errors.
Brooklyn. Trustees. (8296)
Brooklyn. United States Naval Lyceum. see
United States Naval Lyceum, Brooklyn.
Brooklyn. Village Trustees. see Brooklyn.
Trustees.
Brooklyn. Washington Street Church. (43002)
Brooklyn. Water Commissioners. 8321
Brooklyn. Water Committee. 8324, 8327,
8329-8330
Brooklyn. Women's Relief Association. see
United States Sanitary Commission.
Women's Relief Association of Brooklyn.
Brooklyn. Young Men's Bible Society. see
Young Men's Bible Society of Brooklyn.
Brooklyn, Conn. Congregational Church.
104559
Brooklyn and Long Island Fair in aid of the
U. S. Sanitary Commission. 8263
Brooklyn Athenaeum and Reading Room. (8264)
Brooklyn Athenaeum and Reading Room.
Library Committee. (8264)
Brooklyn Auxiliary Society. see New York and
and Brooklyn Auxiliary Society.
Brooklyn City and Kings County record. 8265
Brooklyn city hospital, and the address of
J. C. Hutchinson. 8283
Brooklyn city register for 1848. 8267
Brooklyn Collegiate Institute for Young Ladies.
98489

Brooklyn daily eagle. 83896
Brooklyn daily union. 8285
Brooklyn directory. 8289
Brooklyn directory, for the year 1822. 89598
Brooklyn Female Employment Society. 8334
Brooklyn Industrial School Association, and Home
for Destitute Children. 8334
Brooklyn Library. (8304)
Brooklyn water works and sewers. A descriptive
memoir. 8321
Brooklyn Young Men's Christian Association.
see Young Men's Christian Association,
Brooklyn.
Brooklyn Young Men's Education Society. see
Young Men's Education Society of New
York and Brooklyn.
Brooks, B. F. C. 8335, 47314
Brooks, Charles, 1795-1872. 8336-8340, 85962
see also Society for Ministerial Relief.
Committee of Investigation. Chairman.
Brooks, Charles Timothy, 1813-1883. 8341-
8342
Brooks, David, 1744-1802. (8343)
Brooks, David, fl. 1806. 105040
Brooks, Edward, 1784-1859. 8344-(8345), 42465
Brooks, Erastus, 1815-1886. 8346-8347, (8371),
33593
Brooks, J. 96507
Brooks, J. Tyrwhitt. pseud. see Vizetelly,
Henry.
Brooks, J. W. 48761
Brooks, James, 1810-1873. 8348, 9615
Brooks, James, 1810-1873. supposed author
84162
Brooks, James Gordon, 1801-1841. 49215,
54795
Brooks, James H. 8349
Brooks, Jehiel. 96696 see also U. S.
Commissioners to the Caddo Indians.
Brooks, John, 1752-1825. 8354-8357, 43945,
65821, 101803, 102026 see also Massa-
chusetts. Governor, 1816-1822 (Brooks)
Washington Monument Association, Boston.
President.
Brooks, John P. 34241
Brooks, John W. 8358-8359
Brooks, Maria (Gowen) 1795-1845. 36853,
106371-106372
Brooks, Nathan Covington, 1809-1898. 8360-
8362, 85466, 103352-103353
Brooks, P. 75380
Brooks, P. C. 8363, 2d note after 101499
Brooks, Phillips, Bp., 1835-1893. 8364-8365
Brooks, Preston Smith, 1819-1857. 8366-8367
Brooks, Samuel. 105613A
Brooks, Seth. 8368
Brooks, Sidney, 1813-1887. 102450
Brooks, T. H. 8369
Brooks, William, d. 1778. defendant 105350-
105350A
Brooks, William H. (11118)-11119
Brooks and Sumner. 9311, note after 90461
Brooks Guards, Charleston, S. C. see South
Carolina. Militia. Brooks Guards,
Charleston.
Brooksiana. (8371), 33593
Brooksop, Jone. 8372
Broom, Jacob, 1808-1864. 8373
Broom, Walter William. 8374-8376
Broomall, John Martin, 1816-1894. 8377-8382
Broome, Ralph. supposed author 92842
Broome republican. 88669
Broon, ------. 71444
Brosius, Nicholas. 8383
Bross, William, 1813-1890. 8385-8386
Brossard, Alfred de. 8387

Brossard, Alphonse de. see Brossard, Alfred de.
Brosses, Charles de, 1709-1777. (8388)-8389, 10053, 89444, 89451, 1st note after 94857, note after 99383C
Brossier, ------. 75064 see also Santo Domingo (French Colony) Assemblee Provincial du Nord. President.
Brother. pseud. Commencement, a poem. see Biglow, William.
Brother in the church. pseud. Three communications. 95155
Brother Jonathan. 84162
Brother Jonathan: or, the New Englanders. 8390, 52151
Brother Jonathan: or the "smartest nation in all creation." 63371
Brother Jonathan, the smartest nation in all creation. 63372
Brother Jonathan vs. John Bull. 82128
Brother Jonathan's welcome to Kossuth. 3905
Brother Jonathan's wife. 8391
Brother Mason, the circuit rider. 8393, 45422
Brother of the birch. pseud. Twig of birch for a butting calf. 14000
Br. Ripley's masonic prayer. 71515
Brother series. 72148
Brother soldiers. (72145)
Brother Stoddard's masonic oration. 91925
Brotherhead, William. 1168, 8394-8396, 76403
Brotherhood in the sanctuary. 51614
Brotherhood of nations. 33964
Brotherhood of thieves. 25263
Brotherly Association for the Support of Widows, Philadelphia. 74107
Brotherly love: a discourse. 8392
Brotherly-love. A sermon at a meeting of the Grand Lodge. 50097
Brotherly love . . . a sermon preached before a society of . . . Free . . . Masons. 57107
Brotherly love and faithfulness recommended. 79496
Brotherly love described and directed. 104074
Brotherly love recommended in a sermon. 8170
Brotherly love the duty and mark of Christians. (21241)
Brothers, Thomas. 8397-8398
Brothers (Ship) in admiralty 104223
Brothers. 93410
Brother's boquet for a brother's burial and grave. 61387
Brothers, fugitive and free. 52273
Brothers in Unity, Yale University. see Yale University. Brothers in Unity.
Brothers of St. Patrick, Boston. see Ancient and Most Benevolent Order of the Friendly Brothers of St. Patrick, Boston.
Brothers' Society, Yale University. see Yale University. Brothers in Unity.
Brothers Triplex. pseud. ed. Kaleidoscope. (36983)
Brouez, Prosper, 1786-1861. 8399
Brough, John, 1811-1865. 8400-8402, 52034 see also Ohio. Governor, 1864-1866 (Brough)
Brough, W. 8403
Brougham, Henry Peter. see Brougham and Vaugh, Henry Peter Brougham, Baron, 1778-1868.
Brougham, John, 1810-1880. 8421, 92410
Brougham and Vaux, Henry Peter Brougham, Baron, 1778-1868. 8404-8419, 13496, 15120, 70902, (81892), 81934, 82906, 95661

Broughton, Arthur, d. 1803? 8422, 21901
Broughton, Luke Dennis, 1828-1899. ed. 8426
Broughton, William Robert, 1762-1821. 8423-8425
Broughton's monthly planet reader, and astrological journal. 8426
Broun, Sir Richard, Bart., 1801-1858. plaintiff 8077
Broussonet, -------. tr. (25137)
Brouwer, Hendrick, d. 1643. 8427
Brouwn, Charles. 93870
Brower, Robert F. see Brown, Robert F.
Brown, Colonel. frontiersman 34461
Brown, -------, fl. 1641. 63312
Brown, --------. of Boston 101864
Brown, --------. of Burlington, N. H. 8536
Brown, Aaron Venable, 1795-1859. (8429)-8432, 70481 see also Tennessee. Governor, 1845-1847 (Brown)
Brown, Abiel. 8433
Brown, Abiel, Jr. 97549
Brown, Albert Gallatin, 1813-1880. 8434-8438
Brown, Alexander, 1843-1906. 17425, 70889, 82823, 82832, 94125, 99855, 2d note after 99856, note after 99857, 99858-99859, 99861-99862, 99866, 99870-99872, 99873-99874, 4th note after 99888, 1st note after 99889
Brown, Alexander Campbell. 8439
Brown, Alexander Enos, d. 1865. (8440)
Brown, Alexander M. 8441
Brown, Alfred N. 8442
Brown, Allen. ed. 70710
Brown, Andrew. 20022
Brown, Rev. Andrew. 8443-8445
Brown, Andrew, 1748-1813. 8446
Brown, Andrew W. 8447
Brown, Anson. 65760, 94516
Brown, Anthony. 8448
Brown, Arnold. 66686
Brown, Asa. 8449
Brown, Bedford, 1795-1870. 8450-8451, 8865
Brown, Benjamin B. (8452)
Brown, Benjamin Gratz, 1826-1885. 8453
Brown, C. E. 48768
Brown, Catharine S. 8462
Brown, Charles, a slave. defendant 81920
Brown, Charles. alias see Speckman, Charles.
Brown, Charles, Captain of the Venezuelan Brigade. (8455)
Brown, Charles. defendant (49199), 88670, 96905
Brown, Charles, 1797-1883. 8454
Brown, Charles Barrington. (35584)
Brown, Charles Brockden, 1771-1810. 413, (1205), 1213, 8456-8457, 15513, (21304), 41338, 41490, 42188, 50022, 50182, 77294, 100694, 103888
Brown, Charles Brockden, 1771-1810. supposed author 8126, 8457
Brown, Charles Brockden, 1771-1810. incorrectly supposed author 99449
Brown, Charles Crillon. USN 8458
Brown, Charles H., Captain of the Bark Florida 8459, 93422
Brown, Charles M. 8460
Brown, Clark, 1771-1817. 8461, note just before 69458, 92785
Brown, David Boyer. 8463
Brown, David Paul, 1795-1872. 8465-8466, 27286
Brown, David Stephens. 8467
Brown, David Wolfe. 48728
Brown, Deidamia (Covell) 8464, 17210
Brown, E. 63612
Brown, E. A. (30089), note after 96853

Brown, Edward, of Carleston, S. C.? 8468, 55972
Brown, Elijah. 8469
Brown, Elisha. 103308 see also Rhode Island (Colony) Deputy Governor, 1767 (Brown)
Brown, Ethan Allen, 1766-1852. 56958 see also Ohio. Governor, 1819-1822 (Brown)
Brown, F. G. 8472
Brown, Fenner. (70667)
Brown, Francis, 1784-1820. 8470, 74430
Brown, Francis A. ed. 83120-83121
Brown, Francis Henry, 1835-1917. 8471, 30760, 90500
Brown, Frederick Thomas, 1822-1893. 8473-8474
Brown, Hon. George. 8475
Brown, George. defendant at impeachemnt 48702
Brown, George, of Kentucky. 93230
Brown, George, of Philadelphia. 8478
Brown, George, b. 1792. 8477
Brown, George, 1818-1880. 74556, 74573, (74581)
Brown, George, d. 1819. defendant 96838
Brown, George H. 8479
Brown, George William, 1812-1891. 8480-(8482), (45211A)
Brown, Goold, 1791-1857. 8476
Brown, Harvey S. (8485)
Brown, Helen Tyler. ed. 97617
Brown, Henry, 1789-1849. 8483-(8484), 101157, 101166
Brown, Henry Box. 90864-90865
Brown, Henry T. 66093
Brown, Howard V. illus. 83549
Brown, Hugh, 1811?-1888. (8488)
Brown, Hugh Stowell, 1823-1886. 8486-8487
Brown, Hyrum P. 92685
Brown, Ignatius. 8489, 34582
Brown, Isaac Van Arsdale, 1784-1861. 8490-(8493), 24384
Brown, J. F. 8494
Brown, J. M. ed. 69967
Brown, J. W. ed. 4032
Brown, Jabez. 27052
Brown, Jacob. 8496
Brown, Jacob Jennings, 1775-1828. 96514
Brown, James. 8497
Brown, James. 90668 see also New York and Erie Rail Road Company. Trustees.
Brown, James, Chaplain of the British Garrison at Savannah. 8498
Brown, James, of New Brunswick. 8500
Brown, James, of Virginia. 59725
Brown, James Bryce. 8501
Brown, James D. 8502, 61476
Brown, John. alias. see Syllavan, Owen, alias defendant
Brown, John, fugitive slave. 8516, 8520
Brown, John, of Great Yarmouth. 8512-8515
Brown, John, of Great Yarmouth. incorrectly supposed author 8154, 18487, 50827, 67839, note before 91236, 91240-91241, 91246-91247, 101270
Brown, John, of Orphington, Kent. see Browne, John, of Orphington, Kent.
Brown, John, 1712-1766. 8507
Brown, John, 1722-1787. 8509-8511
Brown, John, 1724-1791. 8504-8505, 8653, 65239-(65240), 1st note after 69428, (75668), 75680, 94115
Brown, John, fl. 1727. 17095
Brown, John, 1735-1788. 31223
Brown, John, 1757-1837. 29765
Brown, John, 1784-1858. 83795

Brown, John, fl. 1796. 100066 see also Virginia. Legislature. Committee to Superintend an Edition of All Legislative Acts Concerning Lands.
Brown, John, 1797-1861. 8517
Brown, John, 1800-1859. 8522, 68528
Brown, John A. appellant 2210
Brown, John Carter, 1797-1874. 82837
Brown, John G. 78994
Brown, John H. defendant 8525
Brown, John H. Hobart. (8508)
Brown, John Mason, 1837-1890. ed. note after 65389
Brown, John Mathias, 1745-1838. 8526
Brown, John Newton, 1803-1868. (36232), (49129)
Brown, John Sullivan. 8495
Brown, John Thompson. 8527
Brown, John W. 8528
Brown, John Young, 1835-1904. 8529
Brown, Jonathan. 8530
Brown, Joseph Emerson, 1821-1894. 8531, 18841, (27053), (27075), 27110, 33150, 78765 see also Georgia. Governor, 1857-1865 (J. E. Brown)
Brown, Joseph Stanley. see Stanley-Brown, Joseph.
Brown, Josephine. 8532
Brown, Leonard, 1837-1914. 8533
Brown, Lewis C. 84285
Brown, Lucian. 86835
Brown, M. 36044
Brown, Mason. 37535
Brown, Milton, 1804-1883. (8534)-8535
Brown, Moses. 3722, 8537, 26007, 51752, 52639, (78487), 80190, 80193 see also Friends, Society of. New England Yearly Meeting. Meeting for Sufferings.
Brown, Moses. supposed author 22115, (78492)-78493
Brown, Mount. 8540
Brown, N. B. 62352
Brown, N. P. ed. 54915
Brown, Nathan. 72816
Brown, Nathaniel. (8541)
Brown, Olympia. petitioner 90404
Brown, Orlando. 8542
Brown, Paul. 67421
Brown, Peter, 1784-1863. 8543
Brown, Peter A. see Browne, Peter Arrell, 1782-1860.
Brown, Rawdon Lubbock, 1803-1883. 8544-8545
Brown, Rebecca (Warren) 8546, note after 92205, 101478-101479
Brown, Robert. tr. 8547-8548, (9501), (20827)
Brown, Robert, 1842-1895. ed. 71430, 71439
Brown, Robert Christopher Lundin. 8549
Brown, Robert F. 8428, 8550
Brown, Robert T. 8551-8552
Brown, Roscoe Conkling Ensign, 1867- 83748
Brown, Samuel, 1769-1830. 8553
Brown, Samuel, fl. 1816. 3598, 36777, 1st note after 90696
Brown, Samuel, fl. 1834. 8554
Brown, Samuel Gilman. 1813-1885. 8555, 12860
Brown, Samuel R., 1775-1817. (8556)-8558
Brown, Solyman, 1790-1876. 8559-(8562), 54459
Brown, Sylvester, b. 1805. 8563
Brown, T. A. H. 91026
Brown, Mrs. T. M. ed. 89882
Brown, T. W. (16823)
Brown, Tarleton, 1757-1846. 8564, 9538
Brown, Thaddeus. 8565
Brown, Rev. Thomas. 8566
Brown, Thomas, Captain. 63519
Brown, Thomas, b. 1740. 63223

Brown, Thomas, 1785-1867. 24885 see also
Florida. Governor, 1849-1853 (Brown)
Brown, Thomas, fl. 1812. (8567)
Brown, Thomas C. 8568
Brown, Thomas Storrow, b. 1803. 8569-8570
Brown, Tom. pseud. Trip to Jamaica. see
Ward, Edward, 1667-1731.
Brown, Uriah. (1116), 81602
Brown, Vandyke. pseud. Vagaries of Vandyke
Brown. see Brannon, William Penn,
d. 1866.
Brown, Rev. W. 8572
Brown, W. R. 10473
Brown, Rev. William. 90444
Brown, William, of Leeds. 8575
Brown, William, fl. 1773. 72992, 101211
see also Gt. Brit. Customs Comptrol-
ler, Savannah, Ga.
Brown, William, fl. 1799. (8574)
Brown, William, fl. 1800. supposed author
8573, 35923
Brown, William A. 8576
Brown, William B. 8577
Brown, William D. 88257
Brown, William H. RN 8579
Brown, William H., 1796-1867. 8580-8581
Brown, William Henry, 1808-1883. 8578
Brown, William Laurence, 1755-1830. 102492
Brown, William Leroy. 8582
Brown, William Linn. incorrectly supposed
author 8583, 102124
Brown, William W. defendant at court martial
8584-8585
Brown, William Wells, b. 1815. 8586-(8596)
Brown, William Young, 1827-1914. (8597)-
8598
Brown. firm see Chipman, Hosmer and Co.
firm
Brown. firm see Stuarts, Edwards & Brown.
firm
Brown & Co. firm see Green, Brown & Co.
firm
Brown, Buckland & Co. firm 90742
Brown Rives et Compagnie. plaintiffs 104223
Brown County, Wisconsin. Board of Super-
visors. 70083
Brown Association, U. S. A. 24454, 82408-
82409
Brown paper. 8602
Brown University. 8602-8603, 8611-8617,
8621, 8625, 8627-8628, 8633, 47005,
70716, 2d note after 93806
Brown University. Agent. (42362) see also
Love, Horace T.
Brown University. Alumni. 8629
Brown University. Chapel. 8620
Brown University. Charter. 8619, 70716,
103255
Brown University. Class of 1774. 5468
Brown University. Corporation. 8629
Brown University. Corporation. petitioners
70716
Brown University. Corporation. Committee
to Raise a Fund of One Hundred Twenty-
Five Thousand Dollars. 8630
Brown University. Delti Phi Society. 8607
Brown University. Executive Board. 8632
Brown University. Faculty. 8601
Brown University. John Carter Brown Library.
99843, 99865, 99868, 99870, 99872
Brown University. Junior Class, 1797. 95519
Brown University. Library. 8604-8605,
8624, 29222
Brown University. One Hundredth Anniversary
Celebration, 1864. 8618

Brown University. Phi Beta Kappa Society.
see Phi Beta Kappa. Rhode Island Alpha,
Brown University.
Brown University. Philermenian Society. 8606,
8609, 8634
Brown University. Students. 8623, 8757
Brown University. United Brothers' Society.
8610, 8634, 97868
Brown University. United Brothers' Society.
Library. 97867
Brown University in the civil war. 9446
Brown University under the presidency of Asa
Messer. 8600
Browne, Albert Gallatin, 1835-1891. 1480,
(8636)-8637
Browne, Alexander E. 8638
Browne, Ansel. (8639)
Browne, Arthur, 1699-1773. 8640-8641, 5th
note after 69412
Browne, Charles. 8642
Browne, Charles Farrar, 1834-1867. (8643)-
8647, 84185-84187
Browne, Charles Hale. 89630
Browne, Daniel Jay, b. 1804. 3420, 8648-(8650),
52046
Browne, David. (8651)
Browne, Dunn. pseud. Experiences in the army.
see Fiske, Samuel.
Browne, George, Archbishop of Dublin, d.
1556. 101877
Browne, George M. 8652
Browne, H. K. illus. 20006, 92441, 92495
Browne, Howe Peter, Marquis of Sligo. see
Sligo, Howe Peter Browne, Marquis de.
Browne, J. Vincent. (37841), 76045 see also
U. S. Customs House, San Francisco.
Appraiser.
Browne, John. defendant at court martial
96839
Browne, John, of Cohasset. see Brown, John,
1724-1791.
Browne, John, of Higham. see Brown, John,
1724-1791.
Browne, John, of Nevis. 8654
Browne, John, of Orphington, Kent. 8655
Browne, John, fl. 1589. 8503
Browne, John Ross, 1817-1875. (8656)-8664,
10029, 44600, (68065) see also U. S.
Special Commissioners on the Mineral
Resources of the U. S.
Browne, John W. 8665
Browne, Joseph. 54602
Browne, Joseph. supposed author 62743
Browne, Junius Henri, 1833-1902. (8666)-(8667)
Browne, Lewis Crebasa. 83585, 83598
Browne, Nathaniel Borodaille, 1819-1875.
8668-8669
Browne, Patrick, 1720-1790. 8670-8671
Browne, Peter Arrell, 1792-1860. 8672-8676,
70191, 70275
Browne, Thomas. tr. 10158
Browne, Sir Thomas, 1605-1682. 8677
Browne, Thomas Egerton. ed. 46870, 104022
see also Louisville daily reporter.
Editor.
Browne, William H. 8679
Browne, William Henry James. illus. 8678
Browne, William M. ed. 88348A
Browne (John W.) firm publishers and book-
sellers 43243, 83865, 93229
Brownell, Charles De Wolf, 1822- 8681
Brownell, George. 62743
Brownell, Henry Howard, 1820-1872. (8682)-
8688, (42879)
Brownell, T. T. see Brownell, Thomas Church,
Bp., 1779-1865.

Brownell, Thomas, d. 1872. 8689
Brownell, Thomas Church, Bp., 1779-1865.
  8690-8691, 52763, 103464
Browne's banking and mercantile table. 8680
Browne's Cincinnati almanac. 93229
Browne's Cincinnati almanac for the year
  1809. 13073
Browne's western calendar, or, the Cincinnati
  almanac. 43243, 93229
Browning, Charles, b. 1765. 8692
Browning, Meshach, b. 1781. (8693)
Browning, O. W. see Browning, Orville
  Hickman, 1806-1881.
Browning, Orville Hickman, 1806-1881. 4256,
  8694-8695, 89214
Browning, Samuel. 8696
Brownings. (29166)
Brownjohn, Bellamy. pseud. No thoroughfare.
  see Dunham, Robert Carr.
Brownlee, William Craig. 8697-8699, 43810,
  66115, 80453
Brownlow, William Gannaway, 1805-1877.
  8701-(8708) see also Tennessee.
  Governor, 1865-1869 (Brownlow)
Brownlow Republicanism vs. Ethridge conserva-
  tism. 5365
Brown's almanac. 8494
Brown's Ferry. 1863. Part I. 84774
Browns of Nottingham. 16655
Brownson, Orestes Augustus, 1803-1876.
  6503, 8709-(8719), 63746, 64692, 69481,
  88909, 90111
Brownson's quarterly review. 6503, (8719),
  69481, 88909
Brownson's review. see Brownson's quarterly
  review.
Brownville, 1st December, 1817. 92227
Bruce, Rev. Archibald. (8720)
Bruce, Archibald, 1777-1818. ed. 1148
Bruce, Benjamin Gratz. 31465
Bruce, David, d. 1830. 8730
Bruce, George. 8722
Bruce, Hamilton. 8723
Bruce, James. see Elgin, James Bruce, 8th
  Earl of, 1811-1863.
Bruce, James C. 8724
Bruce, Lewis. 8725, 83978
Bruce, Peter Henry, 1692-1757. 8726-8727
Bruce, S. D. 8728, 31465
Bruce, V. 8729
Bruchstuck aus einem Reisejournal. 90090
Bruchstuke eines Tagebuchs. (74644)
Brucioli, Antonio. see Rucioli, Antonio.
Bruckmann, Franz Ernst, 1697-1753. 8731,
  89436
Bruckner, G. 8732
Bruckner, J. J. tr. 2522
Brudder Bones. pseud. Brudder Bones' book
  of stump speeches. see Scott, John F.
Brudder Bones' book of stump speeches. 78316
Bruder historie. 17412
Bruder-Mission auf den Danisch-Westindischen
  Inseln. 8733
Brudge, F. illus. 44310
Brudieu, ------. 8734
Brudieu et Lignieres, citoyens arbitrairement
  deportees. 8734
Brudstykker af en dagbog. 74642
Brue, Adrien Hubert. cartographer 8735
Bruen, Matthias, 1793-1829. 8736
Bruere, --------. 8738
Bruere, -------- Boucher de la. see
  Boucher de la Bruere, ------, Fils.
Brug over den oceaan. 35769
Bruges. English merchants. petitioners
  86742, 94070

Brugge, Jacob Segersz van der. see Segersz
  van der Brugge, Jacob.
Bruggemans, A. tr. 49920
Bruguiere, M. L. 68443
Bruin, Abraham de. 8739
Bruin, Servaas de, 1821-1901. tr. 70455
Bruin; or, the grand bear hunt. (69024)
Bruin, ou le chasseur d'ours. 69025
Bruinses, A. G. tr. 92522
Bruised reed bound up. 83794-83795
Bruja, periodico y trata de todo. 48311
Brularet de Sillery, Stephanie Felicite. see
  Sillery, Stephanie Felicite Brularet de,
  Countess de Genlis, 1746-1830.
Brulart, the black pirate. 93418
Brulio, Joachimo. see Brulius, Joachim.
Brulius, Joachim. 8740, 27782
Brulley, C. A. (8741), 9833, 16043, (58163)-
  58165, 65022, 75038, 75178, 86447 see
  also Santo Domingo (French Colony)
  Commissaires.
Brulons, Jacques Savary des. see Savary des
  Brulons, Jacques, 1677-1716.
Brumauld de Beauregard, Jean, Bp. 8742
  see also Orleans, France (Diocese)
  Bishop (Brumauld de Beauregard)
Brumbaugh, Martin Grove, 1862-1930. ed.
  95396
Brumby, Richard T. 8743
Brummelkamp, Anthony. 8744-8746
Brun, ------ de. see De Brun, -------.
Brun, ------ le. see Le Brun, ---------.
Brun, Conrad Malthe. see Malthe-Brun,
  Conrad, i. e. Bruun, Malthe Conrad, 1775-
  1826.
Brun, Jean B. 8747, 1st note after 96990
Brun, Laur. le. see Le Brun, Laur.
Brun, N. le. see Le Brun, N.
Brun, P. le. see Le Brun, P.
Brun, V. A. Malte. see Malte-Brun, A. V.
Brundung von Virginien. 92746
Brune, Frederick W. 8481, 8748
Brunel, Adolphe, i. e. Andre Adolphe Sextius
  Louis, 1810-1871. 8749
Brunel, Andre Adolphe Sextius Louis. see
  Brunel, Adolphe, i. e. Andre Adolphe
  Sextius Louis, 1810-1871.
Brunel, Charles. tr. 41913
Brunel, I. K. 42982
Brunet, E. Sully. see Sully Brunet, E.
Brunet, Gustave, 1807-1896. 64529
Brunet, Louis Ovide, 1826-1876. see Brunet,
  Ovide, i. e. Louis Ovide, 1826-1876.
Brunet, Ovide, i. e. Louis Ovide, 1826-1876.
  8750-8755
Bruning, L. 18722
Brunnermann, K. (8756)
Bruonian. 8623, 8757
Brunot, Felix Reville, 1820-1898. 8758
Bruns, P. F. 8759
Brunson, Alfred, 1793-1882. 8760-8762
Brunswick, Me. 8767
Brunswick, Me. Bowdoin College. see Bowdoin
  College, Brunswick, Me.
Brunswick, Me. Convention, 1816. see Maine.
  Convention, Brunswick, 1816.
Brunswick, Me. Financial and Superintending
  School Committee. 8765
Brunswick, Me. Proprietors. see Pejepscot
  Company.
Brunswick County, Va. Board of Supervisros.
  84970
Brunswick Antimony Company. 8768
Brunswick Canal and Railroad. Charter. 2903
Brunswick County, Virginia. 84970
Brunswick Land Company. (8763)

Brunt, Jonathan. 8769
Brunton, William. 8770
Brush, Conklin. 8772
Brush, Crean, 1725?-1778. 8771
Brush, George Jarvis, 1839-1912. 18424, 82999
Brush, John C. 8773
Brush, Samuel. 8774
Brushfield, Thomas Nadauld, 1828-1910. 67599
Brusle de Montpleinchamp, Jean Chrysostome. 50220
Brusque, Francisco Carlos de Araujo. 58499
   see also Para (Brazilian State)
   President (Brusque)
Brussels. Societe de Colonisation Europeo-
   Americaine au Texas. see Societe de
   Colonisation Europeo-Americaine au
   Texas, Brussels.
Brute de Remur, Simon Guillaume Gabriel,
   Bp., 1779-1839. (4052)
Brute-tamer! 102172
Brutel de la Riviere, ------. 8775
Brutus, fl. 1787. pseud. 102417
Brutus, fl. 1828. pseud. 30055, 70192
Brutus. pseud. Address to the freeholders
   of . . . New York. 53502
Brutus. pseud. Crisis. see Turnbull,
   Robert James, 1775-1833.
Brutus. pseud. Foreign conspiracy. see
   Morse, Samuel Finley Breese, 1791-
   1872.
Brutus. pseud. Letters of Brutus to certain
   celebrated political characters. 8778
Brutus. pseud. Some late pieces. see
   Coram, Robert.
Brutus. pseud. To the public. The present
   General Assembly of this colony. 95978
Brutus. pseud. To the public. Whoever
   seriously considers the impoverished
   state. 95973
Brutus. pseud. Two curious and important
   letters. 97554
Brutus, Junius. pseud. Verzameling van
   stukken tot de dierten Vereenigde Staeten.
   see Kemp, Francois Adriaan van der.
Brutus, Lucius Junius. pseud. Examination
   of the President's answer to the New
   Haven remonstrance. see Coleman,
   William, 1766-1829. supposed author
   and Cranch, William, 1769-1855.
   supposed author
Brutus, Marcus. pseud. see Marcus Brutus.
   pseud.
Brutus; or, the fall of Tarquin. 59288
Bruun, Joh. A. tr. 83255
Bruun, Malthe Conrad. see Malthe-Brun,
   Conrad, i. e. Bruun, Malthe Conrad,
   1775-1826.
Bruyas, Jacques, 1635-1712. 8779
Bruyere, ------ Barbeau de la. see Barbeau
   de la Bruyere, ------.
Bruyere, J. M. 74551, 74555
Bruyere, J.-B.-M.-L. la Reynie de la. see
   La Reynie de la Bruyere, J.-B.-M.-L.
Bruyn, H. de. 8781
Bruzen de la Martiniere, Antoine Augustin,
   1662-1746. 4931-4934, (8783), note
   after 38710
Bruzual, Manual E. 8782
Bry, Dieterichs de. cartographer 55433
Bry, Johann Israel de. (8784)
Bry, Johann Theodor de, 1561-1623? 126,
   2139, 5112, 6161, (8784), 11285, (11608),
   12959, note after 16965, 19152, 22656,
   30122, 30377, 30482-30483, 31506,

31540, 31545, 34160, 36236, 39236, 39634,
   40153, 41356, 41366, 41659, 50723, 55433-
   55434, 55436-(55438), 67355, 67546, 67566,
   67595, 73435, 76212, 77678, 77956, 77961,
   82819, 82823, 82979, 89450, note before
   90036, 92664-92665, note after 99383C,
   99728, note after 102550, 103332, 103395,
   note after 106331
Bryan, Daniel. 8785-8789, 38583
Bryan, E. D. 46901
Bryan, E. T. USA 36377, 84774
Bryan, George J. 8790
Bryan, Hugh, 1699-1753. 8791, 41605
Bryan, James, 1810-1881. 8792-(8793), 62016
Bryan, James W. 8794
Bryan, John A. (7314), (8795)-8796
Bryan, John A. 96703 see also U. S. Com-
   missioner to the Wyandot Indians.
Bryan, John Heritage, 1798-1870. 8797
Bryan, Samuel. 8799-8800, 36360, (60642),
   90746
Bryan, Thomas. 8801
Bryan, Thomas Barbour, 1828-1906. 8802
Bryan, William. 95127, 95132
Bryand, Edouard. see Edwards, Bryan.
Bryant. alias see Williams, George W.
   defendant
Bryant, ------, fl. 1865. 8811
Bryant, Charles S., 1808-1885. 8803
Bryant, Edwin, 1805-1869. (8350), 8804-8805,
   100641, 103893
Bryant, G. J. F. 45721
Bryant, J. 8807, 57544
Bryant, J. R. 34495
Bryant, James Ray M'Corckle, 1802-1866. 8806
Bryant, John Howard. 8808
Bryant, Joseph Decatur, 1845-1914. 84276-
   84277
Bryant, Joshua. 8809
Bryant, Samuel. (8810)
Bryant, William Cullen, 1794-1878. 434, 1125,
   2298, 8812-8826, 9751, 11553, 11996,
   (16573), 16740, 22409, 32707, 33390,
   35221, 49945, 54847, (62692), 63729,
   (70978), 72417, 79003, 84139-84141,
   84143, 84146, 85536, note after 86936,
   94246, 94247, 94258, note before 94463,
   note after 97969, note after 99276, note
   after 99271, 2d note after 106203
Bryant, William M. (8827)
Bryant Festival, New York, 1864. 54137
Bryant Festival at "The Century," November 5,
   M.DCCC.LXIV. 54137
Bryant Homestead-book. 30844
Bryant School, Roslyn, N. Y. (31301)
Bryant's songs from Dixie's land. 8811
Brydges, Sir Samuel Egerton, Bart., 1762-1837.
   8829, 25999, 67599, 79342
Brydone, James Marr. (8830)
Buache, --------. cartographer 51285
Buache, Jean Nicolas, 1741-1825. 8831, (47542)
Buache, Philippe. (8832)-8834
Buache de la Nueville, Jean Nicolas. see
   Buache, Jean Nicolas, 1741-1825.
Buache de l'Isle, Guil. Phil. see Isle, Guil.
   Phil. Buache de l'.
Buade, Louis de, Comte de Palluau et de
   Frontenac, 1620-1698. supposed author
   39650-39651
Bubble, a poem. 8835
Bubble & squeak; or, a dish of all sorts.
   100636, 105178
Bubbles of Canada. 29682-29683
Bucaniers of America: or, a true account.
   23468, (23479), 23481

Bucaniers of America, the second volume. 23468, (23479), 23481-(23482)

Bucareli y Ursua, Antonio Maria, 1717-1779. 8836, 68861, 98490 see also Mexico (Viceroyalty) Virrey, 1771-1779 (Bucareli y Ursua)

Buccaneer. A tale. (8837), 29715

Buccaneer, and other poems. (18438)

Buccaneer, Sir Henry Morgan. 33246

Buccaneers; a romance of our own country. 8838, 36829

Buch, Christian Leopold von, Baron, 1744-1853. 8839

Buch, L. de. 8839, 33733

Buch der Auswanderung. 96791

Buch der Croniken. 77526-77527

Buch der Lehre und Bundnisse der Kirche Jesu Christi. 83222-83224

Buch der Verbrechen. 19485

"Buch der Wilden" im lichte Franzosischer Civilization. 61309

Buch fur Auswanderer. 91208

Buch gehort dem Deutschen Auswanderer. 77665

Buch Mormon. 83124-83130

Buch von der Amerikanischen Nahmaschine. 18666

Buchan, Alexander. defendant 34012

Buchan, David Steuart Erskine, 11th Earl of, 1742-1829. 22789, 101755

Buchanan, Rev. --------. (2792)

Buchanan, A. C. 8840

Buchanan, Archibald. 8841

Buchanan, Claudius, 1766-1815. 8842

Buchanan, David. ed. 82304

Buchanan, Edward Y. (8843)

Buchanan, Franklin. 8844

Buchanan, George, 1763-1808. 8845, (64041)

Buchanan, Harrison Gray. 8846

Buchanan, Isaac, b. 1810. 8847-(8853)

Buchanan, James, British Consul at New York. (8854)-(8860), 21383, (82311), 84616, 85254

Buchanan, James, d. 1778. defendant 105350-105350A

Buchanan, James, Pres. U. S., 1791-1868. 6130, (8860), 8862, 8865, 9943, 12813, 13653, (16860), 22917, 33077, 36542, 37023, 37071, 40330, 40663, 48130-48135, 50955, 52997, 57654, (65356), 70749, (78429), (84616), 85254, note after 87402, 87436, 87438, 86788, 101913 see also U. S. President, 1857-1861 (Buchanan)

Buchanan, James A., of Baltimore. defendant 68042

Buchanan, John. 8866-8867 see also Cumberland County, Pa. Collector of Excise.

Buchanan, Joseph. 105495

Buchanan, Joseph Rodes, 1814-1899. 8868

Buchanan, Robert. (8869), 92341

Buchanan, Robert Williams, 1841-1901. 74982

Buchanan, W. Jefferson. (45252)-45253

Buchanan, William B. 2560, 8870, (45211A)

Buchanan and Breckenridge. 13803

Buchanan and Fillmore compared from the record. 81816

Buchananism not democracy. 2420

Buchele, Karl. 8871

Bucher, T. P. 8872

Buches der Wilden. 47415

Buchler, Johann Ulrich. 8873

Buchner, J. H. 8874

Buchner, Karl. 8875

Buchon, J. A. C. 72014

Buchon, Jean Alexandre, 1791-1846. (1062), 8876

Buc'hoz, Pierre Joseph, 1731-1807. 8877-8879, 47961

Buck, Albert Henry, 1842-1922. 84276

Buck, Anthony. 8880

Buck, Edward, of Boston. 8881-8882

Buck, Ephraim. 8883

Buck, William Joseph, 1825- 8884-8885

Buckalew, Charles Rollin, 1821-1899. 8886, 60468 see also Pennsylvania. Commissioners to Investigate the Affairs of the Bank of Susquehanna County.

Bucke, Charles, 1781-1846. 8887

Buckeye abroad. (17271)

Buckeye blossoms. (64287)

Buckeye Celebration, Hamilton, Ohio, 1835. 30071

Buckholtz, L. von. 8888-8889

Buckingham, --------. defendant 57856, 67255

Buckingham, --------, fl. 1733. 89204

Buckingham, Mrs. --------, fl. 1824. 8912

Buckingham, Edgar. (8890)

Buckingham, Edwin, 1810-1833. (52698), 85433, 95153, note after 103816

Buckingham, George Villiers, 2d Duke of, 1628-1687. 46954

Buckingham, Henry A. (8891)

Buckingham, James Silk, 1786-1855. 8892-8899

Buckingham, John. see Buckingham, Thomas, 1761-1839.

Buckingham, John Albert. 8900

Buckingham, Joseph H., 1806-1880. 8901

Buckingham, Joseph Tinker, 1779-1861. (8902)-8911, 14933, 48852, (52698), 85433, note after 89215, 95153, 103279, note after 103816

Buckingham, Joseph Tinker, 1779-1861. defendant 8911, 96840

Buckingham, Samuel Giles. 8913

Buckingham, Thomas, 1761-1839. 38124

Buckingham, William Alfred, 1804-1875. 15744, 15785, 33150 see also Connecticut. Governor, 1858-1866 (Buckingham)

Buckingham County, Va. 100071

Buckington, Nathaniel. 8914

Buckland, Cyrus. (8915)

Buckland, James. 93906, 105003-105008

Buckland, James. defendant 96945

Buckland, W. 71031

Buckland & Co. firm see Brown, Buckland & Co. firm

Buckle, John. 8916

Buckler, Thomas Hepburn, 1812-1901. 8917

Buckley, --------, of Colchester. 104986

Buckley, Samuel Botsford. 8918

Bucklin, Daniel. 103088

Bucklin, Sylvester Fuller, 1784-1860. (8919)

Buckminster, Edward. 8920

Buckminster, Joseph, 1720-1792. 8923

Buckminster, Joseph, 1751-1812. 8921-8922, 8924-8930, 25233, 47955, 82478

Buckminster, Joseph Stevens, 1784-1812. 8932-8936, 30519

Buckminster, Lydia Nelson (Hastings) b. 1818. 8937

Buckman, Nathan, 1703-1795. 8938-8939

Bucknell University, Lewisburg, Pa. (40870)

Buckner, Aylett, 1806-1869. 8940

Buckner, Henry F., 1818-1882. 8941-8942, (17460), 51585

Buckner, James. ed. 93249

Buckner, John, Bp. of Chichester. 8943

Buckner, Samuel. 8944
Buckner, Simon Bolivar, 1823-1914. (70984)
Bucknor, Robert H. 82247 see also Missis-
sippi. Chancellor.
Bucks County, Pa. Bristol College. see
Bristol College, Bucks, Co., Pa.
Bucks County, Pa. Collector of Excise. 8946,
105676-105678 see also Wyncoop,
Gerardus.
Bucks County, Pa. Constituents. 40513
Bucks County, Pa. Court of Oyer and Ter-
miner. 21019, 1st note after 96847
Bucks County, Pa. Court of Quarter Sessions.
95643
Bucks County, Pa. Lieutenant. 30629 see
also Hart, Joseph.
Bucks County, Pa. Society for the Advance-
ment of General Education. see Society
for the Advancement of General Education
in the County of Bucks.
Bucks County, Pa. Sub-Lieutenant. 8947,
27383, 36970, (38456), 43313, 101085
see also Anderson, Joshua. Gill, John.
Kachline, Andrew. Lacy, John. M'Henry,
William. Wall, George.
Bucks County man. pseud. Narrative of the
modes and measures. 51816
Bucks County man. pseud. True and faithful
narrative. 55104, 2d note after 97901
Bucks have at ye all. 89593
Buckshot war. 93282
Bucktail bards. 99276
Buckwheat cake, a poem. 62628
Bucquoy, J. de. (8948)
Bud, blossom and fruit. 62824
Budan, A. 8949
Budapest. Tudós Társáság. see Tudós
Társaság, Budapest.
Budd, Benjamin. defendant 92736
Budd, George K. (49634)
Budd, Henry. 8950, 54987
Budd, Thomas, d. 1698. 8952-8953, 8955-
8957, 12914, 17510, 37178, 37181,
37185, 37194-(37195), 37205, (37223),
47181, 56650, 86068, note after 94918,
97113
Budd, Thomas, d. 1698. defendant 37203,
(37226), 1st note after 96931, 2d note
after 96956, 2d note after 97284
Budd, Thomas A. 8958
Budd, William. (1771)
Buddingh, Derk. 8959
Budeius, Stephanius Parmenius. 8960
Budge, Richard. petitioner (8961), 53081
Budgell, Eustace, 1686-1737. 8962, 65865,
88185, 88192, 1st note after 99795
Budget. 84162, 85466
Budget. A series of letters on financial,
commercial, and colonial policy. 96233
Budget du Bresil. 92724
Budget for 1860. (54212)
Budget from the saddlebags of a superannuated
itinerant. 81544, 81550, 91480
Budget general des despenses du Ministere de
la Marine. 8963
Budget. Inscribed to the man who thinks him-
self minister. 1659, 8964, 30688,
101118, 103123
Budget of general information. 8265
Budget of legendary, historical, critical, and
sporting intelligence. 40005
Budget; or humble attempts at immortality.
100764
Budgett, Samuel. 8965
Budingen. Laws, statutes, etc. 71405

Budingsche Sammlung. 23094, note after 106352
Budington, William E. see Budington, William
Ives, 1815-1879.
Budington, William Ives, 1815-1879. 8966-8970
Budinjacki, Bozidar. 10301
Buds and flowers, of leisure hours. 8971
Buds, blossoms, and leaves. 79765
Buds of beauty. 12285
Buds of spring. Poetical remains, with addenda.
42756
Buee, William Urban. 8972
Buel, Alexander Woodruff, 1813-1868. (8973)
Buel, C. C. 85374
Buel, David, 1784-1860. 614, 8974-8975
Buel, Jesse, 1778-1839. 8976, (17869), 88654,
90594, 101159
Buel, Samuel. (8977)
Buel, William. 102346
Buel, William Samuel. 105371
Buel's cultivator. (17869)
Buell, Don Carlos, 1818-1898. 8979
Buell, Joseph. 31799
Buell, P. L. 8980
Buell, Samuel, 1716-1798. 8981-8986
Buell, Samuel, 1716-1798. supposed author
106212
Buell Gold Company. see Kip & Buell Gold
Company, Colorado.
Buena de la Rosa, Hipolito. see La Rosa,
Hipolito Buena de.
Buena-Maison, Alonso de. tr. 23471-23474,
(23479), 23481
Buena Ventura, Juan Eustachio. see Bonaven-
tura, Saint, 1221-1274.
Buena vista, and other poems. 18916
Buenacasa, Pedro Martin de. ed. 78772
Buenaventura. Saint see Bonaventura, Saint,
1221-1274.
Buenaventura, F. de San. see San Buenaven-
tura, F. de.
Buenaventura, Gabriel de San. see San Buena-
ventura, Gabriel de.
Buenaventura, J. E. de. 49653
Buenavista, Miguel Perez de Santa Cruz, Mar-
ques de. see Santa Cruz, Miguel Perez
de, Marques de Buenavista.
Buendia, Joseph de. 9047
Buendia, Pedro de Tobar y. see Tobar y
Buendia, Pedro de.
Bueno, Cosme, 1711-1798. 8987-8988, 15884,
87150, 99667
Bueno, Jose Antonio Pimenta. see Pimenta
Bueno, Jose Antonio.
Bueno, Joseph Gonzalez Cabrera. see Cabrera
Bueno, Joseph Gonzalez.
Bueno, Maximano de Souza. see Souza Bueno,
Maximano de.
Buenos Aires. petitioners 9021, (47591)
Buenos Aires. Academia de Medicina. see
Academia de Medicina de Buenos Aires.
Buenos Aires. Aduana. 9025, 9032
Buenos Aires. American Citizens. 41236, 6th
note after 99664
Buenos Aires. Cabildo. (9015), 9029
Buenos Aires. Colegio de Abogados. see
Colegio de Abogados, Buenos Aires.
Buenos Aires. Comision Militar. see Argen-
tine Republic. Comision Militar, Buenos
Aires.
Buenos Aires. Committee of British Merchants.
9037
Buenos Aires. Consulado. 96247
Buenos Aires. Consulado. Charter. 9044
Buenos Aires. Haciendos. petitioners 69974

382

Buenos Aires. Junta de Historia y Numismatica Americana. see Junta de Historia y Numismatic Americana, Buenos Aires.
Buenos Aires. Junta de Observacion, 1815. 9013
Buenos Aires. Justicia Nacional. see Argentine Republic. Justicia Nacional, Buenos Aires.
Buenos Aires. Museo Nacional. 8993
Buenos Aires. Ordinances, etc. (9014), 9021, 9029
Buenos Aires. Real Audiencia. see Rio de la Plata (Viceroyalty) Real Audiencia.
Buenos Aires. Sociedad de Beneficencia de la Capital. see Sociedad de Benefiencia de la Capital, Buenos Aires.
Buenos Aires. Sociedad Economica Empleados de Aduana. see Sociedad Economica Empleados de Aduana, Buenos Aires.
Buenos Aires. Tribunales Ordinarios. 73209
Buneos Aires. Universidad Nacional. Instituto de Investigaciones Historicas. 99460
Buenos Aires (Diocese) 47616
Buenos Aires (Diocese) Bishop (Peralta) 19208-19209, 62441 see also Peralta, Jos. de, Bp.
Buenos Aires (Province) 9003, 9006, 9009, (9015)-9016, (9018)-9019, 9021-9023, 9033-9036, 9045, 14295, 17841, (20441), 38719, (39845), (47752), 58481, (65927), (68829), 68831, 73217
Buenos Aires (Province) Archivo General. 70309
Buenos Aires (Province) Comision de Cuentas. 9017
Buenos Aires (Province) Comision de Inmigracion. 9039
Buenos Aires (Province) Congresso. see Buenos Aires (Province) Legislatura.
Buenos Aires (Province) Convencion Encargada del Examen de la Constitucion Federal, 1859-1860. 9012
Buenos Aires (Province) Diputacion. 9020
Buenos Aires (Province) Fiscal General del Estado. 22812, 47616 see also Agrelo, Pedro Jose, 1776-1846.
Buenos Aires (Province) Gobernador, 1734-1742 (Salcedo y Sierra Alta) 24173 see also Salcedo y Sierra Alta, Miguel de.
Buenos Aires (Province) Gobernador, 1835-1852 (Rosas) 9043, 44278, 44281, 73210, 73215-73217, 93807 see also Argentine Republic. Minister of Foreign Affairs. Rosas, Juan Manuel de, 1793-1877.
Buenos Aires (Province) Laws, statutes, etc. 9013, 51269, 65549, 68385
Buenos Aires (Province) Legacion, Montevideo. 9019, (39845)
Buenos Aires (Province) Legislatura. 44286, note after 95211
Buenos Aires (Province) Legislatura. Camara de Senadores. 9008, 9011, 19102
Buenos Aires (Province) Sala de Representantes. 73221
Buenos Aires (Province) Treaties, etc. 9021, 16166, 58062
Buenos Aires et le peuple Basque. 40204
Buenos Aires y las provincias de la Plata. 58614
Buenos-Ayres. 12347
Buenos Ayres and the Argentine gleanings. (34089)
Buenos Ayres and the province of the Rio de la Plata. 58612-58613

Buenos Ayres duende. see Duende de Buenos Ayres.
Buenos-Ayres et le Paraguay. 19545
Buenos Ayres, Monte Video, and affairs of the River Plate. 44125
Buenos-Ayres reconquistada. 64192
Buenos-Ayres, sa situation presente. (2865)
Buenos Ayres. The trial of Lieutenant General Whitelocke. 103674
Buenos Ayres. Truth and reason. 9002, 103674
Buenos Ayres und die Argentinischen Provinzen. 1462
Buenos-Ayres und die dortige evangelische Gemeinde. 80876
Buenrostro, Antonio Delgado y. see Delgado y Buenrostro, Antonio.
Buff and blue. 91328
Buffalo. Charity Foundation of the Protestant Episcopal Church. see Protestant Episcopal Charity Foundation, Buffalo, N. Y.
Buffalo. Charter. 9063
Buffalo. De Veaux College for Orphan and Destitute Children. see De Veaux College for Orphan and Destitute Children, Buffalo, N. Y.
Buffalo. Citizens. petitioners (22746)
Buffalo. Committee of Public Defense. (9062)
Buffalo. Common Council. 9060
Buffalo. Common Council. Select Committee. 9061, note after 91136
Buffalo. Convention of Delegates from the several Counties of the Holland Purchase, 1827. see Holland Purchase Convention, Buffalo, N. Y., 1827.
Buffalo. Convention of Delegates from the Several Counties Within the Holland Purchase, 1834. see Holland Purchase Convention, Buffalo, N. Y., 1834.
Buffalo. Convention of Delegates of Kansas Aid Societies, 1856. see Convention of Delegates of Kansas Aid Societies, Buffalo, N. Y., 1856.
Buffalo. Convention of Delegates on Title of Holland Land Company, 1834. see Holland Purchase Convention, Buffalo, N. Y., 1834.
Buffalo. Convention of Lake Underwriters, 1856. see Convention of Lake Underwriters, Buffalo, N. Y., 1856.
Buffalo. County Convention of Delegates, from the Several Towns in the County of Erie, 1830. see Holland Purchase Convention, Buffalo, N. Y., 1830.
Buffalo. Court of Oyer and Terminer. see Erie County, N. Y. Court of Oyer and Terminer, Buffalo.
Buffalo, N. Y. East Pembroke Seminary. see East Pembroke Seminary, Buffalo, N. Y.
Buffalo. Educational Convention, 1860. see Educational Convention, Buffalo, N. Y., 1860.
Buffalo. First Presbyterian Church. 9049
Buffalo. First Unitarian Church. 9058
Buffalo. Forest Lawn Cemetery. 25080
Buffalo, N. Y. Forest Law Cemetery Association. see Forest Law Cemetery Association, Buffalo, N. Y.
Buffalo. Fourth of July Celebration, 1865. 9063
Buffalo. Free Soil Party National Convention, 1848. see Free Soil Party. National Convention, Buffalo, N. Y., 1848.
Buffalo. General Aid Society for the Army. see United States Sanitary Commission. General Aid Society for the Army, Buffalo.

Buffalo. Grand Convention of the Mechanics' Mutual Protection of the U. S. A., 1847. see Mechanics' Mutual Protection of the U. S. A. Grand Convention, Buffalo, N. Y., 1847.

Buffalo. Harbor Committee. 9060

Buffalo. Holland Purchase Convention, 1827. see Holland Purchase Convention, Buffalo, N. Y., 1827.

Buffalo. Holland Purchase Convention, 1830. see Holland Purchase Convention, Buffalo, N. Y., 1830.

Buffalo. Holland Purchase Convention, 1834. see Holland Purchase Convention, Buffalo, N. Y., 1834.

Buffalo. Library. see Buffalo Library, Buffalo, N. Y.

Buffalo. Meeting of the Citizens with Reference to the Improvement of the Erie Canal, 1839. see Western Canal Convention, Rochester, N. Y., 1839.

Buffalo. National Liberty Convention, 1848. see National Liberty Convention, Buffalo, N. Y., 1848.

Buffalo. Old Settler's Festival, 1867. see Old Settler's Festival, Buffalo, N. Y., 1867.

Buffalo. Ordinances, etc. 9063

Buffalo. Orphan Asylum. 9063

Buffalo. Protestant Episcopal Charity Foundation. see Protestant Episcopal Charity Foundation, Buffalo, N. Y.

Buffalo. Public Meeting Against Closing the Canal Locks and Stopping the Mails on Sunday, 1858. 65802, 93739

Buffalo. St. Joseph's Cathedral. 75300

Buffalo. St. Louis Church. 9063

Buffalo. Union Anti-Lecompton Mass Meeting of the Citizens of Erie County, 1858. see Erie County, N. Y. Union Anti-Lecompton Mass Meeting, Buffalo, N. Y., 1858.

Buffalo. University. Medical Department. 9063

Buffalo. Washington Street Baptist Church. 9063

Baffalo. Western Literary and Scientifick Academy. see Western Literary and Scientifick Academy, Baffalo, N. Y.

Buffalo. Westminster Presbyterian Church. 84413

Buffalo. Young Men's Association. see Buffalo Library, Buffalo, N. Y.

Buffalo. Young Men's Christian Union. see Young Men's Christian Union, Buffalo, N. Y.

Buffalo (Diocese) Bishop (Ryan) 72935 see also Ryan, Stephen Vincent, Bp.

Buffalo (Diocese) Synod, 1871. 72935

Buffalo Association for the Relief of the Poor. 9063

Buffalo business directory. 9051

Buffalo city directory for 1865. 9056, note after 95451

Buffalo city directory for 1864. 9056, note after 95451

Buffalo city directory for 1867. 9056, 91134, note after 95451

Buffalo city directory for 1863. 9056, note after 95451

Buffalo city sewerage and sanitary science. 91134

Buffalo convention, and the St. Nicholas compact. 11343

Buffalo, Corning and New-York Railroad Company. 9063

Buffalo Creek Reservation, N. Y. Indian Council, 1842. see New York (State) Indian Council, Buffalo Creek Reservation, 1842.

Buffalo daily republic extra. 92874

Buffalo directory for 1865. 9056, (55873), note after 95451

Baffalo Female Academy. see Buffalo Seminary.

Buffalo Gas Light Company. 9063

Buffalo General Hospital. 9063

Buffalo girls. 91843

Buffalo harbor. 9063

Buffalo Historical Society. 69857, 85200, 91135, 102964, 102984, 103454

Buffalo Horticultural Society. 9063

Buffalo in 1836 and 1862. 75791

Buffalo in 1825. 9052

Buffalo Juvenile Asylum. 9063

Buffalo Library, Buffalo, N. Y. 9063, 106158

Buffalo Library, Buffalo, N. Y. Library. 106158

Buffalo medical journal and monthly review of medical and surgical science. 9063

Buffalo, past and present. 9056, note after 95451

Buffalo Presbytery. see Presbyterian Church in the U. S. A. Presbytery of Buffalo.

Buffalo Seminary. 9063

Buffalo Trust Company. 9063

Buffalo, Warren and St. Louis Railroad. 9063

Buffin, John. 9064

Buffinton, James, 1817-1875. 9065

Buffon, Georges Louis Leclerc, Comte de, 1707-1788. (9066), 14267, (41054)

Bufford, J. H. lithographer 84352

Buffum, Arnold, 1782-1859. ed. 66096

Buffum, Edward Gould, 1820-1867. (9067)

Buffum, Gaskill. pseud. Surrejoinder. 93880

Buffum, Jonathan. defendant 79895

Buford, N. D. USA 9068

Bug-Jargal. Claude Gueux. 33614

Bug Jargal, eller negeropstanden paa St. Domingo. (33615)

Bug-Jargal o la rivolta dei negri di San Domingo. (33613)

Bugbee, James McKellar, 1837-1913. (9069), (23273)

Bugbee, Samuel. 9070

Bugg, Francis, 1640-1724? 9071-9072, 66737, 86708

Bugle blast from the army. 9073

Bugle blast; or, spirit of the conflict. 73487

Bugle-call. (73127)

Bugle call. Devoted to the cause of our sick and wounded soldiers. 9074

Buhle, M. 9075

Buhler, J. A. 8215

Buhoup, Jonathan W. 9076

Building associations of Connecticut and other states examined. (9077), 25638

Building meeting-houses, and supporting ministers. 99093

Building of a diocese. 91583

Building of the ship. (41932)

Building Society of the District of Dalhousie, Canada. 66085

Building the tombs of the prophets. 51439

Buisot, J. P. 9078

Buisson, Jean Francois. 9079, note before 95222

Buisson, Paul Ulric du. 9080, 9081-9082, 21036-21039, 29197, 31897, 32106, 92197, 100776

Buist, George, 1770-1808. 9083-9084, 66425

Buist, Henry. 87843

Buist, Robert, 1805-1880. 31683

Buitenland. (9085)

Buitron, Francisco Antonio Lorenzana y. see Lorenzana y Britron, Francisco Antonio, Abp.
Buk of Samz. 67753
Buka no te Paru Haapii. 83230
Buke a Moramona. 83131, 83832-83833
Bula de la Santa Cruzada. 23425, 34836, 93581
Bulas, Juan de. 34819
Bulau, Friedrich, 1805-1859. 3125, 52061-52062
Bulderen, H. v. 9086
Bules, Jaqves. 94351
Bulfinch, Benjamin S. 9087
Bulfinch, Charles, 1763-1844. 9088, 101782
Bulfinch, John. reporter (9089), 96808
Bulfinch, Stephen Greenleaf, 1809-1870. 9090-9091, 63040
Bulfinch, Thomas, 1728-1802. (81388)
Bulfinch, Thomas, 1796-1867. 9092-9093
Bulhoens, Michele de, Bp. (63902), 63904 see also Para (Diocese) Bishop (Bulhoens)
Bulich, J. D. von. 9094
Bulkeley, Gershom, 1635-1713. 9095
Bulkeley, Gershom, 1635-1713. supposed author 9095, 15856, (15860), 86758, note after 96296, 100820
Bulkeley, John. 1639, 9108-9109. 10205, (50834)
Bulkeley, Peter, 1583-1659. (9096)-9097
Bulkley, Charles. 9098
Bulkley, Charles Henry Augustus, 1819-1893. 9099-9101
Bulkley, D. H. ed. 54784
Bulkley, Edward. 103200
Bulkley, Edwin Adolphus, 1826-1905. (9102)-9104
Bulkley, John. see Bulkeley, John.
Bulkley, John, d. 1731. 9105-9107, 101216, 103941
Bulkly, Samuel. 3278, 3290
Bull, ---------, fl. 1834. 101347
Bull, James P. 91146
Bull, Jireh. defendant 12172
Bull, John. ed. 54866
Bull, Marcus. 80679
Bull, Patrick. 9110
Bull for the abolition of the slave trade. 28747
Bull on slavery and the slave-trade. (56653)
Bull Run to Ball's Bluff. 69869
Bull-a. pseud. Beauties of Brother Bull-us. 4205
Bvlla. Bvlla S. D. N. D. Pii Divina Providentia Papae Quarti, super confirmatione oecumeniic [sic] generalis Concilij Tridentini. 63165
Bvlla. Bvlla S. D. N. D. Pii Divina Providentia Papae Quarti, super declaratione temporis obseruadi decreta sacri oecumenici. 63165
Bulla confirmationis et novae concessionis priuilegiorum omnium Ordinum Mendicantium. 63166
Bulla canonizationis S. Rosea de S. Maria Virgine Limanae. 13625
Bulla confirmationis et novae concessionis privilegiorum omnium Ordinum Mendicantium. 9111
Bulla erectionis sanctae metropolitanae ecclesiae Mexiceae. 48312
Bvlla S. D. N. D. Pii Divinia Providentia Papae Quarti, super confirmatione oecumeniic [sic] generalis Consilij Tridentini. 63165

Bvlla S. D. N. D. Pii Divina Providentia Papae Quarti, super declaratione temporis obseruadi decreta sacri oecumenici. 63165
Bullard, Anne Tuttle Jones. 46873
Bullard, Artemas. 9112
Bullard, Edward Fritch, b. 1821. 9113-9114
Bullard, Henry Adams, 1788-1851. 9115-9119, note after 49411
Bullard, Henry Adams, 1788-1851. incorrectly supposed author 5333-5334, 9117
Bullard, Mary Swinton (Legare) 39855
Bullard, O. A. (9120)-9121
Bullarium Latino-Hispanicum Ord. Fratrum Bethlemitarum in Indiis Occidentalibus. 9122
Bullart, Isaac, 1599-1672. 9123
Bullas pontificias. 91117
Bullen, Christians. (9124)
Buller, Charles, 1806-1848. 9125, (71037)
Bulletin colonial. 8126
Bulletin de bouquiniste. 85044
Bulletin de la Societe de Geographie. 2492, 2493A, 7420, 9128, 19741, 36431, 36433, 40764, 76841, 76845, 76848, 77204, 89982, 89990, 101361
Bulletin [de la Societe de Geographie et de Statistique de Mexico] 29148
Bulletin de la Societe Geologique de France. 77205
Bulletin de la Societe Orientale. 70359
Bulletin de la Societe Philomatique. 9127
Bulletin de l'Athenee Oriental. 70375
Bulletin de recherches, observations et decouvertes se rapportant a l'histoire naturelle du Canada. 52049
Bulletin des actes administratifs de la Martinique. 44973
Bulletin du bibliophile et du bibliothecaire. (8784)
Bulletin historique et litteraire de la Societe de l'Histoire du Protestantisme Francais, Paris. 9129, 69745
Bulletin mensuel de la Societe Instituee en 1834 pour l'Abolition de l'Esclavage. 81733, 85816
Bulletin no. 5. [of the Soldiers' Aid Society of Northern Ohio.] 86317
Bulletin of Johns Hopkins Hospital. 84267
Bulletin of the Boston Public Library. 103242
Bulletin of the Bureau of Animal Industry. 84331-84332
Bulletin of the College of William and Mary. 104153
Bulletin of the Essex Institute. 23013
Bulletin of the historical and natural sciences. 67465
Bulletin of the Historical Society of Pennsylvania. 60141, 79148
Bulletin of the Lloyd Library of Botany, Pharmacy and Materia Medicia. 83710, 95605
Bulletin of the Mining Bureau of the Philippine Islands. 84527
Bulletin of the Minnesota Academy of Natural Sciences. 49241
Bulletin of the Museum of Comparative Zoology. 10122
Bulletin of the National Association of Wool Manufacturers. (51934)
Bulletin of the New England Art Union. 52657
Bulletin of the New York Genealogical and Biographical Society. (54779)
Bulletin of the New York Public Library. 37335, 86720, note after 98475, 99362
Bulletin of the New York State Library. 84558
Bulletin of the operations of the Cincinnati Branch of the United States Sanitary Commission. 13097

Bulletin of the proceedings of the National Institution for the Promotion of Science. 51990

Bulletin of the Pottsville Scientific Association. 64694

Bulletin of the Seismological Society of America. 84528

Bulletin of the United States Bureau of Mines. 84296-84297

Bulletin of the University of Oregon. 84532-84533

Bulletin of the University of South Carolina. 83750-83751

Bulletin of the University of Washington. 84295

Bulletin of the Virginia State Library. 91860, 100118

Bulletin officiel de la Guyane Francais. (11618)

Bulletin universel des sciences et de l'industrie. 19648

Bulletins de la Societe d'Anthropologie. 18332

Bulletins of the United States National Museum. 85007

Bullion, L. de. 3707

Bullions, A. B. 9130

Bullions, Alexander. defendant 91610

Bullions, Alexander. defendant before Presbytery and Synod 90516, note after 96840, 1st note after 97091

Bullions, Peter, 1791-1864. ed. 65138

Bullitt, John Christian, 1824-1902. 9131

Bullivant, Benjamin. 9132

Bulloch, -------, fl. 1828. 71995

Bullock, -------, fl. 1878. 83462

Bullock, Alexander Hamilton, 1816-1882. 9133

Bullock, Cynthia, b. 1821. 9134

Bullock, Jonathan Russell, 1815-1899. 9135, 70641, 70643 see also Rhode Island. Commissioner for Adjusting the Accounts of the State Against the United States. Rhode Island. Committee on the Registered State Debt.

Bullock, W. H., 1837- see Hall, William Henry Bullock, 1837-

Bullock, William, fl. 1649. (9145)

Bullock, William, fl. 1808-1828. (9136)-9144, 9219, 48420, 50115

Bullot, -------. 31282

Bulls and bears in Wall Street. 83587-83588

Bulls and bears of New York. 83574

Bulls and the bears. 54138

Bulls and the Jonathans. (59193)

Bull-us, Hector. pseud. Diverting history. see Paulding, James Kirke, 1778-1860.

Bullus, Oscar. USN 9147

Bully. 89119

Bully of the woods. 90009

Bulose, M. 9148A

Bulow, Adam Heinrich Dietrich von. see Bulow, Dietrich, i. e. Adam Heinrich Dietrich, Freiherr von, 1757-1807.

Bulow, Alexander, Freiherr von. 9150-9152, 17016

Bulow, Dietrich, i. e. Adam Heinrich Dietrich, Freiherr von, 1757-1807. 9149

Bulwar, E. L. 93914

Bulwark of truth. 25677

Bulwer, -------, fl. 1850. (52746)

Bulwer, -------, fl. 1868. 94260

Buma, Johannes Acronius van. 9153

Bump, Orlando Franklin, 1841-1884. ed. 34914

Bumper, a country justice. pseud. Americans roused. see Sewall, Jonathan, 1728-1796.

Bumper, a country justice. pseud. Cure for the spleen. see Sewall, Jonathan, 1728-1796.

Bumpus, Amaziah. 9154

Bumstead, George. 9155-9156

Bunce, Oliver Bell, 1828-1890. 9157-9158, 72982-72985

Bunch, -------. 9159, 16887 see also Great Britain. Consulate. Charleston, S. C.

Bundelcund. pseud. Protective system considered. see Burke, Edmund, 1809-1882.

Bundero, Gottlieb. 93112

Bundes-Staatsrecht der Vereinigten Staaten von Nord-Amerika. (49860)

Bundes-Verfassung der Vereinigten Staaten von Nordamerika. 2563

Bundle of facts. 104820

Bundy, Jonas Mills, 1835-1891. (9160), 2d note after 90642

Bungay, George Washington, 1818-1892. 9161-9163

Bungener, Laurence Louis Felix, 1814-1874. (9164)-9166, 41169, (41172)

Bunian, Joh. see Bunyan, John, 1628-1688.

Bunker, Elihu S. 9167

Bunker, Samuel. claimant 51752

Bunker Hill. 84162

Bunker Hill. A poem. 47465

Bunker Hill boy. pseud. Some fresh suggestions. see Griffin, John Q. A.

"Bunker Hill" contest, A. D. 1826. 60944

Bunker Hill declaration. September 10, 1840. 9170, note after 102315

Bunker Hill monument. 9169

Bunker Hill Monument Association. (9174)

Bunker Hill Monument Association. Directors. 9175, 102319 see also Webster, Daniel, 1782-1852.

Bunker Hill Monument Association. President. 9170, note after 102315 see also Webster, Daniel, 1782-1852.

Bunker Hill; or, the death of General Warren. (9271)-9272

Bunker Hill speech. 88910

Bunker Hill Soldiers' Relief Society, Charlestown, Mass. 9172, 12094

Bunker Hill. The monument. 9173

Bunker's Hill. Extract from the third book of 'Washington.' 9168

Bunkley, Josephine M. 9183

Bunn, Alfred, 1796?-1860. (9184)

Bunn, Matthew, b. 1772. (9185)-9186

Bunnell, David C., b. 1793. 9187

Bunner, E. 9188

Bunner, Rudolph, 1779-1837. 9189, 99276

Bunone, Jo. 9094

Bunsen, Christian Karl Josias, Freiherr von, 1791-1860. 9190, 36335

Bunster, Grosvenor. RN 9191

Bunting, R. F. 9192

Buntline, Ned. pseud. see Judson, Edward Z. C., 1822-1886.

Bunyan, John. pseud. Letter to Charles Sumner. 40433

Bunyan, John, 1628-1688. 62847-62849, 71341

Buonaparte in the West Indies. 91235

Buonaparte's campaign. 101236

Buonaventura, F. de San. see San Buenaventura, F. de.

Buoncompagni, Ugo. see Gregory XIII, Pope, 1502-1585.

Buonfiglio Costanzo, Giuseppe, 17th cent. (9193)

Buqcellos. pseud. Beau traites. see Blocquel, Simon.

Buqcellos. pseud. Nouvel abrege. see Blocquel, Simon.
Burbank, Caleb. (9194)-(9195)
Burbank, Caleb, 1761-1869. defendant at court martial (9196)
Burbank, Gardner. 47987
Burbank, Gardner. defendant at court martial 9197
Burcardus. see Brocardus, --------.
Burch, Samuel. (9198)-9199, 15531
Burch, William. 34836
Burchard, ----------, fl. 1844. 95124
Burchard, Charles. 9200
Burchard, Jededeah. (9201)
Burchard, Nathan. (9202)
Burchard, Samuel Dickinson, 1812-1891. 9203
Burchell, William Fitzer. 9204
Burchett, Josiah, 1666?-1746. 9205-9207, 41072
Burck, August. (9208)
Burck, William. see Bourke, William. supposed author
Burcke, Guilermo. see Burke, William, fl. 1805-1810.
Burckhardt, Ed. tr. (48904)
Burd Orphan Asylum of St. Stephen's Church, Philadelphia. see Philadelphia. Burd Orphan Asylum.
Burdell case. 9210
Burden and heat of the day. 88896
Burden of the south. 9309, 9311, note after 90461
Burder, George, 1752-1832. 9211, 46307
Burdett, Charles, b. 1815. (9212)-9214
Burdick, William. 9215-(9216)
Burdick & Co. firm see Erving, Burdick & Co. firm publishers
Burdock, Kenneth B. ed. 103923
Burdon, William, 1764-1818. tr. 23059
Bure, J. J. de. (8784)
Bureau, Allyre. tr. 69029, 69034
Bureau d'Agence de l'Administration des Tontines & Loteries-Immobiliaires. 96173
Bureau d'Agriculture du Bas-Canada. see Quebec (Province) Board of Agriculture.
Bureau of Engraving and Printing and its head. 90579
Bureau of Information and Employment. June 14, 1865. 76617, 76647
Bureau of Ordnance and Hydrography, . . . Washington. (33465)
Buren, ------- van. see Van Buren, ---------.
Buren, Abraham van. see Van Buren, Abraham, 1807-1873.
Buren, J. van. see Van Buren, J.
Buren, John van. see Van Buren, John, 1810-1866.
Buren, Martin van. see Van Buren, Martin, Pres. U. S., 1782-1862.
Buren, W. H. van. see Van Buren, W. H.
Burford, Robert, 1791-1861. 9137, 9218-9219, 48420, 54242, (55114), 67001, 85346
Burgain, F. A. 59516
Burgain, Luis Antonio, 1812-1876. 9220-9221
Burge, William, 1787-1849. 9222-9225
Burger, Ernest Moritz. 9226
Burger, G. U. tr. 25517
Burger, Louis. (9227), 53529 see also U. S. Committee to Investigate the Capacities and Advantages of the New McCarty Gun.
Burger te Amsterdam. pseud. Missive. 49567
Burger van Amsterdam. pseud. Brief. 7910

Burgerkrieg in den Nordamerikanischen Staaten. 77533
Burgerkrieg und das Christliche Leben in Nord-Amerika. (77495)
Burgerlijke en handelkundige geschiedenis. 21903
Burges, Bartholomew. 9228
Burges, Frances. appellant 99975
Burges, Thomas. 79523
Burges, Tristram, 1770-1853. 7060, 9232-9235, 63427, 71751
Burges, Tristram, 1770-1853. petitioner (78855)
Burges, Walter S. 20649, 1st note after 97484
Burgess, Chalon, 1817-1903. 9236
Burgess, Daniel, 1645-1713. 9237-9238, 46501
Burgess, Ebenezer, 1790-1870. (9239)-9241, 19212. 19898, 81778
Burgess, Edward, 1848-1891. 78531
Burgess, G. C. (59557)
Burgess, George, Bp., 1809-1866. 3720, 9242-9243, (20385), 20394-20395, 47243, 66194, 88253
Burgess, George, Bp., 1809-1866. supposed author 92861
Burgess, Sir James Bland, Bart., 1752-1824. supposed author 40603, 2d note after 93312
Burgess, S. A. 83054, 83119
Burgess, Thomas, successively Bp. of St. Davids, and Salisbury, 1756-1837. 81940
Burgess, Wilson. 9244, 10675
Burgess genealogy. 2940
Burgh, James, 1714-1776. 9245-9246, note after 98483
Burgher and Antiburgher Seceders. see Associate-Reformed Synod of North America.
Burghley, William Cecil, Lord, 1520-1598. 90233, 90236-90237, 90246
Burgkmair, Hans, 1473-1531. 90127, 99363
Burgoa, Francisco de, 1605-1681. (9247)-9248
Burgoyne, John, 1730-1792. 1367, 7872, 9250-9260, 9266, 18348, (26320), 27144, 27188, 39708-39710, note after 41332, 66634, 69549, 69717, 87291, 89184, 101481, 101687
Burgoyne, John, 1730-1792. supposed author 9249
Burgoyne, John, 1730-1792. incorrectly supposed author 11304
Burgoyne's surrendery. 86895
Burgtheater, Vienna. see Vienna. Burgtheater.
Burguiza, P. Munoz Ledo y. see Munoz Ledo y Burguiza, P.
Burgwin, H. 9268
Burgy, J. J. 9269
Buried millions. 82806
Buried valley. (47442)
Burk, Edward. 9270
Burk, John Daly, d. 1808. (9271)-9273, 10216
Burk, John Daly, d. 1808. incorrectly supposed author 7184
Burkart, Josef, 1798-1874. 9275-9277
Burke, Aedanus, 1743?-1802? 9278-(9280), 13118, 13128, 56486, 69685, 86138 note just before 87733,
Burke, Andrew. publisher 9281
Burke, Catharine. see Mary St. Thomas, Mother.
Burke, Rev. Edmund. 17594, 69501, 90377
Burke, Edmund, 1729?-1797. 62, 65-66, 1614, 4203, 4385, 5007, 9282-9290, 9292-9295, 9296-9304, 11154, 11157, 11158, (11767), (15052), 17598, 25341, 27209, (28769), 32125, 32162, 42946, (48940), 55518,

56488, 69470, 69549, 80039, 80042,
80577, 89210, 92196, 92842, 95692,
97350, 97353, note after 96403, 98349,
100754, 103959, 104186, 105483
Burke, Edmund, 1729?-1797. supposed author
15030, 23354
Burke, Edmund, 1729?-1797. incorrectly
supposed author 96145
Burke, Edmund, 1809-1882. 9305, (59039),
70725 see also U. S. Patent Office.
Commissioner.
Burke, Edward. 9306
Burke, Edward. tr. 101017
Burke, Emily P. 9307
Burke, Francis. defendant 9308
Burke, Glendy. 88298
Burke, John, 1787-1848. 78640
Burke, John, author of the History of Virginia.
see Burk, John Daly, d. 1808.
Burke, John, d. 1873. 9309-9311, note after
90461
Burke, Peter, 1811-1881. 9312
Burke, Richard, d. 1794. supposed author
9282-9289, 98349
Burke, Thomas A., b. 1828. ed. (9313)
Burke, W. B. defendant 96811
Burke, William, M. D. (9317)-9319, 50469-
50470
Burke, William, 1752-1836. 9316
Burke, William, d. 1898. supposed author
20684, 40263, 40293, 40862, 69470,
98349
Burke, William, fl. 1805-1810. (9209), (9314)-
9315, 100594
Burke, William A. 6943
Burke, William S. 9320
Burke and Alvord memorial. 6943
Burke's guide. 9281
Burke's weekly for boys and girls. (9313)
Burkhard Roslern, W. E. tr. 39582
Burkhart, Gustav Emil. 9321
Burkitt, Henry Lemuel, 1818- (9323)
Burkitt, Lemuel. (9322)-(9323)
Burkitt, William, 1650-1703. 53412
Burlamaque, Frederico Leopoldo Cesar, 1803-
1866. ed. 56370
Burleigh. pseud. Old Colony railroad. see
Smith, Matthew Hale, 1810-1879.
Burleigh. pseud. Sunny side of life insurance.
see Smith, Matthew Hale, 1810-1879.
Burleigh, Charles Calistus, 1810-1878. 9324,
(63463), 95509
Burleigh, Clements. 47436
Burleigh, Joseph Bartlett. (9325)
Burleigh, Walter Atwood, 1820-1896. 9326-
9327
Burleigh, William Henry, 1812-1871. 9328-
9330, 55369, 70023
"Burleigh," of the "Boston journal." pseud.
Caesarism. see Smith, Matthew Hale,
1810-1879.
"Burleigh," of the Boston 'journal.' pseud.
Life insurance illustrated. see Smith,
Matthew Hale, 1810-1879.
Burlesque. 75677
Burlesque account (in verse). (21101)
Burlesque campaign life of Geo. B. McClellan.
note after 43024
Burlesque life of Abraham Lincoln. 41177
Burlesque medley. 93282
Burlseque on Byron. (13435)
Burlseque on 'Symmes' theory of concentric
spheres. (78544)
Burley Grove, the highwayman. alias see
Allen, James. defendant
Burling, Cath. 7879

Burling, Edward. 9331
Burlingame, Anson, 1820-1870. 8910, 9332-
9333, note after 89215
Burlings, E. 103069
Burlington, Iowa. Board of Trade. 9334
Burlington, Mass. School Committee. 9336
Burlington, N. J. College. see Burlington
College, Burlington, N. J.
Burlington, N. J. Court of Bishops Assembled
for the Trial of the Rt. Rev. George
Washington Doane, 1852. see Protestant
Episcopal Church in the U. S. A. House
of Bishops. Court for the Trial of
Bishop George Washington Doane, Bur-
lington, N. J., 1852.
Burlington, N. J. Court of Oyer and Terminer.
96851
Burlington, N. J. Convention, 1776. see New
Jersey. Convention, Burlington, 1776.
Burlington, N. J. Indian Conference, 1758.
see New Jersey (Colony) Indian Confer-
ence, Burlington, 1758.
Burlington, N. J. Library. 28453, 39817,
66735, 66743
Burlington, N. J. St. Mary's Hall. see St.
Mary's Hall, Burlington, N. J.
Burlington, N. J. Supreme Court. see New
Jersey (Colony) Supreme Court, Bur-
lington.
Burlington, Vt. (9338)-(9339), (9341)
Burlington, Vt. Charter. (9339)
Burlington, Vt. First Congregational Church.
9340
Burlington, Vt. Mayor. (9338)
Burlington, Vt. Ordinances, etc. (9339)
Burlington, Vt. Selectmen. (9341)
Burlington (Diocese) Synod. 72936
Burlington almanack for . . . 1776. 53165
Burlington and Mississippi Railroad in Iowa.
35031
Burlington Book Company. publishers 99076-
99077, 99079, 99083, 99094-99096
Burlington College, Burlington, N. J. 9337
Burlington College, Burlington, N. J. Prepara-
tory School. 9337
Burlington College, Burlington, N. J. Social
Library. 9337
Burlington College, Burlington, N. J. Trustees.
9337
Burlington College; as adapted to the training
of pastors. 20391
Burlington Island Association. see Burlington
Island Land Association.
Burlington Island Land Association. 9342
Burlington Island Land Association. petitioners
51925
Burlington Smiths. A family history. 83776
Burlington Social Library. see Burlington
College, Burlington, N. J. Social Library.
Burlington Yearly Meeting. see Friends,
Society of. Burlington Yearly Meeting.
Burman, Johannes, 1706-1779. 3943, 63459
Burmannus, Johannes. see Burman, Johannes,
1706-1779.
Burmeister, German. see Burmeister, Her-
mann, i. e. Karl Hermann Konrad, 1807-
1892.
Burmeister, Hermann, i. e. Karl Hermann
Konrad, 1807-1892. 8993, 9344-9352
Burmeister, Karl Hermann Konrad. see Bur-
meister, Hermann, i. e. Karl Hermann
Konrad, 1807-1892.
Burn, Andrew, 1742-1814. 9353
Burn, Andrew, 1742-1814. supposed author
102865
Burn, David. 9354

Burn, J. (9356)
Burn, J. I. 9355
Burn, John Southerden, 1798-1870. 9357
Burnaby, Andrew, 1734?-1812. 1367, 9358-
9361, 62957
Burnaby, Sir William Crisp Hood, Bart., d.
1853. (9362)
Burnam, C. F. 32553
Burnap, George Washington, 1802-1859. 9363-
9364, (45211A)
Burnap, Jacob, 1748-1821. 9365-(9366), 9368,
note before 89405
Burnap, Uzziah Cicero, 1794-1854. (9367)
(78480)
Burnay, Jacob. see Burnap, Jacob, 1748-
1821.
Burnel, N. N. 9369
Burnell, George Pratt. 9370
Burnet, David Gouverneur, 1788-1870. 94962,
94968, 95023, 95107 see also Texas
(Republic) President, 1836 (Burnet)
Burnet, David Gouverneur, 1788-1870. sup-
posed author 95107
Burnet, Gilbert, Bp. of Salisbury, 1643-1715.
(9371)-9372, note before 14379, 46709,
50546, (78444)-(78445), 78448, 81492,
86717
Burnet, Jacob, 1770-1853. 9373
Burnet, John. 104337
Burnet, John R. (20484)
Burnet, Matthias, 1749-1806. 9375-(9376)
Burnet, William, 1688-1729. 9377, 53199,
78904 see also Massachusetts (Colony)
Governor, 1725-1729 (Burnet) New Jersey
(Colony) Governor, 1720-1725 (Burnet)
Burnet House city guide book, and railroad and
steamboat directory. (9374)
Burnett, ----------. defendant 67822
Burnett, ----------, fl. 1840. 65436
Burnett, Alfred, b. 1823 or 4. 9379
Burnett, H. L. 9381 see also U. S. Judge
Advocate General's Office (Army)
Burnett, Henry Cornelius, 1825-1866. 9380
Burnett, Joseph. 88255
Burnett, Peter Hardeman, 1807-1895. 9382
Burnett, W. I. 1120
Burnett, Ward B. 9384
Burnett, Sir William, 1779-1861. 9383
Burnett, Drake & Co. firm publishers 9385
Burnett, Drake & Co.'s bank note reporter.
9385
Burney, James, 1750-1821. 8427, 9380-9390,
23494, 55448
Burnham, Abraham. 9391
Burnham, Alfred Avery, 1819-1879. 9392
Burnham, Amos Wood. 9393
Burnham, Avis A. see Stanwood, Avis A.
(Burnham)
Burnham, George Pickering, 1814-1902. 9304,
21432, 92751
Burnham, Louis W. 72381
Burnham, Richard, 1711-1752. (9395)
Burnham, William, 1684-1750. 9396
Burnham's Commercial and Mathematical
Institute, Rockford, Ill. 72381
Burnier, L. tr. 2793
Burning and shining light extinguished. 22129
Burning bush. 103510
Burning fen. 72763
Burning of Chambersburg, Pennsylvania.
77731
Burning of Columbia, S. C. 96799
Burning of Schenectady, a poem. 92763
Burning of Schenectady, and other poems.
92764
Burning of Sodom. 83428

Burning of the Ephesian letters. 62772
Burning of the Lexington in Long Island Sound.
40895
Burning of the Maine Asylum. 33867
Burnings bewailed. 47744
Burnley, William Hardin. 9397-9399
Burnouf, --------. ed. 70377-(70378)
Burns, Anthony. defendant 6505, 9404
Burns, David. 9402
Burns, Jabez, 1805-1876. 9403-9404
Burns, James. illus. 72646
Burns, James R. (9405)
Burns, Julia (Flake) 84734, 84910
Burns, Lewis. defendant at court martial
96841
Burns, R. T. 9409
Burns, Robert, 1759-1796. 9407
Burns, Rev. Robert, fl. 1844. 9408
Burns, Robert Ferrier, 1826-1896. (44452)
Burns, W. Scott. 9410
Burns, William W. USA 83789
Burns Celebration. Celebration of the hundredth
anniversary of the birth of Robert Burns.
9407
Burns Club of Boston. 9407
Burns Club of the City of New York. 17965
Burns Club of Washington, D. C. 9407
Burns Club of Washington City. Celebration
of the centennial anniversary of the birth
of Robert Burns. 9407
Burns Ranche Gold Mining Company. (66976)
Burnside, Ambrose Everett, 1824-1881. 2052,
9411-9412, 70602, 70642, 70658 see also
Rhode Island. Governor, 1866-1896
(Burnside)
Burnside, Samuel McGregore, 1783-1850. 9413-
9414, 105360
Burnyeat, John, 1631-1690. note after 7264,
9415-9417, 25363-(25364)
Burpee, E. R. 9418
Burr, Aaron, 1716-1757. 9419-9423, 71320,
(73402)-73404, 93820
Burr, Aaron, 1756-1836. 5906, 7882, 9214,
(9424), 9426, 9430-9431, 9433-(9435),
18864, (34385), note after 53697, 74878,
note after 83791, note before 96930A,
96572, 104541
Burr, Aaron, 1756-1836. defendant 9434,
95607, 104883, 105043
Burr, Charles Chauncey, 1817-1883. 9436-9437,
26773, (41399), 55345, 55967
Burr, David H., 1803-1875. 9438-9439, 19873
Burr, Fearing. (9440)
Burr, Jonathan. 9441
Burr, L. S. (9442)
Burr, Samuel Jones. 9443
Burr, William. 9444
Burr Seminary, Manchester, Vt. 9445, 44223
Burrage, Henry Sweetser, 1837-1926. 9446,
(73290)
Burriel, Andres Marcos, 1719-1762. ed. 98848
Burrill, George Rawson, 1770-1818. 9447-9448
Burrill, James. 2074, 70689
Burrill, Joseph. incorrectly supposed author
6711, 9449, 21088, 42824, 1st note after
99800
Burrill, William. 98474
Burrillville; as it was, and as it is. (37126)
Burrington, George. 9450
Burritt, Elihu, 1810-1879. 9451-9454, 88295-
88296, 92489, 92558, 92572, 93683
Burritt, Elijah Hinsdale, 1794-1838. 83541
Burrough, Edward, 1634-1662. 9445, 9462,
(33362)

Burroughes, Jeremiah, 1599-1646. 9463,
21991, 27952-27954, 51773, (69679),
74624, 91393, 104343 see also Church
of Scotland. General Assembly. Com-
mission.
Burroughs, Charles, 1787-1868. 9456-(9460)
Burroughs, Cornelius. 9461
Burroughs, Eden, 1738-1813. (18879), 99021,
105488
Burroughs, Edward. see Burrough, Edward,
1634-1662.
Burroughs, Jeremy. see Burroughes,
Jeremiah, 1599-1646.
Burroughs, John, 1837-1921. 9464
Burroughs, Peleg. 9465
Burroughs, S. 9468
Burroughs, Stephen, 1765-1840. (9466)-9467
Burroughs, W. 55496
Burroughsian Lyceum. see Medina Academy.
Burroughsian Lyceum.
Burrowes, Edward. 104337
Burrowes, Thomas Henry, 1805-1871. 9469-
9470, 59994, 60075, 60371, 60449
Burrow, E. J. 9471
Burrows, George. 9472
Burrows, John Lansing, 1814-1893. 9473-9476
Burrows, John S. see Burrows, John Lan-
sing, 1814-1893.
Burrows, R. L. 9477
Burrows, Silas E. defendant 9478, 96842
Burrows Brothers Company. firm publishers
95396, 101219
Burr's conspiracy exposed. 104028
Burr's map of New-York. 9439
Burr's moving mirror of the lakes. 9444
Burs, William Pitt. 9479, 15648
Bursted Chase. 95244
Bursting of Pierre Magray's La Salle bubble.
79996
Burt, --------, fl. 1817. note after 99131
Burt, --------, fl. 1858. 57749
Burt, Adam. 9480
Burt, Federal. 9481
Burt, J. 8433
Burt, J. G. 57068
Burt, J. H. 9484
Burt, Jarius, 1795-1857. 9483
Burt, John, 1716-1775. 9482
Burt, Nathaniel Clark, 1825-1874. 9485
Burt, William A. 9486, 38676
Burt, William L. (9487)
Burt. firm publishers see Fay, Davison
and Burt. firm publishers
Burt (A. L.) firm publisher 100482
Burtis, W. R. M. 9488
Burton, ----------. 38184, 95751 see also
Society for the Propagation of the Gospel
in Foreign Parts, London. Secretary.
Burton, ----------, fl. 1845-1855. 84241
Burton, A. D. 76191
Burton, Amos. 9489
Burton, Asa, 1752-1836. (9490)
Burton, C. 9491
Burton, Charles. RN 36695
Burton, Eleanor. 90577
Burton, J. E. 9493
Burton, J. W. ed. 18548
Burton, John, 1696-1771. 9492, 83978
Burton, John Hill, 1809-1881. 9494-9495
Burton, Nathaniel Judson, 1822-1887. 9496
Burton, R. tr. pseud. see Crouch,
Nathaniel, 1632?-1725?
Burton, Richard, 17th cent. pseud. see
Crouch, Nathaniel, 1632?-1725?
Burton, Sir Richard Francis, 1821-1890. 9497-
9498, (44515), 58519, 90060

Burton, Robert, 17th cent. pseud. see Crouch,
Nathaniel, 1632?-1725?
Burton, Robert, fl. 1831. 9503
Burton, Warren, 1800-1866. 9504-(9508), note
after 103490
Burton, William Evans, 1802-1860. 9509,
83778
Burton; or the sieges. (34773)
Burton's gentleman's magazine. 83778
Burt's library of the world's best books.
100482
Burtt, John. 9510
Buruaga, Francisco Solano Asta. see Solano
Asta-Buruaga, Francisco, 1817-1892.
Burunda, Joseph Erazu, de. see Erazu,
Joseph, de Burunda.
Burwell, --------. 100896
Burwell, William Armistead, 1806-1821. 8511-
8512
Burwell, William B. see Burwell, William
Armistead, 1806-1821.
Burwell, William MacCready, 1809-1888. 9513-
(9514), (71194)
Bury, --------. (9517)
Bury, Richard. 9515-9516
Bury, William Coutts Kepel, Viscount. (37598)
Bury's genealogical account of the family of
Leck or Leake. (9517)
Busby, Dr. pseud. State triumvirate. see
Verplanck, Gulian Crommelin.
Busch, Mortiz, 1821-1899. 9518-9520
Busching, Anton Friedrich, 1724-1793. 21748
Buschmann, E. tr. 1945
Buschmann, Johann Karl Eduard, 1805-1880.
9521-9531
Busey, Samuel Claggett, 1828-1901. (9532)
Bush, Charles Peck. 72342
Bush, George, 1796-1859. 9533, 9794, 31732,
52575
Bush, Henry. defendant 96943
Bush, James Smith, 1825-1889. 9534
Bush, Philip. petitioner 73625
Bush in the flame. 79746
Bush that burned with fire. 20387, 20391
Bushe, George. ed. 54814
Bushe, Gervase Parker. supposed author
9637, 11311
Bushee, James. 84971
Bushel, John. 9535
Bushnell, Albert. 9536
Bushnell, Charles Ira, 1826-1883. 4747, 4748,
(5877), 8564, (9537)-9541, (14160), 24719,
(30948), 39861, 47396, (50309)-50311,
(51852), 83998, 93861
Bushnell, Horace, 1802-1876. 9542-9549, 10001,
27409
Bushnell, William. 9550-9551
Bushnell, William H., 1823- 9552-9553
Bushrod Washington. 5473
Business advertiser and general directory of
the city of Chicago. (12639)
Business and diversion inoffensive to God.
78696
Business and literature in account with Ameri-
can education. 4571
Business and resident directory of Leavenworth.
39549
Business arrangements of the Smithsonian
Institution. 85004
Business chart. 83884, 83886
Business chart, showing the course of business.
83885
Business directories of the principal commer-
cial cities. 37301
Business directory. (13677), 54459

Business directory and gazetteer of the towns
and villages on the Albany and Susque-
hanna Railroad. 7103
Business directory and gazetteer to the towns
on the Albany and Susquehanna Railroad.
9555
Business directory, and review of the city of
Burlington, Iowa. 9335
Business-directory and statistics of the city
of Chicago. (12640)
Business directory. 1868-9. 18023
Business directory . . . 1867-8. 54459
Business directory, etc. [of Davenport, Iowa.]
18722
Business directory, &c., . . . of Dedham and
Brighton. 8251
Business directory for 1844 [for Cincinnati.]
13085
Business directory for 1864-65. 19005
Business directory for Portsmouth. 55478
Business directory for the city of Saint John.
75273
Business directory, for the Mississippi valley:
1844. 37761
Business directory for the year 1847. 10117
Business directory of Cayuga Co. 7104
Business directory of Chemung County.
(22359)
Business directory of Chicago. 12619
Business directory of Essex, Hudson and
Union Counties, N. J. 7122
Business directory of Lewiston Falls. 72065
Business directory of . . . Manchester.
44207
Business directory of . . . New Jersey. 53077
Business . . . directory . . . of New York,
Boston, Philadelphia, Baltimore, &c. &c.
(80136)
Business directory of . . . New York, Phila-
delphia, Boston, and Baltimore. 54459
Business directory of over one hundred cities
and villages. 53547
Business directory of St. Louis. 75346
Business directory of [ten] counties of . . .
Pa. 59923
Business directory of the cities of New York,
Philadelphia, Boston, and Baltimore.
(13587)
Business directory of the cities of Richmond,
Petersburg, Norfolk, and Portsmouth,
Virginia. (71174)
Business directory of the city of New York
and vicinity. 8560
Business directory of the city [of Peoria.]
20965
Business directory of the counties of Berks,
Lebanon, Leigh, Northampton, and
Schuylkill, Pa. 7105
Business directory of the five great cities of
California and Oregon. 26813
Business directory of the principal southern
cities. 9554
Business directory of the states and territories.
38131
Business directory of York County [Maine.]
5227
Business done through Buffalo on the Erie
Canal. 3846
Business guide and city directory of Mansfield,
Ohio. 44386
Business guide and history of Richland County.
73437
Business lists of Boston. (16373)
Business man's directory. 13668
Business man's guide. 61837

Business man's guide to the post offices in the
United States. 64502
Business Men of Chicago. see Chicago.
Business Men.
Business men's almanac. 58381
Business mirror. 13085
Business register, map, street directory, etc.
12641
Business register of manufacturers. 9556,
45662
Business register of northern firms. 9554
Business register of the principal manufac-
turers. (13587)
Business sketches. 50243
Business view of the question before us. 45619
Busk, Hans, 1815-1882. 9557
Busk, M. M. 9558
Buss, Franz Joseph, Ritter von, 1803-1878.
9559, 92291
Bussaeus, A. tr. 36637
Busse, Johann Heinrich. tr. 77125
Bussiere, Marie Theodore Renouard, Vicomte
de, 1802-1865. 9560-9561
Bussola, --------. 76897
Bussy, -------. 104002
Bustamante, Antoine Sanchez de. see Sanchez
de Bustamante, Antoine.
Bustamante, Ambrosius de. 86445
Bustamante, Anastasio. 9563-9565
Bustamante, Carlos Maria de, 1774-1848. 714,
6835, 9567-9585, 11613, 27753, 31730,
35318-35319, 39294, 40060, 44189,
(44427), (48310), 48315, 48482, 51444,
52207, 63745, 74945, 74949-74950, 74952,
76277, 76727, 86562, 94846, 2d note after
98255, note after 98763, note after 99675
Bustamante, Javier Aquiler. 9586-9588
Bustamante, Jose Luis, d. 1857. 9589-9593
Bustamante, Jose Maria. 9594
Bustamante Carlos, Calixto. 9566
Bustamante y Guerra, Jose de. 29096 see also
Guatemala (Colony) Gobernador, 1811-1818
(Bustamante y Guerra)
Bustamante, Carlos Maria de. see Bustamante,
Carlos Maria de, 1774-1848.
Bustamante, Fernando Vello de. ed. 27773,
27800
Bustamante, Jose Lopez de. tr. 33720
Bustamente y Tagle, --------. 65931
Busteed, G. W. (9596)-9597
Busteed, Richard, 1822-1898. 9598-9599
Busteed, Richard, 1822-1898. defendant 83872-
83873
Bustillo, Juan Gonzalez. see Gonzalez Bus-
tillo, Juan.
Bustleton Division, No. 173, Sons of Temper-
ance. see Sons of Temperance of North
America. Pennsylvania. Bustleton Divi-
sion, No. 173.
Busto, Alejo Vanegas de. see Vanegas de
Busto, Alejo.
Busto, Francisco Gonzalez de. see Gonzalez
de Bustos, Francisco, fl. 1665.
Busy bees. 52305, 57542, 76692
Bute, John Stuart, 3d Earl of, 1713-1792. supposed
author 20684, 40263, 40293, 60862, 69470
Butel-Dumont, George Marie, 1725-1788. 9601-
9604, 27215, 30794-30795, 34027, 2d note
after 65324, note after 97656
Butel-Dumont, George Marie, 1725-1788. sup-
posed author 35958
Butin, James. 9606
Butler, Andrew Pickens, 1796-1857. 9607
Butler, Arthur Gardiner, 1844- 28401, 71032

Butler, Benjamin Franklin, 1795-1858. 614, 9608-9611, 13621, (43437), (53951), 54707, 66044, 89926 see also Committee of Merchants and Bankers of the City of New York. U. S. Department of Justice.
Butler, Benjamin Franklin, 1795-1858. supposed author 98425
Butler, Benjamin Franklin, 1818-1893. 1481, (6977), 9612-9616, 9621-9622, 19515, 19904-19905, 28909, (39376), 62784
Butler, Caleb, 1776-1854. 1492, (4338), 9623-9626, 28965, 28976, 42460, 60842
Butler, Clement Moore, 1810-1890. 9627-9630, 13562, 85100
Butler, David, fl. 1805-1806. 9631
Butler, David, 1829-1891. 52185 see also Nebraska. Governor, 1867-1870 (Butler)
Butler, Frances Ann (Kemble) see Kemble, Frances Ann, 1809-1893.
Butler, Francis Eugene, 1825-1863. 9636
Butler, Frederick, 1766?-1843. 9634-9635
Butler, George B., fl. 1769. supposed author 9637, 11311
Butler, George Bernard, 1809-1886. 9638-9639
Butler, Henry E. 9640
Butler, J. 96280
Butler, James, 1755-1842? 9641-9642
Butler, James Davie, 1815-1905. (9643)-9645
Butler, James Glentworth, 1821-1916. 9649-9647
Butler, John, successively Bp. of Oxford, and Hereford, 1717-1802. 9648-9650, 97161
Butler, Joseph, successively Bp. of Bristol, and Durham, 1692-1752. (6951)
Butler, Mann, 1784-1852. 9652-9655, 17589
Butler, Mary (Philips) defendant 62457
Butler, Nathaniel. supposed author 82862
Butler, Noble, 1819-1882. (9656)
Butler, Ovid, Bp. 82803.
Butler, P. M. 9658
Butler, Pierce, 1744-1822. 87539
Butler, Pierce, 1807-1867. plaintiff 9657
Butler, Pierce Mason, 1798-1847. 87667 see also South Carolina. Governor, 1836-1838 (Butler)
Butler, Richard. 96598 see also U. S. Commissioners to the Six Nations of Indians.
Butler, Roderick Random, b. 1830? 9659
Butler, Rose. defendant 90183
Butler, Samuel. 9660
Butler, Samuel, 1612-1680. 77887
Butler, Samuel Worcester, 1823-1874. 18872, 47310, 84449
Butler, Thomas. USA 94745
Butler, William. defendant 96847
Butler, William, 17th cent. 104336
Butler, William, fl. 1866. 70609
Butler, William Allen, 1825-1902. 9661-(9663A), (41279), 56223, (67516), 95595,
Butler, William Orlando, 1791-1880. 9664
Butler & Roberts. firm engravers 84237
Butler Hospital for the Insane, Providence, R. I. see Providence, R. I. Butler Hospital for the Insane.
Butman, -------. (51797)
Butron, Jacinto Moran de. see Moran de Butron, Jacinto, 1668-1749.
Butte des morts. 85428, 3d note after 94249
Butter, ---------, fl. 1855. (71174)
Butter, Henry. 102370
Butter's Richmond directory for 1855. (71174)
Butterfield, Carlos. 9666
Butterfield, Carlos. incorrectly supposed author (9667), 81634

Butterfield, Consul Willshire, 1824-1899. (9668)
Butterfield, H. Q. 9669
Butterflies of North America. 21998
Butterfley hunters. (15089)
Butterfly's ball. 59413
Butterworth, William. pseud. Three years' adventures. see Schroeder, Henry. supposed author
Buttner, Johann Gottfried. 8211, 9671-9678
Button, Sir Thomas, d. 1634. 5195, 61246, (74131)
Buttrick, Tilly, b. 1783. 9679
Butts, B. J. 49803
Butts, Isaac, 1816-1874. 9680
Butts, J. T. 43046
Butz, Caspar. ed. 19794
Butze, E. tr. 21403
Buxton, Charles, 1823-1871. (9682), 9684, (9692)
Buxton, Charles, d. 1833. 9681
Buxton, Sir Thomas Fowell, Bart., 1785-1845. 2459A, 9685-9693, 9695, (17963), 43172, 70902, 104012
Buxton, Maine. 68409
Buxtorf, Johannes, 1599-1664. 89546
Buy a lottery ticket. 101273
Buys, J. F. 9696
Buzzell, John R. defendant 12126, 96843-96844
By a law of the state of Connecticut. 105845
By an act of the legislature, passed at Princeton. 94222
By an act of the legislature, passed Jan. 27, 1824. 105342
By authority. 94741
By authority. A full and correct report of the trial. 64131
By authority of the Bureau of Military Record. 53552
By authority. Official message of His Excellency Gov. A. H. Reeder. 68627
By Brigadier General Stanwix, commanding His Majesty's forces in the Southern District of North America. 90452
By Brigadier General Stanwix, commanding His Majesty's forces in the southern provinces of North-America. 90453
By Captain J. Taylour commander of Her Majesty's Ship Litchfield. 54976, 94549
By Captain White, from Barbados, we have the following advices. 103349
By forme van advijs door een Liefhebber van't Vaderlandt. (7981)
By . . . George Thomas, Esq; . . . a proclamation [announcing the declaration of war with France.] (59936), note after 95396
By . . . George Thomas, Esq; . . . a proclamation [of a day of thanksgiving.] 59937, note after 95396
By . . . George Thomas, Esq; . . . a proclamation [relative to the Indians in Lancaster County.] 59935, note after 95396
By George Washington, President of the United States of America; a proclamation. 96583
By His Excelency [sic] Sir Henry Clinton, K. B. 87368
By His Excellency a proclamation . . . given at Fort Charles. 1523
By His Excellency Arthur Fenner, Esq; Governor, Captain-General, and Commander in Chief, of the State of Rhode-Island. 70559
By His Excellency, Benjamin Fletcher. 53672
By His Excellency George Washington, Esquire. A proclamation. 101692

By His Excellency George Washington, Esq:
Captain-General and Commander in
Chief of the forces of the Thirteen
United States. 101691

By His Excellency George Washington, Esquire, Commander in Chief of the Army
of the United Colonies of North-America.
101689

By His Excellency George Washington, Esq;
General and Commander in Chief of all
the forces. 101696

By His Excellency George Washington, Esquire, General and Commander in Chief
of the forces. 101702

By His Excellency Horatio Sharpe, Esq; Governor and Commander in Chief in and
over the province of Maryland. 45095

By His Excellency Isaac Tichenor, Captain
General, Governor, and Commander in
Chief, in and over the state of Vermont.
99070

By His Excellency, Isaac Tichenor, Esquire,
Governour of the state of Vermont.
99071

By His Excellency James Glen, Esq. 87357

By His Excellency John Cotton Smith, Esq.
82936

By His Excellency . . . John Earl of Dunmore,
His Majesty's Lieutenant and Governor
General of the colony . . . of Virginia
. . . a proclamation. 100000

By His Excellency . . . John Earl of Dunmore,
His Majesty's Lieutenant and Governour-
General of the colony . . . of Virginia
. . . a proclamation . . . given under
my hand, on board the ship William.
100003

By His Excellency . . . John Earl of Dunmore,
His Majesty's Lieutenant, and Governor
of the colony . . . of Virginia. 99999

By His Excellency Moses Robinson, Esquire.
99062

By His Excellency John Rutledge, Esq. 87535

By His Excellency Richard Earl of Bellomont,
Captain General and Governour in Chief
of His Majesties province of New-York.
78201

By His Excellency Richard Earl of Bellomont,
Captain General, and Governour in Chief
of His Majesty's provinces of the
Massachusetts-Bay, &c. in America.
78202

By His Excellency Sir William Howe, K. B.
(33338)

By His Excellency the Governor and Council.
45094

By His Excellency, the Governor, Council and
Assembly of the province of the Massachusetts Bay. (19157), 104088

By His Excellency the Right Honourable Lord
Charles-Grenville Montagu. 87358

By His Excellency Thomas Chittenden, Esquire, Captain-General, Governor and
Commander in Chief in and over the
state of Vermont. A proclamation.
99055

By His Excellency Thomas Chittenden, Esq.
Captain General, Governor, and Commander-in-Chief in and over the state
of Vermont. A proclamation. . . . [I]
appoint Thursday the third day of December next. 99067

By His Excellency Thomas Chittenden, Esq;
Captain-General, Governor and Commander in Chief in and over the state
of Vermont. A proclamation. . . . I

. . . do hereby appoint Wednesday.
99057

By His Excellency Tho. Chittenden, Esq; Captain General, Governor and Commander
in Chief, in and over the state of Vermont, a proclamation. The Supreme
Governor of the universe. 99056

By His Excellency Thomas Chittenden, Esq;
Captain-General, Governor and Commander
in Chief in and over the state of Vermont.
A proclamation. Whereas the . . . exertions of the good people. 99051

By His Excellency Thomas Chittenden, Esq;
Captain-General, Governor, and Commander in Chief, in and over the state
of Vermont, a proclamation. Whereas
the General Court. 99058

By His Excellency Thomas Chittenden, Esquire, Captain-General, Governor and
Commander in Chief, in and over the
state of Vermont, a proclamation. Whereas the legislature of this state at their
session in June last. 99054

By His Excellency Thomas Chittenden, Esq.
Captain General Governor, Commander
in Chief, in and over the state of Vermont. A proclamation. 99068

By His Excellency Thomas Chittenden, Esq.
Governor and Commander in Chief in
and over the state of Vermont. A proclamation. . . . [I] appoint Wednesday,
the nineteenth day of April next. 99069

By His Excellency Thomas Chittenden, Esquire,
Governor, and Commander in Chief, in
and over the state of Vermont. A pro-
clamation. . . . I . . . do hereby appoint,
Wednesday, the twentyseventh day of
April next. 99063

By His Excellency Thomas Chittenden, Esquire,
Governor, Captain-General, and Commander in Chief in and over the state of
Vermont, a proclamation. . . . I do hereby
appoint Thursday the first day of December next. 99064

By His Excellency, Thomas Chittenden, Esq;
Governor, Captain-General and Commander in Chief in and over the state of
Vermont. A proclamation. . . . I . . .
do hereby appoint, Thursday the 27th day
of November next. 99061

By His Excellency Thomas Chittenden, Esquire,
Governor, Captain-General and Commander in Chief in and over the state of
Vermont. A proclamation. . . . I do
hereby appoint Wednesday the ninth day
of April next. 99066

By His Excellency Thomas Chittenden, Esq.
Governor, Captain-General and Commander in Chief, in and over the state of
Vermont, a proclamation. . . . I do hereby
appoint Wednesday, the 10th day of April
next. 99065

By His Excellency Thomas Chittenden, Esq;
Governor and Commander in Chief in
and over the state of Vermont, in America, a proclamation. Amid the many
private and public distresses. 99050

By His Excellency Thomas Chittenden, Esq;
Governor, Captain-General and Commander in Chief in and over the state of
Vermont. A proclamation. Whereas
sundry persons, inhabitants of this state.
99053

By His Excellency Thomas Chittenden, Esq.
Governor, Captain-General and Commander in Chief, in and over the state of

Vermont, a proclamation. Whereas the statute laws are now completed. 99059

By His Excellency Thomas Jefferson, Esq. 100198

By His Excellency's command. 101699

By His Maiesties Councell for Virginia. 99881

By His Maiesties Councell for Virginia. God saue the King. 99875

By His Maiesties Councell for Virginia. Whereas sundrie the aduenturers to Virginia. 99870

By His Maiesties Councell for Virginia. Whereas vpon the returne of Sir Thomas Dale Knight. 99874

By His Maiesties Counseil for Virginia. 99877

By His Maiesties Counsell of Virginea. 99865

By His Majesties Commissioners for Virginia. 4th note after 99888

By His Majesties Counseil for Virginia. 99873

By Isaac Tichenor Governor of the state of Vermont. 99072

By . . . James Hamilton, Esq. 59941

By . . . James Hamilton, Esq; . . . A proclamation [against selling liquor to Indians in Pennsylvania.] 59939

By . . . James Hamilton, Esq; . . . A proclamation [against settlers on Indian lands west of the Blue Hills.] 59940

By . . . James Hamilton, Esquire, Lieutenant Governor. 59942

By John Adams, President of the United States. 96590

By . . . John Penn . . . . A proclamation [of a reward for the arrest of two murderers.] 59944

By . . . John Penn . . . . A proclamation [on the Virginia boundary.] 59948

By . . . John Penn . . . . A proclamation [relative to the Connecticut boundary.] 59945

By . . . John Penn . . . . A proclamation [relative to the Maryland boundary.] 59951

By . . . John Penn . . . . A proclamation [relative to the murder of an Indian called Joseph Wipey.] 59950

By . . . John Penn . . . . A proclamation [revoking the preceding.] 59946, (59947)

By . . . John Penn, Esquire . . . . A proclamation [relative to the Maryland boundary.] 59946-(59947)

By . . . John Penn, Esquire . . . . Given the fifteenth day of September 1774. 59949

By-laws . . . see Bylaws . . .

By Mr. Revere, who left Boston on Friday last. 95991

By order of the Congress, Charles Thomson, Secretary. 93439

By order of the Honourable Brigader General Robert Monckton. (49953)

By . . . Patrick Gordon . . . . A proclamation [against abusing the Indians.] 59932

By . . . Patrick Gordon . . . . A proclamation [against riots in Philadelphia.] 59931

By . . . Patrick Gordon . . . . A proclamation [against the murderers of some Indians.] 59933

By . . . Patrick Gordon . . . . A proclamation [to enforce the riot act.] 59934

By request of the Supreme Council of the Order. 86162

By . . . Robert Hunter Morris, Esq; . . . . A proclamation. 59943

By Seneca White. 103453

By Sir William Keith . . . . A proclamation. (59930)

By the Committee of Arrangements. As the President of the United States will honor this town. 101784

By the Counsell of Virginea. Seeing it hath pleased God. 99861

By the Counsell of Virginia. Whereas the good shippe, called the Hercules. 99857

By the following letters, these facts appear unquestionable. 95997

By the Governor, . . . A proclamation. 100220

By the Governor of the commonwealth of Virginia, a proclamation. The President of the United States having been pleased to communicate to me. 100222

By the Governor of the commonwealth of Virginia.—A proclamation. Whereas it is represented to me. 100219

By the Honourable Collonel [sic] John Evans. (59928)

By the Honourable George Clarke, Esq. 98436

By the Honourable, Gurdon Saltonstall Esq. 15823, 75854

By the Honourable Major General Baron de Steuben. 91393

By the Hon. Robert Dinwiddie, Esq. 99992

By the Honourable Robert Hunter Morris, Esq. 50874

By the Honourable Sir William Gooch, Bart. 99987

By the King. A proclamation concerning tobacco. [1624] 99844

By the King. A proclamation concerning tobacco. [1631] 99851

By the King. A proclamation concerning tobacco. [1637] 99852

By the King. A proclamation declaring His Maiesties pleasure concerning Sir Walter Rawleigh. (67547)

By the King. A proclamation, declaring the cessation of arms. 9697

By the King. A proclamation for restraint of the disordered trading for tobacco. 99842

By the King. A proclamation for setling the plantation of Virginia. 99847

By the King. A proclamation for the ordering of tabacco. 99850

By the King. A proclamation for the suppressing a rebellion. 99853

By the King. [A proclamation for the suspension of the lotteries.] 99843

By the King. A proclamation for the vtter prohibiting the importation and vse of all tobacco. 99845

By the King. A proclamation to restraine the planting of tabacco in England and Wales. 99841

By the King. A proclamation touching the sealing of tobacco. 65936, 99849

By the King. A proclamation touching tobacco. [1625] 99846

By the King. A proclamation touching tobacco. [1627] 99848

By the mail which arrived last evening we have received the following. 87419

By the Mayor, Recorder, and Aldermen. (61543)

By the medium of the cirious numerical machine. 61927

By the . . . President and Counsel of the province of Pennsylvania. 59938

By the President of the United States of America, a proclamation [of a treaty with the Cherokee nation.] 96604

By the President of the United States of America, a proclamation [of a treaty with the Creek nation.] 96603
By the President of the United States of America. A proclamation. Whereas, a treaty between the United States of America, and the Potawatamie Tribe of Indians. 96653
By the President of the United States of America. A proclamation. Whereas articles of agreement between the United States of America, and the Winnebago Tribe. 96657
By the Queen, a proclamation. 9698
By the Reverend old Mr. John Cotton, at Salem. 17050
By the Senate, January 20, 1787. 100149
By the Tresuror, Councell and Company for Virginia. 99876
By the United States of America in Congress assembled. 100210
By the Upper House of Assembly, October 28, 1773. 99908
By virtue of the power and authority in me vested by the constitution. 94755
By whom is the world to be converted? 85265
By William Blount, Governor in and over the territory of the United States of America. 94725
By William Keith . . . . A proclamation. 59929
Byam, Edward Samuel, 1788-1869. supposed author 102811
Byam, George. 9699-9703
Byam, William, 1623-1670? 9704, 76501
Bye-laws. . . . see Bylaws . . .
Byepaths of biography. 7979
Byerley, Sir John. (9141)-(9142)
Byerley, T. 71966
Byers, John. 9705-9706
Byers, Leonard. ed. 61583
Byers, William Newton, 1831-1903. 9707
Byeways, backwoods, and prairies. 2166, 29680
Byfield, Nathanael, 1653-1733. 2547, 9708-9709, 52597-52598
Byington, Cyrus, 1793-1868. 9710, 12863, 12865, 12867, 12876, 12878, 89272-89273, 105533, 105535-105540
Bylaagen specteerende tot het berigt. 93837
Bylaagen ter opheldering van de gedenkzuil der vyverklaaring van de dertien Vereenigde Staaten van Noord-Amerika. 41963
By-law for setting up and regulating a public market. 6733
By-law, rules and regulations, acts and solves [of Boston.] 6613
By-laws adopted by the Managers of the New-Jersey State Lunatic Asylum. (53194)
By laws amended and additional since the publication. 86118
By-laws and act of incorporation of the St. Lawrence Co. Mutual Insurance Co. 75316
By-laws and bill of prices of the Lewis County Medical Society. 40868
By-laws and catalogue of library of the Worcester District Medical Society. 105426
By-laws and catalogue of the Burlington Social Library. 9337
By-laws and certificate of incorporation, of the Long Island Historical Society. 41897
By-laws and general rules and regulations of the Board of Education of . . . . New-York. 54121

By-laws, and list of officers and members, of the Chicago Academy of Sciences. 12618
By-laws and orders of the town of Boston . . . now in force. 6608
By-laws and orders of the town of Boston, passed at a legal town-meeting. (6610)
By-laws and orders of the town of Boston, passed at several legal town meetings. 6612
By-laws and ordinances [of Buffalo, N. Y.] 9063
By-laws and ordinances . . . [of New Bedford, Mass.] 52464
Bye-laws and ordinances of the city of Pittsburgh. 63112
By-laws and ordinances of the Mayor . . . of . . . New York. 54139
By-laws and prospectus of the studies purused therein [i. e. the Utica Academy.] 98235
By-laws and regulations for the Suffolk District Medical Society. 93441
By-laws and regulations for . . . Wills' hospital. 62390
By-laws and regulations of the Firewards of New Bedford. 52457
Bylaws and regulations of the Incorporated Proprietors of the Social Library in Salem. 75745
By-laws and regulations of the Mount Vernon Cemetery Company. 51178
By-laws and regulations of the New Bedford Atheneaum. (52465)
By-laws and regulations [of the New-Bedford Port Society.] 85545
By-laws and regulations of the . . . [New York] Hospital. (54481)
By laws and regulations of the Portland Athenaeum. 64357
By-laws and regulations of the Proprietors of the Social Library in Salem. 75745
By-laws and regulations of the Society for the Relief of Poor Widows with Small Children. 85971-85972
By-laws and regulations of the Trinity House of Montreal. 96987
By-laws and report . . . [of the public schools in Marietta, Ohio.] 44567
By-laws and . . . resolutions of the Controllers of Public Schools. 61561
Bye-laws, and rules and regulations, adapted by the Board of Managers [of the Boston Female Asylum.] 6705
By-laws and rules of Good Will Division, no. 17, Sons of Temperance. 87039
By-laws and rules of order of the Grand Division of Eastern New York. 87060
By-laws and rules of order of the Grand Division S. of T., State of Wisconsin. 87097
By-laws and rules of the New Jersey State Society [of the Cincinnati.] 13116
By-laws and rules . . . of the North-Eastern Agricultural Society. 55707
By-laws and standing rules of the Second Division of the Young Men's Society. (62403)
By-laws and statement of property of the Chicago South Branch Dock Co. 12630
By-laws, and system of education, established at Alleghany College. 777
By-laws and town-orders of the town of Boston. 6609
By-laws certificate of incorporation and officers [of the New York Genealogical and Biographical Society.] (54779)
By-laws, confession of faith, covenant, and catalogue of officers and members of the South Church, Springfield, Mass. 89873-89874

By-laws, Dec. 5, 1843 [of the New England Society of Columbus, Ohio.] 14896

By-laws, established by the Trustees of the State Lunatic Hospital, in Worcester, 1848. 46138

By-laws, &c. of the Callaway Mining and Manufacturing Company. (10054)

By-laws, etc., of the New York Association for the Advancement of Science and Art. (54745)

By-laws; . . . etc. [of the town of Chicopee.] 12684

By-laws fixing the rates of assessment for 1847. 50244

By-laws for the government of the state alms-houses. 46134

By-laws for the government of the state alms-houses, together with the general statutes establishing the same. 45663

By-laws for the regulation and government of Mount Vernon Lodge, Boston. 51180

By-laws for the regulation of the officers of the Second Regiment New York State Artillery. 53812

By-laws, manual and sabre exercises of the Roxbury Horse Guard. 73732

By-laws, muster-roll, and papers selected from the archives of the First Troop Philadelphia City Cavalry. 61668

By-laws, . . . names of . . . officers . . . and a list of the pupils [of the New York Institution for the Instruction of the Deaf and Dumb.] 54500

By-laws . . . . Oct. 1837 [of the New Haven Horticultural Society.] 52994

By-laws of Company B (New England Guards.) (52686)

By-laws of Corinthian Lodge. 93829

By-laws of Fairhaven. (23702)

Bye-laws of Federal Lodge. 101939

By-laws of Glenwood Cemetery Company. 61701

By-laws of Groton, relative to schools. (28960)

By-laws . . . [of Groton] reported April 7, 1856. (28960)

By-laws of Kenyon College and Grammar School. 37584

By-laws of Newark College. 54870

By-laws of . . . Norwich, Conn. 55918

By-laws of Revere Lodge, Boston. 70184

By-laws of the Bank of Virginia. 100430

By-laws of the Bay State Granite Company. 72407

By-laws of the Board of Directors . . . [of the Public Schools] for the Third Section, Philadelphia. (61502)

By-laws of the Board of Directors of the Public Schools of the First Section of the First School District. (61502)

By-laws of the Board of Directors of the Sunday School of St. Paul's Chapel. (75462)

By-laws of the Board of Education, and course of study of the public schools of the city of Rochester. 73266

By-laws of the Board of Education, and rules and regulations of the public schools of the city and county of San Francisco. 76074

By-laws of the Board of Managers of the Society for the Reformation of Juvenile Delinquents. 85951

By-laws of the Board of Managers of the Sunbury & Erie Rail Road Company. 93730

By-laws of the Cambridgeport Lyceum. 10147

By-laws [of the Canadian Anti-slavery Baptist Association.] 10404

By-laws of the Canton Run Improvement Company. 10716

By-laws of the Catawissa Railroad Co. 59964

By-laws of the Central Pacific Railroad Company of California. 10023

By-laws [of the Champlain Copper Mining Company.] 11843

By-laws [of the Charlestown Mass. Young Men's Evangelical Union.] (12107)

By-laws of the Chauncy Society for Mutual Improvement. 12342

By-laws of the [Chebucto Gold Mining] Company. 12359

By laws of the city of Hartford relative to fire. 30655

Bye laws of the city of New Haven, in Connecticut. 52961

By-laws of the city of New-Haven, January, 1822. 52961

By laws [of the Columbian Historical Society.] 14865

By-laws of the Connecticut Historical Society. (15710)

By-laws of the Cooper Union for the Advancement of Science and Art. (16596)

By-laws of the Corinthian Lodge [of Concord, Mass.] 15137

By-laws of the Corporation of the New-York Protestant Episcopal Public School. 54529

By-laws of the Dalhousie Lodge. (55088)

By-laws of the . . . Directors of the North Pennsylvania Rail Road Company. 60278

By-laws of the . . . Directors, . . . with the charter of the Pennsylvania Railroad Company. 60358

By-laws of the Discharged Soldiers' Employment Association. 20231

By-laws of the . . . dispensary [in New York City.] 54460

By-laws [of the District Medical Society, of the county of Sussex.] 93940

By-laws of the East Cambridge Lyceum. 10147

By-laws of the First Congregational Church. (54213)

By-laws of the Flint-Steel Mining Company. 24797

By laws of the Franklin Typographical Society of Cincinnati. 13082

By-laws of the Friendship Fire Company. (61682)

By-laws of the Granite Club. 28288

By-laws of the [Great Falls Manufacturing] Corporation. 28446

By-laws of the Lechmere-Point Library Association. 10147

By-laws of the Literary and Historical Society of Quebec: to which is prefixed a copy of the royal charter. 67015

By laws of the Literary and Historical Society of Quebec. To which is prefixed the royal charter. 67015

By-laws of the Lone Star Royal Arch Chapter, no. 3. 95084

By-laws of the Lunenburg Farmers' Club. 42699

By-laws of the . . . Managers for 1839-9 [of the Monument Cemetery.] 61846

By-laws . . . [of the Massachusetts Charitable Fire Society.] 45828

By-laws of the . . . [Massachusetts Medical] Society. 45874

By-laws of the . . . [Massachusetts Rifle] Club. 45889

By-laws of the Mechanics' Mutual Benefit Association. 89866

Bye-laws of the Medical Society of . . . New York. 53762

By-laws [of the Medical Society of South-Carolina.] 87886

By-laws of the Medical Society of South-Carolina, instituted at Charleston. 87878

Bye laws of the Medical Society of the County of New-York. 53458

By-laws of the Merrimack Humane Society. 48012

By-laws of the Merrimack Mutual Fire-Insurance Company. (48013)

By-laws of the Milwaukee and Beliot Rail Road Company. (49165)

By-laws [of the Mohawk Valley Railroad Company.] 49855

By-laws . . . of the Mount Vernon Cemetery Company. 61849

By-laws of the Mystic River Works. 51665

By-laws of the Naval Library and Institute. 12100

By-laws of the New York and African Exchange Company. 54722

By-laws of the . . . [New York Free School] Society. 54285

By-laws of the Newbern Guards. 54886

By-laws of the Norfolk District Medical Society. 55471

By-laws of the North Randolph Church. 55728

By-laws of the Nova Cesarea Harmony Lodge. 56099

By-laws of the Oneida Medical Society. 57341

By-laws of the Ontonagon Copper Company. (57371)

By-laws of the Pennsylvania Horticultural Society. 60326

By-laws of the Pennsylvania State Lunatic Hospital at Harrisburg. 60379

By-laws of the Rutland Marble Co. 74477

By-laws of the Sailors' Snug Harbor. 74977

By-laws [of the St. Patrick Benevolent Society.] 62217

By-laws of the San Francisco Commercial Association. (76091)

By-laws of the Savings Institution in the town of Cambridge. 10152

By-laws of the School Committee, and regulations of the public schools in . . . Providence. 66363

By-laws of the School of Mines of Columbia College. (14812)

By-laws [of the Society for Promoting Theological Education.] 30765

By-laws, of the Society for the Development of the Mineral Resources of the United States. 12159

By-laws of the Society of California Pioneers. 9976

By-laws of the Society of the Friendly Sons of St. Patrick, in the city of New-York. 86143

By-laws of the South Brooklyn Savings Institution. 87345

By-laws of the South-Carolina Canal & Rail Road Company. 87955

By-laws of the South-Carolina Canal and Rail Road Company, adopted by the stockholders, May 13, 1828. 87956

By-laws of the South-Carolina Canal and Rail Road Company, adopted by the stockholders, 12th Jan. 1835. 87957

By-laws of the South Carolina College. 87971

By-laws of the South-Sea Company. 65865, 88189, 88192

By-laws of the South Side R. R. Co. of Long Island. 88210

By-laws of the State Lunatic Hospital, at Taunton, Mass. 46138

By-laws of the State Society of the Cincinnati of Pennsylvania. 86125

By-laws of the Suffolk Club. 93429

By-laws of the Teachers' Association of the Pilgrim Sunday School. (76100)

By-laws of the Theological and Religious Library Association of Cincinnati. 13092

By-laws of the town of Boston. 6611

By-laws of the town of Brookline. 8253

By-laws of the town of Charlestown. (12099)

By-laws of the town of Dorchester. (20628)

By-laws of the town of Gloucester. 27593

By-laws of the town of Groton. 28959

By-laws of the town of New Bedford. 52464

By-laws of the town of Portland. 64343

By-laws of the town of Portsmouth. (64417)

By-laws of the town of Salem, and an act for the regulation of the market. 75641

By-laws of the town of Salem, and the acts, for the regulation of the market and for the solemnization of marriages. 75642

By-laws of the Transylvania University. 96461

By-laws of the Trustees of the Public School Society of New York. 54615

By-laws of the University of South Carolina. 88093

By-laws of the Vermont Lodge, No. I. 99193

By-laws of the village of Cohoes. 14232

By-laws of the Ware Manufacturing Company. 101413

By-laws of the Washington St. Wharf Company. (76102)

By-laws of the Whig Republican Association of Cambridge. (10149)

By-laws, orders, and rules, for the good government of the Corporation of the Governor and Company of Merchants of Great Britain Trading to the South Seas. 88177

By-laws, passed August 8, 1792 [by the Proprietors of the Locks and Canals on Merrimac River.] 48015

By-laws . . . Passed . . . May 6, 1822 [for New Bedford, Mass.] 52464

By-laws, premiums, rules and regulations [of the Lunenburg Farmers' Club.] 42699

By-laws . . . prepared . . . October, 1855. 46135

By-laws, regulations and police of the Center-District New-Hampshire Medical Society. 52878

Bye-laws, resolutions and orders, adopted by the New-York Chamber of Commerce, at a special meeting. 53580

Bye-laws, resolutions and orders, adopted by the New-York Chamber of Commerce, September 18, 1787. 53580

By-laws; revised and passed March, 1840. 98229

By laws, rules and orders of the Trinity-House of Quebec. 96988

By-laws, rules and regulations, certificate of ownership, and act of incorporation [of Erie Cemetery.] 22737

By-laws, rules and regulations of the Corporation . . . for Erecting a Permanent Bridge Over the . . . Schuylkill. 62230

By-laws, rules and regulations of the . . . Louisiana Penitentiary. 42254

By-laws, rules and regulations of the Minnesota Hospital for the Insane. 49277

By-laws, rules and regulations of the new diggings and Shullsburg Mining Co. (52589)

By-baws, [sic] rules, and regulations of the Overseers of Harvard University. (30749)

By-laws, rules and regulations . . . of the [Philadelphia] House of Refuge. 61729

By-laws, rules and regulations . . . of the University Lying-in Hospital, Montreal. 50244

By-laws, rules of order, and principles of discipline. 87072

By-laws, rules of procedure, and catalogue of churches. 52961

By-laws to be observed by the town of Fitchburg. 24591

By-laws, with a list of officers, etc., of the Chicago Historical Society. 13621

By-laws; with rules and regulations for the government of the Asylum for the Insane in Charlestown and the Hospital in Boston. 12101

By-laws . . . with the rules and regulations for the government of the Asylum for the Insane in Charlestown, and the Hospital in Boston. 45846

Byles, Mather, 1707-1788. 6227, 9711-(9718), 21946, 24679, 25397, 65584, 65597, 74633, 78692, 103526, 106229

Byles, Mathew. 65605

Byles, Thomas. 103361

Byll of adventure. Whereas [blank] paid in ready money. 99862

Bylls of adventure, with blankes. 99862

Bylot, ------. (74131)

Byng, John, 1704-1757. 57614, 99249

Byng, John, 1704-1757. defendant at court martial (65839)

Bynum, Alfred. 9719

Bynum, J. W. ed. 88324

Bynum, Jesse Atherton, 1797-1868. 9720

Byrd, William, 1674-1744. (9721)-(9722)

Byrd, William, 1728-1777. 100006 see also Virginia (Colony) Commissioners to the Catawba and Cherokee Indians.

Byrdsall, F. 9723

Byre, James. see Byres, James.

Byres, James. 9724, 78223

Byrn, Marcus Lafayette. 67961-67962

Byrne, A. D. 9728

Byres, James. 9724

Byrne, Bernard Mayles, 1813-1860. 9725

Byrne, Bernard Myles, 1813-1860. defendant at court martial 9726

Byrne, Patrick, d. 1813. defendant (9727)

Byrne, Patrick, fl. 1834. defendant 96939

Byrne, William S. 9728

Byrnes, Daniel. 9729

Byron, George Gordon Noel Byron, 6th Baron, 1788-1824. 5910, (6370), 64007-64008, 85102

Byron, John, 1723-1786. 9730-(9731), 9736-9739, 21211-21215, 29590, 30934-30935, 30937-30945, 31389, 32438, 38022, 52455, 52580, 52591, (54897), 56064, 64396, (69276), 97668, 100836, 101029, 104679

Byron Whipporwill. pseud. Orondalie. see Sturtevant, Peleg. supposed author

Bysonder verhael vander wonderlijcken aert ende het weesen der bevers. (20593)-20594, note after 98474, note after 99310

Bystander. 45096

Bystander; or a series of letters on . . . the "legislative choice." 9740

Bytown and Prescott Railway. 17398

Byvoeging van de walvischvangst. 106374

Bywater, Maurice. 61606

Bywater's Philadelphia business directory. 61606

C

C.·. pseud. Antwoord op deze aanmerkingen. see Cameron, Adam. supposed author

C. pseud. Historical letters. 100480

C., Citoyen. pseud. Reflexions sur un pretendu prodige opere. see Colombel, Noel.

C., ------ de. pseud. tr. see Montucla, ------. tr.

C***, Marquis de. pseud. Lettres d'un citoyen. see Condorcet, Marie Jean Antoine Nicolas Caritat, Marquis de.

C——d, A. pseud. Letter, to the Reverend Mr. Foxcroft. see Cleveland, Aaron. supposed author

C., A. pseud. Morceaux choisis des lettres. see Caillot, Antoine.

C., A. pseud. Tabaco. see Chute, Anthony.

C., A. B. pseud. Letras. 50774

C***, Antoine. pseud. Abrege de l'histoire generale des voyages. see Caillot, Antoine.

C***, Ant. pseud. Nouvelle histoire des naufrages. see Caillot, Antoine.

C., B. pseud. Quakers no apostates. 106101

C., B. pseud. Three letters. see Colman, Benjamin, 1673-1747.

C., C. D. pseud. 93683

C***, C. de St. pseud. see Lammens, ----------.

C., C. M. pseud. 42600

C., D. J. pseud. Catecismo politico. 48330

C., le Comte D. L. pseud. tr. 30036

C., le Sieur D. L. G. D., Avocat en Parlement. pseud. Conduite des Francois justifee. see Lagrange de Checieux, G. A. F. Simon de.

C., D. M. G. pseud. tr. 10655, 99452

C., E. pseud. Sotweed redivivus. see Cook, Edward.

C., E. V. pseud. Letters dedicated to A. H. see Childe, Edward Vernon.

C., F. pseud. Guerre civile en Amerique et l'esclavage. 9741

C***, F., un de ses precedens colons. pseud. Histoire des desastres de Saint Domingue. see Carteaux, J. Felix.

C***, F., un de ses precedens colons. pseud. Soirees bermudiennes. see Carteaux, J. Felix.

C., F. E. pseud. History of the 28th Regt. Massachusetts Vols. see Cushman, Frederick E.

C., F. M. del. pseud. see M. del C., F. pseud.

C., G. pseud. Breaking the line. 9742

C., G. pseud. Fraud and oppression detected. see Carew, George.

C., G. pseud. Victimas del Japon. 99426

C., G., Esq. pseud. Labrador; a poetical epistle. see Cartwright, George.

C., G. A. pseud. tr. 86230

C . . . , I. pseud. Way of the churches of Christ. see Cotton, John, 1584-1652.

C., J. pseud. Further observations intended for improving the culture. see Crockat, or Crockatt, James. supposed author and Leigh, Sir Edward. supposed author

C., J. pseud. Keys of the kingdom of heaven. see Cotton, John, 1584-1652.

C., J. pseud. Observations concerning indigo and cochineal. see Crockat, or Crockatt,

James. supposed author and Leigh, Sir Edward. supposed author

C., J. pseud. Poem occasioned by the death of Jno. Alden. see Cotton, John, 1584-1652.

C., J. pseud. Siege of Penobscot by the rebels. see Calef, John, 1725-1812.

C., J. pseud. Slavery in the south. (9744)

C., J. pseud. Sobre un escrito. see Campino, Joaquin.

C., J. pseud. Twelve cents worth of wit. see Curtis, John, 1744-1823.

C., J. pseud. Twig of birch for Billy's breech. see Cleaveland, John.

C., J., member of the Philadelphia Bar. pseud. reporter Trial of Richard Smith. 83764

C., J. C. pseud. tr. 16848

C., J. J. pseud. Letter, to the Reverend Mr. Foxcroft. 25386

C., J. L. M. pseud. tr. 3255B

C., J. M., Americain, sang-mele. pseud. Precis des gemissements. 9745, 65026

C., J. M. A. pseud. ed. see Castellar, Joao Maria Augusto.

C., J. M. V. pseud. Gloria de la nacion. see Villasenor Cervantes, Jose Maria.

C., J. M. V. pseud. Poesias varias. see Villasenor Cervantes, Jose Maria.

C., J. S. pseud. Pequeno catecismo. see Sierra, Justo.

C., J. T. de. pseud. Comerciante de perlas, novela Americana. 9746

C., L. pseud. Case de l'oncle Tom. 92538

C., L. pseud. Relation d'un voyage. 9038, 9747

C., L. de. pseud. Aanhangsel, behelzende een reize. see Capine, Louis de.

C., Le M. de. pseud. Memoire sur l'esclavage. 9748

C., M. pseud. see Carey, Mathew, 1760-1839.

C**, M. pseud. Traite general du commerce de l'Amerique. see Chambon, -------, fl. 1775.

C., M. B. pseud. Remarks on New-York banking. 9749

C., M. D. L. pseud. Lettre. see La Condamine, Charles Marie de.

C., M. G. T. pseud. Desengano de falsas imposturas. see Toral y Cabanas, Manuel German.

C., M. J. pseud. Ab-sa-ra-ka. see Carrington, Mrs. M. J.

C., M. P. D. L. pseud. Lettres. see Peyroux de la Coudreniere, -----.

C., M. T. pseud. Flowers from the battlefield. 9750

C., M. T. y. pseud. see T. y C., M. pseud.

C., M. W. pseud. Songs of the free. see Chapman, Maria Weston.

C., N. pseud. see Collins, Nathaniel. supposed author

C., N. B. pseud. see Craig, Neville B.

C., N. E. pseud. History of Dungeon Rock. 22565, (48149)

C., N. G. pseud. see Clark, N. G.

C., O. pseud. Letters from the south. 9752

C., O. pseud. To the freemen of this and the neighbouring towns. 95925

C., P. pseud. Short and impartial view. 9753, (78233)

C-----, R------. pseud. Duty of Christians in respect to war. 9754

C., R. pseud. Their voyage to the Massachusets. (51198), note after 104797

C., R., Esq. pseud. Lithobolia. see Cahmberlaine, Richard.

C., R. C. pseud. Trial of episcopacy. see Reed, John. supposed author and Smith, William. supposed author

C., R. E. pseud. Problem of free society. see Colston, R. E.

C., S. pseud. Almanack for the year of Our Lord 1660. see Cheever, Samuel.

C., S. pseud. Almanack for the year of Our Lord 1661. see Cheever, Samuel.

C., S. pseud. Letter to a friend. see Conant, Shubael. supposed author and Hart, William. supposed author

C., S. pseud. Short history of a long travel. see Crisp, Stephen.

C., S. pseud. Truth is no slander. 97264

C., S. D. pseud. tr. 106259-106267

C-----, S----- de. pseud. 67019

C., S. T. pseud. Little fox. 9755

C., T. pseud. Account of a plan. see Crowley, Thomas.

C., T. pseud. Entertaining passages. see Church, Thomas.

C., T. pseud. Scheme to drive the French out. 77555-(77556)

C., T. pseud. To the Right Honovrable Henry Lo: Cary. 80620

C., T. pseud. Youth persuaded to obedience. see Chalkley, Thomas.

C., T. pseud. tr. 40979

C., T., Esq. pseud. Trve discovrse historicall. see Churchyard, Thomas.

C., V. pseud. Resena de los partidos. (70056)

C., V. &. pseud. see V. & C. pseud.

C., V. D. pseud. Examen de l'esclavage. see Cullion, F. Val. de.

C., V. W. pseud. Trou-hertighe onderrichtinge. 9757, 2d note after 97062

C., W. pseud. Anti-slavery in Virginia. see Crane, William.

C., W. pseud. Dutch svrvay. 9758

C., W. pseud. Notice of the late John Revere. 70178

C., W. pseud. Petition. see Castell, William. petitioner

C., W. pseud. Plaine description of the Barmvdas. see Castell, William, d. 1645. supposed author and Courten, Sir William. supposed author

C., W. pseud. Trepidantium malleus intrepidanter malleatus. 106101

C., W. B. pseud. Short sketch. see Crafton, William Bell.

C----- de la B-----, MMe. pseud. see Calderon de la Barca, Frances Erskine (Inglis) 1804-1882.

C. L., A. R. y. pseud. see L., A. R. y C. pseud. tr.

C. S., D. M. Q. pseud. Triunfo de la justicia. see Quiros y Campo Sagrado, Manuel de.

C. y E-----, J. M. pseud. Oracion. see Castaneda y Escalada, Jose Maria.

C. y Sobron, Felix. see Sobron, Felix C. y.

C. A. pseud. see A., C. pseud.

C. A. L. T. de M. pseud. see M., C. A. L. T. de. pseud.

C. A. Roemelings, gewesenen predigers zu Haarburg. 72590

C. A. Z. pseud. see Z., C. A. pseud.

C. B. pseud. see B., C. pseud.

C. B., Gent. pseud. see Brooke, Christopher.

C. B. B. pseud. see Brown, Charles Brockden, 1771-1810.

C. C. pseud. see C., C. pseud.

C

C. C. A. pseud. see A., C. C. pseud.
C. C. A. Bissette homme de couleur de la
  Martinique. 5652
C. C. L. pseud. see Leigh, Charles C.
C. C. The covenanter vindicated from
  perjurie. 91381
C. D. pseud. see D. . ., C. . . pseud
C. D. pseud. see Deane, Charles.
C. D. pseud. see Dove, C.
C. D. pseud. see Dussillion, Charles J.
C. D. pseud. see Weymouth, Mass. South
  Parish. Committee of Inquiry.
C——s D——s. pseud. see Dunham,
  Robert Carr.
C. D. C. pseud. see C., C. D. pseud.
C. D. C. Anastaf de Morales. pseud. see
  San Rafael, Tomas de.
C. D. P. pseud. tr. see P., C. D. pseud.
  tr.
C. de B. pseud. see Beauregard, Couvray
  de.
C. de S. pseud. see Sodre, Francois de.
C. de St. C***. pseud. see St. C***, C. de.
  pseud.
C. F. pseud. see F., C. pseud.
C. F. A. Nobbii litteratura geographiae Ptole-
  maeae. (55376)
C. F. B. pseud. see Briggs, Charles F.
C. Francisco Ibarra gobernador interno a ses
  habitantes, sabed. 66556
C. F. Ph. v. Martius. Seine Lebens- und
  Characterbild. 77968
C. F. Vollneys Reisen durch die Vereinigten
  Staaten. 100689
C. F. Volney's . . . Schilderung der Vereinig-
  ten Staaten. 100690
C. G. pseud. tr. see G., C. pseud. tr.
C. G. A. Oldendorp's Geschichte der Mission
  der Evangelischen Bruder. (57152)
C. G. Klinckhardt's Reise nach Nord-Amerika.
  94639
C. G. Zorgdragers alte und neue Gronlandische
  Fischerei. 106373
C: G: Zorgdragers bloeyende opkomst der
  aloude en hedendaagsche Groenlandsche
  visschery. 106374-106376
C.-G.-D.-B. pseud. see Beaulieu, Charles
  Gillston de.
C. G. P. pseud. see P., C. G. pseud.
C. H. R. pseud. see R., C. H. pseud.
C. H. W. pseud. see Wharton, Charles
  Henry.
C. J. pseud. see J., C. pseud.
C. J. J. pseud. tr. see Jagemann, C. J.
  tr.
C. K. pseud. see K., C. pseud.
C. K. W. pseud. see Whipple, Charles King.
C. L. pseud. see L., C. pseud.
C. L. MacArthur's reliable Troy directory.
  97072
C. L. MacArthur's Troy city directory. 97072
C. L. W. pseud. tr. see W., C. L. pseud.
  tr.
C. Leslie Reilly's Pennsylvania state business
  directory. (69105)
C. M. pseud. see M., C. pseud.
C. M. pseud. see Mather, Cotton, 1663-1728.
C. M. pseud. see Munguia, Clemente de
  Jesus, bp.
C. M. C. pseud. see C., C. M. pseud.
C. M. P. pseud. see P., C. M. pseud.
C. More. pseud. see Smith, Seymour R.
C. Moreira, J. de. see Moreira, J. de. C.
C. N. pseud. see N., C. pseud.
C. P. pseud. see P., C. pseud.
C. P. pseud. see Pusey, Caleb.

C. P. L. P. pseud. see Goens, Rijklof
  Michael van.
C. Roswag ingenieur des mines. 73429
C. S. pseud. see S., C. pseud.
(C. S.) pseud. see MacNemar, Richard.
C. S. pseud. see Saur, C.
C. S. pseud. see Smithsoni, Don Carlos.
C. S. pseud. see Stearns, Charles. aboli-
  tionist
C. S. pseud. see Stearns, Charles, 1788-
  1860.
C. S. A. see Confederate States of America.
C. Sidons. pseud. see Postl, Karl, 1793-1864.
C. Soublette Presidente de la republica a los
  Venezolanos. 87257
C. T. pseud. tr. see T., C. pseud. tr.
C. T. U. S. pseud. see S., C. T. U. pseud.
C. W. pseud. see Wolley, Charles.
Ca da Mosto, Alvise, 1432?-1480? (14362),
  26874-26875, 34100-34107, 50050-50064,
  67730, 67743, 1st-5th notes after 106378
Caaiguarum gentis mores, coepta conuersio.
  4644, 5101, (69246)
Caal, Pedro Alvares. (14362)
Cabalista electoral. 9760
Caballero, Joaquim. 48816 see also Michoa-
  can (Mexican State) Governador (Caba-
  llero)
Caballero, Jose Augustin. 9761
Caballero, Jose de la Luz. 9762
Caballero, Pepe de la Luz. see Caballero,
  Jose de la Luz.
Caballero, Ramon Diosdado, 1740-1829. 9763-
  9764, 70777
Caballero y Ontiveros, Felix. 9765
Caban f'ewythr Tomos. 92620, 92624
Caban f'ewythr Twm. 92623
Caban f'ewyrth Twm. 92621
Cabana del tio Tom. 92419, 92607-92609
Cabana del tio Tomas. 92614
Cabana do pai Thomas. 92598
Cabana indiana. 12249
Cabanas, Agustin. plaintiff 75585
Cabanas, Manuel German Toral y. see Toral
  y Cabanas, Manuel German.
Cabanas, Trinidad, Pres. Honduras, d. 1871.
  32772 see also Honduras. President,
  1852-1855 (Cabanas)
Cabane de l'oncle Tom. 92532, 92536
Cabanis, ------. 77780
Cabeca de Vaca, Alvar Nunez. see Cabeza de
  Vaca, Alvar Nunez, 1490?-1557.
Cabelentz, H. C. von der. 26279-26280
Cabeliau, A. 36636
Cabell, --------, fl. 1845. 88294, 88295-
  88296
Cabell, Edward Carrington, 1816-1896. 9772-
  9773, 86232
Cabell, Joseph Carrington, 1778-1856. 9774,
  (35937)
Cabell, Julia (Mayo) 9775, 42821, (81545)
Cabell, Nathaniel Francis, 1807-1891. 9776
Cabello, F. de. tr. 44655
Cabello, Pedro M. 9777
Cabello y Mesa, Francisco Antonio. ed. 94606
Cabet, Etienne. 9778-9788, 100813
Cabeza de Vaca, Alvar Nunez, 1490?-1557.
  3350, 9767-9771, 16951, 66686, 84383
Cabeza del rey Don Pedro. 24153
Cabezas, J. 9789
Cabichui (gaceta humoristica Parahuaya) 58512
Cabildo de Michoacan, para manifestar que no
  fue arbitraria. 48807
Cabin and parlor. 61229
Cabin book; or, national characteristics. 64537

Cabin book; or, scenes and sketches of the late American and Mexican war. 64538
Cabin book; or, sketches of life in Texas. (64536)
Cabin boy wife. 91290
Cabin on the prairie. 59439
Cabinet. 9791
Cabinet & talisman. 98425
Cabinet conference. (9793)
Cabinet-council. 67598-67599, 82979
Cabinet cyclopaedia. 21287
Cabinet d'antiquites Americaines a Copenhague. 67473-67474
Cabinet de Lecture de Montreal. see Montreal. Cabinet de Lecture.
Cabinet de Mr. Svvammerdam. 95332
Cabinet eloquence. 13554
Cabinet encyclopedia. 16367, 21287, 24087
Cabinet in congress. (17271)
Cabinet library (Bentley's) 29684
Cabinet library (Carter's) Fourth series. 85296
Cabinet library. No. IV. 95591
Cabinet library for schools and families. 27913
Cabinet library of scarce and celebrated tracts. 92296
Cabinet of American authors. 91280
Cabinet of American history. 27999-28000
Cabinet of American literature. 91280
Cabinet of curiosities. 27875
Cabinet of freedom. 9794
Cabinet of general knowledge. 30521
Cabinet of Natural History, New York. see New York Academy of Sciences. and New York State Museum.
Cabinet of natural history, American rural sports. 9795
Cabinet of nature and philosophy. (33901)
Cabinet of portraits. 9796
Cabinet of shells. (33901)
Cabinet of the United States. 52003
Cabinet of variety. 41898
Cabinet officers in congress. 50790
Cabinet; or, a collection of choice things. (9792)
Cabinet theatre. 88544
Cable, Joseph. (9797)
Cable interview between the President and the Queen. (37290)
Cable transatlantique. (9798)
Cabot, George. 9799, 42802, 80587
Cabot, James Elliot, 1821-1903. 506, 1475, 9800-9801
Cabot, Marston. 9802-9803
Cabot, Sebastian, ca. 1474-1557. 19050, 57458-57459, 66686, 67738, (74131), 76897
Cabot, Susan C. 9805
Cabot Institute, Springfield, Mass. 9806
Cabots. firm plaintiffs 96930A
Cabral, Fredrico Augusto de Vasconcellos A. Pereira. 9807
Cabral, Jose Marcellino da Rocha. see Rocha Cabral, Jose Marcellino da.
Cabral, Pedro Alvares, 1460?-1526. 20518, 34100-34107, 50050-50064, 50115, 1st-5th notes after 106378
Cabredo, Rodrigo de. 9810
Cabrer, Jose Maria. 9811
Cabrera, Cayetano. 80981
Cabrera, Christophorus. 9812
Cabrera, Felix. see Cabrera, Paul Felix.
Cabrera, Joseph de. (66574)
Cabrera, Manuel de. 9813, 98932
Cabrera, Michele de. see Cabrera, Miguel.
Cabrera, Miguel. 9814, 44463

Cabrera, Paul Felix. 71445-71447
Cabrera, Rodrigo de. 77289
Cabrera, T. M. 9815
Cabrera Bueno, Joseph Gonzalez. (9816)
Cabrera de Cordoba, L. 94854
Cabrera de Navares, M. 9819
Cabrera Nevares, Miguel. see Nevares, Miguel Cabrera.
Cabrera y Quintero, Cayetano de. 9817-9818
Cabrillo, Juan Rodriguez, d. 1543. 84379
Cabuenas, J. M. de Carballido y. see Carballido y Cabuenas, J. M. de.
Cacao et le chocolat consideres au point de vue botanique. 44249
Caccia, Antonio. 9820
Caceres, Rodrigo de Esquiuel y. see Esquiuel Caceres, Rodrigo de.
Cacho, Jos. M. (Franco Soto) de Rivas. see Rivas-Cacho, Jos. M. (Franco Soto) de.
Cacho, Manuel de Ricas. see Rivas-Cacho, Manuel de.
Cacho Negrete, Modesto. see Negrete, Modesto Cacho.
Cachuto, Juan Agapito Canelo y. see Canelo y Cachuto, Juan Agapito.
Cacique of Ontario; an Indian tale. 9821
Cactaceae. 69946
Cactaceae of the boundary. 22538, 22580
Cada Mosto, Alvise. see Ca da Mosto, Alvise, 1432?-1480?
Cadastres abreges . . . de Trois Rivieres. 66993
Cadastres abreges des seigneuries du District du Montreal. 66993
Cadastres abreges des seigneuries du District de Quebec. 66993
Caddell, Cecilia Mary. (9822)-9823
Caddo Indian treaty. . . . Report [of] the Committee on Indian Affairs. 96696
Caddo Indians. Treaties, etc. 96696
Caddy, J. H. 9824
Cadena, Melchioris de la. 87183
Cadereyta, ------, Conde de. see Alencastro Marona y Silva, Fernando de, Marques de Valdafuentes.
Cadet, J. Marc. 9825-(9826)
Cadet, St. Denis le. pseud. Lottery. see Denison, Edward.
Cadet life at West Point. 92904
Cadets of Temperance. Rhode Island. Franklin Section, no. 3, Pawtucket. 59261
Cadets of Temperance. Rhode Island. Washington Section, no. 2, Providence. (66378)
Cadien, B. see Cadieu, Baptiste. defendant
Cadieu, Baptiste. defendant 96845
Cadieux, J. N. 9827-(9828)
Cadiz. Consulado. 41134, 73866, 98931
Cadiz. Gobernador. 87314
Cadiz. Junta Superior. 36935
Cadiz (Diocese) 66443
Cadiz cases. 102294
Cadmus. 95646
Cadmus est arrive. 77455
Cadogan, George. 9829-9830, 56845, 2d note after 87848
Cadore, Jean Baptiste Nompere de Champagny, Duc de. see Champagny, Jean Baptiste Nompere de, Duc de Cadore.
Cadoret, Eug. (9831)
Cadrana, Rafael Maria de Labra y. see Labra y Cadrana, Rafael Maria de, 1843-
Caduceo, periodico del estado libre de la Puebla. 9832
Cadusch, ---------, Marquis de. 9833
Cadwalader, John, fl. 1730. 50634

Cadwalader, John, 1742-1786. 9836-9837,
   (68568)-68569, (68602), 82725
Cadwalader, John, 1805-1879. 51456, 84728
Cadwalader pamphlet. 82725
Cadwallader, Benjamin. 9834
Cadwallader, Morgan. 7879
Cady, C. W. 34531
Cady, Daniel R. (9838)
Cady, Howard C. 8309
Cady, Louisa. 89518
Caen, Guillaume de. plaintiff 86843
Caerden, Paulus van. 14957-14960, 68455
Caert-thresoor. (9839), 38880, 95757, note
   after 100632
Caerte vande Oost ende West Zee. 104132
Caerte vander zee. 104133
Caesario San Blas, Bachelor. pseud. Voyage
   to the Island of Philosophers. see
   Woodruff, Sylvester. supposed author
Caesarism. General Grant for a third term.
   83575
Caesar's due rendered unto him. (25355)
Caetano da Silva, Antonio Jose, 1817-1865.
   81077
Caetano da Silva, Joaquim. see Silva, Joa-
   quim Caetano da.
Caetano de Almeida Nogueira, Baptista. see
   Almeida Nogueira, Baptista Caetano de.
Caetano de Campos, Luis. see Campos,
   Luis Caetano de.
Caetano Fernandes Pinheiro, Joaquim. see
   Pinheiro, Joaquim Caetano Fernandes.
Cafe. 94839
Caffrey, Andrew. 9840
Cagigal, Francisco Mariano Nipho y. see
   Nipho y Cagigal, Francisco Mariano.
Cagigal, Manuel. 17755
Cagnawaga Indians. see Caughnawaga Indians.
Cahoone, Henry. defendant 103412
Cahoone, Sarah S. 9842, 4th note after 100603
Cahoquia Indians. 84577-84578, 2d-3d notes
   after 97876
Cahumette, Pierre Gaspard. (12296)
Cahun, --------. ed. 70377-(70378)
Caicedo, Jose Maria Torres. see Torres
   Caicedo, Jose Maria.
Caida en Queretaro en 1867. 67096
Caijiga, Ramon. 9864
Cail, -------. (9844)
Cail (J. F.) et Cie. firm 9845
Caillot, Antoine. 9846-9847
Caillout, Antoine. see Caillot, Antoine.
Cain against Abel. (25346)
Cain, and other poems. 81273
Caine, S. C. 9849
Caines, Clement. (9848), 9850-9851
Caines, George, 1771-1825. (9852), 17677,
   (29986), 79011-(79012), note after 98533,
   102037
Cain's lamentations over Abel. 17106
Caird, Sir James, 1816-1892. 9853-9854,
   34111, (34319)
Caird's erroneous view of Canada answered and
   refuted. 34111
Cairnes, John Elliott, 1823-1875. 9855-9857
Cairo, Ignazio Herrera y. see Herrera y
   Cairo, Ignazio, Bp.
Cairo, Ill. 9858, 66075
Cairo, Ill. Citizens. petitioners 47660
Cairo, Ill. Engineers. 66075
Cairo City and Canal Company. 9860-9862
Caius. pseud. Few remarks on Mr. Hamil-
   ton's late letter. 9863
Caius Marius. 83782, 83788
Caja de Ahorros de la Gran Sociedad, Caracas.
   10774, 68854

Cajutenbuch. 64541
Cajutenbuch oder nationale Charakteristiken.
   64534-64535
Cakes and ale at Woodbiney. (14184)
Calabar. Drama en verso. 88787
Calabre Perau, G. L. see Perau, G. L.
   Calabre.
Calado, J. I. Ruiz. see Ruiz Calado, J. I.
Calado, Manoel. 9865-9868
Calageras, Joao Baptista. 9866
Calamity at Richmond. 71169
Calamity, danger, and hope. 105301
Calamy, Edmund, 1600-1666. 3213, 13868,
   80205, 80212, note before 92797, note
   after 92800, 3d note after 103687
Calamy, Edmund, 1671-1732. (9867)-(9868),
   46406
Calancha, Antonio de la. 9870-9873
Calar, N. de Irolo. see Yrolo Calar, Nicolas
   de.
Calar, Nicolas de Yrolo. see Yrolo Calar,
   Nicolas de.
Calart, ------. 58832
Calasiveta, Francisco. 86444
Calatayud y Borda, Cypriano Geronimo. 9874
Calavar. (5550)
Calcano, Jose Antonio. (72784)
Calcott, Alexander. 9875
Calculation of the new scheme. 88178
Calculation, shewing in what time a permanent
   bridge over the River Schuylkill, . . .
   may be built. 61509
Calculations and observations relating to an
   additional duty upon sugar. 46181
Calculations and statements relative to the
   trade. 70155
Calculations on American population. 103909
Calculo astronomico. 75869
Calcutta, Bishop of. see Wilson, Daniel,
   Bishop of Calcutta, 1778-1858.
Caldas, Francisco Jose de. 9876, 79051
Caldas, Sebastian Alvarez Alfonso Rosica de.
   see Rosica de Caldas, Sebastian Alvarez
   Alfonso.
Caldas y Tenorio, Francisco Joseph. ed.
   79054
Caldaza, Antonio Hernandez i. see Hernandez
   i Caldaza, Antonio.
Caldcleugh, Alexander. 9877-9878
Caldeiras Centenera de Villadarias, Manoel
   Durate. see Villadarias, Manoel Durate
   Caldeiras Centenera de.
Calder, David O. 83163
Calderinus, Dominitus. ed. 66470
Calderon, Andres Joseph Roxo y. see Roxo y
   Calderon, Andres Joseph.
Calderon, Andres Rojo y. see Roxo y Calde-
   ron, Andres Joseph.
Calderon, Bernardo Tellez. see Tellez Calde-
   ron, Bernardo.
Calderon, Fern. 9879
Calderon, Francisco. 9880
Calderon, Francisco, fl. 1671. 73850
Calderon, Francisco, fl. 1675. 9881
Calderon, Francisco Garcia. 9882
Calderon, Ignacio. 9883
Calderon, Juan Alonso. (9884)
Calderon, Jose Tellez. see Tellez Calderon,
   Jose.
Calderon, Louisa. plaintiff (9885), 62682-
   62684
Calderon, Pedro. (9886)-(9887)
Calderon, Pedro de Solis. see Solis Calderon,
   Pedro de.
Calderon de la Barca, Frances Erskine (Inglis)
   1804-1882. 9888-9889

Calderon de la Barca, Frances Erskine (Inglis) 1804-1882. supposed author 77459

Calderon de la Barca, Pedro, 1600-1681. (9890)

Calderon de la Varca, Miguel. (9891), note after 96350

Calderon Velarde, Diego. see Velarde, Diego Calderon.

Calderon y Cevallos, A Ventura. see Ventura Calderon y Cevallos, A.

Caldicott, Thomas Ford. 9892, 90777

Caldicott, Thomas Ford. petitioner 90777

Caldovinos, Mucio. 34187, 34189

Caldron, D. Mathias de Peralta. see Peralta Caldron, D. Mathias de.

Caldwell, --------. 93382

Caldwell, Charles, 1772-1853. 3200, 9893-9899, 13079, 17654, 84354, 93167, 96161, 101767, 101797-101799

Caldwell, David. 11169

Caldwell, George Alfred, 1814-1866. 9900

Caldwell, Henry. 9903, 36393, 67023

Caldwell, Henry. plaintiff 9902, 101168

Caldwell, J. (9904)

Caldwell, J. C. USA 76395

Caldwell, John. 9905-9907, 43293, 69400, 90595-90596, 103594 3d note after 103650,

Caldwell, John D. 85896

Caldwell, John H. 9908

Caldwell, John William. (9909)

Caldwell, Joseph. 9910

Caldwell, Joseph. supposed author. 9917, 1st note after 96334, 4th note after 100532

Caldwell, Joseph Blake. 9911

Caldwell, Merritt. 9912

Caldwell, S. T. J. 9916

Caldwell, Samuel B. T. (9913)

Caldwell, Samuel Lunt, 1820-1889. 9914-9915, 51773, 104332-104333

Caldwell, T. supposed author 9917, 1st note after 96334, 4th note after 100532

Caleb D'Anvers, of Gray's Inn, Esq. pseud. see Amhurst, Nicholas. supposed author

Caleb Field. 57185

Caleb Pusie, of Pensilvania. (37180)

Calebius, W. tr. 19446

Caledon, Philo. pseud. Defence of the Scots settlement at Darien. see Fletcher, ------, of Saltoun. supposed author and Ridpath, George. supposed author

Caledonia County, Vt. Grammar School. see Caledonia County Grammar School, Peacham, Vt.

Caledonia County Grammar School, Peacham, Vt. 9921, 59412

Caledonia County Teachers' Institute, Danville, Vt. 9922, 18522

Caledonia Division, no. 90, Sons of Temperance. see Sons of Temperance of North America. Massachusetts. Caledonia Division, no. 90, Boston.

Caledonia; or, the pedlar turn'd merchant. 9919

Caledonia. The declaration of the Council constituted by the Indian and African Company of Scotland. 78197

Caledonia dream. 9924

Caledonia's complaint and resolution. 78203

Calef, Ebenezer. claimant 51752

Calef, John, 1725-1812. 9925

Calef, Robert, 1648-1719. 5196, 9926-9927, (19046), 20884, 27384, 75736, 89927

Calendar and course of study of St. Stephen's College. 75491

Calendar . . . 1818. 77476

Calendar for the Hebrew years 5622-5660. 80774

Calendar of council minutes. 84558

Calendar of King's College, Windsor, Nova Scotia. 37872

Calendar of New York colonial manuscripts. 53556

Calendar of Queen's University and College, Kingston, Canada. 67074

Calendar of St. Mary's College. 75424

Calendar of state papers, Colonial series, America and West Indies 1717-1718. 86730, 2d note after 99911

Calendar of state papers, Colonial series, America and West Indies, 1661-1668. 74980

Calendar of state papers, Colonial series, 1574-1660. 74979

Calendar of the historical manuscripts in the Office of the Secretary of State, Albany, N. Y. 53554

Calendar of the historical mansucripts relating to the war of the revolution. (53555)

Calendar of the journals of the House of Lords. 36756

Calendar of the St. Xavier College, Cincinnati. 75516

Calendar of the University of McGill College. 43273

Calendar of the University of New Brunswick. 52532

Calendar of wealth, fashion and gentility. 6623

Calendar, or New-York and Vermont almanack. 41959

Calendar or the Albany almanac, for . . . 1844. (41376)

Calendar, or western almanac for 1816. 62569

Calendaria manual. (41969)

Calendario. 72811

Calendario arreglado al meridiano de Bogota. (6403)

Calendario de A. D. Solorzano. 86513

Calendario de Guatemala, para el ano de 1842. 29070

Calendario de las fiestas y santos. 15883-15884

Calendario de las senoritas Megicanas. 26463

Calendario de las senoritas Megicanos. (48313)

Calendario manual y guia de forasteros de la isla de Cuba. (17756)

Calendario manual y guia de forasteros de Mexico, para el ano de 1791. 106404

Calendario manual y guia de forasteros de Mexico, para el ano de 1793 [-1821.] 106404

Calendario manual y guia de forasteros de Mexico, para el ano de 1831. 26464

Calendario manual y guia de forasteros en Mexico, para el ano de 1811. 48314, 106404

Calendario Mexicano. (40080)

Calendario para el ano de 1868. (22899)

Calendario para el ano de 1867. (22899)

Calendario y guia de forasteros de la republica Boliviana. 6191

Calendario y guia de forasteros de la republica Peruana para el ano bisieto de 1848. 61083

Calendario y guia de forasteros de la republica Peruana para el ano de 1826. 11037

Calendario y guia de forasteros de Lima. (41081), 62751

Calendarios Mexicanos. 99397

Calender. (33092)
Calender of state papers and manuscripts relating to English affairs. 8545
Calendrier Americain, avec ephemeridies. 9928
Calendrier de Philadelphie. (3335)
Calendrier de Philadelphie, en Pensylvanie. 61511
Calendrier de Philadelphie, ou le moraliste Americain. (61510)
Caleron y Moreira, Jacinto. ed. (47935)
Calheiros de Mello, Roberto. see Mello, Roberto Calheiros de.
Calhoun, Andrew P. 87792, 105943
Calhoun, Charles. 98564 see also Massachusetts. General Court. Senate. Clerk.
Calhoun, George A. 9929
Calhoun, J. S. 9957
Calhoun, James. 95993
Calhoun, James E. 9930
Calhoun, John. 53323
Calhoun, John. USN 9931
Calhoun, John Caldwell, 1782-1850. 4785, 9932-9947, 9954, 10889, 12701, (22237), (23447), 28566, 28944, 30004, 30014, 35343, (36415), (37137), 37854, 57363, 57565, (67132), 83236, 83279, 83288, 87513, 96073, 96635, 97751, note after 100545A, 102283 see also U. S. Commissioner to the Choctaw Indians. U. S. War Department.
Calhoun, Lucia Gilbert. 49818
Calhoun, Samuel H. defendant 28536
Calhoun, Simon H. 9958
Calhoun doctrine, or state nullification discussed. 9938
Calhoun resolution: its basis and its progress. (20611)
Calhoun text book. 9949
Calhoun's address. (22237), note after 100545A
Calhoun's reply to Webster. 9936
Calidades de la provincia. 38381, 56007, (75765)
California. pseud. Diplomat on diplomacy. see Nunes, Joseph Q. supposed author
California (Alta California) Comandancia General Interno. 98384, 98387 see also Vallejo, Mariano Guadalupe.
California (Alta California) Comandante General y Gefe Politico. 24322, 98727 see also Vazquez de Figueroa, Jose.
California (Alta California) Diputacion Territorial. (68884)
California (Alta California) Laws, statutes, etc. (10027), (49897), 76062
California (Spanish Colony) see California (Alta California)
California. 63255-63257, 72430
California. Adjutant General. 10033-10034
California. Attorney General. 10020, 10028
California. Board of Agriculture. 9993
California. Board of State Viticulture Commissioners. 30282 see also Harazthy, A. and Warner, J. J.
California. Comision Especial Sobre la Derivacion y Definicion de los Nombres de los Diferentes Condados del Estado. see California. Commission on the Derivation and Definition of the Names of the Several Counties.
California. Commission on the Derivation and Definition of the Names of the Several Counties. 98386-98387
California. Commission on the Derivation and Definition of the Names of the Several

Counties. Chairman. 98386-98387 see also Vallejo, Mariano Guadalupe.
California. Commissioners on the Culture of the Grape Vine. see California. Board of State Viticulture Commissioners.
California. Comptroller. (10040)
California. Constitution. 1269, 9998, 16113, 33137, 46885, 59488, (66397), 90934
California. Constitutional Convention, 1849. 8660-8661
California. District Court (Fourth Judicial Circuit) 90320
California. District Court (Twentieth Judicial Circuit) 89294
California. Governor. 10037
California. Governor, 1852-1856 (Bigler) 76077 see also Bigler, John, 1805-1871.
California. Governor, 1858-1860 (Weller) 33150 see also Weller, John B., 1812-1875.
California. Governor, 1862-1864 (Stanford) 90212 see also Stanford, Leland, 1825-1893.
California. Governor, 1864-1868 (Low) 42395 see also Low, Frederick Ferdinand, 1820-1894.
California. Laws, statutes, etc. 10001, 10009, 10021-10023, 10029-10030, 22452, 23765, 32276, 52051, 70820-70821, 72430, 74988, 76032, 76043-76044, 76038, 82438, 97445, note after 100812, 103174
California. Legislature. 10006, 10026, 10039
California. Legislature. Committee on Commerce and Navigation. 10037
California. Legislature. Committee on Joint Resolutions to Congress. 10009
California. Legislature. Select Committee in Relation to U. S. Land Commissioners. 10019
California. Legislature. Assembly. 10025, 97497
California. Legislature. Senate. 9993, (10024)
California. Legislature. Senate. Judiciary Committee. 76080
California. Miners. see Miners of California.
California. State Geologist. 10009
California. State Library. 9982
California. State Prison. Directors. 9983
California. State Registrar. (10043)
California. State Reform School. Trustees. 10001
California. Superintendent of Public Instruction. 10001
California. Supreme Court. 67822, 86356
California. Surveyor General. 10019
California. Union League. see Union League of America. California.
California. University. (9996), 10001, 37295, 2d note after 90670
California. University. Alumni. (9996)
California. University. Trustees. 104142
California, Pa. Southwestern Normal College. see Pennsylvania. State Normal School, California.
California: a history of Upper and Lower California. 25035
California: a sermon . . . in . . . Brooklyn. (36320)
California Academy of Natural Sciences. 9961
California Academy of Sciences. 9959-9960
California adventure and vision. 90556
California and her gold regions. (9964)
California and India, in romantic aspects. (58365)
California and its gold mines. 931
California and its gold regions. (72070)

California and its resources. 79633
California and New Mexico. Message from
the President. 9963
California and New Mexico. Speech, in the
House of Representatives. 90434
California and New Mexico. Speech of Hon.
F. P. Stanton. 90408
California and New Mexcio. Speech of Hon.
Joseph M. Root. 73133
California and New Mexico. Speech of Mr.
John A. Rockwell. 72431
California and New Mexico. Speech of Mr.
William B. Preston. (65385)
California and New York Steamship Company.
9965
California and Oregon. 36329
California and Oregon trail. 58801
California and Oregon. . . . with an appendix.
36329
California and the democracy. (8485)
California and the gold mania. 19653
California and the union. 21718
California as I saw it. 43081
California as it is. 47386
California as it is, and as it may be. 103893
California Battalion claim. (20933)
California Borax Company. 62459
California Branch, United States Sanitary Com-
mission. see United States Sanitary
Commission. California Branch.
California characters and mining scenes and
sketches. (9966)
California claims. 20341
California, College of. see California.
University.
California, descrizione geografica, politica e
morale. 24197
California, dess klimat, och guldminor. 9967
California farmer and journal of useful
sciences. 9968
California. Four months among the gold-
finders. 8350, 100641
California, from its discovery by the Spaniards
to the present time. 9969, 3d note after
96480
California girl. 83974
California gold regions. 9970
California guide book. 25836
California: her wealth and resources. 80440
California herald. 10017
California hundred: a poem. 72703
California illustrated. 9971, 40722
California, in-doors and out. 23861
California in 1850. 92776
California, its characteristics and prospects.
9542
California: its gold and its inhabitants. (9972),
33981
California; its history, population, climate.
33595
California; its past history. 9973
California; its situation and resources. 9974
California king. 90212
California Labor Exchange. 10003
California life illustrated. 94547
California magazine. 34045
California Medical Society. 9975
California Medical Society. Convention, Sacre-
mento, 1856. 9975
California miners' almanac for 1864. 59306
California monthly magazine. 62998
California. Outlines of an address. 105322
California ovvero la mania del danario. 21180
California Pioneers grand excursion. 86009
California politics. 28408
California question. 13652

California question, and the ordinance of '87.
37791
California scenery. 9977, 33180
California scenes. 34045
California scrap-book. 80754
California sketches. 9978, 9981, (37946)
California State Agricultural Society. 9993
California state almanac and annual register
for 1855. 9979
California state almanac and hand-book of
statistics for 1863. 9980
California State Teachers Institute. 10001
California, territorial governments, &c. 13618
California text-book. 98117
California: the wonder of the age. 37837,
(37840)
California und seine Goldminen. 9984
California, union, and freedom. 79508
Californian. pseud. Gold stories of '49. see
Smith, Nuima.
Californian Crusoe, a tale of Mormonism.
(11475)
Californian Crusoe; or, the lost treasure found.
9985
Californie. 25969
Californie; beschrijving van dat land. 63328
Californie devoilee. 96779
Californie en zijne bevolking. 77641
Californie et cote du Nord-Ouest. 101350
Californie et les routes interoceaniques. 32497
Californie et Oregon. 73419
Californie, journal des interets generaux de
l'Ocean Pacifique. 9986
(Californie, Maurice, Aden, Madagascar.) 81315
Californie. Recit d'un cercheur-d'or. 9988
Californien. 27186
Californien, dessen Minen, Ackerbau, Handel
und Gewerbe. 9989
Californien, dets nutig og fermtid. 32992
Californien in der Heimath. 3576
Californien, journal de l'industrie et du com-
merce Francais. 9987
Californien. Land und Leute. 77640
Californien. Mexiko. Reisbilder von Madame
Giovanni. 21184
Californien. Mit besonderer Berucksichtigung.
9990
Californien. Ueber dessen Bevolkerung und
gesellschaftliche Zustande. 73982
Californien und seine Verhaltnisse. (57820)
Californien wie es ist oder Hanbuch von
Californien. 102506
Californiens Gegehwart und Zukunft. 32991
Californies. L'Oregon, et les possessions
Russes en Amerique. (68924)
Californische Skizzen. 27172
Californischen Lebensbild aus dem Jahre 1849.
27194
Caligny, Antenor de. 10047, 14347
Calixto de Orihuela, E. Jose. see Orihuela,
E. Jose Calixto de.
Calkins, Matthew. 65495
Calkoen, Hendrik, 1742-1818. 42747-(42749),
94140
Calkoen, Hendrik, 1742-1818. supposed author
102499, 106046
Calkoon, H. see Calkoen, Hendrik, 1742-1818.
Call, ---------. plaintiff 13249
Call, Lamoni. 38114
Call, Richard Keith, 1791-1862. 10048-10049
Call, addressed to British Christians and
philanthropists. 93141
Call and warning from the Lord. 37207-37208
Call for a convention of southern loyalists.
88394

Call for a non-importation meeting of trades-
men. 61512
Call for a public meeting. 61512
Call for a public meeting of manufacturers
and mechanics. 61512
Call for a public meeting to instruct the
representatives. 61512
Call for scripture evidence. 105325
Call from death to life. 5629, 91318
Call from God to the American churches.
76390
Call from heaven. 46645, 46721
Call from heaven to the present and succeed-
ing generations. 46645
Call from Macedonia. 26785
Call from Salem's watch towers. 13654,
57909
Call from the death to the living. 19898
Call from the ocean. 97077
Call of a convention of inventors. 34952
Call of the Gospel applied unto all men.
46244, 46462, 46735, 50296
Call to a professing people to return unto the
Lord. 96385
Call to arms! 96074
Call to arms, or demonstration of the United
Provinces. 3902
Call to humiliation and reform. 21442
Call to my countrymen. 20506
Call to my countrywomen. (20504)
Call to parents, and children. 3471
Call to repentance. 84544
Call to the ministry of the liberal church.
89045
Call to the nobility. 18569
Call to the stockholders. 42325
Call to the tempted. 46646
Call to the unfaithful professors of truth.
23040-23041
Call to the weary & heavy laden. (20054)
Call upon the unemployed talent of the church.
64678
Call upon the stockholders. (31042)
Call vs. Clark. 13249
Callahan. firm publishers see Peoples,
Barnard & Callahan. firm publishers
Callamura. (63411)
Callamy, Edmund. see Calamy, Edmund,
1600-1666.
Callan, John F. 10050-10052
Callander, John, d. 1789. 1629, (8388), 10053,
89452, note after 99383C
Callava, Jose. (10054)
Callaway Mining and Manufacturing Company.
10055
Callcot, Maria (Dundas) Graham, Lady. 28234-
28235
Calle, Juan Diez de la. 10057-10059, 20133
Calle de Don Juan Manuel. (16974)
Calleja, Felix Maria. supposed author 44947,
note after 98949
Callejo, Bernardo Maria del. 10060
Callendar, George. 10061, 52067
Callender, J. engr. 73782
Callender, James Thomson, 1758-1803. 10062-
10071, 13875, 30997, note after 63795,
(78988), (80640), 105044
Callender, James Thomson, 1758-1803.
defendant 10072
Callender, John, 1706-1778. 10073-(10077),
22369, 55044, 70719, 1st note after
94857, 97190, note after 99383C
Callender, John, 1772-1833. 10078
Callender, Tom. see Callender, James
Thomson, 1758-1803.
Caller, James. 102008

Callerholm, S. J. tr. 92616
Callicot, Theophilus C. 10079
Calliopean Society, Yale University. see Yale
University. Calliopean Society.
Calm. 63582, 100804
Calm address to Americanus. 102647
Calm address to our American colonies. 9080-
9081, 23138-(23139), (23141), 24726,
32106, 50452, (57218), 60919, 63771,
70066, 90317, 96184, 97367, 100776,
102647, 105746
Calm address to the Americans. (27219),
63764, 102648, 102676
Calm address to the citizens and voters of
Philadelphia. 61513
Calm address to the citizens of Philadelphia.
61514
Calm address to the inhabitants of England.
(35331), 102649
Calm address to the people of England. 51504
Calm address to the people of the eastern
states. 10854
Calm and dispassionate enquiry. 12485, 42455,
note after 105966
Calm and dispassionate vindication. 4091
Calm and full vindication, &c., relating to Yale
College. 28220
Calm and full vindication of a letter. 26348,
26350
Calm and impartial exposition of the origin and
immediate cause. 62346, note after 97268
Calm and respectful thoughts. 106383
Calm appeal to the citizens of the state of New
York. 88638, 104556
Calm appeal to the friends of American indus-
try. 16142
Calm appeal to the people of the state of Dela-
ware. 19381
Calm discussion of the abolition question.
(16145), 81905
Calm dissuasive against intemperance. 102465
Calm examination of Dr. McMaster's letters.
78249
Calm observer. pseud. American question.
see Joy, George.
Calm observer. pseud. Letter to W. E. Chan-
ning. see Trist, Nicholas Philip. sup-
posed author
Calm review of the measures employed. 12948,
18138
Calomniateurs denonces a la Convention Nation-
ale. 75076
Calomniateurs Le Borgne, Polverel, Sontonax
[sic] et complices. 75077
Calomnies devenues verites. 5652
Calphurnius, Jo. 25088
Caludio de Sequeira, Gabriel. see Sequeira,
Gabriel Caludio de.
Calui, Alessandro. tr. (4832)
Calumet. 10080
Calumet. New series of the harbinger of peace.
10081
Calumnies of Verus. 98924
Calumny exposed. 102724
Calumny refuted. (29314), 25231
Calumny refuted: an answer to the exposition of
Thomas H. Lewis. (7067)
Calumny refuted and truth defended. 94505A
Calumny refuted; or a glance at John Wilbur's
book. 10082
Calvary pastoral. 54140
Calvary—Virginia tragedies. 57755
Calvert, ------. 45069
Calvert, Cecil. see Baltimore, Cecil Calvert,
2d Baron, 1606?-1675.

Calvert, Charles, 1629-1714. see Baltimore, Charles Calvert, 3d Baron, 1629-1714.
Calvert, Charles, 1699-1751. see Baltimore, Charles Calvert, 6th Baron, 1699-1751.
Calvert, Frederick. see Baltimore, Frederick Calvert, 7th Baron, 1731-1771.
Calvert, Sir George. (33263)
Calvert, George Henry, 1803-1889. (10084)-10085, 55028, 100753 see also Newport, R. I. Mayor, 1853-1854 (Calvert)
Calvert and Penn. (47092)
Calvet, Pierre du. see Du Calvet, Pierre, d. 1786.
Calvillo, Juan Bautista Diaz. see Diaz Calvillo, Juan Bautista.
Calvin, -------. 65088, 96801
Calvin, Jean, 1509-1564. 99724
Calvin, John. pseud. At a meeting of the true sons of liberty. 86983
Calvin, Martin V. 2381
Calvin and Calvinism. 74430
Calvin and his enemies. 85266
Calvin and Hopkins versus the Bible and common sense. 65088, 96801
Calvin defended. 85266
Calvin Philanax. pseud. Friendly epistle to Mr. George Keith. see Young, Samuel, nonconformist minister, fl. 1690-1700.
Calvin Phillio's light on masonry and anti-masonry. 62466
Calvinism improved. 92955
Calvinist. 92859
Calvinist Church, Worcester, Mass. see Worcester, Mass. Calvinist Church.
Calvinistic Congregational Church, Sandwich, Mass. see Sandwich, Mass. Calvinistic Congregational Church.
Calvo, Alonso. 10086
Caluo, Andrea. 16950, 56052
Calvo, Carlos, 1824-1906. 10087-(10092)
Calvo, Charles. see Calvo, Carlos, 1824-1906.
Calvo, Nicolas A. tr. 92288
Calvo de la Torre, Juan del Corral. see Corral Calvo de la Torre, Juan del, 1666-1737.
Calvo Iturburu, Atilano. see Iturburu, Atilano Calvo.
Calvo. firm publishers see Harper & Calvo. firm publishers
Calvus. pseud. Letters addressed to Lord Liverpool. 40567
Calyborn, --------. 63312
Calyo's panorama of the Connecticut River. 10094
Calyton, William. 83283
Calzada, Bernardo Maria de, fl. 1784-1807. 10095, 100726
Calzado, Bernardo Maria de. see Calzada, Bernardo Maria de, fl. 1784-1807.
Camac, Turner. supposed author 5959, (10096)
Camacho, R. 10097
Camacho, Sebastian. 10098-10099, (48310)
Camacho, Simon. 44064
Camago, -------. 10101
Camaguey, Cuba (City) see Puerto Principe (City)
Camaguey, Cuba (Province) see Puerto Principe (Province)
Camaleones politicos. 46860
Camalloa, Estevan de Garibay y. see Garibay y Camalloa, Estevan de.
Caman, Vasco di. see Gama, Vasco da, 1469?-1524.
Camara, Manoel Arruda da. 10100

Camare, Eusebio de Queiroz Coitinho Mattoso. see Mattoso Camare, Eusebio de Queiroz Coitinho.
Camargo y Salcedo, Ferdinand. 44553
Cambas, Manuel Rivera. see Rivera Cambas, Manuel.
Cambefort, Joseph Paul Augustin. 10103-(10104), (75171), 96341
Cambell, Duncan. 39797
Cambessedes, Jacques. 10105-10106, (75218), 75222
Cambiagi, -------. (10107)
Cambray, -------. 10108
Cambray, Archbishop of. see Fenelon, Francois de Salignac de la Mothe-, Abp., 1651-1715.
Cambreleng, Churchill Caldom, 1876-1862. 10109-10114, 10889, (31494), 37418, 47878, 77560, 1st note after 92842
Cambrensivm Caroleia. 98691
Cambrensivm Caroleja. 98692
Cambria Iron Company. 10115
Cambridge, John. 10116
Cambridge, Mass. 10123, (10144), (10151)
Cambridge, Mass. Andover Theological Seminary. see Andover Theological Seminary.
Cambridge, Mass. Associate Presbytery. see Presbyterian Church in the U. S. A. Associate Presbytery of Cambridge.
Cambridge, Mass. Board of Aldermen. 10155
Cambridge, Mass. Board of Engineers. 10155
Cambridge, Mass. Board of Health. (10144)
Cambridge, Mass. Botanic Garden. 59493
Cambridge, Mass. Cambridgeport Church. 36467
Cambridge, Mass. Cambridgeport Lyceum. 10147
Cambridge, Mass. Charter. (10144)
Cambridge, Mass. Christ Church. Church Union Auxiliary. (10130)
Cambridge, Mass. Circulating Library. 10147
Cambridge, Mass. Citizens. petitioners 9372, 81492
Cambridge, Mass. City Council. 10155
Cambridge, Mass. Committee of Finance. 10142-10143
Cambridge, Mass. Committee on the West Boston and Canal Bridges. 10124
Cambridge, Mass. Committee to Consider the Expediency of Consolidating Certain Boards of Officers. (10144)
Cambridge, Mass. Committee to Consider the Reorganization of the Public Schools. 10135
Cambridge, Mass. Committee to Investigate the Affairs of the Almshouse. (10144)
Cambridge, Mass. Constitutional Convention, 1779. see Massachusetts. Constitutional Convention, Cambridge, 1779.
Cambridge, Mass. Constitutional Convention, 1779-1780. see Massachusetts. Constitutional Convention, Cambridge, 1779-1780.
Cambridge, Mass. Dowse Institute. 20793
Cambridge, Mass. East Cambridge Female School. 10135
Cambridge, Mass. East Cambridge Lyceum. 10147
Cambridge, Mass. Evangelical Congregational Church. 10131
Cambridge, Mass. Fire Department. (10140)
Cambridge, Mass. First Baptist Church. 10126
Cambridge, Mass. First Church. 10125
Cambridge, Mass. First Church. Committee. 10125

Cambridge, Mass. First Evangelical Congregational Church. 10131

Cambridge, Mass. Friendly Fire Society. see Friendly Fire Society, Cambridge, Mass.

Cambridge, Mass. High School. Library. 10136

Cambridge, Mass. House of Correction. (10144)

Cambridge, Mass. Mayor, 1846. (10141)

Cambridge, Mass. Mayor, 1848. 10142

Cambridge, Mass. Mayor, 1854. (10121)

Cambridge, Mass. Meeting of Citizens in Reference to the Assault on Senator Sumner, June 2, 1856. 93723

Cambridge, Mass. Museum of Comparative Zoology. 10122

Cambridge, Mass. Old Cambridge Division, no. 26, Sons of Temperance. see Sons of Temperance of North America. Massachusetts. Old Cambridge Division, no. 26, Cambridge.

Cambridge, Mass. Ordinances, etc. (10140), (10144)

Cambridge, Mass. Printers' Literary Union. see Printers' Literary Union, Cambridge, Mass.

Cambridge, Mass. Lechmere-Point Library Association. see Lechmere-Point Library Association, Cambridge, Mass.

Cambridge, Mass. Provincial Congress, 1774. see Massachusetts. Provincial Congress, Cambridge, 1774.

Cambridge, Mass. Provincial Congress, 1775. see Massachusetts. Provincial Congress, Cambridge, 1775.

Cambridge, Mass. School Committee. 10135, 10143

Cambridge, Mass. Second Baptist Church. 10133

Cambridge, Mass. Second Evangelical Congregational Church. 10132

Cambridge, Mass. Selectmen. (10144)

Cambridge, Mass. Soldiers' Monument. 86347

Cambridge, Mass. Subscription Fund for the Benefit of the Cambridge Volunteers. see Subscription Fund for the Benefit of the Cambridge Volunteers, Cambridge, Mass.

Cambridge, Mass. Survey of the Roads. (10144)

Cambridge, Mass. Synod, 1641. see Congregational Churches in Massachusetts. Cambridge Synod, 1641.

Cambridge, Mass. Synod, 1648. see Congregational Churches in Massachusetts. Cambridge Synod, 1648.

Cambridge, Mass. Union Temperance Society. see East Cambridge Union Temperance Society.

Cambridge, Mass. University. see Harvard University.

Cambridge, Mass. Washington Benevolent Society. see Washington Benevolent Society. Massachusetts. Cambridge.

Cambridge, Mass. Water Works. 10155

Cambridge, Mass. Whig Republican Association. see Whig Republican Association, Cambridge, Mass.

Cambridge, S. C. Baptist State Convention, 1822. see Baptists. South Carolina. State Convention, Cambridge, 1822.

Cambridge almanac and business directory for the year 1847. 10117

Cambridge and Saybrook platforms of church discipline. 63343

Cambridge chronicle. 41568

Cambridge clergyman. pseud. Mormonism or the Bible? 50757

Cambridge directory. 10118

Cambridge ephemeris. 10119

Cambridge ephemeris. An almanack of coelestial motions and configurations for the year of the Christian epocha, 1687. 62743, 104395

Cambridge ephemeris. An almanack of coelestial motions, configurations &c. for the year of the Christian AEra, 1684. 62743

Cambridge ephemeris an almanack of the coelestial motions, for the year of the Christian AEra, 1685. 62743, 104394

Cambridge essays. 10156

Cambridge Free Soil Club. (10149) see also Free Soil Party. Massachusetts. Cambridge.

Cambridge Humane Society. 10152

Cambridge Humane Society. Agent. 10152

Cambridge man. pseud. Free blacks and slaves. 25705

Cambridge, May [25], 1848. Sir, a collection of books. 88964

Cambridge modern history. 84342

Cambridge platform adopted in 1648. 15486, 69921

Cambridge platform . . . and the confession of faith. (10120)

Cambridge platform of church-discipline. 46439

Cambridge prize poems. 100901

Cambridge Savings Institution, Cambridge, Mass. 10152

Cambridgeport, Mass. see Cambridge, Mass.

Cambridgeport Lyceum. see Cambridge, Mass. Cambridgeport Lyceum.

Cambromyomachia. 65527

Camden, Charles Pratt, 1st Earl of, 1714-1794. 40467, 79246

Camden, Charles Pratt, 1st Earl of, 1714-1794. petitioner 101150

Camden, William. 10157-10159

Camden, N. J. Committee on Bridging the Deleware. 69960

Camden, N. J. Ordinances, etc. 10160

Camden, S. C. Meeting of the Citizens of Kershaw District, 1825. see Kershaw District, S. C. Tariff Meeting, Camden, 1826.

Camden, S. C. Tariff Meeting, 1826. see Kershaw District, S. C. Tariff Meeting, Camden, 1826.

Camden District, S. C. Court of General Sessions of the Peace. Grand Jury. 87468

Camden and Amboy Railroad and Transportation Company. 10162, 10828, (19406), 19416, (31177), note after 91895

Camden and Amboy Railroad and Transportation Company. Executive Committee. 69674

Camden and Amboy Railroad and Transportation Company. Joint Board of Directors. see Joint Board of Directors of the Delaware and Raritan Canal, and Camden and Amboy Railroad Transportation Companies.

Camden and vicinity. 68036

Camden city directory. 10161

Camden journal. 71069

Camden miscellany. 67599

Camel his organization habits and uses. 44735

Camera de Senadores. "Comunicacion de dorotos vasconzelos." (76190)

Cameron, Adam. supposed author 93849

Cameron, Allan. 10164

Cameron, Allen. defendant at court martial 10163

Cameron, Duncan. 40998
Cameron, Hugh. 10166, 1st note after 97062
Cameron, John Hillyard. 10167
Cameron, Malcolm. 10168
Cameron, Simon, 1799-1889. 10169, (78703),
86282, 86289, 89203 see also U. S.
War Department.
Cameron and Lincoln Club, Chicago. 12662
Cameron Hall: a story of the civil war.
(17731)
Cameron's proposed . . . steamers. 10165
Camers, Joannes, i. e. Giovanni Ricuzzi
Vellini, 1448-1546. (63958)-63960,
76838, 86390
Camertus, Joannus. see Camers, Joannes,
i. e. Giovanni Ricuzzi Vellini, 1448-1546.
Camilla. 10170
Camillo Querno. pseud. see Odell, Jonathan,
1738-1818. supposed author and Cock-
ings, George, d. 1802. supposed author
Camillus. pseud. Anti-gallic letters. see
Thom, Adam.
Camillus. pseud. Defence of the treaty of
amity. see Hamilton, Alexander, 1755-
1804.
Camillus. pseud. Enquiry into the evils of
general suffrage. see Henry, J.
Camillus. pseud. Mississippi question fairly
stated. see Duane, William John.
Camillus. pseud. Political rejoinder. see
Hamilton, Alexander, 1755-1804.
Camillus. pseud. To the public. 96001
Caminha e Menezes, Antonio Telles da Silva.
see Telles da Silva Caminha e Menezes,
Antonio, Marquez de Resende, 1790-1875.
Camino de la fortuna. 25586
Camino del cielo en lengua Mexicana. (40080)
Camino verdadero. 75868
Camm, John. 10173, 70255
Cammann, Henry J. 10174
Cammeyer, W. ed. 601
Camoens et Joze India. 19555
Camoens in the hospital. 98242
Camoes, Luiz de, 1524?-1580. 57664
Camp, ------- de. see De Camp, --------.
Camp, David N. 10175
Camp, George Sidney. 10176
Camp, H. ed. 25816
Camp, Hugh J. 10174
Camp, John de. see De Camp, John.
Camp, P. 10177
Camp (J. de) firm publishers see Bell and
De Camp. firm publishers
Camp and field. (17657)
Camp and prison journal. 26020
Camp and the field. 83970
Camp and the field. By one of our chaplains.
10178
Camp Charlotte. A tale of 1774. 10179
Camp de Jackson. 18664
Camp-fire and cotton-field. (38177)
Camp fire companion. 10180
Camp-fire sketches. 6284
Camp-fire songster. 10181
Camp fires and camp cooking. (76394)
Camp fires of the red men. (57728)
Camp Ford (Confederate Military Prison) see
Tyler, Texas. Camp Ford (Confederate
Military Prison)
Camp inspection return. 76542, 76647
Camp inspection returns. 76541, 76647
Camp instruction returns. 34868
Camp Jackson: its history and significance.
20817
Camp jester. 10182
Camp life. 78724

Camp-life in the Adirondacks. 51549
Camp life of a volunteer. 78476
Camp life. The sayings and doings of volun-
teers. 43051
Camp McDonald, the school of instruction of the
Fourth Brigade of Georgia Volunteers.
(10183)
Camp meeting discourse at East Hartford.
48022
Camp-meetings: their history. 64267
Camp songs; a collection of national, patriotic,
and social songs. 10184
Camp songs for the soldier. 31080
Camp stories. 26215
Camp stories and tales of the Crescent City.
86308
Camp tales of Arlington Heights. 42964
Camp, the bivouac, and the battle-field. 26515
Camp Ward journal. (10185)
Campa, Antonio de la. plaintiff 76225
Campagnac, Jean Baptiste Joseph. 11819-11822
Campagne de circumnavigation de la fregate
l'Artemise. 38983
Campagne de l'armee de M. le Cte. de Roch-
ambeau. (72034)
Campagne de l'armee de M. le Comte de
Rochambeau. (72032)-72033
Campagne de l'armee du Potomac. 36406, 1st
note after 97024
Campagne de Mexique. Puebla. (55409)
Campagne du navire l'Espoir de Honfleur 1503-
1505. 27788
Campagne du Potomac. 36408, 1st note after
97024
Campagnes de Francais a St. Domingue. 24001
Campagnes de Virginie et de Maryland en 1862.
39657
Campagnes des Francais a Saint-Domingue.
(39231)
Campagnes du General Americain W. Scott 1847.
4084
Campagnes et croisades dans les etats de
Venezuela et de la Nouvelle Grenada.
10193-10194, note after 94254, note after
98870
Campagnes et croisieres dans les etats de
Venezuela et de la Nouvelle-Grenade.
10193, note before 94254, note 98870
Campagnes militaires du Lieutenant General
Sir William Howe. (33339)
Campaign against Atlanta. 80415
Campaign against Quebec. 31401
Campaign against Savannah. 80415
Campaign document. 67175
Campaign document, no. 14. 41185
Campaign document no. 1, issued by the Demo-
cratic State Central Committee of Louisi-
ana. 91255
Campaign document no. 1, of the Central Union
Club. 8284
Campaign document. No. 1. The Democratic
platform. 10187, 19510
Campaign document, no. 13. 41216
Campaign document, no. 3. (43012)
Campaign document, no. 3. Speech . . . July
24th, 1860. 31703
Campaign document, no. 21. Speech of Gover-
nor Seymour at Philadelphia. (79648)
Campaign document, no. 2. 10187, 15072
Campaign document, no. 2. Issued by the
Democratic State Central Committee of
Louisiana. 42201
Campaign document of 1870. 27019
Campaign document. Speech of D. Reddington.
(68487)

Campaign for president, William H. Harrison. 30575

Campaign in Illinois. 20692

Campaign in Mexico. 78477

Campaign in Mexico, or a glimpse at life in camp. 78476

Campaign in New Mexico with Colonel Doniphan. 10188, 21920

Campaign in northern Mexico in 1846-47. 10189

Campaign in Virginia, in July and August, 1862. 64112

Campaign in Virginia, 1781. 95301

Campaign lives of Seymour and Blair. 17596

Campaign lives of U. S. Grant and S. Colfax. 8012

Campaign of 1856. (20934), (25845)

Campaign of 1860. Comprising the speeches. 10190, 93644

Campaign of 1860. Republican songs for the people. 20935

Campaign of Gen. Scott in the valley of Mexico. 79075

Campaign of Louisbourg. 36392

Campaign of Louisbourg, 1750-'58. 67022

Campaign of 1781 in the Carolinas. (39742), (39750)

Campaign of 1760, in Canada. 67022

Campaign of the armies of the Tennessee, Ohio, and Cumberland. 80413

Campaign of the Sixth Army Corps. (68543)

Campaign on the reserve. 26664

Campaign or Scott and Graham songster. 57880

Campaign poem. 58070

Campaign satire for 1872. 87136

Campaign sketches of the war with Mexico. (31418)

Campaign sketches of Virginia and Maryland. 56214

Campaign songs. 10191

Campaign songs for Christian patriots and true Democrats. (64686)

Campaign through the Carolinas. 80415

Campaign tract for 1864. 10192

Campaign tracts. 8285

Campaigns and cruises in Venezuela. (21638)

Campaigns and cruises, in Venezuela and New Granada. 10193, note after 94254, note after 98870

Campaigns in Virginia, Maryland, &c. 12521

Campaigns of 1862 and 1863. 77504

Campaigns of Lieut.-Gen. N. B. Forrest. 36654

Campaigns of Richmond. 57111

Campaigns of the British Army at Washington. 27571

Campaigns of the First Maine and First District of Columbia Cavalry. (48005)

Campaigns of the Rio Grande and of Mexico. 91522

Campaigns of the Seventeenth Maine. (33159)

Campana contra los Americanos del Norte. Observaciones. 56444, 68932

Campana contra los Americanos del Norte. Primera parte. 10195

Campana de Perote y Oazaca. 71417

Campana del interior. 10196

Campana en ejercito grande. 77067

Campana sin gloria tenida en el recinto de Mexico. 48315

Campanas del General D. Felix Maria Calleja. 9569

Campanas y cruceros. 10193, note after 94254, note after 98870

Campanella, Tommaso, 1568-1639. 10197-10201, (29819)

Campanius Holm, Thomas, d. 1702. 10202-10203, 42726

Campano, Lorenzo. 10204

Campbell, ----------. Chief Justice of Ontario 96883

Campbell, ----------. ed. 1614

Campbell, Mrs. -------- (Bourne) 6925, 93471

Campbell, Albert H. 69946

Campbell, Alexander. 10207-10208

Campbell, Alexander, fl. 1726-1732. 93809, 97097

Campbell, Alexander, fl. 1744. 1639, (50834)

Campbell, Alexander, fl. 1747. 10205

Campbell, Alexander, 1788-1866. 10206, 12904, 36044, 48999, 66674, 91762, 91764, 101063

Campbell, Alexander, fl. 1851. 81954

Campbell, Allen. 10209, 22763, note after 97071

Campbell, Archibald, 1629-1685. see Argyll, Archibald Campbell, 9th Earl of, 1629-1685.

Campbell, Archibald, b. 1787. 10210-10212

Campbell, B. C. 37409-37411

Campbell, Sir C. 56150 see also Nova Scotia. Lieutenant Governor (Campbell)

Campbell, Charles, 1807-1876. 5114, 5867, 10213-10216, 40785

Campbell, Colin, d. 1782. 49954

Campbell, Colin, d. 1782. defendant at court martial 96846

Campbell, D. Forbes. tr. 12595

Campbell, David, 1779-1859. 53633 see also Virginia. Governor, 1837-1840 (Campbell)

Campbell, Duncan G. 96636 see also U. S. Commissioners to the Creek Indians.

Campbell, Eleanor W. (Doak) (10260)

Campbell, F. W. ed. 10634

Campbell, George. 10217

Campbell, George Douglas. see Argyll, George Douglas Campbell, 8th Duke of, 1823-1900.

Campbell, George L. 10218

Campbell, George Washington, 1768-1848. 10219, 94790

Campbell, Henry R. 92416, 92814

Campbell, Hugh Hume. see Marchmont, Hugh Hume Campbell, 3d Earl of.

Campbell, Hugh J. 10220

Campbell, J. A. (48140), 65358 see also Confederate States of America. Peace Commissioners to the Hampton Roads Conference.

Campbell, J. B. 87470

Campbell, J. N. 77736

Campbell, James. 10221

Campbell, Lieut.-Col. James. RA 10222

Campbell, James, Deputy Collector of Customs of the Port of New York. 10224, 94392

Campbell, James Hepburn, 1820-1895. 10223-10224, (78468)

Campbell, John. 10249

Campbell, John, Bookseller, Philadelphia. 10248

Campbell, John, Geologist of Nova Scotia. 12359, (14686), 56109, 81060-81062

Campbell, John, paper dealer, N. Y. 371

Campbell, John, R. A. 10244

Campbell, John, 1678-1743. see Argyll, John Campbell, 2d Duke of, 1678-1743.

Campbell, John, d. 1701. 10226

Campbell, John, 1705-1782. see Loudoun, John Campbell, 4th Earl of, 1705-1782.

Campbell, John, 1708-1775. 102, 10230-10240, 10242, 30483, 71537, 3d note after 102821

Campbell, John, 1708-1775. incorrectly supposed author (5859), 10241, 10243, 28770-28771, 63775, (68962), 88938, 3d note after 103122, note after 106063
Campbell, John, 1764-1867. 10246
Campbell, Sir John, 1776-1847. 56150 see also Nova Scotia. Lieutenant Governor, 1834-1840 (Campbell)
Campbell, John, fl. 1830. 10245
Campbell, John, fl. 1839. 10247
Campbell, John A. 10250
Campbell, John Campbell, Baron, 1779-1861. 31770
Campbell, John D. 68498
Campbell, John Francis. 80595
Campbell, John George Edward Henry Douglas Sutherland. see Argyll, John George Edward Henry Douglas Sutherland Campbell, 9th Duke of, 1845-1914.
Campbell, John Hull, 1800-1868. 10252
Campbell, John L. 10253-10254
Campbell, John N. (10255)
Campbell, John P. 10257-10258, (51879)
Campbell, John Poage, 1767-1814. 92026, 92030
Campbell, John W. Bookseller 10259
Campbell, John Wilson, 1782-1833. (10260)
Campbell, Lewis Davis, 1811-1882. 10261
Campbell, Loomis Joseph. 10262
Campbell, Maria (Hull) (10263)
Campbell, Mary. pseud. Poems and tales. see Blake, Mary E.
Campbell, P. 10264
Campbell, Robert. 10265
Campbell, Rollo. 10266
Campbell, Thomas, 1777-1844. 10267-10270, 10276, 31719, 76381, 92150-92151
Campbell, Thomas, fl. 1840. 10271
Campbell, Thompson. 10272
Campbell, W. H. 28676
Campbell, Lord William, fl. 1776. 87364
Campbell, William Frederick Campbell, 2d Baron. 10273
Campbell, William Henry, 1808-1890. 10274, 74435
Campbell, William W., 1806-1881. 10275-10282, 12480, 37704
Campbell & Richardson. firm publishers 89845
Campbell & Richardson's Springfield city directory. 89845
Campbellism examined. 36093
Campbellism exposed. 94481
Campbellism, its rise, progress, character and influence. 70857
Campbellism re-examined. 36093
Campbellite church at Wellsburg, Virginia. 87096
Campbell's foreign semi-monthly mag. 10932
Campe, Joachim Heinrich, 1746-1818. 10283-10309, (14651), 16273, 72232-72233, note after 100811
Campeador. pseud. Rambling reflections in Greenwood. 28696
Campellos, Joao da Apresentacao. (10310)
Campen, Moses van. see Van Campen, Moses.
Campenon, --------. tr. 72013
Campense, Alberto. 67736
Camphausen, William. illus. 35196
Campi, Pietro Maria. 10311
Campillo, J. illus. (48590)
Campillo, Manuel Ignacio Gonzalez del. see Gonzalez del Campillo, Manuel Ignacio, Bp., 1740-1813.
Campillo y Cosio, Joseph del. 10314, 36661
Campino, Joaquin. 85677

Campo, Est. del. 10315
Campo, Josefo. 10317
Campo, Juan de. 10318
Campo-Sagrado, Manuel de Quiros y. see Quiros y Campo-Sagrado, Manuel de.
Campoamor y Campoosorio, Ramon Maria de las Mercedes de, 1817-1901. 10319
Campo-bell, John Talbot. pseud. Speech. see Robertson, Robert.
Campoosorio, Ramon Maria de las Mercedes de Campoamor y. see Campoamor y Campoosorio, Ramon Maria de las Mercedes de, 1817-1901.
Campos, B. 10320
Campos, Domingo. 10321
Campos, J. G. 10323
Campos, Jose Paulo Rodrigues de. 10324
Campos, Juan de. 10325
Campos, Juan Greg. de. 57422
Campos, Luis Caetano de. 10326
Campos Marin, Juan de. see Marin, Juan de Campos.
Campos Martinez, Juan Gregoria de. see Martinez, Juan Gregoria de Campos.
Campos y Martinez, J. G. de. 24156
Camps, --------. 61065
Camps and prisons. 21152
Campville, J. A. P. 10327
Camstrup, N. J. 77965
Camus, ---------. 46946
Camus, A. G. 10328
Camus de Limare, ------. (8784)
Can a Negro hold office in Georgia? 18815, 27020
Can abolitionists vote or take office? 62528, 81919
Can all professing to be Friends become united? 65434
Can an obligation for the payment of "gold or silver coin" be discharged? 78970
Can India not supply England with cotton? (17122)
Can tell a big lie. pseud. Aurifodia. see Bigly, Cantell A. pseud.
Can the country pay the expenses of the war? 91017
Can we enter into treaty with the new slave trading confederacy? 10329
Canaal van communicatie tusschen Essequebo en Demerary. 22993, 5th note after 102895
Canaan, N. H. Citizens. 52791, note after 98998
Canaan repository of rural knoweldge. 14873
Canaan, Shem and Japheth. 30787
Canada (English Colony, ca. 1625) Charter. 741, 16684, 91853
Canada (Nouvelle France) see New France.
Canada. 8115, 10390, 10402, 10452-(10453), 10521, 10539, (10557), 10588, 10613, 17818, (26252), 39958, (45413), (56766), note after 61176, 69258, (69300), 1st note after 94182, note after 95370, 99753
Canada. Agricultural Society. see Agricultural Society of Canada.
Canada. Assemblee Legislative. see Canada. Parliament. Legislative Assembly.
Canada. Assinniboine and Saskatchewan Exploring Expedition. (31937)
Canada. Attorney General. 88596 see also Southouse, Edward.
Canada. Board of Engineers. see Canada. Geological Survey. Board of Engineers.
Canada. Board of Inspectors of the Provincial Penitentiary. 10551, (10553)

Canada. Bureau of Agriculture and Statistics. (10435)
Canada. Bureau d'Ingenieurs. see Canada. Geological Survey. Board of Engineers.
Canada. Census, 1831. 10400
Canada. Census, 1851-1852. 10401
Canada. Census, 1861. 10400
Canada. Census, 1867. 20325
Canada. Charter. 741
Canada. Columbia River Expedition, 1865. 49776
Canada. Commissaire des Terres de la Couronne. see Canada. Commissioner of Crown Lands.
Canada. Commissaires des Travaux Publics. see Canada. Commissioners of Public Works.
Canada. Commissaires Speciaux, Nomme le 8 de Septembre, 1856. see Canada. Special Commissioners to Investigate Indian Affairs.
Canada. Commission Geologique. see Canada. Geological Survey.
Canada. Commission on the Affairs of the Grand Trunk Railway. (28269)
Canada. Commissioner of Crown lands. (10412), 33551 see also Cauchon, Joseph, 1816-1885.
Canada. Commissioners of Public Works. (10558)-10559, 10561
Canada. Commissioners to Inquire into the Affairs of the University of King's College, and the College of Upper Canada. 10428
Canada. Commissioners to Inquire into the Conduct, Discipline and Management of the Provincial Penitentiary. 10552
Canada. Commissioners to Inquire into the Trade of the West Indies, Mexico, and Brazil. 69782
Canada. Commissioners to Investigate the Origin, etc., of the Epidemic Cholera. 10583
Canada. Commissioners Under the Seigniorial Tenure Act of 1854. 90709
Canada. Courts. 70241, 85421
Canada. Delegates to Negotiate for the Acquisition of Rupert's Land and the North-West Territory. 74149
Canada. Department of Agriculture. 79770
Canada. Department of Indian Affairs. 34464, 67920
Canada. Emigration Agent. 10438, (72878)-72879 see also Rolph, Thomas.
Canada. Forces Charged with the Protection of the Fisheries of the Gulf of St. Lawrence. Commander. 25175-25176 see also Fortin, Pierre.
Canada. Geological Survey. 10457-10460, 26986, 29805, 33893-33894, 33863, 41809-41811, 41815-41816, 84802
Canada. Governor General. 10482, note after (10603)
Canada. Governor General, 1760-1768 (Murray) 67023 see also Murray, James, 1725?-1794.
Canada. Governor General, 1768-1778 (Dorchester) 10904 see also Dorchester, Guy Carleton, 1st Baron, 1724-1808.
Canada. Governor General, 1778-1786 (Haldimand) 52579 see also Haldimand, Sir Frederick, 1718-1791.
Canada. Governor General, 1786-1796 (Dorchester) 67002, 98065C see also Dorchester, Guy Carleton, 1st Baron, 1724-1808.

Canada. Governor General, 1797-1808 (Prescott) 23503 see also Prescott, Robert, 1725-1816.
Canada. Governor General, 1820-1828 (Dalhousie) (10336), 10410, 19456, 58489 see also Dalhousie, George Ramsay, 9th Earl of, 1770-1838.
Canada. Governor General, 1830-1835 (Aylmer) 2519, (5218), (10557A), 4th note after 42522, 67113 see also Aylmer, Matthew Whitmore, 5th Baron, 1775-1850.
Canada. Governor General, 1838-1839 (Seaton) 10517 see also Seaton, John Colborne, 1st Baron, 1778-1863.
Canada. Governor General, 1839-1841 (Sydenham) 42522, 72879 see also Sydenham, Charles Edward Poulett Thomson, 1st Baron, 1799-1841.
Canada. Governor General, 1842-1843 (Bagot) 72879 see also Bagot, Sir Charles, 1781-1843.
Canada. Governor General, 1843-1845 (Metcalfe) 10460, 74568 see also Metcalfe, Charles Theophilus Metcalfe, 1st Baron, 1785-1846.
Canada. Governor General, 1847-1854 (Elgin) 22116-22117, 43350 see also Elgin, James Bruce, 8th Earl of, 1811-1863.
Canada. Governor General, 1854-1861 (Head) 33551 see also Head, Sir Edmund Walker, Bart., 1805-1868.
Canada. Governor in Chief. see Canada. Governor General.
Canada. House of Assembly. see Canada. Parliament. Legislative Assembly.
Canada. Indian Department. 34464
Canada. Inspecteurs du Penitencieur Provincial. see Canada. Board of Inspectors of the Provincial Penitentiary.
Canada. Inspector General. 10418, 10612 see also Hincks, Sir Francis, 1807-1885.
Canada. Inspectors of the Free Ports of Gaspe and Sault Ste. Marie. 26740
Canada. Intercolonial Railway Exploratory Survey, 1864. (24707)
Canada. Laws, statutes, etc. 10331, 10378, 10483, 10539, 14396, 20676, 21337, 26214, 27521, 28476, 28478, 30189, (34389), 38609, 41690, 1st note after 59045, 66390, 67720, 68441, 70241, 73152, 85421, 80709, 93606
Canada. Legislative Assembly. see Canada. Parliament. Legislative Assembly.
Canada. Legislative Council. see Canada. Parliament. Legislative Council.
Canada. Legislature. see Canada. Parliament.
Canada. Library of Parliament, Toronto. see Canada. Parliament. Library.
Canada. Lieutenant Governor, 1782-1785 (Hamilton) 21044 see also Hamilton, Henry, d. 1796.
Canada. Maître-General des Postes. see Canada. Post-Master General.
Canada. Militia. 10519-10520
Canada. Parliament. 10554, 58812, 84792
Canada. Parliament. Canal Committee. 8385
Canada. Parliament. Library. 1578, 10393-10399
Canada. Parliament. Select Committee on the Rights of the Hudson's Bay Company. 33543, 33547, 33550
Canada. Parliament. Special Committee on the Magdalen Islands. 10587

Canada. Parliament. Special Committee to
Enquire and Report as to the Condition,
Management, and Prospects to the Grand
Trunk Railway Company. (28269)
Canada. Parliament. Standing Committee on
Public Accounts. (10453)
Canada. Parliament. Legislative Assembly.
10469, 10487, 10493, 10502, 36757,
57887, 79757, 94187
Canada. Parliament. Legislative Assembly.
Select Committee on the Political State
of Upper and Lower Canada. 10580
Canada. Parliament. Legislative Assembly.
Select Committee on the Public Income
and Expenditures of the Province.
(10451)
Canada. Parliament. Legislative Assembly.
Special Committee on the Seigniorial
Tenure. 10502
Canada. Parliament. Legislative Council.
10493, 21044
Canada. Parliament. Legislative Council.
Select Committee on Accusations Made
Against the Members of the Late Admin-
istration, 1855. (10579)
Canada. Post-Master General. (10548)
Canada. Post Office. (10453), 41690
Canada. Special Commissioners to Investigate
Indian Affairs. 10467, 67924
Canada. Superintendents of Education. (10453)
Canada. Treaties, etc. 69884
Canada. 10367, (26089), 85851
Canada, a battle ground. 86821
Canada: a brief outline. 10368, 22497, 34110
Canada. A descriptive poem. (10370)
Canada: a geographical, agricultural, and
mineralogical sketch. 33892
Canada affairs. 10371
Canada, an encyclopaedia of the country.
84422
Canada. An essay. 32421
Canada and Australia, their relative merits
considered. 72875
Canada and common laws. (28143)
Canada and her resources. (50795)
Canada and Jamaica. 1426
Canada and South Australia. 33891, 72871
Canada and the American revolution. 83469
Canada, and the Canada bill. 72119
Canada and the Canadians. 6330
Canada and the Canadians, in 1846. 6329
Canada and the Continental Congress. (20995)
Canada and the Crimea. 67869
Canada and the empire. 89909
Canada and the Oregon. 96441
Canada and the United States. 16762
Canada and the western states of America
described. 10372
Canada as a field for emigration. 19373
Canada, as it is. 33776
Canada as it was, is, and may be. 6331
Canada at the Universal Exhibition of 1855.
94187
Canada baptist magazine. 10374
Canada Branch of the U.S. Sanitary Commis-
sion, its objects and purposes. 73330
Canada Company. 10609, 44026, note after
90758
Canada Company. Court of Directors. 10584
Canada corn bill. 90303
Canada Correspondent of the London Morning
Post. pseud. Suggestions on the military
resources of Canada. see Roche,
Alfred R.
Canada, courte esquisse de sa position geo-
graphique. 10369

Canada directory . . . . Brought down to
November, 1851. 10416
Canada directory, 1857-58. 10417
Canada directory for 1857-58. 10426
Canada directory . . . . Supplement . . .
brought down to April, 1853. 10416
Canada East at the International Exhibition.
48929
Canada Education and Home Missionary Society,
Montreal. 10433, 50240
Canada educational directory. 32350
Canada: 1849 to 1859. 26452
Canada. Ein kurzer Abriss. 10376
Canada. Eine Darstellung der naturlichen,
socialen und Verkehrsverhaltnisse dieses
Landes. 10375
Canada. Emancipate your colonies. 4765
Canada. Essai auquel le premier prix a ete
adjuge. 32422
Canada, et l'Exposition Universelle de 1855.
94187
Canada Gaurantee Company. Charter. 10378
Canada Gaurantee Company: act of incorporation.
10378
Canada in all shapes. 13635
Canada in 1848, &c. 24181
Canada in 1849. 12943
Canada in 1868. 10377
Canada in 1864. 12552
Canada in 1837-38. 95297
Canada in the years 1832, 1833, and 1834.
10379, (23495)
Canada: is she prepared for war? 19565
Canada: its defences, condition, and resources.
74398-74399
Canada: its financial position and resources.
31931
Canada: its geography, scenery, produce, pop-
ulation. 44304
Canada: its growth and prospects. (41070)
Canada: its present condition. 34111
Canada: its systematic colonization. (10380)
Canada Landed Credit Company. 10556
Canada. Letters from persons who have emi-
grated to Upper Canada. 86184, note
after 98068
Canada, Louisiane, et les terres Anglaises.
47552
Canada medical journal and monthly record of
surgical science. 10381
Canada Mission. 10524
Canada mit besonderer Rucksicht auf dessen
Kolonisation. 10382
Canada (monthly) general railway and, steam
navigation guide. 10384
Canada, moeurs, diverses races, langues,
usages, etc. 10383
Canada, Nova Scotia, New Brunswick, and the
other British provinces. 8895
Canada, Nova Scotia, New Brunswick, Newfound-
land, etc. 10385
Canada; or a view of the importance of the
British American colonies. 1391
Canada papers. 10355
Canada: past, present and future. 84779
Canada. Petition from Lower Canada. 10386
Canada: physical, economical, and social. 41071
Canada pittoresque. 3787
Canada reconquis par la France. 3704
Canada, ses institutions, ressources, produits.
38883
Canada. Sir F. B. Head. Return to an
address. 31138
Canada, son present et son avenir. 25291
Canada sous la domination Anglais. 6845
Canada sous la domination Francaise. 21447

CANADA

Canada. State of political parties. 10387
Canada the land of hope. 10388
Canada under successive administrations.
  10389
Canada Wesleyan Conference. see Wesleyan
  Methodist Church. Canadian Conference.
Canada: why we live in it, and why we like it.
  16693
Canadas. (62620)
Canadas, as they at present commend them-
  selves. (62618)
Canadas as they now are. 10390
Canadas in 1841. 6328, 6332
Canada's thanksgiving . . . . A sermon.
  35995
Canadas, the nature of their existing connection
  with Great Britain discussed. 44117
Canadenser. 10623
Canadensivm plantarvm. (16809)
Canadia, ode Erivikios. 4595
Canadian. pseud. Affairs of the Canadas.
  see Ryerson, Egerton.
Canadian. pseud. Political and historical
  account. see La Terriere, Pierre de
  Salles.
Canadian. pseud. Remarks on the historical
  mis-statements. 69464
Canadian Agricultural Society. see Agricul-
  tural Society of Canada.
Canadian airs. 85619
Canadian almanac, and repository of useful
  knowledge. (10624), 78150
Canadian almanac 1858. 84779
Canadian almanac 1855. 84779
Canadian almanac 1857. 84779
Canadian and other poems. 74452
Canadian Anti-slavery Baptist Association.
  10404
Canadian Anti-slavery Society. see Anti-
  slavery Society of Canada.
Canadian ballads, and occasional verses.
  43260
Canadian boat song. 50445
Canadian, British American, and West Indian
  magazine. 10625
Canadian brothers. 71036
Canadian canals. 37884
Canadian caverns. 27272
Canadian Christian offering. (43265)
Canadian chronicle. 14190, 92649
Canadian church robbery. 100895
Canadian clergy reserves. 100896
Canadian colonization. (10626)
Canadian congregational year book. 84919
Canadian controversy, its origin, nature, and
  merits. 22246
Canadian conveyancer and hand-book of legal
  forms. 73152
Canadian Correspondent of the London Morning
  Post. pseud. Suggestions on the military
  resources of Canada. see Roche,
  Alfred R.
Canadian crisis. 38751, 56368
Canadian customs house guide. 21337
Canadian ferns and wild flowers. 73331
Canadian for-get-me-not for 1837. (81359)
Canadian forests. 82197
Canadian freeholder. 45412
Canadian fruit culturist. (20680)
Canadian gazetteer. 84780
Canadian government not "wide-awake." 79852
Canadian guide book. 10627
Canadian hand-book, and tourists' guide.
  10628, (82198)
Canadian history and Quebec scenery. 40005
Canadian homes. (13634)

Canadian independent. 84919
Canadian inspector. 10629
Canadian Institute. 39843
Canadian Institute. Editing Committee. 85205
Canadian journal. 37007, (37898), 38463,
  82222, 85205
Canadian journal of industry, science, and art.
  10630
Canadian land agency for the investment of
  capital. (10631)
Canadian law courts; a poem. 10414, 17984
Canadian League. (43466)
Canadian literary magazine. 10632
Canadian lyre. 67719
Canadian magazine (1846-   ) 10633
Canadian magazine (1871-   ) (71291)
Canadian medical journal. 10634
Canadian mercantile almanack. 81360
Canadian merchant. pseud. Canadian mer-
  chant's letter on the prospect of British
  shipping. 10635
Canadian merchant's letter on the prospect of
  British shipping. 10635
Canadian merchant's magazine and commercial
  review. 10636
Canadian minstrel. 89154
Canadian naturalist. 8755, 18955, (37334),
  82222
Canadian naturalist, a series of conversations.
  (28061)
Canadian naturalist and geologist. 10637
Canadian newspaper directory. (47403)
Canadian organic remains. Decade II. 41812
Canadian parliamentary companion. (50648)
Canadian patriots and English chartists. 97105
Canadian politicans. pseud. Letters. 10625
Canadian portfolio. 10638
Canadian quarterly agricultural and industrial
  magazine. 10341
Canadian question. 106076
Canadian railways. 10639
Canadian review, and literary & historical
  journal. 10640, (24701)
Canadian scenery. 3786
Canadian scenery, a poem, in two parts.
  43363
Canadian scenery: district of Gaspe. 66864
Canadian settler, late of Portsea, Hants. pseud.
  Emigrant's informant. 98076
Canadian settler's guide. 10643
Canadian Society of Civil Engineers. 84419
Canadian summer evening tales. 89155
Canadian tale. (13634), 40132
Canadian tale; a poem. 34475
Canadian tourist. 10644
Canadian views and studies. 31306
Canadian vine grower. 19207
Canadiana. 84701
Canadiana; containing sketches of Upper Canada.
  102611
Canadiana: containing the crisis. 102611
Canadians of old. 26736
Candicae missionis relatio ab anno 1611.
  36764, note after 69259
Canadien. pseud. Analyse d'un entretien. see
  Viger, Denis Benjamin.
Canadien. pseud. Avis au Canada. see Viger,
  Denis Benjamin.
Canadien, M. P. P. pseud. Considerations
  sur les effets. see Viger, Denis Ben-
  jamin. supposed author
Canadien. 10645
Canadien emigrant. 10646
Canadienne, comedie en un acte et en vers.
  98273
Canadiens. 67622, 97025

414

Canajoharie, N. Y. Central Asylum for the Instruction of the Deaf and Dumb. see New York (State) Central Asylum for the Instruction of the Deaf and Dumb, Canajoharie.

Canajoharie and Catskill Railroad Company. (62617)

Canajoharie and Catskill Railroad Company. Charter. (62617)

Canal, Dom. de la. defendant 57674

Canal, Jose Vallejo de la. see Vallejo de la Canal, Jose.

Canal at Darien. (35109)

Canal contracts. 30834

Canal Convention, Chicago, n. d. petitioners 47709

Canal Convention, Harrisburg, Pa., 1824. see Pennsylvania Canal Convention, Harrisburg, 1824.

Canal de Nicaragua. 37249

Canal guide. 88848

Canal interoceanic par l'isthme de Darien. 10648

Canal interoceanique du Darien. 44168

Canal laws and regulations. 53561

Canal maritime du Darien. (23547)

Canal of Nicaragua. 51764

Canal or railroad between the Atlantic and Pacific Oceans. 72432

Canal policy. 10889

Canal policy of the state . . . [of New York.] (53562)

Canal policy of the state of New-York: delineated in a letter. 13712, 94188, 97067

Canal policy of the state . . . one of progressive enlargement. (53563)

Canal regulations, rates of toll, and names. (53563)

Canale, M. G. 10649

Canals, Tomas. (10650)

Canals of Canada. 37146

Canandaigua, N. Y. Academy. see Canandaigua Academy.

Canandaigua, N. Y. Court. 50684

Canandaigua, N. Y. Ontario Female Seminary. see Ontario Female Seminary, Canandaigua, N. Y.

Canandaigua Academy. 10651

Canaries. 57765

Canas, Ramon Rojas y. see Rojas y Canas, Ramon.

Canauthius, Samuel. (28957), 61293

Canawese Indians. Treaties, etc. 97561

Canby, ---------. USA 87418

Cancelada, Juan Lopez. see Lopez Cancelada, Juan.

Cancellieri, Francesco. 10656

Cancion. 59029

Cancion en elogio de S. Juan de Dios. 76263

Cancion heroica. 11462

Cancion patriotica. 48316

Cancionero spiritual. 39122, (48317)

Canciones funebres a la muerte de D. Christoval de Onate. 51429

Candamo, --------- Gonzalez de. see Gonzalez de Candamo, ---------.

Cande, --------- M. de Maussion. see Maussion Cande, -------- M. de.

Candele, P. le. see Le Candele, P.

Candiche, Monsieur. see Cavendish, Thomas, 1555?-1592.

Candid address to the Episcopalians of Pennsylvania. 63217, 63239-63241, note after 95739

Candid analytical review of the "Sketches of the history of Dartmouth College and Moor's Charity School." 18630, 18633, 58598, note after 99814, note after 103219

Candid and impartial considerations on the nature of sugar trade. 10231, 3d note after 102821

Candid and impartial considerations on the preliminary articles of peace with France and Spain. (10657)

Candid and impartial enquiry into a certain doubtful character. 6814, 27017, 56848

Candid an[d] impartial enquiry into the present dispute. 106121

Candid and impartial narrative of the transactions of the fleet. 10658

Candid animadversions on a petition. 22337, 99771

Candid animadversions respecting a petition. 22337, 99771

Candid answer to a pamphlet. 29038

Candid answer to the "enquiry." 63086

Candid appeal to the American public. (21730)

Candid appeal to the citizens of Massachusetts. 1981

Candid appeal to the citizens of the United States. (13779)

Candid appeal to the moral and religious portion of our countrymen. 21103

Candid appeal to the present ruling party. 10659

Candid appeal to the publick. 99177

Candid considerations of the whole subject. 8327

Candid considerations on libels. 10660

Candid considerations, respecting the canal. 98628

Candid declaration of the church. 97846

Candid defence of administration. (10661)

Candid development of facts. 2900

Candid discussion of some interesting questions. 105248

Candid discussion of the preliminaries of peace. 1776

Candid enquiries. 44202, 58914

Candid examination into the merits of the principal performer. 79095

Candid examination, into the origin of the difference of colour. 36466

Candid examination of certain doctrines. 64477

Candid examination of Dr. Mayhew's observations. 10681, 47130

Candid examination of Mr. Calhoun's report. 13133, 28944

Candid examination of the address. 10662, 59956

Candid examination of the Episcopal Church. 93076, 93080

Candid examination of the facts and arguments. 103123

Candid examination of the mutual claims of Great-Britain. 26422-(26423), 26442

Candid examination of the objections to the treaty. 10663, 84819

Candid examination of the whole affair. 104541

Candid exposition of fact s. (3909)

Candid exposition of the various opinions. 8773

Candid inquiry into the conduct. 103459

Candid merchant of America. pseud. Common sense. see British merchant. pseud.

Candid narrative of the rise and progress of the Herrnhuters. 31583, 71404, 71409

Candid narrative of the rise and progress of the Moravians. 71406, 71408-71409

Candid observations on two pamphlets lately published. 3262

Candid observer. pseud. Poems on America. 63619

Candid opinion given of the nature and tendency of Universalism. 94891

Candid public will recollect. 94663

Candid reflections on the different manner in which the learned and the pious have expressed their conceptions. 30798, 102608

Candid reflections on the expedition to Martinico. 35328

Candid reflections upon the judgment. 10664

Candid refutation of the heresy. 31346

Candid remarks addressed to Christians. (10665)

Candid remarks on Dr. Witherspoon's address. 104930

Candid remarks upon the Rev. Mr. Taylor's discourse. 30150

Candid reply, to "A sermon." 92790

Candid retrospect. 10666, 84564-84565

Candid review of a late publication. 72084

Candid review of the "correspondence in relation to the third church of 1735." 75651, 75655, 2d note after 94170, 105323

Candid statement of facts, in answer to an unwarrantable denunciation. 97592

Candid statement of facts, relative to difficulties. 58080

Candid statement of facts, relative to the concert. 61515

Candid statement of facts, showing the cause of, and the persons who originated the state tax. 60602

Candid statement respecting the Philadelphia County ticket. 61516

Candid thoughts on American independence. 86826

Candid thoughts; or, an enquiry into the causes of national discontents. (10667)

Candid views of facts, in a letter from John B. Colvin. 14903

Candid view of our present difficulties and danger. 55575

Candid view of the presidential question. 60789

Candid Virginian. pseud. Positive facts. 13733

Candidate for the office of Accomptant-General. pseud. Letters. see Integar. pseud.

Candidates, and the doctrines of the two parties. 89493

Candidates book of information. 83697

Candidates for Bachelor's Degree, Nassau Hall, College of New Jersey, 1762. see Princeton University. Class of 1762.

Candidature for the presidency. 9615

Candide. 105490

Candide Anglois. 10668

Candido, Francisco de Paula. see Paula Candido, Francisco de.

Candido, Joao. 10670

Candido Alesna. pseud. Cuatro cartas. see Gutierrez, Manuel Agustin.

Candido lectori. 63957

Candidus. pseud. American independency defended. see Paine, Thomas, 1737-1809.

Candidus. pseud. Letter, addressed to Edward Bacon, Esq. 102843

Candidus. pseud. Letter to Cato. 95920

Candidus. pseud. Letter to Philo Africanus. 40451, 62542

Candidus. pseud. Plain truth. see Chalmers, George, 1742-1825. incorrectly supposed author Galloway, Joseph, 1729?-1803.

supposed author Hamilton, Alexander, 1755-1804. supposed author Inglis, Charles, Bp. of Nova Scotia. supposed author Smith, William, 1727-1803. supposed author

Candidus. pseud. To the printer. 95964

Candidus, Mystagogus. pseud. see Mystagogus Candidus. pseud.

Candish, Thomas. see Cavendish, Thomas, 1555?-1592.

Candish's adventures in the South Seas. 14414

Candler, Allen Daniel, 1834-1910. 38978 91305, 91307, 91313, 91315, 94215

Candler, Isaac. 10672 note after 93608,

Candler, John. 9244, 10673-10675

Candler, Maria. (10676)

Candor. pseud. Letter. 40327

Candor. pseud. To the public. 95983

Candor and good nature of Englishmen exemplified. 43562

Candour of Henry Laurens, Esq. 35984

Canedo, Estanislao. 10677-10678

Canedo, Juan de Dios. 10679

Canelas, Ramon. 10680

Canelo y Cachuto, Juan Agapito. 63349

Caner, Henry, 1700-1792. 4091, (10681)-10684, (32311), 47130

Canfield, E. H. 64642

Canfield, H. 11211

Canfield, Sherman B. 10685

Canfield and Warren. firm publishers 72340

Canfield and Warren's directory of the city of Rochester. 72340

Canisius, A. (3596)

Canizares, Josef. 10686

Canizares, Martin de. plaintiff 56282 see also Augustinians. Provincia del Nuevo Reyno de Granada. Procurador General plaintiff

Cannabich, Johann Gunther Friedrich. 10687, 30815, 101367

Canne, Abednego. (10688)

Canne, J. 35560

Cannelton, Perry County, Ind., at the intersection of the eastern margin of the Illinois coal basin, by the Ohio River. 10689

Canner, Thomas. (10690)

Cannibal Jack. pseud. Run away from home. see Reid, Mayne, i. e. Thomas Mayne, 1818-1883.

Cannibals all! 24617

Canning, E. W. B. (80907)

Canning, George, fl. 1768. 10691, 31911

Canning, George, 1770-1827. 10692-10693, 12489, 16855, 16883, (58464), 101547, 101722

Canning, Josiah D. 10694

Canning, Josiah W. 10695

Cannon, Arthur. reporter 10696, 62051, (71820)

Cannon, Elizabeth. defendant 11005

Cannon, Eugene M. tr. 83144

Cannon, George Q. 64950, 83131, 83133

Cannon, J. S. 10698

Cannon, James. 83804, 84678C

Cannon, John. 10697

Cannon, Richard. 10699

Cannon, Sylvester Q. ed. 83121, 83220

Cannon, William, 1809-1865. 10700, 19389 see also Delaware. Governor, 1863-1865 (Cannon)

Cannon-flashes and pen-dashes. 44851

Cannonade. 13387, 90648

Cannoniers a vos pieces. 2243

Cano, Benito. 9031

Cano, Gabriel de Cardenas Z. anagram see
 Barcia, Andres Gonzalez.
Cano, Juan Sebastian de. 9733, 33660
Cano y Galiano, Antonio Ruiz. see Ruiz
 Cano y Galiano, Antonio.
Cano y Olmedilla, Juan de la Cruz. (10701)
Canoe voyage up the Minnay Sotor. (23958)
Canoe voyage up the Mississippi and around
 Lake Superior. (38916), 38925
Canoeing down 1500 miles of the great River
 Sao Francisco. 9498
Canon for two voices. 94019
Canonazos de un artillero Americano. 86235
Canonheiro, P. A. ed. 24830
Canonicus. pseud. Letter to the Reverend
 Mr. George Whitefield. see Chauncy,
 Charles, 1705-1787. supposed author
Canonicus. pseud. Letters to the Rev. W. E.
 Channing, D. D. see Shedd, William,
 1798-1830.
Canonicus. pseud. Second letter to the Rev-
 erend Mr. George Whitefield. see
 Chauncy, Charles, 1705-1787. supposed
 author
Canonisationis, seu declarationis martyri
 servorum Dei Ignatti Azeuedi. 68434
Canonista de la Sierra. pseud. Coleccion de
 las cartas. 61089
Canonizzazione di Cristoforo Colombo. 76522
Canons for the government of the Protestant
 Episcopal Church in the United States
 . . . also the canons passed. 100511A
Canons for the government of the Protestant
 Episcopal Church in the United States of
 America. 66128
Canons for the government of the Protestant
 Episcopal Church, in this state. 100511
Canons of the Protestant Episcopal Church, in
 the Confederate States of America.
 15262
Canons passed by the Synod of the Diocese of
 Toronto. 10331
Canonsburgh, Pa. Jefferson College. see
 Jefferson College, Canonsburgh, Pa.
Canot, ------. illus. 77467
Canovai, Stanislao. 10702-10708, 99383A, note
 after 99383C
Canovai, Stanislao. incorrectly supposed author
 10705, 51760
Canpo, Florian do. see Ocampo, Florian de.
Casancao, Joao Lins Vieira. see Sinimbu,
 Joao Lins Vieira Cansancao, Visconde de,
 1810-1906.
Canseco, Jose Juan. 29135
Canta Don Jose Maria Villasenor Cervantes.
 99684
Cantabrana, Emanuele. 10709
Cantabrana, Mariana Phelippa de. plaintiff
 34721, 99619
Cantabria vindicada, y demonstrada. 58048
Cantada. 99734
Cantada heroica. 94300
Cantanaei, Io: Mariae. see Cantaneo, Joannes
 Maria.
Cantaneo, Joannes Maria. 11494
Cantate en l'honneur de Son Altesse Royale le
 Prince de Galles. 79086
Cantbrana, Maria P. de. see Cantabrana,
 Maria Phelippa de.
Cantelli, Sansone Bavdrand e. see Bavdrand
 e Cantelli, Sansone.
Canterbury, Archbishop of. see Abbot, George,
 Abp. of Canterbury, 1562-1633. Corn-
 wallis, Frederick, Abp. of Canterbury,
 1713-1783. Decker, Thomas, Abp. of
 Canterbury, Herring, Thomas, Abp. of

Canterbury, 1693-1757. Hutton, Mathew,
 Abp. of Canterbury, 1693-1758. Manners-
 Sutton, Charles, Abp. of Canterbury, 1755-
 1828. Moore, John, Abp. of Canterbury,
 1730-1805. Secker, Thomas, Abp. of
 Canterbury, 1693-1768. Sumner, John
 Bird, Abp. of Canterbury, 1780-1862.
 Tenison, Thomas, Abp. of Canterbury,
 1636-1715.
Canterbury, Conn. School for Colored Females.
 see School for Colored Females, Can-
 terbury, Conn.
Canterbury, N. H. Shakers. see Shakers.
 Canterbury and Enfield, N. H.
Canterbury, N. H. Society of People Commonly
 Called Shakers. see Shakers. Canter-
 bury and Enfield, N. H.
Canterbury, N. H. United Society. see
 Shakers. Canterbury and Enfield, N. H.
Canterbury and the diggins. 34015
Canterbury school. 90705, note before 96855
Cantero, Justo G. 17782
Canti venti. 73264
Cantino. 77803
Cantiques et catechisme en langue Montagnaises
 ou Phipeweyan. 61003
Canto, Francisco del. incorrectly supposed
 author 10710, (67160), 100643
Canto a Bolivar. (49434), note after (57229)
Canto a Cortes. 10712
Canto a la Compana del Ejercito Chileno Liber-
 tador. 10711, note after 96237
Canto al Dr. D. Miguel Cane. (29350)
Canto al primer Presidente popular de la
 republica. 63949
Canto dos alumnos da Sociedad Amante da
 Instruccao. 81296
Canto epico. 42107
Canto heroico. 88718
Canto intitulado Mercurio. 99646
Canto mistico. 11462
Canto patriotico. 58139
Canto patriotico al ciudadano esclarecido J A P.
 10713
Canto premiado. 29375, note after 98270
Canto poetico. 27199
Canto poetico aos faustos annos de S. M. I. o
 Sr. D. Pedro de Alcantara. 27198
Canton, Pedro. 40137
Canton, Mass. 10715
Canton, Mass. School Committee. 10714
Canton, N. Y. St. Lawrence University. see
 St. Lawrence University, Canton, N. Y.
Canton, Ohio. State Convention, 1830. see
 Ohio. Convention, Canton, 1830.
Canton. 39300
Canton Company of Baltimore. (10717)
Canton Company of Baltimore. Committee of
 Stockholders. 3068
Canton Run Improvement Company. 10716
Cantos. 70320
Cantos. Colleccao de poesias. 19963
Cantos de las musas Mexicanas. 4872
Cantos populares. 25100
Cantril, George E. defendant before military
 commission 9381
Cantu, Cesare. 5304, 10718
Cantwell, A. de. tr. 9735
Cantwell, Edward. 10719
Canuto, Don. pseud. Algo de masones. 94577
Canvane, Peter. (10720)
Canvass of the proceedings. 93964, 93966
Canyon City, Colorado, and its surroundings.
 46822
Canzler, Friedrich Gottlieb. tr. 24116
Canzoni eroiche. 12614

Cap, Haiti. see Cap Haitien, Haiti.
Cap Haitien, Haiti. 10750-10751
Cap Haitien, Haiti. Cercle des Philadelphes.
see Cercle des Philadelphes, Cap
Haitien, Haiti.
Cap Haitien, Haiti. Chambre d'Agriculture.
75101, 75112
Cap Haitien, Haiti. Verite Loge. see Free-
masons. Haiti. Verite Loge, Cap
Haitien.
Cap. 39300
Cap au diable. 29257
Capaccio, Giulio Cesare. 10721
Capacho. pseud. sobriquet see Rodriguez
Ucares, Jose.
Capacity of Negroes for religious and moral
improvement. 55353
Capadose, -------. RA 10722
Capanna dello zio Tom. 92418, 92586-92591
Capanna dello zio Tommaso. 92593
Capanna di papa Tom. 92592
Capata, Luys. see Zapata, Luis de.
Capaz, Dionisio. 26112, 44291, 76158, 97717
Capca, Bernardo. 16976
Cape and Canada. 34701
Cape Breton Island. Inhabitants. petitioners
61284
Cape Breton. (49760)
Cape Cod and all along shore. 55460
Cape Cod Association in Boston. 10734
Cape Cod Centennial Celebration, Barnstable,
Mass., 1839. see Barnstable, Mass.
Cape Cod Centennial Celebration, 1839.
Cape Cod Centennial Celebration at Barnstable,
Sept. 3, 1839, of the incorporation of
that town. 10734
Cape Cod harbor. 40811
Cape Francais, Haiti. see Cap Haitien, Haiti.
Cape Francois 17 Since we had the honour
of announcing to you are arrival. 101089
Cape Girardeau, Mo. St. Vincent's College.
see St. Vincent's College, Cape Girar-
deau, Mo.
Cape of Good Hope. Census, 1826. 75410
Cape of Good Hope and its dependencies.
92355
Cape Verde and Hatteras hurricane. 68508
Capel, D. see Capell, D., fl. 1675.
Capel, Rudolf. 10736
Capell, D., fl. 1675. 10735, (25995), 79346
Cappella Imperial, Rio de Janeiro. see Rio
de Janeiro. Capella Imperial.
Capellan, Alexander van der. (10737)
Capellan, Lorenzo de Mendoza. 24814
Capellan, Robert Jasper van der. (10737)
Capellano Maggior de dicta armata a su alteza.
pseud. Itinerario. see Diaz, Juan.
Capellen, Johan Derk, Baron van der. 65455,
97252, 97254
Capelli, D. see Capell, D., fl. 1675.
Capellini, Giovanni. 10738
Capen, Charles J. ed. 45907
Capen, Joseph, 1658-1725. 10740, 65820
Capen, Lemuel. 10741-10743, 2d note after
96962
Capen, Lemuel. petitioner 10743, 20621,
(20626)
Capen, Nahum, 1804-1886. 10744-(10747),
32135, 103304, 105102
Capen, Nahum, 1804-1886. supposed author
(70008)
Capers, Amanda A. P. (52237)
Capers, G. 10748
Capers, William. (10749)
Capilla protestante en Valparaiso. 86241
Capilupus, Hippol. (26502)

Capine, Louis de. (10757), 31360, 31363,
63706
Capistrano de Abreu, Joao. tr. 82720
Capitain John Ross's zweite Nordpolexpedition.
38241
Capitaine Canot. (47094)
Capitaine May et le General de la Vega. 47062
Capitaine Paul. 21182
Capitaine Phillavidas. 4540
Capitaine presentement au Cap-Francais.
pseud. Lettre. 10752
Capital and labor. 38372
Capital against labor. 24536
Capital Committee, St. Louis. see St. Louis
Capital Committee.
Capital de los estados confederados del Rio de
la Plata. (38992), 77063
Capital laws of the Massachusetts Bay. 45664
Capital of West Virginia and the great Kanawha
Valley. 93092
Capital offences in the code of the union.
89066
Capital punishment: a discourse. 8967
Capital punishment. Essays from Poulson's
daily advertiser. 10758
Capital punishment for murder authorized by
God. (21137)
Capital punishment sustained by reason. 59164
Capital punishment. The argument of George
B. Cheever. (12406)
Capital question. Address of the St. Louis
Capital Committee. 75337
Capital University, Columbus, Ohio. 14892
Capitale des Etats Confederes du Rio de la
Plata. 77064-(77066)
Capitalist's guide and railway annual for 1859.
92377
Capitan. pseud. Dialogo entre un abogado y
un capitan. 76747
Capitan Chinchilla. pseud. Ya no cuelo. see
Santamaria, Miguel.
Capitan Don Francisco Solis y Casanova, Pro-
curador General de la Ciudad de Merida
de Yucatan y su provincia. 86442
Capitan Don Iustino de Solorcano, Cauallero del
Orden de Santiago. 86516
Capitan Francisco de Vitoria Baraona. 100624
Capitan Francisco de Vitoria Baraona dize.
100625
Capitan Francisco de Vitoria Baraona, vezino
de la Puebla. 100623
Capitan Gaspar de Villagra para ivstificacion
de las muertes, justicias, y castigos que
el Adelantado Don Iuan de Onate dizen.
99638
Capitan Gaspar de Villagra, para justificacion
de las muertes, y castigos que el
Adelantado Don Iuan de Onate dizen.
99639
Capitan Gaspar de Villagra, para que Su
Magestad la haga merced. 99640
Capitan Jvan Sanchez de la Rocha, vezino de la
ciudad de Los Reyes. 76299
Capitan Mateo de Villerias vezino de Mexico.
99740
Capitan y Almirante Mateo de Vesga Gouernador
y Capitan General que ha sido de las
prouincias de la Nueua Vizcaya en
Nueuaespana, dize. 99326
Capitanes D. Migvel Diez de la Mora, Cavallero
del Orden de Calatrava, y Don Juan de
Larrea del Alcantara, como albaceas
testamentarios. 87160
Capitano Spagnuolo. pseud. Relatione. 1565,
(61097), 67740-67742

Capitaz Ramirez. 21375
Capiteyn Luytenant. pseud. Journael. 77898
Capitol. 74367
Capitol; or, the higher law. 47181
Capitvlaciones de el assiento. 10759
Capitulaciones que el Virrey Don Luys de
Velasco hizo. 98794
Capitulation by the Dutch to the English.
(53570)
Capitulation de Cap, 1803. 43703
Capitulation, or, a history of the expedition
conducted by William Hull. (33641),
57071
Capituli Provincialis celebrati in Imperiali
S. P. N. Dominici Mexicano Conventu.
20581
Capo di Vacca, Alvaro Nunez. see Cabeza
de Vaca, Alvar Nunez, 1490?-1557.
Capoteros, Mexico. petitioners 69972
Cappe, Newcome. 10760
Cappellari, Bartolommeo Alberto. see Gre-
gory XVI, Pope, 1765-1846.
Capper, G. 10761
Capper, H. 10762
Capper, Joseph. 10763, 51773, 52274, 98663A
Cappin, Sir George. 99860
Capponi, -------. ed. 24663
Capron, E. S. (10764)
Capron, Eliab W. 10765
Capse, Charles Francois de, Bp. 10766 see
also Quebec (Diocese) Bishop (Capse)
Captain. pseud. Short address. see Child,
Samuel.
Captain Betagh's observations on the country
of Peru. 62957
Captain Bilton's journal. 5423
Captain Bligh's answer. 5913
Captain Bob, the mountain devil. 25105
Captain Bob-ad-ill. pseud. see Bob-ad-ill,
Captain. pseud.
Captain Bourne's account. 6911
Captain Canot. 47093
Captain Charles S. Montgomery. 13529
Captain Coles and the Admiralty. 14334
Captain Cook's third and last voyage to the
Pacific Ocean. 16256
Captain Cook's three voyages to the Pacific
Ocean. (16269)
Captain Cook's voyages around the world.
16272
Capt. Cowley's voyage round the globe. 18373,
29473
Capt. Dampier's vindication. 18378
Captain Flack. pseud. see Flack, Captain.
pseud.
Capt. Hale's instructions to emigrants. 22500,
86187
Captain Hall in America. (5256)
Captain Hayward's body guard. (31118)
Captain in Gen. Lee's Army. pseud. Jack
Morgan songster. 35338
Captain J. Tasman's discoveries. (72186)
Captain J. Wood's attempt to discovery a
north-east passage to China. (72186)
Captain Johan Stedmans dagbok ofwer sina
falttag i Surinam. 91071
Capt. John Monck's voyage in 1619 and 1620.
13015, 51336
Capt. John Smith, a biography. (31817)
Capt. John Smith, of Willoughby, by Alford,
Lincolnshire. 82855
Capt. John Smith of Willoughby by Alfred,
Lincolnshire. 82856
Captain John Smith's circular. 82823
Capt. John Smith's True travels and adven-
tures. 13015, 82852

Capt. John Wood's lottery. 105048
Captain Kidd. 11650
Capt. Kidd's two commissions. 37701
Captain Le Diable. pseud. Historical sketch
of the third annual conquest of Florida.
(24866)
Captain Leisler's case. 39936, 68277
Captain Lightfoot. alias see Martin, Michael,
d. 1821.
Captain Lightfoot. 44902, 2d note after 101000
Capt. M'Clure's despatches from Her Majesty's
Discovery Ship, "Investigator." 43074
Captain Marry-it, C. B., (Common Bloat)
pseud. Lie-ary on America. (44696)
Captain Maury's letter on American affairs.
46962
Capt. Middleton's defence. 20406
Captain Morgan, or the conspiracy unveiled.
94226
Capt. Munchausen. pseud. see Munchausen,
Capt. pseud.
Captain of H. M. S. Glasgow. see Glasgow
(H. M. Ship) Captain.
Captain of our salvation. 35702
Captain of the British Navy. pseud. Memoirs
of the life and achievements of Lord
Viscount Nelson. 52312
Captain of the Lord's host appearing with his
sword drawn. 13346
Captain of volunteers. pseud. Conquest of
Santa Fe. 15888
Capt. Playfair, R. N. pseud. see Playfair,
Hugh. pseud.
Capt. Partridge's lecture on education. 58962
Capt. Partridge's lecture on national defence.
(56499), (58963)
Captain Ross's voyage to the north pole.
(73383)
Capt. Rutledge. pseud. see Hines, David
Theodore.
Capt. Sharp's journey over the isthmus of
Darien. 18373, 29473
Captain Siden. pseud. History of the Sevarites.
see Vairasse d'Allais, Denis.
Captain Smith and princess Pocahontas. 18848,
82860, 100438, 100467
Captain Stockton's address to the people of
New-Jersey. 91895
Capt. Sutter's account of the first discovery of
gold. 93971
Captain Tasman's discoveries on the coast of
the south terra incognita. 72187
Captain Thomas Philips's voyage to Mountsera-
doe in Africa. 13015
Captain Thomas Wheeler's narrative. 25007,
103200
Captain William Dampier's voyages round the
world. 18373
Captain Wood's attempt to discover a north-
west passage. 72187
Capt. Wood's voyage thro' the streights of
Magellan. 29473
Capt. Wood's voyage through the streights of
Magellan. 18373
Captain's bride. 31580
Captains Drayton and Sayres. 20911
Captive American; containing an account of the
sufferings of Mrs. Johnson. 36326
Captive American, or a narrative of the suf-
ferings of Mrs. Johnson. 36325
Captive boy in Terra del Fuego. 30159
Captive children. 34624
Captive des Mohawks. 22297
Captive of Nootka Sound. 27922
Captive of Patagonia. 6910
Captive of the Harpes. 44802

CAPTIVE

Captive (that hath long been in captivity)
visited. 62919
Captives of Abb's Valley. 10767
Captives of the Norridgewocks. (51551)
Captivity a ballad. 92171
Captivity and deliverance of Mr. John
Williams. 104272
Captivity and deliverance of Mrs. Mary
Rowlandson. 104272
Captivity and sufferings of Gen. Freegift
Patchin of Blenheim. 65485
Captivity & sufferings of Mrs. Mary Smith,
&c. 83535
Captivity in Babylon, and other poems. 13703
Captivity of Father Peter Milet. (80023)
Captivity of General Corcoran. 16755
Captivity of Hans Stade of Hesse. 90060
Captivity of Sieur Mouette in Fez and Moracco.
91538
Captivity of the Moore family. 33301
Captivity of the Oatman girls. 92742
Capture. 25891
Capture a favorite son [sic] in The pirates.
92171A
Capture and escape. (39033)
Capture and shipwreck of the U. S. Brig
Vixon. 105178
Capture and surrender of Mason and Slidell.
(58697)
Capture de l'Alexandre de Bordeaux. 23932
Capture of Black Hawk. 5676
Capture of the American slaver. 12054, 82003
Capture of Ticonderoga in 1775. 29779
Capture of Yankee gunboats, &c. (35421)
Capture, the prison pen, and the escape.
27558
Captured in escaping. (17655)
Capuchins. 68839
Capuchins. Provincia de Sancto Antonio do
Brasil. 70130
Car, Anthony. 86868
Cara Amo y Figueroa, Juan de. 56396, 79138
Carabajal, Juan Leonel de Servantes. see
Servantes Carabajal, Juan Leonel de.
Carabobo (Venezuelan State) 10768
Carabobo (Venezuelan State) Laws, statutes,
etc. 10768
Carabobo (Venezuelan State) Sociedad Patriotica.
see Sociedad Patriotica de Carabobo.
Caracas (Archdiocese) 47803, 2d note after
98873
Caracas (Archdiocese) Archbishop [ca. 1863]
(81131)
Caracas (Archdiocese) Archbishop [ca. 1868]
56450
Caracas (Archdiocese) Archbishop (Mendez)
47803, 67662, 98869, 2d note after 98873,
98874, 98881 see also Mendez, Ramon
Ignacio, Abp., d. 1839.
Caracas (Province) Administrador Principal de
Rentas Municipales. 10779
Caracas (Province) Diputacion Provinvial.
10780-10781, 10785, 32119, 68866
Caracas (Province) Junta de Caminos. 47604
Caracas (Province) Laws, statutes, etc. 10785,
68866
Caracas. Academia de Jurisprudencia. see
Academia de Jurisprudencia, Caracas.
Caracas. Administracion General de Tobaco.
66522
Caracas. Administracion General de Tabaco.
Administrador. 93402 see also Sucre,
Jose Manuel.
Caracas. Administracion General de Tabaco.
Fiel de Almacenes. 93402 see also
Rodriguez, Marcos Jose.

Caracas. Administracion General de Tabaco.
Interventor. 93402 see also Mendivel-
zua, Juan de Dios.
Caracas. Asamblea Popular. 17817
Caracas. Ayuntamiento. (23441)
Caracas. British Chapel and Burial Ground.
(14324), 25090
Caracas. Caja de Ahorros de la Gran Socie-
dad. see Caja de Ahorros de la Gran
Sociedad, Caracas.
Caracas. Carceles. 68882
Caracas. Casa de Misericordia. 10785
Caracas. Catedral. Cabildo. (47807)
Caracas. Catedral. Dean y Cabildo. 10772
Caracas. Catedral. Maestres-Scolia. Charter.
68249
Caracas. Clero. petitioners 47804
Caracas. Cofradia del Glorioso Principe de
los Apostles San Pedro. see Cofradia
del Glorioso Principe de los Apostles
San Pedro, Caracas.
Caracas. Consejo Municipal. 10786
Caracas. Colegio de Chaves. see Colegio de
Chaves, Caracas.
Caracas. Colegio de Ingenieros de Venezuela.
see Colegio de Ingenieros de Venezuela,
Caracas.
Caracas. Colegio de Santa Maria. (76782)
Caracas. Compania Guipuzcoana. see R.
Compania Guipuzcoana de Caracas.
Caracas. Diario de Avisos. see Diario de
Avisos de Caracas.
Caracas. Exhibicion Anual de Bellas Artes
Venezolanas, la., 1872. see Exhibicion
Anual de Bellas Artes Venezolanas, la.,
Caracas, 1872.
Caracas. Gaceta de Venezuela. see Gaceta
de Venezuela.
Caracas. Jurado. 59636
Caracas. Ordinances, etc. 68867
Caracas. Real Audiencia. 47629, 62881
Caracas. Real Audiencia. Presidente. plain-
tiff 62881 see also Pimentel y Soto-
mayor, Francisco. plaintiff
Caracas. Real Compania Guipuzcoana. see
R. Compania Guipuzcoana de Caracas.
Caracas. San Juan Logia, no. 4. see Free-
masons (Scotch Rite) Venezuela. San
Juan Logia, no. 4, Caracas.
Caracas. Sociedad Beneficia y Religiosa de los
Espanoles. see Sociedad Beneficia y
Religiosa de los Espanoles de Caracas.
Caracas. Sociedad de Ciencias Fisicas y
Naturales. see Sociedad de Ciencias
Fisicas y Naturales, Caracas.
Caracas. Sociedad Economica de Amigos del
Pais. see Sociedad Economica de Ami-
gos del Pais, Caracas.
Caracas. Universidad. Charter. 68249
Caracas. Universidad Central. see Venezuela.
Universidad Central, Caracas.
Caracas gaceta. (9209)
Caracas . . . hacia el norte. (40212)
Caracter de la augustisima Isabel Farnecio.
(72295)
Caracter del Pensador Mexicano. 87215
Caracter y costumbres de los Indios. 38381,
56007, (75765)
Caradog, of Llancarvan, d. 1552? 64746
Caraguin. A tale of the Antilles. 10787
Caraibes. (17190)
Caraman, Georges Joseph Victor Riquet, Comte
de. 10788
Caramuru. 21416
Caramaru, ou la decouverte de Bahia. 21417
Carapuceiro. 10789

420

Carassa, Francisco. 85725 see also Socie-
dad de Beneficencia Publica, Lima.
Director.
Carate, Augustin de. see Zarate, Augustin de.
Caravane de sombreros. 4900
Caray, John. (17423)
Carayon, Auguste. (10790)-10792
Carbajal, B. 10793
Carbajal, Francisco. 10795-10797
Carbajal, Francisco Leon. 10794
Carbajal, Miguel de. 69192
Carbajal Espinosa, Francisco. 10798, 22893
Carballido y Cabuenas, J. M. de. 10799
Carballido y Zuniga, Andres Gonzalez de
Barcia. see Barcia Carballido y
Zuniga, Andres Gonzalez de, 1673-1743.
Carbery, Edward. 10800
Carbon County, Pa. Reception to Henry C.
Carey, 1859. 10841, note after 94911
Carbondale, Ill. Southern Normal University.
see Illinois. Southern Normal Univer-
sity, Carbondale.
Carbonell, Ignacio de Ramon. see Ramon
Carbonell, Ignacio de.
Carbonero. pseud. Dialogo primero y segundo
entro un payo y un carbonero. 19923
Carboniferous and Jurassic fossils. 10008
Card. During the last winter, Dr. John Eberle
published. 102326
Card for the sayling of those seas. 35711,
note after 92708
Card. . . . Philadelphia, December 2, 1773.
61517
Card (published by Dr. Knowlton) addressed to
Dr. Crane. 17407
Cardell, William S. 10801
Cardelle, Cora. (19842)
Cardena, Patricio G. (10802)
Cardenas, Alonso de. (47531), 96521, 96526
see also Spain. Legation. Gt. Britain.
Cardenas, Bernardino de, Bp. 10803-10807,
(21763) see also Paraguay (Diocese)
Bishop (Cardenas)
Cardenas, Francisco de. ed. 58072, 106405
Cardenas, Jose Ruiz de Villafranca y. see
Ruiz Villafrancia y Cardenas, Joseph.
Cardenas, Juan de. 10808
Cardenas, Luis Ignatius Penalver y. see
Penalver y Cardenas, Luis Ignatius, Bp.
Cardenas Leon, Carlos Celedonio Velasquez.
see Velasquez de Cardenas y Leon,
Carlos Celedonio.
Cardenas Salazar, Antonio. see Salazar,
Antonio Cardenas.
Cardenas y Leon, Carlos Celedonio Velasquez
de. see Velasquez de Cardenas y Leon,
Carlos Celedonio.
Cardenas y Rodriguez, Jose Maria de, 1812-
1882. 10810-10812
Cardenas Z. Cano, Gabriel de. anagram. see
Barcia, Andres Gonzalez.
Carder, Peter. 10813, 66686
Cardera, Valentin. (10814)
Cardigan, Lady --------, fl. 1763. petitioner
90590
Cardigan, Lord --------, fl. 1763. petitioner
90590
Cardigan, N. H. Citizens. petitioners 52791,
note after 98998
Cardinal, Joseph N. defendant 93241
Cardim, Fernao. 10815
Cardoso Braga, Jose. see Braga, Jose
Cardoso.
Cardozo, J. N. 10816-(10818)
Care, Henry. 10819

Care of health and life in the state of New
York. 84252
Care of religion considered. 23928
Care of the insane. 84068
Care of the insane in the state of New York.
84253
Careaga, Lucas. defendant 75585
Career, last voyage, and fate of Captain Sir
John Franklin. 57760
Career of modern liberty. 44682
Career of the champions. 77402
Career of Tiburcio Vasquez. (71281)
Career, tragedy, and trial of Henry Jumperts.
36896
Careful and free enquiry. 8697-8698
Careful and strict enquiry. 21930
Careful and strict examination. (4486)
Careful research of the earliest records.
84138
Carefully selected collection of poems. 88288
Carefully to observe the signatures of divine
providence. 104313
Carela, Florencio. 98595-98596
Carenzi, C. tr. 3126
Careri, Giovanni Francesco Gemelli. see
Gemelli-Careri, Giovanni Francesco,
1651-1725.
Cares about the nurseries. 46245
Carew, Bampfylde-Moore, 1693-1770? 27615
Carew, Bampfylde-Moore, 1693-1770? supposed
author 93889
Carey, Alice. 10824
Carey, Edward. see Cary, Edward.
Carey, Eustace. (10826)
Carey, Henry Charles, 1793-1879. (2781),
7052, 10827-10840, 10842-10843, (15055),
19412, 45380
Carey, Isaac E. 10844-10846
Carey, James. supposed author 96324-96325
Carey, James P. (10849)
Carey, John. ed. 101726-101733
Carey, John L. 10847-(10848), 11201, 86769-
86770, note before 94159
Carey, Mathew, 1760-1839. 1162-1162A, 1187,
1591, (5459), 9951, 10066, 10842-10843,
(10850)-(10878), 10880-10889, 12053,
13875, 14869, (17294), (18016), 21971,
22987, 22989, 23366, 23640, 23966,
28775, 29979, 30053, 30054, 30414,
1st note after (60039), 60196, 61782,
62252, note after 63795, 66530, 67114,
70218, 73210, (78988), (82420), 84568,
85685, 85856, 85884-85885, 86666, 87818,
note after 87927, note after 92842, 92843,
3d note after 94805, 94884, 95360, note
after 95905, 96073, 96561, 97216, 97407,
note after 97536-97537, 97902, note after
97998-97999, note after 101453, 104186,
104450
Carey, Mathew, 1760-1839. supposed author
2012-2013, 10860, 10889, 23544, 31041,
(39756), 61439, 92843, 97902, 97936
Carey, Mathew, 1760-1839. incorrectly supposed
author 8110, (39756), 92843, note after
94022
Carey, Matthew, Jr. pseud. Democratic
speaker's hand-book. 10890
Carey, S. F. see Cary, Samuel Fenton.
Cary, Thomas. 32182, (32197)
Carey. firm see Johnson & Carey. firm
Carey and Hart. firm publishers 84237
Carey & Hart's library of humorous American
works. 84237
Carey's American atlas. 10855

Carey's American pocket atlas. 10856
Carey's general atlas. 10858
Carey's minor American atlas. (10857)
Carey's miscellanies. 10871
Carey's record of the great rebellion. (10849)
Carey's war-atlas. 10858
Cargos de que le acusa el Sr Fiscal de la
  Superior Junta de Guerra. 29459, 93778
Cargos que le hizo el Senor Licenciado Don
  Pedro de Galuez. 73042
Carib chief. 97543
Caribbeana. 98836
Caribbeana. Containing letters and disserta-
  tions. (37174)
Caribes Inslen, und Neuw Engel Land. 99534
Cariboo. (10896)
Carib's pledge. 3388A
Caricaburu, Arieta & Co. firm appellants
  105476
Caricaburu, Arieta & Company, versus the
  Josefa Segunda. 105476
Caricatura. 96098
Caridad. 73031
Caridad del sacerdote. (72520)
Carigueya, seu marsupiale Americanum.
  97637
Carill, G. defendant 57986
Carillo, Alonso. 10803
Carillo y Perez, Ignacio. see Carrillo y
  Perez, Ignacio.
Carion, H. 92527
Carion, M. L. tr. 92527
Carisius, -------. 51713
Caritat, Marie Jean Antoine Nicolas. see
  Condorcet, Marie Jean Antoine Nicolas
  Caritat, Marquis de,
Carl, Prinz zu Solms-Braunfels. 10898, 86505
Carl Stedman's Geschichte des Ursprungs.
  91056
Carl, the young emigrant. 10899
Carl Werner. 81264
Carl Werner, an imaginative story. 81196
Carleill, J. 10900
Carlet, Joseph Antoine. supposed author
  99542
Carleton. pseud. Following the flag. see
  Coffin, Charles Carleton.
Carleton. pseud. My days and nights on the
  battlefield. see Coffin, Charles Carleton.
Carleton, Charles A. 86095
Carleton, Dudley. see Dorchester, Dudley
  Carleton, Viscount, 1573-1632.
Carleton, George Washington. 10902-10903
Carleton, Sir Guy. see Dorchester, Guy
  Carleton, 1st Baron, 1724-1808.
Carleton, Henry. 42244
Carleton, James Henry. 10905
Carleton, Latham C. 10906
Carleton, Osgood, 1742-1816. 10907, 93499
Carleton's almanac. 10907
Carletti, Francesco. 10908
Carli, Carlo. 31376
Carli, Dionigio. (10909)-(10910), 2d note after
  62591
Carli, Fernando. 10908
Carli, Gian Rinaldo, Comte. 10911-(10914)
Carli, Jean Rinaldo. see Carli, Gian Rinaldo,
  Comte.
Carli V. Imperatoris, historici. 79179
Carlier, Auguste. 10916-10920
Carlile, R. ed. 70018
Carlile, Richard, 1790-1843. 10921
Carlile, Thomas. 10922
Carlin, Thomas. defendant (36456)
Carlisle, -------, fl. 1683. 79781
Carlisle, -------, fl. 1862. 10927

Carlisle, Frederick Howard, 5th Earl of, 1748-
  1825. (10924)-(10925), (14380), 85243,
  102553 see also Gt. Brit. Commissioners,
  to Treat, Consult, and Agree Upon the
  Means of Quieting the Disorders Now
  Subsisting in Certain of the Colonies,
  1778.
Carlisle, Frederick Howard, 5th Earl of, 1748-
  1825. supposed author 97838
Carlisle, George William Frederick Howard,
  7th Earl of, 1802-1864. 33248-33249,
  92493-92494
Carlisle, James H. 88286
Carlisle, James M. 10926
Carlisle, John Snyder, 1817-1878. 10923
Carlisle, Bishop of. see Bradford, Samuel,
  successively Bp. of Carlisle, and Roch-
  ester, 1652-1731. Douglas, John, suc-
  cessively Bp. of Carlisle, and Salisbury,
  1721-1807. Harcourt, Edward, Abp. of
  York, 1757-1847. Law, Edmund, Bp. of
  Carlisle, 1703-1787. Nicolson, William,
  Abp. of Cashel, 1655-1727. Osbaldistun,
  Richard, successively Bp. of Carlisle, and
  London, 1690-1764.
Carlisle, Mass. Congregational Church. (10928)
Carlisle, Pa. Charter. (10929)
Carlisle, Pa. Democratic Party Convention,
  1817. see Democratic Party. Pennsyl-
  vania. Convention, Carlisle, 1817.
Carlisle, Pa. Dickinson College. see Dickin-
  son College, Carlisle, Pa.
Carlisle, Pa. Meeting of Delegates, 1816.
  (47379)
Carlisle, Pa. Ordinances, etc. (10929)
Carlisle, Pa. Schools. (10929)
Carlisle federal republican. 102466
Carlisle gazette. 94520
Carlisle, October, 1798. Fellow-citizens.
  101104
Carlisle Presbytery. see Presbyterian Church
  in the U. S. A. Presbytery of Carlisle.
Carlo Convivio Socio. pseud. see Socio,
  Carlo Convivio, Junr. pseud.
Carlo famoso de Don Luys Capata. 106252
Carlos I, King of Spain, 1550-1588. (11229),
  18782, 22550, 1st note after 39116,
  40902-40904, note after 40960, 94352
  see also Spain. Sovereigns, etc., 1516-
  1556 (Carlos I)
Carlos II, King of Spain, 1661-1700. 39155,
  (42067), 48608, 68231, 68386-68390 see
  also Spain. Sovereigns, etc., 1665-1700
  (Carlos II)
Carlos III, King of Spain, 1716-1788. 16058,
  17808, 19275, 26158, 26483, 29425, 29947,
  (29949), 32428, 32765, 36899, 48334,
  48504, (48613), 48634-48635, 56262,
  (61088), 68022, 68231-68232, 68238,
  (68245), 68247, 68860, 68873, (68890),
  76293, 76312, 88944, 93346, 93778, 96553,
  98019, 98490 see also Spain. Sovereigns, etc., 1759-1788 (Carlos III)
Carlos IV, King of Spain, 1748-1819. 9031,
  17800, 29028, 29094, 29450, (56292),
  56300, 56747, 66596, 67108, 68223,
  68224, (68226), 68228-68229, 76861 see
  also Spain. Sovereigns, etc., 1788-1808
  (Carlos IV)
Carlos, Calixto Bustamante. see Bustamante
  Carlos, Calixto.
Carlos, Jose Martins. defendant 97697
Carlota, Empress of Mexico, 1840-1927. 17157,
  20548
Carlscroon, Jean Dumont, Baron de. see
  Dumont, Jean, Baron de Carlscroon, d.
  1726.

Carlson, August W. tr. 83142
Carlton, Robert, Esq. pseud. New Purchase.
see Hall, Baynard R.
Carlton, Robert, Esq. pseud. Something for
every body. see Hall, Baynard R.
Carlton, Thomas. 82819
Carlyle, Alexander. 10931
Carlyle, Thomas, 1795-1881. 10932-10935
Carman, Thomas. defendant 6326, 1st note
after 96956, 1st note after 97284
Carmany, John H. 10936
Carmel, N. Y. Raymond Institute. see Ray-
mond Institute, Carmel, N. Y.
Carmelites. Provincia de las Indias. 38754,
75984, (74788)
Carmelites. Provincia de las Indias. peti-
tioners 38754
Carmelites. Provincia de las Indias. Dos
Procuradores. 38754
Carmelo Luna, Lino de Monte. see Luna,
Lino de Monte Carmelo.
Carmen Artega, Manuel del. 69332
Carmen (Mexican State) 66387
Carmen Latinum. 68694
Carmen seculare. 33005, 100545
Carmes epistolares de Hugo Foscolo. 81299
Carmes religiosos. 62949
Carmichael, A. C. (28572)
Carmichael, Mrs. A. C. 10937-10938
Carmichael, Sir James, Bart. ed. 85237
Carmichael, John. (10939)
Carmichael, Richard B. petitioner 45275
Carmichael, William. 88969
Carmichael, William M. 10940
Carmichael Smyth, Eliza Ann. see Smyth,
Eliza Ann Carmichael.
Carmichael Smyth, James. see Smyth, Sir
James Carmichael, 1741-1821.
Carmichael Smyth, Robert. see Carmichael
Smith, Robert Stewart, 1800?-1888.
Carmichael Smyth, Robert Stewart, 1800?-1888.
40522, 85258-85261
Carmick. firm see Ramsey and Carmick.
firm
Carmina sacra. 79456
Carmina Yalensia. 26692
Carmona, Antonio Tamariz de. see Tamariz
de Carmona, Antonio.
Carnahan, D. T. 10941
Carnahan, James, 1755-1859. 10942, (36375)
Carnall hypocrite. 32838
Carnavon, Henry Howard Molyneux Herbert,
4th Earl of, 1831-1890. 31458
Carnarvon, Henry John George Herbert, 3d
Earl of, 1800-1849. incorrectly supposed
author 31458
Carnbee, Pieter, Baron Melvill van. see Mel-
vill van Carnbee, Pieter, Baron, 1816-
1856.
Carne, John. (10933)
Carne, William. see Currie, William, 1709-
1803.
Carnegie, James. see Southesk, James
Carnegie, Earl of.
Carnegie Endowment for International Peace.
83376
Carnegie Institute. 100622
Carneiro, Antonio de Mariz. see Mariz
Carneiro, Antonio de.
Carneiro, Nicolao. 85772
Carner, H. (20062)
Carnero, Juan. 10946, 96249
Carnero, Juan. incorrectly supposed author
11450, 56661
Carnes, J. A. 10947
Carnesworth. pseud. Atlantic City. 10948

Carnival of the states. 83548
Carnot, Hippolyte, i. e. Lazare Hippolyte, 1801-
1888. (10949), 28731, 33618
Carnot, Lazare Hippolyte. see Carnot, Hip-
polyte, i. e. Lazare Hippolyte, 1801-1888.
Carnota, John Athelstane Smith, Conte de.
82915-82917
Caro, Manuel de Zequeira y. see Zequeira y
Caro, Manuel de.
Caro, Phelippe Ignacio Zorrilla y. see Zor-
rilla y Caro, Phelippe Ignacio.
Caro, Ramon Martinez. 10950, 44950
Caro de Torres, Francisco. 10951-10952
Carochi, Orazio, d. 1666. 996, 10953-10954,
58285
Caroli Clvsii Atrebatis aleqvot notae in Garciae
aromatum historiam. 13800
Caroli Verardi Caesenatis historiam baeticam.
72023
Carolina almanac. 27050
Carolina and Georgia almanac, for . . . 1800.
87777
Carolina and Georgia almanac for . . . 1799.
87775
Carolina and Georgia almanac, for the year of
Our Lord, 1804. 87781
Carolina and Georgia almanac, for the year of
Our Lord, 1801. 87779
Carolina and Georgia almanac, for the year of
Our Lord, 1807. 87782A
Carolina and Georgia almanac, for the year of
Our Lord, 1806. 87782
Carolina and Georgia almanac, for the year of
Our Lord 1813. 87783
Carolina and Georgia almanac for the year of
Our Lord, 1803. 87780
Carolina and Georgia almanac, for the year of
Our Lord, 1798. 87773
Carolina and Georgia almanac, for the year of
Our Lord, 1797. 87771
Carolina and Georgia almanac, for the year of
Our Lord, 1796. 87769
Carolina and Georgia almanack; or, astronomical
diary for . . . 1787. 87764
Carolina and Georgia almanack, or astronomical
ephemeris for the year of Our Lord 1784.
87762
Carolina and Georgia almanack, or ephemeris,
for the year of Our Lord 1783. 87761
Carolina calendar for 4 years. 10962, 87745
Carolina described more fully than heretofore.
10963, 104685
Carolina housewife, or house and home. (87804)
Carolina in the olden time. 57921, (64842)
Carolina law journal. 10964
Carolina law repository. 10965
Carolina; or a description of the present state
of that country. 2172
Carolina sports, by land and water. 22286-
22287
Carolina tribute to Calhoun. 95427
Caroline County, Va. 100071
Caroline almanack. 10981
Caroline du Nord. see North Carolina.
Caroline du Nord. 101350
Caroline du Sud. see South Carolina.
Caroline du Sud. 101350
Caroline Westerley. 10982
Carolinian. pseud. Comment on a pamphlet by
"A backsettler." 14962
Carolinian. pseud. Enquiry into the causes.
see Goodloe, Daniel R.
Carolinian. pseud. Essays on slavery. see
Worcester, Samuel Melancthon. supposed
author and Palmer, Dr. -------. sup-
posed author

423

Carolinian. pseud. Inquiry into the causes. see Goodloe, Daniel R.
Carolinian. pseud. Question of slavery considered. (67146)
Carolinian. pseud. Slavery in the southern states. see Pringle, Edward J.
Carolinian. pseud. South and the north. 24458
Carolinian. pseud. To their excellencies Richard Viscount Howe. see Drayton, William Henry. supposed author
Carolinian. pseud. Very short and candid appeal. see American. pseud.
Carolinian and Georgian almanac, for the year of Our Lord, 1788. 58328, 87765
Carolinian of eighteen. pseud. Alfred: an historical poem. see Hasell, William Soranzo.
Carolinians convinced by an honourable and eloquent representative. 23545, 84819
Carolinians convinced; or an examination of the objections. 10983
Carolvs Quintus diuina fauente clementia romanoru[m] imperator. 10984, (13624)
Carolvs Verardus de expugnatione regni granatae. 72023
Caron, Francois, ca. 1600-1674. 4935, 4936, (14958)-14960, 105639
Caron, R. E. 10985, 20906-20907
Caron de Beaumarchais, Amelie Eugenie. see Toussaint de la Rue, Amelie Eugenie (Caron de Beaumarchais)
Caron de Beaumarchais, Pierre Auguste Caron de, 1732-1799.
Carondelet, Francisco Luis Hector, Baron de, 1748-1807. 16686
Carothers, Jesse. 89246
Carpe viam. 55085
Carpenter, Davis, 1799-1878. (10987)
Carpenter, E. G. 10988
Carpenter, Frank B. 68049
Carpenter, Francis Bicknell, 1830-1900. 10989, (33170)
Carpenter, George W. 10990-10991
Carpenter, H. ed. 57562
Carpenter, Hugh Smith. 10992-(10994)
Carpenter, J. E. illus. 17936
Carpenter, J. S. reporter 12172
Carpenter, Kinsly. (66295)
Carpenter, Lant. ed. 97385
Carpenter, Matthew Hale, 1824-1881. 10995-(10998), (74136)
Carpenter, Nathanael. 10999
Carpenter, Philip P. 11000-11002
Carpenter, Richard. 16020
Carpenter, Russell Lant. 11003
Carpenter, Stephen Cullen, d. ca. 1820. 11004-11005, 19161, 19591, 50194, 84837, 104632
Carpenter, Thomas. 9433, 11006, 14030, (25961), 96866
Carpenter, W. M. 11016
Carpenter, William. 11007
Carpenter, William Henry, 1813-1899. 2132-(2135), 2997, 11008-(11015)
Carpenter, William W. USA (11017)
Carpenter & Tenney. firm publishers 43749, 90816-90817
Carpenters' Company of Philadelphia. 62118
Carpenters' Company of Philadelphia. Charter. 61518
Carpenters' Hall: the meeting place of the first Continental Congress. 87260
Carpenters' rules of work. 105440
Carpentier, ------. 11018
Carpet-bag. 85515

Carpet-bag of fun. 80482
Carpet manufacture. 23944
Carpin, Jean du Plan de. see Plan de Carpin, Jean du.
Carpio, Lope Felix de Vega. see Vega Carpio, Lope Felix de, 1562-1635.
Carpio, Manuel. (11019)
Carpon, C. J. A. (11020)
Carr, Benjamin, 1768-1831. 84680
Carr, Dabney. 104878
Carr, Ezra S. 11021
Carr, Frank. 104878
Carr, George P. (11022)
Carr, Isaac. plaintiff 104663
Carr, Mrs. Isaac. plaintiff 104663
Carr, John. incorrectly supposed author 2387, 11023, 92782
Carr, John, fl. 1857. 11024, 34461
Carr, Matthew. supposed author 101884
Carr, Spencer. (11025)
Carr, T. 90499
Carr, Thomas B. ed. 45530
Carr, Thomas D. defendant 41001
Carrabasset: a tragedy, in two acts. 19235
Carraby, S. 11026
Carranza, A. J. 11029
Carranza, A. T. ed. 49863
Carranza, B. 75998
Carranza, Domingo Gonzales. see Gonzales Carranza, Domingo.
Carranza, F. Xavier. 11031-11033
Carranza, J. M. (11034)
Carrara, Ubertino. 11035
Carrasco, ------. 85710
Carrasco, Eduardo. 11037, 61083
Carrasco, F. 67317
Carrasco, Jose Matinas. 11038
Carrasco y Encisco, Luis. 11039
Carrasco y Saavedra, Bernardo, Bp. 11036 see also Santiago, Chile (Diocese) Bishop (Carrasco y Saavedra)
Carrazedo, Juan Rodriguez. see Rodriguez Carrazedo, Juan.
Carre, Ezechiel. 11040
Carrega, Francesco. 14662, 79309
Carrel, N. Armand. (11041)
Carrera, Fernando de la. 11042
Carrera, Lorenzo. 11043
Carrera, Manuel J. de. 66589
Carrera, Rafael, Pres. Guatemala, 1814-1865. 34717 see also Guatemala. Presidente, 1844-1865 (Carrera)
Carreri, Giovanni Francesco Gemelli. see Gemelli Careri, Giovanni Francesco, 1651-1725.
Carreras, ---------. 19680
Carrey, Edward. 25970
Carrey, Emile, 1820-1880. (11044)-11046, 26700
Carribbean rover. 51532
Carrie Harrington. 47120
Carriedo, J. B. 11047-(11048)
Carrier. pseud. New-years-day. 53425
Carrier. pseud. Poetical gift. (63645)
Carrier, A. H. 11049-11050
Carrier of the Albany morning express. pseud. see McCall, H. S.
Carrier of the American mercury. pseud. see American Mercury. Carrier. pseud.
Carrier of the American mercury, presents the following to his customers. 100602
Carrier of the New York morning post, and daily advertiser. pseud. Verses. 99286
Carrier of the Ogdensburgh Sentinel. pseud. see Ogdensburgh Sentinel. Carrier. pseud.

Carrier of the Political index. pseud. To
his patrons. 11051
Carrier of the Political index to his patrons,
with the compliments of the season.
11051
Carrier of the Spectator. pseud. Address.
see Smith, William Russell, 1815-1896.
Carrier of the Tuscaloosa Observer. pseud.
Address. see Smith, William Russell,
1815-1896.
Carrier's address to the patrons of the
Spectator. 84896
Carrier's address, to the patrons of the
Ogdensburgh Sentinel. 56827
Carriers' address to the patrons of the Saint
Louis American. (75383)
Carrier's address to the patrons of the "Tus-
caloosa Observer." 84896
Carriers of the Columbian Centinel. pseud.
see Columbian Centinel, Boston. Car-
riers. pseud.
Carriers of the Saint Louis American. pseud.
see Saint Louis American. Carriers.
pseud.
Carriers of the St. Louis Beacon. pseud. see
St. Louis Beacon. Carriers. pseud.
Carrieres d'Amerique. 38447
Carriglio, Alonso. (11052)
Carrignan, Eugene, Prince of Savoie- see
Eugene, Prince of Savoie-Carrignan,
1663-1736.
Carrillo, Crescencio. 11053-11054, (69669)
Carrillo, Fernando Alfonso. (11055), (11693),
66052
Carrillo, Jose. 11058
Carrillo, Jose Baquijano y. see Baquijano y
Carrillo, Jose.
Carrillo, Juan Chumacero y. see Chumacero
y Carrillo, Juan.
Carrillo, Lorenco. plaintiff 86421
Carrillo de Albornos, Mariana de la Puenta.
plaintiff 99484
Carrillo de Aldrete, Martin. see Aldrete,
Martin Carrillo de, Bp.
Carrillo de la Cerda, Concalo. see Cerda,
Goncalo Carrillo de la.
Carrillo Laso de la Vega, Alonso. 17177, 2d
note after 100818
Carrillo y Laso, Alonso. (3253)
Carrillo y Perez, Ignacio. 10897, 11056-11057
Carrington, -------. 16129
Carrington, Charles S. 69919
Carrington, E. 100413
Carrington, Henry Beebee, 1824-1912. 11059,
56917, 84056
Carrington, J. W. 11060
Carrington, M. J. 56640
Carrington, Margaret Irvin (Sullivant) 1831-
1870. (11061)
Carrington, N. 80058
Carrio, Alonso. 9566
Carrio y Morcillo Rubio de Aunon, Alfonso.
50528-50529
Carrion, Alonso de. defendant 51043, 94629
Carrion, Francisco Xavier de la Fita y. see
Fita y Carrion, Francisco Xavier de la.
Carrique, Richard. ed. 69343-(69344)
Carro, Jean de. tr. 81735
Carrol, John. defendant 32362, 96946, 96951,
2d-3d notes after 102623
Carroll, Andrew. 11062
Carroll, Anna Ella. (11063)-11065
Carroll, B. R. 11066-11067, 11766, 27572,
31630, 49086, 57147, 66724, 87349,
1st-2d notes after 87851, 88392, 104685,
106015

Carroll, Charles, 1737-1832. (11068), (45211A)
Carroll, Charles Hobart, 1794-1865. 11069
Carroll, Davis. 11070
Carroll, Elijah A. 3519-3520
Carroll, G. Danielson. 54459
Carroll, J. 11076, note before 89147
Carroll, James, 1791-1873. 45113, (45378)
Carroll, John, Abp., 1735-1815. 442, 7719,
11071-11075, 22702, 30955, 85257, note
after 101769, 103090, 103092 see also
Baltimore (Archdiocese) Archbishop
(Carroll)
Carroll, Joseph Halsted, 1833-1887. 11077-
11078
Carroll, R. W. 11079
Carroll County, Ky. 101067
Carroll College, Waukesha, Wisc. (11080)
Carroll's literary register. 11079
Carroll's New York city directory. 54459
Carruthers, J. 11081
Carruthers, J. J. 11082
Carruthers, William Alexander. see Caruthers,
William Alexander, ca. 1800-1847.
Carry Emerson. 31003
Carryll, Joseph. 3213, note before 92797, note
after 92800, 3d note after 103687
Carson, Ann. defendant 11083, 83764, 96847
Carson, Christopher, 1809-1868. 61190
Carson, J. H. 11084
Carson, James. (11085)
Carson, James. reporter 21750
Carson, Joseph. 11086-11087
Carson, Kit. see Carson, Christopher, 1809-
1868.
Carson, William. 11088-11089
Carson, City, Nev. Constitutional Convention,
1864. see Nevada. Constitutional Con-
vention, Carson City, 1864.
Carstensen, George J. B. 11090
Carstetter, Levi. plaintiff 85129
Carta a Carlos M. Bustamante. 72268
Carta a el buen ciudadano. 94154
Carta a huma senhora. 7530, 56371, 68332
Carta a los editores del Mercurio de Valparaiso.
72505
Carta a los padres superiores. 15907
Carta . . . a sus amigos. 96198
Carta a todos los medicos. 31201
Carta a un amigo. 99794
Carta a un amigo, en que se hacen algunas
observaciones. 74760
Carta a un amigo por ***. 29123, 88736
Carta a un argelino residente en Mejico. 97042
[Carta] a un hermano suyo. 95253
Carta al autor de un manifiesto. 97049
Carta al ciudadano Antonio Guzman Blanco.
38832
Carta al ciudadano Pacifico de San Pedro.
85676
Carta al Don Baltasar de la Cerva. 72288
Carta al D. Juan Domingo Unamunsaga. (11554)
Carta al General de la Compania de Jesus.
(57971)-57974, 98376
Carta al honorable Henrique Clay. 11913
Carta al observador en Londres. 94864
Carta al Pensador Megicano. 97040
Carta al Pensador Mejicano. 96265
Carta al Pensador Mejicano, del ciudadano
amante del bien publico. 94161
Carta al Rey Nuestro Tapatio. 94823
Carta al profesor Perrey. 72788
Carta al Rey Nuestro Senor. 44104
Carta al Sr. D. Francisco Manuel Sanchez de
Tagle. 97041
Carta al redactor da Malagueta. 44087

Carta apologetica de las reflexiones sobre el uso. 50617
Carta apologetica escrita na lingua Castelhana. 99523
Carta apologetica, que escribieron el Lic D. Manuel Antonio Moreno. (40063)-40064
Carta apologetica, que escrive el Doct. Don Miguel de Yturrizara. 106221
Carta athenagorica a la monja poetisa de Mexico. 76775
Carta athenagorica de la Madre Juana Ynes de la Cruz. 11091
Carta blanca sobre el negro folleto. 11092
Carta circular. 73872
Carta circular del D. Manuel Joseph Rubio y Salinas. 73868
Carta circular, dirigida a todos sus amados hijos, y diocesanos. 75971
Carta citatorio a el estado eclesiastico y secular. (72569)
Carta confidencial de Vice-Presidente de la republica. 58138, 1st note after 98873
Carta confidencial que le dirijio el V. P. de la republica. 14621
Carta consolatoria a la ciudad de Guanajuato. 88725
Carta consolatorio a la ciudad de Guanajuato. 24151
Carta constitucional do reino de Portugal. 7556
Carta critica sobre la historia de America. 35298
Carta da costa da provincia do Maranhao. 38620
Carta da provincia de Minas Geraes. 27121
Carta . . . dandoles vna breve noticia. 2475
Carta de Alonso Calvo. 10086
Carta de Antonio Jose de Irisarri. 35076
Carta de consuelo que Ad. Antonio Zabala escribio. 44557A
Carta de Coquimbo. 99785
Carta de D. Carlos de Siguenza y Gongora. 80987
Carta de D. Fedro [sic] Muniz. (51332)
Carta de D. J. Sosa y Lima. 87194
Carta de Don Nicolas Penalver. 21775, (59637)
Carta de Don Sancho de Varaorna. 98593
Carta de edificacion. 23071
Carta de edificacion del P. M. Alvarez de Lava. 39274
Carta de Fray Toribio Motolinia. 84379
Carta de Grazioso Benincasa. 76838
Carta de la deoouverte [sic] faite l'an 1673. 95332
Carta de la muerte, y virtudes del P. Juan de Ledesma. 70788
Carta de la temprana muerte del P. P. Borote. 16824
Carta de la vida del Joseph Maria Genovese. 26966
Carta de la vida del P. Fernando Konsag. 38233
Carta de la vida del P. Juan Gumersbac. 29272
Carta de la vida Pedro Spetiali. 57999
Carta de la vida y virtudes del H. Vicente Gonzalez. 27802, 68248
Carta de Lermin a Tlaucolde. 72245
Carta de Monsieur *** a Monsieur ***. 23342
Carta de N. P. Francisco Picolomini. 62675
Carta de pesame por el fallecimiento del Exmo. Senor Don Bernardo de Galvez. 98599
Carta de Quintino Bocayuva a Pedro Americo. 88731

Carta de relacio embiada a Su. S. Majestad. (16933)
Carta de relacion embiada a su S. Majestad. 16934
Carta de Sebastian Kindelan. 37773
Carta de un Americano a un amigo suyo. 17757
Carta de un Americano a un diputado. 11093, 34423
Carta de un Americano al Espanol. 11094, 48884, 78907, 103421
Carta de un amigo a otro. 11095
[Carta de un ciudadano de Centro-America a los] editores. 32773
Carta de un ciudadano Mexicano. 48318
Carta de un ex-diputado de Nueva Espana. 67362
Carta de un Gallego a Don Toribio. 94155
Carta de un Havanero. 23580
Carta de un Mazon. 56452
Carta de un padre a sus hijos. 76222
Carta de un particular al Jeneral El-Es-Burro. 98321
Carta de un Pensador Tapatio al Pensador Megicano. 94344-94345, note after 96100
Carta de un Peruano a Mr. F. de Brandsen. 68789, 94833
Carta de un sacerdote en el Peru. 97660
[Carta] de una senorita Inglesa. 95253
Carta de varios vecinos de San Francisco de Yare. (49897)
Carta de veinte de Junio de mil ochocientos quince. 99500
Carta del Capitan Don Manuel Coello. (14154)
Carta del Colegial al Pensador Mejicano. 105744
Carta del defensor de tontos. 85676, 98909-note after 98910
Cartas del Doctor Alberdi a sus amigos. 26273
Carta del General de la Merced. Fr. Jose Garcia Palomo. 58389, (63889)
Carta del General Rosecrans. note just before (73261)
Carta del Indio patriota. 977, 16159, 96117
Carta del Indis patriotae. 977, 16159, 96117
Carta del Indus patriota. 977
Carta del ministro . . . del Peru. 96223
Carta del Padre Alonso Bonifacio. 11431
Carta del P. Andreas Velasquez. 98808
Carta del P. Bartholome Braun. 7446, 27535
Carta del Padre Bartolome Tafvr. 94198
Carta del P. D. Manuel Echeverria y Penalver. 21775
Carta del Padre Feliz Antonio de Villagarcia. 99626
Carta del Padre Lozana, etc. 41671
Carta del Padre Luys de Valdiuia. 98327
Carta del Padre Lvys Sotelo. 87202
Carta del P. Pedro Lozano. 42597
Carta del P. Placido Spirembergo. 89466
Carta del Padre Provincial Francisco Zevallos. 106329
Carta del P. Rector Pedro Reales. 27802, 68248
Carta del Prothonotario de Lucena. 57714
Carta del Rey Catholico a Pedro Arias Davila. 18782, 56338
Carta del Rey Fernando V. 86398
Carta del Sagrario de Guadalajara. 57719
Carta del Sr. Andres Bello. (12753)
Carta del Senor Pedro Jose Rojas. 72795
Carta del v. siervo de Dios D. Juan de Palafox y Mendoza. (58281)
Carta dirigida al Escino Sr. Presidente de la republica. 29353

Carta dirigida al Senor Ministro Don Jose Joaquin de Herrera. 98112
Carta dirigida al "Times" por el Sr. Clay. (74180)
Carta dirigida ao . . . D. Romualdo. 11470
Carta dirigida pelo Sr. Theophilo Benedicto Ottoni. (47900)
Carta dirigida por Don Francisco Dias Zapata. 32754
Carta dirijida al Rey de Espana. 58270, 89959
Carta do atlas de Joan Martines. 76838
Carta edificante, . . . da noticia a su provincia Mexicana. (58572)
Carta edificante de la vida de la M. R. M. Maria Josefa de S. Ignacio. 77112
Carta edificante de la vida del P. Martin Larrainzar. 39081
Carta edificante en que el P. Antonio de Paredes. (58572)
Carta edificante, o relacion sumaria de la vida. 74865
Carta edificante que descubre la vida religiosa. (51326)
Carta edificativa. 26553
Carta em resposta a um amigo. (57419)
Carta embiada de la Ciudad de Los Reyes. 96789
Carta, embiada del Brasil a vn cavallero. 7640, note after 96475
Carta en que le da cuenta. 11937
Carta encyclica de edificacion. 47421
[Carta escripta] de huma senhora. 95252
Carta escrita a 5 de Dezembro de 1571. 31382
Carta escrita a Su Majestad D. Carlos Segundo. 73286
Carta escrita a un Americano. 11096, 56244
Carta escrita a un cavalerro de la Ciudad de Los Reyes. (61105)
Carta escrita a seu Irmao. 95252
Carta escrita en al ciudad de Mexico. 99461-99462
Carta escrita pelo mesmo coronel. 38661, 3d note after (69168)
Carta escrita por D. Antonio de Mendoza. 84379
Carta escrita por un regnicola recien. 11097
Carta expresiva de la mas fina lealtad al soberano. 68235
Carta familiar de un sacerdote. 11098
Carta familiar, que para utilidad publica. 86233
Carta gratulatoria del Excmo. e Illmo. Sr. Arzobispo de Mexico. 48319
Carta geral da fronteira do imperio do Brazil. 88810
Carta imparcial sobre el funero del clero. 23060
Carta inedita de Hernan Cortes. 16940
Carta inedita del Felix Varela. 48162
Carta inserta en el Registro oficial. (72279)
Carta instructiva a un predicator moderno. 5024
Carta itineraria Europae. 101025
Carta joco seria, o agri-dulce. 97694
Carta marina. 101017
Carta o diario que escribe D. Jose Eusebio de Llano y Zapata. 41669, 41671
Carta pastoral. 71613, 72539
Carta pastoral a la Venerable Congregacion de San Pedro. (58282), 58290
Carta pastoral a las religiosas de Guadalajara. 72542
Carta pastoral a los curas. 31201
Carta pastoral a los fieles de Guadalajara. 72542

Carta pastora a sus amadas obejas. (41141)
Carta pastoral a todos sus amados diocesanos. 30411
Carta pastoral acompanada de la protesta. 39283
Carta pastoral, advertencias y paternales avisos. 73847
Carta pastoral al clero de Guadalajara. 72542
Carta pastoral al Rector, &c., del Real Colegio de Tepotzotlan. 30411
Carta pastoral . . . con ocasion de haver fundado en la capital de Cordova. 75974
Carta pastoral de D. Francisco Fabian y Fuero. (23593)
Carta pastoral de D. Victoriano Lopez Gonzalo. 27826
Carta pastoral de exhortacion. 99635, 99637
Carta pastoral de exortacion e instrvccion. 99633
Carta pastoral del Illmo. Sr. Arzobispo de Mexico. 26719
Carta pastoral del Illmo Senor Dr. D. Phelippe Ignacio de Truxillo. 97279
Carta pastoral del Illmo. Sr. Obispo de Cuba. (50590)
Carta pastoral del Il[l]ustrisimo Senor Obispo Electo. (67078)
Carta pastoral del Illmo. y Excmo. Sr. Arzobispo de Mexico. 48320
Carta pastoral del Illvst.^{mo} y R.^{mo} Obispo de la Pvebla de los Angeles. 58283
Carta pastoral del P. Hernando de la Rua. 69172
Carta pastoral dirige a todos sus amados diocesanos. 56324
Carta pastoral dirigida a los fieles del Nuevo Reino de Leon. 74746
Carta pastoral do ex.^{mo} e rev.^{mo} Bispo Capellao-mor do Rio de Janeiro. 72500
Carta pastoral escrita desde Roma a todos sus diocesanos. 39284
Carta pastoral-exhortatorio ao clero e Para de Pernambuco. 17011
Carta pastoral. 1799. (23593)
Carta pastoral por Juan A. Huerta, Obispo de Puno. 33561
Carta pastoral, previniendo los animos de los fieles. (58284)
Carta pastoral que dirige a los parrocos. 75972
Carta pastoral que dirige a sus diocesanos. 93284
Carta pastoral que dirige a todos los clerigos. 75975
Carta pastoral que el Illmo. Senor Arzobispo de Mexico. (38617), 39476
Carta pastoral que el Ill° Senor Doctor D. Diego Rodriguez Rivas. 71613
Carta pastoral que el Illmo. Sr. D. Francisco Joseph Diaz de Espada y Landa. 22881
Carta pastoral que el Ilust.° S°ʳ. D. Fray Joseph Antonio de San Alberto, Arzobispo de la Plata, dirige a todos los que en el pasado. 669, 75976
Carta pastoral que el Illmo. Sr. Obispo de Guadalajara dirige. 29019
Carta pastoral que escribe a sus amadas hijas las religiossas. 38810
Carta pastoral, que escribio del D. Diego Ladron de Guevara. 29145
Carta pastoral que el S. D. Manuel Robio de Salinas. 73869
Carta pastoral que los Illmos Sres. Arzobispos de Mejico y Michoacan. 47034
Carta pastoral que sobre las obligaciones del Cristianismo. 57617

Carta pastoral segunda. 75973

Carta pastoral sobre jubileo. 14357

Carta primera de el Pensador Tapatico al
Pensador Mejicano. 94344-94345, note
after 96100

Carta que a los S^{res}. diputados de las cortes
dirige el Intendente de Exercito. 11099,
86819

Carta que Bernabeu escribe al Lopez. 41968

Carta que dirige D. Jose Gonzalez a D. Jose
de Arango. 27807

Carta, que D. Bartholome Goncalez de Poueda.
64742

Carta, qve el Capitan Garcia de Tamayo y
Mendoza, Escrivano Mayor de la Real
Hacienda. 94281

Carta qve el Capitan Garcia de Tamayo y
Mendoza, . . . escriue al Excelentissimo
Senor Principe de Esquilache. 94282-
94283

Carta que el General Jose A. Paez escribio.
(58137)

Carta, que el illustrisimo Senor D. Fr. Joseph
Antonio de San Alberto, Arzobispo de la
Plata, escribio. 75977

Carta qve el Obispo de Areqvipa Fray Don
Pedro de Perea. 60877

Carta, qve el P. Francisco Xavier Rector del
Colegio Maximo de S. Pablo. (11100),
note after 105718

Carta que el Senor Doctor D. Joseph de Antequera y Castro. 58393

Carta que embio a Su Magestad el Senor Don
Fadrique de Toledo. 96110

Carta q[ue] embio Don Barnardino Delgadillo
de Auellaneda. 77289

Carta que embio el Senor Duque de Medina.
(51243), 69235, 2d note after 78907

Carta que en 25 de ultimo dirigio D. Pedro
Celestino Negrete. 56441

Carta que escrivio al Padre Oratio Carochi.
58285

Carta que escrivio del exercito el Padre Fr.
Francisco de Tarazana. 94386

Carta que Gonzalo Coutinho escrivio. 17201,
98711

Carta que la M. R. M. Joachina Maria de
Zavaleta . . . escribe. 106284

Carta que Nuestro Santisimo Padre Clemente
XIV, escribio. (58288)

Carta que o Povo, ou antes o Cura Da Aldea
de S. Francisco Xavier escreveo. 63895

Carta que o Vice-Rei do Brasil D. Jorges
Mascarenhas. 45409

Carta que os membros de Junta do Porto
dirigiram. 57196

Carta que se dirige al Senor D. Ventura de
Arzac. 58435

Carta que sobre los asuntos de Mexico. 59294

Carta relacion de la entrada de la expedicion
Espanola en el Nayar. 86255

Carta respuesta . . . por el Senor D. Fernando
Trvbino. 100637

Carta sediciosa, e fraudulenta. 63895

Carta segunda en que se continua la critica.
51346

Carta sexta de Hernando Cortes. 16943

Carta sobre a nitreira artificial. 98830

Carta, sobre la vida y muerte de la Padre
Doctor Francisco Xavier Lazcano. 26522

Carta sobre lo que debe hacer un principe.
11101

Carta suplicatoria a los Illust. y R. Senores
Arcobispos y Obispos. 63967

Carta tercera de relacio. 16935

Carta universal en que se contiene todo lo que
del mondo. 76838

Carta, y relacion que desde la ciudad de Lima.
94283-94284

Cartegena, Juan. (11102)

Cartegena, Pablo Morillo y Morillo, Conde de.
see Morillo y Morillo, Pablo, Marques
de la Puerta, 1778-1837.

Cartagena, Colombia (Province) Constitucion.
(11133)

Cartagena, Colombia (Province) Gobernador.
2455, 11131-11132, 11134, 1st note after
99245

Cartagena, Colombia (Diocese) Bishop [ca. 1681]
47629

Cartagena, Colombia (Diocese) Bishop [ca. 1730]
56447

Cartaginese, H. 11103

Cartago, Costa Rica. Sociedad Itineraria del
Norte. see Sociedad Itineraria del Norte,
Cartago.

Cartari, Vicenzo. (11104)

Cartas a D. F. M. sobre la variacion de
nuestro sistema gubernativo. 18671,
72266

Cartas a la Ven. Congregacion de S. Francisco
Xavier de Mexico. 76899

Cartas al Abate de Pradt. 36437

Cartas al Br. D. Miguel Sanchez sobre la
historia Guadalupana. 80998

Cartas al R. P. Andrea de Rada. 58286

Cartas Americanas. (10913)

Cartas Americanas, correspondencia con diversas personas. 93812, 99498

Cartas Americanas, politicas y morales.
99472

Cartas de algunas personas. 69202

Cartas de Americo Vespucio. (14362)

Cartas de D. Jose Ramon Pacheco. (58075)

Cartas de Don Juan Bautista Say a M. Malthus.
(77359)

Cartas de Don Luis [i. e. Joseph] de Zuniga.
106403

Cartas de huma Peruviana. 28198

Cartas de Juan Agapito Canelo y Cachuto.
63349

Cartas de Pedro de Valdivia. 12754

Cartas de un Polaco sobre la politica de Chile.
12747

Cartas de una Americano al "Espanol." 48884

Cartas del Canonista de la Sierra. 61089

Cartas del Governador Don Juan de Prado.
16670

Cartas del Sr. Dr. D. Josef Antequera y Castro.
10803

Cartas do Padre Antonio Vieira. 99519

Cartas do P. Antonio Vieyra da Companhia de
Jesu. 99519

Cartas do Padre Antonio Vieyra, da Companhia
de Jesus. 99520

Cartas e outras orbas selectas. 11181

Cartas economico-politicas sobre agricultura
e commercio. 8133

Cartas edificantes, y curiosas. (40705)

Cartas embiadas del Brasil. (16672), 55393

Cartas familiares escritas durante la insurreccion. 15084

Cartas historicas a un amigo. 39096, 58388

Cartas Mejicanas. 51213, 51215

Cartas para servir de introducion. 7422, 7433

Cartas pastorales. 75978

Cartas pastorales del ill^{mo}. fray Francisco
Nunez de la Vega. 56327

Cartas pastorales, y edictos del Illmo. Senor D.
Francisco Antonio Lorenzana y Buitron.
42062

Cartas pehuenches. 47426
Cartas politicas de Erasmo. 7517
Cartas selectas do Padre Antonio Vieira.
99521
Cartas sobre a confederacao dos Tamoyos.
44969
Cartas sobre botanica. 75617
Cartas sobre la America. 44644
Cartas sobre la conquista espiritual de Cali-
fornias. (75870)
Cartas sobre la educacion del bello sexo.
11106
Cartas sobre la variacion de nuestro sistema
gubernativo. 18671, 72266
Cartas y relaciones de Hernan Cortes. 16942
Carte annasse a la tettere de Cte Carlo
Vidua. 99504
Carte coloriee indiquant les progres des
Federales. 79519
Carte de comparaison des plans. 8831,
(47542)
Carte de Diego Ribero, 1529. 76838
Carte de la Bibliotheque de Weimar. 76838
Carte de la lengva Aymara. 96267
Carte de la portion S. O. de l'ile de la
Guadeloupe. 75528
Carte de la temperature des eaux. (75523)
Carte de l'isle de Saint-Domingue. 75172
Carte del Sr. Andres Bello. (12753)
Carte des decouvertes Arctiques provoquees
par la recherche de Franklin. 43044,
44171
Carte des deux Florides et de la Louisiane
interieure. (72039)
Carte des nouvelles decouvertes. 40673
Carte d'etude pour le trace et le profil du
canal. 2768, 26518, note after 95460
Carte du Paraguay nouvellement publiee.
64703
Carte du Texas. 29395, 95072
Carte d'un nouveau monde. 31358
Carte d'un tres grand pais. 31359
Carte d'un tres grands pays. 31359
Carte d'une partie de la Republique Argentine.
57457
Carte enluminee de la Nouvelle-Ecosse.
69671, 96403
Carte geographique. 11620
Carte geologico-topographique dessinee par M.
Poirson. 39603-39604
Carte intitulee Canada, Louisiane, et les
Terres Anglaises. 47552
Carte nouvelle et generale des Etats-Unis.
101358
Carte particuliere de cette colonie MDCCLVI.
19370, 84594
Carte que Concalo Vas Coutino, del Consejo
del Rey Nuestro Senor. 17201, 98711
Carte reduite de Guillaume Levasseur de
Dieppe. 76838
Carte reduite par Jean Dupont de Dieppe.
76838
Carte sobre los ultimos sucesos de Centro-
America. 39075
Carte speciale de l'expedition dressee sur
plan par l'auteur. 5662
Carte tracant l'itineraire exact de la route.
38583, 100811
Carteau, J. Felix. 11107-11111, 74130, 101244
Carteaux, Felix. see Carteau, J. Felix.
Cartee, Cornelius S. 11112
Cartegena, Pablo Morillo, Conde de. 50703
Cartel del certamen poetico con qve celebra
. . . la santa iglesia metropolitana de
Lima. 60856

Cartel del certamen templo del honor y la
virtud. (35821)
Carter, ------. 11126
Carter, Abby (Allin) 961, 11113
Carter, E. (54905)
Carter, James. 11115-11116
Carter, James Gordon, 1795-1849. 11117-11119,
52829, 95259
Carter, John. ed. 66327
Carter, Landon. 70255
Carter, Landon. supposed author 40537, 1st
note after 100484
Carter, Luther Cullen, 1805-1875. 11120
Carter, Nathaniel Hazeltine, 1787-1830. (11121),
53945, note after 92151
Carter, Nicholas. 95118
Carter, Robert. 11122
Carter, St. Leger L. 38823, 56302, 6th note
after 100477
Carter, T. J. 55826
Carter, Thomas. 11123
Carter, Thomas, 1769-1800. (62861), 86904
Carter, William, Lieut., 40th Reg't. of Foot.
11124
Carter, Rev. William. 11125, 34297
Carter, William, fl. 1645. 27954, 80205
Carter, William, fl. 1669. 67599
Carter (Robert) & Brothers. firm publishers
85296
Carter & Minty. firm publishers (54905)
Cartera Cubana. (17758)
Carteret, John. see Granville, John Carteret,
1st Earl, 1690-1763.
Carteret, Philip, d. 1796. 21211-21215, 30934-
30935, 30937-30945, 31389, 32438, 37631,
38022, 50113, 50114, 52455, 52591,
(54897), (69276), 100836, 101029, 104679
Carteret County, N. C. Superior Court. see
North Carolina. Superior Court (Carteret
County)
Carters cabinet library, fourth series. 85296
Carter's Executors. plaintiffs (18203)
Carter's Newburgh city directory. (54905)
Cartes et figures. 30940, (69276)
Cartes generales de tovtes les parties dv monde.
76719
Cartes geographiques et physiques. (33752)
Cartes geologiques. 57457
Cartes marines et portulans posteriores a 1434
76838
Cartes particulieres. 27650, (63966), 68421
Cartes, rapports, estimations, &c. (75311)
Carthage, Ohio. Longview Hospital. see
Hamilton County, Ohio. Longview Hos-
pital, Carthage.
Carthage gazette. note after 94774, 94779
Carthier, James. see Cartier, Jacques, 1491-
1557.
Cartier, G. E. 34041, 69661
Cartier, Jacques, 1491-1557. 11138-11144,
62575, 67740-67742, 80706
Cartilla de Comisarios del Santo Oficio de la
Inquisicion de Mexico. 48321
Cartilla de doctrina Cristiana. 29163
Cartilla de policia. (48322)
Cartilla del federalista. (11145)
Cartilla del nuevo beneficio de la plata. 96225-
96226
Cartilla del pueblo. 5058
Cartilla del sistema metrico-decimal. (74021)
Cartilla de religiosa y sagrada. 72570
Cartilla mayor en lengua Castellana, Latina, y
Mexicana. 48232
Cartilla o silabrio de lengua Maya. 74519

Cartilla o silibario, del uso de letras y raiz de palabras. 74604
Cartilla para el cultivo del cacao en la isla de Cuba. 74909
Cartilla para los gefes y los pueblos en America. 11146
Cartilla y doctrina Christiana. 72811
Cartilla y doctrina espiritual. 76105
Cartledge, Samuel. 102466
Cartridge box. (11147)
Cartter, David Kellogg, 1812-1887. (11148)
Cartuxo, Bruno de Valencuela Monge. see Valenzuela, Bruno de.
Cartwright, ---------. 22263
Cartwright, Charles. 11149
Cartwright, F. D. 11159
Cartwright, George, 1739-1819. 11150-11151, 40641
Cartwright, John, fl. 1599. 66686
Cartwright, John, 1740-1824. 11152-11159
Cartwright, Peter, 1785-1872. 11160-(11163)
Cartwright, Sir Richard John, 1835-1912. 11164
Cartwright, Samuel, M. D. 49650
Cartwright, Samuel Adolphus, 1793-1863. 11165, 78259
Cartwright, William. 11166
Caruthers, Eli Washington, 1793-1865. 11167-11169
Caruthers, J. E. 11170
Caruthers, R. L. 11171
Caruthers, William Alexander, ca. 1800-1847. (11172)-11174, 100443, 100482, 5th note after 100577
Carvajal, Bernardin de, ca. 1456-1523. 11175
Carvajal, Pedro Tellez. see Tellez Carvajal, Pedro.
Carvajal, Rafael. 93419
Carvajal, Tomas Tenorio. see Tenorio Carvajal, Tomas.
Caruajal de Ulloa, Gabriel. 93312
Carvajal y Ribera, Fr. Fernando de. 11177
Carvalhaes, Rodrigo Pinto Pizarro de Almeida. 11178
Carvalho, Hippolyte. 11179
Carvalho, Jorge de. 69171
Carvalho, Manuel de Almeida de, Bp., 1749-1818. 88753 see also Para, Brazil (Diocese) Bishop (Carvalho)
Carvalho, S. N. 11180
Carvalho e Mello, Sebastiao Jose de. see Pombal, Sebastiao Jose de Varvalho e Mello, Marques de, 1699-1782.
Carvalho Silva Leal, Antonio. see Silva Leal, Antonio Carvalho.
Carvalhosa, Manuel Francisco de Barros e Sousa de Mesquita de Macedo Leitao e. see Santarem, Manuel Francisco de Barros e Sousa de Mesquita de Macedo Leitao e Carvalhosa, Visconde de.
Carvallo, Manuel. supposed author 97748
Carvao de pedra no Rio Grande do Sul. 88811
Carver, -------, fl. 1832. 92813
Carver, Hartwell. 11182, 66014
Carver, James. defendant 88951
Carver, James. plaintiff 96888
Carver, John, Esquire, Justice of the Peace and Quorum. pseud. Sketches of New England. see Dodge, N. S.
Carver, Jonathan, 1710-1780. (11183)-11191, 40827, 83623, 96499, 3d note after 96502
Carver, Mary. appellant (11193)-11194
Carver, Robin. 11195
Carver, W. 103191
Carver, William. 11196
Carver, Mass. School Committee. 11197

Carver centenary. 11192
Carwell, H. de W. 11198
Cary, Alpheus. (11199)
Cary, Edward. 25863, 1st note after 96991 see also Committee Appointed by the Passengers of the Oceanus.
Cary, Henry. see Falkland, Henry Cary, Viscount, d. 1633.
Cary, John. 11200
Cary, John L. see Carey, John L.
Cary, Moses. (11202)
Cary, Richard, 1717-1790. 11203, (34627), 95950
Cary, Samuel. 11204-11207, (11209), (25768), 2d note after 97579
Cary, Samuel Fenton. (11210)-11212, 87006, 87010
Cary, Thomas, Jr. 11214
Cary, Rev. Thomas. 11213
Cary, Thomas G. 19662
Cary, Thomas Graves. see Cary, Thomas Greaves.
Cary, Thomas Greaves. 11215-11219, 40392, note after 96512
Cary Improvement Company, Boston. 11220
Caryl, Joseph. (56742), 80200, (80815), 103688
Carzel, Antonio Maria Espinosa y. see Espinosa y Carzel, Antonio Maria.
Casa Barreto, Nicolas Barreto, Conde de. see Barreto, Nicholas, Conde de Casa Barreto.
Casa Yrujo, Carlos Martinez de Yrujo y Tacon, Marques de, 1763-1824. 43815, 56512, note before 88936, 106214-106218 see also Spain. Legacion. United States.
Casa Yrujo, Carlos Martinez de Yrujo y Tacon, Marques de, 1763-1824. supposed author 15004, 56512, note before 88936, note after 94406, note after 106213
Casa de Beneficencia, Havana. see Havana. Casa de Beneficencia.
Casa de Education de Buenavista, Havana. see Havana. Casa de Education de Buenavista.
Casa Consignataria de Alsop y Compania. see Alsop y Compania. firm
Casa de Ninos Expositos, Mexico (City) see Mexico (City) Casa de Ninos Expositos.
Casa del Senor S. Joseph de Ninos Expositos, Mexico (City) see Mexico (City) Casa del Senor S. Joseph de Ninos Expositos.
Casa peregrina. 24819
Casado, D. (11221)-11222
Casafuente, Juan de Acuna, Marques de. see Acuna, Juan de, Marques de Casafuente.
Casal, Manuel Ayres de. see Ayres de Casal, Manuel, b. 1754?
Casamiento de Nazahualcoyotl. 71703
Casanate, Pedro Porter y. see Porter y Casanate, Pedro.
Casanova, Francisco Solis y. see Solis y Casanova, Francisco.
Casapalma, Francisca Fernandez de Cordoba, Condesa de. see Fernandez de Cordoba, Francisca, Condesa de Casapalma.
Casares, Jose Hilario. 11223
Casaretto, Giovanni. 11225
Casarin, Vicente. 11226
Casas, Balthazar de las. see Casas, Bartholome de las, Bp. of Chiapa, 1474-1566.
Casas, Bartholome de las, Bp. of Chiapa, 1474-1566. 11227-11289, 14667, 30525, 31559, 39114-39122, (48317), (49434), 52092, 52098, 57126, 57458-57459, 64130, 66686, 73482, (74830), 2d note after 74844, note before 94570, 98604, 99375 see also Chiapa (Diocese) Bishop (Casas)
Casas, Goncalo de las. 11290

Casas, Las. pseud. see Las Casas. pseud.
Casas, Lucas de las. 11291
Casas, Manuel Maria de Las. 11293
Casas, poeme a trois epoques. 18787
Casasola, Jose Joaquin Trebuesto y. see Trebuesto y Casasola, Jose Joaquin, Comte de Miravalle.
Casasola, Jose Maria. 11294-11295, 75571
Casaus, Bartholome de las. see Casas, Bartholome de las, bp. of Chiapa, 1474-1566.
Casaus, Beatris Bernardina (de Andrada) de Servantes. see Servantes Casaus, Beatris Bernardina (de Andrada) de.
Casaus, R. (11297)
Casaus Torres y las Plazas, Ramon. 86369
Cascadas del Parna. (49434)
Cascades du Niagara et leur marche retrograde. 19751
Cascaliendres, Veremundo Androminas de. 11298
Casco, Rafael. 98648
Cascoigne, John. cartographer 16278, 35966, 35968, (55557)
Casconselos, a romance of the New World. 81271
Case, Albert. 11299
Case, Charles, 1817- 11300
Case, George. 11301
Case, Theodore S. 11302
Case, Thomas. 80205
Case, Wheeler, d. 1793. 11303-11304, 63617, 63622
Case, Wheeler, d. 1793. supposed author 63622
Case, William. 11305
Case. 54701, 97768
Case and claim of the American loyalists. 11306, note after 42561
Case and complaint of Mr. Samuel Osborn. 57756
Case and complaint of Samuel Maxwell. 47053
Case and cure of persons possessed by the devil. 46230
Case and grievance of divers merchants. 105694
Case and opinion of Peter S. Du Ponceau & A. Davezac. 21384
Case and opinion of Theodore W. Dwight. 21544, 76611, 76647
Case and opinion. The trust on which the Sanitary Commission holds its funds. 21544, 76611
Case and petition of His Majesty's loyal subjects. 24847, 102767
Case and points on the part of the plaintiff in error. 102625
Case and proceedings for and against Mr. Jeronimy Clifford. 13687
Case and replication of the legal representatives of Jeronimy Clifford. (13685)
Case and tryal of John Peter Zenger. 106308
Case as it is. (66129)
Case at law. 26269
Case before the House of Lords between Rev. John Horne, plaintiff, and King George III., defendant. 33032
Case before the House of Lords between Robert MacNair and others. 43591
Case before the House of Lords, betwixt the trustees of Andrew Grant, of Grenada, and Douglas Heron & Co. 28294
Case before the House of Lords relative to the ship May. 11307

Case between John Keninon, Esq., and others. 37376
Case between Mr. Whitefield and Dr. Stebbing stated, &c. 26596
Case by both parties. 102175
Case. Court for the Trial of Impeachments and Correction of Errors. 89295
Case de l'oncle Tom. 92414, 92524-92527, 92529, 92531, 92533-92535, 92538-92543
Case de l'oncle Tom; drame en huit actes. (21176)
Case de l'oncle Tome. 92596
Case decided in the District Court of Massachusetts. (11324)
Case decided in the Supreme Court of the United States. 11308
Case du pere Tom. 92531
Case fairly stated. 101268
Case for Southwick. 88639
Case in equity. 44135
Case in Nevis, 1817. 33574
Case (in part) of the seigniors of Lower Canada. 21292
Case in the House of Lords respecting the Scotch estates. 80084
Case, made by the plaintiffs in error. 98616
Case of a soul walking in darkness. 46530, 91833
Case of a troubled mind. (46246), 46328
Case of Abraham Wendell, Jr. 96996
Case of Alexander, Earl and Viscount of Stirling. 91841A
Case of alien enemies considered and decided. (2592), note after 95821
Case of B. Cadien [i. e. Baptiste Cadieu.] 96845
Case of Barbados, for indemnification of losses. 3263
Case of Baptis Irvine. 35112, 3d note after 96883
Case of Benjamin Harris, bookseller. (30463)
Case of Benjamin Withall. 104926
Case of Brailsford & others vs. James Spalding. 7328
Case of Brig. Gen. Alexander Smyth. 85200
Case of C. Sumner. 61042
Case of Captain Abraham Wendell, Jr. 96996, 4th note after 102623
Case of Capt. Geo. Frye. 26102
Case of Charles Brown. 81920
Case of Charles Lord Baltemore. 10083
Case of Chief Engineer Joshua Follansbee. 24952
Case of consicence concerning eating of blood. (46647)
Case of contempt. 35783
Case of contracts for the third and fourth subscriptions. 102179
Case of Cuba. 17759
Case of Dame Dorothy Thomas. 95385
Case of De Witt Littlejohn against Horace Greeley. 17641, 41548
Case of Dr. Bullions fairly stated. 56597, 90512
Case of Dred Scott. In the Supreme Court of the United States, December term, 1854. 78256
Case of Dred Scott in the United States Supreme Court. 78257-(78258)
Case of Edmund Shotwell and others. 80736, 96938
Case of Edward Drewe. 20936
Case of Elizabeth Rutgers versus Joshua Waddington. 74433
Case of F. F. Cavada. 14457

Case of Father McMahon. 57711

Case of Ferdinand Smyth Stuart. 85243

Case of Franz Muller. 51279

Case of General Fremont. 5741, (25845)

Case of George Arnold plaintiff. vs. John Boyle and others. 96814

Case of George M'Intosh, esquire. 43331, 92833

Case of George W. Niven, esquire. 75948, 2d note after 96909

Case of Gibbons against Ogden. 103153

Case of going to war, for the sake of procuring, enlarging, or securing of trade, considered in a new light. 11310, 1st note after 97332, 97346

Case of going to war for the sake of trade. 11310, 1st note after 97332, 97346

Case of Great Britain and America, addressed to the King. 9637, 11311

Case of Hannah Penn. 59672

Case of Heman considered. 65580

Case of hereditary bias. 84787

Case of His Majesty's province of New Hampshire. 52803

Case of His Majesty's province of the Massachusetts Bay in New England. (45666)

Case of His Majesty's province of the Massachusetts Bay touching the dispute. 52847

Case of His Majesty's province of the Massachusetts-Bay, upon two appeals. 45665

Case of His Majesty's subjects having property. 51077, note after 103446

Case of His Majesty's subjects, settled on the coast of Yucatan. 103447, 1st note after 106221

Case of Isaac Hunt, Esq; of Philadelphia. 33862

Case of Isaac Taylor and Elisha Gatchel. 59957, note after 94466

Case of J. Degrave, Francis Minshall, and others. 45977

Case of James Christie, Jun. 12933

Case of Jane Marie. 44560

Case of John Bentley and Isaiah Green. 44898

Case of John Bentley, Gaoler of Baltimore County Gaol, &c. 4771

Case of John Collins, Esq. 54976, 94549

Case of John Dunbar and William Lem. 21236

Case of John Miller. 49027

Case of John Smith. 82900

Case of John Soren. 87137

Case of John Wilmore. 104573

Case of Joseph Segar, of Virginia. (78876)

Case of Lewis Morris. 50847

Case of Lieutenant Flagg. 24657

Case of Mainwaring, Hawes, Payne and others. (44055), 100439, 4th note after 102831

Case of Major John Andre. 1453

Case of merchants and planters trading to, and residing in, Virginia and Maryland. 11312

Case of Messieurs Penn. (59685)

Case of Mr. John Gordon. 27981, 101042

Case of Mr. Law truely stated, in answer. 39310

Case of Mr. M'Leod. 98143

Case of Mr. Workman. 105477

Case of Nathaniel Matson against Nathaniel Thomas. 46875, 95436

Case of Negroes and planters stated. (71969)

Case of our fellow creatures. 4669

Case of Passmore Williamson. 10696

Case of Patrick Roch, Esq. 72287

Case of Peter du Calvert. (21045)

Case of Peter Hasenclever, &c. 30793

Case of Pierce and Bacon. 62707

Case of poor emigrants recommended. 65502

Case of Potter Jackson. (35447)

Case of private and national corruption. (25455)

Case of protestant dissenters in Carolina. 10966, note before 87805

Case of R. W. Meade. 47235

Case of Reilly vs. Huber. (20260), 69106

Case of Richard Budge. 53081

Case of Richard Downing Jennings. 36047

Case of Robert M. Goodwin. 96875

Case of Rollin White. 90389

Case of Samuel A. Worcester vs. the state of Georgia. 105321

Case of Samuel Hanson. 30273

Case of satan's fiery darts. (14525)

Case of Stephen Sayre. 77415

Case of the Agent of Jamaica. 35570

Case of the Agent of the settlers on the coast of Yucatan. (11313), 103448, 2d note after 106221

Case of the annuitants of the redeemable debts. 90602

Case of the annuitants stated. 88197

Case of the appellant. 91849

Case of the battalion stated. 36619

Case of the Belchertown election. 4405

Case of the Black Warrior. 11314

Case of the borrows on the South-Sea loans, stated. 88180

Case of the brig Essex, of Salem. 22999

Case of the British northern colonies. 11315

Case of the British sugar-colonies. 102822

Case of the Canadians at Montreal distressed by fire. 50245

Case of the captors and respondents. 104157

Case of the Caribbs in St. Vincent's. 18727

case of the Caroline. (43530)

Case of the Cherokee Nation against the state of Georgia. 61206

Case of the Church of England in Carolina. 10967, 87359, 87805

Case of the Commissary General of Provisions and Stores. 66994

Case of the commonwealth against Eleazer Oswald. 57828

Case of the creditors of the Royal African Company of England. 73760

Case of the Creole considered. 62465

Case of the crew of the ship "William Engs." 96997

Case of the Danish brig the Hope. 96930A

Case of the defendant in error. (56802)

Case of the Deputies of the Moravian Brethren. 97847

Case of the dissenting ministers. 46915

Case of the Dutch ships considered. 44687

Case of the Episcopal Churches in the United States considered. 103461

Case of the Fanny. 23788

Case of the free-labour British colonies. (11309), 35568, 51929, 81921

Case of the General Assembly of the Presbyterian Church. 39172

Case of the Georgia sales on the Mississippi considered. 27021

Case of the German Protestant Churches settled in . . . Pennsylvania. 59958

Case of the Governor and Company of Connecticut and Mohegan Indians. 45455

Case of the heir-at-law and executrix of the late Proprietor of Pensilvania, etc. 37243, 59959

Case of the holders of reconnoissances given in exchange. 10391

Case of the Honourable James Annesley, Esq.
63222

Case of the Honourable James Annesley,
nobleman. 1601

Case of the Hudson's Bay Company. 25817

Case of the importation of bar-iron. (11316),
2d note after 97332

Case of the incompensated American loyalists.
42562

Case of the inhabitants of East Florida.
24848

Case of the Inhabitants of Pensilvania. 59960

Case of the island of Jamaica. (35569)

Case of the manufacturers of soap and candles.
49737

Case of the mariners and others of the ship
Bristol. 35571

Case of the merchants, and planters, trading
to, and residing in, Virginia, and Maryland. 11312, 100440

Case of the merchants concerned in the West
India trade. 102791

Case of the merchants who have raised a joint
stock. 28638

Case of the Mississippi Territory against
Joseph Pulaski Kennedy. (37434)

Case of the neglected and deserted Negroes.
(1696)

Case of the New York and Harlem Rail Road
Company. (54732)

Case of the people called Quakers in the
province of Pennsylvania. (59961)

Case of the petitioner, Richard Budge. (8961)

Case of the petitioner. (The case on behalf of
the crown.) 99894

Case of the plaintiff in error. (56802)

Case of the planters of tobacco in Virginia.
69714, 99909-99911

Case of the planters of Virginia. 100441

Case of the poor distressed planters. 52427

Case of the Portland city claim. 64382

Case of the present possessors of the French
lands. 75012

Case of the private armed brig of war Gen.
Armstrong. (69090)

Case of the Proprietors of Charles River
Bridge. 12030

Case of the Proprietors of East New-Jersey.
53082

Case of the Proprietors of the province of
Pensilvania. 59962

Case of the protestant dissenters in Carolina.
2169, 10966

Case of the Protestant Episcopal Church, at
New-Brighton, Staten Island. 11439,
52516

Case of the province of Maryland. 45099, 3d
note after 92693

Case of the provinces of Massachusetts-Bay
and New York. 34068

Case of the provinces of Massachusetts Bay
. . . respecting a bill. 45667

Case of the respondents the Governor and
Company of the Colony of Connecticut.
15750-15751

Case of the respondents the landholders.
15750, 15752

Case of the representatives of Major General
the Earl of Stirling. note before 91856

Case of the Right Hon. Alexander Earl of
Stirling and Dovan. 9355

Case of the Right Hon. J. Aislabie. 547

Case of the Right Rev. Henry U. Onderdonk.
57318

Case of the Royal African Company. [ca 1711]
73761

Case of the Royal African Company. [ca 1720]
73762

Case of the Royal African-Company and of the
plantations. 73764

Case of the Royal African Company of England.
[ca 1729] 73756

Case of the Royal African Company of England.
[ca 1730] 73763, (73777), note before
93802

Case of the Royal African Company of England
and their creditors. 73765

Case of the schooner Reward. 92308

Case of the Scotch Presbyterians, of . . . New-
York. (54141)

Case of the seizure of the southern envoys.
11317

Case of the Seneca Indians in the state of New
York. 26253, 79105, 79110, 92978

Case of the ship General Parkhill. (58779)

Case of the ship Nicholas. 55181

Case of the ship Vigilante. 99603

Case of the sinking fund. (66641), 101148

Case of the six mutineers. 35361

Case of the slave-child, Med. 2490

Case of the Somer's mutiny. 43421

Case of the sugar colonies. 14441, 1st note
after 102822

Case of the tobacco planters. 100442

Case of the Trent. (58697)

Case of the Trent examined. 11318

Case of the two vessels. (11319)

Case of the uncompensated American loyalists.
(11320)

Case of the United States Bank. (78742),
100582

Case of the Vigilante. (81922), 99604

Case of the West India Dock Company. 31684-
31685

Case of the West India planters. (59234)

Case of the Whigs who loaned their money.
17966

Case of Thomas C. A. Dexter. 9622, 19904

Case of Thomas Cooper. 16609, 87972

Case of Thomas Kinder. 37774

Case of Thos. Lewis. 40855

Case of Thomas Lord Cochrane. 14082

Case of Thomas Short. 80576

Case of Thomas W. Dorr, explained. 20646, 1st
note after 97484

Case of Vice-Admiral Stirling. 91842

Case of W. Tipton. 95860

Case of war between England and the United
States. 98141

Case of William Atwood. 2346

Case of William H. McCardle. 42984

Case of William L. Chaplin. 11971

Case of Wm. Livingston and . . . other citizens.
19655

Case of William Penn, Esq. as to the proprietary government of Pensilvania. 59686

Case of William Penn, Esq. Proprietary Governor of Pensilvania. 59688

Case of William Penn, Proprietary, and Governor in Chief of the Province of Pennsylvania. 59687

Case of William Ramsay. 67721

Case of William Sharpe. 79853

Case [of William Trent and other traders.]
25595, 34579-34580, 96769, 99584, note
just before 103108

Case of William Vans. 98552

Case of Yale College. 105806

(Case on behalf of the crown.) 99894

Case on behalf of the ladies Ursulines at Quebec. 98170

Case on the part of the appellant. 96762

Case on the part of the appellants. 55717, 96865, 96868, 97879, 98438, 98696

Case on the part of the defendant in error. 96869

Case on the part of the defendants in error. 100996

Case on the part of the plaintiff in error. D. Graham, Jr., for plaintiff in error. 103383

Case on the part of the plaintiff in error. Thomas E. Clark, attorney for plaintiff in error. 104412

Case, on the part of the plaintiffs in error. 96887

Case on the part of the plaintiffs in error. And also on the part of the defendant in error. 100777

Case, on the part of the plaintiffs in error and of the defendants in error. 96885

Case on the part of the respondent. 96869

Case on the part of the respondents. 91365, 100997

Case plainly stated. 22390

Case put & decided by George Fox. 53083

Case referred in pursuance of the Convention of the 29th Sept. 1827. 44046, note before 90764

Case relating to the southern boundary of the Massachusetts Bay. (51547)

Case relative to transactions with Ross and Butler. 73311

Case respecting British debts. 30048

Case stated. 103422

Case stated between the East India Company of the United Netherlands. 17179

Case stated, between the publick and the South-Sea Company. 86619

Case stated on philosophical ground. 11321

Case stated, points of counsel, and the opinion. 102761

Case . . . stated, representing great frauds. 41822

Case stated. The friends and enemies of the American slave. 46186

Case, Trevett against Weeden. 98638

Case upon bill of exceptions. 101425

Case upon the statute for distribution. 105703

Case, William Hunter, in equity. 44630

Caseaux, M. P. tr. (2614)

Caseres y Elorza, Francisco Joseph. 11322

Cases, Emmanuel Dieudonne Marie Joseph, Comte de las. see Las Cases, Emmanuel Dieudonne Marie Joseph, Comte de.

Cases adjudged in the Supreme Court of New-Jersey. 53084

Cases adjudged in the Supreme Court of North Carolina. 94509

Cases and observations. 52962

Cases and queries. 4742, (11323)

Cases decided in the District and Circuit Court. (11324)

Cases determined in the Superior Courts of Law and Equity. 94509

Cases of capture made by France. 83

Cases of compromise with captors. 102295

Cases of conscience concerning evil spirits. (46648)

Cases of conscience concerning witchcrafts and evil spirits. 46687

Cases of contested elections in Congress. 13437

Cases of contested elections in the House of Representatives. 82757

Cases of personal identity. 51361

Cases of Salem witchcraft. 6010

Cases of some English ships taken by the Spaniards. 11325

Cases ruled and adjudged in the Superior Courts of Law & Equity. 94734

Cases ruled and adjudged in the Superior Courts of Law & Equity, Federal Court & Supreme Courts of Errors & Appeals. 94735

Casey, ------. defendant 37808, 97098

Casey, Charles. 11326

Casey, Joseph, 1814-1879. 11327

Casey, Silas, 1807-1882. 11328, 51718

Casgrain, Henri Raymond, 1831-1904. 10455, 11329-11334, (12573), 20892, 39296, (41510), note after 96259

Cash, Caleb. 61409

Cash and credit. 24619

Cashel, Archbishop of. see Nicolson, William, Archbishop of Cashel, 1655-1727.

Casimir, Friedrich, Graf zu Hanau. 11337

Casimire Ortega, J. B. Munoz. see Munoz Casimire Ortega, J. B.

Casket. 11335

Caskie, James. 11336

Casler, Abraham. defendant 11338

Caslo, Anthony. 11339

Caslon, William. 95414

Casmanni, Othonis. 11340

Caso de conciencia. (73165)

Caso do conego Jose Constantino Gomes de Castro. 11458

Casoni, ------. 11341

Casos notables, svcedidos en las costas de la Civdad de Lima. 11342, 41082

Casos raros. 76900

Caspar, F. X. von. tr. 14526, note after 105986

Casparis Barlaei . . . poemata. 3407

Casparis Barlaei, rervm per octennivm in Brasilia. 3408-3409

Casparis Varrerii Lvsitana commentarius de Ophyra Regione. 3597, 64001

Caspersz, W. v. O. 96407

Caspine, Louis de. (10757), 63706

Caspipina, Tamoc. pseud. Letters. see Duche, Jacob.

Caspipina's letters. 21048, 21055

Casqueta, Antonio Joseph Ortiz de, Marques de Altamira. defendant 87193

Casqueta, Bartholome Antonio Joseph Ortiz de, Marques de Altamira. plaintiff 87193

Cass, G. W. 11343

Cass, Lewis, 1782-1866. 11344-11349, (11354), 11356, 23369, 28493, 31699, 32062, (33921), 34481, 34633, 48099, 69446, 69483, (69590), (69691), 70202, 71353, 79582, 89203, 89926, 94662, note after 96593, 96647, 96652-96653, 96657, 96658, 96671, 103696 see also U. S. Commissioner to the Creek Indians. U. S. Commissioner to the Potawatomi Indians. U. S. Commissioners to the Chippewa, Menominee, and Winnebago Indians. U. S. Commissioners to the Michigan Indians. U. S. Commissioners to the Potawatomi Indians. U. S. Commissioners to the Winnebago Tribe and the United Tribes of Potawatomi, Chippewa, and Ottawa Indians.

Cass and Taylor on the slavery question. 7006

Cass platform. 11350

Cassagnac, Adolphe de Granier de. see Granier de Cassagnac, Adolphe de.

Cassandra. pseud. see Cannon, James.

Cassani, Jose, 1673-1750. 1447, 11360-11361

Cassani, Joseph. see Cassani, Jose, 1673-1750.

Casse, ------- du. see Du Casse, --------.
Casseday, Benjamin. (11362)
Casseday, David B. 11363
Cassegrain, Arthur. 11364
Cassell, Johann Philipp. 11365-11366
Cassell. firm publishers 92469
Cassell's edition of Uncle Tom's cabin. 92469
Casserly, Eugene. 11367
Casses de Xalo, Joachin. 11368
Cassette verte de Monsieur de Sartine. 95793
Cassin, John, 1813-1869. 2809, 11369-11370, 27419, 69946
Cassin, Joseph. 11371, 60758
Cassini, Jean Dominique, Comte de, 1748-1845. 8988, (11372), 12003-12004
Cassique of Accabee. 81197
Cassique of Kiawah. (81279), 81198
Cassius. pseud. Address to the freemen. see Burke, Aedanus, 1743?-1802?
Cassius. pseud. Considerations on the society. see Burke, Aedanus, 1743?-1802?
Cassius. pseud. On the citizens making a temporary submission. see Burke, Aedanus, 1743?-1802? supposed author
Cassius. pseud. To the friends of liberty, and commerce. 95930
Cassius M. Clay's appeal. (13532)
Casson, Francois Dollier de. see Dollier de Casson, Francois.
Cassville, Ga. Southern and South-Western Presbyterian Convention, 1840. see Southern and South-Western Presbyterian Convention, Cassville, Ga., 1840.
Cast, J. F. (11373)
Cast away in the cold. 31021
Castaing, -------. 85781
Castaing, -------- de. (11374)
Castalius, P. 48033
Castan, Felipe. 11375
Castanares, Manuel. (11376)
Castaneda, Francisco de Paula. see Paula Castaneda, Francisco de.
Castaneda, Juan Ruiz. 11378
Castaneda de Nagera, Pedro de. 11379, 2d note after 51715
Castaneda y Escalada, Jose Maria. (11380)
Castanheda, Fernao Lopes de. 11381-11391
Castaniga, J. M. 40137
Castanis, Christophorus Plato. 11392
Castaniza de Bascoso, Teresa. 98823, 99687
Castaniza Gonzalez de Aguero, Juan Francisco de. see Gonzalez de Aguero, Juan Francisco de Castaniza.
Castano, Bartholome. 996, 11394
Castano, Diego Nunez. see Nunez Castano, Diego.
Castanos, J. M., fl. 1693. 57421
Castanos, Jose Maria. 11395
Caste: a story of republican equality. 62827-62828, note after 92320
Caste among masons. 31010
Caste and slavery in the American church. 35839, 81923
Castel, Dom. tr. 14269
Castel, Henri Viel. see Viel-Castel, Henri.
Castelazo, Josef Rodrigo de. 48519
Castelfranc, Gideon. 11396
Castell, William, d. 1645. 11397-11398, 57765
Castell, William, d. 1645. supposed author 9759, note after 36681, 100460
Castell della mina von Hollandern erobert. (69296)
Castellamare, Pietro de. 11399
Castellani, Giacomo. tr. 11242-11244
Castellanos, Aaron. 11400
Castellanos, Jose Rafael. (11401)

Castellanos, Juan de. 11402
Castellanos, Manuel. 11403
Castellanos de Losada, Basilio Sebastian. see Losada, Basilio Sebastian Castellanos de.
Castellar, Thomas del. 11404
Castelli, -------. 11405-11408
Castellini, Sebastiano Maria. tr. 60904
Castello de Paiva, A. Herculano e O Barrao do. see Paiva, A. Herculano e O Barrao do Castello de.
Castellon, Feo. see Castellon, Francisco.
Castellon, Francisco. 51080, 55148, 55160 see also Nicaragua. Ministerio de Relaciones Exteriores.
Castelmehor, --------, Conde de. 11409
Castelnau, Francois, Comte de, 1812-1880. (11410)-11412, 19749
Castelu, Antonio Vasquez. see Gastelu, Antonio Vasquez.
Castelverti, J. ed. 91216
Castera, Jean Henri, b. ca. 1755. tr. 25543, 37955, 43416-43417, 77153
Castigar a los ministros no lo haran sus confidentes. 98113
Castigatissimi annali con la loro copiosa tavola. 27518
Castiglioni, Luigi. 11413-11414
Castigo de Deus no anno de 1845. 72501
Castile, Spain. Laws, statutes, etc. 105480
Castile, Spain. Sovereigns, etc., 1504-1506 (Juana) see also Juana, Queen of Castile, 1479-1555.
Castilho, Alexandre Magno de. 7508, 11416-11417
Castillo, Antonio Felician. 11415
Castilla, Joseph de Bravo de Lagunas y. see Bravo de Lagunas y Castilla, Joseph de.
Castilla, Lope Altamirano y. see Altamirano y Castilla, Lope.
Castilla, Miguel de. 11418
Castilla, Pedro Joseph Bravo de Lagunas y. see Bravo de Lagunas y Castilla, Pedro Joseph.
Castilla, Ramon. 12776
Castilla y Zamora, Christoval de, Bp. 16068 see also Guamanga, Peru (Diocese) Bishop (Castilla y Zamora)
Castillero, Andres. defendant 4792, (11419), (52437)
Castillo, -------. (47807)
Castillo, Antonio Diaz del. see Diaz del Castillo, Antonio.
Castillo, Balthasar de. 11420
Castillo, Bernal Diaz del. see Diaz del Castillo, Bernal, 1492-1581?
Castillo, Dom. Lopez de. see Lopez de Castillo, Dom.
Castillo, Felipe del. defendant 11421, 19262 see also Jesuits. Lima Province. Procurador General. defendant
Castillo, Fl. M. del. 11427
Castillo, Geronimo. 11422
Castillo, Jose Antonio de Moral y. see Moral y Castillo, Jose Antonio de.
Castillo, Jose Mariano del. 11425
Castillo, Juan de Torres. see Torres Castillo, Juan de.
Castillo, Juan Joseph de. 11423
Castillo, Luis Maria. 11426
Castillo, Manuel. defendant 27309, (51797), 69915, 93808, 96948
Castillo, Martin del. 69172
Castillo, P. P. del. (11428)-11429
Castillo, Pedro Fernandez del. 76824
Castillo, Pedro Ramirez del. see Ramirez del Castillo, Pedro, d. 1737.

Castillo de Herrera, Alonso de. see Herrera, Alonso de Castillo de.
Castillo Peraza, Joaquin. see Peraza, Joaquin Castillo.
Castillo y San Juan, Pedro Antonio. (11432)
Castine, Me. First Society. Committee. 16861
Castine. 21852
Casting vote of Vice-President Dallas on the tariff of 1846. 18320
Castini, Pedro. 11430
Castle, Joseph. 11433
Castle-builders. 91306
Castle dismal. 81199
Castle of Andalusia. 86925
Castle of Olmutz. 38583, 105186, 105195
Castleman, Alfred L. 11434
Castleman, Richard. 12553-(12555)
Castleman, T. R. 11435-11436
Castlemon, Henry. pseud. see Fosdick, Charles Austin, 1842-
Castlereagh, Robert Stewart, Viscount. see Londonderry, Robert Stewart, 2d Marquis of, 1769-1822.
Castleton, Thomas. (11438)
Castleton, N. Y. St. Paul's Church. Vestry. 11439, 52516
Castleton, Vt. Academy of Medicine. see Castleton Medical College, Castleton, Vt.
Castleton, Vt. Medical Academy. see Castleton Medical College, Castleton, Vt.
Castleton, Vt. Medical College. see Castleton Medical College, Castleton, Vt.
Castleton, Vt. Vermont Academy of Medicine. see Castleton Medical College, Castleton, Vt.
Castleton, Vt. Vermont Medical Institution. see Castleton Medical College, Castleton, Vt.
Castleton grammar school. 99105
Castleton Medical Academy, Castleton, Vt. see Castleton Medical College, Castleton, Vt.
Castleton Medical College, Castleton, Vt. 11440, 48838, 99217-99219, 99231
Castorena y Vrsua, Ivan Ignacio. 17733
Castoreno, J. de. (11441)
Castrillon, A. (11442)
Castrioto Lvsitano parte I. 36088-36089, (67912)
Castriotta, d'Albanie. pseud. Oeuvres choisies. see Zannovich, Stiepan, 1751-1786.
Castro, ------ Bermudez de. see Bermudez de Castro, ------.
Castro, Agustin. (11443)-11447
Castro, Alonso Francisco Moreno y. see Moreno y Castro, Alonso Francisco.
Castro, Alonso Nunez de. see Nunez de Castro, Alonso.
Castro, C. illus. (48590)
Castro, C. A. de Lemos Faria e. see Lemos Faria e Castro, C. A. de.
Castro, Carlos Bermudez de. see Bermudez de Castro, Carlos.
Castro, Eduardo de Sa Pereira de. see Sa Pereira de Castro, Eudardo de.
Castro, Felipe Ferreira de Araujo e. see Araujo e Castro, Felipe Ferreira de.
Castro, Francisco da Silva. 11451-(11452)
Castro, Francisco de. 11450, 56661
Castro, Francisco Paulo de Portugal e. see Portugal e Castro, Francisco Paulo de.
Castro, Gaspar de Zepeda y. see Zepeda y Castro, Gaspar de.
Castro, Geronimo Ortiz de. see Ortiz de Castro, Geronimo.

Castro, Guillen de. (3587)
Castro, Henrique Jose de. 11467
Castro, Henry. 11453, 95120-95121
Castro, Ignacio de, 1732-1792. (11454)-11455, 57422
Castro, Joaquin Machado de. 11456
Castro, Jose. 99407
Castro, Jose Basilio de. alias see Montenegro, Juan. defendant
Castro, Jose Constantino Gomes de. 11457-11458, 88776
Castro, Jose de Antequera Enriquez y. see Antequera Enriquez y Castro, Jose de.
Castro, Jose de Escobar Salmeron y. see Salmeron y Castro, Jose de Escobar.
Castro, Jose de Gama e. see Gama e Castro, Jose de.
Castro, Jose Geronimo Sanchez de. see Sanchez de Castro, Jose Geronimo.
Castro, Joseph Agustin de. 11462
Castro, Joseph de. 11460
Castro, Joseph de Antequera y. see Antequera Enriquez y Castro, Jose de.
Castro, Juan. 66686
Castro, Juan de. 11463
Castro, Juan Gonzalez de. see Gonzalez de Castro, Juan.
Castro, Juan Moreno y. see Moreno y Castro, Juan, Marques de Valle-Ameno.
Castro, Juan Ortiz de. see Ortiz de Castro, Juan.
Castro, Luis Joaquin de Oliveira e. see Oliveira e Castro, Luis Joaquin de.
Castro, M. de. 11468
Castro, Manuel Bermudez de. 4915, 67141
Castro, Manuel Fernandez de. 11464-11465
Castro, Nestor. ed. 85709
Castro, Nicolas de. 11466
Castro, Olegario Herculano de Aquino e. see Aquino e Castro, Olegario Herculano de.
Castro, Pedro de. (6797)
Castro, Pedro Ignacio de. see Ignacio de Castro, Pedro.
Castro, Pedro Munoz de. see Munoz de Castro, Pedro.
Castro, Rafael de. 11469
Castro, Tomas de. 105953 see also Mexico. Fiscales.
Castro, Vicente da Siledade e. see Soledade e Castro, Vicente da.
Castro, Vicente Antonio de. (17758)
Castro a Silva, Manoel de Nascimiento. 69321 see also Brazil. Ministerio da Fazenda.
Castro Andrade y Portugal, Pedro Fernandez de, Conde de Lemos, 1634-1672 40012, 61165, (75986) see also Peru (Viceroyalty) Virrey, 1666-1672 (Castro Andrade y Portugal)
Castro Macedo, Melchor de. see Melchor de Castro Macedo. Fray
Castro Rebello, Francisco Justiniano de. see Rebello, Francisco Justiniano de Castro.
Castro Santa Anna, Jose Manuel de. (48440)
Castro Tavares, Jeronymo Villa de. 11470
Castro-Stadt eine Franzosische Colonie. 95121
Castro-ville, colonie Francaise. 95121
Castro-ville, colonie Francaise, fondee para Henry Castro, le 1er Septembre 1844. 95120
Castrucci, Giuseppe Emanuel. (11471)-11472
Casuisticus, Thomas. pseud. Present way of the country. see A., E. H. M. pseud.
Caswall, Sir George, fl. 1721. 65865, 88192
Caswall, Henry, 9985, 11473-11479
Caswell, Alexis. 11480, 85072

Caswell, Sir George. see Caswall, Sir
  George, fl. 1721.
Cat, C. N. le. see Le Cat, C. N.
Cat-fight; a mock heroic poem. 43344
"Cat let out of the bag." 37356, note after
  95797, 10th note after 95843
"Cat let out of the bag:" a poetical dialogue.
  13883
Cata de un Havanero. 23580
Catagorias de la parte fisco-moral con relac-
  ion al hombre publico. 29420
Cataia. 82979
Catalani, Joseph. ed. 529, (14367)
Cataloga razonado de los manuscritos Espa-
  noles. 56644
Catalogo de alguno varones illustres. (47186)
Catalogo de la Biblioteca de Salva. 75864
Catalogo de las lenguas de las naciones cono-
  cidas y numeracion. 31600
Catalogo de las obras . . . existentes en la
  Biblioteca Nacional. (56267)
Catalogo de las producciones. 29339
Catalogo de los articulos de fondo. (75863)
Catalogo de los arzobispos, y obispos que ha
  tenido la seraphica religion en las
  Indias Occidentales. 96308
Catalogo de los curatos y missiones. 52110,
  (56245)
Catalogo de los individuos que componen la
  Real Sociedad de Amantes de la Patria
  de Guatemala. 29071
Catalogo de los libros antiguos. (75863)
Catalogo de los libros antiguos o escasos.
  (75863)
Catalogo de los libros modernos. (75863)
Catalogo de los libros y otros articulos.
  (75863)
Catalogo de los objetos de bellas artes.
  48324
Catalogo de los medicamentos. 23051
Catalogo de los principales historiadores de
  Mexico. 20101
Catalogo del Museo Historico Indiano. 6833
Catalogo delle lingue conosciute e noticia.
  31600
Catalogodos ill.mos e rev.mos Bispos do Mara-
  hao. 11458
Catalogo dos libros do Gabinete Portuguez de
  Leitura. 71461
Catalogo dos productos naturaes e industriaes.
  71462
Catalogo provisorio dos objectos. 58497
Catalogo y noticia de los literatos. 4871
Catalogue Academiae Yalensis, M.DCC. LXXXI.
  105762
Catalogue alphabetique des arbes et arbisseaux.
  44777
Catalogue . . . an annual announcement of
  lectures. (54000)
Catalogue . . . and announcement of . . .
  lectures. 54514
Catalogue and certain details of Bethany Col-
  lege. 5066
Catalogue and circular of terms of Comer's
  Commercial College, Boston. 14931
Catalogue and circular of the Mount Union,
  Ohio, College and Normal Seminary.
  (51174)
Catalogue and circular of the New England
  Conservatory of Music. (52666)
Catalogue and circular of the Rockland Female
  Institute. (72403)
Catalogue and circular of the S. S. Seward
  Institute, at Florida, Orange County,
  N. Y., 1846. 24905

Catalogue and circular of the S. S. Seward
  Institute, at Florida, Orange County,
  N. Y., under the care of Elizabeth Par-
  sons. 79600
Catalogue and circular of the State and National
  Law School at Ballston Spa, N. Y. 2974
Catalogue and circular of the State & National
  Law School, at Ballston Spa, N. Y.
  (53961)
Catalogue and circular of the State Normal
  School at Framingham, Mass. 46139
Catalogue and circular of the State Normal
  School, at Westfield, Mass. 46139
Catalogue and circular of the State Normal
  School. Bridgewater. 46139
Catalogue and circular of the Strasburg
  Academy. 92723
Catalogue and circulars of the Botanic Garden
  of Transylvania University at Lexington.
  67450
Catalogue and outline of the Steubenville Female
  Seminary. 91469
Catalogue and price-list of maps. 82990
Catalogue and prospectus of St. Mary's Hall.
  (75438)
Catalogue and prospectus of St. Mary's Hall;
  summer term. 75436
Catalogue and prospectus of the winter term,
  1846-7. 20391
Catalogue and register of Racine College.
  67397
Catalogue . . . and regulations . . . December
  1, 1831. 71119
Catalogue and regulations of the Library of the
  Social Reading Rooms, Stamford, Conn.
  90123
Catalogue and rules and regulations of the
  Indiana State Library. 34495
Catalogue, by-laws, and course of study of the
  Woodward College. 105174
Catalogue Caledonia County Teachers' Institute.
  18522
Catalogue chronologique des tremblements de
  terre. 63659
Catalogue, classified and alphabetical. 75369
Catalogue comprising nearly all the flowering
  and filiocid plants. 5311
Catalogue d'arbres. 106129
Catalogue de la Bibliotheque Americaine. 44986
Catalogue de la . . . bibliotheque de D. Jose
  Maria Andrade. 47037
Catalogue de la Bibliotheque de la Legislature
  de Quebec. (66995)
Catalogue de la bibliotheque de F. C. Le Tel-
  lier de Courtanvaux. 40243
Catalogue de la bibliotheque d'un amateur.
  23541
Catalogue de la collection precieuse de livres
  anciens et modernes. 85669
Catalogue de la Guyane Anglaise. 29164
Catalogue de livres, manuscrits et cartes.
  25466
Catalogue de toutes sortes d'insects. 95332
Catalogue des cartes geographiques, des rel-
  ations. (40027)
Catalogue des cartes geographiques, topographi-
  ques & marines. 38394
Catalogue des cartes, plans, etc. 11483
Catalogue des coquilles recueillies a la Guade-
  loupe. (4153)
Catalogue des cryptogames recueillis aux Antil-
  les Francaises. 34032
Catalogue des Jesuites. (8784)
Catalogue des livres anciens Espagnols. (75863)

Catalogue des livres de feu M. l'Abbe d'Or-
leans de Rothelin. 73434
Catalogue des livres et mss. composant la
bibliotheque. 12295
Catalogue des libres et manuscrits de la bib-
liotheque. 94845
Catalogue des livres que se trouvent Chez
Boinod & Gaillard. 61519
Catalogue des meilleures cartes geographiques
& des meilleurs libres. 13018
Catalogue des mineraux envoyes. 12791
Catalogue des objets exposes dans la section
des Etats-Unis d'Amerique. (58595)
Catalogue des officiers et des eleves du
Seminaire de Quebec. 67060
Catalogue des ouvrages relatifs a l'Amerique.
94844
Catalogue des ouvrages relatifs a l'histoire
des Jesuits. (10791)
Catalogue des plantes Canadiennes. 8750
Catalogue des principaux historiens avec des
remarques critiques. 47797
Catalogue des principaux historiens. 40028
Catalogue des produits des colonies Fran-
caises. 14707
Catalogue des produits des colonies Fran-
caises, prevede d'un notice statistique.
(23466)
Catalogue des produits naturels, industriels et
artistiques. 48325
Catalogue des vegetaux ligneux de Canada.
8751
Catalogue descriptif de la collection de cartes.
10457
Catalogue descriptive, biographical and his-
torical. 93289
Catalogue d'ouvrages, etc. 10396
Catalogue d'ouvrages sur l'histoire de
l'Amerique. (23806)
Catalogue d'un choix de livres relatifs a
l'Amerique. 11481
Catalogue d'une collection de livres precieux.
11482
Catalogue d'une collection de livres rares.
5200, 48304
Catalogue . . . 1858 [of Lockport Union
School.] 41744
Catalogue . . . . 1858-9 [of the North Western
University.] 55753
Catalogue, 1854 [of the Hedding Literary
Institute.] 31211
Catalogue, 1857 [of Cincinnatus Academy.]
13136
Catalogue . . . 1857-8 [of Loyola College,
Baltimore.] 42572
Catalogue, 1849[of Falley Seminary.] 23755
Catalogue . . . 1868-9 [of Cornell University.]
16798
Catalogue . . . 1868-9 [of the Western State
Normal School.] 44054
Catalogue, 1866 [of Franklin and Marshall
College.] 25645
Catalogue . . . 1866-67 [of the Homoeopathic
Medical College of Pennsylvania.] 60147
Catalogue . . . 1839-40 [of Kent Academy.]
37482
Catalogue . . . 1833. 74436
Catalogue for 1853 [of Baldwin School.] 2926
Catalogue for 1853-54 [of Newton Theological
Institution.] (55095)
Catalogue for 1848 [of books for sale by O.
Rich.] 70887
Catalogue . . . for . . . 1845-6 [of Mrs. Mead's
School.] 47225
Catalogue for 1868-9 [of the Rochester Theo-
logical Seminary.] 72363

Catalogue for 1864-5 [of the Hudson River
Institute.] 33534
Catalogue for 1861-2 [of the Illinois Normal
University.] 34242
Catalogue . . . for . . . 1839 [of Marietta
Female Seminary.] (44572)
Catalogue . . . for 1839-40 [of Union Village
Academy.] 97823
Catalogue for 1787. Books. 106123
Catalogue for the academic years, 1853-4 &
1854-5. 1707
Catalogue . . . for the academical years, 1842-3
37340
Catalogue for the first, second and third years.
(23052)
Catalogue for the Leither sale, Feb. 15-16,
1933. (62421), 1st note after 96964
Catalogue for the library belonging to the
Spring Street Church Sabbath School.
55032
Catalogue for the sale of Apr. 22, 1919. 101452
Catalogue for the session of 1856-7. 51880
Catalogue . . . for the year ending May 11,
1831. (37770)
Catalogue general des livres. 2815, 11484
Catalogue . . . July, 1866 [of the State Normal
School of Maryland.] (45371)
Catalogue of a bibliographical library. 51362
Catalogue of a cabinet of materia medica.
72705
Catalogue of a choice collection of books.
74677A
Catalogue of a choice collection of valuable
books. 39571
Catalogue of a collection of American birds.
78135
Catalogue of a collection of books belonging to
the Rev. Robert Smith. 83804
Catalogue of a collection of books, consisting
principally of local American history.
(51376)
Catalogue of a collection of books on the his-
tory of America. 70887
Catalogue of a collection of coins and medals.
11730
Catalogue of a collection of manuscripts. 70884
Catalogue of a curious and valuable collection.
11485
Catalogue of a large collection of new and old
books. 61520
Catalogue of a portion of the library belonging
to Mr. Almon W. Griswold. 74678
Catalogue of a portion of the Public Library of
the city of Boston. 6759
Catalogue of a portion of the rare and curious
library. (38652)
Catalogue of a superb private gallery. 83842
Catalogue of a unique and interesting collection.
83017
Catalogue of a valuable collection of books &
pamphlets consisting of the journals.
83309
Catalogue of a valuable collection of books and
pamphlets, illustrating the history & geography. 82326
Catalogue of a valuable collection of books &
pamphlets relating to the history and
geography of North and South America.
83014
Catalogue of a valuable collection of books,
illustrating the history and geography of
North and South America. 83016
Catalogue of a valuable collection of books on
America. 50784
Catalogue of a valuable collection of books,
pamphlets, manuscripts, maps, engravings,
and portraits. 83015

Catalogue of a valuable collection of rare
editions. 369
Catalogue of a valuable portion of the very
interesting collection. 48326
Catalogue of a valuable private library. 74680
Catalogue of additions made to the Library of
Congress. 15579
Catalogue of all books printed in the United
States. 11486
Catalogue of all the books belonging to the
Providence Library. (66330)
Catalogue of American and foreign books.
51363
Catalogue of American and foreign plants.
59493
Catalogue of American books. 70886
Catalogue of American books and periodicals
for sale. 87309
Catalogue of American books, 1859. 91516
Catalogue of American books in the Library of
the British Museum, Christmas, Mdccclvi.
91514
Catalogue of American books in the Library of
the British Museum. Christmas, 1856.
91512-91513
Catalogue of American historical . . . works.
(40110)
Catalogue of American localities of minerals.
18424
Catalogue of American maps in the Library of
the British Museum. 91513-91515
Catalogue of American minerals, with their
localities. 72176
Catalogue of American plays and their authors.
21300
Catalogue of American publications, including
reprints and original works, from 1820 to
1852, inclusive. 73093
Catalogue of American publications, including
reprints and original works, from 1820
to 1848, inclusive. 73091
Catalogue of American publications previous to
the revolution. 95406
Catalogue of Amherst College Library. (1318)
Catalogue of an American library. 51461
Catalogue of an exhibition of portraits. 93160
Catalogue of an extensive and select collection
of choice books. 74679
Catalogue of an extensive collection of books
relating to America. 49026
Catalogue of an extraordinary collection of
books & manuscripts. 24417
Catalogue of an extraordinary collection of
books relating to America. (74675)
Catalogue of an extraordinary collection of
original documents connected with the
British army. (4465), 11487
Catalogue of anatomical preparations. 70492
Catalogue of ancient and modern books of 1787.
65481
Catalogue of animals and plants. 45751
Catalogue of antiquities and curiosities. 23904
Catalogue of articles contained in the Museum
and Curiosity Shop. (54142)
Catalogue of articles to be offered for sale at
the Ladies' Fair. (52658), 75643
Catalogue of authors who have written on Rio
de la Plata. 18335
Catalogue of autograph letters. (49555)
Catalogue of . . . autographs. 33438
Catalogue of Barre Academy, Barre, Vt. 3593
Catalogue of . . . Baylor University. 4073
Catalogue of Bethel Female College, Hopkins-
ville, Ky. (5068)
Catalogue of birds, insects, and squirrels.
73332

Catalogue of books. 77246
Catalogue of books added . . . since 1847.
30678
Catalogue of books added to the library since
1844. 30678
Catalogue of books . . . added to the library
. . . since January, 1839. 54470
Catalogue of books adverse to the Society of
Friends. 83307
Catalogue of books and other publications.
3735
Catalogue of books and pamphlets, belonging to
the Legislative Library. 87725
Catalogue of . . . books and pamphlets relating
to . . . America. 9156
Catalogue of books and pamphlets relating to
the civil war. 3743, 54640
Catalogue of books and papers in the Library
and Reading Room. 13094
Catalogue of books, and rules of the Woodbury
Library Company. 105103
Catalogue of . . . books and tracts. (45445)
Catalogue of books . . . at Bookstore . . . 40
Genesee St., Utica. 98228
Catalogue of books, at the Washington Circulat-
ing Library. 101995
Catalogue of books belonging to Norwich Lib-
rary Company. (55919)
Catalogue of books, belonging to the Association
Library Company of Philadelphia. 61489
Catalogue of books, belonging to the Brothers',
Linonian, and Moral Libraries. Yale
College, November, 1825. 105865
Catalogue of books belonging to the Calliopean
Society, Yale College. 105871-105876
Catalogue of books belonging to the Charleston
Library Society. 12040
Catalogue of books belonging to the Law Asso-
ciation. 61766
Catalogue of books belonging to the Library
Company of Philadelphia. 61784
Catalogue of books, belonging to the Library
Company [of Philadelphia] . . . to which
is prefixed a short account. 61785
Catalogue of books belonging to the Library of
Rhode Island College. 8604
Catalogue of books belonging to the Library of
St. John's College. 75287
Catalogue of books belonging to the Library of
the Adelphic Society. 97789
Catalogue of books belonging to the Library of
the Free Reading Room Association of
Spring Garden. 89818
Catalogue of books belonging to the Library of
the Medical and Chirurgical Faculty, of
Maryland. 45254
Catalogue of books belonging to the . . . Library
of the North Congregational Church. 52467
Catalogue of books belonging to the Library [of
the South Carolina College.] 87997
Catalogue of books, belonging to the Library of
the University of Pennsylvania. 60756
Catalogue of books belonging to the Linonian,
Brothers' and Moral Societies. 105902
Catalogue of books belonging to the Linonian
Society. 105903-105906
Catalogue of books belonging to the Manufactur-
ers and Village Library at Great Falls.
86815
Catalogue of books, belonging to the . . .
[Massachusetts Medical] Library. 45874
Catalogue of books belonging to the New Bed-
ford [Social] Library. 52467
Catalogue of books belonging to the Pittsfield
Library. 63155

Catalogue of books belonging to the Public Library, Reading, Mass. 68206

Catalogue of books belonging to the St. Louis Mercantile Library Association. 75358

Catalogue of books belonging to the Society Library of Rye. 86001

Catalogue of books belonging to the Society of Brothers in Unity. 105886-105868

Catalogue of books belonging to the State Library [of New Jersey.] 53085

Catalogue of books belonging to the Union-Library-Company of Philadelphia. 62353, 2d note after 97808

Catalogue of books belonging to the Wareham Social Library. 101415

Catalogue of books belonging to the Washington Library. 101969

Catalogue of books belonging to the Worcester Social Library. 105437

Catalogue of books belonging to the Young Men's Association of Schenectada. [sic] 106156A

Catalogue of books belonging to the Young Men's Mercantile Association of Cincinnati. 13091

Catalogue of books belonging to the [Young Men's Mercantile Library Association of Cincinnati.] 106175

Catalogue of books . . . classified and alphabetically arranged by titles. 45225

Catalogue of books, consisting of a large collection. 103393

Catalogue of books, consisting of voyages and travels in various parts of the world. 72464

Catalogue of books, &c. belonging to the Library Company of Baltimore. 3023

Catalogue of books, &c. relating to . . . America. 9155

Catalogue of books, &c., sold by Garrat Noel. 55403

Catalogue of books, for sale. 95449

Catalogue of books, for sale by E. and S. Larlin. 39039

Catalogue of books for sale by Isaiah Thomas, Jr. 95415

Catalogue of books for sale either by wholesale or retail. 95451

Catalogue of books, for sale, wholesale and retail. 102718

Catalogue of books, for sale, wholesale or retail, at the bookstore of Thomas, Andrews & Penniman, Albany. 95450

Catalogue of books for school . . . libraries. (70695)

Catalogue of books in history. 55403

Catalogue of books in Social Library, No. I. 85695

Catalogue of books in the Astor Library. 2251, 72586

Catalogue of books in the Baptist Sabbath School Library. 105338

Catalogue of books in the Boston Athenaeum. 6590

Catalogue of books in the Brothers' and Linonian Libraries. 105862-105863

Catalogue of books in the Legislative Library of Prince Edward Island. 65631

Catalogue of books in the Library of Amherst College. 1827

Catalogue of books in the Library of Parliament [of Canada.] 10397

Catalogue of books in the Library of Queen's College. (67066)

Catalogue of books in the library of Stephen Van Rensselaer. 98549

Catalogue of books in the Library of the American Antiquarian Society. 1050

Catalogue of books in the Library of the College of New Jersey. 53088

Catalogue of books in the Library [of the Detroit Young Men's Society.] 19782

Catalogue of books in the Library of the House of Assembly [of Quebec.] 66996

Catalogue of books in the Library of the Legislative Assembly of Canada. 10398

Catalogue of books in the Library of the Literary and Historical Society of Quebec. 67016, 85818

Catalouge of books in the Library of the Maryland Institute. 45225

Catalogue of books in the Library of the Pawcatuck Library Association. 59259

Catalogue of books [in the Library of the Philomathean Society, Union College.] 97797

Catalogue of books in the Library of the Presbyterian Historical Society. 65197

Catalogue of books in the library of the Rev. Dr. Hawks. (21501)

Catalogue of books in the Library of the Second Parish. 105370

Catalogue of books in the Library of the Society for the Promotion of Useful Arts. 85997

Catalogue of books in the Library of the Spring Garden Institute. 89819

Catalogue of books in the Library of the University of Georgia. 27022, 27114

Catalogue of books in the Library of the Worcester Lyceum. 105430

Catalogue of books in the Library of the [Young Men's Association for Mutual Improvement of the City of Albany.] 106155

Catalogue of books in the Library of [the Young Men's Association of the City of Buffalo.] 106158

Catalogue of books, in the Library of Washington College. 102005

Catalogue of books, in the Library of Williams College. 104426-104428, 104430-104431

Catalogue of books in the Library of Yale College. 105898

Catalogue of books in the Library of Yale-College in New-Haven. 13215, 105895

Catalogue of books in the Library of Yale-College, New-Haven. 105896

Catalogue of books in the Library of Yale-College, New-Haven, January 1808. 105897

Catalogue of books in the Linonian, Brothers', and Moral Libraries, Yale College. 105901

Catalogue of books in the Lunenburg Town Library. 42697

Catalogue of books in the Massachusetts Historical Library. 45851

Catalogue of books in the New Haven Social Library. 52963

Catalogue of books, in the Phenix Library. 105907A

Catalogue of books in the Portsmouth Athenaeum. 64425

Catalogue of books in the Richmond Library, Athenaeum Building. 71207

Catalogue of books in the Rio De Janeiro British Subscription Library. 71463

Catalogue of books in the Roxbury Athenaeum. 73725

Catalogue of books in the Sabbath School Library. 101941

Catalogue of books, in the South-Carolina College-Library. 87998

Catalogue of books in the Springfield Library
Company. 89881
Catalogue of books in the State Library [of
Massachusetts.] 46136
Catalogue of books in the Stoneham Social
Library. 92156
Catalogue of books, in the Theological Library.
95311
Catalogue of books in the Troy Library.
97074
Catalogue of books in the United Fraternity's
Library. 18614
Catalogue of books in the Upper Hall of the
Public Library of the city of Boston.
67059
Catalogue of books in Transylvania Library.
96469
Catalogue of books in various languages.
70875, 70878
Catalogue of books, manuscripts, maps and
charts. 97794
Catalogue of books, maps, and charts. 15560
Catalogue of books, maps, plates of America.
51281
Catalogue of books [of the Apprentices Library
Company of Philadelphia.] 61475
Catalogue of books [of the Boston Mercantile
Library Association.] 6745
Catalogue of books [of the Boston Public Lib-
rary.] 6759
Catalogue of books . . . of the late Mr. Rich.
70887
Catalogue of books of the Lexington Library
Company. 40881
Catalogue of books of the New Castle Library
Company. (52565)
Catalogue of . . . books, on masonry. 58975
Catalogue of books on printing and the kindred
arts. (51376)
Catalogue of books on the masonic institution.
26745
Catalogue of books. Part I.—relating to
America. 70887
Catalogue of books presented by him [i. e.
Edward Everett] to the city of Boston.
6759
Catalogue of . . . books principally relating to
America. (51376)
Catalogue of books, printed and published in
America. 102735
Catalogue of books, published by the different
members of the Philadelphia Company of
Printers and Booksellers. (61521), 89650
Catalogue of books published by the Philadel-
phia Company of Printers and Booksellers.
(61521), 89650
Catalogue of books; published in America.
102734
Catalogue . . . of books, relating chiefly to
America. 55871
Catalogue of books, relating principally to
America. (70883)
Catalogue of books relating to America. 790
Catalogue . . . of books relating to America.
(51376)
Catalogue of . . . books relating to America
. . . for sale. 6947
Catalogue of books relating to America, in
various languages. (70877), 70879
Catalogue of books relating to America, in the
collection of Colonel Aspinwall. 2215
Catalogue of books relating to America includ-
ing a large number of rare works. 51280
Catalogue of books relating to America, since
1800. 790

Catalogue of . . . books . . . relating to
American history. 29291
Catalogue of books relating to North and South
America, including also voyages round
the world. 70887
Catalogue of books relating to North and South
America in the library of John Carter
Brown. 22158
Catalogue of books relating to the history and
literature of America. (5199), 91511
Catalogue of books relating to the history of
America. 10396
Catalogue of books sold by Garrat Noel & Co.
55403
Catalogue of books, . . . the by-laws, and a
list of the proprietors [of the Portsmouth
Athenaeum.] 64425
Catalogue of . . . books to be sold at auction.
28159
Catalogue of books to be sold at Francis
Amory's store. 95802
Catalogue of books to be sold by Isaiah Thomas,
at his book-store. 95400
Catalogue of books to be sold by Isaiah Thomas,
at his bookstore. 95402
Catalogue of books to be sold by Thomas, Son
& Thomas. 95452
Catalouge of books, tracts, and manuscripts.
70887
Catalogue of books which may be profitably
read. 7474
Catalogue of books which may be read. 7474
Catalogue of books . . . with a historical
sketch. 37595
Catalogue of Bristol College. 41785
Catalogue of British, colonial, and foreign
postage stamps. 8540
Catalogue of Brown University. 8603
Catalogue [of Burr Seminary, Manchester, Vt.]
9445
Catalogue of . . . Burr Seminary, Manchester,
Vt. June, 1844. 44223
Catalogue of Canadian books. 91513-91514,
91516
Catalogue of Canadian products. 34927
Catalogue [of Canadaigua Academy.] 10651
Catalogue [of Carroll College, Waukesha, Wis.]
(11080)
Catalogue of Catlin's Indian Gallery. 11531,
57375
Catalogue of . . . choice and rare books on
America. (40110)
Catalogue of choice and valuable books. 61522
Catalogue [of Cincinnati college.] (13088)
Catalogue of Clarendon Harris's Circulating
Library. 105386
Catalogue, of Colonel Trumbull's paintings.
97242
Catalogue of Columbia College. (14813)
Catalogue of Concord Literary Institution and
Teacher's Seminary. 15140
Catalogue of congressional documents. 94669
Catalogue of Connecticut election sermons.
83743
Catalogue of Connecticut volunteer organizations.
15785
Catalogue of Contoocook Academy. (16171)
Catalogue of crustacea. 84233
Catalogue of curious and valuable books. 59603
Catalogue of curous books. (8784)
Catalogue of daguerreotype panoramic views in
California. 98437
Catalogue of dahlias. 65621
Catalogue of Delaware Academy. 19419
Catalogue of dictionaries, grammars, and
alphabets. 44718

Catalogue of Dr. Colman's works. 97450
Catalogue . . . of Dr. Dio Lewis's Family School for Young Ladies. 40791
Catalogue of Dr. Warren's works. 101460, note after 101476
Catalogue of drugs and medicines. 84944
Catalogue of drugs, chymical and galenical preparations. 61523
Catalogue of duplicate works in the Library of the New York Hospital. 86152
Catalogue [of Emery College, Oxford, Ga.] 22538
Catalogue of English books in the Library of the Legislative Council [of Quebec.] 66996
Catalogue of English, Scotch, Irish and American books. 95403
Catalogue of Erskine College. (22800)
Catalogue of exotic plants. 8422
Catalogue of fees. 53726
Catalogue of fees established by the Governor and Council. (53570)
Catalogue of 525,000 acres of pine timber lands. 75429
Catalogue of foreign and American books. 66801
Catalogue . . . of Fredonia Academy. 25698
Catalogue of Friends' books. 25362, 83308
Catalogue of Friends' books, ancient and modern. 83309
Catalogue of Friends' books; written by many of the people called Quakers. 103700
Catalogue of Friends' portraits. 83310
Catalogue of fruit and ornamental trees and plants. 65621
Catalogue of fruit and ornamental trees, cultivated at the Union Nurseries. 68219
Catalogue of fruit trees, plants, &c. 65621
Catalogue of . . . Genesee Wesleyan Seminary. 41135
Catalogue [of Gorham Seminary, Me.] (28026)
Catalogue [of Glen Falls Academy, N. Y.] (27577A)
Catalogue [of Gouveneur Wesleyan Seminary.] 28150
Catalogue of Griswold College, Preparatory Department. 28911
Catalogue [of Hampden Sydney College.] 30133
Catalogue [of Hampton Academy, N. H.] 30154
Catalogue [of Hampton Institute.] 30155
Catalogue [of Hanover College.] 30242
Catalogue [of Harvard University.] 17107
Catalogue [of Heidelberg College.] 31239
Catalogue of historical papers. 53825
Catalogue [of Howard University, Washington, D. C.] 33287
Catalogue [of Hudson Female Seminary, N. Y.] (33504)
Catalogue of human crania. 47390
Catalogue of Indian paintings belonging to the government collection. 85090
Catalogue of insects of Pennsylvania. 47470
Catalogue of irregular nouns and verbs. 80654, 80659-80661
Catalogue of James Hammond's Circulating Library. 30093
Catalouge of Jefferson College, Canonsburg, Pa. 35940
Catalogue of John C. Spencer's library. 89359
Catalogue of Johnstown Academy. (36402)
Catalogue of Jonesville Academy, Saratoga Co., N. Y. 36632
Catalogue of . . . Kinderhook Academy. 37775
Catalogue of . . . Kingston Academy. 37913
Catalogue of . . . Kingsville Academy. 37919
Catalogue of . . . Lafayette College. 38586

Catalogue of . . . La Grande College, North Alabama. 38623
Catalogue of Lancaster Town Library. 38791
Catalogue of lands belonging to the American Land Company. 14488
Catalogue of law and miscellaneous books. 92306
Catalogue of law books in the different libraries in Rochester. 72339
Catalogue . . . of . . . Leland Seminary, Townshend, Vt. (39976)
Catalogue of Lincoln Academy. (41269)
Catalogue of . . . Lincoln University . . . 1865-66. 41276
Catalogue of . . . Linden Hall, Litiz, Pa. (41290)
Catalogue of Lombard University, Galesburg, Ill. (41840)
Catalogue of lots comprised in the first plot. 9861
Catalogue of lots from which proprietors may make selections. 51146
Catalogue of lots laid out in the [Mount Auburn] Cemetery. 51146
Catalogue of lots of the Old Marine Hospital Estate. 12417
Catalogue [of McKendree College.] 43401
Catalogue of Madison University, Hamilton, N. Y. 43730
Catalogue of Manhattan College. 44254
Catalogue of manuscripts and relics in Washington's Headquarters, Newburgh, N. Y. 74492
Catalogue of manuscripts and revolutionary relics deposited in Washington's Headquarters, Newburgh. 54900
Catalogue of manuscripts . . . deposited in the New York State Library. 53825
Catalogue of maps and surveys. 53572
Catalogue of Mein's Circulating Library, Boston. 47406
Catalogue of members of the Baldwin Place Baptist Church. 6636
Catalogue of members of the Connecticut Alpha of ♥ BK. 105908
Catalogue of members of the Junior Class, in Rhode-Island College. 95519
Catalogue of members of the late English High School. 75657
Catalogue of members of the Worcester Agricultural Society. 105377
Catalogue [of Mercer University.] 47908
Catalogue of . . . metallick fossils. 55458
Catalogue of Mexican and other Spanish American and West Indian books. 91513-91514, 91517
Catalogue of Milton College, Wis. 49147
Catalogue of mineralogical and geological specimens. 43550
Catalogue of minerals found in the state of Vermont. 29770
Catalogue of minerals, with their formulas, etc. (22053)
Catalogue of Mr. J. H. V. Arnold's library, New York. 50876
Catalogue of Mr. John A. Rice's library. (70839)
Catalogue of Monticello Academy, Sullivan County, N. Y. 50205
Catalogue of Monticello Female Seminary. (50204)
Catalogue of Moore's Hill Male and Female Collegiate Institute. 50461
Catalogue of . . . Mount Holyoke Female Seminary, South Hadley, Mass. 51156

Catalogue of Mount-Washington Collegiate Institute, New York City. 51182

Catalogue of . . . New Ipswich Academy. 53027

Catalogue of New-York State Library: 1856. 53828

Catalogue of . . . Newton Athenaeum. (55091)

Catalogue of 96,046 acres of land. (11489)

Catalogue of North American birds. 2804

Catalogue of North American reptiles. 2808

Catalogue of North Middlesex Circulating Library. 55720

Catalogue . . . of . . . North-Western Christian University. 55739

Catalogue of . . . North-Yarmouth Academy. 55756

Catalouge of notes, accounts, and securities. 5961

Catalogue of novels, tales, . . . in the . . . [New York Mercantile] Library. 54391

Catalogue of . . . Nunda Literary Linstitute. (56317)

Catalogue of Oakland College. 56392

Catalogue of Oakland Female Seminary. 56393

Catalogue of objects in illustration of natural history. 51078

Catalogue of officers and cadets of the American Literary, Scientific, and Military Academy [Middletown, Connecticut.] (48871)

Catalogue of officers & cadets of the American Literary, Scientific, and Military Academy, . . . with the prospectus and regulations. 55931

Catalogue of officers and members of the American Antiquarian Society. 1051

Catalogue of officers and students for 1856 [of Illinois Wesleyan University.] 34245

Catalogue of officers and students for 1843-44 [of Perry-Centre Institute, Perry-Centre.] 61062

Catalogue of officers and students for the year 1853 [of the Military College, Wilmington, Del.] (48956)

Catalogue of officers and students of Dickinson Seminary. 20086

Catalogue of . . . officers and students of Knox Manual Labor College. (38187)

Catalogue of officers and students of Phillips Exeter Academy. 62536

Catalogue of officers and students [of Rensselaer Polytechnic Institute.] 69641

Catalogue of officers and students of South Limington Seminary. 88144

Catalogue of officers and students [of the Michigan Agricultural College.] (48716)

Catalogue of officers and students of the Pacific Methodist College. (58086)

Catalogue of Ohio Female College, Hamilton County, Ohio. 56982

Catalogue of Ohio plants. 71255

Catalogue of oil paintings on exhibition. 60620

Catalogue of old books relating to America. 790

Catalogue of . . . Olivet Institute, Olivet, Eaton County, Mich. 57220

Catalogue of one hundred and seventeen Indian portraits. 34470, 43410

Catalogue of 125,000 acres of valuable pine lands. (75428)

Catalogue of original documents in the English archives. (24964), note after 96789

Catalogue of Pacific coast mosses. 9959

Catalogue of paintings and other works of art. 54143

Catalogue of paintings, belonging to Yale College. 105921

Catalogue of paintings, by Colonel Trumbull, five subjects of the American revolution. 97243

Catalogue of paintings, by Colonel Trumbull; including eight subjects of the American revolution. 97244, 105921A

Catalogue of paintings, by Colonel Trumbull; including nine subjects of the American revolution. 97245

Catalogue of paintings, drawings, statuary, etc. (76637)

Catalogue of paintings . . . etc. of the Art Department. 61705

Catalogue of paintings . . . exhibited by the American Academy of Fine Arts. 54017

Catalogue of . . . paintings [in the Boston Athenaeum Gallery.] 6592

Catalogue of paintings [of the New England Art Union, Boston.] 52657

Catalogue of papers relating to Pennsylvania and Delaware. 11490, 59963

Catalogue of . . . Phipps Union Female Seminary. 62578

Catalogue of pictures and busts, belonging to the Redwood Library. 68534

Catalogue of pictures, in Stanley & Dickerman's North American Indian Portrait Gallery. 90313

Catalogue of pictures in the Gallery of Paintings, at the First Exhibition, Providence, R. I. 66244

Catalogue of Pinkerton Academy, Derry, N. H. 62961

Catalogue of plants collected in a journey to and from the Rocky Mountains. 35692

Catalogue of plants contained in the Botanic Garden at Elgin. 33085

Catalogue of plants found in Oneida County and vicinity. 58188

Catalogue of plants, found in the vicinity of Milwaukee, Wisconsin Territory. 38977

Catalogue of plants. Gathered in August and September, 1857. 68011

Catalogue of plants, growing spontaneously within thirty miles of . . . New-York. 53574

Catalogue of plants growing without cultivation in the vicinity of Amherst College. 32242

Catalogue of plants, growing without cultivation, in the civinity of Troy. 105611

Catalogue of plants . . . in the Botanic Garden, Jamaica. 18460

Catalogue of plants, indigenous and exotic, cultivated in the Elgin Botanic Garden. (33086)

Catalogue of plants, indigenous, naturalized, and cultivated, in Barbados. (47098)

Catalogue of plants indigenous to . . . New York. 53573

Catalogue of plants indigenous to the state of New York. 28526

Catalogue of plants, native and naturalized. 39503

Catalogue of plants, native or naturalized. 17613

Catalogue of plays. 102736

Catalogue of . . . portraits. 23135

Catalogue of postage stamps, American and foreign. 11491, 19892

Catalogue of printed books and manuscripts relating to the conquest of Mexico and Peru. 65261

CATALOGUE

Catalogue of printed books in the Library of
the . . . [New York] Historical Society.
(54471)
Catalogue of prints, and books of prints.
104619
Catalogue of proprietors in the Cemetery of
Mount Auburn. 51146
Catalogue of proprietors [of Greenwood Ceme-
tery.] 28698
Catalogue of provincial copper coins. (79849)
Catalogue of publications in what is now the
United States. 95406
Catalogue of publications of societies. 85005
Catalogue of publications of the Smithsonian
Institution. Corrected to June, 1862.
85006
Catalogue of publications of the Smithsonian
Institution, (1846-1882.) 85007
Catalogue of Randolph Macon College. 67862
Catalogue of rare and valuable books. 91509
Catalogue of rare and valuable books. Being
the greatest part of the library of the
Reverend and Learned Joshua Moodey
and Daniel Gookin. 50299
Catalogue of rare and valuable books . . .
belonging to the late Francis Adrian
Van der Kemp. 98475
Catalogue of rare books. (8784)
Catalogue of recent shells. 35850
Catalogue of regular and honorary members
[of the South Carolina College Clarioso-
phic Society.] 87995
Catalogue of revolutionary relics. (9432)
Catalogue of Richmond College. 71203
Catalogue of Richmondville Union Seminary.
71218
Catalogue of Robinson Female Seminary,
Exeter, N. H. 72240
Catalogue of Rock Hill College, Maryland.
72384
Catalogue of Rutgers Female College. 74443
Catalogue of St. John's College. 75290
Catalogue of St. John's College, at Annapolis,
Maryland. (75286)
Catalogue of St. Stephen's College, Annandale,
1863-4. 75492
Catalogue of sea-books, charts, pilots, &c.
91059
Catalogue of severall fishing voiages which
haue ben performed. 82829
Catalogue of Shelby College. 80117
Catalogue of shells collected at Panama. 175
Catalogue of sins against all the command-
ments. 46313
Catalogue of skulls of man. (51024)
Catalogue of Smithfield Seminary. 84977
Catalogue [of Sodus Academy, Sodus, N. Y.]
86201
Catalogue of southern Methodist books. 88401
Catalogue of Spanish and Portuguese books
with occasional literary and bibliograph-
ical remarks. (75863)
Catalogue of Spanish books. (75863)
Catalogue of Spring Hill College. 89827
Catalogue of Springfield Female College. 89894
Catalogue of State Teachers' Institute . . .
1859. (48772)
Catalogue of statues, busts, &c. 60294
Catalogue [of Steuben Teachers' Institute,
Steuben, N. Y.] 91466
Catalogue of students attending Docts. Marsh
& Armsby's lectures. 99217
Catalogue of subjects contained in the Hubard
Gallery. 33415
Catalogue of telegraph material. (12530)

Catalogue of text, reference and reading books.
(52483)
Catalogue of the Academic Department of North
Illinois University. 55718
Catalogue of the . . . Academical and Theo-
logical Institution, New-Hampton, N. H.
52951
Catalogue of the . . . Academy at Little Falls,
Herkimer County, N. Y. 41534
Catalogue of the Albany Institute Library. 605
Catalogue of the alumni and certain proceedings
of the Society [of the Alumni of the Uni-
versity of Nashville.] 4458
Catalogue of the Alumni Association, of Spring-
field High School. 89865
Catalogue of the alumni of the Divinity School
of the University of Cambridge. 30765
Catalogue of the alumni [of the General Theo-
logical Seminary of the Protestant Epis-
copal Church in the U. S. A.] 26910
Catalogue of the alumni, officers and fellows
of the College of Physicians and Surgeons.
(54000)
Catalogue of the American books in the library
of the British Museum at Christmas
Mdccclvi. 91514
Catalogue of the American Philosophical Society
Library. 1177
Catalogue of the American portion of the library
of the Rev. Thomas Prince. 65582
Catalogue of the American Whig Society, insti-
tuted in the College of New Jersey, 1769.
53088
Catalogue of the Anatomical Museum . . . with
a report. 60756
Catalogue of the animals and plants of Massa-
chusetts. 32243
Catalogue of the Animals of North America.
6468, 25133
Catalogue of the Anti-Secret Confederation.
(1711)
Catalogue of the Appleton Library of Lawrence
University. (39401)
Catalogue of the Apprentices' Library . . . .
Added, an address. 54093
Catalogue of the Arctic collection in the British
Museum. 85553
Catalogue of the Army Medical Museum. 2049
Catalogue of the art exhibition at the Metro-
politan Fair. 54144
Catalogue of the articles contributed to the
Paris Universal Exhibition. 17170
Catalogue of the articles in the museum. 75656
Catalogue of the articles sent to the Universal
Exhibition of Paris. 7571
Catalogue of the Athenaean Library, Bowdoin
College. 7021
Catalogue of the Athenaean Society of Bowdoin
College. 7022
Catalogue of the Athenaeum Library. (66309)
Catalogue of the Belles Lettres Society of
Dickinson College. 20078
Catalogue of the Berkeley Divinity School. 4884
Catalogue of the Berlandier manuscripts. 85008
Catalogue of the Bigelow Association, Clinton,
Mass. 13761
Catalogue of the birds of Chemung County,
N. Y. (28721)
Catalogue of the birds of Connecticut. 41376
Catalogue of the birds of Kansas. 85514
Catalogue of the Blackstone Library Association.
5698
Catalogue of the Board of Education, Board of
Instructors, and School Examiners of
Richmond Public Schools. 71158

444

Catalogue of the books . . . added during . . . 1854. 60378

Catalogue of the books and manuscripts and engravings belonging to William Menzies of New York. 74682

Catalogue of the books and pamphlets issued from the press of Joel Munsell. 51360, 86941

Catalogue of the books, autographs, engravings, and miscellaneous articles, belonging to the estate of the late John Allan. 74681

Catalogue of the books belonging to the Brothers', Linonian, & Moral Libraries. Yale College. 105864

Catalogue of the books belonging to the Company of the Redwood-Library. 68432

Catalogue of the books belonging to the Concord Town Library. 15126

Catalogue of the books belonging to the Incorporated German Society. 60121

Catalogue of the books belonging to the Law Library Company. (61768)

Catalogue of the books belonging to the Library Company of Wilmington. 104582

Catalogue of the books belonging to the Library of Delaware College. 19382

Catalogue of the books belonging to the Library of the Franklin Institute. (25653)

Catalogue of the books belonging to the Library of the Three Monthly Meetings of Friends of Philadelphia. 61524

Catalogue of the books belonging to the Library of the University of Vermont. 99215

Catalogue of the books belonging to the Loganian Library. 61798

Catalogue of the books belonging to the Mercantile Library Association of . . . New-York. 54391

Catalogue of the books belonging to the . . . [New York] Hospital Library. (54482)

Catalogue of the books, belonging to the Redwood Library Company. 55053, 68534

Catalogue of the books belonging to the Salem Athenaeum. 75711

Catalogue of the books contained in the Library [of the Cabot Institute.] 9806

Catalogue of the . . . books, . . . &c., of the late Mr. E. B. Corwin. 16981

Catalogue of the books given by Dr. Bray. 83977

Catalogue of the books in Dartmouth-College Library. 18614

Catalogue of the books in the Apprentices' Library. 54094

Catalogue of the books in the Boston Athenaeum. 6589

Catalogue of the books in the Library of the Lyceum of Natural History. (54365)

Catalogue of the books in the Library of the Philermenian Society. 8606

Catalogue of the books in the Library of the Porcellian Club. 30735

Catalogue of the books in the Library of the Social Fraternity. 85689

Catalogue of the books in the Library of the United Brothers' Society. 97867

Catalogue of the books in the Library of the United Fraternity. 97876

Catalogue of the books in the Mercantile Library of the city of Brooklyn. (8304)

Catalogue of the books in the People's Library, Newport, R. I. 55032

Catalogue of the books in the Portland Athenaeum. 64357

Catalogue of the books in the Social Friend's Library. 18614

Catalogue of the books, . . . in the State Library of New Hampshire. (52804)

Catalogue of the books, manuscripts, maps, drawings and engravings. 74688

Catalogue of the books, maps, and charts. (15562)

[Catalogue of the books of M. de Cisternay du Fay.] (8784)

Catalogue of the books [of the Charleston Apprentices' Library Society.] 12040

Catalogue of the books [of the Easton, Pa., Library Company.] 21698

Catalogue of the books of the Madison Library Association. 43724

Catalogue of the books of the New York Society Library. 54543

Catalogue of the books on bibliography. 53825

Catalogue of the books, pamphlets, autograph letters, original manuscripts, documents, &c., belonging to the late Henry R. Schoolcraft. (77842)

Catalogue of the books, pamphlets, newspapers, charts, manuscripts, &c. in the Library [of the Massachusetts Historical Society.] 45851

Catalogue of the books, tracts, newspapers, maps, charts views, portraits, and manuscripts, in the Library of the . . . [New York] Historical Society. 54470

Catalogue of the Boston Library. (6730)

Catalogue of the bound historical manuscripts collected by Jared Sparks. 88965

Catalogue of the Burlington Social Library. 9337

Catalogue of the Cabinet of Natural History of . . . New-York. 53575

Catalogue [of the Caledonia-County Teachers' Institute, Danville, Vt.] 9922

Catalogue of the California State Library. 9982

Catalogue of the Calliopean Society, Yale College. 105870

Catalogue of the Cambridge Circulating Library. 10147

Catalogue of the Centenary College of Louisiana. 42202

Catalogue of the Central High School of Philadelphia. (61529)

Catalogue of the Charlestown Female Seminary. (12102)

Catalogue of the Cherry Valley Female Academy. 12480

Catalogue of the Chicopee Falls School Library. 12685

Catalogue of the City Library [of Lowell, Mass.] 42475

Catalogue of the City School Library, Lowell, Mass. 42475

Catalogue of the Class of 1812, Dartmouth College. 18615

Catalogue [of the Cleveland Library Association.] 13673

Catalogue of the Cliosophic Society. 53088

Catalogue of the Cohoes District School Library. 14233

Catalogue of the collection of Assyrian, Babylonian, Egyptian, Greek, Etruscan, Roman, Indian, Peruvian and Mexican antiquities. (31598)

Catalogue of the collection of books and manuscripts which formerly belonged to the Reverend Thomas Prince. 65582

Catalogue of the collection of books, manuscripts, and works of art. (65737)

Catalogue of the Columbian College. (14860)

Catalogue of the Congregational Library of the Union Church and Society, Groton. 28963

Catalogue of the corporation, faculty, and students [of Hanover College.] 88138

Catalogue of the corporation, officers and cadets of the Norwich University, for . . . 1843-4. 55927

Catalogue of the corporation, officers, and students of Hamilton College, 1855-56. 30060

Catalogue of the corporation, officers & students of Rutgers College. 74436

Catalogue of the corporation, officers, and students, of the Vermont Literary & Scientific Institution. 99228

Catalogue [of the Cortland Academy, Homer, N. Y.] 16978

Catalogue of the damages for which the English demand reparation. 14492

Catalogue of the Delti Phi Society. 8607

Catalogue of the described coleoptera of the United States. 47469

Catalogue of the described diptera of North America. (56822)

Catalogue of the described lepidoptera of North America. 50842

Catalogue of the different varieties of grapes. 65621

Catalogue [of the East Abingdon Library Association.] 21642

Catalogue of the East Cambridge Female School. 10135

Catalogue of the East Hartford Classical and Grammar School. 72709

Catalogue of . . . the Eliot Sabbath School Library. 55086

Catalogue of the English School [in Marietta, Ohio.] 44571

Catalogue of the Enosionian Society. 14862

Catalogue of the entire collection of the late Mr. John Allan. 74681

Catalogue of the entire library of Andrew Wright, of Philadelphia. 74683

Catalogue of the entire library of the late Rev. Samuel Farmar Jarvis. (74684)

Catalogue of the entire stock in trade of the late Ebenezer Larkin. 103184

Catalogue of the Episcopal Academy of Connecticut. 15726

Catalogue of the esculent vegetable and other seeds. 65621

Catalogue of the Euphradian Society of the South Carolina College. 87996

Catalogue of the exhibition, called Modern Mexico. (9136)

Catalogue of the exhibition of a private collection of works of art. (61525)

Catalogue of the exhibition of the New York Gallery of Fine Arts. 54467

Catalogue of the extraordinary curiosities in the National Institute. 51988

Catalogue of the extraordinary library . . . formed by the late Rev. F. J. Stainforth. 90091

Catalogue of the faculty and students [of Middlebury College.] 48838

Catalogue of the faculty and students of the academical institution of Yale College. 105753

Catalogue of the faculty and students of the College of Physicians and Surgeons. (54000)

Catalogue of the faculty and students of the Medical Institution of Yale College. 105912-105916

Catalogue of the faculty and students of the University [of North Carolina.] 55701

Catalogue of the faculty and students of the Vermont Medical Institution. 99231

Catalogue of the faculty and students of Yale College. 105753

Catalogue of the Fall River Athenaeum Library. 23743

Catalogue of the fauna of South Carolina. 87534

Catalogue of the Fellenberg Academy. 24014

Catalogue of the fifth session of Roanoke College, Salem, Virginia. (75760)

Catalogue of the first annual exhibition of the Maryland Institute. (45224)

Catalogue of the First Church of Christ in Glastenbury. 27554

Catalogue of the first exhibition of paintings, in the Athenaeum Gallery. 6591

Catalogue of the first exhibition of paintings, statuary and other works of art. 70708

Catalogue of the first exhibition of sculpture in the Athenaeum Gallery. 6592

Catalogue of the first exhibition of statuary, paintings, etc. 12647

Catalogue of the first exhibition [of the Albany Gallery of Fine Arts.] 603

Catalogue of the first exhibition [of the Artists' Fund Society of Philadelphia.] (61484)

Catalogue of the First Parish Library, Groton. 28962

Catalogue of the 1st, 2d, 3d, 4th, and 5th regiments Connecticut Volunteers, 1861. 15785

Catalogue of the first Winter Exhibition of the National Academy of Design. 51912

Catalogue of the fishes of the eastern coast of North America. (27385)

Catalogue of the flowering plants and ferns indigenous to, or naturalized in Canada. 33470

Catalogue of the flowering plants and ferns, of Ohio. 54889

Catalogue [of the Flushing Institute.] 24922

Catalogue [of the Fort-Plain Seminary and Female Collegiate Institute.] 25165

Catalogue of the 14th, 15th, 16th, 17th, 18th, 19th, 20th, and 21st regiments. 15785

Catalogue of the Fourth Street . . . School Library. 52467

Catalogue [of the Franklin County Grammar School.] 25652

Catalogue of the Franklin Literary Society of Jefferson College. 35940

Catalogue of the Franklinville Academy. 25669

Catalogue of the fraternity of Φ B K, Alpha of Massachusetts, Harvard University, Cambridge, 1846. 45668

Catalogue of the fraternity of Φ B K, Alpha of Massachusetts, Harvard University . . . 1810. 30765

Catalogue of the fraternity of Phi Beta Kappa, Alpha of New Hampshire. 52805

Catalogue of the fraternity, of Φ B K, Alpha of New-York. 97795

Catalogue of the fraternity of Φ B K, Alpha of Rhode-Island. 8608

Catalogue of the Free Academy of . . . New York. 54284

Catalogue of the Free Public Library, New Bedford, Mass. 52466

Catalogue of the Free Public Library of Lynn, Mass. (42841)

Catalogue of the Friends' Academy, New Bedford, April, 1859. 52469

Catalogue of the Frost Free Library [Marlborough, N. H.] 44635

Catalogue of the geological specimens. 56921
Catalogue [of the Genesee Wesleyan Seminary.] 26924
Catalogue of the Geneva Lyceum. 26941
Catalogue of the Georgia State Library. 27023
Catalogue of the graduates . . . embracing a biographical register. 48834
Catalogue of the graduates of Rutgers College. 74436
Catalogue of the graduates of the Jefferson Medical College of Philadelphia. (35946), 61746
Catalogue of the graduates of Yale College. 105754
Catalogue [of the Green Mountain Liberal Institute.] 28576
Catalogue [of the Greenfield High School for Young Ladies.] 28626
Catalogue of the Groton Public Library. (28961)
Catalogue [of the Hamilton Female Seminary.] 30068
Catalogue of the Hannah More Academy. 61715
Catalogue of the Harris Collection of American poetry. 91873
Catalogue of the Hartford Female Seminary. (30661)
Catalogue of the Hartford Public High School. (30661)
Catalogue of the Haverford Loganian Library. 30906
Catalogue [of the Hazel Green Collegiate Institute.] 31116
Catalogue of the High School Department [of the Richmond Public Schools.] 71158
Catalogue of the High School Library, Charlestown [Mass.] 12095
Catalogue of the hitherto known native and naturalized plants. 51248
Catalogue of the [Hollins] Institute for the sessions of 1863-4. 21885
Catalogue of the honorary and immediate members of the Porcellian Club. 30735
Catalogue of the honorary and ordinary members of the Erodelphian Society. 48682
Catalogue of the Indian Gallery. 40813
Catalogue of the Indiana State Library. 34495
Catalogue of the . . . Institute of 1770. 30727
Catalogue of the Institute Library, with the constitution & by-laws. 89884
Catalogue of the instructors and pupils, in the New Haven Young Ladies' Institute. 52999
Catalogue of the instructors and pupils in the Pittsfield Gymnasium. 63154
Catalogue of the instructors and pupils in the Pittsfield Young Ladies' Institute. (63157)
Catalogue of the instructors and students of St. Johnsbury Academy. 75293
Catalogue of the instructors and students of the State Normal School at Salem. 75748
Catalogue of the invertebrate fossils. 26278
Catalogue of the Jamestown Academy. 35735
Catalogue of the Judson Circulating Library Company. 90125
Catalogue of the Junior Class, Yale-College, 1794. 105757
Catalogue of the kings and emperours of the chiefe nations of the world. 67591
Catalogue of the Lake Forest Academy for 1869-70. 38662
Catalogue of the Lancaster Institute, 1869. 38804
[Catalogue of the] Lasell Female Seminary. (39128)

Catalogue of the Law Department of the Library of Congress. (15576), 47364
Catalogue of the Law Library of Harvard University. 30732, note after 93645
Catalogue of the Law School of the University at Cambridge. 30765
Catalogue of the Lawrence Scientific School, at Harvard College. 30765
Catalogue of the Lenox Academy, January, 1828. 40042
Catalogue of the library and members of the Philermenian Society. 8609
Catalogue of the library and members of the Philermenian Society in Brown University. 8634
Catalogue of the Library and Museum of the Natural History Society of Montreal. 50271
Catalogue of the library, and names of members, of the Athenean Society. 1312
Catalogue of the library, and names of members, of the Philomathesian Society of Kenyon College. 37586
Catalogue of the Library and Reading Room of the Ohio Mechanics Institute. (56989)
Catalogue of the Library and Reading Room of the Young Men's Institute, Hartford. 30678
Catalogue of the Library Association of Skowhegan, Maine. 81666
Catalogue of the library belonging to Mr. Richard W. Roche. 72313, note after (74691)
Catalogue of the library belonging to Mr. Thomas W. Field. 74685
Catalogue of the library belonging to the General Theological Seminary. (66153)
Catalogue of the library belonging to the Society of Brothers in Unity, Yale College. 105869
Catalogue of the library belonging to the Theological Institution in Andover. 1432
Catalogue of the library belonging to Thomas Addis Emmet. 74686
Catalogue of the Library for the [New Haven Young Men's] Institute. 53000
Catalogue of . . . the Library . . . January, 1854 [of the Massachusetts Horticultural Society.] 45862
Catalogue of the Library, January 1860 [of the Bridgeport Library Association.] 7817
Catalogue [of the library of A. E. Douglas.] (74677)
Catalogue of the library of a collector and amateur. 74687
Catalogue of the Library [of Alleghany College.] 777
Catalogue of the Library of Bowdoin College. 7024-7025
Catalogue of the Library of Bowdoin College, in which is added an index of subjects. 7025
Catalogue of the Library of Brown University. 8605
Catalogue of the Library of Congress. 15566-15568, 15571
Catalogue of the Library of Congress. Chapter I. Ancient history. 15578
Catalogue of the Library of Congress. Chapters XVIII-XXIII. Jurisprudence. (15576)
Catalogue of the Library of Congress. December, 1840. 15573
Catalogue of the Library of Congress. December, 1830. (15569)
Catalogue of the Library of Congress in December, 1830. 15570-15571

Catalogue of the Library of Congress, in the capitol. 15572

Catalogue of the Library of Congress. Printed by order of Congress. (15575)

Catalogue of the library of E. G. Squier. 74688

Catalogue of the library of Edwin Forest. 74689

Catalogue of the library of George W. Ordway. 74690

Catalogue of the Library of Harvard University. 30729

Cat. of the library of J. C. Brown. 22158

Catalogue of the library of James Smithson. 84987

Catalogue of the library of Jared Sparks. 88966

Catalogue of the Library of Lawrence Academy, Groton, Mass. 39388

Catalogue of the Library of Lawrence University. (39401)

Catalogue of the Library of Lawrence University, Appleton, Wis. 39400

Catalogue of . . . the Library of Middlebury College. 48832

Catalogue of the Library of Parliament: General Library. (10394)

Catalogue of the Library of Parliament [of Canada.] 10395

Catalogue of the Library of Petersburg. 61216

Catalogue of the library of President Barnas Sears . . . of Brown University. 78631

Catalogue of the library of Rev. Thomas Prince. 65581

Catalogue of the . . . library of T. H. Morrell. (50783)

Catalogue of the Library [of the Academy of Natural Sciences of Philadelphia.] 61405

Catalogue of the Library of the American Geographical and Statistical Society. 1091, note after 92754

Catalogue of the Library of the American Philosophical Society. 1776

Catalogue of the Library of the Athenaeum, in Salem, Massachusetts, 1849. 75711

Catalogue of the Library of the Athenaeum, in Salem, Massachusetts, with the by-laws and regulations. 75711

Catalogue of the Library of the Brooklyn Athenaeum and Reading Room. (8264)

Catalogue of the Library of the Chamber of Commerce . . . [of the State of New York.] (53581)

Catalogue of the Library of the City Library Association . . . [of Springfield, Mass.] 89854

Catalogue of the Library of the College [of New York.] 54198

Catalogue of the . . . library of the Count Mondidier. 49961

Catalogue of the Library of the First Church in Salem. (75661)

Catalogue of the . . . Library of the First Congregational Church. 52467

Catalogue of . . . the Library . . . of the First Presbyterian Church, Newburgh, N. Y. 54901

Catalogue . . . of the Library of the . . . First Universalist Society, of New Bedford. 52467

Catalogue of the . . . Library of the Four Monthly Meetings of Friends of Philadelphia. 61524

Catalogue of the Library of the Franklin Lyceum, Providence. 66263

Catalogue of the Library of the General Court. 45669

Catalogue of the Library of the German Society. 27151

Catalogue of the Library of the Grand Lodge of Iowa. 58975

Catalogue of the Library of the Historical Society [of Pennsylvania.] 60144

Catalogue of the Library . . . of the Institute [for Colored Youth.] 61743

Catalogue of the library of the late Col. William Duane. 20994

Catalogue of the library of the late Dr. Joseph Priestly. (65513)

Catalogue of the library of the late Hon. Sir James Stuart, Bart. 93172

Catalogue of the library of the late Rev. J. S. Buckminster. 103839

Catalogue of the . . .'library of the late Rev. John B. Romeyn. 73048

Catalogue of the library of the late Rev. John Eliot. 22169, 103840

Catalogue of the library of the late Rev. Pascal N. Strong. 93067

Catalogue of the Library of the Law School of Harvard University. (30731)

Catalogue of the Library of the Lyceum and Library Society. 53313

Catalogue of the Library [of the Lynn Library Association.] (42841)

Catalogue of the Library of the Massachusetts Historical Society. 45851

Catalogue of the Library [of the Mattapan Literary Association, Boston.] (46878)

Catalogue of the Library of the Meadville Theological School. 47247

Catalogue of . . . the Library of the Mechanics' Institute [of Montreal.] 50254

Catalogue of the Library of the Medical School of Maine. 7026

Catalogue of the Library of the Middlesex Mechanic Association. (42495)

Catalogue of the Library of the Nantucket Athenaeum. 51751

Catalogue of the Library of the New York Free Academy. 54284

Catalogue of the Library of the New-York Law Institute, July 1, 1842. 54505

Catalogue of the Library [of the Newport Association of Mechanics and Manufacturers.] 55042

Catalogue of . . . the Library of the Northampton Book Club. 55762

Catalogue of the Library of the Patent Office. 59036

Catalogue of the Library of the Peabody Institute, South Danvers, Mass. 18514, 59394

Catalogue of the Library of the . . . [Pennsylvania Horticultural Society.] 60326

Catalogue of . . . the Library of the Philological Society [of Middlebury College.] 48833

Catalogue of the Library of the Philomathean Society [of the University of Pennsylvania.] 60390

Catalogue of the Library of the Portland Athenaeum. 64357

Catalogue of the Library of the Providence Athenaeum. (66309)

Catalogue of the Library of the Rochester Athenaeum and Mechanics' Association. 72355

Catalogue of the . . . Library of the Sabbath School. 52234

Catalogue of the Library of the Salem Athenaeum. 75711

Catalogue of the Library of the School of Mines of Columbia College. 14815

Catalogue of the Library of the South Carolina College. 88000

Catalogue of the Library of the South Carolina College . . . compiled and published by the Library. 87999

Catalogue of the . . . Library of the South Christian Church. 52467

Catalogue of the Library of the State of Maryland. 45369

Catalogue of the Library of the State Street Presbyterian Church Sabbath School. 90649

Catalogue of the Library of the Theol. Seminary in Andover, Mass. 1433

Catalogue of the Library of the Union Theological Seminary. 65644

Catalogue of the Library of the United Brother's Society of Brown University. 8610

Catalogue of the Library of the United States. (15564)

Catalogue of the Library of the U. S. Naval Academy. 1594A

Catalogue of the Library of the University of Alabama. 571

Catalogue of the Library of the University of Michigan. 48804

Catalogue of the Library of the University of Virginia. 100534

Catalogue of the Library . . . [of the Utica Young Men's Association.] 98234

Catalogue of the Library of the Wesleyan University. 102710

Catalogue of the Library of the Young Men's Association of . . . Milwaukee. 49182

Catalogue of the Library of the Young Men's Association of the City of Chicago. 12672

Catalogue of the Library of the Young Men's Institute [of Northampton, Mass.] 55763

Catalogue of the library of . . . Theophilus Parsons. 58906

Catalogue of the . . . library of Thomas Dowse. 45851

Catalogue of the Library of Waterville College, in Waterville, Maine. 102105

Catalogue of the library of Wm. B. Sprague. 89731

Catalogue of the Library of Yale-College in New-Haven. 105894

Catalogue of the library purchased by Congress from Thomas Jefferson. 15565

Catalogue of the Library, with a historical sketch [of the Detroit Young Men's Society.] 19787

Catalogue of the Literary Adelphi of the Academical and Theological Institution, at New Hampton, N. H. 52951

Catalogue of the . . . Literary and Theological Institution, Farifax, Vt. 52951

Catalogue of the lots in Mount Auburn Cemetery. 51146

Catalogue of the Louisiana State Library. 42257

Catalogue of the Louisville Mercantile Library. 42337

Catalogue of the Macedon Academy. 43219

Catalogue of the Maine State Library. 43987

Catalogue [of the Maine State Seminary.] 43989

Catalogue [of the Maine Wesleyan Seminary.] 43991

Catalogue of the Marietta College Library. (44569)

Catalogue of the . . . Manchester Athenaeum. 44212

Catalogue of the Manchester City Library. 44213

Catalogue of the Manchester Library Association, South Manchester, Conn. 88145

Catalogue of the Manufacturers' and Mechanics' Library Association of Lewiston. 40871

Catalogue of the manuscripts, [etc.] and an account of the Library of the Maryland Historical Society. (45211A), 45213

Catalogue of the maps and charts. 30730

Catalogue of the marine, fluviate and terrestrial shells of Massachusetts. 65257

Catalogue of the Marlborough High School. 44636

Catalogue of the Maryland Agricultural College. (45199)

Catalogue of the Maryland State Library. 45370

Catalogue of the Massachusetts State Cabinet. 45900

Catalogue of the Meadville Theological School. 47247

Catalogue of the Mechanics' and Apprentices' Library. 66281

Catalogue of the Mechanics' and Apprentices' Library [Providence, R. I.] 66281

Catalogue of the . . . [Mechanics] Institute. 53149

Catalogue of . . . the Mechanics' Library Association of Newburgh. 54901

Catalogue of . . . the Medford Tufts Library. 47302

Catalogue of the Medical Department of the University [of Missouri.] 49650

Catalogue of the medical graduates . . . with an historical sketch of the . . . Medical Department [of the University of Pennsylvania.] 60756

Catalogue . . . of the Medical Institute of . . . Louisville. 42329

Catalogue of the Medical Institution of Geneva College. 26938, 26940

Catalogue of the Medical Library belonging to the Pennsylvania Hospital. 60328

Catalogue of the Medical Library belonging to the Philadelphia Almshouse. 61455

Catalogue of the Medical Library of the Pennsylvania Hospital. 60328

[Catalogue] of the Medical School of Maine. 7029

Catalogue of the Medical Society in Harvard College. 30765

Catalogue of the medicinal plants. 39715

Catalogue of the members and Library of the Goethean Literary Society. 44815

Catalogue of the members and Library of the Hasty-Pudding Club. 30734

Catalogue of the members and Library of the Peithologian Society. 102711

Catalogue of the members, and Library, of the Philo Literary Society of Jefferson College. 35939

Catalogue of the members and Library of the Philorhetorian Society. 102712

Catalogue of the members and licentiates of the Berkshire Association. 4895

Catalogue of the members and of the Library of the Porcellian Club. 30735

Catalogue of the members during its [i. e. Cayuga County Teachers' Institute's] session at Auburn, 1843. (11635)

Catalogue of the members . . . from its [i. e. First Congregational Church in Vernon's] organization in 1762. 99255

Catalogue of the members, Library and catalogue of the members of the Union Society. 30065

Catalogue of the members of Harvard University, Oct. 1803. 30765

Catalogue of the members . . . of Φ B K, 1806. 30765

Catalogue of the members of the Adelphic Society, instituted in Union College. 97790

Catalogue of the members of the American Legal Association. 1126

Catalogue of the members of the Boylston Medical Society. 30735

Catalogue of the members of the Charles Street Baptist Church. 6638

Catalogue of the members of the Church in the United Society in New Haven. 52964

Catalogue of the members of the Connecticut Alpha of Φ B K. (15727)

Catalogue of the members of the Dialectic Society. 55701

Catalogue of the members of the Equitable Union. 97793

Catalogue of the members of the First Church in New Haven. 52964

Catalogue of the members of the First Church [of Christ, Middleborough, Mass.] 48824

Catalogue of the members of the Hasty-Pudding Club. 30734

Catalogue of the members of the Linonian Society of Yale College. 105899

Catalogue of the members of the Φ B K Society, Alpha of New Hampshire. 52805

Catalogue of the members of the Philo Literary Society of Jefferson College. 35940

Catalogue of the members of the Philomathean Society, instituted in Union College. 97798

Catalogue of the members . . . [of the Philomathean Society of the University of Pennsylvania.] 60390

Catalogue of the . . . members of the Pierian Sodality. 30735

Catalogue of the members of the Troy Female Seminary. 104050

Catalogue of the members of the United Fraternity, Dartmouth College. 97875

Catalogue of the members of the Washington College Athenaeum Society. 102004

Catalogue of the members of the Worcester County Institution for Savings. 105421

Catalogue of the members of the Zelosophic Society. 60756

Catalogue of the members of Yale-College. 105753

Catalogue of the members of Yale-College, in New Haven. 105753

Catalogue of the Memorandum Society in the Mount Holyoke Female Seminary, for five years. 51156

Catalogue of the Mercantile Library Company of Philadelphia. 61836

Catalogue [of the Mercantile Library of San Francisco.] 76057

Catalogue of the Meriden Institute. 47967

Catalogue of the Merrimack Normal Institute, for . . . 1849-50. 48014

Catalogue of the Michigan State Library. 48771

Catalogue of the Michigan State Normal School. (48772)

Catalogue of the microscopical section of the United States Army Medical Museum. 18032

Catalogue of the . . . [Milwaukee Female] College. 49172

Catalogue of the mineralogical collection [of the Literary and Historical Society of Quebec.] 67018

Catalogue of the miscellaneous books in the Pennsylvania State Library. 60378

Catalogue of the Middlesex Mechanic Association, at Lowell, Mass. 48849

Catalogue of the minerals in the cabinet of Benjamin De Witt. 19869

Catalogue of the . . . [Mississippi] State Library. (49490)

Catalogue of the Montreal Library. (50265)

Catalogue of the most valuable varieties of the pear. (44353)

Catalogue of the Mount Airy Agricultural Institute, Germantown, Pa. 51145

Catalogue of the Mount Auburn Young Ladies' Institute. 51153

Catalogue of the Mt. Pleasant Boarding School for Boys. 51168

Catalogue of the Mount-Pleasant Classical Institution. 51169

Catalogue of the Mount Vernon Classical School. 51181

Catalogue of the Museum and Gallery of Art of the . . . [New York] Historical Society. (54471)

Catalogue of the museum of flags, trophies and relics relating to the revolution, the war of 1812, the Mexican war, and the present rebellion; to be exhibited at New York, April 4, 1864. 19617, (54145), (76645)

Catalogue of the museum of flags, trophies, and relics, relating to the revolution, war of 1812, Mexican war, and the present rebellion, . . . to be exhibited at Philadelphia, June 7th, 1864. 61577

Catalogue of the Mystic-Hall Seminary, . . . West Medford, Mass. 51663

Catalogue of the names of the early puritan settlers. 31961

Catalogue of the names of the first puritan settlers. 31961

Catalogue of the names of the trustees, officers, and graduates of the College [of Columbia.] 14830

Catalogue of the . . . Nashua Literary Institution. (51861)

Catalogue of the Natick Town Library. 51903

Catalogue of the National Portrait and Historical Gallery. (59423)

Catalogue of the national portraits in Independence Hall. 61526

Catalogue of the national productions and curiosities which comprise the collections of the Cabinet of Natural History. 19325, 53575, 54146

Catalogue of the Nevada State Library. 52398

Catalogue of the New Bedford Art Exhibition. 52468

Catalogue of the New Haven Gymnasium. 52965

Catalogue of the New Jersey bills of credit. 62487

Catalogue of the New-London Academy, Chester County, Pa. 53265

Catalogue of the . . . New-York Central College. (53804), 54754

Catalogue of the New York Historical Society. 50381

Catalogue of the New York Hydropathic and Physiological School. 54488

Catalogue of the New York State Library. 32734

Catalogue of the New-York State Library: 1855. General Library. 53827

Catalogue of the New-York State Library: 1855. General Library. First supplement. 53827

Catalogue of the New-York State Library: 1855. Law Library. 53829

Catalogue of the New York State Library, 1872. 53830

Catalogue of the New-York State Library: 1865. Law Library: first supplement. 53829

Catalogue of the New-York State Library, January 1, 1850. 53826

Catalogue of the New-York State Library, January 1, 1840. 53826

Catalogue of the . . . New-York Theological Seminary. 54551

Catalogue of the Newark Library Association. 54880

Catalogue of the . . . Newburyport Female High School. 54921

Catalogue of the Newport Reading Room. 55047

Catalogue of the newspapers and periodicals published in the United States. 37433

Catalogue [of the Newton Theological Institution.] (55095)

Catalogue of the Norfolk Law Library. 19215

Catalogue of the North Church, Hartford. (30656)

Catalogue of the . . . North Granville Ladies' Seminary. (55715)

Catalogue of the . . . North-Western Female College. (55742)

Catalogue of the North-Western University, Watertown. 55754

Catalogue of the Northampton Public Library. 55763

Catalogue [of the Northampton Public Library.] With supplements. 55763

Catalogue of the . . . Northfield Institute. 55836

Catalogue of the Nova Scotian Department [of the International Exhibition, 1862.] 34928

Catalogue of the Nova Scotian Department with introduction and appendices. 56127

Catalogue of the numismatic collection formed by Joseph J. Mickley. 48819

Catalogue of the . . . [Oberlin] College. (56415)

Catalogue of the officers, alumni & students of Oglethorpe University. 56850

Catalogue of the officers, alumni, and students, of the University of the City of New-York. (54704)

Catalogue of the officers and alumni and of the honorary and other graduates, of the University of Rochester. 72368

Catalogue of the officers and alumni and of the honorary graduates [of the University of Rochester.] 72368

Catalogue of the officers and alumni of Rutgers College. 74436

Catalogue of the officers and cadets of the American Literary, Scientifick, and Military Academy, Norwich, Vt. note after (58963)

Catalogue of the officers and cadets of the Kentucky Military Institute, 1853-54. (37555)

Catalogue of the officers and cadets of the Maryland Military Academy. 45230

Catalogue of the officers and graduates [of Miami University.] 48682

Catalogue of the officers and matriculates of the University of Virginia. 100536

Catalogue of the officers and [medical] students . . . for . . . 1842-43. 37341

Catalogue of the officers and members . . . including nine branches [of the Massachusetts Peace Society.] 45882

Catalogue of the officers and members of Rensselaer School. 69641

Catalogue of the officers and members of the Boylston Medical Society. 30735

Catalogue of the officers and members of the (Collegiate) Reformed Prot. Dutch Church. 54616

Catalogue of the officers and members [of the Essex Institute.] 23012

Catalogue of the officers and members of the Harvard Natural History Society. 30735

Catalogue of the officers and members of the Hasty-Pudding Club. 30734

Catalogue of the officers and members of the Peucinian Society. 7028

Catalogue of the officers and members of the Rumford Society in Harvard College. 30735

Catalogue of the officers and members of the Social Fraternity of the Academical and Theological Institution at New Hampton, N. H. 85690

Catalogue of the officers and members of Wheaton Female Seminary. 103170

Catalogue of the officers & members of Whitesboro Academy. 103685

Catalogue of the officers and of those who have received any degree in the Ohio University, at Athens. 57015

Catalogue of the officers and pupils of Friends' Boarding School, Providence, R. I. 66266

Catalogue of the officers and pupils of the Michigan Female Seminary. 48763

Catalogue of the officers and students. 44815

Catalogue of the officers and students, and course of instruction in the Boylston Medical School. 7144

Catalogue of the officers and students, and programme of the course of instruction. (45867)

Catalogue of the officers and students, 1840 [of Concord School.] 15129

Catalogue of the officers and students . . . 1867 . . . 1868 [of the Lapham Institute, North Scituate, R. I.] 38980

Catalogue of the officers and students for 1851-2 [of the New York Central College Association.] 54754

Catalogue of the officers and students for 1856-7 [of Iowa University.] 34994

Catalogue of the officers and students for 1864, '65 [of Denison University.] 19575

Catalogue of the officers & students . . . for . . . November 23, 1832 [of Lyndon Academy.] (42826)

Catalogue of the officers and students, for the year 1853-'54, 1854-'55 [of Georgetown College, Kentucky.] 27006

Catalogue of the officers and students in East Tennessee College, Knoxville, Tennessee. 94740

Catalogue of the officers and students in the Collegiate and Commercial Institute, New Haven, Conn. (52966)

Catalogue of the officers and students in the Department of Arts and Sciences, 1843-4 [of the University of Michigan.] 48804

Catalogue of the officers and students in the Medical and Law Departments of Cincinnati College. 93810

Catalogue of the officers and students in the Medical College of Ohio. 56956

Catalogue of the officers and students. In the Western Reserve College. 103014

Catalogue of the officers and students in Yale College. 105753, 105787, 105916

Catalogue of the officers and students [of Alleghany College.] 777

Catalogue of the officers and students of Andrew College. 1483

Catalogue of the officers and students of Bates College. 3951

Catalogue of the officers and students of Beliot College and Seminary. 4590

Catalogue of the officers and students of Berwick Academy. 5032

Catalogue of the officers and students of Bethel College. 5067

Catalogue of the officers and students of Bowdoin College. 7029

Catalogue of the officers and students of Bristol College. 8061

Catalogue of the officers and students of Brown University. 8611

Catalogue of the officers and students of Capital University. 14892

Catalogue of the officers and students of Centenary College. 11680

Catalogue of the officers and students of Centre College. 11688

Catalogue of the officers and students of Clinton Seminary. 13764

Catalogue of the officers and students of Colby University. 14264

Catalogue of the officers and students of Columbia College. 14807

Catalogue of the officers and students of Columbia College, District of Columbia. 14861

Catalogue of the officers and students of Columbia College, with the graduates since 1844. 14814

Catalogue of the officers and students of Dartmouth University. 18616

Catalogue of the officers and students of Dickinson College. 20079

Catalogue of the officers and students of Dummer Academy. 21203

Catalogue of the officers and students [of Franklin and Marshall College.] 25645

Catalogue of the officers and students of Friends' Academy, New Bedford. 52469

Catalogue of the officers and students of Green Mountain Liberal Institute. 88220

Catalogue of the officers and students of Greenland Family School. 63250

Catalogue of the officers and students of Great Barrington Academy. 28431

Catalogue of the officers and students of Groton Academy. 28964

Catalogue of the officers and students of Hanover College. 30240

Catalogue of the officers and students of Hartford University. 30373

Catalogue of the officers and students of Hartwick Theological and Classical Seminary. 30717

Catalogue of the officers and students of Haverford School. 30905

Catalogue of the officers and students of Hobart College. 32313

Catalogue of the officers and students of Illinois College. 34228

Catalogue of the officers and students of Indiana Theological Seminary and Hanover College. 88132

Catalogue of the officers and students of Indiana University. 34518

Catalogue of the officers and students of Iowa College. 34985

Catalogue of the officers and students of Iowa Conference Seminary. 34985

Catalogue of the officers and students of Jefferson College. 35940

Catalogue of the officers and students of Kalamazoo College. (36980)

Catalogue of the officers and students of Kenyon College. 37585

Catalogue of the officers and students of Lawrence Academy. 39388

Catalogue of the officers and students of Lee Academy. 39810

Catalogue of the officers and students [of McKendree College.] 43401

Catalogue of the officers and students [of Marietta College.] (44560)

Catalogue of the officers and students . . . [of Marion College.] 44597

Catalogue of the officers and students . . . [of Marshall College.] (44816)

Catalogue of the officers and students of Meadville Academy. 47246

Catalogue of the officers and students of Middlebury College. 48834

Catalogue of the officers & students of Mount St. Mary's College. (51170)

Catalogue of the officers and students of Newark Academy. 54870

Catalogue of the officers and students of Newark College. 54870

Catalogue of the officers and students of Newbury Seminary. 54910

Catalogue of the officers and students of Peirce Academy. (59557)

Catalogue of the officers and students of Phillips Exeter Academy. 23395

Catalogue of the officers and students of Phillips Exeter Academy. 1783-1869. 62537

Catalogue of the officers and students of Powers Institute. 64807

Catalogue of the officers and students of Richland School. 71119

Catalogue of the officers and students of Ripon College. 71535

Catalogue of the officers and students of Roanoke College. (75760)

Catalogue of the officers and students of Rock River Seminary. 72411

Catalogue of the officers and students of Rutgers College. 74436

Catalogue of the officers and students of St. Francis Xavier's College. 75204

Catalogue of the officers and students of Saint Ignatius' College. 75236, 76085, (76087)

Catalogue of the officers and students of St. John's College, for the academical year 1849-50. 75291

Catalogue of the officers and students of St. John's College, Fordham, New York. 75291

Catalogue of the officers and students of St. Joseph's College. 75301

Catalogue of the officers and students of St. Peter's College. 11809

Catalogue of the officers and students of St. Xavier College, Cincinnati. 75517

Catalogue of the officers and students of Santa Clara College. (76751)

Catalogue of the officers and students of Schoharie Academy. 77763

Catalogue of the officers and students of Shelburne Falls Academy. 80115

Catalogue of the officers and students of Shurtleff College. 80799

Catalogue of the officers and students of Smith-
ville Seminary. 85098

Catalogue of the officers and students of
Starkey Seminary. 90530

Catalogue of the officers and students of the
Bordentown Female College. 6410

Catalogue of the officers and students of the
Caledonia-County Grammar School,
Peacham, Vt. 9921, 59412

Catalogue of the officers and students of the
Chicago Theological Seminary. 12645

Catalogue of the officers and students of the
Clinical School of Medicine, at Woodstock, Vermont. 102104

Catalogue of the officers and students of the
College of New-Jersey. 53088

Catalogue of the officers and students of the
Collegiate Institution, Amherst, Mass.
1319

Catalogue of the officers and students . . .
[of the Farmer's High School.] (60097)

Catalogue of the officers and students [of the
Hamilton Literary and Theological
Institution.] 30069

Catalogue of the officers and students of the
Indiana Asbury University. 34515

Catalogue of the officers and students of the
Iowa Conference Seminary. 34985

Catalogue of the officers and students of the
Law School of Columbia College. 14808

Catalogue of the officers and students of the
Medical Institution of Yale College.
105911

Catalogue of the officers and students of the
Methodist General Biblical Institute.
48195

Catalogue of the officers and students of the
Michigan Central College. 48760

Catalogue of the officers and students of the
Mississippi College. (49526)

Catalogue of the officers and students of the
Moravian College. 50516

Catalogue of the officers and students of the
Nashotah Theological Seminary. 51856

Catalogue of the officers and students of the
New Union Free School and Academy.
54885

Catalogue of the officers and students of the
New York Conference Seminary. 12145,
(54760)

Catalogue of the officers and students of the
New York State Normal School. 53967

Catalogue of the officers and students of the
New-York Theological Seminary. 97819

Catalogue of the officers and students of the
Newton Theological Institution. (55095)

Catalogue of the officers and students of the
Ohio University. 57015

Catalogue of the officers and students of the
Princetown Academy. 65659

Catalogue of the officers and students of the
Protestant Episcopal Theological Seminary, Fairfax County, Virginia. 23689,
100515

Catalogue of the officers and students of the
Rochester Theological Seminary. 72363

Catalogue of the officers and students of the
Rutgers Medical Faculty. 74448

Catalogue of the officers and students of the
St. Lawrence University 1869. 75323

Catalogue of the officers and students of the
St. Lawrence University. Theological
Department. (75324)

Catalogue of the officers and students of the
St. Louis University. 75400

Catalogue of the officers and students of the
Southwestern Normal School, Lebanon,
Ohio. 39576

Catalogue of the officers and students of the
Starling Medical College. 90541

Catalogue of the officers and students of the
Theological Seminary, Andover. 1434

Catalogue of the officers and students of the
Theological Seminary at Columbia, S. C.
14854

Catalogue of the officers and students of the
Theological Seminary, Princeton, New-
Jersey. (65657)

Catalogue of the officers and students of the
University at Lewisburg. (40870)

Catalogue of the officers and students of the
University of Cambridge. 30733

Catalogue of the officers and students of the
University of Chicago. 12646

Catalogue of the officers & students, of the
University of Michigan. 48804

Catalogue of the officers and students of the
University of Mississippi. 49549

Catalogue of the officers and students of the
University of . . . Missouri. 49649

Catalogue of the officers and students of the
University of Rochester. 72368

Catalogue of the officers and students of the
University of Vermont. 99208

Catalogue of the officers and students of the
University of Virginia. 100535

Catalogue of the officers and students of the
Vermont Academy of Medicine. 99218

Catalogue of the officers and students of the
Vermont Medical College. 99229

Catalogue of the officers and students of the
Virginia Baptist Seminary. 100551

Catalogue of the officers and students of the
Wesleyan Academy, Wilbraham, Mass.
102703

Catalogue of the officers and students of the
Wesleyan University. 102709

Catalogue of the officers and students of the
Western Theological Seminary of the
Presbyterian Church. 65230

Catalogue of the officers and students of the
Western University of Pennsylvania.
60783, 103025

Catalogue of the officers and students of Transylvania University, Lexington, Kentucky.
96462

Catalogue of the officers and students of Union
College. 97774

Catalogue of the officers and students of Wabash
College and Teachers' Seminary. 100880

Catalogue of the officers and students of Washington College, 1835-36. 101997

Catalogue of the officers and students of Waterville College, for the academical year
1834-5. 102099

Catalogue of the officers and students of Waterville College, October, 1824. 102099

Catalogue of the officers and students of William
College. 104416

Catalogue of the officers and students of Yale
College. 105753

Catalogue of the officers and students, with
catalogue of the alumni [of the General
Theological Seminary.] 26910

Catalogue of the officers and students with the
charter . . . [of Muhlenberg College.]
51257

Catalogue of the officers, corporation, instructors, graduates and students of the Vermont Academy of Medicine. 99219

Catalogue of the officers, graduates, and students of the Medical Institution of Yale College. 105909

Catalogue of the officers, instructors, and students of the Cheshire County Teacher's Institute. 12516

Catalogue of the officers . . . of Lewiston Falls Academy. 40876

Catalogue of the officers of the Medical Department of Transylvania University. 86470

Catalogue of the officers, professors, and students of the Willoughby University of Lake Erie. 104536

Catalogue of the officers, students and graduates of the Louisville Medical Institute. 42331

Catalogue of the officers, students & scholars of William and Mary College. 104149

Catalogue of the officers, teachers, and pupils. 42840

Catalogue of the officers, teachers, and pupils of the Moravian Young Ladies' Seminary. 50517

Catalogue of the officers, teachers and students of the M'Neely Normal School of Ohio. 43597

Catalogue of the officers, teachers and students of the University of Northern Pennsylvania. 60755

Catalogue of the Ohio Southwestern State Normal School. (57000)

Catalogue of the Ohio State Library. 57007

Catalogue of the Ohio Wesleyan Female College. 57017

Catalogue . . . of the Ohio Wesleyan University. 57018

Catalogue of the Oneida County Seminary. (57340)

Catalogue of the Onondaga Teachers' Institute. 57362

Catalogue of the Ontario Female Seminary, Canandaigua, N. Y. (57369)

Catalogue of the Orange Library Association, Orange, New Jersey. 57428

Catalogue of the . . . Orangeburgh Female College. 57432

Catalogue of the organic remains, which, . . . were presented to the New-York Lyceum of Natural History. 49738

Catalogue of the orthoptera of North America. (78525)

Catalogue of the Oswego City Library. 57837

Catalogue of the . . . Otis Library. (55919)

Catalogue of the Pacific Mills Library. 39393, 58087

Catalogue of the paintings and statuary. 60294

Catalogue of the paintings, engravings, &c. 45214

Catalogue of the palaeozoic fossils of North America. 80764

Catalogue of the Parish Library of St. Andrew's Church. 62206

Catalogue of the Pathological Cabinet of the . . . [New York] Hospital. (54483)

Catalogue of the Pawcatuck Library. 59258

Catalogue of the Pawtucket Library. 59261

Catalogue of the . . . [Pennsylvania State Library.] 60378

Catalogue of the . . . [Pennsylvania State] Library, with index. 60378

Catalogue of the persons admitted to the First Church in New Haven, during the ministry of the Rev. James Pierpont. (18711), 52964

Catalogue of the persons admitted to the First Church in New Haven, from . . . 1758, to . . . 1847. 52964

Catalogue of the persons admitted to the First Church in New Haven. Supplement . . . from . . . 1847, to 1853. 52964

Catalogue of the Peucinian Library, Bowdoin College. 7027

Catalogue of the phenogamous plants and the ferns. (2883), 2d note after 97444

Catalogue of the Philadelphia Circulating Library. 61976

Catalogue of the Philanthropic Society. 55701

Catalogue of the Philorhetorian Society of the Wesleyan University. 102713

Catalogue of the pictures . . . exhibited at the Gallery of the Lyceum Building. 54147

Catalogue of the Pittsburgh Female College. 63133

Catalogue of the Pittsfield Commercial & Classical Boarding School. 63152

Catalogue of the plants found in New Bedford and its vicinity. 31603

Catalogue of the plants of North America. 25135

Catalogue of the Plattesville Academy. 63361

Catalogue of the Plymouth Library, Plymouth, Mass. 63484

Catalogue of . . . the Poughkeepsie Collegiate School. 64713

Catalogue of the principal minerals of Colorado. 82752

Catalogue of the principal officers of Vermont. (19484)

Catalogue of the private cabinet of coins, relics, &c. (81182)

Catalogue of the private library of Samuel G. Drake. 20884

Catalogue of the professors and students of the Union Theological Seminary of the Presbyterian Church. 97820

Catalogue of the Providence Athenaeum Library. (66309)

Catalogue of the Psi Upsilon Fraternity. (54704)

Catalogue of the Public Library of . . . Beverley. 5120

Catalogue of the Public Library of Cincinnati. 64049

Catalogue of the Public Library . . . [of Detroit.] 19785

Catalogue of the Public Library of . . . Medford. 47302

Catalogue of the Public Library of Quincy, Mass. 67293

Catalogue of the Public Library of the city of Charlestown. 12103

Catalogue of the Public Library of the city of Fall River. 23744

Catalogue of the Public Library of the city of Newburyport. 54922

Catalogue of the Public Library, of the town of . . . Beverley. 5121

Catalogue of the Public School Library of Municipality No. Two. 53313

Catalogue of the pupils of St. Joseph's Academy. 75299

Catalogue of the pupils of Spring Lane School. 89828

Catalogue of the Putnam Free School, Newburyport, Mass. 54925

Catalogue of the rare and valuable library of the Right Hon. Edward Lord Viscount Kingsborough. (37801)

Catalogue of the rare, curious, and valuable collection of books, tracts, autographs, MSS., engravings, paintings, &c. (74691)

Catalogue of the Raymond Institute, Carmel, Putnam County, New York. 68071

Catalogue of the Redwood Library. 55053

Catalogue of the Regents of the University and faculty and fellows of the College of Physicians and Surgeons. (54000)

Catalogue of the Regents of the University, and . . . trustees and graduates of the College of Physicians . . . [and Surgeons.] (54000)

Catalogue of the reptilia and amphibia of Michigan. 84797

Catalogue of the resident members of the Church of Christ in Yale College. 105878

Catalogue of the Richmond Female Institute, Richmond, Virginia. 71206

Catalogue of the Rochester Athenaeum and Mechanics' Association. 72355

Catalogue of the Rochester City Library. 72355

Catalogue of the Rochester Commercial Nurseries. (32817)

Catalogue of the Rochester Theological Seminary. 72363

Catalogue of the Rockford Female Seminary. 72382

Catalogue of the St. Johnbury Academy. 75293

Catalogue of the St. Lawrence Academy. 75308

Catalogue of the St. Louis High School. 75390

Catalogue of the St. Louis High School, for the scholastic year, 1862-63. (75391)

Catalogue of the St. Paul Library Association. 75459

Catalogue of the St. Xavier College, Cincinnati, O. 75517

Catalogue of the sale by public auction at Mr. Duplessis' Long-room. 103106

Catalogue of the Salem Mechanic Library. 75730

Catalogue of the Salisbury Mansion School. 75801

Catalogue of the San Francisco Mercantile Library. (76095)

Catalogue of the Sand-Lake Collegiate Institute, N. Y. 76419

Catalogue of the Saratoga Female Seminary, Temple Grove. (76924)

Catalogue of the Schoharie County Teachers' Institute. 77765

Catalogue of the scholars, February, 1826 [at the Boston High School for Girls.] (6713)

Catalogue of the second session of the Memphis Medical College. 47780

Catalogue of the select and most valuable portion of the law library of the late Judge Story. 92320

Catalogue of the Seneca Collegiate Institute. 79101

Catalogue of the several books and pamphlets that have been hitherto published. 18546

Catalogue of the shells, arranged according to the Lamarckian system; together with descriptions. 35851

Catalogue of the shells, arranged according to the Lamarckian system. With their authorities. 35852

Catalogue of the Sigma Phi. 80906

Catalogue of the 6th, 7th, 8th, 9th, 10th, and 11th regiments of infantry. 15785

Catalogue of the Social Law Library, in Boston. 85693

Catalogue of the Society of Brothers in Unity, Tale College. 105860

Catalogue of the Society of Social Friends from 1783 to 1826. 18615, 86089

Catalogue of the Soldiers' Orphans and Widows' Home, St. Joseph. 86350

Catalogue of the Somerset Club. 86805

Catalogue of the Sophimore [sic] Class in Yale-College, 1795. 105759

Catalogue [of the Soule Female College, Nashville.] 87289

Catalogue of the South Carolina College, 1854. 87973

Catalogue of the South Jersey Institute, at Bridgeton, N. J. 88141

Catalogue of the South-Side Institute, Farmville, Virginia. 88209

Catalogue of the Southern Baptist Theological Seminary, Greenville, S. C. 88311

Catalogue of the Southern Female Institute, Richmond, Virginia. 88351

Catalogue [of the Southern Masonic Female College, Covington, Ga.] 88398

Catalogue [of the Southwestern Normal College, California, Pa.] 88620

Catalogue of the Spencertown Academy, Spencertown, N. Y. 89400

Catalogue of the spring course of lectures. 54710

Catalogue of the Spring-Villa Seminary for Young Ladies. 89831

Catalogue of the Starr Institute. 90569

Catalogue of the State Library [of Georgia.] 27023

Catalogue of the State Library of Massachusetts. (46137)

Catalogue of the State Street Presbyterian Sunday School Library. 90650

Catalogue of the State University of Iowa. 34993

Catalogue of the Staunton Baptist Female Institute, Stuanton, Va. 90845

Catalogue of the stock of books of the late firm of West & Blake. 102757

Catalogue of the students, and the rules, etc. [of Johnstown Academy.] (36402)

Catalogue of the students at the Law Institution. 30765

Catalogue of the students in the Law School of the University at Cambridge. 30735

Catalogue of the students in Williams-College. 104415

Catalogue of the students [of St. Ignatius' College.] 75236, 76086

Catalogue of the students . . . [of the Therapeutic Institute of Philadelphia.] (62309)

Catalogue of the students of the University of the City of New York. (54704)

Catalogue of the subscriptions to the fund of one hundred thousand dollars. 105808

Catalogue of the Sunday School Library, belonging to the Second Unitarian Society, in Newton. 55086

Catalogue of the Sunday School Library, of Grace Church, Newton. 55086

Catalogue of the Sunday School Library, of Grace Church Parish. 76035

Catalogue of the Sunday School Library of the First Congregational Church. 76034

Catalogue of the superb collection of engravings the property of Gustavus A. Somerby, Esq. 86788

Catalogue of the teachers and members of the fall session of the Teachers' Institute for Rockingham County. (72385)

Catalogue of the teachers and members of the Rockingham Co. Teachers' Institute. (72385)

Catalogue of the teachers and pupils in the Female Seminary. Washington Ga. 102018

Catalogue of the teachers and pupils of Chapman Hall School. 12002A

Catalogue of the teachers and pupils of Chauncy-Hall School, Boston. 12340

Catalogue of the teachers and pupils of the Charlestown High School. 12095

Catalogue of the teachers and pupils of the Columbia Female Institute. 14855

Catalogue of the teachers and pupils of the Concord School. 15127

Catalogue of the teachers and pupils of the Granville Female Seminary. 28329

Catalogue of the teachers and pupils of the Salem Classical & High School. 75721

Catalogue of the teachers and pupils of the Schenectady Institute. (77600)

Catalogue of the teachers and pupils of the Sing Female Seminary. 81416

Catalogue of the teachers and students of Spring Hill Boarding School. 89826

Catalogue of the teachers and students of the National Normal School. 39575

Catalogue of the teachers and students of the South-Western Normal School and Business Institute, at Lebanon. 88621

Catalogue of the . . . Teachers' Institute, for the County of Kennebec. 37382

Catalogue of the Teachers' Institute in the Second District of Schoharie County. 77765

Catalogue of the teachers, pupils, and patrons of Montgomery Academy. 50162

Catalogue of the Teachers' Seminary, Andover, Mass. 1435

Catalogue of the tenth annual exhibition. 1835 [of the National Academy of Design.] 51913

Catalogue of the terrestrial and fluviatile shells of St. Thomas. 80810

Catalogue of the terrestrial shells in the collection of William A. Haines. 29559

Catalogue of the Territorial Library of Colorado. 14737

Catalogue of the Territorial Library [of Minnesota.] (49242)

Catalogue of the tertiary testacea of the United States. (39484)

Catalogue of the theatrical and miscellaneous library of the late William E. Barton. 74676

Catalogue of the theological and literary bookstore. 105169B

Catalogue of the theological, classical, and miscellaneous book-store. 105170

Catalogue of the Theological Institution, Bangor, Maine. 3157

Catalogue of the . . . Theological School at New Hampton, N. H. 52951

Catalogue of the Theological Seminary and College, 1855-6. 36979

Catalogue of the Theological Seminary at Danville, Ky. 18521

Catalogue of the Theol. Seminary in Andover, Mass. 1433, note after 94525

Catalogue of the Theological Seminary, ... Kenyon College. 37586

Catalogue of the trustees and officers of Tufts College. 97431

Catalogue of the trustees, examiners, faculty and students, of the Vermont Medical College. 99230

Catalogue of the trustees, faculty and students in the University of South Carolina. 88096

Catalogue of the trustees, faculty and students of Geneva College. 26938

Catalogue of the trustees, faculty, and students of Jefferson Medical College . . . for . . . 1841-2. (35946)

Catalogue of the trustees, faculty and students, of the Charleston College. 12033

Catalogue of the trustees, faculty & students of the South-Carolina College. 87974

Catalogue of the trustees, faculty, and students of the Wake Forest Institute for 1836. 100975

Catalogue of the trustees, faculty, and students of Washington College. 102006A

Catalogue of the trustees, instructors and pupils [of the Uxbridge Female Seminary.] 98244

Catalogue of the trustees, instructors, and students, 1838 [of Concord School.] 15128

Catalogue of the trustees, instructors and students of Chatham Academy. 12281

Catalogue of the trustees, instructors, and students . . . [of Monson Academy] for . . . 1839. 50041

Catalogue of the trustees, instructors, and . . . students . . . [of Monson Academy] from its foundation. 50041

Catalogue of the trustees, instructors and students of New-Salem Academy, October, 1827. 53395

Catalogue of the trustees, instructors, and students of St. Johnsbury Academy. 75293

Catalogue of the trustees, instructors, and students of the Putnam Free School, Newburyport, Mass. 66847

Catalogue of the trustees, instructors, and students of Westfield Academy, November, 1824. 103028

Catalogue of the trustees, . . . of the Union Academy, of Philadelphia. 62347

Catalogue of the trustees, officers, and graduates of Franklin College. 25649

Catalogue of the trustees, officers, and students, . . . and of the grammar and charity schools. 60756

Catalogue of the trustees, officers, and students, of Black River Literary and Religious Institute. 102095

Catalogue of the trustees, officers, and students of Indiana University, 1842-3. 34518

Catalogue of the trustees, officers, and students of the Georgia Female College. 27024

Catalogue of the trustees, officers, and students of the Indiana Medical College, Laporte, Ind. 34554

Catalogue of the trustees, officers and students, of the Oberlin Collegiate Institute. (56415)

Catalogue of the trustee, overseers, faculty and students, of the Berkshire Medical Institution. 4896

Catalogue of the trustees . . . students of Leicester Academy. 39902

Catalogue of the trustee, teachers and students connected with the Washington County Grammar School. 102015

Catalogue of the trustees, teachers, and students, 1836 [of Lawrence Academy, Groton, Mass.] 39388

Catalogue of the trustees, teachers, and students, of the Union Village Academy, for the year 1838-9. 97823

Catalogue of the trustees, teachers and students of Worcester County M[anual] L[abor] High School. 105375

Catalogue of the Twelfth and Thirteenth Regiments Connecticut Volunteers. 15785

Catalogue of the Union Institute [of the
McNeely Normal School.] 43597
Catalogue of the unios, alasmodontas and
anodontas of the Ohio River and its
northern tributaries. (56889)
Catalogue of the United Brothers' Society of
Brown University. 8635
Catalogue of the University of Kansas. 37029
Catalogue [of the University of Louisville's
Medical Department.] 42342
Catalogue . . . of the University of Maryland.
(45389)
Catalogue of the . . . University of Nashville.
51880
Catalogue of the University of Notre Dame.
34522
Catalogue of the University of South Carolina.
88092
Catalogue of the University of South Carolina.
1871-1872. 88092
Catalogue of the University of South Carolina,
1872-'73. 88095
Catalogue of the University of South Carolina.
MDCCCLXVII. 88094
Catalogue of the University of South Carolina,
1867-'68-'69. 88102
Catalogue of the Utica Library, incorporated
May 5th, 1825. 98231
Catalogue of the Utica Gymnasium. 98241
Catalogue of the V. A. S. Association. (52868)
Catalogue of the valuable and extensive lib-
rary. 42750
Catalogue of the valuable library of a clergy-
man of New York. 85551
Catalogue of the valuable library of Mr.
Richard W. Roche. 72313, note after
(74691)
Catalogue of the valuable library of the late
J. Troup. 96333
Catalogue of the valuable private library of
the late Lucius Manlius Sargent. 77026
Catalogue of the very choice collection of
books forming the library of Gustavus
A. Somerby. 86789
Catalogue of the Washington collection in the
Boston Athenaeum. 88964
Catalogue of the whole fossil collection. 38194
Catalogue [of the Young Men's Library Asso-
ciation, Springfield, Mass.] 89885
Catalogue of the Young Men's Mercantile Li-
brary Association, of Cincinnati. 13091
Catalogue of theological works. 90217
Catalogue of 35 packages of books. 103328
Catalogue of those who have been educated at
the Theological Seminary in Andover.
(1436)
Catalogue of those who have been educated at
the Theological Seminary of the Presby-
terian Church, in Princeton, N. J.
(65657)
Catalogue of tokens. (12195)
Catalogue of trees. (3867)
Catalogue of 278 lots of land. (48992)
Catalogue of valuable books. 103697
Catalogue of valuable original paintings. 59424
Catalogue of valuable works relating to Amer-
ica. 55871
Catalogue of berbs in common use. 80652
Catalogue of Vermont plants. 56386
Catalogue of volunteer organizations. 15785
Catalogue [of Woodward College, Cincinnati,
O.] 105174
Catalogue of wool manufacturers. 51935
Catalogue of works by the late Henry Inman.
34783

Catalogue of works in refutation of Methodism.
11599
Catalogue of works of art, &c. 89284
Catalogue of . . . works relating to . . .
America. (55866)
Catalogue or alphabetical index of the Astor
Library. (2252)
Catalogue. Philadelphia Art Union. 61480
Catalogue raisonne de la Galerie Indienne de
Mr Catlin. 11530, 57375
Catalogue raisonne du Museum de Mr. C. W.
Peale. 4211, (58327), 59419
Catalogue raisonne d'une collection de livres
sur l'histoire de l'Europe et de l'Ameri-
que. 39647
Catalogue raisonne d'une tres-precieuse col-
lection de livres anciens et modernes.
39647
Catalogue raisonne of the Medical Library
. . . [of the Pennsylvania Hospital.]
60328
Catalogue raisonne . . . of the most important
works. 71239
Catalogue showing the subject or title of every
patent. 1495
Catalogue spring session, 1844 [of Castleton
Medical College.] 11440
Catalogue . . . to which is prefixed a short
account of the institution [i. e. the Red-
wood Library Company.] 55053
Catalogue Universitati Carolinae Septentrionalis.
55701
Catalogue, with officers and students [of Penn-
sylvania College.] 60313
Catalogue, with short titles, of the books now
collected. 2250
Catalogue with the constitution and rules of the
Citizens' Free Library . . . [of Halifax.]
29700
Catalogues and circulars of the Botanical
Garden of Transylvania University.
96468
Catalogues, course of study, &c. [of Hanover
College.] 30241
Catalogues et circulaires du Jardin Botanique
de l'Universite Transylvane a Lexington
en Kentucky. 96468
Catalogues of books on American history.
29304
Catalogues of the Baldwin School. 75453
Catalogues of the silurian fossils of the islands
of Anticosti. (5409)
Catalogues of the trustees, faculty, and stu-
dents for the sessions of 1835-6 . . .
[of the Medical College of South Carolina.]
87873
Catalogues of the very large and valuable law
and miscellaneous library of late Judge
Purviance. 66731
Catalogus Bibliothecae Collegii Alleghaniensis.
(59987)
Catalogus Bibliothecae Harvardianae. 30728
Catalogus Bibliothecae Loganianae. 41797,
61797
Catalogus Bibliothecae per XL annos. (36890)
Catalogus clasis [sic] junioris in Collegio-
Yalensi, M,DCC,XVII. 105755
Catalogus classis juniorum in Collegio Yalensi,
MDCCXCIII. 105756
Catalogus classis sophimorum [sic] in Collegio-
Yalensi. A. D. MDCCXCIV. 105758
Catalogus Collegii Columbiani Neo-Eboracensis.
14816
Catalogus Collegii Harvardini, 1776. 30736
Catalogus Collegii Neo-Caesariensis. 53088

Catalogus curatorum, facultatis sociorum, tutorumque, Collegii Meridionali-Caroliniensis. 87975
Catalogus der Surinaamsche Coloniale Bibliotheek te Paramiabo. (58541)
Catalogus der Surinaamsche Koloniale Bibliotheek. 93871
Catalogus eorum exhibens nomina qui in Collegio Regali Novi-Eboraci. (14717)
Catalogus eorum qui ab anno MDCCXCVII. ad annum MDCCXIX. alicujus gradus laurea donati sunt. 97775
Catalogus eorum qui aliquovis gradu ornati fuerunt. 33506
Catalogus eorum qui in Collegio Harvardino. 30737
Catalogus eorum qui in Collegio Novae Caesareae. 53088
Catalogus eorum qui in Collegio Rhod. Ins. et Prov. Plant Nov.- Anglorum, ab anno 1769. 8613
Catalogus eorum qui in Collegio Rhodiae Insulae quod est Providentiae. 8614
Catalogus eorum [qui in Collegio Yalensi.] 105760
Catalogus eorum qui in Collegio Yalensi, quod est Novi-Porti apud Connecticut. 105760
Catalogus eorum qui in Collegio-Yalensi, quod est Novo-Portu Connecticutensium. 105760
Catalogus eorum qui in Collegio-Yalensi, quod est Novo-Portu Connecticuttensium ab anno MDCCII. 105761
[Catalog]us eorum qui in Gymnasi[ ]o Connecticutensi. 105856
Catalogus florae Ludovicianae. 71255
Catalogus impressorum librorum Bibliothecae Bodleianae. 82833
Catalogus librorum Bibliothecae Collegij Harvardini. 30728
Catalogus librorum in Bibliotheca Cantabrigiensi selectus. 30728
Catalogus monitorius. 105829
Catalogvs patrvm, oratorvm doctorum teologorvm. 63165
Catalogus per triennium eorum qui officia gerunt. 102100
Catalogus personarum et domiciliorum in quibus sub A. R. P. Societatis Jesu. 11493
Catalogus plantarum Americanae Septentrionalis. 51248-51249
Catalogus plantarum quae in insula Jamaica. 82166
Catalogus praesidum et sociorum, cum professoribus, tutoribus, et omnibus, qui in Universitate Brunensi. (8615)
Catalogus Provinciae Marylandiae Societatis Jesu. (45100)
Catalogus recentium. Anno Domini 1771. 105753
Catalogus recentium, in Collegio-Yalensi. 105753
Catalogus recentium, in Collegium-Yalensi admissorum. 105753
Catalogus religiosorum Societate Jesu. 70776
Catalogus senatus academici, eorum qui munera et officia gesserunt . . . in Universitate Transylvaniensi. 96463
Catalogus senatus academici, eorum qui munera et officia gesserunt quique alicujus gradus laurea donati sunt. 1320
Catalogus senatus academici, eorum qui munera et officia gesserunt, quique alicujus gradus laurea donati sunt, in Universitate Harvardiana. 30738
Catalogus senatus academici, eorum qui munero et officia gesserunt, quique alicujus gradus laurea donati sunt in Universitate Brownensi. 8616
Catalogus senatus academici et eorum, qui in Universitate Vermontensi Burlingtoniae, munera et officia gesserunt. 99209
Catalogus senatus academici, et eorum, qui munera et officia academica gesserunt quique alicujus gradus laurea donati sunt. 20080
Catalogus senatus academici, et eorum, qui munera et officia academica gesserunt, quique alicujus gradus laurea exornati fuerunt. 48835
Catalogus senatus academici, et eorum qui munera et officia academica gesserunt, quique aliquo gradu exoranti fuerunt. (30061)
Catalogus senatus academici, et eorum qui munera et officia academica gesserunt, quique aliquovis gradu exornati fuerunt in Collegio Concordiae, Schenectadiae. 97775
Catalogus senatus academici, et eorum qui munera et officia academia gesserunt, quique aliquovis gradu exornati guerunt in Collegio Yalensi. 105763-105782
Catalogus senatus academici, et eorum qui munera et officia academica gesserunt, quique aliquovis gradu exornati sunt. 55701
Catalogus senatus academici et eorum qui munera et officia gesserunt, quique alicujus gradus laurea donati sunt in Collegio Bowdoinensi. 7030
Catalogus, senatus academici, et eorum qui muneribus et officisque functi sunt, et eorum qui alicujus gradus laurea sunt donati, in Universitate Rocestriensi. 72368
Catalogus, senatus accademici, et eorum qui munera et officia accademica gesserunt, quique alicujus gradus laurea exornati fuerunt in Collegio Gulielmo, quod est in oppido Gulielmo Reipublicae Massachusettensis, ab anno MDCCXCV ad annum MDCCXCIX. 104417
Catalogus, senatus accademici, et eorum qui munera et officia accademica gesserunt, quique alicujus gradus laurea exornati fuerunt in Collegio Gulielmo, quod est in oppido Gulielmo Republicae Massachusettensis, ab anno M,DCC,XCV ad annum M, DCCC,II. 104418
Catalogus senatus facultatis eorum qui munera et officia gesserunt, quique alicujus gradus laurea donati sunt in facultate medicinae in Universitate Harvardiana. 30738
Catalogus Universitatis Brownensis. 8617
Catalogus Universitatis Dartmuthensis. 18617
Catalogus Universitatis Harvardinae. 30738
Catalogus van boeken, plaatwerken en kaarten. 51282
Catalogvs mapparvm astronomicarvm et geographicarvm. 32686
Catalogvs scriptorvm Florentinorvm omnis generis. (63505)
Cataloni, Buelik. 23512
Catano y Aragon, Luis de Mendoca. see Mendoca Catano y Aragon, Luis de.
Catastrofe de Don A. de Yturbide. 87297
Catastrophe de Don Aug. de Yturbide. 35288
Catastrophe du 8 Fevrier. 29041
Catastrophe of the Presbyterian Church in 1837. (17564)

Catawba Indians. Treaties, etc. 100006
Catawba Navigation Company. petitioners
  61282
Catawba River, and other poems. 37721
Catawba travellers. 86902
Catawissa Railroad Company. 59964, 60027
Catawissa Railroad Company. defendants
  68169
Catawissa, Williamsport and Erie Rail Road.
  11495
Catawissa Williamsport and Erie Rail Road
  Company. . . . Charter and supplements
  thereto. 59965
Catawissa, Williamsport and Erie Railroad
  Company. 11495, 59965
Catawissa, Williamsport and Erie Railroad
  Company. Charter. 59965
Catbrana, Maria P. de. see Cantbrana,
  Maria P. de.
Catchpoles fallen from twenty to one. (39510)
Catcott, Alexander. 11496
Catechetical exposition of the constitution.
  6004
Catechism. 17107, note after 65546, 79195,
  89121
Catechism agreed upon by the elders at the
  desire of the General Court. (45670)
Catechism and confession of faith. 3366
Catechism and sacred hyms in the Chippewa
  or Santeux language. 4406
Catechism, being an appendix to the foundation
  of the Christian religion. 72110
Catechism, confuting popery, &c., for Chris-
  tians in Maryland. 45101
Catechism for children, exhibiting the promi-
  nent doctrines. 50731
Catechism for children in the Dakota language.
  69649
Catechism for children of four or five years
  old. note after 65546
Catechism for free working men. (11498)
Catechism for the Montagnars Indians. 21435
Catechism for the religious instruction of
  persons of color. 81924
Catechism in the Dakota or Sioux language.
  (63994)
Catechism in the Huron language. 7652
Catechism in the Indian language. 34625
Catechism Iroquois. 35105
Catechism of geography. 8196
Catechism of medical jurisprudence, &c. &c.
  104378
Catechism [of the Assembly of Divines.]
  52715
Catechism of the Church. 66130
Catechism of the history and chronology of
  South Carolina. (71650), 87805A
Catechism of the history of America. 62978
Catechism of the history of New Hampshire.
  (23819)
Catechism of the history of Newfoundland.
  75270
Catechism of the history of South Carolina.
  (71650), 87805A
Catechism of the history of the United States.
  (37625)
Catechism of the Protestant Episcopal Church
  in America. (80663)
Catechism of the United States. 11006
Catechism on the constitution and government
  of Christian churches. 71718
Catechism, or confession of faith and rules of
  discipline. (66916)
Catechism or, the grounds and principles of
  Christian religion. 46775

Catechism, recueil de prieres et cantiques a
  l'usage des sauvages. 33539
Catechism setting forth indisputable facts for
  the consideration of honest, thoughtful,
  and conservative men. 11499
Catechism to be taught orally to those who
  cannot read. (11500)
Catechism which, as with supplies from the
  tower of David, arms Christians of all
  ages. 46589
Catechisme Algonquin avec syllabaire et
  cantiques. (11501), (34626)
Catechisme dans la langue des Abenakis. 4541
Catechisme d'economie politique. 77354, 77361
Catechisme de l'histoire du Canada. 5146
Catechisme du Diocese de Quebec. (75503),
  105708
Catechisme en Bresilien. 5065
Catechisme en Iroquois. 35104
Catechisme en langue Creole. 28151
Catechisme ou abrege de la foi Catholique.
  11502
Catechisme politique. 27137
Catechisme recueil de prieres et de cantiques.
  26669
Catechismo. 98716
Catechismo Brasilico da doutrina Christa. 1890
Catechismo da Diocese do Maranhao. (81118)
Catechismo en lengua Mexicano. (40080)
Catechismo pa uso di Catolicanan di Curacao.
  55291
Catechismo para los Karitis, Indios de Brasil.
  44179
Catechsms. 62978
Catechismus-Mingnek D. M. Lutherim aglega
  innusuinnut innungnullo gum okausianik
  illisimangangitout. 42727
Catechismus ten gebruike der Katholyken van
  Curacao. 55291
Catecismo. 74039
Catecismo breve. 11394
Catecismo breve en el idioma Mejicano.
  (48327)
Catecismo breve, en lengua Mexicana. (48328)
Catecismo breve en lengua Otomi. 49411
Catecismo breve que precisamente debe saber
  el Christiano. 98660
Catecismo da doutrina Christao na lingua
  Brasilica. 44179
Catecismo de economica politica. 77355
Catecismo de la doctrina Christiana, en el
  idioma de los Indios Cairnos. 66579
Catecismo de la doctrina Christiana en lengua
  Zaapoteca. (40732)
Catecismo de la doctrina Cristiana en lengua
  Megicana. 74946
Catecismo de la doctrina Cristiana en lengua
  Mexicana. 59518
Catecismo de la doctrina Cristiana en lengua
  Otomi. 60903
Catecismo de la doctrina Cristiana en lengua
  Timuiquana. 58580
Catecismo de la doctrina Cristiana puesto en
  el idioma Totonaco. (20566)
Catecismo de la geografia de Venezuela. 14115
Catecismo de la historia de Venezuela. 3251
Catecismo de la independencia en siete declo-
  raciones. 39210
Catecismo de la lengva Gvarani. 74028, 74038
Catecismo de los Metodistas. 31305
Catecismo de ortologia dedicada a los alumnos.
  73038
Catecismo de republica. 98601
Catecismo elemental de geografia universal.
  71700

Catecismo elemental de la historia de Mexico. 71701

Catecismo en el idioma Mixteco Montanez. (49771), 98716

Catecismo en idioma Mixteco, segun se habla en los curatos de la Mixteca. (49770), 98716

Catecismo en la lengva Espanola. 67161

Catecismo en la lengua Espanola, y Aymara del Pirv. 96267

Catecismo en lengua Aymara. 2520

Catecismo en lengua Mexicana y Castellana. 970

Catecismo geografico, politico e historico de la republica oriental de Uruguay. 39134

Catecismo geografico-politico e historico de la republica oriental del Uruguay. 87199

Catecismo historico. 74520

Catecismo in idioma Mexicano. 26750, 2d note after 98659

Catecismo Mexicano. 71588

Catecismo para usu de los parrocos hecho por el IV. Concilio Provincial Mexicano. 48329

Catecismo politico arreglado a la constitucion de la monarquia Espanola. 48330

Catecismo politico arreglado a la constitution de la republica de Colombia. (28343)

Catecismo politico de la federacion Mexicana. 48331

Catecismo politico e instructivo, para uso de los habitantes del estado libre de Xalisco. 71698

Catecismo republicano para instruccion popular. 62996

Catecismo y declaracion de la doctrina Christiana en lengua Otomi. 106013

Catecismo y doctrina Cristiana en los idiomas Castellano y Qquechau. 26410, (67162)

Catecismo, y doctrinas Christiana en lengua Lulu, y Tonocote. (43315)

Catecismo y exposicion breve de la doctrina Christiana. (71487)

Catecismo y exposicion breve de la doctrina Cristiana. 71489

Categorias de la parte fisico-moral. 29420

Categorical account of the Female Medical College. 26744

Catel, --------. (12481)

Catel, M. 11503

Cater, Philip. 64962

Cates, J. B. 81740

Cates, Thomas. ed. 9500, 11505, 20828, 20837, 20840-20843, note after 93587-93588

Catesby, Mark, 1679?-1749. 11506-11516, 22090, (41354)

Cathalogus personarum et domiciliorum. 76115

Catharine N. Forrest, respondent, against Edwin Forrest, appellant. 25111

Catharine Robinson, the victim of depravity. 72054

Cathcart, Charles Cathcart, 9th Baron, 1721-1776. 57614, 99249

Cathcart, Charles William, 1809-1888. 11517

Cathcart, Giacomo Leandro. tr. 35893

Cathcart, John. 11518, 17794, 2d note after 99245

Cathecismo breve. 26749

Cathecismo Castellano. 27794

Cathecismo en lengua Castellana, y Timuquana. 58581

Cathecismo en lengua Chuchona y Castellana. (72812)

Cathecismo en lengua Mexicana y Espanola. 36798

Cathecismo na lingua Brasileira. 1889

Cathecismo romano, traducido en Castellano, y Mexicano. 60912

Cathecismo y breve exposicion de la doctrina Christiana. 58582

Cathecismo y examen para los que comulgan en lengua Castellana y Timuquana. 58583

Cathecismo y explicacion de la doctrina Christiana. 71490

Cathedra en concurso de opositores. 55246

Cathemerinon. (66411)

Catherine (Ship) in Admiralty 20982

Catherine Parr. 51245

Catherine II. of Russia. 85158

Catherine, the Iroquois saint. 37949

Catherineau, H. 11519

Catherwood, Frederick. 11520, 91298, 91301

Catholic. pseud. Sons of St. Dominick. 87004

Catholic almanac. 11521

Catholic almanac and ordo. 74827

Catholic and protestant nations compared. 73489

Catholic Benevolent Society, Louisville, Ky. (42315)

Catholic chapter in the history of the United States. 2875, 33589

Catholic Church. (19992), 34361, 34832, 34863, 40959, (42113), 47086, 48335, 48471, 57542, (58520), (58529), (58841), 64914-(64915), 74856, 76464, 86398, 96419, 105708 see also Archicofradia de Ciudadanos de la Santa Veracruz. Archi-Congradia de la Minerva de la Santa Ciudad de Roma. Augustinians. Bridgettines. Cofradia de Santiago, Mexico (City) Cofradia del Glorioso Principe de los Apostoles San Pedro, Caracas. Colegio de Espiritu Santo de Mexico. Colegio de S. Illdefonse de Mexico. Colegio Mayor de S. Maria de Todos-Santos de Mexico. Confrades de Sanctissimo Sacramento. Confradia de la Virgen Maria Nuestra Senora. Congregacion de el Oratorio. Congregacion de Nuestra Senora. Mexico. Congregacion de Nuestra Senora de Aranzazu, Mexico (City) Congregacion de Nuestra Senora de Covadonga. Congregacion de San Pedro. Dominicans. Esclavos Confrades de la Esclavitud de la Santissimo Sacramento, Mexico (City) Franciscans. Hospitalieres. Hospitallers of St. John of God. Mercedarians. Nuestra Senora del Rosario del Indios. Orden de las Religiosas de la Limpia, e Immaculada Concepcion de la Virgen Sant. Nra. Senora. Orden de Santiago. Sagrada Religion de la Charidad, de San Hipolyto Martyr. Society for the Propagation of the Faith. Society for the Propagation of the Faith, Louvain. Society for the Propagation of the Faith, Montreal. Tercer Orden de los Siervos de Maria Santisima de los Dolores, Mexico (City) Trent, Council of, 1545-1563. Vizcainas, Colegio de las. and individual dioceses and ecclesiastical provinces.

Catholic Church. defendants 51041

Catholic Church. Bishops. 86398

Catholic Church. Bulls, etc. 9122, 10984, 11576, (13624), 23039, 23425, 29148, 34836, 36785, (36795), 39893, 40959, (41115), 48312, 51064, 57542, (61164), 63165-63166, (64915), 65990, 68844,

(70785), 72915, 73871, 76132, 76275-
76276, 76315, 90296, 90297, 94186
Catholic Church. Canons, decretals, etc.
72537
Catholic Church. Comissario General de las
Sancta Cruzada. 23425, 87157, 93581
see also Altamirano y Castilla, Lope.
Catholic Church. Congregatio de Propaganda
Fide. 23039
Catholic Church. Congregatio de Propaganda
Fide. petitioners. 93813
Catholic Church. Congregatio Sacrorum
Rituum. (58305), (64173), 74783-(74785),
99503
Catholic Church. Councils. (14367) see also,
Trent, Council of, 1545-1563
Catholic Church. Encyclicals, etc. (38617),
39476
Catholic Church. Indulgences, etc. 522,
33397, 34685, 93581, 93590, 94221,
98724, 106254
Catholic Church. Liturgy and ritual. Brevi-
ary. 93450
Catholic Church. Liturgy and ritual. Gradual.
97004
Catholic Church. Liturgy and ritual. Missal.
19378, 21436, 49460, (58050), 58840,
76885, 93450
Catholic Church. Liturgy and ritual. Prayer-
books, devotionals, etc. 6602
Catholic Church. Liturgy and ritual. Proces-
sional. (67036)
Catholic Church. Pope. 14365, 40959,
(42113), 51445, 64914-(64915), 81117,
93811, 96086
Catholic Church. Pope, 1277-1280 (Nicholas
III) 68841 see also Nicholas III, Pope,
1216?-1280.
Catholic Church. Pope, 1305-1314 (Clement
V) 68841 see also Clement V, Pope,
1264-1314.
Catholic Church. Pope, 1334-1342 (Benedict
XII) 62602 see also Benedict XII,
Pope, 1285-1342.
Catholic Church. Pope, 1458-1464 (Pius II) 63164,
77523 see aslo Pius II, Pope, 1405-1464.
Catholic Church. Pope, 1492-1503 (Alexander
VI) 57542, 65990, (79175), 79179, 90296-
90297 see also Alexander VI, Pope,
1431?-1503.
Catholic Church. Pope, 1523-1534 (Clement
VII) 10984, (13624) see also Clement
VII, Pope, 1478-1534.
Catholic Church. Pope, 1559-1565 (Pius IV)
63165 see also Pius IV, Pope, 1499-
1565.
Catholic Church. Pope, 1566-1572 (Pius V)
9111, 63166-63167, 75884, 76885, 94186
see also Pius V, Pope, Saint, 1504-
1572.
Catholic Church. Pope, 1572-1585 (Gregory
XIII), 75884, 93589 see also Gregory
XIII, Pope, 1502-1585.
Catholic Church. Pope, 1585-1590 (Sixtus V)
42066, 48373-(48374), 76223, 76332, note
after 90828 see also Sixtus V, Pope,
1521-1590.
Catholic Church. Pope, 1592-1605 (Clement
VIII) 51205, 76885 see also Clement
VIII, Pope, 1536-1605.
Catholic Church. Pope, 1623-1644 (Urban VIII)
(68842), 68844, 76885, 98108-98109
see also Urban VIII, Pope, 1568-1644.
Catholic Church. Pope, 1644-1655 (Innocent X)
7704, 34790, 56265, 58280, (77142) see
also Innocent X, Pope, 1574-1655.

Catholic Church. Pope, 1655-1667 (Alexander
VII) 56067, 73990 see also Alexander
VII, Pope, 1599-1667.
Catholic Church. Pope, 1667-1669 (Clement
IX) 24227, 73176 see also Clement
IX, Pope, 1600-1669.
Catholic Church. Pope, 1670-1676 (Clement X)
9122, 13625, 68434 see also Clement
X, Pope, 1590-1676.
Catholic Church. Pope, 1676-1689 (Innocent XI)
23039, 62601, (68842), 68845, 72528,
76275, 93582, 96052 see also Innocent
XI, Pope, 1611-1689.
Catholic Church. Pope, 1691-1700 (Innocent
XII) 68849 see also Innocent XII, Pope,
1615-1700.
Catholic Church. Pope, 1700-1721 (Clement
XI) 68845 see also Clement XI, Pope,
1649-1721.
Catholic Church. Pope, 1721-1724 (Innocent
XIII) 68249 see also Innocent XIII,
Pope, 1655-1724.
Catholic Church. Pope, 1724-1730 (Benedict
XIII) 29148 see also Benedict XIII,
Pope, 1649-1730.
Catholic Church. Pope, 1740-1758 (Benedict
XIV) 14365, (41115), (58529), (61164),
(63902), 63904, 63907, note after 68444,
(68842), 76315, 73871, 1st note after
98174, 99324 see also Benedict XIV,
Pope, 1675-1758.
Catholic Church. Pope, 1758-1769 (Clement
XIII) (48448), 58289, 93811 see also
Clement XIII, Pope, 1693-1769.
Catholic Church. Pope, 1769-1774 (Clement
XIV) 9122, 13626-13627, (58288), 68232,
68247 see also Clement XIV, Pope,
1705-1774.
Catholic Church. Pope, 1775-1799 (Pius VI)
11377, 63168 see also Pius VI, Pope,
1717-1799.
Catholic Church. Pope, 1831-1846 (Gregory
XVI) 22587, 28747, (56653) see also
Gregory XVI, Pope, 1765-1846.
Catholic Church. Pope, 1848-1878 (Pius IX)
26721, (38617), 39284, 39476, 41095,
44559, 48410, 63170-63173, (78909),
79289, (81131), 84193-84200, 84203-
84211, 88911 see also Pius IX, Pope,
1792-1878.
Catholic Church. Pope, 1878-1903 (Leo XIII)
84201 see also Leo XIII, Pope, 1810-
1903.
Catholic Church. Pope, 1903-1914 (Pius X)
(77142) see also Pius X, Pope, 1835-
1914.
Catholic Church. S. Congretio Rituum. see
Catholic Church. Congregation Sacrorum
Rituum.
Catholic Church. Treaties, etc. 44559, 63172,
(81131)
Catholic Church. Venerables Padres Guardianes
del S. Monte Sion, Jerusalem. (16667)
Catholic Church (Mozarabic Rite) 42066,
49459
Catholic Church, St. Augustine, Florida. see
St. Augustine, Fla. Catholic Church.
Catholic Church in Argentina. 47616
Catholic Church in Brazil. 44664, 81117
Catholic Church in Canada. Bishops. (74563)
Catholic Church in Chile. Vicario Apostolica.
100608
Catholic Church in colonial days. 79997
Catholic Church in Cuba. 17812
Catholic Church in England and America.
56836

Catholic Church in Latin America. 41987,
57101, (58841), (61114)
Catholic Church in Latin America. petitioners
47635
Catholic Church in Latin America. Arcobispos
y Obispos de las Indias Occidentales.
petitioners 102866
Catholic Church in Mexico. 26577, 26720,
42102, 44276, (44420)-(44421), 48335,
(48374), (48414), 48471, 48479, 48528,
50611, (51321), 52110, 86399, 86401
Catholic Church in Mexico. petitioners 69985
Catholic Church in Mexico. Jueces Hacedores
de las Rentas Decimales. (78923)
Catholic Church in Mexico. Junta Guadalupana.
9579
Catholic Church in Mexico. Provincial Council,
1st, 1555. (42063)
Catholic Church in Mexico. Provincial Council,
2d, 1566. (42063)
Catholic Church in Mexico. Provincial Council,
3d, 1585. (14367), (23592)-(23593), 42064,
42066, 48373-(48374), 48461, 66551, 76332,
79303, 94221
Catholic Church in Mexico. Provincial
Council, 4th, 1771. 48329, 67637
Catholic Church in Mexico. Provisor. (74861)
Catholic Church in Peru. 57101, (61116), 61161
Catholic Church in Peru. Inquisidor Aposto-
lico. (44359), 98809 see also Manozca,
Juan de. and Quito. Real Audiencia.
Visitador.
Catholic Church in South America. see
Catholic Church in Brazil. and Catholic
Church in Latin America.
Catholic Church in Spanish America. see
Catholic Church in Brazil. and Catholic
Church in Latin America.
Catholic Church in the United States. 34863,
36758, 59019, 79289
Catholic Church in the United States. Apos-
tolic Vice Regent. 6838
Catholic Church in the United States. Manual.
72976
Catholic Church in the United States. Plenary
Council, 1st, Baltimore, 1852. 15107,
59020, 72897, 72937
Catholic Church in the United States. Plenary
Council, 2d, Baltimore, 1866. 15106,
72898-(72899), 79289, 88911
Catholic Church in the United States. Plenary
Council, 3d, Baltimore, 1884. 72900,
84198-84200, 84204-84211
Catholic Church in the United States; pages of
its history. 19201, (80023)
Catholic Church in Venezuela. (81131)
Catholic churches of New York City. 79998
Catholic clergyman. pseud. Address to the
Roman Catholics. see Carroll, John,
Abp., 1735-1815.
Catholic Congregational Society, Bristol, R. I.
8054, 57761, 1st note after 91736
Catholic controversy. 92681
Catholic controversy, maintained in the periodi-
cal publications. 95254
Catholic directory, almanac, and ordo, for
. . . 1867. 74828
Catholic directory, almanac, and ordo for the
year of Our Lord 1876. 79999
Catholic gentleman. pseud. proposed new
plan. 66047
Catholic Historical Society. see United States
Catholic Historical Society.
Catholic history of North America. 43261

Catholic Institute, Dubuque, Iowa. see Dubuque
Catholic Institute.
Catholic laity's directory for 1817. 11521
Catholic Lay Citizens of Philadelphia. 61421
Catholic layman. pseud. Address by a
catholic layman to the Roman Catholics.
(62214)
Catholic layman. pseud. Desultory examina-
tion. see Carey, Mathew, 1760-1839.
Catholic layman. pseud. Rejoinder to the
reply. see Carey, Mathew, 1760-1839.
Catholic layman. pseud. Religious liberty in
danger. 69351
Catholic layman. pseud. Review of three
pamphlets. see Carey, Mathew, 1760-
1839.
Catholic layman's rejoinder. 10889
Catholic liturgy; or forms of prayer. 11522
Catholic mirror. 51171
Catholic mirror's account of the fifty-year
jubilee. 51171
Catholic mission of the Protestant Episcopal
Church. 58734
Catholic missions among the Indian tribes of
the United States. 80010
Catholic principles of civil government.
(37592)
Catholic question at Boston. 6512, (77230)
Catholic question in America. 75949, 2d note
after 96930A, 98520
Catholick question in politics. 37498, 65065
Catholic religion in Canada. 94022
Catholic saved from popery. 89601
Catholic Society of South Carolina. Charter.
87627
Catholic Summer School Extension, Philadelphia.
see Philadelphia. Catholic Summer
School Extension.
Catholic Summer School Extension lectures.
Number 3. 84516
Catholic tracts. No. 11. 95245
Catholic universe. 84195
Catholic view of the public school question.
65379
Catholic work of the Protestant Episcopal
Church in America. 11523
Catholic world. 11524
Catholica, e o Methodista. 76320
Catholicism compatible with republican govern-
ment. By Fenelon [pseud.] (24055)
Catholicism compatible with republican govern-
ment. Lecture by Rev. Joseph F. Berg.
(4835)
Catholicism; or, Christian charity. 73556
Catholicisme dans l'Amerique septentrionale.
79191
Catholick Church of the Holy Cross, in Boston,
is, at present, indebted. 96009
Catholics and the public schools. 78519
Catholics vindicated. 98924
Catholicus. pseud. Few thoughts on the duties.
24244
Catholicus. pseud. Letter to a clergyman.
15818, 40379
Catholicus, Urbanus. pseud. see Urbanus
Catholicus. pseud.
Catholique. pseud. Observations. see
Maguire, Thomas.
Catholisches Christenthum durch die gantze
Welt auszgebreitet. 31114
Catiline, Lucius. pseud. see Lucius Catiline.
pseud.
Catineau-de-la-Roche. see Catineau-Laroche,
Pierre Marie Sebastien, 1772-1828.
Catineau-Laroche, Pierre Marie Sebastien,
1772-1828. 3303, (11525)-11526, (39049)

Catlett, G. C. ed. (75298)
Catlett, H. G. 11527
Catlin, George, 1796-1872. (11528)-11543,
57375, 93143, 96712
Catlin, George Smith, 1808-1851. 11544
Catlin, Jacob. 11545
Catlin, Seth. 12630
Catlin's Indian collection. (11534)
Catlin's Indian gallery of portraits. 11531
Catlin's North American Indian portfolio. (11532)
Catlin's notes of eight years' travels. 11533
Cato. pseud. note after 63244
Cato. pseud. Defence of the national admin-
istration. see Webster, Ezekiel.
Cato. pseud. Examination of the treaty of
amity. see Hamilton, Alexander, 1755-
1804. supposed author and Higginson,
Stephen. supposed author
Cato. pseud. Extract from the second letter.
see Smith, William, 1727-1803.
Cato. pseud. Letters. see Smith, William,
1727-1803.
Cato. pseud. Thoughts on a question of
importance proposed to the public.
95670
Cato. pseud. To the people of the state of
New-York. see Tibbits, George. sup-
posed author
Cato Batavius, de Jonge. pseud. Manifest
van George III. 44266
Cato major; or, a discourse on old age.
13043
Cato major; or, a treatise on old age. 13041
Cato major, or discourse on old age. 13042
Cato major, or his discourse on old-age.
13040
Cato to the people of the state of New-York.
11547, 95781
Catolicismo i la republica. 75910
Catolicismo y la democracia. (23065)
Catolico Ecuatoriano. pseud. Socio de plebe
pauperum. see Bravo, Jose. supposed
author
Catolico. Periodico religioso. 11549
Caton, John Dean, 1812-1895. 5821
Caton, William. 9416, 59660
Catonis disticha moralia. 11548, 13040,
91846
Catorce preguntas del Payo del Rosario.
99696
Cato's letter. 84642
Cato's moral distichs. 11548, 13040
Cato's moral distichs, and Lily's paedagogical
admonitions. 91846
Catrou, P. 32025
Catskill, N. Y. Association. see Catskill
Association.
Catskill almanack. (23850)
Catskill Association. 11551
Catskill Association, formed for the purpose
of improving the town of Catskill, in the
county of Greene. 11551
Catskill mountains and the region around.
72417
Cattaneo, Cagetan. see Cattaneo, Gaetano,
1696-1733.
Cattaneo, Gaetano, 1696-1733. 11554, 51418,
(51423)
Cattanio, Gaetano. see Cattaneo, Gaetano,
1696-1733.
Cattaraugus, N. Y. Indian Council, 1843. see
New York (State) Indian Council, Cat-
taraugus, 1843.
Cattaraugus, N. Y. Indian Council, 1845. see
New York (State) Indian Council, Cat-
taraugus, 1845.

Cattaraugus Baptist Association. see Baptists.
New York. Cattaraugus Baptist Associa-
tion.
Cattaraugus County Agricultural and Horti-
cultural Society. 44302, 46936
Cattaraugus County, N. Y., embracing its
agricultural society, newspapers, civil
list. 44302, 46936
Cattell, Alexander Gilmore, 1816-1894. 11556
Cattemare, Alexander. 53616
Cattermole, William. 11558
Cattle disease in Massachusetts. 5300
Cattle Show and Fair of the Agricultural Society
of Jefferson County, N. Y. see Jefferson
County Agricultural Society. Cattle
Show and Fair. 1st, 1818.
Catto, William C. 11558
Caucaeid. 105521
Cauche, --------, Sieur. 91538
Cauchon, Joseph, 1816-1885. 11559-(11561),
33551 see also Canada. Commissioner
of Crown Lands.
Caucus speech. 22533
Caucuses of 1860. 29924
Caufield, James. ed. 21755
Caughey, James, 1810?-1891. 11562-11564
Caughey, John. 101405
Caughnawaga Bridge Company. Directors.
11565
Caughnawaga Indians. (15440)
Caul, John J. defendant 96821
Caul, Mary. defendant 96821
Caulfield, James. 11569, 21755, 41587
Caulin, Antonio. 11570
Caulkins, Frances Manwaring. 11571-(11574)
Caulkins, Nehemiah. 11575, 102547
Caunter, J. Hobart. ed. (65265)
Causa celebre sobre los asesinos de Don
Florencio Egerton. (22043)
Causa celebre del Hospital Militar de S. Am-
brosio de la Ciudad de la Habana. 44681
Causa criminal en Barancayaco, Territorio de
Cordoba. 16768
Causa criminal instruida al Exmo, Sr. Presi-
dente Constitucional. 98969
Causa criminal segui contra los autores y
complices. (67348)
Causa criminal seguida contra el Coronel
Graduado Apolinar Morillo. (50702)
Causa criminal seguida contra el Ex-Gover-
nador Juan Manuel de Rosas. 73209
Causa de Fernanda Meximiliano de Hapsburgo
y sus generales. 47035
Causa de responsabilidad. (51075)
Causa de Roque Miranda. 49418
Causa formada al Ex-Coronel Juan Yanez y
socios. 105953
Causa Jesuitica de Portugal. 11576
Causa medico criminal. 39063
Causa seguida al D.D.J.C. Argomedo &c. 85677
Causa sobre falsificacion de sellos de franqueo.
(29457)
Causae matrimoniales. 84212
Causas para declarar la guerra a los Estados-
Unidos del Norte. 11577, 48332
Causas que se han seguido y terminado contra
los comprendido en la conspiracion
llamada del Padre Arenas. (1932)
Causas y consecuencias de la guerra de
Mejico. 63746
Causas y efectos de la ultima revolucion de
Megico. (48333)
Cause and circumstances of Mr. Bidwell's
banishment. 5258
Cause and consequences. (37437)
Cause and contrast. 43563

CAUSE

Cause and cure of our national troubles.
36884
Cause and cure of present evils. 45377, note
after 95746
Cause and cure of secession. (49035)
Cause and cure of the rebellion. 81167
Cause and cure of the the [sic] rebellion.
83476
Cause and effect. 81714-81715
Cause and effects of emigration from the
highlands. 35108
Cause and probable results of the civil war
in America. 94548
Cause and progress of the present war.
37142
Cause and the consequence of the election of
Abraham Lincoln. 30879
Cause and the cure of present evils. 72718
Cause celebre coloniale. 5652
Cause de la guerre actuelle 1861-1862. 4084
Cause des esclaves negres et habitans de la
Guinee. 26013
Cause of, and cure for hard times. 11578
Cause of education in Tennessee. 41315
Cause of Freedom. (33603)
Cause of God and his people in New England.
31743,(49658)
Cause of man. 9235
Cause of temperance as connected with home
evangelization. 44745
Cause of temperance the cause of liberty.
102591
Cause of the hard times. 91626
Cause of the heavy burdens of Great Britain.
839
Cause of the present distressed situation.
44703
Cause of the war. Proclamation. 64455
Cause of the war; who brought it on, and for
what purpose? (1388)
Cause of Zion defended. 24444
Cause perdue. 63874
Cause, the crime, and the cure of our national
suicide. 91110
Causeless ground of surmises. (37182)
Causes and consequences of slavery extention.
9099
Causes and consequences of the civil war in
America. 26159
Causes and consequences of the independence
of the south. 1689
Causes and consequences of the late emigra-
tion to the Brazils. 34780, 41329
Causes and danger of delusions in the affairs
of religion. 79193
Causes and effects of war. (22419)
Causes and origin of slavery in the United
States. 11580
Causes and palliatives. 73593
Causes and prevention of idiocy. (33333)
Causes and remedies of national divisions.
101000
Causes and remedies of the present convul-
sions. (42029)
Causes celebres du droit de gens. 44831
Causes et caractere de la derniere guerre
d'Amerique. 43715
Causes et caracteres de la guerre civile aux
Etats-Unis. 39237
Causes, evils, and the remedy, of intemperance.
66839
Causes for national humiliation. 90438
Causes for thanksgiving in the midst of civil
war. 48031
Causes of an unsuccessful ministry. 89744
Causes of declension. 74657

Causes of hostilities of Seminole Indians.
(79065)
Causes of infidelity removed. 84280
Causes of national solicitude. 9203
Causes of our late discontents. 11581
Causes of Scotland's miseries. 78204
Causes of sickness in dwellings. 85494
Causes of steamboat explosions. 82759
Causes of the alienation of the Delaware and
Shawanese Indians. 95562
Causes of the civil war in America. 51103,
69420
Causes of the civil war in the United States.
13869
Causes of the decline of doctrinal preaching.
16338
Causes of the destruction of the American
towns. 43071
Causes of the distress of the British West
India colonies. 11582
Causes of the growth and decline of Amherst
College. 1321
Causes of the Kensington riots explained.
60790
Causes of the present crisis. 11582
Causes of the present distractions in American
explained. 4920
Causes of the progress of liberal Christianity
in New England. 11584, 101053
Causes of the prosperity of new colonies.
82303
Causes of the prosperity of New-York. 5098
Causes of the reduction of American tonnage.
42815
Causes of the war. 11579
Causes, principles and results of the present
conflict. 42140
Causes qui se sont opposees aux progres du
commerce. 94005
Causey, Peter Foster, 1801-1871. 33150 see
also Delaware. Governor, 1855-1859
(Causey)
Causin, John M. S., 1811-1861. 70728
Causten, James H. 11585, 70277
Causten, James H. supposed author 81514,
99552
Caustic, Mrs. pseud. Matrimony. see
Bullard, Anne Tuttle Jones.
Caustic, Christopher. pseud. Caustic's wooden
booksellers. see Fessenden, Thomas
Green, 1771-1837.
Caustic, Christopher. pseud. Democracy
unveiled. see Fessenden, Thomas Green,
1771-1837.
Caustic, Christopher. pseud. Modern philoso-
pher. see Fessenden, Thomas Green,
1771-1837.
Caustick, Pindarick, Hudabrastick poem.
99554
Caustic's wooden booksellers and miseries of
authorship. 24219
Cautelas espirituales. 38511
Caution. 1692, 63577
"Caution." 84246
Caution against our common enemy. 104212
Caution against sedition. 93954
Caution and warning to Great-Britain and her
colonies. (4670), 101276
Caution from New-Englands apostle. 78434
Caution; or reflections on the present contest.
11586
Caution to banks, merchants, &c. 73596
Caution to emigrants. 105612
Caution to erring Christians. 92096
Caution to prevent scandal. 8692, 80910
Caution to sinners. (24927)

464

Caution to the public. 104159
Cautionary hints to Congress. 11587, 105034
Cautionnements donnes par les surintendants d'education. (10453)
Cautions against spirtuall drunkenness. 90261
Cautions to Americans. 4303
Cautions to erring Christians. 30081
Cautions to new settlers. 28291
Cautions to seamen and other voyagers. 57770
Cautions to young persons. 102056
Cautiverio feliz. 12754
Cauwet, Alfred. 11588-11589
Cauxois, Robert Regnault. tr. 125
Cavacio, Alfonso. 11590
Cavada, F. F. 11591
Cavagnal, Pierre Francois de Rigaud. see Vaudreuil de Cavagnal, Pierre Francois de Rigaud, Marquis de.
Cavaliers of Virginia, or the recluse of Jamestown. (11172), 100443, 100482
Cauallero hombre docto, y graduado en derechos. 98764
Cavallier, ------. 96037
Cavalry discipline. 33403
Cavalry discipline. A treatise on the military art. 33403
Cavalry exercises. 33403
Cavalry: its history, management, and uses in war. 72596
Cavalry scout. 36861
Cavanilles, Josef Antonio. 74004
Cavazzi, Giovanni Antonio. 11592
Cave, Jane. 11593
Cave, Sir Stephen, 1820-1880. 58470
Cave of Morar. 63647
Cave of vice. 97548
Cave secret. 77775
Caveat against covetousness. 79406
Caveat against emigration to America. 84697
Caveat against injustice. 80404
Caveat against the new sect of Anabaptists. 68140
Caveat against unreasonable and unscriptural separations. 11594
Caveat on the part of public credit. 11595
Caveat; or considerations against the admission of Missouri. 11596
Cavelier, Jean, 1636-1722. 11597, (80003)
Cavelier, Z. 11598
Cavellero, Maria de Sandoval y. see Sandoval y Cavellero, Maria de.
Cavender, C. H. 11599
Cavendish, Harry. 11600
Cavendish, Sir Henry, Bart. (11601)-11602, 2d note after 105598-9 [sic]
Cavendish, Thomas, 1555?-1592. (8784), 11603-(11608), 14349, 14957, 20829, 31389, 31506, 33660, (54897), note after 65395, 66686, 105624
Caverly, A. M. 11609
Caverly, Robert B. 11610-(11611)
Cavern of Covadonga. 81245
Caverns of Luray. 85009
Cavero y Salazar, Jose. 11612
Caviedes, Juan del Valle y. see Valle y Caviedes, Juan del.
Cavil of Judas. 18269
Cavo, Andres. 11613-11614
Cavo, D. A. 9574
Cawdrey, Daniel. 11615-11616, 17091, 92113, note after 99832
Cawthorne, J. 63291
Caxica, Jacinto de. see Jacinto de Caxica. Fray

"Caxton." pseud. Political letters. 63782
Caxton Club, Chicago. 96172
Cayadutta Division, no. 504, Sons of Temperance. see Sons of Temperance of North America. New York. Cayadutta Division, no. 504.
Cayenme (Colony) Laws, statutes, etc. 11626, note after 98779
Cayet, Pierre Victor. 11627
Cayetano, Hermano Jose San. see San Cayetano, Hermano Jose.
Cayetano de la Torre, Gonzalo. see Torre, Gonzalo Cayetano de la.
Cayetano Portugal, Juan. see Portugal, Juan Cayetano, Abp., 1783-1850.
Cayla, J. M. tr. 92528
Cayley, Arthur, d. 1848. 11630, 67550, 67599
Cayley, C. 11631
Cayley, W. 11632
Caylus, Ernest. 11633
Cayouge Indians. see Cayuga Indians.
Cayuga County, N. Y. Anti-masonic Convention, 1830. see Anti-masonic Party. New York. Cayuga County. Convention, 1830.
Cayuga County, N. Y. Board of Supervisors. 11639
Cayuga County, N. Y. Convention of Delegates, 1819. see Democratic Party. New York. Cayuga County. Convention, Auburn, 1819.
Cayuga County, N. Y. Washington Benevolent Society. see Washington Benevolent Society. New York. Cayuga County.
Cayuga Baptist Association. see Baptists. New York. Cayuga Baptist Association.
Cayuga County Teachers' Institute. (11635)
Cayuga Indians. 49348-49349, 66061 see also Five Nations of Indians.
Cayuga Indians. Treaties, etc. 36337, 60255
Cayuga Lake Academy. 11634
Cayuga Lake, Cayuga bridge, and Taghcanic Falls on the Cayuga. 11636
Cazal, Manoel Ayres de. see Ayres de Casal, Manuel, b. 1754?
Cazauran, A. R. ed. (43241)
Caze, -------- de. see Decaze,——.
Caze, J. F. A. 11642
Cazeau, Fr. 11643
Cazenau, Mrs. William Leslie. supposed author (50135), note after 95118
Cazenove, Leonce de. 11644
Cazenovia, N. Y. Oneida and Genesee Conference Seminary. see Oneida Conference Seminary, Cazenovia, N. Y.
Cazenovia, N. Y. Oneida Conference Seminary. see Oneida Conference Seminary, Cazenovia, N. Y.
Cazique, Indio. defendant. 44289, 79862
Cazo y Estrada, Francisco de Mier, see Mier Cazo y Estrada, Francisco de.
Cazotte, -----------. plaintiff 94390-94391
Ce qui va arriver au Mexique. 64731
Cea, Genaro Rus de. see Rus de Cea, Genaro.
Ceara (Brazilian Province) Eleitos. 88779 see also Souza Martins, Francisco de.
Ceara (Brazilian Province) Escolas Primarias. 88746
Ceara (Brazilian Province) Inspector Geral da Instruccao Publica. 88746 see also Souza Brazil, Thomaz Pompeo de, 1852-
Ceballos, Pedro Ordonez de. see Ordonez de Ceballos, Pedro, d. 1550?
Cebret, ------. 75014

Cecil. pseud. Kansas and the constitution.
see Fisher, Charles Edward.
Cecil, E. 11645-11647
Cecil, Richard. 81579
Cecil, Sir Robert. see Salisbury, Robert
Cecil, 1st Earl of, d. 1612.
Cecil, Thomas. engr. 82851
Cecil, William. see Burghley, William
Cecil, Lord, 1520-1598.
Cecilia Valdes o la loma de angel. 99691
Cecill, T. engr. 76456-76457
Cedar Street Presbyterian Church, New York.
see New York (City) Cedar Street
Presbyterian Church.
Cedula concerniente al teatro de Mexico.
48334
Cedula de el Rey dando gracias a los padres
de la Cia de Jesus. (16665)
Cedula de propiedad y reglamentos adminis-
trativos. (66585)
Cedvla de Sv Magestad. 24067
Cedula de Su Magestad, expedida para que en
la ciudad de San Christoval de la Habana.
16668, 29422
Cedula de Virey de la Nueva-Espana. 29104
Cedula real sobre lo que por punto general se
ha de observar. 61084
Cedula sobre el remate del asiento de la Real
Fabrica y Estampa de Naypes. 56246
Cedula y comission real del Rey. 96475
Cedulario. 66605
Ceely, Christofer. (18236), 20830, (20838)-
20340, 20343, 20855-20856
Cefil. pseud. ed. 89469
Cejudo, Jose. 11648
Celeberrimorum praeliorum. 95777
Celebrated author of Mc.Fingal. pseud.
Progress of dulness. see Trumbull,
John, 1750-1831.
Celebrated commoner. pseud. Celebrated
speech. see Pitt, William, 1st Earl
of Chatham, 1708-1778.
Celebrated jumping frog of Calaveras County.
13623
Celebrated lecture on heads. 91499-91500
Celebrated lecture on heads which has been
exhibited. 91498
Celebrated letter of Joseph Hume. 33779
Celebrated letters of Mr. Jefferson to Benjamin
Austin. 41427
Celebrated letters of Philo-Cato. 62545
Celebrated letters of Phocion. 29948, 84818
Celebrated "moon story." 28839
Celebrated pamphlet on the stamp act. (15202)
Celebrated papers found in Andre's boots.
(1744)
Celebrated poem entitled The art of painting.
105184
Celebrated public writer. pseud. War with
America. (17529), 101267
Celebrated speech of a celebrated commoner.
(63066)
Celebrated speech of the Right Hon. C. Fox.
25337
Celebrated trials of all countries. 11649-11650,
82987
Celebrated women. 27913
Celebration a Nauvoo du septieme anniversaire
du depart. 9778
Celebration at Flushing, of the birth-day of
Linnaeus. 24920
Celebration at North Coventry, March 10, 1859.
55705
Celebration at . . . Salem, July 4, 1862.
42081

Celebration by the Colored People's Educational
Monument Association in Memory of
Abraham Lincoln. 11651
Celebration du 200e anniversaire de la fonda-
tion du Seminaire de Quebec. 67060
Celebration exercises at the one hundred and
fiftieth anniversary of the settled part of
Old Nutfield. 41864
Celebration in Baltimore of the triumph of
liberty in France. 104872
Celebration in Green's Farms. 69367
Celebration in honor of Italian unity. 89554
Celebration in Providence, R. I., of the two
hundred and fiftieth anniversary of congre-
gationalism in this country. 62845
Celebration of Cayuga Lake Academy, July 22d,
1857. 11634
Celebration of Huck's Defeat, Brattonsville,
S. C., 1839. see Brattonsville, S. C.
Celebration of Huck's Defeat, 1839.
Celebration of Jefferson's birth day in Wash-
ington. 35922
Celebration of the Anniversary of the Battle of
Plattsburgh, 1843. see Plattsburgh,
N. Y. Celebration of the Anniversary of
the Battle of Plattsburgh, 1843.
Celebration of the Anniversary of the Glorious
Battle of New-Orleans, by the Personal
and Political Friends of George Mifflin
Dallas, Philadelphia, 1846. (38088)
Celebration of the Anniversary of the National
Independence, New Orleans, 1864. see
New Orleans. Celebration of the Anni-
versary of the National Independence,
1864.
Celebration of the battle of King's Mountain,
October, 1855. 11652
Celebration of the birth day of Linnaeus.
54148
Celebration of the birth-day of Thomas Jeffer-
son, at Salem, Mass. 42082
Celebration of the centenary anniversary of the
settlement of the city of Halifax. (51433)
Celebration of the centennial anniversary of the
birth of George Washington. 54149
Celebration of the centennial anniversary of the
birth of George Washington. New-York,
February 22, 1832. 40838, 101785
Celebration of the centennial anniversary of the
birth of Robert Burns. 9407
Celebration of the Centennial Anniversary of the
Birth of Washington, New York, 1832.
see New York (City) Celebration of the
Centennial Anniversary of the Birth of
Washington, 1832.
Celebration of the centennial anniversary of the
introduction of the art of printing into
New Hampshire. 11653, 52871
Celebration of the Colored People's Education
Monument Association in Memory of
Abraham Lincoln, on the fourth of July,
1865. 41178
Celebration of the 85th anniversary of the
birthday of Thomas Paine, Tammany Hall,
New York. 94296
Celebration of the eighty-sixth anniversary of
the independence of the United States, in
Chicago, July 4th, 1862, 12617
Celebration of the Eighty-Third Anniversary of
American Independence, Boston, 1859.
see Boston. Celebration of the Eighty-
Third Anniversary of American Indepen-
dence, 1859.
Celebration of the 55th anniversary of American
independence, by the Union and State
Rights Party, July 4, 18321. 97752

Celebration of the First Settlement of Ohio, 47th, Cincinnati, 1835. see Cincinnati. Celebration of the First Settlement of Ohio, 47th, 1835.

Celebration of the 45th anniversary of the battle at Put-in-Bay Island. 3967

Celebration of the Forty-Fifth Anniversary of the First Settlement of Cincinnati, 1833. see Cincinnati. Celebration of the Forty-Fifth Anniversary of the First Settlement of Cincinnati and the Miami Country, by Natives of Ohio, 1833.

Celebration of the forty-fifth anniversary of the first settlement of Cincinnati and the Miami Country. 13074, 104448

Celebration of the forty-seventh anniversary of the first settlement of . . Ohio. (56890)

Celebration of the fourth of July at Buffalo, 1865. 9063

Celebration of the fourth of March. 55187

Celebration of the French Revolution, New York, 1830. 51059

Celebration of the golden wedding of Dr. and Mrs. Lowell Smith. 83494

Celebration of the Humboldt Centennial and opening of the Iowa Institute of Science and Arts. 34991

Celebration of the hundredth anniversary [of the American Philosophical Society.] (1175)

Celebration of the hundredth anniversary of the birth of Robert Burns. 9407

Celebration of the hundredth anniversary of the incorporation of Conway, Massachusetts. 16224

Celebration . . . of the independence of the United States, by the American citizens . . . in Melbourne, Australia. 47419

Celebration of the introduction of the water of Cochituate Lake. 6785

Celebration of the Landing of the Pilgrims, St. Louis, 1845. see St. Louis. Anniversary Celebration of the Landing of the Pilgrims, 1845.

Celebration of the Ninetieth Anniversary of American Independence, Geneva, Switzerland, 1866. see Geneva, Switzerland. Celebration of the Ninetieth Anniversary of American Independence, 1866.

Celebration of the ninetieth anniversary of the organization. 60364

Celebration of the one hundred and fiftieth anniversary of the primitive organization of the Congregational Church and Society. 25650

Celebration of the One Hundred and Fiftieth Anniversary of the Settled Part of Old Nitfueld, N. H., 1869. 41864, 43347

Celebration of the one hundredth anniversary of the founding of Brown University. 8618

Celebration of the One Hundredth Anniversary of the Incorporation of the Town of Pawtucket, 1865. see Pawtucket, R. I. Celebration of the One Hundredth Anniversary of the Incorporation of the Town, 1865.

Celebration of the one hundredth anniversary of the incorporation of the town of Princeton, Mass. 65648

Celebration of the one hundredth anniversary of the incorporation of Westminster, Mass. 103035

Celebration of the one hundredth anniversary of the initiation of George Washington, into the order of free masonry. 89049

Celebration of the One Hundredth Anniversary of the Ordination of the Rev. Joseph Lathrop, D. D., West Springfield, Mass., 1856. see West Springfield, Mass. Celebration of the One Hundredth Anniversary of the Ordination of the Rev. Joseph Lathrop, D. D., 1856.

Celebration of the 119th anniversary of the birth-day of Thomas Paine. 58251

Celebration of the quarter-century anniversary [of the Young Men's Association of Buffalo.] 9063

Celebration of the semi-centennial anniversary [of Albany Academy.] 588

Celebration of the semi-centennial anniversary of the I. O. of O. F. 56688

Celebration of the Settlement at Jamestown, Va., 1607, New York, 1860. see Old Dominion Society, New York. Celebration of the Anniversary of the Settlement at Jamestown, Va., 1607, 1st, 1860.

Celebration of the seventy-fifth anniversary, May 1, 1861 [of the Chatham Artillery of Savannah, Ga.] 36475

Celebration of the seventy-fourth anniversary of the signing of the constitution of the United States. (61527)

Celebration of the Triumph of Liberty in France, Baltimore, 1830. see Baltimore. Celebration of the Triumph of Liberty in France, 1830.

Celebration of the twenty-fifth anniversary of . . . [Marietta] College. (44569)

Celebration of the Two Hundred and Fiftieth Anniversary of Congregationalism in This Country, Providence, R. I., 1870. see Providence, R. I. Celebration of the Two Hundred and Fiftieth Anniversary of Congregationalism in This Country, 1870.

Celebration of the two hundred and fiftieth anniversary of the English settlement of Jamestown, Va., May 18, 1857. 35737

Celebration of the Two Hundred and Fiftieth Anniversary of the Landing of the Pilgrims, Plymouth, Mass., 1870. see Pilgrim Society, Plymouth, Mass. Celebration of the Two Hundred and Fiftieth Anniversary of the Landing of the Pilgrims, Plymouth, 1870.

Celebration of the Two Hundred and Seventy-Ninth Anniversary of the Settlement of Dorchester, Mass., 1909. see Dorchester, Mass. Celebration of the Two Hundred and Seventy-Ninth Anniversary of the Settlement of Dorchester, 1909.

Celebration of the two hundredth anniversary of the incorporation of Billerica, Massachusetts. 5403

Celebration of the two-hundredth anniversary of the incorporation of Bridgewater, Massachusetts. 7827

Celebration of the two-hundredth anniversary of the incorporation of Middelborough, Massachusetts. 48225

Celebration of the two hundredth anniversary of the incorporation of the town of Dartmouth. 18609

Celebration of the Two Hundredth Anniversary of the Incorporation of the Town of Marlborough, Mass., 1857. see Marlborough, Mass. Celebration of the Two Hundredth Anniversary of the Incorporation of the Town, 1857.

Celebration of the two hundredth anniversary of the settlement of Hadley, Massachusetts. 29492

Celebration of the Two Hundredth Anniversary
of the Settlement of the Town of Nor-
wich, Conn., 1859. see Norwich, Conn.
Celebration of the Two Hundredth Anni-
versary of the Settlement of the Town,
1859.
Celebration of Washington's birth day at
Hoosick Falls, 1862. 32891
Celebration of Washington's birth-day, 22d of
February, 1851. 54149
Celebrations, . . . of the anniversary of the
battle of Bunker Hill, in 1850 and 1857.
(9174)
Celebre proces de Jean Baptiste Corriveau.
16911
Celebridad y fiestas con que la insigne y
nobilissima Ciudad de los Reyes. 40070
Celer Sealy. pseud. see Sealy, Celer.
pseud.
Celestial magnet. 81669
Celestial wonders and philosophy. 67447
Celiar, leyenda Americana. 11654
Celibacy from the Shaker stand-point. (23152)
Celibato clerical e religioso. 76321
Celio; or, New York above-ground and under-
ground. 25222
Celis, Juan N. defendant at court martial
67340
Cellarius, Christoph, 1638-1707. (2308),
(11655), 51478, 52759, 79124
Cellarius, Franz. 11656
Cellem, Robert. 11657
Celliez, Adelaide de. (11658)-11660
Celsius, Anders, 1701-1744. 46946
Celsius, Olaf, 1670-1756. 91723, 100960
Celtic Society of Upper Canada. see Upper
Canada Celtic Society.
Cementerio General, Havana. see Havana.
Cementerio General.
Cemetery, Philadelphia. see Philadelphia.
Philadelphia Cemetery.
Cemetery Association, Harrisburg, Pa. see
Harrisburg Cemetery Association.
Cemetery of Spring Grove: its by-laws.
89823
Cemetery of Spring Grove: its charter, rules,
and regulations. 89824
Cemetery of the cypress hills. 18217
Cemetery of the Evergreens, New York (City)
see New York (City) Cemetery of the
Evergreens.
Cenchar, A. supposed author 91841A
Cennelles. Choix des poesies indigenes.
38947
Cenni storici sugli Stati Uniti d'America.
13039
Cennick, ------. 72311
Cenotaph; or brief memoirs of eminent
Americans. 42135
Censo de poblacion de la republica de
Colombia. 14560
Censo de poblacion en la republica Argentina.
26109
Censo general de la republica de Chile.
(12748)
Censor. pseud. Appeal to the state. 87792,
87936
Censor. pseud. Appeal to the state continued.
87792, 87936
Censor (Boston) (11661)
Censor (Buenos Aires) 99791
Censor (Schenectady) 97799
Censura. 55255
Censvra del R. P. Fr. Pedro de Arqueta.
76007

Censura del R. P. Francisco Diaz. 76007
Censura eclesiastica de la obra titulada:
Misterios de la inquisicion. 93348
Censura particular &c. 99787
Censura y reforma del codigo de instruccion
publica. 7795
Censure de la Faculte de Theologie de Paris.
(68075)
Censure of that learned and reverend man of
God, Mr. John Cotton. 17051
Censure of the President. 20817
Censure on . . . ungodliness. (46350)
Censure, scandal . . . and things in general.
5347
Census and slavery. 9543
Census and statistical returns of Lower Canada.
10400
Census and statistics. 48724
Census directory for 1811. 60606
Census . . . for 1855 [of New York.] 53577
Census . . . for 1859 [of Iowa.] 34976
Census . . . for 1845 [of New York.] 53577
Census . . . for 1875 [of New York.] 53577
Census . . . for 1865 [of New York.] 53577
[Census] for 1869 [of the state of Iowa.]
34976
[Census] for 1867 [of the state of Iowa.]
34976
Census . . . for 1835 [of New York.] 53577
Census for 1820, being the fourth census.
11664
Census of Canada. 10400
Census of Charleston, S. C., 1848. (18947)
Census of . . . Massachusetts, taken . . . 1855.
(45545)
Census of New Hampshire. (52806)
Census of pensioners for revolutionary or
military services. 11668
Census of . . . Providence, May 1, 1874.
66245
Census of the Canadas. 10401
Census of the city of Charleston. 12034
Census of the city of Providence. 66245
Census of the city of Savannah, together with
statistics relating to the trade, commerce,
mechanic arts and health of the same.
77256
Census of the city of Savannah . . . with
statistics . . . historical notices, and a
commercial directory. 3144
Census of the District of Columbia. 33154
Census of the eastern and western districts
of Pennsylvania. (59966)
Census of the electors and other inhabitants
of the state of New-York. (53576)
Census of the electors, and total population of
the city and county of New York. 54150
Census of the inhabitants of the colony of
Rhode Island. 3737
Census of the new buildings. 30318
Census of the population, and other statistical
returns of Prince Edward Island. 65626
Census of the population and statistical returns
taken in . . . 1841 [of Prince Edward
Island.] 65626
Census of the state of New York, 1821. 512
Census of the state of New York for 1855.
33137
Census of the state of New York, for 1800.
(53576)
Census of the United States. (11663)
Census of the United States and territories,
and of British America. 20325
Census of Upper Canada. (10403)
Census printing and presidential candidates.
84872

Census returns of the different counties [of
Iowa.] 34976
Cent-A-Week Society. see Anti-slavery
Cent-A-Week Society.
Centenaire de l'assaut de Quebec par les
Americains. 66997
Centenary College of Louisiana. see Shrieve-
port, La. Centenary College of Louisiana.
Centenary commemoration of the opening of
Tottenham Court Chapel, London. 71072
Centenary discourse, at Christ's Church,
Norwich. 50690
Centenary discourse before the National
Association of Local Preachers of the
M. E. Church. (71891)
Centenary Discourse of the Rev. John
Callendar. 55044
Centenary fete of the Literary and Historical
Society. 80872
Centenary memorial of Paxton. 59271
Centenary memorial of the dedication of John-
Street Church, New York. (54151)
Centenary of American methodism. note after
91480
Centenary of the Baptists in Nova Scotia.
17388
Centenary of Wesleyan Methodism. 35464
Centenary pictoral album. 71892
Centenary reflections on the providential
character of Methodism. 91474
Centenary sermon. 43364
Centenary sermon . . . December 8th, 1850.
31244
Centenary sermon delivered by him [i. e.
George W. Purefoy] at its one hundredth
annual session. (66707)
Centenary sermon preached before the Newark
Conference. 17404
Centenary sermon, preached before the Phila-
delphia Annual Conference. 11433
Centenary sermon, preached in the Vestry St.
Church. 3168
Centenera, Martin del Barco. see Barco
Centenera, Martin del.
Centenera de Villadarias, Manoel Durate
Caldeiras. see Villadarias, Manoel
Durate Caldeiras Centenera de.
Centennial address at Acton. 33109
Centennial address: being a plea. 2566
Centennial address, by David D. Field.
(24267)
Centennial address. By Samuel L. Southard.
88245
Centennial address, delivered at Franklin,
Mass. 5787
Centennial address, delivered at Upton, Mass.
105021
Centennial address delivered at Trenton, N. Y.
79664
Centennial address, delivered before the St.
Andrew's Society of the City of Charleston.
37824
Centennial address: delivered by Hon. James
S. Rollins. 72857
Centennial anniversary at Athol. 13392
Centennial anniversary of the founding of the
Germantown Academy. 27155
Centennial Association of Connecticut. Women's
Branch. 89488
Centennial birthday of Robert Burns. 17965
Centennial Celebration, Conway, Mass., 1867.
see Conway, Mass. Centennial Celebra-
tion, 1867.
Centennial Celebration, Dublin, N. H., 1852.
see Dublin, N. H. Centennial Celebration,
1852.

Centennial Celebration, New Ipswich, N. H.,
1850. see New Ipswich, N. H. Centen-
nial Celebration, 1850.
Centennial Celebration, Springfield, N. J., 1876.
see Springfield, N. J. Centennial Celebra-
tion, 1876.
Centennial celebration. An account of this
celebration. 98050
Centennial celebration at Cherry Valley, Otsego
Co., N. Y. 12480
Centennial celebration, at Danvers, Mass.
18513, 65949
Centennial celebration at Lebanon, N. H.
39573
Centennial celebration at Lenox, Mass. (72442)
Centennial celebration of Litchfield County,
Conn., 1851. see Litchfield County, Conn.
Centennial Celebration, Litchfield, 1851.
Centennial celebration of . . . Orford, N. H.
(57582)
Centennial celebration of Rutgers College.
74437
Centennial celebration of the Chamber of
Commerce of . . . New York. (53582)
Centennial celebration of the Cumberland
Association of Congregational Ministers.
85224
Centennial Celebration of the First Company
Governor's Foot Guard, Hartford, 1871.
see Hartford, Conn. Centennial Celebra-
tion of the First Company Governor's
Foot Guard, 1871.
Centennial Celebration of the Incorporation of
Derryfield, N. H., 1851. see Manchester,
N. H. Centennial Celebration of the
Incorporation of Derryfield, 1851.
Centennial Celebration of the Introduction of
the Art of Printing into New Hampshire,
Portsmouth, N. H., 1856. 11652, 52871
Centennial celebration of the settlement of
Freyburg, Me. 26104, 88268
Centennial celebration of the South-Carolina
Society. 88036, note after 96180
Centennial celebration of the town of North-
borough, Mass. (55778)
Centennial celebration of the town of Sheffield.
80102
Centennial celebration [of the United States],
Lenox, Mass., 1876. see Lenox, Mass.
Centennial celebration [of the United
States], 1876.
Centennial celebration of Washington's Birthday,
Philadelphia, 1832. see Philadelphia.
Centennial Celebration of Washington's
Birthday, 1832.
Centennial celebration. Proceedings in con-
nection with the celebration at New
Bedford. 18610
Centennial celebration, . . . Sept. 7, 1865 [at
Oxford, N. H.] 58040
Centennial commemoration. A sermon.
(43295)
Centennial Commemoration of the Death of
George Whitefield, Newburyport, Mass.,
1870. see Newburyport, Mass. Centen-
nial Commemoration of the Death of
George Whitefield, 1870.
Centennial commemoration of the death of
George Whitefield, in the Old South
Church, Newburyport, Mass. (54912),
90904
Centennial Committee, Lexington, Mass. see
Lexington, Mass. Centennial Committee.
Centennial discourse, at Andover, Connecticut.
89734

Centennial discourse at the Baptist Church in Stonington. (59354)

Centennial discourse . . . before the First Church . . . in Ipswich. 37750

Centennial discourse . . . before the Providence Annual Conference, in Bristol, R. I. 59115

Centennial discourse. By George Howe, D. D. 33296

Centennial discourse by the present pastor [Ebenezer Burgess.] 9241, 19212

Centennial discourse by the present pastor [of the First Church in Dedham.] 9241, 19212

Centennial discourse, containing a history. (41736)

Centennial discourse, delivered before the Church of Christ. 1491

Centennial discourse, delivered before the Congregational Society. 103409

Centennial discourse, delivered before the First Congregational Society in Chicopee. 11951, 13274

Centennial discourse delivered before the South Church and Society. 21421

Centennial discourse delivered in . . . Newark, N. J. 31326

Centennial discourse delivered in Northborough. 843

Centennial discourse delivered in the First Church. 30921, 30925

Centennial discourse, delivered June 3d, 1864. 35533

Centennial discourse delivered on the one hundredth anniversary. (38778)

Centennial discourse, delivered Sept. 9, 1850. 13460

Centennial discourse delivered to the First Congregational Church and Society in Leominster. 91040

Centennial discourse. History of the First Presbyterian Church. 72423

Centennial discourse, . . . in Williamstown, Mass. (55383)

Centennial discourse, May 18th, A.D. 1853. 11939

Centennial discourse, Oct. 15, 1865. By S. D. Hopkins. 32963

Centennial discourse . . . October 15, 1865, in . . . Nantucket. 33110

Centennial discourse on the one hundredth anniversary of the First Baptist Church, Warren, R. I. 88856

Centennial discourses. 6950

Centennial Exposition, Philadelphia, 1876. see Philadelphia. Centennial Exposition, 1876.

Centennial festival of the Massachusetts Lodge. 45859

Centennial historical sketch of the town of New London. 90568

Centennial history of Licking County, Ohio. 85135

Centennial history of North Bend. 83005

Centennial history of the city of Washington. 84079

Centennial meeting of the descendants of Philip and Rachel Price. 65425

Centennial meeting of the Philadelphia Contributionship for the Insurance of Houses from Loss by Fire. 61986

Centennial memorial of Christian and Anna Maria Wolff. 23649

Centennial memorial of St. Andrew's Lodge. 80319

Centennial memorial, . . . of . . . the one hundredth anniversary of the A. R. Presbyterian Church. 55358

Centennial memorials of the Associate Reformed Presbyterian Church. (41532)

Centennial. One hundred years of progress in the business of banking. 89031

Centennial oration before the society. 74994, note after 95589

Centennial plea for Presbyterian education. 89254

Centennial proceedings . . . historical facts. 94466

Centennial record. (64772)

Centennial report, financial and statistical. 89486

Centennial sermon, . . . at Boston. 58666

Centennial sermon, delivered . . . in Franklin. (82207)

Centennial sermon delivered in St. Luke's Church. 79960

Centennial sermon of the Potomac Baptist Association. 8141

Centennial sermon preached at the rededication of the house of worship, of the First Baptist Church, Pittsfield. 88860

Centennial sermon preached June 7, 1846. 33165

Centennial services of the Stamford Baptist Church. 90117

Centennial, 1766-1866. 11678

Centeno, Carlos de Tapia. see Tapia Zenteno, Carlos de.

Centeno, Juan Francisco. defendant 98730

Centeola; and other tales. 95475

Center District New Hampshire Medical Society. see New Hampshire Medical Society. Center District.

Centerville, Conn. Hancock Division, Sons of Temperance. see Sons of Temperance of North America. Connecticut. Hancock Division, Centerville (Hamden) Connecticut.

Centinel. pseud. Observations on the proposed consitution. 56555

Centinel, Vincent. pseud. Massachusetts in agony. (11679), 45864

Centinel. 14395

Centinel (Boston) 96754

Centinel & Register. see Albany Centinel & Register.

Centinel of the North-Western Territory. 94104

Centinela Federal de Tialpam. 63687

Cento e trienta notas instructivas. 25427

135,000 acres de terres. 96173

Centonicum Virgilianum monimentum mirabilis apparitionis. 71481

Centraal Amerika, uit een geschiedkundig. 29499

Central America (Confederacion de Centro-America, 1823-1840) Comision Especial Reunida de Orden del Poder Ejercitivo. 20114

Central America (Confederacion de Centro-America, 1823-1840) Constitution. 16055

Central America (Confederacion de Centro-America, 1823-1840) Ministerio de Hacienda. 47606

Central America (Confederacion de Centro-America, 1823-1840) Treaties, etc. 58126

Central America (Confederacion de Centro-America, 1853) Junta Preparatoria. 66111

Central America. 59054

Central America and the transit between the oceans. 75940

Central America as it was, is, and may be. 55146

Central America; describing each of the states. 2771

Central America (financial position) . . . 44430

Central American Education Society. 11685

Central Association for the Relief of the Soldiers of South Carolina, Columbia, S. C. 87806-87807

Central Association of Hampshire County, Mass. see Congregational Churches in Massachusetts. Central Association of Hampshire County.

Central Asylum for the Instruction of the Deaf and Dumb, Canojoharie, N. Y. see New York (State) Central Asylum for the Instruction of the Deaf and Dumb, Canojoharie, N. Y.

Central Auxiliary Society for Promoting Education and Industry Among the Indians and Destitute Settlers in Canada, Montreal. 85855

Central basin. 101927

Central Board of Agency for Home Missions, Cincinnati. (13115)

Central Board of Agency for Home Missions. Second annual report. (13115)

Central Church, Worcester, Mass. see Worcester, Mass. Central Church.

Central College, Charlottesville, Va. see Virginia. University.

Central College, McCrawville, N. Y. see New York Central College, McCrawville, N. Y.

Central College Association. 34240

Central College Association of New York. see New York Central College Association.

Central Committee, Appointed by the Legislature Friendly to the Election of John Q. Adams, as President, 1828. see National Republican Party. Massachusetts. Central Committee

Central Committee of Fauquier. see Whig Party. Virginia. Fauquier County. Central Committee.

Central Committee of National Republicans of . . . Baltimore, to the people of Maryland. 45102

Central Committee of the Inhabitants of Upper Canada. 98069

Central Committee of the state, to the Federal electors. 45671

Central Congregational Church, Newtonville, Mass. see Newtonville, Mass. Central Congregational Church.

Central Democratic Club, Philadelphia. see Democratic Party. Pennsylvania. Philadelphia. Central Democratic Club.

Central Dispensary, New York (City) (54142)

Central Executive Committee of Irish Citizens, Washington, D. C. 35083

Central Fremont and Dayton Glee Club of the City of New York. 25816 see also Republican Party. New York. New York City.

Central gold region. (27468)

Central High School of Philadelphia. see Philadelphia. Central High School.

Central Homoeopathic Dispensary, New York (City) see New York Central Homoeopathic Dispensary.

Central Military Tract Railroad Company. 11686

Central Mississippi Citizens' Meeting on the Slavery Question, 1850. see Meeting of the Citizens of Central Mississippi on the Slavery Question, 1850.

Central national highway from the Mississippi River to the Pacific. 4786

Central Pacific Railroad Company. 10023

Central Pacific Railroad Company. Chief Engineer. 36830 see also Judah, Theodore D.

Central Pacific Railroad Company. President. 90210 see also Huntington, Collis Potter, 1821-1900. and Stanford, Leland, 1834-1893.

Central Pacific Railroad Company. Superintendent of Surveys. 11687

Central Pacific Railroad; connecting the great cities of the Atlantic with San Francisco and Puget Sound. 83724

Central Pacific Railroad. Statement made to the President of the United States. 90210

Central park. 54154

Central park album. 54153

Central park photographed. 29219

Central Passenger Railroad Company. 61532, 61880

Central power of the Gospel. 71768

Central Presbyterian. 85341

Central principle. 32943

Central rail road. Report of the Chief Engineer of the Danville and Pottsville Rail Road Company. 59967

Central route to the Pacific. 4106, 31175

Central Synod of Albany, N. Y. see Reformed Church in America. Central Synod of Albany.

Central traveller. 94315

Central Union Club of Brooklyn. 8284

Central water-line from the Ohio River to the Virginia capes. 42103

Centralamerikanische Staat Nicaragua. 89957

Centralamerikanske ambatrae. (56735)

Centralisation Deutscher Auswanderung und Colonisation, Berlin. 2183

Centralization or "state rights." (39963)

Centre College, Danville, Ky. see Danville, Ky. Centre College.

Centro-Americano. pseud. tr. 89962

Centro-Amerika. 11682, 68978

Centuria epistolarum miscellanearum. 106295

Centuriae X. rariora naturae. 61288

Centurial history of the Mendon Association. 5787

Centurial sermon, June, 1836. 104389

Centurial sermon, on the revival of religion A. D. 1740. 104385

Centurie de lepidopteres de l'ile de Cuba. 63668

Centurion, Juan Esteban Squarzafigo y. see Squarzafigo y Centurion, Juan Esteban.

Century and half discourses. 48827

Century Association, New York. 11689-11690, 16080, 54159-(54160)

Century Club, New York. see Century Association, New York.

Century dictionary. 83959

Century discourse, delivered at the anniversary meeting of the freemen. (18414)

Century discourse, delivered in Hamilton. (18172)

Century magazine. 78484, 83740, 83959

Century of episcopacy in Portland. 61051

Century of medicine and chemistry. (81049)

Century of puritanism and a century of its opposites. 16328, 16330

Century of the republic. 84913

Century sermon. 93089

Century sermon, . . . at East Bridgewater. 76472

Century sermon . . . by Rev. Timothy Harrington. 73591

Century sermon, delivered at Danbury. 71842

Century sermon delivered at the South Church, in Portsmouth. 706

Century sermon, delivered in Holliston, Mass. 24565

Century sermon delivered in Hopkinton. 33322

Century sermon: delivered in Philadelphia, at the opening of the Philadelphia Baptist Association. 36600

Century sermon, delivered in Westborough. (72449)

Century sermon, . . . in the East-Parish Meeting House. 58662

Century sermon, Newark, New Jersey. (43681)

Century sermon on the founding of Christ Church. 18191

Century sermon, on the glorious revolution. 104724

Century sermon, or sketches of the history of the eighteenth century. 97180

Century sermon, preached at Deerfield. 94496

Century sermon, preached at Kingston. 71753

Century sermon, preached at Mansfield, January 1, 1801. 102519

Century sermon, preached at the First-Parish in Lancaster. (30457)

Century sermon, preached before the First Church in Windham. 102070

Century sermons. 24452

Centz, P. C. pseud. Davis and Lee. see Bernard J.

Cepeda, Francisco de. 11692-(11695)

Cepeda, Juan Suarez Osorio de. see Suarez Osorio de Cepeda, Juan.

Cepeva, ------. 11696

Cephas. pseud. Familiar dialogue. see Worcester, Noah, 1758-1837.

Cephas. pseud. Inqueries, occasioned by the address. see Worcester, Noah, 1758-1837.

Cepherine; or, the secret cabal. 72133

Cephus Broadluck. pseud. Races of mankind. see Gazlay, Allan W.

Cerca de que los naturales Indios de estas provincias. 16185, (44392)

Cercle des Philadelphes, Cape Francois, Santo Domingo. see Cercle des Philadelphes, Cap Haitien, Haiti.

Cercle des Philadelphes, Cap Haitien, Haiti. 68351, 95349

Cercle des Philadelphes, Port-Au-Prince, Haiti. 47548

Cercle des Philadelphes etabli au Cap-Francois, Isle & Cote St. Domingue. see Cercle des Philadelphes, Cap Haitien, Haiti.

Cerda, ------ Gatica. see Gatica Cerda, ------.

Cerda, Bort de Benavides y de la. see Benavides y de la Cerda, Bort de.

Cerda, Goncalo Carrillo de la. 87157, 93575 see also Congregacion de Nuestro Padre San Pedro, Mexico (City) Abad.

Cerda, Jose de Zuniga y la. see Zuniga y la Cerda, Jose de.

Cerda, Juan Fernandez de Salinas y la. see Salinas y la Cerda, Juan Fernandez de.

Cerda y Rico, Francisco. ed. 75568, 79180

Cerdena, Antonio Machoni de. see Machoni de Cerdena, Antonio.

Cerdena, Antonio Machorie de. see Machoni de Cerdena, Antonio.

Cerdeno y Moncon, Luis. 11698

Cereals. 73958

Ceremonial de la Cour d'Haity. 3885

Ceremonial de las ceremonias del santo sacrificio de la missa. 75814

Ceremonial de las missas cantadas, y rezadas. 86393

Ceremonial dos religiosos Capuchos de Provincia de Sancto Antonio. 70130

Ceremonial para la fiesta nacional del 16 de Sept. de 1866. 47036, 66549

Ceremonial y manual sacado del Missal Romano de Pio V. 76885

Ceremonial y rubricas general con la orden de celebrar las misas. 48335

Ceremonial y rubricas generales, con la orden de celebrar las missas. (58050)

Ceremonies. 4933

Ceremonies and address. 32128

Ceremonies and oration. 101928

Ceremonies at the dedication of the Bigelow Monument. (5329)

Ceremonies at the dedication of the Soldiers' Monument. (55089)

Ceremonies at the laying of the corner stone of the new pioneer hall. 86010

Ceremonies at the unveiling of the statue of William H. Seward. (79599)

Ceremonies attending the introduction of water into the city. (66246)

Ceremonies et coutumes religieuses de tous les peuples du monde. 4931, 62600

Ceremonies et coutumes religieuses des peuples idolatres. 4931, 62600

Ceremonies funebres de toutes les nations. 51442

Ceremonies, . . . New York State Inebriate Asylum. 53821

Ceremonies of the second inauguration of Andrew G. Curtin. 18020

Ceremonies . . . [on laying the corner-stone of the New York] Institution [for the Instruction of the Deaf and Dumb.] 54500

Ceremonies on laying the corner stone of Trinity Church. 101954

Ceremonies on the completion of the monument. (61530)

Ceremonies . . . on the displaying of the national flag. (9174)

Ceremonies on the inauguration of Prof. Richard Somers Smith. 83793

Ceremonies religieuses. 31581

Ceremony and address. 14405, (75466)

Ceremony of laying the corner stone. 10427

Cerero, M. J. 11699

Cerfbeer, A. E. 11700

Cergues, ------ Dufresne de St. see Dufresne de St. Cergues, ------

Cerionem, C. S. ed. 74666

Cerisier, Andoine Marie, d. 1828. 11701-11702, 32012, 55423, 55517, (56478), 58239, 2d note after 93480

Cerisier, Antoine Marie, d. 1828. supposed author 11702

Cerna, D. Jacinto la. see La Cerna, D. Jacinto.

Cernoti, Leonardo. tr. 66506, 66508

Cerqueira e Silva, Ignacio Accioli de. see Accioli de Cerquiera e Silva, Ignacio, 1808-1865.

Cerqueira e Silva, Jose Antonio de. 11708

Cerqueira Pinto, Antonio. see Pinto, Antonio Cerqueira.

Cerralvo, Rodrigo Pacheco Osorio, Marques de. see Osorio, Rodrigo Pacheco, Marques de Cerralvo.
Cerro y Zamudio, Jose Santiago. 97742
Cerro de las Campagnas. 46201
Certain acts of the commonwealth of Virginia, for regulating the militia. 100401
Certain acts of the General Assembly of the commonwealth of Virginia. 100402
Certain agreements and concessions. 27156
Certain articles of agreement and cession. 27072, 95390
Certain aspects of the church. 82941
Certain certificates received from America. 59664
Certain Citizens of Providence, R. I. see Providence, R. I. Citizens.
Certain conditions, or concessions, agreed upon by William Penn. 66223
Certain considerations relating to the Royal African Company. (73766)
Certain errors in navigation. 105574
Certain gentlemen appointed therevnto. pseud. View and survey of such ships. 67574
Certain great man vindicated. 63087
Certain Inhabitants in the Island of Cape Breton. see Cape Breton Island. Inhabitants.
Certain Inhabitants of the County of Westchester. see Westchester County, N. Y. Citizens.
Certain letters written by Mr. Bramham. 104329
Certain Manufacturers, and Others, Philadelphia. see Philadelphia. Meeting of Certain Manufacturers, and Others, 1828.
Certain Members of the Commission on Petigru's Code. see South Carolina. Commission on the Code.
Certain memorial, with remarks, and appendix. 105672
Certain Merchants and Other Inhabitants of Boston. see Boston. Citizens.
Certain Ministers of the Gospel, in Boston. pseud. Defence of evangelical churches. see Mather, Cotton, 1663-1728. and Mather, Increase, 1639-1723.
Certain objections to incorporating the Brookline Horse Railroad Co. 8252
Certain observations on the release of American property. 83826
Certain papers connected with the affairs of the Grand Trunk Railroad Company of Canada. (28269)
Certain papers relating to a svpposed libel. 31947, (32551), 7th note after 97146
Certain Persons of the Town of Minchin-Hampton. defendants see Minchinhampton, England. defendants
Certain phenomena of the great lakes of America. 13724
Certain pieces of this age parabolizd. 78189
Certain Presbyters of St. Louis. pseud. Allegations. 90690
Certain proposals from the scriptures. 104336
Certain propositions relating to the Scots plantation of Caledonia. (78205)
Certain queries. (70107)
Certain queries of the . . . Canal Committee of the Canadian Parliament. 8385
Certain queries tending to accommodadation [sic] between the Presbyterian and Congregationall churches. 17059

Certain queries tending to accomodation and communion of Presbyterian & Congregationall churches. 17052
certain remarks on . . . a letter relating to the divisions. 8505
Certain resolves having been proposed by the Committee of Correspondence. 96024
Certain select cases resolved. 80199-80201, (80257)
Certain Shipowners, Liverpool. petitioners see Liverpool. Certain Shipowners. petitioners
Certain Spanyardes. pseud. Abstract taken out of certain Spanyardes letters. (67551)
Certain statements. 103831
Certain testimony given before the Committee on Banks and Banking. 83857
Certain writings, (never yet printed.) 5629
Certaine epigrams ovt of the first fovre books. (31036)
Certaine errors in nauigation. 106246
Certaine errors in navigation. 105572-105573
Certaine errors in navigation, detected and corrected. 105573
Certaine inducements to well minded people. 11709
Certaine letters written from thence. (45316), 69291-69292, note after 80002, 103353
Certaine pieces of this age paraboliz'd. (78188)
Certaine proposals in order to a new modeling of the laws. 72082
Certaine reasons and arguments of policie. 78361, 78379
Certaine tales of true libertie. 78191
Certainty & suddenness of Christ's coming to judgment. (79507)
Certainty of the facts reported in the Gospel. 20059
Certainty of the world of spirits. 4009
Certainty, the endless duration of future punishment. 92759
Certainty, time, and end of the birth. 3471
Certamen cientifico que el nacional y mas antiguo Colegio de S. Ildefonso de Mexico, dedica. 48336, 76116
Certamen panegyrico historical poetico. 41083
Certamen poetico celebrado para solemnizar la canonizacion. 72815
Certamen poetico con que la Real Vniversidad . . . celebro. 60856
Certamen poetico en el solemne, triunfal recibimiento. 86218-86219
Certamen poetico, palestra de ingenio en la campana del discourso. 76294
Certamen poetico para la noche de navidad de 1741. 73851
Certamen poetico que ofrece . . . la Universidad de Lima. 60856
Certayne questyons, with answeres to the same. 84584
Certificacion acerca del cargo y los diezmos de la Real Compania Guipuzcoana de Caracas. 98765
Certificacion dada a la ciudad de Lima. 62993
Certificacion, que dio el ano de 1666. 94628
Certificate from Mr. Josiah Hewes. 95980
Certificate of civism for Joseph Priestley, Junr. 14012, 92070
Certificate of Daniel Cony. (43923)
Certificate of incorporation and by-laws of the Chamber of Commerce of San Francisco. 76038

CERTIFICATES

Certificates of the efficacy of Doctor Perkins's patent metallic instruments. (60942)
Certified copy from the register of canal boats. (53563)
Certified report of the investigation of the case of Rev. Garret J. Garretson. (26696)
Cerutti, C. F. 11710
Cervantes, Alejandro Magarinos. see Magarinos Cervantes, Alejandro, 1826-
Cervantes, Jose Manuel Ruiz y. see Ruiz y Cervantes, Jose Manuel.
Cervantes, Jose Maria Villasenor. see Villasenor Cervantes, Jose Maria.
Cervantes, Juan Ortiz de. 11716
Cervantes, Juan Ortiz de. petitioner 57718
Cervantes, Nic. Gomez de. see Gomez de Cervantes, Nic.
Cervantes de Salazar, Francesca. see Salazar, Francisco Cervantes.
Cervantes Salazar, Francisco. see Salazar, Francisco Cervantes.
Cesarea (Archdiocese) Archbishop [ca 1848] 66112
Cesi, Prince. (31515)-31516
Cesnola, Louis Palma di. 11717
Cespedes, Andres Garcia de. (11718)
Cespedes, Francisco de Armas y. see Armas y Cespedes, Francisco de.
Cession of Louisiana to the United States. (26794)
Cesso d'Ascoli. 76838
Cest la dedvction du somptueux ordre. 73458
Cesvs a oh Vtes. 72017
Ceur Brandenburg. Laws, statutes, etc. 65730
Ceur Brandenburg. Sovereigns, etc. [ca 1690] 65730
Ceur-Brandenburgse Americaense Compagnie. Charter. 65730
Cevallos, A. Ventura Calderon y. see Ventura Calderon y Cevallos, A.
Cevallos, Fernando. 11719
Cevallos, Pedro Ordonez de. see Ordonez de Ceballos, Pedro, d. 1550?
Ceylon and British Guiana. (29165)
Ch . . . . . , --------. pseud. Guide du l'Amerique. see Chambon, ------, fl. 1755.
Ch******. pseud. Plan de constitution. see Chabanon, Michel Paul Gui de, 1730-1792.
C******, ------ de. pseud. Precis historique. see Chabanon, Michel Paul Gui de, 1730-1792.
Ch., ---------. pseud. tr. 89011
Ch--------, ---------. pseud. tr. 89012
Ch . . . . . e, J . . . . . pseud. Advertisement. 6978, 17481
Chabanon, Michel Paul Gui de, 1730-1792. (11720)-(11721)
Chabert, Daniel de Joncaire. see Joncaire-Chabert, Daniel de.
Chabert, X. 11724-11725
Chabert de Cogolin, Joseph Bernard, Marquis de, 1724-1805. (11723)
Chaboillez, -------. 4268, (9828)
Chace, Benjamin H. 11726
Chace, George Ide, 1808-1885. 4583, 11727, (49210)
Chachereau, -------. 11728, 68741
Chaco, ultimo caudillo de la montonera de los llanos. 77068
Chacon, Luis. 106403 see also Cuba. Governador (Chacon)
Chacon Abarca y Tiedra, Geronymo. see Abarca y Tiedra, Geronymo Chacon.

Chactas. 12248
Chadbourne, B. F. 77031
Chadbourne, Paul A. 11729
Chadbourne, S. H. 11730
Chaffee, Calvin Clifford, 1811-1896. (11733)
Chad's Ford, September 11, 1777. 5 o'clock, P. M. (11731), 101700
Chadwick, James Read. tr. 77755
Chadwick, John. 92832
Chadwick, John W. 90473
Chaff, 81925
Chaffee, Jerome Bunting, 1825-1886. 11734, 90692
Chaffin, William L. 11735
Chagas, Antonio das. 11736, 66386 see also Immaculada Conceycao, Brazil (Ecclesiastical Province) Procurador.
Chagnon, Godefroy. 11737
Chahta alphabet. 104308
Chahta chikasha itatuklo chata palelil pokole tuchena akocha tvlhape bachaya ka tvli hina kvmpeni oke. 63922
Chahta holisso. 105535
Chahta holisso a tukla. 105536
Chahta holisso, it im anumpuli. 12865, note after 105536
Chahta i kana. 105536-105537
Chahta ikhananchi. 12866, 105541
Chahta mikmyt chikasha okla nana akostenecha chi pulla kuk o holisso illvpvt toba hoke. 63921
Chahta mikmvt chikasha okla nana akostanecha chi pulla kuk o kvmpeni illvpvt holisso ha ikbe tok oke. 63922
Chahta na-holhtina. 12868, 105530
Chahta uba isht taloa holisso. 105538
Chahta yakni nan vlhpisa nishkoboka. 105531
Chaille, S. E. 11739
Chaillot, A. tr. 16503
Chain-bearer. 16422, 16525
Chain of Lorenzo. 27025
Chain of tables, for the interchangeable reduction. 105606
Chain, with its concomitants. 20757
Chaine of scripture chronologie. (872)
Chained mother. 30387
Chaines de l'esclavage. (44462)
Chains and freedom. 103198
Chairman and gentlemen of the Joint Committee. 30859
Chairman chastised. 28958
Chairman of the Diocese of New York. pseud. Letter to the Right Rev. Bishop Hobart. 32304
Chaise, Francois d'Aix de la. see La Chaise, Francois d'Aix de.
Chaix, Paul. 11740-(11741)
Chakta chikasha itatuklo chata iklvna tvli hina kvmpeni oke. 63921
Chalas, Alexandre. 11742
Chalesme, ------- de. (11743), 68368
Chalfant, James F. 56377
Chalk, Thomas, (11744)
Chalkley, Thomas. (11745)-11754, 33265, (66742)
Chalkly, Thomas. see Chalkley, Thomas.
Challenge [of M. S. Wilkinson.] 66943
Challenge to Caleb Pusey. (37183)
Challenge to William Pen [sic] and Geor. Whitehead. (37184)
Challen, Howard. 11755, 66534
Challen, James. 11756
Challeux, Nicolas le. see Le Challeux, Nicolas.
Chalmer, Lionel. see Chalmers, Lionel.

Chalmers, George, 1742-1825. 65, (11757)-(11767), 68674-(68675), (69711), 93593, 3d note after 97583

Chalmers, George, 1742-1825. petitioner 93593, 3d note after 105598-9 [sic]

Chalmers, George, 1742-1825. supposed author 57168, 84642

Chalmers, George, 1742-1825. incorrectly supposed author 10671, 11763, (11767), 15526, 51168-51169, note after 63244, 84642

Chalmers, Colonel George, fl. 1801-1818. 11768-11769, (81893), note after 102820

Chalmers, Henry J. 11770

Chalmers, Joseph Williams, 1806-1853. 11771

Chalmers, Lionel. 11772-11773

Chalmers, Thomas, 1780-1847. (11774), 27550, 78514, 89744

Chalmers, W. ed. 18255

Chaloner & Fleming. firm (11775)

Chalumeau de Verneiul, F. T. A. tr. 52105

Chalusset, Abel de. 11776-11777

Chalwill, William G. 11778

Chamber of Commerce, Belfast, Ireland. see Belfast, Ireland. Chamber of Commerce.

Chamber of Commerce, Boston. see Boston. Chamber of Commerce.

Chamber of Commerce, Charleston, S. C. see Charleston, S. C. Chamber of Commerce.

Chamber of Commerce, Cincinnati. see Cincinnati. Chamber of Commerce and Merchants' Exchange.

Chamber of Commerce, Milwaukee. see Milwaukee. Chamber of Commerce

Chamber of Commerce, New Orleans. see New Orleans. Chamber of Commerce.

Chamber of Commerce, New York (City) see New York. Chamber of Commerce of the State of New York.

Chamber of Commerce, St. John, N. B. see New Brunswick. Chamber of Commerce, St John.

Chamber of Commerce, St. Louis. see St. Louis. Chamber of Commerce.

Chamber of Commerce, Saint Paul, Minn. see Saint Paul, Minn. Chamber of Commerce.

Chamber of Commerce, San Diego, Cal. see San Diego, Cal. Chamber of Commerce.

Chamber of Commerce, San Francisco. see San Francisco. Chamber of Commerce.

Chamber of Commerce, Sheffield, England. see Sheffield, England. Chamber of Commerce.

Chamber of Commerce and Merchants' Exchange, Memphis, Tenn. see Memphis, Tenn. Chamber of Commerce.

Chamber of Commerce. Charleston, 13th Nov., 1845. 12035

Chamber of Commerce of Jamaica. see Jamaica. Chamber of Commerce.

Chamber of Commerce of New Brunswick. see New Brunswick. Chamber of Commerce St. John.

Chamber of Commerce of New Orleans. see New Orleans. Chamber of Commerce.

Chamber of Commerce of New York City. see New York. Chamber of Commerce of the State of New York.

Chamber of Commerce of New-York, December, 1858. 53585

Chamber of Commerce of New York State. see New York. Chamber of Commerce of the State of New York.

Chamber of Commerce of Philadelphia. see Philadelphia. Chamber of Commerce.

Chamber of Commerce of St. Paul, Minn. see St. Paul, Minn. Chamber of Commerce.

Chamber of Commerce of San Francisco. see San Francisco. Chamber of Commerce.

Chamber of Commerce of the State of New York. Proceedings, on the burning of the ship Brilliant. 578

Chamber of Commerce. Report of Select Committee on Quarantine. 53583

Chamber of Commerce . . . The committee appointed to consider the condition of the lighthouses of the United States . . . report. 53583

Chamberlain, D. supposed author 86764A

Chamberlain, Daniel Henry, 1835-1907. 32649, 87377, 87401, 87469-87470 see also South Carolina. Attorney General. South Carolina. Governor, 1874-1876 (Chamberlain)

Chamberlain, Ebenezer Mattoon, 1805-1861. (11779)

Chamberlain, H. S. 89309

Chamberlain, J. E. 17118

Chamberlain, James. 11791, 60375 see also Pennsylvania. State Agent at the South West.

Chamberlain, Nathan H. 11780-11784

Chamberlain, Thomas. 95838

Chamberlain, William. 11785

Chamberlain, William Martin. ed. (51970)

Chamberlaine, Richard. 11786

Chamberlayne, Edward, 1616-1703. 11787

Chamberlayne, J. tr. 11788

Chamberlayne, John. 11787, 57435

Chamberlayne, John. supposed author 85939

Chamberlin, ------. 34433

Chamberlin, B. 11789

Chamberlin, E. M. (11790)

Chamberlin, James. see Chamberlain, James.

Chambers, Adam B. 11792, (75341)

Chambers, Ezekiel Forman, 1788-1867. 11793, 45086

Chambers, George. (11794)-11795, 8th note after 96966

Chambers, James M. ed. 86214

Chambers, John, 1797-1875. 11797-(11798)

Chambers, John, 1797-1875. incorrectly supposed author 11799, 17695

Chambers, John, fl. 1818. 11796

Chambers, Jonathan. 84558

Chambers, Richard ed. 13548

Chambers, Robert, 1802-1871. 11800-11801, (35272)

Chambers, Talbot. defendant at court martial (11802)

Chambers, Talbot Wilson, 1819-1896. 7343, 11803-11804

Chambers, Talbott. see Chambers, Talbot.

Chambers, Thomas Jefferson, 1802-1865. 94947, 95079, 95082, 95093

Chambers, William, 1800-1883. 11806-11807, (35272)

Chambers, William, fl. 1853. 11805

Chambers' Edinburgh journal. 85560

Chamber's journal. see Chambers' Edinburgh journal.

Chamber's miscellany. (35272)

Chamber's papers for the people, 2d note after 11684, 65034

Chambers Street Gallery, New York. see American Academy of the Fine Arts, New York. Chambers Street Gallery.

Chambersburg, Pa. Convention, 1839. see Whig Party. Pennsylvania. Convention, Chambersburg, 1839.

Chambersburg, Pa. Democratic Whig State
  Convention, 1839. see Whig Party.
  Pennsylvania. Convention, Chamber-
  sburg, 1839.
Chambersburg, Pa. Whig State Convention,
  1839. see Whig Party. Pennsylvania.
  Convention, Chambersburg, 1839.
Chambersburg in the colony and the revolu-
  tion. (26686)
Chambers's miscellany of instructive & enter-
  taining tracts. (35272)
Chamblit, Rebekah. (11808)
Chambly, Canada. see St. Peter's College.
  see St. Peter's College, Chambly
  County, Quebec.
Chambolle, Adolphe. 11810
Chambolle, Francois Alexis. (11811)
Chambon, --------, fl. 1775. 11812-11814,
  1st note after 96445
Chambre d'Agriculture du Cap. see Cap
  Haitien, Haiti. Chambre d'Agriculture.
Chambre de Commerce d'Aunis. see Aunis,
  France. Chambre de Commerce.
Chambre de Commerce de Normandie. see
  Normandie (Departement) Chambre de
  Commerce.
Chambre des Deputes. Documents communi-
  ques a l'appui du projet de loi. 11815
Chamerovzow, Louis Alexis. ed. 8516
Chamfort, Sebastien Roch Nicolas, called,
  1740?-1794. 11816, 49398
Chamier, Frederick, 1796-1870. ed. 35721
Chamisso, Adelbert von, 1781-1838. 11817-
  (11818), (12884), 38284
Chamisso, Louis Charles Adelbert von. see
  Chamisso, Adelbert von, 1781-1838.
Champ d'Asile, Texas. 40913
Champ d'Asile. 40913, 95071
Champ-d'Asile, au Texas. (18227), 95071
Champ-d'Asile, tableau topographique. 29395,
  40913, 95072
Champ royal specialement co[m]pose par
  maniere de paraphrase. 58825
Champagny, Jean Baptiste Nompere de, Duc
  de Cadore, 1756-1834. 11823-(11826),
  34400, 83815
Champaign County, Ohio. Surveyor. 90555
  see also Taylor, C. W. L.
Champegny, -------. 25853
Champers, John. (81524)
Champe's adventure. 39739
Champion, J. 11829-11830
Champion, Judah, 1729-1810. (11827)-11828
Champion, Richard, 1743-1791. 11831-(11833),
  32637
Champion, Pierre, 1632-1701. 20201, 99507,
  100609
Champion de Villeneuve, A. see Villeneuve,
  A. Champion de.
Champion American. pseud. 19300
Champion; containing a series of papers.
  99257
Champion comic melodist. 79907
Champion of reviling, railing, and slander.
  82478
Champions of freedom. 105179
Champlain, Samuel de, 1567-1635. 11627,
  (11834)-11842, 57425, 66686, 84779
Champlain Cooper Mining Company. 11843
Champlain in the Onondaga valley. 54476
Camplain Valley Horticultural Society. 11844
Champlain's voyages. 65646
Champlin, James. 11845
Champney, J. Wells. illus. 82720
Champney, Julian B. 11846
Champney, W. L. illus. (77336)

Champneys, Benjamin. 11847-11848
Champneys, John. 11849
Champomier, P. A. 11850
Chanca, Diego Alvarez. 14670, 94095-94096
Chance, George I. 8768
Chance for the south. 14974
Chance to get rid of money. 101273
Chancellor, Richard, d. 1556. 29941, 66686
Chancellor out of office. pseud. Letter.
  40269
Chancellor Kent's opinion. 54115, 69689
Chancellor Tucker's opinion. 97308
Chancellor's decree. 98438
Chancellor's memorial to the General Assembly
  of Maryland. 5862, (45103)
Chancellorsville and its results. 19629, 32821
Chancery cases argued and determined in the
  Court of Appeals of South Carolina.
  87454
Chancery cases determined in the Court of
  Appeals of South Carolina. 71403
Chancery of New Jersey, between Joseph
  Hendrickson, complainant, and Thos. L,
  Shotwell and Elizabeth his wife, defend-
  ants. (31332)
Chances of making a million. (39886)
Chandler, --------, fl. 1852. 55827
Chandler, A. 11852
Chandler, Adoniram. 11851
Chandler, Amariah. 11853
Chandler, Charles Frederick, 1836- 11854,
  84277
Chandler, Elizabeth M. 11855-(11856)
Chandler, Isaac. 11857, 11894
Chandler, James. (11858), 11860-(11862),
  97315, 97321-97322
Chandler, John. petitioner 45256
Chandler, John A. (11859)
Chandler, Joseph. (11863)
Chandler, Joseph Ripley, 1792-1880. 4837,
  11864-(11866), (27492), 63063
Chandler, Lucius H. 11867, 78891
Chandler, Peleg Whitman, 1816-1889. 6630,
  11868-11869, 19916, 32362, (33969),
  70231, 83423, 91604, 96946
Chandler, Samuel. tr. 94304
Chandler, Samuel, 1693-1766. 11870
Chandler, Samuel, 1713-1775. (11871)
Chandler, Samuel, fl. 1789. 95917
Chandler, Seth. (11872)
Chandler, T. P. 11884
Chandler, Thomas Bradbury, 1726-1790. 1785,
  6815, 12311, 11873-11875, (11877)-11882,
  11883, 12319, (12326), 16587-16588,
  16590-16591, 26867, 39714, 64328, 78581,
  (78715), 92830-92831, 2d note after
  103119
Chandler, Thomas Bradbury, 1726-1790.
  supposed author 16585, note after 100420
Chandler, Thomas Bradbury, 1726-1790.
  incorrectly supposed author (11881),
  11882, 16590-16591, 29955-29956, 92850,
  2d note after 99553, 2d note after
  103119
Chandler, Will. 11885
Chandler, William Eaton, 1835-1917. 11886,
  89323
Chandler, William Eaton, 1835-1917. reporter
  11886
Chandler, Zachariah, 1813-1879. 11887-11888,
  64249
Chandler (H. C.) & Co. firm publishers
  34209
Chandler's campaign one of slander and libel.
  86837
Chandless, William. 11889

Change: a poem pronounced at Roxbury.
(28413)
Change for the American notes. 20004,
note after 105032
Change of base. 18031, 89487
Change of national empire. (68305)
Changery; an allegorical memoir. 6513,
(11890)
Changes made by the General Convention of
1868. (66131)
Changing base. 23287
Changuion, P. J. 11891-11892
Chani i holisso vhleha chahta anumpa isht
atoshowa hoke. 105532
Chanla, -------- de. pseud. tr. see
Montucla, -------. tr.
Chanler, Isaac. see Chandler, Isaac.
Chanler, Isaac, 1701-1749. (11893)
Chanler, John Winthrop, 1826-1877. 11895
Channel scourge. 63004
Channing, Edward, 1856-1931. ed. 82850
Channing, Edward Tyrrell, 1790-1856. 11896,
55562
Channing, George G. 11897
Channing, Henry. 11898-(11899)
Channing, Walter, 1786-1876. (2482), 11900-
(11905), (52447)
Channing, William Ellery, 1780-1842. 2414-
2415, 11906-(11925), 11932, 30765,
42986, 55862, 64948, 67907, 70190,
80853, 81162, 92829, 93205, 94057,
1st note after 95112, 4th note after
95112, 95141, 96412, 99583, note after
103316, 105131, 105305
Channing, William Ellery, 1818-1901. 11927-
11929, 76249
Channing, William F. 11930
Channing, William Henry, 1810-1884. 11931-
11932, 60956, 65392, 89490, 90752,
102993
Channing Congregational Church, Newton, Mass.
see Newton, Mass. Channing Congregational Church.
Channing Division, no. 5, Sons of Temperance.
see Sons of Temperance of North
America. Rhode Island. Channing
Division, no. 5, Providence.
Channing en face de la nouvelle ecole the-
ologique. 6312
Channing et la mouvement unitaire aux Etats-
Unis. (69597)
Channing sa vie et ses oeuvres. 11907, 11924,
(32513)
Chanson militaire, sur le prise de Dominique.
6878
Chanson nouvelle, d'apres le drame de ce
nom. 92538
Chansonnier Canadien. (10403A)
Chansonnier Canadien, ou nouveau recueil de
chansons. 39265
Chansons populaires du Canada. 26325
Chant de l'independance Mexicane. 69572
Chant royale a la loenge dycelluy. 25190
Chantal, J. B. J. de. 11933-11934
Chantal, Teresa de. see Teresa de Chantal,
Sister.
Chanticleer. 11935, 46830-46831
Chantrans, Justin Girod. see Girod-Chantrans,
Justin.
Chants Canadiens avec accompagnement de
piano. 80296
Chanute, Octave, 1832-1910. 85067
Chanvalon, Jean Baptiste Thibault de. 11936,
5th note after 100802
Chaoone, Sarah S. 9842-9843

Chaparro, Juan Gonzalez. 11937
Chapel-School of St. Barnabas, Dearman, N. Y.
see Dearman, N. Y. Chapel-School of
St. Barnabas.
Chapin, Aaron L. 11938
Chapin, Alonzo B. 11939-11942
Chapin, Calvin. 11943
Chapin, Charles V. 85502
Chapin, E. 11953
Chapin, Edwin Hubbell. 11944-11947
Chapin, George H. 52675
Chapin, H. M. ed. 104796
Chapin, Henry, 1811-1878. 11948, 47819, note
after 90463, 90777
Chapin, Henry, 1811-1878. petitioner 90777
Chapin, Horace B. 11949
Chapin, J. (10826)
Chapin, J. R. (11950)
Chapin, L. 72342
Chapin, Orange. 11951, 13274
Chapin, S. R. 11959
Chapin, Seth. 11954
Chapin, Stephen. 11955-11958
Chapin, W. engr. 12891, 84358-84362, 84365
Chapin, Walter. 11960
Chapin, William. 11961
Chapin, William. supposed author 99630
Chapin Family Meeting, Springfield, Mass.,
1862. see Meeting of the Chapin Family,
Springfield, Mass., 1862.
Chapin gathering. 11952
Chapin genealogy. 11951, 13274
Chapin's Adrian city directory and advertiser.
468
Chapin's city directory of Ann Arbor. 11962
Chapitre de l'histoire de l'abolition. 70290
Chapitre de l'oncle Tom. 92544
Chaplain. pseud. Flag of truce. 24643
Chaplain. pseud. Prison sketches. see
Luckey, John.
Chaplain, Charles L. 11963
Chaplain, John F. 11964
Chaplain Fuller. 26171
Chaplain in the C. S. Army. pseud. Mustered
into service. 88048A
Chaplain of the Conde of St. Malo. pseud.
Voyage to Peru. see Courte de la
Blanchardiere, Rene.
Chaplain of the U. S. Army. pseud. Nation's
sin and punishment. see Hodgman, S. A.
supposed author
Chaplain Smith and the baptists. 82723
Chaplains and clergy of the revolution. 31148
Chaplain's campaign (not) with General Butler.
9618
Chaplain's campaign with Gen. Butler. (33493)
Chaplains of the general government. 36250
Chaplet woven by the friends of the late Mrs.
Osgood. 91034
Chaplin, C. tr. 94939
Chaplin, Daniel. 11965
Chaplin, Ebenezer. 360, 6254, 11967-11968,
3d note after 96741
Chaplin, Jeremiah. (11969)
Chaplin, Joseph. 11970
Chaplin, W. J. ed. 51666
Chaplin, William L. 11971
Chapman, A. W. (11972)
Chapman, C. W. 86349
Chapman, Charles, 1799-1869. 11973
Chapman, Conrad W. illus. 58562
Chapman, Daniel. 11974
Chapman, E. J. 11977-11978
Chapman, Eunice. petitioner 79709
Chapman, Eunice (Hawley) plaintiff 57844,
note after 97893, note after 105575

Chapman, F. W. 11979-11980
Chapman, George T. 11981-(11983)
Chapman, George W. 11984
Chapman, Henry Samuel, 1803-1881. 11985
Chapman, Henry Samuel, 1803-1881. supposed author 103117
Chapman, Isaac A. (11986)
Chapman, J. L. 80104
Chapman, James. 11987
Chapman, James, fl. 1830. 11989
Chapman, John. supposed author 96358, note after 103042
Chapman, John Gadsby, 1808-1889. 11992, 37163, 84154
Chapman, John Grant, 1798-1856. 11990
Chapman, Jonathan. 11991
Chapman, Lucretia. defendant 21019, 1st note after 96847
Chapman, M. I. 11993
Chapman, Maria Weston. 11994-11996, 81909, note after 86936
Chapman, Nathaniel, 1780-1853. 11005, 11997, 59152-(59154), 62010, 94094
Chapman, R. A. 19893, 71527
Chapman, Reuben, 1799-1882. 11998
Chapman, Robert H. 11999
Chapman, Russell. 89199
Chapman, S. (12000)
Chapman, Samuel. 102088
Chapman, T. Ellwood. (12001), 61606, 62050
Chapman, W. R. 12002
Chapman family. 11979
Chapman Hall School, Boston. see Boston. Chapman Hall School.
Chapman's journal of medical and physical science. see Philadelphia journal of medical and physical sciences.
Chappe d'Autreoche, Jean. 12003-12004, 38398
Chappel, Alonzo. illus. 21497-21498, 21500, 77983, 89339-89340
Chappell, Edward. RN (12005)-(12007)
Chappell, W. L. 85616
Chappelsmith, John. 12008, 85072
Chappin, Antoine. 5052
Chappus, ------. 12009
Chappuzeau, ---------, Sieur. 12010-12011, 32022, 32140
Chapter, by Wilson Armistead. 216, 27628
Chapt. XIV. of the revised statutes. 54162
Chapter from the history of the North American & South American States. 27298
Chapter from the history of the Virginia Company of London. 52287
Chapter from the secret history of the war. 51720
Chapter in the early history of South Carolina. 71651
Chapter in the history of abolition at Syracuse. 18712
Chapter in the life of a city pastor. (61374)
Chapter in the life of Jacob Barker. (16042)
Chapter of American history. Five years' progress of the slave power. (12012), 24636
Chapter of American history. Sketches of the revolutionary war. 12013
Chapter of Canadian history. 31932
Chapter of history, or the progress of judicial usurpation. 36166
Chapter of the English colonization of America. 52288
Chapter of the history of the war of 1812 in the northwest. 30840
Chapter on slavery. 31880

Chapter on taverns. 9318
Chapter on the history of Newfoundland. 54978
Chapter on the Indians of the plains. (40996)
Chapter on the lithology. 84531
Chapter on the manufacture of paper from wood. 66093
Chapter I. of the fourth part of the proposed revision. 53596
Chapters and dates of the laws of Massachusetts. (45672)
Chapters from an autobiography. 48919
Character and blessedness of the upright. (79408)
Character and blessedness of those who die in the Lord. 71502
Character and claims of seamen. 22100
Character and death of Abraham Lincoln. 25306
Character and duty of a Christian soldier. 32726
Character and duty of minister and people. 83429
Character and duty of soldiers illustrated. 91755
Character and employment of good angels. 83450
Character and end of the righteous. (21423)
Character and example of a Christian woman. 1852
Character and greatness of Abraham Lincoln. 31954
Character and happiness of a vertuous woman. 46442
Character and hope of the righteous consider'd. 12370
Character and importance of agriculture. 43345
Character and influence of abolitionism. 82173
Character and labours of . . . William Knibb. 55022
Character and overthrow of Laish. 12312
Character and public career of Patrick Henry. 31419
Character and qualifactions of good rulers. 103733
Character and results of the war. 9615
Character and reward of a good and faithful servant of Jesus Christ. (78624)
Character & reward of the faithful & wise minister. (61040)
Character and reward of the faithful ministers of Christ. 79409
Character and reward of the good and faithful servant. 18415
Character and reward of the righteous. (13451)
Character and services of Abraham Lincoln. (42999)
Character and sufferings of the pilgrims. 33789
Character and tendency of colonization. 35867
Character and work of a good ruler. 26782
Character by R. Leighton, Jr. 76250
Character, commendation and reward. 72692, 2d note after 97559
Character &c. of the perfect and upright. 18405
Character of a Christian hero. 101169
Character of a Christian's life and death illustrated. 169
Character of a convent, displayed in the awful disclosures. 49993
Character . . . of a good and faithful servant. (50953)
Character of a good ruler. 104071
Character of a pastor. 79922

Character of a righteous ruler. 17914
Character of a true patriot. 101170
Character of a virtuous and good woman, a discourse. 92953
Character of able ministers of the New-Testament described. 58902
Character of Abraham Lincoln. (33482)
Character of Abraham Lincoln. A discourse. 27604
Character of Abraham Lincoln, and the constitutionality of his emancipation policy. 41179
Character of Abraham Lincoln. By Robert M. Patterson. (59144)
Character of Anna. 25408
Character of Caleb. 65583
Character of Columbus. (5339)
Character of David Brainerd. (21956)
Character of Dr. Barnes. (3512)
Character of Dorcas considered and improved. 71754
Character of Franklin. 27455
Character of Gen. Jackson and Mr. Van Buren. 23237
Character of Hugh Peters. 98043
Character of James Monroe. 95315
Character of Jesus Christ. 89744
Character of John Marshall. 95315
Character of Manlius Stimpson Clarke. 33964
Character of modern science. 90409
Character of Moses illustrated and improved. 61039
Character of Nehemiah. (64233)
Character . . . of preachers. 14217
Character of Rev. Ephraim Peabody. (71769)
Character of Rev. John Eliot, D. D. 25761
Character of some of the fanatics. 44259, 2d note after 102802
Character of the American government. 12014
Character of the candidates for civil government. 24531
Character of the gentleman. 40985
Character of the Godly and faithful. (72712)
Character of the king. 19590
Character of the late honorable Judge Dudley. 79457
Character of the late Thomas Chalmers. 85267 85267
Character of the perfect and upright man. (9717)
Character of the pioneers in the valley of the Ohio. (5337)
Character of the province of Maryland. 963, (80023)
Character of the puritans. 28687
Character of the rebellion. 58688
Character of the Reverend John Murray. 51519
Character of the Reverend Mr. John Wise. 103398
Character of the southern states of America. (55007)
Character of the United Swedish Churches. (13570)
Character of the virtuous Mrs. Abigail Brown. 46581, note after 100591
Character of their phenomena. 78509
Character of Thomas Jefferson. 21535
Character of William Penn vindicated. (59158)
Character, preaching, &c. of the Reverend Mr. George Whitefield. 83430-83433, 103514, 103588, 103601
Character, trials, and security of the church. 92087
Character vocalist. 86220

Characteres generum plantarum. 25134
Characterische Bilder aus dem republikanischen, sogenannt glucklichen Amerika. (37114)
Characteristic sketches of public men. 8894
Characteristic sketches of the people of the United States. 97914
Characteristicks of a good soldier. 42422
Characteristics and claims of the age in which we live. (37470)
Characteristics and prospects of California. 9542
Characteristics of California, Nevada, and other mines. 77762
Characteristics of some previously-described North American coleopterous insects, etc. (30524)
Characteristics of successful benevolent effort. 24435
Characteristics of the age: a discourse. (4616)
Characteristics of the age: an address. 37272
Characteristics of the former, and the recent outrages of the latter. 90867
Characteristics of the minister's work. 71524
Characteristics of the present century. 218
Characteristics of the red race of America. 77852, 77867, 77872
Characteristischen Notizen der vorzuglichsten Theilnahme derselben von F. A. Rocca. 72283
Characters and criticism. 36624
Characters; containing an impartial review of the public conduct. 12015
Characters in Rom. vii. distinctly illustrated. 20059
Characters of its governors and lieutenant-governors. 35585, (35636), 82167
Characters of new tanagers. (78136)
Characters of the old English colonies in America. 42617
Charaib treaty of 1773. 106124
Charakter und Sittengemalde fur die Jungend. (19649)
Charakter und Werth von Washingtons hinterlassenen Schriften. 89014
Charakterbild aus den Jahren 1864-67. 27181
Charakteristiken zur vergleichenden Erd- und Volkerkunde. 66851
Charakterschilderung und Thaten der Sud-Amerikanischen Helden. 6184, 21068
Charault, J. R. 12016, 12067
Charbonnel, Armand Francois Marie de, Bp., 1802-1891. 10420, 74553, 74555 see also Toronto (Archdiocese) Bishop (Charbonnel)
Charcoal sketches. 52162, 52164
Charcoal sketches. Second series. 52163
Chardon, Daniel Marc Antoine. 12017
Charency, Charles Felix Hyacinthe Gouhier, Comte de. see Charency, Hyacinthe, Comte de, 1832-1916.
Charency, Hyacinthe, Comte de, 1832-1916. 1582, 12018-12023, (72812)
Charenton, Joseph Nicholas. tr. 44554
Charge. 71514, 81403
Charge, addressed by the Hon. Peleg Sprague. 89718
Charge addressed to the graduates at the medical commencement. 90833
Charge and inaugural address delivered on occasion of the induction. 32269
Charge and inaugural address on the induction of H. B. Smith. (82712)
Charge, and the right hand of fellowship. 91807
Charge at the ordination of the Rev. James Adams. (37232)

Charge . . . at the triennial visitation . . . 1845. 51187

Charge . . . at the triennial visitation, . . . town of Halifax. (34766)

[Charge at the visitation] . . . June and August, 1803. (34766)

Charge . . . before the clergy of . . . the Diocese of Ohio. 43324

Charge before the Massachusetts Grand Lodge. 30521

Charge [by Bishop Seabury.] 78556

Charge . . . by Rev. Dr. Rodgers. (41630)

Charge, by Rev. John Pierpont. 91372

Charge [by Rev. William Davis Snodgrass.] 85483

Charge, by Samuel Spring, D. D. 105137

Charge, by the Rev. D. Fobes, of Raynham. 76515

Charge, by the Rev. Daniel Thomas. 92259

Charge, by the Rev. Dr. Appleton. 22126

Charge, by the Rev. Gad Hitchcock. 76514

Charge, by the Reverend Increase Mather. (65613)

Charge, by the Rev. James Thompson. 106051

Charge by the Rev. Joseph Lee of Royalston. 92241

Charge, by the Rev. Mr. Appleton. 18110

Charge, by the Rev. Mr. Isaac Backus. 91795

Charge, by the Reverend Mr. Morrill. 71828

Charge, by the Rev. Mr. Niles. 79922

Charge, by the Rev. Peter Powers, of Deer-Island. 89805

Charge, by the Rev. Mr. [Samuel] Wigglesworth. 72713

Charge by the Rev. William Patton. 72067

Charge delivered at his primary visitation held in Christ Church Cathedral, Frederickton. 25697

Charge delivered at the ordination of Josiah Bradshaw. 65701

Charge delivered at the primary visitation of the clergy of the Archdeaconry of Jamaica. 89302

Charge delivered at St. Peter's Church, in Salem. 31878

Charge delivered before the Morning Star Lodge. (4776)

Charge delivered by the Hon. James Wilson. 104626

Charge delivered by the Hon. John Jay, Chief Justice of the State of New York. 35831

Charge, delivered by the Hon. John Jay, Esq., Chief Justice of the United States. 35832

Charge delivered by the Hon. Judge Rush. 74249

Charge; delivered by the Reverend Joseph Bowman. 89793

Charge delivered from the bench to the grand inquest, at a Court of Oyer and Terminer and Gaol Delivery . . . at Philadelphia. 61763

Charge delivered from the bench to the grand inquest, at a Court of Oyer and Terminer and General Gaol Delivery held for the city and county of Philadelphia, April 13, 1736. 41794

Charge delivered from the bench to the grand inquest, at a Court of Oyer and Terminer and General Goal [sic] Delivery, held for the city and county of Philadelphia, April 13th, 1736. 41795

Charge delivered from the bench to the Grand-Jury, at the Court of Quarter Sessions. 41793

Charge delivered in . . . Fredericton, . . . at the second triennial visitation. 47354

Charge delivered in the Cathedral Church of Barbadoes. 58859

Charge, delivered May 17, 1757, at the first anniversary commencement. 84595

Charge, delivered to the Antient and Honorable Fraternity of Free and Accepted Masons, at Boston. 101469

Charge delivered to the brethren of the African Lodge. 29838

Charge delivered to the clergy of Bermuda. (24275)

Charge delivered to the clergy of the Diocese of Guiana. 60872

Charge delivered to the clergy of the Diocese of Montreal, at the primary visitation. 26139

Charge delivered to the clergy of the Diocese of Montreal, at the triennial visitation. 26139

Charge delivered to the clergy of the Diocese of Nova Scotia. (34766)

Charge delivered to the clergy of the Diocese of Toronto at the primary visitation, held in the Cathedral Church of St. James. 92635

Charge delivered to the clergy of the Diocese of Toronto, at the primary visitation, on the 9th Sept. 1841. 92642

Charge, delivered to the Convention of the Protestant Episcopal Church in . . . New-York, . . . October 5, 1808. (50329)

Charge delivered to the graduating class of the Columbian College, D. C. 79466

Charge, delivered to the Grand Juries of Beaufort and Orangeburgh Districts. 87450

Charge, delivered to the Grand Juries of the Circuit Court. 92285

Charge . . . delivered to the Grand Jury . . . at Bristol. 21427

Charge delivered to the Grand Jury at Northampton. 104287

Charge delivered to the Grand Jury for the county of Essex. 79942

Charge delivered to the Grand Jury of the Circuit Court of the United States. 92286

Charge, delivered to the Grand Jury of the county of Worcester. 93068

Charge delivered to the Grand Jury of Wayne Co. 65377

Charge delivered to the Grand Jury, on the fourth . . . of October, 1813. 44898

Charge . . . 1854. 51187

Charge from the President to the graduates at . . . Providence. 44351

Charge given by . . . brother Weeks. 102460

Charge given by the Chief Justice of the province of New-York. 12024

Charge, given by the Rev. Ammi R. Robbins. 92962

Charge, given on that occasion. 102747

Charge lately delivered by the Archdeacon of Colchester. (56601)

Charge of Chief Justice J. De Lancey to the Grand Jury. 19342

Charge of Dr. Norris to the jury. 6150, 12422

Charge of His Hon. C. D. Colden. 2879, 101441

Charge of Hon. William R. Staples. 90477

Charge of ignorance and misrepresentation
proved against "A lover of Cudworth
and truth." 98031
Charge of ignorance and misrepresentation
proved against Rev. George B. Cheever.
98032
Charge of ignorance . . . proved against "A
lover of Cudworth and truth." 98046
Charge of ignorance . . . proved against the
Rev. George B. Cheever. 98046
Charge of Judge Jabez Bowen to the Grand
Jury. 27052
Charge of Judge Maynard to the Grand Jury
of Northampton County. 47167
Charge of Judge Paterson to the jury.
(59056)
Charge of Judge Rogers. 39172
Charge of Judge Thompson. 88951
Charge of Mr. Justice Story. 92287
Charge of St. Paul. (16346)
Charge of the Body Guard at Springfield,
Missouri. 89886
Charge of the Chief Justice of England to the
Grand Jury. (14087)
Charge of the Hon. J. B. Robinson, Chief
Justice of Upper Canada. 72120
Charge of the Honourable James De Lancey
Esq. 19340, 19341, 84557
Charge of the Hon. Judge Snow. 70913,
85563
Charge of the judge to the jury. (43001),
96901
Charge of the Right Reverend Benjamin Moore.
(50329)
Charge of the Sabbath. 80255-(80257)
Charge, on events connected with the organi-
zation. 103465
Charge on the rise of the American empire.
20918
Charge, right hand of fellowship, and address.
90927, 90929
Charge . . . to the African Grand Lodge.
29838
Charge to the clergy. 8691, 52763
Charge to the clergy . . . at the . . . con-
vention. (32301)
Charge to the clergy of the Diocese of Mary-
land. 37338
Charge to the clergy . . . in the state of New
York. (32301)
Charge to the clergy of his diocese. 35801
Charge, to the clergy of his diocess, [sic]
delivered at Derby. 78560
Charge, to the clergy of his diocess [sic],
delivered at Middletown. (15654), 78555
Charge to the clergy of Massachusetts, de-
livered May 16, 1849. 21663
Charge to the clergy of Massachusetts, May 4,
1859. 21553
Charge to the clergy . . . of Pennsylvania.
64617
Charge to the clergy of the Diocese of New
Jersey. 20391
Charge . . . to the clergy of the Diocese of
Ohio . . . in . . . Akron. 43324
Charge . . . to the clergy of the Diocese of
Ohio . . . October 11th, 1851. 43324
Charge . . . to the clergy of the Diocese of
Ohio . . . September 8th, 1843. 43324
Charge to the clergy of the Diocese of Quebec,
delivered at Montreal and at York, Upper
Canada. 91655
Charge to the clergy of the Diocese of Quebec,
delivered at the visitation in Montreal.
91656

Charge . . . to the clergy of the Diocese of
Quebec. . . . 1838. 51187
Charge to the clergy of the Diocese of Rhode
Island. 13385
Charge to the clergy of the Diocese of
Western New York. 19343
Charge to the clergy of the Diocese of Rupert's
Land. 1392
Charge . . . to the clergy of the Protestant
Episcopal Church in the Eastern Diocese.
(28881)
Charge to the clergy of the Protestant Episco-
pal Church in the state of New Jersey.
17581
Charge to the clergy of the Protestant Episco-
pal Church in Virginia. 47242
Charge to the Convention of New-York. 35858
Charge to the first graduates in the said
College [and Academy of Philadelphia.]
84599-84600
Charge to the graduates in the University of
Vermont, at Burlington, at the public
commencement, Sept. 9th, 1807. 76354
Charge to the graduates in the University of
Vermont, at Burlington, at the public
commencement, 29th July, 1812. 76355
Charge to the graduates of Jefferson Medical
College. (21278)
Charge to the Grand Juries of the County
Court of the Fifth Circuit. 376
Charge to the Grand Jury. At a General
Court, held at the capitol. 99777
Charge to the Grand Jury, at the Court of
General Sessions of the Peace. (25771)
Charge to the Grand Jury, at the July term of
the Municipal Court. 32285
Charge to the Grand Jury for the body of this
province. 87356
Charge to the Grand Jury in the District
Court of the United States. 24291
Charge to the Grand Jury in Washington
County. 68502
Charge to the Grand Jury of Edgecombe
Superior Court, 1817. 94509
Charge to the Grand Jury of the county of
Suffolk. 67236
Charge . . . to the Grand Jury of the Criminal
Court of Memphis. 33935
Charge to the Grand Jury of the U. S. Circuit
Court. 92319
Charge to the Grand Jury upon the importance
of maintaining the supremacy of the laws.
(58689)
Charge to the Grand Jury, upon the uncertainty
of the law. 58690
Charge . . . to the jury, in the case of ship
Achorn. 62785
Charge to the pastor . . . by Rev. Dr. Krebs.
32435, note after 89770
Charge to the pastor, by the Rev. E. E. Seelye.
89744
Charge to the people. 85409
Charge to the people by Rev. Dr. Potts.
32435, note after 89770
Charges against Brigadier General Hull.
(33642)
Charges against slavery. 33794
Charges against the Collector and Surveyor of
the Port of Philadelphia. 27286
Charges against the United States Military
Academy. 3482
Charges against Victor Smith. 84483
Charges and banishment of Roger Williams, &c.
6010
Charges, and extracts of charges, on moral
and religious subjects. 74250

Charges and proofs respecting the conduct of
Peter Landis. 38828-38829
Charges and regulations of the . . . Society
of Free . . . Masons. 102460
Charges and specifications of charges against
Lieut. James Glynn. 96872
Charges brought by the Roman Catholics
against the American missionaries
the Sandwich Islands. 76454, 95419
Charges, by Rev. Thomas Smyth, D. D.
85323
Charges delivered on the occasion. 82952
Charges delivered to the clergy of the Diocese
of Barbadoes and the Leeward Islands.
14323
Charges of Hon. James Brooks, of New York,
against Gen. Benjamin F. Butler. 9615
Charges of Mr. John Scoble & Mr. Lewis
Tappan. 67184
Charges of the Board of Trade against the
Phenix Bank. 54266
Charges preferred against Don Joaquin
Velasques de Leon. 76824
Charges preferred against the New-York
Female Benevolent Society. 43188, note
after 103223
Charges, preferred by John White. 103412
Charges to the Grand Jury of the county of
Suffolk. 95187
Charicles: a dramatic poem. 67271
Charisius, --------. petitioner 69585, 2d
note after 102911 see also Deensche
Africaensche Compagnie. Resident.
petitioner
Charitable Baptist Society, Providence, R. I.
66247
Charitable blessed. 21563
Charitable Eye and Ear Infirmary of Massachu-
setts. see Massachusetts. Charitable
Eye and Ear Infirmary.
Charitable Fire Society, Providence, R. I. see
Providence Charitable Fire Society.
Charitable Fire Society of Massachusetts. see
Massachusetts Charitable Fire Society.
Charitable judgment of the opinions and con-
duct of others. 49130
Charitable Mechanic Association, Salem, Mass.
see Salem Charitable Mechanic Associ-
ation.
Charitable Mechanic Association of Maine.
see Maine Charitable Mechanic Associ-
ation.
Charitable Mechanic Association of Massachu-
setts. see Massachusetts Charitable
Mechanic Association.
Charitable plea for the speechless. 50633
Charitable Society, Roxbury, Mass. see
Roxbury Charitable Society, Roxbury,
Mass.
Charitable Society, Instituted by the Franklin
Association of Ministers. see Franklin
Association Charitable Society.
Charitable Society of Franklin County, Mass.
see Franklin Association Charitable
Society.
Charitable Society of Hampshire County, Mass.
see Hampshire Association Charitable
Society.
Charitable Society of Rockingham County, N. H.
see Rockingham Charitable Society, in
New-Hampshire.
Charitable Society of Windham County, Conn.
see Windham County Charitable Society.
Charities of Boston. 756
Charities of New York, Brooklyn and Staten
Island. 10174

Charity: a poem. 93250
Charity and truth. 82942
Charity at home. 70840
Charity considered in a sermon preached at
Charlestown. 91789
Charity Foundation of the Protestant Episcopal
Church in Buffalo. see Protestant
Episcopal Charity Foundation, Buffalo,
N. Y.
Charity Hospital, New Orleans. see New
Orleans. Charity Hospital.
Charity Hospital, Shreveport, La. see
Louisiana. Charity Hospital, Shreveport.
Charity Hospital of Philadelphia. see Phila-
delphia. Charity Hospital.
Charity illustrated and recommended. (39547)
Charity Lodge, Peterborough, N. H. see
Freemasons. New Hampshire. Charity
Lodge, Peterborough.
Charity recommended for the social status of
man. 65562
Charity sermon, delivered at the request of the
Howard Benevolent Society. 89788
Charity sermon, delivered before the Dorcas
Society. 90358
Charity sermon, delivered in . . . Hartford.
68122
Charity sermon, delivered in the North
Presbyterian Meeting-House in Hartford.
(24760)
Charity sermon, in the French Protestant
Church. 37650
Charity supported by orthodoxy. 98033, 98046
Charity to children enforced. 58732
Charity to the distressed members of Christ.
12331
Charland, A. F. Boutron. see Boutron-
Charland, A. F.
Charland, Louis. 100763
Charlatanisme dans l'histoire. (5147)
Charlemagne, Philemon. 12027
Charlemont. (81279)
Charlemont; or, the pride of the village.
(81200)
Charles VI, Emperor of Austria, 1685-1740.
40712, 68792, 102442 see also Austria.
Sovereigns, etc., 1711-1740 (Charles VI)
Charles X, King of France, 1757-1836. (29185),
(57530) see also France. Sovereigns,
etc., 1824-1830 (Charles X)
Charles I, King of Great Britain, 1600-1649.
65936, 95516, 98637, 99849, 100464
see also Great Britain. Sovereigns, etc.,
1625-1649 (Charles I)
Charles II, King of Great Britain, 1630-1685.
46790, 52624, 82797, 87697, 1st note
after 97056, 98511 see also Great
Britain. Sovereigns, etc., 1660-1685
(Charles II)
Charles Edward, The Young Pretender. see
Stuart, Charles Edward Louis Philip
Casimir, 1720-1788.
Charles (Edmund) & Son. firm publishers
12028
Charles Barimore. 25052
Charles C. Jewett. 36109
Charles Chatterton. 74452
Charles Dickens aangeboden snuifje door eene
Amerikaansche dame. (20001)
Charles Doolittle Walcott. 85010
Charles F. Adams platform. 189, (12029)
Charles Guerin. 12344
Charles Hammond and his relations to Henry
Clay. 84788-84789
Charles Henry Cᵗ D'Estaing. 50185, 82379
Charles Hodge Dod. 43164

Charles I. Bushnell. 83998
Charles Morton. 18437
Charles River Bridge Company. firm see
Proprietors of Charles River Bridge.
firm
Charles Sealsfield. pseud. see Postl, Karl,
1793-1864.
Charles Street Baptist Church, Boston. see
Boston. Charles Street Baptist Church.
Charles Summerfield. pseud. see Arrington,
A. W.
Charles Summer. 93689
Charles T. James vs. the Atlantic DeLaine
Company. 35680
Charles the Fifth. 72008
Charles Vernon. 79129
Charles Vincent. 104135
Charleston, S. C. 12043, (12055), 12073,
12090, (30013)
Charleston, S. C. petitioners 10889, (35938)
Charleston, S. C. Agricultural Society of
South Carolina. see Agricultural
Society of South Carolina, Charleston.
Charleston, S. C. Apprentices' Library
Society. see Apprentices' Library
Society, Charleston, S. C.
Charleston, S. C. Bank. see Bank of
Charleston.
Charleston, S. C. Bank of the State of South
Carolina. see Bank of the State of
South Carolina, Charleston.
Charleston, S. C. Bar. 61249
Charleston, S. C. Board of Commissioners
of Free Schools. 12074
Charleston, S. C. Brooks Guards. see
South Carolina. Militia. Brooks Guards,
Charleston.
Charleston, S. C. Board of Trade. 12037,
87934
Charleston, S. C. Celebration of the 55th
Anniversary of American Independence
by the Union and State Rights Party,
1831. see Union and State Rights Party
(South Carolina) Celebration of the
55th Anniversary of American Indepen-
dence, Charleston, 1831.
Charleston, S. C. Celebration of the Fourth
of July, 1831. see Charleston, S. C.
Fourth of July Celebration, 1831.
Charleston, S. C. Census, 1848. 12034,
(18947)
Charleston, S. C. Census, 1861. 12034
Charleston, S. C. Chamber of Commerce.
12035, 12058, 12082, 87934
Charleston, S. C. Charter. 87637, 87710,
87713
Charleston, S. C. Citizens. 12067, 12069,
87938, 88475-88477
Charleston, S. C. Citizens. petitioners
(12059), 12073, 87872
Charleston, S. C. City Council. 12056,
12069, 12075, 85334
Charleston, S. C. City Council. Committee
on Interments Within the City. 12073
Charleston, S. C. City Council. Committee
on the Most Efficient Means to Preserve
the Health of the City. 87879
Charleston, S. C. City Council. Committee
on Ways and Means. 12049
Charleston, S. C. College of Charleston.
12033
Charleston, S. C. College of Charleston.
Faculty. 12033
Charleston, S. C. College of Charleston.
Museum of Natural History. Curator.
12033

Charleston, S. C. Colored People's Convention
of the State of South Carolina, 1865.
see Colored People's Convention of the
State of South Carolina, Charleston,
1865.
Charleston, S. C. Commercial Convention of
the Southern and Western States, 1854. see
Commercial Convention of the Southern
and Western States, Charleston, S. C.,
1854.
Charleston, S. C. Commissioner of the City
Debt. (32604) see also Holmes, James
G.
Charleston, S. C. Committee Appointed by the
Citizens. see Charleston, S. C. Com-
mittee on the Treaty of Amity, Commerce,
and Navigation.
Charleston, S. C. Committee on the Treaty of
Amity, Commerce, and Navigation.
10663, 84819
Charleston, S. C. Congregational Church.
25196
Charleston, S. C. Constitutional Convention,
1775-1776. see South Carolina. Con-
stitutional Convention, Charleston, 1775-
1776.
Charleston, S. C. Convention of Banks, 1841.
see Convention of Banks, Charleston,
S. C. 1841.
Charleston, S. C. Convention of Merchants
and Others for the Promotion of the
Direct Trade, 1839. see Convention of
Merchants and Others for the Promotion
of the Direct Trade, Charleston, 1839.
Charleston, S. C. Co-operation Meeting, 1851.
see Southern Rights and Co-operation
Meeting, Charleston, S. C., 1851.
Charleston, S. C. Court. 37436
Charleston, S. C. Court of Admiralty Sessions.
see South Carolina (Colony) Court of
Vice Admiralty, Charleston, S. C.
Charleston, S. C. Court of Sessions. 92878
Charleston, S. C. Court of Vice Admiralty.
see South Carolina (Colony) Court of
Vice Admiralty, Charleston, S. C.
Charleston, S. C. Customs House. see U. S.
Customs House, Charleston, S. C.
Charleston, S. C. Democratic Party Convention,
1843. see Democratic Party. South
Carolina. Convention, Charleston, 1843.
Charleston, S. C. Democratic Party National
Convention, 1860. see Democratic
Party. National Convention, Charleston,
S. C. 1860.
Charleston, S. C. Eighteen Hundred and Sixty
Society. see Eighteen Hundred and
Sixty Association, Charleston, S. C.
Charleston, S. C. Elliott Society of Natural
History. see Elliott Society of Natural
History, Charleston, S. C.
Charleston, S. C. Fellowship Society. see
Fellowship Society of Charleston, S. C.
Charleston, S. C. Female Domestic Mission-
ary Society. see Female Domestic
Missionary Society, Charleston, S. C.
Charleston, S. C. First Presbyterian Church.
12051
Charleston, S. C. Fourth of July Celebration,
1831. 12068, 88066 see also State
Rights and Free Trade Party of Charles-
ton, S. C. Celebration of the 55th Anni-
versary of American Independence,
Charleston, 1831.
Charleston, S. C. Free Trade Convention,
1831. see Free Trade Convention,
Charleston, S. C., 1831.

Charleston, S. C. General Meeting of the Citizens, in St. Michael's Church, 1795. see Charleston, S. C. Citizens.

Charleston, S. C. Great Southern Co-operation and Anti-Secession Meeting, 1851. see Southern Rights and Co-operation Meeting, Charleston, S. C., 1851.

Charleston, S. C. Immigration Convention, 1870. see Immigration Convention, Charleston, S. C., 1870.

Charleston, S. C. Lazaretto. see South Carolina. Lazaretto, Charleston.

Charleston, S. C. Magnolia Cemetery. 65766

Charleston, S. C. Marine Bible Society. see Marine Bible Society, Charleston, S. C.

Charleston, S. C. Mayor, 1838 (Pinckney) 12077, 85334 see also Pinckney, Henry Laurens, 1794-1863.

Charleston, S. C. Medical College of the State of South Carolina. 87871, 87873, 87874-87875, 87878

Charleston, S. C. Medical College of the State of South Carolina. Board of Trustees. 87872

Charleston, S. C. Medical College of the State of South Carolina. Dean. 87876

Charleston, S. C. Medical College of the State of South Carolina. President. 87872

Charleston, S. C. Medical Convention of South Carolina, 1848. see Medical Convention of South Carolina, Charleston, S. C., 1848.

Charleston, S. C. Meeting of Delegates from the Southern Rights Associations, 1851. see Meeting of Delegates from Southern Rights Associations of South Carolina, Charleston, 1851.

Charleston, S. C. Meeting of the Friends of Co-operation in the Cause of Southern Rights, 1851. see Southern Rights and Co-operation Meeting, Charleston, S. C., 1851.

Charleston, S. C. Meeting of the State Rights Party of South Carolina. 1830. see State Rights and Free Trade Party of Charleston, S. C. Meeting, Charleston, 1830.

Charleston, S. C. Meeting of the Union and State Rights Party. 1832. see State Rights and Free Trade Party of Charleston, S. C. Meeting, Charleston, 1832.

Charleston, S. C. Meeting on the Religious Instruction of the Negroes, 1845. (12071)

Charleston, S. C. Merchants. 50342

Charleston, S. C. New England Society. see New England Society, Charleston, S. C.

Charleston, S. C. Ordinances, etc. 12044, 12048, 12062, 12088, 33049, 57515, 87669, 87710

Charleston, S. C. Orphan House. 12083

Charleston, S. C. Phoenix Rifles. see South Carolina. Militia. Phoenix Rifles, Charleston.

Charleston, S. C. Presbytery. see Presbyterian Church in the United States. Presbytery of Charleston.

Charleston, S. C. Press Conference, 1870. see Press Conference, Charleston, S. C. 1870.

Charleston, S. C. Protestant Episcopal Missionary Society. see Protestant Episcopal Missionary Society, Charleston, S. C.

Charleston, S. C. Public Meeting of the State Rights and Free Trade Party, 1831.

see State Rights and Free Trade Party of Charleston, S. C. Public Meeting, Charleston, 1831.

Charleston, S. C. Reformed Society of Israelites. see Reformed Society of Israelites, Charleston, S. C.

Charleston, S. C. Registrar. 12078

Charleston, S. C. St. Andrew's Club. see St. Andrew's Society of the City of Charleston.

Charleston, S. C. St. Andrew's Society. see St. Andrew's Society of the City of Charleston.

Charleston, S. C. St. John's Lodge, no. 31. see Freemasons. York Rite. South Carolina. St. John's Lodge, no. 31, Charleston.

Charleston, S. C. St. Paul's Agricultural Society. see St. Paul's Agricultural Society, Charleston, S. C.

Charleston, S. C. St. Philip's Church. 87931

Charleston, S. C. Second Presbyterian Church. 85300, 85341

Charleston, S. C. Second Presbyterian Church. Publication Fund. 85331

Charleston, S. C. Select Committee, 1795. 87938

Charleston, S. C. South Carolina Association. see South Carolina Association, Charleston.

Charleston, S. C. South Carolina Society. see South Carolina Society, Charleston.

Charleston, S. C. Southern Rights and Co-operation Meeting, 1851. see Southern Rights and Co-operation Meeting, Charleston, S. C., 1851

Charleston, S. C. State Rights and Free Trade Association. see State Rights and Free Trade Association of South Carolina.

Charleston, S. C. State Rights and Free Trade Convention, 1832. see State Rights and Free Trade Convention, Charleston, S. C. 1832.

Charleston, S. C. State Rights and Free Trade Party. see State Rights and Free Trade Party of Charleston, S. C.

Charleston, S. C. State Rights Celebration, 1830. 12072, 88061

Charleston, S. C. State Temperance Convention, 1844. see South Carolina State Temperance Convention, Charleston, 1844.

Charleston, S. C. State Temperance Convention, 1845. see South Carolina State Temperance Convention, Charleston, 1845.

Charleston, S. C. Sundry Masters of Vessels. see Sundry Masters of Vessels Laying in the Port of Charleston, S. C.

Charleston, S. C. Union and State Rights Party Meeting, 1832. see State Rights and Free Trade Party of Charleston, S. C. Meeting, Charleston, 1832.

Charleston, S. C. Unitarian Book and Tract Society. see Unitarian Book and Tract Society, Charleston, S. C.

Charleston, S. C. Unitarian Church. 12050

Charleston, S. C. Washington Light Infantry. see South Carolina. Militia. Washington Light Infantry, Charleston.

Charleston, S. C. Washington Society. see Washington Society, Charleston, S. C.

Charleston (Diocese) (16085)

Charleston (Diocese) Bishop (England) 22589 see also England, John, Bp., 1786-1842.

Charleston almanac for 1868. 12036

Charleston and her satirists. (81279)
Charleston Association. see Baptists. South
Carolina. Charleston Association.
Charleston Association of Baptist Churches in
the State of South Carolina. see Bap-
tists. South Carolina. Charleston
Association.
Charleston, August 2d, 5809. 87846
Charleston Baptist Association. see Baptists.
South Carolina. Charleston Association.
Charleston Bethel Union. 12092
Charleston Bible Society. 12092
Charleston book. (12038)
Charleston city gazette. 84832, 87866
Charleston College, Charleston, S. C. see
Charleston, S. C. College of Charleston.
Charleston courier. 25675, 28719, 33234,
(52392), 80853, 84828, 85311, 87927,
88074, 1st note after 95112, 99782, note
after 103316, 106004
Charleston courier and the slave trade. 81926
Charleston daily gazette. 97469
Charleston directory, and revenue system.
(12039)
Charleston fee bill. 87878, 87880
Charleston imports. 87920
Charleston Infant School Society. see Infant
School Society, Charleston, S. C.
Charleston, January 19, 1829. 87958
Charleston, July 13, 5809. 87846
Charleston, July 24, 1798. 87537
Charleston Juvenile Missionary Society. 85341
Charleston Library Society, Charleston, S. C.
12040
Charleston, March 9th, 5890. 87848
Charleston, May 27, 1789. (34627)
Charleston medical journal and review. 12041,
81293, 83003
Charleston medical register. 67682
Charleston memorial. 10889, (35938)
Charleston mercury. 12045, 19131, 22985,
69454, 87439, 87856, 96379
Charleston mercury extra. 87439
Charleston observer. Editor. pseud. 98040
Charleston pilot. 87782
Charleston Port Society for Promoting the
Gospel Among Seamen, Charleston, S. C.
12092
Charleston Presbytery. see Presbyterian
Church in the United States. Presbytery
of Charleston.
Charleston press. (3966)
Charleston, South Carolina. A satiric poem.
12042
Charleston, South-Carolina, February 4th 5809.
87846
Charleston South-Carolina. January 8th [i. e.
28th] 5809. 87846
Charleston southern standard. 87856
Charleston standard. 89748-89749
Charleston Union Presbytery. see Presby-
terian Church in the U. S. Presbytery
of Charleston (Union)
Charleston "year book" 1883. 83003
Charlestown, Mass. 12096, 12109, 12112-
12113, (12120), 12123-12124, (50842),
106052
Charlestown, Mass. petitioners 18807
Charlestown, Mass. Associated Pastors. see
Congregational Churches in Massachusetts.
Boston Association.
Charlestown, Mass. Asylum for the Insane.
12101, 45846
Charlestown, Mass. Baptist Meeting-House.
12121, 91812

Charlestown, Mass. Bunker Hill Soldiers'
Relief Society, Charlestown, Mass.
Charlestown, Mass. Charter. 12113
Charlestown, Mass. Citizens. petitioners
95946
Charlestown, Mass. City Council. 12109,
12113, (12120)
Charlestown, Mass. Committee on the Des-
truction of the Ursuline Convent. 12115
Charlestown, Mass. Committee to Consider
the Expediency of Obtaining a City Char-
ter. Majority. 12118
Charlestown, Mass. Edgeworth Chapel. Sunday
School. 12098
Charlestown, Mass. Female Seminary. see
Charlestown Female Seminary, Charles-
town, Mass.
Charlestown, Mass. First Church. 12098
Charlestown, Mass. First Baptist Church.
12098
Charlestown, Mass. First Parish Sabbath
School. 12098
Charlestown, Mass. Free Schools. 12095
Charlestown, Mass. Funeral Ceremonies for
Washington, 1799. 5361, 12114, (50942),
101594, 101777, 101841, 101874
Charlestown, Mass. Grand Rally of the Work-
ingmen, 3d, 1840. see Grand Rally of
the Workingmen of Charlestown, Mass.,
3d, 1840
Charlestown, Mass. High School. 12095
Charlestown, Mass. High School. Library.
12095
Charlestown, Mass. High Street Baptist Church.
12111
Charlestown, Mass. Mayor, 1847. 12108
Charlestown, Mass. Mayor, 1865-1866. (Robin-
son) 72055 see also Robinson, Charles.
Charlestown, Mass. Ministry at Large. 12098,
23286 see also Everett, Oliver Capen.
Charlestown, Mass. Navy Library and Insti-
tute. see Navy Library and Institute,
Charlestown, Mass.
Charlestown, Mass. Ordinances, etc. (12099),
12113
Charlestown, Mass. Public Library. 12103
Charlestown, Mass. Public Library. Trustees.
12103
Charlestown, Mass. School Board. Treasurer.
12095
Charlestown, Mass. School Committee. 12095
Charlestown, Mass. Soldiers' Relief Society.
see Soldiers' Relief Society, Charles-
town, Mass.
Charlestown, Mass. Ursuline Convent. (12110)
Charlestown, Mass. Ursuline Convent. Mother
Superior. 12097, 45038, 68580, 98168
see also Mary Edmond St. George,
Mother.
Charlestown, Mass. Water Works. Chief
Engineer. (12116)
Charlestown, Mass. Water Works. Commis-
sioners. (12116)
Charlestown, Mass. Woodlawn Cemetery.
12109
Charlestown, Mass. Young Men's Charitable
Association. see Young Men's Chari-
table Association of Charlestown, Mass.
Charlestown, Mass. Young Men's Evangelical
Union. see Young Men's Evangelical
Union, Charlestown, Mass.
Charlestown, N. H. Superior Court. 74530
Charlestown. 89557
Charlestown Association for the Reformation
of Morals. 12104

Charlestown chronicle. 77529
Charlestown City Mission and Tract Society. 12098
Charlestown convent; its destruction by a mob. 12105, 26103
Charlestown directory. 12106
Charlestown Female Seminary, Charlestown, Mass. (12102)
Charlestown Gas Company. (12117)
Charlestown, May 27, 1789. 11203, (34627), 95950
Charlestown records. 106052
Charleval, Charles Francois de. supposed author 99506
Charlevoix, P. F. Saverio di. see Charlevoix, Pierre Francois Xavier de, 1682-1761.
Charlevoix, Pierre Francois Xavier de, 1682-1761. 95, 6215, 10330, 12127-12143, 25853, 28448, 61022, 68450, (80023), 84162, 84566, 84701, 84779, note after 98488, 3d note after 99504
Charley Ross. 73344
Charley Temple and his first glass of liquor. 89558
Charlie, the drummer boy. 12144
Charlotte, Empress of Mexico, 1840-1927. see Carlota, Empress of Mexico, 1840-1927.
Charlotte. 73613
Charlotte. A tale of truth. 73604
Charlotte Elizabeth. pseud. Izram, a Mexican tale. see Tonna, Charlotte Elizabeth Brown Phelan.
Charlotte Temple. 73604, 73606, 73608
Charlotte's daughter. 73608
Charlottesville, N. Y. New York Conference Seminary. see New York Conference Seminary, Charlottesville, N. Y.
Charlottesville, Va. Central College. see Virginia. University.
Charlottesville, Va. Democratic Party Convention, 1840. see Democratic Party. Virginia. Convention, Charlottesville, 1840.
Charlottetown, Prince Edward Island. Legislative Library. see Prince Edward Island. Legislative Library, Charlottetown.
Charlton, Dimmock. 12146
Charlton, Edward A. 12147
Charlton, Frederic. 12148
Charlton, H. M. 12149
Charlton, Robert M. 12150-12151
Charlton, Thomas J. 12151
Charlton, Thomas U. P. 12152
Charlton, N. Y. Washington Benevolent Society. see Washington Benevolent Society. New York. Charlton.
Charmilly, -------- Venault de. see Venault de Charmilly, --------.
Charming Betsy (Schooner) in Admiralty (51484)
Charms, Richard de. see de Charms, Richard.
Charnay, Desire. 12153-(12154)
Charnock, John. 12155
Charolais, --------. 12156
Charolais, L. Chauvet. see Chauvet-Charolais, L.
Charpenne, Pierre. 12157
Charpentier, Francois. (69261)
Charrault, J. R. see Charault, J. R.
Charroppin, Ad. 12158
Chart and description of the Boston and Worcester and Western Rail Roads. 29226

Chart and description of the railroad from Boston to New-York. 29227
Chart and memoir, relative to the new discoveries. 40312
Chart, containing the names of senators. 28824
Chart of Boston harbor. 3607
Chart of geology. 23171
Chart of the approaches of Rio de Janeiro. 4854
Chart of the Atlantic Ocean. 88221
Chart of the coast of America. 79030
Chart of the coast of Florida. 24857
Chart of the Colorado River. 9728
Chart of the Diocese of New York. 77988
Chart of the harbour of Boston. 52067
Chart of Mercator's projection. 27722
Chart, or plan of marching, and encamping, laid down. 82771
Charte von den neuen Entdeckungen welche gegen norden der Suder-Meers. (41417)
Charter and act of incorporation of the American Atlantic & Pacific Ship Canal Company. 55139
Charter and amendments. The general mortgage. 55821
Charter, and amendments thereto, of the Planters' Bank. 49532
Charter and by-laws and the deed of endowment of the Protestant Episcopal Society for Promoting Religion and Learning in the State of New York. 85857
Charter and by-laws for the regulation of the Warren Library Society. 101495
Charter and by-laws of Christ Church. 61534
Charter and by-laws of . . . New Haven, June, 1865. 52968
Charter and by-laws of the Alleghany Railroad and Coal Company. 59872
Charter and by-laws [of the American Geographical and Statistical Society.] 1091
Charter and by-laws of the Arch Street Presbyterian Church. 61477
Charter and by-laws of the Artillery Company of . . . Newport. 55034
Charter and by-laws of the Athenaeum [in Philadelphia.] 61496
Charter and by-laws of the Athenaeum, with a list of the members. 54432
Charter and by-laws of the Bank for Savings in . . . New York. 54108
Charter and by-laws of the Bohemian Mining Co. 6141
Charter and by-laws [of the Buffalo Trust Company.] 9063
Charter and by-laws of the Canton Run Improvement Company. 10716
Charter and by-laws of the Chamber of Commerce of . . . New York. 53584
Charter and by-laws of the Charitable Baptist Society, in Providence. 66247
Charter and bye-laws of the city of Montreal. 50246
Charter and by-laws of the Coal Run Improvement and Railroad Company. 59980
Charter and by-laws of the Colored Home, of the City of New-York. 85982
Charter and by-laws [of the Entomological Society of Philadelphia.] 61619
Charter and by-laws of the Franklin Fire Co. 61674
Charter and by-laws of the Franklin Lyceum, Providence, R. I. 66263
Charter and by-laws of the General Society of Mechanics and Tradesmen. 54290

Charter and bye-laws of the General Society of Mechanics & Tradesmen of the City of New-York. 86075

Charter and by-laws of the German Society of the City of New York. (54292)

Charter and by-laws of the German Society, with a list of members. 27152

Charter and by-laws of the Great Western Iron Company. 28476, (35091)

Charter and by-laws of the Howard Fire Insurance Company. (42482)

Charter and by-laws of the Lincoln Institution. 61790

Charter and by-laws of the Long Island College Hospital. (41896)

Charter and by-laws of the Machpelah Cemetery. 61799

Charter and by-laws of the Marine Society of Newport. 55038

Charter and by-laws of the Maryland Anthracite Coal Company. (45203)

Charter and by-laws of the Milwaukee Female College. 49172

Charter and by-laws of the Minneapolis Mill Company. (49232)

Charter and by-laws of the New Bedford Horticultural Society. 52470

Charter and by-laws of the New England Mining and Quarrying Company. 52706

Charter and by-laws of the New Haven County Horticultural Society. 52990

Charter and by-laws of the . . . [New York] Historical Society. (54471)

Charter and by-laws of the . . . [New York] Juvenile Asylum. 54503

Charter and by-laws of the New York Mechanics' and Tradesmen's General Society. 54513

Charter, and bye-laws of the . . . [New York] Society Library. 54545

Charter and by-laws of the . . . [New York State Inebriate] Asylum. 53821

Charter and by-laws of the Newark Library Association. 54880

Charter and by-laws of the Newport Coal Company. 55026

Charter and by-laws of the Ocoee mining Company. (56651)

Charter and by-laws of the Pennsylvania Bible Society. 60304

Charter and by-laws of the Pennsylvania Company for Insurances. 60315

Charter and by-laws [of the Pennsylvania Society for the Prevention of Cruelty to Animals.] (60368)

Charter and by-laws of the Philadelphia and Atlantic Steam Navigation Company. 61943

Charter and by-laws of the Philadelphia Bible Society. 61967

Charter and by-laws of the . . . [Philadelphia] Club. (61981)

Charter and by-laws of the Philadelphia Museum Company. 62020

Charter and by-laws of the . . . [Philadelphia] Society [for Promoting Agriculture.] 62036

Charter and by-laws of the Philadelphia Typographical Society. 62046

Charter and by-laws of the Potomac Copper Company. 64587

Charter and by-laws of the Providence Library Company. 66331

Charter and by-laws of the Rhode-Island Society for the Encouragement of Domestic Industry. (70736)

Charter and by-laws of the Roxbury Gas Light Company. (73731)

Charter and by-laws of the St. Flavien Mining and Smelting Company. 75203

Charter and by-laws of the Society for Promoting the Gospel Among Seamen in the Port of New-York. 85859

Charter and by-laws [of the Society for the Diffusion of Spiritual Knowledge, New York.] 85889

Charter and bye-laws of the Society for the Promotion of the Useful Arts. 85998

Charter and by-laws of the Society of the Friendly Sons of St. Patrick. 86144

Charter and by-laws of the Society of the Lying-In Hospital of the City of New York. 86149

Charter and by-laws of the Society of the Sons of St. George. 62260

Charter and by-laws of the Soldiers' Business, Messenger and Dispatch Company. 86333

Charter and by laws of the Sopori Land and Mining Company. 87134

Charter and by-laws of the South Jersey Cranberry Company. 88140

Charter and by-laws of the Southern Hotel Company of St. Louis. 88374

Charter and by-laws of the Southwestern & Rio Grande Railroad Co. and Shreveport & Southwestern R. R. Co. Consolidated. 88610

Charter and by-laws of the Stony Brook Railroad. 92166

Charter and by-laws of the Stuyvesant Institute. 54685, note after 93289

Charter and by-laws of the Susquehanna and Wyoming Valley Railroad and Coal Company. 93924

Charter and by-laws of the Susquehanna Coal and Coal Mountain Company. 93930

Charter and by-laws of the Union School and Children's Home. 62354, note after 97815

Charter and by-laws of the United States Fire Company. 62357, 97965

Charter and bye-laws of the Vermont Medical Society. 99232

Charter and by-laws of the Warehousing Company of Philadelphia. 62374

Charter and by-laws of the Welch Society. 62378, 102527

Charter and by-laws, rules and regulations of the Providence Association of Mechanics and Manufacturers. 66305

Charter and by-laws, with a history of the Chamber of Commerce of the State of New York. 37784, 53584

Charter and by-laws . . . with an account of the statues, busts, and paintings belonging to the Academy [of Fine Arts.] 54017

Charter and constitution of the Athenaeum Association. 54432

Charter and constitution of the Merchants' and Clerks' Library Association of . . . New-York. 54392

Charter and constitution of the St. George's Society. 43738

Charter and deed of settlement. 61986

Charter and description of the property of the Virginia and New England Mining Company. 100548

Charter and fundamental articles of the Evangelical Reformed Congregation . . . of Philadelphia. 61639

Charter and fundamental laws of the Corporation for the Relief of Widows and Children of Clergymen. 53631

Charter and laws of Iowa City. (35041)

Charter and laws of the colony of New Plymouth. (7962)

Charter and laws of the Missouri Petroleum and Mining Company. 59621

Charter and laws of the states of Ohio, Indiana, Michigan and Illinois. 48768

Charter and laws of the Wake Forest College. 100974

Charter and laws relating to the Long Dock Company. 41889

Charter and ordinance of the New-York Dispensary. 54460

Charter and ordinances of . . . Lowell. 42473

Charter and ordinances of . . . Portland. (64344)

Charter and ordinances of the borough of Carlisle. (10929)

Charter and ordinances of the city of Bangor. 3156

Charter and ordinances of the city of Boston. 6630

Charter and ordinances of the city of Cambridge. (10144)

Charter and ordinances of the city of Chicago. 12650

Charter and ordinances [of the city of Cincinnati.] 13075

Charter and ordinances of the city [of Halifax.] 29701

Charter and ordinances of the city of Lynn. 42834

Charter and ordinances of the city of Mineral Point. 49208

Charter and ordinances of the city of Omaha. 57260

Charter and ordinances of the city of Paterson. 59058

Charter and ordinances of the city of Providence. 66250

Charter and ordinances of the city of Richmond. (71170)

Charter and ordinances of the city of Rockland. 72399

Charter and ordinances of the city of Saco. 74777

Charter and ordinances of the city of Salem. 75645

Charter and ordinances of the city of Schenectady. 77591

Charter and ordinances of the village of Madison. 43736

Charter and ordinances of the village of New Brighton. (52515)

Charter and other acts of the legislature. 88025

Charter and proceedings of the Board of Commissioners. 27235

Charter and project, with a description. 61072

Charter and prospectus of the Opera House. 61458, 61888

Charter and regulations of the Artillery Company of Newport, R. I. 55034

Charter, and remarks of the Committee on Amending the Charter. 54432

Charter and scheme of the Mineral Point Mining Company. (49210)

Charter and statutes of Jefferson College. (35941)

Charter and statutes, of the College of William and Mary. 104150

Charter and supplement to charter of the [Philadelphia] . . . Museum Company. 62020

Charter and supplements . . . with the acts of Assembly. 60358

Charter and the constitution, the by-laws and the regulations. 72355

Charter articles and bye laws, of the Bricklayers Corporation. 61505

Charter, articles, deeds, &c. (76752)

Charter . . . as amended [of Manchester, N. H.] 44208

Charter; being a plain statement of facts. (1235)

Charter, by-laws and act of Assembly. 60338

Charter, by-laws, and list of publications. 62261

Charter, by-laws, and ordinances of the village of Sag Harbor. (74879)

Charter, by-laws, and organization of the Chamber of Commerce. 53584

Charter, bye-laws, and rates of insurance of the Washington Mutual Assurance Company of the City of New-York. 102028

Charter, by-laws and regulations, of the College of Physicians and Surgeons. (54000)

Charter, by-laws and regulations of the Mount Moriah Cemetery Association. 61848

Charter, by-laws and regulations of the Woodlands Cemetery Company. 62394

Charter, by-laws and rules . . . of the Philadelphia Literary Institute. (62011)

Charter, by-laws and rules, of the St. Joseph's Hospital. 62212

Charter, by-laws, and standing resolutions, of the Pennsylvania Academy of the Fine Arts. 60293

Charter, by-laws and statement of property of the Chicago South Branch Dock Co. 12630

Charter, by-laws, &c., of the Blackstone Canal Corporation. 5700

Charter, by-laws, &c. of the Callaway Mining and Manufacturing Company. (10054)

Charter, by-laws, &c., of the Homoeopathic Medical College. 60147

Charter, by-laws, &c., of the Louisville and Portland Canal Company. 42323

Charter, by-laws, &c., of the New York Dispensary. 54460

Charter, by-laws, &c. of the Southern District Medical Society. 88339

Charter, by-laws, officers and members [of the Philadelphia Club.] (61981)

Charter, by-laws, rates of insurance . . . [of the New York Washington Mutual Assurance Company.] 54865

Charter, by-laws, regulations and code of ethnics of the New-Hampshire Medical Society. 52878

Charter, by-laws, rules and regulations, of the Schuylkill Fishing Company. 62232

Charter, constitution and by-laws of the Arizona Historical Society. 1984

Charter, constitution and by-laws of the Athenaeum. (66307)

Charter, constitution, and by-laws of the College [of Physicians, Philadelphia.] 61548

Charter, constitution, and by-laws of the Franklin Institute of Philadelphia, &c. 25654

Charter, constitution and by-laws of the Franklin Society. 75349

Charter, constitution and by-laws of the Home for Aged Women. 66271

Charter, constitution and by-laws of the Law Academy of Philadelphia. (61765)

Charter, constitution and by-laws of the Lyceum of Natural History. (54365)

Charter, constitution and by-laws of the Madison Institute. 43744

Charter, constitution and by-laws of the Mechanics' Institute, of Louisville. 42336

Charter, constitution, and by-laws of the Merchants' Exchange. 52967

Charter, constitution, and by-laws [of the Minnesota Historical Society.] 49275

Charter, constitution and by-laws of the . . . [New York Horticultural] Society. 54479

Charter, constitution, and by-laws of the New-York Mechanic and Scientific Institution. 54512

Charter, constitution and by-laws of the Newport Association of Mechanics and Manufacturers. 55042

Charter, constitution and by-laws of the Numismatic and Antiquarian Society of Philadelphia. 61877

Charter, constitution and by-laws of the . . . [Ohio Mechanics] Institute. (56989)

Charter, constitution and by-laws of the Providence Athenaeum. (66307)

Charter, constitution and by-laws of the St. Nicholas' Society of the City of New York. 75448

Charter, constitution and by-laws, of the Society for the Development of the Mineral Resources of the United States. 12159

Charter, constitution, and by-laws [of the Society of the Alumni of the Law Department of the University of Pennsylvania.] 86092

Charter, constitution and by-laws, with a list of officers, etc., of the Chicago Historical Society. 12621

Charter, constitution and circular of the Rhode-Island Historical Society. 70719

Charter, constitution, and regulations of the Mercantile Library Association of Baltimore. 3024

Charter, constitution, by-laws, and catalogue of the St. Louis Library Association. (75392)

Charter, constitution, &c. and the first annual report of the Executive Committee and Treasurer of the Young Men's Association for Mutual Improvement. 76912, 1st note after 106156

Charter, constitution . . . of the Maryland Institute of Education. (45220)

[Charter, etc. of the] Berlin-Falls Manufacturing Company. (4899)

Charter [etc., of the People's Pacific Railroad Company.] 60828

Charter, &c., of the Submarine Armour Company. 93352

Charter, &c., of the Summit Branch Rail Road Company. 93634

Charter for erecting the said college. 30716, note after 104154

Charter for establishing a hospital . . . in New York. 54163

Charter for establishing an hospital in the city of New-York. 86153

Charter for propagation of the Gospel in New England, &c. 52624

Charter granted by Charles II. to William Penn, Esq. (59968)

Charter granted by His Majesty King Charles the Second, to the colony of Rhode-Island, and Providence-Plantations in America. 70510, 90511

Charter granted by His Majesty, King Charles II. to the Governor and Company of the English Colony of Connecticut in New-England. 15762

Charter granted by His Majesty King Charles II. to the Governor and Company of the English Colony of Rhode Island and Providence-Plantations. 70512, 70514

Charter granted by the state of Nicaragua. 55139

Charter granted by Their Majesties King William and Queen Mary. (45673)

Charter, joint rules and orders, and rules and orders of the Common Council of the city of Portland. (64345)

Charter, laws, and catalogue of books of the Library Company [of Philadelphia.] 61788

Charter, laws and catalogue of books, of the Union Library Company of Hatborough. To which is prefixed a short account of its first establishment. note after 97808

Charter, laws, and catalogue of books of the Union Library Company of Hatborough; with a short account of the first establishment thereof. 30831

Charter, laws and code of ethics of the Philadelphia College of Pharmacy. 61984

Charter, laws and regulations of the Corporation for the Relief of the Widows and Children of the Clergy of the Protestant Episcopal Church in Maryland. 45300

Charter, laws, and regulations of the Literary and Philosophical Society of New-York. 54761

Charter Oak Hall, Hartford, Conn. see Hartford, Conn. Charter Oak Hall.

Charter oak. Its history—its fall. 12160

Charter of Bowdoin College. 7031

Charter of Brown University. 8619

Charter of Canada. 741, 16684, 91853

Charter of Christ Church. 61534

Charter of Columbia College. 14820

Charter of Dartmouth College. 18618

Charter of 1849 [of the Law Association of Philadelphia.] 61766

Charter of Great Salt Lake City. (28464), 75840

Charter of incorporation and by-laws of the Connecticut Historical Society. (15710)

Charter of incorporation and by-laws of the Philadelphia Medical Society. 62017

Charter of incorporation and rules and regulations of the Southern Dispensary. (62266)

Charter of incorporation of the Long Island Water Works Company. 8323

Charter of King's College. 14819

Charter of . . . Lowell. 42472

Charter of Madison University. 43731

Charter of Maryland. (45104)

Charter of Maryland; with an abridgment of the acts of their assembly. 45105

Charter of . . . New-York. 54167, (54169), 54172

Charter of . . . New-York, granted January 15, 1730. 54168

Charter of . . . New-York, John Montgomerie, Esq. Governor. (54170)

Charter of . . . New York. Published pursuant to an order of the Common Council. 54173

Charter of . . . New-York . . . . To which is annexed the act of the Governor confirming the same. 54166

Charter of . . . New York, together with the acts of the legislature in relation thereto. 54171

Charter of . . . New York, with notes. 54175

Charter of . . . New-York, with notes . . . . Also, . . . the journal of the City Convention. 54174

Charter of . . . Newport, R. I. 55033

Charter of Nova Scotia. 741, 16684, 91853

Charter . . . [of Pennsylvania College, Gettysburg.] 60313

Charter of privileges granted by the Honourable William Penn. 59970

Charter of privileges, granted by William Penn, Esq. 59971

Charter of Queen's College, in New Jersey. 52520

Charter of Rhode Island College, granted 1764. 8619

Charter . . . of the American Hose Company. 61457

Charter of "The American Institute . . . of . . . New-York." (54079)

Charter . . . of the . . . [Apprentices Library] Company. 61475

Charter of the Associates of the Jersey Company of Powles Hook. (53089)

Charter of the Bahama Islands. 2716

Charter of the Bank of Kentucky. 37492

Charter of the Bank of Newburgh. 54902

Charter of the Benefit Street [Central] Congregational Society. 66241

Charter of the Boston and Lowell Railroad. 6768

Charter of the Butler Hospital. 66243

Charter [of the Chicago and Rock-Island Railroad Company.] 12665

Charter of the Choctaw and Chickasaw Central Railroad Company. 63921

Charter of the Choctaw and Chickasaw 35th Parallel Railroad Company. 63922

Charter of the city of Albany. 613

Charter of the city of Boston. (6629)

Charter of the city of Brooklyn, and the laws of the state of New-York relating to said city. 8286

Charter of the city of Brooklyn and the special laws relating thereto. 8287

Charter of the city of Chicago. 12650

Charter of the city of Hartford. 30657

Charter of the city of Hudson. (33501)

Charter of the city of Louisville. 42316

Charter of the city of Madison. (43737)

Charter of the city of Milwaukee. 49151

Charter of the city of New-Haven. 52968

Charter of the city of New Orleans. 53314

Charter of the city of New York. 54164

Charter of the city of New-York; printed by order of the Mayor. 54165

Charter of the city . . . [of New York.] With notes . . . . (54176)

Charter of the city of Norwich. 55920

Charter of the city of Philadelphia. 66223

Charter of the city of Providence. 66249

Charter of the city of Salem. 75644

Charter of the College of New-York, in America. 14818

Charter of the College of Physicians and Surgeons in . . . New-York. 54376

Charter of the College of William & Mary. 104152

Charter of the colony of Maryland. 45106

Charter of the Corporation [for the Relief of Poor and Distressed Presbyterian Ministers.] 65129

Charter of the Corporation of Trinity Church defended. 32293, 96982-96983

Charter . . . of the Farmers' Fire Insurance and Loan Company. 54269

Charter of the First Company of the Great Western Turnpike Road. 53597

Charter of the first permanent colony. 91853, 95638

Charter, . . . of the First Universalist Church. 61669

Charter [of the Galena and Chicago Union Railroad.] 26363

Charter [of the Galena Theological Seminary.] 26364

Charter, . . . of the German Reformed Congregation. 61697

Charter of the Girard Life Insurance, Annuity and Trust Company. 61700

Charter of the glebe lands, in the village of Newburgh. (54904)

Charter of the Governor and Company of Merchants of Great Britain, Trading to the South-Sea. 88166

Charter of the Grand Gulf Rail Road and Banking Company. 49491

Charter of the Great Northern Turnpike Company. 28458

Charter of the Honduras Interoceanic Railway. 32755

Charter of the Jersey Bank. (53089)

Charter of the Lake Eire and Mad-River Railroad Company. 38658

Charter of the Lehigh and Delaware Water Gap Railroad Company. 60199

Charter of the Library Company of Philadelphia. (61786)

Charter of the Lordship of Canada. 741, 16684, 91853

Charter of the Louisa Rail Road Company. (42172)

Charter of the Louisville, Cincinnati, and Charleston Railroad Company. 42325

Charter of the Marine Society of . . . Newport. 55038

Charter of the Marine of the City of New York. 54372

Charter of the Massachusetts colony. (45673)

Charter of the Memphis and Ohio Railroad Company. (47778)

Charter of the Merrimack & Connecticut River Railroad. 48010

Charter of the Missouri Juvenile Reform School. 49619

Charter of the Mohawk and Hudson Rail-Road Company. 49853

Charter of the Morris Canal and Banking Company. (50888)

Charter of the Nassau Water Company. 8322

Charter of the New Hampshire Medical Society. 52948

Charter of the New-Hampshire Medical Society. 52878

Charter of the New Haven Water Company. 52998

Charter of the New York and Boston Steamboat Company. 54726

Charter of the "North Philadelphia Plank Road Co." 61868

Charter . . . of the . . . [Northwestern Virginia Railroad] Company. 55856

Charter of the . . . [Pacific Mail Steamship] Company. 58084

Charter of the Philadelphia Fire and Inland Navigation Insurance Company. 61998

Charter of the Philadelphia, Wilmington and Baltimore Railroad Company. 62051

Charter of the Planters and Merchants Bank' of Mobile. 49777

Charter . . . of the Portage Canal and Manufacturing Company. 64189

Charter of the Preston Retreat. 65391

Charter of the Providence Bank. (66312)

Charter of the Providence Franklin Society. 66326

Charter of the province of Pennsylvania. 59969

Charter of the province of the Massachusetts Bay. (45673)

Charter of the Rector and Inhabitants of the City of New-York. 32293, 96982-96983

Charter of the Redwood Library Company. 55053, 68534

Charter of the Rhode-Island Cloth Hall Company. 70715

Charter of the Richmond and Ohio Railroad Company. 71198

Charter of the St. Andrew's Society of Philadelphia. 62207

Charter of the St. Louis Gas-Light Company. 75387

Charter of the Sheboygan and Fond du Lac Road Company. 80064

Charter [of the Society for the Progagation of the Gospel in Foreign Parts.] 101468

Charter of the Society of the New York Hospital. 54484, 86154

Charter of the Somerset Iron and Coal Company of Pennsylvania. 86811

Charter of the South & North Ala. R. R. Co. 87327

Charter of the Southern Bank. 88304

Charter of the Southern Life Insurance and Trust Company. 88388

Charter of the Southern Pacific R. R. Co. of Texas. 88430

Charter of the Swatara and Good Spring Rail Road Company. 94027

Charter of the Texas Railroad. 94991

Charter of the Texas Western Railroad Company. 88431

Charter of the town of Woodstock. 105147

Charter of the trustees of the Fire Association of Philadelphia. 61658

Charter of the Union Academy. 97750

Charter of the Union Bank of Maryland. 45081

Charter of the Union Bank of South-Carolina. 97759

Charter of the United Swedish Lutheran Churches. (52359)

Charter of the village of Greenbush. 28580

Charter of the Warren Insurance Company. 101494

Charter of the Washington Insurance Company in Providence. 102022

Charter [of the Young Men's Association for Mutual Improvement.] 106156

Charter . . . of the Young Men's Association of the City of Milwaukee. 49183

Charter of the Young Men's Christian Association Building. 62401

Charter of Trinity-Church in the city of New-York. 96984

Charter of Trinity Church, Newport. (55056)

Charter of Union College. 97776

Charter of Washington College. 101998

Charter, ordinances, and annual report of the officers of committees of the city of Burlington, Vt. (9339)

Charter, ordinances and regulations [of the New York State Agricultural College, Albany.] 53810

Charter . . . passed June 9, 1832. 30542

Charter, regulations, course of study [of the Theological Seminary of the Protestant Episcopal Church in Kentucky.] (37568), 2d note after 95313

Charter, rules, and regulations for the government of the House of Refuge. 13076

Charter, rules and regulations of the Rosehill Cemetery. (73262)

Charter, supplement and by-laws of the Western Railroad Company. (60279)

Charter, supplement, and by-laws of the Point Breeze Park Association. 63698

Charter, supplements and by-laws [of the Lehigh Valley Rail-road Company.] 60201

Charter, supplements, . . . and . . . officers, of the Philadelphia and Darby Rail Road Company. 61946

Charter, the request, &c. [of the Society for the Propagation of the Gospel in Foreign Parts.] 85934

Charter, transfer, and statutes, of the College of William and Mary. 104151

Charter, trust deed, and by-laws of the Cooper Union for the Advancement of Science and Art. (16596), 55224

Charter with its amendments, and the revised ordinances [of Manchester, N. H.] 44209

Charter with its amendments, and the revised ordinances, of . . . Portsmouth [N. H.] 64418

Chartering of railroad companies. 80372

Charteroak, and other poems. 265

Charters and acts of Assembly of the Province of Pennsylvania. 59972

Charters and acts of Rhode Island. 70560

Charters and general laws of the colony and province of Massachusetts Bay. 45674

Charters and laws . . . [of the Bank of Pennsylvania.] 59910

Charters and legislative documents, illustrative of Rhode-Island history. 70561

Charters and other documents relating to the city of Brooklyn. 8288

Charters granted to the Nashua and Lowell Rail Road Corporation. 51859

Charters of and acts relating to Jersey City. 36066

Charters of California. 2169

Charters of justice, orders in council, &c. 13260

Charters of Massachusetts. 45417

Charters of the British colonies in America. 12162

Charters of the following provinces of North America. 12163, 1st note after 99889

Charters of the province of Pensilvania and city of Philadelphia. 59973

Charters of the Union Potomac Company, and of the Union Company. 97814

Charters, rules, and regulations of the North Carolina Gold-Mining Company. 55651

Charters, statutes, and by-laws [of the University of Pennsylvania.] 60758

Chartier y Olavarria. firm defendants 40951

Charton, Edouard. 12164-12165, note after 99383C

Charts of chronology. 59358

Charts, of some of its most principal ports. 62884

Charts of the coasts and harbors of New England. 32514

Charts of the northern Atlantic ocean. 66700
Chas, Jean. 12166, 39618
Chase, --------, fl. 1867. (30910), 38892
Chase, B. C. 12168
Chase, Benjamin. (12167)
Chase, C. Thurston. 12171
Chase, Carlton, Bp., 1794-1870. 12169-12170
Chase, David T. defendant. 12172
Chase, E. 69342
Chase, Elizabeth. (12173)
Chase, Ezra B. 12174
Chase, Francis. (12175)
Chase, G. B. 12176
Chase, George I. 70676
Chase, George Wingate. 12177, 33217
Chase, H. (12180)
Chase, H. B. reporter 23817
Chase, Horace. (12178)
Chase, Henry. 12179
Chase, Irah. 12181-(12182)
Chase, L. G. 12185
Chase, Leslie. (12183)
Chase, Lucien Bonaparte, 1817-1864. 12184
Chase, Mary M. 12186
Chase, Nahum. 12188
Chase, Owen. 12189
Chase, Philander, Bp., 1775-1852. 12190-
  12194, 37591, 89024, 102726, 102729
Chase, Philemon. see Chase, Philander, Bp.,
  1775-1852.
Chase, Pliny E. (12195)
Chase, Salmon Portland, 1808-1873, 12196-
  12200, 15909, 27969, 33150, 33230,
  52200, (57030), 79584, 82655, 84463,
  88294-88296, 93663 see also Ohio.
  Governor, 1856-1859 (Chase) U. S.
  Supreme Court. Chief Justice. U. S.
  Treasury Department.
Chase, Rev. Samuel. 12208, 12413
Chase, Samuel, 1741-1811. 12206, (25961),
  96866 see also Maryland. Agent for
  the Recovery of the Bank Stock.
Chase, Samuel, 1741-1811. defendant at
  impeachment 11203-11207, 11209,
  30442, 36744
Chase, Stephen. 12210
Chase, Thomas. 12212-12213
Chase, Thomas. ed. 105348
Chase, Thomas, 1827-1892. 12211
Chase, Warren. 12214
Chase, Washington. supposed author 12215,
  (12749), 100814
Chase, William Henry, 1798-1870. 12216,
  60803
Chase. firm see Langford & Chase. firm
Chase. A tale of the sea. (16448)
Chase across the Pampas. 27194
Chase of the rebel steamer of war Oreto.
  12217
Chasles, Philarete, 1798-1873. (12218)-12219,
  19287, 20374
Chasles, Victor Euphemion Philarete. see
  Chasles, Philarete, 1798-1873.
Chassanis, Pierre. 12220, 19728, 95825
Chasse a l'esclave. 23548
Chasse aux chevaux. (69026)
Chasseboeuf, Constantin Francois. see Volney,
  Constantin Francois Chasseboeuf, Comte
  de, 1757-1820.
Chasseriau, Frederic Victor Charles. 12222,
  65024
Chasses dans l'Amerique du Nord. 70329
Chasses et peches de l'autre monde. (70328)
Chasseur. 4266
Chasseur d'Ours. 69025

Chasseur noir. (12573)
Chasseurs de bisons. 69027-(69028)
Chasseurs de chevelures. 69929-69031
Chastain, Elijah Webb, 1813-1874. 12223
Chastellux, Francois Jean, Marquis de, 1734-
  1788. 8017, 8019, (12224)-12232, 33803,
  69508, 81137, 100809
Chastenet, Antoine Hyacinthe Anne de. see
  Puysegur, Antoine Hyacinthe Anne de
  Chastenet, Comte de, 1752-1807.
Chastenet-Destere, G. 12234
Chastisement of war. 85457
Chata wuja Tomasza, czyli zycie niewolnikow
  w zjednoczonych polnocnej Ameryki.
  92595
Chata wuja Tomasza, przez pania. 92596
Chateaubriand, Francois Auguste, Vicomte de,
  1768-1848. 12237-12276, 87129
Chateaubriand illustre. 12252
Chateauneuf, Agricole Hippolyte la Pierre de.
  (12277)
Chatel, Martin Fumee, Sieur de Marley-le-.
  see Funee, Martin, Sieur de Marley-
  le-Chatel, 16th cent.
Chatelain, -------, Chavalier de. tr. (41912)
Chatfield, -------, fl. 1850. 69418
Chatfield, Frederick. (32768), 55145 see also
  Great Britain. Legation. Nicaragua.
Chatham. pseud. Address to the citizens of
  Connecticut. see Webster, Noah, 1758-
  1843. supposed author
Chatham, James. 12278
Chatham, William Pitt, 1st Earl of. see Pitt,
  William, 1st Earl of Chatham, 1708-1778.
Chatham, Mass. 84760
Chatham, Mass. Church. 42037, 92099
Chatham, Mass. School Committee. 12280
Chatham, N. Y. Mutual Insurance Association.
  see Mutual Insurance Association of
  Nassau, Schodack and Chatham, N. Y.
Chatham County, Ga. Inferior Court. Justices.
  103375
Chatham County, Ga. Superior Court. Clerk.
  plaintiff 27020 see also White, Richard
  W. plaintiff
Chatham Academy, Savannah, Ga. 12281
Chatham Artillery of Savannah. 36475
Chatham Anti-slavery Society. see Rochester
  and Chatham Anti-slavery Society.
Chatham controversy. (72416)
Chatham Mining Company. 12282
Chatham-Street Chapel, New York. see New
  York (City) Chatham Street Chapel.
Chatka ojca Toma. 92597
Chattanooga. 12283, 36413
Chattaway, E. D. 91323
Chattel principle. (12284)
Chatterton, Aug. 12285
Chattin, James. 66909
Chaubet, Charles. 48037
Chauca, Jose Joaquin de Avalos y. see
  Avalos y Chauca, Jose Joaquin de.
Chauchard, --------. cartographer 102541
Chaucherprat, F. C. tr. 1701, (73505)-73506
Chaudon, Louis Mayeul, 1737-1817. 27789
Chaudon, Adelaide de Vendel. (12286)-12287
Chaudron, Jean Simon. 12288-12291, 40696,
  note after 101839, 1st note after 101866
Chaudron, Simon. see Chaudron, Jean Simon.
Chaudron's spelling book. 12287
Chaufepie, C. A. de. 12292
Chaufepie, Joan Henn. (12293)
Chauffard, A. tr. 49764
Chaulmer, Charles. 12294
Chaumette, A. 12295

Chaumonot, I. M. (67491)
Chaumonot, Pierre Joseph Marie, 1611-1693.
(12297)-12298, 67018, 2d note after
93480
Chaumont, J. le Ray de. 12299
Chaumont, L. de. (12300)
Chauncey, Charles, of Pennsylvania 12302,
(32986)
Chauncey, Charles, 1777-1849. 12301
Chauncey, Henry. defendant 88828
Chauncey, Nathaniel. (12303)
Chauncy, Charles, 1592-1672. 920, 12304-
(12308), 46779, 49662, 66059, 80261
Chauncy, Charles, 1705-1787. 2561, 13350,
11874-11875, (12309)-12331, 13350,
(21975), 23318-23319, 30530-30531,
34598, (34766), (40382), (41644), 69400,
75875, 90595, 95642, 97569, 2d note
after 99800, 8th note after 100869, 6th-
9th notes after 100870, note after 101077,
102571, 102574, 103563, 103594, 3d note
after 103650, 104735
Chauncy, Charles, 1705-1787. supposed author
25386, 103632-103633, 103649, 105012
Chauncy, Charles, 1707-1787. incorrectly
supposed author 12305, 12316, 12335,
(21935), 67768
Chauncy, Sir Henry. 12339
Chauncy, Isaac, 1632-1712. 12305, 12332-
12335, 104183-104184
Chauncy, Nathaniel. 12336-(12338)
Chauncy, Israel. 62743
Chauncy, Nathaniel. 62743
Chauncy Hall School, Boston. see Boston.
Chauncy Hall School.
Chauncy Society for Mutual Improvement,
Boston. 12342
Chauncy Street Church, Boston. see Boston.
First Church.
Chaunt of life and other poems. (33412)
Chautard, Leon. 12343
Chautauquan. 85091
Chauveau, ------. supposed author 39985,
note after 94187
Chauveau, Pierre Joseph Olivier. 658, (10422),
10455, 12344-12345, 34041, (36708),
(41510), 69284, 69661
Chauveau-Lagarde, N. 12346
Chauvet, Joseph Joachim Victor. 12348
Chauvet-Charolais, L. 12347
Chauveton, Urbain. 4795, 39630, 39634
Chauvin, V. 19557
Chavannes, ------ de. 12349
Chavannes, de la Giraudiere, H. de. 12350
Chave, A. illus. 98107
Chavero, Francisco Martinez de. see
Martinez de Chavero, Francisco.
Chaves, Hieronymo de. 12351, 32684, 74808
Chaves, Jose Francisco, 1833-1904. 12352
Chaves, Joseph Martin de. see Martin de
Chaves, Joseph.
Chazelles, Augustin Jean Baptiste Louis Marie
de, Comte, 1803-1866. 12353-12354,
33474
Chazotte, Peter S. (12355)-12356
Che la platina Americana era un metallo
conosciuto dagli antichi. 51681
Cheadle, Walter Butler, 1835-1910. 24631
Cheap and interesting, new and enlarged
edition. 61064, 94817
Cheap cotton by free labor. 2280
Cheap country and village residences. 71554
Cheap dish for the times. (63431)
Cheap food dependent on cheap transportation.
(67262)

Cheap ocean postage. 93646
Cheap postage. 64478
Cheap Postage Association, Boston. (12357)
Cheap Postage Association, New York. see
New York Cheap Postage Association.
Cheap postage. Remarks and statistics.
39563
Cheap repository. 86663, 87173, 105001
Cheap transportation a public necessity.
71619
Cheap transportation. Delivered before the
American Cheap Transportation Associ-
ation. 88224
Cheat unmask'd. 12358, 59267
Cheatham, or the swamp dragons. 29482
Chebacco narrative. 13592
Chebucto Gold Mining Company. 12359
Checieux, G. A. F. Simon de Lagrange de. see
Lagrange de Checieux, G. A. F. Simon
de.
Checklist of periodical publications. 85011
Checklist of publications [of the Smithsonian
Institution.] 85037
Check list of shells of North America. (39496)
Check list of the invertebrate fossils of North
America. Cretaceous and jurassic.
47369
Check list of the invertebrate fossils of North
America, eocene and oligocene. 15899
Check list of the invertebrate fossils of North
America. Miocene. 47369
Check list of the shells of North America.
12360
Check to the progress of political blasphemy.
14031, 94025
Checkered state of the Gospel church. 103072
Checkley, John. (7850), (12361)-12365, note
after 12879, 20055, (20061), (25402),
25407, 40191, 40192, 46473, 69517,
99800, 101193-101194, 103904
Checkley, Samuel. 12366-(12369), 101016
Checkley, Samuel, Jr. 12370-12371
Checkley family. 20884
Checklist . . . see Check list . . .
Chedel, -------. illus. 21007
Cheerful songster's companion. 85691
Cheesman, D. W. (12372)
Cheetham, James. 9431, 12373-12387, 42881,
52583, 70044, (75956), 2d note after
92859, 1st note after 99571, note after
101455, 105041, 105044, note after 105047,
2d note after 106011
Cheetham, James. supposed author 63828-
63829
Cheetham, James. defendant 41633, (75956),
(75958), note after 96894
Cheever, Charles A. 12388
Cheever, Edward. 12398
Cheever, Ezekiel, 1615-1708. 12390-12393,
46273, 68159, 73398-73400, (73402),
80652, 80654, 80656-80661, 103735-
103737
Cheever, Ezekiel. see Whitman, Ezekiel
Cheever.
Cheever, George. 40852
Cheever, George Barrell. 12394-(12406),
51199, 51201, 54184, 86749, 70009,
98031-98033, 98046
Cheever, George Barrell. defendant 12397,
2d after 97117
Cheever, Henry T. 12407-12410, 15461,
(66632)
Cheever, James. plaintiff (74472), 91108
Cheever, Samuel. 12208, 12412-12413
Cheever, Samuel, 1639-1724. 12411

Cheever, Thomas. 12414
Cheever, Tracy P. 12415
Cheever's Latin accidence. 12392
Chef blanc. 69032
Chefs-d'oeuvre des theatres entrangers. 17876
Cheimonopegnion or, a winter song. 95621-95622
Chelemar, --------, Prince de. 38998, 56001, (74790) see also Spain. Legacion. Portugal.
Chelsea, Mass. 12417
Chelsea, Mass. Board of Water Commissioners. 12417
Chelsea, Mass. Industrial School. see Chelsea Industrial School.
Chelsea, Mass. Joint Special Committee on Introduction of Water. 12417
Chelsea, Mass. Mayor, 1865. 12417
Chelsea, Mass. School Committee. 12417
Chelsea Association for the Improvement of Indigent Girls. 12417
Chelsea directory . . . for 1856. 12416
Chelsea Industrial School. 12417
Chelsea's roll of honor. (12418)
Cheltenham and Willow Grove Turnpike Company. see Willow Grove Turnpike Company.
Cheltnam, Charles S. tr. 29242
Chelys Hesperia. 104683
Chemical analysis and medical properties of the hot mineral waters. 13301
Chemical analysis of the waters of New Lebanon, N. Y. 47237
Chemical and economical essays. (59666)
Chemical examination of the mineral water of Schooley's Mountain. (43607)
Chemical examination of the mineral water of Schooley's Mountain springs. 49739
Chemin de fer de Montreal et Bytown. 50273
Chemin de Fer du Nord. Comite General. see Comite General du Chemin de Fer du Nord, Quebec.
Chemin de fer inter-oceanique de Honduras. 89958
Chemin de la croix et autres prieres. (12420)
Chemins de fer Americains. 64732
Chemist and meteorological journal. 12419
Chemistry and metallurgy of copper. 62808
Chemistry of gold. 47906
Chemung Co., N. Y. Elmira Female College. see Elmira Female College, Chemung Co., N. Y.
Chenango. pseud. Letter. 103281
Chenango almanac. 12423
Chenango Baptist Association. see Baptists. New York. Chenango Baptist Association.
Chenango canal extention. (25022)
Cheney, C. E. ed. 93744
Cheney, Harriet V. Foster. (12425), 59527
Cheney, J. engr. 31643, 91035
Cheney, John M. 12426
Cheney, Martin. 12427
Cheney, T. Apoleon. 12428
Cheney, Thomas. 12546 see also Chester County, Pa. Sub Lieutenant.
Cheney, Timothy C. (12429)
Chenu, J. C. 12430, 15905, 77375
Chepe, -------. pseud?? Dialogo. 76197
Che-quaw-ka-ko. Potawatomi Chief. 96709
Cher, Henry W. B. pseud. Gnaw-wood. 12432
Cherbuliez, ------ Tourte- see Tourte-Cherbuliez, ---------. tr.
Chercheur d'or. pseud. Californie. 9988
Chercheurs d'or. 4521

Cherished memorials of the late Julia A. Parker Dyson. 21607, 39205
Cherokee. 92172-92172B, 92173A, 92176
Cherokee advocate. 12439
Cherokee almanac for the year of Our Lord 1840. 12440
Cherokee alphabet. 12441
Cherokee, an opera. 86907
Cherokee chief. 92698
Cherokee hymns compiled from several authors. 12442, 105317-105321
Cherokee Indians. see Cherokee Nation.
Cherokee Indians. Letter from the Secretary of War. 34628
Cherokee Indians. Memorial of John Ross, and others. 73390
Cherokee Indians of North Carolina. see Cherokee Nation.
Cherokee land lottery. 12444, 82790
Cherokee lands on Walden's Ridge. 12445
Cherokee messenger. 12446, 27915
Cherokee Nation. 12434, 12436, 12473, (55600)
Cherokee Nation. claimants 12477, 90115
Cherokee Nation. petitioners (12466), 47657, 73390
Cherokee Nation. plaintiffs 61206
Cherokee Nation. Constitution. 12450, 12451
Cherokee Nation. Constitutional Convention, New Echota, 1827. 12451
Cherokee Nation. Delegates. 12435, 12449, 12471-12473, (34632), 71280, 73410, 73393 see also Ridge, John R.
Cherokee Nation. Delegates. petitioners 12437, (12466)-12467, 34656, 47637, 47672, 73391
Cherokee Nation. Delegation. see Cherokee Nation. Delegates.
Cherokee Nation. General Convention of Delegates, New Echota, 1827. see Cherokee Nation. Constitutional Convention, New Echota, 1827.
Cherokee Nation. General Council, 1836. 12438
Cherokee Nation. National Council. petitioners 12449
Cherokee Nation. Laws, statutes, etc. (12463), 12450, 39413
Cherokee Nation. Principal Chief. 12468, 73390-73391, 73393 see also Ross, John, Cherokee Chief, 1790?-1866.
Cherokee Nation. Treaties, etc. 12477, 14371, 61206, 90115, 96600, 96604, 96621-96622, 96628, 96697-96698, 100006
Cherokee Nation (Loyal Cherokees) Council. 12473
Cherokee Nation (Southern) 12473
Cherokee Nation (West of the Mississippi) petitioners 34657
Cherokee Nation (West of the Mississippi) Treaties, etc. 96656, 96685
Cherokee phoenix. (6858)-6859, 12439, 12447, 24161, 1st note after 97291
Cherokee physician. 43875
Cherokee primer. 12448
Cherokee question. 34630
Cheraws District, S. C. Court of General Sessions of the Peace. Grand Jury. 87468
Cherrier, G. H. ed. 67045, 73876
Cherrier, Romuald. 34041, 69661
Cherry, -------, fl. 1868. 12478
Cherry, Cummings. 12479
Cherry, F. 66686
Cherry, James. 12479
Cherry, William. (50900)

Cherry Hill, Pa. Eastern Penitentiary. see
Pennsylvania. Eastern Penitentiary,
Cherry Hill.
Cherry Valley, Mass. Methodist Episcopal
Church. Select Committee. 95526
Cherry Valley, N. Y. Centennial Celebration,
1840. 12480
Cherry Valley Female Academy. 12480
Cherubims, cherubims. 72601
Cherubin custodio de el arbol de la Santa
Cruz de Queretaro. (22895)
Chervin, Nicolas, 1783-1843. (12481)-12482,
13645
Chesapeak. 12483
Chesapeake and Delaware Canal Company.
12495, (12497)-12499
Chesapeake and Ohio Canal Company. 12503,
12506, 12510
Chesapeake and Ohio Canal Company. plaintiffs
104870
Chesapeake and Ohio Canal Company. Engi-
neers. 12510
Chesapeake and Ohio Canal Company. General
Committee of the Stockholders. 12507
Chesapeake and Ohio Canal Convention, Wash-
ington, D. C., 1823-1826. 12501, 12504-
12505
Chesapeake and Ohio railroad as a short,
economical, and profitable line. 24522
Chesborough, I. C. 63159
Chesbrough, E. S. 6768, 12511-(12514), 1st
note after 94186 see also Chicago.
Board of Sewerage Commissioners.
Chief Engineer.
Cheshire, H. J. tr. 99367, 99382
Cheshire, Conn. Episcopal Academy. see
Episcopal Academy of Connecticut,
Cheshire, Conn.
Cheshire, Conn. Soldiers' Monument. 12518
Cheshire County, N. H. Benevolent Societies.
see Benevolent Societies in Cheshire
County, N. H.
Cheshire County, N. H. Superior Court of
Judicature. 16784, 96854
Cheshire County Conference of Churches. see
Congregational Churches in New Hamp-
shire. Cheshire County Conference.
Cheshire County Teachers' Institute. 12516
Cheshire Railroad Company. 12517
Chesney, Charles Cornwallis, 1826-1876.
8582, 12520-12521
Chesnut, James, 1815-1885. 12522
Chess book of American literature. (26054)
Chessman, Daniel. 12523, (12525)
Chessman, James. 12524
Chesson, Frederick William, 1833 or 4-1888.
216, 27628
Chessyre, Henry T. N. 12552
Chestatee Hydraulic Company. 5805, 12526
Chester, Albert T. 12527
Chester, Anson G. (37255)
Chester, Anthony. 12528
Chester, Grenville John. (12531)
Chester, John, 1785-1829. 12532-12534
Chester, John, 1785-1829. defendant before
Presbytery (12536), 17909, 97370
Chester, John, 1832-1910. 12537
Chester, Joseph Lemuel. 12538-12541
Chester, Nicholas. 92759, 93240
Chester, S. M. ed. 14782
Chester, Stephen. supposed author 14850
Chester, William F. 12542
Chester (Charles T.) firm (12530)
Chester (J. N.) firm (12530)
Chester, Bishop of. see Blomfield, Charles
James, successively Bp. of Chester,

and London, 1786-1857. Cleaver, William,
successively Bp. of Chester, Bangor, and
St. Asaph, 1742-1815. Dawes, Sir William,
Bart., Abp. of York, 1671-1724. Keene,
Edmund, successively Bp. of Chester,
and Ely, 1714-1781. Porteus, Beilby,
successively Bp. of Chester, and London,
1731-1808.
Chester, England. Society for Promoting
General Inoculation, at Stated Periods,
and Preventing the Natural Small-pox.
see Society for Promoting General
Inoculation, at Stated Periods, and Pre-
venting the Natural Small-pox, Chester,
England.
Chester, N. H. Rockingham Conference of
Churches Annual Meeting, 1851. see
Rockingham Conference of Churches.
Annual Meeting, Chester, N. H., 1851.
Chester, Pa. Court. 50028
Chester, S. C. General Meeting, 1831. 87923
Chester, Vt. Family Reunion of the Descend-
ants of Waitstill Ranney and Jeremiah
Atwood, 8th, 1866. see Family Reunion
of the Descendants of Waitstill Ranney
and Jeremiah Atwood. 8th, Chester, Vt.,
1866.
Chester County, Pa. Citizens. 40513
Chester County, Pa. Collector of Accounts.
12934
Chester County, Pa. Collector of Excise.
17970
Chester County, Pa. Constituents. see
Chester County, Pa. Citizens.
Chester County, Pa. Court of Common Pleas.
President Judge. 102762
Chester County, Pa. Court of Oyer and
Terminer. 104196
Chester County, Pa. Harvest Home Meeting,
Valley Forge, 1828, see Harvest Home
Meeting of Chester and Montgomery
Counties at Valley Forge, July 28, 1828.
Chester County, Pa. Lieutenant. 83805-83807
see also Smith, Robert, 1720-1803.
Chester County, Pa. Meeting of the Free-
holders, 1774. 95944
Chester County, Pa. Public Meeting of Anti-
slavery Citizens, 1835. 12543
Chester County, Pa. Sub Lieutenant. 7102,
12546, 28925, 40760, 83806, 92749,
104678 see also Boyd, Andrew, fl.
1777-1780. Cheney, Thomas. Gronow,
Lewis. Hannum, John. Lewis, Thomas.
Strawbridge, Thomas. Wilson, Robert, fl.
1779.
Chester County, Pa. Washington Association.
see Washington Association, Chester
County, Pa.
Chester County, Pa. Whigs. see Whig Party.
Pennsylvania. Chester County.
Chester County Cabinet of Natural History,
West Chester, Pa. 12545
Chester County Medical Society. 47325
Chester District, South Carolina. Citizens.
petitioners 47661
Chester, September 11, 1777. Twelve o'clock
at night. (11731), 101700
Chester Valley Railroad Company. President.
59974
Chesterfield, Philip Dormer Stanhope, 4th
Earl of, 1694-1773. 90221, 1st note
after 90222-90286
Chesterfield, Philip Dormer Stanhope, 4th
Earl of, 1694-1773. supposed author
20517, note after 74817, 90222

Chesterfield, S. C. Citizens. petitioners
47639
Chesterfield County, Va. Superior Court.
71578
Chesterfield travestie. 12549
Chesterton, George Laval. (12550)-12551
Chestertown, Md. Washington College. see
Washington College, Chestertown, Md.
Chestnut and Walnut Street Railway. 61532
Chestnut Hill. 89904
Chestnut Hill Railroad Company. 61532
Chestnut Street, a poem. 16297
Chestnut tree or a sketch of Brattleborough
(East Village.) 97621
Chetwind, Philip. publisher 71809
Chetwood, William Rufus, d. 1766. supposed
author 12553-12557, 23723, 55285,
88199, 1st-2d notes after 99428, 99429-
99431, note after 99431, note after
100822, 1st note after 100838, 100846
Chetwynd, Sir George, Bart. (79849)
Chevalier, E. 98298
Chevalier, Henry Emile. 12558-12577, 73876,
74884, 74886
Chevalier, J. B. 61913, 103971
Chevalier, Jean Damien. 12578, 40683
Chevalier, Jules. 12579
Chevalier, Michel, 1806-1879. 12580-12597,
21074, (70389), 84478
Chevalier Guisan. 23559
Chevalier Noel Brulart de Sillery. (81022)
Chevaliere, M. Bacon de la. see La Cheva-
liere, M. Bacon de.
Chevaliers: a tale. (5573)
Chevallie, John Augustus. 96342
Chevallier, P. J. 12598
Cheverus, Jean Louis Anne Magdelene Lefebre
de, Cardinal, 1768-1836. 72976 see
also Boston (Archdiocese) Bishop
(Cheverus)
Cheves, E. W. F. (12599)
Cheves, Langdon, 1776-1857. 12600-12603,
33572, 56630, 69706, 87452, 88005,
88496
Chevigni, M. de. 12604
Chevillard, Andre. (12605), 71102
Chevreau, Urbain. (12606)-12609
Chevrier, Antoine. 12610, 18221-18222
Chevrieres de Saint Vallier, Jean Baptiste de
la Croix de. see Saint Vallier, Jean
Baptiste de la Croix de Chevrieres de,
Bp.
Chevrolat, Auguste. 12611
Chew, Jeffrey. defendant 94405
Chew, John H. 12612
Chew, Richard. 83765
Chew, Samuel, 1693-1743. 12613, 86738
Chew, Samuel C. 83664
Chew (Sinnickson) firm publishers 10161
Chew's Camden city directory. 10161
Chi. see Xiu, Gaspar Antonio, also called
Chi or Herrera.
Chiabrera, Gabriello. 12614
Chiapa (Diocese) 34836
Chiapa (Diocese) Bishop (Casas) (11229),
11234-11235, 11239-11235, 11239-11240,
11276, 39115 see also Casas, Barthol-
ome de la, Bp., 1474-1566.
Chiapa y Soconusco (Diocese) Bishop (Nunez
de la Vega) 56327-56328 see also
Nunez de la Vega, Francisco, Bp., d.
1703.
Chiapas, Mexico. Iglesia Catedral. 56451
Chiapas (Mexican State) 48282
Chiapas (Mexican State) Comandante en Gefe
de la Seccion Auxiliar de Chiapas. see

Mexico. Ejercito. Seccion Auxiliar de
Chiapas. Commandante en Gefe.
Chiapas (Mexican State) Vice-Governador.
(34718)
Chiari, Pietro. 12616
Chiave per la capanna dello zio Tom. 92418
Chicago. (12649)
Chicago. Annual Festival of the Sons of Penn,
1850. see Sons of Penn. Chicago.
Annual Festival, 1st, 1850.
Chicago. Bar. 44261
Chicago. Bay State Union. see Bay State
Union, Chicago.
Chicago. Board of Education. 12643-(12644)
Chicago. Board of Public Works. 12652
Chicago. Board of Sewerage Commissioners.
12512, 12653
Chicago. Board of Sewerage Commissioners.
Chief Engineer. 12511 see also
Chesbrough, E. S.
Chicago. Board of Trade. 12636, 12668
Chicago. Board of Water Commissioners.
12654
Chicago. Business Men. 12636
Chicago. Cameron and Lincoln Club. see
Cameron and Lincoln Club, Chicago.
Chicago. Canal Convention, n. d. see Canal
Convention, Chicago, n. d.
Chicago. Caxton Club. see Caxton Club,
Chicago.
Chicago. Celebration of the Eighty-Sixth
Anniversary of the Independence of the
United States, 1862. 12617
Chicago. Charter. 12650
Chicago. Citizens. petitioners 12658,
(47721)
Chicago. Committee on Statistics of the
National Ship Canal Convention, 1863.
see National Ship Canal Convention,
Chicago, 1863. Chicago Committee on
Statistics.
Chicago. Comptroller. (12651)
Chicago. Convention of the Colored Citizens
of the State of Illinois, 1853. see
Convention of the Colored Citizens of the
State of Illinois, 1st, Chicago, 1853.
Chicago. Democratic Party National Convention,
1864. see Democratic Party. National
Convention, Chicago, 1864.
Chicago. Exhibition of the Fine Arts, 1859.
12647
Chicago. Fenian Brotherhood National Con-
vention, 1st, 1863. see Fenian Brother-
hood. National Convention, 1st, Chicago,
1863.
Chicago. Festival of the Sons of Penn, 1850.
see Sons of Penn. Chicago. Annual
Festival, 1st, 1850.
Chicago. First Annual meeting of the North-
western Freedmen's Aid Commission,
1864. see Northwestern Freedmen's
Aid Commission. Annual Meeting, 1st,
Chicago, 1864.
Chicago. Fourth of July Celebration, 1862.
see Chicago. Celebration of the Eighty-
Sixth Anniversary of the Independence of
the United States, 1862.
Chicago. Franklin Society. see Franklin
Society, Chicago.
Chicago. Harbor and River Convention, 1847.
see Harbor and River Convention,
Chicago, 1847.
Chicago. Lind University. see Lind Univer-
sity, Chicago.
Chicago. Medical School of Northwestern
University. see Northwestern University,
Evanston, Ill. Medical School, Chicago.

Chicago. Meeting held at Metropolitan Hall, 1863. 12636
Chicago. Meeting of the Northwestern Freedmen's Aid Commission, 1st, 1864. see Northwestern Freedmen's Aid Commission. Annual Meeting, 1st, Chicago, 1864. 1864.
Chicago. Mississippi Valley Convention, 1847. St. Louis Delegation. 12631, 75343
Chicago. National Convention of the Republic Party, 1860. see Republican Party. National Convention, Chicago, 1860.
Chicago. National Ship-Canal Convention, 1863. see National Ship-Canal Convention, 1863.
Chicago. National Union Party Convention, 1868. see National Union Party. Convention, Chicago, 1868.
Chicago. Northwestern Sanitary Fair, 1865. Department of Arms and Trophies. 55854
Chicago. Ordinances, etc. 12650
Chicago. Presbyterian and Congregational Convention, 1847. see Presbyterian and Congregational Convention, Chicago, 1847.
Chicago. Presbyterian Theological Seminary. (54205)
Chicago. Presbyterian Theological Seminary of the North West. see Chicago. Presbyterian Theological Seminary.
Chicago. Probate Court. 7311
Chicago. Publishing Bureau of the I. W. W. see International Workers of the World. Publishing Bureau, Chicago.
Chicago. Public Meeting Composed of Twenty-Five Clergymen, 1854. see Public Meeting Composed of Twenty-Five Clergymen, Chicago, 1854.
Chicago. Report School. Superintendent. (12670)
Chicago. Republican Party National Convention, 1860. see Republican Party. National Convention, Chicago, 1860.
Chicago. Rosehill Cemetery. (73262)
Chicago. Rosehill Cemetery. Charter. (73262)
Chicago. Rush Medical College. see Rush Medical College, Chicago.
Chicago. Sanitary Commission. see United States Sanitary Commission. Chicago Branch.
Chicago. Superintendent of Public Schools. 13642
Chicago. Triennial Convention of Ministers and Delegates of the Congregational Churches in the Northwest. see Congregational Churches in the Northwest. Triennial Convention of Ministers and Delegates, Chicago, 1858.
Chicago. University. 12646
Chicago. World's Columbian Exposition, 1893. World's Congress. 84790
Chicago. World's Congress Auxiliary to the World's Columbian Exposition, 1893. see Chicago. World's Columbian Exposition, 1893. World's Congress.
Chicago. Young Men's Association. see Young Men's Association of the City of Chicago.
Chicago almanac and advertiser. 12619
Chicago and her churches. 62485
Chicago avant, pendant et apres l'incendie. 25180
Chicago Academy of Sciences. 12618

Chicago after dark. 12622
Chicago and her railroads. 12665
Chicago and Milwaukee Railroad Company. 12665
Chicago and Rock-Island Railroad Company. 12665
Chicago, Burlington and Quincy Railroad Company. 12665
Chicago, Burlington and Quincy Railroad Company. plaintiffs 87300
Chicago business directory for 1859-60. 31253
Chicago Charitable Eye and Ear Infirmary. 12669
Chicago Charitable Eye and Ear Infirmary. Board of Surgeons. 12669
Chicago city directory. 12641
Chicago city directory and business advertiser. 12641
Chicago city directory for 1852 and '53. 12641
Chicago city directory for the years 1861, 1862, 1863, and 1864. 12641
Chicago city directory supplement. 12641
Chicago, Clinton & Dubuque Railroad. see Chicago, Clinton, Dubuque and Minnesota Railroad.
Chicago, Clinton, Dubuque and Minnesota Railroad. 84036
Chicago Convention, 1847. The commerce and navigation of the valley of the Mississippi. 12631, 75343
Chicago copperhead convention. 12662, 89494-89495
Chicago daily democratic press. 61324
Chicago democratic. 83035
Chicago, Dubuque & Minnesota Railroad. see Chicago, Clinton, Dubuque and Minnesota Railroad.
Chicago; her commerce and railroads for 1852. 12620
Chicago. Historical and statistical sketch. 14254
Chicago Historical Society. 12621
Chicago illustrated. 12623
Chicago. Its past, present, and future. (80028), (80031)
Chicago Land Company. 12624
Chicago magazine. 12625
Chicago newsboy. 42672
Chicago Mercantile Association. 12636
Chicago, past, present, future. 105612
Chicago path-finder. (12626)
Chicago platform dissected. (8401)
Chicago record. 12627
Chicago, St. Paul, and Fond du Lac Rail-Road Company. 12666
Chicago, St. Paul, and Fond du Lac Rail-Road Company. Directors. 12666
Chicago sewerage. 12511
Chicago South Branch Dock Company. 12630
Chicago Sunday School Union. publishers 93744
Chicago Theological Seminary. 12645
Chicago to the seaboard. 64183
Chicago tribune. 89494
Chicago tribune as a libeller of men. 22340
Chicago tribune campaign document, no. I. 89494
Chichester, Bishop of. see Buckner, John, Bp. of Chichester. Hare, Francis, successively Bp. of St. Asaph, and Chichester, 1671-1740. Harsnet, Samuel, Abp. of York, 1561-1631. Mawson, Matthias, successively Bishop of Chichester, and Ely, 1683-1770. Williams, John, Bishop of Chichester, 1636?-1709.

Chichorra da Gama, Antonio Pinto. see Gama, Antonio Pinto Chichorra da.
Chickahominy story. 29397, 71610
Chickamauga, the price of Chattanooga. 24586
Chickasaw Indians. 49492
Chickasaw Indians. Treaties, etc. 96596, 96601, 96607, 96619, 96629, 96677, 96694, 96717
Chickering, Jesse. 6614, (12675)-12676, 46145, note after 90315,
Chickering, John W. 12677-12678
Chickering, Joseph. 12678-12680
Chickering and Sons' piano-fortes at the exhibition of 1856. 12681
Chico, J. 12682
Chicopee, Mass. 12683-12684
Chicopee, Mass. School. Library. 12685
Chicopee Falls, Mass. see Chicopee, Mass.
Chicora, and other poems. (28424)
Chicora, and other regions of the conquerors and the conquered. (12684)
Chidlaw, B. W. 12686
Chidley, Katherine. 12687
Chief. A poem. 84873
Chief arts of empire and mysteries of state. 67599
Chief danger of the church in these times. 43324
Chief foundations. 82333
Chief Justice Caton's Seymour letter. 5821
Chief Justice Chase. 62820
Chief Justice's charge to the Grand Jury. 87356
Chief of sinners made a chief of saints. 88044A
Chief of the pilgrims. 91107
Chief officers of the state of South-Carolina. 87785
Chief points in the laws of war and neutrality. 43644
Chief sins of the people. note after (58767)
Chief's daughter. 12688, note after 100443
Chiense, Vincent Justinian. (20580), 29497 see also. Dominicans. Magistro General.
Chifflet, Jean Jacques. 12689
Chigi, Fabio. see Alexander VII, Pope, 1599-1667.
Chihuahua (Mexican State) 12692, 22844
Chihuahua and Sinaloa Gold and Silver Minign Association. 12817
Chilapa, Mexico. Unos Emigrados. pseud. see Unos Emigrados de la Villa de Chilapa. pseud.
Child, ---------, fl. 1789. 95920
Child, ---------, fl. 1827. (46077)
Child, A. B. 12693
Child, Anna P. 12694
Child, Asa. 86753, note after 100786
Child, David Lee, d. 1874. 12695-(12703), 85929, 94059, note after 94937, note just before 95113, note after 98561
Child, David Lee, d. 1874. defendant (12703)
Child, David Lee, d. 1874. supposed author (12696), 19075, 94058
Child, Mrs. David Lee. see Child, Lydia Maria (Francis) 1802-1880.
Child, E. B. ed. 601
Child, Francis James. supposed author 12704, 20884
Child, Hamilton. 35943
Child, Isaac. 12735-(12736), 100599
Child, John. (12705)-12706, 45664, 1st note after 98664, 104797

Child, Sir Josiah, 1630-1699. (12707)-12708, 78984, 78992
Child, Linus, 1803-1870. (12709), (72214)
Child, Lydia Maria (Francis) 1802-1880. 6487, (7722), 12710-(12727), 19232, 35501, (76379), 81821, (81899), 84139-84141, 84143, 84146, 91076
Child, Robert, 1613-1654. 30702
Child, Sir Robert, fl. 1721. 65865, 88192
Child, Samuel. 45360
Child captives. 33107
Child life in Oregon. 74328
Child of adoption. 91287
Child of feeling. 102158
Child of nature. (81026)
Child of Pallas. 65088
Child of song. 27159
Child of the battle-field. 36516
Child of the Cero. 71233
Child of the sun. pseud. Summer-land. 93614
Child, well instructed. 62517
Child wife. 69033
Childe, Alexander. 66686
Childe, Edward Vernon, 1804-1861. 12729, 40650, 76852, 90794
Childe, John. see Child, John.
Childe Harold's pilgrimage. 84915
Childe Harvard. 1308, (12728)
Childe Martin, an epic poem. 68156
Childe Roeliffe's pilgrimage and other tales. 94247
Children of the frontier. 12730, 42690
Children of the future. 83682
Children of the isle. 88661
Children of the kingdom. (72060)
Children well imployed and Jesus much delighted. 62517
Children's Aid Society, New York. 54177
Children's Aid Society, New York. Hudson River Industrial School Association. see Hudson River Industrial School Association.
Children's Aid Society, New York. Italian School. Teacher. 54177
Children's Asylum, New York. see New York (City) Children's Asylum.
Children's Friends' Society, Providence, R. I. 66252
Children's Home, Moyamensing, Pa. see Moyamensing Union School, and Children's Home, Moyamensing, Pa.
Children's Home, Philadelphia. see Philadelphia. Union School and Children's Home.
Children's Home and Home for Aged Females, Roxbury, Mass. see Roxbury Home for Children and Aged Females, Roxbury, Mass.
Children's Home of West Philadelphia. see West Philadelphia Children's Home.
Children's hour. 74609
Children's Primary Association. 85507
Children's Robinson Crusoe. 92339
Childress, George C. 94974 see also Texas (Republic) Legation. United States.
Childs, C. G. illus. (12731), 35199, 99588
Childs, George T. 3950, note after 90573
Childs, H. 12732
Childs, Henry Halsey, 11783-1868. 12733-(12734)
Childs, Isaac. see Child, Isaac.
Childs, Nathaniel. defendant (12737)
Childs, Orville W. 12738-12739, 22586, 34940

Child's anti-slavery book. 81927
Child's book. (80914)
Child's book of American geography. 27922
Child's catechism in Choctaw. 12878, 105534
Child's easy introduction to spelling and
 reading. 95407
Child's first book in geography. 83771
Child's first book in spelling and reading.
 88448
Child's first reading book. 88466
Child's history of England. (6319)
Child's history of the United States. [By
 Charles A. Goodrich.] (27870)
Child's history of the United States. By John
 Gilmary Shea. 80000, (80021)
Child's history of the United States of America.
 (6319)
Child's instructor. 91335
Child's life of Washington. 101846
Child's picture defining and reading book.
 18293, (71344)
Child's portion. 104073
Child's second reading book. 88467
Chile (Spanish Colony) 12775
Chile (Spanish Colony) Consulado. 68223
Chile. 12760, 12765, 12779, 12798, 16849,
 61112, 67318
Chile. Asesor del Consulado. 47811
Chile. Census, 1854. (12748)
Chile. Congreso. 12766
Chile. Constitution. (12757)
Chile. Corte de Apelaciones, Santiago.
 81411
Chile. Corte de Apelaciones, Santiago. Fiscal.
 100608 see also Elizalde, Fernando
 Antonio.
Chile. Ejercito. 7558, 12743
Chile. Ejercito. Ordanza. 12795
Chile. Esposicion Nacional de Agricultura,
 Santiago, 1869. see Esposicion Nacional
 de Agricultura, Santiago, Chile, 1869.
Chile. Exposition Internale, 1875. Commission
 Directrice. (79351)
Chile. Laws, statutes, etc. 12744, (12753),
 12778, 12794-12795, 12801, 66403,
 (68851), (75550), 90775, note after 103224
Chile. Legacion. Bolivia. 87255
Chile. Ministerio de Guerra y Marina. 12782,
 12784 see also Chile. Ministerio de
 Marina.
Chile. Ministerio de Hacienda. 12794, 12801,
 12780, 12785, 17161
Chile. Ministerio de Industria i Obras
 Publicas. 84736
Chile. Ministerio de Justicia, Culto, e Instruc-
 cion Publicia. 12781, 12783
Chile. Ministerio de Marina. 47603 see
 also Chile. Ministerio de Guerra y
 Marina.
Chile. Ministerio de Relaciones Exteriores.
 12759, (12787), 44284 see also Chile.
 Ministerio del Interior y Relaciones
 Exteriores.
Chile. Ministerio del Interior. 12786
Chile. Ministerio del Interior y Relaciones
 Exteriores. 96059 see also Chile.
 Ministerio de Relaciones Exteriores.
 and Tocornal, Joaquin.
Chile. Oficina de Estadistica. 12803
Chile. President, 1831-1841 (Prieto) 12773,
 12789 see also Prieto, Joaquin, Pres.
 Chile, 1786-1854.
Chile. Sala de Comercio. 47811
Chile. Treaties, etc. 12755
Chile. Universidad, Santiago. 12741

Chile. Universidad, Santiago. Consejo. 8013
Chile (Diocese) Bishop (Phelipe) 59522 see
 also Phelipe, Pedro, Bp.
Chile (Diocese) Synod, 1st, 1749. 59522
Chile. 62957
Chile and Peru in 1824. (12749), 100814
Chile and Spain. 12750
Chile con carne. 83970
Chile in 1859. 14084
Chile: its geography, climate, earthquakes.
 27419
Chile mit Beruchsichtigung der Provinz
 Valdavia. 37776
Chilenischer Roman. 27194
Chileno. pseud. Unico asilo de las republicas
 Hispano Americanas. see Carvallo,
 Manuel. supposed author
Chileno instruido en la historia topografica.
 29374
Chili. 101350
Chile et l'Espagne. (12751)
Chili, Paraguay, Uruguay, Buenos-Ayres.
 (23767)
Chili-Peru-Bresil. (67424)
Chili tel qu'il est. (79351)
Chili, the United States and Spain. 33912, 1st
 note after 99449
Chili, through American spectacles. 12752
Chili, von C. Famin. 23768, 102622
Chilidugu sive res Chilensis. (30912)
Chilindrina que sale por cuarta respuesta del
 analisi del llamada Roamnce de Veracruz.
 100695
Chilleau, Marie Charles du. see Airvault,
 Marie Charles du Chilleau, Marquis d'.
Chillicothe, Ohio. Convention, 1802. see
 Northwest Territory, U. S. Convention,
 Chillicothe, 1802.
Chillicothe Presbytery. see Presbyterian
 Church in the U. S. A. Presbytery of
 Chillicothe.
Chilmead, Edward. tr. 10199
Chilton, Edward. 30716, note after 104154
Chilton, James R. 90792
Chilton, Samuel. 23930, 78721, 103287, note
 after 103287 see also Whig Party.
 Virginia. Fauquier County. Central
 Committee.
Chilton, Thomas, 1798-1854. 8862, 12809
Chilula: or the young Mexican. 12810
Chimalpain, Juan Bautista de San Anton Munon.
 ed. and tr. 27753
Chimasia: a reply to Longfellow's Theologian.
 68667
Chimera. (12811)
Chimes of freedom and union. 12812
Chimpan, Daniel. (12818)-(12821)
China and California. 89253
China and Japan. 36367
China and the United States. 89258
China; comprehending a view of the origin,
 antiquity, history. 101135
China Mission Society. see Roberts' Fund
 and China Mission Society.
Chinaman in California. 33108
Chinampa, or island home. 75933
Chinard, Gilbert. 1st note after 100572,
 100837
Chinchilla, Capitan. pseud. El ya no cuela.
 see Santamaria, Miguel.
Chinese. pseud. Wandering Philanthropist.
 25304, 1st note after 101235
Chinese immigration. Speech . . . in the
 Senate of the United States. 76947
Chinese immigration. Speech of Hon. James
 A. Johnson. 36230

Chinese Merchants of San Francisco. see
San Francisco. Chinese Merchants.
Chinese sugar-cane and sugar making. 90368
Chinese sugar-cane; its history, mode of
culture. (34123)
Chiney eye, crooked skin, and Oh, Susannah
songster. 70496
Ching, Lillian. 95776
Chingarora vision, and Fort Hamilton mystery.
90455
Chinigchinich. (10031), 72048
Chinn, Thomas W. 12814
Chiokvyhikoy. pseud. Apocalypse. 12816,
(35102)
Chion du Vergier, -------, Baron Eberstein.
see Eberstein et Chion du Vergier,
--------, Baron.
Chipman, ---------. 5th note after 99205,
99236, 101230
Chipman, C. 12817
Chipman, Daniel. 12820, 88985
Chipman, Daniel. defendant 106058
Chipman, John, 1690?-1775. 2873, 12822,
103934
Chipman, John Logan. 12823
Chipman, Nathaniel, 1752-1843. (12818),
12824, 99132
Chipman, Nathaniel, 1752-1843. supposed author
16144, note after 99172, note after 104629
Chipman, Norton Parker, 1836-1924. (12825)-
12826, 59185, 89300
Chipman, Richard Manning, 1806-1893. 12827-
12828
Chipman, Samuel. 12829
Chipman, Ward. (12830), note after 69528
Chipman, Hosmer and Co. firm 12826,
39406
Chipman, Hosmer, Gilmore & Brown. see
Chipman, Hosmer and Co. firm
Chippewa Club ausgabe. 78404
Chippewa Indians. Treaties, etc. 96599,
96605, 96618, 96630, 96631, 96647,
96652, 96657, 96692, 96716, 96720,
96728 see also Michigan Indians.
Treaties, etc. United Tribes of Pota-
watomi, Chippewa, and Ottawa Indians.
Treaties, etc.
Chippewa Indians (Black River Band) Treaties,
etc. 96704
Chippewa Indians (Saginaw Tribe) see Saga-
naw Tribe of Chippewa Indians.
Chippewa Indians (Swan Creek Band) Treaties,
etc. 96704
Chippeway first lessons in reading and spelling.
35687
Chippeway Indian. 22184
Chippeway primer. 20678
Chippin, -------. 25994
Chippouais. 12569
Chips from the workshop. (35304)
Chirino, Pedro. 12836, 51449
Chiriqui Improvement Company. 52774
Chirridu. pseud. Tambien al Berdugo Azotan.
94286
Chirugijns scheeps-kist. 98929
Chisholm, --------. plaintiff 11308
Chisholm, Colin. 12837-12840
Chisholm (C. R.) firm publishers (33938)
Chisholm (C. R.) & Brothers. firm publishers
12841
Chisholme, David. 12842-12843, 42521, 100872
Chisholm's hand-book of travel. 12841
Chisholm's panoramic guide from Niagara
Falls to Quebec. (33938)
Chislon. pseud. Major Soule. see Nichols,
George Ward. supposed author

Chisolm, J. Julian. 12846
Chispa patriotica. 12847-(12848)
Chissel, John. pseud. Letter. 103224
Chisvs Kilaist chihowa ushi hatak aiokchaya
isht anumpa hoke. 75874
Chittenden, L. E. 12849, 20310, (59046)
Chittenden, Martin, 1769-1840. 55323 see
also Vermont. Governor, 1813-1815.
Chittenden, Nathaniel W. 12850
Chittenden, Thomas, 1730-1797. (12851),
99002, 99008, 99047, 99050-99061,
99073-99076, 99103 see also Vermont.
Governor, 1778-1789 (Chittenden)
Vermont. Governor, 1790-1797
(Chittenden)
Chittenden, W. B. 38519
Chittenden County, N. Y. Washington Benevolent
Society. see Washington Benevolent
Society. New York. Chittenden County.
Chittenden County, Vt. Court. 96810
Chitty, Joseph. 12852
Chivalry of the south. 80552
Chivalry, slavery, and young America. 9310
Chivers, Thomas Holly. 12854
Chivington, J. M. 12855
Chloris boreali-americana. 28369
Chloroform. pseud. Assimilated rank. see
Ruschenberger, W. S. W.
Chlorospermeae. 30782
Choate, Daniel L. defendant. (12856)
Choate, David. 17698
Choate, John, 1697-1765. 2602-2603, 12857,
29853, 34083 see also Massachusetts
(Colony) Commissioners to Treat with
the Eastern Indians, 1749.
Choate, Rufus, 1799-1859. 6519, 7127, 12858,
12860, 18906, 20353, 59446, 67222,
85017, 85055, 85081 see also Smith-
sonian Institution. Board of Regents.
Chocolata Inda opusculum de qualitate et natura
chocolatae. (14543)
Chocorua and other sketches. 1524
Choctaw and Chickasaw Central Railroad Com-
pany. Charter. 63921
Choctaw and Chickasaw 35th Parallel Railroad
Company. Charter. 63922
Choctaw arithmetic. 12868, 105530
Choctaw Bible stories. 12874
Choctaw friend. 105536-105537
Choctaw girl. 12869
Choctaw hymn book. 12867, 105538
Choctaw instructor. 12866, 105541
Choctaw Nation. 49492
Choctaw Nation. petitioners 34658, 63036
Choctaw Nation. Constitution. 105531
Choctaw Nation. Delegates. 63035, 73410
see also Pitchlynn, P. P.
Choctaw Nation. General Council. 12862
Choctaw Nation. Laws, statutes, etc. 12862,
105531
Choctaw Nation. Treaties, etc. 12877, 38815,
48486, 84448, 96596, 96601, 96606,
96624-96625, 96635, 96663, 96697,
96717
Choctaw reader. 12865, note after 105536
Choctaw spelling book. 105535
Choctaw spellingbook. 12870
Choctaw treaty claiming Babbit Creek. 38815
Choctaws and their debts. 12871, 31171
Chodzko, ------. 85791
Chofre, Mateo Morales. defendant 75583
Choice: a discourse, occasioned by the . . .
drought. (43048)
Choice: a poem after the manner of Mr.
Pomfret. 12985, 1st note after 106134

Choice: a tragedy; with other miscellaneous poems. (58115)
Choice and well-selected collection of the most popular, sentimental, patriotic, naval, and comic songs. 58821
Choice collection: inspired by the incidents and scenes of the present war. 86900
Choice collection of about one hundred and seventy of the most popular songs. 97989
Choice collection of all the original songs, as sung in America. 55295
Choice collection of Democratic poems and songs. (16707)
Choice collection of hymns and spiritual songs. 56634, 83419
Choice collection of hymns for social worship. 103505
Choice collection of new songs. 85686
Choice collection of papers relating to state affairs. 12879, 78206
Choice collection of psalm tunes. 84698
Choice collection of psalm-tunes, anthems, and hymns. 42856
Choice collection of popular songs. 52712
Choice collection of songs, anecdotes and witticisms. 82698
Choice collection of songs for the soldier. 10180
Choice collection of the most approved patriotic and other songs. 1224
Choice collection of the most approved patriotic, comic, sentimental, amatory and naval songs. 86951, 86953
Choice collection of the most new and popular American, English, Irish, Scotch, comic, hunting, love, bacchanalian, and sea songs. 54854
Choice dialogue between John Faustus a conjurer, and Jack Tory. 101193
Choice dialogues between a Godly minister and an honest clergyman. (12361), 46473, 101193
Choice drop of honey from the rock Christ. 103965
Choice extracts from a speech of Joseph M. Barr. 3580
Choice farm lands. 34977
Choice gems from Washington Irving. (35219)
Choice memoirs of the history and description of the world. 34033
Choice narrative of Count Gondamor's transactions. 17105, 78362
Choice narrative of the notable exploit of part of the English fleet. 97661
Choice of a profession. 66229
Choice of a rural life. 41647-41648
Choice selection of pieces by our best poets. (5373)
Choice selection of songs. 14332, 82698
Choice songs. 14879
Choice wisdom. 46247
Choicest works of the most popular authors. 91284
Choir. 84041
Choiseul, ------- de. 75041
Choiseul-Praslin, ------- Duc de. 47519
see also Santo Domingo (French Colony) Commissaires.
Choix d'anecdotes ou faits memorables. 14458
Choix de mari. (16514)
Choix de morceaux litteraries. (10348)
Choix de quelques memoires sur les colonies. 98269

Choix de voyages anciens et modernes. 19550
Choix de voyages dans les quartre parties du monde. 42989
Choix de voyages modernes. 225
Choix definitif du point d'escale des transatlantiques. 6880
Choix des letters edifiantes. 50213
Choix des letters historiques. (44563)
Choix des parties les plus remarquables jouees par Paul Morphy en Amerique. 65394
Choix des poesies indigenes. 38947
Choix des relations de voyages les plus interessantes. 12164, note after 99383C
Cholera, a visitation from God. 22788
Cholera at Quebec. 104176
Cholera at the military posts in the harbor of New York. 53598
Cholera beacon. 91831
Cholera in Cincinnati. 39228
Cholera with reference to the geological theory. 39497
Chon, -------. 12880
Chopia d'una letra. 99353, 99374, 99379
Chopin, J. M. 12881-12882
Choppin, Samuel. ed. (53355)
Choquehuanca, Jose Domingo. 12883
Choralmi, Lorenzo di Piero. 99353, 99374, 99379
Choris, Louis. (12884)-12885
Chorister's companion. 36138, 93802
Chorley, J. engr. 12891, 84358-84362, 84365
Chorlton, William. 12886-12887
Chorographia de alguns logares. (3596)
Chorographical and statistical description. 101355
Chorography and topography of all the known parts of the earth. 49905
Chorus for the times. 41530
Choses coloniales. Guadeloupe. 20930
Chotteau, Leon. 12888-12889
Choubard, -------. illus. 42355, (75482)
'Chouk, Tridace-Nafe-Theobrome de Kaout't. pseud. Voyage pittoresque et industriel. see Delmotte, Henri Florent.
Choules, John Overton. 12890-12891, (52144), 84358-84362, 84365
Chouteau, A. P. USA 96719 see also U. S. Commissioners to the Kiowa, Ka-ta-ka, and Ta-wa-karo Nations of Indians.
Chouteau, Auguste. 75357
Chouteau, Henry. plaintiff 83725
Chovel, Rafael. 12892, (48885)
Choza de Tom. 92606, 92610-92611
Choza de Tomas. 92612
Choza del Negro Tomas. 92613
Chrestomathia da lingua Brazilica. 24168, 25426
Chretiens protestants de France a tous leurs freres. 12894
Christ, Potter. pseud. Revelations. see Potter, Arnold.
Christ . . . . A sermon. 59454
Christ a sympathizing savior. 93195
Christ abolishing death. 65584
Christ all. 83306
Christ Church, Boston. see Boston. Christ Church.
Christ Church, Cambridge, Mass. see Cambridge, Mass. Christ Church.
Christ Church, Cincinnati. see Cincinnati. Christ Church.
Christ Church, Elizabeth, N. J. see Elizabeth, N. J. Christ Church.
Christ Church, Hagerstown, Md. see Hagerstown, Md. Christ Church.

Christ Church, Leicester, Mass. see
Leicester, Mass. Christ Church.
Christ Church, New Brighton, N. Y. see
New Brighton, N. Y. Christ Church.
Christ Church, New Brighton, Pa. see New
Brighton, Pa. Christ Church.
Christ Church, New Haven, Conn. see New
Haven, Conn. Christ Church.
Christ Church, New York. see New York
(City) Christ Church.
Christ Church, Philadelphia. see Philadelphia.
Christ Church.
Christ Church, Quincy, Mass. see Quincy,
Mass. Christ Church.
Christ Church, Reading, Pa. see Reading,
Pa. Christ Church.
Christ Church, Upper Merion, Pa. see
Upper Merion, Pa. Christ Church.
Christ Churchl, Wrentham, Mass. see
Wrentham, Mass. Christ Church.
Christ Church. [A circular letter of a com-
mittee.] 67286
Christ Church, Cambridge. One hundredth
anniversary. 10127
Christ Church Hospital, Philadelphia. see
Philadelphia. Christ Church Hospital.
Christ Church Hospital. Extracts from the
will of the founder. 61535
Christ Church Parish, Philadelphia. see
Philadelphia. Christ Church Parish.
Christ Church Parish Ladies' Charitable
Association, New York. see New York
(City) Christ Church Parish Ladies'
Charitable Association.
Christ Church Parish School Association, New
York. see New York (City) Christ
Church Parish School Association.
Christ crucified. 91043
Christ crucified: a sermon preached by
appointment before the General Assembly.
89158
Christ hagonthahninoh nonodagahyot. 79118
Christ, holding the stars. 16347
Christ in the army. (12893)
Christ Protestant Episcopal Church, New York.
New York (City) Christ Church.
Christ . . . Sermon . . . before the General
Assembly of Connecticut. 24437
Christ standing for an ensign of the people.
(14471)
Christ the believer's husband. 103515, 103593
Christ, the believer's refuge. 103510
Christ, the believer's wisdom. 103573
Christ the chief corner stone. 73879
Christ the eternal word. 105216
Christ the foundation. 20794
Christ, the foundation of the salvation of
sinners. 104316
Christ the fountaine of life. (17053)
Christ the glorious builder of the spiritual
temple. 92157
Christ the glory of the temple. 85387
Christ the resurrection. 19875
Christ the son of God. 62793
Christ the theme of the home missionary.
104812
Christ the true victim and conquerer. (80392)
Christ triumphing, and Satan raging. 24386
Christ victorious over the powers of darkness.
79410
Christeligt folkeblad. 13508
Christelijke ervaringen en gesprekken. 7804
Christen Reise nach der Seeligen Ewigkeit.
62848
Christendom in confusion. 51310

Christendoms saga. 74880
Christian V, King of Denmark, 1645-1699.
(18501), 102940 see also Denmark.
Sovereigns, etc., 1670-1699 (Christian V)
Christian VII, King of Denmark, 1749-1808.
37862 see also Denmark. Sovereigns,
etc., 1766-1808 (Christian VII)
Christian, Chief of the Oneida Indians 5880
Christian, Charles. 12895, 54133
Christian, Fletcher, fl. 1789. 12896, (12899)
99601A, 100826
Christian, James. 37593
Christian, Joseph. (12897)
Christian, L. H. 12898
Christian A. B. C. consisting of seven
alphabets. 32496
Christian: a poem. 17432
Christian a stranger and sojourner upon earth.
21052
Christian advices. 86040
Christian advocate and journal. (1235), 89367
Christian advocate; being a continuation of the
Presbyterian magazine. 12899A
Christian advocate. By a Tennesseean. 94814
Christian Alliance, New York. 12900, 54181
Christian Alliance; its constitution. 12900,
54181
Christian almanack. 12901
Christian almanac for Kentucky. 37497
Christian almanac. For Maryland and
Virginia. 12902
Christian ambassador. 25038
Christian ambition. 8900
Christian amendment of the constitution
proposed. (39941)
Christian and civil liberty and freedom
considered. 11828
Christian and literary remembrancer. 104614
Christian and loving animadversions upon
sundry other observable passages in said
brooke. 46781, note before 96158
Christian and the national church. 28687
Christian and worldly contentment. 85603
Christian Anti-slavery Convention, Cincinnati,
1850. 49362
Christian Anti-slavery Convention, Cincinnati,
1851. 49362
Christian Anti-slavery State Convention,
Columbus, Ohio, 1859. see Ohio State
Christian Anti-slavery Convention,
Columbus, 1859.
Christian armed with strength. 46359
Christian armed with strength from above.
46622
Christian Association, Baltimore. see
Baltimore Christian Association.
Christian at his calling. (46248)
Christian awaiting his last change. 6270
Christian ballad. 91918
Christian banner. 12903
Christian baptist. 12904
Christian benevolence. 93954
Christian biography. 97625
Christian bishop: a sermon . . . at . . . New
York. 64608
Christian bishop . . . a sermon preached in
. . . October, A. D. 1827. (32301)
Christian bishop approving himself unto God.
104918
Christian bravery. 13347
Christian benevolence, as illustrated in the
early history of Georgia. 33243
Christian charity. 73556
Christian Church. General Convention, Marion,
N. Y., 1850. 49344

Christian Church, Nashville, Tenn. see
    Nashville, Tenn. Christian Church.
Christian Churches Convention, New Bedford,
    Mass., 1834. see Convention and
    Conference of Ministers and Delegates
    of Christian Churches, New Bedford,
    Mass., 1834.
Christian church's duty to the freemen.
    17924
Christian citizen. 64227
Christian citizen's duty in the present crisis.
    39693
Christian citizenship and honest legislation.
    33963
Christian civilization. A discourse. 8552
Christian civilization. An address. 60955
Christian Commission. A delegate's story.
    9669
Christian Commission For the Army and
    Navy of the United States of America.
    see United States Christian Commission.
Christian commonwealth. 22144
Christian confession. 12906
Christian confidence. 89783
Christian common wealth ought to be well
    instructed & experienced in the military
    art. 71021
Christian commonwealth ought to be well
    instructed and experienced in the military
    art. (71022)
Christian consolation. (68588)
Christian consolation for bereaved parents.
    (23813)
Christian Convention, Aurora, Ill., 1867.
    49363
Christian Convention, Indianapolis, 1859.
    34585
Christian Convention, Newark, N. Y., 1866.
    see New York State Christian Con-
    vention, Newark, N. Y., 1866.
Christian conversing with the great mystery
    of Christianity. 46249
Christian courage. A sermon for the times.
    13241
Christian courage necessary for a Gospel
    minister. 56724
Christian course. 90185
Christian culture. A sermon. 13385
Christian culture in public schools. 85202
Christian cynick. 46250
Christian directions and instructions for
    Negroes. 12907
Christian disciple. see Christian disciple
    and theological review.
Christian disciple and theological review.
    11919, 12908-12909, (26418), 88979,
    90713, 93205, 102563, 105646
Christian doctrine and society of the people
    called Quakers, cleared from the
    reproach. 12913, (66917), note after
    103655
Christian doctrine of human rights and
    slavery. (81928)
Christian doctrine of slavery. 2020
Christian duty of patriotism. 7251
Christian duty of spreading the scriptures.
    90359
Christian duty to emigrants. 29632
Christian education the remedy. 20349
Christian element essential in the truest
    patriotism. 45023
Christian element in the state. 78863
Christian epistle to friends in general of
    weighty concern. 103656
Christian examiner. 2290, (4338), 4344,
    6673, 8340, 9623, 12910, 12911, 12912,

13414, 14732, 16337-16338, 28965, 28976,
    30870, 33625, 42460, 58679, 58757,
    59350, 68723, 69423, 69435, (69703),
    91376, note after 94370, 101057, 101397,
    102091, 103179
Christian examiner and general review. see
    Christian examiner.
Christian examiner and religious miscellany.
    see Christian examiner.
Christian examiner and theological review.
    see Christian examiner.
Christian . . . exemplified. 8509
Christian exhibited as a green olivetree.
    46581, note after 100591
Christian faith of New-England Quakers
    condemn'd. 37185, 37202
Christian faith of the people of God, called in
    scorn, Quakers in Rhode-Island. 12914,
    37185, 37202
Christian fixed in his post. 59602
Christian forbearance in weak consciences.
    92887
Christian fortitude. 18125
Christian funeral. 46251
Christian guardian. 85240
Christian guardian. Editor. 71718
Christian herald. 86271
Christian hero. 17336
Christian hero: his conflicts, virtues, and
    crown. 8598
Christian hero, containing accounts of the
    revival and propagation of religion.
    65577, (65618), note after 103615
Christian history . . . for the year 1744.
    94688, 94709
Christian history: or, a general account of the
    progress of the Gospel. 103616
Christian hymns, poems, and spiritual songs.
    69365
Christian idea of sacrifice. 16764
Christian, in time of national peril, trembling.
    17928
Christian Independents, Gloucester, Mass.
    see Society of Christian Independents,
    Gloucester, Mass.
Christian index. 82073
Christian Indian. 12915
Christian Indians buried at Bethlehem, Pa.
    68992
Christian inquirer. 12916
Christian intelligencer. 92790
Christian intelligencer. see Mutual rights &
    Christian intelligencer.
Christian investigator. 27848
Christian journal. 103472
Christian journal and literary register.
    12917
Christian journal and narrative. 11081
Christian jubliee. 85946
Christian knowledge, and Christian confidence
    inseparable. 89789
Christian labourer. (68558)
"Christian lawyer." A sermon delivered in
    . . . Boston. 81620
Christian lawyer: being a portraiture of the
    life and character of William George
    Baker. 2850
Christian lessons and a Christian life. 84012
Christian letter to Presbyterian, church, &
    Quaker. 12918
Christian liberty. 73563
Christian library. 27415, 102150
Christian life and character of the civil
    institutions of the United States. 50798
Christian life social and individual. 4081

Christian love. 12331
Christian loyalty. (46252)
Christian magazine conducted by members of the Mendon Association. (47820)
Christian magnanimity. 104932-104933, 104947
Christian martyr and child. (48337)
Christian martyrs. (25096)
Christian memorial of two sisters. 43671
Christian memorials of the war. (29475)
Christian merchant. (9474)
Christian messenger. 92031
Christian messenger. see Philadelphia Universalist magazine and Christian messenger.
Christian minister, an ambassador of Christ. 76513
Christian minister commencing his office-work. 84293
Christian minister . . . described. A sermon delivered at the ordination of the Reverend Mr. Joel Benedict. 30632
Christian minister described and distinguished from a pleaser of men. (30631)
Christian ministers commissioned by the great Head of the Church. 18102
Christian ministry. A sermon, at the ordination of . . . Linus Hall Shaw. 14535
Christian ministry. A sermon, preached in . . . Brooklyn. (72424)
Christian ministry. An address delivered at the annual commencement. 89019
Christian ministry. Sermon . . . at the ordination of Rev. Hiram Withington. (29830)
Christian ministry, the wisdom, benevolence and purposes of its appointment. 76508
Christian mirror. 38526
Christian miscellany. 54862
Christian mission. 44813
Christian Missionary Society. 34585
Christian missions. 6018
Christian missions and African colonization. (458)
Christian moderation. (77564)
Christian monitor. 97833
Christian mourning. A discourse . . . at the funeral of Rev. Lucius Bolles. 79783
Christian mourning: a sermon occasioned by the death of Mrs. Isabella Graham. 45463
Christian mourning with hope. 105302, 105306, 105307
Christian news. 3405
Christian obedience to civil government. 71051
Christian observatory, a literary and religious magazine. 43062
Christian observer. 45460, 69480, 98836
Christian officer. 88044
Christian or Bible view of war. 67890
Christian orator. 12919
Christian pantheism. 77425
Christian patriot. A discourse addressed to the graduating class. 3986
Christian patriot. A sermon. 35702
Christian patriot. A sermon . . . at . . . Boston. 51123
Christian patriot. A sermon delivered in Grace Church, Galena. 22016
Christian patriot encouraged. 71052
Christian patriot. Some recollections of the late Col. Hugh Maxwell. 47048
Christian patriotism; a discourse . . . in Augusta, Geo. 9090
Christian patriotism. A sermon delivered in the Reformed Dutch Church. 4991

Christian patriotism. . . . a sermon on occasion of the death of John Adams. 26063
Christian patriotism: a sermon preached in Cumberland-St. M. E. Church. 93629
Christian patriotism. A sermon preached in in St. Clement's Church. (33493)
Christian patriotism. An address delivered in Concord. 6951
Christian patriotism by William Adams. 352
Christian patriot's duty, at the present crisis. 35482
Christian patriot's duty in the present crisis. 21134
Christian patriot's present duty. (67311)
Christian pattern, or the imitation of Jesus Churs. 37343, 1st note after 95453
Christian peace. 19604
Christian people's remembrance of their deceased pastor. 92088
Christian philanthropist. 14224
Christian philanthropy. 64617
Christian Philorthodoxo. pseud. see Philorthodoxo, Christian. pseud.
Christian philosopher. (46253)
Christian piety. 62418
Christian preacher's commission. 18969
Christian psalmody. 85388
Christian pulpit, the rightful guardian of morals. 77719
Christian Quaker. 37186, 37221
Christian-Quaker, and his divine testimony. (59689), note after 103656
Christian Quaker, and his divine testimony vindicated. (59689), note after 103656
Christian radicalism. 104955
Christian rapture. 12920
Christian reader. 56382, 56385, 104083
Christian record (Bloomington, Ind.) 46763
Christian record (Jamaica) 90593
Christian register. see Unitarian register and Universalist leader.
Christian register and Boston observer. see Unitarian register and Universalist leader.
Christian register, and moral and theological review. 12921
Christian religion, epitomized and inculcated. 46527
Christian religion recommended in a letter to his pupils. 92636
Christian reporter. 52807
Christian repository. 99781
Christian retrospect and register. 2784
Christian review (Boston) (12923), 84036
Christian review (New York) (12922)
Christian Rubens. 90090
Christian Sabbath. 6227
Christian Sabbath explained and vindicated. (9718)
Christian sanctuary. 48031
Christian scholar's and farmer's magazine. (12924)
Christian service to the poor in cities. 97385
Christian serving God in his business. 30922
Christian slave. 92504
Christian slaveholders disobedient to Christ. 24610
Christian sobriety. 47150
Christian soldier. A sermon preached at Newbury. 43293
Christian soldier. A sermon . . . before . . . Artillery Company. 26624
Christian soldier. A sermon, preached before the Ancient Honourable Artillery Company. 102745

Christian soldier: a sermon, preached in St. James' Church. 80450
Christian soldier. By Rev. F. Senour. 79141
Christian souldier orderly, and strenuously engaged. 50299
Christian soldier's duties briefly delineated. (34760)
Christian soldier's duty. 84596
Christian spectator. 4344, (12925) 23563, 97594, 99556
Christian statesman: a discourse occasioned by the death of the Hon. James McDowell. 36928
Christian statesman; a portraiture. 51240
Christian stewardship . . . 1863. 82340
Christian submission to civil government. 72169
Christian submission to personal injuries. 79825, 93140
Christian suffering. 64640
Christian system the only source of true peace. 92889
Christian taught of God. 82728
Christian temple. 46254
Christian thank-offering. 46255
Christian thankfulness explained and enforced. 7241, 94361
Christian thanksgiving perpetual. 40846
Christian that was his master in America. pseud. Discourse in way of a dialogue. see Tryon, Thomas.
Christian toleration. 92074
Christian tracts, no. 3. 101392
Christian traveller. 72626
Christian triumphant over death through Christ. 12371
Christian union. 74655, 85516
Christian union. A discourse. (64106)
Christian Union of New York and Brooklyn. 90752
Christian union; or, an argument for the abolition of sects. 98495
Christian unity. 78858
Christian unity, Board of Missions. 35816
Christian visitant. 88640
Christian warfare, victory and crown. (17330)
Christian warrior. A discourse. (81593)
Christian warriour. A sermon . . . in Boston. 43036
Christian warrior crowned. 85276, 85341
Christian watchman. 89372
Christian weapons. (49064)
Christian weekly. 66964
Christian wife and mother. 89262
Christian witness. 85546
Christian witness. Editor. (44318)
Christian womanhood. 23296
Christian work at the south. 47183
Christian world. 85443
Christian year. 84982
Christian year book. 12926
Christiana. December 6. 1771. (12927)
Christiana Bridge, Del. Newark Land and Cash Lottery, 1771. see Newark Land and Cash Lottery, Christiana Bridge, Del., 1771.
Christiana Bridge, July 13. 1771. (12927)
Christiana-Bridge Land & Cash Lottery, in New Castle County, on Delaware. (12927)
Christiana Bridge, March 23. 1772. (12927)
Christiandad del Japon. 80832
Christianesimo felice nelle missioni de' Padre della Compagnia di Gesu nel Paraguai. 51418

Christianis et piis lectoribus. (8784)
Christianity. 71852
Christianity a spirit. (26240)
Christianity and civil government. 353
Christianity and slavery: a review of the correspondence. 29526
Christianity and slavery. Strictures on the Rev. William Hague's review. 47943
Christianity and statesmanship. (29527)
Christianity and the commonwealth. 89920
Christianity and the race problem. 83862
Christianity and war. 72068
Christianity applied to our civil and social relations. 104799-104800
Christianity demonstrated. (46266)
Christianity described. (46347)
Christianity designed and adapted to be a universal religion. 106051
Christianity fitted for universal diffusion. 92119
Christianity: its destined supremacy on the earth. 92266
Christianity of the Quakers asserted. 66918
Christianity tested by eminent men. 9912
Christianity the law of the land. 66757
Christianity the means of civilization. 13829
Christianity, the only source of moral, social and political regeneration. 33593
Christianity the safeguard of civil liberty. 77988
Christianity the source of freedom. 82385
Christianity the wisdom of God. (18419)
Christianity to the life. 46257
Christianity unmasqued. 83610
Christianity, versus treason and slavery. 12931
Christianoyot Mexicanemachtiloni. 71488
Christian's behaviour under severe and repeated breavements. 3471
Christian's best motive for patriotism. 18252
Christians Bullen eines seefahrenden Journal. (9124)
Christians charge. (17087)
Christians Christ's representatives and agents. 85265, 85269
Christian's consolation. 89366
Christian's daily exercise. 46892
Christians daily walk in holy security and peace. 78514
Christian's daily walke in holy securitie and peace. 78511-78513
Christian's duty. 8349
Christian's duty: a sermon. (64646)
Christians duty in the present crisis. 43324
Christian's duty to render to Caesar, the things that are Caesar's. (12930), note after 66918
Christian's employment. 21625
Christians exercise by Satans temptations. 104074
Christian's grand treasure. 73807
Christian's hope. 62780
Christian's looking-glass. (65514)
Christian's magazine, reviewer, and religious intelligencer. (82473)
Christian's magazine. (32301)
Christians may and ought to be influenced. 58900
Christian's new and complete family Bible. 12929
Christian's new hymn book. 86946
Christians on earth and in heaven. 74547
Christian's pocket companion and daily assistant. 82474
Christian's pocket library. 90186

Christian's song. 101865
Christians treated in the quality of souldiers. 68014
Christians tvvo chiefe lessons. 32831
Christian's victory. 26624
Christians warned of temptation. 11860
Christians winter piece. 36919
Christian's work and rest. (72425)
Christianus. pseud. Voice of God. 100664
Christianus per ignem. (46258)
Christie, A. J. 12932
Christie, John. 12934
Christie, Robert, 1788-1856. 12935-12939, 84779
Christie, W. C. 12941
Christie, William. 12940, 65511, 99448
Christio, Gulielmo. see Christie, William.
Christliche Betrachtungen uber die Evanglischen Texte. 102503
Christliche Biographien. 39673
Christlichen vnd frommen Lesern. (8784)
Christlicher Segens-Wunsch. 95208
Christliches Gemuths-Gesprach von dem geistlichen und seligmachenden Glauben. (73102)
Christmas, Henry. ed. 12942-12943
Christmas, J. S. 12944
Christmas and birthday gift. 81368
Christmas and new year's gift for 1829. 29799, 103018
Christmas and new year's gift for young people. 106207
Christmas and new-year's gift, or birth-day present. 99840
Christmas and new-year's present, elegantly illustrated. 88687
Christmas and new year's present. Edited by Hermann Bokum. 6176, note after 92721
Christmas and new year's present. Edited by N. P. Willis. 104516
Christmas and new year's token. 100606
Christmas, and poems on slavery for Christmas, 1843. (81929)
Christmas Bazaar, Rochester, N. Y. see Ladies' Hospital Relief Association, Rochester, N. Y. Christmas Bazaar.
Christmas box. 60325
Christmas discourse . . . December 25th, 1845. (26240)
Christmas, 1863. 6140, 12945
Christmas eve at the White House. 44771
Christmas gift of love. (81253)
Christmas gift to her little southern friends. 13177
Christmas holidays in Rome. 77737
Christmas hymn, composed by the Hon. Royall Tyler. 97616
Chirstmas in 1690. 51638
Christmas, new year, and birthday gift [for 1855.] 85572
Christmas, new-year, and birthday gift, for MDCCCLIV. 85570
Christmas, new-year, and birthday gift, for MDCCLI. 85570
Christmas, new year, and birthday gift [for 1857.] 85572
Christmas, new year, and birthday gift [for 1856.] 85572
Christmas, new-year, and birthday gift, for MDCCCLII. 85570
Christmas, new-year, and birthday gift, for MDCCCLV. 85571
Christmas, new-year, and birthday present, for MDCCCLV. 85571
Christmas offering. 20195
Christmas scenes in New York. 12946
Christmas sermon at Boston. 30494

Christmas sermon at Princeton. 13454
Christmas sermon delivered in Trinity Church, Newark. 64798
Christmas song. 71789
Christmas story for 1869-70. 50630
Christmas tales, for the amusement and instruction of young ladies & gentlemen in winter evenings. 85667
Christmas tales for the amusement and instruction of young ladies and gentlemen, in winter evenings. 65396, 85668
Christmas well kept. 103504
Christnings make not Christians. 104334
Christo, Fabiao de. see Fabiao de Christo.
Christo Rey Seguido y perseguido de las turbas Hebreas. 75609
Christodulus. 46259
Christoforo Colombo, libri VIII. 17007
Christoforo Colombo: discorso. 24076
Christoph Colombo und seine Entdeckungen. 89646
Christoph Colombus. (18362)
Christoph Columbus, der Entdecker der neuen Welt. Ein Volksbuch. 24939
Christoph Columbus der Entdecker der neuen Welt. Historische Erzahlung. 38241
Christoph Columbus, oder die Entdeckung von Amerika. 11659
Christoph Daniel Ebling's Erdbeschreibung und Geschichte von Amerika. 21748
Christoph Gottlieb Murr's Journal. 51480, (51482), 98777
Christophe, Henri, King of Haiti, 1767-1820. 3885, 6978, 17481, 29580, 73830, 98677 see also Haiti. Sovereigns, etc., 1811-1820 (Christophe)
Christophe, Moreau. tr. (60079)
Christophe Colomb, comedie historique. 38756
Christophe Colomb (Cristobal Colon.) 38708
Christophe Colomb et la decouverte du nouveau monde. 4576
Christophe Colomb. Histoire de sa vie et de ses voyages. (73266)
Christophe Colomb, ou la decouverte du nouveau-monde, melodrame historique. 63174
Christophe Colomb, ou la decouverte du nouveau-monde, ode-symphonie en quatre parties. 48037
Christophe Colomb, ou l'Amerique decouverte. 6896
Christophe Colomb, ou notice d'un livre Italien. 38909
Christophe Colomb. Par A. de Lamartine. (38706)
Christophe Colomb. [Par Alphonse Dousseau.] 20732
Christophe Colomb. [Par Emile Deschanel.] 19690
Christophe Colomb par le Comte Roselly de Lorgues. 73267
Christophe Colomb. Par M. le Vicomte H. d'Oulbath. 47906
Christophe Colomb, suivi d'une nouvelle Americaine. (11658)
Christophe Colomb. Traduction de La Bedolliere. 16424
Christophe Colombe. 7980
Christopher. pseud. Remarkable adventures. 69375
Christopher, R. L. 12947
Christopher Caustic. pseud. see Fessenden, Thomas Green, 1771-1837.
Christopher Columbus. 94095
Christopher Columbus: his life, voyages, and discovery. 14647

Christopher Quandary. pseud. see Quandary, Christopher. pseud.
Christopher Whigg. pseud. see Walter, Thomas, 1696-1725.
Christopheri Colom de insvlis nvper inventis in pari Indico. 72023, 77902
Christophers, S. W. 92823
Christophilos. pseud. Review of Rev. Mr. Cushman's "Calm review." 12948, 18138
Christophori a Costa, medici et cheirvrgi, Aromatum & medicamentorum in orientali India nascentium liber. 57666
Christophoro d'Avalos, Felice Antonio de. 12949
Christophorus Cabrera Burgensis ad lectorem. 9812
Christophorus Colom de prima insularem, in mari Indico sitarum. 72023
Christoval Colon. 14930
Christ's agony improved. 30878
Christ's ambassadors allowed neither to usurp the title of "Rabbi and Masters," nor to submit to such usurpation. 103767
Christ's ascension. 12335
Christ's certain and sudden appearance to judgment. 99767
Christ's compassion on the multitudes. 65069, 94067
Christ's famous titles. 21603
Christ's fidelity the only shield. 39443
Christ's First Church, Hempstead, N. Y. see Hempstead, N. Y. Christ's First Church.
Christ's kingdom in the earth. (81652)
Christ's light springing. 24496
Christ's manifestation for the abolition of all kinds of popery! 85126
Christ's mission of the seventy. (13431)
Christ's peaceable reign. 85129
Christ's presence the glory of an house. 100927
Christ's promise to be present. 22221
Christ's promise to the penitent thief. 22121
Christ's rebuke. 39199
Christs satisfaction discussed and explained. 66871
Christ's sermon on the mountain. 79118
Christ's spirit a Christian's strength. 14373, (19437)
Christ's suit to the sinner. 102217
Christ's temptations real facts. 92161
Christ's warning to the churches. 39199
Christus. A mystery. (41932)
Christy, David, b. 1802. 4476, 12950-12954, 22263
Christy, Edwin P. 12955
Christy, William. defendant 12956
Christy's essence of old Kentucky. 12955
Christy's new songster. 12955
Chronica apostolica. 22896
Chronica Beschreibung. 12957, 1st note after 91211
Chronica compendiosissima ab exordio mundi. 994, 106399
Chronica da Companhia de Jesv de Estado do Brasil. 98651
Chronica da Companhia de Jesu do Estado do Brasil. 98653
Chronica da conquista de Guine. 76843
Chronica de la Nueva-Espana. 27752
Chronica de la Provincia de N. S. P. S. Francisco de Zacatecas. (52106)
Chronica de la Provincia de S. Antonio de los Charcas. 47835
Chronica de la Provincia de San Gabriel. 96977

Chronica de la Provincia S. Nicholas de Polentino. 2876
Chronica de la Provincia de San Pedro y San Pablo de Mechoacan. 71697
Chronica de la Provincia del Santissimo Nombre de Jesvs de Gvatemala. 98713
Chronica de la Provincia del Santo Evangelico de Mexico. 99386
Chronica de la Provincia S. Francisco de Zacatecas. 1998
Chronica de la Santa Provincia de San Diego de Mejico. 2987
Chronica de la Santa Provincia de San Diego de Mexico. 47336
Chronica de la seraphica religion del glorioso patriarcha San Francisco de Assis. 96308
Chronica de los mvy altos, y esclarecidos Reyes Catholicos Don Hernando y Dona Ysabel de gloriosa memoria. (66621)
Chronica de Nueva Espana. 27752
Chronica del muy esclavescido Principe y Rey don Alfonso el Onzeno. (56336)
Chronica del Peru. 13044-13046, 27737-27738
Chronica dele vite de pontefici et imperadori Romani. 61290-61292
Chronica do felicissimo Rei D. Manuel de gloriosa memoria. 27687
Chronica do felicissimo Rei Dom Emanvel. 27686
Chronica dos Frades Menores. 34144, 35334
Chronica dos valerosos e insignes feitos del Rey Dom Ioao II. (70063)
Chronica general de las Indias Occidentales. 27726
Chronica general de las Indes. 27725
Chronica litteraria do S. Paulo. 59228
Chronica observantiae strictioris. 44556
Chronica ordinis Sancti Francisci. 12958
Chronica politica y literaria de Lima. (41084)
Chronica seraphica. (22897)
Chronica vniuersal de todas las naciones y tiempos compuesta. (44103)
Chronicas de la Apostolica Provincia de S. Gregorio. 75987
Chroniche che tractano de la origine de Veneti. 74667
Chroniche del uererando padre frate Jacobo Phillipo. 25087
Chroniche di Polonia. 67738
Chroniche vulgare, nouamente dal frate Jacobo Philippo. 24395
Chroniche vulgare nouamente dal venerado patre frate Jacobo Philippo. (25085)
Chronicle, Augusta, Ga. see Augusta Georgia chronicle.
Chronicle, Boston. see Boston chronicle.
Chronicle [by Bartholome de las Casas.] 31559
Chronicle of Boston. 6554, 79004, note after 102419
Chronicle of college scrapes. 16323
Chronicle of Eusebius. 23114
Chronicle of Louisiana. 20584
Chronicle of Louisiana, being an account of Don Diego Rosa. 64881
Chronicle of Paulus Orosius. 26870
Chronicle of Peru. 13057
Chronicle of Poland. 67738
Chronicle of St. John's Berkeley. 81214
Chronicle of secession. 30453
Chronicle of Sirrom. 50887
Chronicle of the Cid. 56618
Chronicle of the Franciscans. 44556

Chronicle of the kingdom of Cassituides. (12961)
Chronicle of the Kings of England. 90222
Chronicle of the valley of the Shenandoah. (16314)
Chronicle of the war. 74451, 75920
Chronicle of the war. By Jessie Benton Fremont. 25834
Chronicler. pseud. tr. 70336
Chronicles of Andrew. 19608, 31915
Chronicles of B***g. 12960
Chronicles of Baltimore. 77507
Chronicles of border warfare. 95720, 104928
Chronicles of Canada. (82199)
Chronicles of Casco Bay. 14336
Chronicles of Cooperstown. 16425
Chronicles of Mount Benedict. 12962
Chronicles of Nathan Ben Saddi. 25413, 74818
Chronicles of Pineville. 12963, 36529, 95542-95543
Chronicles of the children of disobedience. 30662, note after 101993
Chronicles of the city of Gotham. 54182, 59194
Chronicles of the Farmers' and Merchants' Bank of Memphis. 36074
Chronicles of the fire-eaters of the tribe of Mississippi. 12964, 79190
Chronicles of the first planters of the colony of Massachusetts Bay. 13208, 31739, (33445), 46777, 80198, 103397, 105074, 106052
Chronicles of the great rebellion. 78243
Chronicles of the great rebellion against the United States of America. 12965
Chronicles of the great rebellion from the beginning. 78242
Chronicles of the kings of England. 20517
Chronicles of the North American savages. 12966, 34630
Chronicles of the Old Dominion. (71959)
Chronicles of the Old South Church. 6662
Chronicles of the pilgrim fathers of the colony of Plymouth. 18135, (51198), 82837, 104795-104796, note after 104797, 106053
Chronicles of the rebellion of 1861. 73342
Chronicles of the town of Easthampton. 26613
Chronicles of the twenty-first regiment N. Y. S. V. 49108
Chronicles of Turkeytown. 12967, 61198, 84400
Chronicles of Yonkers. 32903
Chronicon. 23114, 73458
Chronicon ad annum MCCCXX. 76838
Chronicon, das ist Beschreibung der Occidentalischen und Indianischen Landern. 12959
Chronicon Ephratense. 49044
Chronique. 74951
Chronique Bresilienne. 6842, (26774)
Chronique orientale et Americaine. 70373
Chroniques judicaries Francaises et etrangeres. 12968
Chronista de la religion de San Benito. 1944, 28739
Chronographica o reportorio de los tiempos, el mas copioso y preciso que hasta ahora ha salido a luz. 12351
Chronologia de rebus Scondiae. 48150
Chronologia hospitalario. 76888
Chronological abridgment or history of discoveries. 3654
Chronological account of the remarkable occurrences from the commencement of the French revolution to Dec. 1815. 12969

Chronological account of the several ages of the world. 37187
Chronological and historical tables. 5747
Chronological and topographical account of Dorchester, Mass. (30506)
Chronological annals of the war. 20415
Chronological biography of the Hon. Zadock Pratt. 64983
Chronological catalogue of the most curious and interesting books. (5198)
Chronological catalogue of twelve hundred books. 83013
Chronological catalogue of works in each class of language. 44718
Chronological detail of all the discoveries made in the 15th century. (4431)
Chronological historian: containing a regular account of all material transactions and occurrences, ecclesiastical, civil, and military, relating to the English affairs from the invasion of the Romans to the death of George I. 75820
Chronological historial: [containing a regular account of all material transactions and occurrences, ecclesiastical, civil, and military, relating to the English affairs] from the invasion of the Romans, to the present time. 75819
Chronological history of America, from its discovery in 1492 to 1806. (32577)
Chronological history of America from its discovery in MCCCXCII to MDCCCVI. 32576
Chronological history of New-England in the form of annals. 28020, 51017, 65585-(65586), 97181
Chronological history of plants. 62624
Chronological history of the Boston watch and police. 77227
Chronological history of the civil war in America. 24486
Chronological history of the discoveries in the South Sea or Pacific Ocean. 9387, 23494, 55448
Chronological history of the north-eastern voyages of discovery. 9386
Chronological history of the people called Methodists. 51645
Chronological history of the United States. 59356
Chronological history of the West Indies. 88568
Chronological history of voyages into the Arctic regions. 3660
Chronological list of the captains of the Royal Navy. 30351
Chronological record: containing . . . the presidents of America. 56852
Chronological record of the American civil war. (32233), 32269
Chronological record of the remarkable public events during the reigns of George III and IV. 12970
Chronological records of the British Royal and commercial navy. 50562
Chronological register of Boscawen. 65422
Chronological sketch of the life of the author. 101651
Chronological table. 6348
Chronological table, containing the principal events. 33634
Chronological table of cyclonic hurricanes. 63660
Chronological table of important events. 3321
Chronological table of the most important events. 45675

Chronological table of the principal events. 67683
Chronological tables. 73412
Chronological tables, exhibiting the most remarkable occurrences. 49775
Chronological tables for every day in the year. 79738
Chronological treatise of the several ages of the world. 37224
Chronological view of the world. 30796
Chronologie de tous les peuples. (75418)
Chronologie der geschiedenis van Suriname. 22316
Chronologie historique de l'Amerique. 25173, 101348-101350
Chronologie neveuaire. 11627
Chronologie novenaire. (47931)
Chronologie septenaire de l'histoire de la paix. 11627
Chronology. A memorial of the deceases at Union-Village, Ohio. 97882
Chronology of history. 85344
Chronology of North Carolina. 4722
Chronology of paper and paper making. 51364
Chronology of the eighteenth and nineteenth centuries. (7137)
Chronology of the principal events as far as they could be ascertained. 9652
Chronology of the reigns of George III. and IV. (4601)
Chronology of the war from 1860 to 1865. 86319
Chronology; or, an introduction and index. 66797
Chrysal: or, adventures of a guinea. 36391
Chrystal fount. 12971
Chrystie, James. supposed author 92838
Chubbuck, Emily. pseud. Alderbrook. see Judson, E. 36863
Chubbuck, Samuel M. defendant 103765
Chugmit Indians. Treaties, etc. 60255
Chugmut Indians. 49348
Chugmut Indians. Treaties, etc. 36337
Chumacero y Carrillo, Juan. 12972
Chumasero, John C. 12973
Chumillas, Julian. 12974
Chuquisaca, Bolivia. Real Audiencia. Presidente. 64742 see also Goncalez de Poueda, Bartholome.
Chuquisaca (Bolivian Department) Ministerio de Interior y Relaciones Esteriores. (47595)
Chur-Pfaltzischer Robinson. 72227
Church, Alonzo. 12975
Church, Benjamin, 1639-1718. (12976)-12977, 12996-12998, 91750, 97190
Church, Benjamin, 1734-1776. (6737), 12978-12981, 12983-12985, 15782, 30754, 40938, (47135), 90138, 2d note after 95839, 103621, 1st note after 106134
Church, Benjamin, 1734-1776. supposed author 12982, 25296, 86684, 3d note after 95765, 2d note after 102065
Church, Edward. supposed author 6927, 12986, 18485
Church, George E. 12987
Church, John Hubbard. 12988-12989
Church, Leman. 15776
Church, Marcus C. C. (12990)
Church, Pharcellus. 12991, 44456
Church, Philip. 12992
Church, R. S. H. 12993
Church, Samuel. 12994
Church, Sandford E. 12995
Church, Thomas, 1674-1746. 12996-12998, 91750

Church, Thomas, 1707-1756. 103565
Church, William. 12999
Church, Biddeford, Me. see Biddeford, Me. Church.
Church, Cambridgeport, Mass. see Cambridge, Mass. Cambridgeport Church.
Church, Chatham, Mass. see Chatham, Mass. Church.
Church, Foxborough, Mass. see Foxborough, Mass. Church.
Church, Hanover, Mass. see Hanover, Mass. Church.
Church, Lancaster, Mass. see Lancaster, Mass. Church.
Church, Malden, Mass. see Malden, Mass. Church.
Church, Medway, Ga. see Medway, Ga. Church.
Church, Middleboro, Mass. see Middleboro, Mass. Church.
Church, North Coventry, Conn. see North Coventry, Conn. Church.
Church, Northampton, N. Y. see Northampton, N. Y. Church.
Church, Rockaway, N. J. see Rockaway, N. J. Church.
Church, Salem, Mass. see Salem, Mass. First Church.
Church, West Brookfield, Mass. see West Brookfield, Mass. Church.
Church, Wrentham, Mass. see Wrentham, Mass. Church.
Church. 71114
Church. Editor. 71114 see also Kent, John.
Church. A discourse. 25016
Church a house of prayer for all. 68586
Church a witness. 90526
Church almanac. (13000)
Church an engine of the state. (13001)
Church and civil government. 13280
Church and Congregation of Machias, Maine. see Machias, Me. Church.
Church and Hospital for British Emigrants Arriving at New York (Proposed) see New York (City) Church and Hospital for British Emigrants Arriving at New York (Proposed)
Church and slavery. By Albert Barnes. 3497
Church and slavery. . . . By Henry A. Rowland. 73564
Church & state. 82947
Church & state. A discourse delivered on Thanksgiving Day. 93747
Church and state. A lecture . . . January 5, 1854. 42965
Church and state: a political union. 5592, 28903
Church and state charities compared. 35309
Church and state in America. 14767
Church and state in America exposed. (42071)
Church and state: or the privileges and duties of an American citizen. 9364
Church and the college. 37976
Church and the country. 13003
Church and the rebellion: a consideration. 90439
Church and the rebellion. Mr. Jay's letter. (35840)
Church and the sword. 13002
Church and the world. A lecture . . . January 31, 1850. 33593
Church Anti-slavery Society. 81930
Church Anti-slavery Society. Proceedings of the convention met at Worcester, Mass. 81930

Church as it is. 62856
Church, . . . as it was, as it is, as it ought to be. 13418
Church Association of Maine (Unitarian) see Unitarian Church Association of Maine.
Church awakened in her duty and her danger. 85270
Church catechism, a morning prayer. 13181, (50765)
Church cause and the church party. 66122
Church Charity Foundation, Brooklyn. 8334
Church, court, and parliament of England. (32957)
Church covenant a perpetual covenant. 17050
Church covenant [of the Baptist Church, Concord, N. H.] 15157
Church covenant [of the Rowe-Street Baptist Church, Boston.] 6671
Church covenants which have been used in the Church of Salem. 75654
Church directory. 32806
Church directory for New York City. 35445, (54444)
Church discipline according to his ancient standard. 7323
Church essential to the republic. 37970
Church establishments defended. (42071)
Church Extension Society. see Methodist Episcopal Church. Church Extension Society.
Church finances. 91551
Church God's peculiar care. 71503
Church government. 18710
Church-government and church-covenant discvssed. 46776
Church history. 83035, 83289
Church history of New England. 2626
Church Home Society, Baltimore. 3028
Church in Canada. 13004, 92643
Church in Canada, no. 2. 13005
Church in the army. (78491)
Church in the colonies, no. 1. 13004, 92643
Church in the colonies, no. 2. 13005
Church in the colonies, no. 3. 13006
Church in the colonies, no. 4. (13007)
Church in the wilderness. 12478
Church in the wilderness. Narrative of a visit. 2749
Church knaviad, or Horace in West Haven. 52969
Church litany of the United Brethren in the Cherokee tongue. 12477
Church manual, and other important items. 88124
Church manual, containing important historical facts. 30422
Church manual, for the members of the Presbyterian Church. 3498
Church manual of the Evangelical Congregational Church . . . Quincy. 67287
Church manual [of the Reformed Dutch Church, Sleepy Hollow, N. Y.] 82124
Church manual: or the history, standing rules, discipline. 78128
Church-member's manual and prayer book. 92155
Church-membership of children, and their right to baptism. 80203-80204
Church-membership of children, and their right to baptisme. 80202
Church memorial, consisting of the history. (51865)
Church Missionary Society. 49475
Church Missionary Society. Secretaries. 51186

Church Missionary Society in England. 81740
Church Missionary Society of Massachusetts. see Massachusetts Church Missionary Society.
Church Missionary Union of Providence, R. I. 66253
Church moves. 103924
Church notes and monumental inscriptions of Jamaica. 72263
Church of Christ (Hendrickite) 83151
Church of Christ (Whitmerite) 83071
Church of Christ, Berlin, Mass. see Berlin, Mass. Church of Christ.
Church of Christ, Dorchester, Mass. see Dorchester, Mass. Church of Christ.
Church of Christ, New York. see New York (City) Church of Christ.
Church of Christ, Newport, R. I. see Newport, R. I. Church of Christ.
Church of Christ, Peacham, Vt. see Peacham, Vt. Church of Christ.
Church of Christ, Roxborough, Mass. see Roxborough, Mass. Church of Christ.
Church of Christ, Williamstown, Mass. see Williamstown, Mass. Church of Christ.
Church of Christ, Wilton, N. H. see Wilton, N. H. Church of Christ.
Church of Christ, Yale University, New Haven, Conn. see Yale University. Church of Christ.
Church of Christ a firm and durable house. 24438-24439
Church of Christ in Fair Street, New York. see New York (City) Fair Street Church of Christ.
Church of Christ one. 92930
Church of Christ under the apostleship, and under the apostacy. 84428-84429
Church of Christ vindicated. 21668
Church of England. 15027, 25090, 45301, 66982, (67003), note after 103616
Church of England. Book of Common Prayer. 6351-6352, 13180-13181, 17456, 57488-57489, 64998-(64999), 79688-79690 see also Church of England in Canada. Book of Common Prayer.
Church of England. Catechisms, etc. note after 65546, 97984
Church of England. Convocation. (2140), 63102
Church of England. Corporation of the Governors of the Bounty of Queen Anne. see Corporation of the Governors of the Bounty of Queen Anne.
Church of England. Liturgy and Ritual. 6349, 69364
Church of England, and in America, compared. 13010
Church of England in America. Book of Common Prayer. see Church of England. Book of Common Prayer.
Church of England in America. Corporation for the Relief of Widows and Children of Clergymen. 86
Church of England in America. Maryland. Commissary. 7470, 7472, 7475, 7477, 105652 see also Bray, Thomas, 1656-1730.
Church of England in America. Massachusetts. (41553)-(41555), 46756, 2d note after 99797
Church of England in America. New Jersey. Clergy. 16585, note after 100420
Church of England in America. New York. 16585, 53683, note after 100420

Church of England in Canada. 13004-(13007)
Church of England in Canada. Book of
Common Prayer. 6352, 57489 see also
Church of England. Book of Common
Prayer.
Church of England in Canada. House of
Bishops. 5574, 34009
Church of England in Canada. Upper Canada
Mission Fund. see Church of England
in Canada. Quebec (Diocese) Bishop of
Quebec's Upper Canada Mission Fund.
Church of England in Canada. Nova Scotia
(Diocese) 56131-56132
Church of England in Canada. Nova Scotia
(Diocese) Halifax Diocesan Committee
of the Society for Promoting Christian
Knowledge. see Society for Promoting
Christian Knowledge, London. Halifax
Diocesan Committee.
Church of England in Canada. Provincial
Synod. 4th Session, 1868. 36742
Church of England in Canada. Quebec
(Diocese) Bishop of Quebec's Upper
Canada Mission Fund. 100897
Church of England in Canada. Toronto
(Diocese) 10331
Church of England in Canada. Toronto
(Diocese) Synod. 6983
Church of England-man. pseud. see S., J.
pseud.
Church of Ephesus arraign'd. 83434
Church of God described. 39199
Church of God, with its officers and govern-
ment. 77317
Church of Ireland in Canada. see Church of
England in Canada.
Church of Jesus Christ of Latter Day Saints.
31992, 47126, (50727), 50729,
50734-50735, 64971, 68683, 70912,
(74796)-74797, 81517, 83035-83036,
83038-83052, 83055-83070, 83072-83073,
83077-83080, 83033-83088, 83091-83094,
83097, 83100-83103, 83105-83107, 83110-
83112, 83114, 83115-83118, 83120-83128,
83130-83131, 83133-83150, 83152-83159,
83161-83165, 83168-83175, 83177-83178,
83181-83183, 83185-83186, 83188-83189,
83192-83194, 83196-83198, 83200-83201,
83207-83209, 83211, 83213-83214, 83215-
83225, 83227-83229, 83246, 83252,
83258, 83259, 83279, 83283, 85168,
89052, 94026 see also Deseret Sunday
School Union, Salt Lake City.
Church of Jesus Christ of Latter Day Saints.
General Board of Young Men's Mutual
Improvement Associations. see General
Board of Young Men's Mutual Improve-
ment Associations.
Church of Jesus Christ of Latter Day Saints.
President. 83163, 83193, 83207-83208,
83211, 83213-83214, 83220, 83223-83225,
83237, 83245, 83283, 83284 see also
Woodruff, Wilford. and Young, Brigham,
1801-1877.
Church of Jesus Christ of Latter Day Saints.
Special Conference of the Elders.
83283
Church of Jesus Christ of Latter Day Saints
(Reorganized) see Reorganized Church
of Jesus Christ of Latter Day Saints.
Church of Leyden. see Leyden, Holland.
Church.
Church of Paramus. see Paramus, N. J.
Church.
Church of Saint Andrew, Philadelphia. see
Philadelphia. Church of St. Andrew.

Church of St. Matthias, Philadelphia. see
Philadelphia. Church of St. Matthias.
Church of Scotland. 66447, (74456), 80715
Church of Scotland. petitioners 78379
Church of Scotland. Commission of the Gen-
eral Assembly. see Church of Scotland.
General Assembly. Commission.
Church of Scotland. General Assembly.
15445, 66446, 80715, 86358, 86364,
94691, 94922, note after 103402
Church of Scotland. General Assembly. Com-
mission. (12861), 15445, 16354, 20223,
51773, (68959), 78221, 80715, 86358,
86364, 104343 see also Bridge, William,
1600?-1670. Burroughs, Jeremiah, 1589-
1646. Goodwin, Thomas, 1600-1646.
Nye, Phillip, 1596?-1672. Simpson,
Sidrach, 1600?-1655.
Church of the Advent, Boston. see Boston.
Church of the Advent.
Church of the Advent, Philadelphia. see Phila-
delphia. Church of the Advent.
Church of the Advent. A salutatory sermon.
6223
Church of the Ascension, New York. see
New York (City) Church of the Ascension.
Church of the colony and town of East Hamp-
ton, L. I. 48031
Church of the Covenant, Philadelphia. see
Philadelphia. Church of the Covenant.
Church of the Disciples, Boston. see Boston.
Church of the Disciples.
Church of the Epiphany, New York. see New
York (City) Church of the Epiphany.
Church of the Epiphany, Philadelphia. see
Philadelphia. Church of the Epiphany.
Church of the Evangelists, Southwark, Pa.
see Southwark, Pa. Protestant Episcopal
Church of the Evangelists.
Church of the future in America. 6224
Church of the Holy Communion, New York
see New York (City) Church of the
Holy Communion.
Church of the Holy Trinity, Lancaster, Pa.
see Lancaster, Pa. Evangelical
Lutheran Church of the Holy Trinity.
Church of the Messiah, New York. see New
York (City) Church of the Messiah.
Church of the Messiah, Philadelphia. see
Philadelphia. Church of the Messiah.
Church of the New Jerusalem. see New
Jerusalem Church.
Church of the Pilgrims, Brooklyn. see
Brooklyn. Church of the Pilgrims.
Church of the Puritans, New York. see New
York (City) Church of the Puritans.
Church of the Redeemer, Milwaukee. see
Milwaukee. Church of the Redeemer.
Church of the Redeemer, Provincetown, Mass.
see Provincetown, Mass. Church of
the Redeemer, Universalist.
Church of the Savior, Brooklyn. see Brooklyn.
Church of the Savior.
Church of the United Brethren and their
missionary labours. 97848
Church offering for all seasons. 23290
Church offerings. 80451
Church organization. (80354)
Church psalmist. 65147
Church polity. 71525
Church polity of the pilgrims the polity of the
New Testament. 19893
Church privilege and obligation on congrega-
tional principles. (58653)
Church Reading Room, Boston. see Boston.
Church Reading Room.

Church record. A weekly paper. 13009
Church record and protestant episcopalian. 13008
Church record; being a concise sketch of the origin and history. 754, 44631
Church register. 102564 see also Protestant Episcopal quarterly review, and church register. and Protestant Episcopalian and church register.
Church renewed covenant, as followeth. 104076
Church review. (1191), 13011, (33801)
Church review and ecclesiastical register. see Church review.
Church, Rome and dissent. 85359
Church Scholarship Society of the Protestant Episcopal Church. see Protestant Episcopal Church in the U. S. A. Church Scholarship Society.
Church Society of the Archdeaconry of New-Brunswick. see Church of England in Canada. Church Society of the Archdeaconry of New-Brunswick.
Church Society of the Diocese of Quebec. 67006
Church—the faith—tradition. 57308
Church, the ministry and the Gospel. 46901
Church the pillar and ground of the truth. 91596
Church Union Auxiliary of Christ Church, Cambridge, Mass. see Cambridge, Mass. Christ Church. Church Union Auxiliary.
Church University Board of Upper Canada. 92637
Church University of Upper Canada. 92637
Church viewed in this relation to the state. 7390
Churches and ministers from 1672-1867. (43935)
Churches and pastors of Washington, D. C. 36251
Churches and sects of the United States. (28034)
Churches Believing in the Salvation of All Men, Philadelphia. see Universalist Church in the United States. Philadelphia.
Churches consisting of saints. 2200
Churches contrasted. 18608, 79727, note after 97880, note after 94924, note after 106196
Churches deliverances. 32838
Churches in New England, 1639. see Congregational Churches in Massachusetts.
Churches in New-England brought to the test. 46407
Churches of New Hampshire. 76239
Churches of the valley. 52420
Churches quarrel espoused. 26753, 103320, 104896, 104897, 104901
Churches resurrection. 17054
Churches warned to stand fast in the liberties. 13012, 104760
Churchill, Amos. supposed author. 33457
Churchill, Awsham, d. 1728. 8427, 10820, 13015-13018, 13419, (14676), 26850, 26851, 31557, 35712, 38975, 50223, 51336, (55278), 55933, 57765, 57972, 59586, (79164), 82852, 94575, 97529
Churchill, C. 106040
Churchill, Charles. 13013
Churchill, George. 13014
Churchill, John. 8427, 10820, 13015-13018, 13419, (14676), 26850, 26851, 31557,

35712, 38975, 50223, 51335, (55278), 55933, 57765, 57972, 29586, (79164), 82852, 94575, 97529
Churchill, John Charles, 1821-1905. 13019
Churchill, John Wesley, 1839-1900. 85208, 85212
Churchill, Juvenal. 13020
Churchill, Silas. 13021-(13022)
Churchill, T. O. 13023
Churchill regenerate. 106040
Churchill's guide through Albany Rural Cemetry. [sic] 13024
Churchman. pseud. 96123, 1st note after 105926
Churchman. pseud. Caste and slavery in the American church. see Jay, John.
Church-man. pseud. George Keith an apostate. 106104
Churchman. pseud. Letter from a churchman to his friend. (40270)
Churchman. pseud. Letter to . . . Bishop Hobart. see Jay, William.
Churchman. pseud. Letter to the Right Hon. Lord Kenyon. 37588, 69396
Churchman. pseud. Progress of Puseyism. 65970
Churchman. pseud. Second defence of church establishments. see Lorimer, John G.
Churchman. pseud. To the clerical and lay members. 45310
Churchman, John. 13026
Churchman. 10825, 66138, (78586), 84746, 90706, 96965
"Churchman." (32305)
Churchman in town. pseud. Review of the "Address of the Lay Association." see Roe, Henry.
Churchman's almanack for 1832. 13027
Churchman's choral companion to his prayer book. 84680
Churchman's defence against its aspersions. 14238
Churchman's monthly magazine. 13028
Churchman's repository. 13029
Churchman's year book. 61060
Church's flight into the wilderness. 80455
Church's forces and faults. 67784
Church's law and the church's liberty. 66875
Church's law of development. 82947
Church's marriage. 21931
Church's mission of reconciliation. 82947
Church's mission to workingmen. 66132
Church's painting. 55382
Church's work. 67784
Churchwell, William Montgomery, 1826-1862. 13030-13031
Churchyard, Thomas. 13032-13034
Churchyarde, Thomas. see Churchyard, Thomas.
Churion, Julian. 13035
Chute, Anthony. 94165
Chute, James Andrew. 42769
Chutes de Magara. 23799
Chwostow, -----. 13036
Chytraeus, Nathane. 13037, 58428
Ciaparro, Giov. Gonzalez. 13038
Cibber, Colley, 1671-1757. tr. 84241
Cibber, Colley. pseud. Life of Edwin Forest. see Rees, James.
Cibo, S. Frenfanelli. 13039
Cicell, Sir E. 78379
Cicero. pseud. 25339
Cicero. pseud. Letter from Cicero to Cataline the Second. see Galloway, Joseph, 1729?-1803.

Cicero. pseud. Letter from Cicero to the Right Hon. Lord Viscount H—e. see Galloway, Joseph, 1729?-1803.
Cicero, Marcus Tullius. 13040-13043, 94092-94093
Ciceronian. 78632
Ciclografia Mexicana. 80987
Cid Campiador. 56618
Cid Hamet Benengeli. pseud. see Benengeli, Cid Hamet. pseud.
Cienca de Leon, Pedro de. 13044-13057, 27737-27738, 91538
Cielo en el parnasso. 60856
Ciencia del Buen Ricardo. 25586
Ciencia para todos. 72779
Ciencia y poesia. 72778
Cienfuegos, Jose. 17772
Cienfuegos, Juan Antonio Velarde y. see Velarde y Cienfuegos, Juan Antonio.
Cifra felix de las dichas imponderables. 13058
Cigana, A. 13059
Cilly, A. Duhaut. see Duhaut-Cilly, A.
Cimber, M. L. pseud. Archives curieuses. 24855, 40178
Cincinnati. 13064
Cincinnati. defendants 90145
Cincinnati. American Reform Tract and Book Society. see American Reform Tract and Book Society, Cincinnati.
Cincinnati. Association for Aged Indigent Women. see Association for Aged Indigent Women, Cincinnati.
Cincinnati. Black Brigade. see Ohio. Militia. Cincinnati Black Brigade.
Cincinnati. Board of Education. (13088), 86697
Cincinnati. Board of Education. defendants 49314
Cincinnati. Board of Trustees and Visitors of the Common Schools. see Cincinnati. Common Schools. Board of Trustees and Visitors.
Cincinnati. Celebration of the First Settlement of Ohio, 47th, 1835. (56890)
Cincinnati. Celebration of the Forty-Fifth Anniversary of the First Settlement of Cincinnati and the Miami Country, by Natives of Ohio, 1833. 13074, 104448
Cincinnati. Celebration of the Forty-Fifth Anniversary of the First Settlement of Cincinnati and the Miami Country, by Natives of Ohio, 1833. Committee of Arrangements. 13074, 104448
Cincinnati. Centinel of the North-Western Territory. see Centinel of the North-Western Territory.
Cincinnati. Central Board of Agency for Home Missions. see Central Board of Agency for Home Missions, Cincinnati.
Cincinnati. Chamber of Commerce and Merchants' Exchange. (13065), 13070-13072, 84725-84727
Cincinnati. Chamber of Commerce and Merchants' Exchange. Superintendent. 84725-84727 see also Maxwell, Sidney D. Smith, Richard, 1823-1898. Smith, William, 1812-1872.
Cincinnati. Charter. 13075
Cincinnati. Christ Church. 57317
Cincinnati. Churst Church. Vestry. 32303, 40545
Cincinnati. Christ Church. Wardens. 32303, 40545
Cincinnati. Christian Anti-slavery Convention, 1850. see Christian Anti-slavery Convention, Cincinnati, 1850.

Cincinnati. Christian Anti-slavery Convention, 1851. see Christian Anti-slavery Convention, Cincinnati, 1851.
Cincinnati. Citizens. 37577, 69859
Cincinnati. Citizens. petitioners 13095, 47662
Cincinnati. Citizens' Committee to Inquire into the Causes of the Explosion of the [Steamboat] Moselle. 13111
Cincinnati. Citizens' Meeting on Improving the Navigation Around the Falls of the Ohio River, 1846. see Meeting Expressing the Sense of the Citizens on Improving the Navigation of the Falls of the Ohio River, Cincinnati, 1846.
Cincinnati. City Auditor. defendant. 90145
Cincinnati. City Council. (13087)
Cincinnati. City Council. Committee on the Ohio and Mississippi Railroad Company. 56968
Cincinnati. City Solicitor. plaintiff. 90145
Cincinnati. College of Professional Teachers. see Western Literary Institute and College of Professional Teachers, Cincinnati.
Cincinnati. Colored People. 12200, 27969
Cincinnati. Colored Public Schools. Board of Trustees. (13088)
Cincinnati. Commercial Hospital and Lunatic Asylum of Ohio. see Cincinnati General Hospital.
Cincinnati. Committee Appointed by the Citizens to Inquire into the Causes of the Explosion of the Moselle. see Cincinnati. Citizens' Committee to Inquire into the Causes of the Explosion of the [Steamboat] Moselle.
Cincinnati. Committee For the Diffusion of Useful Knowledge. see Committee For the Diffusion of Useful Knowledge, Cincinnati.
Cincinnati. Common Schools. Board of Trustees and Visitors. (13087)
Cincinnati. Constitutional Convention, 1850-1851. see Ohio. Constitutional Convention, Cincinnati, 1850-1851.
Cincinnati. Contraband's Relief Commission. see Contraband's Relief Commission, Cincinnati.
Cincinnati. Convention for the Organization of a Peace Party, 1864. see Cincinnati. Peace Party Convention, 1864.
Cincinnati. Convention of Delegates Met to Consult on Missions, 1831. see Convention on Domestic Missions, Cincinnati, 1831.
Cincinnati. Convention of the Colored Freemen of Ohio, 1852. see Convention of the Colored Freemen of Ohio, Cincinnati, 1852.
Cincinnati. Convention on Domestic Missions, 1831. see Convention on Domestic Missions, Cincinnati, 1831.
Cincinnati. Criminal Court. 36388
Cincinnati. Democratic Party National Convention, 1856. see Democratic Party. National Convention, Cincinnati, 1856.
Cincinnati. Eclectic Medical Institute. 8868
Cincinnati. Farmers' College. see College Hill, Ohio. Farmers' College.
Cincinnati. Female Association for the Benefit of Africans. see Female Association for the Benefit of Africans, Cincinnati.
Cincinnati. Fire Department. (13080)

Cincinnati. First New Jerusalem Society.
see New Jerusalem Church. Cincinnati
First Society.
Cincinnati. Franklin Typographical Society.
see Franklin Typographical Society,
Cincinnati.
Cincinnati. General Convention of Western
Baptists, 1834. see General Convention
of Western Baptists, 1st, Cincinnati,
1834
Cincinnati. Great Western Sanitary Fair,
1863. 33438
Cincinnati. House of Refuge. 13076
Cincinnati. House of Refuge. Board of
Directors. 13076
Cincinnati. House of Refuge. Charter. 13076
Cincinnati. Hughes High School. Society of
Alumni. 86002
Cincinnati. Jackson Committee. see Jackson
Committee of Cincinnati.
Cincinnati. Kansas League. see Kansas
League of Cincinnati.
Cincinnati. Lane Theological Seminary. see
Lane Theological Seminary, Cincinnati.
Cincinnati. Lloyd Library of Botany, Phar-
macy, and Materia Medica. see Lloyd
Library of Botany, Pharmacy, and
Materia Medica, Cincinnati.
Cincinnati. McMicken College of Liberal
Arts. see Cincinnati. University.
McMicken College of Liberal Arts.
Cincinnati. McMicken University. see Cin-
cinnati. University. McMicken College
of Liberal Arts.
Cincinnati. Medical Convention of Ohio, 1842.
see Medical Convention of Ohio, Cin-
cinnati, 1842.
Cincinnati. Meeting Expressing the Sense of
the Citizens on Improving the Navigation
Around the Falls of the Ohio River,
1846. see Meeting Expressing the
Sense of the Citizens on Improving the
Navigation Around the Falls of the Ohio
River, Cincinnati, 1846.
Cincinnati. Meeting of the National Board of
Trade, 1868. see National Board of
Trade. Meeting, Cincinnati, 1868.
Cincinnati. Merchants' Exchange. see Cin-
cinnati. Chamber of Commerce and
Merchants' Exchange.
Cincinnati. Methodist Episcopal Church
Annual Conference, 1852. see Methodist
Episcopal Church. Conferences. Cin-
cinnati Annual Conference, 1852.
Cincinnati. Mount Auburn Young Ladies'
Institute. see Mount Auburn Young
Ladies' Institute, Cincinnati.
Cincinnati. National Congress on Penitentiary
and Reformitory Discipline, 1870. see
National Congress on Penitentiary and
Reformitory Discipline, Cincinnati, 1870.
Cincinnati. National Soldier's Historical
Association. see National Soldier's
Historical Association, Cincinnati.
Cincinnati. New England Society. see New
England Society of Cincinnati.
Cincinnati. New Orphan Asylum. see Cin-
cinnati Orphan Asylum.
Cincinnati. Nova Cesarea Harmony Lodge.
see Freemasons. Ohio. Nova Cesarea
Harmony Lodge, Cincinnati.
Cincinnati. Ohio School Library. see Cin-
cinnati. Public Library.
Cincinnati. Ordinances, etc. 13061, 13075,
13076, 13086, (13088), 57513

Cincinnati. Paine Festival, 1840. see Paine
Festival, Cincinnati, 1840.
Cincinnati. Paine Festival, 1856. see Paine
Festival, Cincinnati, 1856.
Cincinnati. Peace Party Convention, 1864.
13081
Cincinnati. Public Library. 13093-13094,
56998, 64049
Cincinnati. Public Meeting on the Subject of
a National Western Armory, 1841. (13104)
Cincinnati. St. Paul's Church. Rector.
69678
Cincinnati. St. Paul's Church. Vestry. 69678
Cincinnati. St. Xavier College. see St.
Xavier College, Cincinnati.
Cincinnati. Southern and Western Liberty
Convention, 1845. see Southern and
Western Liberty Convention, Cincinnati,
1845.
Cincinnati. Southern Commercial Convention,
1870. see Southern Commercial Con-
vention, Cincinnati, 1870.
Cincinnati. Spring Grove Cemetery. 13114-
(13115), 89822-89825
Cincinnati. Spring Grove Cemetery. Charter.
89823-89824
Cincinnati. Spring Grove Cemetery. Lot
Holders. (13115), 89822
Cincinnati. St. Luke's Hospital. 75412
Cincinnati. State Independent Free Territory
Convention of the People of Ohio, 1848.
see State Independent Free Territory
Convention of the People of Ohio, Cin-
cinnati, 1848.
Cincinnati. Superintendent of Common Schools.
(13088)
Cincinnati. Superior Court. 49314
Cincinnati. Theological and Religious Library
Association. see Theological and Re-
ligious Library Association of Cincinnati.
Cincinnati. Tobacco Manufacturers. see
Tobacco Manufacturers of Cincinnati,
Ohio.
Cincinnati. United States Sanitary Commission.
see United States Sanitary Commission.
Cincinnati Branch.
Cincinnati. University. McMicken College of
Liberal Arts. 43576
Cincinnati. University. Medical College of
Ohio. 56956
Cincinnati. Western Academy of Natural
Sciences. see Western Academy of
Natural Sciences of Cincinnati.
Cincinnati. Western Education Society. see
Western Education Society, Cincinnati.
Cincinnati. Western Literary Institute and
College of Professional Teachers. see
Western Liteary Institute and College of
Professional Teachers, Cincinnati.
Cincinnati. Woodward College. see Wood-
ward College, Cincinnati.
Cincinnati. Woodward High School. 105174
Cincinnati. Young Men's Bible Society. see
Young Men's Bible Society of Cincinnati.
Cincinnati. Young Men's Mercantile Associa-
tion. see Young Men's Mercantile
Association of Cincinnati.
Cincinnati. Young Men's Mercantile Library
Association. 13091, 106175
Cincinnati. Young Men's Mercantile Library
Association. Board of Directors. 13090
Cincinnati. Young Men's Mercantile Library
Association. Library. 106175
Cincinnati (Archdiocese) Bishop (Fenwick)
24079 see also Fenwick, Edward
Dominic, Bp., 1768-1832.

Cincinnati (Archdiocese) Archbishop (Purcell) 66673-66676, 72937 <u>see also</u> Purcell, John Baptist, Abp.
Cincinnati (Archdiocese) Silver Jubilee of the Episcopate of the Most Reverend John Baptist Purcell, 1858. 66673
Cincinnati (Archdiocese) Synod. 72937
Cincinnati (Ecclesiastical Province) Council, 1st, 1855. 59021, 66673, (72911)
Cincinnati (Ecclesiastical Province) Council, 2d, 1858. 13101, 66673, 72912
Cincinnati (Ecclesiastical Province) Council, 3d, 1861. (72913), 72937
Cincinnati almanac. 93229
Cincinnati almanac for 1846. 13077
Cincinnati almanac for 1839. 13103
Cincinnati almanac for the year 1809. 13073
Cincinnati almanac, for the year 1806. 43243
Cincinnati almanac for the year 1839. 13077
Cincinnati and Chicago Railroad. 13108
Cincinnati and Lake Superior Copper and Silver Mining Company. (13115)
Cincinnati Angling Club. 65827
Cincinnati as it is, and the way to find it. 13068
Cincinnati as it is in 1853. 13085
Cincinnati Astronomical Society. 13083-13084
Cincinnati at the close of 1826. 13078
Cincinnati Branch of the United States Sanitary Commission. <u>see</u> United States Sanitary Commission. Cincinnati Branch.
Cincinnati Business Directory for 1844. 10385
Cincinnati cemetery of Spring Grove. 89822
Cincinnati cemetery of Spring Grove. Reports, forms, etc. 89825
Cincinnati College. (13088)
Cincinnati College. Law Department. (13088), 93810
Cincinnati College. Medical Department. (13088), 93810
Cincinnati Colonization Society. 13105
Cincinnati, Columbus and Wooster Turnpike Company. Engineer. 104292 <u>see also</u> Williams, John S.
Cincinnati commercial. 5223, last entry under 84727
Cincinnati convention, October 18, 1864. 13081
Cincinnati, Covington, Newport, and Fulton directory. 13085
Cincinnati daily commercial. (33231)
Cincinnati daily gazette. 84147, last entry under 84727
Cincinnati daily press. 68550, 78709
Cincinnati daily times. 59177, 80424
Cincinnati directory, city guide and business mirror. 13085
Cincinnati directory, containing the names. 13085
Cincinnati directory for 1846. 13085
Cincinnati gazette. (8401), 43030
Cincinnati General Hospital. Trustees. (56954)
Cincinnati Historical Society. 13062, 31799
Cincinnati Horticultural Society. 13069
Cincinnati in 1841. 13152
Cincinnati in 1826. 9139, (21813)
Cincinnati Law Library Association. An address. 77447
Cincinnati Literary Gazette. 13079
Cincinnati Medical College. <u>see</u> Cincinnati. University. Medical College of Ohio.
Cincinnati miscellany. 13153
Cincinnati Orphan Asylum. 53378
Cincinnati Orphan Asylum. Board of Trustees. 53378

Cincinnati Ophran Asylum. Managers. (13115)
Cincinnati Orphan Asylum Association. 53378
Cincinnati platform, 1860. (64406)-64407
Cincinnati Presbytery. <u>see</u> Presbyterian Church in the U. S. A. Presbytery of Cincinnati.
Cincinnati price current. 83766, 84725, last entry under 84727
Cincinnati, 1788-90. 42108
Cincinnati, Society of. <u>see</u> Society of the Cincinnati.
Cincinnati Southern Railroad. Argument of Henry Stanbury. 90145
Cincinnati Southern Railway. Trustees. defendants 90145
Cincinnati suburbs in 1870. 47054
Cincinnati Synod. <u>see</u> Presbyterian Church in the U. S. A. Synod of Cincinnati.
Cincinnati to Erie via Columbus & Cleveland. 56994
Cincinnati, Wilmington and Zanesville Railroad, and certain county and city bonds in Ohio. 13110
Cincinnati: with the bye-laws and rules of the New Jersey State Society. 13116
Cincinnati, with the bye laws, rules, etc. of the New Jersey State Society. 86113
Cincinnatus. pseud. <u>see</u> Plumer, William, 1759-1850.
Cincinnatus. pseud. False alarm. 13132, (23757)
Cincinnatus. pseud. Freedom's defence. <u>see</u> Grosvenor, Cyrus Pitt. <u>supposed author</u> <u>and</u> Plumer, William, 1759-1850. <u>supposed author</u>
Cincinnatus. pseud. Reply to A. Hamilton's letter. 13135
Cincinnatus, L. Quincius. pseud. Letter to the freeholders. <u>see</u> Quincy, Edmund, 1703-1788. <u>supposed author</u>
Cincinnatus. 13137
Cincinnatus Academy, Cortland County, N. Y. 13136
Cinco errores capitales de la intervencion. 9592
Cinco libros de la coronica general de Espana. (50496)
Cinco libros de la historia de Portugal. 31538
Cinco libros primeros de la coronica general de Espana. 56621
Cinco meses en los Estados-Unidos de la America del Norte. 74910
Cinco tratados, signe la relacion de las cosas memorables sucedidas. 20135
Cinco ultimos anos de la dominacion Espanola en el Peru. 74608
Cineas. pseud. To Luther Martin, and Robert Lemmon, Esqrs. 95899
Cinha e Figueiredo, Jose Bento da. 60993 <u>see also</u> Pernambuco. Presidente (Cinha e Figueiredo)
Cinq annees de sejour au Canada. 94228
Cinq mois aux Etats-Unis de l'Amerique du Nord. 74911
Cinq pieces, de 1783 a 1788. (58494)
Cinquante nouvelles lettres du R. P. de Smet. 82260, 82271, 82277
Cinque, an African. respondent 274, 2908
Cintero, Andres. 87176-87177
Cintra, Pedro de. (14362), 50050-50064, 1st-5th notes after 106378
Cipolletti, Tommaso Giacento. 13138
Cipriani, -------. illus. 5690
Ciquard, -------. (13139)

Circa spiritualia totus. 2476

Circleville, Ohio. (13140)

Circq, Laurent Saint. see Saint-Circq, Laurent.

Circq, Lorenzo de Saint. see Saint-Circq, Laurent.

Circuit Court of the United States, Massachusetts District. In equity, W. B. Lawrence versus R. H. Dana, Junr. 39377

Circuit Court of the United States. Massachusetts District. In equity, Wilder Holbrook vs. the President, Directors and Company of the Worcester Bank. 105383

Circuit Court of the United States. Massachusetts District, ss. In admiralty. (12856)

Circuit Court of the United States, Northern District of New York. In equity. Robert D. Silliman against the Hudson River Bridge Company at Albany. 81069

Circuit Court of the United States of America, Middle Circuit of the New-Jersey District. The United States, (a.) William Brigstock, otherwise John Jonston. 96837

Circuit rider. 8393, 45422

Circuit-rider days among the Ohio. 82776

Circulaire adresse par M. T. Pacheco. 61096

Circulaire adresse par M. W.-H. Seward. (55610), 79519

Circulaire, Ecole de Medecine de Montreal. 50247

Circulaire van Otto Tank. 57322

Circular. (24327), 88967, 89516, 103436

Circular. A meeting of the Class of 1820 was held. 105882

Circular a todos los sacerdotes de la diocesis. 29020

Circular address. (22174)

Circular address from the Bible Society of Massachusetts. 45647

Circular address of the Importing Committee. 87739

Circular address [of the Society for the Promotion of Theological Education.] (22174), 30765

Circular address on Botany and Zoology. (67448)

Circular address . . . to his [i. e. T. Chilton's] constituents. 12809

Circular address to the people of the United States. 49523

Circular addressed to capitalists. 34008

Circular addressed to the Branches and Aid Societies, tributary to the U. S. Sanitary Commission. May 15, 1865. 76616, 76647

Circular addressed to the Branches and Aid Societies tributary to the U. S. Sanitary Commission. July 4, 1865. 76620, 76647

Circular, addressed to the colonels of different regiments. 76639

Circular addressed to the Governor & Council and members of the Legislature of Vermont. 97591

[Circular addressed] to the ladies of Massachusetts. 19663

Circular addressed to the members of the . . . [Massachusetts] Society [for Suppressing of Intemperance.] (45898)

Circular addressed to the several lodges of Free . . . Masons. (53692)

Circular and act of incorporation [of People's College, Havana, N. Y.] 30867

Circular and address of the National Institution for Promoting Industry in the United States. 51991

Circular and address of the National Society for Promoting Industry in the United States. 52024

Circular and catalogue of Burnham's Commercial and Mathematical Institute. 72381

Circular and catalogue . . . [of Monmouth College.] 50000

Circular and catalogue of Friends' School, Germantown. 61680

Circular and catalogue of Schofield's Commercial College. 77769

Circular and catalogue [of the Buffalo Female College.] 9063

Circular and catalogue of the faculty and students of the College of Physicians and Surgeons of the Western District of the State of New York. 23699, 53605

Circular and catalogue of the . . . Illinois Industrial University. 34235

Circular and catalogue of the Long Island College Hospital. (41896)

Circular and catalogue of the Medical Department of the University of Maryland. 45388

Circular & catalogue of the New Jersey Classical and Scientific Institute. 53171

Circular and catalogue of the Ohio State and Union Law College. 57001

Circular and catalogue of the S. S. Seward Institute. 79600

Circular and catalogue of the Select Family School for Boys. 88216

Circular and catalogue [of the Utica Female Academy.] 98240

Circular and catalogue [of Union College.] 97774

Circular and catalogue [of Woodward College.] 105174

Circular and constitution of the Rhode Island Art Association. 70708

Circular and corresponding letter [of the Vermont Baptist Association.] 99157-99158

Circular and corresponding letters [of the Cumberland Association.] 17880

Circular and market review. 14316

Circular . . . and prospectus . . . of the People's Perpetual Loan Association. 60829

Circular, and the by-laws of the Vermont Mutual Fire Insurance Company. 99235

Circular aos repres.·. do Or.·. Un.·. do Brasil. 88732

Circular, articles of association, resolutions, etc. [of the Rocky-Bar Mining Company, California.] 72456

[Circular blank sent to those who are to examine into the condition and wants of the U. S. Military Hospitals.] 76641

[Circular calling attention to the "Army and Navy Claim Agency," dated, July 15, 1865.] (76688)

Circular charge . . . by James Milnor. 49132

Circular communication, addressed to his constituents. 94256

Circular concerning the Arkansas Road Company. 39500

Circular, constitution and rules of order. 97792

Circular containing proposed amendments. (9487)

Circular, dated Brunswick, Me., Aug. 16, 1832. 43915

Circular de 17 Enero ultimo sobre los ultimos sucesos de San Luis Potosi. 39064, 73169

Circular dedicada aos Srs. Eleitores de Senadores. (57898)

Circular del Excmo. e. Ilustrismo Senor D. Juan Jose Diaz de Espada y Landa. 22882

Circular, 1859 [of East Pembroke Seminary.] 21652

Circular . . . 1859-60 [of the Lasell Female Seminary.] (39128)

Circular, engineers reports and other documents. 9860

Circular, explanatory of the recent proceedings of the Sophomore Class, in Yale College. 105943

Circular for distribution at the Centennial Exhibition, 1876. 85012

Circular. From the Church Reading Room, Boston. 66133

Circular from the Indiana State Board of Agriculture. 34486

Circular from the War Office. 19618

[Circular giving the duties of an associate manager.] 76638

Circular in behalf of the Newburyport Lyceum Institution. 103222

Circular. In Council 8th of January, 1798. 100227

Circular in defence of his conduct. 21695

Circular in reference to American archaeology. 85013

Circular in reference to the degrees of relationship among different nations. 50664

Circular in regard to the company. 30238

Circular . . . in relation to the astronomical expedition to Chile. 27419

Circular instructions—Jamiaca—British Guiana. 58486

Circular issued by the Surveyor General of Kansas and Nebraska. 37022

Circular issued for the purpose of informing the public. 86203

Circular issued to workingmen. 10003

Circular. Lancaster, May 30th, 1799. (59975)

Circular letter. 98578, 100094

Circular letter, addressed in 1794. 45851

Circular letter, addressed to the author. 8526

Circular letter addressed to the state societies of Cincinnati. 13117, 86105

Circular [letter, dated June 4, 1834.] (30752)

Circular letter, from Dr. Benjamin Waterhouse. 102057

Circular letter from General Washington. 101531

Circular letter from George Washington. 101534

Circular letter, from His Excellency George Washington, Commander in Chief of the Armies of the United States of America. 101540-101541

Circular letter from His Excellency George Washington, Commander in Chief of the Armies of the United States of America; addressed to the governors of the several states. 101535-101536

Circular letter from His Excellency George Washington, Commander in Chief of the Armies of the United States of America: addressed to the governors of the United States. 101539

Circular letter from His Excellency George Washington, Commander in Chief of the Armies of the United States of America, dated June 11, 1783. 101538

Circular letter from His Excellency George Washington, Commander in Chief of the Armies of the United States of America: occasioned by his determination to resign the command. 101537

Circular letter from His Excellency George Washington, Commander in Chief of the Armies of the United States of America, to the governors of the several states. 101591

Circular letter from His Excellency George Washington, to the several states. 101531

Circular letter, from His Excellency General Washington. 101544

Circular letter from the Bishop of Toronto. 92638

Circular letter from the Committee of the Society for the Suppression of Vice in the Town of Bedford. 4280, 85987

Circular letter from the Congress of the United States. 15515

Circular letter from the General Republican Committee, of the City of New York. (5982)

[Circular letter from the governor, Edmund Randolph.] 100216

Circular letter from the late committee of this city. 97563

Circular letter from the . . . [Massachusetts Peace] Society. 45882

Circular letter from the Ministers and Messengers of the Woodstock Baptist Association. 105143

Circular letter in behalf of the . . . [Massachusetts Peace] Society. 45882

Circular letter in defence of the United Society of Believers. 79699

Circular letter in the "Minutes of the Warren Association." 2632

Circular letter, June 11, 1783. 14378

Circular letter lately sent to the clergy there, 7473

Circular letter no. I. (61539)

Circular letter no. IV. (61539)

Circular letter no. V. (61539)

Circular letter of General Washington. 101545

Circular letter of Gov. Fayette McMullin. 91523, 2d note after 101924

Circular letter of Joseph M. White. 103423

Circular letter [of the Bowdoinham Baptist Association.] (7040)

Circular letter of the Directors to the ministers and congregations. 98230

Circular letter of the East New Jersey Baptist Association. 24435

Circular letter of the General Assembly. 65217

[Circular letter of the Governor, Edmund Randolph.] 100214

[Circular letter of the Governor, Henry Lee.] 100224

[Circular letter of the Governor, Patrick Henry.] 101212

[Circular letter of the Governor, Robert Brooke.] 100225

Circular letter of the Grand Lodge of Massachusetts. 45760

Circular letter of the Literary and Philosophical Society of New York. 54761

Circular letter of the Massachusetts Historical Society. (56850)

Circular letter of the Philadelphia Baptist
Association. 23143
Circular letter of the Providence Baptist
Association. (66313)
Circular letter of the Sabbath Committee to
the clergy. (74654)
Circular letter [of the Senior Class.] (30752)
Circular letter of the Society of "Friends of
the People." 86072
[Circular letter on steamboat monopoly.]
93515
Circular letter on the all important doctrine
of justification. 72740
Circular letter, relating to lyceums in Massa-
chusetts. 45676
Circular letter relating to the vunerability of
New York. 54696
Circular letter soliciting the co-operation of
the members. 45851
Circular letter to emigrants. 91523, 2d note
after 101924
Circular-letter to his [i. e. Matthew Lyon's]
constituents. 42862
Circular letter to the churches and congre-
gations in the western districts of the
state of Vermont. 99234
Circular letter to the churches and congre-
gations of Vermont. 99234
Circular letter to the clergy of Maryland.
7475, 105652
[Circular letter to the governors of the several
states.] 76530, 76647
Circular letter to the governors of the United
States. 101530
Circular letter to the Literary and Philo-
sophical Society of New York. 13724
Circular letter to the practitioners of physic
and surgery. 54185
Circular letter to the public. 61366
[Circular letter to the public, asking for con-
tributions.] 76529, 76549, 76647
Circular letter to the resident and correspond-
ing members. 45851
Circular [letter to the selectmen of each
town.] 72386
Circular letter to the several congregations of
the Episcopal Church of New Jersey.
56825
Circular letters, containing, an invitation.
(13142)
Circular letters from the Woodstock and
Stonington Baptist Associations. 105144
Circular letters of the Southern Railway and
Steamship Association. 88459-88461
Circular letters to the churches. 26228
Circular letters to the Secretary of War.
47158
Circular memorial to the legislatures and
people. 96284
Circular, misrepresenting Mr. Bartholomew
and his books, answered. 84503
Circular number five. The Salem Leg, under
the patronage of the United States govern-
ment for the use of the army and navy.
75729
Circular no. 5. War Department, Surgeon-
General's Office. 22683
(Circular no. 4.) 104536
Circular number four [of the New England
Historic-Genealogical Society.] (52687)
Circular number four [of the Salem Leg.]
75728
Circular no. 4 of the Surgeon General's
Office. 69920
Circular no. 1. . . . June 10, 1868. 22684

Circular no. 6, Surgeon General's Office.
30116, 57853, 69954
Circular no. 3 of the Surgeon General's Office.
69757
Circular (no. 27) of the Superintendent of the
Insurance Department. 53993
Circular number two of the New England
Historic-Genealogical Society. (52687)
Circular. [Of a committee of the Washington
Benevolent Society of the County of Wor-
cester.] 105416
Circular of a corresponding committee on the
. . . North Branch Canal. 60275
Circular of Castleton Medical College. 11440
Circular of Concordville Seminary. 15159
Circular [of Cooperstown Seminary.] 16649
Circular of Endowment Agent, . . . 1864-5.
(39401)
Circular of Hanover College. 30241
Circular of Hartford Female Seminary. (30661)
Circular [of Hempstead Institute.] (31301)
Circular of Horace T. Love. (42362)
Circular of information. 88097
Circular of James Standefer. 90155
Circular of Liberty Normal Institute. 40945
Circular of . . . members of the faculty of
Yale College. 33458
[Circular of Rockford Female Seminary.]
72383
Circular of St. Ann's Hall. 77988
Circular of terms of Comer's Commercial
College. 14931
Circular of the American Association in
London. 41853
Circular of the Board of Managers of the
Theological School of the Diocese of
Virginia. 100516
Circular of the Board of Missions of the
Diocese of Massachusetts. 45677
Circular of the Book and Pamphlet Society.
6343
Circular of the College of Physicians & Sur-
geons. 53999
Circular of the Commissioners of the Ohio
Canal Fund. (56896)
Circular of the Committee, March 5, 1844.
51990
Circular of the Consolidated Silver Mining
Company. 16039
Circular [of the Democratic League of New
York.] 19504
Circular [of the Democratic Society.] 54240
Circular of the Directors [of the Bunker Hill
Monument Association.] (9174)
Circular of the Directors of the Theological
School. 30765
Circular of the Education Society. 85892
Circular of the Executive Committee [of the
New Jersey Lyceum.] 53179
Circular of the Executive Committee of the
Whitestown and Oneida Institute Anti
Slavery Societies. 103687
Circular of the faculty, June 11, 1834. 30765
Circular of the faculty of physic of the Uni-
versity [of Maryland.] 45387
Circular of the Finance Committee [of the
Martyrs' Monument Association, New
York.] 94461
Circular of the Louisville Medical Institute.
42331
Circular of the McNeely Normal School. 43597
Circular of the Madison Manufacturing Co.
43735
Circular of the . . . [Massachusetts Medical]
College, . . . history. 45874

Circular of the Massachusetts Medical College; with a history. 30765
Circular of the Medical College of South-Carolina. 87874
Circular of the Medical Department of Kemper College. 37339
Circular of the Medical Department of the University of Buffalo. 9063
Circular of the Medical Department of the University of Louisiana. 42310
Circular of the medical faculty of Harvard University. 45874
Circular of the medical institution of Yale College. 105910
Circular of the Medical School of Maine, at Bowdoin College. 7019
Circular . . . of the Mendelssohn Musical Institute. (63151)
Circular of the Mount Pleasant Academy, a military school. 51167
Circular of the National Committee of the Pittsburgh Convention. 51955, 63113
Circular of the . . . [National Medical] College. 52006
Circular of the National Medical College (Department of Columbian College,) Washington. 14859
Circular of the Native Americans of Philadelphia. 61540
Circular of the New England Coal Mining Company. 52665
Circular of the New-Hampshire Medical Institution. 52877
Circular of the New York Fredman's Savings & Trust Co. 54466
Circular of the New-York Gas Regulator Company. 54777
Circular of the [New York] . . . Institution . . . [for the Instruction of the Deaf and Dumb.] 54500
Circular of the New York State Mechanics' Association. 53834
Circular [of the Normal School for Colored Girls, Washington, D. C.] 55492
Circular of the . . . North Western University. 55753
Circular of the People's College. 60820
Circular of the Prisoner's-Friend Association. 45937
Circular of the Quebec School of Medicine. 67050
Circular of the Quebec School of Medicine . . . . 6th session 1854-5. 67050
Circular of the Railroad Commissioners relative to reduction of rates. 90930
Circular of the Rt. Rev. Manton Eastburn. (63248)
Circular of the Rittenhouse Academy. 71590
Circular of the Rutgers Female Institute. 74445
Circular of the . . . School, at Vernon, Oneida County, N. Y. (55911)
Circular of the School Commissioners and Supervisors. 53955
Circular of the School of Medicine at Woodstock, Vermont. 99229
Circular of the shareholders of the Baltimore Library. 3023
Circular [of the Sodus Academy.] 86202
Circular of the South Carolina Female Collegiate Institute. 88004
Circular of the state temperance societies. 105443
Circular of the Superintendent of Common Schools. 53990

Circular of the Temperance Society of the Medical Institution of Yale College. 105919
Circular of the Treasurer of the . . . [Michigan Central Railroad] Company. 48761
Circular of the Union Institute. 43597
Circular of the . . . University of the City of New York. (54704)
Circular of the Van Buren Executive Committee. (62363)
Circular of the Washington Medical College of Baltimore. 102023
Circular. Office of the Auditor of S. C. 87681
Circular on immigration. (10435)
Circular [on instituting a society for the promoting of a taste for music.] 93549
Circular [on the subject of repairs on "the Episcopal Church at Cambridge."] (10129)
Circular or prospectus of his General historie of Virginia. 82823
Circular, or short biography of Col. Ebenezer Allen. 3524
Circular order no. 1. 37938
Circular. Oswego Training School for Primary Teachers. 57831
(Circular.) Perth-Amboy, New-Jersey, 180[6]. 97280
(Circular) Philadelphia, September 22, 1797. 94023
Circular prepared by the mechanics of Boston. 102284
Circular presenting the programme of the proposed society. 86096
Circular. Published weekly by the Oneida and Wallingford Communities. (47337)
Circular que el Provincial de Santo Domingo, dirige. 76878
Circular que el Senor Gobernador de la Sagrada Mitra. (48338)
[Circular relating to the re-establishment of the "free south."] 2756
Circular relative to scientific and literary exchanges. 85014
Circular relative to the provincial exhibition. 50263
Circular [respecting the Bunker-Hill Monument.] 9175, 102319
Circular respecting the publication fund. 60144
(Circular.) Richmond, January 25, 1794. 100223
Circular . . . September 1, 1855. 34993
Circular. Sir, permit us to direct your attention. 89643
(Circular.) Sir, the General Court, in June last. 105367
Circular soliciting subscriptions. (55655)
Circular statement of the condition and prospects of the Michigan Southern Railroad. (48767)
Circular statement of the condition and prospects of the Northern Indiana Rail-road Company. 34571, (55801)
Circular statement, Sept. 1851 [of the Northern Indiana Railroad Company.] 34571, (55801)
Circular. The first report of the Rochester Ladies' Anti-slavery Sewing Society. 72359
Circular. The R. I. Society for the Encouragement of Domestic Industry. (70736)
Circular to advertisers. 73549
Circular to associate members. (76640)
[Circular "To each Inspector of the Sanitary Commission.] 76642

Circular to gentlemen residing in the vicinity of the Erie Canal. 21708
Circular to his [i.e. Charles Anderson Wickliffe's] constituents. 103857
Circular to his [i.e. Spencer Pettis's] constituents. 61303
Circular to holders of municipal bonds. 49152
Circular to members of Congress. 76825
[Circular to regiments.] 76531, 76647
Circular. To southern states citizens in Europe. 88469
Circular to stockholders of the Southern Pacific Railroad Co. 88432
Circular to the bondholders and creditors of said company. 88457
Circular to the bondholders of the Southern Minnesota Railroad Company. 88406
Circular, to the churches of Connecticut. 105922
Circular. To the citizens of the tenth congressional district of Kentucky. 105946
Circular, to the citizens of Tuscaloosa County. 84896
Circular. To the clergymen or other well informed gentlemen. 102343
Circular to the counties requesting friends to solicit the interest of the members of Parliament. (13143)
Circular to the descendants of the British United Empire Loyalists of America. 74560
Circular . . . to the Freemasons of Michigan. 50872
Circular to the . . . House of Representatives. (52683)
Circular to the individual receivers of the doctrines of the New Jerusalem. 13141
(Circular.) To the legatees of Gen. Washington. 101764
Circular. To the members of the Convention for Amending the Constitution of Massachusetts. (5827)
Circular to the members of the Massachusetts Legislature. 52682
Circular to the members of the New-York Φ B K Society. 54835, 97796
Circular, to the people of Florida. 103426
Circular. To the public. 64363
Circular to the stockholders of the American Telegraph Company. 37354
Circular to the stockholders of the Chicago and Rock-Island Railroad Company. 24648
Circular to the voters of the counties of Tuscaloosa, Fayette, Marion, Winston, Walker, Blount and Jefferson. 84896
Circular. To the voters of the second congressional district of Tennessee. (39499)
Circular to the world. (76826)

Circular Washington, May 20, 1824. 96972
Circular, with postscript, issued by the directors. 61943
Circular, with the constitution of the [Defensive] League [of Freedom.] 19263
Circularis inspectionis meteororum libri II. 65940-65941
Circulars, instructions and tables of the Superintendent of Education for Lower Canada. 10433
Circulars 9 and 12 of the Superintendent of Education for Lower Canada. 10433
Circulars [of the Treasury Department, C. S. A.] 15248
Circular-schreiben an die Gouverneure eines jeden Staates. 101542
Circulate. (Published under authority of the National and Jackson Democratic Association Committee.) Read, read. 90765
Circulating library. see Waldie's select circulating library.
Circulating Library, Philadelphia. see Philadelphia Circulating Library.
Circulating Library, Rhinebeck, N. Y. see Rhinebeck, N. Y. Reading Hall and Circulating Library
Circuli sphaerae. (13144)
Circumstances of Boston considered. 46574, 4th note after 98925
Circumstantial account of an attack. 13145
Circumstancial account of her [i.e. Ann Carson's] conspiracy against the late Governor of Pennsylvania. 11083
Circumstancial account of the engagement between the United States Frigate Constellation. 97282
Circumstantial detail of his travels. 92353-92354
Circumstantial narrative of the trial of Lewis Burns. 96841
Circus, Worcester. 105343
Cirilo, Francisco de San. see San Cirilo, Francisco de.
Cirilo, Pedro de San. see Pedro de San Cirilo.
Cish, Jane. 100596
Cisneros, Alonso Vazquez de. see Vazquez de Cisneros, Alonso.
Cisneros, Diego. 13146
Cisneros, Joseph Luis de. 13147-13149
Cisneros, Melchor de Linan y. see Linan y Cisneros, Melchor de, Abp.
Cisneros, Mirano. (13150)
Cisneros y Quixano, Ignacio Beye. 13151
Cist, Charles. 13085, 13152-(13155), 14869, note after 97998
Cist, Lewis J. 13156
Cisternay du Fay, Charles Jerome de. see Du Fay, Charles Herome de Cisternay, 1662-1723.
Cisterne de Courtiras, Gabrielle Anne. see Saint Mars, Gabrielle Anne Cisterne de Courtiras, Vicomtesse de, 1804-1872.
Cisulc uceluswocn agenudasic. 67765

Citadin. pseud. Commerce de l'Amerique par Marseilles. see Chambon, --------.

Citara de Apolo. 75596

Citata in eodem Jos. de Peralta episcopus de Buenos Ayres. 62441

Cites et ruines Americaines Mitla. 12153

Cities in their relation to the world's evangelization. 39174

Citizen. pseud. (70188), 106112

Citizen. pseud. Address to the citizens of New Hampshire. 52795

Citizen. pseud. Address to the freemen of the state of Rhode Island. 70535

Citizen. pseud. Address to the inhabitants of Maine. 43904

Citizen. pseud. Address to the people of Maryland. 45066

Citizen. pseud. Alphabetical analysis of the constitution. see Hickey, William.

Citizen. pseud. Answer. see Stearns, Charles, 1778-1860.

Citizen. pseud. Appeal to the good sense of the legislature. 6597

Citizen. pseud. Appeal to the public. 54092

Citizen. pseud. Brief treatise, on the police of the city of New York. see Christian, Charles.

Citizen. pseud. Cincinnati directory. 13085

Citizen. pseud. Correspondence. see Reynolds, J. N.

Citizen. pseud. Election of a president. 22107

Citizen. pseud. Facts and suggestions in relation to the present state. 52944

Citizen. pseud. Fever. 24228

Citizen. pseud. Few observations on the government. 24235

Citizen. pseud. For the consideration of Congress. 101940

Citizen. pseud. Impositions and frauds in Philadelphia. 61732

Citizen. pseud. Letter to the President of the Board of Trade. see Sherwood, Henry.

Citizen. pseud. Letter to the representatives. see Congdon, James B.

Citizen. pseud. Letter to the Right Honourable W   P   . 40535

Citizen. pseud. Letter to the trustees. see Wilkins, Gouverneur Morris. supposed author

Citizen. pseud. Loud call to mechanics. (42163)

Citizen. pseud. Maine law in the balance. (43976)

Citizen. pseud. Observations on the case of the whig merchants. 56511

Citizen. pseud. Observations on the peculiar case of the whig merchants. see Trumbull, John, 1750-1831.

Citizen. pseud. Old and new tariffs compared. see Winslow, Isaac.

Citizen. pseud. Other side of the question. see Livingston, P.

Citizen. pseud. Pamphlet addressed to the Republicans. (70188), 106122

Citizen. pseud. Plan to lessen and equalize the burthen of taxation. (62066)

Citizen. pseud. Political annals of South Carolina. see De Bow, James Dunworthy Brownson, 1820-1867.

Citizen. pseud. Reflections upon the administration of justice. 60446

Citizen. pseud. Reflections upon the law of libel. see Kimball, Edmund.

Citizen. pseud. Remarks of a citizen upon the condition of our navy. 69390

Citizen. pseud. Remarks on "an act to establish the superior court of the city of Boston." see Quincy, Josiah, 1772-1864.

Citizen. pseud. Reorganized republic. (69658)

Citizen. pseud. Review of the proceedings of the catholics. 70249

Citizen. pseud. Review of the question. see Tappan, Benjamin, 1773-1857.

Citizen. pseud. Review of the revenue system. see Findley, William.

Citizen. pseud. Review of the rise, progress and tendency of the present system of national policy. 70267

Citizen. pseud. The revolution. see Drisko, G. L. supposed author

Citizen. pseud. Short history of late ecclesiastical oppressions in New-England and Vermont. 32178, 80634, 2d note after 99205

Citizen. pseud. Sketches of Springfield. 81571

Citizen. pseud. Some observations . . . on public education. (6764)

Citizen. pseud. Stranger's assistant. 92720

Citizen. pseud. Stricture on the judiciary of Massachusetts. 92827

Citizen. pseud. Supplement to remarks on "an act to establish the superior court of the city of Boston." see Quincy, Josiah, 1772-1864.

Citizen. pseud. Thoughts on emigration, education, &c. 22508

Citizen. pseud. Thoughts on taxation. see Davis, Timothy. supposed author

Citizen. pseud. Thoughts on the destructive influence of quackery. 95699

Citizen. pseud. To His Excellency William Tryon, Esq. 95896

Citizen. pseud. To John M. S   , Esq; Sir, ... 95898

Citizen. pseud. To the citizens of York. 95911

Citizen. pseud. To the members of the Free and Easy Club. 95949

Citizen. pseud. To the people of New-York. 95987

Citizen. pseud. Vindication of the ministry's acceptance of the administration. 99813

Citizen Adet's notes to the Secretary of State. 13884

Citizen and stranger's pictorial . . . directory. 54459

[Citizen bill.] 100047

Citizen. Containing twenty-five discourses. 37239

Citizen of Abbeville. pseud. Signs of the times. 87949

Citizen of Albany. pseud. Calm appeal. see Southwick, Solomon

Citizen of Albany. pseud. No union of church and state. 55373

Citizen of Albany. pseud. Memoirs of John Amiralle. see Southwick, John B.

Citizen of Albany. pseud. Tribute to the memory of De Witt Clinton. see Staats, Cuyler. supposed author

Citizen of Alexandria. pseud. Life of Luther C. Ladd. (38518)

Citizen of America. pseud. Dimension proper for an unit of measures pointed out. 20189

Citizen of America. pseud. Examination into the leading principles of the federal constitution. see Webster, Noah, 1758-1843.

Citizen of America. pseud. Fragments of the history of Bawlfredonia. see Clopper, Jonas.

Citizen of Baltimore. pseud. Battle of New Orleans. 3968

Citizen of Baltimore. pseud. Claims of American citizens against the French republic. 13195

Citizen of Baltimore. pseud. History and description of the Baltimore and Ohio Rail Road. see Smith, William Prescott, 1852?-1872.

Citizen of Baltimore. pseud. Life of Elisha Tyson. see Tyson, John Shoemaker.

Citizen of Baltimore. pseud. Observations on the impressment of American seamen. 56522

Citizen of Baltimore. pseud. Original poems. see Townsend, Richard H.

Citizen of Baltimore. pseud. Protest and argument. 45296

Citizen of Baltimore. pseud. Rail roads in the United States. (67512)

Citizen of Baltimore. pseud. Scenes at Washington. 77460

Citizen of Baltimore. pseud. Sketch of the claims of sundry American citizens on the government of the United States. see Purviance, Robert. supposed author and Causten, James H. supposed author

Citizen of Baltimore. pseud. View of the claims of American citizens. see Causten, James H. supposed author and Purviance, Robert. supposed author

Citizen of Boston. pseud. Declaration of independence; a poem. see Richards, George.

Citizen of Boston. pseud. Essay on American slavery. 22934

Citizen of Boston. pseud. New system of paper money. (53406)

Citizen of Boston. pseud. Ode. 95187

Citizen of Boston. pseud. On the rights and powers of corporations. (57297)

Citizen of Boston. pseud. Particular account of the battle of Bunker, or Breed's Hill. see Bradford, Alden, 1765-1843.

Citizen of Boston. pseud. Proposals [for publishing a history of Boston.] see Snow, Caleb Hopkins, 1796-1835.

Citizen of Boston. pseud. Reality versus fiction. see Derby, Elias Hasket.

Citizen of Boston. pseud. Remarks on banks and banking. see Williams, Henry. of Boston

Citizen of Boston. pseud. Remarks on capital punishments. see Summer, George, 1817-1863. supposed author

Citizen of Boston. pseud. Remarks upon an oration. see Putman, George.

Citizen of Boston. pseud. Review of the speech of Harrison Gray Otis. (70271)

Citizen of Boston. pseud. Thoughts on the laws, government, and morals. 95709

Citizen of Burlington. pseud. see Carey, Henry Charles, 1793-1879.

Citizen of Cambridgeport. pseud. Journal of a tour. see Nason, Daniel.

Citizen of Columbus. pseud. ed. Ohio gazetteer. 37730

Citizen of Connecticut. pseud. Address to the legislature. see Burs, W. Pitt.

Citizen of Connecticut. pseud. History of the discovery of America. see Trumbull, Henry.

Citizen of Connecticut. pseud. Indian wars. see Trumbull, Henry.

Citizen of Connecticut. pseud. Rod for a fool's back. see Webster, Noah, 1758-1843.

Citizen of Danvers. pseud. Biographical sketch. 17712, 75640

Citizen of Edinburgh. pseud. Journal of an excursion. 36702

Citizen of Georgia. pseud. Remarks upon slavery. 69524

Citizen of Hagers-Town, Md. pseud. Memoirs of the illustrious citizen and patriot, Andrew Jackson. see Waldo, Samuel Putnam.

Citizen of Harper's Ferry. pseud. Startling incidents and developments. 8521

Citizen of Havre de Grace. pseud. Narrative. see Wilmer, James Jones.

Citizen of Indiana. pseud. Letter. see Egerton, Joseph K.

Citizen of Iowa. pseud. Reconstruction of the union. (68383)

Citizen of Kentucky. pseud. Plan for conquering treason. 63264

Citizen of Kentucky. pseud. View of the administration of the federal government. 99548

Citizen of Lancaster County. pseud. Sketch of the life, character, and public services of Joseph Ritner. 71584

Citizen of London. pseud. Britain's mistakes. see Merchant and Citizen of London. pseud.

Citizen of London. pseud. Letter to the great man. 40479

Citizen of London. pseud. Wonderful discovery of a hermit. 105003

Citizen of Maine. pseud. Maine law in the balance. see Payson, Edward, 1814-1890.

Citizen of Maine. pseud. Review of Rev. Mr. Lovejoy's 'Lecture on the subject of prohibitory laws.' 42367

Citizen of Maine. pseud. Review of some of the doings of the Legislature. 70217

Citizen of Malden. pseud. Shall we suffocate Ed. Green? see Redpath, James.

Citizen of Mansfield, Conn. pseud. Practical hints. see Robins, Gurdon.

Citizen of Maryland. pseud. Abridgment of Humboldt's statistical essay. (33716)

Citizen of Maryland. pseud. Essay on the policy of appropriations. see Allen, John, fl. 1826.

Citizen of Maryland. pseud. Maryland resolutions. see Maxcy, Virgil.

Citizen of Maryland. pseud. Rambler. 67617

Citizen of Maryland. pseud. Resolutions [relating to the public lands] and the object of them considered. 45354

Citizen of Maryland. pseud. Short history of the public debt of Maryland. 45361

Citizen of Maryland. pseud. Strictures on the letter of Charles J. Ingersoll. 34735, 92851

Citizen of Maryland. pseud. Thoughts on labor. 44298

Citizen of Massachusetts. pseud. Appeal to the good sense of the Democrats. see Phillips, Willard.

Citizen of Massachusetts. pseud. Essex Junto. 23019

Citizen of Massachusetts. pseud. Familiar conversation. see Snell, Thomas, 1774-1862.

Citizen of Massachusetts. pseud. Female review. see Mann, Herman.

Citizen of Massachusetts. pseud. Freemasonry; a poem. 25803

Citizen of Massachusetts. pseud. History of the United States of America. see Prentiss, Charles. supposed author and Sullivan, William. supposed author and Hale, Salma. incorrectly supposed author

Citizen of Massachusetts. pseud. Impartial inquirer. see Lowell, John, 1769-1840. and Higginson, S.

Citizen of Massachusetts. pseud. Letter to William H. Crawford. 17447

Citizen of Massachusetts. pseud. Letters to the Hon. Harrison Gray Otis. 40646

Citizen of Massachusetts. pseud. Memoirs of Andrew Jackson. see Smith, Jerome Van Crowninshield, 1800-1879.

Citizen of Massachusetts. pseud. Merits of Thomas W. Dorr. see Curtis, George Ticknor.

Citizen of Massachusetts. pseud. Opinions respecting the commercial intercourse between the United States. see Bowdoin, James, 1729-1790.

Citizen of Massachusetts. pseud. Path to riches. see Sullivan, James, 1744-1808.

Citizen of Massachusetts. pseud. Remarks on Dr. Channing's slavery. see Austin, James Trecothick, 1784-1870.

Citizen of Massachusetts. pseud. Remarks on state rights. 69430

Citizen of Massachusetts. pseud. Review of a pamphlet. 22270

Citizen of Massachusetts. pseud. Review of Dr. Channing's letter to Hon. Henry Clay. 11913

Citizen of Massachusetts. pseud. Review of the remarks on Dr. Channing's Slavery. see Simmons, George Frederic, 1814-1855.

Citizen of Massachusetts. pseud. Sacred dirges. see Holden, Oliver.

Citizen of Massachusetts. pseud. Temperate examination. see Lowell, John.

Citizen of Massachusetts. pseud. Times. 95843

Citizen of Massachusetts. pseud. Whole truth. see Hancock. pseud.

Citizen of Middletown, Conn. pseud. Indian of New-England. see Barratt, Joseph.

Citizen of Middletown, Conn. pseud. Key to the Indian language of New-Enyland. [sic] see Barratt, Joseph.

Citizen of Milwaukee. pseud. Garangula. 26545

Citizen of nature. 13157

Citizen of New England. pseud. Antigallican. see Cobbett, William, 1763-1835.

Citizen of New England. pseud. Remarks on African colonization. 69408

Citizen of New Haven. pseud. see Sherman, Roger, 1721-1793.

Citizen of New Orleans. pseud. Visit of General La Fayette to Louisiana. 38581

Citizen of New York. pseud. Address on slavery. see Hewlett, Heman.

Citizen of New-York. pseud. Address . . . on the . . . anti-masonic excitement. see Lathrop, John H.

Citizen of New York. pseud. Address to his fellow citizens. 53494

Citizen of New York. pseud. Address to the people of the state of New-York. see Jay, John.

Citizen of New York. pseud. Address to the people of the United States. see Holley, Myron.

Citizen of New York. pseud. Address to the Republicans and people of New York. 441, 53513

Citizen of New-York. pseud. Appeal to the reason and religion of . . . American Christians. see Reese, David M.

Citizen of New York. pseud. Biographical notice of Com. Jesse D. Elliott. see Jarvis, Russell.

Citizen of New York. pseud. Cabinet. (9792)

Citizen of New York. pseud. Commercial conduct of the United States. 14970

Citizen of New York. pseud. Communications on the next election. see Genet, Edmund Charles Edouard, 1763-1834.

Citizen of New-York. pseud. Considerations in favour of the construction of a great state road. see Beck, Nicholas F.

Citizen of New York. pseud. Correct statement. 105041

Citizen of New York. pseud. Essay in defence of slave holding. 22932

Citizen of New York. pseud. Letter to the electors of president. see Genet, Edmund Charles Edouard, 1763-1834.

Citizen of New-York. pseud. Letters about the Hudson River. see Hunt, Freeman.

Citizen of New York. pseud. Measures, not men. 9955, 47273

Citizen of New York. pseud. Memoir of Martin Van Buren. 98425

Citizen of New York. pseud. Memoir on the subject of a General Bible Society. 47505

Citizen of New York. pseud. Narrative of the suppression. see Cheetham, James.

Citizen of New York. pseud. Questions and answers on the presidential elections. 441, 53513

Citizen of New York. pseud. Remarks on that part of the speech. 69431

Citizen of New-York. pseud. Remarks upon a plan for the total abolition of slavery. (69521)

Citizen of New York. pseud. Reply to the report. see Ogilby, Frederick. supposed author

Citizen of New York. pseud. Retrospect of the Boston tea-party. see Hawkes, J. supposed author

Citizen of New-York. pseud. Review of the opinion of Judge Cowen. 17241, 43529

Citizen of New-York. pseud. Serious address to the inhabitants. 79246

Citizen of New York. pseud. Seventeen numbers. see Fisher, R.

Citizen of New-York. pseud. Sketch of our political condition. see Moore, Clement C.

Citizen of New-York. pseud. Strictures on Bishop Watson's "Apology for the Bible." 92836

Citizen of New-York. pseud. Three letters. see Stilwell, Silas M.

Citizen of New-York. pseud. To the people of the United States. 97947

Citizen of New-York. pseud. What is monopoly? see Sedgwick, Theodore, 1811-1859.

Citizen of New York, formerly a U. S. Consul at Lima. pseud. Considerations on the subject of a communication between the Atlantic and Pacific Oceans. 16013

Citizen of Newburyport. pseud. Solemn call. 86361-86362

Citizen of Norfolk. pseud. Address to the citizens. see Ruggles, Nathaniel.

Citizen of North-Carolina. pseud. Considerations relative to a southern confederacy. see Berguin, H. K.

Citizen of North Carolina. pseud. Our currency, some of its evils, and remedies for them. (57917)

Citizen of Northern Pennsylvania. pseud. Appendix. 60275

Citizen of Ohio. pseud. Interior causes of the war. 34906

Citizen of Ohio. pseud. Mysteries of Washington City. see Atwater, Caleb. supposed author

Citizen of Ohio. pseud. Strictures. 92858

Citizen of Otsego County. pseud. Origin and progress of the present difficulties. 57603

Citizen of Pennsylvania. pseud. Dissolution of the union. see Carey, Mathew, 1760-1839.

Citizen of Pennsylvania. pseud. Examination of the causes & effects. 60092

Citizen of Pennsylvania. pseud. Examination of the conduct. see Gallatin, Albert, 1761-1849.

Citizen of Pennsylvania. pseud. Exposition of the late general election. 23456

Citizen of Pennsylvania. pseud. Few plain facts. 60101

Citizen of Pennsylvania. pseud. Few thoughts on intervention. see Reed, William B.

Citizen of Pennsylvania. pseud. Inquiry into the alleged tendency of the separation of convicts. see Packard, Frederic Adolphus.

Citizen of Pennsylvania. pseud. Letter to a friend in a slave state. see Ingersoll, Charles.

Citizen of Pennsylvania. pseud. Letters on the condition of the poor. 61782

Citizen of Pennsylvania. pseud. Notes. see Cleveland, C. D.

Citizen of Pennsylvania. pseud. Rudiments of national knowledge. 73895

Citizen of Pennsylvania. pseud. Strictures on monopolies. 92844

Citizen of Pennsylvania. pseud. Strictures on the proceedings of the General Assembly. 92855

Citizen of Pennsylvania. pseud. Thoughts on the condition and prospects of popular education. see Packard, Frederic Adolphus.

Citizen of Philadelphia. pseud. Politicians. see American, and a citizen of Philadelphia. pseud.

Citizen of Philadelphia. pseud. Common sense. see Carey, Mathew, 1760-1839.

Citizen of Philadelphia. pseud. Considerations on an act of the Legislature of Virginia.

see Swanwick, John. supposed author and Webster, Pelatiah, 1726-1795. supposed author

Citizen of Philadelphia. pseud. Cursory views. see Carey, Mathew, 1760-1839.

Citizen of Philadelphia. pseud. Dissertation on the political union. see Webster, Pelatiah, 1726-1795.

Citizen of Philadelphia. pseud. Essay on credit. see Webster, Pelatiah, 1726-1795.

Citizen of Philadelphia. pseud. Essay on free trade and finance. see Webster, Pelatiah, 1726-1795.

Citizen of Philadelphia. pseud. Essay on the culture of silk. see Webster, Pelatiah, 1726-1795.

Citizen of Philadelphia. pseud. Essay on the seat of the federal government. see Webster, Pelatiah, 1726-1795.

Citizen of Philadelphia. pseud. Essays tending to prove the ruinous effects. see Carey, Mathew, 1760-1839.

Citizen of Philadelphia. pseud. Few political reflections. see Wells, Richard. supposed author

Citizen of Philadelphia. pseud. Fifth essay on free trade and finance. see Webster, Pelatiah, 1726-1795.

Citizen of Philadelphia. pseud. Fourth essay on free trade and finance. see Webster, Pelatiah, 1726-1795.

Citizen of Philadelphia. pseud. Inquiry into the alleged tendency of the separation of convicts. see Packard, Frederic Adolphus.

Citizen of Philadelphia. pseud. Inquiry into the causes and cost of corrup [sic] state legislation. 34798

Citizen of Philadelphia. pseud. Letter on the rebellion. see Rush, Benjamin, 1811-1877.

Citizen of Philadelphia. pseud. Plea for the poor. 63395

Citizen of Philadelphia. pseud. Plea for the poor soldiers. see Webster, Pelatiah, 1726-1795.

Citizen of Philadelphia. pseud. Proposal for altering the eastern front. see Beck, Paul.

Citizen of Philadelphia. pseud. Reasons for repealing the act. see Webster, Pelatiah, 1726-1795.

Citizen of Philadelphia. pseud. Reflections on the system of the Union Benevolent Association. 62349

Citizen of Philadelphia. pseud. Remarks on the address. see Webster, Pelatiah, 1726-1795.

Citizen of Philadelphia. pseud. Second crisis of America. 78725

Citizen of Philadelphia. pseud. Second essay on free trade and finance. see Webster, Pelatiah, 1726-1795.

Citizen of Philadelphia. pseud. Seventh essay on free trade and finance. see Webster, Pelatiah, 1726-1795.

Citizen of Philadelphia. pseud. Sixth essay on free trade and finance. see Webster, Pelatiah, 1726-1795.

Citizen of Philadelphia. pseud. Storm, a poem. see Markoe, Peter. supposed author

Citizen of Philadelphia. pseud. Third essay [on free trade and finance.] see Webster, Pelatiah, 1726-1795.

Citizen of Philadelphia. pseud. To the stock-holders of the Bank of North-America. see Webster, Pelatiah, 1726-1795.

Citizen of Philadelphia. pseud. Views respecting the Chesapeak and Delaware Canal. 99594

Citizen of Philadelphia. pseud. Weaknesses of Brutus exposed. see Webster, Pelatiah, 1726-1795.

Citizen of Pittsburgh. pseud. Republican compiler. see Evans, B. R.

Citizen of Port-Royal in Jamaica. pseud. Letter. 40271

Citizen of Quebec. pseud. Observations on a pamphlet. 56491

Citizen of Rhode-Island. pseud. Principles and men. see Richmond, William E.

Citizen of South-Carolina. pseud. Candid examination. see Smith, William Loughton, 1758-1812. supposed author.

Citizen of South Carolina. pseud. Enquiry into the constitutional authority. see Ford, Timothy. supposed author and Ramsay, David. incorrectly supposed author

Citizen of South Carolina. pseud. Eyes opened. see Smith, William Loughton, 1748-1812. supposed author

Citizen of South Carolina. pseud. Genius of Erin. 14888, 26949

Citizen of South Carolina. pseud. Union and liberty. 97755

Citizen of the cotton country. pseud. Southern chivalry. 88322

Citizen of the country. pseud. Glance at the currency. see Cocke, J. D. supposed author

Citizen of the District of Columbia. pseud. Question of retrocession. 67145

Citizen of the south. pseud. Is slavery a blessing? see Shaw, Charles B.

Citizen of the south. pseud. Question examined. 67143

Citizen of the south. pseud. Sober view of the slavery question. 85664

Citizen of the state of New-York. pseud. Considerations which demand the attention. 16036

Citizen of the state of Tennessee. pseud. Vindication of the measures. see Overton, John.

Citizen of the United States. pseud. tr. 50130

Citizen of the United States. pseud. America. see Everett, Alexander H.

Citizen of the United States. pseud. Connected view of the whole internal navigation of the United States. see Armroyd, George. supposed author and Carey, Mathew, 1760-1839. supposed author

Citizen of the United States. pseud. Columbia and Britannia. see Philophron. pseud.

Citizen of the United States. pseud. Contrast. see Tyler, Royall, 1757-1826.

Citizen of the United States. pseud. Democracy. 19492

Citizen of the United States. pseud. Democracy of Christianity. 19488

Citizen of the United States. pseud. Dissolution of the union. see Carey, Mathew, 1750-1839.

Citizen of the United States. pseud. Essay on money. see Witherspoon, John. and Webster, Pelatiah, 1726-1795. incorrectly supposed author

Citizen of the United States. pseud. Europe. see Everett, Alexander H.

Citizen of the United States. pseud. France and Mexico. (25428)

Citizen of the United States. pseud. Memorial. see Gibbes, George W. petitioner

Citizen of the United States. pseud. Notes on Mexico. see Poinsett, Joel Roberts, 1779-1851.

Citizen of the United States. pseud. Observations on the agriculture. see Coxe, Tench.

Citizen of the United States. pseud. Political sketches. see Murray, William Vans.

Citizen of the United States. pseud. Remarks on a review of Symmes' theory. 70433

Citizen of the United States. pseud. Remarks on Jay's treaty. see Columbus. pseud.

Citizen of the United States. pseud. Remarks on the censures of the government of the United States. see Everett, Alexander H.

Citizen of the United States. pseud. Solution of our national difficulties. 86556

Citizen of the United States. pseud. Thoughts on the state of the American Indians. see Wood, Silas.

Citizen of the United States. pseud. Tour through Upper and Lower Canada. see Ogden, John Cosens.

Citizen of the United States. pseud. Treatise on usury. see Fosdick, David. supposed author

Citizen of the United States. pseud. Tracts on business. see Fosdick, David. supposed author

Citizen of the U. S. pseud. Universal history of the U. S. of America. see Taylor, C. B.

Citizen of the United States. pseud. Vermonters unmasked. see Phelps, Charles.

Citizen of the United States. pseud. View of South-America and Mexico. see Niles, John M.

Citizen of the United States. pseud. War in Texas. see Lundy, Benjamin.

Citizen of the United States of North America. pseud. Vindiciae Americanae. 99832

Citizen of the west. pseud. Braddock's defeat. 7209

Citizen of the west. pseud. Pocahontas. see Owen, Robert Dale, 1801-1877.

Citizen of the world. pseud. America and the Americans. see Boardman, James.

Citizen of the world. pseud. American crisis. 1079

Citizen of the world. pseud. Fragment. see Carey, Mathew, 1760-1839.

Citizen of the world. pseud. Letter 108. 26850

Citizen of these states. pseud. Letter to Major-General Hamilton. 40446

Citizen of this state. pseud. Address to the people of Virginia. see Evans, Thomas.

Citizen of this state. pseud. Our resources. see Hazard, Rowland G.

Citizen of Vermont. pseud. The crisis. (17531), 2d note after 99216

Citizen of Vermont. pseud. Free enquiry. (25709), 3d note after 99216

Citizen of Virginia. pseud. Arator. see Taylor, John, 1753?-1824.

Citizen of Virginia. pseud. Condensed anti-slavery Bible argument. see Bourne, George, 1780-1845.

Citizen of Virginia. pseud. Essays on various subjects. see Tucker, George.

Citizen of Virginia. pseud. History of
Virginia. see Brockenbrough, William
Henry, 1812-1850.
Citizen of Virginia. pseud. Introductory
remarks. 13550
Citizen of Walden. pseud. Shall we suffocate
Ed. Green? see Redpath, James.
Citizen of Washington. pseud. National
money. 52010
Citizen of Washington. pseud. True policy
of the United States. see Mentor.
pseud.
Citizen of Washington, D. C. pseud. Short
biography of the illustrious citizen,
Marquis de Lafayette. 38580
Citizen of Washington Territory. pseud.
Reply. 14288
Citizen of Wayne County, Ind. pseud. History
of the Federal and Democratic parties.
(32169)
Citizen of western New-York. pseud. comp.
Memoirs of General Andrew Jackson.
35377
Citizen of western New-York. pseud.
Thoughts on banking and the currency.
95672
Citizen of Westmoreland County. pseud.
Plain truth. see Lee, Henry. supposed
author
Citizen of Williamsburg. pseud. Letter to
the Rev. Jedediah Morse. see Tucker,
St. George. and Madison, James, Bp.,
1749-1812. supposed author
Citizen Snub. pseud. see Stanwick, John.
supposed author and "Scotch Runaway."
pseud. supposed author
Citizen soldiers at North Point and Fort
McHenry. 3025, 13158, 31704
Citizen south of French Broad and Holston.
pseud. Address to the citizens. 94787
Citizen thereof, whose outward habitation is
Virginia. pseud. Song of Sion. see
Grave, John.
Citizen U. S. N. A. pseud. Book for the
nation and times. 6345
Citizen who pays taxes. pseud. Review of
the new water documents. 8327
Citizens' and strangers' city guide. 6514
Citizens and stranger's guide to the metropolis
of Massachusetts. 7043
Citizens' and Taxpayers' Executive Committee
for . . . Financial Report of the City
. . . of New York. see Executive
Committee of Citizens and Taxpayers
for . . . Financial Report of the City
. . . of New York.
Citizen's appeal in regard to the war with
Mexico. 79677
Citizens assemble at the state-house. 96369
Citizens' Association of New York. 54186-
(54188)
Citizens' Association of New York. Council of
Hygiene and Public Health. (54188)
Citizens' Association of New York. Executive
Council. (54188)
Citizens' Association of New York. An appeal
. . . against the abuses in the local
government. 54186
Citizens' Association of New-York . . . .
Peter Cooper, Chairman. May 20th,
1868. (54188)
Citizens Association of Pennsylvania. 59976
Citizens Association of Pennsylvania. Charter.
59976
Citizens Association of Pennsylvania. Presi-
dent. 59976

Citizens Committee on Obsequies of Abraham
Lincoln in Union Square, New York, April
25, 1865. see New York (City) Citizens
Committee on Obsequies of Abraham
Lincoln in Union Square, April 25, 1865.
Citizens' Committee on Public Honors to Lieu-
tenant-General Grant, New York, 1865.
see New York (City) Citizens Committee
on Public Honors to Lieutenant-General
Grant, 1865.
Citizens Directory and strangers guide through
the city of New York. 54459, 90215
Citizen's duty in the present crisis. 89086
Citizens' Free Library, Halifax. see Halifax,
Nova Scotia. Citizens' Free Library.
Citizen's guide. 105990
Citizens' hand book and voter's manual. 84911
Citizens' hand book for Philadelphia. (61541),
84911
Citizens of Abbeville District, South Carolina.
see Abbeville District, South Carolina.
Citizens.
Citizens of Baltimore. see Baltimore. Citizens.
Citizens of Beaufort District, S. C. see Beau-
fort District, S. C. Citizens.
Citizens of Bennington and vicinity are requested
to meet. 101827
Citizens of Berkshire, Mass. see Berkshire,
Mass. Citizens.
Citizens of Boston. see Boston. Citizens.
Citizens of Boston and Vicinity. Committee.
see Boston. Citizens.
Citizens of Boston Favorable to a Revision of
the Laws in Relation to Debtor and Credi-
tor. see Society for the Promotion of
the Rights and Interests of Bona Fide
Creditors, and the Benefit and Relief of
Honest Debtors, Boston.
Citizens of Boston, Opposed to a Further In-
crease of Duties on Importations. see
Boston. Committee of Citizens Opposed
to a Further Increase of Duties on Im-
portations, 1827.
Citizens of Cairo and Vicinity. petitioners see
Cairo, Ill. Citizens. petitioners
Citizens of Charleston. see Charleston, S. C.
Citizens.
Citizens of Chester District, South Carolina.
see Chester District, South Carolina.
Citizens.
Citizens of Chesterfield, S. C. see Chester-
field, S. C. Citizens.
Citizens of Chicago, Ill. see Chicago.
Citizens.
Citizens of Cincinnati. see Cincinnati.
Citizens.
Citizens of Columbus, Ohio. see Columbus,
Ohio. Citizens.
Citizens of Davenport, Iowa. see Davenport,
Iowa. Citizens.
Citizens of Dona Ana County. see Dona Ana
County, N. M. Citizens.
Citizens of Edgefield, S. C. see Edgefield,
S. C. Citizens.
Citizens of Elizabeth City County, Va. see
Elizabeth City County, Va. Citizens.
Citizens of Englewood, Bergen County, N. J.
see Englewood, N. J. Citizens.
Citizens of Erie County, N. Y., Union Meeting,
1858. see Erie County, N. Y. Union
Anti-Lecompton Mass Meeting, Buffalo,
1858.
Citizens of Fayette County, Ill. see Fayette
County, Ill. Citizens.

Citizens of Franklin County, Ohio, Favorable to the Election of Andrew Jackson. see Democratic Party. Ohio. Franklin County.

Citizens of Georgetown, S. C. see Georgetown, S. C. Citizens.

Citizens of Kanawha County, Va. see Kanawha County, W. Va. Citizens.

Citizens of Kentucky, be upon your guard. 95319

Citizens of Kershaw District, South Carolina. see Kershaw District, S. C. Citizens.

Citizens of Laurens District, S. C. see Laurens District, S. C. Citizens.

Citizens of Louisiana. see Louisiana. Citizens.

Citizens of Maryland. see Maryland. Citizens.

Citizens of Maryland. 101786

Citizens of Massachusetts. see Massachusetts. Citizens.

Citizens of Massachusetts, Purchasers under the Georgia Company. see Massachusetts. Citizens.

Citizens of Mecklenburg County, N. C. see Mecklenburg County, N. C. Citizens.

Citizens of Milwaukee. see Milwaukee. Citizens.

Citizens of Moline, Ill. see Moline, Ill. Citizens.

Citizens of Nevada County, Cal. see Nevada County, Cal. Citizens.

Citizens of New Jersey. see New Jersey. Citizens.

Citizens of New Orleans, Creditors of the Late Republic of Texas. see New Orleans. Citizens, Creditors of the Late Republic of Texas.

Citizens of New York (City) see New York (City) Citizens.

Citizens of New York Having Claims upon France and other European States. see New York (State) Citizens.

Citizens of Newburyport, Mass. see Newburyport, Mass. Citizens.

Citizens of Northern Pennsylvania. petitioners 55823

Citizens of Ohio. see Ohio. Citizens.

Citizens of Pennsylvania. see Pennsylvania. Citizens.

Citizens of Philadelphia. see Philadelphia. Citizens.

Citizens of Pittsburgh. see Pittsburgh. Citizens.

Citizens of Plattsburgh, N. Y. see Plattsburgh, N. Y. Citizens.

Citizens of Plymouth and Kingston, Mass. see Kingston, Mass. Citizens. and Plymouth, Mass. Citizens.

Citizens of Providence. see Providence, R. I. Citizens.

Citizens of Richland District, S. C. see Richland District, S. C. Citizens.

Citizens of Richmond. see Richmond, Va. Citizens.

Citizens of Rock Island, Ill. see Rock Island, Ill. Citizens.

Citizens of Rutland, Vt. see Rutland, Vt. Citizens.

Citizens of St. Louis, Mo. see St. Louis. Citizens.

Citizens of Salt Lake City. see Salt Lake City, Utah. Citizens.

Citizens of San Francisco. see San Francisco. Citizens.

Citizens of the City and County of Philadelphia. see Philadelphia. Citizens.

Citizens of the Counties of St. Lawrence, Franklin and Clinton, N. Y. see Clinton County, N. Y. Citizens. and Franklin County, N. Y. Citizens. and St. Lawrence County, N. Y. Citizens.

Citizens of the County of Albemarle in the State of Virginia. see Albemarle County, Va.

Citizens of the District of Columbia. see District of Columbia. Citizens.

Citizens . . . of the Indiana Territory. see Indiana (Territory) Citizens.

Citizens of the South-End! 87339

Citizens of the State of Maryland. see Maryland. Citizens.

Citizens of the State of New York. see New York (State) Citizens.

Citizens of the United States. see United States. Citizens.

Citizens of Troy, N. Y. see Troy, N. Y. Citizens.

Citizens of Union District, S. C. see Union District, S. C. Citizens.

Citizens of Washington. see Washington, D. C. Citizens.

Citizens of Washington Territory. see Washington (Territory) Citizens.

Citizens of Yuba County, Cal. see Yuba County, Cal. Citizens.

Citizens read!! 60619

Citizen's register for 1807. 43311

Citizens: remember there have been near three hundred of our American vessels. 95364

Citizens Resident and Concerned in the City of Washington. see Washington, D. C. Citizens.

Citizenship: state citizens, general citizens. (5931)

Citlalpopoca, Nicolas Salazar Maxiscatzin. see Salazar Maxiscatzin Citlalpopoca, Nicolas.

Citoyen. pseud. Lettres. see Saintard, P.

Citoyen Americain. pseud. Etats-Unis de l'Angleterre. see Lee, William, 1772-1840.

Citoyen Americain. pseud. Histoire du General de Lafayette. see Ticknor, George.

Citoyen, ancien syndic de la Chambre de Commerce de Lyon. pseud. Dissertation sur les fruits de la decouverte. 20288

Citoyen Andre. pseud. see Andre. pseud. tr.

Citoyen C. pseud. Reflexions sur un pretendu prodige opere. see Colombel, Noel.

Citoyen d'Amsterdam. pseud. Observations. 65049

Citoyen de Geneve. pseud. Bigarures. see Rousseau, Jean Jacques, 1712-1778. supposed author and Wilkes, John, 1727-1797. supposed author

Citoyen de la Haye. pseud. Premiere lettre. 65049

Citoyen de la Plata. pseud. Observations. see O., B. Ey. pseud.

Citoyen de l'Amerique Espagnole. pseud. Revolutions de l'Amerique Espagnole. see Palacio Fajardo, Manuel.

Citoyen de l'Amerique Meridionale. pseud. Esquisse de la revolution. pseud. see Palacio Fajardo, Manuel.

Citoyen de New-York. pseud. Expose des eventualites. 93794, 95081

Citoyen de New-York. pseud. Lettre d'un citoyen de New-York. 93794, 95081

Citoyen de New-York. pseud. Supplement a l'expose. 93794, 95081
Citoyen de Virginie. pseud. Recherches historiques. see Mazzei, Philip, 1730-1816.
Citoyen des Etats Unis. pseud. Essai sur la ville de Washington. 101938
Citoyen des Etats-Unis. pseud. Lettres d'un citoyen. see Condorcet, Marie Jean Antoine Nicolas Caritat, Marquis de.
Citoyen des Etats-Unis. pseud. Reponse aux principales questions. see Bonnet, J. Espirit.
Citoyen des Etats-Unis d'Amerique. 23115
Citoyen Sans-Reproche, homme de couleur. pseud. Reflexions sur le despotisme. (75185)
Citoyens Blancs de Saint Domingue. Treaties, etc. see Santo Domingo (French Colony) Province de l'Ouest.
Citoyens de Couleur de Quatorze Paroisses de la Province de l'Ouest de la Partie Francaise de Saint-Domingue. Treaties, etc. see Santo Domingo (French Colony) Province de l'Ouest. Treaties, etc.
Citoyens de Couleur de Port-au-Prince, Haiti. Treaties, etc. see Santo Domingo (French Colony) Province de Sud. Treaties, etc.
Citoyens de Couleur de Saint Domingue. see Santo Domingo (French Colony) Citoyens de Couleur.
Citoyens de Couleur de Saint Marc, Haiti. see Saint Marc, Haiti. Citoyens de Couleur.
Citoyens de Couleur des Colonies. petitioners 61268
Citoyens de Couleur des Isles et Colonies Francoises. petitioners Adresse. 36424
Citoyens de Couleur, des Isles et Colonies Francoises. Lettre. 40674
Citoyens de Couleur des Isles et Colonies Francoises. petitioners Reclamation. 68373
Citoyens de Couleur des Isles & Colonies Francoises. petitioners Supplique et petition. 93815
Citoyens de Couleur des Isles Francoises. petitioners (61271)
Citoyens Francois, habitants des Etats-Unis de l'Amerique Septentrionale, a leur partie a ses representans. 40181
Citry et de la Guette, S. de Broe, Seigneur de. see Broe, S. de, Seigneur de Citry et de la Guette.
City accounts [of Charleston, S. C.] 12043
City and business directory. 97072
City and business directory of Nashville for 1860-61. 51868
City and country contrasted. 27574
City and poverty. 84068
City and scenery of Newport, Rhode Island. 14442
City and suburban architecture. 82161-(82162)
City architecture. 24285
City Bank, Providence, R. I. Stockholders. 66295
City Bounty Fund Commission, Philadelphia. see Philadelphia. Bounty Fund Commission.
City business directory. 61606
City celebration of the anniversary of the national independence. 53315
City characters. 13159
City charter. . . An act to establish the city of New-Bedford. 52471

City charter and ordinances of . . . Newark 54871
City charter and ordinances of the city of Bangor. (3155)
City charter and ordinances, rules and orders of city council. 23745
City charter proposed for adoption of the freemen of Providence, at a town meeting to be holden October 22, 1831. 66248
City charter, proposed for the adoption of the freemen of Providence, at a town meeting to be holden April 29th, 1829. 66248
City charter, rules and orders of the city council. 52471
City charter; with the joint rules and orders of the city council. (3952)
City Comptroller's third annual statement. (12651)
City Council, July 17, 1832. 87879
City crimes. 54189
City directory Memphis, 1867-8. 47775
City directory of Ann Arbor. 11962
City directory of Leavenworth. 39548
City directory [of Troy.] 97072
City directory, with a supplement. 13085
City document—no. 1. Address of the . . . mayor. 52472
City document—no. 1 [of Boston.] 82805
City document—no. 5 [of Boston.] 82807
City document.—no. 11. City of Boston. 93698
City document. No. 14. . . . Communication of Dr. Henry G. Clark. (13297)
City document.—no. 60. Report of the Committee appointed by the City Council. 12676
City document.—no. 67 [of Boston.] 78674
City document.—no. 92 [of Boston.] 78674
City documents. No. 18 [of Providence, R. I.] 85495
City documents [of Lowell, Mass.] 42474
City documents [of Lynn, Mass.] 42835
City Engineers communication to the Common Council of San Francisco. 76042
City evangelization. 54190
City farce. 105986
City finances. 94429
City gazette (Charleston, S. C.) 87867
City gazette (St. John, N. B.) 40619, 1st note after 98925
City Guard, Roxbury, Mass. see Roxbury, Mass. City Guard.
City guide and business mirror. 13085
City guide to New Haven. 3333
City hall, Boston. 6685
City hall of Lynn; being a history of events. 42836
City hall reporter & New-York law magazine. 96832
City hospitals. 28541
City Institute, Philadelphia. see Philadelphia City Institute.
City intelligencer. 71171
City Library Association, Springfield, Mass. see Springfield City Library Association, Springfield, Mass.
City Mission, Salem, Mass. see Salem City Mission, Salem, Mass.
City Mission, Philadelphia. see Philadelphia City Mission.
City Mission and Tract Society, Charlestown, Mass. see Charlestown City Mission and Tract Society.
City Mission and Tract Society, New York. see New York Mission and Tract Society.
City mission document, no. 9. 35445, (54444)

City Mission Society, New York. see New
York City Mission Society. and New
York Protestant Episcopal City Mission
Society.
City Missionary Society of Portsmouth, N. H.
64419
City missions. 62112
City missions. By Rev. W. A. McVickar.
43680
City-monitor. 74798
City of Cambridge. 10123
City of Charlestown. Documents printed by
order. 12109
City of Charlestown. The inaugural address
of the mayor. 12108
City of Chelsea. Mayor's address. 12417
City of Columbus, Ohio. City documents.
14893
City of God. A sermon. 45447
City of God in the Anglo-Saxon church. 45448
City of Keokuk, in 1856. 13622
City of Louisville, vs. University of Louisville.
(42317)
City of New York and its neighbourhood.
54191
City of New York: its growth, destinies, and
duties. 20338
City of New-York. . . . Representation of the
Commissioners of the Alms-House.
54073
City of New York the greatest missionary field
on the continent. 80495, note after
90579
City of Newburyport. The mayor's address.
54913
City of Philadelphia. By the Mayor, Recorder,
and Aldermen. (61543)
City of Philadelphia, in the state of Pennsyl-
vania. 5530
City of Portsmouth, N. H. Joint resolutions
of the City Council. (64420)
City of refuge. 46260
City of Richmond business directory and city
guide. (71174)
City of Roxbury. Public cemetery. 73668
City of Saco. Mayor's address. 74778
City of Salem. [Report of a committee and
opinion.] 75648
City of Salem. [Report of the Joint Select
Committee.] 75649
City of Salem. [Report on the Browne, Choate,
and Forrester Funds.] (75647)
City of Salem. [Reports of the City Council.]
75650
City of San Francisco demands justice
28444
City of San Francisco vs. the United States.
76046
City of Sonora Tunnel Company. 86977
City of South Bend, Indiana. The South Bend
Hydraulic Company. 87335
City of Superior, Lake Superior. Its position,
harbor, . . . railroads . . . commerce.
71571, note before 93775
City of the dead. 20026
City of the Mormons. 11476
City of the saints and across the Rocky Moun-
tians. 9497
City of the silent; a poem. 81201
City of the silent. A tribute to the Wood-Lawn
Cemetery. 61184
City of Tornoto and the home district com-
mercial directory. 101212
City of Troy: its commerce, manufactures,
and resources. 37282

City of Washington and its neighborhood.
101920
City of Washington, February 10, 1853. 90869
City of Washington in the year of Washington's
inauguration. 84388
City of Washington. The advantageous situation.
101929
City of Watertown, Wisconsin. 67300
City or house divided against itself. 26167
City ordinance for the prevention of fires.
(10140)
City ordinance on cleaning the streets of
Philadelphia. 61544
City Orphan Asylum, Washington, D. C. see
Washington City Orphan Asylum.
City record. 7042
City Registrar's report. 66255
City scenes. 67616
City school. (47991)
City set on a hill. 94537
City taxation. 17262
City Temperance Society, Albany. see Albany
City Temperance Society.
City that was. 84254
City Tract Society, Philadelphia. see Phila-
delphia City Tract Society.
City Treasurer's accounts and other documents.
(66998)
City Treasurer's statement of the receipts.
54914
City's heart. 13160
Ciudad de los huerfanos. (33557)
Ciudad de los Reyes, Peru. see Lima, Peru.
Ciudad de Santa Fe, Nueva Granda. see Santa
Fe, Colombia.
Ciudad de Santiago de Leon de Caracas. see
Caracas.
Ciudadano. pseud. Importante voto de un
ciudadano. 98658
Ciudadano. pseud. Manifiesto que ofrece.
99611
Ciudadano. pseud. Solicitud de un ciudadano.
86387
Ciudadano. pseud. Treuno de la libertad en
Mexico. 97169
Ciudadano. pseud. Voz de la libertad. see
Funes, Gregorio.
Ciudadano amante de bien publico. pseud. see
T., I. J. pseud.
Ciudadano de Centro-America. pseud. Carta.
32773
Ciudadano de los Estados Unidos. pseud.
America. see Everett, Alexander H.
Ciudadano del Estado de Xalisco. pseud.
Contrato de asociacion. 16183
Ciudadano Don Diego Correa al Escmo. Sr.
Capitan General Gefe Superior Politico
&c. &c. &c. 16830
Ciudadano entusiastica de la prosperidad de su
patria. pseud. Projectos de leyes.
65982, 1st note after 98882
Ciudadano imparcial. pseud. Suplemento a la
exposicion breve y sencilla. 93779
Ciudadano Jose Ruiz. 74007
Ciudadano Juan Jose Nieto. 55274
Ciudadano M. B. pseud. see B., M. pseud.
Ciudadano Mexicano. pseud. Carta. 48318
Ciudadano Mexicano. pseud. Manifestacion.
76735
Ciudadano que la subscribe. pseud. Carta.
see Urbina, Thelesforo Jose de.
Ciudadano que no tomo la mas minima parte en
aquellos acontecimientos. pseud. Pro-
nunciamiento de Perote. 65997
Ciudadanos. 48339

Ciudadanos de esta provincia. 73001
Ciudadanos de Morelia, Mexico. see Morelia, Mexico. Ciudadanos.
Ciudadanos! Papel politico. 13161
Civic. pseud. 95979
Civic. pseud. see Civis. pseud.
Civic [sic] avows himself to be the person (supposed to be) alluded to in the publications of Titus Ironicus and Publicus. 95979
Civil and commercial history of the British West Indies. (21904)
Civil and military life of Andrew Jackson. 35363
Civil and military list of Rhode Island. 1800-1850. 83354
Civil and military list of Rhode Island. 1647-1800. 83353
Civil and military lists of Rhode Island. 83355
Civil and military powers. 97439
Civil and natural history of Jamaica. 8670-8671
Civil and political history of New Jersey. 51265-51266
Civil and political history of the state of Tennessee. 31084, 94814
Civil code of Louisiana. 98104
Civil code of Lower Canada. 10477, (42510)
Civil code of the state of Louisiana. By authority. 42204
Civil code of the state of Louisiana; with annotations. 42205
Civil code of the state of Louisiana; with the statutory amendments, from 1825 to 1853, inclusive. 42206
Civil code of the state of Louisiana; with the statutory amendments from 1825 to 1866 inclusive. 42207
Civil engineer and herald of internal improvement. 37731
Civil fund of California. Speech. (39163)
Civil government. 57596
Civil government, a divine ordinance. 6062
Civil government a sacred trust from God. 20391, 86114
Civil government an ordinance of God. A lecture for the times. (36934)
Civil government an ordinance of God. A sermon addressed to the congregation in Franklin, Mass. 88671
Civil government an ordinance of God; a sermon delivered at Concord. 22298
Civil government an ordinance of God. A sermon delivered in Colchester. 18058
Civil government of God. 90440
Civil government of Rhode Island. 70562
Civil government. Reprinted from the Princeton review. 93196
Civil government the foundation of social happiness. 32308
Civil government, the late conspiracy. 74548
Civil law of Spain and Mexico. (77671)
Civil liberty. A sermon preached August 6, 1863. (21443)
Civil liberty. A sermon preached in Farmington. (64291)
Civil liberty asserted, and the rights of the subject defended. 65458
Civil list of forms of government of the colony and state of New York. 34052, (53599)
Civil magistrates must be just. 12313
Civil magistrates power in matters of religion. (13865)
Civil officer or the whole duty of sheriffs. 13162

Civil officer's assistant. 70714
Civil offices and political ethics. (33995)
Civil, political, and mechanical history of the framework knitters. 31434
Civil, political, professional and ecclesiastical history. 91754
Civil policy of the rising kingdom of Jesus Christ. 22144
Civil prudence recommended to the thirteen United Colonies of North America. 13163
Civil, religious, and masonic services. 45846
Civil, religious, and political history of those islands. 5432
Civil rights bill. Mr. H. J. Raymond's remarks. 68044
Civil rights. Speech of Hon. Milton I. Southard. 88234
Civil ruler, a dignify'd servant of the Lord. 19829
Civil rulers an ordinance of God, for the good of mankind. (41753)
Civil rulers are God's ministers, for the peoples good. 105161
Civil rulers Gods by office, and the duties of such considered and enforced. 103456
Civil rulers the ministers of God, for good to man. 96090
Civil rulers raised up by God to feed his people. 65587
Civil service and Jenckes' bill. 13164
Civil service of the United States of America. Report of Mr. Jenckes. 35982
Civil Service Reform Association, Boston. see Boston Civil Service Reform Association.
Civil service reform. Reprinted from the Penn monthly for November. 73281
Civil service reform. Speech of Hon. Henry Snapp. 85366
Civil service reform. Speech of Hon. Thomas J. Speer. 89251
Civil service. Speech . . . April 5, 1869. 35982
Civil service. Speech . . . delivered in the House of Representatives, April 18, 1872. 76947
Civil service swindle exposed. 85367
Civil state compared to rivers. (11966)
Civil tenure act. 89721-89722, 89724
Civil war; a poem. 13165
Civil war and Negro slavery. (22709)
Civil war in America: a lecture. 28163
Civil war in America: an address read at the last meeting. 82675
Civil war in America: by Wm. H. Russell. 74400
Civil war in America: its causes and objects. 13166
Civil war in America: or, the slaveholders' conspiracy. 11931
Civil war in the United States. 50401
Civil war: its causes, its consequences, its crimes, and its compromises. 4326, 13167
Civil war; its nature and end. (7675), 7679
Civil war, no remedy for secession. 64991
Civil wars between the Picarrists and the Almagrians. 98760
Civilian. Review of the proceedings of the Navy Department. 70250
Civilian. pseud. Rights of neutrals and belligerents. 71373
Civilisation et barbarie. 77070
Civilisations inconnus. 14941
Civiliserte Verdens fremtidige Forhold. 77690
Civilizacion i barbarie en las Pampas Arjentinas. (77077)

Civilizacion y barbaria. (68465)
Civilization. (56792)
Civilization and barbarism. 77078
Civilization i barbarie. 77069
Civilization in New York. 47181
Civilization of African and other barbarous
people. 3217
Civilization of the Indian natives. 35413
Civilization, or the Indian chief and the
British pastor. 13168
Civilized America. 28339
Civis. pseud. Appeal to the honorable the
members of the Senate. 53533
Civis. pseud. Dissertation of the nature and
effects of lottery systems. (13170)
Civis. pseud. Following publication. 13171,
24958
Civis. pseud. Letter to the Reverend John
Wesley. 102702
Civis. pseud. Real estate and the betterment
law. (13172)
Civis. pseud. Remarks on the bankrupt law.
(13173)
Civis. pseud. Remarks on the embargo law.
13174, 69461
Civis. pseud. Romanism incompatible with
republican institutions. 72989
Civis. pseud. To the freemen of Pennsyl-
vania. see Mifflin, Thomas. supposed
author
Civis. pseud. To the public. 95979
Civis. pseud. Mr. Webster's Andover address.
see Stuart, Moses.
Civis, G. W. 13169
Civis Anglicus. pseud. Voice from the mother
land. 13175
Civitas Mexicus interior. 11715, (75565)-
75566
Civitates orbis terrarum. 7448, 73000
Cl. Prolemaei Alexandrini, Geographiae libri
octo. 66491
Claar vertooch. 7547
Clack, Franklin Hulse. (13176)
Clack, Louise. 13177-(13178)
Cladera, Christobal. (13179)
Claer licht ofte vertooch. 102886
Claesse, Lawrence. tr. 13180-13181, (50765)
Claeszoon, Aris. 77620
Clagett, Nicholas, successively Bishop of St.
Davids, and Exeter, d. 1746. 13183
Claggett, Clifton. 13182, 13184
Claggett, Nicholas. see Clagett, Nicholas,
successively Bishop of St. Davids, and
Exeter, d. 1746.
Claggett, R. 13185
Claggett, Thomas John, Bp. 13186, 45299,
45304
Claggett, William, fl. 1721. 13187
Claggett, William, 1790-1870. 13188-13190
Claiborne, J. F. H. 13191-13192
Claiborne, William Charles Cole, 1775-1817.
33150, 42211, 42227, 94756 see also
Louisiana (Territory) Governor, 1805-
1812 (Claiborne) Louisiana. Governor,
1812-1816 (Claiborne)
Claim against Holland. 105162
Claim and answer in the case of William
Cunningham & Co. 17975, 84842
Claim and answer; with the subsequent pro-
ceedings in the case of Andrew Allen,
Esq. 782, 84842
Claim and answer with the subsequent pro-
ceedings, in the case of the Right Rev-
erent Charles Inglis. 34761, 84842
Claim for fresh evidence on the subject of the
slave trade considered. 13193

Claim for interest on the advances of Massa-
chusetts in the war of 1812-15. 13194
Claim for military service. 45678
Claim for rent, supplies, etc. (78878)
Claim for the mines and land of New Almaden.
4702
Claim of Amasa Stetson. 91367
Claim of Baron De Kalb and heirs. 7720
Claim of Bertram H. Howell. 48340
Claim of De Beaumarchais' heir against the
United States. (4179)
Claim of Ebenezer Oliver and others. (52708)
Claim of H. Haupt & Co. 30859
Claim of John Livingston. 41621
Claim of Jonas P. Leavy. 17292
Claim of Pelagie Ferribault. 69697
Claim of Richard W. Meade upon the United
States. 47236
Claim of the American loyalists reviewed and
maintained. 26424
Claim of the Church of Rome. 63843
Claim of the colonies to an exemption from
internal taxes. (23375), 38178
Claim of the inhabitants of the town of Newark.
56800
Claim of the North Carolina Indians. (55600)
Claim of the United States to Oregon. 9943,
57565
Claim of the Upper Mississippi Company.
98097
Claim of William Vans. 98553
Claim or title of Mr. James Brown. 8497
Claim to the Lord's table. 67164
Claim, with documents and correspondence.
91366
Claimant. pseud. Sketch of the claims. see
Purviance, Robert. supposed author
Claimants of Land Purchased of Connecticut,
Commonly Called the Gore. petitioners
15683, 47722
Claimants on Mexico. 48341
Claimants under Georgia, &c. petitioners
27069
Claimants Under the Original Patentee of a
Large Tract of Land, in Philips' Upper
Patent. plaintiffs 26969, 101256
Claims against the United States. 13196
Claims against Venezuela. 24666
Claims Agent of the Rhode Island Brigade. see
Rhode Island. Militia. Rhode Island
Brigade. Claims Agent.
Claims and resources of the West Indian
colonies. 90305
Claims for improvements, by the state of
Georgia. 104879
Claims for the use and destruction of private
property. 71573
Claims of abolitionism on the Church of Christ.
37883
Claims of Africa. 49729
Claims of agriculture to be regarded as a
distinct science. 103314
Claims of American citizens against the French
republic. 13195
Claims of Andrew Jackson to the office of
president. 35391
Claims of Beaumarchais' heir against the
United States. 12598
Claims of benevolence upon the young men of
the community. 106161
Claims of Caesar. 61010
Claims of citizens of the United States of
America. 23248
Claims of civil and ecclesiastical history.
21721
Claims of civil government. 22784

Claims of colleges to public favor. 26358
Claims of classical culture. (82463)
Claims of congregational churches. 2566
Claims of "Episcopal bishops," examined. (21137)
Claims of God to recognition in the assassination of President Lincoln. 23876
Claims of Harvard College upon its sons. 58316
Claims of Hobart College for support. 90527
Claims of labor. 14908
Claims of Mexican citizens against the United States for Indian depredations. 48342, (58272)
Claims of New England society upon the young student. 22327
Claims of our country on its literary men. 5076
Claims of past and future generations on civil rulers. 89744
Claims of pastors of churches. 41302
Claims of peace on cities. (13197)
Claims of Peru and Bolivia in regard to this alliance. (58526)
Claims of puritanism. 19854
"Claims of seamen." 28818
Claims of seamen. A sermon. 89324
Claims of the Academy of Natural Sciences of Philadelphia to public favor. 74181
Claims of the Africans. 81931
Claims of the age on the work of the evangelist. (71517)
Claims of the British West Indian colonies. 36646
Claims of the catholics to a portion of the Common School Fund. 54195
Claims of the Christian ministry to an adequate and liberal support. 85272
Claims of the Christian ministry to an adequate support. 85271, 85331
Claims of the Church of England seriously examined. (47141)
Claims of the churchmen and dissenters of Upper Canada. 74549
Claims of the citizens of the United States on Denmark examined. 18084
Claims of the country on American females. 17287
Claims of the Delaware and Raritan Canal. 19411
Claims of the Episcopal Church. (51242)
Claims of the Free Church of Scotland. 85273, 85290
Claims of the Jews to an equality of rights. 39835
Claims of the militia. 81621
Claims of the missionary enterprise on the medical professions. 43277
Claims of the officers of the revolution. 30837
Claims of the Ohio Baptist Book and Tract Society. 56971
Claims of the order on the religious community. 92017
Claims of the poor. 103047
Claims of the Presbyterian Church. 85274, 85331
Claims of the public on the minister. 90095
Claims of the suffering Negroes in America. 71812
Claims of the Tabernacle Church. 75651, 75655, 2d note after 94170
Claims of Thomas Jefferson to the presidency. 8573, 35923
Claims of Tufts College on its first students. 31589

Claims on Mexico. 76827
Claims on Mexico presented before the Board of Commissioners. 17290
Claims on the United States. 53600
Claims thereto of England and America considered. 81339
Claims to the Oregon Territory considered. 95370
Clair, Alexander St. see St. Clair, Alexander.
Clair, Arthur St. see St. Clair, Arthur.
Clair, Henry St. see St. Clair, Henry.
Clair, Thomas Staunton St. see St. Clair, Thomas Staunton.
Clair Roy, -------. 13198
Clairac, ------ de. 13199
Clairaut, ------. 46946
Claire Deville, Charles Joseph Saint. see Saint-Claire Deville, Charles Joseph, 1814-1876.
Clairiere du bois des hogues. 4531
Clairvoyance. 13200
Clajon, William. petitioner 104017
Clamor de amante de los milicianos. 50074
Clamor de la justicia. 98958-98959
Clamor de la justicia, e idioma de la verdad. 98957
Clamor de la verdad al Excmo. Sr. D. Jose de S. Martin. 98791
Clamor de la verdad por un Americano. 98792
Clamor publico. eds. 92607
Clamores de la America. 44540, 94831
Clamorgan Land Association. 94870, 102303, 103424
Clamorgan's case. 103424
Clamorgan's title to land on the Mississippi. 94870, 102303
Clandestine address to the electors. (22680), 97067
Clap, Eliza. 13201
Clap, Nathaniel. 13202-13205, 106289
Clap, Roger, 1609-1691. (13206)-13209, 106052
Clap, Thomas, 1703-1767. (13212)-13220, 18587, (26354), (38374), 104986, 105760, 105826, 105827, 105894, 105895, note after 105924, 3d note after 105937 see also Yale University. President.
Clap, Thomas, 1705-1774. (13210)-13211
Clapp, -------, fl. 1864. 69818
Clapp, A. 13221
Clapp, Alexander Huntington. 13222
Clapp, Charles B. 13223
Clapp, Dexter. 13224
Clapp, Ebenezer. (20619)
Clapp, J. 53519
Clapp, John Bouve. 84781
Clapp, John M. 105848
Clapp, Otis. (13225)-13226
Clapp, Thaddeus. 37289
Clapp, Theodore. 13227-13229
Clapp, Theodore. defendant before Presbytery 13230
Clapp, William Warland. (13231)
Clappier, Hilarion. 13232
Clar de kitchen. 86953
Clara, of Assisi, Saint, d. 1253. 68839
Clara, Sulfras de Santa. see Sulfras de Santa Clara. Fray
Clara Howard. 8457
Clara Moreland. (4723)-(4724)
Clara y sucinta exposicion. 13233
Claramond, Privat Joseph. see Pelet de la Lozere, Privat Joseph Claramond, Comte.
Claraz, George. 31626
Clarck, Banjamin. see Clark, Benjamin.
Clare, Edward. note after 92624
Clare, Marie J. defendant 13234

Claremont, N. H. Soldiers Monument. 13235
Claremont, N. Y. Dale Cemetery. 18302
Clarence, William Henry, Duke of. see
   William IV, King of England, 1765-1837.
Clarence. A drama. 85451
Clarence; or, a tale of our own times. 78769,
   78807
Clarendon, ----------. reporter 79092,
   81932
Clarendon, Edward Hyde, 3d Earl of, 1661-
   1723. 4033, 26145, 53436, 53729,
   53849 see also New York (Colony)
   Governor, 1702-1708 (Clarendon)
Clarendon, George William Frederick Villiers,
   4th Earl of, 1800-1870. 69708, 74366
Clarendon Harris's Circulating Library, Wor-
   cester, Mass. 105386
Clarendon's accurate and copious account of
   the debates in the House of Commons.
   81932
Clarendon's parliamentary chronicle. 79092
Claret de Fleurieu, Charles Pierre, Comte de.
   see Fleurieu, Charles Pierre Claret de,
   Comte de.
Clari. 84786
Clarideo. pseud. Justicia en defensa de la
   verdad. see Verdugo, Manuel Jose.
Clarigny, Athanase Cucheval. see Cucheval-
   Clarigny, Athanase.
Clarimonde. A tale of New Orleans life.
   13237
Clarin Bayames n°. I. 97037
Clarion and Tennessee state gazette. 94786
Clariosophic Society of the College of South
   Carolina. see South Carolina. Uni-
   versity. Clariosophic Society.
Clarissa. pseud. Poetical fate book. see
   Snelling, ----------.
Clarissimo Johanni Adair, Armigero, Guber-
   natori . . . Reipublicae Kentuckiensis.
   96467
Clarissimo viro Bilibaldo Pyrckhaymer Pat-
   ricio Haudno Senatori Norico. 77804
Clark, --------. defendant 79759
Clark, --------. geologist 49247
Clark, A. 3728
Clark, A. B. 85143-85144
Clark, A. N. 13248
Clark, A. S. 13249
Clark, Aaron. 13238-(13240)
Clark, Aaron. reporter (28213)
Clark, Alexander, 1834-1879. 13241-13246,
   63100
Clark, Alonzo. 13247
Clark, Ansel R. 13250
Clark, Appleton P. 13251
Clark, Benjamin. 59710, (59719)
Clark, Benjamin C. 13252-(13254), 26975,
   4th note after 96480
Clark, Benjamin Franklin, 1808-1879. 13255-
   (13256), 33944
Clark, Charles. 10448, 13257-13261
Clark, Charles R. 13262
Clark, Christopher. 13263
Clark, Clinton. 13264
Clark, Daniel, 1766-1813. (13265), 104027
Clark, Daniel, 1809-1891. 13266
Clark, Daniel Atkinson. 1314, 13267-13269,
   21959, note after 102377
Clark, Daniel Wasgatt, Bp., 1812-1871.
   13270-13271, 24380, 82424
Clark, E. B. 11951, 13274
Clark, Eber L. 13272
Clark, Edward. 42982
Clark, Edward L. 13275
Clark, Elijah. 13276

Clark, Emmons. 13273
Clark, Ferdinand. (13277)
Clark, Frederick G. (13278)-13280
Clark, Gaylord J. 13281
Clark, George D. (13282)
Clark, George Edward. (13283)
Clark, George Faber. 13284
Clark, George H. (13285)
Clark, George K. 13286
Clark, George Rogers, 1752-1818. (13287),
   100036
Clark, George Washington, b. 1812. (13288)-
   13291
Clark, Hamlet. 13292
Clark, Harry S. 90321
Clark, Henry. 13293-13295
Clark, Henry Grafton. (13297), 34822, 36581,
   36605, 36647
Clark, Henry James. 85072
Clark, Henry Selby, 1809-1869. 13406
Clark, Hiram C. (13296)
Clark, Horace Francis, 1815-1873. 13298
Clark, Hubert Lyman. 85072
Clark, Hyron H. 13339
Clark, Isaac. (13299)
Clark, J. 77731
Clark, J. V. H. 84484
Clark, J. W., fl. 1842. 13300
Clark, J. W., fl. 1866. ed. 19286
Clark, James. 13301
Clark, Sir James. Bart. 13302
Clark, James C. 13303
Clark, James H. 13304
Clark, Jefferson. 13305
Clark, Joel W. 13306
Clark, John. 35869
Clark, John, fl. 1819. 13309
Clark, John, 1844-1870. 13311
Clark, John, fl. 1856. 13310
Clark, John, fl. 1865. 13312
Clark, John A. 13313
Clark, John Chamberlain, 1793-1852. 13314-
   13315
Clark, John S. cartographer (80023)
Clark, Jonas, 1730-1805. 13316-(13317)
Clark, Jonathan. (13318)
Clark, Rev. Joseph. 13320
Clark, Joseph, 1751-1813. 13321
Clark, Joseph, 1759-1828. 13319
Clark, Joseph G. 13322
Clark, Joseph Henry. 13323
Clark, Joseph S. 13324-13327
Clark, Joshua V. H. (13328)-(13330), 57605,
   84484
Clark, L. M. 13333
Clark, Lewis Gaylord, 1810-1873. 13331-
   13332, 34099
Clark, Lincoln. 13334
Clark, Lot. (13335)
Clark, Mary. 13336-13337
Clerk, Myron Holley, 1806-1892. (36456),
   53616 see also New York (State) Gov-
   ernor, 1855-1857 (Holley)
Clark, N. G. 84929
Clark, N. J. 13323
Clark, Nelson. 13340
Clark, O. 13342
Clark, Orin. (13343)
Clark, Orton S. (13344)
Clark, Peter, 1693-1768. 12331, 13345-13350,
   101218, 102425-102426
Clark, Peter, 1784-1853. (13351)-13352
Clark, Peter H. 13353
Clark, Pitt. see Clarke, Pitt, 1763-1835.
Clark, Robert. 50892

Clark, Rufus W. 13356-13365, 93197
Clark, S. A. 21495
Clark, S. M. 69940 see also U. S.
National Currency Bureau. First
Division. Chief.
Clark, Samuel, fl. 1839. 27924, 94242
Clark, Samuel A. (13366)-(13367)
Clark, Sereno D. 13369
Clark, Stephen Merril. defendant (13370),
96848
Clark, Strong. 13371
Clark, Thaddeus. 13372
Clark, Thomas. plaintiff 53075
Clark, Thomas, fl. 1661. (13373)
Clark, Thomas, 1787-1860. (13374)-13378
Clark, Thomas E. 104412
Clark, Thomas G. (13379)
Clark, Thomas M. 13380-13385
Clark, Uriah. 13386
Clark, W. A. 13387-13388
Clark, William, 1770-1838. 21247, (24507)-
24509, (40825), 62506, 84162, 96499,
96632-96633, 96637, 96638, 96647,
96651, 96662, 96679, 96708, 96675-
96676, 96683 see also U. S. Com-
missioner to the Great and Little Osage
Tribes of Indians. U. S. Commissioner
to the Iowa Tribe of Indians and the
Band of Sacs and Foxes of the Missouri.
U. S. Commissioner to the Kansas
Indians. U. S. Commissioner to the
Shawnee Indians. U. S. Commissioners
to the Confederated Tribes of Sacs and
Foxes, the Mdewakanton, Wahpekute,
Wahpeton and Sisseton Bands or Tribes
of Sioux, the Omahas, Iowas, Oto, and
Missouri Indians. U. S. Commissioners
to the Kaskaskia and Peoria Indians.
U. S. Commissioners to the Kickapoo
Indians. U. S. Commissioners to the
Michigan Indians. U. S. Commissioners
to the Piankshaw and Wea Indians. U. S.
Superintendent of Indian Affairs.
Clark, William Adolphus. 90648
Clark, William H. 9976
Clark, William J. 13389
Clark, William R. 13391-13392, 63162
Clark, Willard. defendant (13390)
Clark, Willis Gaylord. 13332
Clark & Co. firm see Leffingwell, Clark &
Co. firm
Clark (Caleb) publisher 87006
Clark (N. L.) & Co. firm 13341
Clarke, --------. RN 25142
Clarke, --------, fl. 1652. 104333
Clarke, -------, fl. 1756. 106391
Clarke, A. B. 13393
Clarke, Abraham Lynson. 13394-(13395)
Clarke, Adam, 1762?-1832. 82824
Clarke, Bayard, 1815-1884. 13396
Clarke, Calvin. (13397)
Clarke, Carey L. 50400
Clarke, Charles Ezra, 1789-1863. 13398,
37885
Clarke, E. B. 18814, 30130 see also Com-
mittee of Pastors in Hamden County,
Mass.
Clarke, Edward, fl. 1867. 13400
Clarke, Edward, d. 1891. 13399
Clarke, Edward Hammond, 1820-1877. ed.
(13441)
Clarke, F. W. 13401
Clarke, George, 1676-1760. (13402), 98434,
98436 see also New York (Colony)
Council. President.
Clarke, George W. 91043

Clarke, H. C. 13404-13405
Clarke, Henry. 13403
Clarke, Isaac Edwards, 1830-1907. (13407),
84499
Clarke, J. A. 13408
Clarke, J. F. ed. 102993
Clarke, James. petitioner (60307)
Clarke, James Freeman, 1810-1888. (10263),
(13409)-13412, 13414-13418
Clarke, James Freeman, 1810-1888. supposed
author 81836
Clarke, James Stanier. 13419-13421
Clarke, John, Lieut. of Marines 13422
Clarke, John, of Philadelphia 13425
Clarke, John. reporter (18048)
Clarke, John, 1609-1676. 13307-13308, (13865)
Clarke, John, 1687-1734. 73398-73400, (73402)
Clarke, John, 1755-1798. 13423-(13424), 7th
note after 100870, 103423, 105012
Clarke, John, 1755-1798. incorrectly supposed
author 21975, 75875, 8th note after
100870
Clarke, John, fl. 1830. 13427
Clarke, John, fl. 1850. 13426
Clarke, John Hopkins, 1789-1870. (13428)-
(13429)
Clarke, John J. 73649 see also Roxbury,
Mass. Mayor, 1846-1847 (Clarke)
Clarke, Jonathan. defendant 6326, 1st note
after 96956, 1st note after 97284
Clarke, Jonas. 13420-(13431)
Clarke, Joseph S. (13432), 15479
Clarke, L. H. reporter 31715, 49074, 53915,
55375
Clarke, Lewis. (13433)-(13434)
Clarke, Mrs. M. 13436A
Clarke, McDonald, 1798-1842. (13435), (54082),
(69154), (70978), 83665, note before
94463
Clarke, Mary Cowden-, 1809-1898. 13436,
80729
Clarke, Mary Jones (Stimpson) 1785-1866.
(13441)
Clarke, Mary Victoria (Novello) see Clarke,
Mary Cowden-, 1809-1898.
Clarke, Matthew St. Clair. 1228, (12457),
13437-13439, 25053, 90114 see also
U. S. Commissioners to the Cherokee
Indians.
Clarke, Milton. (13434)
Clarke, O. L. 13440
Clarke, Pitt, 1763-1835. 5283, 13354-13355,
(13441)
Clarke, Richard. 13442, 86774
Clarke, Robert, 1829-1899. ed. (22918),
(47016), 82766, 84619
Clarke, S. 18615
Clarke, S. M. 2840, 29386
Clarke, Samuel, 1599-1683. (13443)-13450,
44124
Clarke, Samuel, fl. 1644. 33630
Clarke, Samuel, b. 1721? 92709
Clarke, Samuel, 1791-1859. (13451)-13454
Clarke, Samuel C. 13455-13459
Clarke, Samuel F. 13460
Clarke, Sara J. see Lippincott, Sara J.
(Clarke)
Clarke, Sidney, 1831-1909. 13462-13463
Clarke, Sir Simon Houghton. 95959
Clarke, Sir Simon Houghton. supposed author
86622, 3d note after 102803
Clarke, Thomas. 13464
Clarke, Thomas Curtis. 13465
Clarke, Uriah. 13466
Clarke, Walter. 55846 see also Northumber-
land County, Pa. Sub Lieutenant.

Clarke, Walter, 1812-1871. 13467-13469
Clarke, William. 13470-13471
Clarke, William J. plaintiff 62051 see also
   Delaware. Treasurer. plaintiff
Clarke (Robert) Co. firm publishers 94882
Clarke Institution for Deaf Mutes, Northamp-
   ton, Mass. 13473
Clarke's confederate household almanac.
   13405
Clark's miscellany in prose and verse.
   (13299)
Clarkson, J. G. 60529
Clarkson, Matthew. 13474
Clarkson, Thomas, 1760-1846. 13475-13499,
   20095, 25146, (25478), 34179, (43643),
   70902, 90778, 91011, note after 91132,
   1st note after 93370, note after 93611,
   97154, 100979
Clarkson, Thomas Streatfield. 13500
Clarorum ligurum elogia. 24942
Clarsach Albin, and other poems. 50892
Clarum et venerabile nomen. (5938)
Clary, ------- Le Pelletier du. see Le
   Pelletier du Clary, -------.
Clary, Dexter. 13501
Clary, Timothy Farrar. 13502
Clasen, Jan. 5046
Clason, A. W. (13503)
Clason, Isaac Staar. 13504
Class-book of poetry. 71809
Class book of prose and poetry. 71232
Class book of zoology. 35525
Class depotism. 43334
Class of alumni of Dartmouth College in 1811.
   18619
Class of 1858. 30501
Class of 1814. 105881
Class of 1814—Yale College. 105881
Class of 1861. (80037)
Class of 1831. 64977
Class poem. 104791
Classed catalogue. 10136
Classic. 88628
Classical and Grammar School, East Hartford,
   Conn. see East Hartford, Conn. Clas-
   sical and Grammar School.
Classical and High School, Salem, Mass. see
   Salem Classical and High School, Salem,
   Mass.
Classical and Military Academy, Cooperstown,
   N. Y. see Cooperstown Classical and
   Military Academy.
Classical and Scientific Institute, Hightstown,
   N. J. see New Jersey Classical and
   Scientific Institute, Hightstown, N. J.
Classicos e romanticos. 49989
Classification and synopsis of the trochilidae.
   85072
Classification des peuples anciens et modernes.
   2856
Classification of anatomy and physiology.
   83664
Classification of insects from embryological
   data. 85072
Classification of mankind by the hair and wool
   of their heads. 8676
Classification of mollusca. 50915
Classification of the coleoptera of North
   America. 39662
Classification of the financial report. 76689
Classified arrangement of the doctrinal ser-
   mons. 83256
Classified business directory [of Cincinnati.]
   13085
Classified business mirror for 1864. 14894
Classified catalogue of the birds of Canada.
   73333

Classified catalogue of the lepidoptera of
   Canada. 73334
Classified catalogue of the Mercantile Library
   of San Francisco. 76057
Classified catalogue of the Portland Library.
   64386
Classified index to bills introduced into the
   Assembly. 53601
Classified list of Smithsonian publications.
   85037
Classified mercantile directory for . . . New-
   York and Brooklyn. 54459
Classified statement of the expenditures and
   receipts of the central treasury. 76686
Classified view of the Christian sects. 5728
Classis of Albany. see Reformed Church in
   America. Classis of Albany.
Classis of Geneva. see Reformed Church in
   America. Classis of Geneva.
Classis of Montgomery. see Reformed Church
   in America. Classis of Montgomery.
Classis of New Jersey. see Reformed Church
   in America. Classis of New Jersey.
Classis of New York. see Reformed Church
   in America. Classis of New York.
Classis van Amsterdam. see Nederlandsche
   Hervormde Kerk. Classis van Amsterdam.
Classis van Delft. see Nederlandsche Her-
   vormde Kerk. Classis van Delft.
Classology: an anacreontic ode. (5343)
Classon, -------, fl. 1795. 96447
Claude, William Tell. (13506)
Claude Gueux. 33614
Claudet, M., fl. 1844. engr. 93143
Claudet, M., fl. 1862. 8095, 13507
Claudio Gueux. (33613)
Clavdii Bartholomaei Morisoti. Pervviana.
   (50722)
Clavdii Ptolemaei Alexandrini Geographicae
   enarrationis libri octo. (66483), (66485)
Claudii Ptolemaei Alexandrini Geographiae
   libri octo. 66494
Clavdii Ptholemaei Alexandrini Liber geogra-
   phiae cvm tabvlis. (66477)
Clavdii Ptolemaei Alexandrini Mathematicos
   principis. 66481
Clavdii Ptholemei Alexandrini Philosophi cos-
   mographia. 66470
Clavddii Ptolemaei Geographicae enarrationis
   libri octo. (66482)
Claudii Ptolemaei Tabulae geographicae.
   66498
Claudii Ptolemei viri Alexandrini Mathematice
   discipline. (66478)
Claus, Daniel. ed. 57489
Clausen, A. C. tr. 16508
Clausen, Claus Lauridsen. 13508
Claussen, ---------, Chevalier. (13509)
Clausson, L. J. 13510-13511, 40930 see also
   Santo Domingo (French Colony) Commis-
   saires des Colons [a la Convention Nationale.]
Clausson, Niels Christian, 1724-1794. 13512
Clausura fluvial del Brasil. 7518
Clava del Indio. 74629
Clave. Periodico politico y noticioso. 13513
Clavel, Robert. 13514, 17105
Claverack, N. Y. Hudson River Institute. see
   Hudson River Institute, Claverack, N. Y.
Clavers, Mary. pseud. Emigrant's home. see
   Kirkland, Caroline M. (Stanbury)
Clavers, Mary. pseud. New home, who'll follow?
   see Kirkland, Caroline M. (Stanbury)
Claviere, Etienne, 1735-1793. (8016), 8027,
   8030, 8035, 13515-13517, 40661, 85808
Clavigero, Francisco Javier, 1731-1787.
   13518-13524, (58392), 71989, 71995

Clavis prophetarum. 99529
Clavis, qua mens humana tam in diuinis quam in humanis pertinget. 64521
Clawson, D. L. 90787
Clawson, Isaiah Dunn, 1822-1879. 13525
Claxton, Christopher. (13526)-13528
Claxton, R. Bethel. 13529
Claxton, Timothy. 13530
Clay, Cassius Marcellus, 1810-1903. (13532)-13526, 47179-(47180), 68311, 88295, 95124
Clay, Clement Claiborne, 1819-1882. 13531
Clay, Henry, 1777-1852. (13537)-13551, 13553, 27375, (29314), 35348, 44040, (73530), 81954, 81981, 83279, 89213, 93288, 95067, 95124, 96362, 101069, note after 102304
Clay, Henry, 1777-1852. mediumistic author 58750
Clay, Henry, 1777-1852. supposed author 30833
Clay, James Brown, 1817-1864. 13568-13569
Clay, Jeru Curtis. (13560)
Clay, Joseph. 13571
Clay, Mary Rogers. 84935
Clay, Thomas S. (13572)
Clay and Frelinghuysen. 4623
Clay family. 84935
Clay Lick, Ohio. Celebration of American Independence, 1869. see Licking County Pioneer Society. Celebration of American Independence, Clay Lick, Ohio, 1869.
Clay minstrel. 13555, (41503)
Clay Monument Association of New York State. see New York State Auxiliary Clay Monument Association.
Clayborne, Thomas. 66686
Clayonian lectures. (54872)
Claypool, James. 66926
Claypoole, David C. ed. and publisher 79729, 84620, 101577, 101579-101580, 101686
Claypoole's American daily advertiser. 79729, 84620, 101577, 101579-101580, 101686
Clayton, A. S. comp. 27029
Clayton, Augustin Smith, 1783-1839. 13574, 99823
Clayton, John, fl. 1688. (3808)-3809, (13575), 28923-28924, 49438
Clayton, John Middleton, 1796-1856. (13576), (33581), (69842) see also U. S. Department of State.
Clayton, Powell, 1833-1914. 74138
Clayton, Th. 13579
Clayton, W. 13580-13581
Clayton and Bulwer Convention, 19th April, 1850. 13578
Clayton-Bulwer treaty. 89991
Cle de la connaissance. 73268
Cleansing our way in youth press'd. 25408
Clear and certain truths. 13582
Clear and concise statement. 54196, 70003
Clear and succinct account of North America. 13583
Clear demonstration. (73767)
Clear idea of the genuine and uncorrupted British constitution. 13584, 15516, 48860
Clear light put out in obscure darkness. 24387, 95579
Clear sun-shine of the Gospel. 80205, note before 92797
Clear view of the laws. 16040
Cleare and evident way of enriching the nations. 67599
Clearfield Coal and Lumber Company. 13585, (59977)

Clearing House Association. Boston. see Boston Clearing House Association.
Clearing House Association, New York. see New York Clearing House Association.
Clearing House Association, Philadelphia. see Philadelphia Clearing House Association.
Cleark, John. see Clarke, John, 1609-1676.
Cleary, Nathaniel Greene. 13586
Cleary (William P.) & Co. firm (13587)
Cleaveland, Elisha Lord. 13588-13590, 64304, 89199
Cleaveland, Henry W. 13591
Cleaveland, John, writer on banks and finance 13599-13601
Cleaveland, John, 1722-1799. 13592-(13597), 32316, 47139, 92709, 97539, 103319, 103322
Cleaveland, John, fl. 1812. 13598
Cleaveland, John P. 13602
Cleaveland, Moses. 13603
Cleaveland, Nehemiah, 1796-1877. 13604-(13609), (28695), 28700, 74169
Cleaveland, Parker. 13610-13612, 77910, 85072
Cleaveland. see also Cleveland.
Cleavenger, William S. (13613)
Cleaver, William, successively Bishop of Chester, Bangor, and St. Asaph, 1742-1815. 13614
Cleeve, C. W. 64962
Clef de la case de l'oncle Tom. 92414
Cleland, John. 13615-13616, 2d note after 96139
Cleland, T. H. 33787
Cleland, Thomas, 1778-1858. 92025, 92029
Clemencet, Charles. 101348-101350
Clemencia. 29122
Clemency of the divine government a cause for thanksgiving. 43508
Clemens, Jeremiah, 1814-1865. 13617-13621, 66108
Clemens, Orion. 13622
Clemens, Samuel Langhorne, 1835-1910. 13623
Clement V, Pope, 1264-1314. 68841 see also Catholic Church. Pope, 1305-1314 (Clement V)
Clement VII, Pope, 1478-1534. 10984, (13624) see also Catholic Church. Pope, 1523-1534 (Clement VII)
Clement VIII, Pope, 1536-1605. 51205, 76885 see also Catholic Church. Pope, 1592-1605 (Clement VIII)
Clement IX, Pope, 1600-1669. 24227, 73176 see also Catholic Church. Pope, 1667-1669 (Clement IX)
Clement X, Pope, 1590-1676. 9122, 13625, 68434 see also Catholic Church. Pope, 1670-1676 (Clement X)
Clement XI, Pope, 1649-1721. 68845 see also Catholic Church. Pope, 1700-1721 (Clement XI)
Clement XIII, Pope, 1693-1769. (48448), 58289, 93811 see also Catholic Church. Pope, 1758-1769 (Clement XIII)
Clement XIV, Pope, 1705-1774. 9122, 13626-13627, (58288), 68232, 68247 see also Catholic Church. Pope, 1769-1774 (Clement XIV)
Clement, Charles. (13628)
Clement, Cora. 13629
Clement, F. 101348-101350
Clement, J. 13630
Clement, Jonathan. 13631
Clement, M. A. 77362
Clemente, Claudio. 13632
Clementi, --------. 9586

Clementiae amator. pseud. True description. 13633, 2d note after 97114

Clements, Francis C. 18162

Clements, William J. defendant 18815, 27020

Clements (J.) firm publishers 81217

Clemo, Ebenezer. (13634)-13635

Clemson, Thomas Green, 1807-1888. 85819, 97803

Cleomedes. 65940-65941

Clephane, James O. reporter (30490), 89380

Clerambaut, -------. 48894

Clerc, Lawrent. 13636

Clerc, Pret of Le Pre aux Clercs. pseud. Book of the drama. see Pray, Isaac C.

Clerck, N. de. 13637

Clercq, Christian le. see Le Clercq, Christian.

Clerge Canadien venge par ses ennemis. 10392, 39624, 43857, 99772

Clergy and common schools. 25330

Clergy in Maryland. 807

Clergy not recruiting agents. 13639

Clergy of America. 4399, (13638)

Clergy of New England. petitioners 93655

Clergy of New-York and New-Jersey. see Church of England in America. New Jersey. Clergy. and Church of England in America. New York. Clergy.

Clergy of Philadelphia. see Philadelphia Clergy.

Clergy of the C. S. A. 408

Clergy of Various Denominations, in Philadelphia. see Philadelphia. Clergy of Various Denominations. petitioners

Clergy of Virginia. pseud. Loyal address. 42545, 5th note after 100484

Clergy reserve question. 74550, 96371

Clergy reserves. 92639-92640

Clergy reserves alienation. 19211

Clergy reserves: their history and present position. 41309

Clergy Society of Upper Canada. see Upper Canada Clergy Society.

Clergyman. pseud. ed. 73317

Clergyman. pseud. Full, strong, and clear refutation. (76341)

Clergyman. pseud. ed. The mormons. see F., W. F. pseud. ed.

Clergyman. pseud. Observations on the present state of religion in Maryland. see Duke, William.

Clergyman. pseud. Proposals for the consideration. 66022

Clergyman. pseud. Reign of felicity. see Spence, Thomas. supposed author

Clergyman. pseud. Review of New England politics. see Thomson, Ignatius.

Clergyman. pseud. Sketches for the fireside. 81549

Clergyman. pseud. Some account of Maria Hughes. 86568

Clergyman. pseud. Some questions and answers. 86722

Clergyman. pseud. Spirit of dissent. see Gillmor, William. supposed author

Clergyman in America. pseud. Epistle to the Hon. Arthur Dobbs. see Sterling, James.

Clergy-man in the country. pseud. Letter from a clergy-man in the country. 66929

Clergyman in town. pseud. Cheat unmask'd. 12358, 40302, 59267, 59269, 62218

Clergyman in town. pseud. Letter. 12358, 40302, 59267, 59269, 62218

Clergyman in Virginia. pseud. Poem. 96323

Clergyman of Leicestershire. pseud. Serious and impartial observations. 79252

Clergyman of Massachusetts. pseud. Scripture catechism. 78495

Clergyman of the Church of England. pseud. Letter to the clergy of the Church of England. (72332)

Clergyman of the Church of England. pseud. Strictures on female education. see Bennett, John.

Clergyman of the Episcopal Church. pseud. In perils by my own countrymen. 37039

Clergyman of the Protestant Episcopal Church. pseud. Bishop Hopkins' letter on slavery ripped up. (32928)

Clergyman of the Protestant Episcopal Church. pseud. Scripture doctrine with regard to slavery. see Peyton, William M. supposed author

Clergyman, who resides in a distant part of the kingdom. pseud. Thoughts on the present war. 95720

Clergyman who served Bishop Phelan's last mass. pseud. Life of the Right Reverend Patrick Phelan. (61352)

Clergyman's almanac for 1811. (13640)

Clergyman's daughter. 103478

Clergyman's hymn book. 103337

Clergyman's looking-glass; being a history. (82477)

Clergyman's looking-glass. (No. IV.) 82479

Clergyman's looking-glass, or ancient and modern things contrasted. 82475-82476

Clergyman's looking glass. The champion of reviling. 82478

Clergyman's minor almanac. (13640)

Clergyman's wife and other sketches. 71560

Clergymen of Hanover County, Va. pseud. 27292

Clergymen of the Cumberland Presbyterian Church. see Cumberland Presbyterian Church in the U. S. Clergy.

Clergymen of the Protestant Episcopal Church. see Protestant Episcopal Church in the U. S. A. Clergy.

Clerical and political corruption exposed. 32749

Clerical Benevolent Association of the Diocese of Baltimore. see Baltimore (Archdiocese) Clerical Benevolent Association.

Clerical candidates. A poem. 13641

Clerical directory. 8554

Clerical discipline. 24280

Clerical treatise on the endemic fevers of the West Indies. (23196)

Clericus. pseud. Progressive democracy in religion. 65975

Clerk. pseud. Clerkships in Washington. 13644

Clerk, John, 1728-1812. 103458A-103459

Clerk in Market Street, Philadelphia. pseud. Wanderer. see Rees, James.

Clerk of the California. pseud. Account of a voyage for the discovery of a north-west passage. see Drage, Theodore Swaine. supposed author Drage, William. supposed author Smith, Francis. supposed author

Clerk of the court. pseud. reporter Report of the trial of Levi Weeks. see Coleman, William, 1766-1829. reporter

Clerke, Robert. engr. 82819

Clerke of Oxenford. pseud. Blackwater chronicle. see Kennedy, John Pendleton, 1795-1870.

Clerks in the Executive Departments, at Washington City. petitioners 47668
Clerk's manual of rules, . . . for the regulation of business in the Assembly of the State of New York. 53602
Clerk's manual of rules, forms and laws. 80394
Clerk's magazine. 13643
Clerks of the Executive Departments at Washington. petitioners 47712
Clerkships in Washington. 13644
Clermont-Lodeve, Guillaume Emmanuel Joseph Guilhem de. see Sainte-Croix, Guillaume Emmanuel Joseph Guilhem de Clermont Lodeve, Baron de.
Clero de Honduras. see Honduras (Diocese)
Clero de Mexico. see Catholic Church in Mexico.
Clero del Obispado de la Puebla de los Angeles. see Puebla, Mex. (Archdiocese)
Clero Mexicano. see Catholic Church in Mexico.
Clero ultramontano. 75911
Clerque, Carlos. alais see Belin, Oliberos. plaintiff
Clerque, Gregorio de Molleda y. see Molleda y Clerque, Gregorio de.
Clervin, N. see Chervin, Nicolas, 1783-1843.
Cleveland, Mr. pseud. see Prevost, Antoine Francois, called Prevost d'Exiles, 1697-1763.
Cleveland, --------, fl. 1856. 16661
Cleveland, Aaron. supposed author 25386
Cleveland, Charles. 13646-13649 see also Boston. City Missionary.
Cleveland, Charles Dexter, 1802-1869. 13650-13651, (82076), 88294
Cleveland, Chauncy Fitch, 1799-1887. 13652-13653, 15839, 15841 see also Connecticut. Governor, 1842-1844 (Cleveland)
Cleveland, Mrs. Dorcas C. 13654, 57909
Cleveland, Mrs. E. H. (13655)
Cleveland, Edward. 13656-13657
Cleveland, Henry. 2381, 13658
Cleveland, Henry R. 13659-(13660), 5th note after 96480, 102321
Cleveland, John. 13661-13662
Cleveland, John F. 28493
Cleveland, Orestes, 1829-1896. 13664
Cleveland, Richard J. 13665
Cleveland, S. C. 104032
Cleveland, W. F. 91196
Cleveland, W. S. (13667)
Cleveland, William Neal. 13666
Cleveland. see also Cleavaland.
Cleveland. Adelbert College. see Western Reserve University, Cleveland, Ohio.
Cleveland. Board of Education. 13679-13680
Cleveland. Committee of Citizens in Relation to Steamboat Disasters on the Western Lakes. see Cleveland. Committee on Steam Navigation on the Western Lakes.
Cleveland. Committee on Steam Navigation on the Western Lakes. 65793
Cleveland. Convention of Delegates of Kansas Aid Societies, 1856. see Convention of Kansas Aid Societies, Cleveland, Ohio, 1856.
Cleveland. Convention of United States Assessors, 1863. see Convention of United States Assessors, Cleveland, Ohio, 1863.
Cleveland. Marion Union School. 44598

Cleveland. Medical Convention of Ohio, 1839. see Medical Convention of Ohio. 3d, Cleveland, 1839.
Cleveland. Meeting of Representatives of the Several Railroad Companies, 1854. see Meeting of Representatives of the Several Railroad Companies Between New York, Boston, Philadelphia, and Baltimore, Chicago, Cincinnati, and the Ohio and Mississippi Rivers, Cleveland, 1854.
Cleveland. National Convention of Manufacturers, 1867. see National Convention of Manufacturers, Cleveland, Ohio, 1867.
Cleveland. National Emigration Convention of Colored People, 1854. see National Emigration Convention of Colored People, Cleveland, Ohio, 1854.
Cleveland. National Women's Rights Convention, Celeveland, Ohio, 1853.
Cleveland. Ohio State and Union Law College. see Ohio State and Union Law College, Cleveland.
Cleveland. Perry Statue. 13678
Cleveland. Society for Protection of American Industry. see Society for Protection of American Industry, Cleveland.
Cleveland. Soldiers Aid Society of Northern Ohio. see United States Sanitary Commission. Soldiers Aid Society of Northern Ohio, Cleveland.
Cleveland. State Hospital. see Ohio. State Hospital, Cleveland.
Cleveland. Western Reserve University. see Western Reserve University, Cleveland, Ohio.
Cleveland (Diocese) Synod, 1852. 72938
Cleveland (Diocese) Synod, 1854. 72938
Cleveland (Diocese) Synod, 1857. 72938
Cleveland almanac and business man's directory. 13668
Cleveland and Mahoning Railroad Company. Chief Engineer. 13669
Cleveland and Mahoning Railroad Company. Directors. 13669
Cleveland branch of the United States Sanitary Commission. 76663
Cleveland Branch Sanitary Commission. Soldiers' Aid Soceity of Northern Ohio. 86317
Cleveland city directory. 89108
Cleveland city guide. 89843
Cleveland, Columbus and Cincinnati Rairlaod. 13670-(13671)
Cleveland family. 82516
Cleveland Female Seminary. 13672
Cleveland herald. 78246
Cleveland leader city directory. (13677)
Cleveland Library Association. 13673
Cleveland Mining Company. 13674
Cleveland, O., August 10th, 1865. 85867
Cleveland, Painsville and Ashtabula R. R. Company. 30283
Cleveland, past and present. 13675
Clevelands: showing the influence of a Christian family. 80119
Clever, Charles P. 13682-13683
Clever Jack, and other tales. 7093
Clever stories of many nations. (77336)
Clever young lawyer of Dover. pseud. supposed author Narrative of the life, adventures, travels and sufferings of Henry Tufts. 97416
Clevien, L. F. Jehan de St. see Jehan de St. Clevien, L. F.
Clevin, N. see Chervin, Nicolas, 1783-1843.

Clews, Habicht & Co. firm 90741 see also
    Alabama. Financial Agents.
Clews (Henry) & Co. firm 90741 see also
    Alabama. Financial Agents.
Clibborn, Edward. 13684
Clifford, George de. see Cumberland, George
    de Clifford, 3d Earl of, 1558-1605.
Clifford, J. D. 67462
Clifford, Jeronimy. petitioner (13685)-13688,
    15201, 93853
Clifford, John Henry, 1809-1876. 13689,
    (18939), 64269, 89627 see also Massa-
    chusetts. Attorney General.
Clifford, Nathan, 1803-1881. 13690-13691
Clifford, Peregrine. 13692
Clifford family. 13693
Cliffton, William, 1772-1799. (13694)-13695
Cliffton, William, 1772-1799. supposed author
    14018, note after 95866
Clift, William. 13696
Clifton, Alice. defendant 13697, 96849
Clifton, L. Colfert. 13698
Clifton, William. 13699
Clifton Ladies' Anti-slavery Society. see
    Bristol and Clifton Ladies' Anti-slavery
    Society.
Climacio, Juan. (22811)
Climate and diseases of America. 77755
Climate and diseases of America during the
    revolution. 77555
Climate of Detroit, Mich. An essay. 33418
Climate of Lake Superior. 4048
Climate of the summer of 1853. 5949
Climate of the United States and its endemic
    influences. 25121
Climate, soil, products, timber, water, kind of
    settlers wanted, &c. 34060
Climatology of Buffalo. 75791
Climatology of the United States. 5950
Climax of protection and free trade. 13702
Clinch, Joseph H. 13703
Cline, A. J. 13704
Clingan, George. (13705)
Clingman, Thomas Lanier, 1812-1897. 13706-
    (13707)
Clinical investigations. 64156
Clinical School of Medicine, Woodstock, Vt.
    see Vermont Medical College, Wood-
    stock, Vt.
Clinical School of Medicine of Colby College.
    see Vermont Medical College, Wood-
    stock, Vt.
Clinker Lot Right Men. defendants see
    Elizabeth, N. J. defendants
Clinton, C. A. 13708
Clinton, De Witt, 1769-1828. 1154, 10280,
    13709-13724, 13738-13739, (13747),
    22755, (28481), 30571, (39521), 53766,
    (53775), 53920, 53939, 53959-53960,
    54228, (54232), 54362, 54960, (56974),
    86734A, 1st note after 89220, 93511,
    94188, 2d note after 96480, 2d note after
    96930A, 97067, 98520, 99267, note after
    99831, 105795 see also New York
    (City) Mayor, 1811-1815 (Clinton) New
    York (State) Commissioners on Internal
    Navigation. New York (State) Governor,
    1817-1821 (Clinton) New York (State)
    Governor, 1825-1828 (Clinton)
Clinton, De Witt, 1769-1828. supposed author
    2330, 13721, (56974), 100666, note after
    104454
Clinton, De Witt, 1769-1828. appellant 91365
Clinton, De Witt, 1769-1828. defendant 96865
Clinton, George, 1686?-1761. 13740, 34601,
    53759 see also New York (Colony)
    Governor, 1743-1753 (Clinton)

Clinton, George, 1739-1812. 791, 13741-(13744),
    15590, 53873, 54960, 70350, 1st note
    after 89200, 1st note after 99000, 3d note
    after 99000 see also New York (State)
    Governor, 1777-1791 (Clinton) New York
    (State) Governor, 1801-1804 (Clinton)
Clinton, George William, 1807-1885. 9063,
    13748-13749
Clinton, Sir Henry, 1738?-1795. 4746-4748,
    (10924), (10925), 13750-13754, (14380),
    (16811), 16814, 16854, 27140, 70350,
    87367-87368, 91057, note before 95301,
    95301, 4th note after 99800 see also
    Great Britain. Commissioners to Treat,
    Consult, and Agree, Upon the Means of
    Quieting the Disorders Now Subsisting in
    Certain of the Colonies, 1778. South
    Carolina (British Militiary Governmnet)
    Commander in Chief.
Clinton, Sir Henry, 1738?-1795. supposed
    author 90591
Clinton, Henry L. (13756)
Clinton, Henry Pelham Fiennes Pelham. see
    Newcastle Under Lyme, Henry Pelham
    Fiennes Pelham Clinton, 5th Duke of,
    1811-1864.
Clinton, Jeter. 72134
Clinton, Thomas George. petitioner 13757
Clinton, Maine. Meeting of the Kennebec Con-
    ference of Churches, 1833. see Con-
    gregational Churches in Maine. Kennebec
    Conference.
Clinton, Mass. 13762
Clinton, Mass. Bigelow Association. see
    Bigelow Association, Clinton, Mass.
Clinton, Mass. Cemetery Committee. 13763
Clinton, Mass. Overseers of the Poor. 13763
Clinton, Mass. Selectmen. 13763
Clinton, Mass. Treasurer. 13763
Clinton, Miss. Mississippi College. see
    Mississippi College, Clinton, Miss.
Clinton, N. Y. Clinton Cemetery. 13758
Clinton, N. Y. Clinton Seminary. see Clinton
    Seminary, Clinton, N. Y.
Clinton, N. Y. Hamilton College. see Hamil-
    ton College, Clinton, N. Y.
Clinton County, N. Y. Citizens. petitioners
    (47666)
Clinton County, Ontario. Grammar School.
    Trustees. 28253
Clinton Avenue Church, Brooklyn. see Brook-
    lyn. Clinton Avenue Church.
Clinton Bradshaw. 95391-95392
Clinton correspondence. (13744), 70350
Clinton County Coal Company. 13759
Clinton County Military Association. 63363
Clinton family. 44312
Clinton Hall, New York (City) see New York
    (City) Clinton Hall.
Clinton Hall Association, New York. 54089
Clinton Line Railroad Company. (13760)
Clinton Line Railroad Company. Chief Engi-
    neer. (13760)
Clinton monument. MDCCXLVIII. 13727
Clinton monument, report of the committee on
    the character and location of the monu-
    ment. 13728
Clinton papers. 99054
Clinton Seminary, Clinton, N. Y. 13764
Clinton State Prison, New York. see New
    York (State) Clinton State Prison.
Clintonian meeting. 59978
Clinton's legacy. 13745
Clio. pseud. Converted Indian. see Williams,
    Joseph, of Shrewsbury.
Clio. (60864)

Clio Convivius Socio. pseud. see Socio,
Clio Convivius. pseud.
Cliosophic Society, Princeton University. see
Princeton University. Cliosophic Society.
Clipperton, -------. 31389, (54897)
Clippings from the California press. 13766
Clithoueus, Ludicus. 69130
Clock has struck. 97466
Clock-maker. 29682, 29684, 29695
Clockmaker. 85258-85260
Clocks of Gnoster-Town. (81015)
Clodius. pseud. To the advocates of min-
isterial oppression. 60674, 3d note
after 95905
Clodore, Jean de. 13767-13768, note after
98258
Clogher, Bishop of. see Ash, St. George,
successively Bishop of Cloyne, Clogher,
and Derry. Garnett, John, Bishop of
Clogher.
Clolus, Emile. 13769
Clontarf. 79987
Clopper, Jonas. 13770, note after 95776
Clopton, John. 13771
Cloquet, Jules. 13772-13774
Clos, --------. 6156, 7650, 47525
Close, John. (13775)
Close of a sermon preached on Sunday morn-
ing. 89744
Close of the late rebellion in Rhode Island.
13776, 70563
Closet. [A sermon at the annual autumnal
convention in New Bedford.] 71771
Closet: a sermon preached at the ordination
of Mr. James Francis Brown. 71770
Closing argument for complainant. 35314
Closing argument . . . for the prosecution.
71265
Closing argument in case of the commonwealth
of Pennsylvania, vs. Rev. S. M. Landin.
37740
Closing argument of B. W. Harris. 30465
Closing argument of Charles Edwards. 9210
Closing argument of . . . [Hermann Haupt.]
30859
Closing argument of Hon. Henry Stanbery.
90144
Closing argument of L. D. Latimer. 88914
Closing message of . . . Nathaniel S. Berry.
52808
Closing roll from holy and eternal wisdom.
91701
Closing scenes of the year 1860. (17524)
Closing speech . . . October 7, 1864. 37271
Closing speech of William H. Seward in the
Senate. 79523
Clotel; or, the president's daughter. 8590
Clotelle; a tale of the southern states. 8590
Clothes for a stark naked author. 69528
Cloud, ------- Saint. see Saint Cloud,
--------.
Cloud of human experience. 8729
'Cloud of witnesses' against slavery and
oppression. 2003A
Cloud of witnesses; or the sufferers mirrour.
44124
Cloudesley. 27676
Clough, Ebenezer. defendant 96850
Clough, Joel. defendant 96851
Clough, Samuel. (13777), 52647, 62743,
(66440)
Clough, Simon. 13778-13781, 26141
Clough's farewell almanac. (13777)
Cloven foot. 54960
Cloven-foot discovered. 13782, 80049-80050
Clover, Nathaniel. 13783

Clovernook. 10824
Clowes, J. 13784
Clowes, James. 22935, 102555
Clowes, S. 84558
Clowes, Timothy. 13785-(13787)
Clowes, William J. 13788
Clown song and joke book. 82357
Cloyne, Bishop of. see Ash, St. George,
successively Bishop of Cloyne, Clogher,
and Derry. Berkeley, George, Bishop of
Cloyne, 1685-1753.
Club, Germantown, Pa. see Germantown
Club, Germantown, Pa.
Club, New York. see New York Club, New
York (City)
Club Convened at Boston. see Association of
Laymen, Boston.
Club Jacobino de Francia resucitado en la
capital del Districto del Sud-Oeste del
Departamento de Michoacan. 13789
Club for Colonial Reprints. 52641, note after
100866, 101286, 104336, 104796
Club National de Langue Francaise, New York.
13790
Club national (de langue France), fonde a New
York. 13790
Club of American Merchants. 952, 37244,
66015, 86745, 97575
Club of Laymen, Boston. see Association of
Laymen, Boston.
Club of Odd Volumes. 96155, 104986
Club-room. 13791
Clubb, Henry S. 13792-13794
Clubb, Stephen. 13795
Cluny, Alexander. 13796-13798, 69142, 1st
note after 100846
Cluseret, G. 13799
Clusius, Carolus. 13800-13802, 14355, 57664,
57666, 57670
Cluskey, Michael W. 9436, 13803-13804
Cluster of anecdotes. 32374
Cluste; or memoirs of six deceased members.
102097
Clute, John B. 77602, 2d note after 106156
see also Young Men's Association for
Mutual Improvement in the City of
Schenectada. President.
Clutter, William. defendant 96852
Cluver, Philipp, 1580-1622. (2308), 5013,
13805, 52769, 79124
Cluverius, P. see Cluver, Philipp, 1580-1622.
Clvsio, Carolo. tr. see Ecluse, Charles
de l'. tr
Clyde. firm see Royal & Clyde. firm
publishers
Clyme, James. 100509
Clymer, George, 1739-1813. 94480
Clymer, George, d. 1881. 13806, 2d note after
93829
Clymer, Hiester. 13807
Clytia: a tale of the southern states. 27118
Cnavthivs, Samuel. ed. 61293
Cnopius, L. C. tr. 4519B
Coade, George. 13809
Coahuila and Texas (Mexican State) 13810,
94948
Coahuila and Texas (Mexican State) Congreso
Constituyente, 1827. 94940-94941
Coahuila and Texas (Mexican State) Consti-
tution. 13810, 16084, 39405, 49349,
57349, 94940-94943, 94946, 94948-94949
Coahuila and Texas (Mexican State) Consti-
tutive Congress, 1827. see Coahuila and
Texas (Mexican State) Congreso Consti-
tuyente, 1827.

Coahuila and Texas (Mexican State) Convention, Austin, 1832. 94950
Coahuila and Texas (Mexican State) Convention, Austin, 1833. 94949
Coahuila and Texas (Mexican State) Gobernador (Martinez) 94945 see also Martinez, S. F.
Coahuila and Texas (Mexican State) Laws, statutes, etc. 13810, 16084, 26474, 39405, 93710, note before 94938, 94939, 94944, 94966-94948, 95086, 105111
Coahuila and Texas (Mexican State) Ministerio de Hacienda. 13810, 94948
Coahuila. Laws and decrees of the state of Coahuila and Texas. 13810, 94948
Coal and coal oil. 7049
Coal and iron mines of the Union Potomac Company. 13813
Coal and the coal trade. (7050)
Coal-black maid. 50805
Coal business of the Pennsylvania Railroad. 60358
Coal deposits of Batan Island. 84527
Coal depot side on the Delaware River. 60278
Coal fields of McKean County, Pennsylvania. 80025
Coal-hill, Victoria and Bedford Mines. 13811
Coal, iron, and oil. 18257
Coal: its producers and consumers. 13812
Coal, oil, and petroleum. (22775)
Coal-Owners and Iron-Masters of Richmond. see Richmond, Va. Coal-Owners and Iron-Masters. petitioners
Coal regions of Pennsylvania. 7051
Coal Ridge Improvement and Coal Company. 59979
Coal Run Improvement and Railroad Company. 59980
Coal Run Improvement and Railroad Company. Charter. 59980
Coal trade of British America. (36332)
Coale, Edward J. reporter 30365
Coale, Josiah. 13814-13816, 59660
Coalition. 13819, 62851, 89296
Coalition of the Democracy and the abolitionists. 13818
Coalition: or, an essay on the present state of parties. 13820
Coast and harbour defences. 22209
Coast depot and shipping port. 71475
Coast of Mosquito and the boundary question. 58579
Coast survey. By one who has examined public documents. 13822
Coast survey: its cost, abuses and power. 13823
Coast survey. Reply to the official defence of its cost. (13824)
Coast survey. Review of the operation and results. 13825
Coast survey of the United States. [By F. R. Hassler.] 30816
Coast survey of the United States. By Lieut. C. H. Davis. 18804
Coasting-pilot, a Spanish manuscript. 16303
Coasts of the Pacific Ocean. 24358
Coates, Benjamin. 13827
Coates, Benjamin Honor, 1797-1881. 1183, 13828, 73081
Coates, D. 13829
Coates, Kersey. 13830
Coates, Reynell. 13832, 27664, 39515
Coates, William, fl. 1772. (13835)
Coates-Kinney, -------. see Kinney, Coates, 1826-1904.
Coats, Archibald. respondent 69087
Coats, John. respondent 69087

Coats, William. 3664, 13833
Coats, William, fl. 1772. see Coates, William, fl. 1772.
Coats, William, fl. 1783. 13834 see also Philadelphia County, Pa. Lieutenant.
Cob, Sim., Junior. pseud. see Ward, Nathaniel.
Cobarrubias, Diaz. 13836
Cobarrubias, Josef de. 13837
Cobarruvias Orozco, Seb. de. see Orozco, Seb. de Cobarruvias.
Cobb, Alvan. 13838
Cobb, C. L. 90828
Cobb, Carlos. (53563)
Cobb, Charles. (13839)
Cobb, Edward. 13840, (67748)
Cobb, Enos. supposed author 100729
Cobb, H. (13844)
Cobb, Howell, 1815-1868. 13841-13843, 87548 see also Georgia. Governor, 1851-1853 (Cobb)
Cobb, James, 1756-1818. 86907, 92172
Cobb, Jonathan Holmes. 13847
Cobb, Joseph Beckham, 1819-1858. (13845)-13846, 13848
Cobb, L. 13849
Cobb, L. H. 89897
Cobb, Lyman, 1800-1864. 13850, 102401
Cobb, Lyman, 1800-1864. supposed author 102337
Cobb, Moses Gill. 13851
Cobb, Oliver. 13852-13854
Cobb, Sophia Dickinson. 13855
Cobb, Sylvanus, 1798-1866. 13856-(13857)
Cobb, Sylvanus, 1823-1887. (13857)-(13858)
Cobb, Thomas Read Rootes, 1823-1862. 13859-13861, 27040
Cobb, Thomas Willis, 1784-1830. 13862
Cobbe, Frances Power. 13863-13864, 58741
Cobbet, Thomas, 1608-1685. (13865)-13868
Cobbett, James Paul, 1803-1881. 13869, 14017, 38580
Cobbett, John Morgan, 1800-1887. 14017
Cobbett, William, 1763-1835. 1691, (7258), 8110, 9293, (13870)-13999, 14001-14022, 14026-14027, 14031, (19494A), (24910), 25154-25155, 33627, 38583, 40622, 43429, 44848-44849, 50572, 63374, 64158-(64166), (65512), (78988), 84829, 84832, 86176, 92070, note after 94022, 94025, note after 95800, 12th note after 95843, 2d note after 96805, 98682, 1st note after 99797, 101837, note after 101847, note after 101960, 102401
Cobbett, William, 1763-1835. supposed author 13879, 14018, 95799, note after 95866
Cobbett, William, fl. 1809. 96932
Cobbett against himself. (14024)
Cobbett's annual register. see Cobbett's political register.
Cobbett's political register. 14021, 13878, 84832
Cobbett's weekly register. see Cobbett's political register.
Cobbett's weekly register, for Dec. 13, 1823. 14021
Cobbler politics. 14033
Cobbs, Nicholas H., Bp. 14034
Cobbs, Robert L. 31087
Cobden, Richard, 1804-1865. 12594, 14035-14041, 70902
Cobden, Richard, 1804-1865. supposed author 14036, 100976
Cobes, -------. (56083)
Cobleigh, N. E. 14043

Cobler. pseud. Letter from a cobler to the people of England. 40272
Cobler. pseud. Three letters to the Rev. Dr. Price. 95743
Cobo, Juan Manuel. 99794
Cobourg church. 100896
Coburn, David A. 14044
Coburn, Edward O. defendant 14045
Coburn, John, 1825-1908. 14046
Coburn, Louise Helen. 83486
Coccio, Marco Antonio. see Sabellico, Marco Antonio Coccio, called, 1436-1506.
Cocconato, Gian Francesco Galeani Napione de. see Napione de Cocconato, Gian Francesco Galeani.
Cochabamba. Sociedad de la Union Americana. see Sociedad de la Union Americana de Cochabamba.
Cocheco Railroad Company. Directors. 14047
Cocherel, ------ de. 14048-14059
Cocheris, Hippolyte. 85044
Cochet, Ignacio. 14060
Cochin, Augustin, 1823-1872. 14061-14067, 26734, 27501
Cochin, Pierre Suzanne Augustin. see Cochin, Augustin, 1823-1872.
Cochinchine. 39300
Cochinchinese and Latin dictionary. 1183
Cochituate Lake Water Commission, Boston. see Boston. Cochituate Water Board.
Cochituate-Wasserleitungs-Commission, Boston. see Boston. Cochituate Water Board.
Cochran, J. C. 88012
Cochran, James C. 14068, 69501, 90377
Cochran, John. 89205
Cochran, Thomas B. 85177
Cochran, Thomas F. (14069)
Cochran, William. 14070, 69501
Cochrane, Archibald. see Dundonald, Archibald Cochrane, 9th Earl of, 1749?-1831.
Cochrane, Charles Stuart. 14072-14073
Cochrane, Clark B. 14074-14075
Cochrane, Jacob. defendant 82578, note after 96852
Cochrane, John, 1813-1898. 14076-14077 see also New York (State) Attorney-General.
Cochrane, Thomas, 1775-1860. see Dundonald, Thomas Cochrane, 10th Earl of, 1775-1860.
Cochrane, Thomas, fl. 1789. (13081)
Cochrane, Thomas, fl. 1855. 14080
Cochranism delineated. 14083, 91834-91835
Cochut, Andre. 14084
Cock, S. 14085
Cock, Simon. 56560
Cock, Simon. supposed author 56561
Cockade proclamation. 13884
Cockayne, M. S. 14086
Cockburn, Sir Alexander James Edmund, 1802-1880. (14087)-14088 see also Great Britain. Court of Common Pleas. Chief Justice.
Cockburn, G. F. 14089-14090
Cockburn, Sir George. 23144, note after 101938
Cockburn, James, of Philadelphia 14093
Cockburn, Sir James, Bart., 1723-1809. defendant at court martial 14091-14092
Cockburn, John. 14094-14099, 32703, note after 97744
Cockburn, R. A. 14100
Cockburne, James. see Cockburn, Sir James, Bart., 1723-1809.
Cocke, J. D. supposed author 95088
Cocke, Harrison H. USN (14101)

Cocke, John. 14102
Cocke, John Hartwell, 1780-1866. 1240, 93203
Cocke, R. 66686
Cocke, Richard Ivanhoe. 14103
Cocke, William Archer. 14104
Cocke, William Michael, 1815-1896. 14105-14106, 42822
Cockerell, Richard. 14107
Cockes, R. 66686
Cockings, George. 14108-14110, 101257
Cockings, George. supposed author 1449, 14111
Cockney in America. 14112
Cockran, W. ed. 56416
Cocoa Tree. pseud. Letter. 40328
Cocteau, --------. 14113, 74921-74922
Codazzi, Agustin. 14114-14117, 72786
Codd, --------. RA 65811 see also Great Britain. Consulate. Belize, Honduras.
Codding, Milo Defonz. (14118)
Coddington, David. 14119
Coddington, David S. (14120)
Coddington, William, fl. 1630. (21090), 33698, 78431, 104846
Coddington, William, fl. 1674-1680. 14121, 25363, (25364), 104330
Code. 95185
Code-civil d'Haiti. 29568
Code criminel de l'empire du Bresil. 25275
Code de commerce pour l'etat de la Louisiane. 42208
Code de la Guyane Francaise. 29167
Code de la Martinique. 61263
Code de la Martinique. Nouvelle edition. 44974
Code de la Martinique; par Durand-Molard. 21412
Code de procedure civile adopte a la Guyana Francaise. 29166
Code de procedure civile du Bas Canada. 42511
Code des colons de St. Domingue, avec des notes. 29569, 75078, note after 98577
Code des colons de Saint-Domingue, presentant l'histoire de la legislation de l'ex-colonie. 29569, 75078, note after 98577
Code et reglements de la Societe de Discussion de Quebec. 85802
Code for the government of armies in the field. 40985
Code Henry, loi de commerce, loi penale. 29570
Code Napoleon. (5153)
Code noir et l'additions audit code. (68439), 68459
Code noir, ou edit du Roy, servant de reglement pour le gouvernement & l'administration de justice et la police. 14123
Code de noir ou edit du Roy, servant de reglement pour le gouvernement & l'administration de la justice, police, discipline & le commerce. 14124
Code noir, ou recueil des reglemens rendu. 14125
Code of Alabama. 57632
Code of . . . Atlanta. 44352
Code of Christian the Fifth. (18501)
Code of civil procedure of the state of Ohio. 79125
Code of criminal law. 53086
Code of ethics of the South Carolina Medical Association. 88016
Code of evidence. (41617)
Code of health and longevity. 102056
Code of health ordinances, and rules . . . 1866. 54399

Code of honor. 104661
Code of Iowa. [Edited] by Darwin. (35016)
Code of Iowa, passed at the session of the General Assembly of 1850-51. 35015
Code of laws for the District of Columbia. 20300
Code of laws of the republic of Columbia. 14561
Code of medical ethics adopted by the [San Francisco Medical] Society. 76094
Code of Mississippi. 49492
Code of ordinances of the city of Mobile. (49778)
Code of practice in civil and criminal cases for the state of Kentucky. Prepared by M. C. Johnson. (37531)
Code of practice in civil and criminal cases for the state of Kentucky. With all amendments made prior to January 1, 1867. 37532
Code of practice in civil cases for . . . Louisiana. 42210
Code of practice, in civil cases, for the state of Louisiana. (42209), 98104
Code of procedure, for giving effect to the penal code of . . . Louisiana. 41614
Code of public instruction of the state [of New York.] 53604
Code of reform and prison discipline. (41617)
Code of rules and regulations. 60332
Code of 1650, being a compilation of the earliest laws and orders. 14122
Code of civil procedure and other general statutes of Oregon. 57546
Code of the statute law of South Carolina. 87398
Code of Virginia. (59162)
Code rural a l'usage des habitants tant anciens que nouveaux du Bas-Canada. 42512
Codero, Leon de Febres. 16758
Codes Haitiens annotes. 41381, 64878
Codex Cortesianus manuscrit hieratique des anciens Indiens. 73301
Codex juris gentium diplomaticus. 39893
Codex Telleriano-Remensis. 12022, 73299
Codice diplomatico-Americano de Cristobal Colon. 89647
Codice diplomatico Colombo-Americano. (14644)
Codification of the law of carriers. 104662
Codification of the statute law of Georgia. (27026)
Codification proposal. 4766
Codification. Speech of the Hon. John L. Wilson. 104662
Codigo Brasiliense. 7548
Codigo civil de la Provincia Espanola de Santo Domingo. 75079
Codigo civil de la republica Argentina. 77105
Codigo civil de la republica de Chile. (12753)
Codigo civil del Peru. 61085
Codigo civil [1866]. Libro segundo. 48343
Codigo civil, Sante-Cruz Presidente. 6192
Codigo commercial do imperio do Brasil. 1891
Codigo commercial do imperio do Brasil annotado. (17009)
Codigo commercial do imperio do Brasil pelo Cacharel Annibal Andre Ribeiro. 70793
Codigo criminal do imperio do Brasil. 16757
Codigo criminal do imperio do Brasil, accrescentado com as leis. 81091
Codigo criminal do imperio do Brasil. Augmentado por Josino do Nascimento Silva. 81092

Codigo de comercio de Francia. 14126
Codigo de comercio de la republica del Peru. 61086
Codigo de comercio de Mexico. 48344
Codigo de comercio (de 1 de Junio de 1853.) 56268
Codigo de comercio y de navegacion. 14127
Codigo de instruccion publica del Peru. 61087
Codigo de la legislacion de hacienda publica, navegacion y comercio de Nicaragua. 72291
Codigo de la legislacion de Nicaragua. 72291-72292
Codigo de la restauracion. 48345
Codigo de politica nacional. (14128)
Codigo de procederes Santa Cruz. 76766
Codigo do processo criminal de primeira instancia do imperio do Brasil: augmentado com a lei. 81093
Codigo do processo criminal de primeira instancia do imperio do Brasil, com a disposicao provisoria acerca da administracao da justicia civil. 79306
Codigo do processo criminal de primeira instancia para o imperio do Brazil com annotacoes. 85637
Codigo fundamental de los Estados Unidos Mexicanos. 48346
Codigo general compresivo de las leyes generales, utiles y vivals de las siete partidas. 58417, (72549)
Codigo mercantile Santa Cruz. 76767
Codigo penal Boliviano. (6193)
Codigo penal decretado por las cortes. 48347
Codigo penal Santa-Cruz, del Estado Nor-Peruano. 76768
Codigo Santa Cruz, de procedimientos judiciales del estado Nor-Peruano. 55450, 76769
Codington, Robert. tr. 44536
Codman, Charles R. 14138, 98551, 2d note after 98553
Codman, Francis. 14138, 98551, 2d note after 98553
Codman, John, 1782-1847. (14129)-14138, 97382, 98551, 2d note after 98553
Codman, John, 1814-1890. 14139-14141
Codman, Robert. 12860
Codman, Stephen. 98550, 98562-98565 see also Heirs and Executors of John and Richard Codman.
Codogna, O. see Cotogno, Ott.
Codorniu y Ferreras, Manuel. 14143
Codrington, -----------. 25781
Codrington College, Barbados. 14145-14146, 85947
Codwise, George. plaintiff 96853
Coe, Curtis, 1750-1829. 14147, (78487), 80190
Coe, David B. (14148)
Coe, George S. 14149
Coe, Israel. (55929)
Coe, Jonas. 14150, 43156
Coe, Joseph. (14151)
Coelestinus. 46261
Coelho, A. 99519
Coelho, Jeronimo Francisco. 58502 see also Para (Brazilian State) President (Coelho)
Coelho, Jose Antonio Pereira. 14152
Coelho, Romualdo de Souza. see Souza Coelho, Romualdo de.
Coelho e Mello, Antonio Dias. 69313 see also Sergipe (Brazilian State) Vice-Presidente (Coelho e Mello)
Coelln, Johann von. (41352)
Coello, Duarte de Albuquerque. see Albuquerque Coello, Duarte de, Marques de Basto.
Coello, Manuel. (14154)

Coercion a failure, necessarily and actually.
26189
Coercion completed, or treason triumphant.
30022
Coetlogon, C. de. (14155), 21947
Coeur mort qui bat. (69035)
Coeymans Division, no. 185, Sons of Tem-
perance. see Sons of Temperance of
North America. New York. Coeymans
Division, no. 185.
Coffadwriaeth am y diweddar Barch. 82901
Coffee, John. 96663 see also U. S. Com-
missioners to the Choctaw Indians.
Coffee-house dialogue. 69102, 89288
Coffee-planter. 42530
Coffee planter of Saint Domingo. 38430
Coffee, tea, & chocolate. 75000
Coffey, Titian J. 14156, 89224
Coffey, W. A. 14157
Coffey, William Samuel. (14158)
Coffin, Alexander. 14159-(14160)
Coffin, Amory. 14161
Coffin, Charles, 1779-1851. 14162-14164,
89736, 2d note after 104027
Coffin, Charles Carleton. 14165-14170
Coffin, Ebenezer. 14172
Coffin, Frederick M. illus. 58959, 58961,
84158
Coffin, George G. 41310
Coffin, Isaac. defendant at court martial
49343
Coffin, Isaac. petitioner 49343
Coffin, J. F. 12777, 14173
Coffin, James Henry. 14174, 85072
Coffin, John G. (14175)
Coffin, Joshua, 1792-1864. 14176-14179
Coffin, L. C. 14171
Coffin, N. W. 14180-14181
Coffin, Paul. (14182)-14183
Coffin, Richard. respondent 51752
Coffin, Robert Barry. (14184)
Coffin, Robert Stevenson, 1797-1827. (14185)-
14187, (63618)
Coffin, Roland F. supposed author 52329,
note after 92749
Coffin, Sirson P. (14188)
Coffin, W. H. (14191)
Coffin, William. 14189
Coffin, William F. 14190, 92649
Coffinberry, Andrew. 14192
Coffinieres, ------. 20964
Coffman, W. E. defendant 48146
Cofradia de la Virgen Maria Nuestra Senora.
76275
Cofradia de Santiago, Mexico (City) 48383
Cofradia de Santiago, Mexico (City) Charter.
48635
Cofradia de Santiago en la Ciudad de Mexico.
see Cofradia de Santiago, Mexico (City)
Cofradia del Apostol Santiago en la Ciudad de
Mexico. see Cofradia de Santiago,
Mexico (City)
Cofradia del Glorioso Principe de los Apostoles
San Pedro, Caracas. 16058
Coggeshal, ------, fl. 1748. 24459
Coggeshall, George. 14193-14197
Coggeshall, S. W. 14198
Coggeshall, William T. 14199-14204
Coggeswell, W. H. 15787
Coggin, Jacob. 14205
Coggin, William S. (14206)
Coggshall, William T. see Coggeshall,
William T.
Coghlan, John. 14207
Coghlan, John M. 76947
Coghlan, Margaret (Moncrieffe) 14208-14209

Cogitans, John. pseud. Spiritual mustard pot.
see Morey, Charles.
Cogitata de Cometis. 104851
Cogitations of a convict in the House of Cor-
rection. 67963, 85427
Cogoletto, ------. 4565
Cogolin, Joseph Bernard Chabert de. see
Chabert de Cogolin, Joseph Bernard,
Marquis de, 1724-1805.
Cogolludo, Diego Lopez de. see Lopez de
Cogolludo, Diego.
Cogswell, Elliott C. (14213)-14214
Cogswell, Henry C. 14215
Cogswell, J. S. 2250
Cogswell, James, 1720-1807. 14216-14217,
(21778)
Cogswell, Jonathan. 105531
Cogswell, Joseph Green, 1786-1871. 14218,
54846, 85071, 99281
Cogswell, Nathaniel. 14219
Cogswell, Thomas. 52793
Cogswell, William, of Nova Scotia. (14225)
Cogswell, William, 1787-1850. 1198, 14220-
14224, 22886, 52688, 52886
Cohasset, Mass. 14229
Cohasset, Mass. Overseers of the Poor. 14229
Cohasset, Mass. Second Congregational Church.
14227
Cohasset, Mass. Selectmen. 14229
Cohasset, Mass. Treasurer. 14229
Coheleth. (46262)
Cohen, ------. tr. 78778
Cohen, Alfred A. defendant 90320
Cohen, Bernard. 14230
Cohen, J. Barrett. 88005
Cohen, J. J. 45207
Cohen, M. M. supposed author (14231),
(81536)
Cohen (E. A.) & Co. firm publishers (53347),
61606, 101935
Cohens, ------. plaintiff (30089), note after
96853
Cohen's . . . directory . . . for 1860. 61606
Cohen's New Orleans directory. (53347)
Cohocksink Beneficial Society of Pennsylvania.
59981
Cohoes, N. Y. District School. Library.
14233
Cohoes, N. Y. Ordinances, etc. 14232
Cohos. The wilderness shall blossom as the
rose. 103217
Coignet, ------. (14234), 57691
Coimbra, Manuel. 67331
Coin, Robert L. de. see De Coin, Robert L.
Coindet, Leon. (14235)
Coins, medals, and seals, ancient and modern.
65542
Coins, tokens and medals of Canada. 76412
Coins, tokens and medals of the dominion of
Canada. (74610)
Coit, J. C. 14237
Coit, Thomas Winthrop. 14238
Coitinho Mattoso Camare, Eusebio de Queiroz.
see Mattoso Camare, Eusebio de Queiroz
Coitinho.
Coke, Daniel Parker, 1745-1825. (15052)
Coke, Edward Thomas. 14239
Coke, Henry J. 14240
Coke, Roger. 14241
Coke, Thomas, 1747-1814. 14242-14252, 14338,
48182, 48200, 102644, 102701, 103661,
103663
Coker, Daniel. (14253)
Cokesbury College, Abingdon, Md. 14251
Colahan, W. J. 76119

Colancha, Antonio de la. see Antonio de la
　　Colancha.
Colban, N. A. tr. 4193
Colbert. pseud. Political economy. see
　　Carey, Mathew, 1760-1839.
Colbert, E. 14254
Colbert. 10889
Colborne, Sir John. see Seaton, John Col-
　　borne, 1st Baron, 1788-1863.
Colburn, Samuel W. 14256
Colburn, Zerah. 14257
Colburn's United service magazine, and naval
　　and military journal. 14258
Colburn (Henry) publisher 14258
Colby, Charles. 14259-(14260), 24494, (50912)
Colby, George J. L. (14261)
Colby, H. G. O. 14262
Colby, John. 14263
Colby College, Waterville, Me. 14264, 102199-
　　102102
Colby College, Waterville, Me. Class of 1835.
　　petitioners 102103
Colby College, Waterville, Me. Clinical
　　School of Medicine. see Vermont
　　Medical College, Woodstock, Vt.
Colby College, Waterville, Me. Library.
　　102105
Colby College, Waterville, Me. Manual Labour
　　Association. 102106
Colby College, Waterville, Me. Samaritan
　　Female Society. 102107
Colby University, Waterville, Me. see Colby
　　College, Waterville, Me.
Colchagua (Chilean Province) Intendente.
　　96238-96239, 99790 see also Moreiras,
　　Francisco Javier.
Colchester, Charles Abbott, 2d Baron. 86685
Colchester, Archdeacon of. see Lyall,
　　William Rowe, 1788-1857.
Colchester, Conn. 14265, 1st note after 94219
Colcock, ------. 87453
Cold grapery, from direct American practice.
　　12887
Cold-water-man. 14266, 89906
Cold water melodies. 82178
Cold water melodies, and Washingtonian
　　songster. 62761
Colden, Cadwallader, 1688-1776. 14267-14257,
　　30571, (41354), 54166, (80023), 84566
　　see also New York (State) Governor,
　　1761-1765 (Colden)
Colden, Cadwallader, 1688-1776. supposed
　　author 34882-34884, 100770
Colden, Cadwallader David, 1769-1834. 2879,
　　14277-(14282), 21112, (21117), 55545,
　　72619, 75957, 92149, 93513-93514, 93532,
　　93535, 96876, note after 96922, 101441
　　see also New York (City) Mayor, 1818-
　　1821 (Colden)
Colden, Cadwallader David, 1769-1834.
　　defendant 96888
Cole. pseud. Selection of poems. (78999)
Cole, --------. 72417
Cole, Charles. 64870, 2d note after 102858
Cole, Cornelius, 1822-1922. 14284
Cole, Emma. 14285
Cole, Frederick Wing. 14286
Cole, F. S. (14287)
Cole, George E. 14288
Cole, J. 14290
Cole, John. 14289
Cole, Samuel W., 1796-1851. (14291), 52677
Cole, Thomas. 14292, 104226
Cole, Thomas, 1779-1852. 14293, (55381)-55382
Cole, Timothy. illus. 83740-83741
Cole, W. K. ed. 56694

Cole (A.) & Co. firm (14283)
Colebrooke, Sir George, Bart. petitioner
　　101150
Coleccio regno Jesuitico del Paraguay. 58513
Coleccion de actas, representaciones, y pro-
　　nunciamientos. 98871
Coleccion de amenidades curiosos e instructivos.
　　(51035)
Coleccion de articulos. 57911
Coleccion de articulos de Anselmo Suarez y
　　Romero. 93345
Coleccion de articulos de costumbres. (72804)
Coleccion de articulos escritos y publicados
　　en diversos periodicos. 22195
Coleccion de articulos, relativos a la republica
　　Mexicana. 579, 6834, 48429, 48599
Coleccion de articulos satiricos y de costum-
　　bres. 10810
Coleccion de articulos selectos sobre politica.
　　48259, 48348
Coleccion de articulos sobre la cuestion
　　arzobispo de Caracas y Venezuela. 39087
Coleccion de cartas de privilegios, cedulas y
　　otras escrituras. 89647
Coleccion de cartas escritas por el ciudadano
　　Presidente D. Bernardo Berro. 4988
Coleccion de cartas y planos de las costas de
　　America. 14294
Coleccion de caudros para estadistica general
　　de la republica Mexicana. 48350
Coleccion de causas celebres contemporaneas.
　　26115
Coleccion de certamenes presentados por los
　　colejios y casas de education de la
　　republica de Colombia. 14562
Coleccion de certamenes publicos de doctrina
　　Cristiana. 33553
Coleccion de composiciones escritas por
　　Venezolanos. 24825
Coleccion de composiciones liricas. 71636
Coleccion de composiciones poeticas. (71637)
Coleccion de constituciones de los Estados-
　　Unidos Mexicanos. 48349, 94942
Coleccion de decretos del Congreso Consti-
　　tuyente de Mexico. 48351
Coleccion de decretos expedidos por S. E. el
　　Libertador Presidente de Colombia.
　　14563
Coleccion de decretos, ordenes y circulares
　　espedidas por los gobiernos nacionales
　　de la Federacion Mexicana. (48352)
Coleccion de decretos para el ejercito. 67661
Coleccion de decretos y ordenes de la Primera
　　Legislatura Constitucional del estado
　　libre de San Luis Potosi. 76141
Coleccion de decretos y ordenes del estado
　　libre de Oajaca. 56397
Coleccion de diversas poesias y articulos
　　patrioticos. 87162
Coleccion de documentos antiguos del Archivo
　　del Ayuntamicuto de la Ciudad de
　　Guatemala. 29072
Coleccion de documentos ineditos para la his-
　　toria de Espana. (52099)
Coleccion de documentos ineditos relativos al
　　descubrimiento, conquista y colonizacion
　　de las posesiones Espanolas en America
　　y Oceana. 58072, 106405
Coleccion de documentos officiales sobre la
　　mission. 9003
Coleccion de documentos oficiales con que el
　　gobierno instruye al Cuerpo Legislativo
　　de la provincia. 14295
Coleccion de documentos oficiales de la jefe-
　　tura suprema del Coronel Mariano I.
　　Prado. 61077, 64879

Coleccion de documentos oficiales relativos a la construccion y demolicion del Parian. 48353, (58590)

Coleccion de documentos, opusculos y antiguedades, que publica la Real Academia de la Historia. 47633

Coleccion de documentos para la historia de la guerra de independencia de Mexico. 98806

Coleccion de documentos para la historia de Mexico. 48354

Coleccion de documentos para la historia de Mexico publicada por Joaquin Garcia Icazbalceta. 16939-16940, 34153, 98647

Coleccion de documentos relativos a la conducta del Cabildo Eclesiastico de la Diocesi [sic] de Guadalaxara y del clero misma. 29021

Coleccion de documentos relativos a la vida de Simon Bolivar. 14564

Coleccion de documentos relativos a la vida publica del Libertador de Colombia y del Peru, Simon Bolivar. 14564

Coleccion de documentos relativos a matrimonios civiles. (73163)

Coleccion de documentos relativos al Departmento de Californias. (11376)

Coleccion de E. Merimee. 86471

Coleccion de ensayos i documentos relativos a la union i confederacion de los pueblos Hispano-Americanos. 76857

Coleccion de ensayos i documentos relativos a la union i confederacion de los pueblos Sud-Americanos. 85727

Coleccion de escritos del anterior y presente siglo. (26114), 47936, 61153

Coleccion de escritos sobre los cultivos de la cana. 70457

Coleccion de estampas que representan los principales pasos. 105728

Coleccion de gramaticas de la lengua Mexicana. 94353, 99385

Coleccion de historiadores clasicos del Peru. 98755, 98757

Coleccion de historiadores de Chile. 12754, 93312, 94898-94899, 99469, 106269

Coleccion de historiadores i de documentos relativos a la independencia de Chile. 60804, 96235, note after 97719, 99457

Coleccion de instrucciones pastorales. 670, 75979

Coleccion de laminas de las principales carceles. 74906

Coleccion de las antiguedades Mexicanas. 15196, (34151)

Coleccion de las aplicaciones que se van haciendo de los bienes. (61088)

Coleccion de las cartas del canonista de la Sierra. 61089

Coleccion de las cartas pastorales. 51320

Coleccion de las causas mas celebres. 14296

Coleccion de las ciudades, villas, y lugares. 27813

Coleccion de las composiciones de eloquencia y poesia. 11612

Coleccion de las composiciones poeticas. 14297

Coleccion de las leyes dadas por el Congreso Constitucional. 14565

Coleccion de las leyes de mas frecuente uso. 72545, 72548

Coleccion de las leyes, decretos, circulares y providencias. 59295

Coleccion de las leyes fundamentales que han regido en la Republica Mexicana. 48356

Coleccion de las leyes y decretos de la Neuva Granada. 56280

Coleccion de las leyes y decretos expedidos por el Congreso General. (48357)

Coleccion de las ordenanzas que para el gobierno del Obispado de Michoacan. (67658)

Coleccion de las piezas poeticas. 41409

Coleccion de las publicaciones. 62928

Coleccion de las relaciones de los mas notables. (56731)

Coleccion de las sentencias pronunciadas por los Tribunales Federales. 79055

Coleccion de leyes, decretos, circulares. 48355

Coleccion de leyes, decretos y ordenes publicadas. 61091

Coleccion de leyes y decretos circulares y otros documents. (48288)

Coleccion de leyes y decretos sancionados desde la jura de la independencia. 61090

Coleccion de leyes y decretos sobre justicia nacional. 9004

Coleccion de libros que tratan de America. 105724

Coleccion de libros raros o curiosos. 58294, 58307, 98604, 2d note after 100585, 105717

Coleccion de libros y documentos referentes a la historia del Peru. 99633, 105724

Coleccion de los aranceles. (48511)

Coleccion de los decretos espedidos por el Supremo Gobierno. (48359)

Coleccion de los decretos y ordenes de las cortes de Espana. 48358

Coleccion de los decretos y ordenes del Premer Congreso Constitucional. (67097)

Coleccion de los decretos y ordenes mas importantes. 66550

Coleccion de los dialogos criticos. 94149

Coleccion de los discursos que pronunciaron. (61092)

Coleccion de los documentos mas importantes. (59631)

Coleccion de los documentos mas intersantes. 14298, 48360

Coleccion de los documentos relativos a la navigacion fluviatil del Rio de la Plata. 14299, 38994, note after 93820

Coleccion de los editoriales. 55255

Coleccion de los escritos mas importantes. 67079

Coleccion de los mejores autores Espanoles. 86471, 86473

Coleccion de los mercurios referentes a las misiones. 85681, 97711

Coleccion de los opusculos y articulos. 56453, 106223

Coleccion de los partes publicados desde que se presento. 81474

Coleccion de los partes y otros documentos publicados. 29421

Coleccion de los principales documentos de la guerra. 31566

Coleccion de los recursos de los magistrados despojados. 61093

Coleccion de los tratados de paz, alianza, comercio &c. 14300

Coleccion de los tratados de paz, alianza, neutralidad, garantia, proteccion, tregua, mediacion, accesion, reglamento de limites, comercio-navegacion, &c. 77

Coleccion de los ultimos decretos sobre contribuciones directas. (48359)

Coleccion de los viages y descubrimientos. 52098, 99380, note after 99383C

Coleccion [de Luis Antonio y Cayetano Antonio Torres Tunon.] 9814

Coleccion de macsinas y pesamientos critico-
politico-morales. (47340)
Coleccion de medicamentos indigenas y sus
aplicaciones. 63948
Coleccion de memorias cientificas, agricolas
e industriales. 71646
Coleccion de memorias de historia, literatura,
ciencias y artes. 68835
Coleccion de memorias instructivas. 48361
Coleccion de memorias sobre fisica. 6941
Coleccion de memorias, y noticias del gobierno
general. (75562)
Coleccion de memorias y trabajos de esta
sociedad. 85748
Coleccion de monumentos, trajes y paisajes.
(48590)
Coleccion de obras y documentos relativos a
la historia antigua y moderna de las
provincias del Rio de la Plata. 984,
1537, (2535), 3371, 9811, (11677),
23738, 36347, 69228, 73211, 87305-
87306, 94272, 96247, 96547, 96556,
97447, 97742, 99399, 99515-99517,
99665-99666, 106365
Coleccion de obras y opusculos pertenecientes
a la milagrosa aparicion. 14301
Coleccion de opusculos. 52100
Coleccion de ordenes y decretos de la Sob-
erana Junta Provisional Gubernativa.
48362
Coleccion de papeles cientificos. 74761
Coleccion de papels publicados en aquel reyno.
39525
Coleccion de pensamientos extraidos. 68078
Coleccion de piezas dramaticas. 75912
Coleccion de piezas escogidas. 71699
Collecion de poesias de los mejores poetas.
(58337)
Coleccion de poesias Mejicanas. 48363
Coleccion de poesias originals por Abigail
Lozano. 42589
Coleccion de poesias orijinales, por Jose M.
Sampler Agudelo. (75915)
Coleccion de producciones originales en prosa
y verso. 24826
Coleccion de providencias. 66551
Coleccion de providencias diocesanas dada
por D. Francisco Favian y Fuero.
(23593)
Coleccion de Providencias diocesanas del
Obispado de la Puebla. (23592)
Coleccion de representaciones y protestas.
(51321)
Coleccion de sentencias pronunziadas por los
tribunales y juzgados. 48364
Coleccion de sermones para los Domingos.
74521
Coleccion de todos los documentos. 52247
Coleccion de todos los remitidos. 46187
Coleccion de tratados celebrados por la
republica Argentina. (14302)
Coleccion de tratados celebrados por la
republica de Chile. 12755
Coleccion de tratados con las naciones estran-
jeras. 48365
Coleccion de varias esposiciones. 94191
Coleccion de varios documentos interesantes.
(14303)
Coleccion de varios documentos oficiales.
39523, note after 93820
Coleccion de varios documentos para la his-
toria de la Florida. 84379, 87206
Coleccion de varios escritos presentados por
su apoderado y defensor. 94193
Coleccion de varios papeles relativos a los
sucesos de Buenos-Ayres. 51214

Coleccion de verdades acerca del estado poli-
tico. 17802
Coleccion de viages de los Espanoles. 70884
Coleccion de viajeros y memorias geograficas.
99460
Coleccion diplomatica. 61094
Coleccion eclesiastica Mejicana. 48366
Coleccion escogida de las composiciones.
17766, 86191-86192
Coleccion general de documentos, que contiene
los sucesos. 1668
Coleccion general de documentos tocantes a
la tercera epoca. 10803
Coleccion general de las provincias hasta aqui
tomadas. 14304
Coleccion general de los tratados publicos.
14566
Coleccion legal de cartas, dictamenes, y otros
papeles. 38628
Coleccion polidiomica Mexicana. 48367, 85759
Colecraft, Henry Rowe. sobrequet see
Schoolcraft, Henry Rowe, 1793-1864.
Colector. pseud. Rudo ensayo. (73889)
Colegial. pseud. Recuerdos de 9. de Julio de
1820. see Y., L. J. M. pseud.
Colegii Yalensis, quod est Novo-Portu, Con-
necticutensium, statuta. 105810
Colegio apostolico de Guadalupe, en Zacatecas.
17508
Colegio de Abogados, Buenos Aires. 25104
Colegio de Abogados de Mexico. see Nacional
Colegio de Abogados de Mexico.
Colegio de Abogados de Puebla. 66560
Colegio de Abogados de San Ignacio de Loyola,
Puerto Principe. see Real e Ilustre
Colegio de Abogados de San Ignacio de
Loyola, Puerto Principe.
Colegio de Chaves, Caracas. 68892
Colegio de Escribanos de Cuba. Charter.
17800
Real Colegio de Escribanos de Mexico. 48463
Colegio de Espiritu Santo de Mexico. see
Mexico (City) Colegio del Espiritu Santo.
Colegio de Ingenieros de la Republica de
Venezuela, Caracas. see Colegio de
Ingenieros de Venezuela, Caracas.
Colegio de Ingenieros de Venezuela, Caracas.
68857, (70299)
Colegio de la Independencia Americana, Are-
quipa, Peru. 65960
Colegio de la Paz, Mexico (City) see Mexico
(City) Colegio de la Paz.
Colegio de las Vizcainas. see Vizcainas,
Colegio de las.
Colegio de San Carlos, Havana. see Havana.
Colegio de San Carlos.
Colegio de San Gregorio, Mexico (City) see
Mexico (City) Colegio de San Gregorio.
Real Colegio de S. Ignacio, Puebla, Mexico.
94636
Colegio de San Ignacio de Loyola, Mexico
(City) see Mexico (City) Colegio de
la Paz.
Colegio de San Ildefonso de Mexico. see
Mexico (City) Colegio de San Ildefonso
de Mexico.
Real Colegio de San Luis Gonzaga de Nuestra
Senora de los Zacatecas. 106239
Real Colegio de San Martin, Lima. see Lima.
Universidad de San Marcos.
Colegio de Santa Maria, Caracas. see Cara-
cas. Colegio de Santa Maria.
Colegio de Santa Maria. Directores Angel E.
Ribas Baldwin, Agustin Aveledo. Examen
de 1865. (76782)

COLEGIO

Colegio de Santa Maria, Directores Angel E.
Ribas Baldwin, Agustin Aveledo, exa-
mens de 1866. (76782)
Colegio del Espiritu Santo, Mexico (City) see
Mexico (City) Colegio del Espiritu Santo.
Colegio Mayor de Nuestra Senora del Rosario,
Bogota. see Bogota. Colegio Mayor
de Nuestra Senora del Rosario.
Colegio Nacional, Jalapa, Mexico. see Jal-
apa, Mexico. Colegio Nacional.
Colegio Mayor de Santa Maria de Todos San-
tos, Mexico (City) see Mexico (City)
Colegio Mayor de Santa Maria de Todos
Santos.
Colegio Nacional de Mineria Mexicana. see
Mexico. Colegio Nacional de Mineria.
Colegio Nacional de Mineria, Mexico. see
Mexico. Colegio Nacional de Mineria.
Real Colegio Seminario, Tepotzotlan, Mexico.
see Tepotzotlan, Mexico. Real Colegio
Seminario.
Colegio Seminario de la Santa Iglesia Metro-
politana de Mexico. see Mexico (Arch-
diocese) Colegio Seminario.
Real Colegio Seminario de Lima. see Lima.
Real Colegio Seminario.
Colegio y Escuelas Lancasterianas del Instituto
Literario de Mexico, San Agustin de las
Cuevas. see Instituto Literario de
Mexico. Colegio y Escuelas Lancaster-
ianas, San Agustin de las Cuevas, Mexico.
Coleman, Elihu. 14305
Coleman, Frederick D. plaintiff 81069
Coleman, John. 14306
Coleman, Lyman. 14307-(14308), 52053, note
after 90882
Coleman, Obed. 47561
Coleman, Seth. (14309)
Coleman, Simeon. 51796, 102823
Coleman, Thomas M. illus. 61567
Coleman, William, 1766-1829. 14310-14314,
(23365), 86141
Coleman, William, 1766-1829. supposed author
23981, (40117), 97440
Coleman, William, 1766-1829. defendant
75950, 2d note after 96812
Coleman, William, 1766-1829. reporter
102461
Coleman, William, fl. 1861. 1783A, 14315
Coleman (William T.) & Company. firm 14316
Coleman family. 14307, note after 90882
Coleoptera of Kansas and Eastern New Mexico.
39664, 85072
Coleoptera of Kansas and New Mexico. 39663
Coleopteres du Mexique. 12611
Coleopteres et autres ordres. 21210
Coleraine, George Hanger, 4th Baron, 1751?-
1824. 30226-30227
Coleridge, -------, fl. 1836. 97700
Coleridge, Derwent, 1800-1883. ed. 14317
Coleridge, Hartley. 14317
Coleridge, John. 14321
Coleridge, Henry Nelson. 14318-14320, 2d
note after 102874, 3d note after 102866,
2d note after 106324
Coleridge, S. J. see Coleridge, Samuel
Taylor, 1772-1834.
Coleridge, Samuel Taylor, 1772-1834. 14322,
(40822), 88559-88560
Coleridge, William Hart, Bp. of Barbados,
1789-1849. 14323-(14324), 25090
Coles, Abraham. 14325
Coles, Benjamin C. (14326), 47506
Coles, Edward. 14327
Coles, George. 14328-14330
Coles, J. A. (14331)

Coles, John F. 14332, 82698
Coles, Oscar. 14333
Coleson, Ann. 14335
Colesworthy, Daniel Clement, 1810-1893. 14336
Colesworthy, Daniel Clement, 1810-1893.
supposed author 96320
Colet, John Annesley. 14337-14338, 103663
Coleti, Gian Domenico. 14339
Colfavru, J. C. (14340)
Colfax, R. H. 14341
Colfax, Schuyler, 1823-1885. 14342-14344,
28554, 44863, 60749, 83553
Colgan, William James. (14345)
Colhouer, T. H. 14346
Colignola, Zarrabini de. see Flaminio, Gian
Antonio, 1464-1536.
Coligny, A. de. 14347
Colijn, Michel. 14348-14353, 31540, 31542-
31543, 57901, 67597, note after 102849
Colin, Antoine. 115, 13801, 14355, 49948
Colin, Agusto Frederico. 14356
Colina, Rafael de la. 14358
Colina y Rubio, Carlos Maria. 14357
Colindres, Luys de Rubera y. see Ribera y
Colindres, Luys de.
Colla, Luigi. 14359
Collaert, Adrian, 1560-1618. engr. 92665
Collaert, Joannes, 1566-1628. engr. 92667
Collamer, Jacob, 1791-1865. 14360, 96304
Collamontanus. ed. 66471
Collana di storie e memorie contemporanee.
5304
Collar, Charles B. reporter 3137, 3139,
8705, 23253, 23271, 35354, 51103, 66631,
69420, 87508, 102283
Collecao completa de sortes, versos, etc.
13059
Collecao de noticias para a historia e geografia
das nacoes ultramarinas. 7639, (14362),
85635, note after 99383C
Collecao de noticias ultramarinas. 70794
Collecao de obras originaes. (7603)
Collecao alphabetica e resumida de todos os
avisos. 9760
Collecao chronologica das leis, decretos,
resolucoes, provisoes. 51688
Collecao completa dos tratados celebrados
pelo Brasil. 62986
Collecao contendo a lei da creacao do Supremo
Tribunal de Justicia. 59507
Collecao das disposicioes acerca da arreca-
dacao e escripturacao. 85678
Collecao das mais notaveis composicoes
(7582), 9934
Collecao das melhores poesias dos poetas do
Brasil. 58828
Collecao das obras do ex.^{mo} e rev.^{mo} senhor
D. Romulado Antonio de Seixas. 78952
Collecao de alguns artigos escriptos e publica-
dos no Brasil. 72297
Collecao das leis, alvaras, decretos, cartas
regias, &c. 7548
Collecao das leis do imperio do Brasil. 7549
Collecao das leis e decretos do imperio do
Brasil. (7550)
Collecao das mais nataveis composicoes.
(7582)
Collecao das melhores poesias dos poetas do
Brasil. 58828, 99734
Collecao de libros ineditos da historia Portu-
gueza. 14361
Collecao de monumentos ineditos para a
historia das conquistas. 24023
Collecao de opusculos reimpressos relativos a
historia das navegacoes. (14363), 24895

Colleccao de poesias. 19963, 58830
Colleccao de poesias antiguas e modernas. 60889
Colleccao de poesias diversas de auctores escolhidos. 49440
Colleccao de poesias dos melhores poetas Brasileiros. 60883
Colleccao de receitas, e segredos de utilidade universal. 16048
Colleccao de varias memorias sobre vinte e duas especies de quinas. 98834
Colleccao de vocabulos e frases usados na provincia de S. Pedro do Rio Grande do Sul no Brazil. 14364, 60879, 76904
Colleccao do actos legislativos e executivos. 14356
Colleccao dos breves pontificios e leyes regias, que forao expedidos, e publicadas desde o anno de 1741. 14365, (58529), note after 68444, 99324
Colleccao dos breves pontificios, leyes regias, e officios que se passaram entre as cortes de Roma, e Lisboa. 93811
Colleccao dos principios geraes para o estabelecimiento, conservacao e augmento de um imperio. 88794
Colleccion de documentos. 6185
Colleccion de las leyes de mas frecuente uso. 48906
Colleccion de las leyes vigentes. 48643
Colleccion de las obras del venerable Obispo de Chiapa. (11240)
Colleccion de los principales trabajos. 9997
Colleccion de memorias y documentos. (38718)
Colleccion de vistas de los principales indenios de azucar. 17782
Colleccion escojida de composiciones. 1027
Colleccion general de documentos, tocantes, a la persecucion. 10803, (21763)
Collectanae curiosa. 67599
Collectanea Adamantaea. 102039
Collectanea: displaying the rise and progress of the tariff system. 10889
Collected addresses. 105121
Collected wisdom of ages. 94632
Collected works [of John Wesley.] 102676
Collected works of [Leonard] Woods. 105142
Collected works of Theodore Parker. 58741
Collectio maxima conciliorum Hispaniae a Jos. Aguirre edit. 530
Collectio maxima conciliorum Hispaniae et Novi Orbis. 528
Collectio maxima consiliorum omnium Hispaniae et Novi Orbis. (14367)
Collectio, of versamelinghe, van eenige van de tractaten. 91319
Collectio opusculorum de venerabili servo Dei Gregorio Lopesio. 41978
Collectio un unum corpus librorum. 14366
Collection abrege des voyages. 6897
Collection annotee d'autres classiques Espagnols. 98767
Collection. By G. P. Putnam. (66799), 86327
Collection [by George Hart.] 27113, 91315
Collection, by Joshua Smith. 83409
Collection compendium. 82438
Collection d'anciennes relations inedites. 94843
Collection d'auteurs Francais. 4540, 5135
Collection de decisions de divers tribunaux du Bas-Canada. 70360
Collection de dessins relatifs a leur voyage autour du monde. 6874

Collection de documents dans les langues indigenes. 7423, 7427, 7435, 7437, 38826
Collection de lettres ecrites sur les lieu par l'auteur [N. Bossu.] 6470
Collection de lois maritimes. 58561
Collection de memoires et correspondances officielles. (44145), 98671
Collection de memoires et de relations sur l'histoire ancienne du Canada. 67020, 69256, 1st note after 94271
Collection de memoires pour servir a l'histoire de France sous Napoleon. 99756
Collection de memoires sur les colonies. (44145), 98671
Collection de pieces curieuses d'histoire. (68417)
Collection de precis historiques. 82263, 82271
Collection de quelques ecrits en faveur de la constitution. 23993
Collection de quinze planches. 77153
Collection de renseignements. (11681), 76882
Collection de tableaux. 49832
Collection de tous les voyages faits autour du monde. 4822
Collection des auteurs Francais. 5135
Collection des constitutions. 21119
Collection des differens discours et pieces. 96962
Collection des navires et pirogues. 58593
Collection des relations de voyages. 84560
Collection des relations de voyages en Afrique. 105394
Collection des renseignements. 76882
Collection des voyages de Melchisedech Thevenot. 10328
Collection des voyages et des decouvertes des Espagnols. 14403
Collection des voyages nouveaux les plus estimes. (44156)
Collection d'estampes, representant les evenements de la guerre. 68422
Collection d'ouvrages, ecrits en diverses langues. 101352
Collection du texte des regles. 85813
Collection from the miscellaneous writings of Nathaniel Peabody Rogers. 72716
Collection from the newspaper writings of Nathaniel Peabody Rogers. 72715
Collection geographique cree a la Bibliotheque Royale. 14368
Collection of accurate hydrographique plans. 14369
Collection of acts and parts of acts of Assembly. 3054
Collection of acts or laws passed in the state of Massachusetts Bay. (45679)
Collection of acts passed in the Parliament of Great Britain. 10479
Collection of addresses to His Majesty. 100674
Collection of affidavits and certificates. 46848, (46900), 102024
Collection of all acts and parts of acts of the General Assembly. 35725
Collection of all such acts of the General Assembly. 100403
Collection of all such public acts of the General Assembly. 100392
Collection of all the acts of Assembly, now in force. 100385
Collection of all the acts of Assembly. 55601
Collection of all the . . . acts . . . of Kentucky. 95328
Collection of all the laws of the province of Pennsylvania. 59982

Collection of all the most important documents. 4919, 50683

Collection of all the papers. 44602

Collection of all the public and permanent acts. (37533)

Collection of all the treaties of peace, alliance, and commerce, between Great Britain and other powers, from 1648 to 1784. 19124

Collection of all the treaties of peace, alliance, and commerce, between Great-Britain and other powers, from the revolution of 1688 to the present time. 14371

Collection of all the treaties of peace, alliance and commerce, between Great Britain and other powers, from the treaty of Munster, in 1648, to the treaties signed at Paris in 1783. 14372

Collection of American epitaphs and inscriptions. 705

Collection of ancient and modern British authors. 97032

Collection of anecdotes and incidents of travel. 67514

Collection of authentic discoveries and entertaining voyages. 100821

Collection of authentic documents. 9255

Collection of authentic, useful and entertaining voyages and discoveries. (3655)

Collection of autograph letters. 52346

Collection of British authors. 17935, 90290, 92442, 92462

Collection of calculations and remarks. 86606, 86759

Collection of campaign songs for 1868. 28317

Collection of characters, moral essays and lives. (26181)

Collection of charters and other publick acts. 59983

Collection of charters, treaties, and other documents. 27095, 69760

Collection of Chippeway and English hymns. 36589

Collection of choice things. (9792)

Collection of church music. 4697

Collection of college words and customs. 29734

Collection of composures in metre. 88889

Collection of curious observations. 38729

Collection of debates in Parliament. 2263

Collection of devotional tracts. 14373

Collection of discourses, delivered on public occasions. 90187

Collection of discourses on Christian missions. 92371

Collection of divine hymns, or spiritual songs. 83418

Collection of divine poems from Fr. Quarles. 39820, 1st note after 94666

Collection of doctrines, belonging to the Hopkintonian scheme of orthodoxy. 79272

Collection of documents and letters. 10966, note before 87805

Collection of documents on Spitzbergen & Greenland. 14374

Collection of droll stories. 85468

Collection of earth-quakes. 9516

Collection of esay and instructive lessions. 88466

Collection of 85 curious trees and shurbs. 11507

Collection of elegant eulogies. 36361, note after 101900

Collection of elegiac poems devoted to the memory. 95433

Collection of eloquent and interesting extracts. 12394

Collection of embodied poetical thoughts. 83972

Collection of essays. 102393

Collection of essays and fugitiv [sic] writings. 102344

Collection of essays and miscellanies. 39072

Collection of essays and tracts in theology. 88968

Collection of essays on the subject of episcopacy. (14375), 40570

Collection of essays on various subjects. 24549

Collection of essays on war and peace. 6358

Collection of essays, poems, speeches, histories, and banquets. (29918)

Collection of essays, prose and poetical. 5896

Collection of essays, written in favor of the new constitution. 18934, (23979)-23980, (23991)

Collection of evangelical hymns. 92757

Collection of evidence. 1st note after 98997

Collection of exotics from the island of Antigua. 1697

Collection of extracts from Federal papers. (55313), note after 95351

Collection of extraordinary adventures. 33304

Collection of facts. 69157

Collection of facts and documents relating to ecclesiastical affairs in Groton, Mass. (4338), 9623, 28965, 28976, 42460

Collection of facts and documents relative to the death of Major-General Alexander Hamilton. 14311, 29989, 86141

Collection of facts and documents relative to the project of a bridge. 6598

Collection of facts and interesting anecdotes. 94656

Collection of facts and observations respecting the origin of the yellow fever in this country. 18002

Collection of facts concerning the government of Sir George Prevost. 10629

Collection of facts interspersed with observations. (74427)

Collection of facts, opinions and arguments for freedom. 9329

Collection of facts, relating to the colony of Liberia. 55059

Collection of Fanny Forester's village sketches. 36863

Collection of forms, adapted to the use of justices of the peace. (70564)

Collection of forms of writs, &c. 89384

Collection of forms used by the clerks of the courts. 72117

Collection of fugitive essays, in prose and verse. (65081)

Collection of fugitive pieces from the Philadelphia press. 29814, 62042

Collection of fugitive poems. By J. Mortimer. 50988

Collection of fugitive poems. [By Lewis J. Cist.] 13156

Collection of geographical, moral, religious, biblical, political and other chapters. 89938

Collection of Gospel hymns. 79719, 97893, 4th note after 102601

Collection of his [i. e. Benjamin Franklin's] finest essays. 25534, 102487

Collection of his [i. e. Thomas Chalkley's] works. 11750

Collection of historical letters. 963

Collection of historical tracts. 103352-103353

Collection of histories. 48246

Collection of histories, essays, & novels.
37252, (47869)
Collection of hymns. 104115
Collection of hymns and spiritual songs for
public and private devotion. 75544,
83300
Collection of hymns for public and private
worship. 87915
Collection of hymns for social worship.
103505
Collection of hymns for social worship, with
hymn tunes. 39302
Collection of hymns for the use of native
Christians of the Mohawk language.
(49839)
Collection of hymns, for the use of the Chris-
tian Indians, of the missions of the
United Brethren. 106297
Collection of hymns, for the use of the Chris-
tian Indians of the United Brethren.
50518
Collection of hymns, for the use of the Dela-
ware Christian Indians. 19373, 106298
Collection of hymns for the use of the Pro-
testant Church of the United Brethren.
59984
Collection of hymns for youth. 90188
Collection of hymns, in the Oneida language.
80840
Collection of Indian anecdotes. 34631
Collection of interesting accounts of naval
disasters. (69380)
Collection of interesting and authentic papers.
(32193), (32226)
Collection of interesting and important reports
and papers. 2264
Collection of interesting, authentic papers.
951, 955
Collection of interesting biography. 14376
Collection of interesting fragments, in prose
and verse. 105610
Collection of interesting scenes and events.
17319
Collection of items relative to the history of
the Sunday School. 67779
Collection of legislative enactments. 94992
Collection of letters and state papers. (33263)
Collection of letters, in which the imperfection
of learning . . . and a remedy for it,
are hinted. 44092
Collection of letters on freemasonry. (25794),
89359
Collection of letters sent from the Hovse of
Representatives of the Province of Massa-
chvsetts Bay. 31947, (32551), 7th note
after 97146
Collection of log cabin and patriotic melodies.
95855
Collection of lyrics. 70022
Collection of many select and Christian epis-
tles. 25347
Collection of masonic songs, and others, with
notes. 89428
Collection of masonic songs, odes, &c. 103176
Collection of maxims, morals and miscellanies.
33853
Collection of memorable passages from the
discourses of Henry Ward Beecher. 4318,
50328
Collection of memorables relating to our captives. 46342, 104260
Collection of memorials concerning divers
deceased ministers. 14377
Collection of metrical compositions. 50092
Collection of mining laws of Spain and Mexico.
(29879)

Collection of miscellaneous essays. 36627
Collection of miscellaneous papers. 36627
Collection of miscellaneous pieces in prose
and verse. (77184)
Collection of miscellaneous writings of Pro-
fessor Frisbie. (25978)
Collection of modern and contemporary voy-
ages and travels. 6182, 16771-16772,
19644, 31489, (36696), 37230, 48706,
50230, 60999, (61013), 62507-62508,
76707, 77858, 81047, 81508, 96496
Collection of Moravian hymn-tunes. 75903
Collection of [Mormon] poems, &c. 50740
Collection of most beautiful pieces of music.
86948
Collection of narratives, official reports,
records, &c. 30539
Collection of national, patriotic, and social
songs. 10184
Collection of new, favorite, and national songs.
96368
Collection of observations, hymns, letters, etc.
73140
Collection of occurrences and facts. 31632
Collection of original and select sacred poetry.
84050
Collection of original manuscripts made by the
late Rev. Dr. William B. Sprague. 89732
Collection of original papers relative to the
history of the colony of Massachusetts-
Bay. 33696, 34069, 45706, 51774, 98500
Collection of original pieces in honour of the
arrival of Gen. Lafayette. 38583, 96464
Collection of original poems for the comfort
and encouragement of Christian pilgrims.
(18603)
Collection of original poems on various sub-
jects. 12285
Collection of original poetry. 23537
Collection of original prayers, and divers sen-
tences. 6351
Collection of original sermons. (14877), 22239
Collection of original songs, poems, etc. 89157
Collection of original verse. 66649
Collection of original voyages. 29473
Collection of pamphlets with reference to the
establishment of the Reformed Episcopal
Church. 83518, 83525
Collection of papers and other tracts, written
occasionally. 37239, 37242, 86783
Collection of papers and other tracts, written
occasionally on various subjects. (37238)
Collection of papers by Theodore Janssen,
Bart. 37783
Collection of papers containing the declaration
of independence. 14378
Collection of papers, lately printed in the
Daily advertiser. 103506
Collection of papers [of Sir William Keith.]
86783
Collection of papers on political, literary and
moral subjects. 102345
Collection of papers on the subject of bilious
fevers. 78614, 102346
Collection of papers, printed by order. 85934
Collection of papers relating to the present
juncture of affairs. 81492
Collection of papers, relative to half-pay and
commutation of half-pay, compiled by
permission of His Excellency George
Washington. 101533
Collection of papers, relative to half-pay and
commutation of half-pay, granted by Congress to the officers of the army. 14379,
101533, 101543

Collection of papers, relative to half-pay, and commutation thereof granted by Congress to the officers of the army. 101544

Collection of papers relative to the death and character of General George Washington. 101899

Collection of papers relative to the transactions of the town of Milton. 49146

Collection of papers, respecting a people whose ancestors emigrated from Wales to America, in the year 1170. 9211

Collection of papers, that have been published at different times. (14380)

Collection of passages from the Bible, which show the sin of holding and treating the human species as property. 93762

Collection of passages from the Bible, which show the sin of holding property in man. 93761

Collection of patent cases. 71728

Collection of patriotic and humorous songs and odes. 21615

Collection of patriotic hymns and tunes. (18259)

Collection of patriotic, national, original, and selected songs. 86923

Collection of patriotic songs and heroic poems. 88418

Collection of patriotic songs, in favor of the constitution and the union. 31469

Collection of patriotic songs, original and selected. 58144

Collection of pen portraits and paintings. 71560

Collection of personal and political reminiscences from 1848 to 1876. (72216)

Collection of . . . photographic views. (62587)

Collection of pieces. 100678

Collection of pieces, in prose and poetry. By Ann Welch. 102516

Collection of pieces, in prose and verse, being the exercises of young converts. 100678

Collection of pieces on this subject. 30050, 2d note after 105926

Collection of pieces relating to the French emigrations to Guyana. 29168

Collection of pieces, translated from the French. 104017

Collection of plants of Boston and its environs. 5297

Collection of pleadings and practical precedents. 105999

Collection of poems. 14382, (41932), 51562

Collection of poems. By Eugene Lies. 40994

Collection of poems. By Mrs. M. St. Leon Loud. 42162

Collection of poems. By several hands. (14381)

Collection of poems, chiefly anti-slavery. (26672)

Collection of poems, fables, epigrams, &c. (27411), 57175

Collection of poems for the times. 12812

Collection of poems: inscribed to my valued friend. 60840

Collection of poems, on American affairs. 25892

Collection of poems on different subjects. 36494

Collection of poems, on religious and moral subjects. 14383

Collection of poems, written by William Smith. 84838

Collection of poetical pieces, &c. 65710

Collection of political papers. 105704

Collection of . . . popular, ancient, and modern songs. 39040

Collection of popular and patriotic songs. 41787, 51946, 4th note after 94534

Collection of popular and patriotic songs, . . . dedicated to the friends of Harrison and Tyler. (41786)

Collection of popular, patriotic, national, pathetic, and jolly songs. 10181

Collection of popular songs. 100651

Collection of prayers and exhortations. 2846

Collection of precedents. 38739

Collection of prose and poetry. (13435)

Collection of psalm tunes, hymns, and anthems. 89423

Collection of psalm tunes in three parts. 97421

Collection of psalm tunes, with a few anthems and hymns. 66450

Collection of psalms. 106041

Collection of psalms and hymns. 102650

Collection of psalms, hymns and poems. 104726

Collection of psalms and hymns, in the Mohawk language. 49840

Collection of psalms and hymns. Translated into the language of the York Indians. 45486

Collections of public acts and papers. 14384

Collection of rare and original documents and relations. 58270, 89959

Collection of religious tracts. 4671, 4678

Collection of reminiscent narratives of fishing and coasting trips. 84323

Collection of sacred hymns adopted [sic] to the faith and views of the Church of Jesus Christ, of Latter-Day Saints. 92682

Collection of sacred hymns for the Church of the Latter Day Saints. (72623)

Collection of sacred music. (48842)

Collection of sacred, vocal, and instrumental music. 14864

Collection of scarce acting tragedies. 89398

Collection of scarce and interesting tracts. 14385, 19123, 103122

Collection of scarce and valuable papers. 78206

Collection of scarce and valuable tracts, on the most interesting and valuable subjects. 58061, 67545, 67500, (67585), 67599, 73577, 73579, 78369, 78374, 78376, 3d note after 97555, 98499

Collection of scarce, curious and entertaining pamphlets and tracts. 30394

Collection of select biography. 25677

Collection of select nautical tales. 21109

Collection of sermons by distinguished divines. 89506

Collection of sermons, by eminent divines. 50366

Collection of sermons delivered there by eminent divines. (21141)

Collection of sermons from some of the most eminent preachers. 2401

Collection of sermons on the death of the Right Reverend John Henry Hobart. 32302, 77986

Collection of several commissions. (45413)

Collection of several messages and warnings. 9515

Collection of several pieces of M^r. John Locke. (41726)

Collection of short, correct and easy rules. 34878

Collection of sketches and letters. 13461, note after (41404)

Collection of some memorable passages. 28992

Collection of some papers concerning Mr. Lewis Rou's affair. (73448)

Collection, of some of the many offensive matters. 46263

Collection of some of the most interesting narratives of Indian warfare in the west. 36403, 48166

Collection of some of the most useful acts and ordinances. (10478)

Collection of some writings of the most noted of the people called Quakers. 66919

Collection of songs. 21779, 41355

Collection of songs and odes on the late naval victories. (14875)

Collection of songs, by the inimitable Captain Morris. 50803

Collection of songs for anti-slavery meetings. 8587

Collection of songs, odes, glees, and ballads. 25816

Collection of songs of the American press. 51356

Collection of songs, sentimental, humourous, and patriotic. 90485

Collection of songs, with music. (14386)

Collection of sonnets. 81215

Collection of speeches and addresses. 39749, 50354, 92297, 92299, 104873

Collection of speeches and writings. 14387

Collection of speeches delivered before religious benevolent societies. 12919

Collection of speeches, poems, dialogues, and songs. 14443

Collection of standard American authors. 16452, 16493, (21118), 25537

Collection of state-papers, relative to the first acknowledgement of the sovereignty of the United States of America. 228-229, 14388

Collection of state papers relative to the war against France. 14389

Collection of state tracts. 14390

Collection of statutes relating to the British colonies. 21633

Collection of stories. 12713

Collection of sundry messages. 9516

Collection of sundry publications and other documents. 14391, 69089

Collection of tales and essays. 20996

Collection of tales, poems, and essays, gleaned chiefly from the fugitive literature of the nineteenth century. 76953

Collection of tales, poems, and essays, gleaned from the fugitive literature of the nineteenth centure. 97962

Collection of tears. 84641

Collection of testimonies. 66920

Collection of the acts, deliverances, and testimonies. (2701)

Collection of the acts of Parliament. 14370

Collection of the acts of Virginia and Kentucky relative to Louisville and Portland. 42319

Collection of the acts of Virginia and Kentucky relative to the town of Louisville. (42318)

Collection of the acts, orders, votes, and resolves. 35560

Collection of the addresses. 14393

Collection of the ancient and modern authorities. 3906

Collection of the best psalm tunes. (24654)

Collection of the best discoveries in nature. (46253)

Collection of the British statutes in force in Maryland. 45107

Collection of the celebrated fugitive pieces. 99558

Collection of the constitutions of the thirteen United States of North-America. 16091

Collection of the customs' tariffs of all nations. 54941

Collection of the earliest statistics and judicial proceedings. (15761)

Collection of the early voyages, travels and discoveries of the English nation. 9759, 29599, note after 36681, 100462

Collection of the epistles and works of Benjamin Holme. 32573

Collection of the epistles from the Yearly Meeting of Friends in London. 86041

Collection of the essays on the subject of episcopacy. 41349

Collection of the facts and documents, relative to the death of Major-General Alexander Hamilton. 14311, 86141

Collection of the familiar letters and miscellaneous papers of Benjamin Franklin. (25494), 25507

Collection of the Governor's several speeches. 45108

Collection of the laws of patent privileges. 41961

Collection of the laws of the province of Pennsylvania. 59972, 59985

Collection of the laws. Or legislative acts in force. 94773

Collection of the lives of the most remarkable and most eminent men. 1166, note after 104564

Collection of the military laws of the United States. 87685

Collection of the most admired songs. 49788

Collection of the most celebrated voyages [sic] and travel. 25144

Collection of the most favorite national, patriotic, sentimental and comic ballads of the day. (80486)

Collection of the most important speeches and documents. 70020

Collection of the most instructive and amusing lives. 103541

Collection of the most interesting narratives of Indian warfare. 36403, 48166

Collection of the most interesting tracts, lately published in England and America. 952, 14392, 37244, 66015, 86745, 91132, 97575

Collection of the most modern acting plays. 84783-84784

Collection of the most popular ancient and modern songs. 101272

Collection of the most popular . . . songs. 81417

Collection of the most remarkable narratives. 20874, 73592

Collection of the most select voyages. (63514)

Collection of the native medicinal plants. 5294

Collection of the newest and most approved songs. (52068)

Collection of the noble and praiseworthy deeds. 7293

Collection of the official accounts, in detail. 23940

Collection of the ordinances of the City Council of Charleston. 12044

Collection of the papers of the Sanitary Commission. 76549, 76647

Collection of the penal laws of the commonwealth of Pennsylvania. 59986

Collection of the political censor for 1796. 14005

Collection of the political writings of William Leggett. 39863

Collection of the principal evidence and other documents. (16986), 58408

Collection of the private acts. (55602)

Collection of the proceedings of the Great and General Court of Assembly. (45680)

Collection of the several writings and faithful testimonies. 82734

Collection of the speeches of the President of the U. S. to both houses of Congress. 227

Collection of the speeches of the President of the United States to both houses of Congress, at the opening of every session. 101545

Collection of the state and municipal laws, . . . of Louisville. (42320)

Collection of the statutes now in force. 64479

Collection of the statutes of Charles I. and II. 44198

Collection of the statutes of the Parliament of England. 44870

Collection of the sufferings of the people called Quakers. 66921

Collection of the testimonies of the fathers of New England churches. 52620

Collection of the tracts of a certain free enquirer. 1604, 85685

Collection of the very interesting proclamations. 29578

Collection of the works of that antient, faithful servant of Jesus Christ, Thomas Chalkley. 11747

Collection of the works of Thomas Chalkley. 11746

Collection of the works of William Penn. 59690

Collection of the writings . . . of Mr. Edward Ward. 101285-101286

Collection of thirty-eight psalm tunes. 97421

Collection of XXXVI letters. 1223

Collection of thirty thousand names. (74151)-(74153)

Collection of thoughts from 100 writers. 32279

Collection of thoughts on civil, moral, sentimental and religious subjects. (32278)

Collection of tracts. By John Stanford. 90189

Collection of tracts. By the late John Trenchard, esq: and Thomas Gordon, esq. 86631, 96767, note after 96768

Collection of tracts from the late newspapers, &c. (14394)-14395, 84678C

Collection of tracts in Biblical literature. 65654

Collection of tracts on the subjects of taxing the British colonies in America and regulating their trade. 952, 36244, 38180, 66015, 86745, 97575, 2d note after 103122

Collection of treaties between Great Britain and other powers. (11759)

Collection of treaties, alliances, and conventions. 14397

Collection of treaties, of imperial statutes, and other public acts. 10481, 14396

Collection of treaties of peace and commerce . . . from the Peace of Munster to this time. 14398

Collection of treaties of peace and commerce, manifestos, and public papers. 14399

Collection of treatises relating to the national debts and funds. 34043

Collection of treatises relating to the South Sea stock and scheme. 34043

Collection of upwards of thirty thousand names of German, Swiss, Dutch, French, and other immigrants. 74154

Collection of valuable documents. 14400

Collection of valuable treatises upon metals. 3254

Collection of voyages and travels, consisting of authentic writers in our own tongue. 18774, 26469, 40175, 54979, 57765, 101462, 1st note after 103122

Collection of voyages and travels, in three parts. (17278), 63705

Collection of voyages and travels, some now first printed from original manuscripts. 8427, 10820, 13015-13018, 13419, (14676), 26851, 31557, 35712, 38975, 40175, 50223, 51336, (55278), 55933, 57765, 57972, 59586, (79164), 82852, 94575, 97529

Collection of voyages [by A. van Nispen.] 55355

Collection of voyages, chiefly in the South Atlantic Ocean. 18336

Collection of voyages. In four volumes. 18373, 100940

Collection of voyages to the Southern Hemisphere. 10053, 1st note after 94857, note after 99383C

Collection of voyages undertaken by the Dutch East-India Company. 14401

Collection of words and phrases, supposed to be peculiar to the United States of America. 102363

Collection of words and phrases which have been supposed to be peculiar to the United States. 62637-62638

Collection of writings . . . of Mr. Edward Ward. 101285

Collection out of Sir Matthew Hale's. 15215, 58682

Collectiones peregrinationum in Indiam Orientalem. (8784)

Collections and recollections illustrative of the early settlement and social life of the capital of Ontario. 77433

Collections concerning the Church or Congregation of Protestant Separatists. 33926

Collections concerning the early history of the founders of New Plymouth. 33925

Collections de memoires et correspondances officielles. (44145), 44151

Collection for an essay towards a materia medica. 3804

Collections for charitable and religious purposes. 85275

Collections, historical, and miscellaneous: and monthly literary journal. 7222, 18055, 23837-23838, 36327, 50397, 73592, 94112, 100759

Collections of acts, laws and orders. (23517)

Collections of certain prophecies relating to the present circumstances of New-England. 46277

Collections of the acts passed in the Parliament of Great Britain. 10480

Collections of the American Statistical Association. 1233, 24037

Collections of the Connecticut Historical Society. 9095, 15711, (15860), 15856, 86758, note after 95296, 97181, 104986

Collections of the Dorchester Antiquarian and Historical Society. 577, 13209, 46777

Collections of the Georgia Historical Society. 27027, 27079, 30947, 39327, 45000, 45001, (45003), 50352, (56847), 87900, 94218, 3d note after 106134

Collections of the Illinois State Historical Library. 96172

Collections of the Maine Historical Society.
19195, (43970)-(43971), 58096, 79441,
84343, 90611, 92664, 101005, 104525
Collections of the Massachusetts Historical
Society. 170, 290, 702, 1521-1522,
2357, 3762, 7262-7263, 9260, 12331,
12985, 13307, 13471, 15747, 17042,
17043, (18844), 18895, 19051, (19639),
(20190), 21972, 22129, 22144, 22146-
22147, (22152), 22162, 22166, 23825,
23828, 23836, 25762, 25874, 27832,
27959, 27960, 28017, 28020, (29773),
(30506), 30521, note after 31743, (32581),
32583, 32968, 33925, (36204), (36286),
(36672), 38004, 39641, 40751, (41650),
(43923), 45455, 45652, (45852)-45853,
46642, (47395), 50786, 51201, 51810,
52619, 53249, (58100), 59494, 59619,
60918, 62560, 62575, 62725, (63477),
65296, 65585, 67217, 72102, (73288),
(73981), 75957, 77234, 77246, 77610,
78431, 78438, (79447), 79449, (79835),
80205, 80207-80208, 82815, 82819,
89312, note before 91856, 91945, 92664,
note before 92797, 92801, 93506, 93697,
95632, 97409, 97733, 98034, 99766, note
after 99867, 2d note after 100494, 1st
note after 100508, 100916, 101330,
103689, 104111, 104339, note after
104653, note after 104794-104795, 104797
Collections of the Michigan Historical Society.
84082
Collections of the Minnesota Historical Society.
4607, 83608, 85433
Collections of the New Hampshire Historical
Society. 458-460, 9260, 9481, 16579,
(20190), 23818, 23828, 41883, 46723,
50392, 52872, 59077, 1st note after
65324, 78431, 82801, 101038, 103200
Collections of the New Jersey Historical Society. 1000, 21113, 24291, 25063, 50850,
53058, 53176, 53235, 54882, note after
66024, note before 91508
Collections of the New York Historical Society.
(133), 628, 4744, 10203, 13714, 20594,
20928, 26390, (33084), (37472), 38562,
40419, 49049, (54471)-54474, 66062,
69996, (75021), 78059, 79353, 84566,
84570, 84571, 86744, 88844, 92830,
note after 95562, 96171, note after
98474, 1st note after 98997, 99265,
99281, 99325, 2d note after 99889,
100852, 100853, 102920, 103152
Collections of the Nova Scotia Historical
Society. 84422
Collections of the Pennsylvania Historical
Society. 10203, 21385, 24477, 60142,
97068, 102508
Collections of the Protestant Episcopal Historical Society. 3720, 66194
Collections of the Protestant Episcopal His-
torical Society, for the year 1851. 66193
Collections of the Rhode Island Historical
Society. (10076), 21981, (28046), 64633,
70719, 90475, 104340
Collections of the South Carolina Historical
Society. 82988, note before 87456, 88005
Collections of the Vermont Historical Society.
801, 29781, 34059, 61280, 83679, 1st-2d
notes after 98997, 98999, 99000, 6th note
after 99005, 99014
Collections of the Virginia Historical and
Philosophical Society. 93185
Collections of the Virginia Historical & Philo-
sophical Society, to which is prefixed an
address. 100556

Collections of the Virginia Historical Society.
4th note after 99888, 2d note after 99889,
99994, 100006
Collections of the Wisconsin Historical Society.
20901, 83026, 83029, 92227
Collections on the history of Albany. (51365)
Collections, topographical, historical and bio-
graphical 23837-23838
Collections with regard to the case of the
American loyalists. 14402
Collections with specimens for a series of
memoirs. (3803)
Collectitia. 742, 25318
Collector of Excise, Berks County, Pa. see
Berks County, Pa. Collector of Excise.
Collector of Excise, Cumberland County, Pa.
see Cumberland County, Pa.
Collector of Excise, Bumberland County, Pa. see
Cumberland County, Pa. Collector of Excise
Collector of Excise, Montgomery County, Pa.
see Montgomery County, Pa. Collector
of Excise.
Collector of Excise, York County, Pa. see
York County, Pa. Collector of Excise.
College address. 63925
College almanack, for . . . 1773. 93245, note
after 105846
College almanack, 1761. 93242, note after
105846
College and Academy of Philadelphia. see
Pennsylvania. University.
College and Normal Seminary, Mount Union,
Ohio. see Mount Union, Ohio. College
and Normal Seminary.
College and Theological Seminary, Kalamazoo,
Michigan. see Kalamazoo College and
Theological Seminary.
College exercise. 14404
College Hill, Ohio. Farmer's College. (63390)
College Hill, Ohio. Farmer's College. Com-
mittee on the College. (63390), 70944
College Hill, Ohio. Farmer's College. Com-
mittee on the College. Chairman.
(63390), 70944 see also Richards, Giles.
College Hill, Ohio. Farmer's College. Fac-
ulty. 13137
College Hill, Ohio. Ohio Female College. see
Ohio Female College, College Hill, Ohio.
College life. 57172
College musings. 84871, 84874
College of Agriculture and the Mechanic Arts,
Durham, N. H. see New Hampshire.
College of Agriculture and the Mechanic
Arts, Durham.
College of architecture. (69001)
College of California, Oakland, Cal. see
California. University.
College of Louisiana. see Tulane University
of Louisiana
College of Medicine, Philadelphia. see Phila-
delphia College of Medicine.
College of Music, Philadelphia. see Phila-
delphia College of Music.
College of New Jersey. see Princeton Uni-
versity.
College of New-Jersey. Catalogue of the
officers and students of Nassau Hall.
53088
College of New-York, in America. see Co-
lumbia University.
College of Pharmacy, Philadelphia. see Phila-
delphia College of Pharmacy.
College of Pharmacy of Massachusetts. see
Massachusetts College of Pharmacy.
College of Philadelphia. see Pennsylvania.
University.

College of Physicians and Surgeons, Kansas City, Mo. see Kansas City, Mo. College of Physicians and Surgeons.

College of Physicians and Surgeons, New York. see Columbia University. College of Physicians and Surgeons.

College of Physicians and Surgeons . . . . Catalogue . . . and annual announcement of lectures. (54000)

College of Physicians and Surgeons of the Western District of the State of New York, Fairfield, N. Y. see Albany Medical School.

College of Physicians of Philadelphia. 6282, 61548

College of Physicians of Philadelphia. Charter. 61548

College of Physicians of Philadelphia. 61548

College of Professional Teachers, Cincinnati. see Western Literary Institute and College of Professional Teachers, Cincinnati.

College of St. James, Breathedsville, Md. see Breathedsville, Md. College of St. James.

College of St. James. 51256

College of Saint Paul, Minn. see St. Paul, Minn. College.

College of the Holy Cross, Worcester, Mass. petitioners 69481

College of William and Mary in Virginia. see William and Mary College, Williamsburg, Va.

College poem. 71133

College Point, N. Y. St. Paul's College. see St. Paul's College, College Point, N. Y.

College [proposed] for colored youth. (52970)

College reform. (82553)

College review. see American journal of education and college review.

College roll of honor. 7032

College speeches. 14406

College statement. 43884

College system of education. 55524

College—the bank—the bench. 87897, note after 89935

College, the market, and the court. 18304

Colleges, a power in civilization, to be used for Christ. 92267

Colleges and stability. (32938)

Colleges and the spirit of liberty. 85918

Colleges essential to home missions. 29764

Colleges religious institutions. 61185

Collegian. pseud. Poems. 81246

Collegian (1830) 14407, 30739

Collegian (1866) (14408)

Collegiate addresses. 47005

Collegiate and Commercial Institute, New Haven, Conn. (52965)

Collegiate and theological education at the West. 85913

Collegiate Church, New York. see New York (City) Collegiate Church.

Collegiate Institute, Louisville, Ky. 42340

Collegiate Institute, Marietta, Ohio. see Marietta College, Marietta, Ohio.

Collegiate Institute for Young Ladies, Brooklyn. see Brooklyn Collegiate Institute for Young Ladies.

Collegiate Institution for the Education of Young Ladies, New York. see Abbot Collegiate Institution for Young Ladies, New York.

Collegiate Institution for the Education of Young Ladies. . . . 1853-54. (54199)

Collegiate Institution for Young Ladies, Philadelphia. Young Ladies' Association for the Promotion of Literature and Missions. 106137

Collegiate Reformed Protestant Dutch Church, New York. see New York (City) Collegiate Church.

Collegiate School, Poughkeepsie, N. Y. see Poughkeepsie, N. Y. Collegiate School.

Collegiate School of Connecticut at Saybrook. see Saybrook, Conn. Collegiate School.

Collegido de memorias estrangeiras. 98832

Collegii Yalensis, quod est Novo-Portu Connecticutensium, statuta. 105809, 105811-105812

Collegio de San Luis Potosi, Mexico. see San Luis Potosi, Mexico. Collegio.

Real Collegio de S. Marcos, Lima. see Lima. Universidad de San Marcos.

Collegio del Pueblo de San Luys Potosi. see San Luis Potosi, Mexico. Collegio.

Collens, T. W. reporter 27318

Colleridge, J. see Coleridge, John.

Colles, Christopher. 14409-14411

Collet, ---------. cartographer 1147

Collet, -------, fl. 1758. (14412)

Collet, -------, fl. 1790. 75115

Colleton District, South Carolina. Citizens. 83853

Colley, Thomas. 14413

Colley Cibber. pseud. see Rees, James.

Colliber, Samuel. 14414

Collie, -------. 32863

Collier, -------, fl. 1821. (43001), 96901

Collier, Sir George, 1738-1795. 19775, note after 96363

Collier, John A. 14415

Collier, John Payne, 1789-1883. 14416, 29601, 67554, 67599, 77289, 78597, 82833, 82847

Collier, Mary. 21064

Collier, Robert Laird, 1837-1900. 14417

Collier, Robert R. 14418-14419

Collier, William. 14420

Collier, William R. (14421)-14422

Collin, John Francis, 1802-1889. 14423, 82321

Collin, Nicholas. tr. (133)

Collin, Nils. 14424

Collin de Plancy, Jacques A. S. 100805-100806

Collin and Delia. 92282

Collings, Jesse. 14425

Collings, John. 14426-14427

Collingwood, Cuthbert Collingwood, Baron, 1750-1810. 14428

Collingwood, G. L. Newnham. 14428

Collins, Alexander. 14429

Collins, Charles. (14331), 38548-38549, 57261, (75296)

Collins, Charles, fl. 1858. 14430

Collins, Daniel. 14432

Collins, E. K. 14433, 93819

Collins, Elizabeth. (14435)

Collins, Elizabeth (Ballinger) Mason, 1755-1831. 14434

Collins, Francis. 14436

Collins, Frederick. 60360, 83491

Collins, G. L. 85493

Collins, Gabriel. 42326

Collins, George. 74248

Collins, George C. 14437

Collins, Isaac. 14438, (61792)

Collins, James. 104884

Collins, James C. (70545) see also Rhode Island. Auditor.

Collins, John. petitioner 54976, 94549 see also Newfoundland. Governor, 1709-1712 (Collins) petitioner

Collins, John. illus. 14442, 84081

Collins, John, 1625-1683. 14440

Collins, John, fl. 1792. 14441, 1st note after
102822
Collins, John A. 14443-(14444), 50190
Collins, John Baptist. defendant 97099
Collins, Levi. 14445
Collins, Lewis. 14446, 85376
Collins, N. G. 14447
Collins, Nathaniel. supposed author 74291
Collins, Robert. (14448)
Collins, Ruth. 14449
Collins, S. H. 14450
Collins, Stephen. 14451
Collins, Thad. W. (14452)
Collins, V. L. ed. 104940, 104945-104946
Collins, William, 1818-1878. 14454
Collins, William H. 14455
Collins' business and resident directory of
Leavenworth. 39549
Collins' city directory of Leavenworth. 93548
Collins' Omaha directory. 57261
Collins steamers. 14433
Collinson, Peter. (41354)
Collinson, Sir Richard, 1811-1883. ed. 26000
Collis, Charles H. T. 14457, 86328
Collodion process of photography. 85415
Collom, W. 55544
Colloquia tria, & viginti. 44056
Colloquial poem. 105473
Colloqvios de la paz. 26544
Colloquios en lengua Mexicano. 29249
Colloquios nueuamente. 48236
Colloquy between a citizen of a later New
York and casual visitor. 83851
Collot, A. G. 14458
Collot, George Henry Victor. 14459-14463
Collyer, Isaac J. P. 14464
Collyer, Robert. (14465)-14466
Collyer, Robert H. 14467
Colman, Benjamin, 1673-1747. 14469-14478,
(14480)-(14525), 16630, (16635), 16640-
16641, (17094), 17675, 18698, 20057,
(20271), 40282, 46274, (46522), 46542,
46798, 59601, 59602, 69400, 79194,
79410, 83428, 83430-83433, 90595-90596,
91548, 94707, 94709, 94719, 94916,
95737, 95744, 97450-97451, 100915,
103514, 103588, 103594, 103601, 3d note
after 103650 see also Eight Ministers
Who Carry On the Thursday Lecture in
Boston.
Colman, Benjamin, 1673-1747. supposed author
28052, 28506, 65689, 91945, 105012,
note after 105090
Colman, George, 1762-1836. 14526, note after
105986
Colman, George W. (14527)
Colman, Henry, 1785-1849. 11208, 14528-
14535, 16795, 50030, (69758), 70266,
8th note after 96962, 102319 see also
Massachusetts. Commissioner for the
Agricultural Survey of the State.
Colman, John. 14536-(14538), 40282, 2d note
after 99824, 103900, note after 103907
Colman's monthly miscellany. 84162
Colmar, Johann. 14539
Colmeiro, Manuel. 14540
Colmenar, Juan Alvarez de. 14541
Colmenares Fernandez de Cordova, Felipe.
see Fernandez de Cordova, Felipe
Colmenares.
Colmenero de Ledesma, Antonio. 14542-14545
Colmer, Vicente Martinez. tr. 12267
Colnett, James. RN 14546, 51818
Colocacion de su devotissima imagen. 86429
Cologne, Germany. see Koln, Germany.
Colognesi, Ernesto. 14547

Colom, Jacob. 14548-14550, 102871
Colomb, Christophe. see Colombo, Chistoforo,
1451-1506.
Colomb dans les fers. (38879)
Colomb, ou la terre promise. 39580
Colombeide divisa in canti due. 94287
Colombel, ---------. 14551
Colombel, Noel. 14552-(14554), 98669
Colombia (Viceroyalty) see Nueva Granada
(Viceroyalty)
Colombia. 6135, 6186, 14562, (14571), 14576-
14577, 14581, 14584-(14585), (14600)-
14601, 30572, note after 39087, 51072,
51073, (51075), 52775, 52778, 56275,
61112, 62802, 70104, 99485 see also
Neuva Granada (Viceroyalty) Nueva
Granada (Republic of New Granada, 1832-
1858)
Colombia. Biblioteca Nacional. (56267)
Colombia. Census, 1825. 14560
Colombia. Comision Corografica. 56278
Colombia. Congreso. (14575), 86236
Colombia. Congreso. Camera del Represent-
ates. 14555
Colombia. Congreso de Panama, 1826. see
Congreso de Panama, 1826.
Colombia. Constitution. 14561, 14573-(14575),
14579, 14580, 56272, 57959, note after
95644
Colombia. Ejercito. (14616), (14619), 68850
Colombia. Laws, statutes, etc. 14555, 14561,
14563, 14565, (14575), 14579, 14580,
(14599), (14616), (14619), 29768, 56268,
56279-56281, 56286, 68850, 70013, 98872
Colombia. Legacion. Mexico. 31568 see also
Santamana, Miguel.
Colombia. Milicia. (14619)
Colombia. President, 1819-1830 (Bolivar)
1686, 14563, 14578, 14608, 14612, note
after 39187 see also Bolivar, Simon,
1783-1830.
Colombia. Secretaria de Estado. 14594,
14622, 1st note after 90588 see also
Revenga, Jose R.
Colombia. Secretaria de Estado en el Despacho
de Gobierno. see Colombia. Secretaria
de Gobierno.
Colombia. Secretaria de Estado en el Despacho
de Guerra. see Colombia. Secretaria
de Guerra.
Colombia. Secretaria de Estado en el Despacho
de Hacienda. see Colombia. Secretaria
de Hacienda.
Colombia. Secretaria de Estado en el Despacho
de Marina. see Colombia. Secretaria
de Marina.
Colombia. Secretaria de Estado en el Despacho
de Relaciones Esteriores. see Colombia.
Secretaria de Relaciones Esteriores.
Colombia. Secretaria de Estado en el Despacho
del Interior. see Colombia. Secretaria
del Interior.
Colombia. Secretaria de Gobierno. 56277
Colombia. Secretaria de Guerra. 14586,
14589, 14603, 56277 see also Colombia.
Secretaria de Guerra i Marina.
Colombia. Secretaria de Guerra i Marina.
14583, 56274 see also Colombia.
Secretaria de Guerra. and Colombia.
Secretaria de Marina.
Colombia. Secretaria de Hacienda. 14587,
14604
Colombia. Secretaria de Hacienda i Fomento.
14607
Colombia. Secretaria de Marina. 14588, 14590,
14606 see also Colombia. Secretaria

de Guerra i Marina. and Soublette, Carlos, Pres. Venezuela, 1790-1870.

Colombia. Secretaria de Relaciones Esteriores. 6432, 14576-14577, 14592, 14602, 16905, 56274, 56277, note after 99615 see also Borrero, Eusebio. Colombia. Secretaria del Interior i Relaciones Esteriores. Restrepo, Jose Manuel.

Colombia. Secretaria de Relaciones Esteriores y Mejoras Internas. see Colombia. Secretaria de Relaciones Esteriores.

Colombia. Secretaria del Interior. 14560, 14591, 14605 see also Restrepo, Jose Manuel.

Colombia. Secretaria del Interior y Justicia. 56274

Colombia. Secretaria del Interior i Relaciones Esteriores. 56274 see also Colombia. Secretaria de Relaciones Esteriores.

Colombia. Secretaria del Tesoro y Credito Nacional. 14596, 47596

Colombia. Treaties, etc. 14566, 14625, 52776

Colombia. Vice Presidente, 1824-1828 (Santander) 14609, 14611, 14621, (25459), 58138, 76809, 1st note after 98873 see also Santander, Francisco de Paula, 1792-1840.

Colombia a la America del Norte. (16907)

Colombia: being a geographical, statistical, agricultural, commercial, and political account of that country. 101033

Colombia, comprising its history, geography, and topography. 14567

Colombia constituida. 14568

Colombia e Gujane. 19544

Colombia: its present state. 29768

Colombia o federacion de sus tres secciones. 14570

Colombia: siendo una relacion. 101034

Colombiada. 75572

Colombiade, poema di Madama Du Boccage. 21008

Colombiade poema eroico. (4560)

Colombiade. Poema eroico mitologico. 94288

Colombian monitor. 64979

Colombian navigator. 66692-66696

Colombian phoenix. 24992, 101800

Colombiano. pseud. Bolivar i Washington. see Urdaneta, Amenodoro.

Colombiano. (14572)

Colombie et Guyanes. 19541

Columbien und Guyana, Italien, Aegyptien. 26848A

Colombini, Francesco Maria. 14626

Colombo, Cristoforo, 1451-1506. 1547, (6363)-6364, (8784), 14628-14646, 14654-14655, 14666, 14670-14671, 14675, 18656-18657, (19793)-19793A, 20518, 26874-26875, 31553, 32005, 34100-34107, 38163, 38949, (40041), 41659, 50050-50064, 50115, (50598), 52098, 52103-52105, 56064, 57458-57459, 66686, 67740-67742, 74659, 77901-77902, 82979, 89646-89647, 94096, 98923, 99375, 1st-5th notes after 106378

Colombo, Cristoforo, 1451-1506. supposed author 29396, 49441

Colombo, Diego. see Colon, Diego, 1480-1526.

Colombo, Felipe. 14673

Colombo, Fernando. see Colon, Fernando, 1488-1539.

Colombo de France et d'Italie. 30604

Colombo: melodramma serio in due atti. 14627

Colombo ou o descobrimento da America. 88803

Colombo. Poema. 64398

Colombo poema eroico. 99744

Colombus. (32410)

Colon. pseud. Essays. (19587), 89498

Colon. pseud. Lettre. 93353

Colon. pseud. Memoire sur la colonie. see Vidal, --------.

Colon. pseud. Rencontre d'un colon. see Therou, -------.

Colon, Cristobal. see Colombo, Cristoforo, 1451-1506.

Colon, Diego, 1480-1526. petitioner 65990

Colon, Feliciano Montenegro. 14678, note after 98875

Colon, Feliciano Montenegro. incorrectly supposed author 14679, note after 98871, 105951

Colon, Fernando, 1488-1539. 3350, 13015, (14674)-14677, 30604, 50222, 62957, 106401

Colon, J. M. E. 14680

Colon, Luis, Duque de Veragua, 1521?-1572. 51761

Colon de Larreategui, Mariano. see Larreategui, Mariano Colon de.

Colon. 75572

Colon de Guazacoalco. 12157

Colon de Saint-Domingue. pseud. Discours. see Duval-Sanadon, David.

Colon de Saint Domingue. pseud. Lettre. see Berquin-Duvallon, --------.

Colon de St. Domingue. pseud. Troisieme lettre. see Regnier, --------.

Colon mis hors la loi in 1795. pseud. Cri d'un colon. 17505

Colon. Poema. 10319

Colon. Poema de D. Francisco de Moraes Vasconcelos y Botello. 6798

Colon tres-aise a connoitre. 19300

Colonec, Francisco. 98172

Col. Allston. pseud. see Hines, David Theodore.

Col. Beeston's adjustment of the peace. 79781

Col. Benton. pseud. see Hines, David Theodore.

Colonel Berkley and his friends. 14681

Colonel Boone's autobiography. 30683

Col. Crockett's exploits and adventures in Texas. 17566, 83778

Colonel Daniel Boon's narrative. 24337

Colonel Dambourges. 18363

Colonel de Surville. 93412-93414

Colonel dismounted. 10173, 100444

Col. Fremont not a Roman Catholic. (25845)

Col. Fremont's adventures. 103377

Col. Fremont's religion. (25845)

Col. Fremont's Romanism. 8348

Col. George Rogers Clark's sketch. (13287)

Col. Hamilton. pseud. see Hines, David Theodore.

Colonel Hamilton's second letter. 29965

Col. Hayne. pseud. see Hines, David Theodore.

Col. J. P. Boyd's New Orleans and Carrollton Mass Meeting speeches. (7115)

Col. Jacques. (27453)

Colonel Jesse A. Gore, U. S. A. 21617

Colonel Mason's official dispatches. 10002

Colonel Norwood's voyage to Virginia. 13015, 55933

Colonel of the militia. pseud. Dialogue. 35364

Colonel Paul Revere. 70183

Col. Peter A. Porter. (17322)

Col. Pinckney. pseud. see Hines, David Theodore.

Col. Singleton. pseud. see Hines, David Theodore.

Col. Van Slyck's Milwaukee city directory.
(49154)
Colonel Washington's journal. (41650), note
after 91855
Col. William Campbell and Governor Shelby.
80116
Col. Wm. Dudley's defeat. 14928
Colonel William Smith and lady. 84904
Col. Young's report. 106109
Colonel's conversion. 88044A
Coloney, Myron. 14682, 44358
Coloni, Gio. Pietro. 27473, note after 36086
Coloni ab Anglia ad Americae oram missi.
39160
Coloni, romanzo storico. 16505
Coloniae Anglicanae illustratae. 6209
Coloniaje. 27766
Colonial administration of Great Britain. 4482
Colonial advocate. 22935, 102555
Colonial Agents. 3956
Colonial Agents. petitioners 3956
Colonial almanack. (14683)
Colonial and Asiatic review. 81150
Colonial and international postage. (19672)
Colonial church chronicle. (14685)
Colonial Church Society. 14684
Colonial clergy disabilities bill. 64729
Colonial commerce; comprising an inquiry.
43173
Colonial commerce; or, reflections on the
commercial system. 8439
Colonial constitutions. 49098
Colonial controversy containing a refutation of
the calumnies of the anticolonists. 43641
Colonial crisis. (13526)
Colonial currency reprints. 14536, 14538,
20725, 25770, 34810, 52622, 79377,
86618, 96426, 98355, 4th-5th notes after
98549, 103900, 103902, note after 103907,
104899, 104902, 105085, note after
105456, note after 105459
Colonial documents of New Jersey. 53058
Colonial documents of New York. 20597, note
after 98474, note after 99310
Colonial ecclesiastical establishments. 8842
Colonial empire of Great Britain, especially
in its religious aspect. 42888
Colonial empire of Great Britain: the Atlantic
group. 73544
Colonial history of New Jersey. 83982
Colonial history of Virginia. 5114
Colonial history of San Francisco. 21573
Colonial history of Vincennes, (Indiana.) 39317
Colonial intelligencer. (14687), 33540
Colonial journal. 14688
Colonial Land and Emigration Commissioners.
see Great Britain. Colonial Land and
Emigration Commissioners.
Colonial laws as examined by a Committee of
the House of Commons. 14690
Colonial legislation on the subject of education.
9354
Colonial library. (14319)
Colonial magazine (London) 8893, 90851,
105671
Colonial magazine (Plattsburgh, N. Y.) 14691
Colonial magazine. see Fisher's colonial
magazine.
Colonial magazine and commercial-maritime
journal. 14692
Colonial magazine and East India review.
81150
Colonial magazine and foreign miscellany.
81150
Colonial magazine, or monthly miscellany.
14693

Colonial miscellany. 74991
Colonial Office list for 1862. (14694)
Colonial policy of Great Britain considered.
14695
Colonial policy of Lord John Russell's admin-
istration. (28789)
Colonial policy of Spain. 80163
Colonial policy of the British Empire. 44909
Colonial policy, with hints upon the formation
of military establishments. 14696
Colonial population. 75410
Colonial practice of Saint Vincent. 80270
Colonial records of North Carolina. 87359
Colonial records of Pennsylvania. 19163,
31104, 84604, 91869, 102508
Colonial records of Rhode Island. 32967
Colonial records of Virginia. 2d note before
99889
Colonial reform. (43083)
Colonial register for 1802. 57504
Colonial romance. 81198
Colonial schemes of Popham and Gorges.
95633
Colonial slavery. 14697
Colonial slavery. Defence of the Baptist Mis-
sionaries. 38094
Colonial slavery. Letters to Rt. Hon. Will.
Huskisson. 105996
Colonial sketches. 30565
Colonial Society of Massachusetts. 86696,
104922
Colonial Society of Pennsylvania. 38983
Colonial story. 106369
Colonial system. 5927
Colonial taxes. 83487
Colonias de Santa Fe. 14698
Colonie Belge dans l'Amerique Centrale. 8399
Colonie. Brasilianisches Lebensbild. 27173
Colonie de Guazacoalco . . . au Mexique.
29099
Colonie de Santo-Thomas. 5974, 17835
Colonie du Goazacoalco. 27618
Colonie du Kansas. 5003
Colonie icarienne. (9780)
Colonie icarienne aux Etats-Unis d'Amerique.
(9779)
Colonie icarienne. Situation dans l'Iowa. 9782
Colonie, oder die Harmoniten zu Oeconomie im
Staate Pensylvanien. 67917
Colonie op de wilde kust van America. see
Suriname.
Colonie ou republique icarienne dans les Etats-
Unis d'Amerique. 9781
Colonie St. Maria in Pennsylvanien, N. Amerika.
59988
Colonien in d. nordlichen Amerika. 96191
Colonien und Colonial-System. 42641
Coloniers wonende in de Colonie de Berbice.
see Berbice. Coloniers.
Colonies. 14699
Colonies a sucre et la production indigene.
72470
Colonies, and the present American revolution.
(64883)
Colonies Anglaises. 77743
Colonies Anglaises de 1574 a 1660. 24205
Colonies Angloises. 36944, 68430
Colonies, commerce, agriculture. 14700
Colonies Danoises. 77743
Colonies. Esclavage. Lettre a M. le Ministre
de la Marine et des Colonies. 5652
Colonies Espagnols. (12253)
Colonies et la metropole. (19309)
Colonies et la politique coloniale de la France.
(21479), 21491
Colonies etrangeres et Haiti. 77743

Colonies Francaises depuis l'abolition de l'esclavage. 40127
Colonies Francaises devant la Chambre de Pairs. 21360
Colonies Francaises devant la Chambre des Pairs. Analyse de la discussion generale. 36414
Colonies Francaises en 1852. 6863
Colonies Francaises: essai sur la nature du gouvernement. 14708
Colonies Francaises, future abolition. 49092
Colonies Francaises, geographie, histoire, productions. 67621
Colonies. Note remis au Comite Colonial. 95731
Colonies of England. 72583
Colonisacao do Mucury. (57900)
Colonisation dans l'Amerique Centrale du District de Santo Thomas de Guatemala, por la Communaute de l'Union, fonde par la Compagnie Belge de Colonisation. 14724
Colonisation dans l'Amerique Centrale du District de Santo-Thomas de Quatemala por la Communaute de l'Union. Renseignements generaux. (76883)
Colonisation dans l'Amerique Centrale . . . exploration du pays. (66852)
Colonisation du Bresil. 70387
Colonisation du Canada envisagee au point de vu national. 20888
Colonisation du District de Santo-Thomas. 76884
Colonisation du District de Santo Thomas de Guatemala. Collection de renseignements publies ou recueillis. (11681)
Colonisation du District de Santo-Thomas de Guatemala por la Communaute de l'Union fondee par la Compagnie Belge de Colonisation. 76882
Colonisations-Gesellschaft fur Central-Amerika, Berlin. see Berliner Colonisations-Gesellschaft fur Central-Amerika.
Colonising; or a plain investigation of that subject. 14725
Colonist. pseud. Edinburgh review and the West Indies. 14726
Colonist. pseud. Letter to the members of the imperial Parliament. 40497
Colonist. pseud. Reply to the report of the Earl of Durham. see Haliburton, Thomas Chandler.
Colonist. 77294
Colonist in Augustus 1805. pseud. Kort historisch verhaal. 4809, 38250
Colonist of New Brunswick. pseud. Francis Tamo. 25456
Colonisterne. 16508
Colonists and manufacturers in the West Indies. (2350), (18663)
Colonizadora. see Sociedad Anonima "La Colonizadora," Havana.
Colonizacion en el ysmo de Hoazacoalco e Tehuantepec. 14727
Colonizacion y navegacion del Amazonas. 998, 14728
Colonization. note after 81865
Colonization. A notice of Victor Hugo's views of slavery. 39226
Colonization and abolition. 39226
Colonization and abolition contrasted. 14729
Colonization and Christianity. 33376
Colonization and colonial government: a lecture. 9857
Colonization and subsequent history of New-Jersey. 39378

Colonization [anti-slavery.] 26079
Colonization Association, Cincinnati. see Cincinnati Colonization Association.
Colonization herald. 77725
Colonization herald and general register (1839-   ) 14730
Colonization herald and general register (1848-   ) 14731
Colonization law of the state of Tamaulipas. 13810, 94948
Colonization law of the state of Tamaulipas, and naturalization law of the general congress. 39405
Colonization of America. (5339)
Colonization of Central America. (20611)
Colonization of the free colored population of Maryland. 45245
Colonization scheme considered in its rejection by the colored people. 16806
Colonization Society, Hartford, Conn. see Hartford Colonization Society.
Colonization Society, New York City. see New York Colonization Society.
Colonization Society, Worcester County, Mass. see Worcester County Auxiliary Colonization Society.
Colonization Society of Connecticut. see Connecticut Colonization Society.
Colonization Society of Indiana. see Indiana Colonization Society.
Colonization Society of Kentucky. see Kentucky Colonization Society.
Colonization Society of Louisiana. see Louisiana State Colonization Society.
Colonization Society of Maine. see Maine Colonization Society.
Colonization Society of Maryland. see Maryland State Colonization Society.
Colonization Society of Massachusetts. see Massachusetts Colonization Society.
Colonization Society of New Hampshire. see New Hampshire Colonization Society.
Colonization Society of New Jersey. see New Jersey. Colonization Society.
Colonization Society of New York City. see New York Colonization Society.
Colonization Society of New York State. see New York Colonization Society.
Colonization Society of Ohio. see Ohio State Colonization Society.
Colonization Society of Richmond and Manchester. see Richmond and Manchester Colonization Society.
Colonization Society of the State of Connecticut. see Connecticut Colonization Society.
Colonization Society of the State of Indiana. see Indiana Colonization Society.
Colonization Society of the State of Maine. see Maine Colonization Society.
Colonization Society of Vermont. see Vermont Colonization Society.
Colonization Society of Virginia. see Virginia Colonization Society.
Colonization; . . . with some remarks on small farms. (51757)
Colonizationist and journal of freedom. 14733
Colonize the "fertile belt," which contains forty millions of acres. 68008
Colonnade. 97234
Colonnades. A poem. 5975
Colonne de Bunker Hill. 9176
Colonni, Fabio. (31515)-31516
Colons. pseud. Crie de colons contre un ouvrage de M. l'Eveque Gregoire. 17507

Colons de la Guyane Francaise. see French Guiana. Colons.

Colons de l'Ile de Saint-Domingue. see Santo Domingo (French Colony) Colons.

Colons de Saint-Domingue qui Resident en France. petitioners (75035) see also Colons Francois de Saint-Domingue, Reunis a Paris. petitioners

Colons du Canada. 44701

Colons du Pacifique. (81309)

Colons Francois de Saint-Domingue, Reunis a Paris. petitioners 75039 see also Colons de Saint-Domingue qui Resident en France. petitioners

Colony, a fortress, and a prison. 4907

Colony de Santo-Tomas. 5974

Colony for an Indian reserve in Kansas. 34060

Colony laws, relating to land titles. 23522

Colony of Connecticut, Court of Vice-Admiralty. 81390

Colony of Rhode Island. 101252

Colony or republique of Icaria in the United States of America. 9783

Coloquio de Aristo y de Timandro. 14734

Coloquio dulcisimo entre Jesucristo y el alma. 75868

Coloquio entre Jesus y la alma. 75868

Coloquio tierno y lastimosos ayes de la America. 99731

Coloquios canonico-morales de regulares. 75982

Coloquios dos simples. 57662

Coloquios espirituales y sacramentales y canciones divinas. 27773, 27800

Coloquios o dialogos nueuamente copuestos. 48235

Color guard. 33105

Color line. 84751

Color sergeant. 67809

Colorado (Territory) Governor, 1862-1865 (Evans) 14744, (23154) see also Evans, John.

Colorado (Territory) Governor, 1866 (Cummings) 14740 see also Cummings, --------.

Colorado (Territory) Legislative Assembly. Council. 14745

Colorado (Territory) Legislative Assembly. House. 14746

Colorado (Territory) General Assembly. 14741-14742

Colorado (Territory) Laws, statutes, etc. 14739, 14741-14742, 14747

Colorado (Territory) Territorial Library. see Colorado. State Library, Denver.

Colorado. Board of Trade of Southern Colorado. see Board of Trade of Southern Colorado.

Colorado. State Geologist. 82752-82754 see also Smith, J. Alden.

Colorado. State Library, Denver. 14737

Colorado. 11734

Colorado Agricultural Society. Annual Exhibition, 2d, 1867. 14749

Colorado: . . . its history, geography, and mining. 57110

Colorado: its resources, parks, and prospects. 14735

Colorado of the Pacific. (14736)

Colorado miner. (82236)

Colorado, the Rocky Mountain gem. 23889

Colorado veto reviewed. 14738

Colored American. pseud. Brief inquiry. 75075

Colored American. pseud. Late contemplated insurrection. 12054, 82003

Colored Citizens of Boston. see Boston. Colored Citizens.

Colored Citizens of Norfolk, Va. see Norfolk, Va. Colored Citizens.

Colored Citizens of Oberlin, Ohio. see Public Meeting of the Colored Citizens of Oberlin, Ohio.

Coloured figures and descriptions of exotic ferns. 32866

Colored Home, New York. see New York (City) Lincoln's Hospital and Home.

Colored Home and Hospital, New York. see New York (City) Lincoln's Home and Hospital.

Colored man. pseud. Review of the revolutionary elements. see Putnam, Lewis H.

Colored man round the world. (20639)

Colored man's reminiscences of James Madison. 36045

Colored Men of Philadelphia. petitioners 18856, 81870

Colored National Convention, Rochester, N. Y., 1853. 65829

Coloured patriots of the American revolution. (52301)

Colored People of Cincinnati. see Cincinnati. Colored People.

Colored people of Missouri. see Missouri. Colored People.

Colored People's Convention of the State of South Carolina, Charleston, 1865. 87808

Colored People's Convention of the State of South Carolina, Charleston, 1865. petitioners 87808

Colored People's Educational Convention, St. Louis, 1870. (49629)

Colored People's Educational Monument Association in Memory of Abraham Lincoln, Washington, D. C. 11651, 41183

Colored People's Educational Monument Association in Memory of Abraham Lincoln, Washington, D. C. Board of Directors. 11651, 41183

Colored People's Educational Monument Association in Memory of Abraham Lincoln, Washington, D. C. Fourth of July Celebration, 1865. 11651, 41183

Colored People's Educational Monument Association in Memory of Abraham Lincoln, Washington, D. C. Recording Secretary. 11651, 41183 see also Bell, L. A.

Colored School statistics. 59989

Colored troops and military colonies on southern soil. 14753, 55961

Colors of the United States first raised. 14754

Colosso eloquente que en la solemne aclamacion del agosto monarcha de las Espanas D. Fernando VI. 72533

Coloured . . . see Colored . . .

Colpaert, Emile. 14755

Colportage Board of South Carolina. see South Carolina Colportage Board.

Colportage for 1852-54. (14756)

Colportage in Virginia. (14757), 17656

Colporteur. pseud. Five years in the Alleghanies. (24635)

Colporteur Convention, Pittsburgh, 1852. (14757), 92373

Colporteur Convention, Richmond, Va., 1852. (14757), 92373

Colporteur conventions at Richmond and Pittsburgh. (14757), 92373

Colporteur of the American and Foreign Bible Society. (14757)

Colquhoun, John Campbell. 14758

Colquitt, Walter T. 14759

Colson, Sylvester. alias see Curtis, Winslow. defendant
Colston, E. R. 57880
Colston, R. E. (65741)
Colt, John Caldwell, d. 1842. 14761
Colt, Nelson. (14762)
Colt, Mrs. S. S. ed. 53820
Colton, Benjamin. (14764)-14765
Colton, Calvin, 1789-1857. 13544, 13551, 14766-14784, 17524, 17528, note just before 94393, note after 94395, note after 95065, note after 95143, note after 97028, 100659
Colton, Calvin, 1789-1857. supposed author 14771, 19256, 37408
Colton, Calvin, 1789-1857. incorrectly supposed author 14770, 37284.
Colton, Chauncey, 18100-1876. 14785, (69369)
Colton, George Hooker. 14786
Colton, George W. cartographer 14787-14790, 24490, 57345, 88947
Colton, Henry E. 14791-14792
Colton, Joseph Hutchins, 1800-1893. (14793)-14797, 24486, 24490, 34577, 36182, 82931-82932, note before 90593, 103021
Colton, Phebe W. 103486
Colton, Simeon. 14798
Colton, Walter. USN 14799-14800
Colton (R. & A.) firm publishers 99160
Colton's atlas of America. 14787
Colton's atlas of the world. 14787, 88947
Colton's condensed octavo atlas of the union. 14788
Colton's journal of geography and collateral sciences. 14790
Colton's map of Indiana. 34577
Colton's new and complete statistical gazetteer. 14789
Colton's traveler and tourist's route-book. 24487
Colton's travellers' and tourists' guide-book. (14793)
Coltons' Vermont miniature register. 99160
Columbanus. 46264
Columbeidos, libri priores duo. 91216-91217
Columbi navigatio in Americam. 14648
Columbia, Conn. Congregational Church. (14845)
Columbia, S. C. 81254
Columbia, S. C. Agricultural Committee of South Carolina. see Agricultural Committee of South Carolina, Columbia.
Columbia, S. C. Annual Convention of the State Agricultural and Mechanical Society, 1869. see State Agricultural and Mechanical Society of South Carolina. Annual Convention, Columbia, 1869.
Columbia, S. C. Annual Fair of the State Agricultural and Mechanical Society, 1856. see State Agricultural and Mechanical Society of Society Carolina. Annual Fair, 1st, Columbia, 1856.
Columbia, S. C. Annual Fair of the State Agricultural and Mechanical Society, 1872. see State Agricultural and Mechanical Society of Society Carolina. Annual Fair, 4th, Columbia, 1872.
Columbia, S. C. Bible Convention, 1829. see Bible Convention, Columbia, S. C., 1829.
Columbia, S. C. Bible Convention, 1840. see Bible Convention, Columbia, S. C., 1840.
Columbia, S. C. Bible Convention, 1842. see Bible Convention, Columbia, S. C., 1842.
Columbia, S. C. Bible Convention, 1843. see Bible Convention, Columbia, S. C., 1843.

Columbia, S. C. Bible Convention, 1844. see Bible Convention, Columbia, S. C., 1844.
Columbia, S. C. Central Association for the Relief of the Soldiers of South Carolina. see Central Association for the Relief of the Soldiers of South Carolina, Columbia, S. C.
Columbia, S. C. Conference of Colored Citizens, 1876. see Conference of Colored Citizens, Columbia, S. C., 1876.
Columbia, S. C. Convention, 1832-133. see South Carolina. Convention, Columbia, 1832-1833.
Columbia, S. C. Convention of Delegates from the Various Bible Societies of South Carolina, 1829. see Bible Convention, Columbia, S. C., 1829.
Columbia, S. C. Convention of Teachers, 1850. see Convention of Teachers, Columbia, S. C., 1850.
Columbia, S. C. Convention of the Union and State Rights Party, 1832. State Rights and Free Trade Party of Charleston, S. C. Convention, Columbia, 1832.
Columbia, S. C. Convention of the Various Bible Societies of South Carolina, 1840. see Bible Convention, Columbia, S. C., 1840.
Columbia, S. C. Democratic Party Convention, 1856. see Democratic Party. South Carolina. Convention, Columbia, 1856.
Columbia, S. C. Democratic Party Convention, 1860. see Democratic Party. South Carolina. Convention, Columbia, 1860.
Columbia, S. C. Freemasons Grand Convention, 1809. see Freemasons (York Rite) South Carolina. Grand Convention, Columbia, 1809.
Columbia, S. C. Representative Reform Association. see Representative Reform Association, Columbia, S. C.
Columbia, S. C. Soldiers' Relief Association. see Soldiers' Relief Association, Columbia, S. C.
Columbia, S. C. Southern States Convention of Colored Men, 1871. see Southern States Convention of Colored Men, Columbia, S. C., 1871.
Columbia, S. C. State Rights Meeting, 1830. see State Rights Meeting, Columbia, S. C., 1830.
Columbia, S. C. Tax-payers' Convention, 1871. see Tax-payers' Convention of South Carolina, Columbia, 1871.
Columbia, S. C. Temperance Society. see Columbia Temperance Society, Columbia, S. C.
Columbia, S. C. Theological Seminary. see Theological Seminary, Columbia, S. C.
Columbia, S. C. Union and State Rights Party Convention, 1832. see State Rights and Free Trade Party of Charleston, S. C. Convention, Columbia, 1832.
Columbia, Tenn. Columbia Female Institute. see Columbia Female Institute, Columbia, Tenn.
Columbia County, N. Y. Board of Supervisors. 65824
Columbia County, N. Y. Washington Benevolent Society. see Washington Benevolent Society. New York. Columbia County.
Columbia County, Pa. Reception to Henry C. Carey, 1859. 10841, note after 94911
Columbia. 49816

Columbia, a poetical epistle. 58782
Columbia almanack, for the year of Our Lord 1800. 91978
Columbia almanack, for the year of Our Lord 1801. 91979
Columbia almanack, for the year of Our Lord 1788. 91971
Columbia almanack, for the year of Our Lord 1789. 91972
Columbia almanack, for the year of Our Lord 1787. 91970
Columbia almanack, for the year of Our Lord 1798. 91976
Columbia almanack, for the year of Our Lord 1799. 91977
Columbia almanack, for the year of Our Lord 1791. 91973
Columbia almanack, for the year of Our Lord 1797. 91975
Columbia almanack, for the year of Our Lord 1796. 91974
Columbia and Britannia. 62561
Columbia. Bank secrets of the Bank of Columbia. 14853
Columbia; and address. 16297
Columbia Bridge Company. Board of Managers. 14848
Columbia Bridge Company. Committee of Stockholders. 14848
Columbia Church. see Halcyon Church of Christ in Columbia.
Columbia College, New York. see Columbia University.
Columbia College, Washington, D. C. see George Washington University, Washington, c. C.
Columbia College Library. Report of the Librarian. 14821
Columbia College, 1754-1854. 36627
Columbia daily phoenix. 81254
Columbia, District of. see District of Columbia.
Columbia Female Institute, Columbia, Tenn. 14855
Columbia Gold-Mining Company. (14846)
Columbia-Harvard Freshman Boat Race, New London, Conn., 1895. see Harvard-Columbia Freshman Boat Race, New London, Conn., 1895.
Columbia Historical Society. 39533, 64584, 82954, 101944
Columbia in 1826. 14569
Columbia in mourning for her son. 101790
Columbia. Message from His Excellency the Governor, no. 1. delivered to the Legislature of South-Carolina, on the 29th November, 1808. 87540
Columbia. Message from His Excellency the Governor, no. 1, delivered to the Legislature of South-Carolina, on the 27th of November, 1810. 87542
Columbia Oil Company. Directors. 14847
Columbia Oil Company. President. 14847
Columbia River; or scenes and adventures. 17267
Columbia River Exploration, 1865. Instructions, reports, and journals. 49776
Columbia Temperance Society, Columbia, S. C. 20093, note after 88042
Columbia Temperance Society, Columbia, S. C. Committee on the Influence of Intemperance. 94653
Columbia, the gem of the ocean. 83677
Columbia Typographical Society, Washington, D. C. 28516, 101931, 1st-2d notes after 101931, 101967

Columbia University. 14805, 14807, 14809, (14813)-14814, 14816-(14817), 14822, 14830, 14832, 14841, 14842
Columbia University. Alumni. 54198, 70247
Columbia University Association of the Alumni. 14824
Columbia University. Board of Trustees. 3459, 14811, 14832, (14839), 14842, 14844, 54198, 77672 77674
Columbia University. Board of Trustees. petitioners 84558
Columbia University. Board of Trustees. Committee Charged with an Inquiry into the State of Columbia College. see Columbia University. Board of Trustees. Committee to Inquire into the Condition of the Institution.
Columbia University. Board of Trustees. Committee on the Course of Instruction and Discipline. 14838
Columbia University. Board of Trustees. Committee on the Subject of Appointing a Teacher of Elocution. 14836
Columbia University. Board of Trustees. Committee to Consider and Report on the Subjects of Removal of the College, a Change in the Collegiate Course, the Establishment of a University System, etc. 14834
Columbia University. Board of Trustees. Committee to Inquire into the Condition of the Institution. 14835, 14837, 14842
Columbia University. Board of Trustees. Committee to Inquire into the State of Columbia College. see Columbia University. Board of Trustees. Committee to Inquire into the Condition of the Institution.
Columbia University. Centennial Celebration, 1837. 14802
Columbia University. Charter. 14818-14820, 14830-14831, 54198
Columbia University. College of Physicians and Surgeons. 53999-(54000), (73014)
Columbia University. College of Physicians and Surgeons. petitioners (54000)
Columbia University. College of Physicians and Surgeons. Charter. (54000), 54376, (73014)
Columbia University. College of Physicians and Surgeons. Faculty. Committee. 14843
Columbia University. College of Physicians and Surgeons. Trustees. (54000)
Columbia University. College of Physicians and Surgeons. Trustees. petitioners (54000)
Columbia University. Columbian Peithologian Society. 14801, 14825
Columbia University. Faculty. 14806
Columbia University. Geological Department. 84534
Columbia University. Junior Class, 1851. 69654
Columbia University. Junior Class, 1868. 14842
Columbia University. Law School. 14808
Columbia University. Library. 54198
Columbia University. Library. Librarian. 14821, 36625
Columbia University. Medical College. see Columbia University. College of Physicians and Surgeons.
Columbia University. Peithologian Society. see Columbia University. Columbian Peithologian Society.

Columbia University. Philolexian Society.
14823
Columbia University. President. 3459,
14804-14805, (14810), 14832
Columbia University. St. Stephen's College,
Annandale, N. Y. 42658, 75491-75492
Columbia University, St. Stephen's College,
Annandale, N. Y. Board of Trustees.
75492-(75494)
Columbia University, St. Stephen's College,
Annandale, N. Y. Warden. (75494)
Columbia University. School of Mines.
(14812), 14840, 84535
Columbia University. School of Mines.
Library. 14815
Columbia University. Select Committee on
Prize Scholarships. 73977
Columbia University. Trustees. see Colum-
bia University. Board of Trustees.
Columbia University library. 36625
Columbiad a poem. By Joel Barlow. 3416,
28734-(28735)
Columbiad; a poem. By Archibald Tucker
Ritchie. 71563
Columbiad. A poem. With the last corrections
by the author. 3417
Columbiad: an epic poem. 50405
Columbiad. Esto perpetua. 14842
Columbiad: or, a poem on the American war.
14856, 85590-85592
Columbiad Parnassiad. 78672
Columbiad poems. 79491
Columbiade. 21007
Columbian. pseud. Eulogium on Major Gen-
eral Joseph Warren. 101479
Columbian. 83826
Columbian accountant. 80276
Columbian almanac and agricultural repository.
14858, 44316
Columbian almanack, and magazine of knowl-
edge and fun. 92363
Columbian almanac for . . . 1829. 55544
Columbian almanac for town and country.
14857
Columbian alphabet. (23324)
Columbian calendar: or almanac, for the year
of Our Lord, 1801. 88631
Columbian calendar: or almanac, for the year
of Our Lord, 1806. 88632
Columbian centinel, Boston. 95260, 96575,
96754, 99823
Columbian centinel, Boston. Carriers. 96964
Columbian centinel. Extraordinary. No. 1179.
96575
Columbian Church. see Halycon Church of
Christ in Columbia.
Columbian class book. 42408
Columbian College, Washington, D. C. see
George Washington University, Washing-
ton, D. C.
Columbian eloquence. 12209
Columbian ephemeris and astronomical diary.
(51849)
Columbian grammar. (66017)
Columbian harmonist, no. 1. 68145
Columbian harmonist, or songster's repository.
14863
Columbian harmony. Containing the rules of
psalmody. 92083
Columbian harmony; or, Maine collection of
church music. 71805
Columbian harp. 14864
Columbian historian. 31585
Columbian Historical Society. 14865
Columbian Horticultural Society, Washington,
D. C. 101932

Columbian Horticultural Society, Washington,
D. C. Committee of Arrangement.
101932
Columbian Institute for the Promotion of Arts
and Sciences, Washington, D. C. 88243,
101933
Columbian Institute for the Promotion of Arts
and Sciences. 101933
Columbian kalendar. 26332
Columbian lady's and gentleman's magazine.
14867, 14872
Columbian library. 14868
Columbian magazine (Hudson, N. Y.) (14871)
Columbian magazine (New York) see Colum-
bian lady's and gentleman's magazine.
Columbian magazine; or monthly miscellany
(Kingston, Jamaica) 14870
Columbian magazine; or monthly miscellany
(Philadelphia) 14869, 82974, 82976,
84673, note after 97998
Columbian mercury and Canaan repository of
rural knowledge. 14873
Columbian monitor. 25678
Columbian muse. 14874
Columbian museum. 14869, note after 97998
Columbian naval melody. (14875)
Columbian naval songster. 27396
Columbian observer. 105685
Columbian orator. (5431)
Columbian Order, New York. see Tammany
Society, New York.
Columbian Parnassiad. 14886
Columbian patriot. pseud Observations on
the new constitution. see Warren,
Mercy (Otis)
Columbian Peithologian Society. see Colum-
bia University. Columbian Peithologian
Society.
Columbian phoenix and Boston review. 14876,
24992, 1st note after 101785
Columbian Plutarch. 105167
Columbian preacher. (14877), 22239
Columbian primer. note after 65546
Columbian reader. 10259
Columbian repository of sacred harmony.
32674
Columbian sacred minstrel. (30405)
Columbian Society, Philadelphia. 101929
Columbian Society of Artists, Philadelphia.
Exhibition, 3d, 1813. 14881
Columbian Society of Artists, Philadelphia.
Exhibition, 4th, 1814. 59990
Columbian songster, and freemason's com-
panion. 14878
Columbian songster. Being a large collection
of fashionable songs. 14880
Columbian songster, or jovial companion.
14879
Columbian star. (14882)
Columbian state papers. (14571)
Columbian telescope and literary compiler.
14884
Columbian tragedy. 14885
Columbian traveller and statistical register.
31067
Columbian Union. 104123-140124
Columbianum. 14883
Columbia's freedom. 14888, 26949
Columbia's glory. (65526)
Columbia's lamentation for Gen. Washington.
101833
Columbia's legacy: or, Washington's farewell
address to his fellow-citizens, on his
retiring from the Presidency of the
United States. 101603

Columbia's legacy: or, Washington's farewell address, to his fellow-citizens on his retiring from the Presidency of the United States. To which is added, his last speech in Congress. 101598

Columbia's legacy; or, Washington's valuable advice to his fellow citizens. 101578

Columbia's naval triumphs. 14889

Columbia's wreath. 7418

Columbien und Guyana. 19542, 23770, 102622

Columbien und Guyana von Casar Famin. 23770, 102622

Columbus. pseud. Crisis. see Keteltas, William.

Columbus. pseud. Letters of Columbus. 14898

Columbus. pseud. Origin and true causes of the Texas insurrection. see Lundy, Benjamin. supposed author

Columbus. pseud. Remarks on Jay's treaty. 69414

Columbus, Christopher. see Colombo, Cristoforo, 1451-1506.

Columbus, Diego. see Colon, Diego, 1480-1526.

Columbus, Fernando. see Colon, Fernando, 1488-1539.

Columbus, Ga. Agricultural Society. see Agricultural Society, Columbus, Ga.

Columbus, Miss. Baptist Church. 44412

Columbus, Ohio. 14893

Columbus, Ohio. Asylum for Idiotic and Imbecile Youth. see Ohio. State Hospital, Columbus.

Columbus, Ohio. Capital University. see Capital University, Columbus, Ohio.

Columbus, Ohio. Citizens. petitioners 14895

Columbus, Ohio. Constitutional Convention, 1850. see Ohio. Constitutional Convention, Columbus, 1850.

Columbus, Ohio. Convention of the Ohio Wool Growers' Association, 1864. see Ohio Wool Growers' Association. Convention, Columbus, 1864.

Columbus, Ohio. Esther Institute. see Esther Institute, Columbus, Ohio.

Columbus, Ohio. Deaf and Dumb Asylum. see Ohio State School for the Deaf, Columbus.

Columbus, Ohio. Institution for the Education of the Blind. see Ohio State School for the Blind, Columbus.

Columbus, Ohio. Institution for the Education of the Deaf and Dumb. see Ohio State School for the Deaf, Columbus

Columbus, Ohio. Lunatic Asylum. see Ohio. State Hospital, Columbus.

Columbus, Ohio. New England Society. see New England Society of Columbus, Ohio.

Columbus, Ohio. Ohio State School for the Blind. see Ohio State School for the Blind, Columbus.

Columbus, Ohio. Ohio State School for the Deaf. see Ohio State School for the Deaf, Columbus.

Columbus, Ohio. Public Meeting by the Citizens of Franklin County, Favorable to the Election of Andrew Jackson, 1827. see Democratic Party. Ohio. Franklin County.

Columbus, Ohio. Second Presbyterian Church. 59009

Columbus, Ohio. Starling Medical College. see Starling Medical College, Columbus, Ohio.

Columbus, Ohio. State Christian Anti-slavery Convention, 1859. see Ohio State

Christian Anti-slavery Convention, Columbus, 1859.

Columbus, Ohio. State Convention of the Colored Citizens, 1849. see State Convention of the Colored Citizens of Ohio, Columbus, 1849.

Columbus, Ohio. State Education Convention, 1837. see Ohio State Education Convention, Columbus, 1837.

Columbus, Ohio. State Hospital. see Ohio. State Hospital, Columbus.

Columbus, Ohio. State Library. see Ohio. State Library, Columbus.

Columbus, Ohio. United States Thomsonian Convention, 1832. see United States Thomsonian Convention, Columbus, Ohio, 1832.

Columbus. (32410)

Columbus. A poem. 100901

Columbus almanac for . . . 1822. 14890

Columbus. Amerikanische Miscellen. 14891, 72481

Columbus and Cook. 49935

Columbus and his times. 14649

Columbus and the men of Palos. 80001

Columbus, carmen epicum. 11035

Columbus, Cortez, Pizarro, of de ontdekking van Amerika. 10290

Columbus directory and classified business mirror for 1864. 14894

Columbus directory, city guide, and business mirror. 14894

Columbus directory for 1867-8. 14894

Columbus directory for 1866-7. 14814

Columbus—his first voyage to America. 14650

Columbus im Ausgeblicke der Entdeckung der Neuen Welt. 90090

Columbus in chains. 14652

Columbus memorial. 99374

Columbus no. 1. Convention. 85888

Columbus; oder die Entdeckung von West-Indien. 10283

Columbus: or, a world discovered. 51029

Columbus; or the discovery of America. (17824)

Columbus, or the discovery of America, as related by a father to his children. 10284, (14651)

Columbus; or, the new world. 14656A, 83841

Columbus und seine Weltanschauung. 77915

Columbus's first landing. 63624

Columbus's prayer. 13632

Columella. pseud. Inquiry into the effects of our foreign carrying trade. see Moore, Clement C.

Columna de la constitucion federal de la Republica Mexicana. 48368

Columna rostrata. 14414

Columns on the position of the Old School Presbyterian Assembly. (55074)

Colver, Nathaniel. (14900)-14901, 83464-83465

Colvil, Edward. pseud. Fifteen days. see Putnam, Mary Lowell.

Colville, -------. 76092

Colville, A. 102438

Colvin, John B. 14903-14906, 102396

Colvocoresses, George M. 14907

Colwell, Stephen. 14908-14917, 16703, 17132, (20295), 70170, 70173-70175 see also U. S. Revenue Commission, 1865-1866.

Colyar, A. S. 94184

Colyer, Vincent. 14918-14921

Colyn, Michel. see Colijn, Michel.

Coma, Guglielmo. 94095

Coman, J. M. 14922 see also Bank of Alabama. Decatur Branch. President.

Comanche Indians. Treaties, etc. 96697

Comandante en Gefe de la Division de Operaciones sobre Guadalajara a sus conciudadanos. 72253

Comandante, Gral del Estado de Jalisco a
sus conciudadanos. 35544

Combat naval de Hampton-Roads. (14923)

Combate naval del 21 de Octobre. 26113

Combate of the United Colonies. (28044)

Combats affreux arrives a l'isle St.-Domingue.
75080

Combe, George, 1788-1858. 14924, 33997,
51022

Combier, C. (14925)

Combined directories of Jersey City, Hoboken
and Hudson. (36067)

Combined Petroleum Company. 14926

Combined view of mountains and rivers of the
world. 82380

Combs, Leslie. 14927-(14929)

Combustible; a heroic poem. 78473

Come let us prepare. 86887

Come-out-erism. 27851

Come to Jesus. 72017

Come to the rescue! 32412

Comedia Brasileira em 3 actos. 66903

Comedia de costumbres escolares em 5 actos.
66901

Comedia em um acto. 43301

Comedia famosa. 106275

Comedia nueva en tres actos. 101905

Comedian his own manager. 40771

Comedias de D. Pedro Calderon de la Barca.
(9890)

Comedias de Lope de Vega Carpio. 98772

Comedie. 63020, 67417

Comedie en deux actes. 92544

Comedie en deux actes, et en vers. 100745

Comedie en deux actes et en vers libres.
44656, 100745

Comedie en prose et en trois actes. 96312

Comedie en trois actes. 100745

Comedie en trois actes, a l'usage des colleges. (39578)

Comedie en un acte et en prose. 50511

Comedie en un acte et en vers. 98273

Comedie historique. 38756

Comedie politique aux Etats-Unis. 77109

Comedies, tragi-comedies, with other poems.
11166

Comedy. 46839-46840, 56318, 68826, 77817,
89470, 91152

Comedy, altered by Isaac Beckerstaff. 84241

Comedy. As it is performed at the Theatre
Royal in Drury-Lane. 17876, 77517, 4th
note after 102803

Comedy. By Aham Salem. 51508

Comedy; by Brinsley Sheridan. 80343

Comedy. . . . By C. A. Logan. 41789

Comedy. By John Minshull. 49328

Comedy . . . from the German of Augustus von
Kotzebue. 38279

Comedy in five acts. 28102, 59092, 77816

Comedy in five acts. By George Watterston,
Esq. 102158

Comedy, in five acts. By W. Winstanley.
104818

Comedy, in five acts; by William Charles
White. 103484

Comedy, in five acts. Written in the year
1788. 42405

Comedy, in four acts, founded on fact. 77321

Comedy. In four acts. Written by an American. 97014

Comedy in three acts. 103291

Comedy in two acts, as performed by the Old
American Company. 94614

Comedy—in two acts. By R. Penn Smith.
83787

Comedy. Performed at the Charleston Theatre.
105482

Comedy. . . . Translated from the German of
Kotzebue. 38280

Comella, Luciano Francisco. 14930

Comentario o anotacion de las leyes. 56269

Comentario sobre la constitucion federal.
92288

Comentarios a la Lusiada de Camoes. 23802

Comentarios a las ordenanzas de minas. 26509

Comentarios al codigo de procedimiento judicial de Venezuela. 76701

Comentarios de la constitucion de la Confederacion Arjentina. 77071

Comentarios, dificvltades y discvrsos literales
y misticos. 99672, 99674

Comentarios, dificvltades, y discvrsos lyterales,
morales, y misticos. 99673

Comentarios reales. 98755

Comentarios reales de los Incas. 98755-98757

Comentarios reales que tratan del origen de
los Incas. 98758

Comentarios sobre las rubricas del Missal
Romano. 58840

Comentarios sobre le cuestion de Mejico.
24176

Comer, Braxton Bragg, 1848- 83629 see also
Alabama. Governor, 1907-1911 (Comer)

Comerciante. pseud. Ideas. 34176

Comerciante de perlas, novela Americana.
9746

Comercio. 94193

Comercio de cafe. (43761), 77739

Comercio de esclavos en la isla de Cuba.
8083

Comercio de Megico. petitioners see Mexico.
Comercio. petitioners

Comercio esterior de Mexico. (40139)

Comercio libro vindicado. 14932

Comercio suleto. 76765

Comer's Commercial College, Boston. 14931

Comet. 14934

Comet, by Walter Wildfire. 14933

Cometa. (70775)

Comettant, Oscar. 14935-(14942)

Comfield, Amelia Stratton. 14943

Comfort, George F. (14944)

Comfort bag in the army. 52305, 57942, 76692

Comfort for the afflicted righteous. 96384

Comfort in Christ. 17675

Comfort in tribulation. 81649

Comfort to children. (68488), 2d note after
96107

Comfortable chambers. 46265

Comfortable incouragement. 7996, 16037

Comfortable words. 46356

Comforter of the mourners. (46266)

Comi-heroick thunderclap. 77018, note after
98576

Comic almanac. (52244)

Comic history of the United States. 80443

Comic natural history of the human race.
91293

Comic opera. 44623, (61167)

Comic opera, . . . as it is performed . . . at
the Theatre-Royal, Drury-Lane. (62861),
86904

Comic opera, as originally produced. (35411)

Comic opera, as performed at the New Theatre,
Chestnut-Street. 86925

Comic opera, as performed at the New Theatre,
Philadelphia. 86906

Comic opera; as performed at the Theatre-Royal in Drury-Lane. 86904
Comic opera, as performed with unusual applause. 86905
Comic opera, in three acts, as it is performed by the servants of His Britannic Majesty. 63764
Comic opera in three acts. By Samuel Woodworth. 105181
Comic opera, in two acts. As performed at the New Theatre. 86936
Comic opera, in two acts, wiyh [sic] the words. (64087)
Comic opera or political farce in six acts. 15737
Comic sketches. 40771
Comic song and recitation book. 79908
Comic song, written by Thaddeus W. Meighan. 47386
Comical adventures of Roderick Random. 14945
Comical, quizzical, and tragical adventures of a hossier. (30615)
Comicos aplausos, y reverentes cultos. 36824
Coining age. 68028
Coming battle. 14946
Coming church. 57791
Coming conflict. 50672
Coming contraband. (37994), 56030
Coming financial explosion. 19499
Coming government. 85894
Coming of Christ in his kingdom. 14947
Coming of the mammoth. 31992
Coming struggle among the nations of the earth. 14948
Coming struggle; or, what the people of the Pacific coast think of the Coolie invasion. 90557
Coming woman, a prophetic drama. 18031, 89487
Coming woman or, the spirit of Seventy-Six. 18031, 89487
Comingo, Henry G. 14949
Comins, Lunus Bacon, 1817-1892. (14950)-(14951)
Comision Cientifica que Nombro al Efecto el Empresario D. Jose de Garay. 26550, 60771, 7th note after 94592
Comision de Curas. see Puebla, Mexico (Diocese) Comision de Curas.
Comision de la Junta Civica. 52332 see also Nepomuceno Almonte, Juan.
Comision de la Sociedad Mexicana de Geografia y Estadistica. see Sociedad Mexicana de Geografia y Estadistica. Comision.
Comision del Camino de Nuevitas. see Nuevitas, Cuba. Comision del Camino.
Comision Mixta de Reclamaciones Mexicanas y Americanas. see United States and Mexican Claims Commission, 1869-1876.
Comision Mixta de Reclamaciones Mexicanas y Americanas estableciada Conforme al Tratado de 4 de Julio de 1868 entre Mexico y Los Estados Unidos. Historia de sus trabajos. (72513)
Comision Unidad de Curas de la Mistexa Baja y Montanez. see Puebla, Mexico (Diocese) Comision Unida de Curas de la Mistexa Baja y Montanez.
Comisiones del Ecuador y Nueva Granada en la Cuestion Sobre Limites de Ambos Estados. 21800, (66220)
Comisiones Reunidas de la Real Sociedad Economica, Casa de Benificencia y Demas Dependencias de Aquel Cuerpo, Havana.

69227 see also Havana. Casa de Beni-ficencia. and Sociedad Economica de Amigos del Pais de la Havana.
Comissario General de la Religion de San Francisco, en estas Provincias del Peru, en debido obediecimiento. 87231
Comission, cedulas reales, y arancel. 56247
Comission y poder general del Rey. 56270
Comitatus, Zedekiah. pseud. Reconstruction of "my policy." 14952
Comite Central et Permanent du Comte de Montreal. see Montreal (Comte) Comite Central et Permanent.
Comite Colonial de Saint Domingue, Paris, 1789. 28153, 75119
Comite d'Archeologie Americaine. 14953
Comite des Anciens Proprietaires de Saint Domingue. 22879
Comite des Six. see France. Assemblee Nationale. Comite des Six.
Comite General du Chemin de Fer du Nord, Quebec. 65749
Comite Genevois en Faveur des Esclaves Affranchis. 79270
Comite International d'Etude pour l'Exploration de l'Isthme Americain en Vue de Per-cement d'un Canal Interoceanique. Section Francais. 85803
Comitibus, Natalis de. see Conti, Natale, 1520?-1580?
Comito Venitiano. pseud. Viaggio. 67730
Comly, Isaac. ed. 6121, 14956, 82873
Comly, John, 1773-1850. 6121, (14954)-14956, 82873
Commadore Johann Byron Erzahlung des gros-sen Uglucksfalle. (9731)
Command and government of the army. (26650)
Command in the battle of Bunker Hill. 26080
Commandemens de l'honnete-homme. 78113
Commander Babbit and Consul Trist at Havana. 96998
Commander-in-chief; a defence upon the legal grounds of the Proclamation of emanci-pation. 42534
Commander in the navy. pseud. Sketches by a sailor. (81547)
Commander of said company. pseud. Narra-tive. see Deane, ----------.
Commander Thomas Petigru and the Naval Board. 19131
Commanders and Owners of the Brigs Achilles, Patty and Hibernia. defendants 60582, 94236
Comme on servait autrefois. 86861
Commelin, Isaac. (11608), 14957-14960, 31503, 37691, 55448, 64582, 67558, 68454, 89447, 89447A, 3d note after 100931
Commemoracion hecha por la Sociedad Filo-tecnica. 98611
Commemoration by the Loyal League of Union Citizens. 14961
Commemoration of the Birthday of Washington, Springfield, Mass., 1862. see Spring-field, Mass. Commemoration of the Birthday of Washington, 1862.
Commemoration of the conquest of New Nether-land. (53606)
Commemoration of the Embarkation of the Plymouth Pilgrims from Southampton, England, Plymouth, Mass., 1855. see Plymouth, Mass. Cushman Celebration, 1855.
Commemoration of the faithful departed. 17276
Commemoration of the Fiftieth Anniversary of the Settlement of Rev. John Nelson,

Leicester, Mass., 1862. see Leicester,
Mass. Commemoration of the Fiftieth
Anniversary of the Settlement of Rev.
John Nelson, 1862.
Commemoration of the Fiftieth Anniversary of
the Settlement of Tallmadge, Ohio, 1857.
see Tallmadge, Ohio. Fiftieth Anni-
versary Commemoration, 1857.
Commemoration of the fortieth anniversary of
the consecration of St. Ann's Church,
Lowell. (21877)
Commemoration of the life and death of . . .
William H. Harrison. 39835
Commemoration of the Triumph of Liberty in
France, New York, 1830. see New
York (City) Commemoration of the
Triumph of Liberty in France, 1830.
Commemoration of the twenty-fifth anniversary
of the settlement of John A. Albro, D. D.
10128
Commemoration of the Two Hundredth Anni-
versary of the Incorporation of Mendon,
Mass., 1868. see Mendon, Mass. Two
Hundredth Anniversary Commemoration,
1868.
Commemoration of these poems. (37125), note
after 101268
Commemoration of Washington. 22309
Commemoration of Washington's birth-day.
(66256)
Commemoration sermon. 94109
Commemorative address before the Alumni
Association of Bowdoin College. 85209
Commemorative discourse. 47704
Commemorative discourse . . . at the anni-
versary of his burial. 50687
Commemorative discourse, by Rev. J. P.
Thompson. 47704, note after 95516
Commemorative discourse by Rev. Joachim
Elmendorf. 64235
Commemorative discourse, delivered at Bos-
cawen, N. H. 6952
Commemorative discourse delivered at New-
buryport, Mass. (54912), 90904
Commemorative discourse delivered at the
centennial anniversary of the erection
and the sixtieth of the consecration of
St. Paul's Church. (14158)
Commemorative discourse, delivered in . . .
Baltimore. 9364
Commemorative discourse delivered in Christ
Church, Watertown, Conn. 69010
Commemorative discourse, delivered in St.
Thomas's Church. 4130A
Commemorative discourse delivered in the
New South Church. 22301
Commemorative discourse delivered in the
North Church. 9548
Commemorative discourse in Great Barrington,
May 13, 1866. (21423)
Commemorative discourse, on the completion
of fifty years. 2661
Commemorative discourse on the completion
of the town and spire. (20968)
Commemorative discourse on the death of . . .
Hon. Edward A. Newton. (67783)
Commemorative discourse on the life, character
and services of Rev. Isaac N. Wyckoff.
64235
Commemorative discourse on the Rev. Samuel
Clarke. (31806)
Commemorative discourse pronounced at
Quincy, Mass. 103757
Commemorative discourses. 2660
Commemorative gathering. 19676

Commemorative notices of distinguished Ameri-
can clergymen. 89730
Commemorative of Hon. Edward Southworth.
28979
Commemorative proceedings of the Athenaeum
Club. 54105
Commemorative sermon. 21741
Commemorative sermon on the one hundredth
anniversary of Christ Church. 33000
Commemorative sermon upon the . . . death
of the Rev. Charles Mason. (39823)
Commemorative services at the semi-centennial
anniversary. (62960)
Commemorative services at the twenty-fifth
anniversary of the pastorate. (62821)
Commemorative services held in the West-
minster Church. 84413
Commencement, a poem. 5344
Commencement and distribution of premiums
at St. Vincent's College. 75515
Commencement at Williams-College, 1840.
104419
Commencement at Williams-College, 1838.
104419
Commencement at Williams-College, 1834.
104419
Commencement at Williams-College, 1836.
104419
Commencement at Williams-College. Septem-
ber 6, 1797. 104419
Commencement exercises of the Illinois State
Normal University. 1605
Commencement of a poem. 5344
Commencement of Columbia College August 7,
1799. 14809
Commencement of Columbia College, of New-
York. 14822
Commencement of Kentucky University. 37508
Commencement of St. Joseph's College, Bards-
town, Ky. 75302
Commencement of St. Joseph's College, Perry
County, Ohio. (74304)
Commencement, of St. Mary's College, Marion
County, Kentucky. 75425
Commencement of the Ohio Canal. (56974)
Commencement week. 7035
Commendation of Sir Humphrey Gilberts ven-
trous iourney. 13032
Commendation of the aduenterus viage of the
wurthy captain M. Thomas Stutely. 78597
[Commendations of] Cheever's latin accidence.
12392
Commending the Gospel. 64292
Comment on a pamphlet by "A backsettler."
14963
Comment on some parts of scripture. 94482
Comment upon Christ's last prayer. 32832
Comment upon executive conduct. 63780,
(77040)
Commentaire de l'apoclaypse. 76838
Commentaire ou observations. 31337
Commentaire royal. 98743
Commentaire sur la constitution des Etats-Unis.
92289
Commentaire sur la constitution federale des
Etats-Unis. 92290
Commentaires advenues depuis LXX ans. 93887
Commentaires au traite de la sphere. 76838
Commentaires, de la grammaire Nahuatl.
74951
Commentaires sur les lois du Bas-Canada.
5148
Commentar zu diesem Werke fur gebildete
Laien. 33731
Commentari della Moscovia et della Rvssia.
(67737)

Commentari in Ludovici Vives exercitationes linguae Latinae. (75565)
Commentaria in legum Indicarum recopilationem. 10093
Commentaria in universam Aristotelis logicam. (73860)
Commentarien bearbeitet. 9559
Commentaries d'Alvar Nunex Cabeca de Vaca. 9769
Commentaries of Peru. 66686
Commentaries on American law. By James Kent. 36231, 37473, 37926
Commentaries on American law. By Theophilus Parson. 58908
Commentaries on statute and constitutional law. 82440
Commentaries on the constitution of the United States. 7866, 9559, 60040, 92291-92292, note after 98101, 1st note after 100577, 104627
Commentaries on the constitutions and laws, peoples and history, of the United States. 78604
Commentaries on the criminal law. 5607
Commentaries on the jurisdiction, practice and peculiar jurisprudence. 18035
Commentaries on the laws of England. 5696, 18919, 25416, 40444, (65513), 68564, 97381
Commentaries on the mining ordinances of Spain. 26510
Commentaries upon martial law. 24368
Commentarii ad legem aquvilium. 93324
Commentarii del viaggio in Persia. (67737)
Commentarii rerum urbanorum libri XXXVIII. (43766)
Commentariis Societatis Naturae Curiosorum Lipsiensis. 78104
Commentario a Legislacao Brasileira sobre os bens de defuntos. 85679
Commentario a lei n. 1144. 88730
Commentario critico da lei de 20 de Setembro de 1830. 88766
Commentario en breve compendio de disciplina militar. 51063
Commentariolvs parallelos, sive libellve assertorius. 98222
Commentariolus parallelvs, sive libellus assertorius. (6799)
Commentariorum vrbanorvm. 74659
Commentariorum urbanorum librii XXXVIII. 43764
Commentariorvm vrbanorvm Raphaelis Volaterrani, octo & triginta libri. 43767-43768
Commentariorum urbanorum Raphaelis Volaterrani: octo & tribinta libri cum duplici eorudem indice secondum tomos collecto. 43765
Commentarios de Alvar Nvnez Cabeca de Vaca. 9768
Commentarios . . . de lo sucedido durante su gobierno de Rio de la Plata. 3350
Commentarios, difficvltades, i discvrsos literales, y misticos. 99671
Commentarios reales. 98743, 98747, 98751-98752, 98755, 98757-98758, 98760
Commentarius brevis rerum in orbe gestarum . . . 1500-74. 93883
Commentarivs brevis rervm in orbe gestarvm, ab anno salvtis M. D. vsqve in annvm M. D. LXXIIII. 93884
Commentarivs brevis rervm in orbe gestarvm, ab anno salvtis M. D. vsqve in annvm M. D. LXVIII. 93882

Commentarius de abusu tabaci Americanorum veteri. 59223
Commentarius de lege aquilia. 93324
Commentarius de navigationibus Salomonis. 33567
Commentarius de ophira regione. 3595
Commentarius de ophyra regione. 3597, (34105), 64001,
Commentarius de republic in America Lusitana. 14962
Commentarius in donatum. 99334
Commentarius rerum in orbe gestarum ab a. 1500-1567. 93881
Commentary and review of Montesquieu's Spirit of laws. 96413
Commentary [by Edward Gibbon Wakefield.] 82304
Commentary on common sayings and subjects. 102378-102393
Commentary on that part of the Earl of Durham's report which relates to the disposal of waste lands and emigration. 33891
Commentary on the constitution of the United States. 23992
Commentary on the epistle of the two elders. 43595
Commentary on the insolvent laws of New-York. 19126
Commentary on the laws of Virginia. 97308
Commentary on the new system of naval architecture. 93516
Commentary on the treaties entered into. 95655
Commentary remarks. 71274
Commentatio de lingvis peregrinis atque insvlis ignotis ex scripto manv ipsivs. (28957), 61293
Commentatio de quibusdam Americae Meridianae medicamentis parum cognitis. 57892
Commentatio medica de febre flava Americana. 20121
Commento Antonii Nebrissensis. (66411)
Comments and regulations of the Council of Public Instruction. 56147
Comments by Mr. Samuel Riddle. 60273
Comments, by the "Aboriginal Protection Society." 34675
Comments of the Charleston mercury. 12045
Comments of the N. Y. American. 17471, 35856
Comments on a pamphlet. 42791, 104113, 104117
Comments on a third article in the Princeton review. 58623
Comments on apostolic succession. 64692
Comments on Mr. Jefferson's letter. 31419
Comments on the memorial from Williams College. 89138, 1st note after 104432
Comments on the Nebraska bill. 14964
Comments on the objections of certain Cherokee Delegates. (34632), (71280)
Comments on the policy inaugurated by the President. 5749
Comments on the report of the Select Committee. (53607)
Comments on the trial of Dr. Siah Fuller. 36856
Commercants et Fabricants d'Amiens. see Amiens, France. Commercants et Fabricants.
Commerce and Christianity. 68151
Commerce and industry. 83370
Commerce and navigation. 50197
Commerce and navigation of the upper Mississippi. (14966)

Commerce and navigation of the valley of the Mississippi. 12631, 75343

Commerce and other business of the waterways. 83847

Commerce au dix-neuvieme siecle. 50552

Commerce de la cote occidentale de l'Amerique du Sud. 6451, note after 89323

Commerce de la Grande-Bretagne. 103842

Commerce de la Hollande. 14966A, (79233)

Commerce de l'Amerique par Marseilles. 11812

Commerce decennal compare, 1827 a 1836. (72471)

Commerce defended. 48984

Commerce des Indes Occidentales. 13018

Commerce du coton dans l'Inde. 84006

Commerce in the human species. 6383

Commerce. Industry. Finances. 83703

Commerce, literature and art. (45211A), 47095

Commerce, manufactures, and trade. 22085

Commerce of America with Europe. (8016), 8026, 8028, 8030

Commerce of the lakes. 3846

Commerce of the lakes, and Erie Canal. 3847

Commerce of the ports of the world. 83847

Commerce of the prairies. 28712

Commercial Academy, New York. (25200)

Commercial advertiser. 38076, 79687, 102338

Commercial advertiser directory of the city of Buffalo. 9053

Commercial advertiser's twentieth annual statement. 9054

Commercial, agricultural, manufacturing and mining interests of Pennsylvania. 59991

Commercial and Agricultural Company of the Eastern Coast of Central America. see Eastern Coast of Central America Commercial and Agricultural Company.

Commercial & Classical Boarding School, Pittsfield, Mass. 63152

Commercial and constitutional laws of Brazil. (7551)

Commercial & financial chronicle. (14969), 47920

Commercial and financial legislation of Europe and America. 43281

Commercial and financial strength of the United States. 5951

Commercial and manufacturing advantages of New Albany, Ind. 52429

Commercial and real estate reporter. 55853

Commercial and travelling map of Canada West. 84780

Commercial appendix . . . and a full description of the American trade to Canton. 101135

Commercial Association, San Francisco. see San Francisco Commercial Association.

Commercial associations; their uses and opportunities. 31823

Commercial bank investigation. 100951

Commercial Bank of New Orleans. 53300, 53311

Commercial Bank of New Orleans. President. 53311

Commercial Bank of New Orleans. Water Works Committee. (53369)

Commercial Bank of Troy, Troy, N. Y. 97071

Commercial bulletin. 90087

Commercial chronicle. 98707

Commercial code for . . . Louisiana. (51617)

Commercial conduct of the province of New York considered. (14971), 53620

Commercial conduct of the United States of America considered. 14970

Commercial Convention, Detroit, 1865. 14972, (19790), (31825)

Commercial Convention, Louisville, Ky., 1869. 71619

Commercial Convention, Louisville, Ky., 1869. petitioners 71619

Commercial Convention, Memphis, Tenn., 1869. 47785

Commercial Convention of the Southern and Western States, Charleston, S. C., 1854. 36713

Commercial conventions, direct trade—a chance for the south. 14974

Commercial Correspondent of an Association of Cotton Manufacturers. pseud. Letters. 40597

Commercial dictionary. 50100

Commercial dictionary of trade products. 81146

Commercial directory. 37124

Commercial directory, and a digest of the laws. 51058

Commercial directory; containing, a topographical description. 14975

Commercial directory of the western states and rivers. (14976)

Commercial Exchange of Philadelphia. see Philadelphia Commercial Exchange.

Commercial formalities of Rio de Janeiro. 47059

Commercial gazetteer and business directory of the Ohio River. 57065

Commercial geography. 83375

Commercial guide and continental negotiator. 80272

Commercial herald. Editor. 71718

Commercial Hospital and Lunatic Asylum of Ohio. see Cincinnati General Hospital.

Commercial intercourse of the United States and Great Britain. (14977)

Commercial intercourse with and in states declared in insurrection. 14978

Commercial law, its principles and administration. 40753

Commercial laws of the states. 32693

Commercial-maritime journal. see Colonial magazine and commercial-maritime journal.

Commercial metropolis and American and foreign statistician. 54202

Commercial Navigation Company, of the State of New York. 14979

Commercial products of the vegetable kingdom. 81147

Commercial, railway, and shipbuilding statistics of the city of Portland. 64058

Commercial reasons for the abolition of the slave trade. 14980, 102800

Commercial reference book for . . . Ohio. 56891

Commercial register of prominent New York houses. (16358)

Commercial register of the business men of the city of New York. 31253

Commercial register of the principal merchants and manufacturers in the east and west. 47913

Commercial regulations. 20147

Commercial regulations of the foreign countries. 5239, 14981

Commercial regulations of the United States with all foreign countries. 14982

Commercial relations between the Confederate States and England. 15243, 37838

Commercial relations—letter of the Secretary of State. 14984

Commercial relations of the United States with foreign nations. 14983

Commercial relations with foreign countries. 14985

Commercial relations with the British provinces. 62817

Commercial reports of the principal cities. 7302

Commercial reports received at the Foreign Office. 14986

Commercial review. see Canadian merchant's magazine and commercial review. and Merchants' magazine, and commercial review.

Commercial review of the south and west. 19116

Commercial spirit. 38732

Commercial statistics. (43282)

Commercial statistics of the republics of South America. 77781

Commercial survey of Mexico. 43289

Commercial tariffs and regulations. 43283

Commercial view. 2177

Commercial west. 83900

Commerzielle und finanzielle Starke der Vereinigten Staaten. (5952)

Commettant, Oscar. see Comettant, Oscar.

Commissaire du Bureau General des Terres Publiques. see U. S. Commissioner of Public Lands.

Commissaires des Citoyens de Couleur de Saint Marc. see Saint Marc, Haiti. Citoyens de Couleur. Commissaires.

Commissaires des Colons de St.-Domingue. see Santo Domingo (French Colony) Commissaires des Colons [a la Convention Nationale.]

Commissaires des Colons de St.-Domingue pres la Convention Nationale. 40930

Commissaires des Patriotes de S. Domingue, Deputes Pres la Convention Nationale. 75077

Commissaires & Deputes des Citoyens de Couleur, des Isles & Colonies Francoises. petitioners 93792

Commissaires for the Establishment of a Partition Line of Jurisdiction Between New York and Massachusetts, 1767. see Massachusetts (Colony) Commissioners on the Boundary Between Massachusetts and New York, 1767. and New York (Colony) Commissioners on the Boundary Between New York and Massachusetts, 1767.

Commissao do Madeira. 88722

Commissao Mixta Brasileira e Portugueza na Execucao dos Artigos 6.° e 7.° do Tractado de 29 de Agosto de 1825. 47612

Commissary-General's Office, Philadelphia, October 6, 1777. (14987)

Commissary General's Office, Philadelphia, Oct. 10. (14988)

Commissary Wilson's orderly book. 1311

Commission. 6880

Commission Appointed to Visit Canada, for the Investigation of the Epidemic Cholera, 1832. (35460) see also Harlan, Richard. Jackson, Samuel, 1767-1782. Meigs, Charles D.

Commission Civile. Au nom de la Republique. 87114

Commission d'Enquete du Chemin de Fer de Saint-Etienne, Lyon. see Lyon, France. Commission d'Enquete du Chemin de Fer de Saint-Etienne.

Commission de Geographie Commerciale de Paris. see Paris. Commission de Geographie Commerciale.

Commission for the Survey of the Sounds on the Eastern Shore of Virginia, Maryland and Delaware. 69785

Commission from God. (12406)

Commission Geologique du Canada. Rapport de progres. 41810

Commission institutee pour l'examen des questions relatives a l'esclavage et a la constitution politique des colonies. Proces-verbaux. 14992

Commission of Claims against Mexico. see U. S. Commission of Claims Against Mexico Under Act of Congress of March 3, 1849.

Commission of Claims against Mexico, under act of Congress of March 3, 1849. Treaty . . . of February 2, 1848. 48369

Commission of Claims Under the Convention of February 8, 1853, Between the United States and Great Britain. 48127, 69752

Commission of Inquiry and Advice in Respect of the Sanitary Interests of the United States Forces. see United States Sanitary Commission.

Commission of King James the Second to Sir Edmund Andros. 1521, 35677

Commission of our Blessed Savior to preach and baptize, declared. 75445

Commission on the Survey of the Sounds Lying on the Eastern Shore of Virginia, Maryland and Delaware. see Commission for the Survey of the Sounds on Eastern Shore of Virginia, Maryland and Delaware.

Commission Sanitaire des Etats-Unis son origine. 23191

Commission to Survey the Boundary Between New Hampshire and Maine. 44014, 52900, 52907

Commissioner. pseud. Laws of the United States. (39429)

Commissioner on the Claims of Creditors of the Potawatomi Indians of the Wabash. see U. S. Commissioner on the Claims of Creditors of the Potawatomi Indians of the Wabash.

Commissioners appointed by an act of the Legislature of Maryland, passed at December session, 1821. 93938

Commissioners Appointed by the City Councils of the Cities of Roxbury and Boston, Respectively, On the Union of the Two Cities Under One Municipal Government. (73676)

Commissioners Appointed by the Legislatures of Maryland and Virginia to Run and Mark the Division Line Between Maryland and Virginia, on the Eastern Shore of Chesapeake Bay. see Joint Commission for Marking the Boundary Line Between Maryland and Virginia.

Commissioners Appointed under Chapter 154, Acts of 1861 of New Hampshire. see New Hampshire. Commissioners on the Concord and Sudbury Rivers.

Commissioners for Managing a Treaty of Peace with the Eastern Indians, 1749. see Massachusetts (Colony) Commissioners to Treat With the Eastern Indians, 1749.

Commissioners for Settling the Titles to Land in the County of Onondaga, N. Y. see New York (State) Commissioners for Settling the Titles to Land in the County of Onondaga.

Commissioners For the Adjustment of Claims Under the Convention . . . Between Great Britain and the United States. see

Commission of Claims Under the Convention of February 8, 1853, Between the United States and Great Britain.

Commissioners For the Settlement of Claims under the Treaty with France, Ratified on the 2d of February 1832. 92308

Commissioners for the Zoological and Botanical Survey of the State of Massachusetts. see Massachusetts. Commissioners for the Zoological and Botanical Survey of the State.

Commissioners of Maryland and Virginia Appointed to Survey the Potomac River. 28454, (38470), 45193, (45261), 48083, 64592, 96005

Commissioners of Public Charities. First biennial report. 34217

Commissioners of the Alms-House, vs. Alexander Whistelo. 103312

Commissioners of the Customs, Boston. see Great Britain. Customs Commissioners, Boston.

Commissioners of the Girard Estate. see Girard Estate. Commissioners.

Commissioners of the Public Debt. Circular to holders of municipal bonds. 49152

Commissioners of the Soldiers' National Cemetery Association. see Soldiers' National Cemetery Association. Board of Commissioners.

Commissioners of the State of South Carolina, To the Government at Washington. see South Carolina. Commission to Negotiate with the Government of the United States, 1860-1861.

Commissioners of the States of Delaware, Maryland and Virginia, for the survey of the Sounds Between Cape Charles and Henlopen. see Commission for the Survey of the Sounds on Eastern Shore of Virginia, Maryland and Delaware.

Commissioners of the States of Massachusetts and Rhode Island to Ascertain the True Boundary Line Between the Said States. see Massachusetts. Commissioners on the Boundary with Massachusetts. and Massachusetts. Commissioners on the Boundary with Rhode Island.

Commissioners of the Temporary Lunatic Asylum, Beauport, Quebec. see Beauport, Quebec. Commissioners of the Temporary Lunatic Asylum.

Commissioners of the United Colonies of New England. see United Colonies of New England. Commissioners.

Commissioners' Office, 19th February, 1799. 53609

Commissioners on Cape Cod and East Barbors. see Massachusetts. Commissioners on Cape Cod and East Harbors.

Commissioners, on the Boundary Line Between New Hampshire and Massachusetts. see New Hampshire. Commissioners on the Boundary Line Between New Hampshire and Massachusetts.

Commissioners on the Concord and Sudbury Rivers. see New Hampshire. Commissioners on the Concord and Sudbury Rivers.

Commissioners on the Housatonic Railroad. see Massachusetts. Commissioners on the Housatonic Railroad.

Commissioners on Uniform State Laws in National Conference. see National Conference of Commissioners on Uniform State Laws.

Commissioner's report. 85212

Commissioner's report on . . . matrons and labor. 45681

Commissioners to make reprisal. 99097

Commissioners to Settle the Line Between New Hampshire and Maine. see Commission to Survey the Boundary Between New Hampshire and Maine.

Commissioners to Survey the River Potomac. see Commissioners of Maryland and Virginia Appointed to Survey the Potomac River.

Commissioners to Treat With the Several Tribes of Eastern Indians, 1752. see Massachusetts (Colony) Commissioners to Treat With the Eastern Indians, 1752.

Commissioners Under the Convention of April 1803 with France, Paris. see U. S. Commissioners Under the Convention of April 1803 with France, Paris.

Commissioners Under the Fourth Article of the Treaty of Ghent, Dec. 24, 1814. 14900, 93571

Commissioners Under the Sixth Article of the Treaty of Amity, Commerce, and Navigation. see Board of Commissioners Under Article 6th of the Treaty Between Great Britain and the United States, London, Nov. 19, 1794.

Commissions dv Roy & de Monseigneur l'Admiral au Sieur de Monts. (14933), 50223

Commissions given to the Commissioners to Mark Out the Lines. (45073), 60743, note after 97106

Commissions of President John Cuttss [sic] Esq. 52782

Commitment and detention of the insane in the United States. 84255

Committee Appointed at a Meeting of Episcopalians, in the City of New York, 1857. see New York (City) Meeting of Episcopalians, 1857. Committee.

Committee Appointed at a Meeting of the merchants of Philadelphia, 1824. see Meeting of the Merchants of Philadelphia, 1824. Committee.

Committee Appointed at a Public Meeting to Consider "The Condition of the Public Schools, Rochester, N. Y., 1838. see Rochester, N. Y. Public Meeting to Consider the Condition of the Public Schools, 1838. Committee.

Committee Appointed at Mrs. Vanderwater's, New York, 1784. see New York (City) Committee Appointed at Mrs. Vanderwater's, 1784.

Committee Appointed by a Town Meeting of the Citizens of the City and County of Philadelphia . . . beg leave to report. 85900

Committee Appointed by Certain Citizens, Philadelphia. see Philadelphia. Committee Appointed by Certain Citizens on the Penn Squares of Buildings for the Promotion of Natural Science, Literature, the Fine Arts, and the Mechanic Arts.

Committee Appointed by the Adventurers to Prosecute the Discovery of the Passage to the Western Ocean of America, and Extend the Trade, and Settle the Countries Beyond Hudson's Bay, London, 1749. (51824), 80665

Committee Appointed by the Citizens of Cincinnati to Inquire into the Causes of the Explosion of the [Steamboat] Moselle. see

Cincinnati. Citizens Committee to Inquire into the Causes of the Explosion of the [Steamboat] Moselle.

Committee Appointed by the Citizens of Pittsburgh. see Pittsburgh. Committee on the . . . Railroad from the Western Termination of the Pennsylvania Canal to the Ohio Canal.

Committee Appointed by the Citizens of Providence, Warren and Bristol, on the Providence and Bristol Railroad. 66299

Committee Appointed by the Citizens of the United States, in Charleston, South Carolina. see Charleston, S. C. Committee on the Treaty of Amity, Commerce, and Navigation.

Committee Appointed by the Citizens to Inquire into the State of Manufactures in the City of Pittsburgh. see Pittsburgh. Committee to Inquire into the State of Manufactures in the City, 1817.

Committee Appointed by the Passengers of the Oceanus. 25863, 1st note after 96991 see also Cary, Edward. and French, Justus Clement.

Committee Appointed by the Secretary of the Navy and the Legislature of Connecticut, on the Navy Yard at New London. 39517, 69684, (69688), 69846

Committee Appointed for Relieving the Poor Germans, Who Were Brought to London and There Left Destitute in the Month of August, 1764. see South Carolina (Colony) Committee Appointed for Relieving the Poor Germans, Who Were Brought to London and There Left Destitute in the Month of August, 1764.

Committee Appointed Oct. 6, 1863, At a Meeting of Bank Officers at the New York Clearing House. see New York (City) Meeting of Bank Officers, 1863. Committee.

Committee Appointed on that Part of His Excellency the Governor's Message, No. 1, Which relate[s] to Our Foreign Relations, beg leave to submit the following report. 87509

Committee Appointed on the 14th September, 1793, to Attend to and to Alleviate the Sufferings of the Afflicted with the Malignant Fever, Philadelphia. see Philadelphia. Committee Appointed on the 14th September, 1793, to Attend to and to Alleviate the Sufferings of the Afflicted with the Malignant Fever.

Committee Appointed to Ascertain the Ownership in White-Haven Meeting-House, and for other Purposes, beg leave to report. 103489

Committee Appointed to Conduct the Order of Receiving Their Excellencies Governor Clinton and General Washington, beg leave to inform their fellow-citizens. 101860

Committee Appointed to Consider the Condition of the Lighthouses of the United States . . . report. 53583

Committee Appointed to Consider the Sentence Upon the Right Reverend Benjamin T. Onderdonk. see Protestant Episcopal Church in the U. S. A. Committee Appointed to Consider the Sentence Upon the Right Reverend Benjamin T. Onderdonk.

Committee Appointed to Examine into the Title of the Corporation to the North East

Public Square, . . . and Whether Any . . . Encroachments Have Been Made Thereupon, report. 61549

Committee Appointed to Explore the Western Waters in the State of New York. see New York (State) Committee to Explore the Western Waters.

Committee Appointed to Investigate the Evils of Lotteries, in Pennsylvania. see Pennsylvania. Committee Appointed to Investigate the Evils of Lotteries.

Committee Appointed . . . to Investigate the Ministerial Fund of Lexington, Mass. see Lexington, Mass. Committee to Investigate the Ministerial Fund.

Committee Chamber, December 6, 1774. 14993

Committee Chamber, Philadelphia, May 18, 1776. 61550

Committee, Consisting of Thirty One Gentlemen. 103661, 103665

Committee for Enquiring into the State of Trade, Philadelphia, 1779. see Philadelphia. Committee for Enquiring into the State of Trade, 1779.

Committee for Investigating the Affairs of the Boston and Providence Railroad Corporation. see Massachusetts. Legislature. Committee for Investigating the Affairs of the Boston and Providence Railroad Corporation.

Committee for Promoting the Due Observance of the Lord's Day, Lincoln County, Me. see Lincoln County, Me. Committee for Promoting the Due Observance of the Lord's Day.

Committee for Promoting the Enforcement of the Slave-trade Treaties, Kingston, Jamaica. see Kingston, Jamaica. Committee for Promoting the Enforcement of the Slave-trade Treaties.

Committee for Relief to East Tennessee. New York State Branch. see New York State Committee for Relief to East Tennessee.

Committee for Securing to Colored People in Philadelphia the Right to Use the Street-cars. see Philadelphia. Committee for Securing to Colored People in Philadelphia the Right to Use the Street-cars.

Committee for Tarring and Feathering, Philadelphia. see Philadelphia. Committee on Tarring and Feathering.

Committee for the Abolition of the Slave Trade, London. 69434

Committee for the County of Worcester. see Worcester County, Mass. Committee on the Blackstone Canal.

Committee for the Diffusion of Useful Knowledge, Cincinnati. 91724

Committee for the Relief of Portland, New York. 64372

Committee Having in Charge the Fund Subscribed for the Relief of the Sufferers by the Collision . . . at Camp Hill, July 17, 1856. see North Pennsylvania Railroad Company. Committee Having in Charge the Fund Subscribed for the Relief of the Sufferers by the Collision . . . at Camp Hill, 1856.

Committee in Behalf of Cotton Manufacturers, Providence, R. I. see Cotton Manufacturers, of Providence, R. I. Committee.

Committee in Favor of the Union of Boston and Roxbury. 6769, (73677)

Committee, in the City of New York, Duly Appointed by a Meeting of Officers,

Held on the 13th March, A. D., 1833.
see New York (City) Committee of
Officers of the War of 1812.

Committee man. pseud. Scriptural deacon.
see Nightingale, J.

Committee Meeting, Philadelphia, 1774. see
Philadelphia. Committee Meeting, 1774.

Committee of American Friends of the Great
Western Railroad. see Great Western
Railroad Company, Canada. Committee
of American Friends.

Committee of Arrangements for Federal
Procession, July 4, 1788, Philadelphia.
see Philadelphia. Committee of
Arrangements for Federal Procession,
July 4, 1788.

Committee of Bonholders. see Union Canal
Company of Pennsylvania. Committee
of Bondholders.

Committee of British Merchants, Buenos Aires.
see Buenos Aires. Committee of
British Merchants.

Committee of Both Houses, to whom was
referred the petition praying for the
removal from office of Brigadier-General
David Putnam . . . report. 66773

Committee of Citizens, Appointed at a Public
Meeting, Held Aug. 18th, 1860, On the
Practicability of Manufacturing Railroad
Iron, St. Louis, 1860. see St. Louis.
Committee of Citizens, Appointed at a
Public Meeting, Held Aug. 18th, 1860,
On the Practicability of Manufacturing
Railroad Iron at or Near St. Louis.

Committee of Citizens Appointed to Ascertain
the Feasibility and Cost of Supplying
Water to the City of Concord, N. H. see
Concord, N. H. Committee to Ascertain
the Feasibility and Cost of Supplying
Water to the City.

Committee of Citizens of Cleveland in Relation
to Steamboat Disasters on the Western
Lakes. see Cleveland. Committee on
Steam Navigation on the Western Lakes.

Committee of Citizens of Schenectady. see
Schenectady, N. Y. Committee of Citizens.

Committee of Citizens on the Boz Ball, New
York, 1842. see New York (City) Committee of Citizens on the Boz Ball, 1842.

Committee of Correspondence in Barbados.
see Barbados. Committee of Correspondence.

Committee of Correspondence, in the City of
New-York, Duly Appointed by a Meeting
of Officers, Held on the 15th September,
A. D. 1826. see New York (City) Committee of Officers of the War of 1812.

Committee of Correspondence, Inspection and
Safety, Boston. see Boston. Commit-
tee of Correspondence, Inspection and
Safety.

Committee of Delegates from the Benevolent
Societies of Boston. 6580 see also
Association of Delegates from the Bene-
volent Societies of Boston.

Committee of Devils. pseud. Substance of a
letter. 93364

Committee of Friends of Van Buren of Philadelphia. see Democratic Party. Pennsylvania. Philadelphia.

Committee of Friends this day attended each
house of the Legislature of this state.
61936

Committee of Holders of the Schuylkill Navigation Company's Boat Loan. see

Holders of the Schuylkill Navigation
Company's Boat Loan.

Committee of Holders of Union Canal Bonds.
see Union Canal Company of Pennsylvania. Committee of Bondholders.

Committee of Inspection, Observation, and
Correspondence, Lancaster Co., Pa. see
Lancaster County, Pa. Committee of
Inspection, Observation and Correspond-
ence.

Committee of Internal Improvement, Baltimore.
see Trade Convention, Baltimore, 1835.
Committee of Internal Improvement.

Committee of Investigation on the Rights of
Congregationalists in Knox College. see
Congregational Churches in Illinois.
General Association. Committee of
Investigation on the Rights of Congre-
gationlists in Knox College.

Committee of Investors, Solicitors, and Attorneys. 68269

Committee of its American Friends. see
Great Western Railroad, Canada West.
Committee of American Friends.

Committee of Literary Gentlemen. pseud. eds.
Metropolitan. 48216

Committee of Mechanics, New York. see New
York (City) Committee of Mechanics.

Committee of Merchants, New York. see New
York (City) Committee of Merchants.

Committee of Merchants and Bankers of the
City of New York. 66044 see also
Barney, -------. Butler, Benjamin
Franklin, 1795-1858. Parsons, -------.

Committee of Merchants and Manufacturers on
the Proposed Tariff, Boston, 1824. see
Boston. Committee of Merchants and
Manufacturers, on the Proposed Tariff,
Boston, 1824.

Committee of Merchants and Others, Boston,
1820. see Boston. Committee of
Merchants and Others, 1820.

Committee of Merchants for the Relief of
Colored People Suffering from the Late
Riots, New York. (54633)

Committee of Merchants, Opposed to the
Auction System, New York. see Committee of New York Merchants, Opposed
to the Auction System.

Committee of Mexican Bondholders, London.
(48654)

Committee of Ministers and Laymen. pseud.
eds. Mutual rights. 51612

Committee of New Jersey Bank Officers. 3176,
(8148), 53070

Committee of New York Merchants, Opposed
to the Auction System. 23370, 68302

Committee of Non Episcopalian Denominations
in New York. 103241, 103250

Committee of One Hundred and Fifty, Boston.
see Boston. Committee of One Hundred
and Fifty.

Committee of Officers of the War of 1812,
New York. see New York (City) Committee of Officers of the War of 1812.

Committee of Pastors in Hampden County, Mass.
18814, 30130 see also Clarke, E. B.
Davis, Emerson. Oviatt, George Alexander, 1811-1887.

Committee of Peace in Paris. Member. pseud.
Letter to the American Peace Society.
see Gibbes, George M.

Committee of Philadelphia. see Philadelphia.
Committee.

Committee of Physicians, Norfolk, Va. see
Norfolk, Va. Committee of Physicians.

Committee of Privates, Philadelphia. (60727)

Committee of Relief for Sufferers of the Pemberton Mill. Treasurer. (39392)

Committee of Safety, Philadelphia. see Philadelphia. Committee of Safety.

Committee of Safety of the Colony of New York. see New York (Colony) Committee of Safety, 1775-1776.

Committee of Seven, Philadelphia. see Philadelphia. Committee of Seven.

Committee of Spanish American Bondholders. 90710

Committee of Tarring and Feathering, Philadelphia. see Philadelphia. Committee on Tarring and Feathering.

Committee of Ten on a Proposed University in Brooklyn. 8320, 2d note after 93460

Committee of Anti-Jackson Men of Franklin County, Pa. see National Republican Party. Pennsylvania. Franklin County.

Committee of the Baptist Board of Foreign Missions for the United States. see Baptist Board of Foreign Missions. Committee.

Committee of the Bar of the City of New York. see New York (City) Bar. Committee.

Committee of the Board of Underwriters, New York. see New York Board of Underwriters. Committee.

Committee of the Boston and Worcester and Western Railroad Corporations on Uniting the Two Railroads. 6768

Committee of the Boston Board of Trade "to make . . . Investigation into the Causes of the Recent Monetary Difficulties and Mercantile Embarrassments." see Boston. Board of Trade. Committee "To Make . . . Investigation into the Causes of the Recent Monetary Difficulties and Mercantile Embarrassments."

Committee of the Boston Board of Trade Upon the Cotton Tax. see Boston. Board of Trade. Committee Upon the Cotton Tax.

Committee of the Christian Commission in Charge of the District of Maryland. see United States Christian Commission. Maryland.

Committee of the Citizens of Berkshire County, Mass., on the Removal of Williams College. see Berkshire County, Mass. Meeting on the Removal of Williams College, Pittsfield, 1819. Committee.

Committee of the Citizens of Boston and Vicinity. see Boston. Citizens.

Committee of the Citizens of Boston and Vicinity, Opposed to a Further Increase of Duties on Improtations, 1827. see Boston. Committee of Citizens Opposed to a Further Increase of Duties on Importations, 1827.

Committee of the Citizens of Port Deposite, in Relation to the Proposed Canal from Columbia to Tide. see Port Deposite, Md. Citizens Committee on the Porposed Canal from Columbia to Tide.

Committee of the Citizens to Draft a City Charter, New Bedford, Mass. see New Bedford, Mass. Committee of the Citizens to Draft a City Charter.

Committee of the City's Liberties, Philadelphia. see Philadelphia. Committee of the City's Liberties.

Committee of the Corporation of Brown University. see Brown University. Committee to Raise a Fund of One Hundred Twenty-Five Thousand Dollars.

Committee of the First Parish in Duxbury, Mass. see Duxbury, Mass. First Parish. Committee.

Committee of the Free Trade Convention, 1832. see Free Trade Convention, Boston, 1832. Committee.

Committee . . . of the Friends of Education, Trenton, N. J. 53219

Committee of the Friends of John G. Watmouth. 102127

Committee of the Friends of the Present Administration, Rochester, N. Y., 1842. see Whig Party. New York. Rochester.

Committee of the Greek Fund, New York. 54045

Committee of the Inhabitants of Boston. see Boston. Citizens.

Committee of the Inhabitants of Boston on the Rights of the Colonists, 1772. see Boston. Citizens.

Committee of the Inhabitants of York County, Pa., 1779. see York County, Pa. Committee, 1779.

Committee of the New York Merchants Opposed to the Auction System. 23370, 68302

Committee of the People. see Staten Island, N. Y. St. Andrew's Parish. Committee.

Committee of the Proprietors of St. Paul's Church, Boston. see Boston. St. Paul's Church. Proprietors.

Committee of the Protesting Members of the General Assembly of Vermont. see Vermont. General Assembly. Protesting Members. Committee.

Committee . . . of the Schuylkill Navigation Company, to View the Improvements, . . . of the Navigation of the Connecticut River, report. 78082

Committee of the Several Banks of Philadelphia. (61554)

Committee of the Society for the Suppression of Vice in Bedford, N. Y. see Society for the Suppression of Vice, Bedford, N. Y. Committee.

Committee of the Sons of Liberty, New York. see Sons of Liberty, New York. Committee.

Committee of the Synod of New York and New Jersey. see Presbyterian Church in the U. S. Synod of New York and New Jersey. Committee.

Committee of the Towns of Bozrah, Lebanon and Franklin in the State of Connecticut. 34382

Committee of Those Opposed to the Licence Law. see Massachusetts Committee of Those Opposed to the Licence Law, 1838.

Committee of Twelve on the Proposed Operatic and Dramatic House, Philadelphia. see Philadelphia. Meetings on the Proposed Operatic and Dramatic House, 1839.

Committee of Twenty-Four, Richmond, Va. see Meeting for Devising Means to Suppress . . . Gambling, Richmond, Va., 1833. Committee of Twenty-Four.

Committee of Twenty on the American Coast Survey. see American Association for the Advancement of Science. Committee of Twenty.

Committee of Twenty One. see South Carolina. Convention, Columbia, 1832-1833. Committee of Twenty One.

Committee of Vigilance, New York. see New York Committee of Vigilance.

Committee of Vigilance, Ohio County, Va. see Ohio County, Va. Committee of Vigilance.

Committee of Vigilance, San Francisco. see
San Francisco. Committee of Vigilance.
Committee of Ways and Means 61551
Committee of Ways and Means further report.
87498
Committee of Ways and Means report. 87497
Committee of West India Planters and Mer-
chants. see West India Planters and
Merchants, London.
Committee on a System of Municipal Govern-
ment, Boston. see Boston. Committee
on a System of Municipal Government,
1821.
Committee on Amendments to the City Charter,
Boston. see Boston. Committee on
Amendments to the City Charter.
Committee . . . on as much of the Governor's
address as relates to "the emigration of
young women to the west." (46033)
Committee on Bridging the Delaware, Camden,
N. J. see Camden, N. J. Committee
on Bridging the Delaware.
Committee on Bridging the Delaware, Phila-
delphia. see Philadelphia Committee on
Bridging the Delaware.
Committee on Finance, to which was referred
a resolution of the 30th December, 1829,
directing the Committee to inquire.
83991
Committee on Improvement of the Mississippi
River and Tributaries, St. Louis. see
St. Louis. Committee on Improvement
of the Mississippi River and Tributaries.
Committee on Internal Health, Boston. see
Boston. Common Council. Committee
on Internal Health.
Committee on Mercantile Affairs and Insurance,
to whom was referred the petition of
William Wright, and others, report a
bill. 88215
Committee on Miami University, Oxford, Ohio.
see Oxford Committee on Miami University.
Committee on Public Lands, Boston. see
Boston. City Council. Joint Committee
on Common and Public Grounds.
Committee on Railroads in Austin and Wash-
ington Counties, Texas. 17436, note
before 90804 see also Applewhite, J.
and Crawford, G. W.
Committee on Revolutionary Claims, to whom
was referred a memorial. 82971
Committee on Roads and Canals, to whom was
referred the memorial. 83832
Committee on Spiritualism, Boston, 1857.
42706, 89533 see also Agassiz, Louis,
1807-1873. Gould, B. A. Horsford, Eben
Norton, 1818-1893. Peirce, Benjamin,
1809-1880.
Committee on Statistics, Chicago. see
Chicago. Committee on Statistics.
Committee on Steam Navigation on the Western
Lakes. see Cleveland. Committee on
Steam Navigation on the Western Lakes.
Committee on Tarring and Feathering, Phila-
delphia. see Philadelphia. Committee
on Tarring and Feathering.
Committee on the Boston and Lowell Railroad.
see Massachusetts. Legislature. Com-
mittee on the Boston and Lowell Railroad.
Committee on the Death of General Lafayette,
Boston. see Boston. Committee on the
Death of General Lafayette.
Committee on the Indian and African Company,
Edinburgh. see Company of Scotland

Trading to Africa and the Indies. Committee.
Committee on the Judiciary to whom was
referred the message of the Governor
. . . . (44928)
Committee on the Library, Boston. see
Boston. City Council. Committee on
the Library.
Committee on the North Branch Canal. see
North Branch Canal Committee.
Committee on the Petition of Isaac P. Davis
and Others, Boston. see Boston. Com-
mittee on the Petition of Isaac P. Davis
and Others.
Committee on the Practicability and Utility of
Immediately Constructing a Central Rail-
way, from Pottsville to Sunbury and
Danville, Philadelphia. see
Philadelphia Committee on the Practica-
bility and Utility of Immediately Con-
structing a Central Railway, from Potts-
ville to Sunbury and Danville.
Committee on the Removal of the U. S. Bank
Deposites, Boston. see Boston Com-
mittee on the Removal of the U. S. Bank
Deposites.
Committee on the Washington Funeral Cere-
monies, New London, Conn., 1800. see
New London, Conn. Committee on the
Washington Funeral Ceremonies, 1800.
Committee on the Working Men of Boston.
6572
Committee on the Worcester Co. High School,
presented the following report. 105375
Committee on . . . Transatlantic Steam Navi-
gation, Philadelphia. see Philadelphia
Committee on . . . Transatlantic Steam
Navigation.
Committee Sent to Georgia, to Examine the
Cedar Shoals Water-Power, 1855. see
Massachusetts. Committee Sent to
Georgia, to Examine the Cedar Shoals
Water-Power, 1855.
Committee to Aid in Furnishing Supplies to
the Sick and Wounded Soldiers of Our
Army, New Haven, Conn. see New
Haven, Conn. Committee to Aid in
Furnishing Supplies to the Sick and
Wounded Soldiers of Our Army.
Committee to Ascertain, by Direct Question,
Whether Sundry Persons, Were Purchasing
and Shipping Goods for the Troops at
Boston, New York, 1774. see New York
(City) Committee to Ascertain, by Direct
Question, Whether Sundry Persons, Where
Purchasing and Shipping Goods for the
Troops at Boston, 1774.
Committee to Ascertain Statistics on Intem-
perance, Portsmouth, N. H., 1845. see
Portsmouth, N. H. Committee to Ascer-
tain Statistics on Intemperance, 1845.
Committee to Decide the Controversy Between
Two Parties Claiming a Right in Half a
Share of Land on the Island of Nantucket,
1770. 51752
Committee to Enquire into the Practicability
and Expediency of Establishing Manufac-
tures in Salem, Mass. see Salem, Mass.
Committee to Enquire into the Practica-
bility and Expedience of Establishing
Manufactures in Salem.
Committee to Inquire and Report on the Recent
Arctic Expeditions in Search of Sir J.
Franklin. see Great Britain. Admiralty.
Committee to Inquire and Report on the

Recent Arctic Expeditions in Search of
Sir J. Franklin.
Committee to Investigate the Doings of the
Trustees of the Robinson Female Semi-
nary, Exeter, N. H. see Exeter, N. H.
Committee to Investigate the Doings of
the Trustees of the Robinson Female
Seminary.
Committee . . . to Prevent the Messrs.
Murrays Involving Others in a Breach
of the Association, New York, 1775.
see New York (City) Committee . . .
to Prevent the Messrs. Murrays Involv-
ing Others in a Breach of the Associ-
ation, 1775.
Committee to Promote the Passage of a
Metropolitan Health Bill, New York,
1865. 54047
Committee to Recruit the Ninth Army Corps,
New York. see New York Committee
to Recruit the Ninth Army Corps.
Committee to Revise the City Charter, Boston.
see Boston. City Council. Joint Committee to Revise the City Charter.
Committee to Take into Consideration the
Expediency of Making an Alteration in
the Municipal Government of the Town
of Boston. see Boston. Committee to
Take into Consideration the Expediency
of Making an Alteration in the Municipal
Government of the Town.
Committee to whom was referred the petition
of the President and Fellows of Yale
College, respectfully report. 105798
Committee, to whom was referred the report
of the Secretary of State, to whom was
referred the memorial of Stephen Sayre,
report. (77416)
Committee Who Presented the Report on
Ambulance and Camp-Hospital Corps to
the Authorities in Washington, New York.
see New York (City) Committee who
Presented the Report on Ambulance and
Camp-Hospital Corps to the Authorities
in Washington, 1862.
Committees on the Tornado of 1851, in Med-
ford, West Cambridge, and Waltham,
Mass. see Medford, Mass. Tornado
Committee, 1851. Waltham, Mass.
Tornado Committee, 1851. West Cam-
bridge, Mass. Tornado Committee, 1851.
Committees vindicated. 3094
Commodities of the iland called Manati ore
Long Isle which is in the continent of
Virginia. 14994, note after 44194
Common almanac. 14995
Common apologie of the Chvrch of England.
29818, 72088, 72110
Common Council documents. New city build-
ings. 1860. 61552
Common fallacies and monstrous errors
refuted and exposed. 2978
Common honesty. pseud. Letter. (40329)
Common honesty, C. P. S. pseud. Echo from
the temple of wisdom. see Deane,
Silas, 1737-1789. supposed author
Common law, L. L. D. pseud. Echo from the
temple of wisdom. see Deane, Silas,
1737-1789. supposed author
Common law of Pennsylvania. 79862
Common law procedure act. 81675
Common nature of epidemics, and their relation
to climate and civilization. 84416
Common-place arguments against administration.
95794

Common-place book of prose and poetry.
106146
Common school arithmetic. (36248)
Common school assistant. 14996
Common school controversy. (44318)
Common school education. 71076
Common school history. 27915
Common school history of the United States.
42135
Common school journal. 14997, 44324, (66050),
83572
Common school journal of the state of Penn-
sylvania. 30628, 59993
Common school law and regulations. 53612
Common school law of Kansas Territory.
(37030)
Common school law of the Territory of Colo-
rado. 14739
Common school laws. 60044
Common school laws . . . [of Pennsylvania.]
59994
Common school laws of the state of Kentucky.
37505
Common school library. 95216
Common school system of the state of New
York. (53613), 67800
Common schools. 94510
Common schools. A discourse on the modi-
fications demanded by the Roman Cath-
olics. 9549
Common schools and teachers' seminaries.
92387
Common schools in the United States compared
with those in Europe. 88909
Common schools of New York. 8346
Common schools. Remarks on the school law.
59995
Common schools; the necessity of their im-
provement, and school libraries. 58162
Common sense. pseud. Letters of common
sense respecting the state bank. 40608
Common-sense. pseud. Memorial. 47640
Common sense. pseud. National currency.
(51960)
Common sense. pseud. Oracles of reason.
57424
Common sense. pseud. Privilege of the writ
of habeas corpus. see Kennedy, W. M.
supposed author
Common sense. pseud. Sermon to swine.
79287
Common sense. pseud. Views respecting the
Chesapeak and Delaware Canal. see
Citizen of Philadelphia. pseud.
Common sense, Jr. pseud. Crisis. (17524)
Common sense, Secretary to Foreign Affairs.
pseud. Echo from the temple of wisdom.
see Deane, Silas, 1737-1789. supposed
author
Common sense. 251, 10671, 15526, (58206),
58212-58213, 58215, 58237, note after
63244, (71242), 79187, 84642, 84678C,
note before 95678, 95718, 97119, 97127,
98338, 102144
Common sense addressed to common people.
82156
Common sense: addressed to the inhabitants of
America. 58211, (58214)
Common sense addresses to the citizens of the
southern states. 10859
Common sense, and plain truth. (58214), 84642
Common sense. By "Fabius." 23594
"Common sense" especially addressed to the
most suffering portion of our fellow-
citizens. 47275

Common sense in dishabille. Mr. Sloan's speech. 82152
Common sense in dishabille; or, the farmer's monitor. (23241)
Common sense: in nine conferences. 14998
Common sense versus judicial legislation. (76977)
Common sense; with the whole appendix. (58214)
Common truth, S. S. T. P. pseud. Echo from the temple of wisdom. see Deane, Silas, 1737-1789. supposed author
Common understanding of the effect, and consequence, of an ordinance of secession. 41146
Common understanding of the reason why a state forfeits state rights by its hostility to the United States. 41147
Commoner. pseud. Letter to Viscount Melbourne. 38751
Commoner. pseud. Squatter sovereignty. 89944
Commonwealth in danger. (11155)
Commonwealth of Massachusetts. 8354, 45684
Commonwealth of Massachusetts against the state of Rhode Island and Providence Plantations. 45682
Commonwealth of Massachusetts. Aggregates of polls. (45683)
Commonwealth of Massachusetts. Boston, 25th of May, 1783. 94663
Commonwealth of Massachusetts. By His Excellency John Hancock, Esquire . . . a proclamation. 99007
Commonwealth of Massachusetts. By His Excellency John Hancock, Esquire, Governor of the commonwealth of Massachusetts. A brief. 85865
Commonealth of Massachusetts, complainant, vs. the state of Rhode Island. 45681
Commonwealth of Massachusetts. Essex, SS. November term, 1890. 85212
Commonwealth of Massachusetts. Essex, SS. Supreme Judicial Court. 85212
Commonwealth of Massachusetts. House of Representatives, Jan. 14, 1835. 67908
Commonwealth of Massachusetts. In the year of Our Lord, one thousand seven hundred and eighty-seven. An act. 85864
Commonwealth of Massachusetts. Supreme Judicial Court. 85212
Commonwealth of Massachusetts. Supreme Judicial Court. Essex, SS. 85212
Commonwealth of Massachusetts. Supreme Judicial Court. Essex, SS. In equity. 85212
Commonwealth of Massachusetts. Supreme Judicial Court. Essex, SS. In equity. No. 223. 85212
Commonwealth of Massachusetts. The Attorney-General's report respecting claims for confiscated debts. 5253
Commonwealth of Massachusetts. The committee of both houses, to whom was referred the petition praying for the removal from office of Brigadier-General David Putnam . . . report. 66773
Commonwealth of Massachusetts vs. Ebenezer Clough. 96850
Commonwealth of Massachusetts, vs. Francis O. J. Smith. 82560
Commonwealth of Massachusetts vs. the state of Rhode Island and Providence Plantations. (46151)-46153, 70752
Commonwealth of Pennsylvania. 84397

Commonwealth of Pennsylvania against John Binns. 8466
Commonwealth of Pennsylvania at the relation of Rowland E. Evans vs. the Philadelphia Club. 23184
Commonwealth of Pennsylvania, at the suggestion of Paul Daniel Gonzalve Grande D'Hauteville. 19915
Commonwealth of Pennsylvania vs. Lieut. Richard Smith. (60165), 83762
Common-wealth of Utopia. (50547)
Commonwealth, town & county taxes for Roxbury for 1802. 73637
Commonwealth vs. Buckingham. 57856, 67255
Commonwealth vs. J. T. Buckingham. 8911, 96840
Commonwealth vs. Snelling. 85430
Commonwealth vs. Tench Coxe. 18313
Commonwealth's-man. 82772
Commuck, Thomas. 14999
Communaute de l'Union. Colonisation du District de Santo-Thomas. 76884
Communaute de l'Union, Fondee Par la Compagnie Belge de Colonisation. see Compagine Belge de Colonisation. Communaute de l'Union, Guatemala.
Communicacao entre a Cidade de Bahia e a Villa de Joazeiro. 66422
Communicaciones, entre el Senor Carlos Biddle, Coronel de los E. Unidos del Norte, i la Sociedad Amigos del Pais. 5228, 15000
Communicacoes com os Estados Unidos. (3901)
Communicatie tusschen Essequebo en Demerary. 22993, 5th note after 102895
Communicatie van zekere onderschepte missive van d'Avaux. (39804)
Communication addressed to a Committee of the Board of Directors of the Red Hook Building Company. 68471
Communication addressed to "friends" and all conscientiously scrupulous of bearing arms. 15001
Communication addressed to the Boston Board of Trade. 78675
Communication addressed to the First Religious Society in Newburyport. 54917
Communication addressed to the Hon. S. W. Downs. 77519
Communication addressed to the President . . . of the . . . [Pennsylvania] Railroad, on the cost of transportation. 60358
Communication and other papers. 99597
Communication . . . and report. 53616
Communication between the Atlantic and Pacific Oceans. 50768
Communication . . . by Richard Owen. 6240
Communication by the Proprietors of the New South Meeting-House. (20628)
Communication . . . by William P. C. Barton. 43500
Communication confidentielle adressee a des amis. 15925
Communication faite a la seance du 24 Mai, 1867. (73953)
Communication forwarded from San Felipe de Austin. 95073
Communication from a Committee of the Several Banks of . . . Philadelphia. (61554)
Communication from Adam McAdam. 42927, 43146
Communication from Count Rechberg. (36119)
Communication from E. G. Squier. 89960
Communication from E. Louis Lowe. (42411)

Communication from Henry Snyder. 85601
Communication from His Excellency, Governor McDuffie. 87478
Communication from His Excellency James Y. Smith. 70567
Communication from Hon. Edward Everett. 6759
Communication from Hon. John A. Dix. 20341
Communication from J. S. Green and W. P. Hall. 28532
Communication from James Boorman. 33537
Communication from Judge Stroud. 93099
Communication from Leland Stanford. 90211
Communication from Major General Dix. 53614
Communication from Milton H. Smith. 83629
Communication from Prof. Joseph Henry. 85024
Communication from Sir Charles Brisbane. 8005
Communication from the Agent of the State Prison of the State of New York. 37799
Communication from the Attorney General. 15244
Communication from the Attorney General, . . . relative to the constitutionality of the law abolishing tdls on railroads. 53536
Communication from the Attorney General relative to the suit of Maryland against Virginia. 45090
Communication from the Auditor General. (59903)
Communication from the Auditor General relative to the account of John Dungan. 59905
Communication from the Auditor transmitting a report. 53615
Communication from the Balt. and Ohio R. R. Co. to the Mayor and City Council of Balt. 2992
Communication from . . . the Board of Trade of . . . Oswego. 57832
Communication from the Board of Trade . . . to the Committee on Finance of the Senate of the United States. 61970
Communication from the Brookfield Association to the Ecclesiastical Council. (8247)
Communication from the Canal Commissioners exhibiting the condition of the canals and rail roads. 59952
Communication from the Canal Commissioners, Jan. 5, 1859. 73977
Communication from the Canal Commissioners, relative to the allotment of work on the North Branch Canal. 60275
Communication from the Canal Commissioners relative to the sail of the Main Line of the Public Works of the State. 59955
Communication from the . . . Canal Commissioners, transmitting the reports. (59996)
Communication from the . . . Canal Commissioners, with a report and estimate for avoiding the inclined plane at Philadelphia. note just before 60250
Communication from the City Physician on Asiatic cholera. 68187
Communication from the Commissioner of the Gen. Land Office. 94981
Communication from the Comptroller, in reply to a resolution. (54212)
Communication from the Comptroller, relative to expenditures and receipts of the county. 54211
Communication from the Comptroller to the Commissioners of the Sinking Funds. (54212)

Communication from the Comptroller, transmitting a list of all bills paid by the Auditor. (54212)
Communication from the Comptroller, transmitting his financial estimates. (54212)
Communication from the Department of State at Washington. 70658
Communication from the Director of the Mint to the Secretary of the Treasury. 49330, 85579
Communication from the Executive department. 87479
Communication from the Executive of Delaware. (45109)
Communication from the Executive of South Carolina. 87423
Communication from the First Congregational Society of New Bedford. 26241
Communication from the Governor, accompanied with a communication from the . . . Canal Commissioners. (59996)
Communication from the Governor, accompanied with a report of the . . . Canal Commissioners. (59996)
Communication from the Governor, accompanied with a report of the . . . Canal Commissioners of Pennsylvania. No. 2. (59996)
Communication from the Governor, covering a report. 52809
Communication from the Governor of Georgia. 27028
Communication from the Governor [of Massachusetts.] (32551), 7th note after 97146, 97147
Communication from the Governor of New York. 24430
Communication from the Governor relative to the boundary line. 53616
Communication from the Governor, relative to the geological survey of the state. 53687
Communication from the Governor to the House of Assembly. 75512
Communication from the Governor, transmitting the annual report of the Metropolitan Police. 54400
Communication from the Governor, transmitting the report of the Commissioners of Quarantine. (53885)
Communication from the Grand Lodge of . . . New York. (53692)
Communication from the Hon. Samuel Sewall. (79450)
Communication from the "Local Visiting Committee of Bellevue and Other Hospitals." 86150
Communication from . . . the Mayor in relation to the precautionary measures adopted by him. (54205)
Communication from . . . the Mayor to the City Council. 51869
Communication from the Messrs. Howard and M'Neill. 45110
Communication from the Metropolitan Board of Police and Board of Health. 54400
Communication from the North Pennsylvania R. Road. 62157
Communication from the Postmaster General. 15245
Communication from the President of the American Antiquarian Society. 1052, 95404
Communication from the President of the Ohio & Pennsylvania Rail Road Company. 60358
Communication from the President . . . [of the Union Canal Company] relative to enlarging . . . [the] canal. note after 97766

Communication from the President . . . [of the Union Canal Company] with a report of James D. Harris. 60750, note after 97766

Communication from the President . . . of the West Philadelphia Rail Road Co. note just before 90250

Communication from the President . . . to Thomas Donaldson. 2992

Communication from the Secretary of State, transmitting the census of the state. (53576)

Communication from the Secretary of State, transmitting the report of Mr. Schoolcraft. 77874

Communication from the Secretary of the Commonwealth in relation to census. (60609)

Communication from the Secretary . . . [of the Commonwealth] relative to educating poor children. (60609)

Communication from the Secretary of the Navy, relative to coals of the steamer "Advance." 15312

Communication from the Secretary of the Treasury. Treasury Department C. S. A. 15247

Communication from the Secretary of the Treasury, with an accompanying document. 95048

Communication from the Secretary of War. note after 60249, note after 104493

Communication from the Secretary of War, covering an estimate. 15316

Communication from the Secretary of War in relation to the system of internal improvements. 15002

Communication from the Secretary of War, on the taxes in kind. 15302

Communication from the Secretary of War, relative to operations of the Army of Tennessee. 15311

Communication from the Secretary of War, relative to the number of persons exempted from military service. 15313

Communication from the Select and Common Councils of . . . Philadelphia. 61555

Communication . . . from the Selectmen of . . . Milton [Mass.] 45701

Communication from the State Geologist. 48738

Communication from the State Treasurer. (60639)

Communication from the Street Commissioner. 54684

Communication from the Superintendent of Buildings. 54687

Communication from the Superintendent of the Onondaga Salt Springs. 84484

Communication from the Trustees of the Fourth Ward. 54121

Communication from the Water Commissioners. (54232)

Communication from Thomas Swann. 2992

Communication from W. H. H. Terrell. (34557)

Communication . . . in answer to a resolution. 53616

Communication in relation to a supply of water. (21478)

Communication in relation to the same, from James P. Kirkwood. 8331

Communication in reply to a letter written Gov. Fenton by Hon. John Covode. 35849

Communication made by him [i. e. James G. Carter] to the brethren. 95259

Communication, no. 8. 48054

Communication of A. A. Lawrence. 35680

Communication of Attorney-General Z. Snow. 85562

Communication of Dr. Henry G. Clark. (13297)

Communication of E. F. Chambers. 45086

Communication of Gov. Briggs. 45686

Communication of . . . [H. Haupt.] 30859

Communication of His Excellency Governor Pickens. 87442

Communication of His Excellency the Governor. 45685, 93495

Communication of His Excellency the President. 95009

Communication of His Honor the Mayor. (44210)

Communication of Hon. John B. Floyd. 24913

Communication of Hon. John Cochrane. 14077

Communication of Hon. William H. Seward. 79509

Communication of P. H. Wentworth. 73719

Communication of S. Lawrence and W. W. Stone. 63686

Communication of the Agent of the Foreign Holders of Indiana State Bonds. 34526

Communication of the Comptroller. (54212)

Communication of the Delegation of the Cherokee Nation. 12449

Communication of the . . . Directors of the Panama Railroad Company. 58409

Communication of the Grand Lodge of Massachusetts. 45760

Communication of the Grand Lodge of the State of Maine. (43992)

Communication of the Hon. Jasper Ward. (53929)

Communication of the Mayor, and reports of departments, of the city of Louisville. (42313)

Communication of the Mayor to the City Council. 75652

Communication of the Medical Society of Connecticut. 15783

Communication of the New York Association for Restoration of American Shipping Interests. 54428

Communication of the Pennsylvania Society for the Encouragement of Manufactures and the Useful Arts. 60367

Communication of the report. 94187

Communication of the Secretary of the Treasury. 15246

Communication of the "United Whig Club." 54557

Communication of the Vermont Missionary Society. 99234

Communication officielle de trois lettres de Catineau-Laroche. (39049)

Communication on the improvement of government. 34728

Communication on the language, manners, and customs. 79731

Communication relative to a proposed branch mint at New York. 49330

Communication . . . relative to alleged abuses. 53616

Communication . . . relative to escheats and alleged escheats. 59905

Communication relative to his [i. e. Alfred Brunson's] travels. 8762

Communication relative to the non-destruction of the cotton. 15315

Communication, relative to the subject, from the Selectmen of the town of Milton 17251, 45701, 49146

Communication . . . respecting a system of fire alarms. 11930

Communication respecting the seal of the "Council for New England." (19047)

Communication . . . showing the receipts and expenditures. 59905

Communication, signed D. H. Mulvany. 8239, 62120

Communication to a member of the legislature. 84270

Communication to Board of Directors [of the Southwestern Railroad Company.] 88623

Communication . . . to D. N. Carpenter. 30859

Communication to Dr. Mitchill. (14160)

Communication to Gov. N. Dewey. 38979

Communication to His Excellency Governor Cobb. 87375

Communication to Lord Monteagle. 6889

Communication to the Board of Trustees of the University of Pennsylvania. (59142)

[Communication to the] Chairman and Gentlemen of the Joint Committee. 30859

Communication to the City Council on the subject of introducing water into the city. 6785

Communication to the Commissioners of the Central Park. (28499)

Communication [to the Councils of Philadelphia.] 60278

Communication to the General Assembly of Ohio. 43690

Communication to the General Assembly of Tennessee. 25217

Communication to the Governor of South-Carolina. (26227)

Communication to the Legislature from the minority of the Committee. 8286

Communiation to the Legislature, in reply to a statement. 77604

Communication to the Mayor of New York on prison discipline. 21816

Communication to the Rector, Church Wardens and Vestrymen. 75210

Communication to the Sectional Boards. 61555

Communication to those citizens of the North-Western Territory. 105504

Communication transmitting a copy of the resolution. 101922

Communication . . . transmitting a memorial. 53616

Communication . . . transmitting certain proceedings. 53616

Communication . . . transmitting quarterly statements. 59905

Communication . . . transmitting report of Commissioners. 53616

Communication . . . transmitting the report of Alexander Vattemare. 53616

Communication . . . transmitting the report of State Officers. 53616

Communication . . . transmitting the report of the Board of State Officers. 53968

Communication . . . transmitting the report of the Commissioners Appointed to Locate the Hudson River Asylum for the Insane. 53616

Communication . . . transmitting the report of the Commissioners . . . relative to protecting the harbors and frontiers. 53616

Communications and reports in relation to the survey of Boston Harbor. 6723

Communications and reports, relative to the affairs of the Monument Cemetery. 61846

Communications between the Collector of Customs at Liverpool and Messrs. Klingender and Co. 15003, 55529

Communications concerning the agriculture and commerce of America. 15004, note after 94406, note after 106213

Communications concerning the agriculture and commerce of the United States of America. 92811, 94407

Communications de Mercator. 47890

Communications from Adam McAdam. 42927

Communications from John H. Alexander. 45158

Communications from Messrs. Vogdes & Gerard. 62173

Communications from several states. 15005, 100077

Communications from the Agents of the United States with the governments. 48078

Communications from the Board of Trustees of the Girard College. (27494)

Communications from the London Missionary Society. 15699

Communications from the Mayor of Baltimore. 3027

Communications from the Secretaries of the Treasury and of War. 15309

Communications from the Secretary and Treasurer and the Adjutant-General. 45919

Communications from the Secretary of State. 1498

Communications from the Secretary of the Navy and the Postmaster-General. 15314

Communications from the State Department. 95039

Communications interesting to the public. 95438

Communications of American Ministers. 15006

Communications of "Mercator." 20697

Communications of missionaries in the Cherokee Nation. 1901

Communications of Mr. James R. Hale. 85954

Communications of several states. 100074

Communications [of the British Board of Agriculture.] 101720

Communications of the British Consul. 87501

Communications of the Grand Lodge of the State of Maine. (43992)

Communications of the Rhode Island Medical Society. 70727, 85493

Communications of W. J. M'Alpine and J. B. Jervis, Esqs. 8329

Communications on different subjects. 2717

Communications on the next election for President. 15007, 26928

Communications received at the Foreign Office relative to Hayti. 29571

Communications relative to the progress of Bible Societies in the United States. 15008, 49121

Communications to the Pennsylvania Agricultural Society. (31972), 60296

Communion of churches. 22145

Communion-office, or order of the administration of the Holy Eucharist. (15009), 78561

Communion office. Reprinted in fac-simile. 78561

Como los perros a la luna ladran. 2000

Como seran y como podrian ser en los siglos venideros. 85776-85777

Comonfort, Ignacio, Pres. Mexico, 1812-1863. 48520, 66571, 81474 see also Mexico. President, 1855-1857 (Comonfort)

Comonfort, J. (15011)-15013

Comoto, Florencio Perez y. see Perez y Comoto, Florencio.

Comoza. Potawatomi Indian Chief 96595

Comoza Band of Potawatomi Indians. see Potawatomi Indians (Comoza Band)

Compact, with the charter and laws of the Colony of New Plymouth. (7962)

Compadre. pseud. Signe el tejedor y su compadre. 94598
Compaen, Klaus G. 15015-15016, 23468
Compagne dans l'extreme orient. 21163
Compagne de circumnavigation de la Fregate l'Artemise. 10186
Compagnes et stations. 21163
Compagni, Bartholomew. 76897
Compagnie Belge de Colonisation. (11681), (66852), 66855, 76882
Compagnie Belge de Colonisation. Commission d'Exploration dans l'Amerique Centrale. 66854
Compagnie Belge de Colonisation. Communaute de l'Union, Guatemala. (11681), 14724, 76882-76884
Compagnie de Canada. see Compagnie de la Nouvelle France.
Compagnie de Colonisation Generale a la Guyane Francaise, proposee a l'industrie nationale. 11641, (19139)
Compagnie de Colons de Saint Domingue, Paris. 28153, 75149
Compagnie de Jesus. see Jesuits.
Compagnie de la France Equinoxiale. 11641, 19139, 29169
Compagnie de la Guyane Francaise. see Compagnie de la France Equinoxiale.
Compagnie de la Nouvelle France. (10361), 10529, 55418, 99751
Compagnie de la Nouvelle France. defendants 86843
Compagnie de la Nouvelle France. Directeurs. petitioners 56092
Compagnie de la Nouvelle France. Directeurs et Associez. 10359, 41844
Compagnie de la Nouvelle France. Directeurs et Associez. petitioners (56089)
Compagnie de la Presse a Coton, New Orleans. defendants 87280
Compagnie de New York, Paris. see Company of New York.
Compagnie de Saint Domingue. 40713, 40718-40719, 75095, 75154-75155
Compagnie de Saint Domingue. Charter. 40718, 75154
Compagnie de Wilmington, dans la Caroline du Nord, sur la Riviere de Cape-Fear, aux Etats-Unis de l'Amerique. 104584
Compagnie des Isles de l'Amerique. Charter. 75014, 75016
Compagnie des Indes d'Occident. see Compagnie des Indes Occidentales.
Compagnie des Indes Occidentales. 70119
Compagnie des Indes Occidentales. Charter. (40716)-40717, 68445, 102772-102774
Compagnie des Indes Occidentales. Council. Chief Judge. 103422 see also Boisbriant, --------.
Compagnie des Indes Occidentales (Dutch) see Nederlandsche West Indische Compagnie.
Compagnie des Indes Orientales. Charter. 68444
Compagnie d'Haiti pour la Culture du Cafe et Autres Produits. 29572
Compagnie d'Occident. see Compagnie des Indes Occidentales.
Compagnie Pour le Commerce des Indes Orientales. see Compagnie des Indes Orientales.
Compagnie pour l'exploitation des bois de construction civile et maritime. 29169
Compagnie du Scioto, Paris. 21857, 56913, 78123-78125
Compagnie Franco-Mexicaine de Mines. 49129

Compagnie Franco-Mexicaine pour la repirse de leur exploitation. 49219
Compagnie Generale a Etablir dans les Pays-Bas Autrichiens Pour le Commerce et la Navigation aux Indes. Charter. 40712, 68792, 102442
Compagnie Generalle de la Nouvelle France. see Compagnie de la Nouvelle France.
Compagnie Nommee Par les Colons Residans a Paris. see Compagnie de Colons de Saint Domingue, Paris.
Compagnie Royale de Saint Domingue. see Compagnie de Saint Domingue.
Compagnies devoilees. 19729
Compagnon du per Tom. (31792)
Compagnoni, Giuseppe. 15017-15018, note after 92196
Compan, --------. 15019
Compana de Peru. (41990)
Companhia de Minas de Ouro e Cobre au Sul do Brazil. 88785
Companhia de Navegacao e Commercio do Amazonas. Presidente. 69319 see also Guimaraes, Joaquim da Fonseca.
Companhia do Mucury. (57900)
Companhia do Mucury. Commissao Liquidadora. 69318
Companhia do Mucury. Director. 51229 see also Ottoni, Theophilo Benedicto.
Companhia do Mucury. Historia da empreza. (57900)
Companhia do Queimado. (66077)
Companhia Ferry do Rio de Janeiro e de Nictheroy. Commissao de Exame de Cortas. 71469
Companhia Ferry do Rio de Janeiro e de Nictheroy. Emprezario. 71468 see also Rainey, Thomas.
Companhia Mucury. Relatorio. (57900)
Compania a Cuyo Cargo Este la Conduccion de Tobaccos, Azucar, Corambres, y Otros Frutos, Havana. Charter. 16668, 29422
Compania Aviadora del Mineral del Monte y Pachuca. defendants (44966)
Compania Cosmopolitana Protectoria de la Industria en la Alta-California. (68877)
Compania de Accionistas de Minas de Mexico. 48519
Compania de Almacenes de Santa Catalina. Presidente. (15021)
Compania de Camino de Hierro entre Puerto Principe y Nuevitas. (66585)
Compania de Camino de Hierro entre Puerto Principe y Nuevitas. Charter. (66585)
Compania de Camina de Hierro entre Puerto Principe y Nuevitas. Presidente. 66589
Compania de Cocheros y Lacayos, Mexico (City) see Piadosa Compania de Cocheros y Lacayos, Mexico (City)
R. Compania de Comercio Para las Islas de Santo Domingo, Puerto Rico, y la Margarita. 68236, 1st note after 75184
Compania de Diligencias. petitioners 74745
Compania de Jesus. see Jesuits.
Compania de Minas, Temascaltepec, Mexico. 94634
Compania de Minas Zacatecano-Mexicana. 106240
Compania de Nuevo Almaden. (16906)
Compania de Tobaco, Havana. see Havana. Compania de Tobaco.
Compania del Ferro-Carril de Mexico a Puebla. 48460
Compania del Rio Janeiro. defendants 44290

Compania Ferro-Carril de Copiapo. 16675
Compania Formado en la Provincia de Gui-
puzcoa, para Embiar dos Navios Cada
Ano, con Registro, a la Provincia de
Venezuela. see R. Compania Gui-
puzcoana de Caracas.
Compania General Mexicana para la Exploi-
tacion de la Seda. 48641
R. Compania Guipuzcoana de Caracas. (10782),
15020, 29251, 55998, 68237, 98765
R. Compania Guipuzcoana de Caracas. Direc-
tor. 29251, 68237
R. Compania Guipuzcoana de Caracas. Junta
Jeneral. 10777
Compania Lancasteriana de Mexico. 15022
Compania Mexicana Cientifico-Industrial.
97502-97503
Compania Queretana de Indistria. 67110
Compania Real de Guiana. Charter. 99618
Compania Zacateno-Mexicana. (48370)
Companion and weekly miscellany. 15023
Companion: being a selection of the beauties.
15024
Companion for communicants. 46267, 90160
Companion for the afflicted. (46268)
Companion for the tourist and traveller. 8225,
56749
Companion for traders and travellers. 98274
Companion hand-book of travel. (70959)
Companion to the almanac. 8076
Companion to the American museum. 54498,
78522
Companion to the Bible. 95844
Companion to "the mayflower." 92449
Companion to the "new gospel of peace."
6359, 70160, 103445
Companion to the Rebellion record. 50356
Companion to the Select circulating library.
82983
Companion to the tomb-stone. 90136
Companions in arms! 85184
Compano contra los Americanos del Norte.
15025
Compans, Henri Ternaux. see Ternaux Com-
pans, Henri.
Company for Erecting a Permanent Bridge
Over the Schuylkill At or Near Phila-
delphia. see Schuylkill Bridge Com-
pany.
Company for Making an Artificial Road from
. . . Philadelphia. Charter. (59802)
Company for Propagation of the Gospel in New
England and the Parts Adjacent in Amer-
ica, London. 3213, 22146, 22149, (22152),
49840, 59561, 80205, 80207, note before
85932, note before 92797, note after 92800,
3d note after 103687, note after 104794
see also Corporation for Promoting and
Propagating the Gospel of Jesus Christ in
New England, London.
Company for Propagation of the Gospel in New
England and the Parts Adjacent in Amer-
ica, London. Charter. 52600, 52624
Company for Propagation of the Gospel in New
England and the Parts Adjacent in Amer-
ica, London. Committee. (69725)
Company of Booksellers, Philadelphia. see
Philadelphia Company of Booksellers.
Company of Haberdashers, London. see
Worshipful Company of Haberdashers,
London.
Company of Jesus. see Jesuits.
Company of New York. 19728, 95825
Company of Printers and Booksellers, Phila-
delphia. see Philadelphia Company of
Printers and Booksellers.

Company of Royal Adventurers of England
Trading into Africa. see Royal African
Company of England.
Company of Scotland Trading to Africa and the
Indies. 16081, 18547-18548, (18553),
18554, (18557), 18563-18564, 18566,
18567, (18573)-18574, 58392, 78201-78202,
(78208), (78225)-78226, 78237-78238
Company of Scotland Trading to Africa and the
Indies. petitioners 18570, 78196, 2d
note after 91386
Company of Scotland Trading to Africa and the
Indies. respondents (18573), 78237, note
after 90593
Company of Scotland Trading to Africa and the
Indies. Charter. 18560, 57392, 78220,
78224, 2d note after 98925
Company of Scotland Trading to Africa and the
Indies. Committee. 69786
Company of Scotland Trading to Africa and the
Indies. Council-General. 18554, (18557),
78197
Company of Scotland Trading to Africa and the
Indies. Council-General. petitioners
18566, 69993, (78229), 78231, (78239)
Company of Scotland Trading to Africa and the
Indies. Court of Directors. 18554
Company of Scotland Trading to Africa and the
Indies. Secretary. 78197 see also
Ross, Hugh.
Company of Swiss Settlers. petitioners 47723
Company 1, Fourth Massachusetts Regiment,
nine month volunteers. (43824)
Company, Trading to Mexico and Peru, Liver-
pool. 66073
Company's agreement with the ministers.
106052
Company's instructions to Endicott and his
council. 106052
Company's letters to Higginson and Endicott.
106052
Company's monthly report. 96481
Company's records. 106052
Comparacion general de los territorios. (36806),
97687
Comparaison entre les systems. 33331
Comparatio brevior Germanorum antiquorum
et hodieornarum. 30860
Comparatio inter potiore terrae partes Euro-
pam, Asiam, Africam & Americam. 98390
Comparative advantages between the United
States and Canada. 72876
Comparative anatomy and psychology of the
African Negro. 9344
Comparative and general statistics. 16331
Comparative calculations. 15029, 59997
Comparative chronological statement of events.
57563
Comparative claims of home and foreign mis-
sions. 89325
Comparative footing of the commerce of the
United States. 97910
Comparative importance of foreign and domestic
missions. 30454
Comparative importance of our acquisitions.
15031
Comparative importance of the British and
French islands in the West-Indies. 10231,
3d note after 102821
Comparative importance of the commercial
principles. 15030
Comparative physiognomy or resemblances
between men and animals. 68503
Comparative reflections on the past and present
political, commercial and civil state of
Great Britain. 11831

Comparative state of the public revenues.
90096

Comparative statement of expenditures on
different rail roads. 87959

Comparative statement of mortality in the
Society of Friends. (12195)

Comparative statement of the condition of
the Negroes. 10248

Comparative statement of the English and
American trade. 8121

Comparative statement of the number of
deaths in the city of New York. 50999,
(54206)

Comparative statement of the relative position
and distinctive principles. 5729

Comparative statement of the value of merchandize imported. 56116

Comparative statement with reference to a
British claim against the United States.
81933, 97911

Comparative view and exhibition of reasons.
53617

Comparative view of mild and sanguinary laws.
39051

Comparative view of religion. 103339

Comparative view of the British and American
constitutions. 15032, 99581

Comparative view of the climate of Western
Canada. 31938

Comparative view of the conduct of Lord
Cornwallis and General Howe. 46928,
4th note after 95742

Comparative view of the constitutions of Great
Britain and the United States of America.
535

Comparative view of the constitutions of the
several states with each others. 84820-
84821

Comparative view of the existing tariff of
duties on goods imported from foreign
countries. 15033

Comparative view of the four projected coast-
wise canals. 94408

Comparative view of the mortality in New-York,
Philadelphia, Baltimore, and Boston. 55327

Comparative view of the population of Boston
in 1850. 12676

Comparative view of the punishments annexed
to crime. 94515

Comparative view of the Russian discoveries
with those made by Captains Cook and
Clerke. 17312

Comparative view of the sensorial and nervous
systems in man and animals. 101474

Comparative view of the skulls of various
aboriginal nations of North and South
America. 51022

Comparative view of the wet docks in Wapping,
and in the Isle of Dogs. 102778

Comparative views of the legislative executive
and judiciary departments. (26679)

Comparative views of the most important anthracite collieries in Pennsylvania. 59998

Comparative vocabulary of words in the language of the Pueblo or Civilized Indians
of New Mexico. 81353

Comparatur deportatio in Novam Cambriam
Australem. 31665

Compare the principles, acts and men, of the
two parties. 89493

Comparison between distressed English labourers and the coloured people and slaves
of the West Indies. 102801

Comparison between observant and reflective
age. 74251

Comparison between the British sugar colonies
and New-England. 15026

Comparison between the cereal production of
the United States and other countries.
88354

Comparison between the doctrines taught by
the clergy of the Church of England, and
the doctrines taught by Whitefield. 15027,
note after 103616

Comparison between the internal and foreign
commerce of the United States. 72433

Comparison between the march of the 43rd
Light Infantry. 63370

Comparison between the proposals of the Bank
and the South-Sea Company. 15028,
69523, 96767-96768

Comparison between the tribes of Issachar and
Dan. 7208

Comparison of American and British slavery.
29508

Comparison of experiments on American and
foreign building stones. 36334

Comparison of prayer books. 83518

Comparison of products, population, and
resources. (3908)

Comparison of slavery with abolitionism. 1340

Comparison of the east and the west. (6977)

Comparison of the features of the earth and
the moon. 85072

Comparison of the Fitchburg Railroad, with
other Massachusetts railroads. 29658

Comparison of the practice of the courts of
law. 6012

Comparison of the present with the former
doctrines of the general government.
44758

Comparison of the principles of the Washington
and Jefferson administrations. 35924

Comparison of the social and political state of
both nations. 14036, 100976

Comparison of the state and condition of the
colored people in . . . Philadelphia from
1837 to 1847. 62304

Comparison of the taxes of . . . New York.
54207, note after 94429

Comparison of the wealth, strength, and population of the northern and southern states.
45538

Comparison of the weekly bills of mortality of
New-Orleans and Boston, for 1851. 81293

Comparison of weights and measures, reported
to the Senate of the United States. 30819

Compass. 93691

Compassion to the oppressed. 18104

Compassionate call, and hand reached for the
in tender Gospel love. 29747

Compassionate Samaritane M. S. to A. S. &c.,
examined. note before 17046-17046, 2d
note after 103852

Compassions called for. 46269

Compatriote. pseud. Conseiller du peuple.
see Beaudry, Hercules.

Compend of general history. (63509)

Compend of instructions in military tactics.
92037

Compend of lectures on the aims and duties of
the profession of the law. (79863)

Compend of military instructions. 92037

Compendia della vita, virtu, e miracoli di S.
Francesco Solano. 67526

Compendiaria Asiae, Africae, Europaeque
descriptio. 63164

Compendio breve de la vida, virtudes . . . de
la venerable Francisco de S. Joseph.
67346

Co[m]pe[n]dio breue que tracta d'la manera de como se ha[n] de hazer las p[ro]cessiones. 71101

Compendio chronologico de los privilegios regulares de Indias. (42113)

Compendio da doutrina Christaa na lingua Portugueza, e Brasilica. 5065

Compendio da geographia da provincia do Parana. 25427

Compendio da historia do Brasil. 78

Compendio das eras da provincia do Para. 50101

Compendio da algunas cartas que este ano de 1597. 68329, 72499

Compendio de algunas cosas notables de Espana. 98396

Compendio de algvnas de las muchas y graues razones en que se funda la prudente resolucion. 41085, 98326

Compendio de derecho politica y economica social. 64876

Compendio de geografia fisica. 39212, 1st note after 96217

Compendio de geografia matematica. 59333

Compendio de geographia, adoptado no Collegio de Pedro II. 63950

Compendio de geographia de la republica Mexicana. (26555)

Compendio de gracas e indulgencias. 76783

Compendio de indulgencias concedidas a los ministros. 15036

Compendio de instrucciones gramaticales de la lengua Latina. 76796

Compendio de la Bulla de Cena. 51064

Compendio de la geografia de la isla de Cuba. (63669)-63670

Compendio de la historia de America. 48040

Compendio de la historia de la ciudad de Guatemala. 36817

Compendio de la historia de la Nueva Granada. 63379

Compendio de la historia de las Provinvias Unidas del Rio de la Plata. 44395

Compendio de la historia de los Estados Unidas de America. 15034

Compendio de la historia de Mexico. 71483

Compendio de la historia de Santo Domingo. 26576

Compendio de la historia de Venezuela. 14679, note after 98871, 105951

Compendio de la historia geografica. 49889

Compendio de la historia politica de Centro-America. 89962

Compendio de la istoria sagrada, y de los doctrina Cristiana. 74520

Compendio de la medicina. 98841

Compendio de la vida de el apostol de del Brasil. 4833

Compendio de la vida del V. Padre Cypriano Baraze. 57577

Compendio de la vida del V. P. Juan de Santiago. 50504

Compendio de la vida miravillosa del gloriosissimo Padre S. Francisco de Assis. (22897)

Compendio de la vida y virtudes de N. M. R. M. Maria Ignacia Azlor y Echeverz. 21777, 69226

Compendio de la ystoria general del origen, viajes y monarquia de los Indios. 27479

Compendio de las constituciones. 48371

Compendio de las excelencias, de la Bvlla de la Sancta Cruzada. 36785, 76132

Compendio de las historias de los descubrimientos. 44963

Compendio de las maravillas de la gracia. 76134

Compendio de las noticias que S. M. por su real orden. 97683

Compendio de las tres gracias de la santa Frozada, contra infideles. 60894

Compendio de las vidas de los gloriossimos Santos Elzeario y sus esposa Delfina. 22394

Compendio de lo mvcho qve esta escrito. 86411

Compendio de memorias para escribir la historia de la isla Fernandia de Cuba. 98164

Compendio de navegacion para el uso de los cavalleros Guardias-Marinas. 36801

Compendio de noticias Mexicanas. 74944

Compendio de su [i. e. Peru's] historia. 16780

Compendio de su [i. e. Cypriano Braze's] vida y muerte. 3252

Compendio de terapeutica vejetal de las Antillas. 28942

Compendio del arte de la lengua Mexicana. 10954, 58573

Compendio del arte de navegar. 106245

Compendio del confessionario en idioma Mexicano y Castellano. (15035)

Compendio del despertador de noticias de los Santos Sacramentos. (39678)

Compendio del origin de las esclarecida y milagrosa imagen. 40072

Compendio dell' istorie dell' Indie. 106255

Compendio della guerra nata per confini in America. 2709

Compendio della storia geografica, naturale, e civile del Regno del Chile. 12756, note after 99468, 99469

Compendio della storia universelle. 15017-15018

Compendio della vita del Beato Sebastiano d'Apparizio. 105727A

Compendio della vita, virtu, e miracoli del B. Toribio Alfonso Mogrobesio Arciuecouo di Lima. 98369

Compendio delle chroniche di Polonia. 67738

Compendio do historia da edade media. 9866

Compendio elemental de estadistica. 32759, 55142

Compendio elemental de geographia geral e especial do Brasil. 63951, 88739

Compendio en las excelsias, de la Bulla de la Sancta Cruzada. 36785, 76132

Compendio general de las contribuciones, que en particular ocasionan las mercaderias. 26581

Compendio general de las contribuciones, y gastos que ocasionan todas los efectos. (15037)

Compendio gramatical para la inteligencia del idioma Trahumar. 94615

Compendio historial de la provincia de S. Juan Baptista. 76879

Compendio historial de la vida de la gloriosa S. Rita de Casia. 41425

Compendio historial de las chronicas y universal historia de todos los reynos de Espana. 26666-26667

Compendio historial del descvbrimiento, conquista, y guerra del Reyno de Chile. 105742

Compendio historial, e indice chronologico Peruvano. 72524

Compendio historico, de la Apostolica Provincia de San Gregorio de Philipinas. 75987

Compendio historico de la Cueva Santa de la Santa Cruz. 67098

Compendio historico de la fundacion y progresso de los clerigos seculares. 15038

Compendio historico de la prodigiosa vida, virtudes, y milagros de la venerable sierra de Dios Mariana de Jesus, Flores y Paredes. 27339

Compendio historico de la provincia. 686

Compendio historico (de las misiones) en el Peru. (51590)

Compendio historico del comercio de las Indias. 29360, 73852

Compendio historico del descubrimiento y colonizacion de la Nueva Granada. 117

Compendio historico del origin y progresos de las sociedades secretas. 15039

Compendio historico-politico dos principios da lavoura do Maranhao. 26804, 88775

Compendio narrativo do peregrino da America. 60891

Compendio storico della scoperta di America. 16711

Compendiolum vitae admirabilis et pretiosae mortis B. Roase de S. Maria Limensis Peruanae. (73180)

Compendiosa demonstracion de los crecidos adelantamientos. 23606

Compendious account of the British colonies in North America. 15040

Compendious account of the most important battles. 15043, 93232

Compendious American grammar. 33799

Compendious and complete history of modern geography. 50929

Compendious chronicle of the kingdom of Portugal. 18669

Compendious collection of facts. 32870

Compendious description of the thirteen colonies of British America. 15041

Compendious description of the West-Indies. (35970)

Compendious dictionary of the English language. 102347

Compendious dissertations, respecting social and domestic relations and concerns. (75926)

Compendious exercise for the garrison and field ordnance. (15042)

Compendious exhibition of the most interesting geographical, historical, miscellaneous and theological subjects. (7380)

Compendious extract containing the chiefest articles of doctrine. 86747, 106352, 106361

Compendious flora of the northern states. 28523

Compendious general gazetteer. 49805

Compendious history of Captain Cook's first and second voyages. 16248

Compendious history of Captain Cook's last voyage. 16255

Compendious history of General Washington. 73452, 2d note after 101785

Compendious history of New-England. 50933

Compendious history of New England, designed for schools and private families. 50930, 50932

Compendious history of New England, exhibiting an interesting view of the first settlers of that country. 50931

Compendious history of the British churches in England. 8510

Compendious history of the cotton manufacture. 29140

Compendious history of the First Parish in Dover. 104801

Compendious history of the Goths, Swedes and Vandals. 43832

Compendious history of the Indian wars. 20777

Compendious history of the late war. 15043, 93232

Compendious history of the northern part of the province of New Brunswick. 16397

Compendious history of the principal protestant missions to the heathen. 42020

Compendious history of the rise and progress of the Methodist Church. (47211)

Compendious history of the rise and progress of the reformation. 46790

Compendious history of Yale-College. 105931

Compendious memoirs of the author [i. e. Thomas Branagan.] 7382

Compendious narrative, elucidating the character. 21591

Compendious remonstrance of the present sad state and condition of the English colonie in Virginia. 26760, 2d note after 100516

Compendious system of astrology. 84363-84364

Compendious system of rhetoric, for the use of schools in America. 91847

Compendious system of universal geography. 58599

Compendious treatise, containing a proposal to preserve the noblest of vegetables. 9606

Compendious treatise of the empires. 13449

Compendious view of domestic and foreign missions. 28502

Compendious view of sacred scripture. 84365

Compendious view of some of the most useful modern discoveries and inventions. 24215

Compendious view of the colonies planted by the English on the continent of North America. 44788, note after 101528

Compendious view of the Gospel. 65137, 92031

Compendious view of the trial of Aaron Burr. 95607

Compendious view of universal history. 47184

Compendium. 83176

Compendium and digest of the laws of Massachusetts. 45687, 103484

Compendium cronologicum seculi a Christo nato decimi sexti. (47109)

Compendium evangelicum. 16640

Compendium facultatum, et indulgentiarum, quae religiosis Societatis Jesu. (15044)

Compendium florae Philadelphicae. (3857)

Compendium geographicum. 13692

Compendium historiae plantarum Mexicanarum Francisci Hernandez. 68027

Compendium historiae universalis. 38559

Compendivm ineae. 94818

Compendium in sphaeram. 32681, 74804

Compendium juris canonici ad usum cleri et seminariorum. 84188-84191, 84201-84202, 84208, 84212

Compendium logicae secundum principia D. Renati Cartesii plerumque efformatum. 15045

Compendium memorandorum. 99327

Compendium of American literature. 13650

Compendium of authentic and entertaining voyages. 11128, 20518, 26851

Compendium of Christian duties. 83576

Compendium of church musick. 4050

Compendium of farriery. 36116

Compendium of finance. 14330

Compendium of geography, being a concise description of the various parts of the world. 95278

Compendium of historical facts. 24985

Compendium of information for the use of strangers. 67005

Compendium of information with reference to the wants of merchants and business men. 37301

Compendium of methodism. (64268)

Compendium of military duty. 68016

Compendium of Mr. Clay's speeches. 13539

Compendium of political, philosophical, and moral elements. 67307

Compendium of religious, literary, and philosophical knowledge. 69335

Compendium of slavery as it exists in the United States. 1907

Compendium of the art of surveying. 50321

Compendium of the authentic and entertaining voyages. 20518

Compendium of the Book of Mormon. 58915

Compendium of the English and foreign funds. 24063

Compendium of the enumeration of the inhabitants and statistics of the United States. 11667, 2d note after 15045

Compendium of the faith and doctrines of the Church of Jesus Christ of Latter-Day Saints. 70912

Compendium of the flora of the northern and middle states. 96292

Compendium of the history of all nations. 25678

Compendium of the history of the United States. 91279

Compendium of the impending crisis of the south. (31270), 59563

Compendium of the Indian wars in New England. 97190

Compendium of the law of nations. 44849

Compendium of the laws and decisions relating to mobs. (21757)

Compendium of the laws and government. (18009)

Compendium of the laws and government of England and dominions. 15046

Compendium of the life of Thomas Paine. 98336

Compendium of the minutes of the Warren Baptist Association. 101496

Compendium of the origin, history, principles, rules and regulations. (23152)

Compendium of the principles of the Democratic party. 19516

Compendium of the proceedings of the General Grand Chapter of Royal Arch Masons of the United States. 25850

Compendium of the statistics, historical associations and other matters of interest of every town. 6483

Compendivm vniversi complectens geographicarvm enarrationvm libros sex. 66889

Compensated agency of the U. S. Sanitary Commission explained. 59167

Compensation and Negro suffrage. 18181

Compensation or separation considered. 100679

Compensation to American ship-builders. 51634

Competition between the Sun and the Herald. 4097

Competitive system in government architecture. 84980

Compianta della valle di Wish-ton-wish. 16556

Compilacao alphabetica e chronologia das leis. 24169

Compilacao das leis. (995)

Compilation and digest of the laws. 5259

Compilation and digest of the road laws. 59999

Compilation containing the constitution and canons of the Protestant Episcopal Church. 45301

Compilation containing the Seigniorial Act of 1854. 10495

Compilation from the annual reports and other publications of the Oneida Association. (57337)

Compilation from the annual reports of the Superintendent of Public Instruction. 48725

Compilation from the army regulations. (5989)

Compilation from the writings of the pastors of the Second Church. 57935, 71783

Compilation in which is comprised the constitution of the United States. 42211

Compilation of all the acts. 87686

Compilation of all the general laws. 29553

Compilation of biographical sketches. (24960)

Compilation of laws of the state of New York. 79903

Compilation of military laws. (24849)

Compilation of pensions, pay and bounty lands. 60806, 85618

Compilation of selections from the youth's essay. 92752

Compilation of Spanish and Mexican laws. 72430

Compilation of startling facts. 58658

Compilation of the acts and resolutions. 87688

Compilation of the by-laws and police regulations in force. (50248)

Compilation of the canal and railroad laws of Pennsylvania. 60000

Compilation of the existing ferry leases and railroad grants. 54208

Compilation of the general laws of the city of Nashville. 51870

Compilation of the health laws of Pennsylvania. 60001

Compilation of the insolvent laws of Maryland. 45112

Compilation of the law in relation to elections. 87689

Compilation of the laws in force in the District of Columbia. 20301

Compilation of the laws of Georgia, from 1800 to 1810. 27029

Compilation of the laws of Georgia, passed since 1810. 38703

Compilation of the laws of Massachusetts. (20070)

Compilation of the laws of Pennsylvania, relative to the internal improvements. 60003

Compilation of the laws of . . . Pennsylvania, relative to the poor, from . . . 1700 to 1788. 60002

Compilation of the laws of . . . Pennsylvania, relative to the poor, from . . . 1700, to 1795. 60002

Compilation of the laws of the state of Georgia, passed by the Legislature since the political year 1800. 13574

Compilation of the laws of the state of Georgia, passed . . . since the year 1819 to 1829. 27030

Compilation of the laws of the state of New-York. 18754

Compilation of the laws of the state . . . relating . . . to the city. (54209)

Compilation of the laws of the United States and of states. 8237, 15047

Compilation of the laws of Vermont. 37938

Compilation of the laws regulating taxation in Massachusetts. (45688)

Compilation of the laws, treaties, resolutions, and ordinances. 56898

Compilation of the messages and papers of the Presidents. 104205

Compilation of the penal code of the state of
Georgia. 13842
Compilation of the public laws of . . . New
Jersey. 53090
Compilation of the public laws of the Legis-
lative Council of the Territory of Flor-
ida. 24850
Compilation of the registers of the Army.
(28011)
Compilation of the school laws of Pennsylvania.
60004
Compilation of the several acts of the Legis-
lature of the state and late territory of
Minnesota. 88407
Compilation of the several acts of the Legis-
lature of Wisconsin. 38508, note after
92947
Compilation of the statutes of . . . Illinois.
34279
Compilation of the statutes of South Carolina.
87687
Compilation of the statutes of Tennessee.
11171
Compilation of the tariff act of the Confederate
States of America. 15248
Compiled laws of the state of California.
10021
Compiled laws of the state of Michigan. 48726
Compiled laws of the state of Nevada. 52399
Compiled statutes of the state of New Hamp-
shire. 52810
Compiler's notice. 86943
Complaint. (58595)
Complaint against New England professors.
1722
Complaint against the clergy of the Bay Asso-
ciation. 71053
Complaint and petition. 62310
Complaint for a public hearing. 8956-8957
Complaint of England. (41050)
Complaint of J. Alexander and W. Smith. 729,
84554
Complaint of James Alexander and William
Smith. 729, 84554
Complaint of Mexico. 15048, note after 95073
Complaint: or Britannia lamenting the loss of
her children. 15049
Complaint to the —— of —— against a
pamphlet. 15050
Complaints of Gov. Winthrop, of Massachusetts.
(32842)
Complaints of our supra-inferior-inhabitants.
97288
Complaints of the Negro slaves. 25947, note
after 97286
Compleat body of divinity. 104075
Compleat collection of papers. (9371), 46709
Compleat collection of the laws of Maryland.
45111
Compleat collection of voyages and travels.
5057, (11608), 30482-30483, 55448, 77962,
89452
Compleat description of Carolina. 83978,
86573-86574
Compleat description of the several nations of
the world. 75829
Compleat discourse and description of the four
elements. 7296, note after 94823
Compleat dress for magistrates. (26776)
Compleat fund of literary, political and com-
mercial knowledge. 42153
Compleat geographer. 49905
Compleat history of magic, sorcery, and
witchcraft. 6890, 15051
Compleat history of Spanish America. 10232
Compleat history of the late war. 105602-
105604

Compleat history of the most remarkable
providences. 97495
Compleat library. 97495
Compleat mendicant, or unhappy beggar.
27615, 65465
Compleat minor. 33164
Compleat pilot for the gulf passage. 72995
Compleat souldier. 6375, 22368
Compleat system of geography. (2308)
Complement des ordonnances et jugements.
10482
Complemento de pruebas contra la conducta
publica. 62937
Complete abridgment of the 100 volumes.
14017
Complete account of the John Morgan raid.
(81156)
Complete account of the most remarkable
voyages and travels. 3361
Complete and accurate account of the very
important debate. (15052)
Complete and accurate description of the pro-
cession. 54210
Complete and authentic history of the battle of
Bunker Hill. 7216
Complete and authentic report of all the pro-
ceedings. 4710
Complete and correct annual register. 73796
Complete and elegant map. 72994
Complete and unabridged edition. 41180
Complete business directory of Boston. 6697
Complete catalogue of members from 1776 to
1868. 61965
Complete catalogue of the birds of eastern
Massachusetts. 47162
Complete coiffeur. 105180
Complete coin-book. 61245
Complete collection of all the lavvs of Virginia
now in force. 100381
Complete collection of all the protests of the
peers of Parliament. 15053
Complete collection of forms of procedure.
83708
Complete collection of G. A. R. songs. 84800
Complete collection of songs. 50804
Complete collection of the anecdotes, stories,
and pithy sayings. 41151
Complete collection of the forensic discussions.
26942
Complete collection of the treaties and con-
ventions. 31594
Complete collection of voyages and travels.
5057, (11608), 30482-30483, 55448, 77962,
89452
Complete collection of voyages made into North
and South America. 4508, 21350
Complete constable. 84880
Complete correspondence between union members of Pine St. Presbyterian Church.
75344
Complete description of the American watering
place. 76919
Complete description . . . of the ventilation of
railway carriages. 74491
Complete descriptive and statistical gazetteer
of the United States of America. 30796
Complete descriptive guide of Long Branch.
77562
Complete dictionary of the Chinook jargon.
12815
Complete dictionary of the Indian tongue.
24508, 40832
Complete digest of all such acts of Congress
as concern the United States at large.
28421

Complete digest of the decisions of the Supreme
Court, of the state of Wisconsin. 80096
Complete directory . . . 1859-60. 41742
Complete emigrant's director. 6007
Complete encyclopeadia of music. 50414
Complete ephemeris for 1843. 20769
Complete exercise book, in arithmetic. 91362
Complete expose of the upper ten thousand.
8846
Complete exposure of a pamphlet entitled
,"The Negro." (78545)
Complete faith. 13385
Complete family directory. 98003
Complete farmer and rural economist. 24220
Complete G. A. R. song book. 84800
Complete genealogical, historical, chronological,
and geographical atlas. 39125
Complete geographical dictionary. (78598)
Complete guide. 52320, 55116
Complete guide book and description of the oil
regions. 6298
Complete guide for the day. 34443
Complete guide in all the various methods by
which to capture all kinds of game.
(33940)
Complete guide through the United States.
102324
Complete guide to invalids. 40916
Complete guide to Lake Winnipiseogee. 73501
Complete guide to the gold mines in Kansas
and Nebraska. 15054
Complete guide to their [i. e. Kentucky and
Tennessee's] railroads. (47222)
Complete hand book and guide to the United
States. (22491)
Complete hand-book of the city of Toledo.
(77500)
Complete historical, chronological, and geo-
graphical American atlas. 10843, (15055)
Complete historical record of all events.
(5373)
Complete history and description of the sema-
phoric, electric, and magnetic telegraphs.
(79684)
Complete history of Connecticut. 97190
Complete history of Connecticut, civil and
ecclesiastical. 97181-97182
Complete history of Fairfield County, Ohio.
78272
Complete history of Lake George. (45031)
Complete history of metropolitan life and so-
ciety. (8667)
Complete history of the double murder of Mrs.
Garber & Mrs. Ream. 72374
Complete history of the election in . . . Ken-
tucky. 37563
Complete history of the great rebellion. 50401
Complete history of the late American war.
83616-83617, 83625-83626
Complete history of the late rebellion in
Lower Canada. 10588
Complete history of the late war. 15056,
105602-105605
Complete history of the Marquis de La Fayette.
38569
Complete history of the Mexican War. 8360
Complete history of the most remarkable
transactions at sea. 9205
Complete history of the origin and progress of
the late war. 15057
Complete history of the present civil war.
24099
Complete history of the present war. 15058
Complete history of the United States of
America. 9634

Complete history of the United States to the
present time. 46941
Complete history of the war with Mexico.
(26217)
Complete housewife. 82435
Complete index to Stith's history of Virginia.
91860
Complete index to the ordinances and statutes
of Lower Canada. 42513
Complete introduction to the English and Latin
languages. 73403
Complete introduction to the Latin tongue.
73398-(73402)
Complete key to Smiley's new federal calculator.
(82286)
Complete language used by the Indians of
Oregon. 100644
Complete list of booksellers. 20198
Complete list of Congregational ministers and
churches. 38720
Complete list of the American navy. (15059)
Complete list of the lodges in the United
States. 65383
Complete magazine of entertainment and intelli-
gence. 88052
Complete manual and drill book for the use of
volunteers. 86289
Complete manual for the cultivation of the
strawberry. 58558
Complete manual f or young sportsmen. (31460)
Complete mastication, digestion, and annihilation.
94152
Complete mercantile guide to the continent of
Europe. 73153
Complete merchant's clerk. 103055-103056
Complete military tutor. 96367
Complete mirror of the great metropolis.
83592
Complete New-Hampshire register. 52811
Complete pilot for the West-Indies. 35936
Complete poetical works of the late Miss Lucy
Hooper. 32872
Complete poetical works [of William Words-
worth.] 105466
Complete practical guide to Her Majesty's
Civil Service. (15060)
Complete record of Company "A," 4th Penn'a
Cavalry. 34136
Complete reference gazetteer of the United
States. 11961
Complete refutation of Maria Monk's atrocious
plot. 92133
Complete refutation of the reply of Mr. Joseph
Harvey. 58654
Complete report on the organization and cam-
paigns of the Army of the Potomac.
(43012)
Complete review of all the building associations
established in Connecticut. (9077), 25638
Complete revisal of all the acts of Assembly
of the province of North-Carolina. 55603
Complete series of historical documents and
remarks. (14009)
Complete soldier's pocket companion. 10244
Complete statement of the votes. 63812
Complete system of education. (22174)
Complete system of family registration. 79876
Complete system of geography. (49902)
Complete system of vulgar and decimal frac-
tions, &c. 92721
Complete treatise on the breeding, management
and diseases of sheep. 97788
Complete treaties on the mineral waters of
Virginia. 73457
Complete trial. God gives, and takes away.
60282

Complete trial; or swaggering John. 15061

Complete victory over death. 78323

Complete view of Baltimore, with a statistical sketch. 98629

Complete view of Baltimore, with a statistical sketch of its institutions. 3026

Complete view of episcopacy, as exhibited from the fathers. (12314)

Complete view of the American capital. (62565)

Complete view of the theory and practice of the general and state governments. 44371

Complete vocabulary. 35205

Complete works, in philosophy, politics, and morals. (25495)

Complete works [of Count von Rumford.] 95466

Complete works of Henry W. Longfellow. (41907)

Complete works of Hon. Job Durfee. (21424)

Complete works of John M. Mason. 45465

Complete works of Ralph W. Emerson. 22454

Complete works of Rev. Thomas Smyth. 85263, 85272, 85276, 85292, 85294, 85296, 85303, 85309, 85312, 85314-85315, 85318, 85324, 85326, 85328, 85335, 85339, 85341

Complete works of the Most Rev. John Hughes. 33590

Complete works of the Rev. Daniel Atkinson Clark. 13269

Complete writings of Constantine Smaltz Rafinesque. (67449)

Complete writings of Thomas Say, on the conchology of the Unites States. (77373)

Complete writings of Thomas Say on the entomology of the United States. 77374

Complices de la Conspiracion de Arenas. defendants 106348

Complicity of the Ohio Democracy with treason. 56899

Complimentary banquet. 40213

Complot d'Arnold et de Sir Henry Clinton. 3302, 3d note after 101785

Componimenti poetici d'un Italiano profugo en America. (78873)

Componimento ditirambico in lode della cioccolata. (44091)

Comportement de Villegagnon, en ce pais la. 40148-40149

Composiciones leidas en el teadro de Alarcon. 76142

Composiciones selectas escritas por poetas Sud-Americanos. (29347)

Composition a few days before his death. 91931

Composition and delivery of sermons. 71525

Composition of Asa Stoddard. 91931

Composition of expired air and its effects upon animal life. 85072

Compositions and functions of the Legislative Council. 73347

Composure in death. 90190

Comprehensive and systematic catalogue of photographic apparatus. 85414

Comprehensive atlas, geographical, historical & commercial. 7260

Comprehensive description of Virginia. 44894

Comprehensive geography and history. 27894, 27922

Comprehensive geography, combining mathematical, physical, and political geography. 79897

Comprehensive history, ecclesiastical and civil. (64937)

Comprehensive history of American Methodism. 6915

Comprehensive history of England. 43247

Comprehensive history of Methodism. 64269

Comprehensive history of the iron trade. 78502

Comprehensive history of the southern rebellion. 15062, 88468

Comprehensive index to the merchants' magazine. 33853, 47920

Comprehensive pronouncing and explanatory dictionary. 105236

Comprehensive review of literature, politics, and news. 56158

Comprehensive sketch of his [i. e. Clinton's] life. 13737

Comprehensive sketch of his [i. e. George Washington's] life and character. 101636

Comprehensive story of a farmer's bull. 13899, (65512)

Comprehensive ullage table. 105474

Comprehensive view of the leading and most important principles of natural and revealed religion. 84094

Comprehensive view of the most interesting particulars relative to the geography, &c. 92915

Compressed account of the origin and progress of the said church. 97848

Compressed view of the points to be discussed. (2265)

Compromise bill. Speech of the Hon. John Bell. 4461

Compromise by a compensation. 15063

Compromise measures. Speech . . . in the Senate . . . Dec. 23, 1851. 33195

Compromise measures. Speech of R. Barnwell Rhett. 70479

Compromise necessary. 5750

Compromise, the constitution, and the union. 26268

Compromises of 1850. 52200, 84463, 93663

Compromises of the constitution considered. 15064, 70480

Comptabilite des matieres appartenant au Departement de la Marine des et des Colonies. 15065

Compte de l'examen public du Lycee National. 14552

Compte de Raousset-Boulbon et l'expedition de la Sonore. 38459, 67910

Compte general de l'administration de la justice. 44975

Compte rendu aux Comites de Marine et des Colonies reunis. 95732

Compte-rendu de la Seance Solennelle. 66997

Compte rendu [de l'Academie des Sciences Morales et Politiques, Paris.] (14064)

Compte rendu de son [i. e. G. H. V. Collot's] administration de Saint-Domingue. 14462

Compte-rendu des recettes des depenses des colonies. 15066

Compte-rendu de delegue de la population Francaise. 4516

Compte rendu d'une excursion agricole dans les etats de l'ouest. 61006

Compte rendu d'une mission scientifique en Espagne et en Portugal. 73303

Compte rendu et analyse de l'histoire des nations civilisees du Mexique et de l'Amerique Centrale. (12019)

Compte rendu sur la situation actuelle de la colonie de Saint Domingue. 39611

Compte-rendue a la nation. 75081

Compte rendue a la partie de St. Domingue par les representants. (75082)

Compte rendue [du Congres Geologique International, 1913.] 84533

Compte rendue sur la situation actuelle de Saint-Domingue. 75086

Compte sommaire de l'etat actuel de la colonie de Saint-Domigue. 49419

Comptes definitifs. (15067)

Comptes generaux presentes par le Ministre de la Marine et des Colonies. (15068)

Comptes-rendus des seances de la Societe d'Ethnographie Americaine et Orientale. 70373, 85791

Comptroller's annual report of the revenues and expenditures. (54212)

Comptroller's report, . . . of . . . receipts and expenditures. 53316

Comptroller's statement [of North Carolina.] 55671

Compuestos de Gualeguaychu. 15069

Computation of the French fishery. 10723, 42173, 60841

Comrade. 80865

Comstock, Augustus. 90522

Comstock, Charles. (15070)

Comstock, Daniel D. defendant 105055

Comstock, F. G. 15071, (81012)

Comstock, George Franklin, 1811-1892. 10187, 15072, 15617, 37473

Comstock, J. L. (15073)-15075

Comstock, Joseph. 15076

Comstock, Joshua. 15077

Comstock, William. 15077

Comstock lode. 71227

Comtaeus, Robert. 15079

Comte, Auguste, 1798-1857. 84152

Comte, Charles. 77354, 77360-77361

Comte de M***. pseud. see M***, Comte de. pseud.

Comte de Limonade . . . a ses concitoyens. 41140

Comte de Villanueva et le General Tacon. 18667

Comte d'Eu et la France Nouvelle dans l'Amerique du Sud. 62887

Comte Gaston de Raousset-Boulbon, sa vie et ses aventures. (38700)

Comun bienhechor de todos. 74787

Comun bienhechor predicado en la iglesia de los Carmelitas de Tehuacan. 42068

Comunicacion . . . al supremo gobierno de Costarica. 89961

Comunicacion circular del Ministro de Relaciones. 15080

Comunicacion con el Sumo Pontifice. 99482

Comunicacion de Dorotos Vasconzelos. (76190)

Comunicacion dirigida ultimamente con este motivo al Sr. Encargado de Negocios. 19268, 93785

Comunicacion oficial al Ministro de Relaciones. 39064, 73169

Comunicacion oficial del Exmo. Sr. 76747

Comunicacion oficial que acerca de la conferencias tenidas en Agosto y Setiembre. 58076

Comunicaciones entre el supremo gobierno del Salvador. 76191

Comunicaciones oficiales entre el supremo govierno del estado de Zacatecas y el superior eclesiastico de la Diocesis de Guadalaxara. 15081

Comunicaciones relativas a la agregacion del Departamento de Tejas. 15082, 95074

Comunicado sobre la nacionalidad. 32773

Comunicados y documentos a que se refieren. 15083, 75781

Comyn, Tomas de. 15084

Comyns, Sir John, d. 1740. 85933A

Con O'Regan. 74826

Con preuilegio. Ordenancas y copilacion de leyes. 47833

Con priuilegio coloquios o dialogos. 48235

Con priuilegio de Principe Nuestro Senor. 27728

Con priuilegio. . . . Esta es vna carta. 16941

Con priuilegio imperial . . . Libro llamado Thesoro de virtudes vtil & copioso. note after 27585, 40960, note after 47850

Conanchet eller graendsebeboerne. 16554

Conanchet und die Puritaner in Connecticut. 16555

Conant, Abel. 15085-15086

Conant, Claudius B. 57732

Conant, Gaius. 15088

Conant, Helen S. (15089)

Conant, M. 88415 see also Wisconsin. Commissioners of Public Lands.

Conant, Marshall. 99160, 99233

Conant, Shubael. supposed author 105932

Conant, Sylvanus. 15090-15094

Conant, Thomas Jefferson. 15095

Conant, William C. 15096

Conarroe, George M. 15097

Conart, Louis. 15098

Concada, Balthasar de. (49951)

Concanen, ------. 56843

Conceica, Jose M. da. see Conceicao, Jose Manoel da, 1714-1767.

Conceicao, Apollinario de. see Apollinario de Conceicao.

Conceicao, Claudio de. 15100

Conceicao, Jose Manoel da, 1714-1767. 15101-15102, 44357, 79145

Conceicao Velloso Xavier, Jose Marianno da. see Velloso Xavier, Jose Marianno da Conceicao.

Concejo-Municipal del Departamento Puerto Cabello a la Asamblia Legislativa del Estado de Carabobo. 66583

Concentos fvnebres. 70798

Concentrated account of all the baronies. 3207

Concepcion, Diego de la. see La Concepcion, Diego de.

Concepcion, Joseph Garcia de. see Garcia de Concepcion, Joseph.

Concepcion, Juan de la. see Juan de la Concepcion.

Concepcion, Pedro de la. pseud. Soplos en defensa. see Alva y Astorga, Pedro de.

Concepcion Urtiaga, Pedro de la. see Urtiaga, Pedro de la Concepcion.

Concepcion Valdes, Gabriel de la. see Valdes, Gabriel de la Concepcion.

Concepcion, Chile (Diocese) Bishop (Azua e Yturgoyen) 65553 see also Azua e Yturgoyen, Phelipe de, Abp. Santa Fe, Colombia (Archdiocese) Archbishop (Azua e Yturgoyen)

Concepcion, Chile (Diocese) Synod, 1st, 1744. 65553

Concept van reglement op Brasil. 7552, 7636-7637, note after 89149, note after 102886

Conceptions & means to the end. 83746

Concerning a match. 67599

Concerning baptism. 82475-82476

Concerning marriage and divorce. 72682

Concerning ministers. 82475-82476

Concerning steam boats. 56796

Concerning the church. 82475-82476

Concerning the end for which God has created the world. 21967

Concerning the office and duties of a protestant ministry. 84678C

Concerning the only true God. 72687

Concerning the progressive discovery of North America. 71809

Concert of prayer. 15103

Concesion hecha. note just before (73261)

Concession de la Louisiana a M. Crosat. 42212, 68419

Concessions and compromises. 42275

Concessions to America the bane of Britain. 44703

Concha y de Irihoyen, Jose Gutierrez de la. see Habana, Jose Gutierrez de la Concha y de Irigoyen, Marques de la, 1809-1895.

Conchologist's first book. 63519

Conchyliologie Americaine. 12430, 77375

Concilia Limana, constitvtiones synodales, et alia vtilia monumenta. 50070

Concilia Provincialia Baltimori habita ab anno 1829, usque ad annum 1840. (15105), (72903)

Conciliador. 99482

Conciliation. A discourse at a Sunday evening service. 2662

Concilation and nationality (17271)

Conciliation with America: adapted to the constitutional rights of the colonies. (15108)

Conciliation with America, the true policy of Great Britain. 15109

Conciliator. pseud. Why are we still at war? 15110, 3d note after 103852

Conciliator. 48372

Conciliatory address to the people of Great Britain. 15111

Conciliatory bills considered. 15112

Conciliatory hints, attempting, by a fair state of matters, to remove party-prejudices. 62546, 97383

Conciliatory hints . . . submitted to the consideration of the citizens. 62546

Concilii Mexicani decreta. 33063

Concilii Próvincialis Baltimorensis X. 72910

Concilii Plenarii Baltimorensis II, in ecclesia metropolitana Baltimorensi a die VII ad diem XXI Octobris, A. D. MDCCCLXVI habiti et a sede apostolica recogniti acta et decreta. 15106, 72898

Concilii Plenarii Baltimorensis II, in ecclesia metropolitana Baltimorensi a die VII ad diem XXI Octobris, A. D. MDCCCLXVI habiti et a sede apostolica recogniti, decreta. (72899)

Concilii Provincialis S. Francisci II. 72929

Concilii Provincialis S. Francisci I. 72919

Concilio III. Provincial Mexicano. (48374)

Conciliorum omnium Hispaniae et Novi Orbis. 529

Concilios Provinciales primero, y segundo. (42063)

Concilium Baltimorense Provinciale IX. 72909

Concilium Baltimorense Provinciale VIII. (72908)

Concilium Baltimorense Provinciale primum. 72901

Concilium Baltimorense Provinciale secundum. 72903

Concilium Baltimorense Provinciale VII. 72907

Concilium Baltimorense Provinciale VI. 72906

Concilium Cincinnatense Provinciale II. 72912

Concilium Cincinnatense Provinciale I. (72911)

Concilium Cincinnatense Provinciale III. (72913)

Concilium Limense celebratum anno 1853. 41086

Concilivm Limense. Celebratum anno 1583 sub Gregorio XIII. 41087

Concilivm Limense. Svmario del Concilio Provincial. 41088

Concilium Mexicanum Provinciale III. 42064

Concilium Neo-Aurelianense Provinciale primum. 72914

Concilium Neo-Aurelianense tertium. 72915

Concilium Neo-Eboracense primum. 72916

Concilium Neo-Eboracense III. 72917

Concilium Plenarium Totius Americae Septemtrionalis Foederatae, Baltimori habitam anno 1852. 15107, 72897

Concilium Provinciale Baltimorense V. 72905

Concilium Provinciale secundum. Mense Septembris, A. D. 1858. 72921

Concilium Sanctum Provinciale Mexici celebratum anno 1585. 48373

Concio ad clerum: a sermon . . . [at] Yale-College. (49032)

Concio ad clerum: a sketch of the conditions and prospects of the Christian church. 28395

Concio ad magistratum. Or, a sermon. 92097

Concio ad magistratum. Or an assize sermon. 4403

Concio ad populum. 46270

Concio de passione D. N. J. C. in lingua Aymarensi Indica. 4043

Concio hyemalis. 16640

Concise account of North America. 72723-72724

Concise account of the conduct . . . of Nicholas Manners. 44346

Concise account of the historical events of the Dominican Republic. 8075, 20574

Concise account of the institution, transactions and present condition of the Middlebury College Charitable Society. 48836

Concise account of the life of Thomas Jefferson. (35935)

Concise account of the origin of masonry in America. 100650

Concise account of the present state of Kentucky. 71942

Concise account of the present state of the missions. 97849

Concise account of the religious society of Friends. 23188

Concise account of voyages for the discovery of a North-West Passage. (62660)

Concise account of whatever is most curious and remarkable. 84365

Concise address. 70923

Concise and faithful narrative. 14113

Concise and impartial history. 40023, 84115, 101773

Concise and practical system of geography. 83951-83955

Concise and simple narrative of the controversy. 104283

Concise answer to the general inquiry. 15114, 79700, 97883

Concise biographies and portraits. 90539

Concise but candid relation. 15115

Concise, but plain answewr. 57424

Concise classified lists of . . . bibliography. 2253

Concise description of Schooley's Mountain. 48740

Concise description of the city of New York. 54459, 90215-90216

Concise description of the English and French possessions. (58308)

Concise description of the states of Ohio, Indiana, Illinois. (22486)

Concise description of the various kingdoms. 33435

Concise exposition of the belief. 39612

Concise exposition of the Hopedale Community. 2964

Concise extract, from the sea journal. (51136)

Concise guide. 54319

Concise herbal. 91621

Concise historical account of all the British colonies. 15116, 1st note after 102507

Concise historical account of the judiciary of Connecticut. 18990

Concise historical account of the present constitution. 50519

Concise historical account of the present constitution of the Unitas Fratum. 88928

Concise historical sketch of the several churches. 3551

Concise historical view of the difficulties. 170

Concise history of, and guide through Mount Auburn. 19079

Concise history of High Rock Spring. 43294

Concise history of its [i. e. Paraguay's] rise, and progress. 58521

Concise history of Massachusetts. 13337

Concise history of the autumnal fever. 98685

Concise history of the Baptists in the southern parts of America. 2626

Concise history of the commencement, progress and present condition of the American colonies in Liberia. 104011

Concise history of the Eastern Penitentiary of Pennsylvania. 60078

Concise history of the efforts to obtain an extension of suffrage in Rhode Island. 25966

Concise history of the First Baptist Mariners' Church, New York. 66770

Concise history of the First Church . . . in Ipswich. 35044

Concise history of the First Congregational Church in Ridgefield, Connecticut. 13264

Concise history of the former wars in America. 1024

Concise history of the institution. 105617

Concise history of the introduction of protestantism into Mississippi and the southwest. (36541)

Concise history of the Kehukee Baptist Association, from its original rise down to 1803. (9323)

Concise history of the Kehukee Baptist Association, from its original rise to the present time. (5335)

Concise history of the Kehukee Baptist Association, from its rise to the present time. (9322)

Concise history of the Ketockton Baptist Association. 25983

Concise history of the late revolution. 32123, 40024, 50937

Concise history of the leading events in the old provinces. (82199)

Concise history of the rise, progress, and final dissolution. 40839

Concise history of the Spanish America. 10235

Concise history of the United States, from the discovery of America, till 1807. (43125)

Concise history of the United States, from the discovery of America till 1813. 15118, (43125)

Concise history of the United States, from the discovery of America till 1795. 15117

Concise history of the war. (3617)

Concise history of the war, designed to accompany Perrine's new war map of the southern states. 5611

Concise history of the war in Canada. 83623

Concise history of the woman's war on alcohol. 91100

Concise history of the work of the American Baptist Missionary Union. 84051-84052, 84059

Concise history of those [United] States. 11004

Concise introduction to practical arithmetic. 94664

Concise memorandum of certain articles in the museum. 49749

Concise narrative of General Jackson's first invasion of Florida. 35362, 2d note after 98528

Concise narrative of the barbarous treatment. 51796, 102823

Concise narrative of the proceedings of the Yearly Meeting of Friends of Pennsylvania. 35413

Concise narrative of the rise and progress of the East Tennessee Missionary Society. 94792

Concise narrative of the Seminole campaign. 79066

Concise natural history of East and West Florida. 72992-72993

Concise record of the most important proceedings. 65148

Concise refutation of the claims of New-Hampshire and Massachusetts-Bay to the territory of Vermont. 806, 3d note after 99005

Concise review of a work entitled "American antiquities." 65484

Concise review of the spirit which seemed to govern the time of the late American war. 80769

Concise statement of every important fact, amounting to a presumptive proof of the murder of William Morgan. 88653

Concise statement of every important fact, relating to the masonic outrages on William Morgan and David C. Miller. 88653

Concise statement of facts and reasons. (14308), 52053

Concise statement of the action of Congress. 15119, 53252

Concise statement of the awful conflagration of the theatre. 100862

Concise statement of the construction and of the physical and moral effects of penitentiary principles, on the Auburn principle. 9088

Concise statement of the principles of the only true church. 97884

Concise statement of the proceedings of the Baptist Church at Leverett and Montague. 33421

Concise statement of the question regarding the abolition of the slave trade. 8404, 15120, (81892), 81934

Concise statement of the trial & confession of William Clutter, who was executed on Friday the 8th June, 1810. 96852

Concise summary of the second volume of The olive branch. 824

Concise system of rules of order. (9325)

Concise treatise of rhetoric. 93905

Concise treatise on the practice of the court. 19264, note before 95449, 1st note after 98225

Concise United States calendar. 53836

Concise view of ancient and modern religion. 103338, 103344

Concise view of antient and modern religion. 103339

Concise view of ancient history. 84363-84364

Concise view of Black Rock. (55113)

Concise view of church order or government. 74248

Concise view of . . . Ohio. 56901

Concise view of Oregon Territory. 103376

Concise view of some facts and arguments respecting another bridge. (6599)

Concise view of the American slave law. 89925

Concise view of the critical situation. 78548

Concise view of the controversy between the Proprietors of East and West-Jersey. (53091)

Concise view of the diseases incident to the western climate. 85548

Concise view of the inland navigation of the Canadian provinces. 48024, 102556

Concise view of the late proceedings of the leaders of the Clintonian party. 15121, note before 89139, 1st note after 104983, 105212

Concise view of the most important revolutions and events. 59282

Concise view of the present state of the succession. 91841A

Concise view of the principal points of controversy. 103090

Concise view of the principal religious denominations of the United States. 7378

Concise view of the slavery of the people of colour. 95386

Concise view of the whole world. 104492

Concise vocabulary of the language of Otaheite. 4246, 16242, note after 36695

Concise White Mountain guide. 32077, 89047-89048

Concivis. pseud. Letters to the people of the United States. 15122

Conclave of physicians. 30774

Conclin, George. 15123, (17904), (53393)

Conclin's new river guide. 15123, (53393)

Concluding argument of Conway Robinson. 72063

Concluding argument of Hon. George W. Paschal. (58984)

Concluding chapter on facts. 2186

Concluding tract of the Dean of Gloucester. 97360

Conclusion del sueno del Payo del Rosario. 99697

Conclusion generale de l'ouvrage sur le system. 42605

Conclusion of a ministry in . . . Emanuel Church. 33964

Conclusion of the booke. (18774)

Conclusion of the matter. 85475

Conclusion of the official review of the reports. 69946

Conclusion of the Salem controversy. 75653, note after 98033, 98046

Conclusion to the historical memoirs relating to the Housatunnuk Indians. 32946

Conclusions and orders made and agreed upon. 80205

Conclusions des Prefets de la Loire et du Rhone. 84478

Conclusions on the results on the vegetation of Nova Scotia. 84435

Conclusive exculpation of the Marine Corps in Mexico. 70424

Concord, Mass. 15125, 15136

Concord, Mass. Convention, 1779. see Massachusetts. Convention, Concord, 1779.

Concord, Mass. Corinthian Lodge. see Freemasons. Massachusetts. Corinthian Lodge Concord.

Concord, Mass. Ecclesiastical Council, 1743. see Congregational Churches in Massachusetts. Ecclesiastical Council, Concord, 1743.

Concord, Mass. Fire Department. Chief Engineer. 15136

Concord, Mass. Independent Society for the Culture and Propagation of Learning and Good Manners. see Independent Society for the Culture and Propagation of Learning and Good Manners, Concord, Mass.

Concord, Mass. Indian Conference, 1646. see Massachusetts (Colony) Indian Conference, Concord, 1646.

Concord, Mass. Jackson Convention, 1820. see Jackson Convention, Concord, Mass., 1820.

Concord, Mass. Library. 15126

Concord, Mass. Middlesex County Whig Convention, 1838. see Whig Party. Massachusetts. Middlesex County Convention, Concord, 1838.

Concord, Mass. Overseers of the Poor. 15135-15136

Concord, Mass. School. 15127-15129

Concord, Mass. School Committee. 15124-15125, 15134

Concord, Mass. Selectmen. 15125, 15135-15136

Concord, Mass. Superintendent of Public Grounds. 15136

Concord, Mass. Trinitarian Church. 28551

Concord, Mass. Whig Party Convention, 1838. see Whig Party. Massachusetts. Middlesex County. Convention, Concord, 1838.

Concord, N. H. 15139, (15146)-(15148), 15155

Concord, N. H. Anti-slavery Convention, 1834. see New Hampshire Anti-slavery Convention, Concord, 1834.

Concord, N. H. Asylum for the Insane. see New Hampshire. State Hospital, Concord.

Concord, N. H. Baptist Church. 15157

Concord, N. H. Charter. 15147-(15148)

Concord, N. H. City Council. 15147

Concord, N. H. Committee to Ascertain the Feasibility and Cost of Supplying Water to the City. 15152

Concord, N. H. Constitutional Convention, 1796. see New Hampshire. Constitutional Convention, Concord, 1971.

Concord, N. H. Convention of Congregational Ministers, 1791. see Convention of Congregational Ministers in New Hampshire, Concord, 1791.

Concord, N. H. Exhibition of the New Hampshire Mechanics and Art Association, 1868. see New Hampshire Mechanics and Art Association. Exhibition, 1st, Concord, 1868.

Concord, N. H. First Congregational Church. 6962

Concord. N. H. Great State Convention of Friends of the Administration, 1828. see National Republican Party. New Hampshire. Convention, Concord, 1828.

Concord, N. H. Historical Society. see New Hampshire Historical Society, Concord.

Concord, N. H. Internal Improvements Convention, 1825. see Internal Improvements Convention, Concord, N. H., 1825.

Concord, N. H. Mayor, 1868. 15139

Concord, N. H. National Republican Party Concention, 1828. see National Republican Party. New Hampshire. Convention, Concord, 1828.
Concord, N. H. Ordinances, etc. 15147-(15148)
Concord, N. H. Republican State Convention of Delegates Friendly to the Election of Andrew Jackson, 1828. see Democratic Party. New Hampshire. Convention, Concord, 1828.
Concord, N. H. St. Paul's School. 75470
Concord, N. H. Schools. 15139
Concord, N. H. Special Committee to Ascertain and Define the Boundary Lines of the Several School Districts. 15153
Concord, N. H. State Hospital. see New Hampshire. State Hospital, Concord.
Concord, N. H. Superintending School Committees. 15154
Concord, N. H. Washington Benevolent Society. see Washington Benevolent Society. New Hampshire. Concord.
Concord: a poem delivered before the Lyceum. (3614), 15130
Concord and Boston Oil Company, located in Venango County, Penn. 15138
Concord and religion. 20941
Concord Antiquarian Society. 105074
Concord directory. 15131
Concord directory for 1830. 15141
Concord Female Anti-slavery Society, Concord, N. H. 72714
Concord fight. 3778
Concord fight, April 19, 1775. (70413)
Concord Literary Institution and Teacher's Seminary, Concord, N. H. 15140
Concord pocket almanack for . . . 1810. 15143
Concord Railroad Corporation. 15144
Concordance and reference guide to the Book of doctrine and covenants. (50732), 83160, 83232-83234
Concordance entre les codes civils etrangers et le code Napoleon. 1671
Concordance entre les codes de commerce etrangers et le code de commerce Francais. 1670
Concordance entre les lois hypothecaires etrangeres et Francaises. (1672)
Concordance of the constitution of the United States of America. 90876
Concordance to the constitution of the United States of America. 90875
Concordat de l'Amerique avec Rome. 64885
Concordat, ou traite de paix entre les citoyens blancs et les citoyens de couleur. 75083, 97638
Concordat passe entre les citoyens du Pour-au-Prince & les citoyens de couleur de la meme partie de Saint-Domingue. 75084
Concordato de la America, con Roma. 64886
Concordato de Venezuela celebrado en Roma en Julio de 1862. (81131)
Concordato il la esposicion del Consejo Cantonal de Guayaquil. 29097
Concordia de la discordia. (15158)
Concordia res parvae crescvnt. 97527
Concordville Seminary, Concordville, Pa. 15159
Concours Boucherville. (20733)
Concours General des Lycees et Colleges de Paris et de Versailles, 1854. 63709
Concours simultane de trois causes est necessaire. (48689)
Concurrent resolution New York Legislature, being special act. 19638

Concurrent resolutions of the Legislature of New York. 1415
Concurring opinion of Judge Hook. 84519
Condamine, Charles Marie de la. see La Condamine, Charles Marie de.
Condamnation a mort. 12968
Conde, Francisco. 15160
Conde, Pedro Garcia. 12690, 15161,
Conde y Oquendo, Francisco Xavier. (15162)
Conde y Pineda, Francisco Xavier. 15163
Condemned Negro. 28053, 92943
Condensacion del libro titulado Vidaurre contre Vidaurre. 99499
Condensed American cyclopaedia. 71523
Condensed anti-slavery Bible argument. 6918
Condensed geography and history of the western states. (24786)
Condensed historical examination of the wars of the Indians. 82808, 97196
Condensed history of Cooperstown. (41580)
Condensed history of Mount Union College. 56902
Condensed history of political events from 1811 to 1843. 9954
Condensed history of the early settlements. 17038
Condensed history of the first settlement of Jonesborough. 70343
Condensed history of the Independent Roystering Club. 15164, 34143
Condensed history of the state. 8796
Condensed history of the war. 63929
Condensed memoir of the services of William Henry Harrison. 30576
Condensed octavo atlas of the union. 14788
Condensed physical geography of the Atlantic United States. 24789
Condensed proceedings of the Southern Convention. 88329
Condensed treatise on cotton in all its aspects. 3313
Condensed treatise on meteorology in general. 28920
Condensed treatise on the cotton manufacture. 85385
Condensed universal route book. 19524
Conder, James. 15165
Conder, Josiah. 15166-15170, 29080, 49816-49817
Conder, John. 8791, 41605
Condiciones con que el Gremio de Panaderes de la Ciudad de Vera-Cruz, se obliga a abastecerla de pan. 98905
Condiciones y esmblanzas de los Diputados a Corte. 11092
Condicoes para a encorporacao de uma Companhia de Commercio e Navegacao do Rio Mucury. 57899
Condict, Ira. (15171)
Condict, Lewis, 1773-1862. 325, (15172)
Condie, D. Francis. (15173)-15175
Condie, Thomas. 15176-15179, 37899, 62019, 97202, 101710, 101779, note after 101843, 101851
Condigno llanto de las musas en la muerte del D. B. Galvez. 67360
Condit, Jonathan B. (15180)-15183
Conditien de welcke by de Ed. Groot Mog. Heeren Staten van Hollandt ende West Vrieslandt, etc. (15184), 29170, 99310
Conditien, de welcke by d'Ed. Mog. Heeren Staten van Hollandt ende West-Vrieslandt. 15185
Conditien, die door de Heeren Bvrgermeesteren der Stadt Amstelredam, volgens 't

gemaeckte accoordt met de West-Indische
Compagnie. (15186), 20594, 55280-55281,
note after 98474, note after 99310, 102887
Conditien, tusschen de drie respective leden.
93834
Conditien tusschen de drij respective leden.
93883
Condition and prospects of American cotton
manufactures. 17109, 39345
Condition and fate of England. 40219
Condition and prospects of Canada in 1854.
22116
Condition and prospects of the Protestant
Episcopal Church. (2509)
Condition and prospects of the south. 42409
Condition, elevation, emigration, and destiny
of the colored people of the United State.
[sic] 19353
Condition of American seamen. 96999
Condition of labor. 15187
Condition of peace. 3499
Condition of society. 79701
Condition of the African race in the United
States. 81935
Condition of the apprenticed labourers. 92002
Condition of the Congregational Board of Pub-
lication. 16338
Condition of the country. Speech . . . in the
Senate. 4030
Condition of the country. Speech of Hon. S. L.
Mayham. 47122
Condition of the free people of color in the
United States. 15188
Condition of the Indian tribes. 15188, 20610
Condition of the people of color in . . . Ohio.
(56903)
Condition of the rebel states. 49878
Condition of the slave not preferable to that of
the British peasant. 81936
Condition of the slaves in the British colonies.
102819
Condition of the south; a report. 89214
Condition of the south, and the duty of the
north. 79671
Condition of the south: extracts from the
report. (78024)
Condition of woman in polygamy. 19521, 50733
Condition, prospects, and duties of the American
people. 19860
Conditions for letting or selling. 98631
Conditions for new planters. 53619
Conditions of obedience to the civil government.
(25096)
Conditions of peace. 3794
Conditions of plantation. (45316), 69291, note
after 80002, 103353
Conditions of reconstruction. 58018
Conditions of sale of building lots. 103841
Conditions of success in genealogical investi-
gations. 25323
Conditions of the Magellanic premium. 43818
Conditions propounded by the Right Honorable
the Lord Viscount Falkland. 80620
Condolatory address to his truely noble bena-
factress. 103126-103127
Condolence. 9249
Condorcet, Marie Jean Antoine Nicolas Caritat,
Marquis de. 15190-15194, 23918, 25573,
40687-40688, 41646, 47206, 79151, 96413
Condorcet, Sophie de Grouchy, Marquise de.
tr. 82308, 82317
Condottier; a poem. 15195
Condra, Isidro. ed. 15196, (34151)
Conduct and constancy of the New English
captives. 104261

Conduct and treatment of John Crookshanks,
Esq. 17610, 17611, 22796, (38152)
Conduct, letters . . . addresses. 60005
Conduct of a noble commander in America.
15197, note after 42166
Conduct of a R. Hon. gentleman in resigning
the seals of his office. 63088
Conduct of administration. 15198
Conduct of Admiral Knowles. 38150
Conduct of Admiral Vernon. 99249
Conduct of Cadwallader Colden, Esquire. 14276
Conduct of Dr. Lee. 39889
Conduct of General Jackson. 105495
Conduct of General Washington. (33802)
Conduct of George McDuffie. 43201
Conduct of Great Britain respecting neutrals.
15199
Conduct of His Grace the D-ke of Ar--le. 10227
Conduct of Major Gen. Shirley. 80544, 91854
Conduct of Meriwether Jones. 10063
Conduct of Presbyterian ministers. 47276,
97107
Conduct of the administration. 23227
Conduct of the allies. 15200, 86742, 94069-
94070
Conduct of the British government. 99773
Conduct of the Dutch. 13686, 15201, 93853
Conduct of the French. (35957)
Conduct of the government. 50022
Conduct of the late administration examined.
(15202)-(15203), 95750
Conduct of the late and present ministry com-
pared. 15204
Conduct of the late ministry; or memorial con-
cerning a summary of facts. 15205,
(41650), (47511)-47512, 51661, 101710
Conduct of the ministry compared with its
consequences. 15206
Conduct of the ministry impartially examined;
and the pamphlet entitled, "Consideration
on the present German war" refuted on
its own principles. 15208, (80038),
80043
Conduct of the ministry impartially examined.
In a letter to the merchants of London.
15207
Conduct of the Paxton-Men, impartially repre-
sented. 1663, (15209), 59268
Conduct of the Presbyterian ministers; in re-
lation to a letter addressed to the Arch-
bishop of Canterbury. 47276, 97107
Conduct of the Presbyterian ministers, who
sent the letter to the Archbishop of
Canterbury, considered. 47276, 65149
Conduct of the present Parliament considered.
15210
Conduct of the province of New York considered.
(14971), 53620
Conduct of the society. 8641
Conduct of the Spaniards. 33198-33199
Conduct of the war. Report of the Congressional
Committee. 15212, 69849
Conduct of the war. Speech . . . in the Senate.
11887
Conduct of the war. Speech . . . January 6,
1862. 42369
Conduct of the war. Speech of Hon. W. P.
Sheffield. 80097
Conduct of two B——rs vindicated. 15111
Conduct of Washington. 101786
Conduct of Wm. B. Reed. 90581
Conduct of Wm. Rawle, Esq. (21143)
Conduct pursued by the Rev. J. Knapp. 38064
Conducta del Excelentisimo Senor D. Jose
Iturriguray. 10653, 56248

Conducta del Reverendo Obispo de Michoacan.
(11628)
Conducta injuridica del Juzgado de Presas de
las islas de Bahama. 15213
Conducto del Obispo de Puebla D. Pelagio
Antonio de Lavastida. (6422)
Conductor electrico. 74043, 94286
Conductor generalis. 15215, 58682
Conductor to attractive places in Boston and
vicinity. 15214
Conduite de M. de Santo-Domingo. (76874)
Conduite de Francois a l'egarde de la Nou-
velle France. 38622
Conduite des Francois justifiee. 38622
Conduit des Francois, par rapport a la Nou-
velle France. 35958
Condy, Jeremiah, d. 1768. 15216-15217
Condy, Jeremy. see Condy, Jeremiah, d.
1768.
Condy, Jonathan W. supposed author 93935
Condy, Thomas D. 15218, 87691
Cone, Andrew. 15219
Cone, D. D. 15220-(15221)
Cone, E. W. 15222
Cone, S. W. 15222
Cone, Spencer H. 36848
Conejares, Francisco Alonso y Ruiz de. see
Ruiz de Conejares, Francisco Alonso y.
Conejares, Joseph Ruiz de. see Ruiz de
Conejares, Joseph.
Conelly, Pierce. 14773
Conestaggius, Hieronymius. 77902
Conestoga Indians. Treaties, etc. 97561
Coney, John. 16637
Confederacao dos Tamoyos. Poema. 43793
Confederacion Centro-Americana. see Cen-
tral America (Confederacion de Centro-
America, 1823-1840)
Confederacy and the declaration of Paris.
96788
Confederate. pseud. Greyjackets. 28795
Condererate. 15249, 88112
Confederate confiscation bill. (15250)
Confederate first reader. (15251), 83772-83773
Confederate flag on the ocean. 59495
Confederate hero and his heroic father. 88045
Confederate household almanac. 13405
Confederate loan in England. 19759
Confederate memorial. (15252)
Confederate monitor and patriot's friend.
(35421)
Confederate primer. (15251), 83773-83774
Confederate railroad guide. 31869
Confederate receipt book. 15253
Confederate rhyming primer. 15254
Confederate secession. (37633)
Confederate soldier. 21924
Confederate soldier's prayer book. 51472
Confederate spelling book. 2778
Confederate spelling book, with reading lessons
for the young. 15255, 83774
Confederate states almanac, and repository of
useful knowledge, for 1862. (15256)
Confederate states almanac, and repository of
useful knowledge, for the year 1863.
15257
Confederate states almanac for the year of
Our Lord 1864. 15258
Confederate States Bible Society. (15238)
Confederate States of America. 12449, 15414,
(49317)
Confederate States of America. Adjutant and
Inspector General's Office. see Con-
federate States of America. War Depart-
ment.

Confederate States of America. Agents of
Exchange. see Confederate States of
America. Bureau of Exchange.
Confederate States of America. Army. 2054,
2152-2153, (5989), 7467, 12674, 12846,
15236, 15237, 15241, 15324-15330,
(15332)-15333, 15350, (15359)-15363,
15364-15369, 15386, 15403, 15411, 15424,
(15448)-(15449), 19492, 44410, 56788,
68941, 68963, 88405, 2d note after 100578
Confederate States of America. Army. Adjutant and Inspector General's Office.
see Confederate States of America. War
Department.
Confederate States of America. Army. Andersonville Prison Camp. Surgeon's Office.
1429
Confederate States of America. Army. Cavalry.
15412
Confederate States of America. Army. Conference of General Officers on the Condition of Batteries Wagner and Gregg.
15321
Confederate States of America. Army. Court
of Enquiry Relative to the Fall of New
Orleans. 15337
Confederate States of America. Army. Courts
Martial. 39718
Confederate States of America. Army. De-
partment of South Carolina, Georgia, and
Florida. 15270-15271, 26895
Confederate States of America. Army. De-
partment of the Valley of Virginia.
Smith's Brigade. 15288
Confederate States of America. Army. In-
spector General's Office. see Confeder-
ate States of America. War Department.
Confederate States of America. Army. Judge
Advocate General. 39718
Confederate States of America. Army. Medical
Department. 15353-15354
Confederate States of America. Army. Pay
Department. 58941, 68964
Confederate States of America. Army.
Quartermaster Department. see
Confederate States of America.
War Department.
Confederate States of America. Attorney
General. 15244, (15250), 15371-15373
see also Watts, Thomas Hill, 1819-1892.
Confederate States of America. Bureau of
Exchange. 15323 see also Ould,
Robert, 1820-1882.
Confederate States of America. Commissioner
of Taxes. 15267, 69899
Confederate States of America. Commissioner
to the Indian Nations West of Arkansas.
see Confederate States of America.
Office of Indian Affairs. Commissioner
to the Indian Nations West of Arkansas.
Confederate States of America. Commissioners
to the Hampton Roads Conference. (48140),
65358 see also Campbell, J. A. Hunter,
Robert Mercer Taliaferro, 1809-1887.
Stephens, Alexander Hamilton, 1812-1883.
Confederate States of America. Comptroller of
the Treasury. see Confederate States of
America. Treasury Department. Comptroller.
Confederate States of America. Congress.
395, 4199, 15229, 15231, 15261, 15269,
15324-15330, 15337, (15359), 15363,
15366, 15368, (15401), (15404), 15411,
16865, (21785), 31941, (36376), (49317),
56786, 57656, 74093

Confederate States of America. Congress.
Confederence Committee on the Exemption Bill. 15385
Confederate States of America. Congress.
Joint Special Committee on the Condition and Treatment of Prisoners of War. 69873
Confederate States of America. Congress.
Joint Special Committee to Investigate the Navy Department. 15370
Confederate States of America. Congress.
House of Representatives. (15224), 15336, 15408, 16873, 61325, 70075, 87803
Confederate States of America. Congress.
House of Representatives. Committee of Ways and Means. Minority. 15320
Confederate States of America. Congress.
House of Representatives. Committee on Claims. 15375-15376, 69818, 69909
Confederate States of America. Congress.
House of Representatives. Committee on Deceased Soldiers' Claims. 15377
Confederate States of America. Congress.
House of Representatives. Committee on Elections. Majority. 15284
Confederate States of America. Congress.
House of Representatives. Committee on Foreign Affairs. Majority. 15285-15286
Confederate States of America. Congress.
House of Representatives. Committee on Quartermaster and Commissary Departments. 15384
Confederate States of America. Congress.
House of Representatives. Committee on Salt Supply. (15384A)
Confederate States of America. Congress.
House of Representatives. Committee on the Currency. Minority. (49317)
Confederate States of America. Congress.
House of Representatives. Committee on the Judiciary. Minority. (49317)
Confederate States of America. Congress.
House of Representatives. Committee to Enquire Into the Treatment of Prisoners at Castle Thunder. 15268
Confederate States of America. Congress.
House of Representatives. Committee to Enquire Into the Treatment of Prisoners at Castle Thunder. Majority. (15283)
Confederate States of America. Congress.
House of Representatives. Roanoke Island Investigation Committee. 15389
Confederate States of America. Congress.
House of Representatives. Special Committee on the Pay and Clothing of the Army. (69908)
Confederate States of America. Congress.
House of Representatives. Special Committee on the Recent Military Disasters. 15390-15391, 25018
Confederate States of America. House of Representatives. Special Committee on the Recent Military Disasters. Chairman. 25018, 15390 see also Foote, Henry Stuart.
Confederate States of America. Congress.
House of Representatives. Special Committee to Inquire into Certain Outrages of the Enemy. 15402, 55682
Confederate States of America. Congress.
Senate. 15383, 15407
Confederate States of America. Congress.
Senate. Committee on Finance. 15379-(15381)

Confederate States of America. Congress.
Senate. Committee on Foreign Relations. 15382
Confederate States of America. Senate. Committee on Foreign Relations. Minority. (49317)
Confederate States of America. Congress.
Senate. Committee on the Judiciary. 15383
Confederate States of America. Congress.
Senate. Select Committee on a Portion of the Message of the President of the 13th Inst. [March, 1865.] 15401, 57656
Confederate States of America. Constitution. 15263, 15340-15341, 15417, 16123, (27061), (57514), 87436, 87440
Confederate States of America. Department of State. 4703, 15265, 15286, 16877, 81812 see also Benjamin, Judah Philip, 1811-1884.
Confederate States of America. District Court (Alabama) 15409
Confederate States of America. District Court (Georgia) (27106)
Confederate States of America. District Court (South Carolina) 15410, 79189, 87467
Confederate States of America. Envoy to Great Britain. 16887, 45451 see also Mason, James Murray, 1798-1871.
Confederate States of America. Laws, statutes, etc. 2054, 2152-2153, (5989), 12846, 15225-15229, 15239, (15240)-15241, 15248, (15250), 15266, (15273), 15279, 15288, 15340-15346, (15319), 15348-15358, 15379, (15381), 15383, 15409-15410, 15416-15417, 15420, 21784, (25331), 27106, 39718, (43629), 65724, 88405
Confederate States of America. Navy. 15331, 15355, 15357, 15425, 34855
Confederate States of America. Navy. School-Ship Patrick Henry. 15357
Confederate States of America. Navy Department. 15280, 15312, 15314, (69898) see also Mallory, Stephen Russell, 1813-1873.
Confederate States of America. Office of Indian Affairs. 15397
Confederate States of America. Office of Indian Affairs. Commissioner to the Indian Nations West of Arkansas. 15292
Confederate States of America. Ordnance Department. 15333, 15352, 15358 see also Gorgas, Josiah, 1818-1883.
Confederate States of America. Patent Office. 15374, 15405-15406, 74072 see also Rhodes, Rufus R.
Confederate States of America. Post Office Department. (15234), 15245, 15282, 15314, 15387-15388 see also Reagan, John Henninger, 1818-1905.
Confederate States of America. Postmaster-General. see Confederate States of America. Post Office Department.
Confederate States of America. President. 15230, 15264, 15274, 15289-(15299), 15300-(15318), 15422, 16865, 18837, 18841, 46962, 48146-(48147), 57656, 58700, 65358, 65934, 70203 see also Davis, Jefferson, Pres. Confederate States, 1808-1889.
Confederate States of America. Produce Loan Office. (34851)
Confederate States of America. Secretary of State. see Confederate States of America Department of State.
Confederate States of America. Secretary of the Navy. see Confederate States of America. Navy Department.

Confederate States of America. Secretary of the Treasury. see Confederate States of America. Treasury Department.
Confederate States of America. Secretary of War. see Confederate States of America. War Department.
Confederate States of America. Subsistance Department. see Confederate States of America. War Department.
Confederate States of America. Surgeon General's Office. (15269)
Confederate States of America. Treasury Department. 15246-15248, 15267, 15275-(15276), 15281, 15309, 15310, 15393-15395, 15413, 15415, 15418, (34851), 69899 see also Memminger, Christopher Gustavus, 1803-1888.
Confederate States of America. Treasury Department. Comptroller. (25331)
Confederate States of America. Treasury Department. Second Auditor. (15392), (25331)
Confederate States of America. Treaties, etc. 15417, 15423
Confederate States of America. War Department. 15264, 15270-15272, (15291), 15302, 15309-15311, 15313, 15316, (15349), 15356, 15396-15400, 15419, 16865, 16873, (25331), 26895-26896, 34953, 68941, 68964, 69919, 72174, 78765, 90511 see also Seddon, James Alexander, 1815-1880.
Confederate States of America. War Department. Superintendent of Army Records. (25331) see also Fowler, William C.
C. S. A. and the battle of Bull Run. 3477
Confederate States of America in prophecy. (78671)
Confederate States patent laws. 15259
Confederate States railroad guide. 31870
Confederated Tribes of Sac and Fox Indians. see Fox Indians. and Sauk Indians.
Confederate's assistant to national independence. 35420
Confederation Americaine. 49095
Confederation Argentine. 21160
Confederation Argentine a l'Exposition Universelle de 1867, a Paris. 15427
Confederation considered in relation to the interests of the empire. 30028, (33315)
Confederation considered on its merits. 15426
Confederation du Sud. 5151
Confederation independence annexation Conference fait a l'Institut Canadien de Quebec. 23596
Confederation of British North America. 6242
Confederation of North American republics. (79847)
Confederation of the British North American provinces: the speech of the Rt. Hon. Earl of Carnarvon. 31458
Confederation of the British North American provinces: their past history and future prospects. 68006
Confederation of the provinces of British North America. 6908
Confederation or annexation? 29678
Confederation question considered. 64125
Confederes. 11588
Confederes et federaux. 19425
Conference about the subject and manner of baptism. (46229)
Conference au profit des victimes du tremblement de terre. 15428
Conference between a minister and the prisoner. 46559, 96766

Conference between His Exc. Jonathan Belcher, Esq. 4391, 15429
Conference between Iota and Omega. 85389
Conference between Secretary Stanton, General Sherman and freedmen in Savannah. 15430
Conference between the Commissaries of Massachusetts-Bay, and the Commissaries of New-York. (15431), 45689
Conference Convention, Washington, D. C., 1861. see Washington, D. C. Peace Convention, 1861.
Conference Convention of the Commissioners from the Several States, held, at the request of Virginia. 15434, 59404
Conference fait a l'Institut Canadien de Quebec. 23596
Conference held at Deerfield. (15440)
Conference held at St. George's. 15436
Conference held at the fort at St. George's. 15435
Conference Mr. John Cotton held at Boston. 17055
Conference of Churches, York County, Me. see Congregational Churches in Maine. York County Conference of Churches.
Conference of Colored Citizens, Columbia, S. C., 1876. 87734
Conference of His Excellency the Governor, with the Sachems and Chief Men of the Eastern Indians. (15437), 34654
Conference of . . . Jonathan Belcher, Esq. 4391
Conference of the Governor of Massachusetts Bay with the Sachems of the Eastern Indians. (15437)
Conference on society and manners in Massachusetts. 15438
Conference on the Future of the Smithsonian Institution, Washington, D. C., 1927. 85015
Conference on the future of the Smithsonian Institution, February 11, 1927. 85015
Conference on the occurrences in America. 15439
Conference rights. 78345
Conference sur Franklin. 11026
Conference sur la guerre du Paraguay. 24637
Conference 'twixt a famous Roman causist and an emmissary. 103990
Conference with the Commons. 65862, 88190
Conference with the Eastern Indians, at the further ratification of the peace. 15442, note after (34632)
Conference with the Eastern Indians, at the ratification of the peace. 15441, note after (34632)
Conference with the prisoner. 25397
Conferences de l'Ecole de Droit. 5148
Conferences with George Hammond. 34900, 2d note after 101709
Conferencia publicada sob os auspicios da Maconaria Pernambucana. 88796
Conferencia Tenida Entre los Ministros Plenipotentiarios del Peru y del Ecuador Nombrados Para Transijir las Diferencias que Existen entre Una y Otra Republica, Quito. see Quito, Ecuador. Conferencia Tenida Entre los Ministros Plenipotentiarios del Peru y del Ecuador Nombrados para Transijir las Diferencias que Existen entre Una y Otra Republica.
Conferencias familiares. 14653
Conferencias publicadas na provincia do Maranhao. 88699

Conferencias y comunicaciones tenidas en
Quito. 61095
Confesion de un pecador arrepentido. (73223)-
73224, note after 97019
Confesion publica por D. Juan Echegoyen.
21768
Confesionario general con los tratos y con-
tratos de las Indias. (22889)
Confesiones. 58304
Confesiones del ilustrisimo, excelentisimo, y
v. siervo de Dios Don Juan Palafox y
Mendoza. 99456
Confesor imparcial instriudo. (46871)
Confessario en lengua Mexicano y Castellana.
(40080)
Confession and covenant of the Warwich and
Coventry Baptist Church, Crompton,
R. I. 17602
Confession and declaration of John Hurrin and
Alexander Buchan. 34012
Confession and dying words of John Lechler.
39643
Confession and dying words of Samuel Frost.
105351
Confession and life of C. Gibbs. 27295, 101243
Confession and retractions of the Reverend
Mr. James Davenport. 14496, 18701
Confession de John Wilkes Booth. 6387
Confession, declaration, dying warning and
advice of Patience Sampson. 6471
Confession et penitence de l'Assemblee Gen-
erale. 15443
Confession, &c. of Thomas Mount. 84681-84683
Confession generale. 15444
Confession, history and life of Robert Scott.
78350
Confession, last words, and dying speech of
John Stewart. 91689-91690
Confession of a member. 20360
Confession of Adam Horn. 33012
Confession of Alonzo Phelps. 61359
Confession of Charles Gibbs. 96871
Confession of faith, . . . adopted by the Bap-
tist Association . . . at Philadelphia.
61497
Confession of faith, adopted by the Congrega-
tional Church, in Willimantic. 104496
Confession of faith, adopted by the New-England
churches 1680. 57611, 63342
Confession of faith, adopted in 1680. (10120),
15486, 69921
Confession of faith, agreed upon by the Assembly of Divines at Westminister [sic].
15445
Confession of faith agreed upon by the Church
at Salem. 31744
Confession of faith, and catalogue of members
[of the First Church in Northampton.]
55764
Confession of faith, and catalogue of officers
and members of the Congregational
Church in Rindge, N. H. 71421
Confession of faith and church covenant, approved by the Cumberland Baptist Asso-
ciation. 17881
Confession of faith and church covenant . . .
made . . . by the Church in Middleborough. 48826
Confession of faith and church order. 55103
Confession of faith and covenant, adopted and
used by the Congregational Church in
New Bedford. 52473
Confession of faith and covenant adopted by the
Church of Christ in Berlin. 32292

Confession of faith, and covenant, adopted, by
the Churches in Southampton, Easthampton, and Westhampton. 88227
Confession of faith and covenant, adopted by the
Presbyterian Church of Whitesboro.
103684
Confession of faith and covenant, adopted by
the Presbytery of Oneida. 47334
Confession of faith, and covenant, also a brief
history. 97772
Confession of faith, and covenant, of the Church
in Yale College. 105877
Confession of faith and covenant of the Congre-
gational Church, in Northbridge (Centre)
Mass. (55780)
Confession of faith, and covenant of the Con-
gregational Church in Southington. 88588-
88589
Confession of faith, and covenant of the Con-
gregational Church in Wenham. 102628
Confession of faith, and covenant of the Con-
gregational Church in Westminster East
Parish. 103036
Confession of faith and covenant, of the First
Church in North Yarmouth, Me. (55757)
Confession of faith, and covenant, of the First
Church in Southington. 88587
Confession of faith and covenant of the First
Congregational Church in Vernon, Conn.
99255
Confession of faith and covenant of the Old
South Church. 15453
Confession of faith, and covenant, of the South
Church in Andover. 15451
Confession of faith and covenant of the South
Church, Springfield, Mass. 89875
Confession of faith and covenant of the Union
Church in Worcester. 105373
Confession of faith and covenant, recommended
by the North Western Consociation. 99167
Confession of faith, and covenant, with the
ecclesiastical principles and rules. (10928)
Confession of faith, and form of covenant.
(6663)
Confession of faith, and form of government.
92826
Confession of faith and rules of discipline.
(66916)
Confession of faith, and rules . . . of the First
Free Church, Philadelphia. (61662)
Confession of faith, and the covenant, of the
Evangelical Congregational Church in
Cambridge-port. 10131
Confession of faith, and the covenant, of the
South Church in Dedham. (19216)
Confession of faith, covenant and by-laws of
the Eliot Church, in Newton, Mass. 55086
Confession of faith, covenant, and regulations
of the Congregational Church, Southamp-
ton, Massachusetts. 88228
Confession of faith, covenant and regulations of
the Evangelical Union Church, in Sudbury,
Mass. 93406
Confession of faith, covenant, constitution and
rules of practice. 21649
Confession of faith, covenant, historical notice,
and names. 105146
Confession of faith, &c. [of Samuel Willard.]
28628
Confession of faith, in harmony with the Bible
and common sense. 84762
Confession of faith in the most necessary
things. 15446
Confession of faith [of Moses Taft.] 79922
Confession of faith [of Robert Breck.] 16640

Confession of faith [of the Baptists of Ireland.] 95431

Confession of faith, of the Church of Christ in Peacham, defended. 105241

Confession of faith of the Evangelical Churches. 15454

Confession of faith of the Kirk of Scotland. 80715

Confession of faith of the Second Baptist Church. 26485

Confession of faith of the Second Evangelical Congregational Church. 10132

Confession of faith [of William Cooper.] 14516, 16630

Confession of faith; or a seminary of divinity. 24542

Confession of faith, or a summary of divinity. 15450

Confession of faith owned and consented to by the Elders and Messengers of the Churches in the Colony of Connecticut in New-England. 15447-15448, (77391)-77393

Confession of faith, owned and consented unto by the Elders and Messengers of the Churches assembled at Boston in New-England, May 12, 1680. 15449, 63334-63336, 63342, 104901

Confession of faith owned and consented unto by the Elders & Messengers of the Churches assembled at Boston in New England, May. 12. 1680. Being the second session of that synod. 68013

Confession of faith put forth by the Elders and Brethern of many congregations of Christians. 61557

Confession of faith, put forth by the Elders and Brethren of many congregations of Christians (baptized upon profession of their faith) in London and the country. 87794

Confession of faith, the larger and shorter catechisms. 15445, note after 93573

Confession of faith, the larger and shorter catechisms, with the scripture proofs at large. 80715, 86358, 86364

Confession of George Brown. 96838

Confession of Jereboam [sic] O. Beauchamp. 4160

Confession of Jeroboam O. Beauchamp. 4159

Confession of Jesse Strang, who was convicted. 92689

Confession of Jesse Strang, who was executed. 92690

Confession of John E. Cook. 8519, 16281

Confession of John Loyce, alias Davis. 36782

Confession of Lewis Wilber. 103945

Confession of Michael Martin. (44901)

Confession of Samuel Chapman. 102088

Confession of Sarah E. Littles. 92358

Confession of the murder of William Morgan. 50681

Confession . . . of Thomas Mount. 51144

Confession; or, the blind heart. (81202)-81203, (81279)

Confessionario. (11232), 11235

Confessionario breve en la lengva del reyno de Chile. 42669, 98324

Confessionario breue, en lengua Mexicana y Castellana. 49870, 49872

Confessionario [en la lengua de Michoacan.] 7461

Confessionario en lengua Castellana y Timu-quana. 58584

Confessionario en lengua Mexicana. 3994

Confessionario en lengva Mexicana y Castel-lana. 36132

Confessionario en lengua Mixe. (67320)

Confessionario en lengua Zapoteca. 24105

Confessionario general. 98724

Confessionario mayor, en la lengna [sic] Mexi-cana y Castellana. 49873

Confessionario mayor, en lengua Mexicana y Castellana. (49871)

Confessionario mayor, y menor en lengua Mexi-cana. 48375

Confessionario mvy copioso en dos lengvas. 5021

Confessionario para los cvras de Indios. (15452), 67163

Confessions and execution of the pirates Gibbs & Wansley. 101243

Confessions and experiences of a showman. 8647

Confessions and life of C. Gibbs. 27295

Confessions of a consumptive. 14187

Confessions of a French Catholic priest. 50963

Confessions of a magnetiser. 93755

"Confessions of a magnetiser" exposed! 93755

Confessions of a poet. 57753

Confessions of a Sister of Charity. 22822

Confessions of an inquirer. 35795

Confessions of Nat Turner. 96487

Confessions of Saint Martin. 94237

Confessions of two malefactors Teller and Reynolds. 94617

Confessions, trials, and biographical sketches of the most cold blooded murderers. 15455, 3d note after 96930A

Confessonario [sic] breue. 96268-96269, 100643

Confessonario [sic] breve activo, y passivo. 74650

Confessonario [sic] en lengua Cumanagota. 94346

Confessonario [sic] mas breve. 94346

Confesores de los naturales. 3242

Confidence in time of war. 43200

Confidence-man; his masquerade. 47482

(Confidential) answer to the allegations. (39170)

Confidential disclosures of the Prize Committee. 9661

Confidential memorandum hitherto unpublished. 94495

Confidential message from the President. 15456

Confidential. Theo. S. Fay, to C. C. Jewett, Esq. 90656

Configuracao e descripcao de todos os orgaos fundamentaes. 26490, (75618)

Configuracao e estudo botanico dos vegetaes seculares. 74619

Configuration et nature du sol. 47902

Confirmation of a late epistle. 106098

Confiscated property. (66414)

Confiscation act of the United States. 79189, 87467

Confiscation and emancipation. Speech of Hon. E. G. Spaulding, of New York. Delivered in the House of Representatives, May 23, 1862. 89032

Confiscation and emancipation. Speech of Hon. E. G. Spaulding, of New York, delivered in the House of Representatives, Tuesday, June 17, 1862. 89035

Confiscation and emancipation. Speech . . . May 26, 1862. 29293

Confiscation and emancipation. Speech of Hon. Edward H. Rollins. 72855

Confiscation and emancipation. Speech of Hon. W. E. Lansing. 38941

Confiscation and liberation. 36885

Confiscation; emancipation. 32476

Confiscation of property and emancipation of slaves. 61382

Confiscation of property and emancipation of the slaves of rebels. (22378)
Confiscation of rebel property. Remarks of Hon. Owen Lovejoy. 42369
Confiscation of rebel property. Speech . . . in the House of . . . [Representatives] January 19, 1864. (6977)
Confiscation of rebel property. Speech of Francis P. Blair. 5738
Confiscation of rebel property. Speech of Hon. A. A. Sargent. (76940)
Confiscation of rebel property. Speech of Hon. Ira Harris. 30475
Confiscation of rebel property. Speech of Hon. Rufus P. Spalding. 88915
Confiscation of rebel property. Speech of Hon. William Kellogg. 37302
Confiscation of the property of rebels. 21327
Confiscation or conciliation? (17271)
Confiscation. Speech . . . delivered in the House of Representatives. 22047
Conflagration. 9714
Conflagration. A poem. 15457
Conflagration, a poem, written and published. 44345, (51433)
Conflagration; comprising two poems. (81676)
Conflagration in the city of New-York. 89326
Conflict and truth. 63940
Conflict and the victory. 10846
Conflict between despotism and liberty. 15458
Conflict between "higher law" and the law of the land. 5668
Conflict between religious truths and American infidelity. 27329
Conflict in New Orleans. 68541
Conflict of ages. 91615
Conflict of jurisdiction between state and federal courts. 32558
Conflict of races. 17246
Conflict of the age, a poem. 37722
Conflict of truth. 68591
Conflict of two civilizations. 63353
Conflicting authorities. 56660
Conflicto y armonias de las razas en America. 77087
Conflit Americain et sa solution probable. 62599
Conflit Americain. Le nord et le sud. 15460
Conflit Hispano Chilien. 15459
Conflit Hispano-Peruvien. 61096
Conformists reasons for joining with the non-conformists. 46301
Confrades de Sanctissimo Sacramento. 93590
Confradia del Glorioso Principe de los Apostoles San Pedro, Caracas. 16058
Confusion is fallen. 64680
Confusion of Babel discovered. 77436
Confusion of Tulpehocken. 86746
Confutation of his appendix to his sermons. 82723
Confutation of some grounds for infants baptisme. 62483
Confutation of the arguments. 25747
Confutation of the reply to the speech. 60605, 60645, 93252
Confutation of two tracts. 26753, 103320
Congar, Obadiah. 15461
Congdon, A. W. 105444
Congdon, Charles T. 15462-15464
Congdon, James Bunker, 1802-1880. (15465)-15471, 52474
Congdon, Joseph W. 28523
Conger, A. B. 15472
Conger, Harmon Sweatland, 1816-1882. 15473
Conger, O. T. ed. 62615
Conger, Obadiah. 12407

Conger, Zenas. 101407
Congratulations of the country. 83366
Congratulatory address of the House of Representatives. 92349
Congratulatory epistle to the redoubtable "Peter Porcupine." 14025
Congratulatory letter from a gentleman in the west. (26353), 32309, 105927
Congratulatory letter, to Mr. G———r. 15475
Congratulatory letters. 65011
Congratulatory poem, on the late successes of the British arms. 15476
Congratulatory poem, on the safe arrival of the Scots African and Indian fleet in Calendonia. 78207
Congratulatory poem upon the noble feast made by the ancient and renouned families of the Smiths. 82861
Congregacion de el Oratorio. Mexico (City) 18778
Congregacion de Esclavos del Divinisimo Senor Sacramentado, Mexico (City) see San Jose (Parroquia) Mexico (City) Congregacion del Esclavos del Divinisimo Senor Sacramentado.
Congregacion de Nuestra Senora. Mexico. (48447)
Congregacion de Nuestra Senora de Aranzazu, Mexico (City) 48388
Congregacion de Nuestra Senora de Covadonga. (48384)
Congregacion de Nuestra Padre San Pedro. see Congregacion de San Pedro.
Congregacion de San Pedro. 94354
Congregacion de San Pedro. Mexico (City) 48371, 87157, 93575
Congregacion de San Pedro. Mexico (City) Abad. 87157, 93575 see also Cerda, Goncalo Carrillo de la.
Congregacion del Alumbrado y Vela Continua al Santissimo Sacramento, Mexico (City) see San Sebastian (Parroquia) Mexico (City) Congregacion del Alumbrado y Vela Continua al Santissimo Sacramento.
Congregacion del Esclavos Cocheros del Santiss. Sacramento, Mexico (City) see Salto de Agua (Parroquia) Mexico (City) Congregacion del Esclavos Cocheros del Santiss. Sacramento.
Congregacion del San Joseph. Mexico. 86254
Congregation de Notre-Dame de Quebec. 67054
Congregation des Hommes de Quebec. see Congregation de Notre-Dame de Quebec.
Congregation of God in the Spirit. 2462-2463, 51292-51293, 60766, 60786, 4th note after 97845, note after 106412 see also United Brethren.
Congregation ou une mission chez les Iroquois. 27630
Congregational almanac, 1646. 15477
Congregational Association of Oregon. see Congregational Churches in Oregon. Congregational Association.
Congregational Association of South-Carolina. see Congregational Churches in South Carolina. Congregational Association.
Congregational Board of Publication, Boston. (15478), 95775
Congregational Charitable Society of Massachusetts. see Massachusetts Congregational Charitable Society.
Congregational Church, Augusta, Me. see Augusta, Me. Congregational Church (South Parish)
Congregational Church, Brooklyn, Conn. see Brooklyn, Conn. Congregational Church.

Congregational Church, Carlisle, Mass. see
Carlisle, Mass. Congregational Church.

Congregational Church, Charleston, S. C. see
Charleston, S. C. Congregational Church.

Congregational Church, Columbia, Conn. see
Columbia, Conn. Congregational Church.

Congregational Church, Danbury, Conn. see
Danbury, Conn. Congregational Church.

Congregational Church, Dubuque, Iowa. see
Dubuque, Iowa. Congregational Church.

Congregational Church, Durham, N. H. see
Durham, N. H. Congregational Church.

Congregational Church, East Haven, Conn.
see East Haven, Conn. Congregational
Church.

Congregational Church, Franklin, Conn. see
Franklin, Conn. Congregational Church.

Congregational Church, Greensboro', Vt. see
Greensboro', Vt. Congregational Church.

Congregational Church, Greenwich, N. Y. see
Greenwich, N. Y. Congregational Church.

Congregational Church, Hanover, N. H. see
Hanover, N. H. Congregational Church.

Congregational Church, Homer, N. Y. see
Homer, N. Y. Congregational Church.

Congregational Church, Leicester, Mass. see
Leicester, Mass. Congregational
Church.

Congregational Church, New Bedford, Mass.
see New Bedford, Mass. Congregational
Church.

Congregational Church, North Brookfield, Mass.
see North Brookfield, Mass. Congregational Church.

Congregational Church, Northampton, Mass.
see Northampton, Mass. Congregational
Church.

Congregational Church, Northbridge Centre,
Mass. see Northbridge Centre, Mass.
Congregational Church.

Congregational Church, Pittsfield, N. H. see
Pittsfield, N. H. Congregational Church.

Congregational Church, Plymouth, N. H. see
Plymouth, N. H. Congregational
Church.

Congregational Church, Rehoboth, Mass. see
Rehoboth, Mass. Congregational Church.

Congregational Church, Richmond, Mass. see
Richmond, Mass. Congregational Church.

Congregational Church, Rindge, N. H. see
Rindge, N. H. Congregational Church.

Congregational Church, Rocky Hill, Conn.
see Rocky Hill, Conn. Congregational
Church.

Congregational Church, Rupert, Vt. see
Rupert, Vt. Congregational Church.

Congregational Church, Sanbornton, N. H. see
Sanbornton, N. H. Congregational Church.

Congregational Church, Shelburne, Mass. see
Shelburne, Mass. Congregational Church.

Congregational Church, Shrewsbury, Mass.
see Shrewsbury, Mass. Congregational
Church.

Congregational Church, Somers, Conn. see
Somers, Conn. Congregational Church.

Congregational Church, South Hadley Falls,
Mass. see South Hadley Falls, Mass.
Congregational Church.

Congregational Church, South Norwalk, Conn,
see South Norwalk, Conn. Congregational
Church.

Congregational Church, South Woburn, Mass.
see South Woburn, Mass. Congregational
Church.

Congregational Church, Southampton, Mass.
see Southampton, Mass. Congregational
Church.

Congregational Church, Southbridge, Mass.
see Southbridge, Mass. Congregational
Church.

Congregational Church, Southington, Conn. see
Southington, Conn. Congregational Church.

Congregational Church, Spencer, Mass. see
Spencer, Mass. Congregational Church.

Congregational Church, Springfield, Ohio. see
Springfield, Ohio. Congregational Church.

Congregational Church, Stanwich, Conn. see
Stanwich, Conn. Congregational Church.

Congregational Church, Stockbridge, Vt. see
Stockbridge, Vt. Congregational Church.

Congregational Church, Stratford, Conn. see
Stratford, Conn. Congregational Church.

Congregational Church, Sturbridge, Mass. see
Sturbridge, Mass. Congregational Church.

Congregational Church, Wenham, Mass. see
Wenham, Mass. Congregational Church.

Congregational Church, West Boylston, Mass.
see West Boylston, Mass. Congregational
Church.

Congregational Church, Westfield, Conn. see
Westfield, Conn. Congregational Church.

Congregational Church, Westminster, Vt. see
Westminster, Vt. Congregational Church.

Congregational Church, Whitesboro, N. Y.
see Whitesboro, N. Y. Congregational
Church.

Congregational Church, Willimantic, Conn.
see Willimantic, Conn. Congregational
Church.

Congregational Church, Winsted, Conn. see
Winsted, Conn. Congregational Church.

Congregational Church, Yorktown, N. Y. see
Yorktown, N. Y. Congregational Church.

Congregational Church in Chatham 1720-1920.
84758

Congregational Church in Shelburne, Mass.,
March 12, 1832. 80114

Congregational Church in Westfield. 103027

Congregational church is a catholike visible
church. 92113

Congregational church manual. 28678

Congregational Church of Stratford. 92728

Congregational Churches, Pembroke, Mass.
see Pembroke, Mass. Congregational
Churches.

Congregational Churches (Strict) see Strict
Congregational Churches.

Congregational Churches in Connecticut. 23414,
52621, 77393 see also Presbyterian
Church in the U. S. A. Convention of
Delegates From the Synod of New York
and Philadelphia, and from the Associations of Connecticut, 1766-1775.

Congregational Churches in Connecticut. Associated Churches of Litchfield. see Congregational Churches in Connecticut.
Litchfield Association.

Congregational Churches in Connecticut. Associated Pastors of New Haven Center.
see Congregational Churches in Connecticut. New Haven Center Association.

Congregational Churches in Connecticut. Association of Ministers in the County of Tolland. see Congregational Churches in
Connecticut. Tolland County Association.

Congregational Churches in Connecticut. Asso-
ciation of the County of New Haven. see
Congregational Churches in Connecticut.
New Haven County Association.

Congregational Churches in Connecticut. Asso-
ciation of the South Part of Litchfield
County. see Congregational Churches in
Connecticut. Litchfield South Association.

Congregational Churches in Connecticut.
Association of the Western District of
New Haven County. see Congregational
Churches in Connecticut. New Haven
County Western Association.
Congregational Churches in Connecticut. Consociated Churches of Windham County.
see Congregational Churches in Con-
necticut. Windham County Consociation.
Congregational Churches in Connecticut. Con-
sociation of Litchfield North. see Con-
gregational Churches in Connecticut.
Litchfield North Consociation.
Congregational Churches in Connecticut. Con-
sociation of the County of Windham.
see Congregational Churches in Con-
necticut. Windham County Consociation.
Congregational Churches in Connecticut. Consociation of the Western District of
Fairfield County. see Congregational
Churches in Connecticut. Fairfield
County Western Consociation.
Congregational Churches in Connecticut. Consociation of Windham County. see Congregational Churches in Connecticut.
Windham County Consociation.
Congregational Churches in Connecticut. Convention of Churches in Windham County,
1800. (63288) see also Congregational
Churches in Connecticut. Windham
County Consociation.
Congregational Churches in Connecticut. Convention of the North and South Consociations of Litchfield County, 1852.
41472 see also Congregational Churches
in Connecticut. Litchfield North Consociation. and Congregational Churches
in Connecticut. Litchfield South Consociation.
Congregational Churches in Connecticut. Eastern Association in Fairfield County. see
Congregational Churches in Connecticut.
Fairfield County Eastern Association.
Congregational Churches in Connecticut. Eastern Association of Windham County.
see Congregational Churches in Connecticut. Windham County Eastern Association.
Congregational Churches in Connecticut. Ecclesiastical Council, Danbury, 1764.
23697, 99820, 103374
Congregational Churches in Connecticut. Ecclesiastical Council, Mansfield, 1806.
(80370)-80371, note after 100602, 102522
Congregational Churches in Connecticut. Ecclesiastical Council, New Haven, 1785.
32589
Congregational Churches in Connecticut. Ecclesiastical Council, New London, 1736.
19946, 53253
Congregational Churches in Connecticut. Ecclesiastical Council, New London, 1737.
69488
Congregational Churches in Connecticut. Ecclesiastical Council, Plymouth, 1856.
63470
Congregational Churches in Connecticut. Ecclesiastical Council, Simsbury, 1770.
81389
Congregational Churches in Connecticut. Ecclesiastical Council, Windham, 1813.
90704
Congregational Churches in Connecticut. Ecclesiastical Councils, Stafford, 1781.
73562

Congregational Churches in Connecticut. Ecclesiastical Councils, Wallingford, 1759.
(30647), 96092, 96094
Congregational Churches in Connecticut. Ecclesiastical Councils, West Stafford, 1781.
25232, 73562, 102947
Congregational Churches in Connecticut. Fairfield County Eastern Association. 23697,
99328, 103374, 103628
Congregational Churches in Connecticut. Fairfield County Western Consociation.
28677, 103374
Congregational Churches in Connecticut. Fairfield West Association. (23698)
Congregational Churches in Connecticut.
General Association. 16, 13012, (15636)-
15637, 15715, 15789-15790, 15803-15804,
(15807)-15810, 15813, 15816, 15820,
15822, 15832, 57324, 104760
Congregational Churches in Connecticut.
General Association. Committee. 420,
15646, 2d note after 91736
Congregational Churches in Connecticut.
General Association. Committee on
Home Evangelization. 15825
Congregational Churches in Connecticut. Gen-
eral Association. Committee on the Sin
of Slavery. Minority. (49317), 60952
Congregational Churches in Connecticut.
General Association. Committee to Re-
ceive and Apply Monies Raised by Sub-
scription, to Purchase, or Cause to be
Printed, Suitable Religious Tracts for
Distribution. 104633
Congregational Churches in Connecticut. Hart-
ford County North Association. 94926,
6th note after 103650
Congregational Churches in Connecticut. Litchfield Association. 41469
Congregational Churches in Connecticut. Litchfield North Consociation. 41472, 63916
see also Congregational Churches in
Connecticut. Convention of the North and
South Consociations of Litchfield, 1852.
Congregational Churches in Connecticut. Litch-
field South Association. (28908), 90761
Congregational Churches in Connecticut. Litchfield South Association. Registrar.
(41473)
Congregational Churches in Connecticut. Litch-
field South Consociation. 41471-41472
see also Congregational Churches in
Connecticut. Convention of the North
and South Consociations of Litchfield,
1852.
Congregational Churches in Connecticut. New
Haven Center Association. 52972
Congregational Churches in Connecticut. New
Haven County Association. 7655, 33431,
(52975), 52984, 71829, 91756, 96091,
note after 97187, 103618
Congregational Churches in Connecticut. New
Haven County Association. Scribe.
33431, 52984, note after 97187 see also
Trumbull, Benjamin, 1735-1820.
Congregational Churches in Connecticut. New
Haven County Western Association.
90666, 102965
Congregational Churches in Connecticut. New
Haven East Consociation. 52961
Congregational Churches in Connecticut. North
Association in the County of Hartford.
see Congregational Churches in Con-
necticut. Hartford County North Asso-
ciation.

Congregational Churches in Connecticut.
Ordination Council, Meriden, 1769.
33431-33432

Congregational Churches in Connecticut. Saybrook Synod, 1708. 15447-15448, 15814,
23414, 32307, 63343, (77391)-77394

Congregational Churches in Connecticut. Tolland County Association. 18, 71889, 3d
note after 96123, 104315

Congregational Churches in Connecticut. West
Stafford Association. 25232, 73562,
102947

Congregational Churches in Connecticut. Western Association of New Haven County.
see Congregational Churches in Connecticut. New Haven County Western
Association.

Congregational Churches in Connecticut. Western Consociation in Fairfield County.
see Congregational Churches in Connecticut. Fairfield County Western
Consociation.

Congregational Churches in Connecticut.
Windham County Association. 63946,
(80370)-80371, 91733, note after 100602,
102522, 104759, 2d note after 104760,
104761

Congregational Churches in Connecticut.
Windham County Consociation. (63288),
102523, 104559, 104763

Congregational Churches in Connecticut.
Windham County Convention, 1800.
(63288), 104762

Congregational Churches in Connecticut.
Windham County Eastern Association.
13012, 104760

Congregational Churches in England. 63343

Congregational Churches in Iowa. General
Association. 34978

Congregational Churches in Illinois. General
Association. (34213)

Congregational Churches in Illinois. General
Association. Committee of Investigation
on the Rights of Congregationalists in
Knox College. 2738, 34214, 38188

Congregational Churches in Illinois. Illinois
Association, Quincy. 34297

Congregational Churches in Illinois. Illinois
Association, Quincy. petitioners 11125

Congregational Churches in Kansas. General
Association. 37072

Congregational Churches in Maine. Cumberland Association. 17880, 85224

Congregational Churches in Maine. Ecclesiastical Council, Bloomfield, 1848. 5992

Congregational Churches in Maine. Ecclesiastical Council, North Yarmouth, 1822.
70108

Congregational Churches in Maine. Ecclesiastical Council, Portland, 1812. 49138

Congregational Churches in Maine. Ecclesiastical Council, Portland, 1856. 64379

Congregational Churches in Maine. General
Conference. 44000-44001, (43935),
64985

Congregational Churches in Maine. Kennebec
Conference. 37383

Congregational Churches in Maine. York
County Conference of Churches. 106022

Congregational Churches in Maine. York
County Conference of Churches. Semi-
annual Meeting, Acton, 1839. 106022

Congregational Churches in Maine. York
County Conference of Churches. Semi-
centennial, 1872. 85487

Congregational Churches in Massachusetts.
46160, 46776, 52610, 52621, (63337),
63342, 69921, (75668), 99166 see also
Convention of Congregational Ministers,
Boston, 1759. Convention of Congregational Ministers of Massachusetts. Evangelical Congregational Churches in Massachusetts.

Congregational Churches in Massachusetts.
Barnstable County Ministers. 3554,
103617

Congregational Churches in Massachusetts.
Berkshire Association. 4895, 19848,
24270, 92912

Congregational Churches in Massachusetts.
Berkshire Association. Centennial Commemoration, Stockbridge, Mass., 1863.
32905

Congregational Churches in Massachusetts.
Boston Association. 10743, (14497),
14524, 17675, 18698, 20621, 62774,
94708

Congregational Churches in Massachusetts.
Boston Synod, 1662. 1651, (18703)-18704,
45632, 46103, (46778), 49662, (52609),
57611, 63342, 66059

Congregational Churches in Massachusetts.
Boston Synod, 1662. Dissenting Brethren
and Messengers. 49662, 66059

Congregational Churches in Massachusetts.
Boston Synod, 1679. 46103, (46710)

Congregational Churches in Massachusetts.
Boston Synod, 1680. (10120), 15449,
15486, 57611, 63334-63336, 63342, 68013,
69921, 104901

Congregational Churches in Massachusetts.
Boston Synod, 1716. 46665-46666

Congregational Churches in Massachusetts.
Bristol County Association. 94923

Congregational Churches in Massachusetts.
Brookfield Association. (8247)

Congregational Churches in Massachusetts.
Brookfield Association. Committee.
(8247)

Congregational Churches in Massachusetts.
Cambridge Synod, 1641. (45670)

Congregational Churches in Massachusetts.
Cambridge Synod, 1646. 17059, (70107)

Congregational Churches in Massachusetts.
Cambridge Synod, 1648. (10120), (15486),
46103, 46439, 52632, 57611, 63331-63343,
69921, 104901

Congregational Churches in Massachusetts.
Charlestown Association. see Congre-
gational Churches in Massachusetts.
Boston Association.

Congregational Churches in Massachusetts.
Convention of Ministers, Taunton, 1745.
see Number of Ministers Conven'd at
Taunton, Mass., 1745.

Congregational Churches in Massachusetts.
Council of Six Churches, Woburn, 1746.
see Congregational Churches in Massachusetts. Ecclesiastical Council, Woburn,
1746.

Congregational Churches in Massachusetts.
Ecclesiastical Council, Belchertown, 1723.
64842

Congregational Churches in Massachusetts.
Ecclesiastical Council, Berkley, 1830.
4889B, 65920, 70221, 92834

Congregational Churches in Massachusetts.
Ecclesiastical Council, Bolton, 1773.
6253-6254

Congregational Churches in Massachusetts.
Ecclesiastical Council, Boston, 1723.
22929, (81422), 95162
Congregational Churches in Massachusetts.
Ecclesiastical Council, Boston, 1841.
6652, 101515
Congregational Churches in Massachusetts.
Ecclesiastical Council, Boston, 1866.
70116
Congregational Churches in Massachusetts.
Ecclesiastical Council, Bradford, 1744.
7268, 27584, 103399
Congregational Churches in Massachusetts.
Ecclesiastical Council, Braintree, 1792.
7357
Congregational Churches in Massachusetts.
Ecclesiastical Council, Brimfield, 1801.
7984, 8461, note just before 69458
Congregational Churches in Massachusetts.
Ecclesiastical Council, Concord, 1743.
15137
Congregational Churches in Massachusetts.
Ecclesiastical Council, Danvers, 1852.
70264
Congregational Churches in Massachusetts.
Ecclesiastical Council, Dorchester, 1773.
7095, (20624)-20625, (20628), 69500, note
after 93769
Congregational Churches in Massachusetts
Ecclesiastical Council, Eastham, 1720.
21669
Congregational Churches in Massachusetts.
Ecclesiastical Council, Fitchburg, 1802.
24593-24594, 24600, 105304
Congregational Churches in Massachusetts.
Ecclesiastical Council, Grafton, 1744.
(28200), 103935
Congregational Churches in Massachusetts.
Ecclesiastical Council, Grafton, 1744.
Moderator. (28200), 103935 see also
Wigglesworth, Samuel.
Congregational Churches in Massachusetts.
Ecclesiastical Council, Grafton, 1744.
Scribe. (28200), 103935 see also
Turell, Ebenezer.
Congregational Churches in Massachusetts.
Ecclesiastical Council, Groton, 1826.
(4338), 9623, 28965, 28976, 42460
Congregational Churches in Massachusetts.
Ecclesiastical Council, Greenfield, 1753.
28627
Congregational Churches in Massachusetts.
Ecclesiastical Council, Groton, 1826.
(4338), 9623, 28965; 28976
Congregational Churches in Massachusetts.
Ecclesiastical Council, Ipswich, 1747-
1748. 35047
Congregational Churches in Massachusetts.
Ecclesiastical Council, Ipswich, 1805.
44510, 89813, 99826 see also Spring,
Samuel, 1746-1819.
Congregational Churches in Massachusetts.
Ecclesiastical Council, Ipswich, 1806.
44510
Congregational Churches in Massachusetts.
Ecclesiastical Council, Middleboro, 1822.
58185
Congregational Churches in Massachusetts.
Ecclesiastical Council, New Bedford,
1850. 32627
Congregational Churches in Massachusetts.
Ecclesiastical Council, New Braintree,
1799. 25206
Congregational Churches in Massachusetts.
Ecclesiastical Council, Newton Centre,
1866. 70113

Congregational Churches in Massachusetts.
Ecclesiastical Council, North Wrentham,
1830. 24096, 95158
Congregational Churches in Massachusetts.
Ecclesiastical Council, Northampton,
1750. 21967, 55771
Congregational Churches in Massachusetts.
Ecclesiastical Council, Northampton,
1751. 7663-7664, 21967, 32317
Congregational Churches in Massachusetts.
Ecclesiastical Council, Plymouth, 1832.
70111
Congregational Churches in Massachusetts.
Ecclesiastical Council, Princeton, 1817.
3105, 27695, 70109, 70115
Congregational Churches in Massachusetts.
Ecclesiastical Council, Princeton, 1817.
Minority. 27695, 70109
Congregational Churches in Massachusetts.
Ecclesiastical Council, Reading, 1847.
(68210)
Congregational Churches in Massachusetts.
Ecclesiastical Council, Salem, 1734.
24532, 79415
Congregational Churches in Massachusetts.
Ecclesiastical Council, Salem, 1735.
75669
Congregational Churches in Massachusetts.
Ecclesiastical Council, Salem, 1784.
25038
Congregational Churches in Massachusetts.
Ecclesiastical Council, Salem, 1816.
82895
Congregational Churches in Massachusetts.
Ecclesiastical Council, Salem, 1831.
(75697)
Congregational Churches in Massachusetts.
Ecclesiastical Council, Salem, 1849.
75698-75699
Congregational Churches in Massachusetts.
Ecclesiastical Council, Sandwich, 1817.
(76449)
Congregational Churches in Massachusetts.
Ecclesiastical Council, Stockbridge, 1779.
24528, 33973, 63380
Congregational Churches in Massachusetts.
Ecclesiastical Council, Watertown, 1722.
97093
Congregational Churches in Massachusetts.
Ecclesiastical Council, West Brookfield,
1843. 90691
Congregational Churches in Massachusetts.
Ecclesiastical Council, Woburn, 1746.
35407, 86604, 104972
Congregational Churches in Massachusetts.
Ecclesiastical Council, Woburn, 1746.
Moderator. 35407, 104972 see also
Williams, William, 1688-1760.
Congregational Churches in Massachusetts.
Ecclesiastical Council, Worcester, 1820.
57602, 1st note after 105357, 105358
Congregational Churches in Massachusetts.
Ecclesiastical Council, Wrentham, 1830.
105523
Congregational Churches in Massachusetts.
Ecclesiastical Councils, Greenfield, 1813.
28628, 104118
Congregational Churches in Massachusetts.
Essex South Conference. 75699
Congregational Churches in Massachusetts.
Ex-Parte Council, Hollis Street Church,
Boston, 1839. 6652, 62768
Congregational Churches in Massachusetts.
Ex-Parte Council, 1st-3d, Rehoboth, 1825.
68972, 95524

Congregational Churches in Massachusetts.
Ex-Parte Council, Wareham, 1845.
56049
Congregational Churches in Massachusetts.
Franklin Association. 24280, 25646
see also Franklin Association Charitable Society.
Congregational Churches in Massachusetts.
General Association. 45738, 45739,
45740, 46118, 52768, 66037, 85218
Congregational Churches in Massachusetts.
General Association. Committee. 420,
2d note after 91736
Congregational Churches in Massachusetts.
General Association. Committee of
Correspondence with Southern Ecclesiastical Bodies on Slavery. 82051
Congregational Churches in Massachusetts.
General Association of Massachusetts
Proper. see Congregational Churches
in Massachusetts. General Association.
Congregational Churches in Massachusetts.
General Conference. see Congregational
Churches in Massachusetts. General
Association.
Congregational Churches in Massachusetts.
Hampshire Central Association. 97076
see also Hampshire Association Charitable Association.
Congregational Churches in Massachusetts.
Hampshire County Association. 7656,
(7660)-7661, 21939, (30136), 94626, 6th
note after 103650
Congregational Churches in Massachusetts.
Hampshire County Northern Association.
30142, 79295
Congregational Churches in Massachusetts.
Marlborough Association. 94923
Congregational Churches in Massachusetts.
Mendon Association. (47820)
Congregational Churches in Massachusetts.
Ministers Convened at Taunton, 1745.
see Number of Ministers Conven'd at
Taunton, Mass., 1745.
Congregational Churches in Massachusetts.
Northern Association in the County of
Hampshire. see Congregational
Churches in Massachusetts. Hampshire
County Northern Association.
Congregational Churches in Massachusetts.
Pilgrim Conference. 78129
Congregational Churches in Massachusetts.
South Middlesex Conference of Churches.
63765, note after 88147
Congregational Churches in Massachusetts.
Western Association upon Merrimack
River. 86726, 2d note after 103650
Congregational Churches in Massachusetts.
Weymouth Association. 53311, 92107,
101174
Congregational Churches in Massachusetts.
Worcester Central Association. Auxiliary
Foreign Mission Society. 105335-105336
Congregational Churches in Massachusetts.
Worcester North Vicinity. see Congregational Churches in Massachusetts.
Worcester North Association.
Congregational Churches in Massachusetts.
Worcester North Association. Auxiliary
Foriegn Mission Society. 105337
Congregational Churches in Michigan. General
Association. 48775
Congregational Churches in Minnesota. General Conference. 49296

Congregational Churches in New England.
18710, 46776, 52620, 63343, 63346,
95739 see also Boston. Assembly of
Pastors of Churches in New England,
1743. Convention of Congregational
Ministers of New England.
Congregational Churches in New Hampshire.
see also Convention of Congregational
Ministers in New Hampshire, Concord,
1791.
Congregational Churches in New Hampshire.
Association of Ministers of Piscataqua
River. see Congregational Churches in
New Hampshire. Piscataqua River Association.
Congregational Churches in New Hampshire.
Cheshire County Conference. (12515)
Congregational Churches in New Hampshire.
Council of Ten Churches, Exeter, 1743.
see Congregational Churches in New
Hampshire. Ecclesiastical Council,
Exeter, 1743.
Congregational Churches in New Hampshire.
Ecclesiastical Council, Boscawen, 1833.
6446, 7779
Congregational Churches in New Hampshire.
Ecclesiastical Council, Exeter, 1743.
23391, 70106
Congregational Churches in New Hampshire
Ecclesiastical Council, Exeter, 1743.
Moderator. 23391, 70106 see also
Newmarsh, John.
Congregational Churches in New Hampshire
Ecclesiastical Council, Exeter, 1743.
Scribe. 23391, 70106 see also Prescott, Benjamin, 1687-1777
Congregational Churches in New Hampshire.
Ecclesiastical Council, Exeter, 1842.
23392-(23393), 70110
Congregational Churches in New Hampshire.
Ecclesiastical Council, Haverhill, 1758.
2602-2603, 12857, 29853, 31052
Congregational Churches in New Hampshire.
Ecclesiastical Council, Haverhill, 1759.
2602, 12857, 29853
Congregational Churches in New Hampshire.
Ecclesiastical Council, Holles, 1812.
105235
Congregational Churches in New Hampshire.
Ecclesiastical Council, Portsmouth, 1834.
64431
Congregational Churches in New Hampshire.
General Association. 52823-52824,
(52836), 52851-(52852), 52869, 52895,
105328
Congregational Churches in New Hampshire.
Piscataqua River Association. 64997
Congregational Churches in New Hampshire.
Strafford Conference of Churches.
92668
Congregational Churches in New Hampshire.
Windsor Association. 69458
Congregational Churches in New York. see
also Congregational Convention of Long
Island.
Congregational Churches in New York. Ecclesiastical Council, Brooklyn, 1854.
32116
Congregational Churches in New York. Ecclesiastical Council, New York, 1859.
54184
Congregational Churches in New York. General Association. (53679)
Congregational Churches in New York. Genesee Consociation. (22449), 26921

Congregational Churches in Oregon. Congregational Association. (57557)

Congregational Churches in Pennsylvania. 61557

Congregational Churches in Rhode Island. (70717)

Congregational Churches in Rhode Island. Ecclesiastical Council, Providence, 1792-1793. 104637

Congregational Churches in Rhode Island. Ecclesiastical Council, Providence, 1832. 70112

Congregational Churches in Rhode Island. Ecclesiastical Council, Providence, 1835. 80358

Congregational Churches in Rhode Island. Evangelical Consociation. 70581, 82057

Congregational Churches in Rhode Island. Home Missionary Society. 70581, (70717)

Congregational Churches in South Carolina. Congregational Association. 87809-87810

Congregational Churches in the Northwest. Triennial Convention of Ministers and Delegates, Chicago, 1858. 15485

Congregational Churches in the United States. 52621, (65855) see also National Council of Congregational Churches.

Congregational Churches in the United States. Southwestern Conference. 88611

Congregational Churches in Vermont. 99161, 99166

Congregational Churches in Vermont. Addison Consociation. 99162-99165, 99171, 99172

Congregational Churches in Vermont. Consociation of the Western Districts of Vermont and Parts Adjacent. see Congregational Churches in Vermont. Addison Consociation.

Congregational Churches in Vermont. Ecclesiastical Council, Pomfret, 1792. 63946, 94075, 102523

Congregational Churches in Vermont. Ecclesiastical Council, Rupert, 1815. 74146

Congregational Churches in Vermont. General Convention. 99168-99169, 99170, 99224 see also General Convention of Congregational and Presbyterian Ministers of Vermont.

Congregational Churches in Vermont. Montpelier Congregational Association. 50218

Congregational Churches in Vermont. North Western Consociation. 99167

Congregational Churches in Vermont. Western Districts Consociation. see Congregational Churches in Vermont. Addison Consociation.

Congregational Churches in Vermont. Windham County Association. 94075

Congregational Convention, Chicago, 1847. see Presbyterian and Congregational Convention, Chicago, 1847.

Congregational Convention of Long Island. see also Congregational Churches in New York.

Congregational Convention of Long Island, Brookhaven, N. Y., 1808. (27566)

Congregational Education Society, Boston. see American College and Education Society. American Education Society. Society for the Promotion of Collegiate and Theological Education at the West.

Congregational freedom. 3794

Congregational Home Missionary Society. 1101, 54078, 57914, 61186, 104671

Congregational Home Missionary Society. Executive Committee. 62003

Congregational Library Association, Boston. see American Congregational Association, Boston.

Congregational Library of the Union Church and Society, Groton, Mass. see Groton, Mass. Union Church. Congregational Library.

Congregational manual. 39612

Congregational order. 52621

Congregational polity. 75830

Congregational quarterly. 16479, 18098, 21609, 46666, 85409, 85913, 85220, 85221, 95633, note after 104106

Congregational record. 15480

Congregational register. 16331

Congregational singing. 77673

Congregational Society, Owego, N. Y. see Owego, N. Y. Congregational Society.

Congregational tune book. 51888

Congregational Union in Scotland. 81759

Congregational visiter. 15481

Congregationalism. A discourse. 38772

Congregationalism. A premium tract. (63979)

Congregationalism and church-action. 37162

Congregationalism and Methodism. 30989

Congregationalism and symbolism. 80073

Congregationalism, as contained in the scriptures. (15486)

Congregationalism in America. 66658

Congregationalism in western New-York. (20158)

Congregationalism: its principles and influences. 92268

Congregationalism; what is it. 19894

Congregationalist. pseud. Letter from a congregationalist to a friend. 40273

Congregationalist. 19893, (55072)

Congregationalist minister. pseud. Coming of Christ in his kingdom. 14947

Congregatione Sacrorum Rituum siue Eminent. ac Rev. D. Card. Vidono, Limana beatificationis, et canonizationis serui Dei. (64173), 99503

Congregations in New England. see Congregational Churches in New England.

Congres de Americanistes, 1875. see International Congress of Americanists. 1st, Nancy, France, 1875.

Congres de Panama. Par Mr. G. L. (38383)

Congres de Panama, Par M. de Pradt. 64889

Congres de Verone. Guerre d'Espagne. (12253)

Congres de Vienne, etc. etc. 64901

Congres General de l'Amerique Septenrionale. see U. S. Continental Congress.

Congres Geologique International, 1913. see International Geological Congress. 12th, Toronto, 1913.

Congreso de Panama, 1826. 76828

Congreso de Panama; traducido al Castellano. 64890

Congreso del Estado de Queretaro a sus comitantes. 67099

Congreso ha acordado . . . la siguiente ley. 70013

Congreso y el gobierno estan fueran de la ley. 98114

Congress and the President. Judicially reviewed. 90795

Congress and the President; or, who has hindered reconstruction? 36171

Congress and the President. The political problem of 1866. 15629

Congress at Panama. 15489
Congress between the beasts. 33571
Congress canvassed. 29956, (78562)-78563, 78581, 4th note after 100862
Congress of Albany, 1754. see Albany Congress, 1754.
Congress of nations. (15487)
Congress of nations for the peaceful adjustment of all international disputes. 15599
Congress of New Jersey, 1776. see New Jersey. Congress, 1776.
Congress of Paris, 1856. 44605
Congress of the Commissaries of the Colonies of New York and Massachusetts Bay, on the Establishment of a Partition Line of Jurisdiction Between the Two Provinces, New Haven, Conn., 1767. (15431), 36738, 45689
Congress of the Confederate States. Proceedings on the announcement of the death of Col. Francis S. Bartow. 15261
Congress of the Confederate States. Proceedings on the announcement of the death of Hon. John Tyler. 15260
Congress of the Four Southern Governors, with the Superintendent of that District, with the Five Nations of Indians, Augusta, Ga., 1763. (27056), 36718
Congress of the United States: at the second session. note after 94720
Congress of the United States: at the third session. note after 94720
Congress of the United States. In Senate, January the 20th, 1797. (62648)
Congress of the United States. In Senate, May the 3d, 1794. 15517
Congress of Vienna. see Vienna. Congress, 1814-1815.
Congress of Vienna. By M. de Pradt. 64888
Congress on the Subject of the American Stamp Act, New York, 1765. see Stamp Act Congress, New York, 1765.
Congress zu Verona. 12254
Congressional addresses. 15600
Congressional and cabinet excursion. 15602
Congressional & legislative journal. 90493
Congressional banquet in honor of George Washington. 15601
Congressional chart. (15603)
Congressional directory. (15604)
Congressional directory for the first session of the fifteenth Congress of the United States. 15605
Congressional directory for the first session of the 41st Congress. 15606
Congressional directory for the first session of the thirty-ninth Congress of the United States of America. 64097
Congressional directory for the second session of the thirty-ninth Congress. 64097
Congressional display or Spit and Cudgel. 89923, note after 105176
Congressional document. 1338
Congressional globe. see U. S. Congressional globe.
Congressional legislation. (2068)
Congressional manual. 93958
Congressional railroads, their causes and results. 81469
Congressional register. 15608
Congressional report of Hon. Edward Stanley [sic]. 90329
Congressional reporter. (15609)-15610, (31832)
Congressional sovereignty vs. Democratic faith. 34688

Congressional stenographer. pseud. reporter Report of the trial of Pedro Gilbert. 27309, 69915, 93808, 96948
Congressional Temperance Society, Washington, D. C. (15611), note after 101933, 101934
Congressional test act examined. 51038
Congressional Total Abstinence Society, Washington, D. C. 15612
Conjectures about the Americans. (46668)
Conjuncion magna. (47842)
Conjunct expeditions. 49925
Conjuracion de Mejico. 22842
Conklin, Luther. 15614
Conklin, R. H. 15615
Conkling, Alfred. 15616-(15620)
Conkling, C. 15621
Conkling, Edgar. 15622-15624
Conkling, Edgar. supposed author 15623, 44365
Conkling, Frederick Augustus, 1816-1891. 15625, 52077
Conkling, Henry. 15626
Conkling, Margaret C. (15627)
Conkling, Roscoe, 1829-1888. (15628)-15630
Conley, John L. 27033
Conley, John N. 27014
Conmovido el benefico pueblo. 42106
Connaissance de l'ancien et du nouveau-monde. (20544)
Connaissance de l'huile de petrole. 70383A
Conneaut & Beaver Rail Road. 60007
Connected view of the controversy. 39228
Connected view of the geography and present state of that quarter of the globe [i. e. North America.] 5463
Connected view of the geography and present state of that quarter of the globe [i. e. South America.] 5464
Connected view of the whole internal navigation of the United States. 2012-2013, 10860
Connecticut. pseud. Scripture tract for the times. 78499
Connecticut (Colony) 14122, 15797, 15801, 16747, 24588, 32968, 36351, 36925, 53435, 66519, note after 68297, note after 98296, 98478
Connecticut (Colony) defendants 15748, 36351, 45454, 45455
Connecticut (Colony) respondents 15748-15752
Connecticut (Colony) Census, 1756. (15631)
Connecticut (Colony) Census, 1774. (15631)
Connecticut (Colony) Charter. 1069, 12162-12163, 15634, 15670, 15762, 15766, 15770, (41430), 97189, 1st note after 99889
Connecticut (Colony) Commissioners to the Six Nations of Indians. 34601
Connecticut (Colony) Commissioners to Treat with the Proprietaries of Pennsylvania Respecting the Boundaries. 15685, 93936
Connecticut (Colony) Constitution. 14122
Connecticut (Colony) Council. 15797, 24577, 66519
Connecticut (Colony) Council of War. 25797, 66519
Connecticut (Colony) Court of Vice-Admiralty, New London. 81390
Connecticut (Colony) Election Sermon. see Connecticut. Election Sermon.
Connecticut (Colony) General Assembly. 15754, 16688, (18262), 20987, 100986, 104220
Connecticut (Colony) General Court. see Connecticut (Colony) General Assembly.
Connecticut (Colony) Governor. 31963
Connecticut (Colony) Governor, 1683-1698 (Treat) 15860, note after 95296 see also Treat, Robert, 1622-1710.

Connecticut (Colony) Governor, 1708-1724 (Saltonstall) 15823, 75854 see also Saltonstall, Gurdon, 1666-1724.

Connecticut (Colony) Governor, 1754-1766 (Fitch) 15855, 24589, 77394, 86728 see also Fitch, Thomas, 1700-1774.

Connecticut (Colony) Governor, 1769-1783 (Trumbull) 36925, 93936, 97252-97254, 97290 see also Trumbull, Jonathan, 1710-1785.

Connecticut (Colony) Governor and Company. respondents see Connecticut (Colony) respondents

Connecticut (Colony) Inferior Court of Pleas. 9095

Connecticut (Colony) Landholders. respondents 15750, 15752

Connecticut (Colony) Laws, statutes, etc. 6010, 14122, 15632, 15634, 15674, 15754-15758, 15761-15762, 15765, 39410, 39414, (73483)

Connecticut (Colony) Militia. 63289

Connecticut (Colony) Militia. Third Regiment. 68808

Connecticut (Colony) Secretary. (15860), note after 95296 see also Allyn, John. supposed author

Connecticut (Colony) Treaties, etc. 34601

Connecticut. 15789-15790, (15807)-15810, (15829), 24588, 33149, note after 68297, 74340, 93936

Connecticut. Adjutant General's Office. 15784-15785 see also Ingersoll, Colin Macrae, 1819-1903.

Connecticut. Anti-masonic State Convention, Hartford, 1830. see Anti-masonic State Convention of Connecticut, Hartford, 1830.

Connecticut. Bank Commissioners. see Connecticut. Office of Bank Commissioners.

Connecticut. Board of Agriculture. see Connecticut. State Board of Agriculture.

Connecticut. Board of Commissioners of Common Schools. 3469, 15718, 15722, 15725, 15728

Connecticut. Board of Commissioners of Common Schools. Secretary. 15722

Connecticut. Board of Education. 15719

Connecticut. Board of Education. Secretary. 15719

Connecticut. Census, 1783. 93034

Connecticut. Census, 1854. 15746

Connecticut. Central Asylum for the Education of the Deaf and Dumb. 15694

Connecticut. Commissioner of the School Fund. see Connecticut. School Fund Commissioner.

Connecticut. Commissioners on Idiocy. 15695

Connecticut. Commissioners on the Housatonic Railroad. 33173

Connecticut. Commissioners on the Protection of Fish in the Connecticut River. 15871

Connecticut. Commissioners on the Western Boundary Line Between Connecticut and New York. 15686

Connecticut. Comptroller of Public Accounts. see Connecticut. Comptroller's Office.

Connecticut. Comptroller's Office. 15746, 15842

Connecticut. Constitution. 1269, 1271, 2071, 5316, 6360, 15763, 15775, 16086-16092, 16097, 16099-16103, 16107, 16113, 16118-16120, 16133, (19476), 25790, 33137, (47188), 59711, (66397), 100342, 104198

Connecticut. Convention, 1788. 22233, note after 106002

Connecticut. Delegation to the Constitutional Convention, Philadelphia, 1787. 80405

Connecticut. Democratic State Convention, Middletown, 1828. see Democratic Party. Connecticut. Convention, Middletown, 1828.

Connecticut. Democratic State Convention, Middletown, 1835. see Democratic Party. Connecticut. Convention, Middletown, 1835.

Connecticut. Education Society. see Education Society of Connecticut.

Connecticut. Election Sermon. here are entered all Connecticut election sermons. duplicate entries will be found under respective authors and titles. 195, 2622-2623, (3891), (4496), 6056, 8164, 8690, 9375, 9687, 11828, 12336, (12338), 14216, 18125, 18417, 19829-19830, 20023, 20746, 21563, 21970, 21995, 22004, 22007, 22130, 22137, 22272, 22393, (23025), 23165, 24437, 24579, 25529, 24763, 27883, 27884, 29842, 30637, 31809, 32308, 32812, 32827, 33112, 33836, 33949, (34745), 36322, (39547), 39720, 40810, 41749, 41753, 42012, 42633, 42806, 43230, 44744, 44750-44751, 46207, 46768, 51090, 56041, 60965, 61041, 68128, 71734, 74381, 75846, 75853, 82217, 83743, 91051, 91749-91750, 91758, 91930, 92129, 92937, 92966, 93954, 94525, 95759, 96090, 97183, 100986, 101028, 102520, 102546, 102572, 103066, 103168, 103456, 103699, 103733, 103747, 103760, 103788, 103790, 104073, 104208, 104217, 104316, 104561, 105084, 105088, 105091, 105161, 105508

Connecticut. Federal Legislative Caucus. see Federal Party. Connecticut.

Connecticut. General Assembly. 15675, 15735, 15742-15744, 15746, 15763, 15775, 15776, 15778, 15781, 15788, 15796, 15849-15850, 15852, (18262), 74305, 91398, 97251

Connecticut. General Assembly. Committee of Defence. 15830

Connecticut. General Assembly. Committee on Housatanic Railroad Company. 15800

Connecticut. General Assembly. Committee on Jarvis Divorce Case. 35817

Connecticut. General Assembly. Committee on State Prison. (15793)

Connecticut. General Assembly. Committee on the Baptist Petition. 510

Connecticut. General Assembly. Committee on the Governor's Speech. 15831

Connecticut. General Assembly. Committee on the Insane Poor. (15838)

Connecticut. General Assembly. Committee on the Licence Laws. 15834

Connecticut. General Assembly. Committee on the New Haven Ward Bill. 53011

Connecticut. General Assembly. Committee on the Petition of East Hartford. (21648), 30672

Connecticut. General Assembly. Committee on the Petition of Yale College. 105798

Connecticut. General Assembly. Committee on the Punishment and Reformation of Juvenile Offenders. (15793)

Connecticut. General Assembly. Committee to Inspect the Condition of New-Gate Prison. (15793)

Connecticut. General Assembly. Committee to Visit and Examine the Banks. (15679)

Connecticut. General Assembly. Joint Committee on Capital Punishment. (15793), 15839

Connecticut. General Assembly. Joint Committee on Common Schools. 15718, 15735

Connecticut. General Assembly. Joint Committee on Federal Relations. (69872)

Connecticut. General Assembly. Joint Committee on Hartford Bridge Company. (30658), 30672

Connecticut. General Assembly. Joint Committee on Internal Improvements. 15836

Connecticut. General Assembly. Joint Committee on Public Lands. 15835

Connecticut. General Assembly. Joint Committee on Repudiation of State Debts. 15841

Connecticut. General Assembly. Joint Committee on the Governor's Message, 1834. 15833

Connecticut. General Assembly. Joint Committee on the Governor's Message, as Relates to Capital Punishment, 1850. 15843

Connecticut. General Assembly. Joint Committee on the Proposed Navy Yard at New London. 15844 see also Committee Appointed by the Secretary of the Navy and the Legislature of Connecticut, on the Navy Yard at New London.

Connecticut. General Assembly. Joint Committee on the Tariff. 15840

Connecticut. General Assembly. Joint Standing Committee on Education. 15730-15731

Connecticut. General Assembly. Joint Standing Committee on Prisons. (15793)

Connecticut. General Assembly. Joint Standing Committee on the Public Domain. 15837

Connecticut. General Assembly. House of Representatives. 15740, 15742, 15850, 15852, 27956

Connecticut. General Assembly. Senate. 15741, 15850, 15852, 27956, (69872)

Connecticut. General Hospital Society. see General Hospital Society of Connecticut.

Connecticut. General State Hospital for the Insane. Board of Trustees. (15696)

Connecticut. Geological and Natural History Survey. 60869, 80167

Connecticut. Governor, 1776-1783 (Trumbull) see Connecticut (Colony) Governor, 1769-1783 (Trumbull)

Connecticut. Governor, 1784-1786 (Griswold) 15744 see also Griswold, Matthew, 1714-1799.

Connecticut. Governor, 1811-1813 (Griswold) 15744, 15831-15832, 28889 see also Griswold, Roger, 1762-1812.

Connecticut. Governor, 1813-1818 (Smith) 33150, 82936 see also Smith, John Cotton, 1765-1845.

Connecticut. Governor, 1818-1827 (Wolcott) 10889, 22987 see also Wolcott, Oliver, 1760-1833.

Connecticut. Governor, 1833-1834 (Edwards) 15833 see also Edwards, Henry Waggaman, 1779-1847.

Connecticut. Governor, 1838-1842 (Ellsworth) 22347 see also Ellsworth, William Wolcott, 1791-1868.

Connecticut. Governor, 1842-1844 (Cleveland) 15839, 15841 see also Cleveland, Chauncey Fitch, 1799-1887.

Connecticut. Governor, 1846-1847 (Toucey) 54725 see also Toucey, Isaac, 1796-1869.

Connecticut. Governor, 1850-1853 (Seymour) 15843 see also Seymour, Thomas Hart, 1807-1868.

Connecticut. Governor, 1858-1866 (Buckingham) 15744, 15785, 33150 see also Buckingham, William Alfred, 1804-1875.

Connecticut. Governor's Foot Guard. 1st Company, Hartford. 65764

Connecticut. Laws, statutes, etc. 15633, 15635, (15710), 15725, 15729, 15745, 15760-15761, 15763, 15764, 15766, 15768, 15769-15781, 15783, (15793), 15798, 15806, 15827, 15848, 16078, 18117, 23765, 28722, 30670, 30677, 39414, 39969, 48010, 52051, (52955), 52967-52968, 52990, 52998, 53262, 54839, 55920, 55924, 70820-70821, (81943), 82438, 84464, 85170, 85831, 85870, 91398, 94078, 97177, 101998, 102339, 103710, 105844

Connecticut. Militia. Paymaster General. 15786

Connecticut. Militia. Quartermaster General. 15788

Connecticut. Missionary Society. see Missionary Society of Connecticut.

Connecticut. Office of Bank Commissioners. 15677-15678

Connecticut. School Fund Commissioner. 15735-89346 see also Hillhouse, James.

Connecticut. Secretary of State. 15797, 15846, 31963, 66519, 82936 see also Day, John.

Connecticut. Society for Promoting Agriculture. see Society for Promoting Agriculture in the State of Connecticut.

Connecticut. State Agent for the Care of Soldiers. 15787

Connecticut. State Board of Agriculture. Secretary. 15655

Connecticut. State Librarian. 15851 see also Hoadly, Charles J.

Connecticut. State Normal School. Trustees. 15734

Connecticut. State Prison, Wethersfield. Directors. (15793)

Connecticut. State Prison, Wethersfield. Warden. (15793), 62867 see also Pilsbury, Amos.

Connecticut. State Reform School. Trustees. 15732

Connecticut. Superintendent of Common Schools. 15724

Connecticut. Superior Court. (16211), (73132), 92380, 96922

Connecticut. Supreme Court of Errors. (16211), (73132), 92380

Connecticut. Treasurer. see Connecticut. Treasury Department.

Connecticut. Treasury Department. 15673

Connecticut Academy of Arts and Sciences. 15701-15704, 15858, 21556, 21557, 24273, 50839, 82939, 2d note after 90803

Connecticut Academy of Arts and Sciences. A statistical account of the towns and parishes. (15702)

Connecticut Academy of Arts and Sciences. (Proposals for a statistical history of Connecticut.) 15701

611

Connecticut almanack. 15669
Connecticut almanack, for . . . 1780. 92985
Connecticut almanack, for . . . 1781. 92986
Connecticut almanack, for . . . 1778. (15661), 92983
Connecticut almanack, for . . . 1775. 92980
Connecticut almanack, for . . . 1779. By Hosea Stafford. 93030
Connecticut almanack, for . . . 1779. By the Professor of Mathematics, in Yale College. 92984
Connecticut almanack, for . . . 1777. 92982
Connecticut almanack, for . . . 1776. 92981
Connecticut almanack, or astronomical calendar. 65680
Connecticut and Passumpsic Rail Road, 1847 15799
Connecticut and Passumpsic Rivers Rail Road Company. Directors. 15800
Connecticut Anti-masonic State Convention, Hartford, 1830. see Anti-masonic State Convention of Connecticut, Hartford, 1830.
Connecticut Antimasonic Tract Association. 103825
Connecticut aroused! 37644
Connecticut Association, Massachusetts. 15738
Connecticut Association, Massachusetts. Festival, Boston, 1857. 15738
Connecticut Asylum for the Education and Instruction of Deaf and Dumb Persons, Hartford. see American School for the Deaf, Hartford, Conn.
Connecticut Baptist annual. 92164
Connecticut Baptist Convention. see Baptists. Connecticut. Convention.
Connecticut Bible Society. 15705
Connecticut Bible Society. Directing Committee. (15698)
Connecticut business directory. 15706
Connecticut Centennial Association. see Centennial Association of Connecticut.
Connecticut civil officer. 55318
Connecticut common school journal. 15728
Connecticut Colonization Society. Managers. 15697, 81799
Connecticut courant. 82878, 86895, 91397-91398, 91400, 91405, 93021, 95819, 97210, 97232, 102393
Connecticut diary. 52971, 80401
Connecticut dissenters' strong box. 39969
Connecticut ecclesiastical laws. 39969
Connecticut election sermon, May 14, 1741. (34745)
Connecticut election sermon, May 10, 1781. 46768
Connecticut election sermon, May 10, 1677. 32827
Connecticut evangelical magazine and religious intelligencer. 15707-15708, 69346, 92975
Connecticut farmer. pseud. Remarks on a pamphlet. see Sherman, Roger, 1721-1793.
Connecticut gazette. 91361, 96092, 106117
Connecticut General Hospital Society. see General Hospital Society of Connecticut, New Haven.
Connecticut gentleman. pseud. Plea. see Huntington, Joseph.
Connecticut Gore title. 15681
Connecticut herald. 30050, 96123, 1st-2d notes after 105926
Connecticut historical collections. 3317

Connecticut Historical Society, Hartford. 3317, 9095, (15710)-15711, 15856, (15860), 64324, (71843), 86758, note after 95296, 97181, 104986
Connecticut Historical Society, Hartford. Charter. (15710)
Connecticut journal. (14394)-14395, 90962, note after 92979, 97189, 105712
Connecticut Land Company. (15680), 15712, 103013
Connecticut magazine. 52992, 80405, 97204
Connecticut magazine, or gentleman's and lady's monthly mirror. 15709
Connecticut, Massachusetts, New-York, and Vermont almanack. 15662, 93016
Connecticut Medical Society. 15783
Connecticut Medical Society. Committee. 15783
Connecticut Medical Society. Conventions. 15783
Connecticut Medical Society. Fellows. 15783
Connecticut Medical Society. President. 15783
Connecticut Missionary Society. see Missionary Society of Connecticut.
Connecticut Mutual Life Insurance Company. (81143)
Connecticut, New-Jersey, Hudson's-River, and Quebec weekly advertiser. 71690
Connecticut-Passumpsic Rivers Railroad Convention, Windsor, Vt., 1836. see Convention for Taking Preliminary Measures for a Railroad Through the Valleys of the Connecticut and Passumpsic Rivers to the Saint Lawrence, Windsor, Vt., 1836.
Connecticut pastor. pseud. Plea for religious newspapers. see Hall, J. D.
Connecticut pocket almanac, 1803. 15663
Connecticut pocket almanac, for . . . 1800. 93026
Connecticut register. 7278, 15660, 15665-15667, (15829), 68816
Connecticut register, and United-States calendar. see Connecticut register.
Connecticut register and United-States record. see Connecticut register.
Connecticut register, being a state calendar. see Connecticut register.
Connecticut register, being an official state calendar. see Connecticut register.
Connecticut republicanism. 5590-5591, 5598, 15875, 95742, 102396, 105939
Connecticut Retreat for the Insane. Medical Visitors. 15695
Connecticut, Rhode-Island, Massachusetts, New-Hampshire, Vermont farmers' almanac. 15664
Connecticut River business directory. 48035
Connecticut River Company. 15872
Connecticut River Steam Boat Company. Board of Examiners. 15870
Connecticut River Valley Agricultural Society. Committees. 77314
Connecticut Society for the Promotion of Freedom and the Relief of Persons Unlawfully Holden in Bondage. petitioners 47745
Connecticut Society of Arts and Sciences. 21971
Connecticut soldiers. 55834
Connecticut Soldiers' Relief Association of Washington City, D. C. 15785
Connecticut State Agricultural Society. 15658
Connecticut State Agricultural Society. Annual Cattle Show and Fair, 2d, Hartford, 1855. (15656)

Connecticut State Agricultural Society. County Societies. 15658

Connecticut State Agricultural Society. Executive Committee. 15658

Connecticut State Convention of National Republican Young Men, Hartford, 1832. see Hartford, Conn. State Convention of National Republican Young Men, 1832.

Connecticut State Convention of Sabbath School Teachers, Hartford, 1857. see State Convention of Sabbath School Teachers, 1st, Hartford, Conn., 1857.

Connecticut Temperance Society. Executive Committee. 15700

Connecticut. The Moheagan Indians against the Governor and Company of Connecticut, and others. The case of the respondents the Governor and Company of the Colony of Connecticut. 15751

Connecticut. The Moheagan Indians against the Governor and Company of Connecticut, and others. The case of the respondents the landholders. 15752

Connecticut Theological Institute, East Windsor, Conn. see Hartford Theological Seminary.

Connecticut town-officer. 103710

Connecticut war record. 15713

Connecticut wide awake songster. 15714

Connecticutensis. pseud. Three letters to Abraham Bishop. see Daggett, David. supposed author and Webster, Noah, 1758-1843.

Connecticut's flood. 98059

Connection between liberty and eloquence. 91770

Connection between moral and intellectual improvement. 18399

Connection between the agriculture and manufactures of Canada. 93542

Connection of the Church of England with early American discovery and colonization. 61060

Connection of the city of Cambridge with the Cambridge Water Works. 10155

Connectional centenary documents. 48207

Connell, John. 15876

Connell, John M. USA 15877

Connelley, William Elsey, 1855-1932. 85376

Connelly, Pierce. 15878

Conner, Frances. plaintiff (15879)

Conner, Morgan. USA 101699

Connery, Edward D. 15880

Conness, John, 1821-1909. 15881-15882

Connexion between literature and commerce. 9410

Connexion between the civil and religious state of society. 88953

Connoissance de l'ancien et du nouveau monde. 19359, 3d note after 100846

Connolly, --------. 85243

Connolly, M. 74759

Conocimiento de los tiempos. (8998)

Conocimiento de los tiempos, ephemeride del ano de 1769. 15884

Conocimiento de los tiempos. Ephemeride del ano de 1725. 15883, 41090

Conover, --------. 66001

Conover, O. M. ed. 55745

Conoy Indians. 49348-49349

Conoy Indians. Treaties, etc. 36337, 60255

Conpadre. pseud. Sustos a los regatones. 93942

Conquering republic. 28674

Conquerors. A poem. 15885

Conquerors of the new world and their bondsmen. 31275

Conquest of America, and minor poems. 30850

Conquest of California. (23868)

Conquest of California and New Mexico. (18208)

Conquest of California and travels in Oregon. 23869

Conquest of Canaan; a poem. 21548

Conquest of Canada. 101274

Conquest of Canada; or the siege of Quebec. 14109

Conquest of chivalry in the . . . XIX century. 30762

Conquest of Florida, by Hernando de Soto. 35120

Conquest of Florida, under Hernando de Soto. 35121

Conquest of Kansas. 62532

Conquest of Louisbourg. 15886, (47154)

Conquest of Mexico. 82808, 97196

Conquest of Mexico. An appeal to the citizens of the United States. 48376

Conquest of Mexico, an opera, Italian and English. 6823

Conquest of Mexico: as related by a father to his children. 10285

Conquest of Mexico by Cortes. 14650

Conquest of Mexico. By Hernando Cortez and Francisco Pizarro. (15887)

Conquest of Mexico. By T. C. R. 67382

Conquest of Mexico by the Spaniards. 20979

Conquest of ocean. 7086

Conquest of Peru. 82808, 97196

Conquest of Peru. An account of Pedro de la Gasca. 92228

Conquest of Peru: being a continuation of The discovery of America. (10304)

Conquest of Peru, by Francis Pizarro. 20183

Conquest of Peru [by Hernando Cortez.] 16045

Conquest of Peru by Pizarro. 14650

Conquest of Quebec. A poem. By Joseph Hazard. 31097

Conquest of Quebec: a poem. By Middleton. Howard. 33272, 58036

Conquest of Quebec. An epic poem. 51459

Conquest of Santa Fe and the subjugation of New Mexico. 15888

Conquest of Siberia. 17309

Conquest of the Indies. 20585, 31381

Conquest of the late enemy. 78323

Conquest of the Pequods, Narragansets and Pokanokets. 12714, (76379)

Conqueste de l'empire de la Chine par les Tartares. 4936

Conqueste van Indien. 106257-106258

Conquests and triumphs of grace. 47152

Conquete du Mexique, par C. F. van der Velde. 98818

Conquete du Mexique par Fernand Cortez. Guerre de l'Independance. 51408

Conquete du Mexique par Fernand Cortez; suivie de quelques documents officiels. 15889

Conquete du Mexique. Par J. C. Roche. 72310

Conquete du Mexique, opera en trois actes. (36768), 89596

Conquere du Mexique, poeme en dix chants. 73482

Conquete du Perou. 63175

Conquista, colonizacion, gobiernos coloniales y gobiernos independientes. 27343

Conquista de la Nueva Castilla, poema eroico. 56240, note after 89754

Conquista de las islas Malvcas. 1946
Conquista de Mejico. 27733
Conquista de Mexico, cabeza del imperio septentrional de la Nueva-Espana. 74025
Conquista de Mexico, de Don Fernando de Zarate. 106275
Conquista de Mexico. Segvnda parte de la Chronica General de las Indias Occidentales. 27726
Conquista de Mexico, y de la Nueua Espana. 3350, 27724-27725
Conquista del Megico por Hernan Cortes. 50119
Conquista del Nuevo-Mundo. 86471
Conquista del Peru. 57989, 105723-105724
Conqvista del Perv et provincia del Cusco chiamata la Nuoua Castiglia. 67740
Conqvista del Perv & prouencia del Cuzco de la Indie Occidentali. 105722
Conqvista del Perv & prouincia del Cuzco de la Indie Occidentali. 105721
Conquista del Peru llamada la Nueua Castilla. (61097), 63176
Conquista del Peru. Novela historica original. 58068
Conquista del Peru. Poema heroico. 60852, 63182
Conquista del Peru, y viaje de Hernando Pizarro. 105724
Conquista del Rio de la Plata. 3371, (11677)
Conqvista dell' India Occidentali. 11234-11235, 11248
Conquista espiritual. 74039
Conqvista espiritval hecha por los religiosos de la Compania de Iesus. 74029
Conqvista y antigvedades de las islas de la Gran Canaria. 56337
Conquistador anonimo. 16951
Conquistas de las islas Philipinas. (75996)
Conquistas espirituales y temporales de estos Espanoles dominos. 36799
Conquisto di Messico. 44441
Conqvsta [sic] del Perv et provincia del Cusco chiamata la Nuoua Castiglia. 105724
Conrad, Charles Magill, 1804-1878. 15890, (71426)
Conrad, David Holmes. 15891
Conrad, F. W. 15892-15893
Conrad, I. A. 15894
Conrad, John. (1260)
Conrad, Robert Taylor, 1810-1858. 15895-15898, 26099, 61839, 76400-76403 see also Philadelphia. Mayor, 1854 (Conrad)
Conrad, Timothy Abbott, 1803-1887. (1712), 12430, 15899-15906, 22538, 27419, 38491, 46816, 69946, 77368
Conrade; or, the gamesters. 101457
Conroy, John Joseph, Bp., 1819-1895. 72922 see also Albany (Diocese) Bishop (Conroy)
Consag, Fernando. 15907
Consanguinity of the families of Gibbs and Mitchell. 49667
Conscience, Andre. 15908
Conscience and civil government. 27495
Conscience and the constitution. 13362, 35863, 60952, 82074, 93197
Conscience and the state. 31218
Conscience stricken brigand. 83006
Conscience the best friend upon earth. 93222-93223
Conscript. 29482
Conscrip act. 9638
Conscription. 15909
Conscription act. (43876)

Conscription act vindicated. 31887
"Conscription act." Will laboring men vote for Seymour? 15910
Conscription case. 34727
Conscription reviewed by the people. 20804
Conseca, J. J. (19269)
Consecrated talents. 15911
Consecration of St. John's Memorial Chapel, Cambridge. 21663
Consecration of the flag. 15912
Consecratory exercises. 71654
Consecuencias de la buena y de la mala educacion. 73863
Consecuencias de la revolucion. 99482
Conseil de la Guadeloupe. (29039)
Conseil de Liquidation. Doutes et preventions. 15915
Conseil des colons de Saint-Domingue. 4085
Conseil d'Etat au peuple et l'armee de terre et de mer de Hayti. 15913
Conseil Souvereign de la Martinique. see Martinique. Conseil.
Conseiller du peuple ou reflexions adressees aux Canadiens Francais. 4165
Conseils aux Europeens qui passent dans les pays chauds. (18577)-18578
Conseils aux libreaux. 42898, 1st note after 100806
Conseils de Washington au peuple Americaine. (16121)
Conseils hygieniques en faveur des Europeens destines a passer aux iles. (19694)
Consejo de Espana e Indias a la America Espanola. 15916
Consejo de hombres buenos. 36438
Consejo de la Regencia de Espana y Indias a la America Espanola. 15917
Consejos al pueblo Mexicano. 99658
Conselheiro Francisco Jose Furtado. 26244
Conselheiro Manoel Joaquim do Amaral Gurgel. 29288
Conselhos que da um Brasileiro veterano. 15918, (18234)
Conselumbia. 83548
Consent. 46445
Consequences . . . . De la mer. 46974
Consequences (not before adverted to) that are likely to result. (15919)
Consequences of the bill now depending in favour of the Sugar colonies. 102824
Consequences of trade, &c. 15920
Conservacion de monarqvias y discvrsos politicos. (52108)
Conservador matritense num. 7. y 16. 96506
Conservador, periodico de politica. 15921
Conservadores quieren perder la republica. 56271
Conservative. pseud. Bank bills. 3173
Conservative; a quarterly publication. 15922
Conservative elements of American civilization. 50449
Conservative essays legal and political. (55172), 88002
Conservative Members of the Legislature of Nebraska Territory. see Nebraska (Territory) Legislature. Conservative Members.
Conservative New York merchant. pseud. Political jottings and clippings. 63781
Conservative whig. pseud. Duty of conservative whigs in the present crisis. see Quincy, Josiah, 1772-1864. supposed author and Rogers, Henry B. supposed author
Conservatism and reform. 31213
Considedations [sic] in answer to a pamphlet. 15945

Considerable advantage of a South-Sea trade.
15923
Considerable stock-holder. pseud. Equiry
into the misconduct and frauds. 88181
Consideraciones generales sobre la bondad de
un gobierno. 72269
Consideraciones sobre fronteras y colonias.
(57639)
Consideraciones sobre la navegacion de vapor
y plan para establecarla. 56404
Consideraciones sobre la posibilidad de es-
tableceo uno gno. jeneral en Centro-
America. 32756
Consideraciones sobre la requeza del Peru.
3639
Consideraciones sobre la revolucion seismica.
70169
Consideraciones sobre la situacion politica y
social. (15924)
Consideraciones sobre las leyes de confiscacion
de Colombia. 98872
Consideraciones sobre peligros de independencia.
(67122)
Consideracoes sobre a revolucao Rio-Grandense.
85623
Consideracoes sobre algumas vias de com-
municacao. (57900)
Considerant, Victor. 15925-15928
Consideratie, over de tegenwoordige ghele-
gentheydt van Brasil. 7553
Consideratie, overgeleveret by de Heeren
Bewinthebberen van de Oost-Indische
Compagnie. 15929, note after 102887
Consideratien der Gecommitteerdens uyt de
Hollandsche Raden en Ministers. 47767,
4th note after 102895
Consideratien ende andtwoorden by de Heeren
Bewinthebberen vande Oost-Indische
Compagnie. 69586, 3d note after 102911
Consideratien ende rederen der E, Heeren
Bewind-hebberen vande Geoctroijeerde
West-Indische Compagnie. 15930-15932,
102888
Consideratien op de cautie van Portugael.
15933
Consideratien op de Memorie aan H. H. MM.
geadresseerd door John Adams. 230,
(15934), 98504
Consideratien over de critique toestand der
colonien. 102857
Consideratien tot wederlegginge van de voor-
stellingen door de Heer Mr. Nicholas
Muys van Holy. 15613, 15935, 1st note
after 102888, 102896
Consideratien van Bewinthebberen der Generale
Geoctroyeerde Nederlantse West-Indische
Compagnie. 93854, 2d note after 102888
Consideration of some of the commercial &
manufacturing wants. 12185
Consideration of some unconstitutional measures.
58888
Consideration of the claims and conduct of the
United States. 5924
Consideration of the plans proposed for the
improvement of the Ohio River. 30857
Consideration of the rebellion against the govern-
ment of the United States. 90439
Consideration on the employment of the press,
&c. 15984
Consideration over der directie van der Colonie
van Surinam. 86846
Considerations addressed to all persons of
property in Great Britain. 15936
Considerations addressed to churchmen.
(47245)

Considerations addressed to professors of
Christianity. 15937, 102825
Considerations addressed to the laity of the
Protestant Episcopal Church. 40861
Considerations addressed to the members of
the Yearly Meeting of Friends, of
Philadelphia. 15938, (23142), 61558
Considerations against continuing the great
canal. 15939, note after (63430)
Considerations against laying any new duty upon
sugar. 15940, 1st note after 102825,
102826
Considerations against the admission of
Missouri. 11596
Considerations and arguments. 371
Considerations and documents. 15941
Considerations and remarks. 15942
Considerations, annotations, &c. upon the
Apologetical narrations. (69679)
Considerations de M. Moreau, dit Saint-Mery.
67522
Considerations d'hygiene publique et de police
medicale. 94426
Considerations en faveur de l'organisation de
ce corps. 7786
Considerations, &c., par un Canadien. 1764
Considerations for a new-year's day. 66225
Considerations for and against a South-American
expedition. 15943
Considerations for bankers, and holders of
United States bonds. 89605
Considerations for the American patriot. 2887
Considerations for the people. (65474)
Considerations for the people of Barre. 73832-
73833
Considerations for the stockholders of the
Providence and Worcester Railroad Co.
66301
Considerations generales sur la geologie de
l'Amerique Meridionale. 67935
Considerations generales sur les trois classes.
15944
Considerations generales sur l'Ocean Atlantique.
37619
Considerations generales sur l'Ocean Pacifique.
(37620)
Considerations geographiques et physiques sur
les nouvelles decouvertes. (8832)-(8833)
Considerations geographiques et physiques sur
les terres australes. (8833)
Considerations geographiques sur l'histoire du
Bresil. 2491
Considerations historiques et politiques sur les
republiques de La Plata. 8387
Considerations hygieniques sur la Nouvelle-
Orleans. 95440
Considerations importantes sur l'abolition
generale. 81937
Considerations in favor of the appointment of
Rufus King. 98409
Considerations in favor of the constitutionality
and beneficial operation of a law. 85147
Considerations in favour of the construction of
a great state road. 4235, 15946
Considerations in favor of the Erie Canal.
22742
Considerations in opposition to the petition.
67274
Considerations in reference to the establishment
of a nation school. (15947)
Considerations in regard to the application of
the Shakers. 97885
Considerations in relation to trade considered
69520
Considerations occasion'd by the Craftsman.
86757

Considerations of the sovereignty, independence, trade and fisheries. 53029
Considerations offered to Parliament. 15948
Considerations on . . . a compulsory reduction. 23753
Considerations on an act of the Legislature of Virginia. 94024, note after 100447, note after 102401
Considerations on an insolvent law. 15950
Considerations on behalf of the colonists. 15949, (21200), 57865
Considerations on both sides. 15951
Considerations on Buache's memoir. 18344
Considerations on certain political transactions of the province of South Carolina. 39923-39924, 87790, note after 87810
Considerations on certain remarks on the Negro slavery and abolition questions. note after 92630
Considerations on emancipation. 15952
Considerations on fixing the supplies. 15953
Considerations on keeping Negroes. 105196
Considerations on land-granting and emigration. 6848
Considerations on lowering the value of gold coins. (15954), 95159
Considerations on measures for the discovery and relief of our absent adventurers. (78170)
Considerations on Negro slavery. 43172
Considerations on pure wisdom, and human policy. 105197
Considerations on representative government. 48987
Considerations on slavery. (4673)
Considerations on slavery. Addressed to Christians. 15956, 81938
Considerations on slavery, and the expediency of its abolition. 15955
Considerations on slavery. In a letter to a friend. 1846, 81939
Considerations on slavery in the southern states. 15956, 81938
Considerations on the abolition of slavery. 3377
Considerations on the abolition of slavery and the slave trade. 15957, 81940
Considerations on the abolition of the common law. 15958
Considerations on the African slave trade. 21872
Considerations on the agreement of the Lords Commissioners of His Majesty's Treasury. 101150, note after 103106
Considerations on the alleged necessity of hiring foreign troops. 15959
Considerations on the American inquiry. 15960
Considerations on the American stamp act. 15961
Considerations on the American trade. 15962, 20586, 97095
Considerations on the American war. Addressed to the people of England. (15963)
Considerations on the American war, under the following heads. 104302
Considerations on the appointment of a justice. 7118
Considerations on the approaching dissolution of Parliament. 15964
Considerations on the approaching dissolution of the United States Bank. 2338
Considerations on the approaching peace. 15965
Considerations on the Attorney-General's propositions. 15966

Considerations on the Bank of North-America. 15967, 69398, 104628
Considerations on the Bank of the United States. 106110
Considerations on the bill concerning the British sugar-colonies. (15968)
Considerations on the bill for a general naturalization. 15969
Considerations on the bill now depending before the Honorable House of Commons. 15970
Considerations on the bill now depending in Parliament. 15971
Considerations on the bill now depending in the House of Lords. 15972
Considerations on the bills of credit. 52622, 86618
Considerations on the British commerce. 15973
Considerations on the case of the poor in large cities. 92075
Considerations on the causes, objects, and consequences of the present war. 73227
Considerations on the choice of public rulers. 15974
Considerations on the claims and conduct of the United States. 15975
Considerations on the claims of the "southern tier of counties." 15976
Considerations on the commencement of the civil war in America. 15977
Considerations on the currency and banking system. 26399
Considerations on the Delaware and Raritan Canal. 19410
Considerations on the dependencies of Great Britain. 15978
Considerations on the dispute now depending. 15979, 2d note after 106233
Considerations on the disturbances in North America. 106040
Considerations on the Eastern Diocese. (15980), note before 100964
Considerations on the election of councillors. (15981)
Considerations on the emancipation of Negroes. 15982, (67717), 1st note after 102788
Considerations on the embargo laws. 15983, 96013, 102257
Considerations on the establishment in the Indian Territory. 79042
Considerations on the establishment of a uniform system of bankrupt laws. (15985)
Considerations on the executive government. 105148
Considerations on the expediency of a Spanish War. 104002
Considerations on the expediency of admitting representatives. 45414
Considerations on the expediency of an improved mode of treatment of slaves. 81941
Considerations on the expediency of procuring an act of Parliament. (15986)
Considerations on the fatal consequences of abolishing the slave trade. 15987
Considerations on the foundations, ends and duties of the Christian sabbath. 15988
Considerations on the German war. (40299)
Considerations on the government of the territory of Columbia. 105149
Considerations on the government of the territory of Columbia. Number VIII. 105151
Considerations on the government of the territory of Columbia. Number VII. 105150
Considerations on the great advantages. 22311

Considerations on the great western canal. 29547

Considerations on the importance of Canada. (15989)

Considerations on the imposition of 4 1/2 per cent. 15990

Considerations on the impropriety and in-expediency of renewing the Missouri question. 15991

Considerations on the improvement of northern New-York. 32423

Considerations on the Indian trade. 15992

Considerations on the injustice and impolity of punishing murder by death. 74210

Considerations on the institution and conduct. 1853

Considerations on the jurisprudence of . . . Pennsylvania. 60008

Considerations on the late act. 15993, note after 103935

Considerations on the lawfulness of lotteries. 90357

Considerations on the management of the late secret expeditions. 15994

Considerations on the measures carrying on with respect to the British colonies in North America. 1794, 72151-72153

Considerations on the mode and terms of a treaty of peace. (15995)

Considerations on the national debt. 15996

Considerations on the nature and the extent of the legislative authority. 104629

Considerations on the necessity of establishing an agricultural college. 15997, 19874

Considerations on the Negro cause. (15998), 23077, 1st note after 102801

Considerations on the Order of Concinnati. 9280, (78988)

Considerations on the order of Cincinnatus. 49394-49395

Considerations on the origins of the American war. 24468

Considerations on the past, present and future condition of the Canadas. No. I. 94463

Considerations on the past, present and future condition of the Canadas. No. III. 94464

Considerations on the past, present and future condition of the Canadas. No. II. 94463

Considerations on the penal laws against Roman Catholics in England. 15999

Considerations on the points lately brought into question. 64816, 64821

Considerations on the practicability and utility of immediately constructing a railway. 16000, 60009, 64693

Considerations on the present crisis of affairs as it respects the West India colonies. 16001, (17243), 17527, 2d note after 102825

Considerations on the present dangerous crisis. (57415)

Considerations on the present decline of the sugar trade. 16002, 23078

Considerations on the present German war. 15208, 46916, (80038), 80043, 95722

Considerations on the present peace. 16003

Considerations on the present revolted state of America. 96001

Considerations on the present situation of Great Britain and the United States of America. (11833)

Considerations on the present situation of Great Britain and the United States of North America. 11832

Considerations on the present state of affairs. 18337

Considerations on the present state of public affairs. (66644)

Considerations on the present state of the Indians. 34633

Considerations on the present state of the intercourse between His Majesty's sugar colonies. 834, 91599, 102789

Considerations on the present state of the nation. (38179)

Considerations on the present state of the nation as to publick credit. 16004

Considerations on the present state of the sugar colonies. 102814

Considerations on the present state of Virginia. 55170, 100448-100449

Considerations on the present state of Virginia examined. 55170, 100449

Considerations on the proposed removal of the seat of government. 16006, 30255

Considerations on the propriety and necessity of annexing the province of Texas. 16005, 95075

Considerations on the propriety of imposing taxes. (21170), 19347

Considerations on the provisional treaty with America. (37953)

Considerations on the public expediency of a bridge. 6596, (6600), note after 97401

Considerations on the purity of the principles of William H. Crawford. 13309

Considerations on the questions of the adoption of a constitution. 64632

Considerations on the relative situations. 13317

Considerations on the revival of the Royal-British-Assiento. (64563)

Considerations on the . . . sabbath. 16007

Considerations on the slave trade. 81942

Considerations on the slavery question. 16008, 84444

Considerations on the Society, or Order of Cincinnati. 9279-(9280), 13118, 56486, 69685, 86138

Considerations on the sovereignty. 16009, 53029

Considerations on the state of our northern colonies. 16010

Considerations on the state of the British fisheries in America. 16011

Considerations on the state of the sugar islands. 16012, 2d note after 102788

Considerations on the subject of a communi-cation. 16013

Considerations on the subject of finance. 16014

Considerations on the times. 16015

Considerations on the trade and finances of this kingdom. 103122

Considerations on the trade to Africa. 56657

Considerations on the trade to Newfoundland. 54979, 1st note after 103122

Considerations on the trade with America. 43444, note after 98924

Considerations on the true harmony of mankind. 105198, 105208

Considerations on the value and importance of the British North American provinces. 20682

Considerations on the voyage to Guiana. 67560

Considerations on the war in Brazil. 7536

Considerations on this question, "what should be an honest Englishman's endeavour?" 16016

Considerations on this question; whether the British government acted wisely. 16017

Considerations on trade and navigation. 72083

Considerations on volcanoes. 78505

CONSIDERATIONS

Considerations on war. 4672
Considerations philosophiques et politiques. 3701
Considerations politiques. 86200
Considerations pratiques sur les maladies. (39252)
Considerations preliminary, to the fixing the supplies. 16018, 90097
Considerations presentees aux vrais amis du repos et de bonheur. (50568)
Considerations pressantes sur l'importance de l'isle Saint Domingue. 19525
Considerations relating to a new duty upon sugar. 15940, 16019, 1st note after 102825, 102826-102827
Considerations relating to electorial reform. 67273
Considerations relating to the exclusive grant of rail-road privileges. 52566
Considerations relating to the laying any additional duty on sugar. 16019, 102827
Considerations relative to a southern confederacy. 4862
Considerations relative to an establishment for perfecting the education of young men within the Society of Friends. 28874
Considerations relative to the Library of Harvard University. 30730, 67209
Considerations relative to the North American colonies. 25271
Considerations relative to the subject of the foregoing proposals. 23985, (26248)
Considerations relative to the war. 7554
Considerations respectfully submitted to the citizens of Boston and Charlestown. 7894, 67210
Considerations respecting the commerce of New York City. (54215)
Considerations . . . respecting the duties on wool. 51935
Considerations respecting the lawfulness of war. 16020
Considerations respecting the policy of some recent legislation. 25276
Considerations submitted in defence of the Orders in Council. 99774
Considerations suggested by the establishment of a second college in Connecticut. 15720-15721, 36444, (69512), 1st-2d notes after 101998, 103169
Considerations sur la Guyane Francaise. 16027
Considerations sur la traite du 29 Octubre, 1840. 98596
Considerations sur la traite et l'emancipation des esclaves. 72599
Considerations sur l'admission des navires neutres. 16021
Considerations sur l'Amerique Espagnole. 16022
Considerations sur le commerce colonial de la France. 3303, (11525)
Considerations sur le memoire. 98505
Considerations sur le principe democratique. 64734
Considerations sur le systeme colonial et la tarification des sucres. 93568
Considerations sur le systeme colonial et plan d'abolition de l'esclavage. 93569
Considerations sur l'etat present de la colonie Francaise. 12234
Considerations sur l'emprunt d'Haiti. 94842
Considerations sur les causes, les symptomes, la nature et le traitement de cette maladie. 95440

Considerations sur les classes ouvrieres et la colonisation. 20889
Considerations sur les deserts. (33704)
Considerations sur les differends des courronnes de la Grande Bretagnes et de France. (774), 16023, (47546)-(47547), note after (47740), 47741-47742, note after 96403
Considerations sur les divers methodes a suivre dans l'observations des peuples sauvages. 27117
Considerations sur les effets qu'ont produit en Canada. 1764, 16024, 18160, note after 99596
Considerations sur les finances de France. 60893
Considerations sur les interets politiques et commerciaux. 19528
Considerations sur les limites meridionales de la Guyane Francaise. 8831
Considerations sur les systemes penitentaires en general. 6320
Considerations . . . sur les veritables interets de la Grande-Bretagne. 91247
Considerations sur l'esclavage aux Antilles Francaises. 18228, (21448)
Considerations sur lesquelles le peuple Anglois pourra decider. 68284
Considerations sur l'etat actuel de la question. 16025
Considerations sur l'etat du commerce Francais a l'exterieur. (35239)
Considerations sur l'etat moral et physique de l'Amerique Espagnole. 29235
Considerations sur l'etat present de la colonie Francois. 31897, 75062
Considerations sur l'etat present de l'Amerique du Sud. 16026, 34019
Considerations sur l'etat present du Canada. 67020
Considerations sur l'Ordre de Cincinnatus. 49393
Considerations sur une loi passee en Amerique. 16028
Considerations tending to render the policy questionable. (39323)
Considerations to dispel the clouds. 46313
Considerations touching the new contract for tobacco. 20328, 1st note after 100449
Considerations towards a general plan of measures. 16029
Considerations upon measures proposed. 22400
Considerations upon the act of Parliament. 16030, 102828
Considerations upon the American enquiry. 18321
Considerations upon the art of mining. (37936)
Considerations upon the expediency and the means of establishing a university in . . . New-York. 54216
Considerations upon the expediency of abolishing damages on protested bills of exchange. (43672), 92845
Considerations upon the French and American war. 16032
Considerations upon the invitations of the kings of Great Britain and Prussia for holding a congress. 100667
Considerations upon the nature and tendency of free institutions. 28855
Considerations upon the present state of our affairs. 42889, 64143, 69687, 86737
Considerations upon the present state of the United Netherlands. 93225
Considerations upon the present test-law of Pennsylvania. 60010, 74211

618

Considerations upon the question of communication between the Atlantic and
Pacific Oceans. (22251), (41389)

Considerations upon the question. What should
be an honest Englishman's endeavour?
16033

Considerations upon the rights of the colonists.
16034

Considerations upon the Society or Order of
the Cincinnati. (9280), 13128, 56486

Considerations upon the trade to Guinea.
86764A

Considerations upon the white herring and cod
fisheries. 16035

Considerations which demand the attention of
farmers. 16036

Considerations which may tend to promote the
settlement. 106125

Considerations which tend to prove that a states'
national bank, is necessary. 93517

Considering it the duty of the people of this
district. 90844

Considering there is no publicke action. 99855

Consilia Limana, constitutiones synodales et
alia utilia monumenta. 41089

Consilium in arena. 4886

Consistancy of defensive war, with true Christianity. 94696

Consistencia de el jubileo maximo de el Ano
Santo. 72247

Consistencia de la respuesta. 96277-96278

Consistency. pseud. see Snethen, Nicholas,
1769-1845.

Consistency. 96165

Consistency of discoveries in modern geology.
81048

Consistency of the sinner's inability to comply
with the Gospel. (82213)

Consistent churchman. pseud. Serious call.
see Tucker, Bennet.

Consistent loyalist. pseud. Remarks on a
late pamphlet. (34763), 58833-(58834),
99410-99411

Consociation of Litchfield North. see Congregational Churches in Connecticut. Litchfield North Consociation.

Consociation of the County of Windham. see
Congregational Churches in Connecticut.
Windham County Consociation.

Consociation of the Western District of Fair-
field County. see Congregational
Churches in Connecticut. Fairfield
County Western Consociation.

Consociation of the Western Districts of Vermont and Parts Adjacent. see Congregational Churches in Vermont. Addison
Consociation.

Consociation of Windham County. see Congregational Churches in Connecticut. Windham County Consociation.

Consolation, and advice offered to Christian
parents. 32729

Consolation and confidence afforded by religion.
92321

Consolation: being a replication to Thomas
Paine. 104565

Consolation for our grammar schooles. 7996-
16037

Consolation from Homar. 84684-84685

Consolation in breavement. (17268)

Consolation of the pious widow. 85390

Consolation under affliction. 51121

Consolatory odes. 92278

Consolatory thoughts on American independence.
96076

Consolidacao das leis civis segunda edicao
augmentada. 68335

Consolidacion de la republica Mexicana.
(48377)

Consolidated business directory. 2892

Consolidated index to the reports of the committees. 43627

Consolidated Silver Mining Company. 16039

Consolidated slave law. (35620)

Consolidated statutes for Lower Canada. 10485

Consolidated statutes for Upper Canada. 10484

Consolidated statutes of Canada. 10483

Consolidated Stock and Petroleum Exchange of
New York. 54515

Consolidation. 43205

Consolidation act of the city and county of San
Francisco. 76043

Consolidation act, or charter of the city and
county of San Francisco. 76044

Consolidation. An account of parties in the
United States. 16038, 16610

Consolidation and revision of the statutes.
42213

Consolidation bill. 60011

Consolidation of Buel's cultivator and Genesee
farmer. (17869)

Consortes, Jose Fernandez de Lara y. see
Fernandez de Lara y Consortes, Jose.

Conspectus or clear view of the laws. 16040

Conspectus polygarum florae Guianae Meridionalis. 81288

Conspiracy against civil and religious liberty.
(37780)

Conspiracy against liberty. 15048

Conspiracy against the general freedom of the
people. 16041

Conspiracy against the late Bishop of New-York
unravelled. 71132, 71135

Conspiracy explained and defended. 516

Conspiracy exposed. 94516

Conspiracy exposed, and the Rev. S. S. Latti-
more unmasked. 55070

Conspiracy exposed. Remarks of G. W. Julian
and others. 36886

Conspiracy of Cataline. (60012)

Conspiracy of Colonel Aaron Burr. 9425

Conspiracy of kings. 3418, 3423, 3426, 3436

Conspiracy of leading men of the Republican
Party. 48938

Conspiracy of Pontiac. 50876, 84617, 84619

Conspiracy of the officeholders unmasked.
54775

Conspiracy of the rebels and the peace Democracy. (12663)

Conspiracy to defame John A. Andrews.
(72214)

Conspiracy to defeat the liberation of Gov.
Dorr. (20647), note after 96509

Conspiracy trial. Assassination of President
Lincoln. 41182

Conspiracy trial for the murder of the President. 41181

Conspiracy trials of 1826 and 1827. (16042)

Conspiracy unveiled. A farce, in two acts.
94226

Conspiracy unveiled. The South sacrificed.
33837

Conspiracy contre la republique. 58983

Conspirations trahisons et calomnies devoilees
et denouncees. 16043, 58164

Conspirator. 21397

Constable, Albert, 1805-1855. 16046

Constable, John. defendant at court martial
(37982)-37983, note after 99766, note
after 100901

Constable and Company. firm publishers
16045, 26901, 27660, 71915, 97162
Constable's guide, being a concise treatise.
53621
Constable's guide, with the constitution of
Pennsylvania. (19884)
Constable's miscellany. 16045, 26901, 27660,
71915, 97162
Constables of the city beg leave to present
their respectful compliments. 86605
Constables pocket book. 2557, 16044
Constancio, Francisco Solano. 7626, 9808,
16047-16050
Constancy and uniformity of the divine govern-
ment. 39194
Constancy of Israel. 67913
Constant, ------- de. tr. 92547
Constant, L. 16051
Constant, Louis Rilliet de. see Rilliet de
Constant, Louis, i. e. Frederic Jacques
Louis, 1794-1856.
Constant Charley. 105489
Constant lovers. 97100
Constant preparedness for death a constant
duty. 100908
Constante amie. 10327
Constantia. pseud. Gleaner. see Murray,
Judith (Sargent)
Constantia Neville; or, the West Indies.
102592
Constantia von B. . . . pseud. see B. . . .,
Constantia von. pseud.
Constantin Sander's Geschichte des Burger-
krieges. 76347
Constantine and Eugene. (37324), 3d note after
78761, note after 101786
Constantini, P. L. tr. 12245
Constantino Beltrami da Bergamo. Notizie e
lettere. 73166
Constantinople. Missionaries. see American
Board of Commissioners for Foreign
Missions. Missionaries at Constantinople.
Constanzo, Salvador. (16053)
Constitucao politica do imperio do Brasil.
7555-7556
Constitucao politica do imperio do Brasil
seguida do acto addicional. 7557
Constitucion de la Congregacion de Esclavos
del Divinisimo Senor Sacramentado.
48378
Constitucion de la republica Argentina. 9005
Constitucion de la republica Argentina, sancio-
nada por el Congreso Constituyente. 1951
Constitucion de la republica de Chile. (12757)
Constitucion de la republica de Colombia.
14573
Constitucion de la republica de Tejas. 94975-
94976
Constitucion de la republica de Tejas. Junio,
1841. 95027
Constitucion de la republica federal de Centro-
America. 16055
Constitucion de la Sociedad Democratica de
los Amigos de America. 16056, 85738
Constitucion de las provincias unidas del Rio
de la Plata. 38995
Constitucion de las provincias unidas en Sud-
America. 16059
Constitucion de los Esclavos Cocheros del
Santiss. Sacramento. 48378
Constitucion de N. S. del Rosario de Indios.
73208
Constitucion del Colegio del Espiritu Santo.
(16057)
Constitucion del estado de Cartagena. (11133)

Constitucion del estado de Salvador. 76192
Constitucion del estado de Tejas. 95063
Constitucion federal de los Estados-Unidos de
America. 16050
Constitucion federal de los Estados-Unidos
Mexicanos. 48379
Constitucion, leyes jenerales, &c. de la re-
publica de Tejas. 94976
Constitucion para la nacion Espanola. 23957
Constitucion para la republica Peruana. 61098
Constitucion politica de la Nueva Granada.
56272
Constitucion politica de la republica Boliviana.
6194
Constitucion politica de la republica Boliviana
sancionada por el Congreso Jeneral
Constituyenda de 1839. 6196
Constitucion politica de la republica Boliviana
sancionada por la Asemblea General
Constituyente de 1831. 6195
Constitucion politica de la republica Peruana,
dada por el Congreso Jeneral Consti-
tuyente, el dia 18 de Marzo de 1828.
61099
Constitucion politica de la republica Peruana
dada por el Congreso Jeneral el dia
diez de Noviembre de 1839. 61099
Constitucion politica de la republica Peruana
jurada en Lima. 61099
Constitucion politica del estado de Coahuila y
Texas. 48349, 94942
Constitucion politica del estado de Honduras.
32757
Constitucion politica del estado de Mexico.
(48380)
Constitucion politica del estado de Michoacan.
48808
Constitucion politica del estado de Nicaragua.
55140
Constitucion politica del estado de Queretaro.
67100
Constitucion politica del estado del Salvador.
76193
Constitucion politica del estado libre de Guana-
juato. 29053
Constitucion politica del estado libre de Nuevo
Leon. 56297
Constitucion politica del estado libre de Oajaca.
56398
Constitucion politica del estado libre de S.
Luis Potosi. (76143)
Constitucion politica del estado libre y soberano
de Puebla. 66552
Constitucion politica del estado soberano libre
e independiente de Nicaragua. 55141
Constitucion reformada de la nacion Argentina.
27801
Constitucion reside en las puntas de las bayo-
netas. 99698
Constitucion y leyes organicas . . . [de la
republica Peruava] dadas por el Congreso
de 1860. 61101
Constitucion y leyes organicas de la republica
Peruana dadas . . . [por] la Convencion
Nacional en 1856. (61100)
Constitucional. (48381)
Constitucional. Periodico oficial del gobierno.
(48382)
Constitvciones anadidas por los virreyes.
(41092)
Constituciones de la Archicofradia del Arcangel
San Miguel. 48383
Constituciones de la Cofradia del Apostol
Santiago. 48383
Constituciones de la Confradia del Glorioso
Principe de los Apostoles San Pedro.
16058

Constituciones de la Congregacion de la Purisima Concepcion de Megico. 11430
Constituciones de la Congregacion de Nuestra Senora. (48384)
Constituciones de la Imperial Orden de Guadalupe. 48385
Constituciones de la provincia de San Diego de Mexico. 76023
Constitvciones de la provincia de S. Francisco de Qvito. 76110
Constituciones de la Real y Pontificia Universidad de Mexico. 48662
Constituciones de la Sagrada Religion de la Charidad. 16061
Constituciones de la Universidad. 17768
Constituciones de la Universidad de S. Carlos de Guatemala. (76933)
Constituciones de l'Academia de Jurisprudencia. (48455)
Constituciones de las Senoras de la Ilustre Archicofradia de San Miguel. (48386)
Constituciones del arcobispado. (48387), 98919
Constituciones del Colegio de S. Ignacio de Loyla de Mexico. 48388
Constitvciones del Colegio Mayor de Nuestra Senora del Rosario. 96242
Constituciones del I. y Ven. Congregacion de San Pedro. 94354
Constituciones del primer sinodo diocesano Punense. 33561
Constituciones del Seminario de la Madre Santissima de la Luz. 50090
Constituciones desta Provincia de los Doze Apostoles del Pirv. 61102
Constituciones diaecesanas del Obispado de Chiapa. 56328
Constituciones eclesiasticas para la Diocesis de Santa Fe. 72968
Constituciones formadas para la Junta Tridentina. 56398
Constituciones formadas para el gobierno y direccion. 16062
Constituciones para el Colegio Seminario de la Santa Iglesia Metropolitana de Mexico. 78948
Constituciones para el Colegio Viejo y Mayor de Santa Maria de Todos Santos. 76887
Constituciones para el mejor regimen y govierno. 30411
Constituciones para la contraduria de la Iglesia Cathedral. 58287
Constituciones para la Diocesis en le Peru. 29051
Constituciones que Don Alonso Nunez de Haro y Peralta, Arzobispo de Mexico, formo. 56324
Constituciones, que para el mejor govierno, y direccion de la Real Casa del Senor S. Joseph de Ninos Expositos. 16064
Constituciones sinodales de Merida. 47964
Constitvciones sinodales, hechas por e Ill. y Reuer. Senor Don Fray Damian Lopez de Haro. 30410
Constitvciones synodales de el Obispado de la Civdad de Gvamanga. 16068
Constituciones synodales de la Iglesia Cathedral de Cuba. (58278)
Constituciones synodales del Arcobispado de los Reyes en el Peru. Hechas y ordenadas por el Ill. y Rev. S. D. Bartholome Lobo Guerrero. 16065, 16071, (29131), note a after 41711
Constitvciones synodales del Arcobispado de los Reyes en el Pirv. Hechas, y ordenadas por el Illustrissimo, y Reuerendissimo Senor Doctor Don Fernando Arias de Vgarte. 16067, 16071

Constituciones synodales, del Obispado de Arequipa. 16069
Constitvciones synodales del Obispado de la Civdad de Nvestra Senora de la Paz, en el Perv. 98742
Constitvciones synodales [del Obispado de la Paz]. 72539
Constituciones synodales del Obispado de Venecuela. 3221
Constituciones synodales fechas por el ill° senor D. Pedro de Valencia. 16066, 98346
Constitvciones y ordenanzas antiguas. (41093)
Constitvciones y ordenanzas para el regimen de la Botica del Hospital de los Indios de esta Nuev-Espana. 56249
Constituciones y ordenanzas para el regimen, y govierno del Hospital Real y General de los Indios de esta Nueva-Espana. 56250
Constituciones y reglas municipales. 76881
Constituents of Chester County, Pa. see Chester County, Pa. Citizens.
Constituicao estatutos geraes da Mac: no imperio do Brasil. 16054
Constituicao politica do imperio do Brasil. 72497
Constituciao politica do imperio do Brasil seguida do acto addicional. 16052
Constituicoes e os povos do Rio de Prata [sic]. 88734
Constitutie der republiek Colombia. (14575)
Constitutie eenpariglyk. 16124
Constitutie voor de Vereenigde Staeten van Amerika. 16125
Constitution. pseud. Letter to Edmund Burke. see Cartwright, John.
Constitution. 89614
Constitution a charter of freedom. 9113
Constitution a failure. 16072
Constitution a pro-slavery compact. (43721), 62521
Constitution, act of incorporation, and by-laws, of the Boston Episcopal Charitable Society. 6700
Constitution, act of incorporation, and statutes, of the General Theological Seminary of the Protestant Episcopal Church in the United States. 26910, (66153)
Constitution, addresses and lists of members of the American Association for the Promotion of Social Science. 1058
Constitution. Addresses of Prof. Morse, Mr. Geo. Ticknor Curtis, and Mr. S. J. Tilden. 50958
Constitution . . . adopted by the Convention [of Illinois.] 34219
Constitution adopted by the first Society of Unitarian Christians. 61667
Constitution adopted by the Unitarian Society of Washington. 101955A
Constitution against confiscation and outside reconstruction. 22101
Constitution, agreed upon by the delegates of the people of New Jersey. 53092
Constitution amended. (53622)
Constitution and abstract of principles of the Welsh Neck Baptist Association. 102619
Constitution and abstract of proceedings of the Grand Lodge of Georgia. 45497
Constitution and address of the Baltimore Temperance Society. 83663
Constitution and address of the Bible Association of Friends in America. 86042
Constitution and address of the Bible Society of Salem and Vicinity. 75638

Constitution . . . and address [of the Christian Alliance.] 12900

Constitution and address of the Female Anti-slavery Society of Chatham-Street Chapel. 54270

Constitution and address of the Religious Charitable Society in the County of Worecester, Mass. 105409

Constitution and address of the Rosine Association. 62198

Constitution and address of the Temporary Home Association. (62303)

Constitution and addresses of the Massachusetts Philo-Italian Society. 45884

Constitution and addresses of the National Association for the Amendment of the Constitution of the United States. 51927

Constitution and articles of agreement of the Firemen's Mutual Relief Association. 89860

Constitution and articles of agreement of the Joint Stock Mutual Insurance Merchandizing Company. 71919

Constitution and associate statutes of the Theological Seminary in Andover. 1437, 70224, 95190

Constitution and by laws, act of incorporation, and list of members of the Roxbury Charitable Society. (73726)

Constitution and bye-laws . . . adopted on the fourteenth day of October, 1826. 99214

Constitution and by-laws, as amended, June 12, 1867. 80531

Constitution and by-laws, Dec. 5, 1843. 14896

Constitution and by laws, &c. [of the Columbian Historical Society.] 14865

Constitution and by-laws of Caledonia Division, No. 90, Sons of Temperance. 87035

Constitution and by-law of Cayadutta Division, No. 504. 87064

Constitution and by-laws of Channing Division No. 5. 70568

Constitution and by-laws of Company "A", 23d Regiment, N. C. S. N. Y. 53623

Constitution and by-laws of Corner Stone Division, No. 165. 87036

Constitution and by-laws of East Tennesse Division, No. 18. 87090

Constitution and by-laws of Excelsior Division, No. 16. 87037

Constitution and by-laws of Franklin Section, no. 3. 59261

Constitution and by-laws of Geneva Lake Division, No. 26. 87100

Constitution and by-laws of Gibson Division, No. 21. 87038

Constitution and by-laws of Hancock Division, No. 11. 87023

Constitution and by-laws of Harmony Division, No. 5. 87024

Constitution and by-laws of Henfield Division, No. 2, of the Sons of Temperance, of the state of Massachusetts. 87040

Constitution and by-laws of Henfield Division, No. 2, Sons of Temperance, Salem, state of Massachusetts. 87041

Constitution and by-laws of Hutchinson Division, (No. 63.) 87095

Constitution and by-laws of Independent Division No. III. 87042

Constitution and by-laws of Knoxville Division, No. 3. 87091

Constitution and by-laws of La Grange Division, No. 48. 87092

Constitution and by-laws of Liberty Tree Division, No. 47. 87043

Constitution and by-laws of Massachusetts Division, No. 71. 45839

Constitution and by-laws of Merrimac Division, No. 138. 87044

Constitution and by-laws of New-Albany Lodge, No. 1, I. O. O. F. (52433)

Constitution and by-laws of New Era Division, No. 175. 87045

Constitution and by-laws of Old Cambridge Division, No. 26. 87046

Constitution and by-laws of Olneyville Division, No. 10. 57252

Constitution and by-laws of Philmont Lodge. 62438

Constitution and by-laws of Racine Division, No. 4. 87103

Constitution and by-laws of Richmondville Lodge No. 446. 71217

Constitution and by-laws of Roxbury Division, No. 78. 73730

Constitution and by-laws of Salem Division, No. 61. 87048

Constitution and by-laws of Saltonstall Division, No. 37. 87025

Constitution and by-laws of Social Division, No. 93. 87051

Constitution and by-laws of Shakespeare Division, No. 46. 87049

Constitution and by-laws of Shawmut Division, No. 1. 87050

Constitution and by-laws, of Southport Lodge, No. VII. I. O. O. F. 88597

Constitution and by-laws [of the American Numismatic Society.] (1169)

Constitution and by-laws of the American Statistical Association. 1233

Constitution and by-laws of the Americus Club. 61462

Constitution and by-laws of the Associate Alumni of the General Theological Seminary. (54291)

Constitution and by-laws of the Associated Members of the Bar of Philadelphia. 61486

Constitution and by-laws of the Association and Board of Trustees of the New Orphan Asylum [of Cincinnati.] 53378

Constitution and by-laws of the Association for the Relief of Aged and Destitute Women in Salem. 75635

Constitution and by-laws of the Association for the Relief of Aged, Indigent Women, of Portland. (64341)

Constitution and by-laws of the Battalion of Washington Artillery. 53317

Constitution and by laws of the Board of Trade of . . . Newbern, N. C. 54887

Constitution and by-laws of the Brooks Guards. 8370

Constitution and by-laws of the Cabot Institute. 9806

Constitution and by-laws of the Cambridgeport Lyceum. 10147

Constitution and by-laws of the Central Democratic Club. (61528)

Constitution and by-laws [of the Charlestown Young Men's Evangelical Union.] (12107)

Constitution and by-laws of the Chauncy Society for Mutual Improvement. 12342

Constitution & by-laws of the Church Home Society. 3028

Constitution and by-laws of the Clerical Benevolent Association of the Diocese of Baltimore. 3029

Constitution and by-laws, of the Cohocksink Beneficial Society of Pennsylvania. 59981

Constitution and by-laws [of the Columbian Horticultural Society, Washington, D. C.] 101932

Constitution and by-laws of the Democratic Constitutional Union Party. 54217

Constitution and by-laws of the Discharged Soldiers' Employment Association. 20231

Constitution and by-laws, of the Dubuque Catholic Institute. 21041

Constitution and by-laws of the East Cambridge Lyceum. 10147

Constitution and by-laws of the Endeavour Engine Company. 47468

Constitution and by-laws of the Evangelical Home Missionary Society of Kensington. (61637)

Constitution and by-laws of the Everett Literary Union of . . . New York. 54218

Constitution and by-laws of the Female Humane Association. (71179)

Constitution and by-laws of the First Constitution Club. (60013)

Constitution and by-laws of the First Massachusetts Infantry Veteran Association. 45734

Constitution and by-laws of the Franklin Fire Company. 101942

Constitution and by laws of the Franklin Typographical Society of Cincinnati. 13082

Constitution and by-laws of the Free Reading Room Association of Spring Garden. 89820

Constitution and by-laws of the General Emancipation Society of . . . Missouri. (49595)

Constitution and by-laws of the Geological Society. (60117)

Constitution and by-laws of the Germantown Blues. 61698

Constitution and by-laws of the Good Intent Beneficial Society, of . . . Philadelphia. 61702

Constitution and by-laws of the Grand Lodge, I. O. O. F. 52835

Constitution & by-laws of the Grand Lodge . . . of Free and Accepted Masons, for the state of Rhode Island & Providence Plantations. 70584

Constitution and by-laws of the Grand Lodge of Missouri. 49596

Constitution, and bye laws, of the Grand Lodge of Tennessee. 94797

Constitution and by-laws of the Granite Club. 28288

Constitution and by-laws of the Groton Invincible Club. (28966)

Constitution and by-laws of the Hebrew Benevolent Society. 54310

Constitution and by-laws of the Hebrew Young Men's Literary Association. 54310

Constitution and by-laws of the Historical Society of St. Louis. 75350

Constitution and by-laws of the Home for Friendless Children. 55036

Constitution and by-laws of the Horticultural Society. 60148

Constitution and by-laws of the Hunt Female Beneficial Society. 61731

Constitution and by-laws [of the Independent Company of Cadets.] 34449

Constitution and by-laws of the Infant School Society of . . . New York. 54322

Constitution and by-laws of the Irish American Relief Association of Portland. 64347

Constitution and by-laws of the John Brown Pioneer Radical Republican Club. 53318

Constitution and by-laws of the Junior Association of St. Luke's Hospital. 75415

Constitution and by-laws of the Kansas Emancipation League. 37025

Constitution and by-laws of the Kinderhook Division . . . of the Sons of Temperance. 37775

Constitution and by-laws of the Ladies' Aid and Protection Society. 76051

Constitution and by-laws of the Law Academy [of Philadelphia.] (61765)

Constitution and bye-laws of the Law Institute [of Philadelphia.] (61767)

Constitution and by-laws of the Light Artillery Corps of Washington Grays. (61789)

Constitution and by-laws of the Louisville and Jefferson Co. Horticultural Society. 42322

Constitution and by-laws of the Lyceum of the town of New Bedford. 52474

Constitution and by-laws [of the Manchester, N. H., Athenaeum.] 44212

Constitution and by-laws of the Marblehead Union Moral Society. 44471

Constitution and by-laws of the Maryland Academy of Science and Literature. 45198

Constitution and by-laws of the Maryland Club. 45206

Constitution and by-laws [of the Maryland Institute.] 45225

Constitution and by-laws of the Massachusetts Army Association. 45818

Constitution and by-laws of the Massachusetts Baptist Charitable Society. 45821

Constitution and by-laws of the Massachusetts College of Pharmacy. 45831

Constitution and by-laws of the Massachusetts Dental Society. 45838

Constitution and by-laws of the . . . [Massachusetts Horticultural] Society. 45862

Constitution and by-laws of the Massachusetts Journeymen Shipwright's Union. 45868

Constitution and by-laws of the Massachusetts Teachers' Association. 45907

Constitution and by-laws of the Mattapan Library Association. (46878)

Constitution and by-laws of the May Queen Union, No. 2. 51908

Constitution and by-laws of the Mechanics' Cooperative Association of Roxbury. 73651

Constitution and by-laws of the Medical College of Philadelphia. 61809

Constitution and by-laws of the Medical Society of South-Carolina. 87880

Constitution and by-laws of the Medico-Chirurgical College, at Philadelphia. (61811)

Constitution and by-laws of the Mercantile Library Association of New-Orleans. 53335

Constitution and by-laws of the Middlesex Mechanic Association. 42496

Constitution and by-laws of the Military Orders of the Loyal Legion. 48972

Constitution and by-laws of the Minne-ha-ha Lodge, No. 1. 86995

Constitution and by-laws of the M[ost] W[orthy] Grand Lodge of the State of Indiana. 34550

Constitution and by-laws of the National Academy of Design. 51913

Constitution and by-laws of the National Institution for the Promotion of Science. 51990

Constitution and by-laws of the National Minute Men. 54415

Constitution and by-laws of the National Telegraphic Union. 54417

Constitution and by-laws of the Native American Hall Co. of Cedar Ward. 61861

Constitution and bye-laws of the Natural History Society of Montreal. 50271

Constitution and by-laws of the Needle Pickets of the city of Quincy. 67280

Constitution and by-laws of the New-Bedford Lyceum. 52474

Constitution and by-laws of the New Bedford Martha Washington Total Abstinence Society. 52475

Constitution and by-laws of the New Church Tract Society. 52575

Constitution and by-laws of the New England Historic-Genealogical Society. (52687)

Constitution and by-laws of the New England Society of Orange. 57429

Constitution and by-laws of the New England Society of Quincy. (67279)

Constitution and by-laws of the New England Spiritualists' Association. (52748)

Constitution and by-laws of the New-England Women's Auxiliary Association, Branch of the United States Sanitary Commission. 76661

Constitution and by-laws of the New-Hampshire Historical Society. 52872

Constitution and by-laws of the New Haven Medical Association. 52996

Constitution and by-laws of the New Jersey Historical Society. 53176

Constitution and by-laws of the New Orleans Academy of Sciences. 53338

Constitution and by-laws of the New-York Academy of Medicine. 54423

Constitution and bye-laws of the New York Academy of Sacred Music. 54424

Constitution and bye-laws of the New York Association for the Suppression of Gambling. 54430

Constitution and by-laws of the New-York Athenaeum. 54432

Constitution and bye-laws of the . . . [New York] Historical Society. 54475

Constitution and by-laws of the New York Horicultural Society. 54479

Constitution and by-laws of the New York Mining Stock Board. 54515

Constitution and by-laws of the New York Stock and Exchange Board. (54546)

Constitution and by-laws of the New York Typographical Society. 54552

Constitution and bye-laws of the New-York Washington Military Society. (54555)

Constitution and by-laws of the North-Western Medical Society. 55747

Constitution and by-laws of the Northern Academy of Arts and Sciences. 55785

Constitution and by-laws of the Numismatic Society of Philadelphia. 61878

Constitution and by-laws, of the Orphan Society of Philadelphia. 61909

Constitution and by-laws of the Orphan's Home. 54572

Constitution and by-laws [of the Pennsylvania Horticultural Society.] 60326

Constitution and by-laws of the Pennsylvania Institute. (60335)

Constitution and by-laws of the Pennsylvania Institute of Design. 60336

Constitution and by-laws [of the Pennsylvania Institution for the Deaf and Dumb.] 60338

Constitution and by-laws of the Pennsylvania Seamen's Friend Society. 60362

Constitution and by-laws [of the People's Union Association.] 21646

Constitution and by-laws of the Philolexian Society. 14823

Constitution and by-laws of the Phoenix Hose Company. (62056)

Constitution and by-laws of the Pike Beneficial Society. (62059)

Constitution and by-laws of the Pittsburgh Horticultural Society. 63134

Constitution and by-laws of the Polytechnic Institute of Shrewsbury. 80747

Constitution and by-laws . . . of the Pottsville Scientific Association. 64694

Constitution and by-laws of the Prescott Light Guard. (65301)

Constitution and by-laws of the Protecting Society, New Bedford. 52475

Constitution and by-laws of the Providence Division, No. 2. (66367)

Constitution and by-laws of the Rhode Island Numismatic Association. 70729

Constitution and by-laws of the Ridgway Farm, Agricultural and Coal Co. 71293

Constitution and by-laws of the Sacred Music Society, Madison. 43739

Constitution and by-laws of the Saint Aloysius Juvenile Society. 55055A

Constitution and by-laws of the St. Louis Medical Society of Missouri. 75398

Constitution and by-laws of the St. Louis Prison Discipline Association. (75399)

Constitution and by-laws of the St. Mary's Mutual Benevolent Catholic T. A. Society. 75440

Constitution and by-laws of the St. Nicholas Society, of Nassau Island. 51891

Constitution and by-laws of the St. Stephens Brotherhood in the city of Boston. 75490

Constitution and by-laws of the Samaritan Institute, No. 1. 75898

Constitution and by-laws, of the San Francisco Produce Exchange. 76098

Constitution and by-laws of the School Association of Rensselaer County. 69634

Constitution and by-laws of the Sisters of the Good Samaritan. 81467

Constitution and by-laws of the Society for Savings. 85870

Constitution and by-laws of the Society for the Advancement of Natural Sciences. 85872

Constitution and by-laws [of the Society for the Advancement of Political and Social Science.] 85873

Constitution and by-laws, of the Society for the Development of the Mineral Resources of the United States. 12159

Constitution and by-laws of the Society for the Relief of Orphan and Destitute Children. 37976, 85967

Constitution and by-laws of the Society for the Relief of Poor Widows with Small Children. 85973

Constitution and by-laws of the Society of California Pioneers. 9976, 86011

Constitution and by-laws of the Society of Members of the New York Stock Exchange for Mutual Relief. 86076

Constitution and by-laws of the Society of Regulars. 86078

Constitution and by-laws of the Society of Teachers in the City of Baltimore. 86090

Constitution and bye-laws of the Society of the Sixth Army Corps. 86163

Constitution and by-laws of the Society of the Sons of New England in Pennsylvania. 86999

Constitution and by-laws of the Somerset Club. 86806

Constitution and by-laws of the Sons and Daughters of Delaware. 86982

Constitution and by-laws of the Sons of New-England. 86165

Constitution and by-laws of the Sons of Rhode Island. 87003

Constitution and by-laws of the Southside Sportsmens' Club of Long Island. 88602

Constitution & by laws, of the Southport Anti-secret Association. 88598

Constitution and by-laws of the Springfield Debating Society. 89878

Constitution and by-laws, of the Stafford Western Emigration Company. 90081

Constitution and by-laws of the State Poultry Society. 60638

Constitution and by-laws of the State Union [of Soldiers' and Sailors' of New York.] 86332

Constitution and by-laws of the Statistical Society of Pennsylvania. 60643, note after 90813

Constitution and by-laws of the Supreme Grand Council of the I. O. S. M. 86989

Constitution and by-laws of the Supreme Grand Lodge of the Independent Order of the Sons of Malta. 86992

Constitution and by-laws of the Theological and Religious Library Association of Cincinnati. 13092

Constitution and by-laws of the Typographical Association of New-York. 97632

Constitution and by laws of the Unitarian Home Mission. 53319

Constitution and by-laws of the Union Library Society of Wethersfield. 103063

Constitution and by-laws of the Union Temporary Home for Children. 62356

Constitution and by-laws of the United States Beneficial Society of Philadelphia. 97962

Constitution and by-laws of the United States Naval Lyceum. 97980

Constitution and by-laws of the United Trade Society of Journeymen Sailmakers. 52475

Constitution and by-laws of the Vigilant Fire Company. 99602

Constitution and bye-laws of the Washington Agricultural Society. 101974

Constitution and by-laws of the Washington Association of Chester County. 102036A

Constitution and by-laws [of the Washington Benevolent Society of Pennsylvania.] 60778, 101992

Constitution and by-laws of the Washington Blues. 101994

Constitution and by-laws of the Washington Fire-Engine Company. 42343

Constitution and by-laws of the Washington Military Union of the American Army (67282)

Constitution and bye-laws of the Washington Phoenix Fire Company. 101945

Constitution and by-laws of the Washington Section, No. 2. (66378)

Constitution and by-laws of the West Philadelphia Homestead Association. (62381)

Constitution and by-laws of the Western Association of Ladies for the Relief and Employment of the Poor. 62385

Constitution and by-laws of the Western Library Association of Philadelphia. 62387

Constitution and by-laws of the Whig Republican Association of Cambridge. (10149)

Constitution and by-laws, of the William Penn Beneficial Institution of Pennsylvania. 104158

Constitution and by-laws of the Windham County Agricultural Society. 104758

Constitution and by-laws of the Worcester County Institution for Savings. 105422

Constitution and bye-laws, of the York County Conference of Churches. 106022

Constitution and by-laws of the Young Catholics Friend Society. 106132

Constitution and by-laws of the [Young Men's Association of the City of Buffalo.] 106158

Constitution and by-laws of the Young Men's Central Home Mission. 62400

Constitution and by-laws of the . . . [Young Men's Christian] Association of German-town. 62401

Constitution and by-laws of the . . . [Young Men's Christian] Association [of Philadelphia.] 62401

Constitution and by-laws of the Young Men's Christian Association, of the City of San Francisco. 76103

Constitution and by-laws of the Young Men's Mercantile Library. 63149

Constitution and by-laws of William Penn Division, No. 8. 59261

Constitution and by-laws of Wingaersheek Division, No. 183. 87052

Constitution and by-laws, with a list of officers, etc., of the Chicago Historical Society. 13621

Constitution and canons of 1816. 100512

Constitution and canons of the Protestant Episcopal Church, in Maryland. (45302)

Constitution and canons of the Protestant-Episcopal Church in . . . New York. (53874)

Constitution and canons of the Protestant Episcopal Church, in the Confederate States of America. 15262

Constitution and canons of the Protestant Episcopal Church in the Diocese of Vermont. 99201

Constitution and canons [of the Protestant Episcopal Church in the United States of America.] 66171, note after 103462

Constitution and canons of the Protestant Episcopal Church in the United States of America. Together with the ecclesiastical constitution. 66134

Constitution and canons of the Synod of the Diocese of Toronto. 6983

Constitution and catalogue of books of the Medfield Library. 47299

Constitution and catalogue of Pawlet Library. 59260

Constitution and charter of Home Association. 32706

Constitution and circular of the New York Female Bethel Union. 54464

Constitution and discipline of the Methodist Protestant Church. 48206

Constitution and discipline of the Methodist Protestant Church of British North America. 48207

Constitution and form of government for the state of Massachusetts-Bay. (45690)

Constitution and form of subscription. 96288

Constitution and fourth annual report of the Society for the Employment and Relief of the Poor. 54669

Constitution and frame of government of the free and independent state and commonwealth of New Ireland, &c. 16073, 53029

Constitution and general regulations. 52835

Constitution and government of Harvard-College. 65572

Constitution and government of Harvard College, from its first formation. 30740

Constitution and government of the United States. 30184

Constitution and history of Canada. 104666

Constitution and laws. 16074

Constitution and laws of Maryland in Liberia. 40922

Constitution and laws of . . . New-Hampshire. (54812)

Constitution and laws of Rensselaer School, . . . adopted . . . April 3, 1826. 69641

Constitution and laws of Rensselaer School, in Troy, New-York. 69641

Constitution and laws of the Board of Education. 65141

Constitution and laws of the Boston Marine Society, instituted in 1742. 6734

Constitution and laws of the Boston Marine Society, instituted in the year 1742. 6734

Constitution and laws of the Cherokee Nation. 12450

Constitution and laws of the Choctaw Nation. 105531

Constitution and laws of the Muskokee or Creek Nation. 61063

Constitution and laws of the Orphan Asylum of . . . New-York. (54571)

Constitution and laws [of the Philadelphia Society for the Establishment and Support of Charity Schools.] (62039)

Constitution and laws of the Society for Religious Inquiry. 99216

Constitution and laws, of the Temperance Beneficial Association. 94642

Constitution and laws of the Washington Association to Philadelphia. 101978

Constitution and list of officers and members [of the Union Relief Association, Baltimore.] 3017

Constitution and list of officers of the Young Men's Christian Association, Bristol. 8054

Constitution and list of the members of the Providence Young Men's Temperance Society. (66342)

Constitution and . . . members of the Needham Temperance Society. 52233

Constitution and minutes of the Massachusetts Baptist Convention. 45820

Constitution and Mr. Motley. 23185, 51109

Constitution and nominations of the Subscribers to the Tontine Coffee-House. 54219, note after 96172

Constitution and ordinances of . . . Mississippi. (49493)

Constitution and ordinances of . . . Philadelphia. (61559)

Constitution and other documents in relation to the State Historical Society of Mississippi. (49544)

Constitution and personal liberty. (32591)

Constitution and plan of a Society for Affording Relief to the Families of Deceased Ministers. 16127

Constitution and plan of education for Girard College for Orphans. (27494), 40975

Constitution and plan of organization of the Social Party. 85697

Constitution and proceedings of the M. E. S. G. Royal Arch Chapter of Virginia. 100468

Constitution and proceedings [of the Society for the Suppression of Vice, Bedford, N. Y.] 85988

Constitution and regulations of the Evangelical Lutheran Sunday School Society. 54263

Constitution and regulations of the Grand Royal Arch Chapter of . . . New York. 53624

Constitution and regulations of the Society of Ancient Masons, in Virginia. 100471

Constitution and regulations of the Society of Masons, in Virginia. 31320

Constitution and report of the Managers of the Rosine Association. 62198

Constitution and rules of order of the Evangelical Lutheran Synod of the State of New York. 53659

Constitution and rules of the Associated Pastors of New Haven Center. 52972

Constitution, . . . and rules of the Home for Aged and Infirm Colored Persons. 61724

Constitution and rules of the Monterey Library Association. 50120

Constitution and rules of the St. Andrew's Society. (62208)

Constitution and rules of the South Carolina Rangers. 88031

Constitution and rules of the Welsh Society of Pennsylvania. 102620

Constitution and semi-annual report of the Temporary Home Association. (62303)

Constitution and slavery. 42017

Constitution and standards of the Associate-Reformed Company in North America. 65150

Constitution and statement of the Louisiana Homestead Aid Association. 42252

Constitution and statutes . . . of the University [of the City of New York.] (54704)

Constitution and system of by-laws, for the raising and managing a permanent charitable fund. 1322

Constitution and the clergy. 16075

Constitution and the laws vindicated. 79660

Constitution and the union. Let them together be maintained. 61045

Constitution and the union. Speeches delivered at the American Union Breakfast. 16076

Constitution and third annual report of the Association for the Relief of the Industrious Poor. (54103)

"Constitution as it is." Speech of Hon. J. A. Bingham. (5441)

Constitution, as it is, the only hope of the country. 11065

Constitution, as reported by the Convention of Delegates begun at Philadelphia on the first Monday of May, 1787. (16096)

Constitution, by-laws and . . . catalogue of
the Mercantile Library . . . of Portsmouth, N. H. 64422

Constitution, by-laws, and catalogue of the
Society of Inquiry of Marietta College.
86074

Constitution, by-laws and catalogue of the
Southwark Library Company. 88604

Constitution, by-laws and code of ethics of
the Franklin Medical Association. 25660

Constitution, by-laws, and code of medical
ethics of the Maine Medical Association.
43981

Constitution, by-laws, and general regulations
of the Grand Lodge of Iowa. 58975

Constitution, by-laws, and list of members of
the Georgia Historical Society. 27031

Constitution, by-laws and list of members of
the Mercantile Library Association of
the City of San Francisco. 76058

Constitution, by-laws and list of members of
the Metropolitan Club. 48218

Constitution, by-laws, and list of officers and
members, of the Chicago Academy of
Sciences. 12618

Constitution, by-laws, . . . and members of the
Maryland Historical Society. 45215

Constitution, by-laws, and names of members
of the Portland Society of Natural History.
64369

Constitution, by-laws, and . . . officers, of the
Philadelphia Young Men's Bible Society.
62052

Constitution, by-laws and order of business, of
Philadelphia Degree Temple of Honor,
No. 1. 87088

Constitution, by-laws and regulations of Fraternal Community, No. 1. 32904

Constitution, by-laws, and regulations of the
Louisville Chamber of Commerce. 42324

Constitution, bye-laws, and regulations, of the
. . . [Massachusetts Medical] Society.
45874

Constitution, by-laws, and regulations of the
Mercantile-Library Association of Louisville. 42337

Constitution, by-laws and regulations of the
[Mercantile Library] Association [of New
York.] 54391

Constitution, by-laws and regulations of the
Philharmonic Society of New York.
54523

Constitution, by-laws and rules and orders of
the Steilacoom Library Association,
Washington Territory. 91192

Constitution, by-laws, and rules of Groton
Lodge, No. 71. 45771

Constitution, by-laws and rules . . . of New
York Encampment of Patriarchs, No. 1.
54770

Constitution, by-laws and rules of order, of
Bustleton Division, No. 173. 87078

Constitution, by-laws and rules of order, of
Crystal Fount Division, No. 20. 87079

Constitution, by-laws, and rules of order, of
Delaware Division, No. 22. 87080

Constitution by-laws and rules of order, of Fox
Chase Division, No. 301. 87081

Constitution, by-laws & rules of order, of Grass
River Division, No. 368. 87066

Constitution, by-laws, and rules of order of
Green Bay Division: No. 2. 87101

Constitution, by-laws and rules of order of
Hope Division, No. 3. 87083

Constitution, by-laws and rules of order, of
Lancaster Temple of Honor, No. 48. 87084

Constitution, by-laws, and rules of order, of
Magnolia Division Number 93. 87102

Constitution, by-laws, & rules of order of
Mercantile Division, No. 131. 87085

Constitution by-laws and rules of order, of
Neptune Division, No. 64. 87086

Constitution, by-laws and rules of order, of
Niagara Division, No. 14. 87087

Constitution, by-laws and rules of order, of
Pleasant Grove Division, No. 386. 87089

Constitution, by-laws and rules of order of the
. . . Grand Encampment of Patriarchs.
(53625)

Constitution, by-laws, and rules of order of the
Louisville Pilots' Benevolent Society.
(42333)

Constitution, by-laws, and rules of order of the
New England Protective Union, Division
No. 181. 87336

Constitution, by-laws, and rules of order of the
R. W. Grand Lodge of South-Carolina.
87907

Constitution, by-laws, and rules of order of the
Soldiers' and Sailors' National Union
League. 86323

Constitution, by-laws and rules of order of the
Soldiers' and Sailors' Union. 86330

Constitution, by-laws, and rules of order, of
the Union Fire Company. 101955

Constitution, by-laws and rules of Pakachoag
Division, No. 27. 87047

Constitution, by-laws and rules, of Quinohequin
Lodge. 67176

Constitution, by-laws and rules of Shakespeare
Division No. 37. 87069

Constitution. By-laws and rules of Suffolk
Lodge, Number Eight. 93433

Constitution, by-laws, and rules . . . of the
Everett Club of . . . New-York. 54265

Constitution, by-laws, and rules . . . of the
Massachusetts Tin-plate, Copper, and
Sheet-Iron Worker's Association. 45911

Constitution, by-laws and rules . . . [of the
Pennsylvania Institution for the Instruction
of the Blind.] 60339

Constitution, by-laws and standing rules of the
Philadelphia Young Men's Society. 62053

Constitution, by-laws, &c. and . . . members,
of the Newport Reading Room. 55047

Constitution, &c. of the Auxiliary Protestant
Episcopal Society. 53882

Constitution, by-laws, etc. [of the Boston
Mercantile Library Association.] 6745

Constitution, by-laws, etc. [of the Haverford
School.] 30904

Constitution, by-laws, etc. [of the New York
Book Society.] (54434)

Constitution, by-laws, etc., of the Sunday-School
Union of the Methodist Episcopal Church.
48205

Constitution, by-laws, minutes, circular letter,
articles of faith, and the covenant. 10404

Constitution, by-laws, . . . of Union Lodge, No.
71. 63497

Constitution, by-laws, officers, standing committees, and members of the San Francisco
Medical Society. 76094

Constitution, by-laws, rules and regulations of
the Hopedale Community. 32904

Constitution, by-laws, rules of order, certificates of membership, and receipts for
dues. 90850

Constitution, by-laws, sailing directions, etc.,
of the Eastern Yacht Club. 21667

Constitution, canons, and regulations of the
Protestant Episcopal Church. (60438)

Constitution, charter, and by-laws . . . re-
lating to the . . . [Pennsylvania] Insti-
tution [for the Instruction of the Blind.]
60339
Constitution, confession of faith, & covenant.
(52973)
Constitution construed, and constitutions vindi-
cated. 94486
Constitution, containing a bill of rights. 52813
Constitution de la Compagnie de New York.
95825
Constitution de la Nation Poyaisienne. 64839
Constitution de la republique de Colombia.
14574
Constitution de la republique de Pensylvania.
78114
Constitution de la republique d'Haiti. 29573
Constitution de la Societe Francaise de Bien-
faisance. 62247, 85814
Constitution de la Societe Francaise de Bien-
faisance de New-York. 62247, 85815
Constitution de l'Angleterre. 41646
Constitution de las Provincias Unidas en Sud-
America. 66392
Constitution de l'empire d'Haiti. 29574
Constitution de Massachusetts. 40911
Constitution defended, and the pensioner exposed.
(36296), 78299
Constitution der National-Garde von Louisville.
42338
Constitution der Vereinigten Staaten und die
Constitution vom Staate Pennsylvanien.
101542
Constitution der Vereinigten Staaten von Amer-
ica. 16126
Constitution des Etats-Unis. 98983
Constitution des Etats-Unis d'Amerique.
39589
Constitution des Etats-Unis d'Amerique, par
G. Washington. 25293
Constitution des Etats Unis, suivie de conseils
de Washington. (16121)
Constitution des halos observes a la Havane.
63667
Constitution des Provinces-Unies de l'Amerique
du Sud. 66392
Constitution des Staats Nebraska. 52185
Constitution . . . 1867 [of Michigan.] (48727)
Constitution et organisation de l'armee de terre
des Etats-Unis. 38615
Constitution et reglements de la Societe de
Bienfaisance Franco-Canadienne. 85792
Constitution et reglements ou by-laws de la
Societe Francaise de Bienfaisance de
Philadelphie. 62248
Constitution, &c., of "The Century" adopted
1857, amended 1859. 16080
Constitution, &c., of "The Century" adopted
January 13, 1847. 16080
Constitution, etc., of the Grand Consistory of
the State of Massachusetts. (45759)
Constitution, etc. [of the Horticultural Society
of the Valley of Genesee.] 33065
Constitution, etc. [of the Maryland Historical
Society.] (45211A)
Constitution expounded, respecting its bearing
on the subject, of slavery. 6314, 16077
Constitution federative des Etats-Unis Mexicains.
48389
Constitution for a branch of the Religious
Charitable Society. 105409
Constitution for subordinate lodges. 86993
Constitution for the state of Maine. 43917
Constitution, formularies, and rules and orders
of the Reformed Dutch Church. 68772

Constitution, framed for the administration of
their [i. e. Venezuela's] government.
10775, (34898), note after 98877
Constitution, government, and digest of the laws
of Liberia. 14732
Constitution, government and laws of Liberia.
40922
Constitution guarentees religious freedom.
9333
"Constitution is a dimmycratic machine."
84179, 14182
Constitution is the union. (72610)
Constitution, its origin, function, and authority.
58912
Constitution, list of officers, &c. 34595
Constitution no authority. 89612
Constitution not a compact between sovereign
states. 102283
Constitution not a compact between sovereign
states. An oration. 24290
Constitution. No. 9. 6315
Constitution for a Christian church illustrated.
1854
Constitution of a Society Belonging to Wrentham.
85833
Constitution of a Society for Abolishing the
Slave-Trade. 16078, (81943), 85831
Constitution of a Society, for Detecting Horse-
Thieves, and Recovering Stolen Horses.
85834
Constitution of a Society in the Towns of
Wrentham. 85835, 105526
Constitution of a state agricultural society.
53810
Constitution of Christ Protestant Episcopal
Church. 54180
Constitution of Coahuila and Texas. 94943
Constitution. . . of Coeymans Division, No. 185.
87065
Constitution, . . . of Covenant Lodge. 60752
Constitution of Jamaica. 35572
Constitution of Kansas. 20693
Constitution . . . of Kentucky. 37499
Constitution . . . of Kinderhook Division, No.
164. 87067
Constitution of Massachusetts. 77232
Constitution of Medway Social Library. 47362
Constitution of Michigan. (48727)
Constitution of Minnesota, in the Dakota language
49243, 71323
Constitution . . . of Mutual Alliance Division,
No. 130. 87068
Constitution of nature. 1482
Constitution of New Hampshire. 52814
Constitution of New Hampshire and . . . consti-
tution of Vermont. 52816
Constitution of New Hampshire, as altered and
amended. 52815
Constitution of New Hampshire since it became
an independent state. 52817
Constitution of . . . New York. 53969
Constitution of North Carolina. 55607
Constitution of North Carolina, adopted . . .
1776. 55605
Constitution of . . . North-Carolina, . . . with
the ordinances. (55606)
Constitution of . . . Ohio. 56904
Constitution of . . . Ohio, passed in convention.
56905
Constitution of Pennsylvania. (19884)
Constitution of . . . Pennsylvania. 60018
Constitution of . . . Pennsylvania, as altered
and amended. 60017

Constitution of . . . Pennsylvania, as established by the General Convention. Carefully compared with the originals. (60016)

Constitution of . . . Pennsylvania, as established by the General Convention. To which is added a report. 60015

Constitution of Phillips Academy. 1438

Constitution [of Phillips Exeter Academy.] 62535

Constitution of '76. (16122), 2d note after 100449, 100554

Constitution of societies forming in the states. 70835

Constitution of subordinate divisions. 87031

Constitution of the Agricultural Society in the County of Plymouth. 63492

Constitution . . . of the Albion Society. (61452)

Constitution of the Algic Society. 77843

Constitution of the American Anti-slavery Society. 81824, 88237

Constitution of the American Bible Society. (54075)

Constitution of the American Colonization Society. 104011

Constitution [of the American Historical Society.] 11345

Constitution of the American Home Missionary Society. 54078

Constitution [of the American Literary Association.] 1128

Constitution of the American Society of Free Persons of Colour. 81843

Constitution of the American Society of United Irishmen. 19161

Constitution of the American Sunday-School Union; with the by-laws. 59875

Constitution of the Ancient and Honourable Fraternity of Free and Accepted Masons. 25798, (45498), note after 45694

Constitution of the Ancient Briton's Benefit Society. 45084

Constitution . . . of the Anglo-American Beneficial Society. 61467

Constitution of the Anti-slavery Society of Salem and Vicinity. 75634

Constitution of the Apprentices' Library Society of Charleston, S. C. 12040

Constitution of the Associated Body of House Carpenters of . . . New York. 54220

Constitution of the Associated Churches of Litchfield, Conn. 41469

Constitution of the Associated Mechanics and Manufacturers of Massachusetts. 45643

Constitution of the Association of the Alumni of Columbia College. 14824

Constitution of the Association [of Delegates from the Benevolent Societies of Boston.] 6574, 97387

Constitution of the Auxiliary Bible Society in the County of Worcester. 105388

Constitution of the Auxiliary Unitarian Association. 105389

Constitution of the Aztec Club. 48390

Constitution of the Bay State Union, Chicago. 12662

Constitution of the Benevolent Society in . . . New York. 54114

Constitution of the Benevolent Society of Bloomfield. (5993)

Constitution of the Benevolent Society of the County of Orange. 57429

Constitution of the Berlin Branch of the Washington Benevolent Society. 101984

Constitution [of the Bible Society of Middlesex County, Mass.] 48846

Constitution of the Bible Society, of Union College. 97791

Constitution of the Board of Education of the Presbyterian Church. 65141

Constitution of the Board [of National Popular Education.] 6054

Constitution [of the Boston Mechanics' Institution.] 6743

Constitution of the Boston Sunday School Society. 93743

Constitution of the Boston Tontine Association. 6779, 16079

Constitution of the Brook Farm Association. 8238

Constitution [of the Buffalo Horticultural Society.] 9063

Constitution of the Burroughsian Lyceum. 47350

Constitution [of the California Academy of Sciences.] 9960

Constitution of the Cambridge Free Soil Club. (10149)

Constitution of the Canadas. 104665

Constitution of the Cape Cod Association. 10734

Constitution of the Catholic Benevolent Society of Louisville. (42315)

Constitution of "The Century." 11689

Constitution of the Charitable Society, Instituted by the Franklin Association of Ministers. 25646

Constitution [of the Charlestown Association for the Reformation of Morals.] 12104

Constitution of the Cheap Postage Association. (12357)

Constitution of the Cherokee Nation. 12451

Constitution of the Christian Missionary Society. 34585

Constitution of the Church in the United States of America. (80354)

Constitution of the Church Missionary Union of Providence. 66253

Constitution of the Church of Christ in the Westminister Congregational Society. 66381

Constitution, . . . of the Church of the Messiah. 61538

Constitution of the Church Union Auxiliary of Church. (10130)

Constitution of the Cincinnati Astronomical Society. 13083

Constitution of the Colonization Society of Virginia. 100446

Constitution of the Columbia Typographical Society. 101931

Constitution of the Columbian Peitholological Society. 14825

Constitution of the Columbianum. 14883

Constitution of the common-wealth of Pennsylvania. 60014

Constitution of the Company of Scotland, Trading to Africa and the Indies. 16081, 18547, (78208)

Constitution of the Confederate States. 16123

Constitution of the Confederate States of America. 15263

Constitution of the Congregational Association of South-Carolina. 87809

Constitution of the Congregational Churches. 46475

Constitution of the Connecticut Medical Society. 15783

Constitution of the Convention. 99203

Constitution of the Cumberland Presbyterian Church, in the United States of America. 94789

Constitution of the Cumberland Presbyterian Church, . . . together with the form of government and discipline. 17888

Constitution of the Democratic Association. 61560

Constitution of the Democratic Rescue Association of Philadelphia. (62363)

Constitution of the Democratic Society of Friends of the People. 86073

Constitution of the Democratic Society of the City of New York. 54240

Constitution of the Diocesan Sunday-School Society of Pennsylvania. 60069

Constitution of the Dorchester McClellan Club. (20628)

Constitution of the Education Society of the Presbyterian Church. 65158

Constitution of the Education Society of the Warren Baptist Association. 101497

Constitution of the Educational Monument Association, To the Memory of Abraham Lincoln. 41183

Constitution [of the Episcopal Missionary Association for the West.] 22688

Constitution [of the Essex Historical Society.] 23011

Constitution of the Evangelical Free Church. 88261

Constitution of the Evangelical Lutheran Ministerium. 53658

Constitution of the Evangelical Missionary Society. (45724)

Constitution [of the Evangelical Union Antislavery Society.] 23134

Constitution . . . of the Frame Hose Company. 61651

Constitution of the Farmer's Association at Mount Pleasant. 51165

Constitution of the Federal Tontine Association. 16082

Constitution of the Female Association of Philadelphia, for the Relief of Women. 61655

Constitution of the Female Association of Cincinnati for the Benefit of Africans. 16083

Constitution of the Female Branch, No. I, Temperance Beneficial Association. 94643

Constitution of the Female Society for the Relief of Poor and Distressed Persons in Newark. 54873

Constitution of the First New Jerusalem Society of Cincinnati. 53248

Constitution of the First Regiment of Artillery of Pennsylvania. 60019

Constitution of the First Regiment of Volunteer Artillery of Pennsylvania. 60019

Constitution of the First Society of Unitarian Christians in . . . Philadelphia. 62261

Constitution of the Fraternal Communion. 47821

Constitution of the Free Church Association. (45303)

Constitution of the Free Masons. (45498)

Constitution of the Free Produce Society of Pennsylvania. 60108

Constitution of the Friendly Society of the Town of Haerlem. 29504

Constitution of the Fuel Savings Society. 61689

Constitution of the General Convention of Congregational and Presbyterian Ministers in Vermont. 99168

Constitution of the General Grand Chapter, of Royal Arch Masons. 53680

Constitution of the General Grand Royal Arch Chapter. 25796

Constitution of the General Theological Seminary. 26910

Constitution of the Germantown Society for Promoting Domestic Manufacturers. 27157

Constitution of the "Government by Chiefs." (79106)

Constitution of the government of Newfoundland. 54980

Constitution of the Grand Chapter of . . . New York. 53690

Constitution of the Grand Council of Royal and Select Masters. 87833

Constitution . . . of the Grand Lodge of Iowa. 35022

Constitution of the Grand Lodge of the Independent Order of Odd Fellows. 60160

Constitution of the Grand Lodge of Vermont. 99184

Constitution of the Grand Lodge of York Masons. 55622

Constitution of the Grand Royal Arch Chapter, of the Northern States of America. 45499

Constitution of the Grand Royal Arch Chapter of the United States. 25795

Constitution of the Grand Royal Arch Chapter of Virginia. 100469

Constitution of the "Greene and Delaware Society for the Promotion of Good Morals." 28624

Constitution of the Half Orphan Asylum Society of New-York. 83965

Constitution of the Hampshire Education Society. (30143)

Constitution of the Hartford Auxiliary of the American Colonization Society. 30659

Constitution of the Hartwick Synod of the Evangelical Lutheran Church. 30718

Constitution of the Hawk-Eye Pioneer Association. 19746

Constitution of the Hibernian Providence Association in New York. 54311

Constitution [of the Historical Society of Florida.] 24867

Constitution of the Historical Society of Pennsylvania. 60144

Constitution of the Humane Society of the State [of New York.] 53696

Constitution of the Independent Company of Cadets. 45770

Constitution of "the Indigent Widows and Single Women's Society." 61739

Constitution of the Infant School Society of the Northern Liberties. 61741

Constitution of the Iowa County Agricultural Society. 35042

Constitution . . . of the Irving Library Institute. 61744

Constitution of the K. C. G. 16129

Constitution of the Ladies Society, Established in New-York. 54329, 85974

Constitution of the Lafayette Beneficial Society of Pennsylvania. 60188

Constitution of the Lansdown Land Company. 61762

Constitution of the Light Infantry Company of Winslow Blues. 104815

Constitution of the Lyceum of Natural History. (54365)

Constitution of the Magdalen Society. (61801)

Constitution of the Manual Labour Association. 102106

Constitution of the [Manumission] Society [of Tennessee.] 94801

Constitution of the Marine Bible Society [of Massachusetts.] 36035

Constitution of the Marine Bible Society of New-York. 54373

Constitution [of the Maryland Historical Society.] (45211A)

Constitution of the Maryland Institute. 45225

Constitution of the Maryland Society, for Promoting the Abolition of Slavery. 45241

Constitution of the Massachusetts Army and Navy Union. 45819

Constitution of the Massachusetts Charitable Mechanic Association. 45829

Constitution of the Massachusetts Mechanical Association. 45872

Constitution of the Massachusetts Missionary Society. 45879

Constitution of the . . . [Massachusetts Peace] Society. 45882

Constitution of the . . . [Massachusetts] School [for Idiotic and Feeble-Minded Youth.] 45893

Constitution of the . . . [Massachusetts] Society [for Promoting Christian Knowledge.] 45897

Constitution of the Maternal Association of the First Congregational Church in West-Boylston. 102759

Constitution of the Mechanic Library Society. 52974

Constitution of the Medical Society of . . . Pennsylvania. 60235

Constitution of the Methodist Protestant Church. 48206

Constitution of the Mexican United States. 94943

Constitution of the Mineral Point Guards. 49209

Constitution of the Missionary Society of Connecticut. 15805

Constitution of the Missionary Society of New-Jersey. 53163

Constitution of the Most Worshipful Grand Lodge of Ancient Freemasons of South Carolina. 87839

Constitution of the M. W. Grand Lodge of the State of Mississippi. 49505

Constitution of the Mount Zion Tabernacle, No. 3. 61850

Constitution of the Musical Fund Society of Philadelphia. 61853

Constitution of the Musical Institute. 54408

Constitution of the Mutual Marine Insurance Company. 51611

Constitution of the Mutual Relief Society of . . . New York. 54411

Constitution of the National Council. 88817

Constitution of the National, Grand and subordinate divisions. 87097

Constitution of the National Institute of Letters, Arts and Sciences. 51989

Constitution of the National Institution for the Promotion of Science. 51990

Constitution of the National Musical Convention. 51011

Constitution of the New Bedford Auxiliary Society, for the Suppression of Intemperance. 52475

Constitution of the New Bedford Mechanics' Association. 52476

Constitution of the New Bedford Rural Cemetery. (52477)

Constitution of the New Bedford Young Men's Temperance Society. Adopted February 27, 1836. 52478

Constitution of the New-Bedford Young Men's Temperance Society, adopted July, 1834. 52478, 106188

Constitution of the New England Anti-slavery Society. 52655

Constitution of the New England Guards. (52686)

Constitution of the New England Sabbath School Union. 52741

Constitution of the New-England Society, in the City and State of New-York. (52746)

Constitution of the New England Tract Society. 52750

Constitution of the New-Hampshire Branch of the American Education Society. 52862

Constitution of the New Hampshire Missionary Society. (52879)

Constitution of the New Jersey Abolition Society. 53093

Constitution of the New Jersey Riparian Association. 53188

Constitution of the New Jersey Society for the Abolition of Slavery. 53190

Constitution of the New Jersey Society for the Suppression of Vice and Immorality. 53191

Constitution of the New York African Society for Mutual Relief. 54718

Constitution of the New York City Mission Society. 54445

Constitution of the New-York Dental Protective Association. (54764)

Constitution of the New-York Friars Tontine. 54221

Constitution of the New-York Irish Emigrant Association. 54501

Constitution of the New York Journeymen Shipwrights' Society. (54502)

Constitution of the New-York Lying-In Hospital. (54508)

Constitution [of the New York Mercantile Library Association.] 54391

Constitution of the New York Musical Fund. 54518

Constitution of the [New York Protestant Episcopal City Mission] Society. 54526

Constitution of the New York Protestant Episcopal Sunday-School Society. 54530

Constitution of the New York Society for Promoting Christian Knowledge and Piety. (54536)

Constitution of the New York Society for the Information and Assistance of Persons Emigrating from Foreign Countries. 54538

Constitution of the New York State Horticultural Society. 53819

Constitution of the New York Sunday School Union Society. 54548

Constitution of the New-York Wesleyan Methodist Relief Society. 54556

Constitution of the New-York Young Men's Christian Association. 54561

Constitution of the Newark Bible Society. 54878

Constitution of the Newton Union League. 55096

Constitution of the North-Western Branch of the American Society for Educating Pious Youth for the Gospel Ministry. 55737

Constitution of the North-Western Union Missionary Society. 55752

Constitution . . . of the Northern Home for Friendless Children. (61870)

Constitution, . . . of the Northern Medical Association of Philadelphia. 61871

Constitution of the Northern Missionary Society in the State of New-York. 55812

Constitution of the O. U. A. and sub-constitution of the O. U. A. in Massachusetts. 57495

Constitution of the Order of United Americans, and laws of Archchancery. 57495

Constitution of the O U A laws of Arch-chancery, and constitution of the Chancery, of the State of New York. (56376)

Constitution of the Oneida Bible Society. 98230

Constitution of the Order [of Working Brothers, Mobile.] 19424

Constitution of the Oregon republic. 57547

Constitution of the Orphan Asylum Society. (54571)

Constitution of the Parent Education Society. 32127

Constitution of the Pennsylvania Association of the Defenders of the Country in the War of 1812. 61959, 86175

Constitution of the Pennsylvania Fire Company. 60321

Constitution of the Pennsylvania Society for Promoting the Abolition of Slavery. 60364

Constitution of the . . . [Pennsylvania] Society . . . [for the Encouragement of Manu-factures and Useful Arts.] 60367

Constitution of the [Pennsylvania] Society [for the Promoting of Public Schools.] 60373

Constitution of the . . . [Pennsylvania Coloni-zation] Society. 60314

Constitution of the Philadelphia Anti-slavery Society. 61952

Constitution of the Philadelphia Association of the Defenders of the Country, in the war of 1812. 61959

Constitution . . . of the Philadelphia Asylum for the Deaf and Dumb. (61960)

Constitution of the Philadelphia Company of Booksellers. 61985

Constitution of the . . . [Philadelphia Lying-In Charity. 62012

Constitution of the Philadelphia Orphan Society. 62024

Constitution of the . . . [Philadelphia] Society [for Alleviating the Miseries of Public Prisons.] 62034

Constitution of the Philadelphia Society for the Employment and Instruction of the Poor. 62037

Constitution of the Philadelphia Society, for the Establishment and Support of Charity Schools. (62039)

Constitution of the Philadelphia Unitary Building Association. 62047

Constitution of the Philanthropic Society. 62055

Constitution of the Philological Society in New-York. 54576

Constitution of the Phoenix Rifles. 12047

Constitution of the Pilgrim Society. 63480

Constitution of the Piscataqua Missionary Society. (63025)

Constitution of the Pocomtuck Valley Memorial Association. 63517

Constitution of the Presbyterian Church in the United States of America. 65151

Constitution of the Protestant Episcopal Church Association of . . . New-York. (54611)

Constitution of the Protestant Episcopal Church in the Commonwealth of Massachusetts. 45656

Constitution of the Protestant Episcopal Church in the Diocese of Massachusetts. (45957)

Constitution of the Protestant-Episcopal Church in the Diocese of New York. (53874)

Constitution of the Protestant Episcopal Church in the Eastern Diocese of the United States. 66136

Constitution of the Protestant Episcopal Church in the United States. 66128, 66135

Constitution of the Protestant Episcopal Church in the United States of America. 66135

Constitution of the Protestant Episcopal Church of the Eastern Diocese. (28881)

Constitution of the Protestant Episcopal Clerical Association of the City of New-York. (32305), 99815

Constitution of the Protestant Episcopal Orphan Asylum. 42341

Constitution of the Protestant Episcopal Society for Promoting Christian Knowledge in the Western District. 66200

Constitution of the Protestant Episcopal Society for Promoting Religion and Learning in the State [of New York.] 53882

Constitution of the Protestant Episcopal Society, for the Advancement of Christianity in South-Carolina. 19310, 87932

Constitution of the Protestant Episcopal Sunday School Society. 62105

Constitution of the Protestant Episcopal Tract Society. (66203)

Constitution of the Providence Charitable Fuel Society. 66315

Constitution of the Providence County Temper-ance Society. 66318

Constitution of the Providence Female Society for the Relief of Indigent Women and Children. 66324

Constitution of the Providence Young Men's Christian Association. 66340

Constitution of the Provident Society of New York. 54612

Constitution of the Queen's County Society, for the Promotion of Agriculture and Domestic Manufactures. 67069

Constitution of the Reformed Dutch Church, in the United States of America. (68770)

Constitution of the Reformed Dutch Church of North America. 68771

Constitution of the Reformed Protestant Dutch Church of North America. 68779

Constitution of the Reformed Society of Israel-ites. 68782

Constitution of the Relief Society of New York. 54617

Constitution of the Religious Tract Society. (62114)

Constitution of the republic of Hayti. 29575

Constitution of the republic of Mexico. 16084, 94946

Constitution of the republic of Texas. 94954-94955, 94994

Constitution of the republic of Texas, adopted by the convention. 94972

Constitution of the republic of Texas to which is prefixed the declaration of independence. 94974

Constitution of the Rhode-Island Homoeopathic Society. 70720

Constitution of the Rochester Young men's Christian Association. 72364

Constitution of the Roman Catholic Churches of North Carolina, South Carolina and Georgia. (16085)

Constitution of the S. B. Union for the Sake of the Union. 16128

Constitution of the Sacramento Medical Society. 74793

Constitution of the said state [of Coahuila and Texas.] 13810, 94948

Constitution of the Saint Andrew's Society of the State of New York. 74993

Constitution of the St. George's Society. (75215)

Constitution of the St. Louis Young Men's Christian Association. 75402

Constitution of the St. Patrick Benevolent Society. 62217

Constitution of the St. Patrick's Society of Quebec. 67059

Constitution of the Saint Paul Mercantile Library Association. 75459

Constitution of the Salem Charitable Mechanic Association. 75719

Constitution of the Salem Charitable Mechanic Association, with the names of the officers and members. 75719

Constitution of the Salem Female Charitable Society. 75726

Constitution of the Salem Seamen's Orphan and Children's Friend Society. 75734

Constitution of the Salem Street Academy. 75762

Constitution of the Samaritan Female Society of Waterville College. 102107

Constitution of the San Francisco Mercantile Library Association. (76095)

Constitution of the Scots Thistle Society of Pennsylvania. (62233)

Constitution of the Second Jefferson Benevolent Institution. 60169

Constitution of the Seneca Nation of Indians. 47332, 79107

Constitution of the several independent states of America. 16086-16090

Constitution of the Social Society, instituted at Schenectady. 77601, 85703

Constitution of a Society for Abolishing the Slave-Trade. 16078, (81943)

Constitution of the Society for Detecting Horse Thieves. 85836

Constitution of the Society for Improvement in Practical Piety. 85842

[Constitution of the Society for Improving the Condition, and Elevating the Character of Industrious Females.] 85844

Constitution of the Society for Promoting Religion and Learning in the State of New York. 85857

Constitution of the Society for Promoting the Manufacture of Sugar from the Sugar Maple-Tree. 85861

Constitution of the Society for the Attainment of Useful Knowledge. 62251

Constitution of the Society for the Commemoration of the Landing of William Penn. 85876

Constitution of "the Society for the Defence of the Catholic Religion from Calumny and Abuse." 62252, 85884

Constitution of the Society for the Encouragement of Agriculture, Arts, and Social Intercourse. 2331

Constitution of the Society for the Improvement of the City of Philadelphia. 85901

Constitution of the Society for the Institution and Support of First-Day or Sunday Schools in . . . Philadelphia. 62254

Constitution of the Society for the Mutual Benefit of Female Domestics and the Employers. 85907

Constitution of the Society [for the Promotion of Temperance in South Carolina.] 20093, note after 88042

Constitution of the Society for the Promotion of Theological Education in Harvard University. (30723), 30740

Constitution of the Society for the Relief of Poor Widows. 54673

Constitution of the Society for the Relief of the Destitute. 54674

Constitution of the Society for the Relief of the Widows and Orphans of Deceased Clergymen in the Diocese of Virginia. 85978

Constitution of the Society for Worcester County and Vicinity. 105392

Constitution of the Society of American Republicans. (62256)

Constitution of the Society of Artists of the United States. 62257

Constitution of the Society of Teachers of the City and County of New York. (54678)

Constitution [of the Society of the Alumni of the Hahnemann Medical College of Philadelphia.] 86091

Constitution of the Society of the Alumni . . . [of the University of Pennsylvania.] 60758

Constitution of the Society of the Alumni of Yale College. 105920

Constitution of the Sons of Maine. 86988

Constitution [of the Soul of the Soldiery.] 87263

Constitution of the South Brooklyn Literary Association. 87344

Constitution of the South-Carolina Institute. 88007

Constitution of the South Carolina Rangers' Charitable Association. 88032

Constitution of the [South Carolina] Society [for the Promotion of Temperance.] 20093

Constitution of the Southern Christian Home Missionary Society. 62265

Constitution of the State Agricultural Society. 76240

Constitution of the State Council Sovereigns of Industry of New Hampshire. 88818

Constitution of the State of Alabama. 557

Constitution of the state of Arkansas, . . . adopted . . . 1868. 63923

Constitution of the state of Arkansas, done by the people of Arkansas. 1988

Constitution of the state of California. 9998

Constitution of the state of Deseret. 19731, 98220

Constitution of the state of Deseret, with the journal of the convention. 98219

Constitution of the state of Florida. (24853)

Constitution of the state of Georgia. 27032

Constitution of the state of Georgia, with full marginal notes. 27033

Constitution of the state of Illinois. 34218

Constitution of the state of Indiana. 34502

Constitution of the state of Iowa. 34981

Constitution of the state of Kansas. 37024, 37038, 37070

Constitution of the state [of Maine.] 43918

Constitution of the state of Maine, with marginal references. 43919

Constitution of the state of Maryland. 45113

Constitution of the state of Maryland, . . . adopted . . . April 27, 1864. 45115

Constitution of . . . [the state of] Maryland, . . . adopted by the Convention . . . at . . . Annapolis. 45114

Constitution of the state of Maryland, . . . adopted . . . May 8th, 1867. 45116

Constitution of the state of Maryland, . . . ratified by the people. 45117

Constitution of the state of Massachusetts. 45692

Constitution of the state of Massachusetts . . . April 26, 1853. 45693

Constitution of the state of Michigan, as adopted in convention. (48727)

Constitution of the state of Mississippi. 49495

Constitution of the state of Mississippi, as amended with the orvinances [sic]. (49496)

Constitution of the state of Mississippi, as revised in convention. 49494

Constitution of the state of Missouri. (49585)

Constitution of the state of Nebraska. 52184

Constitution of the state of New-Hampshire. 101982

Constitution of the state of New-York. 53626

Constitution of the state of New-York, adopted in convention. 101650

Constitution of the state of New York, adopted in 1846. 33137

Constitution of the state of New-York as amended. 53626

Constitution of the state of New-York as revised by the Convention of 1846. 53626

Constitution of the state of Rhode-Island and Providence Plantations. Adopted, November, 1842. 70573

Constitution of the state of Rhode Island and Providence Plantations, as adopted by the convention, assembled at Newport, June 21, 1824. 70569

Constitution of the state of Rhode-Island and Providence Plantations, as adopted by the convention, assembled at Newport, September, 1842. 70572

Constitution of the state of Rhode-Island and Providence Plantations, as adopted by the convention assembled at Providence. 70571

Constitution of the state of Rhode-Island and Providence Plantations, as finally adopted by the convention of the people. 70570

Constitution of the state of South-Carolina. 87416

Constitution of the state of South Carolina, adopted April 16, 1868. 87675-87676

Constitution of the state of South Carolina and the ordinances. 87445

Constitution of the state of South-Carolina. We, the delegates. 87415

Constitution of the state of South Carolina, with the ordinances appended. 87675

Constitution of the state of South Carolina, with the ordinances thereunto appended. 87418

Constitution of the state of Tennessee. 94726-94729

Constitution of the state of Texas. 95064-95065

Constitution of the state of Vermont, as established. 99008

Constitution of the state of Vermont, as revised. 99009

Constitution of the State Rights and Free Trade Association. 88063

Constitution of the Subscribers to the Funeral Fund. 66305

Constitution of the Suffolk County Bible Society. 93440

Constitution of the Suffolk Fire Society. 93436

Constitution of the Sunday School Association. 54917

Constitution of the Tammany Society. 94291

Constitution of the Temperance Society, of Fishkill Landing. 94654

Constitution of the Texas San Saba Company. 95126

Constitution of the Theological Seminary of the General Synod of the Evangelical Lutheran Church in the United States. 23127

Constitution of the Thistle Society of the City of New York. 54694, note after 95376

Constitution . . . of the True Republican Society . . . of Philadelphia. 62344, 4th note after 97146

Constitution of the Union Benevolent and Trade Society, of the City of New-Brunswick. 97764

Constitution of the Union Benevolent Association. 62348

Constitution of the Union Congregational Anti-slavery Society. 97800

Constitution of the Union Insurance Company [of Boston.] 97804

Constitution of the Union Insurance Company of Philadelphia. 97807

Constitution of the Unitarian Association in the County of Worcester. 105415

Constitution of the Unitarian Book and Pamphlet Society. 97830

Constitution of the United Mexican States. 94939

Constitution of the United Societies, of Believers (called Shakers.) 97886

Constitution of the United States. 101631, 101648, 101650, 101656, 101662

Constitution of the U. States a study for schools. (2316)

Constitution of the United States, according to the latest amendments. 99011

Constitution of the United States and Massachusetts. 16108

Constitution of the United States and . . . New York. (16109)

Constitution of the United States and of . . . New Jersey. 53094

Constitution of the United States, and of the state of South Carolina. 87417

Constitution of the United States; and revisal of the public acts. 94774

Constitution of the United States & Tennessee. 94730

Constitution of the United States, and the amendments. 20429

Constitution of the United States arranged and epitomized. 84218

Constitution of the United States defended. 101524

Constitution of the United States defined and carefully annotated. 58985

Constitution of the United States: is it pro-slavery or anti-slavery? 20710

Constitution of the United States Naval Benevolent Association. 97978

Constitution of the United States Naval Fraternal Association. 97979

Constitution of the United States of America. 101649

Constitution of the United of America; as proposed by the convention, held at Philadelphia, September 17, 1787. (16094)

Constitution of the United States of America, as proposed by the convention, held at Philadelphia, September 17, 1787, and since ratified. 101643, 101648

Constitution of the United States of America, framed by the General Convention at Philadelphia. 16093

Constitution of the United States of America, the amendments and proposed amendments. 63821

Constitution of the United States of America. To which is prefixed the constitution of the state of Tennessee. 94729

Constitution of the United States of America; with the amendments. 101650

Constitution of the United States of America with the amendments thereto. 16117

Constitution of the United States. The following proposed alterations. 97912

Constitution of the United States, versus slavery. 8007

Constitution of the United States, with a lecture. 25208

Constitution of the United States, with all the amendments. 101630, 101655

Constitution of the United States, with an alphabetical analysis. (31696)

Constitution of the United States (with an index thereunto.) 10051

Constitution of the United States, with its amendments. 101644

Constitution of the United States . . . with the rules and orders of the House of Representatives. 16104

Constitution of the United Working-Men's Trading Society. 97994

Constitution of the University at Cambridge. 30740

Constitution of the Vermont Juvenile Missionary Society. 99226

Constitution of the Veteran Association of Auburn. (2353)

Constitution of the Volunteer Light Infantry Company. 100758

Constitution of the Virginia Society, for the Abolition of Slavery. 100567

Constitution of the Washington Artillery. 101976

Constitution of the Washington Association and United States Insurance Company. 101977

Constitution of the Washington Benevolent Society at Cambridge. 101985

Constitution of the Washington Benevolent Society, of the County of Cayuga. 101986

Constitution of the Washington Benevolent Society of the County of Herkimer. 101990

Constitution of the Washington Benevolent Society of Mount-Holly. 101651

Constitution of the Washington Benevolent Society of Pennsylvania. 60778, 101992

Constitution of the Washington Benevolent Society of the Town of Augusta. 101983

Constitution of the Washington Benevolent Society of the Town of Brookfield. 101984A

Constitution of the Washington Benevolent Society of the Town of Charlton. 101987

Constitution of the Washington Benevolent Society of the Town of Florida. 101607, 101988

Constitution of the Washington Benevolent Society of the Town of Galway. 101989

Constitution of the Washington Bible Society. 101958

Constitution of the Washington City Lyceum. 101960

Constitution of the Washington College Association. 102006

Constitution of the Washington National Monument Society. 102031

Constitution of the Washington Society of Maryland. 45394, 101608, 1st note after 102036A

Constitution of the West Parish Association. 102943

Constitution of the Westchester Agricultural Society. 102950

Constitution of the Western Sunday School Board of Agency. 103019

Constitution of the Widows' Society. (6786), 103886A

Constitution of the Woman's Maryland Branch of the U. S. Sanitary Commission. 45397

Constitution of the Worcester and Middlesex North Sabbath School Union. 105378

Constitution of the Worcester Association of Mutual Aid in Detecting Thieves. 105381

Constitution of the Worcester Female Samaritan Society. 105427

Constitution of the Worcester Lyceum. 105431

Constitution of the Young Man's Institute. 62399

Constitution of the Young Men's Anti-masonic Association for the Diffusion of Truth. 106152

Constitution [of the Young Men's Benevolent Society, Boston.] 106161

Constitution of the [Young Men's Bible Society, of Brooklyn.] 106163

Constitution of the Young Men's Charitable Association of Charlestown. 106166

Constitution of the Young Men's Christian Association. (3030)

Constitution of the Young Men's Christian Association; with a list of officers. 73735

Constitution of the Young Men's Colonization Society. 106168

Constitution [of the Young Men's Missionary Society of New-York.] 106177

Constitution of the . . . [Young Men's Missionary Society of New-York] . . . with an appeal to the friends of Missions. 106176

Constitution of the . . . [Young Men's Missionary Society of South-Carolina.] 106178

Constitution of the Young Men's Unitarian Book and Pamphlet Society. 106193

Constitution [of Vermont.] 99075

Constitution of Vermont. As adopted by the convention. 99013

Constitution of Vermont, as established by convention in the year 1778. 99009

Constitution of Vermont, as established by convention in the year 1778, and revised by convention in June 1786. 99010

Constitution of Vermont, as revised and amended by the Council of Censors. 99012

Constitution, or, articles of agreement of the Washington Building Company. 101957

Constitution or articles of association of the Mutual Fire Society. 105362

Constitution or compact. 14122

Constitution, or form of government, agreed to and resolved upon by the delegates and representatives of the several counties and corporations of Virginia. 100020, 100027

Constitution, or form of government, agreed to, and resolved upon, by the representatives of South-Carolina. 87413

Constitution, or form of government agreed to, and resolved upon by the representatives of the state of North-Carolina. (55604)

Constitution or form of government for the people of Florida. 24851

Constitution or form of government for the people of Florida, as revised and amended. 24852

Constitution, or form of government of the state of Louisiana. 42214

Constitution or form of government of the state of Texas. 94949

Constitution or frame of government, agreed upon. 45691

Constitution or frame of government of the United States of America. (16095)

Constitution, order of business, rules of order, and form. 87098

Constitution our ark in the storm. 25211

Constitution—peace. 35440

Constitution, plan of operation and organization of the Church Union. 2567

Constitution politica de la Republica Dominicana. 20573, (75085)

Constitution politica del estado libre de Coahuila y Tejas. 94941

Constitution, . . . Pride of Oak Lodge. 60752

Constitution, profession of faith, and covenant. (52973)

Constitution public, of the Society of St. Tammany. 94293

Constitution, report and directory of the Young Men's Association of the Madison-Square Presbyterian Church. 54366

Constitution, rules and regulations of the Mutual Assurance Society Against Fire on Buildings in the State of Virginia. 100490

Constitution, rules and regulations of the Stadacona Club. 90034

Constitution, rules and regulations to be adopted and practiced. 95601

Constitution, rules, regulations and by-laws, of Ohio Lodge, No. 1. (56988)

Constitution, state of the funds, and charitable disbursements. 45828

Constitution the true remedy. 17221

Constitution, together with the bye laws. 99183

Constitution; together with the session laws of Oregon. 57548

Constitution universelle. 26328

Constitution upheld and maintained. 30386

Constitution vindicated. 30019

Constitution—wisdom, justice, moderation. 27111, 91254

Constitution, with an address. (26923)

Constitution, with an appeal. 106181

Constitution, with the names of the present members. 6445

Constitutional advocate. 16130

Constitutional amendment. 4653

Constitutional amendment. Letter from Hon. Joseph P. Bradley. 7283

Constitutional amendments. Speech of Hon. Henry J. Raymond. 68045

Constitutional and additional rules of the South-Carolina Society. 88033

Constitutional answer and refutation of an address. (19067), 86193

Constitutional answer to the Rev. Mr. John Wesley's calm address. 102647

Constitutional argument, against American slavery. 82604

Constitutional argument. By a member of the Rock County Bar. (9160), 2d note after 90642

Constitutional arguments indicating the rights and policy. 91488

Constitutional articles and legislative enactments. (30749)

Constitutional articles . . . of the Lincoln Guard. 41271

Constitutional articles of the Pilgrim Society. 63481

Constitutional charts. (26679)

Constitutional class book. 92293

Constitutional Committee on Reform and Progress. 10334

Constitutional considerations on the power of Parliament. 16131

Constitutional convention; its history, powers, and modes of proceeding. 35733

Constitutional convention. Report of the Committee on the Judicial Department. 52818

Constitutional duty of Congress to give the elective franchise. 5608A

Constitutional duty of the federal government to abolish American slavery. (16132)

Constitutional ethics. 56029

Constitutional freedom the genius of our government. 42083

Constitutional friend. pseud. ed. (80344)

Constitutional government against treason. 89103

Constitutional government. By O. W. Brownson. (8712)

Constitutional guide; comprising the constitution of the United States. 51133

Constitutional guide to the objects of the New York State Convention. 53628

Constitutional guide to the people of England. 104248

Constitutional history of England. 58814

Constitutional history of England since the accession of George the Third. (47081)

Constitutional history of the Presbyterian Church. 31866, (32328)

Constitutional history of the United States. 14104

Constitutional inquiry. 35993

Constitutional law and unconstitutional divinity. 58691

Constitutional law. Being a collection of points. (79212)

Constitutional law: being a view of the practice. (79213)

Constitutional law: comprising the declaration of independence. 16133

Constitutional law. Decisions of the Supreme Court. 16134

Constitutional law, relative to credit, currency, and banking. 89606

Constitutional law: with reference to the present condition of the United States. 58692

Constitutional liberty a refuge for the gathering to Shiloh. 28148, (28951)

Constitutional limitations and the contest for freedom. 84788

Constitutional manual for the National American Party. 31110

Constitutional means for putting an end to the disputes. 16135

Constitutional Meeting, Boston, 1850. see Boston. Constitutional Meeting, 1850.

Constitutional notions of the powers of the national and state governments. 97256

Constitutional politicians. 489

Constitutional power of Congress over the territories. (18036)

Constitutional Presbyterian. pseud. Introduction. 73354

Constitutional Presbytery. see Associate Reformed Church in North America. Constitutional Presbytery.

Constitutional principles of the abolitionists. 35849

Constitutional propositions. 45694

Constitutional provisions. 48804

Constitutional queries. 16136

Constitutional question. 96396

Constitutional reform. 16137

Constitutional Reform Association. (10332)

Constitutional reform, in a series of articles. 5302, (37656)

Constitutional reports. 87455

Constitutional reports, Treadway's edition. 87455

Constitutional Republicanism, in opposition to fallacious Federalism. 2395

Constitutional right of Great Britain to tax the colonies. (31912)

Constitutional right of the legislature of Great Britain, to tax the British colonies in America. 1792A, 16138

Constitutional rights of citizens. 16139

Constitutional rights of the states. Speech of J. L. M. Curry. 18007

Constitutional rights of the states. Speech of Hon. J. P. Benjamin. 4701

Constitutional rules of the Society of Unitarian Christians. 62261

Constitutional security to the citizens' rights of property. 16140

Constitutional Society, London. 33032

Constitutional Society of Massachusetts. see Massachusetts Constitutional Society.

Constitutional Society of Pennsylvania, Philadelphia. 60398

Constitutional Society of Pennsylvania, Philadelphia. Chairman. 60398 see also Bache, Richard.

Constitutional text-book: a practical and familiar exposition. 80292

Constitutional text book: containing selections. (16141)

Constitutional Union Party. 16142, 28493

Constitutional Union Party. Convention, 1860. 64407

Constitutional Union Party. Alabama. 69861 see also Bell and Everett Club, Marian, Ala.

Constitutional Union Party. New York. New York City. 54217

"Constitutional Union Party," and "the philosophy of strikes." 82083

Constitutional view of the late war between the states. 91279

Constitutional whig. 95583

Constitutionalist. pseud. Alarm bell. No. 1. 583, 16146

Constitutionalist. pseud. Bigotry exposed. (16145), 81905

Constitutionalist. pseud. Great struggle between democracy and absolutism impending. 28466

Constitutionalist. pseud. Letters to the electors and people of England. 40644

Constitutionalist. 96754

Constitutionalist, addressed to men of all parties. 3852, 16153

Constitutionalist; or amendments of the constitution. 16144, note after 99172, note after 104629

Constitutionalist: or, an enquiry how far it is expedient and proper to alter the constitution of South-Carolina. 87733, 87811

Constitutionalists of Canada. petitioners 95372

Constitutionality and adequacy of Sunday laws. 93745

Constitutionality and construction of the law. 90447

Constitutionality and rightfulness of secession. 36170

Constitutionality of a bridge at Albany. 614

Constitutionality of federal tax. 16147

Constitutionality of slavery. 7007

Constitutionality of the embargo laws. 16148

Constitutionality of the Maine law. 85696

Constitutionality of the Maine liquor law. 77714

Constitutionality, policy, and legality of the late slaves. 27066

Const. Apostolicae sedis. 84193-84200, 84203-84211

Constitutiones dioecesanae ab Illmo ac Rev^mo Domino Joanne Josepho Williams. 72934

Constitutiones dioecesanae in Synodis Philadelphiensibus, annis 1832 et 1842. 72961

Constitutiones dioecesanae in Synodis Philadelphiensibus, annis 1832, 1842, 1847, 1853 et 1855 latae et promulgatae. 72962

Constitutiones dioeceseos Sinus Viridis. 72943

Constitutiones dioecesis Ludovicopolitanae. 72946

Constitutiones ecclesiasticae. 48391

Constitutiones Fratrum Haeremitarum. 98913

Constitutiones Ordinis Fratrum Eremitarum Sancti Augustini. 16063, 48392

Constitutiones Ordinis Fratrum Eremitarum Sancti Augustini, nuper recognitae. 57519

Constitutiones synodales establecidas por el Sr. D. Augustin Rodriguez Delgado. 16070

Constitutiones synodi dioecesanae Detroitensis. 72939

Constitutions and canons of the Protestant Episcopal Church in the United States. 66121

Constitutions de Sancho-Panca. (3335)

Constitutions des principaux etats de l'Europe et des Etats-Unis de l'Amerique. 19327, 38500

Constitutions des treize Etats-Unis de l'Amerique. 16118, 16120, 100342

Constitutions des treize Etats Unis de l'Amerique; avec la declaration de l'independance. 16119

Constitutions d'Europe et d'Amerique. 38588

Constitutions of Great Britain, France, and the United States. 46762

Constitutions of Louisiana. 42215

Constitutions of Pennsylvania. 60020

Constitutions of the Ancient and Honourable Fraternity of Free and Accepted Masons. 25798, 30507, 101471

Constitutions of the Ancient . . . Fraternity of Free . . . Masons in the State of New York. 53627

Constitutions of the Annual Convention of Mechanics' Mutual Protections. 53761

Constitutions of the Company of Scotland, Trading to Africa and the Indies. (78208)

Constitutions of the . . . Fraternity of Free and Accepted Masons. 25798, 30507, 101471

Constitutions of the Free Masons. Containing the history. 1397, 25797

Constitutions of the Free Masons, with the constitution and by-laws. 58975

Constitutions of the Grand Lodge of Massachusetts. 45760, (50333)

Constitutions of the National Division of the Sons of Temperance. 87005

Constitutions of the Publick Academy in the City of Philadelphia. 62108

Constitutions of the several independent states of America. 16092
Constitutions of the several states composing the union. 1269, 1271
Constitutions of the several states of the union and United States. 16113
Constitutions of the sixteen states which compose the confederated republic of America. 16100
Constitutions [of the Sons of Temperance of North America.] 87017
Constitutions of the Tammany Society or Columbian Order. 94294-94295
Constitutions of the United States. 16099, 16103, 16107
Constitutions of the United States; according to the latest amendments. . . . And the bill of rights of the state of Virginia. 16102
Constitutions of the United States, according to the latest amendments: to which are prefixed, the declaration of independence. 16101
Constitutions of the United States, according to the latest amendments. To which is annexed the declaration of independence. 16097
Constitutions of the United States, and of Pennsylvania. 36198, (36199)
Constitutions of the United States and state of New York. 68469
Constitutions republicaines du globe. 2859
Constitutions synodales des conciles de Lima. 30415
Constitutiva de la Federacion Mexicana. 48253
Constituzione della Societa di Mutuo Soccorso di San. Luigi, Mo. 85778
Constituzione della Societa di Unione e Fratellanza Italiana in New-York. 85779
Constituzione della Societa Italiana, di Unione e Benevolenza, in Nueva York. 85780
Constituzione della Societa Italiana in Nuova York. (16149)
Construccion predicable, y predicacion construida. 75990
Construction of the great Victoria Bridge in Canada. 32342
Consudo funerales. 24155
Conseulo, -------. (25110)
Consuelo and Forney letters. (25110)
Consulado de Buenos Aires. see Buenos Aires. Consulado.
Consulado de Cadiz. see Cadiz. Consulado.
Consulado de la Havana. see Havana. Consulado.
Consulado de Lima. see Lima, Peru. Tribunal del Consulado.
Consular establishments. 16150
Consular sea letters, reviewed. 25014
Consulata al Rey, e impugnacion de la obra de Fr. Francisco Ayeta. 76776
Consulta la Excma. Diputacion Provincial. 79185
Consulta del Auditor General. 61103
Consulta del Cabildo Eclesiastico de Guadaljara. 29022
Consulta sobre la necesidad que tenemos de algunas leyes. 99473
Consulta, y representacion hecha al Exmo Senor Marques de Villa Garcia. 61104
Consultas de Seccao de Fazenda do Conselho de Estado. 85680
Consultas morales. 75589
Consultas varias morales y misticas resueltas. (78920)

Consultation de MM. Dalloz, Delegrange, Hennequin, Dupin Jeune, et autres. 18331
Consultus, Juris. pseud. see Juris Consultus. pseud.
Consumers of West India sugar the supporters of West India slavery. 16152, 102829
Consummation: or an end to the old church and old government generally. 104566
Consumption in New England. 6991
Consumption in New England and elsewhere. 6992
Consumptive. pseud. Eleventh hour. see Coffin, Robert Stevenson, 1797-1827.
Consumptives' Home, Boston. see Boston. Consumptives' Home.
Conta dos negocios de reparticao dada a Asemblea Geral Legislativa. 16153
Contador encargado de los sellos, al "Curioso." 58435
Constant d'Orville, Andrew Guillaume. see Corville, Andre Guillaume Contant d'.
Contarini, Ambrosio. 67736
Conte, John L. le. see Le Conte, John Lawrence, 1825-1883.
Conte d'Acadie. 41913
Conte fantastique. 63545
Contemplated secession from the federal republic. 36366
Contemplations on mortality. 39793
Contemplations on the sublime phenomena of creation. (33708)
Contemporain. A. E. Aubry. (11332)
Contemporain. F. X. Garneau. 11333
Contemporain. G. B. Faribault. 11334
Contemporary biography. 66511
Contempory history. 47126, 85168
Contempt on revenge. (74635)
Contes de Pierre Parley sur l'Amerique. (27896), 94248
Contes d'Edgar Poe. (63558)
Contes et equisses. 92430-92431
Contes et fables. (75479)
Contes inedits d'Edgar Poe. 63559
Contes nationaux. 97025
Contest. A military treatise. 73017
Contest; a poem. (11022)
Contest and its duties. 64939
Contest and the crisis. 79512
Contest between Christianity and political Romanism. (11063)
Contest between free and slave labour. (21847)
Contest between the eagle and the crane. 63622
Contest in America. (48985)
Contest in America between Great Britain and France. 49693
Contestacion a Don Miguel Lopez. 75806
Contestacion a este articulo infamatorio. 48582
Contestacion a la carta del Indio patriota. 977, 16159, 96117
Contestacion a la carta publicada por unos accionistas. 16158
Contestacion a la critica que contra dicho metodo dio a luz. 98311
Contestacion a la expresion de agravios. 103966
Contestacion a la memoria sobre la convencion Espanola. (59296)
Contestacion a la protestas que contra el acuerdo del Ve. Cabildo. (47807)
Contestacion a Las observaciones sobre las instrucciones. 63697, 97913, 97925
Contestacion a las reflexiones de J. M. Alvirez. 10097
Contestacion a los observaciones que bajo el nombre de "Unos Peruvanos." 16157

Contestacion a los papeles. 99474
Contestacion a los versos titulados Satira. 16155
Contestacion, a su respuesta dada en el num? XXIV. 78907
Contestacion a un articulo sobre la republica de Chile. 12758, 16156
Contestacion a various articulos y folletos. 94192
Contestacion al alegato presentado por D. J. Suarez Navarro. 93344
Contestacion al articulo comunicado del Senor Coronel Don Pablo Victor Unda. 87167
Contestacion al articulo del Cosmopolitia. 40066
Contestacion al Arzobispo. 73174
Contestacion al avisador y defensor de los gachupines. 95873
Contestacion al Clarin Bayames n̄. I. 97037
Contestacion al comunicado sobre la nacionalidad. 32773
Contestacion al discuros del Senor Huerta. 33560
Contestacion al folieto La oposicion y el gobierno. 48393
Contestacion al folleto que D. Jose de la Lastra dio a luz. 71638
Contestacion al folleto titulado: La guerra de Tejas sin mascara. 95130
Contestacion al impreso del Sr. Conde de Oreilly. (16154)
Contestacion al manifesto que ha dado el Escmo. S. D. Francisco de Arango. (1871), 3611
Contestacion al manifiesto de D. Gabriel Sequeira. 79181
Contestacion al manifiesto que hace a la nacion. 67349
Contestacion al memorandum del Senor D. Eusebio de Salazar y Mazarredo. (59323)
Contestacion al numero septimo del Mensagero semenal de Neuva-York. (74768), 74912
Contestacion al oficio. 76747
Contestacion al papel del Dr. D. Tomas Gutierrez de Pineres. 39298
Contestacion al primer apendice. (66591)
Contestacion al Sr. Alvires. 73159
Contestacion al voto de America. 100789, 105745
Contestacion apacible al ataque brusco. 1876
Contestacion dada en la Habana. 98259
Contestacion dada por el Sʳ. Obispo de Puebla. 66553
Contestacion de la Segunda Comision de Hacienda. 48394
Contestacion de los Gefes del Egercito Unido. 7558
Contestacion de Mucio Valdovinos. 34187, 34189
Contestacion de un Espanol. 11403
Contestacion del Archiduque. 29354
Contestacion del Comisionado por el Ven. Cabildo de Guadalajara. (29023)
Contestacion del Cura de la Aldea. 35545
Contestacion del epilogo de los pasages historicos. 21771
Contestacion del gobierno a el Consul de S. M. B. 76194
Contestacion del Gobierno Provisorio. 55152
Contestacion del Illmo Sr. Arzobispo. (48395)
Contestacion del Ministro Americano, a la escitativa de la Legislatura. 63687
Contestacion del Obispo y Cabildo de la Santa Iglesia Catedral de Oajaca. 56399

Contestacion del S. Secretario de Hacienda. 101294
Contestacion del Sr. Ministro [de Relaciones' Exteriores de la Confederacion Argentina.] 9027
Contestacion documentada al insulso y desalinado folleto. 93300, 94341
Contestacion o sea banderilla. 72270
Contestacion, ou la carta del Indis patriotae. 16159, 96117
Contestacion, ou la carta del Indus patriota. 977, 96117
Contestacion que da a los cargos el ciudadano M. L. Vidaurre. 14601, 99485
Contestacion que da el ciudadano Vicente Sanchez Vergara. 98970
Contestacion que da el Conde de Casa Barreto. 1872, 3612
Contestacion que da el D. D. I. Ortis de Zevallos. 68789, 94833
Contestacion que da Trinidad Moran. 57450
Contestacion rapida al Discurso opinado. 16160
Contestacion remitida al Piloto el Miercoles de la semana pasada. 58435
Contestacion verdadica y formal. 29251, 68237
Contestaciones entre el Gobernador del Estado de Jalisco. 31565
Contestaciones habidas entre el Arzobispo de Mexico. 48396
Contestaciones habidas entre el Supremo Gobierno del Estado de Jalisco. 35546
Contestaciones habidas entre el Supermo Gobierno Mexicano. 48397
Contestaciones que para el mejor govierno y direccion. 56322
Contested election. 30597
Contested elections in Congress. (15518)
Contexacion que da un Eclesiastico. 64101
Contextacion de un Sacerdote Peruano en Chile. 97660
Conti, Armand de Bourbon, Prince de, 1629-1666. 23539
Conti, Michelangelo. see Innocent XIII, Pope, 1655-1724.
Conti, Natale, 1502?-1580? 16161
Conti, Nicolo di. 66686, 67730
Continent of America. note after 99383C
Continental almanac, for the year of Our Lord, 1781. 79775
Continental almanac, for the year of Our Lord, 1782. 79776
Continental almanac; for the year of Our Lord 1793. 90957
Continental Club, New York. 42878
Continental harmony. 5415
Continental hotel. 62342
Continental journal. 95964
Continental key to the liberties of America. 16162, 92709
Continental magazine. 27448
Continental melodist. (41201)
Continental mirror. 95903, 2d note after 97010
Continental money. 16163, 62490
Continental monthly. (16164), 35230
Continental paper money. 62489
Continental Petroleum Company, of Pennsylvania. 60021
Continental pocket almanac for 1781. 79777
Continental pocket almanac for 1782. 79777
Continental rights and relations of our country. (79510)
Continental-System Volker-Seerecht. 42641
Continentaler. pseud. History and horrors of the Helderberg War. 32108
Continentalist, and other papers. 23992

Continente Americano. (16165)
Continuacao das maravilhas que Deus e servido obrar. 98652
Continuacion a la correspondencia. 21775
Continuacion [de la coleccion de los documentos.] 48360
Continuacion de la Coronica general de Espana de Ocampo. (50496)
Continuacion de la historia general de Espana. (49188)
Continuacion de los documentos oficiales. 16166
Continuacion de los materiales para la historia de Sonora. (34155)
Continuacion de los mismos documentos [mas interesantes.] 14298, 48360
Continuacion del despertador de Michoacan. 93403
Continuacion del Pensador. 41666
Contunuacion del tratado sobre las aguas de los valles de Lima. 47937
Continuacion y conclusion del dialogo. 98345
Continuance of an able and Godly minister. 16345
Continuance of correspondence. 54830
Continuance of peace and increasing prosperity. 101376
Continuatio Americae. (8784)
Continuatio der Beschreibung der Landschafft Pensylvanie. 95394
Continuatio labrorum apostolicorum. 79167
Continuatio supplementi catalogi librorum Biblioth. Coll. Harv. 30728
Continuation af relationerne bettreffende den Gronlandske Missions. (22035)
Continuation and progress of a remarkable work of grace. (7340), 85994
Continuation by Henry Boyle. 75419
Continuation, by Mrs. Judith Sargent Murray. 51524
Continuation de la Californie. 101350
Continuation del manifiesto por los oficiales del Batallon Ligero. 16167
Continuation de l'histoire generale des voyages. 65402
Continuation du Chili. 101350
Continuation faite par le citoyen Duchesne. (21061)
Continuation oder Fortsetzung der Beschreibung. 79168
Continuation of a government of fraud. (56793)
Continuation of a monograph of the bivalve shells. 67460
Continuation of a voyage to New Holland. 18377
Continuation of an appendix. 16168
Continuation of an authentic statement, &c. 23088
Continuation of Freedmen's Bureau. 22175
Continuation of Hudibras. 16169
Continuation of letters . . . [concerning the constitution and order of the Christian ministry.] 49052
Continuation of letters from Sussex emigrants, in Upper Canada. 86184-86185, note after 98068, note after 98069, 98070
Continuation of Miss Brewer's adventures. 102742
Continuation of Mr. Ryland's case. 74589
Continuation of Mr. Whitefield's journal. 103535
Continuation of papers presented to Parliament. 16887
Continuation of sketches of the war. 56031
Continuation of the abridgment of all the public acts of Assembly. 100387

Continuation of the account of the Orphan-House in Georgia, from January 1740, to January 1742. 103496 1
   3
Continuation of the account of the Orphan-House in Georgia, from January 1740 to 1742. 103495 1
Continuation of the account of the Pennsylvania Hospital. 25588, 86582
Continuation of the angelical life. 79956-79957
Continuation of the calm and dispassionate vindication. 4092
Continuation of the dialogue. 59728
Continuation of the discovery of America. (10304)
Continuation of the ecclesiastical history [of Worthington.] 70838
Continuation of the essays upon field-husbandry. 22136
Continuation of the exercises in Scurrility Hall. 16070, 84586, 84589, 93366
Continuation of the history of New-York. 84570-84571
Continuation of the history of the Jews. 36666
Continuation of the history of the province of Massachusetts Bay. 49321
Continuation of the journal of a voyage from Gibraltar. 103533
Continuation [of the journal of the Rev. Dr. Coke.] 14242
Continuation of the letters of Collonel Stanhope. 90292
Continuation of the letters of Hermann. 31497
Continuation of the maritime history of Connecticut. 27888
Continuation of the memoirs of Charles Mathews. 46827
Continuation of the messages. 9515
Continuation of the narrative of the Indian Charity School, begun in Lebanon, in Connecticut. 19372, 103210-103212
Continuation of the narrative of the Indian Charity-School, in Lebanon in Connecticut. 103207
Continuation of the narrative of the Indian Charity-School, in Lebanon, on Connecticut. 103208
Continuation of the narrative of the late troubles and transactions in the church at Bolton. 360, 6254, 11968, 3d note after 96741
Continuation of the narrative of the missions to the new settlements. 15810
Continuation of the narrative of the missions to the new settlements, according to the appointment of the General Association of the State of Connecticut: together with an account of the receipts and expenditures of the money contributed by the people of Connecticut. 15809
Continuation of the narrative of the missions to the new settlements, according to appointment of the General Association of the State of Connecticut; together with an account of the receipts and expenditures of money contributed for the support of the missionaries. 15790
Continuation of the narrative of the missions to the new settlements in Connecticut. (15808)
Continuation of the narrative of the state, &c. of the Indian Charity-School, at Lebanon, in Connecticut. 103206
Continuation of the new discovery of a vast country in America. (31372), 95332

Continuation of the proceedings of the representatives of the province of the Massachusetts-Bay. 45695
Continuation of the Reverend Mr. Whitefield's journal, after his arrival at Georgia. 103545
Continuation of the Reverend Mr. Whitefield's journal, during the time he was detained in England by the embargo. 103539-103540
Continuation of the Reverend Mr. Whitefield's journal during the time he was detained in England, by the embargo. Vol. II. 103543
Continuation of the Reverend Mr. Whitefield's journal from a few days after his arrival at Georgia. 103544
Continuation of the Reverend Mr. Whitefield's journal, from a few days after his arrival at Savannah. 103546
Continuation of the Reverend Mr. Whitefield's journal, from a few days after his return to Georgia. 103550
Continuation of the Reverend Mr. Whitefield's journal, from his arrival at London. 103538-103539
Continuation of the Reverend Mr. Whitefield's journal, from his arrival at Savannah, May 7. 103536
Continuation of the Reverend Mr. Whitefield's journal from his arrival at Savannah, to his return to London. 103535, 103539
Continuation of the Reverend Mr. Whitefield's journal, from his embarking after the embargo. 103542-103543
Continuation of the Reverend Mr. Whitefield's journal from his leaving New-England. 103548
Continuation of the Reverend Mr. Whitefield's journal from his leaving Stanford in New England. 103549
Continuation of the Reverend Mr. Whitefield's journal, from Savannah. 103547
Continuation of the state of New-England. (52623), 65324
Continuation of the tabular statistical views of the United States. 102159, 102168
Continuation of travels in the United States. 73818-73819
Continuation to the present time, by Rev. Horatius Bonar. 27414
Continuation of the proceedings of the Humane Society. 45765
Continuation of William Smith's history of New York. 84569, note after 105999
Continued corruption. 6210
Continued life of the believer. 89814
Continuity of the Church of England. (78584)
Continuous record of atmospheric nucleation. 85072
Continuous water line communications. 88325
Continvase de los successos de la Religion Bethlehemitica. 26571
Contistvciones [sic] y ordenancas de la Vniversidad. 41091
Conto original. 67319
Contoocook Academy, Contoocook, N. H. (16171)
Contoocook Valley Plumbago Mine. (16172)
Contostavlos, Alexander. 4041, 16173
Contra antipodes. 41067
Contra el nuevo pacto social. 98265
Contra los frutos caydos que dexo el Obispo de los Charcas. 47420

Contra manifest van Signor Fernando Telles de Faro. 94622
Contraband Christmas. 16174, 67381
"Contraband of war" inapplicable between the United States. 12700
Contrabands and vagrants. 16175
Contraband's Relief Commision, Cincinnati. Committee. 13113
Contract. 60629
Contract between the city of Wheeling and the B. and O. R. Co. 2992
Contract between the Mich. Central R. R. Co. and the Galena and Chicago Union Rail Road. 48761
Contract between the republic of New Granada and the Panama Rail Road Company. 52775
Contract between the town of Boston and the Mill Corporation. 6747
Contract. City of Charlestown, with Woodlawn Cemetery. 12109
Contract d'Association des Iesvites au Trafique de Canada. 16176
Contract entered into between the Executive of the Republic of Mexico and the [sic] David Boyle Blair. 86976
Contract for the purchase of western territory. 27034
Contract of the Mexican government. 18085
Contract of the Ohio Company. (18173)
Contraction or expansion? 10842
Contraction the road to bankruptcy. 37272
Contracto de Sociedade em Commandita Transportes Urbanos na Bahia. 85774
Contracts and specifications for storing reservoir. 52493
Contracts for the cleaning of the streets. 54222
Contracts with the district of West Philadelphia. 62379
Contrast. 16177
Contrast, a comedy. 97617
Contrast. A poem, in two parts. 106068
Contrast, being the speech of King George III. at the opening of his Parliament. 16180, 2d note after 101545, 104459
Contrast between the effects of religion, and the effects of atheism. 105127
Contrast between the effects of the true democratic system. 62691
Contrast. By an old Etonian. 22473
Contrast. By David Young. 106069
Contrast, . . . by S. Patterson. 59146
Contrast, containing sketches of the characters. 46172, note after 103845
Contrast of British America with the United States and Texas. 27868
Contrast of expenses of the government under the present, with those of former administrations. 103265
Contrast of the two speeches. 16182
Contrast; or plain reasons. 16181, 30577
Contrast: or, strictures on select parts. 20483
Contrast, or the Bible and abolitionism. (28230)
Contrast: or William Henry Harrison versus Martin Van Buren. 16181, 31772, 98425
Contrast! Professions and practice of Republican & Democratic statesmen compared. 16178
Contrast taken from an American publication. 22589
Contrast. The Whig and Democratic platforms. 16179

Contrast to the Reverend Nathaniel Whitaker. 26753

Contrato de Associacion para la republica de los Estados Unidos del Anahuac. 16183

Contrato de tobacos para la siembra. 57619

Contratos hechos en los Estados-Unidos. 73025

Contre-guerilla Francaise au Mexique. 16184, (37604)

Contre-guerilla Francaise sur les hauts plateaux. 56298

Contre la reconnaisance. 17191

Contrebande. 42641

Contreras, Christobal Manso de. see Manso de Contreras, Christobal.

Contreras, Francesco Xavier. 16187-16189

Contreras, Francisco de. 93583 see also Franciscans. Province of San Pedro y San Paul de Michoacan. Visitador.

Contreras, Pedro. 98783 see also Mexico (Viceroyalty) Visitador.

Contreras, Pedro Moya de. see Moya de Contreras, Pedro, Abp.

Contreras Gallardo, Pedro de. 16186

Contreras Herrera, Juan de. see Herrera, Juan de Contreras.

Contribucion. [Articulo ministerial. Contribucion personal.] 99482

Contribuciones a la historia antigua de Venezuela. 72782

Contribution among Terre tenants. 5232

Contribution intended to disclose the minute history. 64156

Contribution to the comparative histology of the femur. 85072

Contribution to the Great Central Fair. 52514

Contribution to the history of the fresh-water algae. 85072

Contribution to the history of the war, and a personal vindication. 84769

Contribution to the Metropolitan Fair. (6932)

Contribution to the New York Fair. (6347)

Contribution to the Trinity Church question. 80088, 1st note after 96985

Contributions for the genealogies of the descendants. 59448

Contributions for the genealogies of the first settlers. (59449)

Contributions from the Geological Department of Columbia University. 84534

Contributions of John Lewis Peyton. 6020

Contributions of New England to America. 73937

Contributions of the Maclurian Lyceum. 43557

Contributions [of the Museum of the American Indian.] 96268

Contributions relating to the causation and prevention of disease. 76643

Contributions to a history of the marine algae. 30782

Contributions to American history. (77865)

Contributions to American history, 1858. 16190

Contributions to an insect fauna. 3932

Contributions to botany, iconographic and descriptive. 48890

Contributions to Canadian meteorology. 82222

Contributions to conchology. 176

Contributions to geology. (39486)

Contributions to literature. 27434

Contributions to physical geography of the United States. 22204

Contributions to terrestrial magnetism. 74700

Contributions to terrestrial magnetism, no. V. (74701)

Contributions to terrestrial magnetism, no. XIV. 74704

Contributions to terrestrial magnetism, no. IX. 74703

Contributions to terrestrial magnetism, no. VI. 74702

Contributions to terrestrial magnetism, nos. VII. and VIII. 74703

Contributions to the early history of the northwest. 31795

Contributions to the ecclesiastical history of Connecticut. 15715, 15813

Contributions to the ecclesiastical history of Essex County, Mass. 23002, note after 89921

Contributions to the ecclesiastical history of the United States of America. 30963, (30967), 1st note after 100494, 100513

Contributions to the ethnography and philology of the Indian tribes. (31007)

Contributions to the family history. 27949

Contributions to the fauna of Chili. 27483

Contributions to the financial discussion. 62820

Contributions to the geology and the physical geography of Mexico. 22056

Contributions to the Historical Society of Montana. (50080)

Contributions to the history of ancient families. 66714

Contributions to the history of the ancient families of New York. 66715

Contributions to the history of the Kip Family. 66715

Contributions to the history of the Lackawanna valley. (32554)

Contributions to the ichthyology of Nova Scotia. 36544

Contributions to the improvement of schoolhouses. 3469

Contributions to the natural history of Nova Scotia. 36544

Contributions to the natural history of the acalapgae. 504

Contributions to the natural history of the Bermudas. 36544

Contributions to the natural history of the fresh water fishes. 27482, 85072

Contributions to the natural history of the United States of America. 505

Contributions to the palaeontology of New York. 29804

Contributions to the physical geography of the United States. 22204, 85072

Contributions to the rhymes of the war. 30808, (34112)

Contributions to the statistics, aboriginal history, antiquities and general ethnology of western New-York. 77864

Contributions to the statistics of human growth. 74184

Contributions to the vital statistics of the state of New York. 79877

Contributions towards a flora of South America. (32864)

Contributions towards a grammar and dictionary of Quichua. 44612

Contributions towards the improvement of agriculture. (18951)

Contributor to the "Atlantic." pseud. Ferryboy and the financier. see Trowbridge, John Townsend.

Contributors for Erecting and Establishing a School-House and School, Germantown, Pa. see Germantown, Pa. Contributors for Erecting and Establishing a School-House and School.

Contributors to the Knickerbocker magazine.
see Knickerbocker magazine. Contributors.
Controller-General's statement, March 31, 1863, 27035
Controversial, moral and political essay. 50846
Controversie concerning liberty of conscience in matters of religion. 17056
Controversy between Archbishop Purcell . . . and Thomas Vickers. 66675
Controversy between Armistead Thompson Mason and Charles Fenton Mercer. 45423
Controversy between Caius Gracchus and Opimius. (16191)
Controversy between Dr. Ryerson, Chief Superintendent of Education in Upper Canada, and the Rev. J. M. Bruyere. 74551
Controversy between "Erskine" and "W. M." 19192, 22799
Controversy between Great Britain and her colonies reviewed. (3111), 38180, 2d note after 103122
Controversy between Massachusetts and South Carolina. 16193
Controversy between New Hampshire, New York, and Vermont. 1st note after 98997
Controversy between New York tribune and Gerrit Smith. (28486), 82605
Controversy between Senator Brooks and Archbishop Hughes. (8371), 33593
Controversy between Senator Brooks and " † John," Archbishop of New York. 8347
Controversy between the Canal Commissioners. 30543
Controversy between the First Parish in Cambridge and the Rev. Dr. Holmes. 10125
Controversy between the Rev. Drs. Potts and Wainwright. 64678
Controversy between the Rev. John Thayer, Catholic missionary of Boston, and the Rev. George Lesslie, pastor of a church in Washington, New Hampshire. 95256
Controversy between the Rev. John Thayer, Catholic missionary, of Boston, and the Rev. George Lesslie, pastor of a church in Washington, New-Hampshire. To which are added, several other pieces. 95255
Controversy in St. Peter's Church. 636
Controversy of the Sunday police. 54223
Controversy touching the old stone mill. 8342
Controversy with Fenno. 10889
Controversy with the Creek Indians. 17358
Convalescent. pseud. Spectral visitants. 89147
Convencion relativa a la cuestion de Mosquitos. 51080
Convencion relativa a la Mosquita. 51079
Convendra o no a las neuvas republicas de America? 100789, 105745
Convenio celebredo entre SS. MM. los reges de Espana e Inglaterra. 32773, 51083
Convent, Zelaya, Mexico. see Zelaya, Mexico. Convent (Augustinian)
Convent, Yuririapundaro, Mexico. see Yuririapundaro, Mexico. Convent (Augustinian)
Convent of St. Mary's. 85383
Conventie tusschen de Directeuren van de Societeijt en Gemagtigde. 93839
Conventie tusschen Staaten Generaal der Vereenigde Nederlanden. 96569
Convention, Hartford, Conn., 1814. see Hartford Convention, 1814.

Convention, Kingston Plains, N. H., 1812. see Rockingham County, N. H. Convention, Kingston Plains, 1812.
Convention, New Haven, Conn., 1811. see New Haven Convention, 1811.
Convention, Pittsburgh, 1835. see Pittsburgh Convention, 1835.
Convention, Williamsport, Pa., 1850. see Williamsport, Pa. Convention, 1850.
Convention, Worcester County, Mass., 1779. see Worcester County, Mass. Convention, 1779.
Convention. A poem, in four cantos. 78325
Convention, an excellent new ballad. 16194
Convention and Conference of Ministers and Delegates of Christian Churches, New Bedford, Mass., 1834. 69892
Convention Anti-seigneuriale, Montreal, 1845. 50249
Convention Anti-seigneurial de Montreal au peuple. 50249
Convention at Portland, Maine, and charter of the European and North American Railway. 23109, 63274
Convention Begun and Held at Worcester, in and for the County of Worcester, on the 3d Day of August, 1779. see Worcester County, Mass. Convention, 1779.
Convention between Great Britain and the United States. 90614
Convention between His Most Christian Majesty and the United States. 15493
Convention between the Choctaw and Chickasaw Indians. 96717
Convention between the crowns of Great Britain and Spain. 16195
Convention between the French· republic and the United States. 16196
Convention between the United States, and the Cherokee Nation. 96628
Convention between the United States and the Chiefs and Head Men of the Indian Tribe called the Creeks. 96623
Convention between the United States . . . and the Mexican republic. 48398
Convention between the United States and . . . the Queen. (64480)
Convention, Composed of Delegates from the Thirteen Original United States, Philadelphia, 1852. see Convention of Delegates from the Thirteen Original States, Philadelphia, 1852.
Convention Consisting of the Rev. Grafton Presbytery, Windsor Association, and Others, Cornish, N. H., 1782. see Convention of the Grafton Presbytery, Windsor Association, and Others, Cornish, N. H., 1782.
Convention documents. 87442
Convention entre el Rey Nuestro Senor y el Rey de la Gran Bretana. (16197)
Convention for Bible Missions, Syracuse, N. Y., 1846. (65832)
Convention for Bible Missions, 2d, Albany, 1846. (65832)
Convention for Facilitating the Introduction of Colored Troops into the Service of the United States, Poughkeepsie, N. Y., 1863. 68393
Convention for Organizing the National Convention of Cotton Manufacturers and Planters, New York, 1868. see National Convention of Cotton Manufacturers and Planters.
Convention for Rescuing the Canals from the Ruin with which they are Threatened,

Rochester, 1859. see New York State
Convention for Rescuing the Canals from
the Ruin which which they are Threatened,
Rochester, 1859.

Convention for Rescuing the Canals from the
Ruin with which they are Threatened,
Utica, N. Y., 1859. see New York State
Convention for Rescuing the Canals from
the Ruin with which they are Threatened,
Utica, N. Y., 1859.

Convention for Suppressing Violations of the
Lord's Day, Andover, Mass., 1814. see
Middlesex County, Mass. Convention
for Suppressing Violations of the Lord's
Day, Andover, 1814.

Convention for Taking into Consideration Subjects Connected with the Improvement of
the Navigation of Connecticut River,
Windsor, Vt., 1830. 15868, 99194

Convention for Taking Preliminary Measures
for a Railroad Throught the Valleys of
the Connecticut and Passumpsic Rivers
to the St. Lawrence, Windsor, Vt., 1836.
99195, 104768

Convention for Taking Preliminary Measures
to Effect an Improved Navigation on
Connecticut River, Windsor, Vt., 1825.
15867, 99196

Convention for the liquidation of the Canada
paper money. (10406)

Convention for the Organization of a Peace
Party, Cincinnati, 1864. see Cincinnati.
Peace Party Convention, 1864.

Convention for the Protection of Western Interests, Evansville, Ind., 1850. 65833

Convention for the Revision of the Constitution
of the State of Kentucky, 1849. see
Kentucky. Constitutional Convention,
1849.

Convention, Held for the Promotion of Agriculture and Manufacture, Harrisburg, Pa.,
1827. (16198), 36691

Convention Held on the New-Hampshire Grants,
Cornish, Vt., 1778. see Vermont. Convention, 1778.

Convention in Relation to the Pacific Railroad,
Memphis, Tenn., 1849. (47783)

Convention manual. 53628

Convention Nationale. 87115

Convention Nationale. Compte rendue sur la
situation actuelle de Saint-Domingue.
75086

Convention Nationale. Rapport sur la colonie
de Saint Domingue. (19266)

Convention of Agriculturists and Manufacturers,
Harrisburg, Pa., 1827. see Harrisburg
Convention, 1827.

Convention of agriculturists and manufacturers,
and others. (16198)

Convention of American Instructors of the Deaf
and Dumb. 5th, Jacksonville, Ill., 1858.
65845

Convention of Banks, Charleston, S. C., 1841.
12060

Convention of Baptist Churches for Forming
the New York Association, New York,
1791. see Baptists. New York. Convention for Forming the New York Association, New York, 1791.

Convention of Churches in Windham County,
Conn., 1800. see Congregational Churches
in Connecticut. Windham County Convention, 1800.

Convention of Citizens of the Commonwealth of
Pennsylvania, for Aid to Enlarge the

Union Canal, 1838. see Union Canal
Convention, Pennsylvania, 1838.

Convention of Coloured Citizens of Pennsylvania.
Harrisburg, 1848. see State Convention
of Coloured Citizens of Pennsylvania.
Harrisburg, 1848.

Convention of Colored Men, Lexington, Ky.,
1867. see State Convention of Colored
Men, Lexington, Ky., 1867.

Convention of Committees for the County of
Worcester, Mass., 1775. see Worcester
County, Mass. Non-importation Asso-
ciation.

Convention of Congregational Ministers, Boston,
1759. (46094)

Convention of Congregational Ministers in New
Hampshire, Concord, 1791. (52796)

Convention of Congregational Ministers of
Massachusetts. 32084 see also Congregational Churches in Massachusetts.

Convention of Congregational Ministers of
Massachusetts, Boston, 1657. (20274)

Convention of Congregational Ministers of
Massachusetts, Boston, 1697. 46550,
note after 95360

Convention of Congregational Ministers of
Massachusetts, Boston, 1743. 26831,
(30173), 46160, 65237, 94927

Convention of Congregational Ministers of
Massachusetts, Boston, 1743. Committee.
46160, 94927

Convention of Congregational Ministers of
Massachusetts, Boston, 1743. Moderator.
46160, 94927 see also Eells, Nathaniel.

Convention of Congregational Ministers of
Massachusetts, Boston, 1773. 360, 11968,
56586, 3d note after 96741

Convention of Congregational Ministers of
Massachusetts, Boston, 1795. 45943

Convention of Congregational Ministers of
Massachusetts, Boston, 1799. 45579

Convention of Congregational Ministers of
Massachusetts, Boston, 1830. 45837

Convention of Congregational Ministers of
Massachusetts, Boston, 1849. Committee
on Slavery. 45696, 45817, (82052)

Convention of Congregational Ministers of
Massachusetts, Boston, 1860. 45944

Convention of Congregational Ministers of New
England. see also Congregational
Churches in New England.

Convention of Congregational Ministers of New
England, Boston, 1743. see Boston.
Assembly of Pastors of Churches in New
England, 1743.

Convention of Congregational Ministers of New
England, Boston, 1745. 94922, note after
103402

Convention of Delegates, Brunswick, Me., 1816.
see Maine. Convention, Brunswick, 1816.

Convention of Delegates, Cayuga County, N. Y.,
1819. see Democratic Party. New York.
Cayuga County. Convention, Auburn, 1819.

Convention of Delegates, Appointed by Persons
Interested in the Growth and Manufacture
of Wool, New York, 1831. see Wool
Growers and Manufacturers Convention,
New York, 1831.

Convention of delegates, appointed by public
meetings in the several counties of . . .
Virginia, for the purpose of adopting
measures to prevent the election of
General Jackson . . . assembled . . . in
Richmond. 100499

Convention of Delegates, Chosen by the People of Massachusetts, Without Distinction of Party, to take into Consideration the Proposed Annexation of Texas, Boston, 1845. see Boston. Convention of Delegates on Proposed Annexation of Texas, 1845.

Convention of Delegates, Elected by the Citizens of the Different Districts Interested in the Connexion of the Susquehanna and Lehigh Rivers, by a Canal through the Valley of the Nescopek, and in the Navigation of the Lehigh, Conyngham Town, Pa., 1832. see Nescopeck Canal Convention, Conyngham Town, Pa., 1832.

Convention of Delegates for the Formation of a Domestic Missionary Society, New York, 1822. 97870 see also United Domestic Missionary Society, New York.

Convention of Delegates from all the Towns in Bristol County, Taunton, Mass, 1837. see Whig Party. Massachusetts. Bristol County.

Convention of Delegates from Different Classes and Interests, New York, 1864. see Fiscal Convention, New York, 1864.

Convention of Delegates from Luzerne, Susquehanna and Bradford Counties, Tunkhannock, Pa., 1840. 60406

Convention of Delegates from Several Counties of the Commonwealth, on the Swatara Mining District, Harrisburg, Pa., 1839, see Swatara Mining District Convention, Harrisburg, Pa., 1839.

Convention of Delegates, from Several Moral Societies in the State of New York, Albany, 1819. 96452

Convention of Delegates from Several of the New England States, Boston, 1780 see Boston. Convention of Delegates from Several of the New England States, 1780.

Convention of Delegates from Several States to Nominate a Canadidate for Vice-President, Baltimore, 1832. see Democratic Party. National Convention, Baltimore, 1832.

Convention of Delegates from the Abolition Societies Established in the Different Parts of the United States. see American Convention for Promoting the Abolition of Slavery, and Improving the Condition of the African Race.

Convention of Delegates from the Abolition Societies in Different Parts of the United States. see American Convention for Promoting the Abolition of Slavery, and Improving the Condition of the African Race.

Convention of Delegates from the Abolition Society, New York, 1794. see American Convention for Promoting the Abolition of Slavery, and Improving the Condition of the African Race.

Convention of Delegates from the Counties of Hampshire, Franklin, and Hampden, Northampton, Mass., 1812. 65783

Convention of Delegates, from the Different Counties in the State of New York, Opposed to Free-Masonry, Albany, 1829. see Antimasonic State Convention of New York, Albany, 1829.

Convention of Delegates from the Several Baptist Churches of Central Wisconsin, Milwaukee, 1838. see Baptists. Wisconsin. First Baptist Association of Central Wisconsin.

Convention of Delegates from the Several Counties of New York, Albany, 1828. see

National Republican Party. New York. Convention, Albany, 1828.

Convention of Delegates from the Several Counties of the Holland Purchase, Buffalo, N. Y., 1827. see Holland Purchase Convention, Buffalo, N. Y., 1827.

Convention of Delegates from the Several Counties Within the Holland Purchase, Buffalo, N. Y., 1834. see Holland Purchase Convention, Buffalo, N. Y., 1834.

Convention of Delegates, from the States of Massachusetts, Connecticut, and Rhode-Island, the Counties of Cheshire and Grafton in the State of New-Hampshire, and the County of Windham in the State of Vermont, Hartford, Conn., 1814. see Hartford Convention, 1814.

Convention of Delegates from the Synod of New York and Philadelphia, and from the Associations of Connecticut, 1766-1775. see Presbyterian Church in the U.S.A. Convention of Delegates from the Synod of New York and Philadelphia, and from the Associations of Connecticut, 1766-1775.

Convention of Delegates from the Thirteen Original States, Philadelphia. 1852. 36732, 62164 see also Board of Trustees from the Old Thirteen States, Philadelphia, 1860.

Convention of Delegates from Various Bible Societies of South Carolina, Columbia, 1829. see Bible Convention, Columbia, S. C., 1829.

Convention of Delegates from Twenty Towns and Five Plantations Within the Counties of York, Cumberland, and Lincoln, Portland, Me., 1795. see Maine (District) Convention, Portland, 1795.

Convention of Delegates Holden at Ipswich in the County of Essex, to Take into Consideration the Constitution and Form of Government, 1778. see Essex County, Mass. Convention, Ispwich, 1778.

Convention of Delegates Met to Consult on Missions, Cincinnati, 1831. see Convention on Domestic Missions, Cincinnati, 1831.

Convention of delegates of insurance companies. 53629

Convention of Delegates of Kansas Aid Societies, Buffalo, N. Y., 1856. 37049

Convention of Delegates of Kansas Aid Societies, Cleveland, 1856. 37049

Convention of Delegates of the British American League, Kingston, Ontario, 1849. (8080)

Convention of Delegates of the People of New Jersey, Trenton, 1812. see New Jersey. Convention, Trenton, 1812.

Convention of Delegates of the People of New-Jersey . . . Held by Public Appointment, at Trenton, 4 July, 1812. see New Jersey. Convention, Trenton, 1812.

Convention of Delegates of the Several Moral Societies in the State of New York, Albany, 1820. 65786

Convention of Delegates of the Several Moral Societies in the State of New York, Albany, 1821. 65786

Convention of Delegates on Proposed Annexation of Texas, Boston, 1845. see Boston. Convention of Delegates on Proposed Annexation of Texas, 1845.

Convention of Delegates on Title of Holland Land Company, Buffalo, 1830. see Holland Purchase Convention, Buffalo, N. Y., 1830.

Convention of delegates on title of Holland
Land Company. Two reports, and appeal
to the people of New York. (32516),
84221
Convention of Delegates Opposed to Executive
Usurpation and Abuse, Harrisburg, Pa.,
1834. see Harrisburg, Pa. Convention
of Delegates Opposed to Executive Usurpation and Abuse, 1834.
Convention of Delegates Opposed to Free
Masonry, Le Roy, N. Y., 1828. (65787)
Convention of Delegates Representing the Merchants and Others Interested in Commerce,
Philadelphia, 1820. petitioners 47636
Convention of Delegations from the Diocese of
Mississippi and Alabama, and the Clergy
and Churches of Louisiana, New Orleans,
1835. see Protestant Episcopal Church
in the U. S. A. Convention of Delegations
from the Diocese of Mississippi and
Alabama, and the Clergy and Churches
of Louisiana, New Orleans, 1835.
Convention of Democratic Republican Young
Men, Harrisburg, Pa., 1836. see Demo-
cratic Party. Pennsylvania. Convention
of Young Men, Harrisburg, 1836.
Convention of Democratic Young Men, Reading,
Pa., 1838. see Democratic Party.
Pennsylvania. Convention of Young Men,
Reading, 1838.
Convention of Deputies from the Abolition
Societies in the United States, Philadelphia,
1796. see American Convention for Pro-
moting the Abolition of Slavery, and Im-
proving the Condition of the African
Race.
Convention of drunkards. 27365
Convention of Freedmen of North Carolina,
Raleigh, 1865. (55664)
Convention of Freedmen's Commissions,
Indianapolis, 1864. 25745
Convention of Friends of American Industry.
see Friends of Domestic Industry.
Convention of Friends of the Administration,
Concord, N. H., 1828. see Democratic
Party. New Hampshire. Convention,
Concord, 1828.
Convention of Insurance Companies, New York,
1849. 53629
Convention of Inventors, 1845-1847. (51113)
Convention of Iron Masters, Philadelphia, 1849.
see Ironmasters' Convention, Philadelphia.
1849.
Convention of Iron Workers, Albany, 1849.
35099
Convention of Lake Underwriters, Buffalo,
N. Y., 1856. (3667)
Convention of Laymen of the Methodist Episcopal
Church, New York, 1852. see Methodist
Episcopal Church. Convention of Laymen,
New York, 1852.
Convention of Literary and Scientific Gentlemen,
New York, 1830. 19334, 36734
Convention of Loyal Leagues, Utica, N. Y.,
1863. see Loyal National League of the
State of New York.
Convention of Managers and Superintendents of
Houses of Refuge and Schools of Reform
in the United States. 1st, New York,
1857. 33179
Convention of Managers and Superintendents of
Houses of Refuge and Schools of Reform
in the United States. 2d, New York, 1859.
33179

Convention of Medical Delegates, Northampton,
Mass., 1827. 65788
Convention of Merchants and Others for the
Promotion of the Direct Trade, Charleston,
S. C., 1839. 12070
Convention of Ministers, Richmond, Va., 1863.
81774
Convention of Ministers and Delegates of the
Congregational Churches in the Northwest.
see Congregational Churches in the North-
west. Triennial Convention of Ministers
and Delegates, Chicago, 1858.
Convention of Ministers and Delegates of the
Evangelical Lutheran Churches in New
York, Fordsbuch, 1837. see Evangelical
Lutheran Ministerium of the State of New
York and Adjacent States and Counties.
Convention of Ministers and Delegates,
Fordsbush, 1837.
Convention of National Republican Young Men,
Hartford, Conn., 1832. see National
Republican Party. Connecticut. Conven-
tion of Young Men, Hartford, 1832.
Convention of New England States, Boston, 1780.
see Boston. Convention of Delegates
from Several of the New England States,
1780.
Convention of New Hampshire Publishers,
Editors, and Printers, Wolfeborough, 1868.
52819
Convention of New Hampshire publishers, editors,
and priters, held at Wolfeborough, July 24
and 25, 1868. 52819
Convention of New Jersey, Holden at Trenton,
1787. see New Jersey. Convention,
Trenton, 1787.
Convention of Presbyterian Ministers and Elders,
Hannibal, Mo., 1841. see Presbyterian
Church in the United States. Synod of
Missouri.
Convention of Radical Political Abolitionists,
Syracuse, 1855. 65834
Convention of Republican Antimasonic Delegates,
Ballston Spa, N. Y., 1831. see Anti-
masonic Party. New York. Saratoga
County. Convention, Ballston Spa, 1831.
Convention of Republican Citizens of the County
of Addison, Vt., 1814. see Democratic
Party. Vermont. Addison County. Con-
vention, 1814.
Convention of Republican Delegates from the
County of Norfolk, Dedham, Mass., 1812.
see Democratic Party. Massachusetts.
Norfolk County. Convention, Dedham,
1812.
Convention of Sabbath School Teachers, Hartford,
Conn., 1857. see State Convention of
Sabbath School Teachers, 1st, Hartford,
Conn., 1857.
Convention of Seceding Masons, Le Roy, N. Y.,
1828. 69705, 88653
Convention of Seceding Masons, Le Roy, N. Y.,
1828. Lewiston Committee. 70157
Convention of Teachers, Columbia. S. C., 1850.
87922
Convention of the Anti-masonic Members of
the Legislature of Vermont, 1833. see
Anti-masonic State Convention of Vermont,
Montpelier, 1833.
Convention of the Baptist Denomination, of
Mississippi. see Baptists. Mississippi.
Convention.
Convention of the Church Anti-slavery Society,
Worcester, Mass., 1859. see Church
Anti-slavery Society.

Convention of the Colored Citizens of Ohio, Columbus, 1849. see State Convention of the Colored Citizens of Ohio, Columbus, 1849.

Convention of the Colored Citizens of the State of Illinois, 1st, Chicago, 1853. 34312

Convention of the Colored Freemen of Ohio, Cincinnati, 1852. (13106)

Convention of the Colored People of Virginia, Alexandria, 1865. 40935

Convention of the Commissioners of Appraisement, Montgomery, Ala., 1864. 15335

Convention of the Diocese of Connecticut, Middletown, 1835. see Protestant Episcopal Church in the U. S. A. Connecticut (Diocese) Convention, Middletown, 1835.

Convention of the Friends of African Colonization, Washington, D. C., 1842. see Friends of African Colonization. Convention, Washington, D. C., 1842.

Convention of the Friends of American Industry, Boston, 1832. see Friends of Domestic Industry.

Convention of the Friends of American Industry. Report on the production and manufacture of cotton. 35449

Convention of the Friends of Domestic Industry. see Friends of Domestic Industry.

Convention of the Friends of Education, Mount Holly, N. J., 1847. 69922

Convention of the Friends of John Quincy Adams, Trenton, N. J., 1824. see Democratic Party. New Jersey. Convention, Trenton, 1824.

Convention of the Friends of National Industry, New York, 1819. 65789

Convention of the Friends of Universal Suffrage of Louisiana, 1865. 42284

Convention of the Grafton Presbytery, Windsor Association, and Others, Cornish, N. H., 1782. 69458

Convention of the inhabitants of the New Hampshire Grants in opposition to the claims of New York, 1765-1777. 1st note after 98997

Convention of the Medical Society of Pennsylvania, Lancaster, 1848. see Medical Society of Pennsylvania. Convention, Lancaster, 1848.

Convention of the Ministers of Worcester County, Worcester, Mass., 1837-1838. 105407

Convention of the Ministers of Worcester County, Worcester, Mass., 1837-1838. Minority. 105407

Convention of the Mutual Benefit Societies or Brotherhoods of the Protestant Episcopal Church in the United States, New York, 1853. 66159 see also General Convention of the Brotherhood of the Protestant Episcopal Church.

Convention of the North and South Consociations of Litchfield, Conn., 1852. see Congregational Churches in Connecticut. Convention of the North and South Consociations of Litchfield, 1852.

Convention of the Northern Lines of Railway, Boston, 1850-1851. (55808)

Convention of the Pastors of the Churches in the Province of the Massachusetts-Bay in New-England, Boston, 1743. see Convention of Congregational Ministers of Massachusetts, Boston, 1743.

Convention of the People of Colour. 1st, Philadelphia, 1831. 49342

Convention of the People of Massachusetts, Boston, 1862. see People's Convention, Boston, 1862.

Convention of the People of South Carolina. see South Carolina. Convention, 1832-1833.

Convention of the Protestant Episcopal Church, in the state of Maryland, the the vestries and other members of the said church. 45304

Convention of the Representatives of the New-Hampshire Settlers, Manchester, N. H., 1775. see Vermont. Convention, 1775.

Convention of the Soldiers of the War of 1812, Schuylerville, N. Y., 1856. 65845

Convention of the Soldiers of the War of 1812, Syracuse, 1854. 86348

Convention of the State of Pennsylvania to Propose Amendments to the Constitution, Harrisburg, 1837. see Pennsylvania. Convention to Propose Amendments to the Constitution, Harrisburg, 1837.

Convention of the Stockholders of the Southern Pacific Railroad Company, Memphis, 1858. see Southern Pacific Railroad Company (Texas) Stockholders Convention, Memphis, Tenn., 1858.

Convention of the stockholders of the Southern Pacific Railroad Company, held at Memphis, Sept. 17, 1858. 88433

Convention of the Trustees of a Proposed University for the Southern States, Under the Auspices of the Protestant Episcopal Church, Atlanta, 1857. 65790

Convention of the Various Bible Societies of South Carolina, Columbia, 1840. see Bible Convention, Columbia, S. C., 1840.

Convention of the Young Men of Massachusetts, Friendly to the Cause of Temperance, Worcester, 1836. 65836

Convention of the Young Men of New York, Utica, N. Y., 1828. 53714

Convention of the Young Men's Christian Association of New Hampshire. see Young Men's Christian Association of New Hampshire. State Convention.

Convention of the Whig Party in Massachusetts, Concord, 1838. see Whig Party. Massachusetts. Convention, Concord, 1838.

Convention of Teachers and Friends of Education, Utica, N. Y., 1831. see New York State Convention of Teachers and Friends of Education, Utica, 1831.

Convention of Tobacconists, New York, 1865. 9306

Convention of United States Assessors, Cleveland, 1863. 22425, 23380

Convention of Whig Young Men, Worcester, Mass., 1839. see Whig Party. Massachusetts. Convention of Young Men, Worcester, 1839.

Convention of Wool Manufacturers, 1864. see National Association of Wool Manufacturers. Convention, 1864.

Convention of Worcester County, 1782. see Worcester County, Mass. Convention, 1782.

Convention of Young Men in Rockingham Councillor District, Epping, N. H., 1828. 65752

Convention of Young Men of the County of Washington, Hartford, N. Y., 1830. see Anti-masonic Convention of Young Men of the County of Washington, Hartford, N. Y., 1830.

CONVENTION

Convention of Young Men of the County of
Washington, Opposed to the Masonic
Institution, Hartford, N. Y., 1830. see
Anti-masonic Convention of Young Men
of the County of Washington, Hartford,
N. Y., 1830.
Convention of Young Men of the State of New
York, Utica, 1828. 53714, 1st note after
106151
Convention on Connecting the Pennsylvania and
Ohio Canals, Warren, Ohio, 1833. 60299
Convention on Domestic Missions, Cincinnati,
1831. 49365
Convention on Domestic Missions, Cincinnati,
1831. Committee. 69885
Convention on Domestic Missions, Cincinnati,
1831. Minority. 69885
Convention on Internal Improvement in Virginia,
Lewisburg, [W.] Va., 1831. 100481
Convention on Internal Improvements, Baltimore,
1825. 45287, 45368
Convention of Internal Improvements of Mary-
land, Baltimore, 1836. 45172
Convention on the Great State Road, Newburgh,
N. Y., 1826. (53481)
Convention, on the Improvement of Rivers and
Harbors, Chicago, 1847. see Harbor
and River Convention, Chicago, 1847.
Convention on the Location of the Post Office
in New York, New York, 1836. 54591
Convention on the New Hampshire Grants,
Cornish, N. H., 1778. see Vermont.
Convention, 1778.
Convention on the New Hampshire Grants,
Cornish, N. H., 1779. see Vermont.
Convention, 1779.
Convention on the Proposed Annexation of Texas,
Boston, 1845. see Boston. Convention
of Delegates on Proposed Annexation of
Texas, 1845.
Convention on the Recommendation to Reduce
the Pay for Mail Service to Rail Road
Companies, Baltimore, 1854. 65778
Convention pour l'execution d'un canal maritime
interoceanique sur le territoire de la
Republique de Nicaragua. 16201
Convention Relative to the Observance of the
Lord's Day, and to the Suppression of
Vice, Exeter, N. H., 1815. see Rocking-
ham County, N. H. Convention Relative
to the Observance of the Lord's Day, and
to the Suppression of Vice, Exeter, 1815.
Convention Relative to the St. Lawrence and
Champlain Ship Canal, Saratoga Springs,
N. Y., 1849. 75310
Convention Relative to the St. Lawrence and
Champlain Ship Canal, Saratoga Springs,
N. Y., 1849. American Committee.
75310
Convention Relative to the St. Lawrence and
Champlain Ship Canal, Saratoga Springs,
N. Y., 1849. Canadian Committee.
75310
Convention . . . resolved itself into a com-
mittee of the whole convention. 100033
Convention sermon. 23
Convention speech of Hon. James B. Clay.
13568
Convention to Consider Measures for Re-
forming the Management and Improving
the Trade of the . . . Canals, Rochester,
N. Y., 1870. see State Convention to
Consider Measures for Reforming the
Management and Improving the Trade of
the . . . Canals, Rochester, N. Y., 1870.

Convention to Consider the Expediency of
Establishing a Theological Institute Con-
nected with a System of Manual Labor,
East Windsor, Conn., 1833. 23528
Convention to Deliberate on Internal Improvement in Virginia, Lewisburg, [W.] Va.,
1831. see Convention on Internal Improvement in Virginia, Lewisburg, [W.]
Va., 1831.
Convention to Form a Liturgy for the Episcopal
Churches in the United States. see Protestant Episcopal Church in the U. S. A.
Convention to Form a Liturgy, 1789.
Convention to Form a Supreme Grand Lodge
for the United States, Baltimore, 1847.
see Freemasons. United States. Con-
vention to Form a Supreme Grand Lodge
for the United States, Baltimore, 1847.
Convention to Improve the Condition of the In-
dians in the United States, Boston, 1861.
37660
Convention to Organize a State Anti-slavery
Society, Milton, Indiana, 1838. see In-
diana Convention to Organize a State Anti-
slavery Society, Milton, 1838.
Convention to Promote Common School Education,
Harrisburg, Pa., 1850. see Pennsylvania.
State Convention to Promote Common
School Education, Harrisburg, 1850.
Convention to Propose Amendments to the Consti-
tution of Pennsylvania, Harrisburg, 1837-
1838. see Pennsylvania. Constitutional
Convention, Harrisburg, 1837-1838.
Convention Upon the Subject of an Immediate
Enlargement of the Erie Canal, Rochester,
N. Y., 1837. 22751
Convention vindicated from the misrepresenta-
tions of the enemies of our peace.
(16202), 101144
Conventions in the New Hampshire Grants for
the Independence of Vermont, 1776-1777.
see Vermont. Convention, 1776. and
Vermont. Convention, 1777.
Convento de Corpus Christi, Mexico City. see
Mexico (City) Convento de Corpus Christi.
Convento de la Purisima Concepcion, Puebla,
Mexico. see Puebla, Mexico (City) Con-
vento de la Purisima Concepcion.
Convento de la Santissima Trinidad, Puebla,
Mexico. see Puebla, Mexico (City) Con-
vento de la Santissima Trinidad.
Convento de Nuestra de Bethlem y S. Francisco
Xavier, Mexico (City) see Mexico (City)
Convento de Nuestra Senora de Bethlem y
S. Francisco Xavier (Bethlemite)
Convento de Nuestra Senora de la Concepcion,
Puebla, Mexico. see Puebla, Mexico
(City) Convento de Nuestra Senora de
Concepcion.
Convento de Nuestro Santo Padre Domingo,
Puebla, Mexico. see Puebla, Mexico
(City) Convento de N. S. P. Domingo.
Convento de Religiosas de Jesus Maria, Mexico
(City) see Mexico (City) Convento de
Religiosas de Jesus Maria.
Convento de San Diego, Mexico (City) see
Mexico (City) Convento de San Diego.
Convento de Santa Catarina de Sena, Puebla,
Mexico. see Puebla, Mexico (City)
Convento de Santa Catarina de Sena.
Convento de Santa Clara, Mexico (City) see
Mexico (City) Convento de Santa Clara.
Convento de Santa Ines de Monte Policiano, Pue-
bla, Mexico. see Puebla, Mexico (City)
Convento de Santa Ines de Monte Poli-
ciano.

648

Convento de Sato Antonio, Rio de Janeiro.
see Rio de Janeiro. Convento de Sato
Antonio.
Convento de Senor San Felipe de Jesus, Mexico
(City) see Mexico (City) Convento de
Senor San Felipe de Jesus (Capuchin)
Convento del Maximo Doctor S. Geronimo de
la Puebla de Los Angeles. see Puebla,
Mexico (City) Convento de San Geronimo
(Augustinian)
Convento Real de Jesus Maria, Mexico (City)
see Mexico (City) Convento de Religiosas
de Jesus Maria.
Conventos suprimidos en Mejico. 67657
Conventuum ordinis eremitarum sancti descrip-
tio. (42603)
Converging series expressing the ratio between
the diameter and the circumference of a
circle. 85072
Conversacion de los revolucionarios de Trugillo.
97275
Conversacion de un fuereno con el Pensador
Mexicano. 98258
Conversaciones de Ulloa con sus tres hijos.
97684
Conversation between a mother and her children.
102197
Conversation between a planter and some head-
men. 19945
Conversation between an anti-slavery lecturer
and a lady. 25015
Conversation in a canebrake. 16203
Conversation in heaven. 46261
Conversation in Ireland. (21345)
Conversation of two persons under a window.
97621
Conversation, practical and philosophical.
(16204)
Conversation. Translated from a French
manuscript. 36665
Conversation with Horatio Seymour. 37272
Conversations about the los colonies of Green-
land. (28652)
Conversations . . . about the trees of America.
30962, 1st note after 97724
Conversations and letters on the Sandwich
Islands and Bombay missions. 99628
Conversations at Fairfield on religion and
superstition. 67372
Conversations, discussions and anecdotes of
Thomas Story. 71080, note after 92321
Conversations of a Catholic missionary with
Americans. 61020
Conversations on slavery. 36538
Conversations on some matters to be acted
upon. 37502
Conversations on the Bombay mission. 97515,
97517, 97521-97523
Conversation on the Bombay missions. 99628
Conversations on the Ceylon mission. 97517,
97522-97523
Conversations on the Cherokee missions.
97517
Conversations on the Choctaw mission. 97515
Conversations on the Indian missions. 97518,
97522
Conversations on the Mackinaw and Green Bay
Indian missions. 16205, 97516
Conversations on the mission to the Arkansas
Cherokees. 97517
Conversations on the Sandwich Island missions.
99628
Conversations on the Sandwich Islands. 12673
Conversations on the Sandwich Islands mission.
97516-97517, 97520, 97522-97523

Conversations principally on the aborigines of
North America. (16206), 76378
Conversations round the camp-fire. 69051
Conversations- und Reisebibliothek, Band. VIII.
9518
Conversations with the children about Massa-
chusetts. 97725
Conversations with the children about New York.
(30966), 3d note after 97724
Conversations with the children about the whale
fishery and polar seas. 30971, 2d note
after 97725
Conversations with the children about Virginia.
30970, 2d note after 97726, 2d note after
100480
Conversations with the young people about the
whale fishery and the polar regions.
97726
Conversations with young persons. 30970, 2d
note after 97726, 2d note after 100480
Converse, A. 32360
Converse, Francis. 16207
Converse, Freeman. 16208
Converse, J. K. 16209-16210
Converse, Sherman. 93608
Converse, Sherman. defendant (16211), 92380
Conversion and conduct of John Young. 24664
Conversion and instruction of the free Indians.
34634
Conversion de Piritv. 5852, 74017
Conversion des savvages qvi ont este batizes
en la Novvelle France. 16212, 40167
Conversion of an Indian. (30395), 97269
Conversion of Jonathan the Jew. (76340)
Conversion of Juvenis. 90121
Conversion of Peter Bayssiere. 103985
Conversion of the Reverend John Thayer of
Boston. 95245
Conversion of the world. 85265
Conversion of the world; or, how are the heathen
to be converted. 85291
Conversion of Zaccheus. 103573
Conversion de M.ʳ Thayer et de M.ˡˡᵉ Pitt.
95249
Conversions, reveils, experiences Chretiennes
et entretiens. 7803
Convert instructed in the origin, signification,
and advantages of baptism. 90192
Converted Indian, a poem. 13765, 104301
Converted sinner. 46271
Converted soldier becomes a zealous missionary.
88045A
Conveyances on record in the Register's Office.
78969
Convict. pseud. State prison life. see Banka,
J. Harrie.
Convict in the House of Correction. pseud.
Rat-trap. see Snelling, William Joseph,
1804-1848. supposed author
Convict in Sing Sing State Prison. pseud.
Echoes from the living graves. 21783A
Conviction of slave dealers. (27978)
Convict's visitor. 84686
Convient-il a l'administration de ceder part,
ou de ne rien ceder aux etrangers dans
le commerce de la metropole? 21034
Convite a los verdaderos amantes de la religion
y de la patria. 76222
Convocation of Miletus. 20391
Convocational Congress, Reading, Pa., 1867.
see Protestant Episcopal Church in the
U. S. A. Pennsylvania (Diocese) Convo-
cational Congress, Reading, Pa., 1867.
Convoy, ter gelegenheid van het beloofd en
geweigerd. (16213)

Convulsions of America. 5708
Conway, Cornelius. 16214
Conway, Elias Nelson, 1812-1894. 33150
  see also Arkansas. Governor, 1852-
  1860 (Conway)
Conway, Francis Ingram Seymour. see Hert-
  ford, Francis Ingram Seymour Conway,
  2d Marquis of, 1743-1822.
Conway, H. J. 92408
Conway, Henry Seymour, 1721-1795. (15052),
  16215
Conway, Martin Franklin, 1827-1882. (16216)-
  (16217)
Conway, Moncure Daniel, 1832-1907. 16218-
  16222, 93776
Conway, Thomas W. 16223
Conway, Mass. Centennial Celebration, 1867.
  16224, 70818
Conwell, Henry, Bp. (62214), note after 93765
  see also Philadelphia (Diocese) Bishop
  (Conwell)
Conwell, Russell H. 16225
Cony, Daniel. (43923)
Conybeare, W. H. (16226), 50754
Conyers, Josiah B. 16227
Conyngham, David P. 16228-16229
Conyngham, John N. 16230
Conyngham, Kate. pseud. Sunny South. see
  Ingraham, Joseph H.
Conyngham Town, Pa. Convention of Delegates,
  Elected by the Citizens of the Different
  Districts Interested in the Connexion of
  the Susquehanna and Lehigh Rivers, by a
  Canal Through the Valley of the Nesco-
  peck, and in the Navigation of the Lehigh,
  1832. see Nescopeck Canal Convention,
  Conyngham Town, Pa., 1832.
Conyngham Town, Pa. Lehigh River Navigation
  Convention, 1832. see Nescopeck Canal
  Convention, Conyngham Town, Pa., 1832.
Conyngham Town, Pa. Nescopeck Canal Con-
  vention, 1832. see Nescopeck Canal
  Convention, Conyngham Town, Pa., 1832.
Conyngham Town, Pa. Susquehanna and Lehigh
  Canal Convention, 1832. see Nescopeck
  Canal Convention, Conyngham Town, Pa.,
  1832.
Coock, James. see Cook, James, 1728-1779.
Coody, Abimelech. pseud. Fable for statesmen.
  see Verplanck, Gulian Crommelin.
Coody, Abimeleck. pseud. Letter to the Hon.
  Saml. L. Mitchell. see Verplanck,
  Gulian Crommelin.
Cook, ---------, fl. 1765. RN 16285
Cook, ---------, fl. 1848. USA 58
Cook, ---------, fl. 1862. 60806, 85618
  see also Snyder, Cook and Co. firm
Cook, Ann. see Beauchamp, Ann (Cook)
Cook, Burton Chauncey, 1819-1894. 16232
Cook, Charles. 16233
Cook, Clarence. ed. 53380
Cook, Ebenezer. 16234-(16235), note after
  80002
Cook, Edward. 103040 see also Westmore-
  land County, Pa. Lieutenant.
Cook, Elisha. see Cooke, Elisha.
Cook, Flavius Joseph. (16236)
Cook, G. 16237
Cook, George Hammell, 1818-1889. 16238-
  16239, 53118-53120, 53122-53123 see
  also New Jersey. State Geologist.
Cook, Henry. 16240
Cook, Ichabod. 16241
Cook, J. T. (16280)

Cook, James, 1728-1779. 1147, 4079, 16243,
  (16245)-16249, 16250-16251, 16275-16278,
  21211-21215, 22575, 25131, 25142, 30934-
  (30943), 31389, 32438, 35953-35954,
  35962, 35966, (35967), 36707, 37123,
  38022, (40141), 52455, 52580, 52591,
  (54897), (55557), 56064, (59572), 64396,
  (69276), 69506, 71252, 83981, 101029,
  104679
Cook, James, 1728-1779. incorrectly supposed
  author 4246, 16242, note after 36695
Cook, James M. 90780
Cook, Joel. 16279
Cook, John. defendant 21621
Cook, John E. 8519, 16281
Cook, John H. 11349, 16282
Cook, John Parsons, 1817-1872. 16283
Cook, Joseph. 16284
Cook, M. P. 16288
Cook, Martha (Walker) 16286
Cook, Moody D. (16287)
Cook, Priscilla. 100524
Cook, R. D. 16289
Cook, R. S. 16290-16291
Cook, Samuel. 16292
Cook, Thomas M. ed. 16293, 79652
Cook, Valentine. 91591
Cook, W. H. ed. 88324
Cook, William, 1696-1760. 16294-16296
Cook, William, d. 1876. 16297
Cook, William A. 16298-16299
Cook, Zebedee. 16300
Cook (J. W.) firm publishers 17365
Cook (John) firm publishers 92718
Cook County, Ill. School Commissioner.
  (16301)
Cooke, Charles. (16302)
Cooke, Sir Charles. 37783
Cooke, Capt. Edward. 16303, 31389, (54897)
Cooke, Eleutheros. 16304
Cooke, Elisha. 16305
Cooke, Elisha. supposed author (68724)
Cooke, F. 16306
Cooke, George Frederick. 21306
Cooke, George Lewis. 70629 see also Rhode
  Island. Quartermaster General.
Cooke, George Wingrove, 1814-1865. 16308-
  16309
Cooke, Harriet B. 16310
Cooke, Henry A. 84045
Cooke, Increase. 16311
Cooke, James W. 16312, 31429, 51262, note
  before 90694
Cooke, Jay. 22097
Cooke, John Esten, 1830-1886. (16314)-16323,
  18492, (39543), 2d note after 100578
Cooke, John Henry. (16324)
Cooke, M. C. (16325)
Cooke, McLaurin F. defendant (16326)
Cooke, P. St. George. USA 16339-16340,
  22536
Cooke, Parsons. 16327-16338
Cooke, Phineas. 16341-16342
Cooke, R. L. 16343
Cooke, Samuel, 1687-1747. 16344-16345,
  103628
Cooke, Samuel, 1708-1783. (16346)-16350,
  95642
Cooke, Samuel, fl. 1857. 16351
Cooke, William. see Cook, William, 1696-
  1760.
Cooke, William D. 16352, (30969)
Cooke, William Wilcox. reporter 94736

Cooke (C.) firm publishers 88543, 100719
Cooke (D. B.) & Co. firm publishers 12641
Cook (Jay) & Co. firm 16313, 71939
Cooks Reise omkring Kordkloden i Aarene
  1768-1771. 26273
Cook's voyages. 25134
Cook's [voyages, 1768-1780.] 16270
Cool address to the people of England on the
  slave trade. 346
Cool-minded man. pseud. Few reflections.
  (37509)
Cool reply to a calm address. 90317
Cool thoughts on the consequences to Great
  Britain of American independence. 26425,
  68742
Cool thoughts on the present situation of our
  public affairs. (25496)
Cool thoughts on the subject of the bank.
  60022
Coole, Benjamin. 59737
Coole conference between the cleered re-
  formation and the apologeticall narration.
  91381
Coole conference between the Scottish Com-
  missioners cleared reformation, and the
  Holland Ministers apologeticall narration.
  16354
Cooley, Benjamin Franklin. (16355)-(16356),
  2d note after 93596
Cooley, E. K. (16358)
Cooley, Ebenezer. 16357
Cooley, H. S. 16359, 34249
Cooley, James. 16360
Cooley, James Ewing, b. 1802. 16361
Cooley, James Ewing, b. 1802. supposed
  author 16362, 89058
Cooley, Jonathan. 16363
Cooley, Thomas McIntyre, 1724-1898. 16364,
  48726
Cooley, Timothy Mather, 1772-1859. (16365)-
  16366, 18814, 28327, 30130
Cooley, William Desborough. 16367-16368,
  22771, 47171
Cooley & Keese. firm see Lyman & Rawdon.
  firm
Cooley (J. E.) firm 74683
Coolidge, Austin J. (16369)
Coolidge, Cornelius. petitioner (16370)-16371
Coolidge, George. 6695, 6697, 16372-(16373),
  38548
Coolidge, J. supposed author 100461
Coolidge, James Ivers Trecothiek. (16374)-
  (16379)
Coolidge, Richard D. (34858)
Coolidge, Richard H. 16380-16381
Coolidge, Samuel. 16382
Coolidge, Valorous P. defendant 16384
Coolidge's business lists of Boston. (16373)
Coolie, his rights and wrongs. 35990
Cools, A. de, Baron. 16385-(16388)
Coomans, A. tr. 69020
Coombe, --------. 1382
Coombe, P. 16389
Coombe, Thomas. 16390-(16393)
Coombe, Thomas. supposed author 23389,
  84610
Coombs, Frederick. 16394
Coombs, George. defendant 16395
Coombs, J. J. 16396
Coombs, J. J. reporter (9435)
Cooney, Robert. 16397-16398
Coope, R. 16399
Cooper. pseud. Redvood. see Sedgwick,
  Catharine Maria, 1789-1867.

Cooper, Anthony Ashley. see Shaftesbury,
  Anthony Ashley Cooper, 1st Earl of,
  1621-1683.
Cooper, Benjamin F. reporter 98238
Cooper, C. W. 16400
Cooper, Charles D. defendant (35991), 98547
Cooper, David M. 16401
Cooper, Edward, 1824- 84774 see also New
  York (City) Mayor, 1879-1880 (Cooper)
Cooper, Elizabeth. 16402
Cooper, Ezekiel. (16403)
Cooper, Henry W. plaintiff (71356)
Cooper, J. C. 5869
Cooper, Jacob. 16404
Cooper, James, fl. 1692. 8956-8957
Cooper, James, b. 1826. 16407
Cooper, James, 1810-1863. 16405-16406
Cooper, James Fenimore, 1789-1851. (3559)-
  3562, 11553, 16408-(16572), 17725, (18093)
  32707, 38241, 43426, 72417, 89496, 89934,
  93270, 2d note after 96494, 1st note after
  102052, note after 102637
Cooper, James Fenimore, 1789-1851. plaintiff
  (16421)
Cooper, James Graham, 1830-1902. 10008,
  16574-16576, 69946
Cooper, James M. 16577
Cooper, John, 1765-1845. (16578)
Cooper, John, b. 1806. 16579
Cooper, John H. defendant (16580)
Cooper, Lemuel P. 16579
Cooper, M. 78581
Cooper, Mark Anthony, 1800-1885.
Cooper, Myles, 1735-1785. (3684), (11881),
  (16584)-16589, 26867, 39714, 40514,
  (41634), 92830-92831, 92850
Cooper, Myles, 1735-1785. supposed author
  16585, note after 100420
Cooper, Myles, 1735-1785. incorrectly supposed
  author 11882, 16590-16591, 29955-29956,
  2d note after 99553, 2d note after 103119
Cooper, Peter, 1791-1883. 16592-(16596),
  (54188), 54224
Cooper, S. M. 16607
Cooper, Samuel, 1725-1783. (16597)-16603
Cooper, Samuel, 1725-1783. supposed author
  16603
Cooper, Susan Fenimore, 1813-1894. 16492,
  (16604)-16606, 32707
Cooper, T. J. (16627)
Cooper, T. P. ed. 87687 see also South
  Carolina. Deputy Surveyor.
Cooper, Thomas. defendant (16622)
Cooper, Mrs. Thomas. 16624, (16626), 1st note
  after 102803
Cooper, Thomas, 1759-1839. (3684), 10868,
  16038, 16609-16621, 17283, 17446, (18312),
  (22509), 30566, (34385), note after 53697,
  65511, (68287), 81972, note after 83791,
  note before 87563, 87713, 87968, 87972,
  87976, note after 92827, 2d note after
  95677 see also South Carolina. University. President.
Cooper, Thomas, 1759-1839. defendant 16608
Cooper, Thomas, 1759-1839. supposed author
  47565
Cooper, Thomas, 1791 or 2-1880. (3352),
  16623-(16626), 81972, 1st note after
  102803
Cooper, W. D. 11894, 16582-16584
Cooper, W. H. 16646
Cooper, William, 1694-1743. 2197, 12316,
  14502, 14516, 14523, (16628)-16641,
  17675, 20057, (20271), (21934), 21944,
  (23584), 25397, 46274, 67768, 83428,
  83430-83433, 103514, 103588, 103601

see also Eight Ministers Who Carry on
the Thursday Lecture in Boston.
Cooper, William, 1694-1743. supposed author
46379, 104242
Cooper, William, 1754-1809. (18312), (18312),
69073
Cooper, William, 1754-1809. supposed author
6478
Cooper, William, b. 1775. 16642-16643
Cooper, William, 1798?-1864. 16644
Cooper, William Durrant. 16645
Cooper Institute, New York. see Cooper
Union for the Advancement of Science
and Art, New York.
Cooper Shop Soldiers' Home, Philadelphia.
Managers. (61562)
Cooper Union for the Advancement of Science
and Art, New York. (16596), 54224
Cooper Union for the Advancement of Science
and Art, New York. Charter. (16596),
54224
Cooper Union for the Advancement of Science
and Art, New York. Society of Asso-
ciates. see Society of Associates of the
Cooper Union for the Advancement of
Science and Art, New York.
Cooper vignettes. (18581)
Co-operation. How every man may become
the owner of his home. 84437
Co-operation Meeting, Charleston, S. C., 1851.
see Southern Rights and Co-operation
Meeting, Charleston, S. C., 1851.
Co-operation meeting, held in Charleston, S.
C., July 29th, 1851. 88575
Co-operative stores. 16647, (71220)
Cooper's histories of Greece and Rome. 16582
Cooper's Shop Volunteer Refreshments Saloon,
Philadelphia. 16648
Cooper's select works. 16559
Cooper's stories of the great prairies. 16539
Cooperstown Classical and Military Academy,
Cooperstown, N. Y. 16650
Cooperstown Seminary, Cooperstown, N. Y.
16649
Coos Counsellor Convention. see Grafton and
Coos Counsellor Convention.
Coose Bay Coal Company. 16651
Coote, C. H. ed. 77803, 99363
Coote, Clement T. (16652)
Coote, Richard. see Bellamont, Richard
Coote, 1st Earl of, 1636-1701.
Copalme de l'Amerique Centrale. (56735)
Copartnership directory, for 1860-61. 54459
Co-partnership directory . . . for 1869-70.
54459
Copartnership directory, for 1856-57. 54459
Cope, Edward Drinker, 1840-1897. 29914,
85072
Cope, Gilbert. 16655-16656
Cope, Morris. 16657
Cope, Thomas P., fl. 1797. 95921, 96030
see also American Convention for Pro-
moting the Abolition of Slavery, and Im-
proving the Condition of the African
Race. Secretary.
Cope, Thomas P., fl. 1837. 16658
Copeland, John. 28041, (73483)
Copeland, John. supposed author 52756
Copeland, Robert Morris, 1830-1874. 16659-
16661, 40893
Copenhagen. Groenlandische Gesellschafft.
see Koppenhagen-Groenlandische Gesell-
schafft.
Copenhagen. Groenlandsch Geselschap. see
Koppenhagen-Groenlandische Gesellschafft.

Copenhagen. K. Nordiske Oldskrift-Selskab.
see K. Nordiske Oldskrift-Selskab,
Copenhagen.
Copenhagen. Royal Society of Northern Anti-
quarians. see K. Nordske Oldskrift-
Selskab, Copenhagen.
Copenhagen. Selskabet for Trykkefrihedens
rette Burg. see Selskabet for Trykkefri-
hendens rette Burg, Copenhagen.
Copenhagen. Societe Royale des Antiquaires du
Nord. see K. Nordiske Oldskrift-Selskab,
Copenhagen.
Copernicus. pseud. Rivington's gentleman and
lady's pocket almanac. 71688
Copernicus, Nicolaus, 1473-1543. 16662, 93309
Copey etlicher brieffe so ausz Hispania kumme
seindt. 16663, 63176
Copia augmentada de la carta de edificacion.
23071
Copia da carta que o povo, ou antes o Cura da
Aldea de S. Francisco Xavier escreveo.
63895
Copia da carta sediciosa. 63895
Copia da convencao celebrada entre Gomes
Freire de Andrada, e os Cassiques para
a suspensao de armas. 63895
Copia das instrucc,oens, que os padres, que
governao os Indios. 63895
Copia de carta escrita a Su Majestad D. Carlos
Segundo. 73286
Copia de carta escrita a un cavallero de la
Ciudad de los Reyes. (61105)
Copia de carta, que D. Bartholome Goncalez
de Poueda. 64742
Copia de carta, qve el avtor escrivio a sv hijo.
(72290)
Copia de carta qve el Capitan Garcia de Tamayo
y Mendoza, . . . escriue. 94282-94283
Copia de carta, qve el Capitan Garcia de Tamayo
y Mendoza, Escrivano Mayor de la Real
Hacienda. 94281
Copia de cedula de el Rey dando gracias a los
padres de la Cia de Jesus. (16665)
Copia de los cartas escritas de vn missionero.
16666, 47172
Copia de dos cartas escritas por el Ilmo. y
Excmo. Sr. Dr. D. Juan Antonio de
Vizarron, y Eguiarreta. 100637
Copia de dos cartas muy devotas. (16667)
Copia de hvma carta. 99522
Copia de la carta qve el Obispo de Areqvipa
fray Don Pedro de Perea. 60877
Copia de la carta que Gonzalo Coutinho escrivio.
17201, 98711
Copia de la carta que la M. R. M. Joachina
Maria de Zavaleta. 106284
Copia de la carta respuesta. 100637
Copia de la carte que Goncalo Vas Coutino.
17201, 98711
Copia de la certificacion. 62993
Copia de la espantosa carta. 644
Copia de la lettera per Columbo. 14642
Copia de la real cedula de Su Magestad. 16668,
29422
Copia de la relacion. 87230
Copia de la representacion. 24158
Copia de las sentencias. (44966)
Copia de las tomos XVI y XVII de la coleccion.
(46205)
Copia de reales ordenes, y cartas. 16670
Copia. De Staten Generael der Vereenighde
Nederlanden. 16664, 102889
Copia de tres cartas. 94282-94284
Copia de uma carta sobre a nitreira artificial.
98830

Copia de vna carta del Padre Luys de Valdiuia. 98327

Copia de vna carta, q[ue] embio Don Barnardino Delgadillo de Auellaneda. 77289

Copia de vna carta, y relacion. 94283-94284

Copia de vna certificacion. 94628

Copia de una lettera venuta da Genova. 16671

Copia de unas cartas embiadas del Brasil. (16672), 55393

Copia del informe. 10803

Copia del oficio que los gefes del egercito nacional pasaron. 61331

Copia del primo e del secondo canto del Colombo. 99744

Copia delle lettere del Prefetto della India. 6419-6421, 16669, 54945, (63177)

Copia delle lettere di Francesco Vazquez di Coronado. 67740

Copia der newen Zeytung aus Presillg Landt. (7449)-7560, 22405

Copia di vna letter: che a scritto Luigi Gonzales de Merchado. (63179)

Copia di una lettera del Re di Portogullo. 22408

Copia di una lettera di Syvilia Venuta al Signor Don Lope. 41966, 63180

Copia du vna littera del Re de Portagallo. 22407

Copia eines Briefs von New-Yorck. [sic] 103607

Copia eines Send-Schreibens auss der Neuen Welt. 16673, 27158

Copia fiel de la representacion. 50475

Copia integra de algunos documentos. 94352

Copia van't octroy doer de Hoogh Mog. Heeren Staten Generael der Vanderael der Vereenighde Nederlanden gegeven aen Han Reeps. 16674

Copiapo, Chile. Compania Ferro-Carril. see Compania Ferro-Carril de Copiapo.

Copie de deux lettres envoies dela Novvelle France. 16676, (39991), note after 69259

Copie de la lettre de Messieurs de l'Assemblee Provinciale du Nord de Saint-Domingue. 75087

Copie de la lettre de M. Blanchelande. 5841

Copie de la lettre d'envoi de la municipalite de Saint-Marc. 75102

Copie de la lettre escripte par le R. P. Denys Iamet. note after 69259

Copie de la lettre escrite a Messievrs les Estats Generavx. 100933

Copie de la lettre escrite le 14 Mars 1793. 95733

Copie de la reqveste presentee av Roy d'Espagne. 67356

Copie de qvelqves letres svr la navigation. 99728

Copie de trois lettres. (38679)

Copie des actes de la Legislature de la Caroline du Sud. 16847

Copie des lettres ecrites au Ministre de la Marine. 87115

Copie du traite. (63900)

Copie d'une lettre d'un capitaine presentement au Cap-Francais. 10752

Copie d'une lettre ecrite a M. le Redacteur de la "Gazette de Paris." 14049

Copie d'vne lettre escrite par le Pere Jacques Bigot de la Compagnie de Jesus, l'an 1684. 5353

Copie d'vne lettre escrite par le Pere Jacques Bigot de la Compagnie de Jesus, pour accompagner un collier de pourcelaine. 5352

Copie d'vne lettre missive envoyee aux govuerneurs de La Rochelle. 24855

Copie eens briefs geschreven uyt West-Indien. 62613

Copie eines Schreibens. 100934

Copie. Hoog Mogende Heeren! 102889A

Copie of a letter sent from New-England. 55884

Copie translaet uyt het Portogijs waer in verhaelt wort de vreede dewelcke ghemaeckt. 16677

Copie, van den brief geschreven by Sigismvnd van Shoppe. 77897

Copie van een brief van den Heere Admirael Spil-berghen. 89443

Copie van een missive gheschreven by enn vry man, in Brasil. 7562, 16679

Copie van requesten van de goede gehoorsame Burgeren. (16680), (57320), 1st note after 102889A

Copie vande missive, gheschreven by den Generael Weerdenbvrch. 16678, 100935

Copie vande twee sententien uytgesproocken. 16681, 24085

Copies and abstracts of certain letters and official documents. 105478

Copies and extracts of documents. 16682

Copies and extracts of letters from settlers in Upper Canada. 98071

Copies and extracts of several newspapers printed in New England. 16683

Copies and extracts of sundry ancient charters and papers. 84604

Copies and extracts produced for prosecution. 91841A

Copies and translations of the royal charters. 741, 16684, 91853

Copies des pieces de agens du gouvernement Francais. 16685, 29576

Copies of acts passed by the Legislature of Jamaica. (35621)

Copies of correspondence between members of the government. 10420

Copies of correspondence between the Chief Superintendent of Schools for Upper Canada, and other persons. 10420, 74552

Copies of correspondence in relation to the northeastern boundary. (55710)

Copies of documents produced for the prosecution. 91841A

Copies of documents relating to the Atlantic and Pacific Railroad to Costa Rica. 38354

Copies of extracts from, intercepted and other letters, from John Stuart. 87364

Copies of extracts of despatches relative to North American colonies. 22495

Copies of four letters. 91600

Copies of His Excellency Governor Grant's letters. 72848

Copies of letters from Governor Bruere to Lord Dartmouth. 8738

Copies of letters from settlers in Upper Canada. 98078

Copies of letters from Sir Francis Bernard to the Earl of Hillsborough. 4921

Copies of Mrs. Norton's deeds. 6667

Copies of original letters recently written by persons in Paris, to Dr. Priestley in America. (16687), note after 65502, 92070

Copies of several letters . . . from A. A. Jones. 36447

Copies of several public papers. 60023

Copies of some original papers and other proceedings. 60024

Copies of some records & depositions. 45118

Copies of sundry papers which have passed 60025

Copies of sundry petitions, &c. from George A. Baker. 61563

Copies of sundry petitions, &c. presented by Isaac Austin. 61563

Copies of the decrees. 90775, note after 103224

Copies of the letters which passed. 11131, 1st note after 99245

Copies of the two protests against the bill. 16839

Copies of the power of attorney. 16686

Copies of the proceedings in the several assemblies. 16688

Copies of the proceedings of the court martial. 61047

Copies of the two letters cited by the Rev. Mr. Clap. 21932

Copies of the Virginia resolutions of 1798. 9936

Copies of the treaties lately made between the United States and sundry tribes of Indians. 96592

Copies of treaties, which have lately been entered into. 96591

Copies or extracts of correspondence relative to the affairs of British North America. 8113

Copies or extracts of correspondence respecting the fire. 54985

Copies or extracts of despatches from Sir F. B. Head. 31139

Copies or extracts of despatches relative to the condition of the sugar growing colonies. 16689

Copies or extracts of the answers from the Secretary of State. 31139

Copies, translations, extracts, and lists. 91841A

Copilacao em indice algabetico das disposicoes das leis civis Brazileiras. 72302

Copilacion breue de vn tratado de Sant Buenauentura. 76003

Copious and impartial report. 11006

Copious appendix, containing fifty-one . . . reasons. 10889, 97537

Copious description of Lord Nelson's victory. 91091

Copious extracts from Dr. Wheelock's correspondence. (43066), 1st note after 103214

Copious extracts from the despatches of Sir John Colborne. 10528

Copious extracts from the journal of Thomas Hulme. 31982, 84356

Copithorne, R. (16690), (22611), note after 93420

Copland, P. 66686

Copland, Patrick. 16691, 2d note after 99888

Copland, S. 16692

Copleston, E. A. 10473

Copleston, Edward, *Bishop of Llandaff*, 1776-1849. 16694

Copleston, *Mrs.* Edward. 16693

Copley, Esther. 16695

Copley, Hosiah. 16696

Copley, John Singleton, 1737-1815. *illus.* 168, 28897, 84905, 102133

Copoteros, Mexico (Federal District) *petitioners* 69972

Copp, Joseph A. 16697-16698, 88387

Coppee, Henry, 1821-1895. (16699)-16702, 64623

Copper lands. 25249

Copper mines of Lake Superior. (38670)

Copper mines of the Pacific coast of the United States. 42782

Copper Rock Mining Company. 16704

Copperhead. pseud. Dialogue between an old-fashioned Jackson Democrat and a copperhead. 19931, 42555

Copperhead candidate for vice-president. 59644

Copperhead catechism. 16705

Copperhead conspiracy in the north west. 16706

Copperhead minstrel. (16707)

Copperhead organization and the Knights of the Golden Circle. 5187

Copperheads under the heel of an Illinois farmer. 26212

Copperheads vigorously prosecuting peace. 16708

Coppey, H. 16709

Coppie d'une lettre envoyee de Nouvelle France ou Canada. (56083)

Coppie d'une lettre venant de la Floride. 24854, note after 99605

Coppier, Gvillavme. 16710

Coppin, Ed. *illus.* 23215

Coppin, Pasquale. 16711

Coppinger, John B. 16712

Coppinger, Jose. (16713)

Coppini, Aquilino. 16714

Coppo da Isola, Peter. 16715

Coppuck, -------. 20395

Coppy of a letter from Portsmouth. 74287

Co-Presbyter. pseud. 17270, 90007, note before 96989

Copway, George, *Chippewa chief*, 1818-1863. 16716-(16722), (36972), 56723, 57084, 94682

Copway's American Indian, no. 12. 94682

Copy of a case between Joseph Crosby, of Worcester. 17642

Copy of a case on behalf of the Ladies Ursulines at Quebec. 98170

Copy of a certain memorial. 105672

Copy of a communication and other papers. 99597

Copy of a correspondence. (45087), 95419

Copy of a despatch from Sir F. B. Head. 31138

Copy of a letter addressed by W. J. Curtis. 18068

Copy of a letter addressed to each member of Congress. 61564

Copy of a letter addressed to Judge Yates. 94675

Copy of a letter addressed to the Hon. Daniel Webster. 34635, 5th note after 100864, note after 100928

Copy of a letter found in the study. 4394

Copy of a letter from a Dutch farmer. 100873

Copy of a letter from a gentleman in Guadaloupe. 16723

Copy of a letter from a gentleman in Virginia, to a merchant in Philadelphia. (16724), (40291), 60716, 2d note after 95968, 3d note after 100449, 2d note after 100483

Copy of a letter from a Post Captain. (16725)

Copy of a letter from a young man. (7990)

Copy of a letter from Benjamin Banneker. (3211)

Copy of a letter from Captain Thomas Truxtun. 97282

Copy of a letter from Charles Read. 22192, 40280, 68142-68143

Copy of a letter from ex-president Houston. (33881)

Copy of a letter from General Lee. 39708

Copy of a letter from J. Freeman. 25769

Copy of a letter from James Stuart. 93173

Copy of a letter from Lewis Bollman. 6239

Copy of a letter from Mr. Caleb Spurrier. 89929

Copy of a letter from Quebeck in Canada. 66999

Copy of a letter from Rev. Jacob Duche. 21055

Copy of a letter from Rip Van Dam. 98434

Copy of a letter from that minister, of the 25th of December, 1793. 40343, 87862

Copy of a letter from the Governor of the Territory South of the River Ohio. 69834, note after 94720

Copy of a letter from the Hon. Committee of Congress. 99005

Copy of a letter, from the Honorable Cyrus Griffin. 93937

Copy of a letter from the Rev. Charles Wesley. 102685

Copy of a letter, from the Rev. Mr. Buell. 8981

Copy of a letter from William Penn to George Keith. 92330

Copy of a letter of July 4, 1805. 42372

Copy of a letter of Mr. Cotton of Boston. 17057

Copy of a letter to Alonzo Lewis, Esq. 36032

Copy of a letter to His Excellency Gen. Gage. 97253

Copy of a letter to Stephen R. Bradley. 28228

Copy of a letter to the Rev. John Murray. 105296

Copy of a letter which came from one who hath been a magistrate. (73483), 78753

Copy of a letter which I received. 101746, 101742

Copy of a letter written by Mr. Thomas Parker. 58769

Copy of a letter written from Buffalo. 30820

Copy of a letter written in reply to inquiries. 76644

Copy of a letter written to the President of the United States. 30820

Copy of a manuscript. 91779

Copy of a memorial and petition. 86043, 100522

Copy of a memorial from James Stuart, Esquire. 93174

Copy of a petition from James Stuart, to His Majesty. 93175

Copy of a petition from the British inhabitants. 67000

Copy of a petition from the Governor and Company of the Sommer Islands. 100450, 104190, 104974

Copy of a petition . . . relative to the claim of the officers. 16726

Copy of a petition to the imperial parliament. 98072, 98092

Copy of a relation, &c. 32964

Copy of a relation, or substance of the pleas. 51752

Copy of a remonstrance. 1649

Copy of a remonstrance lately delivered. 27954

Copy of a remonstrance, of the Council. (12851), 99073, 99240

Copy of a report from Reading Howell. 33351, 60026

Copy of a report to His Grace the Duke of Wellington. 85234

Copy of a representation of the Board of Trade. 16727

Copy of a representation of the Lords Commissioners for Trade and Plantations. 54981

Copy of a speech. 95762

Copy of a valedictory and monitory writing. 27859

Copy of a vote of the town at a preceding meeting. 6568

Copy of acts of Assembly and ordinances. 62379

Copy of affidavit. 5321

Copy of an account written by Jordan Seaman. 78612

Copy of an act pass'd in Carolina. 10956, (10958), 10980, 16728, 87347, 87355, 87805, 1st note after 97553

Copy of an act made by Charles Gookin, Esq. 60399

Copy of an address delivered to the students. 94362

Copy of an address to several of the cabinet ministers. 68411

Copy of an authentic Spanish map of America. 28460, 1st note after 94082

Copy of application to the Governor and Senate of New-York. 96510

Copy of Captain Broke's official letter. (50044)

Copy of deed trust. 61973

Copy of documentary evidence. 82904

Copy of General Myer's affidavit. 51630

Copy of his [i. e. James G. Carter's] answer to the vote. 11117

Copy of letters sent to Great Britain. 34071

Copy of Lt. Col. Adam Hubley's journal. 49200

Copy of Major-General Rosecran's report. (73259)

Copy of memorandums addressed by the Commission. 85234

Copy of Mr. Chalmers' letter to the Duke of Portland. 11769

Copy of proposed amendment to the constitution. 45119

Copy of remonstrance against the monopoly of the ships and piers. 54225

Copy of the act authorizing the [California geological] survey. 10009

Copy of the act of Assembly, authorizing the sale. 60358

Copy of the acts and doings. 105799

Copy of the acts . . . passed by the . . . Borough of West Philadelphia. 61565

Copy of the address delivered to the students. 62535, note after 94362

Copy of the address left with His Excellency, Gov. Tryon. 53630, 97291

Copy of the agreement of the New York and Harlem R. R. Co. (54732)

Copy of the answer of Deacon James G. Carter. 11117, 95259

Copy of the articles exhibited by Mr. Freeman. 14144

Copy of the charges made to the United States Senate. 2688

Copy of the charter for propagation of the Gospel in New England. 52624

Copy of the church covenants which have been used. 75654

Copy of the complaint of the House of Representatives of Massachusetts-Bay. 4922

Copy of the constitution and by-laws of the Ridgway Farm, Agricultural and Coal Co. 71293

Copy of the diary of Noahdiah Russell. 74291

Copy of the fifth & sixth articles of the treaty. 96432

Copy of the grants to the Van Rensselaer and Livingston families. 65486

Copy of the information exhibited by the Attorney-General. 37600

Copy of the instructions. 56524, 88939, 97925

Copy of the inventory of his [i. e. Stephen Girard's] personal estate. (27494)

Copy of the King's Majesties charter. 45697

Copy of the last will and testament of the late Robert Richard Randall. 67798, 74977

Copy of the lease. 60133

Copy of the letter of the Bishop of Capsa. 10766

Copy of the letter returned by the ministers of New-England. 55889

Copy of the letters patents. 36762

Copy of the libels or addresses. 4033

Copy of the Lord Glenelg's reply thereto. 31138

Copy of the muster rolls. 7898

Copy of the order of the Virginia Council. 100904

Copy of the original grant of land on the White River. 16686

Copy of the outlines of a plan. 68411

Copy of the petition, in behalf of W. Freeman. 10893

Copy of the petition of William Freeman. 25781

Copy of the poll-list. (54226)

Copy of the proceedings of a court martial, for the trial of Colonel William King. 37854

Copy of the proceedings of a general court martial, held at the Colony House in George Town. 82902

Copy of the proceedings of the court-martial in the trial of General Fitz John Porter. 64247

Copy of the proceedings of the Legislature of the state of South-Carolina. 40343, 87862

Copy of the proceedings on the trial of Lieut. Co. Cockburne. 14092

Copy of the proposals, according to which the Associate-Reformed Synod of North America was erected. 93, (59400), 65121

Copy of the protest of the Cherokee Delegation. 73391

Copy of the record, in the case, Robert Fletcher vs. John Peck. 24736

Copy of the record of the court. 89356, note before 94236A, 1st note after 96929

Copy of the record of the trial of Shelden Braynard. 96835

Copy of the record, transmitted on the appeal of Frances Burges. 99975

Copy of the register of canal boats. (53563)

Copy of the report made to . . . the Lieutenant-Governor. (52533)

Copy of the report of Major D. Fergusson. (24103)

Copy of the report of the Commissioners . . . [on] the northeastern boundary. (55711)

Copy of the report of the Joint Committee of the Legislature. (30658)

Copy of the resolution of the Legislative Assembly. 101922

Copy of the result of the Council at Billingsgate, in Eastham. 21669

Copy of the stenographic report of the hearings before the Visitors. 85212

Copy of the true relation. 102498

Copy of the valuation and taxes . . . for . . . 1855. 42698

Copy of the valuation and taxes . . . of North Brookfield. 55580

Copy of the valuation and taxes of the town of Ashburnham. 2174

Copy of the valuation of taxable property in . . . New Bedford. 52479

Copy of the wills and inventories of the estates. 24781, note after 92069

Copy of those articles. 46235

Copy of three judgments given forth by a party of men, called Quakers. 8956, (37333), 47181, 97113

Copy of three letters. 55240

Copy of two letters. 16729

Copy of verses made by that reverend man of God Mr. John Wilson. 104653

Copy of verses on Mr. Oglethorpe's second voyage to Georgia. 27047, note after 102702

Copy of what was said at giving the right hand of fellowship. (65613)

Copy of writings left by Miss Clarissi Wright. 103936

Copy van een brief aen den Commissaris Generael. (972)

Copy van een brief, so als die tot onse handen quam. 91320

Copy van een brief, soo als die tot onse handen quam. 91319

Copy van Koningh Karel ordere. 91319

Copy van Konink Karel ordre. 91320

Copy van twee brieven, welcke sy-lieden geschreaven hebben, aen het volck des heeren, een weynig voor haere dood. 91320

Copy van twee brieven, welcke sy lieden geschreven hebben, aen het volck des heeren, een weynigh voor haren doodt. 91319

Copye ofte cort ende waerachtigh verhael. 7561, (16739)

Copye, ouergeset wt de Engelsche taele in onse Nederlandtsche spraecke. 11604

Copye van een brief by den selven W. P. geschreven. 59710

Copye, van een brief van den Koningh van Portugael. 16730

Coype van een missive. 16736

Copye van eenen brieff van eenen vriendt aen den anderen. 16737, (57378)

Copye van het mandement von d'Edele Hove van Hollant. 27122

Copye van seker articulen. 16721, 2d note after 102890

Copye. Van't journael gehouden by Gedeon Moris. 50709

Copye van verklaringen op eede voor de achtbaren Magistret. 27123

Copye vande missive geschreven by den Generael Weerdenburgh. 102497

Copye vande resolutie van de Heeren Burgemeesters ende Raden tot Amsterdam. 16732-(16734), 23344, 3d note after 102889A, 7th note after 102890

Copye vande volmacht van Don Iuan. 16735

Copyen. 16738, 102890

Copyen van drie missiven. 50231

Copyright and patent laws of the United States. 39319

Copyright law of the United States. 16740

Copy-right manual. (22349)

Coquerel, ------. 16742

Coquette. 25229, 103731

Coquilles et echinodermes fossiles de Columbie. 57451

Cora, ----------. defendant 37808, 97098
Cora. 8137, 80342
Cora oder die sklavin. 3976
Cora, of de Peruanen. 55419
Corals of the Upper Helderberg and Hamilton groups. 53797
Coraly et Zamore. 16744
Coram, Robert. (16745), 27965, (28024), 28913
Coram, a sketch of one of the Trustees of Georgia. 85819
Corancez, Louis Alexandre Olivier de. see Olivier de Corancez, Louis Alexandre.
Coray, --------. 83496, 83500
Corazo de las Rosas Sepultado. 50078
Corbeau. 63545-63546
Corbet, John. 16746
Corbett, G. O. 16747
Corbett, Henry Winslow, 1827-1903. 16748-16749
Corbett, William. (16750)
Corbiere, Edouard. 16751
Corbin, D. T. 87469-87470
Corbin, William. (16752)
Corbould, ---------. illus. 35158
Corbulacho, Juan Carlos de Apello. 16753
Corcoran, D. (16754)
Corcoran, Michael. defendant at court marital 16755
Corcoran, William W. 62051
Corda, August Carl Joseph. 16756
Cordeiro, Antonio Xavier Rod. 7508
Cordeiro, Carlos Antonio. 16757
Cordeiro, Z. X. R. 11416
Cordeiro da Silva Torres e Alvim, Francisco. see Torres e Alvim, Francisco Cordeiro da Silva.
Cordeiro de Aranjo Lima, Andre. see Aranjo Lima, Andre Cordeiro de.
Cordelier, ---------. ed. 74
Cordell, Eugene Fauntleroy, 1843-1913. 83664
Corderius Americanus. A discourse. 46273
Corderius Americanus. An essay. 46272
Cordero, Manuel Rivero. see Rivero Cordero, Manuel.
Cordeyro, Antonio. 16759
Cordillera. 31626
Cordillera and pampa, mountain and plain. 92669
Cordley, Christopher Minta. 16760
Cordner, John. 16761-16764
Cordoba, A. de. 1729, 16765, 16771-16772, 62509, note after 98611, 98613-98614, 4th note after 100814
Cordoba, Francisca Fernandez de. see Fernandez de Cordoba, Francisca, Condesa de Casapalma.
Cordoba, Jose de. supposed author 32020, 55245, 92200-92201
Cordoba, Juan de, fl. 1578. 16766, 106253
Cordoba, L. Cabrera de. see Cabrera de Cordoba, L.
Cordoba, Manuel Fernandez de. see Fernandez de Cordoba, Manuel.
Cordoba, Pedro Tomas de. 16769, 2d note after 96138, 98367
Cordoba, Tirso Rafael, 1838- (16767)
Cordoba, Tomas de. 16769
Cordoba Salinas, Diego. see Salinas, Diego de Cordova.
Cordoba y Sande, Fernando Fernandez de. see Fernandez de Cordoba y Sande, Fernando.
Cordoba, Mexico. 47032

Cordonnier de Saint Hyacinthe, H. tr. 72218, 99509
Cordova, A. de. see Cordoba, A. de.
Cordova, Buenaventura Salinas y. see Salinas y Cordova, Buenaventura, d. 1653.
Cordoua, Christoual de Moscoso y. see Moscoso y Cordoua, Christoual de.
Cordoua, Didacum von. see Cordova, Diego de.
Cordova, Diego de. 86228-86229
Cordova, Diego Fernandez de. see Fernandez de Cordova, Diego, 1. Marques de Guadalcazar.
Cordova, Felipe Colmenares Fernandez de. see Fernandez de Cordova, Felipe Colmenares.
Cordova, Francisca Fernandez de. see Fernandez de Cordoba, Francisca, Condesa de Casapalma.
Cordova, Francisco Hernandez de. 22086
Cordova, J. de. 16775, (19190)
Cordova, J. M. Fernandez de. see Fernandez de Cordova, J. M.
Cordova, Juan de. see Cordoba, Juan de, fl. 1578.
Cordova, Juan Francisco de Montemayor y. see Montemaior y Cordova de Cuenca, Juan Francisco de, 1620-1685.
Cordova, Matias de. 16774
Cordova, Pedro de. 16777, 70887
Cordova, R. J. de. 16778
Cordova, Seb. de Guzman y. see Guzman y Cordova, Seb. de.
Cordova de Cuenca, Juan Francisco de Montemaior. see Montemaior y Cordova de Cuenca, Juan Francisco, 1620-1685.
Cordova Laso de la Vega, Antonio de. see Laso de la Vega, Antonio de Cordova.
Cordova Salinas, Diego de. see Salinas, Diego de Cordova.
Cordoua y Sande, Fernando de. see Fernandez de Cordoba y Sande, Fernando.
Cordova y Souza, J. A. Fernandez de. see Souza, J. A. Fernandez de Cordova y.
Cordova y Urrutia, Jose Maria. 16779-16780
Cordova, Spain (Diocese) Bishop (Solis) 86398 see also Solis, Francisco de, Bp.
Coreal, Francois. 4937A, 16781-16782, 30483, 67554, note after 98442
Corey, --------. 103012
Corey, Allen. 16783
Corey, Daniel H. defendant 16784, 96854
Corinne Montgomery. pseud. Texas and her presidents. see Cazneau, Mrs. William Leslie. supposed author
Corinth and other poems of the war. 36641
Corinthian Lodge, Concord, Mass. see Freemasons. Massachusetts. Corinthian Lodge, Concord.
Corio, -------. (5849)-5850
Coriolanus. pseud. Remarks on the late infraction. see Smith, William Stephens, 1755-1816.
Cork, Bishop of. see Wetenhall, Edward, successively Bishop of Cork, and Kilmore and Ardagh, 1636-1713.
Corley, Elijah. 104086
Corley, Manuel Simeon, 1823-1902. 16786
Corlies, John. defendant (16787)
Corlies, Patience. 16788
Corliss steam-engine contracts. 89318
Cormach, W. E. 16789
Cormany. firm publishers see Emmert, Shannon & Cormany. firm publishers

Cormere, J. F. Mahy de. see Mahy de
    Cormere, J. F.
Cormier, --------. 16790
Corn Exchange Association of Philadelphia.
    see Philadelphia Commercial Exchange.
Corn laws. (80297)
Corn Plant. Seneca Indian Chief 79109
Cornalia, E. 16791
Cornbury, Edward, Viscount. see Clarendon,
    Edward Hyde, 3d Earl of, 1661-1723.
Corncob, Jonathan. pseud. Adventures. 477
Corne, St.-Luc de la. see La Corne, St.-Luc
    de.
Cornejo, Damian. (22897)
Cornejo, Juan Adrian Fernandez. 16792
Cornejo, Ludouico. ed. 61074
Cornelison, John. 16793
Cornelissen, --------. tr. (21177)
Cornelius. pseud. Extracts from Professor
    Robison's "Proofs of a conspiracy," &c.
    72243
Cornelius, E. E. 1198
Cornelius, Elias, 1794-1832. 16794-16795,
    41538, 62509, 70266, 76707
Cornelius Agrippa. pseud.? see Agrippa,
    Cornelius. pseud.??
Cornelius Gisbert Zorgdragers Beschreibung.
    106377
Cornelius's character. 12331
Cornelius's tour to Virginia. 76707
Cornell, Ezra, 1807-1874. 16796, 26824
Cornell, S. 44730
Cornell, William. 16797
Cornell, William M. 67292
Cornell University, Utica, N. Y. 16798
Cornell University, Utica, N. Y. Library.
    88966
Corner-stone address. 90561
Corner Stone Division, no. 165, Hingham, Mass.
    see Sons of Temperance of North Amer-
    ica. Massachusetts. Corner Stone Divi-
    sion, no. 165, Hingham.
Corner-stone of patriotism, government, and
    nationality. 8428, 8550
Cornet, --------, Comte de. (47421)
Cornette,---------. 16799, 18490, 23098
Cornford, P. H. 16800
Cornhill monthly and literary recorder. 16801
Cornillere, -------, Comte de la. see La
    Cornillere, -------, Comte de.
Cornillon, Charles de. 16803
Corning, Erastus. (41184)
Corning, James Leonard. 16804
Corning, Richard S. 57167
Corning, W. H. 16805
Cornish, F. S. 16806
Cornish, N. H. Convention Consisting of the
    Rev. Grafton Presbytery, Windsor Asso-
    ciation, and Others, 1782. see Conven-
    tion of the Grafton Presbytery, Windsor
    Association, and others, Cornish, N. H.,
    1782.
Cornish, N. H. Convention of the New-Hamp-
    shire Grants, 1778. see Vermont.
    Convention, 1778.
Cornish, N. H. Convention on the New-Hamp-
    shire Grants, 1779. see Vermont.
    Convention, 1779.
Cornish, N. H. Washington Benevolent Society.
    see Washington Benevolent Society.
    New Hampshire. Cornish.
Cornish, N. Y. Meeting of the Inhabitants of
    Saratoga and Warren Counties, 1846.
    see Meeting of the Inhabitants of Sara-
    toga and Warren Counties, Cornish N. Y.,
    1846.

Cornock, Nehemiah. ed. 102681
Cornplanter memorial. 16807, 85580
Cornu, J. Francois. 16808, 75487
Cornut, Jacques Philippe. (16809)
Cornwall, Barry. pseud. see Procter, B. W.
Cornwall, N. E. 16810
Cornwall, P. B. 86008 see also Society of
    California Pioneers, San Francisco.
    President.
Cornwall, Conn. First Congregational Church.
    98140
Cornwall County Jamaica. 70080
Cornwall reflector. 85415
Cornwallis, Charles Cornwallis, 1st Marquis,
    1738-1805. 13751, 13754, (16811)-16814,
    16854, 27140, 82975-82976, note before
    95301, 95301
Cornwallis, Charles Cornwallis, 1st Marquis,
    1738-1805. pseud. Dialogue. see Wills,
    Archibald. supposed author
Cornwallis, Frederick, Abp. of Canterbury,
    1713-1783. 16817
Cornwallis, James Cornwallis, 4th Earl, Bp.
    of Litchfield and Coventry, 1742-1824.
    16818
Cornwallis, Kinahan. 16819-16821
Cornwell, Francis. 17055, 17060
Cornwell, Sir George. pseud. Boston, 25
    January, 1769. A dialogue. 16822
Cornwell S. H. 8267
Cornyn, John K. (16823)
Coroa do Brazil em 1641. 93587
Corochi, Horacio. 58573
Corografia Brazilica ou relacao historico-
    geografica. (2525), 11640
Corografia Parraense. 11703
Corographia historica, chronographica, genea-
    logica, nobiliaria e politica. 47458
Corographia historica do imperio do Brasil.
    7616
Coromina, J. 16824
Corona; a poem. 61295
Corona funebre a la memoria de la celebre
    poetisa Zacatecana. 26884
Corona funebre de Pedro Escobedo. 22838
Corona funebre del malogrado joven Barce-
    lino Palacios. 58275
Corona poetica ofrecida al pueblo Peruano.
    61106
Coronado, Antonio Vazquez. 16825
Coronado, Carlos Vazques. see Vazquez
    Coronado, Carlos.
Coronado, Carlos Vazquez de. see Vazquez
    Coronado, Carlos
Coronado, Francisco Vazquez de. see Vazquez
    de Coronado, Francisco. 1510-1549.
Coronado, Juan. 103673
Coronado, Pedro Jose. 16826
Coronado's march. (81352)
Coronal. 80967
Coronation; or, hypocrisy exposed. 9480
Coronel, Juan Gutierrez. see Gutierrez
    Coronel, Juan.
Coronel, Nicolas Benitez. see Benitez Coro-
    nel, Nicolas.
Coronel, Ricardo Joseph Gutierrez. see
    Gutierrez Coronel, Ricardo Joseph.
Coronel D. Jose Rincon sin excusa ante el
    tribunal de la razon. 71414
Coronensis de cosmographiae. 20210
Coroner's Inquest into the Case of the Explosion
    of the Steamship Empire State, Fall River,
    Mass., 1856. see Fall River, Mass.
    Coroner's Inquest into the Case of the
    Explosion of the Steamship Empire State,
    1856.

Coroner's Jury, Mobile, Ala. see Mobile,
Ala. Coroner's Jury.
Coronica de Aragon. 98286
Coronica de la religiosissima Provincia de
Los Dos Apostoles de Perv. 75780
Coronica de las Indias. 1565, 57989, 105724
Coronica de Ocampo. (50496)
Coronica de S. Augustin en el Peru. 9871
Coronica general de Espana de Ocampo.
(50496)
Coronica moralizada del Orden de San Avgvstin
en el Perv. 9870
Corpancho, Manuel Nicolas. 16827, (57229)
Corpes Belge du Mexique. 7786
"Corporal." pseud. Letters. see Haines,
Zenas T.
Corporal Murray. 51512
"Corporal of the guard." pseud. "High pri-
vate." 31756
Corporation for Promoting and Propagating the
Gospel of Jesus Christ in New England,
London. 22146, 22149, (22152), 22162,
22166, 34625, 52758, note before 92797
see also for Propagation of the Gospel
in New England Company and the Parts
Adjacent in America, London.
Corporation for Propagation of the Gospel in
New England and the Parts Adjacent in
America, London. see Company for
Propagation of the Gospel in America
and the Parts Adjacent in America,
London.
Corporation for Relief of Poor and Distressed
Presbyterian Ministers. 65129
Corporation for Relief of Poor and Distressed
Presbyterian Ministers. Charter. 65129
Corporation for Relief of Poor and Distressed
Presbyterian Ministers. Trustees.
(42384), 66908 see also Alison, Francis.
and Ewing, John, 1732-1802.
Corporation for the Relief of the Widows and
Children of Clergymen, in the Communion
of the Church of England in America.
10880
Corporation for the Relief of the Widows and
Children of Clergymen, in the Communion
of the Church of England in America.
Charter. 84669-84670
Corporation for the Relief of Widows and
Children of Clergymen of the Protestant
Episcopal Church, in Pennsylvania. 60113
Corporation for the Relief of Widows and
Children of Clergymen of the Protestant
Episcopal Church in the Diocese of New
York. 53631
Corporation for the Relief of Widows and
Children of Clergymen of the Protestant
Episcopal Church in the Diocese of New
York. Charter. 53631
Corporation for the Relief of the Widows and
Children of the Clergy of the Protestant
Episcopal Church in Maryland. (54298),
54300
Corporation in England by the Name of the
President and Society for Propagation
of the Gospel in New England. see Com-
pany for Propagation of the Gospel in
New England and the Parts Adjacent in
America, London.
Corporation in England for Promoting the Gos-
pel Among the Indians of New England.
see Corporation for Promoting and Pro-
pagating the Gospel of Jesus Christ in
New England, London.

Corporation in England for Propagating the
Gospel Amongst the Indians. see Cor-
poration for Promoting and Propagating
the Gospel of Jesus Christ in New England,
London.
Corporation laws. 80029
Corporation of Georgetown. see Georgetown,
D. C.
Corporation of Malden Bridge. see Malden
Bridge Corporation.
Corporation of the Governors of the Bounty of
Queen Anne. 90625
Corporation of the New-York Protestant Epis-
copal Public School. 54529
Corporation of the New-York Protestant Epis-
copal Public School. Charter. 54529
Corporation of the United Swedish (Lutheran)
Churches of Wiccacoe, Kingussing, and
Upper Merion, Pa. (62359) see also
Kingussing, Pa. St. James Church.
Upper Merion, Pa. Christ Church.
Wiccacoe, Pa. Gloria Dei Church.
Corporation of the United Swedish (Lutheran)
Churches of Wiccacoe, Kingussing, and
Upper Merion, Pa. Charter. (62359)
Corporation of Trinity Church, New York. see
New York (City) Trinity Church.
Corporation to the reader. note before 92797-
92797
Corps du Commerce, Les Cayes, Haiti. 75101
Corps Franc de rifles. 69034
Corps Legislatif. Conseil de Cinq-Cents.
Rapport fait par Jean-Aime Delacoste.
19324
Corps Legislatif. Conseil des Anciens. Rap-
port fait par Girot-Pouzol. 27511
Corps Legislatif. Conseil des Cinq-Cents.
Discours de J. C. G. Delahaye. 19336
Corps Legislatif. Conseil des Cinq-Cents.
Discours de Villaret-Joyeuse. 99661
Corps Legislatif. Conseil des Cinq-Cents.
Motion d'ordre. 95374
Corps Legislatif. Conseil des Cinq-Cents.
Opinion de Villaret-Joyeuse. 99662
Corps Legislatif. Conseil de Cinq-Cents.
Rapport fait par Eschasseriaux aine.
22823
Corps Legislatif. Conseil des Cinq-Cents.
Rapport fait par Lecointe-Puiraveau.
39656
Corps Legislatif. Conseil des Cinq-Cents.
Rapport fait par Lecomte Puyraveau.
66857
Corps Legislatif. Conseil des Cinq-Cents.
Rapport fait par Sainthorent. 75540
Corps Legislatif. Conseil des Cinq-Cents.
Rapport fait par Villaret-Joyeuse. 99663
Corps Legislatif, le Mexique et la Prusse.
8188
Corps Legislatif. Session de 1863. 39989
Corradi, Juan. tr. 10298
Corral, Felipe Ruiz. 16828
Corral, Joseph del. (72290)
Corral Calvo de la Torre, Juan del, 1666-1737.
10093
Correa, --------. 16832
Correa, Antonio. 16829
Correa, Diego. 16830
Correa, Gaspar. 11385, 62806, note after
90319
Correa, Joao de Medeiros. 16833-16835,
69166
Correa, Juan Nunez. 16836
Correa, Tr. Simao. 16837

Correa de Oliveira, Joao Alfredo. 58501
  see also Para (Brazilian State)
  President (Correa de Oliveira)
Correa do Couto, Antonio. see Couto,
  Antonio Correa do.
Correa Junior, A. P. 16838
Correa. firm see Oliveira Goncalves &
  Correa. firm
Correct account of the capture and sufferings
  of Mrs. Johnson. 34469
Correct account of the piracies in the West
  Indies. 32182, (32197), (36191)
Correct account of the rise and progress of
  the recent popular novements in Lower
  Canada. 10407, (71546)
Correct account of the trials of Charles
  M'Manus. (43564)
Correct and authentic narrative of the Indian
  war in Florida. 3579
Correct annual register for England, Scotland,
  and Ireland for 1767. 73796
Correct copies of the two protests. 16839
Correct copy of his [i. e. Captain Broke's]
  written challenge. (50044)
Correct copy of the charter of the glebe lands.
  (54904)
Correct, full and impartial report. 2483
Correct journal of the landing. 43398
Correct list of all the prizes. 102019
Correct map of Connecticut. 97181
Correct narrative of the celebrated Mammoth
  Cave. 36628
Correct plan of the environs of Quebec.
  67008
Correct poetical account of a tour. 42843,
  70208
Correct report of the trial of Josef Perez.
  60908
Correct statement and review of the trial.
  8911
Correct statement of the defeat and capture.
  104822
Correct statement of the late melancholy affair
  of honor. 104541
Correct statement of the various sources.
  105041
Correct statement of the whole preliminary
  controversy. 79010
Correct view of that part of the United States.
  77609
Correct view of the controversy. (58807),
  87810
Correct woolen table. 3519
Corrected proofs. 102535
Corrected report of the speech of Viscount
  Howick. 33365
Correction of certain errors. 65683
Correction of erroneous statements. 36857,
  54961
Correction of misrepresentations. 97810
Correction of some of the great mistakes.
  38875
Corrector. pseud. Letters addressed to
  Martin Van Buren. see Cochrane,
  James. supposed author
Corrector. pseud. Reply to a letter. see
  Hobart, John Henry, Bp., 1775-1830.
Corrector. pseud. Sketch of the life and
  character. 81522, 103231
Cor-Rector, Philo. pseud. see Philo Cor-
  Rector, Esq. pseud.
Corrector or independent American. (16840)
Corredor del comercio. 48283
Correia, Frederico Jose. 16841
Correio Braziliense ou armazem literario.
  7563

Corrente, Mariano. see Torrente, Mariano.
Correnti, Cesare. 14646
Correo, Atlantico. 16843
Correo de Buenos Aires. 16844
Correo de ultramar. 56289
Correo del Domingo. (16845)
Correo del Peru. 94863
Correo mercantile de Espana y sus Indias.
  16846
Correo. Periodico imparcial. (16842)
Correo semanario de Mexico, por el Pensador
  Mexicano. 48400
Correo, semanario politico y mercantil de
  Mexico. 48399
Correspondance astronomique. 4565
Correspondance avec l'Assemblee Provinciale
  de l'Ouest de S. Domingue. 65980
Correspondance avec ses amis. 35244
Correspondance choisie. 25572
Correspondance de Benjamin Franklin. 38434
Correspondance de Dom Pedre Premier.
  59516
Correspondance de Fernand Cortes. (16953)
Correspondance de la France avec les Etats-
  Unis. 16847
Correspondance de M. le General avec l'As-
  semblee Generale. 75088
Correspondance de M. le Marquis du Chilleau.
  21602
Correspondance de Toussaint-Louverture avec
  Buonaparte. 3885
Correspondance diplomatique. 67142
Correspondance du Comte de Limonade. 3885
Correspondance du General Rochambeau. 99745
Correspondance du Lord G. Germain. 27140
Correspondance entre deux Milords. 62697
Correspondance entre la Legation Extraordi-
  naire du Mexique. 16848
Correspondance entre le Citoyen Genet. 26930
Correspondance entre l'Hon W. H. Draper et
  l'Hon R. E. Caron. 20906
Correspondance entre M. le President de
  l'Assemblee Coloniale. 19366
Correspondance et pensees du Prince de Ligne.
  78916
Correspondance exchangee entre les Ministres
  du Chili. 16849
Correspondance generale. 77361
Correspondance generale avec l'Assemblee
  Generale. 75089
Correspondance inedite de Victor Jacquemont.
  (35515)
Correspondance inedite et secrete du Docteur
  B. Franklin. 25497
Correspondance politique, historique et critique.
  46912
correspondance scientifique et litteraire. 33709
Correspondance secrete de Thom. Boot. 64572
Correspondance secrete des Deputes de Saint-
  Domingue. 75090, 85789
Correspondance secrete entre Milord All'Eye
  et Milord All'Ear. 62695-62696
Correspondance souvenirs et oeuvres inedites.
  38459, 67910
Correspondant. 8188
Correspondant des Etats-Unis. 1291
Correspondant du Canadien. pseud. Excursion
  aux provincies maritimes. see O'Brien,
  J. W.
Correspondence. 97105
Correspondence, addresses, &c., connected
  with the subscriptions of various Indian
  tribes in Upper Canada. 8153, 34636
Correspondence and accompanying papers. 16850
Correspondence and dispatches of the ministers
  to China. 12813

Correspondence and documents relating to the proposals. 16851

Correspondence and documents relative to the attempt. 55375

Correspondence and documents relative to the financial condition. 49586

Correspondence and facts in relation to the appointment. 93951

Correspondence and minutes of the Trustees of the Bank of Maryland. 45078

Correspondence and miscellanies of the Hon. John Cotton Smith. 82937

Correspondence and other papers, relating to Fort Sumter. 87551

Correspondence and other papers, relating to Fort Sumter. Including correspondence of Hon. Isaac W. Hayne. 87552

Correspondence and remarks in regard to Bishop Doane's signature. 5474

Correspondence and remarks on martial law and arrests. 14418

Correspondence and remarks upon Bancroft's history. (78052)

Correspondence and returns. 56117

Correspondence arising out of the conflict between the "Kearsage" and the "Alabama." (37130)

Correspondence between A. Mann, Jr., and Hon. A. C. Flagg. (44305)

Correspondence between Anson Brown, Esq. and others. 65760, 94516

Correspondence between B. F. Stockton and C. Van Rensselaer. 10162

Correspondence between Berkeley Ward. 101281

Correspondence between Bishop Clark and Rev. J. P. Hubbard. 13385

Correspondence between Bishops Chase and McIlvaine. 12170

Correspondence between Citizen Genet. 26929

Correspondence between citizens of New Jersey. 35439

Correspondence between E. S. Chesborough. (12514)

Correspondence between Edward Brooks and John A. Lowell. 8344

Correspondence between Edward Stanly and Harry S. Clark. 90321

Correspondence between Gen. Andrew Jackson and John C. Calhoun. 35343

Correspondence between General Jackson and Mr. Monroe. 35345

Correspondence between General Pope. 64113

Correspondence between General W. T. Sherman. 80411

Correspondence between General Winfield Scott. 78405

Correspondence between George Nicholas. 55166

Correspondence between Gov. Andrew and Major-Gen. Butler. 9616

Correspondence between Governor Brown and the Secretary of War. 78765

Correspondence between Governor Clinton and Governor Williamson. 13747

Correspondence between Governor Thomas of Maryland. (45087), 95419

Correspondence between Great Britain and the United States. 16852

Correspondence between Her Majesty's Government and Messrs. Laird Brothers; and an appendix. (5571)

Correspondence between Her Majesty's Government and Messrs. Laird Brothers respecting the Birkenhead ironclads. 16853

Correspondence between His Excellency Gov. Williams. 104329

Correspondence between His Excellency Sir Henry Clinton. 16854

Correspondence between Hon. John Adams. 232

Correspondence between Hon. Hamilton Fish. (24431)

Correspondence between Hon. Mr. Soule. 87275

Correspondence between Hon. William B. Reed. (68618)

Correspondence between Isaac W. Hayne. 87555

Correspondence between J. N. Reynolds. 70431-70432

Correspondence [between Jacob M. Howard and James Binney.] 33254

Correspondence between James G. Birney. 5575

Correspondence between Jasper Lynch. 42813

Correspondence between John C. Spencer. 89346

Correspondence between John Gladstone. 27524

Correspondence between John Jay and Henry B. Dawson. 18933, 35841

Correspondence between John Quincy Adams. 275

Correspondence between John Ross. 12449

Correspondence between Joseph Smith. 83236

Correspondence between Lt.-Col. Glegg. 27567

Correspondence between Lieut. Rogerson and others. 14092

Correspondence between Lord Brougham and Mr. Clarkson. 13496

Correspondence between Lydia Maria Child. (12727)

Correspondence between Major General Jackson. (35344)

Correspondence between members of the government. 10420

Correspondence between Mr. —— ——. 96088

Correspondence between Mr. Granville Sharp Pattison. 59152, (59154)

Correspondence between Mr. Heckewelder. 1183

Correspondence between Mr. Hulsemann. (33650)

Correspondence between Mr. Monroe and Mr. Canning. 12489

Correspondence between Mr. Ryland and Mr. Murdoch. 74592

Correspondence between Mr. Secretary Canning and the Hon. D. Erskine. 16855

Correspondence [between Mr. Secretary Canning and the Hon. David Erskine,] relating to America. 16883

Corerspondence between Nathan Appleton and John A. Lowell. 1824

Correspondence between Nathan Appleton and John G. Palfrey. 1825

Correspondence between officers of H. M.'s Customs. (5571)

Correspondence between Oliver Johnson and George F. White. 36259

Correspondence between our administration. (15856)

Correspondence between P. A. Adet. 62659

Correspondence between Professor Cairnes. 9857

Correspondence between Reverend David Nelson. 104668

Correspondence between Rev. H. W. Beecher. 76687

Correspondence between Rev. J. Kelly. (37311)

Correspondence between Rev. Nehemiah Adams. 23684

Correspondence between Rev. William Patton. 59164

Correspondence between Right Rev. Alexander Gregg. 24234, 28703

Correspondence between Senhor Jose Silvestre Rebello. 68331

Correspondence between Senor A. Ainsa. 1982

Correspondence between . . . Sir R. W. Horton. 33075, note after 104595

Correspondence between the Agent of the Commonwealth and . . . the Governor. 45698, note before 93483

Correspondence between the . . . Bishop of Massachusetts. 6640

Correspondence between the Board of Trustees of the Clinton County Grammar School. 28253

Correspondence between the British and American plenipotentiaries. 53975, 90639

Correspondence between the British ministry and R. Smith. 16857

Correspondence between the Chairman of the Committee of Ways and Means and the Secretary of the Treasury. 16859

Correspondence between the Chief Superintendent of Schools for Upper Canada. 10420, 74552

Correspondence between the Commissioners for Investigating the Affairs of the Joint Companies, and a citizen of Burlington. 10828

Correspondence between the Commissioners of New York. (53632)

Correspondence between the Commissioners of the State of South Carolina, and the government. (16860), note after 87402, 87436, 87438

Correspondence between the Committee and the Rev. J. Pierpont. 6653

Correspondence between the Committee appointed by the Monthly Meeting of Friends in . . . New York. (54227)

Correspondence between the Committee of the Trinitarian Society. 16861

Correspondence between the Comptroller of the Currency. 44632

Correspondence between the English and American governments. 16862

Correspondence between the envoys of the American states and Monsieur Talleyrand. 16863

Correspondence between the First Church and the Tabernacle Church. 103366

Correspondence between the French government. note after (10603)

Correspondence . . . between the government of Great Britain and . . . the United States. 55712

Correspondence between the governments of the United States and Great Britain, relative to the enlistment of soldiers. (16964)

Correspondence between the governments of the United States and Great Britain; with documents. (22626)

Correspondence between the Governor of Maryland the the Sheriff of Frederick County. 45120

Correspondence between the Governor of New-York and the Governor of Georgia. 79511

Correspondence between the Governor of New York and Virginia. 53633

Correspondence between the Honorable E: Louis Lowe. 2995

Correspondence between the Hon. Ebenezer Foote. 25000, 98297

Correspondence between the Hon. F. H. Elmore. (22361)

Correspondence between the Hon. Horace Mann. 83572

Correspondence between the Hon. John Adams and the late Wm. Cunningham. 62658, 84906

Correspondence between the Hon. John Adams, late President of the United States, and the late William Cunningham. 62658, 84906

Correspondence between the Hon. John C. Spencer. 89347

Correspondence between the Hon. W. H. Draper and the Hon. R. E. Caron. 20907

Correspondence between the International Ocean Telegraph Company. 54830

Correspondence between the Kentucky and Tennessee Commissioners. 37547

Correspondence between the late Commodore Stephen Decatur. 19132

Correspondence between the Legation Extraordinary of Mexico. 102205

Correspondence between the Marquess Wellesley and Mr. Foster. 1012, note after 102574

Correspondence between the Marquess Wellesley and Mr. Morris. 1011, note after 102574

Correspondence between the Mayor and Federal authorities. 53320

Correspondence between the Officers of the Board of Trustees. 21100

Correspondence between the President and Chief Engineer. 60278

Correspondence between the President and General Joseph E. Johnston. 15264, 16865

Correspondence between the President and the Governor of Georgia. 18841

Correspondence between the Property Holders' Union of New Orleans. 90641

Correspondence between the Prophet Joseph Smith. 83279

Correspondence between the Rev. Messrs. Dana and Smyth. 85298

Correspondence between the Rev. Richard Fuller. (26170)

Correspondence between the Rev. Samuel H. Cox. (17269)

Correspondence between the Rev. Stanley Griswold, and the Rev. Dan. Huntington. 5592, 28903

Correspondence between the Rev. W. Crowel. 89369

Correspondence between the Right Rev. Alexander Gregg. 27408

Correspondence between the Right Rev. C. P. McIlvaine. 43322

Correspondence between the Right Rev. George Washington Doane. 20391, (20396), note after 104574

Correspondence between the Right Reverend the Bishop of Massachusetts. 21663

Correspondence between the Roman Catholic Bishop of Toronto. 10420, 74553

Correspondence between the School Committee. (52483)

Correspondence between the Secretary of State, and Col. Peraza. 95040

Correspondence between the Secretary of State and the British Minister. 16866

Correspondence between the Secretary of State; and the French Minister. (70219)

Correspondence between the Secretary of State and the Minister Plenipotentiary of the French Republic. 16867

Correspondence between the Secretary of State for the Colonies. 1697A

Correspondence between the Secretary of War and the President of the Baltimore and Ohio Railroad Company. 2992, 16868

Correspondence between the State Department and the representative of Her Britannic Majesty's government. (16869)

Correspondence between the Treasurer of the W. Shore of Maryland. 45121

Correspondence between the Treasury Department, &c. (17760)

Correspondence between the United States and Great Britain. 16871

Correspondence between the United States of America and Great Britain. 16858, 16870

Correspondence between the War Department and Gen. Lovell. 16873

Correspondence between the Wardens and Vestry. 6676

Correspondence between this government and that of Great Britain. 48095

Correspondence between Thomas Harrison. 87409

Correspondence between . . . Thomas Jefferson. 35883

Correspondence between Thomas Slidell. 93647

Correspondence between Viscount Castlereagh. 1013, (16872)

[Correspondence between Wilkinson, John Randolph, and others.] 104027

Correspondence between William B. Reed. (68602)

Correspondence between Wm. L. Marcy. 44518

Correspondence Committee for Philadelphia. see Democratic Party. Pennsylvania. Philadelphia. Committee of Correspondence.

Correspondence concerning alleged projects of annexation. 17761

Correspondence concerning the insults offered to the flag of the United States. 16874

Correspondence concerning the purchase of naval supplies. 55877, 84955

Correspondence concerning the reasons of Dr. Ryerson's resignation. 74574

Correspondence concerning the system of recruiting volunteers. 1471

Correspondence des Generaux Leclerc. 6978, 17481

Correspondence, despatches, and other papers. 91705

Correspondence, 1843-1851 [of Henry Clay.] 13551

Correspondence, 1801-1852 [of Henry Clay.] 13551

Correspondence, &c. 96405

Correspondence, &c. between E. C. Delavan. 89744

Correspondence, etc. growing out of the seuzure and rescue of Martin Koszta. 48125

Correspondence, &c. in relation to the historical records. 87547

Correspondence, etc., relating to expeditions against the Indians. 34639

Correspondence, &c. To the public. 88851

Correspondence in reference to its original acceptance by the county. 35849

Correspondence in reference to the relief of the sufferers. 75281

Correspondence in regard to the proposed conference. 15317

Correspondence in regard to the right of way. 60278

Correspondence in relation to the British Treaty of 1806. 50011

Correspondence in relation to the capture of the British brigs. 16875, 22270, 96405

Corerspondence in relation to the New Almaden Quicksilver Mine. 52435

Correspondence in relation to the . . . northeastern boundary. 55709

Correspondence in relation to the northeastern boundary . . . of Maine. (55710)

Correspondence in relation to the public meeting at Albany, N. Y. (41184)

Correspondence in relation to the public meeting at Albany, with letter from President Lincoln. 615

Correspondence in relation to the Third Church of 1735. 75651, 75655, 2d note after 94170, 105323

Correspondence . . . with respect to the payment. (44305)

Correspondence laid before the Board of Examiners. 51610

Correspondence of a recent date. 72121

Correspondence of a Society instituted at Halifax. 29703, 2d note after 85847

Correspondence of Amos A. Williams, &c. 104164

Correspondence of Charles, first Marquis Cornwallis. (16812)

Correspondence of Congregation and Vestry with Rev. Noah Hunt Schenck. 77565

Correspondence [of Eleazar Wheelock.] (43066), 1st note after 103214

Correspondence of Eli Whitney. 103756

Correspondence of Gerrit Smith and Albert Barnes. (82606)

Correspondence [of Henry Laurens.] 50360

Correspondence of James Stuart, Esquire. 93176

Correspondence of James W. Bramham. 7372

Correspondence of John A. Graham. 28230

Correspondence of John Adams. (238)

Correspondence of John, fourth Duke of Bedford. 74342

Correspondence of John Quod. 35114

Correspondence of King George the Third. 26994

Correspondence of Lieut. Governor John Graves Simcoe. 98065B

Correspondence of Linnaeus. (41354)

Correspondence [of Martin Van Buren.] 98419

Correspondence of Martin Van Buren and Richard M. Johnson. 98410

Correspondence of Messrs. McLane and Parker. 12813

Correspondence of Miss Adams. 168, 84905

Correspondence of Mr. Munroe, Mr. Madison, and Mr. Rose. 12486

Correspondence of Mr. Pinkney. 48065

Correspondence of Mr. Ralph Izard. (35323)

Correspondence of Palestine tourists. 85504

Correspondence [of Sir Thomas Picton.] 72081

Correspondence of the American revolution. 16876

Correspondence of the Comptroller of the City of New York. 54230

Correspondence [of the Creek Indians.] 76490

Correspondence of the Department of State. 51081

Correspondence of the Department of State, in relation to the British Consuls. 15265, 16877

Correspondence of the French Ministers. 16878

Correspondence of the Honorable John Jay. (35833), 41549

Correspondence of the late John Wilkes.
104003

Correspondence of the late President Adams.
231

Correspondence of the late William Baldwin.
18599

Correspondence of the Marquess Wellesley.
1010, note after 102574

Correspondence of the Office [of Internal
Revenue.] 6975

Correspondence of the Right Hon. Edmund
Burke. 9304

Correspondence of the Rt. Hon. Sir John
Sinclair, Bart. 81394

Correspondence of the Watering Committee.
62371, (78083)

Correspondence of Thomas Jefferson. (5302),
(37656)

Correspondence of William L. Dayton. 19004

Correspondence of William Pitt. 63067

Correspondence of William Wilberforce.
103952

Correspondence officielle. 93807

Correspondence on clergy in North America.
85935

Correspondence on constitutional questions.
56118

Correspondence on the above subject. 93459

Correspondence on the importance and practicability of a railroad. 13739, 54228

Corrspondence on the plunder of the wreck.
16879

Correspondence on the present relations between Great Britain. 16880

Correspondence, on the principles of peace.
28862

Correspondence on the proposed tripartite
convention. (17762)

Correspondence on the relative situation of
France. 16881

Correspondence on the subject between the Rt.
Rev. J. P. K. Henshaw. 16312

Correspondence on the subject of appraise-
ments. (37841), 76045

Correspondence on the subject of the emigration of Indians. 34637

Correspondence on the subject of the removal
of Indians. (34638)

Correspondence on the subjects of mediation.
16882

Correspondence, orders, etc., between Major-
General David Hunter. (33913)

Correspondence particuliere. 9043, 93807

Correspondence passed between the Conference
Committee. 54229

Correspondence poetica i patriotica. (16907)

Correspondence presented to Parliament in
March, 1863. 16887

Correspondence relating to a treaty of peace.
95035

Correspondence relating to America. 16884

Correspondence relating to Chief Justice Kirby
Benedict. 4660

[Correspondence relating to disputed claims.]
101093

Correspondence relating to recent disturbances.
(68475)

Correspondence relating to the boundary.
16885, 55538

Correspondence relating to the civil war.
16886

Correspondence relating to the examination.
60027

Correspondence . . . relating to the foreign
commerce of the United States. 26819

Correspondence relating to the hypothecation.
(1989)

Correspondence relating to the memorial
address. (3132)

[Correspondence relating to] the New-Orleans
Free Library. 53353

Correspondence relating to the operations of
the Massachusetts Mining Company.
45876

Correspondence relating to the post office.
87553

Correspondence relating to the purchase and
fitting out. 16888

Correspondence relating to the reciprocity
treaty. 56119

Correspondence relating to the steamers
"Nashville" and "Tuscarora." 16887,
55534

Correspondence relating to, the wreck of the
Mayflower. (47121)

Correspondence relative to complaints. (33546)

Correspondence relative to difficulties with M.
De Saligny. 95041

Correspondence relative to emigration. 16889

Correspondence relative to . . . establishing
a workhouse. 22733

Correspondence relative to neutral rights.
(16890), 44605

Correspondence relative to surveying the lands.
101924

Correspondence relative to the acceptance for
publication. 85016

Correspondence relative to the American question. 16891

Correspondence relative to the attempted
seizure of M. Fauchet. (48137)

Correspondence relative to the case of Messrs.
Mason and Slidell. 45451

Correspondence relative to the Catawba Indians.
87402

Correspondence relative to the condition and
treatment of slaves at Honduras. (32758)

Correspondence relative to the Corvette Kensington. 37465

Correspondence relative to the discovery of
gold. (16892)

Correspondence relative to the dispute with
America. 16893, 20275

Correspondence relative to the emigration to
Hayti. (16894), (29577)

Correspondence relative to the Falkland Islands.
23733

Correspondence relative to the French decrees.
1014, 16895

Correspondence relative to the insurrection at
Harper's Ferry. 45122

Correspondence relative to the negotiation of
the question. 57549

Correspondence relative to the renewal of
treaties. 16896

Correspondence respecting a proposed settlement. 35574

Correspondence respecting British and American
claims. 16897

Correspondence respecting despatch of letters.
16887

Correspondence respecting instructions given
to naval officers. (16887), (55530)

Correspondence respecting interference with
trade. 2718

Correspondence respecting international maritime law. 16886, (55528)

Correspondence respecting iron-clad vessels.
16887

Correspondence respecting postal improvements.
10744

Correspondence respecting recruitment in Ireland. 16887

Correspondence respecting Russia. 30426, 101161

Correspondence respecting the affairs of Mexico. 48401

Correspondence respecting the "Alabama." 573, 574, 16887, (16898)

Correspondence respecting the "Alabama." (In continuation of papers presented to Parliament in Feb., 1864.) 576

Correspondence respecting the "Alabama." (In continuation of correspondence presented to Parliament in March, 1863.) 575, 16887

Correspondence respecting the assassination. (55530)

Correspondence respecting the bark "Maury." 573

Correspondence respecting the capture of the "Saxon." 16887

Correspondence respecting the conduct of military officers. 35573

Correspondence respecting the enlistment of British seamen. 16886, (37131)

Correspondence respecting the establishment of a Welsh colony. 59032

Correspondence respecting the fire at Saint John's. 54985

Correspondence respecting the Geneva arbitration. 26942

Correspondence respecting the Mosquito Territory. 51082

Correspondence respecting the negotiations with the United States' government. 55535

Correspondence respecting the operations of the commission. 16899

Correspondence respecting the proposed union. 28432

Correspondence respecting the recent Fenian aggression. (10408), 16900

Correspondence respecting the removal of British consuls. 16887

Correspondence respecting the removal of G. W. Gordon. 27977

Correspondence respecting the seizure of Messrs. Masons, Slidell, McFarland and Eustis. 45451, (55530)

Correspondence respecting the seizure of schooner "Will o' the Wisp." 16887

Correspondence respecting the "Tuscaloosa." 16887

Correspondence respecting the visit of Her Majesty's ship "Monarch." (49933)

Correspondence respecting the withdrawal by the government of the United States. 9159, 16887

Correspondence respecting trade with Matamoras. 16887, 46195

Correspondence sustained between the government of Buenos-Aires. 9006

Correspondence, through the "Times" newspaper. 95118

Correspondence to accompany maps and charts of California. 71424

Correspondence to T. Jefferson on constitutional reform. (37656)

Correspondence with . . . distinguished men. 57829

Correspondence with Dr. French. 9283

Correspondence with Gen. James Arlington Bennett. 83288

Correspondence with government. (66860)

Correspondence with W. Jay and Gerritt Smith. 25641

Correspondence with John C. Calhoun. 83288

Correspondence with Mexico. May 19, 1836. 48402

Correspondence with Mr. Adams respecting Confederate agents. 16887

Correspondence with Mr. Adams, respecting neutral rights and duties. 16887, (55531)

Correspondence with Mr. Adams respecting the enlistment of British subjects in the Federal army. 16887

Correspondence with Mr. Mason, Commissioner. 16887

Correspondence with Mr. Mason respecting the blockade. 45451

Correspondence with Mr. Wilson. 10418

Correspondence . . . with Reveredy Johnson and others. (58709)

Correspondence with Richard S. Coxe. 102122

Correspondence with the British Commissioners at Sierra Leone. 58819

Correspondence with the British ministers and agents. 16901

Correspondence with the Chairman of the Committee of the House of Representatives on Naval Affairs. 84956

Correspondence with the Chief of the Bureau of Construction. 84957

Correspondence with the Chief of the Bureau of Ordnance. 84958

Correspondence with the Chief of the Bureau of Steam Engineering. 84959

Correspondence with the Chief of the Bureau of Yards and Docks. 84960

Correspondence with the Collector. 87550

Correspondence with the Colonial Department. 20698

Correspondence with the Ex-committee of the Albany City Temperance Society. 19369, note after 94503

Correspondence with the Executive of Pennsylvania. (45141)

Correspondence with the executive, relative to the rank or command. 78403

Correspondence with the government. 74554

Correspondence with the governments. 16903

Correspondence with the governors and admirals. 8828

Correspondence with the Hon. Daniel Webster. (39344)

Correspondence with the Hon. Henry Clay. 83288

Correspondence with the inhabitants of the moon. 86560

Correspondence . . . with the Mayor and Common Council. 51720

Correspondence with the Russian Emperor. 4768

Correspondence with with the Schuylkill Navigation Company. 61566

Correspondence with the Secretary of the Navy. 26648

Correspondence with the Secretary of War. 101911

Correspondence with the United States on the Order in Council. 16902

Correspondence with the United States respecting Central America. 11683

Correspondencia. 89963

Correspondencia con los Ministros de Inglaterra y de Francia. 9007

Correspondencia de dos Indios naturales del Pire-Mapu. 47426

Correspondencia diplomatica relativa a la cuestion del Paraguay. 58514

Correspondencia diplomatica relativa a la cuestion Espanola. 16904

Correspondencia entre el Exmo. Senor General D. Juan Manuel de Rosas. 34437
Correspondencia entre el General D. Juan Manuel de Rosas. 73210
Correspondencia entre el General D. Juan O-Donoju. (56729)
Correspondencia entre el Jeneral Tomas Cipriani de Mosquera. (51075)
Correspondencia entre el Supremo Gobierno. 76728
Correspondencia entre Jose Manuel de Herrera. 31568
Correspondencia entre la republica de Colombia y D. Jose Villa. 14576
Correspondencia entre la Secretaria de Relaciones Esteriores de la republica de Colombia. 14577, 16905, note after 99615
Correspondencia entre Negrete y Squier. 76195
Correspondencia entre o Exm. Sr. Tenente-General. 88811
Correspondencia entre o sor. Je. Silvestre Rebello. 68332
Correspondencia general del Libertador Simon Bolivar. 6186, 14578, note after 39087
Correspondencia habida entre los abogados de la Compania de Nuevo Almaden. (16906)
Correspondencia literal sequida sobre emprestito. 90474
Correspondencia oficial con el Consul. 9042
Correspondencia oficial e inedita. 2533
Correspondencia que ha mediado. (16908)
Correspondencia recogida a los agentes de Santa-Anna. 26718, 76729
Correspondencia relativa a las indemnizaciones Francescas. 16909
Correspondencias cambiadas. (58515)
Correspondent. pseud. Address to the Rev. Moses C. Welch. see Swift, Zephaniah.
Correspondent. Containing, the publications. 63946, 94075, 102523
Correspondent of the New York times. see New York times. Correspondent.
Correspondent of the Virginia argus. see Virginia argus. Correspondent.
Correspondents abroad receiving publications. 85028
Correspondents of the Society for Promoting Christian Knowledge, London. see Society for Promoting Christian Knowledge, London. Correspondents.
Corresponding Association for the Promoting of Internal Improvements, New York. see New York Corresponding Association for the Promotion of Internal Improvements.
Corresponding Committee on the North Branch Canal. see North Branch Canal Corresponding Committee.
Corresponding epistle for A. D. 1819. 98008
Corresponding Society in New York, with the Baptist Education Society in Philadelphia. see Society of Correspondence in New-York, with the Baptist Education Society in Philadelphia.
Corresponsal del imparcial. 106248
Corrigan, Michael Augustine, Bp. 72954 see also Newark (Diocese) Bishop (Corrigan)
Corriveau, Jean Baptiste. defendant 16911
Corro, Juan del. 16910
Corruption and military despotism exposed. 48952, note after 102946
Corruption in high places. 37308
Corruption of the city government. 54231

Corruptions and frauds of Lincoln's administration. 41185
Corruptions of the age. 91552
Corry, John. 1166, 16912-16916, 37899, 101778, 101781, 101842, note after 104564
Corry, P. 16920
Corry, William M. 16921-16922, 33829, 91841A
Corry O'Lanus. pseud. Corry O'Lanus: his views and experiences. see Stanton, John.
Corry O'Lanus: his views and experiences. 90431
Corsair: a gazette of literature. 16923
Corsair of Sasco Bay. 34776
Corsaire l'Esperance. pseud. Observances. (56574)
Corsaire rouge. 16519
Corsali, Andrea. 67730
Corsario bojo. 16521
Corsario Drake. 94352
Corsaro rosso. 16522
Corse, Barney. defendant (16787), (18542)
Corsini, Filippo. supposed tr. 86486
Corson, G. N. (16924)
Corson, L. E. 60274
Corson, Robert R. 16925
Corson, Samuel. alias see Smith, Samuel, 1792-
Corss, Frederic. see Cross, Frederic.
Cort begryp der caerten ende beschrijvinghen. 38881, note after 100632
Cort begryp van de leven van Rosa. 73181
Cort, bondigh ende waerachtigh verhael. 7564
Cort ende sonderlingh verhael van eenen brief. 86375
Cort ende waerachtich verhael. 7565
Cort ende waerachtigh verhael. 7561, (16739)
Cort ende warachtich verhael. 7573, 16923
Cort verhael, vande ordre die sijne Conincklicke Majesteyt. 45404, 51680
Cort verhael vande voyage. 89747
Corta, Charles Eustache. 16927
Cortambert, -------. 85781, 85791
Cortambert, Eugene, 1805-1881. 16930, 44159
Cortambert, Louis Richard, 1808?-1881. 16928-16929
Cortambert, Pierre Francois Eugene. see Cortambert, Eugene, 1805-1881.
Cortambert, Richard, 1836-1884. 16930
Corte a Fazenda de Santa Fe. 16838
Corte ende warachtige beschrigvinge. 5904
Corte ende waerachtigh verhael van 't gene ghepasseert. 7561
Corte-Real, Diogo de Mendoca. see Mendoca Corte-Real, Diogo de, 1658-1736.
Corte-Real, Gaspar, 1450-1501. 50050-50064, 1st-5th notes after 106378
Corte-real, Joao Pereira, d. ca. 1649. 16931
Cortes, A. (16932)
Cortes, Estefana, Duquesa de Terranoua. defendant 99436
Cortes, Eugenio. defendant at court martial 58565
Cortes, Fernando. see Cortes, Hernando, 1485-1547.
Cortes, Fernando. pseud. Dialogues of the dead. 19948
Cortes, Hernando, 1485-1547. 3350, 6420, 16669, (16933)-16943, 16947-16959, 16961-16965, 20518, 22086, 27750, (34105), 34107, 41659, (42065), 42960, 48287, 48490, 50115, 56064, 56052, 65402, 67740-67742, 76897, 93580, 94220, 3d

note after 96457, note after 99383C,
note after 100840 see also Mexico
(Viceroyalty) Virrey, 1521-1526 (Cortes)
Cortes, Martin, fl. 1551. 16966-16968, 94220
Cortes de Arredondo, Miguel Joseph. 16970,
72809, 73740
Cortes y Larraz, Pedro, Abp. 16969 see
also Guatemala (Archdiocese) Arch-
bishop (Cortes y Larraz)
Cortes y Zedeno, Geronymo Thomas de
Aquino. 16971
Cortes. 106241
Cortes; or the discovery and conquest of
Mexico. 17825
Cortes; or the fall of Mexico. 5550A
Cortez, Ferdinand. pseud. Second dialogue
of the dead. see Johnstone, James.
Cortez; or, the conquest of Mexico. 10285
Cortezero, Diego. ed. 40082
Cortina, Jose Gomez de la. defendant 74888
Cortina, Jose Justo Gomez de la Cortina,
Conde de la, 1799-1860. (16972)-16974
Cortina, Pedro. (52250)
Cortinas, Manuel Diez de las. plaintiff 99653
Cortines Laxe, Joao Baptista. 16977
Cortland, Jacobus van. defendant 58366
Cortland, N. Y. Normal and Training School.
see New York (State) State Normal
School, Cortland.
Cortland, N. Y. Presbyterian Church. (7759)
Cortland, N. Y. State Normal and Training
School, see New York (State) State
Normal School, Cortland.
Cortland, N. Y. State Normal School. see
New York (State) State Normal School,
Cortland.
Cortland County, N. Y. Board of Supervisors.
(16979)
Corland County, N. Y. Cincinnatus Academy.
see Cincinnatus Academy, Cortland
County, N. Y.
Cortland Academy, Homer, N. Y. 16978
Cortland Academy jubilee. 16978
Cortland County and the border wars of New
York. 27942
Cortlandville Academy. see Cortland Academy,
Academy, Homer, N. Y.
Cortlandt, Philip van. see Van Cortlandt,
Philip.
Cortlandt, Pierre van. see Van Cortlandt,
Pierre.
Cortozar, Jose de Lamar y. see Lamar y
Cotozar, Jose de, 1776-1830.
Coruja, Antonio Alvares Pereira. see Pereira
Coruja, Antonio Alvares.
Corver Hooft, G. 102889A
Corvinus, Valerius. pseud. Remarks on the
nature and extent of liberty. see Black-
lock, Thomas. supposed author and
Ferguson, Adam. supposed author
Corwin, Charles Edward, 1868- 83526
Corwin, E. 16980
Corwin, Edward Tanjore. 16982-16983
Corwin, Morris B. 16984
Corwin, Thomas, 1794-1865. 16985, 18830,
74736 see also U. S. Treasury Depart-
ment.
Corwine, Amos B. (16986), 58408 see also
U. S. Legation. Panama.
Corwine, Richard Mortimer, b. 1812. 88506,
88508
Cos, Jose M. Rodriguez y. see Rodriguez y
Cos, Jose Maria, 1823-1899.
Cosa, Juan de la. see De la Cosa, Juan.
Cosas de los Estados Unidos. 16987

Cosas de Mexico. 48403
Cosas del Plata explicadas. (16988)
Coasas notables. 16989
Cosas que jamas se han oido. 99699
Cosas sabidas y cosas por saber. 16990
Cosby, William, 1695?-1736. 53438, (53693A),
53872, 94092 see also New York
(Colony) Governor, 1731-1736 (Cosby)
Cosby, William, 1695?-1736. defendant (53693),
98435 see also New York (Colony)
Governor, 1731-1736 (Cosby) defendant
Cosby, William, 1695?-1736. plaintiff 98429,
98431 see also New York (Colony)
Governor, 1731-1736 (Cosby) plaintiff
Cosco, Aliander de. see Aliander de Cosco.
Cosco, Leander de. see Aliander de Cosco.
Cosecha de trigo. 16991
Cosecheros del Pulque Blanco. plaintiffs
(72561)
Cosens, B. 78201 see also New York
(Colony) Council. Secretary.
Cosenza, Mariano E. tr. note after 99383C,
101017
Cosio, Joaquin Telesforo de Trueba y. see
Trueba y Cosio, Joaquin Telesforo de.
Cosio, Joseph. 16992
Cosio, Joseph del Campillo y. see Campillo
y Cosio, Joseph del.
Cosio, Pedro. 66104 see also Lima. Tri-
bunal del Consulado, y Junta General de
Comercia.
Cosio, Pedro Gutierrez. see Gutierrez Cosio,
Pedro.
Cosme, ------ de St. see Buisson, Jean
Francois.
Cosmogenia. 103389
Cosmographe Espagnol. (73151)
Cosmographei oder Beschreibung aller Lander.
(51387)-51389
Cosmography: das ist, Beschreibung aller
Lander. (51395)
Cosmographey oder Beschreibung aller Lander.
51390-51394
Cosmographeye of Sebastian Munster. (51406)
Cosmographia. 26870, 64531
Cosmographia, autore Abrahamo Peritsol.
60934
Cosmographia. Beschrebug aller Lander.
51386
Cosmographia. Beschreibung aller Lender
[sic]. 51384-51385
Cosmographia, das ist Beschreibung der gantzen
Welt. (51396)
Cosmographia das ist eine schone richtige und
vollkommene Beschreigung. 67977
Cosmographia de Ieronymo Giraua Tarragonez.
1756
Cosmographia de Pedro Apiano. 1756
Cosmographia Francisci Mavrolyci Messanensis
Sicvli. 46957-46958
Cosmographia libri tres. 49773
Cosmographia per Gemmam Frisium correcta.
1747
Cosmographia Petri Apiani. 1748-1750
Cosmographia Pomponii cum figuris. 63955
Cosmographia prosometrica. 71596
Cosmographia, sive descriptio vniversi orbis.
(1751)
Cosmographia. Translated by Jacobus Angelus,
and accompanied by an index. (66474)
Cosmographia. Translated by Jacobus Angelus,
and edited by Nicolaus Donis. (66472)-
66473
Cosmographia. Translated by Jacobus Angelus,
and edited, with the emendations of
Georgius Gemistus. 66470

Cosmographia. [Translated by Jacobus Angelus of Scarparia.] 66469
Cosmographia. Translated by Jacobus Angelus, revised by Hieronymus Manfredus and Petrus Bonus. 66471
Cosmographia vniversale. (51402)-51403
Cosmographia, y geographia. 27504
Cosmographiae disciplinae compendium. 64522
Cosmographiae introductio. 910, 1740, (1741), 1743, 1746, 77803, 77804, 99354-99355, 99358, 99368-99369, 99379-99380, note after 99383C, 101017-101024
Cosmographiae universalis. 51382
Cosmographiae uniuersalis Lib. VI. 51380-51381, (51383)
Cosmographiae uniuersalis Lib. VI. in quibus, iuxta certioris. 51379
Cosmographicae. 91983
Cosmographical glasse. 17971
Cosmographicvs liber Petri Apiani mathematici, iam denuo integritati restitutus per Gemmam Phrysium. 1742
Cosmographicus liber Petri Apiani mathematici studiose collectus. 1738
Cosmographicus liber Petri Apiani mathematici, studiose correctus. 1739, 5260
Cosmographie d'Asaph. 76838
Cosmographie et pelerinage du monde universel. 36681
Cosmographie de Pierre Apian. 1752
Cosmographie, in four books. 31655
Cosmographie, oft beschrijuinghe der gheheelder verelt van Petrus Apianus. 1754
Cosmographie. Ofte beschrijvinge der gheheelder werelt. 1755
Cosmographie . . . par Jean Fonteneau. 100828, 100830, 100833-100834
Cosmographie universelle contenant la situation de toutes les parties du monde. 51398
Cosmographie vniverselle contenant la situation de toutes les parties du monde auec leurs proprietez & appartenances. 51397, 51399
Cosmographie vniverselle d'Andre Thevet. 95535
Cosmographie vniverselle de tovt le monde. 51400
Cosmographie vlauiane. 5715
Cosmographo de su Magestad. pseud. cartographer 76838
Cosmography. 27724
Cosmography and geology. (5968), 76720
Cosmography or, a description of the whole world. 23646
Cosmograupye of Sebastian Munster. 51405
Cosmologie. 100990
Cosmophonography. 28134
Cosmopolis. pseud. Paix en apparence. 91247
Cosmopolita. 40066, 96198
Cosmopolitan Art Association. 16993
Cosmopolitan art journal. 16994
Cosmopolitan ideas on the union. (16995)
Cosmopolite. pseud. Correspondence relative to the dispute with America. 16893
Cosmopolite. pseud. Cry from the wilderness. see Dow, Lorenzo.
Cosmopolite. pseud. Dispute with America. 20275
Cosmopolite. pseud. Miller overthrown. see Tomkins, Abel. supposed author
Cosmopolite. pseud. Plan to reconcile Great Britain & her colonies. 63303
Cosmopolite. pseud. Review of the prosecution against Abner Kneeland. 38091

Cosmopolite. pseud. Tales and sketches. see Lawson, James.
Cosmopolite. 16996
Cosmos; a sketch of the physical description of the universe. 25131, 33729
Cosmos. Essai d'un description physique du monde. 33730
Cosmos: sketch of a physical description of the universe. (33727)
Cosmos philosophicus seu Aristotelicae philosophiae de mundo explanatio. 27266
Coso, Alexandrus de. 72023
Cosquillas. 16997
Cossham, Handel. 16998-17000
Cossio, B. G. de. 17001
Cossio y Guerra, Fermin Aurelio de Tagle. see Tagle Cossio y Guerra, Fermin Aurelio de.
Cost and the consequences. 57566
Cost of Massachusetts government. 8348
Cost of peace. 58024
Cost, revenue, and expenditures of the public works. (60028)
Costa, Agost. Robello da. 17002
Costa, Antonio da. 17003
Costa, Antonio Juliao da. tr. 46989
Costa, Benjamin Franklin De. see DeCosta, Benjamin Franklin.
Costa, Claudio Manoel da. see Manoel da Costa, Claudio.
Costa, Constantino Pereira de. 17004
Costa, Enrique da. see Koster, Henry.
Costa, H. Jose da. 32035
Costa, Isaac. 61606
Costa, Joao Severjano Marciel da. (17005)-17006
Costa, Jose da Silva. see Silva Costa, Jose da.
Costa, Juan Rojo. see Rojo Costa, Juan.
Costa, Lorenza. 17007
Costa, Manoel da. tr. 31382
Costa, Manual de complainant. 47349
Costa, Maria da. 17008
Costa, Nicola. defendant 27309, (51797), 69915, 93808, 96948
Costa, Sallustino Orlando de Aranjo. 1891, (17009), 70793
Costa, Thomas da. 66104 see also Lima. Tribunal del Consulado, y Junta General de Comercio.
Costa Almeida, Antonio Lopes da. 17010
Costa Barros, Pedro Jose de. 24259 see also Maranhao (Brazilian Province) Presidente (Costa Barros)
Costa do Para, Manoel da. defendant 99617
Costa e Lima, Thomas da Encarnacao da. 17011
Costa e Sa, Manoel Jose Maria de. 17012
Costa Honorato, Manoel da. see Honorato, Manoel da Costa.
Costa Mascarenhas, Ignacio Manuel da. see Mascarenhas, Ignacio Manuel da Costa.
Costa Paiva, Antonio da. ed. 98649
Costa Pereira, Jose Saturnino da. 17013
Costa Pereira Furtado de Mendonca, Hypolito Jose da. tr. 3815, 18256
Costa Quintilla, Ignacio da. see Quintilla, Ignacio da Costa.
Costa Rubim, Braz da, 1817- (7493), 73855
Costa Rica. Ministerio de Hacienda. 70014
Costa Rica. Ministerio de Hacienda, Guerra, Marina, y Caminos. 17017
Costa Rica. Ministerio de Relaciones y do lo Interior. 47600
Costa Rica. Ministerio de Relaciones y Gobernacion. 47694

Costa Rica (Diocese) see Nicaragua y Costa Rica (Diocese)
Costa Rica and New Grenada. 49881
Costa-Rica y Nueva Granada. (49880)
Costal, de Indiaan. 4519B
Costal der Indianer. 4519
Costal, l'Indien. 4518, 4520
Costales, Manuel. 50701
Costanso, Miguel. 17019-17020
Costanzo, Giuseppe Buonfiglio. see Buonfiglio Costanzo, Giuseppe.
Costard Sly. pseud. see Sly, Costard. pseud.
Coste, John Francis. 17021
Coste, Nicolas de la. tr. 31547-31550
Coster, G. Van Lennep. see Lennep Coster, G. van.
Costi, Ans. Michelo. 17023
Costilla, Miguel Hildago. 105736
Costly sacrifice. 89917
Costumbres del camp. 93345
Costumbres familiares de los Americanos del norte. 97027
Costume antico e moderno. 24164
Costume of America. 17024
Costumes civils, militaires et religieux du Mxique. 41144
Costumes et moeurs de Mexique. 41143
Costumi, le leggi, et l'usanze di tutti le genti. 6119
Coswell, George. plaintiff 102784
Coswell, John. plaintiff 102784
Cota, Johannes. ed. 66475
Cote occidentale de l'Amerique du Nord. 25936
Cotejo de la conducta de S. M. con la de el Rey Britanico. (16690), 17026, 62442, note after 93420
Cotejo de la conducta del Rey Felipe V. 17025
Cotes, H. 953, (17027), 32177
Cotes, H. supposed author (17027), (36902), 63086, 63089, 80699
Cotes de l'Oregon et du territoire de Washington. 25936
Cotesworth, --------, fl. 1721. 65865, 88192
Cotheal, A. J. 17028
Cothren, William. 17029
Cotogno, Ott. 14142, 17030
Cotolendy, C. tr. 14677
Coton son regime. 70388
Cott, J. M. van. see Van Cott, J. M.
Cotta, Bernhard. 33731
Cottage garden of America. 22097
Cottage library of Christian knowledge, no. III. 105178
Cottage residences. (20773)
Cottages and cottage life. 22260
Cotten, Edward R. 17031
Cotter, Richard. 17032
Cotterel, Francois Frederic. 17033
Cottin, ------. 78774
Cottineau, D. L. (17034)
Cotting, Benjamin Eddy. 17035, 73715 see also Roxbury, Mass. Alms House. Physician.
Cotting, J. R. 17036
Cotting, Uriah. 2398, 17037
Cotton, Alfred Johnson. 17038
Cotton, Anne. 17039, 51810, 2d note after 100494
Cotton, Calvin. ed. 13549
Cotton, Elizabeth (Saltonstall) 46296
Cotton, Henry. 17041

Cotton, John, 1584-1652. 1786, (2219), 2625, 11616, 17042-17081, (17083)-17091, (21090), 22161, 31653, 32861, 33698, (34471), 39934, 45652, 46783, 51773, 52595, 52730, 55888, 58769, 63331, 63515, (70107), 78431, 78434, 81490, 82976, 82978, 92113, note after 99832, 2d note after 103852, 104331, 104333, 104341, 104896, 106052
Cotton, John, 1584-1652. supposed author 18705
Cotton, John, 1584-1652. incorrectly supposed author 17075, 46639, 103396
Cotton, Mrs. John, fl. 1657. 41005, 55881, 55885
Cotton, Sir John, 1679-1731. 67599
Cotton, John, fl. 1687. 17092, 98055
Cotton, John, 1693-1757. 17093-17099, (64276)
Cotton, John, 1712-1789. 10703, 17100-17103, 50996, 71756, 71762, 71830
Cotton, Marigena. see Cotton, Seaborn.
Cotton, Josiah, 1680-1756. 17104, 51013
Cotton, Sir Robert Bruce, Bart., 1571-1631. 17105
Cotton, Sir Robert Bruce, Bart., 1571-1631. supposed author 13514
Cotton, Sir Robert Bruce, Bart., 1571-1631. incorrectly supposed author 78362
Cotton, Rowland. 17106
Cotton, Seaborn. 17107, 52714, 52720, note after 65546
Cotton, Ward. 17108
Cotton—a paper on the growth. 21083
Cotton and common sense. 37370
Cotton as an element of industry. 4086
Cotton commerce, and the southern states. 19115
Cotton crisis. 17110
Cotton cultivation in Africa. 13827
Cotton cultivation in its various details. 27305
Cotton culture. (42792)
Cotton culture and the south considered. (42080)
Cotton famine and the Lancashire operatives. 17111
Cotton fields and cotton factories. (17112)
Cotton fields of Paraguay and Corrientes. 51267
Cotton from the pod to the factory. (17113)
Cotton in the middle states. 22432
Cotton is king. 4476, 12950
Cotton is king, and pro-slavery arguments. 22263, 92870
Cotton: its production and movement. 88352
Cotton kingdom. 2282
Cotton kingdom: a traveller's observations. 57240
Cotton lands the best permanent investment. (36330)
Cotton manufacture. Boston memorial to Congress. 17114
Cotton manufacture. Statistics from the seventh annual report. 17115
Cotton manufacturer. pseud. Cheap cotton by free labor. see Atkinson, Edward.
Cotton Manufacturers' Association of New England. see New England Cotton Manufacturers' Association.
Cotton Manufacturers of Providence, R. I. Committee. petitioners 66282
Cotton Mather and Salem witchcraft. 64042, 64046, 98039
Cotton Mather & witchcraft. 46623, 64043, 98039

Cotton Mather's Wonders of the invisible world. 4009
Cotton plant. 17116
Cotton planter. pseud. Conversation in a canebrake. 16203
Cotton-planter's daughter. 72128
Cotton Planters Convention of Georgia. (36576)
Cotton question. 43308
Cotton question. A portion of the following letter appeared. 17117
Cotton question. An inquiry into the standing. 88353
Cotton question. The production, export, manufacture, and consumption of cotton. 3313
Cotton States Exposition, Atlanta, 1895. 85020
Cotton stealing. A novel. 17118
Cotton supply. 17119
Cotton supply of the United States of America. 43303
Cotton supply question, in relation to the peculiarities and resources of India. 83902
Cotton supply reporter. (17120)
Cotton tables; exhibiting, at a glance, the cost of cotton. (22675)
Cotton tables, tables of cost, quantities received. 89061
Cotton; the chemical, geological, and meteorological conditions. 44132
Cotton trade. 17121
Cotton trade: its bearing upon the prosperity of Great Britain. 43304
Cotton trade of Egypt. 84005
Cotton trade of Great Britain. 84005
Cotton trade of Great Britain: its rise. 44333
Cotton trade of India, being a series of letters. 84005, 84008
Cotton trade of India. Can India not supply England with cotton? (17122)
Cotton's keepsake. 17038
Couch, Paul. 17134-17135
Coucha i Toro, -------. 39151
Coudreniere, ------- Peyroux de la. see Peyroux de la Coudreniere, ----.
Coues, Samuel. 27716
Coues, Samuel Elliott. 17136-(17138)
Coughlan, L. (17139)
Coulanger, A. P. de. tr. 85382
Coulier, Ph. J. 17140
Coulon, ----- Garron. see Garron-Coulon, -------.
Coulter, --------, fl. 1869. 13573, (40970), 85133
Coulter, --------, fl. 1922. 85376
Coulter, John. 17142-17143
Coulter's Executors. defendants 33257
Councell of a father to his sonne. 67599
Councell of Virginia. see Virginia Company of London.
Council and House journal of the Legislative Assembly of Dakota. 18294
Council and House journal of the Territory of Dakota. 18295
Council at Bloomfield. 5992
Council Bluffs' directory. 17144
Council Chamber, January 25, 1794. 100224
Council Chamber, October 20, 1785. 100211
Council-Chamber, Oct. 29, '99. 98059G
Council for New England. 19051, (52625), 68407, 95638
Council for New England. Records. Reprinted from the proceedings. (52625)
Council held at Lancaster August the 28th 1764. 60646, 93361

Council held at Philadelphia, August, 1744. 34640
Council of Congregational Churches, New York, 1859. see Congregational Churches in New York. Ecclesiastical Council, New York, 1859.
Council of Fourteen Churches, Watertown, Mass., 1722. see Congregational Churches in Massachusetts. Ecclesiastical Council, Watertown, 1722.
Council of Nine Churches, Northampton, Mass., 1750. see Congregational Churches in Massachusetts. Ecclesiastical Council, Northampton, 1750.
Council of Prizes, Paris. see France. Council of Prizes, Paris.
Council of Proprietors of East New-Jersey. see Board of Proprietors of the Eastern Division of New Jersey.
Council of Proprietors of the Western Division of New Jersey. 53067, (53091), (53236), (80693), 83892
Council of Proprietors of the Western Division of New Jersey. petitioners 53203
Council of Revision of the State of New York; its history. 92765
Council of Six Churches, Woburn, Mass., 1746. see Congregational Churches in Massachusetts. Ecclesiastical Council, Woburn, 1746.
Council of six churches, conven'd at Woburn, upon the request of the Rev. Mr. Jackson. 35407, 104972
Council of Ten Churches, Exeter, N. H., 1743. see Congregational Churches in New Hampshire. Ecclesiastical Council, Exeter, 1743.
Council of Trent. see Trent, Council of, 1545-1563.
Council-Office. Dec. 29, 1798. 95059C
Council's defence against the charge of certain misdemeanours. 6219
Counseils d'un vieux planteur. 64850
Counsel for emigrants. (17145)
Counsel for parties in the state of New York. 90022
Counsel for the stockholders opposed to the Jay Gould dynasty. pseud. Some suggestions. 86768
Counsel of Ahithophel turned into foolishness. 74363
Counsel of two confederate kings. 12331
Counsel of Washington. 32579
Counsel to the American clergy. 4992
Counsel to the Christian-traveller. 80459
Covnsell of a well-wishing souldier. 78363
Covnsell of Virginia. see Virginia Company of London.
Counsellor at law. pseud. Review of the testimony. see Spencer, John Canfield.
Counsellor-at-law. pseud. ed. Statutes of New York. (53985)
Counsellor, of human life. 29206
Counsellor of peace. 82947
Counsellors and attorneys at law. petitioners 97928
Counsels addressed to young women. 83577
Counsels and cautions. 79784
Counsels and directions to Ebenezer Wales. 101027
Counsels for the new year. 92737
Counsels to the newly converted. 11996
Consul Dean's narrative. 104686
Count, ------- le. see Le Count, --------.

Count Frontenac and New France under
Louis XIV. 58802
Count Johannes. see Jones, George, 1810-
1879.
Count Julian. 81204
Count the cost. (15716), note after 90846
Count Zinzenborf and the Indians, 1742.
68992
Counter-address to the public. 17146, 101143
Counter appeal to an appeal from William
Wilberforce. 44880
Counter declaration published at New York,
1781. (19176)
Counter-irritant. 20506
Counter-letter to the Right Hon. the E—l of
H—ll————gh. 2361, 28749
Counter manifest of the Minister of Foreign
Relations of Chile. 12759
Counter memorial from Jalapa, in Mexico.
(36482)
Counter questions submitted by divers Seign-
iours. 10495
Counter report of a portion of the members.
87510
Counter report of the . . . Committee, on so
much of the Governor's message, as
relates to capital punishment. 45699
Counter report of the Minority of the Commit-
tee. 60029
Counter-statement in support of the petition.
30185
Counter statement of Mr. Packenham. 9943,
57565
Counter statement of the case of Bishop H. U.
Onderdonk. 47238
Counter testimonial. 37188
Covnterblaste to tobacco. 35675, 97551
Counterfeit detector. 12028
Counterpoints in canon law. 84192, 84195,
84197-84211, 84213-84214
Counterpoise. 17147, 2d note after 95643
Countess of Huntington's College. see
Trevecca College, Talgarth, Wales.
Counting-house almanac. 8680
Countrey physitian. pseud. Some observations
made upon the Mexican seeds. 86677
Countries most adapted to emigration. 17148
Country almanack, for 1821. 3885A
Country almanack for the year of Christian
account, 1765. 64090
Country bard. pseud. Epistle to the general
convention. 22699
Country book. 49675
Country boy. pseud. Duet. see Story, Isaac,
1774-1803.
Country clergyman. pseud. Letters. 40582
Country clergyman. pseud. Peace and unity
recommended. 59401
Country curate. pseud. American resistance
indefensible. 1211, 79280
Country dialogue on the present times. 14033
Country editor. pseud. Some adventures of
Captain Simon Suggs. see Hooper,
Johnson J.
Country friend. pseud. Sober dialogue. 85662
Country gentleman. pseud. Candid and im-
partial considerations. (10657)
Country gentleman. pseud. Considerations on
the penal laws. 15999
Country gentleman. pseud. Farther reasons.
(81976)
Country gentleman. pseud. Observations and
reflections. see Polhill, Charles.
Country gentleman. pseud. Parallel drawn
between the administration. 58540

Country gentleman. pseud. Reflexions on a
pamphlet. 68743
Country gentleman. pseud. Short advice to
the counties of New-York. see Wilkins,
Isaac.
Country gentleman. pseud. Thoughts on the
present war, and future peace. 95721
Country gentleman. pseud. Throughts on the
present war: with remarks. 95722
Country gentleman. A journal for the farm.
17150, (17869)
Country gentleman at Boston. pseud. Letter.
6708, 40274
Country gentleman's reasons for voting. 17149
Country journal. 66327
Country life. 16659
Country living and country thinking. 20505
Country love vs. city flirtation. 89406
Country-man Roger. pseud. see Roger.
pseud.
Country-man's companion. 97285, 97288
Country margins. (30110)
Country minister's wife. 61375, note after
93772
"Country parson's" daughter. pseud. Scenes
in our parish. see Holmes, Elizabeth
Emra.
Country pastor. pseud. Stoneridge. see
Smith, Charles A., 1809-1879.
Country printer. 25902, 2d note after 99627
Country school-houses. 36404
Country school master. pseud. Tales and
sketches. see Leggett, William.
Country schoolmaster in love. 71133
Country seats of the United States. 5531
Countryman. pseud. see Sherman, Roger,
1721-1793.
Countryman. pseud. Appeal from a country-
man. see Howe, R. H.
Countryman. pseud. Letter from a country-
man to his friend. 60202
Countryman. pseud. Senator Schurz and his
clock. 78041
Countryman. pseud. To the freeholders and
freemen, in Pennsylvania. 60690
Countryman's lamentations. 17151
Country's welcome to its heroes and defenders.
37974
County and town officer. 45700
County Convention of Delegates from All the
Towns in Bristol County, Taunton, Mass.,
1837. see Whig Party. Massachusetts.
Bristol County.
County Convention of Delegates, from the
Several Towns in the County of Erie,
Buffalo, N. Y., 1830. see Holland Pur-
chase Convention, Buffalo, N. Y., 1830.
County curate. pseud. Poem on the war in
the West Indies. 63592, 99249
County directory. 38189
County Law Reform and Working Men's Con-
vention, Keene, N. H., 1833-1834. 52792
County lyceums. 94560
County of Addison. 99100
County of New York: Surrogate's Court. 58611
County warden, and municipal officer's assist-
ant. (80161)
Coup d'oeil autour du monde. 32701
Coup d'oeil dans la case de l'oncle Tom.
92543
Coup d'oeil d'ensemble sur les differentes
expeditions. 44170
Coup d'oeil geographique et politique sur cette
republique. 39589

Coup-d'oeil historique et statistique sur le Texas. 25288

Coup d'oeil historique sur la projection des cartes. 2492

Coup d'oeil historique sur les evenements qui s'y sont succedes. 39029

Coup-d'oeil impartial sur les decrets. 94422

Coup d'oeil politique sur cette colonie. (17189), (42351)

Coup d'oeil raisonne sur la guerre. 105249

Coup d'oeil rapide sur la republique de Costa Rica. 42907, 49882

Coup d'oeil rapide sur mes differens voyages. 48949

Coup-d'oeil sur Cayenne en 1822. 99605

Coup-d'oeil sur la culture des quelques vegetaux exotiques. 98350

Coup-d'oeil sur la Grand-Bretagne. 17152

Coup d'oeil sur la nation et la langue de Wabis. 7424

Coup d'oeil sur la regime repressif. 38563

Coup d'oeil sur la republique de Costa Rica. 17015

Coup-d'oeil sur la republique de l'Amerique Centrale, et particulierement sur les etats de Nicaragua et Costa Rica. 17153, 19463, 21178

Coup d'oeil sur la republique de l'Amerique Centrale et principalement des etats de Nicaragua et Costa Rica. 17153, 19463, 21178

Coup-d'oeil sur la situation agricole de la Guyane Francaise. 4939

Coup-d'oeil sur la situation des affaires. 17154

Coup-d'oeil sur le commerce homicide de la traite des noirs. 13475

Coup d'oeil sur le voyage de M. Parchappe dans la Republique Argentine. (58557)

Coup d'oeil sur le Yucatan. 44169

Coup-d'oeil sur les differents modes de traiter le tetanos. 98353

Coup d'oeil sur les quatre concours. 68076

Coup-d'oeil sur les ressources productives. (20890)

Coup d'oeil sur l'etat actuel de nos rapports politiques. 23919, 40690

Coup d'oeil sur l'etat actuel des Etats-Unis d'Amerique. 42913

Coup d'oeil sur l'etat de la question d'affranchissement. 77743

Coup d'oeil sur l'etat politique du Bresil au 12 Novembre 1825. 4158

Coup d'oeil sur l'etat politique du Bresil du 12 Novembre, 1823. 7566

Coup-d'oeil sur l'hydrologie du Mexique. 77203

Coup d'oeil sur sa situation actuelle. 7936

Coup-d'oeil sur Saint-Domingue. 12016, 12027

Coup d'lumiere. (17155)

Coup de Saint-Douat, Alexandre. 17156

Coupvent-Desbois, ------. 21216

Cour de Aydes, Rouen. see Rouen, France. Cour de Aydes.

Cour de Rome et l'Empereur Maximilien. 17157

Cour d'Assises, Paris. see Paris. Cour d'Assises.

Cour imperiale de Paris. (6268)

Courage! 20506

Courage and success to the good. 105303

Courage in a good cause. 21138

Courage in doing good. 104764

Courage to the Scotch-Indian-Company. 96428

Courant. 52121

Courazolles, -----. 17158

Courbe, Augustin. (50579), 50724

Courbes, I. de. illus. 40057

Courcelle-Seneuil, I. H. see Courcelle-Seneuil, Jean Gustave, 1813-1892.

Courcelle-Seneuil, Jean Gustave, 1813-1892. 17159-17161, 70301

Courcelles, Jean Baptiste Pierre Jullien de, 1759-1854. 101348-101350, 101352

Courcelles, Jullien de. see Courcelles, Jean Baptiste Pierre Jullien de, 1759-1834.

Courcy, Henri de. see Courcy de Laroche-Heron, Henri de.

Courcy, Richard de. see De Courcy, Richard, 1743-1803.

Courcy de Laroche-Heron, Henri de. (10604), 19201-19202, (80023)

Couret de Villeneuve, L. P. ed. 68418

Coureur des bois. 4521

Courier (New Orleans) 56303

Courier. 17595, 44704

Courier and inquirer. see New York courier and inquirer.

Courier de Boston. 17164

Courier de l'Europe. 17165

Courier politique et litteraire. 17165

Courmont, Felix de. (17166)

Courmont, Ignatius Hungari de la Marche. see Marche-Courmont, Ignatius Hungari de la.

Cournand, Antoine de. (17167), (28733)

Couro, --------. defendant 11223

Courrejolles, -------. 17168

"Courrier de la Martinique" a M. Bayle-Mouillard. 17169

Courrier de Saint-Domingue. 75091

Courrier politique et litteraire du Cap-Francais. 10753, 75092

Cours complet d'economie politique pratique. 77356-(77357)

Cours diplomatique. 44839

Cours d'historie a l'usage des juenes personnes. (81024)-81025

Cours d'historie des etats Europeens. 77753

Cours d'histoire du Canada. 24107

Course of catechising. 7482

Course of catechising to be observed. 7477

Course of empire. (55381)

Course of experiments. 37928

Course of instruction and government of the Natchez Institute. 51897

Course of instruction for undergraduates in Harvard College. 30765

Course of instruction in elocution. 105788

Course of instruction in the Boylston Medical School. 7144

Course of lectures delivered to the Winchester Law School. 97308

Course of lectures, exhibited before the Grand Chapter. 96366

Course of lectures on elocution. 80345

Course of lectures on the constitutional jurisprudence. 21111

Course of lectures on the political history of England. 82689

Course of lectures on the theory of language and universal grammar. 65503

Course of popular lectures. 105588

Course of popular lectures, historical and political. 18639, 105589

Course of sermons on early piety. 46274, 46595, 46629, 65603, 79431

Course of studies, &c. &c. [of Union College.] 97774

Course of study, rules and regulations of the Bowdon Collegiate Institution. 7041

Course of the administration, state of the finances, etc., etc. 26400

Course of theological lectures. 1808
Course of training. 46139
Course on the currency. 2281
Course on the nature and object of America's political institutions. 105589
Courses and distances from Cape-Cod and Cape-Ann. 6025
Coursol, -------. 4710, 74983
Court, J. 17170
Court de Gebelin, Antoine, 1725-1784. (491), (17174)
Court and character of James I. 31654
Court and city kalendar. 17171
Court and city register for England, Scotland, Ireland, and America, for the year 1783. 41855
Court and city register, for England, Scotland, Ireland, and the colonies, for the year 1819. 73796
Court and city register, or gentleman's complete annual kalendar. 17172
Court and reign of Catherine II. 85145-85146, 85155, 85162, 85164
Court circles of the republic. 22215
Court for the Trial of Impeachments, and the Correction of Errors. Andrew Vos & John Boonen Graves, versus the United Insurance Company. 100777
Court martial. 17468
Court martial held at Louisa Courthouse. 105947
Court martial of Charles W. Hall. 29742
Court-martial of Major Daniel Sharp. 79807
Court of Bishops Assembled for the Trial of the Rt. Rev. George Washington Doane, Burlington, N. J., 1852. see Protestant Episcopal Church in the U. S. A. House of Bishops. Court for the Trial of Bishop George Washington Doane, Burlington, N. J., 1852.
Court of Errors and Appeals of the State of Delaware. June term, 1871. 62051
Court of fancy: a poem. 27657
Court of General Sessions, New-York, October term, 1833. 96939
Court of General Sessions. The people vs. John H. Cooper (16580)
Court of Impeachment for the trial of James Prescott. (65250)
Court of Mexico. (38229)
Court of Neptune, and the curse of liberty. 17173
Court of Oyer and Terminer for Lycoming County, Pa. see Lycoming County, Pa. Court of Oyer and Terminer, Williamsport.
Court of Special Sessions of the Peace, Held in and for the City and County of New York. see New York (City) Court of Special Sessions of the Peace.
Court on the Trial of Bishop Onderdonk. see Protestant Episcopal Church in the U. S. A. House of Bishops. Court for the Trial of Benjamin T. Onderdonk, 1844-1845.
Courtanvaux, F. C. le Tellier de. see Le Tellier de Courtanvaux, F. C.
Courtauld, George. see Sourtauld, George.
Courte de la Blanchardiere, Rene. 17176-17177, 2d note after 100818
Courte notice biographique. 93989, 93993
Courte reponse a gros memoire. 4545, 5848
Courte reponse que font les Commissaires de Saint-Domingue. 58164
Courten, Sir William. 7880, 17178-17180
Courten, Sir William. supposed author 9759

Courtenay, E. S. 17181
Courtenay, J. M. de. see De Courtenay, J. M.
Courtenay, James. 17182
Courtenay, Thomas Peregrine. 17183-17184
Courthop, Nathaniel. 66686
Courtier. pseud. Reign of felicity. see Spence, Thomas. supposed author
Courtier. pseud. Three politicians. 95748
Courtiras, Gabrielle Anne Cisterne de. see Saint Mars, Gabrielle Anne Cisterne de Courtiras, Vicomtesse de, 1804-1872.
Courtland, Ala. (50376)
Courtly poets from Raleigh to Montrose. 67599
Courtney, T. E. 17185
Courtney, W. S. 17186
Courtois, -------. 27511 see also France. Corps Legislatif. Counseil des Anciens. Commission.
Courtois, Ferdinand. see Cortes, Hernando, 1485-1547.
Courtonne, Jean Palmyer de. see Paulmier, Jean, d. ca. 1669.
Courtot, Francois. 17187-17188
Courts of Jamaica. 35575
Courtship and marriage. 31436
Courtship of George Howard, Esq. 41018, 64545
Courtship of Miles Standish. 41922
Courtship of Miles Standish, and other poems. 41908
Courtship of Ralph Doughby, Esq. 41018, 64545
Courtship, with a collection of approved songs. 91499
Cousas de C. da Gama nos reynos do Preste Joao. (14363)
Cousen, J. engr. 3784, 3787, 8899, note after 104504, 104505
Cousin, Victor. 94510
Cousin d'Aval, Charles Yvres, called Cousin d'Avalon. (17189), (42351)
Cousin d'Aval, Charles Yvres, called Cousin d'Avalon. supposed author 99513
Cousin d'Avalon, Charles Yvres. see Cousin d'Aval, Charles Yvres, called Cousin d'Avalon.
Cousin d'Amerique. (6936)
Cousin Franck's household. 59441, (63501)
Cousin George. pseud. Sketches of Niagara Falls and River. 81565
Cousin John. pseud. Drummer boy. (20972)
Coussin, J. H. J. (17190)
Coust, ------. 91842
Coustelin, -------. 17191-17193
Coutard, ------. 75187
Coute, Jose Ferrer de. see Ferrer de Couto, Jose.
Couthouy, Joseph P. 17195-17196
Coutinho, Francisco de Sousa. see Sousa Coutinho, Francisco de, 1597?-1660.
Coutinho, Francisco Inocencio de Souza. see Souza Coutinho, Francisco Inocencio de.
Coutinho, Gonzalo. see Vas Coutino, Goncalo.
Coutinho, J. M. Silva. see Silva Coutinho, J. M.
Coutinho, Joaquim Forjaz Pereira. (17199)-(17200)
Coutinho, Jose Joaquim da Cuna de Azeredo. see Cuna de Azeredo Coutinho, Jose Joaquim da.
Coutino, Goncalo Vas. see Vas Coutino, Goncalo.
Couto, Antonio Gorrea do. 17202
Couto, Bernardo, d. 1862. 17203-(17204)
Couto, Diogo de. see Couto, Diego do.

Couto, Diego do. 3646, (3648)
Couto, J. Vieira. 17205
Couto, Jose Bernardo. (11019)
Couto, Jose Ferrer de. see Ferrer de
  Couto, Jose.
Coutto Ferraz, Luiz Pedreira do. see
  Ferraz, Luiz Pedreira do Coutto.
Coutts, W. G. 17206
Couture, Louis. 17207
Couvray, Jean Baptiste Louvet de. see
  Louvet de Couvray, Jean Baptiste.
Covarrubias, Alvaro. 76857
Covarrubias, Alvaro Diaz. 17208-17209
Covarrubias, J. Diaz. see Diaz Covar-
  rubias, J.
Covarruvias, Pedro Lopez de. (48613), 98019
  see also Universidad de Mercaderes de
  Mexico. Consules.
Cove lands. 66257
Covell, Lemuel. 17210
Covenant and membership. 90651
Covenant and official magazine. 56689
Covenant, articles of faith, and rules. 65381
Covenant, doctrinal articles and articles of
  discipline. 25409
Covenant, etc. [of the Bowdoin Square Church,
  Boston.] 18137
Covenant-interest. 40784
Covenant-keeping the way to blessedness.
  104076
Covenant Lodge of the United Ancient Order
  of Druids. see United Ancient Order
  of Druids. Pennsylvania. Covenant
  Lodge.
Covenant [of the Boston First Free Congre-
  gational Church.] 6644
Covenant of Gods free grace. 17058, 17059,
  17085-(17086)
Covenant of grace, discovered in the great
  work. 17059
Covenant of grace not absolute but conditional.
  17211
Covenant of grace opened. 32833
Covenant of nature made with Adam described.
  (66867)
Covenant, of Park-Street Church, Boston.
  6668
Covenant [of the Canadian Anti-slavery Baptist
  Association.] 10404
Covenant, of the Evangelical Congregational
  Church. 10131
Covenant, of the First Church, Charlestown.
  12098
Covenant of the First Church, Groton, Mass.
  28967
Covenant of the First Church of Christ in
  Sutton. 93983
Covenant of the Maverick Church. 6657
Covenant of the New Congregational Church in
  Boston. 6658
Covenant of the Old South Church, Boston.
  15453
Covenant of the Pine-Street Church. (6670)
Covenant, of the South Church in Andover.
  15451
Covenant of the Third Church of Christ in
  Salem. 75755
Covenanter, devoted to the principles of the
  Reformed Presbyterian Church. 17212
Covenanter vindicated from periurie. 91381
Covenants and commandments. 83152, 83163
Covenants and sketch of the history. 105525
Covenants involving moral wrong are not
  obligatory. 59765
Coventry, Alexander. 17213

Coventry, Charles Brodhead, 1801-1875.
  (3909), 17214
Coventry, Conn. First Society. 17-18, 3d
  note after 96123
Coventry, R. I. Baptist Yearly Meeting of the
  Ancient Order of Six Principles of the
  Doctrine of Christ, 1812. see Baptist
  Yearly Meeting of the Ancient Order of
  Six Principles of the Doctrine of Christ,
  Coventry, R. I., 1812.
Coventry Baptist Church, Crompton, R. I. see
  Crompton, R. I. Warwick and Coventry
  Baptist Church.
Coverley, Sir Roger de. pseud. Americans
  roused. see Sewall, Jonathan, 1728-
  1796.
Coverley, Sir Roger de. pseud. Cure for the
  spleen. see Sewall, Jonathan, 1728-
  1796.
Coverly, Nathaniel. ed. 100595
Covill, ------. 14902
Covington, Ga. Southern Masonic Female
  College. see Southern Masonic Female
  College, Covington, Ga.
Covington, Ky. Western Baptist Theological
  Institute. see Western Baptist Theo-
  logical Institute, Covington, Ky.
Covington and Cincinnati Bridge Company.
  defendants (56999)
Covington and Newport directory for 1866-7.
  (17215)
Covlon, ------. ed. 39591
Covode, John, 1808-1871. (17217)-17219, 35849,
  73984
Covode committee. 73984
Covos, Jose Maria. 17220
Cowe chace, a poem in three cantos. 1452
Cow chace: an heroic poem. 1450
Cow chace. In three cantos. 1451
Cow chace, in three cantos, published on
  occasion of the rebel general Wayne's
  attack. 1449
Cow-chase. 21296-21297
Cow pox act. 17251, 45701, 49106
Cowan, Edgar, 1815-1885. 17221, 60376,
  89214, 92011
Cowan, F. W. tr. 23521
Cowan, William. petitioner 100571, 2d note
  after 106003 see also Virginia Yazoo
  Company. Agent. petitioner
Coward. (50628)
Coward's convention. 8041
Coward's curse and patriot's duty. 29323
Cowdell, Thomas. 17222
Cowdell, Thomas D. 17223-17224, 63636
Cowden, J. 17225
Cowden-Clarke, Mary. see Clarke, Mary
  Cowden-, 1809-1898.
Cowdery, Jonathan, 1767-1852. 17226
Cowdery, Oliver. 83038-83039, 83095, 83099,
  83104, 83109, 83129, 83147, 83152
Cowdrey, Peter A. 98616
Cowdrey, Samuel. (17232)
Cowdin, Elliot C., 1819-1880. 17227-17229,
  53595, 2d note after 96963
Cowdin, Mrs. N. G. 17230
Cowdin, Robert. 17231
Cowdry, N. A. 15779
Cowell, Benjamin, 1781-1860. 17233-17235,
  66239
Cowell, Joe. 17236
Cowell, John. 17237-17238, 2d note after
  97081
Cowell, John Welsford. 17239-17240
Cowen, Esek, 1834-1900. 17241, 43529

Cowen, M. V. B. 17242
Cowie, ------. 16001, (17243), 17527, 27567,
    2d note after 102825
Cowles, A. ed. 57190
Cowles, Edwin. 17244
Cowles, Henry. 17245
Cowles, Sylvester. 17246
Cowles. firm see Smead and Cowles. firm
    publisher
Cowley, Captain ------. fl. 1683. 29473,
    31389, (54897)
Cowley, Rev. Dr. see Cooley, Timothy
    Mather, 1772-1859.
Cowley, Charles. 17247-17249
Cowley, R. A. ed. 98165
Cowperthwait, Joseph. 17250, 64187
Cowpland, Jonathan. 90351, 90353
Cox, ------. 40801
Cox, Abraham L. 17252
Cox, Christopher C. 17253, 52008
Cox, Edward Travers, 1821-1907. 17254,
    34253, 34488, 34527, 58014
Cox, Francis Augustus. 17255-(17256)
Cox, Gershom F. 17257
Cox, I. J. ed. 94794
Cox, James. 95993
Cox, Jacob Dolson, 1828-1900. 17259, 20098,
    56936 see also Ohio. Governor, 1866-
    1868 (Cox)
Cox, James E. 17260
Cox, John. 17261
Cox, John Henry. RN (17258), 50985-50986
Cox, John R. 17262
Cox, Leander Martin, 1812-1865. 17263
Cox, Melville B. (17264)
Cox, Paul. 52584
Cox, Richard. 17266
Cox, Sir Richard, Bart. (17265)
Cox, Ross. 17267
Cox, S. A. 78675
Cox, Samuel Hanson, 1793-1881. (17268)-17270,
    (19087), 30843, (35865), 37976, 38861,
    (40147), 49478, 68660, 89783, note after
    95459
Cox, Samuel Hanson, 1793-1881. supposed
    author 17270, 90007, note before 96989
Cox, Samuel Sullivan, 1824-1889. (17271),
    89840
Cox, Sanford C. 17272
Cox, Sun Set. sobriquet see Cox, Samuel
    Sullivan, 1824-1889.
Cox, W. 17273, 23946
Cox, Walter S. 17274
Cox, William. 17309-17312
Cox, William E. 17275
Cox, Zachariah. 94794, 94806
Cox on Quakerism. 40801
Coxe, Miss ------. see Coxe, Margaret.
Cox, Arthur Cleveland, Bp., 1818-1896. 17276-
    17277, (77160), 75294
Coxe, Brinton. ed. 67997
Coxe, Daniel, 1673-1739. (17278)-17281, 25853,
    63705
Coxe, Daniel W. 27509
Coxe, John R. defendant at court martial
    17286
Coxe, John Redman, 1773-1864. 17282-17285
Coxe, Margaret. 17287
Coxe, Richard Smith, 1792-1865. 17288-17292,
    102122-102123
Coxe, Tench, 1775-1824. 17293-17308, (22964),
    23356, 32635, 35933, 56504, 60391,
    63266, 95667-95668, 1st note after 92859,
    95727, 104632
Coxe, Tench, 1775-1824. defendant 17303,
    18313, 60471, note after 96854

Coxe, Tench, 1775-1824. supposed author
    (17297), 43708
Coxe, William. of Philadelphia (17313)
Coxe, William, 1747-1828. (59572), 62957
Coxer, A. C. 9243
Coyer, Gabriel Francis. (17314)-17318
Coyett, Baltazar. 69600
Coyler, Vincent. 7892, 14918
Coyner, David H. 17319
Coyotes de Espana vendran. 99700
Coyuntura todas las fiestas. 57734
Cozier, Ezra S. 98225
Cozine, John. 17320, 30566, (34385), note
    after 53697, (68287), note after 83791
Cozzens, Frederick Swartwout, 1813-1869.
    11690, 17321-17325, 54159, 89026
Cozzens, Issachar. 17326
Cozzens, Samuel W. 17327-17328
Cozzens' wine press. 17325
Crabstick, Deborah. pseud. Auto-biography of
    Sam Simple. see Wilburn, George T.
    supposed author
Cracchus, Caius. pseud. Controversy between
    Caius Cracchus and Opimius. (16191)
Crack in the wall. 57878
Cracked jug. 17329, 52278, 104311
Cracraft, J. W. (17330)
Craddock, Matthew, d. 1641. 106052
Cradlebaugh, John, 1819-1872. 17331
Cradock, Francis. (17332)
Cradock, Thomas, 1718-1770. 17333, 53419
Craesbeecke, Paulus van. 44268
Crafford, John. 17334
Crafton, William Bell. (17335), 80691-80692,
    1st note after 102813
Crafts, F. A. 17336
Crafts, Frederick. 94419
Crafts, George R. ed. (50679)
Crafts, Samuel C. 17337
Crafts, Thomas. (17338)
Crafts, William, 1787-1826. 17339-17346,
    78741, 92878, note after 93564
Crafts, William Augustus. 17347-(17349),
    25078, 73644
Craftsman. 18510, 19251, 32280, 86757, 96427,
    101167
Craftsman; a sermon. 9237
Craftsman extraordinary. 17351
Craftsman's observations on the peace. 101167
Craftsmen. (17350), 84576
Cragg, Saunders. 17352
Craggs, James, 1657-1721. 65865, 88192
Craggs, James, 1657-1721. defendant 65862,
    88190
Craggs, Salisbury. pseud. Landscape. 17353
Cragin, Aaron Harrison, 1820-1898. 17354-
    17355
Cragin, Charles H. (17356)
Cragin, G. ed. 89522
Craig, ------. 17855
Craig, Austin. 17357-(17358)
Craig, Campbell, Lessee of James Annesley,
    Esq., plaintiff 1602
Craig, H. K. USA 17359, 90869, 90874
Craig, Ira. 17360
Craig, J. N. 17361
Craig, Neville B., 1787-1863. 17362-17367,
    47512, 78471, 84618, 84647, 91869,
    101710
Craig, R. H. 17368
Craig, W. B. (17372)-17373
Craig, Wheelock. 17369-17371
Craik, George Lilly. 17374
Craik, Mrs. D. M. Mulock. 85202
Craik, James. 17375-17376, 105116
Cralle, Richard K. ed. 9932, 9936

Cram, Marshal. 17377
Cram, T. J. 17378-17380
Cramer, Carl. (31229)
Cramer, Charles. 17381
Cramer, K. F. tr. 12246
Cramer, P. (17382)-17383
Cramer, Zadok. 17384-17386, (17904), 27389
Cramer. firm publishers 63114
Cramer's Pittsburgh almanack for 1809. 63114
Cramoisy series of Jesuit relations. 5354-
    (5357), 10572, 11597, (12297)-12298,
    18245-18246, (20927), 20929, 28359,
    (28360)-28361, (36143), (36688), 48944,
    58166, 68436, 68828, 69274, note after
    69259, 69303, 74898, 2d note after
    93480
Cramp, John Mocket. (17387)-17388
Crampton, S. W. 45357, 75214
Cranberry, N. J. Washington Benevolent
    Society. see Washington Benevolent
    Society. New Jersey. Cranberry.
Cranberry Indians. Treaties, etc. 53242
Cranch, Christopher Pearse, 1813-1892.
    17389, 102993
Cranch, John. appellant (11193)
Cranch, William, 1759-1855. (17390), 20300,
    (33241), 59041
Cranch, William, 1769-1855. supposed author
    (40117), 97440
Crandall, Prudence. see Philleo, Prudence
    (Crandall) 1803-1890.
Crandall, Reuben, 1805?-1838. defendant
    17393, 96855
Crandall, William Lusk. 17394
Crane, -------, M. D. 12041
Crane, A. Judson. 17395
Crane, C. B. 17396
Crane, Edward. 17397-17398, (73431)
Crane, Isaac Watts. (17400)
Crane, J. C. 97504
Crane, J. T. 17404
Crane, James M. 17399
Crane, John, 1756-1836. 17401-17403, 24429
Crane, Jonathan. (17405)
Crane, S. A. (17406), 65828
Crane, Verner W. 83976, 83978
Crane, William, M. D. 17407
Crane, William, 1790-1866. 81857
Cranebrook, -------. 17408
Cranford, James. 33630, 58770, 91382, 91384
Crania Aegyptiaca. 51022
Crania Americana. 51022
Cranston, Robert B. defendant at court
    martial 17409
Cranston, Samuel, 1659-1727. 99808 see
    also Rhode Island (Colony) Governor,
    1698-1727 (Cranston)
Crantz, David. 17410-17420
Cranz, David. see Crantz, David.
Crapo, Henry H. (17421), (52491)
Crapo, William W. 89672
Crary, Archibald C. 17422
Crary, Isaac Edwin, 1804-1854. 16985, 17424
Crary, John. 91610
Crash, Bank. pseud. Present crisis. see
    Dutton, George.
Crashaw, William, 1572-1626. 17425, note
    after 99858, 2d note after 100502, 103313
Crashaw's sermon. 17425, note after 99858,
    2d note after 100502
Crashavve, W. see Crashaw, William, 1572-
    1626.
Crassus, Lucius. pseud. Examination of Mr.
    Jefferson's message to Congress. see
    Hamilton, Alexander, 1755-1804.

Crassus, Lucius. pseud. Examination of the
    President's message. see Hamilton,
    Alexander, 1755-1804.
Crater. 16474
Crater, or Vulcan's peak. 16426
Cratere, ou le Robinson Americain. 16428
Cratere, ou Marc dans son ile. 15427
Crato, Brazil. Gram Priorado. Presbitero
    Secular. see Presbitero do Gram
    Priorado do Crato. pseud.
Crauliz, Agostino di. see Cravaliz, Agostino
    di.
Cravaliz, Agostino di. tr. 13047, 13050,
    13053-13054, 27734-27736, 27738-27741,
    (27743)-27744
Cravath, J. M. 17427
Craven, Alfred Wingate, 1810-1879. 17428,
    17430
Craven, John J. 17429
Craven, T. T. defendant at court martial
    17430
Cravens, James Addison, 1818-1893. 17431
Crawford, Charles, b. 1752. 8036, 17432-
    17434
Crawford, Elijah. 17435
Crawford, G. W. 17436, note before 90804
    see also Committee on Railroads in
    Austin and Washington Counties, Texas.
Crawford, George Washington, 1798-1872.
    (27061)
Crawford, Ia. 17046
Crawford, J. Agnew. 17438
Crawford, J. Marshall. 17440
Crawford, John. 17437
Crawford, Joseph. 17439
Crawford, Lucy. 17441
Crawford, Martin Jenkins, 1820-1883. 17442
Crawford, Thomas H. 27003
Crawford, W. N. 17449
Crawford, William. 17443
Crawford, William Harris, 1772-1834. 16117,
    17444, 17446, 17448, (44475), note after
    92827
Crawfordsville, Ind. Wabash College. see
    Wabash College, Crawfordsville, Ind.
Crayon, Geoffrey. pseud. see Irving, Wash-
    ington, 1783-1859.
Crayon, Porte. pseud. Adventures of Porte
    Crayon. see Strother, David Hunter,
    1816-1888.
Crayon, Porte. pseud. Virginia illustrated.
    see Strother, David Hunter, 1816-1888.
Crayon. 105847
Crayon miscellany. 35140
Crayon miscellany. . . . no. I. 35139, note
    before 96334
Crayon reading book. 35145
Crayon Rigmarole, Esq. pseud. see Rig-
    marole, Crayon, Esq. pseud.
Crayon sketches. 17273, 23946
Crayon sketches and off-hand takings. (9162)
Crayon sketches of the noticable men of our
    age. (9162)
Crazy trapper. 13698
Creance Americaine. 17503
Creance Jecker. 37605
Creanciers Anglois des Colons de Tobago.
    petitioners 73468-73469, 96047, 96048,
    96078-96080 see also Francklyn,
    Gilbert. petitioner and Tod, William.
    petitioner
Creanciers Anglois des Habitans de la meme
    Isle. see Creanciers Anglois des
    Colons de Tobago.

Creanciers Anglois des Habitans de l'Isle de Tobago. see Creanciers Anglois des Colons de Tobago.
Creanciers des Mr. Lioncey Freres. Syndic. see Syndic des Creanciers des Mr. Lioncey Freres.
Creasy, F. S. 17451
Creation d'un legion pour l'ile St.-Domingue. 75093
Creation et des mysteres devoiles. 85453
Credentials van de Koningin Regente van Portugael. 17452
Credentials of T. M. Jacks and J. M. Johnson. 1994
Credentials of the members of the Convention. 87445
Credentials which he [i. e. Joshua Bradley] exhibited at North-Haven. 96834
Credibility of the Christian doctrine. 14472
Credit mobilier robbery. 89250
Credit of the government made immediately available. 89040
Credit system and the no credit system. 17528
Credit system in France. 10842
Credito mutuo. 64015
Credito publico. (50484)
Creditors of the Island of Tobago. see Creanciers Anglois des Colons de Tobago.
Creditors of the Royal African Company. see Royal African Company. Creditors.
Credo de l'eglise de Jesus-Christ. 5027
Cree, John. 40573
Creecy, James R. (17457)
Creed and covenant of Dartmouth Church. 18612
Creed as related to the life. 82340
Creed of the Liberty Party abolitionists. 91627
Creeds of Christendom. 77494
Creeds without charity. (14911)
Creek first reader. (51587), 72019-72020
Creek Indian. pseud. Speech. 17463, 84624, 84671, 84673
Creek Indians. 27015, 76490
Creek Indians. petitioners 47670, 47675, 51583
Creek Indians. plaintiffs 51583
Creek Indians. Constitution. 61063
Creek Indians. Delegates. 73410
Creek Indians. Laws, statutes, etc. 61063
Creek Indians. Treaties, etc. 33854, 96603, 96609, 96617, 96623, 96636, 96654, 96671, 96686, 96697, 96732
Creek Indians. Message . . . upon the . . . claims. 34641
Creek second reader. 72018
Creeks. Correspondence. 76490
Creery, William R. 17464
Creigh, Alfred. 17465-17466
Creigh, J. J. 17467
Creighton, John Orde. 17468
Creighton, William. 17469, note after 89333
Creisier, Antoine Marie. 11702, 55423, 55517
Crell, J. tr. 25522
Cremony, John C. 17470
Crenne, Jean Rene Antoine, Marquis de Verdun de la. see Verdun de la Crenne, Jean Rene Antoine, Marquis de.
Creola. 62826
Creole (Ship) 17472
Creole blanc et proprietaire de St. Domingue. pseud. Lettre du Cap. (40677)
Creole bride. 75250
Creole case and Mr. Webster's despatch. 17471, 35856

Creole de la Louisiane. pseud. Lettre a Napoleon III. see Musson, Eugene.
Creole; or, siege of New Orleans. (13845)
Creole orphans. 59414
Creole sisters. (64195)
Creoleana. 57504
Creolinden, et billede of livet i Vestindien. 6891
Crequy, ------ de. see De Crequy, -------.
Cresap and Logan. 85141
Cresap, etc. 35908
Crescent almanac. (17473)
Crescent and the cross. 101275
Crescent city directory, 1870. 53352
Crescent city directory for 1867. 53351
Crescent-shine. 27287
Cresey, Noah. 17474
Cresp, Antoine. 17475
Crespel, Emmanuel. (17476)-(17479), 80018
Crespel, Louis. (17476)-17477
Crespigny, Mrs. --------. 64088
Crespin, ------. 45015
Crespo, Benito, Bp. 98359 see also Durango (Diocese) Bishop (Crespo)
Crespo, Jose Maria Blanco y. see White, Joseph Blanco.
Crespo, Joseph Rafel. (17480)
Cressap, Thomas. defendant (59685)
Cresse, Auguste Jean Baptiste Bouvet de. see Bouvet de Cresse, Auguste Auguste Jean Baptiste.
Cresset, Edward, Bp. of Landaff, d. 1755. 17482
Cressey, E. H. 17483
Cresson, -------, fl. 1855. 7052
Cresson, Joshua. 17484
Cresswell, J. A. J. see Creswell, John Andrew Jackson, 1828-1891.
Cresswell, Samuel Gurney. 17490, (43073)
Cresswell unmasked. 17489
Cressy, B. C. (17485)
Cressy, Noah. 17486
Creswell, John Andrew Jackson, 1828-1891. (17487)-17488, 18830
Cretaceous and jurassic. 47369
Cretaceous reptiles of the United States. (39904), 85072
Cretan refugees and their American helpers. 33329
Cretineau-Joly, ------. 17491
Crevxio, Francisco. (21072)
Creuxius, P. see Du Creux, P.
Creuzbaur, R. 17492
Creuze, Michel Pascal. (17493), 58983, 75182
Creuze-Paschal, ------. see Creuze, Michel Pascal.
Crevecoeur, J. Hector St. John, 1735-1813. 2527, 17494-(17502), 24338, 69136, 1st note after 69470, 82979, 98479, 1st note after 100807
Crevecoeur, J. Hector St. John, 1735-1813. supposed author 68739
Crevecoeur, Michel Guillaume Jean de. see Crevecoeur, J. Hector St. John, 1735-1813.
Crevel, ------. 17503
Crew, John L. defendant 53931
Crew, Lemuel. 100524
Crewdson, Isaac. 17504
Crewe, C. supposed author (55298)
Cri de douleur des colons. 87126
Cri de la conscience. 98667
Cri de l'indignation d'un bon citoyen. 69716
Cri des Africains. 13477

Cri des Africains, countre les Europeens.
13475
Cri des colons. 97507
Cri des negres. 21575
Cri d'un colon de Saint-Domingue. 17505
Cricq, Laurent Saint. see Saint-Cricq,
Laurent.
Cricq, Lorenzo de Saint. see Saint-Cricq,
Laurent.
Cridge, Alfred. 17506
Crie de colons. 17507, 97507
Crie de la patrie. 98668
Cries of Africa. 13476
Cries of New-York. 105063
Cries of Philadelphia. 105063
Crignon, Pierre. 58825
Crime, Admonish. pseud. Midsummer's
day-dream. see Richmond, James Cook.
Crime against Kansas. 79130-79131, (81837),
note after 92624, 93647-93648
Crime against the presidency. 5687
Crime and punishment. (25186)
Crime & the doom of the thief declared.
46330
Crime of abolitionists. 82607
Crimean war. 85153
Crimen y expiacion. 67123
Crimenes de la demagogia. 17508
Crimes committed by our government against
the maroons. 27327
Crimes of Washington city. (51657)
Criminal history of the English government.
(68923)
Criminal jurisprudence considered. 75941
Criminal laws that were in force in the prov-
ince of Quebec. 67061
Criminal Procesz wider die Jesuiten in
Spanien. (22821)
Criminal recorder. 103185, 103188
Criminal; the crime; the penalty. 31443
Criminal trials. 67590
Criminal trials supplying copious illustrations.
35784
Criminating complaint, &c. &c. 59147
Crimp, George. defendant 103334
Crippen, William G. 17509
"Cripples Fayette," of Rockingham. 35976
Cripps, John. 8952, 17510, 56650
Crise Americaine. (58210)
Crise Americaine. Recueil de documents.
64717
Crise Americaine, ses causes, ses resultats
probables. (30862)
Crise de l'Amerique. 44236
Crise de l'Europe. 81395
"Crise" Metcalfe and the Fontaine-Baldwin
cabinet defended. 17511, (73346)
Crises commerciales et de leur retour period-
ique. 36871
Crisfield, John Woodland, 1806-1897. 17512-
17513
Crisis. 17519-17520, 34186, 78381
Crisis: a solemn appeal to the President.
10862
Crisis, a work written while with the army.
58218
Crisis Americana. 40733
Crisis: an appeal to a candid world. 14897,
37651
Crisis! An appeal to our countrymen. 17522
Crisis: an appeal to the candid world. 14897,
37651
Crisis. An appeal to the good sense of the
nation. 10861
Crisis. An economic view of the present
contest. 5984, 80445

Crisis, and its claims: a sermon. 32612
Crisis, and its claims upon the church of God.
73046
Crisis and its demands. (78337)
Crisis and its lessons. (23810)
Crisis and our duty. (80144)
Crisis, and the remedy. (66536)
Crisis and the triumph. 4618
Crisis, and what it demands! 63847
Crisis before us, for reading and reflecting
men. 55572
Crisis before us. From the N. Y. herald.
(55574)
Crisis: being an enquiry into the course to be
pursued. 17523
Crisis being deemed by the Parliament of
England a libel. 95996
Crisis. By the author of Plain facts. 17521
Crisis chapter on government. 5817
"Crisis." Closing scenes of the year 1860.
(17524)
Crisis de los Compania de Jesus. 47817
Crisis del ensayo a la historia de la Florida.
75577
Crisis exacta entre los dos manifestos. 71623
Crisis extraordinary. 58219
Crisis facil, y evidente del ensayo chronologica.
75577
Crisis; in answer to The false alarm. 17515
Crisis in Canada. 43350
Crisis in the affairs of the Domestic and
Foreign Missionary Society. 17525
Crisis: its rationale. 81497
"Crisis." Its solution—the causes—their re-
moval. 21719
Crisis met in reply to the Crisis of the coun-
try. 14768, 17526
Crisis. No. I. 17518
Crisis no. I; or thoughts on slavery. 17537,
(31888), 81944
Crisis. Number I. To the people of England
and America. 17514
Crisis, nos. 1-3. (31888), 63502, 100509
Crisis, no. 2. 17537, 31888, 81944
Crisis of affairs. 16001, 17527, 2d note after
102825
Crisis of emancipation in America. 78848
Crisis of freedom. A sermon . . . at . . .
Lynn. 36313
Crisis of freedom. Remarks on the duty.
44486
Crisis of Sir Robert Peel's mission. (8853)
Crisis of the colonies considered. 104246
Crisis of the country. 14768, 17526, 17528
Crisis of the country; the duty of Republicans.
(43387)
Crisis of the dispute with the United States.
(17529), 101267
Crisis of the sugar colonies. 17530, 1st note
after 91235, 2d note after 102829
Crisis of Unitarianism in Boston. 76983
Crisis: on the origin and consequences of our
political dissensions. (17531), 2d note
after 99216
Crisis; on the present state of affairs. 17532
Crisis; or, a defence of administration. 17533
Crisis: or, a discourse representing the most
authentick records. 91151
Crisis or a full defence of the colonies. 16600
Crisis, or a statement of facts. 86870
Crisis: or, essays on the usurpations of the
federal government. 8776, 17534, note
after 97466
Crisis: or immediate concernments of the
British empire. 17535

Crisis, or last trumpet. 66774
Crisis: or nullification unmasked. (17536),
59642
Crisis; or, the enemies of America unmasked.
(39261)
Crisis; or the uncertain doom of kingdoms.
18757
Crisis: relating to the celebrated Massachu-
setts excise bill. 17538
Crisis. Scire volunt, secreta domus atque
inde timeri. (16599)
Crisis. Slavery or freedom. 18202
Crisis . . . the remedy! 45145
Crisis. Think twice ere you speak once.
60030, 60458, 69704
Crisis. To be continued weekly. 17516,
95343
Crisis. To the people of Connecticut. 17539
Crisis. Vol. I. 17517
Crisis—what is resistance? 35418
Crisostomo, M. de S. 17540
Crisp, -------, fl. 1711. 83978, 86573-86574
Crisp, Stephen, 1629-1692. (17541), 53093,
59660, 66926, 79296, 80627-(80631),
99284, 104184
Crisp, Thomas. 17542
Crisp, Tobias. 74459
Crispin, William. 62273 see also Philadel-
phia County, Pa. Collector of Excise.
Crissy, -----. 54459
Cristianesimo e patriottismo estratta dalla
riforma del secolo XIX. 58762
Cristianismo felice. 11554, 18335
Cristianismo y la libertad. 67656
Cristobal Colomb. 17543
Cristobal Colon; et descubrimiento de America.
14653
Cristobal Colon, historia popular. 57579
Cristofero Colombo oder die Entdeckung der
neuen Welt. (73877)
Cristoforo Colombo; tragedia. 7788
Cristoforo Columbo. Documenti & prove della
sua appartebebza a Genoa. 89648
Cristoval, ------, Marques de San. see San
Cristoval, ------, Marques de.
Criswell, Robert. 17544-17545, note after
92624
Criterion: containing portraits of the three
candidates. 17546
Criterion. Literary and critical journal. 17547
Criterion: or, disquisitions on the present
administration. 104303
Critic. A weekly review of literature. 17548
Critic criticised. 76952
Critic criticised, and Worcester vindicated.
17549
Critic of the mustard pot. pseud. see Fidler,
Isaac.
Critica. 93345
Critica que contra dicho metodo. 98311
Critical analysis of a pamphlet entitled "A
review of Mr. Seward's diplomacy."
37771, 2d note after 94129
Critical and candid examination of a late pub-
lication. 92955
Critical and documentary review of two recent
English books. 99363
Critical and faithful extracts from Colonel
Cavallier's memoirs. 95037
Critical and miscellaneous essays. By Thomas
Carlyle. 10932
Critical and miscellaneous essays. To which
are added a few poems. 23228
Critical and miscellaneous writings of Theo-
dore Parker. 58742

Critical chronicle of Ichabod Oculus. 56684
Critical commentary on Archbishop Secker's
letter. 5689, 11878, 17550
Critical dictionary of the English language.
(914)
Critical dictionary of English literature and
British and American authors. 18320
Critical dissertations on the land. 13519
Critical dissertations upon the eloquence of
the ancients. 8418
Critical essay concerning marriage. 17551,
75821
Critical essay on his [i. e. Daniel Webster's]
genius and writings. 68636, note after
102311-102312
Critical essay on the works of Mrs. S. Rowson.
13886
Critical essay: prepared for the Association
of Architects. 48979
Critical examination of our financial policy.
(54936)
Critical examination of the Marquis de
Chatellux's Travels in North America.
8017
Critical examination of the poem entitled "The
vision of Ruberta." 57755
Critical examination of the twelve resolutions
of Mr. Joseph Hume. 58159
Critical history of English sea-affairs. 14414
Critical investigation and research into the
history of the Americans. 71446
Critical journal. see Edinburgh review. and
New York review.
Critical journal of politicks and literature.
57468
Critical miscellany. 95286
Critical moment on which the salvation or
destruction of the British empire depends.
35776
Critical observations on the poem of Mr. Joel
Barlow. (28735)
Critical observations thereon. 106326
Critical review. 41478
Critical review of Noah Webster's spelling-
book. 102337
Critical review of the late speech of Charles
O'Conor. 84084
Critical review of the orthography of Dr.
Webster's series of books. 102401
Critical study. 83467
Critical view of the pamphlet. 46855
Criticism criticised. 17552
Criticism of Mr. Wm. B. Reed's aspersions.
36242
Criticism of the Congregationalist. (55072)
Criticism on Inchiquin's letters. 59215
Criticism on the declaration of independence.
49929, 78977
Criticism on Weem's Life of Washington.
102486
Criticism upon the political account of Trinidad.
(19149), note after 96978
Criticism upon the (so-called) revelation of
July 12th, 1843. 83284
Criticisms, anecdotes, and personal descrip-
tions. 74380
Criticisms of the campaign in the Mountain
Department. (62870)
Criticisms on the declaration of independence.
49929, 78977
Criticorum sacrorum tomus secundus. 3597
Critique. 90888
Critique, by R. Cumberland. 88543
Critique of the Supreme Court of the United
States. 23453, 2d note after 100462

Critique of the Vision of Ruberta. 2466, 57755
Critique on Scott and Gliddon's ethnological
    works. 14325
Critiques & etudes litteraires. (69592)
Critisk undersogelse. 40990
Crito. pseud. Letters to the electors. 17554
Crito's letters to the electors of the United
    States. 17554
Crittenden, John Jordan, 1787-1863. 17555-
    (17556), (70981)
Crittenden, Robert. 96634 see also U. S.
    Commissioner to the Quapaw Indians.
Crittenden, Thomas Leonidas, 1819-1893.
    56422
Crittenden compromise. (78703)
Crittendon, ------. see Crittenden, Thomas
    Leonidas, 1819-1893.
Crivelli, Tomas Moran y. see Moran y
    Crivelli, Tomas.
Croaker. pseud. Poems by Croaker, Croaker
    & Co., & Croaker, Jr. see Drake,
    Joseph Rodman. and Halleck, Fitz-
    Greene, 1790-1867.
Croakers. 20862
Crockat, or Crockatt, James. supposed
    author 17593, 26256, (56466), 87849,
    87904
Crockatt, James. see Crockat, or Crockatt,
    James.
Crocker, A. B. 17557
Crocker, G. G. (17563)
Crocker, H. 38979
Crocker, Hanna Mather. (17558)
Crocker, Samuel L. 17560
Crocker, Uriel H. 17561-(17563)
Crocker, Zebulon. (17564)
Crocker (H. S.) & Co. firm publishers
    17559
Crockett, David, 1786-1836. 17565, 17567,
    17570-17571, (17580), 83668, 84142
Crockett, David, 1786-1836. incorrectly sup-
    posed author 17566, 83778
Crockett, G. F. H. 17577
Crockett, H. C. 17578
Crockett, J. B. 76049
Crockett, Simeon L., d. 1838. defendant
    (17579), note after 100660
Crockett almanack. (17576)
Crockett almanac. Edited by Ben Harding.
    (17576)
Crockitt, ------. see Crockett, David, 1786-
    1836.
Crocus. pseud. History of Pithole. see
    Leonard, Charles C.
Croes, John. 17581, 101749
Croes, Robert B. 17582
Croese, Gerard. 9072, 17583-17584
Croese's mistake concerning W. Penn, etc.
    9072
Croffut, William Augustus, 1835-1915. 17585,
    20902
Croftes, ------. 9500, 20828, 20837, 20840-
    20843, note after 93587, 93588
Crofton, Walter Cavendish. 17586, (17588)
Crofts, James. see Monmouth and Buccleuch,
    James Crofts, Duke of, 1649-1685.
Crofutt, G. A. 17587, 28468-28469
Croghan, George. 17589, (74155) see also
    Great Britain. Deputy Agent for Indian
    Affairs.
Croghan, John. 17590
Croil, James. 17591
Croisieres de l'Alabama et du Sumter. 79078
Croix, ----- de la. see De la Croix, ------.
Croix, A. Pherotee de la. see La Croix, A.
    Pherotee de.

Croix, Carlos Francisco de. 17592, (48663)
Croix, F. D. de la. see De la Croix, F. D.
Croix, Guillaume Emmanuel Joseph Guilhem
    de Clermont-Lodeve, Baron de Sainte.
    see Sainte-Croix, Guillaume Emmanuel
    Joseph Guilhem de Clermont Lodeve,
    Baron de.
Croix, Jacques Vincent de la. see Delacroix,
    Jacques Vincent, 1743-1832.
Croix, M. de la. 237
Croix, Pierre Augustin de Boissier de Sauvages
    de la. see Boissier de Sauvages de la
    Croix, Pierre Augustin de.
Croix de Chevrieres de Saint Vallier, Jean
    Baptiste de la. see Saint Vallier, Jean
    Baptiste de la Croix de Chevrieres
    de, Bp.
Croix dans les deux mondes. 63268
Crokatt, James. see Crockat, or Crockatt,
    James. supposed author
Croke, Sir Alexander. 17594, 69501, 90377
Croker, John Wilson, 1780-1857. 9416, 17595
Croly, David Goodman, 1829-1889. 17596-
    17597, 49433
Croly, George. 17598
Crombie, ------. reporter 96908
Crome, A. F. W. (17599)
Cromelien, Rowland. 17600
Cromelien, Rowland. supposed author 89114
Cromelien on the American rebellion. 17600
Crompton, Sarah. 17601
Crompton, R. I. Warwick and Coventry Baptist
    Church. 17602
Cromwall, Samuel, d. 1842. 86804
Cromwell, ----------. defendant at court
    martial 86804
Cromwell, Henry S. 17603
Cromwell, Oliver, 1599-1659. 78486, 95886
    see also Great Britain. Sovereigns, etc.,
    1649-1658 (Oliver Cromwell)
Cromwell, Ruth N. supposed author 5790,
    51748
Cromwell, Sidney. supposed author 17605,
    43877, note just before 63791
Cromwell. 93410
Cromwell and the protectorate. 92630
Cronica de Espana. 56618
Cronica de la Nueua Espana. 27728
Cronica de la Orden de N. P. S. Augustin.
    (28845)
Cronica de la Orden de N. S. Padre S. Fran-
    cisco. 39024
Cronica de la Orden de S. Augustin. (17606)
Cronica de la Provincia Peruvana del Orden
    de los Ermitanos de S. Agvstin. 96241
Cronica de la Religiosissima Provincia de Los
    Doze Apostoles del Perv. (16770), 75780
Cronica de la villa imperial de Potosi. 67123
Cronica de los Senores Reyes Catolicos Don
    Fernando y Dona Isabel. 66222
Cronica del gran regno del Perv. 13050,
    13053-13054
Cronica del grandissimo regno del Peru. 13047
Cronica del Peru. 13055
Cronica general de Espana. (50496), 56619
Cronica general de la Espana. 45520
Cronica general de las Indias. 94352
Cronica geral de M. A. Cocio Sabelico. 74667
Cronica Hispano-Americana. (38393)
Cronica Mexicana. 95146
Cronica Mexicana. Teoamextli. 9570, (48404)
Cronica. Periodico malicioso. 17607
Cronica serafica del Colegio de Prop. Fide de
    la S. Cruz. 2107
Cronica serafica y apostolica. 22896

Cronica sucinta de Yucatan. 60816
Cronicas de los reyes de Castilla D. Pedro. 41997
Cronise, Titus Fey. 17608
Cronista de Mexico. (48405), 71702
Cronyn, Benjamin, Bp. of Huron, 1802-1871. 5574, 34009, 38844
Crook, William. defendant (23479)
Crooke, William. see Crook, William.
Crooked disciple's remarks. (30398)
Crooked elm. (31738)
Crooker, Turner. petitioner 17609
Crookshanks, John. 17610-17611, 22796, 38152
Crookshanks, John. defendant at court martial 17612
Croom, H. B. 17613-(17614)
Croome, W. 17615
Croome, W. engr. and illus. 26048, 92881
Cropper, James, 1773-1840. 8117, 17616-17624, 24739, 27524, (43643), 70259, 89204, 93137-93138, 99774, 102841, 3d note after 102863
Cropper, James, 1773-1840. supposed author 82097
Crosat, ------. 68419
Crosby, --------, fl. 1865. 5678
Crosby, A. B. 17627
Crosby, Adelphus. 17625-17626
Crosby, Charles Cotesworth Pinckney. 17628, 97991
Crosby, Daniel. 17629
Crosby, Edward N. (17630)-17631
Crosby, Enoch. (3559)-3562
Crosby, Frank. 17632
Crosby, Frances Jane. 17633
Crosby, H. 72402
Crosby, Howard, 1826-1891. (17635)-17636, (44749)
Crosby, Jaazaniah. 17637-17640
Crosby, James L. reporter 17641, 41548
Crosby, Joseph. plaintiff 17642
Crosby, Josiah. 17643
Crosby, Nathan. 17644
Crosby, Platt H. tr. 59341
Crosby, Thomas, d. 1702. 17645
Crosby, U. H. 17646
Crosby Opera House Art Association. 17646
Crosby's Opera House and three hundred paintings. 17646
Crosfield, Joseph. 81872
Crosland, Mrs. Newton. 17647
Crosnier, L. 17648
Cross, --------, fl. 1755. (17666), 84589
Cross, ---------, fl. 1851. 17659
Cross, Major -------. 17660
Cross, Abijah. 17649
Cross, Alejandro. (17650)
Cross, Andrew Boyd, 1809 or 10-1889. 3001, 17651, 45385
Cross, Frederic. 84089
Cross, James Conquest. 17652-17654, 90779
Cross, Jane T. H. (17655)
Cross, Jonathan. (14757), 17656 see also American Tract Society, New York. Superintendent of Colportage.
Cross, Joseph. (17657)
Cross, Joseph Warren. 17658
Cross, Marcus E. 17661
Cross, Nathaniel. 51880
Cross, Robert, fl. 1741. 17662, 62106, 94686, 94700
Cross, Robert, fl. 1822. 17663
Cross, T. illus. 13448
Cross, Truman. (17664)-(17665), 48967

Cross (E. M.) & Co. firm publishers 61606
Cross and a coronet. (13435)
Cross and the church. 20391
Crosse, H. 24425
Crossman, Joseph W. 17667
Crosswell, Andrew. see Croswell, Andrew, 1709-1785.
Crosswell, H. ed. 78573
Croswell, Andrew, 1709-1785. 4497, (17668)-17675, 20056, 46511, 85663, 95316, note after 103614
Croswell, Caleb. 17676
Croswell, Edwin. (62905)
Croswell, Edwin. defendant 53931
Croswell, Harry, 1778-1858. 17667-(17680), 83656
Croswell, Harry, 1778-1858. defendant 17677, (29986), note after 98533, 102037
Croswell, Joseph. 17681-17682
Croswell, S. reporter 53635
Croswell, William. (17683)-17684, (63248)
Croswick Indians. Treaties, etc. 53242
Crotches and quavers. 44524
Crotchett, Timothy. pseud. Infallible scheme. 17685
Crothers, Samuel. 17686, 71558, 86273
Crouch, Nathaniel, 1632?-1725? 8547-8548, 9499-9502, note after 17686, (20827), 20840, (47580)-47581, 99557
Crouch & Gray. firm publishers 88021
Croucher, Richard D. defendant 96856
Crow, --------. RN (19715)
Crow, C. C. see Crowe, C. C.
Crow, Francis. 17687
Crow, William. 17688
Crow Indians. Treaties, etc. 96646
Crowe, C. C. 17689-17690
Crowe, Catharine (Stevens) d. 1876. ed. 92505, 92510-92511
Crowe, Frederick. 17691, 55912
Crowe, William. 17692, 83978
Crowel, William. 89369
Crowell, J. 17693
Crowell, John. 11799, 17695
Crowell, John, 1780-1846. 96654 see also U. S. Commissioners to the Creek Indians.
Crowell, John, 1801-1883. 17693-(17694)
Crowell, Joseph T. 17696
Crowell, Robert. (17697)-17700
Crowell, Seth. 17701
Crowell, William. 17702
Crowell, William J. reporter 62173
Crowley, Ann. 86638-86639
Crowley, Thomas. 17703-17705, (40648), 86638-86639
Crown and the confederation. (43162)
Crown Land Office, 9th February, 1863. 56178
Crown Land Office, 10th February, 1863. 56114
Crown lands. 56114
Crown won but not worn. 28605
Crowning crime of Christendom. 17706
Crowning event. 27333
Crowninshield, Benjamin. 17707
Crowninshield, Francis B. 86807-86808
Crowninshield, Francis B. respondent (12856)
Crowninshield, George. defendant 17708, 2d note after 103741
Crowninshield, Jacob. 17709-17711
Crowninshield, Richard. 17712
Crowninshield catalogue. 91518
Crowns of thorns and coats of thistles. 24661
Crowquill, Alfred. pseud. Goodnatured hints. see Forrester, Alfred Henry.
Crowther, J. 66686
Crowther, Jonathan, 1760-1824. 17713

Croy, Emmanuel, Duc de, 1718-1784. 17714-
17715
Croyate, Thomas. 66686
Croyer, H. P. 17718
Crozat, -------. 36762
Croze, Mathurin Veyssiere de la. see La
Croze, Mathurin Veyssiere de.
Crozet, ------. (17716), 72371
Crozet, Claudius. 17717
Crozier, O. R. L. (17719)
Crtice iz Kolumboca zivota, ili odkrice
Amerike. 10301
Cruautes de la traite des noirs. 8186
Cruautes horribles des conquerants du Mexique.
35319
Cruce, Alphonius a Vera. see Gutierrez,
Alonso.
Cruciferarum, elatinearum, caryphoyllearum
paranychiearumque Brasiliae Meridion-
alis synopsis. 10105
Cruden, John. 17720
Cruel captain. 3403
Cruel nature and injurious effects of the
foreign slave trade. 71924
Cruelties, depredations and illicit trade.
(16690), (22611)
Cruelty of slandering innocent and defenceless
women. 79358
Cruelty of the Spaniards in Peru. 18689
Cruger, -------, fl. 1775. 89210
Cruger, Alfred. 105561
Cruger, Henry N. 87547 see also South
Carolina. Agent for Historical Records.
Cruger, John, 1710-1792. (7884), 17721,
54368, 63210, 95935 see also New
York (City) Mayor, 1781-1782 (Cruger)
New York (Colony) Agents on the Bound-
ary Line Between New York and New
Jersey, 1769.
Cruger, Lewis. 15541, 17722, 90799
Cruice, Robert B. 62212
Cruikshank, George, 1792-1878. illus. 16307,
19285, 21300, 35135, (35148), (42433),
78382-78383, 92470, 92533, 92621,
105010
Cruikshank, Isaac Robert, 1789-1856. illus.
63372, 88546
Cruickshanks, James. 17723-(17724)
Cruillas, -------, Marques de. 98490
Cruise, Peter H. (68468)
Cruise. 10787
Cruise in a whale boat. 70761
Cruise in the Pacific. By a fore-top-man.
41012
Cruise in the Pacific. Edited by Captain F.
Aylmer. (2516)
Cruise in the United States flag ship of the
Gulf Squadron. 94455
Cruise of Admiral D. G. Farragut. 50151
Cruise of H. M. S. Torch. 78339, 96128
Cruise of the Alabama and the Sumter. 79076-
79077
Cruise of the Fire-Fly. 11600
Cruise of the frigate Columbia. (51554)
Cruise of the Midge. 78339
Cruise of the Somers. 17725, 93270
Cruise of the United States flag-ship, Hartford,
1862-'63. 32662, 57742
Cruise of the United States frigate Potomac.
101503
Cruise; or a prospect of the West Indian
archipelago. (21240)
Cruise of Narragansett Bay. 34776
Cruisers; being a letter. 71016
Cruises with Captain Bob. 80482

Cruising in the late war. (61230)
Cruising voyage round the world. 72753-72755
Cruisings, afloat and ashore. (36860)
Crull, T. tr. (19447)
Crumbs for antiquarians. (5877), 8564, 9538,
9540-9541, 39861, 47396, (50309)-50311,
(51852), 83998
Crumbs of comfort for God's dear children.
84025
Crume, Marks. 96678 see also U. S. Com-
missioners to the Potawatomi Tribe of
Indians of the Prairie.
Crumley, William M. 2381
Crummell, Alexander. 1819-1898. 17726-17727,
(68253)
Crump, W. H. 17728
Crusader, a temperance magazine. 87006
Crusaders. 80307
Cruse, Engelhart. 17729
Cruse, Mary A. (17731)
Crush it out! 84465
Crushing review of Little Napoleon's military
career. 43030
Crusius, Martin. 17730
Crusoe, Robinson. pseud. see Robinson
Crusoe. pseud.
Crusoe's island. 8657
Crusoniana. 93946
Crustacea, by Edward J. Miers. 28401, 71032
Crustacea. By James Dana. 18427
Crustacea of the fresh waters of the United
States. 84228
Crustacea of the United States. 77372
Crustacoes, aragnides e insectos. 74921
Crustaces. 29110, 74922
Crustaces; insectes. 57457
Cruz, --------- de la. 17736
Cruz, Ag. da. (4949)
Cruz, Alvaro de Bacan, Marques de Santa.
see Santa Cruz, Alvaro de Bacon,
Marques de.
Cruz, Andres de Santa. see Santa Cruz,
Andres de.
Cruz, Andres Santa. see Santa Cruz, Andres,
Pres. Bolivia, 1794-1865.
Cruz, Antonio Gonsalves da. see Gonsalves
da Cruz, Antonio.
Cruz, Baltasar de Santa. see Santa Cruz,
Baltasar de.
Cruz, Francisco Alonso de la Vera. see
Veracruz, Alonso de.
Cruz, Francisco de la. see Francisco de la
Cruz.
Cruz, Fernando de Santa. see Santa Cruz,
Fernando de.
Cruz, Gabriel Beltran de Santa. see Santa
Cruz, Gabriel Beltran de.
Cruz, Gaspar da. 66686
Cruz, Gervasio Jose da. 17732
Cruz, J. de la. see La Cruz, J. de.
Cruz, Ioaquin de Santa. see Santa Cruz,
Ioaquin de, marques.
Cruz, Juan de la. see De la Cruz, Juan.
Cruz, Juana Ines de la. see Juana Ines de
la Cruz, Sister, 1651-1695.
Cruz, Luis de la, 1768-1828. 29379, 96247,
99399
Cruz, Manuel Fernandez de Sancta. see
Fernandez de Sancta Cruz, Manuel.
Cruz, Mateo de la. 17737
Cruz, Miguel Perez de Santa. see Santa
Cruz, Miguel Perez de, Marques de
Buenavista.
Cruz, Nicolas Maria Santa. see Santa Cruz,
Nicolas Maria.

Cruz, Pedro Agustin Morel de Santa. see
Morel de Santa Cruz, Pedro Agustin, Bp.
Cruz, Rodrigo de la. 17738
Cruz Cano y Olmedilla, Juan de la. see
Cano y Olmedilla, Juan de la Cruz.
Cruz de Marcenado, Alvaro de Navia Osorio,
Marques de Santa. see Santa Cruz de
Marcenado, Alvaro de Navai Osorio,
Marques de, 1684-1732.
Cruz Garcia, Juan de la. see Garcia, Juan
de la Cruz.
Cruz Mendez, ------- de la. see De la
Cruz Mendez, --------.
Cruz Merlin, Mercedes de Santa. see Merlin,
Mercedes de Santa Cruz.
Cruz y Bahamonde, Nicolas de la. tr. 49889
Cruz y Sahagun, Manuel Fernandez de Santa.
see Santa Cruz y Sahagun, Manuel
Fernandez de.
Cruz. 57719
Cruz de Azabache. 23715
Cruzat y Gongora, Ignacia. 74517
Cry from the cotton field. 17739
Cry from the dust. 104950
Cry from the four winds. 17740
Cry from the north. 17741
Cry from the wilderness! (17742), 20757
Cry of Sodom enqvired into. 18476
Cry of the watchmen of Mount Ephraim! 70916
Crynodeb o gaban newyrth Tom. 92622
Cryptogamia: filices. 7193
Cryptogamie. 21216
Cryptogamie; palmiers. 57457
Crystal and masonic journal. 51579
Crystal fount and rechabite recorder. (17743)
Crystal Fount Division, no. 20, Sons of Tem-
perance of North America. see Sons
of Temperance of North America. Penn-
sylvania. Crystal Fount Division, no. 20.
Crystal hunter. 21912
Crystal Palace and its lessons. 28492
Crystal Palace Exhibition, New York, 1853.
see New York (City) Crystal Palace
Exposition, 1853.
Crystal Palace Exposition, New York, 1853.
see New York (City) Crystal Palace
Exposition, 1853.
Crystalline. (80152)
Cuadernito del tramite judicial. 96449
Cuaderno primero y segundo. 21774
Cuaderno que contiene el prestamo hecho a
Colombia. 72271
Cuaderno que contiene las comunicaciones
oficiales. (11176)
Cuaderno que . . . publico. 99783
Cuaderno titulado. 76747
Cuadro de sus adelantos en la poblacion.
74913
Cuadro descriptivo y comparativo de las
lenguas indigenas de Mexico. 51716,
62877-62878, 71411, 72811, 85760
Cuadro estadistico de la siempre fiel isla de
Cuba. 17763, 100633
Cuadro estadistico del Departamento de
Gracias. 32759, 55172
Cuadro historico-critico de los sucesos. 34149,
93910, note after 99718
Cuadro historico de la administracion Montt.
(50227)
Cuadro historico de la revolucion de la
Americana Mexicana. 9571, 9575, 9582,
31730
Cuadro historico politico de la administracion.
106247
Cuadro historico y espantosa de la inquisicion.
17744

Cuadro original de la geographia de las plantas.
79051
Cuadro que demuestra la Division Territorial.
(76231)
Cuadro sinoptico. 59304
Cuadros de la naturaleza Cubana. 93345
Cuadros sociales. (29133)
Cualquiera Zurriago de onde diere. 86256
Cuando el Padre Carrasco lo dice. 89410
Cuarta entrega. (57998)
Cuarta memoria. 81009
Cuarta noticia. 81286
Cuarta parte del semanario judicial. (48637)
Cuarta representacion a la Camara de Diputa-
dos. 67326
Cuarte parte de "Clamor de la justicia."
98958
Cuarto Congreso Constitucional de Tamaulipas,
1831. see Tamaulipas (Mexican State)
Congreso Constitucional, 4th, 1831.
Cuatro cartas que en deshago de su amor.
99783
Cuatro justisimos clamores. (66591)
Cuatro memorias sobre puntos de administra-
cion. (57713)
Cuatro primeras discusiones del Congreso de
Panama. 76828
Cub new lick'd. 12982, 17745, 3d note after
95765, 2d note after 102065
Cuba, Miguel Tacon y Rosique, Marques de
la Union de. see Tacon y Rosique,
Marques de la Union de Cuba, 1777-1854.
Cuba. (29449), 36444, 73454, 93784
Cuba. Academia de la Historia de Cuba. see
Academia de la Historia de Cuba.
Cuba. Academia de Literatura. see Academia
Cubana de Literatura.
Cuba. Aduana de Mar. 34829
Cuba. Alcabalatorio. 17749
Cuba. Colegio de Escribanos. see Colegio
de Escribanos de Cuba.
Cuba. Comision de Gefes y Oficiales. 100633
Cuba. Consejo de Regencia. 68883, 86819
Cuba. Consulado, Havana. 17776, 29450
Cuba. Cuerpo Nacional de Ingenieros. Director
Subinspector Interno. 36962 see also
Justiz, Francisco Jose.
Cuba. Ejercito. 17808
Cuba. Ejercito. Battalion de Malaga. 79183
Cuba. Ejercito. Battalion de Tarrogona.
(44293)
Cuba. Ejercito. Battalion Ligero. 16167
Cuba. Ejercito. Intendente. see Cuba.
Intendente de Ejercito.
Cuba. Ejercito. Junta de Generales. 29425
Cuba. Fiscal. 17779 see also Quiepo, -----.
Cuba. Gefe Superior Politico. see Cuba.
Gobernador.
Cuba. Gobernador, 1703 (Chacon) 106403
see also Chacon, Luis.
Cuba. Gobernador, 1761-1762 (Prado Mayeza
Portocarrero y Luna) 16670 see also
Prado Mayeza Portocarrero y Luna,
Juan de.
Cuba. Gobernador, 1763-1765 (Abarca de Bolea)
29454, (71240) see also Abarca de
Bolea, Ambrosio Funes Villapando, Conde
de Ricla.
Cuba. Gobernador, 1821-1822 (Mahy y Romo)
(34712) see also Mahy y Romo,
Nicolas.
Cuba. Gobernador, 1823-1832 (Vives) 17783
see also Vives, Francisco Dionisio.
Cuba. Gobernador, 1834-1838 (Tacon y Rosique)
17810, 94191-94194 see also Tacon y

Rosique, Miguel, Marques de la Union de Cuba, 1777-1854.

Cuba. Intendencia General de Hacienda. 73454

Cuba. Intendente de Exercito. 11099, 26436, 67636, 86819 see also Ramirez, Alejandro. Roubaud, Rafael Gomez. and Cuba. Superintendente.

Cuba. Junta de Fomento, de Agricultura y Comercio. 17750, 29414

Cuba. Junta de Generales. see Cuba. Ejercito. Junta de Generales.

Cuba. Junta de Guerra. 29458-29459

Cuba. Junta de Guerra. Fiscal. plaintiff 29459, 93778

Cuba. Junta Directiva de la Empresa de los Caminos de Hierro de Cardenas y Jucaro. 34713

Cuba. Junta Superior Contenciosa de Causas de Hacienda. 68855

Cuba. Junta Superior Directiva de Hacienda. 19968, (23515)

Cuba. Laws, statutes, etc. 17749, (17751)-(17752), 17793, 17805, 17808-17809, 17812-17813, 29454, (44951), 51220, (56292), 56294, (66585), 68244, 68868, 68883, 68886, 68891, (71240), 73455, 98259

Cuba. Milicia Nacional. 17805, 68886

Cuba. Renta del Tabaco. 73454

Cuba. Real Audiencia, Havana. Fiscal. 36937 see also Jurado, Juan.

Cuba. Real Audiencia, Havana. Oidor Decano. 70097 see also Ramos, Jose Antonio.

Cuba. Real Audiencia de Cuentas. 98147

Cuba. Supremo Consejo de Regencia. see Cuba. Consejo de Regencia.

Cuba. Superintendente. 26436, 67636 see also Cuba. Intendente de Ejercito. Ramirez, Alejandro.

Cuba. Tribunal y Real Audiencia de Cuentas. see Cuba. Real Audiencia de Cuentas.

Cuba (Diocese) 34836

Cuba (Diocese) Bishop (Garcia de Palacios) (80023), 90830 see also Garcia de Palacios, Juan, Bp.

Cuba (Diocese) Bishop (Hechavarria) 31201, 59014 see also Hechavarria, Santiago Joseph de, Bp.

Cuba (Diocese) Bishop (Morel de Santa Cruz) (50590) see also Morel de Santa Cruz, Pedro Agustin, Bp.

Cuba (Diocese) Synod, 1684. (80023), 90830 see also Florida (Diocese)

Cuba. 101350

Cuba and Africa. 17764

Cuba and Porto Rico. 39213, (57345), 88947

Cuba and the Alabama claims. 24590

Cuba, and the Cubans. (37766)

Cuba. Die Perle der Antillen. (81477)

Cuba en 1858. 26371

Cuba en 1860. 74913

Cuba et les grandes puissances occidentales de l'Europe. 41710

Cuba for invalids. 27276

Cuba: from the Spanish of Don J. M. de la Torre. 39213, (57345), 88947

Cuba in 1851. 36444

Cuba; or the policy of England, Mexico, and Spain. 17765

Cuba poetica. 17766, 86191-86192

Cuba, Puerto Rico y Santo Domingo. 6261

Cuba, ses ressources, son administration, ses population. 67081

Cuba, the United States, and Canada. 51497

Cuba under Spanish rule. 72331

Cuba y America. 99404

Cuba y la emancipacion de sus esclavos. 21402

Cuba y Marzo 15 de 1811. 37773

Cuba y Porto Rico. 17817

Cuba y su gobierno. 17767

Cuban affairs. 8348

Cuban Junta, New York. see New York Cuban Junta.

Cuban question considered. 17764

Cubas, Antonio Garcia de. see Garcia Cubas, Antonio, 1832-1912.

Cubas, Antonio Garcia y. see Garcia Cubas, Antonio, 1832-1912.

Cubbeer burr. 17818, note after 95370

Cubieres, Simon L. P. de, Marquis. 17822-(17823)

Cubillas Don-Yague, Francisco de. tr. (75764)

Cubitt, George. (17824)-17826

Cubus et sphaera geometrice duplicata. 67663

Cuce, Jean-de-Dieu-Raymond de Boisgelin de see De Boisgelin de Cuce, Jean-de-Dieu-Raymond.

Cucheval-Clarigny, Athanase. 17827-(17828)

Cuckoo's trial. 89027

Cucullu, J. S. 17829

Cudena, Pedro, fl. ca. 1634. 17830, 51480, (51482), 98777

Cudesch grands dels Martyrs. 45015

Cudworth, James. (73483), 78753

Cudworth, Warren Handel. (17831)-(17833)

Cudworth, William. 17834

Cudworth defended; and unitarianism delineated. (12406), 86749

Cueba, Juan Diego Gverrero de la. see Guerrero de la Cueba, Juan Diego.

Cueba Ponce de Leon, Alonzo de. see Ponce de Leon, Alonzo de Cueva.

Cuelebrouk, Edouard Blondeel van. see Blondeel van Cuelebrouk, Edouard.

Cuellar, Jose T. de. 17836

Cuenca, Claudio Mamerto. 17837

Cuenca, Juan Francisco de Montemaior y Cordova de. see Montemaior y Cordova de Cuenca, Juan Francisco de, 1620-1685.

Cuendias, Manuel de. 93348

Cuenta carta pastoral. 26719

Cuenta enviada por el ejecutivo al Quinto Congreso de la Union. 48450

Cuenta general de la administracion de las rentas. 61107

Cuenta jeneral de las entradas i gastos fiscales. 12760

Cuenta que da al publico de su Piadosa Comision. 10321

Cuentas de D. Felipe Pardo con el Tesoro del Peru. 58564

Cuentas, gastos, acreedores y otros asuntos del tiempo. 59297

Cuentas generales de la republica. 48406

Cuento Comagueyano. 5060

Cuentos y balades del norte de Europa. 71703

Cuerpo de Invalidos de Nueva Espana. see Mexico (Viceroyalty) Cuerpo de Invalidos.

Cuerpo de leyes de la republica de Colombia, que comprende todas las leyes. 14580

Cuerpo de leyes de la republica de Colombia. Tom. I. 14579

Cuerpo de Patriotas Distinguidos de Fernando Septimo. see Mexico (Viceroyalty) Cuerpo de Patriotas Distinguidos de Fernando Septimo.

Cuesta, Felipe Arroyo de la. see Arroyo de la Cuesta, Felipe.

Cuesta, Gregorio de la. 98858
Cuesta, N. Fernandez. see Fernandez
  Cuesta, N.
Cuestion agricola. 17838
Cuestion de Cuba. 87248
Cuestion de Francia. 48407, 48628
Cuestion de la esclavitud en 1871. 85713
Cuestion de limites entre el Ecuador y el
  Peru. 42916
Cuestion de Mejico y el Conde de Reus. 47838
Cuestion de Mexico. (58075)
Cuestion de Tehuantepec. Contiene las notas.
  17840, 57104, 1st note after 94592
Cuestion de Tehuantepec y representacion.
  17840, 57104, 1st note after 94592
Cuestion de utilidad del ferro-carril de
  Nuevitas a Puerto-Principe. 56290
Cuestion del trabayo agricola. 64860
Cuestion diplomatica. 41094
Cuestion, Dulce-Zulusta-Arguelles. 1962
Cuestion entre el Peru y la Espana. 50625
Cuestion entre la Confederacion Argentina.
  17841
Cuestion Harina de Trigo. 72791
Cuestion Holandesa. 16990
Cuestion Mexicana. 11469
Cuestion papel moneda. 38946
Cuestion Pegones y Tacamahaca. 17842
Cuestion promovida al Ilmo Metropolitano.
  41095
Cuestion promovida por los agentes de
  Francia. 17839
Cuestion social en las Antillas Espanolas.
  85711
Cuestion Talambo ante la America. (61108),
  67380
Cuestiones de Mejico, Venezuela, y America
  en general. 24177
Cuestiones historicas y sociales. 64332
Cuestiones politicas y economicas. 33558
Cueua, Antonia Gregoria de Esquiuel y de la.
  see Esquiuel y de la Cueua, Antonia
  Gregoria de.
Cueva, Antonio de la. ed. 61074
Cueva, Juan Roldan de la. see Roldan de la
  Cueva, Juan.
Cueva, Pedro. 17843
Cueva Ponce de Leon, Alonzo de. see Ponce
  de Leon, Alonzo de Cueva.
Cuevas, J. de J. (17844)-17845
Cuevas, Jose Maria. (17846)
Cuevas, Luis Gonzaga. 17847
Cuevas, Luis Gonzaga. defendant 65926
Cuevas, Manuel Pina y. see Pina y Cuevas,
  Manuel.
Cuevas Aguirre y Espinosa, Jose Francisco
  de. 17848, 24157, 4455B, 78910, 105731
Cuffee, Paul. 17849-17850
Cugnet, Francois Joseph. 17851-17855, (45416)
Cugoano, Quobna Ottobouh. 17856-17858
Cui bono? 97333-97339
Cuijano, Manuel. (43143)
Culbertson, Rosamond. 84030-84032
Culebrina fulminate, para el Senor Bustamante.
  99701
Culinary hints for the soldiers. (76394)
Cullen, Cassius C. 17859
Cullen, Charles. tr. 13519, 13522
Cullen, Edward. 17860
Cullen, R. 102435
Cullion, F. Va. de. 9756, 17862
Cullis, Charles. (17863)
Cullmer, W. 63512
Cullom, Shelby Moore, 1829-1914. (17864)
Cullom, William, 1810-1896. 17867

Cullum, George W. 17865-17866, (17868)
Culpa. Drama en un acto. 44247
Culprit Fay. 37163
Culprit Fay and other poems. 20869
Cultivateur Americain. pseud. Lettres. see
  Crevecoeur, J. Hector St. John 1735-
  1813.
Cultivateur Americain. pseud. Reflexions.
  see Jacquemard, -------. 35511
Cultivateur de New Jersey. pseud. Examen
  du gouvernement d'Angleterre. see
  Livingston, William.
Cultivation and supply of cotton in South
  America. 17123
Cultivation of American grape vines. 89597
Cultivation of cotton. 22085
Cultivation of flax. 10164
Cultivation of the native grape and manufacture
  of American wine. (34031)
Cultivator. 26803
Cultivator, a consolidation of Buel's cultivator
  and Genesee farmer. (17869)
Cultivator, a monthly journal devoted to agri-
  culture. (17869)
Cultivator, a monthly journal for the farm and
  garden. (17869)
Cultivator, a monthly publication designed to
  improve the soil and the mind. (17869)
Cultivator almanac for 1855. 34431, note after
  95426
Cultivator and country gentleman. 17150,
  (17869)
Cultivo del cafe o sea manual teorico practico.
  (43761)
Cultivo del cafeto o arbol que produce el
  cafe. 38431
Cultivo del maiz en Mejico. 73170
Culto festivo pompa solemne conque celebro
  la canonizacion. 67660
Culto festivo y solemne pompa. 76863
Cultura Americana. 62954, 106062
Cultura e opulencio do Brasil. 1715
Cultura ingeniorum. 58989, 64450
Cultura venezolano. 10193, note before 94254,
  note after 98870
Culture et usage de coton. 11814
Culture of cotton. 12950
Culture of Indian corn. (34358)
Culture of silk. 66625
Culture of the beet. (12703)
Culture of the sugar-cane. 2120A
Culture of the vine and emigration. (19206)
Culture, propagation, and management, in the
  garden and orchard. 20774
Culture raisonne des fruits. 66235
Cultuur en behandeling der West-Indischkoffij
  en indigo. 1006
Culver, C. V. 17870
Culver, David. (52915)
Culver, Erastus Dean, 1803-1889. 17871
Culver, J. Horace. 74792
Culver, Nathan. 17872
Cum magnopere. 84204-84211, 84213-84214
Cum priuilegio paesi nouamente retrouati.
  50050, note after 99383C, 4th note after
  106378
Cumarraga, Juan. see Zumarraga, Juan de,
  Bp.
Cumback, Will, 1829-1905. 17873, 33586
Cumberland, George de Clifford, 3d Earl of,
  1558-1605. (16873A)-17874, 66686
Cumberland, Georg, Graaf van. see Cumber-
  land, George de Clifford, 3d Earl of,
  1558-1605.
Cumberland, John. 14526, 51030, 88546, note
  after 105986

Cumberland, Richard, 1732-1811. 17876-17878, 88543, 4th note after 102803, 103051
Cumberland, William Augustus, Duke of. see William Augustus, Duke of Cumberland, 1721-1765.
Cumberland, Md. Special Court of Oyer and Terminer. 94032
Cumberland, Pa. Presbyterian Church. 17888
Cumberland County, Me. Convention, Portland, 1795. see Maine (District) Convention, Portland, 1795.
Cumberland County, Pa. 17889
Cumberland County, Pa. Collector of Excise. 8866-8867, 17889 see also Buchanan, John.
Cumberland County, Pa. Court of Oyer and Terminer. 77758-77759
Cumberland County, Pa. Society for the Promotion of Agriculture and Domestic Manufactures. see Society for the Promotion of Agriculture and Domestic Manufactures in and for Cumberland.
Cumberland Association. (19178), (47286)
Cumberland Association of Churches. see Congregational Churches in Maine. Cumberland Association.
Cumberland Baptist Association. see Baptists. Maine. Cumberland Association.
Cumberland coal district. 17882
Cumberland Coal and Iron Company. 17883
Cumberland College, Nashville, Tenn. 17884
Cumberland Conference of Churches. see Congregational Churches in Maine. Cumberland Association.
Cumberland Presbyterian. 82783
Cumberland Presbyterian Church in the U. S. 94789
Cumberland Presbyterian Church in the U. S. Clergy. 82781
Cumberland Presbyterian Church in the U. S. Synod of Cumberland. 94789
Cumberland Presbyterian pulpit. 82781
Cumberland to the District of Columbia. 71711
Cumberland Valley Rail Road Company. 60031
Cumberland Valley Rail Road Company. Chief Engineer. 60031 see also Roberts, William Milnor.
Cumberland's British theatre. 14526, 51030, 88546, note after 105986
Cuming, David. 93972
Cuming, F. 17890
Cuming, F. H. 100966
Cuming, Hugh. 39487
Cumings, Henry, 1737-1823. 17891-17901, 71810
Cumings, Samuel. 17384, 17902-(17904)
Cumming, Alexander, 1726-1763. 17671, (17905)-17906, 102425
Cumming, Hiram. 17908, 78746
Cumming, Hooper. 17909-17910
Cumming, Hooper. defendant before Presbytery (12536), 17909, 97370
Cumming, Joseph. 78524
Cumming, Kate. 17911
Cummings, ------, fl. 1866. 12479
Cummings, ------. 14740 see also Colorado (Territory) Governor, 1866 (Cummings)
Cummings, A. reporter 21630
Cummings, Alexander. 17912-(17913)
Cummings, Archibald. 17914-17916
Cummings, Asa, 1791-1856. 17917-(17918), (59309)-59310
Cummings, Charles A. 17919
Cummings, Ebenezer E. 17920
Cummings, Jeremiah W. 17921

Cummings, Preston. 17922
Cummings, Samuel. see Cumings, Samuel.
Cummings, Thomas. 11211
Cummings, Thomas S. 17923
Cummins, Alexander G. 17924
Cummins, Ebenezer Harlow. 2775, 17925-17926
Cummins, George D. 17927-(17931)
Cummins, John, carpenter of H. M. S. Wager. 1639, 9108-9109, 10205
Cummins, John, fl. 1854. 17933
Cummins, John D., 1791-1849. 17932
Cummins, John G. see Cummins, John D., 1791-1849.
Cummins, Maria Susanna, 1827-1866. 17934-17940
Cummins, Oliver. defendant 17941, 30345
Cummins, Thomas J. 21336
Cummurrajo, Juan. see Zumarraga, Juan, Bp.
Cumplido, Ignacio. 34350, 48261, 56268
Cumplimiento de la ley por el organo republicano. 49895
Cumpston, Edward H. 17942
Cumulative vote. 8886
Cumulative voting. 8886
Cuncapot. Indian Chief (15440)
Cunha, A. L. da. tr. 101664
Cunha Barbarosa, Januario da. see Cunha Barbosa, Januario da.
Cunha Barbosa, Januario da. 7621, 17933-(17946), 58828, 76845, 99734
Cunha de Azeredo Coutinho, Jose Joaquim de, Bp. (17947)-17955 see also Elvas (Diocese) Bishop (Cunha de Azeredo Coutinho)
Cunha Mattos, Raimundo Jose da. 17956
Cunha Paranagua, Joao Lustosa da. 60991 see also Pernambuco. Presidente (Cunha Paranagua)
Cunha Reis, Manuel Basilio da. 93308
Cunhae Figueiredo, Jose Bento da. 69314, 69327 see also Alagoas (Brazilian Province) Presidente (Cunhae Figueiredo)
Cuningham, William, b. 1531. 17971
Cunnabell, ------. 17957
Cunnabell's Nova-Scotia almanac for 1858. 17957
Cunning, F. H. 17958
Cunning, John P. 17959
Cunningham, Allen. 17960-17961
Cunningham, Andrew. 101871
Cunningham, Emma Augusta. claimant 9210
Cunningham, Ephraim May, 1792-1852. ed. 232
Cunningham, Francis. (17963)
Cunningham, John. 17964-17965
Cunningham, John William. 105490
Cunningham, Letitia. 17966
Cunningham, P. A. 17968
Cunningham, Peter. 17967
Cunningham, Richard. 75949, 2d note after 96930A, 98520
Cunningham, Robert. 17969
Cunningham, Samuel. 17970
Cunningham, Waddel. defendant 25124, 96305
Cunningham, William, b. 1531. see Cuningham, William, b. 1531.
Cunningham, William, d. 1718. defendant 32182, (32197)
Cunningham, William, 1767-1823. 232, 17972-17974, 62658, 84906
Cunningham, William, 1805-1861. (2792)
Cunningham (J. L.) firm 98475
Cunningham (William) & Co. firm claimants 17975-(17976), 56542, 84842

Cunninghams. firm see Dean & Cunninghams. firm
Cunningham's works. 105490
Cunon, J. C. see Cunow, John G. petitioner
Cunow, John G. petitioner 17977, 86170
    see also United Brethren. Directors of
    the Missionary Concerns. petitioners
Cuny, Phil. M. (17978)
Cunynghame, Arthur. 17979
Cuoo, A. 17980-(17981)
Cuoq, -------. tr. (34593), 36969, 46821
Cup of blessing. 76984
Cura. pseud. Patronato dialogo entre un
    cura y un abogado. 59113
Cura, pseud. Tertulia de la aldea. 94895
Cura de Mexico. pseud. Papel sobre el
    verdadero. 58436
Cura de este arzobispado de Lima. pseud.
    Discurso doctrinal. see Ruiz, Santiago
    Jose Lopez.
Cura de la Aldea. pseud. Contestacion.
    35545
Cura de Puebla. pseud. Dictamen. 58436
Cura de Santiago de Queretaro. pseud. A
    sus fieles habitantes. 67101
Cura de Santiago de Queretaro a sus fieles
    habitantes. 67101
Cura del municipio di Bergamo. pseud.
    Costantino Beltrami da Bergamo. see
    Rosa, Gabriele.
Cura del Obispado de Puebla. pseud. Expli-
    cacion clara y sucinta. 23424
Cura del Obispado de Puebla. pseud. tr.
    (64399)
Cura monardes. 99785
Curacao. Heilige Rosa Kirke. Algemeene
    Armenschool. 48227, 66752
Curacao. Ordinances, etc. (68914)
Curacao. Raad Fiscaal. (77501)-77502 see
    also Schagen, Jan van.
Curacao. Santa Rosa. see Curacao. Heilige
    Rosa Kirke.
Curacao, from the Dutch originals of Gerard
    van Keulen. 37659
Curacao. Herinneringen en schetsen. 20277
Curas Beneficiados de la Ciudad de Santa Fee
    Real, y Minas de Guanaxuato. petitioners
    95138
Curate of N——th——t. pseud. see B., J.,
    Curate of N——th——t. pseud.
Curate of the Diocese of Canterbury. pseud.
    Remarks. 102565
Curbed sinner. (46275)
Cure for radicalism. 8398
Cure for the spleen. 1274, 17982, (79396)-
    79397
Cure of sorrow. (46276)
Cures of the diseased, in remote regions.
    103258
Curiae, Amicus. pseud. see Amicus curiae.
    pseud.
Curiae Canadenses. 10414, 17984
Curieuse aenmerckingen der bysonderste Oost
    en West-Indische Verwonderenswaerdige
    dingen. 100854
Curieuse anmerkingen der bysonderste Oost
    en Westindische verwondernswaardige
    dingen. (17985)
Curieuse anmerckungen uber den staat von
    Frankreich. 39308
Curieuse geographia. 28378
Curieuse Nachricht von Pensylvania in Norden-
    America. 23739, 95394
Curieuse und historische Reisen, &c. 11282

Curieuse und warhaffte Erzehlung und
    Beschreibung. (10910)
Curieusen und historischen Reisen, &c. 11282
Curiosa compilacion de documentos. 94846
Curiose Beschreibung der auserlesensten
    Merkwurdigkeiten. 17986
Curiosidades Brasileiras. 47297
Curiositaten der physisch-literarische-
    artistisch-historischen Vor- und Mitwelt.
    (17987)
Curiosites Americaines. 11776-11777
Curiositez de la nature et de l'art. 5582
Curiosities in American history. 83717
Curiosities of American literature. 20276
Curiosities of "American" literature, no. 1.
    82823
Curiosities of common water. 82869-82870
Curiosisites of food. 81148
Curiosities of human nature. 27895, 27913
Curiosities of literature. 20276
Curiosities of nature and art. 17988
Curiosities of savage life. 28691
Curiosities of slavery in the south. 63853,
    (63877)
Curiosity: a poem. 89658
Curiosity of literature and theology. 103924
Curiosity visits to southern plantations. 81945
Curioso parlante. pseud. Matias Campanillas
    y Roque Pechuga. 46860
Cvrioso tratado de la natvraleza y calidad del
    chocolate. 14542
Curious account of Peter Serrano. 93423
Curious account of the cataracts at Niagara.
    3868
Curious account of the Indians. 27079, 3d note
    after 106134
Curious adventures of Captain Stedman. 91072
Curious adventures of Corporal Samuel Stubbs.
    15043, 93232
Curious alphabetical view of the whole world.
    104492
Curious and authentic narratives and anecdotes.
    (81502)
Curious and entertaining voyages. 17989
Curious and interesting dialogue. 98365
Curious and profitable gardener. 17237
Curious book. 25451
Curious calculations. 31028
Curious collection of travels. 54898
Curious collection of trees and shrubs. 11506
Curious collection of voyages and travels.
    105485-105486
Curious directions for cultivating the choicest
    fruits. 17237
Curious facts and anecdotes. 95343
Curious hieroglyphick Bible. (17990)
Curious indictments, 1755 and 1757. 82976
Curious journal of R. Hylkes. 34130
Curious maid. 26961
Curious observations upon the manners. 38730
Curious particulars concerning the Osages.
    49712
Curious secret journal. 95836
Curious traveller. 17991
Curita, -----. 38949
Curren, Benjamin. tr. 56190
Currency; a tract of the times. 21467
Currency and finances. 68582
Currency and the war. 62817
Currency, banking and credit. 73144
Currency. By Joseph S. Ropes. 73145
Currency. By Junius. 14769, 14775
Currency conflict. A review. 77994
"Currency conflict." Address of J. W.
    Schuckers. 77993

Currency debates. (15533)
Currency—funding—gold and silver. (17271)
Currency. Gold the basis, greenbacks the currency. 82299
Currency, its expansion. 8348
Currency—national banks. 78026
Currency of the future. (36960)
Currency, or money; its nature and uses. 17992, 32875
Currency question. A plea for greenbacks. 24286
Currency-question. By G. M. Steele. 91117
Currency question. Four letters to the Hon. Schuyler Colfax. 10842
Currency question, from strictures on the pamphlet of James Gallatin, Esq. 9639
Currency question. Gen. Butler's letter. 9615
Currency. Remarks of Hon. Henry W. Corbett. 16758
Currency—resumption without contraction. 33335
Currency—specie payments. 78025
Currency. Speech . . . December 11, 1867. 50791
Currency. Speech of Hon. James A. Garfield. 26663
Currency; the evil and the remedy. 14770, 26658, 27933, 37284
Currency, the standard of value and the circulating medium. 63354
Currency; what it is, and what it should be. 18881
Current and well-authenticated anecdotes. (5373)
Current expenditures. 105857
Current fictions tested by uncurrent facts, &c. 18933, 35841
Current gold and silver coins of all countries. 44896
Currey, Richard O. 17995
Currey, Samuel, 1806-1878. 17996, 84975
Currie, James. 1756-1805. 17997, 104646
Currie, Margaret Gill. 17998
Currie, William, 1709-1803. 10944, 17999A
Currie, William, fl. 1748. 65118, 79283
Currie, William, 1754-1828. 17999-18003
Currie, William Wallace. 18004
Currier, Edward. 18005, 63811
Currutaco de Lima. pseud. Vica de muchos see Terralla y Landa, Esteban de.
Curry, Daniel, 1809-1889. 11678, 18006, 88560
Curry, George Law, 1820-1878. 57556 see also Oregon (Territory) Governor, 1854-1858 (Curry)
Curry, Jabez Lamar Monroe, 1825-1903. 18007
Curry, John P. 18008
Curry, Otway. ed. 31615
Curry, Thomas. 9119
Cursas medicus Mexicanus. 75776
Curse causeless. 62722
Curse of Canaan rightfully interpreted. 21836
Curse of Christendom. 96318
Curse of cowardice. 18758
Curse of God against political atheism. 12396
Curse of liberty. 17173
Curse of Meroz, in a discourse. 103318
Curse of Meroz; or, the danger of neutrality. 24388
Curse of Minna, and other poems. (55211)
Curse of paper-money. 28074
Curses coming home to roost! 48960
Cursive Christianity. 84256

Curso de derecho constitucional. 76870
Curso de derecho eclesiastico. 99499
Curso de derecho internacional o de gentes. 76871
Curso de derecho natural o de filosofia del derecho. 73164
Curso de derecho Peruano. (76872)
Curso de direito cambial Brazileiro. 88797
Curso de lectura por el metodo de ensenaza nutua. 12761
Curso elemental de derecho de gentes. 60905
Curso elemental de economia-politica. 45419
Curso elemental de geografia universal. 26556
Curso elemental de litteratura nacional. 62950
Curson, H. (18009)
Cursory analytical epistle. 14032, 85597, 94025
Cursory examination of the respective pretensions. 18010
Cursory glimpse of the state of the nation. 18011, 101787
Cursory observations, addressed to the planters. (70444)
Cursory observations relative to the mounting of cannon. 18012
Cursory observations upon Dr. Price's essay on civil liberty. 65459
Cursory reflections on government. 56837
Cursory reflections on the consequences which may ensure. 35926
Cursory reflections on the system of taxation. 10863
Cursory remarks on Dr. Price's Observations on the nature of civil liberty. (65460)
Cursory remarks on men and measures in Georgia. 18013
Cursory remarks on the emancipation of slaves. 18014
Cursory remarks on the importance of agriculture. 38770
Cursory remarks on the laws concerning usury. (80132)
Cursory remarks upon the Reverend Mr. Ramsay's essay. 96054
Cursory review of the "American apology for American accession to Negro slavery." 28246
Cursory review of the Schuylkill coal. 18015
Cursory sketch of the motives and proceedings. 39740
Cursory view of Georgetown. 78658, note after 101799
Cursory view of Spanish America. 72200
Cursory view of the local, social, moral, and political state. (23053)
Cursory view of the peace. 78725
Cursory views of the liberal and restrictive systems. 10889, (18016)
Cursus catecheticus Americanus. 7475
Cursus consummatus. 2476
Curt, ------ de. 18017, 50575, 66214, 93815
Curtained throne. 75921
Curtenius, Peter T. 53473, 54042, 83604
Curths, Carl. 18018
Curtin, Andrew Gregg, 1817-1894. 18019-18020, 27239, 59885, 60249 see also Pennsylvania. Governor, 1861-1866 (Curtin)
Curtin (D.) firm publishers 18023, 41890
Curtins. pseud. Letters. see Grayson, William J.
Curtin's directory of Astoria, Babylon, Bath, Carnarsi, etc. 18023
Curtin's directory of Astoria, East New York, Flatbush. 41890

Curtis, -------, fl. 1856. 13622 see also
   Keokuk, Iowa. Mayor, 1856 (Curtis)
Curtis, Ariana Randolph (Wormeley) 18031,
   89487
Curtis, Benjamin Robbins, 1855-1891. 18024-
   18028, (22293), (37994), 37996, 42534,
   56030, 78257-(78258), 79874
Curtis, Benjamin Robbins, 1855-1891. reporter
   66826
Curtis, C. A. 4355
Curtis, Caleb. 105419
Curtis, Charles Pelham. 18029
Curtis, Mrs. D. S. see Curtis, Ariana
   Randolph (Wormeley)
Curtis, Edward. USA 18032
Curtis, George, fl. 1835. 66250, (70653)
Curtis, George Henry. 92060
Curtis, George Ticknor, 1812-1894. 18033-
   (18040), 20256, 23271, 45711, 50958,
   92068
Curtis, George William, 1824-1892. 18049-
   (18053), 20775, 30477, 78826, 83332
Curtis, John, 1744-1823. 97532
Curtis, John, 1791-1862. 18054
Curtis, John W. 97480
Curtis, Jonah. 6626
Curtis, Jonathan. 18055
Curtis, Josiah. 6626, 18056
Curtis, L. 18058
Curtis, M. A. 55620 see also North Caro-
   lina. Geologist.
Curtis, Martin. see Cortes, Martin, fl. 1551.
Curtis, Moses A. 18059
Curtis, Nathaniel. 18060
Curtis, Newton M. (18061)
Curtis, S. (18062)
Curtis, Samuel D. (38476), 58089
Curtis, Samuel Ryan, 1805-1866. (18064),
   (38476), 58089
Curtis, Stephen. 18063
Curtis, Thomas, fl. 1838. ed. 3153
Curtis, Thomas, fl. 1843. 18066
Curtis, Thomas F. 18067
Curtis, U. (49732)-(49733)
Curtis, W. J. 18068
Curtis, Winslow. defendant 103418
Curtiss, Daniel S. 18069
Curtis's pocket almanack for . . . 1800.
   (18062)
Curtius. pseud. Defence of the measures of
   the administration. see Taylor, John,
   1753?-1824.
Curtius. pseud. Letters. see Thomson,
   John, 1777-1799.
Curtius. pseud. Texas. see Wharton,
   William H.
Curtius. pseud. To the Secretary of the
   Treasury. see Taylor, John, 1753?-
   1824.
Curtius. pseud. Torch light. 96190
Curtius. pseud. Vindication of the treaty.
   see Webster, Noah, 1758-1843.
Curtius to the Secretary of the Treasury of
   the United States. 94487
Curtius's vindication of Mr. Jay's treaty.
   96580
Curvo Semmedo, Joao. see Semmedo, Joao
   Curvo.
Curwen, Maskell E. 18074, 56711, (57030),
   (57046), (57057)
Curwen, Samuel. 18075-18077, 101296
Cusack, George. defendant (18078)
Cushing, Abel. (18079)-18080
Cushing, Caleb, fl. 1745. 18018, 103631

Cushing, Caleb, 1800-1879. 18082-18096,
   30588, 30589, (45880), 47236, 89323,
   93602
Cushing, Christopher. 18097-18098, 85409
Cushing, Daniel. 18099
Cushing, E. L. 18100
Cushing, Eliza Lanesford (Foster) b. 1794.
   supposed author 106048
Cushing, Elmer. 18101
Cushing, J. Stearns. 83468
Cushing, Jacob. 18102-18108
Cushing, Jesse B. 18109
Cushing, John, 1709-1772. 18110
Cushing, John, 1744-1823. 18111-18112
Cushing, John, fl. 1771. 32362, 37712, 96946,
   96951, 2d-3d notes after 102623
Cushing, Jonathan Peter, 1793-1835. 100556
Cushing, Luther Stearns, 1803-1856. 18114-
   18119, (45746), 46081, 98564 see also
   Massachusetts. Legislature. House of
   Representatives. Clerk.
Cushing, Matthew. defendant 102221
Cushing, S. W. 18121
Cushing, T. 18120
Cushing, Thomas. 12341, 18122
Cushing, Thomas H. defendant at court martial
   18123
Cushman, -------. illus. 57780
Cushman, A. S. 18124
Cushman, Elisha. 18125
Cushman, George F. 18126
Cushman, Frederick E. 18127
Cushman, Henry Wayles. (18128)
Cushman, Joshua. 18129-18130, 43906
Cushman, Pauline. 18131
Cushman, R. S. 18136
Cushman, Robert, d. 1625. (18132)-18135,
   19051, 106053
Cushman, Robert W. 12948, 18137-18139
Cushman, W. M. 18141
Cushman Celebration, Plymouth, Mass., 1855.
   see Plymouth, Mass. Cushman Cele-
   bration, 1855.
Cushman Monument, Plymouth, Mass. see
   Plymouth, Mass. Cushman Celebration.
Cushman's discourse. 106053
Cusick, David. 18142
Cussy, Ferdinand de, Baron, 1795-1866. 18143-
   (18144), 30866, 44833
Cussy, Frederic de. see Cussy, Ferdinand
   de, Baron, 1795-1866.
Cust, Sir Edward. 18145-18148
Cust, Nina. 93220
Cust, Reginald John. 18149
Custine, Adam Philippe, Comte de. (18150)
Custis, -------, fl. 1806. 25787
Custis, George Washington Park, 1781-1857.
   18151-(18157), 43659, 101828
Custis, Mary Randolph. see Lee, Mary Randolph
   (Custis) 1806-1873.
Custom house duties. 13646
Custom of Paris. 20676
Customs and anecdotes of the Greenlanders.
   28639
Customs Comptroller, Savannah, Ga. see Great
   Britain. Customs Comptroller, Savannah,
   Ga.
Customs House, Boston. see Great Britain.
   Customs House, Boston.
Customs journal. 34919
Customs, laws. 7566
Customs of all nations. 27913
Customs of New England. (24030)
Customs of service for non-commissioned
   officers. (37119)

Customs of service for officers of the army. 37120
Customs of the Indians. 27913
"Customs of the office" are true as the existance of time. (62196)
Cut-flowers. 80173
Cutbush, Edward. 18158
Cuthbert, Alfred, 1785-1856. 18159
Cuthbert, Ross. 1764, 18160
Cutler, Benjamin C. 18161-18162
Cutler, Calvin. 18163
Cutler, Charles. 18164
Cutler, Ebenezer. 18165-18166
Cutler, Elbridge Jefferson. 18167-(18168)
Cutler, Fanny Thimble. pseud. Journal. (9633)
Cutler, Frank. tr. 83144
Cutler, Mrs. H. M. Tracy. 18169
Cutler, Jervase. 18170, 3d note after 96185
Cutler, Joseph. 18171
Cutler, Manasseh. (18172)-(18177)
Cutler, Nathan, 1775-1861. (44028)-44029
see also Maine. Governor, 1829-1830 (Cutler)
Cutler, Perley. defendant 18178
Cutler, Peter Y. 18179
Cutler, R. King. 18180-18181
Cutler, Rufus Putnam. 18182-18183, 83483
Cutler, Samuel. 18184
Cutler, Timothy. 18185-(18188)
Cutler, William Parker, 1812-1889. 18189-18190
Cutler & Co. firm see Russell, Cutler & Co. firm publishers
Cutter, --------. reporter 4702
Cutter, B. C. 18191
Cutter, Benjamin. 18192
Cutter, Charles Ammi, 1837-1903. 18193
Cutter, Charles W. 18194
Cutter, Edward F. 18195
Cutter, Elizabeth H. tr. 51306
Cutter, G. W. 18196-18197
Cutter, Mary H. 43228
Cutter, O. P. 18198
Cutter, William. 18199-18200
Cutter, William Richard. 18192
Cutting, Francis Brockholst, 1804-1870. 18201, 89221
Cutting, H. P. 18202
Cutting, John Browne. (81203)-81204
Cutting, John Browne. defendant (18203)
Cutting, Sewall S. 18205
Cutting to the quick. 104956
Cutts, Hampden. (18206)
Cutts, James Madison. 18207-(18208), (20690)
Cutts, Mary Pepperrell Sparhawk (Jarvis) 18209
Cuulce, Carsen. (32804)
Cuvero Sebastian, Pedro. (17819)-(17821)
Cuverville, -------- de. tr. 43361
Cuvier, George Leopold Chretien Frederic. see Cuvier, Georges, i. e. Jean Leopold Nicolas Frederic, Baron, 1769-1832.
Cuvier, Georges, i. e. Jean Leopold Nicolas Frederic, Baron, 1769-1832. 2541, (2543), (12884), 18210, 52105, 78689
Cuvier, Jean Leopold Nicolas Frederic. see Cuvier, Georges, i. e. Jean Leopold Nicolas Frederic, Baron, 1769-1832.
Cuvillers, Etienne Felix d'Henin de. see Henin de Cuvillers, Etienne Felix, Baron d', 1755-1841.
Cvya admirable vida. (74995)
Cuyler, Cornelius C. 18221-18212
Cuyler, Henry. 95936

Cuyler, Jacob C. 21238
Cuyler, Theodore L. (18213)
Cuyoano, Ohtabah. pseud.?? Reflexions. 68748
Cuzco, Peru. 97671
Cuzco (Diocese) 51045
Cuzco (Diocese) Bishop [ca 16--] 61133
Cuzco (Diocese) Bishop [ca 1614] 41088
Cuzco (Diocese) Bishop [ca 1720] 97671
Cuzco (Diocese) Bishop (Mendoza) see also 47845 Mendoza, --------, Bp., fl. 1847.
Cuzco (Diocese) Bishop (Moscoso y Peralta) 68838 see also Moscoso y Peralta, Juan Manuel de, Bp.
Cuzco: journal to the ancient capital of Peru. 44613
Cuze. (66554)
Cuzent, Gilbert. 18215
Cycloidal configurations. 57634
Cyclopedia Indiensis. 77844
Cyclopedia of American literature. 7299, 16323, 21505-21506, (24848), 28892, 35819, 84062, 94431
Cyclopedia of American literature, by Evart A. Duyckinck. 28892
Cyclopedia of biography. 30971, 70867-(70868)
Cyclopedia of commerce and commercial navigation. 32595
Cyclopaedia of commercial and business anecdotes. 37998
Cyclopaedia of history and geography. 6436
Cyclopaedia of Methodism. 71365
Cyclopedia of missions. (54931)
Cyclopaedia of religious denominations. 83289
Cyclopaedia of the industry of all nations. 38103
Cyclopedia of universal biography. [By Elihu Rich.] 30971
Cyclopedia of universal biography. By Parke Godwin. 27672
Cyclopaedia of woman's work. 60794
Cyclopaedia; or universal dictionary of arts. 59775, (68634), 102369
Cyd-gordiad egwyddorawl o'r scrythurau. 50634
Cymon. pseud. Hits and dashes. see Somerby, Frederick Thomas, 1814-1871.
Cymon. pseud. Introduction. 38079
Cymon. pseud. Pigmies and the priests. 62811
Cymry of '76. 36445
Cynick. 18216
Cynthia, Ky. Court. 19734
Cypress, J. pseud. Sporting scenes and sundry sketches. see Hawes, William Post.
Cypress River Mining Company. 18218
Cypress River Mining Company: articles of agreement. 18218
Cypress wreath. 28900
Cyprey, ------- Baron Alleye de. see Alleye de Cyprey, -------, Baron.
Cry, N. 18219
Cyran, ------ de Saint. see Saint Cyran, ------ de.
Cyrianci Morelli. pseud. Fasti novi orbis. see Muriel, Domingo.
Cyril Thornton. 30034
Cysatus, R. (18220)
Czarnowsky, Otto von. tr. 37442
Czernickiego, Gustawa. tr. 92406
Czuczor, Gergely. and ed. tr. 89010
Czytelnia domowa. 92406

D***. pseud. Acadiade. see Chevrier, Antoine.

D***. pseud. Lettre de M. D*** a M. D***. 18235

D. pseud. Naufrage. see Dubois-Fontanelle, Jean Gaspard.

D***. pseud. Poemes. see Chevrier, Antoine.

D****. pseud. Voyage de Marseille a Lima. see Durret, --------.

D . . . . , Avocat. pseud. Histoire des naufrages. see Deperthes, Jean Louis Hubert Simon.

D——G. pseud. ed. 88546

D., A. pseud. Guerre civile aux Etats Unis. 18224, 29124

D., A. pseud. Vierge Iroquoise. (18223)

D., A. G. pseud. Writings. see Dole, Anna Greenleaf.

D., B. pseud. Federals and confederates. 18225

D***, B***. pseud. Voyage a la Louisiane. see Baudry de Lozieres, Louis Narcisse.

D., B. G. pseud. see Gerbier, Sir Baltazar, 1592?-1667.

D., B. S. pseud. Isla de Cuba. (18226)

D., C. pseud. ed. see Deane, Charles.

D., C. pseud. Brief and true account. see Dove, Samuel.

D . . . , C . . . pseud. Champ d'Asile au Texas. (18227), 95071

D., C. pseud. Considerations sur l'esclavage. see Dussillion, Charles J.

D., C. pseud. New-England's faction discovered. see Dove, C.

D——S, C——s. pseud. No thoroughfare. see Dunham, Robert Carr.

D., C. pseud. Report of the committee. see Weymouth, Mass. South Parish. Committee of Inquiry.

D*****x, Casimir. Cri des Negres. 21575

D., Ch. J. pseud. Considerations sur l'esclavage aux Antilles Francaises. 18228

D., D. pseud. Au roy. 98928

D***, D***, ci-devant officier d'infantrie. pseud. ed. Epistle dedicatory. 35074

D., E. pseud. Remarks on Dr. Gale's letter. see Dyer, Eliphalet.

D., E. H. pseud. Reality versus fiction. see Derby, Elias Hasket.

D., F. pseud. Epitaphium. see Drake, Francis.

D., G. H. pseud. M. van Buren. 98425

D., H. pseud. Biography of Louis Moreau Gottschalk. 18230

D¹., H. pseud. Considerations sur l'etat present. see Hilliard D'Auberteuil, Michel Rene.

D., H. H. pseud. Betrayal of the cause of freedom. (79596)

D., H. N. pseud. Fifty years of a play-goer's journal. see Ireland, Joseph N.

D., I. pseud. Appendix to the foregoing letters. (22152), note before 92797, note after 104794

D., J. pseud. Almanac for the year 1679. 18232

D., J. pseud. Almanack or register of co-elestial configurations &c. see Danforth, John, 1660-1730.

D., J. pseud. American anti-slavery conventions. see Dunlop, John.

D . . . . , J . . . . . pseud. On Mormonerne. 50751

D., J. pseud. Profession of faith. see Davenport, John.

D., J. pseud. Vindication of the public faith. see Duer, John. supposed author

D., J. B. pseud. Sur Saint-Domingue. see Desmaulants, J. B.

D., J. J. pseud. tr. 98847

D., J. W. pseud. tr. see Caspar, F. X. vo von. tr.

D***, M. pseud. tr. see Demeunier, Jean Nicolas. tr.

D*****, M. pseud. Abrege histoire. see Double, M.

D., M. pseud. Conselhos que da uno Brasileiro veterano. 15918, (18234)

D., M. pseud. Discurso. (18233)

D., M. pseud. Esclavage. see Dumesnil, Marie.

D***, M. pseud. Histoire des naufrages. see Deperthes, Jean Louis Hulbert Simon.

D¹, M. H. pseud. Considerations sur l'etat present. see Hilliard d'Auberteuil, Michel Rene, 1751-1789.

D., M. J. O. pseud. Souvenirs d'un jeune voyagier. see Odolant-Desnos, Pierre Joseph.

D., O. pseud. Unbekante neue welt. see Dapper, Olfert.

D., R. pseud. Sir Francis Drake revived. (18236), 20830, (20838)-20840, 20843, 20855-20856

D., R. pseud. Strange and prodigious religious customs. (18237)

D., R. pseud. Visit to the wild west. (18238)

D., S. pseud. New-England almanack. see Danforth, Samuel, 1626-1674.

D., T. pseud. Manifestation or state and case of the Quakers. 44277

D., T. pseud. Massachusetts. see Dudley, Thomas.

D., T. pseud. Preface. 27270

D., W. pseud. Letters. 95745

D., W. pseud. Ligan. see Duane, William. 20996

D., W. pseud. Plain dealer. see Williamson, Hugh.

D., W. pseud. Second answer to Mr. John Wesley. 18239

D., W. pseud. Summary, historical and politica. see Douglass, William, d. 1752.

D., W. van. pseud. tr. 72325

D. B., B. G. pseud. see Boileau de Bouillon, Gilles, 16th cent.

D. B***, M. pseud. tr. see B***, M. D. pseud. tr.

D. B***, M. pseud. see Buisson, Paul Ulric du.

D. H., T. pseud. Waare en nauwkeurige journael der reize. see Hase, Theodore de. supposed author

D. L. S., M. pseud. see Sauvage, ------- de la.

D. S***, M. R. pseud. Melanges interessans et curieux. see Rousselot de Surgy, Jacques Philibert.

D. S., P. M. pseud. Histoire naturelle. see Rousselot de Surgy, Jacques Philibert.

D. A. J. R. B. F. D. M. pseud. see M., D. A. J. R. B. F. D. pseud. ed.

D. B. pseud. see Daubry des Lozieres, Louis Narcisse.

D. B***. pseud. see Buisson, Paul Ulric du.
D. B. Cooke & Co.'s directory. 12641
D. B. P. F. pseud. see F., D. B. P. pseud.
D. C. T. pseud. see T., D. C. pseud.
D. D. pseud. see D. D. pseud.
D. D. D. Death, the devil and the doctor. 81073
D. de P. y B. pseud. see Vera y Pintado, Bernardo de.
D. E. pseud. see E., D. pseud.
D. G. J. V. D. G. Y. M. pseud. see Guzman y Manrique, Joaquin de.
D. J. A. L. pseud. see L., D. J. A. pseud.
D. J. C. pseud. see C., D. J. pseud.
D. J. E. O. pseud. see O., D. J. E. pseud.
D. J. F. de L. pseud. see Lizardi, Joaquin Fernandez de.
D. J. F. de la V. pseud. see V., D. J. F. de la. pseud.
D. J. M. F. pseud. see F., D. J. M. pseud.
D. J. M. T. pseud. see T., J. M. pseud.
D. K. pseud. see Scott, Thomas.
D. L. pseud. see L., D. pseud.
D. L. pseud. cartographer see L., D. pseud. cartographer
D. L. pseud. see Leeds, Daniel.
D. L. C. pseud. see C., D. L., le comte. pseud.
D. L. G. D. C., sieur, Avocat en Parlement. see Lagrange de Checieux, G. A. F. Simon de.
D. L. M. pseud. see La Martiniere, Pierre Martin de.
D. L. P. pseud. see Poincy, Lonvilliers de.
D. M. pseud. see O'Heguerty, -------, Comte de Magnieres.
D. M. G. C. pseud. see C., D. M. G. pseud.
D..M. Q. C. S. pseud. see Quiros y Campo Sagrado Manuel de.
D. N. pseud. see N., D. pseud.
D. O'C. T. pseud. see Townley, Daniel O'Connell.
D. P. E. P. pseud. see Estala, Pedro.
D. Paredes, Victoriano de. see Paredes, Victoriano de D.
D. Philipp Fermin's Ausfuhrliche historisch-physikalische Beschreibung. (24115)
D. R. pseud. see R., D. pseud.
D. R. pseud. see Russell, Daniel.
D. R. D. P. pseud. see Des Roches de Parthenay, -------.
D. R. S. pseud. see S., D. R. pseud.
D. S. pseud. see Stevens, D. supposed tr.
D . . S . . B . . . . . d. pseud. see B . . . . . . d, D . . S . . pseud.
D. S . . . . de S . . . pseud see Sotomayor, Diego Sanchez de.
D. S. P. D. L. E. pseud. see E., D. S. P. D. L. pseud.
D. T. V. Y. pseud. see Avity, Pierre d', Sieur de Montmartin, 1573-1635.
D. V. pseud. see V., D. pseud.
D. V. A. E. P. pseud. see P., D. V. A. E. pseud.
D. W. pseud. see W., D. pseud.
D. Williams' letters from Mexico. 104188
D'A., Ad. 22923
Daa, Ludvig Kristensen. (18240)
Da Ahna, Charles H. 19013-19014
Da Apresentacao Campellos, Joao. see Campellos, Joao da Apresentacao.
Da Asti, Vittorio Alfieri. see Alfieri da Asti, Vittorio.

Dabadie, F. 18241-18242
D'Abbeville, Adrien Sanson. see Sanson d'Abbeville, Adrien, d. 1708.
D'Abbeville, Claude. see Abbeville, Claude d'.
D'Abbeville, Guillaume Sanson. see Sanson d'Abbeville, Guillaume, d. 1703.
D'Abbeville, Nicolas Sanson. see Sanson d'Abbeville, Nicolas, 1600-1667.
D'Abbeville, Nicolas Sanson. see Sanson d'Abbeville, Nicolas, 1626-1648.
Dabertzhofer, -------. ed. 30177
D'Abienza, ------. 25178
D'Ablancourt, Froncios Fremont. 99522
Dablon, Claude. 18243-(18247), 39998, 25853, note after 69259
Dablon, Claude. supposed author 12298, 1st note after 93480, 95332
Dabney, John Blair. 18248
Dabney, Jonathan P. 18249
Dabney, Richard. 18250-18251
Dabney, Robert L. 18252-18255
Da Boa Vista, Barao. see Boa Vista, Barao da.
Daboll, Nathan, 1750-1818. 15665, 15828, 53257, 62743, 83906, 91361
Daboll's system of arithmetic. note before 83906, 83906
Dabray, -------. 75540 see also France. Corps Legislatif. Conseil des Cinq-Cents. Commission des Colonies.
D'Abreu Medeiros, F. L. see Medeiros, F. L. d'Abreu.
Da Ca da Mosto, Alvise. see Ca da Mosto, Alvise, 1432?-1480?
Da Camara, Manoel Arruda. see Camara, Manoel Arruda da.
Da Carate, Augustin. see Zarate, Augustin de.
Da Cinha e Figueiredo, Jose Bento. see Cinha e Figueiredo, Jose Bento da.
Da Conceica, Jose M. see Conceicao, Jose Manoel da, 1714-1767.
Da Conceicao, Apollinario. see Apollinario da Conceicao.
Da Conceicao, Jose Manoel. see Conceicao, Jose Manoel da, 1714-1767.
Da Conceicao Velloso Xavier, Jose Marianno. see Velloso Xavier, Jose Marianno da Conceicao.
Da Costa, Agost. Robello. see Costa, Agost. Robello da.
Da Costa, Antonio. see Costa, Antonio da.
Da Costa, Antonio Juliao. see Costa, Antonio Juliao da.
Dacosta, Blas. see Acosta, Blas de.
Da Costa, Claudio Manoel. see Manoel da Costa, Claudio.
Da Costa, Enrique. see Koster, Henry.
Da Costa, H. Jose. see Costa, H. Jose da.
Da Costa, Joao Severjano Marciel. see Costa, Joao Severjano Marciel da.
Da Costa, Manoel. see Costa, Manoel da.
Da Costa, Maria. see Costa, Maria da.
Da Costa Almeida, Antonio Lopes. see Costa Almeida, Antonio Lopes da.
Da Costa do Para, Manoel. see Costa do Para, Manoel da.
Da Costa e Lima, Thomas da Encarnacao. see Costa e Lima, Thomas da Encarnaco da.
Da Costa Honorato, Manoel. see Honorato, Manoel da Costa.
Da Costa Mascarenhas, Ignacio Manoel. see Mascarenhas, Ignacio Manoel da Costa.
Da Costa Paiva, Antonio. see Costa Paiva, Antonio da.

Da Costa Pereira, Jose Saturnino. see Costa
Pereira, Jose Saturnino da.
Da Costa Pereira Furtado de Mendonca,
Hypolito Jose. see Costa Pereira
Furtado de Mendonca, Hypolito Jose da.
Da Costa Quintilla, Ignacio. see Quintilla,
Ignacio da Costa.
Da Costa Rubim, Braz. see Costa Rubim,
Braz da, 1817-
Dacotah queen. (21916)
Dacotah scourge. 72079
Da Cruz, Ag. see Cruz, Ag. da.
Da Cruz, Antonio Gonsalves. see Gonsalves
da Cruz, Antonio.
Da Cruz, Gaspar. see Cruz, Gaspar da.
Da Cruz, Gervasio Jose. see Cruz, Gervasio
Jose da.
D'Acugna, Christophe. see Acuna, Christoval
de.
Da Cunha, A. L. see Cunha, A. L. da.
Da Cunha Barbosa, Januario. see Cunha
Barbosa, Januario da.
Da Cunha de Azeredo Coutinho, Jose Joaquim.
see Cunha de Azeredo Coutinho, Jose
Joaquim da, Bp.
Da Cunha Mattos, Raimundo Jose. see Cunha
Mattos, Raimundo Jose da.
Da Cunho Paranagua, Joao Lustosa. see
Cunha Paranagua, Joao Lustosa da.
Da Cunha Reis, Manuel Basilio. see Cunha
Reis, Manuel Basilio da.
Da Cunhae Figueiredo, Jose Bento. see
Cunhae Figueiredo, Jose Bento da.
D'Adda, Gerolamo. see Adda, Gerolamo d'.
Daddow, Samuel Harries. 18257
Daden der zee-helden en ontdeckers van
landen. 18258
Dadmun, J. W. (18259)
Da Drus, Joanna Inger. see Drus, Joanna
Inger da.
Da Empoli, Gioanni. see Empoli, Gioanni da.
Da Encarnacao da Costa e Lima, Thomas.
see Costa e Lima, Thomas da Encarna-
cao da.
Da Fano, Guido Gianetti. see Fano, Guido
Gianetti da.
Da Fonseca, Joaquim Bento. see Fonseca,
Joaquim Bento da.
Da Fonseca, Manuel. see Fonseca, Manuel
da.
Da Fonseca, Yose Gonsalvez. see Fonseca,
Yose Gonsalvez da.
Da Fonseca Guimaraes, Joaquim. see
Guimaraes, Joaquim da Fonseca.
Dag-register, van de reyse die gedaen is door
's landts vloot. 65688
Dag-registers van het Noord-Amerikaansche
Congres. 23510, 55429
Da Gama, Antonio Pinto Chichorra. see
Gama, Antonio Pinto Chichorra da.
Da Gama, Jose Basilio. see Gama, Jose
Basilio da.
Da Gama, Jose da Saldanha. see Saldanha
da Gama, Jose da.
Da Gama, Jose Vicente. see Gama, Jose
Vicente da.
Da Gama, Manuel Jacinto Mogueira. see
Gama, Manuel Jacinto Mogueira da.
Da Gama, Nicolau Antonio Nogueira Valle.
see Gama, Nicolau Antonio Nogueira
Valle da.
Da Gama, Vasco. see Gama, Vasco da, 1469-
1524.
Da Gama Lobo, Ovidio. see Gama Lobo,
Ovidio da.

Dagboek eener expeditie van San Francisco
naar de gouddistricten. 8351, 1st note
after 99534, 1st note after 100641
Dagboek eener reize ter walvisch- en robben-
vangst gedaan in de jaren 1777 en 1778.
37111
Dagboek, gehouden op eene reize langs de
kusten von Chili. 29720
Dagboek van het Britsch ministerie. 18260,
59622, 104991
Dagbok ofwer sina falttig i Surinam. 91071
Dagg, J. L. 18261
Dagge, -------. 25595, 34579-34580, 96769,
99584, note just before 103108
Daggerwood, Sylvester. pseud. see Pangloss,
Peter. pseud.
Daggett, David, 1764-1851. (18262)
Daggett, David, 1764-1851. supposed author
5591, (15651), (15716), 15859, 15875,
note after 90846, note after 90848, 95742,
105939
Daggett, Herman. 18264
Daggett, John, 1805-1885. 18265-18266, 21643
Daggett, Naphtah. 18267-18268
Daggett, O. E. 18269
Daggs, Ruel. plaintiff 18270, 26127
Dagh-register, gehouden by seven matroosen.
78896-78897, 78899-78900
Dagh-register, over de reyse. 23578
Daghelijcx-register van de voyagie na Rio de
Plata. 31228, 57901
Dagnall, John M. 18271
Dagon. 82924
Dagonism exhibited. 104669
D'Agoult, -------, Comte. see Agoult, -----,
Comte d', fl. 1790.
Daguerreian journal. 18272
Daguerreotype of Washington, D. C. 92783
Daguerreotype sketches of the members of the
first Common Council. 61567
D'Aguilar, Jose Francisco. see Aguilar,
Jose Francisco d'.
Dagverhaal eener reize in de Vereenigde
Staaten van Noord-America. 58362
Dagverhaal der lotgevallen van Pichegru.
67626
Dagverhaal der ontdekkings-reis van Mr. Jacob
Roggeveen. 72767
Dagverhaal van eene reis naar Paramaribo.
7747, 93855
Dagverhaal van het verongelukken. 32376
Dagverhaal wegens den opstand. 18273
Dahcotah. 21685
Dahkotah land and Dahkotah life. 52281
Dahl, -------. lithographer 84774
Dahlerup, Hans Birch. 18274
Dahlgreen, C. G. 18275
Dahlgren, J. A. USN 18276-18277
Daigremont, ------. 94179
D'Aigremont, Jean de Laon, Sieur. see Laon,
Jean de, Sieur d'Aigremont.
Dailey, Charlotte F. 18279, 70694 see also
Rhode Island. Commissioner to visit
the Hospitals, 1863.
Dailey, David. ed. 84368
Dailey, J. P. 41187
D'Ailly, Pierre. see Ailly, Pierre d'.
Daily advertiser (Montreal) 103117
Daily Advertiser (New York) see New-York
morning post, and daily advertiser.
Daily advertiser (New York) News-carrier.
pseud. see News-carrier, of the Daily
advertiser. pseud.
Daily advertiser (Philadelphia) see Poulson's
daily advertiser.

Daily American advertiser. 106078
Daily American directory. 72340
Daily campaign record. (18280)
Daily chronicle and convention journal. 60032
Daily chronicle and sentinel. 85357
Daily chronicle of the principle events and history. 13404
Daily Cincinnati gazette. 97272
Daily counsellor. 80195
Daily countersign. 18281
Daily courier. see Portland daily courier.
Daily Democratic press. 70223
Daily eagle. see Brooklyn daily eagle.
Daily evening advertiser. 26811
Daily evening traveller (Boston) (19233), 87439, 93405
Daily gazetteer. 12163, 1st note after 99889
Daily globe (Washington, D. C.) 96362, 101069, 103490A
Daily hand, with truth and a heart in it. 7386
Daily herald. see San Francisco daily herald.
Daily journal of the 192 Regiment Pennsylvania Volunteers. 51632
Daily legislative record. 60033
Daily national intelligencer. (25054), note before 90497
Daily news (London) 92333
Daily news (Newport, R. I.) 93721
Daily northern islander. 92677, 92684, 92686-92687
Daily pocket journal for 1775. 38539
Daily post. 79008
Daily public school in the United Stats. 18282, 58106
Daily publication of the best current and standard literature. 85165
Daily record of the thermometer. 19365
Daily republican. 93219
Daily reveille. 84241
Daily Richmond examiner. 84943
Daily South Carolinian. 96799
Daily times. 92751
Daily transcript. see New York daily transcript.
Daily union vedette. 72134
Dainties and delicacies of different nations. 81148
Dainville, D. (18283)
Daire, E. 77361
Dairo, -------. 68455
D'Airvault, Marie Charles du Chilleau, Marquis. see Airvault, Marie Charles du Chilleau, Marquis d'.
Da Isola, Peter Coppo. see Coppo da Isola, Peter.
Daisy swain. 18271
D'Aix de la Chaise, Francois. see La Chaise, Francois d'Aix de.
Da Jesi, Giovanni Giorgini. see Giovanni Giorgini da Jesi.
Da Jose Maria Rugama, Laenciado. see Rugama, Laenciado da Jose Maria.
Dake, O. C. 18284
Dakin, ---------. illus. 54712, note before 99588
Dakin, Samuel D. defendant 102624, 104412
Dakin & Moody. firm 81532
Dakota (Territory) petitioners 26866
Dakota (Territory) Governor, 1866-1869 (Faulk) 18297 see also Faulk, Andrew Jackson, 1814-1898.
Dakota (Territory) Laws, statutes, etc. 18296, 26866
Dakota (Territory) Legislature. 18297, 26866
Dakota (Territory) Legislature. Council. 18294-18295

Dakota (Territory) Legislature. House. 18294-18295
Dakota A B C wowapi. 71324
Dakota A B C wowapi kin. (71325)
Dakota catechism. 71331
Dakota dowanssi kin. 18285, 69645
Dakota first reading book. 71326
Dokata friend. (18286)
Dokata lapi en. 57380
Dakota lessons. Book I. 18287, 71329
Dakota lessons. Bk. II. 18287, 71330
Dakota Mission, St. Paul, Minn. (18286)
Dakota odowan. 71327-71328
Dakota oyawa wowapi. 71326
Dakota primer for schools. 71345
Dakota tawaxitku kin. (18286)
Dakota tawoonspe. Wowapi I. 18287, 71329
Dakota tawoonspe. Wowapi II. 18287, 71330
Dakota war whoop. 43085
Dakota wiwangapi wowapi. (63994)
Dakota wiwicawangapi kin. 71331
Dakota wowapi wakan kin. 71332
Dalager, Lars. 18298
D'Alaux, Gustave. see Alaux, Gustave d', 1816-1885.
D'Albaredes Portal, Pierre-Barthelemy. see Portal, Pierre-Barthelemy d'Albaredes.
Dalcho, Frederick, 1770?-1836. (18229), (82033), 87837, 87845-87846, 4th note after 88114, 87928
Dale, James W. 18300
Dale, R. (18301)
Dale, Sir Thomas. 52287, 66686, 99866
Dale Cemetery, Claremont, N. Y. see Claremont, N. Y. Dale Cemetery.
Dale Cemetery, (at Claremont, near Sing-Sing.) 18302
Dalei, Bened. pseud. Amerika ohne Schminke. see Egenter, Franz Joseph.
D'Alembert, Alfred. see Almbert, Alfred d', 1813-1881.
Dalen, Corn. van. see Van Dalen, Corn. engr. and illus.
Daley, Dominic. defendant 18303
Dalhousie, George Ramsay, 9th Earl of, 1770-1838. (10336), 10410, 19456, 58489 see also Canada. Governor General, 1820-1828 (Dalhousie)
Dalhousie District, Canada. Building Society. see Building Society of the District of Dalhouse, Canada.
Dalhousie Lodge, Newton, Mass. see Freemasons. Massachusetts. Dalhousie Lodge, Newton.
Dalibard, Thomas F. ed. and tr. 98751
Da Lignano, Jacobo. see Lignano, Jacobo da.
Daling and Bulwer, William Henry Lytton Earle, Baron, 1801-1872. 89975 see also Great Britain. Legation. U. S.
Dall, C. H. (77233)
Dall, Caroline Wells (Healey) 1822-1912. 18304-18306, 18878, 90730
Dall, Charles Henry Appleton. 18307
Dall, William. 14373, (19437)
Dall, William Healey, 1845-1927. 18308, 85072
D'Allais, Denis Vairasse. see Vairasse d'Allais, Denis.
Dallam, James Wilmer, 1818-1847. 94993
Dallas, Mr. supposed author (9261)
Dallas, Alexander James, 1759-1817. 5679, 10883, 16621, 18309-18313, 18319, 23966, 60195, (60609), 93801, 96561 see also Pennsylvania. Secretary of the Commonwealth.
Dallas, Alexander James, 1759-1817. reporter 17303, 18313, (33241), 60471, note after 96854, 104631

Dallas, Angus. 18314
Dallas, Sir George. 18315, (58726)
Dallas, George Mifflin, 1792-1864. 18316-18320, 34735, 72211, 92851, 98425
Dallas, Sir Robert, 1756-1824. 18321
Dallas, Robert Charles, 1754-1824. 18322-18326
Dallas news. see Galveston-Dallas news.
Dallaway, James. 18327
Dalliba, James. (18328)-18329
Dallo y Zavala, M. R. 18330
Dalloz, -------. 18331
Dally, E. 18332
Dalmas, A. 18333
Dalmatie, Nicolas Jean du Dieu Soult, Duc de. see Soult, Nicolas Jean de Dieu, Duc de Dalmatie.
D'Almbert, Alfred. see Almbert, Alfred d', 1813-1887.
D'Almeida e Albuquerque, Francisco de Paula. see Almeida e Albuquerque, Francisco de Paula d'.
D'Almodovar, -------, Marquis. see Almodovar del Rio, Pedro Jiminez de Gongara y Lujan, Duque de, d. 1794.
Dal Rio, Ercole. see Rio, Ercole dal.
Dalrymple, Alexander, 1737-1808. 17020, 18334-18344
Dalrymple, Alexander, 1737-1808. supposed author (5198)
Dalrymple, Campbell. RA 18345, 81142
Dalrymple, E. A. ed. 103353
Dalrymple, John, 1720-1789. see Stair, John Dalrymple, 5th Earl of, 1720-1789.
Dalrymple, Sir John, Bart., 1726-1810. 5378, 18346-18348
Dalrymple, Sir John, Bart., 1726-1810. supposed author 400, 2761, 9266, 18347, 27144-27145, 27188, note after 41286, (62991), note after 71369
Dalrymple, Sir John, Bart., 1726-1810. incorrectly supposed author 18348, 25912, (62991), 90094, 90100 90102
Dalrymple, Samuel B. reporter (71820)
Dalthenus, Petrus, d. 1590. 64003, 66494
Dalton, Benjamin F. defendant 14045
Dalton, Charles H. 83856
Dalton, Edward B. 18349
Dalton, Henry G. (18350), 83640
Dalton, J. C. 76613, 76647
Dalton, James. 18351
Dalton, John. defendant 97443-97444
Dalton, Leonard Victor, 1887- 83640
Dalton, Thomas. ed. 98088
Dalton, William. 18352
Dalvarado, Pietro. see Alvarado, Pedro de.
Dalwig, J. C. 18353
Daly, -------, fl. 1879. 91866
Daly, Augustin, 1838-1899. 18354
Daly, Charles Patrick, 1816-1899. 18355-18358, 28452, 89223
Daly, John Augustin. see Daly, Augustin, 1838-1899.
Da Lylva y Aguiar, Lucas. see Lylva y Aguiar, Lucas de.
Dalziel, Edward, 1817-1905. illus. 8823, 10279, (41909), 41921
Dalziel, George, 1815-1902. illus. 8823, 10279
Dalziel, Thomas. illus. 8823, 10279
Dalzell, J. M. 18359
Dam, Rip van. see Van Dam, Rip.
Dam, W. van Irhoven van. see Irhoven van Dam, W. van.

Dam van Isselt, E. W. van. see Isselt, E. W. van Dam van.
Da Madre de Deus, Manual. see Madre de Deus, Manual da.
Da Mae dos Homens, Francisco. see Homens, Francisco da Mae dos.
Damariscotta Baptist Association. see Baptists. Maine. Damariscotta Baptist Association.
Damas, -------, fl. 1782. 66078
Damas, -------, fl. 1791. 75080
Damaschka, Wilhelm Fr. (18362)
Damaso, Juan San. see San Damaso, Juan.
Dambourges, Francois. 18363
Dames, Wilhelm. 2431
Damiani a Goes eqvitis Lvsitani aliqvot opvscvla. 27960
Dammartin, ------- Moreau de. see Moreau de Dammartin, -------.
Damon, David, 1787-1843. 18364, 105387
Damon, John W. 18365
Damon, Norwood. (18366)-18367
Damon, Samuel C. 18368-18369
Da Montalboddo, Fracanzano. see Fracanzano da Montalboddo.
Da Mosto, Alvise Ca. see Ca da Mosto, Alvise, 1432?-1480?
Da Motta, Vicente Pires. see Motta, Vicente Pires da.
Damotte, C. 18370
Damour, A. 18371
Dampier, Thomas, successively Bishop of Rochester, and Ely, 1748-1812. 18372
Dampier, William, 1652-1715. 18373-18390, 21211-21215, (26213), 29473, 31389, 38163, (54897), 68067, (72761), 78232, 100940, 100943-100944, 100947, 102513
Dampier's Leben und Reise um die Welt. 38239
Dampiers Reise um die Welt. 18390
Dampuille, -------, Duc de. 40691 see also New France. Governor General (Dampuille)
Damrell, -------. 6695-6697, 38548
Damrell, William Shapleigh, 1809-1860. (18391)
Damrell. firm publishers see Ford & Damrell. firm publishers
Damrell & Moore and George Coolidge. firm publishers 6695, 6697, 38548
Damsel of Darien. 81205
Dan (not Bev.) Tucker. pseud. see Tucker, Dan (not Bev.) pseud.
Dan Marble. 23722, 37315
Dan to Beersheba. (18392)
Dana, A. G. 18393
Dana, Amasa, 1792-1867. 18394-18395
Dana, Anderson. petitioner (70351)
Dana, C. W. 18398-18399, (26603)
Dana, Charles Anderson, 1819-1897. 18396-18397, 48674, 52439
Dana, Daniel, 1771-1859. 18400-18405, 18407, 70108
Dana, Daniel, 1771-1859. incorrectly supposed author 18405, (18433)
Dana, David D. 18406
Dana, E. 18407-18408
Dana, Eliza A. 18409
Dana, Francis, 1743-1811. (18411), 88969
Dana, Freeman T. 18412
Dana, J. G. reporter 18431, 79848
Dana, James, 1735-1812. 18413-(18419), 21930, 89736, 105940
Dana, James Dwight, 1813-1895. 1120, 7845, 18420-18427, 44505, 72412
Dana, James Freeman, 1793-1827. 18428

Dana, John Jay. 18429-18430
Dana, Joseph. 18405, (18432)-(18433)
Dana, Joseph. supposed author (18435),
   43376, 79285
Dana, M. M. G. 18436
Dana, Mary S. B. 18437
Dana, Richard Henry, 1787-1879. (18438)-
   18441, 63536, 79003
Dana, Richard Henry, 1815-1882. 18442-18450,
   65470, 89718, note after 97587
Dana, Richard Henry, 1815-1882. defendant
   39377
Dana, Samuel. 18451-(18453)
Dana, Samuel Luther, 1795-1868. 18428
Dana, Samuel Whittelsey, 1760-1830. (18454),
   105940
Dana, Samuel Whittelsey, 1760-1830. supposed
   author 89123
Dana, Stephen, W. 18455
Dana, William B. ed. (2781), (5291), 17109,
   11218-11219, 15624, 24483, 24648,
   (33852), 33853, 34907, 35806, 39345,
   39564, 47919-47920, (64500), 93270
Dana, William C. 18456, 85298
Dana, Mass. Superintending School Committee.
   18457
D'Anania, Gio. Lorenzo. see Anania, Gio
   Lorenzo d'.
Da Natividade Silva, Galdino Augusto. see
   Natividade Silva, Galdino Augusto da.
Danbury, Conn. Congregational Church.
   92111
Danbury, Conn. Congregational Church. Com-
   mittee. 92111
Danbury, Conn. Ecclesiastical Council, 1764.
   see Congregational Churches in Con-
   necticut. Ecclesiastical Council, Danbury,
   1764.
Danbury, Conn. First Church. Committee.
   23697, 99820, 103374
Danbury, Conn. First Society. see Danbury,
   Conn. First Church.
Danbury Baptist Association. see Baptists.
   Connecticut. Danbury Baptist Association.
Dancer, Thomas. 18459-18460
Dancing exploded. 30642
Dancing feather. 34776
Dancing poem, or satyr. 71139
Danckwardt, G. 92573
D'Ancone, Freduci. cartographer 76838
Dande, Jean. tr. 18538, 32008, 40562
Dandelion. 82508
D'Andilly, Arnavld. see Andilly, Arnavld d'.
Dandolo, C. T. 18464-18465
Dandolo, Tullio, Count. tr. (73273)
Dandolo, V. 2246
D'Andrada, Francisco Ladislau Alvares. see
   Andrada, Francisco Ladislau Lavares d'.
D'Andrada e Silva, Jose Bonifacio. see
   Andrada e Silva, Jose Bonifacio de.
D'Andrade, Alonzo. see Andrade, Alonzo de.
D'Andrade, Navarro. see Andrade, Navarro d'.
D'Andrade e Silva, Jose Maria. see Andrade
   e Silva, Jose Maria de.
Dandy, W. G. 18466
Dane, John. 18461
Dane, Nathan, 1752-1835. 18462, (79450)
Dane County, Wisc. 43749
Dane Baptist Association. see Baptists.
   Wisconsin. Dane Baptist Association.
Danemarks und Nordamierkas Streit uber den
   Sundzoll. 23972
Daney, ------ Sidney. see Sidney Daney,
   -------.

Danforth, John, 1660-1730. 17098, 18232,
   (18468)-18470, (19157), 22472, 22929,
   25404, (46340), (46631), 62743, 63597,
   65162, (81422), 95162, 95164, 104088
Danforth, Joshua N. 18471-18472
Danforth, Samuel, 1626-1674. 18473-18477,
   52646, 62743
Danforth, Samuel, 1666-1727. 18478-18479,
   22472, 22929, 37234, (46278), 46701,
   56229, (81422), 95162
Danforth, Thomas. 18480-18481
Danforth, Walter Raleigh. 18482-18483
Danger and duty of the church in the present
   crisis. (26098)
Danger and duty of young people. 73049
Danger and duty pointed out. 92089
Danger and home of the American people.
   89783
Danger of ambition considered. 105115
Danger of America delineated. (43157)
Danger of Arminian principles. 103400
Danger of an unconverted ministry. 94686
Danger of an unqualified ministry. 30170
Danger of apostasie. (14764)
Danger of being over wise. 77007, 89744
Danger of desertion. 32834-32835
Danger of electing an incompetent man as
   president. 26449
Danger of evil company. 89744
Danger of His Majesty's dock-yards. 8514
Danger of infidelity. 20059
Danger of mens taking up with a form of
   godliness. 104098
Danger of miscarrying in point of salvation.
   80189
Danger of misinterpreting and disregarding the
   lessons of calamity. 79490
Danger of neutrality. 24388
Danger of not reforming known evils. 104396
Danger of people's loosing the good impres-
   sions. (16631)
Danger of persecution considered. 94685
Danger of schisms and contentions. (20062)
Danger of speedy degeneracy. 91942, 91963
Danger of taking God's name in vain. 104077
Danger of the country. 8514
Danger of the theatre. 71172
Danger of throwing the election of president
   into Congress. 24274
Danger of tolerating levellers in a civill
   state. 104794
Dangerous and hurtful opinion maintained by
   Samuel Willard. (37179), 37189
Dangerous condition of the country. 18484,
   36263
Dangerous kerosene. 11854
Dangerous situation of England. 72150
Dangerous tendencies of civilization. 42149
Dangerous vice. 6927, 12986, 18485
Dangerous voyage and bold attempts of Captain
   Bartholomew Sharp, & others. (23479)
Dangerous voyage, and bold attempts of Capt.
   Sharp. 23483, 34586-23487, (23489)
Dangerous voyage of Capt. Thomas James, in
   attempting to discover. (17278)
Dangerous voyage of Capt. Thomas James,
   in his intended discovery. 37512
Dangers and defences of New York. 3478
Dangers and duties of the hour. 37272
Dangers and duties of the people. 74567
Dangers and duties of the present hour.
   (29839)
Dangers and duties of the present time. 33818
Dangers and duties. Reconstruction and
   suffrage. 36279, 36885

Dangers du commerce des esclaves Africains. 13483
Dangers d'habiter les bords du Scioto. 35512, 73511
Dangers of a business life. (23813)
Dangers of black-republicanism and the duty of the south. (26714)
Dangers of centralization. (34036)
Dangers of church centralization. 18486
Dangers of extending slavery. 79512
Dangers of Jesuit instruction. 64692
Dangers of our country. 18965
Dangers of our national prosperity. 101028
Dangers of the country. 18487, note before 91236, 91240
Dangers of the country, and the remedies proposed, &c. (64142)
Dangers of the deep. 18488
Dangers of the theatre. (18489)
Dangers of vice. 6927, 12985, 18485
Dangers which threaten the republic. 37739
Dangeul, R. B. Plumard de. see Plumard de Dangeul, R. B.
D'Anghiera, Pietro Martire. see Anghiere, Pietro Martire d', 1455-1526.
Daniel. pseud. Lucia. see Garcia, Eduarda.
Daniel, Charles, 1818-1893. 18490, 23098
Daniel, Charles Travis. defendant 9381
Daniel, Frederick S. (18493), 71205
Daniel, H. defendant 18491
Daniel, Henry, 1786-1873. 18496
Daniel, John Moncure, 1825-1865. (18493), 71205
Daniel, John Moncure, 1825-1865. incorrectly supposed author 18492, 2d note after 100578
Daniel, John Reeves Jones, 1802-1868. 18494
Daniel, Louis. 18495
Daniel, Peter Vivian, 1784-1860. 67818, 69402, 1st note after 99797, 105215
Daniel, Uncle. pseud. Traits of character. see Wrifford, Alison or Anson.
Daniel Boon and the hunters of Kentucky. (6127)
Daniel Boone the pioneer of Kentucky. 31819
Daniel catcher. 91182
Daniel Defoe; his life. 19276
Daniel Leeds, justly rebuked. 66736
Daniel North. 84087
Daniel North of Wyoming Valley. 84086
Daniel O'Connell on American slavery. 12200
Daniel O'Connell upon American slavery. 56652
Daniel O'Connel's [sic] legacy to Irish Americans. 35085, (56653)
Daniel Smith. 85088
Daniel Webster. A discourse. 72627
Daniel Webster, a rhymed eulogy. 41725
Daniel Webster and his contemporaries. 44484
Daniel Webster as a jurist. 58693
Daniel Webster. Eulogy on Daniel Webster. (18890)
Daniel Webster, sa vie et ses oeuvres. 37122
Daniel Webster—speech of Mr. Barnard. 3447
Daniel Webster's memorial. 52200, 84463, 93663
Daniell, W. C. 18497
Daniels, Arthur M. 80821, 86267
Daniels, Edward. 18498
Daniels, Joseph Leonard. 6147
Danielsz, Thomas. 18500
Danischen Quellschriften. 23099, (71434)
Danish African Company. see Deensche Africaensche Compagnie.

Danish Greenland. 71430
Danish inquisition under nine directors. 54468
Danish islands: are we bound in honor to pay for them? 58943
Danish laws. (18501)
Danish massacre. 82108
Danish missions to the East Indies. 18502
Da Nizza, Marco. see Nizza, Marco da.
Danjou, Jean Louis Felix, 1812-1866. ed. 24855, 40178
Dankers, Jaspar. 18503
Dannett, H. 18504
Danon, Pedro. 18505
Dansa dos ossos. 29237
Dansereau, Arthur. 18506
Dansk ugeskrift. 18724
Danske Vestindske oers tilstand i henseende til population, cultur og finance. 58042
K. Danske Videnskabernes Selskabs Skrifter. 40991
Danske West-Indiske og Guineiske Skibe. see West-Indiske og Guineiske Compagnie.
Danson, J. T. 18307
Dantas, Dionizio Rodriguez. (79219) see also Sergipe (Brazilian Province) 2.° Vice-Presidente (Dantas)
Dante Alighieri, 1265-1321. 24174, 92667
Dante de Rinaldi, Piervicentio. see Rinaldi, Piervicentio Dante de.
Danti, A. 18508
Danti, Egratio. 32683
Dantier, Alphonse. 18509
Dantine, Maur-Francois. 101348-101350
D'Anvers, Caleb. pseud. Short view. see Amhurst, Nicholas.
D'Anvers, Caleb, of Gray's-Inn, Esq. pseud. Some further remarks. see Amhurst, Nicholas. supposed author
D'Anvers, Caleb, of Gray's Inn Esq. pseud. Some remarks. see Amhurst, Nicholas. supposed author
Danvers, Sir John, 1588?-1655. 104336
Danvers, John Thierry. 18512
Danvers, Mass. (18518), 74308
Danvers, Mass. Centennial Celebration, 1852. 18513, (55190)
Danvers, Mass. Ecclesiastical Council, 1852. see Congregational Churches in Massachusetts. Ecclesiastical Council, Danvers, 1852.
Danvers, Mass. First Parish. Two Hundredth Anniversary Celebration, 1872. (70819)
Danvers, Mass. Peabody Institute. see Peabody Institute, Danvers, Mass.
Danvers, Mass. Reception and Dinner in Honor of George Peabody, 1856. 18517
Danvers, Mass. School Committee. 18519
Danvers: a poem. 18513, (55190)
Danvers discussion. (18515), 103797
D'Anville, J. B. Bourguignon. see Bourguignon d'Anville, J. B.
Danville, Ky. Centre College. 11688, 37507
Danville, Ky. School for the Deaf. see Kentucky. School for the Deaf, Danville.
Danville, Ky. Theological Seminary of the Presbyterian Church in the U. S. A. 18520-18521
Danville, Pa. State Hospital for the Insane. see Pennsylvania. State Hospital for the Insane, Danville.
Danville, Vt. Caledonia County Teachers' Institute. see Caledonia County Teachers' Institute, Danville, Vt.
Danville and Pottsville Rail Road Company. 60034

Danville and Pottsville Rail Road Company.
Acting Manager. 60034
Danville and Pottsville Rail Road Company.
Chief Engineer. 59967, 60034
Danville and Pottsville Rail Road Company.
Committee. 59967
Danville and Pottsville Rail Road Company.
Engineers. 59967
Danville and Pottsville Rail Road Company.
Managers. 59967
Danville and Pottsville Rail Road Company.
President. 59967
Danville and Pottsville Rail Road Company.
President. petitioner 60034
Danville and Pottsville Rail Road Company.
Superintendent. 60034
Danville, Hazleton & Wilkesbarre Railroad
Company. 60035
Danville quarterly review. 7665, (7675), 7679,
7682, 16404, 18521, (58346)
Danville review. see Danville quarterly re-
view.
Da Paranhos, Silva. see Silva Paranhos,
——da.
Daphnis and Menaleas. 104989
Da Piacenca, D. Carli. see Carli, Dionigio.
Da Ponte, Lorenzo. 64005-64014
Da Pordenone, Odorico. see Odorico da
Pordenone, 1286-1331.
Dapper, Olfert. (18523)-(18524), 50087, 1st
note after 97721
Dappervs exoticvs cvriosvs. (18523)
Da Purificacao, Joao Baptista. see Purifica-
cao, Joao Baptista da.
Daran, ------. 92539
D'Arango, D. A. J. see Arango, D. A. J. d'.
Daranzel; or, the Persian patriot. (23243)
D'Araujo Costa, S. O. see Araujo Costa,
S. O. d'.
Darazzo, Ippolito. supposed author 21418
D'Arbrisselle, J. B. see Arbrisselle, J. B. d'.
Darby, John, 1804-1877. 18525
Darby, John, fl. 1809. 87846, 87848
Darby, Joseph. 18526
Darby, William. (18527)-(18536)
Darcie, A. tr. 10158
D'Arcy, Uriah Derick. (18537)
D'Arcy Dunn. 6376
Darde, Jean. tr. 18538, 32008, 40562
Dardin, Amey. petitioner 18539
Dardis, George. 18540
Dardis, George. supposed author 51871
Dare, Charles P. 18541, 62051
Dare, Virginia. supposed author 30699
Dareste, ------. 67928
Da Resurreicao, Lourenco. see Resurreicao,
Lourenco da.
Darey, P. J. tr. 41810
Darg, John P. (18542)
Dargan, Edmund Strother, 1805-1879. 18543
D'Argensola, Bartolome Leonardo. see
Argensola, Bartolome Leonardo de.
Dargent, ----- Yan'. see Yan' Dargent,
------.
Dargestellt nach authentischen Quellen. (49135)
D'Argoult, Charlotte des Cossas (du Vivier-
Bourgogne) see Argoult, Charlotte des
Cossas (du Vivier-Bourgogne) d'.
D'Argoult, Robert. see Argoult, Robert d'.
D'Argy, ---------, Marquis de Gouy. see
Gouy d'Arsy, Louis Henri Marthe,
Marquis de, 1753-1794.
Da Ribeira de Sabrosa, ------, Baron. see
Ribeira de Sabrosa, ------, Baron da.
Darien Company. see Company of Scotland
Trading to Africa and the Indies.

Darien Indians. 17860
Darien papers. 18548
Darien song in commendation. 78216
Darinel, Pasteur des Amadis. pseud. Sphere
des deux mondes. see Boileau de
Bouillon, Gilles, 16th cent.
Darinel de Tirel. pseud. Sphere des deux
mondes. see Boileau de Bouillon,
Gilles, 16th cent.
Darinel de Tirel, -----. 18576
Daring and heroic deeds of American women.
63002
Daring and suffering. 63100
Daring deeds of American generals. 36001
Daring deeds of American heroes. 7489
Darinnen man sehen kan, wie gross die gantze
Welt? 79674
Dariste, A. J. (18577)-18579
Dark and terrible deeds of George Lathrop.
(39175)
Dark night, and the glorious morning. (21139)
Darkness at noon. 18580
D'Arlach, H. de T. see Arlach, H. de T. d'.
Darley, Felix Octavius Carr, 1822-1888. 15896,
16417, 16430, (16448), 16452, 16502,
(16510), (16528), 16533, 16539, 16559,
(18581)-18583, 20359, 20699, 20859, 26099,
(30969), 33297, 35162, 35165, 35187,
(35193), 35199, (35204), (37668), (41909),
50821, 52164, 57780, (58928), 71729,
79001, 80923, 81503, 81556, 84237,
84239-84240, 86589, 90500, 92751, 94822,
95542, 95543, 95563, 95662, 103101
Darling, Henry. (18584)-18586
Darling, Thomas. 13214, 13220, 18587, 105826-
105827 see also Yale University.
Tutors.
Darling, William Augustus, 1817-1895. 18588-
18590, (54549)
Darling, William Stewart. 18591-(18592)
Darlington, Isaac. 104196
Darlington, James. 19772, 49587
Darlington, L. Lacey. supposed author 84400
Darlington, William, 1782-1863. 14456, (18593)-
18600, 19772, (20167), 54929, 67461,
85094, 4th note after 96966
Darlington, William M. 47070, 82766
Darnall, Henry. 18601
D'Arnay, -------. tr. 72232
Darnell, Elias. 18602
Darnell, Henry Faulkner. (18603)-18604
Darnes, William P. defendant (18605)
Da Rocha, Jose Gomes. see Rocha, Jose
Gomes da.
Da Rocha Cabral, Jose Marcellino. see Rocha
Cabral, Jose Marcellino da.
Da Rocha Ferreira Lapa, Ludgero. see Lapa,
Ludgero da Rocha Ferreira.
Da Rocha Leao, Jose. see Leao, Jose Da
Rocha.
Da Rocha Loureiro, Joao Bernardo. see
Loureiro, Joao Bernardo da Rocha.
Da Rocha Vianna, Antonio. see Rocha Vianna,
Antonio da.
Da Roma, F. Raimondo. see Raimondo da
Roma, F.
Darondeau, ------. 63174
Darondeau, Benoit Henri, 1805-1869. 98298
Da Rosa, Joao Ferreira. see Rosa, Joao
Ferreira da.
Dar que van dando. 97042
Darrach, William, 1796-1865. 18606, 60311
Darragh, Cornelius, 1809-1854. 18607
Darragh, William. reporter 86045
Darrow, David. 18608, note after 97880, note
after 94924, note after 106196

Darsteller der Heiligen der letzten Tage.
82989
Darstellung der Burgerlichen Verhaltnisse in
den Freistaaten von Nordamerika. 58156
Darstellung der Geschichte des Freiheits-
kampfes im Spanischen und Portugiesis-
chen American. 38192
Darstellung der Grundsatze der republikanis-
chen Regierung. 51412
Darstellung der naturlichen, socialen und
Verkehrsverhaltnisse dieses Landes.
10375
Darstellung ihres Glaubens und ihrer Gegen-
wartigen socialen und plitischen
Verhaltnisse. 9519A
Darstellung meines Schicksals in Brasilien.
40993
Darstellung seiner wichtigsten Forschungen.
38049
Darstellung siener wichtigsten Forschungen
von J. Loewenberg. 41777
D'Arsy, Louis Henri Marthe, Marquis de
Gouy. see Gouy d'Arsy, Louis Henri
Marthe, Marquis de, 1753-1794.
Dart, John Sandford. 87415, 87419
Dart, Joseph, 1798?-1879. 9056, note after
95451
Dartmoor massacre. 100885-100888, 100890
Dartmoor prison. (1484), 65713
Dartmouth, Mass. Auditing Committee. 18611
Dartmouth, Mass. Two Hundredth Anniversary
Celebration, New Bedford, Mass., 1864.
18609-18610
Dartmouth. (82338)
Dartmouth Church, Hanover, N. H. see
Hanover, N. H. Dartmouth Church.
Dartmouth College. 18615-18617, 18620,
18625, 18632
Dartmouth College. Alumni. 18619, 18626-
18627
Dartmouth College. Alumni Association.
Dartmouth College. Charter. 18618, 18625
Dartmouth College. Class of 1842. 61233
Dartmouth College. Class of 1849. Perma-
nent Secretary. 90299 see also Stanley,
Clinton W.
Dartmouth College. Library. 18614
Dartmouth College. Member of the Junior
Class. pseud. Home in the west. see
Upham, Thomas Cogswell.
Dartmouth College. Phi Beta Kappa. see
Phi Beta Kappa. New Hampshire Alpha,
Dartmouth College.
Dartmouth College. President. 103219 see
also Wheelock, John.
Dartmouth College. Society of Social Friends.
18615, 96089
Dartmouth College. Society of Social Friends.
Library. 18614
Dartmouth College. Society of the Alumni.
see Dartmouth College. Alumni Associa-
tion.
Dartmouth College. Trustees. 18633, (21281),
(25775), 95535, 103220
Dartmouth College. Trustees. plaintiffs
18613, 18623, 18625, 23887, 31669,
102261
Dartmouth College. United Fraternity. (25888),
97875, 1st note after 97876
Dartmouth College. United Fraternity. Char-
ter. 97875
Dartmouth College. United Fraternity.
Library. 18614, 97876
Dartmouth College and the state of New Hamp-
shire. 52820

Dartmouth College case. 102261
Dartmouth College vs. Woodward. 18613,
18623, 18625
Dartnell, George. (18634)
Dartnell, George R. 18635
Darton, T. G. 18636
D'Arusmont, Frances (Wright) 1795-1852.
18637-18643, (25708), note after 99589-
99590, 105581-105586, 105588-105587-9
[sic], 105747
Darwell, John. (18644)
Darwin, --------. ed. (35016)
Darwin, Charles Robert, 1809-1882. 18645-
18650, 37826, 49654
Da S. Fiora, Paolo Mariani. see Fiora, Paolo
Mariani da S.
Das von den Russen in den Jahren 1765, 66, 67
entdekte nordliche Insel-Meer. 90064
Das von Jesu Christo dem Richter der Leben-
digen und der Todten. 80878
Da Saldanha da Gama, Jose. see Saldanha da
Gama, Jose da.
Da Santo Stephano, Hieronimo. see Santo
Stephano, Hieronimo da.
Das Chagas, Antonio. see Chagas, Antonio
das.
D'Ascoli, Cesso. see Cesso d'Ascoli.
Dascomb, A. B. 18651
Dash into Canada. 20325
Dashes of American humor. 59176
Dashiell, Alfred H. 18652
Dashiell, George. defendant 18653, 45372
Da Silva, ------ Vieira. see Vieira da Silva,
-------.
Da Silva, A. de Moraes. see Moraes da
Silva, A. de.
Da Silva, Antonio Joaquim. see Silva, Antonio
Joaquim da.
Da Silva, Antonio Jose Caetano. see Caetano
da Silva, Antonio Jose, 1817-1865.
Da Silva, Antonio Telles. see Silva, Antonio
Telles da.
Da Silva, Carlos Bento. see Silva, Carlos
Bento da, 1812-
Da Silva, Francisco Gomez. see Silva,
Francisco Gomez da, 1791-1852.
Da Silva, Henrique de Souza de Tavares. see
Souza de Tavares da Silva, Henrique de,
Conde de Miranda.
Da Silva, Innocencio Francisco. see Silva,
Innocencio Francisco da, 1810-
Da Silva, Joao Joaquim. see Silva, Joao
Joaquim da.
Da Silva, Joaquim Caetano. see Silva, Joaquim
Caetano da.
Da Silva, Jose de Seabra. see Silva, Jose de
Seabra da.
Da Silva, Jose Manuel Pereira. see Pereira
da Silva, Jose Manuel, 1819?-1898.
Da Silva, Luis Antonio Vieira. see Silva,
Luis Antonio Vieira da.
Da Silva, Manuel Alves. see Silva, Manuel
Alves da, 1793-
Da Silva, Miguel Antonio. see Silva, Miguel
Antonio da.
Da Silva, Silvestre Ferreira. see Ferreira
da Silva, Silvestre.
Da Silva Araujo e Amazonas, Lourenco. see
Silva Araujo e Amazonas, Lourenco da.
Da Silva Berford, Sebastiao Gomes. see Silva
Berford, Sebastiao Gomes da.
Da Silva Brandao, Luiz. see Silva Brandao,
Luiz da.
Da Silva Caminha e Menezes, Antonio Telles.
see Telles da Silva Caminha e Menezes,
Antonio, Marques de Resende, 1790-1875.

699

Da Silva Castro, Francisco. see Castro, Francisco da Silva.
Da Silva Costa, Jose. see Silva Costa, Jose da.
Da Silva e Sousa, Luis Antonio. see Silva e Sousa, Luis Antonio da.
Da Silva Guimaraes, Aprigio Justiniano. see Silva Guimaraes, Aprigio Justiniano da.
Da Silva Guimaraes, Joao Joaquim. see Silva Guimaraes, Joao Joaquim da.
Da Silva Lisboa, Balthazar. see Lisboa, Balthazar da Silva.
Da Silva Lisboa, Jose. see Lisboa, Jose da Silva.
Da Silva Maia, Jose Antonio. see Maia, Jose Antonio da Silva.
Da Silva Mello, Joaquim Guennes. see Silva Mello, Joaquim Guennes da.
Da Silva Netto, A. see Silva Netto, A. da.
Da Silva Paranhos, ------. see Silva Paranhos, ------ da.
Da Silva Pontes, Rodrigo de Souza. see Souza da Silva Pontes, Rodrigo de.
Da Silva Portilho, Joao Anastacio de Souza Pereira. see Souza Pereira da Silva Portilho, Joao Anastacio de.
Da Silva Porto, Manuel Joaquim. see Silva Porto, Manuel Joaquim da.
Da Silva Ramos, Joaquim Jose Pereira. see Pereira da Silva Ramos, Joaquim Jose, b. 1818.
Da Silva Torres e Alvim, Francisco Cordeiro. see Torres e Alvim, Francisco Cordeiro da Silva.
Da Silveira, Joaquim Lobo. see Silveira, Joaquim Lobo da.
Da Silveira, Manuel Joaquim. see Silveira, Manuel Joaquim da.
Da Silveira, Simao Estaco. see Silveira, Simao Estacio da.
Das Neves e Mello, Antonio Jose. see Neves e Mello, Antonio Jose das.
Da Soledade e Castro, Vicente. see Soledade e Castro, Vicente da.
Da Somma, Agazio. see Somma, Agazio da.
D'Assas, ------ Guillon. see Guillond'Assas, ------.
Dassie, C. R. 18654-18655
D'Atalaya, ------, Cardinal. see Atalaya, ------ d', Cardinal.
Date of Sudbury fight. (6977)
Dates of United States coins. 48819
Dati, Giuliano, Bp., 1445-1524. (14635)-14636, 18656-18657
Dati, Goro. 76838
Dati, Leonardo, d. 1425. 76838
Dati, Leonardo di Stagio. see Stagio Dati, Leonardo di.
D'Atienza, Giovanni. see Atienza, Juan d'.
D'Atienza, Juan. see Atienza, Juan d'.
D'Atondo, Isidore. see Atondo, Isidore d'.
Datos de los trabajos astronomicos y topographicos. 75598
Datos oficiales. 18659
Datos presentados. 12771
Datos para la geografia del imperio Mexicano. 62787
Daubeny, Charles Giles Bridle. (18660)-18662
D'Auberteuil, Michel Rene Hilliard. see Hilliard D'Auberteuil, Michel Rene, 1751-1789.
Daubigny. pseud. Washington. see Baudoin, Jean Marie Theodore.
D'Aubigny, Charles. 68431
D'Aubigny, Charles Francois, 1817-1878. 92536

D'Aubonneau, ------. see Aubonneau, ------ d'.
D'Auborn, A. 25882
D'Aubre, Paul. see Aubre, Paul d'.
D'Audebard, Andre E. J. P. J. F. see Ferussac, Andre E. J. P. J. F. d' Audebard, Baron de.
Daudet, Alexis. 18664
Da Udine, Odorico. see Odorico da Pordenone, 1286-1331.
Daughter. pseud. ed. 47048
Daughter. 83777
Daughter of America. pseud. Women invited to war. 104996
Daughter of Kentucky. pseud. Sunlight upon the landscape. 93772
Daughter of liberty and lover of truth. pseud. Poems, upon several sermons. see Dunlap, Jane.
Daughter of New-York. pseud. City's heart. 13160
Daughter of Pierre Augustin de Beaumarchais. 4175
Daughter's memorial to her mother. 83562
Daughters of Eve. 84137
Daughters of Temperance. Rhode Island. May Queen Union, no. 2, Natick. 51908
Daughters of the prairie. 18665
Daughters of Zion excelling. 82530
D'Augy, --------. see Augy, ------- d'.
Daul, A. 18666
Daum, J. M. 36226
Daumont, Alexandre. 18667
Daumy, Rafael Maria Mendive y. see Mendive y Daumy, Rafael Maria.
Daun, Joao Carlos de Saldanha Oliveira e. see Saldanha, Joao Carlos de Saldanha Oliveira e Daun, 1. Duque de, 1790-1876.
Daunce, Edward. 18668
Dauncey, John. 18669
Dauphin County, Pa. Court of Oyer and Terminer. 96889
Dauphin and Susquehanna Coal Company. 60036, (60844), (71931)
Dauphin and Susquehanna Coal Company. Stockholders. 18670
D'Auriac, Jules Berlioz. see Auriac, Jules Berlioz d', 1820-
Daurico, Maron. pseud. Cartas sobre la variacion. see Roca, Ramon de la.
Daus, Maun-Gwu-. see Maun-Gwu-Daus. Ojibway Indian Chief
D'Auteroche, Jean Chappe. see Chappe d'Auteroche, Jean.
D'Autun, Honore. 76838
Dauxion-Lavaysse, J. J. 18672-18675, note after 39286
Dauxion Lavaysse, Francois. see Lavaysse, Francois Dauxion.
Dauzats, A. 5832, 79139
D'Aval, Charles Yvres Cousin. see Cousin d'Aval, Charles Yvres, called Cousin d'Avalon.
D'Avalon, Cousin. see Cousin d'Aval, Charles Yvres, called Cousin d'Avalon.
Davalos, ------. (18676)
Davalos, A. de Lavastida y. see Lavastida y Davalos, A. de.
D'Avalos, F. A. Christophoro. see Christophoro d'Avalos, Felice Antonio de.
Davalos, Juan Bento Diaz de Gammara y. see Diaz de Gammara y Davalos, Juan bento, 1745-1783.
Davalos, J. E. Hernandez y. see Hernandez y Davalos, J. E.

Davalos, Pelagio Antonio de Labastida y. see Labastida y Davalos, Pelagio Antonio de, Abp., 1816-1891.

Davalos Bracamonte y Espinosa, Pedro Alonso, Conde de Miravalle. plaintiff 98609

Davalos Bracamont y Orozco, Maria Catharina, Condesa de Miraville. plaintiff 98610

D'Avalos y Figueroa, Diego. see Avalos y Figueroa, Diego d'.

Davatz, Thomas. 18677

D'Avaugour, --------, Comte du Parc. see Du Parc d'Avaugour, ------, Comte.

D'Avaux, ------. see Avaux, ----- d'.

Davega, Isaac. 18687

Da Veiga, Evaristo Ferreira. see Ferreira da Veiga, Evaristo.

Da Veiga, Manuel Luis. see Veiga, Manuel Luis da.

Daveis, Charles Stewart. (17682), 20474-20475, (43938), 55708

Daveis, Charles Stuart. supposed author (18679)-(18682), 29649, 55713, note after 97923, note after 100780

Daveiss, Joseph Hamilton. (18683)-(18684)

Davenant, Charles, 1656-1714. 18685-18688, (22976), 69395, 78984

Davenant, Sir William, 1606-1668. 18689-18690

Davenport, A. Benedict. 18691

Davenport, Bishop. 18692-18695

Davenport, D. 18696, 20627, 2d note after 79628

Davenport, Ebenezer. 18697

Davenport, James, 1716-1757. 14496, 18699, 18701, (18716), 104369

Davenport, James J. 53284 see also New Mexico (Territory) Supreme Court. Chief Justice.

Davenport, James R. 18702

Davenport, John, 1597-1670. 17058, (18703)-(18711), 41005, 46776, (46778), 52959, 52964, 55881, 55885, 65369, 66059, 78511-78514

Davenport, John. 18712

Davenport, John J. incorrectly supposed author 18713, 64454

Davenport, John L. 18714

Davenport, John S. (18715)

Davenport, Matthew. (18716)

Davenport, R. supposed author (71346)

Davenport, R. A. 78300

Davenport, Rugus. 18717-18718

Davenport, Thomas. 18719

Davenport & Co. firm see Sampson, Davenport & Co. firm publishers

Davenport, Iowa. Citizens. petitioners 51925

Davenport, Iowa. City Treasurer. 18721

Davenport, Iowa. Griswold College. see Griswold College, Davenport, Iowa.

Davenport, Iowa. Iowa College. see Iowa College, Davenport, Iowa.

Davenport, Iowa. Mayor, 1857. 18721

Davenport, Iowa. Soldiers' Orphans Home. see Iowa Soldiers' Orphans Home, Davenport.

Davenport Brothers, the world renowned spiritual mediums. (18720)

Davenport city directory and advertiser. 89394

Davenport city directory for 1868-9. 18723

Davenport city directory for 1866. 18722

Da Verrazzano, Giovanni. see Verrazzano, Giovanni da, 1485?-1527.

D'Avezac-Macaya, Armand. see Avezac-Macaya, Armand d', 1800-1875.

David, Chr. Georg. Nath. 18724

David, E. W. ed. (60342)

David, Felicien. 48037

David, J. C. 18725

David Cusick's sketches. 18142

David de Parra y Beredenoton. pseud. see Vera y Pintado, Bernardo.

David de Parra y Berdenoton al defensor de tontos. 98909

David Hall, at the new printing-office. 29746

David Hunt, and Malina Gray. 91280

David L. Seymour. 79642

David M. Jones, Harry O'Neill, James Newell. 85173

David M. Reese, M. D. "used up." 73942

David serving his generation, or a discourse. 2079

David serving his generation. Or, a sermon. (46649)

David West's catalogue of books. 102718

David Woodburn, the mountain missionary. (7400)

Da Vide, Sebastiao Monteiro. see Monteiro da Vide, Sebastiao.

Davidge, B. 3112

Davidge, F. H. 18726

Davids danckbaer heyt voor Gods vveldadicheyt. 94580

David's dying charge to the rulers and people of Israel. 14473

David's lamentation over Saul and Jonathan. 64316

Davids elegy. 66431, (66433)-(66434), (66436), (66440), (66442)

Davidson, A. B. 100564

Davidson, G. M. see Davison, Gideon Miner, 1791?-1869.

Davidson, George. 18727

Davidson, H. M. 18730

Davidson, Henry. 18729

Davidson, J. 18731

Davidson, James Ward. 18732

Davidson, John. 18733

Davidson, Lucretia Maria. 18734

Davidson, Margaret (Miller) 1787-1844. 18734-18735

Davidson, Robert, 1750-1812. 18736-18738

Davidson, Robert, 1808-1876. (18739)-18745, 92027, 94159

Davidson, William. 3966, note after 104356

Davidts, L. 79147

Davie, John Constanse. 18746-18747

Davie, William Richardson, 1759-1820. (18748) see also North Carolina. Governor, 1798-1799 (Davie)

Davies, Benjamin. 18749-(18750)

Davies, Benjamin. supposed author 14018, note after 95866

Davies, Charles, 1798-1876. 14806, 18751

Davies, Charles S. (18682), 44013 see also Maine. Agent to Inquire into and Report upon Certain Facts Relating to Aggressions upon the Rights of the Statee, and of Individual Citizens Thereof, by Inhabitants of the Province of New-Brunswick.

Davies, Ebenezer. 18752

Davies, George E. 83828

Davies, Henry E. 18753-18754, 39852

Davies, John, fl. 1665. tr. 18755, 72322

Davies, John, fl. 1825. 18755

Davies, Samuel, 1724-1761. 18757-18770, 24432, 27291, 94691, 100579, 102483

Davies, Samuel, 1724-1761. petitioner 94708

Davies, T. 18773

Davies, William, fl. 1614. (18774), 66686

Davies, William, fl. 1779. 15323, 18775, 69750 see also U.S. Commissioners for Settling a Cartel for the Exchange of Prisoners with Great Britain, 1779.
Daviess, Samuel. defendant 18776
D'Avignon, -------. engr. 26415, (40221)
Davila, -------, fl. 1812. (56729)
Davila, Beatriz Gomes. (42681)
Davila, Diego Quint Fernandez. see Quint Fernandez Davila, Diego.
Davila, Fernando. ed. 61074
Davila, Gil Gonzalez. 18777, 75588
Davila, Julian Gutierrez. 18778-18779
Davila, Manuel Ruiz. see Ruiz Davila, Manuel.
Davila, Quint Fernandez. see Quint Fernandez Davila, Diego.
Davila, Rafael. 18784-18785, 98933
Davila, Rafael. petitioner 69987
Davila, Salvador. 18786
Davila Falcon, Joseph. see Falcon, Joseph Davila.
Davila Morales. J. Antonio. see Morales, J. Antonio Davila.
Davila Padilla, Augustin. 18780-18781
Davila Urrutia y Arana, Juan Antonio Guerrero y. see Guerrero y Davila Urrutia y Arana, Juan Antonio.
David, Diego. tr. (40705)
Davin, F. 18787
Davis, -------, fl. 1830. 27567
Davis, -------, fl. 1851. USA 90671
Davis, -------, fl. 1866. engr. 54071, 96372
Davis, A. (18789)
Davis, A. C. 18797
Davis, Abigail L. 18788
Davis, Andrew Jackson. 18790-18791
Davis, Andrew McFarland. ed. 6711, 9449, 14536, 14538, 21088, 25770, (40332), 42824, 52622, 79377, 86618, 86630, 86716, 96426, 98355, 4th-5th notes after 98549, 1st note after 99800, 103900, 103902, note after 103907, 104536, 104899, 104902, 105085, note after 105456, note after 105459
Davis, Anthony. 102872
Davis, Ashel. 18792-(18795), 54316
Davis, Alex. S. 18796
Davis, C. G. defendant (18802), 1st note after 96812
Davis, Charles Augustus, 1795-1867. 18798-18800, (61178), 84147-84148, 84150, 84155, 84162-84177
Davis, Charles G. defendant 18801
Davis, Charles G. reporter (18802)
Davis, Charles Henry, 1807-1877. (2588), 6723, 12081, 18803-18807, 85072, 87396
Davis, Charles Henry Stanley, 1840-1917. 18808, 18907
Davis, Daniel. 18809-18810
Davis, David. 18811
Davis, E. S. ed. 84821
Davis, Edward, fl. 1683-1702. 100940
Davis, Edwin Hamilton, 1811-1888. 19648, 47813, 70307, 85016, 85072, 89953-89955
Davis, Emerson. 18812-18814, 30130 see also Committee of Pastors in Hamden County, Mass.
Davis, Eugene. reporter 18815, 27020
Davis, Franklin Carsley. 18816
Davis, G. C. 85361
Davis, Garrett, 1801-1872. 18817-18818
Davis, George, fl. 1808. 18819
Davis, George, 1820-1866. 50381

Davis, George, fl. 1856. 18820
Davis, George Lynn Lachlan. (18821), (45211A)
Davis, George R. 18822
Davis, George T. M. 18824
Davis, George Thomas, 1810-1871. 18823, 90870
Davis, Henry. 18825-18826, 89736
Davis, Henry Winter. 18827-18833
Davis, Isaac, 1799-1883. 18835, 41258
Davis, Isaac, fl. 1806. 18834
Davis, Isaac P. petitioner 6748, 69912
Davis, Isaac P. petitioner 69912
Davis, J. A. G. 100538
Davis, J. B. 18855
Davis, J. C. 18856
Davis, J. C. Bancroft. 90668
Davis, J. Lucius. 18857
Davis, James. 62743
Davis, James, Jr. 86807-86808
Davis, Jefferson, Pres. Confederate States, 1808-1889. (4704), 12522, 13621, 15274, 15289-(15318), 15422, 18836-18837, 26126, (27453), 46962, 58700, 65915, 66108, 68322, 69900, 69946 see also Confederate States of America. President. U.S. War Department.
Davis, John. alias. see Joyce, John. defendant
Davis, John. frontiersman 34461
Davis, John, 1550?-1605. see Davys, John, 1550?-1605.
Davis, John, 1761-1847. 51016, 93808, 96929, 101803
Davis, John, 1774-1854. 4965, (18847)-18853, 64472, 82860, note after 96496, 100438, 100467, 101204, 101236
Davis, John, 1787-1854. 297, 5700, 8862, (18844)-18846, 23237, 26126, 29655, 45572, 45920, 45993, 65915, 72483, 90668, note after 105386 see also Massachusetts. Agent for the Prosecution of the Claim Upon the United States, for Militia Services During The Last War, 1841. Massachusetts. Governor, 1834-1835. (Davis) Massachusetts. Governor, 1841-1843 (Davis)
Davis, John, fl. 1851-1852. tr. 83146, 83231, 83278
Davis, John C. 18856, 81870
Davis, John C. B. 18854
Davis, John W. 96678 see also U.S. Commissioners to the Potawatomi Tribe of Indians of the Prairie.
Davis, John W. petitioner 3042
Davis, Jonathan, fl. 1740. 18858
Davis, Jonathan, fl. 1812. 105425 see also Democratic Party. Massachusetts. Worcester County. Convention, Worcester, 1812. President.
Davis, Jonathan, fl. 1841. 13783
Davis, Josiah G. 18859
Davis, Joshua. (18860)
Davis, L. D. 18861
Davis, Matthew Livingston, 1773-1850. (9424), 18862-(18865), 18867-18868, 1st note after 96891, note after 98531
Davis, Matthew Livingston, 1773-1850. supposed author 98531
Davis, Matthew Livingston, 1773-1850. incorrectly supposed author 18866, 98532
Davis, Matthew Livingston, 1773-1850. defendant 3392, 89217-89219, note after 96820, note after 98992
Davis, Mary Elizabeth (Moragne) b. 1815. 50487

Davis, Nathan Smith, 1817-1904. 18871-18872
Davis, Nathaniel W. 18869
Davis, Noah, b. 1804 or 5. 18870
Davis, Noah, 1817-1902. 9477
Davis, Pardon. 18873
Davis, Paris M. 18874-18876
Davis, Phebe B. 18877-18878
Davis, Polly. (18879), 105488
Davis, R. D. 18882
Davis, Rebecca Harding. 44531
Davis, Richard Bingham. 18880
Davis, Robert. 18881
Davis, Samuel, fl. 1781. 25232, 73562, 102947
  see also West Stafford, Conn. Second
  Church. Committee.
Davis, Samuel, fl. 1806. 30510
Davis, Sheldon. 18883
Davis, Solomon. 18884-18885
Davis, Stephen. 18886
Davis, Mrs. Tamar. 18887
Davis, Thomas, 1806-1895. 3694, 8524, 18889,
  note after 89213
Davis, Thomas Treadwell, 1810-1872. (18890)-
  18892, (80907)
Davis, Timothy, fl. 1776-1784. supposed
  author (40279), 94170, 95686
Davis, Timothy, 1821-1888. 18894
Davis, W. A. (20299)
Davis, W. B. (18896)
Davis, W. P. (18899)
Davis, W. W. H. 18900-18905
Davis, Wendell. 18895, (25762)
Davis, William. bibliographer 36391
Davis, William, 1663-1745. 37218
Davis, William, fl. 1821. 95432
Davis, William A. 39425
Davis, William Jackson, 1818-1864. 18941,
  (69567)
Davis, William Morris, 1815-1891. 18897-
  (18898)
Davis, William Watts Hart, 1820-1910. 18905
  see also New Mexico (Territory)
  Governor, 1855-1861 (Davis)
Davis, Woodbury. 18906
Davis and Lee. 11691, (74889)
Davis family record. 18907
Davison, Darias. 18908
Davis, David. tr. 77656
Davison, Gideon Miner, 1791?-1869. 6899,
  18728, 18909, 18910, (23903), (73502),
  76915, 96336, 96487
Davison. firm publisher note after 99131
Davison and Burt. firm publishers see Fay,
  Davison and Burt. firm publishers
Davis's expedition to the golden mines. 18373
D'avitium, Petrum. see Avity, Pierre d',
  Sieur de Montmartin, 1573-1635.
D'Avity, Pierre. see Avity, Pierre d', Sieur
  de Montmartin, 1573-1635.
D'Avrainville, Arthur, see Avrainville,
  Arthur d'.
D'Avrigny, C. J. Loeuillard. see Avrigny,
  C. J. Loeuillard d'.
Davy, Charles William. (18914)
Davy, John, 1790-1868. (5737), 18915
Davy Crockett beaten. 17575
Davy Crockett; or the Nimrod of the west.
  17574
Davy Crockett's almanack, 1845. (17576)
Davy Crockett's 18 almanack. (17576)
Davys, John, 1550?-1605. 18842-(18843),
  66686, (74131)
Dawe, W. plaintiff 30001
Dawes, -------, fl. 1861. 27623
Dawes, Ebenezer. 18917

Dawes, Edward. 61606
Dawes, Henry Laurens, 1816-1903. 18918
Dawes, Matthew. 18919, 40444
Dawes, Rufus. 18920
Dawes, Rufus. supposed author 85358
Dawes, Thomas, 1757-1825. (6737), 18921-
  18924, 2d note after 106134
Dawes, Thomas, fl. 1850. 18924
Dawes, Sir William, Bart., Abp. of York, 1671-
  1724. 18925
Dawkins, Henry. supposed author 22109, 61613
Dawley, T. R. 18926
Dawn of liberty. 87129
Dawn of the millenium 16394
Dawn of the morning. (58103)
Dawnings of music in Kentucky. 31245
Dawnings of the Gospel day. 33360
Daw's doings. (18916), 20651, 70574
Dawson, Aeneas McDonell. 18927
Dawson, C. C. 18928
Dawson, Eli. 18929
Dawson, Henry Barton, 1821-1889. (17743),
  18930-18944, 20948-(20949), (23991),
  28582, (32066), 33217, 35841, 35844,
  note just before 68379, (69567), 74433,
  83423, note after 90644, 1st note after
  98997
Dawson, J. L. 12034, (18947)
Dawson, J. W. 55981
Dawson, John B. 18945
Dawson, John Littleton, 1813-1870. 18946,
  89203
Dawson, John Williams. 18948-18955
Dawson, Mary. plaintiff 2d note after 97056
Dawson, Moses. 18956-18957
Dawson, Reuben. 81792
Dawson, Simon James. 18958, 74298-74299
Dawson, T. M. 18959, 84414
Dawson, William, 1705?-1752. 63621, 104691
Dawson, William Crosby, 1798-1856. 18960,
  27030
Dawson, William McD. 18961
Dawson, William Wirt, 1828-1893. 50468
Dawson's "Foederalist" letter from Mr. Jay.
  35841
Dawydow, -------. 13036
Day, -------, fl. 1641. 50231
Day, Bertha C. illus. 83560
Day, Mrs. C. M. 18963
Day, Charles D. 18962
Day, Charles William. 18964
Day, Mrs. F. H. ed. 31614
Day, George E. 18965-18967
Day, George T. 3694, 8524, note after 89213
Day, Henry Noble, 1808-1890. 47496
Day, Horace H., 1813-1878. 18968
Day, Jeremiah, 1773-1867. 18969, 105787,
  105796, 105800, 105805-105806, 105842
  see also Yale University. President.
Day, Jeremiah, 1773-1867. petitioner 105797-
  105798 see also Yale University.
  President and Fellows. petitioners
Day, Jeremiah Osborn. 89736
Day, John. 82936 see also Connecticut.
  Secretary of State.
Day, L. Madison. 18970-18971
Day, Martha. 18972
Day, Mary L. 18973
Day, Pliny Butts. 18974-18976
Day, S. Sherwood. (62905)
Day, Samuel Phillips. 18977-18978
Day, Sherman. 18979
Day, Thomas, 1748-1789. (18980)-18987
Day, Thomas, 1777-1855. 18988-18991, 96033,
  105844

Day, Thomas, 1777-1855. supposed author 93478, 105785B
Day, Timothy Crane, 1819-1869. (18992)-(18993)
Day, William. 18994
Day (John) and Co. firm 61523
Day and night in 'Dixie.' (66796)
Day and the war. 4468
Day, & the work of the day. 46277
Day at hand. 72426
Day-breaking, if not the sun-rising of the Gospel with the Indians in New-England. 22146-22147, 74696, 80207-80208, note before 92797, 101330, note after 104653
Day in the New York Crystal Palace. 70972
Day of a Godly man's death. (25387)
Day of all saints at New Orleans. 66611
Day of darkness. 12366
Day of doom. 19034-(19035), 103913-103924, 103928
Day of jubilee. 83975
Day of national mourning for Abraham Lincoln. 78938
Day of roads. 9549
Day of small things. A centennial discourse. 843
Day of small things. A sermon. 92245
Day of trial. 88045B
Day of trouble is near. 46650
Day of trouble near. 27960, 30153, note after 95748
Day-star of American freedom. (18821)
Day! The hour, and the man! 52480
Day which the Lord hath made. 18478, (46278)
Dayman, -------. 61065
Daymon, F. tr. 68911
Dayrell, John. 18996, 1st note after 96741
Days and nights in the Shenandoah. 16316
Days and nights of moose-hunting. 30350
Day's bank note list and counterfeit detector. 18995
"Days of adversity." 6953
Days of Columbus. 16478
Days of old; a centennial discourse. 31326
Days of old: or the battle of Hexam. (18997)
Days of Shoddy. 50630
Days of Sixty-three. 18998
Days of Yore. 87812
Day's sport. 91294
Days that are past. 80284
Dayton, Aaron Ogden. (18999)-(19000), 96771
Dayton, Jonathan, 1760-1824. 5906, 19001, 74878
Dayton, William C. 19002
Dayton, William Lewis, 1807-1864. 19003-19004
Dayton, Ohio. Democratic State Convention, 1862. see Democratic Party. Ohio. Convention, Dayton, 1862.
Dayton and Cincinnati (Short Line) Railroad. 19006
Dayton and Michigan Railroad Company. (19007)
Dayton and Western Railroad Company. 19008
Dayton directory and business advertiser. 56711
Dayton directory, city guide, and business mirror. 19005
Dayton Rede des Achtbaren John Brough. 8402
Dayton speech of Hon. John Brough. 8400, 52034
Daza, Diego de Arroyo y. see Arroyo y Daza, Diego de.
D'Azambuja, Jose Bonifacio Nascentes. see Nascentes d'Azambuja, Jose Bonifacio.

D'Azevedo, Joao Ignacio. see Azevedo, Joao Ignacio d'.
Dazille, Jean Barthelemy, 1732 or 3-1812. 19009, 56477
De academiis litteratisqve viris Hispaniae Apologetica narratio. 77902
De aere, aquis, & locis. 7588, 63028
De aeribus, aquis & locis in Brasilia. 3409
De Aethiopibus etiam nonnulla. 6118, 94273
De allagro. 99365
De Amazonibus dissertatio. 61256
De ambiguo Indiae nomine. (8784)
De America. 62588
De America, oratuncula in promotione XXXV. magistrorum anno 1602 habita. 62917
De America priscis cognita. 96782
De Amerigo Vespvcci lettera II. 67730
De Antichristo, libri XI. 44176
De antipodibus. (48687)
De Arabia. 99365
De arte hierogliphum Mexicanorum. 80816
De arte volvntatis libri sex. 55267
De arundine saccharifera. 3409
De auisos prudenciales. 105742
De belli Romani socialis caussis et eventu. 31665
De bello et eventvvm raritate et adparatvm magnificentia nobilissimo. 72023
De bibliotheca eguiarae. 22060
De caffe, chocolatae, herbae thee ac nicotianae natura. 47414
De campain breefa fum Pit Schwefflebrenner und de Brervy, si Alty. 67967
De Chilensium lingua. 7588, 63028
De clarissimo quodam globo Ioannis Schonter. 77804
De coctione ciborum in ventriculo. note after 74241
De colica apud incolas Caribienses endemia. 83473, 83648
De colonia nova Svecia in Americam Borealem deducta historiola. 1941
De confessionibus scrupulosorum brevis tractatus. 75763
De convenientia militaris disciplinae com Christiana religione. (79178)
De convenientia disciplinae militaris com Christiana religione dialogus. 79180
De conversione Indorum & gentilium. 32886
De Cortes valeroso, y Mexicana. 39139
De cortice Peruviano. 30623
De cosmographia disciplina et signorum coelestium vera configuratione. (64523)
De cosmographiae rudimentis duplici editione. 65940-65941
De cosmographiae rudimentis libri duo. 20210
De costumi degli Orinochesi. 27382
De Cultuur van suikerreit. 70455
De decem nationibus Christianorum. 99366
De decouvertes aux terres Australe. 25917
De Deo carmina ad usum scholarum Congregationis S. Philipi Nerii. (51559)
De dictis factilis. 26140
De dictis et factis Alphonse regis Aragonum et Neapolis. 58428
De dimensione terrae. 61311
De dimensione terrae et geometrice. (61312)
De distribution geographica plantarum. 33710
De diva copacavana in Peruano. 44459
De diva virgine. 44675
De diversarum gentium sectis et mundi religionibus. 90127
De dominio maris libri duo. (78971)-(78973)
De effectu detectae Americae in Europam. 93987
De el Sr. Cevallos. 48817

De Europa sub Frederico III. 77523
De examine symboli politici ac militaris plus ultra. 61109
De exortu Maomethis. 62023
De expugnatione regni Granatae. 72023
De extremo Dei judicio et Indorum vocatione. 42675
De facultatibus simplicium. 7588, 63028
De febre biliosa. 104649
De febre flava Indiae Occidentalis. 44637
De fidei Christianae. 70784
De Genea. 99365
De generibus uentorum. 41067
De geographia liber unus. (27536)-27546
De gli habiti dell'America. 98732
De globi terrestris vsv. 77805
De glorieuse martelie. 94576
De gvaiaci medicina et morbo gallico liber vnus. 34095
De Guatemala a Rabinal. 7428
De herba panacea. 23218, 95622
De Hispanicae monarchiae amplitudine oratio. 16714
De i commentarii del viaggio in Persia. 106317
De i commentarii del viaggio in Persia, et delle gverre Persiane. (67737)
De i viaggi di Messer Marco Polo. 67736
De iis, quae ad tollendum servorum Afrorum commercium. 52387
De imagine Guadalupensi Mexicana. 43756
De immacvlata deiparae conceptione. 72289
De immaculate Virginis Mariae conceptioni certitudine. 9873
De imperio militantis ecclesiae libri quattuor. 35264
De imperio Romano liber. 2383
De India ejusque gloriosa huventute sermones. (31955)
De Indiae utriusque re naturali et medicia libri qvatvordecim. (63029)
De Indiarum jvre. 86525-86529, 86534, 86545
De Indis convertendis. (34105)
De Indis et de iure belli relectiones. 100621
De Indis insulanis relactio prior. 100618
De Indis, sive de iure belli Hispanorum. 100618
De insulis. 16948-16949
De insulis apud Americanum. 62588
De insulis epistola Cristoferi Colom. 14629, 98923
De insulis in India. 25083
De insulis Indie supra gangem nuper inuetis. 14628, (14630)-14631, 14633
De insulis inuentis epistola Cristoferi Colom. 14629, 98923
De insulis maris oceani in India. 60934
De insulis meridiani atque indici maris nuper inventis. 94095-94096
De i[n]sulis meridiani atq[ue] i[n]dici maris sub suspicijs inuictis. 94095
De insulis nuper in maro Indico repertis. 98923
De insulis nuper inventis. 62588
De insulis nuper inuentis epistola Christoferi Colom. 14623, 32005, 77901, 98923
De insvlis nvper inventis Ferdinandi Cortensii. 16949
De insulis nuper repertis. (34105)
De inventione mundi novi. 60934
De ipecacuanha Americana. 78010
De judaico isto conatu. 89546
De ivre adhaerendi alterivs appellationis. 93315
De iure, et officiis dominorum in servos. 103882

De jure maritimo et navali. 49924
De iure mercatorum et commerciorum. 44661, 98216
De juris controversia. 40767
De justa Indiarum occidentalium gubernatione. 86526, 86528-86529
De justa Indiarum occidentalium inquisitione. 86525, 86527-86529
De justis belli causis. (79175)-79176
De ivstita distribvtiva & acceptione personarum ei opposita. 106252A
De la aparicion de la milagrosa imagen. 27762
De la baie Pelican. 25936
De la balance du commerce. 2088
De la Californie et des cotes de l'Ocean Pacifique. 95629
De la colonisation du Bresil. 39675
De la colonizacion de la Baja California. 38952
De la constitution Americaine et de l'utilite de son etude. (38433)
De la constitution Americaine, et de quelques calomnies. 4184
De la constitution d'Angleterre. 41646
De la conversion a nuestra santa fe de los Tepeguanes. 70789
De la conversion de los Xumanas. 60876
De la crise Americaine. 74978
De la Danse. 50569
De la decouverte des mines d'or. 91852
De la democracia en la America del Norte. 96060-96061, 96067-96068
De la detention preventive. 13769
De la dette publique en France. (21057)
De la deuda estranjera. 104540
De la devocion y patrocinio de San Miguel. 55266
De la educacion del ciudadano libre. 99482
De la educacion popular. 77072
De la esclavitude en Cuba. 2001
De la expedicion al Gran Chaco. 71450
De la fabrication des sucres aux colonies Francaises. 17475
De la fabrication des sucres en France. (4087)
De la fabrication du sucre au colonies. (9844)
De la fabrication du sucre aux colonies Fran- caises. 75535
Da la fievre jaune. (2975)
De la fievre juane observee aux Antilles. 37610
De la fievre jaune ou typhus d'Amerique. 70463
De la filosofia en la Habana. 48162
De la formation des mots. (73302)
De la France, et des Etats-Unis. 8027, 8035, 13516
De la gerontocratie en Haiti. (27163)
De la guerre actuelle des Etats-Unis d'Amerique. 39659
De la Guyane Francaise de son etat physique. 3303, (11525)
De la Guyane Francaise et de ses colonisa- tions. 38429
De la impiedad de los Negros esclavos. (41141)
De la influencia de los diferentes climas del universo. 7398
De la integridad nacional de la republica Arjentina. 649
De la irregvlaridad de ilegitimidad. 75884
De la legalite des blocus Americaines. 30865
De la libertad del comercio. 50481
De la liberte de conscience et de culte a Haiti. 28725
De la litterature et des hommes de lettres. 98294
De la litterature des Negres. 28727, 38911, 97507

De la machine infernle. 26200
De la Martinique en 1842. 16802, 38493
De la mer. 46974
De la mission de la Sierra de Topia. 70789
De la mission de Parras. 70789
De la mission de San Andres. 70789
De la naturaleza y virtudes de las plantas y
  animales. 31514, 105727
De la navigation de l'Amazone. 1541
De la necessite de differer l'expedition de
  Saint-Domingue. 56369
De la necessite de rendre nos colonies
  Francaises independantes. 4174
De la noblesse de la Peau. 28737
De la oracion y exercicios. (40250)
De la parente de la langue Japonaise. 1582,
  (12020)
De la pluralite des races humaines. 64705
De la presidence du General Jackson. 12596
De la primera entrada de el evangelio a los
  Maynas. 72524
De la primera expedicion contra los Portu-
  gueses de Matogrosso. 71450
De la production des metaux precieux au
  Mexique. 21391
De la protection des nationaux a l'etranger.
  65519
De la prueba por jurados. 36438
De la puissance Americaine. (64735)
De la question de jurisdiction qui s'est pre-
  sentee. 43532
De la question de l'intervention. 12580
De la regla, y constituciones. (40250)
De la regular observancia de N. S. P. S.
  Francisco. (58264)
De la republica de las Indias occidentales.
  72894
De la republique de Haiti. 73522
De la republique des Etats-Unis de l'Amerique
  du Nord. 28187
De la republique d'Haiti. 73084
De la revolution au Mexique. 10677
De la richesse commerciale. 81451
De la richesse dans ses rapports avec la
  population. 81457
De la rupture des glaces du pol Arctique.
  19364
De la salubrite du climat des Andes. 78501
De la societe Americaine. 44942
De la tolerancia. 42904
De la traite du commerce des Negres. 13485
De la traite et de l'esclavage des noirs et
  des blancs. 28737, (81947)
De la vida de la Madre Geronima de la
  Afuncion. (40250)
De l'abolition de l'esclavage dans les colonies
  Francaises. 23934
De l'abolition de l'esclavage aux colonies.
  70369
De l'abolition des droits feodaux et seigneur-
  iaux du Canada. 21194
De l'action du cafe. 74999
De l'agriculture en Europe et Amerique.
  19128
De l'Amerique et des Americains. 1292
De l'Amerique Meridionale dans ses rapports
  actuels. (65954)
De l'Amerique. [Par C. de Bonneville.] 6327
De l'Amerique. Par H. Azais. 2528
De l'aristocratie Anglaise. 23794
De las antigvas minas de Espana. 17177, 2d
  note after 100818
De las batallas en el ocean. 22654
De las calidades particulares de missiones
  entre gentes barbaras. 70789

De las colonias. (64884)
De las elegias de varones illvstres de Indias.
  70789
De las missiones de Cinaloa. 70789
De las nvevas noticias. 72524
De las virtudes maravillosas. 97669
De laudibus & fructu Margarite philosophice.
  69125-69126
De l'avenir et de l'influence des canaux du
  Canada. (37145)
De la sette diuerse genti. 90128
De legatione Babylonica. 34106
De legatione evangelica ad Indos. 31623
De legatione Imperatoris Potentissimi Aethio-
  piae ad Clementem Pontificem VII. 72023
De legatione regis AEthiopiae ad Clementem
  Pontificem VII. 72023
De l'emancipation de Saint-Domingue. 75867
De l'emancipation des esclaves a la Guyane
  Francaise. (73082)
De l'emancipation des esclaves dans les
  colonies Francaises. 16386
De l'emancipation des noirs. 61261
De l'emancipation des noirs et de l'independance
  des Indes-Occidentales. 94500
De l'emigration aux Etats 'Unis d'Amerique.
  47976
De l'emigration Europeenne dans ses rapports
  avec la prosperite. 41379
De l'empire du Bresil. 1570
De l'endemie dysenterique a Saint-Pierre.
  21462
De l'esclavage. 11916
De l'esclavage aux Antilles. 12596
De l'esclavage aux colonies Francaises. 94301
De l'esclavage chez les nations Chretiennes.
  39101
De l'esclavage colonial. (10949)
De l'esclavage dans ses rapports avec l'union
  Americaine. 10916
De l'esclavage des noirs et de la legislation
  coloniale. (77744)
De l'esclavage en general et de l'emancipation
  des noirs. 11406
De l'escavage [sic] et des colonies. 21399
De l'estimation des pierres precieuses. 73297
De l'etat actuel de la marine et des colonies.
  (39615)
De l'etat actuel et de l'avenir de la religion
  en Amerique. 2797
De l'etat de l'instruction primaire et populaire
  en Belgique. 21070
De l'etat des Negres. 81946
De l'etat et du sorte des colonies. 75529-
  75530
De l'etat present et futur des Peaux-Rouges.
  79043
De l'etat social et politique du Mexique. 38407
De l'Europe a l'egard des nouveaux etats du
  Sud de l'Amerique. (17192)
De l'evangelike regne de Jesus Roy des Roys.
  64527-64528
De l'exploitation des suereries. 64850
De l'histoire, comment il conviendrait de la
  faire. 5406
De l'identite de nature des fievres. 13645
De l'importance de la revolution de l'Amerique.
  8035, 13516
De l'indemnite de Saint-Domingue. 98840
De l'influence Angalise. 29239
De l'influence de la revolution d'Amerique sur
  l'Europe. 15194
De l'influence Francaise dans l'Amerique du
  Sud. 34695
De l'influence que le system de Pennsylvania
  exerce. 6320

de lingua Algonkina. 69242
de lingua Brasilicia. 69242
De lingua Brasiliensium. 1371A
De lingua Brasiliensium, e grammatica P.
  Josephi de Anchieta. 7588, 63028
De lingua Caraibica. 69242
De lingua Huronum. 69242
De lingua Mexicana. 69242
De lingua Othomitorum dissertatio. 52131
De lingua Peruana. 69242
De lingua Pocomanica. 69242
De lingua Virginica. 69242
De l'interet de la France. 81450
De lo bevno lo mejor. 26108
De lo q[ue] catolicamente. 105742
De l'oceano. 94402
De locis. 66508
De locis ac mirabilibvs mvndi. 66475-(66476)
De locis ac mirabilibvs mvndi. Et primo de
  tribvs orbis partibvs. (66472)-(66476)
De locis S. scripturae Hebraicis commentarius.
  (3596)
De l'opinion des medecins Americains. 12482,
  13645
De l'ordre de succession observe par les
  Indiens. 94854
De l'origine, de la nature, des progres, et de
  l'inclunce des etablissemens consulaires.
  101356
De l'origine des Americains. (24421)
De los curanderos de los Indios. 38381, 56007,
  (75765)
De los empleos en nvevas redvcciones. 72524
De los nombres. 96269, 100643
De los nombres de Parentesco. 96268
De los problemas y secretos narauillosos de
  las Indias. 10808
De los prodigos de la omnipotencia. 67666
De los pueblos y de los gobiernos. 68078
De los territorios de Californias. 9962
De los tres meses ultimos de la America
  Meridional y del Brasil. 64909
De l'utilite des colonies. 47203
De magnete magneticisque corporibus. 27356
De magnis thesauris spiritualibus ac temporal-
  ibus. 43826
De majoribus oceani insulis. 105632
De manja. 77503
De Martini Frobisseri Angli navigatione.
  25994, 79345
De medicina Brasiliensi. 7588, 63028
De meibloem. 92429
De melle silvestri. 3409
De metheorologicis imp[res]sionibus et mirabil-
  ibus nature operibus. 102560
De mirabilibus novae & veteris urbis Romae.
  661, 665
De miseria hominis. 41067
De Molvccis. 77803
De Molvccis insulis. 47038
De monarchia Hispanica discursus. 10197
De modo procedendi Surinamensi. 31240
De Montcalm en Canada. (44868)
De Montreal a Jerusalem. 64925
De morbis endemiis. 7588, 63028
De morbis gentium libris excerpta. 6118,
  6120, 94273
De moribus ac ritibus gentium. 24162
De mvndo, siue circularis inspectionis meteo-
  rorum libri II. 95940-95941
De natura et indole servitutis. 73838
De natura et moribus anthropophagorum. 61257
De natura et moribus et ceteris id generis
  gentisque. note before 99327, 99336-
  99337, note after 99383C

De natura locorum. 672
De natura Nova Orbis. (8784)
De natvra Novi Orbis libri dvo. 118-120
De nauigatio[n]e a Lusitanis. (66476)
De navigatione Christophori Columbi. (26500)-
  (26502)
De navigatione Gallorum in terram Floridam.
  1761A
De navigatione illustris ac magnanimi equitas
  Aurati Gumfredi Gilberti. 8960
De navigatione in Indiam per Septentrionem
  tentata. 22370
De navigatione libri III. (74642)
De navigatione prima Christophori Columbi
  in Americam. 63203
De nirgua y abuso de los reyes. 59014
De Nova Gallia. 39625
De Novi Orbis natvra. (8784)
De nouis insulis nuper repertis. 8150
De novis insvlis, quomodo, quando, & per quem
  illae inuentae sint. 51379
De Nouo Mundo. note before 99327, 99334,
  99365, 99378, 99383
De Novo Orbe. 5048
De Nouo Orbe conjectanea. 5048
De Nouo Orbe, or the historie of the West
  Indies. 1563, 29600, 45011
De Novo Orbe, sive India Occidentali. 73000
De nuevas conuarsiones de naciones del Rio
  Grande de Zuaque. 70789
De nvper svb D. Carlo repertis insulis. 1553
De occasione et authore hijus historiae. (8784)
De oequinoctiorvm solstitioruque inuentione.
  62809
De officio. 98798-98799
De officio. Auto. 98800
De officio scribae liber unis. 74664
De ophyra regione. (34105), 64001
De optimo reipv. statv. 50543
De ora Antarctica. 99345, 99348
De ora Antarctica per regem Portugallie
  pridem inuenta. note before 99327, 99333
De Orbe Novo decades. 1551, 45010
De Orbe Novo Petri Martyris ab Angleira
  Mediolanensis. 1551, 45010
De Orbe Novo Petri Martyris Angleiri Medio-
  lanensis. (1552), 1st note after 45010
De orbis divisione et insuli rebusque nuper
  inuentis. (26852), 26955-(26956)
De orbis situ, ac descriptione. 25465, 57462
De orbis sitv libri tres. 63957-63960
De orbis terrae concordia libri quatuor. 64524
De orbis terrarvm sitv compendiu[m]. 71582
De orden del Supremo Gobierno. 76196
De origine, ac rebus gestis regum Hispaniae
  liber. 94398
De origine, aditu atque fama genitum American-
  arum. 67386
De origine animalium. 48982
De origine gentium Americanarum dissertatio.
  15079, (28957), 33015, 61293
De origine Maomethis. 62023
De origine seraphicae religionis Franciscanae
  ejusque progressibus. 25934, 27790
De origine Turcarum. 62023
De originibus Americanis, dissertationem Dei
  & superiorum indultu[m]. 100953
De originibus Americanis libri qvatvor. 33014-
  33015
De ornata oris. 38138
De othomitorum lingua. 52132
De par le Roy. (56085)
De Paris a Cayenne. 19426
De Paris au Nouveau Monde et du nouveau a
  Paris. 23097

De partitione orbis. 2383
De peches de M. le Comte de la Luzerne.
38697
De philosophia Canadensium populi in America
Septentrionali. 77969
De plantis Labradoricis libris tres. 48671
De plantis variis Mexicanis. 77645
De ponto occidentali. 39625
De Portvgaliae convinctione. 77902
De praestantia coloniae Geogrio-Anglicanae.
27084, 31209, note after 98130
De praetoris officio liber unis. 74664
De primordiis civitatum oratio. 21235
De principiis astronomiae & cosmographiae.
(26852)-26853, 26855-(26856), 62588
De profundis clamavi. 91110
De providentia numinis, & animi immortalitate.
(67586)
De publico culta erga 40. martyres ante de-
creta. 68434
De quarta . . . gallorum navigatione. (8784)
De IV permaximis insulis. 25088
De quarto gallorum in Floridam navigatione.
(8784)
De quattuor p'maximis insulis. 25086
De quatuor aliis planis. 66479
De Quebec a Lima. 3897
De quelques essais de colonisation Europeene.
75485
De quelques questions relatives aux colonies
Francaises. (59111)
De quinquaginta duobus ex Societate Jesu.
19970, 43776
De radice altili mandihoca. 3409
De ratione paschalis celebrationis. (62810)
De rebvs, Emmanvelis regis Lvsitaniae.
57804
De rebus, et insulis nouiter repertis. 16947-
16949
De rebus gestis Philippi II. 79180
De rebus Hispaniae anacephalaeosis libri
septem. 76316
De rebvs Hispanicis, Lvsitanicis, Aragonicis,
Indicis, et AEthiopicis. 27691, 51646
De rebus Hispanorum gestis. 79180
De rebvs Japonicis. 31016, 38339
De rebvs oceanicis et Novo Orbe. 1558,
(27689)
De rebus omnibus. 63349
De rebvs Pervanis. 96257
De rebus rusticis Brasilicis carminum libri
quatuor. 47462
De regio Petronatu[m] Indiarum. (25687)
De regione et moribus Canadensium. 36766,
note after 69259
De regionibus orientalibus. 59231
De regionibus septentrionalibus. 6117, 106330
De regno. 72023
De religione Gronlandorum naturali disserta-
tiones tres. 33395
De reparatione Latinae linguae libri duo. 74664
De Rio de Janeiro a Cuyaba. 82720
De Roma prisca et nova varii acvtores provt
inseqventi pagella cernere est. 72884
De rusticis Brasiliae rebus carminum libri IV.
47461
De sacro-caesari quod sancerrum vocat
obsidione. 40153
De Saint-Domingue, considere sous les point
de vue de la restauration prochaine.
4960
De Saint-Domingue, de ses guerres, de ses
revolutions. 20963
De Saint-Domingue. Reflexions extraites d'un
memoire. 47205

De sanctitate vitae P. Ignatii. 68434
De secundo ac optando Jehovae-Jesu adventu.
46285
De septem novae legis sacramentis summarium.
39677
De servitute conventionali secundum juris
hodierni rationem. 46188
De servitute in coloniis Americanis tollenda.
12292
De servorum Afrorum commercio. 52230,
(73283)
De simplicibus medicamentis ex Occidentali
India delatis. 49941
De situ Venetae urbis. 74664
De sphaera. 32682, 65940-65941, 74803
De sphaera. Liber vnus. 96108
De sphaera liber I. 65940-65941
De sphera. 32677
De statv religionis Christianae. 40002, 49403
De successu evangelij apud Indios in Nova-
Anglia. (46643), 46699, (46749)
De successu evangelii apud Indios Occidentales.
(39894), 46750
De suis peregrinationibus. (34105)
De sus progresos en la poblacion. 74919
De tabaco exercitationes XIV. 43825
De Tapuiyarum moribus. 7588, 63028
De tellure qua tu Lusitaniru[m] Columbus
obseruauer. (66476)
De terra sub cardine Antarctico per regem
Portugallie pridem inuenta. 99333
De tolerancia. 51324
De totivs Africae descriptione libri IX. (40046)
De tumultibus Americanis deque eorum con-
ciliatoribus meditatio senilis. (4760)-
4761
De universitate seu cosmographia. 64531
De usu globi. 26853, 26855, 62588
De vsv globi astriferi opusculum. (25856)
De vsv globi cosmographici ab eodem editi.
(26856)
De vtilitate tabularum. (46488)
De venematis & antidotis. 7588, 63028
De venetis magistratibus. 84664
De ventis et navigatione, libellvs avttore
Michaele Angelo Blondo. (5518)
De ventis et navigatione libellus, cum accuratis-
sima descriptione. 5517
De vera fuci natantis fructificatione. 73397
De vero novi orbis inventore. 51478, 93251
De veteris quorundum conjecturis Christoforo
Columbo viam monstrantibus. (78099)
De vetustate aquileiae liber sex. 74664
De vi rationum externarum. 66947
De viris Peruvianis. 64930
De vita Antonii Lopezii Portilli. 44242
De vita et moribus sex sacerdotum Paraguai-
corum. 58537, (60857)
De vita et moribus tredecim virorum Paraguai-
corum. 58537
De vita et morte P. Ignatii Azevendi. 64451
De vita Michaelis Gutierii. 44243
De vitimas conuseriones en la Prouincia de
Cinaloa. 70789
De vitis aliquot Mexicanorum aliorumgque.
(44241)
D'E., E. B. pseud. see Engel, Samuel.
De ***. pseud. see Villeneuve, Gabrielle
Suzanne Barbot Gallon de.
De ***, Chevalier. pseud. see ***, Cheva-
lier de. pseud.
De *****, J. M. B. pseud. see Saint Victor,
Jacques Maximilien Benjamin Bins de.
De A., J. S. pseud. see A., J. S. de.
pseud.

De Abad y Queipo, Manuel. see Queipo, Manuel Abad, Bp.
De Abarca, Joseph Mariano. see Mariano de Abarca, Joseph.
De Abascal y Sousa, Jose Fernandez. see Abascal y Sousa, Jose Fernandez de.
De Abraca, J. M. see Abraca, J. M. de.
De Abreu, Antonio Joseph Alvarez. see Abreu, Antonio Joseph Alvarez de, Marquis de la Regalia.
De Abreu, Joao Capistrano. see Capistrano de Abreu, Joao.
De Abrev, Juan. see Abrev, Juan de.
De Abreu de Galindo, Juan. see Abreu de Galindo, Juan de.
De Abreu e Lima, J. J. see Abreu e Lima, J. J. de.
De Abreu y Valdes, Miguel Anselmo Alvarez. see Abreu y Valdes, Miguel Anselmo Alvarez de, Bp.
Deacon, W. F. 19010-19011
Deacon Giles' distillery. 12397
De Acosta, Blas. see Acosta, Blas de.
De Acosta, J. J. see Acosta, J. J. de.
De Acuna, Antonio Gonzalez. see Acuna, Antonio Gonzalez de.
De Acuna, Christoval. see Acuna, Christoval de.
De Acuna, Juan. see Acuna, Juan de, Marques de Casafuente.
De Acuna Bonal, Maria. see Acuna Bonal, Maria de.
De Acusta, Joseph. see Acusta, Joseph de.
Dead are the living. 17270
Dead Christendom reviving. 77426
Dead faith anatomized. 46788
Dead in Christ blessed. 63941
Dead of the cabinet. 97608
Dead of the present war. 42032
Dead on the field of honor. 28025
Dead vicars plea. 63515
Deady, Matthew Paul, 1824-1893. (19012), 57567
Deaf and dumb; a poem. (78340)
Deaf and Dumb Asylum, Columbus, O. see Ohio State School for the Deaf, Columbus.
Deaf and dumb: . . . their education. 44313
Deaf-mutes' Meeting, New York, 1853. see New York (City) Meeting held by Deaf-mutes, 1853.
De Agia, Miguel. see Agia, Miguel de.
De Aguero, Christoual. see Aguero, Christoual de.
De Aguero, Juan Francisco de Castaniza Gonzalez. see Gonzalez de Aguero, Juan Francisco de.
De Aguero, P. see Aguero, P. de.
De Agueros, Pedro Gonzalez. see Gonzalez de Agueros, Pedro.
De Aguerre y Espinosa, Joseph Francisco. see Cuevas Aguierre y Espinosa, Joseph Francisco de.
De Aguiar, Diego. see Aguiar, Diego de.
De Aguiar, Lucas da Lylva. see Lylva de Aguiar, Lucas da.
De Aguiar y Acuna, Rodrigo. see Aguiar y Acuna, Rodrigo de.
De Aguila, Melchor Xufre. see Xufre de Aguila, Melchor.
De Aguilar, G. see Aguilar, G. de.
De Aguilar, Jose. see Aguilar, Jose de.
De Aguilar, Pedro Sanchez. see Sanchez de Aguilar, Pedro.
De Aguilar, Sanchez. see Sanchez de Aguilar, Pedro.

De Aguilar del Rio, Juan. see Rio, Juan de Aguilar del.
De Aguira y Mayora, Jose Mariano. see Aguira y Mayora, Jose Mariano de.
De Aguirre, J. Sanchez. see Aguirre, J. Sanchez de.
De Aguirre, Joseph Saenz. see Saenz de Aguirre, Joseph.
De Aguirre, Miguel. see Aguirre, Miguel de.
De Aguirre Gomendio, Francisco. see Gomendio, Francisco de Aguirre.
De Aguro, Juan Francisco Castaniza Gonzalez. see Castaniza Gonzales de Aguero, Juan Francisco.
De Agurto, Pedro. see Pedro de Agurto.
De Ahumada, Juan Antonio. see Ahumada, Juan Antonio de.
De Alarcon, Hernando. see Alarcon, Hernando de.
De Alba, B. see Alva, B. de.
De Alba, Jose M. Gutierrez. see Gutierrez de Alba, Jose M.
De Albares Serrano, Juan. see Serrano, Juan de Albares.
De Albertinis, Francisco. see Albertinis, Francisco de.
De Albornos, Mariana de la Puenta Carrillo. see Carrillo de Albornos, Mariana de la Puenta.
De Albuerne, Manuel. see Albuerne, Manuel de.
De Albuquerque, Affonso. see Albuquerque, Affonso de, 1453-1515.
De Albuquerque, Antonio. see Albuquerque, Antonio de.
De Albuquerque Coello, Duarte. see Albuquerque Coello, Duarte de, Marques de Basto.
De Alcala, Domingo. see Alcala, Domingo de.
De Alcala, Josef Maria. see Maria de Alcala, Josef.
De Alcantara, Juan de Larrea del. see Larrea del de Alcantara, Juan de.
De Alcazar, Ignacio Antonio. see Alcazar, Ignacio Antonio de.
De Alcedo, Antonio. see Alcedo, Antonio de.
De Alcedo y Herrera, Dionisio. see Alcedo y Herrera, Dionisio de.
De Aldama y Guevara, Joseph Augustin. see Aldama y Guevara, Joseh Augustin de.
De Alday y Aspee, Manuel. see Alday y Aspee, Manuel de.
De Aldrete, Martin Carrillo. see Aldrete, Martin Carrillo de, Bp.
De Aldrey, F. T. see Aldrey, F. T. de.
De Alencar, J. Martiniano. see Martiniano de Alencar, J.
De Alencar Araripe, Tristao. see Araripe, Tristao de Alencar.
De Alencastre, Jose Martins Pereira. see Pereira de Alencastre, Jose Martins.
De Alencastro Marona y Silva, Fernando. see Alencastro Marona y Silva, Fernando de, Marques de Valdafuentes.
Dealers pocket companion. 98275
De Alfaro, ------, Marques de Villahermosa. see Villahermosa de Alfaro, ------, Marques de.
De Alfaro, Diego. see Alfaro, Diego de.
De Alfaro y Beaumont, Isidro Sainz. see Sainz de Alfaro y Beaumont, Isidro.
De Alferes, Barao do Paty. see Paty de Alferes, Barao do.

709

Dealings of God, man, and the devil. (20752)
Dealings of God with Israel and America.
36238
Dealings of God with the nation. 33388
Dealings with the dead. By a sexton of the
old school. 77004
Dealings with the dead ; the human soul.
67851
De Aliste y de Villaflor, Luis Henriquez de
Guzman, Conde de Alva. see Henri-
quez de Guzman, Luis, Conde de Alva
de Aliste y de Villaflor.
De Almarez, Gregorio. pseud. Restauracao
de Portugal prodigiosa. see Escobar,
Manoel de.
De Almedo y Torre, Antonio. see Almedo
y Torre, Antonio de.
De Almeida, Candido Mendes. see Mendes
de Almeida, Candido.
De Almeida, Manuel Antonio. see Almedia,
Manuel Antonio de.
De Almeida, Teodoro. see Almeida, Teodoro
de.
De Almeida, Tito Franco. see Almedia,
Tito Franco de.
De Almeida Carvalhaes, Rodrigo Pinto Pizarro.
see Carvalhaes, Rodrigo Pinto Pizarro
de Almeida.
De Almeida de Carvalho, Manuel. see
Carvalho, Manuel de Almeida de, Bp.,
1749-1818.
De Almeida de Menezes, Jorge. see Menezes,
Jorge de Almeida de.
De Almeida Nogueira, Baptista Caetano. see
Almeida Nogueira, Baptista Caetano de.
De Almiron, Miguel Nieto. see Nieto de
Almiron, Miguel.
De Almodovar, Eduardo Malo de Luque,
Duque. see Almodovar, Eduardo Malo
de Luque, Duque de.
De Almodovar del Rio, Pedro Jimenez de
Gongara y Lujan, Duque. see Aldomovar
del Rio, Pedro Jimenez de Gongara y
Lujan, Duque de, d. 1794.
De Almoguerra, Joannes. see Almoguerra,
Joannes de.
De Altamira, Bartholome Antonio Joseph
Ortiz de Casqueta, Marques. see
Casqueta, Bartholome Antonio Joseph
Ortiz de, Marques de Altamira.
Dealtry, William. 19015
De Alua, Bartholome. see Alua, Bartholome
de.
De Alva de Aliste y de Villaflor, Luis Henri-
quez de Guzman, Conde. see Henriquez
de Guzman, Luis, Conde de Alva de
Aliste y de Villaflor.
De Alva Ixtlilxuchitl, Fernando. see Ixtlilxu-
chitl, Fernando de Alva, ca. 1538-1648.
De Alva y Astorga, Pedro. see Alva y
Astorga, Pedro de.
De Alvarado, Francisco. see Alvarado,
Francisco de.
De Alvarado, Juan. see Juan de Alvarado,
Fray.
De Alvarado, Pedro. see Alvarado, Pedro de
1495?-1541.
De Alvarado y de la Pena, S. see Alvarado
y de la Pena, S. de.
De Alvares, Domingo. see Alvares, Domingo
de.
De Alvear, Diego. see Alvear, Diego de.
De Alvirey, Alexo. see Alvirey, Alexo de.
De Alzate y Ramirez, J. A. see Alzate y
Ramirez, J. A. de.

De Amassa, Juan. see Amassa, Juan de.
De Amati, Bernardino. see Amati,
Bernardino de.
Dean, Amos, 1803-1868. 8976, 19016-19017
Dean, Argus. 19018
Dean, Christopher C. 94022
Dean, Cyrus B. defendant 19019
Dean, Gilbert, 1819-1870. (19020)
Dean, Henry Clay. 19021-19022
Dean, James, 1777-1849. 19023
Dean, Jaspar. see Dean, John, 1679-1761.
Dean, John, 1679-1761. 19024-19029, 46269,
80793, 3d note atfer 97085, 104686
Dean, John, 1831-1888. 85072
Dean, John Ward, 1815-1903. 17604, 18461,
19030-19036, 24401, (32066), 80323
Dean, Jonathan E. (82107)
Dean, Joseph C. 105465
Dean, May (Smith) 84499
Dean, Paul, 1789-1860. 13455, 19037-19038,
70103
Dean, Samuel. see Deane, Samuel, 1784-1834.
Dean, Sarah. 19039
Dean, Sidney. 19040-19041
Dean, William. Quaker 77637
Dean, William, fl. 1791. 33351, 60026 see also
Pennsylvania. Commissioners Appointed to
Explore the Head-waters of the Rivers
Delaware, Lehigh, and Schuylkill, and
North-east Branch of the Susquehanna.
Dean, William Reed. 19068-19070
Dean & Cunninghams. firm 86760
Dean Dudley & Co. firm (71174)
Dean dela Santa Iglesia Catedral de Michoacan.
27344
Dean de la Santa Iglesia Cathedral de Guate-
mala. 19043
Dean le querteron. 27324
Dean of Gloucester. see Sherlock, Thomas,
successively Bp. of Salisbury, and
London, 1678-1761. and Tucker, Josiah,
1712-1799.
Dean y Cabildo de Esta S. Iglesia Metropoli
tana, Mexico (City) see Mexico (City)
Iglesia Metropolitana. Dean y Cabildo.
Dean y Cavildo sedevacante de la Santa Yglesia
Cathedral de Antequera Valle de Oaxaca.
56396, 79138
De Anastaris, Ramon Perez. see Perez de
Anastaris, Ramon.
De Anchieta, Jose. see Anchieta, Jose de,
1533-1597.
De Anchieta, Joseph. see Anchieta, Jose de,
1533-1597.
De Andagoya, Pascual. see Andagoya, Pas-
cual de.
De Andrada, ------- Paes. see Paes de
Andrada, -------.
De Andrada, Antonio Carlos Ribeiro. see
Ribeiro de Andrada, Antonio Carlos.
De Andrada, Beatris Bernardina. see Ser-
vantes Casaus, Beatris Bernardina (De
Andrada) de.
De Andrada, Gomes Freire. see Andrada,
Gomes Freire de.
De Andrada, Martin Francisco Riberio. see
Riberio de Andrada, Martin Francisco.
De Andrada Machado e Silva, Antonio Carlos
Ribeiro. see Ribeiro de Andrada
Machado e Silva, Antonio Carlos.
De Andrade, Alfonso. see Andrade, Alfonso
de.
De Andrade, Alonzo. see Andrade, Alonzo de.
De Andrade Figueira, Antonio Agostinho. see
Figueira, Antonio Agostinho de Andrade.

De Andrade Leitao, Francisco. see Leitao, Francisco de Andrade.
De Andrea, Francisco Jose de Souza Soares. see Souza Soares de Andrea, Francisco Jose de.
De Andueza, D. J. M. see Andueza, D. J. M. de.
Deane, Charles, 1813-1889. 5196, 7262, 18135, 19044-19051, 46385, 51810, 52630, (63477), 68407, 79391, 82816, 82823, 82831, 82834, 82849, 82850, 89927, 90220, 2d note after 100494, 3d note after 100533, 103142, 105077
Deane, E. 19052-19053
Deane, James, 1801-1858. 19054
Deane, John. see Dean, John, 1679-1761.
Deane, Samuel, 1733-1814. 19055-19059, 84352
Deane, Samuel, 1784-1834. 19060-19062, (64147)
Deane, Silas, 1737-1789. 19042, (19063)-19067, 39699-39700, note after 79366, 88969
Deane, Silas, 1737-1789. supposed author 19067, 86193
Deane, William Reed. 89014
Deane Monahan. pseud. see Steele, James William.
De Angelis, Pedro. see Angelis, Pedro de, 1784-1859.
De Angles y Gortari, Mathias. see Angles y Gortari, Mathias de.
De Angliara, Juan. see Anghiera, Pietro Martire d', 1455-1526.
De Angliera, Juan. see Anghiera, Pietro Martire d', 1455-1526.
De Antequera Enriquez y Castro, Jose. see Antequera Enriquez y Castro, Jose de.
De Antequera y Castro, Joseph. see Antequera Enriquez y Castro, Jose de.
De Anzorena, Jose Mariano. see Anzorena, Jose Mariano de.
De Apello Corbulacho, Juan Carlos. see Corbulacho, Juan Carlos de Apello.
De Apodaca, Juan Ruiz. see Ruiz de Apodaca, Juan.
De Aquino, Thomas. see Aquino, Thomas de.
De Aquino e Castro, Olegario Herculano. see Aquino e Castro, Olegario Herculano de.
Dear faithless youth, oh think, what wilt thou do! 92340, 105977
Dear sir, ... 87537
Dear sir: 105886
Dear sir: At a meeting. . . . 105883
Dear sir, at the conculsion of my public employments. 101746
Dear sir, having for the first time in my life. 91368
Dear sir, I find that the people. 104167
Dear sir: the class of 1821, at their third stated meeting. 105883
Dear sir: the undersigned, executive committee 85867
De Araburu, Andres. see Araburu, Andres de.
De Aragao Morato, Francisco Manuel Trigoso. see Morato, Francisco Manuel Trigoso de Aragao.
De Aragon, Manuel Lopez. see Lopez de Aragon, Manuel.
De Aragon, Phelipe. see Aragon, Phelipe de.
De Araguaya, Domingos Jose Goncalves de Magalhanes, Visconde. see Goncalves de Magalhanes, Domingos Jose, Visconde de Araguaya, 1811-1882.
De Arango, Francisco. see Arango, Francisco de.

De Arango, Jose. see Arango, Jose de.
De Arango y Parreno, Francisco. see Arango y Parreno, Francisco de.
De Aranjo Costa, Sallustino Orlando. see Costa, Sallustino Orlando de Aranjo.
De Aranjo Lima, Andre Cordeiro. see Aranjo Lima, Andre Cordeiro de.
De Araujo, Antonio. see Araujo, Antonio de.
De Araujo, Jose Paulo de Figueiroa Nabuco. see Nabuco de Araujo, Jose Paulo de Figueiroa.
De Araujo, Juan Martinez. see Martinez de Araujo, Juan.
De Araujo, Leonardo. see Araujo, Leonardo de.
De Araujo, Manuel do Monte Rodrigues. see Monte Rodrigues de Araujo, Manuel do, Bp., 1798-1863.
De Araujo Brusque, Francisco Carlos. see Brusque, Francisco Carlos de Araujo.
De Araujo e Castro, Felipe Ferreira. see Araujo e Castro, Felipe Ferreira de.
De Araujo e Silva, Domingos. see Araujo e Silva, Domingos de.
De Araujo e Silva, Luis Ferreira. see Araujo e Silva, Luis Ferreira de.
De Araujo Porto-Alegre, Manoel. see Porto-Alegre, Manoel de Araujo.
De Araujo y Rio, Joseph. see Rio, Joseph de Araujo y.
De Arboleya, Jose G. Garcia. see Garcia de Arboleya, Jose G.
Dearborn, Henry, 1751-1829. 14162-14163, 19071, (19074), 35908, 66771-66772, 2d note after 104027
Dearborn, Henry Alexander Scammell, 1783-1851. (12697), 19073-19077, 48980, 73630 see also Roxbury, Mass. Mayor, 1847-1851 (Dearborn)
Dearborn, Henry Alexander Scammell, 1783-1851 supposed author (12696), 19075, 94058
Dearborn, Herman A. 31589
Dearborn, Nathaniel. (19078)-19081
Dearborn, R. F. 76918-76921
Dearborn, W. 19082
Dearborn, W. L. 19083
Dearborn's guide through Mount Auburn. 19079
De Arca, Juan. see Arca, Juan de.
De Arce, Juan Diaz. see Diaz de Arce, Juan.
De Arellano, Diego. see Arellano, Diego de.
De Arellano, Emmanuele Garcia. see Garcia de Arellano, Emmanuele.
De Arellano, R. Ramires. see Ramires de Arellano, R.
De Arena, Thomas Ignacio. see Ignacio de Arena, Thomas.
De Arenas, Pedro. see Arenas, Pedro de.
De Arevalo, Juan Francisco Sahagum. see Sahagum de Arevalo, Juan Francisco.
De Arevalo, Rafael. see Arevalo, Rafael de.
De Argaiz, Gregorio. see Gregorio de Argaiz.
De Argensola, Bartholome Leonardo. see Argensola, Bartholome Leonardo de.
De Arguello, Francisco Suarez. see Suarez de Arguello, Francisco.
De Arguello, Maria de la Soledad Ortega. see Soledad Ortega de Arguello, Maria de la.
De Argumossa y Gandara, Theodoro Ventura. see Ventura de Argumossa y Gandara, Theodoro.
De Arias, Fernando. see Arias, Fernando de.
Dearing, Arthur. 7075, 40818
Dearing tragedy. (65744)
De Arispe, Miguel Ramos. see Ramos de Arispe, Miguel.

De Arizpe, Pedro Joseph Rodriguez. see
    Rodriguez de Arizpe, Pedro Joseph.
De Arjona, Francisco. see Arjona, Francisco
    de.
Dearman, N. Y. Chapel-School of St. Barnabas.
    43679
De Armas, Francisco. see Armas, Francisco
    de.
De Armas, Juan Ignacio. see Armas, Juan
    Ignacio de.
De Arquellada, Ventura. see Arquellada,
    Ventura de.
De Arquellada Mendoza, Domingo Joseph. see
    Mendoza, Domingo Joseph de Arguellada.
De Arqueta, Pedro. see Arqueta, Pedro de.
De Arrangoiz y Berzabal, F. see Arrangoiz
    y Berzabal, F. de.
De Arredondo, Miguel Joseph Cortes. see
    Cortes de Arredondo, Miguel Joseph.
De Arredondo, Nicolas. see Arredondo,
    Nicolas de.
De Arriaga, Pablo Joseph. see Arriaga,
    Pablo Joseph de.
De Arrieta, Francisco Sales. see Arrieta,
    Francisco Sales de, Abp.
De Arroyo Ladron de Guevara, J. see Ladron
    de Guevara, J. de Arroyo.
De Arroyo y Daza, Diego. see Arroyo y
    Dava, Diego de.
Deas, Ann (Izard) (35323)
De Asso y del Rio, Ignacio Jordan. see
    Asso y del Rio, Ignacio Jordan de, 1742-
    1804.
De Astor, Diego. see Astor, Diego de.
Death. pseud. Dialogue between a blind-man
    and death. see Standfast, Richard.
Death. pseud. Speech of death of Levi Ames.
    89186
Death a blessing to the righteous. 71816
Death a duty. 89773
Death: a poetical essay. 64328
Death abolished: a sermon. Occasioned by
    the sickness. 51259
Death abolished. A sermon on occasion of
    the death of Henry C. Parkhurst. 82334
Death and funeral ceremonies of John Caldwell
    Calhoun. 9950, 87480
Death and heaven. 89783
Death and resurrection of the believer. 90003
Death and the grave without any order. 14474
Death chosen rather than life. 102085
Death desirable to the believer. 63980
Death dissolves the nearest and dearest rela-
    tions. 103457
Death God's monitor to the living. 91732
Death in disguise. A temperance poem.
    (13435)
Death in the midst of life deprecated. 82208
Death in the pot. (43359)
Death made easie & happy. 46279
Death of a prophet lamented and improved.
    104397
Death of Abel. 75264
Death of Abraham Lincoln. A discourse
    delivered in the . . . United States
    General Hospital. 44785
Death of Abraham Lincoln. A discourse
    delivered on the day of the national fast.
    36644
Death of Abraham Lincoln. A sermon, ...
    in . . . New Milford. 51434
Death of Abraham Lincoln, President of the
    United States. 74739
Death of an aged servant of God considered
    and improved. 19055

Death of Capt. Nathan Hale. 97191
Death of Christians precious to the Lord.
    89602
Death of Daniel Webster. (81622)
Death of eminent men a public calamity. 59486
Death of Euphemia Mitchell. 90193
Death of General Montgomery, at the siege of
    Quebec. 7185, 50155, (56702), 58640,
    note after 101861
Death of General Montgomery, or the storming
    of Quebec. 14159
Death of General Washington. Tune.—"Death
    of General Wolfe." 101791
Death of Gen. Wahsington, [sic] with some
    remarks. 101788, 101792-101793
Death of General William Henry Harrison.
    (21133)
Death of General Wolfe. 101791
Death of God's saints precious in his sight.
    (14525)
Death of good men. A sermon delivered Feb-
    ruary 23, 1829. 93086
Death of good men compared to a sweet, re-
    freshing sleep. 103733
Death of good men, considered. 46373
Death of great, good and useful men lamented.
    73978
Death of Hilda. 89476
Death of La-Fayette, &c. (13435)
Death of Lincoln, April 15th, 1865. 88670
Death of Lincoln. Proceedings of the Supreme
    Court of Illinois. 41186
Death of Mr. Webster: a sermon. 37844
Death of Moses. A sermon preached . . .
    April 23, 1865. 37151
Death of Moses the servant of the Lord. 22391
Death of President Harrison. 33790
Death of President Lincoln. 71555
Death of President Lincoln; a memorial dis-
    course. 16407
Death of President Lincoln: a sermon delivered
    in . . . Charleston, S. C. (42410)
Death of President Lincoln, a sermon, preached
    in Grace Church. 9534
Death of President Lincoln. A sermon
    preached in Saint Paul's Chapel, New
    York. 20347
Death of President Lincoln. A sermon
    preached in the Presbyterian Church,
    Binghamton. 6064
Death of Rolla. 8137, 80342, 97573
Death of Rolla, a tragedy. 38282
Death of slavery. 16594
Death of the aged. 25440
Death of the Godly. 12367, 101016
Death of the Hon. William Wirt. 104866
Death of the lovely and the useful. 92246
Death of the President of the United States.
    (23811)
Death of the Rev. Habijah Weld. 95169
Death of the righteous, and the birth of Our
    Saviour. 23878
Death of the righteous to be lamented. 328
Death of the saints precious in the sight of
    the Lord. 88881
Death of the soldier of the republic. 75847
Death of the young. 91155
Death of W. H. Harrison. 85505
Death of Washington. 101773, 101789
Death of Washington. A poem. 41336
Death of Washington: or, Columbia in mourning
    for her son. 101790
Death of Washington, with some remarks on
    Jeffersonian policy. 101788, 101792-
    101793
Death of William Irving. 12054, 82003

Death of Wolfe. 101894
Death of young people improved. (46547)
Death speaking from high places. 70412
Death struggles of slavery. 5888
Death the advantage of the Godly. 104219
Death the certain wages of sin to the impenitent. 72691
Death, the Christian's gain. 84043
Death the destroyer of earthly and false hopes. 25408
Death, the devil and the doctor. 81073
Death, the last enemy, destroyed. 65102
Death, the last enemy, destroyed by Christ. 91790
Death, the law of life. 6060
Death unstung. 32286
Death warrant of Negro slavery. 81948
Death's dominion over man considered. 86130
Deaths from 1851-1870. (66238)
De Atienca, Ioan. see Atienza, Juan d'.
De Atienza, Joanne. see Atienza, Juan d'.
De Attelis Santangelo, Orazio Donato Gideon. see Santangelo, Orazio Donato Gideon de Attelis, b. 1774.
Deaubonneau, -----. see Aubonneau, ----- d'.
De Aunon, Alfonso Carrio y Morcillo Rubio. see Carrio y Morcillo Rubio de Aunon, Alfonso.
De Aunon, Pedro Morcillo Rubio. see Morcillo Rubio de Aunon, Pedro.
De Austria, Jose. see Austria, Jose de.
De Avalos y Bracamont, Pedro Alonso. see Avalos y Bracamont, Pedro Alonso de, Conde de Miravalles.
De Avalos y Chauca, Jose Joqauin. see Avalo Avalos y Chauca, Jose Joaquin de.
De Avecilla, Pablo. see Pablo de Avecilla.
De Avellan, Juan. see Avellan, Juan d e.
De Auellaneda, Barnardino Delgadillo. see Auellaneda, Barnardino Delgadillo de.
De Avellaneda, Gertrudis Gomez. see Gomez de Avellaneda, Gertrudis.
De Avendano, Diego. see Avendano, Diego de.
De Auendano y Vilela, Francisco. see Auendano y Vilela, Francisco de.
De Avila, Francisco. see Avila, Francisco de.
De Avila, Juan. see Juan de Avila. fray
De Avity, Peter. see Avity, Pierre d'.
De Ayala, Pedro. see Ayala, Pedro de.
De Ayala, Pedro Lopez. see Lopez de Ayala, Pedro.
De Ayala, T. Ortiz. see Ortiz de Ayala, T.
De Ayala y Aguilar, J. see Ayala y Aguilar, J. de.
De Ayanz, Geronimo. see Ayanz, Geronimo de.
De Ayeta, Francisco. see Ayeta, Francisco de.
De Ayllon, Juan. see Ayllon, Juan de.
De Ayllon Laynez, Juan. see Laynez, Juan de Ayllon.
De Azambuja, Joaquim Maria Nascentes. see Azambuja, Joaquim Maria Nascentes de.
De Azanza, Jose. see Azanza, Jose de.
De Azara, Augustin. see Azara, Augustin de.
De Azara, Felix. see Azara, Felix de.
De Azebedo, Balthasar. see Azebedo, Balthasar de.
De Azeredo Coutinho, Jose Joaquim da Cuna. see Cuna de Azeredo Coutinho, Jose Joaquim da.
De Azero y Aldovera, Miguel. see Azero y Aldovera, Miguel de.

De Azevedo, J. Lucio. see Azevedo, J. Lucio de.
De Azua e Yturgoyen, Pedro Phelipe. see Azua e Yturgoyen, Pedro Phelipe de.
De Azura e Yturgoyen, Phelipe. see Azura e Yturgoyen, Phelipe de, Abp.
De B. pseud. see Barentin de Montchal, Charles Paul Nicolas, Vicomte, 1737-1824.
De B***. pseud. see Behrens, Karl Friedrich.
De B***. pseud. see Brosses, Charles de, 1709-1777.
De B., C. pseud. see Beauregard, Couvray de.
De Baca, Alvar Nunez Cabeza. see Cabeza de Vaca, Alvar Nunez, 1490?-1557?
De Bacan, Alvaro. see Santa Cruz, Alvaro de Bacan, Marques de.
De Backer, -----. see Backer, ----- de.
De Backer, Alois. see Backer, Alois. de.
De Backer, Augustin. see Backer, Augustin de.
De Bacquere, Rumoldus. see Bacquere, Rumoldus de.
De Baeca, G. see Baeca, G. de.
De Baert, Alexandre Balthasar Francois de Paule, Baron. see Baert, Alexandre Balthasar Francois de Paule, Baron de.
De Baides, ------, Marques. see Baides, ------, Marques de.
De Bajamar, ------, Marques. see Bajamar, -----, Marques de.
De Balboa, Vasco Nunez. see Nunez de Balboa, Vasco.
De Balbuena, Bernardo. see Valbuena, Bernardo de.
De Ballesteros, Tomas. see Ballesteros, Tomas de.
De Balmis, Francesco Saverio. see Balmis, Francesco Saverio de.
De Banos y Sotomayor, Diego. see Banos y Sotomayor, Diego de.
De Baptiste, George. see Baptiste, George de.
Debar, J. H. Diss. 19085
De Baranda, Pedro Sainz. see Sainz de Baranda, Pedro.
De Barbacena, --------, Marques. see Barbacena, -----, Marques de.
De Barbazan, E. see Barbazan, E. de.
De Barbe Marbois, Francios. see Barbe-Marbois, Francois de, Marquis, 1745-1837.
De Barberey, ------. see Barberey, ----- de.
De Barcelona, Francisco Xaveiro de Meunrios, Comte. pseud. see Louis XVIII, King of France, 1755-1824.
De Barcelonne, Francisco Xaviero de Meunrios, Comte. see Louis XVIII, King of France, 1755-1824.
De Barcena, Alonzo. see Barcena, Alonzo de.
De Barcia Carballido y Zuniga, Andres Gonzalez. see Barcia Carballido y Zuniga, Andres Gonzalez de, 1673-1743.
De Barco Centenera, Martin. see Barco Centenera, Martin de.
De Baroncourt, ----- Petit. see Petit de Baroncourt, ------.
Debarquement de la flotte Francaise a Saint-Domingue. 19086, (75094)
De Barras, ------. see Barras, ------ de.
De Barreda, Francisco. see Barreda, Francisco de.

713

De Barreda, M. Perez. see Perez de
Barreda, M.
De Barreda, Pedro Perez. see Perez de
Barreda, Pedro.
De Barreda y Vera, Francisco Sanchez. see
Sanchez de Barreda y Vera, Francisco.
De Barrenechea, Juan. see Barrenechea,
Juan de.
De Barriso, J. H. see Barrios, J. H. de.
De Barroetta y Angel, Antonio. see Barroetta
y Angel, Antonio de.
De Barros, Andre. see Barros, Andre de.
De Barros, Joam. see Barros, Joam de.
De Barros, Joao Borges. see Barros, Joao
Borges de.
De Barros, Jose Maurico Fernandes Pereira.
see Pereira de Barros, Jose Maurico
Fernandes.
De Barros, Manuel Francisco de, 2d Visconde
de Santarem. see Santarem, Manuel
Francisco de Barros, 2. Visconde de,
1791-1856.
De Barros Pimentel, Esperidiao Eloy. see
Pimentel, Esperidiao Eloy de Barros.
De Barruel, Augustin. see Barruel, Augustin
de, 1741-1820.
De Barruel-Beauvert, P. A. see Barruel-
Beauvert, P. A. de.
De Bascoso, Teresa Castaniza. see Castaniza
de Bascoso, Teresa.
De Basterot, ------, Vicomte. see Basterot,
-----, Vicomte de.
De Bastide, Jean Francois. see Bastide,
Jean Francois de.
De Basto, Duarte de Albuquerque Coello,
Marques. see Albuquerque Coello,
Duarte de, Marques de Basto.
Debate at the Lane Seminary, Cincinnati.
(19087), 38861, note after 95459
Debate between the Rev'd Mr. Byles. (9718),
106229
Debate between W. G. Brownlow and Rev. A.
Pryne. (8708)
Debate in the Historical Society on "Columbia."
54475
Debate in the House of Commons, June 23,
1825. 93367
Debate in the House of Commons on May 15th,
1823. (81949)
Debate in the House of Commons, on the
abolition of the slave trade. (19088)
Debate in the House of Commons, on the 15th
May, 1835. 98073
Debate in the House of Commons, on the
measures of government. 19089
Debate in the House of Commons on the 22nd
May, 1823. 93362
Debate in the House of Commons on Tuesday
the 1st and on Friday the 11th of June,
1824. 82906
Debate in the House of Commons repsecting
the trial and condemnation of the Rev.
John Smith. 82906
Debate in the House of Lords, 7th March, 1826.
(19091)
Debate in the House of Representatives between
Mr. Butler. 9621
Debate in the House of Representatives of the
Territory of Orleans. (53321), 104030
Debate in the House of Representatives of the
United States, on the Seminole War.
19092, 79067
Debate in the House of Representatives . . .
on Mr. Holgate's resolutions. (60037)
Debate in the Legislature . . . on inviting Gov.
A. Johnson. 60038

Debate in the Massachusetts Senate, on the
bill to incorporate the Boston and Hailfax
Telegraphic Cable Co. (19090)
Debate in the Massachusetts Senate, upon an
act to incorporate the Cambridge Broad-
way Company. (2600)
Debate in the Senate of New York on Mr.
Granger's motion. 28188
Debate in the Senate of the United States,
January 18, 1855. 85017
Debate in the Senate of the United States, on
the memorial of James H. Lane. 89926
Debate in the Senate, on the nomination of
Martin Van Buren. 89211, 98425, 102319
Debate in the Senate on the protection of prop-
erty. (19093), 33195
Debate in the Senate . . . relative to the use
of the Senate Chamber. 60038
Debate in the South Carolina Legislature.
87481
Debate on a motion for the abolition of the
slave trade; in the House of Commons,
. . . April 18 and 19, 1791. 19094
Debate on a motion for the abolition of the
slave-trade, in the House of Commons,
on Monday the second of April 1792.
19095
Debate on Campbellism. 36044
Debate on Christian baptism. 101063
Debate on direct importation to the interior.
51941
Debate on Mr. Ward's resolutions on coloniza-
tion. 101300
Debate on resolutions relative to repeal. 56120
Debate on slavery, at Boston, May, 1841.
13783
Debate on slavery, held in the city of Cincin-
nati. 5825
Debate on sugar duties. 33779
Debate on the bill establishing free schools.
70575
Debate on the constitutional amendment.
(28601)
Debate on the resolution providing for the
publication. 19096
Debate on the resolutions to issue certificates.
(60039)
Debate on the Roman Catholic religion. 66674
Debate proposed in the Temple Patrick Society.
94667
Debates and other proceedings of the conven-
tion . . . convened at Richmond. 100029
Debates and proceedings in the Congress of
the United States. 15519, 84833, 85200,
86193
Debates and proceedings in the convention of
the commonwealth of Massachusetts.
(45703)
Debates and proceedings in the House of
Delegates, of Virginia. (43720)
Debates and proceedings in the Massachusetts
Legislature. 29620
Debates and proceedings in the Massachusetts
Legislature. January, 1856, to June,
1856. (29619), 45704
Debates and proceedings in the New-York
State Convention. 53635
Debates and proceedings of the Constitutional
Convention. 34222
Debates and proceedings of the Constitutional
Convention for the Territory of Minnesota.
49245
Debates and proceedings of the Constitutional
Convention of . . . Michigan. 48728
Debates and proceedings of the Convention of
the State of New York. 53634

Debates and proceedings of the General As-
sembly of Pennsylvania. 10864, 1st
note after (60039)
Debates and proceedings of the General Trien-
nial Convention, 66137, 88394, 96642
Debates and proceedings of the Georgia Con-
vention. 27036
Debates and proceedings of the Honorable the
Legislative Council. 65632
Debates and proceedings of the Legislative
Council, . . . of the province of Nova
Scotia. 56121
Debates and proceedings of the Maryland Re-
form Convention. (45123)
Debates and proceedings of the Minnesota
Constitutional Convention. 49244
Debates and proceedings of the National Coun-
cil of Congregational Churches. 51957
Debates at large between the House of Lords
and the House of Commons. 19098
Debates at the Robin-Hood Society. (54233)
Debates de la Camara de Senadores de Buenos
Aires. 9008, 19102
Debates in both Houses of Parliament. 19099
Debates in Congress. (15607)
Debates in council. 19103
Debates in the Board of Aldermen, of . . .
New York. (54234)
Debates in the British House of Commons.
19100
Debates in the Congress of the United States.
19101
Debates in the Convention for the Revision
and Amendment of the Constitution of
. . . Louisiana. 42217
Debates in the eighty-ninth General Assembly
of . . . New Jersey. 53095
Debates in the federal convention, 25th August,
1787. 93643, 93645
Debates in the General Assembly of . . . New
Jersey. 53096
Debates in the House of Commons in the year
1774. (11601), 2d note after 105598-9
[sic]
Debates in the House of Commons on Mr.
Ryland's case. (74590)
Debates in the House of Commons, on the 15th
May, 1823. 93368
Debates in the House of Commons, on the
present state of colonial slavery. 23524
Debates in the House of Delegates of Virginia.
100104
Debates in the House of Representatives con-
tinued on papers. 14008
Debates in the House of Representatives, of
the United States, during the first session
of the fourth Congress. Part I. 19104
Debates in the House of Representatives, of
the United States, during the first session
of the fourth Congress, upon questions
involved in the British treaty of 1794.
8128
Debates in the House of Representatives of
the United States, 1st session of the 4th
Congress. 15520
Debates in the House of Representatives on
the bills for carrying into effect the
Louisiana treaty. 42216
Debates in the Legislature of Pennsylvania, of
1809-10. 57236, 60041
Debates in the Presbytery of Pennsylvania on
the case of Albert Barnes. 3509
Debates in the Senate in March, 1849. 4785
Debates in the Senate of the United States, on
the judiciary. 19105

Debates in the several state conventions.
22233, 80405, note after 106002
Debates in the third session of the eleventh
Congress. 15521
Debates no Parlamento Brazileiro. 67539
Debates of the Constitutional Convention, 1857
[of Iowa.] 34982
Debates of the Constitutional Convention of
. . . Maryland. 45124
Debates of the Convention, of the State of
Pennsylvania. 60040, 104627
Debates of the House of Clerical and Lay
Delegates. 66138
Debates of the House of Commons, during the
thirteenth Parliament. 11602
Debates of the House of Commons in the year
1774. (11601)
Debates of the Legislature of Pennsylvania in
the case of Gideon Olmstead. (30039),
note after 57236, note before 96910
Debates of the Legislature . . . [of Pennsyl-
vania] of 1810-11. 60042
Debates of the Texas Convention. 94977,
94979
Debates on the adoption of the federal consti-
tution. 22233, 80405, note after 106002
Debates on the bill for abolishing the slave
trade. 93370
Debates on the resolution for abolishing the
slave trade. 93369
Debates on the resolutions providing for the
publication. 19097
Debates on the Trinity Church Bill. (40755)
Debates, resolutions, and other proceedings in
convention, on the adoption of the federal
constitution. 22232, 100029
Debates, resolutions, and other proceedings,
of the Convention of Delegates, assembled
at Portland. (43920)
Debates, resolutions and other proceedings, of
the Convention of the Commonwealth of
Massachusetts. (45702), 74302
Debates which arose in the House of Representatives of South Carolina, on the constitution framed for the United States, by
a convention of delegates, assembled at
Philadelphia. 87511
Debates which arose in the House of Representatives of South-Carolina, on the con-
stitution framed for the United States, by
a convention of delegates assembled at
Philadelphia. Together with such notices
of the convention as could be procured.
87512
Debating Society, Springfield, Mass. see
Springfield Debating Society, Springfield,
Mass.
Debats. (12585), 12596
Debats dans l'Assemblee Legislative sur la
tenure seigneuriale. note after (10603)
Debats entre les accusateurs et les accuses.
19106
Debatten in der 89en Generalversammlung des
Staates New Jersey. 53095
De Bauclas, L. see Bauclas, L. de.
De Baude, Louis. see Baude, Louis de,
Comte de Palluau et de Frontenac, 1620-
1698.
De Bausset-Roquefort, ------, Marquis. see
Bausset-Roquefort, ------, Marquis de.
De Bazancourt, C. see Bazancourt, C. de.
De Beauchamp, Alphonse. see Beauchamp,
Alphonse de.
De Beauchene, Robert. see Beauchene,
Robert de.

De Beaufain, John Henry de Berenger. see
Berenger de Beaufain, John Henry de.
De Beauharnois, -------. see Beauharnois,
------, Seigneur de.
De Beaujoir, Louis Philippe Felix. see
Beaujoir, Louis Philippe Felix de, Baron.
De Beaulieu, Charles Gillston. see Beaulieu,
Charles Gillston de.
De Beaulieu Hues O'Neil, Sieur. pseud. see
Baillet, Adrien, 1649-1706.
De Beaumarchais, Amelie Eugene Caron. see
Toussaint de la Rue, Amelie Eugenie
(Caron de Beaumarchais)
De Beaumarchais, Pierre Auguste Caron. see
Beaumarchais, Pierre Auguste Caron de,
1732-1799.
De Beaumont, ------, Baron. see Beaumont,
------, Baron de.
De Beaumont, Elie. see Beaumont, Elie de,
1798-1854.
De Beaumont, Gustave de la Bonniniere. see
Beaumont de la Bonniere, Gustave
Auguste de, 1802-1866.
De Beaumont, Jean Baptiste Armand Louis
Leonce Elie. see Beaumont, Elie de,
1788-1854.
De Beaumont de la Bonniniere, Gustave
Auguste. see Beaumont de la Bonnin-
ere, Gustave Auguste de, 1802-1866.
De Beauplan, Arthur. see Beauplan, Arthur
de.
De Beauregard, Couvray. see Beauregard,
Couvray de.
De Beauregard, Jean Brumauld. see Bru-
mauld de Beauregard, Jean.
De Beaurepaire, Alezandre Marie Quesnay.
see Quesnay de Beaurepaire, Alexandre
Marie.
De Beaurpaire-Rohan, Henrique. see
Beaurepaire-Rohan, Henrique de, Vis-
conde, 1812-1894.
De Beauvallon, Jean Baptiste Rosemond. see
Beauvallon, Jean Baptiste Rosemond de.
De Beauvart, -------. see Beauvart, -------
de.
De Beauvois, Ambroise Marie Francois Joseph,
Baron Palisot. see Palisot de Beauvois,
Ambroise Marie Francois Joseph, Baron.
De Beck, William L. (1910?)-19108
De Becourt, R. see Becourt, R. de.
De Beliambe, ------. see Beliambe, -------
de.
De Belle-Forest, Francois. see Belle-Forest,
Francois de.
De Bellecombe, Andre. see Bellecombe,
Andre de.
De Bellegarde, Charlotte (Oglethorpe) see
Bellegarde, Charlotte (Oglethorpe) de.
De Bellegarde, Jean Baptiste Morvan. see
Bellegarde, Jean Baptiste Morvan de.
De Bellegarde, Joseph Francois. see Belle-
garde, Joseph Francois de.
De Bellegent, Paul. see Bellegent, Paul de.
De Bellemarre, Louis. see Bellemarre,
Louis de.
De Belleyme, Adolphe. see Belleyme,
Adolphe de.
De Bellgraves, Henrietta. 19109
De Belmont, -------. see Belmont, -------
de.
De Belmonte Bermudez, Luis. see Belmonte
Bermudez, Luis de.
De Benavente, Juan. see Benavente, Juan de.
De Benavente, Toribio. see Motolinia,
Toribio, d. 1568.

De Benavides, Alonso. see Benavides, Alonso
de.
De Benavides, Alphonsus. see Benavides,
Alonso de.
De Benavides, Pedrarias. see Benavides,
Pedrarias de.
De Benavides Cortes, Luis. see Benavides
Cortes, Luis de, Marquis de Fromesta.
De Benavides y de la Cerda, Bort. see
Benavides y de la Cerda, Bort de.
De Benevent, Charles Maurice de Talleyrand-
Perigord, Prince. see Talleyrand-
Perigord, Charles Maurice de, Prince
de Benevent, 1754-1838.
De Berches, C. see Berches, C. de.
De Bercy, ------- Drouin. see Drouin de
Bercy, ------.
De Beratarrechea, D. J. B. see Beratar-
rechea, D. J. B. de.
De Berenger de Beaufain, John Henry. see
Berenger de Beaufain, John Henry de.
De Bernegy, J. A. Sprecher. see Sprecher
de Bernegy, J. A.
De Berniere, Henry. see Berniere, Henry de.
De Beroa, Diego. see Beroa, Diego de.
De Berquen, R. see Berquen, R. de.
De Berredo, Bernardo Pereira. see Berredo,
Bernardo Pereira de.
Deberry, Edmund, 1787-1859. 61016
De Bertier, Ferdinand, Comte. see Bertier,
Ferdinand de, Comte.
De Bertin, Antoine. see Bertin, Antoine de.
De Bertrand, ------. see Bertrand, -------
de.
De Bertrand, Henri Gratien, Comte. see
Bertrand, Henri Gratien, Comte, 1773-
1844.
De Berty, L. Nigon. see Nigon de Berty, L.
De Besiers, Ermangaud. see Besiers,
Ermangaud de.
De Betancourt, J. Ramon. see Betancourt, J.
Ramon de.
De Betancurt y Figueroa, Luis. see Betancurt
y Figueroa, Luis de.
De Beteta, Gregorio. see Beteta, Gregorio
de.
De Bethencourt, Galien. see Bethencourt,
Galien de.
De Bethencourt, Jean. see Bethencourt, Jean
de, d. 1425?
De Bethencourt, Rene Robineau, Sieur. see
Robineau, Rene, Sieur de Bethencourt.
De Betizy, Eugene. see Betizy, Eugene de.
Debidas gracias al Zurriago. 86256
Debido llanto de la Provincia Mexicana de
Redentores de Cautivos. 76853
De Biedma, Luys Hernandez. see Biedma,
Luys Hernandez de.
De Bienvenida, L. see Bienvenida, L. de.
Debilidad del gobierno y embrollos del Padre
Arenas. 89411
De Biluao, Luis. see Biluao, Luis de.
De Binckum, ------. see Binckum, -------
de.
De Biron, Armand Louis de Gontaut, Duc. see
Biron, Armand Louis de Bontaut, Duc de
Lauzun, afterwards Duc de, 1747-1793.
De Biscaie, ------- Acarette. see Acarette
du Biscay, ------.
De Biscay, ------ Acarete. see Acarete du
Biscay, ------.
De Blackford, Dominique. see Blackford,
Thomas.
De Blainville, H. M. Ducrotay. see Ducrotay
de Blainville, H. M.

De Blanchelande, ------. see Blanchelande,
------ de.
De Blaquiere, P. see Blaquiere, P. de.
De Blosseville, Ernest. see Blosseville,
Ernest de.
De Bocanegra, Matea. see Bocanegra, Matea
de.
De Bocayuva, Quintino. see Souza Bocayuva,
Quintino de.
De Boigne, Claude Pierre Joseph Leborgne.
see Leborgne de Boigne, Claude Pierre
Joseph.
De Boileau, Lambert. see Boilieu, Lambert
de.
De Boilieu, Lambert. see Boilieu, Lambert
de.
De Bois, Gualterus, 1666-1751. 73076
De Bois-Mesle, Jean-Baptiste Torchet. see
Bois-Mesle, Jean Baptiste Torchet de.
De Bois-Robert, Joseph Lavallee, Marquis.
see Lavallee, Joseph, Marquis de Bois-
Robert, 1747-1816.
De Boisgelin de Cuce, Jean-de-Dieu-Raymond,
Bp. 68433 see also Aix (Diocese)
Bishop (De Boisgelin de Cuce)
De Boishebert, -------, Sieur. see Bois-
hebert, Sieur de.
De Boislecomte, Andre Olivier Ernest Sain.
see Boislecomte, Andre Olivier Ernest
Sain de, d. 1799.
De Boisneuf, ------- Payen. see Payen de
Boisneuf, ---------.
De Boisneuf, ------ Poyen. see Payen de
Boisneuf, --------.
De Boissier de Sauvages de la Croix, Pierre
Augustin. see Boissier de Sauvages de
la Croix, Pierre Augustin de.
De Boisthibault, ------ Doublet. see Doublet
de Boisthibault, ------.
De Bolea, Ambrosio Funes Villapando Abarca.
see Abarca de Bolea, Ambrosio Funes
Villapando, Conde de Ricla.
De Bologne, Francesco. see Francesco de
Bologne.
De Bomare, ------ Valmont. see Valmont de
de Bomare, ------.
De Bon, Elisabeth. see Bon, Elisabeth de.
De Bona, F. see Bona, F. de.
De Bomare, Jacques Christophe Valmont.
see Valmont de Bomare, Jacques Chris-
tophe, 1731-1807.
De Bondt, Jacob. see Bondt, Jacob de, 1592-
1631.
De Bonelli, L. Hugh. see Bonelli, L. Hugh
de.
De Bonilla, A. A. Montero Prieto. see
Montero Prieto de Bonilla, A. A.
De Bonilla, Joaquin Ignacio Ximenez. see
Ximenez de Bonilla, Joaquin Ignacio.
De Bonilla, Joseph Prieto. see Prieto de
Bonilla, Joseph.
De Bonilla, M. Diez. see Diez de Bonilla, M.
De Bonne-Maison, Alonso. see Buena-Maison,
Alonso de.
De Bonnefoux, Pierre Marie Joseph, Baron.
see Bonnefoux, Pierre Marie Joseph,
Baron de, 1782-1855.
De Bonneville, Benjamin Louis Eulalie. see
Bonneville, Benjamin Louis Eulalie de,
1796-1878.
De Bonneville, Nicolas. see Bonneville,
Nicolas de, 1760-1828.
De Bonneville, Zacherie de Pazzi. see
Bonneville, Zacherie de Pazzi de.
De Bonrepos, -------. see Bonrepos, ------
de.

Deborah Crabstick. pseud. see Wilburn,
George T. supposed author
De Borda, Andres. see Bordas, Andres de.
De Borda, Jean Charles. see Borda, Jean
Charles de, 1733-1799.
De Bordas, Andres. see Bordas, Andres de.
De Borja, Francisco. see Borja y Aragon, Fran-
cisco de, Principe de Esquilache, 1582-1658.
De Borja, Francisco. see Borja, Francisco
de, Saint, 1510-1572.
De Borja y Aragon, Francisco. see Borja y
Aragon, Francisco de, Principe de
Esquilache, 1582-1658.
De Borja y Velasco, Gaspar. see Borja y
Velasco, Gaspar de, Abp.
De Bory, Gabriel. see Bory, Gabriel de.
De Bossay, P. A. Poulain. see Poulain de
Bossay, P. A.
De Botetourt, Norborne Berkeley, Baron. see
Botetourt, Norborne Berkeley, Baron de,
1718?-1770.
De Bouchel, V. 19112
De Boucherville, C. B. see Boucherville,
C. B. de.
De Boucherville, George Boucher. see Bou-
cherville, George Boucher de.
De Bougainville, Hyacinthe Yves Philippe Poten-
tien, Baron. see Bougainville, Hyacinthe
Yves Philippe Potentien, Baron de, 1781-
1846.
De Bougainville, Louis Antoine. see Bougain-
ville, Louis Antoine de, 1729-1811.
De Bouille, Rene, Marquis. see Bouille,
Rene, Marquis de.
De Bouillon, Giles Boileau. see Boileau de
Bouillon, Gilles, 16th cent.
De Boulainvilliers, Henri, Comte. see Bou-
lainvilliers, Henri, Comte de, 1658-1722.
De Bourbon, Armand. see Conti, Armand de
Bourbon, Prince de, 1629-1666.
De Bourbourg, Charles Etienne Brassier. see
Brassier de Bourbourg, Charles Etienne,
1814-1874.
De Bourbourg, E. Beauvois Brasseur. see
Brasseur de Bourbourg, E. Beauvois.
De Bourges, Florentin. see Bourges, Floren-
tin de.
De Bourgoing, Jean Francois, Baron. see
Bourgoing, Jean Francois, Baron de, 1748-
1811.
De Bourgoing, Paul Charles Amable, Baron.
see Bourgoing, Paul Charles Amable,
Baron de, 1791-1864.
De Bovis, --------. see Bovis, ------ de.
De Bow, James Dunworthy Brownson, 1820-
1887. 11669, 11672, 19115-19121, 47490,
49462, note after 87896, 88139, 88298,
88328, 88500 see also U. S. Census
Office. Superintendent.
De Bow's monthly review. see De Bow's review.
De Bow's review. 19116, 74790, 49462, note
after 87896, 88139, 88298, 88328, 88500
De Bow's review, devoted to the restoration of
the southern states. see De Bow's re-
view.
De Bow's review, of the southern and western
states. see De Bow's review.
De Bow's reviews upon the cultivation, commerce, and manufacture of cotton. 19115
De Boye, Emmanuel. see Boye, Emmanuel
de.
De Bradi, -------, Comtesse. see Bradi,
-------, Comtesse de.
De Braga, Bernardo. see Braga, Bernardo
de.

De Braganca, Miguel. see Braganca, Miguel
de.
De Braganza, Miguel Maria Evaristo. see
Miguel I, King of Portugal, 1802-1866.
De Brahm, John Gerar William. see Brahm,
John Gerar William de.
De Brahm, William Gerard. see Brahm,
John Gerar William de.
De Brahm's philosophico-historico-hydrogeog-
raphy of South Carolina. 103051
De Branciforte, Miguel de la Grua Talamanca,
Marques. see Grua Talamanca, Miguel
de la, Marques de Branciforte.
De Brandsen, Carlos Luis Federico. see
Brandsen, Federico, i. e. Carlos Luis
Federico de, 1785-1827.
De Brauw, J. see Brauw, J. de.
De Brebeuf, Jean. see Brebeuf, Jean de,
1593-1649.
De Brebisson, Alphonse. see Brebisson,
Alphonse de, 1798-1872.
De Brehat, Alfred. pseud. Histoires. see
Guezenac, Alfred, 1823-1866.
Debret, J. B. 19122
Debrett, John, d. 1822. 14385, 19123-19124,
103122
De Brez, Guy. see Brez, Guy de.
De Briceno, Mariano. see Briceno, Mariano
de.
De Brie, Jean. see Brie, Jean de.
De Brignoles, -------, Marquis. see
Brignoles, -------, Marquis de.
DeBrij, William J. tr. 83273
De Brisay, Jacques Rene. see Denonville,
Jacques Rene de Brisay, Marquis de,
d. 1710.
De Brito, Bernardo Gomes. see Gomes de
Brito, Bernardo.
De Brito, Francisco Tavares. see Brito,
Francisco Tavares de.
De Brito, J. Jose Rodrigues. see Brito, J.
Jose Rodrigues.
De Brito, Joao Rodgegues. see Brito, Joao
Rodgegues de.
De Brito Freire, Francisco. see Brito
Freire, Francisco de.
De Britto, Anacleto. see Britto, Anacleto de.
De Brivazac, ------ Beaumont. see Beaumont
de Brivazac, --------.
De Broca, Philippe. see Broca, Philippe de.
De Broe, S. see Broe, S. de, Seigneur de
Citry et de la Guette, 17th cent.
De Broglie, Achille Charles Leonce Victor,
Duc. see Broglie, Achille Charles
Leonce Victor, Duc de, 1785-1870.
De Broglie, Albert, i. e. Jacques Victor Albert,
Duc. see Broglie, Albert, i. e. Jacques
Victor Albert, Duc de, 1821-1901.
De Brossard, Alfred. see Brossard, Alfred
de.
De Brossard, Alphonse. see Brossard, Alfred
de.
De Brosses, Charles. see Brosses, Charles
de, 1709-1777.
De Bruin, Servaas. see Bruin, Servaas de.
De Brun, --------. 19125
De Bruyn, H. see Bruyn, H. de.
De Bry, Dieterichs. see Bry, Dieterichs de.
De Bry, Johann Israel. see Bry, Johann
Israel de.
De Bry, Johann Theodor. see Bry, Johann
Theodor de, 1561-1623?
Debt and resources of the United States.
22095
Debtor & creditor's vade mecum. 19126

Debtors' prison. 95315
Debtor's prison. A tale of a revolutionary
soldier. 19127
De Buch, L. see Buch, L. de.
De Bucquoy, J. see Bucquoy, J. de.
De Buena-Maison, Alonso. see Buena-Maison,
Alonso de.
De Buenacasa, Pedro Martin. see Buenacasa,
Pedro Martin de.
De Buenaventura, J. E. see Buenaventura,
J. E. de.
De Buenavista, Miguel Perez de Santa Cruz,
Marques. see Santa Cruz, Miguel Perez
de, Marques de Buenavista.
De Buffon, Georges Louis Leclerc, Comte.
see Buffon, Georges Louis Leclerc,
Comte de, 1707-1788.
De Bulas, Juan. see Bulas, Juan de.
De Bulhoens, Michele. see Bulhoens, Michele
de, Bp.
De Bullion, L. see Bullion, L. de.
De Bure, J. J. see Bure, J. J. de.
De Burgoa, Francisco. see Burgoa, Francisco
de, 1605-1681.
De Burunda, Joseph Erazu. see Erazu, Joseph,
de Burunda.
De Bussiere, Marie Theodore Renaurd, Vicomte.
see Dussiere, Marie Theodore Renaurd,
Vicomte de, 1801-1865.
De Bustamante, Antonio Sanchez. see Sanchez
de Bustamante, Antoine.
De Bustamante, Ambrosius. see Bustamante,
Ambrosius de.
De Bustamante, Carlos Maria. see Bustamante,
Carlos Maria de, 1774-1848.
De Bustamante y Guerra, Jose. see Busta-
mante y Guerra, Jose de.
De Bustamante, Fernando Vello. see Busta-
mente, Fernando Vello de.
De Bustamante, Jose Lopez. see Bustamante,
Jose Lopez de.
De Busto, Alejo Vanegas. see Vanegas de
Busto, Alejo.
De Bustos, Francisco Gonzalez. see Gonzalez
de Bustos, Francisco.
De Butron, Jacinto Moran. see Moran de
Butron, Jacinto, 1668-1749.
Deby, P. N. H. 19128
De C., -----. pseud. see Montucla,
---------.
De C***, Marquis. pseud. see Condorcet,
Marie Jean Antoine Nicolas Caritat,
Marquis de.
De C., J. T. pseud. see C., J. T. de.
De C., L. pseud. see Capine, Louis de.
De C., Le M. pseud. see C., Le M. de.
De C------, S------. pseud. see
C------, S------ de. pseud.
De C. Moreira, J. see Moreira, J. de C.
De Ca de Mosto, Alvise. see Ca da Mosto,
Alvise, 1432?-1480?
De Cabello, F. see Cabello, F. de.
De Cabredo, Rodrigo. see Cabredo, Rodrigo
de.
De Cabrera, Joseph. see Cabrera, Joseph de.
De Cabrera, Manuel. see Cabrera, Manuel de.
De Cabrera, Michele. see Cabrera, Miguel.
De Cabrera, Rodrigo. see Cabrera, Rodrigo
de.
De Cabrera y Quintero, Cayetano. see Cabre-
ra y Quintero, Cayetano de.
Decada terceira da Asia de Ioamo de Barros.
3646
Decade di alberi curiosi ed eleganti piante.
31815

Decade of addresses at Bowdoin College. 891
Decade sermons. 104141
Decade II. Graphtolites of the Quebec group.
10458, 29805
Decadencia del Peru. 3640
Decadencia y restauracion del Peru. 97712
De Cadereyta, -------, Conde. see Alen-
castro Marona y Silva, Fernando de,
Marques de Valdafuentes.
Decades of the Newe Worlde. 1561, 34106,
3d note after 45010, note after 99383C,
106294, 106330-106331
Decades virorum illustrium Paraquariae
Societatis Jesu ex historia ejusdem
provinciae. 94573
Decades virorum illustrium Paraquariae
Societatis Jesu ex instrumentis literariis.
94573
De Cadore, Jean Baptiste Nompere de Cham-
pagny, Duc. see Champagny, Jean
Baptiste Nompere de, Duc de Cadore.
De Cadusch, -------, Marquis. see Cadusch,
-------, Marquis de.
De Caen, Guillaume. see Caen, Guillaume
de.
Decaisne, J. (21355)
De Caldas, Francisco Jose. see Caldas,
Francisco Jose de.
De Caldas, Francisco Juan. see Caldas,
Francisco Juan de.
De Caldas, Sebastian Alvarez Alfonso Rosica.
see Rosica de Caldas, Sebastian Alvarez
Alfonso.
De Caligny, Antenor. see Caligny, Antenor
de.
Decalogium. 102560
Decalogue. 92677
Decalves, Alonso. pseud. 19129-(19130), 2d
note after 96503, note before 98445-
98470, 103225
De Calzada, Bernardo Maria. see Calzada,
Bernardo Maria de, fl. 1784-1807.
De Calzado, Bernardo Maria. see Calzada.
Bernardo Maria de, fl. 1784-1807.
De Camoes, Luiz. see Camoes, Luiz de,
1524?-1580.
De Camp, John. USN 19131
De Camp (J.) firm publisher see Bell and
De Camp. firm publishers
De Campo, Juan. see Campo, Juan de.
De Campoamor y Campoosorio, Ramon Maria
de las Mercedes. see Campoamor y
Campoosorio, Ramon Maria de las Mer-
cedes de, 1817-1901.
De Campos, Jose Paulo Rodrigues. see Cam-
pos, Jose Paulo Rodrigues de.
De Campos, Juan. see Campos, Juan de.
De Campos, Juan Greg. see Campos, Juan
Greg. de.
De Campos, Luis Caetano. see Campos,
Luis Caetano de.
De Campos Marin, Juan. see Marin, Juan
de Campos.
De Campos Martinez, Juan Gregoria. see
Martinez, Juan Gregoria de Campos.
De Campos y Martinez, J. G. see Campos
y Martinez, J. G. de.
De Candamo, ------- Gonzalez. see Gonzalez
de Candamo, -------.
Decandole, -------. 67461
De Canizares, Martin. see Canizares, Martin
de.
De Cano, Sebastian. see Cano, Sebastian de.
De Cantabrana, Mariana Phelippa. see Canta-
brana, Mariana Phelippa de.

De Cantbrana, Maria P. see Cantabrana,
Maria Phelippa de.
De Cantwell, A. see Cantwell, A. de.
Decanver, H. C. anagram see Cavender,
C. H.
De Capine, Louis. see Capine, Louis de.
De Capse, Charles Francois. see Capse,
Charles Francois de, Bp.
De Cara Amo y Figueroa, Juan. see Cara
Amo y Figueroa, Juan de.
De Caraman, Georges Joseph Victor Riquet,
Comte. see Caraman, Georges Joseph
Victor Riquet, Comte de.
De Carate, Augustin. see Zarate, Augustin
de, b. 1514
De Carbajal, Miguel. see Carbajal, Miguel de.
De Carballido y Cabuenas, J. M. see Carballi-
do y Cabuenas, J. M. de.
De Cardenas, Alonso. see Cardenas, Alonso
de.
De Cardenas, Bernardino. see Cardenas,
Bernardino de, Bp.
De Cardenas, Francisco. see Cardenas,
Francisco de.
De Cardenas, Juan. see Cardenas, Juan de.
De Cardenas y Leon, Carlos Celedonio Velas-
quez. see Velasquez de Cardenas y
Leon, Carlos Caledonio.
De Cardenas y Rodriguez, Jose M. see Car-
denas y Rodriguez, Jose M. de.
De Cardenas Z. Cano, Gabriel. pseud. anagram
see Barcia, Andres Gonzalez.
De Carlscroon, Jean Dumont, Baron. see
Dumont, Jean, Baron de Carlscroon,
d. 1726.
De Carmona, Antonio Tamariz. see Tamariz
de Carmona, Antonio.
De Carondelet, Francisco Luis Hector. see
Carondelet, Francisco Luis Hector,
Baron de, 1748?-1807.
De Carpin, Jean du Plan. see Plan de Carpin,
Jean du.
De Carrera, Manuel J. see Carrera, Manuel
J. de.
De Carrion, Alonso. see Carrion, Alonso de.
De Carro, Jean. see Carro, Jean de.
De Carvajal, Bernardin. see Carvajal, Bernar-
din de.
De Carvajal y Ribera, Fr. Fernando. see
Carvajal y Ribera, Fr. Fernando de.
De Carvalho, Jorge. see Carvalho, Jorge de.
De Carvalho, Manuel de Almeida. see Car-
valho, Manuel de Almeida de, Bp., 1749-
1818.
De Carvalho e Mello, Sebastiao Jose. see
Pombal, Sebastiao Jose de Carvalho e
Mello, Marquis de.
De Casa Barreto, Nicolas Barreto, Conde.
see Barreto, Nicholas, Conde de Casa
Barreto.
De Casa Yrujo, Carlos Martinez de Yrujo y
Tacon, Marques. see Casa Yrujo,
Carlos Martinez de Yrujo y Tacon,
Marques de, 1763-1824.
De Casafuente, Juan de Acuna, Marques. see
Acuna, Juan de, Marques de Casafuente.
De Casal, Manuel Ayres. see Ayres de Casal,
Manuel, b. 1754?
De Casapalma, Francisca Fernandez de Cor-
doba, Condesa. see Fernandez de
Cordoba, Francisca, Condesa de Casa-
palma.
De Cascaliendres, Veremundo Androminas.
see Cascaliendres, Veremundo Andro-
minas de.

719

De Casqueta, Antonio Joseph Ortiz. see
  Casqueta, Antonio Joseph Ortiz de,
  Marques de Altamira.
De Casqueta, Bartholome Antonio Joseph Ortiz.
  see Casqueta, Bartholome Antonio
  Joseph Ortiz de, Marques de Altamira.
De Cassagnac, Adolphe de Granier. see
  Granier de Cassagnac, Adolphe de.
Decasse, Nicholas. 95299
De Cassini, Jean Dominique, Comte. see
  Cassini, Jean Dominique, Comte de,
  1748-1845.
De Casson, Francois Dollier. See Dollier
  de Casson, Francois.
De Castaing, -------. see Castaing, -------
  de.
De Castaneda de Nagra, Pedro. see Castan-
  eda de Nagra, Pedro de.
De Castanheda, Fernao Lopez. see Castan-
  heda, Fernao Lopez de.
De Castaniza Gonzalez de Aguero, Juan Fran-
  cisco. see Gonzalez de Aguero, Juan
  Francisco de Castaniza.
De Castelazo, Josef Rodrigo. see Castelazo,
  Josef Rodrigo de.
De Castellamare, Pietro. see Castellamare,
  Pietro de.
De Castellanos, Juan. see Castellanos, Juan
  de.
De Castelmehor, -------, Conde. see
  Castelmehor, -------, Conde de.
De Castelnau, Francois, Comte. see Castel-
  nau, Francois, Comte de, 1812-1880.
De Castilho, Alexandre Magno. see Castilho,
  Alexandre Magno de.
De Castilho, Antonio Felician. see Castilho,
  Antonio Felician de.
De Castilla, Miguel. see Castilla, Miguel de.
De Castilla y Zamora, Christoval. see Castil-
  la y Zamora, Christoval de, Bp.
De Castillo, Bathasar. see Castillo, Bathasar
  de.
De Castillo, Dom. Lopez. see Lopez de
  Castillo, Dom.
De Castillo, Juan Joseph. see Castillo, Juan
  Joseph de.
De Castillo de Herrera, Alonso. see Herrera,
  Alonso de Castillo de.
De Castoreno, J. see Castoreno, J. de.
De Castro, ------- Bermudez. see Berumdez
  de Castro, -------.
De Castro, Alonzo Nunez. see Nunez de
  Castro, Alonzo.
De Castro, Carlos Bermudez. see Bermudez
  de Castro, Carlos.
De Castro, Eduardo de Sa Pereira. see Sa
  Pereira de Castro, Eduardo de.
De Castro, Francisco. see Castro, Francisco
  de.
De Castro, Geronimo Ortiz. see Ortiz de
  Castro, Geronimo.
De Castro, Guillen. see Castro, Guillen de.
De Castro, Henrique Jose. see Castro,
  Henrique Jose de.
De Castro, Ignacio. see Castro, Ignacio de,
  1732-1792.
De Castro, Joaquin Machado. see Castro,
  Joaquin Machado de.
De Castro, Jose Basilio. alias see Montene-
  gro, Juan.
De Castro, Jose Constantino Gomes. see
  Castro, Jose Constantino Gomes de.
De Castro, Jose Geronimo Sanchez. see
  Sanchez de Castro, Jose Geronimo.
De Castro, Joseph. see Castro, Joseph de.

De Castro, Joseph Augustin. see Castro,
  Joseph Augustin de.
De Castro, Juan. see Castro, Juan de.
De Castro, Juan Gonzalez. see Gonzalez de
  Castro, Juan.
De Castro, Juan Ortiz. see Ortiz de Castro,
  Juan.
De Castro, M. see Castro, M. de.
De Castro, Manuel Bermudez. see Castro,
  Manuel Bermudez de.
De Castro, Manuel Fernandez. see Castro,
  Manuel Fernandez de.
De Castro, Nicolas. see Castro, Nicolas de.
De Castro, Pedro. see Castro, Pedro de.
De Castro, Pedro Ignacio. see Ignacio de
  Castro, Pedro.
De Castro, Pedro Munoz. see Munoz de
  Castro, Pedro.
De Castro, Rafael. see Castro, Rafael de.
De Castro, Tomas. see Castro, Tomas de.
De Castro, Vincente Antonio. see Castro,
  Vincente Antonio de.
De Castro Andrade y Portugal, Pedro Fernandez.
  see Castro Andrade y Portugal, Pedro
  Fernandez de, Conde de Lemos, 1634-
  1672.
De Castro Macedo, Melchor. see Melchor de
  Castro Macedo. Fray
De Castro Rebello, Francisco Justiniano. see
  Rebello, Francisco Justiniano de Castro.
De Castro Santa Anna, Jose Manuel. see
  Castro Santa Anna, Jose Manuel de.
De Castro Tavares, Jeronymo Villa. see
  Castro Tavares, Jeronymo Villa.
Decatur, Mrs. S. W. (19135)-19137
Decatur, Stephen, 1779-1820. 19132, 25722,
  1st note after 99448
Decatur, Stephen, 1779-1820. defendant at
  court of enquiry 19133
Decatur, Ala. Bank. see Bank of Alabama.
  Decatur Branch.
Decatur, Ala. Railroad Convention, 1853. see
  Railroad Convention. Decatur, Ala.,
  1853.
Decatur Branch Bank. see Bank of Alabama.
  Decatur Branch.
De Cavagnal, Pierre Francois de Rigaud,
  Marquis de Vandreuil. see Vaudreuil
  de Cavagnal, Pierre Francois de Rigaud,
  Marquis de.
De Caxica, P. Maestro Fray Jacinto. see
  Jacinto de Caxica. Fray
Decay of love to God in churches, offensive &
  dangerous. 74381
Decay of the power of godliness. 103400
De Cazal, Manoel Ayres. see Ayres de
  Cazal, Manuel, b. 1754?
Decaze, -------. 11641, 19139
De Cazenove, Leonce. see Vazenove, Leonce
  de.
De Cea, Genaro Rus. see Rus de Cea, Genaro.
Deceased pastor. 24779
Deceased pastor remembered. 91873
De Ceballos, Pedro Ordonez. see Ordonez de
  Ceballos, Pedro, d. 1550?
Deceit and unreasonableness of self-righteous-
  ness. 82441
Deceitfulnesse of sinne. 32838
Deceiver of the nations discovered. 33361
De Celliez, Adelaide. see Celliez, Adelaide
  de.
Decem conclvsionvm manvs in avgvstissimo
  totivs orbis terrarvm. 86522
Dec. 5, 1723. A most humble proposal.
  51095, 62559

December 30, 1777. All Gentlemen volunteers.
19140
Decennial and farewell sermons. 59167
Decennial catalogue of the class. 71233
Decennial meeting of the class of 1854. 73936
Decennial record; or, digest no II. of the class
of 1859. 53088
Decennial sermon, . . . December 3, 1865.
60935
Decennium luctuosum. 46280
De Cepeda, Francisco. see Cepeda, Francisco
de.
De Cepeda, Juan Suarez Osorio. see Suarez
Osorio de Cepeda, Juan.
De Cerdena, Antonio Machoni. see Machoni
de Cerdena, Antonio.
De Cerqueira e Silva, Jose Antonio. see
Cerqueira e Silva, Jose Antonio de.
De Cerquiera e Silva, Ignacio Accioli. see
Accioli de Cerquiera e Silva, Ignacio,
1808-1865.
De Cerralvo, Rodrigo Pacheco Osorio,
Marques. see Osorio, Rodrigo Pacheco,
Marques de Cerralvo.
De Cervantes, Juan Ortiz. see Cervantes,
Juan Ortiz de.
De Cervantes, Nic. Gomez. see Gomez de
Cervantes, Nic.
De Cespedes, Andres Garcia. see Cespedes,
Andres Garcia de.
De Cevallos, Pedro Ordonez. see Ordonez
de Ceballos, Pedro, d. 1550?
De Ch******. pseud. see Chabanon, Michel
Paul Guy de.
De Chabanon, Michel Paul Guy. see Chabanon,
Michel Paul Guy de.
De Chabert de Cogolin, Joseph Barnard. see
Chabert de Cogolin, Joseph Bernard,
Marquis de, 1724-1805.
Dechado de la castidad. (26412)
Dechado de principes ecclesiasticos. 96249
De Chalesme, -------. see Chalseme,
------ de.
De Chalusset, Abel. see Chalusset, Abel de.
De Chamisso, Adelbert. see Chamisso, Adel-
bert von, 1781-1838.
De Champagny, Jean Baptiste Nompere, Duc
de Cadore. see Champagny, Jean
Baptiste Nompere de, Duc de Cadore.
De Champlain, Samuel. see Champlain,
Samuel de, 1567?-1635.
De Chalna, ------. pseud. see Montucla,
--------.
De Chantal, J. B. J. see Chantal, J. B. J.
de.
De Chantal, Teresa. see Teresa de Chantal.
Sister
De Chanvalon, Jean Baptiste Thibault. see
Chanvalon, Jean Baptise Thibault de.
De Charbonnel, Armand Francois Marie. see
Charbonnel, Armand Francois Marie de,
Bp.
De Charency, Charles Felix Hyacinthe Gouhier,
Comte. see Charency, Hyacinthe,
Comte de, 1832-1916.
De Charency, Hyacinthe, Comte. see Char-
ency, Hyacinthe, Comte de, 1832-1916.
De Charleval, Charles Francois. see Char-
leval, Charles Francois de.
De Charlevoix, Pierre Francois Xavier. see
Charlevoix, Pierre Francois Xavier de.
De Charmilly, ------- Venault. see Venault
de Charmilly, --------.
De Charms, Richard. 19141-19143, 19431
De Charms's tracts for the times. 19141

De Chastellux, Francois Jean, Marquis. see
Chastellux, Francois Jean, Marquis de,
1734-1788.
De Chastenent, Antoine Hyacinthe Anne. see
Pruysegur, Antoine Hyacinthe Anne de
Chastenet, Comte, 1752-1807.
De Chateaubriand, Francois Auguste, Vicomte.
see Chateaubriand, Francois Auguste,
Vicomte de, 1768-1848.
De Chateauneuf, Agricole Hippolyte la Pierre.
see Chateauneuf, Agricole Hippolyte la
Pierre de.
De Chatelain, -------. see Chatelain, -------,
Chevalier de.
De Chaufepie, C. A. see Chaufepie, C. A. de.
De Chaumont, J. le Ray. see Chaumont, J. le
Ray de.
De Chaumont, L. see Chaumont, L. de.
De Chavannes, -------. see Chavannes,
------ de.
De Chavannes de la Giraudiere, H. see
Chavannes de la Giraudiere, H. de.
De Chavero, Francisco Martinez. see Martinez
de Chavero, Francisco.
De Chaves, Hieronymo. see Chaves, Hieronymo
de.
De Chaves, Joseph Martin. see Martin de
Chaves, Joseph.
De Chazelles, Augustin Jean Baptiste Louis
Marie. see Chazelles, Augustin Jean
Baptiste Louis Marie de, Comte, 1803-
1866.
De Checieux, G. A. F. Simon de Lagrange.
see Lagrange de Checieux, G. A. F.
Simon de.
De Chelemar, ---------, Prince. see
Chelemar, -------, Prince de.
De Cheverus, Jean Louis Anne Magdelene
Lefebre. see Cheverus, Jean Louis
Anne Magdelene Lefebre de, Cardinal,
1768-1836.
De Chevigni, -------. see Chevigni, M. de.
De Chevrieres de Saint Vallier, Jean Baptiste
de la Croix. see Saint Vallier, Jean
Baptiste de la Croix de Chevrieres de,
Bp.
De Choiseul, -------. see Choiseul, --------
de.
De Choiseul-Paraslin, -------, Duc. see
Choiseul-Praslin, ------ Duc de.
De Christo, Fabiao. see Fabiao de Christo.
De Christoforo d'Avalos, Felice Antonio see
Christoforo d'Avalos, Felice Antonio de.
De Cieca de Leon, Pedro. see Cieca de Leon,
Pedro de.
Decima tertia pars historia Americanae.
(8784)
Decimal currency. (10453)
Decimal system. 24043
Decimal system, for the arrangement and
administration of libraries. 80775
Decimas al desengano de la vida. 77045
Decimotercio informe anual del Superintendente
de Instruccion Publica. 10001
De Cintra, Pedro. see Cintra, Pedro de.
Decir la verdid de various modos. (78911)
Decision. 103806
Decision. Chancery of New Jersey. (31332)
Decision de la Real Audiencia de los Reyes.
61110
Decision du Conseil Imperial des Prises.
43056
Decision in Chancery of New Jersey. 53097
Decision in the Bourbon Circuit Court. 79759
Decision of Chief Justice Taney. 48029, note
after 94301

Decision of constitutional questions. 18818
Decision of Judge Leavitt, of Ohio. 39565
Decision of the Appeal Court of South-Carolina. 69454
Decision of the arbiter. 104130
Decision of the bishops. 57319
Decision of . . . the case of Dred Scott. 56050
Decision of the Circuit Court of the United States for . . . New Jersey. 53098
Decision of the Commissioners under the Fourth Article of the Treaty of Ghent. 93571
Decision of the Congregational Church in Rupert, Vt. 74146
Decision of the Court of Appeals upon the manor question. 70230
Decision of the Court of Chancery of the state of New Jersey. 80738, 105025-105026
Decision of the General Land Office. 64382
Decision of the King of the Netherlands considered. 19144, 43921, 65017
Decision of the King of the Netherlands, upon the disputed points of boundary. 104131
Decision of the Legislature of Massachusetts. 36735, 82577
Devision of . . . the Lieutenant Governor. (54729)
Decision of the Supreme Court in the Girard will case considered. (27494)
Decision of the Supreme Court, in . . . the Territory of Oregon. (57550)
Decision of the Supreme Court of Pennsylvania, in the ejectments. 60043
Decision of the Supreme Court of Pennsylvania, pronounced in 1799. 9936
Decision of the Supreme Court of Pennsylvania, relative to the after-purchased real estate. 27487
Decision of the Supreme Court of the state of New York. 19145, 39852, 53636
Decision of the Supreme Court, upon the constitutionality of an act. (70576)
Decision of the Supreme Judicial Court of Massachusetts. (8249), note after 91015
Decision of the United States Supreme Court on military commisions. 49087
Decision of the Vice Chancellor. (53637)
Decisiones de la Real Audiencia. (19146)
Decisions and rulings of the Commissioner. 6975, 6977
Decisions de la Audiencia de la isla Espanola. 19147
Decisions des Tribunaux du Bas-Canada. 10495
Decisions in bankruptcy. (60342)
Decisions in Terrett v. Taylor. 31669
Decisions of cases in Virginia. 100230
Decisions of Hon. Peleg Sprague, in admiralty. 89699
Decisions of Hon. Peleg Sprague in maritime, admiralty, and prize causes. 89700
Decisions of the Court of Appeals of the state of Kentucky. 85376
Decisions of the Interior Department in the public land cases. 40230
Decisions of the Superintendent of Common Schools. 60044
Decisions of the Superintendent of Common Schools of the state. 53638
Decisions of the Superintendents of Common Schools of the state of New York. 20341
Decisions of the Supreme Court of Errors and Appeals for the state of Tennessee. 94732

Decision of the Supreme Court of Massachusetts. 65979
Decisions of the Supreme Court of Wisconsin. 26130
Decisions [of the United States Supreme Court.] 2895
Decisions on the tax law. (6977)
Decisive confirmation of the awful disclosures of Maria Monk. 84021, 84023
Decisive conflicts of the late civil war. 19630
De Cisneros, Alonso Vazqeuz. see Vazquez de Cisneros, Alonso.
De Cisneros, Joseph Luis. see Cisneros, Joseph Luis de.
De Cisternay du Fay, Charles Jerome. see Du Fay, Charles Jerome de Cisternay, 1662-1723.
De Citry et de la Guette, S. de Broe, Seineur. see Broe, S. de, Seigneur de Citry et de la Guette.
Decius. pseud. Decius's letters. see Montgomery, James. and Nicholas, John.
Decius. pseud. Letters of Decius. (19148)
Decius. pseud. Letters of Decius, in answer to the criticism. (19149), note after 96978
Decius. pseud. Letters of Decius; or, a few observations. (19150)
Decius. pseud. Letters of Decius to the legislature. 40609
Decius. pseud. Observations on the American treaty. see Courtenay, Thomas P.
Decius's letters. (50137), (55169), 100451
Deck, Isaiah. 19151
Deck and port. 14799
Deck of the Crescent City; a picture of American life. 20352
Deck of the Crescent City. A poem. 20351
Decker, Adolf. 19152, 31501-31510, 33679
Decker, Sir Matthew, Bart., 1679-1749. 65865, 88192
Decker, Sir Matthew, Bart., 1679-1749. supposed author 71086
Deckern, Adolph. see Decker, Adolf.
De Clairac, ------. see Clairac, ------ de.
Declamacion honoraria. 93349
Declamacion oratoria. 98783
Declamacion primera contra el despotismo del poder judicial. 68790, 70097
Declamation del comercio de la Habana. 29423
Declaracion breve de la cartilla que manifiesta. 105736
Declaracion copiosa de las quarto partes mas essenciales. 4450
Declaracion de la doctrina Cristiana. 4610
Declaracion de la independencia hecha por los delegados del pueblo de Tejas. 94976
Declaracion de la regla de S. Francisco. 76286
Declaracion de S. A. con acuerdo de su Consejo manifiestado. (78149)
Declaracion del pueblo de Tejas. 94976
Declaracion del quadrante de las catedrales de Indias. 21767
Declaracion general de las personas que pretenecen. 79159
Declaracion legal de la inocencia del ciudadano Antonio Olarte. 55274, 57103, 1st note after 100684
Declaracion que de orden del Virrei del Peru. 77094
Declaracion que hizo vn soldado del enemigo. 34819
Declaraciones de los indios de los pueblos de Istalguaca. 98593

Declaracon of the presente estate of the English in Virginia. 99871
Declaratie door de Gemagtigden der Vereenigde Colonien van Noord-America. 19153
Declaratie door de Gemagt. der Vereenigden Colonien van Noord-Amerika. 55428
Declaratie, ofte precijse verklaringe van de Plenipotentiarisen ende Ambassadeurs. 19154
Declaratie van Sijn Koninghlijcke Majesteyt van Portugael Don Ioan. 19155
Declaratio coloniae domini Baronis de Baltimoro. 103353
Declaratio specvli orbis compositi. 69130
Declaration. 32287
Declaration adresse au nom du Roi. (23032)
Declaration against prophaneness & immoralities. (19157), 45705, 104088
Declaration against the Penicooke and Eastern Indians. 45705
Declaration and address of His Majesty's loyal associated refugees assembled at Newport, R. I. (19156), 42563
Declaration and constitution of the American Society of United Irishmen. 19161
Declaration and pledge against slavery. 81950
Declaration and principles of the Native Americans of Boston. 8903
Declaration and protest against proceedings of Bishop Hobart. 40545
Declaration and protest of liberty against usurpation and tyranny. 25792
Declaration and protests of the Wardens and Vestry of Christ Church. 32303
Declaration and remonstrance of the distressed and bleeding frontier inhabitants of the province of Pennsylvania. 19163, 19938, 60057, 64448
Declaration and testimony for the doctrine and order of the church of Christ. 19164, 59898
Declaration and testimony [of the General Assembly of the Presbyterian Church in the U. S. A.] 65148
Declaration au Roy. 56084
Declaration by the representatives of the United Colonies in North America. (15522), 19159
Declaration by the representatives of the United Colonies of North-America, now met in General Congress at Philadelphia, setting forth the causes and necessity of their taking up arms. Also an address from the twelve United Colonies. 19159A
Declaration by the representatives of the United Colonies of North America, now met in General Congress at Philadelphia, setting forth the causes and necessity of their taking up arms. The letter of the twelve United Colonies. 19160
Declaration de Messieurs les Directeurs, & Associes en la Compagnie de la Nouuelle France. 99751
Declaration de M. Bissette au sujet de sa derniere brochure. 5652
Declaration de l'auteur [i. e. Boyer-Peyreleau] a ses concitoyens. 7132
Declaration des ambass. d'Espaigne. 19154
Declaration du Roi, concernant les dettes de cargaison des navires. 19166
Declaration du Roy, concernant la regie & perception du droit de capitation. 19167
Declaration du Roy, concernant les cafez provenant des plantations. 19168
Declaration du Roy, concernant les marchandises des colonies Francoises. 19165

Declaration du Roy qui attribue la connoissance des affairs. 75095
Declaration, dying warnings and advice of Rebekah Chamblit. (11808)
Declaration faite a la municipalite de Bordeaux. 5844
Declaration for the certaine time of dravving the great standing lottery. 99872
Declaration from their own publication. 21594
Declaration how the monies . . . were disposed. 99884
Declaration issued by the Yearly Meeting of Anti-slavery Friends of Indiana. 26164
Declaration of a future glorious estate of a church. 34067
Declaration of a number of ministers in Boston and Charlestown. 17675
Declaration of a number of the Associated Pastors of Boston and Charlestown. 14524, 18698
Declaration of American independence. 100075
Declaration of American independence, with a correct fac simile of the signatures. 71976
Declaration of claim in the name and behalf of the proprietors. 95937
Declaration of divine order. (22096)
Declaration of faith and covenant of the Second Baptist Church, Cambridge. 10133
Declaration of faith, compact and platform. 73643
Declaration of faith, published by the Society of Friends. (79616)
Declaration of faith, . . . with rules. 55577
Declaration of faith, with the church covenant. 6671
Declaration of former passages and proceedings. 45706, 51774, 104844
Declaration [of grievances against Rev. W. O. White.] 65094
Declaration of His Highness. 49141
Declaration of his [i. e. James H. Bell's] political views. 4466
Declaration of independence. 19172-19173
Declaration of independence. A candid statement of facts. 97592
Declaration of independence. A discourse. 26232
Declaration of independence; a poem. 70917
Declaration of independence, agreed upon and published. 88653
Declaration of independence and constitution of of the provisional government of . . . Kentucky. 37503
Declaration of independence and constitution of the United States. 19170
Declaration of independence and constitution of the United States of America. (19169), 19177
Declaration of independence, and constitution of the United States of America, with its amendments. (19171)
Declaration of independence, and constitution of the United States of America, with the Amendments; together with the constitution of the state of New-York. 19174
Declaration of independence, and names of the signers. 20429
Declaration of independence, by citizens of Mecklenburg County, (N. C.) (19178), (47286)
Declaration of independence by Congress in 1776. (19176)
Declaration of independence by the citizens of Mecklenburg County. (19178), (47286)

Declaration of independence, by the colony of Massachusetts Bay. 45707

Declaration of independence from the sale of the Democratic Party. 84729

Declaration of independence made at Washington. 94954, 94955

Declaration of independence, made by the delegates of the people of Texas. 95114

Declaration of independence, made in convention, March 2, 1836. 94974

Declaration of independence . . . March 2nd, 1838. 94994

Declaration of independence of Mecklenberg County, N. C. (19178), (47286)

Declaration of independence of the state of South Carolina. 87433

Declaration of independence of the United States of America, 1776. 19175

Declaration of independence, or notes on Lord Mahon's history. (25054)

Declaration of [Michael] Robinson. 72054

Declaration of ministers from divers parts of Massachusetts. 46550

Declaration of ministers in Barnstable County. 3554, 103617

Declaration of New-England Yearly Meeting of Friends. 51789, 52626, 2d note after 92833

Declaration of Ohio Yearly Meeting. 56907

Declaration of one returning from the dates of the grave. 46488

Declaration of principles. 19179

Declaration of religious freedom. 79582

Declaration of remarkable providences. 18461

Declaration of rights. 23194

Declaration of rights, also, the constitution. 94720

Declaration of rights and fundamental rules. 52569

Declaration of rights and wrongs. 87808

Declaration of rights, and the constitution and form of government. (45125)

Declaration of rights and the constitution of Maryland. 45126

Declaration of rights made by the representatives of the good people of Virginia. 100021-100022

Declaration of rights of the inhabitants of the commonwealth of Massachusetts. (45708)

Declaration of sentiment of the American Anti-slavery society. 81825

Declaration sentiments and constitution of the American Anti-slavery Society. (81826)

Declaration of sentiments made by the Synod of Missouri. 64692

Declaration of sentiments of the American Anti-slavery Society. 81825

Declaration of the affairs of the English people. 64974

Declaration of the American citizens on the Mobile. 102008

Declaration of the American Congress. 18347, 27145, note after 41286, note after 71369

Declaration of the Association of the County of New-Haven. (52975), 91756, 103618

Declaration of the company. 88229

Declaration of the Congress at Philadelphia. 34087, note after 92858

Declaration of the Council constituted by the Indian and African Company of Scotland. 78197

Declaration of the county of Essex. 23003

Declaration of the demeanor and cariage of Sir Walter Raleigh. 67548-67550

Declaration of the demeanor of Sir W. Raleigh. 30394

Declaration of the dissatisfied brethren of the church. 78621

Declaration of the doctrine and practice of the church of Christ. 21310, 79717, 92025, note after 97880

Declaration of the faith and doctrine of the Church of the Latter Day Saints. 64971

Declaration of the General Court of Massachusetts. 5628

Declaration of the gentlemen, merchants, and inhabitants of Boston. 9708, 46651, 52597

Declaration of the immediate cause[s] which induce and justify the secession of South Carolina. 87434

Declaration of the immediate causes which induce and justify the secession of South Carolina. 87435-87436

Declaration of the inhabitants of Barbadoes. 3263A, 19162

Declaration of the inhabitants of Boston, and the country adjacent. 46731-46732, 58359, note after 70346, 92350

Declaration of the King of England. 86077

Declaration of the Lord Baltemore's [sic] plantation. 103351

Declaration of the ministers in Barnstable County. 3554, 103617

Declaration of the National Anti-slavery Convention at Philadelphia. 81824

Declaration of the objects and measures of the farmers. 54235

Declaration of the objects of the Liverpool Society. (41582), 81951

Declaration of the people's natural rights. 79808, 79810-79811

Declaration of the reasons and motives for the present appearing in arms. 19180

Declaration of the Rector and Tutors of Yale-College. 13220, 105826

Declaration of the Right Honourable Robert Earle of Warwick. 101508

Declaration of the sad and great persecution. 9455

Declaration of the Seneca Nation of Indians. 79108

Declaration of the society of people (commonly called Shakers.) (19181), 79702, note after 97880, 3d note after 102601

Declaration of the state of the colonie and affaires in Virginia. 55946, 99877-99879, 99882

Declaration of the state of the colony and affaires in Virginia. 99880-99881

Declaration of the state of the colony and affaires in Virginia. With a relation of the barbarous massacre in the time of peace. 99885

Declaration of the supplies. 99879

Declaration of the supplies intended to be sent to Virginia. 99879

Declaration of the true causes of the great troubles. 19182

Declaration of the trustees of that charity. 103207

Declaration of the 1200 masons. 69705

Declaration of the views and objects. 98074

Declaration of the warrantable grounds and proceedings. 53386

Declaration of the whole country. 99976

Declaration of the Yearly Meeting of Friends, held in Philadelphia. 19183

Declaration of the Yearly Meetings of Ohio, Indiana, and Baltimore. 19187

Declaration of trust and articles of agreement and association [of the Saint Lawrence Land Company.] 75317

Declaration of trust and articles of agreement of the New York and Michigan Company. 54736

Declaration of trust, June 1, 1858. 20793

Declaration of views. 7273

Declaration of war [against Great Britain.] 50015

Declaration of war against Spain. 8122

Declaration of war with the law concerning letters of marque. 19184

Declaration of what God has done for our souls. (19185)

Declaration or manifest of the High and Mighty Lords the States General. 19186

Declaration, published by the inhabitants of Boston, and the country adjacent. 46731-46732, 58359, note after 70346, 92350

Declaration, . . . relativement au retour de la princesse. 3294

Declarationis martyri servorum Dei Ignatii Azeuedi. 68434

De Clerck, N. see Clerck, N. de.

De Clermont-Lodeve, Guillaume Emmanuel Joseph Guilhem. see Saint-Croix, Guillaume Emmanuel Joseph Guilhem de Clermont Lodeve, Baron de.

De Clifford, George. see Cumberland, George de Clifford, 3d Earl of, 1558-1605.

Decline and fall of the Hoosac Tunnel. 5540

Decline of popery and its causes. 51539

Declining state of our church-order. 103400

De Clodore, Jean. see Clodore, Jean de.

De Cobarruvias Orozco, Seb. see Orozco, Seb. de Cobarruvias.

De Cocconato, Gian Francesco Galeani Napione. see Napione de Cocconato, Gian Francesco Galeani.

De Cocherel, ------. see Cocherel, ------ de.

De Coetlogon, C. see Coetlogon, C. de.

De Cogolin, Joseph Bernard Chabert. see Chabert de Cogolin, Joseph Bernard, Marquis de, 1724-1805.

De Cogolludo, Diego Lopez. see Lopez de Cogolludo, Diego.

Decoigne City and Canal Company. 19188

De Coin, Robert L. 19189

De Colignola, Zarrabini. see Flaminio, Fian Antonio, 1464-1536.

De Coligny, A. see Coligny, A. de.

De Colmenar, Juan Alvarez. see Colmenar, Juan Alvarez de.

De Comyn, Tomas. see Comyn, Tomas de.

De Conceicao, Apollinario. see Apollinario de Conceicao.

De Conceicao, Claudio. see Conceicao, Claudio de.

De Concepcion, Joseph Garcia. see Garcia de Concepcion, Joseph.

De Condorcet, Marie Jean Antoine Nicolas Caritat, Marquis. see Condorcet, Marie Jean Antoine Nicolas Caritat, Marquis de, 1743-1794.

De Condorcet, Sophie de Grouchy, Marquise. see Condorcet, Sophie de Grouchy, Marquise de.

De Conejares, Francisco Alonso y Ruiz. see Ruiz de Conejares, Francisco Alonso y.

De Conejares, Joseph Ruiz. see Ruiz de Conejares, Joseph.

De Constant, ------. see Constant, ------ de.

De Constant, Louis Rilliet. see Rilliet de Constant, Louis, i. e. Frederic Jacques Louis, 1794-1856.

De Conti, Armand de Bourbon, Prince. see Conti, Armand de Bourbon, Prince de, 1629-1666.

De Contreras, Christobal Manso. see Manso de Contreras, Christobal.

De Contreras, Francisco. see Contreras, Francisco de.

De Contreras, Pedro Moya. see Moya de Contreras, Pedro, Abp.

De Contreras Gallardo, Pedro. see Contreras Gallardo, Pedro de.

De Contreras Herrera, Juan. see Herrera, Juan de Contreras.

De Cools, A. see Cools, A. de, Baron.

De Corancez, Louis Alexandre Olivier. see Olivier de Corancez, Louis Alexandre.

De Cordoba, A. see Cordoba, A. de.

De Cordoba, Francisca Fernandez. see Fernandez de Cordoba, Francisca, Condesa de Casapalma.

De Cordoba, Jose. see Cordoba, Jose de.

De Cordoba, Juan. see Cordoba, Juan de, fl. 1578.

De Cordoba, L. Cabrera. see Cabrera de Cordoba, L.

De Cordoba, Manuel Fernandez. see Fernandez de Cordoba, Manuel.

De Cordoba, Pedro Tomas. see Cordoba, Pedro Tomas de.

De Cordoba, Tomas. see Cordoba, Tomas de.

De Cordoba y Sande, Fernando Fernandez. see Fernandez de Cordoba y Sande, Fernando.

De Cordova, A. see Cordoba, A. de.

De Cordova, Diego. see Cordova, Diego de.

De Cordova, Diego Fernandez. see Fernandez de Cordova, Diego, 1. Marques de Guadalcazar.

De Cordova, Francisca Fernandez. see Fernandez de Cordoba, Francisca, Condesa de Casapalma.

De Cordova, Felipe Colmenares Fernandez. see Fernandez de Cordova, Felipe Colmenares.

De Cordova, Francisco Hernandez. see Cordova, Francisco Hernandez de.

De Cordova, J. see Cordova, J. de, fl. 1858.

De Cordova, J. M. Fernandez. see Fernandez de Cordova, J. M.

De Cordova, Juan. see Cordoba, Juan de, fl. 1578.

De Cordova, Matias. see Cordova, Matias de.

De Cordova, Pedro. see Cordova, Pedro de.

De Cordova, R. J. see Cordova, R. J. de.

De Cordova Laso de la Vega, Antonio. see Laso de la Vega, Antonio de Cordova.

De Cordova Salinas, Diego. see Salinas, Diego de Cordova.

De Cordova y Sande, Fernando. see Fernandez de Cordoba y Sande, Fernando.

De Cordova y Souza, J. A. Fernandez. see Souza, J. A. Fernandez de Cordova y.

De Cormere, J. F. Mahy. see Mahy de Cormere, J. F.

De Cornet, ------, Comte. see Cornet, ------, Comte de.

De Cornillon, Charles. see Cornillon, Charles de.

De Coronado, Carlos Vazquez. see Vasques Coronado, Carlos.

De Coronado, Francisco Vazquez. see Vazquez de Coronado, Francisco, 1510-1549.

De Cosco, Aliander. see Aliander de Cosco.
De Cosco, Leander. see Aliander de Cosco.
De Coso, Alexandrus. see Coso, Alexandrus de.
DeCosta, Benjamin Franklin. 19191-19200, 86264
De Costa, Constantino Pereira. see Costa, Constantino Pereira de.
De Costa, Manual. see Costa, Manual de.
De Costa, Thomas. see Costa, Thomas de.
De Costa Barros, Pedro Jose. see Costa Barros, Pedro Jose de.
De Costa e Sa, Manoel Jose Maria. see Costa e Sa, Manoel Jose Maria de.
De Coulanger, A. P. see Coulanger, A. P. de.
De Courbes, I. see Courbes, I. de.
De Courcelles, Jullien. see Courcelles, Jullien de.
De Courcy, Henri. see Courcy de Laroche-Heron, Henri de.
De Courcy, Richard, 1743-1803. 19203
De Courmont, Felix. see Courmont, Felix de.
De Cournand, Antoine. see Cournand, Antoine de.
De Courtanvaux, F. C. le Tellier. see Le Tellier de Courtanvaux, F. C.
De Courtenay, J. M. (19206)-19207
De Courtiras, Gabrielle Anne Cisterne. see Saint Mars, Gabrielle Anne Cisterne de Courtiras, Vicomtesse de, 1804-1872.
De Courtonne, Jean Palmyer. see Paulmier, Jean, d. ca. 1669.
De Coute, Jose Ferrer. see Ferrer de Couto, Jose.
De Couto, Diogo. see Couto, Diego de.
De Couto, Jose Ferrer. see Ferrer de Couto, Jose.
De Coutto Ferraz, Luis Pedreira. see Ferraz, Luiz Pedreira de Coutto.
Decouverte de Bahia. 21417
Decouverte de l'Amerique. 10286
Decouverte de l'Amerique par les Normands. 67475
Decouverte de l'Amerique pour l'instruction and [sic] l'amusement des enfans et les juenes gens. 10295
Decouverte de l'Isle de Pine's. 82185
Decouverte de quelques pays et nations. 95332
Decouverte des Indes Occidentales par les Espagnols. 11273-(11275), 11282
Decouverte des Indies Occidentales, par les Espagnols. 39117
Decouverte des ruins d'une ancienne ville Mexicaine. 77204
Decouverte des sources du Mississippi. 4604
Decouverte du nouveau-monde. Histoire d'Amerique. (1459)
Decouverte du nouveau-monde, meladrame historique. 63174
Decouverte du nouveau-monde, ode-symphonie en quatre parties. 48037
Decouverte du nouveau monde. Roman historique. 19549
Decouverte du tombeau de Champlain. 39296
Decouverte d'un ancien Volcan. 77217
Decouverte d'un pays plus grand. 4936
Decouverte, l'acquisition, l'etablissement. 24338
Decouvertes dans la mer du sud. 38958
Decouvertes des Francois. 24748
Decouvertes des Scandinaves en Amerique. (4212), 19204
Decouvertes et conquetes du Portugal. 79170

Decouvertes et etablissements de Cavelier de la Salle. 28358
Decouvertes et establissements des Francais. 96172
De Couvray, Jean Baptiste Louvet. see Louvet de Couvray, Jean Baptiste.
De Covarruvias, Pedro Lopez. see Covarruvias, Pedro Lopez de.
De Coverley, Sir Roger. pseud. see Sewall, Jonathan, 1728-1796.
Decow, Stacy. defendant (31332), 80737-80738, 105025-105026
Decow, Stacy. plaintiff 19205, 88244
De Crauliz, Augustino. see Cravaliz, Agostino di.
De Cravaliz, Augustino. see cravaliz, Agostino di.
De Crequy, ------. 102498
Decree. 84738, 89081
Decree (for the complainants). 58366
Decree in the case of Solomon de Medina. 47349
Decree of the Circuit Court of the United States. 92294
Decree of the National Convention. 96340
Decree of the Queen of Portugal. 14378
Decree, on the Admiralty side of the District Court of New York. 20983
Decrees and proceedings in the case of the foreclosure. 83871
Decrees of Senor Benito Juarez. 57679
Decrees of the District Court of the United States. 89224
Decrees of the governments of Peru, Bolivia, and Chile. 90775, note after 103224
Decreet van den Directeur en Raden van Nieuw-Nederlandt. (55282)
De Cresse, Auguste Jean Baptiste Bouvet. see Bouvet de Cresse, Auguste Jean Baptiste.
Decret de la Convention Nationale. 75097
Decret de l'Assemblee Generale de Saint-Domingue. 75096
Decret portant l'organisation du gouvernment de l'isle de St. Barthelemy. 75002
Decreta Concilii Provincialis Orgonesis I. 72918, (80023)
Decreta edita in Synodo Dioecesana 1me celebrada Sinu Viridi. 72944
Decreta Rmi Patris Mag. Regentis Fr. Nicolai Antonii Schiaffinati. 77629
Decreta Synodalia Dioeceseos Sti Pauli de Minnesota. 72969
Decreto constitucional para la libertad de la America Mexicana. 27823, (48380), 48408
Decreto de convocacion de 22 de Marzo de este ano de 1820. 97044
Decreto de la Magestad del Rey Catholico Phelipe V. (19208)
Decreto de Pio IX. 63170
Decreto de 4 de Diciembre de 1860. 48409
Decreto de 28 de Diciembre ultimo [i. e. 1839.] 98259
Decreto del Congreso Granadino. 86236
Decreto del gobierno de Chile de 18 de Deciembre de 1837. 12779
Decreto del P. Ejecutivo sobre pagares afianzados. 101294
Decreto del Sacra Congregazione de' Ritti. (58305)
Decreto del Supremo Gobierno concediendo el pase el breve. 48410
Decreto di Sua Maesta il Re Catolico Filipo V. 19209
Decreto N. 3977 de 12 de Octubre de 1867. 24129

Decreto pontifico expedido en 13 de Diciembre de 1769. (58288)
Decreto sobre extinction de alcabalas en el estado de Mexico. 48411
Decreto sobre la suspension y abolicion de confiscacion. 98872
Decreto sobre uniformidad de las cuotas de alcabala. 19210
Decretos del Congreso Constituyente del estado de Mexico. 48412
Decretos del Congreso Constituyente del estado de Michoacan. 48809
Decretos del Gefe del Estado, Mar. 1827. 29073
Decretos del Rey Don Ferdinando VII. 48413
Decretos del Santo Concilio Tridentino. 57101, 68461
Decretos expedidos desde su restitucion al trone Espanol. 24159
Decrets de l'Assemblee Nationale concernant les colonies. 75098
Decretvm et indvltvm Alexandri Sexti. (79175), 79179
Decretum Oxomem. 58289
Decretum super varias delatas ad regium. 62441
De Crevecoeur, Michel Guillaume Jean. see Crevecoeur, J. Hector St. John, 1735-1818.
De Croix, Carlos Francisco. see Croix, Carlos Francisco de.
De Croy, Emmauel, Duc. see Croy, Emmanuel, Duc de, 1718-1784.
De Croy-Solre, Prince Emmanuel. see Croy, Emmanuel, Duc de, 1718-1784.
De Cruillas, --------, Marques. see Cruillas, -------, Marques de.
De Cuba, Miguel Tacon y Rosique, Marques de la Union. see Tacon y Rosique, Miguel, Marques de la Union de Cuba, 1777-1854.
De Cubas, Antonio Garcia. see Garcia Cubas, Antonio, 1832-1912.
De Cubieres, Simon L. P. see Cubieres, Simon L. P. de, Marquis.
De Cubillas Don-Yague, Francisco. see Cubillas Don-Yague, Francisco de.
De Cuce, Jean-de-Dieu-Raymond de Boisgelin. see De Boisgelin de Cuce, Jean-de-Dieu-Raymond.
De Cuellar, Jose T. see Cuellar, Jose T. de.
De Cuenca, Juan Francisco de Montemayor. see Montemayor y Cordova de Cuenca, Juan Francisco de, 1620-1685.
De Cuenca, Juan Francisco de Montemayor y Cordova. see Montemayor y Cordova de Cuenca, Juan Francisco de, 1620-1685.
De Cuendias, Manuel. see Cuendias, Manuel de.
De Cueva Ponce de Leon, Alonzo. see Ponce de Leon, Alonzo de Cueva.
De Cuevas Aguirre y Espinosa, Jose Francisco. see Cuevas Aguirre y Espinosa, Jose Francisco de.
De Cullion, F. Va. see Cullion, F. Va. de.
De Curt, --------. see Curt, ------ de.
Decus ac tutamen. 46281
De Cussy, Ferdinand. see Cussy, Ferdinand de, Baron, 1795-1866.
De Cussy, Frederic. see Cussy, Ferdinand de, Baron, 1795-1866.
De Custine, Adam Philippe. see Custine, Adam Philippe, Comte de.

De Cuverville, --------. see Cuverville, -------de.
De Cuvillers, Etienne Felix d'Henin. see Henin de Cuvillers, Etienne Felix, Baron d', 1755-1841.
De Cyprey, -------, Baron Alleye. see Alleye de Cyprey, -------, Baron.
De D. Paredes, Victoriano. see Paredes, Victoriano de D.
De Dalmatie, Nicolas Jean de Dieu Soult, Duc. see Soult, Nicolas Jean de Dieu, Duc de Dalmatie.
De Dammartin, ------- Moreau. see Moreau de Dammartin, -------.
De Danguel, R. B. Plumard. see Plumard de Danguel, R. B.
De De Cussy, Ferd. see Cussy, Ferdinand de, Baron, 1795-1866.
De Degrouhette, ------- Pepin. see Pepin de Degrouhette, --------.
Dedekindus de morum simplicitate. 482, 28934
De Delmas, A. see Delmas, A. de.
De Denonville, Jacques Rene de Brisay, Marquis. see Denonville, Jacques Rene de Brisay, Marques de, d. 1710.
De Deos, Gaspar de Madre. see Gaspar de Madre de Deos, 1715-1800.
De Deus, Manual da Madre. see Madre de Deus, Manual da.
De Deux-Ponts, William. see Deux-Ponts, William de.
Dedham, R. C. 19211
Dedham, Mass. (19222)
Dedham, Mass. Citizens' Committee on the Advance of Fares Upon the Boston and Providence Railroad. 19220
Dedham, Mass. Convention of Republican Delegates from the County of Norfolk, 1812. see Democratic Party. Massachusetts. Norfolk County. Convention, Dedham, 1812.
Dedham, Mass. Court. 72744
Dedham, Mass. First Church. (19213), 19221, 38776, note after 90752
Dedham, Mass. Gentlemen. see Gentlemen in Dedham, Massachusetts. pseud. eds.
Dedham, Mass. Medfield Library. see Medfield Library, Dedham, Mass.
Dedham, Mass. Memorial Hall. 19218
Dedham, Mass. Norfolk County Anti-slavery Convention, 1838. see Norfolk County Anti-slavery Convention, Dedham, Mass., 1838.
Dedham, Mass. Norfolk Law Library. 19215
Dedham, Mass. School Committee. (19213)
Dedham, Mass. Selectmen. 19219
Dedham, Mass. South Church. (19216)
Dedham, Mass. Suffolk County Convention, 1774. see Suffolk County, Mass. Convention, Dedham, 1774.
Dedham, Mass. Supreme Judicial Court. see Massachusetts. Supreme Judicial Court.
Dedham patriot. 95157
Dedham pocket almanac and New-England calendar. (19217)
Dedham pulpit. 9241, 19212, 19898
Dedicada a los nuevos refutadores del manifiesto. 96117
Dedicated to "Hon. Martin J. Crawford." 81952
Dedicated the the army. 14092
Dedicated to the British army. Military sketches. (20937)

Dedicated to the genius of war of Delaware.
(3537)
Dedication. 33446, 72811
Dedication address. 18302
Dedication and preface of De Bry. 11285
Dedication;—good believers' character.
106198
Dedication of a soldiers monument, at Clare-
mont, N. H. 13235
Dedication of Antioch College. (19223), 44324
Dedication of Franklin and Marshall College.
25645
Dedication of Green Mount Cemetery. 3031
Dedication of Lyceum Hall. 32997
Dedication of the athenaeum. (66308)
Dedication of the Chapel-School of St. Barnabas.
43679
Dedication of the Lincoln Grammar School
house. 41273
Dedication of the Memorial Hall, in Dedham.
19218
Dedication of the new chapel of Brown Univer-
sity. 8620
Dedication of the New-York State Agricultural
Rooms. 53810
Dedication of the rooms of the . . . [Providence
Young Men's Christian] Association.
66340
Dedication of the soldiers' monument at Che-
shire, Conn. 12518
Dedication of the soldiers' monument at Dor-
chester. (20528)
Dedication of the soldier's monument, October
18, 1866. 28025
Dedication; or an essay on the true modern
Caesar. 19224
Dedication sermon at Charleston, S. C.
32550
Dedication sermon, delivered at the New Brick
Meeting-House. 36610
Dedication sermon, preached in Fayetteville,
North-Carolina. 73568
Dedication sermon—real Christianity. 93207
Dedication sermon . . . Union Presbyterian
Church of St. Louis. (32738)
Dedication services at the opening of Mount
Olivet Cemetery. 3032
Dedication services of the Lowville Rural
Cemetery. 42543
Dedication services. Oxford Presbyterian
Church. (58035)
Dedication to His Excellency Joseph Bloom-
field. 102494
Dedication to the collective body of the people
of England. 64
Dedication to the Marquiss of Rockingham.
106040
Dedication to the said Society [of Scotland for
Propagating Christian Knowledge.] 7339
Dedication to the young gentlemen and ladies
of America. 97532
Dedication with joy. 17637
Dedicator of Mr. Emlyn's "Inquiry." 9422
Dedicatoria que ofrece D. Juan de Cavrera y
Palma. 4844
Dedicatory address at the opening of the
Female Academy. 58118
Dedicatory epistle. 100450, 2d note after
100521, 104974
Dedicatory exercises. 9063
Dedicatory letter. 104969
Dedicatory letter addressed to Washington.
102492
Dedicatory letter to Reymer von Streytperck.
77803

Dedicatory poem . . . Dec. 29, 1868. (16924)
Dedicatory sermon, at the new Meeting-House.
72450
Dedicatory sermon . . . the next day. 30521
Dedicatory services of the new edifice. 63115
Dedicatory speech of President Lincoln.
60592
De Dieu Soult, Nicolas Jean. see Soult,
Nicolas Jean de Dieu, Duc de Dalmatie.
De Dillon, Roger Henri. see Dillon, Roger
Henri de.
De Dios, Jose de la Madre. see Jose de la
Madre de Dios.
De Dios, Juan de la Madre. see Juan de la
Madre de Dios.
De Dios Arias, C. Juan. see Juan de Dios
Arias, C.
De Dios Canedo, Juan. see Canedo, Juan de
Dios.
De Dios Fernandez de Sousa, Juan. see
Fernandez de Sousa, Juan de Dios.
De Dios Mendez, Juan. see Mendez, Juan
de Dios.
De Dios Mendivelzua, Juan. see Mendivelzua,
Juan de Dios.
De Dios Rosal, Juan. see Rosal, Juan de
Dios.
De Dios Salcedo, Juan. see Salcedo, Juan
de Dios.
De Doblas, -------- Gonzalez. see Doblas,
-------- Gonzalez de.
Derick, -------. 51222
De Drummond, Antonio de Vasconcellos Mene-
zes. see Drummond, Antonio de
Vasconcellos Menezes de.
Deduccao chronologica e analytica. 81088-
81090
Deduccas ou manifesto dos factos que na crise
actual suscitao. 19225
Deductie door den Commandeur van St.
Eustatius, J. de Graaf. 49560, 102897
Deductie over de gheime onderhandelingen
tusschen d. Pensionaris van Berkel.
27683
Deductie van den representant van syne door-
lughigste Hoogheid. (19226), (22992), 1st
note after 102890
Dedvctie, waer by onpartijdelijck overvvogen
ende bevvesen vvort. 19227, 2d note
after 102890
Deduction du sumptueux ordre. 19556
Deduction of the case between George Carew.
10823
Deduction of the case between George Carew
and J. Pergens. 10823
Deduction of the title to Harlaem Commons.
78969
Deducation of the title to the Manor of Living-
ston. 93961
Deduzzione abbreviata degli ultimi fatti.
63904
De Echavarri, Bernardo Ibanez. see Ibanez
de Echavarri, Bernardo.
De Echavarry, Ibanez. see Echavarry, Ibanez
de.
De Echave, Balth. see Echave, Balth. de.
De Echevelar, Manuel. see Echevelar,
Manuel de.
De Echeverria, J. see Echeverria, J. de.
De Echeverria, Jose Villegas. see Villegas
de Echeverria, Jose.
De Echeverria, Juan Nepomuceno. see
Echeverria, Juan Nepomuceno de.
De Echeverria, Manuel. see Echeverria y
Penalver, Manuel de.

De Echeverria y Penalver, Manuel. see
 Echeverria y Penalver, Manuel de.
De Echeverria y Vieta, M. F. see Veytia,
 Mariano, 1718-1779.
De Echeverria y Veytia, Mariano Jose Fernan-
 dez. see Veytia, Mariano, 1718-1779.
De Echeverz, Pedro Ignacio. see Echeverez,
 Pedro Ignacio de.
Deed and its results. 58736
Deed of gift. 105195
Deed of gift. A comic opera, in three acts.
 105181
Deed of gift to my dear son, Capt. Mat. Page.
 58157
Deed of horror! 23673
Deed of lease and release of Sarah Derby.
 19669
Deed of settlement of the Mutual Assurance
 Company, for Insuring Houses from Loss
 by Fire in New York. (51605)
Deed of settlement of the Mutual Assurance
 Company, for Insuring Houses from
 Losses by Fire, in . . . Philadelphia.
 (61854)
Deed of settlement of the Society for Insuring
 of Houses, In and Near Philadelphia.
 61568
Deed of the Indians, settling the boundary line
 between the English and Indian lands.
 25595, 34579-34580, 99584, note just
 before 103108
Deed of the Six Nations to the Proprietors of
 Indiana. 22595, 34579-34580, 99584,
 note just before 103108
Deed of trust from Lyne Starling to Robert
 W. McCoy and others. 90541
Deed trust [of the Philadelphia Cemetery.]
 61973
Deedes, H. 19228
Deeds and other documents relating to the
 several pieces of land. 255, 67288
De Eguia, Jose Joaquin. see Eguia, Jose
 Joaquin de.
De Eguiara y Egueren, Juan Joseph. see
 Eguiara y Egueren, Juan Joseph de.
De Eguilaz, Diego. see Eguilaz, Diego de.
De Eguilaz, L. see Eguilaz, L. de.
Deeker, Sir M. see Decker, Sir Matthew,
 Bart., 1679-1749.
De el Rio, A. M. 19229
De Elcio, Philippo. see Elcio, Philippo de.
De Elorza y Rada, Francisco. see Elorza y
 Rada, Francisco de.
Deems, Charles F. 19230
De Encinas, Diego. see Encinas, Diego de.
De Enciso, Martin Fernandez. see Encisco,
 Martin Fernandez de.
Deensche Africaensche Compagnie. Resident.
 petitioner 69585, 2d note after 102911
 see also Charisius, ------. petitioner
Deep placer mining in California. 81050
Deep River Mining and Transportation Company.
 Charter. 19231
Deeper wrong. 7722, note after 12718, 19232,
 35501
De Equiluz, Diego. see Eguilaz, Diego de.
Deer hunters. 44802
Deer Island and the city institutions. (19233)
De Ercilla y Zungia, Alonso. see Ercilla y
 Zuniga, Alonso de.
Deerfield, Mass. petitioners 47691
Deerfield, Mass. Indian Conference, 1735.
 see Massachusetts (Colony) Indian
 Conference, Deerfield, 1735.

Deerfield captive, an Indian story. 93077,
 104274
Deerfield collection of sacred music. 104114-
 104115
De Ericeyra, Luis de Menezes, Conde. see
 Menezes, Luis de, Conde de Ericeyra.
Deering, Sir Edward. (15052)
Deering, N. 19235
Deering, Richard. 19236
De Erreparaz, Joseph. see Erreparaz,
 Joseph de.
Deerslayer. 16460
Deerslayer; or the first war-path. 16430
Deerslayer ou le tueur de daims. (16431)
De Escalante, Bernard. see Escalante,
 Bernard de.
De Escalante, Silvestre Velez. see Velez
 de Escalante, Silvestre.
De Escalante Fontaneda, Hernando. see
 Fontaneda, Hernando de Escalante.
De Escalona Aguero, Gaspar. see Aguero,
 Gaspar de Escalona.
De Escalona y Tamariz, Jose Nicholas. see
 Escalona y Tamariz, Jose Nicholas de.
De Escandon, Juan. see Escandon, Juan de.
De Escobar, Diego Antonio. see Escobar,
 Diego Antonio de.
De Escobar, Diego Lopez. see Lopez de
 Escobar, Diego.
De Escobar, Jose Saenz. see Saenz de
 Escobar, Jose, fl. 1700.
De Escobar, Manoel. see Escobar, Manoel
 de.
De Escobar, Marina. see Escobar, Marina
 de.
De Escobar, Pedro Suarez. see Suarez de
 Escobar, Pedro, Bp.
De Escobar Salmeron y Castro, Jose. see
 Salmeron y Castro, Jose de Escobar.
De Escobar y Llamas, Diego Osorio. see
 Escobar y Llamas, Diego Osorio de, Bp.
De Escoiquiz, Juan. see Escoiquiz, Juan de.
De Escontria, Joseph Gomez. see Escontria,
 Joseph Gomez de.
De Escorza y Escalante, Pedro. see Escorza
 y Escalante, Pedro de.
De Escoyti y Norri, Gabriel Pantaleon. see
 Pantaleon e Escoyti y Norri, Gabriel.
De Escudero, Jose Augustin. see Escudero,
 Jose Augustin de.
De Esealona Aguero, Gaspare. see Aguero,
 Gaspare de Esealona.
De Eslaba, Sebastian. see Eslava y Lazaga,
 Sebastian de.
De Eslava, ------ Goncalez. see Gonzalez de
 Estava, Fernan.
De Eslava y Lazaga, Sebastian. see Eslava
 y Lazaga, Sebastian de.
De Espada y Landa, Francisco Joseph Diaz.
 see Espada y Landa, Francisco Joseph
 Diaz de.
De Espada y Landa, Juan Jose Diaz. see
 Espada y Landa, Juan Jose Diaz de.
De Esparza, M. see Esparza, M. de.
De Esparza, Mariano Ruiz. see Esparza,
 Mariano Ruiz de.
De Espejo, Antonio. see Espejo, Antonio
 de, fl. 1581-1583.
De Espinosa, Antonio Vazquez. see Vazquez
 de Espinosa, Antonio.
De Espinosa, Isidro Felix. see Espinosa,
 Isidro Felix de.
De Espinosa, Josef. see Espinosa, Josef de.
De Espronceda, Jose. see Espronceda, Jose
 de.

De Esquerra, M. see Esquerra, M. de.
De Esquibel, Joseph. see Esquibel Joseph de.
De Esquilache, Francisco de Borja, y Aragon,
    Principe. see Borja y Aragon, Fran-
    cisco de, Principe de Esquilache, 1582-
    1658.
De Esquiuel y Caceres, Rodrigo. see Esquiuel
    y Caceres, Rodrigo de.
De Esquiuel y de la Dueua, Antonio Gregoria.
    see Esquieul y de la Dueua, Antonia
    Gregoria de.
De Esquivel y Vargas, Ildefonso. see Esquivel
    y Vargas, Ildefonso de.
Deesse. (19237)
Deesse, an elssler-atic romance. (19237)
De Estava, Fernan Gonzalez. see Gonzalez
    de Estava, Fernan.
De Estete, Miguel. see Estete, Miguel de.
De Esteyneffer, Hermano Juan. see Steinefer,
    Johann.
De Esteyneffer, Juan. see Steinefer, Johann.
De Estrada, Antonio Nicolas, Duque. see
    Estrada, Antonio Nicolas, Duque de.
De Estrada, Ignacio Francisco. see Estrada,
    Ignacio Francisco de.
De Estrada, Jose Maria Guitterez. see
    Gutierrez y Estrada, Jose María, 1800-
    1867.
De Estrada, Joseph Manuel. see Estrada,
    Joseph Manuel de.
De Estrada, Juan. see Estrada, Juan de.
De Estrada, Sebastian. see Estrada, Sebastian
    de.
De Estrada Medinilla, Maria. see Medinilla,
    Maria Estrada de.
De Estrada y Escouedo, Francisco. see
    Estrada y Escouedo, Francisco de.
De Estrada y Escovedo, Pedro. see Estrada
    y Escovedo, Pedro de.
Deeth, S. G. 72164, 1st note after 97095
De Ezeta, L. G. see Ezeta, L. G. de.
De Ezguerra, Mathías. see Ezguerra, Mathias
    de.
De F., M. R. pseud. see F., M. R. de.
    pseud.
Defaite de l'armee Anglais. 53322
Defaite des savvages Armovchiqvois. 40168
De Faria, Manoel Severim. see Faria,
    Manoel Severim de.
De Faria Rios Sanchez y Zarzosa, Manuel de
    Godoy Alvarez. see Godoy Alvarez de
    Faria Rios Sanchez y Zarzosa, Manuel
    de, Principe de la Paz, 1761-1851
De Faria y Sousa, Manuel. see Faria y
    Sousa, Manuel de.
De Faro, Fernando Telles. see Telles de
    Faro, Fernando.
Defauconpret, Auguste Jean Baptiste, 1767-
    1843. tr. 3661, 16411, 16418, 16427-
    16428, (16431), 16435, 16439, 16451,
    16453, 16462, 16472, 16480, 16482,
    16490, 16496, 16503, 16511, (16514),
    16517, 16519, 16531, 16534, 16550,
    16553, 16560, 16571, 23923, 73377,
    73385
Defauconpret, C. A. tr. 16423, 35174, (35209)
Defeat of Gen. St. Clair. 54476
Defeat of Generals Braddock, Harmer & St.
    Clair. 97192, 97196
Defeats and victories. 18790
Defective state of the administration of justice.
    (61285), 65636, note after 93185
Defects of preachers reproved. 91943-91944
De Felice, G. see Felice, G. de.
Defence against calumny. 22202, 74487

Defence, against King's Attorney and Judge
    Advocate Bille's insidious attack. 6399
Defence against the attacks of the Hon. George
    Brown. 74573
Defence against the charge of treason. 104780
Defence and justification of the conduct of Mr.
    George Pray. 64986
Defence and testimony against an egregious and
    butchering slander. 89314
Defence before a general court-martial. 67490
Defence before the Board of Trustees. 87976
Defence, before the House of Representatives.
    62784
Defence [by Vindex.] (62666)
Defence, containing the author's renunciation of
    universalism. 96096
Defence, delivered before the Classis of Mont-
    gomery. 94677
Defence for fugitive slaves. 89607
Defence in abatement of judgment. 12397
Defence nos. 1 and 2. (43189)
Defence of a book intituled, The snake in the
    grass. (40196)
Defence of a book lately re-printed at Boston,
    entitled A modest proof. 12362, 12364,
    (25402), (25407), 99800, 101194, 103904
Defence of a liberal construction of the powers
    of Congress. 30003, 43202
Defence of a majority of the city of Baltimore's
    Directors. 63126
Defence of a paper, entituled, Gospel-truths.
    59691
Defence of "A true narrative of the origin and
    progress." 103661
Defence of abolition principles. (81953)
Defence of administration against the opposition.
    17533
Defence of Alexander Slidell Mackenzie. 43421
Defence of American Methodism. 46901
Defence of an answer made unto the nine ques-
    tions. 78431
Defence of an essay on dramatique society.
    20979
Defence of an introductory lecture. 58193
Defence of an order of court made in the year
    1637. 98500
Defence of Aristocles letter to Authades.
    (20062)
Defence of Armageddon. 63104
Defence of Baltimore, and death of General
    Ross. 22528
Defence of Bartholomew Las-Casas. 28724
Defence of Brigadier General W. Hull. (33642)
Defence of Brig. Gen'l Wm. A. Hammond.
    (30112)
Defence of Calvin and Calvinism. 74430
Defence of Canada considered as an imperial
    question. (81172)
Defence of capital punishment. By Rev. George
    Cheever. 40852
Defence of capital punishment . . . in a discus-
    sion. (63463)
Defence of Captain Alexander. (15283)
Defence of Captain Digby, concerning Admiral
    Knowles's charges. (20140)
Defence of Capt. Digby Dent. 19609
Defence of Captain Jonas P. Levy. 40763
Defence[of Capt. Middleton.] 20406
Defence of Capt. Richard W. Meade. 47236
Defence of Capt. W. K. Latimer . . . before
    Court of Enquiry, no. 3. (36269)
Defence of Capt. W. K. Latimer, U. S. Navy.
    (39207)
Defence of Christian revelation. 19238
Defence of Christianity. 83667

Defence of church-government. 18708
Defence of Columbia College. (56807)
Defence of Commander Andrew K. Long. 41868
Defence of Commander Cadwalader Ringgold. (71426)
Defence of Commander S. Lockwood. (41754)
Defence of Commodore W. D. Porter. 64322
Defence of country banks. 19245
Defence of Cyrus Barton. 3830
Defence of denominational education. 83855
Defence of Dr. Gould. 21096, 28093
Defence of Dr. Price. 105704
Defence of evangelical churches. 67164
Defence of Fort M'Henry. note before 90497
Defence of Francis W. Edmunds. 21866
Defence of Freemasonry. 64947
Defence of Gen. Henry Dearborn. (19074)
Defence of Gospel-truth. 104183
Defence of himself [i. e. Philander Chase] against the late conspiracy. 12194
Defence of his [i. e. Edmund Randolph's] resignation of that office. 34900, 2d note after 101709
Defence of Hugh Peters. 24034
Defence of injur'd merit unmasked. 19239
Defence of Isaac Davis. 18834
Defence of James W. Parker. 58684
Defence of John Canfield Sterling. 91333
Defence [of John Wilbur.] 94129
Defence of Kansas. 4310
Defence of Kenyon College. 12191
Defence of Lieut. Aug. S. Baldwin. (72747)
Defence of [Lieut. Col.] Burbank. 9197
Defence of Lt. Col. Jno. Geo. Reynolds. 70425
Defence of Lieut. Robert B. Riell. 78352
Defence of Maj. Gen. Caleb Burbank. (9196)
Defence of Major Gen. Pillow. 62853
Defence of Major James W. Ripley. 71527
Defence of masonry. 80300, 80323
Defence of Massachusetts. Speech . . . in the . . . House. 9333
Defence of Massachusetts. Speeches of Hon. Charles Sumner. 93649
Defence of Messrs. Galloway and Wharton. 3d note after 96369
Defence of Methodism. 17713
Defence of Mr. Commissioner Dogy. (6139)
Defence of Mr. Hemphill's observations. 31293, 31297
Defence of Mr. Hervey's dialogues. 17834
Defence of natural, judicial, and constitutional rights. 8769
Defence of Negro slavery. 23046
Defence of New Jersey. 19240
Defence of Ohio congregationalism. 17245
Defence of "our fathers." 22534, 42966
Defence of our naturalization laws. (66653)
Defence of Passed-Midshipman G. H. Bier. 5262
Defence of Power's statue of Webster. 23271
Defence of Presbyterian ordination. 12362, 20055, 101194
Defence of President Fillmore. 8348
Defence of Professor Smyth. 85212
Defence of protection. 28491
Defence of protestantism. 62438, (77444), 98169
Defence of religion, morality & government. (32239)
Defence of religious liberty. 25230
Defence of republicanism. 36237
Defence of Rev. Charles W. Denison. 19562
Defence of Richard W. Meade. 47236

Defence of Richmond against the federal army. 2052A, 19241
Defence of Robert Hodgson. (32364)-32365, note after 96027-96028, note after 103449
Defence of Simon Wilmer. 104575
Defence of slavery: being a review of a letter. (28349)
Defence of southern slavery. 81954
Defence of sundry positions and scriptures. 29402
Defence of that doctrine of justifying faith. (17673)
Defence of that settlement [i. e. Darien.] 18571
Defence of the agency of the Pulteney estate. 29542, 97064
Defence of the alien and sedition laws. note just before 100452, 100583
Defence of the American character. 30367
Defence of the American Congress. 15523, 56060
Defence of the American constitution. 84832
Defence of the American Sunday School Union. (29854)
Defence of the answer and arguments of the Synod. 18704, (46778)
Defence of the answer made unto the nine questions. 921
Defence of the articles on the laboring classes. 8715
Defence of the Baptist missionaries. 38084
Defence of the bill for the abolition of slaves. 44795
Defence of the bill for the registration of slaves. 91236
Defence of the British navy. 35722, 101366
Defence of the character and principles of Mr. Jefferson. 23229
Defence of the character of Thomas Jefferson. 35927, note after 97298, 2d note after 100577
Defence of the clergy of New England against the charges of interfering in our political affairs. (52627)
Defence of the clergy. Speech . . . in the House of Representatives. 47214
Defence of the colonies. (19242), 75099
Defence of the Committee on Government Contracts. 18918
Defence of the conduct of Barbadoes. (3264)
Defence of the conduct of Commodore Morris. 50862
Defence of the constitution and government of the United States of America. (41645), note after 91540
Defence of the constitution of England. 19243
Defence of the constitutions of government of the United States of America. 233, 41646, (63799)
Defence of the constitutions of government of the United States of America against the attack of M. Turgot. 234, 236
Defence of the constitutions of government of the United States of America, against the attack of M. Turgot in his letter. 235
Defence of the Convention of the Protestant Episcopal Church in the State of Massachusetts. 19244, 32933
Defence of the currency of Massachusetts. 15466
Defence of the dialogue between Praelaticus and Eleutherius. 22115, 78493
Defence of the dialogue intitled, A display of God's special grace. 17675, 20056, 95317

Defence of the divine right of infant baptism. 13350

Defence of the doctrine propovnded by the Synode at Dort. (72095), 72110

Defence of the doings of the Reverend Consociation and Association of New-Haven County. 71829, 96091

Defence of the Dutch. 19246

Defence of the Early of Shelburne, &c. 49988, 56437, 69535, (80109)-80110, 90102

Defence of the Elkhorn Association. 96122

Defence of the enquiry. 32280

Defence of the episcopal government of the church. 39530, 102571, 102574

Defence of the experiments. 80679

Defence of the exposition of the middling interest. 93483

Defence of the free state of man in England. 6220, 8069

Defence of the Great Lakes. 19247

Defence of the Halifax libel. 7889

Defence of the Hon. John Rowan and Daniel Clark. 56303

Defence of the itinerary and the conduct of the Reverend Mr. Whitefield. (13597), 32316, (59064), 97539

Defence of the ladies, and others. (71134)

Defence of "the latest form of infidelity" examined. A second letter. 71518

Defence of "the latest form of infidelity" examined. A third letter. 71519

Defence of the legislative constitution. 60045

Defence of the Legislature of Massachusetts. 19248

Defence of the Lehigh Coal and Navigation Company. (39878)

Defence of the "Letter from a gentleman at Halifax." 19249, 29702, 40457

Defence of the liberties of North-America. 16588, (41634)

Defence of the majority of the House of Commons. 41678-41679

Defence of the measures of the administration of Thomas Jefferson. 18070, 94488

Defence of the medical progression of the United States. (58191)

Defence of the merchants of Boston. 27892, 32876

Defence of the Methodist E. Church. 32360

Defence of the minority in the House of Commons. 41678, 96403

Defence of the mission to England. 50012

Defence of the modest proof. 25407, 99800

Defence of the national administration. 102322

Defence of the National Convention of France. (25379)

Defence of the national Democracy against the attack of Judge Douglas. 4701

Defence of the New-England charters. 21197

Defence of the New-Jersey dissent. 19250

Defence of the observations on the Assiento trade. 19251, 96427

Defence of the observations on the charter and conduct. 47130

Defence of the Orangemen, tried in this city. 97722

Defence of the oration. 57874

Defence of the order, containing some remarks. 38074, 76255

Defence of the order, government & economy of the United Society called Shakers. 34961-34962, 79710-79711, note after 97880, 103874

Defence of the organization of the Wesleyan Methodist connection. 39776

Defence of the Orleans Navigation Company. 105479

Defence of the pastoral letter. 87994

Defence of the people of the southern states. 5751

Defence of the planters of the West-Indies. 25002

Defence of the political and parliamentary conduct. 9304

Defence of the prerogative royal. 80059

Defence of the principles of the "Summer-morning's conversation." 13350

Defence of the reconstruction acts of Congress. 39474

Defence of the religious Society of Friends. 3783, 29315

Defence of the remarks of the Plymouth Company. 19252

Defence of the resolutions and address of the American Congress. (19243)

Defence of the Rev. B. T. Roberts. 71879

Defence of the Reverend Mr. Hemphill's observations. (36017)

Defence of the revolutionary history of the state of North Carolina. 36579

Defence of the right and duty of the American union. (73949), 73977

Defence of the Right Honourable the Earl of Shelburne. 56437, 80107

Defence of the right of the public to the batture of New Orleans. 64843

Defence of the Rockingham party. 19254

Defence of the said appeal. 104561

Defence of the Scots abdicating Darien. (18552), 18571, 78206, 78209-78210, (78215), 78234

Defence of the Scots settlement at Darien. 18549, 18571, 78206, 78211-78213, 78234

Defence of the Scots settlement at Darien, answered. 18550

Defence of the settlers of Honduras. 32760

Defence of the shipping interest. 2262

Defence of the slave trade. 19255

Defence of the south!! 31039

Defence of the Surinam Negro-English version of the New Testament. 28625

Defence of the system of solitary confinement. 82592

Defence of the tariff and internal improvement. 97751

Defence of the third article of the Massachusetts Declaration of rights. 45709, 58909

Defence of the title of the late John Leverett Esq. (40748), 101001

Defence of the treaty of amity, commerce, and navigation. 29951

Defence of the truth. 42966

Defence of the union. Speech . . . in the Senate. (39163)

Defence of the use of the Bible in the public schools. 21414

Defence of the Wesleyan Methodist missions. 102148

Defence of the Weselyan petitions. 74580-(74581)

Defence of the West-India-planters. 55354, 74206-74207, (82106), note after 99798, 2d note after 102803

Defence of the Whigs. 14771, 19256, 37408

Defence of their [i. e. the ministers of Hampshire County's] conduct. (7660)

Defence of Thompson Darrah Shaw. 79963

Defence of truth and character. (19257)

Defence of universalism. 105035

Defence of Virginia. 18253
Defence of Washington A. Bartlett. 3780
Defence [of Wesley.] 102647
Defence of William Penn. 23659
Defence of William S. Cleavenger. (13613)
Defence of William S. Fish. 24447
Defence of Young and Minns. 106131
Defence prepared and intended to be delivered.
8802, 101168
Defence read before a general court martial.
96788
Defence upon the legal grounds. 42534
Defenceless . . . situation of our state.
100408
Defences of Maine. 64059
Defences of the north-eastern frontier. 43922
Defendant's counsel. pseud. Trial of Charles
B. Huntington for forgery. see Brady,
James T.
Defenders of the country and its enemies.
(8401)
Defensa canonica de la jurisdiccion. 98130
Defensa canonica por las Provincias de la
Compania de Jesus. (78923)
Defensa canonica y real por las Provincias
de la Compania de Jesus. (19258)
Defensa canonica y real por las Provincias
de los Jesuitas. 19259
Defensa contra la censura. (40063)-40064
Defensa de algunos puntos de la doctrina
Catolica. 22903
Defensa de Don Alejandro Cross. (17650)
Defensa de Don Diego Tabares Caballero del
Orden de Santiago. 28424, note after
94166
Defensa de D. Francisco Lazo Estrada. (23061)
Defensa de D. Gabriel Claudio de Sequeira.
79182
Defensa de D. Ildefonso Villamil. 72587,
99654
Defensa de D. J. Villamil. 72587
Defensa de D. Joaquin Rangel. 70052
Defensa de D. Jose Maria de Ansorena.
34188-34189
Defensa de Eugenio Perez de Cerro. (60909)
Defensa de F. Santillan. 23574
Defensa de J. M. Mora. 50482
Defensa de Jose Maria Rafaeli. (71615)
Defensa de la carta del Sagrario de Guadala-
jara. 57719
Defensa de la causa libral. 29368
Defensa de la jurisdiccion ordinaria de los
obispos. 19261
Defensa de la manifestacion. 26720, (48414)
Defensa de la peticion. 48415
Defensa de la precedencia de los hermanos.
44297
Defensa de la soberania nacional. 99475
Defensa de la viuda e hijos de D. Jose Foribio
Larrain. (12764)
Defensa de las salves de San Pedro. 51349
Defensa de las Senoras Carolina Litchfield de
Liborius. 40951
Defensa de los diez y seis cargos. 19260
Defensa de los tratados de paz. 35077
Defensa de Nuno Nunez de Villavicencio, y
Horozco. 87161
Defensa de San Augustin. 75997
Defensa de Santa-Anna. 76747
Defensa del Archiduque de Austria. 47036,
58273
Defensa del breve de Monsenor Clementi.
9586
Defensa del derecho constitucional. 12762
Defensa del derecho de los llamados a las
capellanias. 87226

Defensa del derecho qve los RR. PP. Provin-
cial absoluto. 86412
Defensa del editor de la obra titulada Los
misterios de la inquisicion. 93348
Defensa del General D. Isidro Reyes. 17203
Defensa del Gobernador politico y militar de
la isla. 93947
Defensa del Homo Attritus. (76030)
Defensa del padre legislativo del Estado de
Nicaragua. 55143
Defensa del voto de America. 100789, 105745
Defensa do Dr. Guilherme Schuch de Com-
panema. 85628
Defensa documentada. 11293
Defensa eclesiastica. (51321)
Defensa Guadalupana, contra la disertacion.
27768
Defensa Guadalupana, escrita por el P. Dr. y
Mtro. D. Manuel Gomez Marin. (44579)
Defensa hecha por el Licenciado Don Manuel
Castellanos. 11403
Defensa juridica de la Senora D. Maria Micaela
Romero de Terreros y Trebuesto. 76223
Defensa juridica de la Sra. Marquesa de S.
Francisco. 76223
Defensa de las exenciones y privilegios regu-
lares. 48416
Defensa de los Americanos. 94158
Defensa del Archiduque de Austria. 47036,
58273
Defensa del articulo "El ministro de la guerra."
60874
Defensa del autor. 96247
Defensa del Cabildo Eclesiastico de Guadala-
jara. (29024)
Defensa del Cura Vicario de Zarate. 67344
Defensa del derecho del Ven. Cabildo de
Oaxaca. 87227
Defensa del Ex-Ministro de Relaciones D. Lucas
Alaman. 48417
Defensa del gobierno de Santa-Fe. 41983
Defensa del Pensador Mexicano. 99702
Defensa dos cidadaos Antonio Carlos Ribeiro
de Andrada Machado e Silva. 88767
Defensa en primera instancia. 74943
Defensa, juridica alegacion, y manifestacion.
48418
Defensa juridica de los albaceas y herederos
de D. Francisco Linares. (76224)
Defensa juridica del P. Felipe del Castillo.
11421, 19262
Defensa juridica que hace D. Francisco Lopez
Solis. 86413
Defensa juridica, que se propone por el derecho.
62944
Defensa juridica, y meritos de justicia. 19912
Defensa legal de D. Antonio de la Campa.
76225
Defensa legal que el Ciudadano Coronel Cirilo
Gomez y Anaya hizo. 27758, 52253
Defensa natural deducida de los mismos autos.
87236
Defensa por medio de la fortificacion de este
grand emporio. 60853
Defensa practicada el dia 19 de los corrientes.
93293
Defensa pronunciada ante el Gran Jurado el 21
de Marzo de 1850. 35066, 93333
Defensa que D. Jose Ramon Pachero ha publi-
cado. 57840
Defensa que el Clero de Honduras hace. 32761
Defensa que hace un pedo al ventoso por Don
Juan Caviedes. 98381
Defensa que hizo el Payo de Rosario. 99703
Defensa que produjo el Dr. D. Juan Jose
Hernandez. 31519

Defensa y demonstracion. 74014
Defensa y satisfaccion. 29425
Defensas de vn ministro afligido. 29105
Defensayo politico. 9587
Defense de constitutions Americaines. 237
Defense contre les attaques calomnieuses.
75834
Defense de Sir J. Yorke. 106045
Defense des emigres Francais. 38694
Defense de Recherches philosophiques sur
les Americains. 59239, 60994
Defense of republicanism. 61038
Defenseur des colonies. 10754
Defensive league of freedom. 19263
Defensive war defended. 94695
Defensive war in a just cause sinless. 36486
Defensor. pseud. Enemies of the constitution
discovered. see Thomas, William.
Defensor de la integridad nacional. 19265
Defensor de los bienes del Marques de Villa-
puente. pseud. Manifestacion. see
Vergara, Augustin de.
Defensor de los bienes del Marques de Villa-
puente. pseud. Manifesto. see Vergara,
Augustin de.
Defensor de tontos. pseud. Carta. see Vera
y Pintado, Bernardo de.
Defensor del pueblo. 55144
Defensores de la integridad del territorio
Mexicano. pseud. Verdad denuda sobre
la guerra de Tejas. 95089, 95130
Defenza de D. Jose Joaquim de Cunha de
Azeredo Coutinho. (17947)
Defenza de los directios del pais. 55145
Defenza perante o Conselho de Guerra. 17006
De Fer, N. see Fer, N. de.
De Fereal, Victor. pseud. see Suberwick,
------- de.
De Fereira, Gaspar Dias. see Fereira,
Gaspar Dias de.
De Feria, Pedro. see Feria, Pedro de.
De Ferminville, -------- La Poix. see La
Poix de Ferminville, --------.
Defermon, --------. (19266)-19267
De Fernandez de Uribe, J. P. see Fernandez
de Uribe, J. P. de.
De Ferussac, Andre E. J. P. J. F. d'Audebard,
Baron. see Ferussac, Andre E. J. P.
J. F. d'Audebard, Baron de.
De Feunleal, S. Ramirez. see Ramirez de
Feunleal, S., Bp.
Deffaudis, ----------, Baron. 19268-19271,
93785
Defi au factieux. 58165
Deficiencies in our history. (9643)
De Figuereido, Manuel. see Figuereido,
Manuel de, 1568-1630.
De Figueiredo e Mello, Pedro Americo. see
Figueriredo e Mello, Pedro Americano
de.
De Figueiroa Nabuco de Araujo, Jose Paulo.
see Nabuco de Araujo, Jose Paulo de
Figuerioa.
De Figueredo, Juan. see Figueredo, Juan de.
De Figuereido, Manoel. see Figuereido,
Manuel de.
De Figueroa, Antonio Vazquez Gastelo el Rey.
see Vazquez Gaztelu, Antonio.
De Figueroa, Christoual Mosquera. see
Mosquera de Figueroa, Christoual.
De Figueroa, Cristobal Suarez. see Suarez
de Figueroa, Cristobal.
De Figueroa, Felix Suarez. see Suarez de
Figueroa, Felix.
De Figueroa, Francisco A. see Figueroa,
Francisco A. de.

De Figueroa, Jose Suarez. see Suarez de
Figueroa, Jose.
De Figueroa, Jose Vazquez. see Vazquez de
Figueroa, Jose.
De Figueroa, Jose Vidal. see Vidal de
Figueroa, Jose.
De Figueroa, Loreco Vidal. see Vidal de
Figueroa, Lorenzo.
De Figueroa, Lorenzo Vidal. see Vidal de
Figueroa, Lorenzo.
De Figueroa, Miguel Suarez. see Suarez de
Figueroa, Miguel.
De Figueroa y Guevara, Baltasar Pardo. see
Pardo de Figueroa y Guevara, Baltasar.
De Figueros, Manuel. see Figueros, Manuel
de.
Definition of parties. (19272), 94489
Definition of the attributes and qualities. 11578
Definitions of all the technical words. (41617)
Definitive treaty. 96545, 96557-96558
Definitive treaty between Great Britain and the
United States of America. 19273, note
before 96570
Definitive treaty of Christian universal and
perpetual peace. 19274, 96545
Definitive treaty of peace and friendship.
19275, 96553
Definitive treaty, signed at Paris, 1783. 96563
De Flacourt, Etienne. see Flacourt, Etienne
de.
De Flassan, Gaetan de Raxis, Comte. see
Flassan, Gaetan de Raxis, Comte de.
De Flavigny, Gratien Jean Baptiste Louis,
Vicomte. see Flavigny, Gratien Jean Bap-
tiste Louis, Vicomte de, 1741-1803? tr.
De Fleurieu, Charles Pierre Claret, Comte
de. see Fleurieu, Charles Pierre Claret
de, Comte de.
De Florencia, Francisco. see Florencia,
Francisco de.
De Florian, Jean Pierre Claris. see Florian,
Jean Pierre Claris de, 1755-1794.
De Flozelles, -------- Henrion. see Henrion
de Flozelles, --------.
De Flurance, R. see Flurance, R. de.
Defoe, Daniel, 1659?-1731. 16303, 19276-
19279, 19281-19291, 19554, 69516, 71086,
note after 72217-72218, 72220-72222,
72228, 78981, 79266, 81423, 87911,
92339, 97330, 97560, 99509-99510,
100613-100614, 105635
Defoe, Daniel, 1659?-1731. supposed author
10966, 12553-12557, 16736, 19277, 22969,
55285, note before 87805, 97083, 1st note
after 99428, 2d note after 99428, 99429-
99431, note after 99431, note after 100822,
1st note after 100838
Defoe, Daniel, 1659?-1731. incorrectly supposed author 10668, (19280), (29384)-
29385, 86785, 105634
De Foigny, Gabriel. see Foigny, Gabriel de.
De Fonseca, Bartolome Agustin Rodriguez.
see Rodriguez de Fonseca, Bartolome
Agustin.
De Fonseca, Fabian. see Fonseca, Fabian
de.
De Fonseca, Geronimo. see Fonseca, Geronimo de.
De Fontaine, Felix Gregory, 1832-1896. 24985
De Fontaine, Felix Gregory, 1832-1896.
reporter 87470
De Fonte, Bartholonew. see Fonte, Bartholo-
mew de.
De Fontpertuis, Adalbert Front. see Front
de Fontpertuis, Adalbert.

Defonz, Milo. see Codding, Milo Defonz.
De Forbin, Louis Nicolas Philippe Auguste, Comte. see Forbin, Louis Nicolas Philippe Auguste, Comte de.
De Forbonnais, Francois de Veron. see Veron de Forbonnias, Francois de.
De Forbonnais, Francois Louis Veron. see Veron de Forbonnais, Francois Louis.
De Forest, Henry. ed. 84556
De Forest, John William, 1826-1906. 19292
De Forest, T. R. 19293, 2d note after 95665
De Forest prize oration of 1859. 91767
Deformed. 83780, 83782, 83785
Deformed gentleman. pseud. Concise view of ancient and modern religion. see Whitcomb, Chapman.
Deformed, or, a woman's trial. 83779
Deformity of a hideous monster discovered in the province of Maine. 19294, (22388)
De Fortia, Marquis. see D'Urban, Fortia.
De Foruile, Pierre Sauorguan. see Foruile, Pierre Sauorguan de.
De Fourt de Pradt, Dominique Georges Frederic de Riom de Prolhiac. see Pradt, Dominique Georges Frederic de Riom de Prolhiac de Fourt de, Abp., 1759-1837.
De Franca Almeida e Sa, Luis. see Franca Almeida e Sa, Luis de.
Defrance, -----. (75100)
Defrance, representant du peuple. (75100)
De Francheville, Joseph du Fresne. see Du Fresne de Francheville, Joseph.
De Francoli, Benito Maria de Moxo y. see Moxo y de Francoli, Benito Maria de.
De Francos, Juan Isidro Pardinas Villar. see Pardinas Villar de Francos, Juan Isidro.
De Fransans, Hippolyte. see Fransans, Hippolyte de.
Defrauded soldier. pseud. Set-off to Mr. Strong's off-set to Mr. Adams's letter!!! 92884
Defrees, John D. 19295-19296
De Frederici, Cesare. see Frederici, Cesare de.
De Freitas, Augusto Teixeira. see Teixeira de Freitas, Augusto.
De Freitas, Joaquim Ferreira. see Ferreira de Freitas, Joaquim.
De Fremery, N. C. see Fremery, N. C. de.
De Frenilly, Auguste Francois Fauveau, Marquis. see Frenilly, Auguste Francois Fauveau, Marquis de, 1768-1848.
De Freville, -------. see Freville, ------- de.
De Freville, A. F. J. see Freville, A. F. J. de.
De Freycinet, Louis Claude Desaulses. see Freycinet, Louis Claude Desaulses de.
De Freytas, Nicolas. (80023)
Defries, Kenneth. defendant (16580)
De Fromesta, Luis de Benavides Cortes, Marques. see Benavides Cortes, Luis de, Marques de Fromesta.
De Fronda, V. see Fronda, V. de.
De Frontenac, Louis de Baude, Comte de Palluau et. see Baude, Louis de, Comte de Palluau et de Frontenac, 1620-1698.
De Frontignieres, --------. see Frontignieres, ------ de.
De Fuente, ------ Villar. see Villar de Fuente, ------.
De Fuentes, Jos. Mor. see Fuentes, Jos. Mor de.

De G. S . . . . . , Edmond. see S . . . . , Edmond de G.
De Gabriac, -------, Comte. see Gabriac, -------, Comte de.
De Gagern, Carlos. see Gagern, Carlos de.
De Galard de Terraube, Louis Antoine Marie Victor. see Galard de Terraube, Louis Antoine Marie Victor de, Marquis, 1765-1840.
De Galardi, Ferdinand. see Galardi, Ferdinand de.
De Galaup, Jean Francois. see La Perouse, Jean Francois de Galaup, Comte de, 1741-1788.
De Galdo Guzman, Diego. see Guzman, Diego de Galdo.
De Galindo, Juan de Abreu. see Abreu de Galindo, Juan de.
De Galliffet, Gaston Alexandre Auguste, Marquis. see Galliffet, Gaston Alexandre Auguste, Marquis de, 1830-1909.
De Galves, --------, Marquis. see Galvez, --------, Marquis de.
De Galvez, Bernardo. see Galvez, Bernardo de.
De Galvez, Jose. see Galvez, Jose de, Marquis de. Sonora.
De Galvez, Josef. see Galvez, Josef de.
De Galuez, Pedro. see Galuez, Pedro de.
De Gama, Jose de Saldanha. see Saldanha da Gama, Jose de.
De Gama, Leonarda Gil. see Gil de Gama, Leonarda.
De Gama e Castro, Jose. see Gama e Castro, Jose de.
De Gamboa, M. Fulgencio. see Gamboa, M. Fulgencio de.
De Gamboa, Pedro Sarmiento. see Sarmiento de Gamboa, Pedro.
De Gammara y Davalos, J. B. Diaz. see Diaz de Gammara y Davalos, Juan Bento, 1745-1783.
De Gamond, Isabelle Gatti. see Gamond, Isabelle Gatti de.
De Gamond, Thomas. see Thome de Gamond, Aime de, 1807-1875.
De Gamond, Thome. see Thome de Gamond, Aime de, 1807-1875.
De Gand, Pierre. see Gand, Pierre de.
De Gandavo, Pero de Magalhanes. see Magalhanes de Gandavo, Pero de.
De Gante, Pedro. see Pedro de Gante.
De Gaona, Joan. see Gaona, Joan de.
De Garay, Jose. see Garay, Jose de.
De Garcia, And. Gonzalez. see Garcia, And. Gonzalez de.
De Garden, Guillaume, Comte. see Garden, Guillaume, Comte de, 1796-1872.
De Garensieres, Theophilus. see Garensieres, Theophilus de.
De Garibay y Camalloa, Estevan. see Garibay y Camalloa, Estevan de.
De Gasparin, Agenor Etienne, Comte. see Gasparin, Agenor Etienne, Comte de, 1810-1871.
De Gaspe, Philippe Aubert. see Gaspe, Philippe Aubert de, 1786-1871.
De Gaspe, Philippe Aubert, Jr. see Gaspe, Philippe Aubert de, d. 1841.
De Gastine, Civique. see Gastine, Civique de, 1793?-1822.
De Gastizabal, Martin Garcia. see Garcia de Gastizabal, Martin.
De-ga-swa-is-doh. see Strong, Nathaniel T.

De Gaubertin, Pierre Boitel, Sieur. see
Boitel, Pierre, Sieur de Gaubertin.
De Gauville, -------, Vicomte. see Gauville,
--------, Vicomte de.
De Gayangos y Arce, Pascual. see Gayangos
y Arce, Pascual de, 1809-1897.
De Gazitua, Joanne. see Gazitua, Joanne de.
De Gaztelu, Dominico. see Gaztelu, Dominico
de.
De Gebelin, Antoine Court. see Court de
Gebelin, Antoine, 1725-1784.
De Gelone, -------- Fernagus. see Fernagus
de Gelone, -------.
Degener, E. 19297
De Genhardt, Charles. see Genhardt, Charles
de.
De Genille et de Marly-le-Chatel, Martin
Fumee, Seigneur. see Fumee, Martin,
Seigneur de Genille et de Marly-le-Chatel,
1540?-1590.
De Genlis, Stephanie Felicite Brularet de
Sillery, Countess. see Sillery, Step-
hanie Felicite Brularet de, Countess de
Genlis, 1746-1830.
De Genlis, Stephanie Felicite Ducrest de Saint-
Aubin, Comtesse. see Saint-Aubin,
Stephanie Felicite Ducrest de, Comtesse
de Genlis.
De Genouilly, Charles Rigault. see Genouilly,
Charles Rigault de.
De Gerrera, Antonio. see Gerrera, Antonio
de.
De Gersdorf, B. see Gersdorf, B. de.
De Gijon y Leon, Thomas. see Gijon y Leon,
Thomas de.
De Giles, Tomas Suarez. see Suarez de Giles,
Tomas.
Degioannis, Giovanni. 19298
De Girardin, Emile. see Girardin, Emile de.
De Girardot, Auguste Theodore, Baron. see
Girardot, Auguste Theodore, Baron de.
De Givre, Gaston Demousseaux. see Demous-
seaux de Givre, Gaston.
Degli elementi e di molti loro notabili effetti.
44434
Degli Oddi, Longaro. see Oddi, Longaro
Degli.
De Goa, Reinoldo Guisco. see Goa, Reinoldo
Guisco de.
De Gobineau, Joseph Arthur, Comte. see
Gobineau, Joseph Arthur, Comte de.
De Godoi, Diego. see Godoy, Diego de, 16th
cent.
De Godoy, Diego. see Godoy, Diego de, 16th
cent.
De Godoy, Manuel. see Godoy Alvarez de
Faria Rios Sanchez y Zarzosa, Manuel
de, Principe de la Paz, 1767-1851.
De Godoy, Nicholas. see Godoy, Nicholas de.
De Goertz, J., Comte. see Goertz, J.,
Comte de.
De Goes, Damiano. see Goes, Damiao de,
1501-ca. 1573.
De Goes, Damiao. see Goes, Damiao de,
1501-ca. 1573.
De Golbert, --------. see Golbert, -------
de.
Degollado, Santos. (19299)
De Gomara, Francisco Lopez. see Gomara,
Francisco Lopez de, 1510-1560?
De Gomberville, -------. see Gomberville,
------ de.
De Goncalez Molguin, Diego. see Gonzalez
Holguin, Diego, d. 1552.
De Gondra, D. G. M. see Gondra, D. G. M.
de.

De Gongara y Lujan, Pedro Jimenez. see
Almodovar del Rio, Pedro Jimenez de
Gongara y Lujan, Duque de, d. 1794.
De Gongora Marmolejo, Alonso. see Marmo-
lejo, Alonso de Gongora.
De Gonneville, Jean Binot Paulmyer de. see
Paulmier, Jean, d. ca. 1669.
De Gontaut, Armand Louis. see Biron,
Armand Louis de Gontaut, Duc de
Lauzun afterwards Duc de, 1747-1793.
De Gonzales, Antonio Teran. see Teran de
Gonzales, Antonio.
De Gorisito, Fr. see Gorisito, Fr. de.
De Gorostiza, Manuel Eduardo. see Gorostiza,
Manuel Eduardo de, 1789-1851.
De Got, Bertrand. see Clement V., Pope,
1264-1314.
Degotti, -------. (36768), 89596
Degouge, -------. 19300
De Gourgues, D. see Gourgues, D. de.
De Gouvest, J. H. Maubert. see Maubert de
Gouvest, J. H.
De Gouy, Louis Marthe. see Gouy, Louis
Marthe de.
De Gouy d'Argy, Louis Henri Marthe, Marquis.
see Gouy d'Arsy, Louis Henri Marthe,
Marquis de, 1753-1794.
De Gouy d'Arsy, Louis Henri Marthe, Marquis.
see Gouy d'Arsy, Louis Henri Marthe,
Marquis de, 1753-1794.
De Goyeneche, Juan. see Goyeneche, Juan de.
De Graaf, Johannes. see Graaf, Johannes de.
De Graaff, Nicolaus. see Graaff, Nicolaus de.
De Grafigny, Frances (d'Isembourg d'Happon-
court) Dame. see Grafigny, Frances
(d'Isembourg d'Happoncourt) Dame de,
1695-1758.
De Grace, --------. see Grace, ------- de.
Degradation of our representative system and
reformation. 24477
Degrading compromise. 19301
De Grafigny, -------. see Grafigny, -------
de.
Degrand, P. P. F. 19302-19305, 58089,
(65854), (76066)
De Grandpierre, ------- Dralse. see Dralse
de Grandpierre, -------.
De Grandmaison, Millin. see Grandmaison,
Millin de.
De Grandpre, L. see Grandpre, L. de.
De Granier de Cassagnac, Adolphe. see
Granier de Cassagnac, Adolphe de.
Degras, C. 21223
De Grasse-Tilly, Alexandre-Francois-Auguste,
Comte. see Grasse-Tilly, Alexandre-
Francois-Auguste, Comte de.
De Grasse-Tilly, Francois Joseph Paul,
Marquis. see Grasse-Tilly, Francois
Joseph Paul, Marquis de, 1722-1788.
Degrave. J. petitioner 54977
De Graville, B. C. Graillard. see Graillard
de Graville, B. C.
Degray, Michael. (19306)
Degree Temple of Honor, no. 1, Philadelphia.
see Sons of Temperance of North
America. Pennsylvania. Philadelphia
Degree Temple of Honor, no. 1.
De Grijalva, Hernando. see Grijalva, Hernando
de.
De Grijalua, Joan. see Grijalua, Joan de.
De Grimaldi, Jeronimo, Marques. see
Grimaldi, Jeronimo, Marques de, 1720-
1786.
De Groot, Olaus. see Magnus, Olaus, Abp.
of Upsala, 1490-1558.

De Grosourdy, Rene. see Grosourdy, Rene de.
De Grote, Olaus. see Magnus, Olaus, Abp. of Upsala, 1490-1558.
De Grouchy, Nicolas. see Grouchy, Nicolas de.
De Grouchy, Sophie. see Condorcet, Sophie de Grouchy, Marquise de.
Degrouhette, ------ Pepin de. see Pepin de Degrouhette, --------.
De Grova, Manuel. see Grova, Manuel de.
De Grudon, Juan Luis. see Grudon, Juan Luis de.
De Guadalajara y Xabierre, Marco. see Guadalajara y Xabierre, Marco de.
De Guadalcazar, Diego Fernandez de Cordova, 1. Marques. see Fernandez de Cordova, Diego, 1. Marques de Guadalcazar.
De Guadalupe, Andres. See Guadalupe, Andreas de.
De Guadalupe Ramirez, Antonio. see Ramirez, Antonio de Guadalupe.
De Gualdo, Diego. see Gualdo, Diego de.
De Guana, Miguel. see Guana, Miguel de.
De Guelen, Auguste. see Guelen, Auguste de.
De Guemes, Pedro Goncalez. see Guemes, Pedro Goncalez de.
De Guemes Pacheo de Podilla, Juan Vicente. see Guemes Pacheo de Podilla, Juan Vicente de, Conde de Revillagigedo.
De Guemes y Horcasitas, Juan Francisco. see Guemes y Horcasitas, Juan Francisco de.
De Guerrico, Jose P. see Guerrico, Jose P. de.
De Guevara, Ant. Landron. see Guevara, Ant. Landron de.
De Guevara, Baltasar Ladron. see Ladron de Guevara, Baltasar.
De Guevara, Cristoval Sanchez. see Sanchez de Guevara, Cristoval.
De Guevara, Diego Ladron. see Guevara, Diego Ladron de, Bp.
De Guevara, J. de Arroyo Ladron. see Ladron de Guevara, J. de Arroyo.
De Gueura, Ioan Ladron. see Gueuara, Ioan Ladron de.
De Guevara, Luis Velez. see Velez de Guevara, Luis.
De Guevara, Miguel. see Guevara, Miguel de.
De Guevara, Miguel Thadeo. see Guevara, Miguel Thadeo de.
De Guevara y Salamanca, Juan Velez. see Velez de Guevara y Salamanca, Juan.
De Guignard, Alexis. see Saint Priest, Alexis de Guignard, Comte de, 1805-1851.
De Guijo, Gregorio Martin. see Guijo, Gregorio Martin de.
De Guines, ------, Comte. see Guines, ------, Comte de.
De Guise, Charles. see Guise, Charles de.
De Guoy, -------. see Guoy, ------- de.
De Gurowski, Adam G., Count. see Gurowski, Adam, Hrabia, 1805-1866.
De Gusmao, Alexandre. see Gusmao, Alexandre de.
De Guzman, Alonzo Enriquez. see Guzman, Alonzo Enriquez de.
De Guzman, Diego Holgado. see Guzman, Diego Holgado de.
De Guzman, Domingo. see Guzman, Domingo de.
De Guzman, Felix Hernandez. see Guzman, Felix Hernandez de.

De Guzman, Gaspar. see Olivares, Gaspar de Guzman, Conde Duque de, 1587-1645.
De Guzman, Jose Maria Vaca. see Vaca de Guzman y Manriquez, Jose Maria.
De Guzman, Luis Henriquez. see Henriquez de Guzman, Luis, Conde de Alva de Aliste y de Villaflor.
De Guzman, Maria Tello. see Tello de Guzman, Maria.
De Guzman, Nuno. see Guzman, Nuno de, 16th cent.
De Guzman, Rui Diaz. see Diaz de Guzman, Rui, 1558?-1629,
De Guzman y Ayala, Sebastian Lopez. see Lopez de Guzman y Ayala, Sebastian.
De Guzman y Cordova, Seb. see Guzman y Cordova, Seb. de.
De Guzman y Gonzaga, Juan Perez. see Guzman y Gonzaga, Juan Perez de.
De Guzman y Manrique, Joaquin. see Guzman y Manrique, Joaquin de.
De Guzman y Manrique, Jose Maria Vaca. see Vaca de Guzman y Manrique, Jose Maria.
De Guzman y Medina, Juan Tello. see Tello de Guzman y Medina, Juan.
De Haas, C. see Haas, C. de.
De Haerne, Le Chanoine. see Haerne, Le Chanoine de.
De Haes Janvier, Francis. see Janvier, Francis de Haes.
De Hamal, Francisco. see Hamal, Francisco de.
De Hamond, Aime Tome. see Tome de Hamond, Aime.
De Hardales, Carlos. see Hardales, Carlos de.
De Haro, Damian Lopez. see Hamo, Damian Lopez de.
De Haro y Peralta, Alonzo Nunez. see Nunez de Haro y Peralta, Alonzo, Abp.
De Haro y Tamariz, Antonio. see Haro y Tamariz, Antonio de.
De Hart, William Chetwood, 1800-1848. 19307
De Hase, Theodore. see Hase, Theodore de.
De Hass, Charles. (59996)
De Hass, Wills, 1818?-1910. 19308
De Haupt, Marie Guerrier. see Haupt, Marie Guerrier de.
De Hauranne, Ernest Duvergier. see Duvergier de Hauranne, Ernest.
De Haut, Marc. see Haut, Marc de.
De Haven, -------. 85145
De Haviland, John. see Haviland, John de.
Dehay, Louis Timothee. (19309)
De Haze, J. see Haze, J. de.
De Hazzi, -------. see Hazzi, ------- de.
De Hechavarria, Santiago Joseph. see Hechavarria, Santiago Joseph de, Bp.
De Heras, Bartolome Maria. see Maria de Heras, Bartolome, Abp.
De Heredia, Mateo. see Heredia, Mateo de.
De Heremite, Jacques. see Hermite, Jacques l'.
De Heres, T. see Heres, T. de.
De Herla, ------- Manuel. see Manuel de Herla, ------.
De Herrada, Martin. see Herrada, Martin de.
De Herrera, A. see Herrera, A. de.
De Herrera, Alonso de Castillo. see Herrera, Alonso de Castillo de.
De Herrera, Antonio. see Herrera y Tordesillas, Antonio de, 1559-1625.
De Herrera, Antonio M. see Herrera, Antonio M. de.

De Herrera, Antonius. see Herrera y
Tordesillas, Antonio de, 1559-1625.
De Herrera, Cypriani. see Herrera, Cypriani
de.
De Herrera, Francisco. see Herrera,
Francisco de.
De Herrera, Hernando Alonso. see Herrera,
Hernando Alonso de.
De Herrera, Jose Joaquin. see Herrera,
Jose Joaquin de, Pres. Mexico, 1792-
1854.
De Herrera, Jose Manuel. see Herrera,
Jose Manuel de.
De Herrera, Jose Sunzin. see Sunzin de
Herrera, Jose.
De Herrera Ascanio, Nicolas. see Herrera
Ascanio, Nicolas de.
De Herrera y Sentmanat, Manuel. see Herrera
y Sentmanat, Manuel de.
De Herrera y Tordesillas, Antonio. see
Herrera y Tordesillas, Antonio de, 1959-
1625.
De Hesse, Joannes. see Hesse, Joannes de.
De Hevia y Valdes, Diego. see Hevia y
Valdes, Diego de, Bp.
Deh-he-wa-mis. 78680-(78682)
De Hindobro, Francisco Garcia. see Hindobro,
Francisco Garcia de.
De Hinojosa, ------ Ortiz. see Ortiz de
Hinojosa, -------.
De Hinojoso, Alonso Lopez. see Lopez de
Hinojoso, Alonso.
De Hoffmanns, -------. see Hoffmanns,
------- de.
Dehon, Theodore. 19310-19314, 87932
De Hondt, Joos. see Hondius, Jodocus,
1546-1611.
De Hondt, P. see Hondt, P. de.
De Hooge, ------ Romyn. see Romyn de
Hooge, ------.
De Hooghe, Romain. see Romyn de Hooge,
-------.
De Hoop Scheffer, J. G. see Scheffer, J. G.
de Hoop.
De Hortega, Jose Diaz. see Diaz de Hortega,
Jose.
De Houtman, Cornelis. see Houtman, Cornelis
de, ca. 1540-1599.
De Hoven, ------- (van Uitenhage de Mist)
see Hoven, Madame -------- (van
Uitenhage de Mist) de.
De Hoyos Santillana, Ignacio. see Santillana,
Ignacio de Hoyos.
De Huerta, Alonso. see Huerta, Alonso de.
De Hverta, Geronomo. see Hverta, Geronomo
de.
De Hutten, Ulrich. see Hutten, Ulrich de.
Dei viaggi e scoperte settentrionali di Nicolo
ed Antonio Zeni. 106411
De Ibarra, Andres. see Ibarra, Andres de.
De Ibarra, Carlos. see Ibarra, Carlos de.
De Ibarra, Francisco. see Ibarra, Francisco
de.
De Ibarra, Miguel. see Ibarra, Miguel de.
Deichmann, L. B. 61223
D'Eichthal, Gustave. see Eichthal, Gustave d'.
De Illescas, Goncalo. see Illescas, Goncalo
de.
Dein, J. R. tr. 20003, 20012
Deisne, And. van. tr. (68536)
De Irigoyen, Jose Gutierrez de la Concha y.
see Habana, Jose Gutierrez de la Concha
y de Irigoyen, Marques de la, 1809-
1895.
De Irisarri, Antonio Jose. see Irisarri,
Antonio Jose de.

De Irisarri, Fermin. see Irisarri, Fermin de.
De Irlanda, Antonio. see Irlanda, Antonio de.
De Irolo Calar, N. see Yrolo Calar, Nicolas
de.
Deisisles, ------ Blanq. see Blanq-Deisisles,
----------.
De Isla, Ruiz. see Isla, Ruiz de.
De Isolanis, Isodorus. see Isolanus, Isodorus
de.
Deist unmasked. 56825
De Itabayana, ------, Visconde. see Itabayana,
------, Visconde de.
De Itauna, Barao. see Itauna, Barao de.
De Itta y Para, J. M. G. see Itta y Para,
J. M. G. de.
De Iturbide, Augustin. see Iturbide, Augustin
de, Emperor of Mexico, 1783-1824.
De Iturrigary, Jose. see Iturrigary, Jose de,
Abp.
D'Ivernois, Sir Francis. see Ivernois, Sir
Francis d'.
De Izco, Wenceslao Ayguals. see Izco, Wen-
ceslao Ayguals de.
De J. Cuevas, J. see Cuevas, J. de J.
De Jauregui, Agustin. see Jauregui, Agustin
de, d. 1784.
De Jauregui, Juan Tomas. see Jauregui, Juan
Tomas de.
De Jaz, Isid. Gil. see Gil de Jaz, Isid.
Dejean, Aug. 19315
Dejean, C. F. G. 19316
Dejean, M. 19317, 34605
Dejean de la Batie, ------. 19318
De Jequitinhonha, -------, Visconde. see
Jequitinhonha, ------, Visconde de.
De Jequitinhonha, -------, Visconde. see
Jequitinhonha, ------, Visconde de.
De Jesu, Antonio. see Jesu, Antonio de.
De Jesus, Alonso. see Alonso de Jesus.
De Jesus, Jose Manual. see Jesus, Jose
Manual de.
De Jesus, Mariano. see Mariano de Jesus.
De Jesus, Marie de Saint Bonaventure. see
Marie de Saint Bonaventure, Mere
Superieure.
De Jesus, Marie de Sainte Bonnaventure. see
Marie de Saint Bonaventure, Mere
Superieure.
De Jesus, Raphael. see Raphael de Jesus.
De Jesus Febles, Manual. see Febles, Manual
de Jesus.
De Jesus Maria, Felix. see Jesus Maria,
Felix de.
De Jesus Maria, Nicolas. see Nicolas de
Jesus Maria.
De Jesus Munguia, Clemente. see Munguia,
Clemente de Jesus, Abp.
De Jesus Puelles, Jose Maria. see Puelles,
Jose Maria de Jesus.
De Jesus Q. Garcia, Jose. see Garcia, Jose
de Jesus Q.
De Jesus Sacedon, Antonio. see Sacedon,
Antonio de Jesus.
De Jesus y Ortega, Alonso. see Jesus y
Ortega, Alonso de.
De Jode, -------. illus. 9870
De Johnstone, James Johnstone, Chevalier.
see Johnstone, James Johnstone,
Chevalier de, 1719-1800?
De Joinville, Francois Ferdinand Philippe Louis
Marie d'Orleans, Prince. see Joinville,
Francois Ferdinand Philippe Louis Marie
d'Orleans, Prince de, 1818-1900.
De Joly, -------. see Joly, -------- de.
De Jomini, Henri. see Jomini, Henri,
Baron de.

De Jonama, -------. see Jonama, -------
de.
De Joncaire Chabert, Daniel. see Joncaire
Chabert, Daniel de.
De Joncourt, Elie. see Joncourt, Elie de.
De Jong, Cornelius. see Jong, Cornelius de.
De Jong, D. see Jong, D. de.
De Jonge, J. C. see Jonge, J. C. de.
De Jonge, J. K. J. see Jonge, J. K. J. de.
De Jonge, John. de Raei see de Jonge, Joh. de.
De Jonnes, Alexandre Moreau. see Moreau
de Jonnes, Alexandre.
De Jorio, M. see Jorio, M. de.
De Jouffroy, Achille, Marquis. see Jouffroy,
Achille, Marquis de.
De Jouy, Victor Joseph Etienne. see Jouy,
Victor Joseph Etienne de.
De Jovenase, ------, Duc. see Chelemar,
-------, Prince de.
De Jovenaso, ------, Duque. see Chelemar,
------, Prince de.
De Juan Martinena, Juan Martin. see Martin-
ena, Juan Martin de Juan.
De Judaeis, Cornelii. see Judaeis, Cornelius
de.
De Junient, Manuel. see Junient, Manuel de.
De Juras Reales, -------, Baron. see Juras
Reales, ------, Baron de.
De Jure, -------. see Jure, ------- de.
De Jussieu, -------. see Jussieu, -------
de.
De Jussieu, Adrien. see Jussieu, Adrien de,
1797-1853.
De Jussieu, Lourenco. see Jussieu, Lourenco
de.
De Kaout't 'Chouk, Tridace-Nafe-Theobrame.
pseud. Voyage pittoresque. see Del-
motte, Henri Florent.
De Kay, James E. 19319-19321, (53783)
Deken, Agatha. supposed author 18260, 59622,
104991
De Keralio, ------ Mantugene. see Mantugene
de Keralio, -------.
De Keratry, Emile, Comte. see Keratry,
Emile de, Comte.
De Keredern, Philippe Regis Denis. see
Trobriand, Philippe Regis Denis de
Keredern, Comte de, 1816-1897.
De Kerguelen Tremarec, Y. J. see Kerguelen-
Tremarec, Y. J. de.
De Kerhallet, Charles Philippe. see Kerhal-
let, Charles Philippe de.
De Kerlerec de Kervasegan, Louis Billouard.
see Kerlerec de Kervasegan, Louis
Billouard de, Marquis.
De Kervasegan, Louis Billouard de Kerlerec.
see Kerlerec de Kervasegan, Louis
Billouard de, Marquis.
De Khanikoff, Nicolas. see Khanikoff, Nicolas
de.
De Klerk, J. see Klerk, J. de.
DeKrafft, F. C. cartographer 101946
De Kroyft, Mrs. S. H. 19322
Del L., J. F. pseud. see Fernandez de
Lizardi, Jose Joaquin, 1776-1827.
De L., M. pseud. see L., M. de. pseud.
De L., M. P. pseud. see L., M. P. de.
pseud.
Del, William. 74459
Del altar. 93316
Del conocimiento de los fosiles. 71443
Del consejo de sa magestad. 58505
Del culto publico en sus relaciones con el
gobierno. 42904, 51324
Del descvbrimiento del Maranon. 72524

Del discacciamento di Christoforo Colombo
Genovese. 73421
Del govierno arbitrario del Piru. (70805)
Del mondo nvovo del Cavalier Tomaso Stigliani.
91728
Del nuevo mundo en la gran capilla del Rosario.
(44464)
Del orden en la observancia de las leyes.
70013
Del origen y milagros de la Santa Cruz. 76779
Del poder municipal. 58429
Del primo scopritore del continente del nuovo
mondo. 14654, (51759)
Del sacramento del matrimonio. 93577
Del segvndo descvbrimiento de las naciones del
Rio Maranon. 72524
Del segvndo estado de la redvcciones del
Maranon. 72524
Del' sito, forma, & misure, dello inferno id
Dante. 27265
Del tolerancia. 42904, 51324
De la Amarillas, --------, Marquesa. see
Amarillas, ------, Marquesa de la.
De la Anunciacion, Domingo. see Domingo de
la Anunciacion.
De la Anunciacion, Juan. see Juan de la
Anunciacion.
De la Balme, --------. 96002
De la Barbinais, Le Gentil. see La Barbinais,
Le Gentil de.
De la Barca, Frances Erskine (Inglis) Calderon.
see Calderon de la Barca, Frances
Erskine (Inglis) 1804-1882.
De la Barca, Pedro Calderon. see Calderon
de la Barca, Pedro, 1600-1681.
De la Barcena, Manuel. see La Barcena,
Manuel de.
De la Barcera y Arce, Manuel. see Barcera
y Arce, Manuel de la.
De la Barra, Justo. see La Barra, Justo de.
De la Barre, --------. see Barre, -------
de la.
De la Barre, Le Febvre. see La Barre, Le
Febvre de.
De la Barrera, Alonso. see Barrera, Alonso
de la.
De la Barreda, Nicholas. see Barreda,
Nicholas de la.
De la Barrera y Troncoso, M. see La
Barrera y Troncoso, M. de.
De la Barreyrie, F. see La Barreyrie, F.
de.
De labarthe, Charles. see Labarthe, Charles
de.
De la Labastida y Davalos, Pelagio Antonio. see
Labastida y Davalos, Pelagio Antonio de,
Abp., 1816-1891.
De la Bastide, Martin. see La Bastide,
Martin de la.
De la Batie, ------- Dejean. see Dejean
de la Batie, -------.
De Labeaume, A.-G. Griffet. see Griffet de
Labeaume, A.-G.
De la Beaumelle, Victor Laurent Suzanne Moise
Angliviel. see Angliviel de la Beau-
melle, Victor Laurent Suzanne Moise.
De la Beche, H. T. 19323
De la Bedolliere, Emile Gigault. see La
Bedolliere, Emile Gigault de.
De la Bettencourt, Jose. see Bettencourt,
Jose de la.
De Labillardiere, Jacques Julien Houton. see
Labillardiere, Jacques Julien Houton de,
1755-1834.
De la Blanchardiere, Rene Courte. see
Courte de la Blanchardiere, Rene.

De la Boirie, ------- Arnault. see Arnault de la Boirie, -------.
De la Boissiere, C. C. Tanguy. see Tanguy de la Boissiere, C. C.
De la Bonniniere, Gustave Auguste de Beaumont. see Beaumont de la Bonniniere, Gustave Auguste de, 1802-1866.
De la Boquette, --------. see Boquette, ------ de la.
De la Borde, -------. see La Borde, ------ de.
De la Borde, Jean Benjamin. see La Borde, Jean Benjamin de.
De Laboulaye, Edouard Rene Lefebvre. see Laboulaye, Edouard Rene Lefebvre de, 1811-1883.
De Labra y Cadrana, Rafael Maria. see Labra y Caldrana, Rafael Maria de, 1843-
De la Bruere, ------ Boucher. see Boucher de la Bruere, -------.
De la Bruyere, ------ Barbeau. see Barbeau de la Bruyere, --------.
De la Bruyere, J.-B.-M.-L, La Reynie. see La Reynie de la Bruyere, J.-B.-M.-L.
De la Cadena, Melchioris. see Cadena, Melchioris de la.
De la Calancha, Antonio. see Calancha, Antonio de la.
De la Calle, Juan Diez de la Calle, Juan.
De la Canal, Dom. see Canal, Dom. de la.
De la Canal, Jose Vallejo. see Vallejo de la Canal, Jose.
De la Carrera, Fernando. see Carrera, Fernando de la.
De la Carrieres, A. C. see La Carrieres, A. C. de.
De Lacerda, Antonio Francisco. see Lacerda, Antonio Francisco de.
De la Cerda, Bort de Benavides y. see Benavides y de la Cerda, Bort de.
De la Cerda, Goncalo Carrillo. see Cerda, Goncalo Carrillo de la.
De Lacerda Werneck, L. P. see Lacerda Werneck, Luiz Peixoto de.
De la Chaise, Francois d'Aix. see La Chaise, Francois d'Aix de.
De Lachapelle, Alfred, Comte. see Lachapelle, Alfred, Comte de, b. 1830.
De Lachartiere, Andre. see Lachartiere, Andre de.
De Lachevalerie, ------ Bacon. see Bacon de Lachevalerie, ------.
De la Clede, ------. see La Clede, ------- de.
De la Colancha, Antonio. see Antonio de la Colancha.
De la Colina, Rafael. see Colina, Rafael de la.
De la Concepcion, Diego. see La Concepcion, Diego de.
De la Concepcion, Juan. see Juan de la Concepcion.
De la Concepcion, Pedro. pseud. Soplas en defensa. see Alva y Astorga, Pedro de.
De la Concepcion Urtiaga, Pedro. see Urtiaga, Pedro de la Concepcion.
De la Concepcion Valdes, Gabriel. see Valdes, Gabriel de la Concepcion.
De la Concha, J. see Concha, J. de la.
De la Concha y de Irigoyen, Jose Gutierrez. see Habana, Jose Gutierrez de la Concha y de Irigoyen, Marques de la, 1809-1895.
De la Condamine, Charles Marie. see La Condamine, Charles Marie de.

De la Corne, St.-Luc. see La Corne, St.-Luc de.
De la Cornillere, ------, Comte. see La Cornillere, ------ Comte de.
De la Cortina, Jose Gomez. see Cortina, Jose Gomez de la.
De la Cortina, Jose Justo Gomez. see Cortina, Jose Justo Gomez de la Cortina, Conde de la, 1799-1860.
De la Cosa, Juan. 76838
De Lacoste, Henri, Comte Verdier. see Verdier de Lacoste, Henri, Comte.
Delacoste, Jean-Aime. 19324-19325, 53575, 54146
De la Coste, Nicolas. see Coste, Nicolas de la.
De la Coudreniere, ------- Peyroux. see Peyroux de la Coudreniere, ------.
Delacour, Adolphe. 19326
De la Crenne, Jean Rene Antoine, Marquis de Verdun. see Verdun de la Crenne, Jean Rene Antoine, Marquis de.
De lacretelle, --------. see Lacretelle, ------- de.
De la Croix, ------. 237
De la Croix, A. Pherotee. see La Croix, A. Pherotee de.
De la Croix, F. D. defendant (21256), (26336)
De Lacroix, Francois Joseph Pamphile. see Lacroix, Francois Joseph Pamphile, Vicomte de, 1774-1842.
De Lacroix, Irenee Amelot. see Lacroix, Irenee Amelot de.
Delacroix, Jacques Vincent, 1743-1832. 19327-(19329), 38500-38503
De Lacroix, Louis Antoine Nicolle. see Lacroix, Louis Antoine Nicolle de, 1704-1760.
De la Croix, Pierre Augustin de Boissier de Sauvages. see Boissier de Sauvages de la Croix, Pierre Augustin de.
De la Croix de Chevrieres de Saint Vallier, Jean Baptiste. see Saint Vallier, Jean Baptiste de la Croix de Chevrieres de, Bp.
De la Croze, Mathurin Veyssiere. see La Croze, Mathurin Veyssiere de.
De la Cruz, -------. see Cruz, ------- de la.
De la Cruz, Francisco. see Francisco de la Cruz.
De la Cruz, J. see La Cruz, J. de.
De la Cruz, Juan. 36800
De la Cruz, Juana Ines. see Juana Ines de la Cruz, Sister, 1651-1695.
De la Cruz, Luis. see Cruz, Luis de la, 1768-1828.
De la Cruz, Mateo. see Cruz, Mateo de la.
De la Cruz Cano y Olmedilla, Juan. see Cano y Olmedillo, Juan de la Cruz.
De la Cruz Garcia, Juan. see Garcia, Juan de la Cruz.
De la Cruz Mendez, ------. (6199)
De la Cruz y Bahamonde, Nicolas. see Cruz y Bahamonde, Nicolas de.
De la Cueba, Juan Diego Gverrero. see Gverrero de la Cueba, Juan Diego.
De la Cuesta, Felipo Arroyo. see Arroyo de la Cuesta, Felipe.
De la Cuesta, Gregorio. see Cuesta, Gregorio de la.
De la Cueua, Antonia Gregoria de Esquiuel y. see Esquiuel y de la Cueua, Antonia Gregoria de.
De la Cueva, Antonio. see Cueva, Antonio de la.

De la Cueva, Juan Roldan. see Roldan de la Cueva, Juan.
De Lacunza, J. M. see Lacunza, J. M.
De la Drevetiere, Louis Francois Deslisle. see Deslisle de la Drevetiere, Louis Francois.
De la Encina, Louis Gonzaga. see La Encina, Louis Gonzaga de.
De la Erizeira, Francisco Xavier de Meneses, Conde. see Meneses, Francisco Xavier de, Conde de la Erizeira.
De la Escosura, P. see Escosura, P. de la.
De la Estela Escalante, Francisco. see Escalante, Francisco de la Estela.
De Laet, Joannes, 1593-1649. see Laet, Joannes de, 1593-1649.
De Laet, Juan. see Laet, Joannes de, 1593-1649.
De la Falissoniere, --------. see Falissoniere, ------- de la.
De la Farelle, F. see La Farelle, F. de.
De Lafargue, Etienne. see Lafargue, Etienne de.
Delafaye Brehier, Julie. 19330, 38567
De Lafayette, Marquis. pseud. Epistle from Marquis de La Fayette. see Bannerman, Anne. supposed author and Hamilton, George. supposed author and Hamilton, Hugh. supposed author
De Lafayette, Marie Jean Paul Roche Yves Gilbert du Motier, Marquis. see Lafayette, Marie Jean Paul Roche Yves Gilbert du Motier, Marquis de, 1757-1834.
Delafield, Edward. 19331
Delafield, John, 1786-1853. 84571-84572
Delafield, John, 1812-1865 or 6. 19332-19334
Delafield, Richard, 1798-1873. 62051, 103089
De la Fita y Carrion, Francisco Xavier. see Fita y Carrion, Francisco Xavier de la.
De la Fontaine, Jean. see La Fontaine, Jean de.
Delafosse, J. M. Lemonnier. see Lemonnier Delafosse, J. M.
Delafosse de Rouville, --------. 19335
De la Fruston, Fr. see La Fruston, Fr. de, 1806-1864.
De la Fuente, Francisco. see Fuente, Francisco de la.
De la Fuente, G. see Fuente, G. de la.
De la Fuente, Juan Fernandez. see Fernandez de la Fuente, Juan.
De la Fuente, Romualdo. see Fuente, Romualdo de la.
De la Fuente, Vicente. see Fuente, Vicente de la.
De la Galissoniere, -------. see Galissoniere, -------- de la.
De la Gandara, Juan Zorrilla. see Zorrilla de la Gandara, Juan.
De la Gandara, Salvador. see Gandara, Salvador de la.
De la Garza, Juan Jose. see Garza, Juan Jose de la.
De la Garza, Lazaro. see Garza, Lazaro de la, Abp.
De la Garza y Ballesteros, Lazaro. see Garza y Ballesteros, Lazara de la, Abp.
De la Gasca, Pedro. see Gasca, Pedro de la.
De la Giraudiere, H. de Chavannes. see Chavannes de la Giraudiere, H. de.
De la Gracerie, --------. see Gracerie, ------ de la.
Delagrange, --------, fl. 1829. 18331

Delagrange, --------, fl. 1860. 81660
De Lagrange de Checieux, G. A. F. Simon. see Lagrange de Checieux, G. A. F. Simon de.
De la Grua Talamanca, Miguel. see Grua Talamanca, Miguel de la, Marques de Branciforte.
De la Guard, Theodore. pseud. Mercurius anti-merchanicus. see Ward, Nathaniel.
De la Guard, Theodore. pseud. Simple cobler of Agagawam in America. see Ward, Nathaniel.
De la Guarda, Manuel. see Guarda, Manuel de la.
De la Guarden, Theodore. pseud. Mercurius anti-merchanicus. see Ward, Nathaniel.
De la Guardia, Antonio Jos. Garcia. see Garcia de la Guardia, Antonio Jos.
De la Guardia, Heraclio Martin. see Guardia, Heraclio Martin de la.
De la Guette, S. de Broe, Seigneur de Sitry et. see Broe, S. de, Seigneur de Citry et de la Guette, 17th cent.
Del Aguila, Melchora. see Aguila, Melchora del.
De Lagunas, Juan Baptista. see Lagunas, Juan Baptista de.
De Lagunas y Castilla, Pedro Joseph Bravo. see Bravo de Lagunas y Castilla, Pedro Joseph.
De la Habana, Jose Gutierrez de la Concha y de Irigoyen, Marques. see Habana, Jose Gutierrez de la Concha y de la Irigoyen, Marques de la, 1809-1895.
De La Harpe, Benard. see La Harpe, Benard de.
De la Harpe, Jean Francois. see La Harpe, Jean Francois de.
De la Haute-Vienne Jourdan, --------. see Jourdan, ------- de la Haute-Vienne.
Delahay, M. W. 58852
Delahaye, --------. illus. 6982
Delahaye, J. C. G. 19336
De la Haye, Jean. tr. 95757
De la Hera, Jose Santos. see Hera, Jose Santos de la.
De la Hermosa y Salcedo, Francisco Ugarte. see Ugarte y de la Hermosa y Salcedo, Francisco.
De la Higuera y Amarilla, Bernabe. see Higuera y Amarilla, Bernabe de la.
De la Hontan, N., Baron. see La Hontan, N., Baron de.
De la Hure, V. L. Baril, Comte. see Baril, V. L., Comte de la Hure.
De l'Ain, L. F. see L'Hertier, Louis Francois.
De la Laguna, Joseph de Rivera Bermudez, Conde de Santiago. see Rivera Bermudez, Joseph de, Conde de Santiago de la Laguna.
De la Lande, J. J. see La Lande, J. J. de.
De la Lastra, Jose. see Lastra, Jose de la.
De la Campa, Antonio. see Campa, Antonio de la.
De la Llana, Francisco Murcia. see Murcia de la Llana, Francisco.
De la Llosa, M. E. see Llosa, M. E. de la.
De la Loza, L. Rio. see Loza, L. Rio de la.
De la Lozere, Privat Joseph Claramond, Comte Pelet. see Pelet de la Lozere, Privat Joseph Claramond, Comte.
De la Luz, Jose. see Luz, Jose de la.
De la Luz Caballero, Jose. see Caballero, Jose de la Luz.

De la Luz Caballero, Pepe. see Caballero, Jose de la Luz.

De la Luz Hernandez, Jose. see Hernandez, Jose de la Luz.

De la Luzerne, Cesar Henri, Comte. see La Luzerne, Cesar Henri, Comte de, 1737-1799.

De la Madalena, Juan. pseud. tr. see Estrada, Juan. tr.

De la Madelene, Henry. see La Madelene, Henry de.

De la Madre de Dios, Jose. see Jose de la Madre de Dios.

De la Madre de Dios, Juan. see Juan de la Madre de Dios.

De Lamadrid, Gregorio Araoz. see Lamadrid, Gregorio Araoz de.

De la Madriz, Pedro Fernandez. see Fernandez de la Madriz, Pedro.

De la Magdalena, Augustin. see Magdalena, Augustin de la.

De la Maillardiere, Charles Francois, Visconte. see Maillardiere, Charles Francois, Visconte de la.

De Lamar y Cortozar, Jose. see Lamar y Cortozar, Jose de, 1776-1830.

Delamarche, C. F. cartographer 71865-71866, 71868-71870

De la Marche-Courmont, Ignatius Hungari. see Marche-Courmont, Ignatius Hungari de la.

De Lamarck, Jean Baptiste Pierre Antoine de Monet. see Lamarck, Jean Baptiste Pierre Antoine de Monet de, 1744-1829.

Delamardelle, Guillaume-Pierre-Francois. 19337, 22628

De Lamartine, Alphonse Marie Louis. see Lamartine, Alphonse Marie Louis de, 1790-1869.

De la Martiniere, Antoine Augustin Bruzen. see Bruzen de la Martiniere, Antoine Augustin, 1662-1746.

De la Martiniere, Pierre Martin. see La Martiniere, Pierre Martin de.

De la Maza Arredono, Fernando. see Arredono, Fernando de la Maza.

De Lambertie, Charles. see Lambertie, Charles de.

De Lamberty, L. B. T. see Lamberty, L. B. T. de.

De la Mijst, Gerardus. see Mijst, Gerardus dela.

De la Montagne, J. see Montagne, J. de la.

De la Mora, Miguel Diez. see Diez de la Mora, Miguel.

De la Morandiere, ------- Turmeau. see Turmeau de la Morandiere, --------.

De la Moriniere, Simon Barthelemi Joseph Noel. see Noel de la Moriniere, Simon Barthelemi Joseph.

De la Mota, J. J. see Mota, J. J. de la.

De la Mota, Manuel. see Mota, Manuel de la.

De la Mota Padilla, Matias. see Mota Padilla, Matias de la.

De la Mothe-Fenelon, Francois de Salignac. see Fenelon, Francois de Salignac de la Mothe-, Abp., 1641-1715.

De la Mothe le Vayer, --------. pseud. see La Peyrere, Isaac de, 1594-1676.

De la Motta, Jacob. 19339

De la Motte, ------- Douin. see Douin de la Motte, -----------.

De la Movila, F. see Movila, F. de la.

De la Nassy, D. see Nassy, David de Isaac Cohen.

De la Natividad Saldanha, Jose. see Saldanha, Jose de la Natividad.

De Lancey, --------, fl. 1769. 103241

De Lancey, James, 1703-1760. 14818, 19340-19342, 54198, 84577, 97479 see also New York (Colony) Lieutenant Governor, 1753-1755 (De Lancey) New York (Colony) Supreme Court of Judicature. Chief Justice.

De Lancey, William Heathcote, Bp., 1797-1865. 19343-19345

De Lanciego y Eguilaz, Joseph. see Lanciego y Eguilaz, Joseph de, Abp.

De Lancival, Luce. see Lancival, Luce de.

Delancy, ---------. supposed author. 20044

Delancy, Anne. defendant 96885

De Lancy, James. 19346

De Landa, Ambrosius Cerdan. see Landa, Ambrosius Cerdan de.

De Landa, Carlos. see Landa, Carlos de.

De Landa, Diego. see Landa, Diego de.

De Landaluze, Victor Patricio. see Landaluze, Victor Patricio de.

De Landres, J.-R. Frey. see Frey de Landres, J.-R.

De la Nevfville, Legeuen. see La Nevfville, Legeuen de.

De la Neuville, Jean Nicolas Buache. see Buache, Jean Nicolas, 1741-1825.

Delaney, Oliver. incorrectly supposed author 19347, (21170)

De Langeac, N. de l'Espinasse, Chevalier. see Espinasse, N. de l', Chevalier de Langeac.

De Langres, Bruno. 79993

Delano, Amasa. 19348-19349

Delano, Christopher. 19350

Delano, Columbus, 1809-1896. 19351-(19352)

Delano, Judah. 101936-101937

De la Noue, Pierre. see Noue, Pierre de la.

De Lanoye, Ferdinand Tugnot. see Tugnot de Lanoye, Ferdinand, 1810-1870.

De Lansegue, ---------. 80612

De Lanuza, V. Blasco. see Lanuza, V. Blasco de.

Delany, Martin Robinson. 19353-19354

Delany, Oliver. 19347

De Laon, Jean. see Laon, Jean de, Sieur d'Aigremont.

De la P., L. J. see P., L. J. de la. pseud.

Delap, Francis. defendant 19355

De la Palata, Melchor de Navarra y Rocaful, Duque. see Navarra y Rocaful Melchor de, Duque de la Palata.

De la Paleen, -------. see Paleen, -------- de la.

De la Parra, Francisco. see Parra, Francisco de la.

De la Parra, Isaac. see Parra, Isaac de la.

De la Parra, Jacinto. see Parra, Jacinto de la.

De la Parra, Jose Gomez. see Gomez de la Parra, Jose.

De la Parra, Samuel Henrico. see Parra, Samuel Henrico de la.

De la Paz, Francisco Santos. see Santos de la Paz, Francisco.

De la Paz, Juan Bautista Orendayn, Marques. see Orendayn, Juan Bautista, Marques de la Paz.

De la Paz Villaverde, Cirilo Simon. see Villaverde, Cirilo Simon de la Paz.

De la Pedrosa, J. see Pedrosa, J. de la.

De Lepelin, ---------. see Lapelin, ------- de.

De la Pena, Andres Saenz. see Saenz de la Pena, Andres.
De la Pena, Antonio. see Pena, Antonio de la.
De la Pena, D. M. see La Pena, D. M. de.
De la Pena, Francisco. see Pena, Francisco de la.
De la Pena, Francisco Javier. see Pena, Francisco Javier de la.
De la Pena, Francisco Sains. see Sains de la Pena, Francisco.
De la Pena, Gertrudis. see Pena, Gertrudis de la.
De la Pena, Ignacio. see Pena, Ignacio de la.
De la Pena, J. see Pena, J. de la.
De la Pena, Josepho Antonio. see Pena, Josepho Antonio de la.
De la Pena, Juan Nunez. see Nunez de la Pena, Juan.
De la Pena, Manuel. see Pena, Manuel de la.
De la Pena, S. de Alvarado y. see Alvarado y de la Pena, S. de.
De la Pena Montenegro, Alonso. see Pena Montenegro, Alonso de la, Bp.
De la Pena y Garcia, J. M. see Pena y Garcia, J. M. de la.
De la Pena y Pena, Manuel. see Pena y Pena, Manuel de la.
De la Pena y Villar, Blas. see Pena y Villar, Blas de la.
De la Perouse, Jean Francois de Galaup, Comte. see La Perouse, Jean Francois de Galaup, Comte de, 1741-1788.
De la Peyrere, Isaac. see La Peyrere, Isaac de, 1594-1676.
De la Peza, Ignacio. see Peza, Ignacio de la.
De la Pezuela, Jacobo. see Pezuela, Jacobo de la.
De la Pezuela, Joaquin. see Pezuela, Joaquin de la.
De la Pezula y Sanchez Munoz de Velasco, Joaquin. see Pezula y Sanchez Munoz de Velasco, Joaquin De la, 1. Marques de Viluma, 1761-1830.
De la Place, Pierre Simon, Marquis. see Laplace, Pierre Simon, Marquis de, 1749-1827.
Delaplain, Sophia. pseud. Thrilling and exciting account. 19356
Delaplaine, Joseph, 1777-1824. 9899, 19357-19358
Delaplaine's prospectus of national panzographia. 19358
Delaplaine's repository of the lives and portraits. 9899, 19358
De la Plaza, Eugenio. see Plaza, Eugenio de la.
De la Poepe, Claude. see La Poepe, Claude de.
De la Poix Ferminville, M. J. see La Poix Ferminville, M. J. de.
De la Popeliniere, --------, Sieur. see La Popeliniere, -------, Sieur de la, fl. 1630.
De la Popeliniere, Lancelot Voisin. see La Popeliniere, Lancelot Voisin, Sieur de, 1541-1608.
De la Pordilla, Pedro. see Pordilla, Pedro de la.
De la Porte, Joseph. see Laporte, Joseph de, 1713-1779.
De la Porte, Luc. see Porte, Luc de la.

De la Porte, Lucas. see Porte, Lucas de la.
De la Portilla, Anselmo. see Portilla, Anselmo de la.
De la Portilla, J. see Portilla, J. de la.
De la Portilla, Pedro. see Portilla, de la.
De la Poterie, Claud Florent Bouchard. see Bouchard de la Poterie, Claud Florent.
De la Potherie, Claude Charles le Roy Bacqueville. see Bacqueville de la Potherie, Claude Charles le Roy, b. ca. 1668.
De Laprade, Victor. see Laprade, Victor de.
De la Providencia, Josepha. see Josepha de la Providencia.
De la Puenta, Juan Gonzalez. see Gonzalez de la Puenta, Juan.
De la Puenta Carrillo de Albornos, Mariana. see Carrillo de Albornos, Mariana de la Puenta.
De la Puente, Antonio Hay. see Hay de la Puente, Antonio.
De la Puente, Francisco. see Puente, Francisco de la.
De la Puente, Grimaneza. see Puente, Grimaneza de la.
De la Puente, Joseph Martinez. see Martinez de la Puente, Jose, fl. 1681.
De la Puente Ibanez, Juan Joseph. see Puente Ibanez, Juan Joseph de la.
De la Puerta, Pablo Morillo y Morillo, Marques. see Morillo y Morillo, Pablo, Marques de la Puerta, 1778-1837.
De la Pylaie, A. J. M. Bachelot. see Bachelot de la Pylaie, A. J. M.
De Lara, -------- Leon. see Leon de Lara, --------.
De Lara, Alonso Perez. see Perez de Lara, Alonso.
De Lara, Jacob. see Lara, Jacob de.
De Lara, Jose Fernandez. see Lara, Jose Fernandez de.
De Lara, Jose Mariano Beristain de Souza Fernandez. see Beristain de Souza, Jose Mariano, 1756-1817.
De Lara, Jose M. see Lara, Jose M. de.
De Lara, Juan Jose Fernandez. see Lara, Juan Jose Fernandez de.
De Lara, Mariano Aniceto. see Lara, Mariano Aniceto de.
De Lara Fernandez, Antonio Ferreira. see Fernandez, Antonio Ferreira de Lara.
De Lara Galan, Joseph. see Lara Galan, Joseph de.
De Lara y Consortes, Jose Fernandez. see Fernandez de Lara y Consortes, Jose.
De la Rada y Delgado, Juan de Dios. see Rada y Delgado, Juan de Dios de la.
Delaram, Francis. engr. (76455), 82823-82824, 82826
Del Arco, Francisco Sanchez. see Sanchez del Arco, Francisco.
De Larea, Bernardo. see Larea, Bernardo de.
De la Regalia, Antonio Joseph Alvarez de Abreu, Marques. see Abreu, Antonio Joseph Alvarez de, Marques de la Regalia.
De la Reintrie, Henry Ray. see La Reintrie, Henry Ray de.
De la Renaudiere, Philippe Francois. see La Renaudiere, Philippe Francois, 1781-1845.
De la Resurreccion, Francisco. see Francisco de la Resurreccion.
De la Revilla, Jose. see Revilla, Jose de la.
De la Richardiere, Gilles Boucher. see Boucher de la Richardiere, Gilles, 1733-1810.

De la Sabliere, Trudaine. see Trudaine de la Sabliere, --------.
De la Sagaga, Juan Lucas. see Lasaga, Juan Lucas de.
De la Sagra, ------ Ramon. see Ramon de la Sagra, -------.
De la Riestra, Isabel Garcia. see Riestra, Isabel Garcia de la.
De la Ripia, Juan. see Ripia, Juan de la.
De la Riva Aguero, Jose. see Riva Aguero, Jose de la.
De Larivas, Juan. see Larivas, Juan de.
De la Rivas, Manuel Joseph. see La Rivas, Manuel Joseph de.
De la Riviere, ------ Brutel. see Brutel de la Riviere, -------.
De la Roca, J. J. see Roca, J. J. de la.
De la Roca, Ramon. see Roca, Ramon de la.
De la Rocha, Jesus. see Rocha, Jesus de la.
De la Rocha, Juan Ignacio. see Rocha, Juan Ignacio de la.
De la Rocha, Juan Sanchez. see Sanchez de la Rocha, Juan.
De la Rocha, Pedro Francisco. see Rocha, Pedro Francisco de la.
Delaroche, Peter. 19362
De la Roche, Pierre Marie Sebastian Catineau. see Catineau-Laroche, Pierre Marie Sebastien.
De la Roche Gallichon, F. C. see La Roche Gallichon, F. C. de.
De Laroche-Heron, Henri de Courcy. see Courcy de Laroche-Heron, Henri de.
De la Roche-Tillac, Jean Charles Poncelin. see Poncelin de la Roche-Tillac, Jean Charles, 1746-1828.
De la Rochefoucauld, Francois, Duc. see La Rochefoucauld, Francois, Duc de, 1613-1680.
De la Rochefoucauld-Liancourt, Francois Alexandre Frederic, Duc. see La Rochefoucauld-Liancourt, Francois Alexandre Frederic, Duc de, 1747-1827.
De la Rochelle, Jean Francois Nee. see Nee de la Rochelle, Jean Francois, 1751-1838.
De la Rocque, -------. see La Rocque, ------ de.
De la Roquette, Jean Baptiste Marie Alexandre Dezos. see La Roquette, Jean Baptiste Marie Alexandre Dezos de, 1784-1868.
De la Rosa, Agustin. see Rosa, Agustin de la.
De la Rosa, Hipolito Buena. see La Rosa, Hipolito Buena de.
De la Rosa, Jose. see Sierra, Jose de.
De la Rosa, Jose Nicolas. see Rosa, Jose Nicolas de la.
De la Rosa, Luis. see Rosa, Luis de la.
De la Rosa, Manuel. see Rosa, Manuel de la.
De la Rosa, Manuel Toribio Gonzalez. see Rosa, Manuel Toribio Gonzalez de la.
De la Rosa Figueroa, Francisco Antonio. see Figueroa, Francisco Antonio de la Rosa.
De la Rosa Toro, Agustin. see La Rosa Toro, Agustin de.
De Larra, Victor. pseud. Echos democraticos. see Souza Pinto, Antonio de.
De Larranaga, B. J. see Larranaga, B. J. de.
De Larrazabal, Antonio. see Larrazabal, Antonio de.
De Larrea del de Alcantara, Juan. see Larrea Del de Alcantara, Juan de.
De Larreategui, Mariano Colon. see Larreategui, Mariano Colon de.
De Larrey, P. J. see Larrey, P. J. de.

De la Rua, Hernando. see Rua, Hernando de la.
De la Rue, --------, fl. 1799. (1534), (27337)
De Larue, --------. see Larue, -------, Chevalier de, fl. 1821.
De la Rue, Amelie Eugenie (Caron de Beaumarchais) Toussaint. see Toussaint de la Rue, Amelie Eugenie (Caron de Beaumarchais)
De la Rue, Warren. 19363
De la Rynaga Salazar, Juan. see Rynaga Salazar, Juan de la.
De la Sagra, Ramon. see Sagra, Ramon de la.
De la Salle, A. see La Salle, A. de.
De la Salle, Antoine. see La Salle, Antoine de.
De la Salle, Robert Cavelier, Sieur. see La Salle, Robert Cavelier, Sieur de, 1643-1687.
De la Salle de l'Estang, Simon Philibert. see La Salle de l'Estang, Simon Philibert de, d. 1765.
De la Sauvage, --------. see Sauvage, ------ de la.
De las Casas, Balthazar. see Casas, Bartholome de las, Bp. of Chiapa, 1474-1566.
De las Casas, Bartholome. see Casas, Bartholome de las, Bp. of Chiapa, 1474-1566.
De las Casas, Goncalo. see Casas, Goncalo de las.
De las Casas, Lucas. see Casas, Lucas de las.
De las Cases, Emmanuel Dieudonne Marie Joseph, Comte. see Las Cases, Emmanuel Dieudonne Marie Joseph, Comte de.
De Lascaux, Paul. see Lascaux, Paul de.
De las Cortinas, Manuel Diez. see Cortinas, Manuel Diez de las.
De la Selva, Juan. see Selva, Juan de la.
De la Serna, Juan. see Serna, Juan de la, Abp.
De la Serna, Juan Perez. see Serna, Juan Perez de la.
De la Serre, ------- Barbier, Chevalier. see Barbier, -----, Chevalier De la Serre.
De las Heras, Bartolome Maria. see Heras, Bartolome Maria de las, Bp.
De las Nieves Robledo, Maria. see Robledo, Maria de las Nievas.
De la Soledad Ortega de Arguello, Maria. see Soledad Ortega de Arguello, Maria de la.
De la Sota, Juan Manuel. see Sota, Juan Manuel de la.
De la Source, Dominique Antoine Thaumur. see Thaumur de la Source, Dominique Antoine.
De Lassaga, Juan Lucas. see Lassaga, Juan Lucas de.
De Lasteyrie, Ferdinand, Comte. see Lasteyrie, Ferdinand, Comte de.
De las Torres, -------, Marquesa. see Torres, -------, Marquesa de las.
De la Tega, R. see Tega, R. de la.
De Lates, Bonet. see Bonet, de Lates, 16th cent.
De la Tombe, Joseph. see Letombe, Joseph.
De Lato-Monte, Ludovici. see Lato-Monte, Ludovici de.
De la Torre, -------. see Torre, -------, de la, fl. 1825.
De la Torre, Antonio Teran. see Teran de la Torre, Antonio.
De la Torre, Geronimo Alonso. see Torre, Geronimo Alonso de la.

De la Torre, Gonzalo Gayetano. see Torre, Gonzalo Cayetano de la.
De la Torre, Jose Maria. see Torre, Jose Maria de la.
De la Torre, Juan del Corral Calvo. see Corral Calvo de la Torre, Juan del, 1666-1737.
De la Torre, Luis. see Torre, Luis de la.
De la Torre, Manuel. see Torre, Manuel de la.
De la Torre, Manuel Ortiz. see Ortiz de la Torre, Manuel.
De la Torre, Martin. 80976
De la Torre, Matias Rubin. see Rubin de la Torre, Matias.
De la Torre, Miguel. see Torre, Miguel de la.
De la Torre, Pedro. see Torre, Pedro de la.
De la Torre, Pedro Bermudes. see Bermudez de la Torre y Solier, Pedro Joseph.
De la Torre, Pedro Jose Bermudez. see Bermudez de la Torre, Pedro Jose.
De la Torre, Rafael Martinez. see Martinez de la Torre, Rafael.
De la Torre, Ramond. see Torre, Ramond de la.
De la Torre Lloreda, Manuel. see Torre Lloreda, Manuel de la.
De la Torre Miranda, Antonio. see Torre Miranda, Antonio de la.
De la Torre Rezzonico, Carlo. see Clement XIII, Pope, 1693-1769.
De la Torre y Solier, Pedro Joseph Bermudez. see Bermudez de la Torre y Solier, Pedro Joseph.
De la Torres, Duque de Medina. see Olivares, Gaspar de Guzman, Conde Duque de, 1587-1645.
De Latouanne, -------, Vicomte. see Latouanne, ------, Vicomte de.
De la Touche, Louis Charles le Vassor. see Le Vassor de la Touche, Louis Charles.
De la Tour, ------ Leschenault. see Leschenault de la Tour, ------.
Delatour, A. J. 19365
De la Tour, Bertrand. see La Tour, Bertrand de.
De la Tour, Charles de Saint Estienne, Seigneur. see Saint Estienne, Charles de, Seigneur de la Tour.
De la Tour, Louis Brion. see Brion de la Tour, Louis.
De la Tour, Serres. see Tour, Serres de la.
De Latour Dufay, L. Pierre Dufay. see Dufay de Latour Dufay, L. Pierre, Marquis.
De Latreiche, Antoinette Francois Anne Symon. see Drohojowska, Antoinette Francois Anne Symon de Latreiche, Comtesse.
De la Trinidad, Bernardo. see Bernardo de la Trinidad. Fray
De la Trinidad, Juan. see Trinidad, Juan de la.
De Lattre, Ph.-Albert. see Lattre, Ph.-Albert de.
De Laudonniere, Rene Goulaine. see Laudonniere, Rene Goulaine de.
De Laudun, ------ Vallette. see Vallette de Laudun, -------.
De Laujon, A. see Laujon, A. de.
De L'Aulnaye, F. H. S. see Aulaye, F. H. S. de l'.
De l'Aulne, Anne Robert Jacques Turgot, Baron. see Turgot, Anne Robert Jacques, Baron de l'Aulne, 1727-1781.
Delaunay, Ferd. ed. 70355

De L'Aunay, Mosneron. see L'Aunay, Mosneron de.
De Launay de Valery, Cordier. see Launay de Valery, Cordier de.
De Laune, Thomas, d. 1685. 62812, 78732
Delauney, ------. 32029
De la Union de Cuba, Miguel Tacon y Rosique, Marques. see Tacon y Rosique, Miguel, Marques de la Union de Cuba, 1777-1854.
De Laura, Miseno. see Laura, Miseno de.
De Lauraguais, ------, Comte. see Lauraguais, -------, Comte de.
De Laurnaga, Pablo. see Laurnaga, Pablo de.
De Lauzun, Armand Louis de Gontaut, Duc. see Biron, Armand Louis de Gontaut, Duc de Lauzun, afterwards Duc de, 1747-1793.
De la V., D. J. F. pseud. see V., D. J. F. de la. pseud.
De Lava, Alvarez. see Lava, Alvarez de.
Delaval, ------. 19366 see also Santo Domingo (French Colony) Assemblee Generale. President.
De Laval, Antoine Jean. see Laval, Antoine Jean de.
De Laval, Francois Pyrard. see Pyrard, Francois, ca. 1570-1621.
De Laval de Montmorency, Francois. see Laval de Montmorency, Francois de.
De la Valette, -------. see Valette, ------- de la.
De Lavalette, Antoine. 94126
De la Valiniere, Pierre Huet. see Valiniere, Pierre Huet de la.
Delavall, John. 19367, 37209
De la Valle, -------. see Valle, ------- de la.
De Lavalle, Jose A. see Lavalle, Jose A. de.
Delavan, Edward C. 19368
Delavan, Edward C. defendant 19369, 89744, 94503-note after 94503
Delavan, James. supposed author 10036
De la Vara, Francisco Antonio Velasco. see Velasco de la Vara, Francisco Antonio.
De la Varca, Miguel Calderon. see Calderon de la Varca, Miguel.
De la Vega, Alonso Carillo Laso. see Carillo Laso de la Vega, Alonso.
De Lavega, Antonio. see Lavega, Antonio de.
De la Vega, Antonio de Cordova Laso. see Laso de la Vega, Antonio de Cordova.
De la Vega, Bernardo. see La Vega, Bernardo de.
De la Vega, Dionisio Martinez. see Martinez de la Vega, Dionisio.
De la Vega, Feliciano. see Vega, Feliciano de la.
De la Vega, Francisco Nunez. see Nunez de la Vega, Francisco.
De la Vega, Garcilaso. see Garcilaso de la Vega, Called el Inca, 1539-1616.
De la Vega, Jos. Antonio Garcia. see Garcia de la Vega, Jos. Antonio.
De la Vega, Gonzalez. see La Vega, Gonzales de.
De la Vega, Jose Maria Gonzalez. see Gonzalez de la Vega, Jose Maria.
De la Vega, Joseph. see Vega, Joseph de la.
De la Vega, Manuel. see Vega, Manuel de la.
De la Vega, Matheo. see Vega, Matheo de la.
De la Vega, Nicolas del Valle y. see Valle y de la Vega, Nicolas de.
De la Vega, Pedro. see Vega, Pedro de la.
De la Vega, R. see La Vega, R. de.
De la Vega, Silvestre Diaz. see Vega, Silvestre Diaz de la.

De la Vega, Ventura. see Vega, Ventura de la.

De la Vera Cruz, Francisco Alonso. see Veracruz, Alonso de.

De la Vigne, Charles. see Vigne, Charles de la.

De la Vigne, Magdeleine (Buree) see Vigne, Magdeline (Buree) de la

De la Ville, Jean Ignace. 19370, (47547)-(47548), 84594

Delaville de Mirmont, Alexandre Jean Joseph. 19371

De Lavison, Etienne Rufz. see Rufz de Lavison, Etienne, 1806-1884.

Delaware, Thomas West, 3d Lord. see De La Warr, Thomas West, 3d Lord, 1577-1618.

Delaware (Colony) 11490

Delaware (Colony) plaintiffs (59685)

Delaware (Colony) General Assembly. see Pennsylvania (Colony) General Assembly.

Delaware (Colony) Governor, 1693-1694 (Fletcher) 53435, 53671-53672 see also Fletcher, Benjamin.

Delaware (Colony) Laws, statutes, etc. 19391, 39410, 39414-39415

Delaware. 52569

Delaware. Commission for the Survey of the Sounds Between Cape Charles and Henlopen. see Commission for Survey of the Sounds on Eastern Shore of Virginia, Maryland and Delaware.

Delaware. Commission on the Survey of the Sounds Lying on the Eastern Shore of Virginia, Maryland, and Delaware. see Joint Commission on the Survey of the Sounds Lying on the Eastern Shore of Virginia, Maryland and Delaware.

Delaware. Commissioners on the Boundary Lines of the States of Maryland, Pennsylvania and Delaware. see Joint Commissioners on the Boundary Lines of the States of Maryland, Pennsylvania, and Delaware.

Delaware. Constitution. 1269, 1271, 2071, 5316, 6360, 16086-16092, 16097, 16099-16103, 16107, 16113, 16118-16120, 16133, (19576), 25790, 33137, (47188), 52569, (66397), 100342, 104198

Delaware. Constitutional Convention, 1791. 19386, 19395

Delaware. Constitutional Convention, 1792. (19396)

Delaware. Convention, Newcastle, 1776. 52569

Delaware. Convention, Newcastle, 1776. Clerk. 52569 see also Booth, James.

Delaware. Convention, Newcastle, 1776. President. 52569 see also Read, George, 1733-1798.

Delaware. Convention, 1787. 22233, note after 106002

Delaware. Court of Errors and Appeals. 62051

Delaware. General Assembly. 19404

Delaware. General Assembly. Committee in Regard to the Interference by United States Troops with the General Election, 1862. 69812

Delaware. General Assembly. House of Representatives. 13579

Delaware. General Assembly. House of Representatives. Committee to Investigate the Loan Made by this State to the Philadelphia, Wilmington and Baltimore Rail Road Company. 62051

Delaware. General Assembly. Senate. 13579, 19390

Delaware. Governor, 1814-1817 (Rodney) 33150 see also Rodney, Daniel, 1764-1846.

Delaware. Governor, 1833-1837 (Bennett) (45109) see also Bennett, Caleb P., 1758-1836.

Delaware. Governor, 1855-1859 (Causey) 33150 see also Causey, Peter Foster, 1801-1871.

Delaware. Governor, 1863-1865 (Cannon) 10700, 19389 see also Cannon, William, 1809-1865.

Delaware. Joint Commissioners on the Boundary Lines between the States of Pennsylvania, Delaware and Maryland. see Joint Commissioners on the Boundary Lines between the States of Pennsylvania, Delaware and Maryland.

Delaware. Laws, statutes, etc. 19379, 19387, 19392, 23765, 39414, 52051, (52565), 70820-70821, 82438, 87538, 89066, 104581, 104586

Delaware. Treasurer. plaintiff 62051 see also Clarke, William J. plaintiff

Delaware, Ohio. Ohio Wesleyan Female College. see Ohio Wesleyan University, Delaware, Ohio.

Delaware, Ohio. Ohio Wesleyan University. see Ohio Wesleyan University, Delaware, Ohio.

Delaware, Ohio. State Sunday School Convention, 1865. see Ohio State Sunday School Convention, Delaware, 1865.

Delaware County, N. Y. Delaware Academy. see Delaware Academy, Delaware County, N. Y.

Delaware County, Pa. Institute of Science. 19420, (82584)

Delaware Abolition Society. Committee. 58482

Delaware Academy, Delaware County, N. Y. 19419

Delaware and Hudson Canal Company. 19405, 19409

Delaware and Raritan canal. 19407

Delaware and Raritan Canal Company. 10162, 10828, (19406), (19408), 19411, 19416, (53099)

Delaware and Raritan Canal Company. Board of Directors. see Joint Board of Directors of the Delaware and Raritan Canal, and Camden and Amboy Rail Road Transportation Companies.

Delaware and Schuylkill Basin Company. Charter. 61569

Delaware and Schuylkill Canal Company. see Delaware and Schuylkill Canal Navigation.

Delaware and Schuylkill Canal Company. (19418) see also Schuylkill and Susquehanna Navigation Company. and Union Canal Company of Pennsylvania.

Delaware and Schuylkill Canal Navigation. petitioners 60046, 60725, 78072, 84648

Delaware and Schuylkill Canal Navigation. Committee. (19418), 39219, 60046, 60451, 62116, 84648

Delaware and Schuylkill Canal Navigation. Committee. petitioners 39219, 84647

Delaware and Schuylkill Canal Navigation. President and Managers. 50865, 84620-84621

Delaware and Schuylkill Canal Navigation. Stockholders. 60046

Delaware Association for the Moral Improvement and Education of the Colored People of the State. 19401

Delaware Coal Company. 94460
Delaware College, Newark, Del. 54870
Delaware College, Newark, Del. Library.
19382
Delaware College, Newark, Del. Newark
Academy. 54870
Delaware County Medical Society. 47325
Delaware courant. 102337
Delaware Division, no. 22, New Hope, Pa.
see Sons of Temperance of North
America. Pennsylvania. Delaware
Division, no. 22, New Hope.
Delaware Division Canal Company of Penn-
sylvania. (60047)
Delaware express. 73967
Delaware farmer's union almanac for the year
1865. 19383
Delaware first book. 19374
Delaware gazette. (16745), 27965
Delaware Historical Society. 19398, 83864,
84091, 84969
Delaware Indian and English spelling book.
106299
Delaware Indians. 34640, 36337, 49248-49249,
86037
Delaware Indians. Treaties, etc. (48062),
60255, 96591, 96599, 96605, 96614,
96618, 96620, 96660, 96661, 96675,
97561, 99605
Delaware, Lackawanna, and Western Railroad
Company. 72662
Delaware, Lehigh, Schuylkill and Susquehanna
Railroad Company. Charter. 60048
Delaware lottery for the College of New Jersey.
19397
Delaware register and farmer's magazine.
(19384)
Delaware Society of Paper Makers. see
Society of Paper Makers of Pennsylvania
and Delaware.
Delaware state directory. 19380
Delaware waggoner. pseud. Investigation of
that false, fabulous and blasphemous
misrepresentation of truth. see Nelson,
D. supposed author
Delawariad; or, a second part of the Wilming-
toniad. 19421
De la Warr, Thomas West, 3d Lord, 1577-1618.
66686, 92664, 102756 see also Virginia
(Colony) Governor, 1610-1618 (De la Warr)
De Layseca, Francisco Martin. see Layseca,
Francisco Martin de.
De Lazerne, W. see La Luzerne, Cesar
Henri, Comte de, 1737-1799.
Del Barco Centenera, Martin. see Barco
Centenera, Martin del.
Del Barrio, Paulino. see Barrio, Paulino del.
Delbas, Antonio Fernando. (2229), 19422
Del C., F. M. pseud. see M. del C., F.
pseud.
Del Callejo, B. M. see Callejo, B. M. de.
Del Campillo, Manuel Ignacio Gonzalez. see
Gonzalez del Campillo, Manuel Ignacio,
Bp., 1740-1813.
Del Campillo y Cosio, Joseph. see Campillo
y Cosio, Joseph del.
Del Campo, Est. see Campo, Est. del.
Del Canto, Francisco. see Canto, Francisco
del.
Del Carmen Artega, Manuel. see Carmen
Artega, Manuel del.
Del Castellar, Thomas. see Castellar, Thomas
del.
Del Castillo, Antonio Diaz. see Diaz del
Castillo, Antonio.

Del Castillo, Bernal Diaz. see Diaz del
Castillo, Bernal, 1492-1581?
Del Castillo, Felipe. see Castillo, Felipe del.
Del Castillo, Fl. M. see Castillo, Fl. M. del.
Del Castillo, Jose Mariano. see Castillo, Jose
Mariano del.
Del Castillo, Martin. see Castillo, Martin
del.
Del Castillo, P. P. see Castillo, P. P. del.
Del Castillo, Pedro Fernandez. see Castillo,
Pedro Fernandez del.
Del Castillo, Pedro Ramirez. see Ramirez
del Castillo, Pedro, d. 1737.
Delchamps, J. J. (19423)-19424
Del Corral, Joseph. see Corral, Joseph del.
Del Corral Calvo de la Torre, Juan. see
Corral Calvo de la Torre, Juan del, 1666-
1737.
Del Corro, Juan. see Corro, Juan del.
Del de Alcantara, Juan de Larrea. see Larrea
del de Alcantara, Juan de.
De Leao, Bartholameu. see Leao, Bartholameu
de.
De Leaumont, Laurent Marie. see Leaumont,
Laurent Marie de.
De Lebrija, Elio Antonio. see Lebrija, Elio
Antonio de, 1441?-1522.
De Lebrixa y Pruna, Manuel. see Lebrixa y
Pruna, Manuel de.
Delecluze, Charles. 19426
Delectus florae et faunae Brasiliensis. 48911
De Ledesma, Antonio Colmenero. see Col-
menero de Ledesma, Antonio.
De Ledesma, Clemente. see Ledesma, Cle-
mente de.
De Ledesma, Ph. Rod. see Ledesma, Ph. Rod.
de.
De Legaspi, Michael Lopez. see Lopez de
Legaspi, Michael.
Delegate to the Anti-slavery Convention of
American Women, Held in Philadelphia,
May, 1838. pseud. see Lovell, Laura
H.
Delegates Appointed at a Meeting of the Free
Colored People of Baltimore to Visit
British Guiana and the Island of Trinidad,
1839. see Baltimore. Meeting of the
Free Colored People, 1839. Delegates to
Visit British Guiana, and the Island of
Trinidad, for the Purpose of Ascertaining
the Advantages to be Derived by Colored
People Migrating to those Places.
Delegates Appointed by Various Sections of the
District of Columbia. see District of
Columbia. Delegates. petitioners
Delegates from the General Aid Society for the
Army, at Buffalo, N. Y. see General
Aid Society for the Army, Buffalo, N. Y.
Delegates.
Delegates of Georgia. pseud. Observations
upon the effects of certain late political
suggestions. see Few, W. and Howly,
R. and Walton, George, 1740-1804.
Delegates of the Banks of New York, to the
Bank Convention, New York, 1837. see
Bank Convention, New York, 1837. Dele-
gates of the Banks of New York City.
Delegates of the people. pseud. Present state
of Maryland. see Maryland. General
Assembly. House of Delegates.
Delegate's story. 9669
Delegates to the Chicago Convention, St. Louis,
1847. see St. Louis. Delegates to the
Chicago Convention, 1847.

747

Delegates to the National Convention of Business Men, Philadelphia, 1837. see National Convention of Business Men, Philadelphia, 1837. Philadelphia Delegates.

Delegation Appointed By the Commissioners of Public Schools of Baltimore to Represent the Board in the National Convention of the Friends of Common School Instruction, 1849. see Baltimore. Commissioners of Public Schools. Delegation to the National Convention of the Friends of Common School Instruction, 1849.

Delegation of the Cherokee Tribe of Indians. see Cherokee Nation. Delegates.

Delegation to Washington. (56122)

De Legazpi, Garcia. see Legazpi, Garcia de.

De Leiba, Diego. see Leiba, Diego de.

De Lejarza, Juan Jose Martinez. see Lejarza, Juan Jose Martinez de.

De Lemos, Pedro Fernandez de Castro Andrade y Portugal, Conde. see Castro Andrade y Portugal, Pedro Fernandez de, Conde de Lemos, 1634-1672.

De Lemos Faria e Castro, C. A. see Lemos Faria e Castro, C. A. de.

De Lemos y Andrada, Conde -------. see Lemos y Andrada, ------, Conde de.

De Lemus, Diego. see Lemus, Diego de.

De Leon, A. J. Rodriguez. see Rodriguez de Leon, A. J.

De Leon, Alonzo de Cueva Ponce. see Ponce de Leon, Alonzo de Cueva.

De Leon, Antonio. see Leon, Antonio de, Bp.

De Leon, Antonio Rodriguez. see Rodriguez de Leon, Antonio.

De Leon, Edwin. see Leon, Edwin de, 1828-1891.

De Leon, F. Ponce. see Ponce de Leon, F.

De Leon, Francisco Ponce. see Ponce de Leon, Francisco.

De Leon, Francisco Ruiz. see Ruiz de Leon, Francisco.

De Leon, Gabriel. see Leon, Gabriel de.

De Leon, Joaquin Velasquez. see Velasquez de Leon, Joaquin.

De Leon, Jose Socorro. see Leon, Jose Socorro de, 1831-1869.

De Leon, Joses Mariano Ponce. see Ponce de Leon, Joses Mariano.

De Leon, Joseph Antonio. see Leon, Joseph Antonio de.

De Leon, Joseph Antonio Eugenio Ponce. see Ponce de Leon, Joseph Antonio Eugenio.

De Leon, Juan Bautista Ponce. see Ponce de Leon, Juan Bautista.

De Leon, Juan Recio. see Recio de Leon, Juan.

De Leon, Luis. see Leon, Luis de.

De Leon, Martin. see Leon, Martin, fl. 1612.

De Leon, Moses Pereira. see Pereira de Leon, Moses.

De Leon, Nicolas Suarez Ponce. see Suarez Ponce de Leon, Nicolas.

De Leon, Pedro de Cieza. see Cieza de Leon, Pedro de.

De Leon, Rodriguez. see Leon, Rodriguez de.

De Leon, Pinelo, Antonio Rodriguez. see Leon Pinelo, Antonio Rodriguez de, d. 1660.

De Leon Pinelo, Didacus. see Leon Pinelo, Diego, fl. 1660.

De Leon Pinelo, Diego. see Leon Pinelo, Diego, fl. 1660.

De Leon y Gama, Antonio. see Leon y Gama, Antonio de.

De Leon y Messia, Franciso Garabito. see Garabito de Leon y Messia, Francisco.

De Leon y White, Diaz. see Leon y White, Diaz de.

De Lerry, Jean. see Lerry, Jean de.

Delery, Ch. 19425

De Lery, Jean. see Lery, Jean de, 1534-1611.

De Lesaga, Juan Lucas. see Lesaga, Juan Lucas de.

De l'Espinasse, N. see Espinasse, N. de l', Chevalier de Langeac.

De l'Espine, H. see L'Espine, H. de.

Del Espiritu Sancto, Antonio. see Antonio del Espiritu Sancto.

De Lesseps, Jean Baptiste Barthelemy, Baron. see Lesseps, Jean Baptiste Barthelemy, Baron de, 1766-1834.

Delessert, Benjamin. 19427

Delerssert, Edouard, 1828-1898. 19428, 37009

Delessert, Eugene. 19429

De l'Estang, Simon Philibert de la Salle. see Salle de l'Estang, Simon Philibert de, d. 1765.

De Letona, Bartolome. see Letona, Bartolome de.

Deleware Indians. see Delaware Indians.

De Lewis, Denis. see Richel, Dionisio.

De Leyba, Diego. see Leyba, Diego de.

De Lezama, Juan. see Lezama, Juan de.

De Lezamis, Jose. see Lezamis, Jose de.

De Lezay-Marnezia, Cl. Fr. Ad. see Lezay-Marnezia, Cl. Fr. Ad. de.

Delft, Netherlands. Classis. see Nederlandsche Hervormde Kerk. E. Classis van Delft.

Delgadillo de Auellaneda, Barnardino. see Auellaneda, Barnardino Delgadillo de.

Delgado, Augustin Rodriguez. see Rodriquez Delgado, Augustin, Bp.

Delgado, Evarista. (34684)

Delgado, Juan de Dios de la Rada y. see Rada y Delgado, Juan de Dios de la.

Delgado y Buenrostro, Ant. 19430

Delharms, R. 19431

Delhi, N. Y. Court. (25259), 73045

Delhinor, E. 19432

Del Hoyo, Joseph. see Hoyo, Joseph del.

De Lhuys, Edouard Drouyn. see Drouyn de Lhuys, Edouard, 1805-1881.

De Liancourt, -------. see Liancourt, ------- de.

Deliberation de la Chambre d'Agriculture du Cap. 75101

Deliberation du Conseil Colonial de la Guiane Francaise. 29171

Deliberation; or the substance of that may be spoken. 19433

Deliberations de la paroisse du Fond-des-Negres. 75113

Deliberations et avis des conseils speciaux. 67154

De Liborius, Carolina Litchfield. see Liborius, Carolina Litchfield de.

De Licana, Bernardo. see Licana, Bernardo de.

De Liceaga, Jose Maria. see Liceaga, Jose Maria de.

Delices et annales de l'Espagne et du Portugal. 14541

De Lignac, Joseph Adrien le Large. see Lignac, Joseph Adrien le Large de.

Deligne, ------. 19434

De Ligne, Charles Joseph. see Ligne, Charles Joseph, Prince de, 1735-1814.

De Liguori, Alfonso Maria. see Liguori, Alfonso Maria de, Saint, 1696-1787.

De Lima Felner, R. J. see Felner, R. J. de Lima.
De Limare, ------ Camus. see Camus de Limare, -------.
De Limonade, Julien Prevost, Comte. see Limonade, Julien Prevost, Comte de.
De Linan y Cisneros, Melchor. see Linan y Cisneros, Melchor de, Abp.
De Linarez y Pacheco, Wenceslo. see Linares y Pacheco, Wenceslo de.
De L'Incarnation, Marie. see Marie de l'Incarnation. Mother Superior.
De Linda, Lucae. see Linda, Lucae de.
Delineated description and history. 106370
Delineated Presbyterian play'd hob with. 2464A, 69528
Delineation of different classes of Christians. 36094
Delineation of the causes. 63619
Delineation of the characteristic features. 8167
Delineation of the laws and government of the state of Kentucky. 34354, 34356-34357
Del Infantado, Rodrigo Diaz de Vivar, 6. Duque. see Infantado, Rodrigo Diaz de Vivar, 6. Duque del.
De Linieres, Eduardo Enrique Teodoro de Turreau. see Turreau de Linieres, Eduardo Enrique Teodoro de.
De Linieres, Louis Marie Turreau. see Turreau de Linieres, Louis Marie, Baron, 1756-1816.
Delinquent tax bill. 61570
De Liri, Antonio. see Liri, Antonio de.
De Lirio, Sebastian. see Lirio, Sebastian de.
Delirium of my childhood. 19435
De Lisboa, Diego. see Lisboa, Diego de.
De Lisboa y Lyon, Diego Lopez. see Lisboa y Lyon, Diego Lopez de.
De Lisle, --------. see Lisle, -------- de, fl. 1784.
Delisle, --------. cartographer 40312, 40673, 51285, (72759), note after 93778
De Lisle, Eduardo. 19268, 93785
De l'Isle, Guillaume. see L'Isle, Guillaume de, 1675-1726.
De l'Isle, Guil. Phil. Buache. see Isle, Guil. Phil. Buache de l'.
De l'Isle, J. N. see Isle, J. N. de l'.
Delisle de la Drevetiere, Louis Francois. 13616, note before 96140
De Liste, --------. see Liste, -------- de.
Delitsch, Otto. 19436, 91197
Delius, Edouard. supposed author (42157), note after 101236
Delius, Goduridus. 66062
Deliverance. 63582, 100804
Deliverance from the furnace. 5915
Delivered April 2, 1835. 73120
Deliverer of his country. 101866
De Lizana y Beaumont, Francisco Xavier. see Lizana y Beaumont, Francisco Xavier de.
De Lizardi, Jose Joaquin Fernandez. see Fernandez de Lizardi, Jose Joaquin, 1776-1827
De Lizarraga Vengoa, -------, Conde. see Lizarraga Vengoa, -------, Conde de.
Dell, William, d. 1670? 14373, (19437)-19439
Dell' America, canti cinque. 86842
Dell dart. 91162
Dell' eccellenze di St Pietro. 58291
Dell' Hercole e stvdio geografico. 55258
Dell' historia de i semplici, aromati, et altre cose. 57668-57669
Dell' historia de i semplici aromati. Et altre cose che vengono portate dall' Indie Orientali. 57670

Dell' historia della China. 27778-27779, 47828
Dell' historia di i semplici, aromati, et altre cose. 57667
Dell' historia ecclesiastica di Piacenza di Pietro Maria Campi. 10311
Della chiesa cattolica negli Stati Uniti d'America. 19440
Della China et delle altre sue specie nouvamente scoperte. 73991
Della cose che vengono portate dall' Indie Occidentali. 49939
Della descrittione dell' Africa. 67730
Della generale et natvrale historia delle Indie. 67740
Della historia del Signor Giovan de Barros. 67731
Della istoria Vinitiana. 4620
Della origine e della patria di Cristoforo Colombo. 89648
Della patria di Cristoforo Colombo. 14654, 51758-(51759), 51762
Della patria di Colombo. 10705, 51760
Della religione e delle lingue degli Orinochesi. 27382
Della scoperta dell' America. 10915
Della selva di varia lettione. 48239
Della storia geografica e naturale della provincia dell' Oronoco. 27382
Della vita del ven. servo di Dio P. Guiseppe Anchieta. 1374, 56697, 100610
De Llaguno Amirola, Eugenio. see Llaguno Amirola, Eugenio de.
Della Madre di Dio, Giuseppe. see Jose de la Madre de Dios.
De Llano y Valdes, F. see Llano y Valdes, F. de.
De Llano y Zapata, Joseph Eusebio. see Llano y Zapata, Joseph Eusebio de.
Dellatly, -------. 26845, 83796
Delle cose, che vengono portate dall' Indie Occidentali. 49940
Delle cose della Moscovia. 67736
Delle due trombe i primi fiati. 4632
Delle historie memorabili. 106333
Delle lettere Americane. 10911
Delle navigationi et viaggi in molti Lvoghi corretta, et ampliata. 67731
Delle navigationi et viaggi nel qval si contiene la descrittione. 67730
Delle navigationi et viaggi raccolto da M. Gio. Batt. Ramvsio. 16951, (67733)-67735, 67739, 67742, note after 99383C
Delle navigationi et viaggi raccolto gia da M. Gio. Battista Ramvsio. 67732
Delle nvove isole in qual modo et quando furono trouate. (51402)
Delle relationi vniversali. 6803
Delle relationi vniversali di Giovanni Botero. 6801
Delle sigle usate da C. Colombo nella sua firma. 76522
Delle sollevationi di stato accadute ne' nostri tempi. 106333
Dellet, James, 1788-1848. 19441
Delleville, Philippes. 19442
Delli viaggi di Enrico Wanton alle terre australi. 79229
Dellmann, Fr. (19443)
Dello scoprimento dell' isola Frislanda. (67737)
Dello stato e della sorte delle colonie degli antichi popoli. 75531
Dellon, C. 19444-(19447)
Del Luoco, Francese. see Luoco, Francese del.
Delmar, Alexander. (19448)-19451, 54853

Delmas, A. de. tr. (7164)
Delmira. pseud. Dialogo. (18233)
Del Molino Torres, Julian. see Torres,
 Julian Del Molino.
Delmonte y Tejada, Antonio, 1783-1861. 19452,
 50093
Delmotte, Henri Florent. 19453
Del Nino Jesus, Pablo Antonio. see Pablo
 Antonio del Nino Jesus.
De Loaisa y Quinones, Pedro. see Loaisa y
 Quinones, Pedro de.
De Loaisaga, Manuel. see Loaisaga, Manuel
 de.
De Lohenschiold, Ottonis Christi. see Lohen-
 schiold, Ottone Christiano de.
De Lolme, Jean Louis. see Lolme, Jean
 Louis de, 1740-1806.
Del Olmo, Joseph Vicente. see Olmo, Joseph
 Vicente del.
De Lomenie, Ch. F. see Lomenie, Ch. F. de.
De Long, C. E. 68945 see also U. S.
 Legation. Japan.
De Longchamp, ---------. see Longchamp,
 -------- de, fl. 1720.
De Longchamps, Pierre. see Longchamps,
 Pierre de, d. 1812.
De Longperier, Adrien. see Longperier,
 Adrien de.
De Lorea, Antonio. see Lorea, Antonio de.
De Lorento, ------- Penalver, Conde de Santa
 Maria. see Penalver, -------, Conde
 de Santa Maria de Lorento.
De Lorgues, Antoine Francois Felix, Comte
 Roselly. see Roselly de Lorgues,
 Antoine Francois Felix, Comte, 1805-
 1898.
De Lorito, Antonio Ardoino, Marquis. see
 Ardoino, Antonio, Marques de Lorito.
Delorme, Emile Nouette. see Nouette-Delorme,
 Emile.
De Lorra Baquio, Francisco. see Lorra Ba-
 quio, Francisco de.
De los Hoyos, Juan. see Hoyos, Juan de los.
De Los Monteros, Ignacio Espinosa. see
 Espinosa de los Monteros, Ignacio.
De los Olivos, Alonso Vascallero. see Vas-
 callero de los Olivos, Alonso.
De los Reyes, Jose Maria. (26589)
De los Reyes Angel, Gaspar. see Reyes
 Angel, Gaspar de los.
De los Rios, A. F. 40741
De los Rios, Epitacio J. see Rios, Epitacio
 J. de los.
De los Rios, J. P. see Rios, J. P. de los.
De los Rios, Jose Amador. ed. 57990
De los Rios, Thomas Theran. see Theran de
 los Rios, Thomas.
De los Rios y Rosas, Antonio. see Rios y
 Rosas, Antonio de los, 1808-1873.
De Losa, Francois. see Loza, Francisco.
De Losada, Basilio Sebastian Castellanos.
 see Losada, Basilio Sebastian Castel-
 lanos de.
De Losada, Juan Miguel. see Losada, Juan
 Miguel de.
De Lotbiniere, Joly. see Lotbiniere, Joly de.
De Loureiro, Lorenco Trigo. see Loureiro
 Lorenco Trigo de.
De Lourmel, Felix Esprit. see Lourmet,
 Felix Esprit de.
Del Oviedo, Gonzolo Ferdinando. see Oviedo,
 Gonzolo Ferdinando del.
De Lowencourt, F. see Lowencourt, F. de,
 Sieur de Vauchelles.
De Lowenorn, P. see Lowenorn, P. de.

De Loza, Augustin Joseph Mariano del Rio.
 see Rio de Loza, Augustin Joseph
 Mariano del.
Del Penon Blanco, -------- Salinas. see
 Salinas del Penon Blanco, ------.
Delpeux, -------. tr. 35147
Delphian evening. 102121
Delphine. pseud. Solon. see Baker, Delphine
 Paris. supposed author
Del Pinto, Joseph Gonzalez. see Gonzalez del
 Pinto, Joseph.
Del Pozo, Antonio. see Pozo, Antonio del.
Del Puerto, Domingo. see Puerto, Domingo
 del.
Del Puerto, Juan. see Puerto, Juan del.
Del Raso, Antonio. see Raso, Antonio del.
Del Real Transporte, ------, Marques. see
 Real Transporte, -----, Marques del.
Del Rey, Fermin. see Fermin del Rey.
Del Rey, Firmin. see Fermin del Rey.
Del Ribero, Pedro Bravo. see Ribero, Pedro
 Bravo del.
Del Rincon, Antonio. see Rincon, Antonio del.
Del Rincon, Lucas. see Rincon, Lucas del.
Del Rio, Alphonso Mariano. see Rio, Alphonso
 Mariano del.
Del Rio, Andres. see Rio, Andres del.
Del Rio, Andres Manuel. see Rio, Andres
 Manuel del.
Del Rio, Antonio. see Rio, Antonio del.
Del Rio, Antonio Ferrer. see Rio, Antonio
 Ferrer del.
Del Rio, Guillermo. see Rio, Guillermo del.
Del Rio, Ignacio Jordan de Asso y. see Asso
 y del Rio, Ignacio Jordan de, 1742-1804.
Del Rio, J. Garcia. see Garcia del Rio, J.
Del Rio, Juan de Aguilar. see Rio, Juan de
 Aguilar del.
Del Rio, Manuel. see Rio, Manuel del.
Del Rio, Manuel Rojo. see Rojo del Rio,
 Manuel, 1708-1764.
Del Rio, Pedro Jimenez de Gongara y Lujan,
 Duque de Almodovar. see Almodovar
 del Rio, Pedro Jimenez de Gongara y
 Lujan, Duque de, d. 1794.
Del Rio de Loza, Augustin Joseph Mariano.
 see Rio de Loza, Augustin Joseph
 Mariano del.
Del Rio Laubyan y Vieyra, E. R. see Laubyan
 y Vieyra, E. R. del Rio.
Del Rivero, Eladio Ramon. see Rivero,
 Eladio Ramon del.
Del Rivero, Luis Manuel. see Rivero, Luis
 Manuel del.
Del Rodo, Juan Lope. see Rodo, Juan Lope
 del.
Del Rosario, Payo. pseud. see Villavicencio,
 Pablo de.
Del Salvador, Jos. see Salvador, Jos. del.
Del Salvatore, Michele. see Salvatore,
 Michele del.
Del Santo Sacramento, Lorenzo. see Lorenzo
 del Santo Sacramento. Fray
Del Sesso e di Venafro, Ambrogio Spinola,
 Marchese. see Sesso e di Venafro,
 Ambrogio Spinola, Marchese del.
Del Soccoro Rodriguez, Manuel. see Rodriguez,
 Manuel del Soccoro.
Del Solar, Fidelis Pastor. see Solar, Fidelis
 Pastor del.
Del Solar, Mercedes Marin. see Solar,
 Mercedes Marin del, 1804-1866.
Delta. pseud. Letter from Delta to Senex.
 19456
Delta. pseud. Spurious reprints of early books.
 see Deane, Charles, 1813-1889.

Delta de los rios Uruguay, Parana y Plata. 77131
Del Techo, Nicolas. see Techo, Nicolas del, Originally du Toict, 1611-1685.
Del Tepeyac, Juan Diego. see Tepeyac, Juan Diego del.
Delti Phi Society, Brown University. see Brown University. Delti Phi Society.
Del Toro, J. Rodriguez. see Rodriguez del Toro, J.
De Lucy, Richard. see Lucy, Richard de.
Deluge. A semi-serious poem. 82290, 83788
De Lugo, Bernardo. see Lugo, Bernardo de.
De Lumina, ------ Poullin. see Poullin de Lumina, -------.
De Luna, J. G. see Luna, J. G. de.
De Luna y Arellano, Miguel. see Luna y Arellano, Miguel de.
De Luque, Eduardo Malo. pseud. Histoire politica. see Almodovar de Rio, Pedro Jimenez de Gongara y Lujan, Duque de, d. 1794.
De Lurcy, Gabriel Lafond. see Lafond de Lurcy, Gabriel.
De Lurieu, G. see Lurieu, G. de.
Delure, John van. pseud. see Decalves, Alonso. pseud.
Delusion; or the witch of New England. 19457
Delisions dispelled in regard to interoceanic communication. 34939
Delusive and dangerous principles of the minority exposed and refuted. 19458
De Lussaga, J. Lucas. see Lassaga, Juan Lucas de.
De Lussan, ------ Raveneau. see Raveneau de Lussan, ------, Sieur.
Deluvium ignis. 46285
De Luxembourg, Raphael. see Luxembourg, Raphael de.
Deluzy, Leon. (44859)
Del Valle, ---------, Marques. see Valle, -------, Marques del.
Del Valle, Jose Cecilio. see Valle, Jose Cecilio del.
Del Valle, Jose Z. Gonzalez. see Gonzalez del Valle, Jose Z.
Del Valle, Juan. see Valle, Juan del.
Del Valle, Zarco. see Valle, Zarco del.
Del Valle y Caviedes, Juan. see Valle y Caviedes, Juan del.
Del Valle y de la Vega, Nicolas. see Valle y de la Vega, Nicolas del.
Del Valle y Gozman, Francisco. see Valle y Gozman, Francisco del.
Del Valle y Portillo, Manuel. see Valle y Portillo, Manuel del.
Del Villar, Francisco de Paula. see Villar, Francisco de Paula del.
Del Villar, Pedro. see Villar, Pedro del.
D'Elville, Rinaldo. 105178
Delvin, George. see Dillwyn, George.
De Lyra, J. M. see Lyra, J. M. de.
De M***, le Comte. pseud. see M***, Comte de. pseud.
De M., C. A. L. T. pseud. see M., C. A. L. T. de. pseud.
De M., L. B. pseud. see M., L. B. de. pseud.
De Mably, Gabriel Bonnot. see Mably, Gabriel Bonnot de, 1709-1785.
De Macedo, Antonio. see Macedo, Antonio de.
De Macedo, Antonio de Souza. see Souza de Macedo, Antonio de.
De Macedo, Ignacio Jose. see Macedo, Ignacio Jose de.

De Macedo, Joaquim Manoel. see Macedo, Joaquim Manoel de.
De Macedo, Joaquim Teixeira. see Macedo, Joaquim Teixeira de.
De Macedo, Jose Agostinho. see Macedo, Jose Agostinho de.
De Macedo, M. A. see Macedo, M. A. de.
De Machault, Jacques. see Machault, Jacques de.
De Mackau, -------, Baron. see Mackau, -------, Baron de.
De Madraoz, D. P. see Madraoz, D. P. de.
De Madre de Deos, Gaspar de. see Gaspar de Madre de Deos, 1715-1800.
De Madrid, Jose Fernandez. see Fernandez de Madrid, Jose.
De Madriga, Pedro. see Madriga, Pedro de.
De Magalhanes, Domingo Jose Goncalves. see Goncalves de Magalhanes, Domingos Jose, Visconde, de Araguaya, 1811-1882.
De Magalhanes de Gandavo, Pero. see Magalhanes de Gandavo, Pero de.
De Magnieres, Domingo O'Heguerty, Comte. see O'Heguerty, Domingo, Comte de Magnieres, 1699-1790.
De Maillet, B. see Maillet, B. de.
De Maires, P. see Maires, P. de.
De Mairobert, Matthieu Francois Pidansat. see Pidansat de Mairobert, Matthieu Francois.
De Majorada, -------, Marques. see Majorada, -------, Marques de.
De Malet du Gravier, ------, Comte. see Malet du Gravier, -----, Comte de.
De Mallery, Carel. see Mallery, Carel de, 1571-1635. engr.
De Malves, Gua. see Malves, Gua de.
De Man, Jan Willem Engelbert. see Man, Jan Willem Engelbert de.
De Mancera, Pedro de Toledo y Leiva, Marques. see Toledo y Leiva, Pedro de, Marques de Mancera, 1585-1654.
De Mancy, Adrien (Le Breton) Jarry. see Jarry de Mancy, Adrien (Le Breton)
Demand of William Vans, on Stephen Codman. 98558
Demand of William Vans, on the heirs of John and Richard Codman. 98568
Demanda promovida en Guanajuato, Mina de la Luz. 73864
Demanda promovida en Guanajuato por los herederos. 73864
De Mandauilla, Joanne. see Mandauilla, Joanne de.
Demande en grace pour Adele. 5653
De Mandeville, ------- Marigni. see Marigni de Mandeville, ------.
Demands of freedom. 93640
Demands of the age on colleges. 44324
De Manero, Jose Mariano. see Manero, Jose Mariano de.
De Manne-Vilette, Dapres. see Manne-Vilette, Dapres de.
De Manoncourt, Charles Nicolas Sigisbert Sonnini. see Sonnini de Manoncourt, Charles Nicolas Sigisbert, 1751-1812.
De Manozca, Juan. see Manozca, Juan de.
De Manozca, Ivan. see Mendoza, Juan de, Abp.
De Manozca, Juan Saenz. see Saenz de Manozca, Juan.
De Manuel y Rodrigues, Miguel. see Manuel y Rodrigues, Miguel de, fl. 1780.
De Manzaneda y Encinas, Diego Miguel Bringas. see Bringas de Manzaneda y Encinas, Diego Miguel.

De Manzaneda y Enzinas, Diego Bringas de.
see Bringas de Manzaneda y Encinas,
Diego Miguel.
De Marbois, ----- Barbe. see Barbe Mar-
bois, Francois de, Marquis, 1745-1837.
De Marcay, ------. see Marcay, ------ de.
De Marcenado, Alvaro de Navia Osorio, Mar
ques de Santa Cruz. see Santa Cruz
de Marcenado, Alvaro de Navia Osorio,
Marques de, 1684-1732.
Demarchais, ------. (19459)
De Marcilla, Pedro Garces. see Marcilla,
Pedro Garces de.
De Marconnay, H. Lablanc. see Marconnay,
H. Lablanc de.
Demarest, David D. 19460
Demarest, G. I. 51524
Demarest, James. 19461-(19462)
Demarest, William. 25972
De Maria, Isidoro. see Maria, Isidoro de.
De Mariana, Juan. see Mariana, Juan de.
De Marianela, Juan de Meneses y Padilla,
Marques. see Meneses y Padilla,
Juan de, Marques de Marianela.
De Mariz, Pedro. see Mariz, Pedro de.
De Mariz Carneiro, Antonio. see Mariz
Carneiro, Antonio de.
De Marles, J. see Marles, J. de.
De Marley-le-Chatel, Martin Fumee, Sieur.
see Fumee, Martin, Sieur de Marlet-
le-Chatel, 16th cent.
De Marmont, Auguste Frederic Louis Viesse.
see Marmont, Auguste Frederic Louis
Viesse de.
De Marquetz, -------. 44668
De Marre, J. see Marre, J. de.
De Marsy, Francois Marie. see Marsy,
Francois Marie de.
De Martens, Charles. see Martens, Charles
de.
De Martius, Car. Fr. Ph. see Martius, Karl
Freidrich Philipp von, 1794-1868.
Demartray, Alonzo. 17153, 19463-19464,
21178-21179
De Mata, Nicolas Urbano. see Urbano de
Mata, Nicolas.
De Mattos, Jose Ferreira. see Mattos, Jose
Ferreira de.
De Mauny, ------, Comte. see Mauny,
------, Comte de.
De Maupertuis, Pierre Louis Moreau. see
Maupertuis, Pierre Louis Moreau de.
De Mauvillon, E. see Mauvillon, E. de.
De Mauvillon, M. see Mauvillon, M. de.
De Maye, John Cornelitz. 89444
De Mayerne-Turquet, Louis. see Mayerne-
Turquet, Louis de.
De Mayorga, Francisco Xavier Tello. see
Tello de Mayorga, Francisco Xavier.
De Mayorga, Martin. see Mayorga, Martin
de.
De Mayre, Jacobo. see Le Maire, Jacob,
1585-1616.
De Maza, Manuel Vicente. 99791
De Mazariegos, Mariano Robles Dominguez.
see Robles Dominguez de Mazariegos,
Mariano.
De Mazarredo, Josef Salazar. see Salazar
de Mazarredo, Josef.
Demby, J. M. 19465
Demeanor of Sir W. Raleigh. 78994
De Meaux, Jean Mocquet. see Mocquet de
Meaux, Jean.
De Medeiros Correa, Joao. see Correa,
Joao de Medeiros.

De Medici, Giulio. see Clement VII, Pope,
1478-1534.
De Medina, Antonio. see Medina, Antonio de.
De Medina, Balthasar. see Medina, Balthasar
de, d. 1697.
De Medina, Bernardo. see Medina, Bernardo
de.
De Medina, Cristobal Gutierrez. see Gutierrez
de Medina, Cristobal.
De Medina, Eduardo. see Medina, Eduardo
de.
De Medina, Francisco. see Medina, Francisco
de.
De Medina, Francisco G. see Medina, Fran-
cisco G. de.
De Medina, Ivan Vazquez. see Vazquez de
Medina, Ivan.
De Medina, Pedro. see Medina, Pedro de.
De Medina, Solomon. see Medina, Solomon
de.
De Medina de la Torres, Duque. see Olivares,
Gaspar de Guzman, Conde Duque de,
1587-1645.
De Medina Rincon, Juan. see Medina Rincon,
Juan de.
De Medina y Saravia, Joseph Diego. see
Medina y Saravia, Joseph Diego de.
De Medine, Pierre. see Medina, Pedro de.
De Medinilla, Maria Estrada. see Medinilla,
Maria Estrada de.
De Medrano, Petro. see Medrano, Petro de.
De Medrano, Sebastian Fernandez. see Med-
rano, Sebastian Fernandez de.
De Mejorda, -------, Marques. see Mejorada,
-------, Marques de.
De Melgar, Esteban Sancho. see Melgar,
Esteban Sancho de.
De Mella, Nicolas Romero. see Romero de
Mella, Nicolas.
De Mello, Emilio Xavier Sobreira. see
Sobreira de Mello, Emilio Xavier, d.
1885.
De Mello, Francisco Freire. see Mello,
Francisco Freire de.
De Mello, Francisco Manoel. see Mello,
Francisco Manuel de, 1608-1666.
De Mello, Francisco Manuel. see Mello,
Francisco Manuel de, 1608-1666.
De Mello, Jose Rodrigues. see Rodrigues de
Mello, Jose, 1704-1783.
De Mello, Josephi Rodrigues. see Rodrigues
de Mello, Jose, 1704-1783.
De Mello, Roberto Calheiros. see Mello,
Roberto Calheiros de.
De Mello, Urbano Sabino Pessoa. see Pessoa
de Mello, Urbano Sabino.
De Mello Freier, Paschoal Jose. see Mello
Freire, Paschoal Jose de.
De Mello Moraes, A. J. see Mello Moraes,
Alexandre Jose de, 1816-1882.
De Melo, Matias Saurez. see Suarez de Melo,
Matias.
De Mena, Pedro. see Mena, Pedro de.
De Mendana, Alvarez. see Mendana, Alvarez
de.
De Mendez y Lachica, Tomas. see Mendez
y Lachica, Tomas de.
De Mendibil, Pablo. see Mendibil, Pablo de.
De Mendieta, Alphonso. see Mendieta,
Alphonso de.
De Mendieta, Geronimo. see Mendieta,
Geronimo de.
De Mendive, R. Maria. see Mendive, R.
Maria de.
De Mendizabal, L. see Mendizabal, L. de.

752

De Mendizabal, Pedro Josef. see Mendizabal, Pedro Josef de.

De Mendizbal, L. see Mendizabal, L. de.

De Mendoca, Antonio. see Mendoca, Antonio de.

De Mendoca, Juan Gonzalez. see Gonzalez de Mendoza, Juan, Abp., 1571-1639.

De Mendoca, Lorenco. see Mendoca, Lorenco de.

De Mendoca Catano y Aragon, Luis. see Mendoca Catano y Aragon, Luis de.

De Mendoca Corte-Real, Diogo. see Mendoca Corte-Real, Diogo de.

De Mendoca Furtado, Tristao. see Mendoca Furtado, Tristao de.

De Mendonca, Antonio Pedro Lopes. see Mendonca, Antonio Pedro Lopes de.

De Mendonca, Francisco Maria de Souza Furtado. see Souza Furtado de Mendonca, Francisco Maria de.

De Mendonca, Hypolito Jose da Costa Pereira Furtado. see Costa Pereira Furtado de Mendonca, Hypolito Jose da.

De Mendonca, Joao Jacyntho. see Mendonca, Joao Jacyntho de.

De Mendonza, Al. see Mendonza, Al. de.

De Mendosa Jardinas, Tristan. see Mendosa Jardinas, Tristan de.

De Mendosse Jardis, Tristan. see Mendosa Jardis, Tristan de.

De Mendoz, Lopez. see Mendoz, Lopez de.

De Mendoza, A. see Mendoza, A. de.

De Mendoza, Antonio. see Mendoza, Antonio de, Conde de Tendilla.

De Mendoza, Diego. see Mendoza, Diego de.

De Mendoza, Garcia Hurtago. see Mendoza, Garcia Hurtago de.

De Mendoza, Javier. see Mendoza, Javier de.

De Mnedoza, Juan. see Mendoza, Juan de, Abp.

De Mendoza, Juan Gonzales. see Gonzalez de Mendoza, Juan, Abp., 1571-1639.

De Mendoza, Juan Lopez. see Mendoza, Juan Lopez de.

De Mendoza, Juan Suarez. see Suarez de Mendoza, Juan.

De Mendoza, Lorenco Hurtago. see Mendoza, Lorenco Hurtago de.

De Mendoza, Luis Torres. see Torres de Mendoza, Luis.

De Mendoza, Pedro Salazar. see Salazar de Mendoza, Pedro.

De Mendoza Ayala, Juan. see Mendoza Ayala, Juan de.

De Mendoza Capellan, Lorenzo. see Capellan, Lorenzo de Mendoza.

De Mendoza y Luna, Juan. see Mendoza y Luna, Juan de, Marques de Montesclaros.

De Meneses, Duart. see Meneses, Duart de.

De Meneses, F. see Meneses, F. de.

De Meneses, Francisco Tello. see Tello de Meneses, Francisco.

De Meneses, Francisco Xavier. see Meneses, Francisco Xavier de, Conde de la Erizeira.

De Meneses Bracamonte, Bernardino. see Meneses Bracamonte, Bernardo de.

De Meneses y Padilla, Juan. see Meneses y Padilla, Juan de, Marques de Marianela.

De Menezes, Francisco Xavier. see Menezes, Francisco Xavier de.

De Menezes, Jorge de Almeida. see Menezes, Jorge de Almeida de.

De Menezes, Luis. see Menezes, Luis de, Conde de Ericeyra.

De Menezes, Manuel. see Menezes, Manuel de.

De Menezes, Manuel Jacome Bezerra. see Menezes, Manuel Jacome Bezerra de.

De Menezes, Manuel Joaquim. see Menezes, Manuel Joaquim de.

De Menil, Alexander Nicolas, 1849-1928. 84241

De Monoville, Nicolas Joseph Thiery. see Thiery de Menonville, Nicolas Joseph.

Demons egomet. pseud. Greatest sermon that ever was preached. 104382

Demerara. Court. 31398

Demerara. Courts martial (Smith) 82898-82899, 82902-82905, 82910

Demerara. Laws, statutes, etc. 19466, 22996-22998, 31398

Demerara. 44938

Demerara & Essequibo vade-mecum. 19466

Demerara. Further papers. 82903

Demerara. Further papers; viz. 82904

Demerara after fifteen years of freedom. 19469

Demerara memorial. 19468

Demerara. Return to an address from the Honourable the House of Commons. 82902

Demerary, transition de l'esclavage a la liberte. 49092

De Merchado, Luigi Gonzales. see Gonzales de Merchado, Luigi.

De Marian, ------, Baron. see Merian, ------, Baron de.

De Merino, Fernando A. see Merino, Fernando A. de.

De Merlhiac, G. see Merlhiac, G. de.

Demersay, Alfred, d. 1891. 19471-19474

Demersay, L. M. Alfred. see Demersay, Alfred, d. 1891.

De Mescua, Antonio Mira. see Mira de Mescua, Antonio.

Demesle de l'espirit et du judgement. 40126

De Mesquita, J. J. see Mesquita, J. J. de.

De Mesquita, Martinho. see Martinho de Mesquita.

De Messia, P. see Mexia, Pedro, 1496?-1552?

Demetrius, Junior, the silversmith. pseud. Mormonism exposed! 50756

Demetz, ------. 19475

De Metz, Gauthier. see Metz, Gauthier de.

Demeunier, Jean Nicolas. 16261, (19476)-19478, 62574, 98441

De Meunrios, Francisco Xaviero. pseud. see Louis XVIII, King of France, 1755-1824.

Demeur, Adolphe Louis Joseph. 19479

De Mexia, Pedro. see. Mexia, Pedro, 1496?-1552?

Demica [sic] tertia pars historiae Americanae. (8784)

De Michel, ------. see Michel, ------ de.

De Middelgeest, Simon. see Middlegeest, Simon de.

De Mier, ------. see Mier, ------ de.

De Mier, Manual. see Mier, Manual de.

De Mier Cazo y Estrada, Francisco. see Mier Cazo y Estrada, Francisco de.

De Mier Noriega y Guerra, Jose Servando Teresa. see Mier Noriega y Guerra, Jose Servando Teresa de, 1765-1827.

De Mier Quatemoc zin, Juan Rosillo. see Mier Quatemoczin, Juan Rosillo de.

De Mier y Guerra Servando, Jose. see Mier y Guerra Servando, Jose de.

De Mier y Teran, Manuel. see Mier y Teran, Manuel de.

De Miggrode, Jacques. see Miggrode, Jacques de.
De Mijangos, Juan. see Mijangos, Iaon de.
Demilt Dispensary, New York. 54236
Demilt Dispensary, New York. Charter. 54236
De Miltitz, Alex. see Miltitz, Alex. de.
De Mina, Carolino Estrados. see Mina, Carolino Estrados de.
De Mina, Francisco Xavier. see Mina, Francisco Xavier de.
Deming, Calvin. 99232
Deming, Ebenezer. 13085, 19480, 104013
Deming, Henry Champion, 1815-1872. (12161), 14763, 19481-19483, 30669, 65765, 78460
Deming, Leonard. (19484)
Demi-Quaker. pseud. Observations on the sermons of Elias Hicks. 31714
De Miqueorena, A. see Miqueorena, A. de.
De Mira, Jose Joaquin. see Mira, Jose Joaquin de.
De Mirabeau, Honore Gabriel Riquetti, Comte. see Mirabeau, Honore Gabriel Riquetti, Comte de, 1749-1791.
De Mirabeau. Victor Riquetti, Marquis. see Mirabeau, Victor Riquetti, Marquis de. 1715-1789.
De Miranda, Francisco. see Miranda, Francisco de.
De Miranda, Henrique de Souza de Tavares da Silva, Conde. see Souza de Tavares da Silva, Henrique de, Conde de Miranda.
De Miranda, Joao Antonio. see Miranda, Joao Antonio de.
De Miravalle, Jose Joaquin Trebuesto y Casasola, Conde. see Trebuesto y Casasola, Jose Joaquin, Conde de Miravalle.
De Miravalle, Maria Catharina Davalos Bracamont y Orozco, Condesa. see Davalos Bracamont y Orozco, Maria Catharina, Condesa de Miraville.
De Miravalle, Pedro Alonso Davalos Bracamonte y Espinosa, Conde. see Davalos Bracamonte y Espinosa, Pedro Alonso, Conde de Miravalle.
De Miravalles, Pedro Alonso de Avalos y Bracamont, Conde. see Avalos y Bracamont, Pedro Alonso de, Conde de Miravalles.
De Mirbeck, Frederic Ignace. see Mirbec, Frederic Ignace de.
De Mirmont, Alexandre Jean Joseph Delaville. see Delaville de Mirmont, Alexandre Jean Joseph.
De Mirtilo Nortes, Josephinas. see Nortes, Josephinas de Mirtilo.
De Mirval, C.-H. see Mirval, C.-H. de.
Demi-serious poem, canto the first. 82290
De Missy, Jean Rousset. see Rousset de Missy, Jean.
De Mist, ------- van Uitenhage. see Hoven, Madame ------ (van Uitenhage de Mist) de.
Demme, Wilhelm Ludwig. 19485
Demmin, Auguste. 19486
Democracy. 14775
Democracy, a lecture. 20583
Democracy. An address delivered before the Jacksonville Mechanic's Union. 93278
Democracy: an epic poem. 41608
Democracy and Dred Scott. (2277)
Democracy and progress. (42071)
Democracy and the church. 84069

Democracy and the nation. 50629
Democracy at National Hall, Feb. 8, 1858. 90411
Democracy. By George Sidney Camp. 10176
Democracy, constructive and pacific. 27672
Democracy displayed. 19487
Democracy in America. 21074, 96061-96065
Democracy in 1968. 82514
Democracy in the United States. 27402
Democracy, law, order, and the will of the majority. 35271
Democracy of Christianity. 19488
Democracy or, the fundamental principles of democracy. 19492
Democracy, the climax of political progress. 51105
Democracy. The old and the new. 31703
Democracy under constitutional limitations. 84516
Democracy unmasked. 20659
Democracy unveiled, in a letter to Sir Francis Burdett. 345
Democracy unveiled; or, tyranny stripped of the garb of patriotism. (24212)
Democracy vindicated and Dorrism unveiled. 67776
Democrat. pseud. Few words to Democrats. (24248)
Democrat. pseud. Reasons why the United States government should be upheld. 68304
Democrat; or intrigues and adventures of Jean le Noir. 19493, 66861
Democrat of Maryland. pseud. Plain facts for plain people. 63220
Democrat of the old school. pseud. Programme of peace. 65962
Democrat who opposed Governor Johnston. pseud. State debt. 90586
Democrata. Periodico politico, literario y comercial. 19494
Democrates. 79176-(79178)
Democrates secundus, sive de justis belli causis. 79176
Democrates, sive de conventia disciplinae militaris. 79180
Democratiad: a poem. 13879, 13885, (19494A), (78988), 95799
Democratic absolutism. (3899)
Democratic address at Indianapolis, 10 Feb. 1838. 58024
Democratic address in opposition to the special deposite schemes. 53639
Democratic age. 19495
Democratic almanac and political compendium for 1868. 19496
Democratic and Republican platforms. 19497
Democratic Anti-abolition State Right Association of New York. 53640, 54237 see also Democratic Party. New York.
Democratic Anti-masonic Party. see Anti-masonic Party.
Democratic Association, Gloucester, Co., N. J. 27599 see also Democratic Party. New Jersey. Gloucester County.
Democratic Association, Philadelphia. 61560 see also Democratic Party. Pennsylvania. Philadelphia.
Democratic Association, Washington, D. C. 88496, 96362, 101069 see also Democratic Party. Washington, D. C.
Democratic catechism. 19498
Democratic catechism of Negro equality. 19499
Democratic celebration in Independence Square. (61571)

Democratic clarion and Tennessee gazette. 94784

Democratic Constitutional Union Party. see Constitutional Union Party.

Democratic convention, held at the Cooper Institute, New York. 54238

Democratic convention. Proceedings of the national Democratic convention, convened at Charleston. 19500

Democratic dirge, a poem. 13885, (78988)

Democratic documents for the campaign. 19501

Democratic falsehoods exposed. (19502)

Democratic fellow citizens of western Pennsylvania. 60049

Democratic free press. 39890, 98981

Democratic General Committee of . . . New-Hampshire: nomination of Gen. Houston, Oct. 11. 52821

Democratic gospel of peace, according to St. Tammany. (19503)

Democratic hand-book recommended by the Democratic National Committee. 13803

Democratic Hickory Club, Philadelphia. 61572 see also Democratic Party. Pennsylvania. Philadelphia.

Democratic judge. (13880)

Democratic League, New York. 19504-19505, 80445 see also Democratic Party. New York. New York City.

Democratic League. Circular. 19504

Democratic League. . . . The slaveholders' conspiracy. 19505, 68242

Democratic Legislative Convention, Boston, 1840. 94388 see also Democratic Party. Massachusetts.

Democratic Legislative Convention, Boston, 1840. Committee to Prepare the Address. 94388

Democratic medley. 61573

Democratic meeting in the park, New-York City. 54239

Democratic member of the Common Council. pseud. Brief investigation of the causes. (54131)

Democratic memories. (13876)

Democratic National Committee. 13803 see also Democratic Party.

Democratic national convention. 47007

Democratic national convention at Baltimore, June, 1852. 19506

Democratic National Executive Committee. see Democratic Party (Southern) National Committee, 1860-1864.

Democratic Party. 392, 10187, 16179, 19497, 19510, 19516, 20429, (23627), 28493, 30204, (32928), 36262, (36267), 41185, 41216, 51993, 58450, 73984, 81794, 85887, 91524, 94790, 96032 see also Democratic National Committee. National and Jackson Democratic Association. National Johnson Club.

Democratic Party. National Convention, Baltimore, 1832. 36692

Democratic Party. National Convention, Baltimore, 1835. 98425

Democratic Party. National Convention, Baltimore, 1840. 65886

Democratic Party. National Convention, Baltimore, 1852. 19506, 20428, 63347, 65840, 65886

Democratic Party. National Convention, Cincinnati, 1856. 13100, 13803, (65353)

Democratic Party. National Convention, Baltimore, 1860. see Democratic Party

(Southern) National Convention, Baltimore, 1860.

Democratic Party. National Convention, Charleston, 1860. 19500, 56777, (64406)-(64407), 65351, 65837, 65840

Democratic Party. National Convention, Chicago, 1864. 12662, 63348, 68234, 89494-89495

Democratic Party. National Executive Committee. 414, 19490, 51971, 65837, note after 91521

Democratic Party. Alabama. Tuscaloosa County. Executive Committee. 84896

Democratic Party. Connecticut. 97814

Democratic Party. Connecticut. Convention, Middletown, 1828. 15652

Democratic Party. Connecticut. Convention, Middletown, 1835. (15650)

Democratic Party. Connecticut. General Committee. 15638, 104980

Democratic Party. Connecticut. New Haven. Committee of Publications. 86732

Democratic Party. Delaware. New Castle County. Committee. 52563

Democratic Party. Indiana. Convention, Indianapolis, 1836. 98425

Democratic Party. Indiana. Convention, Indianapolis, 1866. (34523)

Democratic Party. Illinois. State Central Committee. 34197

Democratic Party. Kentucky. Louisville. 42339

Democratic Party. Louisiana. State Central Committee. 42201, 91255

Democratic Party. Maine. (43902)

Democratic Party. Maryland. 45051-45052 see also Jackson Central Committee of Maryland.

Democratic Party. Maryland. Convention, Baltimore, 1827. 45053

Democratic Party. Maryland. State Central Committee. 45145

Democratic Party. Maryland. State Executive Committee. 45131

Democratic Party. Maryland. Baltimore. 35391

Democratic Party. Massachusetts. 45576, 45585, 46088, 46090 see also Democratic Legislative Convention, Boston, 1840.

Democratic Party. Massachusetts. Convention, Boston, 1860. (45880), (45947)

Democratic Party. Massachusetts. Convention of the Ward and County Committees of Boston and Suffolk, 1855. 81875

Democratic Party. Massachusetts. General Committee. 15847, 104980

Democratic Party. Massachusetts. General Committee. Clerk. see also 15847, 104980 Jones, Levi. Jr.

Democratic Party. Massachusetts. State Central Committee. (45972)

Democratic Party. Massachusetts. Barnstable County. 97413

Democratic Party. Massachusetts. Boston. 6553, 45636, 81875 see also Democratic Party. Massachusetts. Convention of the Ward and County Committees of Boston and Suffolk, 1855.

Democratic Party. Massachusetts. Dorchester. see also Dorchester McClellan Club.

Democratic Party. Massachusetts. Norfolk County. Convention, Dedham, 1812. 55468

Democratic Party. Massachusetts. Suffolk County. 45636, 81875 see also

Democratic Party. Massachusetts. Convention of the Ward and County Committees of Boston and Suffolk, 1855.

Democratic Party. Massachusetts. Worcester County. Committee. 105411-105413

Democratic Party. Massachusetts. Worcester County. Convention, Worcester, 1812. 105425

Democratic Party. Massachusetts. Worcester County. Convention, Worcester, 1812. President. 105425 see also Davis, Jonathan.

Democratic Party. Massachusetts. Worcester County. Convention, Worcester, 1812. Secretary. 105425 see also Gilbert, Daniel.

Democratic Party. New Hampshire. General Committee. 52821

Democratic Party. New Hampshire. Rockingham County. Convention, 1812. 72390

Democratic Party. New Jersey. Central Committee. (53056)

Democratic Party. New Jersey. Convention, Trenton, 1824. 96770

Democratic Party. New Jersey. Convention, Trenton, 1828. 53205, 96771

Democratic Party. New Jersey. Gloucester County. 27599 see also Democratic Association, Gloucester County, N. J.

Democratic Party. New Mexico. 53285

Democratic Party. New York. 53476, (53478), 53486, 53488, (53490), 53500, 53639-53640, 53963, 53980, 69417, 2d note after 90684 see also Democratic Antiabolition State Right Association, New York. New York (State) National Democratic Volunteers.

New York Democratic Association of Washington. New York Democratic Vigilent Association

Democratic Party. New York. Convention, Syracuse, 1836. (53641), 69723

Democratic Party. New York. Convention, New York, 1840. 106111

Democratic Party. New York. Convention, Albany, 1848. (53866)

Democratic Party. New York. Convention, Utica, 1848. 53484

Democratic Party. New York. Convention, Rome, 1849. 53472, (53846), 53867

Democratic Party. New York. Convention, Syracuse, 1855. 65910

Democratic Party. New York. Convention, Syracuse, 1856. 53862

Democratic Party. New York. Convention, Albany, 1861. 53868

Democratic Party. New York. Convention, New York, 1862. 54238

Democratic Party. New York. General Committee. 53489, 53497, 53512, (60684) see also Democratic Party. New York. New York City. General Committee.

Democratic Party. New York. National Democratic Committee. 54057

Democratic Party. New York. Young Men's General Committee. 53483

Democratic Party. New York. Albany. 627, 26908, 100693

Democratic Party. New York. Albany. Corresponding Committee. 586, 54002, 92865, note after 99543, 101159

Democratic Party. New York. Albany. Corresponding Committee. Chairman. 26908, 54002, 92865, note after 99543, 100693 see also James, William. Stringer, Samuel.

Democratic Party. New York. Albany. Corresponding Committee. Secretary. 26908, 54002, 92865, note after 99543, 100693 see also Van Ingen, James. York, Joseph.

Democratic Party. New York. Albany. Legislative Meeting, 1834. 96417

Democratic Party. New York. Albany County. Convention, 1828. 322, note after 92864

Democratic Party. New York. Albany County. Meeting, 1810. 626

Democratic Party. New York. Albany County. Meeting, 1853. 611

Democratic Party. New York. Colonie. Meeting, 1810. see Democratic Party. New York. Albany County. Meeting, 1810.

Democratic Party. New York. Cayuga County. Convention, Auburn, 1819. 11638

Democratic Party. New York. New York City. 10187, 15072, 54058, 54130, 54217, 54229, 54239, 54240, 54265, 54455, 54605, 54703, 65751 see also Democratic League, New York. Democratic Republican Association, New York. Democratic Society, New York. Everett Club, New York. German Democratic Central Club, New York. German Democratic Union Party. New York. New York City. McClellan Legion, New York.

Democratic Party. New York. New York City. Convention, 1840. 9936

Democratic Party. New York. New York City. General Committee. (5982), 37444, 54603, 71303 see also Democratic Party. New York. General Committee.

Democratic Party. New York. New York City. Merchants Great Democratic Meeting, 1856. (54609)

Democratic Party. New York. New York City. Merchants Great Democratic Meeting, 1856. Committees. (45609)

Democratic Party. New York. New York City. Young Men's General Comittee. 35391, 54049-54050

Democratic Party. New York. New York County. 69723

Democratic Party. New York. Newburgh. Mass Meeting, 1852. 89205

Democratic Party. North Carolina. Executive Committee. 55589

Democratic Party. Ohio. Convention, Dayton, 1862. 57021

Democratic Party. Ohio. Executive Committee. 88236

Democratic Party. Ohio. Cincinnati. 35373 see also Jackson Committee of Cincinnati.

Democratic Party. Pennsylvania. 59838-59839, 60542, 60686-60687, (61539) see also State Rights Democratic Party. Pennsylvania.

Democratic Party. Pennsylvania. Central Committee of Correspondence. 59834, 59837

Democratic Party. Pennsylvania. Convention, Carlisle, 1817. 60481

Democratic Party. Pennsylvania. Convention, Harrisburg, 1824. 60409

Democratic Party. Pennsylvania. Convention, Harrisburg, 1828. 60412

Democratic Party. Pennsylvania. Convention, Harrisburg, 1832. 60412, 60763

Democratic Party. Pennsylvania. Convention, Harrisburg, 1835. 60413

Democratic Party. Pennsylvania. Convention, Harrisburg, 1856. 60425

Democratic Party. Pennsylvania. Convention, Harrisburg, 1859. (60415)

Democratic Party. Pennsylvania. Convention, Harrisburg, 1866. (60052)

Democratic Party. Pennsylvania. Convention of Young Men, Harrisburg, 1836. 60414

Democratic Party. Pennsylvania. Convention. of Young Men, Reading, 1838. 60404

Democratic Party. Pennsylvania. General Committee of Correspondence. 59838

Democratic Party. Pennsylvania. State Central Committee. 59837, 59844, 60619

Democratic Party. Pennsylvania. State Committee of Correspondence. 39888, 59843

Democratic Party. Pennsylvania. Adams County. 59862

Democratic Party. Pennsylvania. Cumberland County. 59978

Democratic Party. Pennsylvania. Harrisburg. see also Harrisburg National Democratic Union Club.

Democratic Party. Pennsylvania. Montgomery County. Young Men's Meeting, 1838. 60053

Democratic Party. Pennsylvania. Philadelphia. (61571)-61572, (61574)-61575, 62018, 62077, 62193, 62203, (62363), 103855 see also Democratic Association, Philadelphia. Democratic Hickory Club, Philadelphia. Democratic Rescue Association of Philadelphia. Democratic Society, Philadelphia. Jackson Club of the City and County of Philadelphia. Major General Geo. B. McClellan Club, Philadelphia. Society of Independent Democrats, Philadelphia.

Democratic Party. Pennsylvania. Philadelphia. Central Democratic Club. (61528)

Democratic Party. Pennsylvania. Philadelphia. Committee. 62227, 60603, (61663), 61844, 62227, 65349

Democratic Party. Pennsylvania. Philadelphia. Committee of Delegates of the Several Wards. 61424

Democratic Party. Pennsylvania. Philadelphia. Committee of Correspondence. (40566), 60603, 61423, 61425, 61427

Democratic Party. Pennsylvania. Philadelphia. Meeting, 1844. 92007

Democratic Party. Pennsylvania. Philadelphia County. 103855 see also Jackson Club of the City and County of Philadelphia.

Democratic Party. Pennsylvania. Pittsburgh. Committee. 13726

Democratic Party. Pennsylvania. Washington County. 102011

Democratic Party. Pennsylvania. Washington County. Committee. 102011

Democratic Party. Rhode Island. 64635, (70598), 70725, 70728

Democratic Party. Rhode Island. Convention, Providence, 1841. (70521)

Democratic Party. Rhode Island. Convention, Providence, 1845. 70539, 106194

Democratic Party. South Carolina. Convention, Charleston, 1843. 87813

Democratic Party. South Carolina. Convention, Columbia, 1856. 87814

Democratic Party. South Carolina. Convention, Columbia, 1860. 87815

Democratic Party. South Carolina. Convention, Columbia, 1860. 87816

Democratic Party. South Carolina. State Central Executive Committee. 30152, 87791, 87817

Democratic Party. Tennessee. Central Corresponding Committee. 81794, 94790

Democratic Party. Tennessee. Nashville. 35373 see also Jackson Committee of Nashville.

Democratic Party. Vermont. petitioners 82367

Democratic Party. Vermont. Convention, Montpelier, 1828. 99173

Democratic Party. Vermont. State Committee. 98525

Democratic Party. Vermont. Addison County. Convention, 1814. 99174

Democratic Party. Virginia. 99807, 100421, 100452, 100531, note after 100544, note after 104322

Democratic Party. Virginia. Committee. (23627)

Democratic Party. Virginia. Convention, Fredericksburg, 1836. 100453

Democratic Party. Virginia. Convention, Suffolk, 1837. 100456

Democratic Party. Virginia. Convention, Richmond, 1839. 70036, 100455

Democratic Party. Virginia. Convention, Charlottesville, 1840. 100454

Democratic Party. Virginia. Goochland County. 100457

Democratic Party. Washington, D. C. 101949-101952 see also Democratic Association, Washington, D. C. Granite State Lincoln Club, Washington, D. C. Jackson Democratic Association, Washington, D. C.

Democratic Party (Free) see Free-soil Party.

Democratic Party (Southern) National Convention, 1860-1864. (19491)

Democratic Party (Southern) National Convention, Baltimore, 1860. 56777, (64406)-64407, 65351, 65837, 65840

Democratic Party (Southern) National Convention, Baltimore, 1860. Committee on Accreditation. Minority. 91524

Democratic party a disunion party. 90381 (18992)

Democratic party as it was and as it is! 30386

Democratic party: . . . speech . . . June 22nd, 1859. 30386

Democratic Party. The record of 1860-1865. 19508

Democratic party. Words of counsel to men of business. 19509

Democratic peace offered for the acceptance of Pennsylvania. 60050

Democratic platform. 20429

Democratic platform. General McClellan's letter of acceptance. 10187, 19510

Democratic platform of 1852. (23627)

Democratic platform. People's resolutions. 19511, 80444

Democratic peom, dedicated unto youth. 72647

Democratic policy in regard to the canals. 43586

Democratic position illustrated by Frank P. Blair, Jr. 51020

Democratic presidential campaign songster, no. 1. 19512, 43030

Democratic press. 16617, 17446, (39890), 65354, note after 92827, 97592, 99448

Democratic principles exemplified by example. (13876)

Democratic principles illustrated by example. 64162

Democratic protests against the Lecompton fraud. 19513

Democratic record. (64146)

Democratic reformer. 19514

Democratic regenerator. 79365

Democratic Republican. pseud. ed. "Address of the General Committee of Whig Young Men." 103283

Democratic Republican. pseud. Calhoun doctrine. 9948

Democratic Republican Association, New York. 54048 see also Democratic Party. New York. New York City.

Democratic Republican Convention of Young Men of Pennsylvania, Harrisburg, 1836. see Democratic Party. Pennsylvania. Convention of Young Men, Harrisburg, 1836.

Democratic Republican Party. see Democratic Party.

Democratic Rescue Association of Philadelphia. (62363) see also Democratic Party. Pennsylvania. Philadelphia.

Democratic review. see United States magazine and democratic review.

Democratic Society, New York. 54240 see also Democratic Party. New York. New York City.

Democratic Society, Philadelphia. (61574)-61575 see also Democratic Party. Pennsylvania. Philadelphia.

Democratic Society, Philadelphia. Committee. 60051

Democratic Society of Friends of the People. see Society of Friends of the People, Philadelphia.

Democratic soldier's speech. 84386

Democratic speaker's hand-book. 10890

Democratic state convention. (53641)

Democratic state convention, for nomination of governor. (60052)

Democratic statesmen and generals to the loyal sons of the union. 19515

Democratic tax payer, of the Jefferson school. pseud. State debt. 90586

Democratic text book. 19516

Democratic times. 19517

Democratic Vigilent Association, New York. see New York Democratic Vigilent Association.

Democratic Whig Association of the City and County of Philadelphia. (51576) see also Whig Party. Pennsylvania. Philadelphia.

Democratic Whig National Convention, Harrisburg, Pa., 1839. see Whig Party. National Convention, Harrisburg, Pa., 1839.

Democratic Whig Party. see Whig Party.

Democratic young lady. pseud. Reply. 17353

Democratic Young Men's General Committee, New York. see Democratic Party. New York. New York City. Young Men's General Committee.

Democratic Young Men's Meeting, Montgomery County, Pa., 1838. see Democratic Party. Pennsylvania. Montgomery County. Young Men's Meeting, 1838.

Democratic young men's meeting of Montgomery County. 60053

Democraticus. pseud. Jeffersoniad. 19518

Democratischen Republikaner in Adams County. see Democratic Party. Pennsylvania. Adams County.

Democrats and the war. 64285

Democrats! Be not deceived. 88440

Democrat's handbook. 19487

Democrat's rule. (36945)

Democritus. pseud. History of an old fringed petticoat. 32126

Democritus. pseud. Standard of liberty. see Brackenridge, Hugh Henry, 1748-1816.

De Mofras, Eugene Dulfot. see Duflot de Mofras, Eugene, 1810-1884.

De Moine Navigation and Railroad Company. see Des Moines Navigation and Railroad Company.

Demoiselle Angloise a que il a faite faire son abjuration. pseud. Lettre. see Pitt, --------.

Demokratiet i Nordamerika, efter Tocqueville. 18724

De Molina, Alonso. see Molina, Alonso de, d. 1585.

De Molina, Camillo Quintanilla y Malo. see Quintanilla y Malo de Molina, Camillo.

De Molina, Jose Ignacio. see Molina, Jose Ignacio.

De Molina, Luis. see Molina, Luis de.

De Molina, Tirso. pseud. see Tellez, Gabriel, 1571?-1648.

De Molleda, Gregorio. see Molleda, Gregorio de, Bp.

De Molleda y Clerque, Gregorio. see Molleda y Clerque, Gregorio de.

De Moncada, Balthasar. see Moncada, Balthasar de.

De Monchy, Solomon. see Monchy, Solomon de.

De Monardes, Nicoloso. see Monardes, Nicoloso de.

Demond, Charles. 19519

De Monderie, Thiebault. see Monderie, Thiebault de.

De Mondragon, Alonso. see Mondragon, Alonso de.

De Mondragon, Carlos Ximenez. see Ximenez de Mondragon, Carlos.

De Monet de Lamarck, Jean Baptiste Pierre Antoine. see Lamarck, Jean Baptiste Pierre Antoine de Monet de, 1744-1829.

De Monglave, Eugene. see Monglave, Eugene de.

De Monmonier, Charles. see Monmonier, Charles de.

Demonology and witchcraft. 78382-78383

De Monroy, Antonius. see Monroy, Antonius de.

De Monsalve, Miguel. see Monsalve, Miguel de.

Demonstracao do desenho original. 93832

Demonstracao do maior jubilo no fausto dia 12 de Marco de 1769. 88790

Demonstracao politica sobre os extinctos direitos. 17004

Demonstracion compendiosa y evidente. 58078

Demonstracion de gozo en las fiestas por el nacimiento del Principe D. Carlos Clemente. 42573

Demonstracion de gozo que a obsequio del Senor D. Carlos Clemente de Burbon. 41832

Demonstracion de la impericia del Mariscal del Campo D. Juan Maria Echeverri. 78912

Demonstracion de las eficaces virtudes. 2980

Demonstracion de las facultades coactivas y represivas. (1877)

Demonstracion de las proporciones e improporciones. 27811

Demonstracion de las proposiciones o defectos. 27811

Demonstracion de los motivos que han originado los rezagos. 98147

Demonstracion generosa de la mas agradecida piedad. 26562

Demonstracion y lamentable muerte del Conde de Galvez. 26477

Demonstratio historico-geographica. 25983
Demonstration de la Compagnie des Indes
    Occidentales. 47825
Demonstration de l'existence de Dieu. 86590
Demonstration de toutes les religions & here-
    sies. 73318
Demonstration of the duty and importance of
    infant baptism. 92930
Demonstration of the insidious views of republi-
    can France. 103116
Demonstration of the right to the navigation.
    93518
Demonstration of true love unto you. 14121
Demonstration on the advantages and necessity
    of free competition. (31775), 32129
Demonstrations in favor of Dr. Cheever, in
    Scotland. (12406)
Demonstrative proofs from scripture. (18707)
De Montalembert, Charles Forbes, Comte.
    see Montalembert, Charles Forbes,
    Comte de.
De Mont-Serrat, E. see Mont-Serrat, E. de.
De Montalvan, Perez. see Montalvan, Perez
    de.
De Montalvao, Jorge Mascarenhas, Marquez.
    see Mascarenhas, Jorge, Marquez de
    Montalvao.
De Montalvo, Luis Berrio. see Montalvo,
    Luis Berrio de.
De Montauban, ------, Sieur. see Montauban,
    ------, Sieur de.
De Montbeillard, -------. see Montbeillard,
    ------ de.
De Montcalm Saint-Veran, L. J. Marquis.
    see Montcalm Saint-Veran, Louis Joseph,
    Marquis de, 1712-1759.
De Montchal, Charles A. Louis Barentin. see
    Barentin de Montchal, Charles Paul
    Nicolas, Vicomte, 1737-1824.
De Montchal, Charles Paul Nicolas, Vicomte
    Barentin. see Barentin de Montchal,
    Charles Paul Nicolas, Vicomte, 1737-
    1824.
De Montchal, Louis Barentin. see Barentin
    de Montchal, Charles Paul Nicolas,
    Vicomte, 1737-1824.
De Monte Carmelo Luna, Lino. see Luna,
    Lino de Monte Carmelo.
De Monte Mayor, Geronimo. see Monte
    Mayor, Geronimo de.
De Montemaior de Cuenca, Juan Francisco.
    see Montemaior y Cordova de Cuenca,
    Juan Francisco de.
De Montemaior y Cordova de Cuenca, Juan
    Francisco. see Montemaior y Cordova
    de Cuenca, Juan Francisco de.
De Montemayor y Belena, -------. see
    Montemayor y Belena, ------ de.
De Montemayor y Cordova, J. F. see
    Montemaior y Cordova de Cuenca, Juan
    Francisco de.
De Montenegro, A. C. see Montenegro, A.
    C. de.
De Monterey, Gaspar de Zuniga y Acevedo,
    Conde. see Zuniga y Acevedo, Gaspar
    de, Conde de Monterey.
De Monteroyo Mascarenhas, Jose Freire.
    see Mascarenhas, Jose Freire de Monero-
    yo.
De Montes, Jose Varela. see Varela de
    Montes, Jose.
De Montesclaros, Juan de Mendoza y Luna,
    Marques. see Mendoza y Luna, Juna de,
    Marques de Montesclaros.
Demontesinos, Fernando. see Montesinos,
    Fernando de.

Demontezon, Fortune. 10522, 10573, 11620,
    19520, 44869, note after 69259
De Montezuma, Jose Sarmiento Valladares,
    Conde. see Valladares, Jose Sar-
    miento, Conde de Montezuma.
De Montfaucon, Bernard. see Montfaucon,
    Bernard de.
De Montagaillard, Juan Gabriel Maurice Roques.
    see Montgaillard, Juan Gabriel Maurice
    Roques de.
De Montgolfier, Adelaide. see Montgolfier,
    Adelaide de.
De Montigny, -------. see Buisson, Jean
    Francois.
De Montiguy, ------ Dumont. see Dumont de
    Montiguy, ------, Lieutenant.
De Montiguy, Gabriel Lucas. see Lucas de
    Montiguy, Gabriel, b. 1782.
De Montirat, ----------. see Montirat,
    ------- de.
De Montlezun, -------, Baron. see Montlezun,
    -------, Baron de.
De Montluc, A. see Montluc, A. de.
De Montmorency, Francois de Laval. see
    Laval de Montmorency, Francois de.
De Montoya, Antonio Ruiz. see Ruiz de
    Montoya, Antonio.
De Montoya, Juan. see Montoya, Juan de,
    fl. 1602.
De Montpleinchamp, Jean Chrysostome Brusle.
    see Brusle de Montpleinchamp, Jean
    Chrysostome.
De Montrol, F. see Montrol, F. de.
De Montrond, Maxime. see Montrond, Maxime
    de.
De Monts, -------, Sieur. see Monts,
    -------, Sieur de.
De Montserrat, Guillaume. see Montserrat,
    Guillaume de.
De Montufar, Alonso. see Montufar, Alonso
    de, Abp.
De Montufar, Lorenco. see Montufar, Lorenco
    de.
De Montule, Edouard. see Montule, Edouard
    de.
De Montuval, -------, Marquis. see Montuval,
    -------, Marquis de.
Demophilus. pseud. Genuine principles.
    26964
Demophilus. pseud. Propriety of independency.
    see Paine, Thomas, 1737-1809.
De Mora, J. A. see Mora, J. A. de.
De Mora, Jose Joaquin. see Mora, Jose
    Joaquin de, 1783-1864.
De Mora, Juan Gomez. see Gomez de Mora,
    Juan.
De Moraes, Eduardo Jose. see Moraes,
    Eduardo Jose de.
De Moraes, Emanuel. see Moraes, Emanuel
    de.
De Moraes da Silva, A. see Moraes da Silva,
    A. de.
De Moraes Navarra, Jose Gregorio. see
    Moraes Navarra, Jose Gregorio de.
De Moraes y Vasconcelos, Francisco Botello.
    see Botello de Moraes y Vasconcelos,
    Francisco.
De Moral y Castillo, Jose Antonio. see
    Moral y Castillo, Jose Antonio de.
De Morales, Ambrosio. see Morales,
    Ambrosio de.
De Morales, C. D. F. Anastaf. pseud. Vida
    de Hernan-Cortes. see San Rafael,
    Tomas de.
De Morales, Francisco Jose. see Morales,
    Francisco Jose de.

De Morales Valverde, Juan. see Morales
Valverde, Juan de.
De Morales y Ugalde, Jose. see Morales y
Ugalde, Jose de.
Demoralizing doctrines and disloyal teachings
of the Mormon hierarchy. 19521, 50733
De Morande, Theveneau. see Morande,
Theveneau de.
De More, Juan. see More, Juan de.
De Morga, Antonio. see Morga, Antonio de.
De Morgues, Jacob le Moyne. see Le Moyne
de Morgues, Jacob.
De Morineau, A. see Morineau, A. de.
De Morlaix, Bernard Barrere. see Barrere
de Morlaix, Bernard.
De Mornay, Edward. see Mornay, Edward de.
De Morveau, Louis Bernard, Baron Guyton.
see Guyton de Morveau, Louis Bernard,
Baron, 1747-1816.
Demos in council. (19522), note after 93549
De Moscoso y Cordoua, Christoual. see
Moscoso y Cordoua, Christoual de.
De Moscoso y Peralta, Juan Manuel. see
Moscoso y Peralta, Juan Manuel de, Bp.
De Mosloy, Louis Guillaume, Otto, Comte.
see Otto, Louis Guillaume, Comte de
Mosloy, 1754-1817.
De Mosquere, J. see Mosquera, Manuel Jose,
Abp.
De Mosquera, Tomas Cipriano. see Mosquera,
Tomas Cipriano de, 1798-1878.
De Mosto, Alvise de Ca. see Ca da Mosto,
Alvise, 1432?-1480?
Demoticus Philalethes. pseud. see Philalethes,
Demoticus. pseud.
De Motier, Gilbert. see Motier, Gilbert de.
De Motolinia, Toribio. see Motolinia, Toribio,
d. 1868.
De Motta, Vicente Pires. see Motta, Vicente
Pires da.
De Mouneville, --------. see Mouneville,
------- de.
De Moura, Antonio Bonifacio. see Souza,
Bernardo Xavier Pinto de.
De Moura, Caetano Lopes. see Lopes de
Moura, Caetano, 1780-1860.
De Moura e Limos, Luis Antonio Innocencio.
see Moura e Limos, Luis Antonio In-
nocencio de.
De Mousseaux, Henry Roger Gougenot. see
Gougenot de Mousseaux, Henry Roger.
Demousseaux de Givre, Gaston. 19523
De Moussy, V. Martin. see Martin de Moussy,
V.
De Movilla, Gregorio. see Movilla, Gregorio
de.
De Moxo, Benito Maria. see Moxo, Benito
Maria de, Abp.
De Moxo y de Francoli, Benito Maria. see
Moxo y de Francoli, Benito Maria de.
De Moya, Juan. see Moya, Juan de.
Dempsey, J. M. 19524
Demun, J. J. 19525
Demund, Isaac S. 19526-(19527)
De Munibe, Jose Maria. see Munibe, Jose
Maria de.
De Munon, Sancho Sanchez. see Sanchez de
Munon, Sancho.
De Mura, Pedro. see Mur, Pedro de.
De Mura, Pierre. see Grand, Pierre de.
De Muros y Salazar, Salvador Jose. see
Someruelos, Salvador Jose de Muros y
Salazar, Marques de, 1754-1813.
De Murr, M. see Murr, M. de.
Demurrer. 31595
Demuthige Vorstellung. 96549

De Myst, Gerardus. see Mijst, Gerardus
de la.
De N., N. pseud. see N, N. de. pseud.
Den, H. 13867
Den, John. plaintiff (17400)
Denacoes da fazenda. 68809
De Nadaillac, Jean Francois Albert du Pouget,
Marquis. see Nadaillac, Jean Francois
Albert du Pouget, Marquis de, 1818-
1904.
De Nagera, Alonzo Goncalez. see Goncalez
de Nagera, Alonzo.
De Nagera Yanguas, Diego. see Nagera
Yanguas, Diego de.
De Nagra, Pedro de Castaneda. see Cas-
taneda de Nagra, Pedro de.
Denain, A. 19528-19529
Denais, -------. 38632
De Najera Yanguas, Diego. see Nagera
Yanguas, Diego de.
Denance, L. V. 19530-19534
De Nantes, Bernardo. see Nantes, Bernardo
de.
De Nantes, Martin. see Martin de Nantes.
pere
De Narte, Sejo Amira. pseud. Clamores de
la America. see Teran, Jose Maria.
De Nascimento Castro a Silva, Manoel. see
Castro a Silva, Manoel de Nascimento.
De Navara, J. I. Maria. see Navara, J. I.
Maria de.
De Navares, M. Cabrera. see Cabrera de
Navares, M.
De Navarra y Rocaful, Melchor. see Navarra
y Rocaful, Melchor de, Duque de la
Palata.
De Navarrete, Eustaquio Fernandez. see
Fernandez de Navarrete, Eustaquio,
1820-1866.
De Navarrete, Martin Fernandez. see Navarrete,
Martin Fernandez de, 1765-1824.
De Navia Osorio, Alvaro. see Santa Cruz de
Marcenado, Alvaro de Navia Osorio,
Marques de, 1684-1732.
De Naxera, M. see Naxera, M. de.
Den Bergh, L. Ph. C. van. see Bergh, L. Ph.
C. van den.
Den Bergh, S. J. van. see Bergh, S. J. Van
den.
Denberry, Ed. 90338
Den Biesen, J. J. van. see Biesen, J. J. van
den.
Den Bos, Lambertus van. see Bos or Bosch,
in Latin, Sylvanius, Lambertus van den.
Den Bosch, -------- van. see Bosch,
------- van den, fl. 1822.
Den Bosch, J. van. see Bosch, J. van den.
Den Bosch, Lambertus van. see Bos or Bosch,
in Latin, Sylvanius, Lambertus van den.
Den Brandhof Ez, A. van. see Brandhof Ez,
A. van den.
Den Broeck, Matheus van. see Broeck, Matheus
van den.
Den Broeck, Pieter van. see Broeck, Pieter
van den.
Den Broek, Reinier van. see Van den Broek,
Reinier.
Den Broek, Wilhelm van. see Borek, Wilhelm
van den.
Dencausse, ------. (19535)
Dencke, C. F. tr. 19377
Denckmahl gottlicher Gut und Vororge. 33622
Denckwurdige reyse nach ost Indien. 6340
Dendy, W. 13312
De Nebrija, Antonio. see Lebrija, Elio
Antonio de, 1441?-1522.

De Nebrija, Elio Antonio. see Lebrija, Elio
Antonio de, 1441?-1522.
De Nebrixa, Antonio. see Lebrija, Elio
Antonio de, 1441?-1522.
De Necker, Noel Joseph. see Necker, Noel
Joseph de, 1729-1793.
De Negreiros, Andrea Vidal. see Vidal de
Negreiros, Andrea.
De Negreiros, Antonio Thomaz. see Thomaz
de Negreiros, Antonio.
De Neimeyer Bellegarde, Henrique Luis. see
Neimeyer Bellegarde, Henrique Luis de.
De Nemours, Pierre Samuel du Pont. see
Du Port de Nemours, Pierre Samuel.
Denen Schriften so Hr. Daines Barrington in
London. (22574)
De Neufchateau, Nicolas Louis Francois de,
Comte. see Neufchateau Nicolas Louis
Francois de, Comte de.
De Neufville, J. see Neufville, J. de.
De Neuville, -------. see Neuville, -------
de.
De Neuville, A. see Neuville, A. de.
De Neuville, J. G. Hyde, Baron. see Hyde
de Neuville, J. G., Baron.
De Neuville, Jean Nicolaus Bauche. see
Bauche de Neuville, Jean Nicolas.
De Neve y Molina, Luis. see Neve y Molina,
Luis de.
De Neyn, P. see Neyn, P. de.
Denham, Sir James Steuart, 1712-1780. 91387
Den Huevel, Jacob Adrien van. see Van
Huevel, Jacob Adrien.
Den Heuvell, H. H. van. see Heuvell, H. H.
van den.
De Nicolai, Nicolas. see Nicolai, Nicolas de.
Denio, Hiram. 19536, (53951)
Denio and Philips. firm publishers 104113
Denis, Alexander. 19537
Denis, Alexandre. 19538
Denis, Ed. 19539
Denis, Ferdinand, 1798-1890. 19540-19557,
44151, 44249, (68924), 73458, 85781,
94416-94417, 102622, 106227
Denis, Jean Ferdinand. see Denis, Ferdinand,
1798-1890.
Denis le Cadet, St. pseud. Lottery. see
Denison, Edward.
Denis McArthy. 19558
Denison, ---------, fl. 1836. 58034
Denison, Andrew Clark. 19559
Denison, Mrs. C. W. see Denison, Mary A.
Denison, Charles Wheeler. 19560-19562,
59762, note after 94332
Denison, Daniel. 19563
Denison, Edward. 42154, 75034
Denison, Frederick. (19564)
Denison, George T. 19565-(19570)
Denison, Henry Mandeville. 19571
Denison, Jesse. 19608, 31915
Denison, John L. (19572)
Denison, Joseph. 19573
Denison, Mary A. (19574)
Denison & Co. firm. see Spear, Denison &
Co. firm publishers
Denison University, Granville, Ohio. 19575
Denison University, Granville, Ohio. Trustees.
28328
Denke, C. F. see Dencke, C. F.
Denkschrift die volkswirthschaftlichen Bestim-
mungen. 73083
Denkschrift uber die Nothwendigkeit. 19576
Denkschriften der K. Akademie der Wissen-
schaften, Munchen. 4000
Denkschriften der K. Akademie der Wissen-
chatfen, Wien. 5209-5210

Denkschriften der Russischen Geographischen
Gesellschaft. 19577
Denkwurdige Ereignisse im Leben des Andreas
Bernardus Smolnikar. 85107-85109
Denkwurdige Erinnerungen aus einer vierjah-
rigen Reise. 74647
Denkwurdige und aus fuhrliche Erzehlung.
22558, (74507)
Denkwurdigkeiten aus dem offentlichen Leben.
35289
Denkwurdigkeiten des Hauptmanns Bernal Diaz
del Castillo. 19986
Denkwurdigkeiten einer Reise nach dem
Russischen Amerika. 38024
Denkwurdigkeiten uber seinen dreissihjahrigen
Aufenthalt. 35685, 94328
Denman, Joseph, 1810-1874. 19578
Denman, Thomas Denman, 1st Baron, 1779-
1854. 19579-19580, 91234, note after
92624
Denmark. Laws, statutes, etc. (18501), 37862,
102934, 102936-102937
Denmark. Mediators for the Treaty of Breda
Between Great Britain and the Netherlands,
1667. 96524
Denmark. Minister to the Netherlands. 38031,
5th note after 102893
Denmark. Sovereigns, etc., 1648-1670 (Frederik
III) 7915, 38031, 5th note after 102893
see also Frederik III, King of Denmark,
1609-1670.
Denmark. Sovereigns, etc., 1670-1699
(Christian V) (18501), 102940 see also
Christian V, King of Denmark, 1646-
1699.
Denmark. Sovereigns, etc., 1766-1808 (Chris-
tian VII) 37862 see also Christian VII,
King of Denmark, 1749-1808.
Denmead, Adam. plaintiff 45163, 45328
Denne, H. 74459
Denne, John. 19581
Dennery, Adolphe Philippe, called. see Ennery
Adolphe Philippe, called d'.
Dennet. firm see Tappan and Dennet. firm
publishers
Dennett, Frederick. 19582, 100925
Dennett, W. B. 49782
Denney, Charles. defendant 96939
Dennie, -------, fl. 1769. 90612
Dennie, James. (19584), 19771
Dennie, James. defendant 19583, (69415)
Dennie, Joseph, 1786-1912. 16964, 19071,
19585-(19587), 29813, (32499) 57215,
(64182), 67377, 73248, 89498
Dennis, John. 19588-(19589)
Dennis, Jonas. 19590
Dennis, L. P. 45064
Dennis, Richard. defendant 19591
Dennis, William L. 19592
Dennison, Goldsmith. (19594)
Dennison, William, 1815-1882. 1253, 19593
Denniston, Gwalterus. 78199
Denny, Austin. 19595
Denny, E. 68399
Denny, Ebenezer. 19596
Denny, Francis P. 19597
Denny, Joe. defendant 19598
Denny, John F. (19599), 60087, 81963
Denny, Nathaniel P. 19600, 105416
Denny, William H. 19596, 19601
Dennys, N. B. 19602
De Noailles, --------, Sieur. see Noailles,
------, Sieur de.
De Noboa, Pedro Vasquez. see Vasquez de
Noboa, Pedro.
De Nodal, Bartholome Garcia. see Nodal,
Bartolome Garcia de.

De Nodal, Goncalo. see Nodal, Goncalo de.
De Nogales, Miguel Roman. see Roman de
Nogales, Miguel.
Denombrement des habitations de Granade.
28750
Denombrement des plantes. 3603
Denominational colleges. 93279
Denominational education in parochial schools.
85277
Denominational education: its necessity and its
practicability. 85278
Denonciation aux Etats Generaux. 25289
Denonciation contre M. le Comte de Pey-
ronnet. 5652
Denonciation contre . . . Peyronnet. 5653
Denonciation de buveurs de sang. 95325
Denonciation de ces memes commissaires.
(75185)
Denonciation de M. de la Luzerne. 38698,
42753, note after 93793
Denonville, Jacques Rene de Brisay, Marquis
de, d. 1710. 51806, (55421)
De Noort, Juan. see Noort, Juan de.
De Noort, Olivier. see Noort, Olivier de.
De Nores, Jason. see Nores, Giasone di.
De Normandie, James, 1836-1924. 19604-
(19605)
De Noranha, Juana Manso. see Manso de
Noronha, Juana.
De Noronha Freire, Joao. see Santa Teresa,
Giovanni Gioseppe di.
De Notaris, J. see Notaris, J. de.
De Nouvion, Victor. see Nouvion, Victor de.
De Novion. pseud. Sermon. see Sullivan,
James, 1744-1808.
Denslow, Van Buren. 19606
Denson, -------. 47774
Denson, A. C. 19607
Denson, Jesse. 19608
Denson's Memphis directory, for 1865. 47774
Dent, Digby. 19609
Dent, George. 19610
Dental Society of Massachusetts. see Massa-
chusetts Dental Society.
Denton, Daniel. 19611-19612
Denton, Samuel. appellant 31299
Denton, William. 19613
D'Entrecasteaux, Joseph Antoine Bruni. see
Entrecasteaux, Joseph Antoine Bruni d'.
De Nuix, Josef. see Nuix, Juan, 1740-1783.
De Nuix y de Perpina, Josef. see Nuix, Juan
1740-1783.
Denuncia de los autores del asesinato del Jose
Govin. 28162
De Nursia, Benedictus. see Benedict, Saint,
Abbot of Monte Casino.
Denver, -------, fl. 1866. 33609-33610
Denver, Colo. Board of Trade. 19614
Denver, Colo. State Library. see Colorado.
State Library, Denver.
Denver and Rio Grande Railway Company.
88158
Denver illustrated. 84399
Denver Real Estate and Stock Exchange,
Denver, Colo. 84399
Den Vondel, Joost van. see Vondel, Joost
van den.
Denying suffrage even to soldiers! (82608)
Denys, Ferdinand. see Denis, Ferdinand,
1798-1890.
Denys, Marie Jean Leon, Marquis d'Hervey
de Saint. see Hervey de Saint-Denys,
Marie Jean Leon, Marquis d', 1823-
1892.

Denys, Nicolas, 1598-1688. 19615-19616,
(31357)
De O., P. M. pseud. see Olive, Pedro Maria
de.
Deo opt. max. 76464-76467
De Obando, Manuel A. Solis. see Solisde
Obando, Manuel A.
De Oca, ------ Montes. see Montes de Oca,
-------.
De Oca, Ignacio Montes. see Montes de Oca,
Ignacio.
De Oca, J. J. Montes. see Montes de Oca,
J. J.
De Oca, Juan Evanhelista Montes. pseud.
Carta de un particular. see Valdes,
Rafael.
De Ocampo, Andres Sanchez. see Sanchez
de Ocampo, Andres.
De Ocampo, Diego Gomez. see Ocampo, Diego
Gomez de.
De Ocampo, Florian. see Ocampo, Florian de,
1499?-1555?
De Ocariz, Jose Volante. see Volante de
Ocariz, Jose.
De Ocariz, Juan Florez. see Florez de
Ocariz, Juan.
De Ochoa, D. Durama. see Durama de Ochoa,
D.
De Ochoa, Juan Ignacio. see Ochoa, Juan
Ignacio de.
De Ochoa y Ronna, Eugene. see Ochoa y
Ronna, Eugene de, 1815-1872.
De Ochoa y Ronna, Eugenio. see Ochoa y
Ronna, Eugenio de, 1815-1872.
Deodatensus, Gualterus Lud. see Lud,
Gualterus, 1448-1527.
De Odriozola, Manuel. see Odriozola, Manuel
de.
De Olabarrieta Medrano, Miguel. see Olabar-
rieta Medrano, Miguel de.
De Olaguibel, M. see Olaguibel, M. de.
De Olaneta, J. A. see Olaneta, J. A. de.
De Olavarria, Carolina Liborius. see Liborius
de Olavarria, Carolina.
De Olave, A. S. see Olave, A. S. de.
De Olavide, Pablo. see Olavide, Pablo de.
De Olea, Nicolao. see Olea, Nicolao de.
De Oliva, Fernan Perez. see Perez de Oliva,
Fernan, 1495?-1533.
De Oliva, Manuel Perez. see Perez de Oliva,
Manuel.
De Olivan, Juan. see Olivan, Juan de.
De Olivares, Gabriel. see Olivares, Gabriel
de.
De Olivares, Gaspar de Guzman, Conde Duque.
see Olivares, Gaspar de Guzman, Conde
Duque de, 1587-1645.
De Olive, Pedro Maria. see Olive, Pedro
Maria de.
De Oliveira, Antonio Rodrigues Velloso. see
Velloso de Oliveira, Antonio Rodrigues.
De Oliveira, Candido Baptista. see Oliveira,
Candido Baptista de.
De Oliveira, Francisco Manuel. see Oliveira,
Francisco Manuel de.
De Oliveira, Joao Alfredo Correa. see Correa
de Oliveira, Joao Alfredo.
De Oliveira, Jose Alvares. see Alvares de
Oliveira, Jose.
De Oliveira, Manoel Lucas. see Oliveira,
Manoel Lucas de.
De Oliveira Bastos, Manuel Jose. see Oliveira
Bastos, Manuel Jose de.
De Oliveira e Castro, Luis Joaquin. see
Oliveira y Castro, Luis Joaquin de.

De Oliveira e Daun, Joao Carlos de Saldanha.
see Saldanha, Joao Carlos de Saldanha
Oliveira e Daun, 1. Duque de, 1790-1876.
De Oliveira Mendes, Luis Antonio. see Men-
des, Luis Antonio de Oliveria.
De Oliveira Pinto, Basilio Jose. see Pinto,
Basilio Jose de Oliveira.
De Olmedo, J. J. see Olmedo, J. J. de.
De Olmedo y Sossa, Isidoro. see Olmedo y
Sossa, Isidoro de.
De Olmedo y Torre, Antonio. see Olmedo y
Torre, Antonio de.
De Olmos, Andres. see Olmos, Andres de,
ca. 1491-1571.
De Olmos, Didac. see Olmos, Didac. de.
De Olmoz, Andres. see Olmos, Andres de,
ca. 1491-1571.
De Ona, Pedro. see Ona, Pedro de.
De Onate, Alonso. see Onate, Alonso de.
De Onate y Salazar, Juan. see Onate y
Salazar, Juan de.
Deo-nieh-doh. see Pierce, Benjamin.
De Onis, Luis. see Onis, Luis de, 1769-
1830.
De Orcolaga, Diego Ambrosio. see Orcolaga,
Diego Ambrosio de.
De Ordaz, Jose. see Ordaz, Jose de.
De Orduna, Luis. see Orduna, Luis de.
De Ore, Luis Geronimo. see Ore, Luis
Geronimo de.
De Orellana, Antonio. see Orellana, Antonio
de.
De Orellana, Estevan. see Orellana, Estevan
de.
De Orellana, Francisco Pizarro. see Pizarro
de Orellana, Francisco.
De Orihuela, E. Jose Calixto. see Orihuela,
E. Jose Calixto de.
De Oronsoro, Pedro. see Oronsoro, Pedro
de.
De Orrantia, Tomas. see Orrantia, Tomas de.
De Orrio, Francisco Xavier Alexo. see Alexo
de Orrio, Francisco Xavier.
De Orsuna, Bravo. see Orsuna, Bravo de.
De Orta, Garcia. see Orta, Garcia de, 16th
cent.
De Ortega, Casimiro. see Ortega, Casimiro
de.
De Ortega, Fernando. see Ortega, Fernando
de.
De Orteaga, Jos. Joachin. see Orteaga, Jos.
Joachin de.
De Ortega, Jose. see Ortega, Jose de.
De Ortega, Juan Gualberto. see Gualberto de
Ortega, Juan.
De Ortega Montanez, J. see Ortega Montanez,
J. de.
Deos, Gaspar de Madre de. see Gaspar de
Madre de Deos, 1715-1800.
De Soma, J. I. see Osma, J. I. de.
De Osorio, Juan Prudencio. see Osorio, Juan
Prudencio de.
De Osorio y Balcon, Juan Prudencio. see
Osorio y Balcon, Juan Prudencio de.
De Ossav y Tovar, Joseph Pellicer. see
Pellicer de Ossav y Tovar, Joseph.
De Ossera y Estella, Joseph Miguel. see
Ossera y Estella, Joseph Miguel de.
De Ossoli, Sarah Margaret (Fuller), Marchesa.
see Ossoli, Sarah Maraet (Fuller)
Marchesa de, 1810-1850.
De Otalora, Francisca Arce. see Otalora,
Francisca Arce de.
De Oteiza, Juan Jose. see Oteiza, Juan Jose
de.
De Oteiza y Vertiz, Joaquin Maria. see
Oteiza y Vertiz, Joaquin Maria de.

De Otero, Jose Mateo. see Mateo de Otero,
Jose.
De Otero, Juan. see Otero, Juan de.
De Otero y Baldillo, Jos. Ant. E. de. see
Otero y Baldillo, Jos. Ant. E. de.
De Ovalle, Alonso. see Valle, Alonso de.
De Oviedo, Antonio. see Oviedo, Antonio de.
De Oviedo, Consaluo Fernando. see Oviedo,
Consaluo Fernando de.
De Oviedo, Juan Antonio. see Oviedo, Juan
Antonio de, 1670-1757.
De Oviedo y Banos, Diego Antonio. see
Oviedo y Banos, Diego Antonio de.
De Oviedo y Banos, Joseph. see Oviedo y
Banos, Joseph de.
De Oviedo y Herrera, Luis Antonio. see
Oviedo y Herrera, Luis Antonio de.
De Oviedo y Valdes, Gonzalo Fernandez. see
Oviedo y Valdes Gonzalo Fernandez de,
1478-1557.
De Oviedo y Valdez, Gonzalo Hernandez. see
Oviedo y Valdes, Gonzalo Fernandez de,
1478-1557.
De Oxendi, Juan. see Oxendi, Juan de.
De Oyanzabal, Juan. see Oyanzabal, Juan de.
De Oyarvide, Andres. see Oyarvide, Andres
de.
De Ozaeta y Gallaiztegui, Joseph Hippolito.
see Ozaeta y Gallaiztegui, Joseph
Hippolito de.
De Ozaeta y Oro, Joseph Francisco. see
Ozaeta y Oro, Joseph Francisco de.
De P***, -------. pseud. see Pauw, Corne-
lius de.
De P., Mademoiselle. pseud. see P.,
Mademoiselle de. pseud.
De P., A.-D. pseud. see P., A.-D. de.
pseud.
De P. Orta, Fr. see Orta, Fr. de. P.
De P. Santander, -------- Francisco.
see Francisco de P. Santander, ------.
De P. Serrano, Francisco. see Serrano,
Francisco de P.
De P. T., F. pseud. see T., F. de P.
pseud.
De P. y B., D. pseud. see Vera y Pintado,
Bernardo de.
De Padilla, Juan. see Padilla, Juan de.
De Padron, Antonio Josef Ruiz. see Ruiz de
Padron, Antonio Josef.
De Pagan, Blaise Francois. see Pagan, Blaise
Francois de.
De Pages, Pierre Marie Francois. see Pages,
Pierre Marie Francois.
De Paiva, Octaviano Jose. see Paiva, Octaviano
Jose de.
De Paiva, A. Herculano e O Barrao do Cas-
tello. see Paiva, A. Herculano e O
Barrao do Castello de.
De Palacio, Diego Garcia. see Garcia de
Palacio, Garcia, fl. 1576-1587.
De Palacios, Juan Garcia. see Garcia de
Palacios, Juan, Abp.
De Palafox y Mendoza, Joannis. see Palafox
y Mendoza, Juan de, Abp., 1600-1659.
De Palafox y Mendoza, Juan. see Palafox y
Mendoza, Juan de, Abp., 1600-1559.
De Palluau et de Frontenac, Louis de Baude,
Comte. see Baude, Louis de, Comte
de Palluau et de Frontenac, 1620-1698.
De Palma, Ramon. see Palma, Ramon de.
De Palos, J. F. see Palos, J. F. de.
De Pando, J. M. see Pando, J. M. de.
De Pandolfi, Ubaldus. see Pandolfi, Ubaldus
de.
De Pansey, Henrion. see Pansey, Henrion de.

De Paravey, Charles Hippolyto. see Paravey, Charles Hippolyto de.
De Paredes, Antonio. see Paredes, Antonio de.
De Paredes, Ignacio. see Paredes, Ignacio de.
De Paredes, Robert, Comte. see Paredes, Robert, Comte de.
De Paradis, Jean Michel de Venture. see Venture de Paradis, Jean Michel de, 1739-1799.
De Parisio, Math. see Parisio, Math. de.
De Parra, Jacinto. see Parra, Jacinto de.
De Parra y Bedernoton, David. see Vera y Pintado, Bernardo.
Depart de la Perouse, ou les navigateurs modernes. 2500
Depart du Temple, pour Cayenne. 21459
Depart pour la Californie. (39578)
Departamento del Interior. 9009
Departed heroes, and the soldier's dream. (74303)
Departed of a year. 85202
Departed spirit. pseud. What is sauce for a goose. see Williamson, Hugh.
Departement de la Gironde. see Gironde (French Department)
De Parthenay, ------- des Roches. see Des Roches de Parthenay, -------.
Department for Supplying the City with Water. Report on the experiments. 62370
Department of Agriculture, and United States Agricultural Academy. 85446
Department of Arms and Trophies, Great Central Fair. Catalogue. 61577
Department of Arms and Trophies, Metropolitan Fair. 19617, (54145), (76645)
Department of Massachusetts, proceedings of the . . . Grand Army of the Republic. 45758
Department of New Jersey, proceedings of the . . . Grand Army of the Republic. 53100
Department of Special Inspection of the General Hospitals of the Army. First report to the Commission. 76581, 76647
Department of Special Inspection of the General Hospitals of the Army. Second report to the Committee. 34822, 76591, 76647
Department of the Special Inspection of the General Hospitals U. S. A. Third (preliminary) report to the Committee. 76605, 76647
Department of the West. Fremont. 33227
Department of War. December 5th, 1794. 19618
Departmental clerk. pseud. Tale of the rebellion. see Penfield, A.
Departure and character of Elijah considered and improved. 46793
Departure of Elijah lamented. A sermon occasioned by the great & publick loss. (65588)
Departure of Elijah lamented. A sermon preached at the funeral. 7658
Departure of the Senior Class, July 31, 1811. 30765
De Pas, C. see Pas, C. de.
De Pascua, -------- Flores. see Flores de Pascua, -------.
De Pascual, A. D. see Pascual, A. D. de.
De Paternina, Estevan. see Paternina, Estevan de.
De Patot, Simon Tyssot. see Tyssot de Patot, Simon.

De Paul, Marie Joseph Vincent. see Vincent de Paul, Marie Joseph.
De Paula Arias, Anselmo. see Arias, Anselmo de Paula.
De Paula Candido, Francisco. see Paula Candido, Francisco de.
De Paula Castaneda, Francisco. see Paula Castaneda, Francisco de.
De Paula D'Almeida e Albuquerque, Francisco. see Almeida e Albuquerque, Francisco de Paula d'.
De Paula de Sancta Gertrudes Magna, Francisco. see Gertrudes Magna, Francisco de Paula de Sancta.
De Paula del Villar, Francisco. see Villar, Francisco de Paula del.
De Paula Garcia Pelaez, Francisco. see Pelaez, Francisco de Paula Garcia.
De Paula Menezes, Francisco. see Menezes, Francisco de Paula.
De Paula Quadrado y De-Roo, Francisco. see Quadrado y De-Roo, Francisco de Paula.
De Paula Rodriguez Velasco, Francisco. see Rodriguez Velasco, Francisco de Paula.
De Paula Santander, Francisco. see Paula Santander, Francisco de.
De Paula Sosa, Francisco. see Sosa, Francisco de Paula.
De Paule, Alexandre Balthasar Francois. see Baert, Alexandre Balthasar Francois de Paule, Baron de.
De Paulo Pardo, Francisco. see Pardo, Francisco de Paulo.
De Paulo Toro, Francisco. see Paulo Toro, Francisco de.
De Pauly, T. see Pauly, T. de.
De Pauw, Corneille. see Pauw, Cornelius de.
De Pauw, Cornelius. see Pauw, Cornelius de.
De Pauw University, Greencastle, Indiana. 34515
De Paz, Jose. see Paz, Jose de.
De Paz, Joseph Manuel. see Paz, Joseph Manuel de.
De Pazos, Manuel Antonio. see Pazos, Manuel Antonio de.
De Pazzi de Bonneville, Zacherie. see Bonneville, Zacherie de Pazzi de.
Depeche de M. Calhoun a M. King, a Paris. (36415)
Depeche ecrite le 16 Janvier 1797. 95305
Depeches arrivees de Saint-Domingue le 29 Septembre 1790. 75102
Depeches du . . . Comte d'Elgin et Kincardine. 22117
De Pedraca, Julien. see Pedraza, Julien de.
De Pedraza, Julien. see Pedraza, Julien de.
De Pedroso, Pedro Josef Rodriguez Saenz. see Rodriguez Saenz de Pedroso, Pedro Josef.
De Peiresc, ------. see Peiresc, ------ de.
De Pelterie, T. see Pelterie, T. de.
De Penalosa y Mondragon, Benito. see Penalosa y Mondragon, Benito de.
De Penalver, Fernando. see Penalver, Fernando de.
Dependence of Science upon religion. 102183
Dependence of the fine arts. 11215
Dependent and criminal population of Pennsylvania. 59976
Depenses du recensement. (10453)
De Peralta, Alfonso. see Peralta, Alfonso de.
De Peralta, Antonio. see Peralta, Antonio de.
De Peralta, Guiseppe. see Peralta, Guiseppe de.
De Peralta, Jos. see Peralta, Jos. de, Bp.
De Peralta, Juan Suarez. see Suarez de Peralta, Juan.

De Peralta, Pedro. see Peralta, Pedro de.
De Peralta Barneuvo Rocha y Benavides,
  Pedro. see Peralta Barneuvo Rocha y
  Benavides, Pedro de.
De Peralta Caldron, D. Mathias. see Peralta
  Caldron, D. Mathias de.
De Peralta y Pujadas, Maria Geronyma Lopez.
  see Lopez de Peralta y Pujadas, Maria
  Geronyma.
Deperditarum. 58412
De Perea, Estevan. see Perea, Estevan de.
De Perea, Pedro. see Perea, Pedro de, Bp.
De Pereda Palacio, Manuel. see Pereda
  Pelacio, Manuel de.
De Peredo, Agustin Suarez. see Suarez de
  Peredo, Agustin.
De Peredo, Vicente del Nino Jesus Suarez.
  see Suarez de Peredo, Vicente del Nino
  Jesus.
De Perez Galvez, Francisca de Paula. see
  Galvez, Francisca de Paula de Perez.
De Perpina, Josef de Nuix y. see Nuix, Juan,
  1740-1783.
De Perpina, Juan de Nuix y. see Nuix, Juan,
  1740-1783.
De Perre, J. van. see Perre, J. van de.
Deperthes, Jean Luis Hubert Simon, 1730-1792.
  23567, 19619-19621, note after 32202,
  32152, 68486
De Peyreleau, Eugene Edouard, Baron de
  Boyer. see Boyer de Peyreleau, Eugene
  Edouard, Baron de.
De Peysac, ------- de Vins, Marques. see
  Vins, ------ de, Marques de Peysac.
Depeyster, Arent Schuyler. (19622)
De Peyster, Frederick. 19623-19626
De Peyster, John Watts. 19627-19638, 32821
De Piccolomini, Enea Silvio. see Pius II,
  Pope, 1405-1464.
De Peirola, F. A. see Pierola, F. A. de.
De Pierola, Nicolas Fern. see Pierola,
  Nicolas Fern. de.
De Pina Leitao, Antonio Jose Osorio. see
  Leitao, Antonio Jose Osorio de Pina.
De Pineda y Bascunan, Franzisco Nunez. see
  Pineda y Bascunan, Franzisco Nunez de.
De Pineres, Jerman G. see Pineres, Jerman
  G. de.
De Pinerez, Tomas Gutierrez. see Pinerez,
  Tomas Gutierrez de.
De Pinillos, Claudio Martinez. see Martinez
  de Pinillos, Claudio.
De Pinto, -------. see Pinto, ------ de.
De Pinto, Isaac. see Pinto, Isaac de, 1715-
  1787.
De Pinto, J. see Pinto, Isaac de, 1715-1787.
De Pixerecourt, R. C. Guilbert. see Pixere-
  court, R. C. Guilbert de.
De Pizarro y Gardin, Jose. see Pizarro y
  Gardin, Jose de.
De Plancy, Jacques A. S. Collin. see Collin
  de Plancy, Jacques A. S.
De Planitz, C. B. see Planitz, C. B. de.
De Plaza, Jose Antonio. see Plaza, Jose
  Antonio de.
Deplorable state of New-England. (19639),
  note after 31743, (79447)
Deploration sur la nort desditz Parmentiers.
  58825
De Pluma, Joaquin. see Pluma, Joaquin de.
De Poblete, Juan Millan. see Millan de
  Poblete, Juan.
De Podilla, Juan Vicente de Guemes Pacheo.
  see Guemes Pacheo de Podilla, Juan
  Vicente de, Conde de Rivillagigedo.
De Poggi, A. C. see Poggi, A. C. de.

De Poincy, Lonvilliers. see Poincy, Lon-
  villiers de.
De Pointi, --------. see Pointis, J. B. D. de.
De Pointis, J. B. D. see Pointis, J. B. D. de.
De Poisy, ---------. see Poisy, ---------
  de.
De Polignac, Camille Armand Jules Marie.
  see Polignac, Camille Armand Jules
  Marie de.
De Pombal, Sebastiao Jose de Carvalho e
  Mello, Marquis. see Pombal, Sebastiao
  Jose de Carvalho e Mello, Marquis de.
De Pombo, Lino. see Pombo, Lino de.
De Ponlevoy, Armand. see Ponlevoy, Armand
  de, 1812-1874.
Depons, F. J. see Pons, Francois Raymond
  Joseph de, 1751-1812.
De Pons, Francois Raymond Joseph. see Pons,
  Francois Raymond Joseph de, 1751-1812.
De Pontalba, -------, Baronne. see Pontalba,
  -------, Baronne de.
De Pontille, Charles Guiot. see Guiot, Charles.
De Porres, Martini. see Porres, Martini de.
Deportation et naufrage de J.-J. Aime. 544
Deportation et naufrage de J. J. Ayme. 2521
Deporte. pseud. Veilles de Cayenne. see
  Soave, Francesco. supposed author
Deporte a Cayenne. 36941
De Portegueda, Juan Bentura. see Portegueda,
  Juan Bentura de.
Deportes a la Guyane. pseud. Anecdotes
  secretes. (1534), 67625
De Portes e Infantes, Tomas. see Portes e
  Infantes, Tomas de, Abp.
De Porto Mauricio, Leonardo. see Porto
  Mauricio, Leonardo de.
De Porto Seguro, Francisco Adolfo de Varnhagen,
  Conde. see Varnhagen, Francisco Adolfo
  de, Conde de Porto Seguro, 1816-1878. see
De Portugal e Castro, Francisco Paulo. see
  Portugal e Castro, Francisco Paulo de.
De Posada, Melchor Diaz. see Diaz de Posada,
  Melchor.
Deposit of agricultural flint implements in
  southern Illinois. 67966
Deposition. 28506
Deposition in relation to the claims of Prof.
  Samuel F. B. Morse. 28097
Deposition of Andrew Oliver. 45940
Deposition of Batholomew Green. 28052,
  28506, 65689
Deposition of Daniel Clark. 104027
Deposition of Edward Stow. 92376
Deposition of John Allen and Timothy Green.
  28052, 28506, 65689
Deposition of Mary Dyer. 11976
Deposition of Massey Herbeson. 44258, 105687,
  note after 105687, note after 105689-note
  after 105690
Deposition of Michael Mallespine. 95299
Deposition of Moses B. Ives. 35214
Deposition of Simeon Bordon. 6407
Deposition respecting a letter. 13276
Depositions of John Mico & Zecharaiah Tuthill,
  merchants. 28052, 28506, 65689
Depositions of Thomas Brattle. 28052, 28506,
  65689
Depositions of witnesses. 45090
Depositions taken before the committee. 3072
Depositions taken by order of Congress.
  26318, 51804
De Posos, J. see Posos, J. de.
De Possada, Melchior Diaz. see Possada,
  Melchior Diaz de.
De Poterat, -------, Marquis. see Poterat,
  -------, Marquis de.

De Poutrincourt, --------. see Poutrincourt, -------- de.
De Poueda, Bartholome Goncalez. see Goncalez de Poueda, Bartholome.
De Pozobueno, ------, Marques. see Pozobueno, ------, Marques de.
De Pozos Dulces, Francisco Frias y Jacott, Conde. see Frias y Jacott, Francisco, Conde de Pozos Dulces, 1809-1877.
Depping. pseud. Voyages. see Navarre, P.
Depping, George Bernhard, 1784-1853. 4607, 19647-(19650)
Depping, M. 52092, note after 100836
Depping's evening entertainments. (19650)
De Prada, Francisco. see Prada, Francisco de.
De Prade, N. see Prade, N. de.
De Prado, Joseph Garcia. see Garcia de Prado, Joseph.
De Prado, Marcos Ramirez. see Ramirez de Prado, Marcos.
De Prado, Pablo. see Prado, Pablo de.
De Prado Mayeza Portocarrero y Lina, Juan. see Prado Mayeza Portocarrero y Lina. Juan de.
De Pradt, Dominique Georges Frederic de Riom de Prolhiac de Fourt. see Pradt, Dominique Georges Frederic de Riom de Prolhiac de Fourt de, Abp., 1759-1837.
Depravity of slavery. (21579)
Depreciation of the currency. 83027
De Prefontaine, -------. see Prefontaine, ------- de.
De Proisy, ------, Chevalier. see Proisy, ------, Chevalier de.
De Prolhiac de Fourt de Bradt, Dominic Georges Frederic de Riom. see Pradt, Dominique Georges Frederic de Riom de Prolhiac de Fourt de, Abp., 1759-1837.
De Propiac, Catherine Joseph Ferdinand Girard. see Propiac, Catherine Joseph Ferdinand Girard de, 1759-1822.
De Prouville, Alexandre, Marquis de Tracy. see Prouville, Alexandre de, Marquis de Tracy.
De Provins, Pacifique. see Provins, Pacifique de.
Depth of the divine thought. 18185
De Pueirredon, Juan Martin. see Pueryredon, Juan Martin de.
De Puga, Vasco. see Puga, Vasco de.
Depvis que cette relation a paru au lour. (67492)-67493
De Pulgar, Ferdinand. see Pulgar, Hernando de, 1436?-1492.
De Pulgar, Hernando. see Pulgar, Hernando de, 1436?-1492.
Deputes de Saint-Domingue a l'Assemblee Nationale. see Santo Domingo (French Colony). Deputes a l'Assemblee Nationale.
Deputes des Manufactures & du Commerce de France. see France. Deputes des Manufactures et du.Commerce de France.
Deputies of the Moravian Brethren. see United Brethren. Great Britain. Deputies.
Deputies of the United Moravian Churches. see United Brethren. Great Britain. Deputies.
Deputies of Their High Mightinesses for the City of New York. pseud. To the agents. 95906
Deputy commissary's guide within the province of Maryland. 93360, 98392
De Puy, Henry W. (19651)-(19652)
De Puydt, Remi. see Puydt, Remi de, 1789-1844.

De Puysegur, Antoine Hyacinthe Anne Chastenet, Comte. see Puysegur, Antoine Hyacinthe Anne Chastenet, Comte de, 1752-1807.
De Queilhe, L. le Meynard. see Meynard de Queilhe, L. le.
De Queiros, Pedro Fernandes. see Queiros, Pedro Fernandes de, d. 1615.
De Queiros Coitinho Mattoso Camare, Eusebio. see Mattoso Camare, Eusebio de Queiros Coitinho.
De Quens, Jean. see Quens, Jean de.
De Querbeuf, Y. M. M. see Querbeuf, Y. M. M. de.
De Querion, Anne Gabriel Meusnier. see Meusnier de Querion, Anne Gabriel, 1702-1780.
De Quesada, Conzalo Ximenez. see Quesada, Conzalo Ximenez de.
De Quesada, Manuel. see Quesada, Manuel de.
De Quesada, Rafael. see Quesada, Rafael de.
De Quevedo, H. G. see Quevedo, H. G. de.
De Quevedo, J. H. Garcia. see Quevedo, J. H. Garcia de.
De Quincey, Thomas, 1785-1589. 19653
De Quintana, Andres Nario. see Quintana, Andres Nario de.
De Quintana, Augustin. see Quintana, Augustin de.
De Quintana y Guido, Antonio. see Quintana y Guido, Antonio de.
De Quintanilla, Angel Miguel. see Quintanilla, Angel Miguel.
De Quintela, Augustin. see Quintela, Augustin de.
De Quintero, Mariana Yuste. see Quintero, Mariana Yuste de.
De Quir, Pedro Fernandes. see Queiros, Pedro Fernandes de, d. 1615.
De Quir, Petrus Fernandez. see Queiros, Pedro Fernandes de, d. 1615.
De Quir, Pierre Ferdinand. see Queiros, Pedro Fernandes de, d. 1615.
De Quiroga, Diego Gonzales. see Quiroga, Diego Gonzales de.
De Quiroga, Vasco. see Quiroga, Vasca de, Bp., ca. 1470-1565.
De Quiroga y Lossada, Diego. see Quiroga y Lossada, Diego de.
De Quiros, Blas. see Quiros, Blas de.
De Quiros, Fernand. see Quiros, Fernand de.
De Quiros, Pedro Fernandez. see Queiros, Pedro Fernandes de, d. 1615.
De Quiros y Campo-Sagrado, Manuel. see Quiros y Campo-Sagrado, Manuel de.
Der in dem Wilden America. (42897)
Der in der Americanischen Wildnusz. 102510
De Rada, Joseph Lorenz. see Rada, Joseph Lorenz de.
De Raei de Jonge, Joh. see Raei de Jonge, Joh. de.
Deraggis, ------. 19654
De Rainville, Cesar. see Rainville, Cesar de.
De Ramezay, Jean Baptiste Nicolas Roch, Sieur. see Ramezay, Jean Baptiste Nicolas Roch, Sieur de, 1708-1777.
De Ramon Carbonell, Ignacio. see Ramon Carbonell, Ignacio de.
De Ransonnet, M. see Ransonnet, ------ de.
De Raousset-Boulbon, Gaston. see Raousset-Boulbon, Gaston de, Comte.
De Rayneval, J. M. Gerard. see Rayneval, J. M. Gerard de.
Derbigny, ------. 21383
Der Broeck, P. van. see Broecke, Pieter van der, 1575-1641.

Der Broecke, Pieter van. see Broecke, Pieter van der, 1575-1641.
Der Brugge, Jacob Segersz van. see Segersz van der Brugge, Jacob.
Derby, Charles Stanley, 8th Earl of. 90296-90297
Derby, Edward George Geoffrey Smith Stanley, 14th Earl of. 90303-90304
Derby, Edward Henry Stanley, 15th Earl of. 90305-90307
Derby, Elias Hasket, 1803-1880. 11219, 19655-19659, (19661)-19662, 21357, 64447, 103006
Derby, Mrs. Elias Hasket. 19663
Derby, George. 19664
Derby, George Horatio, 1823-1861. (19665), 83706, 97652, note after 98848
Derby, John Barton, 1793?-1867. 19666-19668
Derby, Sarah. 19669
Derby, W. illus. 84357
Der Capellan, Robert Jasper van. see Capellan, Robert Jasper van der.
Der Capellen, Johan Berk, Baron van. see Capellen, Johan Berk, Baron van der.
Derde discovrs. By forma van missive. 19670, 3d note after 102890
Derde discovrs. VVaer in by forme van missive. 19671, 4th note after 102890
Derde en vierde brief wegens een uitstorting des Heigligen Geestes in de Vereenigde Staten van Amerika. 7920
Derde verclaringe aengaende de goude ende silvere mijne aenghewesen door den Ridder Balthasar Gerbier. 27132
Der Donck, Adriaen van. see Donck, Adriaen van der, d. 1655.
De Rebolledo, Juan. see Rebolledo, Juan de.
De Recabarren, Martin. see Recabarren, Martin de.
Derecho constitucional de las republicas Hispano-Americanas. 14540
Derecho de las iglesias metropolitanas de las Indias. 5063
Derecho de las iglesias metropolitanas, i catedrales de las Indias. 5064
Derecho del Illmo. Sr. Obispo de Michoacan. 51325
Derecho international teorico y practico de Europa y America. (10088)
Derecho natural o filosofia del derecho. 76873
Derechos adquiridos y los actos de la dictadura de Peru. 61111
Derechos de Fernando VII. al trono del imperio Mexicano. 96199
Derechos y obligaciones del ciudadano. 97043
Derecourt, Henry. (19672)
De Regiomonte, Espitola J. see Regiomonte, Espitola J. de.
De Reinhard, Charles. defendant 69111, 81378, note after 96856
De Remonville, -------. see Remonville, ------ de.
De Remur, Simon Guillaume Gabriel Brute. see Brute de Remur, Simon Guillaume Gabriel, Bp., 1779-1839.
De Remusat, Charles Francois Marie, Comte. see Remusat, Charles Francois Marie, Comte de, 1797-1875.
De Renne, George Wymberley Jones, 1827-1880. 7325, (36505), (77034), 101211
De Rennefort, Urbain Souchu. see Rennefort, Urbain Souchu de, ca. 1630- ca. 1689.
De Renneville, Rene Augustin Constantin. see Renneville, Rene Augustin Constantin de.

De Renovales, Mariano. see Renovales, Mariano de.
De Requena, Martin. see Requena, Martin de.
D'Eres, Charles Dennis Rouso. see Rouso d'Eres, Charles Dennis, b. 1761.
De Resende, Angelo Andrea. see Resende, Angelo Andrea de.
De Resende, Antonio Telles da Silva Caminha e Menezes, Marquez. see Telles da Silva Caminha e Menezes, Antonio, Marquez de Resende, 1790-1875.
De Resende, Garcia. see Resende, Garcia de.
De Reste, Bernard. see Reste, Bernard de.
De Retana, J. G. see Retana, J. G. de.
De Reveira Bastos, Jose. see Bastos, Jose de Reveira.
De Revello, F. J. Bovo. see Revello, F. J. Bovo de.
De Revillagigedo, Juan Vicente de Guemes Pacheo de Podilla, Conde. see Guemes Pacheo de Podilla, Juan Vicente de, Conde de Revillagigedo.
De Reynaud, ------, Comte. see Reynaud, -------, Comte de.
De Reynoso, Diego. see Reynoso, Diego de.
De Pezabal y Ugarte, Joseph. see Rezabal y Ugarte, Joseph de.
Der Gabelentz, H. C. von. see Gabelentz, H. C. von der.
Der Gon Netscher, A. D. van. see Netscher, A. D. van der Gon.
Der Groben, J. van. see Groben, J. van der.
Der Hagen, ------- van. see Hagen, ------- van der.
Der Hagen, Et. van. see Hagen, Et. van der.
Der Hagen, Steven van. see Hagen, Steven van der.
De Rham, Henry C. petitioner 19673
Derham, W. ed. (13575), 49438
Derhoven, Orrin van. see Van Derhoven, Orrin.
De Rianzuela, ------, Marques. see Rianzuela, ------, Marques de.
De Ribadeneyra, Diego Portichuelo. see Portichuelo de Ribadeneyra, Diego.
De Ribadeneyra y Barrientos, Antonio Joaquin. see Ribadeneyra y Barrientos, Antonio Joaquin de.
De Ribas, Alonso Rubio. see Rubio de Ribas, Alonso.
De Ribas, Andres Perez. see Perez de Ribas, Andres.
De Ribas, Antonio Perez. see Ribas, Antonio Perez de.
De Ribas, Diego Rodriguez. see Rodriguez de Ribas, Diego, Bp., d. 1771.
De Ribera, Antonio. see Ribera, Antonio de.
De Ribera, Antonio Flores. see Flores de Ribera, Jose Antonio.
De Ribera, Diego. see Ribera, Diego de.
De Ribera, F. Payo. see Payo de Ribera, F.
De Ribera, J. B. see Ribera, J. B. de.
De Ribera, Jose Antonio Flores. see Flores de Ribera, Jose Antonio.
De Ribera, Miguel P. see Ribera, Miguel P. de.
De Ribera, Payo Henriquez. see Ribera, Payo Henriquez de, Abp.
De Ribera Florez, Dionysio. see Ribera Florez, Dionysio de.
De Ribera y Colindres, Luys. see Ribera y Colindres, Luys de.
De Richelieu, Armand Jean du Plessis, Cardinal, Duc. see Richelieu, Armand Jean du Plessis, Cardinal, Duc de, 1585-1642.

De Ricla, Ambrosio Funes Villapando Abarca
de Bolea, Conde. see Abarca de
Bolea, Ambrosio Funes Villapando,
Conde de Ricla.
De Riedesel, ---------. see Riedesel,
Frederica Charlotte Louise (von Massow)
Baronness von. and Riedesel, Friedrich
Adolphus, Freyherr von.
De Rigaud, Pierre Francois. see Vaudreuil
de Cavagnal, Pierre Francois de Rigaud,
Marquis de.
De Rinaldi, Piervicentio Dante. see Rinaldi,
Piervicentio Dante de.
De Rio-Frio, Miguel Maria. see Rio-Frio,
Miguel Maria de.
De Riofrio, Bernardo. see Riofrio, Bernardo
de.
De Riom de Prolhiac de Fourt de Pradt, Domini-
que Georges Frederic. see Pradt,
Dominique Georges Frederic de Riom de
Prolhiac de Fourt de, Abp., 1759-1837.
De Ripalda, Geronimo. see Ripalda, Geronimo
de.
De Ripperda, Joan Willem van, Duque de.
see Ripperda, Joan Willem van, Duque,
d. 1737.
De Rivadeneira, Pedro. see Ribadeneira,
Petrus.
De Rivarol, P. see Rivarol, P. de.
De Rivas, Andres-Perez. see Ribas, Andres-
Perez de.
De Rivas-Cacho, Jos. M. (Franco Soto) see
Rivas-Cacho, Jos. M. (Franco Soto) de.
De Rivas-Cacho, Manuel. see Ricas-Cacho,
Manuel de.
De Rivera, Antonio. see Rivera, Antonio de.
De Rivera, Jos. see Rivera, Jos. de.
De Rivera, Pedro. see Rivera, Pedro de.
De Rivera Bernardes, I. de. see Rivera
Bernardez, Joseph de, Conde de
Santiago de La Laguna.
De Rivera Bernardez, Joseph. see Rivera
Bernardez, Joseph de, Conde de
Santiago de la Laguna.
De Rivera Marquez, Pedro. see Rivera
Marquez, Pedro de.
De Rivera Villalon, Pedro. see Rivera
Villalon, Pedro de.
De Rivero, Joseph Bravo, see Rivero, Joseph
Bravo de.
De Rivero, Mariano Eduardo. see Rivero,
Mariano Eduardo de.
De Rivero y Ustariz, Mariano Eduardo. see
Rivero y Ustariz, Mariano Eduardo de.
De Rivero y Zavala, Andres Bravo. see
Rivero y Zuvala, Andres Bravo de.
De Rivero y Zavala, Diego Miguel Bravo.
see Rivero y Zavala, Diego Miguel
Bravo de.
De Rives, Eugene. pseud. Notice biographique.
see Casgrain, H. R.
Derk, Johan. see Capellen, Johan Derk,
Baron van der.
Der Kemp, Francis Adrian van. see Kemp,
Francois Adriaan van der.
Derkinderen, James. 19674
Der Linden, Johannes van. see Linden,
Johannes van der, 1756?-1835.
Der Maelen, Ph. van. see Maelen, Ph. van
der.
Dermer, Thomas. 66686
Der Meulen, M. E. van. see Meulen, M. E.
van der.
Dermott, L. 102460
Der Myle, Arnold van. see Mylius, Arnold,
1540-1604.

Der Mylius, Arnold van. see Mylius, Arnold,
1540-1604.
Derne, --------. 83978
Dernier chef des filibustiers. 62677
Dernier de Mohicans. 16453
Dernier des Abencerrages. (12250)
Dernier des serviteurs de Jesus-Christ.
pseud. see Last servant of Jesus
Christ. pseud.
Dernier mot sur le Guazacoalco. 21022
Dernier voeu de la justice. 39847
Dernier wigwam des Pawnies. 6306
Derniere guerre des betes. (23929)
Derniere lettre a l'empereur Alexandre.
93988
Derniere response de M. de. Cocherel.
14050
Dernieres annees de la colonie Francaise.
(44868)
Dernieres decouvertes dans l'Amerique
Septentrionale. 96172
Dernieres observations pour les Sieurs Thomas
Walpole & consorts. 101149
Dernieres observations pour Thomas Walpole
& consorts. 101149
Derniers Iroquois. 12558
De Roa, Alonso. see Roa, Alonso de.
De Roberval, ------. see Roberval, ------
de.
De Robles, Antonio. see Robles, Antonio de.
De Robles, Ivan. see Robles, Juan de.
De Rochambeau, Donatien Marie Joseph de
Vimeur, Vicomte. see Rochambeau,
Donatien Marie Joseph de Vimeur,
Vicomte de.
De Rochambeau, Jean Baptiste Donatien de
Vimeur, Comte. see Rochambeau,
Jean Baptiste Donatien de Vimeur,
Comte de, 1725-1807.
De Roche, ------. see Roche, ------ de.
De Rochefort, Cesar. see Rochefort, Cesar
de.
De Rochefort, Charles. see Rochefort, Charles
de.
De Rochelle, Jean Baptiste Gaspard Roux. see
Roux de Rochelle, Jean Baptiste Gaspard,
1762-1849.
De Rochemore, ------. see Rochemore,
------ de.
De Rochemore, Vincent-Gaspard-Pierre, Sieur.
see Rochemore, Vincent-Gaspard-Pierre
de, Sieur.
De Roches, V. see Roches, V. de.
Derocho apologetico por la justicia de el
Capitan Don Andres Patino Lastellanos.
59068
De Rochon, Alexis Marie. see Rochon, Alexis
Marie de, 1741-1817.
De Rocoles, Jean Baptiste. see Rocoles, Jean
Baptiste de.
De Rodrigues, Pierre. see Rodrigues, Pedro,
1542-1628.
De Rojas y Rocha, Francisco. see Rojas y
Rocha, Francisco de.
Derome, F. M. 34041, 69661
De Ron, Antonio Joseph Alvarez. see Ron,
Antonio Joseph Alvarez de.
De Ronde, Lambertus. see Ronde, Lambertus
de.
De-Roo, Francisco de Paula Quadrado y. see
Quadrado y De-Roo, Francisco de Paula.
De Roos, Frederick Fitzgerald. 19677
De Roquefeuil, Camille. see Roquefuil,
Camille de.
De Rosal, Juana Albares. see Pinto de Ulloa,
Juana (Albares de Rosal) de Valverde.

De Rosales, Diego. see Rosales, Diego de.
De Rosamel, ------. see Rosamel, ------
de.
De Rosas, Juan Manuel. see Rosas, Juan
Manuel de.
De Rosende, Antonio Gonzalez. see Gonzalez
de Rosende, Antonio, 17th cent.
De Rosiers, --------, Comte. see Rosiers,
--------, Comte de.
Derosne, Ch. (9844)
De Rosnel, Pierre. see Rosnel, Pierre de.
De Rosny, Leon. see Rosny, Leon de.
De Rosny, Lucien. see Rosny, Lucien de.
De Rossal, J. A. see Rossal, J. A. de.
De Rossel, --------. see Rossel, ------- de.
De Rossel, Elisabeth Paul Edouard. see
Rossel, Elisabeth Paul Edouard de.
De Rossett, Lewis Henry. 84564
De Rostoff, Alexandre Labanoff. see Labanoff
de Rostoff, Alexandre.
De Rotalde, Francisco. see Rotalde, Francisco
de.
De Rothelin, ------- d'Orleans. see Rothe-
lin, -------.
De Rottermund, -------, Comte. see Rot-
termund, -----, Comte de.
De Roussignac, Jacques. see Roussignac,
Jacques de.
De Rouville, ------ Delafosse. see Delafosse
de Rouville, -------.
De Roxas, Alonso. see Roxas, Alonso de.
De Roxas, Francisco. see Roxas, Francisco
de.
Deroy, -------. illus. 48916, 73935
De Roy, Albert. 30852
De Rozas, Manuel Gaspar. see Rozas,
Manuel Gaspar de.
De Rozoi, ------. see Farmin de Rosi,
known as Durosoi.
De Rozot, ------. see Rozot, ----- de.
Der Plaats, ----- van. see Plaats, ------
van der.
Derradeiro Mohicano. (16565)
Derrick and drill. 50812
Derrota del General Morazan. 29075
Derrotas de la America Occidental. (55395)
Derrotero de la expedicion en la provincia de
los Texas. 59626
Derrotero de las Antillas. 66694
Derrotero de las costas de Espana. 98306
Derrotero de las Islas Antillas. (1700), 19678-
19679, 48419, 99439
Derrotero general de las republicas del Peru,
Colombia, Buenos-Ayres y Chile. 19680
Derrotero jeneral de las republicas del Peru,
Buenos-Ayres, Colombia y Chile. 61112
Derroteros y viajes a la ciudad encantada.
72776
Derry, Joseph T. 2381
Derry, Bishop of. see Ash, St. George,
successively Bishop of Cloyne, Clogher,
and Derry. Nicolson, William, Archbishop
of Cashel, 1655-1727.
Derry, N. H. Old Nutfield Celebration, 1869.
see Celebration of the One Hundred and
Fiftieth Anniversary of the Settled Part
of Old Nutfield, N. H., 1869.
Derry, N. H. Pinkerton Academy. see
Pinkerton Academy, Derry, N. H.
Derryfield, N. H. Centennial Celebration, 1851.
see Manchester, N. H. Centennial
Celebration of the Incorporation of Derry-
field, 1851.
Der Schley, J. van. see Schley, J. van der.
Der Sloot, F. W. van. see Sloot, F. W. van
der.

Der Steere, Dionysius van. see Steere,
Dionysius van der.
Der Straten-Ponthoz, Gabriel Auguste van.
see Straten-Ponthoz, Gabriel Auguste
van der.
De Rubalcava, Joseph Gutierrez. see
Rubalcava, Joseph Gutierrez de.
De Rubriquis, William. see Ruysbroek,
Willem van.
De Rubruck, Guillaume. see Ruysbroek,
Willem van.
De Ruhliere, Claude Carloman. see Ruhliere,
Claude Carloman de.
De Ruusscher, Melchior. see Ruusscher,
Melchior de.
De Ruyter, Michael Adrian. see Ruyter,
Michael Adrian de.
Der Veer, C. van. see Van der Veer, C.
Der Vegt, A. Helmig van. see Helmig van
der Vegt, A.
Der Velde, Karl Franz van. see Velde,
Karl Franz van der.
Der Vlag, M. M. van. pseud. see Vlag,
M. M. van der. pseud.
Der Water, Guillelmus van der. see Water,
Guillelmus van der.
Der Worm, A. W. van. see Worm, A. W.
van der.
De S., C. pseud. see Sodre, Francois de.
De S . . . ., D. S . . . . pseud. see
Sotomayor, Diego Sanchez de.
De S., M. B . . . . pseud. see S., M.
B . . . . de. pseud.
De S. Bernardino Botelho, Jose. see Botelho,
Jose de S. Bernardino.
De S. Benoit Dinouart, Chanoine. see Dinouart,
Chanoine de S. Beniot.
De S. Crisostomo, M. see Crisostomo, M.
de S.
De S. Jose, Rodrigo. see Rodrigo de S. Jose.
De S. Thomas, ------ Domingo. see Domingo
de S. Thomas, ------.
De S. Jose Muro, Antonio. see Muro, Antonio
de S. Jose.
De S. Joseph, Marcelo. see Marcelo de S.
Joseph.
De S. Juan Hermoso, Faustino. see Hermoso,
Faustino de S. Juan.
De S. Michel, Mavrile. see Mavrile de S.
Michel.
De S. Miguel, Juan Rodriguez. see Miguel
Juan Rodriguez de S.
De S., P. pseud. see Souza, Bernardo
Xavier Pinto de.
De S. Pierre, -------, Comte. see S.
Pierre, ------, Comte de.
De S. Pierre, Louis. see Pierre, Louis de
S.
De S. S., J. Norberto. pseud. see Souza
Silva, Joaquim Norberto de, 1820-1891.
De S. Teresa, Gio. Gioseppe. see Santa
Teresa, Giovanni Gioseppe di.
Des bateaux a vapeur. (36680)
Des betes a laine des Andes. 14755
Des bords de la Saone a la baie de San
Salvador. 21162
Des ceremonies observees autrefois par les
Indiens. 94854
Des colonies et de la legislation sur les sucres.
30118
Des colonies, et de la revolution actuelle de
l'Amerique. 23915, (40684), 64882
Des colonies et de la traite des negres.
(4611)
Des colonies, et particulierement de celle de
Saint-Domingue. 44114

Des colonies; et particulierement de la Guyane
  Francaise. 74985
Des colonies Francaises. 5652, 77745
Des colonies Francaises et en particulier de
  l'ile de Saint-Domingue. 22878
Des colonies modernes sous la zone torride.
  3592, 75506
Des emigrations Europeennes dans l'Amerique
  du Sud. (64697)
Des emigres Francais. 40728
Des Etats-Unis d'Amerique. (65954)
Des Etats-Unis, de la guerre du Mexique
  et de l'ile de Cuba. (17166)
Des institutions republicaines. (39470)
Des interets reciproques de l'Europe et de
  l'Amerique. (64699)
Des isles marquises et des colonies de la
  France. (38603)
Des iles et q. il possess en Aphrique.
  25190
Des moeurs et coutumes religieuses. 4933
Des moyens de conserver la sante des blancs
  et des Negres. 5011
Des orden del Director Supremo del estado de
  Nicaragua. 55159
Des pays & isles nouvellement trouvez. 50059,
  99379
Des petitions de quelques ouvriers et ouvrieres
  de Paris. 36420
Des peuples et des gouvernments. 68077
Des premieres relations entre l'Amerique et
  l'Europe. 105741
Des prisons de Philadelphie. 39053, 50576
Des remarques sur la navigation du Detroit de
  Belle-Isle. 4550
Des savvages, ov, voyage de Samvel Champlain.
  (11834)
Des services a vapeur transatlantiques. 4816
Des traitez curieux touchant la haut Ethyopie.
  36944, 68430
Des vrais povrtraits. 95341
De Sa, S. J. Ribeiro. see Ribeiro de Sa, S.
  J.
De Sa de Menezes, Francisco. see Menezes,
  Francisco de Sa de.
De Sa e Albuquerque, A. C. see Sa e Albuquer-
  que, A. C. de.
De Sa e Menezes, Estacio. see Sa e Menezes,
  Estacio de.
De Saavedra, Francisco Javier Venegas. see
  Venegas de Saavedra, Francisco Javier.
De Saavedra, Marcos. see Saavedra, Marcos
  de.
De Saavedra Guzman, Antoine. see Guzman,
  Antoine de Saavedra.
De Saba, Onuphrio Prat. see Prat de Saba,
  Onuphrio.
De Sabroso, ------, Baron de Ribeira. see
  Riberia de Sabrosa, -----, Baron de.
De Sacro Bosco, Joannes. see Sacro Bosco,
  Joannes de, fl. 1230.
De Sacy, Claude Louis Michel. see Sacy,
  Claude Louis Michel de.
Desaggravo do clero e do povo catholico
  flumiense. 76322
Desague del valle de Mexico. 64726
De Sahagun, Bernardino. see Sahagun,
  Bernardino de.
De Saillet, Alexandre. see Saillet, Alexandre
  de.
De Saint-Adolphe, J. C. R. Milliet. see
  Milliet de Saint-Adolphe, J. C. R.
De St Albin, Jacques. pseud. see Collin
  de Plancy, Jacques A. S.
De Saint-Allias, Nocolas Viton. see Saint-
  Allias, Nicolas Viton de, 1773-1842.

De Saint-Amant, Ch. see Saint-Amant, Ch. de.
De Saint-Andre, Dupin. see Saint-Andre, Dupin
  de.
De Saint-Aubin, Stephanie Felicite Ducrest.
  see Saint-Aubin, Stephanie Felicite Du-
  crest de, Comtesse de Genlis.
De Saint-Aurele, De la Guadeloupe Poirie. see
  Poirie de Saint-Aurele, De la Guadeloupe.
De Saint Blin, -------- Duverger. see Saint
  Blin, Duverger de.
De Saint Bonaventure, Marie. see Marie.
  de Saint Bonaventure, Mere Superieure.
De Saint Bonaventure de Jesus, Marie. see
  Marie de Saint Bonaventure, Mere
  Superieure.
De St. C**, C. pseud. see Lammens,
  --------.
De St. Cergues, ------ Dufresne. see Du-
  fresne de St. Cergues, -------.
De Saint Circq, Lorenzo. see Saint-Circq,
  Laurent.
De St. Clevien, L. F. Jehan. see Jehan de
  St. Clevien, L. F.
De St. Cosme, ------. see Buisson, Jean
  Francois.
De Saint Cyran, -------. see Saint Cyran,
  ------- de.
De Saint-Denys, Marie Jean Leon, Marquis
  d'Hervey. see Hervey de Saint-Denys,
  Marie Jean Leon, Marquis d', 1823-1892.
De Saint-Douat, Alexandre Coupe. see Coupe
  de Saint-Douat, Alexandre.
De Saint Estienne, Charles. see Saint Estienne,
  Charles de, Seigneur de la Tour.
De Saint Fargeau, ------ Le Pelletier. see
  Le Pelletier de Saint Fargeau, -------.
De Saint-Gelays, Melin. see Saint-Gelays,
  Melin de.
De Saint-Genois, J. see Saint-Genois, J. de.
De Saint-Hilaire, Auguste Francois Cesar
  Prouvencal. see Saint-Hilaire, Auguste
  Francois Cesar Prouvencal de, 1779-1853.
De Saint-Hilaire, Edme-Jean-Hilaire Filleau.
  see Filleau de Saint-Hilaire, Edme-Jean-
  Hilaire.
De Saint Hyacinthe, H. Cordonnier. see
  Cordonnier de Saint Hyacinthe, H.
De St. Ignace, Francoise Juchereau. see
  Juchereau de St. Ignace, Francoise.
De Saint-Joseph, Francois Anthoine. see
  Anthoine de Saint-Joseph, Francois,
  Baron.
De Saint Mars, Gabrielle Anne Cisterne de
  Courtiras, Vicomtesse. see Saint
  Mars, Gabrielle Anne Cisterne de Courtiras,
  Vicomtesse de, 1804-1872.
De Saint-Martin, Baillot. see Baillot de Saint-
  Martin, ------- .
De St.-Memin, M. see St.-Memin, M. de.
De Saint-Mery, Mederic Louis Elie Moreau.
  see Moreau de Saint-Mery, Mederic
  Louis Elie, 1750-1819.
De Saint-Mesmin, E. Menu. see Menu de
  Saint-Mesmin, E.
De Saint-Paul, P. see Saint-Paul, P. de.
De Saint Pierre, Jacques Henri Bernardin.
  see Saint Pierre, Jacques Henri Bernar-
  din de, 1734-1814.
De Saint Pierre, Louis. see Saint-Pierre,
  Louis de.
De Saint-Prest, Jean Yves. see Saint-Prest,
  Jean Yves de.
De Saint Priest, Alexis de Guignard, Comte.
  see Saint Priest, Alexis de Guignard,
  Comte de, 1805-1851.
De Saint-Quentin, Alfred. see Saint-Quentin,
  Alfred de.

De Saint-Quentin, Auguste. see Saint-Quentin, Auguste de.

De Saint-Quentin, Edouard. see Saint-Quentin, Edouard de.

De Saint-Quentin, Eugene. see Saint-Quentin, Eugene de.

De Saint-Quentin, J. Bellon. see Bellon de Saint-Quentin, J.

De St. Real, Joseph Remi Vallieres. see Vallieres de St. Real, Joseph Remi.

De Saint-Remey, R. Lepelletier. see Lepelletier de Saint-Remy, R.

De Saint Robert, -----------. see Saint Robert, -------, Chevalier de.

De Saint Sauveur, Jacques Grasset. see Grasset de Saint Sauveur, Jacques.

De St. Valier, --------, Sieur Joly. see Joly de St. Valier, ------, Sieur.

De Saint Vallier, Jean Baptiste de la Croix de Chevrieres. see Saint Vallier, Jean Baptiste de la Croix de Chevrieres de, Bp.

De Saint-Victor, J. B. see Saint-Victor, J. B. de.

De Saint Victor, Jacques Maximilien Benjamin Bins. see Saint Victor, Jacques Maximilien Benjamin Bins de.

De Saint Vincent, Jean Baptiste Georges Bory. see Bory de Saint Vincent, Jean Baptiste Georges, 1778-1846.

De Sainte Bonnaventure de Jesus, Marie. see Marie de Saint Bonaventure, Mere Superieure.

De Sainte-Croix, Carloman Louis Francois Felix Renouard. see Sainte-Croix, Carloman Louis Francois Felix Renouard de, Marquis.

De Sainte-Croix, Guillaume Emmanuel Joseph Guilhem de Clermont-Lodeve, Baron. see Sainte-Croix, Guillaume Emmanuel Joseph Guilhem de Clermont-Lodeve, Baron de.

De Saintonge, Alfonse. see Fonteneau, Jean.

De Saintrac, Louis Nadal. see Nadal de Saintrac, Louis.

De Salamanca, Ignatius. see Salmanca, Ignatius de.

De Salas, Joseph Prefecto. see Salas, Joseph Prefecto de.

De Salas, Pedro. see Salas, Pedro de.

De Salas y Quiroga, Jacinto. see Salas y Quiroga, Jacinto de.

De Salas y Valdes, Juan. see Salas y Valdes, Juan de.

De Salazar, A. see Salazar, A. de.

De Salazar, Domingo. see Salazar, Domingo de.

De Salazar, Francesca Cervantes. see Salazar, Francisco Cervantes.

De Salazar, Joseph. see Salazar, Joseph de.

De Salazar, Juan Joseph. see Salazar, Juan Joseph de.

De Salazar, Juan Velazquez. see Velazques de Salazar, Juan.

De Salazar y Mazarredo, Eusebio. see Salazar y Mazarredo, Eusebio de.

De Salazar y Olarte, Ignacio. see Salazar y Olarte, Ignacio de.

De Salazar y Vicuna, Manuel. see Salazar y Vicuna, Manuel de.

De Salazar y Zevallos, Alonso Eduardo. see Salazar y Zevallos, Alonso Eduardo de.

De Salcedo y Sierra Alta, Miguel. see Salcedo y Sierra Alta, Miguel de.

De Saldanha da Gama, Joao. see Saldanha da Gama, Jose da.

De Saldanha da Gama, Jose. see Saldanha Da Gama, Jose de.

De Saldanha Oliveira e Daun, Joao Carlos. see Saldanha, Joao Carlos de Saldanha Oliveira e Daun, 1. Duque de, 1790-1876.

De Saldana y Ortega, Antonio. see Saldana y Ortega, Antonio de.

De Sales, Francisco. see Francois de Sales. Saint

De Sales, Francois. see Francois de Sales. Saint

De Sales la Terriere, Peter. see Sales la Terriere, Peter de.

De Salignac de la Mothe-Fenelon, Francois. see Fenelon, Francois de Salignac de la Mothe-, Abp., 1641-1715.

De Salinas, Juan. see Salinas, Juan de.

De Salinas, Luis de Velasco, Marques. see Velasco, Luis de, Marques de Salinas, 1534-1617.

De Salinas y La Cerda, Juan Fernandez. see Salinas y La Cerda, Juan Fernandez de.

De Salles, Eusebe Fr. see Salles, Eusebe Fr. de.

De Salles, Jose Agostinho. see Salles, Jose Agostinho de.

De Salles la Terriere, Pierre. see La Terriere, Pierre de Salles.

De Salluste, Guillaume. see Du Bartas, Guillaume de Salluste, Seigneur, 1544-1590.

De Salm-Salm, Felix. see Salm-Salm, Felix de.

De Salm Salm, Ines. see Salm, Salm, Ines de.

De Salontha, ------. see Salontha, ------- de.

De Salvandy, Narcisse Achille. see Salvandy, Narcisse Achille de.

De Salvatierra, Andres Vernal. see Salvatierra, Andres Vernal de.

De Salzedo, Joseph. see Salzedo, Joseph de.

De Samaniego, Francisco. see Samaniego, Francisco de.

De Sambrano, Joseph. see Zambrano Bonilla, Jose.

De Sampajo, Francisco Xavier Ribeiro. see Ribeiro de Sampajo, Francisco Xavier.

De San Alberto, Jose Antonio. see San Alberto, Jose Antonio de, Abp., 1727-1804.

De San Anastasio, Juan. see San Anastasio, Juan de.

De San Anton Munon Chimalpain, Juan Bautista. see Chimalpain, Juan Bautista de San Anton Munon.

De San Antonio, Francisco. see San Antonio, Francisco de.

De San Antonio, Juan Francisco. see San Antonio, Juan Francisco de.

De San Antonio Moreno, Martin. see San Antonio Moreno, Martin de.

De San Antonio Ortega, J. see Ortega, J. de San Antonio.

De San Augustin, Andres. see San Augustin, Andres de.

De San Augustin, Gaspar. see San Augustin, Gaspar de.

De San Bartolome, Jose. see San Bartolome, Jose de.

De San Bernardo, Juan. see Juan de San Bernardo.

De San Buenaventura, F. see San Buenaventura, F. de.

De San Buenaventura, Gabriel. see San Buenaventura, Gabriel de.

De San Cirilo, Francisco. see San Cirilo, Francisco de.

De San Cirilo, Pedro. see Pedro de San Cirilo.
De San Cristoval, --------, Marques. see San Cristoval, ------, Marques de.
De San Fermin, Antonio. see San Fermin, Antonio de.
De San Francisco, Juan. see San Francisco, Juan de.
De San Francisco, Maria Micaela Romero de Terreros y Trebuesto, Marquesa. see Terreros y Trebuesto, Maria Micaela Romero de, Marquesa de San Francisco.
De San Ignacio, Maria Anna Agueda. see San Ignacio, Maria Anna Agueda de.
De San Jose, A. M. see San Jose, A. M. de.
De San Jose, Baltasar. see San Jose, Baltasar de.
De San Jose, Francisco. see Francisco de San Jose, d. 1701.
De San Jose, Juan. see Juan de San Jose. Fray
De San Jose, Prudencia. see San Jose, Prudencia de.
De San Jose Muro, Antonio. see Muro, Antonio de San Jose.
De San Joseph, Francisco. see Francisco de San Jose, d. 1701.
De San Joseph Betancur, Pedro. see Betancur, Pedro de San Joseph.
De San Juan Bautista, Elias. see San Juan Bautista, Elias de, d. 1605.
De San Juan Bautista, Matias. see San Juan Bautista, Matias de.
De San Leopoldo, Jose Feliciano Fernandes Pinheiro, Visconde. see Fernandes Pinheiro, Jose Feliciano, Visconde de San Leopoldo, 1774-1847.
De San Martin, Jose. see San Martin, Jose, 1778-1850.
De San Miguel, Andres. see San Miguel, Andres de.
De San Miguel, Juan Rodriguez. see Rodriguez de San Miguel, Juan.
De San Miguel, Matias Sanz. see San Miguel, Matias Sanz de.
De San Miguel, N. A. Diez. see Diez de San Miguel, N. A.
De San Miguel, Phelipe Sico. see Sico de San Miguel, Phelipe, Bp.
De San Miguel, Vicente Tofino. see Tofino de San Miguel, Vicente.
De San Miguel, Ysidro. see San Miguel, Ysidro de.
De San Milian, Francisco Lorenzo. see Lorenzo de San Milian, Francisco.
De San Nicolas, Andres. see San Nicolas, Andres de.
De San Nicolas, Gabriel. see Gabriel de San Nicolas.
De San Pedro, Diego Antonio Menedez. see Menedez de San Pedro, Diego Antonio.
De San Pedro, Francisco. see San Pedro, Francisco de.
De San Pedro, Nicolas. see San Pedro, Nicolas de.
De San Rafael, Tomas. see San Rafael, Tomas de.
De San Roman, Antonio. see San Roman, Antonio de.
De San Salvador, Agustin Pomposo Fernandez. see San Salvador, Agustin Pomposo Fernandez de.
De San Salvador, Fernando Fernandez. see Fernandez de San Salvador, Fernando.
De San Vicente, Juan Manuel. see San Vicente, Juan Manuel de.

De San Vicente, Nicolas Garcia. see Garcia de San Vicente, Nicolas.
De San Xavier, ------, Conde. see San Xavier, ------, Conde de.
De Sancere, Adelaide. see Sancere, Adelaide de.
De Sancta Anna, Joaquim. see Sancta Anna, Joaquim de.
De Sancta Anna Esbarra, Joaquim Jose. see Esbarra, Joaquim Jose de Sancta Anna.
De Sancta Cruz, Manuel Fernandez. see Fernandez de Sancta Cruz, Manuel.
De Sancta Gertrudes Magna, Francisco de Paula de. see Gertrudes Magna, Francisco de Paula de Sancta.
De Sancta Maria, Goncalo Garcia. see Garcia de Sancta Maria, Goncalo.
De Sancta Maria Jaboatam, Antonio. see Jaboatam, Antonio de Sancta Maria.
De Sancta Rita Bastos, Francisco Xavier. see Sancta Rita Bastos, Francisco Xavier de.
De Sande, J. van. see Sande, J. van de.
De Sandi, Francisco. see Sandi, Francisco de.
De Sandoval, Geronimo. see Sandoval, Geronimo de.
De Sandoval, Prudencio. see Sandoval, Prudencio de.
De Sandoval y Cavellero, Maria. see Sandoval y Cavellero, Maria de.
De Sandoval y Guzman, Sebastian. see Sandoval y Guzman, Sebastian de.
De Santa Anna, Antonio Lopez. see Santa Anna, Antonio Lopez de, Pres. Mexico, 1795-1876.
De Santa Clara, Sufras. see Sufras de Santa Clara. Fray
De Santa Cruz, Andres. see Santa Cruz, Andres de.
De Santa Cruz, Baltasar. see Santa Cruz, Baltasar de.
De Santa Cruz, Fernando. see Santa Cruz, Fernando de.
De Santa Cruz, Gabriel Beltran. see Santa Cruz, Gabriel Beltran de.
De Santa Cruz, Ioaquin. see Santa Cruz, Ioaquin de, Marquez.
De Santa Cruz, Manuel Fernandez. see Fernandez de Santa Cruz, Manuel.
De Santa Cruz, Miguel Perez. see Santa Cruz, Miguel Perez de, Marques de Buenavista.
De Santa Cruz, Pedro Agustin Morel. see Morel de Santa Cruz, Pedro Agustin, Bp.
De Santa Cruz Merlin, Mercedes. see Merlin, Mercedes de Santa Cruz.
De Santa Cruz y Sahagun, Manuel Fernandez. see Santa Cruz y Sahagun, Manuel Fernandez de.
De Santa Ines, Melchior Oyanguren. see Oyanguren de Santa Ines, Melchior.
De Santa Isabel, Gonsalo. see Santa Isabel, Gonsalo de.
De Santa Maria, Agostinho. see Santa Maria, Agostinho de.
De Santa Maria, Bernardo. see Bernardo de Santa Maria. Fray
De Santa Maria, Juan. see Santa Maria, Juan de.
De Santa Maria, Miguel. see Santa Maria, Miguel de.
De Santa Maria, Pedro. see Pedro de Santa Maria.
De Santa Maria de Lorento, ------ Penalver, Conde. see Penalver, ------, Conde de Santa Maria de Lorento.

De Santa Maria Iaboatam, Antonio. see
Jaboatam, Antonio de Sancta Maria.
De Santa Maria Maraver, Juan. see Santa
Maria Maraver, Juan de.
De Santa Rita Durao, Jose. see Durao, Jose
de Santa Rita.
De Santa Rosa Maria, Pedro Beltran. see
Beltran de Santa Rosa Maria, Pedro.
De Santa Teresa, Giovanni Gioseppe. see
Santa Teresa, Giovanni Gioseppe di.
De Santa Teresa, Luis. see Santa Teresa,
Luis de.
De Santa Teresa, Manuel. see Santa Teresa,
Manuel de.
De Santalla, Thirso Goncalez. see Goncalez
de Santalla, Thirso.
De Santander, J. see Santander, J. de.
De Santander, Juan. see Santander, Juan de.
De Santarem, Manuel Francisco de Barros, 2.
Visconde. see Santarem, Manuel Fran-
cisco de Barros, 2. Visconde de, 1791-
1856.
De Santayana y Spinosa, Rodrigo Saenz. see
Sanez de Santayana y Spinosa, Rodrigo.
De Santiago de la Laguna, Joseph de Rivera
Bermudez, Conde. see Rivera Ber-
mudez, Joseph de, Conde de Santiago
de la Laguna.
De Santisteuan Osorio, Diego. see Osorio,
Diego de Santisteuan.
De Santo Domingo, ------. see Santo-Domingo,
------ de.
De Santo Domingo, Garcia. see Santo Domingo,
Garcia de.
De Santo Thomas, Diego. see Santo Thomas,
Diego de.
De Santo Tomas, Domingo. see Domingo de
Santo Tomas.
De Santo Tomas, Manuel. see Santo Tomas,
Manuel de.
De Santo Tomas, Miguel Rodriguez. see
Rodriguez de Santo Tomas, Miguel.
De Sanvitores, Diego Luis. see Sanvitores,
Diego Luis de.
De Sao Leopoldo, ------, Visconde. see
Sao Leopoldo, ------, Visconde de.
De Sard, Antonio. see Sard, Antonio de.
De Sarria, Juan. see Sarria y Alderete,
Juan.
Desarrollo y desenlace de la cuestion Francesa.
98596
De Sartiges, E. see Sartiges, E. de.
De Sartines, ------. see Sartines, ------ de.
Desastres de la Guadaloupe. 29040
De Saules, Carlos Luiz. see Saules, Carlos
Luiz de.
Desaulses de Freycinet, Louis Claude. see
Freycinet, Louis Claude Dessaulses de.
De Saumarez, James Saumerez, 1st Baron
73373
De Saussure, Henri Louis Frederic. see
Saussure, Henri Louis Frederic de,
1829-1905.
Desaussure, Henry William, 1763-1839. 1655,
12034, 19682-19683, 87866, 3d note be-
fore 87733, 87733, 87902, 87970
Desaussure, Henry William, 1763-1839. reporter
87457
Desaussure, Henry William, 1763-1839. sup-
posed author 55969, 87902
De Saussure, W. F. 27093, 27102, 87436,
87443 see also South Carolina. Con-
vention, 1860-1862. Committee on the
Address to the Southern States. Chairman.
Desaussure, Wilmot Gibbes, 1822-1866. 87907

De Sauvages de la Croix, Pierre Augustin de
Boissier. see Boissier de Sauvages de
la Croix, Pierre Augustin de.
De Sauvigny, Louis Edme Billardon. see
Billardon de Sauvigny, Louis Edme.
De Saxe, Maurice, Comte. see Saxe, Maurice,
Comte de, 1696-1750.
De Sayve, ---------, Comte. see Sayve,
-------, Comte de.
Desbarats, George E. (19684)
Desbarres, Joseph Frederick Wallet. 3606,
3608, 19685, 35969, 84697
Desbois, ------- Coupvent. see Coupvent-
Desbois, -------.
Desbordes-Valmore, Marceline. 19681
Desborow, Charles. 19686-19687
Des Brulons, Jacques Savary. see Savary des
Brulons, Jacques, 1677-1716.
De Scalona Aguero, Gaspar. see Aguero,
Gaspar de Escalona.
Descalves, Alonso. pseud. see Declaves,
Alonso. pseud.
Descalzo, Recoleto Augustino. see Juan de la
Concepcion. Fray
Descamps, Ant. Ign. 19688
Descant on the present state of the nation.
36949
Descant on the times. 40241
Descendant. pseud. Genealogical memoir. see
Rogers, Augustus Dodge.
Descendant. pseud. Proposals for publishing.
see Smyth, John Ferdinand Dalziel, 1745-
1814.
Descendant. pseud. Salkeld family of Penn-
sylvania. (75803)
Descendant. pseud. Tribute to the principles.
see Chambers, George.
Descendant of the Huguenots. pseud. Indians.
34659
Descendants of Chas. Norton. 55857
Descendants of Hans Hansen Bergen. 4845
Descendants of John Phoenix. (62583)
Descendants of John Read. 55020, (68173)
Descendants of Jonathan Padelford. 55020
Descendants of Joseph Loomis. 41953
Descendants of Lieut. William Pratt. (11980)
Descendants of Matthew Griswold. 28887
Descendants of Nathaniel Foote. (27948)
Descendants of Peter Hill of York County,
Maine. 58918
Descendants of Rev. John Lathrop. 39204
Descendants of Rev. Thomas Jenner. 36036
Descendants of Richard Gardner of Woburn.
26652, 28673
Descendants of Robert Chapman. 11979
Descendants of Samuel Hayward. (33261)
Descendants of the Rev. John Robinson. 72110
Descendants of Thomas Olcott. 27947
Descendants of William Ames. 1298
Descerpz, Francois. 19689, 86432
Deschamps, Isaac. defendant at impeachment
94546
Deschanel, Emile. 19690
Deschausse, Placide Augustin. 21482
De Schweinitz, Edmund Alexander, 1825-1887.
19691, 50520, 78101-78102
De Schweinitz, Lewis D. see Schweinitz,
Lewis David von, 1780-1834.
D'Escobar, Jerome. see Escobar, Jerome d'.
Descobrimento da America. 88803
Descobrimento da ilha da Madeira anno 1420.
679-680, 32051, 69287
Descourtilz, J. Theodore. 19692-19693
Descourtilz, Michael Etienne, 1775-1835.
19693-(19695)

Descourtilz, Michael Etienne, 1775-1835.
supposed author 3312, 75129
Descripcao da cidade do Porto. 17002
Descripcao da ilha de Itaparica. 88718
Descripcao das cartas da America Meridional.
(73500)
Descripcao fisica, historica, e politica. 11703
Descripcao topographico e politica do Rio de
S. Francisco. 11706
Descripcio de las funerales exequias, y sermon.
78766
Descripcion breve de la muy noble y leal
ciudad de Zacatecas. 4950, (71629),
76862
Descripcion breve de los svcessos examplares.
99388
Descripcion chorographica del terreno, rios,
arboles, y animales. 19696, (42598)
Descripcion de algunos objetos del Museo
Nacional de Antiguedades. 67642
Descripcion de cada uno de los departamentos
del estado del Salvador. 86961
Descripcion de Callao. 71450
Descripcion de diferentes piezas de historia
natural. 58835
[Descripcion] de Guayaquil. 71450
Descripcion de la Bahia de Santa Maria de
Galve. 80971
Descripcion de la Casa Fabricada en Lima.
19697, (49951)
Descripcion de la cordilleras de la America
Meridional. (49434)
Descripcion de la funcion dada en el mes de
Mayo del presente ano de 1826. 85721
Descripcion de la Iglesia parroquial de Ntra.
Sra. de Guadalupe. 29426
Descripcion de la isla y ciudad de Puerto-
Rico. 94352
Descripcion de la nueva provincia de Otuquis
en Bolivia. 2585, 57902
Descripcion de la prouincia de Cinaloa.
70789
Descripcion de la provincia de los Quixos.
40013
Descripcion de la provincia de Mato-Grosso.
6462
Descripcion de la serrania de Zacatecas.
9594
Descripcion de la solemnidad funebre. 58074
Descripcion de la solemnidad y aparatos.
106239
Descripcion de las demonstraciones. 67308
Descripcion de las fiestas que se hicieron en
la solemne dedicacion. 76790
Descripcion de las fiestas que hicieron los
Diputados de la ciudad de Tehuacan.
87154
Descripcion de las fiestas y corridas de toros.
75871
Descripcion de las funciones que con motivo de
la nueva constitucion han celebrado.
66586
Descripcion de las Indias Occidentales. 31539-
31541, 31546
Descripcion de las islas, y tierra firme del
mar oceano. 31545
Descripcion de las misiones. 94272
Descripcion de las provincias de el Peru.
8987
Descripcion de las provincias del Arzobispado
de la Plata. 15884
Descripcion de los costumbres y usos. 19698
Descripcion de los festivos aplausos. 24156
Descripcion de los ornatos. 73002
Descripcion de Patagonia. 23738
Descripcion de su presente estado moral
politico, intelectual &c. 96434

Descripcion de su presente estado, y esperanzas
de su condicion futura. 48582, 86434
Descripcion de su [i, e. Diego de Alvear's]
viage desde Buenos-Aires. 9190
Descripcion de todas las provincias. 6810,
(68338)
Descripcion del aerolito de Yanhuitlan. 42588
Descripcion del arco triunfal. (11443)
Descripcion del cemeterio general. 41096
Descripcion del feniz renacido. 75606
Descripcion del Rio Paraguay. 67347
Descripcion del seno da Sta. Maria de Galve.
80971
Descripcion e historia del Paraguay y del Rio
de la Plata. 2534
Descripcion en verse castellano. (75597)
Descripcion en verso de los dos terremotos.
93394
Descripcion exacta de las provincias de Vene-
zuela. 13147
Descripcion expressiva de la plausible pompa.
86441
Descripcion fiel de la demonstracion. 41097
Descripcion general de los reynos. 99686
Descripcion geografica de un nuevo camino.
87305
Descripcion geografica del Departamento de
Chiapas y Soconusco. 62929
Descripcion geografica del territorio.
70396
Descripcion geografica, historica, y estadistica
de Bolivia. 57452
Descripcion geografica, y derrotero de la
region Avstral Magallanica. (78960)
Descripcion geografica y estadistica de la
provincia de Santa Cruz de la Sierra.
99516
Descripcion geografica y pintoresca. 40741
Descripcion historial de la provincia y archipie-
lago de Chiloe. 524, 27822
Descripcion historica de la antigua provincia
del Paraguay. 49863
Descripcion historica del triunfo funebre.
29427
Descripcion historica y cronologica de las los
piedras. 40059-40060
Descripcion historia y moral. 24805
Descripcion historico de las cuatro milagrosas
imogenes. 21776, note after 99395
Descripcion historique d'un monstre symbolique.
19705
Descripcion orthographica universal. (40061)
Descripcion panegirica de la fvente qve en la
plaza mayor de Lima. 87240
Descripcion panegirica del nuevo templo de
Santa Teresa la Antigua. 76892
Descripcion sacro politica de las grandezas.
(21765)
Descripcion verdadera. 86440
Descripciones de plantas. 39091
Descripciones y laminas. 73993
Descriptio ac delineatio geographica detectionis
freti. 33490-33491, 67355
Descriptio admirandi itineris a Guillielmo
Schouten Hollando peracti. (8784)
Descriptio Americae excepta ex tabulis geo-
graphicis P. Bertij. (14350)-(14351),
31539-31543
Descriptio contracta navigationvm trium admiran-
darum, a Belgis. 77559
Descriptio Guineae. 41366
Descriptio Indiae Occidentalis. (8784), 31540,
44057
Descriptio mundi et totius orbis terrarum.
27583, 102623
Descriptio omnium quotquot in hunc usque
diem. (14350)-(14351), 31539-31543

Descriptio orbis & omnium ejus rerum publicarum. 41288
Descriptio orbis habitabilis. 65940-65941
Descriptio primi itineris. (8784)
Descriptio provinciae Moxitarum in regno Peruano. 21830, 44085
Descriptio terrae sanctae exactissima. 8150
Descriptio totivs Brasiliae. 3410
Descriptio totivs Gvineae tractvs. 19699, 41366
Descriptio uberior graminum et plantarum calamariarum. 51249
Description abregee de la Guyane Francaise. 39603
Description abregee de l'etat present de la Caroline Meridionale. 66723
Description abregee des Etats Unis de l'Amerique. 8001
Description abregee des possessions Angloises et Francoises. 58309
Description abregee des possessions des Anglois. 19700
Description abregee du territoire & gouvernment des Etats-Unis. 56908
Description and catalogue of the University of Michigan. 11962
Description and history of Newton. (32727)
Description and history of the island of Jamaica. 1427
Description and history of new sugar islands. 10231
Description and natural history of the islands. 12143
Description and use of the globes. 28783
Description and use of the sphaere. 105574
Description botanique du Chironthodendron, arbre de Mexique. 38678, 39092
Description breve de la muy noble y leal ciudad de Zacatecas. 4950, (71629)
Description de Buenos-Ayres. 9038, 9747
Description de cette grande partie du monde. 1295
Description de deux magnifiques aurores boreales. 63667
Description de la Brasil. 60988
Description de la cote du Perou. (39103)
Description de la France Eqvinoctiale. (38403)
Description de la Grande Java. 68455
Description de la Guyane Francaise. 39604
Description de la Louisiane. 19616, (31347)
Description de la Louisiane nouvellement decouverte. (31348)
Description de la Nouvelle-Californie geographique, politique et morale. 24198
Description de la Nouuelle Espagne. (27748)-27749
Description de la Pensylvanie & de Philadelphia sa capitale. 12554, note after 99431, 1st note after 100838
Description de la province de Guatemala. 94853
Description de la reprise de la ville de S. Salvador. (76213)
Description de l'admirable voyage de Guillaume Schouten Hollandois. 77947
Description de l'Amerique. 5014
Description de l'Amerique en Arabe. (19703A)
Description de l'Amerique et des Indes Occidentales. 19703
Description de l'Amerique & des parties d'icelle. 19701, 41372-(41373), 49497
Description de l'Amerique Meridionale. (19702), 6th note after 97689

Description de l'empire du Pretre-Jean. 36944, 68430
Description de l'isle de la Jamaique. 4937A, 36944, 68430
Description de l'isle de la Jamaique et des differents objets. 62946
Description de l'isthme de Darien. (58403)
Description de l'univers. 44130
Description de Nieuw Netherland. (36143)
Description de Quebec et de ses environs en 1608. 10620
Description de todas las provincias. 6810
Description de tout l'univers. (76721)
Description de toutes les parties du monde. 44159
Description de toutes les plants des forets. (66234)
Description del reyno de Chile. 63969
Description des anchorages. 18655
Description des anciennes mines d'Espagne. 17176
Description des animaux, des chasses, des danses, des jeux. 11776-11777
Description des animaux, plantes, fruits, et autres curiosities. 24114
Description des cinq parties de la terre. (77481)
Description des cotes de l'Amerique Meridionale. 73498-73499
Description des cotes orientales de l'Amerique du Nord. 6028
Description des cotes, rades, harvres, rochers, bas-fonds, isles, caps, aiguades, criques, anses. 72757-(72758), note after 93778
Description des crustaces nouveaux de la cote occidentale du Mexique. 77206
Description des debouquemens qui sont au nord de l'isle de Saint-Domingue. 4552, 75103
Description des especes de silures du Suriname. 5900
Description des Indes Occidentales, contenant dix-huict liures. (38558)
Description des Indes Occidentales, qu'on appelle aujourdhuy le Novveau Monde. (14352), 31543
Description des isles et terres du roi d' Angleterre. (5969), 57158
Description des isles et terres que l'Angleterre possede. 5970
Description des merveilles d'une partie de l'Asie. 68443
Description des moeurs, coutumes, et usages. 6899
Description des moeurs, & des prouinces de tous les sauuages. 7133
Description des monuments de l'Ohio. 12272
Description des pays arroses par la Mississipi. 14460
Description des pays moeurs des habitans richesses des forces le gouvernement la religion et le princes. 19704
Description des plantes de l'Amerique. 36455
Description des plantes principales de l'Amerique Septentrionale. 12135
Description des possessions Neerlandaises dans la Guyane. 4737
Description des principales especes nouvelles de la flore du Bresil. (75217)
Description des prisons de Gand, Philadelphia, Ilchester, and Milbank. (17963)
Description des quartres parties du monde. (1460)

Description des ruins decouvertes pres de Palenque. 68443
Description des ses quatre parties. 18911-18912
Description des terres Magellaniques et des pays adjacens. 23737
Description du Bresil. 66879
Description du filon et des mines de Veta-Grande. 9276
Description du gouvernement du Perou. 68455
Description du Kentucky et de Genesy. 7802
Description du marveillevx voyage de Gvilliavme Schovten. 77948-77951
Description du Mississippi. 6335
Description dv penible voyage fait entovr de l'vnivers ov globe terrestre. 55436, (55438)
Description du royaume de Juda. 28273
Description du royaume de Quito. 94853
Description du sol. 18176
Description du Texas. 95076
Description du Tombechbe. 29395, 95072
Description d'un meteore. 62680
Description d'un recueil exquis d'animaux rares. 100783
Description d'un volcan eteint. 77205
Description d'un voyage au Bresil. (47023), 47024
Description d'une nouvelle espece qui doit porte le nom d'Hypnoides. 75235
Description en vers. 7715
Description et colonisation de l'isthme de Tehuantepec. 27471
Description et histoire naturelle du Groenland. 22027
Description, &c. of the Molucco and Philippine Islands. 91538
Description ethnographique des peuples de la Russe. (59233)
Description exacte de la pesche de molues. 19615
Description exacte des objets precieux. 78689
Description exacte des regions & des lieux. 12010, 32022
Description from the Franklin journal. 93519
Description generale de l'Amerique. 18911-18912, 26858, note after 69259
Description generale de l'Europe. 8000
Description generale des costes de l'Amerique. 18654
Description generale, historique, geographique, et physique de la colonie de Surinam. (24112), 24117
Description, geographical, historical, and topographical. 15169, 29080
Description geographique de debouquemens qui sont au nord de l'isle de Saint Dominque. 4552
Description geographique de la Guyane. 4551
Description geographique de l'Amerique Septentrionale. 4550
Description geographique des isles Antilles. (4553)
Description geographique et historique des costes de l'Ameriqve Septentrionale. 19615
Description geographique et historique du Bresil. 101357
Description geographique et pittoresque. 44172
Description geographique et statistique de la Confederation Argentine. 44923
Description geographique, politique et civile du Paraguay. 2541
Description geographie, politique et historique du royaume de Paraguay. 58516

Description geologique du Chili. 12763
Description historica de las cuatro milagrosas imagens. (24140)
Description historique d'un monstre symbolique. 48226
Description nautique de la cote du Labrador. (46929)
Description nautique des cotes de la Martinique. 50001
Description novvelle des merveilles de ce mo[n]de. 58825
Description of a cheap, durable rail road. 93528
Description of a direct route for the Erie Canal. 67807
Description of a good character. 30637
Description of a great sea-storm. 19706
Description of a new chart of history. 65504
Description of a new genus and new species. 27665
Description of a new genus of the family Melaniana. 39487
Description of a new genus . . . of the family Melanidae. (39496)
Description of a new mollusk. (39496)
Description of a new species of Triquetra. (39496)
Description of a new sub-genus of Naiades. (39496)
Description of a plantation. 75908
Description of a prison. 53642
Description of a railroad route. 19083
Description of a rare Scarabaeus. 25434
Description of a sub-marine aqueduct. 93520
Description of a view of . . . New York. 54242
Description of a view of the city of Quebec. 67001
Description of a view of the falls of Niagara. 9218, (55114)
Description of a view of the north coast of Spitzbergen. 89540
Description of a visit to the West Indies. 30932
Description of active and extinct volcanos. (18660)
Description of all the circvmnavigations of the globe. 66686
Description of all the parts of the world. 44166
Description of American land shells. 5500
Description of an hermaphrodite orang-outang. (30393)
Description of an invention for aerial navigation. 28465
Description of ancient and modern coins. 85581
Description of an ancient sepulchral mound near Newark, Ohio. 44757
Descriptions of ancient works in Ohio. 103822
Description of, and critical remarks on the picture of Christ healing the sick. 72116
Description of, and specific for, a religious hydrophobia. 14083, 91834
Description of and statement of the property of the East Boston Company. 6699
Description of Banvard's geographical painting. 3224
Description of Banvard's panorama of the Mississippi River. 3223
Description of Bayne's gigantic panorama. 4083
Description of Boston. 85489
Description of British Guiana. (77782)
Description of Brunswick in letters by a gentleman of South Carolina. 66803

Description of Callao and Lima before their destruction. (42593), 97102

Description of Calycophyllum Stanleyanum. note after 77796

Description of Calyo's panorama of the Connecticut River. 10094

Description of Canadian lake and river scenery. 10628

Description of central Iowa. (34984)

Description of Christ's navy in New England. 52628

Description of Clifton, Staten Island, and the narrows. 13700

Description of Col. Long's bridges. 41886

Description of Deerfield. 20071

Description of Don Pedro Hibbert. (51797)

Description of each state and territory in the union. (49716)

Description of East and West Florida. 47428

Description of East-Florida. 92222

Description of fair virtue. 39820

Description of Fulton Market House. 54243

Description of Georgia. 27037

Description of Greenland. (22028)-22029

Description of Greenland, 1553-1622. 66686

Description of Guinea. 66686

Description of Gunae Island, &c. 19707

Description of improved farms in the state of Tennessee. 94791

Description of insects. 77381

Description of its [i. e. Boston's] Cochituate Water Works. 7277

Description of its [i. e. Jefferson County, Missouri's] products. 35942

Description of J. Souther's patent self-operating fire extinguisher. 88267

Description of Kansas. (22474), (37026), 37054

Description of Kentucky. (19708), 96327

Description of Keokuk. 68649

Description of . . . Lawrence, Van Buren County . . . Iowa. 39387

Description of light houses. 19709

Description of Louisiana. (79995), (80023)

Description of Maj. Dades massacre. 3579

Description of Marshpee. 25767

Description of Massachusetts. 106052

Description of Master Robert Evelin. 19724, 63310

Description of . . . medals strucks. 47266

Description of Mero District. (13299)

Description of Messrs. Marshall's grand peristrephic panorama. 89541

Description of mineral-bearing rocks. 77762

Description of Mr. Healy's picture. 31172

Description of Mount Auburn Cemetery. 30209

Description of New Brighton, on Staten Island. 101296

Description of New England. 82815-82816, 82819-82821, 82823-82824, 82855, 91853

Description of New England in general. 52629

Description of New-England. Published by John Seller. (79026)

Description of New-Found-Land. 103332

Description of New Netherland in 1642-3. (36142)

Description of new North American Insects. 77376

Description of new species of Coleoptera from California. 39666

Description of new species of Coleopterous Insects. (77377)

Description of new species of Curculionites of North America. 77378

Description of new species of fossils. 43003

Description of new species of Hymenoptera. (77379)

Description of . . . New York. 72464

Description of North-America. 19710

Description of north and south Guinea and Angola. 13015

Description of northern Wiskonsan [sic]. 8760

Description of Nova Scotia. (49760)

Description of Ohio. 58360

Description of one hundred cities. 19713

Description of one hundred thousand acres of oil. 19711

Description of Oregon and California. 9999, 19712

Description of Patagonia. 23734, 49894

Description of Peale's portrait of Washington. 101794

Description of Pensylvania and Philadelphia. 99429, note after 100822

Description of persons and events connected with Canadian Methodism. 11076, note before 89147

Description of Peru. (42593), 97102

Description of Peter Plancius's universal map. 6024

Description of Pitcairn's Island and its inhabitants. 3663

Description of plan for the improvement of Fairmount Park. 61650

Description of Prince Edward Island. 10116

Description of remains of extinct mammalia and Chelonia. 39903

Description of several cases of disease. 95605

Description of several new and interesting animals. (29607)

Description of several Spanish territories in America. 55068

Description of shells from the Gulf of California. 28089

Description of Siberia, Samoieda, and Tingoesia, 1612. 66686

Description of singing birds. 86947

Description of Smith's patent street-sweeping machines. 83846

Description of some grasses and sedges. note after 77796

Description of some new fossil shells. 39485

Description of some new species of organic remains. (51024)

Description of South Carolina. 27572, note after 87817

Description of southern plants. 18525

Description of Tartaria. 66686

Description of that adorable personage, Jesus Christ. 91817

Description of that part of New France. 40175-40176, 57765

Description of the American electro magnetic telegraph. 98292

Description of the American marine rail-way. 93521

Description of the American yellow fever. 12837, 41333

Description of the animal and vegetable productions. 44717

Description of the antiquities discovered in the western country. 2332, (2336)

Description of the Bay Todos los Santos in Brazil. 66686

Description of the Bermudas or Somers' Islands. (24357)

Description of the book presented to General La Fayette. 38583

Description of the Borough of Reading. 90089

Description of the Boston Water Works.
32446

Description of the botanical character. 5310

Description of the bounty lands in the state of
Illinois. 18407

Description of the Brattleboro' Hydropathic
Establishment. (7443)

Description of the British possessions in North
America. 19714, 47429

Description of the business of Nashua and
Nashville. (37760)

Description of the Butler Hospital for the
Insane. 68024

Description of the canals and rail roads.
94316

Description of the cartoon of Sebastian Cabot.
9804

Description of the Champlain Canal. 99559

Description of the ceremony of dedication of
the statue. 78826

Description of the characters and habits of
Troglodytes Gorilla. 77249

Description of the cities, townships, . . . and
settlements. 54244

Description of the City Hospital of Boston.
(6692)

Description of the city of Boston. 58245

Description of the city of New-York; containing
its population. 30319

Description of the city of New York: with a
brief account. 32533

Description of the city of Philadelphia. 12553,
2d note after 99428

Description of the climate, soil, production and
advantages. 26651

Description of the coast. (19715)

Description of the conflagration of the theatre
at Richmond. 71173

Description of the country, and a particular
account of the Scots colony. 18549,
18571, 78211-78213, 78234

Description of the country—its soil—climate &
resources. 58852

Description of the country of the Mississippi.
26144

Description of the Convention of the People of
Ohio. 56930

Description of the Croton Aqueduct. 36071

Description of the Daily Evening Traveler
Building. 6515

Description of the dedication of the monument.
(29878)

Description of the designs. 33888

Description of the different routes to California.
(9991)

Description of the district of Maine. 16919

Description of the Dowse Library. 20793

Description of the eastern coast of the county
of Barnstable. 18895, (25762)

Description of the Eastern Penitentiary of
Pennsylvania. 74612

Description of the elephant tortoise. (30393)

Description of the Elizabeth Islands. (22194)

Description of the empires, kingdoms, states,
and colonies. 62959

Description of the English and French territories. 19716

Description of the English plantations in
America. 15046

Description of the English province of Carolana.
[sic] (17278)-17281, 25853

Description of the Esquimeaux. 62509

Description of the fishes inhabiting the waters.
32455

Description of the forest trees indigenous to
the United States. (8649)

Description of the forest trees of the United
States. 48694-48695, 56351

Description of the fossils and shells collected
in California. 5802

Description of the four parts of the world.
19717-19718

Description of the four pictures. 97246

Description of the Franklin medallion. 28982

Description of the Genese country. 53643,
104441

Description of the Genesee country, in the state
of New York. 50009, 51355, 99573

Description of the Genesee country, its rapidly
progressive population and improvements.
53643, 104441

Description of the genus Pinus, illustrated with
figures. 38727

Description of the genus Pinus, with descriptions.
(38726)

Description of the geology of . . . New Jersey.
53114

Description of the geology of the state of New
Jersey. 72656

Description of the Girard College for Orphans.
27493, 101199

Description of the gold box. 37597

Description of the golden islands. (19719)

Description of the grand fete given at Washington Hall. 38583

Description of the great and last judgment.
103915-103916

Description of the great tree. 19720

Description of the great Tulare Valley. 11084

Description of the Great Western Canal. 19721

Description of the great western lakes. 8558

Description of the hereticks and sectaries.
31483

Description of the Hydrarchos Harlani. 38193

Description of the hydraulic power. 104021

Description of the Incas of Peru. 19722

Description of the indigenous and naturalized
plants. (3857)

Description of the influence of the slavery
party. 46842

Description of the insects of North America.
77371

Description of the iron lands. 75421

Description of the island of Cape Breton.
10729

Description of the island of Jamaica. 5966-
5967, note after 41144

Description of the island of Nevis. 74598

Description of the . . . island of St. Domingo.
(47566)

Description of the island of St. John. 75278

Description of the jail distemper. 85232

Description of the land and fresh water shells.
77380

Description of the lands and mines of the
Great Western Copper Mining Co. of
Lake Superior. 25248

Description of the largest ship in the world.
(28462), 43360

Description of the last judgment. 59479

Description of the last voyage to Bermudas.
30354

Description of the leading firms. 27621

Description of the Malone Quarry. (44144)

Description of the Mammouth Cave in Kentucky.
7763, (19723)

Description of the Maryland Marble Company.
45229

Description of the medals of Washington.
85582

Description of the Mexican people and country.
78306

Description of the mine of Potozi. 101116

Description of the Missourium, or Missouri Leviathan. 38194

Description of the Missourium Theristocaulodon. 38195

Description of the Mount Vernon School in 1832. 51181

Description of the Murichi. 77783

Description of the natives. 104465

Description of the new and flourishing city of Cincinnati. 9139

Description of the new Ledger Building. 61578

Description of the new school house. 4720

Description of the New World. 26659

Description of the New York Central Park. (54155)

Description of the New-York Croton Aqueduct. 77967

Description of the numerical telegraph, etc. 14411

Description . . . of the Oakland and Ottawa Railroad. 56390

Description of the observatory. 6288

Description of the Panama and Nicaragua routes. 9971

Description of the panorama of the suberb city of Mexico. 9137, 9219, 48420

Description of the Persian monarchy now being. 31471

Description of the Philipsburg Estate. 62461

Description of the picture of the home of Washington. 73425

Description of the physical geography of California. 25842

Description of the piers of the new railroad bridges. 50027

Description of the Pittsburgh and Baltimore Coal, Coke & Iron Co's lands. 63124

Description of the plans for a new building for the Congressional Library. 84980

Description of the positive self-graduating warp delivery motion. 85384

Description of the Prattsville Tannery. 64983

Description of the present state of that country. 2172

Description of the present system of bank note engraving. 57634

Description of the principal cities of the island of Cuba and of Mexico. 84768

Description of the principal establishments. 40973

Description of the principal fruits of Cuba. 28089, 28681

Description of the principal paintings in Mr. Vanderlyn's exhibition. 98483

Description of the principles and plan of proposed establishments. 24066

Description of the property and mine. (63205)

Description of the province and bay of Darien. 5705, 78214

Description of the province and city of New York. 49026, (80023)

Description of the province of New Albion. 19724, 59667, 63310-63311

Description of the province of New Sweden. 10203

Description of the province of South Carolina. 66724

Description of the province of VVest-Jersey in America. 59692, 102942

Description of the purtrayture and shape of those strange kinde of people. 79343

Description of the railroad across the Blue Ridge at Rock Fish Gap. 22209

Description of the recently discovered petroleum region. 10000, 81051

Description of the reptiles inhabiting the United States. (32453)-32454

Description of the Reveille quartz lode in Humboldt. 81052

Description of the river Saguenay. 42527

Description of the river Susquehanna. 93935

Description of the roads in the United States. (19725), 47437

Description of the rock formations. 21702, (53688), 3d note after 98549

Description of the Rock River country in northwestern Illinois. 72412

Description of the ruins of an ancient city. 71446

Description of the scenery. (53844)

Description of the Schuylkill County Prison. 78074

Description of the seat of war. 47437

Description of the settlement of the Genesee country. 59284, 104442, 104444

Description of the shortest and only all rail road route to Kansas. 15054

Description of the silver mines in Huantajaya, in Peru. 33414

Description of the situation, climate, soil and productions. (43923)

Description of the sliding-rule. 24459

Description of the soil, productions, commercial, agricultural and local advantages of the Georgia western territory. 50934

Description of the south Indies. 29820

Description of the Spanish islands. (35959)-(35960), 102830

Description of the spirituall temple. 17060

Description of the springs. 29214, 2d note after 100478

Description of the state capitol of Tennessee. 18540

Description of the state of Tenasee. [sic] (34358)

Description of the strategic plans. 24586

Description of the sword. 80412

Description of the teeth of a new fossil animal. (27281)

Description of the Tennessee State Capitol. 51871

Description of the terraqueous globe. 18736

Description of the town and harbour of Boston. 6516

Description of the Tremont House. 22178A

Description of the unique exhibition. 9138

Description of the United States lands in Iowa. 104241

Description of the universal mappes and cardes. 6022

Description of the various silver ores and minerals. 5803

Description of the water power. 23328

Description of the West Indies. 66686

Description of the West-Indies. A poem, in four books. 81424-81425

Description of the western territory. 34357

Description of the whole world. 23646

Description of the Windward Passage. 19726, 24857

Description of the Wisconsin Territory. 8125, 104885

Description of . . . the world. 44165

Description of the world, in all its kingdoms. 50535

Description of three hundred animals. 19727

Description of three new meteoric irons. 83003

Description of Trenton Falls. 80366

Description of Trinidad, Guiana, and the river of Orenoco in 1602. 66686

DESCRIPTION

Description of true religion. (78282)
Description of twenty-five new species of
exotic Uniones. (39496)
Description of twenty-six counties of south-
west Missouri. 55164
Description of two islands in the South Sea.
(77892)-77893
Description of two new species of fossil shells.
(51024)
Description of upper Louisiana. 7207
Description of valuable coal, iron ore, lumber,
and farm lands. 86814
Description of views in South America. 57943
Description of Virginia. 4889
Description of Virginia by Captaine Iohn Smith.
82832
Description of Virginia, New Netherland, New
England and the islands of Bermuda.
5045
Description of Washington monument. 3033
Description of Wier's cave. 36460
Description of William Wells Brown's original
panoramic views. 8591
Description of Wisconsin, Illinois, and Iowa.
18069
Description of works relating to America
published between the years 1492 and
1551. 24933, 30599
Description of works relating to America
published between the years 1492 and 1551.
Additions. 30600
Description of Wyer's Cave, Augusta, Va.
16343
Description partiallere de l'Asie. 16930
Description statistique, historique et politique.
101358
Description succincte du Tombechbe. 29395,
95072
Description succincte, naturelle et mediciale
de l'etat de la Louisiane. 25292
Description succincte des terres dont les
Jesuites Espagnoles se sont empares.
7458
Description topographique de la province du
Bas Canada. 6850
Description topographique de la Virginie.
(34055)
Description topographique de six cents acres
de terres. 19728
Description topographique et politique de la
partie Espagnole de l'isle Saint-Domingue.
50570
Description topographique, physique, civille,
politique et historique de la partie
Francaise de Saint-Domingue. 50571
Description what God, &c. (72095)
Descriptione terrae Samoiedarum & Tingoe-
siorum. 33490-33491, 67355
Desc. Terrae Sanctae. 1553
Descriptionem trivm itinervm nobillissimi et
fortissimi eqvitis Francisci Draken.
(8784)
Descriptiones et icones graminum in America
et in insulis Philippinis et Marianis
collectiae. 65360
Descriptiones, et icones plantarum Peruvianarum,
et Chilensium. 73995
Descriptiones plantarum praesertim Americae
Meridionalis. 98287
Descriptiones plantarum quarundam Surinamen-
sium. 73442
Descriptionis Ptolemaicae augmentum. 105699
Descriptionis Ptolemaicae augmentum, siue
occidentis notitae breui commentario
illustrata. 105697-105698

Descriptionis Ptolemaicae avgmentvm, siue
occidentis notitia breui commentario
illustrata sutdio et opera. 105696
Descriptions and a historical sketch. 54154
Descriptions and figures of new and little-
known species. 5410
Descriptions and figures of the eggs of North
American birds. (7760)
Descriptions and notices of some of the land
shells of Cuba. 28089
Descriptions by ――――― Perkins. 29219
Descriptions et d'anecdotes sur la vie militaire
et politique de Georges Washington.
4022
Descriptions et figures des coquilles du nord
de l'Amerique. 77375
Descriptions et figures de toutes les especes
et varietes de chenes. 48691
Descriptions geographical, statistical, and
historical. 14784
Descriptions of ancient works in Ohio. 85072
Descriptions of designs for the Central Park.
(54155)
Descriptions of eight new species of Unionidae.
(39496)
Descriptions of five new species of Anodontae.
39487
Descriptions of four new species of exotic
Uniones. (39496)
Descriptions of invertebrates. 34253
Descriptions of Leutze's picture. (19919)
Descriptions of new fossils. 80765
Descriptions of new North American Coleopter-
ous insects. 77382
Descriptions of new organic remains. Collected
in Nebraska Territory. 47370
Descriptions of new organic remains from
north-western Kansas. (47371)
Descriptions of new species and genera of
fossils. (47371)
Descriptions of new species of Heteropterous
Hemiptera. 77383
Descriptions of new species of mollusca and
shells. 17195
Descriptions of new species of North American
insects. (77384)
Descriptions of new species of Pupadae. 50915
Descriptions of new species of shells. (39496)
Descriptions of new species of the family
Unionidae. 39490
Descriptions of Niagara. 3378
Descriptions of plants. 34253
Descriptions of plants collected by Col. J. C.
Fremont. 85072, 96297
Descriptions of portions of the collection.
5806
Descriptions of Puerto Bello and the island
Cuba. 97661
Descriptions of remarkable manufactories at
the present time. 5606
Descriptions of Russia, Catay, etc. 66686
Descriptions of several new discovered coun-
tries. 4246
Descriptions of shells and mollusks. (28085)
Descriptions of six new species of the genus
Unio. (39496)
Descriptions of some new and interesting in-
sects. 39666
Descriptions of some new terrestrial and
fluviatile shells. 77385
Descriptions of species based chiefly on the
collections. 2805
Descriptions of the insects of North America.
77369-77370
Descriptions of the most common plants in the
middle and northern states. 15075

Descriptions of the shells of North America. 77368

Descriptions of twelve new species of Unioniadae. (39496)

Descriptions of twenty-seven new species of Uniones. (39496)

Descriptions of vertebrates. 34253

Descriptionum et iconum rariores et pro maxima parte. 73441

Descriptionum plantarum praefectura Fluminensi. 98833

Descriptive account of my collection. 25567, 91509-91511

Descriptive account of the city of Peoria. 60831

Descriptive account of the discipline. 89056

Descriptive account of the island of Jamaica. 4248

Descriptive account of the island of Trinidad. 44131

Descriptive account of the remains of land animals. 18950

Descriptive and historical view of Burr's moving mirror. 9444

Descriptive and moral. 1692, 63577

Descriptive and statistical account of Canada. 72877

Descriptive and statistical account of the British empire. 43126

Descriptive book of the tour of Europe. 83008

Descriptive catalogue. 83991

Descriptive catalogue (in part) of the fishes of New Brunswick and Nova Scotia. 60982

Descriptive catalogue of a collection of the economical minerals. 41813

Descriptive catalogue of books and pamphlets. 29736

Descriptive catalogue of books in the iron safe. 56123

Descriptive catalogue of Catlin's Indian collection. (11534)

Descriptive catalogue of flags. 53644

Descriptive catalogue of Friends' books. 25362, 83307-83308, 83312-83313

Descriptive catalogue of fruit and ornamental trees, . . . at the Wachusett Nurseries. 52481

Descriptive catalogue, of fruit and ornamental trees, shrubs, vines, plants, &c. 65621

Descriptive catalogue of Mexican antiquities. 48420

Descriptive catalogue of minerals. 46990

Descriptive catalogue of . . . minerals . . . sent to the London . . . Exhibition for 1862. 26986

Descriptive catalogue of . . . premiums! 17646

Descriptive catalogue of strawberries. 65621

Descriptive catalogue of the books in the library. 75354

Descriptive catalogue of the collection of flags. (76646)

Descriptive catalogue of the fishes of Nova Scotia. (38127)

Descriptive catalogue of the known species of tanagers. 78145

Descriptive catalogue of the Nova Scotia Department for the International Exhibition. (56124)

Descriptive catalogue of the pictures, . . . from the most celebrated masters. 50963

Descriptive catalogue of the tracts published by the South Carolina Tract Society. 88045C

Descriptive catalogue of the Warren Anatomical Museum. 30741

Descriptive catalogue of those maps, charts, and surveys. 38212

Descriptive catalogue of . . . trees. (17421)

Descriptive circular, of the Columbia Springs. 14851

Descriptive essays contributed to the Quarterly review. 31142

Descriptive guide. 55040, 2d note after 94219

Descriptive handbook of America. 2648

Descriptive, historical, and geographical account of the dominions of Spain. 6333

Descriptive, historical, chemical and therapeutical analysis. (75796)

Descriptive key, to accompany the "Outline map of New England." 5936

Descriptive legend. 64623

Descriptive letter press to accompany the engraving. (63475)

Descriptive list of carboniferous plants. 18954

Descriptive narrative of the wonderful petrification of a man. 19350

Descriptive notices, by Cornelia W. Walter. 51149, 74169

Descriptive notices [of Greenwood Cemetery.] 28700

Descriptive pamphlet of Smith's leviathan panorama. 83009

Descriptive poem, representing the voyage to America. 55526

Descriptive poem, written at Quebec, 1805. (10370)

Descriptive poems. (43460)

Descriptive sketch of Philadelphia, for 1832. 61579

Descriptive sketch of the present state of Vermont. 28229

Descriptive sketch of West Point. 92904

Descriptive sketches and statistics of Cuba. (17769)

Descriptive sketches of Nova Scotia. 25420

Descriptive sketches of the natural history. 97657

Descriptive tale. 96083, note after 105147

Descriptive work of the business metropolis of Indiana. (71858)

Descrittione compendiosa della Prusia. 67738

Descrittione del mappamondo. (64149)

Descrittione dell' America, o dell' India Occidentale. 66506

Descrittione dell' isola d'Elandia. 64151

Descrittione dell' isola et terra di Santa Croce. (64149)

Descrittione dell' Istria. 64151

Descrittione della geografia vniversale con tavole qvarantadve. 66507

Descrittione della gran citta e isola Temistitan. (64149)

Descrittione della Sarmatia Evropea. 67738

Descrittione delle provincie ouer Palatinati di Lituania. 67738

Descrittione di tvtta Italia. 659

Descrittione di tvtto'l mondo terreno al piv moderno stile del nostro tempo. 66506

Descrizione dell' entrata della Sereniss. Reina Giouanna d'Austria. (47453)

Decrizione del viaggio a Rio de Janeiro. 72508

Descrizione della Lvigiana. 31356

Descrizione delle Pensilvania e di Filadelfia sua capitale. (12555)

Descrizione geografica, politica, istorica del regno del Paraguay. 51424, (58517)

Descrizzione di tutta Italia. 660

Descubes, Paul. 19729

Descubierto el caracter de la pluma impia.
87216
Descubrimiento de America. 17543
Descubrimiento de America por los Normandos.
67476
Descubrimiento de la aguja nautica. 58993
Descubrimiento de los terros y riquezas.
19730
Descubrimiento del camino que la ciudad de
Quit. 98790
Descubrimiento y conquista de la America.
10298
Descvbridores, conqvistadores, y pacificadores
del Puvlento. (63189)
Desdunes, ------- Rossignol. see Rossignol
Desdunes, --------.
De Seabra da Silva, Jose. see Silva, Jose de
Seabra da.
De Segovia, Gaspar Ibanez. see Ibanez de
Segovia, Gaspar.
De Seguin, Pascasio. see Seguin, Pascasio
de.
De Segur, Louis Gaston. see Segur, Louis
Gaston de.
De Segur, Comte Louis Philippe. see
Segur, Louis Philippe, Comte de, 1753-
1832.
De Segur-Dupeyron, P. see Segur-Dupeyron,
P. de.
De Segura, Nicolas. see Segura, Nicolas de.
De Seixas, Manuel Justiniano. see Seixas,
Manuel Justiniano de.
De Seixas, Romualdo Antonio. see Seixas,
Romualdo Antonio de, Abp.
De Seixas y Lovera, Francisco. see Seixas
y Lovera, Francisco de.
De Selys-Longchamps, Walthere. see Selys-
Longchamps, Walthere de.
De Semalle, Rene. see Semalle, Rene de.
Desempenar con todo el llego de las leyes.
100903
De Sena, Manuel Garcia. see Garcia de Sena,
Manuel.
Desengano a los indios, haciendoles ver lo que
deben a los Espanoles. 98254
Desengano a los pueblos de Bresil. 7696
Desengano de falsas imposturas. 96188
Desengano del hombre. (66618)
Desenganos que a los insurgentes de N. Espana
seducidos. 24146, 60902, 76217
Desenhos dos vegetaes. (75618)
De Senovert, ------. see Senovert, -------
de.
De Sentmanat, Antonio. see Sentmanat,
Antonio, Cardinal de.
Deseos patrioticos de un Habanero. 1878
De Sept-Fontaines, H. C. Emmery. see
Emmery de Sept-Fontaines, H. C.
De Septenville, Edouard. see Septenville,
Edouard de.
De Sepulveda, Gines. see Sepulveda, Gines
de.
De Sequeira, Gabriel Claudio. see Sequeira,
Gabriel Claudio de.
De Sequeira e Sa, Manoel Tavares. see
Sequeira e Sa, Manoel Tavares de.
Deseret. see also Utah.
Deseret. Constitution. 98219-98220
Deseret. Constitutional Convention, 1849.
98219-98220
Deseret. Laws, statutes, etc. 98220-98221
Deseret. Legislature. 98219
Deseret evening news. 83038
Deseret first book. 83050
Deseret news. 83163, 83245, 83259, 83283
Deseret news extra. 83163, 83259, 83283

Deseret second book. 83050
Deseret sunday school catechism no. 1. 83281
Deseret Sunday School Union, Salt Lake City.
83281 see also Church of Jesus Christ
of Latter-Day Saints.
De Serionne, Joseph Accarias. see Accarias
de Serionne, Joseph, 1706-1792.
De Serqueira, Thomas Jose Pinto. see
Serqueira, Thomas Jose Pinto de.
Desert. (69035)
Desert and the promised land. 29625
Desert et le monde sauvage. 44250
Desert home. 69036-69037, 69039
Deserted bride; and other poems. 50821
Deserter. 86927
Deserter's daughter. 31580
Deserts de l'Amerique Septentrionale. (12573)
De Servantes Carabajal, Juan Leonel. see
Servantes Carabajal, Juan Leonel de.
De Servantes Causas, Beatris Bernardina
(De Andrada) see Servantes Causas,
Beatris Bernardina (De Andrada) de.
De Servastanoff, Pierre. see Servastanoff,
Pierre de.
Des Essars, ------- de Vieufville. see
Viefville des Essars, ------ de.
Des Essarts, Alfred Stanislaus Langlois, 1811-
1893? 19732, 20007
De Sesse, Josepe. see Sesse, Josepe de.
Desestanco del tabaco. 72792
Deseves, F. X. supposed author 58495, 94638
Desfosses, -------- Romain. see Romain-
Desfosses, --------.
Desfourneaux, -------. 59480
Desgeorge, -------. 19733
Desgranges, J. Poisle. see Poisle Desgranges,
J.
Desgraz, C. (21224)
Desgrifiad o diriogaeth Wisconsin. 104886
Desha, Isaac B. defendant 19734, note after
95447
Desha, Joseph, 1768-1842. 37548 see also
Kentucky. Governor, 1824-1828 (Desha)
Deshalles, --------. 19735
De Sibouette, -------. see Sibouette, -------
de.
Desiderius. 46282
De Siebold, Philipp Franz. see Siebold,
Philipp Franz von, 1796-1866.
De Sierra, Jose. see Sierra, Jose de.
De Sierragorda, ---------, Conde. see
Sierragorda, ------, Conde de.
Design and advantages of the House of Refuge.
61729
Design and advantages of the South Sea trade.
19736, 97083
Design and benefits of instrumental musick.
42806
Design and blessedness of the Gospel. 71504
Design and duty of a church. 85279
Design and nature of atonement. 69569
Design and utility of free-masonry considered.
71505
Design for Fairmount Park. 77193
Design for the Butler Hospital for the Insane.
4471
Design of Jehovah in building the temple.
90205
Design of the Christian ministry. 91103
Design of the institution of the Gospel-ministry.
(28383)
Design, rights, and duties of local churches.
4329, 4344
Designs for a marine hospital. 19737
Designs for monuments and mural tablets.
82981

Designs for the gateways of the southern entrances to the Central Park. 33888

Designs for villas, cottages and farm houses. 82163

Designs of the Republican Party. (72061)

Designs of the southern conspirators and their northern allies. 19738

De Siguenza y Gongora, Carlos. see Siguenza y Gongora, Carlos de, 1645-1700.

De Siles, Francisco. see Siles, Francisco de.

De Silhouette, ------. see Silhouette, ------- de.

De Sillery, Stephanie Felicite Brulaert. see Sillery, Stephanie Felicite Brularet de, Comtesse de Genlis, 1746-1830.

De Silva, Juan. see Silva, Juan de.

De Silva Lisboa, Bento. see Lisboa, Bento de Silva.

Desilver, Robert. (19739), 61606, 84218

Desilver's annual almanac. (19739)

Desilver's Philadelphia directory and stranger's guide. 61606

Desilver's United States almanac. 84218

De Sinimbu, Joao Lins Vieira Cansancao, Visconde. see Sinimbu, Joao Lins Vieira Cansancao, Visconde de, 1810-1906.

Desirableness of the divine providence with civil rulers. 24529

Desirade. 101350

Desireable man describ'd. 46282

Desires and wishes of England. 78372-(78373), 78379, 2d note after 100788

Desires of piety. 46457

Desires that Joshua's resolution may be revived. (79411)

De Sismondi, Jean Charles Leonard Simonde. see Sismondi, Jean Charles Leonard Simonde de, 1773-1842.

Desjardins, Ernest. 19740-19741

Desjardins, G. 19742

Des Kaskaskia, H. see Kaskaskia, H. des.

Deslandes, ------. 19743

Deslandes, Andre Francois Boureau, 1690-1757. 19744

Deslisle de la Drevetiere, Louis Francois. 13616, 2d note after 96139

Deslonchamps, Eugene Eudes. see Eude Deslonchamps, Eugene, 1830-1889.

Des Lozieres, Louis Narcisse Baudry. see Baudry des Lozieres, Louis Narcisse.

Desmadryl, Narciso. illus. 49757

Desmarest, --------. ed. 78689

Desmarquet, Jean Antoine Samson. 44668, 47541

Desmaulants, J. B. (19745), note after 93825

D'Esmenard, J. B. see Esmenard, Jean Baptiste d', 1772-1824.

De Smet, Peter John. see Smet, Peter John de, 1801-1872.

Des Minieres, Ernest Bellot. see Bellot des Minieres, Ernest.

Des Moines County, Iowa. Hawk-Eye Pioneer Association. see Hawk-Eye Pioneer Association, Des Moines Co., Iowa.

Des Moines Navigation and Railroad Company. 19748

Des Moines register. 84786

Des Moines River land grant. 19747

Desmon. pseud. Old Toney and his master. 82029

Des Murs, O. 19749, 21354

Desnos, Pierre Joseph Odolant. see Odolant-Desnos, Pierre Joseph.

Des Nos, Sophie. see Nos, Sophie des.

Desnoyers, Charles Louis Francois. 19750, (38607)

De Sobolewski, Serge. see Sobolevskii, Sergiei Aleksandrovich, 1803-1870.

De Sobrino, Rodrigo Alvarez. see Alvarez de Sobrino, Rodrigo.

De Sodre, Francois. see Sodre, Francois de.

De Soelen, Johan Gijsbert Verstolk. see Verstolk de Soelen, Johan Gijsbert, d. 1845.

De Sola y Fuente, Geronimo. see Sola y Fuente, Geronimo de.

Desolacion de la ciudad de Lima. 41098

De Solano, Jose Maria Diez. see Diez de Solano, Jose Maria, Bp., 1820-1881.

Desolation of America: a poem. (18980)-18981

Desolation of Eyam. 33379

De Solchaga, Juan. see Solchaga, Juan de.

De Soles, Martin. see Soles, Martin de.

De Solignac, Armand. see Solignac, Armand de.

De Solis, Alonso Suarez. see Suarez de Solis, Alonso.

De Solis, Antonio. see Solis y Ribadeneyra, Antonio de, 1610-1686.

De Solis, Francisco. see Solis, Francisco de.

De Solis, Francisco Lopez. see Solis, Francisco Lopez de, d. 1664.

De Solis, Gaspar Jose. see Solis, Gaspar Jose de.

De Solis, Hernando. see Solis, Hernando de.

De Solis, Juan Diaz. see Solis, Juan Diaz de.

De Solis Aguirre, Ambrosio. see Solis Aguirre, Ambrosio de.

De Solis Calderon, Pedro. see Solis Calderon, Pedro de.

De Solis Holguin, Gonzalo. see Solis Holguin, Gonzalo de.

De Solis Osorio, Francisco. see Solis Osorio, Francisco de.

De Solis Valderabano i Bracamonte, Alonso. see Solis Valderabano i Bracamonte, Alonso de.

De Solis Vango, Juan Prospero. see Solis Vango, Juan Prospero de.

De Solis y Alcazar, Francisco. see Solis y Alcazar, Francisco de.

De Solis y Barbosa, Antonio Sebastian. see Solis y Barbosa, Antonio Sebastian de.

De Solis y Haro, Marcelino. see Solis y Haro, Marcelino de.

De Solis y Quinones, Pedro. see Solis y Quinones, Pedro de.

De Solis y Ribadeneyra, Antonio. see Solis y Ribadeneyra, Antonio de, 1610-1686.

De Solis y Ulloa, Matias. see Solis y Ulloa, Matias de.

De Solis y Valenzuela, Pedro. see Solis y Valenzuela, Pedro de.

De Sologuren, Juan. see Sologuren, Juan de.

De Solorcano, Bernardino. see Solorzano, Bernardino de.

De Solorcano, Justino. see Solorzano, Justino de.

De Solorzano, Bernardino. see Solorzano, Bernardino de.

De Solorzano, Justino. see Solorzano, Justino de.

De Solorzano Paniagua i Trexo, Gabriel. see Solorzano Paniagua i Trexo, Gabriel de.

De Solorzano Pereira, Juan. see Solorzano Pereira, Juan de, 1575-1655.

De Solorzano Pereyra, Juan. see Solorzano Pereira, Juan de, 1575-1655.

De Solorzano y Salcedo, Juan. see Solorzano y Salcedo, Juan de.

De Solorzano y Velasco, Alonso. see Solorzano y Velasco, Alonso de, d. 1680.
De Someruelos, Salvador Jose de Muros y Salazar, Marques. see Someruelos, Salvador Jose de Muros y Salazar, Marques de, 1754-1813.
De Somonte y Velasco, Jose Balthasar. see Somonte y Velasco, Jose Baltasar de.
De Somoza, Jeronimo Suarez. pseud. see Andrade, Alfonso de.
De Sonora, Jose de Galvez, Marques. see Galvez, Jose de, Marques de Sonora.
Desor, Edouard. 19751
Desordres des guerres civiles. 47107
De Soria, Domingo. see Soria, Domingo de.
De Soria, Francisco. see Soria, Francisco de.
De Soria, Francisco Joseph. see Soria, Francisco Joseph de.
De Soria, Gabriel. see Soria, Gabriel de.
De Soria Briviesca, Alvaro. see Soria Briviesca, Alvaro de.
De Soria Velasquez, Jeronimo. see Soria Velasquez, Jeronimo de.
De Soria y Mendoza, Manuel Ignacio. see Soria y Mendoza, Manuel Ignaciode.
De Sosa, Antonio. see Sosa, Antonio de.
De Sosa, Diego. see Sosa, Diego, 1696-1767.
De Sosa, Fernando. see Sosa, Fernando de.
De Sosa, Francisco. see Sosa, Francisco de.
De Sosa, Miguel. see Sosa, Miguel de.
De Sosa, Pedro. see Sosa, Pedro de, 1556-
De Sosa, Miguel Feyjoo. see Feyjoo de Sosa, Miguel, d. 1784.
De Sosa Troncoso, Antonio. see Sosa Troncoso, Antonio de.
De Sosa Victoria, Jose. see Sosa Victoria, Jose de.
De Sosa Victoria, Nicolas. see Sosa Victoria, Nicolas de.
De Sossa, Pedro. see Sosa, Pedro de, 1556-
De Soto, --------. see Soto, ------ de, fl. 1552.
De Soto, Basil Varen. see Soto, Basil Varen de.
De Soto, Bernardo. see Soto, Bernardo de.
De Soto, Francisco. see Soto, Francisco de.
De Soto, Hernando. see Soto, Hernando de, 1500 (ca)-1542.
De Soto, Juan. see Soto, Juan de.
De Soto, Pedro. see Soto, Pedro de.
De Soto Loria, Jose. see Soto Loria, Jose de.
De Soto y Marne, Francisco. see Soto y Marne, Francisco de.
De Soto Zevallos Aranguren, Ignacio. see Soto Zevallos Aranguren, Ignacio de.
De Sotomayor, Alonso. see Sotomayor, Alonso de.
De Sotomayor, Antonio Valedares. see Valledares de Sotomayor, Antonio.
De Sotomayor, Diego Sanchez. see Sotomayor, Diego Sanchez de.
De Sotomayor, Fernando. see Sotomayor, Fernando de.
De Sotomayor, Juan. see Sotomayor, Juan de.
De Sotomayor, Juan F. see Sotomayor, Juan F. de.
De Sotomayor, Juan Gomez Tonel. see Tonel de Sotomayor, Juan Gomez.
De Sotomayor, Juliana (de Truxillo) Tonel. see Tonel de Sotomayor, Juliana (de Truxillo)
De Sotomayor, Urbano Feijoo. see Sotomayor, Urbano Feijoo de.
De Soto's expedition. 25853
De Soto's narrative. 7754

De Soto's voyage to Florida. 66686
De Souillac, Jose Sourryere. see Sourryere de Souillac, Jose, 1750-1820.
De Sourigny, --------. see Sourigny, ------- de.
De Sousa, Jose Carlos Pinto. see Pinto de Sousa, Jose Carlos.
De Sousa, Pedro Lopes. see Lopes de Sousa, Pedro.
De Sousa Azevedo Pizarro e Araujo, Jose. see Azevedo Pizarro e Araujo, Jose de Sousa.
De Sousa Brazil, Thomaz Pompeo. see Sousa Prazil, Thomaz Pompeo de.
De Sousa Coutinho, Francisco. see Sousa Coutinho, Francisco de, 1597?-1660.
De Sousa Franco, Bernardo. see Franco, Bernardo de Sousa.
De Sousa Maldonado, Theodoro. see Maldonado, Theodoro de Sousa.
De Sousa Silva, Joaquim Norberto. see Sousa Silva, Joaquim Norberto de.
De Souza, Antonio Ennes. see Souza, Antonio Ennes de.
De Souza, Antonio Jose. see Souza, Antonio Jose de.
De Souza, Augusto Fausto. see Souza, Augusto Fausto de.
De Souza, Bernardo Xavier Pinto. see Souza, Bernardo Xavier Pinto de.
De Souza, Domingo. see Souza, Domingo de
De Souza, Feliciano Joaquim. see Souza Nunes, Feliciano Joaquim de.
De Souza, Francisco. see Souza, Francisco de.
De Souza, Francisco Bernardino. see Souza, Francisco Bernardino de.
De Souza, Gabriel Soares. see Soares de Souza, Gabriel.
De Souza, Jose Mariano Berstain. see Beristain de Souza, Jose Mariano, 1756-1817.
De Souza, Juan. see Souza, Juan de.
De Souza, Paulino Jose Soares, 1807-1866. see Soares de Souza, Paulino Jose, Visconde do Uruguay, 1807-1866.
De Souza, Paulino Jose Soares, 1834- see Soares de Souza, Paulino Jose, 1834-
De Souza, Pedro Lopes. see Souza, Pedro Lopes de.
De Souza Azevedo Pizarro e Araujo, Jose. see Azevedo Pizarro e Araujo, Joze de Sousa.
De Souza Bandeira, Antonio Herculano. see Souza Bandeira, Antonio Herculano de.
De Souza Bocayuva, Quintino. see Souza Bocayuva, Quintino de.
De Souza Brazil, Thomaz Pompeo. see Souza Brazil, Thomaz Pompeo de, 1852-
De Souza Bueno, Maximiano. see Souza Bueno, Maximiano de.
De Souza Coelho, Romualdo. see Souza Coelho, Romualdo de.
De Souza Coutinho, Francisco. see Souza Coutinho, Francisco de.
De Souza Coutinho, Francisco Inocencio. see Souza Coutinho, Francisco Inocencio de.
De Souza da Silva Pontes, Rodrigo. see Souza da Silva Pontes, Rodrigo de.
De Souza de Macedo, Antonio. see Souza de Macedo, Antonio de.
De Souza de Tavares da Silva, Henrique. see Silva, Henrique de Souza de Tavares da.
De Souza e Mello, Felisardo. see Souza e Mello, Felisardo de.
De Souza e Oliveira, Saturnino. see Souza e Oliveira, Saturnino de, 1824-

De Souza Fernandez de Lara, J. M. Meristain. see Beristain de Souza, Jose Mariano, 1756-1817.
De Souza Ferreira, Joao Carlos. see Souza Ferreira, Joao Carlos de, 1831-
De Souza Franca, Manoel Jose. see Souza Franca, Manoel Jose de.
De Souza Furtado de Mendonca, Francisco Maria. see Souza Furtado de Mendonca, Francisco Maria de.
De Souza Gayoso, Jose. see Souza Gayoso, Raymundo Jose de.
De Souza Martins, Antonio. see Souza Martins, Antonio de.
De Souza Martins, Francisco. see Souza Martins, Francisco de.
De Souza Mello e Alvim, Miguel. see Souza Mello e Alvim, Miguel de.
De Souza Mello e Netto, Ladislau. see Souza Mello e Netto, Ladislau de.
De Souza Menezes, Agrario. see Souza Menezes, Agrario de.
De Souza Menezes, Rodrigo Ignacio. see Souza Menezes, Rodrigo Ignacio de.
De Souza Monteiro, Joze Maria. see Souza Monteiro, Joze Maria de.
De Souza Nunes, Feliciano Joaquim. see Souza Nunes, Feliciano Joaquim de.
De Souza Paraizo, Francisco. see Souza Paraizo, Francisco de.
De Souza Pereira de Silva Portilho, Joao Anastacio. see Souza Pereira da Silva Portilho, Joao Anastacio de.
De Souza Pinto, Antonio. see Souza Pinto, Antonio de, 1843-
De Souza Pinto, Jose Maria Frederico. see Souza Pinto, Jose Maria Frederico de.
De Souza Rego, Antonio Jose. see Souza Rego, Antonio Jose de.
De Souza Ribeiro, Antonio. see Souza Ribeiro, Antonio de.
De Souza Silva, Joaquim Norberto. see Souza Silva, Joaquim Norberto de, 1820-1891.
De Souza Soares de Andrea, Francisco Jose. see Souza Soares de Andrea, Francisco Jose de.
De Souza y Amador, Augustin. see Souza y Amador, Augustin de.
De Soza, Juan. see Souza, Juan de.
Des P., M. O. T. pseud. see P., M. O. T. des. pseud.
Despacho para que la justicia de la jurisdiccion de luego q[ue] lo reciva lo haga publicar. 93313
Despacho requissitorui de D. Fr. Benito Garret, y Arlovi. 72531
Despachos y cartas de govierno. 61113
Despair of science. 76960
Despard, Edward Marcus. 3209
Despard, G. P. 19752
Despatch from Her Majesty's Minister at Washington. 19753, (23505), 55527
Despatch from Lord Bathurst to . . . Sir Henry Warde. 3282
Despatch from Lord Bathurst to the governor. 3956
Despatch from . . . Lord Glenelg. (28300)
Despatch from Lord Lyons. 42876
Despatch from Sir F. B. Head. 31338
Depatch [of Daniel Webster.] 17471, 35856
Despatch [of Morshead.] 59031
Despatch of Senor Salazar y Mazarredo. 11710
Despatch of the 9th of July. 8005
Despatch to Mr. Stewart. 452
Despatches. 43022

Despatches from Admiral Squib. 23543, note after 89945
Despatches from Her Majesty's Disvovery Ship, "Investigator." 43074
Despatches laid before the Legislature. (67517)
Despatches of Capt. Sir Edward Belcher. 1918, (43072)
Despatches of Hernando Cortes. 16964
Despatches of Sir John Colborne. 10528
Despatches of the . . . Earl of Elgin and Kincardine. 22116
Despatches relative to North American colonies. 22495
Despatches relative to the condition of the sugar growing colonies. 16689
Despatches to the Governor of the province. 16285
Despedida de un religioso. 86496
Despedida del General Santa-Anna. 76730
Desperado: a tale of the ocean. 39833
Desperrieres, ------- Poissonnier. see Poissonnier-Desperrieres, -------.
Despertador. 9221
Despertador de Michoacan. 93403
Despertador republicano. 50774
Despertador sobre el comercio, agricultura, y manufacturas. 98896
De Spinola, H. see Spinola, H. de.
Despinosa, A. Vazquez. see Vazquez de Espinosa, Antonio.
Despised race. 58676
Deplaces, A Thoisnier. see Thoisnier-Desplaces, A.
Despojo a mano armado. 19755-(19756)
Despojo de los bienes eclesiasticos. (19757)
Desponding lovers. 105178
Despones, ------- Garcia. see Garcia Despones, -------.
Desportes, Felix. 19758
Desportes, J. B. R. Pouppe. see Pouppe-Desportes, J. B. R.
Despotic doctrines. 33267
Despotism and democracy at necessary, eternal, exterminating war. 27955
Despotism at Richmond. 19759
Despotism in America. 31773-31774
Despotism of Episcopal Methodism. 3879
Despotism of freedom. 12695
Despotism; or the last days of the American republic. 34966
Desprez, Adrien. 19760
Desprez, Hippolyte. 40234
Despves de lo qve doctissimamente otros mejores sujetos tienen informado. 86414
Desrais, --------. illus. 27140
Des Rivieres Beaubien, Henry. 19761
Des Roches de Parthenay, -------. tr. 22027
Des Rotours, Noel Francois Arnot. (19762)
Dess Robins Sect. 54944
Dessalles, Adrien. 19763-19764
Dessaulles, L. A. 19765-19769
Desseins de Son Excellence le Cardinal de Richelieu. (12605)
Desseins du Cardinal Richelieu sur l'Amerique. 71102
Dessen Bericht vom Ursprung der Abgotterey. 73324
Dessen gleichzeitigen Erzahlung bearbeit von der Uebersetzerin des Vassari. 19987
Dessen letzte Reise durch Amerika in den Jahren 1824 und 1825. 40736
Dessert to the true American. 61580
Dessourtilz, Michel Etienne. supposed author 75129
D'Estaing, Charles Hector, Comte. see Estaing, Charles Hector, Comte d'.

D'Estaing eclipsed, or Yankee Doodle's defeat. (64855)
Destere, G. Chastenet. see Chastenet-Destere, G.
Destierro para las Yndias. 64914
D'Estimauville, Robert. see Estimauville, Robert d'.
Destin del l'Amerique. 11702, 55423, 55517
Destined efficiency of juvenile missionary effort. 85280
Destinee de Sir J. Franklin devoilee. 43044, 44171
Destiny; a poem. (82448)
Destiny and fortitude. 85243-85244
Destiny of America. 79513
Destiny of Nicaragua. 55146
Destiny of our country. 37995
Destiny of Pittsburgh. (71922)
Destiny of rebellious nations. 92059
Destiny of the people of color. 82793
Destiny of the races of this continent. 5739
Destiny of the United States. 79513, 79534
Destiny. Progress. 11219
Destruccion de las Indias. 98604
Destruccion del imperio del Peru. 44655
Destruction de l'empire du Perou. (44652), 56299
Destruction d'une ville sans defence. 6258
Destruction of democratic republicanism. 50314
Destruction of eight hundred and forty-two slaves. 81991
Destruction of New Mexico. (80023)
Destruction of republicanism the object of the rebellion. 50314
Destruction of the American carrying trade. (21844)
Destruction of the empire of Peru. 44653
Destruction of the republic. 50315
Destruction of the union is emancipation. 40639, 43617
Destruction of the Willey family, a ballad. 98051
Destructive art of healing. 20092
Destructive operation of foul air. (14160)
Destutt de Tracy, Antoine Louis Claude. see Tracy, Antoine Louis Claude Destutt de, Comte.
De Suberwick, -------. see Suberwick, ------- de.
De Subia, Juan. see Subia, Juan de.
De Suckau, W. see Suckau, W. de.
De Sucre, Antonio Jose. see Sucre, Antonio Jose de, Pres. Bolivia, 1795-1830.
Desultory account of the yellow fever. 10865
Desultory examination of the reply. 10889
Desultory facts and observations. 19770
Desultory observations on the abuses of the banking system. (73914)
Desultory observations, on the situation. 91992
Desultory pieces in prose and verse. 38380
Desultory poem. 9328
Desultory reflections, excited by the calamitous fate of John Fullerton. 10889
Desultory reflections on the new political aspects. (19584), 19771
Desultory reflections on the political aspects. 24074
Desultory reflections upon the ruinous consequences. 10889
Desultory remarks on the question of extending slavery. 19772, 49587
Desultory sketches and tales of Barbados. 3266, 19773

Desultory thoughts on educational science. 61400
De Sousa, Juan De Dios Fernandez. see Fernandez de Sousa, Juan de Dios.
De Superunda, Joseph Antonio Manso de Velasco, Conde. see Manso de Velasco, Joseph Antonio, Conde de de Superunda.
De Surgy, Jacques Philibert Rousselot. see Rousselot de Surgy, Jacques Philibert.
De Surville, J. F. see Surville, J. F. de.
De Survillier, Charlotte Julie (Bonaparte) Comtesse. see Survillier, Charlotte Julie (Bonaparte) Comtesse de.
De Suzannet, -------, Comte. see Suzannet, -------, Comte de.
Desvergers, --------. 23093, note after 98620
De Syria, Pedro. see Syria, Pedro de.
De Taboada, M. E. Nunez. see Nunez de Taboada, M. E.
De Tagle, Domingo Ruyz. see Ruiz de Tagle, Domingo.
De Tagle, Jose Bernardo. see Tagle y Portocarrero, Jose Bernardo de, Marques de Torre-Tagle.
De Tagle Cossio y Guerra, Fermin Aurelio see Tagle Cossio y Guerra, Fermin Aurelio de.
De Tagle Isasaga, Pedro Matias. see Tagle Isasaga, Pedro Matias de.
De Tagle y Portocarrero, Jose Bernardo. see Tagle y Portocarrero, Jose Bernardo de, Marques de Torre-Tagle.
Detail and conduct of the American war. 19774, 99558
Detail historique des tentatives qui ont ete (22313)
Detail of a plan for the moral improvement of Negroes. (13572)
Detail of Captain Stout's travels through the deserts of Caffraria. 92355
Detail of some particular services. 19775, note after 96363
Detail of the siege of ninety six. 43431, 94397
Detail sur la navigation. (12235)
Detailed account of the battle of San Jacinto. 33189, 94961
Detailed account of the battle of San Jacinto, with a complete list of officers. 95077
Detailed account of the embarkation. 6505
Detailed account of the receipts into, and expenditures from the treasury. 45710
Detailed account of the various modes of duck shooting. 49338
Detailed and practical information for intending emigrants. 8501
Detailed directions to emigrants. 8840
Detailed report of the proceedings. (43035)
Detailed report of the state treasurer. 60443
Detailed statement of an excursion. 98629
Detailed statement of the receipts and disbursements. 56909
Details and proceedings of the exhibition of 1867. 89880
Details der Communication zwischen England. 19777
Details intimes sur l'etat des lieux. 13232
Details of an unpaid claim on France. 58848
Details of real prison life at Richmond and Danville. 74319
Details of the commercial transactions. 47300
Details of the military and naval operations. (8556)
Details of the naval operations in China. 4390
Details of the proposed plans and improvements. 82956

Details sur le General Moreau. 93989
Details sur l'emancipation des escalves.
    81955
Details sur les derniers moments du General
    Moreau. 93988, 93990
Details sur quelques uns de evenemens qui ont
    eu lieu en Amerique. (19776)
Detall de las operacions ocurridas en la de-
    fensa de la capital. (19778)
Detall y algunos documentos relativos al triunfo
    alcanzado. 67910
De Talleyrand-Perigord, Charles Maurice.
    see Talleyrand-Perigord, Charles
    Maurice de, Prince de Benevent, 1754-
    1838.
De Talvera, Gabriel. see Talvera, Gabriel de.
De Tapia, Andres. see Tapia, Andres de.
De Tapia, Diego. see Tapia, Diego de.
De Tapia, Francisco. see Tapia, Francisco
    de.
De Tapia, Juan Antonio. see Tapia, Juan
    Antonio de.
De Tapia, Mathias. see Tapia, Mathias.
De Tapia Centeno, Carlos. see Tapia Zenteno,
    Carlos de.
De Tapia Zenteno, Carlos. see Tapia Zenteno,
    Carlos de.
D'Etaples, Jacques Le Fevre. see Le Fevre,
    Jacques, d'Etaples, d. 1537.
De Taranaltos, F. see Taranaltos, F. de.
De Tarazana, Francisco. see Tarazana,
    Francisco de.
De Tassy, ------- Garcin. see Garcin de
    Tassy, -------.
De Tavares da Silva, Henrique de Souza. see
    Souza de Tavares da Silva, Henrique de,
    Conde de Miranda.
De Tebar, Pedro. see Tebar, Pedro de.
Detection detected. 26845, 83796
Detection of a conspiracy formed by the United
    Brethren. (13881)
Detection of the errors of M. J. Hector St.
    John. 2527, (17497), 1st note after
    69470
Detection of the false reasons and facts.
    (19779), 29044, note after (68287)
Detection of the proceedings and practices of
    the Directors of the Royal African Com-
    pany of England. (19780), 73768-73769
Detection of the proceedings of the directors
    of the Royal African Company from 1672
    to 1848. (19780), 73768
Detection of the state and situation of the pre-
    sent sugar planters. (3265), 22641, 3d
    note after 102832
Detection of the state and situation of the sugar
    planters of Barbadoes. 3291, note before
    93803
Detective's manual and officer's guide. 11953
Detector detected. 73769
De Tejada, Bernardo. see Tejada, Bernardo
    de.
De Tejada, Miguel Lerdo. see Lerdo de
    Tejada, Miguel.
De Tejada, Sebastian Lerdo. see Lerdo de
    Tejada, Sebastian, Pres. Mexico,
    1824-1889.
De Tejado, Fran Lerdo. see Lerdo de Tejado,
    Fran.
De Tembra y Simanes, Jose Javier. see
    Tembra y Simanes, Jose Xavier de.
De Tempore, Disciplus. see Tempore,
    Disciplus de.
De Tendilla, Antonio de Mendoza, Conde.
    see Mendoza, Antonio de, Conde de
    Tendilla.

De Teran Rubin, Pedro. see Teran Rubin,
    Pedro de.
Determinacion de la posicion geografica de
    Mexico. 17208
Determinacion fisico-geografica de la ciudad de
    Mexico. (16972)
Determination of the case of Mr. Thomas Story.
    6106, 92322
Determination of the ratio (x) of the specific
    heats. 85072
De Teron y Prieto, Jose. see Teron y Prieto,
    Jose de.
De Terralla y Landa, Esteban. see Terralla y
    Landa, Esteban de.
De Terranoua, Estefana Cortes, Duquesa. see
    Cortes, Estefana, Duquesa de Terranoua.
De Terraube, Louis Antoine Marie Victor de,
    Marquis Galard. see Galard de Terraube,
    Louis Antione Marie Victor de, Marquis,
    1765-1840.
De Terrones, Lorenzo. see Terrones, Lorenzo
    de.
De Terreros y Trebuesto, Maria Micaela Romero.
    see Terreros y Trebuesto, Maria Micaela
    Romero de, Marquesa de San Francisco.
De Tesillo, Santiago. see Tesillo, Santiago de.
De Tessan, U. see Tessan, U. de.
De Texeda, Antonio. see Texeda, Antonio de.
De Texada, J. Lerdo. see Lerdo de Texada,
    J.
De Texada, J. Prudencio Moreno. see Moreno
    de Texada, J. Prudencio.
De Texada, Manuel Saenz. see Saenz de
    Texada, Manuel.
De Texada y Guzman, Juan. see Texada y
    Guzman, Juan de.
De Texeda, Pedro Alexandro. see Texeda,
    Pedro Alexandro de.
De Theca, Marcos. see Theca, Marcos de.
De Thome de Gamond, Aime. see Thome
    de Gamond, Aime de, 1807-1875.
De Thoron, Enrique, Vicomte Onffroy. see
    Onffroy de Thoron, Enrique, Vicomte.
De Tierrafirme, D. see Tierrafirme, D. de.
De Tirel, ------ Darinel. see Darinel de
    Tirel, --------.
De Tivoli, J. see Tivoli, J. de.
De Tobar, Mateo. see Tobar, Mateo de.
De Tobar, Pedro. see Pedro de Tobar.
De Tobar y Buendia, Pedro. see Tobar y
    Buendia, Pedro de.
De Toca Velasco, Jose Ignacio. see Toca
    Velasco, Jose Ignacio de.
De Tocqueville, Alexis Charles Henri Maurice
    Clerel. see Tocqueville, Alexis Charles
    Henri Maurice Clerel de, 1805-1859.
De Toledo, Domingo Albarez. see Albarez de
    Toledo, Domingo.
De Toledo, F. Alvarez. see Alvarez de
    Toledo, F.
De Toledo, Fadrique. see Toledo Osorio y
    Mendoza, Fadrique de.
De Toledo, Francisco. see Toledo, Francisco
    de, 1532-1596.
De Toledo, Francisco. see Toledo, Francisco
    de, d. 1584.
De Toledo, Joaquim Floriano. see Toledo,
    Joaquim Floriano de.
De Toledo, Jose Alvarez. see Toledo y Dubois,
    Jose Alvarez de.
De Toledo, Juan Baptista Alvarez. see Alvarez
    de Toledo, Juan Baptista, Bp.
De Toledo, Luys Tribaldos. see Tribaldos de
    Toledo, Luys.

De Toledo Osorio y Mendoza, Fadrique. see
 Toledo Osorio y Mendoza, Fadrique de.
De Toledo y Dubois, Jose Alvarez. see
 Toledo y Dubois, Jose Alvarez de.
De Toledo y Leiva, Pedro. see Toledo y
 Leiva, Pedro de, Marques de Mancera,
 1585-1654.
De Tollo, Luis B. see Tollo, Luis B. de.
De Tolosan, J. see Tolosan, J. de.
De Tonti, Henri. see Tonti, Henri de, d.
 1704.
De Torija Ortuno, Francisco. see Torija
 Ortuno, Francisco de.
De Tornos, Alberto. see Tornos, Alberto de.
De Toro, Francisco Rodriguez. see Toro,
 Francisco Rodriguez de.
De Toro Zambrano y Ureta, Mateo. see Toro
 Zambrano y Ureta, Mateo de.
De Torquemada, Juan. see Torquemada,
 Juan de.
De Torre-Tagle, Juan Bernardo de Tagle y
 Portocarrero, Marques. see Tagle y
 Portocarrero, Jose Bernardo de, Marques
 de Torre-Tagle.
De Torres, Antonio. see Torres, Antonio de.
De Torres, Bernardo. see Torres, Bernardo
 de.
De Torres, Cristobal. see Torres, Cristobal
 de.
De Torres, Francisco. see Torres, Fran-
 cisco de.
De Torres, Francisco Caro. see Caro de
 Torres, Francisco.
De Torres, Ignacio. see Torres, Ignacio de.
De Torres, Jose. see Torres, Jose de.
De Torres, Joseph. see Torres, Joseph de.
De Torres, Joseph Julio Garcia. see Garcia
 de Torres, Joseph Julio.
De Torres, Juan. see Torres, Juan de.
De Torres, Ludovico Antonio. see Torres
 Tunon, Luis Antonio.
De Torres, Luis. see Torres Tunon, Luis
 Antonio.
De Torres, Manuel Gaytan. see Gaytan de
 Torres, Manuel.
De Torres, Miguel. see Torres, Miguel de.
De Torres, Nicolas. see Torres, Nicolas de.
De Torres, Pedro Antonio. see Torres,
 Pedro Antonio de.
De Torres, Simon Perez. see Perez de
 Torres, Simon.
De Torres Bollo, Diego. see Torres Bollo,
 Diego de.
De Torres Palacios, Jose Gregorio. see
 Torres Palacios, Jose Gregorio de.
De Torres Rubio, Diego. see Torres Rubio,
 Diego de.
De Torres Vargas, Diego. see Torres Var-
 gas, Diego de.
De Torres y Morales, Rodrigo. see Torres
 y Morales, Rodrigo de.
De Torres y Vergara, Jose. see Torres y
 Vergara, Jose de.
De Torrontegui, Jose Manuel. see Torronte-
 gui, Joseph Manuel de.
De Toulza, Philippe. see Toulza, Philippe de.
De Tous, -------, Marquis. see Tous,
 -------, Marquis de.
De Tovar, Balthasar. see Tovar, Balthasar
 de.
De Tracy, Alexandre de Prouville, Marquis.
 see Prouville, Alexandre de, Marquis
 de Tracy.
De Tracy, Antoine Louis Claude Destutt. see
 Tracy, Antoine Louis Claude Destutt de,
 Comte.

De Tres-Palacios y Verdeja, Felipe Jose. see
 Tres-Palacios y Verdeja, Felipe Jose
 de, Bp.
De Tripoli, Guillaume. see Tripoli, Guillaume
 de.
De Trobriand, Philippe Regis Denis de
 Keredern, Comte. see Trobriand,
 Philippe Regis Denis de Keredern, Comte
 de, 1816-1897.
Detroit. Bar. Supper, 1857. (21131)
Detroit. Board of Education. (19792)
Detroit. Board of Trade. Special Committee.
 (19791)
Detroit. Board of Water Commissioners.
 19783, (19792)
Detroit. Board of Water Commissioners.
 Engineer. (19792)
Detroit. Board of Water Commissioners.
 Secretary. (19792)
Detroit. Board of Water Commissioners.
 Superintendent. (19792)
Detroit. Citizens' Meeting on the Southern
 Boundary of Michigan, 1836. see Detroit.
 Meeting of the Citizens on the Southern
 Boundary of Michigan, 1836.
Detroit. Commercial Connvention, 1865. see
 Commercial Convention, Detroit, 1865.
Detroit. Common Council. 19789
Detroit. Meeting of the Citizens on the South-
 ern Boundary of Micihgan, 1836. 88314
Detroit. National Labor Congress, 1869. see
 National Labor Congress, Detroit, 1869.
Detroit. Ordinances, etc. (19792)-19793
Detroit. Public Library. 19785
Detroit. Public Schools. (19792)
Detroit. St. Paul's Church. Former Member
 of the Vestry. pseud. Statement of facts.
 see Waterman, J. W.
Detroit (Diocese) Synod, 1859. 72939
Detroit (Diocese) Synod, 1862. (72940)
Detroit advertiser. 19784
Detroit and Milwaukee Railroad Company.
 (33280)
Detroit city directory. 19786
Detroit free press. 92687
Detroit gazette. 15992, 34479
Detroit journal and Michigan advertiser. 88691
Detroit, June 3, 1869. 43494
Detroit Ladies Industrial School Association.
 (19792)
Detroit Manufacturers' Association. Committee.
 70993
Detroit Young Men's Society. 19782, 19787
Detroit Young Men's Society. Board of Direc-
 tors. 19782
Detroit Young Men's Society. Charter. 19782
Detroit Young Men's Society. Library. 19782,
 19787
De Tronchoy, ------ Gautier. see Gautier
 du Tronchoy, -------.
De Trueba y Cosio, Joaquin Telesforo. see
 Trueba y Cosio, Joaquin Telesforo de.
De Truxillo, Juan Ignacio. see Truxillo,
 Juan Ignacio de.
De Truxillo, Juliana. see Tonel de Sotomayor,
 Juliana (de Truxillo)
De Truxillo y Guerrero, Felipe Ignacio. see
 Truxillo y Guerrero, Felipe Ignacio de,
 Bp.
De Tschudi, Juan Diego. see Tschudi, Johann
 Jakob von.
Dette du Mexique et les obligations Mexicaines.
 4996B
De Tupac-Amaru, Jose Gabriel. see Tupac-
 Amaru, Jose Gabriel de.
Detur digniori. 46283

De Turpin, -------. see Turpin, ------- de.
De Turreau de Linieres, Eduardo Enrique
Teodoro, see Turreau de Linieres,
Eduardo Enrique Teodoro de.
De Tussac, F. R. see Tussac, F. R. de.
Deuber, Franz Xavier Anselm. (19793)-
19793A
Deuber's, Dr. U. Prof., Geschichte der
Schiffahrt. (19793)
Deuda y credita publico. 48431
Deudo de Acosta. pseud. Horrible ley mer-
cantil y sus ejecutores. 98877
De Ugarte, Benito. see Ugarte, Benito de.
De Ugarte, Fernando Arias. see Ugarte,
Fernando Arias de, Abp.
De Ugarte-Videa, Francisco. see Ugarte-
Videa, Francisco de.
De Ugarte y Sarabia, Agustin. see Ugarte y
Sarabia, Agustin de, Bp.
De Ugarteche, Felix. see Ugarteche, Felix
de.
De Ugartechea, Domingo. see Ugartechea,
Domingo de.
De Ulibarri y Olasso, Jose Manuel Velez.
see Velez de Ulibarri y Olasso, Jose
Manuel.
De Ulloa, Alfonso. see Ulloa, Alfonso de.
De Ulloa, Antonio. see Ulloa, Antonio de,
1716-1795.
De Ulloa, Bernardo. see Ulloa, Bernardo de.
De Ulloa, Gabriel Caraujal. see Caraujal de
Ulloa, Gabriel.
De Ulloa, Gonzalo Astete. see Gonzalo de
Ulloa, Astete.
De Ulloa, Juana (Albares de Rosal) de Valverde
Pinto. see Pinto de Ulloa, Juana
(Albares de Rosal) de Valverde.
De Ulloa, Toscano Alfonso. see Ulloa, Tos-
cano Alfonso de.
De Ulua, San Juan. see Ulua, San Juan de.
De Unzueta, Juan Antonio. see Unzueta, Juan
Antonio de.
De Urbina, Thelesforo Jose. see Urbina,
Thelesforo Jose de.
De Urcullu, Jose. see Urcullu, Jose de.
De Urdinola, Francisco. see Urdinola,
Francisco de.
De Uribe, Francisco. see Uribe, Francisco
de.
De Uribe, J. P. de Fernandez. see Fernandez
de Uribe, J. P. de.
De Urizar y Bernal, Antonio Joaquin. see
Urizar y Bernal, Antonio Joaquin de.
De Urizar y Estrada, Juan. see Urizar y
Estrada, Juan de.
De Urquinaona y Pardo, Pedro. see Urguin-
aona y Pardo, Pedro de.
De Urquiza, Justo Jose. see Urquiza, Justo
Jose de.
De Urruha Montoya, Ignacio Joseph. see
Urrutia y Montoya, Ignacio Jose de.
De Urrutia, Carlos. see Urrutia, Carlos de.
De Urrutia, Fernando. see Urrutia, Fer-
nando de.
De Urrutia, Francisco Xavier Maria. see
Urrutia, Francisco Xavier Maria de.
De Urrutia, Juan Antonio. see Urrutia, Juan
Antonio de.
De Urrutia, Manuel Jose. see Urrutia,
Manuel Jose de.
De Urrutia y Montoya, Ignacio Jose. see
Urrutia y Montoya, Ignacio Jose de.
De Urrutigoyti, Miguel Antonio Francisco.
see Urrutigoyti, Miguel Antonio Fran-
cisco de.
De Urtassum, Juan. see Urtassum, Juan de.

De Uruena, Antanasio Jose. see Ureuna,
Atanasio Jose de.
Deus, Manual da Madre de. see Madre de
Deus, Manual de.
Deus nobiscum. A narrative of a great deliver-
ance at sea. 36336
Deus nobiscum. A very brief essay. (46284)
Deussen, P. tr. 70291
De Ustariz, Geronymo. see Uztariz, Geronymo
de.
Deutliche Vorstellung. 106316
Deutsch, R. Manuel. cartographer 51379
Deutsch-Amerikanisch Wahlverwandtschaften.
64539
Deutsch-Amerikanische Bibliothek. 86384
Deutsch-Amerikanische Monatshefte fur Politik.
19794
Deutsch-Amerikanisches Freiheitbund. 19795
Deutsch-Brasilianisches Leben und Treiben.
22579
Deutsch-Evangelischen Kirche, Baltimore. see
Baltimore. Deutsch-Evangelischen Kirche.
Deutsche Ansiedelung in Mittel-Amerika. 1623
Deutsche Ansiedelung in Texas. 78005
Deutsche Auswanderer-Zeitung. (19796)
Deutsche Auswanderung nach Chile. (20522)
Deutsche Auswanderung und ihre culturhis-
torische Bedeutung. 25989
Deutsche Bevolkerung der Vereinigten Staaten.
19797
Deutsche Briefe aus den Vereinigten Staaten
von Nordamerika. 19798
Deutsche Colonisirungs-Projekt an der Mosquito-
Kust. 38316
Deutsche Gesellschaft, New York. see Deutsche
Gesellschaft der Stadt New York.
Deutsche Gesellschaft der Stadt New York.
(9676), 54325, 101242
Deutsche Gesellschaft in dem Staate von Neu-
York. see Duetsche Gesellschaft der
Stadt New-York.
Deutsche Gesellschaft von Pennsylvanien, Phila-
delphia. 60054-60055, (62305), 68801,
77972
Deutsche Gesellschaft von Pennsylvanien, Phila-
delphia. Charter. 59815
Deutsche Gesellschaft von Pennsylvanien,
Philadelphia. Library. 60121
Deutsche in Amerika. (6131)
Deutsche in Nord America. 26243
Deutsche Knabe in Amerika. 3577
Deutsche Kirchenfreund. 77496
Deutsche Kolonie Blumenau. (6013)
Deutsche Kolonie Dona Francisca. (39135)
Deutsche Kolonie in der Sudbrasilischen
Provinz Sta. Katharina. (6014)
Deutsche Kossuth-Versammlung in Boston.
38269
Deutsche Pionier. 19799
Deutsche Schaubuhne. 100720
Deutschen. pseud. Bilder aus dem geselligen
Leben. 5367
Deutschen Ackerbau-Kolonien in Santa
Catharina. 38224
Deutschen aus Nord-America. pseud. Brief
von Duetschen. (7931)
Deutschen aus Nord-Amerika. pseud. Brief
eines Duetschen. 7924
Deutschen Auswanderer fahrten und Schicksale.
20130, 27174
Deutschen Auswanderern gewidmet. 3974
Deutschen Colonien in der Nahe des Saginaw-
Flusses. (38202)
Deutschen Colonisten an den Ufern des Colo-
rado. 4522

Deutschen Gesellschaft der Stadt New-York.
see Duetsche Gesellschaft der Stadt
New-York.
Deutschen Hulfstruppen im Nord-Amerikanischen
Befreiungskriege. (22001)
Deutschen im Staate New York. 37094
Deutschen in Amerika. 32525
Deutschen in Nordamerika. 31582
Deutschen in Spanien und Portugal. 92806
Deutschen Minenarbeiter. 9989
Deutscher Verein, Saint Paul, Minn. see Saint
Paul Deutscher Verein.
Deutschen, vornemlich die zum Wahlen
Berechtigten. pseud. An die Deutschen.
(61464)
Deutscher Landsknecht. 90039
Deutschern Hohen Schule, Lancaster, Pa. see
Lancaster, Pa. Deutschern Hohen Schule.
Deutschlands Weltberuf. 90130
Deutschmann, K. tr. 35087
Deutz, J. 19800, 65956
Deux adresses de l'Assemblee Legislative.
10502
Deux adresses de l'Honorable Assemblee
Legislative. 10502
Deux albums prepares par M. Viger. (57399)
Deux Ameriques. (23549)
Deux amiraux. 16543
Deux amis, contre Iroquois. (35106)
Deux annees au Bresil. 5134
Deux ans de sejour dans les deserts de
l'Amazonie. 93273
2 cartes du Senegal et de Madagascar. (21479)
Deux cartes generales de la republique de
Bolivia. 57457
Deux chasseurs noirs dans les forets de
l'Amerique. 19532
Deux cinq cent martyrs du Japon. 6123
Deux deputes. pseud. Dialogue. 19940
Deux egorgeurs de Saint-Domingue. pseud.
Dialogue. see Theoru,——.
Deux episodes de l'histoire de Saint-Domingue.
(21025)
Deux expeditions contre le Fort Fisher. 19802
Deux histoires. 93413
Deux histoires, 1772-1810. 93412, 93414
Deux intendants du Canada sous Louis XIV.
(67969)
Deux lettres. 75838
Deux lettres envoies dela Novvelle France.
16676, (39991), note after 69259
Deux lettres sur le decouverte des Saults en
Canada. (55404)
Deux lettres sur les desastres de la Guade-
loupe. 39581
Deux memoires de M. le Docteur Rufz. 13645
Deux mots sur une note de M. V. Schoelcher.
5652
Deux notices sur l'esclavage. 9694
Deux oceans. 1863
Deux precis de Don Jose Domingo Diaz. 50703,
note after 96221
Deux seules blanches conservees a Saint-
Domingue. 58063
Deux soldats Americans. 19803
II. expose de M. Staempfli. IV. L'"Alabama."
90066
Deuxieme lettre [a M. le Duc de Broglie.]
61262
2me lettre du delegue de la population Francaise
de Grey-Town. 3681, 28797-28798
Deuxieme supplement [a la] catalogue de la
Bibliotheque de la Legislature de Quebec.
(66995)
Deuz-Ponts, William de. 19801

De Uztariz, Geronymo. see Uztariz, Geronymo
de.
De V***, ——. pseud. see V***, ——
de. pseud.
De V., B. L. M. pseud. see Villarroel,
Hipolito. supposed author
De V., S. pseud. see Vries, Simon de.
De V. y M., J. B. pseud. see V. y M., J. B.
de. pseud.
De Vaca, Alvar Nunez Cabeza de. see Cabeza
de Vaca, Alvar Nunez, 1490?-1557.
De Vadillo, Jose Manuel. see Vadillo, Jose
Manuel de.
De Vagad, Gaubert Fabricius. see Vagad,
Gaubert Fabricius de.
De Valades, ———. see Valades, ——— de.
De Valasco, Luis. see Valasco, Luis de.
De Valcarcel, Francisco. see Valcarcel,
Francisco de.
De Valdafuentes, Fernando de Alencastro Marona
y Silva, Marques. see Alencastro Marona
y Silva, Fernando de, Marques de
Valdafuentes.
De Valdenebro, J. see Valdenebro, J. de.
De Valdeosera, Miguel Gonzales. see Gonzales
de Valdeosera, Miguel.
De Valdes, Garcia Ossorio. see Valdes,
Garcia Ossorio de.
De Valdes, Juana. see Valdes, Juana de.
De Valdes, Rodrigo. see Valdes, Rodrigo de.
De Valdes, Rodrigo Garcia Flores. see Flores
de Valdes, Rodrigo Garcia.
De Valdespino, Juan. see Valdespino, Juan de.
De Valdivia, Luis. see Valdivia, Luis de,
1561-1642.
De Valdivia, Pedro. see Valdivia, Pedro de.
De Valdivieso y Torrejon, Miguel. see
Valdivieso y Torrejon, Miguel de.
De Valencia, Jose. see Valencia, Jose de.
De Valencia, Martin. see Martin de Valencia.
De Valencia, Pedro. see Valencia, Pedro de,
Bp.
De Valencia, Salvador. see Valencia, Salvador
de.
De Valencuela Monge Cartuxo, Bruno. see
Valenzuela, Bruno de.
De Valenzuela, Francisco. see Valenzuela,
Francisco de.
De Valenzuela, Francisco Ramiro. see
Valenzuela, Francisco Ramiro de.
De Valenzuela, Ramio. see Valenzuela, Raimo
de.
De Valero, Baltazar de Zuniga Guzman
Sotomayor y Mendoza, Marques. see
Zuniga Guzman Sotomayor y Mendoza,
Baltazar de, Marques de Valero.
De Valery, Cordier de Launay. see Launay
de Valery, Cordier de.
De Valladolid, Diego. see Valladolid, Diego
de.
De Valladolid, Juan Francisco. see Valladolid,
Juan Francisco de.
De Vallarna, Francisco Maria. see Vallarna,
Francisco Maria de.
De Vallarta, Joseph Mariano. see Vallarta,
Joseph Mariano de.
De Valle, Alonso. see Valle, Alonso de.
De Valle-Ameno, Juan Moreno y Castro,
Marques. see Moreno y Castro, Juan,
Marques de Valle-Ameno.
De Valle Hernandez, Antonio. see Hernandez,
Antonio de Valle.
De Valsequa, Gabriell. see Valsequa, Gabriell
de.

De Valtanas, Domingo. see Valtanas, Domingo de.
De Valverde, Fernando. see Valverde, Fernando de.
De Valverde, Juana (Albares de Rosal) see Pinto de Ulloa, Juana (Albares de Rosal) de Valverde.
De Valverde y Rosal, Maria Theresa. see Valverde y Rosal, Maria Theresa de.
De Vane: a story of plebeians and patricians. (31890)
De Varahinca, Domingo. see Varahinca, Domingo de.
De Varaorna, Sancho. see Varaorna, Sancho de.
De Varga, ------ Ramirez. see Ramirez de Varga, -------.
De Varga y Ponce, Jose. see Varga y Ponce, Jose de.
De Vargara, Augustin. see Vargara, Augustin de.
De Vargas, Alonso Ramirez. see Ramirez de Vargas, Alonso.
De Vargas, Jose Mariano. see Vargas, Jose Mariano de.
De Vargas, Juan. see Vargas, Juan de.
De Vargas, Juan Tapia. see Tapia de Vargas, Juan.
De Vargas, Luis. see Vargas, Luis de.
De Vargas, Manuel Antonio. see Vargas, Manuel Antonio de.
De Vargas, Melchior. see Vargas, Melchior de.
De Vargas, Tomas Tamayo. see Tamayo de Vargas, Tomas.
De Vargas Machuca, Bernardo. see Vargas Machuca, Bernardo de.
De Vargas Machuca, Juan. see Vargas Machuca, Juan de.
De Vargas Machuca, Pedro. see Vargas Machuca, Pedro de.
De Vargas y Ponce, Jose. see Vargas y Ponce, Jose de.
De Varnhagen, ------. see Varnhagen, ------- de.
De Varnhagen, Adolfe. see Varnhagen, Francisco Adolfo de, Conde de Porto Seguro, 1816-1878.
De Varnhagen, Francisco Adolfo. see Varnhagen, Francisco Adolfo de, Conde de Porto Seguro, 1816-1878.
De Varrerius, J. see Barreiros, Gaspar.
De Varthema, Ludovico. see Varthema, Ludovico de.
De Vasconcellos, J. M. Pereira. see Pereira de Vasconcellos, J. M.
De Vasconcellos, Simao. see Vasconcellos, Simao de.
De Vasconcellos A. Pereira Cabral, Fredrico Augusto. see Cabral, Fredrico Augusto de Vasconcellos A. Pereira.
De Vasconcellos & Souza, Aloysius. see Vasconcellos & Souza, Aloysius de.
De Vasconzelos, Mariano. see Vasconzelos, Mariano de.
De Vastey, Pompee Valentine. see Vastey, Pompee Valentine, Baron de.
De Vaublanc, Vincent Marie Vienot, Comte. see Vaublanc, Vincent Marie Vienot, Comte de.
De Vauchelles, F. de Lowencourt, Sieur. see Lowencourt, F. de, Sieur de Vauchelles.
De Vaudreuil, ------, Comte. see Vaudreuil, ------, Comte de.

De Vaudreuil de Cavagnal, Pierre Francois de Rigaud, Marquis. see Vaudreuil de Cavagnal, Pierre Francois de Rigaud, Marquis de, 1698-1765.
De Vaugondt, Didier Robert. see Robert de Vaugondy, Didier, 1723-1786.
De Vaugondy, Gilles Robert. see Robert de Vaugondy, Gilles, 1688-1766.
De Vaul, Jacques. see Vaul, Jacques de.
De Vaux, Charles Grant, Vicomte. see Grant, Charles, Vicomte de Vaux.
Devaux, Vve. ed. 73310
De Vaucelles, Simon Jerome Bourlet. see Vauxcelles, Simon Jerome Bourlet de.
De Vazquez, F. P. see Vazquez, F. P. de.
De Veaux, Samuel, 1789-1852. 19804-19805
De Veaux College for Orphans and Destitute Children, Buffalo, N. Y. 19806
Deved. firm publishers see Edwards, Greenough & Deved. firm publishers
De Vedia, Augustin. see Vedia, Augustin de.
De Vedia, Enrique. see Vedia, Enrique de. ed.
De Veen, Corneille. see Veen, Corneille de.
De Veer, -------. see Veer, ---- de.
De Veer, Gerart. see Veer, Gerrit de.
De Veer, Gerrit. see Veer, Gerrit de.
De Vega, Juan. see Vega, Juan de.
De Vega Bazan, Estanislao. see Vega Bazan, Estanislao de.
De Vega Carpio, Lope Felix. see Vega Carpio, Lope Felix de, 1562-1635.
De Vega y Vec, Joseph. see Vega y Vec, Joseph de.
De Veir, G. see Veir, G. de.
De Veitia Linaje, Jose. see Veitia Linaje, Jose de, 162-?-1688.
De Velasco, Alonso Alberto. see Velasco, Alonso Alberto de.
De Velasco, Baltasar de Zurita. see Zurita de Velasco, Baltasar de.
De Velasco, Diego. see Velasco, Diego de.
De Velasco, Ignacio Alonso. see Velasco, Ignacio Alonso de.
De Velasco, J. Banos. see Velasco, J. Banos de.
De Velasco, Joaquin de la Pezula y Sanchez Munoz. see Pezula y Sanchez Munoz de Velasco, Joaquin de la, 1. Marques de Viluma, 1761-1830.
De Velasco, Jo. Fernandez. see Velasco, Jo. Fernandez de.
De Velasco, Joseph Antonio Manso. see Manso de Velasco, Joseph Antonio, Conde de Superunda.
De Velasco, Juan. see Velasco, Juan de.
De Velasco, Luis. see Velasco, Luis de, Marques de Salinas, 1534-1617.
De Velasco, Lvdovico. see Velasco, Lvdovico de.
De Velasco, Pedro. see Velasco, Pedro de.
Developement du sophisme de Thomas Jefferson. 26328
Developement of facts appertaining to the arbitrary and oppressive proceedings of the North Association of Litchfield County. 58656
Development of our resources. 91015
Development of the idea of human freedom. (72175)
Development of the locomotive. 84419
Developpement des causes des troubles et desastres. 19807

Developpement et caractere du systeme colonial. 63709

Developpement parfait du mystere de la generation. (24121)

De Vendrel Chaudron, Adelaide. see Chaudron, Adelaide de Vendel.

Devens, Charles. 19808

Devens, Samuel Adams. (19809)

De Venture de Paradis, Jean Michel. see Venture de Paradis, Jean Michel de, 1739-1799.

De Ver, Gerhart. see Veer, Gerrit de.

De Vera, Francisco. see Vera, Francisco de.

De Vera, Juan Ansaldo. see Ansaldo de Vera, Juan.

De Vera y Pintado, Bernardo. see Vera y Pintado, Bernardo de.

De Veracruz, Alonso. see Gutierrez, Alonzo.

De Vergua, Luis Colon, Duque de. see Colon, Luis, Duque de Veragua, 1521?-1572.

De Verdier, Antoine. see Verdier, Antoine de.

De Verdun de la Crenne, Jean Rene Antoine, Marquis. see Verdun de la Vrenne, Jean Rene Antoine, Marquis de.

De Vere, Maximilian Schele. see Schele de Vere, Maximilian, 1820-1898.

Devereux, ------. illus. 83734

Devereaux, ------, fl. 1804. 5906, 74878

Devereaux, John C. 19811

Deverell, Robert. 19810

Devereux, H. 103366

Devereux, N. defendant 98238 see also Utica and Schenectady Railroad Company. Commissioners. defendants

Devereux, Rachel. 19812

Devereux, Robert. see Essex, Robert Devereux, 2d Earl of, 1566-1601.

De Vergara, Antonio Urrutia. see Urrutia de Vergara, Antonio.

De Vergara, Augustin. see Vergara, Augustin de.

De Vergara, Miguel. see Vergara, Miguel de.

De Vergara y Estrada, Manuel Urrutia. see Urrutia de Vergara y Estrada, Manuel.

De Vergennes, ------. see Vergennes, ------ de.

De Vergennes, Charles Gravier. see Vergennes, Charles Gravier de.

De Vering, Josephus. see Vering, Josephus de.

De Vermon de Forbonnais, Francois. see Vernon de Forbonnais, Francois de.

De Verneuil, Enrique Leopoldo. see Verneuil, Enrique Leopoldo de.

De Verneuil, F. T. A. Chalumeau. see Chalumeau de Verneuil, F. T. A.

De Verre, Pierre Alexandre Jacques. see Verre, Pierre Alexandre Jacques de.

De Verrier Prestre, Jean. see Prestre, Jean de Verrier.

De Verteuil, Louis Antoine Aime Gaston, b. 1807. 19813

De Vertiz, Pedro. see Vertiz, Pedro de.

De Verze, ------ Briand. see Briand de Verze, -------.

De Vesga Lopez, Mateo. see Vesga Lopez, Mateo de.

De Vetancurt, Augustin. see Vetancurt, Augustin de.

D'Eveux de Fleurieu. see Fleurieu, Charles Pierre Claret de, Comte de.

De Veytia Linage, Joseph Fernandez. see Veytia Linage, Joseph Fernandez de.

Deveze, -----. 19814-19815

De Viana Zavala Saenz de Villaverde, Francisco Leandro. see Viana Zavala Saenz de Villaverde, Francisco Leandro de.

De Victoria, Francisco. see Victoria, Francisco de, fl. 1633.

De Victoria, Paulo. see Victoria, Paulo de.

De Victoria, Pedro Gobeo. see Victoria, Pedro Gobeo de.

De Vidaurrazaga, Aparicio. see Vidaurrazaga, Aparicio de.

De Vidaurre, Felipe Gomez. see Vidaurre, Felipe Gomez de.

De Vidaurre y Encalada, Manuel Lorenze. see Vidaurre y Encalada, Manuel Lorenzo de.

De Viedma, Antonio. see Viedma, Antonio de.

De Viedma, Francisco. see Viedma, Francisco de.

De Viefville des Essars, ------. see Viefville des Essars, ----- de.

De Viera, Juan. see Viera, Juan de.

De Vievigne, ----- Petit. see Petit de Vievigne, -----.

Devil and his subjects in Hartford. 98835

Devil at work in the church. 75306

Devil discovered. 46603

Devil done over. 102466

Devil in America. (38475)

Devil in Dixie. 19816

Devil is in the camp! 25815

Devil let loose . . . . A discourse. 57771

Devil let loose; or, a wonderful instance of the goodness of God. 19817

Devil let loose, or the wo occasioned in the inhabitants. 19818

Devil on politics. 2876

Devil turned doctor. 104664

Devil turn'd roundhead. 94477

De Vilaplana, Hermenegildo. see Vilaplana, Hermenegildo de.

De Villa Flor, ------, Conde. see Villa Flor, ------, Conde de.

De Villa Real, Christoval. see Villa Real, Christoval de.

De Villa Sanchez, Juan. see Villa Sanchez, Juan de.

De Villa Senor y Sanchez, Joseph. see Villa Senor y Sanchez, Joseph de.

De Villadarias, Manoel Duarte Caldeiras Centenera. see Villadarias, Manoel Durate Caldeiras Centenera de.

De Villaflor, Luis Henriquez de Guzman, Conde de Alva de Aliste y. see Henriquez de Guzman, Luis, Conde de Alva de Aliste y de Villaflor.

De Villafranca y Cardenas, Jose Ruiz. see Ruiz Villafranca y Cardenas, Joseph.

De Villagarcia, Feliz Antonio. see Villagarcia, Feliz Antonio de.

De Villagomez, Pedro. see Villagomez, Pedro de, Abp.

De Villagra, Gaspar. see Villagra, Gaspar de.

De Villagra, Gaspar Perez. see Villagra, Gaspar Perez de.

De Villagutierre Soto-Mayor, Juan. see Villagutierre Soto-Mayor, Juan de, fl. 1701.

De Villahermosa de Alfaro, ------, Marques. see Vallahermosa de Alfaro, -------, Marques de.

De Villahumbrosa, ------, Duque. see Villahumbrosa, ------, Duque de.

De Villalobos, Arias. see Villalobos, Arias de.

De Villalobos, Baltasar. see Villalobos, Baltasar de.

De Villalobos, Joachin Antonio. see Villalobos, Joachin Antonio de.

De Villalobos, Juan. see Villalobos, Juan de.

De Villalobos, Juan Julian. see Villalobos, Juan Julian de.

De Villalpando, Luis. see Villalpando, Luis de.

De Villalta, Jose Garcia. see Villalta, Jose Garcia de.

De Villalva, Jose Arcadio. see Villalva, Jose Arcadio de.

De Villamor, Pedro Pablo. see Villamor, Pedro Pablo de.

De Villarreal, Juan Joseph. see Villarreal, Juan Joseph de.

De Villaroel, Gaspar. see Villaroel, Gaspar de.

De Villars, ------- Miette. see Miette de Villars, -------.

De Villars, Charles Hautin. see Hautin de Villars, Charles.

De Villasenor y Sanchez, Jose Antonio. see Villasenor y Sanchez, Jose Antonio de.

De Villaurrutia, Jacobo. see Villaurrutia, Jacobo de.

De Villaurrutia y Puente, Wenceslao. see Villaurrutia y Puente, Wenceslao de.

De Villauscencio, Nunez. see Villauscencio, Nunez de.

De Villaverde, Francisco Leandro de Viana Zavala Saenz. see Viana Zavala Saenz de Villaverde, Francisco Leandro.

De Villavicencio, Johannes a Malo. see Villavicencio, Johannes a Malo de.

De Villavicencio, Juan Joseph. see Villavicencio, Juan Joseph de.

De Villavicencio, Pablo. see Villavicencio, Pablo de.

De Villavicencio Nunez, Jos. Philippus. see Nunez, Jos. Philippus de Villavicencio.

De Villavicencio y Horozco, Nuno Nunez. see Villavicencio y Horozco, Nuno Nunez de.

De Villavicensio, Damian. see Villavicensio, Damian de.

Deville, Charles Joseph Sainte Claire. see Saint Claire Deville, Charles Joseph, 1814-1876.

De Villebrune, ------ Le Febvre. see Le Febvre de Villebrune, -------.

De Villegagnon, Nicolas Durand. see Villegagnon, Nicolas Durand de, 1510-1571?

De Villegas, Alonso. see Villegas, Alonso de.

De Villegas, Antonio Claudio. see Villegas, Antonio Claudio de.

De Villegas, Manuel Jose. see Villegas, Manuel Jose de.

De Villeneuve, ----- Belin. see Belin de Villeneuve, ------.

De Villeneuve, A. Champion. see Villeneuve, A. Champion de.

De Villeneuve, Gabrielle Suzanne Barbot Gallon. see Villeneuve, Gabrielle Suzanne Barbot Gallon de.

De Villeneuve, Jerome Petin. see Petin de Villeneuve, Jerome.

De Villeneuve, L. P. Couret. see Couret de Villeneuve, L. P.

De Villerias, Mateo. see Villerias, Mateo de.

De Villers, Charles. see Villers, Charles de.

De Villeveque, ------ Laisne. see Laisne de Villeveque, -------.

De Villiers, -------. see Villiers, ------ de.

De Villiers, Sir John Braham Jacobs, 1863-1931. ed. 89452

Devil's comical oldmanick. 95078

Devil's confession in his dying hour. 19819, 21430

Devil's hole. (14762)

Devil's race course. 20482

Devil's visit to "Old Abe." 5523

De Viluma, Joaquin de la Pezula y Sanchez Munoz de Velasco. 1. Marques. see Pezula y Sanchez Munoz de Velasco, Joaquin de la, 1. Marques de Viluma, 1761-1830.

De Vimeur, Donatien Marie Joseph. see Rochambeau, Donatien Marie Joseph de Vimeur, Vicomte de.

De Vimeur, Jean Baptiste Donatien. see Rochambeau, Jean Baptiste Donatien de Vimeur, Comte de, 1725-1807.

De Vincent, -------. see Vincent, ------- de.

Devine, -------. reporter 97630

De Vinne, Daniel, 1793-1883. 19821

De Vins, -------, Marques de Peysac. see Vins, ------ de, Marques de Peysac.

Devises, bequests and grants to the corporation. 61581

De Vitoria, Paulo. see Victoria, Paulo de.

De Vitoria, Pedro Gobeo. see Victoria, Pedro Gobeo de.

De Vitoria Baraona, Francisco. see Vitoria Barahona, Francisco.

De Vivanco, Diego. see Vivanco, Diego de.

De Vivar, Andres. see Vivar, Andres de.

De Vivar, Rodrigo Diaz. see Infantado Rodrigo Diaz de Vivar, 6. Duque del.

De Vizarron y Eguiarreta, Juan Antonio. see Vizarron y Eguiarreta, Juan Antonio de.

Devlin, B. complainant 38769, 74983

Devlin, John E. 101418

Devlin, John S. defendant at court martial 19822, 70424

Devocion en honra de la purisima leche. 76112

Devocion, y novena de la Esclarecida Virgen. 36792

Devocionario a todos los santos. 76122

Devocionario de Nuestra Senora de Itzmal. 40961

Devocionario en Mejicano. (48327)

Devocionario hecho por un sacerdote. 79320

Devocionario sacerdotal. 86391

Devocionarios para el culto de las imagenes milagrosas. 76287

Devociones varias sacadas de las obras. 76113

De Voe, Thomas Farrington, 1811-1892. 19823-19824

DeVoe, W. M. illus. 90555

De Volafan, Genero H. pseud. ed. see Varnhagen, Francisco Adolfo de, Conde de Porto Seguro, 1816-1878.

De Volney, Constantin Francois Chasseboeuf, Comte. see Volney, Constantin Francois Chasseboeuf, Comte de, 1757-1820.

De Voltaire, Francois Marie Arouet. see Voltaire, Francois Marie Arouet de, 1694-1778.

Devon, W. A. 19826

Devonshire, Charles Blount, Earl of, 1563-1606. 67545

Devonshire, Wills Hill, 1st Marquis of, 1718-1793. 101150

Devot, ----------. supposed author 19827, 27619

Devoted legions. A poem. 18982

Devoted ministry. 26536

Devoted servant of Christ. 12989

Devotedness to Christ. 62717
Devoti, Felix. 19828, 41103, 99659
Devotion, Ebenezer. 19829
Devotion, John. 19830
Devotion and fidelity of a woman. (12573)
Devotion to the Blessed Virgin Mary in North
    America. 43546
Devotional somnium. 2846
Devotions of God's people. 26785
Devoto de santo. pseud. Eustaquidos. see
    Souza, Francisco de.
Devoto instruido en la santo sacrificio de la
    misa. (38950)
Devout and humble enquiry into the reasons
    of . . . the death of good men. 14475
Devout contemplation. 14475
Devout exercises. 80720
Devout exercises of the heart. 73540
De Vouves, P.-L.-C.-F. Rezard. see Rezard
    de Vouves, P.-L.-C.-F.
D'Evreux, Yves. see Yves d'Evreux. Pere
De Vria, Nicolas Ambrosio. see Vria,
    Nicolas Ambrosio de.
De Vries, David Pietersz. see Vries, David
    Pietersz. de.
De Vries, J. V. Ouwerkerk. see Ouwerkerk
    de Vries, J. V.
De Vries, Simon. see Vries, Simon de.
De Vrij, J. E. see Vrij, J. E. de.
Devyr, Thomas Ainge. (13832)
Devyr, Thomas Ainge. petitioner (19831)
Dew, Thomas Roderick. 19833-19836, 65736,
    81240, 82091, 7th note after 88114
Dew-drops of the nineteenth century. 84139-
    84141, 84143, 84146, 84162
De Wailly, Leon. see Wailly, Leon de.
De Waldeck, Jean Frederic Maximilien, Comte.
    see Waldeck, Jean Frederic Maximilien,
    Comte de.
De Walden, Thomas Howard, 1st Baron Howard.
    see Suffolk, Thomas Howard, 1st Earl
    of, 1561-1626.
De Walderande, J. B. see Walderande, J. B.
    de.
De Warrdenau, D. 19837
Dewart, Edward Hartley. ed. 19838
De Warville, Anacharsis Brissot. see Brissot
    de Warville, Anacharsis.
De Warville, Jacques Pierre Brissot. see
    Warville, Jacques Pierre Brissot de.
De Weert, Sebald. see Weert, Sebald de.
Dewees, Jacob. 19839-19841
Dewees, Samuel. 30231, 62274 see also
    Philadelphia County, Pa. Sub-Lieutenant.
Dewees, W. B. (19842)
Dewees, W. P. ed. 62010
Dewees, Watson W. 103058
De Wegmann, Ferdinande. see Wegmann,
    Ferdinand de.
De Welderen, ------, Comte. see Welderen,
    ------, Comte de.
D'Ewes, J. 19843
De Wette, Ludwig. see Wette, Ludwig de.
De Wette, Wilhelm Martin Leberecht. see
    Wette, Wilhelm Martin Leberecht de.
Dewey, Adolphus. 96360
Dewey, Benoni. 18632, 1st note after 97087,
    2d note after 103214 see also Hanover,
    N. H. Congregational Church. Commit-
    tee.
Dewey, Chester, 1784-1867. 19844-19848,
    24270, 92912 see also Massachusetts.
    Zoological and Botanical Survey.
Dewey, Dillon Marcus. 19849, 72340
Dewey, Daniel Perkens. 19850
Dewey, J. J. 38189

Dewey, Mary E. (78782)
Dewey, Orville, 1794-1882. 19852-19862,
    28427, 63162
Dewey, Sherman. (19863)
Dewey, William. 19864-19865
Dewey (D. M.) firm publisher 72340
Dewey's county directory. 38189
Dewey's Rochester city directory. 72340
Dewherst, Henry William. (19866)
De Wimpffen, Francois Alexandre Stanislaus,
    Baron. see Wimpffen, Francois Alexandre
    Stanislaus, Baron de.
De Wind, S. see Wind, S. de.
De Windt, Carolina Amelia (Smith) ed. 168,
    84905
Dewing, Francis. engr. 85489
De Wintton, ------. 19867
Dewis, J. P. 19868
De Wit, Frederick. see Wit, Frederick de.
    cartographer
De With, Witte Cornelisszoon. see With,
    Witte Cornelisszoon de, 1599-1658.
De Witt, Benjamin, 1774-1819. 19869-(19871),
    32053, 54021, 94298
Dewitt, Clinton. 3707
De Witt, Cornelis. see Witt, Cornelis de.
De Witt, Francis. 1st-2d notes after (19871)
De Witt, Johan. see Witt, Johan de.
De Witt, John, fl. 1740. 78992
De Witt, John, fl. 1835. 19872
De Witt, Simeon, 1756-1834. 15997, 19873-
    19874
De Witt, Thomas, 1791-1874. 19875-19877,
    21338, 25972, 37943, (38166), 89736
De Witt, Wallace. 60378
De Witt, William Radcliffe, 1792-1867. 19878-
    19880, 30544, 80768
De Witt (Clinton T.) firm publisher 80849,
    84786
DeWitt (R. M.) firm publishers 25105
De Witt Clinton and the late war. 13729,
    30187
De Witt Guard. see New York (State) Militia.
    Fiftieth Regiment. Company A (De Witt
    Guard)
De Witt's acting plays (number 263) 84786
De Witt's special report. 80849
De Wolf, L. E. (19884)
De Wolf, Thaddeus K. 19885
De Wrangell, ------. see Wrangel, Ferdi-
    nand Petrovich, Baron von.
Dewry, Joseph. 104986
Dewsbury, William, 1621-1688. 19886, 79296,
    84552
De Xaintoigne, Jean Alfonce. see Xaintoigne,
    Jean Alfonce de, i. e. Jean Fonteneau,
    known as.
De Xalo, Joachin Casses. see Casses de
    Xalo, Joachin.
De Xanctoigne, Jean Alfonce. see Xaintoigne,
    Jean Alfonce de, i. e. Jean Fonteneau,
    known as.
De Xanctoigne, Jean Alfonse. see Xaintoigne,
    Jean Alfonce de, i. e. Jean Fonteneau,
    known as.
D'Exauvillez, Andre Philippe Octave Boistel.
    see Boistel d'Exauvillez, Andre Philippe
    Octave.
De Xeres, Francisco. see Xerez, Francisco
    de, b. 1500.
De Xerez, Francisco. see Xerez, Francisco
    de, b. 1500.
D'Exiles, Antoine Francois Prevost. see
    Prevost d'Exiles, Antoine Francois.
De Xivrey, J. B. see Xivrey, J. B. de.
Dexter, --------, fl. 1850. 19909

Dexter, Andrew. 19887
Dexter, Charles. 19888
Dexter, E. 19889
Dexter, Edward. plaintiff 89104
Dexter, Franklin, 1793-1857. 275, 6688,
    19890-19891, (30195), 34959, 85430
Dexter, Franklin Bowditch. 1842-1920. ed.
    note after 91736, 91750
Dexter, George. 11491, 19892
Dexter, Henry Martyn, 1821-1890. 7263,
    (12976)-12977, 15479, 19893-19896,
    51200, 74795, 104334
Dexter, John H. 19897
Dexter, Mary. 96306
Dexter, O. P. (77233)
Dexter, Samuel. respondent 44135
Dexter, Samuel, 1700-1755. 19898-19899
Dexter, Samuel, 1761-1816. 19900-19903,
    41648, (79012)
Dexter, Thomas C. A. defendant before mili-
    tary commission 9622, 19904-19905
Dexter, Timothy, 1747-1806. 19906-(19908),
    38079, 86840
Dexter, Asylum, Providence, R. I. see Provi-
    dence, R. I. Dexter Asylum.
Dexter genealogy. 55017-(55018)
Dexter's pickle for the knowing ones. 38079
De Yangues, Manuel. see Yangues, Manuel
    de.
De Yarza, Joseph Antonio. see Yarza, Joseph
    Antonio de.
De Yarza, Remigio. see Yarza, Remigio de.
Deye, Thomas Cockey. 45279
Deynoodt, Francois. 82277
Deynoot, W. T. Gevers. see Gevers Deynoot,
    W. T.
De Yramategui, Juan. see Yramategui, Juan
    de.
De Yrolo Calar, Nicolas. see Yrolo Calar,
    Nicolas de.
De Yrujo y Tacon, Carlos Martinez. see
    Casa Yrujo, Carlos Martinez de Yrujo
    y Tacon, Marques de, 1763-1824.
De Ysla, Ruy Diaz. see Ysla, Ruy Diaz de.
De Yta y Parra, Bartolome Felipe. see Yta
    y Parra, Bartolome Felipe de.
De Yturbide, Agustin. see Iturbide, Agustin
    de, Emperor of Mexico, 1783-1824.
De Yturrigaray, Joseph. see Yturrigaray,
    Joseph de.
De Yturrizara, Miguel. see Yturrizara,
    Miguel de.
De Yunibarbia, Bernardo. see Yunibarbia,
    Bernardo de.
De Yzaguerri, Francisco. see Yzaguerri,
    Francisco de.
Deza y Ulloa, Antonio. plaintiff 19912
Deza y Ulloa, Clara. 19912
De Zaldivar y Mendoca, Vicente. see Zaldivar
    y Mendoca, Vicente de.
De Zanartu, Miguel Jose. see Zanartu,
    Miguel Jose de.
De Zapata, Luis. see Zapata, Luis de.
De Zarate, Augustin. see Zarate, Augustin
    de.
De Zarate, Fernando. see Zarate, Fernando
    de.
De Zarate, J. see Zarate, J. de, Bp.
De Zavala, L. see Zavala, L. de.
De Zavala, Lorenzo. see Zavala, Lorenzo de.
De Zavala Fanarraga, Juan. see Zavala
    Fanarraga, Juan de.
De Zavala y Aunon, Miguel. see Zavala y
    Aunon, Miguel de.
De Zavaleta, Antonio Fernando Maria. see
    Zavaleta, Antonio Fernando Maria de.

De Zavaleta, Joachina Maria. see Zavaleta,
    Joachina Maria de.
De Zayas, Juan Suarez. see Suarez de Zayas,
    Juan.
De Zeltner, A. see Zeltner, A. de.
De Zepeda, Juan. see Zepeda, Juan de.
De Zepeda, y Castro, Gaspar. see Zepeda y
    Castro, Gaspar de.
De Zequeira y Arango, Manuel. see Zequeira
    y Arango, Manuel de.
De Zequeira y Caro, Manuel. see Zequeira y
    Caro, Manuel de.
De Zevallos, Ciriaco. see Zevallos, Ciriaco
    de.
De Zecallos, D. I. Ortis. see Ortis de
    Zevallos, D. I.
De Zizur, Pablo. see Zizur, Pablo de.
Dezos de la Roquette, Jean Baptiste Marie
    Alexandre. see Roquette, Jean Baptiste
    Marie Alexandre Dezos de la.
Dezoteux, ------. 19913
De Zubiria, Jose Antonio Lopez. see Lopez
    de Zubiria, Jose Antonio.
De Zuelta, Pedro. defendant 19914
De Zumarraga, Juan. see Zumarraga, Juan
    de, Abp.
De Zuniga, Diego Ortiz. see Ortiz de Zuniga,
    Diego.
De Zuniga, Luis. see Zuniga, Joseph de.
De Zuniga Guzman Sotomayor y Mendoza,
    Baltazar. see Zuniga Guzman Sotomayor
    y Mendoza, Baltazar, Marques de Valero.
De Zuniga y Acevedo, Gaspar. see Zuniga y
    Acevedo, Gaspar de, Conde de Monterey.
De Zuniga y la Cerda, Jose. see Zuniga y
    la Cerda, Jose de.
De Zuniga y Ontiveros, Felipe. see Zuniga
    y Ontiveros, Felipe de.
De Zuniga y Ontiveros, Mariano. see Zuniga
    y Ontiveros, Mariano de.
De Zurita, Alonso. see Zurita, Alonso de.
De Zurita de Velasco, Baltasar. see Zurita
    de Velasco, Baltasar de.
D'Hachette, ----- Fourquet. see Fourquet-
    D'Hachette, -------.
D'Happoncourt, Francoise d'Isembourg. see
    Grafigny, Francois (d'Isembourg d'Happon-
    court) de, 1695-1758.
D'Harponville, Gustave, Vicomte d'Hespel. see
    Hespel d'Harponville, Gustave, Vicomte d'.
D'Hauteriver, -------, Comte. see Hauteriver,
    -----, Comte d'.
D'Hauteville, Ellen (Sears) Grand. defendant
    19915-19916, 49067, 70231
D'Hauteville, Paul Daniel Gonzalve Grand.
    plaintiff 19915-19916, 49067, 70231
D'Henin de Cuvillers, Etienne Felix. see
    Henin de Cuvillers, Etienne Felix, Baron
    d', 1755-1841.
D'Heguerty, -----. see O'Heguerty, Domingo,
    Comte de Magnieres, 1699-1790.
D'Helf, Josephine Lebassu. see Lebassu
    d'Helf, Josephine.
D'Hervey de Saint-Denys, Marie Jean Leon,
    Marquis. see Hervey de Saint-Denys,
    Marie Jean Leon, Marquis d', 1823-1892.
D'Hespel d'Harponville, Gustave, Vicomte. see
    Hespel d'Harponville, Gustave, Vicomte d'.
D'Homergue, Jean. see Homergue, Jean d'.
Dhormoys, Paul. 19917-19918
Dhu, Helen. pseud. Stanhope Burleigh. see
    Black, Helen. supposed author and
    Lester, Charles Edward. supposed author
Di Fernando Cortese la seconda relatione della
    Nvova Spagna. 67740

Di M. Gio. Battista Ramvsio discorso sopra il libro del Signor Hayton Armeno. 67736

Di M. Gio. Battista Ramvsio prefatione. 67736-67739

Di Marco Polo e degli altri viaggiatori Veneziani. 106411

Di Messer Iosafa Barbaro gentil'hvomo Venetiano. 67736

Di orbis divisione ac insulis. 26853, 62588

Di Pietro d'Alvarado a Fernando Cortese lettere. 67740

Di qvarta relatione di Fernando Cortese della Nvova Spagna. 67740

Dia 5 de Julio del ano 14 en la Habana. 6302

Dia de Lima. 44394

Dia deseado. 24143

Dia festivo proprio para el culto. 35285

Dia natalico do Muito Alto e Muito Poderoso Senhor D. Pedro IV. 44107

Dia que no se contrar entre los de Colombia. (76806)

Diable, Captain. pseud. see Captain Le Diable. pseud.

Diablo en Mexico. 13836

Diablo predicador. (48041)

Diabolo suelto y predicador. 41977

Diadochus, Proclus. 91983

Diagrams and plans. 104029

Diagrams of the floor. (19919)

Diagrams of the townships in Upper Canada. 10415

Dial: a magazine for literature, philosophy, and religion. 19920, 71523

Dial; a monthly magazine for literature, philosophy, and religion. 19921

Dialectic Society of the University of North Carolina. see North Carolina. University. Dialectic Society.

Dialectica resolutio cum textu Aristotelis. 98912

Dialogi di Academio Mexicana. 11715, (75565)

Dialogisirte Skizze. 101901

Dialogo. 94597, 105740

Dialogo Chileno-Hispano muy curioso. 23968

Dialogo constitucional Brasileiro. 51687

Dialogo critico joco-serio, en que entre varios interlocutores. 87234

Dialogo critico joco-serio, cobre las observaciones. 87233

Dialogo de doctrina Christiana en la lengua de Mechuaca. (27358)

Dialogo de la dignidad del hombre. 75567-75568

Dialogo de los editores del Argos. 61128

Dialogo de un Indio. 76747

Dialogo del conpadre [sic] y su amigo. 93942

Dialogo dela dignidad del hombre. 75567

Dialogo di Giovanni Stamlerno Augustense. 90128

Dialogo entre A. y B. 96506

Dialogo entre Celso y su padre. 11226

Dialogo entre Clarideo y Rosa. 98958

Dialogo entre D. Chepe y D. Nacho. 76197

Dialogo entre Don Tecla y D. Canuto. 94577

Dialogo entre D. Toribio y D. Venancio. 29430, 96194

Dialogo entre dos hermanos Paulino y Rosa. 98957

Dialogo————entre el enthusiastica libral y el filosofo rancio. 96117

Dialogo entre el veijo chapeton D. Diego Rota. 98345

Dialogo entre Marcina e Delmira. (18233)

Dialogo entre un abogado y un capitan. 76747

Dialogo entre un militar y un paisano. 94143

Dialogo entre una senorita y un Indio. 19922

Dialogo llamado Democrates. 79177

Dialogo, metrico-heroyco. (55349)

Dialogo muy curioso entre un dragon. 98254

Dialogo primero y segundo. 19923

Dialogo 2 entre Paulino y Rosa. 98959

Dialogo sobre el comercio de los reinos de Castilla con las Indias. 93114

Dialogo sobre la independencia. 977, 16159, 96117-note after 96117

Dialogos criticos-jocoserios entre un cohetero y un tamborilero. 18785

Dialogos de la doctrina Christiana en lengua Mexicana. (70807)

Dialogos de varia historia. 44608

Dialogos en lengua Mexicana. 3995, (76133)

Dialogos en que se explican el Kalendario Romano. 72463

Dialogos entre un cohetero y un tamborilero. 18784

Dialogos militares. 58268

Dialogos nueuamente compuestos. 48235

Dialogos o colloquios nueuamente corregidas. 48236

Dialogos segundo. 35078

Dialogue. 18944, 19421, 23387, 35082, 61547, note after 90644, 90896, 97552, 104590

Dialogue and a poem. 91810

Dialogue and ode. 84606-84607

Dialogue and two odes. 23389, 61547, 84610

Dialogue between A and B. 19924

Dialogue between a barrister and a juryman. 30976

Dialogue between a beggar and a divine. 83975

Dialogue between a blind-man and death. 90157-90159

Dialogue between a Christian and a Quaker. 59728

Dialogue between a colonel of the militia, and a militia-man. 35364

Dialogue between a father and son. 71195

Dialogue between a Federalist and a Republican. 1655

Dialogue between a Jesuite and a recusant. (65743)-67544

Dialogue between a merchant and a planter. 25724, 87830

Dialogue between a merchant and a planter. Part II. 19925, 88064

Dialogue between a minister and a non-professor. 13002

Dailogue between a minister and his neighbour about the times. 97454

Dialogue between a minister and his people. 74633

Dialogue between a minister and one of his parishioners. 20053

Dialogue between a miser and a spendthrift. 63585, 104539

Dialogue between a noble lord and a poor wood-man. 19930

Dialogue between a one thousand-dollar clerk. 19932

Dialogue between a protestant and a catholic. 87004

Dialogue between a southern delegate, and his spouce. 19933, 4th note after 98269

Dialogue between Academicus and Sawney, and Mundungus. 20724, 101195

Dialogue between Adam and Eve. 98493

Dialogue between an abolitionist and a West Indian. 81964, 4th note after 102832

Dialogue between an Episcopalian and a Presbyterian. 19927, 54245

Dialogue between an Indian and a white man. 2478

Dialogue between an old constable and a new.
2557, 16044
Dialogue between an old-fashioned Jackson
Democrat and a copperhead. 19931,
42555
Dialogue between an uncle and his kinsman.
97723
Dialogue, between Andrew Trueman, and
Thomas Zealot. 19926, 79242, 97168
Dialogue between Christ, a youth, and the
devil. note after 65546
Dialogue between Col. Paine and Miss Clorinda
Fairchild. 63622
Dialogue between death, the soul, body, world
and Jesus Christ. 102530
Dialogue between Do Justice and professing-
Christians. 26693
Dialogue, between Eusebius and Eleutherius.
103067
Dialogue between Franklin and the gout. 62425
Dialogue between Freeman and Trusty. 60056,
60204
Dialogue between General Arnold and Lord
Cornwallis. 63585, 104539
Dialogue between George Fox a Quaker.
106099
Dialogue between George the Third of Great-
Britain, and his ministers. 67955
Dialogue between George III and his ministers.
19928
Dialogue between Marat and Peter Porcupine.
14025
Dialogue between Mr. Ebenezer Eastlove and
Giles Homespun. 52261
Dialogue between Mr. Robert Rich, and Roger
Plowman. (70897)
Dialogue between old England and new. 7296,
note after 94823
Dialogue between Praeleticus and Eleutherius.
(78491)-78493
Dialogue between Rusticus and Academicus.
(74419)
Dialogue between S. & B. 21609, note after
104106
Dialogue between self and the soul. 41039
Dialogue between Simon and Timothy. 67995
Dialogue between Sir George Cornwell. 16822
Dialovue between Telemachus and Mentor.
19934, note after 94609
Dialogue between the famous Roman casuist
Escabar. 103645
Dialogue between the ghost of General Mont-
gomery. (58214), 58220
Dialogue between the giant Polypheme and his
son Jack Nothing. 19929
Dialogue between the Observator and his
country-man Roger. 56596, 67997
Dialogue between the professor and Sir John
Brute. 16170
Dialogue between the pulpit and the deading-
desk. 85206-85207
Dialogue between Thomas Sweet-Scented,
William Oronoco. 100458
Dialogue between two gentlemen in New York.
19935
Dialogue between two great ladies. 19936
Dialogue between two Negroes in South Carolina.
75900
Dialogue betwixt a Quaker and a hireling
priest. 9237
Dialogue betwixt General Wolfe and the Marquis
Montcalm. 19937
Dialogue . . . by Eunice Smith. (82541)
Dialogue [by Mr. Hart.] 32955
Dialogue by Mr. Nat. Evans. 23388, 61547

Dialogue, by the same hand. (32953), note
after 102754
Dialogue concerning the half-way covenant.
4497
Dialogue concerning the slavery of the Africans.
19939, (32948), (81956)
Dialogue containing a compendious discourse.
102831
Dialogue, containing some reflections. 19938,
60057, 64448
Dialogue en vers, avec des notes. 6894, 4th
note after 100806
Dialogue entre deux deputes. 19940
Dialogue entre la goutre et Franklin. 25596
Dialogue entre les deux egorgeurs de Saint-
Domingue. 87116, 95326
Dialogue, &c. (61582), 84610
Dialogue exhibited on the stage. 93478,
105785B
Dialogue, exhibiting some of the principles.
92247
Dialogue in Hades. 67022
Dialogue, in one act. 87132
Dialogue in the shades, between General Wolfe.
19947, note after 96403
Dialogue in three parts. (75899)
Dialogue in verse between a patriot, a courtier,
and their friend. 95748
Dialogue occasioned by the recent duel at
Washington. 105232
Dialogue of the backwoodsman and the dandy.
20488-20489
Dialogue on cheap postage. 64478
Dialogue on commonwealths. 67421
Dialogue on democracy. 51129
Dialogue on peace, an entertainment. 19942
"Dialogue on the actual state of Parliament."
19941, 56508
Dialogue on the Christian sacraments. 4487
Dialogue, on the effectual means of separating
free masonry. 90895
Dialogue on the honourable nature of military
study. 79176
Dialogue on the penitentiary system. (19943)
Dialogue on the principles of the constitution
and legal liberty. 19944
Dialogue I. Washington, Alfred and William
Tell. 1081A, 101770
Dialogue or conversation between a planter
and some headmen. 8105, 19945
Dialogue, or discourse between James Freeman.
(55502), note after 87925
Dialogue, or discourse between Mary & Martha.
82542
Dialogue, or, representation of matters of fact.
19946, 53253
Dialogue, or the sum of a conference. 51017,
106053
Dialogue shewing the sentiments. 45412
Dialogue shewing, what's therein to be found.
60058, 97997
Dialogue tusschen een Hollander Engelsman en
Fransman. 38028, 3d note after 102893
Dialogue II. Washington, Hamilton, and Fisher
Ames. 1081A, 101770
Dialogues against Mr. Bellamy's Theron.
17834
Dialogues between an Ethiopian. 25947, note
after 97286
Dialogues de Monsieur le Baron de la Honton.
38633-83634
Dialogues de Monsieur le Baron de Lahontan.
29142, (38643)
Dialogues in the shades. 19947, note after
96403
Dialogues of devils. (34693)

Dialogues of the American dead. 1081A, 101770
Dialogues of the dead. 19948
Dialogues on slavery. 32592
Dialogues, or third conference. 52630
Dialogues pittoresques dans lesquels on developpe la cause. 11702
Dialogus, of t' samen-sprekinge. 24340
Diamond: a full exposition. 92684
Diamond: being the law. 92683
Diamond atlas. (14260)
"Diamond murder." 67965
Diamond Point. A national poem. 9121
Diamond wedding. 91065
Diana of the Ephesians. 86635
Diana's shrines turned into ready money. 66232
Diannyere, Antoine. tr. 68748
Di Araujo, Manuel do Monte Rodrigues. see Monte Rodrigues de Araujo, Manuel do, Bp., 1798-1863.
Diarial account. (65989)
Diaries and correspondence of the Right Hon. George Rose. (73240)
Diaries of George Washington. 101710
Diaries of the Rev. Seth Williston. 104533
Diarii biographici tomus secundus. 104961
Diario constitucional de 9 de Julio de 1820. 93783
Diario da navagacao da armada. 88726
Diario da navegacao de Pedro Lopes de Souza. 88727
Diario da viagem que em visita e correicao. 70794
Diario de avisos de Caracas. 7796
Diario de avisos de religion. 48421
Diario de Californias. 1768, 38234, 57680
Diario de Caracas. 64015
Diario de comercio de Paris. 99834
Diario de documentos del gobierno. 12765
Diario de D. Luis de la Cruz. 96247
Diario de gobierno de Megico. 19268, 93785
Diario de la Comision Nombrada para Establecer la Nueva Linea. 73211
Diario de la expedicion de 1822. (26589)
Diario de la expedicion del Mariscal de Campo D. Juan Ramirez. (689)
Diario de la expedicion hecha en 1774. 46869
Diario de la expedicion reduccional del ano de 1780. 1973
Diario de la guerra de los guaranies. 10803
Diario de la guerra del Paraguay. 58513
Diario de la Habana. 1887, 74769, 94191
Diario de la Junta Nacional instituyente del imperio Mexicano. (49422)
Diario de la marina de la Habana. 11465, 50527
Diario de la navegacion empredida en 1781. 19665.
Diario de la navegacion que hizo Juan Rodriguez Cabrillo. 84379
Diario de la navegacion y reconocimiento del Rio Tebicuari. (2535)
Diario de la primera expedicion al Chaco. 16792
Diario de la segunda division de limites. 9010
Diario de las noticias de Lima. 41099
Diario de las operaciones contra la plaza de Panzacola. 26475
Diario de las operaciones de la expedicion contra la plaza de Panzacola. 19949
Diario de las operaciones del ejercito federal. 26386
Diario de las operaciones militares. 98152

Diario de las sesiones de la Soberana Junta Provisional. 48423
Diario de las sesiones del Congreso del estado de Jalisco. 35548
Diario de Lima. 41100
Diario de los ninos. 19950
Diario de los viages de mar y tierra. 17019
Diario de Mexico. 48424
Diario de sesiones de la Camara de Senadores. 9011
Diario de sesiones de la Convencion del estado de Buenos-Aires. 9012
Diario de todo lo occurido. 19951, 22877
Diario de un reconocimiento de las guardias y fortines. 2536
Diario de un soldado. 86257
Diario de un viage a la costa de Patagonia. 99515
Diario de un viage a Salinas Grandes. 26590
Diario de una expedicion a Salinas. 106365
Diario de Veracruz. 94154, 95851, 98906
Diario de viage de la Comision de Limites. 12982, (48885)
Diario de viaje de D. Ramon de la Sagra. 74910
Diario del Gobierno Constitucional de la Habana. 93784
Diario del gobierno de Megico. 93785
Diario del imperio. 48425
Diario del pilota de la Real Armada. 99666
Diario del viage de los cincos misioneros. 98173
Diario general de todo lo sucedido en Espana. 19952
Diario historico das celebridades que na cidade de Bahia. 46905
Diario historico de la Compana da Apure de 1837. 19953
Diario historico de la rebelion y guerra. 31341
Diario historico del sitio, indefension, perdida, y saco. 98388
Diario historico del ultimo viaje. 36761
Diario literario de Mexico. 48426
Diario militar del General Jose Urrea. 98152
Diario notable de la Marquesa de las Amarillas. 19954, 48427
Diario official. (48440)
Diario official del gobierno de la republica Mejicana. 48478
Diario oficial de Mexico. 67910
Diario oficial del Jueves 12 de Octubre. 93788
Diario oficial. Estados Unidos de Colombia. 14581
Diario philosophico. 26374
Diario politico, literario, noticioso y mercantil. 70310
Diario politico, literario y comercial. 34446, 70340
Diario que escribe D. Jose Eusebio de Llano y Zapata. 41669, 41671
Diario satirico-burlesco. (38808)
Diario y derrotero de lo caminado. 19955
Diario y observaciones del presbitero Jose Cortes Madriaga. 43693
Diarium biographicum. 104961
Diarium, vel descriptio laboriosissimi, & molestissimi itineris. 77958-77961
Diary. 40603, 2d note after 99312
Diary and autobiography of Edmund Bohun, Esq. 6144
Diary and correspondence of the late Amos Lawrence. 39384
Diary and narrative of travel. 88549

Diary and other writings of Mrs. Almira Torrey. 96280
Diary, by Pigafetta. 47042, 1st note after 99406
Diary, 1863, '64, '65. (29320)
Diary for 1841. 91707
Diary for 1869. 48831
Diary. Four months of prison life. 19956
Diary, from March 4, 1861, to November 12, 1862. 29319
Diary, from November 18, 1862, to October 18, 1863. 29319
Diary in America. (44697)
Diary in America, with remarks on its institutions. (44696)
Diary kept at Valley Forge. 100999
Diary kept upon the overland route to California. (38904)
Diary of a Bull Run prisoner, at Richmond. 47981
Diary of a journey from the Mississippi. 49915
Diary of a lady of Gettysburg, Pennsylvania. 19957, 27232
Diary of a milliner. 105122
Diary of a physician in California. 97640
Diary of a Samaritan. 19958, 72213
Diary of a soldier. (25043)
Diary of a southern refugee during the war. (19959), 43297
Diary of a staff-officer. (55199)
Diary of American events. 7965, 40590, 41029, (43011), 43370, 50356, 50368, note after 69327, 74401, 89506, 89687-89688
Diary of an American physician. 99427
Diary of an excursion to Abo Quarra and Gran Quivira. 10905
Diary of an expedition from San Francisco. (8350), 100641-1st note after 100641
Diary of Battery A. 68980
Diary [of Col. Winthrop Sargent. (77034)
Diary [of Cotton Mather.] 91833, 91945, 104243
Diary [of Daniel Wadsworth.] 100927
Diary of David How. 33217
Diary of David Zeisberger. note after 106301
Diary of D. Ant. de Robles. (48440)
Diary of D. Gregorio Martin de Guijo. (48440)
Diary of D. Jose Manuel de Castro Santa Anna. (48440)
Diary of Fanny Newell. 54951
Diary [of George Washington.] 7754, 101710
Diary of George Washington, from 1789 to 1791. (80023)
Diary of Isaiah Thomas, 1805-1828. 2d note after 95414
Diary [of John A. Sutter.] 84946
Diary [of John Adams.] 26445
Diary of John Hull. (33637)
Diary of Jose Gomez. (48440)
Diary of John Buell and John Matthews. 31799
Diary [of Moses Abbot.] (16628)
Diary of Nathan Hale in 1775 and 1776. 93163
Diary of Salado exploration in 1862 and 1863. (34089)
Diary of Samuel Sewall. 79449
Diary of some religious exercises and experience. (78355)
Diary of the American revolution. 50357
Diary of the debates in the Congress. 22233
Diary of the deceased [i. e. Pitt Clarke.] 5283
Diary of the great rebellion. 19960
Diary of the late George Bubb Doddington. 20516
Diary of the late Samuel Emlin. 22514

Diary of the Rev. Solomon Spittle. (77005), 89539, note before 96475
Diary of the siege of Detroit. 19788, 33138, (72725)
Diary of the war for separation, a daily chronicle. 13404
Diary of the war for separation . . . to the battle of Shiloh. 13405
Diary of the wreck of H. M. S. Challenger. (19961)
Diary of Thomas Robbins, D. D. (71843)
Diary of unwritten history. 11434
Diary of war for separation. 15257
Diary of sketches and reviews. 20511
Dias, Antonio Goncalves. see Goncalves Dias, Antonio, 1823-1864.
Dias, Jose Domingo. 68466
Dias Coelho e Mello, Antonio. see Coelho e Mello, Antonio Dias.
Dias de Arce, Juan. 1898, 19964-19965
Dias de Fereira, Gaspar. see Fereira, Gaspar Dias de.
Dias do Quintal, Joao. see Quintal, Joao Dias do.
Dias Zapata, Francis. see Zapata, Francis Dias.
Diatriba de signo filii hominis. 46652
Diatribe of the same M. Hooker. 11615
Diaz, Francisco. 76007
Diaz, J. 94854
Diaz, Jose Domingo. 10783, (19966)-19967, 36437, 50703, 68466, 96221-note after 96221, 3d note after 98882.
Diaz, Jose Francisco. 19968, (23515)
Diaz, Juan. 98643-98647
Diaz, N. Ant. 19969
Diaz, Pedro. 18658, 19970, 19971, 43776, 44963-44965, 89536-note after 89538
Diaz, Ramon. 3249-3250
Diaz, Sose A. 19972
Diaz Calvillo, Juan Bautista. 19973-(19974), 56012
Diaz Covarrubias, J. (19975)
Diaz de Espada y Landa, Juan Jose. see Espada y Landa, Juan Jose Diaz de.
Diaz de Espada y Landa, Francisco Joseph. see Espada y Landa, Francisco Joseph Diaz de.
Diaz de Gammara y Davalos, Juan Bento, 1745-1783. 26498-26499
Diaz de Guzman, Rui, 1558?-1629. (29149), (29378)-29379
Diaz de Hortega, Jose. 19976
Diaz de la Vega, Silvestre. see Vega, Silvestre Diaz de la.
Diaz de Possada, Melchior. see Possada, Melchior Diaz de.
Diaz de Solis, Juan. see Solis, Juan Diaz de.
Diaz de Vivar, Rodrigo. see Infantado, Rodrigo Diaz de Vivar, 6. Duque del.
Diaz de Ysla, Ruy. see Ysla, Ruy Diaz de.
Diaz del Castillo, Bernal, 1492-1581? 2002A, 16964, 19977, 19978-19987, 26874-26875, 27752, 74951, 80987
Diaz Freile, Juan. see Freile, Juan Diaz.
Diaz Noriega, Jose Maria. 19988
Diaz Pimienta, Francisco. see Pimienta, Francisco Diaz.
Diaz Quintero, Francisco. see Quintero, Francisco Diaz.
Diaz Salcedo, Bruno. see Salcedo, Bruno Diaz.
Diaz Tano, Francisco. 19989
Diaz y Tarado, Jos. Atan. 19990
Dibble, Sheldon. 19991-(19992)

Dibble, Sheldon. supposed author (19992), 76454, 96419
Dibblee, Albert. 76036 see also San Francisco Chamber of Commerce. President.
Dibdin, Charles, 1745-1814. 86906, 92176A, 94132
Dibdin, Thomas John, 1771-1841. 88542
Di Caman, Vasco. see Gama, Vasco da, 1469?-1524.
Diccionario. 74017
Diccionario bibliografico-historico de los antiguos reinos. 51354
Diccionario bibliographico Portuguez. (81083)
Diccionario Chileno-Hispano. 23970
Diccionario da lingua geral dos Indios do Brasil. 81107
Diccionario da lingua Tupy chamada lingua geral dos indigenas do Brazil. (19962)
Diccionario de Chilenismos. 86250
Diccionario de derecho internacional. 67649
Diccionario de la legislacion Peruana. 9882
Diccionario de la lengua de los Indios Cummanagotos, y Palenques. 105954
Diccionario de la lengua Maya. 60910
Diccionario de plantas. 50587
Diccionario Espanol y Mexicano. (48428)
Diccionario geografico universal, que comprehende la descripcion de las quatro partes del mundo. 50217
Diccionario geografico universal, que contiene la descripcion de todos los paises. 44158
Diccionario geografico de las diversas ciudades. (68852)
Diccionario geografico, estadistico, historico de Espana. 43751
Diccionario geografico, estadistico, historico de la isla de Cuba. 61327
Diccionario geografico-historico de las Indias Occidentales to America. 682
Diccionario geographico das provincias. 88789
Diccionario geographico, historico e descriptivo do imperiodo Brasil. 49085
Diccionario Hispano Chileno. 23969
Diccionario historico, biografico y monumental de Yucatan. 11422
Diccionario historico e geographico da provincia de S. Pedro. 1892
Diccionario jeografico de la republica de Chile. 86242
Diccionario Mayo-Hispano e Hispano-Mayo. 76007
Diccionario para el pueblo. 22901
Diccionario Portuguez e Brasiliano. 19993, 81107, 98831
Diccionario Portuguez Tupico. 81100
Diccionario provincial casi-razonado de voces Cubanas. 62603
Diccionario provincial, de voces Cubanas. 17770
Diccionario topografico, estaidstico o historico. 32788
Diccionario topographico do imperio do Brasil. 17013
Diccionario topographico e estadistico da provincia do Ceara. 63952, 88740
Diccionario topographico, historico e descriptivo da comarca. 81099
Diccionario Tupico-Portuguez. 81100
Diccionario universal de historia y de geografica. 589, 6834, 48429, 48599
Di Censola, Louis Palma. see Cesnola, Louis Palma di.
Dicey, Edward. 19994
Di Charlevoix, P. F. Saverio. see Charlevoix, Pierre Francois Xavier de, 1682-1761.

Dichos, y hechos del Senor Rey Don Felipe Segundo. 64171-64172
Dichtgedachten. (38325)
Dichtstuk. 35269
Dichtwerken. (5370)
Dick, -------. illus. (46835)-46836
Dick, A. L. engr. 84163
Dick, Elisha C. 749, 105116
Dick Boldhero. 27922
Dick Farmer. pseud. Whereas great quantities of English copper half-pence. 103247
Dick Retort. pseud. Tit for tat. see Cobbett, William, 1763-1835. supposed author
Clifton, William. supposed author Davies, Benjamin. supposed author
Dick Shift; a political tale. (19995), 99276
Dick Twiss: a poem. 17320
Dick Wilson, the rumseller's victim. (16823)
Dickens, Charles, 1809-1870. (6319), 11217, 19680, 19996-20013, 40392, 52162, 54960, 64034, 84144, 91234, note after 92624, note after 105032
Dickenson, Jonathan, d. 1822. 20014-20017
Dickermann, -------. 90313
Dickerson, Edward N. 20018
Dickerson, Mahlon, 1770-1853. 20019, 33150, 70431-70432 see also New Jersey. Governor, 1815-1817 (Dickerson)
Dickerson, Thomas. 20020
Dickerson, William R. 36918, 61781
Dickertova, A. tr. 99367, 99382
Dickeson, Montroville Wilson. (20021)-20022, 69864
Dickey, -------. 88294-88296
Dickey, John, 1794-1853. 20023
Dickie, -----. 34758
Dickins, Asbury. 20024-(20025)
Dickins, Asbury. supposed author 35923
Dickins, J. W. 3950, note after 90573
Dickinson, Andrew. 20026
Dickinson, Anna E. 20027, 61445
Dickinson, Austin. 20028
Dickinson, Daniel Stevens, 1800-1866. 20029-20031, 28472, 56238
Dickinson, J. R. 20030
Dickinson, James. 20033-20034
Dickinson, James Taylor, 1806-1884. 20035-20036
Dickinson, John, 1732-1808. 405, 3262, 4479, 5220, (20037)-20052, 25576-25577, (26444), (59888), (66215), 84586-84587, 84678C, 90137, 91785, 104455
Dickinson, John, 1732-1808. supposed author (74423)
Dickinson, John, 1732-1808. incorrectly supposed author (5859), 10243, 28770-28771, 3d note after 103122
Dickinson, Jonathan, 1688-1747. 4095, 12362, (12363), 13350, 17675, 20053-(20062), (20271), 22115, (32311), 66216, 69515, 69522, (78491)-78494, 95316, 95581, 101194
Dickinson, Jonathan, 1688-1747. supposed author 20014, 31296, 69518
Dickinson, Mahlon H. 60466
Dickinson, Moses. (20062)-20063
Dickinson, N. S. (20065)
Dickinson, Nodes. 20064
Dickinson, P. 9837
Dickinson, Pliny, 1777-1834. (20066)-20067
Dickinson, Richard W. 20069
Dickinson, Rodolphus, 1787-1863. 20068, (20070)-20073, (24292)
Dickinson, S. G. (20065)
Dickinson, Samuel F. (20074)-20075

Dickinson, Thomas. RN 20076
Dickinson, Timothy. 20077
Dickinson, William. (50990)
Dickinson College, Carlisle, Pa. 20079-20080, 20084-20085
Dickinson College, Carlisle, Pa. Belles Lettres Society. 20078
Dickinson College, Carlisle, Pa. Board of Trustees. 20081, 99393
Dickinson College, Carlisle, Pa. Board of Trustees. Committee. 20081, 99393
Dickinson College, Carlisle, Pa. Union Philosophical Society. 20082-20083
Dickinson Seminary, Williamsport, Pa. 20086
Dicks, John. defendant (34042), 64251, 2d note after 96883
Dickson, George. RN 64396
Dickson, James H. (20087)-20088
Dickson, John, 1783-1852. 20089-20090
Dickson, Joseph. (32506)
Dickson, M. F. 20091, 77466
Dickson, Samuel. 20092
Dickson, Samuel Henry. 20093, 87872, note after 88042
Dickson, William. 20094-20095, 24461, 49755, note after 91132
Dickson, William Jonathan. (20096)
Dickson, William M. (20097)-20098
Dickson, William Steel. 20099
Dickson's letters to Clarkson. 20095, 49755, note after 91132
Dickson's narrative of an attack. 20100
Dicon, James. petitioner 20372
Di Conti, Nicolo. see Conti, Nicolo di.
Di Coronado, Francesco, Vazquez. see Vazquez de Coronado, Francisco, 1510-1549.
Di Courcelles, Jean. see Courcelles, Jean Baptiste Pierre Jullien de, 1759-1834.
Di Crauliz, Agostino. see Cravaliz, Agostino di.
Dictador en Mexico confundiendo. 48430
Dictadura de O'Higgins. (1002A), 56857
Dictamen . . . algunas ideas sobre la historia y manera de escribir la de Mexico. 20101, (39076)
Dictamen aprobado en la Camara de Diputados. 68681
Dictamen de la Comision de la Camara de Senadores. 20104
Dictamen de la Comision de Credito Publico de la Camara de Diputados, sobre el arreglo de la dueda Inglesa. 20102
Dictamen de la Comision de Credito Publico de la Camara de Diputados, sobre arreglo de la deuda interior de la nacion. 48432
Dictamen de la Comision de Credito Publico sobre el arreglo de la deuda Inglesa. 48431
Dictamen de la Comision de Hacienda. 20103
Dictamen de la Comision de Negocios Esclesiasticos. (20105)
Dictamen de la Comision de Puntos Constitutionales. 20106
Dictamen de la Comision Especial de la Camara de Diputados del Congreso General. 26550
Dictamen de la Comision Especial de Convocatoria para un Nuevo Congreso. 20108
Dictamen de la Comision Especial de Tehuantepec de Senado. 26550
Dictamen de la Comision Especial sobre el mismo asunto. 26550
Dictamen de la Comision Nombrada para Proponer Medias Conducentes al Bien y Felicidad de Ambas Americas. 20107

Dictamen de la Comision Nombrada por la Sociedad Mexicana de Geografia y Estadistica. 62878, 85760
Dictamen de la Comision Primera de la Camara de Representates. 48433
Dictamen de la Comision Segunda de Puntos Constitucionales. 76144
Dictamen de la Comision y acuerdo del Cabildo Metropolitano de Mexico. 48434
Dictamen de la Comision y acuerdo del Illmo. Cabildo Metropolitano de Mexico. 50096
Dictamen de la Primera Comision de Hacienda de la Camara de Diputados. 20110
Dictamen de la Segunda Comision de Guerra. 20111
Dictamen de la Segunda Comision de Hacienda. 20110
Dictamen de las Comisiones Eclesiastica y de Relaciones, acerca de las instrucciones al enviado a Roma. 68678
Dictamen de las Comisiones Eclesiastica y de Relaciones sobre las instrucciones que deben darse a nuestro enviado a Roma. 20109
Dictamen de las Comisiones Eclesiasticas y de Relaciones del Senado, sobre las instrucciones que deben darse al enviado. 66567
Dictamen de las Comisiones Unidas de Industria y Primera de Hacienda, sobre las propuestas. 20112
Dictamen de las Comisiones Unidas de Relaciones y Guerra. 20113
Dictamen de las Sesiones Unidas del Gran Jurado. 76747
Dictamen de una Comision Especial reunida de orden del poder ejecutivo. 20114
Dictamen del Doctor Don Antonio Josef Ruiz de Padron. 74043
Dictamen del Excmo. Consejo de Estado. (20115)
Dictamen del Fiscal General del Estado. 22812
Dictamen del Procurador General. 20116
Dictamen leido y presentado en el Consejo de Castilla. (29358)
Dictamen noticia historica de Soconusco. (48435)
Dictamen presentado a la Camara de Senadores. 106224
Dictamen presentado a la Sociedad de Geografia y Estadistica de Mexico por el Lic. D. Manuel Larrainzar. 39078
Dictamen presentado a la Sociedad de Geografia y Estadistica de Mexico sobre la obra de Brasseur de Bourbourg. 48436
Dictamen presentado a la Sociedad Mexicana de Geografia y Estadistica por la mayoria de la Comision. 85761
Dictamen que de orden del Rey comunicada por el Marques de Majorada. 34177, 47417, 86398
Dictamen, que la Comision de Negocios Eclesiasticos presento. 56443
Dictamen que la Junta Departamental de Queretaro. 67102
Dictamen que las Comisiones Reunidas presentaron a la Camara de Senadores. 48604
Dictamen sobre diezmos y vacantes. 48810
Dictamen sobre establecimiento de aduanas maritimas y fronterizas. 20117
Dictamen sobre lalangosta. (20118)
Dictamen sobre los pactos celebrados por la Convencion de Nacaome. 32773
Dictamen sobre provision de beneficios eclesiasticos. 20119

Dictamen sobre reformas del arancel general. 20120

Dictamen teologico. 29132

Dictamen y articulos de las Comisiones Eclesiastica y de Relaciones. 98952

Dictamenes dados al Ministerio de Justicia y Negocios Eclesiasticos. 59633

Dictamenes theologico-legales de ninos expositos. 41101

Dictates of reason. 105252

Dictionaire. (66881)

Dictionaire Caribe-Francois. (7739)

Dictionaire de la langue Huronne. 74881, 74883-74884, 74886

Dictionare Francois-Caraibe. 7740

Dictionarie of the Indian language. 92664

Dictionaries in the Boston Mercantile Library. 64049

Dictionarium Gallice, Latine et Galibi. (65038), (74627), 1st note after 77220

Dictionarium geographicum. 67431

Dictionarium Groenlandico-Danico-Latinum. (22032)

Dictionary, geographical, statistical, and historical. 43127, 43130, 83926

Dictionary of all officers. 26638

Dictionary of all religions. 211

Dictionary of America and the West Indies. 95512

Dictionary of American biography. 85433

Dictionary of Americanisms. 3738-3739, 38221

Dictionary of arts and sciences. 78985

Dictionary of arts and sciences, and miscellaneous literature. 32123, 40024, 50937

Dictionary of Baptist biography. (31058)

Dictionary of books relating to America. 74692-(74694)

Dictionary of congregational usages and principles. 17922

Dictionary of contemporaries. (47791)

Dictionary of dates. 31015, 66800-667

Dictionary of dates and universal reference. 31014

Dictionary of freemasonry. 50872

Dictionary of geographical knowledge. 26812

Dictionary of geography, ancient and modern. 15168

Dictionary of geography, descriptive, physical, statistical, and historical. (36352)

Dictionary of the Abnaki language. 67942

Dictionary of the Algonkine language. 38644

Dictionary of the arts and sciences and miscellaneous literature. 22555

Dictionary of the Book of Mormon. 83038

Dictionary of the Chinook jargon. 27301

Dictionary of the county of Placer. 91146

Dictionary of the English language. 80346

Dictionary of the English language: in which the words are deduced from their originals. 73616, 102360

Dictionary of the Hudson's Bay Indian language. 7098

Dictionary of the Indian tongue. 24509

Dictionary of the most uncommon wonders. (30320)

Dictionary of the photographic art. 85414

Dictionary of the Ptchipwe language. 3247

Dictionary of the United States Congress. 38917

Dictionary of trade products. (81149)

Dictionary, practical, theoretical, and historical. 32695, 43128

Dictionnaire a la mode. 56307

Dictionnaire biographique. 5149, (5153)

Dictionnaire Caraibe-Francais. 39648

Dictionnaire complet de tous les lieux. 3337

Dictionnaire de la langue du mesme pais. 5269

Dictionnaire de la langue [Galibienne.] 7133

Dictionnaire de la langue Huronne. 74882

Dictionnaire de la langue Nahuatl ou Mexicaine. 81139

Dictionnaire de la litterature Danois, Islandaise et Norwegienne de Nyerup. 42882

Dictionnaire de la penaltie dans toutes les parties du monde connu. 75197

Dictionnaire de linguistique et de philologie comparee. 35977

Dictionnaire de medecine therapeutique. 93271

Dictionnaire de ouvrages relatifs a l'histoire de la vie publique. (56739)

Dictionnaire du comerce et des marchandises. 74918

Dictionnaire Francois-Onontague. 80007

Dictionnaire Galibi. (65038), (77219)-77220, 1st note after (74627)

Dic. gen. de la politique. 12590

Dictionnaire historique des hommes illustres. 5149, (5153)

Dictionnaire mythologique universel. 35494

Dictionnaire universel de Commerce. (77272)-77274

Dictionnaire universel de Commerce, d'histoire naturelle, d'arts et metiers. 77271

Dictionnaire universel de commerce: d'histoire naturelle, & des arts & metiers. 77275

Dictionnaire universel de geographie maritime. 44120

Dictionnaire universel de la France ancienne et moderne. 77156

Dictum, Obiter. pseud. see Obiter Dictum. pseud.

Dic Verum. pseud. see Your wellwisher, Dic Verum. pseud.

Did General McClellan ever intend to hurt the rebels? 43030

Did the First Church of Salem originally have a confession of faith? 24037

Didactic poem in four books. 101305

Didactics: social, literary, and political. 101162

Diderot, Denis, 1713-1784. 68081

Didier, Const. 20121

Didier, Eugene L. ed. 88489

Didier, Eugene L. reporter 92013

Didimus, H. 53340

Di Dio, Giuseppe Della Madre. see Jose de la Madre de Dios.

Didot, Jules. illus. 35026

Didricksen, D. tr. 77690

Die in Texas und Virginien gelegenen. (49909)

Diefenborf, Oliver. (26892), 56435

Dieffenbach, Er. 18650

Diego y Villalon, Juan San. see San Diego y Villalon, Juan.

Diego de Torres breue relacion del fruto. 96259

Dieguez, Manuel Solorzano. see Solorzano Dieguez, Manuel.

Diejenigen anmerkungen. 106352, 106361

Dielitz, Theodor. 20122-20125

Dienstich voor stierlieden. 14550

Diepenbeck, Rudolph. 20126

Dieperink, H. H. (20127)

Dieppe (City) 47541

Dieren palleys. 99366

Diereville, -----. (6876), (20128), 69148

Dies canicvlares seu colloquia tria, & viginti. 44056

Dies i seis remedios. 40902

Dies irae du Mexique. 78712

Diesseits und Jenseits des oceans. 57894

Dieterich, Veit. 66466
Diether, ------. 16961
Diether, Andrea. tr. 16957
Diether, Christoph Ludwig. (25461)
Dietrich, Ew. Chr. Vict. 20129
Dietrich, Ludwig. 20130
Dietrich Knickerbocker's humeristische
    Geschichte von New-York. (35167)
Dietrichson, Johannes Vilhelm. 20131
Dieu Soult, Nicolas Jean de. see Soult,
    Nicolas Jean de Dieu, Duc de Dalmatie.
Diez, Pierre. see Diaz, Pedro.
Diez de Bonilla, M. defendant 65926
Diez de la Calle, Juan. 20133-20135
Diez de la Mora, Miguel. respondent 87160
Diez de las Cortinas, Manuel. see Cortinas,
    Manuel Diez de las.
Diez de San Miguel, N. A. 20136-20137
Diez de Solano, Jose Maria, Bp., 1820-1881.
    20138, 93348 see also Leon, Mexico
    (Diocese) Bishop (Diez de Solano)
Diez Navarro, Luis. see Navarro, Luis Diez.
Diez Pimienta, Francisco. see Pimienta,
    Francisco Diez.
19 de Abril. (11428)
Diez y ocho sermones, predicados a diversos
    assumptos. 94900
16 retratos de la dinastia imperial de Marco
    Ccapac. 74955
"Diez y siete anos de desgracias." 96222
Dieze, Johann Andreas. tr. 97689
Diezmann, August, 1805-1869. tr. (4538),
    21214-21215, 57456
Diezmann, Johann August. see Diezmann,
    August, 1805-1869.
Difensa d'Amerigo Vespuccio. 10702
Difere[n]cias de libros q[ue] ay en [e]l
    vniuerso. 98502
Diferencias de libros q[ue] ay en el vniuerso.
    98501
Diferentes acreedores. defendants 34720
Difference between Jack and his captain.
    98425
Difference between money and capital. 63767
Difference between the Christian and Anti-
    christian church. 17055
Difference between the Royal African Company
    and the separate traders. 20139
Difference between vegetable and mineral
    medicines. 95588
Differences between the inhabitants of Salem-
    Village. 9926
Different gentlemen. pseud. Nature displayed.
    98634
Different hands. pseud. trs. 5108
Different hands. pseud. Appendix. 44314,
    note after 75924
Different hands. pseud. East and west.
    21641, note after 90311
Different political parties. 93674
Different practitioners. pseud. Letters and
    essays. 67169, 1st note after 102848
Different schools of opinion in the church.
    82947
Different systems considered. 87334
Different systems of penal codes in Europe.
    (76485)
Different tracts and surveys. 85243
Different writers. pseud. Strictures. 92849
Differentes constitutions des trieze provinces.
    (19476)
Differentes races de l'Amerique. 17736
Differents actes politiques. 6160
Difficulties, . . . of Christ's ministers con-
    sidered. 58649

Dificultad imaginada y facilidad verdadera.
    74859, 106407
Digby, ------. (20140)
Digest. Being a particular and detailed account.
    36448
Digest, compiled from the records. (65152)
Digest for 1847. 66825
Digest in force January 1, 1856. 61583
Digest no. II. of the class of 1859. 53088
Digest of accounts of manufacturing establish-
    ments. (20141)
Digest of acts of assembly relating to the
    Kensington District. 61590
Digest of acts of assembly, relating to the . . .
    Northern Liberties. 61592
Digest of acts of assembly, the codified ordi-
    nance of the city of Pittsburgh. 63116
Digest of acts of the Legislature, incorporating
    the city of Mobile. 49779
Digest of all the laws and ordinances. 54246
Digest of all the ordinances of the city of
    Savannah. 77257
Digest of all the reports in equity. 66826
Digest of American cases. 39320
Digest of canal claims presented to the legis-
    lature. (53563)
Digest of cases adjudged in the Circuit Court
    of the United States. 103111
"Digest of cases" in the Supreme Court.
    102624
Digest of claims. (53563)
Digest of common law and admiralty reports.
    66826
Digest of county laws. (60059)
Digest of current literature, British, American,
    French, and German. 53391
Digest of election cases. 82757
Digest [of law reports, by Metcalf.] 66825
Digest of laws relating to . . . Philadelphia,
    from . . . 1854, until . . . 1865. 61585
Digest of laws relating to . . . Philadelphia,
    from . . . 1854, until . . . 1866. (61586)
Digest of laws relating to . . . Philadelphia,
    from its territorial extension. 61584
Digest of laws relating to the British provinces.
    21634
Digest of laws respecting real property. 41835
Digest of M. Victor Cousin's report. 94510
Digest of opinions of the Judge Advocate
    General of the Army: . . . between
    September, 1862, and July, 1868. 20143
Digest of opinions of the Judge Advocate
    General of the Army, including opinions
    given since the issue of the digest of
    1865. 20142
Digest of patents. 20144, (22344)
Digest of political methods in vogue. 84391
Digest of returns from the Agricultural
    Societies. 43908
Digest of select British statutes. (60060),
    71916
Digest of taxation in the state. 53972
Digest of the act of Congress establishing the
    Smithsonian Institution. 85018
Digest of the act to provide a national currency.
    20145
Digest of the acts of assembly and a code.
    63116
Digest of the acts of assembly, and of the
    ordinances . . . of the District of Spring
    Garden. (61589)
Digest of the acts of assembly, and of the
    ordinances of the inhabitants and Com-
    missioners of the District of Spring
    Garden. 89817

Digest of the acts of assembly and ordinances of Councils. 1939

Digest of the acts of assembly and ordinances of the District of Moyamensing. 61591

Digest of the acts of assembly, and the ordinances of the . . . Incorporated District of the Northern Liberties. 61587

Digest of the acts of assembly, and the ordinances, . . . of the Kensington District. 61588

Digest of the acts of assembly, ordinances and resolutions of the inhabitants and Commissioners of the District of Spring Garden. 62300

Digest of the acts of assembly relating to . . . Philadelphia. 61593

Digest of the acts of assembly relative to the Board of Health. 60061

Digest of the acts of assembly relative to the First School District. 60062

Digest of the acts of the commonwealth . . . relating to the . . . [Massachusetts Medical] Society. 45874

Digest of the acts of the General Assembly . . . of a general nature. 60063

Digest of the acts of the Supreme Judicatory. 65153

Digest of the American, English, Scotch and Irish reports. 79859

Digest of the canons for the government of the Episcopal Church. 20146

Digest of the canons for the government of the Protestant Episcopal Church. 66140

Digest of the canons . . . of the Protestant Episcopal Church. 66139

Digest of the cases decided and reported. 82244

Digest of the cases reported. 87455

Digest of the charter and revised ordinances of the city of St. Louis. 75345

Digest of the charters, statutes, and ordinances. (32400), 54351

Digest of the civil laws now in force. 42218

Digest of the commercial regulations. 20147

Digest of the common law. 20072

Digest of the common school system of the state of New York. 53645, 67801

Digest of the decisions, construing the statutes of Maryland. 47113

Digest of the decisions of the Board of Discipline. 87073

Digest of the decisions of the courts of the U. S. 20148

Digest of the decisions of the Grand Lodge I. O. of O. F. 33861

Digest of the decisions of the Supreme Court of the United States. 103154

Digest of the English statutes in force in the state of Georgia. 77652

Digest of the existing regulations of foreign countries. 20149

Digest of the general laws of Kentucky. (37536)

Digest of the law of evidence. 94078

Digest of the law of maritime captures and prizes. (74252), 103155

Digest of the laws, and rules of exercise and discipline. 69641

Digest of the laws, containing all statutes. 27038

Digest of the laws . . . containing the rules and decisions. (53101)

Digest of the laws of Alabama. 47368

Digest of the laws of Castile and the Spanish Indies. 105480

Digest of the laws of Connecticut. 15779

Digest of the laws of Georgia, from 1755 to 1800, inclusive. (44475)

Digest of the laws of . . . Georgia . . . previous to . . . December, 1837. 27039

Digest of the laws of Maryland. 31596

Digest of the laws of Mississippi. 49498

Digest of the laws of New-Hampshire. 52822

Digest of the laws of . . . Odd-Fellows. (56696)

Digest of the laws of Pennsylvania brought down to 28th April, 1851. (60064), 60065

Digest of the laws of Pennsylvania, for . . . 1854 and 1855. 59882

Digest of the laws of Pennsylvania from April 7, 1830, to April 15, 1835. 60065

Digest of the laws of Pennsylvania from 1700 to 1840. (60064)-60065

Digest of the laws of Pennsylvania from 1700 to 1846. (60064)-60065

Digest of the laws of Pennsylvania from 1700 to 1824. (60064)-60065

Digest of the laws of Pennsylvania, of a general nature. 60066

Digest of the laws of South-Carolina. 87690

Digest of the laws of Texas: containing a full and complete compilation. 94993

Digest of the laws of Texas: to which is subjoined an appendix. 30694

Digest of the laws of the corporation of the city of Washington. (9198)

Digest of the laws of the Independent Order of Odd Fellows. 60159

Digest of the laws of the state of Alabama. 96328

Digest of the laws [of the state of Connecticut.] 94078

Digest of the laws of the state of Georgia. 25197

Digest of the laws of the state of Missouri. (49588)

Digest of the laws of the United States & the state of South-Carolina. 87691

Digest of the laws of the United States, including an abstract. 27994

Digest of the laws of the United States of America, from March 4th, 1789. 34739

Digest of the laws of the United States of America, . . . now in force. 31597

Digest of the laws . . . relating to the police of . . . Philadelphia. 61594

Digest of the military and naval laws of the Confederate States. 15266

Digest of the military laws of the United States. (63726)

Digest of the militia law of the state of New-York. 33071

Digest of the militia law of Massachusetts. 46148, 92038-92039

Digest of the mining laws of Pennsylvania. (79771)

Digest of the minutes of the Synod of the Presbyterian Church of Canada. (37334)

Digest of the most important decisions. 30403

Digest of the ordinances and resolutions of the Second Municipality; and of the General Council of the city of New-Orleans. 88593

Digest of the ordinances and resolutions of the Second Municipality of New-Orleans, in force May 1, 1840. 53323

Digest [of the ordinances of Philadelphia.] 61596

Digest of the ordinances of . . . Philadelphia, and the acts of assembly relating thereto. 61596

Digest of the ordinances of the Borough of Frankford. (61597)

Digest of the ordinances of the city of Charleston. 12048
Digest of the ordinances of the said city [of Cincinnati.] 13061
Digest of the ordinances, resolutions, by-laws and regulations. 53324
Digest of the penal law of the state of Louisiana. 72156
Digest of the principal decisions in the S. J. Court of Massachusetts. 13162
Digest of the principal ordinances of Cincinnati. 13086
Digest of the productive resources. (43282)
Digest of the resolutions and decisions. 87093
Digest of the revenue laws of the United States. 15524
Digest of the road-law. 87692
Digest of the road laws and election laws. 60067
Digest of the rules of proceeding. (16106)
Digest of the statistics of manufactures. 20150
Digest of the statute law of Kentucky. 37534
Digest of the statute law of the state of Florida. (25883), 2d note after 95517
Digest of the statute laws of Kentucky. 37535
Digest of the statute laws of the state of Georgia. 27040
Digest of the statutes of Arkansas. 28115
Digest of the statutes of the Mississippi Territory. 49499, 96328
Digest of the statutory and constitutional constructions. (53102)
Digest of the treaties and statutes of the United States. 27995
Digested index of the statute law of South Carolina. 1837 to 1857. 87694
Digested index of the statute law of South Carolina, from the earliest period. 70864, 87693
Digested index to certain of the reports and resolutions. 87689
Digested index to the executive documents and reports. 20151
Digested index to the reported cases in Lower Canada. 67720
Digested index to the reported decisions of the several courts of law in the United States. 18989
Digested index to the reported decisions of the several courts of law in the western and southern states, 1824. 103111
Digested summary and alphabetical list. (20152)
Digesto teorico-practico. 72537
Digests of the acts of assembly. (27494)
Digges, Sir Dudley, 1583-1639. 5195, 61246
Digges, Sir Dudley, 1583-1639. supposed author (22976), 67599
Digitus Dei. 78378-78379
Digitus Dei: nevv discoveryes. 95650
Dignity and duty of the civil magistrate. 102620
Dignity and encouragement of independent labor. 70828
Dignity and importance of the Gospel ministry. 38162
Dignity and importance of the military character illustrated. (25039)
Dignity of human nature. 9245
Dignity of man, a discourse. 22522
Dignity of man, especially as displayed in civil government. 97183
Dignity of man. Proposals of Isaiah Thomas, Jun. 95416

Dignity of teaching. 72628
Dignity of the agricultural occupation. 44804
Dignity . . . of the Gospel. 21563
Dignowity, Anthony M. 20153
Digression tendant a prouver que l'Amerique a ete connue des anciens. 59172
Di Gvsman, Nvnno. see Guzman, Nuno de, 16th cent.
Di Horticosa, Petrii. see Horticosa, Petrius di.
Dike, Samuel F. 20154
Diligence in the work of God. 72364
Diligencia que el Alcalde de Mapimiha practicado. (44450)
Diligencias practicadas para averiguar un hecho criminal. 22833
Diligent hand. pseud. True relation. 97143
Diligent observer of the said disputation. pseud. Moro-mastix. 50773
Diligent servant excited. 51517
Dilke, Sir Charles Wentworth, Bart., 1843-1911. 20155-20156
Dill, ------. (20157)
Dill, James H. (20158)
Dillard, Ryland T. (20159)
Dillaway, Charles Knapp. 20160
Dillaye, Stephen D. 20161-20162
Dille, Goszwin Theodor von. tr. 99526, 99530
Dillin, Peter. 21211-21215
Dillingham, J. H. 20163
Dillingham, Paul. 20164 see also Vermont. Commissioner on the National Cemetery at Gettysburg.
Dillingham, William H. 14456, 20165-(20167), 4th note after 96966
Dillingham. firm publishers 2108A, note after 93619
Dillon, ------. 8015
Dillon, Arthur. 20168-20170
Dillon, Augustus. 20171
Dillon, John B. 20172-20174
Dillon, Sir John Talbot, Bart., 1740?-1805. (59572)
Dillon, Sir Peter. RN 20175-20177
Dillon, Robert. defendant at court martial (20178), 96857
Dillon, Roger Henri de. 20179
Dillwyn, George. (20180), 77279, 77285-77287
Dillwyn, William. ed. 17484
Dilly, ------. ed. 25514, 25516
Diluvio constitucional. 20181
Dilworth, H. W. 20182-20185, 23486
Dilworth, Thomas. note after 65546
Diman, James. 20186
Diman, Jeremiah Lewis, 1831-1881. 17044, 20187-20188, 51773, 104337
Dimas Rangel, Joseph Francisco. see Rangel, Joseph Francisco Dimas.
Dime American comic songster. 79907
Dime comic speaker, no. 4. 4101
Dime knapsack songster. 4101
Dime military song book. 4101
Dime military song book and songs for the war. 4101
Dime patriotic speaker. 4101
Dime patriotic speaker, no. 3. 4101
Dime song book. 4101
Dime speakers nos. 1 & 2. 4101
Dime tales, traditions, and romance of border and revolutionary times. 4101, 22297
Dime union song book. 4101
Di Mendozza, Antonio. see Mendoza, Antonio de.

Di Mendozza, Giouanni Gonzalez. see Gonzalez de Mendoza, Juan, Abp., 1571-1639.
Dimension proper for an unit of measures pointed out. 20189
Di Micheovo, Mattheo. see Micheovo, Mattheo di.
Di Michiel, Nicolo. see Michiel, Nicolo di.
Dimick, Augustus. reporter 39779
Diminution of crime by suppression of Sunday liquor traffic. 93745
Dimision del ministerio. 48437
Dimmick, Luther Fraseur. 20190-20193
Dimmick, Robert A. 20194
Dimmock, McLellan & Co. firm publishers 92756
Dimock, J. Judson. 15776
Dimond, Elizabeth. 20195
Dimond, William. 20196
Dimostrazione della verita del passo all' America Settentrionale. 96311
Dindimus, King of the Brachmans. 69333, 105218
Dingley, Amasa. 20197
Dingman, John H. 20198-20199
Di Nica, Marco. see Nica, Marco di.
Dinmore, R. 20200
Dinner at the La Pierre House. 10841, note after 94911
Dinner, Boston, July 5, 1858. see Boston. Dinner, July 5, 1858.
Dinner for Louis Kossuth, Washington, D. C., 1852. 38269
Dinner given by Mr. George Peabody. 59367, 1st note after 91507
Dinner Given by Mr. George Peabody to the Americans Connected with the Great Exhibition at London, 1851. see London. Dinner Given by Mr. George Peabody to the Americans Connected with the Great Exhibition, 1851.
Dinner Given by the Americans in Paris, to Professor S. F. B. Morse, Paris, 1858. 50963
Dinner Given by the Bar of New Jersey. see New Jersey. Bar. Dinner Given to Thomas H. Dudley, 1868.
Dinner given by the Citizens of Brooklyn to the Hon. Henry C. Murphy, 1857. 8311
Dinner given by the Philadelphia Bar to the judiciary. 61598
Dinner Given to Charles Dickens, Boston, 1842. 20005, 69854
Dinner Given to Professor List, Philadelphia, 1827. see Pennsylvania Society for the Encouragement of Manufactures, Philadelphia. Dinner Given to Professor List, 1827.
Dinner Given to the Hon. Daniel Webster by the Reform Convention of Maryland, Annapolis, 1851. see Maryland. Constitutional Convention, 1850-1851. Webster Dinner, 1851.
Dinner in Honor of the Centennial Anniversary of Washington, Washington, D. C., 1832. see Public Dinner in Honor of the Centennial Anniversary of Washington, Washington, D.C., 1832.
Dinner of the Hide and Leather Trade of the City of New York, 1859. see Annual Dinner of the Hide and Leather Trade of the City of New York, 1859.
Dinner of the New England Society, with the speeches. (52746)
Dinner to Charles Peabody, Salem, Mass., 1856. see Salem, Mass. Dinner to Charles Peabody, 1856.

Dinner to Senor Matias Romero, New York, 1864. see New York (City) Dinner to Senor Matias Romero, 1864.
Dinner to Senor Matias Romero, Envoy Extraordinary and Minister Plenipotentiary from Mexico. 73026
Di Nores, Giasone. see Nores, Giasone di.
Dinouart, Chanoine de S. Benoit. 20201, 99507, 100609
Dinsmoor, Robert. 20202
Dinsmore, J. 20203-(20204)
Dinsmore, Richard. ed. 52003
Dinsmore, Samuel P. 93476
Dinsmore genealogy, from about 1620 to 1865. 20203
Dintero, Edmondo. (63019)
Dinwiddie, Robert, 1693-1770. 99905, 99923, 99990-99994, 101710 see also Virginia (Colony) Governor, 1751-1758 (Dinwiddie)
Dinwiddie County, Va. 100071
Dinwiddie County, Va. Society of Friends. see Friends, Society of. Dinwiddie County, Va., Meeting.
Dio, Giuseppe della Madre di. see Jose la Madre de Dios.
Diocesan Missionary Society of the Protestant Episcopal Church in Pennsylvania. see Protestant Episcopal Missionary Society in Pennsylvania.
Diocesan missions and its trumpet calls. 91570
Diocesan missions of Pennsylvania. 20206
Diocesan register and New-England calendar for the year 1812. 20207, 52631
Diocesan Sunday-School Society of Pennsylvania. see Protestant Episcopal Sunday-School Society of Pennsylvania.
Diocese of Guiana, a journal of the Bishop's visitation in 1851. (13007)
Diocese of Maryland. Amendments proposed for the constitution. 45127
Dioceseseos Albanensis statuta. 72922
Dioddefiadau, etc. 35576
Diodorus Siculus. pseud. Letter to the members. 20208, 87857
Dioecesanan Baltimorensis, mense Junio 1857 habita. 72927
Diomede: from the Iliad of Homer. 84896
Dionysii Aphride totivs orbis situ. 20210
Dionysius, Africanus. see Dionysius, Periegetes.
Dionysius, Afrus. see Dionysius, Periegetes.
Dionysius, Lybicus. see Dionysisus, Periegetes.
Dionysius, Periegetes. (20209)-20211, 65940-65941
Dionysius Lybicvs poetae de sitv habitabilis orbis. 20211
Dios, Jose de la Madre de. see Jose de la Madre de Dios.
Dios, Juan de la Madre de. see Juan de la Madre de Dios.
Dios Arias, C. Juan de. see Juan de Dios Arias, C.
Dios Canedo, Juan de. see Canedo, Juan de Dios.
Dios Fernandez de Sousa, Juan de. see Fernandez de Sousa, Juan de Dios.
Dios Mendez, Juan de. see Mendez, Juan de Dios.
Dios Mendivelzua, Juan de. see Mendivelzua, Juan de Dios.
Dios Rosal, Juan de. see Rosal, Juan de Dios.
Dios Salcedo, Juan de. see Salcedo, Juan de Dios.
Dios del sigla. 75555

Dios prodigioso en el jvdio mas obstinado. (75995)

Di Osma & di Xara & Zegio, Pietro. see Osma & di Xara & Zegio, Pietro di.

Di Palafox, Giovanni. see Palafox y Mendoza, Joannis de, Bp.

Diphtheria. 52277

Di Piero Choralmi, Lorenzo. see Choralmi, Lorenzo di Piero.

Diplomacy and commerce. No. I. 98142

Diplomacy and retrenchment. 89840

Diplomacy of the revolution. 96783

Diplomacy of the United States. 42796-(42797)

Diplomat on diplomacy. (20212), 56319, (68603)

Diplomatic and consular act of August 18, 1856. 20213

Diplomatic and consular bill. 89840

Diplomatic and consular officers of the United States. 20213

Diplomatic blunderbuss. 13884

Diplomatic code of the United States of America. 22234

Diplomatic correspondence. 20214

Diplomatic correspondence for 1861-1865. 5307

Diplomatic correspondence of the American revolution. 88969

Diplomatic correspondence of the republic of Texas. note before 95044, 103113

Diplomatic correspondence of the revolution. 102208

Diplomatic correspondence of the United States. 20215

Diplomatic correspondence. Official edition. 67135

Diplomatic history of the administrations of Washington and Adams. 96784

Diplomatic history of the war for the union. 79595

Diplomatic policy of Mr. Madison unveiled. In a series of essays. 42451

Diplomatic policy of Mr. Madison unveiled: in strictures. 42446

Diplomatic relations with Austria. 11349

Diplomatic talents of John Quincy Adams. 277, 96755

Diplomatic year. 34725, 68604

Diplomatische Geschichte des Portugiesischen Beruhmten. (13179), 51478

Diplomatisches Archiv fur die Zeit- und Staatengeschichte. 20216

D'Ippocrate, Lvoghi. see Lvoghi d'Ippocrate.

Diptera Americae Septentrionalis indigena. 42398

Diputacion Americana a las Cortes de Espana. see Spain. Cortes. Diputacion Americana.

Diputacion para la Junta de Gobierno de la Casa de Beneficencia. 20217

Diputacion Patriotica, Puerto Principe. see Puerto Principe (Province) Diputacion Patriotica.

Diputacion Permanente, Jalisco. see Jalisco (State) Diputacion Permanente.

Diputado de las Cortes Reunidas en Cadiz. pseud. Manifesto. see Toledo y Dubois, Jose Alvarez de.

Diputado [de Valladolid, Mexico.] see Valladolid, Mexico. Diputado.

Diputados de America. see Spain. Cortes. Diputacion Americana.

Diputados del Ultramar. pseud. Exposicion. see Ramirez, Miguel.

Di Quebrada, Innez. see Quebrada, Innez di.

Dirck, -------. 98973

Dirckinck, Constant. 20218

Dirckinck-Holmfeld, Carl. tr. 23972

Direccion general de cartas de Espana a sus Indias. 31394

Direct taxes! Loans! Fruits of commercial restrictions! 105397A

"Direct trade." 4072

Direct trade——a chance for the south. 14974

Directeurs des Compagnies d'Orient. see Nederlandsche Oost-Indische Compagnie. Bewinthebberen. and Nederlandsche West-Indische Compagnie. Bewinthebberen.

Direction des glaces deduite des relations de Ross et de Parry. (9826)

Direction for a public profession in the church assembly. 31744

Direction pour la culture du tabac. 77699

Directions. 95092

Directions and regulations relative to Yale College wood and woodyards. 105838

Directions for a candidate for the ministry. 46400, 46532

Directions for a close and comfortable walk with God. 20059

Direction for adventvrers with small stock. 63312

Directions for breeding silk-worms. 57895

Directions for bringing over seeds and plants. 22319

Directions for Buzzards Bay and New Bedford. 80035

Directions for exact spelling, reading, and writing. 92976

Directions for making botanical collections. 71255

Directions for making calcined or pearl-ashes. 20219

Directions for manouvres. (61599)

Directions for medicine chests. 93166

Directions for meteorological observations. 85019

Directions for navigating the gulf and river of St. Lawrence. (35961), 75318

Directions for navigating the west and south-coast of Newfoundland. 16276

Directions for preserving the health of soldiers. 74212-74213

Directions for sailing in and out of Plymouth harbour. 63476

Directions for sailing into the harbours of Salem, Marblehead, Beverly and Man-chester. 6996

Directions for sailing through the gulf of Florida. 72995

Directions for silk-worm nurseries. (58982)

Directions for spelling. note after 52712

Directions for spelling, reading 92977

Directions for the breeding and management of silk-worms. 6163, 20220

Directions for the gulph and river of St. Lawrence. 75319

Directions for the making of bread in private families. 86653

Directions for the officers of His Majesty's General Court and Session of Oyer and Terminer. 27041, note after 91992

Directions for the proper management of American . . . singing birds. 44329

Directions for the transplantation and manage-ment of young thorn and other hedge plants. 43994

Directions for the use of the mineral water and cold bath. (20221), 74214

Directions how to employ the liesure [sic] of the winter. (46599)

Directions how to hear a sermon. 103516

Directions how to hear sermons. 103507

Directions. Smith County Old Settlers Home-
coming Association. 84962
Directions to Army surgeons on the field of
battle. 30113, 76536, 76647, 76657
Directions to assayers, miners, and smelters.
(40986)
Directions to emigrants. By D. Griffiths, Jr.
28833
Directions to emigrants. By Samuel Brown.
8558
Directions to his people, &c. 17672, 97454-
97455
Directions to his people with relation to the
present times. 97455
Directions to mankind how they may be happy.
104606
Directions to sail into and up Delaware Bay.
19385
Directions to slaveholders revived. (4011)
Directions to such as are concern'd, to obtain
a true conversion unto God. 104398-
104399
Directions to the American loyalists. 20222
Directions with regard to the improvement of
temporal blessings. 59126
Directoire Francais et guide des affaires en
Amerique. 46930
Director. pseud. Journey on the Mississippi
River. 49551
Director . . . 1868-9 [of Milwaukee.] (49154)
Director of the city of Columbus for the year
1848. 14894
Director of the inhabitants, etc. of Lafayette.
38584
Director to Indianapolis, for 1869. 34582
Director to . . . Milwaukee, for 1865. (49154)
Director to the city of Indianapolis for 1865-6.
34582
Director to the inhabitants, etc., in Freeport.
25818
Director to the inhabitants, etc., in the cities
of New Albany and Jeffersonville, for
1865-6. 52432
Director to the inhabitants, etc. of Madison,
for 1867. 43725
Director to the inhabitants, institutions, incorporated companies, manufacturing establishments, business, business firms, &c.,
in the city of St. Louis. 75346
Directoribus Societatis tum Orientalis tum
Occidentalis. see Nederlandsche Oost-
Indische Compagnie. Bewinthebberen.
and Nederlandsche West-Indische Compagnie. Bewinthebberen.
Directories for Lowell, Salem, and other cities.
87340
Directorio de artes, comercio e industrias de
la Habana, 1860. 29428
Directorio de banqueiros, extrahido dos mel-
hores autores. 52251, 95457
Directorio de confesores principiantes y de
nuevos ministros. 75588
Directorio de la ciudad de la Habana. (29429)
Directorio de religiosas. (75764)
Directorio espiritval en la lengva Espanola.
58069, 64880
Directorio general de los supremos poderes.
48906, 72550
Directorio maritimo. 71632
Directorio para informaciones de los pretend-
ientes de Santo Habito de N. Seraphico
P. S. Francisco. 52107
Directors of the Joint Companies, and of the
several railroad and cnaal companies of
the state. 53065

Directors of the Western and Northern Inland
Lock Navigation Companies, respectfully
report. 69857, 102964
Directors of the Western Inland Lock Navigation
Company, order. 102982
Directors' report [of the Newport, R. I., Free
Library.] 55046
Directors submit this their annual report.
88207
Directory and business advertiser for 1868.
26343
Directory and business advertiser for 1867-68.
(26344)
Directory and gazetteer for 1867-68. 8059
Directory and gazetteer of the city of Rochester,
for 1844. 72340
Directory and guide for persons emigrating to
the United States. (22486)
Directory and register for 1844. (49781)
Directory, and register for the year 1814.
104580
Directory . . . and sketches of Randolph County.
(50048)
Directory and statistics of Quincy, Illinois, for
1864-5. 67281
Directory . . . by Dean Dudley & Co. (71174)
Directory, containing names, places of business,
and residence. 101991
Directory, 1855-6. 54459
Directory . . . 1859-60. 54459
Directory, 1868-9. (49154)
Directory for all the rail road and stage routes.
6483
Directory for Augusta and vicinity, including
Hamburg. 66616
Directory [for Columbus, Ohio.] 14894
Directory, for . . . 1811. 54459
Directory . . . for 1858 and '59. 49899
Directory . . . for 1851-52. (33502)
Directory for 1857-8, with various historical
sketches. 48873
Directory for 1856-'57, of Pittsburgh. 63128,
3d note after 95774
Directory, for 1853-4. 54459
Directory for 1870. 57261
Directory . . . for 1860. 61606
Directory for 1867. 34582
Directory . . . for 1867. 34582, 75454
Directory for 1820-21. 54459
Directory for 1823. 61606
Directory for family-worship. 80715
Directory for justices of the peace. 95470
Directory for the city and suburbs of Phila-
delphia. (61601)
Directory, for the city of London, C. W.
(41863)
Directory for the navigation of the Pacific
Ocean. 24358
Directory for the public worship. 15445, 20223,
80715
Directory for the use of the white sulphur
water. 50466, 50469
Directory for the village of Buffalo. 9055
Directory for the village of Poughkeepsie. 64710
Directory for the village of Rochester. 72340
[Directory] for the year ending May 1, 1860.
12641
Directory for Virginia City, Gold Hill, Silver
City and American City. (14431)
Directory for visitors [to Greenwood Cemetery.]
(13607)
Directory of a city [i. e. Pittsburgh.] 36603
Directory of all mines. 42104
Directory of Astoria. 41890
Directory of booksellers. 20199

Directory of Brewer. (3152)
Directory of Camp Massachusetts. 92627
Directory . . . of Concord Centre Village. (15142)
Directory of East Davenport. 89394
Directory of Elizabeth, Rahway, and Plainfield. 22191
Directory of emigrants, &c. 5962
Directory of Greene County for 1855-6. 85375A
Directory of Jersey City & Hoboken for 1856-7. (36068)
Directory of Lancaster County. 38797
Directory of . . . Lawrence . . . 1848. 39394
Directory of . . . Lynn. 42837
Directory of Malone. 44143
Directory of . . . Mineral Point. 49209
Directory of . . . Minneapolis. (49232)
Directory of Nevada Territory. 37309
Directory of Newark. (54874)
Directory of Newburyport. 54915
Directory of . . . Norwich and . . . parts of Preston. 55925
Directory of . . . Oshkosh. 57795
Directory of Pittsburgh and Allegheny cities. 63128
Directory of Pittsburgh & vicinity. 63128
Directory of Potsdam Village. 64597
Directory of prominent business men. 61606
Directory of Reading, Allentown, Easton, Pottsville, and Bethlehem (Pa.) 27963
Directory of Richmond, and historical sketch. (71174)
Directory of Richmond city, and a business directory of about fifty counties of Virginia. (71174)
Directory of Richmond city, and a business directory of Norfolk, Lynchburg, Petersburg, and Richmond. (71174)
Directory . . . [of Rutland, Vt.] 74467
Directory of Saginaw City. 21653
Directory of . . . Saint Anthony. 74997
Directory of Sandusky, O. (76443)
Directory of Saratoga Springs, for 1868-9. 76913
Directory of Springfield, Illinois, and Sangamon County. 89849
Directory of the city and town of Norwich. 91085
Directory of the city of Cleveland. 13676
Directory of the city of Council Bluffs. 9320
Directory of the city of Hudson, for the years 1852-53. 91969
Directory of the city of Kingston. 37908
Directory of the city of Kingston, for 1857-1858. 37909
Directory of the city of Lancaster. (38794)
Directory of the city of Lexington. 40882
Directory of the city of Milwaukee for . . . 1847-48. (49154)
Directory of the city of Mobile for the year 1866. 49782
Directory of the city of New Brunswick. (52521)
Directory of the city of Newark. (54874)
Directory of the city of Reading, 1870-71. 68213
Directory of the city of Rock Island. 72393
Directory of the city of Rochester. C. and M. Morse, publishers. 72340
Directory of the city of Rochester, for 1845-6. 72340
Directory of the city of Rochester for 1838. 72340
Directory of the city of Springfield. 89889
Directory of the fifty-eighth General Assembly. 56910

Directory of the Grass Valley Township for 1865. 9728
Directory of the inhabitants, etc., in the city of Chicago. 12641
Directory of the Monongahela and Youghiogheny valleys. 50005, 4th note after 95774
Directory of the Protestant Episcopal Church and church institutions in Philadelphia. 62101
Directory of the public officers. 25059
Directory of the Roxbury Charitable Society. (73726)
Directory of the Sons of Temperance of North America. 87007
Directory of the trades in Albany. 51366
Directory of the village of Geneva. (26936)
Directory of Weatherford. 85356
Directory of soldiers' register of Wayne County, Indiana. 64770
Directory series. 89891
Directory to the principal objects of interest in New York. 27623
Direito administrativo Brasileiro. 70790
Direito publico Brasileira. 8989
Direitos e deveres dos estrangeiros no Brasil. 26494
Dirge. 95175, 101867
Dirge, or sepulchral service. 32475, 51578, note after 74795, note after 101879, 104278
Dirge sung at the chapel in Natchez on February 22. 61335
Dirom, Alexander. 95726
Dirrhaimer, Ulric. 20224
D'Irujo, ------, Marquis. see Casa Yrujo, Carlos Martinez de Yrujo y Tacon, Marques de, 1763-1824.
Disabilities of Charleston for complete and equal taxation. 12049
Di Sacrobusto, Giovanni. see Sacro Bosco, Joannes de, fl. 1230.
Di Santa Teresa, Giovanni Gioseppe. see Santa Teresa, Giovanni Gioseppe di.
Disappointment. 3801
Disappointments of youth. 102161
Disasters of an emigrant. 14018
Disbrow, Levi. 20225, (54070), note before 93512, 93538
Disbursements by the Treasurer of Yale College. 105857
Disbursement to Indians. 34642
Disbursements to the Indians. (34643)
Discarded daughter. 88661
Discharged Soldiers' Employment Association. 20231
Disciple of the old school philosophy. pseud. Moral education. (50494)
Disciple of the Washington school. pseud. Arguments. 1970
Disciple of the Washington school. pseud. Oregon. 57566
Disciple warming of himself and owning of his Lord. (46258)
Disciples of Christ. Rhode Island and Massachusetts Conference. 81836
Discipline. 83302
Discipline and rules of the First Moravian Church. (61664)
Discipline for seamen. 75325
Discipline, harmony and efficiency of the navy. 52123
Discipline of the Society of Friends, of Indiana Yearly Meeting. 34497
Discipline of the Society of Friends of New-York Yearly Meeting. 54246A

Discipline of the Society of Friends, of Ohio
Yearly Meeting. 56911
Discipline of the Trinitarian Church in Concord,
Mass. 28551
Discipline of the Yearly Meeting of Friends,
held in Baltimore. (20232)
Discipline of the Yearly Meeting of Friends,
held in New York. 86044
Discipline practiced in the churches of New
England, containing a platform of dis-
cipline. 52632
Discipline practiced in the churches of New
England, containing the principles owned.
46286
Discipulus libertatis atque humanitatis. pseud.
Intellectual Flambeau. see Torrey,
Jesse.
Disclosure—no. I. (20226), 20476, 31849,
(37852), (37853), 37856, 104779
Disclosure of the real parties to the purchase
and sale. 96431
Disclosures. note after 101315
Disclosures of convent life. 22822
Disclosures relating to the "A. B. C." affair.
25799
Disclosures relating to the "A. B. C." affair.
From the Essex register. 20227
Disclosures relating to the "A. B. C." affair
of Capt. Jeb. King. 37810
Discord in union. 97788
Discord of the grand Quakers among them-
selves. 70894
Discordia de la concordia. 63968
Discorse des temps. 23036
Discorsi apologetici. (11052)
Discorsi (messaggio) del Sig. Tommaso
Jefferson. 35893
Discorsi, nelli qvali si tratta brevemente
dell' eternita del euo. 73198
Discorso. 24076
Discorso apologetico di Lorenzo da Ponte.
64014
Discorso del Lodevole K. R. Ingersoll. 34749
Discorso della nobilita. 73194
Discorso di Carlo Passi. 1559, 2d note after
45010
Discorso di Jason Denores. 55466
Discorso di M. Gio. Battista Ramvsio. 67741-
67742
Discorso di M. Gioseppe Moleto. 66505
Discorso di M. Gioseppe Moleto medico. 66505
Discorso d'vn gran capitano di mare Francese.
67740
Discorso filosofico. 27791
Discorso intorno ad alcune regole principali.
51762
Discorso intorno alla carta da navigare.
(64149)
Discorso intorno alle tauole astronimiche.
106256
Discorso istorico-critico-artistico. 73421
Discorso . . . por Jose Manuel Mestre. 48162
Discorso sopra alcvne lettere, et navigationi.
67730
Discorso sopra gli scritti di Giouanmaria
Angiolello. 67736
Discorso sopra il crescor del fivme Nilo.
67730
Discorso sopra il discoprimento et conqvista
del Perv. 67740
Discorso sopra il libro del Signor Hayton
Armeno. 67736
Discorso sopra il libro di Messer Alvise da
Ca da Mosto. 67730
Discorso sopra il libro di Odoardo Barbessa.
67730

Discorso sopra il terzo volume. 67740
Discorso sopra il tre viaggi subseqventi.
67741
Discorso sopra il viaggio dell Ethiopia. 67730
Discorso sopra il viaggio di Nearcho capitano
di Alessandro. 67730
Discorso sopra il viaggio di Nicolo di Conti
Venetiano. 67730
Discorso sopra il viaggio fatto da gli Spagnovli.
67730
Discorso sopra la navigatione del mar Rosso.
67730
Discorso sopra la navigatione di Hannone
Carthaginese. 67730
Discorso sopra la prima et secunda lettera.
67730
Discorso sopra la relation di Nvnno di Gvsman.
67740
Discorso sopra la relatione di Francesco
Vlloa. 67740
Discorso sopra la terra ferma delle Indie
Occidentali. 67740
Discorso sopra l'adone del marino. 86842
Discorso sopra lo itinerario di Lodovico
Barthema. 67730
Discorso sopra vari viaggi per liqvali sono
state condotte. 67730
Discorso vniversale di M. Gioseppe Moleto
matematico. 66504
Discorso vniversale di M. Gioseppe Moleto
mathematico. 66503
Discours. 25173
Discours a la Societe Militaire Federale.
(39660)
Discours a l'Assemblee Nationale, prononce
par M. William Henry Vernon. 99254
Discours a l'occasion de la victoire remportee
par les forces navales. 63417
Discours a l'occasion du service solemnel.
(67388)
Discours a Sa Majeste. 75039
Discours a trois jeunes Haitiens. 2360
Discours aux representans de la nation. 81946
Discovrs by forme van remonstrantie: vervan-
tende de noodsaeckelickheyd vande Oos-
Indische navigatie. 98192
Discovrs by forme van remonstrantye: verva-
tende de nootsaeckelickheydt vande Oost-
Indische navigatie. 98193
Discours daer in kortelijck ende grondigh
werdt. 20233, 5th note after 102890
Discours de J. C. G. Delahaye. 19336
Discours de l'Amerique. (24642)
Discovrs de l'histoire de la Floride. 39633
Discovrs de l'histoire de la Floride, contenant
la cruaute des Espagnols. (39632)
Discovrs de l'histoire de la Floride, contenant
la trahison. 39631
Discours de l'Hon. L. J. Papineau. 65748
Discours de . . . Louis Joseph Papineau.
(58488)
Discours de M. Berryer. 4996A
Discours de M. de Bertrand. 5028
Discours de M. Calvert Rogniat. 72771
Discours de M. Corta. 16927
Discours de M. Gaston Demousseaux de Givre.
19523
Discours de M. le Duc de Broglie. 8186
Discours de M. Pierre Soule de la Louisiane.
87276
Discours de Mr. J. Hancock, M. Francklinn,
&c. 25583
Discours de Nicolas Barre. 3589
Discours de S. Exc. M. Billault. 5392-5393
Discours de Son Excellence Monsieur Jean
Hancock. 30176, 78114

Discours de Villaret-Joyeuse, depute de Morbihan. 99661
Discours des pais. 6119
Discours d'un fidele sujet du Roy. (69261)
Discours d'un soi-disant bon Hollandois. (56478), 2d note after 93480
Discovrs du tabac. 2758
Discours du Tres Honorable E. G. Stanly. (10535)
Discovrs dv voyage des Francois avx Indes Orientales. 66879
Discovrs dv voyage fait par le Capitaine Iaqves Cartier. 11140
Discours en vers. 33803
Discours ende beschrijbinge van het groot eylandt Canaria. 31227
Discours et faits memorables du General La Fayette. (5093)
Discours et projet de loi pour l'affranchisse-ment des Negres. 99518
Discours fait a l'Assemblee Nationale. 75104
Discours, fait par Monsieur de Sousa de Macedo. 88759
Discours funebre prononce a la memorie de M. President Lincoln. 27503
Discours historico juridico del origen y fundacion del hospital. 7462
Discours historique sur la cause et les desastres. (58163)
Discovrs of voyages into ye Easte & West Indies. (41374)
Discovrs op verscheyde voorslaghen rakende d'Oost en VVest-Indische trafyken. 20235, 6th note after 102890
Discovrs over de gelegentheyt van Nieuw Nederlandt. (20593)-20594, note after 98474, note after 99310
Discovrs over den Nederlandtschen vrede-handel. 20236
Discours . . . par P. Duponceau. 21356
Discours politiques sur la nature du gouverne-ment. 75518
Discours populaires. 38446
Discours preliminaire, de remarques sur l'histoire naturelle, &c. 60996
Discours preliminaire, par M. Charles Farcy. 23795, 40038
Discours preliminaire, par M. D. B. Warden. 40038
Discours prononce a la Cathedrale de Saint-Louis. 73476
Discours prononce a la seance d' ouverture du Comite d'Archeologie Americaine. 4502
Discours prononce a la translation du corps de Messiere Girouard. 68061
Discours prononce a l'Assemblee Nationale, le 2 Octobre 1790. 75105
Discours prononce a l'Assemblee Nationale par les Deputes de l'Assemblee Provin-ciale. 75106
Discours prononce a l'ouverture de la premiere seance publique. 2126
Discours prononce au Corps Legislatif de 10 Prairial. 96348
Discours prononce dans la discussion du projet de loi. 5652
Discours prononce dans la seance du 10. Prairial dernier. 39289
Discours prononce devant la Societe Litteraire de Quebec. 63254
Discours prononce le . . . 18 Juillet 1855. 12345
Discours prononce le 4 Decembre 1849. (38433)

Discours prononce par C. Lavaux. 39285
Discours prononce par le Gen. Chaumette. (12296)
Discours prononce par le Ministre de la Marine. (75107)
Discours prononce par M. Somis. 86841
Discours prononce par Sonthonax. 87116
Discours prononce sur l'abolition de l'esclavage. 50065
Discours prononcee par M. le Duc de Broglie. 8187
Discours prononces a Quebec, en 1852. 58586
Discours prononces a Saint Roch de Quebec. 67389
Discours prononces dans la discussion de l'adresse. 39989
Discours prononces . . . les 22 et 23 Juillet 1867. 4996B
Discours prononces par M. Poivre Commissaire du Roi. (63715)
Discours sur cette question. 44239
Discours sur la colonie de St.-Domingue. 98679A
Discours . . . sur la conduite du General Lafayette. 96196
Discours sur la constitution de l'esclavage. 75452
Discours sur la constitution et le gouvernement des Etats-Unis. 3306
Discours sur la disette du numeraire. (52384)
Discours . . . sur la grandeur et l'importance de la revolution qui vient de s'operer dans l'Amerique Septentrionale. 43885
Discours sur la grandeur & l'importance de la revolution qui vieut de s'operer dans l'Amerique Septentrionale; sujet propose par l'Academie. 19743
Discours sur la guerre civile. (4019)
Discours sur la necessite de maintenir le decret. 9078
Discours sur la necessite d'etablier a Paris. (20229)
Discours sur les ameliorations des gouverne-ments. 100811
Discours sur les Americains. 5840
Discours sur les antiquites Americaines, Mexicaines, &c. 23795
Discours sur les avantages ou les desavantages. (12224)
Discours sur les causes. 59110
Discours sur les colonies. 39247
Discours sur les commerce en general. 39251
Discours . . . sur les principaux navigateurs. 58789
Discours sur les revolutions de la surface du globe. 18210
Discours sur les troubles de Saint-Domingue. 61250
Discours sur l'esclavage des Negres. 20228, 21484
Discours sur l'etat de Saint-Domingue. 98680
Discours sur l'Institut Canadien. 19765
Discours sur un projet de decret. 8018
Discours van Pieter en Pauwels. 20230
Discours daer in kortelijk ende grondigh werdt. 20233
Discours de la paix. 20234
Discourse. 17675, (19527), 21043, 24779, 25408, 31429, (44749), 50800, (64671), 67992, 89744
Discourse about civil government. 18705
Discourse about the day of judgment. 46690
Discourse about the war with the Peqvods. 33446
Discourse about the warre with the Pequods. (33445)

Discourse adapted to the awful visitation. 104736

Discourse adapted to the present day. 33971

Discourse, adapted to the present situation. (22299)

Discourse addressed by a New-England pastor to his flock. 63344

Discourse addressed by appointment. (21261)

Discourse addressed to a congregation in Hackney. 65446

Discourse addressed to His Majesty's provincial troops. 78576

Discourse, addressed to the alumni of Jefferson College. 2790

Discourse addressed to the alumni of the Princeton Theological Seminary. 89733

Discourse, addressed to the alumni of Yale College. 89743

Discourse addressed to the Baptist Church in Portland. 71533

Discourse addressed to the candidates for the baccalaureate. 24568

Discourse addressed to the congregation in Franklin. 21977, 22525

Discourse addressed to the congregation in Franklin, upon the occasion of their receiving from Dr. Franklin. 22522

Discourse addressed to the congregation in the Presbyterian Church on University Place, New York. 89744

Discourse addressed to the Congregational Church and Society in Pembroke, N. H. 9391

Discourse addressed to the First Parish in Hingham. 71054

Discourse addressed to the First Presbyterian Congregation in Elizabeth, N. J., February 10, 1861. 89744

Discourse, addressed to the First Presbyterian Congregation of Elizabeth, N. J., October 9, 1867. 89744

Discourse addressed to the graduating class of Pennsylvania College. 3986

Discourse addressed to the members of Concordia Lodge. (48931)

Discourse, addressed to the Norfolk Auxiliary Society. 22525

Discourse addressed to the Plymouth and Norfolk Bible Society. 14535

Discourse addressed to the Religious Society of Young Men in Dorchester. 30508

Discourse addressed to the Roxbury Charitable Society. 17901

Discourse . . . addressed to the Second Congregational Church. 30637

Discourse addressed to the Second Presbyterian Congregation, Albany. 89744

Discourse, addressed to the Sons of Liberty. 20237

Discourse addressed to the United Presbyterian Congregation, Troy. 89744

Discourse addressed to Washington Lodge, No. 7. (76356)

Discourse . . . after the death of Theodore Parker. 31446

Discourse, . . . after the decease of Mr. Richard Friend. 47181

Discourse . . . after the decease of Mrs. S. C. E. Mayo. 47181

Discourse, after thirty years' ministry. 3794

Discourse, against conferences. 3105

Discourse against life-taking. 43430

Discourse against speaking evil of rulers. (43388)

Discourse . . . Albany, . . . 1858. 47181

Discourse, American Education Society. 30889

Discourse, and correspondence with varied learned jurists. 75955

Discourse and discovery of Nevv-Fovnd-Land. 103330-103332, 104786

Discourse and proceedings at the dedication. 12050

Discourse and proofe that Madoc Ap Owen-Gwyned first found. 21471

Discourse and view of Virginia. 4889, 100459

Discourse . . . Andover, June 25, 1852. 58625

Discourse, . . . anniversary of the Massachusetts Humane Society. 22465

Discourse . . . annual meeting of the American Baptist Home Mission Society. 34171

Discourse, . . . April 8, 1812. 21563

Discourse, . . . April 11, 1806. 22525

Discourse . . . April 15, 1858. 11784

Discourse . . . April 2, 1868. 45435

Discourse . . . April 17, 1859. (26240)

Discourse . . . April 16th, 1857. 26060

Discourse . . . April 3d, 1849. (41884)

Discourse . . . April 13, 1808. 39187

Discourse . . . April 12, 1797. (49064)

Discourse . . . April 28, 1861. 3794

Discourse at a public lecture in Boston. (14525)

Discourse at a Sunday evening service. 2662

Discourse . . . at a time, when the author has newly seen repeated strokes of death, on his own family. 46233

Discourse . . . at an evening lecture, in Portsmouth, N. H. 25867

Discourse at Amherst, Mass. Jan. 1781. 7659

Discourse at Attleborough, Jan. 21, 1811. 21977

Discourse at Attleborough, July 19, 1808. 22525

Discourse . . . at Auburn. 39201

Discourse . . . at . . . Augusta. 36841

Discourse . . . at Barnstable on the third of September, 1839. (58318)

Discourse . . . at Barnstable, Sept. 30, 1801. (3512)

Discourse at Belchertown, Mass., June 24, 1861. 27703

Discourse . . . at Borckville, Elizabethtown, April 27, 1815. 82239

Discourse . . . at Boston. 62517

Discourse . . . at Braintree, . . . April 9, 1818. 33950

Discourse at Braintree, April 23, 1738. 30174

Discourse at Bridgewater. 30521

Discourse at Bristol on the landing of the pilgrims. (44330)

Discourse . . . at Bristol, on the public thanksgiving. 40809

Discourse at Brookfield, Mass. 30521

Discourse. . . . at Buffalo, November 27, 1862. 5436

Discourse . . . at Burlington, before the literary societies of the University of Vermont, August 5th, 1845. (80079)

Discourse . . . at Burlington before the literary societies of the University of Vermont, August 1st, 1838. 3454

Discourse at Burlington, 29 April, 1813. 76357

Discourse . . . at Byfield, fast day, July 23, 1812. 58605

Discourse . . . at Byfield on the annual fast. 58609

Discourse . . . at Byfield on the annual thanksgiving. 58600

Discourse . . . at Byfield, on the public fast. (58601)

Discourse at Cambridge in the hearing of the University. 57778

Discourse, . . . at Canaan, March 23, 1815. (58655)

Discourse . . . at Canterbury. 42013

Discourse . . . at Canton, Jan. 30, 1822. 62733

Discourse at Castleton on the organization of the Mount Vernon Institution. 3941

Discourse at Castleton, Vt., Sept. 16, 1818. 3941

Discourse at Christ-Church, Cambridge, Aug. 21, 1764. 1857

Discourse at Christ-Church, Cambridge, on the death of Mrs Anne Wheelwright. 1852

Discourse . . . at Cohasset. 24771

Discourse . . . at Concord, N. H. 6957

Discourse . . . at Dedham . . . Dec. 21, 1851. 38776

Discourse . . . at Dedham, July 19, 1857. 38776

Discourse . . . at Dedham, June 14, 1857. 38776

Discourse . . . at Dedham, May 14, 1841. 38776

Discourse at Dorchester, June 11, 1817. 21977

Discourse at Dorchester, March 5, 1813. 30521

Discourse at Dorchester, Mass., May 10, 1864. (39830)

Discourse . . . at Dorchester, October 10, 1804. 30521

Discourse . . . at Dorchester, on 17 June, 1830. 62726

Discourse at Dumbarton, New Hampshire. 30528

Discourse at Dunstable, N. H. 9365, note before 89405

Discourse at Elizabeth Town and New York. 2405

Discourse . . . at Ellsworth. 37347

Discourse at Free Masons' Hall, St. Louis. (37764)

Discourse at Freehold, N. J. Dec. 1. 1723. 50661

Discourse at funeral of Mrs. Mary Sexton. 14445

Discourse at Goshen in Lebanon. 25299

Discourse, . . . at Goshen, January 17th, A. D. 1768. (54947)

Discourse . . . at Hackensack, N. J. 48998

Discourse . . . at Hallowell and . . . Augusta. 27401

Discourse at Hallowell. Thanksgiving, March 21, 1811. 27401

Discourse . . . at Hanover, . . . February 19, 1795. (47448)

Discourse, . . . at Hanover, . . . June 24th, 1793. 47449

Discourse . . . at Harwinton, on the 5th day of January, 1797. (28881)

Discourse . . . at Hingham . . . at the Association of . . . Ministers. 47447

Discourse . . . at Hingham, May 20, 1818. 55866

Discourse . . . at Hinsdale, July 29, 1892. 26777

Discourse at Hopkinton, March 24, 1776. 24570

Discourse at Hopkinton, Mass. Oct. 5, 1791. 7238

Discourse . . . at Hopkinton, (N. H.) 82490

Discourse at Lebanon, 4 March, 1805. 20507

Discourse, . . . at Liverpool, N. Y. 54969

Discourse . . . at Lyme, Feb. 4th, 1741, 2. (58894)

Discourse . . . at Marblehead, December, 1846. (39348)

Discourse . . . at Marblehead, June 24, 1822. 30521

Discourse at Marblehead, Mass. June 20, 1819. 3734

Discourse, . . . at Marlborough, March 24th, 1773. 47446

Discourse . . . at Medfield, . . . July 4, 1799. 65103

Discourse . . . at Medfield, October, 1797. 62733

Discourse . . . at Middlebury, on the annual fast. 3941

Discourse, . . . at Milford, August 20th, 1812. (50391)

Discourse . . . at Milford, N. H., January 12, 1815. (50391)

Discourse . . . at Milton, January 30, 1853. 50893

Discourse . . . at Milton, October 3d, 1804. 39187

Discourse . . . at Montpelier. 49729

Discourse at New Haven, before a special convention. 35801

Discourse at New Haven, Oct. 20, 1790. (18419)

Discourse at New-Town, Connecticut, Jan. 12, 1752. 36859

Discourse . . . at . . . Newbury-Port, Nov. 4th, 1779. (51518)

Discourse at Newburyport, August 12, 1779. (40210)

Discourse . . . at Newport, April 30, 1811. (63009)

Discourse . . . at Newport, Rhode Island. 30633

Discourse at North Coventry. 9

Discourse . . . at Northfield, Mass. 45483

Discourse . . . at Norwich, Conn., Nov. 14, 1865. 58369

Discourse at Philadelphia, June 2, 1828. 2969

Discourse . . . at Pittsfield, Mass., January 4, 1861. 33794

Discourse at Plymouth. 10

Discourse . . . at Plymouth, Dec. 20, 1828. 28555

Discourse . . . at Plymouth, Dec. 22d. 1808. 30521

Discourse . . . at Plymouth, December 22, 1815. 24772

Discourse, at Plymouth, July 14, 1799. 79967

Discourse at Plymouth, Mass., on the . . . anniversary of the landing of the pilgrims. (28387)

Discourse, . . . at Portland, May 5, 1814. (59309)

Discourse . . . at Princeton, June 18, 1817. 62733

Discourse . . . at Providence, August 5, 1836. (63049)

Discourse at Providence, Jan. 1, 1784. (57213)

Discourse . . . at Quincy. 42714

Discourse . . . at . . . Roxbury, January 4th, 1861. 54992

Discourse . . . at St. Paul's in Narraganset. 1759, 43664, (52608)

Discourse at Saybrook, Nov. 3, 1793. 33129

Discourse . . . at Southborough, May 15, 1757. 58798

Discourse . . . at Springfield, October 30, 1805. 39195

Discourse . . . at Stoughton, before the Rising Star Lodge. 30521

Discourse . . . at Taunton, (Mass.) July fourth, 1809. 82491

Discourse . . . at the anniversary meeting of the Kappa Alphi Phi Society. 43595

Discourse . . . at the Bromfield Street M. E. Church. 54993

Discourse . . . at the celebration. 59143

Discourse . . . at the commemoration of the landing of the pilgrims in Maryland, celebrated May 15, 1843. 16920

Discourse . . . at the commemoration of the landing of the pilgrims of Maryland, . . . May 11, 1846. 43659

Discourse at the completion of the first century of the Warren Association. 9914

Discourse at the dedication of a new church on Church Green. 95189

Discourse at the dedication of a new meeting house. 21449

Discourse . . . at the dedication of the Advent Chapel. (57799)

Discourse . . . at the dedication of the Bethlehem Church. 38776, 39441

Discourse . . . at the dedication of the church on Arlington Street. 26536

Discourse . . . at the dedication of the Congregational Church. 47986

Discourse, . . . at the dedication of the First Congregational Unitarian Church, Philadelphia. 26233

Discourse at the dedication of the Franklin Street Church. 19896

Discourse . . . at the dedication of the meeting-house erected by the Independent Congregational Society in Ipswich. 26536

Discourse . . . at the dedication of the meeting-house . . . in Ipswich, October 23, 1833. 26536

Discourse . . . at the dedication of the meeting-house of the First Congregational Society, Burlington, Vt. (62727)

Discourse . . . at the dedication of the new academy in Fryeburg. 64290

Discourse . . . at the dedication of the New Divinity Hall. (29753)

Discourse . . . at the dedication of the new hall, . . . New York. (17358)

Discourse . . . at the dedication of the new meeting house. 51614

Discourse at the dedication of the Seminary Hall in Saugus. 22448

Discourse . . . at the dedication of the Stone Church of the First Parish. 55201

Discourse . . . at the dedication of the . . . Union Church. 62742

Discourse . . . at the dedication of the Union Meeting-House. 48926

Discourse . . . at the dedication of the Unitarian Meeting-House. 41558

Discourse . . . at the first public meeting. 59364

Discourse at the Freeman's Meeting. 33951

Discourse . . . at the French Meeting-House in School-Street. 17671

Discourse . . . at the funeral of . . . Alpheus Spring. 43050

Discourse . . . at the funeral of Caleb Butler. 55299

Discourse at the funeral of Col. Benj. R. Hoagland. 44231

Discourse at the funeral of Dea. Tyler Batcheller. 18097

Discourse . . . at the funeral of Elisha Cowles Jones. 64303

Discourse, . . . at the funeral of Franklin C. Vadsworth. 77252

Discourse . . . at the funeral of John Adams, LL. D. 27605

Discourse [at the funeral of John Wesley.] 94539

Discourse at the funeral of Joseph Cummings. 60935

Discourse at the funeral of Lieut. Edgar M. Newcomb. 47255

Discourse at the funeral of Madam Abigail Stearns. 79451, 90905

Discourse at the funeral of Mr. Henry Lyman. (76359)

Discourse . . . at the funeral of Mr. Ichabod Pease. 29866

Discourse . . . at the funeral of Mr. Luther B. Lincoln. (50471)

Discourse . . . at the funeral of Mrs. Cornelia Higinbotham. 55203

Discourse . . . at the funeral of Mrs. D. W. V. Fiske. 33794

Discourse at the funeral of Mrs. Emily Jewett. 76358

Discourse at the funeral of Mrs. Harriot Putnam. 25875

Discourse at the funeral of Mrs. Julia Ann Balch. 70953

Discourse [at the funeral of Moses Stuart.] 93213

Discourse at the funeral of N. Eells. 30637

Discourse, at the funeral of Nehemiah Strong. 102071

Discourse . . . at the funeral of Professor Moses Stuart. 58625

Discourse . . . at the funeral of Rev. Abraham Burnham. 56212

Discourse at the funeral of Rev. David Sanford. 21977

Discourse . . . at the funeral of Rev. John Pierce. 38060

Discourse . . . at the funeral of Rev. Lucius Bolles. 79783

Discourse . . . at the funeral of Rev. Joseph Bennett. 12678

Discourse . . . at the funeral of Rev. Leonard Woods. (39348)

Discourse . . . at the funeral of Rev. Levi W. Leonard. 39536

Discourse . . . at the funeral of Rev. Samuel N. Steele. 55310

Discourse . . . at the funeral of Rev. Thomas Jones. 46181

Discourse at the funeral of the Rev. Thomas Snell. 85409

Discourse . . . at the funeral of Richard W. Flournoy. (50450)

Discourse, . . . at the funeral of Samuel Taylor. (50450)

Discourse . . . [at] the . . . funeral of the Hon. John C. Calhoun. 48932

Discourse . . . at the funeral of the Rev. D. M. Miller. 51539

Discourse . . . at the funeral of the Rev. Elisur Goodrich. 21563

Discourse at the funeral of the Rev. John Prince. 98034

Discourse . . . at the funeral of the Rev. John Smith. 63941

Discourse . . . at the funeral of the Reverend Mr. Peter Clarke. 3489

Discourse . . . at the funeral of the Rev. Philip Colby. 33951

Discourse at the funeral of the Rev. Thomas Snell. 18098, 85409

Discourse at the funeral of the Reverend Timothy Stone. 30636

Discourse . . . at the funeral of the Right Rev. William White. 57317

Discourse, . . . at the funeral of William B. O. Peabody. 26536

Discourse . . . at the inauguration of the author. (28670)

Discourse at the inauguration of William H. Green. 36605

Discourse at the installation of Dr. M'Auley. 85482

Discourse . . . at the installation of Rev. Alfred P. Putnam. 26536

Discourse . . . at the installation of Rev. George Whitney. 42714

Discourse . . . at the installation of Rev. John Jay Putnam. 41558

Discourse at the installation of Rev. Thomas Williams. 21977

Discourse at the installation of Rev. William Henry Channing. 4575

Discourse . . . at the installation of the Rev. Andrew Bigelow. 7495

Discourse . . . at the installation of the Reverend Daniel Marsh. 64213

Discourse . . . at the installation of the Rev. John Parkman. 26536

Discourse . . . at the installation of the Rev. Mellish Irving Motte. 11924

Discourse . . . at the installation of the Rev. Thomas Williams. 22525

Discourse at the installation of Theodore Parker. 58748

Discourse . . . at the institution of Warren Lodge. (37664)

Discourse . . . at the interment of Rev. John Boddily. 18400

Discourse, . . . at the interment of the Rev. Samuel Haven. 8930

Discourse . . . at the Music Hall, Boston. 62528

Discourse at the officers general hospital. 44785

Discourse . . . at the Old South Church in Boston. 32588

Discourse at the 150th anniversary of the incorporation of Abington. 21588

Discourse . . . at the opening of the Christian Chapel. 50693

Discourse, at the opening of the convention of clerical and lay-delegates. 84688

Discourse at the opening of the Presbyterian Church in the Northern Liberties. (28505)

Discourse at the opening of the Presbytery of New York. 3210

Discourse at the opening of the Synod of New Jersey. (21141)

Discourse . . . at the opening of the Tabernacle Baptist Church. 39174

Discourse at the ordination of Joel Barker. 22433

Discourse . . . at the ordination of Mr. Daniel M. Stearns. note after 42429

Discourse . . . at the ordination of Reverend Abiel Holmes. (30631)

Discourse . . . at the ordination of Rev. Amos D. Wheeler. 59354

Discourse . . . at the ordination of Rev. Artemas B. Muzzey. 26536

Discourse . . . at the ordination of Rev. Henry Emmons. 59354

Discourse . . . at the ordination of Rev. Walter S. Alexander. 58625

Discourse . . . at the ordination of the Rev. Abel Flint. (32257)

Discourse, . . . at the ordination of the Rev. Calvin Chapin. 60966

Discourse . . . at the ordination of the Rev. Charles E. Hodges. (26240)

Discourse, . . . at the ordination of the Rev. Eli Smith. 22525

Discourse . . . at the ordination of the Rev. Enoch Pond. 63983

Discourse . . . at the ordination of the Rev. Frederick A. Farley. 11924

Discourse . . . at the ordination of the Rev. George Putnam. 19862

Discourse . . . at the ordination of the Rev. James Harvey Hotchkin. (64216)

Discourse at the ordination of the Reverend John Wilder. 30637

Discourse . . . at the ordination of the Rev. Jonathan Ellis. 39696

Discourse . . . at the ordination of the Rev. Leonard Woods. 57778

Discourse at the ordination of the Rev. Mr. Amos Chase. 30637

Discourse . . . at the ordination of the Rev. Nathaniel W. Taylor. 21563

Discourse at the ordination of the Rev. Stephen Chapin. 22525

Discourse at the ordination of the Rev. Timothy Symmes. 33111

Discourse . . . at the ordination of the Rev. William Newell. 28687

Discourse . . . at the ordination of T. W. Higginson. 11932

Discourse at the ordination of Walter Harris. 22525

Discourse . . . at the organization of the Church of Christ, at Utica. 63441

Discourse . . . at the organization of the Second Presbytery of Philadelphia. 52293

Discourse . . . at the organization of the Trinitarian Congregational Church, in Taunton, Mass. 33950

Discourse . . . at the Paine Celebration in Cincinnati. 51540

Discourse at the . . . Pennsylvania College. 59135

Discourse at the public lecture in Boston. 3471

Discourse at the re-dedication of the Centre Church. 33091

Discourse . . . at the request of the Female Charitable Society. 33950

Discourse at the semi-centennial celebration of the First Congregational Church, Glover, Vt. 60974

Discourse . . . at the seventh anniversary of the Society for the Promotion of Collegiate and Theological Education at the West. 81640

Discourse . . . at the thirty-fifth anniversary of the American Institute. 18358

Discourse at the Thursday Lecture, March 16, 1797. 6517, 20238, 39183

Discourse . . . at the United States General Hospital. 44785

Discourse . . . at Trinity Church, Boston. 26624

Discourse . . . at Upton. 24427

Discourse at Wardsborough, Vt. 22525

Discourse . . . at . . . Washington, D. C. 51703

Discourse at Washington, N. H. 4350

Discourse at Waterford. (13775)

Discourse . . . at Weathersfield July 27, 1755. 41749

Discourse . . . at Wellfleet. 47444

Discourse . . . at West Dedham. 38776

Discourse . . . at Wethersfield, December 11th, 1783. 44742

Discourse . . . at Williamsburgh, January 24, 1836. 42722

Discourse . . . at Williamsburgh, Va. 82399

Discourse . . . at Winslow. 18129

Discourse . . . at Windsor . . . Vermont. 3105

Discourse at Worcester, April 28, 1824. 3105

Dsicourse at Worcester, March 28, 1775. 24428

Discourse at York. 8930

Discourse . . . August 8, 1858. 26527

Discourse . . . August 9, 1832. 58317

[Discourse] August 22, 1812. 4630

Discourse . . . Aug. 26, 1826. 43472

Discourse before a missionary meeting. 12991

Discourse . . . before . . . Caleb Strong, Esq. 38002

Discourse before His Excellency . . . and the Legislature of Massachusetts. 62731

Discourse . . . before the African Society in Boston. (30512)

Discourse . . . before the African Society . . . on the abolition of the slave trade. 19038

Discourse . . . before the alumni [of the University of the City of New York.] (45429)

Discourse before the alumni of Yale College. 2675

Discourse before the American Baptist Publication Society. 52170

Discourse before the American Board of Commissioners for Foreign Missions. 52310

Discourse . . . before the American Education Society, May 28, 1855. 80074

Discourse, before the American Education Society, . . . May 24, 1859. 44350

Discourse . . . before the American Home Missionary Society. 79920

Discourse before the American Institute. (28387)

Discourse . . . before the Ancient and Honorable Artillery Company, June 1, 1840. (79789)

Discourse . . . before the Ancient and Honorable Artillery Company, June 1, 1846. 22309

Discourse . . . before the Ancient and Honorable Artillery Company, June 3d, 1839. 81621

Discourse . . . before the Ancient and Honourable Artillery Company, June 7, 1841. 32234

Discourse . . . before the Ancient and Honorable Artillery Company of Massachusetts. 62772

Discourse . . . before the Ancient and Honorable Artillery Company, on its CXCVIIth anniversary. 58325

Discourse . . . before the Ancient and Honorable Artillery Company, on their CCXII anniversary. (37845)

Discourse before the Ancient . . . Artillery Company, June 5th, 1843. 48928

Discourse . . . before the Annual Convention of . . . Ministers of Massachusetts. 57778

Discourse before the Association of the Alumni. 71518-71519, 71521

Discourse before the baptism of R. J. Morris. (14525)

Discourse before the Baptist Church in Abington. 29847

Discourse before the Benevolent Fraternity of Churches. 11924

Discourse, . . . before the Berkshire Medical Institution. 32250

Discourse . . . before the Bible Society of Pennsylvania College. 43519

Discourse before the Bible Society of Salem and Vicinity. (18177)

Discourse . . . before the Boston Baptist Association. 44096

Discourse, . . . before, . . . the Boston Female Asylum, September 20th, 1805. 22465

Discourse . . . before the . . . Boston Female Asylum, September 21, 1804. 39187

Discourse . . . before the . . . Boston Female Asylum, September 26, 1806. 2921

Discourse, before the . . . College of New Jersey. 10942

Discourse . . . before the Conference of Baptist Ministers, May 25, 1841. 52170

Discourse . . . before the Congregation Mikve Israel. 50489

Discourse . . . before the Congregational Library Association . . . Boston. 32943

Dsicourse . . . before the Congregational Library Association, May 25, 1858. 80073

Discourse . . . before the Convention of the Congregational Ministers of Massachusetts. 58617

Discourse, delivered before the Erosophic Society. 64202

Discourse . . . before the Essex Agricultural Society. 62659

Discourse . . . before the . . . Female Charitable Society of Newburyport. (49136)

Discourse . . . before the First Congregational Society of Cincinnati. 60955

Discourse . . . before the First Parish in Cambridge. 54967

Discourse . . . before the . . . Free . . . Masons. 33983

Discourse before the General Assembly, May 7th, 1858. 33293

Discourse before the General Assembly of South Carolina. 58343

Discourse, . . . before the General Assembly, of the Presbyterian Church. (35751)

Discourse . . . before the General Convention of the Protestant Episcopal Church. 19314

Discourse . . . before . . . the Governor . . . Council, etc. 47994

Discourse . . . before the graduating class in the University of Vermont. 59457

Discourse before the graduating class of the University of North Carolina. (58346)

Discourse . . . before the Grand Chapter of the State of New York. 65095

Discourse . . . before the Howard Benevolent Society. 64210

Discourse, before the Humane Society, in Boston. 39187

Discourse . . . before the Humane Society of . . . Massachusetts, . . . June 11th, 1805. 28412

Discourse . . . before the Humane Society . . . of Massachusetts, June 10, 1806. 30510

discourse, before the Humane Society, of the Commonwealth of Massachusetts, Boston, June 14, 1808. 18480

Discourse . . . before the Law Academy of Philadelphia. 42976

Dicourse before the Literary and Moral Society of Ripley College. 5824

Discourse . . . before the Literary and Philosophical Society of New Jersey. (49064)

Discourse . . . before . . . the Literary School in Sharon. 58656

Discourse . . . before the literary societies of Amherst College. 80082

Discourse . . . before the literary societies of Union College. 44737

Discourse . . . before the Maine Historical Society. 24965

Discourse before the Maryland Historical
Society . . . January 25, 1855. 50844

Discourse . . . before the Maryland Historical
Society, . . . 20 June, 1844. (45211A),
(47106)

Discourse before the Massachusetts Charitable
Fire Society. 39187

Discourse . . . before the Massachusetts
Convention of Congregational Ministers.
38772

Discourse before the Massachusetts Historical
Society. (18844)

Discourse . . . before the Massachusetts
Horticultural Society. (30524)

Discourse . . . before the members of the
Salem Female Charitable Society. 6232

Discourse before the Merrimac Bible Society.
(50979)

Discourse before the Michigan Historical
Society in 1831. 77846

Discourse . . . before the New-England
Historic-Genealogical Society. (51883)

Discourse before the New Hampshire Colonization Society. 18405

Discourse . . . before the New Hampshire
Volunteers. 26323

Discourse . . . before the New-York Historical
Society . . . 19th of April, 1832. 39383

Discourse . . . before the New York Historical
Society, . . . November 20, 1866. (57789)

Discourse . . . before the New-York Historical
Society, . . . 6th December, 1812.
50832

Discourse before the New York Missionary
Society, April 1st, 1800. 41348

Discourse before the Pennsylvania Academy
of the Fine Arts. 27458

Discourse . . . before the Pennsylvania Colonization Society. 43271

Discourse . . . before the . . . Phi Beta Kappa
Society at Cambridge. 44737

Discourse . . . before the Phi Beta Kappa
Society of Amherst College. 31875

Discourse before the Phi Beta Kappa Society
of Brown University. Delivered September fourth, 1833. 47008

Discourse before the Phi Beta Kappa Society
of Brown University. Delivered September third, 1834. (71741)

Discourse before the Philadelphia County
Medical Society. 35459

Discourse before the Philomathean Society.
34750

Discourse before the Philomathesian Society.
44737

Discourse . . . before the Piscataqua Association of Ministers. 38875

Discourse before the Portsmouth Female
Asylum. 1808

Discourse before the Presbyterian Church at
Ballston Spa, N. Y. 43567

Discourse, before the public renewal of covenant. 8506

Discourse before the Reformed Society of
Israelites. 30294

Discourse . . . before the Rhode-Island Historical Society. (29751)

Discourse before the R. I. State Temperance
Society. 24971

Discourse before the Roxbury Charitable
Society. 3734

Discourse . . . before the Salem Female
Charitable Society. 65562

Discourse . . . before the Second Congregational Society. 3095

Discourse before the Senate of Union College.
3454

Discourse before the senior class of the
Divinity School. 12124

Discourse before the societies of St. Mary's
College. 8466

Discourse . . . [before] the Society for Instruct-
ing the Deaf and Dumb. 49749

Discourse before the Society for Propagating
the Gospel among the Indians and Others
in North America, delivered November
5th, 1807. (64241)

Discourse before the Society for Propagating
the Gospel among the Indians and Others
in North America, delivered Nov. 7, 1805.
21789

Discourse, before the Society for Propagating
the Gospel among the Indians, and Others,
in North America. Delivered on the 1st
of November, 1804. 25979

Discourse before the Society for "Propagating
the Gospel among the Indians, and Others,
in North-America." Delivered on the 19th
of January, 1804. 39177

Discourse before the Society for Propagating
the Gospel among the Indians and Others,
in North America, November 4, 1830.
7218

Discourse before the Society for Propagating
the Gospel among the Indians and Others
in North America: . . . Nov. 9, 1820.
42424

Discourse before the Society for Propagating
the Gospel among the Indians and Others
in North America . . . November 6, 1806.
3491

Discourse . . . before the Society for the
Commemoration of the Landing of William
Penn. 34729

Discourse before the Society for the Promotion
of Christian Education in Harvard University. 7495

Discourse before the Society for the Promotion
of Collegiate and Theological Education
at the West . . . at Springfield. 4618

Discourse before the Society for the Promotion
of Collegiate and Theological Education
at the West, delivered in High Street
Church. 92267

Discourse before the Society of the Sons of
New England. 7667

Discourse . . . before the Temperance Society
in Woburn. 52307

Discourse . . . before the Temperance Society
of the University of Vermont. 80071

Discourse . . . before the Trustees, faculty,
and students. (79200)

Discourse . . . before the Trustees of Hamilton College. 55524

Discourse . . . before the Unitarian Society
of Germantown. 54969

Discourse before the United Brothers' Society.
52161

[Discourse] before the united literary societies
of New Hampton Institution. 5308

Discourse . . . before the Universalist Societies. 56678

Discourse, before the University of Cambridge.
101751

Discourse . . . before the . . . University of
Vermont. 59457

Discourse before the Vermont Colonization
Society. 16209

Discourse before the Virginia Alpha of the
Phi Beta Kappa Society. (28844)

Discourse . . . before the Virginia Historical Society. 33928

Discourse . . . before the Warren Association. 48151

Discourse before the Young Catholic Friends' Society. 79588

Discourse before the Young Men's Christian Association of Richmond. (71660)

Discourse before the Young Men's Colonization Society. 97644

Discourse between Mary & Martha. 82542

Discourse by Alexander M'Leod. 43528

Discourse by Brantz Mayer, at the dedication. 47095

Discourse by Brantz Mayer; delivered in Baltimore. 47104

Discourse . . . by Brantz Mayer . . . . 8 April, 1852. (47092)

Discourse. By Daniel Sharp. 79794

Discourse, by David McKinny. 43467

Discourse . . . by David Tappan. 94368

Discourse . . . by Dr. William E. Channing. 42986

Discourse. By Edward D. Mansfield. 44376

Discourse by F. W. Sprague, of Newport. 89669

Discourse, by Frederick Frothingham. 26059

Discourse by George W. Burnap. 9364, (45211A)

Discourse by Gerrit Lydekker. 80901

Discourse . . . by Gerrit Smith, in Peterboro, Feb. 21st, 1858. (82669)

Discourse by Gerrit Smith, in Peterboro, November 20, 1864. 82603

Discourse, by Gerrit Smith, in Peterborough, July twenty-second, 1860. 82652

Discourse by Gordon Hall. 29777

Discourse. By H. Fuller. 26159

Discourse by J. G. Forman. (25096)

Discourse by James Banks, Esq. 43364

Discourse by Job R. Tyson. (27492)

Discourse. . . . By Nehemiah Hobart. (32306)

Discourse by President Nott of Union College. 89695, 3d note after 96966

Discourse, by Rev. D. F. Robertson. 71945

Discourse by Rev. David Root. 73122

Discourse by Rev. Dr. C. B. Boynton. 52032

Discourse. By Rev. E. P. Rogers. 72636

Discourse by Rev. Francis C. Clements. 18162

Discourse by Rev. J. S. Buckminster. 30519

Discourse. By Rev. John C. Lord. (42029)

Discourse by Rev. Nathan Strong. 101824

Discourse by Rev. Rufus P. Stebbins. 31864, 84013, 91049

Discourse . . . by Rev. Thomas Worcester. 68540

Discourse, by Rev. William Neal Cleveland. 13666

Discourse, by Richard Storrs. 50041, 92272

Discourse . . . by Rt. Rev. Dr. Onderdonk. 4032

Discourse [by Robert Cushman.] 106053

Discourse by S. F. Streeter. (45211A), 92793

Discourse . . . by the late . . . Mr. Ebenezer Pemberton. (59699)

Discourse by the Reverend and learned Mr. Solomon Stoddard. 91958

Discourse . . . by the Rev. Jedediah Morse. 12104

Discourse by the Rev. S. J. Buckminster. 8932

Discourse, by the Rev. Thomas Smyth. 85311

Discourse by the same author [i. e. John Augustin Smith.] 82921

Discourse, by W. B. Randolph. (67859)

Discourse [by Wayland.] (70542)

Discourse [by Z. Ely.] 22392, 97205

Discourse . . . Charlestown . . . state fast. 30880

Discourse . . . Cincinnati, O. 16222

Discourse, commemorating . . . Daniel Webster. 47165

Discourse commemorating the anniversary of the Church of the Ascension. 4274

Discourse commemorative of Abiel Chandler. 42040

Discourse commemorative of Amos Lawrence. 32939

Discourse commemorative of B. Waugh. (50878)

Discourse commemorative of Benjamin Holt Rice. (77587)

Discourse commemorative of Charles Brickett Haddock. 8555

Discourse, commemorative of forty years in the Christian ministry. 20192

Discourse, commemorative of forty years ministry. 6954

Discourse commemorative of General Samuel P. Strong. 88866

Discourse commemorative of Isaac Newton. 29530

Discourse commemorative of James Hunnewell. (48931)

Discourse commemorative of John Newton Putnam. 8555

Discourse commemorative of John W. Crafts. (39653)

Discourse commemorative of Major Charles Jarvis. 37765

Discourse, commemorative of Nathan Jackson. 32943

Discourse commemorative of Nathaniel Chapman. 35459

Discourse commemorative of our illustrious martyr. (21922)

Discourse commemorative of . . . Professor T. D. Mutter. (58416)

Discourse commemorative of Rev. Benjamin Tappan. (80178)

Discourse commemorative of Rev. Frederick Starr. 52309

Discourse commemorative of Rev. Joseph Vaill. 90981

Discourse commemorative of the character and career of Hon. John Parker Hale. 88867

Discourse commemorative of the death of Abraham Lincoln, delivered by Rev. Henry E. Butler. 9640

Discourse commemorative of the death of Abraham Lincoln, sixteenth President of the United States. 9103

Discourse; commemorative of the death of General George Washington. 43063

Discourse commemorative of the death of President Lincoln. 30977

Discourse commemorative of the distinguished service. 88869

Discourse commemorative of the fiftieth anniversary. 67779

Discourse commemorative of the heroes of Albany. 13358

Discourse commemorative of the history of the Bridge Street Church. 4994

Discourse, commemorative of the history of the Church of Christ in Yale College. 24464

Discourse commemorative of the Hon. Thomas Kinnicult. (31806)

Discourse commemorative of the late Hon. Ambrose Spencer. 89744

Discourse commemorative of the late Major-Gen. William Moultrie. 86131

Discourse commemorative of the late Rev. John M. Krebs. 89744

Discourse commemorative of the late Rev. Robert Baird, D. D. 89744

Discourse commemorative . . . of the late Rev. Samuel Miller. 6066

Discourse commemorative of the late William E. Horner. 35459

Discourse commemorative of the life and character of Abraham Lincoln. (5938)

Discourse commemorative of the life and character of Hon. Richard Fletcher. 27970

Discourse commemorative of the life and character of Mrs. Mary Kelley. 88857

Discourse, commemorative of the life and character of Rev. John Maltby. 63981

Discourse commemorative of the life and character of the Hon. Joseph Story. (28669)

Discourse commemorative of the life and character of the Rev. John Overton Choules. 29530

Discourse, commemorative of the life and ministry of Rev. Zephaniah Willis. 64105

Discourse commemorative of the life and services of Abraham Lincoln. (2700)

Discourse commemorative of the life and services of Josiah Willard Gibbs. 24465

Discourse commemorative of the life and services of the late Dr. Dan King. 11726

Discourse commemorative of the life and services of the Rev. Stephen Jewett. 4131

Discourse commemorative of the life, character and labors of the Rev. Thomas Smyth. 85341

Discourse commemorative of the Rev. John Knox. 19877

Discourse commemorative of the Rev. Joseph Fish. 33464

Discourse, commemorative of the Rev. Samuel Miller. 89744

Discourse commemorative of the Rev. Thomas Chalmers. 89744

Discourse commemorative of the Rev. W. Croswell. 20391

Discourse commemorative of the Rev. William Croswell. 20391

Discourse commemorative of the talents, virtues and services. 15616

Discourse commemorative of the twenty-second anniversary. 82950

Discourse commemorative of the virtue and attainments. (12406)

Discourse concerning chocolata. 93224

Discourse concerning comets. 46696

Discourse concerning congregational churches. 46791

Discourse concerning earthquakes. (46653)

Discourse concerning episcopacy. 12365, 101194

Discourse concerning faith and fervency in prayer, and the glorious kingdom of the Lord Jesus Christ. 46654

Discourse concerning faith and fervency in prayer, especially respecting the glorious visible kingdom of our Lord Jesus Christ. 35890, (46655)

Discourse concerning kindness. 25408

Discourse concerning paper money. 102246

Discourse concerning plantations. 78992

Discourse concerning prejudice in matters of religion. 94105, 97420

Discourse concerning the conversion of the heathen Americans. 84597-84598, 84601

Discourse concerning the covenant. 46496

Discourse concerning the currencies. 20721, 56481, 84538

Discourse concerning the death of the righteous; at Lyme. (46210)

Discourse concerning the death of the righteous. Occasioned by the death of the Honourable, John Foster Esqr. (46656)

Discourse concerning the design'd establishment. 51194

Discourse concerning the difficulty & necessity. (46789)

Discourse concerning the existence and the omniscience of God. 46657

Discourse concerning the $4\frac{1}{2}$ per cent. duty paid in Barbados. 6012, note just before (69427)

Discourse concerning the general conversion of the Israelitish nation. 46707

Discourse concerning the grace of courage. (46658)

Discourse concerning the influence of America on the mind. 34730

Discourse concerning the institution and observation of the Lord's-Day. 18478, (46278)

Discourse concerning the maintenance due to those that preach the Gospel. (46659)-46660

Discourse concerning the materials. 2627

Discourse concerning the nature and power of the holy angels. 46630

Discourse concerning the nature of regeneration. (30648)

Discourse concerning the origin and properties of wind. 6146

Discourse concerning the parts and progress of that work. 96301

Discourse concerning the publick reading. 32737

Discourse concerninge the Spanishe Fleete. 97661

Discourse concerning the subject of baptisme. 46661

Discourse concerning the uncertainty of the times of men. (46662)

Discourse concerning the witnesses. 32811

Discourse concerning Theodore Parker. 13412

Discourse concerning unlimited submission. 47131, 95642

Discourse, concerning what faith is saving. 92106

Discourse concluding with a dialogue. 50301

Discovrse containing a loving invitation. 103331, 103333, 104786

Discourse, containing an historical sketch of the First Congregational Church in North Brookfield. 85391

Discourse, containing an historical sketch of the town of North Brookfield. 85391

Discourse, containing some fragments of the history. 44303

Discourse containing two sermons. 97473

Dsicourse, death of J. Ashmun. 2675

Discourse . . . death of J. H. Castner. (48159)

Discourse . . . death of John Quincy Adams, 1848. 39201

Discourse, . . . death of R't Rev. S. Seabury. 35801

Discourse . . . death of Honorable Jabez Hamlin. 33957

Discourse . . . death of the Hon. John Quincy Adams. (29528)

Discourse . . . death of the Rev. Joseph Jackson. 18103

Discourse, . . . December 16, 1807. (59317)
Discourse, . . . December 6th, 1850. 64194
Discourse . . . December 10, 1843. 6961
Discourse . . . December 31, 1858. 37752
Discourse . . . Dec. 20, 1836. 30925
Discourse . . . December 25, 1859. 64463
Discourse . . . Dec. 25, 1870. 26536
Discourse . . . December 22d, 1850. (42363)
Discourse . . . Dec. 22, 1861. 26236
Discourse, declaring not onely [sic] the lawfulness, but also the necessity of the heavenly ordinance. 66430
Discourse declaring not only the lawfulness, but also the necessity of the heavenly ordinance. (66428)
Discourse . . . Dedham . . . Society for the Suppression of Intemperance. 14200
Discourse . . . dedication of Presbyterian Church, Hamptonburgh. 36373
Discourse delivered after the annual commencement. 99275
Discourse delivered . . . after the interment. 38005
Discourse delivered April 11, 1798. 82502
Discourse, delivered April 5, 1804. 102077
Discourse delivered April 5, 1803, 104280
Discourse delivered . . . April 19, 1837. 13280
Discourse delivered April 10, 1851. 80130
Discourse, delivered April 3, 1814. 71056
Discourse delivered . . . April 13. 97737
Discourse delivered April 30, 1863, at Brownsburg, Indiana. 8552
Discourse delivered April 30, 1863. By Rev. Chauncey Giles. 27367
Discourse delivered . . . April 28, 1850. (26240)
Discourse, delivered April 25, 1799. 102532
Discourse delivered April 29, 1849. 31108
Discourse delivered April 23d, 1865, at . . . Jacksonville, Ill. 27604
Discourse delivered April 23, 1865. By Rev. E. Hingeley. 31954
Discourse, delivered at a funeral. 102072
Discourse delivered at a lecture in Lebanon. 104359
Discourse, delivered at a public meeting in Hornby. 76257
Discourse delivered at a quarterly meeting of the German United Brethren. 85440
Discourse, delivered at Ackworth. 16342
Discourse, delivered at Amherst. (4776)
Discourse delivered at an occasional lecture in Andover. 94119
Discourse, delivered at Andover. 16329
Discourse, delivered at Ashburnham. 18111
Discourse, delivered at Attleborough. 103981
Discourse, delivered at Augusta (Maine.) 92034
Discourse delivered at Bedford. 90968
Discourse, delivered at Berkshire. 97075
Discourse, delivered at Berlin. 66602
Discourse delivered at Bolton. 21834
Discourse, delivered at Boscawen. 105061
Discourse delivered at Boston, before the Humane Society. 95197
[Discourse] delivered . . . at Boston . . . December 20, 1854. 4784
Discourse delivered at Boston, in the presence of His Excellency the Governor. 21245
Discourse delivered at . . . Boston, . . . June 27. 1742. 42008
Discourse delivered at Boston, on July 11, 1726. 83435
Discourse delivered at Bradford. 21450
Discourse delivered at Brookfield. 92089

Discourse delivered at Brookline . . . and . . . Roxbury. 64240
Discourse delivered at Brookline, 24 November, 1805. 62725
Discourse delivered at . . . Brooklyn. 4311, 4322
Discourse delivered at Brunswick, (Maine.) 17917
Discourse delivered at Bulfinch Street. 19038
Discourse delivered at Cainhoy. 83453
Discourse, delivered at Cambridge, February 22, 1800. 32579
Discourse delivered at Castleton, May 27, 1830. 89744
Discourse delivered at Charlestown. 103047
Discourse: delivered at Chelsea. 30637
Discourse delivered at Chicago, December 4th, 1859. 59167
Discourse delivered at Chicago, upon the landing of the pilgrims of Plymouth. 81618
Discourse delivered at Clayville. 43267
Discourse, delivered at Clearspring. 30287
Discourse, delivered at Colrain. 94204
Discourse, delivered at Concord, before the . . . Legislature. 64288
Discourse delivered at Concord, July 6th, 1791. 102065
Discourse delivered at Concord, October the fifth, 1825. 7939
Discourse, delivered at Conway, N. H. 64289
Discourse, delivered at Cornish (N. H.) 4449
Discourse delivered at Dedham, at the consecration of Constellation Lodge. 22170
Discourse, delivered at Dedham, before Constellation Lodge. (71055)
Discourse, delivered at Dedham, on the day of public thanksgiving. 19899
Discourse, delivered at Derby, Conn. (8343)
Discourse delivered . . . [at] Dorchester, at the funeral of . . . Rev. Richard Pike. 29827
Discourse, delivered at Dorchester, Dec. 29, 1799. 20623, 30509, 1st note after 101877
Discourse delivered at Dorchester, March 29, 1813. 30521
Discourse delivered at East-Hampton (Long-Island), Lord's-Day, July 22, 1798. 18264
Discourse delivered at East Hampton, Long Island, November 28, 1861. 48031
Discourse delivered at East-Hartford. 104214
Discourse delivered at East Machias. 92121
Discourse, delivered at Easton. (23160)
Discourse delivered at Fairfield. 102570
Discourse delivered at Fitchburg. 56234
Discourse . . . delivered at George-Town. 4005
Discourse delivered at Gettysburg. 77719
Discourse delivered at Hackensack. 41343
Discourse delivered at Halifax. 71114
Discourse delivered at Halifax in the County of Plymouth, February 2d 1757. 2867
Discourse delivered at Hallifax in the county of Plymouth, July 24th, 1766. 59121
Discourse, delivered at Hallowell, April 25th, 1799. 27398
Discourse delivered at Hallowell, at the opening of the academy. 7217
Discourse delivered at Hallowell, on the day of the annual thanksgiving. 27401
Discourse delivered at Hamilton Centre. 90032
Discourse delivered at Hanover. 16294
Discourse, delivered at Hartford, Feb. 22, 1800. 24761

Discourse delivered . . . at Hartford, . . . May 23, 1852. 13384

Discourse, delivered at Haverhill, (Massachusetts). 71505

Discourse, delivered at Haverhill, N. H. 93954

Discourse delivered . . . at Harvard. 59446

Discourse, delivered at Hebron. 92890

Discourse delivered at Hillsburgh. 17388

Discourse, delivered at his [i. e. Alva Woods'] inauguration. 105119

Discourse delivered at Hollis. 18976

Discourse, delivered at Honolulu. 18369

Discourse delivered at Hopkinton. 7308

Discourse delivered at Jefferson Hall. 82480

Discourse delivered at Kensington. 18416

Discourse delivered at Lebanon, N. H. 16341

Discourse, delivered at Lexington. 104166

Discourse delivered at Malden, January 8, 1800. (28498)

Discourse delivered at Mansfield, Sept. 23. 1742. 104367

Discourse, delivered at Marshfield. (79966)

Discourse, delivered at Mendon, June 14, 1810. 37347

Discourse delivered at Methuen. 74718

Discourse delivered at Middleborough. (15091)

Discourse, delivered at Montpelier, October 17, 1834. 25330

Discourse, delivered at Montpelier, on the evening of October 20, 1852. 89744

Discourse delivered at New-Ark in New-Jersey. 9419

Discourse delivered at New-Haven, Feb. 22, 1800. 21549

Discourse delivered at New-Haven, September 10th, 1741. (21934)

Discourse delivered at New-London. 349

Discourse delivered at . . . Newbury. By Jonathan Parsons. 58893

Discourse delivered at Newbury, March 26th, 1793. 102420

Discourse, delivered at Newbury-Port, North Meeting House. 55387

Dsicourse delivered at Newport, R. I. 3886

Discourse delivered at Norfolk. 22104

Discourse delivered at Northampton at the time of the late wonderful revival there. 21947

Discourse delivered at Northampton, N. H. 25872

Discourse delivered at Northampton, on the fourth of July, 1827. 89744

Discourse, delivered at Northborough. 103768

Discourse delivered at Owego Village. 91617

Discourse delivered at Oxford. (14206)

Discourse, delivered at Peacham, (Vermont,) March 31, 1839. 105244

Discourse, delivered at Philadelphia. 85295

Discourse delivered at Pittsfield, January 4, 1861. 33794

Discourse, delivered at Plymouth, December 22, 1820. 102262

Discourse, delivered at Plymouth, February 22d, 1800. 37364

Discourse delivered at Plymouth, Dec. 22, 1808. 30511

Discourse delivered at Plymouth, Mass., Dec. 22, 1832. 25437

Discourse, delivered at Plymouth, (North Carolina.) 102077

Discourse, delivered at Plymouth, 22 December, 1806. 32588

Discourse delivered at Pomfret. 104371

Discourse, delivered at Portsmouth. 8922

Discourse delivered at Princetown. (30458)

Discourse delivered at Providence. 13394

Discourse delivered at Quincy, October 19, 1811. 103772

Discourse, delivered at Quincy, September 19, 1804. 103773

Discourse delivered at Quebec. 18929

Discourse, delivered at Reading February 22, 1800. 92047

Discourse delivered at Reading, North Parish. 92048

Discourse, delivered at Reading, on the day of the national fast. 92049

Discourse, delivered at Rome. 2399

Discourse, delivered at Rupert, February 23, 1813. 102458

Discourse delivered at Rye, . . . January 1, 1801. 64256

Discourse, delivered at Rye, June 5th, 1803. 64255

Discourse, delivered at Saco, on the dedication of the new meeting house. 103345

Discourse delivered at St. Paul's Church, Shadwell. 33863

Discourse delivered at Salem. 65560

Discourse, delivered at Salisbury, Conn., on the day of the annual thanksgiving. 68999

Discourse delivered at Salisbury, West Church, Mass. 2866

Discourse delivered at Schenectady. 13724

Discourse, delivered at Scipio. 104530

Discourse delivered at South Canaan, Conn. 27934

Discourse delivered at South Hingham. 7491

Discourse delivered at South Parish in Scituate. 3510

Discourse delivered at Spencertown. 89744

Discourse delivered at Stanford, Lord's-Day. 102571

Discourse delivered at Stillwater. 9631

Discourse delivered at Stoughton, Mass. 92248

Discourse, delivered at Stow. 95258

Discourse delivered at the anniversary Dudleian-Lecture at Harvard-College in Cambridge. 12331

Discourse delivered at the anniversary Dudleian-Lecture at Harvard-College, . . . May 12. 1762. 12331

Discourse, delivered at the anniversary meeting of the freemen. 97184

Discourse, delivered at the anniversary of the Derby Academy, in Higham, May 19, 1847. (26240)

Discourse, delivered at the anniversary of the Derby Academy, in Hingham, May 21, 1828. 25440

Discourse, delivered at the annual election. 19037

Discourse delivered at the camp of the 8th Connecticut Vols. 83644

Discourse, delivered at the celebration of the nativity. 105022

Discourse delivered at the celebration of the two hundredth anniversary. 94442

Discourse delivered at the Christian Chapel, West Seventeenth St. 7761

Discourse delivered at the commemoration of the landing of the pilgrims of Maryland. 42412

Discourse, delivered at the consecration of the synagogue . . . in . . . New-York. 55375

Discourse delivered at the consecration of the synagogue of the Hebrew Congregation, Mikva Israel. 19339

Discourse delivered at the constitution of Rising-Sun Lodge. 106019-20 [sic]

Discourse delivered at the constitution of the Seventh-Day Baptist Church. 47046

Discourse delivered at the dedication of the new house of worship, at West Boxford. 21736

Discourse delivered at the dedication of Divinity Hall. 11924

Discourse, delivered at the dedication of Lawrence Church. 90031A

Discourse, delivered at the dedication of Manning Hall. 102183

Discourse, delivered at the dedication of the American Asylum. 26409

Discourse delivered at the dedication of the Baptist Church in Bowdoin Square. 29530

Discourse delivered at the dedication of the chapel. 13418

Discourse delivered at the dedication of the Church of the Messiah. 19855

Discourse delivered at the dedication of the First Meeting-House. 22302

Discourse delivered at the dedication of the meeting-house of the First Baptist Church in Barnstable. 63851

Discourse delivered at the dedication of the meetinghouse of the Keene Congregational Society. 93544

Discourse, delivered . . . at the dedication of the new brick meeting house. 70918

Discourse delivered . . . at the dedication of the new church, Jan. 1, 1846. 24779

Discourse delivered at the dedication of the new church of the First Parish in Concord. 26015

Discourse delivered at the dedication of the new congregational meetinghouse. (32252)

Discourse delivered at the dedication of the North Meeting House in Braintree. 92251

Discourse delivered at the dedication of the North Meeting House in Weymouth. 4753

Discourse, delivered at the dedication of the Reformed Dutch Church in Chittenango. 105989

Discourse delivered at the dedication of the Second Congregational Church, Scituate. 19060

Discourse delivered at the dedication of the Second Congregational Society in Worcester. (31806)

Dsicourse delivered at the dedication of the Unitarian Church, Montreal. 26536

Discourse delivered at the dedication of the Unitarian Congregational Church in Newport. 11924

Discourse, delivered at the dedication of the Universalist Meeting House in Beverly. 13856

Discourse delivered at the dedication of the Winthrop Church. 74323

Discourse delivered at the dedication of Westminster Church in Providence. 23812

Discourse delivered at the first meeting of the Historical Society of Michigan. 11344

Discourse, delivered at the fourth anniversary of the Warren Street Chapel. (25376)

Discourse: delivered at the funeral obsequies of the late Hon. Edward W. Fox. 75831

Discourse delivered at the funeral of Hon. Solomon Foot. (78683)

Discourse delivered at the funeral of Hon. William M. Richardson. 13631

Discourse, delivered at the funeral of Mr. Samuel Rockwood. 22525

Discourse, delivered at the funeral of Mrs. Bathsheba Sanford. 22525

Discourse delivered at the funeral of Mrs. Julia R. Sikes. 90982

Discourse, delivered at the funeral of Mrs. Marshall Mason. (67878)

Discourse delivered at the funeral of Mrs. Mary Woodward. 80789

Discourse delivered at the funeral of Mrs. Rachel Lewis. 90207

Discourse delivered at the funeral of Mrs. Rachel Roome. 90201

Discourse delivered at the funeral of Rev. Chester W. Carpenter. 92778

Discourse delivered . . . at the funeral of Richard George, Esquire. (20599)

Dsicourse, . . . delivered at the funeral of the Rev. David Sanford. 22525

Discourse delivered at the funeral of the Rev. I. S. Spencer. 89783

Discourse, delivered at the funeral of the Rev. John Cleaveland. 22525

Discourse delivered at the funeral of the Rev. Robert Breck. 39199

Discourse delivered at the funeral of the Rev. Thomas Fessenden. (20066)

Discourse, delivered at the funeral of the Rev. Timothy Dickinson. 22525

Discourse delivered at the funeral of William Roe. 82934

Discourse delivered at the funeral service. 103357

Discourse delivered at the Furman Theological Institution. 70428

Discourse delivered at the installation of J. K. Karcher. 26075

Discourse delivered at the installation of Rev. David Fosdick. 66780

Discourse, delivered at the Jewish Synagogue. 67913

Discourse delivered at the Lowell Institute in Boston. (18045)

Discourse delivered at the meeting-house in Fayette-Street. 90209

Discourse delivered at the M. E. Church in Adrian. 82235

Discourse delivered at the New Chapel in City-Road. 103662

Discourse delivered at the New Church, Boston. 25761

Discourse delivered at the new edifice of the Baptist Church. (36955)

Discourse delivered at the New Universalist Chapel. 62626

Discourse, delivered at the North Church of Newburyport. 80790

Discourse delivered at the obsequies of Gen. Zachary Taylor. 91571

Discourse, delivered at the one hundredth anniversary of the organization of the Baldwin Place Baptist Church. 92368

Discourse delivered at the one hundredth anniversary of the organization of the First Baptist Church. 58339

Discourse delivered at the opening of a session of the Presbytery of Baltimore. 104624

Discourse delivered at the opening of the Christian Meeting House. 13780

Discourse delivered at the opening of the church erected. (21702)

Discourse delivered at the opening of the Medical Institution. 18158

Discourse delivered at the opening of the New Almshouse. 32588

Discourse, delivered at the opening of the New Baptist Meeting-House. 12121, 91812

Discourse, delivered at the opening of the Providence Athenaeum. 102184

Discourse delivered at the opening of the twentieth convocation. 77478

Discourse delivered at the opening of the Westminster Presbyterian Church. 2634

Discourse, delivered at the ordination, of Brother Thomas Barnes. (70928)

Discourse delivered at the ordination of the Rev. David Lawrence Morrill. 30792

Discourse, delivered at the ordination of the Rev. Ebenezer Coffin. 14183

Discourse delivered at the ordination of the Rev. J. S. Buckminster. 8930

Discourse, delivered at the ordination of the Rev. James W. Thompson. 106051

Discourse, delivered at the ordination of the Rev. James Wilson. 76514

Discourse delivered at the ordination of the Reverend Jonathan Gould. (32257)

Discourse delivered at the ordination of William J. Potter. (26240)

Discourse, delivered at the public lecture in Boston. 6517, 39183

Discourse delivered at the re-opening and dedication of the North Church in Portsmouth. (32647)

Discourse delivered at the re-opening of St. Peter's Church. 4131A

Discourse, delivered at the request of the American Revolution Society. (7064)

Discourse, delivered at the request of the Massachusetts Charitable Fire Society. 97402

Discourse delivered at the request of the officers of the Second Presbyterian Church. 78397

Discourse, delivered, at the Roman Catholic Church in Boston. 95256

Discourse delivered at the School House. 75030

Discourse, delivered at the sixteenth anniversary of the Society for the Promotion of Collegiate and Theological Education at the West. 90910

Discourse, delivered at the Tabernacle in Salem. 105303

Discourse delivered at the Third Church in Brookfield. 92086

Discourse delivered at the Third Parish in Newbury. 94364

Discourse, delivered at the twelfth anniversary of the New-York Baptist Theological Seminary. 90204

Discourse delivered at the Unitarian Chapel. (37247)

Discourse delivered at the united service of the seven Presbyterian congregations of Buffalo. 5435

Discourse, delivered at the Universal Meeting-House. 70916

Discourse, delivered at the Universalist Meeting-House in Charlestown, Mass. April 13, 1815. 97478

Discourse delivered at the Universalist Meeting-House in Charlestown, Mass. on thanksgiving day, December 3, 1818. 97476

Discourse, delivered at the Universalist Meeting-House in Charlestown, Mass. September 14, 1815. 97479

Discourse, delivered at the University Hall in Philadelphia. 65502

Discourse delivered at the University of North Carolina. 9910

Discourse delivered at the West Church in Boston. 8504

Discourse, delivered at Topsfield. 7365

Discourse delivered at Wallingford. (18419)

Discourse, delivered at Watertown. 105159

Dsicourse delivered at Welles. 31287

Discourse, delivered at Westford. 89808

Discourse delivered at Winslow. 18130

Discourse delivered at Wintonbury. 73558

Discourse delivered at Woodbury. 17581, 101749

Discourse delivered at Woodstock. 102582

Discourse delivered at Worcester, December 11, 1825. (27702)

Discourse delivered August 18, 1847. 21892

Discourse delivered August 2, 1864. 89744

Discourse delivered . . . August 6, 1862. 31679

Discourse, delivered August 10, 1795. 22525

Discourse delivered Aug. 23, 1863. 3676

Discourse delivered . . . Baltimore on the 14th January, 1815. (38173)

Discourse delivered before a Brigade of Continental Troopers. 23162

Discourse delivered before . . . Governor, . . . Council, etc., of . . . Vermont. (9490)

Discourse delivered before Hiram Lodge, No. 72. 90208

Discourse delivered before His Excellency Thomas Chittenden. 104345

Discourse, delivered before His Honour Paul Brigham. 103708

Discourse delivered before the alumni of the University of Pennsylvania. 103108

Discourse, delivered before the American Academy of the Arts. 13713

Discourse, delivered before the American Education Society. 92022

Discourse delivered before the Ancient and Honorable Artllery [sic] Company, in Boston, 1 June, 1818. 14528

Discourse delivered before the Ancient and Honorable Artillery Company, in Boston, June 1, 1807. 2915

Discourse, delivered before the Ancient and Honorable Artillery Company, June 6, 1831. 3619

Discourse delivered before the Ancient and Honorable Artillery Company, on its CCXXIII. anniversary, June 3, 1861. 42140

Discourse delivered before the Ancient & Honorable Artillery Company on their CCXI anniversary. (11383)

Discourse delivered before the Baptist Church and Society of Wheatland. 48864

Discourse, delivered before the Benevolent Fraternity of Churches. 26536

Discourse delivered before the Bible Society of Pennsylvania College. 83345

Discourse delivered before the Boston Children's Friend Society. 92075

Discourse, delivered before the . . . Boston Female Asylum. (21792)

Discourse delivered before the Boston Mechanics' Institution. 92303

Discourse delivered before the Boston Mercantile Association. 93550

Discourse delivered before the Boston Young Men's Total Abstinence Society. 26536

Discourse delivered before the Charitable Female Society. 11965

Dsicourse delivered before the Colporteur Convention. 92373

Discourse delivered before the Congregation Shearit Israel. 67913

Discourse, delivered before the Congregational Ministers of the colony of Rhode Island. 73556

Discourse, delivered before the Congregational Society in Berkeley. (1526)

Discourse delivered before the Connecticut Alpha of φ . B. K. 33794

Discourse delivered . . . before the consolidated constitution of New Hampshire. 16342

Discourse delivered before the Convention of Congregational Ministers of Massachusetts. 3105

Discourse delivered before the Delaware Historical Society. 68170

Discourse delivered before the faculty, students and alumni of Dartmouth College. 12858

Discourse, delivered before the First Parish in Hingham. 71052

Discourse delivered before the General Assembly of the Presbyterian Church in the United States. 89783

Discourse delivered before the General Assembly of the Presbyterian Church in the United States of America. 70841

Discourse delivered before the General Association of Connecticut. 31644

Discourse delivered before the General Association of New York. 92268

Dsicourse delivered before the General Convention of the Baptist denomination April 28th, 1841. 26169

Discourse delivered before the General Convention of the Baptist denomination in the United States. 92369

Discourse delivered before the Georgia Historical Society, . . . February 12, 1840. 39327

Discourse delivered before the Georgia Historical Society, Savannah. 91572

Discourse delivered before the Georgia Historical Society, 12th February, 1845. 12975

Discourse delivered before the Georgia Historical Society . . . 12th February, 1844. 22278

Discourse, delivered before the Grand Lodge. 94689

Discourse delivered before the Hartford Temperance Society. 89815

Discourse delivered before the Historical and Philosophical Society of Ohio. 94356

Discourse delivered before the Historical Society of Louisiana. 9116

Discourse delivered before the Historical Society of Pennsylvania: March 26, 1850. 37011

Discourse delivered before the Historical Society of Pennsylvania, November 19, 1828. 61305

Discourse delivered before the Historical Society of Pennsylvania, October 24, 1831. 97642

Discourse, delivered before the Historical Society of Pennsylvania, on the 28th day of April, 1834. 13828

Discourse, delivered before the Historical Society of Pennsylvania, the ninth day of April, 1836. 24476

Discourse delivered before the Historical Society of the American Lutheran Church. 70452

Discourse delivered before the Historical Society of the State of Pennsylvania, on New Year's Day, 1827. 98699

Discourse delivered before the Honourable the Mayor and Corporation of the city of New-York. 90198

Discourse delivered before the Humane Society, at their anniversary, May, 1817. 97405

Discourse delivered before the Humane Society of . . . Massachusetts, . . . June 8, 1802. 64245

Discourse delivered before the Humane Society of . . . Massachusetts . . . June 10, 1794. (3490)

Discourse delivered before the Humane Society of . . . Massachusetts, . . . June 12, 1804. (33258)

Discourse delivered before the Humane Society of . . . Massachusetts, 9th June, 1795. (8355)

Discourse delivered before the Humane Society of the commonwealth of Massachusetts, at the semiannual meeting twelfth of June, 1798. 101201

Discourse delivered before the Humane Society of the commonwealth of Massachusetts, at their semiannual meeting, June 14th, 1796. 71735

Discourse, delivered before the Humane Society of the commonwealth of Massachusetts, . . . eleventh of June, 1793. (13424)

Discourse delivered before the Indiana Historical Society. 105661

Discourse delivered before the legislative departments of Massachusetts. 761

Discourse delivered before . . . the Legislature of Massachusetts. 7368

Discourse delivered before the Legislature of New York. (72637)

Discourse delivered before the Legislature of Vermont, on the day of general election, at Montpelier. 105112

Discourse delivered before the Legislature of Vermont, on the day of general election, October 14, 1830. 34742

Discourse delivered before the Literary and Philosophical Society of Hampden Sydney College. 70842

Discourse delivered before the Maine Historical Society. 9243

Discourse delivered before the Massachusetts Horticultural Society. (74346)

Discourse delivered before the Massachusetts Society for the Suppression of Intemperance. 93551

Discourse, delivered before the members of the Boston Female Asylum. 91791

Discourse delivered before the members of the "Old Guard," of St. Louis. (22178)

Discourse delivered before the members of the Portsmouth Female Charity School. 8930

Discourse delivered before the Merrimack Humane Society. 1503

Discourse, delivered before the Methodist Society and citizens of Bangor. 94590

Discourse, delivered before the New-England Historic, Genealogical Society, Boston, March 18, 1870. 81693

Discourse delivered before the New-England Society in the City of New York, December 22, 1851. 31872

Discourse delivered before the New-England Society of the City and State of New-York, Dec. 22, 1822. 103228

Discourse delivered before the New England Society in the City of New York, December 22, 1847. 29816

Discourse delivered before the New England Society of the City of New York, December 22, 1841. (29484)

Discourse delivered before the New Hampshire Historical Society. 6960

Dsicourse . . . delivered before the New-York Alpha of the Phi Beta Kappa Society. 36668

Discourse delivered before the New York Historical Society, . . . December 19, 1839. 68607

Discourse delivered before the New York Historical Society, December 6th, 1828. 54469

Discourse delivered before the New-York Historical Society . . . November 17, 1863. 4652

Discourse delivered before the New York Historical Society . . . November 20, 1845. 7234

Discourse delivered before the New York Historical Society, on the 20th of December, 1859. 24963A

Discourse, delivered before the New-York Historical Society, on Thursday, December 28, 1820. 103152

Discourse delivered before the New-York Historical Society . . . 6th December, 1811. 13714

Discourse delivered before the North-British Society. 8443

Discourse delivered before the officers and members of the Humane Society of Massachusetts. (79943)

Discourse, delivered before the Ohio Historical and Philosophical Society, at Columbus. 101080

Discourse, delivered before the Pennsylvania Academy of the Fine Arts. 32985

Discourse delivered before the Phi Beta Kappa Society at Harvard University. 89007

Discourse delivered before the Phi Beta Kappa Society of Bowdoin College. 89744

Discourse delivered before the Phi Beta Kappa Society of Harvard University. 31875

Discourse delivered before the Phi Beta Kappa Society of Rhode Island. 11480

Discourse delivered before the Phi Beta Kappa Society of the University of Georgia . . . February 22d, 1852. 7414

Discourse delivered before the Philomathean Society of the University of Pennsylvania. 61306

Discourse delivered before the Pilgrim Society, at Plymouth. 93552

Discourse: delivered before the Presbyterian Board of Foreign Missions. 85478

Discourse delivered before the Presbyterian Historical Society. (18744)

Discourse delivered before the Rhode Island Historical Society, December 27, 1865. 77082

Discourse delivered before the Rhode-Island Historical Society, . . . February 8, 1849. 28596

Discourse, delivered before the Rhode-Island Historical Society, . . . February 16, 1852. (58917)

Discourse delivered before the Rhode Island Historical Society, . . . January 18th, 1848. (31099)

Discourse delivered before the Rhode-Island Historical Society . . . January 13, 1847. (21425)

Discourse delivered before the Rhode-Island Historical Society, on the evening of January 17, 1853. 2082

Discourse, delivered before the Roxbury Charitable Society, . . . September 15, 1800. 22465

Discourse delivered before the Roxbury Charitable Society September 14th, 1795. 64245

Discourse, delivered before the Roxbury Charitable Society . . . Sept. 24, 1817. (14129)

Discourse delivered before the St. Nicholas Society of Manhattan. 32390

Discourse, delivered before the Senate of Union College. 78839

Discourse delivered before the Society for Promoting Collegiate and Theological Education at the West, in . . . Newark. 3506

Discourse delivered before the Society for Promoting Collegiate Education at the West, in . . . New Haven. 15181

Discourse delivered before the Society for Propagating the Gospel among the Indians and Others in North America, at their anniversary meeting in Boston, November 3, 1808. 32580

Discourse delivered before the Society for Propagating the Gospel among the Indians and Others in North America, 6th November, 1823. 30513

Discourse delivered before the Society for the Commemoration of the Landing of William Penn. 3395

Discourse delivered before the Society for the Prevention of Pauperism . . . Jan. 8, 1854. 13365

Discourse delivered before the Society of the Alumni of Harvard University. 92295

Discourse delivered before the State Historical Society of Wisconsin. 84860

Discourse, delivered before the Synod of New York and New Jersey. (73565)

Discourse delivered before the Triennial Convention of the Protestant Episcopal Church in the United States of America. 78564

Discourse delivered before the Union Baptist Church, Jersey City, N. J. 1800

Discourse delivered before the Virginia Historical Society. 28843

Discourse delivered before the Washington Benevolent Society in Exeter. 31766

Discourse delivered before the Young Men's Christian Association of St. Paul, Minnesota. 89257

Discourse delivered before Theodore Parker's Society. (26240)

Discourse delivered . . . Boston, on Fast Day. 3620

Discourse, delivered, by appointment, at Oakland College. 104740

Discourse delivered by Benjamin Thurston. 95774

Discourse, delivered by Geo. Wm. Brown. 8480

Discourse, delivered by Micah Stone. 92092

Discourse delivered by Presidents Joseph Smith and Brigham Young. 83237

Discourse delivered by request of the Executive Committee of the Board of Foreign Missions. 89744

Discourse delivered by Rev. G. W. Samson. 75963

Discourse delivered by Rev. I. H. T. Blanchard. 5822

Discourse delivered by Rev. J. S. Backus.
3636, 37583

Discourse delivered by Rev. James Smither.
84964

Discourse, delivered by Rev. Richard Fuller.
26167

Discourse delivered by Rev. Robert Norton.
(44452)

Discourse, delivered by Revd Thomas Armitage. 2009

Discourse, delivered by Rev. Thomas Gallaudet.
26405

Discourse delivered by Samuel Spring. 89789

Discourse, delivered by the desire and in the
presence of the Female Beneficient
Society. 92953

Discourse delivered by the Rev. T. H. Barr.
3582

Discourse delivered by the Rev. William J.
Hoge. (32434)

Discourse delivered by the Rev. William Scott.
78390

Discourse, delivered . . . Cambridgeport and
in Charlestown. 22309

Discourse delivered . . . Canton, Mass. 31605

Discourse, delivered Dec. 1, 1808. 102081

Discourse delivered Dec. 2, 1860. 59009

Discourse delivered Dec. 17th, 1840. (81644)

Discourse, delivered December 3, 1824. 66840

Discourse, delivered December 31, 1816.
90975

Discourse delivered December 12, 1850, on
occasion of the public thanksgiving.
92269

Discourse delivered . . . December 12, 1850,
the day of the annual thanksgiving. 6065

Discourse delivered December 29, 1799; occasioned by the melancholy death of
George Washington. (25236)

Discourse, delivered December 29, 1799, the
Lord's-Day immediately following the
melancholy tidings of the loss. 57774

Discourse delivered, 1813, Nov. 11, in Salem,
New-Hampshire. 82894

Discourse, delivered extempore. 67806

Discourse, delivered . . . February 8, 1863.
9475

Discourse delivered Feb. 11th, 1803. 92050

Discourse delivered Feb. 15, 1818. 3941

Discourse, delivered February 15, 1795. 92274

Discourse delivered February 19, 1795; being
the day of national thanksgiving. 75927

Discourse delivered February 19, 1795, the
day . . . for a national thanksgiving
through the United States. 57772

Discourse delivered February 10th, 1867.
58650

Discourse, delivered February 25, 1849. 89634

Dsicourse, delivered . . . February 22, 1852.
9629

Discourse, delivered Feb. 22, 1819. 23024

Discourse delivered February 23, 1840. 84921

Dsicourse, delivered 14th January, 1810.
70946

Discourse delivered in . . . Albany. 13364

Discourse delivered in . . . Amherst, Mass.
33790

Discourse delivered in Ashby. 67777

Discourse delivered in . . . Baltimore. 34768

Discourse delivered in Bath, June 20, 1852.
(24548)

Discourse, delivered . . . in Boscawen. 65423

Discourse delivered . . . in Boston, April 9th,
1835. 11924

Discourse, delivered in Boston, April 13,
1815. (39182)

Discourse delivered in Boston, August 11, 1861.
21805

Discourse delivered . . . in . . . Boston, before
the Ancient and Honourable Artillery
Company, June 7, 1847. 42710

Discourse, delivered in Boston, before the
Humane Society of Massachusetts, 9 June,
1812. 14535

Discourse delivered in . . . Boston, December
31, 1820. 42423

Discourse, delivered . . . in Boston . . .
February 24, 1850. 26556

Discourse, delivered in Boston, July 17, 1836.
23784

Discourse delivered in . . . Boston . . . June
11, 1837. 14535

Dsicourse delivered . . . in Boston, . . . June
11th, 1799. 33987

Discourse delivered in Boston, March 1, 1826.
3840

Discourse delivered . . . in Boston, 19th April,
A. D. 1795. (13424)

Discourse, delivered in Boston, on the day of
public thanksgiving. 39187

Discourse delivered in Bowdoin Square Church.
18138

Dsicourse delivered in Bowdoin Street Church,
Boston. 92846, 104805

Discourse delivered in Bowdoin-Street Church
. . . June 16, 1839. 104802

Discourse delivered in . . . Bradford, December 22, 1820. 61030-61031

Discourse delivered in Brookline. (62724)

Discourse delivered in . . . Brooklyn, N. Y.
66757

Discourse . . . delivered . . . in Buffalo.
74010

Discourse delivered . . . in Burlington. 59376

Discourse, delivered . . . in Canadaigua.
21803

Discourse delivered in Central Church, Boston,
Oct. 19, 1851. (70931)

Discourse, delivered in Central Church, Boston,
October 17, 1852. (70939)

Discourse delivered in Central Church, Boston,
13 August, 1851. 70930

Discourse delivered in . . . Charlestown. 22309

Discourse delivered in Chelsea. 37850

Discourse delivered in Chepachet, R. I. 20746

Discourse, delivered in Chester. 83726

Discourse delivered in Christ's Church at
Norwich-Landing. 84687

Discourse delivered in Cincinnati, December
11, 1861. 72068

Discourse delivered in . . . Claremont, January
4, 1861. 12169

Discourse delivered in Clinton, N. Y. 24501

Discourse delivered in Cohasset. 8340

Discourse in commemoration of the . . .
anniversary of the Mite Society. 35416

Discourse delivered in Concord, N. H. 42991

Discourse, delivered . . . in Dedham, May 29,
1803. 65102

Discourse delivered in . . . Dedham, . . .
July 31, 1864. 26536

Discourse delivered . . . in . . . Detroit,
Mich. 31676

Discourse, delivered in different churches.
98589

Discourse delivered in Dr. Heron's Church.
73123

Discourse delivered in Dorchester. (29830)

Discourse delivered in Dover. (28403)

Discourse delivered in Dublin, N. H. at the
consecration of Altemont Lodge. 4350

Discourse, delivered in Dublin, N. H., September 7, 1845. 40112

Discourse delivered in . . . East Medowbrook, Mass. 74394

Discourse delivered . . . in . . . East Saginaw. (50584)

Discourse delivered in Eastport, on the dedication of the First Congregational Meeting-House. 5274

Discourse delivered in . . . Elizabeth, N. J. 43819

Discourse delivered in Fairfax County, Virginia. 104732

Discourse delivered in . . . Finsbury. (3535)

Discourse delivered in Fitzwilliam, N. H. 26802

Discourse delivered in . . . Fort Wayne. 42537

Discourse delivered in . . . Frankfort, Ky. 17376

Discourse delivered in Franklin. 17403

Discourse, delivered in Grace Church, in the city of New York. (71153)

Discourse delivered in Grace Church, Philadelphia. 93407

Discourse delivered in Hanover, N. H. 29483

Discourse delivered in Harvard Church, Charle Charlestown, July 14, 1839. 101054

Discourse delivered in Harvard Church, Charlestown, June 13, 1869. 22309

Discourse delivered in Harvard Church, Charlestown, on Sunday. 22303

Discourse delivered in Harvard Church, Charlestown, on thanksgiving Day. 22308

Discourse delivered in Haverhill, Jan. 31, 1805. 91792

Discourse, delivered in Haverhill, March 22, 1805. 64134

Discourse delivered in Hollis Street Church, Boston. 62762

Discourse delivered in Ipswich, October 8, 1856. (37751)

Discourse delivered in Kingston, U. C. 74548

Discourse delivered in . . . Lancaster, Pa. 15892

Discourse, delivered in Lebanon. 22392, 97205

Discourse, delivered in . . . Litchfield. 26177

Discourse . . . delivered in Liverpool. 11932

Discourse delivered in . . . Lowell, Mass. 67881

Discourse delivered . . . in Manchester, N. H. 19896

Discourse, delivered in Mansfield, Oct. 3, 1841. 92065

Discourse delivered in Marlborough, Mass. 18965

Discourse delivered in Middleboro, Mass. 3397

Discourse delivered in Murray Street Church. 85482

Discourse delivered in New Haven, Dec. 30, 1860. 2669

Discourse, delivered in . . . New Orleans. 78394

Discourse delivered in . . . N. York, before . . . the American Tract Society. 73047

Discourse delivered in . . . New-York, on the . . . 10th of March, 1833. 73537

Discourse delivered in . . . Newark, N. J. 540

Discourse delivered in Newburyport, July 4, 1814. 18405

Discourse delivered . . . in Newburyport . . . Nov. 19, 1844. 18401

Discourse, delivered in Newport, Rhode-Island. 19311

Discourse delivered in Norfolk, Conn. 22104

Discourse delivered in North Church, Weymouth, Mass. 22468

Discourse delivered in Orrington. 63980

Discourse delivered in Philadelphia, August 15th, 1824. 79933

Discourse delivered in Philadelphia, . . . Feb. 9, 1851. (26240)

Discourse delivered in Philadelphia, July 18, 1854. 13228

Discourse delivered in . . . Philadelphia, June 29, 1862. 26232

Discourse delivered in . . . Philadelphia, November 6th, 1864. 6062

Discourse delivered in . . . Philadelphia, Nov. 23, 1848. 64609

Discourse delivered in . . . Philadelphia, on . . . November 26th, 1863. 33320

Discourse delivered in Plymouth, at the Cushman Festival. 18139

Discourse delivered in Plymouth Church, Brooklyn. 32269

Discourse delivered in . . . Portsmouth, December 14, 1800. 8925

Discourse delivered in . . . Portsmouth, November 15, 1898. 8924

Discourse delivered in . . . Potsdam, N. Y., June 29, 1856. 67880

Discourse delivered in presence of His Excellency Thomas Chittenden. 80809

Discourse delivered in . . . Princeton. 43151

Discourse delivered in Providence, in the Colony of Rhode Island, on the 25th day of July, 1768. 20767

Discourse delivered in . . . Providence, on the occasion of the third jubilee. 31429

Discourse delivered in Providence, September 6, 1804. 19314

Discourse delivered in Quincy, at the interment of John Adams. 103774

Discourse delivered in Quincy, March 11, 1848. 42711

Discourse delivered in . . . Quincy, March 7, 1843. 42714

Discourse delivered in . . . Quincy, . . . Sept. 15, 1850. (42713)

Discourse, delivered in . . . Richmond, Va. . . . April 8th, 1864. 20526

Discourse delivered in . . . Richmond, Virginia, . . . 4th July, 1833. 63040

Discourse delivered in Roxbury, October 12, 5796. (4776)

Discourse delivered in . . . Roxbury, on fastday, April 8, 1847. (7008), 66782

Discourse delivered in . . . Roxbury, on fast day, April 6, 1843. 66785

Discourse delivered in said [i. e. Christ] Church. Church. (21711)

Discourse delivered in said [i. e. Trinity] Church. 73881

Discourse, delivered in St. Albans, at the funeral of Dea. Horace Janes. 84922

Discourse, delivered in St. Albans, Vt. 67881

Discourse delivered in St. James' Church, in New-London. (78565)

Discourse delivered in St. John's Church, Brooklyn. 36209

Discourse delivered in St. John's Church, in Portsmouth. (78566)

Discourse delivered in St. John's Church, Jamaica Plain. 81692

Discourse delivered in St John's Church, Providence. 84690

Discourse delivered in St. John's (Lutheran) Church. (78944)

Discourse delivered in . . . St. Louis. (22178)

Discourse delivered in St. Luke's Church. 78583

Discourse delivered in St. Matthew's Church. 3682

Discourse, delivered in St. Mark's Church, Liverpool. 102727

Discourse delivered in St. Paul's Church, Troy. 14238

Discourse delivered in St. Paul's Evangelical Lutheran Church. 2378

Discourse delivered in St. Peter's Evan. Luthern Church. 22069

Discourse delivered in St. Philip's Church. 104323

Discourse . . . delivered . . . in Salem. 7495

Discourse delivered in . . . Salisbury, Conn. 68996

Discourse delivered in Sansquoit, May 5, 1861. 43268

Discourse delivered in . . . Savannah, Georgia, July 4th, 1858. 64226

Discourse delivered . . . in . . . Schenectady. 68590

Discourse delivered in . . . South Salem. 41311

Discourse delivered in Springfield, Ohio. 78459

Discourse delivered in Stephentown and Troy. 4618

Discourse delivered in Stokesley Church. 102728

Discourse, delivered in Stoneham, (Mass.) April 8, 1813. 91546

Discourse delivered in Stoneham, (Mass.) April 8, 1813. Being the day of the state fast. 91544

Discourse delivered in Stoneham, (Mass.) April 7, 1814. 91545

Discourse delivered . . . in Sudbury, Mass. 18367

Discourse, delivered in Suffield 1st Society. 101000

Discourse delivered in the Adelaide Street Wesleyan-Methodist Church. 74547

Discourse delivered in the Ancient Meeting-House of the First Congregational Society in Hingham. 31805

Discourse delivered in the Baptist Church, Keeseville, N. Y. 5308

Discourse delivered in the Baptist Meeting House, Franklin, Indiana. 2752

Discourse delivered in the Brick Church, Montpelier, Vt. 28802

Discourse delivered in the Brick Meeting House in Danvers. 100921

Discourse delivered in the Chapel of Harvard-College. 97326

Discourse delivered in the Chapel of the Hamilton Literary and Theological Institution. 21721

Discourse delivered in the Chapel of the New Alms-House in Portsmouth. 9458

Discourse: delivered in the Chapel of Yale College. (24569)

Discourse delivered in the Church of Epiphany. 29741

Discourse delivered in the Church of the Puritans, New York. 12396

Discourse delivered in the Church on Church Green. 106056

Discourse delivered in the Circular Church, Charleston. 39961

Discourse, delivered in the city of New Haven. 18413

Discourse, delivered in the city of New-York. 33036

Discourse delivered in the city of Washington. 82951

Discourse delivered in the College Street Church. 92903

Discourse delivered in the Conference on the Second Advent Near, at Boston. 101299

Discourse delivered in the Congregational Church at Hansom. 25759

Discourse, delivered in the Congregational Church in Purchase Street. 71523

Discourse, delivered in the Congregational Church in Rutland, Vermont. 78684

Discourse delivered in the Congregational Church of Manchester, Vermont. 18136

Discourse delivered in the Council House, at Greenville. 70470

Discourse, delivered in the Court-House of Prince George County, Virginia. 89603

Discourse, delivered in the Dutch Church, in Albany. 82922

Discourse delivered in the English Lutheran Church. 77726

Discourse delivered in the Federal-Street Meeting House. (26535)

Discourse delivered in the First Baptist Church, Richmond. 9476

Discourse delivered in the First Baptist Meeting-House in Boston. 13571

Discourse delivered in the First Baptist Meeting-House in Providence. 79788

Discourse delivered in the First Baptist Meeting House, Lawrence, Mass. 71048

Discourse, delivered in the First Church, Beverly. 95227

Discourse delivered in the First Church in Boston. 102061

Discourse delivered in the First Church of Christ at Portsmouth. 8921

Discourse delivered in the First Church of Dover. 88868

Discourse delivered in the First Congregational Church, Albany. 58371

Discourse delivered in the First Congregational Church in Northampton. 89744

Discourse delivered in the First Congregational Church in West Springfield. 89744

Discourse delivered in the First Congregational Unitarian Church. 26231

Discourse delivered in the First Constitutional Presbyterian Church. 21333

Discourse delivered in the First Constitutional Presbyterian Church, May 7, 1865. 21332

Discourse delivered in the First Parish Church, Gloucester. 100972

Discourse . . . delivered in the First Parish of Hingham. 26784

Discourse delivered in the First Presbyterian Church, at Oakland. 92939

Discourse delivered in the First Presbyterian Church, in Augusta, Georgia. 72626

Discourse delivered in the First Presbyterian Church in Rochester. 21997

Discourse delivered in the First Presbyterian Church, in the city of Milwaukee. 89262

Discourse delivered in the First Presbyterian Church, Newark, N. J. December 8th, 1831. 30046

Discourse, delivered in the First Presbyterian Church, Newark, N. J., on Thanksgiving Day, Dec. 12, 1850. 90907

Discourse delivered in the First Presbyterian Church of Detroit. 21136

Discourse delivered in the First Presbyterian Church of Easton. 9472

Discourse delivered in the First Presbyterian Church of Penn Yan. 90549

Discourse delivered in the First Presbyterian Church of Philadelphia. 5753

Discourse, delivered in the First Presbyterian Church, Penn Yan. 90550

Discourse, delivered in the First Presbyterian Church, Philadelphia. 3507

Discourse delivered in the First Presbyterian Church, Troy, N. Y. 4618

Discourse delivered in the First Presbyterian Church, Troy, New York, on Thanksgiving Day. 4615

Discourse delivered in the Fisrt Protestant Reformed Dutch Church of Albany. 105994

Discourse delivered in the First Reformed Church, New-Brunswick. 91157

Discourse delivered in the First Reformed Presbyterian Church, New York. 91113

Discourse, delivered in the First Society of Killingsworth. 73978

Discourse delivered in the Fourth Baptist Meeting House, Providence. (82551)

Discourse: delivered in the Fourth Congregational Church of Norwich. 90445

Discourse delivered in the Fourth Presbyterian Church, Albany. (18584)

Discourse, delivered in the "Free Church," Clinton, N. Y. 84290

Discourse, delivered in the German Reformed Church in . . . New York. 20941

Discourse delivered in the Howard Presbyterian Church, San Francisco. 78520

Discourse delivered in the Meeting House of the Second Baptist Society. 92375

Discourse delivered in the M. E. Church. 9236

Discourse delivered in the Methodist Protestant Church Wentworth-St. 85443

Discourse delivered in the mines at Symsbury. 4015, note after 97633

Discourse delivered in the morning at Quincy. 103775

Discourse delivered in the New Dutch Church, Nassau Street. 21325

Discourse delivered in the New Meetinghouse at Chelsea. 97602

Discourse delivered in the New Road, and Brunswick-Place Chapels. 102719

Discourse, delivered in the New-York City Hospital. 90181

Discourse, delivered in the North Church, Newburyport. 20193

Discourse delivered in the North Church of Christ. 8930

Discourse delivered in the North Congregational Church New-Bedford. 84407

Discourse, delivered in the North Dutch Church, in Albany. 72640

Discourse, delivered in the North Meeting-House in Bridgewater. 92923

Discourse delivered in the North Presbyterian Church, in Chicago. 71084

Discourse delivered in the North Reformed Dutch Church. 19876

Discourse delivered in the Old South Church, Reading, Mass., March 2, 1862. 3678

Discourse, delivered in the Old South Church, Reading, Mass., December 28, 1862. 3680

Discourse, delivered in the Orphan Asylum, New-York. 90190

Discourse delivered in the Presbyterian Church, Brooklyn. (76492)

Discourse delivered in the Presbyterian Church, Honesdale, Penn. 73563

Discourse delivered in the Presbyterian Church in Caldwell, N. J. 89683

Discourse delivered in the Presbyterian Church in Cedar-Street. 73532

Discourse, delivered in the Presbyterian Church, in Georgetown. 84116

Discourse delivered in the Presbyterian Church, in the city of Baltimore. (928)

Discourse delivered in the Presbyterian Church, New Scotland. 78648

Discourse delivered in the Presbyterian Church of Frankfort. 83700

Discourse delivered in the Protestant Episcopal Church. 44982

Discourse delivered in the Protestant Reformed Dutch Church. 44231

Discourse delivered in the Reformed Dutch Church, Jamaica, L. I. 26695

Discourse delivered in the Reformed Dutch Church, Stapleton, S. I. 81650

Discourse delivered in the Second Congregational Church, Dorchester, Ms. 92249

Discourse, delivered in the 2d Congregational Church, Newport, . . . [after] the interment of Doctor Isaac Senter. 59126

Discourse, delivered in the 2d Congregational Church, Newport, December 29th, 1799. 69122

Discourse delivered in the Second Presbyterian Church, Albany, April 16, 1865. 89744

Discourse delivered in the Second Presbyterian Church, Albany, December 3, 1865. 89744

Discourse delivered in the Second Presbyterian Church, Albany, September 4, 1864. 89744

Discourse delivered in the Second Presbyterian Church, Albany, November 28, 1861. 89744

Discourse delivered in the Second Presbyterian Church in Brooklyn. 89326

Discourse delivered in the Second Presbyterian Church, New-Brunswick. 79760

Discourse, delivered in the Second Presbyterian Church, of Lafayette. 104667

Discourse, delivered in the Second Unitarian Church, and also in the First Parish Church. 103739

Discourse, delivered in the Second Unitarian Church, Sunday, December 31, 1837. 103740

Discourse delivered in the South Church, at Montreal. 86858

Discourse delivered in the South Church, Salem, Mass. 22421

Discourse delivered in the South Congregational Church, Middletown. 21084

Discourse, delivered in the South Meeting-House in Andover. 94365

Discourse delivered in the South Reformed Church, October 19, 1873. 72632

Discourse delivered in the South Reformed Church on Thanksgiving Day, November 26th, 1874. 72631

Discourse, delivered in the Synagogue in New York, on the ninth of May, 1798. 78949

Discourse delivered in the town of Versailles. 94399

Discourse delivered in the . . . United States Hospital. 44785

Discourse delivered in the Universalist Church, Albany, N. Y. 84291

Discourse delivered in the Universalist Church at New Bedford. (75268)

Discourse delivered in the West Parish of Brookfield. 85409

Discourse delivered in Trinity Church, in Newport. 19313

Discourse delivered in Trinity Church, New-York. 77979

Discourse, delivered in . . . Troy, July fourth, 1841. 4618

Discourse delivered in . . . Troy, N. Y. on Thanksgiving Day. (4616)

Discourse, delivered in . . . Troy, October 15, 1843. 4618

Discourse, delivered in Troy, Sabbath evening, January 17. 97369

Discourse delivered in two parts. 18405, (18433)

Discourse delivered in Utica, New York, July 28, 1861. (25316)

Discourse delivered in . . . Washington, D. C. 12404

Discourse delivered in . . . Washington, D. C. on Thanksgiving Day. 9630

Discourse delivered in Washington, D. C., on the day of humiliation and prayer. 33388

Discourse delivered . . . in Watertown. 25440

Discourse delivered in . . . West Bridgewater, Mass. 25097

Discourse, delivered . . . in West Cambridge, Mass. 18367

Discourse delivered in West Newbury, Mass. 23863

Discourse, delivered in Wilbraham, May 12, 1799. 104963-104964

Discourse delivered in Wilbraham, November 17, 1805. 104962

Discourse delivered in Williamsburg, New-York. 27850

Discourse delivered in Wilmington, Delaware. 39693

Discourse delivered in Windham, N. H. 26295

Discourse delivered in . . . Worcester. 59355

Discourse delivered in Zanesville. 68572

Discourse delivered January 18, 1794. 88950

Discourse, delivered January 18, MDCCXCIV. 88949

Discourse delivered Jan. 5, 1816. 100918

Discourse delivered January 1, 1850. 37365

Discourse delivered January 1st, 1841. 10940

Discourse, delivered January 1, 1802. 43474

Discourse delivered . . . January 14, 1827. 62626

Discourse . . . delivered Jan. 14, 1759. (9718)

Discourse delivered January 4, 1861. (21137)

Discourse, delivered Jan. 12, 1815. 97309

Discourse delivered Jan. 12, 1825. 72739

Discourse delivered January 28th, 1741, 2. 7300

Discourse delivered January 29th, 1865. 9496

Discourse delivered January 22, 1811. 22525

Discourse delivered July 4, 1806. 20749

Discourse delivered July 4, 1833. 11853

Discourse, delivered . . . July 4th, 1825. (65534)

Discourse delivered, July 5, 1802. 22525

Discourse delivered . . . July 3, 1859. (26240)

Discourse delivered July 30, 1823. 100922

Discourse delivered June 20, 1813. 1803

Discourse, delivered, . . . July 23, 1812. (26622)

Discourse delivered . . . June 5th, 1833. 11900

Discourse, delivered March 4, 1814. 3941

Discourse delivered March 14, 1846. 24779

Discourse, delivered March 9, 1807. 78323

Discourse, delivered . . . March 17, 1844. (26240)

Discourse delivered March 13, 1808. 89791

Discourse delivered March 31, 1805. 18405

Discourse . . . delivered . . . May 5, 1802. 57778

Discourse delivered . . . May 1, 1853. 33964

Discourse, delivered May 9, 1798. Being the day of fasting and prayer. 22525

Discourse, delivered May 9, 1798, on the importance of special humiliation. 103982

Discourse delivered May 16, 1779. 33279

Discourse delivered . . . May 3, 1840. 58800

Discourse, delivered . . . May 31, 1809. 57775

Discourse delivered near York in Virginia. 23161

Discourse delivered November 18, 1872. (64302)

Discourse delivered November 19, A. D. 1820. 100926

Discourse, delivered November 17, 1847. 84923

Discourse delivered November 10, 1861. (12406)

Discourse delivered November 10, 1779. 104348

Discourse, delivered November 20, 1814. 22525

Discourse, delivered November 25, 1813. 22525

Discourse delivered Nov. 24, 1864. 58823

Discourse delivered November 27, 1862. 4617

Discourse, delivered Nov. 23, 1794. 18405

Discourse delivered . . . October, 1825. (32301)

Discourse delivered (Oct. 16, 1862). 13222

Discourse, delivered October 21st. 1792. 104349

Discourse delivered October 10, 1841. 64934

Discourse, delivered, October, 13, 1813. 22525

Discourse, delivered, October 22, 1806. 82886

Discourse . . . delivered . . . on a special occasion. 52212

Discourse, delivered on a special occasion at Weymouth. 40856

Discourse delivered on board the Transport Ship Java. 46853

Discourse delivered on fast day. 11947

Discourse delivered on fast day, April 15, 1858. 92059

Discourse delivered on fast day, April 2, 1846. 79792

Discourse, delivered on fast day, April 6, 1843. 79692

Discourse, delivered on fast day, entitled God and our country. (7008)

Discourse delivered on fast day, in the Third Baptist Meeting House in Boston. 79803

Discourse delivered on Friday, December 12, 1862. 89744

Discourse, delivered on Friday, December 27, 1799. 92954

Discourse delivered on occasion of the death of George Washington, late President. 2403, 97766, note after 101874

Discourse delivered on occasion of the death of John Boynton. 89089

Discourse delivered on occasion of the first commencement. 85316

Discourse delivered on occasion of the fortieth anniversary. 76507

Discourse delivered on occasion of the late national fast. 35508

Discourse delivered on relinquishing the pastoral care. 104814

Discourse delivered on Sabbath evening, August 17, 1845. 89744

Discourse, delivered on Sabbath evening, January 3, 1830. 85483

Discourse delivered on Sabbath evening, July 19, 1846. 89744

Discourse, delivered on Sabbath evening, March 17, 1833. 89744

Discourse delivered on Saturday, February 22, 1800. 22271

Discourse, delivered on Saturday, the 10th day of August, 1769. 104677

Discourse delivered on Sunday evening, March 25, 1849. 89744

Discourse delivered on Thanksgiving Day. 27367

Discourse delivered on Thanksgiving Day, at West Galway. (49700)

Discourse delivered on Thanksgiving Day, December 12th, 1850. 82455

Discourse delivered on Thanksgiving Day, November 28, '61. 70934

Discourse delivered on Thanksgiving-Day, November 24th, 1853, by N. A. Boardman. 6074

Discourse delivered on Thanksgiving Day, November 24, 1853, in the First Presbyterian Church. 93748

Discourse, delivered on Thanksgiving Day, November 24, 1864. (74954)

Discourse delivered on Thanksgiving Day, November 29, 1860. 16804

Discourse delivered on Thanksgiving-Day, November 26th, 1846. 84928

Discourse, delivered on Thanksgiving Day, Nov. 26, 1863. 24435

Discourse delivered on Thanksgiving Day, November 23, 1854. 93747

Discourse delivered on the anniversary of the association of the First Parish in Hingham. 98035

Discourse, delivered on the anniversary of the Historical Society of Michigan, June, 1831. 103692

Discourse delivered on the anniversary of the Historical Society of Michigan, June 4, 1830. 77845

Discourse delivered on the annual fast, 1847. 7369

Discourse, delivered on the annual fast in Massachusetts. 22525

Discourse delivered on the annual fast in Massachusetts, April 7, 1808. 27399

Discourse, delivered on the annual thanksgiving, 1846. 9549

Discourse delivered on the day appointed by the President of the United States, Jan. 4, 1861. 68141

Discourse delivered on the day of annual thanksgiving. 33843

Discourse, delivered on the day of fasting, humiliation and prayer. 90438

Discourse delivered on the day of national humiliation. 7677, 7679

Discourse delivered on the day of national thanksgiving. 10685

Discourse delivered on the day of public thanksgiving, December 12, 1860. 82339

Discourse delivered on the day of public thanksgiving through the United States of America. 100917

Discourse delivered on the day of the annual provincial thanksgiving. 8653

Discourse delivered . . . on the day of the annual thanksgiving. (21571)

Discourse delivered on the day of the funeral of President Lincoln. 43046

Discourse delivered on the day of the national fast. 36644

Discourse delivered on the day preceding the annual commencement. 99264

Discourse delivered on the death of Capt. Paul Cuffee. 104324-104325

Discourse, delivered on the death of John Fillis. (71564)

Discourse, delivered on the dedication of the new lecture room. 85300

Discourse, delivered, on the 18th day of December, 1777. 23159

Discourse, delivered on the 18th of October, 1797. 84691

Discourse delivered on the . . . erection in the church. (26240)

Discourse, delivered on the fast day. 21260

Discourse delivered on the . . . fifth anniversary of the organization. 42541

Discourse delivered on the fiftieth anniversary of his installation. 89767

Discourse, delivered on the first centennial anniversary of the Tabernacle Church. 105324

Discourse, delivered on the fourth of July, 1825. 29301

Discourse delivered on the fourth of July, 1827. 22382

Discourse delivered on the . . . national fast, April 30, 1863. 68997

Discourse, delivered on the national fast, at Franklin. 22525

Discourse, delivered on the national fast, August 20th, 1812. 95521

Discourse delivered on the national fast day. 38737

Discourse delivered on the . . . National fast, January 4, 1861. 27605

Discourse delivered on the national fast, Sept. 26, 1861. 39825

Discourse delivered on . . . the 19th of February, 1795. note after 43706

Discourse, delivered on the occasion of organizing a Catholic Total Abstinence Association. 77735

Discourse delivered on the occasion of the birth of Washington. 82387

Discourse delivered on the occasion of the centenary jubilee. 77477

Discourse delivered on the occasion of the death of John Vaughan. (26240)

Discourse, delivered on the occasion of the death of Gen. Zachary Taylor. 89392

Discourse delivered on the occasion of the funeral obsequies of President Lincoln. 68583

Discourse delivered on the occasion of the national and state thanksgiving. 19604

Discourse delivered on the occasion of the national fast, September 26, 1861 . . . . By Rev. Ichabod Simmons. 81165

Discourse delivered on the occasion of the national fast, September 26th, 1861, in . . . Philadelphia. 26235

Discourse delivered on the occasion of the opening . . . the building erected by the Consistory of the Reformed Prot. Dutch Church. 19877

Discourse delivered on the occasion of the twenty-second anniversary of the N. Y. Academy of Medicine. 82691

Discourse delivered on the public thanksgiving day. 21790

Discourse delivered on the Sabbath after the Commencement of the year 1802. 22269

Discourse, delivered on the Sabbath after the decease of the Hon. Timothy Pickering. 98036

Discourse delivered on the Sabbath evening after the death of the late President Harrison. 89774

Discourse delivered on the 17 March, 1828. 40759

Discourse delivered on the Sunday after the disaster of Bull Run. 9546

Discourse, delivered on the Sunday morning after the murder of President Lincoln. 6060

Discourse, delivered on the 12th June, 1818. 98536

Discourse, delivered on the twenty-fifth anniversary. 36583

Discourse [delivered on the 25th of May, 1856.] 80775, 89767

Discourse, delivered on the twenty-fourth of October, 1826. 103109

Discourse delivered on the 22d of February, 1797. 84095

Discourse, delivered on the 26th of November, 1795. 41348

Discourse delivered on the 29th of December, upon the close of the year 1799. 65561

Discourse delivered on 22d November 1804. 6126

Discourse, delivered on Wednesday evening, the 16th of May, 1798. 90840

Discourse delivered one hundred and fifty years ago. 102450

Discourse delivered Sabbath afternoon, July 4th, 1841. 77247

Discourse, delivered Sabbath day, August 9, 1812. 105303

Discourse, delivered Sabbath morning, September 3, 1865. 89744

Discourse, delivered . . . September 2, 1807. (4776)

Discourse, delivered September 3, 1850. 89744

Discourse delivered . . . September 30th. 6072

Discourse deliver'd September 24th, 1763. (48178)

Discourse delivered . . . 16th of January, 1855. 7159

Discourse delivered Sunday morning, April 7, 1861. 89744

Discourse, delivered . . . Thanksgiving Day, December 12th, 1850. 81642

Discourse delivered Thanksgiving Day, November 28, 1867. 70405

Discourse, delivered the next Lord's Day after the interment of Deacon Peter Whiting. 22525

Discourse delivered to the Barton-Square Society at Salem. 38086

Discourse delivered to the church and congregation in Franklin. 82210

Discourse delivered to the class of the Kentucky School of Medicine. 24782

Discourse, delivered to the congregation in Franklin. 22525

Discourse delivered to the congregation of the Southern Parish in Ipswich, March 20th. 1755. 103929

Discourse delivered to the congregation of the Southern Parish in Ipswich, May 25th. 1755. 103929

Discourse delivered to the Congregational Church and Society in West Woodstock, Conn. 97737

Discourse delivered to the Congregational Society in Foxborough. 62471

Discourse delivered to the Congregational Society in Woburn. 12679

Discourse, delivered to the Evangelical Society in Brookfield. 92091

Discourse delivered to the First Church and congregation in Marblehead. 103837

Discourse delivered to the First Religious Society in Braintree. 92252

Discourse delivered to the freemen collected in the Second Society in Saybrook. 5547

Discourse delivered to the pupils of the Episcopal Academy. 4131B

Discourse delivered 27th June, 1847. 37294

Discourse delivered unto some part of the forces. 46526

Discourse, delivered unto the Commissioners. (46367)

Discourse designed to comfort the afflicted. 33943

Discourse designed to commemorate the discovery of New-York. 49049

Discourse dilivered [sic] July 11, 1811. 5976

Discourse . . . Dorchester . . . Jan. 22, 1865. (29830)

Discourse, Education Society of the Saratoga British Association. 27616

Discourse, Edwards Church, Thanksgiving Day, November 27, 1856. 29777

Discourse . . . 1844. 28878

Discourse . . . eleventh anniversary. 21803

Discourse, embracing the civil and religious history of Rhode-Island. (73341)

Discourse . . . fast-day, April 8, 1852. 26536

Discourse . . . February 8th, 1857. 38776

Discourse . . . February 11, 1838. (28881)

Discourse . . . February 15. 1787. 13423, 7th note after 100870

Discourse . . . February 1, 1852. 42032

Discourse . . . February 4, 1803. 57778

Discourse . . . February 9, 1823. 37366

Discourse . . . Feb. 17th, 1861. 4575

Discourse . . . February 10, 1869. (29830)

Discourse, Feb. 22, 1857. 22309

Discourse, First Congregational Church. 13229

Discourse for city missions. (18213)

Discourse for 1850. 26381

Discourse for home missions. 9549

Discourse for Thanksgiving. 10846

Discourse for the divine institution of water-baptism. 103655

Discourse for the fast. 81434

Discourse, for the month of April, A. D. 1816. 104383

Discourse for the time . . . January 4, 1851. (26240)

Discourse for the times, delivered in . . . St. Louis. 22177

Discourse for the times, delivered in the Braodway Church. 16697

Discourse IV, on the science of government. 92203

Discourse, fourth of July, 1828. 72701

Discourse . . . 4th of July, 1824. 64465

Discourse from Acts xiii. 27. 2632

Discourse from Deut. XXIX. 19, 20, 21. 94705

Discourse from I Kings, viii. 13, 27, 57, 60. 84599-84600

Discourse, from . . . [I. Thess. ii. 13] in which is shewn. 17675

Discourse from Judges the XXth the 28th. 22792-22793

Discourse from Ps. CXXII. I. (14525)

Discourse from Psalm XXV. 7. 22441

Discourse from Rev. XXI. 8. 104275

Discourse . . . funeral of . . . Silas Wright. 36220A

Discourse: given in the First Universalist Church. 75267

Discourse given on a day of prayer. 46414

Discourse, given on . . . national fast. 4573

Discourse giving the right hand of fellowship. (25976A)

Discourse, had by him [i. e. Joseph Stevens] at Cambridge. 91548

Discourse had in the College-Hall at Cambridge. 14477

Discourse, historical and commemorative. (43541)

Discourse, historical of St. Thomas' Church. (4754)

Discourse how those parties and countries. (48248)

Discourse . . . in . . . Albany, before the Ladies' Society. 56034

Discourse . . . in . . . Albany, March 19th, 1854. 29530

Discourse . . . in . . . Albany, occasioned by the . . . death of General Alexander Hamilton. 56035

Discourse . . . in . . . Albany, the fourth of July, 1801. 56036

Discourse . . . in Amsterdam Village. (27840)

Discourse . . . in Augusta, Geo. 9090

Discourse . . . in Baltimore. 9364

Discourse in behalf of a law prohibiting the traffic. (3496)

Discourse in behalf of African colonization. 63884

Discourse in behalf of the American Home Missionary Society, preached in the cities of New York and Brooklyn, May, 1855. 93277

Discourse in behalf of the American Home Missionary Society, preached in the cities of New York and Brooklyn, May, 1857. 93277

Discourse in behalf of the American Home Missionary Society, preached in the cities of New York and Brooklyn, May, 1853. (31707)

Discourse in behalf of the American Home Missionary Society, preached in the city of New York. (21571)

Discourse in behalf of the Children's Friend Society. (29753)

Discourse in behalf of the ministry at lagre. 33964

Discourse in behalf of the sufferers of Norfolk and Portsmouth, Va. 17930

Discourse . . . in . . . Boston, . . . after the death of George Peabody. (24021)

Discourse . . . in Boston before the Pastoral Association. 58618

Discourse . . . in Boston . . . Feb. 16, 1868. 26536

Discourse . . . in Boston, July 14, 1808. (50953)

Discourse . . . in . . . Boston, . . . July 4, 1858. 51439

Discourse, . . . in . . . Boston, June 9, 1852. 49196

Discourse . . . in Boston, March 16, 1807. 2921

Discourse . . . in Bridgewater, . . . June 30th, A. L. 1797. (57653)

Discourse, . . . in . . . Brookfield, Vt. (58653)

Discourse . . . in . . . Brookline, on fast day. (31216)

Discourse . . . in . . . Brookline, on . . . Thanksgiving. 51438

Discourse . . . in . . . Brooklyn, on Thanksgiving Day. 36208

Discourse in Burlington. 76360

Discourse . . . in Cambridge, . . . [after] the death of Mr. Andrews Norton. 54967

Discourse . . . in Cambridge, . . . after the death of Mrs. Harriet F. Webster. 54967

Discourse . . . in Cambridge, August 1, 1847. 51614

Discourse in . . . Cambridge, . . . December 31, 1848. 54967

Discourse . . . in Cambridge . . . February 19, 1795. (24557)

Discourse . . . in Cambridge, . . . May 27, 1855. 54966

Discourse . . . in Cambridge, on the . . . annual fast. 54967

Discourse . . . in Cambridgeport, March 31, 1861. (81593)

Discourse . . . in Cambridgeport, Thanksgiving Day. 58101

Discourse . . . in . . . Charleston, on the 27th December, 1815. 39961

Discourse, . . . in . . . Charleston, S. C., November 19, 1863. 48679

Discourse . . . in . . . Cincinnati, O. 42993

Discourse . . . in Chohasset. (57783)

Discourse . . . in Colebrook. 39720

Discourse in commemoration of Rev. William Parsons Lunt. (71772)

Discourse, in commemoration of the bicentenary anniversary of that body. 85297

Discourse in commemoration of the extinction of slavery. 4124

Discourse in commemoration of the glorious reformation. 77720

Discourse in commemoration of the fifty-third anniversary. (25445)

Discourse in commemoration of the founding of the Academy of Natural Sciences. 25277

Discourse in commemoration of the landing of the pilgrims, delivered at Plymouth. 104908

Discourse in commemoration of the landing of the pilgrims of Maryland. 48924

Discourse in commemoration of the life and character of Rev. Henry Ware. (71773)

Discourse, in commemoration of the life and character of the late George W. Bethune. 24190

Discourse in commemoration of the life, character and services of the Rev. Thomas H. Gallaudet. 3469

Discourse in commemoration of the lives and services of John Adams and Thomas Jefferson. 102269

Discourse in commemoration of the martyrdom of the Rev. Elijah P. Lovejoy. (28510)

Discourse in commemoration of the pilgrim fathers. (64470)

Discourse in commemoration of the Rev. Robinson Potter Dunn. 20187

Discourse in commemoration of Washington's birthday. 19191

Discourse, in consequence of the late duel. 89807

Discourse . . . in Dedham. 38776

Discourse, . . . in . . . Duxbury. 50416

Discourse in English, by David Tappan. 104054

Discourse . . . in Fair Haven. 30620

Discourse in favour of the abolition of slavery.
33607

Discourse . . . in Freeport (Maine) 36035

Discourse . . . in . . . Hamilton College,
June 25, 1849. 55524

Discourse . . . in . . . Hamilton College,
March 10, 1852. 55524

Discourse . . . in . . . Hamilton College,
Sept. 13th, 1849. 55524

Discourse . . . in . . . Hamilton, N. Y. 37372

Discourse . . . in . . . Hamilton, O. 43141

Discourse . . . in Hartford . . . December 9th,
1844. 30925

Discourse, . . . in . . . Hartford, . . . November 20, 1856. 51439

Discourse, . . . in Hollis Street Church, . . .
January 27, 1839. 62772

Discourse . . . in Hollis St. Church, . . . 24th
November, 1839. 62772

Discourse . . . in Jamaica Plain. 27971

Discourse in King's Chapel, Boston. 37366

Discourse . . . in Kingston, Nov. 22, 1846.
(64106)

Discourse in . . . Lafayette, Ind. 70823

Discourse in Lebanon, October 14, 1810. 22939

Discourse . . . in . . . Lee, Mass. (26359)

Discourse . . . in Lowell. 67876

Discourse . . . in . . . Ludlow, Mass. (47196)

Discourse in Lyndeborough, February 26, 1801.
(24539)

Discourse . . . in Madison, Wis. 22052

Discourse . . . in Marietta, Ohio. (32938)

Discourse in Medway, West Parish. 34175

Discourse . . . in memory of David Kimball
Hobart. 3794

Discourse in memory of Edward Everett.
57790

Discourse in memory of Hon. Teunis Van
Vechten. 72641

Discourse in memory of John Abbot Emery.
59384

Discourse in memory of Kendall O. Peabody.
77253

Discourse in memory of Melvin A. Pingree.
37708

Discourse in memory of Mrs. A. B. Talcott.
72629

Discourse in memory of Rev. Thomas Starr
King. 3794

Discourse in memory of the late Rev. Andrew
W. Black. (43541)

Discourse in memory of the life and character
of the Hon. Geo. E. Badger. 28240

Discourse in memory of Thomas Harvey
Skinner. 65090

Discourse in memory of William Darrach.
(80464)

Discourse in memory of William Hague.
84044

Discourse, . . . in Milford, (Mass.) 41870

Discourse, . . . in . . . New Bedford. 58676

Discourse . . . in New Haven. 61396

Discourse . . . in New Market. (49135)

Discourse . . . in . . . New Orleans. (58345)

Discourse . . . in . . . New York, before the
Grand Lodge of Free and Accepted
Masons. (49064)

Discourse . . . in New York, March 23, 1806.
48998

Discourse . . . in . . . Newburyport. 32813

Discourse . . . in Newington. 60968

Discourse, . . . in Norfield. (56224)

Discourse . . . in Norwich. 6276

Discourse . . . in . . . Orono, Me. 40108

Discourse . . . in . . . [Paris.] 37976

Discourse . . . in . . . Philadelphia . . . April
11, 1858. (26240)

Discourse, . . . in Philadelphia, February 27,
1848. (26240)

Discourse . . . in . . . Philadelphia, on Thanksgiving Day. 33320

Discourse in . . . Philadelphia, . . . on the
national fast day. 21808

Discourse . . . in . . . Portsmouth, May 29th,
1808. (50979)

Discourse . . . in Preston . . . Dec. 29, 1799.
(30635)

Discourse . . . in . . . Quincy, . . . January
8, 1854. 42709

Discourse . . . in Quincy, . . . Thanksgiving
Day. 42712

Discourse in reference to the decease of the
late Governor of Illinois. 59486

Discourse . . . in Rhode Island. (28881)

Discourse . . . in Richmond, Virginia. 20524

Discourse in . . . Rochester, N. Y. (21996)

Discourse . . . in . . . Rockford, Ill. (36256)

Discourse . . . in Rowley. 62824

Discourse in St. Luke's Church, Rochester.
13529

Discourse . . . in Salem, before the Bible
Society of Salem & Vicinity. 65562

Discourse . . . in . . . Salem . . . February
19, 1843. 45427

Discourse . . . in Saybrook. (46210)

Discourse . . . in Schenectady. 64617

Discourse . . . in Sharon, Connecticut. 43496

Discourse in Shirley, Feb. 1, 1841. (11872)

Discourse in . . . Shrewsbury, Massachusetts.
43274

Discourse . . . in Somerville, Mass. 42409

Discourse, . . . in . . . South Danvers. (51513)

Discourse in Sutton, 2d Parish, January 17,
1773. (11966)

Discourse . . . in Taunton. 5279

Discourse . . . in the Chapel of Hamilton College, june 23, 1850. 55524

Discourse . . . in the Chapel of Harvard-College. 47150

Discourse . . . in the Chapel of Rhode Island
College. 48151

Discourse . . . in the Chapel of the University
at CRmbridge. 32258

Discourse . . . in the Chespeake General
Hospital, . . . national fast, April 30th,
1863. 44785

Discourse . . . in the Chespeake General
Hospital, . . . Thanksgiving. 44785

Discourse in the Choctaw language. 12878,
104306

Discourse . . . in the Church of the Messiah.
57791

Discourse, . . . in the Congregational Church,
Rowley. (62822)

Discourse, . . . in the Congregational Church,
Rowley, on the twenty-second anniversary
of his settlement. 62823

Discourse . . . in the First Baptist Church,
New Haven. 61397

Discourse in the First Baptist Church, . . .
November 26, 1829. 28944

Discourse in the First Presbyterian Church of
Penn Yan, New york. 90551

Discourse in the North Meeting-House in
Bridgewater. 33947

Discourse . . . in the Second Baptist Meeting-House in Boston. 2916

Discourse . . . in the Unitarian Church, Montreal. 16763

Discourse . . . in the . . . United States
Military Academy. (58808)

Discourse . . . in the Universalist Church in Hudson. 62626

Discourse . . . in Trinity Church, Boston. 58732

Discourse, in two parts, . . . December 1820. 37752

Discourse, in two parts. Delivered in Leominster. 26644

Discourse, in two parts; delivered in Paris, (N. Y.) 91115

Discourse in two parts, delivered July 23, 1812. 21552

Discourse in two parts, from Ps. ii. 8. 84599, 84600

Discourse . . . in Watertown, Mass. 50324

Discourse in way of dialogue. 97287

Discourse in way of dialogues between an Ethiopian. 25947, note after 97286

Discourse . . . in . . . West Church, in Boston. 42425

Discourse . . . in . . . West Roxbury. 39264

Discourse . . . in . . . West Springfield. 25211

Discourse . . . in Westminster, Mass. 56687

Discourse, . . . in Wethersfield. (44741)

Discourse, in which is considered the history. 82132

Dsicourse . . . in Worcester. (31806)

Discourse, . . . Indianapolis, October 10, 1861. 42536

Discourse, intended to commemorate the discovery of America. (4431)

Discourse intituled An overture. 69515

Discourse introductory to a course of lectures. (59418)

Discourse introductory to the course of lectures. 70176

Discourse . . . January, 1859. 50975

Discourse, Jan. 8, 1769. 25003

Discourse . . . January 15, 1862. 39686

Discourse . . . January 19, 1840. 26234

Discourse . . . January 17, 1856. 32467

Discourse . . . January 7, 1827. 62626

Discourse . . . Jan. 6, 1853. 36842

Discourse . . . January 10, 1864. (26240)

Discourse, July 4, 1858. 26175

Discourse, July 17, 1836. 28512

Discourse . . . July 17, 1794. 43800

Discourse . . . July 28th, 1797. 58116

Discourse . . . June 24th, 1870. 36035

Discourse, . . . Kentucky State Medical Society. 24782

Discourse, . . . Lancaster, . . . September 5th, 1756. (30459)

Discourse lately had by him [i. e. Increase Mather] to young people. 46274

Discourse . . . Law Academy of Philadelphia. 37006

Discourse . . . Louisville, Ky. 31671

Discourse . . . Lynn, on the . . . death of William Henry Harrison. 16332

Discourse . . . Macon, Ga. 72448

Discourse made on the burning of the effigy of the St—pm-n. 20239

Discourse made unto the General Court of the Massachusetts colony. 46504

Discourse . . . Marbledead. 3734

Discourse . . . March 19, 1817. note after 42429

Discourse . . . March 17, 1844. (26240)

Discourse . . . March 7, 1859. 43153

Discourse, . . . March 6, 1853. 49196

Discourse . . . March 13, 1859. (26529)

Discourse, . . . March 20, 1854. 26536

Discourse . . . March 20th, 1859. (26240)

Discourse . . . March 23, 1862. 67881

Discourse . . . May 14th, 1841. 5273

Discourse . . . May 3, 1827. 50957

Discourse . . . May 12, 1844. 11945

Discourse . . . May 12, 1817. (61018)

Discourse . . . May 12, 1861. 50672

Discourse . . . May 28, 1854. (12406)

[Discourse] May 29, 1813. 4630

Discourse . . . May 22d, 1751. 10684

Discourse . . . Middlebury College. (44736)

Discourse . . . Middlebury, Vermont. 65681

Discourse . . . national fast day. 18743

Discourse. New Year's Day at Shrewsbury, Mass. 844

Discourse . . . New York, on Thanksgiving Day. 38314

Discourse, . . . Newark, N. J., Oct. 29, 1851. 61185

Discourse . . . 19th April, A. D. 1795. (13424)

Discourse . . . 9 November, 1817. 62728

Discourse, . . . November 14, 1862. 21134

Discourse . . . November 7th, 1838. 43567

Discourse, Nov. 6, 1814. (24774)

Discourse, . . . November 3, 1819. 24779

Discourse Nov. 3, 1790. 22525

Discourse . . . November 12, 1837. 11924

Discourse . . . November 25, 1860. (26240)

Discourse . . . November 24, 1819. 60969

Discourse, . . . Nov. 29. 1857. 47181

Discourse . . . November 27, 1845. (3508)

Discourse . . . Nov. 27, 1828. 32250

Discourse occasionally made on burning the effige of the ST-PM-N. 40938, 90138

Discourse occasioned by the assassination of Abraham Lincoln. (21583)

Discourse occasioned by the assassination of President Lincoln. 5437

Discourse occasioned by the bill for the government. 71085

Discourse occasioned by the Boston Fugitive Slave Case. (26240)

Discourse occasioned by the burning of the theatre. 94568

Discourse occasioned by the burning of the theatre in Richmond. (721)

Discourse occasioned by the centennial anniversary of Hon. Timothy Farrar. 13502

Discourse occasioned by the death, and delivered at the funeral. 103787

Discourse occasion'd by the death of a young woman at Malden. 22436

Discourse occasioned by the death of Abraham Lincoln. 30847

Discourse, occasioned by the death of Brigadier General M'Pherson. 9083

Discourse, occasioned by the death of Capt. Amos Hawes. 22525

Discourse occasioned by the death of Charles Beck. 54967

Discourse occasioned by the death of Col: James Morrison. 32527

Discourse, occasioned by the death of Daniel Webster, delivered in Central Church, Boston. 70932

Discourse, occasioned by the death of Daniel Webster, preached at the Melodeon on Sunday. 36924, 58744, note before 90886

Discourse occasioned by the death of Dea. Moses Little. 24543

Discourse occasioned by the death of Deacon Samuel Williams. (72712)

Discourse, occasioned by the death of Doctor Abijah Everett. 22525

Discourse occasioned by the death . . . of Dr. Joseph Torrey. 20540

Discourse occasioned by the death of Dr.
Warren F. Chamberlin. 26323
Discourse occasioned by the death of Dr.
William Coffin. 31768
Discourse, occasioned by the death of General
George Washington. At Mount-Vernon,
Dec. 14, 1799. (13395)
Discourse occasioned by the death of General
George Washington. Delivered Dec. 29,
1799. (38001), 101686
Discourse, occasioned by the death of General
George Washington . . . delivered in
Warren. 34026
Discourse occasioned by the death of George
Gibbs. 19312
Discourse occasioned by the death of . . .
George II. (47134)
Discourse, occasioned by the death of His
Excellency Jonathan Trumbull. 21551
Discourse occasioned by the death of Hon.
Daniel Webster, preached in Newburyport.
22009
Discourse occasioned by the death of Hon.
Daniel Webster, preached October 31,
and repeated November 14, 1852. 13588
Discourse occasioned by the death of Hon.
Elisha Boane. 24442
Discourse, occasioned by the death of Hon.
Jabez W. Huntington. 2015
Discourse occasioned by the death of Hon. John
A. Rockwell. . . . Norwich, Ct. 6270
Discourse, occasioned by the death of Hon.
John A. Rockwell, delivered in Norwich,
Ct. (6273)
Discourse occasioned by the death of James
Freeman Curtis. 28682
Discourse occasioned by the death of Jared
Sparks. 54967
Discourse, occasioned by the death of John
Coyle. (43484)
Discourse occasioned by the death of John
Hall, Esq. 103791
Discourse occasioned by the . . . death of
John Hall . . . son of Elihu Hall, Esq.
(18419)
Discourse occasioned by the death of John
Quincy Adams. 58743
Discourse occasioned by the death of Julius
R. Friedlander. (26240)
Discourse occasioned by the death of Justin
Ely, Esq. 89744
Discourse, occasioned by the death of Miss
Mirey Tufts. 26157
Discourse occasioned by the death of Mr.
Archibald Sloan. (6083)
Discourse . . . Occasioned by the . . . death
. . . Mr. Eph. Avery. 19830
Discourse occasioned by the death of Mr.
George Livermore. 2699
Discourse occasioned by the death of Mr.
Jacob Bell. 30843
Discourse . . . occasioned by the death of Mr.
John Loring. 42091
Discourse, occasioned by the death of Mr.
Russell Hubbard. 6272
Discourse; occasioned by the death of Mrs.
Elizabeth Lathrop. 39187
Discourse occasioned by the death of Mrs.
Elizabeth Livingston Budington. 5722
Discourse occasioned by the death of Mrs.
Hannah Richards. 30887
Discourse occasioned by the death of Mrs.
Knox. 43225
Discourse, occasioned by the death of Mrs.
Margaretta Willoughby. 41733

Discourse occasioned by the death of Mrs.
Mary Augusta Greene. 18162
Discourse occasioned by the death of Mrs.
Mary Gideon. 82948
Discourse occasioned by the death of Mrs.
Mary Harris Ely. 28946
Discourse occasioned by the death of Mrs.
Mary Hooker. (29271)
Discourse occasioned by the death of Mrs.
Mary Lathrop. 39187
Discourse occasioned by the death of Mrs.
Sarah Thayer. 3795
Discourse, occasioned by the death of Mrs.
Susan Bemis. 4628
Discourse occasioned by the death of Rev.
Isaac Allen. 78637
Discourse occasioned by the death of Rev.
James Flint. 13224
Discourse, occasioned by the death of Rev.
Samuel Washburn. 30843
Discourse, occasioned by the death of Richard
Hazen Ayer. 26157
Discourse occasioned by the death of that pious
and afflicted gentlewoman, Mrs. Martha
Gerrish. (1827), 27166
Discourse occasioned by the death of the Hon.
Daniel Edwards. (20640)
Discourse occasioned by the death of the Hon.
Henry Wheaton. (29753)
Discourse occasioned by the death of the Hon.
Jobez Huntington. 30637
Discourse occasioned by the death of the Hon.
James McDowell. 36928
Discourse occasioned by the death of the Honor-
able John Winthrop. 103910
Discourse occasioned by the death of the Hon.
Joseph Story. 54967
Discourse, occasioned by the death of the Hon.
Josiah Quincy. 26528
Discourse occasioned by the death of the Hon.
Roger Wolcott. 61039
Discourse occasion'd by the death of the Honour-
able Samuel Sewall. 79425
Discourse occasioned by the death of the Hon.
Samuel Summer Wilde. 59360
Discourse occasioned by the death of the Hon.
Silas Wright. 89744
Discourse occasioned by the death of the
Honourable Stephen Sewall. 47133
Discourse occasioned by the death of the
Honourable William Williams. 22393
Discourse occasioned by the death of the late
Rev. Erskine Mason. (17268)
Discourse occasioned by the death of the Rev.
Follen. 11924
Discourse occasioned by the death of the Rever-
end Dr. Joseph Sewell. 12331
Discourse occasioned by the death of the Rev.
Edward Wigglesworth. 1829, 94517
Discourse, occasioned by the death of the
Reverend George Whitefield. 89912
Discourse, occasioned by the death of the
Reverend Gideon Mills. 92932
Discourse occasioned by the death of the
Reverend John Ewing. (41337)
Discourse occasioned by the death of the
Reverend Jonathan Mayhew. 12331
Discourse occasioned by the death of the Rev.
Joseph Buckminster. 58716
Discourse occasioned by the death of the Rev.
Joseph Tomkinson. 46903
Discourse occasioned by the death of the
Reverend Mr, Nathaniel Clap. 10074
Discourse, occasioned by the death of the Rev.
President Stiles. 59126

Discourse occasioned by the death of the Rev. Samuel Checkley. 7066

Discourse occasioned by the death of the Reverend Thomas Foxcroft. 12331

Discourse occasioned by the death of the Rev. Aalmon Tobey. 35416

Discourse occasioned by the death of William Ellery Channing, D. D. 4569

Discourse occasioned by the death of William Ellery Channing. Preached . . . Oct. 16, 1842. (62764)

Discourse occasioned by the death of William Ellery Chauncey. (29753)

Discourse occasioned by the death of Wm. Henry Harrison. 64207

Discourse occasioned by the destruction of the Steam Packet Pulaski. 65381

Discourse, occasioned by the drought. (43048)

Discourse occasioned by the early death of seven young ministers. 46579, 1st note after 99604

Discourse . . . occasioned by the earthquake in November 1755. 47132

Discourse occasion'd by the earthquake. Preached at Boxford. 72694

Discourse occasioned by the late desolating fire. (8926)

Discourse occasioned by the late distressing storm. 197

Discourse, occasioned by the loss of a number of vessels. 103838

Discourse occasioned by the mournful catastrophe. 43801

Discourse occasioned by the much lamented death of the Rev. Edward Wigglesworth. 1829, 94517, 104056

Discourse, occasioned by the murder of the late Warden. 8967

Discourse occasioned by the news of peace. 24762

Discourse occasioned by the present crisis. (78643)

Discourse, occasioned by the proclamation of peace. 104384

Discourse, occasioned by the recent duel in Washington. 101387

Discourse occasioned by the rendition of Anthony Burns. (28380)

Discourse, occasioned by the sudden death of three young persons. 90836

Discourse occasioned by the sudden death of two young men. 102422

Discourse occasioned by the trial and execution of John W. Webster. (37973)

Discourse occasionly made on burning the effigie of the st--pm-n. 15782

Discourse . . . October 1, 1851. 37396

Discourse, . . . October 9, 1842. 79786

Discourse, . . . October 16, 1828. 50995

Discourse, . . . October 10, 1810. 60968

Discourse . . . October 31, 1856. 47443

Discourse . . . October 28, 1860. 38776

Discourse . . . October 21, 1860. 26536

Discourse . . . October 21st . . . in Quincy. 42714

Discourse of a discouerie for a new passage to Cataia. 27351

Discourse of Cotton Mathers. 37209

Discourse of Dr. Waterland's. (71910)

Discourse [of George Best.] 5051, 25994

Discourse of husbandry used in Brabant and Flaunders. 30702

Discourse of mistakes concerning religion. 14373

Discourse of Mr. Benton. 4784

Discourse of New-Found-Land. 103332

Discourse of old-age. 13040

Discourse of R. J. Breckenridge, D. D. 7677, 7679

Discourse of . . . Rev. Lemuel Briant. 55332

Discourse of Rev. Mr. Carey. 10845

Discourse of set forms of prayer. 17070

Discourse [of Sir Robert Montgomerie.] (19719)

Discourse of demand and supply in church and state. 38085

Discourse of that which happened in the battell fought. 20240

Discourse of the absolute freedom. 92106

Discourse of the cacao-nut-tree. 33605

Discourse of the Dukedom of Modena. 49798

Discourse of the duties on merchandize. 20242

Discourse of the function of a teacher of religion. note after (58767)

Discourse of the glory to which God hath called the believers by Jesus Christ. 49655-49656

Discourse of the late judgement. 103705

Discourse of the life and character of the Hon. Francois Xavier Martin. 9115

Discourse of the plantation trade. (22976)

Discourse of the pleasure of religious worship. (14525)

Discourse of the principle questions incident to the governmental polity of the United States. 81619

Discourse of the Queenes Maiesties entertainement. 13032

Discourse of the Rev. Jonathan Parsons. 97319

Discourse of the sea and navigation. 29522

Discourse of the state of health in the island of Jamaica. 96473

Discourse of the variation of the cumpas. 55496

Discourse of trade. (12707)

Discourse of trade-winds. 18375

Discourse of Virginia. 19051

Discourse of what happened in the battell fought. 76755

Discourse offered to a numerous assembly. (58889), 79747, 97319

[Discourse] on a day of public thanksgiving. 92094

Discourse on a day of thanksgiving. 2675

Discourse on . . . a pillar of salt. 26785

Discourse on Acts XX. 17, 18, 19, 20, 21. 97312

Discourse on Acts ii. 42. In which the practice of owning the covenant is examined. 92892

Discourse on Acts II. 42. In which the practice of owning the covenant, is particularly examined. 92891

Discourse on adversity. 84601

Discourse on African colonization. 73925

Discourse on agricultural chemistry. 81671

Discourse on agriculture. (61205)

Discourse on American independence. 16240

Discourse on . . . American slavery. 2965

Discourse on America's duty and danger (51518)

Discourse, on . . . animation. 3734

Discourse on baptism. 91591

Discourse on brotherly love. 78567

Discourse on celestial marriage. 82585

Discourse on Christian charity. 71216

Discourse on Christian politics. 13416

Discourse on Christian union. 103724

Discourse on church extension in cities. (77586)

Discourse, on church musick. (25239)

Discourse on . . . classical learning. 35117

Discourse on colonial slavery. 28131

Discourse . . . on commencing the lectures in Jefferson Medical College. (59154)

Discourse on congregationalism. 64467

Discourse on conversion. 3105

Discourse on dancing. 72701

Discourse on dancing delivered in the Central Presbyterian Church. 70857

Discourse on death of Rev. William Worthington. 22140

Discourse . . . on decease of Calhoun, Clay and Webster. 42032

Discourse on divine providence. 83803

Discourse; on divine providence, in special reference to the memory, character and death of the late Gen. George Washington. 104539

Discourse on divine sovereignty. 71832

Discourse on educated manhood. 90983

Discourse on education. 72701

Discourse on education: . . . at . . . Providence. (32257)

Discourse on education, at the dedication and opening of Bristol Academy. (20529)

Discourse on education delivered at Westfield. 79515

Discourse on education, delivered before the Legislature of the state of Indiana. 105662

Discourse on education, delivered before the Trustees of the Derby Academy. (3512)

Discourse on Edward Everett. 31215

Discourse on episcopacy. 69517

Discourse on fast day, April 2, 1846. 3794

Discourse . . . on . . . fast [day], in . . . Chelsea. 57237

Discourse on I. Chron. 28.9. 104406

Discourse on I. Cor. XV. 58. 13203

Discourse on General Washington. Delivered in the Catholic Church of St. Peter, in Baltimore. 11073

Discourse on government and religion, calculated for the meridian of the 30th of January. 20241

Discourse on government and religion, delivered July 4, 1810. 82481

Discourse on Heb. XI. 7. 104405

Discourse on Henry Clay and Daniel Webster. 2907

Discourse on Hosea xiv. 9. 30892

Discourse on intemperance, . . . April 5, 1827. 58325

Discourse on intemperance . . . March 1st, 1828. 29825

Discourse on Jeremiah 8th, 20th. 64655

Discourse on Jer. 4. I. 104398-104399

Discourse on John VI. 44. 70950

Discourse on John VI. 67, 68. 46208

Discourse on Judges V. 23. 103317, 103324

Discourse on Judges 5th 23. 103318

Discourse on knowing and trusting God. 89789

Discourse on legal education. 21380

Discourse on liberty and slavery. (8562)

Discourse on liberty. 72489

Discourse on Luke vii. 42. 17675

Discourse on Luke XXIII. 39,-43. 13204

Discourse on masonry. 45500

Discourse on means of a revival. 20182

Discourse on Methodist Church polity. 50877

Discourse on miracles. 19862

Discourse on missions. (82386)

Discourse on mistakes concerning religion. 8192, 30696

Discourse on national sins. 41348

Discourse on natural religion . . . May 8. 1771. 22129

Discourse on natural religion . . . September 3, 1795. 3493

Discourse on occasion of the death of Dr. Price. (65513)

Discourse . . . on occasion of the death of Jonathan Goodhue. 4575

Discourse, on occasion of the death of Mr. Eldridge Packer. (76362)

Discourse, on occasion of the death of the Rev. Johathan Edwards. 83808

Discourse, on occasion of the death of William Coit. 76361

Discourse on occasion of the interment of . . . L. Cutler. 92250

Discourse on old age. 13042-13043

Discourse on opening the new building in the House of Refuge. 90194

Discourse on our national affairs. 84540

Discourse on pastoral duty. 14535

Discourse on planting the sciences. 84601

Discourse on popular education. (47902)

Discourse on preparation for sudden death. 17645

Discourse on Prov. 2. 1-6. 104405

Discourse on Psalm CXVII. 18, 19. 97314

Discourse on Psal. cxii. 7. 1826

Discourse on recovery from sickness. 46412

Discourse on regeneration. (20062)

Discourse on relative and federal holiness. (13775)

Discourse on resignation. 46360

Discourse on revealed religion. 66604

Discourse on sacramental occasions. 46663

Discourse on St. Mark. 1511

Discourse on saving knowledge. 91737

Discourse on sea ports. 67599

Discourse on 2 Cor. II: 15, 16. (28443)

Discourse on II. Tim. iii. 16. 78568

Discourse on secret prayer. 32736

Discourse on serious piety. 24576

Discourse on slander. 76363

"Discourse" on slavery. 103169

Discourse on slavery and the annexation of Texas. 19856

Discourse on slavery, by G. W. Blagden. 5725

Discourse on slavery: before the Anti-slavery Society. 104697

Discourse on slavery in the United States. 47075

Discourse on some events of the last century. 21550

Discourse on some of the principal desiderata in natural distory. 3805

Discourse on some points of difference. 93692

Discourse on Sunday morning, April 23, 1865. 11735

Discourse on sympathy with the afflicted. 64260

Discourse on temperance. 72701

Discourse on temperance, April 6, 1848. 62479

Discourse on temperance, and of the applicability of stimulants. 3836

Discourse . . . on . . . Thanksgiving at the Church of the Messiah. 60930

Discourse . . . on . . . Thanksgiving Day, December 2, 1830. 26536

Discourse . . . on Thanksgiving Day, Dec. 7, 1837. 41558

Discourse, . . . on Thanksgiving Day, December 12, 1844. 9364

Discourse on Thanksgiving Day, Nov. 19, 1840. (2667)

Discourse . . . Thanksgiving day, Nov. 24, 1842. 798u

Discourse . . . on . . . Thanksgiving . . . November 27, 1828. 42074

Discourse on that subject . . . by Mr. Ross. 36859

Discourse on the aborigines of the valley of the Ohio. 30571

Discourse on the agriculture of the state of Connecticut. 33815

Discourse, . . . on the anniversary election. 24773

Discourse on the anniversary of St. John the Evangelist. (78628)

Discourse, on the anniversary of the Ancient and Honorable Artillery Company. 98037

Discourse on the anniversary thanksgiving, delivered in Andover. (25871)

Discourse . . . on the annual thanksgiving in Massachusetts, November 29, 1804. 22525, 27401

Discourse on the aspects of the war. 13410

Discourse on the assassination of Abraham Lincoln. 55163

Discourse on the assassination of President Lincoln. 64459

Discourse on the Cambridge Church-gathering in 1636. 54964

Discourse on the causes of national prosperity. 32251

Discourse on the character and death of General George Washington. (18432)

Discourse . . . on the character and death of the Rev. John Murray. 19038

Discourse on "the character and influence of abolitionism." 82173

Discourse on the character and public services of Dewitt Clinton. (69652)

Discourse on the character and scientific attainments of De Witt Clinton. 49742

Discourse on the character and services of John Hampden. 71661

Discourse on the character and services of Thomas Jefferson. 49741

Discourse on the character and virtues of General George Washington. (18402)

Discourse on the character and writings of Rev. William Ellery Channing. 19862

Discourse on the character, life, genius, and death of Daniel Webster. 78392

Discourse on the character of Daniel Webster. 3447

Discourse on the character of King George the Third. 92641

Discourse on the character of Mr. John Hawes. 10741

Discourse on the character of the late Chester Averill. (68589)

Discourse on the character of the late Stephen Chase. 42045

Discourse on the character of the Right Reverend John Henry Hobart. (77980)

Discourse on the character proper to a Christian society. 14535

Discourse on the characteristics of the Puritans. 21584

Discourse on the Christian union. 91738-91740

Discourse on the completion of fifty years service. 48036

Discourse on the conduct of the government of Great Britain. 14372, 19124, 36023

Discourse on the constitution and government of the United States. 9932, 9936

Discourse on the covenant with Judas. (62863)

Discourse, . . . on the day of fasting. (58346)

Discourse . . . on the day of humiliation and prayer. 9091

Discourse, . . . on the day of national thanksgiving, December 7, 1865. 82384

Discourse . . . on the day of national thanksgiving for peace. (64135)

Discourse, . . . on the day of publick thanksgiving. 39187

Discourse . . . on the day of . . . thanksgiving. 57773

Discourse, on the day of the annual fast, in Massachusetts. 22525

Discourse on the day of the annual thanksgiving, in the state of New-York. 89783

Discourse on the death of Abraham Lincoln. 92939

Discourse on the death of Abraham Lincoln. By J. McLowne. 43549

Discourse on the death of Abraham Lincoln, delivered at Buenos Aires. 27856

Discourse on the death of Abraham Lincoln. Delivered in . . . Philadelphia. 58130

Discourse, on the death of Abraham Lincoln, delivered in the 1st Presbyterian Church in Bloomington. 32970

Discourse on the death of Abraham Lincoln, delivered in the Greenhill Presbyterian Church. 71815

Discourse, on the death of Abraham Lincoln, late President. 35303

Discourse on the death of Abraham Lincoln, preached in . . . Charlestown. 67879

Discourse on the death of Abraham Lincoln, President of the United States. (14527)

Discourse on the death of an unfortunate youth. 90195

Discourse . . . on the death of Caleb A. Buckingham. (30456)

Discourse on the death of Captain Farmer. 33863

Discourse . . . on . . . the death of Charles U. Fosdick. 2511

Discourse on the death of Daniel Webster. 45427

Discourse . . . on . . . the death of Dr. George C. Sha uck. [sic] 3794

Discourse, on the death of General George Washington; delivered at the North Congregational Church in Newburyport. 89796

Discourse on the death of General George Washington, delivered in the township of Northampton. (39109)

Discourse on the death of Gen. Joseph R. F. Mansfield. 21085

Discourse, on the death of General Washington. 43706

Discourse on the death of Gen. Zachary Taylor. (33786)

Discource on the death of George Vanderpool. 90184

Discourse on the death of Helen Elizabeth Lawson. 36578

Discourse, on the death of Hon. Daniel Webster. (39348)

Discourse on the death of Hon. Heman Ely. 28946

Discourse on the death of Hon. John Fairfield. 850

Discourse on the death of Hon. John Quincy Adams, delivered Feb. 27, 1848. 849

Discourse . . . on the . . . death of Hon. John Quincy Adams . . . March 5, 1848. 41556

Discourse on the death of Hon. William Sullivan. 76985

Discourse . . . [on] the death of Mrs. Elizabeth Howard. 33279

Discourse on the death of Mrs. Lucy Waldo. 12331

Discourse on the death of Oliver Shepherd, of Wrentham. 21977

Discourse on the death of President Abraham Lincoln. (66709)

Discourse on the death of President Harrison, . . . at Wareham. (56044)

Discourse on the death of President Harrison, delivered in Concord. 6955

Discourse, on the death of President Lincoln, . . . Pittsburgh, Pa. 36219

Discourse on the death of President Lincoln, preached at Stillwater, N. Y. 36350

Discourse on the death of President Lincoln, preached in the Orthodox Congregational Church, in Dedham. 2575

Discourse on the death of Rev. Gilbert R. Livingston. 18212

Discourse . . . on the death of Rev. Norris Bull. 42032

Discourse on the death of the Hon. Daniel Webster. 37971

Discourse on the death of the Hon. Gordon Saltonstall. 198

Discourse . . . on the death of the Hon. Samuel Wilkenson. 42032

Discourse on the death of the Honourable Thomas Jefferson. 90196

Discourse on the death of the President. 90984

Discourse [on] the death of the Rev. Edward Dorr Griffin. 32943

Discourse, on the death of the Rev. Francis Asbury, late Bishop of the Methodist Episcopal Church in the United States. 85435

Discourse on the death of the Rev. Francis Asbury, late Bishop of the Methodist Episcopal Church in the United States of America. 85436

Discourse on . . . the death of the Rev. James Boyd. 64679

Discourse on the death of the Rev. Samuel Brown Wylie. 43539

Discourse on the death of the Rev. Thomas Priestley. 4597

Discourse on the . . . death of the Right Rev. Nathaniel Bowen. (26287)

Discourse on the death of W. H. Harrison, delivered before the citizens of New Haven. 2663

Discourse on the death of W. H. Harrison, Late President of the United States. 5077

Discourse on the death of W. H. Harrison, late President of the United States, at Eastville, Northampton County, Virginia. 17942

Discourse on the death of Wilber Fish. 3168

Discourse on the death of Wm. H. Harrison. By Rev. Palmer Dyer. 21600

Discourse on the death of William H. Harrison, President of the United States. (17680)

Discourse on the death of William Henry Harrison, . . . delivered before the two houses of the Legislature. 64641

Discourse on the death of William Henry Harrison; . . . delivered . . . on the day of the national fast. 31214

Discourse on the death of William K. Townsend. 30619

Discourse on the death of Zachary Taylor, by John O. Fiske. 24547

Discourse: on the death of Zachary Taylor . . . President of the United States. 38315

Discourse . . . on . . . the decease of F. L. D'Wolf. (28881)

Discourse, on the decease of Mrs. Martha Russell. 76364

Discourse on the decease of S. B. Wylie. 43569

Discourse, on the dignity and excellence of the human character. 32253

Discourse on the divine appointment of the Gospel ministry. (20062)

Discourse on the doctrine of the Trinity. 71852

Discourse on the duty of a patriot. 5078

Discourse on the duty of Christians with regard to the use of distilled spirits. 88594

Discourse on the duty of civil government. 104554

Discourse on the duty of sustaining the laws. 91370

Discourse on the early constitutional history of Connecticut. 2664

Discourse on the early history of Pennsylvania. 21379

Discourse on the earthquake. 24576

Discourse . . . on the 8th day of October, 1834. 9189

Discourse on the ends and uses of a liberal education. 37924

Discourse on the English constitution. 20243

Discourse on the epidemic cholera morbus. 83359

Discourse on the evidence of the American Indians. 55374

Discourse; on the evils and the end of war. 104384

Discourse on the evils of intemperance. 84757A

Discourse on the existing state of mrals. 13589

Discourse on the extent and evils of the Sunday liquor traffic. 44746

Discourse on the family as an element of government. 65426

Discourse . . . on the Festival of Saint John the Baptist. 36035

Discourse on the fiftieth anniversary of his [i. e. Allen M'Lean's] ordination. 43509

Discourse on the first centennial celebration of the birth-day of Washington. 9894

Discourse on the formation and development of the American mind. 7676

Discourse on the formation and progress of the First Methodist Episcopal Church in Lynn. 13391

Discourse on the forty-seventh anniversary. (43223)

[Discourse on the fourth commandment, by Rev. Aaron Bancroft.] 63992

Discourse on the 4th July, 1798. 36238

Discourse on the funeral of Hubert Morrill Perham. 85522

Discourse . . . on the . . . general election. 59491

Discourse on the genius and character of the Rev. Horace Holley. 9895

Discourse on the genius of the federative system. 97372

Discourse on the good education of children. 46273

Discourse on "the good news from a far country." 12315, 95642

Discourse on the great American idea. 89263

Discourse on the greatness and power of faith in the world's history. 64468

Discourse on the greatness, and praise of the Lord. 80901

Discourse on the guilt and folly of being ashamed of religion. 84096, 84121

Discourse on the history, character, and prospects of the west. 20819

Discourse, on the history of the First Christian Church and Society. 18452

Discourse on the history of the town [of Mason, N. H.] 31845

Discourse on the holiness of the Sabbath day. 21198

Discourse on the horrid murder of Captain James Purrington's family. 48022

Discourse on the imperative duties of the hour. (28380)

Discourse on the importance of character and education. 28875

Discourse on the influence of diseases on the intellectual and moral powers. 83360

Discourse on the institution and observation of the Lord's Day. 18478

Discourse on the invention of ships. 68598

Discourse on the late Rev. Professor Ware. 58800

Discourse on the Laton outrage. 105242

Discourse on the law of retaliation. 39187

Discourse on the life of Calvert. (37410)

Discourse on the life and character of Daniel Webster. 6067

Discourse on the life and character of Dea. Joseph Otis. 6271

Discourse on the life and character of De Witt Clinton. 38084

Discourse on the life and character of Dr. Luther V. Bell. (68025)

Discourse on the life and character of Francis R. Shunk. 19878, 80768

Discourse on the life and character of George Calvert. 37409-(37410), (45211A)

Discourse on the life and character of Hon. James Richardson. 38776

Discourse on the life and character of Hon. Joseph Lyman. 22327

Discourse on the life and character of Howard Townsend. 13359

Discourse on the life and character of John Barker, D. D. 3946

Discourse on the life and character of John Quincy Adams. (23813)

Discourse on the life and character of Joseph Brown Smith. 31671

Discourse on the life and character of Rev. Charles Hall. 82335

Discourse on the life and character of Rev. Irah Chase. 29530

Discourse on the life and character of Rev. Jason Whitman. (20645)

Discourse on the life and character of Rev. Joseph C. Smith. 48928

Discourse on the life and character of Samuel Bard. 49749

Discourse on the life and character of Samuel Putnam. 3794

Discourse on the life and character of Sir Walter Raleigh. 30480, (45211A)

Discourse on the life and character of the Hon. George Mathews. 102171

Discourse on the life and character of the Hon. Littleton Waller Tazewell. (28842)

Discourse on the life and character of the Hon. Nathaniel Bowditch. 106055, 106057

Discourse on the life and character of the late Hon. Leverett Saltonstall. 7494

Discourse on the life and character of the late John A. G. Davis. 49315

Discourse on the life and character of the Rev. Aaron Bancroft. (31806)

Discourse on the life and character of the Rev. Charles Follen. 47078

Discourse on the life and character of the Rev. Henry V. D. Johns. 83387

Discourse on the life and character of the Reverend Henry Ware. 58325

Discourse on the life and character of the Rev. Hezekiah G. Leigh. 84740

Discourse on the life and character of the Rev. Jeremiah Chamberlain. 92738

Discourse on the life and character of the Reverend John Thornton Kirkland, D. D., . . . June 5, 1840. 58325

Discourse on the life and character of the Reverend John Thornton Kirkland, D. D. L L. D. 106054-106055

Discourse on the life and character of the Rev. Nathaniel Thayer. 31804

Discourse on the life and character of the Rev. Samuel Jennings. 91914

Discourse on the life and character of Rev. William R. DeWitt. 72193

Discourse on the life and public services of the late Jacob Burnet. 23043

Discourse on the life and services of Daniel Webster. 31671

Discourse on the life and services of the late Gulian Crommelin Verplanck. 30622

Discourse on the life, character, and genius of Washington Irving. 8814

Discourse on the life, character, and public services of Ambrose Spencer. 3448

Discourse on the life, character, and public services of James Kent. 21105

Discourse on the life, character, and services of Daniel Drake, M. D. 28937

Discourse on the life . . . of Hon. Henry Clay . . . at . . . Gettysburg. 38310

Discourse on the life of Honorable Henry Clay. By W. H. MacFarland. (43245)

Discourse on the life of John Lowell, Jr. 58322

Discourse on the life . . . of Rev. John Pierpont. (29830)

Discourse on the life . . . of William Wirt. 37412

Discourse on the life, services, and character of Stephen Van Rensselaer. (3449)

Discourse on the lives and characters of Thomas Jefferson and John Adams. 104873

Discourse . . . on the Lord's Day, 17 May, 1812. 39187

Discourse on the love of our country. 104346

Discourse on the man of sin. 16603

Discourse on the medium of commerce. 37239

Discourse on the modifications demanded by the Roman Catholics. 9549

Discourse on the moral influence of Railroads. 20190

Discourse, on the moral, legal and domestic condition of our colored population. 16210

Discourse on the national crisis. 23316

Discourse . . . on the national fast. (71269)

Discourse on the national fast, April 30. By Henry W. Bellows. 4575

Discourse . . . on the . . . national fast, April 30, 1863. (50319)

Discourse . . . on the national fast day, January 4th, 1861, . . . in . . . Boston. 45427

Discourse . . . on . . . the national fast day, January 4, 1861, in . . . Washington, D. C. 29741

Discourse on the national fast, delivered in Yale-College Chapel. 21563

Discourse; on the . . . national fast, September 26th, 1861. (50384)

Discourse on the national thanksgiving, April 13, 1815. By Jonathan Edwards. (21976)

Discourse, . . . on the national thanksgiving, April 13, 1816. [By Nathaniel Emmons.] 22525

Discourse on the nature and benefits of Christ's intercession in Heaven. (62794)

Discourse on the nature and danger of small faults. 84097, 84121

Discourse on the nature and importance of church discipline. 18264

Discourse on the nature and reasonableness of fasting. 84098

Discourse on the nature and study of law. 68000

Discourse on the nature, and the danger. 46788

Discourse on the nature of faith. 90567

Discourse on the nature, properties, and conversion of the soul. (81499)

Discourse on the nature, the proper subjects, and the benefits of baptism. (84099)

Discourse on the navigation which the Portugales doe make. 22813

Discourse on the Nebraska bill. 51286

Discourse on the necessity and importance of wisdom and knowledge. 4054

Discourse on the necessity and the means of making our national literature independent. 21383

Discourse on the objects and importance of the National Institution for the Promotion of Science. 63688

Discourse, on the occasion of forming the African Mission School Society. 100964

Discourse . . . on the occasion of the death of Bishop Dehon. (26286)

Discourse on the occasion of the death of General George Washington. (7069)

Discourse on the occasion of the death of James H. Perkins. 31088

Discourse on the occasion of the death of James Jing. (10255)

Discourse on the occasion of the death of President Lincoln. (81331)

Discourse, on the occasion of the death of the Hon. Augustin S. Clayton. 84542

Discourse, on the occasion of the death of William Henry Harrison. 66781

Discourse on the occasion of the fall of Richmond. 27333

Discourse [on] the opening of a new theatre in Boston. 37976

Discourse . . . on the . . . opening of the Reformed . . . Church. 38165

Discourse on the order and propriety of divine inspiration and revelation. 79703

Discourse on the origin of evil. 105296

Discourse on the origin, progress, and design of Freemasonry. 3767

Discourse, on the original diversity of mankind. 84103-84106

Discovrse on the originall and fundamentall cause. 67561, 67587, 67598

Discourse on the past history. 92296

Discourse on the peace. (39179)

Discourse on the power and malice of devils. 46528

Discourse on the preparation of the body for the small-pox. 95559

Discourse on the present state and duty of the church. 6051

Discourse on the present state of education in Maryland. (38174)

Discourse on the present state of the British plantations. 37239

Discourse on the present vileness of the body. (9717)

Discourse, on the preservation of documents. 9457

Discourse on the principle of vitality. 102055

Discourse on the privileges of the church of Jesus Christ. 79161

Discourse on the professional character and virtues of the late William Wirt. 88246

Discourse on the progress of Philosophy. 97299

Discourse on the progress of science and literature. 1173, 92297

Discourse on the proper character of religious institutions. 14529

Discourse on the proposed repeal of the Missouri Compromise. 52315

Discourse on the prospects of letters and taste in Virginia. (30561)

Discourse on the province and uses of Baptist history. 18205

Discourse on the public duties of medical men. 83361

Discourse on the qualifications and duties of an historian. 37824

Discourse on the religion of the Indian tribes of North America. (35812)

Discourse on the Rev. Simon Gabriel Brute. 42965

Discourse on the Right Revd. Benedict J. Fenwick. 92159

Discourse on the rightfulness and expedience of capital punishments. (21571)

Discourse on the Sabbath following the funeral of Miss Elizabeth P. Hooker. (32816)

Discourse on the second appearing of Christ. 79703

Discourse on the settlement and progress of New-England. 64293

Discourse on the slavery question . . . by Francis Gillette. 27409

Discourse on the slavery question. Delivered in the North Church, Hartford. 9544

Discourse on the social and moral advantages of the cultivation of local literature. 14202

Discourse on the social influence of Christianity. 18095

Discourse on the state and prospects of American literature. 49749

Discourse on the state of the country. 91371

Discourse on the state of the German population in the United States. 6175

Discourse on the study of the law of nature and nations. 43470

Discourse on the subjects of national gratitude. 84102

Discourse, on the subjects of national gratitude, delivered in the Third Presbyterian Church in Philadelphia. 84100-84101

Discourse on the surviving remnant of the Indian race. 97645

Discourse on the terrible, irresistible, yet sublime logic. 76258

Discourse on the third Sunday after Easter. 78585

Discourse [on the 31st of October, 1858.] 89767, 89775

Discourse on the times. (20244)

Discourse on the times. Delivered in the West Spruce St. Presbyterian Church. 7698

Discourse on the traffic in spirituous liquors. 2665

Discourse on the transient and permanent in Christianity. note after (58767)

Discourse on the trial by jury. (65427)

Discourse on the true idea of the state as a religious institution. (40851)

Discourse . . . on the 12th of September, 1866. 37942

Discourse on the twentieth anniversary of his [i. e. William P. Lunt's] installation. 42714

Discourse on the twentieth anniversary of his [i. e. John T. Gilman Nichols'] ordination. 55209

[Discourse] on the 20th of August. 39185

Discourse on the twenty-fifth anniversary of his [i.e. Alonzo Hill's] ordination. (31806)

[Discourse] on the 23d of July, 1812. 39185

Discourse on the true nature of freedom and slavery. 19142, 19431

Discourse on the two witnesses. (31745)

Discourse on the urim and the thummim. 90197

Discourse on the uses and importance of history. 71662

Discourse on the utility of history. 44376

Discourse on the validity of ordination. (65613)

Discourse on the validity of Presbyterian ordination. 32588

Discourse on the vanity and mischief of presuming on things. 33973

Discourse of the verity and validity of infants baptisme. 62483

Discourse on the virtues and public services of the late Judge Hay. (12406)

Discourse on the war . . . at Exeter, N. H. 51888

Discourse on the western Autumnal disease. 99394

Discourse on the wickedness and folly of the present war. 3893

Discourse . . . on Theodore Parker. 3791

Discourse on . . . Thomas Addis Emmet. 49749

Discourse on trade, more particularly on sugar and tobacco. 20245

Discourse on true magnanimity. 89744

Discourse on vaccination. 78617

Discourse on victory and its dangers. 18974

Discourse [on Washington.] 20623

Discourse on Wigglesworth. 94517

Discourse on witchcraft. 46407, 46528

Discourse on woman. 51114

Discourse: . . . opening of the new hall. 25448

Discourse or sermon, shewing what is wisdom. 100677

Discourse . . . Pittsburgh, Pa. . . . June 1st, 1865. 38310

Discourse . . . Pittsburgh, Pa. on Thanksgiving Day, Nov. 26, 1857. (38309)

Discourse pointing out the advantages. 33865

Discourse pointing out the reciprocal advantages. 33966

Discourse . . . "politics in the pulpit." 57250

Discourse, Portsmouth, June 24, 1806. 4350

Discourse preached April 23d, 1865. 89098

Discourse preached at Auburn, N. Y. 24036

Discourse, preached at . . . Boston . . . February 21, 1813. 39187

Discourse preached at Canton, Mass., April 16, 1857. 11782

Discourse, preached at his [i. e. Thomas Sumner Winn's] funeral. 104785

Discourse preached at Hollis, N. H. 18859

Discourse . . . preach'd at King's-Chapel in Boston. 10683

Discourse preached at Lancaster, Sunday, March 19, 1843. 78638

Discourse preached at Lancaster, the last Sabbath in the year. 78644

Discourse preached at Needham, October 24, 1841. 71579

Discourse preached at New London. 78572

Discourse preached at Newport. 62721

Discourse preached at . . . Roxbury, June 10, . . . 1860. 54993

Discourse preached at South Kingston. (13395)

Discourse, . . . preached at the commencement of the nineteenth century. 39181

Discourse preached at the dedication of Suffolk Street Chapel. 76986

Discourse preached at the dedication of the Church of the Messiah. 16764

Discourse preached at the dedication of the First Congregational Church. 22176

Discourse preached at the dedication of the House of the Thirteenth Congregational Church. 16378

Discourse preached at the dedication of the New Congregational Church. 80264

Discourse preached at the dedication of the Second Congregational Unitarian Church. 11909

Discourse preached at the funeral of the late Mr. Samuel Fessenden. 25097

Discourse preached at the installation of Rev. Erastus Dickinson. 13467

Discourse preached at the installation of the Rev. John Gosman. 5083

Discourse preached at the ordination of the Rev. Samuel Shepard. 92896

Discourse, preached at the request of the Episcopal Education Society of Pennsylvania. 97626

Discourse preached at the Unitarian Convention at Baltimore. 22309

Discourse preached at West Winstead, Conn. 9099

Discourse preached at Whitehall, New York. 16805

Discourse preached at Wilmington, Delaware. (37280)

Discourse, preached before the Ancient and Honorable Artillery Company. 103727

Discourse preached before the Barnstable Conference. [sic] 13324

Discourse preached before the Benevolent Fraternity of Churches. 23327

Discourse preached before the General Synod. (77727)

Discourse preached before the members of the Boston Female Asylum. 30521

Discourse, preached before the Second Church and Society in Boston. 71774

Discourse, preached before the Society for Propagating the Gospel among the Indians and Others in North America. 97386

Discourse preached before the West Baptist Church and Society. 37582

Discourse preached by Rev. A. B. Dascomb. 18651

Discourse preached by the appointment of the General Assembly of the Presbyterian Church. 89783

Discourse preached December 15th 1774. Being the day recommended by the Provincial Congress; and afterwards at the Boston Lecture. 28005-(28007), 95642

Discourse preached, December 15th, 1774.
Being the day recommended by the Provincial Congress, to be observed in
thanksgiving. (39178)

Discourse, preached Dec. 22. [by George B.
Cheever.] (12406)

Discourse preached Dec. 22d, 1850 . . . on
occasion of the anniversary. (12406)

Discourse, preached fast day, April 8, 1841.
(11946)

Discourse preached from Psalm XC. 12.
80266

Discourse preached in . . . Albany. (64646)

Discourse preached in behalf of the U. S. Christian Commission. 82700

Discourse, preached in Boston, before the
Massachusetts Baptist Missionary Society.
91793

Discourse preached . . . in Boston, . . .
June 8, 1856. (26534)

Discourse preached . . . in Boston, . . . June
11, 1854. (18042), 26531

Discourse preached in Bradford, Sept, 11, 1804.
89793

Discourse preached in Chelsea, 1858. 16698

Discourse preached in . . . Chicago. 73747

Discourse preached in Christ Church. 43804

Discourse preached . . . in Concord. 25440

Discourse preached in . . . Hartford, Conn.,
. . . October 7, 1855. 59167

Discourse preached in Harvard Church. 22309

Discourse preached in Medwat, Mass. (34174)

Discourse. Preached in New Bedford, May
13th, 1860. 64667

Discourse preached in . . . New Haven. 13589

Discourse preached in Providence. 31218

Discourse preached in St. Paul's Church.
102076

Discourse preached . . . [in] Salem, Mass.
7495

Discourse preached in the city of Washington.
19862

Discourse preached in the First Church, Dorchester. 29657, 29828

Discourse preached in the First Presbyterian
Church, New Albany. 2326

Discourse preached in the Old South Church
before the Howard Benevolent Society,
December 11, 1853. 22327

Discourse preached in the Old South Church
before the Howard Benevolent Society,
December 15, 1850. 92021

Discourse, preached in the Second Parish,
Plymouth. 91379

Discourse preached in Wethersfield, Nov. 29,
1827. 94815

Discourse preached in Worcester. (31806)

Discourse preached Jan. 7, 1846. 30454

Discourse preached . . . June 7, 1857. (16377)

Discourse preach'd lately in the Royal Chappel
at Boston. 30785

Discourse preached March 21st, 1844. (21835)

Discourse, preached May 14, 1841. 89781

Discourse preached Nov. 1st, 1868. 22051

Discourse preached November 29, 1860.
(43163)

Discourse preached November 27, 1862. 18436

Discourse preached October 2d, 1864. 89096

Discourse preached on January 30, 1780.
72169

Discourse, preached on March the fifth, 1778.
39180

Discourse, preached on Nov. 9, 1856. 16222

Discourse preached on occasion of the appointment by the now sectionalized General
Assembly. 85339

Discourse, preached on Sunday, Feb. 15, 1863.
89056

Discourse preached on the day of the national
fasting. 85264A

Discourse preached on the day of the national
funeral of President Lincoln. 36314

Discourse preached on the death of Rev. Francis
C. Clements. 18162

Discourse preached on the death of Zachary
Taylor. 70412

Discourse preached on the first Sunday after
the arrival of the intelligence of the fall
of Sebastopol. 71114

Discourse preached . . . on the first Sunday of
the year. 33964

Discourse, preached on the fourth of July, 1798.
21553

Discourse preached on the national Thanksgiving
Day. 10846

Discourse preached on the occasion of leaving
the Old Meeting House. (70413)

Discourse preached on the occasion of the
annual thanksgiving. 90443

Discourse preached on the occasion of the day
of humiliation and prayer. 85324

Discourse preached on the occasion of the state
fast. 29776

Discourse preached on the Sabbath following
the assassination of the President. 12537

Discourse preached on the twenty-fifth anniversary. 6964

Discourse, preached on Tuesday, February 11,
1812. (74670)

Discourse preached September 29, 1861. 83339

Discourse preached to the Congregational Society
in Norton. (20529)

Discourse preached to the Third Congregational
Society in Chelsea. 71835

Discourse preparatory to the choice of a minister. 25408

Discourse prepared for the national fast day.
808

Discourse, Presbyterian Historical Society,
1858. 25152

Discourse pronounced at Burlington, Vermont.
76365

Discourse, pronounced at Schenectady, July 22,
1845. 64610

Discourse pronounced at the capital of the
United States . . . before the American
Historical Society. 11345

Discourse pronounced at the capitol of the
United States, in the Hall of Representatives. 105099

Discourse pronounced at the funeral obsequies
of John Hooker Ashmun. 92298

Discourse pronounced at the inauguration of the
author. (24040)

Discourse pronounced at the request of the
Essex Historical Society. 92299

Discourse, pronounced before His Excellency,
John Brooks. 95257

Discourse, pronounced before His Excellency
William Eustis. 79785

Discourse pronounced before the class of
Starling Medical College. 84070

Discourse pronounced before the Euglossian
and Alpha Phi Delta Societies. (31388)

Discourse pronounced before the Hartford
County Peace Society. (31388)

Discourse pronounced before the Middlesex
Martial Band. 25214

Discourse pronounced before the Phi Beta
Kappa Society. 92300

Discourse pronounced before the Phi Sigma
Nu Society. (31388)

Discourse pronounced before the Rhode-Island Alpha of the Phi Beta Kappa Society. 28617

Discourse pronounced before the Young Men's Association of New-Brunswick. 39378

Discourse pronounced in the first Presbyterian Church in Augusta. 72627

Discourse pronounced July 30, 1844. 89744

Discourse, pronounced on Sabbath evening, July 4, 1852. 1643

Discourse, pronounced on the twenty-third of November, 1844. 78395

Discourse pronounced upon the inauguration of the author. 92301

Discourse proving that the Christian religion, is the only true religion. 46664

Discourse publickly delivered by a female Friend. 86045

Discourse putting Christians in mind. 196

Discourse, read before the New Jersey Historical Society. 24291

Discourse, read before the Rhode-Island Medical Society. 97485

Discourse . . . reasons for law with special reference to the traffic in intoxicating drinks. 44721

Discourse relating to the present times. 95529

Discourse relative to the subject of animation. 24686

Discourse representing from the most authentick records. 91151

Discourse reviewing a ministry of fifty years. 52293

Discourse, . . . Richmond, Virginia. (50450)

Discourse, sacred to the memory of George Washington. (7101)

Discourse. . . . Second Baptist Church . . . Salem. 28944

Discourse . . . Sept. 18, 1861. 29323

Discourse . . . September 12th, 1858. 42960

Discourse, . . . September 2d, MDCCXCIII, Franklin. 22525

Discourse, . . . Semptember 3d, MDCCXCII, . . . Franklin. 22525

Discourse . . . September 30th, 1855. (29830)

Discourse, Sept. 20, 1857. (25228)

Discourse . . . September 20, 1846. 33964

Discourse . . . September 28, 1862. (26240)

Discourse shewing Christ's tender care of his mother. 24682

Discourse, shewing how duties on some sorts of merchandize may make the province of New-York richer. 34882-(34884), 97562, 100770, 106314

Discourse shewing that God dealeth with men. 47123

Discourse shewing that the real first cause of the straits and difficulties of this province. 58203

Discourse shewing the cause and effects of the increase of building. 1765

Discourse shewing the grace of love in a believer. 104091-2 [sic]

Discourse shewing the nature and discipline. 59722

Discourse shewing the nature and necessity of an internal call. 2624

Discourse, shewing the necessity of a well-governed trade. 96426

Discourse, shewing what cause there is to fear. 46694

Discourse shewing, who is a true pastor of the church of Christ. 69571, 101194

Discourse shewing who is a true preacher of the church of Christ. 12365

Discourse showing the certainty of Christ's personal appearance. 24444

Discourse . . . Society for the Promotion of Collegiate and Theological Education at the West. 29764

Discourse, . . . South-Carolina College, July 4th, A. D. 1819. 47005

Discourse, . . . Springfield, Illinois. 59486

Discourse, . . . Sterling Centre. 71936

Discourse, suggested by the burning of the Steamer Henry Clay. 79490

Discourse suggested by the death of Hon. J. C. Calhoun. 84546

Discourse. Sympathy, its foundation and legitimate exercise. 37403

Discourse, thanksgiving. By A. T. Hopkins. (32907)

Discourse . . . Thanksgiving Day. 48996

Discourse . . . Thanksgiving Day . . . 1866. 43184

Discourse. Thanksgiving Day . . . Nov. 18, 1858. 16804

Discourse, . . . Thanksgiving Day, Nov. 28, 1850. 22009

Discourse, . . . Thanksgiving Day, Nov. 25, 1858. 51439

Discourse . . . Thanksgiving Day, November 29, 1866. 50454

Discourse . . . Thanksgiving Day, November 20, 1856. 33953

Discourse, . . . Thanksgiving, December 12, 1850. 65093

Discourse, Thanksgiving, 1867. 25037

Discourse . . . Thanksgiving, November 28, 1844. 29530

Discourse . . . Thanksgiving, November 24th, 1864. 41511

Discourse . . . Thanksgiving, November 30, 1837. 63963

Discourse. The American Anti-slavery Society at war with the church. 13469

Discourse the day after the reception of the tidings. 58673

Discourse . . . the day of the national fast. 57771

Discourse (the substance of which was) delivered at Westchester. (81637)

Discourse the substance of which was delivered in Woodbridge. 8736

Discourse III. 92303

Discourse . . . 13th September, 1814. 8139

Discourse . . . 31st of December, 1808. 28396

Discourse to commemorate the rendition of Thomas Simms. (58740)

Discourse to prove a passage by the northwest. (29594)

Discourse to the Congregational Church and Society, in Stockbridge, Mass. 22052

Discourse to the Federal Military Society. 39661

Discourse to the graduating class of Wesleyan University. 57174

Discourse to the people of Taunton, etc. 18479

Discourse . . . to the . . . St. Alban's Lodge. (44330)

Discourse to the . . . Society for the Manumission of Slaves. (54851)

Discourse to the students of Phillips' Exeter Academy. 31768

Discourse touching a marriage, etc. 67598

Discourse touching a match, etc. 67598

Discourse touching the Jews' synagogue. 17062

Discourse touching the propagating the Gospel of Christ Jesus. 28944, 104338

Discourse touching the Spanish monarchie. 10198

Discourse . . . 24 June, 1802. 40111

Discourse . . . 22d February, 1846. 80121

Discourse II. 92303

Discourse, under the title of An after-thought. (79098)-79100

Discourse, upon Acts XX. 17, —21. 97312

Discourse upon agriculture. 18600

Discourse upon baptism. 66754

Discourse upon death. 46279

Discourse upon . . . eloquence. 25415, 35146, 72485

Discourse upon evangelical repentance. 5118

Discourse upon governments. 14237

Discourse upon Negro-slavery. 97633

[Discourse] upon occasion of the condemnation of Benjamin Goad. 18476

Discourse upon occasion of the death of James Adger. 85328

Discourse upon President Lincoln. 18742

Discourse upon the death of Her . . . Majesty Wilhelmina Dorothea Carolina. 46796

Discourse upon . . . the death . . . of Mr. Moses Abbot. (16628)

Discourse upon the duration of future punishment. 73924

Discourse upon the duties of the Christian citizen. 90440

Discourse upon the entended voyage to the hethermoste parts of America. 10900

Discourse upon the good work. (30171)

Discourse upon gracious and wondrous restraints. (46275)

Discourse upon the institution of medical schools in America. 50650

Discourse upon the lawfulness of war. 77436

Discourse upon the life and character of Stephen A. Douglas. 37694

Discourse upon the life, character and services, of James Madison. 98440

Discourse upon the life, character, and services of the Honorable John Marshall. 92302

Discourse upon the life, services, and death of Abraham Lincoln. 17718

Discourse upon the true and unfeigned repentance of Job. 73075

Discourse utter'd in part at Ammauskeeg-Falls. 78696

Discourse . . . Washington City . . . September 16, 1855. 16222

Discourse . . . Washington, D. C. , January 26, 1856. 16222

Discourse . . . Western District Literary . . . Association. 38463

Discourse . . . Weymouth, Feb. 3, 1811. 55879

Discourse, Weymouth, Jan. 5, 1851. 22535

Discourse wherein is showed that the great care and endeavour of every Christian ought to be. 2079

Discourse wherein the danger of, and by, unprofitable hearing. 101174

Discourse wherein the state of all our towns is considered. (46556), note after 96368

Discourse wherin [sic] is shewed, I. That the children of Godly parents are under special advantages. 46645

Discourse, which was written, on board a ship at sea. 78702, note after 102094

Discourse . . . Winchester, Va. . . . June 8th, 1851. 38310

Discourse . . . with . . . remarks on the present miserable situation. 33864

Discourse . . . with remarks on the writings of Mr. Sandeman. 2632

Discourse. . . . Written by Cotton Mather. 46442

Discourse written by Sir George Downing. 20779

Discourse de Oost-Indische Vaert en de coopmanschap betreffende. 31505

Discourses after the half-century, Norwich, 1778. 42007

Discourses and addresses at the installation. 1323, 90998

Discourses and addresses on subjects of American history. 99266

Discourses and dialogues of the late Rev. Samuel Porter. 64315

Discourses and essays. 80075

Discourses and letters commemorative of Emily Lane Symth. 85229

Discourses and reviews, principally upon subjects of political economy. 39379

Discourses, and speeches. 50041, 92272

Discourses at the dedication of the Calvinist Church. 2425

Discourses at the inauguration of the Rev. Alexander T. M'Gill. 65658

Discourses at the inauguration of the Rev. James W. Alexander. 65658

Discourses at the inauguration of the Rev. William Henry Green. 65658

Discourses at West Hartford, Conn. (50855)

Discourses . . . before the Cincinnati Medical Library Association. 20825

Discourses between an Indian philosopher and a missionary. 43892, note after 94626

Discourses, by Abiel Abbot Livermore. (41557)

Discourses by Moses Wall. 44194

Discourses, charges, addresses, pastoral letters. 64611

Discourses, comprising a history of the First Congregational Church in Providence. 29752

Discourses, dedicatory and historical. 32449

Discourses . . . delivered at the Thursday Lecture in Boston. 1828

Discourses delivered by Dr. Spring on the closing of the old church. 89767, 89775

Discourses delivered by William Savery. 77280

Discourses delivered in Murray Street Church. 85483

Discourses delivered in the celebration of the two hundredth anniversary. 29525

Discourses, delivered in the College of New Jersey. 28501

Discourses delivered in the island of Barbadoes. 32481

Discourses delivered on that occasion. (2990)

Discourses . . . illustrating the principles. 30514

Discourses in commemoration of Abraham Lincoln. 2342

Discourses in memory of Robert Waterston. 26537

Discourses . . . in the New North Church. 58799

Discourses, . . . July 19, 1835. (29830)

Discourses. Memorial of Abraham Lincoln. 41187

Discourses on celestial marriage. 64950

Discourses on Davila. 239

Discourses on his [i. e. Charles G. Ives'] fiftieth anniversary. 35305

Discourses on human life. 19862

Discourses on passages of scripture. 76338

Discourses on prophecy. 1857

Discourses on public occasions in America.
84599-84600, 84614-84615, 84626, 84641,
84664, 84678C
Discourses on religious subjects. 94066
Discourses on several important subjects.
78570
Discourses on several public occasions during
the war in America. 84580, 84585,
84595, 84597, 84601
Discourses on several subjects. 78569, 78571
Discourses on tea. (80571)
Discourses on the apostolic succession. 84577
Discourses on the glorious characters. 46548
Discourses on the life and character of John
Thornton Kirkland. 106054-106055,
106057
Discourses on the parable of the ten virgins.
97450
Discourses on the philosophy of religion.
71523
Discourses on the progress of science and
literature. 92297, 92303
Discourses on the public revenues, and on the
trade of England. 18686, (22976), 69395
Discourses on the signs of the times. 41344
Discourses on the Song of Solomon. 94697
Discourses on the whole LVth chapter of Isaiah.
101171
Discourses on topics suggested by the times.
4314
Discourses on various important subjects.
21933
Discourses on various subjects. By Jacob
Duche. 21050
Discourses on various subjects. [By Orville
Dewey.] 19862
Discourses on various subjects, intended to
have been delivered. 65505
Discourses preached in Swanton. 61037
Discourses preached in the First Congregational
Church, East Bloomfield. 15614
Discourses, reviews, and miscellanies. 11908
Discourses upon a recovery from sickness.
80568
Discourses upon Christian duties. 50686
Discourses upon I. Tim. I. 15. 97318
Discourses upon the nature, the design, and
the subject of the Lords Supper. 46267
Discourso com que o Presidente da Provincia
do Para fez a abertura. 88812
Discourso sobre elecciones por el ciudadano
Manuel Vidaurre. 99480
Discourso sobre o estado actual das minas do
Brazil. 17948
Discoverers and pioneers of America. 58671
Discoverers, pioneers and settlers of North
and South America. 8683
Discoverie and conqvest of the Prouinces of
Peru. 106272
Discoverie of the large, rich, and bevvtifvl
empire of Gviana. (67551)-67553
Discoverie of the large, rich, and bevvtifvl
empyre of Gviana. 16781, 67554
Discoveries by the English. 62957
Discoveries in the South Seas. 8427
Discoveries made in exploring the Missouri.
21247, (40825)
Discoveries made in Hudson's Bay. 28460,
1st note after 94082
Discoveries of ancient American records.
83287
Discoveries of Columbus and of the English in
America. (21340)
Discoveries of John Lederer. 39676
Discoveries of Seb. Cabot. 14414

Discoveries of the French in 1768 and 1769.
24749
Discoveries of the Spaniards in America.
66686
Discoveries of the world from their first
original to the year of Our Lord 1555.
26470
Discoveries of the world from their first
originall vnto the yeere of Our Lord
1555. 13419, 26469, 26470, 47765
Discoveries of the Zeni. 66686
Discoveries of the origin. 68662
Discoveries, purchases of land, &c. 37259
Discoveries, rights and possessions of France.
9602, 30794-30795, 34027, 2d note after
65324
Discoveries, rights and possessions of Great
Britain. 9602, 30794-30795, 34027, 2d
note after 65324
Discoveries to the northwest. 66686
Discovery, a poem. (36483)
Discovery and colonization of America. 23249
Discovery and conquest of Mexico. 17825
Discovery and conquest of Peru. 17826
Discovery and conquest of Terra Florida.
24858, (24864)
Discovery and conquest of the Molucco and
Philippine Islands. (1948)
Discovery and conquest of the northwest.
101710
Discovery and examination of the mistakes.
31656
Discovery and explanation of the source.
(72358)
Discovery and exploration of the Mississippi
Valley. 80002
Discovery and settlement of Missouri Territory.
49589
Discovery by Columbus. 82808, 97196
Discovery of a large, rich, and plentiful country.
(20247), 31373
Discovery of a nation of Welshmen. 34896
Discovery of all known heresies in all ages
and places. 73315-73317
Discovery of America: a poem. 31146
Discovery of America, as related by a father
to his children. 10284, (14651)
Discovery of America by Christopher Columbus.
(43332)
Discovery of America by Columbus. 2445
Discovery of America. By George Cubitt.
(17824)
Discovery of America by Madoc ap Owen
Gwyneth. 31472
Discovery of America by the Norsemen. 9800
Discovery of America by the Northmen. 37697,
67477
Discovery of America by the Northmen in the
tenth century. By Joshua Toulmin Smith.
83425
Discovery of America by the Northmen in the
tenth century. Comprising translations.
83426
Discovery of America by the Northmen, in the
tenth century, with notices of the early
settlements of the Irish. (4117), 81698
Discovery of America by the Welsh. 21
Discovery of America by the Welsh more than
300 years before . . . Columbus. (58011)
Discovery of America, conquest of Mexico, and
conquest of Peru. 63022
Discovery of America. Ein Lesebuch fur An-
fanger. 10297
Discovery of America, for the use of children
and young persons. (10304)

Discovery of America, Kamtchatka and the Aleutian Islands. 67489
Discovery of America, with an enquiry into the rise and progress of the contest there. 20246
Discovery of and voyages to Virginia. 62957
Discovery of Astoria, Babylon, Bath, Carnarsi, etc. 18023
Discovery of California and northwest America. 94437
Discovery of Columbus. 82808
Discovery of Fonseca in a voyage to Surranam. 20248, (74617)
Discovery of gold in California. 21232
Discovery of gold plates. 63959
Discovery of . . . Guiana. 67560, 67598
Discovery of Humboldt Bay. 105053
Discovery of infinite treasvre. 63360
Discovery of modern anaesthesia. 90888
Discovery of Nevv Brittaine. 52518-52519, 104191
Discovery of New-found-land. 103332
Discovery of New France. 62957
Discovery of northern New York. 32470
Discovery of some materials. (20628)
Discovery of subterraneall treasure. 63360
Discovery of the aforesaid Master Prynne. 103441
Discovery of the Barmvdas. 100460
Discovery of the great west. 58802
Discovery of the island Frivola. (17314)
Discovery of the large, rich, and beautiful empire of Guiana. 67552, 67554-67555
Discovery of the Mississippi. 31374
Discovery of the New World. 29820
Discovery of the north-west passage. 1918, (43072)
Discovery of the north-west passage by H. M. S. "Investigator." (43073)
Discovery of the polar regions. 52321
Discovery of the sources of the Mississippi. 4606
Discovery of the sources of the Mississippi River. 77878
Discovery of the true nature of schism. 24401
Discovery of this mystery of iniquity. 37185, 37194, 37202
Discovery of true religion. 79956-79957
Discovery, purchase, and settlement of the country of Kentuckie. 24624
Discovery, settlement and present state of Kentucke. 24436, 84936
Discovery, settlement, and present state of Kentucky. 24337, (34358)
Discriminating duties. 20249
Discriminating preacher. 89783
Discription of what God hath predestinated. (72095)
Discurrido por un Espanol Americano. 99676
Discurriolo el Bachiller Ignacio de Torres. 96245
Discurso a la Convencion Nacional. 39131
Discurso biografico del Senor Lino Ramirez. 87164
Discurso biografico-necrologico, recitado na Academia Imperial. 47851
Discurso breve, en defensa, de la justi[cia], e, ynnocencia. 98721
[Discurso breve en defensa de su justicia e enocencia.] 98721
Discurso civico, en elogio de Exmo. Sr. D. Agostin de Iturbide. 35290
Discurso, civico, pronunciado. 73085
Discurso cometologico, y relacion del nueva cometa. 75818

Discurso con motivo de la apertura y benedicion solemne. 31455
Discurso contra el fanatismo y la impostura de los rebeldes. 70398
Discurso contra la memoria sobre la seda silvestre. 79327
Discurso cuarto contra el caso septimo. 99476
Discurso de Ambrosio de Morales. 75568
Discurso de apertura al curso anual de botanica agricola. 74914
Discurso de Ioan de Montoya cantabro. 69210
Discvrso de la enfermedad serampion experimentada. 72813
Discurso de la engermedades de la Compagnie de Jesus. (44555)
Discurso de la vida, meritos, y trabajos del Ilvstrissimo Senor Obispo del Paraguay. 76025
Discurso de M. Pierre Soule. 87277
Discurso del ciudadano Manuel Vidaurre. 99477
Discurso del Diputado Manuel Vidaurre. 99478
Discurso del Doctor Antonio Flores. 24820
Discurso del D. D. Anjel Pachecho. 58071
Discurso del General Prim. (65521)
Discurso del Hortelano. 98147
Discurso del libertador. 6205, (66401)
Discurso del R. P. M. F. Martin Sarmiento. 77092
Discurso del tercer aniversario de la apertura del Instituto de Jalisco. (41426)
Discurso di Cesare Correnti su Colombo. 14646
Discurso doctrinal sobre la obediencia debida al soberano y a sus magistrados. 41102, 41998, 74012-74013
Discurso dogmatico sobre la potestad eclesiastica. 60878
Discurso . . . el dia 22 de Julio de 1824. 98824
Discurso . . . en el solemne aniversario de los patriotas difuntos. 96227
Discurso en la alameda 16 de Setiembre 1846. 73174
Discurso en las juntas generales de la Real Sociedad Patriotica. 99690
Discurso en las capitulares elecciones de la Provincia de S. Pedro et Pablo de Michoacan. 98719
Discurso en profesion de cuarto voto hecha p. J. M. Castaniga y Pedro Canton. 40137
Discurso . . . en que se muestra la obligacion. 20250, 63188
Discurso, en que se preueua la proposicion. 98711
Discurso en verso del estado de la misma ciudad. 48603
Discurso escrito en honor de Diego Morcillo Rubio de Aunon. 60856
Discurso etheorologico. 72506
Discurso exhortatorio. 2811
Discoure fisico sobre la formacion de las auroras boreales. 67867
Discurso funebre del Luis de Cortazar y Rabago. 81004
Discurso funebre nas exequias celebradas. (17946)
Discvrso genealogico. 88814
Discurso geologico leido en el acto de mineralogia. 71442
Discurso gratulatorio ao comprir annos a Serenissima Princeza do Brazil. 64439
Discvrso hecho sobre la significacion de dos impressiones meteorologicas. 74516
Discvrso hercotectonico. 60853

Discurso historico civico pronunciado en cele-
bridad del 27 de Setiembre de 1821.
88729
Discurso historico, geographico, genealogico,
politico e encomiastico. 35333
Discurso historico-juridico del origin, fundacion,
redificacion, derechos, y extenciones del
Hospital de San Lazaro de Lima. 38629
Discuros historico moral sobre la fundacion
y progresos. 73003
Discurso historico sobre el nuevo camino del
Callao. 97713
Discurso historico sobre los progresos que ha
tenido en Espana. 52101
Discurso historico . . . 29 de Setembro 1858.
47459
Discvrso, i alegacion en derecho. 86531
Discurso inaugural pronunciado en la reinstala-
cion del Circulo de Amigos de las Letras
de Santiago. 39150
Discurso instruct. sobre las ventajas que puede
conseguir la industria. 2125
Discurso jvridico-historico-politico, en defensa
de la jurisdicion real ilvstracion de la
prouision de 20 de Febrero del ano
1684. 41987, (61114)
Discurso juridico, historico-politico, en defensa
de la jurisdicion real sobre las obenciones
a los Indios. 41987, (61114)
Discurso juridico que propugna e informa el
derecho. (42681)
Discvrso ivridico sobre que pertenece a la
dignidad arcobispal. 99635
Discvrso legal de la obligacion qve tienen los
reyes. (63189)
Discvrso legal, e informacion en derecho.
86548
Discvrso legal militar. 51042
Discurso legal, politico, y moral. 97277
Discurso legal que en defensa de la menor
Dona Grimaneza de la Puente. 74649
Discvrso legal theologico-practico. (61115)
Discvrso legal y politico. 20250, 63188-(63189)
Discurso leido en la apertura publica. 74915
Discurso leido por Don Ramon Sotomayor
Valdes. 87253
Discurso metrico, moral y politico. 57465
Discurso moral sobre como deben haverse los
buenos vasallos. (72520)
Discurso moral sobre la augusta dignidad del
sacerdocio. 73072
Discurso panegirico del Santisimo Nombre de
Maria. 72806
Discurso para ser lido na augusta presenca de
sua magestade. 88833
Discurso patriotico, pronunciado en la santa
iglesia catedral de esta ciudad. 87209
Discurso patriotico, pronunciado en Puebla.
57102
Discurso pela fausta acclamacao d'elrei Nosso
Senhor. 66708
Discurso politico, en que se manifiesta el es-
tado del reyno. (11432)
Discvrso politico: historico juridico del derecho.
50106
Discurso politico-moral y Cristiano. 88724
Discurso politico sobre o se haver de largar
a coroa de Portugal. 39940
Discurso preliminar. 41676, 96235, 99397,
99515
Discurso preliminar historico. 47802
Discurso preliminar por Don Ventura de la
Vega. 11654
Discurso primiado por la Sociedad Patriotica
de la Habana. (73004)

Discurso proferido na Assemblea Provincial
do Rio de Janeiro. 43212
Discurso proferido na Camara dos Srs. Depu-
tados. 85655
Discurso proferido na sessao de 23 de Agosto
de 1871. 85649
Discurso pronunciado a la oficialidad por el
Senor Don Rafael Vasco. 98648
Discurso pronunciado al poner la piedra angular.
102267
Discurso pronunciado ante el Supremo Consejo
de la Guerra. 58565
Discurso pronunciado el dia 19 de Junio de
1864. 12682
Discurso pronunciado el 14 Dic. de 1862.
11426
Discurso pronunciado el 20 de Octubre del
corriente ano. 72530
Discurso pronunciado el 27 de Setiembre de
1845. (52113)
Discurso pronunciado en el Congreso de la
Union. 87210
Discurso pronunciado en el Palacio de Miramar.
29354
Discurso pronunciado en el Senado de los Estados
Estados-Unidos. (43186)
Discurso pronunciado en la alameda de esta
capital. 67326
Discurso pronunciado en la ciudad de Charcas.
96252
Discurso pronunciado en la festividad civica
del 16 de Setiembre de 1861. 41984
Discurso pronunciado en la festividad civica
de Toluca. 31480
Discurso, pronunciado en Mexico el 16 de
Setiembre de 1838. 80890
Discurso pronunciado en Mexico, el 27 de
Setiembre de 1838. 96316
Discurso pronunciado improviso por el Diputado.
99482
Discurso pronunciado por D. Jose Isidro Yanez.
105952
Discurso pronunciado por el ciudadano Andres
Quintana Roo. 73085
Discurso pronunciado por el cuidadano Jose
Rivera y Rio. 71634
Discurso pronunciado por el ciudadano Lic.
Jose Maria Perez y Herenandez. 31521
Discurso pronunciado por el Dr. D. Jose
Augustin Caballero. 9761
Discurso pronunciado por el Ministro del
Interior. 96059
Discurso pronunciado por el Presidente de la
Republico Mexicana. 31567
Discurso pronunciado por el Presidente de los
Estados-Unidos Mexicanos. 31567
Discurso pronunciado por el Senor Senador
Presidente. 76198
Discurso pronunciado por el Sr. Vidaurre.
99482
Discurso pronunciado por M. L. de Vidaurre.
99479
Discurso que dirige a la nacion el hero de
Nueva-Espana. 7074
Discurso que dirige a su grey D. Bart. Maria
de Heras. 44541
Discurso que dirige los elejidos del Pueblo
Chileno. 51407
Discurso que el dia 9 de Diciembre de 1814.
105738
Discurso que el dia I. de Enero de 1813.
50607
Discurso que en la abertura del estudio de
botanica. 39091
Discurso que en la Catedral de Longrono
pronuncio. (48041)

Discurso que en la misa de gracias celebrada. 96228

Discurso que en la plaza principal de las capital de Puebla. (70392)

Discurso que en la solemne funcion de la bandera del batallon. 10793

Discurso que fizeram duas senhoras Portuguezas. (18233)

Discurso que por encargo de la junta patriotica pronuncio. 80891

Discurso que pronuncio Augustin de la Rosa. 73160

Discurso que pronuncio el ciudadano Dr. Juan Jose Quinones. 67309

Discurso que pronuncio el dia 14 de Marzo. 96215

Discurso que pronuncio . . . el dia 27 de Setiembre de 1808. 51217

Discurso que pronuncio el Escmo. Senor General D. Jose Maria Tornel y Mendivil. 96200

Discurso que pronuncio el 1° de Setiembre de 1865. 16826

Discurso que pronuncio el Tesorero General de Tentas del Estado. 70403

Discurso que pronuncio en la colocacion en Santa Paula. 80892

Discurso que pronuncio en la sesion del 9. de Diciembre. 57187, 98176

Discurso que recitou o Bispo do Para. 88750

Discurso que se leyo en junta ordinaria de la Sociedad Patriotica. 56747

Discurso recitado no acto da inhumacao dos restos mortaes. 81297

Discurso recitado pelo Exm. Snr Doutor Joao Antonio de Miranda. 49414

Discurso sobra a utilidada da instituicao de jardins. 10100

Discurso sobre a confirmacao dos bispos. 76323

Discurso sobre a organizacao da bibliotheca popular do Maranhao. 88700

Discurso sobre as matriculas dos estudantes das escholas-medicas. (81298)

Discurso sobre el cementerio general. 19828

Discurso sobre el establecimiento de una escuela publica. (11034)

Discurso sobre el panteon. 97714

Discurso sobre imprentas y libelos escrito en Porto Principe. 99496

Discurso sobre imprentas y libelos que presede a la proposicion. 99481

Discurso sobre la acta de navegacion. 99482

Discurso sobre la centinela del reyno de Chile. 47805

Discurso sobre la constitutcion de la iglesia. (17204)

Discurso sobre la defensa de Zaragoza contra los Franceses. 73005

Discurso sobre la historia real y sagrada del Illmo. Sr. Palafox. 72557

Discurso sobre la importancia, y disposicion de leyes de las Indias. 40051

Discurso sobre la insurreccion de America. 20251, 67370

Discurso sobre la intolerancia religiosa. 96118

Discurso sobre la legislacion de las antiguos Mexicanos. 10794

Discurso sobre la lengua, y sobre el modo en que pasaron los primeros pobladores. (36806), 97687

Discvrso sobre la nvlidad del capitvlo provincial. 94819

Discurso sobre las mitas de America. 57228

Discurso sobre las ocurrencias del estado de Veracruz. 98899

Discurso sobre los males que puede causar la desunion. 19973

Discurso sobre los medios de connaturalizer y propagar en Espana. 58836

Discurso sobre los medios de fomentar. (47722)

Discurso sobre los obstaculos. 73006

Discurso sobre los tribunales militares. 93339

Discurso sobre o melhoramento de economica rustica do Brazil. 50486

Discurso sopra la navigatione. 67730

Discurso teologico-politico sobre la tolerancia. 75613

Discurso theojuridico. 80897

Discurso, y alegacion juridica por el Venerable Dean, y Cabildo de la Santa Iglesia Cathedral Metropolitana. 93331

Discursos academicos de J. V. Lastarria. 39149

Discursos de apertura en los sesiones. 12766

Discursos de J. Scoble e de J. J. Gurney. (78153)

Discursos de Jose del Valle. 98378

Discursos de la antiguedad de la lengua Cantabra Bascongada. 21764

Discursos das costas aromaticas. 25418A

Discursos del ciudadano M. L. Vidaurre. 99482

Discvrsos espiritvales. 58290

Discursos historicos, leidos en la Academa del Colegio de S. Juan de Letran. 38512

Discursos leidos ante la Real Academia de la Historia. 61328

Discursos parliamentares. 60881

Discursos politico-morales que hace el amante del Cristianismo. 100630

Discursos politicos-moraes, comprovados com vasta erudicao. 88791

Discursos populares de D. F. Sarmiento. 77087

Discursos proferidos na Camara dos Deputados. 85654

Discursos proferidos na Camara dos Senhores Deputados. 85638

Discursos proferidos no Senado nas Sessoes. 85651

Discursos pronunciados en la Camara de Representates. 63689

Discursos pronunciados en la Real Universidad de San Marcos. 41103, 99659

Discursos pronunciados en la sesion dedico a la memoria. 85762

Discursos pronunciados en las festividades celebradas. 47036

Discursos pronunciados en Mexico. 24142

Discursos que em defesa das prerogativas da Camara dos Deputados. 85650

Discursos que en ella se pronunciaron. 85751

Discursos que pronunciaron los Senores Diputados de America. (61092)

Discursos sacro-politico-morales. 105739

Discursos sobre la navegacion de los naos. 16931

Discursos sobre la propiedad de los empleos. 10796

Discursos sobre los comercios de las dos Indias. (27759)

Discvrsvm super Ophyra regione. (34105)

Discursus politicus de incrementis imperiorum. 5048

Discursus von der Spanischen monarchia. 10200

Discursz an Ihr Jon. Maj. in Spanien. (33666)

Discusion que huvo en las Cortes Espanoles. 20252

Discussao do orcamento do Ministerio do Imperio. 85651

Discussion and defence of the Lord's Day of sacred rest. (36934)

Discussion [at Danvers, Mass.] 103802

Discussion . . . between Elder John Taylor. 64962

Discussion . . . between Elder William Gibson. 64962

Discussion between Rev. Joel Parker, and Rev. A. Rood. 58705

Discussion between Rev. John L. Shinn of the Universalist Church. 80497

Discussion des petitions pour l'abolition complete. 81957

Discussion . . . do the scriptures teach the doctrine of endless punishment, etc. 80104

Discussion d'un article de M. R. de F. 62599

Discussion et le detail des chefs d'accusation. (38696), 47528

Discussion held in Lebanon, Pa. 91199

Discussion in the Senate. (1231), note after 93362

Discussion of its historical claims. 64133

Discussion of the great point in divinity. 55882, (66867), 66871

Discussion of the civill magistrates power. 17059

Discussion of the Greek question. 20253, 102264

Discussion of the harvester case. 84519

Discussion of the lawfulness of a pastor's acting. 46771

Discussion of the magnetic and meteorological observations made at the Girard College Observatory, Philadelphia. Part I. 2588, 85072

Discussion of the magnetic and meteorological observations made at the Girard College Observatory, Philadelphia. Parts 7-12. 85072

Discussion of the magnetic and meteorological observations made at the Girard College Observatory, Philadelphia. [Parts II-VI.] 85072

Discussion of the question, is the Roman Catholic religion inimical to civil or religious liberty. 33594

Discussion of the water boundary question. 76131

Discussion of the West India cyclone. 21678

Discussion on American slavery, between George Thompson. 95493

Discussion on American slavery, in Dr. Wardlaw's Chapel. 95494

Discussion on finances. 20254

Discussion on Methodist Episcopacy. 29945

Discussion on slaveholding. 20255

Discussion on the order of the Sons of Temperance. 19880

Discussion on the question, whether inhabitants of the United States born there before the independence. 68674-(68675), 3d note after 97583

Discussion ou dissertation abregee. 58549

Discussion relative to the Buffalo Hospital of the Sisters of Charity. 42032

Discussion sommaire sur les anciennes limites de l'Acadie. (47547), (56129), 62694, note after 96403

Discussion with Robert Dale Owen of the law of divorce. 28491

Discussion with two clergymen. 91677

Discussion on slavery. 7690

Discussions on the constitution proposed. 20256, 45711

Discvssionvm historicarvm libri duo. 3597, 64001

Dise figur anzaigt vns das volck vnd insel die gefunden. 20257, note before 99327, 99361-99362

Disease among Texas cattle. 83367

Diseases in the American stable. 43076

Diseases incident to armies. 94063

D'Isembourg d'Happoncourt, Francoise, Dame de Grafigny. see Grafigny, Francoise (d'Isembourg d'Happoncourt) Dame de, 1695-1758.

Disendowment condemned by the Supreme Court of America. 31669

Disensions de las republicas. 20280

Disenthralled. 26755

Disertacion academica sobre el poder temporal. 73033

Disertacion canonica. 75885

Disertacion contra la tolerancia religiosa. 42911, 50499

Disertacion critico-theo-filosofica. (59069)

Disertacion de D. Juan Bautista Munoz. (44579)

Disertacion de J. B. Munoz. 27768

Disertacion en que se manifiesta que el primer autor de todo lo expuesto. 58993

Disertacion fisica. 40062

Disertacion historica sobre la aparicion. (15162)

Disertacion historico-critica sobre la aparicion de Nuestra Senora en Tepeyac. 9579

Disertacion historico-legal sobre la memorable historia. 75998

Disertacion juridica. 76297

Disertacion leida en la Sociedad Mexicana de Historia Natural. 62880

Disertacion por Jose Maria Moreno. 50609

Disertacion que manifiesta la propriedad. 20258

Disertacion sobre el cultivo, comercio y virtudes de la famosa planta del Peru. 97715

Disertacion sobre el decreto de Tuicion. 56273

Disertacion sobre el uso medicinal. 76267

Disertacion sobre la aparicion Guadalupana, comprobada con la refutacion del argumento negativo. 9567

Disertacion sobre la aparicion Guadalupana, y con notas. 74945

Disertacion sobre la concepcion de Nra. Sra. (11454)

Disertacion sobre la fiebre maligna. 73007

Disertacion sobre la historia de la nautica. 52102

Disertacion sobre la lengua Othomi. 52130

Disertacion sobre la raiz de la ratanhia. 73992

Disertacion sobre la restitucion de los bienes eclesiasticos. 20259

Disertacion sobre que los terceros de una orden pueden serlo. 76273

Disertaciones sobre la historia de la republica Megicana. 580

Disertaciones sobre la navigacion de las Indias Orientales. 3973

Disertation [sic] on the laws of excise. 61607

Disestablished church in the republic. 32807

Disfranchisement of deserters. (20260), 69106

Disfranchisement of the inhabitants of New London. 53254

Dish no. 3. 19424

Dish of all sorts. 100636, 105178
Dish of frogs. 87303
Dishonorable peace with rebellion! 19517
Di Sigur, --------, Conte. see Sigur,
    --------, Conte di.
Disinfectants. 85495
Disinterested benevolence. 51101
Disinterested hand. pseud. Modest enquiry.
    49822
Disinterested love. 2425
Disinterested witness. pseud. Remarks upon
    Mr. Appleton's remarks on currency and
    banking. 1818
Dislere, --------. 20261
Disloyal democracy and the war. 20262
Disloyale acting of the Bermudas Company in
    London, etc. (71362)
Dismal swamp. 92410
Dismal Swamp Canal Company. Directors.
    (20263)-(20264)
Dismal Swamp Canal Company. President.
    (20263)-(20264)
Dismissal of Major Granville O. Halley.
    29886
Dismissed usher. pseud. Echoes from the
    school-room. see Reed, William.
Disney, Daniel. defendant 20265, 96858
Disney, David Tiernan, 1803-1857. 20266-
    20267
Disney, John. 5690, 20268
Disobedient lady reclaimed. 65953
Disorganization and disunion. 43631
Disosway, Gabriel P. (20269), 82281
Disowned; a tale a country life. (49699)
Disowned; or the prodigals. 83779-83780
Dispassionate inquiry into the reasons.
    (42452)
Dispassionate thoughts on the American war.
    20270, 26440, 97340
Dispatch to the governors of the colonies.
    69417
Dispatch written the 16th. January 1797.
    94304
Dispatches and other official documents.
    75200
Dispensary, Lowell, Mass. see Lowell Dis-
    pensary, Lowell, Mass.
Dispensary, New York. see New York Dis-
    pensary, New York.
Dispensary, Philadelphia. see Philadelphia
    Dispensary.
Dispensary, Providence, R. I. see Providence
    Dispensary, Providence, R. I.
Dispensary, Salem, Mass. see Salem Dispen-
    sary, Salem, Mass.
Dispensary and Vaccine Institution, Portland,
    Me. see Portland Dispensary and Vac-
    cine Institution, Portland, Me.
Dispensations of divine providence. 11965
Dispensatory, etc. 23314
Display of Gods sovereign grace. 96302
Display of God's special grace. 17675, 20056-
    20057, (20271), 95316
Display of religious principles. (59899)
Display of the characters of such flag officers.
    52070
Display of the honors. 65392
Display of the specific distinctions. 18725
Disposall of the vessell. 88229
Disposiciones commerciales vijentes en repub-
    lica Boliviana. 6197
Disposiciones legales y otros documentos.
    (20272)
Disposiciones relativas a los colegios naciona-
    les. 98873

Disposition of the commisioned ships of the
    British Navy. 91092
Disposition of the mineral lands. (30384)
Disposition of the public domain. 72734
Dispositions concernant le voyage de la colonie
    Suisse. 20273
Dispuestos por los nobles caballeros D. Jos.
    Martin de Chaves. 44893
Disputa. 11234-11235, 11237, 11239, 11285
Disputatio aduersus Aristotelez Aristo Telicosq3
    sequaces. (31564)
Disputatio de parricidii crimine. 86528
Disputatio geographica de vero Californiae situ
    et conditione. (26849)
Disputatio geographico-historica. 67386
Disputatio historica, de America. 99537
Disputatio historica secunda. 99538
Disputatio historico-geographica. 25985
Disputatio theologica de conversione Indorum &
    Gentilium. 32885
Disputatio theologica de missionibus in Indias.
    77676
Disputation concerning church-members and
    their children. (20274)
Dispvtationem de Indiarvm ivre. 86525
Disputationes ad morborum historiam et
    curationem facientes. 83648
Dispvtationvm de Indiarvm ivre. 86526
Dispute between General Greene and Governor
    Gerard. 97439
Dispute between the northern colonies and the
    sugar islands. 102832
Dispute between the northern settlements and the
    sugar colonies. 97146
Dispute that has lately arisen in this place.
    95981
Dispute touching scandall and church libertie.
    74455
Dispute with America. 16893, 20275
Disputes between Great Britain and her Ameri-
    can colonies. 41716
Disputeur, Guillaume le. pseud. see
    Guillaume-le-Disputeur. pseud.
Disquisicion historico-critica de esta tradicion.
    (67641)
Disquisitio. 59231
Disquisition concerning angelical-apparations.
    46630
Disquisition concerning ecclesiastical councils.
    46665-46666
Disquisition concerning the state of the souls
    of men. 46667
Disquisition on ancient India. 71978
Disquisition on faith. 67421
Disquisition on government. 9932, 9936
Disquisition on imprisonment for debt. (33286)
Disqusition on the evils of using tobacco.
    25315
Disquisition on the great sin of self-righteous-
    ness. 64663
Disquisitions on the present administration.
    104303
Disraeli, Benjamin. see Beaconsfield, Benjamin
    Disraeli, 1st Earl of, 1804-1881.
Disruption and fall of these states. 1342
Dis[s] buchlin saget wie die zwe[n] durchluch-
    tigsten Herre[n]. note before 99327,
    99356-99357, 99377, 102623
Dissatisfied Brethren of the Church, &c. see
    Boston. New North Church. Dissatisfied
    Brethren.
Dissecting of the sixteenth section of his book.
    50773
Dissel, S. van. 20277
Disseminator of useful knowledge. 20278

Dissensions des republiques de la Plata.
20279, note after 38995
Dissent from the Church of England, fully
justified. 96356, 99418, 103403
Dissent [of certain merchants and other inhabi-
tants of Boston.] 96754
Dissent of the minority, of the House of Repre-
sentatives of the commonwealth of Penn-
sylvania. 60070
Dissenter. pseud. Dissenter's petition. 39969
Dissenter's petition. 39969
Dissenting gentleman. pseud. Answer to the
Reverend Mr. White's three letters.
see Towgood, Micaiah.
Dissenting gentleman. pseud. Three letters
and postscript. see Towgood, Micaiah.
Dissenting gentleman's answer. 96357, 103403
Dissenting gentleman's three letters. 96356,
103403
Dissenting minister in England. pseud. Letter.
55240
Dissenting opinion of Judge Sanborn. 94519
Dissenting petition. 94719
Dissenting protestant. pseud. Letter to a
gentleman. 40387
Dissertacao historica. 11704
Dissertacao sobre as plantas da Brasil. 10101
Dissertacao sobre o actual governo. 17202
Dissertacion canonica regular. 86426
Dissertacion canonica sobre los justos motivos.
29074
Dissertacion historica y geographica. 36802,
1st note after 97684
Dissertacion sobre el origen de la esclavitud.
1702
Dissertacion sobre la facilidad de ordenar.
64101
Dissertaciones sobre la tierra. 13520
Dissertatio altera de origine gentium Ameri-
canarum. (28957)
Dissertatio brevis de principiis botanicorvm
et zoologorvm. 49694
Dissertatio de cortice Peruviano. 61226
Dissertatio de dysenteria contagiosae. 3844
Dissertatio de effectu detectae Americae in
Europam. 93987
Dissertatio de elephantiasi Surinamensi. 4352
Dissertatio de generatione et metamorphosibus
insectorum Surinamensium. (47958)
Dissertatio de linguis Americanis. 69242
Dissertatio de modo probabiliori quo primae
in Americam Septentrionalem immigra-
tiones sunt. (41825), (52385)
Dissertatio geographica de terra Australi.
(78049)
Dissertatio geographica de vero Californiae
situ et conditione. 30705
Dissertatio gradualis de plantatione ecclesiae
Svccanae in Amerika. 5664, 28916,
89174
Dissertatio gradualis de Svionum in America
colonia. 94037
Dissertatio historica, de America. 91228
Dissertatio historico-critica. 51478, 93251
Dissertatio historico politica de statu regiminis
Americanorum. 93770
Dissertatio inavgvralis medica de serpentaria
Virginiana. 27626
Dissertatio medica de cortice Geoffreae Sur-
namensis. 6293
Dissertatio medica de febre maligna biliosa
Americanae. 51140
Dissertatio medica inauguralis de abortu.
68521

Dissertatio medica inauguralis, de colica apud
incolas Caribienses endemia. 83473,
83648
Dissertatio medica inauguralis, de febre maligna
biliosa Americae. (51141)
Dissertatio medica inauguralis, de febribus
intermittentibus. 64681
Dissertatio medica inauguralis, de febribus
intermittentibus, quas, annuente Deo Ter
Opt. Max. 82773
Dissertatio medica inauguralis, de fluore albo.
(35826)
Dissertatio medico-botanica, sistens specificia
Canadiensium. 27682
Dissertatio medico inauguralis quaedam de
cantharidum natura et sus complectens.
(31033)
Dissertatio philologico-historica. 11365
Dissertatio physica inauguralis de coctione
ciborum in ventriculo. note after 74241
Dissertatio sistens specifica Canadensium.
(41352)
Dissertation a la tete sur la meme reviere.
72757, (72759), note after 93778
Dissertation against persecution. 93100
Dissertation at the public commencement at
New Haven. 52976
Dissertation, . . . before the New York State
Medical Society. (42974)
Dissertation by Dr. John Stearns. 105991
Dissertation by Francis Hopkinson. 25279,
84611-84612
Dissertation by John Morgan. 25279, 84611-
84612
Dissertation by Joseph Reed. 25279, 84611-
84612
Dissertation canonica sobre los justos motivos.
29074, 72541
Dissertation concerning inoculation of the small-
pox. 7142, 20722, 37493
Dissertation concerning political equality.
(12375)
Dissertation concerning the future conversion
of the Jewish nation. (46668)
Dissertation concerning the most venerable
name of Jehovah. 46807
Dissertation concerning the nature of true
virtue. 32955, (30648)
Dissertation critique par Dom. Pernetty.
59241
Dissertation critique par Dom Pernety. [sic]
59244, 59246
Dissertation historique et geographique sur le
meridien de demarcation, 36803, 2d
note after 97684
Dissertation, in answer to a late lecture.
(31889)
Dissertation inaugurale sur la freure jaune.
(11811)
Dissertation inaugurale sur les medicamens
Bresiliens. 59564
Dissertation of the nature and effects of lottery
systems. (13170)
Dissertation on a congress of nations. 38523
Dissertation on a north west passage. 14401
Dissertation on epidemic diseases. 96290
Dissertation on his [i. e. George Whitefield's]
character. 103588
Dissertation on Indian treaties. 84432-84433
Dissertation on letters. 57867
Dissertation on liberty and necessity. 25498
Dissertation on light and vision. 83865
Dissertation on mans fall. 51295
Dissertation on oaths. 40801
Dissertation on pure love. (24054)

Dissertation on slavery. 97375
Dissertation on the altar of brass. 104729
Dissertation on the autumnal remitting fever. 18003
Dissertation on the canon and feudal law. 240, 32551, 7th note after 97146, 97147
[Dissertation] on the circumnavigation of Africa by the ancients. (4431)
[Dissertation] on the colour of the native Americans. (4431)
Dissertation on the currencies. (34073)
Dissertation on the discovery of the Hudson River. 19198
Dissertation on the freedom of navigation. 3853
Dissertation on the image of God. (14525)
Dissertation on the liberty of the subject. 37239
Dissertation on the manner of acquiring the character and privileges. (20281), 67684
Dissertation on the manners, governments, and spirit, of Africa. (32546)
Dissertation on the methods and economies of tanning. 78006
Dissertation on the mineral waters of Saratoga. 78615-78616
Dissertation on the mixed fever. (39453)
Dissertation on the nature and character of the Chinese system of writing. 1183
Dissertation on the nature and extent of the jurisdiction. 12380
Dissertation on the nature of true virtue. 32955
Dissertation on the Oleum Palmae Christi. (10720)
Dissertation on the origin of languages. 82314
Dissertation on the plants. (43236)
Dissertation on the poetry. 93351
Dissertation on the political abilities of the Earl of Abingdon. 5008
Dissertation on the political union. 59397, 80405, 102402
Dissertation on the present conjuncture. 20283
Dissertation on the progress of medical science. 3762
Dissertation on the prophecies. (82531)
Dissertation on the prophecies relative to anti-Christ and the last times. (82531)
Dissertation on the puerperal fever. 75766
Dissertation on the qualifications necessary to a lawful profession. 3712
Dissertation on the querulousness of statesmen. 20284
[Dissertation] on the question, whether the honey-bee is a native of America? (4431)
Dissertation on the questions which arise from the contrariety of the positive laws. 41578
Dissertation on the resources and policy of California. 102640
Dissertation on the right and obligation of the civil magistrate. 2637
Dissertation on the rise, progress, views, strength, interests and characters. (20285)
Dissertation on the rule of faith. 89783
Dissertation on the same subject. (32301)
Dissertation on the salutary effects of mercury. 93167
Dissertation on the seventy weeks of Daniel. 25199
Dissertation on the source of epidemic and pestilential diseases. 43006

Dissertation on the sources of the malignant bilious, or yellow fever. 11778
Dissertation on the subject of a congress of nations. 20286
Dissertation, on the subject of procuring the education. 20287
Dissertation physique a l'occasion de Negre blanc. 46945
Dissertation shewing the necessity of asserting the principles of liberty. 78595-(78596)
Dissertation sur la caffe. 38396
Dissertation sur la commerce des colonies. (11720)
Dissertation sur la fievre jaune. 98512
Dissertation sur la fievre jaune, qui a regne epidemiquement a Saint-Domingue. 99758
Dissertation sur la fievre jaune qui regna a Philadelphia en 1793. 19815
Dissertation sur la generation et les transformations des insectes. 47960
Dissertation sur la maladie que les medecins de Saint-Domingue ont appelle fievre jaune. (4999)
Dissertation sur la question s'il est permis d'avoir en sa possession des esclaves. (24113)
Dissertation sur la riviere des Amazones. 151
Dissertation sur la traite des Negres. 4564, 81958
Dissertation sur la traite et le commerce des Negres. 4564, 81958
Dissertation sur l'Amerique et les Americains, contre les Recherches philosophiques de Mr. de P[auw.] 60994
Dissertation sur l'Amerique & les Americains, par Dom Pernety [sic]. 49239, 49242-49243
Dissertation sur le canon de bronze. 5001
Dissertation sur le fameaux crapaud de Surinam. (24121)
Dissertation sur le noisetier de St.-Domignue. 8877
Dissertation sur le quinquina. 8878
Dissertation sur le recoulier. 8879
Dissertation sur les avantages que le commerce de l'empire doit tirer de la stipulation. 42895, 101246
Dissertation sur les fruits de la decouverte de l'Amerique. 20288
Dissertation sur les races qui composaient l'ancienne population du Perou. 28058
Dissertation sur l'origine de la maladie venerienne. 76268
Dissertation sur l'origine de l'ancienne population. 23795, 40038, 101364
Dissertation sur l'origine des langues. 82317
Dissertation upon extraordinary awakenings. 68122
Dissertation upon . . . liberty and slavery. 42426
Dissertation upon tea, explaining its nature, properties, and natural history. 80572
Dissertation upon the constitutional freedom of the press. 20289, 93496
Dissertation, wherein the strange doctrine lately published. (46669), 46737, 91941, 91945
Dissertationem Dei & superiorum indultu. 100953
Dissertationem Hvgonis Grotii de origine gentium Americanarum. 38561
Dissertationem secundam Hvgonis Grotii. 38562
Dissertationes scholasticae de S. Joseph. 60846

Dissertations and discussions. 48986
Dissertations: being the preliminary part of a course. 37474
Dissertations les plus rares. 3255A
Dissertations on government. 58221
Dissertations on servitude. 77316
Dissertations on the English language. 102341, 102348
Dissertations on the grand dispute. 20290
Dissertations on the licence system and Maine liquor law. 7940
Dissertations on the prophecies. 23860
Dissertations on the statute adopting the common law of England. 99132
Dissertations sur le droit public. 20291, 61251
Dissertations upon various subjects. 39531, 80391
Dissertationum marinarum decas. 993
Dissertationum miscellanearum. 1371, (38646), 69242
Dissertazione. 51681, 106411
Dissertazione critico-espositiva. 36883
Dissertazione del P. Giambattista Toderini. 96099
Dissertazione giustificativa. 10704
Dissertazione intorno ai viaggi e scoperte settentrionali. 106409
Dissertazione sopra il primo viaggio d'Amerigo Vespucci. 10703
Dissertazione storico-geografica del Padre F. Giuseppe Torrubia. 96311
Dissertazioni. 106411
Dissertazioni epistolario bibliografiche. 10656
Dissertazioni sulla terra. 13518
Dissipation; a sermon. 26536
Dissolution of earthly monarchies. 39726
Dissolution of the American union question. 23628
Dissolution of the . . . [Public School] Society [of New York.] 54615
Dissolution of the union. 19517
Dissolution of the union. A sober address. 10889, 87818
Dissolution of the union, and its inevitable results. 23884
Dissolution of the union. Serious reflections. 87818
Dissolution of the union. Speech at the anniversary of the New York Young Men's City Anti-slavery Society. 8665
Dissolution of the union. The past, the present, and the future. 20292
Dissolving views of Richmond. 20293
Dissuasion to Great-Britain. 20294, 94006
Dissvasive from the errours of the time. (4059), 17091
Disswasive against swearing. 23
Disswasive from the errors of the time. 2762
Di Stagio Dati, Leonardo. see Stagio Dati, Leonardo di.
Distelvink. 91166
Distilled spirits and the influence of taxes. (20295)
Distinct and seuerall opinions of the late and best phisitions. 94165
Distinct claims of government. 31346
Distinct narratives of their personal adventures. 5461
Distinction between the English and Irish flag. (65308), 104247
Distinctive character and claims of Christianity. 97399
Distinctive characteristics of the pilgrims. 55324

Distinctive principles of the Presbyterian Church. 65154
Distinctive principles of the Reformed Presbyterian Church. 78250
Distinguished Calvinists and Hopkinsians. pseud. Views of religion. 99589
Distinguished citizen of "Ould Newberry." pseud. Introductory preface. 19906
Distinguished citizens of Tennessee. pseud. Letters and documents. see Blythe, S. K. Erwin, Andrew. Greene, H. Jackson, Andrew, Pres. U. S., 1767-1845. M'Nairy, Boyd. Tannehill, Wilkins. Weakley, R.
Distinguished Georgians. pseud. Speeches, letters, &c. 27111, 91254
Distinguished historian. pseud. History of the flag. 37693
Distinguished individuals. pseud. Letters. 52826, 92068
Distinguished southern journalist. pseud. Early life, campaigns and public services of Robert E. Lee. see Pollard, Edward A.
Distinguishing marks of a work of the spirit of God. 12316, (21934)-(21935), 67768, note after 102650, 102651
Distinguishing reward in heaven. 81636
Distinta descrittione della citta di Constantinopoli. 64153
Distress and adventures of John Cockburn. 14094
Distress for rent in Virginia. 100461
Distressed and bleeding frontier inhabitants of the province of Pennsylvania. petitioners see Gibson, J. petitioner and Smith, M. petitioner
Distressed damsel. 96474
Distressed people entertained with proposals. 46270
Distressed state of the town of Boston considered. 14536-(14538), 40282, 2d note after 99824, 103900, note after 103907
Distressed state of the town of Boston once more considered. 14537
Distresses of the frontiers. 59268
Distressing calamity. 71175
Distressing dangers. 80793
Distressing narrative of the loss. 39021
Distribe contra a Timonice, etc. 57735
Distribucion de las obras ordinarias y extraordinarias del dia. 56325
Distributing resevoir. 52493
Distribution des eaux. 74902
Distribution methodique de la famille des Graminees. 33765
Distribution of surplus funds. 63836
Distributive co-operation. 88819
[District court bill.] 100043, 100052
District Court of the United States for the Southern Division of Iowa. 26127
District Medical Society, Sussex Co., N. J. 93940
District of Columbia. see also Georgetown, D. C. and Washington, D. C.
District of Columbia. Board of Metropolitan Police. see District of Columbia. Police Department.
District of Columbia. Board of Registrators. defendants 89380
District of Columbia. Census, 1867. 33154
District of Columbia. Circuit Court. see U. S. Circuit Court (District of Columbia)
District of Columbia. Citizens. 48962
District of Columbia. Delegates. petitioners 20314

District of Columbia. Free Soil Association.
see Free Soil Association of the District
of Columbia.
District of Columbia. Judge of Election.
defendant 89380
District of Columbia. Laws, statutes, etc.
82086, 85445
District of Columbia. National Training School
for Boys. 20307
District of Columbia. Penitentiary. see
Washington, D. C. Penitentiary of the
District of Columbia.
District of Columbia. Police Department.
20314
District of Columbia. Reform School. see
District of Columbia. National Training
School for Boys.
District of Columbia. Supreme Court. 89380
District of Columbia. Supreme Court. Bar.
Members. see Members of the Bar of
the Supreme Court of the District of
Columbia and the United States Court of
Claims. pseud.
District of Columbia Free Soil Association.
see Free Soil Association of the District
of Columbia.
District of Columbia Ladies' Relief Association.
see Ladies' Relief Association of the
District of Columbia.
District of Columbia National Freedman's Re-
lief Association. see National Freedman's
Relief Association of the District of
Columbia.
District of Columbia Temperance Union. see
Temperance Union, Washington, D. C.
District of Gaspe. 66864
District of Maine. 93499
District of Niagara, Ontario. see Niagara
(District), Ontario.
District of the Northern Liberties, Pa. see
Northern Liberties (District), Philadelphia.
District school. 94511-94512
District school as it was. 9504-9505, (9508),
note after 103490
District school journal of education of . . .
New-York. 53646
Distrito del Peten Itza. 20315
Distrito federal, capital de los Estados Unidos
de Colombia. 60900
Distruzione del Peru. 44654
Disturnell, John. 20316-20325, 26970, 53389,
58809, 53818, note after 55831, 89905,
2d note after 96991
Disturnell's guide through the middle, northern,
and eastern states. 20318
Disturnell's United States national register and
calendar. 20325
Disunion and its results to the South. (20326),
32335
Disunion, and a Mississippi Valley Confederacy.
20327
Disunion and slavery. 68046
Disunion conspiracy. 43631
Disunion Convention, Worcester, Mass., 1857.
see Massachusetts State Disunion Con-
vention, Worcester, 1857.
Disunion document, no. 1. 8366
Disunion letter. 88496
Disunion our wisdom and our duty. 32338
Disunion policy of the administration. 31573
Disuni-on [sic] sentiment in Congress in 1794.
94495
Disunion; two discourses at Music Hall. 62528
Disunionist. 24299
Disunited states, January 1, 1834. 96073

Ditchfield, Edward. 20328, 1st note after
100449
Ditterline, T. 20329
Dittocheon. (66411)
Diuhsawahgwah gayadoshah. 20330, 105544
Diurnal and crepuscular lepidoptera. 50845
Diurnal vnd historische Beschreybung. 19152
Di Vacca, Alvaro Nunez Capo. see Cabeza
de Vaca, Alvar Nunez, 1490?-1557.
Diven, Alexander Samuel, 1809-1896. 20331
Di Venafro, Ambrogio Spinola, Marchese del
Sesso e. see Sesso e Di Venafro, Am-
brogio Spinola, Marchese del.
Divers apercus sur l'industrie de la glace.
(8149)
Divers churches in London, owning personal
election. 90613-80614
Divers documens. [sic] 99598
Divers documents addressed to the Honorable
Louis Joseph Papineau. 99598
Divers documents et communications addresses
a l'Honorable Louis Joseph Papineau.
99598
Divers epistles of the same author [i. e. Joseph
Estaugh.] 23040-23041
Divers epistles to friends in Great Britain and
America. 25270
Divers extraits relativement au lieu de l'hiver-
nement. 10620
Divers freemen of the said commonwealth.
petitioners see Pennsylvania. Citizens.
petitioners
Divers freemen of the said commonwealth beg
leave to shew. 60723
Divers Friends deceased. pseud. Letters.
40618
Diuers instructions of speciall moment. (7730)
Divers letters from America relating to Penn-
sylvania. 41762, 63318
Divers memoires touchant les Indes Orientales.
68455
Divers ministers. pseud. Sermons on sacra-
mental occasions. 79292
Divers ministers of the province. pseud.
Address. 45633
Divers of the gentry, merchants, and others,
your Majesties most loyal and dutiful
subjects. petitioners see Boston.
Citizens. petitioners Charlestown, Mass.
Citizens. petitioners Massachusetts
(Colony) Citizens. petitioners
Divers renseignements sur l'etat actuel da la
Californie. 8805
Divers sentimens et aduis des peres qui sont
en la Novvelle-France. 39950-39951,
note after 69259
Divers sermons preached for the help of dark
souls. 104107
Divers sermons preached on, Psalm XXXII.
104109
Divers views. 41718
Divers voyages faits pour la correction de la
carte. 39276
Divers voyages, touching the disouerie of
America. 29592-29593, 70792, 99281
Divers weighty and serious considerations.
20332
Divers witches, at Salem. defendants 46563,
2d note after 97085
Diversas declamaciones. (59637)
Diversas memorias del Ministerio de Rela-
ciones Exteriores. 14299, note after
93820
Diverses lecons d'Antoine du Verdier. 48245
Diverses lecons de Pierre Messie. (48243)-
48244

Diuerses lettres escrites par aucuns de ladite
Compagnie. 32027

Diverses personnes. pseud. Notes et critiques
de diverses personnes sur Atala. (12261)

Diversi avisi particolari dal' Indie di Porto-
gallo riceuuti. (20333)

Diversis litteria missionariorum. 103353

Diversity. pseud. Essays on taxation and
reconstruction. see Scott, William B.

Diversse projecten, geïnventeert door Jan van
Schagen. (77501)

Diverting history of John Bull and Brother
Jonathan. 4205, 59195

Dividing line between federal and local authority.
20691

Di Vinadio, Cesare Balbo, Conte. see Balbo,
Cesare, Conte di Vinadio, 1789-1853.

Divine, W. J. ed. (30540)

Divine (William J.) & Co. firm (71174)

Divine afflations. (46287)

Divine agency. 97477

Divine and supernatural light. 21936

Divine appointment, . . . duties, and . . .
qualifications. (49064)

Divine appointment of the seventh day. 51007

Divine arrangement respecting revivals. 89680

Divine authenticity of the Book of Mormon.
64951

Divine authority, or the question, was Joseph
Smith sent by God? 64952

Divine benevolence to the poor. 90198

Divine book of holy and eternal wisdom. 79704

Divine command and a Christian duty. (21443)

Divine compassion magnified. (14525), (46522)

Divine compassions new every morning.
(14525)

Divine condescension. 90837

Divine conduct vindicated. 27291

Divine cosmographer. (32367)

Divine discourse, representing the soul of a
believer. 41769

Divine faithfulness. 82949

Divine favours gratefully recollected. 882

Divine glory displayed in the late war with
Great Britain. 8168

Divine goodness displayed, in the American
revolution. 72473

Divine goodness to the United States of
America. A discourse. 84100-84102

Divine goodness to the United States of America,
particularly in the course of the last year.
43473

Divine government. 84416

Divine grace display'd. (7340), 85994

Divine grace illustrious. 104220

Divine help implored under the loss of Godly'&
faithful men. 8506, 94115

Divine hymns, or spiritual songs. 83398-83417,
83419

Divine institution of congregational churches.
12335

Divine institution of preaching the Gospel,
considered. (65529)

Divine judgments upon tyrants. 18104

Divine love, the source of all Christian virtue.
68122

Divine management of Gospel churches by the
ordinance of councils. 22145

Divine meditations and prayers fitted for morning and evening services. 83397

Divine mercy a cause for humiliation. 29776

Divine ordeal of the American republic. 83607

Divine organic law. (21137)

Divine origin and uninterrupted succession of
Episcopacy maintained. 80744

Divine original & authority of civil government
asserted. 96090

Divine original and dignity of government asserted. 59600

Divine poem by Mr. Addison. 103502

Divine poem, on Pharaoh to Jacob. 94891A

Divine poem, on the three persons in the Holy
Trinity. 102043

Divine promises considered and the duty of
Christians. 65589, note after 104226,
note after 104404

Divine providence ador'd justify'd. 25408,
101016

Divine providence asserted and some objections
answered. 31612

Divine providence historically illustrated.
68152

Divine providence illustrated and improved.
(73557)

Divine providence in American history and
politics. 79760

Divine providence (to appearance) visibly engaged. 44488

Divine providences noticed. 64256

Divine rebuke, being a discourse. (21133)

Divine right of Church-government and excommunication. 74455

Divine right of deacons. 25388

Divine right of episcopacy. 96123, 1st note
after 105926

Divine right of infant baptism. 18969

Divine right of infant baptism examined and
disproved. 13350

Divine right of infant-baptisme asserted and
proved. (46670)

Divine right of government. 42714

Divine right of presbyterian ordination. (25392),
78494, 103067

Divine right of presbyterian ordination and
government. (78491)-(78492)

Divine right of presbyterian ordination asserted.
102571

Divine right of presbyterianism. 96123, 1st
note after 105926

Divine right of private judgment. . . . A reply.
(24469)

Divine right of private judgment. A sermon.
83442

Divine right of private judgment vindicated.
(24469)-24470, 83436

Divine rite of immersion. (13597)

Divine song of praise. note after 65546

Divine songs, extracted from Mr. J. Hart's
hymns. 105017

Divine sov'reignty, displayed and adorned.
46571

Divine sovereignty in the salvation of sinners.
16344

Divine teaching to be sought. 16640

Divine visitations. 104967

Divine warnings. 104405

Divinity minister in England. pseud. [Letter]
from a divinity minister. 16729

Divinity of the scriptures. 59640

Divinity School of the University at Cambridge.
see Harvard University. Divinity School.

Divino narcisso. 36815

Division de la ciudad de S. Luis Potosi en
quarteles. (75600)

Division de los Aztecas. 71703

Division de los obispados de Guamanga y
Arequipa. (61116)

Division de territorio en Yucatan. 55255

Division del estado de Mexico. 87210

Division eclesiastica de este reyno. 52110,
56245

Division in Parliament on peace with America. 229
Division on labor in schools. 18120
Division of Roxbury. (73638)
Division, supineness and slavery. 86869
Divisions in the Society of Friends. 89062
Divo Maximiliano Saesari Avgvsto Martinvs Ilacomilvs. 101017
Divoll, Willard. 20335
Divorce. 83788
Dix, Dorothea. see Dix, Dorothy Lynde, 1802-1887.
Dix, Dorothy Lynde, 1802-1887. 20336-(20337), 60242
Dix, Elijah. 105366-105367
Dix, John Adams, 1798-1879. 19515, 20337-20341, 40611, 53614, 53638, 53689, 59651, 70242, 73464, 89205, 93659 see also New York (State) Department of Public Instruction. New York (State) Secretary of State.
Dix, John Adams, 1798-1879. defendant 29713
Dix, John Ross. (20342)-20346, 5th note after 96452
Dix, Morgan. 20347-20349
Dix, William. 20350
Dix, William Giles. 20351-20353
Dix-Douglas oration. 59651
Dix-huit ans chez les sauvages. 24126-24127
Dix-huit mois dans le Nouveau Monde. 57225
XVII. dialogues courts & intelligibles. 104692
Di Xara & Zegio, Pietro di Osma &. see Osma & di Xara & Zegio, Pietro di.
Di Xerez, Francesco. see Xerez, Francesco di.
Dixie. 83677
Dixie elementary spelling book. 50426
Dixie farmer. 88334
Dixie primer. 50426
Dixie reader. 50426
Dixie speller. 50426
Dixmont, Pa. Western State Hospital. Managers. 69782
Dixon, --------. supposed author 73931, 4th note after 96452
Dixon, B. Homer. (20354)-20357
Dixon, Edward H. 20358-20360, 77439
Dixon, George, 1755?-1800. 20361-20367, (47257), 52580, 64389-(64392), 64395-64396
Dixon, James, 1788-1871. (20369)-20370
Dixon, James, 1814-1873. 20368, 42865
Dixon, John. ed. 100464, 100501
Dixon, John. petitioner 100046, 100049, 100053
Dixon, Nathan F. 20371, (70667)
Dixon, S. H. 85231
Dixon, T. P. reporter 52560
Dixon, William. petitioner 20372
Dixon, William Hepworth. 20373-20378
Dixon and Nicolson. Firm publishers 100332-100334
Dixon, Ill. Annual Meeting of the North-Western Fruit Growers Association, 2d, 1852. see North-Western Fruit Growers Association. Annual Meeting, 2d, Dixon, Ill., 1852.
Dixwell, John, d. 1689. 11569
Dixwell, John, fl. 1823. 20379, 45760
Dizac, F. 20380
Di Zarate, Agostino. see Zarate, Augustin de.
Dizionario storico-geographico dell' America Meridionale. 14339

D-Ken, Agatha. see Deken, Agatha.
Dmfy, DL. (20371)
Do Justice. pseud. Dialogue. see Garretson, Freeborn, d. 1827.
Do the scriptures teach the doctrine of endless punishment, etc. 80104
Do the times demand a southern confederacy? (42869)
Doak, Johanney W. 20382
Do Amaral, Deffim Augusto Maciel. see Amaral, Delfim Augusto Maciel do.
Do Amaral, Melchior Estacio. see Estacio do Amaral, Melchior.
Do Amaral E Silva, Antonio Luiz. see Amaral e Silva, Antonio Luiz do.
Do Amaral Gurgel, Manoel Joaquim. see Gurgel, Manoel Joaquim do Amaral.
Doane, --------. defendant 29638, 1st note after 90723
Doane, A. Sidney. tr. (68923)
Doane, George Washington, Bp., 1799-1859. 5474, 20383-20393, 20395-20397, (32305), (75434)-75435, 86114, 2d note after 94139, 103093-103094, note after 104574
Doane, George Washington, Bp., 1799-1859. defendant at church court (20385), 20394, 47243, 88253
Doane, Gustavus C. 20398
Doane, Hannah. 21669
Doane, Richard, 1755-1797. defendant 92970
Doane, Richard B. 20399
Doane, Thomas. 20400
Doane, William Croswell, Bp., 1832-1913. 20401, 86114
Doane's Administrators. defendants 29638, (59653), 1st note after 90723
Dobbin, James Cochrane, 1814-1857. 20402
Dobbing, J. C. 20403, 50806
Dobbins, Peter. pseud. Political farrago. see Fessenden, William.
Dobbs, Arthur, 1689-1765. 20404-20407, (27056), 35254, 36718, 40312, 40673, 48855-48858 see also North Carolina (Colony) Governor, 1754-1765 (Dobbs)
Dobbs, Arthur, 1689-1765. supposed author 20408
Dobb's narrative of the unfortunate voyage. 20408
Dobbs family in America. 20409
Dobereiner, Philipp. ed. (79097)
Doblas, ------- Gonzalez de. 29379
Dobrizhoffer, Martin. 20412-(20414), (60857), 79162
Dobson, John. 20415
Dobson, Thomas. 22555, 32123, 40024, 50937
Dobson (Thomas) bookseller (65513)
Do Campo, Florian. see Ocampo, Floran de.
Do Castello de Paiva, A. Herculano e O Barrao. see Paiva, A. Herculano e O Barrao do Castello de.
Docimasia. 3255C
Dockham, C. A. ed. 54915
Dockstader, Jacob. 105630
Do Colitario, A. C. Tavares Bastos. see Tavares Bastos, Aureliano Candido, 1839-1875.
Do Couto, Antonio Correa. see Couto, Antonio Correa do.
Do Couto, Diego. see Couto, Diego de.
Do Coutto Ferraz, Luiz Pedreira. see Ferraz, Luiz Pedreira do Coutto.
Docteur Americain. 70330
Dr. Addington's narrative. 63082
Doctor Alonso Vazquez de Cisneros Oydor de la Real Audiencia de Mexico. Dize. 98722

Doctor Alonso Vazquez de Cisneros Oydor de
la Real Audiencia de Mexico, suplica a
V. Sonoria. 98721

Dr. Bell's letter. 4471A

Dr. Brandreth. pseud. see Hines, David
Theodore.

Dr. Breckenridge's statement. (7678)

Dr. Breviloq. pseud. Curious and interesting
dialogue. see Valiniere, Pierre Huet de
la.

Dr. Broadcloth. pseud. United States' political
looking-glass. 97983

Doctor Brownlee, versus the Bible. 80453

Dr. Busby. pseud. Edition of the Bucktail
Bards. see Verplanck, Gulien Crommelin.

Dr. Busby's edition of the Bucktail Bards.
99276

Dr. Cleaveland's statement. 13589

Dr. Codman's speech. 14137

Dr. Colman's return. 14478, 79194

Dr. Conant's letter. 15095

Dr. Cooper's defence. 87976

Dr. Cotton Mather's student and preacher.
46532

Dr. Cowdery's journal in minature. 17226

Dr. Dio Lewis's Family School for Young
Ladies, Lexington, Mass. 40791

Doctor D. Alonso de Solorzano y Velasco,
abogado de la Audiencia de Lima. 86547

Dr. D. Antonio de Texada, nacio del legitimo
matrimonio. 95136

Dr. D. Antonio Joachin de Urizar, Y Bernal,
Colegial Huesped en el Mayor, y Viejo
de Santa Maria. 98129

Dr. D. Antonio Joachin de Urizar, y Bernal.
Colegial Huesped mas antiguo. 98128

Doctor Don Baltazar Maziel, Primer Cance-
lario de los estudios publicos. 29341

Dr. D. Fermin Aurelio de Tagle, Cossio, y
Guerra, Colegial que fuel. 94213

Doctor Don Francisco de Sosa, del Consejo de
Sv Magestad. 87176

Dr. D. J. M. Solano y Marcha . . . presenta
a V. Esc. 86247

D. D. Joannis de Solorzano Pereira, Juris
utriusque Doctoris, ex Equestri Militia
D. Jacobi, et in Supremis Castellae, et
Indiarum Consiliis Senatoris; de Indiarum
jure. 86528-86529

Dr. D. Joseph Maria Solano y Marcha, originario
de esta ciudad. 86248

Dr. D. Joseph Xavier de Tembra, y Simanes,
como vno de los oppositores. 94635

Doctor D. Ivan de Solorzano Pereyra, Cavallero
del Orden de Santiago. 86524

D. D. Lvdovico de Velasco huius noui orbis pro-
regi candidissimo. 96218

Doctor Don Luis de Mendoca Catano y Aragon,
suplica a V. Excelnica. (47831)

Dr. D. Pedro Alexandro de Texeda clerigo
presbytero originario. 95139

Dr. Dwight's dissertation on the poetry.
93351

Dr. Edmund Halley's two voyages. 18336

Doctor Federico Rivas como administrado de
la hacienda del Tigre. 71614

"Dr. Francia," dictator of Paraguay. 10932,
(10933)

Dr. Francis Lieber's English verson. 40985

Doctor Gale's letter. 26351-26352

Dr. Gardiner versus James Flagg. 26630A,
95968

Dr. Gordon in search of his children. 28130

Dr. Hamilton. pseud. see Hines, David
Theodore.

Dr. has again intruded himself. 84822

Dr. Haynes. pseud. see Hines, David
Theodore.

D. Henrici Glareani Poetae Lavreati De geographia. (27536)

Dr. Hobart's system of intolerance exemplified.
36461

Dr. Howe's report on the case of Laura Bridgman. 33332

Dr. Houstoun's memoirs of his own life-time.
33198

Doctor in medicine. 84257

Dr. Inglis's defence. (34763), 58833-(58834),
99410-99411

Dr. J. Tongo's Infirmary for the Cure of Deaf-
ness. 96106

Doctor Ioan de Solorzano Pereira, Fisca del
Real Conseio de las Indias. 86523

D. Io. Davidis Schoepf. (77756)

D. Ioannis de Solorzano Pereira I. V. D. et in
regio, ac svpremo Indiarvm Senatv Consili-
arii. 86526

D. Joannis de Solorzano Pereyra, Juris utrusque
Doctoris, ex Equestri Militia Divi Jacobi.
86538-86539

D. Ioannis Svarez de Mendoza Ivrisconsvlti
Hispani. 93324

Dr. John Williams' last legacy, and useful
family guide. 104252, 104254

Dr. John Williams' last legacy, or the useful
family herb bill. 104251

Dr. John Williams' last legacy, or the useful
family herbal. 104253

Dr. John Williams' last legacy to the people
of the United States. 104249

D. Johannis Mitchell dissertatio brevis. 49694

Dr. Johns: being a narrative of certain events.
49673

Dr. Kane, and Christian heroism as seen in
Arctic voyaging. 11782

Dr. Kane's arctic voyage. 36999

Dr. Knox's new year's discourse of St. Christopher. 38162

Doctor Lorenzo de Terrones, Oyador de la
Real Audiencia de Santa-Fe. 94885

Dr. Mahan's speech. 43867

Doctor Mariano Galvez, sobre la cuestion de
Tehuantepec. 26848

Dr. Mason's speech. 45463

Docton Mondschein. 18031, 89487

Dr. Moore. 85392

Dr. Nassy's account of the same fever. 10883

Dr. Newton's columns. (55074)

Doctor of law. pseud. Appendix to a letter to
Dr. Shebbeare. see Baillie, Hugh.

Doctor of Laws. pseud. Appendix to a letter
to Dr. Shebbeare. see Baillie, Hugh.

Doctor of physick in the countrey. pseud.
Some observations made upon the Angola
seed. 86672

Doctor of physick in the countrey. pseud.
Some observations made upon the Bermudas berries. see Pechey, John. supposed author and Trapham, Thomas.
supposed author

Doctor of physick in the countrey. pseud.
Some observations made upon the Virginian nutts. see Pechey, John. supposed
author

Dictory of physick in the countrey. pseud.
Some observations made upon the wood
called Lignum Nephriticum. see Pechey,
John. supposed author

Doctor Oldham at Greystones. (31388)

Dr. Palmer's address and Mr. Street's poem.
92771

Dr. Poedagogus. pseud. Sketch of the life.
see Whelpley, Samuel.
Dr. Porcher. pseud. see Hines, David
Theodore.
Doctor Price's notions of the nature of civil
liberty. (28397)
Dr. Price's observations on civil liberty.
(4284)
Dr. Quackenburgius. pseud. Trial of Jonathan
Syntax. 96805
Dr. Ryerson's letter in reply. 74556
Dr. Ryerson's letters in reply. 74555
Dr. Ryerson's reply to the recent pamphlet.
74583
Dr. Smith's answer to Mr. Blatchford's letter.
84692
Dr. Smollett's account. 35753
Dr. Snell's historical and centennial discourses.
85391
Dr. Snodgrass' address before the Alumni
Association. 85476
Dr. Snodgrass' discourse at the installation of
Dr. M'Auley. 85482
Dr. Snow's address. 85485
D. Solomoni Schvveigkero Sultzensi, qui Con-
stantinopoli in aula legati. 17730
Dr. Spear on the Maine law. 89087, 89093
Dr. Sprague's appeal to the public. 89744
Dr. Sprague's reply. 89744
Dr. Springwater, of North America. pseud.
Cold-water-man. see Quaw, James E.
supposed author
Dr. Stearns's petition. 90962
Dr. Stearns's tour from London to Paris.
90963, 90965
Dr. Stillman's fast sermon. 91801
Dr. Stillman's thanksgiving sermon. 91808
Dr. Sullivan's poem. 93538
Dr. Syntax, Jr. pseud. New "Sartor resartus."
see Kimber, S.
Doctor Thacher's sermon. 95175, note after
102616
Dr. Thomson's academical discourse. 95559
Dr. Tucker's sermon. 97324
Dr. Tyng and others against Trinity Church.
50655
Dr. Underhill's testimony. 41298
Dr. Watt's second catechism. 69649
Dr. Williams's half-century sermon. 104360
Doct. y Maestro Don Antonio Terreros, Ochoa
. . . en el pleito. 94874
Doctria Xpiana en lengua Misteca. (24132)
Doctrina. 72811-(72812)
Doctrina a los Indios. 20420
Doctrina breve sacada del catecismo Mexicana.
58574
Doctrina breve sacada del catecismo Mexicano.
76430
Doctrina Christiana. 72811, 74946, 74953, 2d
note after 99650
Doctrina Christiana en Castellano y Mexicano.
1725
Doctrina Christiana en la misma lengua. 24105
Doctrina Christiana en lengva Chinanteca.
3594
Doctrina Christiana en le[n]gua Espanola y
Mexicana. 20416
Doctrina Christiana en lengua Mexicana muy
necessaria. 49874
Doctrina Christiana en lengua Mixteca. 24130-
(24132)
Doctrina Christiana en lengua Utlatleca. 44694
Doctrina Christiana (en Quichua y Aymara)
20417, 67161, 67163
Doctrina Christiana mvy cvmplida. 36796
Doctrina Christiana, muy vtil. 98603

Doctrina Christiana of 1584. 20417, 67161
Doctrina Christiana, y cathecismo aprobado.
42669, 98324
Doctrina Christiana, y cathecismo del Concilio
de Lima. 98324-98325, 98334
Doctrina Christiana y cathecismo en lengua
Mexicana. 49875-(49878)
Doctrina Christiana y confesionario. 84380
Doctrina Christiana y confesionario en lengua
Nevome. 2124, 84380
Doctrina Christiana: y explicacion de sus mis-
terios. 20418
Doctrina Christiana y platicas doctrinales.
20419, 57386
Doctrina Cristiana breve para ensenanza de
los ninos. 106400
Doctrina Cristiana en la lengua Abigira. 93306
Doctrina Cristiana en lengua Mexicana. 59519
Doctrina Cristiana en lengua Opata. (57387)
Doctrina Cristiana en Mexicano. 74947
Doctrina Cristiana, oraciones, confesionario,
arte y vocabulario. 57681
Doctrina Cristiana por el Dr. D. Sancho San-
chez de Munon. (76300)
Doctrina Cristiana traducida en Aymara.
76937
Doctrina Cristiana y cathecismo en la lengua
Allentiac. 98328-98329, 98334
Doctrina de la lengua de Naolingo. 106244
Doctrina en lengua Misteca. 24131
Doctrina extractado de los catecismos Mexi-
canos. 996
Doctrina Monroe. note just before (73261)
Doctrina pequena en Mexicano. 20421
Doctrina Xtiana breue y copendio. 20563
Doctrina, y ensenanca en la lengua Macahua.
51716, note after 105953A
Doctrina y oraciones Cristianas en lengua
Moseteca. 31572
Doctrinal articles, the covenant, and articles
of order and discipline. 66375
Doctrinal articles and covenant of the Richmond-
Street Congregational Church. 66362
Doctrinal controversy between the Hopkintonian
and the Universalist. 72084
Doctrinalis fidei in Mechvacanensivm Indorvm
lengva. 47341, note after (71415)
Doctrine and covenants, of the Church of Jesus
Christ of Latter-Day Saints. 83168-83174,
83177-83178, 83181-83183, 83185-83186,
83188-83189, 83192-83194, 83196-83198,
83203-83204
Doctrine and covenants of the Church of Jesus
Christ of the Latter Day Saints. 83039,
83048, 83054, 83070, 83112-83113, 83147,
83152-83154, 83156, 83200-83201, 83207-
83208, 83211, 83213-83214, 83258, 83259,
83270, 83282, 83283
Doctrine and covenants of the Church of Latter-
Day Saints. 83208
Doctrine and discipline of the United Brethren
in Christ. 97864-97865
Doctrine and formula for the government and
discipline of the Evangelical Lutheran
Church. 20422
Doctrine and glory of the Saint's resurrection.
83437
Doctrine and law of the holy Sabbath. (14525)
Doctrine and mission of Jesus Christ. (18419)
Doctrine and principles of the people called
Quakers. 104522
Doctrine Chrestienne. (39682)
Doctrine de Monroe. 11633
Doctrine du siecle dore. 64527-64528
Doctrine of a particular providence. 95610

Doctrine of a providence, illustrated and applied. 101045

Doctrine of absolute reprobation. 21657

Doctrine of baptism. 14373

Doctrine of baptisms. 19438

Doctrine of believer's baptism. 82722

Doctrine of Christian perfection and sanctification. 82776

Doctrine of Christianity. 92972-92973

Doctrine of Christianity, as held by the people called Quakers. 82872-82873, 82982, 94694-94695

Doctrine of continuous voyages. (30298)

Doctrine of convictions set in a clear light. 24387, 95579

Doctrine of divine providence opened and applied. (46671)

Doctrine of earthquakes. 58204

Doctrine of election . . . a sermon. 8641

Doctrine of election defended and supported. 103508

Doctrine of eternal misery reconcileable with the infinite benevolence of God. 92955

Doctrine of grace. 85206-85207, 103574

Doctrine of grace: a sermon. 89107

Doctrine of instituted churches. 67164

Doctrine of instituted churches explained and proved. 91945

Doctrine of justification . . . explained and vindicated. 26596

Doctrine of life, or of mans redemtion. (32666)

Doctrine of living unto God. 25478

Doctrine of merit exploded, and humility recommended. 919

Doctrine of nullification examined. 20423, 56849

Doctrine of original sin defended. 21967

Doctrine of particular election and final preseverance. 2632

Doctrine of perpetual allegiance considered. 57711

Doctrine of predestination truly & fairly stated. 5754

Doctrine of predestination unto life. 16632

Doctrine of regeneration. 88881

Doctrine of singular obedience. (46672)

Doctrine of sovereign grace opened and vindicated. 2628

Doctrine of the church. (17061)

Doctrine of the covenant of redemption. 104078

Doctrine of the cross, the only Gospel. 67746

Doctrine of the holy apostles & prophets. 37190

Doctrine of the last judgment. 24928

Doctrine of the new birth. 57350

Doctrine of the Prince of Peace and His servants. 82482

Doctrine of the Sabbath. 80255-(80257)

Doctrine of the saints' perseverance . . . &c. 68122

Doctrine of the Trinity confuted by scripture. 97836

Doctrine of the unity of the human race. 2612

Doctrine which is according to Godliness. 12335

Doctrines and discipline of the African Methodist Episcopal Church. 48181

Doctrines and discipline of the Methodist Episcopal Church. 48184

Doctrines and discipline of the Methodist Episcopal Church in America. 48182

Doctrines and discipline of the Methodist Episcopal Church South. 48183

Doctrines and discipline of the people called Quakers. 78347

Doctrines and policy of the Republican Party. 20424

Doctrines et alliances de l'Eglise de Jesus-Christ des Saints des Derniers Jours. 83221

Doctrines of Christianity made easy to the meanest capacities. 104690

Doctrines of glorious life unfolded. (11893)

Doctrines of the "abolitionists" refuted. 97639

Doctrines of the Democratic and abolition parties contrasted. 5668

Doctrines of the Latter Day Saints. 71919

Doctrines of the Society of Friends. 92323

Doctrines of the strictures vindicated. 92030

Documens communiques a l'appui du projet de lois. 20425, 27274, 96445

Documens hieroglyphiques. (58550)

Documens officiels publies par le noticioso de ambos mundos. 48593

Documens relatifs au commerce des nouveaux etats de l'Amerique. 20426, 75029

Documens sur le commerce exterieur. 20427

Document accompanying report of the Commissioners on the Georgia-Mississippi Territory. 27043

Document and analysis of facts. 89387

Document containing the correspondence, orders, &c. 50734, 83238

Document for the canvass. 20428

Document for the people. 20429, 59002, 93657

Document from the Hampshire Central Association. 97076

Document issued by the Conference of Friends. 86046

Document No. — referred to in the Governor's message. 87547

Document no. 18. 41229, 70036

Document no. 11 of the New York Sabbath Committee. 93745

Document no. 15. (43013)

Document no. V [of the New York Sabbath Committee.] 93740

Document no. 1. 87423

Document no. 7. 71283

(Document No. XXIX.) 88350

Document no. XXVI [of the New York Sabbath Committee.] 77493

Document no. XXIII [of the New York Sabbath Committee.] 86277

Document no. II. 54128

Document of the Pilgrim Conference of Churches 78129

Document pour servir a l'histoire de l'intervention Europeenne dans la Plata. 85639

Document recently printed by order of the House of Representatives. 96996, 4th note after 102623

Document submitted to the Committee. 33528

Document III. -VIII. 51921

Document 21 [of the McClellan Legion.] 78745

Document XVII [of the New York Sabbath Committee.] 77492

Documentary evidence. 82904

Documentary history of Rhinebeck. 82456

Documentary history of slavery in the United States. 81959

Documentary history of Suffield. 80124

Documentary history of the American revolution. (27277)

Documentary history of the destruction of the Gaspee. 90476

Documentary history of the Maine law. 20431, (43977)

Documentary history of the Milwaukee and Rock River Canal. 38978

Documentary history of the Protestant Episcopal Church in the Diocese of Vermont.
99204

Documentary history of the Protestant Episcopal Church, in the United States of America.
30973

Documentary history of the public affairs of the United States. 20432

Documentary history of the revolution. (25788), 87858

Documentary history of the state of Maine. (43971), 90611

Documentary history of the state of New York. (22754), 24582, 51355, 53647, (56665), 61280, 69741, (73448), 74124, 74126, 74129, 99573, 1st note after 98997, 2d note after 98997, 99573, 102983, 104441, 104442

Documentary history of the United States. 13439

Documentary introduction by William F. Goodwin. 68409

Documenti prove della sua appartebbza a Genoa. 98648

Documento curioso sobre los acontecimientos de Venezuela. 58138, 1st note after 98873

Documento importante para la illustracion de algunas de las cuestiones. 86786

Documento para la historia. 86240

Documentos. 47593, 70104, 96967

Documentos authenticos, bulas, leyes relaes. 11576

Documentos autograficos e ineditos. 98861

Documentos creados sobre platicas de paz. 55147

Documentos de la memoria de lo interior. 20433

Documentos diplomaticos presentados por el Gobierno Espanol. (20434)

Documentos diplomaticos relativos a la detencion. (20435), 38719

Documentos en que justifica la ilegalidad de la expropiacion. (20436)

Documentos estatisticos. 7568

Documentos historicos del Peru. 60804, note after 97719, 100850

Documentos imparciales y justificativos. 100640

Documentos importantes, tocantes a la representacion. 20437

Documentos importantes tomados del espediente instruido. 48438

Documentos ineditos. 16965

Documentos ineditos, siglos XV y XVI. 94352

Documentos interceptados. 20438

Documentos interesantes relativos a Caracas. 10775, (34898), note after 98877

Documentos interesantes sobre el atentado cometido. 51084

Documentos interesantes y decretos. 98622

Documentos interessantes para saber el origen. 20439

Documentos justificativos. 9564, 98379

(Documentos justificativos) 94210, 96230

Documeritos justificativos de la conducta de A. M. Moreno. 50602

Documentos justificativos de la conducte observado. 23762

Documentos justificativos de la conducta que ha observado. 52114

Documentos justificativos de los servicios. 41988

Documentos justificativos e imparciales. 20440

Documentos justificativos sobre la expedicion libertadora del Peru. 61117

Documentos literarios del Peru. 61118

Documentos oficiales de la Comandancia General del Estado de Jalisco. 35549

Documentos oficiales de la revolucion de Jalisco. 35547

Documentos oficiales publicados sobre el Asunto de Malvinas. 44177

Documentos oficiales que dan el justo concepto. 47803, 2d note after 98873

Documentos oficiales que se publican par orden del Supremo Gobierno. 48439

Documentos oficiales relativos a la conversion de la deuda Mexicana. 51475

Documentos oficiales relativos a los incidentes. (20441), 38719

Documentos oficiales relativos al estranamiento. 41982

Documentos, opusculos y antiguedades. (44650)

Documentos para la biografia e historia. 51065

Documentos para la historia de la sublevacion. 97447

Documentos para la historia de la vida publica. 98879

Documentos para la historia de Mexico. 34154-(34156), 48287, (48440), 56008, 80985, 93580, 99397, 99646

Documentos para manifestar la justicia. 76199

Documentos parlamentarios. 12766

Documentos politicos. 49931

Documentos que accompanham o relatorio. 51122

Documentos que bastam para o publico formar o juizo. 88751

Documentos que demuestran la justicia. 98900

Documentos que ilustran el reclamo de . . . Santiago Webster. 102327

Documentos que justifican el pronuciamiento verificado. 20442

Documentos que manifiestan la conducta que observo. 43217

[Documentos que refieren a su separacion del Ministerio.] 96201

Documentos que verificam a boa ou ma conducta do Bispo do Mara. 88752

Documentos relativos. 85729

Documentos relativos a la admision. (77474)

Documentos relativos a la cuestion de limites y navegacion. 20443

Documentos relativos a la deneyacion de pasaporte. 26572

Documentos relativos a la dimision que el Jeneral Santa Cruz hizo. 76770

Documentos relativos a la historia nacional. 12754

Documentos relativos a la instalacion del Presidente. 48441

Documentos relativos a la intervencion de los bienes eclesiasticos. (66554)

Documentos relativos a la legacion de los estados de Nicaragua y Honduras. 55148

Documentos relativos a la mision del Hon. Sr. D. Tomas Samuel Hood. 32803

Documentos relativos a la mision politica. 47036

Documentos relativos a la primera exposicion del flores. 48442

Documentos relativos a la reunion en esta capital. (48443)

Documentos relativos a la sublevacion del General D. Juan Alvarez. 48444

Documentos relativos a las conferencias en Jalapa. 35539

Documentos relativos a las operaciones. 10196

Documentos relativos a las ultimas ocurrencias.
(20444), 56251

Documentos relativos a lo ocurrido en el
puerto de San Juan del Norte. 76129

Documentos relativos a lo ocurrido ultimamente.
57840

Documentos relativos a los reclamos de la
Legacion de Buenos Aires. 9019,
(39845)

Documentos relativos a reclamos al gobierno
del Peru. (61119)

Documentos relativos al armisticio preliminar.
(55149)

Documentos relativos al expediente sobre
establecimiento. 20445

Documentos relativos al fondo piadoso de
missiones. 72543

Documentos relativos al ingreso y a la separacion. 48445

Documentos relativos al promovido por D.
Eustaquio Barron. 36872

Documentos relativos al tumulto de 1624.
99397

Documentos relativos y narracion del viaje
de nuestros soberanos. 47032

Documentos sobre el contrato de conversion.
61120

Documentos sobre la historia. (26779)

Docvmentos vtiles, Christianos, y politicos.
96217

Documentos verdaderos acerca de la capilla y
San Cruz. (20446)

Documentos verificativos de los servicos.
22653

Documentos y ordenes del Correo General.
20447

Documents accompanying a bill for the relief
of Anthony Buck. 8880

Documents accompanying a bill for the relief
of Harry Caldwell. 9901

Documents accompanying a bill making compensation. 40823

Documents accompaying a bill . . . providing
for the accomodation of the General Post
Office and Patent Office. (64481)

Documents accompanying a memorial of the
President and Directors of the Baltimore
and Ohio Railroad Company. 2992

Documents accompanying a message from the
President. 20449

Documents accompanying report of Secretary
of the Treasury. 15267

Documents accompanying the bill for the relief
of Isaac Briggs. (7950)

Documents accompanying the Governor's message . . . 1822. 45133

Documents accompanying the Governors message
to the Legislature. 45128

Documents accompanying the journal of the
House of Representatives of the state of
Michigan. (48730)

Documents accompanying the journal of the
Senate of . . . Michigan. 48729

Documents accompanying the message of the
President, Dec. 5, 1821. 24859

Documents accompanying the message of the
President of the United States, to the two
houses of Congress, at the opening of the
first session of the twelfth Congress.
20450

Documents accompanying the message of the
President of the United States, to the
two houses of Congress, at the opening
of the second session of the eleventh
Congress. November 29th, 1809. Printed
by order of the Senate. 83809

Documents accompanying the message of the
President of the United States, to the two
houses of Congress, at the opening of the
second session of the eleventh Congress.
November 29th, 1809. Read, and referred
to a committee. 83810

Documents accompanying the President's message at the second session of the eleventh
Congress. 83811

Documents accompanying the President's message
to Congress, Nov. 29, 1809. 34400,
83814, 83816

Documents . . . accompanying the report of the
Commissioners. 27042

Documents accompanying the report of the
Committee, on Roads, Bridges and Inland
Navigation. 60071

Documents accompanying the report of the
Secretary of State. 53956

Documents accompanying the report of the
Secretary of the Navy. 20451

Documents anciens et nouveau. 3584

Documents Americains. Annexion du Texas.
(36415)

Documents Americains. Troisieme serie.
36416

Documents and annual reports. 34509

Documents and facts illustrating the origin of
the mission to Japan. 58340

Documents and facts relating to military events
during the late war. 20452

Documents and facts, relative to military events
during the late war. 7114, 20453

Documents and facts showing the fatal effects
of interments. (20454)

Documents and letters. 57313

Documents and letters and papers showing
the nature of the services. 24046,
62051

Documents and official reports. 20455

Documents and other papers. 20456

Documents and papers. (31177), note after
91895

Documents and plans submitted by the Water
Committee. 8324

Documents and proceedings relating to the
formation and progress. 20457

Documents and records. 6965

Documents communicated to the Senate and
House of Representatives. (48730)

Documents concerning Liberia. 14732

Documents concerning recent measures of the
Vestry. 77978, note after 96981

Documents connected with the history of South
Carolina. 103051

Documents connected with the late controversy.
95079, 95093

Documents connected with the liturgy of the
Church of England. 6349, 69364

Documents containing the correspondence.
83238

Documents containing the reason. (10742)

Documents de statistique. 38719

Documents demonstrating beyond the possibility
of doubt. 20459

Documents, depositions and brief of law points.
76046

Documents destinees aux Chambres. 19270

Documents diplomatiques. 1866. 48258

Documents diplomatiques relatifs a l'annexion
aux Etats-Unis. 20430

Documents ecrits de l'antiquite Americaine.
73303

DOCUMENTS

Documents, elucidating the nature and character
of the opposition. 25220
Documents et notes bibliographiques. 19556
Documents, &c. 29575
Documents exhibiting the political sentiments
of the late and present collectors of
New Bedford. 97413
Documents explaining the failure of the northern
campaign. 20460
Documents . . . for a charter for Manhattan
College. 54247
Documents . . . from a secret agent of the
British government. 48068
Documents from the heads of departments.
95010
Documents furnished by the British government.
20461
Documents, historical and explanatory. 1667
Documents in proof of the climate and soil of
Florida, particularly East Florida. 24861
Documents in proof of the climate and soil of
Florida, particularly the southern section.
24860
Documents in relation to charges preferred.
97497
Documents in relation to difficulties existing.
34644
Documents in relation to Mark Langdon Hill.
(20226), (37853), 37856, 104779
Documents in relation to the application.
33507
Documents in relation to the attack on the
private armed brig. 26869
Documents, in relation to the Canada road.
43924
Documents in relation to the claim of James
Johnson. 36228
Documents in relation to the claim of the
executor of John J. Burlow, Jr. 20462
Documents in relation to the comparative
merits of canals and railroads. 33268
Documents in relation to the differences which
subsisted. 22270
Documents in relation to the dismissal of
David G. Seixas. 60338
Documents in relation to the European and
North American Railway Company.
(23110)
Documents in relation to the examination of
banks. (43912)
Documents in relation to the management of
affairs on the Boston Station. 96807
Documents in relation to the return of Santa
Anna. 73135
Documents in support of the right of the inhabi-
tants. 20481, 28362
Documents in the case of James Richards.
70951
Documents in the case of Thomas Brownell.
8689
Documents inedits et d'un long memoire.
34945, note after 48507
Documents inedits sur l'empire des Incas.
(38406)
Documents, legislative and executive. 1228
Documents of Anthony J. Bleecker. 5897
Documents of Major Gen. Sam. Houston.
33189, 94961
Documents of the Assembly . . . fifty-fourth
session, 1831. 53649
Documents of the Board of Aldermen. (54248)
Documents of the Board of Councilmen.
(54249)
Documents of the Board of Education. 54121
Documents [of the Cherokee Indians of North
Carolina.] 12443

Documents of the City Convention, 1846. 54250
Documents of the city of Boston. 6518
Documents of the constitution of England and
America. (7056)
Documents of the Convention of . . . New-York,
1846. (53650)
Documents of the Convention of . . . New-York,
1867-68. (53651)
Documents of the General Assembly of Indiana.
34504
Documents of the General Assembly of Louisiana.
42220
Documents of the House of Delegates for 1840.
45129
Documents of the House of Delegates of Mary-
land. 45128
Documents of the House of Representatives of
the United States. 20463
Documents of the Massachusetts Reform School
for . . . 1849. 45903
Documents of the New York Sabbath Committee.
54279
Documents of the New York Sabbath Committee,
1857-1867. 54533, 77492-77493, 86277,
93745
Documents of the ninety-second Legislature [of
New Jersey.] 53103
Documents [of the St. Louis Church, Buffalo,
N. Y.] 9063
Documents of the . . . second Legislature of
the state of Louisiana. (42219)
Documents of the Senate and House of Repre-
sentatives of the commonwealth of Massa-
chusetts. (34074)
Documents of the Senate of Indiana. 34503
Documents of the Senate of Maryland. 45130
Documents of the Senate of . . . New-York.
53652
Documents of the U. S. Sanitary Commission.
76647
Documents officiels. (70048)
Documents officiels en forme de depeches.
24677, 28133
Documents officiels exchanges entre les Etats-
Unis et l'Angleterre. (20464), 89991
Documents officiels rec. dans la secret. privee
de Maximilien. (39838), 47036
Documents officiels sur le chemin de fer
inter-oceanique. 59583
Documents officiels sur le Penitencier de
l'Est. (60079)
Documents on Indian affairs. 95011
Documents on the matter of application. 44254
Documents on the relations of the United States.
20465
Documents on the subject of British impress-
ments. 16682
Documents on the subject of the Salem Alms
House. (75708)
Documents, ordered by the Convention of the
People of South Carolina, to be trans-
mitted. 48097, 87420, 87422-87423,
87427-87428
Documents, papers and proofs. 53648
Documents prepared and submitted to the
General Court. 45712
Documents presented by Charles C. Harper.
77448
Documents presented to the General Assembly.
34558
Documents presented to the Legislature of the
state of New York. 41894
Documents printed by order of the City Council
[of Charlestown, Mass.] 12109
Documents printed by order of the Constitutional
Convention. 45713

Documents printed by order of the House of Representatives. 45714

Documents printed by order of the Legislature. 43925

Documents printed by order of the Senate of the commonwealth of Massachusetts. 45715

Documents printed by order of the Valuation Committee. (45716)

Documents publies sur cette question. 26518, note after 95460

Documents referred to in the President's speech. 20466

Documents referring to the controversy. 60072

Documents relatifs a la protection des sujets entrangers. (48446)

Documents relatifs a tous les phases. 6321

Documents relatifs au bill sur l'usure. 42222

Documents relatifs au meme traite. 27274

Documents relatifs aux tremblements de terre au Chili. 61008

Documents, relating to a recent call of a minister. 6654

Documents relating to certain calumnies against the Hon. Henry Clay. 78393

Documents relating to dividend. 53311

Documents relating to grants of lands. 104548

Documents relating to Harvard College. 30765

Documents relating to its [i. e. the Maine liquor law's] principles. 43978

Documents relating to land-grant extension. 12667

Documents relating to steam navigation in the Pacific. 43150, 104607

Documents relating to the affairs of Rhode Island. 70577

Documents relating to the Atlantic and Pacific Railroad to Costa Rica. 38354

Documents relating to the Board of Health. 54124

Documents relating to the boundary between Georgia and Florida. 27044

Documents relating to the boundary line and disputed territory. 20468, 45717, 70578

Documents relating to the boundary line between Maine and New Brunswick. 20469, 43926

Documents relating to the capture and destruction of the Frigate Philadelphia. 62408

Documents relating to the case of Christ Church. 52516

Documents relating to the city of Cairo. 9862

Documents relating to the claim of Joshua Shaw. (79938)

Documents relating to the Clergy Reserves. 10571

Documents relating to the Coal-Hill, Victoria, and Bedford Mines. 20470, (69557)

Documents relating to the colonial history of . . . New Jersey. 83979

Documents relating to the Connecticut settlement in the Wyoming Valley. 84605

Documents relating to the conveyance of land. 41891

Documents relating to the deepening of the ship canal. 75471

Documents relating to the dissolution. 25196

Documents relating to the Dominguez Grant. 20471, 95079A

Documents relating to the Galveston Bay and Texas Land Company. 16084, 94946

Documents relating to the improvement of the navigation. 49550

Documents relating to the Indians. 49850

Documents relating to the life of Gen. Jose. A. Paez. 58139

Documents, relating to the Maine boundary. 43927

Documents relating to the manufacture of iron in Pennsylvania. 60073

Documents relating to the manufactures in the United States. (20472)

Documents relating to the negotation. 34204

Documents relating to the New York contest. 20473

Documents relating to the north eastern boundary, communicated by the Governor of Maine. 84038

Documents relating to the north eastern boundary of the state of Maine. (18682), 20474-20475, (43938), 55708

Documents relating to the organization. 34318

Documents relating to the Portsmouth Company. 64435

Documents relating to the Potomac and Alleghany Coal and Iron Manufacturing Company. (64586)

Documents relating to the presidential election. 4037, 20458

Documents relating to the publication of anti-slavery tracts. (81844)

Documents relating to the resignation of the Canadian ministry. 10418

Documents relating to the separation of Maine from Massachusetts. 43929

Documents relating to the State Reform School. 46141

Documents relating to the State Prison. 45719

Documents relating to the state survey. 45718

Documents relating to the Ursuline Convent. (12110)

Documents relating to trespassers on the public lands. (43920)

Documents relating to violations and evasions of the laws. (20226), 20476, 31849, (37852)-(37853), 37856, 104779

Documents relating to Washington College. (15815)

Documents relative to a communication. 60074, 63117

Documents relative to acts of retaliation. 20477

Documents relative to an attack. 35478

Documents relative to Central American affairs. 11684, 20478

Documents relative to Dartmouth College. 18620

Documents relative to Indian affairs. 79109

Documents relative to Mr. Ryland's claim on government. (74591)

Documents relative to savings banks. 20480, 54670

Documents relative to the claim of Mrs. Decatur against the government. 19136

Documents relative to the claim of Mrs. Decatur, with her earnest request. 19137

Documents relative to the claims of Mrs. Decatur. (19135)

Documents relative to the Coast Survey. 30816

Documents relative to the colonial history of . . . New-York. 53653

Documents relative to the construction of a bridge. 33509

Documents relative to the controversy. 12051

Documents relative to the dismissal of Post-Captain Edwin W. Moore. 95005

Documents relative to the dismission of Loring D. Dewey. 19851

Documents relative to the dispute between the Trustees of Union College. 97777

Documents relative to the House of Refuge. 30640

Documents relative to the Indian trade. 34645

Documents relative to the investigation, by order of the Secretary of the Navy. 5465

Documents relative to the investigation of banks. 42195

Documents relative to the McDonogh bequest. 43177

Documents relative to the Marshpee Indians. 44819, 45720

Documents relative to the negotiation of a loan. 50890

Documents relative to the negotiations for peace. 20479

Documents relative to the separation. (56912)

Documents relative to the southern and western boundaries of this state. 45090

Documents relative to the submission to arbitration. 36462

Documents relative to the survey and improvement of the rapids. 35807

Documents relative to the usury bill. 42221, (71971)

Documents respecting Capt. Sprague's book. 86232, 89686

Documents respecting the application of Caramalli. 29944

Documents respecting the bridge. 10161

Documents respecting the claim of the persons. 34505

Documents respecting the Protestant Episcopal Theological Education Society. 53884

Documents respecting the resolutions. 5324

Documents, selected from several others. 24616

Documents shewing that Mecklenburg County. (47287)

Documents showing the division of the public lands. 43946

Documents showing the testimony given. 83239

Documents submitted by the Baltimore and Ohio Railroad Company. 2992

Documents sur le commerce exterieur. 20427

Documents sur les tremblements de terre au Perou. 61008

Documents sur les tremblements de terre . . . des Isles Aleutiennes. 61008

Documents tending to prove the superior advantages. 91539

Documents upon the "merits," etc. 46068

Documents which accompanied the message of the President of the United States at the opening of the second session. 34398, 83812

Documents which accompanied the message of the President of the United States, to Congress. 83817

Documents without comments. 56796

Documunts [sic] referred to in the speech. 13550

Docwra, E. H. 20482

Dodd, A. Charles. 20483

Dodd, Bethuel L. (20484)

Dodd, Daniel. reporter 72160

Dodd, Harrison H. defendant before military commission 96953

Dodd, Stephen. 11304, 20485-30486

Doddridge, ------, fl. 1848. 30597

Doddridge, Joseph. 20488-20491, 37611, 97028

Doddridge, Philip, 1702-1751. 7339, 83419

Doddridge, Philip, 1772-1832. 20492

Dodge, ------. see Kimball & Dodge. comps.

Dodge, Allen W. (20494)

Dodge, Augustus Caesar, 1812-1883. 20493

Dodge, David Low, 1774-1852. 20495, 47645

Dodge, G. M. (20496)

Dodge, Henry, 1782-1867. (20497), 96706, 96712-96713, 96720 see also U. S. Commissioner to the Chippewa Indians. U. S. Commissioner to the Confederate Tribes of Sauk and Fox Indians. U. S. Commissioner to the Menominee Indians. U. S. Office of Indian Affairs. Wisconsin (Territory) Governor, 1841-1848 (Dodge)

Dodge, J. G. 20498

Dodge, Jacob Richards, 1823-1902. 20499-20500, 50196

Dodge, John. 20501

Dodge, John. plaintiff 96859

Dodge, Joshua. 20502

Dodge, Mary Abigail, 1833-1896. 20503-20506, 52305, 57942, 76692

Dodge, Mary Elizabeth (Mapes) 1831-1905. (75446), 83959

Dodge, Nehemiah. 20507

Dodge, N. S. (20508)

Dodge, Oliver. 63946, 94075, 102523

Dodge, Paul. 20509

Dodge, Peter. petitioner 97898

Dodge, Robert. 20510-20511, (45211A)

Dodge, W. B. (3754)

Dodge, W. C. (20512)

Dodge, William Earl, 1805-1883. 20513-20514

Dodge, William Sumner. 20515-20516, 32159

Dodington, George Bubb. see Melcombe, George Bubb Dodington, Baron, 1691-1762.

Dods, J. B. plaintiff 83585

Dodsley, Robert, 1703-1764. 1614, 11128, 20517-20518, 26851

Dodsley, Robert, 1703-1764. supposed author 20517, 25413, note after 74817-74818, 90222, note before 90250-90286

Dodson, Charles W. 20519

Dodsworth, Edward. 66686

Doe, John. pseud. Letter to John Jones. 61779

Doedes, J. I. 20520

Doeg, the Edomite. 3500

Doehn, R. 20521

Doell, -----. (20522)

Does it answer? Slavery in America. 73089

Does matter do it all? 76966

Does slavery Christianize the Negro? 31755

Does the Bible sanction polygamy! 64953

Does the Bible sanction American slavery? 82676

Does the Bible sanction slavery? A discourse. 22104

Doues the Bible sanction slavery? . . . Examination into the Egyptian, Mosaic, and American systems of service and labor. 59464

Does the constitution of the United States sac sanction slavery? 43141

Does the country require a national armory? (20523)

Doesticks, Q. K. Philander. pseud. Doesticks what he says. see Thomson, Mortimer, 1832-1875. and Underhill, Edward Fitch, 1830-1898.

Doesticks, Q. K. Philander. pseud. History and records of the Eliphant Club. see Thomson, Mortimer, 1832-1875. and Underhill, Edward Fitch, 1830-1898.

Doesticks what he says. 95592

Dog and the sportsman. 81614

D'Oge, Mort. 94901

Doggett, David Seth, 1810-1880. 20524-20526, 66968

Doggett, John, Jr. 20527-20528, 54298, 54459

Doggett, Simeon. (20529)

Doggett, Thomas. 20530

Doggett, Theophilus P. 20531

Doggett's New York city directory. 54459

Doggett's New York city street directory. 54459

Doggett's United States railroad and ocean steam navigation guide, for 1848. 54459

Doggett's United States railroad & ocean steam navigation guide, illustrated with a map. 20528

Dogherty, Roger. (80868)

Dogma socialista de la Asociacion Mayo. 21772

Doheny, Michael, 1805-1862. 20532-20533

D'Ohsson, ------. see Ohsson, ------ d'.

Doige, ------. (50260)

Doings of the American Commissioners at Paris. (20534)

Doings of the Council at their sitting at Fort George, Dec. 19, 1727. 20536

Doings of the Council at their sitting at Fort George, Nov. 25, 1727. 20535

Doings of the Council of the Massachusetts Temperance Society. 45909

Doings of the first Editors and Publishers' Convention in Maine. 32471

Doings of the fourth National Exhibition of Horses. 89858

Dr. A. Petermanns Mitteilungen. 99362

Dr. Heinrich Berghaus' physikalischer Atlas. 4857

Dr. Karl Follen. 8875

Dr. Martin Luther sie klein Katechismus. 64913

Dr. von Spiz und Dr. von Martius Reise in Brazilien. Zur Belehrung und Unterhaltung fur die Jugend. 38241

Dr. von Spiz und Dr. von Martius Reise in Brasilien . . . fur die Jugend. 89548

Do Lago, Antonio Bernardino Pereira. see Lago, Antonio Bernardino Pereira do.

D'Olarte, D. see Olarte, D. d'.

Dole, Anna Greenleaf. 20537

Dole, Benjamin. 20538-20539

Dole, George T. 20540

Dole, Isaiah. (20541)

Dole, Richard. 97311

Doleances d'un citoyen. 47202

Doleful state of the damned. (50312)

Doleful tragedy of the raising of Jo. Burnham. 37356, note after 95797, 10th note after 95843

Dolfus, A. 20542

D'Oliveira, H. V. see Oliveira, H. V. d'.

D'Oliveyra, Francisco Xavier. see Oliveyra, Francisco Xavier d'.

Dollar, William. 104840

Dollar magazine. 84982

Dollar weekly magazine. 73524

Dollier de Casson, Francois. supposed author 67023

Dolores: a historical novel of South America. 30606

Dolores: a tale of disappointment and distress. 72053

Dolores. Novela historica. 27755

Dolph, Eliza. 23841, 92191

Dolphia (Ship) in Admiralty 5097, 61179

Dom. M. Manni de Florentinis inventis commentarium. 44348

Dom Pernety's [sic] historical journal. 6870

Domairon, Louis. 20543-(20544), note after 68456

Domairon, Louis. supposed author 19359-19361, 3d note after 100846

Domby. pseud. No thoroughfare. see Dunham, Robert Carr.

Domenech, Emanuel. 20545-20556, 47415, 61309-61310, 85781

Domenen las reyes soberanas a los jueces prevaricadores. 87217

Domenichi, L. tr. 27478

Domestic and Foreign Missionary Society of the Protestant Episcopal Church in the U. S. 12891, 84358, 84359-84362, 84365

Domestic and foreign relations of the United States. 58694

Domestic and political tragedy. (2818), 19455, 86512

Domestic drama, in six acts. 92513

Domestic history of the American revolution. 22210

Domestic legend. 81199

Domestic life of Thomas Jefferson. (67854)

Domestic manners and social condition. 10937

Domestic manners, etc., of the West Indies. (28572)

Domestic manners of the Americans. 97028

Domestic manners of the Americans; or, characteristic sketches. 97914

Domestic Missionary Society, Franklin County, Mass. see Franklin County Domestic Missionary Society.

Domestic Missionary Society, Providence, R. I. see Providence Domestic Missionary Society.

Domestic Missionary Society of Massachusetts. see Massachusetts Domestic Missionary Society.

Domestic Missionary Society of Richmond, Va. see Richmond Domestic Missionary Society.

Domestic Missionary Society of South Carolina. see South Carolina Domestic Missionary Society.

Domestic Missionary Society of Vermont. see Vermont Domestic Missionary Society.

Domestic missions of the Protestant Episcopal Church. 66143

Domestic narrative, illustrating the peculiar doctrines of George Fox. 28915

Domestic narrative of the life of Samuel Bard. 43673

Domestic romance. 74170

Domestic scenes in Greenland and Iceland. 20557, 28640

Domestic Secretary of the United Foreign Missionary Society. see United Foreign Missionary Society. Domestic Secretary.

Domestic service illustrated. 78786-78787

Domestic slavery considered as a scriptural institution. (26170), 82785

Domestic story. (81202)-81203

Domestic tale from real life. 1025924A-102593

Domestic tale of the present time. 58961

Domesticus. pseud. Letter. 98980

Domeyko, Ignacio. 20558-(20561)

Domination Espagnole et guerre d'independance. 4084

Doming Y Ramirez, Manuel Maria. see Ramirez, Manuel Maria Doming y.

Domingo de la Anunciacion. 1725, 20563

Domingo de la Calzada, Saint, d. 1109? 67652

Domingo de Santo Tomas. 20564-(20565)

Domingo de Santo Tomas. incorrectly supposed
   author 100643
Domingo, Antonio Santo. see Santo Domingo
   Antonio.
Domingo, Garcia de Santo. see Santo Domingo,
   Garcia de.
Domingo. 20562
Dominguez, Francisco. (20566)-20567, 106244
Dominguez, Francisco Eugenio. 20568
Dominguez, J. F. 20569
Dominguez, Jose. 25104
Dominguez, L. 49757
Dominguez, Luis L. 20570-20571, 98596
Dominguez de Mazariegos, Mariano Robles.
   see Robles Dominguez de Mazariegos,
   Mariano.
Dominic, Saint. see Domingo de la Calzada,
   Saint, d. 1109?
Dominica, from an actual survey. 20572
Dominicain de la Martinique. pseud. Lettre.
   44977
Dominican Republic. 75191
Dominican Republic. Constitution. 20573,
   (75085)
Dominican Republic. Laws, statutes, etc.
   20576, 75156-75157
Dominican Republic. Legislature. (20578)
Dominican Republic. President, 1846. 20576
Dominican Republic and the Emperor Soulouque.
   8075, 20574
Dominicans. 20576, (20580)-20581, 29497,
   40686, 64859, 68895, 68937-68938,
   98642
Dominicans. petitioners 68895
Dominicans. Magistro General. see also
   (20580), 29497 Chiense, Vicent Justinian.
Dominicans. Vicar General. defendant 96417
   see also Valdespino, Juan de. defendant
Dominicans. Mexico. (20580), 29497, 65401,
   66544, 86411 see also Dominicans.
   Province of Gvaxaca. Dominicans.
   Province of San Hipolyto Martyr de
   Oaxaca. Dominicans. Province of
   Santiago.
Dominicans. Mexico. plaintiffs 86421
Dominicans. Mexico. Procurador General.
   petitioner 106408
Dominicans. Mexico. Provincial. 65401
   see also Barreda, Domingo.
Dominicans. Province of California. 38381,
   56007, (75765)
Dominicans. Province of Gvaxaca. Juez
   Conservador. plaintiff 106003A see
   also Ybanes, Diego. plaintiff
Dominicans. Province of Lima. 61074
Dominicans. Province of San Antonio de el
   Nuevo Reyno de Granada. plaintiffs
   96052
Dominicans. Province of San Antonio de el
   Nuevo Reyno de Granada. Provurador
   General. plaintiff 96052 see also
   Tobar, Pedro de. plaintiff
Dominicans. Province of San Hipolyto Martyr
   de Oaxaca. plaintiffs 56403, 86409,
   86418
Dominicans. Province of San Juan Bautista del
   Peru. Procurador General. petitioner
   87224-87225 see also Soto, Pedro de.
   petitioner
Dominicans. Province of Santiago de Mexico
   86417
Dominicans. Province of Santiago de Mexico.
   Abogado. 86417 see also Solis, Fran-
   cisco Lopez de, d. 1664.

Dominicans. Province of Santiago de Mexico.
   Procurador General. plaintiff 96417
   see also Bezerra, Hernando. plaintiff
Dominicans. Province of the Indies. 29497
Dominicans. Province of Toulouse. 40686
Dominie Nicholas Aegidius Oudenarde. pseud.
   Book of Saint Nicholas. see Paulding,
   James Kirke, 1778-1860.
Dominikus, J. tr. 2090
Dominio temporal del Papa. 14547
Dominion of providence over the passions of
   men. 104931, 104934
Dominion of the Prince of Peace. 744
Dominique. 26009
Dominus Jesvs. 50108
Do Monte Rodrigues de Araujo, Manuel. see
   Monte Rodrigues de Araujo, Manuel do,
   Bp., 1798-1863.
Domschcke, Bernhard. (20582)
Domus, Victor. 20583
Don, David, 1799-1841. 38727
D. Alonso de la Cueva, Ponze de Leon en los
   autos. 63968
Don Alonso de Sotomayor, dize, que las tierras.
   87237
Don Alonso de Sotomayor, dize que son tan
   fuertes y concluyentes. 87238
Don Alvarez, oder die Entdeckung von Brasilien.
   9809
Don Alvaro Velazquez. 98816
Don Augustin Arambul, su biografia. 86380
D. Bartholomaei de las Casas, Episcopi Chai-
   pensis. 11237, 39118
Don Bonifacio. (48993)
Don Carlos, sa vie et sa mort. 65295
Don Diego Rosa. 20584
Don Experientia. pseud.?? 93872
D. F. Michele de Bulhoens dell' Ordine de
   Predicatori. (63902), (63904)
Don Fadrique, Gran Maestre de Santiago.
   29058
Don Francisco de Solis Ossorio, Vezino, y
   Procurador General. 86438
Don Francisco de Varas y Valdes. 98594
D. Francisco Dionisio Vives, Caballero Gran
   Cruz de la Real Orden Americana del
   Isabel la Catolica . . . habitantes de la
   isla de Cuba. 100634
Don Francisco Dionisio Vives, Caballero Gran
   Cruz de la Real Orden Americana del
   Isabel la Catolica . . . Mariscal de Campo.
   100635
Don Francisco Xavier Maria de Urrutia. 98155
Don Francisco Xavier Venegas de Saavedra,
   . . . Virey, Gobernador y Capitan General
   de esta N. E. . . . Ayamo moyolpachi-
   huitia. 98850
Don Francisco Xavier Venegas de Saavedra
   . . . Virey, Gobernador y Capitan General
   de esta N. E. . . . Entre los infames
   medios. 98851
Don Francisco Xavier Venegas de Saavedra
   . . . Virey, Gobernardor y Capitan
   General de esta Nueva Espana . . .
   Habiendo llegado a mis manos. 98853
Don Francisco Xavier Venegas de Saavedra
   . . . Virey, Gobernardor y Capitan
   General de esta N. E. . . . Habiendo
   tenido los rebeldes. 98852
Don Felipe el Prvdente. 30079
Don Giovanni. 64014
Don Henriquez de Castro. 20585, 31381
D. Ioan de Solorzano Pereyra, Cavallero del
   Orden de Santiago, del Consejo de Sv
   Magestad en el Svpremo de Castilla, y

de las Indias, Ivnta de Gverra dellas, y
de las Minas. Obras posthvmas. 86542
D. Ioan de Solorzano Pereyra, Cavallero del
Orden de Santiago, del Consejo de Su
Magestad en el Supremo de Castilla, y
de las Indias, Junta de Guerra dellas, y
de las Minas. Obras varias. 86543
Don John further display'd. 15962, 20586
Don Jose Ildefonso Suarez. 93301
Don Jose Maria Villasenor Cervantes. 99677
D. Joseph Antonio de Yarra. [sic] 105987A
D. Joseph de Araujo y Rio. 71451
D. Joseph de Yturrigaray. 106220B
D. Juan Antonio Velarde, y Cienfuegos. 98785
Don Juan Bautista Munoz Geschichte der Neuen
Welt. 51344
Don Juan, cantos XVII. and XVIII. 13504
Don Juan Martin Munoz. 86379
Don Juan Perez de Guzman. 79781
Don Junipero. (36901)
Don Lucas Alaman. 71448
Don Luys de Velasco, Cauallero de la Orden
de Sanctiago. 98796
Don Lvys de Velasco, Causallero [sic] de la
orden de Sanctiago. 98795
Don Manuel Abad Queipo . . . Obispo . . . de
Michoacan: a todos sus habitantes pas y
salud. (67080)
Don Manuel Abad Queipo . . . Obispo . . . de
Michoacan, a todos sus habitantes salud
y paz. (67080)
Don Manuel Abad Queipo . . . Obispo Electo.
(67080)
Don Manuel Solorzano Dieguez. 86517
Don Pablo de Olavide. 39280
Don Paez, and other poems. 65438, 3d note
after 100577
D. Pedro Alonso Davalos, Bracamonte, y
Espinosa. 98609
Don Pedro de Toledo y Leyva. 96119
Don Pedro Quaerendo Reminisco. pseud.
Life in the Union Army. 41019
D. Petri de Villagomez. 99634
Don Phelipe . . . Por quanto en atencion a las
repetidas instancias. (76858)
Don Quixote. pseud. Ichneumon. see Tupper,
------.
Don Quixote at college, &c. 101339
Don Quixots at college. 20587, note after
97428
Don Quizotes at college. 20587, note after
97428
D. Salvador Jose de Muros y Salazar. 86817
D. Santos Degollado. (19299)
Don-Yague, Francisco de Cubillas. see
Cubillas Don-Yague, Francisco de.
Dona Ana County, N. M. Citizens. defendants
76778
Dona Clara Verdad. pseud. Coleccion de los
dialogos criticos. see T., G. pseud.
Dona Juana Valiente. pseud. Coleccion de los
dialogos criticos. see T., G. pseud.
Donaldson, ------. plaintiff 130160
Dolandson, Arthur. supposed author 96039
Donaldson, J. L. 20588
Donaldson, James, fl. 1700. 20589
Donaldson, James, fl. 1706. 69520
Donaldson, John I. 45058
Donaldson, Nanna (Smithwick) ed. 85099
Donaldson, Paschal. ed. (56695)
Donaldson, S. J. tr. 88698
Donaldson, Thomas. 20590, (45211A)
Donaldson, W. 20591, 55526
Donallan, John Whiting. 20592
Donance, Phelim. 94518

Do Nascimente Silva, Josino. see Silva, Josino
do Nascimento.
Donation hymn. 105557
Donations. 102680
Donativo de miedo de pesos. 51351
Donck, Adriaen van der, d. 1655. 5045,
(15186), (20593)-20597, 47472, 69996,
83982, note after 98474, note after 99310,
102887
Donde vamos a parar? 26765
D'onder-aardse wereld. 37968
Doney, T. engr. 84905
Dongan, Thomas. see Limerick, Thomas
Dongan, Earl of, 1634-1715.
Dongo, Joachin Antonio. 44893
Doniphan, A. W. (82343)
Doniphan County Kansas, history and directory.
83736
Doniphan's campaign. 10188, 21920
Doniphan's expedition. (33596)
Donis, Nicolaus. cartographer (66472)-(66476),
(66478)
Donkin, R. 20598
Donn, J. W. 84774
Donna Florida. A tale. 81206
Donnant, D. F. (20599)
Donnavan, C. 20600
Donne, John, 1573-1631. (20601), 1st note after
99888
Donne, M. A. 77457
Donne, W. Bodham. ed. 26994
Donnelly, Ignatius, 1831-1901. 20602
Donnelly, James P. defendant 20603
Donnelly, T. J. 20603
D. D. Dissertatio medico-botanica. 27682
Donoho, Joy, & Co. firm 20604
Donop, Wilhelm Gottlieb Lev., Freiherr.
20605
Donoso, Justo, Bp., 1800-1868. 20606
'Don't give up the ship.' 24788
Doolittel, Thomas. 20607
Doolittle, A. illus. 36666, 97181
Doolittle, James Rood, 1815-1897. 1253, 15188,
19593, 20609-(20611), 52127, 78028,
83029, 89214
Doolittle, Benjamin. 20608
Doolittle, Mark, d. 1855. 20612, 105842
Doolittle, Thomas. 20613-20614
Doom of slavery in the union. 20615, note
after 96378
Doom of the crescent. 95476
Doom of the tory's guide. (18061)
Doomed chief. 95476
Doomed hunter. 7061
Doomed ship. (34021)
Doop-boek. 77592
Door, E. P. 9056, note after 95451
Door, Mrs. J. C. R. 37278
Door County, Wisc. Board of Supervisors.
70083
Door of heaven opened and shut. 25370
Door opened for equal Christian liberty. 2632
Do Para, Manoel da Costa. see Costa do
Para, Manoel da.
D'operations trigonometriques. (33757)
Dopler, Carl Emile, 1824-1905. illus. 32741-
81066
Doppelung. 64600
Do Quintal, Joao Dias. see Quintal, Joao Dias
do.
Dorado, Manuel. 6200
Dorado; being a narrative. 98513
Doran, J. 20616
Dorat, ------. 20617
Doraway, Jeffrey. 47467

D'Orbigny, Alcide. see Orbigny, Alcide d'.
Dorcas Society, Philadelphia. see Philadelphia.
Tenth Presbyterian Church. Dorcas
Society.
Dorcas Society of the Tenth Presbyterian Church,
Philadelphia. 61608
Dorchester, Dudley Carleton, Viscount, 1573-
1632. 10901
Dorchester, Guy Carleton, 1st Baron, 1724-
1808. 10904, 67002, 98065C see also
Canada. Governor General, 1768-1778
(Dorchester) Canada. Governor General,
1786-1796 (Dorchester)
Dorchester, Mass. 20623, (20628), 1st note
after 101877
Dorchester, Mass. Antiquarian and Historical
Society. see Dorchester Antiquarian and
Historical Society, Dorchester, Mass.
Dorchester, Mass. Auditor. (20628)
Dorchester, Mass. Barnard Freemen's Aid
Society. see Barnard Freemen's Aid
Society, Dorchester, Mass.
Dorchester, Mass. Board of Health. (20628)
Dorchester, Mass. Celebration of the Two
Hundred and Seventy-Ninth Anniversary
of the Settlement of Dorchester, 1909.
103397
Dorchester, Mass. Church of Christ. 7095,
(20624)-20625, (20628), 69500, note after
93769
Dorchester, Mass. Ecclesiastical Council,
1773. see Congregational Churches in
Massachusetts. Ecclesiastical Council,
Dorchester, 1773.
Dorchester, Mass. First Parish. (20628)
Dorchester, Mass. Gibson Division, no. 21,
Sons of Temperance. see Sons of
Temperance of North America. Massa-
chusetts. Gibson Division, no. 21, Dor-
chester.
Dorchester, Mass. Historical Society. see
Dorchester Historical Society, Dorchester,
Mass.
Dorchester, Mass. Industrial School for Girls.
see Massachusetts. Industrial School
for Girls, Dorchester
Dorchester, Mass. July Fourth Celebration,
1855. (20618)
Dorchester, Mass. Mount Hope Cemetery.
(20628), (51160)
Dorchester, Mass. New South Meeting House.
Proprietors. 10743, 20621, (20626),
(20628)
Dorchester, Mass. Ordinances, etc. (20628)
Dorchester, Mass. Proceedings Relative to
the Death of Washington, February 22,
1800. 20623, 23285, 101594, 101810, 1st
note after 101877
Dorchester, Mass. School Committee. (20628)
Dorchester, Mass. Second Church and Parish.
20622, (20626)
Dorchester, Mass. Selectmen. (20628)
Dorchester, Mass. Soldiers' Monument.
(20628)
Dorchester, Mass. Special Committee on
Schools. (20628)
Dorchester, Mass. Union Lodge. see Free-
masons. Massachusetts. Union Lodge,
Dorchester.
Dorchester and Quincy directory, for 1868-9.
67294
Dorchester Antiquarian and Historical Society,
Dorchester, Mass. 5777, 13209, 46777
Dorchester Antiquarian and Historical Society,
Dorchester, Mass. Committee. (20619)

Dorchester-Cemetery memorial. 18696, 20627,
2d note after 79628
Dorchester Company. 95638
Dorchester day, celebration of the two hundred
and seventy-ninth anniversary of the
settlement of Dorchester. 103397
Dorchester Historical Society, Dorchester, Mass.
103397
Dorchester in 1639, 1776, and 1855. (20618)
Dorchester, Jan. 15, 1822. 91368
Dorchester McClellan Club. (20628) see also
Democratic Party. Massachusetts.
Dorchester.
Dorchester Mining Company. (20628)
Dorchester, past and present. 47251
Dorchester Temperance Society. (20628)
Dordrecht, Netherlands. 35653
Dore, Gustave, 1832-1883. Illus. 12238,
12241, 44160, 69048, 69075
Dore, James. 20629
Do Rego Abranches, Antonio Manuel. see
Rego Abranches, Antonio Manuel do.
Do Rego Barreto, Luis. see Rego Barreto,
Luis do.
Doremus, J. C. 20630
Doremus, Noah. defendant 96945
Doren, Isaac van. see Van Doren, Isaac.
Doriol, -------. 20631
Dorion, A. A. 20632
Dorking emigrants, who went to Upper Canada.
pseud Letters. 3355, 98083
D'Orleans, Francois Ferdinand Philippe Louis
Marie. see Joinville, Francois Ferdinand
Philippe Louis Marie d'Orleans, Prince
de, 1818-1900.
D'Orleans de Rothelin, -------. see Rothelin,
-------.
Dormant powers of the government. 9113
Dormenon, Pierre. 20633
Dorn, Earl van. see Van Dorn, Earl.
Dorn, Robert C. defendant 20634
Dornier, -------. 75173
Do Rosario, Antonio. see Rosario, Antonio do,
d. 1703.
Do Rosario, Paulo. see Paulo do Rosario.
Dorph, N. V. tr. 17877
Dorr, Benjamin. 20635-20638, 61535, 62093
Dorr, David F. (20639)
Dorr, E. P. 9056
Dorr, Edward. (20640)-20641
Dorr, Elisha. 95942
Dorr, F. W. 84774
Dorr, Herbert C. 20642
Dorr, James A. 20643-(20644)
Dorr, Theodore H. (20645)
Dorr, Thomas Q. (70653)
Dorr, Thomas Wilson, 1805-1854. defendant
20646-(20647), 20649, 70508, 70537, note
after 96509, 1st note after 97484
Dorr, Thomas Wilson, 1805-1854. plaintiff
(20647), note after 96509
Dorrance, ---------. defendant (59056)
Dorrance, John. defendant 20652
Dorrance, John. plaintiff 20652
Dorriad. 20653
Dorr-ianna. 20654
Dorset, John Frederick Sackville, 3d Duke of,
1745-1799. 38137
Dorsey, Anna Hanson. 20655
Dorsey, Clement, 1778-1846. 20656, 45150,
45271
Dorsey, Dennis B. 20657
Dorsey, J. 102641
Dorsey, John L. 20658-20659
Dorsey, Sarah A. 20660
Dort (Synod) (72095), 72110

D'Orto, Garcia. see Orto, Garcia d'.
Dorval; or the speculator. 105057
D'Orville, Andre Guillaume Contant. see
Orville, Andre Guillaume Contant d'.
Dorvo-Soulastre, ------. 20661
Do Sacramento, Leandro. see Leandro do
Sacramento.
Dosal, Juan Bautista. 76105
Dos anos de gobierno en America. 51843
Dos anos en Mejico. 20662
Dos cartas escritas de vn Missionero. 16666,
47172
Dos cartas escritas por el Ilmo. y Excmo.
Sr. D. Juan Antonio de Vizarron, y
Eguiarreta. 100637
Dos cartas mesajeres a los reyes. 57714
Dos cartas muy devotas. (16667)
Dos cartas pastorales. 94275
Dos discursos del General Washington. 16060
Dos Guimaraens Peixoto, Ribeiro. see Peixoto,
Ribeiro dos Guimaraens.
Dos ilustres sabios vindicados. 59330
Dos Indios naturales del Pire-Mapu. pseud.
Cartas pehuenches. see Milillanca y
Guanalcoa, --------.
Dos libros, en vno que trata de todas las
cosas. 49936
Dos manifiestos. 35299
Dos pactos religioso i politico. 76699
Dos palabras a los Espanoles de Cuba. 86381
Dos palabras al Escmo. Presidente de la
republica. 58174
Dos palabras en honor de Queretaro. (67103)
Dos palabritas al oido a los malos escritores.
94150
Dos poetas. 58338
Dos politicas en candidatura. (20663)
Dos relaciones hechas al mismo cortes. 3350
Dos Robinsones. 38402
Dos sermones. 75612
(Dos sermones) predicado 23 de Marzo y 18 de
Mayo de 1698. 75609
Dosal, Juan Bautista. 76105
Dose for the doctor. 84822
Dos Homens, Francisco da Mae. see Homens,
Francisco da Mae dos.
Dos Reis Quita, Domingos. see Quita, Domin-
gos dos Reis.
Dos Sanctos, Joao. see Joao dos Sanctos.
fray
Dos Sanctos, Luis Goncalves. see Sanctos,
Luis Goncalves dos.
Dos Sanctos e Silva, Thomas Antonio. see
Sanctos e Silva, Thomas Antonio dos.
Dos Santos Marrocas, F. J. see Sanctos
Marrocas, F. J. dos.
Dos Santo, Francisco. see Santo, Francisco
dos.
Dos Santos Barretto, Joao P. see Santos
Barretto, Joao P. dos.
Do Silva Castro, Francisco. see Castro,
Francisco da Silva.
Do Solitario, A. C. Tavares Bastos. see Tava-
res Bastos, Aureliano Candido, 1839-1875.
Dossie, Robert, d. 1777. (20664), 86653
Dostie, A. P. 20665-20666
Dosyowah ganokdayah, tgaisdaniyont. 105557
Dotrina breue muy [pro]uechosa. 106398
Dotrina xpiana pa instrucion & informacio.
16777, 70887
Dottings on the roadside. 62871
Dotty Dimple out west. 47079
Doty, Duane. 90763
Doty, Elihu. 4734
Doty, James. 69946

Doty, James Duane, 1799-1865. (20667), 1st
note after 104889
Doty, James Duane, 1799-1865. plaintiff 96860
Doty, John. 20668
Doty, L. L. 53553 see also New York (State)
Bureau of Military Statistics. Chief.
Dou, Jan Pieterssoon. illus. 63419
Douai, Adolf. 20669-20670
Douat, Alexandre Coupe de Saint. see Coupe
de Saint-Douat, Alexandre.
Douay, ------. 25853
Douay, Anastase. 80002
Double, M. (20671)
Double conspiracy. 97206
Double delusion. 20672
Double honor. 4147
Double-runner Club. 80482
Doubleday, Edward. 28401, 71032
Doubleday, Ulysses. (70188), 106112
Doublet de Boisthibault, -------. 20673
Doubtful gentleman. pseud. Tales of the good
woman. see Paulding, James Kirke,
1778-1860.
Doubting Christian encouraged. 14034
Doubts concerning the battle of Bunker's Hill.
33477
Doubts concerning the legality of slavery. (20674)
Doubts on the abolition of the slave trade.
(20675)
Douce demeure. 94385
Doucet, J. N. P. 20676
Dougall, James. (20680)
Dougherty, Daniel. 20677
Dougherty, John. 96714, 96730 see also
U. S. Commissioner to the Iowa Indians.
U. S. Commissioners to the Oto, Missouri,
Omaha, and Yankton and Santee Bands of
Sioux. U. S. Office of Indian Affairs.
Dougherty, Peter, 1805-1894. 20678-20679,
26378
Dougherty, Roger. 12431, (81868)
Doughty, John. 83978
Douglas, -------, fl. 1838. 20688
Douglas, -------, plaintiff. 7328
Douglas, -------. supposed author 101235
Douglas, A. B. Clinton. 20681
Douglas, D. 94215-94218
Douglas, George B. tr. 40807
Douglas, Sir Howard, Bart. 20682
Douglas, J. H. 76582, 76647
Douglas, James. 20683
Douglas, James. defendant 29534
Douglas, John, surgeon in the British Army.
20686
Douglas, John, successively Bishop of Carlisle,
and Salisbury, 1721-1807. 20684-(20685),
40293, 60862, 68700, 69470, note after
96403
Douglas, John, successively Bishop of Carlisle,
and Salisbury, 1721-1807. supposed
author 1661, 26900, 29043, 40263,
40479, 68296
Douglas, John, fl. 1859. 20687
Douglas, Neil. supposed author 95680
Douglas, R. 68698
Douglas, Mrs. R. (20689)
Douglas, Stephen Arnold, 1813-1861. 5679,
18207, (20690)-20694, (20696), 24767,
28493, (35369), 36266, 37040, 41156,
52180, 52200, note after 69421, (71617),
(81907), 84463, 88323, 89203, 89205,
89926, 93662
Douglas, Sylvester. 91849
Douglas, Thomas, 5th Earl of Selkirk. see
Selkirk, Thomas Douglas, 5th Earl of.
Douglas, Thomas, 1790-1855. 20705-20706

Douglas an enemy to the north. 41148
Douglas and popular sovereignty. 78027-78028
Douglas' doctrine of popular sovereignty in the territories. (20696)
Douglas farm. (7283A)
Douglas Heron & Co. firm defendants 28294
Douglas Houghton Mining Company. Trustees. 20730
Douglas Monument Association. (20696)
Douglasism exposed and republicanism vindicated. (78044)
Douglass, ---------. USA (64590)
Douglass, David B. (20707)-20708, 37590
Douglass, Frederick, 1817?-1895. (17269), 20709-20717, 22713, 61445, 76191, note before 90885
Douglass, Sir Howard. 70156
Douglass, Isaac S. 75949, 98520, 2d note after 96930A
Douglass, J. H. 20718
Douglass, John T. 96718 see also U. S. Commissioner to the Potawatomi Indians.
Douglass, Margaret. (20719)
Douglass, Robert. 50892
Douglass, S. H. (19792)
Douglass, William, 1691?-1752. 5691, 7142, 20720-20724, 20726-20728, (31657), 34810, (34791), 34793, 46744, 51709, 56481, 62743, 64570, 65025, 84538, 3d note after 93596, 96191, 4th note after 98549
Douglass, William, 1691?-1752. incorrectly supposed author 20725, 5th note after 98549
Douglass, William, fl. 1862. 20729
Douin de la Motte, -------. (20731)
D'Oulbath, H. see Oulbath, H. d', Vicomte.
D'Oultreman, Pierre. see Oultreman, Pierre d'.
Dounton, Nich. 66686
Dous discursos gratulatorias. 64439
Dous discursos sobre a philosophia. 78959
Dousman, -------. 38979
Dousseau, Alphonse. 20732
Doutes et preventions relativement a la restitution. 15915
Doutre, Joseph. (20733)-20735
Douttos Cochrane ao respeitavel e sensato poro Brasileiro. 14080
D'Outreman, J. 4829
Douville, Jean Baptiste. 20736-20737
Douvily, Balthazar Gerbier, Baron. see Gerbier, Sir Baltazar, 1592?-1667.
Douze apotres et leur femmes. 12565
D'Ovalle, Alonso. see Ovalle, Alonso de.
Dove, ------. 84586
Dove, C. 18229, 52757
Dove, David James. 69495
Dove, David James. supposed author 2464A, 41946, 66932-(66933), 69495
Dove, H. W. 7394
Dove, John. 20738-20740
Dove, P. Edward. ed. 93657
Dove, Samuel. 7855, 18229, 52757
Dove in safety. 46608, note after 105465
Dover, Joseph Yorke, Baron, 1724-1792. 30708, 35876, (36569), (49566), 63286, 65049, 67155, 94140, 96569, 106043-106046 see also Great Britain. Legation. Netherlands.
Dover, Del. Committee of Arrangement. 99833
Dover, Mass. Berwick Academy. see Berwick Academy, Dover, Mass.
Dover, N. H. 20743, 20745
Dover, N. H. First Church. 20742

Dover, N. H. July Fourth Celebration, 1865. 20744
Dover, N. H. Mayor, 1868. 20745
Dover, N. H. One Hundredth Anniversary of the National Independence Celebration, July 4, 1876. 67313
Dover, N. H. Public Schools. 20745
Dover, N. Y. Meeting of Landholders, 1838. see Meeting of Landholders, Dover, N. Y., 1838.
Dover. 89557
Dover and Great Falls directory. 20745
Dover Baptist Association. see Baptists. Virginia. Dover Baptist Association.
Dover directory. 91556
Dover directory, containing the names. 91554
Dover directory, march—1833. 91555
Dover, January 1, 1771. 20741
Dover land and cash lottery &c. 20741
Dover Manufacturing Company. 52785
Dover pulpit during the revolutionary war. 88869
Doves flying to the windows of their Saviour. 46264
Dow, Jr. pseud. Short patent sermons. 20760
Dow, -------. 64373, 71823 see also Portland, Me. Mayor, 1855 (Dow)
Dow, Daniel, 1772-1849. 20746, 85409, 98479, note after 105520
Dow, George Francis, 1868- 85380
Dow, J. Warren. 20748
Dow, Jabez. (20747)
Dow, John. 20749
Dow, Jonathan. supposed author 84162
Dow, Joseph. 20750
Dow, Lorenzo. (17742), 20751-20757, 86766, 96361
Dow, Moses. (20758)
Dow, Neil. USA 89215
Dow, Peggy. (20752), 20757, 20759
Dow, Ulysses. spurious author 89511
Dowanpi kin. 18285, 69645
Dowdall, P. S. 20761
Dowdell, James F. 20762
Dowe, Henry. 63580
Dowe, William. 20763
Dowie, Marie Muriel, ed. 94233
Dowler, Bennett. 20764-20765, 25302
Dowley, -----. 20766
Dowling, John. (20752)
Dowling, Joseph A. 32426, 104958
Dowling, William, d. 1718. defendant 32182, (32197)
Down-east commentator. 42426
Down-easters, &c. &c. &c. 52152
Down in Tennessee. 27449
Down south. 18977
Down with the black flag of confiscation. 11895
Downame, John. 58769, 80205
Downer, Silas. 20767
Downes, John. 85072
Downes, John, 1799-1882. 20769
Downey, Stephen W. 20770
Downfal of Hadgi-Ali-Bashaw. 83032
Downfal of mystical Babylon. 2405
Downfall of Babylon. 84022, 84034
Downfall of despotism. 20770
Downfall of freemasonry. 66668
Downfall of Jacobism and despotism. 59477
Downie, Murdo. 91090
Downing, Andrew Jackson. 20772-(20776), (33066)
Downing, Charles. 20774
Downing, Clement. 20777
Downing, Elizabeth Hedding. 20778
Downing, Elijah. ed. 20789

Downing, Elijah H. 20778
Downing, Sir George, Bart., 1623-1684. 20779-(20787), note after 98954 see also Great Britain. Legation. Netherlands.
Downing, George T. 20788, 1st note after 79756
Downing, Hugh. defendant 18028
Downing, Majer Jack. pseud. 84184
Downing, Major J., Downingville Militia, Second Brigade. pseud. see Davis, Charles Augustus, 1795-1867.
Downing, Major Jack. pseud. 84178-84183, 84185-84187
Downing, Major Jack, pseud. see Davis, Charles Augustus, 1795-1867. and Smith, Seba, 1792-1868.
Downing, Major Jack, of the Downingville Militia. pseud. 84177
Downing, John. 31047
Downing, Joshua. pseud. see Smith, Seba, 1792-1868.
Downing, Joshua Wells. 20789
Downing, Lewis. 12464, 20790
Downing, "Sargent" Joel. pseud. see Smith, Seba, 1792-1868.
Downing gazette. 84142, 84145, 84162
Downs, Solomon Weathesbell, 1801-1854. 20791
Downton, Nic. see Dounton, Nich.
Dowse, Thomas. 20792
Dowse Institute, Cambridge, Mass. see Cambridge, Mass. Dowse Institute.
Dowse Institute, Cambridge. Declaration of trust. 20793
Dowse library. 20793
Dox, H. L. 20794
Dox, Peter Myndert, 1813-1891. 20795
Doxology of the angels. (66441)
Doy, John. 20796
Doyle, C. A. illus. 16270, 47794
Doyle, John Andrew. 20797
Doyle, Martin. pseud. Hints on emigration. see Hickey, William.
Doyle, Thomas. pseud. Five years in a lottery office. see More, John J.
Doyle, William. 20799
Doylestown, Pa. Court of Oyer and Terminer. see Bucks County, Pa. Court of Oyer and Terminer.
D'Oyley, Edward. (51808) see also Jamaica. Governor, 1657-1662 (D'Oyley)
D'Oyley, Daniel. 20880-20801
Doze Apostoles del Peru (Ecclesiastical Province) 61102
Doze comedias de Lope de Vega Carpio. 98767
12 vistas do Rio de Janeiro. 89133
Dozy, ------. 20802
D'Pauta, -------. see Pauta, ------ d'.
D'Peyster, Johannes. petitioner 90020
Drack, F. see Drake, Sir Francis, 1540?-1596.
Dracut, Mass. Selectmen. (20803)
Draft arrangement of the genus Thamnophilus. 78137
Draft of a bill for declaring the intentions of the Parliament. 20806
Draft of a bill for the suppression of the traffic. 53843
Draft of a bill to provide internal revenue. 34920
Draft of a city charter. 52482
Draft of a constitution. 70579
Draft of a revised common school law. 60075
Draft of an act to provide internal revenue. 20807
Draft of an overture for the government. 65155

Dr. of protest. 84558
Draft; or conscription reviewed by the people. 20804
Draft riots in New York, July, 1863. 3513
Drafting; being the complete militia law. 53654
Drafts of a proposed memorial to Congress. 79104
Drage, Theodore Swaine. supposed author 20808, 28460, 82549, 1st note after 94082
Drage, William. supposed author 20808, 28460, 82549, 1st note after 94082
Dragge, William. see Drage, Theodore Swaine. and Drage, William.
Dragon. pseud. Desengano a los Indios. see V., A., el Mexicano. pseud.
Dragon de la reine. 4520
Dragon: that old serpent. 90030
Dragontea de Lope de Vega Carpio. 98768
Dragoon. pseud. Dragoon campaigns. see Hildreth, James.
Dragoon campaigns in the Rocky Mountains. 31769
Dragoon's bride. 35317
Drainage of land. 6889
Drake, Benjamin. 9139, 20810-(20813), 96082
Drake, C. ed. 47327
Drake, Charles Daniel, 1811-1892. (20814)-20817, 20824, (49576)
Drake, Daniel, 1785-1852. 20818-20825, 84074, 102992
Drake, Daniel, 1785-1852. supposed author 5677, 60822
Drake, Edward Cavendish. 20826
Drake, F. 20857
Drake, Sir Francis, 1540?-1596. (3667), 8547-8548, (8784), 11605-11607, 14349, 14957, (18236), 20518, 20828, 20830, 20837-20843, 20850, 28701, 31389, 33660, 38163, 38347, (38494), 52580, (54897), 57765, 64396, 66686, 71906, 77218, 93588, 97103, 100827
Drake, Sir Francis, Bart., fl. 1600. (18236), 20830, (20838)-20840, 20843, 20855-20856
Drake, Francis Samuel, 1825-1885. 77854, 86107, 86111
Drake, G. R. 23321
Drake, J. 95393
Drake, John H. 20858
Drake, Joseph Rodman, 1795-1820. 20859-20862, 29876, 37163
Drake, Morgan L. 20863
Drake, Richard. 20865
Drake, Samuel Adams. 1833-1905. 84062
Drake, Samuel Gardner, 1798-1875. 4065, 9927, 12998, 20866-20884, 26055, 30266, 33453, 39069, 46280, 46675, 46693, 52445, (52623), 52638, 55892, (62471), 65324, (65586), 67599, 73592, 91853, 97085, 101454
Drake, Samuel Gardner, 1798-1875. supposed author 12704, 20884
Drake, Sir T. 20832
Drake, W. E. reporter 46896, 59924
Drake, William C. (35028)
Drake & Co. firm see Burnett, Drake & Co. firm.
Draker, Sir William. (36911)
Drake's expedition to Cadiz, &c. 14414
Dralse de Grandpierre, -------. (20885), 28272, 69260
Dralymont, I. D., Lord of Yarleme. tr. 69752

Drama. 38583, 55296, 62447, 72133, 77171, (79867)
Drama. By D. J. Snider. 85451
Drama dividido en tres actos. 57223
Drama doble de lectura i de representacion. 76700
Drama em verso, e em 5 actos. 88787
Drama en cinco actos y en verso original. 11711
Drama en caracteres en cinco actos. 76700
Drama en cuatro actos. 29058
Drama en 4 actos y en verso. 29058
Drama en Quichua. 55398
Drama en tres actos. 60916
Drama en tres jornadas y en verso. 72512
Drama en un acto. 44247
Drama epico-historico Americano. 93587
Drama esclavagiste prologue. 12576
Drama, founded on a portion of Uncle Tom's cabin. 92504
Drama heroico. 11708
Drama historico. 55499
Drama historico em tres actos. 43301
Drama historico en cinco actos. 62935
Drama historico . . . en tres actos y en verso. (71449)
Drama, in five acts. 105968
Drama, in five acts. As performed at the Charleston Theatre. 103415
Drama in five acts. By E. G. Holland. 32501
Drama: in five acts. Written by David Trumbull. 97191
Drama, in four acts, founded on the novel. 92408
Drama in Pokerville. 24282
Drama, in three acts. 43613
Drama, in three acts, as performed at the New-York Park Theatre. 38583, 105186, 105195
Drama, in three acts, by George Lionel Stevens. 91504
Drama, in three acts. By Richard Penn Smith. 83781
Drama in three acts. By William Leman Rede. 68489
Drama in three acts. Founded on the events of the revolutionary war. 55375
Drama in two acts. By Felix Megia. 47381
Drama, in two acts, (from Mrs. Beecher Stowe's popular novel.) 92409, note after 93950
Drama lyrico em quatro actos. 81300
Drama of Obi. 86903
Drama of secession. 3531
Drama original Brasileiro en 5 actos. 77162
Drama original en tres actos i en prosa. (75916)
Drama original en verso y en tres actos. 29122
Drama original Portuguez em quatro actos. 43301
Drama politica en tres actos i en prologo. 63725
Drama. Por Galvan Ygnacio Rodriguez. 72511
Drama. The victory of San Jacinto, or the liberation of Texas. 100871
Drama. Three first acts of things amongst us. 34946
Drama. Written & exhibited in the United Fraternity. (25888), 1st note after 97876
Draman, M. P. (18515)
Dramas de Nueva-York. (71635)
Dramas, discourses, and other pieces. (31885)
Dramatic and poetical works. 9250

Dramatic authors of America. 68637
Dramatic censor. 49429
Dramatic dialogues for the use of schools. 90854
Dramatic entertainment. 50793
Dramatic entertainment in three acts. 13616, 2d note after 96139
Dramatic historical piece. 38280
Dramatic jeu d'esprit, in three acts. 78541
Dramatic novel. 26797
Dramatic piece. By a citizen of the United States. 62561
Dramatic piece on the battle of Bunker's-Hill. 7185, 50155
Dramatic piece. Written by an American. 63819
Dramatic poem. 65647, 67272, 73783, 77132, 84892, 96299
Dramatic poem. By James Rees. (68638)
Dramatic poem. By Mrs. Elizabeth Record. 68391, 71250
Dramatic poem. By Samuel B. H. Judah. 36828
Dramatic poem. By the author of Lyteria. 67271
Dramatic poem, in five acts. 71250
Dramatic poem on the present disputes in Europe and America. 8067
Dramatic poems of Harriette Fanning Read. 68150
Dramatic prelude. 74251
Dramatic satire. (38475)
Dramatic selections, for . . . schools, academies, and families. 42379
Dramatic sketch. 87303
Dramatic sketch, and other poems. 62499
Dramatic sketch, commemorative of the tragedies. (41525)
Dramatic sketch in one act. 2466, 57755
Dramatic sketch, in two acts. 95304
Dramatic story in five acts. 31281
Dramatic works. 57755
Dramatic works of Aaron Hill. 100719
Dramatic works of George Colman the Younger. 14526, note after 105986
Dramatic works of Mrs. Aphra Behn. 4369
Dramatic piece in four acts. (81026)
Dramatick miscellany. 95330
Dramatisches Gedicht. (77729)
Drame. 36976
Drame en cinq actes. (38607)
Drame en cinq actes et neuf tableaux. 92546
Drame en deux actes. 23093, note after 98620
Drame en huit actes. 92539
Drames de l'Amerique du Nord. 12570
Drames du Nouveau-Monde. 70331
Dramma. 64014
Dramma eroicomico. 64014
Drane, A. defendant at court martial 20886
Drane, R. B. 20887
Drapeau, Stanislaus. 20888-20892
Draper, ----------. (52746)
Draper, Andrew Sloan. 84897
Draper, Bourne Hall. (20893)
Draper, Edward A. 20894
Draper, Henry. 85072
Draper, James. 20895
Draper, John William, 1811-1882. 20896-20809, 54710
Draper, Lyman Copeland, 1815-1891. 20900-20902 see also Wisconsin. Superintendent of Public Instruction.
Draper, Simeon. 20903
Draper, W. G. 20905
Draper, W. H. 20906-20907

Draper, Sir William. 20904, note before
95670, 5th note after 96481, note after
99409

Drapier, Ariel. reporter 34493

Drapier, W. H. reporter 34493

Draudius, G. (20908)

Draught of a bill, for declaring the intentions
of Parliament. 20909

Draught of a bill proposed to be brought into
Parliament. 11124

Draught of a constitution of government.
19386

Draught of a fundamental constitution . . . of
Virginia. 35894, 1st note after 100461,
2d note after 100504

Draught of a letter of requisition to the
colonies. 89172

Draught of a plan of education. 104583

Draught of a plan of government and discipline.
65156, 104935

Draught of an overture. (20910)

Draught of Boston-Harbor. 88221

Draught of constitution. 99202

Draught of New-England. 88221

Draught of statutes for Columbia College.
14826

Draught of the form of the government. 65157,
104936

Draught of the harbour of Lewisbourg. 88221

Draughts of such bills. 100058-100059

Drawback du sucre indigene. (40128)

Drawing-books. 84500

Drawing in public schools. 84502

Drawing in public schools by the use of the
Smith books condemned. 84501

Drawing in the public schools of the city of
Boston. 84492

Drawing near to God. 104376

Drawings and tintings. 92766

Drawings of Mitla. 46101

Drayton, Daniel. 20912

Drayton, John, 1766-1822. 20913-(20915),
87509, 87541-87542 see also South
Carolina. Governor, 1808-1810 (John
Drayton)

Drayton, Michael, 1563-1631. 20916

Drayton, William, 1776-1846. 20917, 28860,
(31042), 88061

Drayton, William, 1776-1846. supposed author
88214

Drayton, William Henry, 1732-1779. 20918-
(20919), (25787)-(25788), (87588), 87858,
87865 see also South Carolina. Supreme
Court. Chief Justice.

Drayton, William Henry, 1732-1779. supposed
author 20920, 39224, 87790

Drayton; a story of American life. 20921

Dreadful hurricanes in Barbados. 4051

Dreadful murder. 89626

Dreadful sound with which the wicked are to be
thunderstruck. 46559, 96766

Dream. 55003

Dream and the reality. 50762

Dream of a day, and other poems. 60865

Dream of the highlands. 101488

Dream or the true history of Deacon Giles'
distillery. 12397

Dream that was dreamed above forty years
ago. 92709-92710

Dreamer. pseud. Way of the world. see
Wardwell, Joseph.

Dreams of a pew holder. 66633

Dreams of dulocracy. 7821

Dreams of the pound master. 104715

Drebing, Gustav L. 20922

Dreby, ------. tr. 82303

Dred. 46842, 92396-92407, 95867

Dred: a tale of the Dismal Swamp. 92409, note
after 93950

Dred; a tale of the Great Dismal Swamp.
92408

Dred: or, the Dismal Swamp. 92410

Dred Scott case—what the court decided.
(69606)

Dred Scott decision. 82110

Dred Scott decision. Opinion of Chief Justice
Taney. 78259

Dred Scott . . . vs. John F. A. Sandford.
(18036)

Drees, J. W. 20923

Drei Berichte des General Kapitans von Neu-
Spanien. 16959

Drei Jahre in Amerika 1859-1862. 2698

Drei Jahre in der Potomac-Armee. (2167)

III. Nahrichten von Kentucky. 85251

Dreijahrigen Beobachtungen wahrend einer Reise.
9350

Dreiullette, Gabriel. ed. 20929, 68436

Dreizehnte Fortsetzungen. 78013

Dresser, Amos. 20924

Dresser, Horace Erastus, 1841- 20925, (53409)

Dresserus, Matthaeus. 20926

Dreuillette, Gabriel. (20927)-20929

Drevetiere, Louis Francois Deslisle de la.
see Deslisle de la Drevetiere, Louis
Francois.

Dreveton, Theodore. 20930

Drew, Benjamin. (20931)

Drew, C. C. (55092)

Drew, Charles. 77702, note after 85148-85149

Drew, S. S. (20933)

Drew, Samuel, 1765-1833. 20932, 103588

Drew, Thomas. 8518, (20934)-20935, (25845)

Drewe, Edward. 20936-20938

Drews, Johannes. 20939

Drexel & Co. firm 20940

Drey newe relationes. (54943)

Drey vnd zwantzigste Schiffahrt. (33676)

Dreyer, John H. 20941

Dreyhundert auserlesene Amerkianische Gewachse
nach linneischer Ordnung. 2440, 20942,
35519

Dreyjahrige Reise Georg von Spilbergen. 89452

Dreys, Nicolas. (20943)-20944, 56000

Dreysehente Schiffart. 30112, note after (33666)

Dreyzehente Schiffahrt. 30122, (30666)

Drezzanio, Fra[n]cois. 20945

Drie Babels. 12575

Drie jaren in Noord Amerika. 93168

Drie leeraren uit de Presbyteriaansche Kerk.
pseud. Mededeeld. 7804

Drie missiven. 50231

Drie predicatien. 98491

Drie scheeps-togten na het goud-rijke koningrijk
Guiana. (67556)

[Drie] scheeptogten van Kolumbus. 31553

Drie seldsame scheeps-togten. 25998

Drie togten ter zee en te land. 31555

Drie voyagien gedaen na Groenlandt. 28641,
51334

Dried plants. 27419

Driedubbeld Harnas. 104990

Driejarig berblijk in de Vereenigde Staten.
97035

Driesen, L. 20946

Driessen, Petrus van. see Van Briessen,
Petrus.

Drietal van uitmuntende dichtstukjse. 55427

Drift of the war. 8881

Drifting about. 46175

Driggs, John Fletcher, 1813-1877. 20947

Drilling in stone without the use of metals. 67966

Dring, Thomas. 20948-(20949), 28582, note just before 68379

Drinker, John. 20950, 56528, 60579, 60712, 61936, 69999, 1st note after 96428 see also Friends, Society of. Philadelphia Yearly Meeting. Clerk.

Drinking usages of society. 64617

Drinkwater, Anne J. 20951

Drinkwater, D. F. 20952

Drinkwater Bethune, C. R. ed. 26470, 30958

Driscoll, Frederick. 20953-20954

Drisden Harwood, Esq. 102473

Drisko, G. L. supposed author 70343

Drisler, Henry. 20955

Dritte Fortsetzung der Nachricht. 78013

Dritte Theil der Newen Welt. 1762-1762A

Dritten Buch Americae. (8784)

Dritten Confernz der Evangelischen Religionen Teutscher Nation in Pennsylvania. 4th note after 97895, note after 106412

Driver, ------- fl. 1841. 23684, 87341

Droeshout, Martin. engr. 82851

Droevig Verhaal z. ongel. reis. 30552

Droguet, Marc Juline. 20956

Drohojowska, Antoinette Francoise Anne Symon de Latreiche, Comtesse. (20957)

Droit de souverainete de France. 75108

Droit des gens. 5137

Droit des gens maritime universel. (36680)

(Droit des neutres.) 65413

Droit des neutres sur mer. 27229

Droit et necessite des garanties. 16385

Droit public. 14709, 61252

Droits de la Grande-Bretagne etablis. 18348, (25912)

Droits des gens. (5153)

Droll descriptions of town and country. 50630

Drone. 102394

Droom van Californie. (40033)

Droop, Henry Richmond. 20958

Droppings from the heart. 43399

Drops of myrrh. 72112

Drouet, -------, fl. 1768. ed. 21149, note before 40028-40028

Drouet, Henri, 1829- (20959)-20963

Drouin de Bercy, ------. 20961-20963

Drouyn de Lhuys, Edouard, 1805-1881. 19004, 20964

Drown, S. De Witt. 20965, (60833)

Drowne, Solomon. 20966-20967

Drowne, T. Stafford. (20968), 81607

Drown'd wife of Stephens's Creek. 102474

Druck om geluck. pseud. (31660)-(31661)

Drucke und Holzschnitte des XV. und XVI. Jahrhunderts in getreuer Nachbildung 99354, 99363, 99378, 101017

Druecker, John. plaintiff 10997

Drugulin, William E. 3125, 3556, 17936, (21118), 63552, 92561

Druids, United Ancient Order of. see United Ancient Order of Druids.

Drukee, S. 45874

Drum for the ears of the drowsy. 20969

Drumm, John H. 20970

Drummer boy. 12144

Drummer boy. A story of the war. (20972)

Drummer, of New York clerks and country merchant. 20971

Drummond, Antonio de Vasconcellos Menezes de. 20973

Drummond, Sir Gordon. 12935

Drummond, Robert. respondent 91849

Drummond, Robert Blackley. 20974

Drummond, Robert Hay, Abp. of York, 1711-1776. 20976, 77122, 84646

Drummond, Thomas. 20975

Drummond, William H. ed. and illus. 73527

Drunkard. A moral domestic drama. 84785

Drumkard: or the fallen saved. 84781

Drunkard: or the fallen saved; a moral domestic drama. 84782

Drunkard; or, the fallen saved. A moral domestic drama in five acts. 84783-84784, 84786

Drunkard's heart and the devil's palace. (44749)

Drunkard's looking glass. 102467-102468, 102472, 102476, 102491

Drunkenness reproved by a beast. 89175

Drury, Amos. 99161

Drury, Luke. 20977

Dury, P. Sheldon. ed. 90576

Drus, Joanna Inger da. 34186

Dry dock at California. 102960

Dry dock in California. 102960

Dry dock—New York harbor. 51462

Dry Goods Importers, Philadelphia. see Philadelphia. Dry Goods Importers.

Dry goods trade. 20978

Dryandrius, Johannes. see Eychman, Joannes.

Dryden, John, 1631-1700. 20979-20980

Drysdale, Isabel. (20981)

Du Bresil. (26416)

Du camp de General Waginston [sic]. 96990

Du climate de Phernambuco. 44520, 51319

Du climat et des maladies de Bresil. (80899)

Du commerce des colonies, ses principes et ses lois, appliques aux colonies Francaises de l'Amerique. 14968

Du commerce des colonies, ses principes et ses lois, la paia est le temps de regler & d'agrandir le commerce. 14967

Du commerce des neutres en temps de guerre. 38771

Du commerce et de la Compagnie des Indes. 21389

Du Congres de Vienne. 64887

Du droit politique en Amerique et en Suisse. 42701

Du gouvernement de Saint Domingue. 73839

Du Gynobase considere dans les Polypetales. 75235

Du libre travail. 12158

Du mal rouge observe a Cayenne. 4849

Du mariage et du contrat de mariage en Angleterre. (14340)

Du Mexique avant et pendant la conquete. 12589

Du passage de Venis sur le soleil. 38677

Du pin maritime. 6165

Du perfectionnement de l'industrie sucriere aux Antilles. 55253

Du principe federatif et de la necessite de reconstituer. 66231

Du progres et de l'etat actuel de la reforme penitentiaire. 21071

Du projet de loi. 93570

Du projet Mackau. 5652

Du role et de l'importance des colonies. 63709

Du seul partie a prendre a l'egard de Saint-Domingue. 99755

Du systeme penitentiaire Americain en 1836. 36892

Dy systeme penitentiaire aux Etats-Unis. 4190, 1st note after 96068

Du systeme penitentiaire en Europe et aux Etats-Unis. 42605

Du tabac au Paraguay. 19472

Du travail libre et du travail esclave. 36422
Du typhus d'Amerique. (2975)
Du voyage des peres Jesuites. 5136, 69268,
(69300)
Duae constitutiones Vaticanae. 72915
Duae navigationes Dn. Americi Vesputii.
(8784)
Dual government in South Carolina. 88005
Dual revolutions. 36316
Duane, --------. 9199, 15531
Duane, James, 1733-1797. 792, 20987, 54168,
51825-51826, 90629, 4th-5th notes after
98997 see also New York (City) Mayor,
1776-1777 (Duane) New York (City)
Mayor, 1784-1789 (Duane)
Duane, Richard B. 20983-20984
Duane, William, 1760-1835. 20985-20986,
20988-20994, 44767-44768, 61583, 97270,
75924, 80560, 2d note after 94138, 94304,
note after 97549, 3d note after 102203,
105044
Duane, William, 1760-1835. supposed author
(20989), 20994, (74488), note after 96799-
96800, 97270, note before 101837
Duane, William, 1760-1835. incorrectly sup-
posed author 20987, 90629
Duane, William, 1808-1882. ed. 13043,
(20995), 20996
Duane, William John, 1780-1865. 3189,
10172, 11796, 20997-21002, (23921),
25614, 39425, 56521, 93538
Duane, William John, 1780-1865. defendant
21002
Duane's collection. 94304
Duane's tracts. 20994
Duarte y Zenea, Antonio. 21003
Du Barry, Edmund L. tr. 64736
Du Bartas, Guillaume de Salluste, Seigneur,
1544-1590. (30701), 76838
Du Bellet, Paul Pecquet. see Pecquet du
Bellet, Paul.
Duben C. von. 21004
Dubh, Scian. pseud. see Scian Dubh. pseud.
Dubigeon, --------. defendant 47527
Du Biscay, -------- Acarete. see Acarete
du Biscay, ---------.
Dublar, L. J. 21005
Dublin, Archbishop of. see Browne, George,
Archbishop of Dublin, d. 1556.
Dublin. Public Meeting Concerning the Protes-
tant Episcopal Diocese of Ohio, 1828.
102729
Dublin. Royal Irish Academy. see Royal
Irish Academy, Dublin.
Dublin. Society for Promoting the United and
Scriptural Education of the Poor in Ire-
land. see Society for Promoting the
United and Scriptural Education of the
Poor in Ireland, Dublin.
Dublin. Society of United Irishmen. see
Society of United Irishmen, Dublin.
Dublin. University. 10645, 84677
Dublin, N. H. 21006
Dublin, N. H. Centennial Celebration, 1852.
40114
Dublin, N. H. Schools. 21006
Dublin, N. H. Superintending School Committee.
21006
Dublin chronicle. 105985
Dublin Friends' Tract Association. 105204,
105206
Dublin review. 84021
Dublin suit: decided in the Supreme Judicial
Court of New Hampshire. 21006
Dublin Suit. Supreme Judicial Court. 18100
Dublin University magazine. 10645

Dubocage, Marie Anne. see Duboccage, Marie
Anne.
Duboccage, Marie Anne. 21007-21008
Dubois, Benjamin. 98289
Dubois, E. 21009
Dubois, F. E. 21010
Du Bois, Gualterus, 1666-1751. 38208, 73073,
73076
Dubois, Jose Alvarez de Toledo y. see
Toledo y Dubois, Jose Alvarez de.
Dubois, Lucien. (21011)
Du Bois, Henry A. 21012
Du Bois, T. K. (21013)
Du Bois, William Ewing. 21014-21019, 21786-
21788, 23332, 1st note after 96847
Dubois-Fontanelle, Jean Gaspard. 21020,
99412-99420
Dubos, J.-B. supposed author 98172
Du Bosque, -------. 21021
Dubouchet, Charles. 3245B, 21022-21023
Dubourg, Jacques Barbeu. see Barbeu-Dubourg,
Jacques.
Dubourg, Clemente. 21024
Dubourg, J. Huen. see Huen Dubourg, J.
Duboy, Alexandre. (21025)
Duboys, P. M. 21026
Dubroca, Louis. 10655, 21027-21031, (24993),
note after 96377, 99452, note after
101800
Dubuc, Jean Baptiste. 21032
Dubuc-Duferret, ------. 21033
Dubucq, -------. 21034-21035, 56579, 65031,
69719
Dubucq, ------. supposed author 21035,
68752
Du Buisson, Paul Ulric. see Buisson, Paul
Ulric du.
Dubuque, Iowa. Board of Education. 21041
Dubuque, Iowa. Congregational Church. 21041
Dubuque, Iowa. Institute of Science and Arts.
see Iowa Institute of Science and Arts,
Dubuque.
Dubuque, Iowa. Masonic Festival, 1867. see
Freemasons. Iowa. Masonic Festival,
Dubuque, 1867.
Dubuque, Iowa. Mississippi River Improve-
ment Convention, 1866. see Mississippi
River Improvement Convention, Dubuque,
Iowa, 1866.
Dubuque, Iowa. Northern Iowa Sanitary Fair,
1864. 55803
Dubuque, Iowa. Northern Iowa Sanitary Fair,
1864. Treasurer. 55803
Dubuque, Iowa. Northwestern Ship Canal Con-
vention, 1864. see Northwestern Ship
Canal Convention, Dubuque, Iowa, 1864.
Dubuque, Iowa. Public Schools. 21041
Dubuque (Diocese) Bishop (Smyth) 72941 see
also Smyth, D. Clement, Bp.
Dubuque (Diocese) Synod, 1871. 72941
Dubuque and Pacific Railroad. 21042
Dubuque and Sioux City Railroad. 21042
Dubuque Catholic Institute. 21041
Dubuque city directory for 1868-9. (21040)
Dubuque claim case. 83725
Dubuque Emigrant Association. 35029
Dubuque; its history, mines, Indian legends,
etc. 38906
Duc, Eugene Emmanuel Viollet le. see Viollet
le Duc, Eugene Emmanuel, 1814-1879.
Duc, Saint-Germain le. 8876
Duc, W. G. le. see Le Duc, W. G.
Duc de la Rochefaucault's travels. 46984,
102540
Ducachet, Henry William. 1144, 21043

Du Calvert, Peter. see Du Calvert, Pierre, d. 1796.
Du Calvert, Pierre, d. 1796. 21044-(21045)
Du Casse, ----------. supposed author 69286
Ducatel, Julius T. 45153, 45155, (45156)
Duchalet, Henry William. 23317
Duchassing, P. (21046)
Duche, Jacob, 1738-1798. 21047-21055, 23387, 61547, 84608, 84641, 84678C, 101739-101740
Ducher, G. J. A. D. 21056-21059
Duchesne, ------. 21060-(21061)
Du Chilleau, Marie Charles. see Airvault, Marie Charles du Chilleau, Marquis d'
Duck, Stephen. 21064
Duckers duck'd. 106100
Duclairon, Antoine Maillet. see Maillet Duclairon, Antoine.
Du Clary, -------- Le Pelletier. see Le Pelletier du Clary, --------
Duclaux, E. 85072
Duclesmeur, -----. 44594
Duclos, Francis. (21065)
Ducoeur Joly, S. J. 21066
Du Coudray, -------- Troncon. see Troncon du Coudray, --------.
Ducoudray-Holstein H. La Fayette Villaume, 1763-1839. 6184, 21067-(21069), 32643-(32644)
Ducpetiaux, Ed. 21070-21071
Ducrest de Saint-Aubin, Stephanie Felicite. see Saint-Aubin, Stephanie Felicite Ducrest de, Comtesse de Genlis.
Ducreux, ------. (21072)
Ducrotay de Blainville, H. M. 9127
Dudas acerca de la ceremonias sanctas de la missa. (48447)
Duden, Gottfried. 21073-21076
Dudevant, Amandine Aurore Lucie (Dupin) 1804-1876. see Sand, George, pseud. of Mme. Dudevant, 1804-1876.
Dudgeon, Thomas. (21077)
Dudleian Lecture, Harvard University. 23, 173, 891, 3470, 3471, 3489, 3493, 12331, 13350, 16603, 22169, 24553, 22129, (26783), 30892, 31768, (31895), 32258, 32588, 38776, 38875, 57778, 62733, 66604, 97326, 102574, 103907, 103908
Dudley, B. W. 17653, 90779
Dudley, Dean. 6694, (21078)-21081, 20745, 56755, 64426
Dudley, Edward Bishop, 1787-1855. (55644) see also North Carolina. Governor, 1837-1841 (Dudley)
Dudley, John. 21082
Dudley, John G. 21083
Dudley, John L. 21084-21085
Dudley, John William Ward, 1st Earl of, 1781-1833. 21093
Dudley, Joseph. 62743
Dudley, Joseph, 1647-1720. (19157), 45633, 45705, 46127, 52601, 67086, 104088 see also Massachusetts (Colony) Governor, 1702-1715 (Dudley)
Dudley, Joseph, 1648-1720. incorrectly supposed author 49822, 62560
Dudley, Mary. 21086, 51733, note after 78497
Dudley, Paul. 9709, 9711, (21087)-21088, (40332), 42824, 78667, 1st note after 99800
Dudley, Robert. illus. (74396)
Dudley, Sir Robert, styled Duke of Northumberland and Earl of Warwick, 1574-1649. 21089

Dudley, Thomas, 1576-1663. (21090), 33698, 78431, 104846, 106052
Dudley, Thomas, fl. 1690. supposed ed. (21090), 33698, 78431, 104846
Dudley, Thomas, d. 1814. 3493
Dudley, Thomas P. 21092
Dudley & Co. firm. see Dean Dudley & Co. firm
Dudley & Greenough. firm publishers 8059, 8251, 64426, 86830
Dudley genealogies and family records. (21078)
Dudley Observatory, Albany, N. Y. see Albany, N. Y. Dudley Observatory.
Dudley Observatory and the Scientific Council. 21097
Dudley Observatory: meeting of the Board of Underwriters. 21100
Dudley Street Baptist Church, Roxbury, Mass. see Roxbury, Mass. Dudley Street Baptist Church.
Dudley's letter to the Countess of Lincoln. 106052
Dudot, S. (21460)
Dve altri libri parimente di qvelle che si portano. 57667
Dve altri libri parimente di quelle cose che si portano. 57670
Due ammiragli. 16544
Due antichi monumenti di architetura. 44673
Due consideration of, and preparation for our latter end. 79497
Due Europaische Entwickelung. 21076
Due funffte kurtze wunderbare Beschreibung. 67564
Due glory to be given to God. 97473
Due lettera ad rem del Sig. T. Matthias all' autore. 64014
Due lettre di Monsig. Fleming. (24703)
Dve libri dell' historia de i semplici, aromati, et altre coes. 57668-57669
Dve libri dell' historia di i semplici, aromati, et altre cose. 57667
Due preparation. 27960, 30153, note after 95748
Due relazioni del regno del Cile. 23776
Due right of presbyteries. 17091, (74456)
Due right of presbyters. 46782
Due sistemi d'economia politica. 81452
Due sonora. 21376
Due viaggi del Beato Odorico da Vdine. (67737)
Due West, S. C. Erskine College. see Erskine College, Due West, S. C.
Duel or no duel. (21101)
Duelist. 21103
Duell, Rodolphus Holland, 1824-1891. 21104
Duelling explained from philanthropic motives. 90446
Duellists looking glass. 102472
Duellum Britanicum. 78189
Duelo de la inquisicion. 94824, 95998
Duelo vindicado. 70093
Duenas, Francisco, Pres. Salvador, d. 1875. 65346 see also Salvador. President, 1863-1871 (Duenas)
Duende de Buenos Ayres. 6187, 22660
Duer, John. 21105-21108, (53951), 99276
Duer, John. supposed author 21107, 99287, 99821
Duer, John K. 21109
Duer, William, 1747-1799. 21110
Duer, William Alexander, 1780-1858. 14281-(14282), 21111-(21117), 38577
Duet, or Colin and Delia. 92282
Dufau, Pierre Armand. 21119-21120

Du Fay, -------, fl. 1798. 21122
Du Fay, Charles Jerome de Cisternay, 1662-
   1723. (8784)
Dufay, Jules. 21121
Dufay, L. Pierre Dufay de Latour. see Dufay
   de Latour Dufay, L. Pierre, Marquis.
Dufay de Latour Dufay, L. Pierre, Marquis.
   75086
Duferret, ------ Dubuc. see Dubuc-Duferret,
   -------.
Dufet, L. (21123)
Dufey, P. J. S. 21124-21128
Duff, Henry J. petitioner 21129, 80410
Duff, Mountstuart E. Grant. 21130
Duff (Ship) (49480)-49482
Duffay, ------. 75126, 87116
Duffield, D. B. (21131)
Duffield, Edward. 90356
Duffield, George, 1732-1790. 21132
Duffield, George, 1794-1868. (21133)-(21137),
   48777, 69536
Duffield, George, 1818-1888. 21138-21140
Duffield, John Thomas, 1823-1901. ed.
   (21141), 65653
Duffield, S. P. (75394)
Duffield on regeneration. 69536
Duffin, P. W. defendant 21142
Duflocq, ------. 92539
Duflos, -------. illus. (4932)
Duflot de Mofras, Eugene, 1810-1884. 9990,
   12790, 21144, 51734, 55986, 81475
Dufour, Adolphe Hippolyte. (21145), 38418
Dufour, El. tr. 56738
Dufour, Ph. S. 21146
Dufour de Pradt, Dominique. see Pradt,
   Dominique Georges Frederic de Riom
   de Prolhiac de Fourt de, Abp., 1759-
   1837.
Dufranc, ------ 75153
Dufrenoy, ------. 67935
Du Fresne de Francheville, Joseph. (21147)-
   21148, 69298
Dufresne de St. Cergues, ------. 21412
Du Fresnoy, Charles. see Fresnoy, Charles
   du.
Du Fresnoy, Nicolas Lenglet. see Lenglet
   Dufresnoy, Nicolas, 1674-1755.
Dufruit, Th. pseud. tr. see Cabet, Etienne.
Dufur, A. J. 21151
Duganne, Augustine J. H. 2948, 21152-21156,
   (31631)
Dugdale, Richard, ed. 78366
Dugdale, Robert. 21157
Duggan, George. (21158)
Dugoujon, ------. 21159
Du Graty, Alfred M. 21160-21161
Du Gravier, ------, Comte de Malet. see
   Malet du Gravier, ------, Comte de.
Dugrivel, A. 21162
Du Guay-Trouin, -------. see Guay-Trouin,
   ------ du.
Dugue, Ferdinand. (6895)
Du Hailly, Ed. 21163
Du Halde, -------. tr. 40697
Du Hameau, -----. 75061
Duhaut-Cilly, A. 21164-21165
Duhousset, -----. 70373
Duhring, Henry. (21166)
Duitsch Godegeleerd Seminarium in Noord-
   Amerika. 103081
Du Jarric, Pierre. see Jarric, Pierre du.
Duke, Basil W. 21167
Duke, Seymour R. (81242)
Duke, William, fl. 1741-1743. 3278, 3290
Duke, William, fl. 1795. 45272

Duke, William, fl. 1816. supposed author
   94101
Du Keere, Pierre. see Keere, Pieter van der.
Dukes, Joseph. tr. 21168
Dukes, Joseph H. 21169
Du Lac, F. M. Perrin. see Perrin du Lac,
   F. M.
Dulaney, Daniel. see Dulany, Daniel, 1721-
   1797.
Dulany, Daniel, 1721-1797. 19347, (21170)-
   21171, 56542, 84842
Dulce. 1962
Dulces, Francisco Frias y Jacott, Cunde de
   Pozos. see Frias y Jacott, Francisco,
   Conde de Pozos Dulces, 1809-1877.
Dulcisimos amores. 76222
Dulen, Jacob W. 21172
Dulien, J. 21173
Dullaart, H. tr. 72320
Dulles, Joseph Heatly, 1853- 83738, 83759
Dulmanhorst, Salomon Davidssoon van. illus.
   63419
Dulon, Jacob W. see Dulen, Jacob W.
Dulon, Rudolph. 21174
Dumail, F. 21175
Dumanoir, Philippe Francois Pinel, called,
   1806-1865. (21176)-(21177), 92539
Du Martineau, Mathurin Eyquem. see Eyquem,
   Mathurin, Sieur de Martineau.
Dumartray, Alonzo. see Demartray, Alonzo.
Dumas, --------, fl. 1768. tr. 84618-84619
Dumas, Alexander J. pseud. Col. Crockett's
   exploits. see Smith, Richard Penn, 1799-
   1896.
Dumas, Alexandre, 1802-1870. 21180-21187,
   27477
Dumas, Charles G. F. tr. (51287), 84647
Dumas, G. 21188
Dumas, M. 88969
Dumas, Mathieu. 21189-21191, 67627
Dumay, Louis, d. 1681. 21192, 47073
Dumbar, Gerhard. (21193)
Dumeril, --------. 21354
Dumesle, ------ Herard. see Herard-Dumesle,
   -------.
Dumesnil, Clement. 21194-21195
Du Mesnil, Emilio Mangel. see Mesnil, Emilio
   Mangel du.
Dumesnil, Marie. 21196
Dumfries, Va. District Court. 36994, 94411,
   note after 96882, 3d note after 96891
Dumfries and Galloway courier. 94730
Dummer, Jeremiah. 21197-(21200)
Dummer, Jeremiah, supposed author 15949,
   (21200), 57865
Dummer Academy, South Byfield, Mass.
   21202-21203
Dummer Academy, South Byfield, Mass. Trus-
   tees. 21201
Dumon, -------. 21204
Dumond, Annie (Hamilton) Nelles, 1837- 52304
Dumond, D. L. ed. 102550
D'Umons, Charles E. Micoud. see Micoud
   d'Umons, Charles E.
Dumont, Ebenezer, 1814-1871. (21205)-(21206)
Dumont, Georges Marie Butel. see Butel
   Dumont, Georges Marie, 1725-1788.
Dumont, Henry. (21207)
Du Mont, J. see Mont, J. du.
Dumont, Jean, Baron de Carlescroon, d.
   1726. 21208
Dumont, Jose. 96251
Dumont, Pieter. 25755, 25974, 98572
Dumont de Montiguy, --------, Lieutenant.
   (9605), 25853, note after 42913

Dumont d'Urville, Jules Sebastien Cesar. (6153), 21209-21219, 36014, 56064
Du Montellier, --------, Sieur. 21220
Dumorter, E. 21221
Du Motier, Marie Jean Paul Roche Yves Gilbert. see Lafayette, Marie Jean Paul Roche Yves Gilbert du Motier, Marquis de, 1757-1834.
Du Moulin, -------. 21641, 84945
Du Moulin, John F. supposed author 21222, (22945), 30996
Dumoulin, Vincendon. 21216, 21223-(21224)
Dumoutier, F. A. C. 21216, (24937), 2d note after 93879
Dun, Barlow & Co. firm publishers 21225
Dunand, Charles. 21226
Dunant, J. Henry. 21227
Dunbar, Asa. 21228
Dunbar, Edward E. 21229-21232, note after 90732, note after 94370
Dunbar, Elijah. 21233-21234
Dunbar, H. C. 5625
Dunbar, James. 21235
Dunbar, John D. 21237
Dunbar, Reuben. defendant 21238
Dunbar, Robert N. (21239)-(21240)
Dunbar, Samuel. (21241)-(21246)
Dunbar, W. petitioner 69844
Dunbar, William. 21247, 40824-40828, 49827
Dunbarton, N. H. Centennial Celebration, 1865. 21248
Duncan, Alexander. 86205 see also Sodus Canal Company. Treasurer.
Duncan, Alexander, 1788-1853. 21249-21250
Duncan, Archibald. 21251-21252
Duncan, David. 21253
Duncan, Francis. 21254
Duncan, Greer B. (21256)
Duncan, Henry, 1735?-1814. 20363, (21257)
Duncan, Joseph Henry, 1793-1869 (21258)
Duncan, John Mason, 1790-1851. 21260-21261, 90334
Duncan, John Morison. 21259, (74653), 84305-84306, 84309, 84313, 94228, 94331
Duncan, Peter. 21263
Duncan, William, 1760-1827. 61703
Ducan, William, fl. 1792. 54458
Ducan, William, fl. 1869. 21264, 47174
Duncan, William Garnett, 1800-1875. (21255)
Duncan & Co. firm (21265)
Duncan, Sherman & Co. firm (21265)
Duncan, Sherman & Co. firm plaintiffs 64285
Duncan Adair. (17655)
Duncan Dunbar. (11969)
Duncanson, Alexander. 21266
Duncombe, C. 21268
Duncombe, C. petitioner 31138
Duncombe, Charles. 21267
Duncombe (John) publisher 91843-91844
Duncombe's edition of the British theatre. 91843-91844
Dumcombe's free banking. 21267
Dundas, Henry. 21269-21270
Dundas, Robert. 21271
Dundas, or a sketch of Canadian history. 17591
Dundee advertiser. 69680
Dundee northern star. 18638, 105587
Dunderhead, Von. pseud. see Von Dunderhead. pseud.
Dundertjahrige Calender. 33830
Dundonald, Archibald Cochrane, 9th Earl of, 1749?-1831. 14071
Dundonald, Thomas Cochrane, 10th Earl of, 1775-1860. 14078-14079, 21273-21275, 61117
D'Unger, Robert. (21276)

Dunglas, P. M. (21277)
Dunglison, Robert. (21278)
Dunham, --------, fl. 1841. 23684, 87341
Dunham, Cyrus Livingston, 1817-1877. 21279
Dunham, J. M. 100650
Dunham, Jacob. 21280
Dunham, Josiah, 1769-1844. (21281)-21284, 101803
Dunham, Robert Carr. 55372
Dunham, S. A. 21287
Dunham, Samuel. 21286
Dunham and True. firm publishers 21284, 97633
Dunham and True's almanac. 21284
Dunham Copper Company. 21288
Dunigan & Bros. firm publishers 21289
Dunigan's American catholic almanac for 1858. 21289
Dunkin, Benjamin Fanueil. (21290)
Dunkin, Christopher. 21291-21292
Dunkin, George. defendant 6326, 1st note after 96956, 1st note after 97284
Dunlap, Andrew. 21293
Dunlap, G. W. 21294
Dunlap, James. ed. 84842
Dunlap, Jane. 103641, 103643
Dunlap, John. 21295
Dunlap, Robert Pinckney, 1794-1859. 43940 see also Maine. Governor, 1834-1838 (Dunlap)
Dunlap, William, 1766-1839. 18258, 21296-21309, (82501), 84620, 84678C, 84651, 95362, 94614, 98481, 105957, 106078
Dunlap and Hayes. firm publishers petitioners 100410
Dunlap and Claypoole's American daily advertiser. see Claypoole's American Daily advertiser.
Dunlap Society. 97617
Dunlap's Pennsylvania packet. (80702)-80703, 84839, 84842, 86638, 93430, 93439, 102405, 102417, 102599, 104632
Dunlavy, John, 1769-1826. 21309-21310, (43605)-43606, 52324), 56493, 79717, 89893, 92025, 92031, note after 97880
Dunlevy, A. H. 21311
Dunlop, ---------. RN 21313
Dunlop, Alexander. 21312
Dunlop, Charles. 21314
Dunlop, James, fl. 1777. plaintiff 21315
Dunlop, James, 1795-1856. 21316
Dunlop, John, fl. 1800. plaintiff 104223
Dunlop, John, fl. 1846. 81822, (81839)
Dunlop, Robert Glasgow. (21317)
Dunlop, William, 1792-1848. 10610, 21318, 78247, 90813
Dunmore, John Murray, 4th Earl of, 1732-1809. 54162, 85243, 86153, 99971-99973 99999-100004 see also New York (Colony) Governor, 1770 (Dunmore) Virginia (Colony) Governor, 1771-1775 (Dunmore)
Dunmore, John Murray, 4th Earl of, 1732-1809. petitioner 93593, 3d note after 105598-9 [sic]
Dunn, Ballard S. 21319
Dunn, George H. (34548)
Dunn, Henry. 21320
Dunn, John. 21321-21322
Dunn, John. tr. 38729
Dunn, John, fl. 1841. 21323
Dunn, L. A. 23874
Dunn, Nathan. 21324, 104773
Dunn, Thomas. 21325
Dunn, William McKee, 1814-1887. 21327-21329, 42371
Dunnel, Henry Gale. 21330
Dunning, H. 21331-21333

Dunning, H. N. (21334)-(21335)
Dunogan, William. defendant 101087
Dunphy, Thomas. 21336
Dunscombe, J. W. 21337
Dunshee, ------. 96939
Dunshee, Henry Webb. 21338-21339
Dunster, H. P. (21340)
Dunster, Henry. 66431-(66441)
Dunster, Isaiah. 21341
Dunt, Detlef. 21342
Duntautoogoe. Indian Chief (15440)
Dunton, John, 1659-1733. 21343-(21345), 22148, 46244, 57765, 65646
Dunton, John, 1659-1733. supposed author (19280), 86795-86798
Dunton, Larkin. ed. 83633
Dunton's conversation in Ireland. (21345)
Duny, ------. 96447
Duo itinera. (8784)
Duo lettere. 14654, (51759)
Duodecennium luctuosum. 46289
Duodecim fragmenta. 44175
Dupaix, -------. (37800), 40038
Dupanloup, Felix Antoine Philibert, Bp. 21346, 57624 see also Orleans, France (Diocese) Bishop (Dupanloup)
Du Parc d'Avaugour, -------, Comte. 21347
Du Pare, ------- Lenoir. see Lenoir de Pare, -------.
Du Pasquier, H. 21348
Du Perier, -------. 4508, 21349-21351, (26880)
Duperre, B. 50002
Duperre, Victor Guy, Baron, 1775-1846. 12222, 21352, 65024, (81719)-81721 see also France. Ministre de la Marine et des Colonies.
Duperrey, Louis Isidore. 21211-21215, 21353, 56064
Dupetit-Thouars, Abel Aubert, 1793-1864. 1862, 21354-(21355), 75235
Dupetit-Thouars, Aristide Aubert. 61260
Dupeyron, P. de Segur. see Segur-Dupeyron, P. de.
Dupin, ------, fl. 1791. 5844
Dupin, -------, fl. 1829. 18331
Dupin, Andre Marie Jean Jacques, 1783-1865. 21356
Dupin, Charles, Baron, 1784-1873. 21357-21360
Du Pin, L. Ellies. 21361
Dupin, Pierre Charles Francois. see Dupin, Charles, Baron, 1784-1873.
Du Pin e Almeida, Miguel Calmon. see Pin e Almeida, Miguel Calmon du.
Du Pinet, Antoine. see Pinet, Antoine du.
Du Plan de Carpin, Jean. see Plan de Carpin, Jean du.
Duplessis, -------. 21366
Duplessis, ---------. auctioneer 103106
Duplessis, -------. illus. 85819
Duplessis, ------ Mauduit. see Mauduit-Duplessis, --------.
Du Plessis, Armand Jean. see Richelieu, Armand Jean du Plessis, Cardinal, Duc de, 1585-1642.
Duplessis, Paul. 21367-21376
Du Plessis, Salomon. see Plessis, Salomon du.
Duplessis's memoirs. 21366
Duplicate letters. 276
Duplicity and treachery of Josiah A. Noonan. 41023, 66706
Dvply to M. S. alias two brethren. 91382, 91384
Duply to the two brethern. 91382

Duplyque op seeckere replyque. 20786, note after 98953
Du Ponceau, Peter Steven, 1760-1844. 1183, (8860), 21356, 21377-21385, (22159), 31206, 58877, (68001), 81459, 85877, 87696, 91393, note before 91395, 91428, 103110, 106301
Du Ponceau, Pierre Etienne. see Du Ponceau, Peter Steven, 1760-1844.
Dupont, -------, Chevalier. 21386
Du Pont, ------, fl. 1604. 32015
Dupont, ------, fl. 1763. (38696), 47528
Dupont, Emilien. 21387
Dupont, Jean. 76838
Du Pont, S. F. 21388
Dupont, St. Clair. 21391
Du Pont de Nemours, Pierre Samuel, 1739-1817. 21389-21390, 21883, 25583, 41646, note after 93823
Du Pont-Graue, --------. see Pont-Graue, ------ du.
Du Pont's artesian wells. 82992
Du Pouget, Jean Francois Albert. see Nadaillac, Jean Francois Albert du Pouget, Marquis de, 1818-1904.
Duprat, L. 21393
Du Pratz, ------ Le Page. see Le Page du Pratz, -------.
Dupre, L. 21394-21395
Dupressoir, ------. illus. 48916
Du Puget, R. see Puget, R. du.
Du Puis, F. Mathias. 21396
Dupey, A. E. 21397-21398
Du Puynode, Michael Gustave Pastoureau. 21399
Du Quoine Female Seminary. An argument. 21401
Durable riches. (46290)
Durama de Ochoa, D. 21402-(21404)
Duran, Diego. 21405
Duran, Diego. supposed author 118
Duran, Jos. Miguel. (21406)
Duran, Nicolas. 21407-21408
Duran, R. 976
Durand, Asher Brown, 1796-1886. (14279), 42808, 84143
Durand, B. 21409
Durand, Cyrus. 89131
Durand, D. 99363
Durand, E. 69946
Durand, J. ed. 16987
Durand, James R. 21411
Durand, P. tr. (40693)
Durand, Ursin. 101348-101350
Durand-Brager, ------. illus. 44250
Durand de Villegagnon, Nicolas. see Villegafon, Nicolas Durand de, 1510-1571?
Durand-Molard, -------. 21412, 44974
Durand & Co. firm engrs. 84154
Durand & Co. firm see Wright (C. C.) Durand & Co. firm
Durang, Charles. 21413
Durango (Mexican State) 48282
Durango (Diocese) Bishop (Crespo) plaintiff 98359 see also Crespo, Benito, Bp. plaintiff
Durango (Diocese) Bishop (Lopez de Zubiria) 41982 see also Lopez de Zubiria, Jose Antonio, Bp.
Durant, C. F. (12514), 64851, 92135
Durant, Henry F. 21414
Durant, Thomas J. 21415, 88471
Durao, Jose de Santa Rita. 21416-21417
Durate Caldeiras Centenera de Villadarias, Manoel. see Villadarias, Manoel Durate Caldeiras Centenera de.

Durazzo, Ippolito. supposed author 21418
D'Urban, Fortia. 101348-101350
Durbin, John P. (61307)
Durch Europam Lauffende. 104838
Durch seine Excellenz. (33338)
Durchaus verstandliches Lesebuch fur Jedermann. 27210, 51555
Durchleuchtiger hochgeborner Furst. (8784)
Durchstich der Amerikanischen Landenge. 4579
De Redouer, Mathurin. see Redouer, Mathurin du.
Durell, Philip. 21419
Durell, William. 84553
Duresme, Bishop of. see Durham, Bishop of.
Duret, -------. (21420)
Durfee, ---------. ed. (21424)
Durfee, Calvin. 21421-(21423)
Durfee, Job. 20650, (21424)-21427
Durfee, Joseph. 21428
Durfee, Thomas. reporter 70696
Durgin, Clement. 21429
Durham, A. A. 19819, 21430
Durham, Ebenezer. 60707
Durham, John George Lambton, 1st Earl of, 1790-1840. 29693, 33891, 38746-38751, 58489, (71037)
Durham, Terry. (70540)
Durham, Bishop of. see Barrington, Shute, successively Bp. of Salisbury, and Durham, 1734-1826. Butler, Joseph, successively Bp. of Bristol, and Durham, 1692-1752. Egerton, John, successively Bp. of Bangor, Litchfield and Coventry, and Durham, 1721-1787. Monteigne, George, Abp. of York, d. 1628. Thurlow, Thomas, successively Bp. of Lincoln, and Durham, 1727-1787. Trevor, Richard, successively Bp. of St. Davids, and Durham, 1707-1771. Van Mildert, William, successively Bp. of Llandaff, and Durham, 1765-1836.
Durham, N. H. College of Agriculture and the Mechanic Arts. see New Hampshire. College of Agriculture and the Mechanic Arts, Durham.
Durham, N. H. Congregational Church. 91152A
Durham, N. Y. First Presbyterian Church. 21431
Durieu, Jean-Louis. supposed author 100807
Du Rieux, L. see Rieux, L. du.
During the last winter, Dr. John Eberle published. 102326
Durivage, Francis Alexander. 21432, 92751
Durkee, Charles, 1805-1870. 21433
Durkee, S. 45874, note after 89212
Durnford, Mary. 21434
Duro, Fernandez. (76810)
Durocher, -------. 21435-21436
Durosoi. see Farmian de Rosoi, known as Durosoi.
Durr (A.) firm publishers 16452, 15493, (21118), 25537
Durret, ------. 21437, note after 100808, 3d note after 102871
Durrett, Reuben Thomas, 1824-1913. 84934-84936
Durrie, Daniel Steele. (21438)-21440, 83029
Durroc, ------. (21441)
Durruy, V. 6852
D'Urville, Jules Sebastien Cesar Dumont. see Dumont d'Urville, Jules Sebastien Cesar.
Dury, John, 1596-1680. 55889, 95650
Duryea, C. see Duryee, C.
Duryea, Joseph T. 21442-(21443)
Duryee, C. 21444

Dusch und Eiselein, Al. von. tr. 40161
Dusen, Increase McGee van. see Van Dusen, Increase McGee.
Dusen, Maria van. see Van Dusen, Maria.
Dusenbery, Benjamin M. 21445, 94403
Du Simitiere, Pierre Eugene. see Simitiere, Pierre Eugene du.
Dussen Muilkerk, W. E. J. Berg van. see Berg van Dussen Muilkerk, W. E. J.
Dussey, R. D. 94650
D'Ussieux, Louis. see Ussieux, Louis d'.
Dussillion, Charles J. 18228, (21448)
Dust and ashes. 46291
Dust to earth. 25440
Dutch, Ebenezer. 21449-21450
Dutch almanack. 53674
Dutch at the North Pole. (19631)
Dutch dignity. (13435)
Dutch divine. pseud. Sermon. see Hellenbrock, Abraham.
Dutch dominie of the Catskills. 51435
Dutch farmer. pseud. Melancholy case of Mrs. Acherman. see W., Z. pseud.
Dutch Guiana. (56663), 93842-93843, 93861 see also Societeit van Suriname.
Dutch Guiana. British Commissioner. see Great Britain. Consulate. Paramaribo.
Dutch Guiana. Charter. 27126, (56682), 102903
Dutch Guiana. Gouverneur Generaal, 1742-1751 (Mauritius) 68458, 93844, 1st note after 93862 see also Mauritius, Johan Jacob.
Dutch Guiana. Gouverneur Generaal, 1742-1751 (Mauritius) defendant 68458 see also Mauritius, Johan Jacob. defendant
Dutch Guiana. Gouverneur Generaal, 1783-1784 (Matroos) 93845 see also Matroos, Wolphus Johan Beeldsnijder.
Dutch Guiana. Hove van Civile Justitie. 93846
Dutch Guiana. Hove van Politie en Crimineele Justitie. 93847
Dutch Guiana. Koloniale Bibliotheek. see Paramaribo. Surinaamsche Koloniale Bibliotheek.
Dutch Guiana. Laws, statutes, etc. 6453, 46681, 68633, 68913, note after 93841, 1st note after 93850
Dutch Guiana. Minister van Kolonien. 93848
Dutch Guiana. Raad van Politie. 93836, 93841
Dutch Guiana. Raad van Politie en Crimineele Justitie. 68458, 93844, 1st note after 93862 see also Plessis, Salomon du.
Dutch in Maine. 19636
Dutch manifesto. (56516), 69459
Dutch philosophical transactions. 49952
Dutch pilgrim fathers and other poems. 32993
Dutch proceedings at Amboyna against divers Englishmen. 66686
Dutch Reformed Church. see Nederlandsche Hervormde Kerk.
Dutch sailor. pseud. Authentic relation. 21451
Dutch survey. 9758
Dutch Vespucius. note before 99327, 99370
Dutch West Indies. Laws, statutes etc. 48961-48962
Dutcher, Dea. L. L. 24152
Dutcher, George Matthew, 1874-85357
Dutcher, J. W. 21453
Dutcher, Salem. 21454, 85357
Dutchess County, N. Y. Citizens. petitioners 47642
Dutchess County, N. Y. Society for the Promotion of Agriculture. see Society of

Dutchess County for the Promotion of Agriculture, Poughkeepsie.
Dutchess County and Poughkeepsie Sanitary Fair, 1864. see Poughkeepsie, N. Y. Dutchess County and Poughkeepsie Sanitary Fair, 1864.
Dutchman's fireside. 59190, 59196, 59216
Dutchmen and yankees. 30044
Dutens, Jean Victoire. (59572)
Du Tertre, Jean Baptiste. 21457-21458, 57458-58459, 72314
Duties and adngers of those who are born free. 59381
Duties and dignities of American freemen. (35436)
Duties and responsibilites of the Christian ministry. 84924
Duties and responsibilities of the rising generation. (21117)
Duties and the comforts of good men. (46268)
Duties connected with the present commercial distress. 2666
Duties of a banker. 36162
Duties of a church advocate. 27362
Duties of a fast, in time of war. 91545
Duties of a theologian. 58625
Duties of American citizens: a discourse. 59486
Duties of American citizens. Position of New Jersey. 2508
Duties of an American citizen. 102185
Duties of educated men; an oration. 5079
Duties of educated men [especially in America.] 3777
Duties of educated young men. 18955
Duties of hard times. 26074
Duties of justice, as they affect the individual and the state. (64646)
Duties of literary men. 71266
Duties of Massachusetts. A sermon. 13411
Duties of Massachusetts at this crisis. 93651
Duties of masters to servants: three premium essays. 43667, note before 93267
Duties of masters to their servants. 43667, note before 93267
Duties of parents in aid of the teacher. 47254
Duties of piety and loyalty recommended. 88954
Duties of teachers. 74388
Duties of the citizen soldier. 9364
Duties of the colored inhabitants of the District of Columbia. 59280
Duties of the hour. (37280)
Duties of the ministry. 91709
Duties of the north and south. 16222
Duties of the ransomed. 59280
Duties of the Regents of the University. (54000)
Duties of the rich. 105128
Duties of the times. (24191)
Duties of the watchman upon the walls of Zion. 66228
Duties of tonnage. 21461
Duties on woollens. 18846
Duties payable on goods, wares, and merchandise, imported into the United States . . . 1816. 21444
Duties payable on goods, wares and merchandise, imported into the United States after the last day of June, 1794. 21461
Duties payable on goods, wares and merchandise, imported into the United States after the 30th September, 1797. 21461
Duties payable on goods, wares and merchandise, imported into the United States of America from June 1792. 12461

Duties payable upon importation of goods. 91089
Duties suggested by the national grief. (31445)
Dutifull advice of a loving son to his aged father. 67578
Dutifull advice of a loving sonne to his aged father. 67599
Dutiful advice to a loving son. 67598
Dutillois, A. engr. 85819
Du Toict, Nicolas. see Techo, Nicolas del, originally du Toict, 1611-1685.
Du Tronchoy, ------ Gautier. see Gautier du Tronchoy, ------.
Dutroulau, -------. 21462
Duttenhofer, A. 21463-21464
Dutton, Aaron. 21465
Dutton, Anne. 21466
Dutton, George. 21467
Dutton, Henry, 1796-1869. 15763, 15778-15779, 21468, 94078
Dutton, John. 21343, 65646
Dutton, Sir Richard. defendant 30273
Dutton, Samuel W. S. 2675, 13589, 21469-21471, 80281
Dutton, Warren. 8363, 21472, 2d note after 101499
Duty, advantages, and pleasure of public worship. 82879
Duty, and a mark of Zion's children. 50661
Duty and advantages of singling praises unto God. 94119
Duty and importance of making the scriptures the rule. 362
Duty and importance of calling upon God illustrated. 88897
Duty and interest identical in the present crisis. 4575
Duty and interest of a people. 104398-104399
Duty and interest of early piety. A sermon. 103509
Duty and interest of the people to sanctify the Lord of Hosts. 19830
Duty and manner of propagating the Gospel shewn. 102176
Duty and manner of singing in Christian churches. 31219
Duty and obligation of Christians to marry. 102752
Duty and privilege of all to believe in Christ. 85335
Duty & property of a religious householder. 39444
Duty and reward of honouring God. 73050
Duty and reward of loving our country. 18405, (18433)
Duty and reward of propagating principles of religion. 9492
Duty and the interest of contributing to the promotion. 17581
Duty, character and reward of Christ's faithful servants. 79412
Duty of a Christian citizen. 92903
Duty of a Christian minister. 89744
Duty of a freeman. 21474
Duty of a minister. 7239
Duty of a people respecting their deceased ministers. 95539, 104112
Duty of a people that have renewed their covenant with God. 104079
Duty of a people, to . . . lament the death of a good king. (12368)
Duty of a people to stand in awe of God. 79413
Duty of a people, under dark providences. 104214

Duty of a people, under the oppression of man. (31894)

Duty of abstaining from the use of West India produce. 21473

Duty of all. 47445

Duty of all Christians urged. 13203

Duty of alms-giving. 92739

Duty of America enforced. (43157)

Duty of America to her emigrant citizens. 57741

Duty of American Christians. 14137

Duty of American women. 4289

Duty of Americans. 78504

Duty of Americans, at the present crisis. 21553

Duty of Americans to preserve civil and religious liberty. (39540)

Duty of an apostatizing people. 42084

Duty of benevolence and public spirit. 26230

Duty of British Christians in reference to colonial slavery. 102719

Duty of children. 79358

Duty of children whose parents have pray'd for them. 46292, 46673

Duty of Christian freemen to elect Christian rulers. 22382

Duty of Christian soldiers, when called to war. 104359

Duty of Christians, both ministers and people. 104360

Duty of Christians in respect to war. 9754

Duty of Christians in the present crisis. 29243

Duty of Christians to civil government. 80196

Duty of Christians to pray for the missionary cause. 64228

Duty of Christians to propagate their religion. 18759

Duty of Christ's ministers to be spiritual labourers. 21242

Duty of citizens in the work of reconstruction. 18189

Duty of civil rulers to be the nursing fathers. 20641

Duty of Columbia College to the community. 70247, (73950), 73977

Duty of commemorating the deeds of our fathers. 67877

Duty of committing our souls to Christ. 59605

Duty of congregationalism to itself. 85218

Duty of Congress. 32624

Duty of conservative Whigs in the present crisis. 12859, (67211), 72651

Duty of considering our ways. 78572

Duty of disobedience to the fugitive slave act. (12727)

Duty of disobedience to wicked laws. 4297

Duty of electors. 11965

Duty of every man to be always read to die. 79414

Duty of God's people to pray for the peace of Jerusalem. 22

Duty of God's people when engaged in war. 12371

Duty of Gospel ministers . . . Sermon. (25204)

Duty of Gospel-ministers to preserve a people from corruption. 91946

Duty of Gospel-ministers, to take heed to themselves. 27882

Duty of fasting and prayer. 13272

Duty of interesting children in the missionary cause. 85281

Duty of living for the good of posterity. 11955

Duty of loyal men. 20031

Duty of magnifying the work of the Lord. 101511

Duty of men's serving their generation. 92090

Duty of ministers . . . . A sermon preach'd at Norton. 47447

Duty of ministers . . . . A sermon preached at the ordination. 12331

Duty of ministers in relation to American slavery. 91103

Duty of ministers of the Gospel to guard. 32667

Duty of ministers, to testify. 21243

Duty of ministers to work the works of Him that sent them. 101016, 102218

Duty of moral reflection. 90923

Duty of nations. 43568

Duty of our nation to the world. 20391

Duty of parents in educating their children. 18976

Duty of parents, to instruct their children. 83438

Duty of parents to pray for their children, and especially to ask God. (14525)

Duty of parents to pray for their children, opened & applyed in a sermon. 46673

Duty of parents to transmit religion. 104406

Duty of patient submission to every condition. 46598

Duty of Pennsylvania concerning slavery. 60076

Duty of people to pray for and praise their rulers. 26785

Duty of praising the works of God. 103768

Duty of prayer for rulers. 21082

Duty of praying for our rulers. 78394

Duty of promoting Christianity by the circulation of books. 101386

Duty of prompt and complete abolition of colonial slavery. 104038

Duty of public spirit recommended. 17692

Duty of public usefulness. (41524)

Duty of renewing their baptismal covenant. (28224)

Duty of resignation. (50953)

Duty of Republican citizens. 8927, 8931

Duty of Republicans. (43387)

Duty of rulers . . . . A sermon. 56041

Duty of rulers and teachers in unitely leading God's people. 105508

Duty of singing considered. 92931

Duty of standing fast in our spiritual and temporal liberties. 21051

Duty of supporting the government. Arbitrary arrests. 68057

Duty of supporting the government in the present crisis. 23271

Duty of supporting the ministry. 84851

Duty of survivors to remember and to follow. 102224

Duty of sustaining the government. 89681

Duty of the American scholar to politics and the times. 18049

Duty of the American scholar to the literature. (26054)

Duty of the church in these times. 68585

Duty of the Christian minister. 51187

Duty of the citizen to the law. 26074

Duty of the educated young men of this country. 89016

Duty of the free states. 11924

Duty of the free states. Second part. 11924

Duty of the General Assembly to all the church. 33028

Duty of the Godly. (25387)

Duty of the good and faithful soldier. 104057

Duty of the hour: an oration delivered at Jamaica. (43102)

Duty of the hour. By Rev. Samuel T. Spear. 89088

Duty of the hour. The great issue. 21475, 28451, (35097)

Duty of the king and subject. 21476

Duty of the legislature of Nova Scotia. 25119

Duty of the people to take and keep the oath of allegiance. 62517

Duty of the Presbyterian Church. (35751)

Duty of the present. 36885

Duty of the present generation to evangelize the world. 21477, 76451

Duty of the south. (58346)

Duty of the southern patriot and Christian. 58259

Duty of the time. 3794

Duty of union in a just war. 91546

Duty of women to promote the cause of peace. (38524)

Duty of worshiping God in his house. 92108, 97741

Duty of young people to give their hearts to God. (14525)

Duty on lumber paid by Canadians. 24200

Duty on paper. (58438)

Duty on railroad iron. 79516

Duty . . . on tobacco. 100517

Duty, the measure, and the mode of honouring the Lord. 80451

Duty to God not to be overlooked. 26292

Duty to government and to God. (81623)

Du Val, ------. 66882

Duval, Alfred. (21478)

Duval, John P. 24850

Duval, Jules. (21479), 21480, 21491

Du Val, Marcus. (21481)

Du-Val, Pierre, 1618-1683. 21468, 21482

Du Val, S. 45381 see also Maryland. Agent of the Western Shore.

Duval-Sanadon, David. 20228, 21484-21485, 68974

Duvall, William Pope, 1784-1854. 43385

Duvallon, ------ Berquin. see Berquin-Duvallon, ------.

Duval's magazine. see Haddy and Duval's Magazine.

Duvaux, J. illus. 69046

Du Verdier, Antoine. see Verdier, Antoine de.

Duverger de Saint Blin, ------. see Saint Blin, ----- Duverger de.

Du Vergier, ------, Baron Eberstein et Chion. see Eberstein et Chion du Vergier, ------, Baron.

Duvergier, Jean Baptiste. 21119-21120

Duvergier de Hauranne, Ernest. 21489

Duvernay, Ludgar. plaintiff 96930

Duvernois, Clement. 21490, 34945, note after 48507

Duvert, ------. 100745

Duvivier, Franciade Fleurus. 21488

Du Vivier-Bourgogne, Charlotte des Cossas. see Argoult, Charlotte des Cossas (du Vivier-Bourgogne) d'.

Du Vivier-Bourgogne, Marie-Anne (Godefroy) see Bourgogne, Marie-Anne Godefroy du Vivier-.

Dux, Adolf. tr. 21368

Duxal, Jules. see Duval, Jules.

Duxbury, Mass. First Parish. Committee. 21492, 103045 see also Moore, Josiah.

Duxbury, Mass. School Committee. 21494

Duy, Albert William. (13367), 21495

Duyckinck, Evart Augustus, 1816-1878. 1927, 7299, 16323, 21496-21506, (24948), 25901, 28892, 35223, 41499, 42645, 73234-73235, 84062, 84317, 94431, 95819

Duyckinck, George Long, 1823-1863. 21505, 28892, 41499, 42645

Duyckinck, Henry. 21507

Duycks, W. C. tr. 38415

Duyn, Nicolaas. 21508

Duyrcant, A. (31660)-(31661)

Dwarf, a dramatic poem. (68638)

Dwarris, Sir Fortunatus. 21509-21510, 102869 see also Gt. Britain. Commissioner on Civil and Criminal Justice in West Indies.

Dweller in the temple. pseud. Philosophy of modern miracles. 62563

Dwellings and schools for the poor. 55874

Dwenger, Joseph, Bp. 72942 see also Fort Wayne (Diocese) Bishop (Dwenger)

Dwerhagen, Herman C. 21511

Dwight, ------. 21514

Dwight, Benjamin Woolsey. 21512-21513

Dwight, Edmund. 21515-21516

Dwight, Edward S. 21517

Dwight, Harrison Gray Otis. 21518, 82471

Dwight, Henry. (21519)

Dwight, Henry W. 104433

Dwight, Jasper, of Vermont. pseud. Letter to George Washington. see Duane, William, 1760-1835. supposed author and Treziulney, ------. supposed author

Dwight, John S. ed. 21520

Dwight, Josiah. (21521)

Dwight, Nathaniel. 21522-21524

Dwight, Sereno Edwards, 1786-1850. 21525-21528, 21974, 21953, 92259

Dwight, Theodore, 1764-1846. 965-(966), 15791, 21529-21534, (21778)

Dwight, Theodore, 1796-1866. (18536), 21535-(21542), 51070, (55833), 84163, 95352

Dwight, Theodore William, 1822-1892. 14828, 21543-21545, (71356), 76611, 76647, 85212

Dwight, Timothy, 1752-1817. (15702), 15643, 15858, (21542), 21546-21554, 21556-21563, 21566, 24273, (82501), 90122, 2d note after 90803, 93351, note after 97007, 97126, note after 98342, 105785C, 105786, 105940, 105929 see also Yale University. President.

Dwight, Timothy, 1752-1817. supposed author (21555), (50944)

Dwight, Timothy, 1828-1916. 92514

Dwight, Wilder. (21567)

Dwight, Mrs. Wilder. (21567)

Dwight, William T. 21527, (21569)-(21571)

Dwight's journal of music. 21520

Dwinell, Israel E. 21572

Dwinell, Israel E. supposed author 89534

Dwinelle, John W. 21573

D'Wolf, John, 1779-1872. 19882-19883

Dwyer, Charles P. 21574

Dyalogus. Iohannis Stamler. Augustn. 90127

Dyas et trias. 44505

Dyce, ------. ed. 78597

Dyck, Abraham van. see Van Dyck, Abraham.

Dyck, Henry van. see Van Dyck, Henry.

Dyckman, J. G. (21576)

Dydacki, Franciszek. 92595

Dye, Deacon. 21578

Dye, John Smith. (21579)-(21580)

Dyer, Alexander B. defendant at court of inquiry 21581

Dyer, Charles E. 67391

Dyer, Charles George. 21582

Dyer, David. (21583)-21586

Dyer, E. Porter. 21588

Dyer, Eliphalet, 1721-1807. 21587

Dyer, Eliphalet, 1721-1807. supposed author 26351-26352

Dyer, Elisha, 1811-1890. 33150 see also
  Rhode Island. Governor, 1857-1859
  (Dyer)
Dyer, George. 21589
Dyer, Hernan. 21590
Dyer, Joseph. 21591
Dyer, J. C. (21592)
Dyer, Mary M. see Marshall, Mary M. (Dyer)
  fl. 1818.
Dyer, John. 9353
Dyer, Oliver. 21599, 54836, 89212
Dyer, Palmer. 21600
Dyer, Sydney. 21601-21602
Dyer, William. 21603
Dyers' assistant. (105176A)
Dye's bank note plate delineator. (21580)
Dying address of the three thayers. 95263
Dying Christian's retrospections and anticipations.
  89089
Dying confession of Alexander White. 103349A
Dying confession of Lewis Wilber. 103946
Dying criminal: a poem. 106090-106091
Dying declaration of James Buchanan. 105350
Dying exercises of Mrs. Deborah Prince.
  65590
Dying expressions of a young man who embraced
  the same principles. 86655
Dying fathers last legacy to an onely child.
  61191
Dying fathers last legacy to an onely child.
  61192
Dying in peace. (14480)
Dying legacy of a minister to his . . . people.
  46674
Dying legacy of an aged minister. 46794
Dying legacy to the people of his beloved
  charge. 51539
Dying mother's advice. 104310
Dying Negro, a poem. 18987
Dying prayer of Christ. (65591)
Dying prostitute; a poem. 17434
Dying robber. 88046
Dying speech and confession of William Linsey.
  105355
Dying speeches of several Indians. 22148
Dying testimony to the sovereign grace of God.
  46684
Dying words. 105467
Dying-words of Ockamickon, an Indian king.
  105218
Dying words of William Fletcher. 24743
Dying words of the criminal [i. e. Jeremiah
  Meacham.] 13202
Dyke, Henry J. van. see Van Dyke, Henry J.
Dyke, Thomas. 21604
Dykes, George Parker, d. 1888. tr. 83124-
  83128
Dymond, Jonathan. 21605-21606
Dymond on slavery. 21605
Dynastie des Lopez avant en pendant la guerre
  actuelle. 39982
Dynes, J. engr. 84779
Dyottsville Apprentices' Library Company.
  61609
Dyottsville Glass Factory. 61609
Dyottsville Glass Factory. Committee to Inves-
  tigate the Internal Regulations. 61609
Dyson, John. 101527
Dyson, Julia A. Parker. 21607, 39205

E

E * * * pseud. tr. see Eidous, Marc
  Antoine. tr.

E., A. pseud. ed. 96179
E., A. B. C. D. pseud. Pretty story. see
  Hopkinson, Francis.
E., B. I. D. P. pseud. Recherches sur
  l'origine du despotisme oriental. see
  Boulanger, Nicolas Antoine.
E., D. pseud. Verses addressed to Ferdinand
  Smyth Stuart. 85244
E., D. S. P. D. L. pseud. Jubilos de Lima.
  36824
E., E. B. d'. pseud. Essai sur cette question.
  see Engel, Samuel.
E., F. W. pseud. ed. Ethan Allen's captivity.
  797
E——g, J. pseud. Address of thanks. see
  Ewing, John.
E., J. pseud. Justice of the present war.
  see Ellis, Johnathan.
E., J. pseud. Logic primer. see Eliot, John,
  1604-1690.
E., J. pseud. Slow horses made fast. see
  Elderkin, John.
E., J. A. pseud. Sketch of the rise and pro-
  gress of Grace Church. see Eames,
  Mrs. Jane Anthony.
E., J. M. C. y. pseud. Oracion. see Cas-
  taneda y Escalada, Jose Maria.
E., M. pseud. tr. see Eidous, Marc
  Antoine.
E., M. B. J. L. et. pseud. see L. et E.,
  M. B. J. pseud.
E., M. le B. pseud. Memoir sur la navigation.
  see Engel, Samuel.
E., M. y. pseud. see M. y E. pseud.
E., N. pseud. Antiquarian researches. 86033
E——, O——, a young student. pseud. On
  the death of the Reverend Benjamin Col-
  man. see Seccombe, Joseph, 1706-1760.
E., P. pseud. Some miscellany observations.
  see Willard, Samuel, 1640-1707.
E., P. pseud. tr. see Erondelle, P. tr.
E., P. P. pseud. see Estala, Pedro,
  presbitero. ed. and tr.
E., S. pseud. Further quaeries upon the pre-
  sent state. 21610-21611, 52640
E., W. pseud. Interesting detail of the opera-
  tions. see Eaton, William, 1764-1811.
E., W. pseud. New-England's present suffer-
  ings. see Wharton, Edward.
E. A. pseud. see Atkinson, Edward.
E. A. W. pseud. see Walker, Edward Ashley.
E. A. W. H. pseud. see H., E. A. W. pseud.
E. B. pseud. tr. see B., E. pseud. tr.
E. B. pseud. see Burrough, Edward.
E—— B——. pseud. see Burke, Edmund,
  1729?-1797. incorrectly supposed author
E——ce B—— g——l. pseud. see Budgel,
  Eustace, 1686-1737.
E—st—— ce B——g——11. pseud. see Bud-
  gel, Eustace, 1686-1737.
E. B. d'E. pseud. see Engel, Samuel.
E. B. G. pseud. see Greene, Edward Burn-
  aby.
E. B. R. pseud. see R., E. B. pseud.
E. B. S. pseud. see Seabrook, E. Bayard.
E. B. V. W. pseud. see W., E. B. V. pseud.
  ed.
E. C. G. pseud. see G., E. C. pseud. ed.
E. C. M. J. D. M. pseud. see M., E. C. M.
  J. D. pseud.
E. C. S. pseud. see Stanton, Elizabeth (Cady)
  1815-1902.
E. C. Smyth, Appelant. 85212
E. D. pseud. see Dyer, Eliphalet. 1721-
  1807.
E. D. K. pseud. see Kendall, E. D.

E. D. N. pseud. see Neill, Edward Duffield.
E. F. pseud. see F., E. pseud.
E. F. pseud. see Weymouth, Mass. South Parish. Committee of Inquiry.
E. Foxton. pseud. see Palfrey, Sarah Hammond.
E. G. pseud. see G., E. pseud.
E. G. pseud. see Gardiner, Edmund.
E. G. pseud. see Grimstone, Edward. supposed tr.
E. G. Happelii Grosseste Denkwurdigkeiten der Welt. (30277)
E. G. S. pseud. see Squier, Ephraim George, 1821-1888.
E. George Squier, Nicaragua, y Henri Lytton Bulwer. 89964
E. Gerry for Governor. 46090
E. H. pseud. see Harrison, Edward.
E. H. pseud. see Hickeringill, Edmond.
E. H. M. A. pseud. see A., E. H. M. pseud.
E. H. S. pseud. see Derby, Edward Henry Stanley, 15th Earl of.
E. J. T. pseud. see T., E. J. pseud.
E. L. pseud. see L., E. pseud.
E. Lockett versus the Merchants' Insurance Company. 82144
E. M. pseud. see M., E. pseud.
E. M. pseud. see Musson, Eugene.
E. M., of Antwerp. see M., E., of Antwerp.
E. M. Cross & Co.'s Philadelphia business directory. 61606
E. M. Institute. see Cincinnati. Eclectic Medical Institute.
E. N. L. pseud. see Lockerby, Elizabeth N.
E. P. pseud. see P., E. pseud.
E. P. pseud. see Parkman, Ebenezer.
E. P. pseud. see Penington, Edward.
E. P. U. pseud. see Nye, G.
E. R. pseud. see Rawson, Edward.
E. R. pseud. see Ritchie, Elizabeth.
E. S. pseud. see Stinchfield, Ephraim.
E. S. S. pseud. see Seward, Edward S.
E. S. T. pseud. see T., E. S. pseud.
E. Snow's reply to the self-styled philanthropist. 85509
E. T. pseud. see T., E. pseud.
E. T. W. pseud. see W., E. T. pseud.
E. V. C. pseud. see Childe, Edward Vernon.
E. W. pseud. see MacNemar, Richard.
E. W. pseud. see Wharton, Edward.
E. W. pseud. see Winslow, Edward.
E. W., Gent. pseud. see Williams, Edward, fl. 1650.
E. W. S. pseud. see S., E. W. pseud.
E. Wright. pseud. see MacNemar, Richard.
E nel fine l'historia vera. 10311
E Pluribus Unum. pseud. see Unum, E Pluribus. pseud.
E pluribus unum. The address at Burlington College. 20391
E pluribus unum. The articles of confederation vs. the constitution. 65568
E pluribus unum. British cruelty, oppression, and murder. 30178
Ea continens. 2476
Eachard, L. see Echard, Laurence.
Eacker, George I. (21612)-(21613)
Eads, James B. 34324
Eads, James D. comp. (34998)
Eager, Samuel W. 21614
Eager, William. plaintiff 102600
Eagle, Brattleboro, Vt. see Brattleboro semi-weekly eagle.
Eagle and hawk. 21615

Eagle Fire Company, New York. defendants (72621), note after 96921
Eagle Fire Company, New York. Charter. 54251
Eagle library, no. 4. 83896
Eagle of the Mohawks. 80067
Eagle of the south. (55074)
Eagle of Washington. 55006
Eagle pass. 50132
Eagleson, Jonathan. 84583
Eakin, C. M. 62383
Eakin, H. M. 83721
Eames, Benjamin T. ed. 70700
Eames, C. 3924
Eames, H. H. 49247
Eames, J. H. 21616
Eames, Jane Anthony. 21617-21618
Eames, Jonathan. 21619
Eames, Theodore. 21620
Eames, Wilberforce. 2d note after 87347, note before 99075, 2d note after 103846, 104274
Earhart, T. J. 21621
Earl, John. see Earle, John.
Earl of Albion's proclamation. 52434
Earl of Buchan's address. 22789
Earl of Harrington on the Maine-law. 39895
Earl of Selkirk's pamphlet. 20704, (22080)
Earl Rupert, and other tales and poems. (51698)
Earl Russell and the slave trade. 74343
Earle, A. B. (21623)
Earle, Augustus. 21624
Earle, J. 21625
Earle, John. 21622, 81461
Earle, John Milton. 21626
Earle, Oliver. plaintiff (21627)
Earle, Pliny, 1809-1892. 21628, (54117)
Earle, Thomas, 1796-1849. 21629
Earle, Thomas, fl. 1845. 88295
Earle, William, Jr. 56420, 4th note after 95756
Earles, John. defendant 21630
Earliest churches of New England and its vicinity. (20269)
Earliest books in the new world. 106398
Earliest diplomatic documents on America. 96515
Earliest printed sources of New England history. 82835
Early, Jubal Anderon, 1816-1894. (21631), 88369
Early, Peter, 1773-1817. 49073
Early American children's books. 102376
Early American Indian history. 95216
Early and modern democracy reviewed. 28872
Early and real Godliness urged. 46292
Early attempts at Rhode Island history. 70719
Early Baptists of Virginia. (33352)
Early biography, travels and adventures. 11845
Early buds. (69621)
Early Catholic missions in the North West. 88910
Early Chatham settlers. 84759
Early churchmen of Connecticut. 11940
Early conversion of islanders. 90218-90219
"Early day" in the north-west. 12660, (37941)
Early days at Prairie du Chien. 85433
Early days at Racine, Wisconsin. 67391
Early days in the Society of Friends. 37328
Early days of California. A comedy. 56318
Early days of California; embracing what I saw and heard there. 23865
Early days of the church in the Hilderberg. 26173
Early days of Thomas Whittemore. 103803

Early discoveries by Spaniards in New-Mexico. (7162)
Early English colonies. 97149
Early friend. pseud. ed. Memoirs of Mrs. Susan Huntington. see Wisner, Benjamin Blydenburg.
Early Friends (or Quakers) in Maryland. (45211A), 55504
Early history and present state of the city and island of Montreal. 6793
Early history of agriculture in Virginia. 9776
Early history of Bennington, Vt. 36041
Early history of Boston. 6564, 97079
Early history of cartography. 91866
Early history of Dunbarton. 29488
Early history of Florida. 23668
Early history of Grand Island and Ararat. 9056, note after 95451
Early history of Ithica. (37804)
Early history of Michigan. 80119, note after 91676
Early history of Narragansett. 64633, 70719
Early history of New England; being a relation. 46675
Early history of New England, illustrated by numerous interesting incidents. 94022, 103387
Early history of Omaha. 87143
Early history of Palmyra, New York. 21722
Early history of Presbyterianism in South Carolina. 33292
Early history of Rhode Island. (10076)
Early history of Rochester. (72341)
Early history of St. Louis and Missouri. 80176
Early history of South Carolina. 1902
Early history of Southampton. 33347
Early history of Suffolk County, L. I. (55256)
Early history of the American Philosophical Society. 59143
Early history of the church in Georgia. 91583
Early history of the falls of Skuylkill. 29520
Early history of the Iroquois. 92154
Early history of the Lutheran Church in America. 77479
Early history of the Lutheran Church in the state of New York. 41383
Early history of the Maumee Valley. 33102
Early history of the medical profession. 693
Early history of the New Hampshire Medical Institution. 83654
Early history of the northwestern states. 29731
Early history of the original charter. 24356
Early history of the Pease families in America. 59455
Early history of the southern states. 30964, 2d note after 100461
Early history of the town [of Watertown, Mass.] (6283)
Early history of the University of Virginia. (35937)
Early history of Waterbury. 58650
Early history of western Pennsylvania. (74155), 84617, 101710
Early Indian trails. 83689
Early investment. 88487
Early Jesuit missions in America. 40006
Early Jesuit missions in North America. 37949
Early Kansas history. 84037
Early lays. 81207
Early life and complete trial of Mary, alias Polly Bodine. 6112
Early life and professional years of Bishop Hobart. 43675

Early life, campaigns and public services of Robert E. Lee. 63854
Early life of Washington. 101795-101796
Early Massachusetts press. 91182-91183
Early meeting of the American Medico-Psychological Association. 84258
Early Methodism within the . . . Old Genesee Conference. (59471)
Early New England marriage dower. (78338)
Early New York business tokens. 9538
Early notices of Toronto. (77427)
Early offerings best accepted. 80187
Early peopling of America. 55012
Early piety again inculcated. (14525)
Early piety encouraged. 22436
Early piety exemplified in Elizabeth Butcher of Boston. 46294
Early piety, exemplified in the life and death of Mr. Nathanael Mather. 46293, (46505)
Early piety . . . illustrated. 62824
Early piety joyful to beholders. 16640
Early piety recommended. 12331
Early piety the basis of elevated character. 57174
Early Presbyterian immigration into South Carolina. 33293
Early recollections of Newport, R. I. 11897
Early recollections of the Californian mines. 11084
Early records of the city and county of Albany. (59450)
Early records of the Grand Lodge of the State of Vermont. 99192
Early religion recommended. 90916
Early religion, urged in a sermon. 46295
Early reminiscences: a poem. 78335
Early reminiscences of Quincy. 37684
Early scenes in Cumberland. 23101
Early scenes in Kentucky. 72572
Early schools and school-books of New England. 102336
Early settlement & progress of Philadelphia & Pennsylvania. 102142
Early settlement, rise and progress of Vincennes. 39316
Early settlers in the West. A poem. (73523)
Early settlers of Hingham, New England. 18099
Early sketches, latter settlements, and further developments. 5604
Early southern tracts. 16234, (45316), 69292, note after 80002, 103353
Early sunset. 91156
Early times in middle Tennessee. 11024
Early times in the Massachusetts. 78775-78776
Early times on the Susquehanna. (60949)
Early use of cavalry in this country. 36469
Early voyages of discovery. 32470
Early voyages up and down the Mississippi. 11597, (80003)
Early western travels. 96381, 102508, 102514, 105125, 105629
Early years in the far west. 29729
Early years of the late Bishop Hobart. 43674, 43679
Earnest address to such of the people called Quakers. 21632
Earnest address to the colonies. 84585
Earnest address to the people of Great-Britain and Ireland. 63089
Earnest and affectionate address to the people called Methodists. 104691
Earnest appeal for peace. (24909)
Earnest appeal on behalf of the missing Arctic expedition. (62873)

Earnest appeal to the patriotism and good
sense of the citizens. (41201)
Earnest appeal to the people of Maryland.
45131
Earnest call. 61610
Earnest discussion of momentous themes.
78940
Earnest exhortation to the children of New-
England. 46676
Earnest exhortation to the inhabitants of New-
England. 46640, 46677
Earnest expostulation. 59657
Earnest expostulation with those professed
members. 86047
Earnest Grey: or, the sins of society. 47052
Earnest persuasive to the frequent receiving
of the Holy Communion. 78573
Earnest plea of laymen of the New School
Presbyterian and Congregational Churches.
(54252)
Earnest well-wisher to the truth. pseud.
Vindiciae clavium. see Cawdrey, Daniel.
Earnest word . . . in behalf of the church
institutions. 43324
Earnshaw, W. 21633-21634
Earth and man. 31949
Earth delivered from the curse. 12331
Earth devoured by the curse. 14496
Earth twice shaken wonderfully. 73496
Earthly care, a heavenly discipline. 92453-
92454
Earthquake a divine visitation. 25389
Earthquake dangers. 73594
Earthquake of Caraccas. 10193, (21638), note
before 94254, note after 98870
Earth-quake of Jamaica. 97509
Earthquake of Juan Fernandez. 21639, 93948,
93950
Earthquakes a token of the righteous anger of
God. 12331
Earthquakes and volcanoes. 64018
Earthquakes explained and practically improved.
20607
Earthquakes in Oregon. 84528
Earthquakes: instrumentalities in the divine
government. 21837
Earthquakes the effects of God's wrath. 9482
Earthquakes the works of God. 65592-65593
Earth's felicities. 91182
East, David J. 13312
East, Sir E. H. supposed author 21640,
80683, 2d note after 102866
East Abingdon, Mass. Library Association.
21642
East and the west. (74967)
East and the west; our doings with our neigh-
bours. 21641, note after 90311
East and west. 47181
East and west. A novel. 95392
East and west: an inaugural discourse. 16218
East and West India Sugar. (42951), 86736,
1st note after 102832
East and west; or, the beauty of Willard's
Mill. 3637
East Anglian. pseud. Letters. see Wells,
William Benjamin. supposed author
East Boston, Mass. 6556 see also Boston.
East Boston, Mass. Charter. 6556
East Boston Company. 6699, 21644
East Boston ferries. 83858
East Boston Ferry Company. petitioners
78515
East Bridgeport directory. 7815
East Bridgewater, Mass. School Committee.
21645

East Bridgewater, Mass. Selectmen. 21645
East Cambridge, Mass. People's Union As-
sociation. 21646
East Cambridge Female School, Cambridge,
Mass. see Cambridge, Mass. East
Cambridge Female School.
East Cambridge Lyceum. see Cambridge, Mass.
East Cambridge Lyceum.
East Cambridge Union Temperance Society.
Committee. 10153
East coast . . . from Cape St. Roque to Cape
San Antonio. 87325
East Evangelical Church, Ware, Mass. see
Ware, Mass. East Evangelical Church.
East Florida. Governor, 1764-1771 (Grant)
72848 see also Grant, James.
East Grenwich, R. I. 65828
East Hartford, Conn. (21648)
East Hartford, Conn. petitioners (21648),
30672
East Hartford, Conn. Classical and Grammar
School. 72709
East Haven, Conn. Congregational Church.
21649
East Haven, Conn. Saltonstall Division, no. 37.
see Sons of Temperance of North America.
Connecticut. Saltonstall Division, no. 37,
East Haven.
East-Haven register: in three parts. 20485
East India Company (British) 65865, (74131),
88192
East India Company (Dutch) see Nederlandsche
Oost-Indische Compagnie.
East India Marine Society, Salem, Mass.
75656
East India Marine Society, Salem, Mass. Char-
ter. 75656
East India Marine Society, Salem, Mass.
Museum. 75656
East India Marine Society of Salem. 75656
East India review. see British and colonial
magazine and East India review.
East Jersey. see New Jersey (Colony)
East Jersey under the proprietary governments.
78186, 83982
East Kingston, N. H. Auditor. 21651
East Kingston, N. H. Superintending School
Committee. 21651
East Lansing, Mich. State Agricultural College.
see Michigan. State University, East
Lansing.
East Lansing, Mich. State University. see
Michigan. State University, East Lansing.
East New Jersey Baptist Association. see
Baptists. New Jersey. East New Jersey
Baptist Association.
East Pembroke Seminary, Buffalo, N. Y.
21652
East Riding Anti-slavery Association. see
Hull and East Riding Anti-slavery As-
sociation.
East River Fire Insurance Company of . . .
New-York. Charter. 54253
East River Industrial School for Girls, New
York. 54254
East Saginaw city directory. 21653
East Saginaw courier. 90819
East Tennessee College. see Tennessee.
University.
East Tennessee Missionary Society. 94792
East Tennessee Relief Association, Knoxville.
21656, 33782
East Tennessee Relief Association, Knoxville.
General Agent. 21656, 33782 see also
Humes, Thomas L.

East Tennessee Relief Association, Knoxville, Proceedings Commemorative of the Death of Edward Everett, 1865. 21656

East Tennessee University. see Tennessee. University.

East Tennessean. pseud. Secession. 78710

East Windsor, Conn. Convention to Consider the Expediency of Establishing a Theological Institute Connected with a System of Manual Labor, 1833. see Convention to Consider the Expediency of Establishing a Theological Institute Connected with a System of Manual Labor, East Windsor, Conn., 1833.

East Windsor, Conn. First Church of Christ. 86640

East Windsor, Conn. First Congregational Church. 68408

East Windsor, Conn. Theological Institute. see Hartford Theological Institute.

East Windsor Institute. see Hartford Theological Institute.

Eastburn, Benjamin. 21657

Eastburn, James Wallis. 21659, 89130

Eastburn, Manton, Bp., 1801-1871. 1676, 14802, 17684, 21660-21663, (63248), 11th note after 96966

Eastburn, Robert. 21664, 94709

Eastburn (James) & Co. firm 21658, 93522

Eastburn, Kirk & Co. firm 21658

Easter, Hamilton. defendant 71258

Easter Fair of the Washington Light Infantry. 88104

Easter sermon. 71778

Easter services. 66758

Easterbrooks, Joseph, fl. 1705. 21665, 23023

Eastern and middle states, and the British provinces. 70961

Eastern and western states of America. (8896)

Eastern argus. 65002, 84162, 94571

Eastern Association in Fairfield County. see Congregational Churches in Connecticut. Fairfield County Eastern Association.

Eastern Association in Windham County. see Congregational Churches in Connecticut. Windham County Eastern Association.

Eastern Auxiliary Foreign Missionary Society of Rockingham County, New-Hampshire. 72387

Eastern boundary of New Hampshire. 37471, (52943)

Eastern coast of Central America. 1381

Eastern Coast of Central America Commercial and Agricultural Company. Charter. 7907, (29069)

Eastern Dispensary, New York. 54255

Eastern Dispensary, New York. Charter. 54255

Eastern District New Hampshire Medical Society. see New Hampshire Medical Society. Eastern District.

Eastern Indians (Massachusetts) see Norridgewock Indians. and Penobscot Indians.

Eastern Lunatic Asylum of Kentucky. see Kentucky. Asylum for Insane, Lexington.

Eastern mail, Waterville, Me. 59446

Eastern Market Company. Charter. 60077

Eastern New-Brunswick Baptist Association. see Baptists. New Brunswick. Eastern New Brunswick Baptist Association.

Eastern oriel opened. (77428)

Eastern Penitentiary, Cherry Hill, Pa. see Pennsylvania. Eastern Penitentiary, Cherry Hill.

Eastern Pennsylvania Fruit Growers' Society. see Fruit Growers' Society of Eastern Pennsylvania.

Eastern Railroad Company. (21666)

Eastern Railroad Company. Directors. (21666)

Eastern Subordinate Synod. see Reformed Presbyterian Church in North America. Eastern Subordinate Synod.

Eastern tourist. 20325

Eastern townships of Lower Canada. 8079

Eastern township's scenery, Canada East. 33936

Eastern, western, and southern business directory. 37758

Eastern, western & southern circular. 61606

Eastern Yacht Club, Boston. 21667

Eastham, Mass. Ecclesiastical Council, 1720. see Congregational Churches in Massachusetts. Ecclesiastical Council, Eastham, 1720.

Eastham, Mass. South Church. 21668

Eastlacke, Francis. (21671)

Eastland, Thomas. ed. 32047, 104738

Eastlove, Ebenezer. pseud. Negro emancipation. 52261

Eastman, Charles G. (9201), (21672)

Eastman, Daniel. 21673

Eastman, Edwin. (79352)

Eastman, F. S. (21675)-21676

Eastman, H. 21677

Eastman, J. R. 21678

Eastman, Jacob W. 21679

Eastman, Lucius Root. 21680

Eastman, Luke. 21681

Eastman, Mary H. 21682-(21686)

Eastman, Seth, 1808-1875. illus. 21682, 21685, 77839, 88755

Eastman, Samuel C. 21687

Eastman, Thomas. 21688

Eastman, Thomas. defendant at court martial 21689

Eastman, Tilton. 21690

Eastman, Z. (21691), 82072

Eastman National Business College, Poughkeepsie, N. Y. 64711

Easton, Hosea. (21692), 21723

Easton, James. 21693

Easton, John. 21694

Easton, Rufus. 21695

Easton, W. 19880

Easton, William C. (21696)

Easton, Mass. School Committee. 21697

Easton, Mass. Selectmen. 21697

Easton, Mass. Treasurer. 21697

Easton, Pa. Indian Conference, 1756. see Pennsylvania (Colony) Indian Conference, Easton, 1756.

Easton, Pa. Indian Conference, 1758. see Pennsylvania (Colony) Indian Conference, Easton, 1758.

Easton, Pa. Indian Conference, 1761. see Pennsylvania (Colony) Indian Conference, Easton, 1761.

Easton, Pa. Lafayette College. see Lafayette College, Easton, Pa.

Easton, Pa. Library Company. 21698

Eastport, Mass. Friendly Botanic Society. see Friendly Botanic Society at Eastport, Mass. and Portsmouth, N. H.

Eastport and Passamaquoddy. 103048

Eastwick, Edward B. 21699

Easy, Edward. 15023

Easy and compendious system of short-hand. 77059

Easy and pleasant guide to the art of reading. 52715, note after 65546, 73806

Easy essays of the hermit. (19587), 89498

Easy instructor. 84698

Easy introduction to the study of geography. 82284

Easy method of finding the distance of an object. 82327-(82328)
Easy Nat: or Boston bars and Boston boys. 21700
Easy Nat; or, the three apprentices. 91825, 91828
Easy plan for restoring quiet. (17666), 84589-84593
Easy plan of discipline for a militia. 62649
Eaton, ------, fl. 1648. 74459
Eaton, ------. defendant 30048
Eaton, A. K. 8331
Eaton, Amos, 1776-1842. 617, 21701-21710, 26985, 44408, (53688), 67461, 1st-3d notes after 98549, 3d note after 103741
Eaton, Asa, 1778-1858. (21711), (45842)
Eaton, B. A. 21712
Eaton, Cyrus. (21713)-(21714)
Eaton, Daniel C. (11972)
Eaton, Dea. M. 21716
Eaton, Dorman Bridgman, 1823-1899. 21715, 84254
Eaton, Edward. (21717)
Eaton, Edward Byron. 21718-21719
Eaton, F. W. 21721
Eaton, Francis Brown, 1825-1904. 21720, 85227-85229
Eaton, H. Hurlbert. 21725, (80563)
Eaton, Horace, 1810-1883. 21722, (21724)
Eaton, Horace. 1810-1883. incorrectly supposed author (21692), 21723
Eaton, Isaac. 21726
Eaton, Jacob. 21727
Eaton, John. 21728-21729, 25746 see also U. S. Bureau of Refugees, Freedmen, and Abandoned Lands. Department of Tennessee and Arkansas. General Superintendent.
Eaton, John Henry, 1790-1856. (21730)-21732, note after (69016), 96663-96664, 96694 see also U. S. Commissioner to the Chickasaw Indians. U. S. Commissioners to the Choctaw Nation. U. S. Commissioners to the Menominee Indians. U. S. War Department.
Eaton, Lilley. (24776), 68207
Eaton, Moses. 21735
Eaton, Peter. 21736-21737
Eaton, Rebecca. (21738)
Eaton, Samuel. 29402
Eaton, Samuel J. W. 21739-21740
Eaton, Theodore. 21741
Eaton, Thomas. 21742
Eaton, W. W. (21747)
Eaton, William. 21745-21746
Eaton, William, 1764-1811. 21743-(21744), 65083
Ebanhelio hezu Clizto zan Lucas. 74522
Ebeling, Christoph Daniel, 1741-1817. 1287, 9361, 21747-21748
Eben, Karl Theodor, 1836- 6173, 17632, 85148
Eben Caldwell Stanwood. 90458
Eben Ezer; or a monument of thankfulness. 26818
Ebenezer Beriah Kelly, an auto-biography. (37060)
Ebenezer Eastlove. pseud. see Eastlove, Ebenezer. pseud.
Ebenezer Kimball Sanborn. A memorial. 76236
Ebenezer: or, a faithful and exact account. 102450
Ebenezer: or Jehovah the helper of America. (43154)
Ebenezer S. Snell. 85386
Ebenezer's dream. 21749, 104309

Eberle, Frederick. defendant 21750
Eberle, John, 1787-1838. 1144, 47328, 83654, 83664, 102326
Eberstein et Chion du Vergier, --------, Baron. 69538
Ebert, Adolf. ed. 35536
Ebling, Christoph Daniel. 1287, (3818), 21748
Eblu de fidste dages hellige. 50752
Eboracus. pseud. Great and grave questions. see Broom, W. W.
Ebony idol. 21751
Eburne, Richard. 21752
Eby, P. 21753
Ecarte. 71041, 100881
Ecce ecclesia. 88660
Ecce iterum crispinus! 84822
Eccentric and wonderful persons. 27913
Eccentric biography. 21754
Eccentric magazine. 21755
Eccentricites Americaines. 23550
Ecclesiae monilia. (17040), 46296
Ecclesiastes. 46297
Ecclesiastical biography. 59497
Ecclesiastical catechism of the Presbyterian Church. 85282-85287, 85290, 85297, 85312, 85314, 85331
Ecclesiastical Council, Belchertown, Mass., 1723. see Congregational Churches in Massachusetts. Ecclesiastical Council, Belchertown, 1723.
Ecclesiastical Council, Berkley, Mass., 1830. see Congregational Churches in Massachusetts. Ecclesiastical Council, Berkley, 1830.
Ecclesiastical Council, Bloomfield, Me., 1848. see Congregational Churches in Maine. Ecclesiastical Council, Bloomfield, 1848.
Ecclesiastical Council, Bolton, Mass., 1773. see Congregational Churches in Massachusetts. Ecclesiastical Council, Bolton, 1773.
Ecclesiastical Council, Boscawen, N. H., 1833. see Congregational Churches in New Hampshire. Ecclesiastical Council, Boscawen, 1833.
Ecclesiastical Council, Boston, 1723. see Congregational Churches in Massachusetts. Ecclesiastical Council, Boston, 1723.
Ecclesiastical Council, Boston, 1841. see Congregational Churches in Massachusetts. Ecclesiastical Council, Boston, 1841.
Ecclesiastical Council, Boston, 1866. see Congregational Churches in Massachusetts. Ecclesiastical Council, Boston, 1866.
Ecclesiastical Council, Bradford, Mass., 1744. see Congregational Churches in Massachusetts. Ecclesiastical Council, Bradford, 1744.
Ecclesiastical Council, Braintree, Mass., 1792. see Congregational Churches in Massachusetts. Ecclesiastical Council, Braintree, 1792.
Ecclesiastical Council, Brimfield, Mass., 1801. see Congregational Churches in Massachusetts. Ecclesiastical Council, Brimfield, 1801.
Ecclesiastical Council, Brooklyn, 1854. see Congregational Churches in New York. Ecclesiastical Council, Brooklyn, 1854.
Ecclesiastical Council, Concord, Mass., 1743. see Congregational Churches in Massachusetts. Ecclesiastical Council, Concord, 1743.
Ecclesiastical Council, Danbury, Conn., 1764. see Congregational Churches in Connecticut. Ecclesiastical Council, Danbury, 1764.

Ecclesiastical Council, Danvers, Mass., 1852.
see Congregational Churches in Massachusetts. Ecclesiastical Council, Danvers, 1852

Ecclesiastical Council, Dorchester, Mass.,
1773. see Congregational Churches in
Massachusetts. Ecclesiastical Council,
Dorchester, 1773.

Ecclesiastical Council, Eastham, Mass., 1720.
see Congregational Churches in Massachusetts. Ecclesiastical Council, Eastham,
1720.

Ecclesiastical Council, Exeter, Mass., 1743.
see Congregational Churches in Massachusetts. Ecclesiastical Council, Exeter,
1743.

Ecclesiastical Council, Exeter, N. H., 1842.
see Congregational Churches in New
Hampshire. Ecclesiastical Council, Exeter, 1842.

Ecclesiastical Council, Fitchburg, Mass., 1802.
see Congregational Churches in Massachusetts. Ecclesiastical Council, Fitchburg, 1802.

Ecclesiastical Council, Grafton, Mass., 1744.
see Congregational Churches in Massachusetts. Ecclesiastical Council, Grafton,
1744.

Ecclesiastical Council, Grenfield, Mass., 1753.
see Congregational Churches in Massachusetts. Ecclesiastical Council, Grenfield,
1753.

Ecclesiastical Council, Groton, Mass., 1826.
see Congregational Churches in Massachusetts. Ecclesiastical Council, Groton,
1826.

Ecclesiastical Council, Haverhill, N. H., 1758.
see Congregational Churches in New
Hampshire. Ecclesiastical Council,
Haverhill, 1758.

Ecclesiastical Council, Haverhill, N. H., 1759.
see Congregational Churches in New
Hampshire. Ecclesiastical Council,
Haverhill, 1759.

Ecclesiastical Council, Holles, N. H., 1812.
see Congregational Churches in New
Hampshire. Ecclesiastical Council, Holles,
1812.

Ecclesiastical Council, Ipswich, Mass., 1747-
1748. see Congregational Churches in
Massachusetts. Ecclesiastical Council,
Ipswich, 1747-1748.

Ecclesiastical Council, Ipswich, Mass., 1805.
see Congregational Churches in Massachusetts. Ecclesiastical Council, Ipswich,
1805.

Ecclesiastical Council, Mansfield, Conn., 1806.
see Congregational Churches in Connecticut. Ecclesiastical Council, Mansfield,
1806.

Ecclesiastical Council, Middleboro, Mass., 1822.
see Congregational Churches in Massachusetts. Ecclesiastical Council, Middleboro, 1822.

Ecclesiastical Council, New Bedford, Mass.,
1850. see Congregational Churches in
Massachusetts. Ecclesiastical Council,
New Bedford, 1850.

Ecclesiastical Council, New Braintree, Mass.,
1799? see Congregational Churches in
Massachusetts. Ecclesiastical Council,
New Braintree, 1799?

Ecclesiastical Council, New Haven, Conn., 1785.
see Congregational Churches in Connecticut. Ecclesiastical Council, New
Haven, 1785.

Ecclesiastical Council, New London, Conn.,
1736. see Congregational Churches in
Connecticut. Ecclesiastical Council, New
London, 1736.

Ecclesiastical Council, New London, Conn.,
1737. see Congregational Churches in
Connecticut. Ecclesiastical Council, New
London, 1737.

Ecclesiastical Council, New York, 1859. see
Congregational Churches in New York.
Ecclesiastical Council, New York City,
1859.

Ecclesiastical Council, Newton Centre, Mass.,
1866. see Congregational Churches in
Massachusetts. Ecclesiastical Council,
Newton Centre, Mass., 1866.

Ecclesiastical Council, North Wrentham, Mass.,
1830. see Congregational Churches in
Massachusetts. Ecclesiastical Council,
North Wrentham, 1830.

Ecclesiastical Council, North Yarmouth, Me.,
1822. see Congregational Churches in
Maine. Ecclesiastical Council, North
Yarmouth, 1822.

Ecclesiastical Council, Northampton, Mass.,
1750. see Congregational Churches in
Massachusetts. Ecclesiastical Council,
Northampton, 1750.

Ecclesiastical Council, Northampton, Mass.,
1751. see Congregational Churches in
Massachusetts. Ecclesiastical Council,
Northampton, 1751.

Ecclesiastical Council, Plymouth, Conn., 1856.
see Congregational Churches in Connecticut. Ecclesiastical Council, Plymouth,
1856.

Ecclesiastical Council, Plymouth, Mass., 1832.
see Congregational Churches in Massachusetts. Ecclesiastical Council, Plymouth. 1832.

Ecclesiastical Council, Pomfret, Vt., 1792.
see Congregational Churches in Vermont.
Ecclesiastical Council, Pomfret, 1792.

Ecclesiastical Council, Portland, Me., 1812.
see Congregational Churches in Maine.
Ecclesiastical Council, Portland, 1812.

Ecclesiastical Council, Portland, Me., 1856.
see Congregational Churches in Maine.
Ecclesiastical Council, Portland, 1856.

Ecclesiastical Council, Portsmouth, N. H.,
1834. see Congregational churches in
New Hampshire. Ecclesiastical Council,
Portsmouth, 1834.

Ecclesiastical Council, Princeton, Mass., 1817.
see Congregational Churches in Massachusetts. Ecclesiastical Council, Princeton, 1817.

Ecclesiastical Council, Providence, R. I., 1792-
1793. see Congregational Churches in
Rhode Island. Ecclesiastical Council,
Providence, 1792-1793.

Ecclesiastical Council, Providence, R. I., 1832.
See Congregational Churches in Rhode
Island. Ecclesiastical Council, Providence,
1832.

Ecclesiastical Council, Providence, R. I., 1835.
see Congregational Churches in Rhode
Island. Ecclesiastical Council, Providence,
1835.

Ecclesiastical Council, Reading, Mass., 1847.
see Congregational Churches in Massachusetts. Ecclesiastical Council, Reading,
1847.

Ecclesiastical Council, Rupert, Vt., 1815. see
Congregational Churches in Vermont.
Ecclesiastical Council, Rupert, 1815.

Ecclesiastical Council, Salem, Mass., 1734.
see Econgregational Churches in Massachusetts Ecclesiastical Council, Salem,
1734.

Ecclesiastical Council, Salem, Mass., 1735. see
Congregational Churches in Massachusetts.
Ecclesiastical Council, Salem, 1735.

Ecclesiastical Council, Salem, Mass., 1784.
see Congregational Churches in Massachusetts. Ecclesiastical Council, Salem,
1784.

Ecclesiastical Council, Salem, Mass., 1816.
see Congregational Churches in Massachusetts. Ecclesiastical Council, Salem,
1816.

Ecclesiastical Council, Salem, Mass., 1831.
see Congregational Churches in Massachusetts. Ecclesiastical Council, Salem,
1831.

Ecclesiastical Council, Salem, Mass., 1849.
see Congregational Churches in Massachusetts. Ecclesiastical Council, Salem,
1849.

Ecclesiastical Council, Sandwich, Mass., 1817.
see Congregational Churches in Massachusetts. Ecclesiastical Council, Sandwich, 1817.

Ecclesiastical Council, Sandy Hill, N. Y., 1860.
see Baptists. New York. Ecclesiastical
Council, Sandy Hill, 1860.

Ecclesiastical Council, Simsbury, Conn., 1770.
see Congregational Churches in Connecticut. Ecclesiastical Council, Simsbury, 1770.

Ecclesiastical Council, Watertown, Mass.,
1722. see Congregational Churches in
Massachusetts. Ecclesiastical Council,
Watertown, 1722.

Ecclesiastical Council, West Brookfield, Mass.,
1843. see Congregational Churches in
Massachusetts. Ecclesiastical Council,
West Brookfield, 1843.

Ecclesiastical Council, Windham, Conn., 1813.
see Congregational Churches in Connecticut. Ecclesiastical Council, Windham,
1813.

Ecclesiastical Council, Woburn, Mass., 1746.
see Congregational Churches in Massachusetts. Ecclesiastical Council, Woburn,
1746.

Ecclesiastical Council, Worcester, Mass., 1820.
see Congregational Churches in Massachusetts. Ecclesiastical Council, Worcester, 1820.

Ecclesiastical Council, Wrentham, Mass., 1830.
see Congregational Churches in Massachusetts. Ecclesiastical Council, Vrentham,
1830.

Ecclesiastical Councils, Greenfield, Mass., 1813.
see Congregational Churches in Massachusetts. Ecclesiastical Councils, Greenfield, 1813.

Ecclesiastical Councils, Stafford, Conn., 1781.
see Congregational Churches in Connecticut. Ecclesiastical Councils, Stafford,
1781.

Ecclesiastical Councils, Wallingford, Conn.,
1759. see Congregational Churches in
Connecticut. Ecclesiastical Councils,
Wallingford, 1759.

Ecclesiastical Councils, West Stafford, Conn.,
1781. see Congregational Churches in
Connecticut. Ecclesiastical Councils,
West Stafford, 1781.

Ecclesiastical councils viewed from celestial
and satanic stand-points. 105621

Ecclesiastical disruption of 1861. 90441
Ecclesiastical government. 71844
Ecclesiastical history. 99822, 99825
Ecclesiastical history, from the commencement
of the Christian era. 74719
Ecclesiastical history of New England & British
America. 91750
Ecclesiastical history of New England; com-
prising not only religious, but also moral
and other relations. 24031
Ecclesiastical history of New-England, from
its first planting. 5631, 46392
Ecclesiastical history to 1853. 70837-70838
Ecclesiastical law of the state of New York.
32405
Ecclesiastical legislation on slavery. 12954
Ecclesiastical manual. 39776
Ecclesiastical memoir of Essex Street Religious
Society. (74720), 97772A
Ecclesiastical peace recommended. 11
Ecclesiastical persons. 84201-84202
Ecclesiastical proceedings relative to the Third
Presbyterian Church. 62310
Ecclesiastical punishments. 84209-84211
Ecclesiastical record. 88159
Ecclesiastical register. see Church review.
Ecclesiastical register. 18729
Ecclesiastical register of New Hampshire.
23820
Ecclesiastical republicanism. 85284-85285,
85287, 85290, 85297, 85314, 85325
Ecclesiastical tenures. (66816)
Ecclesiastical trials. 84203-84208
Ecclesiastical usurpation and strange in-
consistency exposed. 105326
Eclesiastico de la Diocesis de Popayan. pseud.
Contextacion. 64101
Ecclesiasticum. 12335
Ecclesiastique originaire de cette mesme terre.
pseud. Memoires. see Gonneville, Jean
Binot Paulmyer de.
Ecclesine, J. B. 21756-(21757)
Eccleston, Samuel, Abp., 1801-1851. 379,
70228 see also Baltimore (Archdiocese)
Archbishop (Eccleston)
Eccleston, T. 21758
Ecclestone, -------, fl. 1721. 65865, 88192
Ecco das vozes saudosas. 99523
Ecco sonoro da clamorosa voz. 1759A
Echaiz, Jesus. 21759
Echantillon. 47550
Echantillon de la doctrine que les Jesuites
enseignent. 11040
Echard, Laurence, 1670?-1830. 21760-21761
Echard, Laurence, 1670?-1730. supposed ed.
67542
Echasseriaux, -------. 21762
Echaurren, Gregorio. 97672
Echavarri, Bernardo Ibanez de. see Ibanez de
Echavarri, Bernardo.
Echave, Balth. de. 21764
Echave y Assu, Francisco. (21765)
Echeagaray, -------. 21766
Echeagaray, Martin. 21767
Echegoyen, J. I. (23443)
Echegoyen, Juan. 21768
Echevelar, Manuel de. 21770, (55395)-(55396)
Echeverria, Estevan. 21772-(21773)
Echeverria, J. de. 14568
Echeverria, Jose Antonio. ed. 63320
Echeverria, Juan Nepomuceno de. 21774
Echeverria, Manual de. see Echeverria y
Penalver, Manuel de.
Echeverria y Penalver, Manuel de. 21771,
21775, (59637) see also Albacea Fidu-
ciario del Ilmo. Sr. Dr. Don Luis de
Penalver.

Echeverria y Veitia, Mariano Jose Fernandez de. see Veytia, Mariano, 1718-1779.
Echeverria y Veytia, Mariano Jose Fernandez de. see Veytia, Mariano, 1718-1779.
Echeverz, Pedro Ignacio de. 21777, 69226
Echinodermata. 80764
Echo. (21778), 97240
Echo. A collection of songs. 21779
Echo, and other poems. 21534
Echo d. neuester Englischen Tagespresse. 16475
Echo from the army. 21781
Echo from the temple of wisdom. (19067), 86193
Echo of truth to the voice of slander. 64728
Echo: or, a satirical poem on the virtuous ten. 21780
Echo, or borrowed notes for home circulation. 32384
Echo; or, the battle of the shells. 21782, 63005
Echo to the groans of an expiring faction. 19518
Echo, with other poems. (966)
Echoes from the backwoods. 40757
Echoes from the cabinet. 21783
Echoes from the garrett. (78600)
Echoes from the living graves. 21783A
Echoes from the school-room. 68596
Echoes from the South. 21784, 63881
Echoes of a belle. (79680)
Echoes of devotion. 46298
Echoes of Harper's Ferry. (68524)
Echoes of song. 81392
Echoes of the cabinet. 21783
Echoes of the fort-hills [sic]. 30650
Echols, John. (15359), (21785)
Echos aus dem Urwandern oder Skizzen trans-atlantischen Lebens. 27194
Echos democraticos. 88795
Echo's of devotion. 46620
Echt historisch Verhaal van drie zeelieden. 28642
Echt historisch verhaal zo uit de mond als pen. (32804)
Echt uittrekset uit het politiek vertoog. 98506
Eckart, Anselm. 51480, (51482), 98777
Eckerlin, Israel. 71229, 106363
Eckfeldt, Jacob R. 21786-21788
Eckford, Henry. defendant 3392
Eckley, Joseph. 21789-(21792), 101868, 101870, 102747
Eclaireur, devoted to the army and militia. 19632
Eclaircissemens historiques. 94619
Eclaircissemens sur les positions geographiques. (27520)
Eclaircissements sur la demande de Messieurs les Deputes. 75109
Eclectic Medical College, New York. see New York. see New York (City) Eclectic Medical College.
Eclectic Medical College of Pennsylvania. see Philadelphia University of Medicine and Surgery.
Eclectic Medical Institute, Cincinnati. see Cincinnati. Eclectic Medical Institute.
Eclectic Medical Society of New York. (53655)
Eclectic museum. 10932
Eclectic review. 3096, 35606, 52749, (81854), note after 95491
Eckley, ------. 101868, 101870
Eclipse. 21793
Eclipse de sol. 97685
Ecloga pastoril. 57194

Ecloga tragico-pastoril na morte do Senhor D. Jose. 10324
Eclogae Americanae seu descriptiones plantarum. 98287
Eclogue. And other papers. 68185
Eclogue. Attempted by O——E—— a young student. (14525), 21608, 78697
Eclogue occasioned by the death of Reverend Alexander Comming. 17907
Eclogue sacred to the memory of the Rev. Dr. Jonathan Mayhew. 28546
Eclogue. 16390
Ecluse, Charles de l'. tr. 49941-49943, 49948
Ecole de Medecine, Montreal. 50247
Ecole Militaire de Quebec. 42721
Ecoles de droit aux Etats-Unis. 46863
Economia della vita humana. 64014
Economic views of the present contest. 5984, 80445
Economica: a statistical manual. 5956
Economica poletica aplicada a la propriedad territorial en Mexico. 62879
Economical almanack. (23241)
Economical causes of slavery in the United States. 21794, (48861), 1st note after 88112
Economical geology. 45750-45751, 45755
Economical observations on military hospitals. 95834
Economical School, New York. 54257
Economical value of the semi-bituminous coal. 67886
Economics. 48524
Economics and crime. 84067
Economie politique. 93480
Economie politique sur la balance des con-sommations. 81453
Economistes modernes. (70389)
Economy and policy of a Christian education. (30473)
Economy is the watchword. 84124
Economy of human life. 90282, 90284-90285
Economy. Thoughts on a plan of economy. 5957
Ecos de los Andes. 75913
Ecos del Espiritu Santo. 16187
Ecrit publie par la Compagnie des Indes Oc-cidentales. 47824
Ecrit traitant cette question. 42895, 101246
Ecritures figuratives et hieroglyphiques. 73304
Ecrivains Canadiens. 23597
Ecsamen de las facultades. 21795
Escposicion que hace el comdanate [sic]. 98384
Ecuador. Comision a la Exposicion Universal, Paris, 1867. 70049
Ecuador. Comision de fomento. 65718
Ecuador. Comisiones del Ecuador y Nueva Granada en la Cuestion Sobre Limites de Ambos Estados. see Comisiones del Ecuador Y Nueva Granada en la Cuestion Sobre Limites de Ambos Estados.
Ecuador. Ministerio de Hacienda. 21799
Ecuador. Ministro Plenipotentiario Nombrado para Transijir las Diferencias que Existen entre Peru y Ecuador. 61095 see also Quito, Ecuador. Conferencia Tenida entre los Ministros Plenipotentiarios del Peru y del Ecuador Nombrados para Transijir las Diferencias que Existen entre Una y Otra Republica.
Ecuador. Treaties, etc. 21800, (66220)
Ecuador und die Ecuador-Land-Compagnie. 21798
Ecumeur de mer, ou la sorciere des eaux. 16546
Ecumeurs de mer. 70331

Eddis, William. 21801
Eddowes, Ralph. (21802), 42526
Eddy, Ansel Doan, 1798-1875. 21803, 28818
Eddy, Caleb. 21804 see also Middlesex
Canal Corporation. Agent.
Eddy, Daniel C. 21805-21808
Eddy, George S. 90137
Eddy, Isaac. illus. 74289
Eddy, J. cartographer 82815
Eddy, John. 21809, 62743
Eddy, R. H. (21813)
Eddy, Richard. 21810-21812
Eddy, Samuel. 21814-21815
Eddy, Thomas, 1758-1827. 21816, 38080,
(54026), 86586
Eddy, Thomas, 1758-1827. supposed author
(54026), (54481)
Eddy, Thomas Mears, 1823-1874. 21817-21818,
32428
Eddy, William. defendant 6326, 1st note after
96956, 1st note after 97284
Eddy, Zachariah. 21819-21820, 70221
Ede, Charles R. N. 21821
Edelman, George W. (21822)
Eden, Sir Frederick Morton. 21823-21824,
99777
Eden, John. 21825
Eden, Morton. see Henley, Morton Eden, 1st
Baron, 1752-1830.
Eden, Richard, 1521?-1576. 1561-1563, (16967)-
16968, (21826), 3d note after 45010,
54011, (54104), 62803, 44220, note after
99383C, 102837, 2d note after 104134,
106294, 106330-106331
Eden, Sir Robert, d. 1784. 45290 see also
Maryland (Colony) Governor, 1769-1776
(Eden)
Eden, William. see Auckland, William Eden,
1st Baron, 1744-1814.
Eden in Virginia. 21829
Eder, Franc. Xav. 21830, 44085
Edes, Edward H. 21831
Edes, Henry. 21832
Edes, Peter. 93899
Edes, Richard S. 21834-(21835), 47070
Edes and Gill. firm publishers 21833, 91308
Edes and Gill's North-American almanack and
Massachusetts register. 21833
Edewakenk. Indian Chief 4391, 15429
Edgar, Alexander. plaintiff 90724
Edgar, Cornelius H. 21836-21839
Edgar, John G. 21840
Edgar, Patrick Nisbett. 21841
Edgar Huntly. 8457
Edgar Wentworth. 27942
Edgardo Poe. 63563
Edgarton, L. C. (78334)
Edgarton, Sarah C. see Mayo, Sarah C.
(Edgarton)
Edgcomb, Mass. petitioners (61266)
Edge, Frederick Milnes. 21842-(21847), 55300
Edge, Thomas. 66686
Edge Hill, or the family of the Fitzroyals.
21848, 4th note after 100577
Edgecome County, N. C. Superior Court. Grand
Jury. 94509
Edgefield, S. C. Citizens. petitioners 47663
Edgefield advertiser. 74481, 87946
Edgerton, Joseph Ketchum, 1818-1893. 21849,
22047, (40350)
Edgerton, Sidney, 1818-1900. 21850
Edgerton, Walter. 21851
Edgeville, Edward. 21852
Edgeworth, Maria, 1767-1849. 71806
Edgeworth Association, Malden, Mass. (44099)

Edgeworth Chapel, Charlestown, Mass. see
Charlestown, Mass. Edgeworth Chapel.
Edicion de "La Sociedad." 47032, 71704
Edicion de tres obras clasicas. 56299
Edict against the protestants in France. 25882
Edict du Roy pour l'etablissement de la Nouuelle
France. 56086
Edicto del Arzobispo de Mexico. (48448)
Edicto del Exmo. e Illmo. Senor Obispo de
Puebla. 66555
Edicto en que Ilustrisimo Senor Doctor Don
Felipe Joseph de Tres-Palacios y Verdeja
. . . corrige. 96781
Edicto instructivo. (67080)
Edicto para la publicacion del Santo Jubileo.
26721
Edicto pastoral con notivo de la presente
guerra. 41104
Edicto pastoral sobre diezmos. 73972
Edicto pastoral sobre jubileos. 73872
Edicto pastoral sobre los dias festivos. 78947
Edictus adversus omnes Catholicos sui regni.
22188
Edifying and curious letters. 21853, 40697
Edifying and curious letters from some mission-
ers. 21853
Edinburgh. Aungervyle Society. see Aunger-
vyle Society, Edinburgh.
Edinburgh. Court of Session. 104487
Edinburgh. Election sermon. 22793
Edinburgh. High Court of Justiciary. 33827-
33829, 91841A, 94849, note after 97471
Edinburgh. Society. see Society, Edinburgh.
Edinburgh. Society for Promoting the Mitiga-
tion and Ultimate Abolition of Negro
Slavery. see Society for Promoting the
Mitigation and Ultimate Abolition of Negro
Slavery, Edinburgh.
Edinburgh. Voluntary Church Association. see
Voluntary Church Association, Edinburgh.
Edinburgh annual register. 88550
Edinburgh cabinet edition. 32050
Edinburgh cabinet library. 97657
Edinburgh encyclopedia. 102166
Edinburgh evening courant. 93169
Edinburgh magazine. 5708
Edinburgh medical and surgical journal. 90519
Edinburgh new philosophical journal. 78182
Edinburgh review. 1217, 13496, 13499, 14726,
(16226), 19657, (21854), (21855), (35602),
35662, 37018, (43643), 46989, 50754,
67599, 79130-79131, (81837), 84304-84306,
84313, 84321, note after 90597, note after
92624, 93648, 95661, 102798
Edinburgh review and the West Indies. 14726,
(21855)
Edinburgh reviewers. 99809
Edinburgh weekly magazine. 1399
Edington, ------. (21856)
Edit du Congres de Etats-Unis pour les terres
dependantes des etats. 21857, 56913,
78124
Edit du Congres des Etats-Unis de l'Amerique.
21857, 56913, 78124
Edit du Roi; portant creation des princes.
21858
Edit du Roi, du mois de May 1664. 102773
Edit du Roy, portant revocation de la Compagnie des Indes Occidentales. 102774
Edit du Roy, povr l'etablissement de la Com-
pagnie des Indes Occidentalles. 21859,
102772
Edit du Roy, qui ordonne une fabrication
d'espices d'argent. 21860

Edit du Roy, servant de reglement pour le gouvernement & l'administration de justice et la police des isles Francoises. 14123

Edit du Roy, servant de reglement pour le gouvernement & l'administration de la justice, police, discipline & le commerce. 14124

Edit, portant revocation de la Compagnie de Saint Domingue. 75154

Editeur de l'An 2440. pseud. ed. see Jacob, Gerard. and Mercier, Louis Sebastien.

Edition du monde illustre 13. 100745

Edith Allen, or sketches of life in Virginia. 47483, (52419)

Edito pastoral formado con el objeto de procurar la pacificacion. (38553)

Editor. pseud. Account of Col. Crockett's glorious death at the Alamo. 17570

Editor. pseud. Annexation of Texas. see Minor, B. B.

Editor. pseud. Case upon the statute for distribution. see Wythe, George.

Editor. pseud. Explanatory and critical notes. 63094

Editor. pseud. Introduction to the whole. (32953), note after 102754

Editor. pseud. Letters from Nahant. see Wheildon, William Willder.

Editor. pseud. Notes. 81848

Editor. pseud. Noticia del editor. 55999

Editor. pseud. Postscript, addressed to Sir W******* H***. 40506

Editor. pseud. Preface. 63294

Editor. pseud. Supplement. see Pringle, Thomas.

Editor and Proprietor of the New-York morning post and morning star. pseud. see New-York morning post and morning star. Editor and Proprietor.

Editor of a quarterly review. pseud. Notes, critical and explanatory. see Deacon, W. F.

Editor of "Life in Normandy." pseud. Short American tramp in the fall of 1864. see Campbell, John Francis.

Editor of the "Aurora." pseud. see Duane, William John, 1780-1865.

Editor of the Boston daily advertiser. pseud. Remarks on the practicability. see Hale, Nathan.

Editor of the Canadian freeman. pseud. Abridged view of the alien question unmasked. see Collins, Francis.

Editor of the "Eclectic review." pseud. Jamaica; who is to blame? 35606

Editor of the Journal of the Franklin Institute. pseud. Remarks. 89118

Editor of the Louisville journal. pseud. Prenticeana. see Prentice, George D.

Editor of the Masonic mirror. pseud. Masonic character and correspondence. see Moore, Charles W.

Editor of the Morning chronicle. pseud. Preface. 2549

Editor of the "National." pseud. Life of Thomas Paine. see Holyoake, G. J.

Editor of the New-York morning post and morning star. pseud. see New York Morning post and morning star. Editor.

Editor of the Newport mercury. pseud. Newport illustrated. see Mason, George Champlin.

Editor of the North Carolina Christian advocate. pseud. see North Carolina Christian advocate. Editor.

Editor of the Port folio. pseud. Memoirs of eminent persons. see Hall, John E.

Editor of the Protestant. pseud. Secret institutions of the Jesuits. 78747

Editor [of the speeches of John Wilkes.] pseud. Notes. 104008-104009

Editor of the Standard bearer. pseud. Correspondence. see Rodman, Washington.

Editor of the Standard bearer's correspondence with the Dean. 72491

Editores del Argos. pseud. see Argos. Editores.

Editores del "Salvador rejenerado." 32773

Editorial article in the New York journal of commerce. (70273)

Editorial article in the Providence journal. (71146)

Editorial Association of Ohio. see Ohio Editorial Association.

Editorial de El Libreral de 15 de Enero de 1848. 72793

Editorial introduction by Richard B. Kimball. 37767

Editorials from the New York daily bulletin and auction record. 89111

Editorials from the New York daily bulletin. Reprinted by request. 89111

Editorials of the Knoxville whig. 8702

Editors are furnished with the remaining documents. 34400, 83815

Editors having been favoured with the late correspondence. 34400, 83814

Editors of the "Acta Columbiana," 1875-6. pseud. eds. 86933

Edits, ordinances, declarations and decrees. (10603)

Edits, ordonnances royaux, declarations et arrets. 10486

Edmands, J. Cushing. defendant at court martial 21861

Edmands, James M. 58089

Edmands, John Wiley, 1809-1877. 21862, 93269

Edme, B. Saint. pseud. Dictionnaire. see Bourg, Edme Theodore.

Edme Billardon de Sauvigny, Louis. see Sauvigny, Louis Edme Billardon de.

Edmerton, Jonathan. (21863)

Edmeston, --------. RA 21864

Edmonds, Cyrus R. 21865

Edmonds, James. 83450

Edmonds, John H. 88221

Edmonds, John Worth, 1799-1874. 21867-21868, 37977, 53983, 74795 see also U. S. Commissioner on the Claims of Creditors of the Potawatomi Indians of the Wabash.

Edmonds, S. Emma E. (21869)

Edmondson, ------. 104337

Edmondson family and the capture of the Schooner Pearl. 92411

Edmund Burke: a historical study. 50725

Edmund Burke's Jahrbucher der neuern Geschichte. 9287

Edmund Burkes Leben. 5649

Edmund Burke's Reden. 9297

Edmund Charles & Son's New York Bank note list. 12028

Edmund Kirke. pseud. see Gilmore, James R.

Edmund Randolph: a memoir. 67819

Edmund the Wanderer. pseud. Minstrelsey. see Spence, Robert T.

Edmunds, Francis W. 21866

Edmunds, Edward. 21870

Edmunds, George Franklin, 1828-1919. 21871

Edmunds, J. M. 70005

Edmunds, Lucy. 21872

Edmundson, William, d. 1712. 21873, 25363-(25364), note before 91980

Edsall, Benjamin B. 21874, 93939, note after 97514

Edson, George L. 90681

Edson, John. 90581

Edson, Theodore, 1793-1883. (21875)-(21877), (66153)

Educacion. 93345

Educacion cientifica, moral, y literaria, del bello sexo. 79052

Educacion comun. 77073

Education, a poem. 5349

Education after the war. (36783)

Education. An address, delivered at Leicester. 105617

Education: an address . . . to the Constitutional Convention of the state of Virginia. 78632

Education and evangelism. 81640

Education and labour. 15725

Education and Missionary Society of the Protestant Episcopal Church in the State of New York. Board of Managers. (54126), 66144

Education and morality in America. 84509

Education and progress. 38315

Education at the west. 15181

Education, by Henry Barnard. 22085

Education Convention to Examine into a System of Primary Instruction, Oswego, N. Y., 1862. (65843)

Education, emigration, and supremacy. 33632

Education for an agricultural people. 56050

Education for the ministry in the American Episcopal Church. 66145

Education in Castleton, Staten Island. 58735

Education in Massachusetts. 22428

Education in South Carolina. 88005

Education in the two Andovers. 26174

Education of daughters. 85443

Education of divine providence. 27925

Education of females. 74389

Education of idiots. 61611, 64617

Education of Indian youth. (5636)

Education of officers. 33819

Education of teachers in the south. 21885

Education of the heart. 82716

Education of the poor. 51187

Education of the XVIIth century. 21882

Education of woman. 78593

Education papers. No. 1. 65141

Education. Part I. 77674

Education reform. (25200)

Education Society of Connecticut. (15723)

Education Society of New England. see New England Education Society.

Education Society of the Presbyterian Church, Philadelphia. see Philadelphia Education Society of the Presbyterian Church.

Education Society of the Presbyterian Church in the United States. 65158-65159 see also Presbyterian Church in the United States. Board of Education. Presbyterian Education Society.

Education Society of the Warren Baptist Association. see Baptists. Rhode Island. Warren Baptist Association. Education Society.

Education Society of the Young Men of Boston. 104356

Education Society of the Young Men of Boston. Treasurer. 104356

Education we want. 78395

Educational addresses. (61354)

Educational arrangements and college life at Oberlin. (23676)

Educational biography. 3465

Educational Commission for Freedmen. see New England Freedmen's Aid Society.

Educational Convention, Boston, 1860. Baltimore Delegation. see Baltimore. Delegates to the Educational Conventions of Buffalo and Boston, 1860.

Educational directory. 102447

Educational institutions of the United States. (81007)

Educational labors of William Russell. 74392

Educational laws of . . . Iowa. 34986

Educational manual for Upper Canada. 32350

Educational miscellany. 85386

Educational Monument Association, to the Memory of Abraham Lincoln, Washington, D. C. see Colored People's Educational Monument Association in Memory of Abraham Lincoln, Washington, D. C.

Educational museum and school of art and design. 74557

Educational powers of our present national troubles. 73886

Educational system of the state of New-York. 37681

Educational systems of the puritans and Jesuits compared. 64299

Educational tracts, by Henry Barnard. 3469

Educational wants of Georgia. 13859

Educator. 89076

Edulcorator. 46299

Edward VI, King of England, 1537-1553. note after 52712

Edward VI, King of England, 1537-1553. spirit author 78374-78375, 100799

Edward VII, King of Great Britain, 1841-1910. 658, 69284 see also Great Britain. Sovereigns, etc., 1901-1910 (Edward VII)

Edward, an American prisoner in England. pseud. Epistle. 22691

Edward, David B. 21886, 95090

Edward, W. N. 21887

Edward Bates against Thomas H. Benton. 3929

Edward Colvil's journal. 66833

Edward Everett. A sermon occasioned by the death. 66759

Edward Everett in the ministry of reconciliation. 29632

Edward Lincoln Atkinson. 84507

Edward Meltons Engelsch Edelmans zeldzamme en gedenkwaardige zee-en land reizen. 47472-47473

Edward Meltons zee en land reizen. 47472

Edward Myers. 16485

Edward Sydenham. pseud. Man of two lives. see Boarden, James.

Edward Terry's voyage to the Easterne India. 66686

Edward William Sidney. pseud. Partisan leader. see Tucker, Nathaniel Beverley.

Edwardean. pseud. Letters on the present state. 40627

Edwards, -------, fl. 1836. (72166)

Edwards, A. F. (74754)

Edwards, Alexander. 12062

Edwards, Bela Bates, 1802-1852. 1198, 21888-21892

Edwards, Brian, 1743-1800. (21893)-21910, note after (35559), 65382, 75196, 91599, 94565, 98837-98838, 106128

Edwards, C. L. (21916)

Edwards, Mrs. C. M. 21917

Edwards, Charles, 1797-1868. 9210, 21912, 21914

Edwards, Charles Lee. 21915
Edwards, D. 21918
Edwards, Edward, 1812-1886. 21919, 67599
Edwards, Frank S. 10188, 21920
Edwards, George. 21921
Edwards, George, 1694-1773. 11508-11509
Edwards, Henry L. (21922)
Edwards, Henry S. tr. 41846
Edwards, Henry Waggaman, 1779-1847. 15833
  see also Connecticut. Governor, 1833-
  1834 (Edwards)
Edwards, Isaac. 89273
Edwards, J. P. 21926, note after 92624
Edwards, John, 1749-1790. 94132
Edwards, John, fl. 1822. defendant 21923
Edwards, John Ellis, 1814-1891. 21924
Edwards, John N. 21925
Edwards, Jonathan, 1703-1758. 4497, (7340),
  7342, 12687, 13216-(13218), 21316,
  21927-21949, 21951-21967, 24432, (30648),
  32955, note just before 51834, 55771,
  59608, 64945, 67768, 69346, 75875,
  85210, 85213, 85222, 85994, 93291, 8th
  note after 100870, note after 102650,
  102651, 102653, 102684, note after
  102697, 104399, 105826
Edwards, Jonathan, 1703-1758. defendant at
  church council 7663, 21967
Edwards, Jonathan, 1745-1801. 21968-(21975),
  56636
Edwards, Jonathan, 1817-1891. 21978
Edwards, Jonathan, 1820-1894. (21976)-21977,
  22525
Edwards, Justin, 1787-1853. 1240, 21979,
  93203 see also American Temperance
  Society. Corresponding Secretary.
Edwards, Milne. (24424)
Edwards, Morgan. 21981-21983
Edwards, Munroe. defendant 95142
Edwards, N. W. (21984)
Edwards, Newton. 64278
Edwards, Ninian, 1775-1833. 21985
Edwards, Ogden. 3392, note after 96820-96821,
  96945, note after 98992
Edwards, Pierpont, 1750-1826. 21986, (34385),
  note after 53697, note after 83791
Edwards, Richard. ed. (49153), 75346
Edwards, Richard, of St. Louis. (21987)
Edwards, Richard, of Virginia. 21988-(21990)
Edwards, T. (21975)
Edwards, Thomas, fl. 1650. 21991-21992,
  27952
Edwards, Thomas, fl. 1812-1827. reporter
  21993, 29517, 2d note after 92630
Edwards, Thomas McKey, 1795-1875. 21994
Edwards, Timothy. 21995
Edwards, Tryon, 1809-1894. 4497, (21996)-
  21997
Edwards, William H. 21998-21999
Edwards & Boyd. 34582
Edwards & Brown. firm see Stuart, Edwards
  & Brown. firm
Edwards, Greenough & Deved. firm publishers
  12641, 25818, 34582, 34584, 42326,
  43725, (49154), 52432, 75346
Edwards' annual director . . . [to Milwaukee,
  for] 1868-9. (49154)
Edwards' annual director to . . . Milwaukee,
  for 1865. (49154)
Edwards' annual director to the inhabitants,
  etc., in Freeport. 25818
Edwards' annual director to the inhabitants,
  etc., in the cities of New Albany and
  Jeffersonville, for 1865-6. 52432
Edwards' annual director to the inhabitants,
  etc. of Lafayette. 38584

Edwards' annual director to the inhabitants, etc.
  of Madison. 43725
Edwards' annual director to the inhabitants,
  institutions, incorporated companies,
  manufacturing establishments. 75346
Edwards' annual directory of the inhabitants,
  etc., in the city of Chicago. 12641
Edwards Church, Saxonville, Mass. see Saxon-
  ville, Mass. Edwards Church.
Edwards's on revivals. 21937
Edwards's annual director to Indianapolis, for
  1869. 34582
Edwards's annual director to the city of Indian-
  apolis for 1865-6. 34582
Edwards's annual directory . . . for 1857 [to
  Indianapolis.] 34582
Edwards's great west and her commercial
  metropolis. (21987)
Edwards's monthly. (21987)
Edwardsville Baptist Association. see Baptists.
  Illinois. Edwardsville Baptist Association.
Edwin, -------. engr. 84677
Edwin, D. illus. 63894
Edwin & Angelina. A tale. 103847
Edwin and Angelina; or the banditti. 82503
Edwin and Eltrude. 104227
Edwin Bartlett, died at Annandale, N. Y. 74185
Edwin: or the emigrant. 16390
Edwin R. Purple. 66720
Edwy and Elgiva. 34735
Eeenige advijscit ende verklaringhen uyt Brasi-
  lien. 7502
Eel River Indians. Treaties, etc. 96605, 96620,
  96655, 99605
Eelking, Max von. (22001)-22003
Eells, Cushing. 101041
Eells, Edward. 22004, 96092, 96094, 104316
Eells, Myron. 85041
Eells, Nathaniel. 22005-(22007), 26831, 46160,
  94921, 94927, note after 103633 see also
  Convention of Congregational Ministers of
  Massachusetts, Boston, 1743. Moderator.
Eells, Samuel. 22008
Eells, W. W. 22009
Eendracht maakt macht. 77593
Eenen die daer mede in de vlote ghewesst is.
  pseud. Beschryvinge. 11605-(11606),
  note after 65395
Eenige advijsen ende verklaringhen uyt Brasil.
  (7573A)
Eenige aanmerkingen op het libel. 22001
Eenige aenteekeningen verrijkt. 6872
Eenige maanden in de Vereenigten Staten van
  Noord-Amerika. 28275
Eenige miscontentierde participanten vande
  Oost-Indische Compagnie. pseud. Extract
  wt een tegen-vertooch. 19671, 4th note
  after 102890
Eenige predicatien. (25971)
Eenige requesten, vertoogen, deductien, enz.
  (38253), 106291
Eenige woordern ter aanprijzing van den Mais-
  bouw in de Kolonie Suriname. 67410
Eensgezinheid in de devisie, te Suriname.
  46193
Eer der regeering van Amsterdam. 22012
Eerezang voor het Fransche volk. (22013)
Eerste deel van den spiegel der Spaensche
  tyrannye. 11257
Eerste deel van het brandende veen. Verlich-
  tende alle de vaste kusten ende eylanden
  van geheel West-Indien. (72762)
Eerste deel van het brandende veen, verlich-
  tende geheel West-Indien. (72762)
Eerste godsdienstoefening d. puriteinen in Noord
  Amerika. 93191

Eerste maandags relaes. 22014
Eerste scheeps-togt ter verdere ontdekkinge van de West-Indien. 86427
Eerste schip-vaert gedaen van de Hollanders. 74833
Eerste shceeps-togt [sic] ter verder ontdekking van de West-Indien. 86428
Eerste vervolg der vaderlandsche merkwaerdigheden in het wonderjaar 1783. 98277
Eerstelingen van Surinaamsche Mengelpoezy. 73099
Eersten dagen van het Mexicaansche Keizerrijck. 63887
Efectos de la facciones en los gobernos nacientes. 99483
Efectos estranjeros. 99482
Efemerides Americanas desde el descubrimiento del Rio de la Plata. 56331
Efemerides astronomicas del sol y de la luna. 76280
Efemerides de la guerra de los guaranies, 1754. 58513
Efemerides de los deguellos. 34435
Efemerides de los hechos notables acaecidos en la Republica de Centro-America. 45018
Effect of an alteration of the sugar duties. 38654
Effect of incorporated coal companies upon the anthracite coal trade. 94459
Effect of incorporated coal companies upon the coal trade. 94460
Effect of proscriptive or extreme legislation. (62709)
Effect of secession on the relation of the United States. 5608
Effect of secession upon the commercial relations. 42018, 57245, 64054
Effect of slavery on the American people. note after (58767)
Effect of the nitrous vapour. 85232-85233
Effect on Negro race and on slavery. 8348
Effecting account of the tragical death of Major Swan. 94000
Effects . . . of a material increase . . . of the money metals. (30805)
Effects of discord. 30072
Effects of divine fury. 83450
Effects of drunkenness. 102468
Effects of holiday Sunday illustrated. 93745
Effects of high duties on imports. 29648
Effects of intemperance upon national wealth. 64692
Effects of naval reform. 44138
Effects of Negro-slavery. 92866
Effects of romance. 39042
Effects of secluded and gloomy imprisonment. 1183
Effects of sixteen years of freedom on a slave colony. 5305
Effects of slavery, &c. 102397
Effects of slavery on morals and industry. 102349
Effects of the battle-axe. 102088
Effects of the continental blockade. 35301
Effects of the gold standard. 84801
Effects of the introduction of ardent spirits and implements of war. 103180
Effects of the late colonial policy of Great Britain described. (3351)
Effects of the new system of free trade. 2285
Effects of the passions. 99412
Effects of the state on the manners of a people. (29697)
Effects of the war of the revolution. 26175

Effectual method to augment small livings. 94404
Effeitos beneficos das machinas e do combustibel. 93284
Effeitos das machinas e suas vantagens. 93285
Effen, J. van. tr. 72218, 99509
Effets des passions. 12265
Effets des passions, ou memoires de M. de Floricourt. 99412
Effets du blocus continental. 35300
Efficacy of the fear of hell. 91947
Efficiency of primitive missions. 92369
Efficient ministry. 13385
Effigies of Bishop Sherlock. 80352
Effigies regvm ac principum. 58995
Effingham, C. pseud. Virginia comedians. see Cooke, John Esten, 1830-1886.
Effort and failure to civilize the aborigines. 52288
Effort to refute the opinion. (30369)
Effusions. 78968
Effusions of female fancy. 106140
Effusions, religious, moral, and patriotic. 91360
Efterretning om de Danske Vestindiske oers St. Croix's. 102639
Efterretning om Engellaendernes og Nordamerikanernes fart. 36939
Efterretninger om Gronland. 22034
Efterretninger om Island, Gronland og Strat Davis. 1406
Egalite, Messrs. 1'. pseud. see L'Egalite, Messrs. pseud.
Egan, Charles. (22015)
Egan, Howard. defendant 70913, 82585, 85563
Egana, Juan. 47599, 103421
Egar, John H. 22016-22017
Egbert C. Smyth, appellant from a decree. 85212
Egbert C. Smyth, appellant from a decree of the Visitors of the Theological Instititon in Phillips Academy in Andover. 85212
Egbert C. Smyth, appellant, on appeal from the Visitors of the Theological Institution in Phillips Academy. 85212
Egbert C. Smyth, appellant, v. the Visitors of the Theological Institution in Phillips Academy in Andover, appellee. 85212
Egbert C. Smith [sic], appellant, vs. the Visitors of the Theological Institution in Phillips Academy in Andover. Brief of appellant. 85212
Egbert C. Smyth, appellant, vs. the Visitors of the Theological Institution in Phillips Academy in Andover. C. T. Russell, William Gaston, Counsel for appellant. 85212
Egbert C. Smyth, appellant, vs. the Visitors of the Theological Institution in Phillips Academy in Andover. Commissioner's report. 85212
Egbert C. Symth, appellant, v. the Visitors of the Theological Institution in Phillisp Academy in Andover. Supplementary brief. 85212
Egbert, C. Smyth, vs. the Visitors of the Theological Institution in Phillips Academy in Andover. Outline of brief. 85212
Egbert C. Smyth vs. Visitors of the Theological Institution in Phillips Academy in Andover. 85212
Egede, Hans, 1686-1758. 6110, 22018-22031, 22036
Egede, Hans, 1686-1758. incorrectly supposed author (20030)
Egede, Johannis. see Egede, Hans, 1686-1758.

Egede, Paul, 1708-1789. (22032)-22041,
(22849), 42727, 56343, 95618
Egelmann, Charles F. 84219
Egenolff, Christian. supposed author 12947,
1st note after 91211
Egenter, Franz Joseph. (22042)
Egeria. (81208)
Egerton, Charles Calvert. 36705
Egerton, Florencio. Illus. 22044
Egerton, Francis. see Ellesmere, Francis
Egerton, 1st Earl of, 1800-1857.
Egerton, Henry, Bp. of Hereford, d. 1746.
22045
Egerton, John, successively Bishop of Bangor,
Litchfield and Coventry, and Durham,
1721-1787. 22046
Egerton, Joseph K. see Edgerton, Joseph
Ketchum, 1818-1893.
Egerton, W. H. 95080
Egerton's views in Mexico. 22044
Eggede, ----. see Egede, Hans, 1686-1758.
Egger, Karl. (24746)
Eggerling, H. W. E. 22048
Eggers, H. P. 22049
Eggers, J. L. C. tr. (3618)
Eggleston, Benjamin. plaintiff (77406)
Eggleston, C. M. 22050
Eggleston, Nathaniel H. 22051-22052
Egle, William H. 31105, note after 60301,
85177
Egleston, Thomas. 1067, (22053)-22055, 86814
Eglise de Jesus-Christ des Saints-des-Derniers-
Jours. see Church of Jesus Christ of
Latter Day Saints.
Eglise Protestante Francais du Saint-Spirit,
New York. see New York (City) French
Church du Saint-Spirit.
Egloffstein, F. W. von. 22056
Egloga. En alabanza del Exmo. S. D. Jose
Mariano de Almansa. 97038
Egloga . . . por Don Bruno Francisco Larran-
aga. 39082
Egmet, Demens. pseud. see Demens Egmet.
pseud.
Egmont, John Percival, 1st Earl of, 1683-
1748. 60861, 86573, 91305, 91307
Egmont, John Percival, 2d Earl of, 1711-1770.
supposed author 20684, 23367, 23610,
40263, 40293, 45001, (60681), 60862,
69470
Egnatius, Ioannis Baptista. 72023
Egrede, P. see Egede, Paul, 1708-1789.
Egron, Peter. 22057, 40744
Egte stukken en vewyzen door Salomon du
Plessis. 68458, 1st note after 93862
Egueren, Juan Joseph de Eguiara y. see
Eguiara y Egueren, Juan Joseph de.
Eguia, J. Garus y. see Garces y Eguia,
Jose.
Eguia, Jose Garces y. see Garces y Eguia,
Jose.
Eguia, Jose Joaquin de. 22058, 47610
Eguia y Moro, J. P. 22059
Eguiara y Egueren, Juan Joseph de. 22060-
22066
Eguiarreta, Juan Antonio de Vizarron y. see
Vizarron y Eguiarreta, Juan Antonio de.
Eguilaz, Diego de. 22068, 22715
Eguilaz, Joseph de Lanciego y. see Lanciego
y Eguilaz, Joseph de, Abp.
Eguilaz, L. de. 22067
Egusquiza, Jose Maria. defendant at court
martial 58565
Egypt and the Holy Land. 89339
Egyptian in New York. pseud. Letters.
(40587)

Ehakeun okaga. (69644)
Ehle, George L. supposed author 89467
Ehmals verdorrete nun aber wieder grunende
und Frucht-bringende Ruthe Aarons.
106364
Ehrehart, Charles J. 22069
Ehrenberg, Christian Gottfried, 1795-1876.
22070, 77780
Ehrenberg, H. 22071-22072
Ehrenkreutz, V., Freiherr. (22073)
Ehret, George Dionysius. illus. 8671, 33582
Ehrmann, Theophil. Fridrich. tr. 4964, (8038),
18323, 22074, 41297, 43457, 48707, 72988,
100690
Ehrwurdige Leben und vil [sic] werther Tod.
62982
Ehrwurdigen Pater Emanuel Crespels mer-
wurdige Reisen. 17478
Eibergen, Rutgerus. 22075, note after 94086
Eich, Hans Jacob Zur-. pseud. Landtschafft
fetu in Africa. see Muller, W. J.
Eichhoff, Frederic Gustave, 1799-1875. 70375,
85791
Eichthal, Gustave d', 1804-1886. 22076-(22077),
98106
Eick, Coanrod Ten. see Ten Eick, Coanrod.
Eidous, Marc Antoine. 9284, (29277), (38303),
71990, 82315, 84573, 98843
Eidrag til Verstindiens geographie-natur- og
folkehistorie. 38370
Eigen levensbeschryving. 27683
Eigendliche Beschreibung des Landes Guiana.
29112
Eigenen Beobachtungen und den neuesten Quellen
geschildert. 8871
Eigener Anschauung und mit besonderer Bezu-
gnahme. 9151
Eigener Bericht an Raphael Sanxis. (19793)
Eigenhandigen Brief van den eerw. Heer
Neerinckx R. C. Priester. (52239)
Eigenheiten der Englischen Sprache in Nord-
amerika. 38221
Eigentliche Beschreibung des an dem grossen
Flusse. 22079
Eigentliche Beschreibung des Lands Guiana.
22078
Eigentliche Furbildung aller newen fermden
seltsamen Historien und Geschichten.
4801
Eigentliche vnnd warhaftige Beschreibung, der
wunderbahre Reiz vnd Schiffart. 33670,
89452
Eigentliche und warhafftige Beschreibung der
wunderbarlichen Schiffarth (der Hollander).
55437
Eight days in New Orleans. 62667
Eight dollars reward. 93972
Eight essays upon important subjects. 46569,
note after 98241
Eight-hour law. Speech. 50791
Eight lectures delivered. 71260
Eight lectures on geology. 42764
Eight letters on . . . the commerce and manu-
factures of Great Britain. 21824
Eight letters on the subject of the Earl of
Selkirk's pamphlet. 20704, (22080)
Eight letters, six whereof, directed to a gentle-
man. (65236)
Eight men in Greenland, 1630. 20518
Eight Ministers Who Carry on the Thursday
Lecture in Boston. pseud. Course of
sermons. 46274, 46595, 46629, 65603,
79431 see also Colman, Benjamin,
1673-1747. Cooper, William, 1694-1743.
Foxcroft, Thomas. Mather, Cotton, 1663-
1728. Prince, Thomas, 1687-1758. Sewall,

Joseph, 1688-1769. Wadsworth, Benjamin. 1669-1737. Webb, John. and Thursday Lecture, Boston.
Eight months in Illinois. 57214
Eight months in prison and on parole. 63876
Eight months in Washington. 37308
Eight practical treatises. 22081
Eight severall arguments. 13308
Eight years experience and observation. 103753
Eight years in British Guiana. 65050
Eight years in Canada. (71037)-71038
Eight years in Congress. (17271)
Eight years in the far west. 6221
Eight years on the stage. 51026
Eight years' residence in British Guiana. 22082
Eighteen essays. 20986, 3d note after 102203
1855. Wm. N. Seymour's Madison directory. 43741
1851 & 1852. Prince's supplementary catalogue. 65621
1856-7. Portsmouth city book and directory. 64426
1856. Traveller's guide to Montreal and its vicinity. (50291), note after 96490
1852-'53. First report to the General Assembly. (70634)
1845. 1870. 87082
1844, New-York State Agricultural Society. 53811
1844; or, the power of the "S. F." 22606
1846. 73647
1846. January 1. Carriers' address to the patrons. (75383)
Eighteen Hundred and Sixty Association, Charleston, S. C. publishers (20696), 30101, 96379, note after 97063
Eighteen hundred and thirty. (58363)
Eighteen months in Dixie. 24461
Eighteen months in the polar regions. 57760
Eighteen months in the Somers' Island. 4907
Eighteen Presbyterian Ministers, in America. pseud. Letter to the Archbishop of Canterbury. 40455, 47276, 65149, (78736), 97107 see also Finley, James. Rogers, John. Tennent, Charles. Tennent, Gilbert. Tennent, William.
Eighteen rules. 9463
Eighteen sermons and a charge. 25763
Eighteen sermons preached by the late Rev. George Whitefield. 103510
1870. Public ledger almanac. (66518)
1879 guide to Leadville. (82236)
1876. Some points relating to grain. 88357
1873-74. City documents. No. 18. 85495
1868. 1869. Doniphan County, Kansas. 83736
1867. Fourth of July in Charleston. 80843
1860-61. The Portsmouth directory. 64426
1860. Twelfth annual report of the Young Men's Mercantile Library Association. 63149
1835 and 1836. Nursery of William Kenrick. 37463
1831. 1888. History of the First Presbyterian Church. 83700
1833-1883. In memoriam. 83364
1812 General catalogue of the Theological and Literary Book-Store. 105171
1812: the war, and its moral. 14190, 92649
1820. 1870. Semi-centennial of the Providence journal. 66364
1826. To be continued annually. 84218
Eighteenth and nineteenth reports of the Directors of the African Institution. 81966
Eighteenth annual report . . . see Report . . .
Eighteenth Congress, Jan. 1824. 102264

Eighteenth Massachusetts Regiment. 19191
Eighteenth Ward Republican Festival, New York, 1860. 1424, 40940 see also Republican Party. New York. New York City.
Eighth and ninth annual reports of the Newcastle District Committee. 85852
Eighth and ninth annual reports [of the United States Bureau of Animal Industry.] 84332
Eighth and ninth letters to the Rev. Samuel Miller. 88970
Eighth and ninth report of the same committee. 10411
Eighth, and ninth reports [on the noxious, beneficial and other insects, of the state of New York.] 24562
Eighth annual catalogue . . . see Catalogue . . .
Eighth annual report . . . see Report . . .
Eighth . . . debate. 55840
Eighth half-yearly report of the San Francisco Savings Union. 76099
[Eighth letter to the Rev. Samuel Miller.] (49063)
Eighth of a series of lectures. 104001
Eighth of January, a drama. 83779-83781
Eighth report . . . see Report . . .
Eighth supplement [to the public laws of Rhode Island.] 70700
Eights, James. 22083-22084, 54735
89th anniversary of the national independence. 20744
Eighty original poems. 43590
Eighty second anniversary of American independence. 6519
Eighty years and more. 90405
Eighty years. Embracing a history of Presbyterianism in Baltimore. 83388
Eighty years of republican goverment in the United States. 36043
Eighty years progress in British North America. 31939
Eighty years' progress of the United States. 22085
Eilfften Theils Americae. (8784)
Ein vnd zwantsigste Schiffart. 7567, 33674
Eindelyk de reize. 55285, 1st note after 99428
Eine mit ausslandischen Raritaten und Geschichten. 30279
Einem als erwehnter Gesellschaft. pseud. Erbauliche und angenehme Geschichten. 12835, 24138, 1st note after 98488
Einem Stuck der Warnungs-Predigt von Hn. Johann Tribecko, &c. 98990
Eines ist Noth. 86110
Einfache Worte an einfache Leute von einem einfachen Mannen. 22087, 38332
Einfaltiges Reim-Gedichte. 77196
Einfuhrungsrede von D. F. Schaffer. 77717
Eingefuhrt durch zwei Briefe. 49913
Eingehuhrt von Amexander von Humboldt. 49914
Eingestreuten historischen, statistischen, und andern Bemerkungen. 7898
Einheit und Freiheit. 67487
Einhorn, D. (22088)-(22089)
Einige advijsen uyt Brasilien. (7568A)
Einige Anmerkungen uber Nord-Amerika. 107
Einige Anmerkungen und verbesserungen der Nachrichten der Verfassers. 97689
Einige Anweisungen fur Auswanderer. 67975
Einige Bemerkungen uber Amerikanisch-Mexikanische Geographie und Geologie. 6862
Einige Blatter des Werkes. 21075
Einige Beobachtungen uber die Temperatur der See-Oberflache. 38205

Einige Extract den Zustand der Eben Ezerischen Gemeinde. 98134

Einige wechtige Ansiedelungsgebiete in Texas. 6826

Einige Worte an die Heiligen der letzten Tage. 82989

Einige Worte uber die Industrie-Austellung in New-York. 54258

Einladung zu einer Zusammenkunst. 85120

Einleitung. 103607

Einleitung in die Kenntniss der Reiche und Staaten der Welt. 6104

Einleitung uber den dermaligen Stand. 8520

Einleitung uber die Sklaverei. 92565

Einleitung und 4 Illustrationen von Wilhelm Heine. 43352

Einleitung von Friedrich Kapp. 89335

Einleitung zur leichten Verstehen. 85109

Einleitung zur Statistik dieser Lander. 30814

Eiselein, Al. von Dusch und. see Dusch und Eiselein, Al. von.

Eisenach, Karl Bernhard, Herzog zu. see Karl Bernhard, Herzog zu Sachsen-Weimer-Eisenach.

Eisenbahnen in Europa una Amerika. 68491

Eisenberger, N. F. 11512, 11515, 22090

Eisenhabn zur Verbindung des Atlantischen Oceans. 32763

Eisner, H. (12250)

Either great destruction of human life and property. 85111

Ejaculations. 7919, note just before 53081

Ejectment: the people of the State of New York vs. the Rector, &c. of Trinity Church. 49046

Ejecucion de justicia. 99704

Ejecucion del decreto. 58139

Ejemplos morales. 73863

Ejercecio del Santa Via Crucis Puerto en lengua Maya. 47086

Ejercicio del Santo Viacrucis Puesto en lengua Maya. 86494

Ejercito Imperial Mexicano. 44671

Ejolfssine, Ejnare. 2058, (28646), 74880

Ejolfsson, E. tr. 36637

Ekins, Charles. 22091, 103458A, 103459

Ekkoes from Kentucky. 41719

El que dicto esta carte. pseud. Suplemento al Espiritu publico. see Tornel, Jose Maria.

El que sigue empachado con la merienda y con sintomas de apoplegia. pseud. Tercera amonestacion al muy reverendo fray "Americano." see Paula Castaneda, Francisco de.

El que suscribe. pseud. Satisfaccion. see Trevino, Ignacio.

Ela, Jacob Hart, 1820-1884. 22092

Ela, Richard. reporter 96867

Elaborate description. 37453

Elaborate review. 16515, 43426

Elcio, Philippo de. 86444

Elcock, Ephraim. 22093

Elder, G. A. M. plaintiff 70848

Elder, Joshua. (38801) see also Lancaster County, Pa. Lieutenant.

Elder, William. 22094-22097

Elder, William Henry, Bp. 51898, 72950, (72952) see also Natchez (Diocese) Bishop (Elder)

Elder in an Old School Presbyterian Church. pseud. Letter. 40323

Elder of the Church of Latter-Day Saints. pseud. Timely warning. 95839

Elder tenents in the bay. 28926

Elderhorst, William. 22098

Elderkin, John. (22099), 82192

Elders and messengers from the various societies believing the doctrine of the universal love of God in Christ to the children of men. 98012

Elders and Messengers of the Churches Assembled at Boston in New-England, 1680. see Congregational Churches in Massachusetts. Boston Synod, 1680.

Elders and Messengers of the Churches Assembled in the Synod at Boston in New-England, Sept. 10. 1679. see Congregational Churches in Massachusetts. Boston Synod, 1679.

Elders and Messengers of the Churches Assembled at the Synod at Cambridge in New England, 1648. see Congregational Churches in Massachusetts. Cambridge Synod, 1648.

Elders and Other Messengers of the Churches Assembled at Boston in the Year 1662. see Congregational Churches in Massachusetts. Boston Synod, 1662.

Elders in the Province of the Massachusetts Bay, Who Assisted at the Ordination of the Rev. Mr. John Hubbard. pseud. Letter. see Ballantine, John Breck, Robert. Lathrop, Joseph.

Elders journal of the Church of the Latter Day Saints. 50735, 83289

Elders of the Several Churches in New England. see Congregational Churches in New England.

Eldership of the Presbyterian Church. 85288-85289, 85331

Eldorado of the north. 83599

Eldorado, or adventures in the path of empire. 94440

El-Dorado. Schilderung einer Reise nach Californien's Goldminen. 38241

Eldred, J. 66686

Eldred Grayson. pseud. Standish, the puritan. see Hare, Robert. supposed author

Eldredge, Charles Augustus, 1820-1896. 22101

Eldridge, -------. ed. 88421

Eldridge, -------. engr. 84081

Eldridge, Azariah. 22100

Eldridge, John. defendant 24083, note after 97149

Eldridge, Joseph. 22103-22104

Eldridge, Robert D. defendant 85129

Eldridge. firm publishers see Thayer & Eldridge. firm publishers

Eleanor Winthrop's diary. 48831

Eleazer Cary family with affiliated lines. 83600

Eleazar Wright. pseud. see MacNemar, Richard.

Elecciones. 99482

Elecciones de Toluca. 96127

Elecciones proscimas. 76200

Electing love. 73573

Election. 22106

Election, a medley. (61612)

Election, a poem. (22105)

Election and re-election ode. 24925, 83790

Election ballad. 5584

Election case in the Eleventh (Norfolk) District. (5541)

Election. Federal Republican candidates. 105406A

Election. Humbly inscribed to the Saturday-Night Club. 22109, 61613

Election law of New York of 1842. 53656

Election law of . . . Pennsylvania. 60082

Election law of Rhode Island. 70580

Election laws of Illinois. 34280
Election laws of Pennsylvania. 60084
Election laws . . . of Pennsylvania, relating to . . . Philadelphia. (60083)
Election laws of the state of Maryland. (45138)
Election laws of the state of Maryland, . . . with such portions of the constitution as relate to the elective franchise. 45139
Election of a black Republican president an over act of aggression. 32466
Election of a president of the United States, considered. 22107
Election of judges by the people. 77714
Election of Mr. Lincoln. 17827
Election of President of the United States. 22108
Election sermon. see Connecticut. Election sermons. Edinburgh. Election sermons. Massachusetts. Election sermons. New Hampshire. Election sermons. Vermont. Election sermons. and Artillery election sermons.
Election sermon, April 29, 1668. 65607
Election sermon, . . . at Hartford. 51090
Election sermon . . . before the . . . Senate and House . . . of New Hampshire. 58673
Election sermon, delivered at Concord. 105250
Election sermon; delivered before the Honorable Legislature of the State of Vermont. (25203)
Election sermon, Hartford. 29842
Election sermon, Mass., May 26, 1813. 892
Election sermon . . . May 4. 1692. 50299
Election sermon, May 9, 1811. 91061
Election-sermon . . . May 30. 1705. 23023
Election sermon, N. H., June 2, 1814. 32656
Election sermon, preached at Hartford. 9375
Election sermon preached before the General Court of New Hampshire. 30892
Election sermon, preached before the General Court, of New-Hampshire, at Portsmouth. 4432
Election sermon, 1786. 30637
Election sermon. MDCCLXXXIII. 91749
Election sermon, 1705. 21665
Election sermon, . . . 1748. (50312)
Election sermon, 1749. 2870
Election sermon, 1671. 58029
Election sermons of J. Barnard and N. Appleton. 12313
Election the foundation of obedience. 89462
Elections by the Select and Common Councils. 61614
Elective judiciary. 39968
Elector. pseud. Remarks on the constitution of Maine. 69450
Elector. pseud. Review and exposition. see Young, Samuel, 1789-1580.
Elector. pseud. Review of the constitution of Maine. 44038
Elector. pseud. To the public. 96010
Elector of Finsbury. pseud. Facts relative to colonial slavery. 81971
Elector of Herkimer. pseud. To the public. 95914
Electoral ticket for Virginia—1828. 100499
Electors of Worcester County: 105397A
Electric telegraph. 74737
Electro magnetic telegraphs. 50963
Electro-magnetism. 18719
Electron; or, the pranks of the modern puck. (70973)
Electuarium novum Alexipharmacum. 30785
Elegant extracts in prose and poetry. 16311
Elegant James Oneale. 102470

Elegant lessons. 103711
Elegant representation illustrated. 28977
Elegia a la muerte del Excmo. Sr. D. Jose Maria Morelos. 50599
Elegia in laudem S. Virginis Cristinae. 4548
Elegia na morte do Serenissimo Senhor D. Jose Principe do Brasil. [Por Antonio Jose Osorio de Pina Leitao.] 39939
Elegia na morte do Serenissimo Senhor D. Jose, Principe do Brasil, por Fr. Theodoro de Sousa Maldonado. 44112
Elegiac epistle, addressed to a friend. (20937)
Elegiac epistle from Lieut. Gen. B-rg-yne. 9249
Elegiac epistles on the calamities of love and war. 22110
Elegiac ode. 32901
Elegiac ode on the death of Mr. Ephraim May. 103144
Elegiac pieces, commemorative of distinguished characters. 7185, 50155
Elegiac poem. 101416
Elegiac poem. Dedicated to the citizens of Philadelphia. 24228
Elegiac poem on James G. Percival. 71811
Elegiac poem, on the death of Dr. Benjamin Rush. 74242
Elegiac poem on the death of G. Whitefield. 103130
Elegiac poem on the death of General George Washington. 101798
Elegiac poem on the death of General Washington. 9896, 101797
Elegiac poem, on the death of George Washington. 101799
Elegiac poem, on the death of that celebrated divine, and eminent servant of Jesus Christ, the Reverend and Learned George Whitefield. 103126-103128
Elegiac poem, on the death of that celebrated divine and eminent servant of Jesus Christ the Rev. Geo. Whitefield. 59606, 103131
Elegiac poem, on the death of the Rev. Mr. Whitefield. 103129
Elegiac poem or ode. 32987
Elegiac poem; sacred to the memory of the Rev. George Whitefield. 103619
Elegiack poem, sacred to the memory of the Rev. Nathaniel Pitcher. 63033
Elegiac poem to the memory of Mr. Davies. 18766
Elegiac sonnets. 82403
Elegiac sonnets, and other poems. (82404)
Elegiac tale, occasioned by the death of Prince **** 1708. 65697
Elegiack tribute to the sacred dust. 96157
Elegiack verse, on the death of the pious and profound grammarian. 101172
Elegiac verses, on the decease of His Late Excellency. 7858, note after 101799
Elegiac verses to a young lady. 72143
Elegiack . . . see Elegiac . . .
Elegiacvm. 25994, 79345
Elegiarvm et miscellaneorvm Carminvm. 3407
Eleg. et epigramm. 70787
Elegias de varones illvstres de Indias. 11402
Elegie sur la mort de Washington. 38863
Elegie upon the death of the Reverend Mr. Thomas Shepard. 56381
Elegies Americaines. 99741
Elegies Bresiliennes. 16751
Elegy. 97619, 101867, 103091
Elegy, addressed to Mr. Israel Keith. 90857
Elegy "by a friend." 93236
Elegy. By a student of Harvard University. 30520, 93243

Elegy by Benjamin Francis. 25436
Elegy by the Reverend Mr. John Danforth. (46340)
Elegy composed upon the death of Mr. John Woodmancy. 96153
Elegy exhibiting a brief history of the life. 38130
Elegy inscribed to . . . Benjamin Franklin. 15049
Elegy, occasion'd by the death of Major-General Joseph Warren. 101479
Elegy occasioned by the dismission of the Right Honorable William Pitt. 8068
Elegy occasioned by the rejection of Mr. Wilberforce's motion. 22111
Elegy on Captain Cook. (79474)-79475, 79477-79479, 79486-79487
Elegy on his [i. e. Peter Porcupine's] death. 64158
Elegy on the author [i. e. Samuel Clough.] (13777)
Elegy on the death of a virtuous young lady. 102068
Elegy on the death of Capt. Annanias Valentine. 95212-95213
Elegy on the death of Colonel Dan Shaw. 79902
Elegy on the death of Doct. Nathaniel Scudder. 65527
Elegy on the death of John Wesley. 104720
Elegy on the death of John Winthrop. (52761), 96156
Elegy on the death of Michael Young. 63585, 104539
Elegy, on the death of Mr. Buckingham St. John. 97207, 2d note after 105927
Elegy, on the death of Mr. Daniel Parish. 96401
Elegy on the death of Mr. Moses Brown, Jr. 2074
Elegy, on the death of Mrs. Ann Belding. (4413)
Elegy on the death of Mrs. Magdalen Hunt. 33856
Elegy, on the death of Mrs. Margaret Stebbins. 91028
Elegy on the death of the late glorious Duke of Marlborough. 27586
Elegy on the death of the Rev. John Wesley. 90964
Elegy on the death of the Reverend Jonathan Mayhew. 12979, (47135)
Elegy on the death of the Rev. Mr. John Wesley. 104721
Elegy on the deaths of the people. 90936
Elegy on the execution of Huggins and Mansfield. 105354
Elegy on the late Honorable Titus Hosmer. 3419
Elegy on the late Reverend George Whitefield. 102642
Elegy on the much lamented death of the ingenious and well-beloved Aquila Rose. 73234
Elegy on the much lamented death of the Reverend Mr. George Whitefield. 103620
Elegy on the much-to-be-deplored death of that never-to-be-forgotten person, the Reverend Mr. Nathanael Collins. 46300, 46462
Elegy on the times. 22112, 97208
Elegy sacred to the memory of that great divine the Reverend and Learned Dr. Samuel Cooper. (61199), note after 103131
Elegy, to Miss. Mary Moorhead. 103132

Elegy to the infamous memory of Sr. F———B———. 4926
Elegy to the memory of Captain James King. 46986
Elegy to the memory of Miss Sarah Hart. 30644
Elegy to the memory of Mrs. Mary Wharton. 103091
Elegy to the memory of that pious and eminent servant of Jesus Christ, the Reverend Mr. George Whitefield. 12980, 103621
Elegy upon Messrs. John and Charles Wesley. 104722
Elegy upon the deaths of those excellent and learned divines. (62510)
Elegy upon the much lamented deaths of two desireable brothers. 102459
Elegy upon them. 46579, 1st note after 99604
Elegy written among the ruins of an abbey. 36061, 105979
Elegy written in a country church yard. 100663
Elegy written in a country meeting house. (63794)
Eleicao de 40 distrito da provincia do Ceara. 88741
Elemens de geographie moderne. 85790
Elemens de la langue Angloise. 81444
Elemens d'ideologie. 96415
Elemens du droit public. 27137
Elementa fidei Christianae lingua Groenlandica. 22033
Elementa medicinae. 31223
Elementa philosophica. 36291
Elementary arithmetic. (36248)
Elementary book of the Ioway language. 30040
[Elementary book, with a few hymns and reading lessons.] 98575
Elementary catechism on the constitution of the United States. 90360
Elementary geography for Massachusetts children. 25298
Elementary geography in the Dakota language. (71338)
Elementary geology. 32250
Elementary geology. With an appended catalogue. 45755
Elementary history of the United States. 66885
Elementary instruction. An address. 8340
Elementary reader. 103012
Elementary treatise on advanced-guard. 43862
Elementary treatise on mineralogy and geology. 13611
Elementary treatise on the rights and duties of citizens. 83396
Elementary treatise on the structure and operations. 45428
Elemento servil. Estudo por Theodoro Parker. (58745)
Elemento servil; projecto elaborado. 85773
Elemento vasco en la historia de Venezuela. 72780
Elementos de botanica. 67525
Elementos de direito ecclesiastico. 72502
Elementos de estatistica. 85624
Elementos de geografia fisica. 47970
Elementos de geografia general. 27821
Elementos de geographia offerecidos a mocidade Cearense. 88742
Elementos de gramatica Quichua. 55397
Elementos de los beligerantes organizacion. 57597
Elementos de mineralojia. 20559
Elementos de orictognosia. 71443
Elementos del gobierno republicano. 98601
Elements and evidences of national permanence. 21839

Elements de la grammaire Othomi et vocabu-
laire. 12021
Elements de la grammaire Othomi, traduits
de l'Espagnol. 52411
Elements de l'agriculture. 82786
Elements of a bank charter. 73070
Elements of anatomy and physiology. 74197
Elements of arithmetick. 72087
Elements of artillery. 96339
Elements of botany. 74197
Elements of botany, or outlines of the natural
history of vegetables. 3806
Elements of chemistry. 81048
Elements of civil and religious liberty. 73563
Elements of commerce, and theory of taxes.
97341
Elements of commerce, politics and finance.
50991
Elements of conchology. 74197
Elements of constitutional law. 68038
Elements of constitutional law and of political
economy. 68039
Elements of discord in secessia. 744
Elements of discord in secessia. Vulgarity of
treason. 22113
Elements of ecclesiastical law. 84188-84191,
84192-84214
Elements of empire in America. (79517)
Elements of entomology. 74197
Elements of general history. 3318
Elements of geographical and astronomical
science. 4142
Elements of geography, adapted for use in
British America. 69012
Elements of geography. [By Benjamin Work-
man.] 105474
Elements of geography. [By Thomas Smith.]
84363-84364
Elements of geography. . . . On a new plan.
(50935)
Elements of geology. By Alonzo Gray. 28364
Elements of geology. [By W. S. W. Ruschen-
berger.] 74197
Elements of geology, for popular use. (39716)
Elements of geology, for the use of schools.
46810
Elements of geology, with an outline. 49683
Elements of gesture. (78388)
Elements of herpetology and ichthyology. 74197
Elements of history and chronology. 42666
Elements of ideology. 96415
Elements of industrial management. 83371
Elements of international law. 39377
Elements of international law and laws of war.
29880
Elements of international law: with a sketch.
103156
Elements of leadership. 21818
Elements of mammology. 74197
Elements of mechanics. 69654
Elements of mineralogy. (15073)
Elements of moral science on the subject of
slavery. 94538
Elements of morality, for the use of children.
75881
Elements of natural greatness. 12398
Elements of natural philosophy. (80068)
Elements of oratory, briefly stated. 91847
Elements of ornithology. 74197
Elements of perspective. 105046
Elements of philosophy. 84678C
Elements of physical and political geography.
11112
Elements of political economy. By Francis
Wayland. 102186

Elements of political economy. In two parts.
68040
Elements of power in public speaking. 81641
Elements of seamanship. 58777
Elements of success. 18139
Elements of the etiology and philosophy of
epidemics. 83362
Elements of the law and practice. 18115
Elements of the laws. 84401-84402
Elements of the philosophy of the human mind.
91676
Elements of useful knowledge. 102350
Elements of war. 44154
Elenchus. (8784)
Elenore, a drama. 79866-(79867)
Ελεοϳρίαμβος. (39794)
Elephanstius, G. T. Galbano. see Galbano
Elephanstius, G. T.
Elephantiasis. 31336
Elespuru, J. B. 22114
Eletrajzi, Ország, es Nepismertető Munkák
Gyüjteménye. 89010
Eleusinian mysteries revived. 57649
Eleutheria. 46301
Eleutheria, a hymn to liberty. 90260
Eleutheria: or, an idea of the reformation.
46301, 46790
Eleutherius. pseud. Eleutherius enervatus.
see Wetmore, James.
Eleutherius. pseud. Scripture bishop. see
Dickinson, Jonathan, 1688-1747.
Eleutherius. pseud. Scripture-bishop vindicated.
see Dickinson, Jonathan, 1688-1747.
Eleutherius enervatus. 22115, (25392), 78493,
103067
Eleutherus, Philalethes. pseud. see Philale-
thes Eleutherus. pseud.
Elevatio relationis Montezinianae. 89546
Elevation et la chute de l'Empereur Maxi-
milien. 37606
Eleven letters from the Revd Mr. Smith.
84563
Eleven Ministers in Boston. pseud. 51516
Eleven reasons for believing. 89138, 1st note
after 104432
Eleven seceeding members. pseud. Free
masonry revealed and exposed. see
Morgan, William.
Eleven sermons in reply. 81624
Eleven years among the Shakers at Enfield.
(22198)
Eleventh annual catalogue . . . see Catalogue
. . .
Eleventh annual discourse after the half-
century. 42007
Eleventh annual fair of the Rutland County
Agricultural Society. (74475)
Eleventh annual report . . . see Report
. . .
Eleventh Army Corps. 3965
Eleventh hour. 14187
Eleventh report . . . see Report . . .
Eleventh series. 30054
Elfie Grafton. (31421)
Elgin, James Bruce, 8th Earl of, 1811-1863.
22116-22117, 43350 see also Canada.
Governor General, 1847-1854 (Elgin)
Elguero, Hilario. (44966)
Elhuyar, Fausto. 22118-(22119)
Eli, Alfred. (22120)
Eli the priest dying suddenly. 25390
Elias de San Juan Bautista. see San Juan
Bautista, Elias de, d. 1605.
Elias, D. A. Alrich y. see Alrich y Elias,
D. A.

Elias Monitor. pseud. Stranger's apology. see Worcester, Noah, 1758-1837. supposed author
Elihu's reply. 96353
Elijah's mantle. 12411
Elijah's mantle. A faithful testimony. 49657-(49658), 92351
Eliot, ------, fl. 1766. 6215
Eliot, Andrew, 1718-1778. 1307, 22121-22129
Eliot, Andrew, fl. 1819. 22130
Eliot, Ephraim. 6660, 22132
Eliot, George. pseud. 40774
Eliot, James. 22133, 23952, 38583, 51101
Eliot, Jared. (22134)-22140
Eliot, John, 1604-1690. 3213, 4012-4013, (4076), 22141-22145, 22148-22166, 27413, 32496, 34625, 49739, (49660), 54860, (56742), 59541, (66428)-66430, 66445, 69242, 80205-80206, 80217, (80815), 82975-82976, note just before 85867, note just before 85932, note before 92797-92801, 95639, 95652-95653, note before 101232, 1st note after 102552, 103688, 3d note after 103679, 103840, 2d note after 103846, note after 104794
Eliot, John, 1604-1690. supposed author 105074-105077
Eliot, John, 1604-1690. incorrectly supposed author 22146-22147, 74696, 80207-80208, 101330, note after 104653
Eliot, John, 1754-1813. 22168-22169, 101469
Eliot, John Fleet. 86917
Eliot, R. R. see Eliot, Richard B.
Eliot, Richard B. 22170
Eliot, S. 23271
Eliot, Samuel, 1821-1898. 22171-(22172), (79670)
Eliot, Samuel Atkins, 1798-1862. 19890, 22173-(22174), 22238, (30195), 30765, 31432-31433, note after 92624, 102944
Eliot, Thomas Dawes, 1808-1870. 22175
Eliot, William Greenleaf, 1811-1887. 22176-(22178), 102993, note after 103016
Eliot, William Harvard, 1796-1831. 22178A
Eliot, William Horace, 1824-1852. 22179
Eliot Church, Newton, Mass. see Newton, Mass. Eliot Church.
Eliot Church, Roxbury, Mass. see Roxbury, Mass. Eliot Church.
Eliot Orthodox Congregational Church, Newton Corner, Mass. see Newton Corner, Mass. Eliot Orthodox Congregational Church.
Eliot Sabbath School, Roxbury, Mass. see Roxbury, Mass. Eliot Sabbath School.
Eliot Sabbath School Library, Newton, Mass. see Newton, Mass. Eliot Sabbath School Library.
Eliot School case. 21414
Eliot School rebellion. 21414
Eliot tracts. 22142, 22146, 22149, 22151-(22152), 22155, 52758, 52759, 80205, 80207, note before 85932, note before 85867, note before 92797, 103688, note after 104794
Elippihw, Augusto Revilo. pseud. Nine letters. see Whipple, Augustus Oliver.
Elisa ou un chapitre de l'Oncle Tom. 92544
Elisabeth Seton et les commencements de l'Eglise Catholique. 18509
Eliseo, ------. (22181)
Elisha, Patrick. 22182
Elisha, Patrick N. I. 59045
Elisha lamenting after the God of Elijah. 25391
Elixir magnum. (22183)

Elixir of gold. 101417
Elixir of moonshine. (13435)
Eliza et Maria. 44660
Eliza H. Sperry. 89405
Eliza. The Chippeway Indian. 22184
Eliza Woodson. 22185
Elizabeth I, Queen of England, 1533-1603. 22188, 68259 see also Great Britain. Sovereigns, etc., 1558-1603.
Elizabeth I, Queen of England, 1533-1603. spirit author 78374-78375, 100799
Elizabeth, d. 1797 or 8. 57613
Elizabeth (Ship) 100439
Elizabeth, N. J. defendants 5378, (53066)
Elizabeth, N. J. Caldwell Monument. 9918
Elizabeth, N. J. Christ Church. 22193, 32397
Elizabeth, N. J. Christ Church. Rector. 22193, 32397 see also Hoffman, Eugene Augustus.
Elizabeth, N. J. Proprietors. defendants 5378, (53066)
Elizabeth Canning in America. 100592
Elizabeth City County, Va. Citizens. 98413
Elizabeth Hamilton (Ship) in Admiralty 21621
Elizabeth in her holy retirement. 22186, 46302, (46621)
Elizabeth (N. J.) directory for 1865. 22190
Elizabeth; or, the exiles of Siberia. 78744
Elizabeth T. Stone. 92055
Elizabethae Angliae Reginae edictum adversus omnes catholicos sui regni. 22188
Elizabethae Angliae Reginae haeresim Calviniam propugnantis. (58903)
Elizabethtown, Md. see Hagerstown, Md.
Elizabethtown, N. J. see Elizabeth, N. J.
Elizabethtown Presbytery. see Presbyterian Church in the U. S. A. Presbytery of Elizabethtown.
Elizaga, Lorenzo. 22195
Elizalde, Fernando Antonio. 100608 see also Chile. Corte de Apelaciones. Fiscal.
Elizaphan of Parnach. pseud. Liberty and property vindicated. see Church, Benjamin, 1734-1776.
Elking, Henry. 22196, 28659, note after 99559-99560
Elking, William. (22198)
Elkington, T. 66686
Elkins, Hervey. 22197
Elkswatawa. 25864
Ella Barnwell. (4724)
Ella Cameron. (22199)
Ella Lincoln. (29388)
Ella V——. 94453
Elleanor's second book. 103302
Ellegood, Jacob. (22200)
Ellen Clayton. (34113)
Ellen; or, the chained mother. 30387
Ellen; or, the fanatic's daughter. 17230
Ellenborough, Edward Law, Baron, 1750-1818. 102784
Ellery, Abraham Redwood. 22201
Ellery, Christopher. 22202, 74487
Ellesmere, Francis Egerton, 1st Earl of, 1800-1857. 29211
Ellet, Charles. 19018, 22203-22209, 58448, 68214, (72576), 85072
Ellet, Elizabeth Fries (Lummis) 22210-22215
Ellice and Co. petitioners see Inglis, Ellice and Co. petitioners
Ellicott, Andrew. (22216)-22217, 22219 see also U. S. Commissioner for Determining the Boundary Between the United States and the Possessions of His Catholic Majesty in America, 1796-1800.

Ellicott, Andrew. incorrectly supposed author 22218, 39533, 64584, 101944
Ellicott, James. 69746
Ellicott, Thomas. 22220, 45368, 93938 see also Maryland. Suszuehannah Commissioners.
Ellicott, William M. defendant 45079
Ellicott & Co. firm see Poultney, Ellicott & Co. firm
Ellicott City, Maryland. Rock Hill College. see Rock Hill College, Ellicott City, Md.
Ellie, or the human comedy. 16323
Elliner, and other poems. 95564
Ellington, Edward. 22221-22222
Ellington, George. pseud. Women of New York. 22223
Ellington, John W. 22224
Ellingwood, N. D. 22225
Elliot, -------. botanist 67461
Elliot, -------. engr. 81486
Elliot, -------. illus. 77467
Elliot, Mrs. ------, fl. 1824. 82905
Elliot, C. S. 22226
Elliot, Daniel Girard. 22227-22229, 85072
Elliot, James. 22230
Elliot, Jonathan. 22231-(22237), 80405, note after 100545A, note after 106002
Elliot, Nathan. ed. (14877), 22239
Elliot, R. 22240
Elliot, S. H. 22244, 52755
Elliot, Samuel, 1777-1845, 22241-22243, 22273
Elliot, Seth. 22245
Elliot, T. F. 22246
Elliot, William. 22247-22249, 101965-101966, 102166
Elliot, William, Jr. 22250
Elliot, William, Jr. incorrectly supposed author (22251), (41389)
Elliot (W.) firm publishers 54459
Elliot & Crissy's . . . directory. 54459
Elliot's improved New York double directory. 54459
Elliot's Panama, Nicaragua, and Tehuantepec. (22251), (41389)
Elliot's Washington pocket almanac. 22238
Elliott. pseud. Remarks on the Bunker-Hill monument. see Coues, Samuel Elliott.
Elliott, A. B. (22252)
Elliott, Benjamin, 1786-1836. 22253, 87704
Elliott, Charles, 1792-1869. 22254-22257, (26284)
Elliott, Charles Wyllys. 22258-22260
Elliott, Clark. 62743
Elliott, David, 1787-1874. 22261, 64315
Elliott, E. N. 22263, 92870
Elliott, Ezekiel Brown, 1823-1888. 22262, 76571, 76647
Elliott, Franklin Reuben. 22264-(22266)
Elliott, J. H. 22267
Elliott, James Thomas, 1823-1875. (22268)
Elliott, Jehi. 22269
Elliott, Jesse Duncan, 1782-1845. 3828, 8458, 16875, 22270, 61047, 96405
Elliott, John. RN 2459
Elliott, John, 1768-1824. 22271-22272
Elliott, Mary. (61419)
Elliott, Robert J. 42316
Elliott, Samuel. 22274
Elliott, Samuel. incorrectly supposed author 22242, 22273
Elliott, Samuel M. 22275
Elliott, Stephen, 1771-1830. 22276
Elliott, Stephen, Bp., 1806-1866. 22277-22283, 57309, 63846
Elliott, Thomas Odingsell. 22285
Elliott, Wallace W. 84946-84947

Elliott, William 22286-22287
Elliott, William, 1788-1863. 87518 see also South Carolina. Commissioner to the Universal Exhibition at Paris, 1855.
Elliott Joyce, L. E. see Joyce, L. E. Elliott.
Elliott. firm. see Smith & Elliott. firm
Elliott Society of Natural History, Charleston, S. C. 12052, 22288, 84914
Ellis, -------, fl. 1890. 85380
Ellis, Anthony, Bp. see Ellys, Anthony, Bp. of St. Davids, 1690-1761.
Ellis, C. 22290
Ellis, Charles. 89209
Ellis, Charles Edward. see Edwards, Charles.
Ellis, Charles Mayo, 1818-1878. 8910, 18028, 22291-(22293), 75374, note after 89215
Ellis, Chesselden, 1808-1854. 22294
Ellis, Daniel. 22295
Ellis, Edward Sylvester, 1840-1916. 4101, 22296-22297
Ellis, Ferdinand. 22298-(22299)
Ellis, G. A. 22299
Ellis, George Edward, 1814-1894. 22300-22309
Ellis, George Edward, 1814-1894. supposed author 22309, 40657, note after 95099
Ellis, George W. 22310
Ellis, H. W. R. 22316
Ellis, Henry. 22311-22315
Ellis, J. V. 22324
Ellis, James. 22316A
Ellis, John, 1606-1681. 33496
Ellis, John, 1718-1776. 22317, 22319
Ellis, John, fl. 1720. 22318
Ellis, John B. 22320
Ellis, John F. 22321
Ellis, John Harvard. ed. 7299, note after 94823
Ellis, Jonathan, 1717-1785. 22322, 36951
Ellis, Jonathan, 1762-1827. 22323
Ellis, Robert. defendant 96924
Ellis, Rowland. tr. 66608
Ellis, Rufus. 22325-22327
Ellis, Samuel. (22328), 95127, 95132
Ellis, T. 22329-22330
Ellis, Thomas T. 22331
Ellis, V. 22332
Ellis, W. 22333-22334
Ellis, W. H. illus. (25106)
Ellis, William, fl. 1659. supposed author 55064
Ellis, William, 1794-1872. 22335, (76380), 91665-91666, 91669-91670, 91672
Ellis, William, fl. 1837. 13829
Ellis, William H. C. 22336
Ellison, -------, fl. 1777. (63615)
Ellison, Patrick. see Allison, Patrick.
Ellison, Robert. plaintiff 101149
Ellison, Thomas, 1833-1904. (22338), 84005
Elliston, Thomas. 22339
Ellithorpe, A. C. 22340
Ellmaker, E. E. 22341
Ellolie. pseud. Poems. see Smith, Zoda G.
Ellson, William. 22342
Ellsworth, A. A. pseud. 67420
Ellsworth, E. E. 22343
Ellsworth, Henry Leavitt, 1791-1858. 20144, (22344)-(22345), (34260), 59037, 59040, 59043, 96684-96686, 96688, 96691, 96693 see also U. S. Commissioner to the Four Confederated Bands of Pawnees. U. S. Commissioner to the United Bands of the Otos and Missouris. U. S. Commissioners to the Cherokee Nation of Indians, West of the Mississippi. U. S. Commissioner to the Muskogee or Creek

Nation of Indians. U. S. Commissioners to the Seminole Indians. U. S. Commissioners to the Seneca and Shawnee Indians. U. S. Patent Office. Commissioner.

Ellsworth, Henry William. (22346)

Ellsworth, Oliver. 30048

Ellsworth, P. W. 84449

Ellsworth, William Wolcott, 1791-1868. 22347-(22349), (30666), 84396 see also Connecticut. Governor, 1838-1842 (Ellsworth)

Ellsworth and his Zoauves. 1239

Ellwood, Thomas. 22350-22353, 37214, 105653

Ellys, Anthony, Bishop of St. Davids, 1690-1761. 22289

Ellyson, H. K. (71174)

Ellyson, M. ed. (71174)

Ellyson's Richmond directory. (71174)

Elmacin, George. 66682

Elmendorf, J. J. 22354

Elmendorf, Joachim. 64235

Elmendorf, L. 22355

Elmer, Jonathan. 22356, 57749

Elmer, Lucius Quintius Cincinnatus, 1793-1883. 22357, (53101)

Elmer, W. ed. (55551)

Elmes, James. 22358

Elmira and Williamsport Railroad Company. 60027, 60085

Elimra and Williamsport Railroad Company. Managers. 60085

Elmira directory. (22359)

Elmira Female College, Chemunga County, N. Y. 22360

Elmira tragedia en cinco actos. 63031

Elmore, E. C. (15224)

Elmore, F. H. (22361), 89311

Elmsley, John. 92645

Elmwood, Elnathan. pseud. Yankee among the nullifiers. see Greene, Asa.

Eloge civique de Benjamin Franklin. 23918

Eloge de Captitaine Cook. 5815

Eloge de Franklin. 15194

Eloge de M. Franklin. 15190, 23918

Eloge de M. Thiery de Menonville. 95349

Eloge de Washington. 21027

Eloge du tabac en poudre. 40126

Eloge funebre de M. l'Abbe L. J. Casault. 39108

Eloge funebre de S. M. Don Pedro. 59516

Eloge funebre de Washington. 24992, 101800

Eloge funebre du Comte d'Ennery. 19337, 22628

Eloge funebre du General de Division Lamarre. 74742

Eloge funebre du prelate. 39279

Eloge funebre du President A. Lincoln. 31017

Eloge funebre du President Lincoln. 3133

Eloge historique de la Soeur Marguerite Bourgeoys. 77202

Eloge historique du Chev. Mauduit-Duplessis. 19335

Eloges funebres de Washington. (24993), note after 96377, note after 101800

Elogi storici di Christoforo Colombo. 21418

Elogi vite brevemente scritte d'huomini illustri di guerra. 27478

Elogia a la muerte de J. M. Morelos. 29134

Elogia et nomenclator clarorum Hispaniae scriptorum. 77900

Elogia militaria. 33068, 73225

Elogia selecta ab Alumnis Academiae S. Philippi Neri elaborata. 76027

Elogia selecta e varijs. 26564

Elogia virorum bellica virtute illustrium. 36773

Elogio a Cristoforo Colombo. 4133

Elogio a la hermosura de Amarillis. 75886

Elogio a los patriotas. 100605

Elogio a nacao Portugueza. 88794

Elogio al Coronel Jos. Joaq. Marquez Donallo. 38404

Elogio al ejercito Trigarante. 98256

Elogio ao commercio. 43209

Elogio Castellano de Carlos IV. Rey de Espana. (77113)

Elogio d'Amerigo Vespucci. 10704

Elogio de Carlos IIII. Rey de Espana y de las Indias. 98319

Elogio de Cristobal Colon. (57673)

Elogio de D. Jose de Arango y Castillo. 2609

Elogio de la Bienaventurada Catarina de Riccis. 87195

Elogio de la concepcion de la Madre de Dios. 76173

Elogio de la concepcion de Nuestra Senora. 86425

Elogio de la concepcion inmaculada de Maria. (76011)

Elogio de la concepcion purisima de la Virgen. 76169

Elogio de la concepcion purisima de Maria. (72293)

Elogio de la Congregacion Hospitalaria de los Belemitas. 75612

Elogio de la glorioso Santa Catarina de Sena. 17737

Elogio de la inmaculada concepcion de la Santisima Virgen Maria. 73990

Elogio de la immaculada concepcion de la Virgen Maria. 72250

Elogio de la neuva orden religiosa de Belemitas. 75612

Elogio de la Santa Cruz. (78929)

Elogio de los militares y Espanoles difuntos. (72520)

Elogio de Maria Santisima en su admirable imagen. 76795

Elogio de Maria Santisima jurada patrona de la Nueva Espana. 74009

Elogio de Nuestra Senora de Guadalupe de Mexico. 78931

Elogio de Ntra. Sra. de Guadalupe [por Francisco de San Cirilo.] 76012

Elogio de Nostra Senora de Guadalupe [por J. E. Estrada.] 23066

Elogio de S. Bernardo Abad. 76187

Elogio de S. Felipe de Jesus. 76288

Elogio de S. Felipe Neri. 76868

Elogio de San Felipe Neri en la Iglesia de su congregacion de Mexico. 62607

Elogio de S. Francisco de Asis. 76134

Elogio de S. Ignacio de Loyola. 72250

Elogio de S. Juan de Dios en las fiestas de su canonizacion. 76135

Elogio de S. Juan de Dios [por Juan de Santa Maria Maraver.] 76791

Elogio de S. Juan de Dios [por Pablo Salceda.] 75599

Elogio de S. Pedro Apostol. 78930

Elogio de S. Salvador de Horta. 76278

Elogio de Santa Teresa de Jesus. (76165)

Elogio del apostol S. Pedro. 75612

Elogio del Beato Felipe de Jesus. 79301

Elogio del Dr. D. Eusebio Valli. (73009)

Elogio del eruditissimo Canonigo de la Puebla de los Angeles. 75887

Elogio del Exemo e Illmo Senor D. D. Bart. Maria de las Heras. 39097

Elogio del Excmo. Sr. Dr. Manuel Gomez Maranon. (72514)

Elogio del Exc. Senor D. Ambrosio O. Higgins. (56858)

Elogio del Excel. Senor D. Jose de San Martin y Matorras. 46864

Elogio del Excelentisimo Senor Don Luis de las Casas y Aragorri. 73008

Elogio del Excmo. Sr. Marques de Someruelos. 24335

Elogio del glorioso martir S. Pedro de Verona. 75592

Elogio del gran padre y Doctor de la Iglesia S. Agustin. 72529

Elogio del Ilust. senor Dr. D. Manuel J. Gonzalez de Acuna. 27819

Elogio del Marques de Santa Cruz. 51063

Elogio del maximo Dr. S. Geronimo. 80836

Elogio del medico mas sabio y martir invicto, S. Pantaleon. 73079

Elogio del mismo seminario al Excmo. Senor Don J. T. Abascal y Sousa. 68235

Elogio del p. eterno predicado en Mexico. 76229

Elogio del P. Francisco Clavijero. 11444

Elogio del precursor de Cristo, S. Juan Bautista. 76891

Elogio del Principe de los Aposteles, S. Pedro. [Por Antonio Salazar.] 75558

Elogio del Principe de los Apostoles, S. Pedro. [Por Matias Santillan.] 76867

Elogio del Senador Don Juan Egana. 44575

Elogio del Sr. D. Alfonso de Viania y Ulloa. 63437

Elogio del Sr. D. Ignacio Montalbo. (1879)

Elogio di Amerigo Vespucci. (24396), (39154)

Elogio di Giovanni da Verrazzano. 99280

Elogio dirigido a amisade, e esplendida companhia. 81114

Elogio do Padre D. Luiz Caetano de Lima. 5131

Elogio do Senador e Conselheiro d'Estado Jose Clemente Pereira. (79307)

Elogio funebre de Ilust. Sen. D. Francisco Xavier de Aldazaal. 75601

Elogio funebre de la amiable Reina de Espana. (73078)

Elogio funebre de la celebre poetisa Mexicana. 80987

Elogio funebre de la ilustre Madre, Antonia de S. Jacinto. 72250

Elogio funebre de la M. R. M. Marcela Estrada y Escobedo. 72522

Elogio funebre de la M. R. M. Sebastiana del Espiritu Sto. 76013

Elogio funebre de la Ven. M. Jacinta, de S. Antonio. 76816

Elogio funebre de la V. M. Sebastiana Josefa de la SSma. Trinidad. 75608

Elogio funebre de los militares difuntos Espanoles. 77101

Elogio funebre de los 21 religiosos de la Regular Observencia de S. Francisco. 77046

Elogio funebre del Capitan D. Diego de Medrano. 76174

Elogio funebre del Capitan D. Manuel Raboso de la Plaza. (76815)

Elogio funebre del Dr. D. Pedro Otalora y Carvajal. 75610

Elogio funebre del D. Man. J. Gonzalez del Campillo. 98714

Elogio funebre del Exmo. e. Ilmo. Senor D. Manuel Ignacio Gonzales del Campillo. 47815, 86368, 98715

Elogio funebre del Excmo. Sr. D. Francisco Sandoval Padilla y Acuna. 75888

Elogio funebre del Exmo. Sr. Duque de Linares. 76163

Elogio funebre del Illmo. Sr. D. Domingo Pantaleon Alvarez de Abreu. 73039

Elogio funebre del Illmo. Sr. D. Feliciano de la Vega. 86431

Elogio funebre del Illmo. Sr. D. Manuel Escalante. 76283

Elogio funebre del Illmo. Sr. D. Manuel Rubio y Salinas. 72509

Elogio funebre del Ilustrisimo Senor Doct. Gregorio Francisco de Campos. 22717

Elogio funebre del joven eclesiastico D. Fernando de Cordova y Bocanegra. (75570)

Elogio funebre del M. R. P. Mtro. Fr. Hortensio Felix Palavicino. 72558

Elogio funebre del muy excelso, muy poderoso y muy amable Senor Don Carlos III. (79319)

Elogio funebre del P. Luis Felipe Neri de Alfaro. 26498

Elogio funebre del Principe D. Baltasar Carlos de Austria. (75783)

Elogio funebre del Rmo. P. M. Fr. Francisco Xavier Vasquez de Sandoval y Romero. 11375

Elogio funebre del Sr. Carlos II. Rey de Espana. 76175

Elogio funebre del Senor Don Carlos IV. 72800

Elogio funebre del Sr. D. Carlos III. 80837

Elogio funebre del Sr. D. Pedro Ramon Romero de Terreros. 72799

Elogio funebre del Sr. Felipe III. de Espana. 73873

Elogio funebre del Sumo Pontifice Benedicto XIII. 76817

Elogio funebre del Ven. P. Fr. Cristobal Munoz. 77047

Elogio funebre dell Illmo R. D. Nicolas Gomez de Cervantes. 11058

Elogio funebre do Ser.mo Sr. D. Jose, Principe de Brasil. 51195

Elogio funebre en las exequias de Melchor de Moriega. (22924)

Elogio funebre na morte do Sr. D. Jose, Principe do Brasil. 14152

Elogio funebre pronunciado el 26 de Abril de 1849. 45401

Elogio funebre, pronunciado en sus magnificias ecsequias. 29135

Elogio funebre que dixo D. Francisco Pablo Vasquez. 10313

Elogio funebre que en las honras de D. Juan Joseph Yandiola y el Campo. 52089

Elogio historico. 52217

Elogio historico da Princeza do Brazil D. Maria Francisca Benedicta. 50513

Elogio historico da Sua Magestade Imperial o Sr. D. Pedro. 94620

Elogio historico de Maria Santisima de Guadalupe de Mexico. 98598

Elogio historico del Excelentissimo Senor Don Antonio de Escano. 66895

Elogio historico del S. D. J. A. del Castillo y Llata. 26577

Elogio historico do Finado Marquez de Abrantes. 48950

Elogio historico e noticia. 29288

Elogio historico-funebre. (72295)

Elogio historico por Antonio Felician de Castilo. 11415

Elogio patriotico. 58419

Elogio sepulcral en las solemnas exequias. 59630

Elogios a las valientes tropas Espanolas Americanas. 105713

Elogios de muchos hermanos coadjutores de la Compania de Jesus. (58000)

Elogios dos reverendissimos padres DD. Abbades
Geraes. 1861
Elogios en loorde los tres famoses varones.
39138
Elogios funebres con que la Santa Iglesia
Catedral de Guadalaxara ha celebrado la
buena memoria del Fr. Antonio Alcade.
29025
Elogios funebres con que la Santa Iglesia
Catedral de Guadalaxara ha celebrado la
buena memoria du su prelado el Illmo.
y Rmo. Senor Mtro. D. F. Antonio Al-
calde. 22362
Elogios funebres del Excelentisimo Senor D.
Luis de las Casas y Aragorri. 11292,
(39123), 73008, 85742
Elogios funebres: oratio y sermon funebre.
24824
Elogios funebres, que la Pontifical y Rl. Uni-
versidad de Mexico dedico. 52090
Elogios Latino y Castellano. 41660
Elogium R. P. Adriani Knudde dicti Crespi.
4644, 5101, (69246)
Elogium R. P. Cornelii Beudin dicti Godinez.
4644, 5101, (69246)
Elogj Italiani. 73853
Elogue du tabac en fumee. 40126
Elogue historique de Monsieur le Marquis de
Montcalm. 50090
Elohi nulistanitolv kanohesgi. 27915
Elopement. (23688)
Eloquence and liberty. 43841
Eloquence of nature. 61398
Eloquence of the British senate. (31124)
Eloquence of the colonial and revolutionary
times. 43837
Eloquence of the United States. 72468, 84837,
92297, 96420, 101477, 101478, 102269,
104526
Eloquent and instructive passages. 4400
Eloquentia libertatis Vindex. 101418
Elorriaga, C. Fr. (22363)
Elorriaga, Francisco. tr. 48589
Elorza, Francisco Joseph Caseres y. see
Caseres y Elorza, Francisco Joseph.
Elorza y Rada, Francisco de. (22365), 55377
Eloy de Barros Pimentel, Esperidiao. see
Pimentel, Esperidiao Eloy de Barros.
El Rey de Figueroa, Antonio Vazquez Gastelu.
see Vazquez Gaztelu, Antonio.
Elsemore, Moses. 22364
El-Shaddai. A brief essay. 46303
Elsie's stars. 54829
Elsner, Chrysostom H. 22366
Elsner, Heinrich. ed. 22366
Elstracke, -------. engr. 67560, (78188)
Elton, J. F. 22367
Elton, Richard. 6375, 22368
Elton, Romeo, 1790-1870. (10076), 22369,
46999, 47001, 47005, 70719
Elvas (Diocese) Bishop (Cunha de Azeredo
Coutinho) 17955 see also Cunha de
Azeredo Coutinho, Jose Joaquim de, Bp.
Elvas, Gentleman of. pseud. see Knight of
Elvas. pseud.
Elvas, Gentleman of the town of. pseud. see
Knight of Elvas. pseud.
Elvas, Knight of. pseud. see Knight of Elvas.
pseud.
Elves of Ginnistian. pseud. Sprite. 89907
Elville, Rinaldo d'. see D'Elville, Rinaldo.
Elvira de Oquendo o los amores de una Guajira.
98827
Elvias, P. 22370
Elwes, Mrs. Alfred W. supposed author
64589

Elwes, Robert. 22371-22372
Elwin, Alfred L. (22374)
Elwood, J. L. 72340
Elworth, Thomas. (22373)
Elwyn, Thomas. 22375, 67181, 79401
Elwyn, Pa. Training School for Feeble Minded
Children. see Pennsylvania Training
School for Feeble-Minded Children, Elwyn.
Ely, A. engr. 94019
Ely, Alfred, 1778-1866. 22376-22377
Ely, Alfred, 1815-1892. (22378)
Ely, Alfred B. (22379)-22381
Ely, Ezra Stiles. 22382-22384, 66971, 97087,
103443
Ely, Isaac M. 22385
Ely, John. 22386
Ely, John, Jr. Complainant 97779-97781,
97785
Ely, Richard. 22387
Ely, S. 54647
Ely, S. W. 22390
Ely, Samuel. 19294, (22388)
Ely, Smith. 22389
Ely, Zebulon. 22391-22393, 97205
Ely, Bishop of. see Dampier, Thomas,
successively Bp. of Rochester, and Ely,
1748-1812. Felton, Nicholas, succes-
sively Bp. of Bristol and Ely, 1556-1626.
Fleetwood, William, successively Bp. of
St. Asaph, and Ely, 1656-1723. Gooch,
Sir Thomas, Bart., successively Bishop
of Bristol, Norwich, and Ely, d. 1754.
Green, Thomas, successively Bp. of
Norwich, and Ely, 1658-1738. Keene,
Edmund, successively Bp. of Chester,
and Ely, 1714-1781. Mawson, Matthias,
Successively Bishop of Chichester, and
Ely, 1683-1770. Moore, John, succes-
sively Bp. of Norwich, and Ely, 1645?-
1714. Turner, Francis, successively
Bp. of Rochester, and Ely, 1638?-1700.
Yorke, James, successively Bp. of
Gloucester, and Ely, d. 1808.
Elze, Karl. 2306, 88987
Em. C. L. pseud. see L., Em. C. pseud.
Emancipate your colonies. 4765, 4767
Emancipated labor in Louisiana. 3206
Emancipated slave face to face with his old
master. 43371
Emancipatie der slaven. 28777
Emancipatie der slaven. Bijdrage tot eene
nadere beschouwing. 94584
Emancipatie der slaven in Nederlandsche Indie.
32379
Emancipatie der W. I. slaven. 22395
Emancipatie door centralisatie. 22396, 38934,
2d note after 93855
Emancipation. 22397
Emancipation; a poem. 22399
Emancipation and enrollment of slaves. 78809
Emancipation and its results. (17271)
Emancipation and the church. 20255
Emancipation and the war. (27864)
Emancipation and war. 3405
Emancipation Anglaise jugee par ses resultats.
36422
Emancipation as a state policy. 8453
Emancipation aux Antilles Francaises. 28075
Emancipation: by William E. Channing. 11910
Emancipation Convention, Jefferson City, Mo.,
1862. 49630
Emancipation der sklaven auf Cuba. 21403
Emancipation des esclaves. 5652
Emancipation des esclaves aux colonies Fran-
caises. 75536
Emancipation des noirs. (36415)
Emancipation des serfs en Russie. 22398

Emancipation immediate et complete des esclaves. (24009)
Emancipation in disguise. 22400
Emancipation in India. 37769
Emancipation in Kentucky. 64923
Emancipation in Louisiana. (31906)
Emancipation in Maryland. 45140
Emancipation in Missouri. A discourse delivered in . . . St. Louis. (22178)
Emancipation in Missouri. Speech of Samuel T. Glover at the ratification meeting, St. Louis. 27611
Emancipation in Missouri. Speech of Samuel T. Glover, Esq., . . . St. Louis. 27612
Emancipation in peace. 58024
Emancipation in the British W. Indies. 47078
Emancipation in the West Indies. A six months' tour. 95460
Emancipation in the West Indies. By F. B. Sanborn. 76248
Emancipation in the West Indies, in 1838. (81960), 2d note after 102832
Emancipation; its condition and policy. 22097
Emancipation: its justice, expediency and necessity. (6977)
Emancipation, its necessity and means of accomplishment. 3168
Emancipation League, Boston. 23618
Emancipation League of Kansas. see Kansas Emancipation League.
Emancipation of Negro apprentices. 8419
Emancipation of South America. (9314)
Emancipation of the Negro slaves. (22402)
Emancipation; or practical advice to British slave-holders. 104782
Emancipation oration, by Dr. Ezra R. Johnson. 36210
Emancipation problem in Maryland. 22401, 47105
Emancipation proclamation. 89850
Emancipation proclamation and arbitrary arrests. (19020)
Emancipation proclamation. By Hon. A. Andrus and W. H. Brand. 1528
Emancipation Society, Glasgow. see Glasgow Emancipation Society.
Emancipation Society, Paisley, Scotland. see Paisley Emancipation Society, Paisley, Scotland.
Emancipation transformation. 12353
Emancipation unmask'd. 7822
Emancipation——white and black. 55244
Emancipator. 22404, 93138
Emancipator extra. Tract no. 2. 71360
Emancipirte Sklave und sein fruherer Herr. 43372
Emanuel I, King of Portugal, 1469-1521. 22405-22408, 34100-34107, 56407, 99335 see also Portugal. Sovereigns, etc., 1495-1521 (Emanuel I)
Emanuel Timonius. pseud. see Timonius, Emanuel. pseud.
Embargo acts, 1808. 22410
Embargo and non-importation laws. 22411
Embargo laws. 22412
Embargo, (on common sense) "taken off." 1793, 2d note after 98175
Embargo, or sketches of the times. 8815, 22409, 2d note after 106203
Embassy to the eastern courts of Cochin-China, Siam, and Muscat. 71884
Embers from poverty's hearth. 22156
Emblemas de los geroglificos y poesias. 75604
Emblemas regio-politicos. 86540
Emblemas yeroglificas y poesias. 75603

Emblemata centvm, regio politica. 86538-86539, 86545
Emblematic tree. 48021
Embryonic development of Planocera Elliptica. 27484
Embury, Emma C. 22414
Emendatione temporum. 6118, 94273
Emerald. A collection of tales. 76953
Emerald, or miscellany of literature. 22415
Emeressio, Ormildo. pseud. Ammiraglio dell' Indie. see Alvise, Querini.
Emerick, Albert G. 22417
Emerson, A. L. 22418
Emerson, Brown. (22419)-22421
Emerson, Charles N. 22422-22425
Emerson Eleanor. 105302, 105306
Emerson, Enoch. (32426)
Emerson, Ezekiel. 22427
Emerson, G. ed. 52291
Emerson, George Barrell, 1797-1881. 22428-22492, 44324, 93558
Emerson, Gouverneur, 1796-1874. 22430-22432, 36201
Emerson, J. D. 85487
Emerson, J. E. 13365
Emerson, John. 22433
Emerson, Joseph, 1700-1767. 22435-22443
Emerson, Joseph, 1724-1775. (22444)-(22447)
Emerson, Joseph, 1777-1833. 22448-(22449), 26921, 105098
Emerson, Mrs. M. Farley. (22450)
Emerson, P. 45059
Emerson, Ralph. 22461
Emerson, Ralph. tr. 22452
Emerson, Ralph Waldo, 1803-1882. 19920, 22453-22460, 41167, note before 94542, 101395
Emerson, Reuben. 22461, 75698
Emerson, Samuel. 22462-(22463)
Emerson, Sylvanus. defendant 62482
Emerson, W. D. 22466
Emerson, William. 22464-22465
Emerson (J. M.) & Co. firm publishers 22467, (66843), 84151, 84162
Emerson as a lecturer. 67423
Emerson's Female Seminary, Weathersfield, Conn. see Joseph Emerson's Female Seminary, Weathersfield, Conn.
Emerson's internal revenue guide, 1867. 22423
Emerson's magazine and Putnam's monthly. 22467, (66843), 84151, 84162
Emerson's United States magazine. 84162
Emerson's United States register. (66843)
Emerton, M. P. ed. 82304
Emery, John L. reporter 50681
Emery, Joshua. 22468-22469
Emery, Louis. (22470)
Emery, Marcellus. 43915
Emery, Moses. 22471, 87270
Emery, Rush. 35003
Emery, Samuel Hopkins, 1815-1901. 22472, 95162
Emigracion Alemana al Rio de la Plata. (77074)
Emigracion de los Aztecas hacia el Anahuac. 71703
Emigrado observador. 56648
Emigrant. pseud. Letter to the Right Hon. E. G. Stanley. see Thom, Adam.
Emigrant. 33379, 72648
Emigrant: a contrast. 22473
Emigrant, a poem. 103693
Emigrant Aid Company of Massachusetts. 45735
Emigrant Aid Company of Massachusetts. Committee. 52198

Emigrant. An ecloque. 16390
Emigrant and traveller's guide to and through
    Canada. 51525
Emigrant. By Sir Francis B. Head, Bart.
    (31132)
Emigrant churchman. 12943
Emigrant churchman in Canada. 12942
Emigrant, etc. 16391
Emigrant farmer. pseud. Memoranda of a
    settler. see Abbott, J.
Emigrant farmer. 22475
Emigrant farmer of twenty-five years' experi-
    ence. pseud. Emigrant to North America.
    22476
Emigrant-Foreningen i Stockholm. 57259
Emigrant guide to the west for 1866. 17144
Emigrant Hospital of New York State. see
    New York (State) Emigrant Hospital.
Emigrant, just returned to England. pseud.
    Things as they are. 95351
Emigrant, late of the United States. pseud.
    History of Texas. see Stille, --------.
Emigrant, late of the United States. pseud.
    Texas in 1840. see Stille, --------.
Emigrant life in the new world. 74826
Emigrant, or reflections while descending the
    Ohio. 95393
Emigrant Society, Philadelphia. see Phila-
    delphia Emigrant Society.
Emigrant squire. (51635)
Emigrant to North America. 22476
Emigranten, et uafhaengigt demokratist blad.
    13508
Emigrantin. pseud. Ansiedlungen in den
    Urwaldern von Canada. see Traill,
    Catherine Parr (Strickland)
Emigrants. pseud. Important extracts from
    recent letters. 34401
Emigrants; a tale. (18592)
Emigrant's and traveller's guide to the west.
    2594, note after 94327, 99586
Emigrant's and traveller's guide to the west,
    with a view of the Mississippi Valley.
    22477
Emigrant's assistant. 12932
Emigrants aux Bresil. 25937, (77894)-77895
Emigrant's companion and guide. 102721
Emigrant's complete guide to Canada. 9660
Emigrant's complete guide to Canada; con-
    taining the most recent information.
    44336
Emigrant's complete guide to the United States
    of America. (44337)
Emigrant's directory and guide to obtain lands.
    23150
Emigrant's directory; containing a general
    description. 102980
Emigrant's directory. Containing a geographical
    description. 8558
Emigrant's directory; containing different
    routes. 91141-91143
Emigrant's directory: containing general des-
    criptions. 91145
Emigrant's directory to the western states.
    1349
Emigrants en Amerique. 39287
Emigrants, &c., or the history of an expatriated
    family. 34353
Emigrant's, farmer's and politician's guide.
    21886, 95090
Emigrant's five years in the free states of
    America. 30192
Emigrant's friend. 22478
Emigrant's friend in Canada. 73287
Emigrant's Friend Society, Philadelphia.
    Directors. Executive Committee. 61615

Emigrant's guide. 14797, 91145, 102980
Emigrant's guide; a description of Wisconsin.
    18069
Emigrant's guide and state directory. 54997
Emigrant's guide; being the information published.
    98075
Emigrants guide. By George Henry. 31390
Emigrant's guide. Comprising advice and
    instruction. 22483
Emigrant's guide; containing a correct des-
    cription. 54998
Emigrant's guide; containing general descriptions.
    91144, 2d note after 96483
Emigrant's guide; in ten letters. 13882
Emigrant's guide, or a picture of America.
    (22479)
Emigrant's guide; or, pocket gazetteer of the
    surveyed part of Michigan. (23821)
Emigrant's guide, or pocket geography. 22480
Emigrant's guide overland. 10253
Emigrant's guide through the states of Ohio,
    Michigan. 14797, 82931-82932, 103021
Emigrant's guide through the western states.
    22481
Emigrant's guide to and description of the
    United States of America. 14450
Emigrant's guide to Australia and Canada.
    22484
Emigrant's guide to California, containing every
    point of information. 101405
Emigrant's guide to California, describing its
    geography. 10002
Emigrant's guide to New Mexico. 20325
Emigrants' guide to Oregon and California.
    30824
Emigrant's guide to Texas. 95087
Emigrants' guide to the Canadas. 102154
Emigrant's guide to the gold fields. 8095
Emigrant's guide to the gold mines. 81347
Emigrant's guide to the gold mines of Upper
    California. 79643
Emigrants' guide to the gold regions of the
    west. 9320
Emigrant's guide to the new republic. 95091,
    95122
Emigrant's guide to the state of Michigan.
    22482, note after 95567
Emigrant's guide, to the United States of
    America; including the substance of the
    journal of Thomas Hulme. 84355
Emigrant's guide to the United States of
    America; . . . the latest information.
    32485
Emigrant's guide to the United States: who
    should and who should not emigrate.
    22485
Emigrant's guide to the western and south-
    western states. (18527)
Emigrant's guide to the western states of
    America. 68798
Emigrant's guide to Upper Canada. 82226,
    93133
Emigrant's guides. 34111
Emigrant's hand book, and guide to Wisconsin.
    25777
Emigrant's hand-book, and new guide for
    travellers. 82926
Emigrant's hand-book. By Samuel Stewart.
    91706
Emigrant's hand-book of facts. 9660
Emigrant's hand-book; or, a directory and
    guide. (22486)
Emigrant's hand book to the United States.
    22487
Emigrant's home; or, life in the far west.
    37986

Emigrant's home; or, real life in the west.
37986, 37988
Emigrant's informant. 98076
Emigrant's introduction to the acquaintance
with the British American colonies.
31860
Emigrant's journal. (80862)
Emigrants; (la colonie du Kansas) 5003
Emigrants' letters; being recent communi-
cations. (22489)
Emigrants' letters from Canada and South
Australia. 22488, note after 93911
Emigrants' letters, written in 1832. 86184,
note after 98068
Emigrant's location. 84225
Emigrant's location, being a guide to the
selection. 84224
Emigrant's manual; containing, Australia, New
Zealand, America, and South Africa.
9494
Emigrant's manual, particularly addressed to
the industrious classes. (72878)
Emigrant's narrative. 84714
Emigrant's note book and guide. 50662
Emigrants; or first and final step. 79637
Emigrant's or stranger's guide to the Valley
of the Mississippi. (55833)
Emigrant's pocket companion. 51241
Emigrant's progress from the old world to the
new. (74336)
Emigrants' settlers', and travellers' guide.
29761
Emigrant's vade-mecum. 59155
Emigrating Indians. 17459, note after 94645
Emigration a la Guyane Anglaise. 49093
Emigration. A letter to a member of Parlia-
ment. 86186, 1st note after 98076
Emigration a Monte Video y a Buenos Ayres.
3602
Emigration and colonization. 72879
Emigration circular. (22491)
Emigration colonies. 10762
Emigration, colonisation dans l'Amerique.
47475
Emigration colonization dans l'Amerique Cen-
trale. 48228
Emigration commission. 22499
Emigration considered. 22492
Emigration, emigrants, and know-nothings.
22493
Emigration et les divers projets du Canal de
Jonction. (58064)
Emigration Europeenne. Rapport par M. Huer-
tier. 31624
Emigration Europeenne, son importance.
39870
Emigration fields: North America, the Cape,
Australia, and New Zealand. 46884
Emigration for the million. 17167
Emigration from Europe during the present
century. (36656)
Emigration from Ireland. 10889
Emigration guide to Kanzas [sic]. 13792
Emigration; its advantages to Great Britain
and her colonies. 43187
Emigration. Letters from Sussex emigrants.
22500, 40594, 86187, 2d note after 98076
Emigration (North American colonies) 22495
Emigration of free and emancipated Negroes
to Africa. 78396
Emigration of the emancipated Negores to
British Guiana. 22490
Emigration, or no emigration. 62639
Emigration. Practical advice to emigrants.
22501
Emigration practically considered. 8840

Emigration. Prince Edward Island. 40769
Emigration Society, Petworth, England. see
Petworth Emigration Society, Petworth
England.
Emigration to America. 22496, 71241
Emigration to Brazil. 7569
Emigration to Canada. Canada: a brief outline.
10368, 22497, 34110
Emigration to Canada. Narrative of a voyage
to Quebec. 43159
Emigration to Canada. The eastern townships
of Lower Canada. 8079
Emigration to Canada. The Province of Ontario.
10436
Emigration to Texas. Proposals for colonizing
certain extensive tracts. 95080
Emigration to Texas. Texas. 94937
Emigration to the United States of North America.
22498, 51018
Emigration to the United States, upon a new
and practical plan. 32392
Emigration: where to go. 34015
Emigration: with advice to emigrants. 43478
Emigration, with special reference to Min-
nesota. (68007)
Emigrations-Geschichte von denen aus dem
Ertz-Bissthum Saltzburg Vertriebenen
Lutheranern. 27627
Emigrations-Monographie. (59595)
Emigres Francais dans la Louisiane (1800-1804)
22510, (64540)
Emile Carrey. 11046
Emilio, -----. 22511
Emily Hamilton, a novel. 99422
Eminent American poet. pseud. Marriage: an
epic poem. 102439
Eminent Americans. 42115, 42121, 42127
Eminent barrister. pseud. reporter 103674
Eminent citizen. pseud. Full, clear, and
succinct discussion. 26149
Eminent citizen of Virginia. pseud. Letters
of Algernon Sydney. see Leigh, Ben-
jamin Watkins.
Eminent dead. 59543
Eminent lawyer of Connecticut. pseud. Letter.
see Hooker, John.
Eminent merchant. pseud. Mr. Chase's finan-
cial scheme. 12201
Eminent merchant. pseud. Proposal. 99553
Eminent physicians and surgeons. pseud.
Testimonies and cases. 94912
Eminent reporter. pseud. Trial of Capt.
Henry Whitby. see Sampson, William.
supposed author
Eminent senator. pseud. To the people of the
United States. 97946
Eminent woolgrowers. pseud. Letters. 50781
Eminent women of the age. 22513, 58944
Eminent writers. pseud. Men of history.
47789
Eminently good and vseful men. 199
Emion, Francis. tr. 84006
Emitting and redeeming money. 99082
Emlen, Samuel. 22514
Emlen Institution for the Education of Children
of African or Indian Descent, Phila-
delphia. Trustees. (61616)
Emlyn, Thomas, 1663-1741. 9422, 93820
Emma Cobbett. 22515, (64975)
Emma Corbett. 22515, (64975)
Emma Willard School, Troy, N. Y. 104050
Emmanuel Church, Baltimore. see Baltimore.
Emmanuel Church.
Emmerson, -----, fl. 1821. 94733
Emmerson, Thomas. ed. 94808

Emmert, Shannon & Company. firm publishers 88380

Emmery de Sept-Fontaines, H. C. tr. 91590

Emmet, ------, fl. 1809. 75957, note after 96922

Emmet, ------, fl. 1826. 21108

Emmet, Thomas Addis. petitioner 97941

Emmett, ------, fl. 1804. 5906, 74878

Emissary. pseud. Wiles of popery. 103990

Emmitsburg, Md. Mount St. Mary's College. see Mount St. Mary's College, Emmitsburg, Md.

Emmons, Charles P. (22517)

Emmons, Ebenezer, 1799-1863. 22518, 46069, 46082, 51980, 53791, 53794, 55592, 55614-55619 see also North Carolina. Geologist.

Emmons, George F. USN 22519

Emmons, Henry. 22520

Emmons, Henry, fl. 1809. 22521

Emmons, Nathaniel, 1745-1840. (10120), 22522-22526, 26141, 63344, 73140, 95888

Emmons, Nathaniel 1745-1840. supposed author 21977, 22525

Emmons, Richard. (22527)-22530

Emmons, William. 22531-22533

Emmons's oration on Lexington battle. 22531

Emogene. 51455

Emory, John, Bp., 1789-1835. 22534, 33398, 42966, 89002, 102150, 102681

Emory, Joshua. 22535

Emory, William D. 22538, 22580

Emory, William Helmsley, 1811-1887. 22536-22538, 25836-25837, 25846, 69900, 69946

Emory, Va. Emory and Henry College. see Emory and Henry College, Emory, Va.

Emory and Henry College, Emory, Va. 88470

Emory College, Oxford, Ga. 22539

Emott, James, 1771-1850. (22540)-(22541)

Empenos de Santa Isable en su Casa. 73200

Emperador Napoleon III. y la Inglaterra. 51765

Empereur du Mexique. (22542)

Empereur Maximilien. (37607)

Emperor Nicholas I. 85155, 85158, 85159, 85162

Empire almanac. 22543

Empire aux Mexique. 20546

Empire City. (41392)

Empire du Bresil. 3380

Empire du Bresil a l'Exposition Universelle de 1867. (7572)

Empire et l'intervention. 48502

Empire Francaise et les Etats-Unis. 6130

Empire Mexicain. 20547

Empire Mexician, histoire des Tolteques. 9561

Empire of Brazil at the Paris International Exhibition of 1867. 7570

Empire of Brazil at the Paris International Exhibition of 1867. With an appendix. 7571

Empire of Christ is peace. (22544)

Empire of reason. 22545

Empire Spring. 22518

Empires and dominions of this world. 71734

Employee of the Bureau. pseud. Starling disclosures! 90579

Employers and the employed. (25316)

Employment of the Indians by the English. 54476

Employment of the people and capital. 85258-85260

Employment of women. 60794

Employment Society, Providence, R. I. 66258

Empoli, Gioanni da. 67730

Emporium of arts & sciences. 17283

Emporium R. E. & M. Company, Cincinnati. firm 82956

Empresarios, de Fabricas Nacionales de Hilados y Tegidos de Algodon. petitioners 22546

Emprestino Brasileiro contrahido em Londres em 1863. 22547

Emprestito de Chile. 35079

Empson, Charles. (22548)

Empty sleeve. 47213

En Amerique, en France et ailleurs. 14935

En Amerique et en Europe. 44642

En Cour d'Appel. 99598

En defensa de la Real Hacienda. 98358

En defensa del Excmo. Sr. Virey, Conde del Venadito. 106242

En el expediente instruido en esta Real Audiencia. 86518

En el nombre de Dios, Amen. 2234

En el pleyto que es entre partes. 99464

En el elogio de Don Luis de Velasco. 98802

En la ciudad de Lima. 94627

En la gloriosa inauguracion de Augustin Primero. 96279

En la Junta de Sociedad Patriotica de 24 de Noviembre de 1796. 56746

En la inauguracion del Conservatorio Nacional de Declamacion de Mexico. 11648

En steamer d'Europe aux Etats-Unis. 4817

En verdadero patriota. (11428)

Enactments [by the Rector and Visitors of the University of Virginia.] 100537

Enactments by the Rector and Visitors of the University of Virginia, for constituting, governing and conducting that institution. 100537

Enamiad o Nanagatawenda Mowinan. 37115

Enault, Louis. tr. 92529

Encalada, Manuel Lorenzo de Vidaurre y. see Vidaurre y Encalada, Manuel Lorenzo de.

Encargado de la Presidente de la republica, a la nacion. 49930

Encarnacao da Costa e Lima, Thomas da. see Costa e Lima, Thomas da Encarnacao da.

Encarnacion, or the prisoners in Mexico. 78306

Encarnacion prisoners. 22549, 65708

Encensoir des dames. 100745

Enchanted rock. 75251, 75253-75254

Enchiridon cosmographicvm. (66890)-66891

Enchiridion de los tiempos. 98863-98865

Enchiridion geographicum. 74625

Enciclica de Ntro. Santisimo Padre el Senor Pio IX. (38617), 39476

Enciclopedia de viajes modernos, etc. 24141

Enciclopedia juridica. 23718

Enciclopedia popular Mejicana. 58004

Encina, Louis Gonzaga de la. see La Encina, Louis Gonzaga de.

Encinas, Diego de. ed. 22550, note after 40960

Encinas, Diego Miguel Bringas de Manzaneda y. see Bringas de Manzaneda y Encinas, Diego Miguel.

Encisco, Luis Carrasco y. see Carrasco y Encisco, Luis.

Enciso, Martin Fernandez de. 22551-22553, note after 93574

Encomiastic advertisement of the work. 30003, 43202

Encomium on the ladies . . . at Sutton. (29824)

Encounter between a white man and two savages. 44258, 105687-note after 105690

Encourage domestic industry. 85896
Encouragement for seamen and mariners.
  23281
Encouragement of foreign commerce. 80137
Encouragement to colonies. 739, 73797, 81697,
  91853
Encouragement to holy effect. 71833
Encouragements for such as shall have inten-
  tion. 27967, 41715
Encouragements to religious effort. 102187
Encroachments and depredations of the French.
  9602, 30794-30795, 34027, 2d note after
  65324
Encroachments and exactions of slavery. 92379
Encroachments of the slave-power. 22554,
  90866
Encyclopaedia. see Encyclopedia.
Encyclopedia. 77380
Encyclopaedia Americana. 22556, 62635,
  (70885), 84062, 103911
Encyclopaedia Britannica. (14620), 23255,
  41673, (78330), 97654-97655, 99801
Encyclopedia containing descriptions of the
  most famous and memorable land battles
  and sieges. 60859
Encyclopedia. Containing everything necessary.
  13804
Encyclopaedia metropolitana. 102370
Encyclopaedia of geography . . . . By Thomas
  T. Smiley. 82285
Encyclopedia of geography: comprising a com-
  plete description of the earth. (51499)
Encyclopaedia of the country. 84422
Encyclopedia of the trade and commerce of the
  United States. 19117-19118
Encyclopaedia of United States history. note
  after 99383C
Encyclopaedia of wit and humor. 84241
Encyclopaedia; or dictionary of arts and
  sciences. 22555, 32123, 40024, 50937
Encyclopedie des voyages. 16808, 75487
Encyclopedie methodique. (19477)
End of life persued. 46488
End of strife. (33885)
End of the irrepressible conflict. 22557,
  34180
End of the miserable world. 45399
End of the world. 83579
End of the world about 1864-69. 4008
End of time. 74292
End to the old church and old government
  generally. 104566
End to the slavery controversy. (79744)
End why Christ gave himself. 32848
Enda vag till salighet. 85525
Endeavour after the reconcilement. 17062
Endeavour Engine Company, Melrose, Mass.
  47468
Endeavours used by the Society for the Propa-
  gation of the Gospel in Foreign Parts.
  54259
Endechas en la muerte de D. Tomas de
  Iriarte. 73905
Endecot, John. see Endicott, John, 1588-1665.
Endecott, John. see Endicott, John, 1588-1665.
Endemic influence of evil government. 24973
Enderica, Antonio. 26824
Endhoven, Jan van. 22558
Endicott, Charles M. 22559-22561
Endicott, G. illus. 76914
Endicott, John, 1588-1665. 3213, 4013, 9455,
  33695, 33696, note before 92797, note
  after 92800, 3d note after 103687 see
  also Massachusetts (Colony) Governor,
  1654-1664 (Endicott)

Endicott & Co. firm publishers (6347)
Endicott's picture of Saratoga for 1843. 76914
Endless life the inheritance of the righteous.
  91113
Endlicher, Stephan Friedrich Ladislaus, 1804-
  1849. 22562, 63628
Endowment. 98493-98494
Endowment, as it was acted by upwards of
  twelve thousand. 22563
Ends and objects of Burlington College. 20391
Enduran, L. 22564
Endurance, individual and national. 55361
Ene niyoh raodeweyena. (50765)
Eneas Espanol. 98162
Enemies of America unmasked. (39261)
Enemies of the constitution and the union.
  13281
Enemies of the constitution discovered. 19264,
  note before 95449, 1st note after 98225
Enemy of delusion. pseud. Political craft.
  63760
Enemy to creeds. pseud. Review of a pamphlet.
  34498, 70194
Enemy to human diseases. pseud. Formula of
  prescriptions. see Plinth, Octavius.
Enemy to the villains of every denomination.
  pseud. Faithful account. (23712)
Enemy's territory and alien enemies. (18444)
Enesee. pseud. History of Dungeon Rock.
  see C., N. E. pseud
Enfaldiga tankar om nyttons om England kan
  hafva af Sina Nybyggen i Norra America.
  (36990)
Enfans & Heritiers de Messiere Charles de
  Saint Estienne Seigneur de la Tour.
  petitioners (47523)
Enfant perdu. 6295
Enfants de bois. 69038
Enfermedades politicas. 9582, 2d note after
  98255, note after 99675
Enfield, Eward. 22566
Enfield, N. H. Citizens. 52791, note after
  98998
Enfield, N. H. Society of People Commonly
  Called Shakers. see Shakers. Canter-
  bury and Enfield, N. H.
Enfield, N. H. United Society. see Shakers.
  Canterbury and Enfield, N. H.
Enforced contraction of the currency. 58196
Enforcement of fifteenth amendment. Speech of
  Hon. George E. Spencer. 89319
Enforcement of fourteenth amendment. Speech
  of Hon. George F. Edmunds. 21871
Enforcement of fourteenth amendment. Speech
  of Hon. Oliver P. Snyder. 85605
Enforcement of the fifteenth amendment. Speech
  of Hon. Carl Schurz. 78029
Enforcement of the fourteenth amendment—Ku
  Klux legislation. (71941)
Enforcement of the fourteenth amendment.
  Speech . . . April 5th and 12th, 1871.
  64024
Enforcement of the fourteenth amendment.
  Speech of Hon. Samuel Shellabarger.
  (80138)
Enforcing bill. 69479, 6th note after 88114
Enfranchisement of labor. 74310
Engagement between the American sloop of
  war Wasp. 102038
Engagement between the Chesapeake and Shannon.
  102206
Engagement on the White Plains. 50185, 82379
Engel, --------. cartographer 8831, (47542)
Engel, Landvogt. tr. 62575
Engel, M. tr. 12597
Engel, Samuel. 22567-22576

915

Engeland in de agttiende eeuw. 103890
Engelands dwaashied. 22577
Engelen, Jacobus Voegen van. see Voegen
van Engelen, Jacobus.
Engelhard, Georg Heinrich. tr. 98965
Engelhardt, -------. 105518
Engelhardt, G. tr. 105519
Engelhardt, N. (22578)
Engell-Gunther, Julia. 22579
Engelmann, George, 1809-1884. 22538, 22580,
35308, 69946, 103032
Engelmann, Henry. 34253
Engels, L. 22581
Engelsche dog. 77976
Engelsche en Amerikaansche kaart-spel.
(77512)
Engelsche hond is dol. (77977)
Engelsche syllogismen of verzameling van alle
de bewyzen der beste schryveren. 22583
Engelschen duyvel ontdeckt in twafflt artykelen.
22582
Engelschen in Amerika. 16457
Engelsman. pseud. Klachte der West-Indische
Compagnie. 38028, 3d note after 102893
Enghuysen, Jan Outghersz van. 22584
Enginae Societatis Poeta. pseud. Rebelliad.
30755
Engineer and artillery operations against the
defences. (27422)
Engineer and artillery operations . . . with a
supplement. 27423
Engineer upon that expedition. pseud. Short
account. see Moncrief, ---------. RA
Engineering. 84419
Engineers' and mechanics' companion. 78481
Engineer's and mechanic's pocket book. 30830
Engineers,' contractors,' and surveyors' pocket
table-book. 78481
Engineer's opinion of the marine railway.
(22585)
Engineer's report and charter of the New-
London, Willimantic and Springfield Rail-
road Company. 53262
Engineer's report . . . . For . . . 1850 [of
the Milwaukee and Mississippi Rail Road
Company.] 49167
Engineers' report for supplying the city of
Rochester with water. 72369, 93145
Engineer's report of the cost of constructing
the ship canal. 12738, 22586
Engineer's report . . . of the . . . direct route.
61617
Engineer's report [on the Lehigh Luzerne Rail-
road Company.] 60200
Engineer's report [on the New York and Boston
Railroad Company.] 54725
Engineers' report on the Niagara Ship Canal.
55115, 93146
Engineer's report [on the proposed canal from
Baltimore to the Potomac.] 45098
Engineer's report [on the practability of a
canal.] 3066
Engineer's report [on the Springfield, Mount
Vernon & Pittsburg Railroad Company.]
89900-89901
Engineer's report on the survey from New
Haven city. 52977
Engineer's report to the Jeffersonville As-
sociation. 35950
Engineers reports and other documents. 9860
England, John, Bp., 1786-1852. 22587-22589
see also Charleston (Diocese) Bishop
(England)
England. for governmental entries, see under
Great Britain.
England among the nations. 38695

England and America. (33076)
England and America; a comparison of the
social and political state of both nations.
14036, 100976
England and America. A discourse . . . Dec.
22, 1861. 26236
England and America: a lecture. 82677-82678
England and America. From the Princeton re-
view. (32329)
England and America: speech of Henry Ward
Beecher. (4312)
England and France, or the contrast. 22589
England and France—some advice for John Bull.
96396
England and her subject-races with special
reference to Jamaica. 73475
England and Russia. 29941
England and the disrupted states of America.
28340
England during the reigns of James I and
Charles I. 85105
England enslaved by her own slave colonies.
22590, 91237, 95563
England, her colonies and her enemies. 22591
England in the new world. 101275
England, Ireland, and America. 14035, 14038
England needs to soothe America. 82621
England, the civilizer. 22592
England, the north, and the south. 32895,
(32896), 32898
England, the United States, and the southern
confederacy. 76967
England und der Continent. 42641
England und die Anglo-Sachsische Staatenbildung
in Amerika. 31247
England under seven administrations. (24975)
England victorious. (50044)
Englandischen Pflanzstadte in Nord-America.
22598
Englands alarm. 97590
England's benefit and advantage by foreign trade
demonstrated. (71909)
England's danger and her safety. 21845
England's defiance. 22593
England's duty. 24679
England's-exchequer. 29522
England's folly in the present war. 22577
Englands forewarner. (67586)
England's former gothic constitution censored
and opposed. 97364
England's grandeur, and way to get wealth.
97286
England's improvement. 14241
England's improvement reviv'd. 82864-82865
Englands interest asserted. 67599
England's interest considered. 59677
Englands interest mestaken en [sic] the present
war. 98172
England's interest; or, a discipline for seamen.
75325
Englands joy. 78379
England's liability for indemnity. 42075
Englands monarchs. 99557
England's perfect school-master. 92976-92977
England's present interest considered. 59677
England's present interest discover'd. 59693
England's remembrancer. (32044)
England's safety, in trade's increase. 72083
England's safety: or, a bridle to the French
King. 75324
Englands shame. 106018
England's sympathy with America's inability.
22594
England's treasure by foreign trade. 44184
England's triumph: or Spanish cowardice
expos'd. 22595, (35988)

England's triumph over the Spaniards. 22596
England's true interest considered. 59693
England's western, or America's eastern shore. 22597
England's worthies. 67599
Engle, Jacob. 62276 see also Philadelphia County, Pa. Sub-Lieutenant.
Englehardt, Z. 106398
Engleheart, G. D. 22600
Englemann, George. 22538, 22580
Engles, William M. 22601-22602, 97087
Englewood, N. J. Citizens. 90753
Englische Held und Ritter Franciscus Drake. 8547, (9501), (20827)
Englische Philologie in Nordamerika. 24916
Englische, Schottische und Nord-Amerikanische Strafverfahren. (49763)
Englischen Amerikaners von Philadelphia. pseud. Bericht. 4864
Englischen Fraulein. pseud. Briefe. 95250
Englischer Freihandel ein Betrug. 85897, 91010
English, Henry. 22603
English, Stephen. ed. 34874
English, Thomas C. 22604
English, Thomas, Dunn. 22605-22606
English, William Hayden, 1822-1896. 22607-22608
English acquisitions. 99557
English address. 59563
English alternative of 1641-41, old or new England? 42619
English America. 5971
English America: or pictures of Canadian places and people. 18978
English American. pseud. Letter to Lord Dartmouth. see Paine, Thomas, 1737-1809.
English American. pseud. To the regular soldiery of Great-Britain. 96018
English-American his travail by sea and land. 5390, (26298)-(26299), note after 98597
English ancestry of Rev. John Cotton of Boston. 86790
English and American intelligencer. (22609)
English and American rebellion compared and contrasted. 55082
English and Choctaw definer. 9710
English and Dakota vocabulary. 22610, 71322
English and French journal. 31286
English and French neutrality. 7146-(7147)
English and Irish budget. 1125
English and Latine exercises for school-boys. 4055
English Branch, United States Sanitary Commission. see United States Sanitary Commission. English Branch.
English Branch of the United States Sanitary Commission. The motive of its establishment. 24457, (76648)
English civilization undemonstrative. 77429
English clergyman. pseud. Letter to a member of the Congress. 40408
English colonization in America. 64060
English colonization of America during the seventeenth century. 52282
English combatant. pseud. Battle fields of the south. 3963
English cotejo. (16690), (22611)
English country gentleman. pseud. Address. see Knox, W. supposed author
English country gentleman's address to the Irish members. 81961
English cricketers' trip to Canada. (41076)
English cyclopedia. 38105

English discoveries towards the north and north-east. 66686
English duelist. pseud. Dialogues of the dead. 19948
English editor. pseud. Introduction. 49193
English editor. pseud. Preface. 29948
English emigrants, now in America. pseud. Several authentic and most interesting letters. 13882, 14450
English empire in America. 99557
English empire in America: or a prospect of His Majesties dominions. 9499
English enlistment question. 74366
English Evangelical Lutheran Church in New York. 92757
English exile. 45006
English family Robinson. 69036, 69039
English farmer. pseud. Few plain directions. 10447, 10541, note after 98077
English farmer. pseud. Inquiries of an emigrant. see Pickering, Joseph.
English farmer. pseud. Plain directions. 10447, 10541, note after 98077
English freeholder. pseud. Address. see Zouche, Henry. supposed author
English freeholder's address to his countrymen. 22612, 106378A
English gentleman. pseud. tr. 12229
English gentleman. pseud. Excursion through the United States. see Blane, William Newham, 1800-1825.
English gentleman. pseud. No rum, no sugar. 55368
English gentleman in China. pseud. see Chesterfield, Philip Dormer Stanhope, 4th Earl of, 1694-1773.
English gentleman now residing in China. pseud. see Chesterfield, Philip Dormer Stanhope, 4th Earl of, 1694-1773.
English gentleman, now residing in Pekin. pseud. see Chesterfield, Philip Dormer Stanhope, 4th Earl of, 1694-1773.
English gentleman residing in China. pseud. see Chesterfield, Philip Dormer Stanhope, 4th Earl of, 1694-1773.
English gentlemen. pseud. Relations. 23480
English grammar on the productive system. note before 83906, 83918-83920
English green box. 22613
English guide to American literature. (42403)
English heptarchy and the American union. 73951
English hermit. 66951
English hero, or Sir Francis Drake. 8547
English heroe. 9500
English-Hidatsa vocabulary. 80015
English High School, Salem, Mass. see Salem, Mass. English High School.
English High School Association, Salem, Mass. see Salem English High School Association, Salem, Mass.
English in America. (29685)
English lady. pseud. Notes and letters on the American war. see Bayman, Mrs. A. Phelps. and Bayman, Robert.
English lady. pseud. Sketch of the life of the illustrious Washington. see Saint-George, Mrs. A.
English lady, four years resident in the United States. pseud. Fanny Kemble in America. 37332
English language in America. 10156
English lawyer. pseud. Remarks on the trial of the Earl of Stirling. 33829, 91841A
English layman. pseud. Recent recollections. 68345

English liberties. 10819
English library. 63556
English literature for schools series. 82852
English lyricks. 85344
English man. pseud. Justification of the
   present war. see Stubbe, Henry, 1632-
   1676.
English merchant. pseud. Narrative of two
   months residence. 51838
English merchant. pseud. Some modern
   observations upon Jamaica. see Wharton,
   Philip Wharton, Duke of.
English merchant. pseud. Spanish empire in
   America. see Campbell, John, 1708-1775.
English merchants. 6922
English Merchants at Bruges. petitioners see
   Bruges. English Merchants. petitioners
English Mercury. pseud. Discovery of the
   new world. see Hall, Joseph.
English minister. pseud. Epistle to the
   Christian Indians. see Mather, Cotton,
   1663-1728.
English missionary to the coast of Guinea.
   pseud. Memoirs. see Thompson,
   Thomas, 1708?-1773.
English neptune. 79027
English neutrality. 22614, 42534
English officer. pseud. Tecumseh. see
   Richardson, John.
English officer at Canada. pseud. Letter
   from an English officer at Canada.
   48965
English opinion on the American rebellion.
   2138
English orphans. 32617
English party's excursion to Paris. 22615
English pilot. 95631
English pilot. The fourth book. (22617)-22619,
   88221
English practice. 22620, 78819
English Presbyterian Church, Amsterdam.
   see Amsterdam. English Presbyterian
   Church.
English question. 95115
English reprints. 35675, (67585)
English resident in the United States. pseud.
   Anticipations of the future. see Ruffin,
   Edmund.
English sailer. pseud. see English Sailor.
   pseud.
English sailor. pseud. State of the navy
   consider'd. 90621
English sailors, tragedy. 87802
English scholar's library. 82855
English School, Marietta, Ohio. see Marietta,
   Ohio. English School.
English seamen under the Tudors. 6923
English ship for righting herself. 102351
English Society for Promoting Christian Knowl-
   edge, London. see Society for Promoting
   Christian Knowledge, London.
English sportsman in the western prairies.
   4883
English traveller. pseud. Letters. 19857
English travellers. pseud. Abraham Lincoln's
   character. see Broom, W. W.
English universities in the North American
   review. 70898
English voyages to the East Indies. 66686
English Wesleyan Conference. see Wesleyan
   Methodist Church. English Conference.
English West Indies. (22621), 101821
English woolen manufacturer. pseud. Essay
   presented. see Webb, Daniel, English
   woolen manufacturer
English workman. pseud. London v. New York.
   41862

Englishman. pseud. American civil war.
   1075
Englishman. pseud. Common sense. (58214)
Englishman. pseud. Cuba. 17765
Englishman. pseud. Englishman's answer.
   see Lind, Jonathan. supposed author
Englishman. pseud. Few remarks. 35917
Englishman. pseud. Five years' residence in
   Buenos Ayres. (9014)
Englishman. pseud. Francis, Lord Bacon.
   (25455)
Englishman. pseud. Information for emigrants.
   34701
Englishman. pseud. Inquiry into the present
   state of the British navy. 34814
Englishman. pseud. Letter to a noble Lord.
   40419
Englishman. pseud. Morality of public men.
   see Harcourt, William George Granville
   Vernon.
Englishman. pseud. Present state of liberty.
   65321
Englishman. pseud. Reply to an "American's
   examination" of the "right of search."
   see Ouseley, Sir William Gore.
Englishman. pseud. Right of search. see
   Ouseley, Sir William Gore.
Englishman. pseud. Yankeeland in her trouble.
   see Stocqueler, Joachim Heywood.
Englishman. 22622, 94793
Englishman directed in the choice of his religion.
   96358, note after 103042
Englishman deceived. 22632
Englishman in Kansas. 27528
Englishman resident in Upper Canada. pseud.
   Warning to the Canadian Land Company.
   101450
Englishman, traveling through the United States
   as a spy. pseud. Englishman. 22622,
   94793
Englishman's adventures in the county of the
   Incas. 37904
Englishman's answer, to the address. 22624,
   note after 41286
Englishman's correspondence during the war.
   91923
Englishman's duty to the free and the enslaved
   American. 103881
Englishman's experience at the seat of the
   American war. 18977
Englishman's right. 30876
Englishman's sketch-book. (22625)
Englishman's thoughts on the crimes of the
   south. 8374
Englishman's travels in America. (4788)
Englishman's view of the battle. 21843
Englishmen, in the United States. pseud.
   Letters. (38117)
Englishwoman. pseud. American slavery.
   81840
Englishwoman. pseud. Some facts. 86642
Englishwoman. pseud. Views of society and
   manners in America. see D'Arusmont,
   Frances (Wright) 1795-1852.
Englishwoman in America. (5544)-5545
Englishwoman in America. By Sarah Mytton
   Maury. 46976
Englishwoman's experience in America. 24354
Engraved work of Timothy Cole. 83740
Engravings of plans, profiles and maps. 53657
Engrossed bill for enabling the British merchants
   to recover their debts. 100084
Enio instruido. 75606
Enjoyment of a glorious Christ, proposed.
   46445
Enlargement of canal locks of New York. (22378)

Enlargement of Christ's kingdom. 82922
Enlargement of geographical science. 61044
Enlargement of the locks on the Erie Canal. (66091)
Enlargement of the Schuylkill Navigation. 78084
Enlargement of the State House, in Boston. 45721
Enlistment and Central-American questions. (22626)
Enneades Marci Antonii Sabellici ab inclinatione R. Imperii. 74659
Enneades Marci Antonij Sabellici ab orbe condito. 74658
Enneadis Septimae. 74658
Ennemoser, Joseph. 22627
Ennery, Adolphe Philippe, called d'. (21176), - (21177), 92339
Ennes de Souza, Antonio. see Souza, Antonio Ennes de.
Ennis, Jacob. 22629
Enon, John of. pseud. Watery war. see Benedict, Noah.
Enormity of the slave trade. 22630
Enormous charges on western produce. 2214
Enosionian Society, George Washington University, Washington, D. C. see George Washington University, Washington, D. C. Enosionian Society.
Enough of war. 17194, 24178
Enquete de M. Blondeel van Cuelebrouk. 5974, 17835
Enquete sur le serpent. 73927
Enquete sur le serpent de la Martinique. 73928
Enquetes. (39638)
Enquetes du Parlement Anglais. 81721
Enquetes parlementaires et documents divers. (81720)
Enquire at Amos Giles' distillery. 12397
Enquirer. pseud. True nature and cause of the tails of comets. see Perkins, John.
Enquirer after truth. pseud. Brief exposition of the fanaticism. 79698, note after 97880
Enquiries and doubts respecting animal magnetism. 25579, 92135
Enquiries concerning the books of Capt. Marryat and Mr. Dickens. 11217
Enquiries historical and moral. 51503
Enquiries into the necessity of assuming exclusive legislation. (22631)
Enquiries into the necessity or expediency of assuming exclusive legislation. 20302, 105152
Enquiries into vulgar errors. 8677
Enquiries . . . proposed by the Philadelphia Society for Promoting Agriculture. 59850
Enquiries relative to middle Florida. (43612)
Enqviries tovching the diuersity of langvages. (7732)
Enquiring of the fathers. 58799
Enquiry. see also Inquiry.
Enquiry as to the causes and consequences of the late ministerial resignations. 10597
Enquiry concerning the first discovery of America. 104276
Enquiry concerning the grant of the Legislature of Connecticut. 15682, (15736)
Enquiry concerning the intellectual and moral faculties. (28728)
Enquiry, concerning the liberty, and licentiousness of the press. 95584
Enquiry, concerning the materials. 78985
Enquiry concerning the power of increase in the numbers of mankind. 27676
Enquiry concerning the promises of the Gospel. 32955

Enquiry how far it is expedient. 87811
Enquiry, how far the Americans are bound to abide by, and execute, the decisions of the late Continental Congress. 11882, 16590-16591, 2d note after 22626
Enquiry how far the charges against them. 63395
Enquiry how far the punishment of death is necessary in Pennsylvania. 7265
Enquiry into and observations upon the causes and effects of the disease which raged into Philadelphia. 19814
Enquiry into, and remarks upon the conduct of Lieutenant General Burgoyne. 9260
Enquiry into enthusiasm. 20608
Enquiry into Mr. B. Nooley's conduct. 55424
Enquiry into public abuses. 53104
Enquiry into public errors. 9246
Enquiry into the Caledonian project. 18551, 7th note after 95843
Enquiry into the causes of frequent failure among men of business. 11215
Enquiry into the causes of national discontents and misfortunes. (10667)
Enquiry into the causes of our ill success in the present war. 22632
Enquiry into the causes of our naval miscarriages. 74972
Enquiry into the causes of the alienation of the Delaware and Shawanese Indians. 95562
Enquiry into the causes of the failure of the late expedition. 10732
Enquiry into the causes of the miscarriage of the Scots colony at Darien. (18552), 78206, 78209, (78215)
Enquiry into the causes of the present commercial embarrassments. 22633
Enquiry into the causes which have retarded the accumulation of wealth. (81962)
Enquiry into the chymical character and properties. 22634
Enquiry into the condition and influence of the brothels. 61618
Enquiry into the condition and prospects of the African race. (22635)
Enquiry into the conduct of a late Right Honourable commoner. (17027), (36902), 63086, 63090, 80699
Enquiry into the conduct of General Putnam. (12696), 19075, 94059
Enquiry into the conduct of our domestick affairs. 101148
Enquiry into the conduct of our domestick affairs, from the year 1721, to the present time. 22636, note after (66641)
Enquiry into the conduct of Pitt. 28774
Enquiry into the conduct of the President of the United States. 22637
Enquiry into the conduct of two B******. 22638
Enquiry into the constitutional authority of the Supreme Federal Court. 22639, 2d note after 88111, 93501
Enquiry into the doctrine . . . concerning libels. 2d note after 104010
Enquiry into the effects of public punishment. 67712, 74215
Enquiry into the effects of spirituous liquors. note after 74241
Enquiry into the evil consequences of a fluctuating medium of exchange. 80404
Enquiry into the evils of general suffrage. 10171, 10441, (31394)
Enquiry into the excise laws of Connecticut. 15672, 102339, 105672

Enquiry into the existence of the living principle and causes of animal life. 77322

Enquiry into the expediency of establishing cotton manufactures. 28719

Enquiry into the extent of the power of juries. 45415

Enquiry into the grounds and reasons for the present dislike. 19777, 22969

Enquiry into the late essay on the bilious fever. 104245

Enquiry into the law-merchant of the United States. (9852)

Enquiry into the law of Negro slavery. 13860-13861

Enquiry into the merits of the supposed preliminaries of peace. 22640

Enquiry into the methods that are said to be now proposed. 22641, 3d note after 102832

Enquiry into the misconduct and frauds committed. 88181

Enquiry into the moral and religious character of the American government. (22642)

Enquiry into the natural history of medicine. 74237

Enquiry into the nature and causes of the present disputes. 22643

Enquiry into the nature and necessity of a paper currency. 22644

Enquiry into the nature of the British constitution. 15969

Enquiry into the nature of true holiness. 32955

Enquiry into the objects. 17530, 1st note after 91235, 2d note after 102829

Enquiry into the origin of the American Colonization Society. 81810

Enquiry into the origin of the Cherokees. 12452

Enquiry into the origin of the late epidemic fever in Philadelphia. 10876, 74216

Enquiry into the origin, progress, and present state of slavery. (22645)

Enquiry into the political grade of the free coloured population. 60087, 81963

Enquiry into the present system of medical education. (22646), 43595

Enquiry into the principles and tendency of certain public measures. 22647, 94486, note after 94489

Enquiry into the principles on which a commercial system for the United States should be founded. 17295

Enquiry into the propriety of granting charters of incorporation. 87819

Enquiry into the reasons of the conduct of Great Britain. 32280, 86721

Enquiry into the right of American slavery. 70419

Enquiry into the right to change the ecclesiastical constitution. 22648

Enquiry into the rights of the British colonies. (5859)

Enquiry into the state of bills of credit. 22649

Enquiry into the state of the British West Indies. 42417

Enquiry into the truth of the tradition. 104276

Enquiry into the validity of Methodist episcopacy. 37663

Enquiry on freedom of will. 21930

Enquiry relative to the moral & political improvement of the human species. 58351

Enquiry respecting the capture of Washington by the British. (22650), 89139, note after 101937, 104746

Enquiry whether the absolute independence of America is not to be prefered. 22651

Enquiry whether the act of Congress. 22652

Enquiry, whether the guilt of the present civil war in America. (72580)-72582

Ευρηκα. (46308)

Enrico, John. 95080

Enrico Wanton. pseud. see Seriman, Zaccaria.

Enrique Wanton. pseud. see Seriman, Zaccaria.

Enriquez, Pedro. 22654

Enriquez y Castro, Jose de Antequera. see Antequera Enriquez y Castro, Jose de

Enrollment laws of the United States. 22655

Ens, Gaspar. 22656-(22657), 46956, 66496, 1st note after 102874, note after 102948

Ensaio corografico do imperio do Brasil. 47459

Ensaio corographico do impero do Brasil. 11705

Ensaio da Brasiliense. 52416

Ensaio estadistico da Provincia do Veara. 88743

Ensaio historico-juridico-social. 60873

Ensaio historico sobre as letras no Brasil. (7582), 9934

Ensaio para, pela primeira vez, indicar. 58073

Ensaio sobre a historia e estatistica da Provincia do Espirito-Sancto. 60889

Ensaio sobre o direito administrativo com referencia. 85640

Ensaio sobre o fabrico do assucar. 62888

Ensaio sobre os melhoramentos de Portugal. (25483), 85657

Ensaios, etc. 76848

Ensay sobre las libertades de la Iglesia Espanola. 22661

Ensayo biografico de Don Crescencio Carrillo. 87179

Ensayo biografico y critico de Don Wenceslao Alpuche. 87180

Ensayo cronologico, para la historia general de la Florida. 3349, 75577, 80971, 98745, 98758

Ensayo de clasificacion de las lenguas de Mexico. 57641

Ensayo de clasificacion de las mismas lenguas. 57641

Ensayo de estadistica completa de la Provincia de Azangaro. 22658

Ensayo de estadistica completa de los ramos economico politicos. 12883

Ensayo de la biblioteca Espanola. 26385

Ensayo de la historia civil del Paraguay. 26211, 44174

Ensayo de metalurgia. 77100

Ensayo de un estudio de derecho Romano y del derecho publico. 59304

Ensayo de una alocucion patriotica. 66259

Ensayo de una biblioteca de traductores Espanoles. 59590

Ensayo de una constitucion. 56649

Ensayo de una historia anecdotica de Mexico. 71702

Ensayo de una teoria del magnetismo terrestre en el Peru. (59327)

Ensayo de vera seismologia del Valle de Mexico. 63661

Ensayo economico sobre o comercio. 17949

Ensayo epico in trece cantos. 73567

Ensayo estadistico sobre el estado de Chihuahua. 12690, 15161

Ensayo estadistico sobre el territorio de Colima. 14354

Ensayo filosofico-critico. 97696

Ensayo historico de la defensa de Buenos-Aires. (9591)

Ensayo historico de la isla de Cuba. 61329
Ensayo historico de las revoluciones de Megico. 106277
Ensayo historico por el Lic. Don Alejandro Arango y Escandor. 40079
Ensayo historico, por M. Payno. 48888
Ensayo historico sobre el origin de la enfermedad venerea. 58133
Ensayo historico sobre la revolucion de los comuneros del Paraguay. (23067)
Ensayo historico sobre la revolucion del Paraguay. (69612)
Ensayo historico sobre la vida del Exmo. Sr. D. Juan Manuel de Rosas. 73212
Ensayo historico sobre las revoluciones de Yucatan. 3244
Ensayo literario sobre el Libertador de America. 75573
Ensayo para la materia medica Mexicana. 48449
Ensayo politico. El systema colombiano. (72272)
Ensayo politico sobre e reino de la Nueva Espana. 33769
Ensayo politico sobre el reyno de Nueva-Espana. 33714
Ensayo politico sobre la isla de Cuba. 33720
Ensayo politico sobre . . . la Nueva-Espana. 33718
Ensayo sobre Chile. 73204
Ensayo sobre el Bejuco-Guaco en Tabasco. 94167
Ensayo sobre el cultivo de la cana de azucar. 70453
Ensayo sobre el cultivo del cafe. 31513
Ensayo sobre el nuevo systema de carceles. 72273
Ensayo sobre el verdadero estado de la cuestion. 57840
Ensayo sobre la administracion public de Mexico. 73171
Ensayo sobre la civilizacion Americana. 67656
Ensayo sobre la conducta del General Bolivar. 6187, 22660
Ensayo sobre la doctrina de Edmundo Richer. 71109
Ensayo sobre la historia de la literatura Ecuatoriana. 31570
Ensayo sobre la interpretacion de la escritura hieratica. 73306
Ensayo sobre la necesidad de una federacion jeneral. 50094
Ensayo sobre la topografia de los Rios Plata. 21511
Ensayo sobre las glorias Franciscanas. 76934
Ensayo sobre las revoluciones politicas. (75914)
Ensayo sobre los intereses politicos. 19529
Ensayo sobre tolerancia religiosa. 29132, 72274
Ensayos biograficos y de critica literaria. 96260
Ensayos de un conocimiento. 31626
Ensayos poeticos. 60858
Ensayos poeticos. Por Jose M. Rodriguez y Cos. 72568
Ensayos poeticos, prededidos de varios juicios escritos en Europa y America. 16827
Ensayos politicos. 22195
Ensayos politicas y literarias. (16053)
Ensayos sobro estudios de literatura i ciencias. 4914
Ense, Rubeo. 70787
Enschede (J.) & Sons. firm publishers (32028)

Ensign, Bridgman & Fanning. firm publishers 22662
Ensign, Bridgman & Fanning's lake and river guide. 22662
Ensign of liberty, and the wicked one revealed. 36652
Ensign of liberty of the church of Christ. 50736
Ensign of the army. pseud. Tears of the foot guards. 1664A, 94569
Ensl, Gaspar. see Ens, Gaspar.
Ensley, E. 94790
Enslin, Theodor Christian Friedrich. 22663
Entdeckung America's durch die Normannen. 67478
Entdeckung Amerikas. Achter Auflage. Dritter Theil: Pizarro. 10302
Entdeckung Amerikas in zehnten Jahrhundert. 67479
Entdeckung Amerikas. Nach den altesten Quellen geschichtlich dargestellt. 38347
Entdeckung der Neuen Welt. (73877)
Entdeckung der Nordwestl. Durchfahrt durch MacClure. 25633
Entdeckung einer Erstandt und Sud-Amerika. (17987)
Entdeckung und Eroberung von Mexico. Von Karl Ritter. 71594
Entdeckung und Eroberung von Mexiko, nach dessen gleichzeitigen Erzahlung bearbeitet. 19987
Entdeckung von America. (31499)
Entdeckung von Amerika. 10293
Entdeckung von Amerika. Christoph Columbus. (18362)
Entdeckung von Amerika. Ferdinand Cortez oder die Eroberung von Mexico. 19432
Entdeckung von Amerika. Nach dem Franzosischem. 11659
Entdeckung von Amerika. Nach den neuesten Quellen der Jugend erzahlt. (32410)
Entdeckung von West-Indien. 10283
Entdeckungen der Carthager und Griechen. 39977
Entdeckungsreise der koniglichen Schiffe Isabella und Alexander. 73378
Entdeckungsreise in das Stille Meer. 8425
Entdeckungs-Reise in die Sud-See und nach der Berings-Strasse. 11817, 38284
Entdeckungs reise nach den nordlichen Polargegenden. 58870
Entdeckungsreise nach den Sudlandern. 61000
Entdeckungsreise nach der Sudsee 1776-80. 16267
Entdeckungsreise um die Baffins-Bay. 73379
Entel, W. ten. tr. 77641
Enterpreza e restauracao de Pernambuco. 36088
Enterprise and art of man. 27913
Enterprise beyond the Rocky Mountains. 35130
Enterprising adventures of Pizarro. 8137, 80342
Enterprize, benevolence, and Christian conduct exemplified. 17849
Enterre vif. (69035)
Entertainer. 22663
Entertaining account of all the countries. 22665
Entertaining anecdotes of Washington. 101801
Entertaining and marvellous repository. (22666)
Entertaining histories, for the amusement and instruction. 85668
Entertaining histories for young ladies and gentlemen. 65396, 85668
Entertaining moralist. (63412)

Entertaining passages relating to Philip's War. 12996-12997
Entertaining traveller. (25670)
Entertaining travels of the Sieur Mouette. 91537
Entertainment for a winter's evening. 28547
Entertainment given by the late candidates. 48964
Entertainment Given in Honor of Duncan McIntosh, Baltimore, 1809. 43330, 96962
Enthaltend Abbildungen und ausfuhrliche Beschreibung. 9351
Enthaltend: Auslandische, nach geographischen Rucksichten geordnete Natur-Gegenstande. 5369
Enthaltend eine allgemeine Volkertafel. (4858)
Enthaltsamkeits-Vereine. 9675
Enthullung des Erdkreises. 104702-104703
Enthusiasm. 31145
Enthusiasm described and caution'd against. 12331
Enthusiasms of Methodists and papists compar'd. 103595
Entick, John. 22667-22670, 26882
Entire correspondence of the French Ministers. 88969
Entire correspondence of William P. Tebbs and Benjamin G. Orr. 94572
Entire internal revenue laws. (6977)
Entire message of the President. 1016
Entire new plan for a national currency. 47799
Entirely new system of grammar. 80368
Entomologia boreali Americana. 37963, 71029
Entomological Society of Philadelphia. (57824), 61619, 78532
Entomological Society of Philadelphia. Charter. 61619
Entomologie du voyage. 42613
Entomology. 77386
Entrada a su noble Exercicio obra politica. 57811
Entrada del Padre Cypriano Baraze. 3252A
Entre el Cura, el Alcalde, y un Vecina de ella. 94895
Entre los infames medios. 98851
Entre los remedios q[ue] do[n] Fray Bartolome de las Casas. (11229), 11235, 11283, 11289, 1st note after 39116
Entre Rios (Argentine Province) Treaties, etc. 16166
Entrecasteaux, Joseph Antoine Bruni d'. 21211-21215, (22671)-22672
Entrennes d'Apollon. (42849)
Entrepots reels. 40129
Entretenimientos de un prisionero. 51215
Entretenimientos phisicos-historicos. (36806), 97687
Entretiens de Guillaume de Naussau. (22673), 50156
Entretiens des voyageurs sur la mer. 22674
Entretiens d'un philosophie Indien. 43891
Entrevue sur la route d'Espagne. 87118, note after 97172
Entschulidigungen wegen des Verbrechens. 93686
Entstehung und umstandliche Barstellung. 72283
Entstehung und Verbreitung des Methodismus. 88554
Entstehungsgeschichte der freistadtischen Bunde. 38263
Entstehungageschichte und gegenwartiger Zustand. 95122
Entusiasta liberal. pseud. Dialogo. 977, 16159, 96117-note after 96117
Entwerffung von Eroberung. 41848

Entwisle, Joseph. ed. 104695
Entwurf einer Deutschen Kolonial-Politik. 38323
Entwurf einer physischen Weltbeschreibung. 33726
Entwurf eines Planes zur Einrichtung einer Deutschen Kolonisations-Gesellschaft. 8202
Entz, J. F. (22675)-22676
Enumerantur que in hoc ope dicto Margarita phylosophica contineantur. (69122)
Enumeratio diagnostica quarundam orchidearum Surinamensium. 24936
Enumeratio muscarum omnium Austro-Americanorum auctori hucusque cognitorum. 49762
Enumeratio plantarum in deserto Atacamense. 62452
Enumeratio plantarum in Guiana cresentium. 81289
Enumeratio synoptica plantarum phanerogamicarum. 44850
Enumeratio systematica plantarum. 35520
Enumeration and account of some remarkable natural objects. 67465
Enumeration des especes zoologiques et botaniques. 74916
Enumeration des genres de plantes. (8752)
Enumeration des observations horaires faites a l'Observatoire Physico-Meteorique de la Havane. 63667
Enumeration of some of the . . . instances in which the . . . constitution has been violated by our national government. 71381
Enumeration of the inhabitants of the United States. 11665
Enumeration of the inhabitants of the United States, as corrected. (81491)
Environs of Boston from Corey's Hill. 71004
Envois d'or et d'argent. 94854
Envoy, from free hearts to the free. 22677, note after 103302
Envy wishes, then believes. 105129
Enzinas, Diego Bringas de Manzaneda y. see Bringas de Manzaneda y Encinas, Diego Miguel.
Eolopoesis. 5295
Eoneguski, or, the Cherokee chief. 92698
Epaminondas. pseud. Address of Epaminondas. see Granger, Gideon.
Epaminondas. pseud. Answer to a clandestine address. (22680), 97067
Epaminondas. pseud. Considerations on the government. see Woodward, Augustus Brevoort.
Epaminondas. pseud. Epaminondas on the government. see Woodward, Augustus Brevoort.
Epaminondas on the government of the territory of Columbia. 105152
Epaminondas: originally published in numbers. (22678), 105152
Epaphroditus. pseud. Observations on the trial. 58795
Epes Sargent . . . and his descendants. 89539
Epeysodio da historia patria. 58988
Ephemera. (70831)
Ephemerides generales de los mouimientos de los cielos. 93309
Ephemeris. 106404
Ephemeris, &c. for the year . . . 1774. 25375
Ephemeris expeditionis Norreysij et Draki in Lusitaniam. (20834), 101423
Ephemeris, for 1682. 95820

Ephemeris of coelestial motions, aspects, eclipses &c. 62743

Ephemeris of the coelestial motions, aspects, and eclipses, &c. for the year . . . MDCCX. 72025

Ephemeris of the coelestial motions, &c., for the year 1709. 32668

Ephemeris of the coelestial motions for the year of the Christian epocha 1672. 62743

Ephemeris of the planet Neptune for the date of the Lalande observations. 85072

Ephemeris of the planet Neptune for the year 1850. 85072, 101074

Ephemeris of the planet Neptune for the year 1851. 85072, 101074

Ephemeris of the planet Neptune for the year 1852. 85072, 101074

[Ephemeris of the planet Neptune for the years 1846, 1847, 1848, and 1849.] 101074

Ephemeron. 46608, note after 105465

Eph. Peters. 30044

Epic-doggerel, in six books. 88322

Epic poem. 68156, 102439

Epic poem. By Aquiline Nimble-Chops, Democrat. 41608

Epic poem by Robert B. Caverly. 11610

Epic poem, by Robert Southey. 88555

Epic poem. In eight books. 51459

Epic poem. In four cantos. 97216-97217

Epic poem on the discovery of America. 50405

Epick poem on the late war of 1812. 22529

Epic poems. 88556

Epic story of the Island of Manhattan. 57755, 3d note after 100601

Epicedio ivridico, dialectico, politico, y moral. 93335

Epicedio nas sentidissimas e lamentaveis. 88834

Epick . . . see Epic . . .

Epictetus. 22682

Epictetus, his morals done out of the original Greek. 22682

Epicure. pseud. Salad for the solitary. see Saunders, Frederic.

Epicure. pseud. Salad for the solitary and the social. see Saunders, Frederic.

Epidemic cholera. 22683

Epidemic cholera and yellow fever. 22684

Epidemic cholera, its history, &c. 17214

Epidemic of 1858. 53330

Epidemic of 1853. 53330

Epidemic of the nineteenth century. (7126)

Epidemics considered with relation to their common nature. 84416

Epidemie de la Guadeloupe. 18215

Epigrammata. 2383, (27824)

Epigrams and other small parcels, both morall and divine. 31037

Epilogata da l'Abate Gio: Battista Pacichelli. 73185

Epilogo de las entradas. 97711

Epilogo metrico de la vida de Fray Sebastian de Aparicio. 1728

Epilogue by R. Horace Pratt. (7653)

Epilogue by R. T. Paine, Jnr. Esq. 103478

Epilogue to the late peace. (22685)

Epilogue. Written by R. T. Paine, Jun. Esq. 103484

Episcopacy examined. 82523

Episcopal Academy of Connecticut, Cheshire, Conn. 15726

Episcopal address at the Convention . . . May 30, 1838. 20391

Episcopal address at the Convention . . . May 29, 1833. 20391

Episcopal address at the Convention . . . May 22, 1834. 20391

Episcopal address to the . . . Convention of . . . Western New York. 19345

Episcopal and the Assembly of Divines' catechism. note after 65546

Episcopal Book Society, Philadelphia. see Protestant Episcopal Book Society, Philadelphia.

Episcopal charge. 103462

Episcopal Charitable Society, Boston. 6700-6701

Episcopal Church Association of New York. see Protestant Episcopal Church Association of New York.

Episcopal Church at the south. (52272)

"Episcopal Church defended" reviewed. 6222, 91104

Episcopal Church defended, with an examination. 6222, 91104

Episcopal Church in the American colonies. (13366)

Episcopal claims calmly considered. 104638

Episcopal Clerical Association of the City of New York. see Protestant Episcopal Clerical Association of the City of New York.

Episcopal Clergy of Connecticut. see Protestant Episcopal Church in the U. S. A. Connecticut (Diocese) Clergy.

Episcopal doctrine of apostolic succession examined. 64692

Episcopal Education Society of Pennsylvania. 97626

Episcopal Education Society of Pennsylvania. Managers. 22687, 60088

Episcopal family monitor. 66146

Episcopal magazine. 22686

Episcopal manual. 104576

Episcopal Methodism, as it was and is. 28035

Episcopal Methodism; or Dagonism exhibited. 104669

Episcopal minister. pseud. Coming battle. 14946

Episcopal Ministers of Maryland. petitioners see Protestant Episcopal Church in the U. S. A. Maryland (Diocese) Clergy. petitioners

Episcopal Mission to Seamen in the Port of New York. see Protestant Episcopal Mission to Seamen, New York.

Episcopal Mission to Seamen in the port of New-York. 54260

Episcopal Missionary Association for the West. Board of Managers. 22688, 66147

Episcopal Missionary Society of Massachusetts. see Massachusetts Episcopal Missionary Society.

Episcopal Missionary Society of Philadelphia. see Philadelphia Episcopal Missionary Society.

Episcopal quarterly. 82947

Episcopal recorder. 90719

Episcopal recorder (extra) 89018

Episcopal register. 69422

Episcopal School of North Carolina, Raleigh. 55669

Episcopal Society for Promoting Christian Knowledge in the Western District of the State of New York. see Protestant Episcopal Society for Promoting Christian Knowledge in the Western District of the State of New York.

Episcopal Society for Promoting Religion and Learning in the State of New York. see Protestant Episcopal Society for Promoting Religion and Learning in the State of New York.

Episcopal Society for the Advancement of Christianity in South Carolina. see Protestant Episcopal Society for the Advancement of Christianity in South Carolina.

Episcopal Society for the Increase of the Ministry. see Protestant Episcopal Society for the Increase of the Ministry.

Episcopal Society for the Promotion of Evangelical Knowledge, New York. see Protestant Episcopal Society for the Promotion of Evangelical Knowledge, New York.

Episcopal Society for the Religious Instruction of Freedmen. see Massachusetts Episcopal Society for the Religious Instruction of Freedmen.

Episcopal Society in Western New York for the Promotion of Evangelical Knowledge. see Protestant Episcopal Society in Western New York for the Promotion of Evangelical Knowledge.

Episcopal Sunday School Society, New York. see Protestant Episcopal Sunday School Society, New York.

Episcopal Sunday-School Society of Pennsylvania. see Protestant Episcopal Sunday-School Society of Pennsylvania.

Episcopal Sunday School Society Union, New York. see General Protestant Episcopal Sunday School Union, New York.

Episcopalian. pseud. Answer to Bishop Hobart's pastoral letter. 32296

Episcopalian. pseud. Comments upon apostolic succession. 64692

Episcopalian. pseud. Dialogue. 19927, 54245

Episcopalian. pseud. Letters to John H. Hopkins, D. D. see Sargent, Lucius M.

Episcopalian. pseud. Plain address. 63208

Episcopalian. pseud. Resolutions of certain Episcopalians. (70071)

Episcopalian. pseud. Review of a sermon. 64692

Episcopalian of the city of New-York. pseud. Notes. 32293, 96982-96983

Episcopalian of . . . Maryland. pseud. Enquiry into the validity. see Kewley, John.

Episcopalian of Maryland. pseud. Some remarks on a pamphlet. 43324

Episcopus. pseud. 78581

Episode de la colonisation du Canada. (12571)

Episode de la guerre d'Amerique. 23093, note after 98620

Episode de la guerre servile. 12577

Episode de la revolution de Saint-Domingue. 19531

Episode de la vie Californienne. (34129)

Episode de l'emigration Belge en Virginia. 24205

Episode de l'histoire d'Haiti. 43703

Episode d'un voyage dans l'Amerique Centrale. 7328

Episode d'un voyage en Californie. 6306

Episode emprunta a la domination Francaise en Amerique. 26690

Episode in the colonization of Canada. (12573)

Episode of a journey through California. 6307

Episode of city life. (9663A)

Episode of the border. (65066)

Episode of the colonization of Canada. (12572)

Episodes de la guerre des Etats-Unis d'Amerique. (31254)

Episodes of live in New York. 28102

Episodio de 1863. 77068

Episodio de la guerra de la independencia. 72990

Episodio de la revolucion de Marzo de 1858. 22689

Episodio della guerra Americana ossia la spia. 16536

Episodio historico del gobierno dictatorial. 15010, 64333

Episodios de la trajicomedia del siglo XIX. 67158

Episodo do genie do Christianismo. (12268)

Epistle. (36061), 105976, 106979, 105981, 105982, 105985

Epistle an Audubon. 25822

Epistle and dedication to Lord N—. 32126

Epistle and testimony, from the Yearly Meeting of Friends, held in New York. 54262, 58904, (70195)

Epistle, by Mather Byles. 78692

Epistle, by Thomas Goodwin, and Philip Nye. 32828

Epistle. [By Thomas Nicholas.] 27752

Epistle [by William Penn.] (66925)

Epistle congratulatory to the Bishop. 18827

Epistle congratulatory to the Rt. Rev. the Bishops. 34099

Epistle containing some further reasons. 95581

Epistle dedicatorie. 33630, 66678-66679, 78377, 100801, 103313

Epistle dedicatory. 28052, 32286, (46655), (46789), 78209, 82823, 91945, 103688, 104896, note after 105090

Epistle dedicatory of the Union Press. 105576

Epistle dedicatory [to] Mrs. Catharine Hodson. 17059

Epistle for general service. 104545

Epistle from a young lady. (22690)

Epistle from Baltimore Yearly Meeting. 86048

Epistle from Benjamin Holme. 32574

Epistle from Edward, an American prisoner in England. 22691

Epistle from Hakluyt to Sir Walter Raleigh. (1552), 1st note after 45010

Epistle from John Burnyeat to Friends in Pennsylvania. 9415

Epistle from Oberea, Queen of Otaheite. (3204)

Epistle from our general spring meeting of ministers and elders. 61621

Epistle from our yearly meeting at Burlington. 22692, 61622

Epistle from our yearly-meeting, held at Philadelphia. 22693, 61624

Epistle from our yearly-meeting, held at Philadelphia, from the 24th . . . 9th month, to the 1st of the 10th month. (61623)

(Epistle) from our yearly meeting of Women Friends. 100523

Epistle from the Honourable Charles Fox. 95795

Epistle from the Marquis de La Fayette. (30010), 38570, 101802

Epistle from the Meeting for Sufferings, of the people called Quakers. 66922

Epistle from the Meeting of Sufferings, held in Philadelphia. 61625

Epistle from the Monthly Meeting of Friends of Philadelphia. 86049

Epistle from the three Monthly Meetings of Friends of Philadelphia. 61626

Epistle from the Yearly Meeting . . . held in Philadelphia. 61628

Epistle from the Yearly-Meeting, in London, held by adjournments. 86051

Epistle from the Yearly-Meeting in London, held . . . from the 27th of the fifth month to the 1st of the sixth month, 1776. 61627

Epistle from the Yearly Meeting of Friends, for New England. (52634)

Epistle from the Yearly Meeting of Friends, held at New Garden. 55608

Epistle from the Yearly Meeting of Friends held in New York. 86052

Epistle from the Yearly Meeting of Friends, held in Philadelphia, . . . 1829. (61630)

Epistle from the Yearly Meeting of Friends, held in Philadelphia . . . 1827. (61629)

Epistle from the Yearly Meeting of Friends, held in Philadelphia, . . . 15th of the fourth month . . . 1861. 61632

Epistle from the Yearly Meeting of Friends, held in Philadelphia, to the Yearly Meeting of Friends, held in London. 61631

Epistle from the Yearly Meeting [of Philadelphia.] 86050

Epistle from the Yearly Meeting of the people called Quakers. (66923)

Epistle from Thomas Janney. 35763

Epistle from Timoleon. 6211, 4th note after 95843

Epistle from Yarico to Inkle. (36061), 105979

Epistle from Yarico to Inkle, together with their characters. 105983

Epistle from Yarico to Inkle, with their characters. 105984

Epistle from Yarrico to Inkle, after he had left her in slavery. 92340, 105977

Epistle general. (22694)

Epistle in verse. 94401

Epistle in verse from the country. 70135

Epistle in verse, with other poems. 1008, 94401

Epistle, in verse, written from America. 94401

Epistle issued by a meeting of the followers of Elias Hicks. 31717

Epistle of advice from the Yearly Meeting of Friends. 100524

Epistle of caution and advice concerning the buying and keeping of slaves. 22695

Epistle of . . . caution and counsel, addressed to its members. 61634

Epistle of caution to Friends. 61633

Epistle of Demetrius, Junior. 60756

Epistle of John Burnyeat's. note after 7264

Epistle of love. 5631

Epistle of love and caution. 29747

Epistle of love and tender caution. 5460

Epistle [of Mr. Ilmestone.] 17051

Epistle of Paul, the Apostle, to the Ephesians. 12454

Epistle of Paul to the Ephesians. 49842

Epistle of Paul to the Galatians. 49842

Epistle of Paul to the Romans. 67765

Epistle of Paul . . . to the Romans, in the Mohawk language. 49841

Epistle of tender caution and counsel. 22696, 61635

Epistle of the two elders. 43595

Epistle [of William Penn.] (66925)

Epistle of Yarico to Inkle. (22697), 105978, 105985

Epistle, or salutation of Gospel love. (14954)

Epistle pacificatory to the brethren dissenting in this way. 17091

Epistle perfixed, [sic] by the Reverend Dr. Increase Mather. 91951

Epistle prefixed, by the Reverend Dr. Increase Mather. 91950, 91952-91953

Epistle sent from God to the world. (72683)

Epistle to a member of the General Court of Massachusetts. (22697A), 45722

Epistle to Alexander Pope. 87820

Epistle to all my dear friends. 25348

Epistle to all planters. 25349

Epistle to all professors in New England. 25350

Epistle to all who conscientiously suffer for not paying them. 41763

Epistle to Dr. Mead respecting the bite of a viper. 94710

Epistle to Dr. Richard Mead. 94711

Epistle to Friends. 21758

Epistle to Friends and tender-minded people in America. 32575

Epistle to Friends briefly commemorating the gracious dealings. 22350

Epistle to Friends, &c. 37214

Epistle to Friends in Gravesend in Long-Island. 18073

Epistle to Friends in Great Britain. 55234

Epistle to Friends in Maryland. 4454

Epistle to Friends in New-England. 13816

Epistle to Friends in Pennsylvania. (28341)

Epistle to Friends of Knaresborough Monthly-Meeting. 29747

Epistle to Friends of the quarterly and monthly meetings. 86053

Epistle to Friends to be read in their monthly meeting. (66925)

Epistle to Gov. Belcher by Rev. Mr. Biles. 65584

Epistle to his [i. e. Samuel Fothergill's] brethren. 25272

Epistle to Joseph T. Buckingham. (14185)

Epistle to Lord George Germaine, in verse. (27141)

Epistle to Mr. Jackson. 28552

Epistle to Rev. Stephen H. Tyng. (63414)

Epistle to Sir Walter Raleigh. (1552)

Epistle to the Bishops of the Episcopal Court at Camden. 20391

Epistle to the Christian Indians. 22698, 46304

Epistle to the churches of Christ, call'd Quakers. 72682-(72683), 72687

Epistle to the clergy of the southern states. (28856)

Epistle to the General Convention. 22699

Epistle to the Hon. Arthur Dobbs. 20405, 91330

Epistle to the Honourable Charles Price, Esq. 104245

Epistle to the inhabitants of Amsterdam. 59615, 94925

Epistle to the inhabitants of South-Carolina. (33781)

Epistle to the members of the yearly meeting of Friends. 61636

Epistle to the National Meeting of Friends, in Dublin. 62825, 95752

Epistle to the people called Quakers. 70892

Epistle to the quarterly and monthly-meeting of Friends in Pennsilvania [sic]. 86054

Epistle to the quarterly and monthly meetings of Friends. 105199, 105208

Epistle to the quarterly and monthly meetings, within the limits of the New-England Yearly Meeting. (52634)

Epistle to the Reverend Mr. Ebenezer Turell. (14513), 97451

Epistle to the Right Honourable and Right Worshipful the Governour, Councell, and Companie for Virginia. 7996, 16037

Epistle to the Right Honourable Lord G— G——. 28765

Epistle to the Right Honourable Lord N****. 28435

Epistle to the Scots reader. (21934)

Epistle to the reader. (17066), 46501, 72682, 78511, (79411)

Epistle to the said E. Smith. 80191

Epistle to the yearly-meeting at Philadelphia. 61627

Epistle to William Wilberforce, Esq. on the rejection of the bill. 3300

Epistle to William Wilberforce, Esq., written during the disturbances in the West Indies. 103959

Epistle to Zenas. A poem. 22700, 26624, 93506

Epistle written in Barbado's. 60121

Epistles addressed by the Yearly Meeting of Friends. 86055

Epistles and discourses betwixt Alexander the Conqueror. 105218

Epistles and testimonies issued by the yearly meetings of Friends. 86056

Epistles dedicatory. 56218

Epistles domestic, confidential, and official. 101742-101743

Epistles, odes, and other poems. 50445

Epistles of Brevet Major Pindar Puff. 99276

Epistles of George Fox. (25353)

Epistles of John, translated into the Chanta language. 105532

Epistles of John translated into the Cherokee language. 12453

Epistles of (Mr. Robert Rich) to the seven churches. 70893

Epistles of Mohammed Pash. 58990

Epistles of Paul. 49842

Epistles of Pindar Puff. 99276

Epistles to the barnburners. 65645

Epistola. 73990

Epistola a los missionarios de Mexico. 3601

Epistola a Prospero. 58419

Epistola ad auditores Virgilius Wellendarffer Saltzburgensis. 102560

Epistola ad bonos Pensilvaniae cives Christo non inimicos. 106356

Epistola ad fratrem eius ab ipso scripta. 95251

Epistola ad Paulum III. 24663

Epistola ad praepositum generalem Societatis Jesu. 98375

Epistola ad provincialem Flandriae. 59520

Epistola ad Reuerendissium Patre & Dominu[m] Bessarionem Carlinalem Nicenum. 66479

Epistola al muy illustre Senor do Hernando Crotes. 75567

Epistola Albericij. De nuuo mundo. note before 99327, 99334, 99378

Epistola alia, quam ad eum scripsit puella quaedam sectae Anglicanae. 95251

Epistola ao Serenissimo Sr. D. Jose. (6795)

Epistola Christoferi Colom (cui etas nostra tum debet: de insulis. . . .) 14628, (14630)-14631, 14633

Epistola, de admirabili & nouissima Hispanoru[m] in Orientem nauigatione. 47039-47040

Epistola de duodecim sociis. 31382

Epistola de insulis de nouo repertis. 41632

Epistola de insulis noui ter repertis. 14633

Epistola de rebus Indicis a quodam Soc. Jesu Presbyter Italice scripta. 26283

Epistola de vita et morte P. Alphonsi Aragonii Societatis Jesu. 4956

Epistola dedicatoria. 45011, (77903), 2d note after 102836

Epistola di Massimiliano Transilvano. 67730

Epistola dos Inglezes residentes no Imperio do Brazil. 22701

Epistola encyclica quanta cura. 72915

Epistola & globus geographicus. 77800, 77807

Epistola ex Portu-Regali in Acadia. note after 69259

Epistola Gasparis Dias Fereira. (24086)

Epistola Ill. D. Archiepiscopi Baltimorensis. 22702

Epistola nvncvpatoria. (49871), 66484, 66486-(66488)

Epistola, qua eorum quae priori epistola quaesita sunt. 98283

Epistola Rev. P. Gabrielis Dreuillettes. (20927)

Epistola reverendissimis patribus et comprovincialibus. 79303

Epistola Vadiani. (63958)-63960

Epistolae ad Pium Sixtum. 22703

Epistolae duae de LII Jesuitis interfectis in Brasilia. 19971

Epistolae duae M. Canum. 79180

Epistolae duae Petri Diazii. 19970, 43776

Epistolae familiares et alia quaedam miscellanea. 5108

Epistolae-Ho-Elianae. (33348)

Epistolae Indicae, de stvpendis et praeclaris rebus. 22704

Epistolae Indicae et Japonicae de multarum gentium. (36082)

Epistolarum familiarum liber duo. 97006

Epistolarum libri XII. 74664

Epistolary correspondence between the Rev. John C. Ogden. 56814

Epistolary declaration . . . of Friends. (52633)

Epistolary disquisition on college morality. 3779

Epistolary lament. 22705

Epistolica exercitatio. 61109

Epistolicall discourse of Mr. Iohn Dury. 95650

Epistolium typographi ad lectorem. (68936)

Epistre a l'Archivesque de Rheims. 74885

Epitaficos Latinos y Castellanos. 99644

Epitaficos originales. (67330)

Epitaph, &c. 22706, note before 102432

Epitaph. Here lie the mutilated and disjointed remains. 87821

Epitaph of P. Heyn. 32382

Epitaph on a certain great man. 78475, 104455

Epitaph on Benjamin Thompson. 78987

Epitaph on the United States of America. 87822

Epitaph on William Penn. 71244

Epitaphia Hippol. Capilupi in Chr. Columbum. (26502)

Epitaphs and elegies. 22707

Epitaphs from Copp's Hill Burial Ground, Boston. 7836

Epitaphs from King's Chapel Burial Ground. 7837

Epitaphs from the cemetery on Worcester
  Common. 3864
Epitaphs from the old burying-ground in Cam-
  bridge. 30535
Epitaphs from the old burying-ground in Water-
  town. 30536
Epithalame. 18576
Epitom [sic] of . . . lectures. 30773
Epitome and vindication of the public life.
  (35920), 97904
Epitome breve de la vida, y mverte del ilvstris-
  simo Doctor Don Bernardino de Almansa.
  86499, note after 98357
Epitome Chileno, ideas contra la paz. 94897
Epitome cronicorum seculi moderni. (47110)
Epitome de inuentis nuper Indiae populis idolola-
  tris ad fidem Christi. 16949
Epitome de la bibliotheca oriental i occidental,
  nautica i geografica. (40052)
Epitome de la bibliotheca oriental, y occidental,
  nautica, y geografica. 40053
Epitome de la relacion del viage de algunos
  mercaderes. 3350
Epitome de la vida de S. Juan de la Cruz.
  76797
Epitome de la vida del V. P. Juan de Viana de
  la Compania de Jesus. 94574
Epitome de las historias portvguesas. 23803
Epitome de les seconde et tierce narrationes.
  (16952)
Epitome de lo que debe saber, y entender el
  Christiano. 67638
Epitome de los principios fondamentales de la
  economica politica. 77364
Epitome del computo eclesiastico. 87241
Epitome des principes fondamentaux de l'econ-
  omie politique. 77362
Epitome du theatre de l'univers d'Abraham
  Ortelius. 57691
Epitome dv theatre dv monde d'Abraham
  Ortelivs. (57688)
Epitome et totius himani corporis fabrica.
  57817
Epitome historica da vida do Arcebispo da
  Bahia. (10310)
Epitome hist. & cron. mundi. 76906
Epitome of all historical passages. 67599
Epitome of American history. 92334
Epitome of commerce north and south. 99504
Epitome of history. 59282
Epitome of its [i. e. United States of America's]
  finances. 80487
Epitome of Mr. Forsyth's treatise on the cultiva-
  tion and management of fruit-trees. 25154
Epitome of Mr. John Speed's theatre of the
  empire of Great Britain. 89228
Epitome of mythology. 84363-84364
Epitome of proceedings at a telegraphic soiree.
  29317
Epitome of some exhortations delivered by the
  Indians. 22149
Epitome of spirit-intercourse. 17506
Epitome of . . . the chief events. 38786
Epitome of the faith and doctrines of the Re-
  organized Church of Jesus Christ of
  Latter Day Saints. 50737
Epitome of the laws of Nova Scotia. (51433)
Epitome of the life & character of Thomas
  Jefferson. 97904
Epitome of the Massachusetts and Rhode Island
  boundary question. 25315
Epitome of the opinions and practice of the most
  celebrated. 105993
Epitome of the stocks and public funds. 25179
Epitome of the West India question. 81964, 4th
  note after 102832

Epitome of United States history. 84336
Epitome of universal chronology. 30000
Epitome of Workman's geography. 105474
Epitome panegyrico de la vida admirable.
  88760
Epitome rervm gestarvm in India a Lusitanis.
  70060
Epitome theatri Orteliani. 57689-(57690)
Epitome topographica totivs orbis. 98278
Epitome trivm terrae partivm. 98279-98282,
  note after 102155
Epitomical history of the Christian era. (77437)
Epitomy of such exhortations as these Indians . . .
  did deliver. 66445
Epitre a M. Desforges Boucher. 5010
Epitre a Son Altesse Royale le Prince de Galles.
  28984
Epitre a Son Altesse Royale le Prince Ernest
  Albert. 28984
Epitre a Victor Hugo. (42625)
Epitre adressee a Mademoiselle F. Wright.
  72986
Epitre de M. le Mquis de la Fayette. 96990
Epitre dedicatoire. 95349
Epitres, satires, chansons, epigrammes. 5158
Epochs of transition. 77566
Epopee au Bresil. 73906
Epopeya postuma de D. Carlos de Siguenza y
  Gongora. 80969
Epoque de la mort du P. Garaze. 3252A
Epoque de l'establissement des Europeens.
  27650, (63966), 68421
Epoque glaciaire temporaire commencement de
  l'age de bronze. (7437)
Epoques memorables, traits interessants,
  moeurs, usages, coutumes. (18283)
Epoques remarquables. (20169)
Epouse du Republican Lavaux. 39286
Epouse d'un Mormon. pseud. Femme chez les
  Mormons. 23215
Eppes, John Wayles, 1773-1823. 22708
Epping, J. P. M. (22709)
Epping, N. H. Convention of Young Men in Rock-
  ingham Councillor District, 1828. see
  Convention of Young Men in Rockingham
  Councillor District, Epping, N. H., 1828.
Epping, N. Y. Selectmen. 22710
Epplen Hartenstein, Clara von. see Gerstner,
  Clara (von Epplen Hartenstein) von.
Eppler, Christoph Friedrich. 22711
Equal liberty of the press. (13880)
Equal rights. pseud. Report of the pamphlet
  of "Oswego." (22766)
Equal rights for the rich and poor. 29711
Eqaul rights for women. (18053)
Equal rights for women. A speech. (18053)
Equal rights of man asserted. 102582
Equal suffrage and the material development
  of the country. (25866)
Eqvall wayes of God. 32836
Equality and the new constitution. (22712)
Equality before the law. 93642
Equality of all men before the law. 22713,
  note before 90885
Equality of citizenship. 63937
Equality of civil rights amid native and
  naturalized citizens. 69350
Equality of mankind and the evils of slavery.
  103164
Equality of white men! 17355
Equality, the first principle of government.
  91617
Equality of soldiers' bounties. 86324
Equateur, scenes de la vie Sud-Americaine.
  32498

Equiano, Olaudah. 10763, 22714, 52274, 98661-98664, 103139

Equisse historique sur son origin et sa marche. 62248

Equisse sur l'histoire religieuse des premiers temps. 11329

Equisses historiques des hommes d'etat. 8407

Equisses historiques, statistiques, administratives, commerciales et morales. 26117

Equitable Mining Company. 75347

Equitable Mining Company. Charter. 75347

Equity and wisdom of administration. 22790

Equity in Pennsylvania. 68004

Equiluz, Diego de. see Eguilaz, Diego de.

Er det klogskab eller galskab af foli i Danmark at udvandre til Amerika? 87140

Erasmi Francisci Guineischer und Americanischer Blumen-Busch. (25461)

Erasmo. pseud. Ao imperador. 7517

Erasmus. pseud. Plea for reason. 22716

Erasmus, Desiderius, d. 1536. 98278

Erato. 26382

Erazu, Joseph, de Burunda. 22717

Erbauliche Gedanken von der Nachtigal. 98133

Erbauliche Lieder-Sammlung. 66467

Erbauliche und angenehme Geschichten derer Chiquitos. 12835, 24138, 1st note after 98488

Erben, M. Merians. 1917

Ercilla y Guniga, Alonso de, 1533-1594. 22718-(22729), 49893, 56299, 57300, 57629, (57801)-57803, 93311

Erdbeschreibung und Geschichte von Amerika. 21748

Erde und ihre Bewohner. 106334, 106336, 106339, 106345

Erdmann, Charles. tr. 10888, 31268

Ere nouvelle. (48595)

Ereignisse in Amerika in ihrer Ruckwirkung auf Deutschland. (22730)

Eres, Charles Dennis Rouso d'. see Rouso d'Eres, Charles Dennis, b. 1761.

Erfahrungen, Reisen und Studien. 25988

Erfindung und Offenbahrung der Newen Welt. (8784), note after 106331

Erganzungen nach Duflot de Mofras und Fremont. 9990

Erhard-Schieble, -------. engr. 75528

Erhardt, Joel B. 84774

Erholungen fur die gebildte Jungend. 9075

Ericeyra, Luis de Menezes, Conde de. see Menezes, Luis de, Conde de Ericeyra.

Erichson, -------. 77780

Ericsson, J. (22732)

Erie, Pa. Cemetery. 22737

Erie, Pa. Cemetery. Charter. 22737

Erie, Pa. Cemetery. Managers. 22737

Erie, Pa. Penn Industrial Reform School. see Penn Industrial Reform School, Erie, Pa.

Erie County, N. Y. Bar. 8790

Erie County, N. Y. Board of Supervisors. 22733

Erie County, N. Y. Convention, Buffalo, 1830. see Holland Purchase Convention, Buffalo, N. Y., 1830.

Erie County, N. Y. Convention of Delegates, from the Several Towns, Buffalo, 1830. see Holland Purchase Convention, Buffalo, N. Y., 1830.

Erie County, N. Y. Court of Oyer and Terminer, Buffalo. 95263-95277

Erie County, N. Y. Penitentiary. 22734

Erie County, N. Y. Union Anti-Lecompton Mass Meeting, Buffalo, 1858. 22735

Erie Canal Company of Pennsylvania. 60089

Erie Canal Company of Pennsylvania. Charter. 60089

Erie Cemetery, Erie, Pa. see Erie, Pa. Cemetery.

Erie County Penitentiary. 22734

Erie directory for 1867-68. 22736

Erie war. 22768

Erienensis. pseud. Sketches of the thirteenth Parliament. see Crofton, Walter Cavendish.

Erindringer fra et ophold i Amerika. 86851

Erindringer fra Polarlandene optegnede af Carl Petersen. 61223

Erindinger om mit ophold og mine reiser i Brasilien. 4581

Erinneringen uit eene driejarige dienst. 14582

Erinnerungen. (20582), 40992

Erinnerungen an Brasilien. 2470

Erinnerungen aus Amerika. 20545

Erinnerungen aus dem Leben von Anna Jane Linnard. (2800)

Erinnerungen aus Italien, England und Amerika. 12271

Erinnerungen aus Sud-Amerika. 5212

Erizeira, Francisco Xavier de Meneses, Conde de la. see Meneses, Francisco Xavier de, Conde de la Erizeira.

Erkelens, Dirk. 94163, note after 101819, 3d note after 101888

Erkenvkv hall coyvte. 72017

Erklarung der Charte von den neuen Entdeckungen. (41417)

Erklarung der Unabhangigkeit. 102481

Erklarung des Baues der beruhmtesten und merkwurdigsten alteren. 6103

Erklarung seines systems in seinem Praxis, oder Gewohnheit. 95599

Erlanger, Arman. defendant 47527

Erlauterung der Frey-Maurerey. 50680

Erlauterung fur Herrn Caspar Schwenckfeld. 60090

Erlauterungen zur Fauna Brasiliens. 9351

Erlebnisse auf meiner Wanderungen. 20130

Erlebnisse eines jungen Auswanderers in Virginien. 4532

Erlendsson, Haukr. ed. 74880

Erler, Christian August. 22769

Erma, -----------. 32597

Ermahnungs-Schreiben an die Bereits dahin verreisste Teutsche. 2390, 32377, 98990

Erman, George Adolf, 1806-1877. 22770-22771, 32991-32992

Ermatinger, Edward. 22772-(22773)

Ermine in the ring. (22774), 60945

Ermite de Niagara. 47935

Ermite du Chimboraco. (49431)

Ermordung Abraham Lincoln's 37118

Ernest Linwood. 31436

Erni, Henri. (22775)

Ernsliche Betrauchtung des gegenwartigen Zustandes. 25522-25563

Ernst, Adolf, 1832-1899. 22776-(22778), 58925

Ernst, F. 22781

Ernst, John Frederick. (22779)-22780

Ernsthaffte Christen Pflicht. (73102)

Ernstige beschouwing van d. tegenwoord. staat. 95324

Eroberer und Sclaven der neuen Welt. 22782

Eroberung Mexico's durch Hernandez Cortez. 18018

Eroberung von Mexico. 19432

Eroberung von Mexico und Peru. 22783
Eroberung von Mexico, von C. F. von de
Velde. 98820
Eroberung von Mexiko durch Ferdinand
Cortez. 38241
Eroberung von Mexiko. Ein historisch-
romantisches Gemalde. 98819
Erodelphian and Union Literary Societies,
Miami University, Oxford, Ohio. see
Miami University, Oxford, Ohio.
Erodelphian and Union Literary Societies.
Erodelphian Society, Miami University, Oxford,
Ohio. see Miami University, Oxford,
Ohio. Erodelphian Society.
Eroismo di Ferdinando Cortese. 9764
Erondelle, P. tr. 40175-40176
Erorterungen uber Secession. 89280
Erpenius, Thomas. tr. 66683
Errand to the south in the summer of 1862.
44118
Errata behorende tot het bericht. 1st note
after 102890
Errata; or, the art of printing incorrectly.
22785, 91385
Errata; or, the works of Will. Adams. A tale.
52153
Erratic poems. 80337
Erreparaz, Joseph de. (52106)
Errers que se padecen en las causales de su
cadencia. 97690
Errett, Isaac. 22784
Erroneous view of Canada answered and
refuted. 34111
Error and duty in regard to slavery. 95775
Error book. 83019, 101435, 103686
Error confundidado y la verdad demonstrada.
(22786)
Error exposed and truth upheld. 51223
Errores que contiene la memoria sobre la
decadencia de las misiones Jesuiticas.
44426
Errors and blasphemies of the Gortinians.
97736
Errors in Butter's Scholar's companion.
102370
Errors in education. 25440
Errors in English grammar. 102370
Errors in fact, advanced by Senator Hayne.
31041
Errors in Richardson's dictionary. 102370
Errors of Anna Braithwaite. 7359
Errors of Hopkinsianism detected and refuted.
3168
Errors of modern infidelity. 85170
Errors of the American Congress demonstrated.
94433
Errors of the British Minister. 22787
Errors of the Quakers. 104522
Erskine. pseud. Controversy between
"Erskine" and "W. M." 16192, 22799
Erskine, David Montague, 1776-1855. 16883,
22797, (58464), 83809-83817 see also
Great Britain. Legation. United States.
Erskine, David Steuart. see Buchan, David
Steuart Erskine, 11th Earl of, 1742-1829.
Erskine, Ebenezer. 22788
Erskine, John, 1721-1803. 22790-22793,
65615, 78983, 80911, 83802, 84096
Erskine, Ralph. (22794)-(22795)
Erskine, Robert. 22796
Erskine, Thomas, Baron, 1750-1823. 22798,
(37437), 91849, 96910, 96913-969147
96916-96917
Erskine, William. (33338)

Erskine College, Due West, S. C. (22800)
Erskines, -------. (17673)
Erst Theil dieses Weltbuchs. 25471
Erstaunliche Geschichten und unheimliche
Gebebenheiten. 63565
Erste Amerikaner in Texas. 95104
Erste Botschaft von Gouverneur David Butler.
52185
Erste Reise am die Erde. (9208)
Erste Reise nach dem Nordlichen Amerika.
59182
Erste und zweite Verhor von John Fries.
25961, 96866
Erste und Zweyte Reise von Ochotsk in
Sibirien. (77539), 91218
Erster Jahres Bericht des Stadts Superintenden-
ten. 45137
Erster Kriegszug der Spanier durch Florida.
98744
Erster Nummer. Der Goldne Ring meiner
Mutter. (77017)
Erster Theil, der Reiszbeschreibung. 79166
Erstes Lesebuch. 90129
Erstes Uebungsbuechlein fuer Kinder. 91209
Erudiccion politica. 98896
Erudita & elegans explicatio quaestitionis
vtrum reges vel principes. 11237,
39118
Erudito Americano. pseud. Musa Americana.
51558
Ervendberg, L. C. 22801
Erving, Thomas. (56974)
Erving, Burdick & Co. firm publisher
(49154)
Erving, Burdick & Co.'s Milwaukee city
directory. (49154)
Erwarde Classis van Amsterdam. see Neder-
landsche Hervormde Kerk. Classis van
Amsterdam.
Erweckungsrede, welche an Die in Jena
angekommene Saltzburg. 100989
Erweiterung dess Privilegii so der allerdurch-
leuchtigste, grossmachtigste Furst vnd
Heer Gustavus Adolphus. 98186
Erwerbsweige, Fabrikwesen und Handel der
Vereinigten Staaten von Nordamerika.
(24693)
Erwiederung in Bezung auf die Verhaftung
Vallandigham's. 41154
Erwin, ------. 22802
Erwin, Andrew. 40575, 93797, 94799
Erwin, John B. 87803
Erwin County, N. Y. (proposed) 22803
Erzahlung ans Sud-Amerika. 27192
Erzahlung aus dem Amerikanische Befreiung-
kriege. 38241
Erzahlung aus dem Amerikanischen Wald- und
Indianer-Leben. (6431)
Erzahlung aus dem grossen Dismal-Sumpfe.
92400
Erzahlung aus dem grossen Schreckensmoore.
92404
Erzahlung aus dem grossen Wustermoore.
92401
Erzahlung aus dem grozen Schreckenssumpfe.
92403
Erzahlung aus dem Jahre 1757. 16456
Erzahlung aus dem Sudlichen Californien und
Neu-Mexico. 49916
Erzahlung aus dem Westlichen Nordamerika.
49911
Erzahlung aus den Amerikan. Sumpfen. 92402
Erzahlung aus den Zeiten des Kriegszuges.
49912
Erzahlung aus der Kirchengeschichte. 35087
Ezrahlung aus Neu-Mexico. 49910

Erzahlung der unglucksfalle Die. 9737
Erzahlung fur die Christliche Jugend. 44332
Erzahlung fur die Jugend. 27194
Erzahlung fur die Jugend von Wilhelm Hoffmann. 32411
Erzahlung fur Kinder bearbeitet. 92575
Erzahlung nach Cooper fur die Jugend. 38241
Erzahlungen aus dem Character und Handlungen Joseph des Zweyten. 101877
Erzahlungen aus dem fernen Westen. 49916
Erzahlungen eines Auswanderers. 21187
Erzahlungen fur die Jugend von Mrs. Beecher Stowe. 92580
Erzahlungen und Beschreibungen aus Amerika. 22804
Erzahlungen und Bilder aus Amerika. 22805
Erzahlungen und Schilderungen aus dem Westlichen Nordamerika. 49916
Erzahlungen von den Sitten und Schiksalen der Negersklaven. (22806)
Erzahlungen von . . . der Negersklaven. 38226
Erzahlungen von Obern-See. 38214
Erzahlungsbibliothek fur Jedermann. 92570
Erzehlung der wunderbaren Zufalle. 38974, note after 100853
Erzehlung dessen Reisen nach denen Bis dass noch unbekannten Sudlichen Welt-Theilen. 1669
Erzehlungen von Maria Le Roy und Barbara Leininger. 73752
Es por la que se interesa el amigo de esta. 98935
Esa, aplyng this systm to the education of a stat r nation. (70874)
Esame critico del primero viaggio d'Amerigo Vespucci. (57812)
Esame critico del primo viaggio di Amerigo Vespucci. 10705, 51760
Esame de principj di Adam Smith. 81452
Esame della pastorale emanata del Sinodo della Chiesa. 66148
Esbarra, Joaquim Jose de Sancta Anna. 22807-(22809)
Esboco biographico do mesmo afferecido. 15101
Esboco biograph. e necrolog. de Conselheiro Jose Bonifacio de Andrada e Silva. 22810
Esboco historico das estradas de ferro do Brazil. 57896
Esboco ou primeiros tracos da crise commercial. 85625
Escabar. pseud. Short trip to Rome. 103645
Escadon y Llera, Mariano. 34185, (48815), (76183) see also Michoacan (Diocese) Comisionados para el Funeral y Exequias del Antonio de San Miguel Iglesias.
Escala espiritual para llegar al cielo. (22811)
Escalada, Jaime Sosa. see Sosa Escalada, Jaime, 1846?-1906.
Escalada, Jose Maria Castaneda y. see Castaneda y Escalada, Jose Maria.
Escalada, Mariano. 22812
Escalafon general que comprende a los Sres. Capitan General. 48458
Escalala, an American tale. 4098
Escalante, Bernard de. 22813
Escalante, Feliz M. 22814
Escalante, Francisco de la Estela. 22815
Escalante, Pedro de Escorza y. see Escorza y Escalante, Pedro de.
Escalante, Silvestre Velez de. see Velez de Escalante, Silvestre.
Escalante, Thomas. (22816)-22817
Escalante Fontaneda, Hernando de. see Fontaneda, Hernando de Escalante.

Escalera, Evaristo. 22818
Escalona, Gaspar de. 520, 22819, 22820
Escalona Aguero, Gaspar de. see Aguero, Gaspar de Escalona.
Escalona y Tamariz, Jose Nicolas de. 98803
Escandon, Domingo Trespalacios y. see Trespalacios y Escandon, Domingo.
Escandon, Juan de. (22821)
Escandon, M. petitioner 98901
Escandon y Compania. firm 98900
Escandor, Alejandro Aranho y. see Arango y Escandor, Alejandro.
Escape from Cayenne. 12343
Escape from the Mormons. 5694
Escape of Sainte Frances Patrick. 84021, 84023
Escape; or, a leap for freedom. A drama. 8592
Escape or loiterings amid the scenes of story and song. 43238
Escaped from the prison in Worcester. 105364
Escaped nun. 22822
Escarbot, M. see Lescarbot, M.
Escenas de la vida Mejicana. 25689
Escenas de la vida militar en Mexico. 24196
Escesos del gobierno le reclutan enemigos y atacan la libertad. 89412
Escesos del Senor Molinos y castigo que merece. 89413
Eschasseriaux, --------. 22823, 75540 see also France. Corps Legislatif. Conseil des Cinq-Cents. Commission des Colonies.
Eschoscholtz, ------. 38288
Eschricht, D. F. 22824
Eschwege, L. W. von. 22825-22827
Eschwege, W. C. von. 22828
Eschwege, W. L. von. 22829-22830
Esclaritud y emancipacion de los Aztecas en Colhuacan. 71703
Esclavage. 21196
Esclavage a Cuba. 74762
Esclavage aux Etats-Unis. Dean le quarteron. 27324
Esclavage aux Etats-Unis et la loi. 77746
Esclavage aux Etats-Unis: tableau des moeurs Americaines. 4188
Esclavage chez les Musulmans. 21227
Esclavage dans l'antiquite. (19684)
Esclavage dans les etats confederes. 22832
Esclavage des Americains et des Negres. 74811
Esclavage en Amerique. 40742
Esclavage et la traite a Cuba. 67137
Esclavage et liberte. 71273
Esclavage et traite. 26727
Esclavage. Lettre a M. le Ministre de la Marine et des Colonies. 5652
Esclavage, poeme. 21196
Esclave. (20957)
Esclave blanc, nouvelle peinture de l'esclavage en Amerique. (31792)
Esclaves. 27692
Esclaves des colonies Francaises au clerge Francais. 5652
Esclavitud. 11917
Esclavitud de la Santissimo Sacramento, Mexico (City) see Esclavos Confrades de la Santissimo Sacramento, Mexico (City)
Esclavos Cocheros del Santiss. Sacramento, Mexico (City) see Salto de Agua (Parroquia) Mexico (City) Congregacion del Esclavos Cocheros del Santiss. Sacramento.

Esclavos Confrades de la Esclavitud de la Santissimo Sacramento, Mexico (City) 93581
Escobar, Desiderio. 22833
Escobar, Diego Antonio de. 22834
Escobar, Diego Lopez de. see Lopez de Escobar, Diego.
Escobar, Jerome d'. 94853
Escobar, Jose Saenz de. see Saenz de Escobar, Jose, fl. 1700.
Escobar, Manoel de. 22835
Escobar, Manuel de. 22836-(22837)
Escobar, Marina de. 68844
Escobar, Pedro Suarez de. see Suarez de Escobar, Pedro, Bp.
Escobar Salmeron y Castro, Jose de. see Salmeron y Castro, Jose de Escobar.
Escobar y Llamas, Diego Osorio de, Bp. 66573 see also Peubla, Mexico (Archdiocese) Bishop (Escobar y Llamas)
Escobar y Llamas, Diego Osorio de, Bp. plaintiff 66573 see also Puebla, Mexico (Archdiocese) Bishop (Escobar y Llamas)
Escobedo, -------. 36791
Escobenda, Pedro. 22838
Escoiquiz, Juan de. 22839
Escola mercantil. 98776
Escolapios, P.-P. ed. 12242
Escontria, Joseph Gomez de. 22840
Escorza y Escalante, Pedro de. 22841, (70795)
Escosura, P. de la. 22842
Escouedo, Francisco de Estrada y. see Estrada y Escouedo, Francisco de.
Escovedo, Pedro de Estrada y. see Estrada y Escovedo, Pedro de.
Escoyti y Norri, Gabriel Pantaleon de. see Pantaleon de Escoyti y Norri, Gabriel.
Escribiala, N. J. Torres. see Torres Escribiala, N. J.
Escriptos ao povo por Joao de Saldanha da Gama. 75614
Escritativa de la Legislatura del Estado de Mexico. 63687
Escrito evacuando el Sr. Comandante Jose Jesus Vallenilla. 98389
Escrito legal sobre la vacante que el Cabildo de Michoacan publico. 73043
Escrito presentado al Consejo de Guerra. 67340
Escritor de los pelados. 96959
Escritos politicos, economicos y literarios. 98596
Escritos presentados a esta comandancia. 75774
Escritura de Asociacion de la Compania de Minas Zacatecano-Mexicana. 106240
Escriuano Carrillo, Fernando Alfonso. see Carrillo, Fernando Alfonso Escruiano.
Escudero, Jose Augustin de. (22843)-22844, 62980
Escudo de armas de Mexico. 9817, 80981
Escuela de la Inmaculada Concepcion, Vera Cruz (Parroquia) see Vera Cruz (Parroquia), Mexico (City) Escuela de la Inmaculada Concepcion.
Escuela de la razon: enio instruido. 75606
Escuela Practica de Minas. see Mexico. Colegio Nacional de Mineria.
Escuelas. (77075)
Escursion a los Indios Ranqueles. 44390
Esealona Aguero, Gaspare de. see Aguero, Gaspare de Esealona.
Esenbeck, C. G. Nees von. see Nees von Esenbeck, C. G.

Esercitato Accademico della Crusca. pseud. Lettera. 40560
Esfera, forma del mundo con una breve descripcion del mapa. 49191, note after 98817
Eskimaux and English vocabulary. 101906
Eskimo. pseud. illus. 71430, 71439
Eskimo stories. 83549
Eskimoiske eventyr og sagn med supplement. 71432
Eskimoiske eventyr og sagn oversatte efter de indfodts fortaelleres opskrifter og meddelelser. 71431
Eskimoiske eventyr og sagn. Supplement indeholdende et tillaeg. 71432
Eslaba, Sebastian de. see Eslava y Lazaga, Sebastian de.
Eslava, ------ Goncalez de. see Gonzalex de Estava, Fernan.
Eslava y Lazuga, Sebastian de. 11131-11132, 11134, 19951, 22877, 1st note after 99245 see also Nueva Granada (Vice-royalty) Virrey, 1740-1748 (Eslava y Lazaga)
Esmangart, Charles. 22878-22879
Esmenard, Jean Baptiste d', 1772-1824. ed. 27668
Esmenard, Joseph Etienne, 1767-1811. 22880, (36768), 89596
Espada y Landa, Francisco Joseph Diaz de. 22881
Espada y Landa, Juan Jose Diaz de. 22882
Espada de la justicia. 98257
Espada de San Fernando. 22067
Espagne et l'esclavage dans les isles de Cuba et de Porto-Rico. 14067
Espagnoles Americanos Residentes en Esta Ciudad. petitioners see Valladolid, Mexico. Espagnoles Americanos Residentes en Esta Ciudad. petitioners
Espana, M. 29031
Espana en Mexico. 64332
Espana libre. Poema. 106322
Espana sagrada. 24834
Espana y America. 72796
Espana y la republica de Mejico. 5855
Espana y las republicas de la America del Sur. 650
Espana y Venezuela. 24974
Espanaphoras de varia historia Portugueza. 69287
Espano y Mejico en el asunto de la convencion Espanola. 22883
Espanol. pseud. Contestacion de un Espanol. 11403
Espanol. pseud. Tardes Americanas. 29255
Espanol. 11094, 22884, 48884, 78907, 103421
Espanol Americano. pseud. Alla va eso y tope donde topare. see Villasenor Cervantes, Jose Maria.
Espanol-Americano. pseud. Colombia con-stituida. 14568
Espanol Americano. pseud. Incitativa. (34431)
Espanol en Philadelphia. pseud. Reflexiones sobre el comercio. 68734
Espanol Europeo. pseud. Reflexiones. 68730
Espanol que acaba de regresar de Mejico. pseud. Representacion. 69979
Espanola. see Santo Domingo (Spanish Colony)
Espanoles Americanos. pseud. Representacion y manifiesto. 69991
Espanoles en Chile. 9600, (27798)
Esparza, Marcos de. 22885-22886

Esparza, Mariano Ruiz de. ed. 87242, 87244
Especifico celestial. 61121
Especifico y unico remedio de la pobreza del imperio Mexicano. 86397
Especulacion astrologica. 23207
Espedicion de Mexico. 67303
Espediciones piraticas de ciudadanos Americanos. 63746
Espediente de la cuenta enviada por el Ejecutivo. 48450
Espediente formado sobre la suspension. 67104
Espeio. see Espejo, Antonio de, fl. 1581-1583.
Espeio de vida Christiana. 93310
Espeio divino en lengva Mexicana. (48908)
Espejo, Antonio de, fl. 1581-1583. 53293, 66686, 69210
Espejo crystalino de paciencia. 50479
Espejo de aprovechados y perfectos. 87151
Espejo de doctrina Cristiana. 24321
Espejo de exemplares obispos. 11418
Espejo de mi tierra. 22887
Espejo de variedades, 1575. 94853
Espejo juridico informe. (22888)
Espejo para el alma pecadora. 74045
Espejo para todos los reyes. 76175
Esperance, poeme. 75507
Esperanza: or, the home of the wanderers. (7094)
Esperienze intorno a diverse cose naturali. 68516
Esphera Mexicana. 67648
Espinas del hombre Dios. 10946
Espinasse, N. de l', Chevalier de Langeac. 1531, (38878)-(38879)
Espine, H. de l'. see L'Espine, H. de.
Espino, Luis. 89410-89419
Espinosa, Antonio Vazquez de. see Vazquez de Espinosa, Antonio.
Espinosa, C. see Espinosa, Juan.
Espinosa, Francisco Carbajal. see Carbajal Espinosa, Francisco.
Espinosa, Gilberto. tr. 99641
Espinosa, Isidro Felix de. (22895)-22898
Espinosa, J. M. (22900)
Espinosa, Jose Dolores. (22899)
Espinosa, Jose Ignacio. defendant 582, (65925)
Espinosa, Josef de. 681, (69221)
Espinosa, Jose Francisco de Aguerre y. see Cuevas Aguerre y Espinosa, Joseph Francisco de.
Espinosa, Joseph Francisco de Cuevas Aguirre y. see Cuevas Aguirre y Espinosa, Joseph Francisco de.
Espinosa, Juan. 22890-(22892), 22901-22902
Espinosa, Pedro, Abp., 1793-1866. 22903-22904, 31565, 56464 see also Guadalajara (Archdiocese) Archbishop (Espinosa) Jalisco (Diocese) Bishop (Espinosa)
Espinosa, Pedro Alonso Davalos Bracamonte y. see Davalos Bracamonte y Espinosa, Pedro Alonso, Conde de Miravalle.
Espinosa de los Monteros, Ignacio. 22894
Espinosa Rendon, Jose D. ed. (69669)
Espinosa y Carzel, Antonio Maria. ed. 57717
Espinosa y Tello, Josef. 22905
Espion Americain in Europe. 22906
Espion Anglais. 62697
Espion Anglois. 62696
Espion des sauvages en Angleterre. 22907
Espion d'un nouvelle espece. 32029
Espion Indien. 22297
Espion noir. 12577
Espion roman nouveau. 16534

Espion serrano. 58046
Espirit du sisteme politique de la regence d'Amsterdam. 98507
Espirito Sancto, (Brazilian Province) Presidente (Nascentes d'Azambuja) 51844 see also Nascentes d'Azambuja, Jose Bonifacio.
Espiritu Sancto, Antonio del. see Antonio del Espiritu Sancto.
Espiritu. 12758, 16156
Espiritu constitucional. 92860
Espiritu de los mejores diarios que se publican. 22908
Espiritu publico. 12758, 16156, 93786-93787
Espiritu Santo Bay. 87205
Espiritu y condiciones de la historia en America. 77076
Espiritus fuentes descubren. 99467
Espiritvs Sanctus illuminet sensus. 87177
Esplicacion de algunos tratados de fisica. 74763
Esplicacion de la doctrina Cristiana. 55247
Esplicacion de las laminas pretencientes. 65268
Esplorazione delle regioni equatoriali. (57767)
Espos y Mina, Lino Amalia. defendant 21019, 1st note after 96847
Espos y Mina, Lucretia. see Chapman, Lucretia. defendant
Esposicion a los Senores del Imperio. 72544
Esposicion a su gefe los Senores de la Comision de Policia. 98304
Esposicion al Soberano Congreso. 36816
Esposicion de la conducta politica. 63690
Esposicion de la Tareas Administrativas del Gobierno. 61122
Esposicion de las causas que hacian indispensables. 11469
Esposicion de las ventajas. 97506
Esposicion de Jose R. Revenga. 14594
Esposicion de los motivos. 22911
Esposicion de los sentimientos de los funcionarios publicos. (14585)
Esposicion de los servicios. 22909
Esposicion del estado de los departamentos. 14593
Esposicion del gobierno del estado de Chiapas. 57433
Esposicion del Presidente del Estado de Honduras. 32764
Esposicion del Secretario de Estado, en el Despacho del Interior. 56274
Esposicion del Secretario de Guerra i Marina. 14583
Esposicion del Secretario de la Guerra al Congreso, 1824. 14589
Esposicion del Secretario de Marina. 14590
Esposicion del Secretario de Ralaciones Esteriores. 56274
Esposicion del Sr. Gobernador de la Mitra. (29026)
Esposicion dirijida a las Camaras del Congreso General. 33551
Esposicion dirigida al Exmo. Sr. Gen. Presidente. 76747
Esposicion dirigida al Supremo Gobierno. 22914
Esposicion documentada de la instalacion y estado actual. 99623
Esposicion hecha a la Camara de Diputados. 93340
Esposicion hecha al Exmo. St. General d. Epitacio Huerta. (48811)
Esposicion hecha por los individuos de la Corte Marcial. 67845
Esposicion Nacional de Agricultura, Santiago, Chile, 1869. 17209

Esposicion publica. (27966)

Esposicion que dirije al Congreso del Estado. 40067

Esposicion que dirige al Congreso General. (52096)

Esposicion que dirige al pueblo. (35550)

Esposicion que dirige desde la fortaleza. 76747

Esposicion que dirige Jesus Lopez Portilla. (64334)

Esposicion que el Cabildo Metropolitano de Mexico ha elevado. 48451

Esposicion que el Gobernador del Obispado de Oaxaca dirije. 56400

Esposicion que el Ministro Secretario de Estado en el Despacho de Relaciones Esteriores del gobierno de la republica, presenta. 56274

Esposicion que el Ministro Secretario de Estado en el Despacho del Interior y Justicia del gobierno de la republica presenta. 56274

Esposicion que el Secretario de Estado del Despacho del Interior hiro. 14591

Esposicion que el Secretario de Estado en el Despacho de Marina hace. 14588

Esposicion que el Secretario de Estado en el Despacho de Relaciones Esteriores de la republica de Colombia hace. 14592

Esposicion que el Secretario del Interio i Relaciones Esteriores del Gobierno de la Nueva Granada, hace. 56274

Esposicion que eleva al Supremo Gobierno. 26519

Esposicion que elevan al Congreso de la Union. 22910

Esposicion que en cumplimiento del articulo 83 de la constitucion. 56400

Esposicion que hace a la Camara de Diputados del Congreso. 94274

Esposicion que hace a los pueblas. 94618

Esposicion que hace a sus conciudadanos. 58577

Esposicion que hace con el objeto de escitar el patriotismo. 50498

Esposicion que hace el Jeneral Blanco al Supremo Gobierno. 22912

Esposicion que hace el Praecid. Provision de la Repub. 61123

Esposicion que los Conservadores de la Provincias dirigen. 48452

Esposicion que por las exenciones de la Provincia Carmen hace. 22915

Esposicion que presenta a las Camaras Legislativas de la Nueva Granada. 56274

Esposicion que presenta en Bolivia al Ministro de Estado, en el Despacho del Interior. (29335)

Esposicion sobre la ocurrido en la hacienda de Aguatepec. 97730

Esposicion sobre las analogias i diferencias que se versan. 107230

Esposicion sobre el estado de los bancos. 50127

Esposiciones verificadas en 1850. (48453)

Espositione di M. Gio. Battista Ramvsio. 67736-67739

Espositioni et introdvttioni vniversali, di Girolamo Rvscelli sopra totta la geografia. 66505, 66507

Espositioni et introdvttioni vniversali, di Girolamo Rvscelli sopra tutta la geografia. 66503, 99504

Espostulory letter. 97358

Espoussete des armories de Villegaignon. 99725

Espoz y Mina, Francisco, 1781-1836. 49185

Espresiones de sincero y tierno efecto. 74638

Esprit blanc. 4901

Espronceda, Jose de. 22916

Espry, James Pollard, 1795-1830. 22917, (68512)

Espry, John Pollard. see Espry, James Pollard, 1795-1830.

Espry, Josiah. (22918)

Esquemeling, John. see Exquemelin, Alexandre Olivier.

Esquerra, M. de. 22920

Esquerra, Mathias. 22919

Esqvibel, Joseph de. 98884

Esquibel y Vargas, Agustin Francisco. 22921

Esquilache, Francisco de Borja y Aragon, Principe de. see Borja y Aragon, Francisco de, Principe de Esquilache, 1582-1658.

Esquimaux Christian. 51542

Esquire. pseud. Reign of felicity. see Spence, Thomas. supposed author

Esquisse biographique. 82277

Esquisse biographique sur Chevalier de Lorimier. 23598

Esquisse biographique sur Mgr. de Laval. 7425

Esquisse de evenements militaires et politiques. 39658

Esquisse de la constitution Britannique. 100851

Esquisse de la revolution de l'Amerique Espagnole. 58266

Esquisse de la vie et des travaux apostolique. 39279

Esquisse d'un poeme sur l'Independance de l'Amerique. 38759

Esquisse d'un tableau historique des progres de l'esprit humain. 15191

Esquisse d'une classification des chaines de montagnes. 44505

Esquisse geographique. 44173

Esquisse geologique du Canada, pour servir a l'intelligence de la carte geologique. 41818

Esquisse geologique du Canada suivie d'un catalogue. 10457

Esquisse historique des principaux evenemens. 17033

Esquisse historique et geographique. (21224)

Esquisse interessante du tableau fidele. 22922

Esquisse morale et politique des Etats-Unis de l'Amerique du Nord. 51413

Esquisses Americaines, ou tablettes d'un voyageur. 22923

Esquisses Americaines. Souvenir d'un sejour chez les planteurs du sud. 39153

Esquisses historiques, politiques et statistiqeus de Buenos-Ayres. 56332

Esquisses morales et litteraires. 35147

Esquisses sur les moeurs Anglaises et Americaines. 35212

Esquivel, J. M. 22925

Esquiuel y Caceres, Rodrigo de. plaintiff 98314

Esquiuel y de la Cueua, Antonia Gregoria de. defendant 98314

Esquivel y Vargas, Ildefonso de. (22924)

Essai analytique sur les principes des judgements. 82317

Essai anthropologique. 64705

Essai auquel le premier prix a ete adjuge. 32422

Essai couronne. De l'avenir et de l'influence des canaux du Canada. (37145)

Essai critique par l'auteur de la Bibliotheca Americana vetustissima. 30602

Essai de comparaison entre la France et les Etats-Unis. 106335

Essai de conciliation. 39610

Essai de grammaire. Par M. D. L. S. (65038)

Essai de grammaire sur l'idiome usite dans les colonies Francaises. 28151

Essai de l'hygiene militaire des Antilles. 50553

Essai de restitution et d'interpretation d'un passage de Scylax. 68443

Essai d'instructions pour voyageur utilement. 4935-4936

Essai d'un monographie du Rio-de-la-Plata. 64698

Essai d'une climatologie medicale de Monte-Video. 77200

Essai d'une description physique du monde. 33730

Essai d'une faune des Myriapodes du Mexique. (77207), 77211

Essai d'une instruction pour les Indiens. 104692

Essai geognostique sur la gisement des roches. 33711

Essai historique et philosophique. 75877

Essai historique sur la colonie de Surinam. (40086), (51894), 3d note after 93855

Essai historique sur la revolution du Paraguay. 4815, 69611

Essai historique sur les sources de la philologie Mexicaine. 7426

Essai historique sur l'ile de Cuba. (4002)

Essai historique sur Louisiane. 26790

Essai historique sur la colonie de Surinam. (40086)

Essai politique sur la royaume de la Nouvelle-Espagne. 33713, (33756), 81454

Essai politique sur l'ile de Cuba. (33719)

Essai statistique et politique sur les Etats-Unis d'Amerique. 50706

Essai statistique sur le royaume de Portugal et d'Algarve. 2857

Essai sur cette question. 22568

Essai sur Henri-Christophe. 75481

Essai sur la cochenille et le nopal. (8741)

Essai sur la colonie de Sainte Lucie. 12017

Essai sur la colonisation. 100907

Essai sur la construction navale des peuples extra-Europeens. 58593

Essai sur la culture de la canne a sucre. 70456

Essai sur la discipline des prisons. 33331

Essai sur la fievre jaune d'Amerique. 95440

Essai sur la fievre jaune observee a la Martinique. 99282

Essai sur la geographie des plantes. 33759

Essai sur la marine ancienne des Venitiens. 25095

Essai sur la nature du gouvernement. 14708

Essai sur la poesie, la musique, la danse et l'art dramatique. 7427

Essai sur la population des colonies a sucre. (6437), 22927

Essai sur la question coloniale a la Guyane Francaise. 19316

Essai sur la route aux Indes par le Nord. 22571

Essai sur la situation de Saint-Domingue a cette epoque. 19335

Essai sur la theogonie Mexicaine. 94848

Essai sur la topographie de l'isle de Sainte-Lucie. 66619

Essai sur la transportation comme recompense. (50211)

Essai sur la veritable liberte civil. 23426

Essai sur la vie de Robertson. 72013

Essai sur la vie de Marquis de Bouille. 6879

Essai sur la vie et les doctrines de Channing. 11915

Essai sur la vie et les ouvrages de l'auteur [i. e. J. H. Campe.] 10296

Essai sur la ville de Washington. 101938

Essai sur l'admission des navires neutres dans nos colonies. 99260

Essai sur l'administration de St. Domingue. 68079

Essai sur l'administration des colonies Francoises. 22926

Essai sur l'administration des colonies. Par M. le Comte de Mauny. (46944)

Essai sur l'ancien Cundinamarca. 81287, 94847

Essai sur le commerce et les interets de l'Espagne. 12949

Essai sur le systeme silurien de l'Amerique Septentrionale. (11410)

Essai sur l'empoissonement par les miasmes de marais. 43701, 71251

Essai sur les avantages a retirer de colonies nouvelles. 94260

Essai sur les causes de la revolution. 14553, 98669

Essai sur les colonies Francaises. Par M. Antenor de Caligny. 10047, 14347

Essai sur les colonies francoises; ou discours politiques. 75518

Essai sur les dechiffrement de l'ecriture hieratique de l'Amerique Centrale. 73305

Essai sur les desavantages politique de la traite des Negres; trad. de l'anglais. (13482)

Essai sur les desavantages politiques de la traite des Negres; traduit par Gramagnac. 13481

Essai sur les Etats-Unis. (19477)

Essai sur les insectes et les maladies qui effectle ble. 21387

Essai sur les interets du commerce maritime. 31236, (56856)

Essai sur les langues d'Amerique. (17174)

Essai sur les mollusques terrestriales et fluviatiles. (20959)

Essai sur les moyens d'extirper les prejuges des blancs. 41380

Essai sur les principes de l'Ecole Americaine. 35890

Essai sur l'etablissement des colonies en general. 100905

Essai sur l'etat actuelle de l'administration de la colonie. 44976

Essai sur leur distribution geographique dans ces iles. 34032

Essai sur l'histoire de la cosmographie. 76839

Essai sur l'histoire de la geographie. 71871

Essai sur l'histoire des communautes religieuses. (10604)

Essai sur l'histoire naturelle de la France Equinoxiale. 3603

Essai sur l'histoire naturelle de l'Isle de Saint-Domingue. 55259

Essai sur l'histoire naturelle du Chili. 49890

Essai sur nos colonies. 47

Essai sur Washington. 12880

Essai (I) sur les plantes usuelles de la Jamaique. 105627

Essaie sur l'histoire des communautes religieuses de femmes. 19202

[Essais a la] Societe Philotechnique. (5153)

Essais de biographie et de critique. 65260

Essais de Nicolas Freeman. 35825

Essais historiques et critiques sur la marine de France. 39129

Essais historiques et politiques sur la revolution de l'Amerique Septentrionale. (31899)

Essais historiques et politiques sur les Anglo-Americains. 999, (31899)-31900

Essais poetiques. (39987)

Essais politiques. 38436

Essais politiques sur l'etat actuel de quelques puissances. 74486

Essais statistiques sur les possessions Portugaises. 76848

Essais sur les isles fortunees et l'Antique Atlantide. 6438

Essais sur les rapports de la constitution federal. 42701

Essais sur l'esprit des lois colonies. 6985

Essais sur l'histoire naturelle des quadrupedes. 2537

Essais sur l'organisation progressive de la marine. 21358

Essaix philosophiques. 47930

Essars, ------ de Viefville des. see Viefville des Essars, ------- de.

Essarts, Alfred Stanislaus Langlois des. see Des Essarts, Alfred Stanislaus Langlois, 1811-1893?

Essay. 31755, (44330)

Essay at a picturesque voyage in North America. 93992

Essay . . . at the exhibition of the English High School. 33216

Essay before the literary societies of the State Normal School. 77612

Essay; being an enquiry into the late proceedings of Great-Britain. 96074

Essay by a friend to the constitution. (22928)

Essay, by a L.L.B. of Harvard College. 70898

Essay, by a western man. 24683, 50344

Essay. By Bela Hubbard. 33418

Essay . . . by Edwards A. Park. 58619

Essay. By James Shannon. 79764

Essay, by Prof. John M'Crady. 87738

Essay by Rev. Abijah P. Marvin. 45023

Essay . . . By S. P. Parker, D. D. 58734

Essay, by several ministers of the Gospel. 22472, 22929, (81422), 95162

Essay by Stephen Watts. 25279, 84611-84612

Essay [by T. W. Field.] 39651

Essay concerning . . . domestic manufactures. (55313)

Essay concerning gratitude. 46807

Essay concerning marriage. 75822

Essay concerning obedience to the supreme powers. 28790, 79243

Essay, concerning silver and paper currencies. 20723, 34810, 4th note after 98549

Essay concerning slavery, and the danger Jamaica is expos'd to from the too great number of slaves. 22930, 1st note after 96764

Essay concerning the Perkiomen Zinc Mine. 105107

Essay concerning the true original, extent, and end of civil government. 41727

Essay delivered in a competition. 13571

Essay, delivered to the Literary and Philosophical Society of Charleston. 36341

Essay directing persons under sadness. (46276)

Essay, directing them that are young. 46616

Essay, first published in the Religious herald. 92868-92869

Essay for discharging the debts, improving the lands. 8070

Essay for discharging the debts of the nation. 22931

Essay for our awakening out of a sinful sleep. 46414

Essay for regulating and improving the trade and plantations. (4730)

Essay for reviving religion. 103930

Essay for the cure of ungodly anger. 46328

Essay for the recording of illustrious providences. 46678-46680

Essay for the times. 45480

Essay for the undoing of heavy burdens. (46266)

Essay from the Virginia argus. 58933, 71187

Essay in defence of slave holding. 22932

Essay in verse. (44610), 82075

Essay in vindication of the continental colonies of America. 22933

Essay made in a few words. 46352

Essay. New Brunswick, as a home for emigrants. 9488

Essay, . . . October 27, 1863. 27974

Essay of a Delaware-Indian and English spelling book. 106300

Essay of G. C. Swallow. 39842

Essay of profitable reflections. 46269

Essay offered on a new-years-day. 46431

Essay offered unto a society of young men. 47487

Essay on a congress of nations. 38525

Essay on a course of liberal education. (65513)

Essay on a disease of the jaw bones. (80427)

Essay on a uniform orthography for the Indian languages. 62631

Essay on American poetry. 8559

Essay on American slavery. 22934

Essay on an ancient prophetical inscription. 44657

Essay on apostolic succession. 71114

Essay on Asiatic cholera. (55080)

Essay on banking. 21267

Essay, on bitters and astringents. 105106

Essay on calcareous manures. 73915

Essay on canals and inland navigation. 22935, 102555

Essay on canon and feudal law. 229, 241, 14388, (32634)

Essay on church government. (49006)

Essay on church polity. note after 91480

Essay on comets, in two parts. 57199

Essay on common school education. 71967

Essay on commonwealth. 22936

Essay on comparative agriculture. 9493

Essay on constitutional reform. 30822

Essay on civil and religious liberty. (22943)

Essay on colonization. 100905

Essay on comets, in two parts. 57199, 104858

Essay on contagions and infections. (80068)

Essay on credit. (22938), 102403

Essay on currency and banking. (22938), 84367

Essay on currents at sea. 47224

Essay on dancing. 106095

Essay on demonology. 95149

Essay on digestion. 83664

Essay on diseases incidental to Europeans. (41277)

Essay on dueling. (21102), (22939)

Essay on dying man. 46573

Essay on education. 105784

Essay on epidemics. (80425)

Essay on equity in Pennsylvania. (39267)

Essay on faith. 73436

Essay on fevers, the rattles, & canker.
101215

Essay on flogging in the navy. 22940

Essay on free trade and finance. 102404

Essay on "free trade," written in the autumn
of 1849. 85614

Essay on freedom. 87108

Essay on genius and education. 33198-33199

Essay on hereditary titles. 22941

Essay on his [i. e. James Richards'] character.
70950

Essay on his [i. e. Jonathan Edwards'] genius
and writings. 21974

Essay on honour. 31801

Essay on import duties and prohibitions.
(22941)

Essay on Indian bibliography. 74685

Essay on Indian corn. 8676

Essay on industry. 84130, 1st note after
95758

Essay on inoculation for the small pox.
(74428)

Essay on its [i. e. odd fellowship's] practical
influence. 14901

Essay on its [i. e. the culture of silk's]
rational practice and improvement.
66625

Essay on Junius and his letters. 102058

Essay on labor and subsistence. 55311

Essay on liberty and slavery. 5892, 5894,
79900

Essay on maritime power and commerce.
19744

Essay on medical education. 74698

Essay on meteorological observations.
(55257)

Essay on ministers negating the votes of the
church. 360, 11967, 3d note after
96741

Essay on modern martyrs. (9261), 18321

Essay on modern reformers. 98077

Essay on money, as a medium of commerce.
22944, note after 102409, 104937

Essay on monumental architecture. 83734

Essay on "national government." 82001

Essay on naturalization and allegiance.
21222, (22945), 30996

Essay on naval establishments. 98266

Essay on Negro emancipation. (66863)

Essay on Negro slavery. 57097

Essay on organic remains. 27466

Essay [on patriotism.] (12401)

Essay on perfect intonation and the euharmonic
organ. (64035)

Essay on plantations. 78992

Essay on plantership, &c. 22946

Essay on political society. 22947

Essay on printing in South America. 95406

Essay on professional ethics. 79864

Essay on remarkables in the way of wicked
men. 46305

Essay on republican principles. 1500

Essay on salt. 98541

Essay on scripture-prophecy. 9377

Essay on sea coast crops. 932

Essay on separate and congregate systems
of prison discipline. 33330

Essay on sheep. 41636

Essay on shooting. 89637-89639

Essay on slavery. 22948

Essay on slavery and abolitionism. 4290,
28854, 31771

Essay on slavery. By Thomas R. Dew.
19833

Essay on slavery in the light of international
law. 22263

Essay on slavery, proving from scripture its
inconsistency. 79823

Essay on slavery; re-published from the
Boston recorder & telegraph. 99610,
note after 105324

Essay on songs among thorns. 46432

Essay on state rights. 23147

Essay on sugar. 22949, 5th note after 102832

Essay on temperance. 32250

Essay on the abolition, not only of the African
slave trade. 22950

Essay on the abolition of slavery. 4004

Essay on the administration of church government. 52635

Essay on the advantages and disadvantages
which respectively attend France and
Great Britain. 97342

Essay on the African slave trade. (22951),
(25499)

Essay on the agitations of the sea. 22952

Essay on the agricultural capabilities of South
Carolina. 78549

Essay on the amendments proposed. 44727

Essay on the American crisis. 43563

Essay on the antiquities of Great Britain and
Ireland. (44093)

Essay on the apprenticeship system. 44389

Essay on the art of adorning natural, and
creating artifical, beauty. 105180

Essay on the art of making muscovado sugar.
2838

Essay on the art which makes a man happy
in himself. 90233, 90236-90237, 90246

Essay on the beauties and excellencies of
painting. 103218

Essay on the best way of developing improved
political and commercial relations.
39561

Essay on the bibliography of the councils.
80004

Essay on the bilious epidemic fever. 105991

Essay on the bilous fever. 104245

Essay on the bilious, or yellow fever of
Jamaica. 104244-104245

Essay on the bilious or yellow fever of
Jamaica: collected from the manuscript
of a late surgeon. 5908

Essay, on the care taken in the divine providence for children. 46443

Essay on the causes and cure of the usual
diseases. 49952

Essay on the causes of the decline of the
foreign trade. 71086

Essay on the causes of the revolution and
civil wars of Hayti. 98670

Essay on the causes of the variety of com-
plexion and figure of the human species.
84103, 84105-84106

Essay on the character and condition of the
African race. 7075, 40818

Essay on the character, manners, and genius
of women. 95376

Essay on the character of Capt. Thomas Coram.
65728

Essay on the character of Washington. 29263

Essay on the Chippeway languages. 35687

Essay on the climate of the state of New York.
33154

Essay on the climate of the United States.
22953

Essays on the coal-formation and its fossils.
60119, 72657

Essay on the commerce and products of the
Portuguese colonies. 17951

Essay on the comparative cost and productive-
ness of free and slave labour. 15170

Essay on the comparative efficiency of regulation. 13478

Essay on the congress of nations. 65732, 103738

Essay on the consolations of God whereof, a man whom his mother comforteth. 46404

Essay on the constitution and government of the United States. 33935

Essay on the constitutional power of Great-Britain. 20040, 84678C

Essay on the conversion of the Negro slaves. (27313)

Essay on the courses pursued by Great Britain. 22954

Essay on the creation. 73543

Essay on the cultivation and manufacturing of that article of West-India commerce. 42530

Essay on the culture and management of forest trees. 62975

Essay on the culture of silk and raising white mulberry trees. 102410

Essay on the currency. (14421)

Essay on the death of Capt. Josiah Winslow. 46299

Essay on the death of Mrs. Mary Brown. (46308)

Essay on the disease called yellow fever. 3112

Essay on the diseases of the internal ear. 83664

Essay on the dissolution of the union. 10889, 87818

Essay on the doctrine of the Trinity. note after 101417

Essay on the domestic debts of the United States. 43089

Essay on the earthquake of 1755. (22955)

Essay on the eclipse. 42374

Essay on the education of a young British nobleman. 37239

Essay on the effects of slavery. 22956

Essay on the eminent services and illustrious character of Henry Clay. (24908)

Essay on the enlargement of the Erie Canal. 30982

Essay on the epidemics of the winters of 1813 and 1814. 44866

Essay on the episcopate of the Protestant Episcopal Church. 23157

Essay on the erratic rocks of North America. 12951

Essay on the establishment of a chancery jurisdiction in Massachusetts. 22957, 45723, 2d note after 105499

Essay on the evils of intemperance. 91628

Essay on the expediency and practicability of improving or creating home markets. 95782

Essay on the expediency of inoculation. 43521

Essay on the fall of angels and men. 21930

Essay on the formation of rocks. 43551

Essay on the fugitive law of the U. S. Congress of 1850. 7075, 40818

Essay on the future progress and prospects of Dayton. 85615

Essay on the future state of Europe. 30426, 101161

Essay on the geology of the Hudson River. 551

Essay on the golden streets of the Holy City. (46545), note after 95317

Essay on the good effects which may be derived. 26338

Essay on the Gospel's relations to the civil law. 16338

Essay on the government of dependencies. 40804

Essay on the ground and reason of punishment. 40852

Essay on the heating and ventilation of public buildings. 84978

Essay on the history and growth of the Mercantile Library Company. 61836

Essay on the history and nature of original titles to land. (34038)

Essay, on the holy employments which are proper. 46479

Essay on the human mind and its education. 70422

Essay on the illegality of kidnapping and the slave trade. 104483

Essay on the impolicy of the African slave trade. 13479-13480

Essay on the important purpose of the Universal Redeemer's destination. 8498

Essay on the improvement in the manufacture of sugar. 36845

Essay on the increasing growth and enormities of our great cities. 36949

Essay on the influence of religion in civil society. (68663)

Essay on the influence of tobacco upon life and death. 51595

Essay on the insects and diseases injurious to the wheat crops. 31938

Essay on the inspection laws of Virginia. 73920

Essay on the intellectual, moral and religious instruction. 22958

Essay on the interest of money. 19836

Essay on the interests of Britain in regard to America. (22959)

Essay on the invention or art of making very good iron. (22134)

Essay on the inventions of both ancients & moderns. 50623

Essay on the judicial history of France. 79620

Essay on the late institution of the American Society for Colonizing the Free People of Color of the United States. (22960)

Essay on the law of God. 90199

Essay on the law of grand juries. 34740

Essay on the law of patents and new inventions. (24216), 24220

Essay on the laws of trade. 22205

Essay on the legality of impressing seamen. 22961

Essay on the liberty of the press. 84678C

Essay on the liberty of the press, respectfully inscribed. 30997

Essay on the liberty of the press, shewing that the requisition of security. 30997

Essay on the life and character of Dick Hairbrain. 97237

Essay on the life and times of the author [i. e. Samuel Davies.] 18766

Essay on the life, character and writings of John B. Gibson. 64318

Essay on the life of George Washington. 3096

Essay on the life of the Honourable Major General Israel Putnam. 24022, 33804-33805, 86106, 94058

Essay on the life of the Right Reverend Theodore Dehon. (26288)

Essay on the literary institution best adapted. 87977

Essay on the malignant pestilential fever. 12837-12838

Essay on the management of slaves. 78550

Essay on the management of the present war with Spain. 22962

Essay, on the manufacture of straw bonnets. (22963), note after 90316

Essay on the manufacturing interest of the United States. 17296, (22964)

Essay on the means of maintaining the commercial and naval interests. 22965

Essay on the means of preventing war. (4993)

Essay on the merchandise of slaves and souls of men. (21087), 78667

Essay on the military policy and institutions of the British Empire. (58992)

Essay on the mineral properties of the sweet springs of Virginia. 3090

Essay on the ministry of the holy angels. 46261

Essay on the mode of teaching the surd or deaf. 95646

Essay on the more common West-India diseases. 28248, 6th note after 102832

Essay on the natural boundaries of empires. 24353

Essay on the natural history of Guiana. 3106, 4th note after 93855

Essay on the natural history of mankind. 56040

Essay on the natural history of the prognathous race. 78259

Essay on the nature and foundation of moral virtue and obligation. 13216

Essay on the nature and glory of the Gospel. 4488

Essay on the nature and methods of carrying on a trade. 962

Essay on the nature and principles of public credit. 26361

Essay on the nature and principles of true freedom. 79269

Essay on the nature of a public spirit. 37239

Essay on the nature of a publick spirit. (37238)

Essay on the nature of colonies. 49397

Essay on the nature, source, and extent of moral freedom. 60958, note after 95318, 8th note after 102552

Essay on the nature, symptoms, and treatment, of Asiatic cholera. 104798

Essay on the necessity of correcting the errors. 23045

Essay on the necessity of improving our national forces. 96159

Essay on the oppression of the exiled sons of Africa. (7379)

Essay on the Oregon question. (47942)

Essay on the origin and uses of petroleum. 80757

Essay on the origin, progress and establishment of national society. 80042

Essay on the origins, habits, &c., of the African race. 24907

Essay on the Pacific railway. 24572

Essay on the paramount unwritten law. 25963

Essay on the penal law of Pennsylvania. 97646

Essay on the pernicious nature and destructive effects. 1619

Essay on the phenomena of dreams. (66863)

Essay on the philosophical character of W. E. Chaning [sic]. 31101

Essay on the piety which by remembering the many days of darkness, will change them. (46388)

Essay on the plurisy. 94712

Essay on the policy of appropriations. 838

Essay on the political grade of the free colored population. (19599)

Essay on the practice of duelling. (78874)

Essay on the prairies of the western country. (5563)

Essay on the present condition of the Lutheran Church in the United States. 44338

Essay on the present state of parties. 13820

Essay on the present state of the English language. 62638

Essay on the present state of the province of Nova-Scotia. 56125

Essay on the prevailing fever of 1817. (80068)

Essay on the prevailing, or yellow-fever, of 1817. (80065)

Essay on the principal branches of trade. 3170, 22966, 40532

Essay on the principles and properties of the electric fluid. (80068)

Essay on the principles of civil government. (15620)

Essay on the prize-question. 93198

Essay on the propagation of the Gospel. 17433

Essay on the rate of wages. 10842

Essay on the Red Sulphur Springs, of Virginia. 74622

Essay on the reformed mode of spelling. 102348

Essay on the registry laws of Lower Canada. 6308

Essay on the Rhustoxicodendron. (711)

Essay on the right of authors and inventors to a perpetual property. 89610

Essay on the right of conquest. 22967

Essay on the right of a state to tax a body corporate. 1543

Essay on the rights and duties of nations relative to fugitives. 1793, 23242, 2d note after 98175

Essay on the rights and duties of the Christian pulpit. 63827

Essay on the rights of government. 35484

Essay on the rights of man. 20757

Essay on the rights of neutral nations. 102369

Essay on the seat of the Federal government. (20303), 102411

Essay on the slave trade. 22968, note after 95622

Essay on the slavery and commerce of the human species. 13484

Essay. On the soiling of cattle. 67212

Essay on the south sea trade. 19277, 22969

Essay on the stage. 93291

Essay on the Star Spangled Banner and national songs. 75798

Essay on the state of England. 11200

Essay on the state of the dead. (46523)

Essay on the subject of the yellow fever. 92876

Essay on the summer and autumnal fevers of south Alabama. 93726

Essay on the tariff. (14191)

Essay on the trade, commerce, and manufactures of Scotland. 41716

Essay on the trade of the northern colonies of Great Britain. 22970

Essay on the theory of the earth. 18210

Essay on the treatment and conversion of African slaves in the sugar colonies. 67713, 67715, 67718, 82760, 96054

Essay on the treatment and management of slaves. (14448)

Essay on the trial by Jury. 89608

Essay on the true modern Caesar. 19224
Essay on the unconstitutionality of slavery.
62524
Essay on the unity of the human family.
13190
Essay on the use and advantages of the fine
arts. 22971, 97209
Essay on the value of the mines. 101116
Essay on the varieties of human species.
51022
Essay on the wages paid to females for their
labour. 97397
Essay, on the warrant, nature and duties.
49050
Essay on the ways and means of raising
money to support the present war.
(51674)
Essay on the writ of habeas corpus. 5484,
48675
Essay on the use and advantages of the fine
arts. 22971
Essay on the very seasonable & remarkable
interpositions. 46417
Essay on the warehousing system and govern-
ment credits. (22972)
Essay on the yellow fever, as it has occurred
in Charleston. 81328
Essay on the yellow fever of Jamaica.
(28302)
Essay on those acts of compliance which all
calls to piety are to be entertained
withal. 46620
Essay on toleration. 57171
Essay on trade and commerce. 22973
Essay on universal redemption. 82868
Essay on wages. 25962
Essay on war. Proving that the spirit of war.
102596
Essay on war; shewing, that the spirit of war
existing. 102597
Essay on ways and means. (22976), 67599
Essay on winter management of bees.
(49205)
Essay on wounds of the intestines. 84354
Essay on yellow fever. 55233
Essay presented. 102210
Essay . . . . Produced by the premature and
much lamented death of Mr. Joshua
Lamb. 46515
Essay read before the National Sabbath Con-
vention. 77493
Essay read before the Third Methodist State
Convention. 72643
Essay, read by W. H. Wallace. 87988
Essay read to the Pastoral Convention of New
Hampshire. 76243
Essay revealing new facts. 30874
Essay . . . seasonably to be presented.
46335
Essay showing our whole duty. (19840)
Essay; submitted . . . to the Teachers' Asso-
ciation of . . . Washington. (2316)
Essay tending to promote reformation. 55890
Essay tending to promote the kingdom of our
Lord Jesus Christ. 4404
Essay to a more correct Blason. 27284
Essay to assist the serious. 46610, note after
105468
Essay, to awaken people. 46530, 91833
Essay to block up the sinful wayes of young
people. 50303
Essay, to bring a dead soul into the way.
46529, 89479
Essay to bring the Indian language into rules.
22157, 22158

Essay to consider the sanctifying work of
grace. (46266)
Essay to convey religion into the Spanish
Indies. 46481
Essay, to defend some of the most important
principles. 13593
Essay, to demonstrate that the soldiers and
other public creditors, who really and
actually supported the burden of the late
war, have not been paid! 102412
Essay, to describe and bespeak those gracious
influences. (46287)
Essay to describe and commend the good works
of a vertuous woman. 46536
Essay to direct the frontiers of a countrey
exposed. 46332
Essay to discover the principal causes.
(26702)
Essay to do good. 25941
Essay, to dry up a fountain of, confusion and
every evil work. 46514, note after
85661
Essay to excite and assist religious approaches.
46419
Essay to excite and assist . . . the instruction.
46426
Essay, to manage an act of trespass. (46341)
Essay to prepare a pious woman for her lying-
in. 22186, 46302, (46621)
Essay to prove, that when God once enters
upon a controversie. 104208
Essay to prove the interest of the children of
believers. 104400
Essay to render parents and children happy in
one another. 46324
Essay to revive and encourage military
exercises. 59374
Essay, to revive the true and ancient mode of
singing. 94117
Essay, to shew the nature, causes, and effects.
94105
Essay to silence the outcry that has been
made. (21521)
Essay to solve the difficulties. 65573
Essay to the translation of Virgil's AEneis.
57984, 76458
Essay, to which, . . . was awarded. (60795)
Essay: to which was awarded the first prize.
32421
Essay toward forming a more complete repre-
sentation. 38894
Essay toward the vindication of the Committee
of Correspondence. 3262
Essay towards a brotherly peace & union.
35063
Essay towards a catalogue of the phaenogamous
plants. 18595
Essay towards a method of preserving the
seeds of plants. 66626
Essay towards a new course of national farm-
ing. 67791
Essay towards a plan for the more effectual
civilization. 64326
Essay towards an analysis of the principles by
which men naturally judge. 82314
Essay towards an improved register of deeds.
(28847)
Essay towards an Indian bibliography. 24294
Essay towards an instruction for the Indians.
104690-104691
Essay towards giving some just ideas. 71407
Essay towards promoting all necessary and
useful knowledge. 7476
Essay towards propagating the Gospel. 34646
Essay towards the establishing the fishery of
Great Britain. (77191)

Essay towards the most ancient histories. (25414)

Essay towards the topography. 24336, 34355, (34358)

Essay towards the vindication of the Committee of Correspondence. 3267

Essay . . . under the signature of Oglethorpe. 20423, 56849

Essay, upon a case too commonly calling for consideration. 46491

Essay upon a Christian considered as a temple. 46254

Essay upon a late expedient for taking away all impositions. (17332)

Essay upon, a happy departure. (46362), 101016

Essay upon field husbandry in New England. 22135

Essay upon government. 22974

Essay upon incurables. 46368

Essay upon plantership. 44920

Essay upon repentance to the last. 46291

Essay upon that case. 46492

Essay upon that paradox. 12362, 101194

Essay upon the act of the General Assembly of Virginia. 100462

Essay upon the advantages to be derived from new colonies. 47492, 94259

Essay upon the blessings and comforts reserved for pious children. 46446

Essay upon the constitutional rights as to slave property. 22975, 72064

Essay upon the existence of a north-west passage. 20405

Essay, upon the Godly and glorious improvements. (46558), 2d note after 96762

Essay upon the good education of children. 46272

Essay upon the good, that is to be devised and designed. 46238, 46305

Essay upon the government of the English plantations. (22976)

Essay upon the idolatry. 46364

Essay upon the king's friends. 22977

Essay upon the methods of conversing with a glorious Christ. 46357

Essay upon the mighty shakes. 46507

Essay upon the origin and progress, mental and physical, of the Negro race. 31027

Essay upon the origin of free masonry. 95315

Essay upon the peace of 1783. 24725

Essay upon the principles of political economy. (63766)

Essay upon the raising and breeding of sheep. 8676

Essay upon the silk worm. 3375

Essay upon the wines and strong drinks of the ancient Hebrews. 93199

Essay upon withering flowers. 46583

Essay, upon the Godly. (46558)

Essay, with memorial of the artists and manufacturers of Philadelphia to Congress. 44431

Essayes and religious meditations of Sir Francis Bacon. 39820, 1st note after 94666

Essayes; or, observations divine and morall. 72096-72097

Essayist, or literary cabinet. 93238

Essays about the poor, manufacturers, trade, plantations. 4542

Essays against the repeal of the bankrupt law. 22978

Essays, agricultural and literary. 28399

Essays: and a drama in five acts. 32501

Essays and lectures. 43661

Essays and letters on various political subjects. 105480-105481

Essays and notes on husbandry and rural affairs. (6414)

Essays and observations physical and literary. (22979)

Essays and reviews chiefly on theology, politics, and socialism. (8713)

Essays and reviews. Selected from the Princeton review. (32330)

Essays, being introductions drawn from the Baconian philosophy. 11165

Essays by different hands. 21641, note after 90311

Essays [by John Foster.] (25241)

Essays by Sydney Smith. 84304-84306, 84321

Essays chiefly philological and ethnographical. 39167

Essays commercial and political. 22980

Essays concerning iron and steel. 33031

Essays designed to elucidate the science of political economy. 22981, 28492

Essays ecclesiastical and social. (16226)

Essays ethnological and linguistic. 37398

Essays for summer hours. 38918

Essays for the forecastle. 82122

Essays from Poulson's Daily advertiser. 10758

Essays from the desk of Poor Robert the Scribe. 64080

Essays, historical, moral, political and agricultural. 44436

Essays, humorous, moral, and literary. 25500, 25534, 25536, 102487

Essays, humorous, moral & literary, chiefly in the manner of the Spectator. (25600), 102487

Essays; including biographical and miscellaneous pieces. 63351

Essays, literary and political. 11924

Essays, literary, moral & philosophical. 74217

Essays, literary, moral and philosophical. 74223

Essays mainly written in hot countries. 75547

Essays, moral, dramatic, poetical. 84137

Essays of Howard. 33237

Essays of Philanthropos on peace & war. 38526

Essays of Phocion. 97915

Essays [of Ralph Waldo Emerson.] 22455

Essays on American silk. 32731

Essays on astronomy. 91585

Essays on asylums for inebriates. 105166

Essays on asylums for persons of unsound mind. 26459

Essays on banking. 10889

Essays on capital punishments. 62431-62432

Essays on domestic industry. 28719

Essays on fevers. 49203-49204, 1st-2d notes after 97444

Essays on human rights and their political guaranties. 33997

Essays on husbandry. 30651

Essays on husbandry, addressed to the Canadian farmers. 28479-(28480)

Essays on imprisonment for debt. 89065-89066

Essays on Italy and Ireland. 65746

Essays on lay representation and church government. 85442

Essays on malaria and temperance. 9899

Essays on natural history. 102094

Essays on political economy. 10866

Essays on political organization. 22982

Essays on political society. (22983)
Essays on practical education. 77887
Essays on property and labour. (40976)
Essays on railroads. 10889
[Essays] on regeneration. 5746
Essays on select passages of sacred composition. 93351
Essays on several subjects. 5999
Essays on slavery. 2640
Essays on slavery; re-published from the Boston recorder & telegraph. 99610
Essays on some important subjects. 68783
Essays on taxation and reconstruction. 20334, 78401
Essays on Texas. 30194, note after 95080
Essays on the American system. 94090
Essays on the coal-formation and its fossils. 72657
Essay on the confusion of tongues. 36525
Essay on the cultivation of the tea plant. 83460
Essay on the elective franchise. 30186
Essays on the following subjects. 106079
Essays on the foreign relations of England. (34933)
Essays on the liberty of the press. (44479)
[Essays] on the means . . . of grace. 5746
Essays on the natural equality of man. 102492
Essays on the origin of pauperism and crime. 22984
Essays on the origin of the federal government. 22985
Essays on the preaching required by the times. 91475
Essays on the present crisis in the condition of the American Indians. 23200
Essays on the principles of political economy. (22986)
Essays on the progress of nations. 78604
Essays on the progress of nations, in civilization. 78606-78607
Essays on the progress of nations, in productive industry. 78605
Essays on the protecting system. 10889, 22987
Essays on the public charities of Philadelphia. 10871, 10889
Essays on the punishment of death. 89066
Essays on . . . the Sacraments. 5746
Essays on the soiling of cattle. (67213)
Essays on the spirit of Jacksonism. 1978, (43402)
Essays on the U. S. Constitution. 80405
Essays on the use of distilled spirits. 96287
Essays on the usurpations of the Federal government. 8776, 17534, note after 97466
Essays on the "will of the people." 92855
Essays on trade and navigation. 7778
Essays on various subjects in morals and literature. (12270)
Essays on various subjects, notes and queries, etc. 34794
Essays on various subjects of medical science. 33089
Essays on various subjects of taste, morals, and national policy. 97300
Essays on woman's true destiny. 44855
Essays, originally published in the Connecticut herald. 96123, 1st note after 105926
Essays, philanthropic and moral. 11855
Essays, political, economical, and philosophical. 95466
Essays, political, historical, and miscellaneous. 770

Essays social and political. 84309-84310, 84313
Essays, social and political, 1802-1825. 84307, 84312
Essays, social and political. Second series. 84308, 84311
Essays tending to prove the ruinous effects of the policy. 10867
Essays to do good. 46307, 46469
Essays upon authors and books. 36627
Essays upon field-husbandry in New-England. 22136
Essays upon French spoliations. 24629
Essays upon popular education. 11117
Essays upon the making of salt-petre and gun-powder. 22988, 1st note after 96762
Essence and unitie of the Church Catholike Visible. 33495
Essence of agriculture. 98632
Essence of old Kentucky. 12955
Essence of slavery. 17360
Essential principles of the art of war. 44651
Essential requisites to form the good ruler's character. 103760
Essential rights and liberties of protestants. 22990, 104221
Essential rights of the Americans. 836, 81586-81588, 94006
Essentials in Church history. 83349
Essequibo (Colony) Laws, statutes, etc. 22996-22998
Essex, Robert Devereux, 2d Earl of, 1566-1601. 66686
Essex, (Brig) 22999
Essex, N. H. Phillips Exeter Academy. see Phillips Exeter Academy, Essex, N. H.
Essex County, Mass. Bar. (23009)
Essex County, Mass. Convention, Ipswich, 1778. 58906, 99826
Essex County, Mass. Convention, Ipswich, 1812. 23003
Essex County, Mass. Grand Jury. 79942
Essex County, Mass. House of Correction. 23008
Essex County, Mass. Meeting of Delegates from the Several Towns, Topsfield, 1808. (23007)
Essex County, N. J. Court of Common Pleas. 72620, note after 96880
Essex County, N. Y. Board of Supervisors. 23017
Essex County, Va. 100071
Essex Agricultural Society. (23004)-23005, 74345, 97257
Essex Agricultural Society. Trustees. 97257-97258
Essex almanack for the year . . . 1773. 23006, 62743
Essex almanack, for the year of the Lord Christ, 1770. 62540, 62743
Essex almanack for the years 1770 and 1771. (25776)
Essex Baptist Association. see Baptists. New York. Essex Baptist Association.
Essex Company, Lawrence, Mass. 23000
Essex County directory for the year . . . 1866. 23001
Essex County Natural History Society. (23010)
Essex County Washingtonian extra. 62781
Essex gazette. (65236), 86867, 94006
Essex gazette. News boy. see Weeden, Job.
Essex harmony . . . by Jacob Kimball, Jun. 37756
Essex harmony; containing a collection of psalm tunes. 4050
Essex Historical Society, Salem, Mass. 23011

Essex Institute, Salem, Mass. 7947, 23012-
23016, 65006, (71882), (78526), 88922,
92784
Essex Institute, Salem, Mass. Charter.
23015
Essex Institute, Salem, Mass. Committee on
the First Church of the Pilgrims.
23016, 75688
Essex Institute historical collections. 7947,
23014, 65006
Essex journal. 95255
Essex junto and the British spy. 23020,
(31399)
Essex junto exposed. (30196), 103851-103852
Essex junto, or Quixotic guardian. 23019
Essex memorial, for 1836. 54994
Essex register. 20227, 83826
Essex, SS. Supreme Judicial Court. 85212
Essex-Street Church, Boston. see Boston.
Essex-Street Church.
Essex Street Religious Society, Boston. see
Boston. Union Church.
Esslingen, ------- Mayer von. see Mayer
von Esslingen, --------.
Essordio. 67736
Esta es vna carta que el muy ilustre Senor
Don Hernando Cortes. 16941
Esta inguena expresion. 99677
Esta presente el oficial aprendiz. 94598
Establecimiento cientifico. 41330
Establecimiento de la Inquisicion en el nuevo
mundo. 93348
Establecimiento i progresos de las misiones.
(34155)
Establidad permanente del gobierno religioso.
106283
Established or Parochial Schoolmasters in
Scotland. Commissioner. petitioner
84628 see also Smith, William, 1727-
1803.
Establishing of courts of judicature. 54975
Establishments of protestant missionaries and
schools. (2320)
Establishment of the English colonies in
America. 6210
Establissements philanthropiques aux Etats-
Unis. 4998
Estabrook, A. 52202
Estabrook, Hobart. (23021)-23022
Estabrook, Joseph. see Easterbrooks, Joseph,
fl. 1705.
Estabrook, Joseph, fl. 1819. 23024
Estabrook, Samuel. (23025)
Estabrooks, Henry L. (23026)
Estacio do Amaral, Melchior. 23027
Estadas que acompanan la memoria. 48454
Estadistica bibliografica de la literatura
Chilena. 8013
Estadistica comercial de la republica de Chile,
correspondiente al ano de 1866. 12769
Estadistica comercial de la republica de Chile,
correspondiente al primer semestre del
ano de 1857. 12768
Estadistica comercial de la republica de Chile
correspondiente al primer trimestre de
1844. 12767
Estadistica de Espana. (50554)
Estadistica de la republica de Chile Provincia
del Maule. (12770)
Estadistica de la republica Mejicana. 31522
Estadistica de Yucatan. (68805)
Estadistica del Colegio de Abogados. (48455)
Estadistica del imperio Mexicano. (48456)
Estadistica general de la provincia de Caracas.
10776

Estadistica general de la republica del
Salvador. 76201
Estadistica, historica, geografica, etc. de los
pueblos. 16779
Estadistica jeneral de la Nueva Granada.
56275
Estadistico de Ialisco. 35552
Estado actual de Chihuahua. 12691
Estado actual de la isla de Cuba. 17771
Estado de Antioquia. 60990
Estado de Bolivar. 60990
Estado de Boyaca. 60990
Estado de colectura y tesoreria. 23030
Estado de Cundinamarca. 60900
Estado de Magdalena. 60900
Estado de Occidente. 23208
Estado de Panama. 60900
Estado de Santander. 60900
Estado de Tolima. 60900
Estado de Veracruz a toso los Federacion
Megicana. 76747, 96967
Estado del Colegio de Ocopa. 85681, 97711
Estado del Convento de Goatemala [sic].
50036
Estado del Hospital Gral de S. Juan de Dios
de Guatemala. 29076
Estado demonstrativo o indice alfebetico.
(48457)
Estado general de la isla de Cuba. 67636
Estado general de la poblacion de la isla en
1817. 17772
Estado general de las misiones de la provincia
de California. 38381, 56007, (75765)
Estado general de las misiones que tiene a
su cargo. 23029
Estado general que presenta al Ministerio de
Fomento. 38625
Estado Mayor General del Ejercito. 48458
Estado militar de la isla de Cuba. 17773
Estado presente de la Comision de Residencia
del Gobierno. 106232
Estado politico de Guatemala. 29075
Estado politico del reyno del Peru. 61124
Estado provisional del imperio Mexicano.
48459
Estado que manifiesta los bienes que posee
cada una. 38381, 56007, (75765)
Estados de America. 13837
Estados Unidos de Colombia. see Colombia.
Estados Unidos de Colombia . . . . Comprende
la jeografia. 60900
Estados varios. 29413
Estados y constituciones relaes de la Imperial
y Regia Universidad de Mexico. 48662
Estafas escandalosas. 29430, 96194
Estafette. 16184, (37604), 72547
Estaing, Charles Hector, Comte d'. (23031)-
23034
Estaing, Charles Hector, Comte d'. supposed
author 23034, 28331
Estala, Pedro. Presbitero ed. and tr.
19360, 23580, 99403
Estancelin, L. 23035
Estang, Simon Philibert de la Salle de l'. see
La Salle de l'Estang, Simon Philibert de,
d. 1765.
Estas si con claridades. 76747
Estat de l'eglise avec le discorse des temps.
23036
Estat general des debtes passives. (56087)
Estat present de l'eglise. 23037, 38506,
66978
Estate, Miguel de. see Estete, Miguel de.
Estate of Charles S. Boker. defendants 50152
Estatera juridica balanza. 75880

Estatistica do commercio maritimo do Brazil. 85626

Estatistica historica-geographica da Provincia da Maranhao. (38621)

Estats, esquels il est discouru du prince. 24917

Estatua del General San Martin. 76156

Estatuto de recolcimento de M. S. de Gloria de logar de Boa-Visita de Pernambuco. (17200)

Estatuto provisional dado. 61125

Estatuto provisional para la direccion y administracion. 9013

Estatutos da Companhia do Queimado. (66077)

Estatutos da Provincia de S. Antonio do Brasil. 75989

Estatutos da Sociedade Commercio da Provincia da Bahia. 85769

Estatutos de California. 10030

Estatutos de la Compania del Ferro-Carril de Mexico a Puebla. 48460

Estatutos de la Real Academia de San Carlos de Nueva-Espana. 68220

Estatutos de la Real Sociedad Economica . . . aprobados por el Rey. 85743

Estatutos de la Real Sociedad Economica de la Habana. 85744

Estatutos de la Santa Iglesia de Mexico, 1585, revisados. 48461

Estatutos de la Sociedad Anomina Denominada Banco Industrial. 23038, 29431

Estatutos de la Sociedad Anomina Titulada: La Colonizadora. 85716

Estatutos de la Sociedad de los Amigos del Bien Publico. 85732

Estatutos de la Sociedad Economica de Mexico. 48462

Estatutos de la Sociedad Patriotica de la Havana. 85745

Estatutos del Real Colegio de Escribanos de Mexico. 48463

Estatos del Real e Ilustre Colegio de Abogados de Puerto Principe. 66587

Estatutos del Real e Ilustre Colegio de Abogados de San Ignacio de Loyola. 66587

Estatutos do Instituto Historico e Geographico Brasileiro fundado no Rio de Janeiro. 71464

Estatutos do Instituto Historico e Geographico Brasileiro, installado no Rio de Janeiro. 7574

Estatvtos generales de Barcelon. 48464, 57469, 76105

Estatutos municipaes da Provincia da Immaculada Conceycao do Brazil. 11736, 66386

Estatutos novos do Instituto Historico e Geographico Brasileiro. 71464

Estatutos y constituciones del Colegio de Abogados. (48465)

Estatvtos y constitvciones hechsa con comission particvlar. 58292, 86444

Estatvtos, y constitvciones reales de la Imperial, y Regia Vniversidad de Mexico. 58292, 86444

Estatutos y ordenanciones segun la bulas. 23039

Estatutos y reglamento interior. 85733

Estatutos y reglamento interno. 85757

Estaugh, John. 23040-23041

Estava, Fernan Gonzalez de. see Gonzalez de Estava, Fernan.

Estcourt, J. H. 4319, (23042)

Este, D. K. 23043

Este es vn co[m]pe[n]dio breue. 71100-71101

Este es vn trotado quel Obispo dele ciudad real de Chiapo do Fray Bartholome de las Casas, o Casaus compuso. 11230, 11235, 11245-11247, 11267, 11289

Este si es papel. 95368

Estee, C. F. 23044

Estefas escandalosas. 23943

Estela Escalante, Francisco de la. see Escalante, Francisco de la Estela.

Estella, Joseph Miguel de Ossera y. see Ossera y Estella, Joseph Miguel de.

Esten, ------. 85421

Esten, Cornelius. 60714, 95967

Esterbrooks, -------, fl. 1793. (18879), 105488

Esterly, George. supposed author 89112

Esterretning om Rudera eller Levninger. 95614

Estes, Benjamin H. 23045

Estes, Matthew. 23046

Estete, Miguel de. 105724

Esteva, Gonzalo A. (23047), 69596

Esteva, J. Y. see Esteva, Jose Ignacio.

Esteva, Jose Ignacio. 23048-23050

Estevan, Ricardo. supposed author 86259

Esteves, -------. plaintiffs 25480

Estevez, Pablo. supposed author 39250

Esteyneffer, Hermano Juan de. see Steinefer, Johann.

Esteyneffer, Juan de. see Steinefer, Johann.

Esther. (53426)

Esther, and other poems. 36853, 106372

Esther Institute, Columbus, Ohio. (23052)

Esthetics in collegiate education. (14944)

Estill, William. 87818

Estimate for deepening the bar of Sullivan's Island. (2588), 12081

Estimate of certain expenses. 10450

Estimate of commercial advantages. 94794

Estimate of revenue and expenditure. (56126)

Estimate of the comparative strength of Great Britain. 11760

Estimate of the financial effect of the proposed reservation. (73397)

Estimate of the political crisis. 24095

Estimate of the probable amount of the expense. 85234

Estimate of the public services. 57732

Estimate of the receipts and expenditures. 66259

Estimate of the revenue. 96319

Estimate of the temperature of different latitudes. 38013

Estimates for the enlargement of the aqueduct. (50241)

Estimates of appropriations. (34647)

Estimates of the . . . interoceanic ship canal. 12739

Estimation de la temperature. 38014

Estimauville, Robert d'. (23053)

Estimauville, Robert d'. supposed author 100851

Estirpe Vespasiana. 40076

Estlacke, Francis. (23054)

Estlin, J. B. (23055)-23056, (81913)

Esto es esperanza de Israel. (44191)

Esto pertetua. 14842

Eston, Lilley. 68207

Estourneau, J. tr. 93887

Estracto alphabetico. 29432

Estracto de las sesiones. 85767

Estracto de noticias. 76009

Estracto de varias cedulas y cartas del Rey. 94352

Estrada, Alvaro Florez. see Florez Estrada, Alvaro, 1766?-1854?

Estrada, Antonio Nicolas, Duque de. 55247
Estrada, Francisco. 23060
Estrada, Francisco de Mier Cazo y. see
  Mier Cazo y Estrada, Francisco de.
Estrada, Francisco Lazo. defendant (23061)
Estrada, Ignacio Francisco de. plaintiff
  64176, 99624
Estrada, J. E. 23066
Estrada, J. M. Guitterez de. see Guitterez
  de Estrada, Jose Maria, 1800-1867.
Estrada, Jose Manuel. (23065), (23067)-
  (23068), 70298
Estrada, Joseph Manuel de. (23069)
Estrada, Juan de. 23062
Estrada, Juan de Urizar y. see Urizar y
  Estrada, Juan de.
Estrada, Manuel Urrutia de Vergara y. see
  Urrutia de Vergara y Estrada, Manuel.
Estrada, Sebastian de. 23071
Estrada de Medinilla, Maria. see Medinilla,
  Maria Estrada de.
Estrada Medinilla, Maria de. see Medinilla,
  Maria Estrada de.
Estrada y Escouedo, Francisco de. (69218)
Estrada y Escovedo, Pedro de. 23070
Estrada y Lecler, M. D. (23072)
Estrado, T. Maria. 55143
Estrados de Mina, Carolino. see Mina,
  Carolino Estrados de.
Estrange, A. G. l'. see L'Estrange, A. G.
Estrange, Hanson l'. see L'Estrange, Hanson.
Estrange, Sir Roger l'. see L'Estrange, Sir
  Roger, 1616-1704.
Estranjeros. 99482
Estrato de varias cartas dirigidas al soberano.
  94352
Estratto dall' antologia. (28181)
Estrella de el norte de Mexico. 24806-
  24807
Estrella del Norte de Mexico. 24808
Estrella de Lima. (21765)
Estrella mas hermosa. 93327
Estreum fulmen in Batavorum. (44967)
Estrille de Nicolas Durand. 99725
Estrille, pour blason d'armoiries. 99725
Estrup, H. F. J. 23073
Estudantes da Bahia. 66901
Estvdio. note after 99383C
Estudio de la filosofia y riqueza de la lengua
  Mexicana. 73161
Estudio de los animales. (39067)
Estudio geologico-historico. 72785
Estudio geologico presentado a la Sociedad de
  Ciencias Fisicas y Naturales de Caracas.
  72783
Estudio geologico sobre los terremotos y
  temblores de tierra. 72781
Estudio historico. 62942
Estudio historico de Bolivia. 87251
Estudio historico sobre la raza indigena de
  Yucatan. 11053
Estudio seismologico. 70169
Estudio sobre a colonisacao Brasileira.
  70810
Estudio sobre las minas de oro de la isla de
  Cuba. 11464
Estudios biografico-bibliograficos. 85683
Estudios biograficos, historicos y arqueologicos.
  67657
Estudios biograficos y criticos sobre algunos
  poetas. 29342
Estudios economico-politicos. 23074
Estudios estadisticos. 26109
Estudios historicos. (67124)
Estudios historicos, politicos y sociales.
  11713, (43798)

Estudios historicos sobre la revolucion
  Argentina. 49756
Estudios historicos, y estadisticos del estado
  Oaxaqueno. 11047
Estudios indigenas. 72782
Estudios preparatorios. 12771
Estudios progresivos. 70457
Estudios recreativos, historicos y morales.
  (4904)
Estudios sobre a emancipacao dos escravos
  no Brasil. 52356
Estudios sobre as primeiras tentativas para a
  independencia nacional. 55452, 88804
Estudios sobre la America. 27343
Estudios sobre la aplicacion de la justicia
  federal. 26586
Estudios sobre la constitucion Argentina de
  1853. 651
Estudios sobre la constitution de los Estados-
  Unidos. 28435
Estudios sobre las Quiebras. 50609
Estudios sobre los Estados Unidos. (31478)
Estudios sobre los partidos. 7796
Estudo de direito constitucional. 7598
Estudo por Theodoro Parker. (58745)
Estudos de Innocencio Francisco da Silva.
  (81083)
Estudos praticos. 85641
Estudos sobre a emancipacao dos escravos no
  Brazil. (81111)
Estudos sobre o credito rural. 38453
Estudos sobre o ensino publico. 81106
Estudos sobre reforma administrativa. (3901)
Estvan, B. 23075-23076
Estwick, Samuel. (15998), 16002, 23077-
  23079, 1st note after 102801
Estwick, Samuel. supposed author 44259, 2d
  note after 102802
Estwick Evans for the presidency. (23149)
Esty, William C. 85386
Eszler, Jacobus. ed. (66478)
Et sicut illud statutum est hominibus. 33134
Etado [sic] de Filipinas en 1810. 15084
Etablissement de la Compagnie du Canada.
  10442
Etaples, Jacques le Fevre d'. see Le Fevre,
  Jacques, d'Etaples, d. 1537.
Etat actuel des lettres dans l'Amerique. 11924
Etat actuel des populations indigenes dans les
  diverses colonies Europeennes. 79044
Etat actuel des transactions dans les
  principales contrees. 50552
Etat d'Alabama. 29556
Etat de Costa-Rica. (64716)
Etat de Georgie. 101350
Etat de la cause. 94126
Etat de la partie Espagnole de Saint-Domingue.
  (3305)
Etat de la question. (23547)
Etat des colonies et du commerce des Europeens.
  (61313)
Etat des finances de Saint-Domingue, contenant
  le resume des recettes & depenses de
  toutes les caisses, depuis le 1er Janvier
  1789. 65980
Etat des finances de Saint-Domingue, contenant
  le resume des recettes et depenses de
  toutes les caisses publiques, depuis le
  10 Nov. 1785. 3304
Etat des finances de Saint-Domingue, contenant
  le resume des recettes et depenses de
  toutes les caisses publiques depuis le
  1er Janvier 1788. (3305)
Etat des finances de Saint Domingue depuis
  Janvier 1789. 63714

Etat des finances de Saint-Domingue [depuis le 1er Janvier 1788.] 75110
Etat des isles Danoises aux Indes Occidentales. 58043
Etat des sommes depensees a mem l'octroi de £30,000. 6944
Etat du personnel de la marine et des colonies. 23080
Etat et avenir du Canada en 1854. 22117
Etat et ses limites. 38436
Etat general de la marine et des colonies. 23081
Etat militaire de la Grande Bretagne. 28433
Etat physique, politique, ecclesiastique & militaire de l'Amerique. 941
Etat physique, politique, ecclesiastique et militaire de l'Asie. 941
Etat present de la Caroline Meridionale. 66723
Etat present de la Grande-Bretagne. (23082)
Etat-present de la Louisiane. 11824
Etat present de la Pensylvanie. 19370, 84594
Etat present de l'eglise et de la colonie Francoise. 66978
Etat present du pais. 5115-5117, 2d note after 100478
Etats Confederes d'Amerique visites en 1863. 23083, (27480)
Etats Confederes et l'esclavage. 76968
Etats des colonies Francaises pour 1837. 14710
Etats du nord-west et Chicago. 25970
Etats, empires, et principautes du monde. 18913, 41288, note after 105742
Etats ou empires du monde. 18911
Etats-Unis. 24125
Etats-Unis. A M. Casimir Delavigne. 11810
Etats-Unis d'Amerique. Apercu statistique. 27897
Etats-Unis d'Amerique en 1863. 5303
Etats-Unis d'Amerique et l'Angleterre. 36416
Etats-Unis d'Amerique. Histoire de la guerre civile Americaine. 16929
Etats-Unis d'Amerique. Les etats du nord-west et Chicago. 25970
Etats-Unis d'Amerique. Moeurs, usages et coutumes politiques. 64737
Etats-Unis d'Amerique, ou tableau de l'agriculture. 8048
Etats-Unis d'Amerique. Par M. Roux de Rochelle. 73516
Etats-Unis de l'Amerique. 23085
Etats-Unis de l'Amerique a la fin du XVIIIe siecle. 6323
Etats-Unis de l'Amerique. Pieces officielles. 23085, 59593, 62702, 103848
Etats Unis de l'Amerique Septentrionale. 47107
Etats-Unis de l'Amerique Septentrionale, leurs origines. 26088
Etats-Unis de l'Angleterre. 39803
Etats-Unis, depuis 1812 jusqu'a nos jours. (68924)
Etats-Unis en 1800. 93272
Etats-Unis en 1865. 44115
Etats-Unis en 1866. 23086
Etats-Unis en 1861. Par Georges Fisch. 24415
Etats-Unis en 1861. Un grand peiple qui se relevo. 26728
Etats-Unis et autres pays du nord de l'Amerique. 4641
Etats-Unis et la France. 38436-(38437)
Etats-Unis et la Havana. 42505
Etats Unis et l'Angleterre. 39803

Etats-Unis et le Mexique. 21348
Etats-Unis et le Russie. (24694)
Etats-Unis et l'Europe. (56053)
Etats-Unis, jusqu'en 1812. 73517
Etats-Unis il y a quarante ans. 10788
Etats-Unis, le self-gouvernement et le Cesarisme. 64191
Etats-Unis pendant la guerre (1861-1865) 39238
Etats-Unis. Suite de la correspondance relative aux affaires de Mexique. 48258
&c. 93221
Etches, John. 23087-23088
Etchings by Samuel Lover, Esq. 43846
Etchings from the Naval Academy. 4711
Etchings from the sketch-book of a country pastor. 82389
Etchings of a whaling cruise. 8658
Eternal salvation on no account a matter of just debt. 82214
Eternal truths. 36971
Eternity of God. 917
Eternity of hell torments. 103511
Ethan Allen and the Green-Mountain heroes of '76. (19651)
Ethan Allen; or, the King's men. 805, (47484)
Ethan Allen papers. 801, 6th note after 99005
Ethan Allen's captivity. 797
Ethan Allen's narrative of the capture of Ticonderoga. 799
Ethel Somers. 23089, 35357, (45041)
Ethelyn's mistake. 32616
Ether and chloroform. 5293
Ether controversy. 6998
Ether discovery. 90329
Etheridge, Emerson, 1819-1902. 23090
Etheridge, Robert. (35584)
Etherization; with surgical remarks. 101475
Ethic strains. 56722
Ethica: or the first principles of moral philosophy. 36293
Ethica, or things relating to moral behavior. 36291
Ethical essay. 32673
Ethices elementa. 23091, 36294
Ethics and policy of the American civil war. 33441
Ethics of American slavery. 23092, 1st note after 95517
Ethics of mursing. 84259
Ethiopean or Negro-slave. pseud. Discourse in way of dialogue. see Tryon, Thomas.
Ethiopia. Ambassador to the Vatacan. 67730 see also Alvarez, Francesco, 16th cent.
Ethiopia: her gloom and glory. 12952
Ethiopian drama, no. 11. 83022
Ethiopian manifiesto. 106097
Ethiopian melodies. (76462)
Ethnographisch und mit ausfuhrlicher Berucksichtiging des culturgeschichtlichen Stoffes. 37164
Ethnographische Skizzen. 32572
Ethnographischen Archiv, Jena. 7389, 9143, 14073, 73378, 91691, 94230, 101113
Ethnography and philology. 29635
Ethnography of the Gran Chaco. 5933
Ethnological and philological essays. 37399
Ethnological and philological table. (67442)
Ethnological memoir. 85016
Ethnological researches, based upon the ancient monuments. 56040
Ethnological researches, respecting the red men in America. 77849
Ethnological Society, London. 36721

Ethnology. 68476
Ethnology of the British colonies and dependencies. 39164
Ethridge's record exposed. 5365
Etienne, -------. 23093, note after 98620
Etienne, Sylvian Saint. see Saint-Etienne, Sylvian.
Etliche Anmerkungen uber den Zustand und Gemuths-Beschaffenheit. 89175
Etliche zu dieser Zeit. 23094, note after 106352
Etlicher Brieff so ausz Hispania kumme seindt. 16663, 63176
Etna van de noir. (30191)
Etoiles filantes observees a la Havane. 63667
Etourneau, -------. 23095-23097
Etranger. pseud. Paraguay. 58525
Etrennes Americaines. 64179
Etrennes d'Apollon. (42849)
Etshitt thlu sitskai thlu siais thlu sitskaisitlinish. 101041
Etter, Joseph. 81582
Ettwein, John. 86174, 97862
Etude biographique. Le Chevalier Noel Brulart de Sillery. (81022)
Etude biographique, par M. de la Roquette. (73151)
Etude d'archeologie Americaine comparee. 73310
Etude de l'emancipation. (39638)
Etude de l'ouvrage Hollandais du Dr. W. R. van Hoevell. 86209
Etude de moeurs contemporaines. 27692
Etude de moeurs electorales. 77109
Etude de moeurs et coutumes Americaines. 14939
Etude economique, politique et financiere. 44342
Etude economique sur le mate ou the du Paraguay. 19471
Etude et solution nouvelle de la question Haitienne. 40129
Etude fait devant le Cabinet de Lecture de Montreal. (19684)
Etude historique Canadienne. 18363
Etude historique et critique des Cayes (Haiti) 6160
Etude historique et critique, suivis de notes. 42355, (75482)
Etude historique et d'economie politique. 64737
Etude historique et economique au point de vue de l'etat actuel. 44343
Etude historique par M. Alphonse Dantier. 18509
Etude litteraire sur Chateaubriand. (12261)
Etude monographique et historique. 75483
Etude sur la revolution des Etats-Unis. 77423
Etude sur le droit de visite. 8387
Etude sur le Perou. 14755
Etude sur les explorations Arctiques de McClure. 40008
Etude sur les rapports de l'Amerique. 26294
Etude sur l'esclavage aux Etats-Unis. 11916
Etude sur l'industrie huitriere des Etats-Unis. (8149)
Etude sur l'ouvrage. 92527
Etude sur l'union projetee des provinces Britanniques. 11559
Etude sur Mirabeau, par Victor Hugo. 49399
Etude technique et administrative. 93234
Etudes ante-historiques. 72775
Etudes biographiques et litteraires. 38910
Etudes d'artillerie navale. 959

Etudes de theologie. 18490, 23098
Etudes. Des interets reciproques de l'Europe et de l'Amerique. (64699)
Etudes des sciences sociales. (81455)-81456
Etudes d'ethnographie et d'archeologie Americaines. 73310
Etudes d'histoire religieuse. (69597)
Etudes economiques sur l'Amerique Meridionale. 19472
Etudes et avant-projet d'un institution financiere. 39636
Etudes et considerations sur ce pays. 64727
Etudes et recherches biographiques. 81021
Etudes geographiques et historiques. (44646)
Etudes Hispano-Americaines. (74917)
Etudes historiques et statistiques. 73929
Etudes historiques sur le Mexique au point de vue politique et social. 38382, 48466
Etudes historiques. Voyage en Amerique. 12255
Etudes philologiques sur quelques langues sauvages. 17980
Etudes physiognomiques sur la vegetation. 4834
Etudes politiques. 23794
Etudes speciales sur les fleurs de la Guyane Francaise. 39599
Etudes sur la colonisation. (20890)
Etudes sur la famille des Vespides. 77208
Etudes sur la Guianne Francaise. 73514
Etudes sur la litterature et les moeurs des Anglo-Americains. (12218)
Etudes sur la societe en France. (41845)
Etudes sur l'Amerique Espagnole. 38602
Etudes sur le Bresil au point de vue. 11179
Etudes sur le developpement de la colonisation. 20891
Etudes sur le developpement de la race Francaise. 67622
Etudes sur le systeme graphique et la langue de Mayas. (44433), 49464
Etudes sur l'emancipation dans les colonies. 12579
Etudes sur les colonies agricoles et mendiants. 42715
Etudes sur les constitutions des peuples libres. (81455)-81456
Etudes sur les dernieres explorations du globe. (21011)
Etudes sur les fruits de la Guyane Francaise. 39600
Etudes sur les maladies des colonies. (40730)
Etudes sur les mollusques terrestres et fluviatiles. 24425
Etudes sur les myriapodes. 77213
Etudes sur les origines bouddhiques de la civilization Americaine. (22077)
Etudes sur les reformateurs contemporains. 70390
Etudes sur les reformateurs ou socialistes modernes. 70390
Etudes sur les travaux. (57969)
Etudes sur l'esclavage aux Etats-Unis. 5267
Etudes sur l'histoire d'Haiti. 1928
Etudes sur l'histoire primitive des races Oceaniennes et Americaines. 22076
Etudes sur l'isle de la Guadeloupe. 71253
Etudes sur l'instruction publique chez les Canadiens Francais. 51648
Etudes topographiques, medicales et agronomiques sur le Bresil. 69608
Etudiant. pseud. Voyages d'un etudiant. see Navarre, P.
Etwas uber den gegenwartigen Zustand. 42741
Etwas ueber die Natur-Wunder in Nord-Amerika. 17381

Etzel, Anton von. tr. 23099, (71434)
Etzler, J. A. 23100
Eucleia, works by Rev. William Cook. 16297
Eudes Deslonchamps, Eugene, 1830-1889. ed. 78689
Eudromia. 16297
Eugene, Prince of Savoie-Carrignan, 1663-1736. 86742, 94070
Eugene de Cerceil, or les Caraibes. (17190)
Eugenia Marshall. 23101
Eugenics and new social consciousness. 84069
Eugenie, ou la vierge du Canada. 23102
Eugenio. pseud. Letters between Theophilus and Eugenio. see Franklin, Benjamin, 1706-1790. supposed author
Eugenius. pseud. Yorick's sentimental journey continued. see Hall-Stevenson, John.
Eugir. Vetromile datlias. 958
Eugubini, J. Gabrielius. see Gabrielius Eugubini, J.
Eulalie. pseud. Buds, blossoms, and leaves. see Shannon, Mary Eulalie (Fee)
Eulalius. 23103-23105
Eulogical poem on Gen. George Washington. 22323
Eulogies and orations on the life and death of General George Washington. (6049), 82800, 83303, 93693, 101803
Eulogies delivered in the Senate and House of Representatives. 23106
Eulogies delivered on the occasion of the announcement of the death of Hon. Edwin M. Stanton. 90394
Eulogies of two distinguished members of the Philadelphia bar. 27712, 95821-95822
Eulogies read by W. J. Hoppin, and Fred. S. Cozzens. 16690, 54159
Eulogio, por J. B. Baquijano. (35821)
Eulogium. (25601)
Eulogium, by Doctor Albigence Waldo. 103763
Eulogium by George M. Dallas. 18320
Eulogium, commemorative of the exalted virtues. (18262)
Eulogium delivered by General James Tallmadge. 38583
Elogium, delivered to a large concourse of respectable citizens. 99833
Eulogium in commemoration of Doctor Caspar Wistar. 95822
Eulogium in commemoration of the Hon. Bushrod Washington. 32983
Eulogium in commemoration of the Hon. William Tilghman. 21383
Eulogium in honor of the late Dr. William Cullen. 17861, 74218
Eulogium in memory of the late Dr. Benjamin Rish. 90838
Eulogium, intended to perpetuate the memory of David Rittenhouse. 74219
Eulogium of M. Fauchet. 25573
Eulogium of that renowned hero. 58057, 104989
Eulogium of the brave men. 7186
Eulogium of Thomas Jefferson and John Adams. 104019
Eulogium, on Adams and Jefferson. (25148)
Eulogium on Benjamin Franklin. 84602-84603, 84678C
Eulogium on Capt. James Lawrence. 68149
Eulogium on Caspar Wistar. 9899
Eulogium on Chief Justice Marshall. 8806
Eulogium on De Witt Clinton. (44299)
Eulogium on Doctor William Shippen. 104919

Eulogium on General George Washington, pronounced on the 22d of February, 20024
Eulogium, on General George Washington; spoken at Tolland. 90883
Eulogium on General Lafayette. 43511
Eulogium on . . . Hon. Theodore Gaillard. (38805)
Eulogium on Keating Lewis Simons. (17342)
Eulogy on Lafayette, delivered at Concord. 98047
Eulogium on La Fayette; delivered in . . . Washington City. (21696)
Eulogium on Major General Joseph Warren. 101479
Eulogium on Mr. George Lee. 9899
Eulogium on Nathan Smith. 38119, 83653-83654
Eulogium on Rev. J. Smith. 42045
Eulogium on Robert J. Turnbull. 30016
Eulogium on Stephen Elliott. (51139)
Eulogium on the capture of Washington. 77438
Eulogium, on the character of Benjamin Ridgway Smith. 98700
Eulogium on the character of Brother John Crawford. 102119
Eulogium, on the character of Gen. George Washington. 22356, 57749
Eulogium on the character of General Washington. (35472)-35473, 101748-101749
Eulogium on the character of Washington. 101724
Eulogium, on the death of General George Washington. By a member of the Senate of the United States. 101804
Eulogium on the death of Gen¹ George Washington Commander in Chief of the armies of America. 5621
Eulogium on the death of George Washington. 5622
Eulogium on the late General George Washington. 101805
Eulogium on the late Gen. Washington. 103897
Eulogium on the late Gov. John A. King. (28114)
Eulogium on . . . the late John Sargent. 47948
Eulogium on the late Wright Post. 82918
Eulogium on the life and character of Horace Binney. 93085
Eulogium on the life and character of Rev. Henry Holcombe. 70469
Eulogium on the life and character of the late Honorable Thomas Morris. 8008
Eulogium on the life and character of Thomas Clarkson. 17726
Eulogium on the life and character of Thomas S. Grimke. 82791
Eulogium on the life and character of William Wilberforce. 33578
Eulogium on the life and services of Simeon De Witt. 4237
Eulogium on the Rev. John Smith. 103219
Eulogium on Thomas C. Brinsmade. (33423)
Eulogium on Thomas Jefferson. 5240
Eulogium on William Shippen. 104920
Eulogium, or tribute of gratitude. 16252, (69383)
Eulogium, . . . pronounced at the request of the Pennsylvania Society of the Cincinnati. 35473, 101748
Euolgium, pronounced before the citizens of Eastport, Maine. 43624
Eulogium, pronounced by the Hon. James Strong. 92917

Eulogium pronounced on account of the death of Brother Amos Haines. 44328

Eulogium pronounced 23d January 1835. 219

Eulogium sacred to the memory of Major General Warren. 101479

Eulogium, spoken on the delivery of the medal. 25279, 84611-84612

Eulogium to the memory of Dr. Samuel Cooper. 9899

Eulogium to the memory of General George Washington. 61335

Eulogium to the memory of the Rev. Gershom Mendes Seizas. 62504

Eulogium upon Antony Laussat. 36571

Eulogium upon Benjamin Rush. 67685

Eulogium upon Gen. Andrew Jackson. 10048

Eulogium upon James Knox Polk. 64271

Eulogium upon the Hon. Charles Ewing. 88247

Eulogium upon Hon. William Tilghman. 5475

Eulogium upon the life and character of James Barbour. 3341

Eulogium upon the life, professional labors and public services of Joseph Mather Smith. 71930

Eulogium upon the Rev. John F. Greer. 60799

Eulogium upon Wilberforce. 8466

Eulogium upon William Rawle. 8466

Eulogy at Belfast, Me. 36165

Eulogy, . . . at his [i. e. Joseph McKeen's] funeral. (43391)

Eulogy at Norwich, Vt. 32915

Eulogy, at the dedication of the statue of Daniel Webster. 23271

Eulogy, at the funeral of General Gideon Foster. 37791

Eulogy, . . . at the funeral of . . . Horace Clark. (55011)

Eulogy . . . at the funeral of Rear Admiral George Washington Storer. 59354

Eulogy . . . at the funeral of the late Silas Bowen. 55217

Eulogy before the Legislature of New York. 316

Eulogy by Amos Dean. 8976

Eulogy, by another author. (24390)

Eulogy by Edward Everett. 20793

Eulogy by Elliot C. Cowdin. 53595, 2d note after 96963

Eulogy, by Gen. J. Huntington. 33974, 101813

Eulogy by Hon. Geo. Bancroft. 36007

Eulogy, by Judge Minot. 39749

Eulogy by Professor Webber. 39187, note after 102250, 104056

Eulogy by R. S. Storrs, Jun., D. D. 41219

Eulogy, by the Hon. Brother Timothy Bigelow. 101870

Eulogy, by the Hon. George Richards Minot. 101868

Eulogy delivered, at Anamisa, Iowa. 30117

Eulogy delivered at Louisville, Ky. 84403

Eulogy delivered at Lunenburg, on . . . the 22d of February 1800. 17973

Eulogy, delivered at the funeral of the Hon. William Gorham. (31895)

Eulogy, delivered at the grave. 95229

Eulogy delivered . . . at the interment of James Hervy Pierrepont. (9460)

Eulogy delivered before the Legislature of New York. 79533

Eulogy, delivered by appointment of the officers and members of the Fayetteville Bar. 92700

Eulogy, delivered in the Chapel of Brown University, on Mr. Ezra Bailey. 3842

Eulogy, delivered in the Chapel of Brown University, on Mr. Henry Smith. 74332

Eulogy, delivered in the Chapel of Brown University, on Mr. Isaac Fuller. 89667

Eulogy . . . delivered in the House of Representatives of South Carolina. 96788

Eulogy, delivered June 29, 1796, at the meeting-house in Charlestown. 95175, note after 102616

Eulogy, illustrative of the life. 36031

Eulogy . . . in . . . Boston. 38084

Eulogy . . . in commemoration of Rev. and R. W. Thaddeus Mason Harris. 33982

Eulogy in commemoration of the sublime virtues of General George Washington. (7219)

Eulogy . . . in Wiscasset, April 22, 1841. 80308

Eulogy moralized on the illustrious character of the late General George Washington. 25040

Eulogy occasioned by the death of General Washington. 79389

Eulogy of Abraham Lincoln. 18195

Eulogy of Andrea d'Oria. 21418

Eulogy of Captain James Cook. 27267

Eulogy of Columbus. 21418

Eulogy of Gen. Chs. Cotesworth Pinckney. 26600

Eulogy of Hon. George Bancroft. 36008

Eulogy of Hon. Geo. Bancroft, delivered at Washington, D. C. 35377

Eulogy of Hon. Stephen A. Douglass [sic]. (17271)

Eulogy of J. K. Polk. 26671

Eulogy of the Hon. Ira Perley. 60980

Eulogy of William Henry Harrison. 59361

Eulogy on Abraham Lincoln, . . . before the New England Historic-Genealogical Society, Boston. 51884

Eulogy on Abraham Lincoln, by George W. Briggs. 7946

Eulogy on Abraham Lincoln, by Henry Champion Deming. 19481

Eulogy on Abraham Lincoln, delivered in Portsmouth, N. H. (59128), 64412

Eulogy on Abraham Lincoln, late President of the United States. 23238

Eulogy on Abraham Lincoln, late President of the United States, pronounced at Springfield, Mass. 32510, 89868

Eulogy on Abraham Lincoln sixteenth President of the United States. 78810

Eulogy on Alexander Metcalf Fisher. 37892

Eulogy on Andrew Jackson. By Hon. Milton Sawyer. (77323)

Eulogy on Andrew Jackson, . . . Columbus, O. (77405)

Eulogy on Charles Carroll of Carrollton. 79201

Eulogy on Charles Henry Griffin. (73547)

Eulogy on Charles Sumner. By Charles Schurz. 78030

Eulogy on Charles Sumner: delivered in the Assembly Chamber. 89308

Eulogy on Col. Boon, and choice of life. (6370)

Eulogy on Daniel Webster, . . . at the New England Festival. 50896

Eulogy on Daniel Webster, delivered before the students and friends of the Albany Medical College. 68005

Eulogy on Daniel Webster, delivered before the students of Bowdoin College. 32266

Eulogy on Daniel Webster, delivered before the students of Phillips Academy. 76241

Eulogy on Daniel Webster, delivered in Syracuse, N. Y. (18890)

Eulogy on Daniel Webster: pronounced before the Chelsea Library Association. 12415

Eulogy on Dr. Godman. 79467

Eulogy on Gen. Alexander Hamilton. 47854

Eulogy on General George Washington. A sermon. 36239

Eulogy on Gen. George Washington, late President of the United States. 2270

Eulogy, on General George Washington, pronounced at Boston. 18845

Eulogy on General George Washington, pronounced . . . in presence of the Grand Lodge of South Carolina. (58198)

Eulogy on General George Washington: who departed this life December 14th, 1799, in the 68th year of his age. 1504

Eulogy on Gen. George Washington, who died Dec. 14, 1799. 77229

Eulogy, on General George Washington, who died on the 14th of Dec. 1799. 20623, 23285, 1st note after 101877

Eulogy on General George Washington; written at the request of the inhabitants of Marblehead. 33154, 92304

Eulogy on General George Washington; written by a gentleman of Georgetown. 101806

Eulogy on General Jackson, . . . July 9, 1845. 47987

Eulogy, on General Washington. 8356

Eulogy on General Zachary Taylor, late President of the United States, delivered . . . Cambridge, August 13, 1850. 4472

Eulogy on Gen. Zachary Taylor, late President of the United States, delivered October 2d, 1850. 34746

Eulogy on George Washington. By Francis Kinloch. 37923

Eulogy on George Washington. By Jonathan Allen. 841

Eulogy on George Washington . . . . By Thomas Paine. 58253

Eulogy on George Washington, Esq. 37922, 1st note after 101806

Eulogy on George Washington, first President of the United States. 95198

Eulogy on George Washington, late Commander-in-Chief of the American armies. 28507

Eulogy on George Washington, late Commander-in-Chief of the armies. 24970

Eulogy on George Washington, late Commander of the armies. 64242, 101686

Eulogy on George Washington the great and the good. 62729, 101686

Eulogy on George Washington, who died at Mount Vernon, December 14th, 1799. 103367

Eulogy on George Washington, . . . who died December 14, 1799. (49322)

Eulogy on Hon. James Alfred Pearce. (2588)

Eulogy on Hon. John Wheelock. 867

Eulogy on Hugh Swinton Legare. 65387

Eulogy on James Madison. 103310

Eulogy on John Adams and Thomas Jefferson . . . August 2, 1826. 79929

Eulogy on John Adams and Thomas Jefferson . . . in Newburyport. (18086)

Eulogy on John Adams and Thomas Jefferson; pronounced . . . [at] Albany. (21117)

Eulogy on John Adams and Thomas Jefferson, pronounced August 10, 1826. 89690

Eulogy on John Adams and Thomas Jefferson, pronounced in Hallowell, July, 1827. 89701

Eulogy on John Adams, delivered September 14, 1826. 25071

Eulogy on . . . John Doane Wells. (12734)

Eulogy on John Hubbard. (58602)

Eulogy on John W. Francis. (26637)

Eulogy on Joseph S. Hubbard. 28094

Eulogy on King Philip. 1734

Eulogy on Lafayette, delivered . . . at Boston. 23250

Eulogy on La Fayette, delivered at Concord. 63435

Eulogy on Lafayette, delivered in Bloomington. 105663

Eulogy on Lafayette, delivered in . . . Dartmouth College. 28710

Eulogy on Lafayette, delivered in the Masonic Temple, Boston. 4062

Eulogy on La Fayette, pronounced at the request of the young men of Dover. 18087

Eulogy on La Fayette, pronounced before the Society of Cincinnati. (19000)

Eulogy on Maj. Gen. J. Morton and E. W. King. (31578)

Eulogy on Mr. Chase. 77996

Eulogy on Mr. John Leckie. (45429)

Eulogy on Mr. Samuel Smith Adams. 24524

Eulogy on Nathaniel Appleton Haven. 84703

Eulogy on Nathaniel Bowditch. (62632)

Eulogy on President Lincoln. (14120)

Eulogy on Prof. Alexander Dallas Bach. 31403

Eulogy on . . . Rev. Dr. Frederick A. Rauch. 52422

Eulogy on Rev. Jeremiah Chaplin. 59156

Eulogy on Samuel McClellan. 5884

Eulogy on Silas Wright. 27456

Eulogy on the character and services of the late Daniel Webster. 904

Eulogy on the character of George Washington. 57749, 22356

Eulogy on the character of John Warren. 35425

Eulogy on the character of the late Gen. George Washington. Delivered before the inhabitants of the town of Worcester. 3098

Eulogy on the character of the late Gen. George Washington: the pride of America, the glory of the world. 47987

Eulogy . . . on the character of Thomas Smith Webb. 19038

Eulogy on the death of Abraham Lincoln. 6974

Eulogy on the death of Capt. Abraham Van Olinda. 79869

Eulogy on the death of Henry Clay. (39192)

Eulogy on the excellent character of George Washington. 100919

Eulogy on the glorious virtues of the illustrious Gen. George Washington. 92279

Eulogy on the Hon. Benjamin Russell. 4063

Eulogy, on the Honourable James Bowdoin. 42442

Eulogy on the Hon. John Campbell. 81379

Eulogy on the Honorable John Quincy Adams. (24041)

Eulogy on the Hon. Levi Woodbury. (67901)

Eulogy on the Honourable Thomas Russell. 101470

Eulogy on the Hon. William H. Woodward. 60941

Eulogy on the illustrious character of the late General George Washington. 25980

Eulogy on the illustrious George Washington. 93693

Eulogy on the illustrious life and character of George Washington. 12, 101686

Eulogy, on the intellectuality of Daniel Webster. (76259)

Eulogy on the late Brevet Major-General Joseph G. Totten. (3479)

Eulogy on the late Daniel Webster. (37645)

Eulogy on the late Edward Post. (51529)

Eulogy on the late General George Washington. 7366

Eulogy on the late General Washington. 79398

Eulogy on the late Hon. William Jay. 20716

Eulogy on the late John P. Curran Sampson. 42657

Eulogy on the late John W. Francis. 51119

Eulogy on the late Keating Lewis Simons. 26293

Eulogy on the late President Washington. 17891

Eulogy on the late Solomon Metcalf Allen. (29771)

Eulogy on the late Valentine Mott. 64452

Eulogy on the late Washington Irving. note after 103316

Eulogy on the late William Henry Harrison. 10992

Eulogy on the life and character of Abraham Lincoln. 13266

Eulogy on the life and character of General Andrew Jackson. 5669

Eulogy on the life and character of Gen. Zachary Taylor. 65091

Eulogy on the life and character of Henry Clay. 8555

Eulogy, on the life and character of His Excellency George Washington. 40795

Eulogy on the life and character of James Madison. 278

Eulogy on the life and character of James Monroe. 279-280

Eulogy on the life and character of John Marshall. 5476

Eulogy on the life and character of John Quincy Adams. 23251

Eulogy on the life and character of Layafette. 56821

Eulogy on the life and character of Nathaniel Bowditch. 103368

Eulogy on the life and character of Oliver Whittlesey. 25850

Eulogy on the life and character of P. G. M. Henry G. Lawrence. 83959

Eulogy on the life and character of Rev. Zachariah Greene. 57539

Eulogy on the life and character of the Hon. Richard Biddle. (71566)

Eulogy on the life and character of the Hon. Samuel Latham Mitchill. (58982)

Eulogy on the life and character of the Hon. Thomas J. Rusk. 31291

Eulogy on the life and character of the late Hon. Robert M. Charlton. 30309

Eulogy on the life and character of the late Judge Jesse Buel. 19017

Eulogy on the life and character of the late President James K. Polk. 18317

Eulogy on the life and character of the late Zachary Taylor. 67263

Eulogy on the life and character of the Reverend John H. Livingston. 98591

Eulogy on the life and character of Theodoric Romeyn Beck. 30008

Eulogy on the life and character of Thomas Clarkson. (68253)

Eulogy on the life and character of Thomas Wildey. 71288

Eulogy on the life and character of Wm. Henry Harrison . . . delivered at . . . Chicago. (4187)

Eulogy on the life and character of William Henry Harrison, late President of the United States. 4978

Eulogy on the life and character of William Rufus King. 92699

Eulogy on the life and character of William Wirt. (80434)

Eulogy on the life and character of Yelverton Peyton Page. 25850

Eulogy on the life and character of Zachary Taylor. 22380

Eulogy on the life and public services of the Hon. Henry Clay. 10748

Eulogy on the life and services of Henry Clay. 35989

Eulogy on the life and services of James S. Wadsworth. 33002

Eulogy on the life and services of President Lincoln. 13294

Eulogy on the life, character and public services of the Hon. John C. Calhoun. 14237

Eulogy on the life, character and public services of the late President Lincoln. (17831)

Eulogy on the life, character, and services of Brother George Washington. 5325

Eulogy on the life of Gen. George Washington, late Commander in Chief of the Armies. 97603

Eulogy on the life of General George Washington . . . . Written at the request of the citizens of Newburyport. 58199

Eulogy on the memory of General George Washington. 95203

Eulogy, on the occasion of the death of William Henry Harrison. 1569

Eulogy on . . . the re-interment of his [i. e. Frederick Augustus Rauch's] remains at Lancaster, Pa. 52422

Eulogy on the Rev. Joseph McKean. 31220

Eulogy on the Rev. Joshua Bates. 33294

Eulogy, on the virtues of General George Washington. 103832

Eulogy on Thomas Crawford. 31722

Eulogy on Thomas Dowse. 23252

Eulogy on Thomas Jefferson, and John Adams, &c. 7183, note after 105507

Eulogy on Thomas Jefferson, delivered at the Columbian College. (35708)

Eulogy on Thomas Jefferson, delivered August 3d, 1826. (36340)

Eulogy on Thomas Watson, Jr. 90915

Eulogy on Washington. 72114

Eulogy on . . . Wm. Crafts. 17181

Eulogy on William Henry Harrison . . . at Ann Arbor. 13602

Eulogy on William H. Harrison. By R. B. Haughton. 30855

Eulogy on . . . William Henry Harrison . . . 14th of May, 1841. 44376

Eulogy on William Ladd. 4261

Eulogy on William Wilberforce. 103297

Eulogy on Zachary Taylor. 41514

Eulogy pronounced at Salem. 39355, 92329

Eulogy pronounced before the citizens of Windsor, Vt. (70954)

Eulogy pronounced before the Connecticut Historical Society. 82937

Eulogy, pronounced in Brunswick (Maine). 36035

Eulogy pronounced in Providence, July 17, 1826. 95828

Eulogy pronounced in the City Hall, Providence. 19040

Eulogy pronounced July 20, 1810. 101377

Eulogy, pronounced on the 22d of February, 1800. 59553

Eulogy to the memory, of the Honourable Nathaniel Gorham. 95175

Eulogy upon General Thomas L. Hamer. 88916, 88918

Eulogy upon John Quincy Adams. 37789

Eulogy upon President Lincoln. 80407

Eulogy upon Stephen A. Douglas. 80030

Eulogy upon the character and services of Abraham Lincoln. 17560

Eulogy upon the character of George Swan. 9642

Eulogy upon the Hon. George Mifflin Dallas. 5230

Eulogy upon the late Gov. Barbour, of Virginia. 51001

Eulogy upon the late Stephen A. Douglas. 25102

Eulogy upon the life and character of George Eustis. 73427

Eulogy upon the life and character of James K. Polk. 25020

Eulogy upon the life and character of the Hon. Chas. J. McDonald. (35417)

Eulogy upon the life and character of the late Robert Y. Hayne. 43203

Eulogy, upon the life and public services of Daniel Webster. 64120

Eulogy upon the life, character, and death of Gen. Andrew Jackson. 13334

Eulogy upon the life, character, and public services of General Zachary Taylor. 927

Eulogy upon the life, character and services of Henry Clay. 84083

Eumenes. 28829

Euphradian Society of the College of South Carolina. see South Carolina. University. Euphradian Society.

Euphrasen, Bengt And. (23107)

Eureka. 63521

Eureka: a prose poem. 63520

Europ. Foljetongen. 92446, 92616

Europa ed America scene della vita dal 1848 al 1850. 9820

Europa en Amerika. (77691)

Europa og America. 77690

Europa und Amerika. 77687

Europa und Deutschalnd von Nordamerika. 21076

Europa und Nordamerika im Lichte der Gegenwart. 7451

Europa y la America en 1821. (64894)

Europae totius orbis terrarum partis. 66892

Europaisch-Amerikanischen Colonisationsgesellschaft in Texas. see Societe de Colonisation Europeo-Americaine au Texas, Brussels.

Europaische Bibliothek der neuen belletristchen Literature. 4522, 4529, 16473, 20130, 21184, 92403, 92444, 104891

Europaische Staats-cantzeley. 4847A

Europaischen Besitzungen. 91197

Europe and America. 62581, 77689

Europe and America in 1839. 23108

Europe and America, in 1821. 64893

Europe and America or the relative state of the civilized world. 77689

Europe et l'Amerique comparees. 20961

Europe et l'Amerique, depuis le Congres d'Aix-la-Chapelle. 64891

Europe et l'Amerique en 1821. 64892

Europe et l'Amerique en 1822 et 1823. 64895

Europe et l'Amerique, ou les rapports futurs du monde civilise. 77688

Europe et ses colonies. 4195

Europe: or a general survey. 23224, (23230)-(23231), 23235

Europea intervencion en Mexico. 48467

European. pseud. On the prisons of Philadelphia. see La Rochefoucauld-Liancourt, Francois Alexandre Frederic, Duc de, 1747-1827. and Moreau de Saint-Mery, Mederic Louis Elie, 1750-1819. incorrectly supposed author

European and colonial sugar manufacturer. pseud. On sugar cultivation. 57281

European and colonial sugar manufacturer. pseud. Sugar question. (40073), 57281, 93456

European and North America Railway Company. 23109-(23110), 50993, 63274, 66087

European and North American Railway Company. petitioners 54062, 64064

European and North American Railway Company. Charter. 23109, 63274

European and North American Railway Convention, Portland, Me., 1850. 23109, 63274

European Branch, United States Sanitary Commission. see United States Sanitary Commission. European Branch.

European Branch of the United States Sanitary Commission, Bureau, No. 21, Rue Martel, Paris. (7076), (76649)

European colonies. 33367

European colonization in Texas. 15927

European commerce. 73153

European delineation of the American character. (23111)

European history. 27913

European immigration to the United States. 37101

European magazine, and London review. 23112, 50185, 80062, 82379, 86565

European mail. 35605

European settlements on the west coast of Africa. 31635

European stranger in America. 23564

European traveller. pseud. European traveller in America. 23113

European traveller in America. 23113

European. pseud. Des prisons de Philadelphie. see La Rochefoucault-Liancourt, Francois Alexandre Frederic, Duc de, 1737-1827. and Moreau de Saint-Mery, Mederic Louis Elie, 1750-1819. incorrectly supposed author

Europeen au President Abraham Lincoln. (56054)

Europeens et Negres. 73935

Europeer in Philadelphia. pseud. Gevangenhuizen van Philadelphia. (27250)

Europeis magazyn der byzondere zaken. (58518)

Europeo. pseud. Manifiesto. see Herrera, Antonio Maria.

Europe's glory. 33163

Evsebii Caesariesis Episcopi chronicon. 23114

Eusebius. pseud. Eleutherius enervatus. see Wetmore, James.

Eusebius. pseud. [Essays.] 96123, 1st note after 105926

Eusebius Pamphili, Bp. of Caesarea. 23114, 44124, 73458, 99365

Eusebius ineramatus. (25392), 103067

Eusebius Philadelphus. pseud. Baptismus redivivus. 75445

Euskildta lefeverne ofwersattn. 25618

Eustace, Jean-Skey. 23115, 23117-23119 see also Georgia. Adjutant and Inspector General.

Eustace, Thomas. 23120

Eustache, an account of a faithful Negro slave of San Domingo. 85819

Eustacius Swammerdam. pseud. see Swammerdam, Eustacius. pseud.

Eustaquidos. 88718

Eustaquidos: poema sacro e tragi-comico. 88719

Eustis, William, 1753-1825. 23121, (68946), 85187-85188, 93720, 97413 see also Massachusetts. Governor, 1823-1825 (Eustis) U. S. War Department.

Eustis, Dr. William, fl. 1776. 23122

Eutaw. (81279)

Eutaw; a sequel to The forayers. 81209

Eutaxia. 23124

Euthanasia. 46309

Eutopian. pseud. Humours of Eutopia. 33784

Eva Effingham, of schetsen van Amerikaansche zeden. 16436

Eva Effingham, or home. 16434

Eva Effingham. Traduit . . . par A. J. B. Defauconpret. 16435

Eva Labree. 51656

"Evaculation day," 1783. 71388

Evaculation of Texas. 24323

Evaluation des especes. 2093

Evangelho politico dos Estados Unidos d'America. 101664

Evangelia und episteln auf alle Sonntage. 100688

Evangeliad. 36842

Evangeliarium epistolarium et lectionarium Aztecum. 74948

Evangelica quatuor. (28849)

Evangelical Alliance. Secretaries. 59164

Evangelical almanac. 23126

Evangelical bishop. 22005

Evangelical Church, Bolton, Mass. see Bolton, Mass. Evangelical Church.

Evangelical Church, Brookfield, Mass. see Brookfield, Mass. Evangelical Church.

Evangelical Church, Lancaster, Mass. see Lancaster, Mass. Evangelical Church.

Evangelical Church, Quincy, Mass. see Quincy, Mass. Evangelical Church.

Evangelical Church, Sterling, Mass. see Sterling, Mass. Evangelical Church.

Evangelical Church, Stow, Mass. see Stow, Mass. Evangelical Church.

Evangelical conference. 77567

Evangelical Congregational Church, Cambridgeport, Mass. see Cambridge, Mass. Evangelical Congregational Church.

Evangelical Congregational Church, Quincy, Mass. see Quincy, Mass. Evangelical Congregational Church.

Evangelical Congregational Churches in Massachusetts. see also Congregational Churches in Massachusetts.

Evangelical Congregational Churches in Massachusetts. Barnstable Conference. 3551, 59462

Evangelical Congregational Churches in Massachusetts. Barnstable Conference. Committee. 3551, 59462

Evangelical Consociation of Rhode Island. see Congregational Churches in Rhode Island. Evangelical Consociation.

Evangelical Education Society of the Protestant Episcopal Church. 66149

Evangelical Education Society of the Protestant Episcopal Church. Board of Managers. 66149

Evangelical Education Society of the Protestant Episcopal Church. . . . Its students and its principles. 66149

Evangelical family library. 21928, 70844

Evangelical Free Church, Globe Village, Mass. see Southbridge, Mass. Evangelical Free Church.

Evangelical Free Church, Southbridge, Mass. see Southbridge, Mass. Evangelical Free Church.

Evangelical guardian and review. 23133

Evangelical Home Missionary Society of Kensington, Pa. (61637)

Evangelical intelligencer. 53398, (65167), 65185, 94719

Evangelical Knowledge Society of South Carolina. 87823

Evangelical Library, Salem, Mass. see Salem Evangelical Library, Salem, Mass.

Evangelical Lutheran Church, Lockport, N. Y. see Lockport, N. Y. Evangelical Lutheran Church.

Evangelical Lutheran Church of St. John, Philadelphia. see Philadelphia. Evangelical Lutheran Church of St. John.

Evangelical Lutheran Church of the Holy Trinity, Lancaster, Pa. see Lancaster, Pa. Evangelical Lutheran Church of the Holy Trinity.

Evangelical Lutheran Ebenezer Church, Albany, N. Y. see Albany, N. Y. Evangelical Lutheran Ebenezer Church.

Evangelical Lutheran General Synod of the United States of America. see General Synod of the Evangelical Lutheran Church of the United States of America.

Evangelical Lutheran intelligencer. 23128

Evangelical Lutheran Ministerium of Pennsylvania and Adjoining States. 25919, 27148, 37965, 60120, 65035, 75905, 77972, 78013-78014

Evangelical Lutheran Ministerium of the State of New York and Adjacent States and Counties. 49385, 53658-53659 see also Hartwick Synod of the Evangelical Lutheran Church in the State of New York.

Evangelical Lutheran Ministerium of the State of New York and Adjacent States and Counties. Convention of Ministers and Delegates, Fordsbush, 1837. 53864

Evangelical Lutheran Missionary Institute, Selin's Grove, Pa. 79014

Evangelical Lutheran Sunday School Society, New York. 54263

Evangelical Lutheran Synod of Hartwick, N. Y. see Hartwick Synod of the Evangelical Lutheran Church in the State of New York.

Evangelical Lutheran Synod of Maryland and Virginia. 23128-23129, 49382, 66221, 100485

Evangelical Lutheran Synod of New York. see Evangelical Lutheran Ministerium of the State of New York and Adjacent States and Counties.

Evangelical Lutheran Synod of North Carolina and Bordering States. 55702

Evangelical Lutheran Synod of Pennsylvania.
see Evangelical Lutheran Ministerium
of Pennsylvania and Adjoining States.
Evangelical Lutheran Synod of Pittsburgh.
see Pittsburgh Synod of the Evangelical
Lutheran Church.
Evangelical Lutheran Synod of Tennessee.
see Evangelical Lutheran Tennessee
Synod.
Evangelical Lutheran Synod of Virginia. see
Evangelical Lutheran Synod of Maryland
and Virginia.
Evangelical Lutheran Tennessee Synod. 94795
Evangelical magazine. 6855, 82901, 93719
Evangelical ministry, the security of a nation.
(45438)
Evangelical Missionary Society for Young
Men, New York. see New-York Evan-
gelical Missionary Society for Young
Men.
Evangelical Missionary Society of Massa-
chusetts. (45724)
Evangelical Missionary Society of Massa-
chusetts. Trustees. (45724), 45648
Evangelical obedience described and demanded.
46215
Evangelical perfection. (79448), note after
98054, 104082
Evangelical plan. (64276)
Evangelical preacher. 83795
Evangelical preacher. A sermon. 26785
Evangelical preaching. 18405
Evangelical record and western review.
(23131)
Evangelical Reformed Congregation, Philadel-
phia. see Philadelphia. Evangelical
Reformed Congregation.
Evangelical repository. 69356
Evangelical review. 23132, 91986
Evangelical review of modern genius. 81281
Evangelical Seamen's Friend Society, Provi-
dence, R. I. see Providence Evangelical
Seamen's Friend Society.
Evangelical Tract Society, Hartford, Conn.
see Hartford Evangelical Tract Society.
Evangelical Union Anti-slavery Society of the
City of New York. 23134, 54264,
(81780)
Evangelical Union Church, Sudbury, Mass.
see Sudbury, Mass. Evangelical Union
Church.
Evangelico liberal. 29368
Evangelina; poeme. (41912)
Evangeline. (39987), 41911
Evangeline, a tale of Acadie. (41909)
Evangeline, a tale of Acadie; the belfrey of
Bruges. 41910
Evangeline; conte d'Acadie. 41913
Evangeline traduction du poeme Acadien.
41914
Evangeline und Neger Tom. 92571
Evangelio de Jesu Christo. 59345
Evangelio de S. Lucas. 23125
Evangelios en Tarasco. 27359
Evangelisch-Lutherisch Kirche in den Vereinig-
ten Staaten. see Evangelical Lutheran
Ministerium of Pennsylvania and Adjoin-
ing States.
Evangelisch-Lutherischen Gemeinen in Nord-
Amerika. see Evangelical Lutheran
Ministerium of Pennsylvania and Adjoin-
ing States.
Evangelisch-Lutherischen Synod fur Nord-
Carolina und Angranzende Staaten. see
Evangelical Lutheran Synod of North
Carolina and Bordering States.

Evangelisch-Lutherischen Synode von Mary-
land und Virginien. see Evangelical
Lutheran Synod of Maryland and Virginia.
Evangelisch-Lutherischen Tennessee Synode.
see Evangelical Lutheran Tennessee
Synode.
Evangelische Allianz und ihre Generalversamm-
lung in New-York. 89440
Evangelische Mission unter den Eskimo's in
Gronland und Labrador. 9321
Evangelische Mission unter den Indianern in
Nord- und Sud-Amerika. 9321
Evangelische Mission unter den Negern in
Westindien und Sudakerika. 9321
Evangelischen Arbeiter in Pennsylvania. see
Congregation of God in the Spirit.
Evangelischen-Lutherischen General-Synode in
der Vereinigten Staaten von Nord-Amerika.
see General Synod of the Evangelical
Lutheran Church in the United States of
America.
Evangelischen Religionen Teutscher Nation in
Pennsylvania. see Congregation of God
in the Spirit. and United Brethren.
Evangelischen Religionen Teutscher Nation in
Pennsylvania. Dritten Conferenz. see
United Brethren.
Evangelisches Zeugnuss. 106384
Evangelisk-Kirke i Danmark. 35772
Evangelist, and other poems. 17272
Evangelist in Brasilien. 5421
Evangelium Okausek tussarnersok Gub niarnanik
Innungortimik. (22037)
Evangelium S. Johannis. 22850
Evans, ------, fl. 1788. 23177
Evans, A. E. 23135
Evans, A. J. 23136
Evans, Alexander. 90329
Evans, Ann. 23137
Evans, B. R. 70025, 85577
Evans, Caleb, 1737-1791. 21539, 23138-
(23141), 24726, (57218), 97367
Evans, Charles, 1802-1879. 11204, 15938,
(23142), 59900, 61558
Evans, D. 23143
Evans, David E. petitioner 53566
Evans, David Morier, 1819-1874. (23145),
25179
Evans, De Lacy. 23144, note after 101938
Evans, Elwood. 23146
Evans, Estwick, 1787-1866. 23147-(23149),
24411
Evans, Estwick, 1787-1866. petitioner 52934
Evans, Evan. 37218
Evans, Francis A. 23150
Evans, Frederick White. 23151-(23152)
Evans, George, 1797-1867. 23153
Evans, H. B. (23155)-23156
Evans, H. Smith. 23158
Evans, Henry. defendant 96861
Everett, Horace, 1799-1851. (23282)
Evans, Hugh Davey. 23157, 45180
Evans, Israel. 23159-23165
Evans, J. D. 23171
Evans, J. H. 104808
Evans, James, 1784-1872. (23166), (23283),
36589, 85207
Evans, James W. ed. 31761
Evans, John, fl. 1703-1731. (59928) see also
Pennsylvania (Colony) Governor, 1703-
1707 (Evans)
Evans, John, fl. 1754. 22695
Evans, John, fl. 1807. 23167
Evans, John, fl. 1811. defendant 23168, note
before 105987

Evans, John, fl. 1811. plaintiff 23168,
  32936, 69768, note before 105987
Evans, John, fl. 1811. reporter 23168, note
  before 105987
Evans, John, 1814- 11734, 14744, (23154),
  90692 see also Colorado (Territory)
  Governor, 1862-1865 (Evans)
Evans, John, fl. 1819. 23170
Evans, John, fl. 1864. (23172)
Evans, Jonathan. 23173, 77282, 99822,
  99825
Evans, Joshua, 1731-1798. ed. 6121, 14956,
  82873
Evans, Josiah James, 1786-1858. 23169,
  87692
Evans, Lemenuel Dale, 1810-1877. 23174
Evans, Lewis, 1700?-1756. 23175-23176,
  35953-35954, 35962, (40141), (64835),
  69064, 64832, 100426
Evans, N. (27658)
Evans, Nathaniel, 1742-1767. (23178)-23179,
  23388, 61547, 84610, 84678C
Evans, Oliver, 1755-1819. 23180-(23182),
  95317, 96991
Evans, Oliver, 1755-1819. petitioner (23182)
Evans, Richard. 13184, 23183
Evans, Rowland E. 51109
Evans, Rowland E. plaintiff 23184-23185
Evans, S. ed. (45523)
Evans, S. B. 85041
Evans, T. E. tr. 21120
Evans, Thomas. 21873, 22352, 23188-
  (23190), (25956), 67116, 77453, note
  before 91980, 100425, 103560, 103622,
  103644-103645, 105653
Evans, Thomas. of Virginia supposed
  author 23186, 94189
Evans, Thomas J. 87093
Evans, Thomas W. 23191-23192
Evans, W. J. 23195-(23196)
Evans, Warren F. 23193
Evans, William. 10341, 21873, 22352, (25956),
  77453, note before 91980, 105653
Evans, William B. 23194
Evans (T. C.) publisher 23187
Evans' advertising hand-book. 23187
Evanston, Ill. North-Western Female College.
  see North-Western Female College,
  Evanston, Ill.
Evanston, Ill. Northwestern University. see
  Northwestern University, Evanston, Ill.
Evansville, Ind. Board of Trade. 23198
Evansville, Ind. Convention for the Protection
  of Western Interests, 1850. see Con-
  vention for the Protection of Western
  Interests, Evansville, Ind., 1850.
Evansville directory for 1866. 23197
Evansville: her commerce and manufactures.
  (71858)
Evansville, Indianapolis, and Cleveland
  Straight-Line Railroad Company. Direc-
  tors. 23199
Evarts, Jeremiah, 1781-1831. (20626), 23200-
  (23201), note after 70279, 105305
Evarts, William Maxwell. 10190, (23202)-
  23205, (54732), 77996, 93644
Evasion de Pichegru, Ramel, &c. (1534),
  (27337)
Eve, Paul F. 23206
Eveleth, Samuel. (41260)
Evelin, Robert. 19724, 63310, 63312
Evelina. 103484
Evelino, G. J. 23207
Evelyn, John, 1620-1706. 23208, 71086,
  78981, 97330

Evenemens deplorables de la guerre desastr-
  euse. 19086, (75094)
Evenements de la Guadeloupe en 1814. 7134
Evening advertiser (London) 97351
Evening amusement, for all ages and sizes.
  103294
Evening and morning star. 83147, 83289
Evening at Mount Vernon. (37324), 3d note
  after 78761, note after 101786
Evening book. 37987
Evening chronicle (Philadelphia) 91499
Evening entertainments. (19650)
Evening excursion. 71156
Evening Free School, Salem, Mass. see
  Salem Evening Free School, Salem,
  Mass.
Evening journal (Albany) 10190, 93644
Evening journal (Philadelphia) 68625
Evening journal (Pittsfield, Mass.) 83323
Evening journal tracts. 10190, 93644
Evening Lecture, Boston. (9717), 59375
Evening lecture, February 16, 1812. 70927
Evening post (Baltimore) (55313)
Evening post (Boston) see Boston evening
  post.
Evening post (New York) see New York
  evening post.
Evening post documents. (73952), 78405,
  89203, 93659
Evening post extra. Evening post documents.
  89203, 93659
Evening post extra. History of the canal
  policy. 53660
Evening post extra. Is a law against slavery
  in the territories necessary? (73952)
Evening prayer. 79195
Evening press (Hartford) 84446
Evening readings in history. 80967
Evening schools and district libraries. 61640
Evening service of Roshashanah, and Kippur.
  (23209)
Evening star. 79982
Evening telegraph (Boston) 92067
Evening with the chaplain. 39034
Evenings at Woodlawn. 22214
Evenings in Boston. 4204, (5780), (34604),
  67665
Evenings peep into a polite circle. (76703),
  101487
Evenings with the sacred poets. 77175
Evens, Joseph. 23210-23211
Eventful day in the Rhode Island rebellion.
  23212, 93998
Eventful Friday. 67373
Eventful history of the mutiny and piratical
  seizure. 2662, 23213
Eventful life and curious adventures of Peter
  Williamson. 104468
Eventful narrative of Capt. William Stockwell.
  91877
Eventful voyage of H. M. Discovery Ship
  "Resolute." 43183
Events in Indian history. 23214
Events in the history of James W. C. Penning-
  ton. 59764
Events of a military life. (31417)
Events of an important nature having recently
  taken place. 105941
Events which have taken place since the first
  settlement. 52743
Eveque de Bardstown et Louisville. (24645)
Everard, Charles. tr. 23215
Everard, Giles. 23216
Everard, John. (23217)
Everartus, AEgidius. 23218, 95622
Everest, Charles W. (23219), 85564

Everest, Robert. 23220-23221
Everet, John. 59726
Everett, Alexander Hill, 1790-1847. 8118,
23222-23237, 42448, 55562, (69411),
note before 92845, 92886
Everett, Amherst. 70641 see also Rhode
Island. Commissioner on the Registered
State Debt.
Everett, Charles Carroll, 1829-1900. 23238-
(23240)
Everett, David. 1793, 4405, (23241)-(23243),
45992, 2d note after 98185, 103479
Everett, Edward, 1794-1865. 1469, 6477,
6759, 7840, 13791, (17762), 19515,
(20618), 20793, 23344-23271, 23933,
(25794), 27231, (27248), 28493, 30765,
32655, 35221, 38583, 39785, 45572,
45582, (45858), 56064, 48851, 50368,
52200, 55562, 58322, 55099, 60592,
64990, note after 68327, 69386, 69537,
60887, 71351, 77265, (79670), 84463,
85071, 89359, 90330, 93663, 104863
see also Boston. Public Meeting for
the Relief of the Greeks, 1823. Com-
mittee. Secretary. Massachusetts.
Governor, 1836-1840 (Everett)
Everett, Edward F. 23279
Everett, Erastus, 1813-1900. 23280, 65648
Everett, George. 23281
Everett, John. (23283A)
Everett, L. S. 51524
Everett, Moses. 23284
Everett, Oliver. 20623, 23285
Everett, Oliver Capen. 12098, 23286 see
also Charlestown, Mass. Ministry at
Large.
Everett, Robert. 92623
Everett, Thomas. 34461
Everett, William. 23287
Everett, William. supposed author 86366
Everett Club, New York. 54265 see also
Democratic Party. New York. New
York City.
Everett Literary Union, New York. 54218
Everett massacre. 84489
Everett School, Boston. see Boston. Everett
School.
Evergreen. 105348
Evergreen. A repository of religious, literary
and entertaining knowledge. 23288
Evergreen. An offering for all seasons.
23289
Evergreen Cemetery, Brighton, Mass. see
Brighton, Mass. Evergreen Cemetery.
Evergreen, or church offering for all seasons.
23290
Evergreen, or monthly church magazine.
23291
Everhard, Sir Richard. (60861), 91305
Everitt, John L. 69934
Everlasting deliverance from British tyranny.
96502
Everlasting God. 88886
Everlasting Gospel. 46310, 46349
Everlasting Gospel, commanded to be preached
by Jesus Christ. (80879)
Everlasting Gospel preached unto the nations.
(46394)
Everlasting oracle of fate. 90495
Everndon, Thomas. (37195)
Everpoint. pseud. Drama in Pokerville.
see Field, J. M.
Evershaw, Mary. 23294
Eversz, Emil. 2431
Eversz, Louis. 2431
Everts, Herman. 23295

Evertson, Isaac. defendant (38467)
Every-body's almanac and diary. 23297
Every child, rich or poor. 13251
Every-day book; containing biographical
sketches. 23298
Every day book of history and chronology.
51367
Every-day life in the wilds of North America.
2952
Every lady her own flower gardener. 36255
Every man his own doctor. 23299, 24459,
94713
Every man his own fattener. 23300
Every man his own guide to Niagara Falls.
36212
Every man his own guide to the falls of
Niagara. 33634
Every man his own house painter & paper
hanger. 84372
Every man his own property. 40408
Every man's right to live. 40843, 106353
Every Philadelphian's book. 61641
Every place in Canada and how to get to it.
10473
Every stranger his own guide to Niagara
Falls. 33634
Every thing beautiful in his own time. (42713)
Everyboddy's [sic] friend. 79909
Everybody's hand-book. 84953
Evesque de Petree. see Arabia Petraea
(Diocese) Bishop.
Eveux de Fleurieu, ---- d'. see Fleurieu,
Charles Pierre Claret de, Comte de.
Evidence (after-discovered) in support of
appeal. 64249
Evidence against the vices of the abolitionists,
&c. 14341
Evidence and report of the Investigating Com-
mittee. 43079
Evidence before a Committee of the House of
Commons. 68673
Evidence before the Committee of Council.
23301, (81744)
Evidence before the Congressional Committee.
80414
Evidence before the House of Commons.
23525
Evidence before the Street Railway Commis-
sioners. 45725
Evidence contained in the report. 23301,
(81744)
Evidence delivered before a Select Committee.
81745-81746, 93600
Evidence delivered on the petition. 23302,
(27606), (27610)
Evidence delivered to a Committee of the
Honourable House of Commons. 28609
Evidence demonstrating the falsehoods of
William L. Stone. 50250
Evidence from scripture and history. (49077)
Evidence given before a Committee of the
House of Commons on Aborigines.
13829
Evidence given before the Committee of the
Privy Council. 67744
Evidence given by Thomas Irving. (35122)
Evidence given in a cause depending. 94405
Evidence in relation to land titles. 94963
Evidence in the case, John Atkins, Appellant.
76505
Evidence in the case of the United States, vs.
Andres Castillero. (11419)
Evidence in the contested election. (71284)
Evidence of Lord M'Cartney. (57146), 99320,
note after 99776

Evidence of sundry persons on the slave
   trade. 13494, 1st note after 93370
Evidence of the common and statute laws of
   the realm. 23303
Evidence of the existence of God. 86591
Evidence of the linnen trade with America.
   41322
Evidence of the validity of the will of Oliver
   Smith. 7127
Evidence reported to the Senate. 82881
Evidence taken at Port of Spain. (9885)
Evidence taken before the Committee of the
   House of Commons. 10443
Evidence taken before the Committee of the
   House of Representatives. 15268,
   23304
Evidence taken by the Committee of Investiga-
   tion. 87482
Evidence taken in the Pennsylvania contested
   election. 60091
Evidence taken in the trial of Mr. Smith.
   83240
Evidence to show that Beale's survey is
   correct. 43255
Evidence upon oath. 23305
Evidences of Christianity. 20059
Evidences of the superiority of the present
   administration. 14905, 102396
Evident advantages to Great Britain and its
   allies. 23306
Evident approach of a war. 23307
Evident tokens of salvation. 46311
Evil and adulterous generation. 22122
Evil and the remedy. 49201
Evil and the remedy. Discourse . . . on the
   . . . national fast. (50319)
Evil designs of men made subservient by God
   to the public good. 363
Evil effects of a high tariff. 23308
Evil, its own destroyer. (50584)
Evil moral principles. 94491
Evil of lying. 105219
Evil of rebellion, as applicable to American
   conduct, considered. (51432)
Evil tendencies of corporal punishment.
   13850
Evils and abuses in the naval and merchant
   services exposed. 43592
Evils and remdy of lewdness. (32907)
Evils and remedy of using promises to pay
   as a measure of value. 28571
Evils and the remedy of using "promise to
   pay the bearer on demand." (56598)
Evils of democracy exemplified. 345
Evils of intemperance. A discourse. 62626
Evils of intemperance. A sermon. 27401
Evils of intemperance. By Reybold Snethen.
   85444
Evils of long credits. 92035
Evils of slavery, and the cure of slavery.
   (12727)
Evils of slavery, method of its removal.
   note after 92624
Evils of the revolutionary war. 23309,
   103300
Evils of the work now prevailing. 40573
Evils suffered by American women and Ameri-
   can children. 4291
Evis, William, alias see Livers, William.
Evolution of a state or recollections of old
   Texas days. 85099
Evolution of the foot. 53271
Evolution for the cavalry and artillery. 104819
Evolutions of a brigade, and corps d'armee.
   11328

Evreux, pere Yves d'. see Yves d'Evreux.
   Pere
Evrie, J. H. van. see Van Evrie, J. H.
Ewald, Schack Herrmann. tr. 156, 23736
Ewart, David. 23310
Ewbank, Henry. (1299), 23311
Ewbank, J. S. 54459
Ewbank, Thomas. 19504, 23312-(23313),
   27419, 69946
Ewbank, Thomas. supposed author 103034
Ewell, James. 23314
Ewer, Charles. incorrectly attributed author
   23315, 91932
Ewer, F. C. 23316-23317, 62998
Ewer, John, successively Bishop of Llandaff,
   and Bangor, d. 1774. 12318-12319,
   23318-23319, (34766), 41642-(41644),
   3d note after 99800
Ewes, J. d'. see D'Ewes, J.
Ewh oomenwahjemoowin owh Tawanemenuung
   Jesus Christ. 57265
Ewige evangelium. 91211
Ewing, Andrew, 1813-1864. 23320
Ewing, Charles. 23321, (74136)
Ewing, Edward H. (23322)
Ewing, Grenville. 23323
Ewing, James. (23324)-23325
Ewing, John, 1732-1802. 23327, (42384),
   61470, 66980, 84678C see also Corpora-
   tion for the Relief of Poor and Distressed
   Presbyterian Ministers. Trustees.
Ewing, John, 1732-1802. supposed author
   20049
Ewing, John Hoge, 1796-1887. 23326
Ewing, M. C. 23328
Ewing, Presley Underwood, 1822-1854.
   23329
Ewing, Stephen S. (23330)
Ewing, Thomas, 1789-1871. 8441, 23331,
   84743, 88935, 90380, 102287
Ewing, William. (23333)
Ex- . . . see Ex. . .
Ex Clavdii Ptolemaei geographicis libris octo.
   66497
Ex parte statement of Mrs. McFarland.
   (43241)
Ex primo rapsodiae historiarvm libro. 74658
Exact abridgment of all the public acts of
   Assembly of Virginia. 100390
Exact abridgment of all the public acts of
   Assembly, of Virginia, in force and use.
   Together with sundry precedents.
   100386
Exact abridgment of all the tryals. 37702
Exact account of all the circumstances. 4003
Exact account of Sir Hen. Morgan's voyage to,
   and famous siege and taking of Panama
   from the Spaniards. 35649
Exact and authentic narrative of the events.
   3034, 95885
Exact and impartial account of the most im-
   portant events. 27669
Exact and true account. 11786
Exact copies of advertisements of persons.
   23334
Exact description of the West-Indies. 51678,
   102816
Exact epitome of the four monarchies. 7296,
   note after 94823
Exact list of all the men, women, and boys.
   (18553)
Exact list of Parliament. 23335
Exact model or platform of good magistracy.
   33178
Exact narrative of the proceedings at Turners
   Hall. (37191)

Exact relation of the most execrable, attempts of John Allin. 9704
Exact survey of the tide. 3413
Exact table. 45726
Exact table to bring old tenor into lawful money. 45726
Exact time when the whole American debt will be entirely paid off. 23336
Exact transcripts of inscriptions. 7839
Exacta descripcion. 76227
Exacto descripcao das ilha dos Acores. 7645
Exaltacion de la . . . rosa Americana jerico. 11468
Exaltacion magnifica de la Betlemitica Rosa. 23337, 51352
Exame critico do parecer que deu a Commissao Especial das Cortes. 42345
Exame das causes, que allegou o gabinete das Thuilherias. 85658
Examen analitico del informe. 74764
Examen apologetico. 3350
Examen canonico-legal. 23338, 96309
Examen comparatif de la question des chemins de fer. 64738
Examen comparativo de la monarquia y de la republic. 23339
Examen comparativo de la tarifa i lejislacion aduanera. 17159
Examen confectionis pacificae. 12305, 12335
Examen critico-apologetico de los escritores del dia. 86383
Examen critico de un opusculo sobre el huano. 3642
Examen critico del diario de D. Luis de la Cruz. 96247
Examen critico del libelo publicado en la imprenta del comercio en Lima. 51068
Examen critico-legal de la Real orden. 17774
Examen critique de l'histoire de la geographie. 33722, 99383B
Examen critique de l'histoire et de la geographie du nouveau continent. 33753
Examen critique des voyages dans l'Amerique Septentrionale. 8019
Examen critique du memoir lu par M. d' Avezac. 30604
Examen critique du prejuge contre la couleur des Africains. (77740)
Examen critique du voyage de Roggeween. 24751, note just before 44492
Examen critique d'une nouvelle histoire. 2491
Examen de cette question. 44146
Examen de la conduite de Sonthonax, Polverel, et Nilhaud. 28286
Examen de la cuestion de Cuba. (17775)
Examen de la cuestion de limites. (49880)
Examen de la question aujourd'huis pendante. 11347
Examen de la reponse de M. N..... 50595
Examen de las indulgencias. 76272
Examen de las penitenciarias de los Estados Unidos. 23340, (59328)
Examen de l'esclavage en general. 9756, 17862
Examen de l'expose des motifs. (64896)
Examen de los derechos con que se establecieron los gobiernos popula. 1880
Examen de 1865. Concurso a premios. (76782)
Examen de pilotos com os reteiros de Portugal para o Brasil. (24316)
Examen del estado actual de los esclavos. 24799

Examen del merito que puedan tener los fundamentos. 105492, 106013A
Examen del plan presentado a las cortes. 64898
Examen des assertions contenues dans un opuscule. 76840
Examen des avantages que les plus grandes victoires. 97337-97338
Examen des droits des Etats-Unis. 41611, 95344
Examen des operations des ministres d' Angleterre. 36426
Examen des operations des ministres en Angleterre. (36425)
Examen des projets de communication maritime. 50769
Examen des questions de jurisdiction. 23341
Examen des recherches philosophiques. 60995
Examen du gouvernement d'Angleterre. 41646
Examen du plan presente aux cortes. 64897
Examen du projet financier. 22398
Examen du rapport. 75111
Examen du sentiment d'un pretendu patriote. (22243)
Examen d'un ecrit de M. le Marquis de Barbe-Marbois. (11525)
Examen d'un pamphlet. 14553, 98669
Examen et reponse. 47824
Examen general de la situacion politica. 23225
Examen historico-critico. 94564
Examen historicum. 31656
Examen historique. (76269)
Examen imparcial de les dissensiones. 23058
Examen imparcial de la respuesta. 97044
Examen impartial du jugement. 77647
Examen impartial d'un ouvrage. 50210
Examen ingeniorum Ioannis Huartis expenditur. 64450
Examen over het vertoogh tegen het ongefonde-erde ende schadelijck sluyten. 7575
Examen over het vertoogh teghen het onghe-fondeerde ende schadelijck sluyten. 7576, 99308
Examen politique des colonies modernes. 11111, 101244
Examen politique des colonies modernes, dans le but les plus particulier. 11107, 101244
Examen publico. 72523
Examen: quels avantages les Anglois ou les Americains? 97339
Examen rapide des deux projets. 5652
Examen rapide du cahier de doleances de la colonies. 11728
Examen sobre la Franca comunication. 2094, 58404
Examen sucincto. 23342
Examen vande valsche resolutie van de Heeren Burgemeesters ende Raden tot Amster-dam. 16732-16734, 23344, 3d note after 102889A, 7th note after 102890
Examens de 1866. (76782)
Examination and confutation of several errors. 24387, 95579
Examination and explanation of the South-Sea Company's scheme. 88182
Examination and explanation of the South-Sea scheme. 69523
Examination and refutation of Mr. Gilbert Tennent's remarks. 94700
Examination and rejection of Tho. Ledie Birch. 5529
Examination and review of a pamphlet. 102205

Examination by chemical analysis and otherwise. 23345

Examination by Robert D. Smith. 83857

Examination [by Roger Williams.] 17077

Examination into the causes of explosions.
43488

Examination into the conduct of Mr. P———.
63091

Examination into the conduct of the delegates.
29956, (78562)-78563, 4th note after
100862

Examination into the conduct of the present
administration. 23346

Examination into the claims of Methodist
episcopacy. 6222

Examination into the Egyptian, Mosaic, and
American systems. 59464

Examination into the expediency of establishing a Board of Agriculture. 29548,
53661

Examination into the leading principles.
102352

Examination into the legality and propriety.
64783

Examination into the principles, conduct, and
designs of the Earl of Shelburne.
80108

Examination into the principles, conduct, and
designs, of the minister. 23347

Examination into the principle, capabilities,
and terms of union. 15426

Examination into the prospective effects.
23348

Examination into the rights of the Indian
nations. 23349, 63221, 1st note after
103107

Examination into the true cause of the Gulf
Stream. 91090

Examination into the validity of the New
Jersey senatorial election. (53105)

Examination of a case. 1st note after 100510,
100584

Examination of a French prisoner. 4035

Examination of a pamphlet, entitled "Calumny
refuted." 35231

Examination of a pamphlet, entitled "His
Catholic Majesty's manifesto." (23350)

Examination of a pamphlet entitled Republican
economy. 102396

Examination of a pamphlet . . . on Dr.
Horner's . . . notice. 33037

Examination of a person. 67164

Examination of a recent pamphlet. 90878

Examination of "A reply to 'Hints on the reorganization of the navy.'" 31978, 74187,
69696

Examination of a tract. 10868

Examination of an article. (69590)

Examination of an epistle. 31717

Examination of an some answer to a pamphlet.
7661

Examination of Beachamp Plantagenet's description. 59667

Examination of Cadwallader D. Colden's book.
14278

Examination of certain charges against Lemuel
G. Arnold. (1665), 2077

Examination of certain charges preferred
against the medical class. (60757)

Examination of certain proceedings and
principles. 3930

Examination of certain proceedings of the
Board of Superintendents. 98496

Examination of certain remarks, &c., in a
letter. 8505, (65240)

Examination of certain remarks on . . . a
letter. 8505, (65240)

Examination of certain reviews. 73834

Examination of charges against the American
missionaries. 23351

Examination of Col. Aaron Burr. 9426

Examination of Col. Trumbull's address.
50959

Examination of Dr. Bascom's review. 59472

Examination of Dr. Beecher's sermon. 103798

Examination of Doctor Benjamin Franklin,
before an august assembly. 25501

Examination of Doctor Benjamin Franklin,
relative of the repeal of the American
stamp act. (25502)

Examination of Dr. Bond's rejoinder. (33569)

Examination of E. L.'s "Review of the causes
and course." 25219

Examination of five varieties of cabbage.
75793

Examination of General Wilkinson's conduct.
104028

Examination of Joseph Galloway, Esq., by a
Committee of the House of Commons.
(26428), note after 79366

Examination of Joseph Galloway, Esq; late
Speaker. 26427

Examination of Lieutenant General the Earl
Cornwallis. 16813

Examination of M. Hudson his vindication.
92113

Examination of Mr. Barnes reply. 71285

Examination of Mr. Bradish's answer. 25641

Examination of Mr. Harris's scriptural
researches. 18504

Examination of Mr. Huskinson's system of
duties on imports. 10889, (18016)

Examination of Mr. Jefferson's message to
Congress. 17426

Examination of Mr. Randolph's vindication.
96446

Examination of Mr. Rantoul's report. 25039

Examination of Mr. Stephen's "Slavery of the
British West India colonies." (3352)

Examination of Mr. Thomas C. Brown. 8568

Examination of nine sermons on Matth. 16. 18.
2629, 2629, 24439

[Examination of officers.] 76554, 76647

Examination of phrenology. 79468

Examination of Professor Agassiz's sketch.
2612

Examination of "remarks," on a second college
in Connecticut. 15721, 36334, note
before 101999

Examination of Rev. Augustus Littlejohn.
41546

Examination of seven sermons. 2425

Examination of some of the anthracites.
36334

Examination of some of the provisions. 23352,
91879

Examination of some statements concerning
Major-General Greene. 28600

Examination of statements respecting Barbados.
(3268)

Examination of subjects who are in the House
of Refuge. 85952

Examination of sundry scriptures. 29402

Examination of that part of Mr. Blair's
affidavit. 55222

Examination of the accout lately published by
Mr. E. Smith. 80191

Examination of the Age of reason. 100977

Examination of the alleged expediency. 23353,
49088

Examination of the banking system of Massachusetts. 1813, 19245, (69692)

Examination of the Boston report on free trade. 10889

Examination of the British doctrine which subjects to capture. 4549, 43707, 101270

Examination of the case of Dred Scot. 25009

Examination of the causes & effects. 60092

Examination of the causes of the differences. 10842

Examination of the Chancellor's opinion. 41638

Examination of the charges of Mr. John Scoble & Mr. Lewis Tappan. 67184

Examination of the charges of the Board of Trade. 54266

Examination of the Charleston memorial. 10889, 12053

Examination of the Charleston memorial.—No. 1. (35938)

Examination of the Charleston memorial. No. V. 12053

Examination of the charter and proceedings. 24609

Examination of the Cherokee question. 12455

Examination of the claim of the United States. 95345

Examination of the claims and assertions of Emanuel Swedenborg. 55347

Examination of the claims of Mr. Van Buren and Gen. Harrison. 95536

Examination of the commercial principles of the late negotiation between Great Britain and France in MDCCLXI. 23354

Examination of the commercial principles of the late negotiation in 1761. 15031

Examination of the company's mineral lands. (1960)

Examination of the conduct of Great Britain, respecting neutrals. (17297), 43708

Examination of the conduct of Great Britain towards the neutral commerce of America. 3384

Examination of the conduct of the executive. 23355, (26388), 2d note after 101806

Examination of the Connecticut claim to lands in Pennsylvania. 84604-84605

Examination of the constitution for [sic] the United States. 23356, 104632

Examination of the constitutionality of the embargo laws. (5766)

Examination of the controversy between Georgia and the Creeks. 23357

Examination of the controversy between the Greek deputies. 21108

Examination of the decision of the Commissioners. 93571

Examination of the decision of the Supreme Court. (5576)

Examination of the difficulties between those powers. (25428)

Examination of the doctrine declared and the power claimed. 35311-35312

Examination of the doctrines and principles. 104523

Examination of the executive proceeding. 102116

Examination of the evidence before Select Committee. 23358

Examination of the expediency and constitutionality. 6039

Examination of the false assumptions. (36932)

Examination of the falsely-assumed equality. 10248

Examination of the financial problems of the day. 68549

Examination of the fourth volume. 28792

Examination of the grounds or causes. 23359, 59659

Examination of the justice, legality, and policy of the new system. (57502)

Examination of the late proceedings in Congress. 29952, 94490

Examination of the late Rev. President Edwards' "Enquiry on freedom of will." 21930

Examination of the law of burial. 73961

Examination of the legality of the general orders. (23360), (74188), 1st note after 93829

Examination of the letter addressed by Edward Potter, M. P. 26105

Examination of the levy for 1864. 54446

Examination of the licence law of . . . Massachusetts. 77015, 2d note after 98269

Examination of the line of the Great Erie Canal. 22743

Examination of the measure of Mr. James G. Holmes. 12049

Examination of the memoirs and writings of Joseph John Guerney. (32368)

Examination of the memorial. 23361

Examination of the message. 102586

Examination of the Mosaic laws of servitude. 35867

Examination of the new tariff. 10109, 10889, 1st note after 92842

Examination of the objections to the British treaty. 10983

Examination of the operations of the British ministers. (36427)

Examination of the opinion. 23362, note after 102973

Examination of the origin, policy, and principles. 96190

Examination of the pamphlet entitled, "The actions of the councils vindicated in the case of Olivet Church." 88660

Examination of the power of the fraternity. 91957

Examination of the power of the President to remove from office. 23364, (29394)

Examination of the pretended charters of . . . New York. 54267

Examination of the President, Cashiers and Directors of the United States Bank. 3189

Examination of the President's answer to the New-Haven Remonstrance. (40117)

Examination of the President's message. 29953

Examination of the President's reply to the New-Haven Remonstrance. 14312, (23365), 97440

Examination of the pretentions of Martin Behaim. (4431)

Examination of the pretentions of New England. 10889, 23366

Examination of the pretentions of Thomas Jefferson. 84829

Examination of the principles, and an enquiry. (23367), (60861)

Examination of the principles and boasted disinterestedness. 41680

Examination of the principles of peace and war. 23368

Examination of the principles of the slave registry bill. 36647

Examination of the proceedings on the presentment. 100681

Examination of the prophecies. 95315

Examination of the proposed union. 44799

Examination of the question, "how far the common law of England is the law of the federal government of the United States?" 97376

Examination of the question now in discussion. 11346, 23369, (69691), 71353

Examination of the question of Anaesthesia. 84441, 84445-84446

Examination of the question, who is the writer? 20985, (74488)

Examination of the reasons. 23370, 68302

Examination of the relations between the Cherokees. (12456)

Examination of the remarks made by a curate. 102565

Examination of the "remarks" on considerations suggested by the establishment of a second college in Connecticut. 15720-15721, 36444, (69512), note before 101999, 103169

Examination of the remarks on the report of the Commissioners. (53977), 69497, (73230)

Examination of the report of a Committee of Citizens. 23363

Examination of the report of the Berbice Commissioners. 44704

Examination of the report of the Committee of Investigation. (22650), 89139, note after 101937, 104796

Examination . . . of the reports of explorations for railroad routes. 69900, 69946

Examination . . . of the reports of explorations . . . in 1853-'54. 69900, 69946

Examination of the Rev. Mr. Barstow's "Remarks." 3094

Examination of the Reverend Mr. Burke's letter. 17594, 69501, 90377

Examination of the Rev. Mr. Harris's scriptural researches. 67714

Examination of the Rev. Mr. Tyler's second pamphlet. 68122

Examination of the review of the reports. 6763, 77770

Examination of the "Review of the trial and acquital." 84739

Examination of the right of secession. 23371

Examination of the rights of the colonies. 23372

Examination of the Russian claims. 93270

Examination of the strictures in the New-England journal. 49203-49204, 1st-2d notes after 97444

Examination of the strictures upon the American Education Society. 93200

Examination of the system of Universalism. 83596

Examination of the telegraphic apparatus and the processes. 50963

Examination of the theory and the effect of laws. 32877

Examination of the third volume. 28792

Examination of the three French prisoners. 66062

Examination of the treaty of amity. (29954), (31747)

Examination of the validity of the pretended charters. 74603

Examination of the various charges exhibited against Aaron Burr. 98529-98530

Examination of the water question. (8325)

Examination of Thomas Paine's Age of reason. 91818

Examination of witnesses before George W. Miller. 54826

Examination of usury. (82697)

Examination papers for . . . 1865-66. (45867)

Examination papers of the New York Free Academy. 54284

Examinations of Doctor Marriott, and Messrs. Maseres and Hey. 44688

Examinations of the judgment rendered. (28363)

Examinator. pseud. Critical review. see. Cobb, Lyman. supposed author

Examiner. pseud. Causes of the present crisis. 11583

Examiner. pseud. Reading Railroad Company. 68214

"Examiner." pseud. [Remarks on the sedition law.] 57860

Examiner. 93543

Examiner and chronicle. 84051

Examiner and journal of political economy. 23373, 67501

Examiner; containing political essays. 23374

Examiner examined. Letter from a gentleman in Connecticut. (23375), 38178

Examiner examin'd. Or, an answer to the Rev. Mr. Prescott's examination. 8505, (65240)

Examiner, examined, or Gilbert Tennent, harmonius. 30172, 62419, 94687

Examiner examined. Remarks on a piece wrote by Mr. Isaac Backus. 2627, 24439

Examiner, or Gilbert against Tennent. 30172, 62419, 94687

Examiner, or New-York recorder and Baptist register. 23376

Example for Scotchmen in Canada. 85470

Example of Christ. 97313

Example of justice in the tryal. 42737, 88270

Example of life and death. 80917

Example of Washington. 698

Example to youth. 25616

Examples from the eighteenth and nineteenth centuries. 90816

Examples of household taste. 84493

Examples of the revolution. 86114

Exauvillez, Andre Philippe Octave Boistel d'. see Boistel d'Exauvillez, Andre Philippe Octave.

Ex-Cadet. pseud. Life of Lieut. Gen. T. J. Jackson. (35467)

Ex-Cadet. pseud. Life of Thomas J. Jackson. 35468

Exceeding danger of men's deferring their repentance. 46690

Exmo. Sor. El Comissario General de la Religion de San Francisco. 87231

Exmo. Senor. el Dr. D. J. M. Solano y Marcha. 86247

Excelent.mo Senor. El Doctor Don Luis de Mendoca Catano y Aragon. (47831)

Ex.mo Senor. Por condicion expresa del assiento ajustado. 99618

Excellence of the Gospel. 58609

Excellencie of Christ Jesvs, treated on. 32841

Excellency and advantage of doing good. 95612

Excellency and advantages of religion. 31610

Excellency and usefulness of the common-prayer. 86617

Excellency of a good name. 18267

Excellency of a public spirit. 46681, 46686

Excellency of a publick spirit discoursed. 46681
Excellency of faith. 103941
Excellency of our Christian polity. (73565)
Excellency of the Christian religion. 8641
Excellency of the divine commandment. 3471
Excellency of the Gospel-message. 103931
Excellency of the righteous. 24442
Excellent act concerning preaching. 94922, note after 103402
Excellent charge to the jury. 96819
Excellent collection of hymns. (82499)
Excellent discourse which sheweth by cleare and strong arguments. 31510, 1st note after 97141
Excellent help to multiplication. 104997
Excellent observations and notes. 67561
Excellent sermon preached in St. Paul's Church. 56408
Excellent song. 94432
Excellent speech for the defendant. 96913
Excellent spirit forms the character of a good ruler. 102520
Excellent work, published some years ago. 105227
Excellentissimo Senor. Por el Coronel de Cavalleria Don Francisco de Aguirre Gomendio. 98018
Excelsior Division, no. 16, Boston. see Sons of Temperance of North America. Massachusetts. Excelsior Division, no. 16, Boston.
Excelsior series. 84305
Exceptions, in a second letter. 13350
Exceptions of Mr. Solomon Williams. 17675
Excerpta ex relatione. 96969
Excessive cruelty to slaves. 103668
Exchange, Boston. see Boston. Exchange.
Exchange. A home and colonial review of commerce. 23377
Exchange alley. 23378
Exchange and cotton trade. 22676
Exchange Company, Philadelphia. see Philadelphia Exchange Company. firm
Exchange tables of British sterling. 24949
Exchequer and currency. (31425)
Excise journal. 34918
Excise tax law. An act to provide internal revenue. 23379
Excise tax law. Approved July 1, 1862. 23044
Excise tax laws. 23380
Excitations to the constant and diligent exercise. (79411)
Excitement. 50311
Exciting crisis. (29622)
Exciting story of army and high life in New York in 1776. (9212)
Exclamacion y declamacion funeral de el D. Juan de Veytia. 19229
Exclusion of non-communicants. 82919
Exclusively paper currency inconsistent. 50791
Exclusivism. 3501
Ex-Colonel of the Adjutant-General's Department. pseud. Baked meats of the funeral. see Halpine, Charles Graham.
Ex-colons, refugies a la Jamaique. pseud. Expose de l'etat actuel des choses. 65420
Excommunication of M. Phelps from the Congretational Church. (61383)
Excvbationes semicentvm ex decicisionibvs. 50107
Excursion au Canada. 14936

Excursion au Rio-Salado et dans la Chaco. 35516
Excursion aux Indes Occidentales. 20380
Excursion aux Provinces Maritimes. 56433
Excursion certificate. 88462
Excursion chez les Peaux-Rouges. 81307
Excursion dans l'Amerique du Sud. 23381
Excursion d'un touriste au Mexique. 27485, 73751
Excursion into Bethlehem & Nazareth. (56815)
Excursion made by the executive and legislatures. 23382
Excursion of the dog cart, a poem. (23383)
Excursion of the Portland Light Infantry to Montreal, C. E. 90504
Excursion of the Putnam Phalanx to Boston. 23384
Excursion of the Putnam Phalanx to Mount Vernon. 13248
Excursion on the River Connecticut. (15865)
Excursion through the slave states. 23960
Excursion through the United States and Canada during the years 1822-23. (5872), 84305-84306, 84309, 84313, 96503
Excursion to California. 37321
Excursion to Montauk. 92741
Excursion to the Mammoth Cave. (18739)
Excursion to the Oregon. 96382
Excursion to the springs. 23385
Excursion to the United States. 101240
Excursions dans l'Amerique Meridionale. 102093
Excursions d'un naturaliste en France. 20960
Excursions in and about Newfoundland. 36877
Excursions in North America. 100980, 100981-100983
Excursions to Cairo, Jerusalem, Damascus and Balbec. 36499
Excursions to Murray Bay. 23386
Ex-diputado de Nueva Espana. pseud. Carta. see Quiros y Millan, Jose Maria.
Execution of John Brown. 59167
Execution of Casey and Cora. 37808, 97098
Execution of five professional gamblers. 33250, note before 91708
Execution of laws in Utah. 17354
Execution of seventeen innocent persons! 89067
Execution of United States laws. 20693
Executive acts of Ex-President Fillmore. (24332)
Executive address of . . . Fairbanks. 23666
Executive and legislative documents. 55609
Executive committee of citizens and taxpayers. 54090
Executive committee of the Association respectfully submit. 89645
Executive Committee on Auction Regulations, New York. 69439
Executive communication . . . inclosing the correspondence. (45141)
Executive communication to the General Assembly. 45142
Executive communication to the House of Delegates. 45143
Executive Council Chamber, of the Province of Upper Canada. 98059B
Executive Department, Columbia, S. C., Nov. 26, 1852. 87548
Executive Department, November 28, 1836. 87545
Executive Department of Texas. 94957

Executive documents, first session, seventeenth Congress. 15525

Executive documents . . . for . . . 1860. 49246

Executive documents, Letter to the collector. 87724

Executive documents. No. 5. 87555

Executive documents. No. 4. 87554

Executive documents. No. 1. 87550

Executive documents. No. 3. 87553

Executive documents. No. 2. Correspondence and other papers, relating to Fort Sumter. 87551

Executive documents. No. 2. Correspondence and other papers, relating to Fort Sumter. Including correspondence of Hon. Isaac W. Hayne. 87552

Executive influence. 27329

Executive journal of the Senate of . . . Michigan. (48731)

Executive message of . . . William F. M. Arny. 53277

Executive message on the western boundary of the state. 45090

Executive officers &c. of the Confederate States government. 87786, 87788-87789

Executive organization of the U. S. Sanitary Commission. 76650

Executive power. 18027, 42534

Executive power of appointment and removal. 1277A

Executive power of removal. 72748

Executive proceedings of the Senate of the United States. 58405

Executive proclamations and licence. 14978

Executive protest, prerogatives, and patronage. 4104

Executive record. 74353

Executive usurpation. 4030

Executive vetoes. 82365

Executor and Heirs of John and Richard Codman. see Heirs and Executors of John and Richard Codman. and Codman, Stephen.

Exec. of D. Rittenhouse. defendant 7970

Executor of William Cecil. defendant see William Cecil's Executor. defendant

Executors of Andrew Fresneau. defendants 47349

Executors of Stirk. defendants 7328

Executors of the Last Will and Testament of Samuel Hughes, Deceased. 96442

Executrix's sale. 74681

Exegesis regi Hispaniae facta. 33491, 67355

Exemplar bullo. 745

Exemplar duarum litterarum. (8784)

Exemplar libelli supplicis. 67355

Exemplar vida de la muy Rev. Madre so Maria Josefa Sina. 26499

Exemplar vida y gloriosa muerte en odio de la fe. 24809

Exemplare der zu Rostock von Hermann Barckhusen. 99378

Exemplary pastor. 89793

Exemplary wife. (73614)

Exemplification of several distinguished American characters. 105167

Exemplo, que segun la costumbre de los sabados de Quaresma. 39478

Exequias celebradas por el S. C. de Mier y Trespalacios. (48887)

Exequias de Abrahao Lincoln, com um esboco biographico. 44327

Exequias de Abrahao Lincoln. Presidente dos Estados da America. 15101

Exequias de D. Manuel Ignacio Gonzalez del Campillo. 10313

Exequias de el Illust. Senor Dr. D. Manuel Antonio Roxo, Rio, y Vieyra. 72809, 73740

Exequias de la Marquesa de las Torres de Rada. (11032)

Exequias de la Reyna de Maria de Austria en Mexico. 23576

Exequias de la Reyna Dona Margarita de Austria. 46859

Exequias de la Reyna D. Maria de Austria celebradas en Lima. 41105

Exequias de la Reyna Dona Mariana de Austria. 22919

Exequias dedicadas el dia 4 de Noviembre de 1817. 98910

Exequias del Rey Felipe III. 70051

Exequias do Senhor D. Miguel de Brahanca. 7319

Exequias del Senor D. Manuel Ignacio Gonzalez del Campillo. (27818)

Exequias hechas al Ilustrisimo Senor Doctor Mariano Fernandez Fortique. 25177

Exequias honorarias. 57818

Exequias militar. 48468

Exequias mitologicas. 76264

Exequias que por muerte de D. J. C. Ruiz de Cabanas y Crespo. 9766

Exequias reales celebradas en la Santa Iglesia Catedral de Mexico. 48468

Exequias reales en Mexico. (48468)

Exercice 1830. (15068)

Exercicio practico de la voluntad divina. 76777

Exerciciso divinos revelados al Venerable Nicolas Eschio. 93885-93886

Exerciciso poeticos. 49989

Exercise, consisting of a dialogue and ode. 84607

Exercise, containing a dialogue and an ode. 32978

Exercise, containing a dialogue and ode on peace. 23388, 61547

Exercise, containing a dialogue and ode on the accession. 23387, 61547, 84608

Exercise, containing a dialogue and ode sacred to the memory. 84606

Exercise, containing a dialogue and two odes performed at the public commencement, in the College of Philadelphia, May 20th, 1766. 61643, 84610

Exercise, containing a dialogue and two odes, performed at the public commencement in the College of Philadelphia. November 17, 1767. 23389, 61547, 84610

Exercise; containing, a dialogue and two odes set to music. 61642, 84609

Exercise delivered at the public commencement at Nassau-Hall. 7190

Exercise for garrison and field ordnance. 23390

Exercise for the militia. 45727, 1st note after 48978

Exercise of the musket. 45727

Exercise, performed at the public commencement. 84610

Exercise at the consecration of the flag. 6664

Exercises at the consecration of Mount Hope Cemetery. (20628)

Exercises at the dedication of the new city hall. 89859

Exercises at the fourth annual commencement and distribution of premiums. 75236, (76987)

Exercises at the reunion of the Young Ladies' High School. 66383
Exercises commemorating the two-hundredth anniversary. 85222
Exercises, containing eight treatises. 6023
Exercises, contayning eight treatises. 6024
Exercises held at the celebration. (53692)
Exercises in English reading. 64034
Exercises in history, chronology, and biography. 73609
Exercises of commencement day. 9337
Exercises on the hundredth anniversary of the incorporation. 59271
Exercises on the . . . inauguration of Daniel Read. 68147
Exercises on the 150th anniversary of . . . Old Nutfield. 43347
Exercises on the ter-centenary celebration. 42493
Exercises philosophiques et litteraires. 67060
Exercises, political and others. 95532-95533
Exercises publiques des etudians du Petit Seminaire de Quebec. 67060
Exercitacao na qual plenamente se prova. 47460
Exercitation on Numb. XXXII. 10, 11, 12. (21087)
Exercitationes. (75565)
Exercitationum academicarum maxima. 104959
Exeter, Richard. 104548
Exeter, Bishop of. see Clagett, Nicholas, successively Bishop of St. Davids, and Exeter, d. 1746. Keppel, Frederic, Bishop of Exeter, 1729-1777. Ross, John, Bishop of Exeter, 1719-1792.
Exeter, Mass. Church. 72616
Exeter, N. H. Committee to Investigate and Report the Doings of the Trustees of the Robinson Female Seminary. 72240
Exeter, N. H. Convention Relative to the Observance of the Lord's Day, and to the Suppression of Vice, 1815. see Rockingham County, N. H. Convention Relative to the Observance of the Lord's Day, and to the Suppression of Vice, Exeter, 1815.
Exeter, N. H. Council of Ten Churches, 1743. see Congregational Churches in New Hampshire. Ecclesiastical Council, Exeter, 1743.
Exeter, N. H. Ecclesiastical Council, 1842. see Congregational Churches in New Hampshire. Ecclesiastical Council, Exeter, 1842.
Exeter, N. H. Library Society. see Exeter Library Society, Exeter, N. H.
Exeter, N. H. Robinson Female Seminary. see Robinson Female Seminary, Exeter, N. H.
Exeter, N. H. Rockingham County Teacher's Institute. see Rockingham County, N. H. Teacher's Institute, Exeter.
Exeter Library Society, Exeter, N. H. (23394)
Ex.-Gov. Lowe's letter to the Virginia Legislature. 46962
Ex.-Gov. Lowe's letter to the Virginia Legislature, dated, Ashland, Virginia. 42413
Exhaustive argument of A. J. Mullane, Esq. (51276)
Exhibicion Anual de Bellas Artes Venezolanas, la., Caracas, 1872. 89284
Exhibit concerning the improvement of the Cayuga Marshes. 88873

Exhibit in relation to the present condition of the Springfield and Mansfield Railroad Company. 89900
Exhibit in relation to the present condition of the Springfield, Mount Vernon & Pittsburg Railroad Company. 89901
Exhibit of affairs of the Bellefontaine and Indiana Railroad Company. 4504
Exhibit of condition [of the Burlington and Mississippi Rail Road in Iowa.] 35031
Exhibit of the affairs of the Cincinnati and Marietta Railroad. 13109
Exhibit of the affairs of the Pittsburgh, Maysville and Cincinnati Railroad Company. 63137
Exhibit of the affairs of the Seaboard and Roanoke Railroad Company. 78543
Exhibit of the Catawissa, Williamsport and Erie Railroad Company. 59965
Exhibit of the condition of the South Western Railroad Company. 88627
Exhibit of the conditions and prospects of the Iron Mountain Railroad Company. (35096)
Exhibit of the Fox and Wisconsin Improvement Company. 25383
Exhibit of the Lake Superior Iron Company. 38671
Exhibit of the losses sustained. 23396
Exhibit of the manufacturing and commercial industry. 49233, note before 96959
Exhibit of the Milwaukee & Horicon Railroad Company. 49166
Exhibit of the . . . [Milwaukee and Mississippi Rail Road] Company. 49167
Exhibit of the present condition of the . . . [Milwaukee, Waukesha, and Mississippi Rail Road] Company. 49177
Exhibit of the shocking oppression and injustice suffered. 10889
Exhibit of the Smithsonian Institution at the Cotton States Exposition, Atlanta, 1895. 85020
Exhibit of the value and importance of the coal mines. (51154)
Exhibit of the views and spirit of the Episcopal press. 97125
Exhibit representative in a measure of the collection. 83739
Exhibit, showing the success of cotton factories. 23397
Exhibition catalogue of paintings of the National Gallery. 51985
Exhibition, 1845 [of the Buffalo Horticultural Society.] 9063
Exhibition intelligencer. 23900
Exhibition. Jesus Christ crucified and put to an open shame. 105928
Exhibition of Antique Relics, &c., Held by the Ladies' Centennial Committee, Salem, Mass., 1875. see Salem, Mass. Ladies' Centennial Committee. Exhibition of Antique Relics, &c., 1875.
Exhibition of 1853. 23399
Exhibition of facts. 42093, (45728)
Exhibition of Fine Arts, Chicago, 1859. see Chicago. Exhibition of Fine Arts, 1859.
Exhibition of fine arts. Catalogue of the first exhibition. 12647
Exhibition of Industry, New-York, 183. 23398
Exhibition of Ingenuity and Design, Philadelphia, 1857. see Pennsylvania Institute of Design. Exhibition, 1st, Philadelphia, 1857.
Exhibition of Leutze's . . . picture. 40729

Exhibition of Oil Paintings for the Benefit of
the Soldiers' and Sailors' Home,
Philadelphia, 1865. 60620
Exhibition of rare old paintings. 77108
Exhibition of Rhode Island College and Brown
University. 8621
Exhibition of some of the dishonorable means.
102253A
Exhibition of the advantages and disadvantages.
90965
Exhibition of the Charleston Apprentices'
Library Society. 12040
Exhibition of the Columbian Society of Art-
ists. 14881
Exhibition of the Dismal Swamp Canal.
(20264)
Exhibition of the Industry of All Nations,
New York, 1853-1854. see New York
(City) Exhibition of the Industry of All
Nations, 1853-1854.
Exhibition of the Lawrence Academy, July
20, 1858. 39388
Exhibition of the Linonian Society. 105900
Exhibition of the National Academy of Design.
M.DCCC.XXX. The fifth. 54412
Exhibition of the National Academy of Design.
1831. The sixth. 51913
Exhibition of the Pennsylvania Academy of the
Fine Arts, . . . 1838. 60294
Exhibition of the rigorous morals. (15761)
Exhibition of the Society of Artists of the
United States. 1811. 86006
Exhibition of the Society of Artists of the
United States, and the Pennsylvania
Academy. 60616
Exhibition of the University Grammar School.
66377
Exhibition of the unjust and oppressive opera-
tion. 23340
Exhibition of the Works of Industry of All
Nations, London, 1851. see London.
Great Exhibition of the Works of Industry
of All Nations, 1851.
Exhibition of Tom Thumb. 96131
Exhibition of wolves in Sheep's clothing.
23401
Exhibitions of paintings, etc. during 1848-58.
(45211A)
Exhibitor of the Lecture on heads. pseud.
Exhibitor of the Lecture on heads,
having received an advertisement. see
Stevens, George Alexander.
Exhibitor of the Lecture on heads, having
received an advertisement signed W, X,
Y, Z. 91499
Exhibits accompanying the answer. 12206
Exhibits of the condition and prospects of the
Cleveland, Columbus and Cincinnati
Railroad. (13671)
Exhibits of the Smithsonian Institution and
United States National Museum at the
Alaska-Yukon-Pacific Exposition, Seattle,
Washington, 1909. 85021
Exhibits of the Smithsonian Institution and
United States National Museum at the
Jamestown Tercentennial Exposition,
Norfolk, Virginia, 1907. 85022
Exhibits of the Smithsonian Institution at the
Panama-Pacific International Exposition,
San Francisco, California, 1915. 85023
Exhortacion a la submission y concordia.
50608
Exhortacion a los habitantes del Nuevo Mundo.
23402
Exhortacion a los fieles de la ciudad de la
Havana. 29433

Exhortacion de paz. 40908
Exhortacion del Exmo. Illmo. Sr. Don
Francisco Xavier de Lizana y Beaumont.
41661
Exhortacion del Ilmo. Senor Obispo de Mallorca.
44136
Exhortacion hecha en la Catedral de la ciudad
de La Plata. 94867
Exhortacion pastoral. 97278
Exhortacion patriotica a la milicia nacional.
67327
Exhortacion patriotica a los habitantes de la
isla de Cuba. (1881)
Exhortacion patriotica-sagrada. (60897)
Exhortacion pronunciada en la Iglesia Parro-
quial de Guadalupe. 60914
Exhortacion que dirige a los habitantes de la
provincia de Valladolid. 98371
Exhortation. 46735
Exhortation adressee a tous les Chretiens.
27311
Exhortation & caution to Friends. 37193,
86057
Exhortation at Cooperstown. (43157)
Exhortation, delivered to the people. 2131
Exhortation or call to a professing people.
96385
Exhortation to a condemned malefactor,
delivered March 6th, 1685-6. 46244
Exhortation to a condemned malefactor
delivered March the 7th, 1686. 50296
Exhortation to all. 18477
Exhortation to be with God. 103699
Exhortation to his [i. e. Sir Henry Vane's]
children and family. 80993
Exhortation to his [i. e. Joseph Emerson's]
people. 22437
Exhortation to the clergy of Pennsylvania.
(17915)
Exhortation to the freemen of America.
97557
Exhortation to the inhabitants of the province
of South-Carolina. 33780
Exhortation to the Roman Catholick clergy of
Ireland. 4880
Exhortation to the United Friends. 86627,
note after 104031
Exhortation to young and old. 102245
Exhortation to youth. (47454)
Exhortation unto reformation, amplified.
96301
Exhortations to faith and obedience. 81337
Exile of Ireland. 104835
Exile of Major-General Eustace. (23116)
Exiled Irish patriots. 79518
Exiles, Antoine Francois Prevost d'. see
Prevost d'Exiles, Antoine Francois.
Exiles. A tale. 72189, 2d note after 94271
Exiles dans la foret. 69040
Exiles in Virginia. 27464
Exiles lay. 23403
Exiles of Florida. 27327
Exiles of Siberia. 78744
Exile's return. 81175, 81177
Exile's return; or a narrative of Samuel Snow.
85537
Existence de l'homme et des societes en
harmonie. 71273
Existence of the United States foretold in the
Bible. (2910)
Existing desecration. 74657
Existing difficulties in the government of the
Canadas. 72584
Existing revolution. 62670
"Existing vacancy." 5534

Ex-member of Congress. pseud. Ella
   Cameron. (22199)
Ex-member of Congress. pseud. My ride
   to the barbecue. 51622
Ex-member of the Philadelphia Bar. pseud.
   Finger-post to public business. (24366)
Ex-ministro de relationes. pseud. Exposi-
   cion. 23435
Exodus, Deuteronomy, Job, Ezra, Nehemiah,
   Esther, Ruth. (22851)
Exodus of the Church of Scotland. 85290
Exodus of the western nations. (37598)
Ex-orderly sergeant a veteran of the Na-
   tional Guard. pseud. Recollections of
   the early days. see Mason, John.
Exortacion del D. D. Antonio Camilo Vergara.
   98968
Exotic case of taxation. 94935
Exotic ornithology. 78138
Exotici curiosi continuatio. (18524)
Ex-parte Council, Hollis Street Church,
   Boston, 1839. see Congregational
   Churches in Massachusetts. Ex-parte
   Council, Hollis Street Church, Boston,
   1839.
Ex-parte Council, Newton Centre, Mass.,
   1866. see Congregational Churches in
   Massachusetts. Ecclesiastical Council,
   Newton Centre, 1866.
Ex-parte Council, Providence, R. I., 1832.
   see Congregational Churches in Rhode
   Island. Ecclesiastical Council, Provi-
   dence, 1832.
Ex-parte Council, Rehoboth, Mass., 1825.
   see Congregational Churches in Massa-
   chusetts. Ecclesiastical Council, 1st-
   3d, Rehoboth, 1825.
Ex-parte Council, Wareham, Mass., 1845.
   see Congregational Churches in Massa-
   chusetts. Ex-parte Council, Wareham,
   1845.
Expected dissolution of all things. (47136)
Expedicion Goicuria. 86257
Expedicion hecha en Tejas. 104992
Expediency and means of establishing a uni-
   versity in . . . New-York. 40840
Expediency and utility of war. 171
Expediency of securing our American colonies.
   23404
Expediente instruido en el Ministerio de
   Relaciones Esteriores. 23405
Expediente instruido por el Consulado de la
   Habana. 17776
Expediente seguido en Junta Extraordinaria de
   Tribunales. 23406
Expeditio Francisci Draki Eqvitis Angli.
   20828, 93588
Expeditio in Floridam. 39634
Expedition against Carthagene, 1741. 20518
Expedition Belge au Mexique. 19479
Expedition dans les parties centrales de
   l'Amerique du Sud. 11411
Expedition du General Banks dans la Riviere
   Rouge. 2306A
Expedition du General en Chef Leclerc. 40011
Expedition du Mexique. Par Edgar Quinet.
   67302
Expedition du Mexique. Par M. Michel
   Chevalier. 12581
Expedition du Mexique. . . . Seance du 7
   Fevrier 1863. 5393
Expedition du Mexique. . . . Seance du 26 Juin
   1862. 5932
Expedition Francaise . . . 1861-1863. 51408
Expedition into the interior of British Guayana.
   77793

Expedition of Captain Fisk. 24526
Expedition of Capt. John Lovewell. (37711),
   94112
Expedition of Diego Dionisio de Penalosa.
   (80023)
Expedition of Gen. Anthony Wayne. 85142
Expedition of Gonzalo Pizarro to the land of
   Cinnamon. 44614
Expedition of Major General Braddock to
   Virginia. 7210, 1st note after 100462
Expedition of Orsua. 88550
Expedition of P. Le Moyne d'Iberville to
   Louisiana. (25854)
Expedition of Pedro de Ursua & Lope de
   Aguirre. 81285
Expedition to Santa Fe. 23724
Expedition to the gold mines. 100940
Expedition to the Great Salt Lake of Utah.
   90370
Expedition to the North-West Indians. (77847)
Expedition to the valley of the Great Salt Lake
   of Utah. 90371
Expeditionis navalis. 44968
Expeditions into the valley of the Amazons.
   44614
Expeditions of Capt. John Lovewell. (37711),
   94112
Expeditions of the United States government.
   22262
Expeditions that have been carried on jointly.
   49925
Expences of the town of Salem. 75658
Expenditures of government from 1843, to
   July, 1858. 36504
Expenditures of the general government.
   80373
Expenditures of the town of Fitchburg. 24592
Expenditures of the town of Groton. 28968
Expenses Cayuse Ware, Oregon. 85230
Expenses of . . . Lynnfield. (42846)
Expenses of the town of Newbury. 54908
Expenses of the town of Scituate. 78130
Expenses of the war. 26399
Expenses of Virginia. 82968
Ex-pension agent. pseud. Spur of Monmouth.
   see Morford, Henry. supposed author
Experience. pseud. Treatise on the cotton
   trade. 23407, 96745
Experience and ministerial labors of Rev.
   Thomas Smith. 84368
Experience and personal narrative of Uncle
   Tom Jones. (36611)
Experience and trials of Edward D. Tippett.
   95857
Experience by a Green Mountain girl. 99175
Experience of a Confederate States prisoner.
   (23408)
Experience of an early settler. 92810
Experience of an Indian man. 104520
Experience of an officer's wife on the plains.
   (11061)
Experience of another together with poems.
   99175
Experience of five Christian Indians. 1737
Experience of George A. Spywood. 89939
Experience of life insurance companies.
   (3838)
Experience of Nancy Welch. 102525
Experience of the author [i. e. James A.
   Brents.] 7729
Experience of Thomas Jones. (36611)
Experience of William Apes. (1733)
Experience, or, folly as it flies. 103833
Experience preferable to theory. 23409
Experience the best teacher. 37719

Experience the test of government. 20986, 3d note after 102203

Experienced carver. pseud. New York by slices. see Foster, G. G.

Experienced dyer. pseud. Methods of improving the manufacture of indigo. see Ledyard, John.

Experienced farmer, an entire new work. 58784

Experienced farmer's tour of America. (58785)

Experienced hand. pseud. His Majesties property and dominion. see Clavel, Robert.

Experienced member of the Philada. Bar. pseud. Letters of Junius. see Dickerson, William R.

Experienced physician. pseud. Traveller's pocket medical guide. 96494

Experiences and observations of a chaplain. 72702

Experiences and travels of the Rev. Richard Whatcoat. 62582, note after 103120

Experiences faites en Angleterre et aux Etats-Unis. 26200

Experiences of a prisoner of war. 11591

Experiences of a scientific expedition. (51183)

Experiences of God's gracious dealing. 103381

Experiences of Mexican travel. 94440

Experiences of pioneer life. 101060

Experiences of Sampson Maynard. 47168

Experiences sur les ombres prismatiques. 63667

Experiencia abolicionista de Puerto-Rico. 85714

Experientia, Don. pseud. ??? see Don Experientia. pseud. ???

Experiment. 67870

Experimenta circa res diversas naturales. (68517)

Experimenta et melentemata de plantarum generatione. (41796)

Experimental discoverie of Spanish practices. 88936

Experimental dissertation on the chemical and medical properties. 7327

Experimental dissertation on the Rhus-Vernix. (33049A)

Experimental enquiry into the chemical properties. 47237

Experimental inquiry into the modus operandi of mercury. 96161

Experimental proofs that the lues venerea, or gonorrhoea, are two distinct forms of disease. 96161

Experimental School for Teaching and Training Idiotic Children, Boston. see Massachusetts. Walter E. Fernald State School, Waltham.

Experimentall discoverie of Spanish practices. 78379

Experimentall discoverie of Spanish practices or the covnsell of a well-wishing souldier. 78363

Experiments and considerations on the generation of plants. (41796)

Experiments and observations on American potashes. 40857

Experiments and observations on electricity made at Philadelphia. 25505-25506, 25559

Experiments and observations on the mineral waters. 74220

Experiments at Columbia College. 74705

Experiments in aerodynamics. 84072

Experiments on the freezing of sea water. 3632

Experiments on the red and quill Peruvian bark. 35119

Experiments of spiritual life & health. 104335

Experiments with ionized air. 85072

Expert artilleryman. 6375, 22368

Expert in the art of exhumation of the dead. (74245)

Expilly, Charles. 23410-(23412)

Explanation. 23421

Explanation and answer to Mr. John Braithwaite's supplement. 73370

Explanation and history of the Book of common prayer. 23413

Explanation and history of the mysterious communion with spirits. 10765

Explanation and vindication of Samuel Leggett. 39862

Explanation and vindication of the course pursued. (53692)

Explanation, by John L. Sullivan. 93522

Explanation for the new map of Nova Scotia. (28537), (35963)

Explanation, lately published by Dr. Priestley. 14012, 92070

Explanation of a project for navigating the River Magdalena. (47071)

Explanation of a steam engine. 74125

Explanation of Captain Sabine's remarks. 73371

Explanation of Say-brook Platform. 77394

Explanation of that opinion in 1786. 40451, 62542, 92694

Explanation of the Apocalypse. 82324, 85200

Explanation of the bill now before Congress. 55818

Explanation of the case. 23415, (75201)

Explanation of the conduct of the French government. 23416

Explanation of the difficulty between Lieut. Kenner Garrard. 26688

Explanation of the first principles of the doctrine. 85527, 85529

Explanation of the first, second, and third heats. 23417

Explanation of the frontispiece. 84630

Explanation of the internal tax bill. 50791

Explanation of the magnetic atlas. 13026

Explanation of the map of the city and liberties of Philadelphia. 68854

Explanation of the map which delineates that part of the federal lands comprehended between Pennsylvania west line, the Ohio and Scioto Rivers & Lake Erie. 18174

Explanation of the map which delineates that part of the federal lands, comprehended between Pennsylvania west line, the Rivers Ohio and Scioto, and Lake Erie. 18174

Explanation of the meaning of prohibitory terms. 23457

Explanation of the names Smyth and Stuart. 85243

Explanation of the painting by James Burns. 72646

Explanation of the plate in the first page. 102051

Explanation of the principles and issues involved. 79750

Explanation of the proceedings of Eunice Chapman . . . against the . . . Shakers. 57844, note after 97893, note after 105575

Explanation of the prophecies. 85129

Explanation of the prospective-plan of the battle. 23418

Explanation of the Quipoes. 92882, 95532

Explanation of the Saybrook Platform. 15814, 23414, 32307
Explanation of the solemn advice. 24577
Explanation of the views of the situation. 23419
Explanation of the views of the Society for Employing the Female Poor. (23420)
Explanation of the views of the Society for Employing the Poor. 85837
Explanation of the words purpose, elect, and election. 82492
Explanation of votes. 49644
Explanation, or eighteen hundred and thirty. (58363)
Explanation to the policy-holders. 54826
Explanations, and biographical notes. (24720)
Explanations and sailing directions. 46963
Explanations of manual exercise. 23421
Explanations of prepositions, in English, and other languages. 102370
Explanations of the temperance map. 104698
Explanatory and practical observations. 74558
Explanatory article. 23422
Explanatory catalogue of voyages from Churchill's collection. 13419
Explanatory charter. 45729
Explanatory letter to the Honourable Burgher Council of St. Croix. 4396, 4398
Explanatory map. 50865, 84620
Explanatory note by Capt. A. A. Humphreys. 69946
Explanatory notes by Dr. John Farmer. (20190)
Explanatory notes from the Roman history. 13041
Explanatory notes upon the articles of the general rule. 96086
Explanatory pastoral letter. 43322
Explanatory preface, by a merchant of the old school. (17529), 101267
Explanatory preface, notes, &c. 30050, 2d note after 105926
Explanatory remarks on the Assembly's resolves. 23423
Explanatory remarks to a sectional plan. 8290
Explanatory report. 28376
Explicacion clara y sucinta de los principales misterios. 23424
Explicacion de el arco erigido en la puerta de el palacio arzobispal. 48469, 73870
Explicacion de la Bula de la Santa Cruzada. 23425
Explicacion de la doctrina que compuso el Cardenal Belarmino. 51205
Explicacion de la primera regla. 67310
Explicacion de las sagrados ceremonias. 74046
Explicacion de las sesenta y cinco proposiciones. 72528
Explicacion de los adornos simbolicos y poeticas del arco de triunfo, que para la entrada publica y solemne de D. Ant. Maria de Bucareli y Ursua. 40078, note before 98814
Explicacion de los adornos simbolicos y poeticas del arco de triunfo, que para la entrada publica y solemne de Joaquin de Monserrat. (40077), 98814
Explicacion de los libros quarto, y quinto. 52204
Explicacion de una parte de la doctrina Cristiana. 71249
Explicacion del eclypse de sol. 26573
Explicacion del libro quarto conforme a las reglas. 52204
Explicacion del libro quinto de Nebrija. 72536

Explicacion para sacar por las reglas. 75869
Explicacion previa de los carros y mascara. (41106)
Explicacion que el P. Fr. Manuel de Quesada hace. 67119
Explicacion, y reflexions sobre la ultima proclama. 87314
Explicatio quaestionis utrum reges. 11238
Explicatio terminorum. 75983
Explication and analysis of the Assembly's shorter catechism. 84713
Explication de la carte des nouvelles decouvertes au nord. 35253, (41417)
Explication de la pierre de Taunston [sic]. 50566
Explication des lettres-patentes du Roi. 11812
Explication des premieres causes d'action. 14269
Explication du plan de l'isle de la Granade. (28750A)
Explication d'une prophetie de Nostradamus fait en 1545. 55935
Explication of the first causes of action in matter. 14267-14268
Explication of the twenty-fourth chapter of Isaiah. (2219)
Explications demandees par le Roi. (69722)
Explicit avowal of nothingarianism. 104382
Exploits and adventures of Le Grand. 23483-23484, 23486-23487, (23489)
Exploits and triumphs. (50775)
Exploits of faction. 71548
Exploits of . . . his secretary. (36527)
Exploits of Robinson Crusoe. 19284
Exploits of ye distinguished attorney and general. 9619
Exploracion oficial. (48710)
Exploration. (11681), 76882
Exploration and survey. 90372
Exploration dans l'isthme de Darien. 6893
Exploration de Quebec au Lac St. Jean. 61006
Exploration du territoire de l'Oregon. 21144, 51734
Exploration mineralogique. 29231
Exploration of the Colorado River of the West. 64753, note after 85023
Exploration of the northwest coast. 55848
Exploration of the Red River of Louisiana. (44512)
Exploration of the valley of the Amazon. 31524
Explorations in Ecuador. 65717
Explorations in the interior. 31933
Explorations of the aboriginal remains of Tennessee. 85072
Explorations of the Arctic regions. 37002
Explorations on a voyage. 4257
Explorations scientifiques au Bresil. 40915
Explorations, surveys and reports from Belfast to Quebec. 29808
Exploratory travels through the western territories. (62837)
Explorer. pseud. Few remarks. 24240
Exploring Expedition, 1846. see United States Exploring Expedition, 1846.
Exploring expedition. Correspondence. 70431-70432
Exploring expedition to the Rocky Mountains. 25842
Exploring the highlands of the Brazil. 9498
Expocicio do Marquez de Barbacena. 3293
Exponent of democracy. 84508
Exports and imports. 2828
Expose. 83958
Expose and review of the vindication. 94933
Expose de la conduite de M. Santo-Domingo. 76875

Expose de la conduite politique. 88777
Expose de la situation actuelle. 14711
Expose de la situation politique et militaire.
(55610), 79519
Expose de l'etat actuel des choises dans la
colonie. 65420
Expose de l'etat de la question penitentiaire.
42606
Expose de M. Staempfli. 90065-90066
Expose de M. Staempfli relativement aux
croisseur le "Sumter." 90067
Expose de sa conduite avant et depuis qu'il
a quittee la France. 36430
Expose des droits de Sa Majeste Tres-Fidele,
Donna Maria II. 101225
Expose des droits des colonies Britanniques.
23426
Expose des eventualites et des consequences
d'une guerre. 93794, 95081
Expose des faits par suit desquels M. de
Turpin. (19762)
Expose des faits qui justifient leur [i. e. Azaza
and O'Farrill's] conduite. 2530
Expose des faits qui ont accompagnes l'agres-
sion des Francais. 23427
Expose des motifs de la conduite de Sa Majeste
Tres Chretienne. 27283
Expose des motifs de la conduite du Roi de
France. 44282
Expose des motifs de la conduite du Roi Tres-
Cretien. 23428
Expose des motifs et projets d'organisation.
11405
Expose des moyens curatifs employes dans les
Antilles. 93271
Expose des moyens de mettre en valeur.
40163
Expose des poursuites vexatoires du gouverne-
ment Britannique. 91841A
Expose general des resultats. 14712
Expose historique. 61126
Expose of facts concerning recent transactions.
(23420), 1st note after 102945
Expose of facts, . . . relating to the conduct
of Winslow Lewis. 47478
Expose of his [i. e. Oliver H. Smith's] admin-
istration. 83696
Expose of Joe Smith and Mormonism. (4733)
Expose of odd-fellowship. 60495
Expose of polygamy in Utah. 91222
Expose of some of the misrepresentations.
78283, 78289
Expose of the Atlantic and Pacific Railroad
Company. 59524
Expose of the Baltimore Custom House frauds.
3035
Expose of the case of the Commonwealth, or,
John W. Sims & Co. vs. McEwen & Shee.
43234
Expose of the condition of the North American
phalanx. 55558
Expose of the court party of Kentucky. 3174
Expose of the vidence in the case of the
Parkman murder. 5331
Expose of the existing dissensions between
Chili and the Peru-Bolivian Confeder-
ations. 12772
Expose of the Know Nothings. 94083
Expose of the operations. 105995
Expose of the origin. 46901
Expose of the relief system. 103865
Expose of the Secret Order of Know Nothings.
23431
Expose of the vice of gaming. 85425
Expose on the dissentions of Spanish America.
101220

Expose ou examen des operations des ministres
d'Angleterre. 36426
Expose ou examen des operations des ministres
en Angleterre. (36425)
Expose sommaire de la constitution des Etats
Unis d'Amerique. 21378
Expose sommaire des possessions de la repub-
lique sous l'equateur. 49978
Expose suceinct des nations Indiennes. 24338
Expose, to Oliver H. Smith. 83696
Exposer of "sectarian stratagem" exposed.
91592
Expose des motifs, rapports, et debats. 23429
Exposicao analytica e justificativa da conducta.
71480
Exposicao do procedimento do desembargador
Francisco de Souza Paraizo. 88793
Exposicao do procedimento politico do Consul
Geral de Portugal. 88777
Exposicao fiel sobre a negociacao do emprestimo.
35274
Exposicao historica da maconaria no Brasil.
47859
Exposicao Paraense, Para, Brazil, 1866. see
Para, Brazil. Exposicao Paraense, 1866.
Exposicion a la Seccion des Gran Jurado de la
Camara de Senadores. 22885
Exposicion agricola-rural Argentina en 1859.
1953
Exposicion al Soberano Congreso Mexicano.
47335
Exposicion al Supremo Gobierno. 26520
Exposicion al Tribunal Superior del Distrito
Federal. 62889
Exposicion astronomica de el cometa. 37936
Exposicion breve y sencilla. 66588, 93779
Exposicion con motivo de la comunicacion
oficial que acerca de las conferencias
tenidas. 58076
Exposicion con que la Comision. 23432
Exposicion contra las observaciones del Pen-
sador Mexicano. (40136)
Exposicion de Don Jose de la Riva Aguero.
523
Exposicion de la Audiencia. 76145
Exposicion de la conducta politica de Jose de
la Riva-Aguero. 71603
Exposicion de la fiesta de gracias. 29435
Exposicion de las conferencias con el Comis-
ionado de los Estados-Unidos. 23433
Exposicion de las honras funebres. 29434
Exposicion de los fines que se propone. 85768
Exposicion de los sentimientos de los funcion-
arios publicos, asi nacionales como de-
partamentales y municipales. 6135
Exposicion de los sentimientos de los funcion-
arios publicos, hecha para ser presentada
al Libertador. 14584
Exposicion de mi dictamen. 35049
Exposicion de Objetos Naturales e Industriales,
2a., Toluca, Mexico, 1851. 48655
Exposicion de una persona residente en la
republica Mexicana. 23434
Exposicion de varias personas de Mexico.
48473
Exposicion del ex-Juez Letrado Don Andres
Torres. 99790
Exposicion del ex-Ministro de Relationes.
23435
Exposicion del ex-Ministro que la suscribe.
48470
Exposicion del Flores, Arbustos, Frutas, la.,
Mexico City, 1849. see Mexico (City)
Exposicion del Flores, Arbustos, Frutas,
la., 1849.

Exposicion del Intendente de Ejercito al publico de la Habana. 29436

Exposicion del origen y naturaleza de mi deuda. 1882

Exposicion del pequeno catecismo. 48471

Exposicion del Provincial de la Compania de Jesus. 22913, 76111

Exposicion del Secretario de Estado, del Despacho de Negocios Eclesiasticos al Congreso General Constituyente del Peru. 50500

Exposicion del Senor Obispo de Popayan. 86236

Exposicion des parties de la terre. 24933, 58546

Exposicion dirigida a las Provincias Unidas del Rio de la Plata. 38996

Exposicion dirigida al Cuerpo Legislativo de la nacion Peruana. 50625

Exposicion dirigida al Supremo Gobierno de la nacion. 51325

Exposicion documentada. 80893

Exposicion General de Industria, Mexico (City), 1853. (48453)

Exposicion hecha por la Comision Especial de Mineria. 48472

Exposicion presentada a las Cortes por los Diputados del Ultramar. 23436, 67655

Exposicion publica. 49413

Exposicion que a la Legislatura Nacional presenta. (23437)

Exposicion, que al Soberano Congreso del Peru. 97716

Exposicion que da al publico el ciudadano Andres Torres. 96238

Exposicion que del resultado de las visitas a la oficinas de Correos. 96243

Exposicion que dirije a la Legislatura Nacional en 1865. 23440

Exposicion que dirige a sus compatriotas en general. 73857

Exposicion que dirige al Congreso de Venezuela. 23445

Exposicion que dirijen al Congreso Nacional. 23439

Exposicion que el Congreso Nacional presenta. 23438

Exposicion que el ejercutivo dirige. (48474)

Exposicion que el Illmo Fr. Arzobispo de Lima. 41107

Exposicion que el Presidente de la republica Ioaq. Prieto dirige. 12773

Exposicion que el Provincial del Carmen hizo. 66387

Exposicion que el Secretario de Estado del Despacho del la Guerra hace. 14586

Exposicion que ha dirigido al augusto Congreso Nacional. (23441)

Exposicion que hace al publico la Junta de Senoras. 23442

Exposicion que hace el Battalon de Malaga. 79183

Exposicion que hace el Secretario de Estado en el Despacho de Haicenda. 14587

Exposicion que hace el Senor Brigadier D. Carlos Alvear. 982

Exposicion que la Honorable Legislatura del Estado. 76146

Exposicion que los Conservadores de los Provincias dirigen. 23444

Exposicion que Octaviano Munoz Ledo dirige. 39685, 51350

Exposicion que por las exenciones de la Provincia del Carmen. 66387

Exposicion que presenta a este sensato publico. (23443)

Exposicion presentada al Presidente de la republica. 104993

Exposicion que publica Gabriel Pantaleon de Escoyti y Norri. 58430

Exposicion sencilla del modo. 77364

Exposicion sobre diezmos que hace el Arzobispo de Caracas. 98874

Exposicion sobre el juicio a que le sujeto. 40135

Exposicion sobre el proyecto de lei. 28174

Exposicion su Ministro de Hacienda. 23048

Exposicion sucinta y sencilla de la Provincia del Nuevo Mexico. 62979

Exposicion y protesta. 76789

Exposiciones de la Sociedad Abolicionista Espanola. 85714

Exposiciones de la Suprema Corte de Justicia. 23446

Expositio catechismi Gronlandici. 95615

Exposition. 94307

Exposition, addressed to the United Provinces of the River Plate. 50613

Exposition and defence of Earl Bathurst's administration. 33073, 104594

Exposition and protest. (23447), 87513

Exposition before the New Jersey Historical Society. 31403

Exposition, by Albert M. Lea. 39500

Exposition by the Council of the University of . . . New-York. 54705

Exposition concerning the mineral coal of Michigan. 38940

Exposition des primiers principes de la doctrine de l'Eglise. 85531

Exposition des principes du gouvernement republicain. (51414)

Exposition, historical and legal. 49669, 103424A

Exposition of a congressional caucus. 32138

Exposition of a most villainous attempt at extortion. 105992

Exposition of a pamphlet. 23448

Exposition of a part of the frauds. 32318

Exposition of animal magnetism. 64851

Exposition of certain abuses. 41243

Exposition of errors. 93523

Exposition of evidence in support of the memorial to Congress. 10889, 39753, (39766), 92843

Exposition of evidence on the sugar duty. 10889, 39753, (39756), 92843

Exposition of facts. (3841)

Exposition of facts and arguments. 23449, 39754

Exposition of facts relating to the rise and progress. 93946

Exposition of facts relative to the administration. 10743

Exposition of Mackinaw City and its surroundings. 15623, 44365

Exposition of motives. (50021)

Exposition of official tyranny in the United States Navy. 76260

Exposition of part of the patent law. 23180

Exposition of Revelation xiii, 11-17. 84470

Exposition of Rev. 13: 11-17. 84469, 84471

Exposition of Romans III., 20, 21, 22, 23. 1845

Exposition of sentiments. 60093

Exposition of some errors. 68595

Exposition of some facts. 17298

Exposition of some of the evils arising from the auction system. 23450, 68302

Exposition of some of the reasons. 94382

Exposition of the absurdity of sending Albert Gallitan. 64165

Exposition of the administration of the Maine State Prison. 86820

Exposition of the advantages of a railroad. 23451

Exposition of the affairs of the Medical Society. 87881

Exposition of the African slave trade. 23452

Exposition of the Assemblies' catechism. 24678

Exposition of the boundary differences. 98142

Exposition of the causes and character of the late war. 18310

Exposition of the causes and character of the late war with Great Britain. 18309, (18311), 93801

Exposition of the causes and consequences of the boundary differences. 98143

Exposition of the causes which led to the secession. 37369

Exposition of the ceremony of the initiation. 86997

Exposition of the commerce of Spanish America. 96248

Exposition of the conduct and character of Dr. John Augustine Smith. 44300

Exposition of the conduct of Charles Henry Foster. 25202

Exposition of the conduct of France towards America. 27719

Exposition of the conduct of Rev. Isaac Jennison. 43507

Exposition of the conduct of the Hon. Francis James Jackson. 34400, 83816

Exposition of the conduct of the two houses. 4041

Exposition of the constitution of the United States. 24669

Exposition of the controversy. 69392

Exposition of the course pursued by the School Committee. 37836

Exposition of the criminal laws of the Territory of Orleans. (37629)

Exposition of the dangers during a malignant yellow fever. (58982)

Exposition of the difficulties between T. B. Lawrence and his wife. 39372

Exposition of the differences existing between presses. 82561

Exposition of the documents and claim of Amasa Stetson. 91369

Exposition of the evidence. 39753, 92843

Exposition of the facts and circumstances. 64217

Exposition of the facts sustaining the claim. 103060

Exposition of the failure of the Franklin Bank, N. Y. (3865)

Exposition of the faith of the religious society of Friends. 23189

Exposition of the fatally successful arts of demagogues who exalt themselves. 32091, 75929-75930, note after 79739

Exposition of the federal constitution. 23453, 2d note after 100462

Exposition of the fifth kingdom. 4838

Exposition of the forms and usages observed. (43722)

Exposition of the government of the Methodist Episcopal Conference. 23454

Exposition of the Houmas land grant. (23455), (30625)

Exposition of the J. D. & M. Williams fraud. 27889

Exposition of the late controversy in the Methodist Episcopal Church. 36049

Exposition of the late general election in New-York. 23456

Exposition of the law, accompanied by remarks. (60094)

Exposition of the lottery system in the United States. 50540

Exposition of the meaning of the clause. 5161

Exposition of the memorial of sundry presbyters. 23458, 51252

Exposition of the motives of the conduct. 27282

Exposition of the mysteries. 24021

Exposition of the natural position of Mackinaw City. (44366)

Exposition of the objects and plans. 23459

Exposition of the objects of the institution of the New England Mutual Life Insurance Company. 52709

Exposition of the objects of the . . . [Massachusetts Health Insurance] Company, Boston. 45847

Exposition of the origin, objects and principles of the Knights of the Golden Circle. 74671

Exposition of the part taken by T. J. Chambers. 95082

Exposition of the peculiarities, difficulties, and tendencies. 23460

Exposition of the penitentiary system of punishment. 23461

Exposition of the plan and objects of the Greenwood Cemetery. 28700

Exposition of the political character and principles. 34754

Exposition of the political Jesuitism of James Madison. 70028

Exposition of the pretended claims of William Vans on the estate of John Codman. 14138, 98551, 2d note after 98553

Exposition of the principles and regulations of the Shakers. 23462

Exposition of the principles and views of the middling interest. (6520)

Exposition of the proceedings of John P. Darg. (18542)

Exposition of the proceedings of the faculty of the University of Virginia. 100538

Exposition of the reasons for the resignation. 54705, note after 99392

Exposition of the relationship. 92877

Exposition of the scheme of distribution. 7055

Exposition of the Secret Order of the Sons of Temperance. 92629

Exposition of the signs of the times. (29622)

Exposition of the situation, character, and interests. 28864

Exposition, of the 16. chapter of Revelation. 17074

Exposition of the spirit manifestation. (16355)

Exposition of the system of instruction and discipline. 99210-99211

Exposition of the system pursued by the Baptist missionaries. 23463

Exposition of the three orders in Council. 24912

Exposition of the transactions. (54000)

Exposition of the treatment of slaves. 7781, 23464

Exposition of the unconstitutionality of the law. 23465

Exposition of the views of the Baptists. (26227)

Exposition of the Virginia resolutions of 1798. 100463

Exposition of the weakness and inefficiency of the government. 47900

Exposition of Thomas H. Lewis. (7067)

Exposition of Thomas W. Bartley. 17260

Exposition, or a new theory of animal magnetism. 92135

Exposition succincte de l'origine. 59682, 59694

Exposition Universelle, Paris, 1855. see Paris. Exposition Universelle, 1855.

Exposition Universelle, Paris, 1867. see Paris. Exposition Universelle, 1867.

Exposition Universelle de 1867. (23466)

Exposition Universelle de 1867, a Paris. Comite des Poids et Mesures. (73953)

Exposition Universelle de 1867. Catalogue of the Nova Scotian Department. 56127

Exposition upon I. Cor 12. 7. 72682

Exposition upon several places of scripture. 72682-(72683)

Exposition upon the thirteenth chapter of the Revelation. 17063

Exposition upon Tit. 2. 11. 72682

Exposition with observations. (17076)

Exposition with Thomas Lloyd. 8956-8957

Expositions of the must eminent statesmen and jurists. 9437

Expositor. pseud. Letter to the citizens of Charleston. see Leland, Aaron W.

Expositor. pseud. Western Maryland Railroad. 45396

Expositor. (37363)

Expositor of Popery. 66115

Expositor of certain newspaper publications. 8622

Expositor, or many mysteries unravelled. 62891

Ex-post-facto laws. 23457

Expostulation to Lafayette. 38583

Expostulation with Samuell Jenings. (37223)

Expostulation with the Christians of that land. 46186

Expostulatory address to Abbe Mably. 53021

Expostulatory address to saints and sinners. 94705

Expostulatory and pacific letter. (30173)

Expostulatory epistle to Will. Penn. 95527

Expostulatory letter, addressed to Nicholas Lewis, Count Zinzendorff. 130512

Expostulatory letter from the Rev. Mr. Edwards. 21938

Expostulatory letter to George Washington. (74281), 3d note after 101806

Expostulatory letter to George Washington, of Mount Vernon. 74280

Exposure of a few of the many misstatements. 17362

Exposure of an attempt recently made. (81965), 7th note after 102832

Exposure of Dr. McMaster's "Brief enquiry." 78251

Exposure of facts. 100795

Exposure of Jamaican justice. 91339

Exposure of Maria Monk's pretended abduction. 49995

Exposure of Miller's letter. 30381, 2d note after 96986

Exposure of . . . missstatements and misrepresentations. 44709

Exposure of some of the numerous misstatements. 44705

Exposure of statements by the Rev. J. G. Lorimer. 104001

Exposure of the erroneous opinions. 70251

Exposure of the fraudulent origin of the "Book of Mormon." 50748

Exposure of the principles of Mormonism. 94506A

Exposure of the Schuylkill Navigation Company. (78085)

Exposure on board the Atlantic & Pacific car of emancipation. (58104)

Exposure, or examination of the operations of the British ministers. (36427)

Expounder expounded. (36054), 103591

Exprecion panegirica solemne demonstracion de las festivas reales. 56646

Ex-President Mahan's letters. 28492

Ex-Presiding Elder. pseud. Bishop's council. 5627

Expresion gratulatoria al Rey Nuestro Senor. 98861

Expresiones del dolor del Cristiano David. (72520)

Express directory and railway forwarder's guide. 26833, 28702

Express just arrived from General Washington. 101690

Express messenger. 91825

Express office hand-book and directory. 91826

Expression de Michoacan. 48812

Expression of sentiments. 24959

Expugnatio de Tyri ab Alexandro Macedone. 23718-23719

Exprgnatio regni Granatiae. 72023

Expulsion of free Negroes from the state. (7266)

Expulsion of Senator Bright. 30476

Expulsion; the best earthly conservative of peace. (24909)

Exquemelin, Alexandre Olivier. 9387, 23468-23494, note after 23576, 36192, 67985-(67986)

Ex-settler. pseud. Canada in the years 1832, 1833, and 1834. 10379, (23495)

Ex-steward. pseud. Prairie mud circuit. 64921

Extempore preaching. 84548

Extension and increase of slavery. 68057

Extension correspondence. 1864. 56165

Extension of boundaries. Speech . . . February 25, 1869. (32882)

Extension of Ku Klux Act. Speech of Hon. John Scott. 78310

Extension of slavery . . . . Speech . . . June 6, 1860. 50791

"Extension of slavery." The official acts of both parties. 15862

Extension of the Ku Klux act. Speech of Hon. George E. Spencer. 89320

Extension of the slave power. 1801

Extensive charity, in a small compass. 103073

Extensive commerce from the continent of America. 101088

Extensive system of emigration considered. 79899

Extent and value of the possessory rights. 17291

Extent and character of Sunday theatricals. 93745

Extent and perpetuity of the Abrahamic covenant. (76254)

Extent and reasonableness of self-denial. 103586

Extent of the missionary field. 66228

Extinct mammalian fauna. 39905

Extincta servitute apud insulas occidentales. (23496)

Extinction of slavery a national necessity. 5941

Extinction of the American Colonization Society. 17616

"Extinguisher" extinguished! 73942

Extinguisher for the royal faction of New-England. (23979), 104279

Extirpacion de la idolatria. 2106

Exortacion a virtud. 48236

Exortacion para el juramento. 29289

Extortionate charges for messages. 24904

Extra. Full particulars of the assassination. (70986)

Extra official state papers. 38181

Extra quarterly communication. 60129

Extra report of the Board of Directors. 102557

Extra sheets from Spaulding's History of legal tender. 89033

Extract. 103644

Extract and value of the possessory rights. 33541

Extract aus des Conferenz-Schreibers Johann Jacob Mullers Registratur. 51293, 4th note after 97845

Extract aus Unsers Conferenz-Schreibers Jahann Jacob Mullers Gefuhrten Proto-coll. 51292, 4th note after 97845

Extract dan seeckeren Brief. 23514

Extract en copye van verklaringen. 27123

Extract ende copye, van verscheyde brieven end schriften. 7577

Extract for the information of the concerned. 57145, 88116

Extract from a biographical sketch of Gen. George Washington. 101634

Extract from a despatch to Mr. Steward. 452

Extract from a discourse by President Nott. 89695, 3d note after 96966

Extract from a discourse by Rev. J. S. Buck-minister. 30519

Extract from a discourse by the Rev. J. S. Buckminster, preached in the church in Brattle Square. 8932

Extract from a discourse, delivered August 10, 1785. 22525

Extract from a discourse delivered Sunday, December 29, 1799. 859

Extract from a document. 96996, 4th note after 102623

Extract from a funeral sermon. (21792)

Extract from A. H. Stevens' speech in Georgia. 10192

Extract from a late sermon on the death of Rev. Samuel Moodey. 50303

Extract from a late sermon on the death of the Reverend Mr. Joseph Emerson. (22444)

Extract from a letter by a Massachusetts man. 13776, 70563

Extract from a letter from a gentleman in London. (18761)

Extract from a letter from the Reverend Solomon Stoddard. 79441

Extract from a letter of Father De Smedt. (34468), 82261

Extract from a letter to a gentleman in Mary-land. 79820

Extract from a letter written by a pious lawyer. 51492

Extract from a manuscript collection of annals. 100464

Ectract from a manuscript journal. 67022

Extract from a manuscript journal relating to the siege of Quebec. 25684

Extract from a message of Governor Wolcott. 10889, 22987

Extract from a poem entitled Old Virginia georgics. 94257

Extract from a printed account of the confla-gration. 71172

Extract from a proposed act for the limitation of actions. 99022

Extract from a protest against the nomination of candidates. 23497

Extract from a reply to the observations of Lieut. General William Howe. 23499, 26429, 26442, note after 102651

Extract from a report, made by a Committee of the House. 60095

Extract from a report made to the Yearly Meeting of Friends. 53662

Extract from a report of a military recon-naissance. 69946

[Extract from a] report on the medical topo-graphy and epidemics. (41807)

Extract from a report to the Trustees of the Apalachicola Land Company. 5878

Extract from a representation of the injustice and dangerous tendency of tolerating slavery. 79818-79819

Extract from a representation of the injustice of slavery. 4689

Extract from a sermon delivered at the Bul-finch-Street Church, Boston. (28388)

Extract from a sermon delivered in the Church of the Holy Innocents. 68586

Extract from a sermon preach'd at the South Church, in Boston. 65595

Extract from a sermon preached . . . Aug. 7, 1842. note after 42429

Extract from a sermon, preached on Sunday, April 23, 1865. 9476

Extract from a speech delivered at South Hoosick. 2942

Extract from a treatise by William Law, M. A. called, The spirit of prayer. (39324)

Extract from a treatise by William Law, M. A. . . . with some thoughts. 39325

Extract from a treatise on Chili. 44682

Extract from a treatise on the subject of prayer. (4673)

Extract from "American slavery as it is." 11575

Extract from an account of the country of Accadie in North America. 40707, note after 96500

Extract from an address, by James B. Congdon. 15471

Extract from an address delivered on the morn-ing of May 31, 1826. 101378

Extract from an address in the Virginia gazette. 23500, 100465

Extract from an address to his [i. e. Samuel Thayer Spear's] people. 89087, 89093

Extract from an eulogium on the late Gen. Washington. 103897

Extract from an eulogium on William Shippen. 104920

Extract from an excellent work, published some years ago. 105227

Extract from an unpublished manuscript on Shaker history. 23501, 79705

Extract from Dr. C. Nisbet's address. 73361

Extract from Edward Colvil's journal. 66833

Extract from Gov. Clinton's speech in the Legislature of New-York. 105795

Extract from Mr. Bruge's printed letter. 9222

Extract from Mr. Prince's sermon, on Job. I. 21. 65594

Extract from Mr. Whitefield's journal, Dec. 24, 1738. 103504

Extract from Mr. Whitefield's tracts. 27415

Extract from remarks of R. W. Russell. 74365

Extract from report . . . in relation to light houses, beacons, &c. 13826

Extract from report of Lieutenant Colonel Emory. 69900, 69946

Extract from Rev. Prof. Mckee's lecture. 43382

Extract from Rev. T. Snell's sermon. 85492

Extract from Senator Benton's speech. 4787

Extract from the accqunt of East Florida. 92223

Extract from the American citizen. (32927)

Extract from the annual report of the Commissioner of Indian Affairs for the year 1868. 34648, note before 94525

Extract from the charge of Judge Maynard. 47167

Extract from the epistle of the Meeting for Sufferings in London. 86058

Extract from the executive record, comprehending the messages of the president in relation to the nomination of Albert Gallatin. 23502

Extract from the executive record, comprehending the messages of the President of the United States. 74353

Extract from the inaugural address of His Honor, George B. Richmond. 71130

Extract from the journal of Francis Asbury. (2163)

Extract from the journal of proceeidngs. 53139

Extract from the journal of the annual convention of the Diocese of Connecticut. (15815), 101999

Extract from the journal of the Honble House of Representatives. 45730

Extract, from the journal of the proceedings. 15526, note after 63244, 84642

Extract from the journal of the Rev. Dr. Coke. 14242

Extract from the journals of Congress. (23526)

Extract from the laws of William Penn. 59695

Extract from the letter of the Rev. Nathan Lord. (31378)

Extract from the memoirs of Stephen B. Stedman. 91070

Extract from the minutes of Congress. (40489)

Extract from the minutes of Council. 23503

Extract from the minutes of the Commission of the Synod. (31294)

Extract from the minutes of the General Association of Connecticut. 15816

Extract from the minutes of the Grand Consistory. 53691

Extract from the minutes of the Worcester Baptist Association. 105375

Extract from the minutes of the Yearly Meeting of Women Friends. 86059

Extract from the New-England farmer. 83824

Extract from the Political state of Great Britain. (23504), 63808

Extract from the private writings of Mr. Hirst. (14490)

Extract from the proceedings of the Democratic meeting. 100457

Extract from the proceedings of the Grand Lodge of Louisiana. 42259

Extract from the proceedings of the New York State Society, of the Cincinnati. 13119

Extract from the proceedings of the South Carolina Tazoo Company. 88054

Extract from the records of the town of Lynn. 42838

Extract from the register of the decrees. 96568

Extract from the report of Alexander Hamilton. 97751

Extract from the report of Benjamin Wright, Esq. 98088

Extract from the report of Hartman Bache. note after 60249, note after 104493

Extract from the report of the Commissioner of Indian Affairs. (79113)

Extract from the report of the Directors [of the Massachusetts State Prison.] 45902

Extract from the report of the Managers [of the Society for Employing the Poor, Boston.] 85837

Extract from the report of the Secretary of the Interior. 20314

Extract from the Reverend and Learned Mr. Peirce's vindication. (59550)

Extract from the Rev. J. Marsden's journal. 44713

Extract from the Rev. Mr. John Wesley's journal, from August 9, 1779. 102672

Extract from the Rev. Mr. John Wesley's journal. From January 1, 1776. 102671

Extract from the Reverend Mr. John Wesley's journal, from July 20, 1749. 102661

Extract from the Reverend Mr. John Wesley's journal, from November 25, 1746. 102660

Extract from the Rev. Mr. John Wesley's journal with regard to the affidavit made by Captain Robert Williams. 102652

Extract from the second letter. 10671, 15526, note after 63244, 84642

Extract from the secred debates of the federal convention. (26931), 40471

Extract from the speech of Hon. J. A. Meriwether. (47975)

Extract from the speech of Mr. Garrett Davis. 18818

Extract from the twenty-second annual report. 45894

Extract from the will of George Cheyne Shattuck. 79870

Extract of a despatch from Her Majesty's Minister. 19753, (23505), 55527

Extract of a letter, dated Philadelphia, January 2. 1755. 84590

Extract of a letter from a gentleman in America to a friend in England. 16611, 16615, (22509), 2d note after 95677

Extract of a letter from a gentleman in Maryland. 23506

Extract of a letter from a minister in Boston. 103622

Extract of a letter from a western citizen. 95116

Extract of a letter from an Indian chief. 89206

Extract [sic] of a letter from an officer. 87824

Extract of a letter from an officer, who arrived at Philadelphia. 101697

Extract of a letter from Dr. Benjamin Rush. 74221

Extract of a letter from General Washington to Congress. 101697

Extract of a letter from Lieut. Christopher Claxont. 13527

Extract of a letter from Mr. Mather. 46723, 1st note after 65324

Extract of a letter from Mr. Randolph to the printer. 1st note after 99797

Extract of a letter, from President Jefferson, to President Adams. 103776

Extract of a letter from several Friends in Philadelphia. 61644

Extract of a letter from the House of Representatives of Massachusetts-Bay. 23507

Extract of a letter from the Reverend Mr Wright. 105601

Extract of a letter from Vice Admiral Townshend. 96404

EXTRACT

Extract of a letter from "Vindex." 20657
Extract of a letter to the Right Honourable
  Lord Viscount H**e. 33327, note after
  102652
Extract of a letter to the Right Honorable
  Lord Viscount Howe. 33327, note after
  102652
Extract of a report. 29976
Extract of a sermon. (2670)
Extract of a translation. 10203
Extract of an act of the General Assembly for
  raising £100,000. (53663)
Extract of an act of the General Assembly of
  New York for raising a supply of
  £100,000. 23508
Extract of certaine letters written from thence.
  (45316), 69291, 103353
Extract of my pamphlet, n°. 8. (70901)
Extract of remarks of Mr. Rives. 71656
Extract of some accounts. 46458
Extract of some letters sent him. 103513
Extract of sundry passages taken out of Mr.
  G. Tennent's sermon. 67117
Extract of sundry passages taken out of Mr.
  Whitefield's printed sermons. 67116,
  103560, 103622, 103644-103645
Extract of the justificative pieces . . . cited.
  96340
Extract of the life of the late Rev. Mr. David
  Brainerd. 102653
Extract of the minutes of Council. 23503
Extract of the preface to the Reverend Mr.
  Whitefield's account. 103513
Extract of the proceedings of a committee of
  the whole Council. 67002
Extract of the proceedings of the adjourned
  Superior Court. 99074
Extract of the proceedings of the New York
  State Society, of the Cincinnati. 13119
Extract of the report made to the Directing
  Senate. 90063
Extract of the Revd. Mr. John Wesley's jour-
  nal, from August 12, 1738. 102656
Extract of the Rev. Mr. John Wesley's jour-
  nal, from Feb. 1, 1737-8. 102655
Extract of the Rev. Mr. John Wesley's jour-
  nal, from February 16, 1755. 102663
Extract of the Rev. Mr. John Wesley's jour-
  nal from his embarking for Georgia.
  102654
Extract of the Reverend Mr. John Wesley's
  journal, from July XX, 1750. 102662
Extract of the Rev. Mr. John Wesley's journal,
  from June 17, 1758. 102664
Extract of the Rev. Mr. John Wesley's journal,
  from June 28, 1786. 102674
Extract of the Rev. Mr. John Wesley's journal,
  from May 14th, 1768. 102668
Extract of the Rev. Mr. John Wesley's journal,
  from May 6, 1760. 102665
Extract of the Rev. Mr. John Wesley's journal,
  from May 27, 1765. 102667
Extract of the Rev. Mr. John Wesley's journal,
  from October 29, 1762. 102666
Extract of the Reverend Mr. John Wesley's
  journal, from October 27, 1743. 102659
Extract of the Rev. Mr. John Wesley's journal,
  from Sept. 4, 1782. 102673
Extract of the Rev. Mr. John Wesley's journal,
  from Sept. 2, 1770. 102669
Extract of the Revd. Mr. John Wesley's journal,
  from Sept. 3, 1741. 102658
Extract of the Rev. Mr. John Wesley's journal,
  from September 13th, 1773. 102670
Extract of the Rev. Mr. John Wesley's journals.
  102675

Extract of the Reverend Mr. Wesley's journal.
  102657
Extract of the spirit of prayer. 14373
Extract oft kort verhael wt het groote journael.
  55432
Extract our of the letter. 102912A
Extract our of the regicter [sic] of the States
  General. 20779
Extract uit de dag-registers van het Noord-
  Amerikaansche Congres. 23510, 55429
Extract uit dezelve maniere van procedeeren.
  93846
Extract uit het register der resolutien. 102889A
Extract vnd. Augsszug. der grossen vn. wun-
  derbarlichen Schiff-farth. 23512
Extract uyt d'articulen van het tractaet. 23509,
  102891
Extract uyt de Heer Matthias Becks. 49559,
  2d note after 102897
Extract uyt de missive vanden President ende
  Raden. 7578
Extract uyt den brief van den E. Generael
  Pieter Pietersz. Heyn. 31658
Extract uyt den brief vande politycque Raeden
  in Brasil. 7579, note after 102891
Extract uyt een brief gheschreven in Maurits-
  Stadt de Pernambuco. 23511
Extract uyt het register resolutien van de Ho'.
  Mog. Heeren Staten Generaal. 93836
Extract uyt het register der resolutien van de
  Hoog Mog: Heeren Staten Generaal der
  Vereenigde Nederlanden. Jovis, den 28
  December, 1713. 93834
Extract uyt het register der resolutien van de
  Hoog Mog: Heeren Staten Generaal der
  Vereenigde Nederlanden. Sabbathi, den
  5 October, 1686. 93834
Extract uyt register der resolutien van de
  Hoog Mog. Heeren Staten Generaal der
  Vereenigde Nederlanden. Veneris, den
  28 July, 1713. 93834
Extract uyt het register der resolutien van
  haer Hoogh Moog. 486, 102877
Extract uyt het register der resolutien van
  Ridderschap en Steden. 93834
Extract uyt 't register. 41356
Extract uytte missive by den voornoemden
  Directeur. 102912
Extract uyttet register der resolutien vande
  Hoogh Mogh. Heeren Staten Generael.
  23513
Extract wt een tegen-vertooch. 19671, 4th note
  after 102890
Extracten uyt het register der resolutien.
  102982
Extracto alfabetico. 19968, (23515)
Extracto . . . de la causa criminal. (48475)
Extracto de la causa formada al ex-Coronel
  Juan Yanez y socios. 105953
Extracto de la conquista de el Ytza en la Nueva
  Espana. (22365), 55377
Extracto de la gramatica Mutsun. 2117
Extracto de un discurso del R. P. M. F. Martin
  Sarmiento. 77092
Extracto de una relacion sobre el antiguo reyno
  de Guatemala. 52118
Extracto de varias cartas. 97671
Extracto del diario de observaciones. 33486
Extracto del hecho, y breves apuntes de derecho.
  48476
Extracto del libro de D. Geronimo Uztariz.
  97690
Extracto dos debates no Parlamento Brazileiro.
  67539
Extracto historial del expediente que pende.
  23516

Extracto o relacion de los autos de recono-
cimiento. 27811
Extracto, o relacion methodica. 29077
Extracto puntual de todas las pragmaticas.
76293
Extractos dos discursos de J. Scoble e de J.
J. Gurney. (78153)
Extracts and collections of acts. (23517)
Extracts and copies of letters. 102630
Extracts and records of the First Ecclesiastical
Society. 2660
Extracts and remarks on the subject of pun-
ishment. 23518, 85832
Extracts for the information of the concerned.
57145, 88116
Extracts from a charge delivered to the clergy
of the Diocese of Toronto. 92642
Extracts from a charge delivered to the Grand
Jury. 104287
Extracts from a diary of Salado Exploration.
(34089)
Extracts from a discourse delivered at Pitts-
field. 33794
Extracts from a discourse on the late Rev.
Professor Ware. 58800
Extracts from a journal kept by the author.
29193
Extracts from a journal kept during a voyage.
35332
Extracts from a journal of a settler. 10607,
2d note after 98090
Extracts from a journal of Dr. Lavagnino.
39275
Extracts from a journal of the Bishop of
Honolulu. 90108
Extracts from a journal of travels in North
America. 768, 38071
Extracts from a journal, written on the coasts
of Chili. 29718
Extracts from a lecture on insanity. 17214
Extracts from a letter of William H. Smith.
84807-84808
Extracts from a letter on the mode of Choos-
ing the president. 86827
Extracts from a letter written to the President
of Congress, by the Hon. Arthur Lee,
Esq. 39699
Extracts from a letter written to the President
of Congress, by the Honorable Arthur
Lee, Esquire. 39700
Extracts from a military essay. 18345, 81142
Extracts from a "Narrative of privations and
sufferings." 34341, 76651
Extract from a pamphlet, entitled The friend
of peace, with six letters from Omar to
the President. (23519)
Extract from a pamphlet, entitled The friend
of peace: containing a special inter-
view. 105251
Extracts from a pamphlet published by the
Rev. Benjamin Fawcett. 30768, 102608
Extracts from a poem of nearly 2000 lines.
103924
Extracts from a private journal. 96381
Extracts from a report made to the Board of
Council. 64428
Extract s from a report made to the Maryland
and New York Coal and Iron Company.
81034
Extracts from a report made to the Maryland
Mining Company. 81033
Extracts from a report to the Trustees of the
Ascension Association. 82943
Extracts from a review of the parliamentary
and forensic eloquence. 23520

Extracts from a sermon occasioned by the fall
of the brave Captain John Lovewell.
94111
Extracts from a speech . . . containing some
account. 11219
Extracts from a speech . . . in the Missouri
House of Representatives. 8453
Extracts from a supplementary letter from the
Illinois. 5565
Extracts from a tragic comedy. 43638
Extracts from a treatise on the constitution of
the United States. 6316
Extracts from a West India plantation journal.
91238
Extracts from a work called "Breeden Baedt."
23521
Extracts from all the notable speeches. 12662,
89494-89495
Extracts . . . from American authors. 81673
Extracts from an address before the people of
Orange, N. J. 8348
Extracts from an address delivered before the
inhabitants of the town of Caroline, N. Y.
89234
Extracts from an address, delibered July 4,
1832. 14422
Extracts from an address . . . in . . . Lime,
N. H. (38027)
Extracts from an article in the North American
review. 88971, 88973
Extracts from an article published in the Wor-
cester daily spy. 92867
Extracts from an essay concerning obedience.
28790
Extracts from an oration delivered before the
authorities of the city of Boston. 93652
Extracts from an oration delivered by Onson
Burlingame. 9333
Extracts from an oration delivered by Elihu
Palmer. 63790
Extracts from an unpublished farce. 97788
Extracts from, and enclosures in, the letters
of Mr. Monroe. 43713
Extracts from Antonie Galvano's discoveries of
the world. 66686
Extracts from authentic papers. 58932, note
after 75175
Extracts from Baron de Steuben's regulations.
91448
Extracts from certain laws of . . . Massa-
chusetts. 12104
Extracts from Chief Justice William Allen's
letter book. 84586
Extracts from Colonel Tempelhoffe's history
of the Seven Years War. 41301
Extracts from colony laws. 23522
Extracts from different letters. 103353
Extracts from evidence before the House of
Commons. 23525
Extracts from Federal papers, &c. (55313),
note after 95351
Extracts from General Halleck's work on
international law. (29881)
Extracts from General John A. Sutter's diary.
84946
Extracts from Genesis and the psalms. 18288,
69646
Extracts from his [i. e. Walter Brodie's] pri-
vate journal. 8181
Extracts from his [i. e. Benjamin Silliman's]
report and from report of John Campbell.
(14686), 81061
Extracts from humbuggiana. 56833
Extracts from, intercepted and other letters.
87364
Extracts from Jack Tar's journals. 59477

Extracts from journals of expeditions to the north of California. 8759

Extracts from letters and other pieces. (35446)

Extracts from letters, from an English resident. 73912

Extracts from letters from the Navy Department. 91900

Extracts from letters of teachers and superintendents of the New-England Educational Commission for Freedmen. 23523, 25685, 25739

Extracts from "Letters on the Colonization Society." 10889

Extracts from Locke and others. 8769

Extracts from manuscripts. 47402

Extracts from Mr. Webster's speeches, in 1832. 102281

Extracts from Mr. Webster's speeches, in the Senate. 102292

Extracts from newspapers. 28862

Extracts from ordinances relative to the interment of the dead. 54268

Extracts from original letters. 20757

Extracts from pamphlets originally published in England. 102729

Extracts from papers, printed by order of the House of Commons. 102833

Extracts from Professor Robinson's "Proofs of a conspiracy," &c. 72243

Extracts from Propertius and Strabo. 67730

Extracts from R. C. Taylor's report. 94527, 94529

Extracts from rebel organs. 22113

Extracts from records relating to his history and objects. 85961

Extracts from "Remarks on Dr. Channing's Slavery," with comments. (11920)

Extracts from renunciations of seceding masons. 90897

Extracts from report of New-York society. 10889

Extracts from reports made by P. M. Butler. 9658

Extracts from reports of E. F. Beale. 88607

Extracts from reports of Gold Commissioner of Nova Scotia. (14686), 81061

Extracts from reports of Missions to the Cherokees. 34650

Extracts from reports of the [Boston Female] Society [for Missionary Purposes.] (6706)

Extracts from reports of the Gold Commissioner of Nova Scotia. (14686), 81061

Extracts from Richmond journals. 55834

Extracts from Solorzano's Politica Indiana. 86544

Extracts from some letters. (19257)

Extracts from some of the depositions for the claimants. 80420

Extracts from the act authorizing the town of Cambridge to establish a Board of Health. (10144)

Extracts from the act of the Legislature of New York. 53664

Extracts from the address of John Quincy Adams. 311

Extracts from the annual messages. 933, 87499

Extracts from the army regulations, etc. 49711

Extracts from the Boston memorial of 1842. 6498

Extracts from the catalogue of General Jackson's juvenile indiscretions. 35386

Extracts from the coffee planter of St. Domingo. 38430

Extracts from the correspondence and minutes of the Trustees of the Bank of Maryland. 45078

Extracts from the correspondence: British West Indies. 85936

Extracts from the correspondent of the New York Times. 55402

Extracts from the crisis. 10889

Extracts from the debates in the House of Commons. 23524

Extracts from the diary and correspondence of the late Amos Lawrence. 39384

Extracts from the diary of an American physician. 99427

Extracts from the diary of the deceased [i. e. Pitt Clarke.] 5283

Extracts from the diary of the late Samuel Emlin. 22514

Extracts from the doop-boek. 77592

Extracts from the editorial columns of the "New Orleans picayune." (23525)

Extracts from the eighteenth and nineteenth reports of the Directors of the African Institution. 81966

Extracts from the Gospels of Matthew, Luke & John. 18289, 69647

Extracts from the itineraries and other miscellanies. 91750

Extracts from the journal of Captain Harry Gordon. (64835)

Extracts from the journal of Job Scott. 78284

Extracts from the journal of John Candler. 10674

Extracts from the journal of Marshal Soult. (38072)

Extracts from the journal of proceedings. 53106

Extracts from the journal of the annual convention of the Diocese of Connecticut. (15815), 101999

Extracts from the journal of the writer. 79371, 88478

Extracts from the journals and proceedings of the General Assembly. 99023

Extracts from the journals kept by the Rev. Thomas Smith. 84350

Extracts from the journals of Congress. 15527

Extracts from the journals of the first branch of the City Council. 63126

Extracts from the journals of the Provincial Congress of South-Carolina. Held at Charles-Town, February 1st, 1776. 87363

Extracts from the journals of the Provincial Congress of South Carolina held at Charles-Town June 1st to 22d, 1775. 87361

Extracts from the journals of the Provincial Congress of South Carolina. Held at Charles-Town, November 1st to November 29, 1775. 87365

Extracts from the journals of the Provincial Congress of South-Carolina. Published by order of the Congress. 87360

Extracts from the laws. 8226

Extracts from the letters and journal of Daniel Wheeler. 103181-103182

Extracts from the log of Capt. Middleton. 3664, 13833

Extracts from the Madison papers, etc. 62521

Extracts from the manuscript of Kooch's blue book. 38235

Extracts from the manuscript writings of Barnaby Nixon. 55359

Extracts from the marine practice of physic and surgery. 94063

Extracts from the memorandums of Jane Bettle. 5092

Extracts from the militia laws of Massachusetts. 48981

Extracts from the minutes and papers of the Transylvania Presbytery. 96458

Extracts from the minutes and proceedings of the Assembly of New Jersey. 53107

Extracts from the minutes and votes of the House of Assembly. 53108

Extracts from the minutes . . . at an occasional meeting held at New-York, December 28th, 1809. 97975

Extracts from the minutes . . . at an occasional meeting held at Washington, January 30, 1808. 97975

Extracts from the minutes of Council. 10351

Extracts from the minutes of Daniel Cushing of Hingham. 18099

Extracts from the minutes of our yearly meeting. (45364)

Extracts from the minutes of the acts and proceedings of the Associate-Reformed Synod. 65160

Extracts from the minutes of the Associate Synod of North America, at their meeting at Pittsburgh. 65162

Extracts from the minutes of the Associate Synod of North America, relative to the above union. 98181

Extracts from the minutes of the Council of the province of New-York. 53665

Extracts from the minutes of the convention assembled at East Windsor. 23528

Extracts from the minutes of the General Assembly of the Presbyterian Church. 65163

Extracts from the minutes of the General Association of Congregational Ministers in Massachusetts. 45739

Extracts from the minutes of the General Association of New Hampshire. 52823

Extracts from the minutes of the General Association of Massachusetts Proper. 45738

Extracts from the minutes of the General Convention of Congregational and Presbyterian Ministers in Vermont. 99169

Extract from the minutes of the Indiana Yearly Meeting. 34498

Extracts from the minutes of the New England Yearly Meeting of Women Friends. 52636

Extracts from the minutes of the proceedings of the Congress. 23533, 45731

Extracts from the minutes of the proceedings of the First General Synod of the Associate-Reformed Church in North-America. 65161

Extracts from the minutes of the Synod of New-York and New-Jersey. A. D. 1811. 53666

Extracts from the minutes of the Synod of New-York and New-Jersey, A. D. 1809. 65164

Extracts from the minutes of the Synod of the Evangelical Lutheran Ministerium. 53658

Extracts from the minutes of the Third Session of the Hartwick Synod and Ministerium of the Evangelical Lutheran Church. 53658

Extracts from the minutes of the United States Military Philosophical Society. 97975

Extracts from the minutes of the Yearly Meeting of Friends, held in New York. (53667)

Extracts from the minutes of the Yearly Meeting of Friends, held in Philadelphia. 61645

Extracts from the North American review. 14732, (55563)

Extracts from the note-book. 1648

Extracts from the Nubian geography. 66686

Extracts from the Olive branch, no. 3. 10889

Extracts from the oratory of Judge Joseph Holt. 59099

Extracts from the papers and proceedings of the Aborigines Protection Society. 34649

Extracts from the . . . penal code. 41614

Extracts from the (preliminary) report of Lieut. A. W. Whipple. 69946

Extracts from the proceedings and reports of the Rhode-Island State Total Abstinence Society. 70738

Extracts from the proceedings for 1839 [of the Grand Chapter of Freemasons of Vermont.] 99179

Extracts from the proceedings for 1828 [of the Grand Chapter of Freemasons of Vermont.] 99179

Extracts from the proceedings for 1829 [of the Grand Chapter of Freemasons of Vermont.] 99179

Extracts from the proceedings for 1827 [of the Grand Chapter of Freemasons of Vermont.] 99179

Extracts from the proceedings for 1826 [of the Grand Chapter of Freemasons of Vermont.] 99179

Extracts from the proceedings of His Majesty's Council. 94546

Extracts from the proceedings of the American Continental Congress. 23530

Extracts from the proceedings of the Board of Regents of the Smithsonian Institution. 85024

Extracts from the proceedings of the Committee of Observation. 45144

Extracts from the proceedings of the Convention at Concord and Boston. 23531

Extracts from the proceedings of the Convention at Concord, Mass. 15132

Extracts from the proceedings of the Court of Vice-Admiralty in Charles-Town, South-Carolina. 23532, 39925, 1st note after 87356, note after 87824, note after 96924

Extracts from the proceedings of the first U. States Anti-masonic Convention. 50682, 97958

Extracts from the proceedings of the General Association of New-Hampshire. 52824

Extracts from the proceedings of the Grand Chapter of . . . New York. 53690

Extracts from the proceedings of the Grand Chapter of the State of Vermont, at its annual communication. 99179

Extracts from the proceedings of the Grand Chapter of the State of Vermont, held at Rutland. 99180

Extracts from the proceedings of the Grand Lodge, of . . . New-York. (53692)

Extracts from the proceedings of the High Court of Vice-Admiralty, in Charlestown, South Carolina, upon six several informations. 33926-33927, 1st note after 87356, note after 87824

Extracts from the proceedings of the Meeting for Sufferings in London. 26254, 26255, 34651

Extracts from the proceedings of the Yearly Meeting of Philadelphia. 26255, 34652

Extracts from the Providence journal. 35313

Extracts from the public jorunals. 39305

Extracts from the quarterly special relief report. 76615, 76647

Extracts from the records of Colchester. 14265, 1st note after 94219

Extracts from the records of New-England Yearly Meeting Boarding School. 52637

Extracts from the records of the Church, in Foxborough. 104387

Extracts from the records of the Grand Lodge of Virginia. 100472

Extracts from the records of the Provincial Congress, held at Cambridge. 23533, 45731

Extracts from the records of the Synod of Mississippi. 49500

Extracts from the report of Committee on Fairmount Park Contribution. 61650

Extracts from the report of His Majesty's Commissioners. 23527

Extracts from the report of Major-General Carl Schurz. (78024)

Extracts from the report of Mr. Justus Ludwig Von Uslar. 98183

Extracts from the report of the International Committee on Weights, Measures, and Coins. 23534

Extracts from the report of the survey. (38466)

Extracts from the report on the survey of the Lackawanna and Lanesboro' Railroad. 60187, note after 96479

Extracts from the report . . . on weights, measures, and coins. (58595)

Extracts from the reports of the Canal Commissioners. (53563)

Extracts from the reports of the Paris International Exhibition of 1855. 10445

Extracts from the resolutions of the stockholders. 60046

Extracts from the Rev. Mr. Marsh's sermon. 4102

Extracts from the revised statutes. 28969

Extracts from the "Rules and regulations." 74080

Extracts from the second report of the Committee. (81967)

Extracts from the several treaties subsisting. 23535

Extracts from the special report concerning the rebel hospitals. 71178

Extracts from the speech of the Hon. Alex. H. Stephens. 91255

Extracts from the speech . . . on the Kansas question. 4707

Extracts from the state laws. 23703

Extracts from the treatise between Great-Britain and other kingdoms. 28069

Extracts from the true grandeur of nations. 93653

Extracts from the unpublished journal of Job Scott. 78285

Extracts from the votes and proceedings of the American Continental Congress, held at Philadelphia on the 5th of September 1774. (15528), note after 23535

Extracts from the votes and proceedings of the American Continental Congress, held at Philadelphia, 10th May, 1775. 23536

Extracts from the votes and proceedings of the Hon. the Assembly. 3269

Extracts from the votes of the House of Assembly of the province of Nova-Scotia. (56128)

Extracts from the votes of the House of Assembly, of the province of Pennsylvania. 60096

Extracts from the works of Dr. Tucker. 66648

Extracts from the writings and speeches of Daniel Webster. 102313

Extracts from the writings of D. Phillips and Wm. Penn. (62478)

Extracts from the writings of friends on the subject of slavery. 81968

Extracts from the writings of John Dunlavy. 21310

Extracts from the writings of Mrs. Bethune. (5080)

Extracts from the writings of the Abbe Raynal. 4688

Extracts from the writings of William Law and Judge Hale. 59699

Extracts from the Yearly Meeting minutes about Indian concerns. (56914)

Extracts from the Yearly Meeting of Friends, held . . . in the city of Baltimore. 86060

Extracts from Thos. Jefferson. 81857

Extracts from three letters lately received from America. 13422

Extracts from treasury regulations, etc. 8723

Extracts from two letters relating to the subject. 93591

Extracts from two letters, wrote originally in German. 87146

Extracts from various writers on emigration to Canada. 22500, 40594, 86187, 2d note after 98076

Extracts in prose and verse. 23537

Extracts, magazine articles, and observations. (38424)

Extracts of despatches relative to North American colonies. 22495

Extracts of letters from an officer. 7210, 1st note after 100462

Extracts of letters &c. Published by order of Congress. 87364

Extracts of letters from L. M. S. to E. C. D. 77006

Extracts of letters from poor persons. (10444), 78506

Extracts of letters lately received from the West Indies. (10676)

Extracts of letters received by the Educational Commission, Boston. 23529

Extracts of letters, written by the relations, friends, and contemporaries of Washington. 101794

Extracts of private letters from London. 94142

Extracts of sermons. 98181

Extracts of several letters. 97454

Extracts of several papers, written by several persons. 46295

Extracts of several treatises wrote by the Prince of Conti. 23539

Extracts of some letters occasioned by the proceedings. 23538

Extracts of the journals of Mr. Commissary Von Reck. 68369

Extracts of the journals of the Rev. Dr. Coke's five vistis. 14243

Extracts of the journals of the Rev. Dr. Coke's three visits. 14243

Extracts of the subject of slavery. 105200

Extracts taken out of the report. 56494

Extradition proceedings. 51279

Extraict ov recveil des isles nouuellement truuees. 1554

Extrait de la bulletin de la Societe de Geographie. 19741
Extrait de la correspondance du General Rochambeau. 99745
Extrait de la description topographique. 50571
Extrait de la Gazette de Quebec du 11 Janvier 1827. 43858, 84701, 99766
Extrait de la geographie physique. 46971
Extrait de la lettre de M. F. Bremond. (7716)
Extrait de la relation des avantures et voyages de Mathieu Sagean. 58166, 74898
Extrait de la relation des missions. 4935-4936
Extrait de la realtion d'un voyage fait par ordre de S. M. Danoise. 42504
Extrait de la "Revue colonial." 21462
Extrait de la revue du monde colonial. 87308
Extrait de l'histoire de Philippe II. 94854
Extrait de l'histoire d'Ethiopie. 36944, 68430
Extrait de mes tablettes d'outre-mer. (19535)
Extrait des actes de la Societe Philologique. (72812)
Extrait des annales d'Afrique. 96345
Extrait . . . des annales generales des sciences physiques. 67458
Extrait des annales maritimes et coloniales. 70357
Extrait des annales maritimes et coloniales de 1823. 42504
Extrait des deliberations de la Chambre d' Agriculture du Cap. 75112
Extrait des deliverations de la paroisse du Fond-des-Negres. 75113
Extrait des enquetes. 94854
Extrait des lois et des ordonnances concernant la piraterie. 36192
Extrait des memoires de la Societe des Ingenieurs Civils. 24638
Extrait des nouvelles annales des voyages. 89976
Extrait des pieces deposees aux Archives de l'Assemblee Generale. 75114
Extrait des pieces justificatives a l'appui de la denonciation. 28152
Extrait des pieces justificatives qui constantent la conduite de M. de Damas. 68366
Extrait des registres de l'Assemblee Provinciale . . . de l'Ouest. 75116
Extrait des registres des deliberations de l'Assemblee Provinciale du Sud de Saint-Domingue. 75115
Extrait des registres des deliberations de l'Assemblee Provinciale du Sud et de la seance du 1er Mai 1790. 75117
Extrait des registres du Conseil d'Etat. 75057, 75059
Extrait des registres du Conseil d'Estat. (56085), 56091
Extrait des registres du Conseil d'Estat. "Le Roy ayant par son arrest." 56090
Extrait des registres du Conseil d'Estat . . . le Roy s'estant fait. 41843
Extrait des registres du Conseil d'Estat. Sur la requeste. (65089)
Extrait des registres du Conseil Ppiue du Roy. 56088, 72043
Extrait des registres du Parlement. 68074
Extrait des voyages de Christophe Colomb. 30849
Extrait des voyages les plus recents. 6259
Extrait des voyages recents. 38632
Extrait du catalogue de la bibliotheque. 23541
Extrait du dictionnaire du comerce et des marchandises. 74918
Extrait du Journal de physique. 105627

Extrait du journal de sa navigation. 37618
Extrait du journal d'un officier de la marine. 23033
Extrait du memoire justificatif du citoyen Larchevesque-Thibaud. 39018
Extrait du pamphlet Americain. 102144
Extrait du pamphlet publie par le gouvernement. 79770
Extrait du proces-verbal de l'assemblee. (75118)
Extrait du rapport adresse au Directoire Executif. (42350), 96343
Extrait du recueil des divers memoirs Anglois. 34862
Extrait du registre des deliberations de la Deputation de Saint-Domingue. 75120
Extrait du registre des deliberations du Comite Colonial de Saint Domingue. 75119
Extrait du registre des Etats Generaux des Pais Bas Unis. (68750)
Extrait du second voyage de Byron. 9735
Extrait du voyage de M. J. M. Duncan. 94228, 94231
Extrait du voyage d'exploration en Californie. 74986
Extrait du voyage geologique aux Antilles. 75524
Extrait d'une lettre de Baltimore. 98105
Extrait d'une lettre de l'Assemblee Generale. 56096
Extrait d'une lettre d'un jeune refugie Francais. 95105
Extrait d'une lettre, sur les malheurs de Saint-Domingue. (10755), 23540
Extrait . . . 1841. (55990)
Extrait ou recueil des isles nouvelles trouvees. 23542
Extrait ov recveil des isles nouuellement trouuees. (16952)
Extrait particulier des registres de deliberations. 85787
Extrait raisonne de l'histoire philosophique des deux Indes. (68072)
Extrait relatif au Canada. 72030
Extraite du discours de M. le Duc de Broglie. 8186
Extraites de quatre lettres de M. de Blanchelande. 5844
Extraites des ouvrages du Baron de Humboldt. 33732
Extraits de la relation abregee. 63907, 1st note after 98174
Extraits des auteurs et voyageurs. (56097)
Extraits des edits, declarations, ordonnances et reglemens. 17851
Extraits des journaux publies en Amerique. 5205
Extraits des minutes du Conseil. 10352
Extraits des rapports et documents officiels. 38563
Extraits des regitres du Conseil Superieur. 17851
Extraites des titres des anciennes concessions. 100763
Extraits du rapport sur l'Exposition de Paris. 10445
Extraits plus ou moins rapides. 6847
Extraits raisonnes des voyages. 22569
Extraordinaire Kayserliche Reichs-post-zeitung. 27160, 101420
Extraordinaria ocurrencia. 62937
Extraordinary account of a young woman. 93893
Extraordinary adventures & discoveries of several famous men. 9502

Extraordinary adventures of Arthur Gordon
Pym. 63526
Extraordinary adventures of M. Duportail.
42357
Extraordinary adventures of William Montgomery.
50159
Extraordinary and singular law case of Joseph
Parker. (58712)
Extraordinary assembly of the Grand Lodge
of . . . New York. (53692)
Extraordinary bravery of a woman. 44258-
note after 105690
Extraordinary career of a New York physician.
63013
Extraordinary case providentially prepared
for judges. 85116
Extraordinary conversion. 71498
Extraordinary disclosure of arbitrary power.
95858
Extraordinary disclosures! 68324
Extraordinary displays of the divine majesty
& power. 49769
Extraordinary events the doings of God. 65596
Extraordinary gazette. 23543, note after 89945
Extraordinary men. 74395
Extraordinary museum. 42166
Extraordinary narrative. 7718
Extraordinary proceedings at . . . New York.
58783, 2d note after 97255
Extraordinary prosperity of Great Britain.
23544
Extraordinary remarks concerning the raising
of flowers from seed. 17237
Extraordinary revelation of the deceit and
treachery practiced. (22199)
Extroardinary trial of the Rev. John Seys.
79673
Extra-territorial incidents of colonial legislation.
28378
Extravagance: a sermon for the times. 3794
Extravagance will not be tolerated. 84124
Extremadura en America. 105724
Extreme injustice and hardships. 85243
Eychman, Joannes. (8784), 25472, 77677-77678,
90036-90039, 105680
Eydoux, Fortune, 1802-1841. 98298
Eydoux, Joseph Fortune Theodore. see
Eydoux, Fortune, 1802-1841.
Eye and the wing. 81190
Eye Infirmary, New York. see New York
Eye Infirmary.
Eye Infirmary and Orthopaedic Institution,
Peoria, Ill. see Peoria Eye Infirmary
and Orthopaedic Institution.
Eye-opener! a real liberty song. 5818
Eye-opener for the people. 89944
Eye-slave, or a watch-word from our Lord
Iesus Christ. 80263, 95195
Eye-witness. pseud. Bastille in America.
(3899)
Eye-witness. pseud. Brief and perfect journal.
see S., I., an eye-witness. pseud.
Eyewitness. pseud. Col. Crockett's exploits.
see Smith, Richard Penn, 1799-1854.
Eye-witness. pseud. Extract from an un-
published manuscript on Shaker history.
23501, 79705
Eye-witness. pseud. Hurricane. see Burk,
Edward
Eye witness. pseud. Last days of Gordon.
27986
Eye-witness. pseud. Last night of the session.
10018

Eye witness. pseud. Narrative of the late
awful and calamitous earthquake.
51811
Eye-witness. pseud. Narrative of the revolt
and insurrection. see Turnbull,
Gordon.
Eye witness. pseud. Pictures of the "peculiar
institution." 62690
Eye-witness. pseud. Portrait of what are
called "new measures." 64404
Eye witness. pseud. reporter Report of the
trial of an action for libel. 96898
Eye witness. pseud. Riot and outrage of the
9th June, in Montreal. 50285
Eye-witness to the facts related. pseud.
Second address to the people of Great
Britain. see Burn, Andrew, 1742-
1814. supposed author
Eyes and ears. 4313
Eyes opened, or Carolinians convinced. 10063,
23545, 84819
Eygentliche Erzehlung. (22657), 1st note after
102874, note after 102948
Eyghentlijcke beschryvinge van West-Indien.
14348
Eyghentlijcke beschryvinghe van West-Indien.
14352
Eyles, Sir John, fl. 1721. 65865, 88192
Eylffte Schiffart, oder Kurtze Beschreibung
einer Reyse. 33665
Eylffter Schiffart ander Theil. 33665
Eylffter Theil Americae. (8784)
Eyma, Xavier. 23546-23558
Eynard, Charles. 23559
Eyndhoven, Jan van. 23578, (74507)
Eyquem, Mathurin, Sieur Du Martineau. 23560
Eyre, Edward John, 1815-1861. 23562,
(35643) see also Jamaica.
Governor, 1862-1866 (Eyre)
Eyre, Edward John, 1815-1901. defendant
23561, 24371
Eyre, G. 99894
Eyre, John. 23563-23566, 42586
Eyres, Jean Baptiste Benoit, 1767-1846. 7432,
(7438), 7441, 8424, 19619, 19621,
23567, 31802, (33704), 38332, 38982,
(46949), 46993, (47043), (51196),
55954, 56093, 57458-57459, 76833,
76838, 76844, 89976, 94228, 94843,
94847-94848, 94851, 95146
Eyring, Heinrich. tr. 83222-83224
Eyron, Pierre. ed. 23568, 55357, 93480
Eyth, -------. 23569
Eytinge, Sol. illus. 91067
Eyton, ------. 23570
Ez, A. van den Brandhof. see Brandhof Ez,
A. van den.
Eyzaguirre, J. J. 23572-(23593)
Eyzaguirre, Jose Ignacio Victor. 23571
Ezekiel Gobble and Co. pseud. Some account
of an existing correspondence. 86566
Ezeta, L. G. de. 23574-23575
Ezguerra, Mathias de. 23576
Ezra Phillips, jun., Executor, vs. Sylvanus
Emerson. 62481
Ezra White, vs. the people of the State of New
York. 103382-103383

F

F. pseud. Americains coureurs des bois.
(23577)
F------. pseud. spurious author Animadversions. 96145

F. and G. pseud. Proposals for traffick and commerce. 66039

F., A. pseud. Journal. 23578

F***, A. pseud. Precis historique. 23579

F., A. J. pseud. Ventajas de la independencia. 98892

F., A. O. pseud. Wreath for the Rev. Daniel Dow. see Kemp, Francis Adriaan van der.

F., A. R. pseud. Agua ligada para ayudar. 86395

F., B. psued. [Dedication.] see Fisher, Benjamin. supposed author

F., B. pseud. Idea of the English school. see Franklin, Benjamin, 1706-1790.

F., C. pseud. tr. 44268

F., D. B. P. pseud. Carta de un Habanero. 23580

F., D. J. M. pseud. ed. 86968

F., E. pseud. Report of the Committee. see Weymouth, Mass. South Parish. Committee of Inquiry.

F., E. pseud. True state of the case. 71082

F., G. pseud. Answer to several new laws and orders. see Fox, George, 1624-1691.

F., G. pseud. Caesar's due rendered unto him. see Fox, George, 1624-1691.

F., G. pseud. Here is declared the manner of the naming of children. see Fox, George, 1624-1691

F......n, G...n. pseud. Heroine du Texas. 31532

F——n, G——n. pseud. Heroine du Texas. (23581), note before 95090

G., G. pseud. Queries for the New England priests. see Fox, George, 1624-1691.

F., G. pseud. Secret workes of a cruel people. see Fox, George, 1624-1691.

F., G. pseud. Woord voor der Konink. see Fox, George, 1624-1691.

F., G. de. pseud. Terre australe connue. see Foigny, Gabriel de.

F., I. pseud. tr. 105221

F., I. pseud. tr. see Florio, John. tr.

F., J. pseud. Letter to Rev. Thomas Foxcroft. 23582

F., J. pseud. Letter to the Rev. Mr. William Hobby. 23583

F., J. pseud. Remarks on the American universal geography. see Freeman, James.

F., J. pseud. Remarks on the Rev. Mr. Cooper's objections. (23584)

F., J. pseud. Remarks on the Rev. Mr. Joshua Gee's letter. 23585

F., J. pseud. 1678. An almanack. see Foster, John.

F., J., Moderator. pseud. Testimony and advice. 94917

F., M. A. R. pseud. Carta segunda. 51346

F., M. R. de. pseud. Question Americaine. 62599

F., Mrs. P. pseud. Short account. 80742

F*****, P. pseud. Tabac. 94164

F——, Philip. pseud. American independence. see Freneau, Philip Morin, 1752-1832.

F., R. pseud. Present state of Carolina. 23586, 87919

F., R. A. pseud. Promtuario de la constitucion. 23587

F., T. pseud. Advertisement. see Foster (Theodore) firm publishers

F., T. pseud. Funeral sermon. see Foxcroft, Thomas, 1697-1769.

F., T. pseud. Letters on the West India question. 99775

F., W. F. pseud. ed. Mormons. 50762

F. de L., J. pseud. see Fernandez de Lizardi, Jose Joaquin, 1776-1827.

F. A. pseud. see A., F. pseud.

F. A. pseud. see Dummer, James. supposed author

F. A. pseud. see Otis, James. supposed author

F——s A——n. pseud. see Alison, Francis.

F. A. R. pseud. tr. see R., F. A. pseud. tr.

F. A. V. Z. pseud. see Z., F. A. V. pseud.

F. B. pseud. tr. see Brooke, Francis,

F—— B——. pseud. see Bernard, Sir Francis, 1712-1779.

F---l B--t. pseud. see B--t, F----l. pseud.

F. C. pseud. see C., F. pseud.

F. C***. pseud. see Carteaux, Felix.

F. C. J. pseud. see J., F. C. pseud.

F. D. pseud. see Drake, Sir Francis, 1540?-1596.

F. D. G. pseud. see Fernagus de Gelone, ------.

F. de P. T. pseud. see T., F. de P. pseud.

F. E. C. pseud. see Cushman, Frederick E.

F. Freiligrath's Epistle an Audubon. 25822

F. G. pseud. see G., F. pseud.

F. G. pseud. see Adair, James Makittrick. supposed author

F. G. M. R. pseud. see R., F, G. M. pseud.

F. H. W. pseud. see McDougall, Frances Harriet (Whipple) Greene.

F. J. N. pseud. see N., F. J. pseud.

F. L. pseud. see L., F. pseud.

F. L. pseud. see Leypoldt, F.

F. L. pseud. see Palmer, John.

F. L. pseud. see Sales, Luis.

F. L***, ancien consul. pseud. see L***, F., ancien consul. pseud.

F. L. M. pseud. see Mortimer, F. L.

F. L. S. pseud. see Sales, Luis.

F. M. pseud. see M., F. pseud.

F. M. pseud. see Molina, Felipe.

F. M. M. pseud. see M., F. M. pseud.

F. M. T. pseud. see T., F. M. pseud.

F. Marten's observations made in Greenland. (72186)

F. Marten's voyage to Spitzbergen and Greenland. 72187

F. O. pseud. see O., F. pseud.

F. Prevost et P. Pecquet. 65413

F. S. pseud. see S., F. pseud.

F. V. pseud. see V., F. pseud.

Fabens, Joseph Warren. 23588-23590

Faber, Conrad W. petitioner (23591)

Faber, F. W. (73193)

Faber, G. S. 89744

Faber, Johannes, ca. 1570-ca. 1640. (31515)-31516

Fabian, Peter. (31919)

Fabian y Fuero, Francisco, Bp. (23592)-(23593), 66551 see also Puebla, Mexico (Archdiocese) Bishop (Fabian y Fuero)

Fabiao de Christo. Fray 1759A

Fabie, A. M. 98604

Fabien, -------. 5653-5654

Fabien, -------, fils. 5653, 5655-5656

Fabius. pseud. Common sense. 23594

Fabius. pseud. Letters. 23595

Fabius Maximus, Q. 24340

Fable for critics. 42434

Fable for statesmen and politicians. 99267

Fable for the people. 20642

Fable of the bees. 67175

Fable on two cats and a monkey. 63585, 104539

Fable pour servir a l'histoire du 18e siecle. (23929)

Fable to suit the times. (78708)

Fables. 105598-9 [sic]

Fables and legends of many countries. 77337

Fables de Lafontaine, travesties en patois Creole. 38608

Fables et chansons. (75479)

Fabre, -------. tr. see Faure, Louis Joseph, 1760-1837. supposed tr.

Fabre, Hector. 23596-23598

Fabre, Jacques Antoine. tr. 62803

Fabrega, Jose. (16986), 58408 see also Panama (Province) Gobernador, 1856 (Fabrega)

Fabricius, Johann Albert, 1668-1736. 23599

Fabricius, Johann Friedrich, b. 1800. 23600

Fabricius, Otho, Bp., 1744-1822. (5164), 22852, 22859, 22864, 22873, 23601-23604, 37963

Fabricius: or, letters to the people of Great Britain. 26430

Fabricus Videns. pseud. see Videns, Fabricus. pseud.

Fabrius, Jacobus, Stapulensis. see Le Fevre, Jacques, d'Etaples, d. 1537.

Fabronius, Hermann, 1570-1630. 23605

Fabrus, Ulricus, Straubingensis. see Schmidel, Ulrich, 1510?-1579?

Fabry, Joseph Antonio. 23606

Fabula enim ex miris constituitur. (78188)-78190

Fabula politica. Los animales en cortes. 23607, 97045

Fabulas de Juan Nepomuceno Troncoso. 97046

Fabulas politicas de Juan Nepomuceno Troncoso. 52334

Fabulas politicas y militares de Ludovico Lato-Monte. (39211)

Fabulas politicas dedicadas al pueblo libre. 29352

Fabyan y Fuero, Francisco. see Fabian y Fuero, Francisco, Bp.

Faca; an army memoir. 44490

Facias, Scire. plaintiff 105479

Facileque omnium principus, in Procli Diadochi. 91983

Facilitated carrying. (15145), 15156, (52825), note after (52943)

Facio, J. S. defendant (57673)

Facio, Jose Antonio. defendant 582, (65925)

Facsimile atlas. 91866

Fac-simile autograph names. 21783

Fac-simile copy of the recently discovered American tune. 90498

Facsimile des autographes des gouverneurs. 23609

Facsimile letter of Washington. 39614

Facsimile letters of the signers. 8395

Facsimile of a Cherokee phoenix newspaper. 24161

Facsimile of a journal. 1921

Fac-simile of a paper in imitation of print. 47085

Facsimile of an unique broadsheep containing an early account. 99383

Fac simile of the autographs. 61646

Fac-simile of the "Dutch Vespucius." note before 99327, 99370

Fac simile of the handwriting and composition. 7835

Facsimile of the Illustrated Artic [sic] news. 23608

Fac-simile of the original draught of 'America.' 84041

Fac simile of Washington's accounts. 101546-101546A

Fac simile privately printed for John William Wallace. 7264

Fac simile reprint of Dr. George Buchanan's oration. (64041)

Fac-similes of church documents. 102700

Fac similes of letters from His Excellency George Washington. 101547

Fact and fiction. (81242)

Fact and fiction: a collection of stories. 12713

Faction, a sketch. 29391

Faction and ambition. 78191

Faction Anglaise, ses projets. 75121

Faction detected, by the evidence of facts. 23610, (60861), 70279

Faction the cause of all the confusion. 20672

Factor of New-England. pseud. News from New-England. 18229, 52757, 55060-55062

Factor to the South Sea Company. pseud. Answer to a calumny. 1653, note after 35564

Factors of London. see Merchants or Factors of London.

Factory-bell. (71235)

Factory girl. pseud. Cotton famine and the Lancashire operatives. 17111

Factory hand, of Waltham. pseud. Review. see Bigelow, Josiah.

Factory life as it is. 23611

Factory system, in its hygienic relations. 28544

Factory tracts. 23611

Facts about Cuba. 23612

Facts about peat as an article of fuel. (39567)

Facts about Santo Domingo. 23588

Facts [about the Sons of Temperance.] 87054

Facts: addressed to the landholders, stockholders, merchants. 96174, 100755

Facts against fancy. 4972-4973, 2d note after 96984

Facts against rumor. 90786

Facts and accusations set forth in a late pamphlet. 22796

Facts and arguments against the election of General Cass. 35810

Facts and arguments in favor of adopting railways in Pennsylvania. 67611

Facts and arguments in favour of adopting railways in preference to canals, in Pennsylvania, &c. (23613), 82593

Facts and arguments in favor of the removal of the national capital. (68307)

Facts and arguments. Letters from the Hon. Abbott Lawrence. (39344)

Facts and arguments relative to the presidential election. 81554

Facts and arguments respecting the great utility of an extensive plan. 5959, (10096)

Facts and authorities on the suspension of the privilege of the writ. (23615)

Facts and calculations respecting the population. (23616)

Facts and circumstances relative to the sufferings. 23617

Facts and conditions of progress in the north west. 26381

Facts and conjectures relative to the ancient condition. (3803)

Facts and considerations for the Democracy of the Empire State. 23619, 53668

Facts and considerations relative to duties on books. 36108

Facts and documents bearing upon the legal and moral questions. 90785

Facts and documents connected with the late insurrection. 35577

Facts and documents, exhibiting a summary view of the ecclesiastical affairs lately ransacted in Fitchburg. 24593-24594, 24600, 105304

Facts and documents in relation to Harvard College. 30765

Facts and documents in the case of Rev. Charles Morgridge. 25878

Facts and documents on the ecclesiastical affairs of Fitchburg. 24593-24594, 24600, 105304

Facts and documents relating to a second ex-parte council. 68972, 95524

Facts and documents, relating to a third ex-parte council. 68972, 95524

Facts and documents, relating to an ex-parte council. 68972, 95524

Facts and documents respecting Capt. Joseph Loring. 42094

Facts and duties of the times. (60950)

Facts and elucidations as connected with the management. 59094

Facts and estimates relative to the business. 66301

Facts and fallacies. 16998

Facts and fancies, for school-day reading. 78770

Facts and fancy—As you like it—Go on, or stop. 100893

Facts and features of the late war in Oregon. 4360

Facts and figures concerning the Hoosac Tunnel. 63006

Facts and figures exhibiting its advantages and resources. 32615, (68522)

Facts and figures for Fremont and freedom. 15615

"Facts and figures for the hour." 64750

Facts and figures from the standpoint of a departmental clerk. 59652, 1st note after 94241

Facts and figures, relating to the state of the controversy. (23620), 101807

Facts and figures relating to Vancouver Island. (59618)

Facts and law in the case of the ship Harvey Birch. (23639)

Facts and observations briefly stated. (3110)

Facts and observations concerning the organization. 105039

Facts and observations, illustrative of some recent transactions. 62436

Facts and observations, illustrative of the past and present situation and future prospects of the United States; embracing a view of the causes of the late bankruptcies in Boston. 10869

Facts and observations illustrative of the past and present situation and future prospects of the United States. With a sketch of the restrictive system. 10869, 23640

Facts and observations in relation to the origin and completion of the Erie Canal. 22744

Facts and observations justifying the claims of John Browne Cutting. 18204

Facts and observations, justifying the claims of the Prince of Luxembourg. 87825

Facts and observations on the culture of vines. (12355)

Facts and observations on the merits of the memorial. 22355

Facts and observations relative to the nature and origin of the pestilential fever. 61548

Facts and observations relative to the participation of American citizens in the African slave trade. 23641, 81969

Facts and observations respecting Canada. (28480)

Facts and observations, respecting the country. 103107

Facts and official documents. 256, 35365

Facts and opinions respecting Mr. John Quincy Adams. 315

Facts and opinions touching the real origin. 91011

Facts and principles connected with the claims. 88404

Facts and reasons in support of a bill. 75202

Facts and statements concerning the Cleveland and St. Louis Railroad. 23638

Facts and statistics in regard to the wealth. (13140)

Facts and suggestions, biographical, historical, financial, and political. 28514

Facts and suggestions in relation to the present state of the times. 52944

Facts and suggestions relating to the New-York and Albany Railroad. 54723

Facts and suggestions relative to finance & currency. (28515)

Facts and their consequences. 90098

Facts are stubborn things. 32482

Facts as to the metropolitan excise law. 23614

Facts [by Mr. Morgan.] 98574

Facts concerning quartz and quartz mining. 44257

Facts concerning the American indians. 82147

Facts concerning the bonds and stock. (74754)

Facts concerning the freedmen. 23618

Facts concerning the navy. (52124)

Facts concerning the rebellion. 44740

Facts connected with the application of the Connecticut River Company. 15866

Facts connected with the cruise. 26967

Facts connected with the inquisition. 75659

Facts connected with the presentment of Bishop Onderdonk. (35842)

Facts designed to exhibit the real character. 82579

Facts explaining the nature of the slavery of the blacks. 23621

Facts for Americans. 64128

Facts for Baptish churches. 25187

Facts for emigrants. A description of twenty-six counties of south-west Missouri. 55164

Facts for emigrants and capitalists. 55695, 2d note after 93999

Facts for emigrants. Northern Missouri. 55723

Facts for emigrants to California. 10003

Facts for families. 20092

Facts for farmers. 72181

Facts for the consideration of ship builders. 23622

Facts for the consideration of the legal voters of Boston. 6521

Facts for the laboring man. 23623, 31111

Facts for the people. 19501-(19502), 92412

"Facts for the people." 83690

Facts for the people. Ben Wade on McClellan. 43030

Facts for the people: containing a comparison and exposition of votes. 25967

Facts for the people, G. Bailey, editor. 23625

Facts for the people. No. X. Address, of the National Anti-slavery Convention. (23624)

Facts for the people of Barre. 73833

Facts for the people of the south. 81970

Facts for the people . . . Philadelphia, September, 1832. 61647

Facts for the people. Republican and Democratic management. 90582

Facts for the people, showing the relation of the United States government to slavery. Compiled from official and authentic documents. (50317)

Facts for the people; showing the relations of the United States government to slavery, embracing a history of the Mexican War. 50316

Facts for the people. The abolition leaders convicted. 23626

Facts for the people. The address adopted by the Democratic State Convention. (34523)

Facts for the people. The Massachusetts anti-liquor law no failure. (45732)

Facts for the people. The various charges against General W. H. Harrison briefly stated and refuted. 103285

Facts for the present crisis. (23627)

Facts for the shore owners of . . . New Jersey. 53109

Facts for the tax payers. 79649

Facts for the times. 28762

Facts for the times. Dissolution of the American union question. 23628

Facts gathered from a personal examination. 12829

Facts illustrating the unrighteous prejudice existing. 2186

Facts illustrative of freemasonry. (51668)

Facts illustrative of the character of the anthracite, or Lehigh coal. 23629, (39879)

Facts illustrative of the condition of the Negro slaves in Jamaica. 16623

Facts important to be known. 23630

Facts in reference to the Society for the Promotion of Collegiate and Theological Education at the West. 85914

Facts in reference to the aspersions. 84906

Facts in regard to African colonization. 42255

Facts in relation to the bank. 59910

Facts in relation to the introduction of gas light. 61648

Facts in relation to the official career of B. F. Isherwood. (35249)

Facts in relation to the . . . prospects. 61649

Facts in the life of General Taylor. 90863, 90866

Facts involved in the Rhode Island controversy. 23631

Facts, observations, and conjectures. 3807

Facts of its [i. e. Spiritualism's] history classified. 75965

Facts of the case of the Rev. Albert Barnes. 65165

Facts on congregational intolerance. (61241)

Facts, principles, and progress. 23632

Facts relating to north eastern Texas. 3672

Facts relating to slavery. (27525)

Facts relating to the bridge question. 55025

Facts relating to the capture of Washington. 23144, note after 101938

Facts relating to the early history of Chester, N. H. 4450

Facts . . . relating to the endowments. 57014

Facts relating to the state of the St. Maurice bridges. 75443

Facts relating to the trade. 96151

Facts relative to colonial slavery. 81971

Facts relative to the brief statement. 24595

Facts relative to the campaign on the Niagara. 23634, 55425, 71500

Facts relative to the Canadian Indians. (23634A)

Facts relative to the conduct of the war. 21269

Facts relative to the expulsion of the Mormons. 28606

Facts relative to the first mortgage loan. 60278

Facts . . . relative to the negociation of the first mortgage loan. 60278

Facts relative to the political and moral claims. 71144

Facts relative to the present state of the British cotton colonies. 23635

Facts relative to the Session . . . of the Reformed Presbyterian Church. 20683

Facts respecting slavery. (23636)

Facts respecting the captures property. (23637)

Facts respecting the treatment of Americans. 8088

Facts serving to shew the comparative forwardness. 5296

Facts shewing the right of certain companies. (27045)

Facts tending to prove that General Lee was never absent. 27506

Facts tending to prove the identity of Louis XVII. 30267, 104213

Facts verified upon oath. 16624, (16626), 81972, 1st note after 102803

Facts versus fancies. 23774, 3d note after 88547

Facts versus Lord Durham. 38750

Facts, views, &c., relating to the British and American steamers. 14433, 93819

Facts, views, statements, and opinions. 93819

Facts which are now history. 8285

Facts which were presented by citizens of New York. 54135

Facts without fiction. 23642

Factum de M. Schoelcher intitule: La verite. 5652

Facultades de los supremos poderes federales. 98623

Faculte de Theologie, Paris. see Paris. Faculte de Theologie.

Faculty, requisites for admission, terms, &c. 1705

Facundo Quiroga, Juan. see Quiroga, Juan Facundo.

Facundo. (77077)

Facundo Quiroga et Aldao. 77070

Faded flower. 54933

Faded hope. 80918

Faden, William. cartographer 23643, 62063, 83981, 94397

Faehtz, E. F. M. 23644

Faes, Jose Estevan. 23645

Fage, Robert. 23646

Fagel, G. (39804), 49568

Fages, E. 23647

Fahey, James. 23648

Fahnestock, George Wolff. 23649

Fahrten und Abenteuer des Kapitain John Ross. 73388
Fahrten u. Schicksale eines Deutschen in Texas. 22071
Faillon, -------. 23650-23655, 39588, 4th note after 99504
Failure of free society. 24168
Fair, G. Y. 23656 see also Bank of the State of Alabama. Montgomery Branch. President.
Fair, Rockingham Co., N. H. see Rockingham County, N. H. Fair.
Fair, Utica, N. Y., 1853. see Oneida County Agricultural Society. Annual Fair, Utica, N. Y., 1853.
Fair account of the late unhappy disturbance. 6735, 45940
Fair American, a comic opera. (62861), 86940
Fair American. Exemplifying the peculiar advantages. 106061
Fair and candid examination of the last discourse. 4095
Fair and correct account of facts. 104771
Fair and full view of the votes. 78009
Fair and rational vindication. 6788
Fair dealing between debtor and creditor. 46312
Fair epistle from a little poet. 100889
Fair, fat, and forty. 81269
Fair for the Soldiers' and Sailors' Home, Philadelphia, 1865. see Soldiers' Home, Philadelphia. Fair, 1865.
Fair for the Soldiers' and Sailors' Home. 86336
Fair Harvard. 23657
Fair inquirer. pseud. Few remarks on an address. see Hawkins, John.
Fair maid of Wyoming. 31719
Fair narrative of the proceedings of the Presbytery. 55, 50462, 58896
Fair of the New England and Vermont State Agricultural Societies, Brattleborough, Vt., 1866. 65051
Fair of the Rutland County Agricultural Society. (74475)
Fair pilgrim. 94250
Fair play. pseud. True state of the American question. 23658, 3d note after 97148
Fair play! Or, a needful word. 13350, 102425
Fair play to women. 42705, 58758, 67423
Fair representation of His Majesty's right to Nova-Scotia or Acadie. (47547), (56129), note after 96403
Fair stating of the claims. 7286
Fair-Street Church of Christ, New York. see New York (City) Fair-Street Church of Christ.
Fair traders objections, against the bill. 100466
Fair view of both sides of the slavery question. 17545, note after 92624
Fair warning to Lord Baltimore. 38886, 92940
Fair weather. 46313
Fairbairn, Henry. 23659-23660
Fairbairn, Robert B. (23661)
Fairbank, -----. 103012
Fairbank, Drury. 23662
Fairbank, Thaddeus. 97477
Fairbanks, Cassie. 23663
Fairbanks, Charles. 23664
Fairbanks, Charles R. 23665, note after 69942
Fairbanks, Ebenezer. 23673

Fairbanks, Erastus, 1792-1864. 23666-23667 see also Vermont. Governor, 1860-1861 (Fairbanks)
Fairbanks, George F. 23668-23670
Fairbanks, Gerry. (23671)
Fairbanks, Jason. defendant 23672-23673, 96862
Fairbanks, John. 23674
Fairbanks, Stephen. 64990
Fairburn, John ed. 8999, 62682, 66951
Fairburn's edition of the English hermit. 66951
Fairburn's edition of the trial of Thomas Picton. 62682
Fairchild, Ashbel G. 23675
Fairchild, David. 85095
Fairchild, E. R. 73567
Fairchild, Helen Lincklaen. ed. 98479
Fairchild, James Harris, 1817-1902. (23676)-23679
Fairchild, Joy Hamlet, 1790-1859. (23680)-(23682), 87341, 103792
Fairchild, Joy Hamlet, 1790-1859. defendant before Church Council 23683-23684
Fairclough, Joseph W. 23685
Fairfax, Bryan Fairfax, 8th Baron. 52283, 92856
Fairfax, Ferdinando, 1766-1820. 23687
Fairfax, Ferdinando, 1766-1820. petitioner (23686)
Fairfax, George William. 55283
Fairfax, L. (23688)
Fairfax, Thomas Fairfax, 6th Baron, 1692-1782. petitioner 99894
Fairfax, William. 52283
Fairfax, Vt. Literary and Theological Institution. see Literary and Theological Institution, Vairfax, Vt.
Fairfax County, Va. Court. 101636, 101751-101755, 101756-101758, 101760-101764, 101899
Fairfax County, Va. Court. Clerk. 101757
Fairfax County, Va. Protestant Episcopal Theological Seminary. see Alexandria, Va. Protestant Episcopal Theological Seminary in Virginia.
Fairfax correspondence. 23690
Fairfax; or, the master of Greenway Court. (16314)
Fairfaxes of England and America. 52283
Fairfield, Edmund B. 23691
Fairfield, Jane. (23692)-23693
Fairfield, John, 1797-1847. 23694
Fairfield, Sumner Lincoln. (23692), 23695, 55549, 55561
Fairfield, Conn. Superior Court. see Connecticut. Superior Court, Fairfield.
Fairfield, N. Y. College of Physicians and Surgeons of the Western District of the State of New York. see Albany Medical School.
Fairfield County, Conn. Consociation of the Western District. see Congregational Churches in Connecticut. Fairfield County Western Consocation.
Fairfield, Conn. Eastern Association. see Congregational Churches in Connecticut. Fairfield County Eastern Association.
Fairfield County Western Consociation. see Congregational Churches in Connecticut. Fairfield County Western Consociation.
Fairfield West Association. see Congregational Churches in Connecticut. Fairfield West Association.
Fairfield gazette. 40318, 80391

Fairhaven, Mass. Ordinances, etc. 23701-23703, 23707
Fairhaven, Mass. School Committee. 23701, 23704-23705, 23707
Fairhaven, (Ontario Bay,) the terminus. (23700)
Fairholt, F. W. 23708
Fairman, G. 101660
Fairman, W. Blennerhasset. (23709)
Fairmount Park contribution. 61650
Fairmount Park contribution. Sedgely Park Estate. 61650
Fairmount Park. Sketches of its scenery. 37695
Fairplay, Oliver. pseud. Proposals. see Jefferson, Thomas, Pres. U. S., 1743-1826.
Fairplay & Co. pseud. Letter to John Wurtz. 105641
Fairservice, James. pseud. Plain dealing. 23711
Fairy extravaganza. 70830
Fairy of the stream, and other poems. (23816)
Fairy's search. (82525)
Fait historique en trois actes et en prose. 98956
Faith absolutely necessary. 17916
Faith and doctrines of the Church of the Ternal Son. 92781
Faith and fancy. 77237
Faith and freedom in America. 57788
Faith and order of the Protestant Episcopal Church. 32934
Faith and patience. 7697
Faith and prayer of a dying malefactor. 80794
Faith and testimony of the martyrs. 32480
Faith at work. 46314
Faith encouraged. 46315
Faith kept. 104670
Faith in divine providence the great support. 47997
Faith of Christ's ministers an example for His people. (77587)
Faith of the fathers. 46316
Faith of the martyrs in New England vindicated. 8654
Faith once delivered to the saints. 4331
Faith the principle of a holy life. 84123
Faith, the principle of missions. 85291
Faithful abstract of Lord Chatham's last speech. 63068
Faithful account of that singular imposition and delusion. (33290)
Faithful account of the discipline professed and practiced. 46464
Faithful account of the distresses and adventures of John Cockburn. 14097, note after 97744
Faithful account of the French prophets. 105011-105012
Faithful account of the massacre of the family. 35433
Faithful account of the whole of the transactions. (23712)
Faithful advice from several ministers. 46587, note after 101451
Faithful advice from several ministers of the Gospel. 46682
Faithful and exact account of God's great goodness. 102450
Faithful and most comfortable incouragement. 1996, 16037
Faithful and pathetic expostulation to the women. 79251

Faithful and true relation of the persecution. 13308
Faithful bishop. 19344
Faithful, but melancholy account of several barbarities. 62560
Faithful collection of signs, wonders and prodigies. 52342
Faithful couple. 50440
Faithful covenanter. 32837
Faithful evangelist. 12332
Faithful exposition of the causes that have produced the civil war. 10638
Faithful Federalist. pseud. Letter to Mr. Roger B. Taney. 40450
Faithful hand. pseud. ed. Sermon by Hugh Peters. 61196
Faithful history of remarkable occurrences in the captivity and deliverance of Mr. John Williams. 104262-104267, 104269-104271, 104274
Faithful history of the Cherokee Tribe of Indians. (12457), 90114
Faithful instructor. (45410), 46403
Faithful lover. 2108A, note after 93619
Faithful man abounding with blessings. 46795
Faithful man described and rewarded. A sermon. 46318
Faithful man, described and rewarded. Some observable & serviceable passages. 46317
Faithful minister. 62795
Faithful minister the glory of Christ. 32317
Faithful minister's course finished. 106385
Faithful minister's monument. 104352
Faithful ministers of Christ mindful of their own death. 14481
Faithful minister's parting blessing. 103510
Faithful minister's trials. 81636
Faithful minister's work. 96121
Faithful missionary. 68070
Faithful monitor. pseud. Solemn warning. see Everett, William, supposed author.
Faithful monitor. 45733, 46319
Faithful narrative, derived from official documents. 4051, 25287
Faithful narrative of Elizabeth Wilson. 104617
Faithful narrative of remarkable occurrences in the captivity and deliverance of Mr. John Williams. 104268
Faithful narrative of remarkable occurrences in the captivity of the Reverend Mr. John Williams, &c. 104264
Faithful narrative, of the distresses and adventures of John Cockburn. 14098, note after 97744, 104096
Faithful narrative of the horrid and unexampled massacres. 11288
Faithful narrative of the life and character of the Reverend Mr. Whitefield. 103623
Faithful narrative of the many dangers and sufferings. 21664, 94709
Faithful narrative of the proceedings of the Ecclesiastical Council. 24532, 79415
Faithful narrative, of the proceedings, of the First Society and Church in Wallingford. (30647), 96092, 96094
Faithful narrative of the proceedings of the North American colonies. 12163, 1st note after 99889
Faithful narrative of the remarkable revival of religion. 8982-8983
Faithful narrative of the surprising work of God. 21937, 21939, (21956), 102684

Faithful narrative of the unfortunate adventures of Charles Cartwright. 11149
Faithful narrative of the unparalleled sufferings. 82297-82298
Faithful narrative of the wicked life and remarkable conversion. (6472)
Faithful narrative of the wonderful dealings of God towards Polly Davis. (18879), 105488
Faithful narrative of transactions noticed at a camp-meeting. 89140
Faithful pastor. 66226
Faithful pastors angels of the churches. 14482
Faithful picture of the political situation of New Orleans. 53325, 104030, note after 105480
Faithful preacher. A sermon. 89159
Faithful relation of a multitude of acts of horrid barbarity. 13873
Faithful relation of some late, but strange occurrences. 46269
Faithful relation of the extremities the company was reduc'd to. 19029, 3d note after 97085
Faithful report of matters uttered by many. 46552, note after 95669
Faithful report of the trial of Doctor William Little. 96894
Faithful report of the trial of the cause of Philip I. Arcularius. 75950, 2d note after 96812
Faithful representation of the Indian war dance. 59169, 64408
Faithful ruler described and excited. 12336
Faithful servant. 65597, 65617
Faithful servant approv'd at death. 65597
Faithful servant in the joy of his Lord. 14483
Faithful servant of Christ call'd up to glory. 73558
Faithful servant of Christ, described and rewarded. 103899
Faithful servant of Jesus Christ. pseud. Writings of a pretended prophet. 50696, 105629-105630
Faithful servant rewarded: a sermon. (72474)
Faithful servant rewarded. By Nathanael Chauncy. 12337
Faithful serving of God in our generation. 18268
Faithful steward. (22123)
Faithful testimony, to New-England. (49658), 92351
Faithful testimony, to the cause and work of God. 49657, 92351
Faithful warnings to prevent fearful judgments. 46320
Faithful witness for magistracy & ministry. (24361), 105669
Faithless Briton. (79484)
Faithorne, -------. illus. 80993, note after 98499
Faits et idees sur Saint-Domingue. 75122
Faits explicatifs de la nature de la traite des Noirs. 23713
Faits historiques sur Saint-Domingue. 28981
Faits memorables, saillies et bon-mots. 14458
Faits relatifs aux troubles de Saint-Domingue. (6423)
Fajardo, Heraclio. C. 17837, 23714-23716, 68460
Fajardo, Manuel Palacio. see Palacio Fajardo, Manuel.
Fal lal la. A favorite Welsh air. 92172A-92172B
Falck, N. 23718
Falckner, Justus. 23719

Falcon, J. C. 27816
Falcon, Joseph Davila. 38271
Falconar, Harriet. 23720
Falconar, Maria. 23720
Falconbridge. pseud. Dan Marble. see Kelly, Jonathan F.
Falconbridge, Alexander. 23721, 55077
Falconer, Richard. 23723, 100846
Falconer, Thomas. 23724-23728, (28630), (28632), 96172
Falconer, William. 92225, 99418
Falconetti, A. F. tr. 19544
Faldo, John. 59708, 59727
Fales, William R. 23729
Falissoniere, ------ de la. (47547)-(47548)
Falken aus der Falken-Hohle. 5555
Falkenstein, Charles. see Falkenstein, Christian Karl.
Falkenstein, Christian Karl. (23730)-23731
Falkland, -------. tr. 38441
Falkland, Henry Cary, Viscount, d. 1633. 80620
Falkland, Lucius. (23732), 31044
Falkland Islands, &c. &c. 103714
Falkland's Islands. 36302
Falkner, John Blake, 1832- 5778
Falkner, Thomas, 1707-1784. 23734-23738, 29379, 49894
Falknern, Daniel. 23739, 95394
Fall, Robert. 23740
Fall: a sermon . . . Nov. 27, 1864. 3794
Fall of angels and men. (82499)
Fall of Aztalan. (724)
Fall of Babylon. 46332, 46589
Fall of Bexar. 81239
Fall of British tyranny. 39512
Fall of Burgoyne. 63622
Fall of Chicago. 71046
Fall of Delhi. 100861
Fall of empires. 84842
Fall of faction. 63647, note after 94220
Fall of Fort Morgan. A poem. 26643
Fall of Fort Sumter. 23741
Fall of Iturbide. 92907
Fall of man, and recovery by Christ. 85550
Fall of Mexico. 48477
Fall of Mexico. A poem. (36060)
Fall of Mexico. A romance. 5550A, 5553
Fall of Palmyra. 105619
Fall of Peter Pindar. 100757
Fall of Ray Potter. 64662
Fall of San Antonio. 100884
Fall of Sumter. 30984
Fall of Tarquin. 59288
Fall of the confederacy. 32923
Fall of the great republic. 79366
Fall of the Indian. 43524, 106005
Fall of the Indian, with other poems. 43523
Fall of the mighty lamented. 46796
Fall of the Nau Soung. 49856
Fall of the sugar planters of Jamaica. 35578, 65686
Fall of wicked nations. 103229
Fall River, Mass. 20468, 45717, 70578
Fall River, Mass. petitioners 46051
Fall River, Mass. Athenaeum. Library. 23743
Fall River, Mass. Charter. 23745, 23748
Fall River, Mass. Citizens. 30407
Fall, River, Mass. City Council, 23745, 23748
Fall River, Mass. Committee on the South Boundary. 23749
Fall River, Mass. Coroner. 69890

Fall River, Mass. Coroner's Inquest in the Case of the Explosion of the Steamship Empire State, 1856. 69890

Fall River, Mass. Mayor, 1858 (Borden) 23742 see also Borden, Nathaniel B.

Fall River, Mass. Ordinances, etc. 23745, 23748

Fall River, Mass. Public Library. 23744

Fall River, Mass. Public Library. Trustees. 23744

Fall River, Mass. School Committee (23750)

Fall River, an authentic narrative. 104172

Fall River; an historical sketch. 23747

Fall River directory. 23746

Fall River Female Anti-slavery Society. 82049

Fall River Lithograph Company. firm publishers 89510

Fall-River monitor. 92834

Falla recitada na abertura da Assemblea Legislativa da Bahia. 81431

Falla recitada pelo Excellentissimo Senhor Antonio Pinto Chichorra da Gama. 60989

Fallacies of freemen. (23752)

Fallacy detected, by the evidence of facts. 23753

Fallacy detected, in a letter to the Rev. Mr. Wesley. 102676

Fallacy of free-trade doctrine. 23754

Fallacy of neutrality. 32650

Fallen brave. 80005

Fallen saved. 84781-84786

Fallen sinners of men able to do well. 25231

Falley Seminary, Fulton, N. Y. 23755

Fallon, Christopher. 93732 see also Sunbury & Erie Rail Road Company. President.

Falls of Montmorency. 24392

Falls of Niagara: . . . a complete guide. 52320

Falls of Niagara and the vicinity. 55116

Falls of Niagara, as seen from the Table Rock. 55117

Falls of Niagara, or tourist's guide. 19804

Falls of Niagara, sketches by the way. 55118

Falls of Passaic. 33856

Falls of Taughannock. 29921

Falmouth, --------. defendant 45709, 58909

Falmouth, Me. 84350 see also Portland, Me.

Falmouth, Mass. Indian Conference, 1732. see Massachusetts (Colony) Indian Conference, Falmouth, 1732.

Falmouth, Mass. Indian Conference, 1749. see Massachusetts (Colony) Indian Conference, Falmouth, 1749.

Falmouth, Mass. Indian Conference, 1754. see Massachusetts (Colony) Indian Conference, Falmouth, 1754.

False accusers accused. 23756

False alarm. (36296), 36302, 78299

False alarm, addressed to the Right Honourable Richard Rigby, Esq. 13132, (23757)

False alarm: or, the American mistaken. 23758

False friendship. 78191

False hopes discovered. 42088

False judgment of a yearly meeting. 37185, 37194, 37202

False judgments reprehended. (37195)

False nation and its "bases." 58967

False news from Garth rejected. 66737

False pretences. 18269

False prophet! 46896

False prophet confounded. 96147

False shame: or the American orphan in Germany. 38279

Falsedades que contiene el cuaderno titulado: Despojo a mano armada. (19756)

Falsehood and forgery detected and exposed. 23759

Falsehood exposed. 96507

Falseness of the hopes of many professors. 91948

Falsenhart, J. see Felsenhart, J.

Falses on all sides. 23760

Falvel, M. J. reporter 94964

Fama posthuma del Senor . . . Juan Dom. Gonzales de Reguera. 68935

Fama postuma del D. Juan Domingo Gonzalez de la Reguera. 39025

Fama postuma del Excelentisimo e Ilust. Senor D. D. J. D. Gonzalez de la Reguera. 4911, 27812

Fama postuma dell Excell. Senor Doctor Don Juan Domingo Gonzalez de la Regure y oracion funebre. 4911, 27812, 39025

Fama, y obras posthumas del fenix de Mexico. 17734, note after 34687

Fama, y obras posthumas de fenix de Mexico, secima musa. 36814

Fama, y obras posthumas del feniz de Mexico. 17733, 17735

Fame and fancy, or Voltaire improved. 100729

Fame and glory. 93654

Fame and glory of England vindicated. 8543

Fame: and other poems. (80532)

Fame Hose Company, Philadelphia. 61651

Fameux marins du XVe siecle 1461-1492. 30604

Familiar conversation upon an old subject. 95393

Familiar conversations upon the constitution of the United States. 29616

Familiar conversational history. 23761

Familiar dialogue between a minister, a gentleman of his congregation. (20271)

Familiar dialogue between a minister & a gentleman of his congregation. 20057

Familiar dialogue, between Cephus & Bereas. 105252

Familiar dialogues between Americus and Britannicus. (44888)

Familiar dialogues on Shakerism. 43206

Familiar discourse by way of a dialogue. (17066)

Familiar epistle to Robert J. Walker. 43305

Familiar epistles, and other miscellaneous pieces. 4108

Familiar exposition of the constitution of Pennsylvania. 26158

Familiar exposition of the constitution of the United States. 92305

Familiar history of the birds of the United States. 2754

Familiar lectures on botany. 41241

Familiar lectures on botany, practical, elementary, and physiological. 61353

Familiar letters and miscellaneous papers of Benjamin Franklin. (25494), 25507

Familiar letters domestic and forren [sic]. (33348)

Familiar letters, illustrating the scenery. 81488, 2d note after 100605

Familiar letters, in answer to the Rev. John Sherman's treatise. 98479, note after 105520

Familiar letters [of Charles Francis Adams.] 84633

Familiar letters [of William Smith.] 84678C

Familiar letters on public characters, and public events. 93553

Familiar letters to a friend. 94074-94075, 102523

Familiar letters to a gentleman. 20058

Familiar letters to Henry Clay of Kentucky. 29309, 29311-29312

Familiar letters to his [i. e. John Sanderson's] friends. 76405

Familiar letters to John B. Fitzpatrick. (24623)

Familiar letters upon a variety of religious subjects. 20059

Familiar letters, written by Mrs. Sarah Osborn. 57757

Familiar notes of thought and life. 57787

Familiar scenes in town. 13159

Familiar sermons. (67748)

Familiar sketch of William Wilberforce. (29314)

Familiar talk about monarchist and Jacobins. 84791

Familie Wharton. 38241

Familien-Roman. 91198

Familienbuch. 27187

Familietafereel uit het Surinamsche volsleven. 77503

Famille Americaine ou l'Amerique il y a soixante ans. 78771

Famille Ameriquaine. Comedie en prose et en trois actes. 96312

Famille de Martel le planteur. 19531

Famille Littlepage. 16529

Famille Need. 4998

Family Aegis. 69438

Family affairs. 78750

Family almanac for . . . 1859. (50582)

Family and personal history of Henry Adolph. 63038

Family and slavery. 81973-81974

Family anecdotes. 46862

Family assistant. (82472)

Family book; containing discourses on various subjects. 25042

Family book of history. 57249

Family Christian almanac for the United States. 23762

Family compact. 33865

Family companion: containing rules and directions. 78759

Family companion; or the oeconomy of human life. 90250

Family edition. 92491

Family education and government. 12878, 104306

Family encyclopedia of useful knowledge and general literature. (5782)

Family gathering of the family of Pease. 59461

Family genealogies. 36843

Family history. 52155

Family history and fifty-two years of preacher life. 84541

Family history. By J. L. McConnel. 43086

Family history. By R. Morris Smith. 83776

Family library (Harper's) 9188, 18448, 82726, 95216, 92132, 97658, note after 97587

Family library (Murray's) 21865, 35160, (35207), 78382

Family library magazine. 59073

Family magazine, devoted to education. 88474

Family magazine or general abstract of useful knowledge. 23763

Family Meeting of the Descendants of Charles Kellogg, Boston?, 1858. 37279

Family meeting of the descendants of Charles Kellogg, of Kelloggville, N. Y. 37279

Family memoirs. 99240

Family memorial. A history and genealogy of the Kilbourn family. 37734

Family memorial. Part I. 95230

Family memorials. (6283)

Family miscellany. 69353

Family notices collected by William Gibbs. 27307

Family of John Webster. 102354

Family of Leck, of Bedlington. 39644

Family of Rev. David D. Field. 24276

Family of the Fitzroyals. 21848, 4th note after 100577

Family physician. 50026

Family prayer not to be neglected. 2632

Family reader. 84162

Family recollections of Lieut. Genl. E. W. Durnford. 21434

Family record. 79857

Family record of Daniel Dodd. 20486

Family record of the ancestors of Ephraim and Abigail Robbins. 71818

Family record, of the descendants of John Spofford, and Elizabeth, his wife. 89561

Family records of the descendants of John Spofford, who emigrated from England. 89562

Family records. 96449

Family records and lineage of Isaac Otis. 57862

Family records and recollections. 82449, 83606

Family records of the early settlers of West Simsbury. 8433

Family records: or genealogies of the first settlers of Passaic Valley. 41502

Family register. (23764), 57879, 101278

Family register of the descendants of Edward Farmer. 23822

Family register of the descendants of Nathaniel Smith, Jr. 82418

Family register. Taken from recollections. 103486

Family register; with a collection of marriage rites. 23765

Family relation, as affected by slavery. (47241), 81975, 93816

Family-religion, excited and assisted. 46321

Family religion urged. 46322

Family Reunion of the Descendants of Waitstill Ranney and Jeremiah Atwood, 8th, Chester, Vt., 1866. 67896

Family sacrifice. (46323)

Family tablet: containing a selection of original poetry. 23766, 91750, 91778

Family tree book. 84734, 84910

Family tourist. 27869

Family visitor, and silk culturist. (21542)

Family well-ordered. 46324

Famin, Cesar. 19541, 19544, (23767)-23771, 102622

Famine and the sword. 33964

Famine at home. 88345

Famous American Indians. 27913

Famous Americans of recent times. 58945

Famous boys. (23772)

Famous discoverer. 91067

Famous Faneuil Hall proceedings. 7256

Famovs historie of the Indies. 1564, 45011, 106330

Famous Maine-law discussion. 90304

Famous men of modern times. 27913

Famous old charter of Rhode-Island. 70582

Famous old people. 30990

Famous Roman causist. pseud. Wiles of popery. 103990

Famous Roman causist Escabar. pseud. Short trip to Rome. see Escabar. pseud.

Famous voyage of Sir Francis Drake into the South Sea. note after 65395

Famous voyage of Sir Francis Drake, with a particular account. 20829, 105624

Famous voyages & travailes of Vincent Le Blanc, or White. 39593

Fan for Fanning, and a touchstone for Tryon. (55611), 68970

Fanal, del imperio Mexicano. 23773

Fanarraga, Juan de Zavala. see Zavala Fanarraga, Juan de.

Fanaticism, and its results. 23774, 3d note after 88547

Fanaticism; its source and influence. 98337

Fanaticism of the Democratic Party. 42367

Fanatic's daughter. 17230

Fancourt, Charles St. John. 23775

Fancy. pseud. Travels of fancy. 96500

Fancy ball. A sketch. 1723

Fane, John. see Westmoreland, John Fane, 10th Earl of, 1759-1841.

Fanelli, Antonio Maria. 23776

Faneuil, Benjamin. petitioner 26145

Faneuil Hall address. 23777

Faneuil Hall Committee on Water Supply, Boston. see Boston. Faneuil Hall Committee on Water Supply.

Faneuil Hall Meeting, Boston, 1820. see Boston. Free Trade Meeting, 1820.

Faneuil Hall Meeting, Boston, 1821-1822. see Boston. Faneuil Hall Meeting, 1821-1822.

Faneuil Hall Meeting, Boston, 1854. see Boston. Faneuil Hall Meeting, 1854.

Faniel, Benjamin. see Faneuil, Benjamin.

Fanning, David. 23778-23779

Fanning, Edmund. 23780-23781, (23783), 37812

Fanning, Nathaniel. 23782-(23783), 51795

Fanning, T. 23784

Fanning, Thomas W. (23785), 29562

Fanning, firm see Ensign, Bridgman & Fanning. firm publishers

Fanning & Co. firm see Phelps, Fanning & Co. firm publishers

Fanning's illustrated gazetteer of the United States. (23786)

Fanny. (29869)

Fanny; a poem. (29870)

Fanny: a poem. With notes. 29872

Fanny, continued. 29873

Fanny Fern. pseud. see Parton, Sarah Payson Willis.

Fanny Grant among the Indians. 57216

Fanny Hunter's western adventures. 23787, 33916

Fanny Kemble in America. 37332

Fanny: with other poems. 29871

Fano, Guido Gianetti da. 76897

Fantaisie Americaine. 2244

Fantasia of Bos Bibens. 44259, 2d note after 102802

Fantasma. pseud. Solo en Durango. 86506

Fantasque. 23789

Far north: explorations in the Arctic regions. 37002

Far off. 50984

Far west, a sketch of the Illinois and other states. (23791)

Far west; or, a tour beyond the mountains. (23790), 24651

Far west; or, the emigrant's progress from the old world to the new. (74336)

Far west record. 83147

Far-west scenes. 71729, 94822

Far west songster. 74378

Faran, James John, 1808-1892. 23792

Faraud, Henry, Bp. 24126-24127

Farbigen. 64544

Farce. 5945, (50168), 70464, 73619, 77815, 79739, 101481

Farce, accompanied by an interlude. 20314, 94403

Farce: as lately acted, and to be re-acted. 101483

Farce, in one act and a beautiful variety of scenes. 79709

Farce, in one act. By E. Stirling, Esq. 91844

Farce, in one act. By X, author of nothing. 67870

Farce, in three acts. 101092

Farce, in three acts, both serious and comic. 94160

Farce, in three acts . . . by who d'ye think? 94543, note before 95353

Farce: in three acts. Respectfully dedicated. 94542

Farce in three acts. Written for the St. Louis Thespians. 103065

Farce in two acts. 94227, 98180

Farce in two acts, as it was performed Theatre Royal, Covent Garden. 25884, note after 91499

Farce, in two acts. As performed at the theatre in Boston. 89592-89593

Farce, in two acts. By C. S. Talbot. 94226

Farce, of domestic origin. 96968

Farce, Published for the entertainment of the curious. 51110, 101485

Farce. Translated from the original French. 59270

Farcical tragedy. 23793

Farcy, Charles. 23794-23795, 40038

Farewel . . . see Farewell . . .

Farewell, William. 23902, 90998

Farewell. 100804

Farewell: a sermon preached to the First Church. 26064

Farewell address . . . before the . . . City Council. 42478

Farewell address. . . . [By Lemuel Capen.] (10742)

Farewell address. By the Rev. Noah Hunt Schenck. 77567

Farewell address. [By William Hogan.] 32426

Farewell address delivered at Haverford College. 20163

Farewell address delivered in . . . Waterford. 5881

Farewell address, delivered to the Church and Congregation. 101283

Farewell address in facsimile. note after 101547

Farewell address [of Andrew Jackson.] (14151), 21445

Farewell address of Andrew Jackson to the people of the United States: and the inaugural address of Martin Van Buren. 98411

Farewell address of Andrew Jackson, to the people of the United States. Delivered March 4, 1837. 35347

Farewell address of Elisha Tyson. 97638

Farewell address of Gen. George Washington. 101630

Farewell address of Gen. George Washington, to the people of the United States, on the 17th September, 1796. 101613

Farewell address, of Gen. Geo. Washington, to the people of the United States. September 17, 1796. 101604

Farewell address of George Washington. 449, 5361, 12114, 15601, 20623, (20989), 32784-32785, 45394, (50942), 59107-59108, 60778, 63586-63588, 65359, 77766, (78703), 78997, (79403), 89198, 89200, 92817, note after 96799-96800, 97202, note after 99300, 101418, note after 101593, 101594, 101597, 101611, 101631, 101648, 101650, 101653, 101660, 101662, 101686, 101777, note before 101837, 101841, note after 101843, 101846A, 1st, 3d and 5th notes after 101872, 101874, 2d note after 101883, 6th note after 101885, 4th note after 101886, 101982, 101992, 101998, 1st note after 102036A, 102746

Farewell address of George Washington, President of the United States. 101600

Farewell address of George Washington to the people of the United States. 101685

Farewell address of the Chaplain. 13648

Farewell address of the Hon. Wm. Drayton. 28860

Farewell address on occasion of taking temporary leave. 73533

Farewell address to his [i. e. Andrew Bigelow's] flock. (5276)

Farewell address, to his [i. e. George Washington's] fellow-citizens. 101598, 101603

Farewell address to missionaries. 54969

Farewell address to the army. 104140

Farewell address to the citizens of the United States. 101627

Farewell address to the Payson Church, South Boston. (23680)

Farewell address to the people of the United States. 101605, 101607-101608, 101612, 101614, 101617, 101619-101626, 101628-101629, 101634-101641, 101643-101646, 101649-101651, 101654-101660, 101667, 101686, 101724, 101725

Farewel [sic] address to the people of the United States, on his [i. e. George Washington's] resignation. 101565

Farewell address to the people of the United States, September 19, 1796. 101681

Farewell address to the people of the United States. September 1796. 101661, 101668

Farewell address to the people of the United States. September 17, 1796. 101663

Farewell address to the people of the United States, together with his [i. e. Andrew Jackson's] proclamation. 35347

Farewell address to the people upon leaving them. 104373

Farewell address to the Rev. Mr. James Ramsay. 96055

Farewell address to the . . . Society. 34742

Farewell address to the students of Hamilton College. 18826

Farewell address to the Unitarian Society in Nashua. 57791

Farewell address to the youths of, and final adieu to the state of Massachusetts. 102741

Farewell addresses of Washington and Jackson. (14151)

Farewell addresses presented to H. E. Sir C. T. Metcalfe. 35579

Farewell almanac, 1708. (13777)

Farewell banquet to Mr. John Bigelow. 5307

Farewell discourse at North Coventry. 81602

Farewell discourse [by Joseph Emerson.] 22451

Farewell discourse. [By Joseph Priestley.] (65513)

Farewell discourse, by Rev. N. Scott. 78342

Farewell discourse. By Silas Ketchum. (37647)

Farewell discourse, Columbia, South Carolina. 31415

Farewell discourse delivered at the Thirteenth Congregational Church. 16376

Farewell discourse, delivered before the Congregation of St. Peter's Church. 40220

Farewell discourse, delivered Sunday, October 8th, 1854. 104163

Farewell discourse, delivered to the Church and Society of the First Parish in West Springfield. 98993

Farewell discourse delivered to the Congregational Church. 71520

Farewell discourse, delivered to the Purchase Street Congregation. 16375

Farewell discourse . . . in Eastport. (5275)

Farewell discourse . . . Jan. 5, 1845. 30330

Farewell discourse: preached in St. Stephen's Church. 21172

Farewell discourse, preached in the Central Church, Boston. (70933)

Farewell discourse, preached in the First Church, Charlestown. 8968

Farewell discourse, preached to the Congregational Church. 105600

Farewell discourse read before the Channing Congregational Society. 83321

Farewell discourse to his [i. e. Joseph Priestley's] congregation. (65513)

Farewell discourse . . . to his [i. e. George Trask's] late charge. note before 96475

Farewell discourse to the children. 101055

Farewell discourse . . . to the . . . Congregational Church. 37851

Farewell discourse, to the Congregational Church . . . Rutland. 24462

Farewell discourse to the First Church and Society. (28587)

Farewell discourse to the Free Presbyterian Churches. 58706

Farewell discourse . . . Washington, May 12, 1844. 9091

Farewell discourses delivered, September 26, 1847. 71015

Farewell doctrinal discourse. (39806)

Farewell entituled to Sir Iohn Norris and Syr Frauncis Drake. 59526

Farewel-exhortation [sic] to the church and people. 46779

Farewell hymn, on leaving the old meeting-house. 24775

Farewell hymn; on the death of Miss Polly Child. 104806

Farewell lecture to the friends of temperance. 11003

Farewell letter, addressed to the American Presbyterian Society. 12944

Farewell letter to his [i. e. S. Remington's] last charge. (69559)

Farewell letter . . . to the vestry and congregation. 19345

Farewell letters to a few friends in Britain and America. 101345

Farewell Meeting for Dr. Massie, of London,
New York, 1863. see New York State
Anti-slavery Society. Farewell Meeting
for Dr. Massie, of London, New York,
1863.
Farewell message, and obituary notices.
14034
Farewell orders of General Washington. 101591
Farewell orders, to the armies of America.
101545
Farewell orders to the armies of the United
States. 101530
Farewell: pastoral letter to the people. 47791
Farewell sermon. A sermon, preached at
Rochester. 33211
Farewell sermon addressed to the First
Presbyterian Church. 18405
Farewell sermon and address. (20667)
Farewel [sic] sermon, and postoral charge.
86583
Farewell sermon at Bridgewater, 1811. 47363
Farewell sermon . . . at Cooperstown, N. Y.
52293
Farewell sermon . . . at Kingston. 42995
Farewell sermon, . . . at Milford, N. H.
(50391)
Farewell sermon at St. John's, at Nevis.
31611
Farewell sermon at Tinmouth, Oct. 28, 1787.
(57744)
Farewell sermon . . . August 20, 1843. 48933
Farewell sermon, Boiling Spring Church, Oct.
18, 1802. 20382
Farewell sermon [by Sylvester Sage.] 74897
Farewell sermon, by the Rev. John Taylor.
94498
Farewell sermon [by William W. Spear.] 89106
Farewell sermon, delivered April 7, 1844.
9630
Farewell sermon, delivered at Haverhill, N. H.
82533
Farewell sermon, delivered before the Con-
gregational Church. 103216
Farewell sermon, delivered in Grace Church.
9630
Farewell sermon delivered in the Edwards
Church. 72630
Farewell sermon, delivered September 26th,
1802. 36240
Farewell sermon . . . Geneva, N. Y. (9102)
Farewell sermon . . . in Barre, Mass. 50349
Farewell sermon . . . in . . . Boston. 38064
Farewell sermon . . . in . . . Brooklyn.
40859
Farewell sermon . . . in Colebrook. 39720
Farewell sermon . . . in the Church of the
Mediator. 63353
Farewell sermon . . . in the Eliot Church.
39568
Farewell sermon . . . in the Unitarian Church.
51515
Farewell sermon in Zion Church, N. Y. 17266
Farewell sermon, . . . January 20, 1833.
43392
Farewell sermon . . . June 22, 1750. 21947
Farevvell sermon of Mr. Thomas Hooker.
32834-32835
Farewell sermon of Rev. Henry B. Shermer.
80423
Farewel [sic] sermon, preached at New-Haven.
93201
Farewel-sermon [sic], preached at Plainfield.
73561
Farewell sermon, preached at Rowe. 83727

Farewell sermon, preached at St. George's
and St. Paul's Chapels. (34766)
Farewell sermon preached at South Natick.
(2578)
Farewel-sermon [sic] preached at the first
precinct. (21941)
Farewell sermon, preached by Rev. Henry M.
Storrs. 92231
Farewell sermon, preached in Christ Church,
Troy. 90528
Farewell sermon preached in St. John's Church.
103895
Farewel-sermon [sic] preach'd in the Church
of St. Catharine. 96958
Farewell sermon preached July 1, 1860.
(25185)
Farewell sermon preached March 15, 1835.
(66808)
Farewell sermon, preached May 28, 1809.
28817
Farewell sermon, preached October 20, 1850.
25209
Farewel [sic] sermon preached on board Whitaker.
103598
Farewell sermon, preached September 10th,
1815. 65380
Farewell sermon preached to the Protestant
Episcopal Congregation. 89362
Farewell sermon preached to the Third Con-
gregational Society. 90924
Farewell sermon preached to the Winnisimeet
Congregational Church. 38905
Farewel [sic] sermon to the Congregation in
Tottenham-Court Chapel. 86583
Farewell sermon to the Congregation of St.
Stephens. 72574
Farewell sermon, to the First Utica Presby-
terian Society. (21519)
Farewell sermon to the people of Windham,
N. H. (30498)
Farewel [sic] 1702. 62743
Farewell speech in the Senate of the U. S.
13550
Farewell to his lady. 67599
Farewell to old Scotland. 78230
Farewell to Pittsburg and the mountains.
100865
Farewell to the Antilles. (8687)
Farewell to the friends and patrons of the
Sprite. 89907
Farewell to the graduating class. 49725
Farewell to the subscribers of the Charleston
mercury. 70487
Farewell words. 36985
Farfan, Agostin. 23796-(23797)
Fargeau, ------ Le Pelletier de Saint. see
Le Pelletier de Saint Fargeau, -------.
Fargo, F. F. 23798
Fargues, H. 23799-23800
Faria, Manoel Severim de. (3648)
Faria e Castro, C. A. de Lemos. see Lemos
Faria e Castro, C. A. de.
Faria Rios Sanchez y Zarzosa, Manuel de Godoy
Alvarez de. see Godoy Alvarez de Faria
Rios Sanchez y Zarzosa, Manuel de,
Principe de la Paz, 1767-1851.
Faria y Sousa, Manuel de. 23801-23803,
(64154)
Faria y Sousa, T. 23804
Farias, Ignacio. 23805
Fariaz, Benito Gomez. see Gomez Fariaz,
Benito.
Faribault, G. B. 11141, 11143, (23806),
47556, 67019-67021, 69256, 1st note after
94271

Faribault, Minn. Bishop Seabury Mission.
see Bishop Seabury Mission, Faribault,
Minn.
Faribault, Minn. Institution for the Education
of the Deaf and Dumb. see Minnesota.
School for the Deaf, Faribault.
Faribault, Minn. Minnesota State Sabbath
School Association Annual Convention,
10th, 1868. see Minnesota State Sabbath
School Association. Annual Convention,
10th, Faribault, 1868.
Faribault, Minn. School for the Deaf. see
Minnesota. School for the Deaf, Faribault.
Farine, Charles. 23807
Farinholt, B. F. 15386, (23808)
Farissol, Abraham. 60934
Farist Community. 23809
Farley, Charles A. (23810)
Farley, Frederick A. (23811)-(23813)
Farley, George F. (13256)
Farley, H. ed. 42491, 2d note after 95375
Farley, Harriet. 23814, 42491, (52711), 2d
note after 95375
Farley, Stephen. 23815, 92790
Farm for sale. 84764
Farm school. (13647)
Farm within the reach of every man. 71294
Farmer. pseud. Address from a farmer to
the honest men. see Burges, Thomas.
Farmer. pseud. Address to the farmers of
Rhode Island. 70529
Farmer. pseud. Farmer's and Monitor's
letters. see Dickinson, John, 1732-1808.
Farmer. pseud. Farmer's letters to the
people. see Lincoln, Levi.
Farmer. pseud. Five letters addressed to
the yoemanry. see Laughan, ------.
and Logan, George, supposed author
Farmer. pseud. Free thoughts. see Seabury,
Samuel, Bp., 1729-1796. and Wilkins,
Isaac.
Farmer. pseud. Historic progress of civil
and rational liberty. see Whipple,
Oliver.
Farmer. pseud. Letter, containing some candid
observations on mankind. 40267
Farmer. pseud. Letter from a farmer to his
friend. 40275
Farmer. pseud. Letter from a farmer [on
the conduct of the eighteen Presbyterian
ministers.]. 47276, 97107
Farmer. pseud. Letters addressed to the
yeomanry. see Laughan, -------.
Farmer. pseud. Letters of a farmer to the
people of Georgia. 27066
Farmer. pseud. Letters to the people. see
Lincoln, Levi.
Farmer. pseud. Letters under the signatures
of "Senex," and of "A farmer." 40656,
79122
Farmer. pseud. Reign of felicity. see Spence,
Thomas. supposed author
Farmer. pseud. Sentiments on what is freedom.
see Dickinson, John, 1732-1808.
Farmer. pseud. Serious address to the rulers
of America. (79248)-(79250)
Farmer. pseud. Three voices. see Funk,
Isaac.
Farmer. pseud. To the farmers of Rhode
Island! 70755
Farmer. pseud. To the public. 96012
Farmer. pseud. Treatise on the law and the
Gospel. see B . . . . d, D. . S. .
pseud.
Farmer, ---------- defendant at Court Martial
23840, 24893

Farmer, A. W. pseud. Congress canvassed.
see Seabury, Samuel, Bp., 1729-1796.
and Wilkins, Isaac.
Farmer, A. W. pseud. Free thoughts. see
Seabury, Samuel, Bp., 1729-1796. and
Wilkins, Isaac.
Farmer, A. W. pseud. View of the con-
troversy. see Seabury, Samuel, Bp.,
1729-1796.
Farmer, C. M. (23816)
Farmer, Daniel Davis. defendant 23817
Farmer, Dick. pseud. see Dick Farmer.
pseud.
Farmer, Hugh. 92161
Farmer, John, 1789-1838. (4437), 7222, 15141,
18055, 18629, 23818-23839, 36327, 50392,
50397, 52884, 52885, 73592, (77233),
78431, 94112, 100759
Farmer, John, 1836-1901. 17936
Farmer, Miles. plaintiff 23841, 92191
Farmer, William. 8586, (8596)
Farmer: a comic opera, in two acts. 86936
Farmer and gardener. 23842
Farmer and his son's return from a visit to
camp: together with The rose tree.
105961-2 [sic]
Farmer and his son's return from a visit to
the camp. 105959
Farmer and landholder of Jessup's Cut, Md.
pseud. Address to the people of Maryland.
45060
Farmer and mechanic. 23843
Farmer (and once a grand juror) of Orange
County. pseud. To the General Assembly.
95931
Farmer and soldier. 80919
Farmer and the man. 31930
Farmer boy. 31170
Farmer in Ohio. pseud. Brief an einen Farmer
in Ohio. see Carey, Henry Charles,
1793-1879.
Farmer in Pennsylvania. pseud. Letters.
see Dickinson, John, 1732-1808.
Farmer in the country of Rockingham. pseud.
Letter. 40275
Farmer, in the state of the Massachusetts-Bay.
pseud. Some remarks. 86743
Farmer Jackson in New York. 35391, 94809
Farmer of New Jersey. pseud. Observations
on government. see Livingston, William.
incorrectly supposed author and Stevens,
John, 1749-1838.
Farmer of New-Jersey, a tale. 101236
Farmer of Windham County. pseud. Present
state of our country considered. 99200
Farmer refuted. 29955
Farmers' accountant and instructions for over-
seers. 93479
Farmer's almanac. 93230
Farmer's almanack, and annual register, for
. . . 1828. 89578
Farmer's almanack; and annual register [for
1824.] 89576, 89582
Farmer's almanack, and annual register, for
. . . 1829. 89585
Farmer's almanack, and annual register, for
. . . 1826. 89577
Farmer's almanack; and annual register [for
1823.] 89576, 89582
Farmer's almanac for . . . 1818. 79844
Farmer's almanack, for . . . 1859. 47912
Farmer's almanac, for . . . 1851. (47161)
Farmer's almanac, for . . . 1841. 89589
Farmer's almanack . . . for . . . 1846. 82914
Farmer's almanack, for . . . 1830. 54730
Farmer's almanac for . . . 1822. 79472

Farmer's almanac . . . for . . . 1793. 23844,
2d note after 95414, 95447
Farmer's almanack, for the middle states.
89586
Farmer's almanack; or an astronomical diary.
89576, 89582
Farmer's allminax from 1870 to 1880. 79910
Farmer's allminax for the year ov Our Lord
1874. 79910
Farmer's and emigrant's handbook. 44805
Farmers' and mechanics' almanac for 1866.
78461
Farmers and Mechanics Bank, Philadelphia.
see Philadelphia. Farmers and
Mechanics Bank.
Farmer's and Monitor's letters to the in-
habitants. 20052
Farmers' and planters' friend. 23845
Farmers, . . . and other working men, of the
city and county of New York. 54235
Farmer's assistant. 55227
Farmer's Association, Mount Pleasant, N. Y.
51165
Farmers' Bank, Geneva, N. Y. 26935
Farmers' Bank of Kentucky. 37494
Farmers' Bank of Kentucky, October, 1850.
37494
Farmer's Brother. Seneca Indian Chief 89175,
89187, 89206
Farmer's calendar. 23849
Farmer's calendar, or New York and Vermont
almanack. 23846
Farmer's calendar, or northern almanac.
23848
Farmer's calendar, or Utica almanack. (23847)
Farmer's catechism. 102353, 102367, note
after 102396
Farmers' Club, Lunenburg, Mass. see
Lunenburg Farmers' Club.
Farmers' College, College Hill, Ohio. see
College Hill, Ohio. Farmers' College.
Farmers' College, Hamilton County, Ohio. see
College Hill, Ohio. Farmers' College.
Farmer's companion. 8976
Farmer's daily register. (39555)
Farmer's dialogue, for Nantucket. (52343)
Farmer's diary, or Catskill almanack. (23850)
Farmer's encyclopaedia. 36201
Farmer's fall. 43638
Farmers' Fire Insurance and Loan Company,
New York. Charter. 54269
Farmer's fireside. 1216, 98049
Farmer's friend. 32254
Farmer's fruit book. 82204
Farmers, Gardeners and Silk Culturists National
Convention, New York, 1846. see Na-
tional Convention of Farmers, Gardeners
and Silk Culturists, New York, 1846.
Farmer's guide. A description of the business
of Nashua and Nashville. (37760)
Farmer's guide, and western agriculturist.
102961
Farmers' guide to the orchard and fruit garden.
27878
Farmer's hand book. 23851
Farmers' High School of Pennsylvania. see
Pennsylvania State College.
Farmer's journal. (10342)
Farmer's letters to the people. 23852, 41255
Farmer's library and monthly journal of agri-
culture. 23853
Farmers' Loan & Trust Company, New York.
75456

Farmer's magazine. see Christian scholar's
and farmer's magazine. Delaware register
and farmer's magazine.
Farmer's manual. see Silk culturist and
farmer's manual. Silk-grower and farmer's
manual.
Farmer's manual. [By J. H. Sheppard.] (80297)
Farmers, mechanics, and laborers need pro-
tection. 37272
Farmers', mechanics' and servants' magazine.
23854
Farmer's, mechanic's, manufacturer's, and
sportman's magazine. 23855
Farmer's monitor. (23241)
Farmer's monthly museum. 74171, 101012
Farmer's monthly visitor. (23856), (31832),
64621
Farmer's museum, or lay preachers' gazette.
(19587), 89498
Farmer's Mutual Fire Insurance Company.
50219
Farmers . . . of the County of Kent. petitioners
see Kent County, R. I. Farmers.
petitioners
Farmer's question. 10842
Farmer's register. 23857
Farmers' register. Supplement. (9721)
Farmers' souvenir. 101722
Farmer's useful and entertaining companion.
23858
Farmian de Rosi, known as Durosoi. 23859,
73846
Farming as it is! 62964
Farming for boys. 50813
Farmington, Me. State Normal and Training
School. see Maine. State Normal and
Training School, Farmington.
Farmington, Me. Western State Normal School.
see Maine. State Normal and Training
School, Farmingto.
Farmville, Va. Longwood College. see Long-
wood College, Farmville, Va.
Farmville, Va. South Side Institute. see
Longwood College, Farmville, Va.
Farnese, Francisco. 82851
Farnham, Benjamin. 23860
Farnham, Eliza W. 23861-23862, 75945
Faro, Fernando Telles de. see Telles de
Faro, Fernando.
Farnham, Henry. 82355, 104222 see also
Meeting of Working-Men and Other
Persons Favorable to Political Principle,
Albany, N. Y., 1830. Assistant Chairman.
Farnham, Luther. 23863-23864
Farnham, Robert. (29617)
Farnham, Thomas J. 23865-23872
Farnsworth, Benjamin F. 105356
Farnsworth, Frederick. 101428
Farnsworth, Frederick. supposed author
104447
Farnsworth, John Franklin, 1820-1897. 23873
Farnsworth, J. H. 23874
Farnsworth, Oliver. ed. 101841, 101852
Farnum Preparatory School. see New Jersey.
State Normal School. Farnum Preparatory
School.
Faro, Fernando Telles de. see Telles de
Faro, Fernando.
Farol Indiano, y gvia de curas de Indios.
60913
Farol. Periodico semanario de la Puebla de
los Angeles. (23875)
Farola de la Habana. 29437
Faron, James J. see Faran, James J.
Farquhar, John. 23876
Farquhar, R. T. (23877)

Farr, Jonathan. 23878
Farra, Eliza Rotch. 23883
Farrago plantarum quarundam Indicarum &
Americanarum. 68027
Farragut, David Glasgow, 1810-1870. 23879
Farragut and our naval commanders. 31149
Farragut testimonial. 23880
Farrand, -----. tr. 24338
Farrand, William P. ed. (65157), 65185
Farrar, -------. 83876
Farrar, C. C. S. 23881
Farrar, Eliza Ware (Rotch) 23383, 92339,
106147
Farrar, John. (23882)
Farrar, Mrs. John. see Farrar, Eliza Ware
(Rotch)
Farrar, N. 23884
Farrar, T. (23888)
Farrar, Timothy. reporter 23887
Farrar, Timothy, 1788-1874. 23885-23886
Farrell, N. E. 23889
Farren, -------. 23890
Farrent, J. 23891
Farrer, John. cartographer 2d note after
100557, 104101, 104193
Farrer, Sir Thomas. 83876
Farrer, Virginia. cartographer 2d note after
100557, 104191
Farrier, Arthur. defendant 17941, 30345
Farrington, E. F. 23892
Farrow, Henry. 49782
Farrow, Henry P. 23892
Farther account of the great diversions.
(23894)
Farther adventures of Robinson Crusoe.
(19283)
Farther appeal to men of reason and religion.
102685
Farther appeal to the unprejudiced judgment
of mankind. 23895, (26248)
Farther brief and true narrative of the late
wars. 52638
Farther considerations on the present state of
affairs. 23896-(23897)
Farther defence of Col. William Lovetruth
Bluster. 23898
Farther discovery of the present state of the
Indians. note before 92797
Farther discovery ofthe present state of the
Indians in New-England. note before
92797, 103688-103689
Farther discovery of the present state of the
Indians . . . manifested by letters. 103689
Farther discussion of that great point in
divinity. 66868
Farther examination and explanation. 23899
Farther facts connected with the West Indies.
90306
Farther observations, on the discovery of
America. 104277
Farther proceedings concerning the case of
Rip Van Dam. 98431
Farther relation of the cruel and bloody suffer-
ings. 5631
Farther supplement to the act. (60098)
Farwell, J. H. 23900
Farwell, T. F. 23900
Farwell, W. B. 23901
Farwell, Willard B. 86010
Farwell, William. 23902
Fascicvlvs geographicvs. 66893
Fasciculus Viventium. 46325
Fasel, G. W. illus. 54153
Fashion and famine. 91281, 91288

"Fashion of this world passeth away." A
sermon. 84412
Fashion of this world passeth away. By Mrs.
S. Henderson Smith. 84133
Fashion, or life in New-York. 51206
Fashion, or the art of making breeches. 35088
Fashionable business directory. 54288
Fashionable miscellany. 55122
Fashionable songs for 1798. 15024
Fashionable tour. A guide to travellers.
(23903), 96487
Fashionable tour, and guide to travellers.
18909
Fashionable tour in 1825. 96487
Fashionable tour: or, a trip to the springs.
76915, 96487
Fashion's analysis. 5887, 1st note after 104829
Fashions and follies of Washington life. 65397
Fast, Edward G. 23904
Fast, Simon Hold. pseud. see Hold-Fast,
Simon. pseud.
Fast and the feast. 15614
Fast day discourse, by Daniel Foster. 25210
Fast-day discourse, delivered August 21st, 1863.
9192
Fast day discourse . . . in Philadelphia.
(35996)
[Fast day proclamation. April, 1779.] 99052
[Fast day] proclamations. 99049
Fast day sermon. 51703
Fast-day sermon . . . April 30th, 1863. 11964
Fast day sermon at Greencastle, July, 1812.
(37438)
Fast-day sermon. By James Harvey. 30777
[Fast-day sermon.] By the Rev. Samuel Blair.
5755
Fast day sermon, delivered in Northampton.
21820
Fast day sermon, delivered in the city of Flint.
82233
Fast day sermon, delivered January 4, 1861.
57891
Fast-day sermon on the declaration of war with
Great Britain. 11545
Fast day sermon, preached April 30, 1863.
8349
Fast day sermon preached in Boston in January,
1636-37. 103223
Fast day sermon, preached in . . . New Haven.
13589
Fast day sermons. (23907)
Fast folks. 56318
Fast implies a duty. (64208)
Fast in the ice. 23906
Fast men and grass widows. 54287
Fast of God's chusing, plainly opened. 95195
Fast of the pilgrims. 89600
Fast sermon. April 25, 1799. 91801
Fast sermon, . . . at Bath, Me. (58372)
Fast sermon at Brookline. 918
Fast sermon at Merrimack, N. H. (9366)
Fast sermon . . . at North-Yarmouth, April 7,
1814. 8470
Fast sermon at Portland, Me. 4618
Fast sermon at Sullivan. 17893
Fast sermon, civil war, Demopolis, Ala.
31312
Fast sermon, delivered in the North Presby-
terian Meeting House. 92956
Fast sermon on slavery. 73120
Fast sermon, preached at ------ Feb. the 10th,
1799. (23905)
Fast sermon, preached at Fitchburg, July 23,
1812. 3850, 93905

[Fast] sermon preached in the church at Falmouth. 14070

Fast sermon, 12 April, 1764. 3456

Fast which God hath chosen. 14484

Fast sermon, [Wrentham, Mass.] Aug. 20, 1812. 13598

Fastes de la gloire. 29395, 40913, 95072

Fasti Novi Orbis et ordinationum apostolicarum. 51445

Fasti Societatis Jesu. 20939

Fastos de la dictadura del Peru. 61127

Fastos militares de iniquitad. 57620

Fasts of Nineveh and the fasts of Connecticut. (7957)

Fatal armour. 105178

Fatal consequence of a people's persisting in sin. 3471

Fatal consequences of the unscriptural doctrine. (80879)

Fatal curiosity. 104462

Fatal effects of ardent spirits. (64233)

Fatal effects of vicious company. 91070

Fatal error, a tragedy. (39960)

Fatal feud. [By G. A. Raybold.] 68037

Fatal feud [by John Tait.] 63647, note after 94220

Fatal jest, and other poems. 78341

Fatal patent. A metrical romance. 100562

Fataler Schiffs-Capitain. 1669

Fate of blood-thirsty oppressors. 13316

Fate of Franklin. 5695

Fate of Major Frederick D. Mills. 49103

Fate of the freemen. (17271)

Fate of the union. 23089, 85357

Fate, or the prophecy, a tragedy. 23908

Father. pseud. Book for Massachusetts children. see Hildreth, Hosea.

Father. pseud. Book for New-Hampshire children. see Hildreth, Hosea.

Father. pseud. Columbus, or the discovery of America. (14651)

Father. pseud. Hog. 32417

Father. pseud. Richmond alarm. 71195

Father. pseud. Son in the army. 86864

Father. pseud. Stories about whale-catching. see Tuttle, George.

Father Abbey. pseud. Father Abbey's will. see Seccome, John, 1708-1793.

Father Abbey's will. (78690)-78691

Father Abbot, or, the home tourist. 81210

Father Abraham. pseud. Speech to a good number of people. see Franklin, Benjamin, 1706-1790.

Father Abraham's almanack. 23909

Father Abraham's speech to a good number of people. 25508, 70906

"Father Clark" or the pioneer preacher. 59482

Father Cyril, in Georgia. 88486

Father departing. 46326

Father Girard and Miss Cadiere. 83610

Father Henson's story of his own life. 31433, note after 92624

Father Hutchins revived. 23910

Father Jouges' account of the captivity. (80023)

Father Kemp and his old folks. (37336)

Father Larkin's mission to Jonesville. (55215)

Father Marest's journey. 37949

Father Mathew: a biography. 43855

Father of a nation will restore it to peace. 78627

Father of Candor. pseud. Enquiry into the doctrine. 2d note after 104010

Father of Candor. pseud. Letter concerning libels. 2d note after 104010

Father; or, American shandy-ism. 23912

Father Sawyer's centennial. 88269

Father Smith's advice respecting diseases and their cure. 83709-83710

Father Tammany's almanack. 23911

Father Ward's letter to Professor Stuart. 101311

Father's advice to his son. 86864

Father's legacy to his daughters. 90238, 90240, 90244

Father's legacy to his two daughters. 90234

Fathers of New England. A sermon. 74721

Fathers of New England. An oration. (9545)

Fathers of the desert. 73924

Fathers of the German Reformed Church. 30284

Fathers of the New Hampshire ministry. (6956)

Father's story of Charley Ross. (73343)

Fatigas y descanso de Jesucristo en la conversion de la Samaritana. 76162

Fatio, L. C. F. 23913

Fatio, Philip. supposed author 106216

Fatti accaduti nel Messico in seguito dell' intervento Francese. 23914

Fauchat, ------. 23915

Fauche, Pierre Francois. 23916

Faucher, J. S. (23917)

Fauchet, Claude, 1744-1793. 23918, 25573, (25601)

Fauchet, Joseph, Baron, 1761-1834. 16878, 23919-(23921), 34900, 40690, 2d note after 101709 see also France. Legation. U. S.

Faucon, Emma. 23922

Fauconpret, C. A. de. see Defauconpret, C. A.

Fauconpret, A. J. B. see Defauconpret, A. J. B.

Faugeres, Margaretta V. (Bleecker) 5896, (23924), 106080

Faulk, Andrew Jackson, 1814-1898. 18297 see also Dakota (Territory) Governor, 1866-1869 (Faulk)

Faulkner, Charles James. 23924-(23926)

Faulkner, T. C. (23927)

Faulkner on slavery. (23926)

Faulkner's history of the revolution. (23927)

Faults on both sides. 23928

Faults on both sides, Federal and Democratic. 10851, (10877)

Fauna Americana. 30390, (30393), 37665

Fauna Boreali-Americana. 37963, 71026-71029

Fauna Boreali Americana, part IV. 37963, 71029

Favna Groenlandica. 23602, 37963

Fauna und Flora Guiana's. 77780

Faune entomologique de l'Ocean Pacifique. (6153), 21210

Fauno, Lucio. tr. 6119

Faunstelter, Georg. ed. 672

Fauque, ------. (23929)

Fauquier, Francis, 1704?-1768. (51674), 99906, 99924, 99995-99998 see also Virginia (Colony) Governor, 1758-1768 (Fauquier)

Fauquier County, Va. Central Committee. see Whig Party. Virginia. Fauquier County. Central Committee.

Faure, Louis Joseph, 1760-1837. supposed tr. 41646

Faussell, B. 23931

Faustino, L. A. 84529

Fausto de Souza, Augusto. see Souza, Augusto Fausto de.

Fausto. Impresiones del gaucho Anastasio el Pollo. 10315

Faustus, John. pseud. Choice dialogue. see Walter, Thomas, 1696-1725.

Fauveau, Auguste Francois. see Frenilly, Auguste Francois Fauveau, Marquis de, 1768-1848.

Fauvel, -------. engr. 27650, (63966), 68421

Fauvel-Gouraud, Francois. 28134

Fauvel Gouraud, J. B. G. 23932, 24677, 28133, 35677

Faux, U. 23933

Favard, -----. 23934

Favez, ------. 91222

Favolius, Hugo. 23935

Favorite ballad of the poor black boy. 92173

Favorite country dance compos'd by Dibdin. 92176A

Favorite duett song. 92174D

Favorite of heaven described. 46370

Favorite song. 92170

Favorite song, at the American camp. 101815

Favorite son [sic] in the Pirates. 29171A

Favorite song of the Black bird. 105966

Favorite song translated from the German. 86371

Favorite toasts and sentiments. 100654

Favorite Welsh air. 92172A-92172B

Favoritism unveiled. 87897, note after 89935

Fawcett, Benjamin. 30798, 102608

Fawcett, J. 21939

Fawcett, Wynne. defendant at Court Martial 96863

Fawn of the pale faces. 7160

Faxardo, E. M. plaintiff 48476

Faxardo, Francisco Palma. see Palma Faxardo, Francisco.

Faxon, John, 1763-1826. defendant 96895, 101476

Faxon, William. 23936

Faxton, Theodore S. (23937)

Fay, ----- du. see Du Fay, ------, fl. 1798.

Fay, Charles Jerome de Cisternay du. see Du Fay, Charles Jerome de Cisternay, 1662-1723.

Fay, Cyrus H. 23938

Fay, Eli. 69157

Fay, Francis B. 23939

Fay, H. A. 23940

Fay, J. D. 12739

Fay, Jonas. 806, 34059, 1st note after 98997, 3d note after 99005, 99014 see also Vermont. Constitutional Convention, Windsor, 1777. Clerk. Vermont. Conventions, 1776-1777. Clerk.

Fay, Joseph. 803, 806, 7286, 2d and 4th notes after 99005, 99047 see also Vermont. General Assembly. Secretary. Vermont. Secretary. Vermont. Supreme Executive Council. Secretary.

Fay, Joseph Dewey, 1779-1825. 33237, (33286)

Fay, Josiah. 93898, note after 99131

Fay, Louis. (23941)

Fay, Richard S. 23942-(23943)

Fay, Samuel. 23944

Fay, Samuel P. P. 12097, 23945, 45038, 75208, 2d note after 98167-98168

Fay, Theodore S. 17273, 23946-(23949), (49780), 54712, 90656, note before 94094, note before 99588

Fay, W. F. 23950

Fay, Warren. (23951), (75697)

Fay, Davison and Burt. firm publishers note after 99131

Faye, M. H. tr. 33730

Faye Brehier, J. de la. see Delafaye Brehier, Julie.

Fayette County, Ill. Citizens. (23953)

Fayette County, Pa Collector of Excise. 23954, 28238 see also Adams, Samuel, fl. 1783-1785. Graham, William.

Fayette in prison. 22133, 23952, 38583, 51101

Fayetteville advertiser. see North-Carolina minerva, and Fayetteville advertiser.

Fayrweather, Hannah. respondent 101002

Fayrweather, John. respondent 101002

Fazanas del Quijote de Michoacan. 76218

Fazendeiro do Brazil criador. 98832

Fe del Christiano. (46327), 46481

Fe, la religion, la iglesia, la real potestad, la America. 105737

Fear of an oath. 104080

Fear of God an antidote against the fear of man. 22445

Fear of God restraining men. 95168

Fearful condition of the Church of England. 38844

Fearful issue to be decided in November next. 23955

Fearne, Charles. (38151), note after 96893

Fearon, Henry Brandshaw. 23956-23957, 84304-84036, 84320-84321

Fears and hopes for the nation. (36246)

Feast of the dedication! 70918

Feathers from a moulting muse. 76973

Feathers from my own wings. (21913)

Featherston, Winfield Scott, 1820-1891. 23958

Featherstonhaugh, George William. 1115, (23959)-23964, 50166

Featherstonhaugh, Sir Harry, Bart. petitioner 101150

Featherstonhaugh, J. W. 90792

Featly, Daniel. 7996, 16037

Featly, John. 23965

Feature of the times. 71775, (71802)

Features of Federalism. 66527

Features of inauguration of the Franklin Statue. 38157

Features of Mr. Jay's treaty. 10883, 23966, 96561

Features of sundry great personages. (65019)

Febles, Manuel de Jesus. 23967

Febres, Andres. 23968-23971

Feb. 17, 1838. Mr. Deberry . . . made the following report. 61016

February 6, 1777. Additional information for John Wedderburn. 102435

February 22, 1833. 97934

February 20, 1776. Note of authorities quoted. 102436

Febure, ---- Le. see Le Febure, ------.

Febvre de Villebrune, ----- Le. see Le Febvre de Villebrune, -------.

Fecunda nube del cielo Guadalupano. 29120

Feddersen, Fr. 23972

Federacion Colombiana. 16990

Federacion y Tejas. 95083

Foederal advertiser. see Middlesex gazette, or foederal advertiser.

Federal American monthly. 16999, 23973

Federal and state constitutions. note after 94720, note after 94725

Federal and state laws. 29892, (34686)

Federal arithmetic. 56217

Federal arithmetic, improved. 77030

Federal calculator. 83913-83914

Federal calculator, and American ready reckoner. 104037

Federal catechism, being a short and easy explanation. 102367, note after 102396
Federal catechism; containing a short explanation of the constitution. 102367, note after 102396
Federal catechism metamorphosed. 23974
Federal Committee of Albany. see Federal Party. New York. Albany. Committee.
Federal constitution and Washington for ever. 15024
Federal constitution for the United States of America. 23975
Federal constitution: its claims upon the educated men. 24472
Federal constitution of the United States. 24938
Federal farmer. pseud. Additional number of letters. see Lee, Richard Henry, 1732-1794.
Federal farmer. pseud. Letters. see Lee, Richard Henry, 1732-1794.
Federal farmer. pseud. Observations leading to a fair examination. see Lee, Richard Henry, 1732-1794.
Federal gazette. 102120
Federal gazette and daily advertiser. 96422
Federal government: its nature and character. 7866, 92291, note after 98101, 1st note after 100577
Federal government; its officers and their duties. 27403
Federal harmony; containing in a familiar manner. 4695
Federal harmony: in three parts. 94014-94017
Federal judiciary. (6068)
Federal Legislative Caucus, Connecticut. see Federal Party. Connecticut.
Federal Lodge, no. 15, Washington, D. C. see Freemasons. Washington, D. C. Federal Lodge, no. 15.
Federal monthly. 29996
Federal or new ready reckoner. 23977
Federal orrery. 23976, (26623)
Federal papers, &c. (55313), note after 95351
Federal Party. 28493
Federal Party. Connecticut. 15644, note after 102333
Federal Party. Connecticut. Chairman. 15644, note after 102333 see also Ingersoll, Jonathan.
Federal Party. Connecticut. Clerk. 15644, note after 102333 see also Smith, Sam.
Federal Party. Connecticut. New Haven. 14312, (23365), (40117)
Federal Party. Massachusetts. 45618, 105461-105462
Federal Party. Massachusetts. Central Committee. 45671
Federal Party. Massachusetts. Boston. 97413
Federal Party. Massachusetts. Hampshire County. 92884
Federal Party. Massachusetts. Hampshire County. Committee to Prepare an Address, 1809. 30139
Federal Party. Massachusetts. Plymouth County. Committee. (63491), 95432
Federal Party. Massachusetts. Worcester County. 105397A-105398, 105406-105406A
Federal Party. Massachusetts. Worcester County. Committee. 105401-105406
Federal Party. Massachusetts. Worcester County. Convention, 1812. 45581, 105399
Federal Party. Massachusetts. Worcester County. South Senatorial District Convention, 1812. 105400

Federal Party. New Hampshire. Rockingham County. 93487
Federal Party. New Jersey. Burlington County. 254, 5674
Federal Party. New York. (53507)
Federal Party. New York. Convention, Albany, 1812. 53865
Federal Party. New York. Albany. Committee. 602, 619, 35929
Federal Party. New York. New York City. General Committee. 13725, 54039, 54051
Federal Party. Pennsylvania. (59975), (60676), (60685)
Federal Party. Virginia. 100422
Federal Politician. (66617)
Federal prisoners (privates) in Richmond, Tuscaloosa, New Orleans, and Salisbury, N. C. pseud. Stars and stripes in rebeldom. 3950, note after 90573
Federal pye. 31891
Federal ready reckoner. 23978
Federal relations. 102112
Federal republican. pseud. Address to the citizens. see Desaussure, Henry William, 1763-1839.
Federal republican. pseud. Politics of Connecticut. see Richards, -----. supposed author
Federal republican. pseud. Review of the constitution. 70225
Federal republican. 30257, (30261)
Federal republican candidates. 105406A
Federal Republican Party. see Federal Party.
Federal republicanism displayed in two discourses. (58117)
Federal Street Meeting House, Boston. see Boston. Arlington Street Church.
Federal Tontine Association. 16082
"Federal union, it must be preserved!" 45145
Federalism: or the question of exclusive power. 37819
Federalism triumphant in the steady habits of Connecticut alone. 15737
Federalism turned inside out! (55313), note after 95351
Federalism unmasked. 27861
Federalist. pseud. Answer to certain parts of a work. 10879
Federalist. pseud. Letter to General Hamilton. see Webster, Noah, 1758-1843. and Van Ness, William Peter. supposed author
Federalist. 18933, 18934, (23979)-23993, 29987, 30022, 35841, 35844, 96754
Federalist: a collection of essays. (23979)-23980, (23991)
[Federalist] circular. Lancaster, May 30th, 1799. (59975)
Federlist: containing some strictures. 23994, 84832
Federalist of 1788, and still (1833) a constitutionalist. pseud. Constitution of the United States. 97912
Federalist, on the new constitution. 23981-23988, 23990
Federalist republican. pseud. Reply to A. Hamilton's letter. see Cincinnatus. pseud.
Federalista. 49931
Federalista, publicado em inglez por Hamilton. 23996
Federaliste. 23993
Federals and confederates. 18225
Federative union of the British North American provinces. 80436

Federmann, Nicolas. 23997-23999
Fedix, P. A. 24000
Fedon, Bury. 24001
Fedric, Francis. 24002
Fee, John Gregg, 1816-   24003-24005,
    88294-88296
Fee, N. 84418
Feeble attempt to promote the felicity. 103074
Feeding the lambs. 73641, note after 95465
Feer, ------. ed. 70375
Feigned apparation of Sir Walter Rawleigh.
    67599
Feijo, Diogo Antonio. 76329
Feijoo de Sosa, Miguel. see Feyjoo de Sosa,
    Miguel, d. 1784.
Feirabend, Sigismund. (8784), 77677
Feith, Rhijnvis. supposed author 101893
Felch, Adelpheus, 1804-1896. 24005
Felch, Alpheus, 1806-   48739 see also
    Michigan. Governor, 1846-1847 (Felch)
Felch, Cheever. 24007
Feld, Gefangniss und Flucht. 70985
Feldner, W. Chr. G. von. 24008
Feldzuge der Armee des Hrn. Grafen Roch-
    ambeau. 72037
Felice, G. de. (24009)
Felicidad de Mexico en el establecimiento de
    la V. Orden Tercera. 77114
Felicidad de Mexico, en el principio y milagroso
    origen. 4216
Felicidad de Mexico en su mayor congoja por
    el dichoso natalicio de la senorita.
    99732
Felicitacion a sus estimados conciudadanos.
    6303
Felicitation for the West-Indian fleet. 32382
Felicity of the times. 1855
Felipe II, King of Spain, 1527-1598. 22550,
    42066, 56201, 57483, 64171-64172,
    76223, 76332, note after 90828, 94352
    see also Spain. Sovereigns etc., 1556-
    1598 (Felipe II)
Felipe III, King of Spain, 1578-1621. (48613),
    56338, 70095, 98019 see also Spain.
    Sovereigns, etc., 1598-1621 (Felipe III)
Felipe IV, King of Spain, 1605-1665. 10759,
    (41092), 44267, 45404, (48613), 51680,
    (57477), 57480, 59305, 61135, 64628,
    65039, 65048, 65977, 96475, 98019,
    98825, 99441-99442, 106408 see also
    Spain. Sovereigns, etc., 1621-1665 (Felipe
    IV)
Felipe V, King of Spain, 1683-1746. (9891),
    (16665), 16668, (16690), 17026, 19208-
    19209, 28422, 29359, (37863)-37864,
    (48613), 48618, 56003, 56293, (56589),
    61084, 62441-62443, 66408, 68231, 68238,
    68249, (70381), 70382, 72044, 73852,
    (76858), 79140, 86398, 88181, note after
    93420, note after 96350, 96541, 98019,
    99618 see also Spain. Sovereigns, etc.,
    1700-1746 (Felipe V)
Felipe V, King of Spain, 1683-1746. plaintiff
    105732 see also Spain. Sovereigns,
    etc., 1700-1746 (Felipe V) plaintiff
Felipe el Grande en Jerusalen. 44104
Feliu, Ramon Olaguer. 24010
Felix de Jesus Maria. see Jesus Maria,
    Felix de.
Felix y Adela, novela Cubana. 50982
Feliz y solemne pompa. 94834
Felizardo Fortes, Ignacio. see Fortes,
    Ignacio Felizardo.
Fell, Frederick S. (24011)
Fell, Lydia. 24012
Fellechner, A. 24013, 51076

Fellenberg Academy, Greenfield, Mass. 24014-
    (24015)
Fellenberg; or, an appeal to the friends of
    education. (24016)
Feller, Francois Xavier. 24017
Fellkampff, J. L. 24018
Fellow citizen. pseud. "Is the north right!"
    35235
Fellow-citizen. pseud. Narrative, &c. 87898
Fellow citizen. pseud. Political establishments
    of the United States of America. 63776
Fellow citizen. pseud. Tribute to the American
    people. see Porter, David, 1780-1843.
Fellow citizens. 3115, 95933, 96972
Fellow citizens! 95919
Fellow-citizens: 96971
Fellow citizens:—. 94563
Fellow-citizens, a memorial to Congress.
    102201
Fellow citizens, after an absence of sixteen
    months. 95938
Fellow citizens, and countrymen. (61652)
Fellow citizens and fellow voters. 100786
Fellow citizens—As the time approaches.
    85198
Fellow-citizens—At a very large and respectable
    meeting. 102013
Fellow citizens, friends to liberty and equal
    commerce. 93244
Fellow citizens, I am a freeman of this city.
    105454
Fellow-citizens, in a gouvernment like ours.
    94758
Fellow citizens . . . In the absence of the
    executive. 101923
Fellow citizens of Jefferson and Oldham
    Counties. 89229
Fellow citizens of Pennsylvania. (60099)
Fellow citizens. Please read this narrative.
    98554
Fellow citizens—representatives of the people.
    98555
Fellow citizens! Since our last address to you.
    94676
Fellow citizens! The approach of every im-
    portant election. 94674
Fellow-citizens, the present sheriff's time
    being about to expire. 101104
Fellow citizens, your sense of humanity have,
    the last evening. 95998
Fellow of Harvard College. pseud. Essay to
    solve the difficulties. see Prince,
    Nathan.
Fellow of the Massachusetts Medical Society.
    pseud. Remarks on the dangers and
    duties of sepulture. 69453
Fellow of the Royal Geographical Society.
    pseud. Cotton supply. 17119
Fellow of the Royal Society. pseud. Angel
    of Bethesda. see Mather, Cotton, 1663-
    1728.
Fellow of the Royal Society. pseud. Coheleth.
    see Mather, Cotton, 1663-1728.
Fellow of the Royal Society. pseud. Natural
    history of those parts. 100940
Fellow of the Royal Society. pseud. Voyages
    of Lionel Wafer. 18373
Fellow student. pseud. Reminiscences. 35427
Fellow-student. pseud. Slavery in the gentile
    churches. 82095
Fellow-sufferer. pseud. Address to the
    citizens of Massachusetts. see Park,
    John.
Fellow workers. Two sermons. 4271
Fellowes, Francis, 1803-1888. ed. 15778,
    31385

Fellowes, William Dorset. 24019
Fellows, Francis. 15778
Fellows, Sir John, fl. 1721. 65865, 88192
Fellows, John, 1759-1844. 24021-24022, 94058
Fellows, John, d. 1785. (24020)
Fellows, John, fl. 1810. ed. 95315
Fellows, John W. defendant 12172
Fellows of the . . . [Massachusetts Medical]
  Society. 45874
Fellows of the . . . [Massachusetts Medical]
  Society, 1787 to 1854. 45874
Fellowship Society of Charleston, S. C.
  12084, 85311
Felner, R. J. de Lima. 24023
Felon's account of fourteen years' transporta-
  tion. (24024)
Felsenhart, J. 24025
Felsenthal, B. 24026
Felt, George H. defendant at Court of Inquiry
  24027
Felt, Joseph Barlow, 1789-1869. 24028-24037,
  55889
Feltman, William. 24038
Felton, Mrs. ------. 24044
Felton, Cornelius Conway, 1807-1862. 24039-
  (24040), 35221, (69425)
Felton, Franklin Eliot. 24041
Felton, John Brooks. 24042
Felton, John H. 24043
Felton, Nicholas, successively Bishop of
  Bristol, and Ely, 1556-1626. 103332
Felton, Samuel Morse. 24045-24046, 34391,
  62051 see also Philadelphia, Wilmington
  & Baltimore Railroad Company.
  President.
Felton, U. M. 84285
Feltus, Henry. (24047)
Feltus, Jenry J. (79395)
Female Academy, Albany, N. Y. see Albany
  Female Academy, Albany, N. Y.
Female Academy, Buffalo, N. Y. see Buffalo
  Seminary.
Female Academy, Cherry Valley, N. Y. see
  Cherry Valley Academy.
Female Academy, Utica, N. Y. see Utica
  Female Academy.
Female American. 104781
Female Anti-slavery Society, Boston. see
  Boston Female Anti-slavery Society.
Female Anti-slavery Society, Concord, N. H.
  see Concord Female Anti-slavery Society,
  Concord, N. H.
Female Anti-slavery Society, Fall River, Mass.
  see Fall River Female Anti-slavery
  Society.
Female Anti-slavery Society, Glasgow. see
  Glasgow Female Anti-slavery Society.
Female Anti-slavery Society, Philadelphia.
  see Philadelphia Female Anti-slavery
  Society.
Female Anti-slavery Society of Boston. see
  Boston Female Anti-slavery Society.
Female Anti-slavery Society of Chatham-Street
  Chapel, New York. see New York (City)
  Chatham-Street Chapel. Female Anti-
  slavery Society.
Female Association, New York. 54271
Female Association for the Benefit of Africans,
  Cincinnati. 16083
Female Association for the Relief of Women,
  Philadelphia. see Female Association
  of Philadelphia, for the Relief of Women.
Female Association of Cincinnati for the Benefit
  of Africans. see Female Association
  for the Benefit of Africans, Cincinnati.

Female Association of Philadelphia, for the
  Relief of Women. 61653
Female Asylum, Boston. see Boston Society
  for the Care of Girls.
Female Auxiliary Bible Society, New York.
  see New York Female Auxiliary Bible
  Society.
Female Beneficent Society, Hartford, Conn.
  92953
Female Benevolence Society, New Haven, Conn.
  105929
Female benevolent Society. 105929
Female Benevolent Society, New York. see
  New York Female Benevolent Society.
Female Benevolent Society, Providence, R. I.
  see Providence Female Benevolent
  Society, Providence, R. I.
Female Bethel Union, New York. see New
  York Female Bethel Union.
Female Bible Society, Poughkeepsie, N. Y.
  see Poughkeepsie Female Bible Society.
Female Bible Society of Philadelphia. see
  Philadelphia Female Bible Society.
Female biography; containing notices of dis-
  tinguished women. 38073
Female biography; or, memoirs of illustrious
  and celebrated women. 31061
Female blueberard. 93415
Female Branch, no. I, of the Temperance
  Beneficial Association, Southwark, Pa.
  see Temperance Beneficial Association,
  Southwark, Pa. Female Branch, no. I.
Female captive. 58670
Female Cent Institution. see New Hampshire
  Female Cent Institution and Home
  Missionary Union.
Female Charitable Society, Salem, Mass. see
  Salem Female Charitable Society.
Female charity an acceptable offering. 100920
Female Classical Seminary, Worcester, Mass.
  105356
Female Classical Seminary, at Worcester,
  Mass. 105356
Female College, Milwaukee, Wisc. see Mil-
  waukee Female College.
Female College, Pittsburgh, Pa. see Pittsburgh
  Female College.
Female College, Springfield, Ohio. see Spring-
  field Female College, Springfield, Ohio.
Female Collegiate Institute, Barhamville, S. C.
  see South Carolina Female Collegiate
  Institute, Barhamville, S. C.
Female Domestic Missionary Society, Charleston,
  S. C. 12092
Female Domestic Missionary Society, Pro-
  vidence, R. I. Missionary. 66237
Female Domestic Missionary Society, Phila-
  delphia. (61655)
Female drummer. 86899
Female drummer: and the blue bell of Scotland.
  105959
Female education. An address . . . anniversary
  . . . of the Newark Institute for Young
  Ladies. 64798
Female education. An address . . . dedication
  of the Ohio Female College. 24503
Female Education Society of New Haven.
  (15723)
Female education. Tendencies of the principles.
  51157
Female emigration as it is and as it may be.
  80861
Female Employment Society, Brooklyn. see
  Brooklyn Female Employment Society.
Female Friend. pseud. Discourse publicly
  delivered. 86045

Female friend. pseud. To the Reverend Mr.
James Davenport. see Moorhead, Sarah
(Parsons)
Female hand. pseud. Christian pattern.
37343, 1st note after 95453
Female hand. pseud. History of Joseph. see
Rowe, Elizabeth.
Female heorism exemplified. 84129-84130,
note after 93109, 1st note after 95758
Female High School, New York. see New
York (City) Female High School.
Female Hospital Society, Philadelphia. (61656)
Female Hospital Society, Philadelphia. Charter.
(61656)
Female Humane Association, Richmond, Va.
(71179)
Female in the Northern Liberties of Phila-
delphia. pseud. Three remarkable
dreams. see Ashburn, Rebecca.
Female Institute, Richmond, Va. see Rich-
mond Female Institute, Richmond, Va.
Female life among the Mormons. 24185, note
after 101315
Female marine, or adventures of Miss Lucy
Brewer. 102742
Female marine, or adventures of Miss Lucy
Brewer, a native of Plymouth County,
Mass. 102742
Female Medical College, Philadelphia. 60100
Female Medical College of New England. see
New England Female Medical College.
Female Medical Education Society. 24049,
(52683) see also New England Female
Medical College.
Female Medical Education Society, and the
New-England Female Medical College.
24049
Female Missionary Society of the Western
District of New York. Trustees. 24050
Female Moral Reform Society of New England.
see New York Female Moral Reform
Society.
Female of Vermont. pseud. Appeal to the
females of the north. 81877
Female Oneida Missionary Society. Trustees.
57342
Female Orphan Asylum, Baton Rouge, La.
see Baton Rouge, La. Female Orphan
Asylum.
Female patriot, a farce. 73619
Female poets of America. 28893
Female poets of America. With portraits.
68174
Female policy detected. 101286
Female preaching defended. 102113
Female prisoner. 60962
Female prose writers of America. 20628
Female Quixotism. 94816
Female review. 44314, note after 75924
Female Samaritan Society, Worcester, Mass.
see Worcester Female Samaritan Society.
Female Seamen's Friend Society, Philadelphia.
60362
Female Seminary, Bethlehem, Pa. see
Bethlehem Female Seminary, Bethlehem,
Pa.
Female Seminary, Charlestown, Mass. see
Charlestown, Mass. Female Seminary.
Female Seminary, Cleveland, Ohio. see
Cleveland Female Seminary.
Female Seminary, Granville, Ohio. see
Granville Female Seminary.
Female Seminary, Marietta, Ohio. mee
Marietta Female Seminary.
Female Seminary, New Hampton, N. H. see
New Hampton Female Seminary.

Female Seminary, North Granville, N. Y. see
North Granville Female Seminary, North
Granville, N. Y.
Female Seminary, Saratoga Springs, N. Y. see
Saratoga Female Seminary, Saratoga
Springs, N. Y.
Female Seminary, Sing Sing, N. Y. see Sing
Sing Female Seminary, Sing Sing, N. Y.
Female Seminary, Steubenville, Ohio. see
Steubenville Female Seminary, Steubenville,
Ohio.
Female serenaders! 91843
Female shipwright. 38517
Female slave. pseud. Autobiography. see
Griffiths, Mattie.
Female slave. 91074
Female Society, New York. 54275
Female Society for Missionary Pruposes,
Boston. (6706)
Female Society for the Relief of Indigent
Women and Children, Providence, R. I.
see Providence Female Society for the
Relief of Indigent Women and Children.
Female Society for the Relief of Poor and
Distressed Persons, Newark, N. J.
54873
Female Society of the Presbyterian Congregation
in Cedar Street for the Support of
Theological Students, New York. see
New York (City) Cedar Street Presbyterian
Church. Female Society for the Support
of Theological Students.
Female spy. (59221)
Female Tract Society, Philadelphia. see
Philadelphia Female Tract Society.
Female Tract Society, Providence, R. I. see
Providence Female Tract Society.
Female Union Society, New York. see New
York Female Union Society.
Female visitor to the prisoners of the Eastern
Penitentiary. pseud. Address. 60080
Female volunteer. 5411
Female wages and female oppression. 10889
Female warrior. 80851
Females Actively Employed in the Mills,
Lowell, Mass. see Lowell, Mass.
Females Actively Employed in the Mills.
Femme chez les Mormons. 23215
Femme d'un missionaire. pseud. Journal.
36687
Femmes d'Amerique. 4509
Femmes du Nouveau Monde. 23551
Femmes et leurs moeurs du Bresil. 23411
Fendall, Philip R. (24051), 98425, 101950
Fendall, Philip R. supposed author 24052,
2d note after (69432), 93573
Fenderich, Charles. illus. 24053
Fendigraphia. 24951
Fenelon. pseud. Catholicism compatable with
republican government. (24055)
Fenelon, Francois de Salignac de la Mothe-,
Abp., 1651-1715. (12268), (24054),
86590-86591
Fenety, George E. 24056-24057
Fenian Brotherhood. (24058)
Fenian Brotherhood. Investigating Committee.
24059
Fenian Brotherhood. National Convention, 1st,
Chicago, 1863. (24061)
Fenian Brotherhood. National Convention, 7th,
Philadelphia, 1868. 24060
Fenian Brotherhood. New York. New York
City. Committee of the Management.
24059
Fenian Brotherhood of America. Official report.
24059

Fenian raid on Fort Erie. 19566
Fenix. 24062
Fenix de el amor. 22921
Fenix de la America. 80987
Fenix de los mineros ricos de la America.
　105730
Fenix de Occidente. 80987
Fenn, Eleanor (Frere) Lady, 1743-1813. 96146
Fenn, Harry. illus. 84041
Fennenherg, F. F. von. 24064
Fennell, James. 24065-24066, 52331, 86836
Fenner, Arthur, 1745-1805. 70559 see also
　Rhode Island. Governor, 1790-1805
　(Fenner)
Fenner, Arthur, 1771-1846. defendant 20652
Fenner, Arthur, 1771-1846. plaintiff 20652
Fenner, E. D. 24067-(24068), 53354
Fenner, Robert. 24071
Fenning, Daniel. 23977, 68217
Fenning, John. 24073
Fenno, Miss J., of Boston. see Fenno,
　Jenny.
Fenno, J. W. 24074
Fenno, Jenny. 24075
Fenno, John, 1751-1798. 101577
Fenn's compendium. 24063
Fenocchio, Antonio. 24076
Fenton, Elijah. 70733
Fenton, Joseph. (36362)
Fenton, Reuben Eaton, 1819-1885. 24077-
　24078, 53616, (53885), 82591 see also
　New York (State) Governor, 1865-1869
　(Fenton)
Fenwick, Benjamin Joseph, Bp., 1782-1846.
　72885 see also Boston (Archdiocese)
　Bishop (Fenwick)
Fenwick, Benedict K. (24080)
Fenwick, Edward Dominic, Bp., 1768-1832.
　24079 see also Cincinnati (Archdiocese)
　Bishop (Fenwick)
Fenwick, G. E. ed. 10634
Fenwick, John. 24081-24083, (36281)
Fenwick, John. plaintiff 24083, note after
　97149
Fenzl, Eduard, 1808-1879. 44988
Fer, N. de. 25062
Ferdinand II, King of Bohemia, 1578-1637.
　69589 see also Bohemia. Sovereigns,
　etc., 1617-1619 (Ferdinand II)
Ferdinand, King of Sicily, 1452-1516. see
　Fernando V, King of Spain, 1452-1516.
Ferdinand, d. 1797 or 8. 57613
Ferdinand Joseph Maximilian. see Maximilian
　I, Emperor of Mexico, 1832-1867.
Ferdinand de Quir, Pierre. see Queiros,
　Pedro Fernandes de, d. 1615.
Ferdinand and Elizabeth. 101236
Ferdinand & Elmira. 105058
Ferdinand and Isabella. 4918
Ferdinand Cortes, peome. 73519
Ferdinand Cortez oder die Eroberung von
　Mexico. 19432
Ferdinand von Soto. 98744
Ferdinandi Cortesii. Von dem Newen His-
　panien. 16957
Ferdinandia die Mexicanische Insul. (24084)
Fereal, Victor de. pseud. Misterios de la
　inquisicion. see Suberwick, ------ de.
Fereal, Victor de. pseud. Mysteres de l'in-
　quisition. see Suberwick, ----- de.
Fereira, Gaspar Dias de. defendant 16681,
　24085-(24086)

Fereira, J. de Solorzano. see Solorzano
　Pereira, J. de.
Ferencz, ------. tr. (67481)
Fergus, Henry. 24087
Ferguson, Adam. 24088-24090, 1st note after
　96400
Ferguson, Adam. supposed author 69475
Ferguson, Bradbury. defendant 64621
Ferguson, Edward A. defendant 90145
Ferguson, Elizabeth (Graeme) 23179
Ferguson, George. (35734)
Ferguson, J. 102437
Ferguson, J. B. 24092-24095
Ferguson, James. 24091
Ferguson, John. 24096-(24097), 95158
Ferguson, R. 24098
Ferguson, Robert. 9407
Ferguson, Robert, d. 1814. (18552), 18571,
　(32340), 78206, 78209-78210, (78215),
　note after 78219, 78234, 7th note after
　95843
Ferguson, T. 24099
Ferguson, W. E. 88627
Ferguson, W. F. 24101
Ferguson, William. 24100
Fergusson, Adam. 24102
Fergusson, David. (24103)
Fergusson, James. 24104
Feria, Pedro de, Bp., 1524-1586? 24105
Feria de la caridad en 183. 5060
Ferland, Jean Baptiste Antoine, 1805-1865.
　10455, (12573), 24106-24110, (41510)
Ferlus, L. D. (24111)
Fermerius, Bernardus. 66494
Fermeture des fleuves sous pretexte de l'
　ouverture de l'Amazone. 7615, 63832
Fermier de Pensylvanie. pseud. see Dick-
　inson, John, 1732-1808.
Fermin, Philippe. (24112)-(24121), 8th note
　after 93855
Fermin del Rey. 24122, 24402
Ferminville, M. J. de la Poix. see La Poix
　Ferminville, M. J. de.
Fern, Fanny. pseud. see Parton, Sarah
　Payson Willis.
Fern leaves from Fanny's port-folio. 58959
Fernagus de Gelone, ------. 24123-24124
Fernambuco. see Pernambuco.
Fernan, ------. (24160)
Fernan Cortez, comedie. 63020
Fernand, Jacques. 24125
Fernand-Michel, ------. 24126-24127
Fernand Colomb sa vie, ses oeuvres. 30602
Fernand Cortes, tragedie en 5 actes et en
　prose. 20980
Fernand Cortez, ou la conquete du Mexique,
　opera en trois actes. (36768), 89596
Fernand Cortez, ou la conquete du Mexique.
　Par J. L. Roche. 72310
Fernandes, Antonio Ferreira de Lara. see
　Fernandez, Antonio Ferreira de Lara.
Fernandes, Duarte. 88727
Fernandes de Queiros, Pedro. see Queiros,
　Pedro Fernandes de, d. 1615.
Fernandes de Quir, Pedro. see Queiros,
　Pedro Fernandes de, d. 1615.
Fernandes Pereira de Barros, Jose Maurico.
　see Pereira de Barros, Jose Maurico
　Fernandes.
Fernandes Pinheiro, Joaquim Caetano, 1825-
　1876. 62949-62951, 88551, 98650
Fernandes Pinheiro, Jose Feliciano, Visconde
　de S. Leopoldo, 1774-1847. 40118,
　62952-62955, 106062

Fernandes Vieira, Joao. see Vieira, Joao Fernandes.

Fernandes Vieira, ou Pernambuco libertado. 9220

Fernandez, Augustin Pomposo. tr. (10913)

Fernandez, Alonso. 24128

Fernandez, Antonio Ferreira de Lara. 24129

Fernandez, Benito. 24130-(24132)

Fernandez, Diego. 24133

Fernandez, Emilio. tr. 84332

Fernandez, Francisco Emilio. 65964

Fernandez, Francisco Rodriguez. see Rodriguez Fernandez, Francisco.

Fernandez, J. 24134

Fernandez, Juan Patricio, d. 1672. 12835, 24135-24139, 31535, 52380, 1st note after 98488

Fernandez, Manuel Felix. see Victoria, Manuel Felix Fernandez Guadalupe, Pres. Mexico, 1789-1843.

Fernandez, Mariano. supposed author 21776, (24140), note after 99395

Fernandez Cuesta, N. 24141

Fernandez Davila, Diego Quint. see Quint Fernandez Davila, Diego.

Fernandez de Abascal y Sousa, Jose. see Abascal y Sousa, Jose Fernandez de.

Fernandez de Castro Andrade y Portugal, Pedro. see Castro Andrade y Portugal, Pedro Fernandez de, Conde de Lemos, 1634-1672.

Fernandez de Cordoba, Francisca, Condesa de Casapalma. defendant 88723, 96051

Fernandez de Cordoba, Manuel. 24142

Fernandez de Cordoba y Sande, Fernando. plaintiff 96050-96051

Fernandez de Cordova, Diego, 1. Marques de Guadalcazar. 98331 see also Peru (Viceroyalty) Virrey, 1622-1629 (Fernandez de Cordova)

Fernandez de Cordova, Felipe Colmenares. 24143

Fernandez de Cordova, J. M. defendant 88723

Fernandez de Cordova y Souza, J. A. see Souza, J. A. Fernandez de Cordova y.

Fernandez de Echeverria y Veitia, Mariano Jose. see Veytia, Mariano, 1718-1779.

Fernandez de Echeverria y Veytia, Mariano Jose. see Veytia, Mariano, 1718-1779.

Fernandez de Enciso, Martin. see Enciso, Martin Fernandez de.

Fernandez de la Fuente, Juan. 57674, 74858

Fernandez de la Madriz, Pedro. defendant 96243

Fernandez de la Santa Cruz, Manuel, Bp. 24149, 66568

Fernandez de Lara, Jose. see Lara, Jose Fernandez de.

Fernandez de Lara, Jose Mariano Beristain de Souza. see Beristain de Souza, Jose Mariano, 1756-1817.

Fernandez de Lara, Juan Jose. see Lara, Juan Jose Fernandez de.

Fernandez de Lara y Consortes, Jose. defendant 34710

Fernandez de Lizardi, Jose Joaquin, 1776-1827. 41663-41666, 48400, 56448, 74043, 87216, 94823, 94908, 98936

Fernandez de Madrid, Jose. (24144), 43757-43759

Fernandez de Medrano, Sebastian. see Medrano, Sebastian Fernandez de.

Fernandez de Navarrete, Eustaquio, 1820-1866. (52094)

Fernandez de Navarrete, Martin. see Navarrete, Martin Fernandez de.

Fernandez de Oviedo y Valdes, Gonzalo. see Oviedo y Valdes, Gonzalo Fernando de, 1478-1557.

Fernandez de Quir, Petrus. see Queiros, PEdro Fernands de, d. 1615.

Fernandez de Quiros, Pedro. see Queiros, Pedro Fernandez de, d. 1615.

Fernandez de San Salvador, Agustin Pomposo. see San Salvador, Agustin Pomposo Fernandez de.

Fernandez de San Salvador, Fernando. 76223-76226

Fernandez de Sancta Cruz, Manuel. ed. 26746, 1st note after 98659

Fernandez de Santa Cruz, Manuel. 24149-24150

Fernandez de Santa Cruz y Sahagun, Manuel. see Santa Cruz y Sahagun, Manuel Fernandez de.

Fernandez de Sousa, Juan de Dios. 24151

Fernandez de Uribe, J. P. de. 24152

Fernandez de Velasco, Jo. see Velasco, Jo. Fernandez de.

Fernandez de Veytia Linage, Joseph. see Veytia Linage, Joseph Fernandez de.

Fernandez del Castillo, Pedro. see Castillo, Pedro Fernandez del.

Fernandez Guadalupe Victoria, Manuel Felix. see Victoria, Manuel Felix Fernandez Guadalupe, Pres. Mexico, 1789-1843.

Fernandez Navarrete, Domingo, Abp., fl. 1689. 52095 see also Santo Domingo (Archdiocese) Archbishop (Fernandez Navarrette)

Fernandez Navarrete, Pedro. (52108)

Fernandez Nodal, Jose. see Nodal, Jose Fernandez.

Fernandez Perdones, Luciano. 93308

Fernandez Piedrahita, Lucas. see Piedrahita Lucas Fernandez.

Fernandez y Gonzalez, M. Amparo. 24153

Fernandi Tellii oratio habita in Senatu Apostolico VI. 94623

Fernando V, King of Spain, 1452-1516. 18792, 22550, 39893, note after 40960, 56338, 86398, 89647, 94352 see also Sicily. Sovereigns, etc., 1468-1516 (Fernando V) Spain. Sovereigns, etc., 1479-1516 (Fernando V)

Fernando VI, King of Spain, 1713-1759. 96515, 96544, 96546 see also Spain. Sovereigns, etc., 1746-1759 (Fernando VI)

Fernando VII, King of Spain, 1784-1833. 17749, 17774, 17799, 17801, 24159, 29029, 48358, 48413, (48613), 66587, 68227, 68230, 68233, 68244, 68250, (68384), (70383), 72430, 98650 see also Spain. Sovereigns, etc., 1814-1833 (Fernando VII)

Fernando Cortes: tragedie. 63021

Fernando Cortez. Historischer Roman. 16960

Fernando the Gothamite. pseud. Copperhead catechism. see Wilson, Montgomery. supposed author

Fernando Wood unmasked! (54317)

Fernly, J. F. 102083

Fernon, Thomas F. 60358

Fernon, Thomas S. 60278

Fernow, Berthold, 1837-1908. ed. 84558

Ferns. (11972)

Fero, Elisha B. defendant 64203

Ferrall, S. A. 24161

Fernnan, John. 30699

Ferrande, Pierre Gracie, called. see Gracie,
Pierre, called Ferrande, ca. 1435-ca.
1520.
Ferrar, Alexander Sardi. 24152
Ferrara, Italy. Biblioteca. 69331
Ferrari, Felipe. see Ferrarius, PHilippus,
d. 1626.
Ferrario, Giuseppe, 1802-1870. 24164
Ferrarius, Philippus, d. 1626. 24163, 40879
Farraro, Giuseppe, 1846-1907. ed. 69331
Farraz, Luiz Pedreira de Coutto. 24165,
38224 see also Brazil. Ministerio das
Relacoes Exteriores.
Ferreira, Antonio Jose Domingues. 24166
Ferreira, Joao Carlos de Souza. see Souza
Ferreira, Joao Carlos de, 1831-
Ferreira, Manoel Jesuino. 24169
Ferreira, Ramon. 1959, 24170
Ferreira, Silvestre Pinheiro. 24171-24172,
(44840)
Ferreira da Rosa, Joao. see Rosa, Joao
Ferreira da.
Ferreira da Silva, Silvestre. 24173
Ferreira da Veiga, Evaristo. 79218 see also
Sergipe (Brazilian Province) Presidente
(Ferreira da Veiga)
Ferreira de Araujo e Silva, Luis. see Araujo
e Silva, Luis Ferreira de.
Ferreira de Freitas, Joaquim. 47607
Ferreira de Lara Fernandez, Antonio. see
Fernandez, Antonio Ferreira de Lara.
Ferreira de Mattos, Jose. see Mattos, Jose
Ferreira de.
Ferreira e Souza, Bernardo Avellino. 24167
Ferreira Franca, Ernesto. see Franca,
Ernesto Ferreira.
Ferreira Lapa, Ludgero da Rocha. see Lapa,
Ludgero da Rocha Ferreira.
Ferreira Lagos, Manoel. see Lagos, Manoel
Ferreira.
Ferreira Penna, Dominges Soares. see Penna,
Dominges Soares Ferreira.
Ferrel, William. 85072
Ferrer, Antonio. defendant 27309, (51797),
69915, 93808, 96948
Ferrer, Jaime. 24174
Ferrer, Manuel Tossiat. see Tossiat Ferrer,
Manuel.
Ferrer, Miguel Rodriguez. see Rodriguez-
Ferrer, Miguel.
Ferrer de Couto, Jose. 17194, 24175-24178
Ferrer del Rio, Antonio. see Rio, Antonio
Ferrer del.
Ferreras, Manuel Codorniu y. see Cordorniu
y Ferreras, Manuel.
Ferretti, Giovanni Maria Mastai. see Pius
IX, Pope, 1792-1878.
Ferri-Pisani, M. V. P. C. 24180, 63023
Ferriar, J. ed. 88547
Ferribault, Pelagie. claimant 69697
Ferrie, Adam. 24181
Ferrin, -----. 84403
Ferrin, Mary Upton. 24182
Ferris, Benjamin, 1780-1867. 24183
Ferris, Benjamin G. 24184
Ferris, Mrs. Benjamin G. 24185-24186
Ferris, Charles G. 24187
Ferris, David. defendant at Court of Inquiry
24188
Ferris, David, 1707-1779. 24189
Ferris, Mrs. G. B. see Ferris, Mrs.
Benjamin G.
Ferris, George Titus, 1840-   84041
Ferris, Isaac. 24190-(24191)
Ferris, Jacob. 24192

Ferris, John A. 24193
Ferris (Benjamin) firm booksellers 95752
Ferriss, Orange, 1814-1894. 24194
Ferro, ------ Gil Gelpi y. see Gil Gelpi y
Ferro, -------
Ferro-carril central de la isla de Cuba. 11465
Ferro-carril central transandino. 41108
Ferrocarril interoceanico, ultimas comunica-
ciones cambiadas. note just before
(73261)
Ferrocarriles, carta del General Rosecrans.
note just before (73261)
Ferrocarriles. La concesion hecha. note just
before (73261)
Ferrufino, Juan Baptista. 24195
Ferry, Gabriel. pseud. see Bellemarre,
Louis de.
Ferry, I. 24197-24198
Ferry, J. C. tr. (23234)
Ferry, Orris Sanford, 1823-1875. 24199
Ferry, Thomas White, 1827-1896. 24200
Ferry-boy and the financier. 97070
Ferst reding buk in Mikmak. 67754
Ferussac, Andrew E. J. P. J. F. d'Audebard,
Baron de. 24201, 78689
Fescourt, ------. 24202
Fessenden, Benjamin. 24203
Fessenden, Caleb Page. (24204)
Fessenden, Guy Mannering, 1804-1871. 24205-
24206
Fessenden, John M. 6768, (21666), (24207)
Fessenden, Samuel. 24208
Fessenden, Samuel Clement, 1815-1882. 24209-
24210
Fessenden, Thomas, 1739-1813. 24211, 69458
Fessenden, Thomas Green, 1771-1837. (24212)-
24220, 52676, 52679, 62855, note after
94875, 95185
Fessenden, William. 24221
Fessenden, William. supposed editor 15178
Fessenden, William Pitt, 1806-1869. 24222-
24223
Fessenden & Co. firm 1047
Fest und Fasting. 32321
Festin hecho por las Morenas Criollas de la
. . . ciudad de Mexico. 99400
Festiva pompa. (47422), 73182
Festival at Leicester Academy. 39902
Festival at the Exchange, in Honor of the
Russian Achievements over their French
Invaders, Boston, 1813. see Boston.
Festival at the Exchange, in Honor of the
Russian Achievements over their French
Invaders, 1813.
Festival discourse. (43681)
Festival Given to the National Unitarian Con-
vention, New York, 1865. see National
Unitarian Convention, New York, 1865.
Festival Held in the City of Cincinnati, 1840.
see Paine Festival, Cincinnati, 1840.
Festival in celebration of the 25th anniversary
of the arrival. 86017
Festival of Anacreon. 50804
Festival of song. 77176
Festival of the Connecticut Association, Boston,
1857. see Connecticut Association.
Festival, Boston, 1867.
Festival of the Connecticut Association, at the
Revere House, Boston. 1867.
Festival of the Mitchell Family, South Britain,
Conn., 1858. see Mitchell Family
Festival, South Britain, Conn., 1858.
Festival of the Pilgrim Society, Dec. 22, 1820.
63482
Festival of the Pilgrims, Boston, 1842. 6539

Festival of the Sons of New Hampshire, 1st,
Boston, 1849. see Sons of New Hamp-
shire. Festival, 1st, Boston, 1849.
Festival of the Sons of New Hampshire, 2d,
Boston, 1853. see Sons of New Hamp-
shire. Festival, 2d, Boston, 1853.
Festival of the Sons of New Hampshire: with
the speeches. 52826, 92068
Festivaliad. 93253
Festivals, games and amusements. 82726
Festivas aclamaciones de la ciudad de Mexico.
24157, 44557B
Festivas aclamaciones de Xalapa. 99678
Festivo, Justo. pseud. Soliloquio. see
Quesada, Rafael.
Festgabe zur XXV. Versammlung Deutscher
Philologen Orientalisten und Schulmanner
in Halle a. d. S. (64601)
Festschrift zur ersten Sakularfeier der
Vereinigten Staaten. 66398
Festus, Rufus. see Rufus Festus. paraphraser
Festus, Sextus Pompeius. (20209)
Fete Bresilienne, Rouen, France, 1550. see
Rouen, France. Fete Bresilienne, 1550.
Fete Bresilienne, celebree a Rouen en 1550.
19556, 73458
Fete civique. 61259
Fete des chasseurs. (69041)
Fete Donnee a Mr. Ducan M'Intosh, Baltimore,
1809. see Entertainment Given in Honor
of Duncan McIntosh, Baltimore, 1809.
Fete extraordinary. M. Van Buren's last letter.
88669
Fete funebre de Washington celebree a
Amsterdam. 101808
Fettyplace, William. petitioner 92308
Feuille, Louis, 1660-1732. (24224)-24226,
(25925), 25930, note after 94101
Feuille de la Guyane Francaise. (29173),
47870
Feuille hebdominaire. 35074
Feuilley, Jean Baptiste. 27793, (73189),
(73193)
Feuillet, Jean Baptiste. supposed author
24227, 73176
Feuilletean, W. petitioner 103112
Feunleal, S. Ramirez de. see Ramirez de
Feunleal, S., Bp.
Feutry, -----. 78113
Feutry, A. A. Jos. 72219
Fever. 85072
Fever: an elegaic poem. 24228
Fevers in the West Indies. 25313
Fevillee, R. P. see Feuille, Louis.
Fevre, C. F. le. see Le Fevre, C. F.
Fevre, Jacques le. see Le Fevre, Jacques,
d'Etaples, d. 1537.
Few, W. 101211
Few are ignorent. 95974
Few brief facts. 24230
Few brief remarks on Mr. Graham's answer.
26349, 28221
Few brief remarks touching Mr. C. O. Shepard.
(39192)
Few chapters to Brother Jonathan. 62438,
(77444), 98169
Few characteristical notes. 1566
Few considerations for reflecting voters.
56221
Few considerations in relation to the choice
of president. 24229
Few cursory remarks. 30765
Few days ago I was at my neighbor's. 96012
Few days at Nashotah. 37950
Few days in Athens. 105590

Few eccentric poems. 69008
Few extracts from 'The whore of Babylon
unmasked.' 105575
Few facts and considerations for business men.
60358
Few facts and documents. 24231
Few facts and feelings. 29236, (39828)
Few facts and observations. 1402
Few facts and reasons why Orange and Ulster
Counties should not be divided. (24232)
Few facts and thoughts on American slavery.
92069
Few facts from the record of patriotic services.
52302
Few facts, pertaining to currency and banking.
90885
Few facts plainly stated for the citizens.
62340
Few facts regarding the geological survey of
Pennsylvania. (24233), (40189)
Few facts relating to petroleum. 4355
Few facts respecting the American Colonization
Society. 81977, 90703
Few friends. pseud. Additional sketches.
27429
Few hints for the reading public. 63920
Few hints humbly offered for the perusal of
the legislators. 98636
Few hints on guard duty. 63736
Few hints to such artizans, mechanics,
labourers, farmers and husbandmen.
(41943)
Few hints to the creditors of Mexico. 95119
Few hints to the wise. 102987
Few historic records. 27408
Few historical facts concerning the murderous
assault. 92687
Few historical facts respecting the establish-
ment. 24648
Few historical records of the church. 24234,
28703
Few hymns translated by the Rev. James Evans
and George Henry. 36589
Few imperfect rhymes. 82924
Few introductory observations. 58999
Few introductory remarks in answer to a
pamphlet. 43205
Few months in America. 71954
Few more words on the chivalry of the south.
80553
Few more words, on the freedom of the press.
84642, 2d note after 96428
Few more words, on the freedom of the press
in America. 97366
Few more words upon Canada. 13258
Few notes and observations. 37865
Few notes on certain passages. (23231)
Few notes on the Jesuit relations. 56609
Few notes respecting the United States of
America. 91995, note after 97915
Few notes upon the history of the constitution.
83515
Few observations, lately published by Jonthan
Cowpland. 90351
Few observations on Canada. (10446)
Few observations on Mr. Foster's divine rite
of immersion. (13597)
Few observations on some of the principles.
13840, (67748)
Few observations on the government of the
state of Rhode Island. 24235
Few observations on the importation of slave
grown sugar. 24236
Few observations on the natural history of the
sperm whale. 4108

Few observations on the politics of the present time. (19150)

Few observations on the reality of wooden pavements. 98577

Few observations on the utility of wooden pavements. 98577

Few observations regarding the tariff. (57751)

Few observations upon the value and importance of our North American colonies. (57153)

Few of her particular friends. pseud. eds. Letters of Martha Smith. 83527

Few pages for Americans. 32985, 6th note after 103115

Few "patriotic" contemplations. (31246)

Few personal recollections of Mr. Thackeray. 68606

Few plagiarisms. 102342

Few plain directions for persons. 10447, 10541, note after 98077

Few plain facts, addressed to the people of Pennsylvania. 60101

Few plain facts for gas consumers! 62336

Few plain facts, shewing the necessity of immigration into British Guiana and the West Indies. 102820

Few plain thoughts on emigration and colonization. 81133

Few plain words to England and her manufacturers. 32699

Few plain words with the rank and file of the Union armies. 24237

Few political reflections submitted to the consideration of the British colonies. 24238, 102599

Few practical hints to intending emigrants. 9974

Few practical words of advice. (68313)-(68314)

Few prefatory remarks. 93253

Few queries in answer to the scruples. 7143, 86588

Few questions with respect to the Episcopal mission. 90105

Few raps over the knuckles of the present age. 77730

Few reasons in favor of the annexation of a part of the town. 14181

Few reasons in favor of the restoration of the original policy. 24239

Few reasons in favour of vendues. (25509), 61657

Few reflections of a cool-minded man. (37509)

Few reflections on the conduct of that enterprize. 7301

Few remarks about sick children in New York. (54277), note after 91682

Few remarks by an Englishman. 35917

Few remarks by Dr. Rush. 79268

Few remarks by Robert Hurnard. 4058

Few remarks on an address to the Roman Catholics. 30955

Few remarks in reply to the anonymous scribbler. 51057

Few remarks on Doctor Benjamin Trumbull's . . . appeal. 97179

Few remarks on Mr. Hamilton's late letter. 9863

Few remarks on religion, manners, customs, and political state. 102812

Few remarks on religious corporations and examples of them. 74559

Few remarks on the cultivation of the sugar cane. 42226

Few remarks on the operations of the companies. 24240

Few remarks on the peculiar trials of our day. 32369

Few remarks on the recommendatory preface. 12331, 13350

Few remarks on the remarks, etc. 28221

Few remarks on the state of her defences. 19565

Few remarks recommended to the consideration of the creditors. 73770

Few remarks upon "Four papers from the Boston courier." 58758

Few remarks upon Quaker-politicks. 104452-104453

Few remarks upon some of the votes and resolutions. 15529, 15597, 28391, 2d note after 97553

Few remarks upon the late writings of Dr. Hemmenway. 2632

Few remarks, upon the ordination of the Rev'd Mr. James Dana. (30647), 96092

Few remarks upon the subject of a railroad to the Pacific. 24241

Few reminiscences of Salem, Mass. (19667)

Few revolutionary facts. (6977)

Few sea officers of both line and staff. pseud. Suggestions upon naval reform. 93477

Few serious questions for reason and conscience to decide. 105327

Few short remarks on Dr. O'Gallagher's reply. 103090

Few statements relative to the commerce of the Canadas. 6768, 12513, 1st note after 94186

Few suggestions for thoughtful and patriotic men. (44755), (57296)

Few suggestions on the slave trade. 81978

Few suggestions to the Young Men's Sodality, of St. Louis, Mo. 86194

Few suggestions with regard to nonintervention between European states. 1416

Few strictures on liberty of conscience. 81587

Few thoughts for a young man. 44324

Few thoughts for tax payers and voters. 89931

Few thoughts on intervention. (24242), 68605

Few thoughts on the artillery. 24243

Few thoughts on the confiscation act. 52326

Few thoughts on the duties, difficulties, and relations. 24244

Few thoughts on the foreign policy of the United States. 96785

Few thoughts on the hard times. 24245

Few thoughts on the powers and duties of woman. 44324

Few thoughts on three subjects of public interests. (24246)

Few thoughts on volunteering. 33094

Few thoughts to be thought of before proceeding. 57245

Few verses by the late Reverend Mr. Killinghall. 4395

Few verses for a few friends. (24300)

Few words about John Tyler. 63777, 63816

Few words concerning the life of a Christian. 80459

Few words for honest Pennsylvania Democrats. 24250, 60102

Few words for the American crisis. 49808

Few words in behalf of the loyal women of the United States. 24251

Few words in vindication of the action of the Court of Bishops. (39694)

Few words of a letter to John Cotton. 37212

Few words of intelligence. 97261

Few words of warning to New Yorkers. 8042

Few words on Sunday morning, April 16th, 1865. (19605)

Few words on the Central Park. 16661

Few words on the crisis. (24247)

Few words on the Hudson's Bay Company. (33542)

Few words on the nature of the slave trade. 24252

Few words on the objects and prospects of the Bolivian Association. 24253

Few words on the subject of Canada. 10448, 13257

Few words relating to the present aspect of Republicanism. (76234)

Few words to Democrats. (24248)

Few words to emigrants. (24249)

Few words to His Excellency the Hon. C. F. Adams, &c. 12993

Few words to loyal Democrats. 24254

Few words to the thinking and judicious voters. 24255

Few words touching a late pamphlet. 26713

Few words upon Canada. 10449

Fewsmith, Joseph. see Smith, Joseph Few, 1816-1888.

Feyerabend, Sigismund. see Feirabend, Sigismund.

Feyjoo de Sosa, Miguel, d. 1784. 24256, 71450

Fhelgum, ----- Murk van. see Murk van Fhelgum, ------.

Ffirth, John. supposed author 97269

Fiancee du ministre. 92443

Fiances de Caracas. 44919

Fibbleton, George. pseud. Travels in America. see Greene, Asa.

Fibra salvage. (29350)

Fibre plants of India, Africa, and our colonies. 20088

Fibrilia substitut pratique et economique du coton. (24257)

Fibufugium. 46328

Fick, J. G. C. tr. 5649

Ficklin, Orlando Bell, 1808-1886. 24258

Fidanza, Giovanni. see Bonaventura, Saint, 1221-1274.

Fiddle—D. D. 36358

Fidel. pseud. Viajes de orden suprema. see Prieto, Guillermo.

Fidele sujet du Roy. pseud. Discours. see Charpentier, Francois.

Fidelis of the cross. 84510

Fidelissimo echo. 99529

Fidelitas, Philo. pseud. see Philo Fidelitas. pseud.

Fidelity, and other poems. 61398

Fidelity approved and rewarded. 101289

Fidelity Division, no. 2, Trenton, N. J. see Sons of Temperance of North America. New Jersey. Fidelity Division, no. 2, Trenton.

Fidelity in Christian ministers. (71506)

Fidelity of ministers to themselves. (28383)

Fidelity of the Gospel ministry. 23327

Fidelity to Christ. 14485

Fidelity to duty. 88857

Fidelity to our political idea. 48928

Fides, religio, & mores Aethiopum. 6118, 94273

Fides, religio, moresque AEthiopum. 77902

Fides, religio, moresqve Aethiopvm svb imperio preciosi Ioannis. 27688

Fidfaddy, Frederick Augustus. pseud. Adventures of Uncle Sam. 479, 24260

Fidler, Isaac. 24261, 28585, 36358

Fidler, James M. 24262

Fiebre y sabandijas en Venezuela. 98875

Field, Miss ------. 32707

Field, Albert S. defendant 24263

Field, Alfred R. 24264

Field, Anson. petitioner 82206

Field, Aylwin. 83008

Field, B. ed. 100606

Field, Charles. defendant 80738, 105025

Field, Cyrus West, 1819-1892. 24265, 74365

Field, David Dudley. 19848, 24266-24274, 2d note after 90803, 92912, note after 99270, 99274

Field, Edward, Bp. of Newfoundland, 1801-1876. (24275)

Field, Edwin W. 16880

Field, Henry M. 24276-24277

Field, J. M. 24282

Field, James. plaintiff 80738, 105025

Field, John, 1648-1723. 24278-24279

Field, John, fl. 1838. 25179

Field, Joseph. 24280-24281

Field, Joseph E. 24283

Field, Levi A. 24284

Field, M. 24285

Field, M. C. 84237

Field, Maunsel B. tr. 49974

Field, Moses W. 24286-24287

Field, Osgood. 24288

Field, R. engr. 79729

Field, R. M. defendant 96304

Field, Richard S. 24289-24291

Field, Robert S. defendant 29890, note after 96863

Field, Samuel. (24292)

Field, Stephen J. complainant 97497

Field, Thomas P. 53255

Field, Thomas W. (24293)-24295, 26599, 39651

Field, Timothy. 24296

Field and garden vegetables of America. (9440)

Field book of the revolution. 5220

Field engineer. 13199

Field, forest, and garden botany. (28370)

Field genealogy. 24276

Field, gunboat, hospital, and prison. 29400

Field manual of courts martial. (16699)

Field Negro. 63624

Field notes of geology. 57743

Field notes of thirteen leagues of land. 85455

Field of mars. 24297

Field of the green banner. 79987

Field of war. 53286

Field officer. pseud. Bermuda. 4907

Field officer. pseud. Life of a soldier. see Lewin, Ross.

Field officer. pseud. Manual of the lance. 44415

Field officer on the staff. pseud. Narrative of the operations. 51819

Field Officers of the Fourteenth Division of the Massachusetts Militia. see Massachusetts. Militia. Fourteenth Division. Officers.

Field record of the officers. 24298

Field Relief Corps, United States Sanitary Commission. see United States Sanitary Commission. Field Relief Corps.

Field sports of the United States and British provinces. (31461)

Field sports on the prairie. 24641

Fielder, Herbert. 24299

Fielding, Henry, 1707-1754. 99257

Fielding, John. 93906, 105003
Fielding, Newton. illus. 90312
Fielding, T. engr. 102850
Fields, James T. (24300)-24301
Fields, R. 24302
Fields, William. 24303
Fiennes Pelham Clinton, Henry Pelham. see
  Newcastle Under Lyme, Henry Pelham
  Fiennes Pelham Clinton, 5th Duke of,
  1811-1864.
Fiery cross. 24304, (31081)
Fiery tryal no strange thing. 104081
Fiesco. 50121, 56608
Fiestas de la ciudad de Lima. 41109
Fiestas de precepto para los Indios. 96269,
  101643
Fiestas en la beatification de Santa Rosa de
  Santa Maria. 24305
Fiestas, entierros y exequias de los Indios.
  38381, 56007, (75765)
Fiestas nacionales. 24306
Fievre jaune a la Havane. 4591
Fievre jaune en general. 77269
Fievre jaune que a regne a la Martinique.
  (12481)
Fievre jaune, sa maniere d'entre. 47925
Fife coast garland. 36566
Fifield, Noah. 24307
Fifteen days. 66833
Fifteen discourses for the liberties of the
  churches. 47447
Fifteen discourses on the marvellous works
  in nature. 68982
Fifteen gallon jug. 17329, 104311
Fifteen gallons. 24308
Fifteen minutes around New York. (25223)
Fifteen proposals of the ministers. 104336
Fifteen sermon, preached on various important
  subjects. 83433, 103514
Fifteen years among the Mormons. 28553,
  83550-83552
Fifteen years in Canada. 30914
Fifteen years in the senior order of Shakers.
  22197
Fifteen years' observations among the theatres
  of New York. 55758
Fifteen years of prayer. (65540)
Fifteen years' residence with the Mormons.
  83555
Fifteenth amendment to the constitution. (28601)
Fifteenth annual account of the missionary
  labors. 15812
Fifteenth annual catalogue of the Rockford
  Female Seminary. 72382
Fifteenth annual report . . . see Report . . .
Fifteenth report . . . see Report . . .
Fifteenth semi-annual report . . . see Report
  . . .
Fifth and last letter to Mr. Burke. 69501,
  90377
Fifth & sixth articles of the treaty of neutrality.
  96432
Fifth anniversary of the Congressional Tem-
  perance Society. (15611), note after
  101933
Fifth anniversary of the ex-officers union.
  54391
Fifth annual address. 32397
Fifth annual address of the Rector of Christ
  Church. (7783)
Fifth annual announcement of the New York
  Medical College for Women. (54806)
Fifth annual catalogue of the officers and
  students of Green Mountain Liberal In-
  stitute. 88220

Fifth annual catalogue of the students. (62309)
Fifth annual report . . . see Report . . .
5th Army Corps memorial. 86142
Fifth biennial report . . . see Report . . .
Fifth book of records of the town of Southampton.
  88230
Fifth census. 11665
Fifth collection of papers. 81492
Fifth Congregational Church, Providence, R. I.
  see Providence, R. I. Fifth Congrega-
  tional Church.
Fifth . . . debate . . . October 3, 1864. 55840
Fifth essay on free trade and finance. 102407
Fifth general report of the . . . Chesapeake
  and Delaware Canal Company. 12499
Fifth letter, by the author of four former
  letters. 80043
Fifth letter of Hernan Cortes. 16965
Fifth letter to convicts in state prisons.
  (20336A)
Fifth letter to Daniel Dulany. 31313
Fifth letter to the Earl of Carlisle. 21828
Fifth letter to the people of England. (80044)
[Fifth letter to the Rev. Samuel Miller.]
  (49063)
Fifth of March oration. 16603
Fifth narrative [of George Keith.] 103703
Fifth narrative, of his [i. e. George Keith's]
  proceedings. (37191)
Fifth National Sunday-School Convention, held
  at Indianapolis. 52025
Fifth report . . . see Report . . .
Fifth series of historical documents. 67025
Fifth supplement [to the public laws of Rhode
  Island.] 70700
Fiftieth anniversary address before the First
  Baptist Sunday School. 41253
Fiftieth anniversary celebration of the . . .
  [New York Mercantile Library] Associa-
  tion. 54391
Fiftieth anniversary of a marriage-day. 30306
Fiftieth anniversary of the founding of the
  . . . [New York] Historical Society.
  54477
Fiftieth anniversary of the marriage of James
  and Mary North. 55519
Fiftieth anniversary of the marriage of John
  J. and Sarah A. Knox. 38168
Fiftieth anniversary of the organization of the
  First Congregational Church. 35736
Fiftieth anniversary of the Second Presbyterian
  Church. 83339
L. [i. e. fifty] 87730
Fifty arguments in favor of sustaining. 13360
Fifty days on board a slave-vessel. (31852)
Fifty dollar act. 95470
$50 reward. 85422
Fifty female sketches. 82774
Fifty-eighth anniversary celebration. (52746)
Fifty-fifth annual report . . . see Report . . .
Fifty-fourth annual report . . . see Report
  . . .
Fifty notable years. 84292
Fifty-one reasons against any alteration what-
  ever. 10889
Fifty-one substantial reasons. 10889
Fifty reasons why Henry Clay should be elected.
  14437
Fifty reasons why the Hon. Henry Clay should
  be elected. 13556
Fifty-second annual catalogue of Pinkerton
  Academy. 62961
Fifty-second annual report . . . see Report
  . . .
Fifty-sixth annual report . . . see Report . . .

FIFTY

Fiftytwo [sic] sermons on the dignity of man. 95416

Fifty years among the Baptists. 4649

Fifty years at the Litchfield County Bar. 78814

Fifty years history of the temperance cause. 91026

Fifty years in both hemispheres. 55412

Fifty [i. e., fifteen] years in chains. 83552

Fifty years in chains; or, the life of an American slave. 24309

Fifty years in New-York. 46844

Fifty years in the itinerant ministry. (38842)

Fifty year's ministry. 66809

Fifty years of a play-goer's journal. (18231), 24310, 35057

Fifty years of public life. 84811

Fifty years of slavery in the southern states of America. 24002

Fifty years' progress. 101441

Fifty years since. 32881

Fifty years social. 33857

Fifty years with the Revere Copper Co. 95541

Figaro. 76522

Fight for Missouri. 85374

Fight for the flag. 54899

Fight for the union. A poem. 25453

Fighting Joe. 358

Fighting Quakers. 21153

Fighting Quaker's expedition in Pensilvania. 23734

Fighting sailor turned peaceable Christian. 42716

Figsbee, -----. 24311

Figueira, Antonio Agostinho de Andrade. 52217

Figueira, Luiz, 1573-1643. 24313-24314

Figueiredo, Jose Bento da Cunhae. see Cunhae Figueiredo, Jose Bento da.

Figueiredo, Jose Bento da Cinha e. see Cinha e Figueiredo, Jose Bento da.

Figueiredo, Manuel de, 1568-1630. (24316), (73433)

Figueiredo e Mello, Pedro Americo de. 24315, 95628A

Figueiroa Nabuco de Aranjo, Jose Paulo de. see Nabuco de Araujo, Jose Paulo de Figueiroa.

Figueredo, Juan de. 96270-96271

Figueroa, Antonio Vazquez Gastelu el Rey de. see Vazquez Gaztelu, Antonio.

Figueroa, Christoual Mosquera de. see Mosquera de Figueroa, Christoual.

Figueroa, Cristoval Suarez de. see Suarez de Figueroa, Cristoval.

Figueroa, Diego d'Avalos y. see Avalos y Figueroa, Diego d'.

Figueroa, Francisco A. de. 24318

Figueroa, Francisco Antonio de la Rosa. 24321

Figueroa, Francisco de. 24319-24320

Figueroa, Felix Suarez de. see Suarez de Figueroa, Felix.

Figueroa, Garcia Silva. 66686

Figueroa, Jose. see Vazquez de Figueroa, Jose.

Figueroa, Jose Suarez de. see Suarez de Figueroa, Jose.

Figueroa, Jose Vazquez de. see Vazquez de Figueroa, Jose.

Figueroa, Jose Vidal de. see Vidal de Figueroa, Jose.

Figueroa, Juan de Cara Amo y. see Cara Amo y Figueroa, Juan de.

Figueroa, Loreco Vidal de. see Vida de Figueroa, Lorenzo.

Figueroa, Luis de Betancurt y. see Betancurt y Figueroa, Luis de.

Figueroa, Manuel Mosquera y. see Mosquera y Figueroa, Manuel.

Figueroa, Miguel Suarez de. see Suarez de Figueroa, Miguel.

Figueroa y Guevara, Baltasar Pardo de. see Pardo de Figueroa y Guevara, Baltasar.

Figueros, Manuel de. 99619

Figura de gentiu[m] i[n] Armenica. 99365, 99383

Figure de la terre. (6876)-6877

Figure of the earth. 46946

Figures, Nicolao. tr. 44175

Figures and descriptions of Canadian organic remains. 10458, 29805

Figures or types of the Old Testament. (46785)-(46786)

Filantropicos. pseud. Denuncia de las autores. 28162

Filho, Jose de Saldanha da Gama. see Gama Filho, Jose de Saldanha da.

Filho do Compadre do Rio de Janeiro. pseud. Justa retribuicao. 76326-76327

Filial tribure. 79451, 90905

Filices a leiboldo in Mexico lectae. 38349

Filices exoticae. 32866

Filices: including Lycopodiaceae and Hydropterides. 7193

Filicetum Americanum. 63456

Filicum, polypodiorum, adiantorum, etc. 63456

Filii, quum legisset, gratulatio. 46400

Filipe Segundo. 94854

Filisola, Vincente. 24323-24326

Fille de chambre. 73613

Fille des Indiens rouges. (12560)

Filleau de Saint-Hillaire, Edme-Jean-Hilaire. supposed author 14720, 94850, 95786

Fillebrown, Thomas. (24327)

Filley, William. 24328

Fillmore, John. (24329)-24330

Fillmore, Millard, Pres. U. S., 1800-1874. (17792), (24332)-24333, 36885, 48118-48122, 53049, 91278 see also U. S. President, 1850-1853 (Fillmore)

Fillmore state address. 24333

Fillpot, an inn-keeper. pseud. Amusement for a winter's evening. see Sewall, Jonathan, 1728-1796.

Fillpot, an inn-keeper. pseud. Cure for the spleen. see Sewall, Joanthan, 1728-1796.

Filmer, William. 39394

Filmore, Joseph. see Pilmore, Joseph.

Filomeno, Francisco. 24335

Filosofia del derecho. 76873

Filosofia Frankliniana. 96099

Filosofo Inglese. 65410

Filosofo rancio. pseud. Contestacion. 977, 16159, 96117-note after 96117

Filosophia rancio. pseud. Contestacion. 977, 16159, 96117-note after 96117

Filotea de la cruz. 76775

Fils. pseud. Lettres d'un fils a son pere. 40689, note after 93857

Fils de l'oncle Tom. 70331

Filson, John. 24336-(24339), 24624, 30683, 34355, (34358), 84936

Filson Club publications. 84834-84935

Filson Society, Louisville. 84934-84935

Filter, Urbanus. pseud. New England magazine. see Mecom, Benjamin, b. 1732.

Fin de la guerre. 24340

Fin de la monarchie en Amerique. 20737

Fin du monde miserable. 45400

Finaeus, Orontius. see Fine, Oronce.

Final answer. 62665
Final controversia diplomatica. 56284
Final diplomatic controversy relating to the occurrences that took place at Panama. 51072, 52778
Final effort of the Society for the Promotion of Collegiate and Theological Education at the West. 85915
Final emancipation inevitable. 82179
Final memoirs of a staff officer. 16318
Final peace. 18186
Final philosophy. 80465
Final proceedings and general report. 88346
Final protest. 93655
Final reply to the libels of E. Poulteney. (36272)
Final reply to the numerous slanders. 59153
Final report . . . see Report . . .
Final settlement of the claim. 30859
Final triumph of equity. 10993
Final word of the alliance. 28082
Finan, P. 24341
Finance. 83703
Finance. A letter addressed to the House Committee. 24342, 29929
Finance and hours of labour. (31100)
Finance bill. (43876)
Finance, no. 3. Should the interest on the national debt be forced? 29929
Finance.—No. II.—Bill—synopsis—and explanatory reports. 24343
Finance of cheap postage. 39564
Finance. Speech . . . January 27, 1869. 43119
Finances and policy of New-York. 99268
Finances & resources of the United States. 91018
Finances and trade of Canada at the beginning of 1855. 11632
Finances de 1812. 20734
Finances et les banques des Etats Unis depuis la guerre. 14084
Finances, faith & credit of the state. (32398)
Finances of the canal fund. 95783
Finances: panics and specie payments. 77995
Financial and political facts of the eighteenth century. 42941
Financial and superintending School Committee's reports. 8765
Financial aspects of the rebellion. 73146
Financial Commission of New Orleans. see U. S. Army. Department of the Gulf. Financial Commission of New Orleans, 1864.
Financial condition and resources of the United States. 24345, (38907)
Financial condition and restricted charitable operations. 54484
Financial condition of the country. 50780
Financial condition. Speech of William Sprague. 89723-89724
Financial considerations. 74615
Financial considerations, no. 2. 74615
Financial credit of the United States. 24346
Financial crisis. 71824
Financial crisis: its evils and their remedy. 62820
Financial economy of the United States Illustrated. 24193
Financial economy of the United States, with suggestions. 26403
Financial estimates, or budget for 1860. (54212)
Financial history and condition of Lane Seminary. 38861
Financial measures of the United States government. 24347

Financial necessities and policy of the national government. 68057
Financial policy of Massachusetts. 19658
Financial problem. (24348)
Financial problem: being suggestions. 47891
Financial question of the day. 57711
Financial register of the United States. 24349
Financial report of . . . North Reading. 55729
Financial report of the city of Brooklyn. (8292)
Financial report of the Mayor, . . . [of Montreal.] 50251
Financial report of the U. S. Sanitary Commission. (76609), 76647
Financial returns. . . . 1867. (56130)
Financial review. (24350)
Financial scheme for the government. 24351
Financial secret worth knowing. (58508)
Financial situation. 24352
Financial statement of the Auditor of the Canal Department. 53557
Financial statement of the city of Chicago. (12649)
Financial. The currency, the standard of value. 63354
Financiers A, B, C, respecting currency. 32748
Finanzen und die Finanzgeschichten der Vereinigten Staaten. (32323)
Finch, Francis Miles. 23205
Finch, Heneage. see Winchilsea, Heneage Finch, 2d Earl of.
Finch, John, fl. 1812. 86301
Finch, John, fl. 1835. 24353
Finch, Marianne. 24354
Finch, Richard. 66686
Finch, Robert Pool. 24355
Finch, W. 66686
Finck, Jonas. (66003)
Fincke, F. Gustav. 24356
Finden, ------. illus. (25624), 25627, 28235, (42853), 73385
Finding list of books in the Portland Institute. 64363
Findings and conclusions of the Court of Inquiry. 83319
Findlay, -------. engr. 91844
Findlay, Alexander G. (24357)-24359, 66695-66696, 66700, 66703-66704
Findley, William. (24360)-(24363), 70265, 105669
Fine, John. (24364)
Fine, Orance. (34101), 63960, 69130-69132, 76897
Fine Arkansas gentleman who died before his time. (41036), 62816
Fine arts. A reply to article X. 50960
Fine arts in the United States. 37296
Fine wool sheep husbandry. 67790
Fines, Charles. (21090), 33698, 78431, 104846
Finest part of America. 24365, note after 98632
Finger-point from Plymouth Rock. 93656
Finger-post to public business. (24366)
Finishing stroke to Mr. Wesley's Calm address. 51504
Fink, Gottlob. tr. 7710, 12720, 28716, 77741
Fink, W. W. 24367
Finlason, W. F. 24368-(24373)
Finlason, W. F. reporter 23561
Finlay, Alexander. plaintiff 85190
Finlay, D. L. 24374
Finlay, Hugh. 24375
Finlay, Hugh. supposed author 67024
Finlay, John B. 24376
Finley, E. L. 24377
Finley, Isaac J. 66838

Finley, James. 40455, 47276, 65149, (78736), 97107 see also Eighteen Presbyterian Ministers, in America. pseud.
Finley, James B. (24378)-24382, (49704), 92378, 92824
Finley, R. 24383
Finley, Robert. 95695
Finley, Samuel, 1715-1766. 18766, 24386-24391, 26845, 50633, 71320, (73402), 73404, 83796, 95579
Finn, Henry J. 24392, 36356, 103296
Finn, W. G. 82041
Finney, ------. 46902
Finney, C. G. 24393, 97073
Finney's lectures on human governments reviewed. 46902
Fino, Alemanio. 4620
Fiora, Paolo Mariani da S. 24394
Fiorauante, Christoforo. 67736
Fiorentino, Francesco C. 24395, (25085)
Fiorentino, Mauro. 32677-32684
Fiori di maggio. 92437
Fire and hammer of God's word. (12399)
Fire Association, Newark, N. J. see Newark Fire Association.
Fire Association of Philadelphia. Trustees. Charter. 61658
Fire departments of the United States. 18406
Fire fiend, and other poems. 26607-26608
Fire insurance: 1868-1869. 35006
Fire insurance register and index to the resources. 89146
Fire marshall almanac. 8334
Fire marshall almanac and reference book. (4442)
Fire marshall Rufus R. Belknap's semi-annual report. 4444
Fire on the hearth in Sleepy Hollow. 32994
Fire Society, Worcester, Mass. see Worcester Fire Society, Worcester, Mass.
Firelands Historical Society. 24397
Firelands pioneer. 24397
Fireman. 18406
Fireman's almanac. 4443
Fireman's liturgy. 16297
Fireman's own book. 41516
Firemen's Insurance Company of Washington. Charter. 101942
Firemen's Mutual Relief Association, Spring-field, Mass. 89860
Firemen's songster. 61661
Fires and fire systems. 5548
Fireside book. A miscellany. 100998
Fireside companion. 103940
Fireside poetical readings. (37796)
Fireside preacher. 89531
Fireside reading. 13271
Fireside review. see Mentor and fireside review.
Fireside talks on morals and manners. 37987
Firey, Lewis P. 24398
Firm, Henry. 24399
Firm and immoveable courage to obey God. 104361
Firm union of a people presented. 18187
Firmamento religioso de Lvzidos Astors. 55270
Firmin, Giles. 24400-24401
Firmin, M. C. (24403)
Firmin del Rey. see Fermin del Rey.
Firsch, Valentin Marquard von. 102874
First a bitt and a knock for vnder-sheriffs. (39510)
First account of the "Spanish Association of Kentucky." 5906

First address of the Whig Central Committee of Vigilance of Fauquier County. 23930, 78721, note after 103287
First adventures, particularly Ferdinand De Soto. 20183
First American in Texas. 41018, 64545
First and final step. 79637
First and great commandment. 79416
First and last fundamental constitutions. 10980, 87347, 87355, 1st note after 97553
First and last fundamfntal [sic] constitutions. 10980, 87347, 87355, 1st note after 97553
First and last annual festivals. 86981
First and second annual report . . . see Report . . .
First and second annual reports . . . see Reports . . .
First and second books of Samuel. 12872
First and second epistles of Nathaniel Very. 99318
First and second letters of the Provincial Council. 66673
First and second parts of the adventures of Mrs. West. 102741
First and second report . . . see Report . . .
First and second reports . . . see Re-ports . . .
First and second speaker. 85507
First and second statements on the part of Great Britain. 44046, note before 90764
First and secondary justification. 20059
First anniversary address before the Associa-tion of American Geologists. 32250
First anniversary of the abolition of slavery. 91697
First anniversary of the Home for Jewish Widows and Orphans. 53329
First anniversary of the Massachusetts Church Missionary Society. 45830
First anniversary of the New York Peace Society. (54421)
First anniversary of the . . . [New York State Woman's] Hospital. 53978
First anniversary of the opening of the Girard College for Orphans. (27492)
First anniversary of the proclamation of freedom in South Carolina. 87826
First anniversary sermon. 6576
First annual address, . . . before the Hartford Peace Society. 41378
First annual address before the New-Jersey Historical Society. 20391
First annual address . . . before the Public School Teachers' Association. 17464
First annual address, read before the Religious Historical Society. 105668
First annual address to the Philadelphia Annual Conference. (59285)
First annual announcement . . . see Announce-ment . . .
First annual catalogue . . . see Catalogue . . .
First annual circular . . . see Circular . . .
First annual discourse . . . see Discourse . . .
First annual exhibition of the Society of Artists of the United States. 86006
First annual meeting of the Association for the Improvement of Common Schools in Indiana. 34506
First annual meeting of the Massachusetts Episcopal Society for the Religious in-struction of Freedmen. (45843)

First annual meeting . . . Proceedings of the Commissioners of the Soldiers' National Cemetery Association. 27233, 65830

First annual message . . . see Message . . .

First annual register of the officers and students for 1854-5. 61061

First annual report . . . see Report . . .

First annual reports . . . see Reports . . .

First annual review of Pierce County, Wisc. 62748

First annual statement . . . see Statement . . .

First attempt, or something new. 105182

First attempts to establish a colony in Canada. 32470

First Baltimore Battalion. see Maryland. Militia. First Baltimore Battalion.

First Baptist Association of Central Wisconsin. see Baptists. Wisconsin. First Baptist Association of Central Wisconsin.

First Baptist Church, Boston. see Boston. First Baptist Church.

First Baptist Church, Cambridge, Mass. see Cambridge, Mass. First Baptist Church.

First Baptist Church, Charlestown, Mass. see Charlestown, Mass. First Baptist Church.

First Baptist Church, New Bedford, Mass. see New Bedford, Mass. First Baptist Church.

First Baptist Church, New York. see New York (City) First Baptist Church.

First Baptist Church, Philadelphia. see Phialdelphia. First Baptist Church.

First Baptist Church, Providence, R. I. see Providence, R. I. First Baptist Church.

First Baptist Church, South Kingstown, R. I. see South Kingstown, R. I. First Baptist Church.

First Baptist Church, Southbridge, Mass. see Southbridge, Mass. First Baptist Church.

First Baptist Church, Springfield, Mass. see Springfield, Mass. First Baptist Church.

First Baptist Church, Warren, R. I. see Warren, R. I. First Baptist Church.

First Baptist Church, Waterville, Me. see Waterville, Me. First Baptist Church.

First Battalion of Pennsylvania Loyalists. 60662

First biennial report . . . see Report . . .

First Bishop of Toronto. (77430)

First book. (34471)

First book for children. 4694

First book for Indian schools. 105545

First book in arithmetic. 83910

First book in geography. note before 83906, 83937-83945, 83948, 83951-83955

First book of geography. 95545

First book of history. 27922

First book of records of the town of Southampton. 88230

First book of the American chronicles of the times. 24404

First book of the chronicles of the children of disobedience. 30662, note after 101993

First book of the constitution. 80293

First book of the "Washington Benevolents." 101993

First book of the art of metals. 3254

First booke of the historie of the discouerie and conquest. 11391

First books of natural history. 74197

First branch journal. 17262

First California story book. 97724

First campaign. 39512

First catalogue . . . see Catalogue . . .

First catalogues . . . see Catalogues . . .

First Cattle Show and Fair, of the Agricultural Society of Jefferson County, N. Y. see Jefferson County Agricultural Society. Cattle Show and Fair. 1st, 1818.

First celebration by the Old Dominion Society. 35738, 57125, 93623

First census instructions of Kansas. (37021)

First centenary of the North Church and Society. (75660)

First centennial anniversary of the College of New Jersey. 53088

First centennial report. 89486

First century of Columbia College. 36627

First century of Drummer Academy. (13605)

First chapter of the lamentation of Burgoyne. 63622

First charge. 78556

First charge, to the clergy of his diocess [sic]. (15654), 39529, 78555-78556

First charter and the early religious legislatuion. (58695)

First charter granted by the King. 10969

First Christian Party of Oneida Indians. see Oneida Indians (First Christian Party)

First Church, Beverly, Mass. see Beverly, Mass. First Church.

First Church, Boston. see Boston. First Church.

First Church, Braintree, Mass. see Braintree, Mass. First Church.

First Church, Charlestown, Mass. see Charlestown, Mass. First Church.

First Church, Danbury, Conn. see Danbury, Conn. First Church.

First Church, Dedham, Mass. see Dedham, Mass. First Church.

First Church, Dover, N. H. see Dover, N. H. First Church.

First Church, Gloucester, Mass. see Gloucester, Mass. First Church.

First Church, Groton, Mass. see Groton, Mass. First Church.

First Church, Ipswich, Mass. see Ipswich, Mass. First Church.

First Church, Mansfield, Conn. see Mansfield, Conn. First Church.

First Church, Middleboro, Mass. see Middleboro, Mass. First Church.

First Church, New Haven, Conn. see New Haven, Conn. First Church.

First Church, New London, Conn. see New London, Conn. First Church.

First Church, North Yarmouth, Me. see North Yarmouth, Me. First Church.

First Church, Northampton, Mass. see Northampton, Mass. First Church.

First Church, Orange, N. J. see Orange, N. J. First Church.

First Church, Portland, Me. see Portland, Me. First Church.

First Church, Salem, Mass. see Salem, Mass. First Church.

First Church, Simsbury, Conn. see Simsbury, Conn. First Church.

First Church, South Hadley, Mass. see South Hadley, Mass. First Church.

First Church, Southington, Conn. see Southington, Conn. Congregational Church.

First Church, Stamford, Conn. see Stamford, Conn. Congregational Church.

First Church, Windham, Conn. see Windham, Conn. First Church.

First Church, Woburn, Mass. see Woburn, Mass. First Church.

First Church, Worcester, Mass. see Worcester, Mass. First Church (Old South)

First Church (Unitarian), Boston. see Boston. First Church (Unitarian)

First Church and Parish, Dedham, Mass. see Dedham, Mass. First Church.

First Church and Society, Wallingford, Conn. see Wallingford, Conn. First Church and Society.

First church in Buffalo. 13468

First Church in Dover, N. H. see Dover, N. H. First Church.

First Church in Middleborough, Mass. 48827

First Church in New Haven, Conn. see New Haven, Conn. First Church.

First Church in Newark. 90906

First Church in Northampton. Confession of faith, and catalogue. 55764

First Church in Salem, Mass., 1634. 75662

First Church of Christ, Boston. see Boston. First Church of Christ.

First Church of Christ, East Windsor, Conn. see East Windsor, Conn. First Church of Christ.

First Church of Christ, Glastonbury, Conn. see Glastonbury, Conn. First Church of Christ.

First Church of Christ, Hingham, Mass. see Hingham, Mass. First Church of Christ.

First Church of Christ, Middleboro, Mass. see Middleboro, Mass. First Church of Christ.

First Church of Christ, Pomfret, Conn. see Pomfret, Conn. First Church of Christ.

First Church of Christ, Portsmouth, N. H. see Portsmouth, N. H. First Church of Christ.

First Church of Christ, Salem, Mass. see Salem, Mass. First Church.

First Church of Christ, South Windsor, Conn. see South Windsor, Conn. First Congregational Church.

First Church of Christ, Springfield, Mass. see Springfield, Mass. First Church of Christ.

First Church of Christ, Sutton, Mass. see Sutton, Mass. First Church of Christ.

First Church of Christ Weymouth, Mass. see Weymouth, Mass. First Church of Christ.

First Church of Gloucester, Mass. See Gloucester, Mass. First Church.

First Church of Universalists, Boston. see Boston. First Church of Universalists.

First Church, Orange, N. J. 56427

First circular. 34993

(First-class standard reader.) 76966

First colonization of New England. 64061

First commander of Kent Island. 92793

First commencement of the College of New Jersey. 84555

First communication of the Grand Lodge of the State of Maine. (43992)

First Company of the Great Western Turnpike Road. Charter. 53597

First Congregational Church, Berlin, Mass. see Berlin, Mass. First Congregational Church.

First Congregational Church, Bolton, Mass. see Bolton, Mass. First Congregational Church.

First Congregational Church, Burlington, Vt. see Burlington, Vt. First Congregational Church.

First Congregational Church, Concord, N. H. see Concord, N. H. First Congregational Church.

First Congregational Church, Cornwall, Conn. see Cornwall, Conn. First Congregational Church.

First Congregational Church, East Windsor, Conn. see East Windsor, Conn. First Congregational Church.

First Congregational Church, Grand Rapids, Mich. see Grand Rapids, Mich. First Congregational Church.

First Congregational Church, Hillsborough, Ill. see Hillsborough, Ill. First Congregational Church.

First Congregational Church, Ludlow, Mass. see Ludlow, Mass. First Congregational Church.

First Congregational Church, Madison, Wis. see Madison, Wis. First Congregational Church.

First Congregational Church, Middleborough, Mass. see Middleborough, Mass. First Congregational Church.

First Congregational Church, New Bedford, Mass. see New Bedford, Mass. First Congregational Church.

First Congregational Church, New York. see New York (City) First Congregational Church.

First Congregational Church, Northampton, Mass. see First Congregational Church, Northampton, Mass.

First Congregational Church, Norwich, Conn. see Norwich, Conn. First Congregational Church.

First Congregational Church, Rockport, Mass. see Rockport, Mass. First Congregational Church.

First Congregational Church, St. John, N. B. see St. John, N. B. First Congregational Church.

First Congregational Church, San Francisco. see San Francisco. First Congregational Church.

First Congregational Church, South Adams, Mass. see South Adams, Mass. First Congregational Church.

First Congregational Church, South Hadley Falls, Mass. see South Hadley Falls, Mass. Congregational Church.

First Congregational Church, Spencerport, N. Y. see Spencerport, N. Y. First Congregational Church.

First Congregational Church, Springfield, Mass. see Springfield, Mass. First Congregational Church.

First Congregational Church, Stamford, Conn. see Stamford, Conn. First Congregational Church.

First Congregational Church, Suffield, Conn. see Suffield, Conn. First Congregational Church.

First Congregational Church, Sutton, Mass. see Sutton, Mass. First Congregational Church.

First Congregational Church, Vernon, Conn. see Vernon, Conn. First Congregational Church.

First Congregational Church, Wellfleet, Mass. see Wellfleet, Mass. First Congregational Church.

First Congregational Church, West Boylston, Mass. see West Boylston, Mass. First Congregational Church.

First Congregational Church, Westbrook, Me. see Westbrook, Me. First Congregational Church.

First Congregational Society, New Bedford, Mass. see New Bedford, Mass. First Congregational Society.

First Congregational Society, Philadelphia. see Philadelphia. First Congregational Society.

First Constitution of New Hampshire. 52827

First Constitution Club of the State of Pennsylvania. (60013)

First council in Jerusalem. 89020

First cruise of the United States Frigate, Essex. 65006

First declaration of His Highness William Henry. 104143

First directory of Nevada Territory. 37309

First discourse . . . before the Maryland Historical Society. (47106)

First discovery of America. 38324

First discovery of the 'Golden Islands or America.' 1560

First Dixie reader. 50426

First duty of the citizen. 24405

First duty of the citizen. The grandeur of the struggle. 24406

First Ecclesiastical Society, New Haven, Conn. see New Haven, Conn, First Ecclesiastical Society.

First edition. Fifth thousand. 71571, note before 93775

First edition of Steward's Healing art. 91621

First epic of our country. (80006)

First epistle general of John. 17455

First epistle of Paul. 49851

First establishment of the faith in New France. (80023)

First Evangelical Congregational Church, Cambridge-Port, Mass. see Cambridge, Mass. First Evangelical Congregational Church.

First exhibit . . . of the condition and prospects. (19007)

First exhibition and fair . . . held . . . in . . . Portland. 43966

First exhibition and fair of the Massachusetts Charitable Mechanic Association. 45829

First exhibition at Concord, N. H. 52876

First exhibition of the Charleston Apprentices' Library Society. 12040

First familiar conference. 4095, 78730

First field of the west; a poem. 7209

First fifty years of Cazenovia Seminary. 85202, 85348

First five books of Ovid's Metamorphosis. (76455)

First five years of the Sabbath reform. 54279

First forty years of Washington society. 83509, 83511, note after 84079

First forty years of Wesleyan evangelism. (59471)

First four voyages of Americus Vespuccius. II. note before 99327, 99377

First four voyages of Americus Vespucius. note before 99327, 99377

First four voyages of Amerigo Vespucci reprinted in facsimile. note before 99327, 99374

First four voyages of Amerigo Vespucci. Translated from the rare original edition. note before 99327, 99372

First four years of a settler's experience. 79668

First Free Church, Philadelphia. see Philadelphia. First Free Church.

First Free Congregational Church, Boston. see Boston. First Free Congregational Church.

First Free Presbyterian Church, New York. see New York (City) First Free Presbyterian Church.

First fruits. 9337

First fruits, in a series of letters. (32464)

First fruits of the Maine law. 88667

First fugitive slave case of record in Ohio. 84791

First general announcement. 16798

First General Baptist Church, Warwick, R. I. see Warwick, R. I. First General Baptist Church.

First Great South-Western Turnpike Road Company. petitioners 47673

First Great South-Western Turn-Pike Road Company. President and Directors. petitioners 22355

First half-yearly report . . . see Report . . .

First impressions. By Harvey Rice. 70832

First impressions of the new world. 24407, note after 97060

First inaugural message of Gov. John Hancock. 64028

First Independent Church, St. Louis. see St. Louis. First Independent Church.

First Independent Presbyterian Church, Oakland, Cal. see Oakland, Cal. First Independent Presbyterian Church.

First inhabitants of Central America. (18793)

First initiatory catechism. 26378

First issue. Frank Swick's resident and business directory. 75297

First jubilee of American independence. (24408)

First jubilee of the Newark Mechanics' Association. 54881

1st July, 1856. 10384

First Latin book. 85355

First lecture before the Protestant Alliance. (37780)

First lecture on popular education. 94513

First lessons in Delaware. 47377

First lessons in the history of the United States. 24409

First lessons in the history of the United States: compiled for the use of the junior classes. 95225

First letter [by Samuel Worcester.] 96412

First letter of Mr. Jenyns. 95315

First letter . . . on Negro slavery. (33074), note after 104595

First letter to R. F. Buxton. (13526)

First letter to the citizens of . . . Pennsylvania. (61663)

First letter to the people of England. 80045

First love of Aaron Burr. 9214

First Lutheran Church, Albany. see Albany. First Lutheran Church.

First map of Kentucky. 84936

First Massachusetts Infantry Veteran Association. 45734

First measures necessary. 24410

First meeting. 75715

First Methodist Episcopal Church in New Haven, Conn. 84325

First minister of the Dutch Reformed Church in the United States. 48688

First monthly report of the Merchants' Union Law Company. 47923

First Moravian Church, Philadelphia. see Philadelphia. First Moravian Church.

First mortgage, convertable bonds. 12666

First mortgage loan of the Southern Pennsylvania Iron and Rail Road Company, $625,000. 88441

First mortgage of the South Carolina Rail Road Company. 88026

First mortgage, sinking fund, gold bonds, seven per cent. interest. 89899

First National Bank, St. Albans, Vt. see St. Albans, Vt. First National Bank.

First New England Temperance Convention, Boston, 1866. see New England Temperance Convention, 1st, Boston, 1866.

First New Jerusalem Society of Cincinnati. see New Jerusalem Church. First Society, Cincinnati.

First of a series of a work. 24411

First of a series of American tales. 12915

First of August. Abolition of the apprenticeship. 95495

First of August, 1838. 35582

First of patriots gathered to his grave. (4629)

First of the Knickerbockers: a tale of 1673. 51636, 59197

First organization of colored troops in the state of New York. (53670), 57594

First Parish, Dorchester, Mass. see Dorchester, Mass. First Parish.

First Parish, Danvers, Mass. see Danvers, Mass. First Parish.

First Parish, Duxbury, Mass. see Duxbury, Mass. First Parish.

First Parish, Portland, Me. see Portland, Me. First Parish.

First Parish, Salem Village, Mass. see Salem Village, Mass. First Parish.

First Parish and Congregational Society, Berlin, Mass. see Berlin, Mass. First Congregational Church.

First Parish Church, Cambridge, Mass. see Cambridge, Mass. First Parish Church.

First Parish Church, Needham, Mass. see Needham, Mass. First Parish Church.

First Parish Library, Groton, Mass. see Groton, Mass. First Parish Library.

First Parish Sabbath School, Charlestown, Mass. see Charlestown, Mass. First Parish Sabbath School.

First part of a general treatise on the slavery question. 36571

First part of a series of letters. 97621, 3d note after 105973

First part of the Burning fen. 72763

First part of the North American pilot. (35967)

First part of the synoptical flora Telluriana. 67451

First part of the dvply [sic] to M. S. 91384

First pastoral letter. 92683

First patent for the plantation of Virginia in 1606. 66686

First planters of New-England. (21090), 33698, 78431-78432, 104846, 106052

First Plymouth patent. 19051, (63477)

First Presbyterian Church, Albany. see Albany. First Presbyterian Church.

First Presbyterian Church, Asylum, Pa. see Asylum, Pa. First Presbyterian Church.

First Presbyterian Church, Buffalo, N. Y. see Buffalo, N. Y. First Presbyterian Church.

First Presbyterian Church, Charleston, S. C. see Charleston, S. C. First Presbyterian Church.

First Presbyterian Church, Durham, N. Y. see Durham, N. Y. First Presbyterian Church.

First Presbyterian Church, Hudson, N. Y. see Hudson, N. Y. First Presbyterian Church.

First Presbyterian Church, Milwaukee. see Milwaukee. First Presbyterian Church.

First Presbyterian Church, New York. see New York (City) First Presbyterian Church.

First Presbyterian Church, Newburgh, N. Y. see Newburgh, N. Y. First Presbyterian Church.

First Presbyterian Church, Newburyport, Mass. see Newburyport, Mass. First Presbyterian Church.

First Presbyterian Church, Philadelphia. see Philadelphia. First Presbyterian Church.

First Presbyterian Church, Portsmouth, Ohio. see Portsmouth, Ohio. First Presbyterian Church.

First Presbyterian Church, Utica, N. Y. see Utica, N. Y. First Presbyterian Church.

First Presbyterian Church, Stamford, Conn. see Stamford, Conn. First Presbyterian Church.

First Presbyterian Church, Stamford, Conn. Covenant and membership. 90121

First Presbyterian Church, Troy, N. Y. see Troy, N. Y. First Presbyterian Church.

First Presbyterian Church of Southwark. 61666

First Presbytery of the Eastward. pseud. Bath-kol. see Murray, John.

First principles of human knowledge. (36292)

First principles of moral philosophy. 23091, 36293-36294

First principles of New-England. (46683)

First principles of popular education. (67802)

First principles of the doctrine of Christ. 24578

First principles of the oracles of God. 80199-80201, (80257)-80258

First proceedings of the Society for the Encouragement of Arts, Manufactures, and Commerce established in Barbadoes, 1781. 34825

First productive spelling book. 83651

First proposals made in America. 7264

First Protestant Dutch Church, Schenectady, N. Y. see Schenectady, N. Y. First Protestant Dutch Church.

First quarter century of the Winslow Church. 5788

First quarterly report . . . see Report . . .

First quinquennial register and circular. 53967

First reader for southern schools. (24412)

First reading book in the Micmac language. 67755

First record of Connecticut. 6010

First records of Anglo-American colonization. 95634

First reflections on reading the President's message. 29932

First Reformed Dutch Church, Hudson, N. Y. see Hudson, N. Y. First Reformed Dutch Church.

First Reformed Dutch Church, Schenectady, N. Y. see Schenectady, N. Y. First Reformed Dutch Church.

First relation of Iames Carthier. 11144, 80706

First religious general with his army. 56206

First Religious Society, Newburyport, Mass. see Newburyport, Mass. First Religious Society.

First report . . . see Report . . .

First republic. 99855

First re-union a great success. 87000

First reunion of the Sons of Vermont. 87111

First ripe fruits. 45463

First Sabbath School Society in Massachusetts. 12098
First School Society, Hartford, Conn. Board of School Visitors. (30661), 53021
First, second, and third books of history. (27914)
First, second, third, and fourth voyages of Columbus. (14655)
First, second, third and fourth years of the war. 94085
First reader for the use of primary schools. (12286)
First semi-annual report . . . see Report . . .
First semi-centennial anniversary of the Philomathean Society. 62552
Ist series. No. 217. 91044
First sermon in St. Mary's Church, Burlington. 20391
First sermon preached in the New Meeting-House of the First Parish. 37752
First set of the fundamental constitutions. 11067, 31630, 1st note after 87851
First settlement of New England. 12988
First settlers. 100467
First settlers of New-England. 12714, (76379)
First settlers of Southold. (28811)
First settlers of Virginia. 18849, 100467, 101204
First Society, Castine, Me. see Castine, Me. First Society.
First Society, Coventry, Conn. see Coventry, Conn. First Society.
First Society, Danbury, Conn. see Danbury, Conn. First Society.
First Society of Unitarian Christians, Philadelphia. see Unitarian Church. Philadelphia. First Society.
First speech, . . . delivered in 1818. 8466
First speech on the report. 67832
First State Exhibition by the Mass. Board of Agriculture. 45824
First steamship pioneers. 86018
First step in crime leads to the gallows. (19107)
First step to the art of reading. note after 65546
First steps to geography. 105096
First supplement . . . see Supplement . . .
First supplementary catalogue of the Athenaeum Library. (66309)
First supplementary catalogue of the Library of the Providence Athenaeum. (66309)
First Sussex centenary. 21874, 93939, note after 97514
First Texan novel. 51651
First three English books on America. 99366, note after 99383C
First trial of A. Morhouse. 96907
First triennial catalogue . . . see Catalogue. . . .
First triennial register of the . . . State Normal School. 53195
First Trinitarian Congregational Church of Christ, Scituate, Mass. see Scituate, Mass. First Trinitarian Congregational Church of Christ.
First trip on the Great Pacific Railroad. 33685
Firts Troop Philadelphia City Cavalry. see Pennsylvania. Militia. Philadelphia City Cavalry. First Troop.
First twenty years of my life. 71120
First Unitarian Church, Buffalo, N. Y. see Buffalo, N. Y. First Unitarian Church.

First Unitarian Church in Buffalo: its history and progress. 9058
First Unitarian Church of Christ, Roxbury, Mass. see Roxbury, Mass. First Unitarian Church of Christ.
First Unitarian Congregational Society, Nashua, N. H. see Nashua, N. H. First Unitarian Congregational Society.
First Universalist Church, Philadelphia. see Philadelphia. First Universalist Church.
First Universalist Society, New Bedford, Mass. see New Bedford, Mass. First Universalist Society.
First Universalist Society, Roxbury, Mass. see Roxbury, Mass. First Universalist Society.
First victory of the southern troops. (3966)
First visit of La Salle to the Senecas, in 1669. 44807
First visit to Washington. 97070
First voyage round the world, by Magellan. 62806, note after 90319
First voyage to the coast of California. 94437
First voyages to divers parts of America. 66686
First war-path. 16430
First white man of the west. 24785
First wife of William Starkie Bliss. pseud. Sketches of the life and character. 5940
First year of the war. 63855-63857
First year of the war in America. 63858
First year of Winthrop's journal. 104847
First years of Minnesota. 5604
Firth, Son & Co. firm publishers 86268
Fiscal Convention, New York, 1864. 24413
Fiscal Convention. Hints for the people, &c. 24413
Fiscal de la Ilustrisima Corte de Apelaciones. pseud. Vista del Fiscal. see Elizalde, Fernando Antonio. supposed author
Fiscal history of Texas. (28071)
Fisch, G. 24414
Fisch, Georges, 1814-   24415-24416
Fischer, Augustin. 5200, 24417, 48304
Fischer, Christian August, 1771-1829. 4382, 16583, (24418)-24420, (59572)
Fischer, Emil. 60328
Fischer, J. ed. 101017
Fischer, Jean-Eberhard. (24421)
Fischer, Johann G. 24422
Fischer, Johannes Jacob Gottlob. 2098, 24423
Fischer, P. (24424)-24425
Fisco i los derechos sobre la azucar. 87252
Fiset, Louis Joseph Cyprien. ed. 10455, (12573), (41510)
Fish, Allen. 101141
Fish, Elisha. 24426-24429, 25199
Fish, F. G. (8318), note after 93743
Fish, Hamilton, 1808-1893. 24430-(24431), 53616 see also New York. Governor, 1849-1851 (Fish)
Fish, Henry Clay, 1820-1877. 24432-24436
Fish, Jesse. 27981, 101042
Fish, Joseph. 2627, 2629, 24437-24441
Fish, Phineas. 24442-(24443)
Fish, Samuel. 24444, 33691
Fish, T. G. (8318), 24445, note after 93743
Fish, W. H. 24446
Fish, William S. defendant 24447
Fish and fishing in the United States. (31463)-31464
Fish, by J. Richardson. 31945
Fish. By John Richardson. 71028
Fish. [By Sir John Richardson.] 71033
Fish, by the Rev. Leonard Jenyns. 18649

Fish caught in his own net. 2627, 2629, 24439
Fish culture compared in importance with agriculture. 73106
Fish hatching and fish catching. 73107
Fishback, James. (24449), 96122
Fishback, William M. 24450
Fisher, -------. (24495)
Fisher, Abiel, 1787-1862. 24451-24452
Fisher, Alexander. 24453, 62509
Fisher, Allen. 42006
Fisher, Benjamin. 92914
Fisher, C. M. 24454, 82143
Fisher, Charles. 24455
Fisher, Charles Edward. (24456)
Fisher, Christian August. see Fischer, Christian August, 1771-1829.
Fisher, E. T. tr. 69745
Fisher, Edmund Crisp. 24457, (76648) see also United States Sanitary Commission. English Branch. Agent.
Fisher, Ellwood. 24458, 51593
Fisher, George. pseud.?? 24459, 94713
Fisher, George. tr. 95063
Fisher, George, b. 1795. 24460
Fisher, George Adams. 24461
Fisher, George E. 24462, 88127
Fisher, George J. 24463
Fisher, George Park, 1827-1909. 2675, 24464-24465
Fisher, George Purnell, 1818-1899. (24466)
Fisher, George S. 24467
Fisher, H. D. 63939
Fisher, Herbert W. 24468
Fisher, Hugh. (24469)-24470, 83436
Fisher, J. 35966
Fisher, Jacob. 24471
Fisher, James H. 24472
Fisher, John. 86351
Fisher, Jonathan. (24473)
Fisher, Joshua. cartographer 16278, 35966, 35968, (55557)
Fisher, Joshua, M. D. 24474
Fisher, Joshua Francis, 1807-1873. 21385, 24475-24477, 84678C
Fisher, L. P. 24478
Fisher, M. P. (4153)
Fisher, Miles. 61935
Fisher, Nathaniel, 1742-1812. 24479-(24480), 101882
Fisher, Peter. 24481
Fisher, R., fl. 1737. 24484
Fisher, R., fl. 186-? (24482)
Fisher, Redwood S., 1782-1856. ed. 23363, 24483, (39756), (51999)
Fisher, Richard Swainson. 14787, 14789, 24485-24494, 36182, 37429, 39213, (57345), 88947
Fisher, Samuel, 1605-1665. 24496
Fisher, Samuel, fl. 1793. 61935
Fisher, Samuel, fl. 1808-1839. 24497
Fisher, Samuel H. 24498
Fisher, Samuel W. defendant 24499, 62134
Fisher, Samuel Ware, 1814-1874. 14286, 24500-24503, 30063
Fisher, Sydney George, 1856-1927. 24504-24506, 27155, 39336
Fisher, Thomas Jefferson. 89360
Fisher, William. (24507)-24509, 40832, 96499
Fisher, William A. 45396
Fisher, William Logan. (24510)-24512
Fisher. firm. see Turner & Fisher. firm publishers
Fisher (C. J. B.) publisher 89508
Fisher (James) publisher (17576)

Fisher and Inman. firm publishers 89508
Fisher in small streams. pseud, Scribblings and sketches. see Watmough, Edward Coxe. and Brown, William Linn. incorrectly supposed author
Fisheries, 1826-1830. 42382
Fisheries of Cape Ann. 84323
Fisheries of Gloucester. (65942)
Fisheries of Massachusetts. 94007
Fisherman. pseud. Letter to the West India merchants. see B., M. pseud.
Fisher-man's calling. 46329
Fishermen's memorial and record book. (65942)
Fishermen's own book. (65942)
Fisher's advertiser's guide. 24478
Fisher's colonial magazine. 3218
Fisher's Crockett almanac. (17576)
Fisher's magazine and industrial record. 24483
Fisher's River (North Carolina) scenes and characters. 94255
Fishes. 53786, 69946
Fishes, by Charles Girard. 69946
Fishes, by John Richardson. 28401, 71032
Fishes. By Sir John Richardson. 28401, 71032
Fishes of Guiana. 77788
Fishing bounties. 42
Fishing in American waters. (78267)
Fishkill-Landing, N. Y. Temperance Society. see Temperance Society of Fishkill Landing, N. Y.
Fisico Christiano parte primera. 57811
Fisk, Mrs. ------. defendant before church council 24528, 33973, 63380
Fisk, Amasa. (24514)
Fisk, Charles B. 24515, 60750
Fisk, Clinton B. 24516
Fisk, Elisha, fl. 1766. 24517
Fisk, Elisha, 1769-1851. 24518-24519
Fisk, Ezra. (24520)
Fisk, Fidelia. 24521
Fisk, H. 24522-24523
Fisk, Isaac. 24524
Fisk, James L. 24526
Fisk, L. R. (24527)
Fisk, Phineas. 24529
Fisk, Richmond. 24530
Fisk, Samuel. 24531-24534, 75666, 79415
Fisk, Theophilus. 24535-24536, (51958)
Fisk, W. 2486, 1st note after 99826
Fisk, Wilbur. (24537)
Fiske, -------, fl. 1872. (71791)
Fiske, Abel. 24538-(24539)
Fiske, Albert A. 24540-(24541)
Fiske, Ann. 24542
Fiske, Calvin. 105417
Fiske, D. T. 24543
Fiske, Daniel Willard. 24544
Fiske, E. R. ed. 57562
Fiske, John. 24545-24546
Fiske, John O. 24547-(24548)
Fiske, Nathan. 24549-24553
Fiske, Oliver. 24554
Fiske, Samuel. (24555)
Fiske, Thadeus. 24556-(24557)
Fiske, Theophilus. see Fisk, Theophilus.
Fisler, L. F. (24558)
Fist, Samuel. 75666
Fita, Juan Salcedo. see Salcedo Fita, Juan.
Fita y Carrion, Francisco Xavier de la. 77141
Fitch, -------. 66686
Fitch, -------. illus. 32822-32823, 32866

Fitch, Mrs. ------. 49682
Fitch, A. 24560
Fitch, A. petitioner 24561
Fitch, Abel F. defendant 24559, 48784
Fitch, Asa. 24562-24563
Fitch, Charles. 24564-24565
Fitch, Charles E. 24566-24567
Fitch, Ebenezer, 1756-1833. 24568, 105896
Fitch, Eleazar Thompson, 1791-1871. 18972, (24569), 105842
Fitch, Elijah. 24570
Fitch, Henry S. 24571-24572
Fitch, J. P. 102096
Fitch, Jabez, 1672-1746. 24573-24576, 63394, 80794
Fitch, James, 1622-1702. 24577-24579
Fitch, James, fl. 1842. 24580
Fitch, Jeremiah. 103184
Fitch, John, of Alton, Ill. 24585-(24587)
Fitch, John, 1743-1798. 3521, 24582, 74126, 82974, 82976
Fitch, John, 1770-1827. 24583-24584
Fitch, L. W. 60868
Fitch, Ralph. 66686
Fitch, Thomas, 1700-1774. 15801, 15855, 24588-24589, note after 68296, 77394, 86728 see also Connecticut (Colony) Governor, 1754-1766 (Fitch)
Fitch, Thomas, 1838-1923. 24590
Fitch Brothers & Co. firm 24560-24561
Fitchburg, Mass. 24592
Fitchburg, Mass. Auditing Committee. 24602
Fitchburg, Mass. City Council. 85491
Fitchburg, Mass. Ecclesiastical Council, 1802. see Congregational Churches in Massachusetts. Ecclesiastical Council, Fitchburg, 1802.
Fitchburg, Mass. Northfield Institute. see Northfield Institute, Fitchburg, Mass.
Fitchburg, Mass. Ordinances, etc. 24591
Fitchburg, Mass. School Committee. 24602
Fitchburg, Mass. Selectmen. 24602
Fitchburg, Mass. Trinitarian Church. 24601
Fitchburg, Mass. Washington Benevolent Society. see Washington Benevolent Society. Fitchburg.
Fitchburg almanac, directory and advertiser. 8494
Fitchburg almanac, directory, and business advertiser for 1871. 24596
Fitchburg and Worcester Railroad Company. 24598
Fitchburg directory. 24597
Fitchburg Railroad. 24599
Fitchburg Railroad. Committee of Investigation. 24599
Fitchburg Railroad. Directors. Committee. 24599
Fitten, J. H. ed. 88341
Fittler, ------. engr. 13420
Fitton, James. (24603)
Fitts, James Hill. 24604
Fitz, Daniel. 24605-24606
Fitz, Henry. ed. 84281
Fitz, John. 24607
Fitz-Geffrey, Charles. 24608
Fitz-Gibbon, ------. 63302
Fitz-Herbert, Humphrey. 66686
Fitz-James, Zillah. (24621)
Fitz-Green Halleck: a memorial. (17323)
Fitze-Greene [sic] Halleck. 21496
Fitzers, William. (8784)
Fitzgeorge's narrative. 102206
Fitzgerald, Edward. 24611
Fitzgerald, J. B. 77599

Fitzgerald, James Edward. 24609
Fitzgerald, John, fl. 1854. 24610
Fitzgerald, John, fl. 1864. 57835
Fitzgerald, Ross. see Ross, Fitzgerald.
Fitzgerald, Thomas. 27047, note after 102702
Fitzgerald, W. 24613
Fitzgerald, W. N. P. 90022
Fitzgerald, W. P. N. 24614
Fitzgibbon, J. 24615-25616
Fitzharris, James Howard, Viscount. see Malmesbury, James Howard, 3d Earl of.
Fitzherbert, Sir William. supposed author 41286, 1st note after 95742
Fitzhugh, Augustine. engr. 88221
Fitzhugh, George. 24617-24618
Fitzhugh, William Henry. 24619-(24620)
Fitzhugh's copy, 1694. 88221
Fitzmaurice, Henry Petty. see Lansdowne, Henry Petty Fitzmaurice, 3d, Marquis of, 1780-1863.
Fitzmaurice, William Petty. see Lansdowne, William Petty Fitzmaurice, 1st Marquis of, 1737-1805.
Fitzpatrick, Sir Jeremiah. (24622)
Fitzpatrick, John C. ed. 98409, 98425, 101546A, 101696, 101700, 101702, 101710, 101767
Fitzpen or Phippen, and allied families. 62570
Fitzroy, Alexander. 24624
Fitzroy, Augustus Henry. see Grafton, Augustus Henry Fitzroy, 3d Duke of, 1735-1811.
Fitzroy, James. see Monmouth and Buccleuch, James Fitzroy, Duke of, 1649-1685.
Fitzroy, Robert, 1805-1865. (18647), (24625)-(24628), 26558, 37826, 87325, 89971
Fitzsimmons, Thomas. pseud. Essays upon French spoliations. 24629
Fitzsimmons, Thomas. (61975)
Fitzsimons, Thomas, 1741-1811. 75018
Fitzwilliam, Charles William Wentworth Fitzwilliam, Earl, 1786-1857. ed. 9304
Fitzwilliam, William Wentworth. see Milton, William Fitzwilliam, Viscount, 1839-1877.
Five acres too much. 73108
Five and twenty years ago. 34864
Five answers to my Neighbor Parley's five letters. 17329, 24632, (27898), 52278, 104311
Five articles originally published in the Evening post. 24274
Five Cent Savings Bank, Lowell, Mass. see Lowell Five Cent Savings Bank, Lowell, Mass.
Five . . . clergymen. pseud. Recommendatory preface. 12331, 13350
Five cotton states and New York. (14909)
Five dialogues on the grounds and causes of the division. 84761
Five discourses. . . . By Thomas D'Arcy McGee. 43261
Five discourses. Containing a careful enquiry. 91114
Five discourses on contrary subjects. 64680
Five discourses on the truth and inspiration of the Bible. 2623
Five dissertations on the scripture account. 12331
Five essays, on the laws and politics of our country. 59085
Five government tests. 32542
Five hundred curious and interesting narratives and anecdotes. 97914
Five hundred pounds reward. (44641)
560,000 acres pine lands. 75430

Five hundred thousand strokes for freedom.
40946

Five Indian Nations of Canada. Treaties, etc.
14273-14275

Five last protests enter'd on the journals.
65862, 88190

Five lessons for young men. 88641

Five letters addressed to the yeomanry of the
United States. (39242)

Five letters, by Patrioticus. 74294

Five letters from a gentleman in Guadaloupe.
29044, note after (68267)

Five letters from Job Scott. 78286

Five letters from Scotland. 9372, 81492

Five letters to a friend in Great Britain.
94610

Five letters to Governor Hamilton. 30016

Five letters to my neighbor Smith. 17329,
24632, (27898), 52278, 104311

Five letters to Rev. Eli Smith. 105234

Five letters to the Hon. M. C. Cameron.
74583

Five letters upon different moral subjects.
37305

Five letters, with remarks. 82483

Five love adventures of S. Slug. (71719)

Five minutes answer to Paine's letter. 58228,
101809

Five months among the Yankees. 37169

Five months in Labrador and Newfoundland.
97297

Five months in rebeldom. 47981

Five months in the New York State Lunatic
Asylum. 24633

Five Nations of Indians. 66061 see also
Cayuga Indians. Mohawk Indians. Oneida
Indians. Onondaga Indians. Seneca
Indians.

Five Nations of Indians. Treaties, etc. 24712,
(27056), 36718, (58936), (60733)

Five occasional lectures. (26136)

Five per cent. impost act considered and
recommended. 97439

Five Points House of Industry, New York. see
New York (City) Five Points House of
Industry.

Five Points Mission, New York. see New
York (City) Five Points Mission.

Five points monthly record. 24634, 54419

Five Professional Gamblers, Vicksburg, d.
1835. defendants 33250, note before
91708

Five sermons and a prayer. 77281

Five sermons and appendix. 30172, 62419,
94687

Five sermons. . . . By Charles Chauncy.
12331

Five sermons on several subjects. [By Increase Mather.] 46684

Five sermons on several subjects. [By
Jonathan Mayhew.] 47150

Five sermons on the following subjects. 103515

Five sermonson the strongman . . . armed.
(14525)

Five sermons preached before the Corporation
for the Relief of the Widows and Children
of Clergymen. 84570

Five sermons, viz I. The wise and foolish
virgins. 103516

Five sermons: viz. The first on Septemb. 30.
1711. 100709

Five short sermons. 83434

Five strange wonders of the world. 104194

5,000 dollars! By authority. 94741

Five travel scripts commonly attributed to
Edward Ward. 101285-101286

Five years among the Indians! 92742

Five years before the mast. (31121)

Five years' church work in the kingdom of
Hawaii. 90106

Five years in a lottery office. 50540

Five years in Pennsylvania. 23294

Five years in the Alleghanies. (24635)

Five years in Trinidad and St. Vincent. 10938

Five years' ministry. (9100)

Five years of ministerial life. 59009

Five years of prayer, with the answers.
(65539)

Five years on the Erie Canal. 21716

Five years' progress of the slave power.
(12012), 24636

Five years' residence in Buenos Ayres. (9014)

Five years' residence in the Canadas. 94229

Five years' residence in the West Indies.
18964

Five years within the golden gate. 77347

Fix, Theodore. 24637

Flaccus. pseud. Passaic. see Ward, Thomas,
1807-1873.

Flaccus, Horatius. pseud. see Horatius
Flaccus. pseud.

Flachat, Jules. 24638

Flack, Captain. (24639)-24641

Flacourt, Etienne de. (24642)

Flag of the United States. 90573

Flag-ship. 94456

Flag of truce. By the chaplain. 24643

Flage of truce. Dedicated to the Emperor of
the French. 24644

Flaget, ------. (24645)

Flagg, Azariah C. 24647-24648, 33537, 34907,
(44305)

Flagg, Charles E. B. 24649, 87694

Flagg, Edmund, 1815-1890. 14982, 24650

Flagg, Edward. (23790), 24651

Flagg, Henry C. (24652)

Flagg, James. 26630A, 95968

Flagg, Josiah. (24654)

Flagg, Melzer. 24653

Flagg, William. 24655

Flagg, William Joseph, 1818-1898. 24656-
24658

Flagg, Wilson. 24659-24662

Flake, Osmer D. 84734, 84910

Flamant, Manuel M. tr. 12249

Flamen, Catholique zele, demeurant a Londres.
pseud. Lettre. 11603

Flameng, Leopold. illus. 4576

Flaming sword! Methodists in trouble. 85538

Flaming sword, or a sign from heaven. 101083

Flaminio, Gian Antonio, 1464-1536. 24663

Flaminius. see Flaminio, Gian Antonio, 1464-
1536.

Flanagan, Christopher. 24664

Flanagan, James Winright, 1805-1887. 24665

Flanaga, John J. 24666

Flanders, Charles W. 24667-24668

Flanders, Henry, 1826-1911. 24669-24673

Flanerie Parisienne aux Etats-Unis. (716),
946

Flaneur. pseud. Fantasque. Journal redige.
see Aubin, N.

Flanigan, J. H. 24674

Flassan, Gaetan de Raxis de, Comte. 24675

Flatbootmann. 27177

Flatbush County, N. Y. Court of Oyer and
Terminer. 65442

Flatlands, N. Y. Census, 1864. 24676

Flauvel Gouraud, J. B. G. see Fauvel
Gouraud, J. B. G.
Flavel, John, 1630?-1691. 24678-24682,
44124
Flavell, John. see Flavel, John, 1630?-1691.
Flavigny, Gratien Jean Baptiste Louis,
Vicomte de, 1741-1803? tr. (16953),
16958, 16962, 16964
Flax movement. (13509)
"Flea in the ear." 12622
Fleckno, Richard. see Flecknoe, Richard.
Flecknoe, Richard. 24684
Fleeming, John. 24685, 47407, 62743 see
also Meir and Fleeming. firm
publishers
Fleeming's register. 24685, 62743
Fleet, J. (24688)
Fleet, John. 24686
Fleet, Samuel. ed. 54771-54773
Fleet, Simon. ed 41898
Fleet, Thomas. (24687)-(24688), 86617
Fleet, William Henry. 24689
Fleet (J.) firm publishers see Fleet (T. & J.)
firm publishers
Fleet (T. & J.) firm publishers (24688), 45887
Fleet's pocket almanack. (24688)
Fleet's register and pocket almanack. (24688)
Fleetwood, William, successively Bp. of St.
Asaph, and Ely, 1656-1723. 24690
Fleetwood, or the stain of birth. 76954
Fleharty, S. F. 24691
Fleischauer, ------. (24692)
Fleischmann, Charles L. (9202), (24693)-
(24697)
Fleishman, S. L. (24698)
Fleming, Monseigneur --------. 24702-
(24703)
Fleming, Ann Cuthbert. see Knight, Ann
Cuthbert.
Fleming, Caleb. 12319
Fleming, Elizabeth, fl. 1756. 20016, 24708,
51833
Fleming, Francis Anthony. 98924
Fleming, Rev. John. 24700
Fleming, John, 1786?-1832. (24701)
Fleming, Peter. 24704-24705, 49853
Fleming, R., fl. 1701. 101877
Fleming, Sandford. 24706-(24707)
Fleming, William, M. D. 24709
Fleming, William, fl. 1756. 20016, 24708,
51833
Fleming, firm see Chaloner & Fleming.
firm
Fleming & Torrey. firm 72393
Fletcher, --------, of Saltoun. supposed
author 18549, 18571, 78211-78213,
78234
Fletcher, Judge ------. 24731
Fletcher, -------, fl. 1848. 12106
Fletcher, A. 92477
Fletcher, A. J. 70037
Fletcher, Abel. 24710
Fletcher, Alexander. (24711)
Fletcher, Benjamin. 4035, 24712-(24714),
53435, 53671, 53672 see also Delaware
(Colony) Governor, 1693-1694 (Fletcher)
New York (Colony) Governor, 1692-1697
(Fletcher) Pennsylvania (Colony) Governor,
1693-1694 (Fletcher)
Fletcher, Charles Fosdick. (24715)-24716
Fletcher, Cyrus. 24717
Fletcher, Ebenezer, 1761-1831. 9538, 24718-
24719
Fletcher, Edward H. (24720)-24721

Fletcher, Francis. (18236), 20830, (20838)-
20840, 20843, 20853-20856
Fletcher, Giles. 66686
Fletcher, Henry Charles. (24722)
Fletcher, James C. 7591, 24723, 37709,
53586
Fletcher, John. reporter 24728
Fletcher, Rev. John. 23140, (23141), (24724)-
24727, 97367
Fletcher, John, 1576-1625. note after 88547
Fletcher, John, fl. 1852. 24729
Fletcher, Joseph. 24730
Fletcher, Miriam. 24723
Fletcher, Nathaniel H. 24733
Fletcher, Reuben. 24734
Fletcher, Richard, 1788-1869. 24735, 75648
Fletcher, Robert. plaintiff 24736-24737
Fletcher, Silas S. 24738
Fletcher, Thomas. 24740
Fletcher, Thomas, fl. 1822. 24739
Fletcher, Thomas Clement, 1827-1899. 24741-
(24742), (49584), 64113 see also
Missouri. Governor, 1865-1869 (Fletcher)
Fletcher, William, d. 1699. 24743, 78661
Fletcher, William, fl. 1753. plaintiff 24744,
note before 90598, 2d note after 98664
Fletcher, William L. (64045)
Fletcher genealogy. 24721
Fletcher's Charlestown directory. 12106
Fleur de Mai. 92430-92432
Fleur-des-bois. 16526
Fleur des bois, ou les peaux rouges. 16526
Fleuriau, -------, fl. 1831. 5652
Fleuriau, Bertrand Gabriel. 24745-24747
Fleurieu, Charles Pierre Claret de, Comte de.
24748-24752, note just before 44492
Fleurr, ------. 74520
Fleurs d'Amerique, poesies nouvelles. (73479)
Fleurs des Antilles: poesies. 27497
Fleury, --------. USA 87696, note after
91395, 91428
Fleury, Jules Raymond Lame. see Lame
Eleury, Jules Raymond, 1797-1878.
Flibustier, [sic] poem en trois chants. (63707)
Flibustiers [sic] Americains. 55135
Fliegende Vogel no. 1. 19795
Fliegenden Menschen. note after 104017
Flight of a thousand converts to the West India
islands. 55878
Flight of popery from Rome to the west.
84024
Flight to America. 68489
Flinders, Matthew. RN. 21211-21215, (24758)
Flinn, Albert. 85300
Flinn, Andrew. (24759), (37232)
Flinn, J. William. ed. 85276
Flinn, Jean Adger. ed. 85276
Flint, ------. incorrectly supposed author
(23790), 24651
Flint, Mr., an independent gentleman. pseud.
Boston, 25 January, 1769. 16822
Flint, Abel, 1765-1825. (24760)-24763, 92958
Flint, Austin, 1812-1886. 9063, 24764, 76643
Flint, Charles, Louis, 1824-1889. 22085,
(24765)-24766, (30524)
Flint, H. see Flynt, H.
Flint, Henry M. 24767-24769
Flint, J. B. 47321
Flint, Jacob. (24770)-24771
Flint, James, Scotchman. 24780
Flint, James, 1779-1855. 24772-24779, 68207
Flint, John. 24781, note after 92069
Flint, Joshua Barker. 24782
Flint, Josiah. 23386, 62743
Flint, Micah P. 24783

Flint, Nelson. 24781, note after 92069
Flint, Robert F. 24781, note after 92069
Flint, Timothy. 24784-(24795), 59150, 80735, 100998, 102997
Flint, Waldo. (24796)
Flint & Pere Marquette Rail Road. 32230, 74900
Flint family. 24781, note after 92069
Flint-Steel Mining Company, Lake Superior. 24797
Flinter, George Dawson. (24798)-24801
Flip, Frank. pseud. Cockney in America. 14112
Flirtations in America. 64551
Floating drydocks. 93148
Floating flowers, from a hidden brook. 74634, note after 91914
Floating ideas of nature. 98633
Flood. A sermon. 47076
Flor, -------, Conde de Villa. see Villa Flor, ------, Conde de.
Flor, Charles, Charles O'Squarr. tr. (69041)
Flora Americae Septentrionalis. 6466
Flora Americae Septentrionalis; or, a systematic arrangement. 66728
Flora and fauna within living animals. (39906), 85072
Flora Antarctica. 32822
Flora Barbadensis. (47089)
Flora Boreali-Americana; or, the botany of the northern parts. (32865)
Flora Boreali-Americana, sistens caracteres plantarum. (48690)
Flora Brasilia exhibens characteres generum et specierum plantarum. 81290
Flora Brasiliae Meridionalis. (75218)
Flora Brasiliensis, ou histoire et description de toutes les plantes. (75219)
Flora Brasiliensisseu enumeratio plantarum. (44987)
Flora Brasiliensis sive enumeratio plantarum in Brasilia hactenus delectarum. 22562
Flora Brasiliensis sivi enumeratio plantarum in Brasilia. 44988
Flora Carolinaeensis. 80066
Flora Caroliniana. 101198
Flora Cestrica: an essay towards a catalogue. 18595
Flora Cestrica: an herborizing companion. 18596
Flora fossilis Arctica. (31229)
Flora Jamaicensis. 76420
Flora Lyndsay. 50304
Flora Marchitas. (75915)
Flora medica; a botanical account. 41293
Flora medica y util de las Antillas. 69601
Flora of Jamaica. (43236)
Flora of North America: containing abridged descriptions. 96293
Flora of North America. Illustrated by coloured figures. (3858)
Flora of north western Mexico. 78865
Flora of the British West Indian islands. 28879
Flora of the lower country of South Carolina reviewed. 84914
Flora of the northern and middle sections of the United States. 96294
Flora of the southern United States. (11972)
Flora of the state of Louisiana. 72031, (72039)
Flora of the state of New-York. 53788, note after 96294
Flora of western Eskimaux-Land. 78865
Flora Peruviana, et Chilensis. 73995
Flora Telluriana. 67451, 67464

Flora Virginica. (3808)-3809, 28923-28924
Florae Americae Septentrionalis. 25135
Florae Columbiae terrarumque adiacentium specimina selecta. 37104
Florae Columbianae prodromus. 7731
Florae Fluminensis. 98833
Florae Peruvianae, et Chilensis prodromus. 73993-73994
Florae Philadelphicae prodromus. 3859
Florae Scandinaviae prodromus. (70151)
Floral department. 84140-84141
Floral home. 5604
Floral magazine and botanical repository. 38847
Floral medical y util. 28942
Flora's dictionary. 104867-104868
Flora's interpreter, or fortuna flora. 29670
Flora's interpreter: or, the American book of flowers. 29670
Floran, Juan. tr. 97027
Flore Canadienne. (66234)
Flore de Antilles. 97508
Flore de terre nueve. 2605, 24802
Flore des jardins du Roy des Pays Bas. 1580
Flore Louisiane. 72031, (72039)
Flore medicale des Antilles. 19693
Flore pittoresque et medicale des Antilles. 19693
Florance, Thomas B. 24803, 51972
Florence, Ala. Wesleyan University. see Florence Wesleyan University, Florence, Ala.
Florence Company. (24804)
Florence Murray. (51498)
Florence Percy. pseud. Forest buds. see Allen, Elizabeth (Chase) Akers, 1832-1911.
Florence, the parish orphan. (39731)
Florence Wesleyan University, Florence, Ala. Dialectical Society. 88324
Florence Wesleyan University, Florence, Ala. LaFayette Society. 88324
Florencia, Francisco de. 24805-24819, 80987, 99450
Florencia, Francisco de. supposed author 24818, 29033, 39891
Florent Bouchard de la Poterie, Claud. see Bouchard de la Poterie, Claud Florent.
Florentine gazette. 35933, note after 92859
Flores, --------, fl. 1624. 69233
Flores, Alonzo. 24823
Flores, Antonio. 24820
Flores, Francisco Fernando de. (24821)
Flores, Luis. 24822
Flores, Venancio. 24829
Flores Alatorre, Juan Jose. (48665), 98823, 1st note after 99783
Flores de Ribera, Antonio. see Flores de Ribera, Jose Antonio.
Flores de Ribera, Jose Antonio. 24824, (70796)
Flores de Pascua, -------. 24825-24826
Flores de Valdes, Rodrigo Garcia. 24828
Flores Estrada, Alvaro, 1766?-1854? 23057-23059
Flores y Aguilar, Nic. (24827)
Flores de mar. 29045
Flores del destierro. 71636
Flores do Lima. (4949)
Flores Guadalupanas. 63305
Flores illustrium epitaphiorum. 24830
Flores singelas. 58135
Flores y lagrimas. 25101
Floresta. 24831
Floresta de la Santa Iglesia. 73168
Floresta Espanola Peruana. (24832)

Florez, Dionysio de Ribera. see Ribera
    Florez, Dionysio de.
Florez, Fr. Henrique. 24833-24834
Florez, Pedro Celestino. 24836
Florez, Palacido. 24837
Florez de Ocariz, Juan. 24835, 56624
Floriad. 24838, 97799
Florian, Jean Pierre Claris de, 1755-1794.
    (79484)
Florian claim. 24839
Floriano de Toledo, Joaquim. see Toledo,
    Joaquim Floriano de.
Florianus, Ioannis. see Florio, John, 1553?-
    1625.
Florida (Spanish Colony) see also East
    Florida. West Florida.
Florida (Spanish Colony) Gobernador, 1699-1706
    (Zuniga y la Cerda) 106403 see also
    Zuniga y la Cerda, Jose de.
Florida (Territory) 24847-24848, 99607
Florida (Territory) Constitutional Convention,
    St Joseph, 1838. (24870)
Florida (Territory) House of Representatives.
    Bank Committee. 97757
Florida (Territory) House of Representatives.
    Judiciary Committee. 97757
Florida (Territory) Laws, statutes, etc. 24843,
    24849, 24850, 24877, 24880, 24892,
    72430, 103434
Florida (Territory) Legislative Council. 24873,
    97757
Florida (Territory) Senate. 24875
Florida (Territory) Superior Court. 83356
Florida. complainant 27048
Florida. Constitution. 1269, 5316, 16113,
    24851-(24853), 33137, (66397)
Florida. Constitutional Convention, 1861.
    24852
Florida. Constitutional Convention, 1868.
    (24853), 24871
Florida. General Assembly. 24844-(24845),
    34926
Florida. General Assembly. Committee to
    Investigate the Actions of Governor
    Harrison Reed, 1868. 24868
Florida. General Assembly. House of Repre-
    sentatives. 24872
Florida. General Assembly. Senate. (24874)
Florida. Governor, 1849-1853 (Brown) 24885
    see also Brown, Thomas, 1785-1867.
Florida. Governor, 1857-1861 (Perry) 33150
    see also Perry, Madison S.
Florida. Governor, 1865 (Marvin) 45035 see
    also Marvin, William, 1808-1892.
Florida. Governor, 1868-1872 (Reed) (24890),
    68544 see also Reed, Harison, 1813-
Florida. Laws, statutes, etc. 23765, 24842,
    24844-(24845), 24876, 24880, (24883),
    52051, 70820-70821, 82438, 89066, 2d
    note after 95517
Florida. Lieutenant Governor, 1868-1872
    (Gleason) (24890) see also Gleason,
    ------.
Florida. Supreme Court. (24890)
Florida. Union Bank. see Union Bank of
    Florida.
Florida (Diocese) see also Cuba (Diocese)
    Louisiana and the Floridas (Diocese)
Florida (Diocese) Synod, 1684. (80023), 90830
Florida, N. Y. S. S. Seward Institute. see
    S. S. Seward Institute, Florida, N. Y.
Florida, N. Y. Washington Benevolent Society.
    see Washington Benevolent Society. New
    York. Florida.
"Florida." 90065

Florida als Auswanderung-Kolonie. 18353
Florida and the game water-birds. (73109)
Florida colonist. 24862
Florida contested election of United States
    Senator. 90391
Florida del Ynca. 3349, 98744-98745, 98752
Florida en Mexico. 106334
Florida Historical Society, Saint Augustine.
    23668, 24867
Florida: its climate, soil, and productions.
    24862
Florida mirror. 92221
Florida; or, the iron will. (19574)
Florida Peninsula Land Company. 24846
Florida pirate. 24863
Florida reef. 16450
Florida Telegraph Company. 24904
Florida Telegraph Company. petitioners
    69676, 84773
Florida und Mexico. 106336
Floride. 101350
Florido, Silvester. ed. 29029
Floridus. see Lambertius, -------.
Florilegio da poesia Brazileira. (7582), 99734
Florilegio medicinal. 23051, note after 91199
Florilegio romantico serie ottava. 92586
Florio, John, 1553?-1625. 11144, (40046),
    80706, 99866
Floris, P. Williamson. 66686
Florist and horticultural journal. 24906
Florula Atacamensis. 62452
Florula Bostoniensis. 5297
Florula Columbiana. (20305)
Florula Columbiensis. 20304
Florula Guatimalensis. 5015
Florula Lancastriensis. 5311
Florula Ludoviciana. 72031, (72039)
Florule Louisvillensis. (43587)
Floss, Ph. von Roesgen von. see Roesgen
    von Floss, Ph. von.
Flotta auss Engelland nach Virginia. (69296)
"Floure of souvenance." 51724
Flourish of the annual spring. (9717)
Flournoy, John Jacobus. 24907-(24909)
Flournoy, John James. see Flournoy, John
    Jacobus.
Flower, Benjamin. 24911
Flower, Richard. (24910)-24911, 34730
Flower, Samuel. (37134)
Flower-du-luce. (41932)
Flower of Shenandoah. 18271
Flowerdew, D. C. 24912
Flowering reed. pseud. Dedicated to "Hon.
    Martin J. Crawford." 81952
Flowers, C. reporter 43648
Flowers from the battle-field. 9750
Flowers of hope and memory. Poems. 36642
Flowers of literature, being a compendious
    exhibition. (7380)
Flowers of literature, wit and sentiment.
    11335
Flowers of modern history. 223
Flowers of modern travels. 224
Flowers of melody. 28225
Flowers plucked by a traveller on the journey
    of life. 15462
Flowery legend of Our Lady of Guadalupe.
    20616
Flowret. A collection of poems. 84838
Floy, Michael. 41291
Floy, -------. USA 49073
Floyd, B. (42476)
Floyd, John, 1783-1837. 87423 see also
    Virginia. Governor, 1830-1834 (Floyd)

Floyd, John Buchanan, 1807-1863. 3926, 24913-(24914), 40362, (54609), 88350 see also U. S. War Department. Virginia. Governor, 1850-1852 (Floyd)

Floyd, John G. (24915)

Floyd, Mary Faith. see McAdoo, Mary Faith (Floyd)

Floyd's acceptances. (21265)

Flozelles, ------ Henrion de. see Henrion de Flozelles, -------.

Fluch und Segen der Auswanderungen. 2438

Fluchtinge. (4724)

Fluchtling. 49910

Flucker, Thomas. pseud. Thomas Gage's proclamation versified. see Trumbull, John, 1750-1831.

Fluctuations in the price of middling and fair New Orleans cotton. 50657

Flug durch die Vereinigten Staaten. 51672

Flugel, Felix. 24916

Fluminense, a poem, suggested by scenes in the Brazils. 98242

Flup answurts gemadote Reize. 7178

Flurance, R. de. 24917

Flurkarte. 71221

Flush times of Alabama and Mississippi. 2898

Flushing, N. Y. Board of Education. 24919

Flushing, N. Y. Institute. see St. Paul's College, Flushing, N. Y.

Flushing, N. Y. Linaean Botanic Gardens & Nurseries. see Linaean Botanic Gardens & Nurseries, Flushing, N. Y.

Flushing, N. Y. St. Ann's Hall. see St. Ann's Hall, Flushing, N. Y.

Flushing, N. Y. St. Paul's College. see St. Paul's College, Flushing, N. Y.

Flushing Institute, Flushing, N. Y. see St. Paul's College, Flushing, N. Y.

Flushing, past and present. 44230

Flusser, Charles T. (24923)

Flusspiraten des Mississippi. 27194

Fluvia, Francisco Xavier. 1768, 98849

Fluviatulis Piscator. pseud. Business and diversion inoffensive to God. see Seccombe, Joseph, 1706-1760.

Fly sheet. 85444

Flying artillerist. 36516

Flying bird from Missouri. (24925)

Flying Dutchman. 77338

Flying-post. 69442, 86759

Flying regiment. 28308

Flying roll, brought forth. 46330

Flying roll; or, the miscellaneous writings of Redemptio. 24925, 83790

Flying spider. 85210

Flying visits to the city of Mexico and the Pacific coast. 83475

Flynn, Thomas. 37909

Flynt, Henry. (24926)-24930, 103899

Foache, Stanislas. supposed author 21035, 68752

Fobes, D. 76515

Fobes, Perez. 24931-24932

Focard, Jacques. 24933, 58546

Focher, Joae. (24934)

Focht, D. H. 24935

Focke, H. C. 24936-(24937), 2d note after 93879

Focus. 105495

Fodere, P. Pradier. see Pradier-Fodere, P.

Foedera. 31095, 67547

Foederal . . . see Federal . . .

Foederalist . . . see Federalist . . .

Foerster, Fr. 24939

Foes of liberty. (23952)

Fogg, Christopher. defendant at court martial (37982)-37983, note after 99766, note after 100901

Fogg, Jeremiah. (20747)

Fogg, Thomas Brinley. 24940

Fogg, William. 22180, 24941

Foggy night at Newport. 55035

Fogie, Francis. pseud. Introductory chapter. 67982

Foglietta, Uberto. 24942

Fogueras, Juan. 24943

Foi portee au Nouveau Monde. Poeme. 21007

Foignet, ------. 5652-5653

Foigny, Gabriel de. 74819-(74823)

Fok: a Greenlander's travels in Europe. 24944

Fokkens, F. 24945

Folch, Vicente. see Folch y Juan, Vicente.

Folch y Juan, Vicente. 102764 see also West Florida. Governor, 1796-1812 (Folch y Juan)

Folcon, ------. 47292

Fold for Christ's sheep. 83975

Foley, Daniel. 24946

Foley, Fanny. pseud. Romance of the ocean. 24947

Folgen hernacher eigentliche Furbildung. (8784)

Folgen hernacher eigentlicke vnd warhafftige Furbildungen. (8784)

Folgen nun die Figuren. (8784)

Folgen nun die Figuren vnd Kupfferstuck. (8784)

Folgen nun die Figuren, welche ins siebende Theil. (8784)

Folger, Brazillai. claimant 51752

Folger, L. B. cartographer 84936

Folger, Peter. (24948)

Folger, Robert M. 24949

Folhinha da guerra. 24950

Folhinha a da Braz Gomes. 7583

Folie philosophique en un act. 100745

Folieta, Ubertus. see Foglietta, Uberto.

Folix, ------. tr. 98844

Folkingham, W. 24951

Follansbee, Joshua. defendant at court martial 24952

Follansbee Association. 82410

Follen, Charles. 24953

Follen, Eliza Lee. 24954-24955

Folletin [sic] del diario official del gobierno. 48478

Folleto critico-burlesco de las arenas del Uruguay. 23716

Folleto que D. Jose de la Lastra dio a luz. 71638

Follett, Frederick. (24956)

Follies of the day. 84995

Folliott, George. defendant (56802)

Following account has been compiled by N. Webster. 102354

Following account of Washington College, in the state of Connecticut, is contained in the appendix. 103167

Following act came to hand. 94142

Following address, and particular instances as to the duties. (24957)

Following address was read. 61670

Following anonymous letter was some nights ago thrown in. 86865

Following are copies of letters. 98078

Following bills, together with a letter from Governor Tryon. 97290

Following compilation from the writings of Washington. 94929, 2d note after 101745

Following composed of the lamented death of Michael Griswold. 94566

Following declaration was reported. 100021

Following eulogium on General Washington was pronounced. 101559

Following impartial work was undertaken. 98999

Following interesting intelligence, we received yesterday. 88944

Following is a dispensation. 70596

Following is a narrative of part of the transactions. 104136

Following is a true and faithful account. 66713

Following is an account of the religious experience. 104518

Following is respectfully submitted to the Senate. 93951

Following is the most particular account. 102203

Following late transactions, with some remarks on them. 87898

Following laws, supplemetary to those in the last edition. 105819-105820

Following letters are printed for private use only. 94810

Following letters are published by order. 101688

Following letters of sympathy and aid. 90172

Following lots and parts of lots in the county of Onondaga. 102132

Following memorial has been presented. 93742

Following memorial was presented. 93921

Following narrative of the exercise and experience. 104519

(Following notice of the death and character of Edward C. Upham.) 98038

Following pages are a fac-simile copy of the original history. 72721, 106070

Following paper having been much misrepresented. (68570)

Following paper was read before the Columbian Institute. 71854

Following particulars of the action between the militia &c. 104136

Following pastoral letter is so fitting. 92634

Following persons are nominated. 86984

Following petition . . . was prepared. 93180

Following portion of the warden's report is published. (75494)

Following proposed alterations or additions. 97912

Following publication, which shews the rancorous disposition. 13171, 24958

Following remonstrance, was this day presented. (59611), 61671

Following review of the origin and causes. 14899, (57604), 95108

Following speech was delivered in a public council. 89187

Following the flag. 14165

Following treatise contains a brief account. 6226

Following treatise . . . is approved of. 7286, 4th note after 99005

(Following vindication was published.) 99822, 99825

Following was wrote by an officer. 104753

Following written to the young people. 94566

Following wrote by an officer. 104750

Folly and a crime. 34748

Folly and danger of presuming on time to come. (79966)

Folly and falsehood of the Golden Book of Mormon. 89052

Folly and perjury of the rebellion in Scotland display'd. 8641

Folly as it flies. 103833

Folly as it flies; hit at by Fanny Fern. 58961

Folly of our speculations. 28013

Folly of rejecting revealed religion. 85600

Folly of sinning, opened & applied. (46685)

Folsom, Abby H. 24959

Folsom, Benjamin. (24960)

Folsom, Charles. 24961, 85071

Folsom, Charles L. 24962

Folsom, David. 89272

Folsom, George. 16943, 16964, 24963-24967, 38562, note after 86789

Folsom, George F. (24968)

Folsom, James M. 24969

Folsom, Nathaniel Smith. 24971

Folsom, Peter. 24970

Folsom's new pocket almanac for the year. 1789. 24972

Foltz, J. M. 24973

Folwell, Charles H. (54874)

Folwell, Richard. 15179, 89504

Folwell, S. illus. 44258, 105687-note after 105689, note after 105690

Folwell (Charles H) & Co. firm publishers (54874)

Fombono, Evaristo. 24974

Fonblanque, Albany. (24975)

Fond de Cale. 69042

Fonda, Sebastian F. 24976

Fondation de la republique des Etats-Unis d' Amerique. 89011-89012

Fondey, William H. (24977)

Fonfrede, J. B. Boyer. see Boyer-Fonfrede, J. B.

Fonseca, Bartolome Agustin Rodriguez de see Rodriguez de Fonseca, Bartolome Agustin.

Fonseca, Fabian de. (24978)

Fonseca, Geronimo de. defendant 86541

Fonseca, Joaquim Bento da. 24979-24980

Fonseca, Manuel da. (24981)

Fonseca, Yose Gonsalvez da. 24892

Fonseca Guimaraes, Joaquim da. see Guimaraes, Joaquim da Fonseca.

Font, Antonio Jugla y. see Jugla y Font, Antonio.

Fontaine, D. A. la. see La Fontaine, D. A.

Fontaine, Edward. 24984

Fontaine, Felix G. reporter 80849

Fontaine, Felix Gregory de. see De Fontaine, Felix Gregory, 1832-1896.

Fontaine, James. 24986-24987

Fontaine, Jean de la. see La Fontaine, Jean de.

Fontaine, L. H. la. see La Fontaine, L. H.

Fontaines, H. C. Emmery de Sept-. see Emmery de Sept-Fontaines, H. C.

Fontana, Felix. 24988-(24990)

Fontane, Marius. 24991

Fontaneda, Hernando de Escalante. 87205

Fontanedo. 24894, note after 94854, 94856

Fontanelle, Jean Gaspard Dubois. see Dubois-Fontanelle, Jean Gaspard.

Fontanes, L. 24992-(24993), note after 96377, 101800-note after 101800

Fontani, A. D. 24994

Fonte, Bartholomew de. 8834, 20404, 28460, 1st note after 94082

Fonte, Pedro Jose, Abp. 24995, 48651, see also Mexico (Archdiocese) Archbishop (Fonte)

Fontenay, Marie. 24996

Fonteneau, Jean. see Xaintoigne, Jean Alfonce de, i. e. Jean Fonteneau, known as.
Fonticello, Antonio. 24997
Fontpertuis, Adelbert Front de. see Front de Fontpertuis, Adalbert.
Food of fresh-water fishes. 84229
Foolishness of preaching. 89342
Foos, Conrad. (24998)
Foos, Joseph. (24999)
Foot, Ebenezer. see Foote, Ebenezer.
Foot, George. 25001
Foot, George F. 25008
Foot, J. B. (58880)
Foot, Jesse. 25002
Foot, John, 1742-1813. 25003
Foot, John, fl. 1862. petitioner (25004)
Foot, Joseph I. 25005-25007, 103200
Foot, Joseph J. 25008
Foot, Solomon, 1802-1866. 25010-25012, 85064
Foot, Samuel A. 25009
Foote, Mrs. -----. 25025
Foote, Andrew H. (25013)-25014
Foote, C. C. 25015
Foote, Caleb. petitioner 75691
Foote, Ebenezer. 25000, 89297
Foote, Henry. 25016
Foote, Henry G. (25017)
Foote, Henry Stuart, 1804-1880. 15285, 15390-15391, 25018-25020, 39671 see also Confederate States of America. Congress. House. Special Committee on the Recent Military Disasters.
Foote, Henry W. (25021)
Foote, J. S. 85072
Foote, James. (80215)
Foote, John J. (25022)
Foote, John P. 25023-25024
Foote, Samuel Augustus, 1780-1846. 3832, (23732), (31043)-31044
Foote, Sarah. see Smith, Sarah (Foote) 1829-
Foote, Thomas M. 25026
Foote, William Henry. 25027-25029, 85333
Foote family. (27948)
Footfalls on the boundary of another world. 58024
Foot-prints of a letter-carrier. (68639)
Footprints of a Presbyterian to spiritualism. 82552
Foot-prints of an itinerant. (26285)
Footprints of famous men. 21840
Footprints of Miles Standish. 19192
Foot-prints of Roger Williams. 51237
Footprints of travellers. 25030
Footprints of truth, or voice of humanity. (29511)
Footsteps of our forefathers. 48681
For a believer. 99285
For gratuitous distribution. 26787
For many years you have seen your country oppressed. 85199
For peace. . . . 35816
For President, Abraham Lincoln. 65894
For promoting military discipline. 104754
For sale, by subscription. 104841
For sale: one million acres of the finest agricultural and mineral lands. 88151
For the afflicted. 79196
For the benefit of the widows and orphans of the army. 25031
For the celebration of the close of the second century. (26072)
For the colony in Virginea Britannia. 99866
For the consideration of Congress. 101940
For the constitution and the laws. 105363
For the contemplation of honourable and just legislators. 25032

For the conversion of the French. 34135, 102677-102679
For the encouragement of the raising and well-curing and dressing of flax within this province. 85839
For the great empire of liberty, forward! (78031)
For the liberty of choosing our own religion. 5468
For the loyal Americans. 34135, 102677-102679
For the people. The public debt: what to do with it. 68549
For the plantation in Virginia or Nova Britannia. 99856
For the Right Honourable the Lord Elesmore. 82819
For the satisfaction of the adventurers. 46191
For the service of truth, against George Keith. 46933
For the use of the militia of Pennsylvania. 91396
For whom ought you to vote? 25033
For whom should our suffrages be given? 79692
For whom will you vote? 25033
Foraminiferas. 74921
Foraminiferes. 74922
Foraminiferes de l'ile de Cuba. (57453)
Forasmuch as notwithstanding the late publication of our purpose. 99865
Forasmuch as there have been many disputes and controversies. (69482)
Forastero. pseud. Crisis del Ensayo a la historia de la Florida. see Salazar, Joseph de.
Forayers. (81279)
Forayers, or, the raid of the dog-days. 81209, 81211
Forbes, --------. defendant 31398
Forbes, Abner. (25034), 46109
Forbes, Alexander. 25035
Forbes, Alexander C. supposed author 25047, 2d note after 96992
Forbes, Charles, M. D. 25036
Forbes, Charles. see Montalembert, Charles Forbes, Comte de.
Forbes, Darius. 25037
Forbes, E. (25043)
Forbes, Edward, 1815-1854. 36879, 71033
Forbes, Eli. 25038-25042
Forbes, J. G. reporter 25045, 33645
Forbes, James Grant. 25046
Forbes, M. 25044
Forbes, Robert. 7288
Forbes, Robert B. 25048-25051
Forbes, Playfair, W. W. Smith, Percy and Hunt. 36879
Forbin, Louis Nicolas Philippe Auguste, Comte de. 25052
Forbonnais, Francois de Vernon de. see Vernon de Forbonnais, Francois de.
Force, Peter, 1790-1868. 1521, 4366, 4889A, (9145), 9708, 9759, 11397, (12705), 13439, (13575), 17039, 17042, 19724, (20190), (24896), 25053-25059, 26274, (27018), 27037, 27113, (28046), 30102, (30701), 31739, (31919), 35677, (36286), 39425, 41460, 44080, 45000, 46642, 46732, 51028, 51810, 51194, 52595, (52617)-52618, 53249, 54971, 55933, 56098, 60918, 63310, 63311, 66724, 67574, 68369, note after 70346, 78431, 80748, 82820, 82836, 85072, 86574, 91316, 92350, 94218, 1st note after 99856, 3d note after 99856, 99860, 99866, note after

99867, 99881, 100460, 100464, 2d note after 100494, 1st note after 100507, 100547, note after 100560, 101328, 101942A, 102552, 103352-103353, 103397, 104190, 1st note after 105510, 106015

Force, W. Q. 2042, 25060-25061

Force bill. Speech of Hon. Henry C. Burnett. 9380

Force of accident. (36148)

Force of credulity. 3801

Force of right purpose. 71776

Forces de l'Europe. 25062

Ford, -------. 7052

Ford, David. 25063

Ford, Francis Clarke. 70047 see also Great Britain. Legation. Buenos-Aires. Secretary.

Ford, Henry. 25064

Ford, Henry A. 25065

Ford, J. 10118

Ford, John. 25066

Ford, John. defendant 85486

Ford, Paul Leicester, 1865-1902. 67681, 80405, 83604, 84586, 84787, 84835, note before 87733, 2d note after 87733, 90137, 91785, 93611, note after 101485, 102352, 102354, 102417, 104632

Ford, Philip. 25067

Ford, Sir Richard. supposed author 89592-89593

Ford, S. H. 25068

Ford, Sally R. 25069

Ford, Thomas. 59528, note after 93777

Ford, Thomas, 1800-1850. 25070, 83288 see also Illinois. Governor, 1842-1846 (Ford)

Ford, Timothy, 1762-1830. 25071, 87733

Ford, Timothy, 1762-1830. supposed author 22639, 87733, 22639, note after 88111, 93501

Ford, William. 25072

Ford, Worthington Chauncey, 1858- 80594, 82832, 84904, 85376, 86730, 89186, 2d note after 99911, 101710, 101726, 101767

Ford & Damrell. firm publishers 89491

Fordham, New York (City) St. John's College. see Fordham University Fordham, New York (City) St. John's College.

Fordham, New York (City) University. see Fordham University, Fordham, New York (City)

Fordham University, Fordham, New York (City) 75291

Fordham University, Fordham, New York (City) St. John's College. 75291

Fordsbush, N. Y. Convention of Ministers and Delegates of the Evangelical Lutheran Churches in New York, 1837. see Evangelical Lutheran Ministerium of the State of New York and Adjacent States and Counties. Convention of Ministers and Delegates, Fordsbush, N. Y.

Fordyce, W. defendant 104485, 104487

Fordyce (Baillie W) and Company. firm 104476

Fordyce, Grant & Co. firm 91658

Fore and act. 61399

Foregleams of immortality. 78644

Foreign affairs: a series of articles. 55008

Foreign affairs of the Argentine Confederation. 1954

Foreign author. pseud. Substance of two letters. 93378

Foreign commerce courses, John Franklin Crowell, Director. 83381

Foreign conspiracy against the liberties of the United States. 8777, 50961

Foreign countries. 83370

Foreign debt of Mexico. 72016

Foreign Emigrant Society. (25073)

Foreign enlistment act. 27297

Foreign Holders of Indiana State Bonds. Agent. see Agent of the Foreign Holders of Indiana State Bonds.

Foreign loans and their consequences considered. 41709

Foreign loans, or valuable information. 93949-93950

Foreign miscellany. 81150

Foreign missionary chronicle. (65229), note after 102979

Foreign Missionary Society of New York and Brooklyn. 89090, 92266

Foreign paupers and naturalization laws. 74321

Foreign quarterly review. 32384

Foreign relations of Great Britain. 8405

Foreign semi-monthly magazine. 10932

Foreign slave trade, a brief account of its state. 25074, note after 92002

Foreign slave trade. Abstract of the information. (81979)

Foreign slave trade the source of political power. 89748

Foreign travel and life at sea. 72417

Foreign traveller in New-York. pseud. European delineation of American character. (23111)

Foreigner. pseud. Emigration, emigrants, and Know-Nothings. 22493

Foreigner. pseud. Letters from Washington. see Watterston, George.

Foreigner., pseud. Sentiments. see Raynal, Guillaume Thomas. 68105

Foreigner in 1817-18. pseud. Constitution and laws. 16074

Foreigner's protracted journey. 23566

Foreigner's scribble for amusement. 97256

Foreman, Richard. 43875

Foreman, Walter. defendant 102781

Forende stater, nationeres under, dets fortids, nutids og fremtids historie. 84476

Forende staters historie. 3127

Forensic dispute on the legality of enslaving the Africans. 25075, (81980), note after 97552

Forenta staterna. 84475

Forenta staterna beskadede i profetians ljus. 84474

Forenta staterna och Canada. 1942

Forerunners and competitors of the pilgrims and puritans. 82815, 82823

Foresight, Ned. pseud. Vermont almanack. note after 99139

Foresight in 1819. 19435

Forest, Francois de Belle. see Belle-Forest, Francois de.

Forest, Henry de. see De Forest, Henry.

Forest, John William de. see De Forest, John William, 1826-1906.

Forest, P. 25076

Forest, T. R. de. see De Forest, T. R.

Forest. A sequel to Alban. 33970

Forest and shore. 34345

Forest stream hand-book for riflemen. 90552

Forest Arcadia of Northern New York. 25077

Forest boy. 51238

Forest buds. 60871

Forest exiles. 69043

Forest exiles; or, the adventures of a Peruvian family. (69045)

Forest exiles; or the perils of a Peruvian family amid the wilds of the Amazon. 69044
Forest flowers of the west. 71238
Forest garrison. 22297
Forest Hills Cemetery, Roxbury, Mass. see Roxbury, Mass. Forest Hills Cemetery.
Forest Hills Cemetery; its establishment, progress, scenery, monuments, etc. 17347, 25078, 73644
Forest hymn. 8816
Forest Improvement Company. Agents. petitioners 60455
Forest Lawn Cemetery, Buffalo, N. Y. see Buffalo, N. Y. Forest Lawn Cemetery.
Forest Lawn Cemetery Association, Buffalo, N. Y. 25080
Forest life. 37986, 37988
Forest life and forest trees. 89837
Forest life in Acadie. 30349
Forest lodge. A romance of Indian life. 89833
Forest Mining Company. 25081
Forest Mining Company. Charter. 25081
Forest Mining Company. Directors. 25081
Forest minstrel. 59562
Forest of Rosenwald. 91998
Forest pictures in the Adirondacks. 33391, 92775
Forest pilgrims, and other poems. 5351
Forest rose; a tale of the frontier. (4724)
Forest rose, or American farmers. 105183
Forest scenes and incidents, in the wilds of North America; being the diary of a winter's route. 31143
Forest scenes and incidents in the wolds of North America,,being a winter's route from Halifax to the Canadas. 25082
Forest Sheperd's report. (57371)
Forest tragedy and other tales. 13461, 41401
Forest tree culturist. (26156)
Foreste or collection of histories. 48246
Forester. pseud. see Paine, Thomas, 1737-1809.
Forester, Fanny. pseud. Alderbrook. see Judson, E.
Forester, Frank. pseud. see Herbert, Henry William.
Foresters, a poem, descriptive of a pedestrian journey to the falls of Niagara. 104600
Foresters; a poem, descriptive of a pedestrian journey to the falls of Niagara, in the autumn of 1804. 104599, 104601
Foresters; an American tale. 4433
Foresti, Jacobo Philippo. 24395, 25083-25088, 36987, 74659
Forestiers du Michigan. 2388, 4902
Forests of Canada. 33995
Foretaelling af Victor Hugo. (33615)
Forethought. 84810
Foretier, Marie Ambale. see Viger, Marie Amable (Foretier)
Foretokens of the pestilence and sickness. 61672
Fore-top-man. pseud. Life in a man-of-war. 41012
Forets interieures. 96441
Forets vierges. 69046
Forets vierges de la Guyane Francaise. 29174, 56210
Foreword [by David Moore.] 101936
Forfaits de Sonthonax, Victor Hugues et Lebas. (28285)
Forfaits des Jesuites au Paraguay. 25089
Forfatning. 58042

Forfeiture and confiscation of rebel property. 17221
Forge and the pulpit. 59181
Forged American certificates. 8514
Forgery detected. 20407, 48855
Forget and forgive. 44081
Forget-me-not. 89492
Forget-me-nots from New Drop Dale. 74418
Forgetfulness of God. 73880
Forgiveness. 59354
Forgotten village. 27720
Forgues, Paul Emile Daurand. tr. 16368, 92414, 92533
Forklaring ofver begynnelselaran i "Jesu Christi de siste-dagers heliges kyrka." 85525
Forlani, --------. 5000
Forlorn hope of slavery. 62856
Form for genealogical records. (54779)
Form for the solemnization of matrimony. 85292
Form . . . for the 27th of February, 1778. (25091)
Form of a legacy. 101276
Form of admission, articles of faith and covenant. 6646
Form of church government. 15445
Form of consecration of the British Chapel and Burial Ground. (14324), 25090
Form of constitution and by-laws for auxiliary societies [of the Emigrant Aid Company of Massachusetts.] 45735
Form of constitution and by-laws, for auxiliary societies [of the New England Emigrant Aid Society.] (52673)
Form of covenant adopted by the First Presbyterian Church, Buffalo. 9049
Form of covenant of the Old-South Church, Boston. (6665)
Form of covenant, of the Old-South Church, in Boston, Mass. (6663)
Form of discipline . . . of the Methodist Episcopal Church in America. 48185
Form of government for the people of Florida. 24851-24852
Form of government of the state of Louisiana. 42214
Form of government of the state of Texas. 94949
Form of passing laws. 99095
Form of prayer and thanksgiving for the blessings of civil liberty. 53110
Form of prayer and thanksgiving for the victory. 30930
Form of prayer and thanksgiving to Almighty God. 66982, (67003)
Form or prayer, ... for a general fast. (25091)
Form of prayer, for a general fast, &c., on 5th February, 1812. (25091)
Form of prayer, for a general fast, &c., on 10th March, 1813. (25091)
Form of prayer for a perpetual fast to be observed. 35580
Form of prayer, for fast day, Nova Scotia, February 23, 1810. 56132
Form of prayer for Feb. 27th, for a general fast. (25091)
Form of prayer for the fast, May 7, 1762. (25091)
Form of prayer, proper to be used in the churches in the province of New York, 13 July 1757, for a general fast. (25091)
Form of prayer, proper to be used in the churches throughout the province of New-York, on Friday the twelfth of May. (25091)

Form of prayer to be used in all churches and chapels in Ireland. (25091)

Form of prayer to be used in all churches and chapels, on the general fast. (25091)

Form of prayer, to be used in all the churches, on May 10, 1793. 56131

Form of prayer, . . . to be used in the churches throughout the province of New York. 53683

Form of prayer to be used in the Diocese of New York. 53673

Form of prayer to be used . . . November 30, 1863. 53673

Form of prayer . . . 21 Feb., 1781. (25091)

Form of Presbyterian church-government. 80715

Form of public Christian confession. 85293, 85331

Form of thanksgiving used on the occasion. 88958

Form of the declarations for assurance. 100491

Forma administrandi infirmis sacramentum Eucharistiae. 76007

Forma brev. administr. ap. Indios S. baptismo sacramentum. 48479

Forma breve de administrar los sacramentos a los Indios. 51205

Forma de el nvevo beneficio de metales de plata. 16910

Forma, y modo breve para tener a punto de guerra. 25093

Forma y modo de fundar las confradias del cordon de N. P. S. Francisco. 26092

Formacion del diccionario Hispano-Americano. 87253

Formal opening of Franklin and Marshall College. 25644

Formal opening of the Pittsburgh, Washington and Baltimore Railroad. 63126

Formaleoni, Vincenzio Antonio, 1752-1797. 25094-25095, 92197, 94571

Forman, -------, fl. 1725. 25098

Forman, Aaron. 84948-84950

Forman, J. G. (25026)-25027, 86298, note after 103016

Forman. firm see Smith & Forman. firm publishers

Formas caracteristicas de la flora Venezolana. 58925

Formation of a corps of artillery. 91568

Formento, Domingo Balcarcel y. see Balcarcel y Formento, Domingo.

Former French Roman Catholic. pseud. Startling disclosure of the secret workings of the Jesuits. 90578

Former glory of the African race. 16308

Former member of the vestry. pseud. Statement of facts. see Waterman, J. W.

Former resident of the south. pseud. Leaven for dough faces. 39546

Former review of the speeches. (78726)

Formidable obsticle to the conversion of the world. 27850

Formose negligee. 68455

Forms and regulations established by the Commissioner of Internal Revenue. 6975

Forms, general regulations and instructions. 10424

Forms of daily prayer. 83397

Forms of doxology and benediction with concluding prayers. 85294

Forms of government, containing an abstract of the original charter of Maryland. 45146

Forms of government of all the states in the world. 25099

Forms of issuing letters-patent by the crown of England. 19048

Forms of minority representation. 90460

Forms of prayer. 11522

Forms of prayer, hymns, &c. for little children. 89799

Forms of prayer to be used in the island of Jamaica. 35581

Forms of procedure, in the courts of Pennsylvania. 83707

Formula for the government and discipline. 23199

Formula of prescriptions. 63422

Formulario geometrico-judicial. 26466

Formulary, of a preamble for private subscriptions. 95164

Formulieren van gebeden by de staten van Hollandt ende West-Vrieslandt. 70069

Fornaris, Jose. 17766, 25100-25101, 86191-86192

Fornel, J. Maria. 57620

Forney, -------. (25110)

Forney, John W. 25102

Fornication binds the criminal parties to marry. 74146

Fornier, -------. petitioner 75613, 99242

Foro, B. supposed author 94825

Foro, de la Habana y sus ministerios. 25103

Foro. Revista de legislacion y jurisprudencia. 25104

Forrest, Catharine N. plaintiff 25109-(25110), 25112-25113

Forrest, Catharine N. respondent 25111

Forrest, Christopher. 25105

Forrest, Edwin. 74689

Forrest, Edwin. appellant 25111

Forrest, Edwin. defendant 25109-(25110), 25112-25113

Forrest, Mary. 25114

Forrest, Michael. 25115

Forrest, Robert. 25116

Forrest, William S. 25117-(25118), 55478

Forrest rangers. 14192

Forrester, Alexander. 25119

Forrester, Alfred Henry. 25120

Forrester, James. 90230, 90233, 90236-90237, 90246

Forry, Samuel. 25121-25122, (54786)

Fors, Luis Ricardo. 25123

Forsaken. 83777

Forsaken. A tale. 83782

Forschungen uber die Lage der Auswanderer. 92725

Forscutt, Mark H. 75544, 80497, 83300

Forsey, Thomas. plaintiff 25124

Forskjellinge, -------. tr. 16565

Forslag af nagra Nord-Amerikas trad. 14424

Forsøg i de skiønne og nytting videnskaber. note before 100709

Forsog til en forbedret Gronlandsk grammatica ved Otho Fabricus. 23603

Forsok til et biographiskt lexicon ofver namnkunnige. 27255

Forstall, E. J. 25125

Første brev til mine venner og landsmard i Danmark. 87141

Forste missionair paa Gronland. 42685

Forster, Charles. tr. 23731

Forster, Georg. tr. 5912, 16274, 41880, 47264, (64394), 69146, 89763

Forster, Johann Georg Adam, 1754-1794. 25126-25135, 101031

Forster, Johann Reinholt, 1729-1798. 1370, 6446, 6468, (6469), 25129, 25132-25142, (31184)-31185, 34359, 36989, 43808, (64392), 89763

Forster, Josiah. 25143, 49339, (55655)

Forster, L. G. ed. (27208)

Forster, R. P. 25144

Forster, Thomas Gales. 25145

Forster, W. E. 25146-25147, 82683

Forster, William. (78847)

Forsyth, John. 106029-106030 see also York County, Pa. Collector of Excise.

Forsyth, John, 1780-1841. (25148)-25151, 64808 see also Georgia. Governor, 1827-1829 (Forsyth) U. S. Legation. Spain.

Forsyth, John, 1810-1886. 25152

Forsyth, John, fl. 1840-1848. (25153), 95313

Forsyth, William, M. A. (25156)

Forsyth, William. petitioner 10577

Forsyth, William. surveyor 25157

Forsyth, William, 1737-1804. 25154-25155

Fort, G. 25158

Fort, L. Th. tr. 4526

Fort Braddock letters. 7331

Fort Braddock letters; or, a tale of the French and Indian wars. 25160

For Duquesne. 68828

Fort Duquesne, 1754, by Robert Stobo. 91869

Fort Edward Institute magazine. 25162

Fort Fillmore Silver Mining Company, New Mexico. 89685

Fort Fisher. 39346

Fort George. Council. 20535-20536

Fort Lafayette, N. Y. see Lafayette, Fort, N. Y.

"Fort-La-Fayette life." (24163)

Fort Pitt. see also Pittsburgh.

Fort Pitt. Indian Conference, 1768. see Indian Conference, Fort Pitt, 1768.

Fort Plain Seminary and Female Collegiate Institute, Montgomery County, N. Y. 25165

Fort Riley & Santa Fe Steam Traction Engine Company. 25166

Fort Stanwix, N. Y. Indian Conference, 1768. see New York (Colony) Indian Conference, Fort Stanwix, 1768.

Fort Stanwix captive. 65487

Fort Wayne, Ind. Land Office. Receiver. see U. S. General Land Office. Receiver, Fort Wayne, Ind.

Fort Wayne (Diocese) Bishop (Dwenger) 72942 see also Dwenger, Joseph, Bp.

Fort Wayne (Diocese) Synod, 1874. 72942

Fort Wayne directory for 1866-67. 25169

Fortaelling. 36870

Fortaelling af det Amerikanske colonistliv. (5558)

Fortanell, Ignacio. defendant 75571

Forten, James. 25170

Fortes, Ignacio Felizardo. tr. 4156

Fortescue, William. 25171, 81375

Fortesque, Thomas. tr. 48246

Fortgang der West Indianischen Compagnia. 102893

Forthcoming. pseud. President Holly not the Transylvania University. 25172, 96466

Fortia d'Urban, Agricola Joseph Francois Xavier Pierre Espirit Simon Paul Antoine, Marquis de. ed. 25173, 101358-101352

Fortier, ------. 56471

Fortieth anniversary. A discourse. 20192

Fortieth anniversary sermon. A sermon . . . at Rockaway. 37782

Fortieth anniversary sermon, May 14, 1865. 11797

Fortificaciones y ruinas de la ciudad de Puebla. 66557

Fortin, Pierre. 25175-25176 see also Canada. Forces Charged with the Protection of the Fisheries of the Gulf of St. Lawrence. Commander.

Fortique, Mariano Fernandez, Bp. 25177

Fortnightly review. 67590, 82685

Fortress of the lakes and its surroundings. 92821

Fortress of the rebellion. (17719)

Fortsetzung der Beschreibung deren denck-wurdigeren Paraquarischen Sachen. 79168

Fortsetzung der Historie von Gronland. 17414

Fortsetzung der Zeytungen. 18658, 25178

Fortsetzung von David Cranzens Bruder historie. 17412

Fortsetzung von "Viola." (4724)

Fortuna flora. 29670

Fortunate contractor. 5944

Fortunate discovery. 106142

Fortunati nimium sua si bona norunt Eboracenses. 80594

Fortune, E. F. T. 25179

Fortunes and misfortunes of the famous Moll Flanders. 19278

Fortune's favorite. 1603

Fortunes of a colonist. 74505

Fortunes of a New England boy. 909, 78829

Fortunes of Mr. Mason's successors. 55904

Fortunio. pseud. Chicago avant, pendant et apres l'incendie. 25180

Forty etchings from sketches. 29721

Forty-fifth annual report . . . see Report . . .

XLV. chapter of the prophecies of Thomas the Rhymer. 95453

44 years of his [i. e. Edward D. Tippett's] life. 95857

Forty-fourth annual report . . . see Report . . .

Forty photographs. (41053)

Forty-Seventh Celebration of the First Settlement of Ohio, Cincinnati, 1835. see Cincinnati. Celebration of the First Settlement of Ohio, 47th, 1835.

Forty-six select scripture narratives. (19375)

Forty-sixth anniversary of the Rensselaerville Baptist Association. 69642

Forty-third regiment United States Colored Troops. 25181, note after 48819

[42] Message from the President of the United States. (35378)

Forty years an evangelist. 83892

Forty years' experience in Sunday Schools. 97629

Forty years full practice at the Philadelphia Bar. 8465

Forty years in phrenology. (81496)

Forty years in the wilderness. 89375

Forty years in Trinity Parish. 17678

Forty years of American life. 55214

Forty years of pioneer life. 2574, 59487

Forty years of the Boston Baptist Bethel. 84045

Forty years of Washington society. 83510

Forty years' residence in America. 95610

Forty years with the Sioux. 71339

Foruile, Pierre Sauorguan de. tr. 1554

Forum concientiae sive pastorale internum. 98166

Forum; or, forty years full practice. 8465
Forward, Walter. 25182, 34735, 92851
Forward or backward? 59577
Forward with the flag. (72147)
Forwood, W. Stump. 14325, (25183)
Forze del regno di Francia. (6800)
Foscari, or, the Venetian exile. 103413
Foscolo, Hugo. 81299
Fosdick, Blanchard. (25186)
Fosdick, Charles Austin, 1842- 11437
Fosdick, Daniel. 25184-(25185)
Fosdick, David. supposed author 96411
Fosdick, H. M. (69769) see also Quebec
    and Saguenay Railway. Chief Engineer.
Fosiles. 74921
Foss, A. T. 25187
Foss, Daniel. 25189
Foss, John. (25188)
Fossetier de la glorieuse victoire. 25190
Fossey, Mathieu de. 25191-25192
Fossil fishes of the Devonian rocks of Ohio.
    (54890)
Fossil foot-marks in the red sandstone. 39488
Fossil mammalia. 18649
Fossil mammals, by J. Wyman. 27419
Fossil mammals. By Sir John Richardson. 71033
Fossil plants of the coal measures of the United
    States. (40206)
Fossil shells, by T. A. Conrad. 27419
Fossile Flora de Polarlander. (31229)
Fossils. 69946
Fossils of the Medial Tertiary of the United
    States. 15900
Fossils of the Miocene formation of the United
    States. (15901)
Fossils of the Tertiary formations of the
    United States. 15902
Foster, Aaron. 25193
Foster, Abiel. 25194
Foster, Alexander W. 63116 see also Pitts-
    burgh. City Solicitor.
Foster, Amos. 25195
Foster, Andrew. 40224, 99383A, 99383C-note
    after 99383C
Foster, Anthony. 25196
Foster, Arthur. 25197
Foster, Sir Augustus John, Bart., 1780-1848.
    1010, 1013, (16872), (25198), (48069),
    50015, note after 102754 see also Great
    Britain. Legation. U. S.
Foster, Benjamin, 1750-1798. (13597), 25199
Foster, Benjamin Franklin. (25200)-25201
Foster, Birket. illus. (41909), 41919, 41922
Foster, Dan, fl. 1789. (25203), 9 2955
Foster, Daniel, 1751-1795. (25204)-25206
Foster, Daniel, fl. 1850. 25207-25210
Foster, E. K. 89199
Foster, Eden Burroughs. 25211-(25213)
Foster, Edmund. 25214-25216
Foster, Edward H. 88230
Foster, Ephraim Hubbard, 1795?-1824. 25217-
    25218, 94803
Foster, Ethan. 25219
Foster, Ezekiel. claimant 92312
Foster, Festus. 25220-(25221)
Foster, G. G. 25222-25227
Foster, G. L. (25228)
Foster, Hannah. 25229, (52668), 103731
Foster, Isaac. 25230-25233, 73562, 102947
    see also West Stafford, Conn. Second
    Church. Pastor.
Foster, J. Heron. 25235
Foster, J. R. tr. 8033
Foster, James. (4687), (33641), 57071
Foster, Jared B. 15776
Foster, Jeremiah J. 80737, 105026

Foster, Joel. 25234
Foster, John, of Groton, Conn. 25240
Foster, John, of Portalnd, Me. 25242
Foster, John, fl. 1680. 62743
Foster, John, 1763-1829. (25236)-(25239)
Foster, John, 1770-1843. (25241)
Foster, John Gray, 1823-1874. (33913), 51720,
    69870
Foster, John W. 25250
Foster, John Welch, 1789-1852. (25243)-(25244),
    59349
Foster, John Wells, 1815-1873. 25245-25249,
    48738
Foster, John Y. 25251
Foster, Josiah. 92736
Foster, Lafayette Sabine, 1806-1880. 25251,
    42865
Foster, Lillian. 25253-25254
Foster, Luke B. 25255
Foster, N. G. 25256
Foster, Nathan. defendant (25259), 73045
Foster, Nathan W. 25257
Foster, Nathaniel. (25258)
Foster, Nathaniel. defendant see Foster,
    Nathan. defendant
Foster, Nicholas. 25260
Foster, R. B. (25261)
Foster, R. S. 82427
Foster, Stephen Clark, 1799-1872. 25262-25263
Foster, Theodore. 95921 see also American
    Convention for promoting the Abolition of
    Slavery, and Improving the Condition of
    the African Race. President.
Foster, Theodore. supposed author 2108A,
    93617-note after 93619
Foster, Thomas. 3463, 25264
Foster, Thomas Flournoy, 1790-1848. 25265
Foster, Turner H. (51874)
Foster, Vere. (25266)
Foster, W. E. 13491
Foster, William, 1740-1780. 25267
Foster, William, fl. 1857. 25268
Foster, William B. 55578, 60275-60276 see
    also North Branch Canal Company.
    Engineer.
Foster, William C. 25269
Foster (Theodore) publisher 96061
Fosteriana. (25241)
Fostina Woodman, the wonderful adventurer.
    90456
Fote, Philip. 82832, note after 92664, 2d
    note after 100510
Fortherby, Robert. 66686
Fotherby, Robert. supposed author 89542
Fothergill, John, 1676-1744. 25270
Fothergill, John, 1712-1786. 25271, 58788
Fothergill, Samuel, 1715-1772. 25272-25273,
    64996, 69660
Fothergill. 89407
Fotheringham, ------. ed. 85527
Foucaud, Edouard. (25274)
Foucher, Louis Charles. defendant at impeach-
    ment 96864
Foucher, Victor, 1802-1866. 25275, 36892
Foudras, M. A. tr. 2530
Foul charges of the Tories. 20994, 97270
Foulke, William Parker. 25276-25277
Foullouze, James. reporter 42287
Foulquier, ------, fl. 1782. 66078
Foulquier, ------, fl. 1865. illus. 44250
Foundation and other poems. 8817
Foundation of Calvinism and priesthood shaken.
    82482
Foundation of religious liberty displayed. 5697
Foundation of success. 91105
Foundation of the American colonies. 82679

Foundation of the Christian religion. 72091-72094, 72110

Foundation of the Massachusetts professorship of natural history. 30765

Foundations and statutes of the professorships. 30765

Foundations, effects and distinguishing properties. 59375

Foundations for the U. S. Government Post Office and Custom House Building. 84898

Foundations of civil order and political life. (51264)

Foundations of nationality. 16763

Founder and destroyer of the first Huguenot settlement. 84390

Founder of Mormonism. 83038

Founders of the Massachusetts Bay Colony. 84138

Founder's letters and the papers. 59391

Founders of New England in the reign of James the first. 3789

Founders of New York. 56810

Founders of the Institute. 82464

Founders of the nation. 86117

Founding of Massachusetts. 103397, 104847

Founding of Virginia. A poem. 31880

Foundling of the forest. 20196

Foundling of the prairie. 36582

Fountain and the bottle. 25278

Fountain opened. 79444, (79448), 91940, note after 98054, 104082-104083

Fountain rock. 71427

Fouque, ------. plaintiff 94390-94391

Fouquier, -------. ed. 40234

Four acts of despotism. (43876)

Four amendments to the constitution of the United States. 76483

Four articles on the state of the country. 7679

Four centurions. (78391)

Four Christian ministers, recently returned from the colonies. pseud. Testimony. 101433A

Four claims against Mexico. 48533

Four conclusions touching the faith and order. 13307

Four Confederated Bands of Pawnees. see Pawnee Indians.

Four crisis letters to the ladies. 97813

Four days at the falls of Niagara. 24709

Four discourses, accomodated unto the designs of practical Godliness. 46513

Four discourses intended to have been delivered in Philadelphia. 65506, 65511

Four dissertations, connected with various parts of the discourse. (4431)

Four dissertations, on the reciprocal advantages of a perpetual union. 25279, (68570), 84611-84612

Four episodes of Wisconsin pioneering. 84132

Four essays. By a clergyman of the Church of England. 92839

Four essays on colonial slavery. 36056

Four essays on the right and prioprety of secession. (25280)

Four essays: the science of political economy. 48862

Four Gospels and the Acts of the Holy Apostles. 25281

Four great powers. (7147), (7150)

Four Indian kings. pseud. Speech. (25283), 89182

Four Indian Kings speech to Her Majesty. London, April 20. 1710. 89182

Four Indian Kings' speech to Her Majesty on the 20th April. (25283)

Four Indian princes. pseud. Speech. 89182

Four kings of Canada. 25282

Four letters addressed to Lord Liverpool. 14011

Four letters addressed to Mr. Adams. 42925

Four letters: being an interesting correspondence. 242

Four letters. By a friend of the Anglo-Saxons. 57559

Four letters. By Rev. Jeremiah Hallock. (29905), 51841

Four letters concerning the flourishing condition. 4732

Four letters, concerning the slavery of the colliers. 91600

Four letters, . . . containing a statement of facts. 43146

Four letters, &c. Taken from the London weekly history of the progress of the Gospel. 83439, note after 103623

Four letters, from a citizen of Washington. 97137

Four letters, from the London weekly history of the progress of the Gospel. 25284

Four letters on important national subjects. 97343-97345

Four letters on interesting subjects. 25285

Four letters to a friend. 95691

Four letters to an English friend. 103499

Four letters to the Earl of Carlisle. (21827)

Four letters to the Honourable Harrison Gray Otis. 40048, 70067

Four letters to the Hon. Schuyler Colfax. 10842

Four letters to the people of Pennsylvania. 56592, (74232)-74233

Four letters to the people. 45147

Four letters to the Rev. Dr. Humphrey. (45962)

Four letters to the Reverend James Caughey. 36383

Four letters to the Right Hon. Henry Addington. 17530, 1st note after 91235, 2d note after 102829

Four letters written by him [i. e. Abraham Morhouse.] 50696, 105629

Four letters, written by the prophet, after his detection. 105630

Four months among the gold-finders. 100641

Four months among the goldfinders in Alta California. (8350), 100641, 1st note after 100641

Four months in Libby. 36364

Four months in the mines of California. 103053-103054

Four months of prison life of 1st Maryland Regiment. 16656

Four necessary cases of conscience of daily use. 80209

Four of us. pseud. Whimwhams. see Finn, Henry J. Miller, James W. Whitney, Moses. Wyman, Oliver C.

Four papers from the Boston courier. 42705, 58758, 67423

Four physicians. pseud. Statement. 90673

Four poems. 38308

Four principal battles of the late war. 18874

Four proposals to the Honoured Parliament. 13307

Four propositions sustained. 61186, 104671, 104673

Four questions considered. 30923

Four questions for the people. 51106

Four Russian sailors. pseud. Narrative of the extraordinary adventures. 29385, 89543

Four Russian sailors. pseud. Surprising
adventures. 89544
Four Russian sailors. pseud. Voyage au
Spitzberg. 89545
Four scouts of the Waccamaw. 31324
Four select tales from Marmontel. 79358
Four sermons. [By Benjamin Colman.]
(14525)
Four sermons. [By George Hutton.] 34108
Four sermons, delivered at Cavendish, Vt.
81653
Four sermons delivered before the First Con-
gregational Society. 64669
Four sermons, delivered May 9, & 16, 1830.
104907
Four sermons on important subjects. 56825
Four sermons on the following important
subjects. 91794
Four sermons preached by the Rev. J. Caughey.
11563
Four sermons, preach'd to the Church of Christ.
16632
Four sermons. 1714. (14525)
Four sermons: the two former delivered at the
Tuesday-Evening Lecture. 79419
Four sermons . . . to a society of young men.
(17096)
Four sermons, upon the great and indispensable
duty of all Christian lasters and mis-
tresses. 2685, 2687, 3d note after 97579
Four sermons upon the XXth chap. of the
Revelations. 83975
Four sermons, viz., I. The glorious throne.
46686
Four sermons. . . . With a preface by Mr.
Foxcroft. (20062)
Four sheet map of the United States. 94310
Four thousand British planters settled in New
England. 91738, 91740
Four tracts, on political and commercial sub-
jects. 97347-97348
Four tracts. Reflections on the present state
of England. 18983
Four tracts, together with two sermons, on
political and commercial subjects. 11310,
1st note after 97332, 97346, 97352, 97353,
97366
Four volumes of Lorenzo's journal. 20757
Four weeks in the rebel army. 58349
Four years among the Spanish Americans.
30812
Four years at Yale. (25286)
Four years in British Columbia and Vancouver
Island. 47174
Four years in Paraguay. 71961
Four years in Parliament. 61006
Four years in secessia. (8666)
Four years in the Government Exploring Expedi-
tion. 14907
Four years in the Pacific. 101142
Four years in the saddle. 27445
Four years of fighting. 14166
Four years of personal observations. 71204
Four years' residence in the United States and
Canada. 8575
Four years residence in the United States.
4051, 25287
Four-years' resident. pseud. Views of Canada
and the colonists. 10618
Four years voyages of Capt. George Roberts.
(71888)
Fourcroy, ------. 88905
Fovre . . . treatises. 32838
Fournel, Henri. 25288
Fournier, -------. petitioner (2765), 75163

Fournier, C. 25289
Fournier, Jacques. see Benedict XII, Pope,
1285-1342.
Fournier, Jules. 25290-25291
Fournier, L. M. 25292
Fourquet-d'Hachette, --------. 25293
Fourt de Pradt, Dominique Georges Frederic
de Riom de Prolhiac de. see Pradt,
Dominique Georges Frederic de Riom
de Prolhiac de Fourt de, Abp., 1759-1837.
Fourteen agricultural experiments. 41790
Fourteen Ioway Indians. 11535
Fourteen months in American bastiles,
25294, (33247)
Fourteen months in southern prisons. 18730
Fourteen objections answered. 83914
Fourteen spirited resolutions. 9911
Fourteen views of Rio de Janeiro and neighbor-
hood. 50586
Fourteen years in the interior of North America.
97133
Fourteenth anniversary of the Stephenstown
Baptist Association. 91326
Fourteenth annual report . . . see Report
. . .
Fourteenth report . . . see Report . . .
Fourth and fifth letters to the Rev. Samuel
Miller. 88972
Fourth and fifth reports . . . see Reports
. . .
Fourth annual address before the Agricultural
Society of Warren County. 68170
Fourth annual and final report of the Woman's
Central Association of Relief. 76634
Fourth annual catalogue of the Spring-Villa
Seminary. 89831
Fourth annual commencement, of St. Mary's
College. 75425
Fourth annual exhibition of the Maryland
Institute. (45223)
Fourth annual fair of the Saint Louis Agricul-
tural and Mechanical Association. 75381
Fourth annual message . . . see Message
. . .
Fourth annual report . . . see Report . . .
Fourth biennial report . . . see Report . . .
Fourth book of records of the town of South-
hampton. 88230
Fourth book of "Washington benevolents,"
otherwise called, the book of knaves.
25295, 101993
Fourth centennial anniversary of the Moravian
Church. 50520
Fourth charge to the clergy. 8691, 52763
Fourth collection of papers. 81492
Fourth Congregational Church, Hartford, Conn.
see Hartford, Conn. Fourth Congrega-
tional Church.
Fourth Congregational Church, Providence,
R. I. see Providence, R. I. Fourth
Congregational Church.
Fourth . . . debate. Mr. Northrop's reply.
55840
Fourth dialogue between a minister and his
parishioner. 78734
Fourth edition of the letter to William Wilber-
force. 95658
Fourth essay on free trade and finance. 102406
Fourth . . . exhibition of the Columbian Society
of Artists. 59990
Fourth journal [of George Whitefield.] 102565
Fourth letter . . . [by John Henry Hopkins.]
(32931)
Fourth letter [from Sir John Dalrymple.]
18348

Fourth letter to the citizens of . . . Pennsylvania. (61663)
Fourth letter to the people of England. (26147), (80046)-80048
[Fourth letter to the Rev. Samuel Miller.] (49063)
Fourth memorial. 103717
Fourth meteorological report of Prof. James P. Espy. 22917
Fourth narrative, of his [i. e. George Keith's] proceedings. (37191)
Fourth National Quarantine and Sanitary Convention, Boston, 1860. see National Quarantine and Sanitary Convention. 4th, Boston, 1860.
Fourth of July. 19526
Fourth of July Celebration, Charleston, 1831. see Charleston, S. C. Fourth of July Celebration, 1831.
Fourth of July, 1850, at Burlington College. 9337
Fourth of July in Charleston. 80843
Fourth of July orations in 1803 and 1812. 98537
4th of July reminiscences and reflections. 103485
Fourth of July sermon. 39502
Fourth of July, to the patriotic citizens of Pompton Plains. (19527)
Fourth paper, presented by Maior Butler. 104336
Fourth part of Dr. Priestley's lectures on history. 105938
Fourth part of the General English pilot. (22617)
Fourth part of the synoptical flora Telluriana. 67451
Fourth party in the field! 10137
Fourth Presbyterian Church, Washington, D. C. see Washington, D. C. Fourth Presbyterian Church.
Fourth quarterly report . . . see Report . . .
Fourth report . . . see Report . . .
Fourth semi-annual report . . . see Report . . .
Fourth supplement [to the public laws of Rhode Island.] 70700
Fourth triennial charge to the clergy. 13385
Fourth voice from America. 24393
Fourth Ward Industrial School for Girls, New York. see New York (City) Fourth Ward Industrial School for Girls.
Fourth Ward Industrial School for Girls. First annual report. 54281
Fourty-four [sic] years of the life of a hunter. (8693)
Fowle, D. supposed author (15954), 95159
Fowle, Daniel. 12982, 25296
Fowle, Robert. 25297
Fowle, William. 25313
Fowle, William A. 86789
Fowle, William Bentley, 1795-1865. 14997, 25298, 44324, (66050), 83572
Fowler, Mr. see Fowle, William.
Fowler, Amos. 25299
Fowler, Andrew. 25300
Fowler, Asa. ed. 52884
Fowler, Bancroft. 25301
Fowler, Bernard. see Dowler, Bernard.
Fowler, Daniel W. (25303)
Fowler, Francis M. 25079
Fowler, George. ed. 25304, 1st note after 101235
Fowler, H. reporter 91226
Fowler, Henry. ed. 12186

Fowler, Henry, 1824-1872. 25305-25307
Fowler, James H. (25308)
Fowler, John. (25309)-25310, 1st note after 93591, 1st note after 96048
Fowler, John, Jr. 25311
Fowler, Mrs. L. F. 54488
Fowler, M. Field. 25312
Fowler, Orin. (25314)-25315
Fowler, P. H. (25316)
Fowler, Reginald. 25317
Fowler, Robert. 25318
Fowler, S. W. (25321)
Fowler, Samuel M. 25319
Fowler, Samuel P. (19046), 25320, 75736, 89927
Fowler, Theodosius. plaintiff 88951
Fowler, Theodosius. defendant 96888
Fowler, Thomas. 25322
Fowler, W. see Fowler, Daniel W.
Fowler, W. B. ed. 14997
Fowler, William C. (25331) see also Alabama. Agent to Adjust the Claims of Deceased Soldiers. Confederate States of America. War Department. Superintendent of Army Records.
Fowler, William Chauncey. 25323-25330
Fowler, William H. 22824
Fowler, William Worthington. (25332)
Fowler, Kirtland & Co. firm. see Janes, Fowler, Kirtland & Co. firm
Fox, Charles. 25333
Fox, Sir Charles. supposed author 36897
Fox, Charles. pseud. Epistle. see Tickell, Richard. supposed author
Fox, Charles Barnard. (25334)
Fox, Charles James, 1749-1806. 4203, (15052), 25335-25337, 25341, 52930, 101559
Fox, Charles James, 1811-1844. 25342, 52861
Fox, D. R. ed. 89496
Fox, Ebenezer. 25343-25344
Fox, George, 1624-1691. 25171, 25345-25358, 25363-25365, 28453, 28794, 28926, 32025, 39817, (44754), 53083, 66735, 66743, 70894, 78753, 81375, note after 100596, 103883, 105221, 106101, 106221
Fox, George, 1624-1691. incorrectly supposed author 25357, 37228, note after 100596
Fox, George, a Quaker. pseud. Dialogue. see Young, Samuel, fl. 1690-1700.
Fox, George Townshend. 25366
Fox, H. R. 25367
Fox, Henry Stephen, 1791-1846. see also 43927 Great Britain. Legation. U. S.
Fox, James. 7099, 25368
Fox, John, 1678?-1756. 25369-25370
Fox, John, 1834 or 5-1856? defendant 25372
Fox, John, fl. 1838. 25371
Fox, Joseph. defendant 97771
Fox, Luke. (74131)
Fox, Margaret. see Kane, Margaret (Fox)
Fox, S. M. 88022, 91702
Fox, Samuel M. defendant 25374
Fox, Thomas. 25375
Fox, Thomas B. (25376)
Fox, William. 429, 25378-(25380), 80582, 80692, 93600, 1st note after 102813, 102868
Fox, William. supposed author 81745, 81746, 93600
Fox, William B. 105414
Fox Alden, T. J. see Alden, T. J. Fox.
Fox Bourne, H. R. see Bourne, H. R. Fox.
Fox and Hoyt. firm publishers 25382
Fox. (27416)
Fox and Hoyt's quadrennial register. 25382

Fox and Wisconsin Improvement Company. 25383-25384
Fox Chase Division, no. 301, Sons of Temperance. see Sons of Temperance of North America. Pennsylvania. Fox Chase Division, no. 301.
Fox from the north-west passage. 25410
Fox Hunting Club, Gloucester, Pa. see Gloucester Fox Hunting Club.
Fox Indians. Chief. see Keokuk, Chief of the Sauk and Fox Indians
Fox Indians. Treaties, etc. 96591, 96616, 96633, 96647, 96662, 96674, 96708, 96712-96713, 96722 see also Michigan Indians. Treaties, etc.
Fox out of the pit. 70065
Fox turned preacher. 74623
Foxborough, Mass. Church. 104387
Foxborough, Mass. Society for Detecting Horse-Thieves, and Recovering Stolen Horses. see Society for Detecting Horse-Thieves, and Recovering Stolen Horses, Wrentham, Franklin, Medway, Medfield, Walpole, Foxborough, Mansfield, and Attleborough, Mass.
Foxborough, R. I. Church. 25409
Foxcroft, Frank. (25385)
Foxcroft, James. see Foxcroft, Thomas, 1697-1769.
Foxcroft, Thomas, 1697-1769. 12325, 12362, 12364, 17675, 20057, (20062), (20271), 21946, 25386-25408, 46274, 59604, 99800, 101016, 101171, 101194, 103067, 103900, note after 103907 see also Eight Ministers who carry on the Thursday Lecture in Boston.
Foxe, John, 1516-1587. 25381, 44124
Foxe, Luke. 25410
Foxonian quakers, dunces, lyars, and slanderers. 106101
Fox's martyrs. 25381
Foxton, E. pseud. Herman, or young knighthood. see Palfrey, Sarah Hammond.
Foyer Canadien. Recueil litteraire et historique. 10455, 12345, (12573), (41510)
Fra Graenlandi. 7706
Frac-Mazon. pseud. Monitor o guia de los Franc-Mazones utilisimo. see Webb, Thomas Smith.
Fracanzano da Montalboddo. 50050-50064, 99369, 99379, note after 99383C, 1st-5th notes after 106378
Fracastorius, Hieronymus. 25411, 67730
Fracker, George. 25412, 3d note after 100818
Frades Menores. see Franciscans.
Fragmens de politique et de litterature. 44236
Fragmens du poeme de Las-Casas. 73482
Fragmens d'un voyage dans l'Amerique meridionale. 59253
Fragmens pour servir a l'histoire de la guerre presente. 100730
Fragment. 40985, 62966, 72496, 103392
Fragment. Addressed to all whom it may concern. 12986
Fragment. Addressed to the sons and daughters of humanity. 10889
Fragment. By Robert Knox. (38172)
Fragment de Xenophon nouvellement trouve. 8138, 105719
Fragment des memoires de M. Marc-Gabriel Hurt-Binet. 34018
Fragment du XVIe siecle. 19556, 73458
Fragment d'un voyage au centre de l'Amerique Meridionale. (57454)

Fragment d'un voyage dans le Chili et au Curco. 26778
Fragment d'un voyageur Americain. 100691
Fragment, inscribed to the married ladies of America. 19933, 4th note after 98269
Fragment of a journal of a sentimental philosopher. 25415, 35146, 72485
Fragment of a letter on the slavery of Negroes. 18983-18984, 18987
Fragment of a political burletta. 46917
Fragment of a sermon. 89360
Fragment of a sermon on the great American sin. 84447
Fragment of a tale. 81177
Fragment of an essay. (25414)
Fragment of an original letter. 18983-18984, 18987
Fragment of Col. Auguste Chouteau's journal. 75357
Fragment of political science. 40985
Fragment of the chronicle of Nathan Ben Saddi. 25413, 74818
Fragment of war history. 30570
Fragment on government. 25416
Fragment; or, letters and poems. 46881
Fragment, poem. 97788
Fragment sur la geologiede la Guadelupe. (40164)
Fragment sur les colonies en general. 82301
Fragmenta entomologia. 39666
Fragmentary sketches of the early history. 83743
Fragmenten uit een dagboek. (22030), (74645)
Fragmento de la historia antigua. 80987
Fragmentos. 98868
Fragmentos de ciencia politica sobre nacionalismo e internacionalismo. 50985
Fragmentos de la historia general y natural de las Indias. 94352
Fragmentos de la vida, y virtudes del V. Illmo. y Rmo. Sr. Dr. D. Vasco de Quiroga. 47952, 50611
Fragmentos de proceso de residencia. 67646
Fragments. 16297
Fragments de sagas Irlandais. [sic] (4212), 19204
Fragments de sages Islandaises. (4212), 19204
Fragments d'une histoire du commerce et de l'industrie. 78919
Fragments et opuscules inedits. 77361
Fragments from the study of a pastor. 55200
Fragments in prose and verse. 82505
Fragments of family and contemporary history. 72194
Fragments of political science. 40985
Fragments of the history of Bawlfredonia. 13770, note after 95776
Fragments of the history of Newton. 32728
Fragments of the natural history of Pennsylvania. 3809
Fragments of voyages and travels. (29722)
Fragments of the confederation of the American states. 25417
Fragments sur l'Inde, sur le General Lalli. 38693
Fragmentum synopseos plantarum phanerogamarum. 63627
Fragoso, Joanne. (25418), 26005
Frai Domingo de Nyra. 29343
Frai Francisco Xavier Vazquez Peruano. 98718
Fraile. (69334)
Fraile o un Gachupin? 93445
Frailities of humanity. 84801

Frailty and misery of man's life. 104362
Fraley, Frederick, 1804-1901. 7052, 25419, 30546, 60799
Frame, Eliza. 25420
Frame, Richard. 25421
Frame of government of the province of Pennsylvania. (60104)
Frame of the government of the province of Pennsilvania in America. 59697
Frame of the government of the province of Pennsilvania, 1682, 1683, 1696. 66223
Frame of the government of the province of Pennsylvania in America: together with certain laws agreed upon in England. 59696
Frame work of liberty. 73566
Framery, Nicolas Etienne. 97025
Framingham, Mass. 25422
Framingham, Mass. Normal School. see Massachusetts. State Normal School, Framingham.
Framingham, Mass. Quarter-Centennial Celebration of the Establishment of Normal Schools in America, 1864. see Quarter-Centennial Celebration of the Establishment of Normal Schools in America, Framingham, Mass., 1864.
Framingham, Mass. School Committee. 25424
Framingham, Mass. State Normal School. see Massachusetts. State Normal School, Framingham.
Framingham, Mass. Treasurer. 25423
Framingham Academy, Lowell, Mass. Trustees. 96836
Frammento di un viaggio fatto nelle due Americhe. (57767)
Frampton, John. tr. 22813, 47347, 49944-49946
Franca, Ernesto Ferreira. 24168, 25425-25426
Franca, Jose Pedreira. (57584)
Franca, Manoel Jose de Souza. see Souza Franca, Manoel Jose de.
Franca Almeida e Sa, Luiz de. 25427
Franca y Cardenas, Jose Ruiz de Villa. see Villafranca y Cardenas, Jose Ruiz de.
Franca Exposicao dos acontecimentos que tiveram logar. 72294
Francais. pseud. Considerations sur les differends. 16023
Francais a Mexique. 21009
Francais en Amerique. Acadiens et Canadiens. 67622
Francais en Amerique. Le Canada. (2608ᴜ)
Francais Refugies de St. Domingue, Baltimore. 43330, 96962 see also Entertainment Given in Honor of Duncan McIntosh, Baltimore, 1809.
Francais qui en merit le nom. pseud. Relation d'un traversee. 69252
France. 454-456, (774), 1014, 1225, 2446, 2460, 4512, 6257, 6258, 10442, 10513, note after (10603), 11812-11814, 15066, (15067), 15205, 16847, 16856, (16890), 16878, 16895, 16896, 16903, 17365, 20427, (20464), 21459, 23920, 25497, 26821-26822, 26929-26930, (29582), 34399, 34400, 38563, (38735), 40319, 40576, (41650), 42443-42444, 44605, 46762, (47511)-47512, 47516-47517, (48137), 51661, 56505, 59593, 62702, 64938, 67142, 68283-68284, 69499, 69530, note after 80055, 83813, 83815, note after 91855, 1st note after 93806, 94387, 99303, note

after 99383C, 101170, 1st note after 102785, 103848
France. Administration des Douanes. see France. Direction Generale des Douanes.
France. Administration des Finances. 75173
France. Agence Centrale des Banques Coloniales, Paris. 3222
France. Agens. 16685, 29576
France. Armee. 15056, 38164, 75088, 101710, 105602-105605
France. Armee. Marechal de Camp. 23119 see also Eustace, Jean Skey.
France. Assemblee Nationale. 23920, 25429, (36682), 39675, 48102, 56776, 74144, 75043, 75048, 75098, 75106, (75107), 75148, (75174), 75176, 75183, 75476, 94422, 99254, 101723
France. Assemblee Nationale. Chambre des Deputes. 11815, (65757), 86816, 96071, 96445
France. Assemblee Nationale. Chambre des Pairs. 85816
France. Assemblee Nationale. Comite d'Agriculture. 3494, 34844
France. Assemblee Nationale. Comite de Commerce. 3494, 34844
France. Assemblee Nationale. Comite de Constitution. 3494, 34844
France. Assemblee Nationale. Comite de Defence Generale. 67927
France. Assemblee Nationale. Comite de la Marine. 14713, 34844
France. Assemblee Nationale. Comite de la Marine et des Colonies. 44826
France. Assemblee Nationale. Comite des Colonies. 3494, 28153, 34844, 75054, 75149, 85174
France. Assemblee Nationale. Comite des Six. 14056-14057
France. Assemblee Nationale. Presidente. 101723 see also Sieyes, Em.
France. Avocat General. 94126 see also Le Pelletier de Saint Fargeau, --------
France. Bibliotheque Nationale, Paris. see Paris. Bibliotheque Nationale.
France. Bureau de Commerce et des Colonies. 20426, 75029
France. Bureau de la Marine. Archives, Paris. 67020-67021
France. Bureau des Affaires Indiennes. Chef. (32746)
France. Chambre des Comptes. 21859, 102772, 102774
France. Comite Colonial. see France. Assemblee Nationale. Comite des Colonies.
France. Comite de Defence Generale. see France. Assemblee Nationale. Comite de Defence Generale.
France. Comite de Marine et des Colonies. see France. Assemblee Nationale. Comite de la Marine et des Colonies.
France. Comite des Six. see France. Assemblee Nationale. Comite des Six.
France. Commissaires de la Colonie de Saint Domingue. see Santo Domingo (French Colony) Commissaires.
France. Commission a Saint Domingue. see France. Commission aux Iles Sous le Vent.
France. Commission aux Isles Francais de l'Amerique. see France. Commission aux Isles Sous le Vent.
France. Commission aux Isles Sous le Vent. (42350), 73471, 75149, 78720, 87114-87116, 87120, 87123, 96343 see also

Ailhaud, --------. Polverel, --------.
Raimond, Julien. Roume, Philippe Rose.
Sonthonax, Leger Felicite, 1763-1813.
France. Commission Chargee de l'Examen du
Magnetisme Animal. 25579, 82987,
92135 see also Franklin, Benjamin,
1706-1790.
France. Commission Chargee de Presenter
les Lois Organiques de la Constitution
dans les Colonies. 21762
France. Commission Chargee d'Examiner le
Projet de Loi Relatif au Traite du 4
Juillet 1831. 21204
France. Commission de Colonisation de la
Guyane. (29189)
France. Commission d'Education. 84504
France. Commission des Colonies. 19366,
22823, 26685, 98682 see also Proissy,
--.
France. Commission du Commerce de la
Martinique. 56471
France. Commission Etablie dans l'Affaire du
Canada. 10550
France. Commission Institutee Pour l'Examen
des Questions Relatives a l'Esclavage et
a la Constitution Politique des Colonies.
728, 14717, 14992, (67930)
France. Commission National-Civil Delegue
aux Isles Sous le Vent. see France.
Commission aux Isles Sous le Vent.
France. Commission Speciale. 67931
France. Commission sur les Limites de St.
Lucie et de l'Acadie. (774), 16023,
(47511)-47512, note after (47740), 47741-
47742, (47546)-(47548), (56129), 69463,
69671, 91869, note after 96403 see also
Galissoniere, ------- de la. Silhouette,
-------- de. Valle, ------- de la.
France. Commissioners, Charged by the King
of France, With the Examination of the
Animal Magnetism, as now Practiced at
Paris. see France. Commission Chargee
de l'Examination du Magnetisme Animal.
France. Comptroller General. (38735) see
also Lambert, M.
France. Conseil Colonial. 22831, 67154
France. Conseil de Liquidation. 15915, 81658
France. Conseil des Prises, Paris. 27719,
43056
France. Conseil d'Etat. 4510, 10351-10352,
10356, 10486, 14702-14706, 15913,
15914, 29159, (38735), 40001, (40680)-
(40681), 41843, 56058-56078, (56085),
56088-56091, 56472, 57904, 68431, 68918-
68919, 70119, (73809)-73816, 74011,
75056-75060, 75409
France. Conseil d'Etat. Commissaires pour
la Regie de la Compagnie des Indies.
57526
France. Conseil du Commerce. Deputes.
14052, 14059, 16742, 69852
France. Conseil du Commerce. Deputes.
petitioners 47744
France. Conseil du Roi. 57904, 72043, 75160,
86843
France. Conseil Special. 22831, 67154
France. Constitution. 28921
France. Consulat. Buenos Aires. 9027-9028,
9042, 9045-9046, 72604 see also Roger,
Aime. France. Legation. Buenos Aires
(Province)
France. Consulat. Cartegena. (3651), 11135,
62802 see also Barrot, Adolf.
France. Consulat. Philadelphia. 65342 see
also France. Legation. United States.

France. Convention Nationale. 26685, 28132,
75086, 75097, 75182, 87120, 96340
France. Convention Nationale. Comite de
Salut Public. (19266)-19267, 96568
France. Convention Nationale. Commission
des Onze. 28132
France. Corps Legislatif. Conseil des Anciens.
96167-96168
France. Corps Legislatif. Conseil des Anciens.
Commission. 27511 see also Courtois,
--------. Girot-Pouzol, --------.
Ligeret, ----------.
France. Corps Legislatif. Conseil des Cinq-
Cents. 19324, 19336, 22823, 66857,
87117, 95374, 98680-98682, 99661-99663
France. Corps Legislatif. Conseil des Cinq-
Cents. Commission des Colonies. 22823,
75540 see also Bergoing, -------------.
Dabray, ----------. Eschasseriaux,
---------. Gregoire, ----------. Lyon,
--------. Porte, ---------. Sainthorent,
-------. Salicetti, --------.
France. Corps Legislatif. Conseil des Cinq-
Cents. Commission des Colonies
Occidentales. 39656
France. Cour de Cassation. 68431
France. Department de Marine. see France.
Ministere de la Marine.
France. Departement de la Marine et des
Colonies. see France. Ministere de
la Marine.
France. Depot des Cartes et Plans de la
Marine. 34862, 52337, 75172
France. Direction Generale des Douanes.
14722, note just before 94176
France. Directoire Executif. 23085, (26931),
59593, 62702, 99663, 99745-99746,
103848
France. Directoire Executif. Agens Parti-
culiers. 99745-99746
France. Etats-Generaux, 1789. (68072)
France. Institut National des Sciences et
Arts, Paris. see Paris. Institut
National des Sciences et Arts.
France. Laws, statutes, etc. 1014, 8037,
10486, 11814, 14123-14126, (14340),
14709, 16895, 17852, 18724, 20291,
20427, 20676, 24892, 25882, 27274,
31095, 36762, (38735), 40001, (40680),
(40681), 40686, 40691, 40713-40720,
42212, 56776, 57526-57528, (57530)-
57531, 57904, 61251, (66984), (66985),
(67031), (67061), 67720, 68074, 68373,
68419-(68420), 68431, 68438, (68439),
68441, 68444-68445, (68447), 68459,
(68461), 68898, (68900)-68910, 68915-
68921, 69480, 70119, 73469, 73741,
(73809)-73817, 75011, 75014, 75016,
75055-75060, 75062, 75064-75065, 75081,
75088, 75095, 75097, 75098, 75153-
75155, 75159, 75175, 75409, 75476,
79096, 81658, 89126, 94422, 96047,
96048, 96055, 96340, 96445, 1st note
after 96445, 99618, 103763, 102772-
102774, 103429, 103434
France. Legation. Argentine Confederation.
9003, 9006-9007
France. Legation. Brazil. 85639 see also
Saint-Georges, --------.
France. Legation. Buenos Aires (Province)
9021 see also France. Consulat.
Buenos Aires.
France. Legation. Mexico. 19268, 35539-
35540, 93785 see also Baudin, --------.
France. Legation. Nicaragua. 2506

France. Legation. United States. 454-456, 2460, 16850, 16867, 16878, 26929-26930, 34900, 40343, 40690, 62653, 62659, (70219), 87862, 88969, 100797, 2d note after 101709 see also Adet, Pierre Auguste, 1763-1832. Genet, Edmund Charles Edouard, 1763-1834. Fauchet, Joseph. La Luzerne, Cesar Henri, Comte de, 1737-1799. and France. Consulat. Philadelphia.

France. Marine. 38164

France. Marine. Capitaines des Galleres. 24855

France. Marine. Rear-Admiral Commanding the French Naval Forces on Station of Brazil and of the South Seas. 9043, 93807 see also Leblanc, L.

France. Mediators for the Treaty of Breda Between Great Britain and the Netherlands, 1667. 96524

France. Ministere de la Marine. 1360, 5028, (8149), 8963, 14054, 14717, 14718, 14720, (15068), 15459, 25125, 27274, (26931), 29182, (29187)-(29189), 38697, 38698, 42753, (44145), 44602, 47509, 49975, (62965), 72241, 74966, 75172, 76081, (75107), (81719)-81721, 91186, 94850, 95786, 98298, 98450, 99745 see also Bertrand, -------- de. Duperre, Victor Guy, Baron, 1775-1846. La Luzerne, Cesar Henri, Comte de, 1737-1799. Malouet, V. P. Rochermore, -------- de. Rosamel, ---------- de. Roville, ----------.

France. Ministere de la Marine. Bibliotheque. 11484

France. Ministere de la Marine et des Colonies. see France. Ministere de la Marine.

France. Ministere des Affairs Etrangeres. 16863, 20425, 27274, 45451, (56773), 59593, 62702, 94261, 96445, 99303, 103848, 103868 see also Talleyrand-Perigord, Charles Maurice de, Prince de Benevent, 1754-1838. Thouvenel, Edouard Antoine, 1818-1866.

France. Ministere des Colonies. see France. Ministere de la Marine.

France. Parlement (Paris) 21859, 40691, 40718, 50223, 68074, 68898, 75154, 102772-102774

France. Parlement (Paris) Avocat. pseud. Patriote Anglois. see Le Blanc, Jean Bernard. supposed author

France. Parlement (Rouen) (40681)

France. Premiere Chambre d'Appel. (6268)

France. Procureur General. 10550, (38696), 40956, 47528, 59429 see also Boucly, ---------.

France. Protestant Ministers. see Protestant Ministers of France.

France. Societe Americaine. see Societe Americaine de France.

France. Societe des Antiquaires. see Societe Nationale des Antiquaires de France.

France. Societe Entomologique. see Societe Entomologique de France, Paris.

France. Societe Geologique. see Societe Geologique de France.

France. Societe Nationale des Antiquaires. see Societe Nationale des Antiquaires de France.

France. Sovereigns, etc. 10486, 17851-17855, 31095, (40701), (66984), (68420), 68438-(68439), 68444-68445, 68459, 103429

France. Sovereigns, etc., 1589-1610 (Henri IV) (14991), 50223 see also Henri IV, King of France, 1553-1610.

France. Sovereigns, etc., 1610-1643 (Louis XIII) 10360, 56079, 75014, 75016 see also Louis XIII, King of France, 1601-1643.

France. Sovereigns, etc., 1643-1715 (Louis XIV) 2144, 2148, 2151, 21859, 25882, 36762, 40691, 41843-41844, 42212, 42389, 50223, 56084, 56086, 56090, 57904, 68419, 68908, 68909, 70119, note before 96521, 96526, 96535, 99618, 102772-102774 see also Louis XVI, King of France, 1638-1715.

France. Sovereigns, etc., 1715-1774 (Louis XV) 4512, 10357, 19165-19168, 21860, 40686, 40713-40720, 52528, 57527, 57531, (68420), (68439), 68898, (68900), 68902, (68904)-68907, 68910, 68915-68917, 68920-68921, 73817, 75055, 75095, 75153-75155, 89126 see also Louis XV, King of France, 1710-1774.

France. Sovereigns, etc., 1774-1792 (Louis XVI) 57531, (62864), 68901, (68903), 68918, 68919, (69722), 75175, 96055, 96566 see also Louis XVI, King of France, 1754-1793.

France. Sovereigns, etc., 1804-1815 (Napoleon I) 42355, (75482) see also Napoleon I, Emperor of the French, 1769-1821.

France. Sovereigns, etc., 1815-1824 (Louis XVIII) 21858 see also Louis XVIII, King of France, 1755-1824.

France. Sovereigns, etc., 1824-1830 (Charles X) (29185), (57530) see also Charles X, King of France, 1757-1836.

France. Sovereigns, etc., 1830-1848 (Louis Philippe) 728, 14717, 17992, (67930) see also Louis Philippe, King of France, 1773-1850.

France. Sovereigns, etc., 1850-1870 (Napoleon III) see also Napoleon III, Emperor of the French, 1808-1873.

France. Treaties, etc. 2144, 2148, 2151, 2447-2449, 3557, (6361), 9021, 9080, 11815, 12689, 13768, 14372, 14378, 15493, 16086-16090, 16119, 16196, 16201, 19274, 19275, 20425, (21123), (22015), 24675, 25729, 26872-26873, 27274, 30866, 35779, 39155, 40104, 41843, 42054, 42211, 42227, 42895, 42308, 42309, 47516-47517, (47531), (48060), 56502, 56530, 56582, 65044, 65046, (65757), 68441, 68452, 68453, 68792, 75534, 77548, 78919, 80700-80701, 85648, 91091-91093, 94777, 2d note after 96185, 86516, note before 96521-96521, 96526, 96529-96532, 96533-96540, 96543-96545, 96548-96553, 96557, 96559-96562, 96565-96568, note after 98258, 98596, 99303, 99585, 101147, 101167, 101246, 102442

France. Voyage d'Exploration en CAlifornie et en Oregon, 1851-1852. 74986

France; atlas des quatre-vingt-six departements. (21145)

France aux colonies. 67622

France and England in North America. 58802

France and Mexico. (25428)

France en Amerique. 38436

France Equinoxiale. 49978

France et Amerique. (39470)

France et Bresil. (21460)

France et colonies. 9126

France et l'Amerique du Sud. (64699)
France et le Mexique. 4547
France et les Etats Confederes. 17239
France et les Yankees. 5137
France et Mexique. 22564
France et ses colonies. 44172
France; its king, court, and government. 11349
France, le Mexico, et les Etats Confederes.
    25429
France, l'emigration, et les colons. 64899
France, Mexico, and the Confederate States.
    12582
France protestante . . . . (29405)
France rendue florissante par la Guyane.
    21347
Francesco d'Assisi, Saint. 67652, 68841
Francesco de Bologne. 25435, 94854
Francfort, E. 25430
Franchere, Gabriel. 25431-25432
Francheville, Joseph du Fresne de. see Du
    Fresne de Francheville, Joseph.
Franchi, Vicenzo. tr. 98602
Francia, Thomas. 25433
Francia. (80174)
Francia's reign of terror. 71962, 71964
Francillon, John. 25434
Francis, of Assisi, Saint. see Francesco
    d'Assisi, Saint.
Francis, -------. see Haley, Thomas.
Francis, Benjamin. 25436
Francis, Convers. 25437-25440, 91372
Francis, James B. 25441
Francis, John Wakefield, 1789-1861. 25442-
    25448, 31577, 33083, 35221, 2d note after
    52014, 54803-(54804), 84441, 84445,
    84571, 84572
Francis, Sir Philip, 1740-1818. 25449, 58778
Francis, Samuel W. (25450)-25452
Francis, Valentine Mott. 25453
Francis. firm see Sever & Francis. firm
    publishers
Francis (C. C.) & Co. firm publishers
    (54282)
Francis Abbot, the recluse of Niagara. (5546)
Francis Adams. pseud. Voyages et aventures.
    see Cabet, Etienne.
Francis Adrian Van der Kemp, 1752-1829, an
    autobiography. 98479
Francis and Eliza (Ship) 81933, 97911
Francis Berrian, or the Mexican patriot.
    24787, (24795), 80735
Francis Herbert. pseud. Talisman. see
    Bryant, William Cullen, 1794-1878. Sands,
    Robert Charles, 1799-1832. Verplanck,
    Gulian Crommelin, 1786-1870.
Francis Herbert, a romance of the revolution.
    92905
Francis Lister Hawks, D. D. 50687
Francis, Lord Bacon. (25455)
Francis' new guide to . . . New York and
    Brooklyn. (54282)
Francis Spinoza. pseud. see Spinoza, Francis.
    pseud.
Francis Tamo. 25456
Francis W. Sabine. 74717
Francis Walsingham. pseud. Free Briton
    extraordinary. see Arnall, William.
Franciscan Convent, Talmanaco, Mexico. see
    Talmanaco, Mexico. Franciscan Convent
Franciscans. 9111, 12958, 25092, 29148,
    34823, 48464, 57469, 63166-63167, 63168,
    68841, 68843, 76105, 76106, 76885,
    93450, 94186, 97278, 98737
Franciscans. defendants 99442

Franciscans. Master General, 1579-1587
    (Gonzaga) 48464, 57469, 76105-76106
    see also Gonzaga, Francisco, Bp.
Franciscans. Master General. defendant
    105732
Franciscans. Indies. (76812)
Franciscans. Indies. Comissario General.
    (76812), 97278 see also Santander, J.
    de. Truxillo, Manuel Maria.
Franciscans. Mexico. 7748, 40958, 44419,
    47867, 66544, (68897), (69643), 76286,
    86406, 86411, 86414, 86416 see also
    Franciscans. Province of San Diego.
Franciscans. Province of San Pedro y
    San Paul de Michoacan. Tercer Orden
    de los Siervos de Maria Santisima de los
    Dolores. Mexico.
Franciscans. Mexico. plaintiffs. 86421,
    98773
Franciscans. Mexico. Comissairo General.
    petitioner 4636, 75785, (76810) see also
    Salinas y Cordova, Buenaventura, d. 1653.
    petitioner Santander, Juan de. petitioner
Franciscans. Mexico. Procurador General.
    73848, 73850 see also Heredia, Mateo
    de.
Franciscans. Mexico. Procurador General.
    petitioner 65347, 106408 see also
    Heredia, Mateo de. petitioner
Franciscans. Mexico. Procurador General.
    plaintiff 66561, (66574), 98773 see also
    Heredia, Mateo de. plaintiff
Franciscans. Peru. Comissario General.
    petitioner 76110, 87231 see also
    Herrera, Francisco de. petitioner
Franciscans. Philippines. (69643)
Franciscans. Spain. 76106
Franciscans. Province of Brazil. 34144
Franciscans. Province of Los Charcas del
    Reyno del Peru. 99730
Franciscans. Province of Los Doze Apostoles
    de Lima. 99730
Franciscans. Province of San Augustin de
    Quito. Definidor y Procurador General.
    petitioner 96757 see also Herera,
    Francisco de. petitioner
Franciscans. Province of San Diego. 44419,
    98737 see also Franciscans. Mexico.
Franciscans. Province of San Diego. Provin-
    cial. 19261
Franciscans. Province of San Francisco de
    Quito. Visitador. 76110 see also
    Gueuara, Ioan Ladron de.
Franciscans. Province of San Pedro y San
    Paul de Michoacan. 93583 see also
    Franciscans. Mexico.
Franciscans. Province of San Pedro y San
    Paul de Michoacan. Visitador. 93583
    see also Contreras, Francisco de.
Francisci, Erasmus, 1627-1694. 6441, 7407,
    25430-25465, 57462, note after 98470
Francisci Ceruantis Salazari Toletai, ad
    Ludouici Viuis Valentini exercitationem.
    (75565)
Francisci de Victoria Theologi Hispani celeber-
    rimi relectiones. 100621
Francisci Hernandi Medici atque historici
    Philippi II. Hisp. 31517
Francisci Plante Brugensis Mavritiados libri
    XII. 63319
Francisci Taraphae Barcinonem. De origine,
    ac rebus gestis. 94398
Franciscia, Julia. 25457
Francisco de Vitoria, 1486?-1546. 100618-
    100622

Francisco de la Cruz. Fray 87224-87225

Francisco de la Resurreccion. defendant 56282

Francisco de San Jose, d. 1701. 25458, (76126)

Francisco de San Joseph. see Francisco de San Jose, d. 1701.

Francisco, Juan de San. see San Francisco, Juan de.

Francisco, Maria Micaela Romero de Terreros y Trebuesto, Marquesa de San. see Terreros y Trebuesto, Maria Micaela Romero de, Marquesa de San Francisco.

Francisco, Melchor San. see San Francisco, Melchor.

Francisco, Pedro San. see San Francisco, Pedro.

Francisco de P. Santander, -------. (25459)

Francisco de Salles, Eusebe. see Salles, Eusebe Francisco de.

Francisco Balduini Commentaris de lege aquilia. 93324

Fr. de Gonzaga De origine seraphicae religionis Franciscanae. 27790

Francisco de Miranda and the revolutionizing of Spanish America. 83640

Francisco de Vrdinola, Gouernador y Capitan General de la Nueua Vizcaya por Su Magestad. 98121

Francisco Gallardo Solano, his deeds, and success. 86230

Francisco Pizarro, drama historico. (71449)

Francisco Solano, Gefe de las Tribus de esta frontera abusado del poder. 98385

Franciscus de Victoria. see Francisco de Vitoria, 1486?-1546.

Franck, -------, fl. 1860. 85791

Franck, A. 25466

Franck, H. (69296)

Franck, R. 25467

Franck, Sebastian. (25468)-25473, 77677-77678, 90039

Francke, A. H. 25474, 46805

Francke. firm see List & Francke. firm

Franckean Evangelic Lutheran Synod. 25476

Francken, G. tr. 8351, 74533, 1st note after 99534, 1st note after 100641

Franckenberg, Hans von. (25476)

Franckland (Tennessee) see Tennessee (Franklin Governmental District)

Francklin, Thomas. 25477, 83978

Francklin, William, 1763-1839. (59572), 62957

Francklyn, Gilbert. petitioner (25478)-25479, 73468-73469, 96047-96048, 96078-96080 see also Creanciers Anglois des Colons de Tabago. petitioners

Francklyn, Gilbert. supposed author 93365

Franco. pseud. see Simeon, el Franco. pseud.

Franco, A. 25480

Franco, Abraham. 25481

Franco, Abraham. plaintiff 25481

Franco, Bernardo de Sousa. 25482

Franco, Fernandez. ed. 79176

Franco, Francisco Soares. see Soares Franco, Francisco.

Franco, Giacomo. engr. 76897

Franco, Harry. pseud. Bankrupt stories. see Briggs, Charles F.

Franco, Jacob. plaintiff 25481

Franco de Almeida, Tito. see Almeida, Tito Franco de.

Franco Soto, Jos M. see Rivas-Cacho, Jos. M. (Franco Soto) de.

Franco-Americain. pseud. Verite sur le projet de chemin de ferinteroceanique. 32773

Franco-Canadian annexionists of Elmira, N. Y. 9827

Francois. pseud. Fragment de Xenophon. see Brizard, Gabriel.

Francois. pseud. Lettres. see Moreau, -------.

Francois. pseud. Notes. see Butel-Dumont, -------. supposed author

Francois. pseud. Voyages d'un Francois. 1st note after 100572, 100837

Francois de Sales. Saint 75763-(75764)

Francois, Armand le. see Le Francois, Armand.

Francoli, Benito Maria de Moxo y de. see Moxo y de Francoli, Benito Maria de.

Francos, Juan Isidro Pardinas Villar de. see Pardinas Villar de Francos, Juan Isidro.

Frank, Elizabeth. 51534

Frank before Vicksburg. 11437

Frank Forester. pseud. see Herbert, Henry William.

Frank Forester and his friends. (31462)

Frank Forester's field sports. (31461)

Frank Forester's fish and fishing in the United States. (31463)-31464

Frank Forester's horses and horsemanship. 31465

Frank Freeman's barber shop. 29727

Frank in the woods. 11437

Frank Leslie's pictorial history. 40199, note after 89964

Frank Myrtle. pseud. Poems. see Spencer, Caleb Lynn.

Frank Nelson. 30162

Frank on the lower Mississippi. 11437

Frank on the prairie. 11437

Frank, or, who's the croaker. 25485

Frank Rande, the tramping tragedian. 84246

Frank Swick's resident and business directory. 75297

Frank Wildman's adventures on land and water. 27178

Frankenstein, Jacob August. 25488

Frankenstein, John. 25486

Frankford, Pa. Asylum for the Relief of Persons Deprived of . . . Reason. see Philadelphia. Friends' Asylum for the Insane.

Frankford, Pa. Charter. 61904

Frankford, Pa. Ordinances, etc. (61597), 61904

Frankford, Pa. St. Mark's Church. 62213

Frankford (District), Philadelphia. see Frankford, Pa.

Frankfort, Ky. Institution for the Education of Feenle-Minded Children. see Kentucky. Institution for the Education of Feeble-Minded Children, Frankfort.

Frankfort, Ky. National Republican Party Convention, 1830. see National Republican Party. Kentucky. Convention, Frankfort, 1830.

Frankfort, Ky. Southern Rights Party Convention, 1861. see Southern Rights Party of Kentucky. Convention, Frankfort, 1861.

Frankfort (Borough), Philadelphia. see Frankford, Pa.

Frankfort Literary Society. 25488

Frankfurt am Main. Gesellschaft fur Anthropologie, Ethnologie und Urgeschichte.

see Frankfurter Gesellschaft fur Anthro-
pologie, Ethnologie und Urgeschichte.
Frankfurt am Main. Stadtbibliothek. 99378
Frankfurter Gesellschaft fur Anthropologie,
Ethnologie und Urgeschichte. 90036,
105680
Franking privilege. 68668
Franklin. pseud. Address to the country over
the signature of Franklin. 15653
Franklin. pseud. Address to the people of
Pennsylvania. 59859
Franklin. pseud. Examination of Mr.
Dradish's answer. 25641
Franklin. pseud. Fellow citizens of Pennsyl-
vania. (60099)
Franklin. pseud. Letters of Franklin.
(13895), (14009), 25640, 101838, note
after 101847
Franklin. pseud. To the freemen of Vermont.
99206
Franklin. pseud. To the people of Virginia.
99807, note after 100544
Franklin, -------. defendant (17400)
Franklin, A. W. ed. 25489
Franklin, Benjamin, 1706-1790. 108, 1604,
5691, 13040-13043, 13470-13471, (17987),
(23951), 23807, 23491-25510, 25512-
25527, (25529)-25557, 25559-25560,
25562-25574, 25576-25577, 25579-25590,
(25592)-(25594), 25596-25608, 25611,
25615, 25617-25618, 25668, 26445,
(26887), 30571, 31198, 31295, 31296,
(32145), (34358), 34792, 34891, (35450),
38434, note after 38799, 41024, 52386,
56487, 56583, (59888), 60181, 60329,
(60436), 60754, 61201, 61203, 61299,
61522, 61657, 61783, 62425, 63506,
64822, 65025, 65678, (66215), 66394,
66648, 68692, 68693, 69499, 70006,
70906, 73061, 74092, 74168, 76966,
78109-78118, 78729, 79369, 79604, 82400,
82974, 82976, 82978-82979, 82987, 84583,
84586, 84587, 84589, 84602, 84614,
84643, 85685, 86264, 86582, 88824,
88969, 88982-88984, 90312, 92135, 94554,
94663, 96091, 96191, 2d note after 96428,
2d note after 97091, 97106, 6th note after
97146, 97158, note after 97166, 97167,
97352, 97565, 101047, 101479, 102182,
102348, 102394, 102487, 102488, 103107,
103121, 104455, 1st note after 104563,
1st note after 105132 see also France.
Commission Chargee de l'Examen du
Magnetisme Animal. Pennsylvania (Colony)
Commissioners to the Ohio Indians.
Pennsylvania. Supreme Executive Council.
President. U. S. Legation. France.
U. S. Peace Commissioners, Paris, 1782-
1783.
Franklin, Benjamin, 1706-1790. supposed author
(491), 6569, 22595, 25490, 25511, 25528,
25558, (25561), (25575), 25578, 25591,
25595, 34579-34580, 34809, (35450),
39706, 60646, 60742, 63221, 65678,
89384, 93361, 95675, 96191, 96769,
97090, note before 97095, 99584, note
after 103106, 1st note after 103107, note
just before 103108
Franklin, Benjamin, 1706-1790. incorrectly
supposed author 1783, 25558, (39697)-
39698, 65499, (79890), 83984, note after
95316, 97567, 101150, 102351
Franklin, Benjamin, 1706-1790. petitioner
101150

Franklin, Benjamin, 1706-1790. spirit author
36665, 38845, 71149
Franklin, Benjamin, 1706-1790. spurious author
89403
Franklin, H. (53894)
Franklin, Henry. pseud. Excursions in North
America. see Wakefield, Priscilla (Bell)
Franklin, J. 25623
Franklin, James, fl. 1785. 25620
Franklin, James, fl. 1828. (25621)-(25622)
Franklin, James. supposed author 100759
Franklin, Lady Jane (Griffin) 1792-1875.
25634
Franklin, John, fl. 1786. (59830), 105686A,
105693A
Franklin, Sir John, 1786-1847. 19582, (25624)-
25630, 25633, 31601, 50115, 74730,
85145-85146, 100825
Franklin, Mathew. 71369
Franklin, S. F. 25635
Franklin, Thomas. plaintiff 96765
Franklin, W. S. ed. 15592, 70076
Franklin, W. T. 35339
Franklin, William, of Connecticut. (9077),
25638
Franklin, William, ca. 1730-1813. 25636-
25637 see also New Jersey (Colony)
Governor, 1763-1776 (Franklin)
Franklin, William, ca. 1730-1813. petitioner
93593, 3d note after 105598-9 [sic]
Franklin, William, ca. 1730-1813. supposed
author 25512, 60646, 93361
Franklin, William B. 25639
Franklin, William Temple. 25491, 25523,
25545-25546, 25550, 25569, 25571-25572
Franklin (Benjamin) & Co. firm 84583
Franklin (James) firm publisher 62743,
70701-(70702)
Franklin and Hall. firm publishers 90137
Franklin (State) see Tennessee (Franklin
Governmental District)
Franklin, Conn. Committee. see Committee
of the Towns of Bozrah, Lebanon and
Franklin in the State of Connecticut.
Franklin, Conn. Congregational Church. 25650
Franklin, Mass. 25661
Franklin, Mass. petitioners 16140
Franklin, Mass. School Committee. (25657)
Franklin, Mass. Society for Detecting Horse-
Thieves, and Recovering Stolen Horses.
see Society for Detecting Horse-Thieves,
and Recovering Stolen Horses, Wrentham,
Franklin, Medway, Medfield, Walpole,
Foxborough, Mansfield, and Attleborough,
Mass.
Franklin County, Ky. Circuit Court. 18431,
79848
Franklin County, Mass. Agricultural Society.
see Franklin County Agricultural Society.
Franklin County, Mass. Benevolent Societies.
see Benevolent Societies of Franklin
County, Mass.
Franklin County, Mass. Medical Association.
see Franklin Medical Association.
Franklin County, Mass. Washington Benevolent
Society. see Washington Benevolent
Society. Massachusetts. Franklin County.
Franklin County, N. Y. Board of Supervisors.
25651
Franklin County, N. Y. Citizens. petitioners
(47666)
Franklin County, N. Y. Court of Oyer and
Terminer. 99501
Franklin County, Ohio. Citizens Favorable to
the Election of Andrew Jackson. see

Democratic Party. Ohio. Franklin County.

Franklin County, Pa. Committee of the Anti-Jackson Men. see National Republican Party. Pennsylvania. Franklin County.

Franklin County, Pa. Treasurer. (13705)

Franklin County, Vt. Grammar School. 25652

Franklin. (5522), 85819

Franklin Agricultural Society. see Hampshire, Franklin and Hampden Agricultural Society.

Franklin almanac and diary, for 1868. 25643

Franklin almanac for 1819. 25642

Franklin. An address delivered . . . on Franklin's birth-day. 2844

Franklin and Hall work-book. 90137

Franklin and Hampden Agricultural Society. see Hampshire, Franklin and Hampden Agricultural Society.

Franklin and Marshall College, Lancaster, Pa. 25644-25645

Franklin Association. see Congregational Churches in Massachusetts. Franklin Association of Ministers.

Franklin Association Charitable Society. 25646 see also Congregational Churches in Massachusetts. Franklin Association of Ministers.

Franklin Association Charitable Society. Committee. 25646

Franklin Association of Ministers. see Congregational Churches in Massachusetts. Franklin Association of Ministers.

Franklin Baptist Association. see Baptists. New York. Franklin Baptist Association.

Franklin before the Privy Council. (25510)

Franklin Cemetery, Philadelphia. see Philadelphia. Franklin Cemetery.

Franklin cemetery. 61673

Franklin College, Athens, Ga. 25649

Franklin comedie historique en cinq actes et en prose. 5050

Franklin County Agricultural Society. 25662

Franklin county register. 44928

Franklin der Philosoph und Staatsmann. 48668

Franklin Domestic Missionary Society. 25659

Franklin expedition. (78170)

Franklin expedition from first to last. 37797

Franklin-Expedition und ihr Ausgang. 25633

Franklin family primer. note after 65546

Franklin Fire Company, Philadelphia. 61674

Franklin Fire Company, Philadelphia. Charter. 61674

Franklin Fire Company, Washington, D. C. 101942

Franklin Fire Company, Washington, D. C. Charter. 101942

Franklin Fire Insurance Company. 61675

Franklin Fire Insurance Company. Charter. 61675

Franklin Fire Insurance Company. . . . The public are . . . informed. 61675

Franklin Fire Society, Boston. see Franklin United Fire Society, Boston.

Franklin Fund, Boston. 6707

Franklin— his genius, life, and character. 36115

Franklin. . . . Horace Mann. 38446

Franklin Institute, New Haven, Conn. 52978

Franklin Institute, Philadelphia. 12584, 25654, 25656, 60106, (68512), 89118, 93519, 93521

Franklin Institute, Philadelphia. Committee on Premiums and Exhibitions. 25656

Franklin Institute, Philadelphia. Committee on Investigations. 93521

Franklin Institute, Philadelphia. Committee on Publications. (25655)

Franklin Institute, Philadelphia. Corresponding Secretary. 25656

Franklin Institute, Philadelphia. Editor of the Journal. pseud. see Editor of the Journal of the Franklin Institute. pseud.

Franklin Institute, Philadelphia. Library. (25653)

Franklin Institute of the State of Pennsylvania. see Franklin Institute, Philadelphia.

Franklin journal, and the American mechanics' magazine. (25655), (30393), 98697 see also Journal of the Franklin Institute.

Franklin lectures. 24953

Franklin Library Association, Lawrence, Mass. see Lawrence, Mass. Franklin Library Association.

Franklin library edition, series 1-2. 96128

Franklin Lyceum, Providence, R. I. see Providence, R. I. Franklin Museum.

Franklin Medical Association. 25660

Franklin Mining Company. Directors. 25663

Franklin ore and iron. 25664

Franklin Pierce's Leben und Wirken. 62715

Franklin Rail Road. A report of the Chief Engineer. 60107

Franklin Rail Road Company. 25665

Franklin Rail Road Company. Chief Engineer. 60107

Franklin Rail Road Company. Managers. 60107

Franklin Rail Road Company. President. 60107

Franklin Section, no. 3, Cadets of Temperance. see Cadets of Temperance. Rhode Island. Franklin Section, no. 3, Pawtucket.

Franklin Society, Chicago. 80033

Franklin Society, Providence, R. I. see Providence Franklin Society, Providence, R. I.

Franklin Society, St. Louis. 74349

Franklin Society, St. Louis. Charter. 75324

Franklin Society publications, I. 80033

Franklin Square library. 100482

Franklin Street Church, Boston. see Boston. Franklin Street Church.

Franklin the apprentice. 25610

Franklin, the apprentice boy. 32

Franklin Typographical Society, Boston. Librarian. 90012 see also Squire, Henry.

Franklin Typographical Society, Boston. Printers' Festival, 1848. 25666, 65770

Franklin Typographical Society, Cincinnati. 13082

Franklin und Washington. 3985

Franklin United Fire Society, Boston. 97872

Frankliniana. (25668)

Franklin's aefi. (25593), 97526

Franklin's autobiography. 25537

Franklin's footsteps. (44615)

Franklin's Leben. (25540), 25556A

Franklin's legacy. 25667

Franklin's letter to his kinsfolk. 25511

Franklinville Academy, Franklinville, N. Y. 25669

Frankreich und die Freistaaten von Nordamerika. 106337

Frankreichs Handlung-Bilanz und auswartige Handlungs-Beziehungen. 2091

Frankreichs Verfahren gegen Amerika. 99303

Franks, David. 54456

Franquez, Gonzalo. defendant (34719)
Fransham, John. (25670)
Fransioli, Joseph. 25671
Fransman. pseud. Klachte der West-Indische
  Compagnie. 38028, 3d note after 102893
Fransoni, Domenico, Marchese. supposed
  author 14657, note after 98906
Frantic conduct of John Bull. 25672
Frantic maid. 25673
Frantzius, A. von. tr. 58271
Franz, Hermann. tr. 97030
Franz Xavier Veigl vormaliger Missionar der
  Gesellschaft Jesu. 51480, (51482),
  98777
Franzoia, Matteo, Conte. tr. 100725
Frappaz, -------. tr. 46834
Frasans, Hippolyte de. 25674, (29042)
Fraser, A. reporter 8415
Fraser, Charles. 25675
Fraser, Donald, fl. 1797. 25676-25678, 68341
Fraser, Donald, 1826-1892. 25679
Fraser, Eliza. 25880
Fraser, James. 25682
Fraser, John. (25683)
Fraser, Malcolm, 1733-1815. 25684, 67022
Fraser, Thomas. 25685
Fraser (James) publisher 10645, (25681),
  (48985), 58455
Fraser and Co. firm. see M'Tavish, Fraser
  and Co. firm.
Fraser mines vindicated. 100899
Fraser's magazine. 10645, (25681), (48985),
  58455
Frasso, Pedro, fl. 1675. (25687), 70803 see
  also Guatemala (Spanish Colony) Real
  Audiencia. Fiscal.
Frast, Johann. ed. (59173)
Frater Alphonsvs a Vera Crvce Ordinis
  Heremitarum Sancti Augustini Magister.
  98913
Fraternal affection and neighbourly kindness.
  102077
Fraternal appeal and other documents. (45148)
Fraternal appeal to the American churches.
  77721
Fraternal appeal to the friends of the Evan-
  gelical Alliance. 77721
Fraternal Communion, Mendon, Mass. 47821
Fraternal intercessory cry of faith and love.
  18470
Fraternal tribute of respect. 20623, 101810,
  1st note after 101877
Fraternity, Boston. 58768, 12th note after
  96966
Fraternity lectures . . . Boston, Oct. 4, 1859.
  62528
Fraternity of Gentlemen. see Yale University.
  Fraternity of Gentlemen. eds.
Fratris Ioannis Capato, y Sandoval Avgvstiniani.
  106252A
Fratris Nicolai Hortvlani Epigramma. 77804
Fratrium Mendicantium. see Franciscans.
Fraud and oppression detected and arraigned.
  10622
Fraud exposed. 90739
Fraud! Fraud! Fraud! 83284
Fraud upon the people. (5680)
Frauds and corruption in the Navy Department.
  29641
Frauds in District of Columbia. (73110)
Frauds in Kansas illustrated. 90410
Frauds in naval contracts. (80374)
Frauds of neutral commerce. 101270
Frauds of the Indian Office. 18797

Frauds of the neutral flags. 8514, 18487,
  50827, 67839, note before 91236, 91240-
  91241, 91246-91247, 101270
Frauds of the New York city government
  exposed. 26965
Frauds on the revenue. 77577
Frauds on the treasury. 32571
Fraudulent Mexican land claims in California.
  32439
Frauenfahrt um die Welt. 61336
Frauenleben unter den Mormonem. note after
  101315
Fraunces, Andrew G. 25688
Fraxinellae plantarum familiae naturalis.
  52240
Fr. Bernardino de Solorcano, Procurador
  General. 86515
Fr. Bernardo Manetense, Capuch., Catechismo
  para los Karistis. 44234
Fray Matias Ruiz Blanco, de la Regular
  Observancia de N. P. San Francisco.
  74019
Fray Mateo de Heredia de la Orden de S.
  Francisco. 73850
Fray Pedro de Sosa, de la Orden de San
  Francisco. Dize, ... 87185
Fray Pedro de Sosa de la Orden de San
  Francisco por el Reyno de Chile. Dize,
  87184
Fray Pedro de Sosa Guardian del Conuento de
  S. Fransisco de Santiago. 87188
Fray Pedro de Sossa de la Orden de. S.
  Francisco, Guardian del Couento de S.
  Francisco de la ciudad de Santiago.
  87186
Fray Pedro de Sossa de la Orden de S.
  Francisco, Predicador y Guardian del
  Conuento de la misma orden de Santiago.
  87187
Fray Serapio, escenas de la vida Mejicana.
  25689
Frazee, Bradford. (25890)
Frazee, George. reporter 18270, 26127
Frazee, John. 25691
Frazer, J. F. ed. (25655)
Frazer, John, fl. 1789. 25692
Frazer, John, fl. 1850. 83706
Frazer, William Clark. 25693
Frazier, -------. (19702), 6th note after
  97689
Frazier, Elihu. defendant 18270, 26127
Frazier, James A. (72376)-72377
Frazier, Thomas W. defendant 25694
Frazier & Randolph. firm. (72376)
Freaks of Columbia. 20314, 94403
Freble, Thomas M. see Preble, Thomas M.
Fred Shaw's American diadem. 79907
Fred Shaw's champion comic melodist. 79907
Fred Shaw's dime American comic songster.
  79907
Frederici, Cesare de. (67734)-67735, 67742
Frederick, Francis, d. 1819. defendant (41584),
  96944, 104281-note after 104281
Frederick Augustus Fidfaddy. pseud. see
  Fidfaddy, Frederick Augustus. pseud.
Frederick, Md. State School for the Deaf.
  see Maryland. State School For the
  Deaf, Frederick.
Frederick County, Md. Agricultural Society.
  see Frederick County Agricultural Society.
Frederick County, Md. St. Joseph's Academy.
  see St. Joseph's Academy, Frederick
  County, Md.
Frederick County, Md. Sheriff. 45120

Frederick County, Md. Young Men's Bible Society. see Young Men's Bible Society of Frederick County, Maryland.

Frederick County Agricultural Society. Committee on Essays. (68058)

Frederick de Algeroy, the hero of Camden Plains. 26808

Fredericksburg, Va. Democratic PArty Convention, 1836. see Democratic Party. Virginia. Convention, Fredericksburg, 1836.

Fredericksburg, Va. Mary Washington College. see Mary Washington College, Fredericksburg, Va.

Fredericksburg, Va. Southern Female Institute. see Mary Washington College, Fredericksburg, Va.

Fredericton, Bishop of. see Medley, John, Bishop of Fredericton, 1804-1892.

Fredericton, N. B. University. see New Brunswick. University.

Frederik III, King of Denmark, 1609-1670. 7915, 38031, 5th note after 102893 see also Denmark. Sovereigns, etc., 1648-1670 (Frederik III)

Frederike, Caesar. 66686

Fredonia, N. Y. Academy. see Fredonia Academy, Fredonia, N. Y.

Fredonia Academy, Fredonia, N. Y. 25698

Fredonia Academy, Fredonia, N. Y. Reunion, 1867. 25698

Fredoniad. 22529

Fredrik Martens naukeurige beschryvinge van Groenland en Spitsbergen. 44836

Fredrik Martens nauwkeurige beschryvinge van Groenland of Spitsbergen. 44835

Free Academy, New York. see New York (City) City College.

Free Academy, Rochester, N. Y. Principal. 72366

Free-agency of man. 68122

Free and calm considerations. (65236)

Free and candid address to the Right Hon. William Pitt. 25699

Free and candid disquisitions. (26248)

Free and candid reflections. 37333

Free and candid remarks on a late celebrated oration. 25700

Free and candid review, of a tract. 32636

Free and easy. (76703), 101487

Free and friendly remarks on a speech. (29314), 81981

Free and impartial examiner. 25701

Free and impartial examination. 25702

Free and impartial remarks. 25703

Free and independent elector. pseud. Sentiments. 99828

Free and natural inquiry into the propriety of the Christian faith. 106081

Free and slave labour. 93452

Free appeal to the people of Great Britain. 25704, 95750

Free appeal to the people on the conduct of the present administration. 25704, 95750

Free Associate Presbytery of Miami. 48683

Free banking. 21267

Free banks. 89113

Free banks and chartered banks compared. 42195

Free blacks and slaves. 25705

Free-born subject's inheritance. 10819

Free Briton. pseud. Free Briton's memorial. see Bollan, William.

Free Briton. pseud. Free Briton's supplemental memorial. see Bollan, William.

Free Briton. pseud. Occasional thoughts. 56631

Free Briton extraordinary. 101167

Free Briton's memorial. 6212

Free Briton's supplementary memorial. 6213

Free Christian state and the present struggle. 65093

Free Church Association of the Diocese of Maryland. see Protestant Episcopal Church in the U. S. A. Maryland (Diocese) Free Church Association.

Free church circular. (25706), 89516

Free Church of St. Mary, for Sailors, Boston. see Boston. Free Church of St. Mary, for Sailors.

Free Church of St. Mary, for Sailors. Rev. John P. Robinson, Rector. 72136, 75420

Free churches. 25707

Free citizens. pseud. To the public. 95988

Free Citizens of Color in Pittsburg and its Vicinity. see Pittsburgh. Free Citizens of Color. petitioners

Free collegiate education. 8868

Free commerce between the states. 26664

Free communion of all Christians. 85542-85544

Free constitutionalists. pseud. Address. see Spooner, Lysander.

Free Convention, Rutland, Vt., 1858. 65853

Free cotton. (32629)

Free cotton and free cotton states. 76486

Free Democratic document. No. 10. 93658

Free Democratic Meeting, Boston, 1852. see Free Soil Party. Massachusetts. Boston.

Free Democratic Party. see Free-Soil Party.

Free disputation against the pretended liberty of conscience. (74457)

Free education in Pittsfield, Mass. 83333

Free enquirer. (25708), 52953, 62439

Free enquiry into the causes. (25709), 3d note after 99216

Free Evangelical Congregational Church, Providence, R. I. see Providence, R. I. Free Evangelical Congregational Church.

Free examination of the critical commentary. 11878

Free forgiveness of spiritual debts. 17675

Free flag of Cuba. (30325)

Free government in England and America. (36317)

Free grace. 103517, 103556

Free grace indeed! 103517

Free-grace, maintained & improved. 46331

Free Holders' Bank of Upper Canada. Charter. 98079

Free homes for free men. (28994)

Free justification thro' Christ's redemption. 17671

Free labor in the colonies. 25710

Free lands of Iowa. 26192

Free Library, New Orleans. see New Orleans. Free Library.

Free Library, Newton, Mass. see Newton, Mass. Free Library.

Free-masonry an agent in the civilization of man. 72448

Free-masonry in reply to anti-masonry. 25805

Free masonry. Its pretentions exposed. 45501, 96366

Free masonry revealed and exposed, by eleven seceeding members. (50678)

Free masonry unmasked. 25807, note after 91560

Free-mason's annual anthology. 39190

Free mason's calendar, and continental almanac. 90957

Free-mason's daughter. 84328
Free-mason's vocal assistant. 25812, 52255, 87840
Free military school for applicants for commands. (25711)
Free navigation of the St. Lawrence. (8973)
Free man. pseud. Brief and impartial history. see Snelling, William Joseph, 1804-1848.
Free Negro question in Maryland. 25712, (25497A)
Free Negroes and mulattoes. 42798, (45736)
Free Negroism. 25713, (81982)
Free parliaments. 56508
Free-people bestrided in their persons, and liberties. 27713
Free people of color of the United States. pseud. Opinions. 91011
Free Presbyterian Church. 72118
Free Produce Association of Friends, New York. see New York Free Produce Association of Friends.
Free Produce Association of Friends, Philadelphia. see Philadelphia Free Produce Association of Friends.
Free Produce Society of Pennsylvania. 60108
Free public libraries. 25714
Free Public Library, Lynn, Mass. see Lynn, Mass. Free Public Library.
Free Public Library, New Bedford Mass. see New Bedford, Mass. Free Public Library.
Free Public Library, Art-Gallery, and Museum, Providence, R. I. see Providence, R. I. Free Public Library, Art-Gallery, and Museum.
Free Public Library, Art-Gallery, and Museum, in . . . Providence. 66265
Free School, New York. see New York (City) Free School.
Free Reading-Room, Spring Garden (District), Philadelphia. see Spring Garden Institute, Philadelphia.
Free Reading Room Association of Spring Garden. see Spring Garden Institute, Philadelphia.
Free Reading-Room of Spring Garden, for young men and apprentices. 62270
Free religion. 25715
Free remarks on the spirit of the federal constitution. 25716, 2d note after 101162
Free school law, by-laws, ordinances, &c. 72366
Free School of 1645 in Roxburie. 20160
Free School Society, New York. 44414, 54285
Free School Society, New York. Committee on the State of the Society. 54285
Free School Society, New York. Trustees. 54285
Free School Society, New york. Trustees. Committee on the Distribution of the Common School Fund. 54285
Free schools for the south. 86341
Free-schools in Virginia. 16219
Free schools vs. state schools. 74551
Free Society of Traders in Pennsylvania. 59897
Free Soil Association of the District of Columbia. 20314, (81761) see also Free Soil Party. Washington, D. C.
Free Soil Club, Cambridge, Mass. see Cambridge Free Soil Club.
Free soil, free democracy, free ideas. (37677)
Free soil minstrel. 25717
Free Soil Party. 20428-20429, 28493, (52182)
Free Soil Party. National Convention, Buffalo, 1848. 21599, 63347

Free Soil Party. National Convention, Pittsburgh, 1852. 63347
Free Soil Party. Massachusetts. Boston. 8910, note after 89215
Free Soil Party. Massachusetts. Cambridge. (10149) see also Cambridge Free Soil Club.
Free Soil Party. New York. Convention, Rome, 1849. 53867
Free Soil Party. Washington, D. C. 20314, (81761) see also Free Soil Association of the District of Columbia.
Free Soil Party in Wisconsin. 84337
Free soil songs for the people. 25718
Free-soiler from the start. pseud. Remarks on the proposed state constitution. see Palfrey, John Gorham.
Free speech: by Elizabeth Cady Stanton. 90400
Free State Party. Louisiana. 42282
Free State Topeka Convention, Topeka, Kansas, 1857. 37016
Free sugar. Speech . . . February 5, 1867. 14344
Free territory. 82227
Free thinker. pseud. Few remarks. 97179
Free thinker. pseud. Random sketches. see Crocker, A. B.
Free, thought private New-England-Man. pseud. Voice of the people. 100672
Free thoughts communicated to free thinkers. 11748
Free thoughts, &c. (78562)-78563, 78580
Free thoughts on despotic and free governments. 25719
Free thoughts on politics and politicians in Michigan. (41950)
Free thoughts on the American contest. 1399
Free thoughts on the continuance of the American war. 25720
Free thoughts on the present ciritical conjuncture. 90620, note before 93779, note after 93808
Free thoughts on the present state of public affairs. 96354, 102676
Free thoughts, on the proceedings of the Continental Congress. 78574-78575, 78581, 4th note after 100862
Free town libraries. 21919
Free trade advocate, and journal of political economy. 67502
Free trade and farmer's rights. 25721
Free trade and protection. 96396
Free trade and protection. By S. L. Fleishman. (24698)
Free trade and sailors' rights. 25722, 1st note after 99488
Free Trade and State Rights Association. see State Rights and Free Trade Association of South Carolina.
Free trade and the American system. 25724, 87830
Free Trade Convention, Philadelphia, 1831. 10889, 30052, 36724
Free Trade Convention, Philadelphia, 1831. Committee to Prepare and Present a Memorial to Congress. petitioners (26399), (47498), 47669 see also Gallatin, Albert, 1761-1849. petitioner
Free Trade Convention, Boston, 1832. petitioners 10889, 39753, (39766), 92843
Free Trade Convention, Boston, 1832. Committee. 23400, (39756), 92843
Free trade falsehood that "a tariff is a tax" exposed. 91012

Free trade in money. 103304
Free trade in Negroes. (25723)
Free Trade Meeting, Boston, 1820. see
Boston. Free Trade Meeting, 1820.
Free trade policy. 25725
Free trade: remarks . . . at the Workingmen's
Institute, Boston. (11790)
Free trade versus reciprocity. 84007
Free-trader. 25726
Free-trader; or, the cruiser of Narragansett
Bay. 34776
Free Whig Republican Democrat. pseud.
Squint at parties in Massachusetts.
90008
Free White Schools, Richmond, Va. Superin-
tendent. see Soldiers' Memorial Society,
Boston. Free White Schools, Richmond,
Va. Superintendent.
Free-Will Baptist register for 1847. 25727
Free-Will Baptists. North America. General
Conference. (25728)
Free-Will Baptists. Pawtucket, R. I. 64665
Freebetter, Edmund. 52649, 53257, 62743
Freebooters. (31118)
Freeborn Englishman's unmasked battery.
25729
Freed boy in Alabama. 49666
Freed-man. 25736
Freedley, Edwin T. (25730)-(25733)
Freedman, John J. (25734)-25735
Freedman soldier. 59445
Freedman's book. (12715)
Freedman's harp. 25741
Freedman's Bureau. Speech 20602
Freedman's Saving and Trust Company, New
York. 25744, 54466
Freedman's Saving and Trust Company, New
York. Charter. 25737
Freedman's Saving and Trust Company. 25744,
25737
Freedman's Saving and Trust Company. Speech
of Hon. Elisha D. Standiford. 90163
Freedman's Union Commission. see American
Freedman's Union Commission.
Freedmen at Fortress Monroe. 37938
Freedmen in America. 39919
Freedmen of Louisiana. 16223
Freedmen of Port Royal, South Carolina.
62710
Freedmen of South Carolina. An address . . .
by J. Miller M'Kim. 43455
Freedmen of South Carolina; some account of
their appearance. 55462
Freedmen of the south. 81702
Freedmen of the war. 34171
Freedmen's Aid Society, New England. see
New England Freedmen's Aid Society.
Freedmen's bulletin. 25740
Freedmen's Bureau. see United States. Bureau
of Refugees, Freedmen, and Abandoned
Lands.
Freedmen's Bureau. Reports of Generals
Steedman and Fullerton. 91088
Freedmen's Bureau. Speech . . . delivered in
the House. 11895
Freedmen's Convention, Annapolis, Md., 1864.
45149
Freedmen's Convention, Raleigh, N. C., 1866.
67600
Freedmen's Convention at Annapolis, July, 1864.
45149
Freedmen's code. 87715
Freedmen's journal. 25742
Freedmen's record. 25742
Freedom; a poem. (68253)

Freedom and franchise inseparable. 8453
Freedom and largeness of the Christian faith.
(66760)
Freedom and love. 8185
Freedom and protection are its best support.
103121
Freedom and protection, the policy. 97916
Freedom and public faith. 79520
Freedom and slavery. 79750
Freedom and slavery in the United States.
65739
Freedom and slavery in the United States of
America. . 55399
Freedom and the union. 79521
Freedom and war. 4314
Freedom for Missouri. 8453
Freedom from civil and ecclesiastical slavery,
the purchase of Christ. (58889), 79747,
97319
Freedom in Kansas. 79522-79523
Freedom in Jamaica. 35582
Freedom national; slavery sectional. Speech
of Hon. Charles Sumner, of Massachu-
setts. 59002, 93657-93659
Freedom national—slavery sectional. Speech
of Hon. John J. Perry. 61038
Freedom national—slavery sectional. Speech
. . . on the Governor's message. 30109
Freedom of commerce of the subjects of the
Netherlands. 25747
Freedom of speech and writing upon public
affairs, considered. 6214, 25748, 93387
Freedom of speech. Speech of Hon. James S.
Rollins. 72858
Freedom of speech vindicated, defended, and
maintained. 13099, 38000
Freedom of speech vindicated. Speech . . .
on the President's message. 27329
Freedom of the mind, demanded of American
freemen. 56045
Freedom of the press wantonly violated.
(44466)
Freedom of the pulpit. 70410
Freedom of thought, the true mean. 92921
Freedom or slavery in the United States.
81406
Freedom policy and reconstruction. 6005
Freedom takes no step backwards. 5772
Freedom the first of blessings. (25749),
42376
Freedom vs. slavery. Address of Dr. A. P.
Dostie. 20665
Freedom versus slavery. Letters from Henry
B. Pearson. 59446
Freedom vs. slavery. Speech of . . . John
Hutchins, of Ohio. (34047)
Freedom's banner. 33209
Freedom's bower. 72648
Freedom's defence. 13133, 28944
Freedom's early sacrifice. 81179-81181
Freedom's gift. 81983
Freedom's journal. (25750)
Freedom's songster. 35393
Freedom's triumph. 104542
Freeholder. pseud. Account of some particu-
lars. see Smelt, Leonard.
Freeholder. pseud. Appeal to the people of
the United States. 1784, 25751
Freeholder. pseud. Equity and wisdom of
administration. see Erskine, John.
Freeholder. pseud. Freeholder to the free-
holders, etc.,of Philadelphia. 61676
Freeholder. pseud. Freeholder's address to
the freeholders in the southern district.
25752

Freeholder. pseud. Freeholder's address to the Honourable House of Representatives. see Wise, John.
Freeholder. pseud. Inquiries of a freeholder. 26680
Freeholder. pseud. Reflections on the rise. see Erskine, John.
Freeholder. pseud. To the freeholders, merchants, tradesmen and farmers. 62320, 62337
Freeholder. pseud. To the inhabitants of Pennsylvania. 60706
Freeholder. pseud. To the public. As it is generally imagined. 95970
Freeholder. pseud. To the public. I was sorry to observe. 96006
Freeholder of South-Carolina. pseud. Humble enquiry. see Zubly, John Joachim.
Freeholder of Suffolk. pseud. Two letters. 97564
Freeholder to the freeholders, etc. 61676
Freeholder's address to the freeholders. 25752
Freeholder's address to the Honourable House of Representatives. 104898
Freeholders and Inhabitants, Philadelphia. see Philadelphia. Freeholders and Inhabitants.
Freeholders, and other electors . . . are requested to attend. 61677
Freeholders Meeting, Philadelphia, 1817. see Meeting of the Freeholders From . . . the State, Philadelphia, 1817.
Freeholders of the Somers-Island Company in London. see Bermuda Company.
Freeholder's political catechism. 25753
Freeland, William H. 25754
Freeman. pseud. Address to the deputies of North America. (15511)
Freeman. pseud. Address to the freemen of Massachusetts. see Allen, George.
Freeman. pseud. Address to the freemen of Rhode Island. 70530
Freeman. pseud. Calm and respectful thoughts. see Zubly, John Joachim.
Freeman. pseud. Dialogue between Freeman and Trusty. 60056
Freeman. pseud. Freeman on freemasonry. (25800)
Freeman. pseud. Freeman's address to the North Americans. (25789)
Freeman. pseud. Hints to the farmers of Rhode Island. 31986, 103115
Freeman. pseud. Letters of Freeman, &c. see Drayton, William Henry. Gadsden, Christopher. Mackenzie, John. Wragg, William.
Freeman. pseud. Principles and acts of Mr. Adams' administration vindicated. see Moore, Jacob Bailey.
Freeman. pseud. Question of a south ferry to Long Island. see Warner, Henry Whiting.
Freeman. pseud. Strictures upon the observations. 52933
Freeman. pseud. To the public. 95987
Freeman, Mr. ------. pseud. 60181, 97167
Freeman, -------, fl. 1715. tr. 13181, (50765)
Freeman, -------, fl. 1806. 25787
Freeman, Bernardus. 25755
Freeman, Edward A. 25756
Freeman, Frederick, 1799-1883. 25757-25759
Freeman, Frederick, fl. 1860-1862. (25760)
Freeman, H. C. 34253
Freeman, J. 25769

Freeman, James, 1759-1835. 4596, (11209), 18895, 25761-25767, (25768), (41553), 96412, 2d note after 97579
Freeman, James. pseud. Profitable advice for rich and poor. see Norris, John.
Freeman, Mylo. pseud. Word in season. 25770, note after 105456
Freeman, Nathaniel. (25771)
Freeman, Nehemiah. 25772, 94182
Freeman, Nicolas. pseud. Glaneur. see Jay, Antoine.
Freeman, Nilekaw. pseud.??? Preface. 97090
Freeman, O. S. pseud. Letters on slavery. see Rogers, Edward Coit.
Freeman, Peyton Randolph. 25774-(25775)
Freeman, Philo. pseud. Essex almanac for the year . . . 1773. 23006
Freeman, Philo. pseud. Essex almanack for the years 1770 and 1771. (25776)
Freeman, Q. illus. 44250
Freeman, Sambo. 81587
Freeman, Samuel. 25777
Freeman, Samuel, 1743-1831. 45869, 84350
Freeman, Samuel, d. 1805. defendant 102521
Freeman, T. Bampfylde. 95331
Freeman, Theophilus. pseud. General epistle. see Matthews, William.
Freeman, Theresa J. 25778
Freeman, Thomas, fl. 1736. 25779, 60181, note after 97166
Freeman, Thomas, fl. 1806. (25780)
Freeman, W. petitioner 10893
Freeman, William. 25782-25784
Freeman, William, owner of a Plantation in St. Christopher. petitioner 25781
Freeman, William, 1824-1847. defendant 25785, (79503)
Freeman, William P. 25786
Freeman L. Usher. pseud. Signal. see Worcester, Noah, 1758-1837.
Freeman of Massachusetts. pseud. Remarks and documents. see Daggett, John.
Freeman of South Carolina. pseud. Letter from a freeman of South Carolina. (40277), 86648
Freeman of South Carolina. pseud. Letter of freeman of South Carolina. see Drayton, William Henry.
Freeman of the United States. pseud. Address to the people. 35391
Freeman of this city. pseud. Word in season. 105454
Freeman on freemasonry. (25800)
Freeman's address to the North Americans. (25789)
Freeman's Dutch almanack. 53674
Freeman's guide. 25790
Freeman's journal. 13118
Freeman's New York almanack for 1767. 53674
Freeman's New York pocket almanack. 53674
Freeman's New York royal sheet almanack. 53674
Freeman's oath. 25791, 59555, 62743
Freemantle, Arthur James. 25832
Freemason; a monthly magazine. 25801
Freemason; a masonic monthly journal. 25802
Freemasonry, a covenant with death. 76257
Freemasonry; a poem. 25803
Freemasonry and the war. 25804
Freemasonry at the present time. 50872
Freemasonry illustrated. 94309
Freemasonry in New York. 25806

Freemasonry practically illustrated. 95474, note before 99222
Freemasonry, the healer of the nation's wounds. 33820
Freemasonry unmasked. 25807
Freemasons. 1397, 25797-25798, 30507, 35022, 36660, note after 45694, (45498), 45508, (49356), 55811, 58975, 99145, 102460
Freemasons. Alabama. Grand Lodge. 28261
Freemasons. Connecticut. Grand Lodge. (65871)
Freemasons. Connecticut. Knights Templars. Grand Encampment. 65857
Freemasons. Connecticut. St. John's Lodge, Bridgeport. 23317
Freemasons. Cuba. Scottish Rite. Havana. 68891
Freemasons. District of Columbia. Grand Lodge. 65872
Freemasons. Georgia. 87840
Freemasons. Georgia. Grand Lodge. 45497, 72447
Freemasons. Georgia. Grand Royal Arch Chapter. 65859
Freemasons. Georgia. York Rite. Grand Lodge. 87846
Freemasons. Haiti. Verite Lodge, Cap Haitien. 94176
Freemasons. Idaho. Grand Lodge. (34169)
Freemasons. Indiana. Grand Lodge. 34550, 34553
Freemasons. Indiana. Royal and Select Masters. Grand Council. 34552
Freemasons. Iowa. Grand Chapter. 35022
Freemasons. Iowa. Grand Lodge. 35022, 58975
Freemasons. Iowa. Grand Lodge. Library. 58975
Freemasons. Iowa. Masonic Festival, Dubuque, 1867. 47678
Freemasons. Kentucky. 50871
Freemasons. Kentucky. Grand Lodge. 37542, 45520, 50400
Freemasons. Kentucky. Grand Royal Arch Chapter. 37543
Freemasons. Louisiana. Committee on Foreign Correspondence. 42259
Freemasons. Louisiana. Grand Lodge. 42259
Freemasons. Louisiana. Grand Lodge. Committee. 45503
Freemasons. Louisiana. Louisiana Relief Lodge, New Orleans. 42259
Freemasons. Maine. Grand Lodge. (43992)
Freemasons. Maine. Grand Lodge. petitioners (43992)
Freemasons. Maine. Grand Lodge. Committee on Foreign Correspondence. (43992)
Freemasons. Maine. Grand Royal Arch Chapter. 43993
Freemasons. Maine. Lewy's Island Lodge, no. 138, Princeton. Committee on History. 77031
Freemasons. Maryland. 45200
Freemasons. Maryland. Grand Lodge. 45159
Freemasons. Massachusetts. 45760, 101868, 101870, 101872
Freemasons. Massachusetts. Grand Lodge. 25798, 30507, 31180, (45498), (45508), note after 45694, 45760, (50333), 90173, 101471
Freemasons. Massachusetts. Grand Lodge. Chairman. 25798, 30507, 101471 see also Warren, John, 1753-1815.

Freemasons. Massachusetts. Grand Lodge. Charity Fund. 45760
Freemasons. Massachusetts. Grand Royal Arch Chapter. 45761
Freemasons. Massachusetts. Knights Templars. (28259), 47500
Freemasons. Massachusetts. Knights Templars. Grand Encampment. 38133 see also Freemasons. Rhode Island. Knights Templars. Grand Encampment.
Freemasons. Massachusetts. Corinthian Lodge, Concord. 15137, 93829
Freemasons. Massachusetts. Corinthian Lodge, Concord. Charter. 93829
Freemasons. Massachusetts. Dalhousie Lodge, Newton. (55088)
Freemasons. Massachusetts. Montgomery Lodge, Milford. 90468
Freemasons. Massachusetts. Mount Vernon Lodge, Boston. 51180
Freemasons. Massachusetts. Revere Lodge, Boston. 70184
Freemasons. Massachusetts. St. Alban's Lodge, Wrentham. Committee. 105522
Freemasons. Massachusetts. St. Andrew's Lodge, Boston. (45508), 80319
Freemasons. Massachusetts. Union Lodge, Dorchester. 101810
Freemasons. Mexico. York Rite. 68865
Freemasons. Michigan. Royal and Select Masters. Grand Council. (48765)
Freemasons. Minnesota. Grand Lodge. 49299
Freemasons. Mississippi. Grand Lodge. 49505
Freemasons. Missouri. Grand Lodge. 49596
Freemasons. Missouri. Grand Royal Arch Chapter. 49596
Freemasons. New Hampshire. Grand Lodge. 52835
Freemasons. New Hampshire. Grand Lodge. Grand Chaplain. 70922 see also Richards, George.
Freemasons. New Hampshire. Grand Royal Arch Chapter. 52935
Freemasons. New Hampshire. Knights Templars. Grand Commandery. 52895
Freemasons. New Hampshire. Altemont Lodge, Peterborough. 89049
Freemasons. New Hampshire. Bethel Lodge, Peterborough. 89049
Freemasons. New Hampshire. Celebration of the One Hundredth Anniversary of the Initiation of George Washington, Peterborough, 1852. 89049
Freemasons. New Hampshire. Charity Lodge, Peterborough. 89049
Freemasons. New Jersey. Grand Lodge. 53126, 83526
Freemasons. New York. 53627, (53692)
Freemasons. New York. Convention of Seceding Masons, 1828. see Convention of Seceding Masons, Le Roy, N. Y., 1828.
Freemasons. New York. District of Albany. District Grand Committee. (53962)
Freemasons. New York. General Grand Chapter. 53680, 53690
Freemasons. New York. Grand Consistory. 53691
Freemasons. New York. Grand Encampment of Northern New York. (53692)
Freemasons. New York. Grand Lodge. (53692), 69675
Freemasons. New York. Grand Lodge. Special Committee on the Riotous Proceedings, 1849. (53962)

Freemasons. New York. Grand Royal Arch Chapter. 53624, (53692)
Freemasons. New York. Grand Stewards' Lodge. (53692)
Freemasons. New York. Masonic Board of Relief. (53692)
Freemasons. New York. Masters and Past Masters, New York City. 54037
Freemasons. New York. Rising-Star Lodge, no. 393, Yonkers. 106019-20 [sic]
Freemasons. New York. St. John's Grand Lodge. (53692)
Freemasons. North Carolina. 52255
Freemasons. North Carolina. Grand Lodge. 55666, 55683 see also Freemasons. North Carolina and Tennessee. Grand Lodge.
Freemasons. North Carolina. Grand Lodge. Masonic Seminary. Trustees. 55683
Freemasons. North Carolina. York Rite. Grand Lodge. 55622
Freemasons. North Carolina and Tennessee. Grand Lodge. (55623) see also Freemasons. North Carolina. Grand Lodge. Freemasons. Tennessee. Grand Lodge.
Freemasons. Ohio. Grand Encampment. 57023
Freemasons. Ohio. Grand Lodge. 57024, 92822
Freemasons. Ohio. Grand Royal Arch Chapter. (56941)
Freemasons. Ohio. Knights Templars. Grand Commandery. 57022
Freemasons. Ohio. Nova Cesarea Harmony Lodge, Cincinnati. 56099
Freemasons. Oregon. Grand Lodge. (57568)
Freemasons. Pennsylvania. 27240
Freemasons. Pennsylvania. Grand Chapter. 60129
Freemasons. Pennsylvania. Grand Holy Arch Chapter. 59870
Freemasons. Pennsylvania. Grand Lodge. 18320, 49703, 59870, 60128-60129, 84584, 84668
Freemasons. Pennsylvania. Knights Templars. Grand Commandery. 60184
Freemasons. Pennsylvania. Royal Arch Chapter. 60129
Freemasons. Pennsylvania. Friendship Lodge, no. 73, Philadelphia. 40696, note after 101839
Freemasons. Pennsylvania. Loge l'Amenite no. 73. see Freemasons. Pennsylvania. Friendship Lodge, no. 73, Philadelphia.
Freemasons. Pernambuco. 88976
Freemasons. Rhode Island. 70596
Freemasons. Rhode Island. Grand Lodge. 70584
Freemasons. Rhode Island. Knights Templars. (28259), 47500
Freemasons. Rhode Island. Knights Templars. Grand Encampment. 38133 see also Freemasons. Massachusetts. Knights Templars. Grand Encampment.
Freemasons. Rhode Island. Washington Lodge, no. 3, Warren. Charter. 101493
Freemasons. South Carolina. 52255, 87835, 87840
Freemasons. South Carolina. Ancient York Masons. Grand Lodge. see Freemasons. South Carolina. York Rite. Grand Lodge.
Freemasons. South Carolina. Grand Lodge. (43445), 87834-87835, 87837-87839, 87841-87844, 87846

Freemasons. South Carolina. Grand Lodge. Committee. 87846
Freemasons. South Carolina. Grand Lodge. Committee of Correspondence. 87846
Freemasons. South Carolina. Grand Lodge. Grand Chaplain. 87841
Freemasons. South Carolina. Grand Lodge. Grand Master. 87841
Freemasons. South Carolina. Grand Lodge. Select Committee. 87836
Freemasons. South Carolina. Grand Royal Arch Chapter. 87832
Freemasons. South Carolina. Royal and Select Masters. Grand Council. 87833
Freemasons. South Carolina. York Rite. Grand Convention, Columbia, 1809. 87846
Freemasons. South Carolina. York Rite. Grand Lodge. 87841, 87845-87847
Freemasons. South Carolina. York Rite. Grand Lodge. Committee. 87846
Freemasons. South Carolina. York Rite. Grand Lodge. Committee of Correspondence. 87846
Freemasons. South Carolina. York Rite. St. John's Lodge, no. Charleston. Corresponding Committee. 87848
Freemasons. Tennessee. Grand Lodge. 94797-94798 see also Freemasons. North Carolina and Tennessee. Grand Lodge.
Freemasons. Tennessee. Grand Royal Arch Chapter. 94796
Freemasons. Texas. Grand Lodge. 74462, 95085
Freemasons. Texas. Lone Star Royal Arch Chapter, no. 3. 95084
Freemasons. United States. 25797, 33576
Freemasons. United States. Convention to Form a Supreme Grand Lodge ofr the United States, Baltimore, 1847. (65792)
Freemasons. United States. Egyptian Rite of Memphis. (71600)
Freemasons. Uinited States Egyptian Rite of Memphis. Sovereign Sanctuary (95) of the Valley of Chicago. (71600)
Freemasons. United States Egyptian Rite of Memphis. Sovereign Sanctuary (95º) of the Valley of Chicago. (71600)
Freemasons. United States. General Grand Chapter. 25813
Freemasons. United States. Grand Lodge. 45504
Freemasons. United States. Knights Templars. Grand Encampment. (28259), (38134)
Freemasons. United States. National Masonic Convention, Baltimore, 1843. (65891)
Freemasons. United States. Northern Jurisdiction. Supreme Grand Council. (49356), 55811
Freemasons. United States. Royal Arch Masons. General Grand Chapter. 25795, 25850, 53680
Freemasons. United States. Royal Arch Masons. General Grand Chapter (Northern States) 25796, 45499
Freemasons. United States. Scottish Rite. 62815
Freemasons. United States. Supreme Council of the Grand Inspectors General of the 33d Degree. 45507
Freemasons. Venezuela. Scottish Rite. Grand Lodge. 68893
Freemasons. Venezuela. Scottish Rite. San Juan Logia, no. 4, Caracas. 68893

Freemasons. Vermont. Convention, Middlebury, 1819. Committee. 99176
Freemasons. Vermont. Grand Chapter. 99179-99180
Freemasons. Vermont. Grand Royal Arch Chapter. 99178, 99181-99192
Freemasons. Vermont. Craftsbury Lodge. 99177
Freemasons. Vermont. Concord Lodge. 99177
Freemasons. Vermont. Lyndon Lodge. 99177
Freemasons. Vermont. Peacham Lodge. 99177
Freemasons. Vermont. Royal Arch Chapter, Danville. 99177
Freemasons. Vermont. St. Johnbury Lodge. 99177
Freemasons. Vermont. Vermont Lodge, no. I. 99193
Freemasons. Vermont. Waterford Lodge. 99177
Freemasons. Virginia. 31320, 101471
Freemasons. Virginia. Grand Lodge. 68161, 101471-101475
Freemasons. Virginia. Grand Lodge. Committee. 25804
Freemasons. Virginia. Grand Royal Arch Chapter. 100468-100470
Freemasons. Washington, D. C. Federal Lodge, no. 15. 101939
Freemasons. Constitution of the General Grand Royal Arch Chapter. 25796
Freemason's companion. 14878
Freemason's journal. 26772
Freemasons' magazine. (25809)
Freemasons' magazine and general miscellany. 25808
Freemason's manual. 91698
Freemasons' monitor. (25810)
Freemason's monitor; or illustrations of masonry. 102232-102242
Freemasons' monthly magazine. 80321
Freemasons' repository. 25811
Freemen. pseud. Letters of freemen. see Drayton, William Henry.
Freemen. 61919
Freemen, awake!! Declaration and protest of liberty. 25792
Freemen, awake! The devil is in the camp. 25815
Freemen of . . . Philadelphia are desired to attend. 61678
Freemen's advocate. (55830)
Freemen's glee-book. 25816
Freemen's guide to the polls. 64687
Freeport, Andrew. 25817
Freerman, Bernardus. see Freeman, Bernardus.
Freese, A. G. F. tr. 28066
Freese, Jacob R. 25820
Freidlander, Julius R. 25821
Freie Auswanderung als Mittel der Abhulfe der Noth im Vaterlande. 8202
Freie Burgerthum. 7450
Freigio, Joannis Thomas. tr. 5053, 25994-(25995), 79345-79346
Freigium, Joan. Tho. see Freigio, Joannis Thomas.
Freihandels Heiland und dessen Apostel. 71307
Freiheit in den Vereinigten Staaten. (12587)
Freiheit und Sklaverei unter dem Sternenbanner. 28807
Freiheitskampf im Spanischen Amerika. 58267
Freiheitskampf in Sud-Amerika. 72482
Freiheitskampf in Texas im Jahre 1836. 22072

Freiherrn von Wimpffen neueste Reisen nach Saint Domingo. 104708
Freijlinghausen, Theodorus Jacobus. see Frelinghuysen, Theodorus Jacobus, 1691-1747.
Freile, Juan Diaz. 36787
Freiligrath, F. 25822
Freimuthiges Wort an alle Deutsche. 34159
Freire, Domingo. tr. 73188
Freire, Francisco de Brito. see Brito Freire, Francisco de.
Freira, Joao de Noronha. see Santa Teresa, Giovani Gioseppedi.
Freire, Jose Rodrigues. 25824, 72555
Freire, Jose Rodriguez. see Freire, Jose Rodrigues.
Freire, Manuel Gomes. see Santa Maria, Agostinho de.
Freire, Paschal Jose de Mello. see Mello Freire, Paschoal Jose de.
Freire Allemao, F. 88782
Freire de Andrada, Gomes. see Andrada, Gomes Freire de.
Freire de Mello, Francisco. see Mello, Francisco Freire de.
Freire de Monteroyo Mascarenhas, Jose. see Mascarenhas, Jose Freire de Monteroyo.
Freisach, Karl. 25823
Freisleben, Ed. tr. 35126
Freistaat Costa Rica. 17016
Freistaat Nicaragua in Mittel-Amerika. 9151
Freistaat von Nord-Amerika. 9149
Freitas, Augusto Teixeira de. see Teixeira de Freitas, Augusto.
Freitas, Joaquim Ferreira de. see Ferreira de Freitas, Joaquim.
Frejes, Francisco. 25825
Frelagh, J. H. 25826
Freligh. firm see Hutton & Freligh. firm publishers
Frelinghuysen, Frederick, 1753-1804. 1795, 25827, note after 53697, note after 83791
Frelinghuysen, Frederick Theodore, 1817-1885. 25828
Frelinghuysen, Theodore, 1787-1862. 2788, (2800), 25829-(25831), (30593), 89216, note after 102276
Frelinghuysen, Theodore, 1787-1862. supposed author 101439
Frelinghuysen, Theodore, fl. 1745-1761. 25940
Frelinghuysen, Theodore Jacobus, 1691-1747. 25755, (25971)-25974, 98572
Fremery, N. C. de. tr. 10887
Freminville, M. J. de la Poix de. see La Poix de Freminville, M. J. de.
Fremond, Sarah Parker. 25833
Fremont, Jessie (Benton) 1824-1902. 25834-25835
Fremont, John Charles, 1813-1890. 5306, 9990, 25836-25837, 25839-25846, 69143, 77710, 85161, 91904, 102502, 105656
Fremont, John Charles, 1813-1890. defendant at Court Martial 25840
Fremont, John Charles, 1813-1890. petitioner 25844
Fremont d'Ablancourt, Francois. see D'Ablancourt, Francois Fremont.
Fremont. 33227
Fremont a catholic!! (25845)
Fremont, a poem. 16297
Fremont a protestant! (25845)
Fremont & Dayton Central Club of the City of New York. (25845) see also Republican Party. New York. New York City.

Fremont and his speculations. (5680)
Fremont and McClellan. 19606
Fremont and McClellan, their political and
  military careers reviewed. (25845),
  43025
Fremont estate. (32393)
Fremont songs for the people. (20934),
  (25845)
Fremont, the conservative candidate. (24431)
"Fremont's hundred days in Missouri."
  Speech of Hon. F. P. Blair. (5740)
Fremont's hundred days in Missouri. Speech
  of Schuyler Colfax. 14342
Fremont's principles exposed. 42047
Fremont's Romanism established. (25845)
French, Mrs. A. M. (25847)
French, Asa. 85212
French, B. (25848)
French, Benjamin Brown. 25849-25850
French, Benjamin Franklin. 9116, (9605),
  11824, 18246, 24852-24854, (24896),
  25851-25856, 25892, 70792, 80002,
  87205, 87206, 95332, 96172, note after
  99605, 3d note after 99856, 1st note after
  105510
French, Ebenezer. 25857
French, Edward W. 25858
French, George, fl. 1717-1719. 25859-25860
French, George, fl. 1793. 102020
French, George, fl. 1834. defendant 96939
French, Henry F. (25861)
French, J. H. 25862
French, J. W. see French, J. H.
French, James Clark. see French, Justus
  Clement.
French, James S. 25864-(25865)
French, John R. (25866)
French, Jonathan. comp. 25876
French, Jonathan, 1740-1809. 25867-(25870)
French, Jonathan, 1778-1856. (25871)-25875
French, Justus Clement. 8386, 25863, 1st note
  after 96991
French, L. Virginia. 25877
French, Rodney. 25878
French, S. G. USA 36377, 84774
French, T. P. 25879 see also Ontario.
  Crown Land Agent.
French, William. 3213, note before 92797,
  note after 92800, 3d note after 103687
French (Samuel) publisher 8421, (16551),
  84784, 92410, 92513, note after 102637
French abbot. pseud. Account of the customs.
  94
French and American tariffs compared. 10842
French and Indian cruelty. 104467-104472
French and Indian cruelty exemplified. 104473-
  104474
French and Indian cruelty exemplified in the
  adventurous life. 104475
French arrogance. 13883
French Benevolent Society of the City of New
  York. see Societe Francaise de Bien-
  faisance, New York.
French Canadian Missionary Society. 10523
French-Canadians in New-England. 85211
French captive. 21155
French Catholic priest. pseud. Confessions.
  50963
French Church du Saint Spirit, New York. see
  New York (City) French Church du Saint
  Spirit.
French Citizens of the County of Wayne, Indiana.
  petitioners see Wayne County, Ind.
  French Citizens. petitioners

French claims. To the people of the United
  States. 25881
French commerce and manufactures. 39382
French convert. 25882
French counsellor of state. pseud. Interesting
  account of the project. 34889
French counsellor of state. pseud. Memorial,
  on the war of St. Domingo. 42188
French counsels destructive to Great Britain.
  18511
French domination. 26793
French encroachments exposed. 25883, note
  after 59281
French evening post. 17165
French flogged. 25884, note after 91499
French gentleman. pseud. Extract of an
  account. 40707, note after 96500
French gentleman. pseud. Short history of
  Muscovy. (38714)
French Guiana. (11618), 44975
French Guiana. Colons. plaintiffs 29177
French Guiana. Conseil Colonial. 29171
French Guiana. Laws, statutes, etc. (11625),
  29166-29167, (29185), 29195
French-Illinois dictionary. note after 80015
French influence upon English counsels.
  25885
French interference in Mexico. 43185
French intervention in America. 37893
French King's declaration relating to the
  situation of Negroes. 96055
French King's late declaration concerning
  religion. 89126
French memorial of justification. (47511),
  68283-68284, note after 80055
French memorials concerning the limits of
  Acadia. (47547), 69463, note after 96403
French mission life. 11123
French nation defended. 93492-93493
French officer on board the Chezine Frigate.
  pseud. Journal. 26630
French Officers in the fleet of Court d'Estaing.
  pseud. Siege of Savannah, in 1779.
  36481, 80874
French-Onondaga dictionary. 80007
French original letters. 23919
French originals of all the documents. 25886
French policy. 104302
French policy defeated. (25887)
French Protestant Church, New York. see
  New York (City) French Church du Saint
  Spirit.
French Protestant Refugees Inhabiting the
  Province of New-York Generally.
  petitioners 26145
French protestants of Abbeville District, S. C.
  88005
French Reformed Protestant Church, New York.
  see New York (City) French Church du
  Saint Spirit.
French revolution; including a story. (25888),
  1st note after 97876
French revolution of 1848. 74269
French spoliations. 52980
French spoliations prior to 1800. 25889
French spoliations prior to 1800. Report of
  E. Everett. 23271
French teacher, no. II. 101888
French trader. pseud. 72726-72727, 84616-
  84618, 85254
French Universal Exposition for 1867. 25890
French view of the Grand International Ex-
  position of 1876. 81308
French way of paying national debts. (12811)

French West India Company. see Compagnie des Indes Occidentales.
Frenchman in Virginia. 1st note after 100572, 100837
French's American drama. 8421, 92410
French's modern standard drama. (16551), note after 102637
French's standard drama. 84784, 92410, 92513
French's village in Bath. 3953
Freneau, Peter. 87507 see also South Carolina. Secretary of State.
Freneau, Philip Morin, 1752-1832. 6571, 7190, 25891-25904, 26319, 72035, (82501), 94235, 96129, 96502, 2d note after 99627, 1st note after 100818, 101437
Freneau, Philip Morin, 1752-1832. supposed author 97240
Freneau, Philip Morin, 1752-1832. incorrectly supposed author (62911), 97380
Freneau s gazette. 97380
Frenilly, Auguste Francois Fauveau, Marquis de, 1768-1848. 25906
Freno. Dialogo de los editores del Argos. 61128
Frenzel, --------. (25905)
Frere ****. pseud. Apologie des Franc-Macons. 25793
Frere, Hookham. see Frere, John Hookham, 1769-1846.
Frere, J. 25907
Frere, John Hookham, 1769-1846. 3281, (3288)-3289, 98839
Frere, T. engr. 84886
Freret, William. (17760)
Freschot, Casimiro. tr. 31356
Fresenius, --------. 23094, 4th note after 97845, note after 106352
Fresh advices from Virginia. 100476
Fresh antidote against neonomian bane and poyson. 12335
Fresh catalogue of southern outrages upon northern citizens. 25908
Fresh discovery of some prodigious new-wandring-blasing-stars. (66417), 103441
Fresh leaves. 58960
Fresh leaves from western woods. 99432
Fresh news, just arrived from Gen. Wooster. 105223
Fresh water and land shells of Vermont. 178
Fresh water fish. 82196
Fresne de Francheville, Joseph du. see Du Fresne de Francheville, Joseph.
Fresnel, R. F. 25909-25910
Fresnoy, Charles du. 105184
Fresnoy, Nicolas Lenglet du. see Lenglet Dufresnoy, Nicolas, 1674-1755.
Freville, A. F. J. de. tr. (3201)-(3202), 6864, 6867, 15589, 18344, 18348, (25912)-25914, 41282, 93292, note after 93794, 2d note after 100806
Frey, Alfred A. 25915
Frey, Andrew. 71406, (71410)
Frey, C. F. 78672
Frey, J. S. C. 36121
Frey de Landres, J.-R. ed. (58329)
Frey-Mauren. pseud. Erlauterung der Frey-Maurerey. see Morgan, William.
Freyburg, Me. Centennial Celebration, 1863. 26104
Freycinet, Louis. 60998-60999
Freycinet, Louis Claude Desaulses de. 21211-21215, 25916-25917, 56064
Freyhalter und Einwohner der Stadt und County Philadelphia. pseud. An Freyhalter und Einwohner der Stadt und County Philadelphia, Deutscher Nation. 61456

Freyheit die treue Liebe. (25918)
Freyheits Brief der Deutschern Hohen Schule (College) 38795
Freylinghausen, Gotlieb Anastasius. 25919, 78013
Freymaurerey. 36660
Freyre, Domingos. 25920
Freyre, Ramon. 25921
Freyreiss, Georg Wilhelm. 25922
Freystaaten von Nordamerika. 42529
Freytag, Gustav, 1816-1895. 86385
Freytag, Jean David, 1765-1832. 25923
Freytas, Nicolas de. see De Freytas, Nicolas.
Frezier, Amedee Francois. 25924-25930
Friars of the Franciscan Convent of Talmanaco. see Talmanaco, Mexico. Franciscan Convent.
Friars Tontine, New York. see New York Friars Tontine, New York.
Frias, Felix. (25930)
Frias, Jose Antonio Ximenez y. see Ximenez y Frias, Jose Antonio.
Frias, Josef Antonio Gimenez. see Ximenez y Frias, Jose Antonio.
Frias y Jacott, Francisco, Conde de Pozos Dulces, 1809-1877. 64860
Fribert, Lauritz Jacob. 25932
Fric, Karel. 25933
Friccius, Valentinus. 25934
Fricius, V. see Friccius, Valentinus.
Frick, William. 90852
Frick, William, 1790-1855. 25935
Frickmann, A. 25936
Friday Lecture, Boston. (14525), 79433
Friderick Martens von Hamburg Spitzbergensche oder Groenlandische Reise. 44834
Friedel, Louis. 25937, (77894)
Friedenberg, Gottfried. tr. 16419, 16520, 16547, 16555
Friedenschotschaft an alle Volker. 85112
Friedlander, Julisu R. 9344, 25938, 60399
Friedmann, S. 25939
Friedner, Rud. tr. 35180
Friedrich II, King of Prussia, 1712-1786. 100667 see also Prussia. Sovereigns, etc., 1740-1786 (Friedrich II)
Friedrich Martens von Hamburg Spitzbergische oder Groenlandische Reise Beschreiben. 14374
Friedrick der Grosse und die Vereinigten Staaten von Amerika. 37101
Frielenhuysen, Theodorus. see Frelinghuysen, Theodorus, fl. 1745-1761.
Friend. pseud. ed. 21055, 103384
Friend. pseud. publisher see Harlakenden, Richard.
Friend. pseud. Additional notices [of Miss Hannah Adams.] 213
Friend. pseud. Beacon to the Society of Friends. 19187
Friend. pseud. Biographical sketch of Dr. James W. Stone. 92068
Friend. pseud. Biography of General Lewis Cass. (11351)
Friend. pseud. Brief continuation. 51524
Friend. pseud. Elegy. 93236
Friend. pseud. Elegy on the death of Colonel Dan Shaw. 79902
Friend. pseud. Experience of Thomas Jones. (36611)
Friend. pseud. Few hints to the wise. 102987
Friend. pseud. Historical account of the rise and establishment. 32055
Friend. pseud. Inquiries. 73391
Friend. pseud. Letter from a friend. see Davis, Timothy.

Friend. pseud. Letter to a clergyman. 15818
Friend. pseud. Memorial of Colonel John A. Bross. 8384
Friend. pseud. Memorials of Margaret Elizabeth. (47740)
Friend. pseud. ed. Narrative and writings of Andrew Jackson. 35392, 51778
Friend. pseud. Nautical education. 52064
Friend. pseud. Poem. 37660
Friend. pseud. Serious call to the Quakers. see Keith, George, 1638?-1716.
Friend. pseud. Sorrowful poem. 87168
Friend. pseud. Three politicians. 96748
Friend. 25941, 32369, 52612, (81886), 86033, 86035, 88264, 88264, 98098, 104544, 105671
Friend. A religious and literary journal. 25943, 83829
Friend, an independent monthly. 25942
Friend at J——— ———. pseud. Letter. see Smith, James, of Kingston, Jamaica.
Friend in America. pseud. Letter. 78283, 78289
Friend . . . In England. pseud. Letter to the Negroes lately converted. 8798, 40504
Friend in London. pseud. Letter to an American planter. 40425
Friend in London. pseud. Reading mo preaching. 68202
Friend in New England. pseud. Letter. 91318
Friend in the country. pseud. Considerations upon the present state of our affairs. see Lyttelton of Frankley, George Lyttelton, 1st Baron, 1709-1773.
Friend in the country. pseud. Mr. Sandeman refuted by an old woman. 76339
Friend in the north. pseud. Letter. (40278)
Friend in the north. pseud. South. see Colwell, Stephen.
Friend in the west. pseud. Answer. see Clap, Thomas, 1703-1767.
Friend indeed. pseud. Answer to "Questions addressed to Rev. T. Parker." see Sargent, John T.
Friend of American liberty. pseud. Observations. see Green, Jacob. supposed author
Friend of both countries. pseud. American vindicated. (1030)
Friend of Christ, and of his people. 14486
Friend of domestic economy. pseud. Summary of the practical principles. see Cushing, Caleb.
Friend of education. pseud. State education not radically wrong. 45137
Friend of his [i. e, Gershom Bulkeley's] in the bay. pseud. Letter. 9095
Friend of improvement. pseud. Boston common. 6689
Friend of John Fitch, deceased. pseud. Examination of Cadwallader D. Colden's book. 14278
Friend of knowledge. 67445
Friend of liberty. pseud. Maryland scheme of expatriation examined. 45239
Friend of men of all colours. pseud. On the slave trade. see Gregoire, Henri.
Friend of merit, wherever found. pseud. Defence of Injur'd merit unmasked. 19239
Friend of peace. pseud. Dissertation on the subject of a congress of nations. 20286
Friend of peace. (23519), 25944, 50233, 105256-105258, 105260, 105265, 105269-105270, 105291
Friend of peace, containing a review of the arguments of Lord Kames. 105260

Friend of peace: containing a special interview between the President of the United States and Omar. 105262
Friend of peace: containing, a special interview between the President of the United States, and Omar, an officer dismissed for duelling; six letters from Omar to the President. 105253, 105257, 105260, 105263
Friend of peace: containing a special interview between the President of the United States and Omar, an officer dismissed for duelling; with six letters from Omor to the President. 105251
Friend of peace, in a series of numbers. 105261, 105265
Friend of peace, no. II. 105254-105255
Friend of peace, to which is prefixed a solemn review. 105259
Friend of progress. 25945
Friend of religious toleration. pseud. Account of the conflagration of the Urseline Convent. 12093, 1st note after 98167
Friend of seamen. pseud. Accounts of shipwreck and other disasters at sea. see Allen, William, 1784-1868.
Friend of that college. pseud. Review of Dr. Morse's "Appeal to the publick." see Lowell, John.
Friend of the Aborigines Protesction Society. pseud. Young patriot. see Burtt, John.
Friend of the Anglo-Saxons. pseud. Oregon controversy reviewed. 57559
Friend of the artist. pseud. Review of the "biographical sketch." 98491
Friend of the Christian examiner, and a lover of truth. pseud. Some remarks. see Prince, John.
Friend of the college, the church and his country. pseud. Letter to an honourable gentleman. pseud. see Baldwin, Ebenezer. supposed author and Trumbull, Benjamin. supposed author
Friend of the colonel. pseud. Davy Crockett. 17574
Friend of the drama. pseud. Enquiry into the condition and influence of the brothels. 61618
Friend of the order. pseud. 10512
Friend of the people. pseud. Banks and paper currency. see Ronaldson, James.
Friend of the south. pseud. Friend of the south in answer to Remarks on Dr. Channing's Slavery. see Pratt, Minot. supposed author and Swett, Samuel, 1782-1866. supposed author
Friend of the south in answer to remarks on Dr. Channing's Slavery. (11920), 64948, 94057
Friend of the union. pseud. Henry Clay and the administration. 13557
Friend of truth. pseud. Chebacco narrative rescu'd. see Cleaveland, John.
Friend of truth. pseud. Correct view of the controversy. see Parks, L. D.
Friend of truth. pseud. Washington miracle refuted. 46848, (46900), 102024
Friend of truth, and of honorable peace. pseud. Conduct of Washington. 101786
Friend of truth and of honourable peace. pseud. Facts and documents. (23620), 101807
Friend of truth, and of honorable peace, free trade and sailor's rights. pseud. Conduct of Washington. 101786
Friend of truth and peace. pseud. True. interests of the European powers. see Walton, William, 1784-1857.

Friend of truth and sound policy. pseud.
Strictures on a voyage to South America.
see Irvine, Baptis. supposed author
Friend of union and liberty. pseud. Dissolu-
tion of the union. see Carey, Mathew,
1760-1839.
Friend of youth. pseud. Early life of
Washington. 101795-101796
Friend to all mankind. pseud. Wrongs of
Almoona. 105631
Friend to American literature. pseud. To the
friends of American literature. 102401
Friend to American manufactures. pseud.
Valuable collection of arts and trades.
98400
Friend to an able ministry. pseud. Outline
of a plan. see Going, Jonathan.
Friend to British manufactures. pseud. Con-
ciliation with America. 15109
Friend to Carolina. pseud. Observations
concerning indigo and cochineal. see
Crockat, or Crockatt, James. supposed
author and Leigh, Sir Edward. supposed
author
Friend to church and state. pseud. Spy.
89935
Friend to civil and religious liberty. pseud.
98911
Friend to commerce and humanity. pseud.
Thoughts on colonization. 95673
Friend to equal rights. pseud. Nativism.
(52040)
Friend to freedom. pseud. Address to the
people of the eastern states. 81793,
88423
Friend to freedom. pseud. Southern oppression.
81793, 88423
Friend to general improvements. pseud.
Remarks on steamboats. 93515
Friend to general improvements, regrets that
the inventor of the steam towboat, has
not explained. 93515
Friend to genius and art. pseud. Notice of
sculpture. 70911
Friend to Great Britain. pseud. Address to
the rulers of state. 443
Friend to Great Britain. pseud. Letter.
33340
Friend to harmony. pseud. Candid consider-
ations on libels. 10660
Friend to him [i. e. John Cotton.] pseud. ed.
17063
Friend to his country. pseud. Brief, decent,
but free remarks. (7862)
Friend to his country. pseud. Serious appeal
to the wisdom and patriotism. 22767
Friend to innocent mirth. pseud. Whim wham.
103294
Friend to justice, and courts of justice. pseud.
Answer to a seditious and scandalous
pamphlet. see Starling, Samuel.
Friend to Justice and merit. pseud. Notices
of the Rideau Canal. 55994
Friend to liberty. pseud. Vindication of the
planters of Martinique & Guadaloupe.
99817
Friend to mankind. pseud. Address to the
inhabitants of . . . Philadelphia. 61438
Friend to Maryland. pseud. Answer to the
queries. see Calvert, --------.
Friend to Maryland. pseud. Remarks upon a
message. 45318
Friend to national industry. pseud. Facts and
arguments. see Blodget, William.
incorrectly supposed author and Camac,
Turner. supposed author

Friend to national industry. pseud. Thoughts
on inland navigation. see Blodget,
William. supposed author
Friend to native simplicity. pseud. Laws of
Siasconset. 80812
Friend to New-Jersey. pseud. Take care!!
94222
Friend to order. pseud. To the publick.
95998
Friend to our happy establishment in church
and state. pseud. Voice of God. see
Christianus. pseud.
Friend to peace. pseud. Thoughts upon the
conduct. see Lowell, John.
Friend to peace and good order. pseud. Few
remarks upon some of the votes. see
Gray, Harrison.
Friend to peace and good order. pseud. Two
congresses cut up. see Gray, Harrison.
Friend to political equality. pseud. Pill for
Porcupine. 14029
Friend to posterity and mankind. pseud.
Review of the American contest. see
Paine, Thomas, 1737-1809.
Friend to rational liberty. pseud. Jacobin
looking-glass. 35495
Friend to real religion. pseud. Vindication
of the religion of Mr. Jefferson. see
Knox, Samuel. supposed author
Friend to reform. pseud. Plan of reform.
see Omicron. pseud.
Friend to regular government. pseud. British
honour and humanity. see Swanwick,
John. supposed author and Carey, Mathew,
1760-1839. incorrectly supposed author
Friend to revivals. pseud. Strictures on a
sermon by Edward D. Griffin. 28818,
92835
Friend to science. pseud. Useful essays.
98178
Friend to So. Ca. College. pseud. Letter
to Hon. James Hamilton. 30016, 87984
Friend to state rights. pseud. Examination
of the right of secession. 23371
Friend to suffering humanity. pseud. Mrs.
Willard reviewed. 104049
Friend to Texas. pseud. Strictures on " A"
letter." 29829, 4th note after 95112
Friend to the administration. pseud. Import
duties considered. (34394)
Friend to the British flag. pseud. Some
material and very important remarks.
86656
Friend to the cause. pseud. Sketch of the
origin and progress. 82062
Friend to the churches. pseud. Plea for the
ministers of the Gospel. see Mather,
Increase, 1639-1723.
Friend to the civil and religious liberties of
man. pseud. Letter to the Roman
Catholics of Philadelphia. 40539
Friend to the constitution. pseud. Essay.
(22928)
Friend to the constitution. pseud. Short
history of late administrations. 80633
Friend to the constitution. Nos I. to V.
25946
Friend to the constitutional rights of the
citizen. pseud. Letters. 103752
Friend to the fair. I. S. pseud. Mirror of
merit and beauty. see Smith, James,
d. 1812.
Friend to the King and country. pseud. View
of the moral and political epidemic.
99568

Friend to the liberty of his country. pseud.
Liberty and property vindicated. see
Church, Benjamin, 1734-1776.
Friend to the navy. pseud. Exploring Expe-
dition. Correspondence. see Dickerson,
Mahlon.
Friend to the Negro. pseud. Garland of
freedom. see Armistead, Wilson.
Friend to the Negroes. pseud. Two points
of the West India question considered.
97578
Friend to the Parliament, city, and ministery
of it. pseud. Word to Mr. Peters. see
Ward, Nathaniel.
Friend to the people and their liberties. pseud.
Full and impartial examination. 102647
Friend to the prosperity of the British empire.
pseud. Patriot known by comparison.
59084
Friend to the public. pseud. Delusive and
dangerous principles. 19458
Friend to the public. pseud. Remarks on the
report. (69498)
Friend to the public. pseud. tr. Some
modern directions. 86658
Friend to the public welfare. pseud. Steady
habits vindicated. see Daggett, David.
supposed author and Sampson, -------.
supposed author
Friend to the "public worship of the Deity."
pseud. Some remarks on the "toleration
act" of 1819. see Smith, William, 1799-
1830.
Friend to the rights of the constitution. pseud.
Civil liberty asserted. 65458
Friend to the south. pseud. Introduction.
(30338)
Friend to the union. pseud. Remarks upon
the controversy. see Ward, S. D.
Friend to the West India colonies, and their
inhabitants. pseud. Cursory remarks.
see Tobin, James. pseud.
Friend to toleration. pseud. [Essays.] 96123,
1st note after 105926
Friend to trade. pseud. To the merchants
and other inhabitants of Pennsylvania.
60708
Friend to truth. pseud. Candid enquiries . . .
relative to the difficulties. see Parsons,
Tyler.
Friend to truth. pseud. Charter of the
Corporation of Trinity Church defended.
see Hobart, John Henry, Bp., 1775-1830.
Friend to truth. pseud. Correct view of the
controversy. see Parks, L. D.
Friend to truth. pseud. Full vindication of
the R. H. General's conduct. 33340
Friend to truth. pseud. History of facts.
see Thomas, Moses.
Friend to truth. pseud. Religious colloquy.
48192
Friend to truth. pseud. Strictures on Dr. John
M. Mason's plea. see Chrystie, James.
supposed author
Friend to truth. pseud. Whereas on the late
examination. 103254
Friend to truth, and lover of mankind. pseud.
Observations on the doctrines. see
Tucker, John.
Friend to truth and peace. pseud. Brief
narration of the practices of the churches
of New-England. (52617)
Friend to truth and peace. pseud. Brief
narration of the practices of the churches
of New-England, in their solemne worship
of God. 52618

Friend unknown. pseud. Paper to William
Penn. 58444
Friend . . . W. P. pseud. Spirit of truth
vindicated. see Penn, William, 1644-
1718.
Friend who is now no more. pseud. Brief
account of the prominent points. 64562
Friendly address to all Americans. Also some
remarks. (81904)
Friendly address to all reasonable Americans,
on the subject of our political confusions.
(3684), (11881), 16587-16588, 26867,
39714, (41634), 92830-92831, 92850
Friendly address to the honourable women of
the United States. 104996
Friendly advice to all shareholders and friends.
9757
Friendly advice to the gentlemen-planters of the
East and West Indies. 25947, note after
97286
Friendly advcie [sic] to the gentelmen-[sic]
planters of the East and West Indies.
97287
Friendly advice to the inhabitants of
Pensilvania [sic]. 55500
Friendly American mediation move. (36119)
Friendly Association for Mutual Interests,
Philadelphia. 61679
Friendly Association for Preserving Peace with
the Indians. see Friendly Association
for Regaining and Preserving Peace with
the Indians by Pacific Measures, Phila-
delphia.
Friendly Association for Regaining and
Preserving Peace with the Indians by
Pacific Measures, Philadelphia. 34589,
59831, 60729 see also Friends, Society
of. Philadelphia Yearly Meeting.
Friendly Association for Regaining and
Preserving Peace with the Indians by
Pacific Measures, Philadelphia. Treasurer.
34589, 59831, 60729
Friendly Association for Regaining and
Preserving Peace with the Indians by
Pacific Measures, Philadelphia. Trustees.
34589, 59831, 60729
Friendly, Aunt. pseud. see Aunt Friendly.
pseud.
Friendly Botanic Society at Eastport, Mass
and Portsmouth, N. H. 95601
Friendly Brothers of St. Patrick, Boston. see
Ancient and Most Benevolent Order of the
Friendly Brothers of St. Patrick, Boston.
Friendly check, from a kind relation. 25948,
104899
Friendly, Christian advice. 102705
Friendly debate; or, a dialogue between
Rusticus and Academicus. (74419)
Friendly debate; or, a dialogue, between
Academicus; and Sawny & Mundungus.
20724, 101195
Friendly dialogue between Philalethes and
Toletus. 62422, 89794
Friendly dialogue between Theophilus and
Philadelphius. 96353
Friendly dialogue, in three parts. 89794,
89797, 94368
Friendly discussion of party politics in 1860-1.
(44759)
Friendly epistle to Mr. George Keith. 106102
Friendly epistle to neighbour John Taylor of
Norwich. 370
Friendly epistle to the reverend clergy, and
nonconforming divines. 106103
Friendly examination of the pacifick paper.
12305, 12335

Friendly expostulation. 4093-(4094), 102569

Friendly Fire Society, Boston. 74075

Friendly Fire Society, Cambridge, Mass. 10153

Friendly hint to Missouri. 83288

Friendly influence of religion and virtue. (37232)

Friendly letter from London. 18551, 7th note after 95843

Friendly letter . . . on the pro-slavery influences. (25096)

Friendly letter to a membery of the Episcopal Church. 97837

Friendly letter to a Trinitarian brother in the ministry. 105334

Friendly letter to parents and heads of families. 25949

Friendly letter to the Rev. Mr. Cumings. 71810

Friendly letter to the Reverend Thomas Baldwin. 2914, 105248, 105266

Friendly letters to a Universalist. 103724A

Friendly remarks on result of council. 2603

Friendly remarks to the people of Connecticut. 25950, 105930

Friendly Society of the Town of Haerlem, New York. 29504

Friendly triall of the grounds tending to separation. 2938

Friendly visitant. 90778

Friendly voice from England on American affairs. 14037

Friendly warning to all persons. 42626, 60224

Friendly word to the Rev. Francis L. Hawks. 26134

Friendly writer and register of truth. 14449

Friends. pseud. North star: the poetry of freedom. 55730

Friends, Washington. 25952

Friends' Academy, New Bedford, Mass. 52469

Friends and Admirers of Lord Metcalf. Meeting, Montreal, 1847. see Meeting of the Friends and Admirers of Lord Metcalf, Montreal, 1847.

Friends and brethren. 101689

Friends and countrymen, the business and profession of a soldier. 95018

Friends and countrymen, the critical time is now come. 20041, 90137

Friends and enemies of the American slave. 46186

Friends and fellow citizens. 96010

Friends and fellow citizens, a paper addressed. 95769

Friends and fellow citizens, pursuant to appointment. 99005

Friends and fellow-countrymen, pursuant to instructions. 99004

Friends' Association of Philadelphia for the Relief of Colored Freedmen. Executive Board. 61490, 62294 see also Friends, Society of. Philadelphia Yearly Meeting.

Friends' Asylum for the Insane, Philadelphia. see Philadelphia. Friends' Asylum for the Insane.

Friends' Boarding School, Providence, R. I. 66266

Friends, brethren, and countrymen, &c. (25953)

Friends, countrymen, and fellow-electors. 61681

Friends discourse delivered at an yearly meeting. 66924

Friends Historical Society. 83315

Friends in council. A colloquy. 15470

Friends' Institute, London. see London Friends' Institute.

Friends' library. 7097, (7492), 9416, 11751, 13025, 14434, 20033, 21873, 22351, 22352, 25361, (25956), (28341), (28825), 33091, (36651), 52167, 69371, 71023, 73504, (77452), (78355), 79612, 80490, 88884, 90388, note before 91980, 92324, 95375, 104689, 105203, 105653

Friends miscellany. 6121, 14956, 82873

Friends of a National Bank, Boston, 1841. 3181

Friends of a Railroad to San Francisco, Boston. Public Meeting, 1849. 19303, 58089, (65854), (76066)

Friends of African Colonization. petitioners 37404

Friends of African Colonization, Convention, Washington, D. C. 1842. 14732

Friends of African Colonization. Meeting, Baltimore, 1827. 14732, 45245, (65800) see also Maryland State Colonization Society.

Friends of America in England. 16999

Friends of American Industry. see Friends of Domestic Industry.

Friends of Civil and Religious Liberty, Baltimore. Meeting, 1837. see Great Meeting of the Friends of Civil and Religious Liberty, Baltimore, 1837.

Friends of Co-operation in the Cause of Southern Rights. Meeting, Charleston, S. C., 1851. see Southern Rights and Co-operation Meeting, Charleston, S. C., 1851.

Friends of David Henshaw. pseud. Refutation. (31423)

Friends of Domestic Industry. 398, (16200), 17127, 17131, 35449, (53675), (55313), 104020

Friends of Domestic Industry. petitioners 53770, 53769

Friends of Domestic Industry. Committees. (53675)

Friends of Education. Convention, Mount Holly, N. J., 1847. see Convention of the Friends of Education, Mount Holly, N. J., 1847.

Friends of Education. National Convention, Philadelphia, 1849. see National Convention of the Friends of Education, Philadelphia, 1849.

Friends of Education, Trenton, N. J. Committee. see Committee . . . of the Friends of Education, Trenton, N. J.

Friends of freedom. pseud. Liberty hall. 40942

Friends of General Jackson, Lousiville, Ky., 1827. see Democratic Party. Kentucky. Louisville.

Friends of Human Progress, Waterloo, N. Y. (25954)

Friends of John G. Watmouth. Committee. see Committee of the Friends of John G. Watmouth.

Friends of Judge Yates, New York. Special Committee. see Special Committee Appointed by the Friends of Judge Yates in the City of New York.

Friends of Liberty, New York. 103251

Friends of liberty and equality. pseud. Address to the people of North Carolina. (55591)

Friends of liberty and justice think it necessary. necessary. (25955)

Friends of literature, who wish to encourage
the art of printing. 95401
Friends of Rev. John Pierpont. pseud. Reply.
(62777) see also Boston. Hollis Street
Church. Meeting of Friends of Rev.
John Pierpont, 1839.
Friends of temperance and the statute of 1838.
pseud. Address to the people of
Massachusetts. 45615
Friends of the Administration. Convention,
Concord, N. H., 1828. see National
Republican Party. New Hampshire.
Convention, Concord, 1828.
Friends of the American Colonization Society,
Worcester County, Mass. see Worcester
County Auxiliary Colonization Society.
Friends of the General Administration Meeting,
Greensburgh, Pa., 1827. see National
Republican Party. Pennsylvania. Green-
sburgh. National Republican Party.
Pennsylvania. Westmoreland County.
Friends of the late Mrs. Osgood. pseud.
Laurel leaves. 91034
Friends of the late Mrs. Osgood. pseud.
Memorial. 31653, 91035
Friends of the Troy and Greenfield Rail Road.
pseud. Boston and the west. 6485
Friends of the Union, Baltimore. Public
Meeting, 1861. see Baltimore. Public
Meeting of the Friends of the Union,
1861.
Friends of the Union and the Constitution,
Portland, Me. Meeting, 1835. see
Meeting of the Friends of the Union and
the Constitution, Portland, Me., 1835.
Friends of Universal Education. publishers
77886
Friends of Universal Suffrage of Louisiana.
Convention, 1865. see Convention of the
Friends of Universal Suffrage of
Louisiana, 1865.
Friends of Washington! Look here!! 101772
Friends of William Vans. publishers 98560
Friends' pocket almanac, for 1852. 25957
Friends' School, Germantown, Pa. 61680
Friends' School, Providence, R. I. 52637
Friends, Society of. 24279, 23188-23189,
(25956), (26877), 32055, 32936, (41049),
(44820), 49341, 52602, 59703, 66904,
66910-66911, (66916), 66919, 66921,
(66925), 79105, (79616), 86038, 86062-
86063, 86067-86070, 2d-3d notes after
94928, 95752, 96142, 100959, 2d note
after 105986
Friends, Society of. petitioners 37818
Friends, Society of. American Bible Associ-
ation. see Bible Association of Friends
in America.
Friends, Society of. Associated Executive
Committee on Indian Affairs. 34608
Friends, Society of. Associated Executive
Committee on Indian Affairs. Meeting,
1st, Mt. Pleasant, Ohio, 1870. 34608
Friends, Society of. Association for the Free
Instruction of Adult Colored Citizens.
see Association of Friends for the Free
Instruction of Adult Colored Persons.
Friends, Society of. Bible Association in
America. see Bible Association of
Friends in America.
Friends, Society of. Committee to Assist in
the Complete Abolition of the Slavery of
the Blacks. 23621
Friends, Society of. Committee to Complete
the Abolition of Trade in Blacks. 23713

Friends, Society of. Conference, Baltimore,
1849. 86046
Friends, Society of. Conference of the Com-
mittees of the Yearly Meetings of New
York, New England, Baltimore, North
Carolina, and Indiana, Baltimore, 1851.
86927
Friends, Society of. General Committee
Representing the Yearly Meetings of
Genesee, New York, Philadelphia, and
Baltimore. see General Committee
Representing the Yearly Meetings of
Genesee, New York, Philadelphia, and
Baltimore.
Friends, Society of. Historical Society. see
Friends Historical Society.
Friends, Society of. Joint Committee Appointed
by the Society of Friends, Constituting
the Yearly Meetings of Genesee, New York,
Philadelphia, and Baltimore. see Joint
Committee Appointed by the Society of
Friends, Constituting the Yearly Meetings
of Genesee, New York, Philadelphia, and
Baltimore, for Promoting the Civilization,
and Improving the Condition of the Seneca
Nation of Indians.
Friends, Society of. Joint Committee on
Indian Affairs of the Four Yearly Meetings
of Friends of Genesee, New York, Phila-
delphia, and Baltimore. see Joint Com-
mittee on Indian Affairs of the Four Yearly
Meetings of Friends of Genesee, New
York, Philadelphia, and Baltimore.
Friends, Society of. Joint Delegation Appointed
by the Committee on the Indian Concern
of the Yearly Meetings of Ohio and Genesee.
see Joint Delegation Appointed by the
Committee on the Indian Concern of the
Yearly Meetings of Ohio and Genesee.
Friends, Society of. Joint Delegation on the
Committee on the Indian Concern of the
Yearly Meetings of Baltimore, Philadelphia,
and New York. see Joint Delegation of
the Committee on the Indian Concern of
the Yearly Meetings of Baltimore, Phila-
delphia and New York, to Visit the Indians
Under the Care of Friends, in the
Northern Superintendency, State of
Nebraska, 1869.
Friends, Society of. Baltimore Yearly Meeting.
3783, (20232), 26255, 29315, 34652,
(45364), (47582), 65919, 66924, (70201),
86048, 86060, 86062, 90754 see also
Baltimore Association of Friends to Advise
and Assist Friends in the Southern States.
Friends, Society of. Conference of the Com-
mittees of the Yearly Meetings of New
York, New England, Baltimore, North
Carolina, and Indiana, Baltimore, 1851.
General Committee Representing the
Yearly Meetings of Genesee, New York,
Philadelphia, and Baltimore. Joint Com-
mittee Appointed by the Society of Friends,
Constituting the Yearly Meetings of
Genesee, New York, Philadelphia, and
Baltimore, for Promoting the Civilization,
and Improving the Condition of the Seneca
Nation of Indians. Joint Committee on
Indian Affairs of the Four Yearly Meetings
of Friends of Genesee, New York, Phila-
delphia, and Baltimore.
Friends, Society of. Baltimore Yearly Meeting.
petitioners 47690
Friends, Society of. Baltimore Yearly Meeting.
Committee for Promoting the Improvement

and Civilization of the Indian Natives.
see Friends, Society of. Baltimore
Yearly Meeting. Committee on Indian
Affairs.
Friends, Society of. Baltimore Yearly Meeting.
Committee on Indian Affairs. 7849,
26254, 34602, 34651 see also Joint
Committee on Indian Affairs, of the
Four Yearly Meetings of Friends of
Genesee, New York, Philadelphia, and
Baltimore.
Friends, Society of. Baltimore Yearly Meeting.
Committee on Indian Affairs. petitioners
47620, 95389
Friends, Society of. Baltimore Yearly Meeting.
Committee on the Indian Concern. 34672,
94539 see also Joint Delegation of the
Committee on the Indian Concern of
Yearly Meetings of Baltimore, Philadel-
phia, and New York, to Visit the Indians
Under the Care of Friends, in the
Northern Superintendency, State of
Nebraska, 1869.
Friends, Society of. Baltimore Yearly Meeting.
Committee on the Indian Concern. Sub-
Committee. 69746
Friends, Society of. Boston Yearly Meeting.
(40299)
Friends, Society of. Boston Yearly Meeting.
Meeting for Sufferings. (52642)
Friends, Society of. Burlington Monthly
Meeting. 91249, 105211
Friends, Society of. Burlington Yearly Meeting.
15446, 22692, 30235, 61622 see also
Friends, Society of. New Jersey Yearly
Meeting. Friends, Society of. Philadel-
phia Yearly Meeting.
Friends, Society of. Cincinnati Yearly Meeting.
see Friends, Society of. Ohio Yearly
Meeting.
Friends, Society of. Delaware Yearly Meeting.
59841, note after 66906, 81764, 86037
see also Friends, Society of. Philadel-
phia Yearly Meeting.
Friends, Society of. Delaware Yearly Meeting.
petitioners 77451
Friends, Society of. Dinwiddie County, Va.,
Meeting. 20205
Friends, Society of. Dublin, Ireland, Meeting.
see also Dublin Friends' Tract Associ-
ation.
Friends, Society of. Ferrisburgh Monthly
Meeting. 91491
Friends, Society of. Genesee Yearly Meeting.
(47582) see also General Committee
Representing the Yearly Meetings of
Genesee, New York, Philadelphia, and
Baltimore. Joint Committee Appointed
by the Society of Friends, Constituting
the Yearly Meetings of Genesee, New
York, Philadelphia, and Baltimore, for
Promoting the Civilization, and Improving
the Condition of the Seneca Nation of
Indians. Joint Committee on Indian
Affairs of the Four Yearly Meetings of
Friends of Genesee, New York, Philadel-
phia, and Baltimore. Joint Delegation
Appointed by the Committee on the Indian
Concern of the Yearly Meetings of Ohio
and Genesee.
Friends, Society of. Gravelley Run, Va.,
Yearly Meeting. 100524
Friends, Society of. Great Britain. 9244,
10675, (81880), (81889) see also Friends,
Society of. London Yearly Meeting.
Friends, Society of. Manchester,

England, Yearly Meeting. Friends,
Society of. Yorkshire Quarterly Meeting.
Friends, Society of. Great Britain and Ire-
land. (47626), 81787, 81806 see also
Friends, Society of. Dublin, Ireland,
Meeting.
Friends, Society of. Gwynedd, Pa., Monthly
Meeting. 66608
Friends, Society of. Indiana Yearly Meeting.
19187, 21851, 34497-34498, 34591, (47582),
70194, 86056, 94919 see also Friends,
Society of. Conference of the Committees
of the Yearly Meetings of New York, New
England, Baltimore, North Carolina, and
Indiana, Baltimore, 1851.
Friends, Society of. Jericho, N. Y., Monthly
Meeting. 31718, note before 94920
Friends, Society of. London Yearly Meeting.
4676, 26254, 30235, 34651, 34674,
(37191), 37192, 49339, (49341), 61627,
61685, 65774, (66923), 68343, 69883,
86070, (81777), (81873), 86024, 86041,
86051, 90754, 3d note after 94928 see
also Friends, Society of. Great Britain.
London Friends' Institute. Tract Associ-
ation of the Society of Friends, London.
Friends, Society of. London Yearly Meeting.
Committee on the Distress Existing in
Ireland. 86026
Friends, Society of. London Yearly Meeting.
Committee on the Fugitive Slaves in
America. 81872
Friends, Society of. London Yearly Meeting.
Committee on the Negro and Aborigines
Fund. 86065
Friends, Society of. London Yearly Meeting.
Committee on the Ship Vigilante. (81922),
99604
Friends, Society of. London Yearly Meeting.
Committee to Promote the Total Abolition
of the Slave Trade. (34699)
Friends, Society of. London Yearly Meeting.
Meeting for Sufferings. 26254, 34651,
34652, 34674, 34676, 34705, 52258,
61687, 69883, 82043-(82045), 82053-(82045),
82053-82054, 86058, 93601
Friends, Society of. London Yearly Meeting.
Meeting for Sufferings. petitioners 47727
Friends, Society of. London Yearly Meeting.
Meeting for Sufferings. Aborigines Com-
mittee. (23634A), 26255, 34652, 34667,
86572
Friends, Society of. London Yearly Meeting.
Sub-Committee for Managing the Donation
Fund. 61494, 81896
Friends, Society of. Manchester, England,
Yearly Meeting. 49339 see also Friends,
Society of. Great Britain.
Friends, Society of. Maryland Yearly Meeting.
26255, 37185, 37194, 37202 see also
Friends, Society of. Baltimore Yearly
Meeting. Friends, Society of. Maryland
and Virginia Yearly Meeting. Friends,
Society of. Philadelphia Yearly Meeting.
Friends, Society of. Maryland Yearly Meeting.
Committee for Promoting the Improvement
and Gradual Civilization of the Indian
Natives in Some Parts of North America.
60613
Friends, Society of. Maryland and Virginia
Yearly Meeting. 34652 see also Friends,
Society of. Maryland Yearly Meeting.
Friends, Society of. Virginia Yearly
Meeting.
Friends, Society of. New England Yearly
Meeting. (21627), 26255, 34652, 47739,

51789, 52604, 52606-(52607), 52612-
52614, 52626, (52633), (52634), 53754,
(70000), (74099)-74100, (81886), 86021,
86039, 86047, 86064, 86069, (81886),
2d note after 92833, 2d note after 94928,
99591 see also Friends' School,
Providence, R. I. Friends, Society of.
Conference of the Committees of the
Yearly Meetings of New York, New
England, Baltimore, North Carolina, and
Indiana, Baltimore, 1851.
Friends, Society of. New England Yearly
Meeting. petitioners 93676
Friends, Society of. New England Yearly
Meeting. Meeting for Sufferings. 8537,
26007, 52639
Friends, Society of. New England Yearly
Meeting. Meeting for Sufferings. Clerk.
8537, 26007, 52639 see also Brown,
Moses.
Friends, Society of. New Jersey Yearly
Meeting. 22692, 53071, 59841, 61622,
note after 66906, 81764, 81969 see also
Friends, Society of. Burlington Yearly
Meeting. Friends, Society of. Philadel-
phia. Yearly Meeting.
Friends, Society of. New Jersey Yearly
Meeting. petitioners 77451
Friends, Society of. New Jersey Yearly
Meeting. Committee for Promoting the
Improvement and Gradual Civilization
of the Indian Tribes. 7848, (34617)
Friends, Society of. New London Monthly
Meeting. (19185)
Friends, Society of. New York Monthly
Meeting. 86025
Friends, Society of. New York Monthly
Meeting. defendants 90735, 93607
Friends, Society of. New York Monthly
Meeting. Committee to Correspond with
the Orthodox Party of Friends. (54227)
Friends, Society of. New York Monthly
Meeting. Committee to Take Charge of
the Defence of the Suit in Chancery,
Instituted by the Orthodox Party of
Friends. 90735
Friends, Society of. New York Monthly Meeting.
Property Committee. complainants
104500 see also Griffen, Solomon.
complainant Underhill, Joshua S. complainant Wood, John. complainant
Friends, Society of. New York Monthly
Meeting. Trustees. complainants 104500
see also Murray, Lundley, fl. 1833. complainant Willis, John R. complainant
Friends, Society of. New York Yearly Meeting.
16020, 26255, 34652, 36355, (47582),
47738, (53667), 45060, 54246A, 54262,
(54559), 58904, 61631, (70195), 81768,
(81781), 86023, 86044, 93591, 95624
see also Friends, Society of. Conference
of the Committees of the Yearly Meetings
of New York, New England, Baltimore,
North Carolina, and Indiana, Baltimore,
1851. General Committee Representing
the Yearly Meetings of Genesee, New York,
Philadelphia, and Baltimore. Joint Committee Appointed by the Society of Friends,
Constituting the Yearly Meeting of Genesee,
New York, Philadelphia, and Baltimore,
for Promoting the Civilization, and Improving
the Condition of the Seneca Nation of Indians.
New York Association of Friends for the
Relief of Those Held in Slavery. New York
Free Produce Association of Friends.
Tract Association of Friends, New York.

Friends, Society of. New York Yearly Meeting.
Committee on the Indian Concern. 34602,
51793 see also Joint Committee on
Indian Affairs, of the Four Yearly Meetings.
of Friends of Genesee, New York, Phila-
delphia, and Baltimore. Joint Delegation
of the Committee on the Indian Concern
of the Yearly Meetings of Baltimore,
Philadelphia, and New York, to visit the
Indians Under the Care of Friends, in the
Northern Superintendency, State of Nebraska,
1869.
Friends, Society of. New York Yearly Meeting.
Committee on the Indian Concern.
petitioners 47620
Friends, Society of. New York Yearly Meeting.
Committee Upon the Condition and Wants
of the Colored Refugees. 14752, (54559)
Friends, Society of. New York Yearly Meeting.
Committees. 53662
Friends, Society of. New York Yearly Meeting.
Meeting for Sufferings. 53779, 97938
Friends, Society of. Nine-Partners Monthly
Meeting. 95625
Friends, Society of. North America. 86056
Friends, Society of. North Carolina Yearly
Meeting. 55587, 55608 see also Friends,
Society of. Conference of the Committees
of the Yearly Meetings of New York, New
England, Baltimore, North Carolina, and
Indiana, Baltimore, 1851.
Friends, Society of. Ohio Yearly Meeting.
19187, 26255, 34652, (47582), 56876,
56907, 56911, (56912), (56914), 57042,
65774, 69746
Friends, Society of. Ohio Yearly Meeting.
petitioners 56967
Friends, Society of. Ohio Yearly Meeting.
Committee on the Indian Concern. 34602
see also Joint Delegation Appointed by the
Committee on the Indian Concern of the
Yearly Meetings of Ohio and Genesee.
Friends, Society of. Ohio Yearly Meeting.
Committee on the Indian Concern. Sub-
Committee. 69746
Friends, Society of. Ohio Yearly Meeting.
Meeting for Sufferings. 86056, 94919
Friends, Society of. Pennsylvania and New-
Jersey Yearly Meeting. see Friends,
Society of. New Jersey Yearly Meeting.
and Friends, Society of. Philadelphia
Yearly Meeting.
Friends, Society of. Pennsylvania Yearly
Meeting. see Friends, Society of. Phila-
delphia Yearly Meeting.
Friends, Society of. Philadelphia Monthly
Meeting. 8956, 22696, 37178, 37200,
37205, 60712, (61419), 61449, 61626,
61635, 80460, 86049, 86068, 90387-90388,
90682, note after 94918, 97059, 97113
see also Philadelphia. Library of the
Three Monthly Meetings of Friends.
Philadelphia. Library of the Four Monthly
Meetings of Friends.
Friends, Society of. Philadelphia Yearly
Meeting. (1771), 1773, 8956, 19183,
19187, 21632, 22692-22693, 23168, 23452,
23641, 26006, 26255, 26261, (26877),
34622, 34652, 36337, 37185, 37200, 37202,
37210, (37333), 47181, (47582), 47336-
(47337), 48711, 57908, 59612-59614, 59703,
59840-59841, 59845, 60579, 60599, (60600),
60624, 60769, 61429, 61469, 61495,
61621-61624, 61628-61635, 61644-61645,
61683-61684, 62202, 66906-note after
66906, note after 66909, 66912, 66918,

(66925), 69768, 69999, 74101-74102, 81968-81969, 96028, 86031, 86035, 86037, 86040, 86050, 86053, 86054-86055, 86652, 91764, 92948, 94920, 95739, 97113, 99574 see also Association of Friends at Philadelphia and Vicinity, for the Relief of Colored Freedmen. Friendly Association for Regaining and Preserving Peace with the Indians by Pacific Measures, Philadelphia. Friends, Society of. Burlington Yearly Meeting. Friends, Society of. Delaware Yearly Meeting. Friends, Society of. Maryland Yearly Meeting. Friends, Society of. New Jersey Yearly Meeting. General Committee Representing the Yearly Meetings of Genesse, New York, Philadelphia, and Baltimore. Joint Committee Appointed by the Society of Friends, Constituting the Yearly Meetings of Genesee, New York, Philadelphia, and Baltimore, for Promoting the Civilization, and Improving the Condition of the Seneca Nation of Indians. Philadelphia Association of Friends for the Education of Poor Children. Philadelphia Free Produce Association of Friends. Tract Association of Friends, Philadelphia.

Friends, Society of. Philadelphia Yearly Meeting. petitioners (55961), 60579, 61936, 77451, 82979

Friends, Society of. Philadelphia Yearly Meeting. plaintiffs 23168, 32936, note before 101987

Friends, Society of. Philadelphia Yearly Meeting. Clerk. 59614, 61936, note after 66909, 86691 see also Drinker, John. Pemberton, James. Pemberton, John. John.

Friends, Society of. Philadelphia Yearly Meeting. Committee for Promoting the Improvement and Gradual Civilization of the Indian Natives in Some Parts of North America. 7848, (34617), (34669), 34679, 60613, 86037 see also Joint Committee on Indian Affairs, of the Four Yearly Meetings of Friends of Genesee, New York, Philadelphia, and Baltimore. Joint Delegation of the Committee on the Indian Concern of the Yearly Meetings of Baltimore, Philadelphia, and New York, to Visit the Indians Under the Care of Friends, in the Northern Superintendency, State of Nebraska, 1869.

Friends, Society of. Philadelphia Yearly Meeting. Committee on Indian Affairs. 26254-26255, 34602, 34651-34652

Friends, Society of. Philadelphia Yearly Meeting. Committee on Indian Affairs. petitioners 47620

Friends, Society of. Philadelphia Yearly Meeting. Committee on the Establishment of Schools. 86691

Friends, Society of. Philadelphia Yearly Meeting. Committee to Have Charge of the Subject of Slavery. 81802

Friends, Society of. Philadelphia Yearly Meeting. Committees. 53662

Friends, Society of. Philadelphia Yearly Meeting. Meeting for Sufferings. 59613, (59854), 60759, 61625, 61687, 62161, 62312, 65902, 66922, note after 95901, 86056, 95909, 99574

Friends, Society of. Philadelphia Yearly Meeting. Meeting for Sufferings. Clerk. 62312, note after 95901 see also Pemberton, John.

Friends, Society of. Pyrmont, Westphalia (Germany) Monthly Meeting. 59615, 94925

Friends, Society of. Purchase Monthly Meeting. 28815

Friends, Society of. Rhode Island Quarterly Meeting, 70522

Friends, Society of. Rhode Island Yearly Meeting. Meeting for Sufferings. (52642)

Friends, Society of. Scipio Quarterly Meeting. 86022

Friends, Society of. Steubenville, Ohio, Monthly Meeting. defendants 28119, note after 96937

Friends, Society of. Virginia Yearly Meeting. 26255, 34652, 100526 see also Friends, Society of. Maryland and Virginia Yearly Meeting. Friends, Society of. Philadelphia Yearly Meeting.

Friends, Society of. Virginia Yearly Meeting. petitioners 3922, 47619, 47622-47623, 47687, 86042-86043, 100522, 101522, 101525, 101527-101527A

Friends, Society of. Virginia Yearly Meeting. Meeting for Sufferings. 55359

Friends, Society of. Yorkshire Quarterly Meeting. 105211

Friends, Society of (Anti-slavery) Clear Lake Monthly Meeting. 57745

Friends, Society of (Anti-slavery) Indiana Yearly Meeting. 26164

Friends, Society of (Congregational) New York Yearly Meeting. (65918)

Friends, Society of (Hicksite) New York Yearly Meeting. 86052

Friends, Society of (Hicksite) Philadelphia Yearly Meeting. 31717

Friends, Society of (Keithian) Philadelphia Monthly Meeting. 37193, 86057

Friends, Society of (Orthodox) New York. (53637)

Friends, Society of (Orthodox) New York. plaintiffs 90735

Friends, Society of (Orthodox) New York. Committee to Correspond with the New York Monthly Meeting of Friends. (54227)

Friends, Society of (Progressive) Pennsylvania Yearly Meeting. 24512, 60093, (60386)

Friends, Society of (Rogers Sect) 64973

Friends, Society of (Women Friends) New England Yearly Meeting. 52636

Friends, Society of (Women Friends) Philadelphia Yearly Meeting. 86059

Friends, Society of (Women Friends) Virginia Yearly Meeting. 100523

Friends, these are to satisfie you. 24081

Friends' Tract Association, Dublin. see Dublin Friends' Tract Association.

Friends' Tract Association, London. see Tract Association of the Society of Friends, London.

Friendship Division, no. 19, Philadelphia. see Sons of Temperance of North America. Pennsylvania. Friendship Division, no. 19, Philadelphia.

Friendship Fire Company, Philadelphia. (61682)

Friendship in death. 73541

Friendship Lodge, no. 73, Philadelphia. see Freemasons. Pennsylvania. Friendship Lodge, no. 73, Philadelphia.

Friendship with Britain. 84837

Friendship with Britain the true interest of America. 84823
Friendship's offering. 102069
Frierson, Madison S. 25958
Fries, E. 25959
Fries, Georg. tr. (22030), (74644)-74646
Fries, George, 1799-1866. (25960)
Fries, John. defendant 25961, 96866
Fries, Lorenz, of Colmar, 1490 (ca.)-1531. 25964-25965, 66481, 1st note after 98183, 98184
Friese, Philip C. 25962-25963
Friesen verugde over het vrij verklaaren van Amerika. 91730
Friess, Laurentius. see Fries, Lorenz, of Colmar, 1490 (ca.)-1531.
Frieze, Jacob. 25966-25967, 70739
Frieze, Robert. 25968
Frignet, Ernest. 25969-25970
Frilinghuisen, Theodorus Jacobus. see Frelinghuysen, Theodorus Jacobus, 1691-1757.
Frimodig provelse af den Engelske Admiralitetsrets dom. 77648
Frink, Samuel. 25975
Frink, Thomas. (25976)-(25977)
Frinkle Fry. pseud. see Fry, Frinkle. pseud.
Frio, Miguel Maria de Rio. see Rio-Frio, Miguel Maria de.
Frisbie, Barns. 25977
Frisbie, Levi, 1783-1822. 19372, (25978)-(25981), (55864), 63590, 103208, 103211-103212
Frisch, P. 25982
Frisia seu de viris rebusque Frisiae illustribus. 29937
Frisius, Gemma Reinerus. see Gemma, Reinerus, Frisius, 1508-1555.
Fristoe, William. 25983
Fritsch, Joanne Gottlob. 25984-25985
Fritz, Johann Friedrich. 25986, 78007
Frobel, Julius. 25987-25993
Frobisher, Sir Martin, 1535?-1594. 25994-26000, 28641, (38973)-38974, 51334, 62957, 68419, (74131), (79344), 79346, note after 100853, note after 100854
Frobisher's three voyages, 1576-78. 62957
Frobisher's three voyages in search of a passage. 26000
Frobisser, Martin. see Frobisher, Sir Martin, 1535?-1594.
Froger, F. 26001-(26004)
Frogoso, J. see Fragoso, Joanne.
Frolics of fancy. 2284
Froloff, N. tr. 33726
From a folio manuscript. 13442
From a just view of their dependence. 82936
From Canada. An address and caution to the public. 10456
From Cape Cod to Dixie and the tropics. 43453
From Chattanooga to Petersburg. 84769
From dawn to daylight. 4327
From everglade to canon. 72467
From Gettysburg to Appomatox. 83420
From gipsy tent to pulpit. 83893
From Liverpool to St. Louis. (29834)
From Montreal to the maritime provinces and back. (27346)
From Nauvoo to the penitentiary. 85535
From New-York to Boston. 89903
From New York to Delhi. 49337
From our general spring meeting of ministers and elders. 61683

From our meeting for sufferings. 61687
From our yearly-meeting, held at Philadelphia, for Pennsylvania and New-Jersey. 26006, 61684
From our yearly meeting held at Philadelphia . . . thee 2d of the ninth month. 61685
From our yearly-meeting, held in London. 61686
From our yearly meeting of Women Friends. 100523
From the American journal of science and arts. 72476
From the Atlantic surf to the Golden Gate. 33685
From the General Committee of Conference. 60109
From the gold fields to the land of the midnight sun. 83599
From the hub to the Hudson. 27523
From the London gazette. 93962
From the Meeting of Sufferings for New England. 8537, 26007, 52639
From the Meeting for Sufferings, in London. 61687
From the merchants and traders of Philadelphia. 61688
From the New-York journal. 77413
From the Overland monthly. 90931
From the proceedings of the American Ethnological Society. 106326
From the public news-papers. Boston, July 14. & 17. 1766. 104852
From the Richmond enquirer, of March 6th, 1860. 78888
From the St. Lawrence River to the Gulf of Mexico. 84424
From the 2d of August 1784, to the 6th of August 1785. 38802
From the United States gazette. 26008
From the Washington globe, 25th ult. 94790
From 25th February, till 21st Sept. 1786. 38802
From Wisconsin to California, and return. 73365
Fromelden. pseud. Clergy not recruiting agents. 13639
Fromentin, Eligius, d. 1822. (35378)
Fromentin, Eugene, 1820-1876. 26009
Fromesta, Luis de Benavides Cortes, Marques de. see Benavides Cortes, Luis de, Marques de Fromesta.
Frond, Victor, 1821- ed. (70809)
Fronda, V. de. 19260
Front view of Yale-College. 105931
Frontaura, Placido Rico. see Rico Frontaura, Placido.
Frontenac, Louis de Baude, Comte de Palluau et de. see Baude, Louis de, Comte de Palluau et de Frontenac, 1620-1698.
Frontenac. A poem. 92767
Frontenac Lead Mining Company . . . in Bedford. 26010
Frontenac, Lennox & Addington. 16400
Frontenac: or the Atotarho of the Iroquois. 92768
Frontier, a magazine of the northwest. 101041
Frontier life. 30344
Frontier maid. 26011, 1st note after 105691
Frontier missionary. 3720, 66194
Frontier sketches. 26012
Frontiers well defended. 46332, 46589
Frontiersmen of New York. 81183
Frontignieres, ------ de. tr. (23475), 23478
Frontispice [sic] explaned [sic]. 78189
Frontispiece for a meeting house. (21863)

Frossard, Benjamin Sigismond. 26013-26014
Frost, -------. defendant 8466
Frost, Barzillai. 26015-26017
Frost, Daniel. 26018
Frost, Edward. 87489
Frost, Griffin. 26020
Frost, Henry R. 87875
Frost, J. ed. (77823)
Frost, Mrs. J. Blakeslee. (26021)
Frost, J. H. (39724)
Frost, John, 1800-1859. (25274), 26022-26055,
  34460, 50455, 51827, 71983-71984,
  79511
Frost, John, 1800-1859. supposed author
  3694, 31526, 35380, 92215
Frost, John, 1800-1859. incorrectly supposed
  author 52242, 2d note after 95758
Frost, Joseph H. (39724)
Frost, Samuel, d. 1793. defendant 105351
Frost Free Library, Marlborough, N. H. see
  Marlborough, N. H. Frost Free Library.
Frothingham, Charles W. 26057
Frothingham, Ebenezer, 1717?-1798. 2632,
  26058, 79161
Frothingham, F. E. 26061
Frothingham, Frederick. 26059-(26060)
Frothingham, Nathaniel L. 26063-26074, 7th
  note after 96966
Frothingham, O. B. 21153, 26075-26079, note
  after 81865
Frothingham, Richard. 26080-26087, (37846)
Froudfit, Alexander. 25152
Frout de Fontpertuis, Adalbert. 26088-(26089)
Frowd, J. G. Player. see Player-Frowd,
  J. G.
Fruchte der Einsamkeit. 59700
Frue, William B. 88156 see also South
  Pewabic Copper Company. Mine.
  Superintendent.
Fruhauf, Daniel. 26090
Fruhbeck, F. J. (26091)
Fruhlings-Kuren. 47409
Fruit book. 22264
Fruit, flower, and kitchen garden. 52291
Fruit Growers National Convention, New York,
  1848. see National Convention of Fruit
  Growers, New York, 1848.
Fruit Growers' Society, of Eastern Pennsylvania,
  60110
Fruit in old age. 32943
Fruitful bough. 17404
Fruitful retrospect. 70952
Fruitfull and usefull discourse. 13866
Fruitfulness in old age. 72427
Fruits and fruit trees of America. 20774
Fruits of a father's love. 59698
Fruits of America. 33206
Fruits of colonization. (26092)
Fruits of commercial restructions! 105397A
Fruits of congregationalism. 37750
Fruits of leisure. 66649
Fruits of retirement. A collection of pieces.
  102516
Fruits of retirement, or miscellaneous poems.
  49922
Fruits of solitude. 59699, (59734)
Fruits of the liquor trade. 91053
Fruston, Fr. de la. see La Fruston, Fr. de,
  1806-1864.
Frutas do Brasil. 73206
Fruteful and pleasant worke of the beste state.
  50544
Frutefull pleasaunt, & wittie worke. 50545
Fry, Alfred A. 10589
Fry, Benjamin St. James. 26093

Fry, Edmund. 26094
Fry, F. (26095)
Fry, Frinkle. pseud. "Wooden nutmegs" at
  Bull Run. 26096
Fry, Henry. 81708
Fry, Henry. petitioner (26097)
Fry, J. 601
Fry, Jacob. (26098)
Fry, James B. (15628)
Fry, Joseph Reese, 1811-1865. 15896, 26099,
  102996
Fry, Lewis. (26100)
Fry, W. H. 26101
Fry, William. 65043
Frye, George. defendant at impeachment
  26102 see also Montserrat. President
  of the Council. defendant at impeachment
Frye, Isaac W. 12105, 26103
Frye, T. C. 94112
Fryer, Alfred. 26105
Frying pan for poor sinners. 97778
Fry's travellers' guide and descriptive
  journal. (26095)
Fuchsius, S. 26106
Fudge family in Washington. (25107), 55341
Fueillet, Jean Baptiste. supposed author
  24227, 73176
Fuel Savings Society of the City and Liberties
  of Philadelphia. 61689
Funebro aparato a las exequias que en la
  cicudad de Santiago. 58433
Fuente, Ant. Gutierrez de la. see La Fuente,
  Ant. Gutierrez de.
Fuente, Francisco de la. 26108
Fuente, G. de la. 26109
Fuente, Geronymo de Sola y. see Sola y
  Fuente, Geronymo de.
Fuente, Juan Fernandez de la. see Fernandez
  de la Fuente, Juan.
Fuente, Romualdo de la. 26110
Fuente, Vicente de la. 26111, (70780)
Fuente, Villar de. see Villar de Fuente,
  _____.
Fuentes, ------- Alvarez. see Alvarez
  Fuentes, -------.
Fuentes, Jos. Mor. de. 26113
Fuentes, Manuel A. (26114)-26120, 47936,
  61153
Fuentes, P. 26121
Fuentes y Guzman, ------. 26817
Fuerbilde der Heilsamen Worten von Glauben
  und Liebe. 69151
Fuereno. pseud. Ironico hablador. see V.,
  F. pseud.
Fuero, Francisco Fabian y. see Fabian y
  Fuero, Francisco, Bp.
Fugitive blacksmith. 59764
Fugitive hand-bill has lately been addressed
  to you. 103262
Fugitive pieces. 18938
Fugitive poems of Miss Amanda A. P. Capers.
  (52237)
Fugitive poetry. 104506
Fugitive political essays which have appeared.
  26123
Fugitive slave act of 1793. 16113
Fugitive slave bill. 26124
Fugitive slave bill. . . . A sermon. (14900)
Fugitive slave bill; its history and unconstitu-
  tionality. 26125
Fugitive slave case. A statement of the facts.
  2406
Fugitive slave case. District Court of the
  United States for the Southern District of
  Iowa. 18270, 26127

Fugitive slave law. A discourse. 25097
Fugitive slave law, and its victims. 26128
Fugitive slave law as a "finality." 21433
Fugitive slave law: its character fairly stated. 81984
Fugitive slave law of 1850. 16112, 20429-20429, 26129
"Fugitive slave law" of the United States. 90864
Fugitive slave law. Speech of Hon. Robert Rantoul. (67902)
Fugitive slave law. The religious duty of obediency. 89327
Fugitive slave law too bad for southern Negroes. (81727)
Fugitive slave law. Unconstitutionality of the fugitive slave act. 26130
Fugitive slave laws. 8237, 15047
Fugitive slaves. 47947
Fugitive slaves: a sermon . . . in . . . Winchendon. 45024
Fugitive slaves. N. Y. Court of Appeals. 26131, 40003
Fugitive tales, no. 1. 7331
Fugitive thoughts on the African slave trade. 26132
Fugitives; or, a trip to Canada. 38850
Futigives: or, the Quaker scout of Wyoming. 22297
Fugitt, James Preston. 26133-26134
Fugl, Ulrich Nicolai. 26135
Fuhrer fur Auswanderer nach Amerika. 62641
Fulcherius Carnotensis. 66686
Fuldstaendigt udtog af Christian Georg Andreas Oldendorp's Missions-Historie. (57151)
Fulfilling of the prophecies. 104044
Fulfilment of a promise. 104044
Fulfilment of modern prophecy. 64957
Fulford, Francis, Bp. of Montreal, 1802-1868. (26136)-26139, 31255
Fulgencio de Gamboa, M. see Gamboa, M. Fulgencio de.
Fulgosis, Baptista. 26140
Full account of his [i. e. Robert Blake's] glorious achievements. 5791
Full account of many of the great battles. (5373)
Full account of the actions of the late famous pyrate. 37704
Full account of the assassination plot. 28440
Full account of the attempted insurrection at Harper's Ferry. 8519
Full account of the burning of the Richmond theatre. 71180
Full account of the captivity and truely wonderful escape. 51574
Full account of the case of Jeronimy Clifford. 15201
Full account of the celebration of the said revolution. 51059
Full account of the centennial celebration, June 17, 1842. 6734
Full account of the dangerous voyages. 9500
Full account of the duel. 13060
Full account of the gold and diamond mines. 9498
Full account of the great calamity. 71181
Full account of the great fire at Pittsburgh. 25235
Full account of the late dreadful earthquake. 35559, (42593), 64185, 97102
Full account of the late expedition to Canada. 101050, 101051
Full account of the life and dealings of God. 103518

Full account of the murders of James King, of Wm., of Dr. Randall. 76047
Full account of the proceedings in relation to Capt. Kidd. 37703
Full account of the richness and extent. 2951
Full account of the sporting along our seashores and inland waters. 73111
Full account of this wholesale outrage. 5987
Full analysis of the credit system. 14917
Full and accurate report of the judicial proceedings. 46898
Full and authentic account of the debate which will take place. 1686
Full and authentic account of the murders. 71693
Full and authentic expose of the Ku-Klux-Klan. 38341
Full and authentic report of a lecture. 93139
Full and authentic report of the brilliant speech. (11866)
Full and authentic report of the debates in Faneuil Hall. 26141
Full and authentic report of the testimony. (70981)
Full and candid answer to "Considerations." 46916
Full and complete account of the Herberton tragedy. 31200
Full and complete account of the late awful riots. 61690
Full and complete description of the Covington and Cincinnati suspension bridge. 23892
Full and complete exposure of all the swindles. 72772
Full and correct account of the battle of Bunker Hill. 9177
Full and correct account of the chief naval occurrences. 35717
Full and correct account of the military occurrences. 35718
Full and correct account of the testimony given before the Joint Committee. 60111
Full and correct report of the trial of Sir Home Popham. 64131
Full and exact collection of all the considerable addresses. 18555
Full and exact account of the proceedings. 18554
Full and faithful report of the debates in both Houses of Parliament. 26142, 97349
Full and faithful account of the life of James Bather. 3954
Full and free inquiry into the merits of the peace. 26143
Full and impartial account of the Company of the Mississippi. 26144
Full and impartial answer to a letter in the Gazetteer. 28751
Full and impartial examination of the Rev. Mr. John Wesley's address. 102647
Full and impartial history of the trial of the petition. 35817
Full & just discovery of the weak & slender foundation. 26145
Full and particular account of all the circumstances. (26146), 103190
Full and particular account of an invasion. (87848A)
Full and particular account of the lives and tragical deaths. 4162
Full and particular account of . . . the loss. (40896)
Full and particular account of the trial of Francisco dos Santo. 86863
Full and particular answer to all the calumines. (26147), 80048

Full and true account of the life and death of Nathanael Bacon Esquire. 92716, 100488, 3d note after 100527A

Full and true history of the conquest of Mexico. 19982

Full and true relation of the Count Martini. 60112

Full and true statement of the examination and ordination of Mr. Arthur Carey. 10825

Full annals of the revolution in France, 1830. 51059

Full answer to a late pamphlet. 20407

Full answer to some notes and observations upon the votes. 55945, 55952

Full answer to the Apologeticall narration. 21991, 27952

Full answer to the King of Spain's late manifesto. 26148, 32765

Full answer to the late pamphlet. 80621

Full answer to the observations. 25637

Full answer to the pamphlet intitled A brief state. 60742, note after 97095

Full answer to the pamphlet intitled "A short vindication." 26630A

Full, clear, and succinct discussion. 26149

Full defence of the colonies. 16600

Full defence of the Rev. John Wesley. (57218)

Full description of the great mineral resources. 57075

Full description of the Oregon Territory. (31952)

Full description of the origin and progress. 91026

Full description of the saint and sinner. 82441

Full description of the soil. 98590

Full description of the Sunday Transcript Building. 67172

Full description . . . of the White Mountains. 4247

Full directory, for Washington City. 101935

Full expose. 38343

Full exposition of a pamphlet. 26150

Full exposition of the Clintonian faction. 105042

Full exposition of the law of God. 92684

Full exposure of Dr. Chas. T. Jackson's pretentions. 37353

Full exposure of the conduct of Dr. Charles T. Jackson. 35403

Full exposure of the Southern traitors. 36968

Full genealogical record. 84299

Full instructions relative to the cultivation. 88355

Full instructions to emigrants. 36329

Full justification of the people of Boston. 11152

Full length picture of universalism. 79305

Full length portrait. 83958

Full-length portrait of Washington Irving. 64765

Full manifestation of what Mr. Henry Laurens falsely denominates candour. 35985

Full metrical, juridical, and analytical report. 57390

Full narrative of the mysterious disappearance. 72362

Full opinions of Chief Justice Taney. 78257-(78258)

Full particulars as far as known. 72708

Full particulars of the assassination of Albert D. Richardson. (70986)

Full particulars of the two late awful shipwrecks near Sandy Hook. 93727

Full pedigrees of all the imported thorough-bred stallions. 8728

Full proceedings in the Senate [of Pennsylvania.] (60444)

Full proceedings [of the Pennsylvania Democratic State Convention.] (60052)

Full redemption, not interfering with free grace. 82214

Full refutation of an invidious pamphlet. 80699

Full relation of another voyage into the West Indies. 20830, 20840

Full reply to a late pamphlet. (66641), 101148

Full reply to Lieut. Cadogan's Spanish hireling. 9830, 56845, 2d note after 87848

Full report, embracing all the evidence and arguments. 71578

Full report of the action of the Grand Committee of Twenty. 2381

Full report of the arguments . . . in the case. (27985)

Full report of the case of Stacy Decow. 19205

Full report of the highly interesting breach of promise case. 96821

Full report of the proceedings at the meetings. 95496

Full report of the proceedings including speeches. (57388)

Full report of the proceedings of its [i. e. Hawk-Eye Pioneer Association's] first annual restival. 19746

Full report of the proceedings of the special convention. 53208

Full report of the speeches at the meeting of citizens in Cambridge. 93723

Full report of the trial of Ephraim K. Avery. 29887

Full report of the trial of John Gordon and William Gordon. (27983)

Full report of the trial of W. P. Darnes. (18605)

Full report of the trial of William Smith for piracy. 51456, 84728

Full sketches of other prisons. (37300)

Full state of the dispute. 26151, note after 87347

Full statement of the reasons offered. 26152

Full statement of the reasons . . . why there should be no penal laws. (45737)

Full statement of the trial and acquittal of Aaron Burr. 105043

Full, strong, and clear refutation of Mr. Sandeman's pernicious doctrines. (76341)

Full survey of Sion and Babylon. 26314

Full vindication of the measures of the Congress. 29956, (48562)-78563, 78574-78575, 78580-78581, 4th note after 100862

Full vindication of the R. H. General's conduct. 33340

Fullarton, William. 26153-26155

Fuller, ------, fl. 1803. 32951

Fuller, Allen C. 34306 see also Illinois. Adjutant General.

Fuller, Andrew S. (26156)

Fuller, Arthur B. (18259), 26157, 57813, 57816

Fuller, Daniel. 25168

Fuller, H. 26159

Fuller, Henry M. (26160), 36542

Fuller, Henry W. 26161

Fuller, Hiram. 26162-(26163)

Fuller, James Cannings. 26164

Fuller, Jane Gay. (26165-(26166)

Fuller, Margaret. see Ossoli, Sarah Margaret (Fuller), Marchesa de, 1810-1850.

Fuller, Metta Victoria. see Victor, Metta
Victoria (Fuller)
Fuller, Nicholas. 79443
Fuller, Richard, 1804-1876. 26167-(26170),
28944, 29526, 30099, 47943, 82096,
82795
Fuller, Richard B. 26171
Fuller, Robert. 26172
Fuller, Samuel. 26173-26178, 66656
Fuller, Siah. defendant 36856
Fuller, Stephen. 26180, 35618, 35626, 35627,
35640, 35659, 35666-35667, 82058,
89793, note after 97578 see also
Jamaica. Agent.
Fuller, Stephen. petitioner (26179), 35570
Fuller, Thomas, 1608-1661. (26181), 44124
Fuller, Thomas James Duncan, 1808-1876.
26183
Fuller, Timothy, 1739-1805. 26184
Fuller, Timothy, 1778-1835. (26185)-26188
Fuller. firm see Scammon, McCagg &
Fuller. firm
Fuller, Jeter, Yates. 84852
Fullerton, Alexander. 26189
Fullerton, J. S. USA 91088
Fullmacht for William Ussling. 98194
Fullner, G. tr. 4539
Fullom, S. W. 26191
Fullonton, Joseph. 26190
Fulness of joy in the presence of God. 30785
Fulness of life and joy in the presence of God.
65598
Fulton, A. R. 26192
Fulton, H. defendant 32558
Fulton, Hamilton. 55593
Fulton, J. D. 65899
Fulton, James Alexander. 25193
Fulton, John. supposed author 36316-36319,
88479
Fulton, Justin D. 26194-26195
Fulton, Philo. pseud. To the citizens of the
United States. see Carey, Mathew,
1760-1839. supposed author
Fulton, Robert, 1765-1815. 22740, 26196-
26203, 50826, 54581, 71349, 81394,
82974, 82976, note after 97065
Fulton, Robert, 1765-1815. plaintiff 41637-
41638
Fulton, Robert, 1765-1815. respondent 95903
Fulton, Ill. Illinois Soldiers' College. see
Illinois Soldiers' College, Fulton, Ill.
Fulton, Mo. Institution for the Deaf and Dumb.
see Missouri School for the Deaf, Fulton,
Mo.
Fulton, Mo. School for the Deaf. see
Missouri School for the Deaf, Fulton,
Mo.
Fulton, Mo. State Hospital. see Missouri.
State Hospital, Fulton.
Fulton, Mo. State Lunatic Asylum. see
Missouri. State Hospital, Fulton.
Fulton, N. Y. Falley Seminary. see Falley
Seminary, Fulton, N. Y.
Fulton County, N. Y. Auxiliary Bible Society.
see Auxiliary Bible Society of the Counties
of Montgomery, Fulton and Hamilton,
N. Y.
Fulton County, Pa. Board of Supervisors.
26205
Fulton. 85819
Fulton County Auxiliary Bible Society. see
Auxiliary Bible Society of the Counties
of Montgomery, Fulton and Hamilton,
N. Y.
Fulton Georges et Robert Stephenson. 35758

Fulton Township, Pa. Pleasant Grove Division,
no. 386. see Sons of Temperance of
North America. Pennsylvania. Pleasant
Grove Division, no. 386, Fulton Township.
Fulton Steam-Boat Company. respondents
93524
Fume, Joseph. pseud. Paper of tobacco.
58443
Fumee, Martin, Sieur de Marley-le-Chatel,
16th cent. tr. 27746-27749, 102836
Fun for the camp. (26206)
Fun, sentiment and adventure. 88291
Funch, Johan Christian Vilhelm. 26207
Funcion dramatica en el Palacio Imperial de
Mexico. 48480
Funck, Heinrich. supposed author 89431-89432
Function and place of conscience. note after
(58767)
Functions of a city. 22171
Fund for the Education of Teachers in the
Protestant Episcopal Church, St. Paul's
College, N. Y. see St. Paul's College,
College Point, N. Y. Fund for the
Education of Teachers in the Protestant
Episcopal Church.
Fund for the education of teachers in the
Protestant Episcopal Church, at St. Paul's
College. 75467
Fund for the Relief of East Tennessee. 23271
Fund publication, no. 3. 45216
Fund publications of the Maryland Historical
Society. 83976, 92793, 103352-103353,
105651
Fundacion de la cicudad de Buenos Aires.
26550
Fundacion de la obra pia. 27340
Fundacion de Mexico. 71703
Fundacion e indulgencias de la Orden de la
Merced. 47894
Fundacion y descripcion de la Santa Iglesia
Catedral de Guadalajara. 29027
Fundacion y primero siglo del . . . Convento
de S. Joseph. 27763
Fundacion y summario de indulgencias del
Sacro Orden de Nuestra Senora de la
Merced. 74799, 98897-98898
Fundament und klare Anweisung. 81284
Fundalmental by-laws and tables of rates.
60113
Fundamental constitutions of Carolina. (10971),
(41726)
Fundamental constitutions of Carolina, in
number a hundred and twenty. 10970
Fundamental doctrines of Christianity. 85295
Fundamental laws, charter of incorporation,
and supplement thereto. 62102
Fundamental laws, statutes, and constitutions.
75450
Fundamental principles of democracy. 19492
Fundamental principles of the laws of Canada.
20676
Fundamental rules and regulations of the
stockholders. 61691
Fundamental rules for administration of
general estate. 43177
Fundamentos con que el Senor Fiscal de
Consejo de Indias remitido. 70092
Fundamentos de hecho y de derecho. 26208
Fundamentos legales. 97672
Funding. 94491
Funding bill. 10872
Funding bill. Speech . . . in the Senate.
31319
Funding bill. Speech . . . March 3, 1868.
50791

Funding bill. Speech of Hon. Henry W.
Corbett. 16749
Funding bill. Speech of Hon. John Sherman,
of Ohio. (80375)
Funding system of the United States and of
Great Britain. 22235
Funds of Yale College. 105796
Funebre parentacion. 105730
Fvnebre panegirico. 86497
Fvenbre pompa, demonstracion doliente.
(60848)
Funebre pompa, magnificas, exequias. 57676
Fvnebres demonstraciones. (77048)
Funebris declamatio in solemni funere. 72536
Funeral address and discourse by Rev.
Edward K. Alden. 696
Funeral address . . . at the interment of
Right Rev. Benjamin Moore. (32301)
Funeral address, . . . Burlington, . . . 13
April, 1841. 20391
Funeral address, by Rev. William Adams.
(17268)
Funeral address, delivered at . . . Charleston.
27435
Funeral address delivered at the burial of
President Lincoln. 81366
Funeral address delivered at the interment
of the Hon. John Nicholas. (13343)
Funeral address, delivered in the German
Lutheran Church, Lancaster. 84613
Funeral address, delivered on Sunday, April
30, 1865. 20974
Funeral address on the death of Abraham
Lincoln, delivered in the Church of the
Covenant. (9628)
Funeral address on the death of Abraham
Lincoln, late lamented President of the
United States. 78646
Funeral address on the occasion of the
execution of Peter. 44658
Funeral address . . . on the twenty-sixth of
May, 1818. 33089
Funeral Ceremonies in Honor of Calhoun,
Clay and Webster, New Orleans, 1852.
see New Orleans. Funeral Ceremonies
in Honor of Calhoun, Clay and Webster,
1852.
Funeral ceremonies of Mr. King. 37808,
97098
Funeral dirge. 101289
Funeral dirge on the death of General
Washington. 101811
Funeral discourse after the decease of the
Reverend Mr. William Welsted. (46806)
Funeral discourse . . . at Rye, August, 1800.
64260
Funeral discourse, . . . Buffalo, June 28,
1862. 42032
Funeral discourse, by Rev. Evarts Scudder.
78510
Funeral discourse: . . . by the author of Two
discourses. 64996
Funeral discourse [by William D. Snodgrass.]
85483
Funeral discourse commemorative of Dr. John
Porter. 50416
Funeral discourse commemorative . . . of the
late Hon. Stephen Van Rensselaer. 3442
Funeral discourse deliver'd at Marlborough.
94067
Funeral discourse, delivered at North-Haven.
97188
Funeral discourse delivered at Portland, May
31, 1795. 19055

Funeral discourse, delivered at the interment
of the Hon. Josiah Bartlett. 95229
Funeral discourse, delivered at the interment
of the Rev. Nathaniel Noyes. 89795
Funeral discourse, delivered at the residence
of the Hon. Josiah Quincy. 71816
Funeral discourse, delivered December 27,
1836. (65424)
Funeral discourse deliver'd in Charlestown.
83437
Funeral discourse delivered in . . . Harvard.
58681
Funeral discourse, delivered in . . . Salem
. . . after the death of Major General
John Fiske. 4773
Funeral discourse, delivered in . . . Salem
. . . 15th April, 1804. (4776)
Funeral discourse, delivered in the Presbyterian
Church of New-Brunswick. (15171)
Funeral discourse delivered in the Third
Presbyterian Church. 5757
Funeral discourse, for Rev. Daniel H. Mansfield.
(38171)
Funeral discourse in memorial of Robert C.
Morse. 43340
Funeral discourse, May 4th, 1845. (26240)
Funeral discourse, . . . Newburyport. (9460)
Funeral discourse occasioned by the death of
John Brown. 54993
Funeral discourse occasion'd by the death of
Mrs. Hannah Williams. 65589, note after
104226, note after 104404
Funeral discourse, occasioned by the death of
Rev. Andrew Yates. 10274
Funeral discourse, occasioned by the death of
Sir Knight Joseph Foster. 36130
Funeral discourse occasioned by the death of
the Hon. Abraham Van Vechten. 98994
Funeral discourse occasioned by the death of
the Honourable John Appleton. 72692,
2d note after 97559
Funeral discourse, occasioned by the death of
the Hon. Stephen Van Rensselaer. 98995
Funeral discourse, occasioned by the death of
Thomas Sewall. (50300)
Funeral discourse occasioned by the deaths in
the Congregational Society. 85202
Funeral discourse of C. C. Beatty. 14949
Funeral discourse of J. H. Livingston. 19872
Funeral discourse of Rev. R. W. Patterson.
44261
Funeral discourse on David Perkins Page.
33962
Funeral discourse of Hugh Brady. (22137)
Funeral discourse, on occasion of the death
of Mrs. J. A. Barry. 71112
Funeral discourse on the death of Abraham
Lincoln. 27932
Funeral discourse on the death of Allison
Remington Bowen. 73413
Funeral discourse on the death of Gov. Richard
Dobbs Spaight. 35123
Funeral discourse . . . on the . . . death of
. . . J. Muir. (30554)
Funeral discourse on the death of Joseph J.
Stuart. 14429
Funeral discourse on . . . the death of Mrs.
Betsy Coningham. 77422
Funeral discourse on the death of Rev. James
Reid. (51702)
Funeral discourse, on the death of that eminent
man. (16403)
Funeral discourse on the occasion of the death
of Hon. Ephraim Cutler. 1493

Funeral discourse on the occasion of the death of Rev. Hezekiah G. Leigh. 84741

Funeral discourse on Wm. Crounse. (18899)

Funeral-discourse, preached after the death of the Honorable Francis Foxcroft, Esq. 1832

Funeral discourse preached by the Rev. H. W. Spalding. 88881

Funeral discourse, preached in memory of Capt. Ayres C. Barker. 22050

Funeral discourse preached on the occasion of the death of . . . Prince Frederick Lewis. 46797

Funeral discourse preached on the death of the Rev. Mr. George Whitefield. 22240

Funeral discourse, sacred to the memory of Mr. Joseph Moody. 83440

Funeral discourse . . . September 18th, 1842. 38315

Funeral discourse suggested by the death of the late Colonel Edward Brooks. 82954

Funeral discourse upon . . . the death of . . . Major General Denison. 33442

Funeral discourse upon the death of the Honourable Thomas Hutchinson. 46795

Funeral-discourses, occasioned by the death of several relatives. (46405)

Funeral discourses on the Reverend Mr. Stiles's death. 103786

Funeral elegy by way of a dialogue. 102531

Funeral elegy by way of dialogue. 102528-102529

Funeral elegy dedicated to the memory. 95820

Funeral elegy for 22d February. 101812

Funeral elegy of the death of General George Washington. 105017-101518, 103771

Funeral elegy on the Rev. and Renowned George Whitefield. 103626

Funeral elegy, on the Revd. and Renowned George Whitefield. 103624, 103627

Funeral elegy, on the Rev'd. and Renowned George Whitefield. 103625

Funeral elegy vpon the death of that excellent and most worthy gentleman John Winthrop Esq. 104850

Funeral eulogium on the Reverend Mr. Aaron Burr. (41641)

Funeral eulogium, pronounced at New-Milford on on the twenty-second of February, 1800. 28905

Funeral eulogy and oration. 33974, 101813

Funeral eulogy and prayer. 33915

Funeral eulogy at the obsequies. 80465

Funeral eulogy by General J. Hutington. 33974, 101813

Funeral eulogy, occasioned by the death of General Washington. (41345)

Funeral eulogy, on the characters of Thomas Jefferson and John Adams. 91489

Funeral gratitud con que la religiosa communidad del Convento de N. S. P. San Francisco. 26209

Funeral gratitud del Conventu de S. Franc. 34781

Funeral hymn, composed by that eminent servant. 103519-103520

Funeral hymn, made by the Rev. George Whitefield. 102643

Funeral hymns, 1st series. 102643

Funeral march to the memory of Abraham Lincoln. 41187

Funeral masonic oration. 81408

Funeral obsequies of the late Dr. Kane. 37004

Funeral observances . . . by the German, English and American ministers. 41188

Funeral Observances in Honor of Abraham Lincoln, New London, Conn., 1865. see New London, Conn. Funeral Observances in Honor of Abraham Lincoln, 1865.

Funeral observances at New London, Connecticut. 53255

Funeral of time, and other poems. 31992

Funeral: or grief a-la-mode. 91152

Funeral oration. 39744, note after 101813

Funeral oration at the obsequies of . . . Thomas Wildey. 58733

Funeral oration by Ephraim H. Foster. 25218

Funeral oration. By Wilson M'Candless, Esq. (63107)

Funeral oration commemorative of the illustrious virtues of the late great and good General Washington. (38174)

Funeral oration deliver'd at the opening of the annual meeting. (42377)

Funeral oration, delivered before the city government and citizens. 1421

Funeral oration: delivered . . . Boston. 24953

Funeral oration, delivered in Danville. 91337

Funeral oration, delivered in . . . Rhode Island College. 32570

Funeral oration, delivered in the Brick Presbyterian Church. 45459

Funeral oration delivered in the Chapel of Rhode-Island College, on Friday, 13th of November, 1795. 81319

Funeral oration, delivered in the Chapel of Rhode-Island College, on Wednesday the 29th of March, 1797. 95519

Funeral oration, delivered on the death of Benjamin French. 97488

Funeral oration delivered over the body of the Hon. Jonathan Cilley. 13060

Funeral oration, in honour of the memory of George Washington. (39745)-39746, (49322)

Funeral oration in memory of George Washington. 25693

Funeral oration in memory of Mr. Jonathan Lyman. (42786)

Funeral oration in memory of the Hon. James M. Vernon. 20967

Funeral oration in remembrance of George Washington. 73051

Funeral oration . . . in St. Louis. 20817

Funeral oration, occasioned by the death of Ephraim Simonds. 102255

Funeral oration, occasioned by the death of Gen. George Washington. 4040

Funeral oration. Occasioned by the death of General George Washington. Written at the request of the Boston Mechanic Association. 96388

Funeral oration occasioned by the death of General Washington. 97399

Funeral oration, occasioned by the death of Thomas Cole. 8818

Funeral oration on Brother Geo. Washington. 12289

Funeral oration, on General George Washington. (74348)

Funeral oration on George Washington. 21282

Funeral oration, on the character, life, and public services of Henry Clay. 1387

Funeral oration, on the death of Gen. George Washington. 72308

Funeral oration on the death of General Washington. 39747

Funeral oration, on the death of George Washington: delivered in . . . Albany. 33134

Funeral oration on the death of George
  Washington, late President. 39749
Funeral oration on the death of Hon. Daniel
  Webster. 43108
Funeral oration on the death of Jonathan
  Lyman. 2884
Funeral oration on the death of Mr. Elizur
  Belden. 32265
Funeral oration on the death of President
  Giddings. (20159)
Funeral oration on the death of Samuel
  Gurley. 56043
Funeral oration on the death of Samuel Hyde.
  7485
Funeral oration, on the death of Simeon
  Bristol. 19573
Funeral oration on the death of Thomas
  Jefferson. 97609
Funeral oration on Washington. 98479
Funeral oration, to the . . . memory of Mr.
  Henry E. Dwight. 63183
Funeral oration upon the death of General
  George Washington. 29284
Funeral oration over Jonathan Cilley. 68650
Funeral oration, pronounced at St. Petersburg.
  93996
Funeral panegyric on George Washington.
  35053
Funeral poem by the Reverend John Danforth.
  25404
Funeral procession. New-York. 101814
Funeral sermon. A sermon, delivered at
  Hartford. 92957
Funeral sermon . . . at Plymouth. 37366
Funeral sermon . . . at the obsequies of
  Colonel E. E. Ellsworth. (33796)
Funeral sermon . . . August 4, 1773. 106385
Funeral sermon. By Charles T. Torrey.
  96281
Funeral sermon. By Newman Hall. 29835
Funeral sermon, by Rev. John Hopkins. 57182
Funeral sermon by Rev. O. B. Forthingham.
  21153
Funeral sermon by the Rev. Edward H. Krans.
  21507
Funeral sermon, by the Rev. Mr. Searl.
  58895
Funeral sermon, commemorative of the death
  of the Rev. L. Blackman. 89366
Funeral sermon, . . . December 17, 1817.
  47005
Funeral sermon delivered at Newbury-port.
  (78625)
Funeral sermon delivered by the Rev. Elijah
  W. Stoddard. 91934
Funeral sermon, delivered in January, 1809.
  (21792)
Funeral sermon, delivered in St. Paul's
  Church. 91573
Funeral sermon, delivered in the Presbyterian
  Church. 98540
Funeral sermon, delivered Thursday, July 26,
  1787. 91741
Funeral sermon for Mrs. Anne Lord. 42013
Funeral sermon [for Mrs. Sarah Leveret.]
  40746
Funeral sermon, for that venerable and
  memorable servant of Christ. 46433
Funeral sermon for the Honorable Hezekiah
  Huntington. 42013
Funeral sermon for the Reverend Mr. John
  Wesley. 104723
Funeral sermon, in commemoration of the
  virtues of General Washington. 103084
Funeral sermon . . . in Holme's Harbour.
  40102

Funeral-sermon, . . . in Lancaster. 47447
Funeral sermon . . . in memory of Mrs. Mary
  Patten. 51261
Funeral sermon . . . in the Baptist Meeting-
  House in Providence. 47000
Funeral sermon . . . January 28th, 1802. 39199
Funeral sermon. Obituary notices and testi-
  monials of respect. 25012
Funeral sermon, occasioned by his [i. e. Thomas
  Baldwin's] death. 12523
Funeral sermon occasion'd by several mournful
  deaths. (25393)
Funeral sermon, occasioned by the assassination
  of President Lincoln. 28015
Funeral sermon occasioned by the death of
  Frank A. Brown. (33942)
Funeral sermon occasioned by the death of
  Mr. Ebenezer Little. 58895
Funeral sermon, occasioned by the death of
  Mrs. John Sampson Bobo. 47005
Funeral sermon occasioned by the death of
  Mrs. Alicia Blatchford. 68592
Funeral sermon, occasioned by the death of
  Mrs. Ann McClure. 20687
Funeral sermon, occasioned by the death of
  Mrs. Mary Bowers. 82877
Funeral sermon, occasioned by the death of
  Mrs. Sarah Bowen. (32257)
Funeral sermon, occasioned by the death of
  Mrs. Sarah Leveret. (46418)
Funeral sermon occasioned by the death of
  Rev. Joseph Green. 10740
Funeral sermon occasioned by the death of
  . . . Rev. Joseph Priestly. (65514)
Funeral sermon . . . occasioned by the death
  of the Hon. John Chandler Williams.
  11981
Funeral sermon: occasion'd by the death of the
  Honourable Spencer Phips. 1830
Funeral sermon, occasioned by the death of the
  late Adj't Myron W. Smith. 83502
Funeral sermon, occasioned by the death of
  the Rev. Isaac Eaton. (46601)
Funeral sermon, occasioned by the death of the
  Rev. Jonathan Parsons. (78624)
Funeral sermon occasion'd by the death of the
  Reverend Mr. John Rowland. 94688
Funeral sermon . . . occasion'd by the death
  of the Rev. Mr. Samuel Russel. 73979
Funeral sermon, occasioned by the death of the
  Rev. Philip Melancthon Whelpley. 89783
Funeral sermon, occasioned by the death of
  three little boys. 105114
Funeral sermon occasioned by the death of
  W. H. Harrison. 31429
Funeral sermon, occasioned by the much
  lamented death of John Kekyll. 65462
Funeral sermon occasioned by the much
  lamented death of the Reverend Mr.
  Willard. 95539, 104112
Funeral sermon . . . October 25, 1796. 39199
Funeral sermon of Capt. Joseph R. Toy. 81164
Funeral sermon of Hugh Aikman. 89085
Funeral sermon of John C. Lord. 8790
Funeral sermon . . . of Miss Sarah Coffin
  Whitney. (29307)
Funeral sermon of Mrs. Lydia Whitney. 39187
Funeral sermon of the Rev. C. M. Butler.
  13562
Funeral sermon of the Rev. Dr. Stone. 49131
Funeral sermon on Eliphalet Kimball. 841
Funeral sermon . . . on . . . Hon. William
  R. King. (63359)
Funeral sermon, on Michael Morin. (26210),
  50705

Funeral sermon on Mrs. Clark. 36243
Funeral sermon on resignation. 27939
[Funeral sermon on Rev. A. Mitchell.] 94815
Funeral sermon on Rev. Benj. Brigham, June
14, 1790. 39773
[Funeral sermon on Rev. Samuel Austin.]
94816
Funeral sermon on the death of Abraham
Becker. (79973)
Funeral sermon on the death of General
George Washington. 29252
Funeral sermon on the death of Governor
Madison. 82469
Funeral sermon, . . . [on] the death of Henry
Clay. 55229
Funeral sermon . . . [on] the death of James
Edgar Moore. 52442
Funeral sermon on the death of Jeduthan
Baldwin. (25203)
Funeral sermon on the death of John Adams
and Thomas Jefferson. (41524)
Funeral sermon on the death of Mr. Daniel
Kellogg. (34016)
Funeral sermon . . . on the death of Rev.
John Summerfield. 48036
Funeral sermon on the death of Rev. John
Williams. 12335
Funeral sermon on the death of Rev. Thomas
Bernard. 94118
Funeral sermon on the death of . . . Samuel
Holden. 14483
Funeral sermon on the Honourable Mrs.
Katherine Drummer. (9717)
Funeral sermon, on the death of the Hon.
Richard Stockton. 84107
Funeral sermon on the death of the Rev.
Elisha B. Cook. 71845
Funeral sermon on the death of the Rev.
George Whitefield. 106386
Funeral sermon, on the death of the Reverend
George Whitefield, who died suddenly at
Newbury-Port. 103321
Funeral sermon, on the death of the Rev. Jacob
R. Hardenbergh. 93236
Funeral sermon, on the death of the Rev.
Joseph McKean. 26074
Funeral sermon on the death of the Rev. Mr.
George Whitefield, . . . who died . . .
at Newbury Port. 59981
Funeral-sermon on the death of the Reverend
Mr. George Whitefield, . . . who died
. . . at Newbury Port, . . . Sept. 30th,
1770. 58890
Funeral sermon on the death of . . . the
Reverend Mr. Samuel Willard. 59601
Funeral sermon on the death of the Rt. Rev.
John Prentiss Kewley Henshaw. 43340
Funeral sermon on the Honorable William
Drummer. (9717)
Funeral sermon on the late Hon. Christopher
Gove. 28683
Funeral sermon on the mournful occasion of
the death. 103398
Funeral sermon, . . . on the occasion of the
death of Nathaniel Rogers. 12527
Funeral sermon on the Reverend Mr. Nathanael
Williams. (65599)
Funeral sermon preached after the death of
Mr. Nathanael Cotton. 17093
Funeral sermon preach'd at Boston. 25931
Funeral sermon preached at Bradford. 8506,
94115
Funeral sermon preached at Dorchester. 32550
Funeral sermon, preached at Elizabeth-Town.
62795

Funeral sermon preached at Newfane. 94466
Funeral sermon preached at the burial of the
crew. 48031
Funeral sermon, preached at the interment.
9420
Funeral sermon preached by F. Gilbert.
(27349)
Funeral sermon, preached December 25, 1863.
(9838)
Funeral sermon preached (for him) at Maldon.
46317
Funeral sermon, preached in Newark. (43681)
Funeral sermon, preached in the First Presby-
terian Church. 90363
Funeral sermon, preached on that occasion, the
14th March, 1819. 88956
Funeral sermon preached on Walterhouse
Fernley. 26450
Funeral sermon preached upon the death of
the Honourable Charles Frost. 104894
Funeral sermon preached upon the death of the
truly vertuous and religious Grove Hirst.
(14490)
Funeral sermons, preached at King's Chapel,
Boston. (25768)
Funeral sermons, preached . . . New-York.
16351
Funeral service of the Free . . . Masons of
. . . California. 45502
Funeral services at Christ Church, Cambridge.
(10138)
Funeral services at the burial of Lieut. Gen.
Leonidas Polk. 63846
Funeral Solemnities in Honor of Gen.
Washington, Philadelphia, 1799. see
Philadelphia. Funeral Solemnities in
Honor of Gen. Washington, 1799.
Funeral tribute to the honourable dust of that
most celebrated Christian. 96152
Funerales del Sr. Carlos II. Rey de Espana.
76168
Funeraria moerenti Mexicanae minervae
declamatio. 58390
Funereal address, on the death of the late
General George Washington. (51625)
Funes, Gregorio. 26211, 44174, 100848
Funes Villapando Abarca de Bolea, Ambrosio.
see Abarca de Bolea, Ambrosio Funes
Villapando, Conde de Ricla.
Funestos recuerdes del Libertador de Mexico.
19988
Funestos recuerdos del Libertador de Mexico.
44142
5 Ansichten nach der Natur aufgenommen und
in Stahlstich ausgefuhrt. 7921
Funfachter Jahres-Bericht. 75366
Funff vnd zweyntzigste Schifffahrt. 8427,
33678
Funffte kurtze wunderbare Beschreibung.
67565-67566
Funffzehende Schiffart. 33668
Funfzehnte Fortsetzung. 78013
Funfzig Jahre in beiden Hemispharen. 55411
Fungi Caroliniani exsiccati. (67987)
Fungi of Carolina. (67987)
Fungorum species nova Surinamenses. 50043
Funk, -------, fl. 1860. 26212
Funk, Isaac. 95753
Funnell, William. (26213), 18373, 18378
Fuqua, James P. 42207, 42210
Fur Auswanderungslustige ! 87148
Fur die Einheit des Vaterlandes ! 78050
Fur die Freiheit aller ! 78050
Fur, fin, and feather. 26214
Fur hunters of the far west. 73327

Furber, George C. 26215-(26217)
Furent presens en leurs personnes par deuant le notaire. 71103
Furieuse defaite des Espagnols. 31508-31509
Furley, --------. 60445
Furlong, Lawrence. (2588), 6025, 26218-26219, 87364, 101284
Furman, Charles E. 72342
Furman, Gabriel, 1800-1854. 8288, 19612, 26220, 79709
Furman, Gabriel, 1800-1854. plaintiff 74603
Furman, Garrit, 1782-1848. (26221)-(26222), 68513, 74425
Furman, Guido. 26223
Furman, J. C. 28676
Furman, Moore, 1728-1808. 26224, 103944
Furman, Richard, 1755-1825. 26225-(26227), 86130, 87795
Furman, Wood. 26228
Furman Club. publishers 105070
Furnace (British Ship of War) 48858
Furnace of affliction. 103510
Furnald, Amos. defendant 96867
Furneaux, John. RN (16245), 16248, 26229
Furneaux, Philip. 26230
Furness, William Henry, 1802-1896. 3401, 26231-(26240), 62614, 81851
Furst, A. tr. 32099
Furst, Moritz. (26242)
Furstenwarther, Moritz, Freiherr von. 26243
Furtado, Emanuel. defendant 97099
Furtado, Tristao de Mendoca. see Mendoca Furtado, Tristao de.
Furtado de Mendonca, Francisco Maria de Souza. see Souza Furtado de Mendonca, Francisco Maria de.
Furtado de Mendonca, Hypolito Jose da Costa Pereira. see Costa Pereira Furtado de Mendonca, Hypolito Jose da.
Further accompt of the progress of the Gospel. 22149, 22155, 59561
Further account of God's dealings. 103521-103522
Further account of New Jersey. 26245, 30710
Further account of that young gentlewoman. (46578), 3d note after 99448
Further account of the progress of the Gospel. 22151
Further account of the province of Pennsylvania. 26246, 59701-59702
Further account of the tryals of the New-England witches. 46607, 46687
Further address to friends. (14954)
Further appeal to the unprejudiced judgment. 23895, (26248)
Further and still more important suppressed documents. 26247
Further consideration of the dangerous condition of the country. (26250), 36264
Further considerations for encouraging the wollen manufactures. 26249
Further considerations for the stockholders. 66301, 70757
Further considerations on our insurance of the French commerce. 26251
Further continuation. 14242
Further correspondence. 39002
Further correspondence [in relation to the New Almaden Quicksilver Mine.] 52435
Further correspondence [relating to the civil war in the United States.] 16886
Further correspondence respecting the enlistment of British seamen. 16886, (37131)
Further correspondence respecting the enlist-ment of British subjects. 16887

Further correspondence respecting the proposed union. 8115, (26252)
Further development of some of the internal and distinctive views. 91999
Further disclosures of Maria Monk. (49997), 84021
Further discovery of that spirit of contention & division. 22351
Further discovery of the spirit of falsehood. 37196
Further examination of our present American measures. 72154
Further facts with reference to the character of Joseph Reed. 68571
Further hints, on the expediency of a rail road. 91540
Further illustration of the case of the Seneca Indians. 26253, 79105, 79110, 92978
Further information respecting the aborigines, containing extracts from the proceedings. 26254, 34651
Further information respecting the aborigines, containing reports of the Committee on Indian Affairs at Philadelphia. 26255, 34652
Further justification. 93225
Further letter from a gentleman of Barbadoes. (66041)
Further letters on King Philip's War. 83760
Further manifestation of the progress of the Gospel. 22150
Further narrative of the progress of the Gospel. 22166
Further objections relating to whirlwind storms. (68512)
Further observations in support of the right. 64844
Further observations intended for improving the culture and curing of indigo, &c. 17593, 26256, 87849
Further papers and returns. 26257
Further papers relating to American loyalists. 26258
Further papers [relative to the disturbances in Jamaica.] 35645
Further papers relative to the [expedition and region] and thence to the Pacific Ocean. 58332
Further papers [relative to the recent Arctic expeditions.] 25633
Further papers respecting the arrest and imprisonment. 43317
Further papers respecting the union of British Columbia. 8091
Further papers; viz. further return to an address. 82904
Further papers, viz. Return to an address. 82903
Further particulars respecting the Moravian missions. 97850
Further proceedings of the . . . House of Assembly of Jamaica. 35583
Further proceedings of the Joint Committee. 79111
Further proceedings on the trial of John Horne. 96175
Further quaeries upon the present state of the New-English affairs. 21610, 52611, 52640
Further reasons for inlarging the trade to Russia. 100477
Further reasons of a country gentleman. (81976)
Further reflections upon the state of the currency. 182
Further refutation on Dr. Price's statement. 18347, 27145, note after 71369

Further remarks, &c., on the late trials for
    conspiracy. 3392
Further remarks on the memorial of the
    officers of Harvard College. (42447)
Further remarks on the report of the Secretary
    of the Treasury. 72434
Further remarks on the voyages of John
    Meares. 20363
Further reply [of Robert Wickliffe.] 103873
Further reply [to Breckenridge's third defence.]
    103873
Further report from the Committee of Secrecy,
    appointed to enquire into the conduct of
    Robert, Earl of Orford. 26260, 57581,
    101148
Further report from the Committee of Secrecy,
    appointed to enquire into the conduct of
    Robert, Earl of Oxford [sic: i.e., Orford.]
    58031
Further report to the Committee Appointed 8th
    July to Prepare and Report Articles of
    Impeachment. 6000
Further report of the Committee on that part
    of the President's message. 26259
Further report of the Finance Committee of
    the state. 70583
Further return to an address. 82904
Further salutation of brotherly love. 26261
Further statement of facts and circumstances.
    20708
Further supplement to an act entitled An act
    to incorporate. 97808
Further supplement to an act . . . to incorpo-
    rate . . . Philadelphia. 60114
Further testimony against the scandalous
    proceedings. (46648), (46688)
Further thoughts concerning the bank. 17305,
    60391, 63266, 95667
Further traces of the ancient Northmen in
    America. 50902
Fusee d'Aublet, Jean Baptiste Christophe. see
    Aublet, Jean Baptiste Christophe Fusee.
Fusion in Pennsylvania. (43059)
Futhey, J. Smith. supposed author 84400
Future. A poem. (55207)
Future civilization of the south. 29632
Future destinies of America. 49474
Future duty. 83644
Future glory of America discovered. 27710
Future great city of the world. 68312
Future intentional addition of its constitution.
    79361
Future of America. (44460)
Future of Christianity. 89090
Future of nations. 38269
Future of the colored race in America. 541
Future of the country. 26262
Future of the northwest. 58019
Future of Vallejo. 86226
Future retribution. 83582
Future state of man. 74292
Future supply of cotton. 2282
Future wealth of America. 6342
Fyens stifts-avis. 13508
Fyfe, Alexander Gordon. 26263
Fyfe, J. Hamilton. 26264-26265
Fywyd Negroaidd yn America. 29622
Fywyd yn mhlith yr Iselradd. 29623